JEAN M.

JEAN M.

THE GREAT GEOGRAPHICAL ATLAS

GEOGR

THE GREAT GEOGRAPHICAL ATLAS

MITCHELL BEAZLEY in association with

ISTITUTO GEOGRAFICO DE AGOSTINI and

RAND McNALLY & COMPANY

THE GREAT GEOGRAPHICAL ATLAS
© 1982 Mitchell Beazley Publishers,
Istituto Geografico De Agostini
and Rand McNally & Company

Encyclopaedia Section edited
and designed by Mitchell Beazley
International Ltd.,
87–89 Shaftesbury Avenue,
London W1V 7AD
© 1982 Mitchell Beazley Publishers
and Rand McNally & Company

International Map Section edited
and designed by Istituto Geografico
De Agostini, Novara, Italy
© 1982 Istituto Geografico
De Agostini

United Kingdom and Ireland Map
Section edited and designed by
Rand McNally & Company,
Chicago, Illinois, USA, from
The International Atlas
© 1982, 1980, 1969 Rand McNally
& Company

Printed in the United States of America
by Rand McNally and Company

ISBN 0 85533 386 3

Askja volcano, Iceland

Gerard Mercator (1512-1594), the cartographic genius of the world's great age of exploration, first coined the word atlas to describe a collection of maps (although Abraham Ortelius published the first modern atlas, at Antwerp in 1570). Mercator took the name of Atlas from the mythological figure, who symbolized for him the sum of terrestrial and celestial knowledge. When Mercator's *Atlas* was published in its fullest form, after his death, it consisted of the largest collection of maps yet assembled in book form, but it nevertheless fell short of the great cartographer's original and ambitious plan.

Mercator's intention had been to map the known world and to describe its creation and subsequent story. This is also the aim of *The Great Geographical Atlas*, which consists of an entirely new and complete collection of maps, a compendium of current geographical knowledge, and an account of the origin, development and present state of the Earth.

The major atlases of the world, from Mercator's time onwards, have been published to satisfy a need for new information. As the rate of information gathering increased, so did the need for assimilating that information and making it available to the public. Current technology is at a point where man can survey the planet in the minutest detail. The resultant information explosion is in danger of overwhelming the ordinary atlas user. In *The Great Geographical Atlas*, this mass of information is organized and presented in the fullest, clearest and most elegant way. To achieve this objective, three major international publishers of cartographic and Earth science material pooled their talents and resources: Istituto Geografico De Agostini of Italy, Mitchell Beazley of the United Kingdom, and Rand McNally of the United States. The result is an atlas that reflects the ambition of Mercator, the original atlas-maker, by bringing together the conclusions of our current scientific and cartographic revolution. It marks the latest stage of internationality in map coverage and Earth science studies.

The spirit of the great atlases has always been international, although until very recently the Western countries were particularly emphasized. This internationality is implicit throughout the atlas, from the choices of projection to the coverage of Earth science subjects in the Encyclopaedia Section. In one important way, however, the present atlas extends the international tradition, for it supplies to every country in which the atlas is published a special regional section of larger-scale maps, complete with local name forms and a separate index. This special map section offers a unique and satisfying solution to the needs of atlas users for definitive map coverage of the world, together with detailed maps of their own particular region. It honours and expands the spirit of internationality, and it serves the local requirements of individual users.

We believe that *The Great Geographical Atlas* is the definitive atlas to carry us forward into the 21st century, in terms not only of cartographic but also of encyclopaedic excellence, and that it combines visual elegance with scientific authority and clarity in a fashion that has yet to be matched by any other work of a similar nature.

JAMES MITCHELL
Mitchell Beazley Publishers

ACHILLE BOROLI
Istituto Geografico De Agostini

ANDREW MCNALLY IV
Rand McNally & Company

PUBLISHING ADVISORY GROUP

Adrian Webster
Mitchell Beazley Publishers

Adolfo Boroli
Istituto Geografico De Agostini

Charles C. Bronson
Rand McNally & Company

MITCHELL BEAZLEY PUBLISHERS

Editorial Director
Iain Parsons

Art Director
Ed Day

Senior Executive Art Editor
Michael McGuinness

Executive Editor
James Hughes

ISTITUTO GEOGRAFICO DE AGOSTINI

Product Director
Marco Drago

Cartographic/Geographic Director
Giuseppe Motta

Cartographic Editor
Vittorio Castelli

Geographic Research
Giovanni Baselli
Marta Colombo

Cartographic Production
Francesco Tosi

RAND McNALLY & COMPANY

Product Director
Russell L. Voisin

Creative Director
Chris Arvetis

Managing Editor
Jon M. Leverenz

Geographic Research
V. Patrick Healy

Research Co-ordinator
Susan K. Eidsvoog

Cartographic Production
Ronald F. Peters

Complete list of contributors
and consultants:
Encyclopaedia Section page 104
International Map Section page 112

Sahara Desert, Souf, Algeria

THE GREAT GEOGRAPHICAL ATLAS essentially consists of three self-contained but interrelated parts. First, an Encyclopaedia Section provides an authoritative survey of current scientific knowledge concerning Earth's structure, organization and life, from its origins to its present state. Next, the International Map Section contributes a newly created collection of maps, using the latest cartographical technology and presenting a detailed picture of the world, including its most recently mapped or modified areas. Finally, there is a special section of larger-scale maps specifically related to the country in which the edition is published. Thus the local and regional, as well as the international, requirements of the modern atlas user are met. The three sections have their own indexes and are supplemented by a digest of the latest geographical information.

INTERNATIONAL MAP SECTION
This full-scale production of a new set of maps of every part of the world is designed to satisfy a number of different needs. It provides new information on those areas of the world that have undergone political, demographic or infrastructural change. It makes use of the latest scientific and technological developments to give a more detailed picture of areas that have only recently been mapped. And it modifies the presentation of the maps in response to the new needs of atlas users. For such needs have greatly changed, both through the expansion of tourism and communications, and also through the influence of the media, so that today a new awareness of the world is emerging. **An international character** is the hallmark of these maps, reflecting as it does the international context in which the mass of information presently available, geographical or otherwise, is increasingly collected and evaluated. For this reason, the planning, editing and production of the maps have all been undertaken to transcend the limitations of the traditional Western point of view. As a first step, every place-name or named geographical feature is given in its local form, using where necessary international systems of transcription and transliteration, or systems proposed by the countries concerned.

Secondly, the tendency to assign a major proportion of the maps to specific national areas has been discarded in favour of a more balanced coverage of every region in the world. Map scales have also been selected to reflect the importance—economic, cultural, historical and social—of all parts of the world. The international nature of the maps is further reinforced by the use of the metric system for such measurements as heights and depths. The sequential order of the maps gives a logical arrangement to each region, both in the internal

relationship of its parts and in its global context.

Following a principle generally accepted in works of an international nature, *The Great Geographical Atlas* records the contemporary *de facto* disposition of states, boundaries and frontiers. It does not attempt to interpret *de jure* situations in contentious areas, or the territorial claims of contending parties. However, the application of this principle does not imply that the publishers necessarily accept or approve the political status recorded on the maps.

The reader's requirements have also been carefully considered, in conjunction with those that are consistent with a truly international approach. On continental and global maps, whether physical or political, all name forms relating to major geographical features—countries, oceans, seas, mountains, etc—appear in the English language; place-names for the most important towns and cities appear in English versions as well as in local forms. These same English-version names from the continental

THE MAKING OF THE ATLAS

maps recur on the larger-scale maps alongside the local forms. In addition, to satisfy the local and regional requirements of the reader, a special section of large-scale maps of the United Kingdom and Ireland, complete with its own index, follows the International Map Section.

For ease of reference, continental maps giving separate coverage of physical and political features are juxtaposed. These are followed by larger-scale maps that combine both physical and political aspects, thus bringing together natural and man-made features. The larger-scale maps offer a wide range of physical detail, using hill shading and a graded range of colour tints to indicate heights. They also provide political details such as settlements, administrative boundaries, and many other political and cultural features.

At each stage of production, the maps have been submitted to a rigorous process of research and updating to ensure that all data used are valid, accurate and fully up-to-date. Special care has been taken in the selection of the information shown, and map projections have been chosen to minimize distortion. A data bank was established to ensure consistency throughout the thousands of place-names used. **Projections** chosen for the maps reflect the particular requirements of the various areas, and a computer and table plotter were used for their development, ensuring a degree of accuracy of 0.1 mm. For global maps, the projection chosen as best suited for representing the

whole Earth was Hammer's Equivalent Azimuthal with Wagner linear pole. However, the global map showing "Transportation and Time Zones" has been drawn on the grid of Mercator's cylindrical projection. Maps of continents and other extensive areas follow Lambert's Equivalent Azimuthal Projection, since this is particularly suitable for representing continental areas with a minimum of shape and scale distortion. This projection enables the reader to compare the areas of different regions of the world, since the area scale is consistent throughout.

For the large-scale maps of such areas as the United States, European countries, etc, Delisle's Equidistant Conic Projection has been generally employed. Whenever possible, the same projection has been used for all maps relating to the same world area, so that they may be regarded as sections of a single map or as parts of a single whole. For example, all the maps of European countries that are scaled to 1:3,000,000 have been drawn on a single Delisle Equidistant Conic Projection which was developed on the latitudes 60° and 40° North, these being areas of minimum distortion. This technique allows distances to be calculated with extremely fine accuracy throughout the area.

Map scales have as far as possible been limited in number and employed according to the relevant needs—the more detail required, the larger the scale—and to enable comparisons to be made from area to area. For global maps the scales are 1:75,000,000 and 1:90,000,000; for continental maps 1:30,000,000, apart from Europe, which is scaled at 1:15,000,000; for the major geographical or political regions the scales are 1:12,000,000 and 1:9,000,000. Larger-scale maps giving details of more important areas are scaled at 1:6,000,000, 1:3,000,000 and 1:1,500,000. Numerical scales always follow the metric system; graphic scales are given both in metric and in statute mile systems.

The map coverage has been organized to show a physical or political unit in its entirety on a single spread. The relatively extensive areas of overlap between maps on adjacent pages is designed to maintain continuity and interrelation of locality from page to page.

Terrain is shown with the maximum detail and precision that the scale will allow. Relief and elevation have been depicted in a unique style, combining altimetric tinting and specially detailed shading techniques. The tints used show elevation and depth in a harmoniously graded range of colours. A refined hill-shading technique complements the tints, giving a three-dimensional appearance while showing the overall configuration of the area.

Hydrographic features such as rivers, lakes

and coasts have been clearly differentiated. Permanent rivers, for instance, are distinguished from intermittently flowing rivers; saltwater lakes are distinguished from freshwater lakes; defined shorelines are distinguished from undefined shorelines.

Place-name selection is of fundamental importance in any large atlas seeking to illustrate both the physical and the political–administrative aspects of the world. A suitable balance needs to be struck between names of natural and of manmade features if the continual interaction of the two is to be correctly recorded. The place-names are given in a wide variety of typefaces and typesizes to reflect the geographical, economic, demographic and historical importance of the subjects, and to give a unified and balanced picture of the human habitat and of man's relation to his territory.

Name forms have been standardized according to the principle, now internationally accepted and well established in reference atlases, of printing names and geographical terms in the language of the country concerned, and avoiding phonetic or traditional forms that may vary from country to country. The systems for transliteration and transcription are either those devised by internationally recognized geographical organizations or those that have been proposed by the countries concerned. For example, Russian, Bulgarian or Serb placenames originally in Cyrillic script have been transliterated according to the system established by the *Organisation Internationale de Normalisation*, and Chinese names have been transcribed according to the Pinyin system proposed by the Chinese government. Diacritical signs in each language or system of transliteration have been retained throughout.

Lettering and graphics have been designed to ensure quick and easy consultation. The more important features are represented in an integrated fashion appropriate to the varying needs of reference and research. To ensure that the large quantity of information on the maps is clearly legible, care has been taken in selecting typefaces that allow visual clarity. Eleven different typefaces have been used to indicate a broad range of physical and man-made features, with the size and weight of the characters reflecting the importance of the item. In accord with current cartographic practice, the typesizes for towns and cities are related to population densities and arranged in accordance with the map scales.

Geographical information of the most detailed kind has been assembled to accompany the international maps, together with a glossary of geographical terms used in the atlas. These appear in a separate section preceding the International Map Index. Documentation and data for these were drawn from original sources

Nepal, aerial view

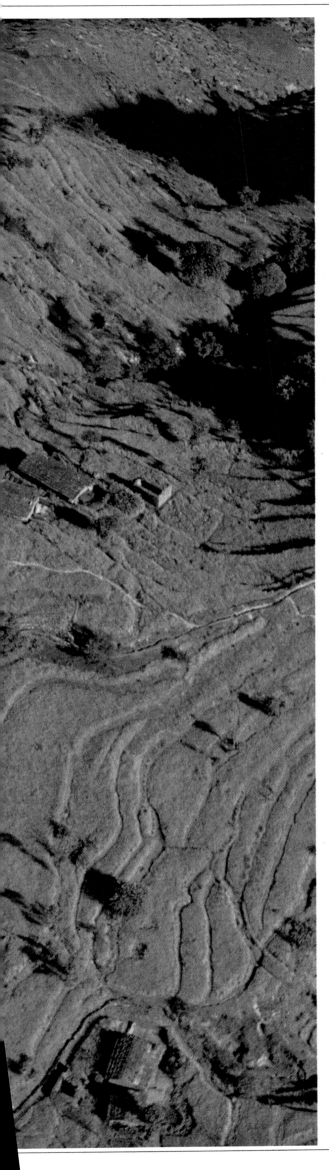

and from an extensive range of recent publications. In addition to cartographic sources, use was made of statistical surveys, census returns, geographical publications, special research projects in different parts of the world, analysis of satellite photographs, and many other information systems. All the information thus obtained has been evaluated, reviewed and compared in collaboration with the appropriate official bodies of the countries concerned.

The map indexes of *The Great Geographical Atlas* are twofold. One index relates to the larger-scale United Kingdom and Ireland Map section, and is placed immediately after this section. The other, which comes at the end of the atlas, includes all names found in the International Map Section. This index carries an Introduction explaining its various unusual features, system of cross-references and graphic symbols, which are designed to provide the reader with maximum information regarding the nature and precise location of every entry.

ENCYCLOPAEDIA SECTION

Recent decades have seen revolutionary changes in virtually all branches of the Earth sciences—those that relate to our planet and the life it supports. With this great increase in our knowledge has come an even greater demand on Earth's resources, as human populations soar and their needs multiply. The Encyclopaedia Section of *The Great Geographical Atlas*, written by leading authorities in their fields and illustrated with original creative artwork, brings together the latest discoveries and conclusions of science regarding the Earth: its origins in the universe; its structural components and dynamics; its creation and evolution of life; its rich variety of habitats; its natural and physical resources; and its widespread and increasing modifications at the hands of man. The Section is divided into five parts, of which the first four are concerned directly with aspects of Earth science. The fifth part discusses the representation of the Earth's surface in graphic form—the art and science of mapping—and leads into the International Map Section with a precise explanation of how to make maximum use of the maps.

The Earth and the Universe, Part 1 of the Encyclopaedia Section, places the Earth in its context within the cosmos. Recent advances in astronomy have led to an extraordinary increase in our knowledge of the heavens, including the discovery of background radiation that may mark the origin of the universe itself. This first part of the Section, compiled and authenticated by leading astronomers, interprets the discoveries of the space age.

Making and Shaping the Earth, Part 2 of the Encyclopaedia Section, brings together the latest conclusions of geology to describe both the structure and the formation of our planet and also the forces that have provided the fine detailing of individual landscapes, with particular reference to the role played by man. Each of these subjects is discussed and illustrated with integrated artwork complementing the text—a unique feature that characterizes the treatment of all the subjects covered in the Encyclopaedia Section.

The Emergence of Life, Part 3 of the Encyclopaedia Section, is concerned with the origin, evolution and development of life on Earth. The sciences of biology and palaeontology have shared the information explosion affecting all the Earth sciences, and it is now possible to give a coherent account of the emergence, flourishing and disappearance of life forms throughout Earth's history. The section goes on to describe the zoogeographical regions of the world, with a full description of the various species as they have adapted to their ecological niches. Finally, there is an account of the origin, distribution and adaptation of the world's dominant species—man.

The Diversity of Life, Part 4 of the Encyclopaedia Section, describes the range of habitats provided by Earth, from the polar regions to the equatorial forests. Each of these is seen both in terms of its natural life and with special reference to the needs and activities of man. Man's interaction with his habitat in terms of food, population, resources, communications, settlement patterns, urbanization and industrialization forms a key part of this section, and has been contributed by Professor Michael Wise, one of the world's leading authorities on these questions and the general consultant for the whole Encyclopaedia Section. Illustrations and diagrams based on the most recent available statistics complement this authoritative text. The juxtaposition of natural and "man-made" habitats within each of the world's living communities, or biomes, reflects an awareness of the need to preserve the ecological balance while meeting the urgent demands of expanding populations and sophisticated social systems.

Understanding Maps is the title of the last part of the Encyclopaedia Section, and it has been contributed by the Map Librarian of the British Library, Dr Helen Wallis. Pointing out that map-making appears to be an innate activity in human beings, the author provides an illuminating account of the development of map-making from the earliest times to the present day, with its advanced techniques of satellite photography and photogrammetrics. She then describes the language of mapping and its structure, the means whereby a three-dimensional world is translated into symbols on a two-dimensional surface. Finally, she explains how to read maps, with particular reference to the maps contained in *The Great Geographical Atlas*.

STRUCTURE OF THE ATLAS

The Great Geographical Atlas is arranged according to the following structure:

I–XVI	Preliminary pages
1–103	Encyclopaedia Section
104–111	Encyclopaedia Section Acknowledgments and Index
112–240	International Map Section
241–249	United Kingdom and Ireland Map Section
250–256	United Kingdom and Ireland Map Index
A·1–A·24	Geographical Information
A·25–A·144	International Map Index

CONTENTS OF ENCYCLOPAEDIA SECTION

Part 1

THE EARTH AND THE UNIVERSE

2–3	The Making of the Universe
4–5	Earth in the Solar System
6–7	Earth as a Planet
8–9	Man Looks at the Earth

GRAPHICAL ATLAS

Part 2

MAKING AND SHAPING THE EARTH

10–11	Earth's Structure
12–13	Earth's Moving Crust
14–15	Folds, Faults and Mountain Chains
16–17	Rock Formation and History
18–19	Earth's Minerals
20–21	Earthquakes and Volcanoes
22–23	The Oceans
24–25	Landscape-makers: Water
26–27	Landscape-makers: Ice and Snow
28–29	Landscape-makers: The Seas
30–31	Landscape-makers: Wind and Weathering
32–33	Landscape-makers: Man

Part 3

THE EMERGENCE OF LIFE

34–35	The Source of Life
36–37	The Structure of Life
38–39	Earliest Life Forms
40–41	The Age of Reptiles
42–43	The Age of Mammals
44–45	Spread of Life
46–47	Spread of Man

Part 4

THE DIVERSITY OF LIFE

48–49	Earth's Natural Regions
50–51	Climate and Weather
52–53	Resources and Energy
54–55	Population Growth
56–57	Human Settlement
58–59	Trade and Transport
60–61	Polar Regions
62–63	Tundra and Taiga
64–65	Temperate Forests
66–67	Man and the Temperate Forests
68–69	Mediterranean Regions
70–71	Temperate Grasslands
72–73	Man and the Temperate Grasslands
74–75	Deserts
76–77	Man and the Deserts
78–79	Savannas
80–81	Man and the Savannas
82–83	Tropical Rainforests
84–85	Man and the Tropical Rainforests
86–87	Monsoon Regions
88–89	Mountain Regions
90–91	Freshwater Environments
92–93	Man and the Freshwater Environments
94–95	Seawater Environments
96–97	Man and the Seawater Environments

Part 5

UNDERSTANDING MAPS

98–99	Mapping, Old and New
100–101	The Language of Maps
102–103	How to Use Maps
104–111	Acknowledgments and Index

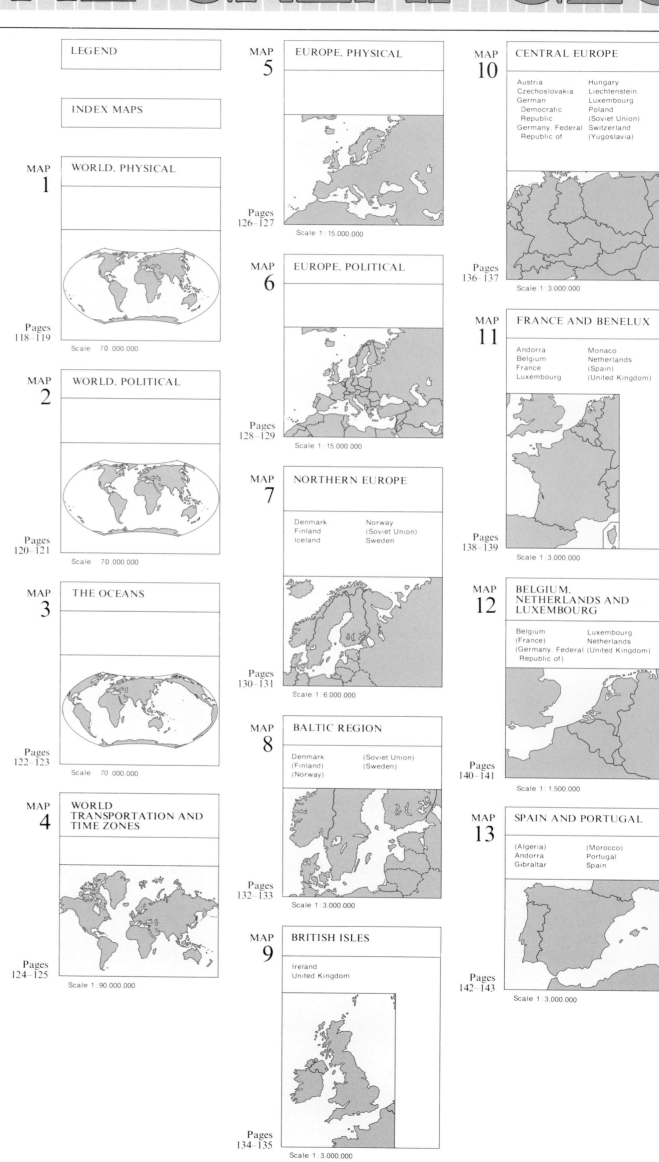

LEGEND

INDEX MAPS

CONTENTS OF INTERNATIONAL MAP SECTION

PAGES		MAPS
114–115	Legend	
116–117	Index maps	
118–125	World maps	1–4
126–155	Europe	5–20
156–173	Asia	21–29
174–189	Africa	30–37
190–213	North America	38–51
214–223	South America	52–56
224–237	Australia and Oceania	57–65
238–240	Antarctic and Arctic	66–67

An alphabetical list of major entities appears on page XVI.

MAP 1 — WORLD, PHYSICAL
Pages 118–119
Scale 70.000.000

MAP 2 — WORLD, POLITICAL
Pages 120–121
Scale 70.000.000

MAP 3 — THE OCEANS
Pages 122–123
Scale 70.000.000

MAP 4 — WORLD TRANSPORTATION AND TIME ZONES
Pages 124–125
Scale 1:90.000.000

MAP 5 — EUROPE, PHYSICAL
Pages 126–127
Scale 1:15.000.000

MAP 6 — EUROPE, POLITICAL
Pages 128–129
Scale 1:15.000.000

MAP 7 — NORTHERN EUROPE
Denmark   Norway
Finland   (Soviet Union)
Iceland   Sweden
Pages 130–131
Scale 1:6.000.000

MAP 8 — BALTIC REGION
Denmark   (Soviet Union)
(Finland)   (Sweden)
(Norway)
Pages 132–133
Scale 1:3.000.000

MAP 9 — BRITISH ISLES
Ireland
United Kingdom
Pages 134–135
Scale 1:3.000.000

MAP 10 — CENTRAL EUROPE
Austria   Hungary
Czechoslovakia   Liechtenstein
German   Luxembourg
  Democratic   Poland
  Republic   (Soviet Union)
Germany, Federal   Switzerland
  Republic of   (Yugoslavia)
Pages 136–137
Scale 1:3.000.000

MAP 11 — FRANCE AND BENELUX
Andorra   Monaco
Belgium   Netherlands
France   (Spain)
Luxembourg   (United Kingdom)
Pages 138–139
Scale 1:3.000.000

MAP 12 — BELGIUM, NETHERLANDS AND LUXEMBOURG
Belgium   Luxembourg
(France)   Netherlands
(Germany, Federal   (United Kingdom)
  Republic of)
Pages 140–141
Scale 1:1.500.000

MAP 13 — SPAIN AND PORTUGAL
(Algeria)   (Morocco)
Andorra   Portugal
Gibraltar   Spain
Pages 142–143
Scale 1:3.000.000

GRAPHICAL ATLAS

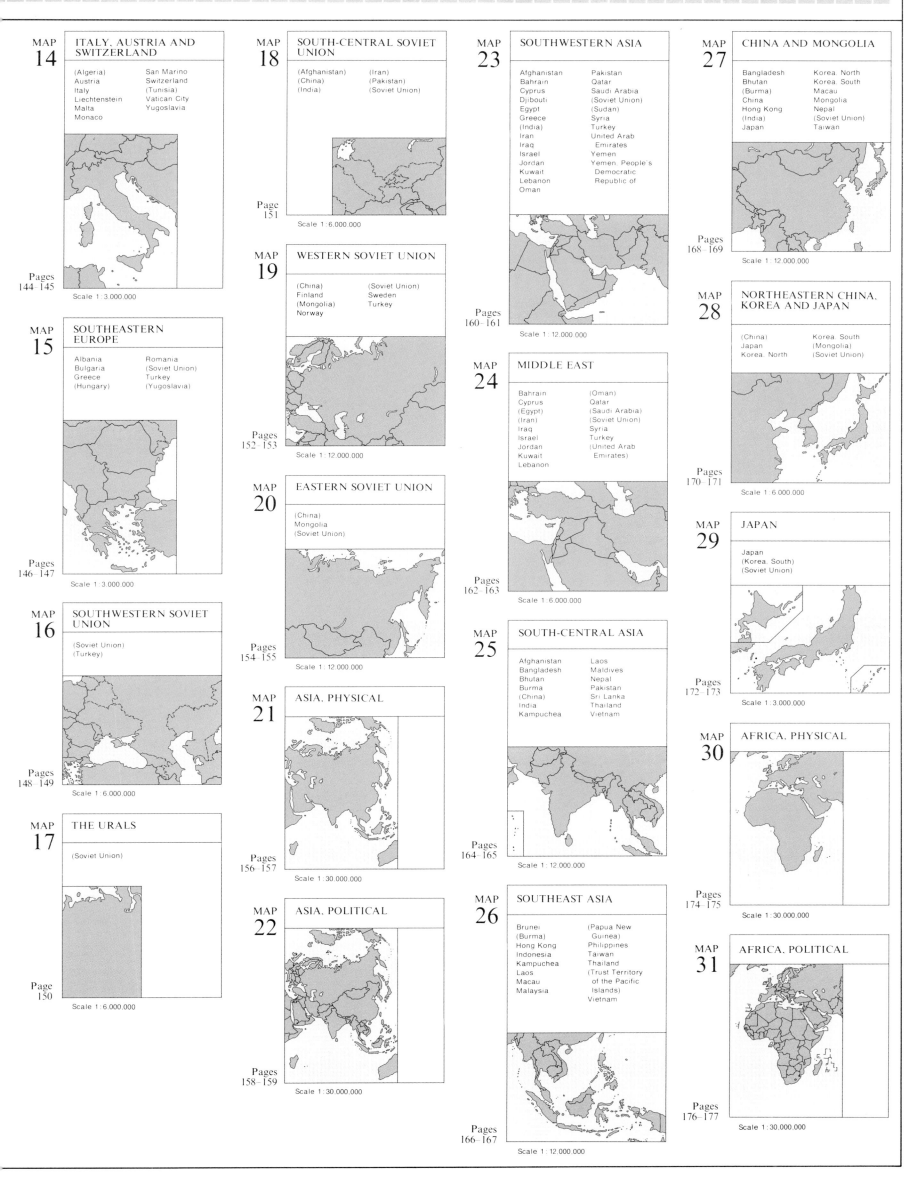

MAP
14
ITALY, AUSTRIA AND SWITZERLAND

(Algeria)   San Marino
Austria   Switzerland
Italy   (Tunisia)
Liechtenstein   Vatican City
Malta   Yugoslavia
Monaco

Pages
144–145
Scale 1:3.000.000

MAP
15
SOUTHEASTERN EUROPE

Albania   Romania
Bulgaria   (Soviet Union)
Greece   Turkey
(Hungary)   (Yugoslavia)

Pages
146–147
Scale 1:3.000.000

MAP
16
SOUTHWESTERN SOVIET UNION

(Soviet Union)
(Turkey)

Pages
148–149
Scale 1:6.000.000

MAP
17
THE URALS

(Soviet Union)

Page
150
Scale 1:6.000.000

MAP
18
SOUTH-CENTRAL SOVIET UNION

(Afghanistan)   (Iran)
(China)   (Pakistan)
(India)   (Soviet Union)

Page
151
Scale 1:6.000.000

MAP
19
WESTERN SOVIET UNION

(China)   (Soviet Union)
Finland   Sweden
(Mongolia)   Turkey
Norway

Pages
152–153
Scale 1:12.000.000

MAP
20
EASTERN SOVIET UNION

(China)
Mongolia
(Soviet Union)

Pages
154–155
Scale 1:12.000.000

MAP
21
ASIA, PHYSICAL

Pages
156–157
Scale 1:30.000.000

MAP
22
ASIA, POLITICAL

Pages
158–159
Scale 1:30.000.000

MAP
23
SOUTHWESTERN ASIA

Afghanistan   Pakistan
Bahrain   Qatar
Cyprus   Saudi Arabia
Djibouti   (Soviet Union)
Egypt   (Sudan)
Greece   Syria
(India)   Turkey
Iran   United Arab
Iraq   Emirates
Israel   Yemen
Jordan   Yemen, People's
Kuwait   Democratic
Lebanon   Republic of
Oman

Pages
160–161
Scale 1:12.000.000

MAP
24
MIDDLE EAST

Bahrain   (Oman)
Cyprus   Qatar
(Egypt)   (Saudi Arabia)
(Iran)   (Soviet Union)
Iraq   Syria
Israel   Turkey
Jordan   (United Arab
Kuwait   Emirates)
Lebanon

Pages
162–163
Scale 1:6.000.000

MAP
25
SOUTH-CENTRAL ASIA

Afghanistan   Laos
Bangladesh   Maldives
Bhutan   Nepal
Burma   Pakistan
(China)   Sri Lanka
India   Thailand
Kampuchea   Vietnam

Pages
164–165
Scale 1:12.000.000

MAP
26
SOUTHEAST ASIA

Brunei   (Papua New
(Burma)   Guinea)
Hong Kong   Philippines
Indonesia   Taiwan
Kampuchea   Thailand
Laos   (Trust Territory
Macau   of the Pacific
Malaysia   Islands)
                   Vietnam

Pages
166–167
Scale 1:12.000.000

MAP
27
CHINA AND MONGOLIA

Bangladesh   Korea, North
Bhutan   Korea, South
(Burma)   Macau
China   Mongolia
Hong Kong   Nepal
(India)   (Soviet Union)
Japan   Taiwan

Pages
168–169
Scale 1:12.000.000

MAP
28
NORTHEASTERN CHINA, KOREA AND JAPAN

(China)   Korea, South
Japan   (Mongolia)
Korea, North   (Soviet Union)

Pages
170–171
Scale 1:6.000.000

MAP
29
JAPAN

Japan
(Korea, South)
(Soviet Union)

Pages
172–173
Scale 1:3.000.000

MAP
30
AFRICA, PHYSICAL

Pages
174–175
Scale 1:30.000.000

MAP
31
AFRICA, POLITICAL

Pages
176–177
Scale 1:30.000.000

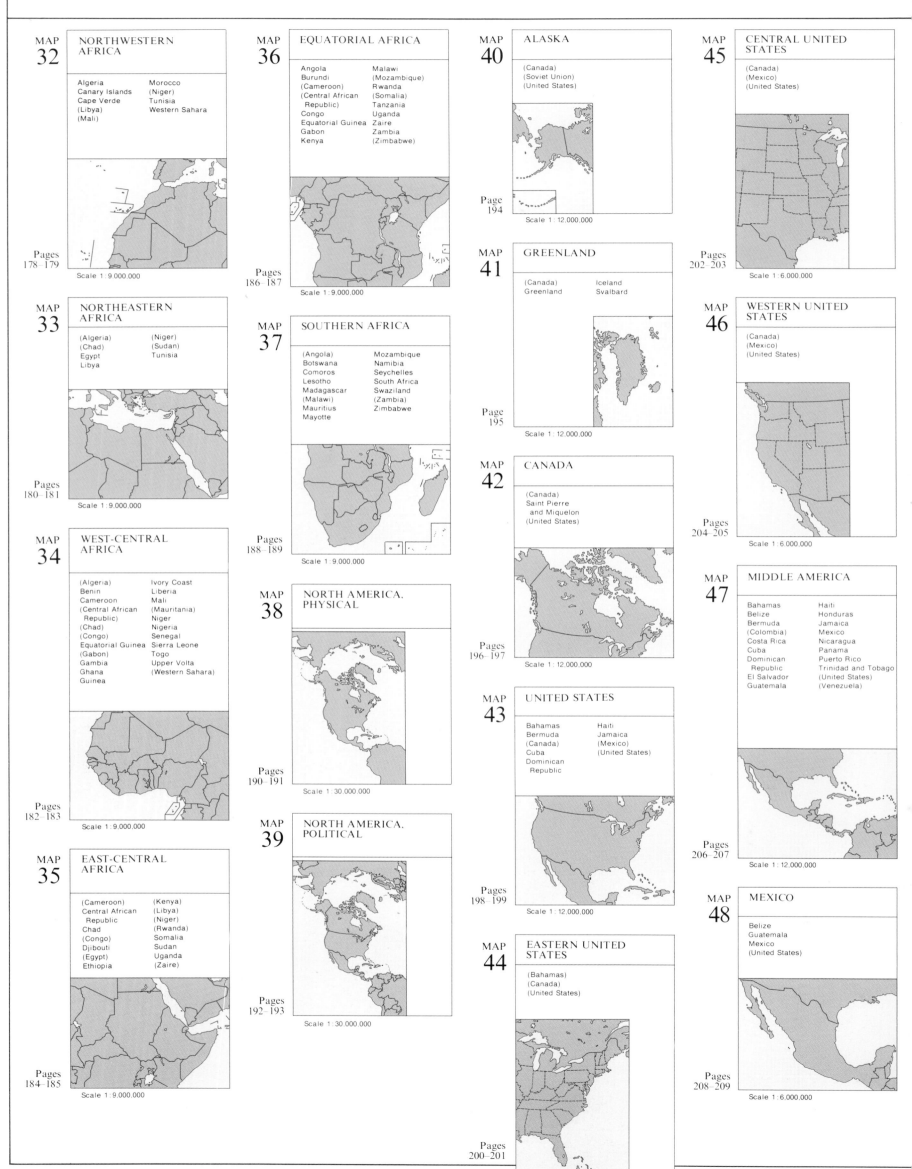

MAP 32 — NORTHWESTERN AFRICA

Algeria
Canary Islands
Cape Verde
(Libya)
(Mali)
Morocco
(Niger)
Tunisia
Western Sahara

Pages 178–179
Scale 1:9.000.000

MAP 33 — NORTHEASTERN AFRICA

(Algeria)
(Chad)
Egypt
Libya
(Niger)
(Sudan)
Tunisia

Pages 180–181
Scale 1:9.000.000

MAP 34 — WEST-CENTRAL AFRICA

(Algeria)
Benin
Cameroon
(Central African Republic)
(Chad)
(Congo)
Equatorial Guinea
(Gabon)
Gambia
Ghana
Guinea
Ivory Coast
Liberia
Mali
(Mauritania)
Niger
Nigeria
Senegal
Sierra Leone
Togo
Upper Volta
(Western Sahara)

Pages 182–183
Scale 1:9.000.000

MAP 35 — EAST-CENTRAL AFRICA

(Cameroon)
Central African Republic
Chad
(Congo)
Djibouti
(Egypt)
Ethiopia
(Kenya)
(Libya)
(Niger)
(Rwanda)
Somalia
Sudan
Uganda
(Zaire)

Pages 184–185
Scale 1:9.000.000

MAP 36 — EQUATORIAL AFRICA

Angola
Burundi
(Cameroon)
(Central African Republic)
Congo
Equatorial Guinea
Gabon
Kenya
Malawi
(Mozambique)
Rwanda
(Somalia)
Tanzania
Uganda
Zaire
Zambia
(Zimbabwe)

Pages 186–187
Scale 1:9.000.000

MAP 37 — SOUTHERN AFRICA

(Angola)
Botswana
Comoros
Lesotho
Madagascar
(Malawi)
Mauritius
Mayotte
Mozambique
Namibia
Seychelles
South Africa
Swaziland
(Zambia)
Zimbabwe

Pages 188–189
Scale 1:9.000.000

MAP 38 — NORTH AMERICA, PHYSICAL

Pages 190–191
Scale 1:30.000.000

MAP 39 — NORTH AMERICA, POLITICAL

Pages 192–193
Scale 1:30.000.000

MAP 40 — ALASKA

(Canada)
(Soviet Union)
(United States)

Page 194
Scale 1:12.000.000

MAP 41 — GREENLAND

(Canada)
Greenland
Iceland
Svalbard

Page 195
Scale 1:12.000.000

MAP 42 — CANADA

(Canada)
Saint Pierre and Miquelon
(United States)

Pages 196–197
Scale 1:12.000.000

MAP 43 — UNITED STATES

Bahamas
Bermuda
(Canada)
Cuba
Dominican Republic
Haiti
Jamaica
(Mexico)
(United States)

Pages 198–199
Scale 1:12.000.000

MAP 44 — EASTERN UNITED STATES

(Bahamas)
(Canada)
(United States)

Pages 200–201
Scale 1:6.000.000

MAP 45 — CENTRAL UNITED STATES

(Canada)
(Mexico)
(United States)

Pages 202–203
Scale 1:6.000.000

MAP 46 — WESTERN UNITED STATES

(Canada)
(Mexico)
(United States)

Pages 204–205
Scale 1:6.000.000

MAP 47 — MIDDLE AMERICA

Bahamas
Belize
Bermuda
(Colombia)
Costa Rica
Cuba
Dominican Republic
El Salvador
Guatemala
Haiti
Honduras
Jamaica
Mexico
Nicaragua
Panama
Puerto Rico
Trinidad and Tobago
(United States)
(Venezuela)

Pages 206–207
Scale 1:12.000.000

MAP 48 — MEXICO

Belize
Guatemala
Mexico
(United States)

Pages 208–209
Scale 1:6.000.000

ENCYCLOPAEDIA SECTION

Part 1

THE EARTH AND THE UNIVERSE

How the universe began · Earth's place in the Solar System
How the Earth became fit for life
Man looks at Earth from outer space

CREATION AND DESTRUCTION

Violent activity pervades our universe and has done so ever since the primordial fireball of creation. Evidence of violence comes from radio telescopes scanning the farthest reaches: entire galaxies may be exploding, torn apart by gravitational forces of unimaginable power. Some very large stars may burst apart in supernovas, spraying interstellar space with cosmic debris. From this violence new stars and new planets are constantly being formed throughout the universe.

The Big Bang theory (left) of the origin of the universe envisages all matter originating from one point in time and space—a point of infinite density. In the intensely hot Big Bang all the material that goes to make up the planets, stars and galaxies that we see now began to expand outwards in all directions. This expansion has been likened to someone blowing up a balloon on which spots have been painted. As the air fills and expands the balloon, the spots get farther away from each other. Likewise, clusters of galaxies that formed from the original superdense matter began, and continue, to move away from neighbouring clusters. The Big Bang generated enormous temperatures and the remnants of the event still linger throughout space. A leftover, background radiation provides a uniform and measurable temperature of 3°C. It is generally believed that the universe will continue to expand into complete nothingness.

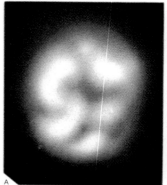

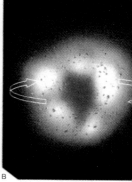

Stars vary enormously in size, temperature and luminosity. The largest, so-called red giants like Antares (1)—the biggest yet known—or Aldebaran (2), are nearing the end of their lives: diminishing nuclear "fuel" causes their thinning envelopes to expand. Rigel (3) is many times brighter than our Sun (4)—a middle-aged star—but both are so-called main-sequence stars. Epsilon Eridani (5) is rather like the Sun. Wolf 359 (6) is a red dwarf.

Our Solar System was formed from a collapsing cloud of gas and dust (A). Collapse made the centre hotter and denser (B) until nuclear reactions started. Heat blew matter from the heart of the now flattened, spinning disc (C). Heavier materials condensed closest to the young Sun, now a hot star, eventually forming the inner ring of planets; the lighter ones accumulated farther out, making up the atmosphere and composition of the giant outer planets (D).

Billions of galaxies exist outside our own Milky Way, each thousands of light-years across and filled with millions of stars. Found in clusters, they are either elliptical or spiral in form. The clusters recede from each other following the space-time geometry, as established by Hubble in 1929, proving that the universe is expanding.

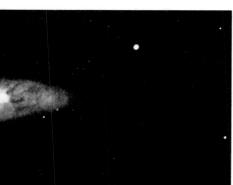

The "exploding" galaxy M82 may be an example of the violence of our universe. Clouds of hydrogen gas, equivalent in mass to 5,000,000 suns, have been ejected from the nucleus at 160 km (100 miles) per second. Black holes may cause the explosions, when gravity sucks in all matter, so that even light cannot escape.

The Making of the Universe

Most astronomers believe that the universe began in a great explosion of matter and energy – the "Big Bang" – about 15,000 million years ago. This event was implied by Einstein's theory of general relativity, as well as by more recent astronomical observations and calculations. But the clinching evidence came in 1965, when two American radio astronomers discovered a faint, uniform, background radiation which permeated all space. This they identified as the remnants of the primordial Big Bang.

The generally accepted explanation for the so-called "cosmic microwave" background, detected by American astronomers Arno Penzias and Robert Wilson, is indeed that it is the echo of the Big Bang itself, the radio noise left over from the fireball of creation. In recognition of their discovery, Penzias and Wilson shared a Nobel Prize in 1978.

The Big Bang has also been identified by astronomers in other ways. All the evidence shows that the universe is expanding, and its constituent parts—clusters of galaxies, each containing thousands of millions of stars like our Sun—are moving away from each other at great speeds. From this and other evidence scientists deduce that long ago the galaxies must have been closer together, in a superdense phase, and that at some time in the remote past all the material in the universe must have started spreading out from a single point. But this "single point" includes not only all three-dimensional matter and space but also the dimension of time, as envisioned in Einstein's revolutionary concept of space-time. Einstein's theory of relativity describes the phenomenon, not in terms of galaxies moving through space in

then re-used to form new stars and planets.

Thus, from the debris of such explosions new stars can form to repeat the creative cycle, and at each stage more of the heavy elements are produced. Today's heavenly bodies are very much the products of stellar violence in the universe, and indeed the universe itself is now seen to be an area of violent activity. During the past two decades the old idea of the universe as a place of quiet stability has been increasingly superseded by evidence of intense activity on all scales. Astronomers have identified what appear to be vast explosions involving whole galaxies, as well as those of individual stars.

Black holes

The evidence of just why these huge explosions occur is often hard to obtain, because the exploding galaxies may be so far away that light from them takes millions of years to reach telescopes on Earth. But it is becoming increasingly accepted by astronomers that such violent events may be associated with the presence of black holes at the centres of some galaxies.

These black holes are regions in which matter has become so concentrated that the force of gravity makes it impossible for anything—even light itself—to escape. As stars are pulled into super-massive black holes they are torn apart by gravitational forces, and their material forms into a swirling maelstrom from which huge explosions can occur. Collapse into black holes, accompanied by violent outbursts from the maelstrom, may be the ultimate fate of all matter in the universe. For our own Solar System, however, such a fate is far in the future: the Sun in its present form is believed to have enough "fuel" to keep it going for at least another 5,000 million years.

A star is born

The origins of the Earth and the Solar System are intimately connected with the structure of our own galaxy, the Milky Way. There are two main types of galaxies: flattened, disc-shaped spiral galaxies (like the Milky Way), and the more rounded elliptical galaxies, which range in form from near-spheres to cigar shapes. The most important feature of a spiral galaxy is that it is rotating, a great mass of stars sweeping around a common centre. In our galaxy the Sun, located some way out from the galaxy's centre, takes about 225 million years to complete one circuit, called a cosmic year.

New stars are born out of the twisting arms of a spiral galaxy, with each arm marking a region of debris left over from previous stellar explosions. These arms are in fact clouds of dust and gas, including nitrogen and oxygen. As the spiral galaxy rotates over a period of millions of years, the twisting arms are squeezed by a high-density pressure wave as they pass through the cycle of the cosmic year. With two main spiral arms twining around a galaxy such as our own, large, diffuse clouds get squeezed twice during each orbit round the centre of the galaxy.

Even if one orbit takes as long as hundreds of millions of years, a score or more squeezes have probably occurred since the Milky Way was first formed thousands of millions of years ago. At a critical point, such repeated squeezing increases the density of a gas cloud so much that it begins to collapse rapidly under the inward pull of its own gravity. A typical cloud of this kind contains enough material to make many stars. As it breaks up it collapses into smaller clouds—which are also collapsing—and these become stars in their own right.

Our own Solar System may have been formed in this way from such a collapsing gas cloud, which went on to evolve into the system of planets that we know today.

Our own cluster of galaxies (below), the Local Group (A), consists of about 30 members, weakly linked by the force of gravity. Earth lies in the second-largest galaxy, the Milky Way (B)—here shown edge-on and at an angle—which is a spiral galaxy of about 100,000 million stars. Its rotating "arms" are great masses of clouds, dust and stars that sweep round a dense nucleus. In the course of this new stars are regularly created from dust and gas. Our Sun (S)

lies 33,000 light-years from the nucleus and takes 225 million years to complete an orbit. The Andromeda Galaxy (C), known to astronomers as M31, is the largest of our Local Group. It too is a spiral, and lies about two million light-years away. Roughly 130,000 light-years in diameter, it appears as a flattened disc, and indicates how our galaxy would look if viewed from outside. Two smaller elliptical galaxies, M32 and NGC 205, can also be seen.

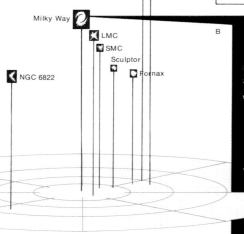

Leo II
Leo I
Milky Way
B
LMC
SMC
Sculptor
NGC 147 NGC 185
Fornax
NGC 6822
M31
M33
C
M32 NGC 205
IC 1613
A

Nucleus (N)   Sun (S)
100,000 light-years

the expansion, but as being carried apart by the expansion of space-time itself. Space-time may be imagined as a rubber sheet speckled with paint blobs (galaxies), which move apart as the rubber sheet expands.

Galaxies consist of star systems, dust clouds and gases formed from the hot material exploding outwards from the original cosmic fireball. Our own Milky Way system, the band of light that stretches across the night sky, is typical of many galaxies, containing millions of stars slowly rotating around a central nucleus.

Exploding space

The original material of the universe was hydrogen, the simplest of all elements. Nuclear reactions that occurred during the superdense phase of the Big Bang converted about 20 per cent of the original hydrogen into helium, the next simplest element. So the first stars were formed from a mixture of about 80 per cent hydrogen and 20 per cent helium. All other matter in the universe, including the atoms of heavier elements such as carbon and oxygen—which help to make up the human body or the pages of this book—has been processed in further nuclear reactions. The explosion of a star—a relatively rare event called a supernova—scatters material across space, briefly radiating more energy than a billion suns and ejecting matter into the cosmic reservoir of interstellar space. This is

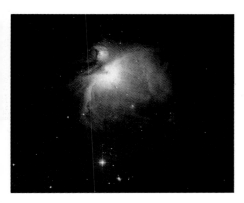

Stars are being born (left) in the Great Nebula of Orion, visible from Earth. The brilliant light comes from a cluster of very hot young stars, the Trapezium, surrounded by a glowing aura of hydrogen gas. Behind the visible nebula there is known to be a dense cloud where radio astronomers have detected emissions from interstellar molecules, and have identified high-density globules. These probably indicate that stars are starting to form.

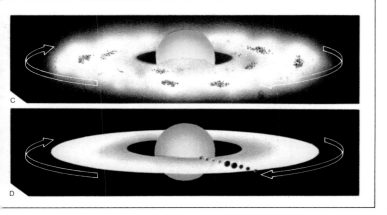

C

D

Earth in the Solar System

The Sun is an ordinary, medium-sized star located some two-thirds of the way from the centre of our galaxy, the Milky Way. Yet it comprises more than 99 per cent of the Solar System's total mass and provides all the light and heat that make life possible on Earth. This energy comes from nuclear reactions that take place in the Sun's hot, dense interior. The reactions convert hydrogen into helium, with the release of vast amounts of energy – the energy that keeps the Sun shining.

Nuclear reactions in the Sun's core maintain a temperature of some 15,000,000°C and this heat prevents the star from shrinking. The surface temperature is comparatively much lower —a mere 6,000°C. Thermonuclear energy-generating processes cause the Sun to "lose" mass from the centre at the rate of four million tonnes of hydrogen every second. This mass is turned into energy (heat), and each gramme of matter "burnt" produces the heat equivalent of 100 billion electric fires. The Sun's total mass is so great, however, that it contains enough matter to continue radiating at its present rate for several thousand million years before it runs out of "fuel".

The Sun's retinue
The Solar System emerged from a collapsing gas cloud. In addition to the Sun there are at least nine planets, their satellites, thousands of minor planets (asteroids), comets and meteors. Most stars occur in pairs, triplets or in even more complicated systems, and the Sun is among a minority of stars in being alone except for its planetary companions. It does seem, however, that a single star with a planetary system offers the greatest potential for the development of life. When there are two or more stars in the same system, any planets are likely to have unstable orbits and to suffer from wide extremes of temperature.

The Solar System's structure is thought to be typical of a star that formed in isolation. As the hot young Sun threw material outwards, inner planets (Mercury, Venus, Earth and Mars) were left as small rocky bodies, whereas outer planets (Jupiter, Saturn, Uranus and Neptune) kept their lighter gases and became huge "gas giants". Jupiter has two and a half times the mass of all the other planets put together. Pluto, a small object with a strange orbit, which sometimes carries it within the orbit of Neptune, is usually regarded as a ninth planet, but some astronomers consider it to be an escaped moon of Neptune or a large asteroid.

Planetary relations
Several planets are accompanied by smaller bodies called moons or satellites. Jupiter and Saturn have at least 17 and 22 respectively, whereas Earth has its solitary Moon. Sizes vary enormously, from Ganymede, one of Jupiter's large, so-called Galilean satellites, which has a diameter of 5,000 km (3,100 miles), to Mars' tiny Deimos, which is only 8 km (5 miles) across.

The Earth's Moon is at an average distance of 384,000 km (239,000 miles) and has a diameter of 3,476 km (2,160 miles). Its mass is $\frac{1}{81}$ of the Earth's. Although it is referred to as the Earth's satellite, the Moon is large for a secondary body. Some astronomers have suggested that the Earth/Moon system is a double planet. Certain theories of the origins of the Moon propose that it was formed from the solar nebula in the same way as the Earth was and very close to it. The Moon takes 27.3 days to orbit the Earth—exactly the same time that it takes to rotate once on its axis. As a result, it presents the same face to the Earth all the time.

Our planet's orbit around the Sun is not a perfect circle but an ellipse and so its distance from the Sun varies slightly. More importantly, the Earth is tilted, so that at different times of the year one pole or other "leans" towards the Sun. Without this tilt there would be no seasons. The angle of tilt is not constant: over tens of thousands of years the axis of the Earth "wobbles" like a slowly spinning top, so that the pattern of the seasons varies over the ages. These changes have been linked to recent ice ages, which seem to occur when the northern hemisphere has relatively cool summers.

Patterns of time
The Earth's movements on its axis and around the Sun give us our basic measurements of time—the day and the year—as well as setting the rhythm of the seasons and the ice ages. One rotation of the Earth on its axis—the time from one sunrise to the next—originally defined the day, and the time taken for one complete orbit around the Sun defined the year. Today, however, scientists define both the day and the year in terms of time units "counted" by precision instruments called atomic clocks.

A third basic rhythm is set not by the Sun but by the Moon, which runs through a cycle of phases $29\frac{1}{2}$ days long. This is the basis of the calendar month. But just as the modern calendar cannot cope with months $29\frac{1}{2}$ days long, so too it would have trouble with the precise year, which is, inconveniently, just less than $365\frac{1}{4}$ days long. This is the reason for leap years, by means of which an extra day is added to the month of February every fourth year.

Even this system does not keep the calendar exactly in step with the Sun. Accordingly, the leap year is left out in the years which complete centuries, such as 1900, but retained when they divide exactly by 400. The year 2000 will, therefore, be a leap year. With all these corrections, the average length of the calendar year is within 26 seconds of the year defined by the Earth's movements around the Sun. Thus the calendar will be one day out of step with the heavens in the year 4906.

Cosmic rubble
The other planets are too small and too far away to produce noticeable effects on the Earth, but the smallest members of the Sun's family, the asteroids, can affect us directly. Some of them have orbits that cross the orbit of the Earth around the Sun. From time to time they penetrate the Earth's atmosphere: small fragments burn up high in the atmosphere as meteors, whereas larger pieces may survive to strike the ground as meteorites. These in fact provide an echo of times gone by. All the planets, as the battered face of the Moon shows, suffered collisions from many smaller bodies in the course of their evolution from the collapsing pre-solar gas cloud.

Eclipses occur because the Moon, smaller than the Sun, is closer to Earth and looks just as big. This means that when all three are lined up the Moon can blot out the Sun, causing a solar eclipse. When the Earth passes through the main shadow cone, or umbra, the eclipse is total; in the area of partial shadow, or penumbra, a partial eclipse is seen. A similar effect is produced when Earth passes between the Moon and the Sun, causing a lunar eclipse. At most full moons, eclipses do not occur; the Moon passes either above or below the Earth's shadow, because the Moon's orbit is inclined at an angle of 5° to the orbit of the Earth.

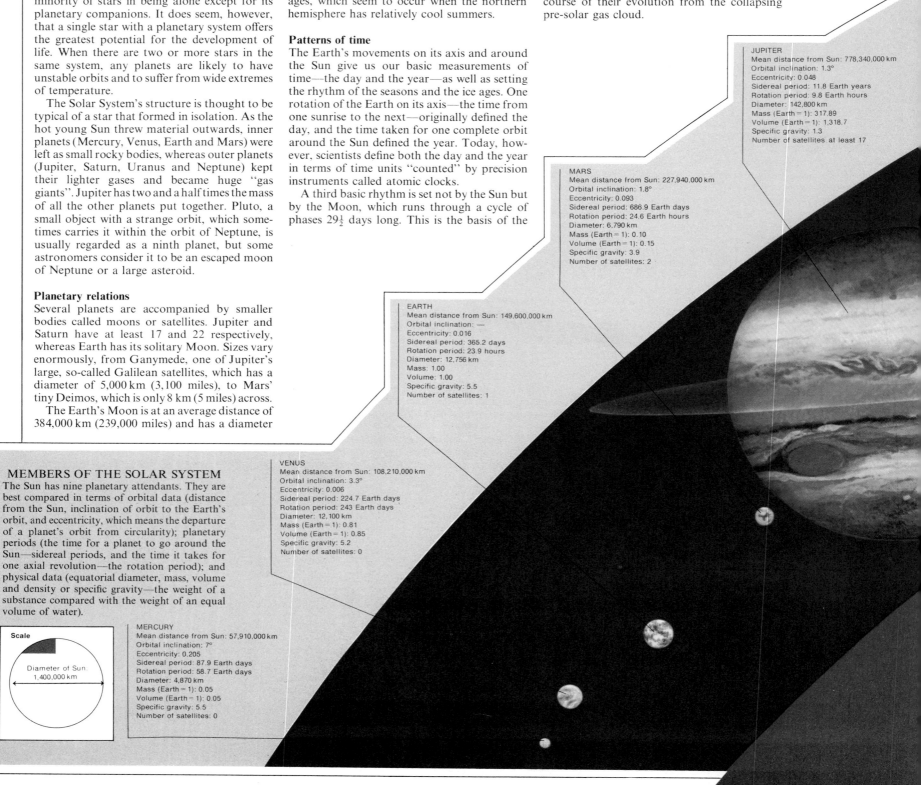

JUPITER
Mean distance from Sun: 778,340,000 km
Orbital inclination: 1.3°
Eccentricity: 0.048
Sidereal period: 11.8 Earth years
Rotation period: 9.8 Earth hours
Diameter: 142,800 km
Mass (Earth = 1): 317.89
Volume (Earth = 1): 1,318.7
Specific gravity: 1.3
Number of satellites at least 17

MARS
Mean distance from Sun: 227,940,000 km
Orbital inclination: 1.8°
Eccentricity: 0.093
Sidereal period: 686.9 Earth days
Rotation period: 24.6 Earth hours
Diameter: 6,790 km
Mass (Earth = 1): 0.10
Volume (Earth = 1): 0.15
Specific gravity: 3.9
Number of satellites: 2

EARTH
Mean distance from Sun: 149,600,000 km
Orbital inclination: —
Eccentricity: 0.016
Sidereal period: 365.2 days
Rotation period: 23.9 hours
Diameter: 12,756 km
Mass: 1.00
Volume: 1.00
Specific gravity: 5.5
Number of satellites: 1

VENUS
Mean distance from Sun: 108,210,000 km
Orbital inclination: 3.3°
Eccentricity: 0.006
Sidereal period: 224.7 Earth days
Rotation period: 243 Earth days
Diameter: 12,100 km
Mass (Earth = 1): 0.81
Volume (Earth = 1): 0.85
Specific gravity: 5.2
Number of satellites: 0

MEMBERS OF THE SOLAR SYSTEM
The Sun has nine planetary attendants. They are best compared in terms of orbital data (distance from the Sun, inclination of orbit to the Earth's orbit, and eccentricity, which means the departure of a planet's orbit from circularity); planetary periods (the time for a planet to go around the Sun—sidereal periods, and the time it takes for one axial revolution—the rotation period); and physical data (equatorial diameter, mass, volume and density or specific gravity—the weight of a substance compared with the weight of an equal volume of water).

Scale

Diameter of Sun:
1,400,000 km

MERCURY
Mean distance from Sun: 57,910,000 km
Orbital inclination: 7°
Eccentricity: 0.205
Sidereal period: 87.9 Earth days
Rotation period: 58.7 Earth days
Diameter: 4,870 km
Mass (Earth = 1): 0.05
Volume (Earth = 1): 0.05
Specific gravity: 5.5
Number of satellites: 0

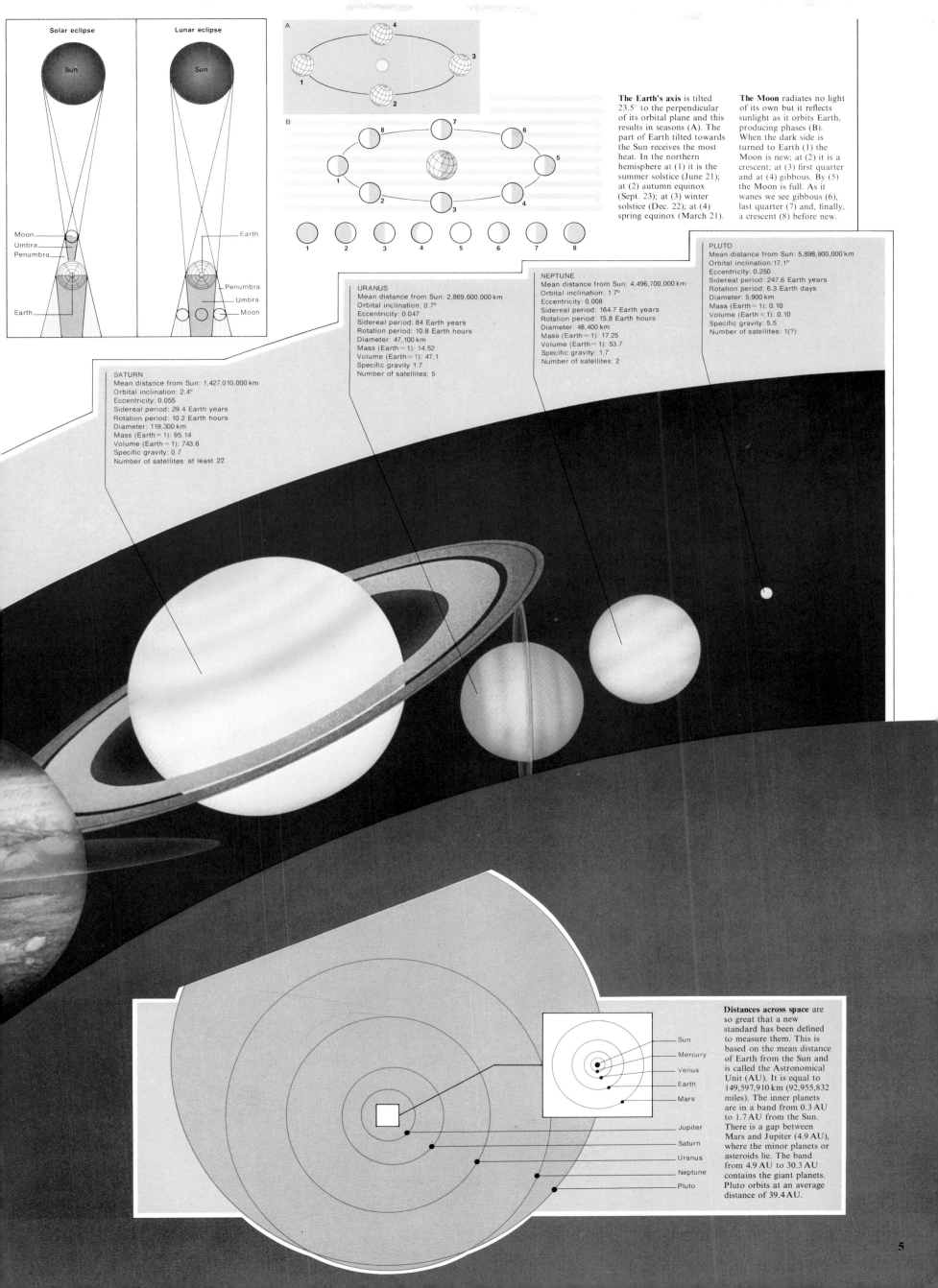

Solar eclipse

Lunar eclipse

Sun

Sun

Moon
Umbra
Penumbra

Earth
Penumbra
Umbra
Moon

Earth

The Earth's axis is tilted 23.5° to the perpendicular of its orbital plane and this results in seasons (A). The part of Earth tilted towards the Sun receives the most heat. In the northern hemisphere at (1) it is the summer solstice (June 21); at (2) autumn equinox (Sept. 23); at (3) winter solstice (Dec. 22); at (4) spring equinox (March 21).

The Moon radiates no light of its own but it reflects sunlight as it orbits Earth, producing phases (B). When the dark side is turned to Earth (1) the Moon is new; at (2) it is a crescent; at (3) first quarter and at (4) gibbous. By (5) the Moon is full. As it wanes we see gibbous (6), last quarter (7) and, finally, a crescent (8) before new.

SATURN
Mean distance from Sun: 1,427,010,000 km
Orbital inclination: 2.4°
Eccentricity: 0.055
Sidereal period: 29.4 Earth years
Rotation period: 10.2 Earth hours
Diameter: 119,300 km
Mass (Earth = 1): 95.14
Volume (Earth = 1): 743.6
Specific gravity: 0.7
Number of satellites: at least 22

URANUS
Mean distance from Sun: 2,869,600,000 km
Orbital inclination: 0.7°
Eccentricity: 0.047
Sidereal period: 84 Earth years
Rotation period: 10.8 Earth hours
Diameter: 47,100 km
Mass (Earth = 1): 14.52
Volume (Earth = 1): 47.1
Specific gravity 1.7
Number of satellites: 5

NEPTUNE
Mean distance from Sun: 4,496,700,000 km
Orbital inclination: 1.7°
Eccentricity: 0.008
Sidereal period: 164.7 Earth years
Rotation period: 15.8 Earth hours
Diameter: 48,400 km
Mass (Earth = 1): 17.25
Volume (Earth = 1): 53.7
Specific gravity: 1.7
Number of satellites: 2

PLUTO
Mean distance from Sun: 5,898,900,000 km
Orbital inclination: 17.1°
Eccentricity: 0.250
Sidereal period: 247.6 Earth years
Rotation period: 6.3 Earth days
Diameter: 5,900 km
Mass (Earth = 1): 0.10
Volume (Earth = 1): 0.10
Specific gravity: 5.5
Number of satellites: 1(?)

Sun
Mercury
Venus
Earth
Mars
Jupiter
Saturn
Uranus
Neptune
Pluto

Distances across space are so great that a new standard has been defined to measure them. This is based on the mean distance of Earth from the Sun and is called the Astronomical Unit (AU). It is equal to 149,597,910 km (92,955,832 miles). The inner planets are in a band from 0.3 AU to 1.7 AU from the Sun. There is a gap between Mars and Jupiter (4.9 AU), where the minor planets or asteroids lie. The band from 4.9 AU to 30.3 AU contains the giant planets. Pluto orbits at an average distance of 39.4 AU.

Earth as a Planet

Viewed from space, the Earth appears to be an ordinary member of the group of inner planets orbiting the Sun. But the Earth is unique in the Solar System because it has an atmosphere that contains oxygen. It is the nature of this surrounding blanket of air that has allowed higher life forms to evolve on Earth and provides their life-support system. At the same time the atmosphere acts as a shield to protect living things from the damaging effects of radiation from the Sun.

Any traces of gas that may have clung to the newly formed Earth were soon swept away into space by the heat of the Sun before it attained a stable state powered by nuclear fusion. Farther out in the Solar System, the Sun's heat was never strong enough to blow these gases away into space, so that even today the giant planets retain atmospheres composed of these primordial gases—mostly methane and ammonia.

The evolution of air

Until the Sun "settled down", Earth was a hot, airless ball of rock. The atmosphere and oceans—like the atmospheres of Venus and Mars—were produced by the "outgassing" of material from the hot interior of the planet as the crust cooled. Volcanoes erupted constantly and produced millions of tonnes of ash and lava. They also probably yielded, as they do today, great quantities of gas, chiefly carbon dioxide, and water vapour. A little nitrogen and various sulphur compounds were also released. Other things being equal, we would expect rocky planets, like the young Earth, to have atmospheres rich in carbon dioxide and water vapour. Venus and Mars do indeed have carbon dioxide atmospheres today, but the Earth now has a nitrogen/oxygen atmosphere. This results from the fact that life evolved on Earth, converting the carbon dioxide to oxygen and storing carbon in organic remains such as coal. Some carbon dioxide was also dissolved in the oceans. The Earth's oxygen atmosphere is a clear sign of life; the carbon dioxide atmospheres of Venus and Mars suggest the absence of life. Why did the Earth begin to evolve in a different way from the other inner planets?

When the Sun stabilized, Earth, Venus and Mars started off down the same evolutionary road, and carbon dioxide and water vapour were the chief constituents of the original atmospheres. On Venus the temperature was hot enough for the water to remain in a gaseous form, and both the water vapour and carbon dioxide in the Venusian atmosphere trapped heat by means of the so-called "greenhouse effect". In this process, radiant energy from the Sun passes through the atmospheric gases and warms the ground. The warmed ground re-radiates heat energy, but at infra-red wavelengths, with the result that carbon dioxide and water molecules absorb it and stop it escaping from the planet. Instead of acting like a window, the atmosphere acts like a mirror for outgoing energy. As a result, the surface of Venus became hotter still. Today the surface temperature has stabilized at more than 500°C.

Mars, farther out from the Sun than Earth, was never hot enough for the greenhouse effect to dominate. The red planet once had a much thicker atmosphere than it does today, but, being smaller than the Earth, its gravity is too weak to retain a thick atmosphere. As a result, the planet cooled into a frozen desert as atmospheric gases escaped into space. Mars then, in fact, suffered a climatic change. At one time—hundreds of millions of years ago—there must have been running water because traces of old river beds still scar the Martian surface. Today, however, Mars has a thin atmosphere of carbon dioxide and surface temperatures below zero.

Earth—the ideal home

On Earth conditions were just right. Water stayed as a liquid and formed the oceans, while some carbon dioxide from outgassing went into the atmosphere, and some dissolved in the oceans. The resulting modest greenhouse effect

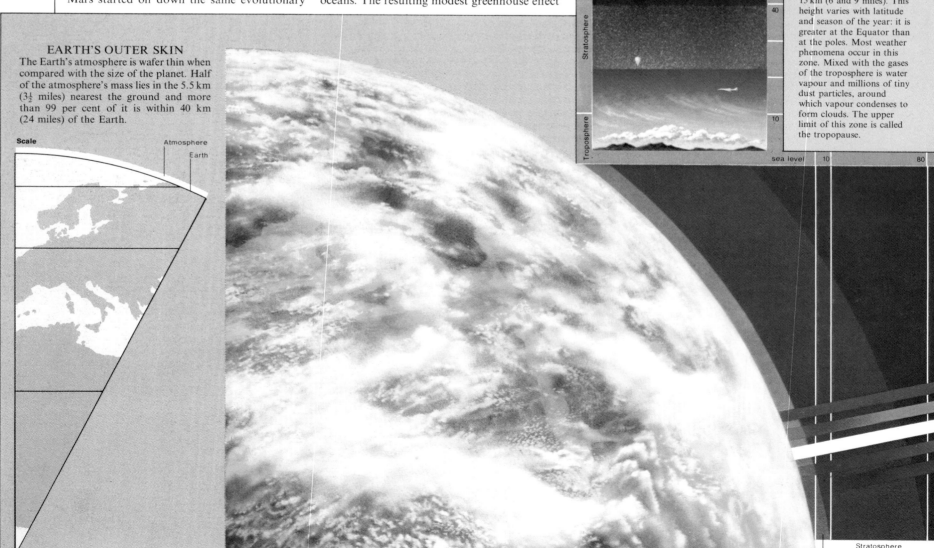

The thermosphere extends from 80 km (50 miles) up to 400 km (250 miles). Within this zone temperatures rise steadily with height to as much as 1,650°C (3,000°F), but the air is so thin that temperature is not a meaningful concept. At this height the air is mostly composed of nitrogen molecules to a height of 200 km (125 miles), when oxygen molecules become the dominant constituent.

The mesosphere is between 50 and 80 km (30 and 50 miles) above ground level. The stratopause is its lower limit and the mesopause its upper. This zone of the atmosphere is mainly distinguished by its ever decreasing temperatures and, unlike the stratosphere, it does not absorb solar energy.

The stratosphere is the level above the troposphere and extends as far as 50 km (30 miles). The chemical composition of the air up to this height is nearly constant and, in terms of volume, it is composed of nitrogen (78%) and oxygen (20%). The rest is mostly argon and other trace elements. The percentage of carbon dioxide (0.003) is small but crucial because this gas absorbs heat. There is virtually no water vapour or dust in this region of the atmosphere, but it does include the ozone layer, which is strongest between 20 km (12 miles) and 40 km (24 miles) high.

The troposphere extends from ground level to a height of between 10 and 15 km (6 and 9 miles). This height varies with latitude and season of the year: it is greater at the Equator than at the poles. Most weather phenomena occur in this zone. Mixed with the gases of the troposphere is water vapour and millions of tiny dust particles, around which vapour condenses to form clouds. The upper limit of this zone is called the tropopause.

EARTH'S OUTER SKIN

The Earth's atmosphere is wafer thin when compared with the size of the planet. Half of the atmosphere's mass lies in the 5.5 km (3½ miles) nearest the ground and more than 99 per cent of it is within 40 km (24 miles) of the Earth.

Scale

Atmosphere
Earth

Earth's radius: 6,378 km

Earth reduced by 90% in proportion to this scale

Stratosphere and Mesosphere

Troposphere

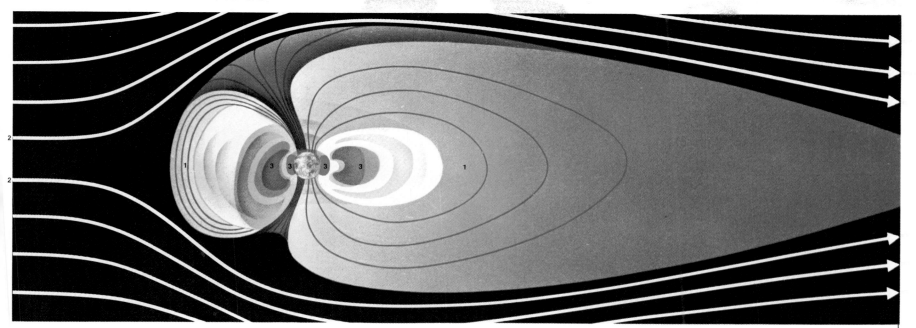

was compensated for by the formation of shiny white clouds of water droplets which reflected some of the Sun's radiation back into space. Our planet stabilized with an average temperature of 15°C. This proved ideal for the emergence of life, which evolved first in the seas and then moved on to land, converting carbon dioxide into oxygen as it did so.

In any view from space, planet Earth is dominated by water—in blue oceans and white clouds—and water is the key to life as we know it. Animal life—oxygen-breathing life—could only evolve after earlier forms of life had converted the atmosphere to an oxygen-rich state. The nature of the air today is a product of life as well as being vital to its existence.

An atmospheric layer cake
Starting at ground level, the first zone of the atmosphere is the troposphere, kept warm near the ground by the greenhouse effect but cooling to a chilly −60°C at an altitude of 15 km (9 miles). Above the troposphere is a warming layer, the stratosphere, in which energy from the Sun is absorbed and temperatures increase to reach 0°C at an altitude of 50 km (30 miles). The energy—in the form of ultraviolet radiation—is absorbed by molecules of ozone, a form of oxygen. Without the ozone layer in the atmosphere ultraviolet rays would penetrate the

The Earth's magnetic field behaves as if there were a huge bar magnet placed inside the globe, with its magnetic axis tilted at a slight angle to the geographical north–south axis. The speed of rotation of the liquid core differs from that of the mantle, producing an effect like a dynamo (below). The region in which the magnetic field extends beyond the Earth is the magnetosphere (1). Streams of charged particles (2) from the Sun distort its shape into that of a teardrop. Zones of the magnetosphere include the Van Allen Belts (3), which are regions of intense radioactivity where magnetic particles are "trapped".

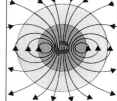

ground and sterilize the land surface: without life, there would be no oxygen from which an ozone layer could form.

Above the stratosphere, another cooling layer, the mesosphere, extends up to 80 km (50 miles), at which point the temperature has fallen to about −100°C. Above this level the gases of the atmosphere are so thin that the standard concept of temperature is no real guide to their behaviour, and from the mesosphere outwards the atmosphere is best described in terms of its electrical properties.

In the outer layers of the atmosphere, the Sun's energy is absorbed by individual atoms in such a way that it strips electrons off them, leaving behind positively charged ions, which give the region its name—the ionosphere. A few hundred kilometres above the Earth's surface, gravity is so feeble that electromagnetic forces begin to determine the behaviour of the charged particles, which are shepherded along the lines of force in the Earth's magnetic field. Above 500 km (300 miles), the magnetic field is so dominant that yet another region, the magnetosphere, is distinguished. This is the true boundary between Earth and interplanetary space.

The magnetosphere has been likened to the hull of "spaceship Earth". Charged particles (the solar wind) streaming out from the Sun are deflected around Earth by the magnetosphere

like water around a moving ship, while the region of the Earth's magnetic influence in space trails "downstream" away from the Sun like the wake of a ship. The Van Allen Belts, at altitudes of 3,000 and 15,000 km (1,850 and 9,300 miles) are regions of space high above the Equator where particles are trapped by the magnetic field. Particles spilling out of the belts spiral towards the polar regions of Earth, producing the spectacle of the auroras—the northern and southern lights. The Earth and Mercury are the only inner planets with magnetospheres such as this. The cause of the Earth's magnetism is almost certainly the planet's heavy molten core, which is composed of magnetic materials.

The Earth's atmosphere exhibits a great variety of characteristics on a vertical scale. As well as variations of temperature and the electrical properties of the air, there are differences in chemical composition—in the mixture of gases and water vapour—according to altitude. The Earth's gravitational pull means that air density and pressure decrease with altitude. Pressure of about 1,000 millibars at sea level falls to virtually nothing (10^{-42} millibars) by a height of 700 km (435 miles) above the Earth. All these factors, and their interrelationships, help to maintain the Earth's atmosphere as a protective outer covering or radiation shield and an essential life-support system.

The ionosphere is another name for the atmospheric layer beyond 80 km (50 miles). The region is best described in terms of the electrical properties of its constituents rather than by temperature. It is here that ionization occurs. Gamma and X-rays from the Sun are absorbed by atoms and molecules of nitrogen and oxygen and, as a result, each molecule or atom gives up one or more of its electrons, thus becoming a positively charged ion. These ions reflect radio waves and are used to bounce back radio waves transmitted from the surface of the Earth.

The exosphere is the layer above the thermosphere and it extends from 400 km (250 miles) up to about 700 km (435 miles), the point at which, it may be said, space begins. It is almost a complete vacuum because most of its atoms and molecules of oxygen escape the Earth's gravity.

The magnetosphere includes the exosphere, but it extends far beyond the atmosphere—to a distance of between 64,000 and 130,000 km (40,000 and 80,000 miles) above the Earth. It represents the Earth's external magnetic field and its outer limit is called the magnetopause.

The atmosphere protects the Earth from harmful solar radiation and also from bombardment by small particles from space. Most meteors (particles orbiting the Sun) burn up in the atmosphere, but meteorites (debris of minor planets) reach the ground. Of all incoming solar radiation, only visible light, radio waves and infra-red rays reach the surface of Earth. X-rays are removed in the ionosphere, and ultraviolet and some infra-red radiations are filtered out in the stratosphere. Studies of such radiations have therefore to be made from observatories in space.

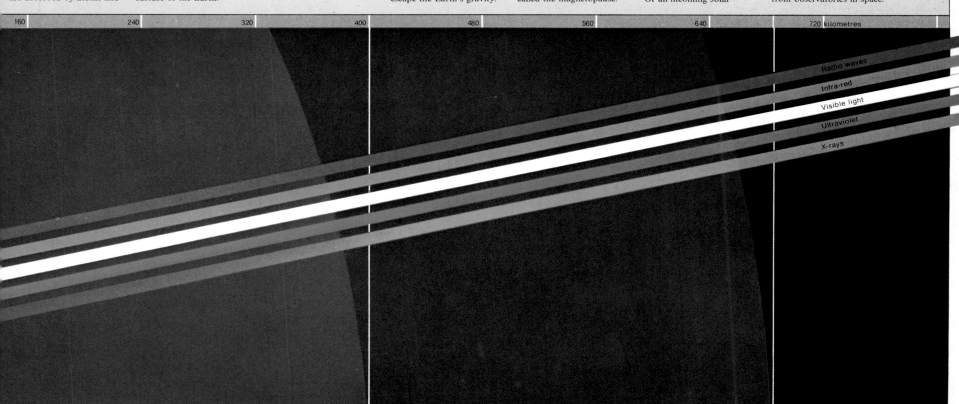

160   240   320   400   480   560   640   720 kilometres

Radio waves
Infra-red
Visible light
Ultraviolet
X-rays

Thermosphere/Ionosphere   Exosphere/Magnetosphere   Space

Man Looks at the Earth

Orbiting satellites keep a detailed watch on the Earth's land surface, oceans and atmosphere, feeding streams of data to meteorologists, geologists, oceanographers, farmers, fishermen and many others. Some information would be unobtainable by any other means. Surveys from orbit are quicker and less expensive than from aircraft, for example, because a satellite can scan a much larger area. And, surprisingly enough, certain features on the ground are easier to see from space.

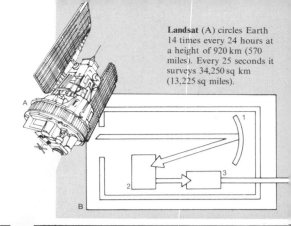

Landsat (A) circles Earth 14 times every 24 hours at a height of 920 km (570 miles). Every 25 seconds it surveys 34,250 sq km (13,225 sq miles).

MAPPING AND MEASURING
Man has been looking at Earth from satellites since the beginning of the 1960s, and has firmly established the value of surveys from space to those engaged in a variety of earthly pursuits. Chief of these activities are resource management, ranging from monitoring the spread of deserts and river silting to locating likely mineral deposits; environmental protection, which includes observing delicate ecosystems and natural disasters; and a whole range of mapping and land-use planning.

Satellites give us a greater overview of numerous aspects of life on Earth than any earthbound eye could see.

Of all the information gleaned from satellites, accurate weather forecasts are of particular social and economic value. The first weather satellite was Tiros 1 (Television and Infrared Observation Satellite), launched by the United States in 1960. By the time Tiros 10 ceased operations in 1967, the series had sent back more than half a million photographs, firmly establishing the value of satellite imagery.

Tiros was superseded by the ESSA (Environmental Science Services Administration) and the NOAA (National Oceanic and Atmospheric Administration) satellites. These orbited the Earth from pole to pole, and they covered the entire globe during the course of a day. Other weather satellites, such as the European Meteosat, are placed in geostationary orbit over the Equator, which means they stay in one place and continually monitor a single large region.

Watching the weather
In addition to photographing clouds, weather satellites monitor the extent of snow and ice cover, and they measure the temperature of the oceans and the composition of the atmosphere. Information about the overall heat balance of our planet gives clues to long-term climatic change, and includes the effects on climate of human activities such as the burning of fossil fuels and deforestation.

Infra-red sensors allow pictures to be taken at night as well as during the day. The temperature of cloud tops, measured by infra-red devices, is a guide to the height of the clouds. In a typical infra-red image, high clouds appear white because they are the coldest, lower clouds and land areas appear grey, and oceans and lakes are black. Information on humidity in the atmosphere is provided by sensors tuned to wavelengths between 5.5 and 7 micrometres, at which water vapour strongly absorbs the radiation.

To "see" inside clouds, where infra-red and visible light cannot penetrate, satellites use sensors tuned to short-wavelength radio waves (microwaves) around the 1.5 centimetre wavelength. These sensors can reveal whether or not clouds will give rise to heavy rainfall, snow or hail. Microwave sensors are also useful for locating ice floes in polar regions, making use of the different microwave reflections from land ice, sea ice and open water.

Satellites that send out such pictures are in relatively low orbits, at a height of about 1,000 km (620 miles), and they pass over each part of the Earth once every 12 hours. But to build up a global model of the Earth's weather and climate, meteorologists need continual information on wind speed and direction at various levels in the atmosphere, together with temperature and humidity profiles. This data is provided by geostationary satellites. Cloud photographs taken every half-hour give information on winds, and computers combine this with temperature and humidity soundings to give as complete a model as is possible of the Earth's atmosphere.

Increasing attention is also being paid to the Earth's surface, notably by means of a series of satellites called Landsat (originally ERTS or Earth Resource Technology Satellites), the first of which was launched by the United States in 1972. The third and current Landsat is in a similar pole-to-pole orbit as the weather satellites, but its cameras are more powerful and they make more detailed surveys of the Earth. Landsat rephotographs each part of the Earth's surface every 18 days.

How to map resources
The satellite has two sensor systems: a television camera, which takes pictures of the Earth using visible light; and a device called a multi-spectral scanner, which scans the Earth at several distinct wavelengths, including visible light and infra-red. Data from the various channels of the multi-spectral scanner can be combined to produce so-called false-colour images, in which each wavelength band is assigned a colour (not necessarily its real one) to emphasize features of interest.

An important use of Landsat photographs is for making maps, particularly of large countries with remote areas that have never been adequately surveyed from the ground. Several countries, including Brazil, Canada and China, have set up ground stations to receive Landsat data directly. Features previously unknown or incorrectly mapped, including rivers, lakes and glaciers, show up readily on Landsat images. Urban mapping and hence planning are aided by satellite pictures that can distinguish areas of industry, housing and open parkland.

Landsat photographs have also proved invaluable for agricultural land-use planning. They are used for estimates of soil types and for determining land-use patterns. Areas of crop disease or dying vegetation are detectable by their different colours. Yields of certain crops such as wheat can now be accurately predicted from satellite imagery, so that at last it is becoming possible to keep track of the worldwide production of vital food crops. Freshwater, too, is one of our most valuable resources, and knowing its sources and seasonal variation is vital to irrigation projects.

Finally, the geologist and mineral prospector have benefited from remote sensing. Features such as fault lines and different types of sediments and rocks show up clearly on Landsat pictures. This allows geologists to select promising areas in which the prospector can look for mineral deposits.

Another way to study the Earth is by bouncing radar beams off it. Radar sensing indicates the nature of soil or rock on land and movement of water at sea, for example. This was not done by Landsat, but by equipment aboard the United States' Skylab and by a short-lived American satellite called Seasat. The Soviet Union has included Earth surveying in its Salyut programme, and resource mapping is also a feature of the spacelab aboard the American space shuttle. All these activities help man to manage the limited resources on our planet and to preserve the environment.

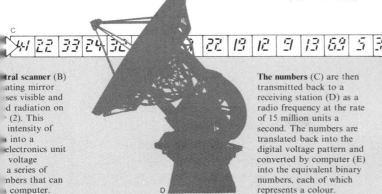
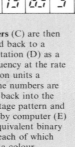

spectral scanner (B) oscillating mirror focuses visible and infra-red radiation on to (2). This records intensity of light into an electronics unit as a voltage — a series of numbers that can go to a computer.

The numbers (C) are then transmitted back to a receiving station (D) as a radio frequency at the rate of 15 million units a second. The numbers are translated back into the digital voltage pattern and converted by computer (E) into the equivalent binary numbers, each of which represents a colour.

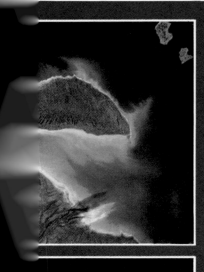

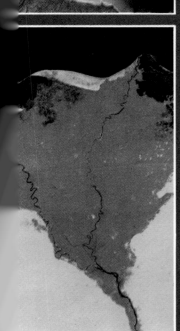

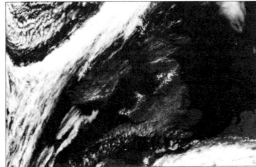

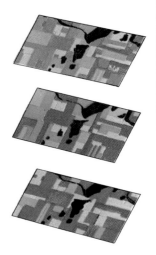

A Landsat image is made up of very many points, each of which is obtained by means of the procedure described above. Each number in the image (F) represents the radiation from a small area of land, or pixel, 0.44 hectares (1.1 acres) in size. A computer then translates the numbers into different colours, or different shades of one colour, which are projected on to a TV screen (G) and the image is seen for the first time. Finally, photographs of this false-colour image are produced (H). This picture, showing a forest fire in the Upper Peninsula, Michigan, is of use to those engaged in forest management. Other satellite data of use in forestry include types of trees, patterns of growth and the spread of disease.

Observation of waterways and coastal areas (above) shows pollution and deposition of sediments. This is of importance to the fishing industry. Fish congregate in areas where upwelling brings nutrients to the surface, for example. The large yellow-orange halo around Akimiski Island in James Bay (A)— a southern extension of Hudson Bay in Canada— is fine sediment resulting from wave action on a silty shore. Seeing the sediment in this way helps to determine current patterns in the Bay. In a predominantly desert area, the Nile delta (B) stands out dramatically. The red is an intensively cultivated area: cotton is the main crop. The larger irrigation canals can be seen on the photograph. Thermal imagery, or heat capacity mapping, is used to identify rocks, to study the effects of urban "heat islands", to estimate soil moisture and snow melt,

and to map shallow ground water. In this photograph of the northeast coast of North America (C) purple represents the coldest temperatures—in Lakes Erie and Ontario. The coldest parts of the Atlantic Ocean are deep blue, whereas warmer waters near the coast are light blue. Green is the warmer land, but also the Gulf Stream in the lower right part of the image. Brown, yellow and orange represent successively warmer land surface areas. Red is hot regions around cities and coal-mining regions found in eastern Pennsylvania (to the upper left of centre in the picture); and, finally, grey and white are the very hottest areas—the urban heat islands of Baltimore, Philadelphia and New York City. Black areas in the upper left are cold clouds. The temperature range of the image is about 30°C (55°F).

The Earth seen from space shows phases just like the Moon, Mercury and Venus do to us. These dramatic photographs were taken from a satellite moving at 35,885 km (22,300 miles) above South America at 7.30 am (1), 10.30 am (2), noon (3), 3.30 pm (4) and at 10.30 pm (5), and clearly show the Earth in phase.

Weather satellite imagery can save lives and property by giving advance warning of bad weather conditions, as well as providing day-to-day forecasts. This Tiros image (left) shows a cold front moving west of Ireland with low-level wave clouds over southern and central England. There are low-pressure systems over northern France and to the northwest of Ireland.

LANDSAT AND THE FARMER

Sep	Oct	Nov	Dec	Jan	Feb	Mar	Apr	May	Jun	Jul	Aug
sown	grows		dormant			grows			ripe	harvest	

Agriculturists benefit from "multitemporal analysis" by satellites (left). This is the comparison of data from the same field recorded on two or more dates. It is also able to differentiate crops, which may have an identical appearance, or signature, on one day, but on another occasion exhibit different rates of growth. The pattern of growth is different for small grains than most other crops. A "biowindow" is the period of time in which vegetation is observed. These three biowindows (right) show the emergence and ripening (light blue to red to dark blue) of wheat in May, July and August.

Part 2

MAKING AND SHAPING THE EARTH

The structure and substance of the Earth
Forces that move continents · Forces that fashion Earth's landscapes
How man has changed the face of the Earth

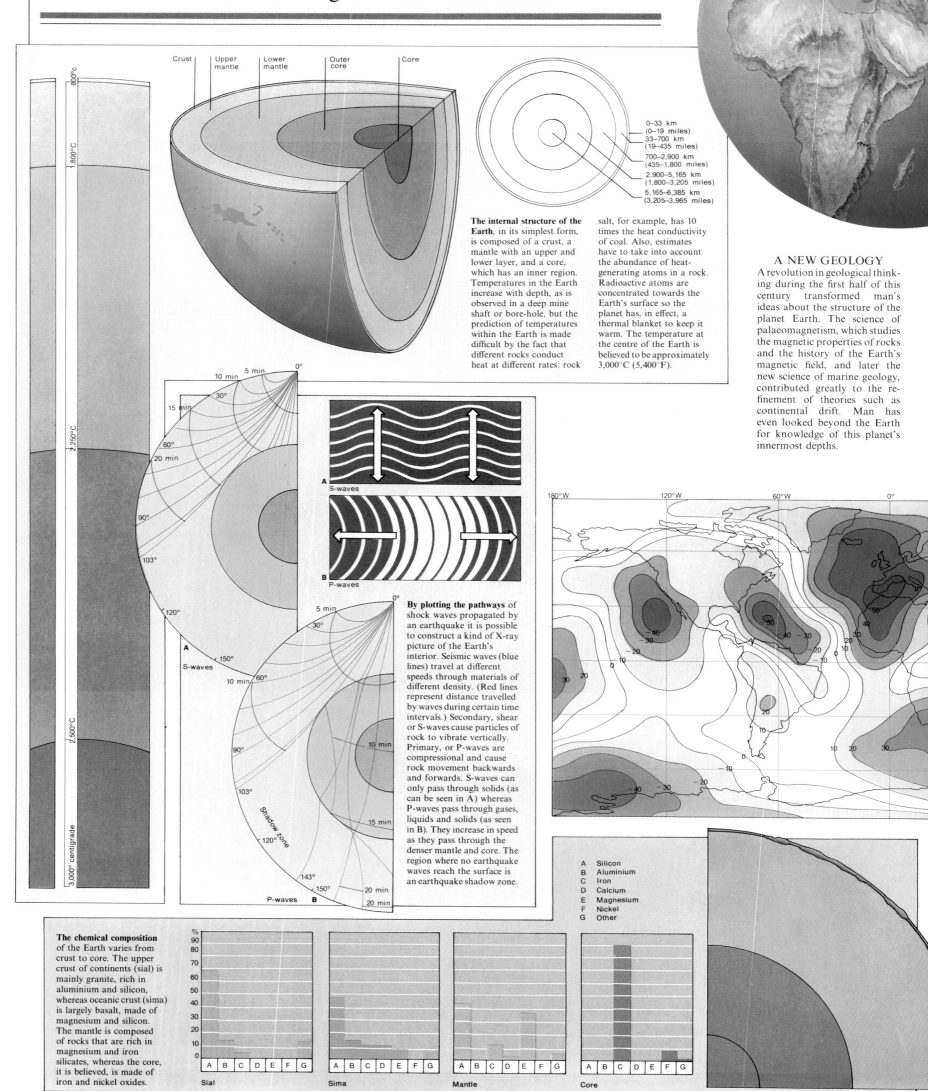

Crust | Upper mantle | Lower mantle | Outer core | Core

0–33 km
(0–19 miles)
33–700 km
(19–435 miles)
700–2,900 km
(435–1,800 miles)
2,900–5,165 km
(1,800–3,205 miles)
5,165–6,385 km
(3,205–3,965 miles)

The internal structure of the Earth, in its simplest form, is composed of a crust, a mantle with an upper and lower layer, and a core, which has an inner region. Temperatures in the Earth increase with depth, as is observed in a deep mine shaft or bore-hole, but the prediction of temperatures within the Earth is made difficult by the fact that different rocks conduct heat at different rates: rock salt, for example, has 10 times the heat conductivity of coal. Also, estimates have to take into account the abundance of heat-generating atoms in a rock. Radioactive atoms are concentrated towards the Earth's surface so the planet has, in effect, a thermal blanket to keep it warm. The temperature at the centre of the Earth is believed to be approximately 3,000°C (5,400°F).

A NEW GEOLOGY

A revolution in geological thinking during the first half of this century transformed man's ideas about the structure of the planet Earth. The science of palaeomagnetism, which studies the magnetic properties of rocks and the history of the Earth's magnetic field, and later the new science of marine geology, contributed greatly to the refinement of theories such as continental drift. Man has even looked beyond the Earth for knowledge of this planet's innermost depths.

By plotting the pathways of shock waves propagated by an earthquake it is possible to construct a kind of X-ray picture of the Earth's interior. Seismic waves (blue lines) travel at different speeds through materials of different density. (Red lines represent distance travelled by waves during certain time intervals.) Secondary, shear or S-waves cause particles of rock to vibrate vertically. Primary, or P-waves are compressional and cause rock movement backwards and forwards. S-waves can only pass through solids (as can be seen in A) whereas P-waves pass through gases, liquids and solids (as seen in B). They increase in speed as they pass through the denser mantle and core. The region where no earthquake waves reach the surface is an earthquake shadow zone.

A Silicon
B Aluminium
C Iron
D Calcium
E Magnesium
F Nickel
G Other

The chemical composition of the Earth varies from crust to core. The upper crust of continents (sial) is mainly granite, rich in aluminium and silicon, whereas oceanic crust (sima) is largely basalt, made of magnesium and silicon. The mantle is composed of rocks that are rich in magnesium and iron silicates, whereas the core, it is believed, is made of iron and nickel oxides.

Sial | Sima | Mantle | Core

Earth's Structure

The Earth is made up of concentric shells of different kinds of material. Immediately beneath us is the crust; below that is the mantle; and at the centre of the globe is the core. Knowledge of the internal structure of Earth is the key to an understanding of the substances of Earth and an appreciation of the forces at work, not only deep in the centre of the planet but also affecting the formation of surface features and large-scale landscapes. The workings of all these elements are inextricably linked.

A 17th-century diagram of the Earth shows an internal structure of fire and subterranean rivers.

Our knowledge of the Earth is largely restricted to the outer crust. The deepest hole that man has drilled reaches only 10 km (6 miles)—less than 1/600th of the planet's radius—and so our knowledge about the rest of the Earth has had to come via indirect means: by the study of earthquake waves, and a comparison between rocks on Earth and those that make up meteorites—small fragments of asteroids and other minor planetary bodies that originated from similar materials to the Earth.

The Earth's crust
The outermost layer of the Earth is called the crust. The crust beneath the oceans is different from the material that makes up continental crust. Ocean crust is formed at mid-ocean ridges where melted rocks (magma) from the mantle rise up in great quantities and solidify to form a layer a few kilometres thick over the mantle. As this ocean crust spreads out from the ridge it becomes covered with deep-ocean sediments. The ocean crust was initially called "sima", a word made up from the first two letters of the characteristic elements—silicon and magnesium. Sima has a density of 2.9 gm/cc (1 gm/cc is the density of water).

Continental crust was named "sial"—from silicon and aluminium, the most abundant elements. Sial is lighter than sima with a density of 2.7 gm/cc. The continental crust is like a series of giant rafts, 17 to 70 km (9–43 miles) thick. As a result of numerous collisions and breakages, these continental rafts have been bulldozed into their present shape, but they have been forming for at least 4,000 million years. The oldest known rocks, in Greenland, are 3,750 million years old, which is only about 800 million years younger than the Earth itself. The complex history of the continents' evolution over this vast time span makes construction of an ideal cross-section difficult, but the rocks of the lower two-thirds of the crust appear to be denser (2.9 gm/cc) than the upper levels.

The Moho, or Mohorovičić discontinuity, discovered in 1909, marks the base of the crust and the beginning of the mantle rocks, where the density increases from 2.9 to 3.3 gm/cc. The Moho is at an average depth of 10 km (6 miles) under the sea and 35 km (20 miles) below land.

The mantle
Our knowledge of the mantle comes from mantle rocks that are sometimes brought to the surface. These are even more enriched in magnesium oxides than the sima, with lesser amounts of iron and calcium oxides. The uppermost mantle to a depth of between 60 and 100 km (40–60 miles), together with the overlying crust, forms the rigid lithosphere, which is divided into plates. Below this is a pasty

layer, or asthenosphere, extending to a depth of 700 km (435 miles). The upper mantle is separated from the lower mantle by another discontinuity where the density of the rock increases from 3.3 to 4.3 gm/cc.

Scientists now believe that the mantle is the planetary motor force behind the movements of the continents. By studying in detail the chemistry of the volcanic rocks that have come directly from the mantle, they have gathered much information about this mantle motor. The rocks that come up along oceanic ridges and form new oceanic crust reveal by their chemical composition that they have formed from mantle that has undergone previous melting. By contrast, islands such as Hawaii and Iceland have formed from mantle material that, for the most part, has never been melted before. One explanation for these chemical observations is that, while the top 700 km (435 miles) of the mantle region is moving in accordance with movement of the plates, the mantle beneath it is moving independently and sending occasional rivers of unaltered material through the surface to form islands like volcanic Hawaii.

The core
Structurally, the most important boundary in the Earth lies at a depth of 2,900 km (1,800 miles) below the surface, where the rock density almost doubles from about 5.5 to 9.9 gm/cc. This is known as the Gutenberg discontinuity and was discovered in 1914. Below this level the material must have the properties of a liquid since certain earthquake waves cannot penetrate it. Scientists infer from the composition of meteorites, some of which are composed of iron and nickel, that this deep core material is composed largely of iron, with some nickel and perhaps lighter elements such as silicon. The processes involved in the formation of a planet have been compared to the separation of the metals (the core) from the slag (the mantle and crust) in a blast furnace.

The core has a radius of 3,485 km (2,165 miles) and makes up only one-sixth of the Earth's volume, yet it has one-third of its mass. In the middle of the liquid outer core there is an even denser ball with a radius of 1,220 km (760 miles)—two-thirds the size of the Moon—where, under intense pressure, the metals have solidified. The inner core is believed to be solid iron and nickel and is 20 per cent denser (12–13 gm/cc) than the surrounding liquid.

Electric currents in the core are the only possible source of the Earth's magnetic field. This drifts and alters in a way which could arise only from some deeply buried fluid movement. At the top of the core, the pattern of the field moves about 100 m (330 ft) west each day. Every million years or so during the Earth's history, the north–south magnetic poles have switched so that compasses pointed south, not north.

The dynamo that generates magnetism and its strange variations is still not fully understood. Motion in the core may be powered by giant slabs of metal that crystallize out from the liquid and sink to join the inner core. Our knowledge of the Earth's structure has increased greatly over the last 50 years, but many intriguing questions remain to be answered.

The Earth is not a sphere but an ellipsoid (below) that is flattened at the poles, where the radius is 6,378 km (3,960 miles), and bulging at the Equator, where the radius is 6,536 km (4,060 miles). This results from the Earth's rapid rotation. But, rather than a perfect ellipsoid, the true shape is a "geoid"—the actual shape of sea level—which is lumpy, with variations away from ellipsoid of up to 80 m (260 ft) (left). This reflects major variations in density in Earth's outer layers.

The Earth as a Geoid

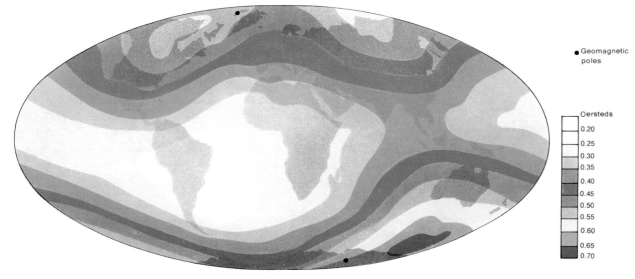

Geomagnetic poles

Oersteds
0.20
0.25
0.30
0.35
0.40
0.45
0.50
0.55
0.60
0.65
0.70

The Earth's magnetic field is strongest at the poles and weakest in equatorial regions. If the field were simply like a bar magnet inside the globe, lines of intensity would mirror lines of latitude; but the field is inclined at an angle of 11° to the Earth's axis. The geomagnetic poles are similarly inclined and they do not coincide with the geographic poles. In reality, the field is much more complex than that of a bar magnet. In addition, over long periods of time, the magnetic poles and the north–south orientation of the field change slowly. The strength of the Earth's magnetic field is measured in units called oersteds.

Earth's Moving Crust

The top layer of the Earth is known as the lithosphere and is composed of the crust and the uppermost mantle. It is divided into six major rigid plates and several smaller platelets that move relative to each other, driven by movements that lie deep in the Earth's liquid mantle. The plate boundaries correspond to the zones of earthquakes and the sites of active volcanoes. The concept of plate tectonics – that the Earth's crust is mobile despite being rigid – emerged in the 1960s and helped to confirm the early twentieth-century theory of continental drift proposed by Alfred Wegener.

THE DYNAMIC EARTH

As early as the 17th century, the English philosopher Francis Bacon noted that the coasts on either side of the Atlantic were similar and could be fitted together like pieces of a jig-saw puzzle. Three hundred years later Alfred Wegener proposed the theory of continental drift, but no one would believe the Earth's rigid crust could move. Today, geological evidence has provided the basis for the theory of plate tectonics, which demonstrates that the Earth's crust is slowly but continually moving.

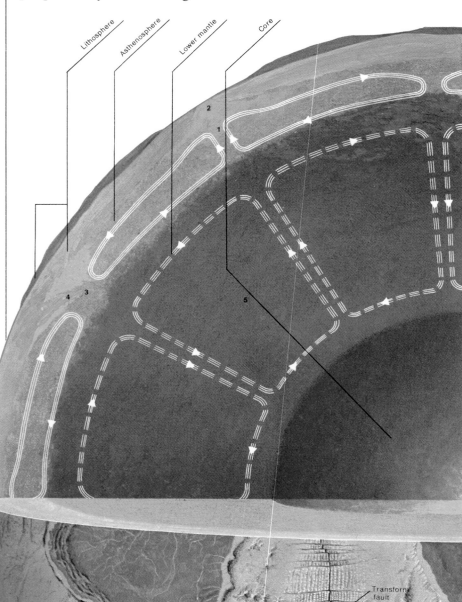

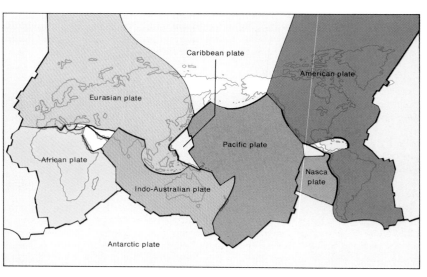

Earth's lithosphere—the rocky shell, or crust—is made up of six major plates and several smaller platelets, each separated from each other by ridges, subduction zones or transcurrent faults. The plates grow bigger by accretion along the mid-ocean ridges, are destroyed at subduction zones beneath the trenches, and slide beside each other along the transcurrent faults. The African and Antarctic plates have no trenches along their borders to destroy any of their crust, so they are growing bigger. This growth is compensated by the subduction zone that is developing to the north of the Tonga Islands and subduction zones in the Pacific. Conversely, the Pacific and Indo-Australian plates are shrinking. Along the plate boundaries magma wells up from the mantle to form volcanoes. Here, too, are the origins of earthquakes as the plates collide or slide slowly past each other.

The motor that drives the lithospheric plates is found deep in the mantle. The simplified model at the top of the globe shows how this may work. Due to temperature differences in the mantle, slow convection currents circulate. Where two current cycles move upwards together and separate (1), the plates bulge and move apart along mid-ocean ridges (2). Where there is a downward moving current (3), the plates move together and sometimes one slips under the other to form a subduction zone (4). Another model proposes that the convection currents are found deep in the mantle (5). Only time and more research, however, will reveal the true mechanism of plate movement.

Subduction zones are the sites of destruction of the ocean crust. As one plate passes beneath another down into the mantle, the ocean floor is pulled downward and a deep ocean trench is formed. The movement taking place along the length of the subduction zone causes earthquakes, while melting of the rock at depth produces magma that rises to create the volcanoes that form island arcs.

An oceanic ridge is formed when two plates move away from each other. As they move, molten magma from the mantle forces its way to the surface. This magma cools and is in turn injected with new magma. Thus the oceanic ridge is gradually forming the newest part of Earth's crust.

Transform, or transcurrent, faults are found where two plates slide past each other. They may, for example, link two parts of a ridge (A, B). A study of the magnetic properties of the sea bed may suggest a motion shown by the white arrows, but the true movements of the plates are shown by the red arrows. The transform fault is active only between points (2) and (3). Between points (1) and (2) and between (3) and (4) the scar of the fault is healed and the line of the fault is no longer a plate boundary.

The early evidence for continental drift was gathered by Alfred Wegener, a German meteorologist. He noticed that the coastlines on each side of the Atlantic Ocean could be made to fit together, and that much of the geological history of the flanking continents—shown by fossils, structures and past climates—also seemed to match. Wegener compared the two sides of the Atlantic with a sheet of torn newspaper and reasoned that if not just one line of print but 10 lines match then there is a good case for arguing that the two sides were once joined. Yet for 50 years continental drift was generally considered to be a fanciful dream.

Sea-floor spreading
In the 1950s the first geological surveys of the oceans began, and a 60,000 km (37,200 mile) long chain of mountains was discovered running down the centre of the Atlantic Ocean, all round the Antarctic, up to the Indian Ocean, into the Red Sea and up the Eastern Pacific Ocean into Alaska. Along the axis of this mid-ocean ridge system there was often a narrow, deep rift valley. In places this ridge was offset along sharp fractures in the ocean floor.

The breakthrough in developing the global plate tectonic theory came with the first large-scale survey of the ocean floor. Magnetometers, which were developed during World War II for tracking submarines, showed the ocean floor to be magnetically striped. The ocean floor reveals magnetic characteristics because the ocean crust basalts are full of tiny crystals of the magnetic mineral magnetite. As the basalt cooled, the magnetic field of these crystals aligned itself with the Earth's magnetic field. This would be insignificant if it were not for the fact that the magnetic pole of the Earth has switched from north to south at different times in the past. Half the magnetite compasses of the ocean floor point south rather than north.

In the middle 1960s, two Cambridge geophysicists, Drummond Matthews and Fred Vine, noticed that the pattern of stripes was symmetrical around the mid-ocean ridge. Such an extraordinary and unlikely symmetry could mean only one thing—any two matching stripes must originally have been formed together at the mid-ocean ridge and then moved away from each other as newer crust formed between them to create new stripes. It was soon calculated that the North Atlantic Ocean was growing wider by about 2 cm (¾ in) a year. At last, drifting continents was accepted.

Consumption of the sea floor
Sea-floor spreading soon became included in an even more sensational model—plate tectonics. If the oceans are growing wider, then either the whole planet is expanding or the spreading ocean floor is consumed elsewhere. In the late 1950s a global network of seismic stations had been set up to monitor nuclear explosions and earthquakes. For the first time the positions of all earthquakes could be accurately defined.

It was found that the zones of earthquake activity were predominantly narrow, following the mid-ocean ridges and extending along the rim of the Pacific, beneath the island arcs of the

West Pacific and beneath the continental margins in the East Pacific as well as underlying the Alpine-Himalayan Mountain Belt. The seismic zones around the Pacific dipped away from the ocean and continued to depths as great as 700 km (430 miles). They intercepted the surface at the curious arc-shaped deep-ocean trenches. It had been known for 20 years that the pull of gravity over these trenches is strangely reduced, so to survive they must continually be dragged downwards. Here was the site of ocean-floor consumption—now known as a subduction zone. Subduction zones must be efficient at consuming ocean crust because no known ocean crust is older than 200 million years—less than five per cent of Earth's lifetime.

The oceanic lithosphere (the Earth's rocky crust) is extraordinarily rigid. Even where the oceanic lithosphere becomes consumed within subduction zones it still maintains its rigidity. As it bends down into the Earth it tends to corrugate, forming very long folds. These corrugations give rise to the pattern of chains of deep-ocean trenches and chains of volcanic islands formed above the subduction zone.

As oceanic lithosphere grows older it cools, contracts and sinks. From the depth of the ocean floor it is possible to make an accurate estimate of the age of the crust beneath. Even the steepness of the subduction zone is a function of the age, and therefore the density, of the lithosphere. The oldest crust provides the strongest downward pull and hence the steepest angle of dip of the subduction zone.

As well as the spreading ridges (constructive margins) and the subduction zones (destructive margins) there is one other kind of plate boundary (conservative margins), where the plates slip past one another along a major fault such as the San Andreas Fault of California.

The past positions of the continents
Continental drift is thus the result of the creation and destruction of oceanic lithosphere, but only the continents can record the oceanic plate motions taking place more than 200 million years ago. The discovery of ancient lines of subduction zone volcanoes can testify to the destruction of long gone oceans. One particularly important technique for finding the positions of the continents is to study the magnetism of certain rocks, particularly lavas, that record the position of the north-south magnetic poles at the time when the rock cooled. If the rock "compass" points, for example, west, then the continent must have rotated by 90°. The vertical dip of the rock compass can reveal the approximate latitude of the rock at its formation (the dip increases from horizontal at the Equator to vertical at the magnetic poles).

As longitude is entirely arbitrary (defined on the position of Greenwich) one can only hope to gain the relative positions of the continents with regard to one another. The best additional information is provided by studies of fossils—if the remains of shallow-water marine organisms are very different then they must have been separated by an ocean. The full impact of continental drift on the development of land animals and plants is only beginning to be realized.

Magnetic surveys of the sea bed helped build the plate tectonics theory. Research vessels equipped with magnetometers sailed back and forth over a mid-ocean ridge and recorded the varying magnetism of the sea bed. The Earth's magnetic pole has switched from north to south at different times in the past, and this mapping revealed a striped magnetic pattern on the sea bed. It was noticed that the stripes on either side of the ridge were symmetrical. The explanation was that the matching stripes must have formed together and moved apart as more crust was injected between them—a notion that was subsequently supported by dating of the sea floor.

3   2   1   0   1   2   3

Time in millions of years

THE DRIFTING CONTINENTS
It is now accepted that the continents have changed their positions during the past millions of years, and by studying the magnetism preserved in the rocks the configuration of the continents has been plotted for various geological times. The sequence of continental drifting, illustrated below, begins with one single landmass—the so-called supercontinent Pangaea—and the ancestral Pacific Ocean, called the Panthalassa Ocean. Pangaea first split into a northern landmass called Laurasia and a southern block called Gondwanaland, and subsequently into the continents we see today. The maps illustrate the positions of the continents in the past, where they are now and their predicted positions in 50 million years' time.

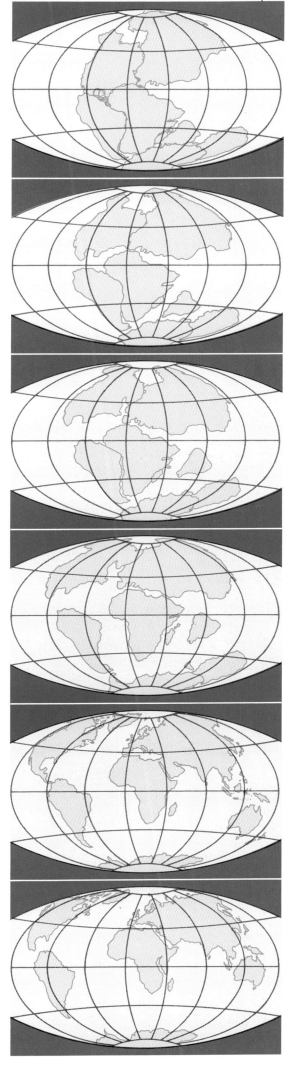

225 million years ago one large landmass, the supercontinent Pangaea, exists and Panthalassa forms the ancestral Pacific Ocean. The Tethys Sea separates Eurasia and Africa and forms an ancestor of the Mediterranean Sea.

180 million years ago Pangaea splits up, the northern block of continents, Laurasia, drifts northwards and the southern block, Gondwanaland, begins to break up. India separates and the South American-African block divides from Australia-Antarctica. New ocean floor is created between the continents.

135 million years ago the Indian plate continues its northward drift and Eurasia rotates to begin to close the eastern end of the Tethys Sea. The North Atlantic and the Indian Ocean have opened up and the South Atlantic is just beginning to form.

65 million years ago Madagascar has split from Africa and the Tethys Sea has closed, with the Mediterranean Sea opening behind it. The South Atlantic Ocean has opened up considerably, but Australia is still joined to the Antarctic and India is about to collide with Asia.

The present day: India has completed its northward migration and collided with Asia, Australia has set itself free from Antarctica, and North America has freed itself from Eurasia to leave Greenland between them. During the past 65 million years (a relatively short geological span of time) nearly half of the present-day ocean floor has been created.

50 million years in the future, Australia may continue its northward drift, part of East Africa will separate from the mainland, and California west of the San Andreas Fault will separate from North America and move northwards. The Pacific Ocean will become smaller, compensating for the increase in size of both the Atlantic and Indian oceans. The Mediterranean Sea will disappear as Africa moves to the north.

Folds, Faults and Mountain Chains

The continents are great rafts of lighter rock that float in the mantle of the Earth. When drifting continents collide, great mountain chains are thrown up as the continental crust is forced to thicken to absorb the impact of the collision. The highest mountains are formed out of thick piles of sediment that are built up from the debris of erosion constantly washed off the land and deposited on the continental margins. Through the massive deformations of rock faults and folds these remains of old mountains become recycled, thus building new mountains from the remains of old ones.

For the formation of **mountain ranges** such as the Appalachians or the Himalayas, or the Caledonian mountain chain of Norway, Scotland and Newfoundland, the pattern of development is very much the same. First, a widening ocean with passive margins is located between two continents.

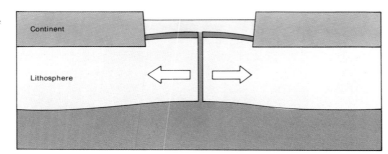

As more **ocean floor is created** the continents move farther apart, and at the edge of each continent sediment accumulates from the debris of erosion. These piles of thick sediment are known as sedimentary basins.

For the formation of the **Appalachians**, the ancestral Atlantic Ocean began to close, a subduction zone was formed at the ocean–continent boundary, and the oceanic lithosphere began to be absorbed into the mantle. Magma intruded to form granite "plutons" and volcanoes, and much of the sedimentary basin was metamorphosed.

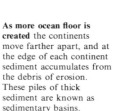
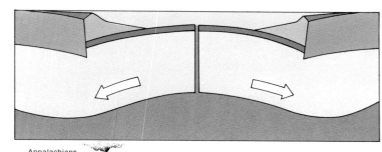

The ocean **continued to close** until North America and Africa were joined together, further compressing the sediments in the sedimentary basin at the passive ocean margin. The two continents were joined like this between 350 and 225 million years ago.

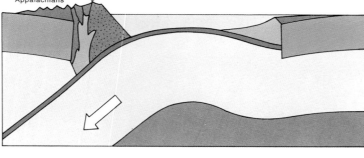

About 180 **million years ago**, after the original Appalachians had been worn down in size, the present Atlantic Ocean opened along a new break in the continental crust, offset from the line of the original mountains. As the continents split, so the crust became stretched along great curved faults.

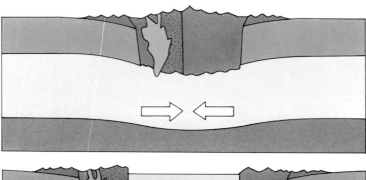

Parts of the **ancient Appalachian mountains** have been eroded to sea level, leaving the Appalachians, that formed on the edge of the old continent, inland.

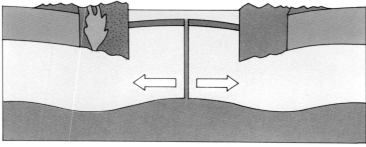

 Continental shelf
 Granite
Metamorphic rock
Sediment
Ocean crust

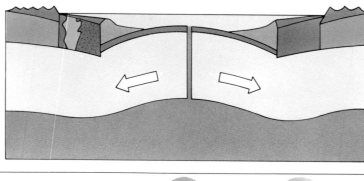

BIRTH AND DEATH OF A MOUNTAIN

Mountains are thrust upwards by the pressure exerted by the moving plates of the Earth's crust, and are formed out of the sediments that have been eroded from the continental masses. Young mountains are lofty and much folded, but the agents of erosion and weathering soon begin to reduce their height, and over many millions of years the mountain range is eroded to sea level. This eroded material accumulates in the sea at the edge of the continents and becomes the building material for another phase of mountain building.

ISOSTASY

The continents float in the Earth's mantle, and because they are only slightly less dense (2.67 g/cc compared to 3.27 g/cc), 85% of their bulk lies below sea level. Thus the higher the mountain the deeper the mountain root. And as the crust can exist only to a maximum depth of about 70 km (43 miles) before it is liquefied in the mantle, mountains can never rise above a maximum of 10 km (6 miles) above sea level.

Folds are generally related to underlying faults. The commonest simple folds are monoclines, formed when a single fault exhibits underlying movement. With continued movement a simple symmetrical anticline (1) may fold unevenly to form an asymmetric anticline (2). More movement bends the strata further into a recumbent fold (3) and eventually the strata break to form an overthrust fold (4). Over a long period an overthrust fold may be pushed many kilometres from its original position to form a nappe (5). Faults are generally of three kinds: faults of tension known as normal faults, when one block drops down (6); faults of horizontal shear (7), known as strike-slip faults; and faults of compression (8), known as thrust faults.

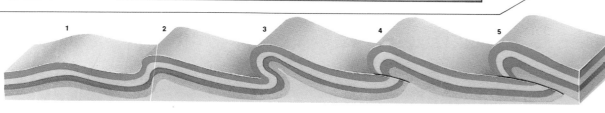

Continents float in the Earth's mantle like icebergs in the sea—more than four-fifths of their bulk lies beneath the surface. The continental crust is 28 km (17 miles) thick at sea level, and where mountains rise above this level there is a corresponding thickening in the crust beneath. The maximum thickness of crust is 70 km (43 miles), so mountains can only ever rise to a maximum height of approximately 10 km (6 miles) above sea level. This relation between upper and underlying crust is known as isostasy, or state of equal pressure.

As mountains become eroded, the process of isostatic rebound allows them to recover about 85 cm (34 in) for every 1 metre (40 in) removed. When, after about 100 million years, a major mountain range has been eroded down to sea level, the rocks exposed at the surface are those that were 15–25 km (9–15 miles) underground when the mountains were at their highest. Such rocks are coarsely crystalline, and make up the fabric of the old, tough continental crust.

Sedimentary basins
As early as the nineteenth century it was noticed that the biggest mountains formed where there had previously been the thickest pile of sediments. According to the principle of isostasy, a thick pile of sediments can form only where the Earth's crust is thin and sinking. The Aegean Sea in the eastern Mediterranean, for example, is at present being pulled apart, and therefore becoming thinner. Over the next few million years, as the Aegean crust sinks, a thick pile of sediments—a sedimentary basin—will accumulate. Most sedimentary basins are at present shallow seas, and form the continental shelves. The depth of water over these shelf seas has been determined by the erosion that accompanied the lowest sea levels of the past 100 million years—about 140 m (460 ft) below the present sea level.

Mountain building
When continents collide, it is the regions of stretched crust that are the first to absorb some of the impact. Such a former sedimentary basin is being turned into the Zagros Mountains of southwestern Iran as Arabia advances northeastwards into Asia. The individual blocks of continental crust appear to be sliding back along curved faults, and the sediments that have built up over the thinned crust are now being forced into folds.

Early in the life of such a sedimentary basin sea water may become cut off from the ocean and evaporate to form extensive deposits of salt. Such salt deposits reduce friction and allow the folded pile of sediments overlying the continental blocks to become disconnected and to slide up to 100 km (62 miles) away from the collision zone. In the Zagros Mountains this process has only just begun, but in older mountain ranges, such as the Canadian Rockies or the European Alps, the formation of nappes—disconnected sediment piles forced ahead of the main compression zone—has been widespread.

As mountain ranges often form out of the sedimentary basins along the boundaries between a continent and the ocean, new mountains tend to add on to the fringes of the continents. In North America, for example, the oldest remnants of ranges that make up large tracts of the Canadian shield are found in the centre of the continent, while the process of mountain building is continuing in the west.

Other continents show a more complex pattern of mountain ranges through subsequent phases of splitting and amalgamation, and the Himalayas and the Urals have formed where smaller continents have come together to make up the continent of Asia.

The boundary between the continent and the ocean along the western coast of the Atlantic Ocean is not a plate boundary and is therefore termed passive, in contrast to active boundaries such as the eastern coast of the Pacific Ocean, where the ocean plate is moving down into the mantle at a subduction zone beneath the Andean mountain chain. The highest Andean mountains are tall volcanoes of andesite (formed from magmas pouring off the underlying subduction zone). The bulk of the mountain range consists of enormous underground batholiths, in which the magma has solidified before being able to erupt, and compressed and uplifted sedimentary basins formed along the continental margin.

The crustal region immediately beyond the volcanoes that form above subduction zones, however, is very often in tension, and in the process of being pulled apart. This appears to be caused by mantle material being dragged down with the oceanic lithosphere. Small ocean basins, such as the Sea of Japan, may open up under such conditions.

Folds and faults
When movement of the Earth's crust has taken place along a planar fracture through sedimentary rocks, it can be easily identified by the breaks in the layers, and such planes of movement are known as faults. Folds form where rock layers bend rather than break. Generally, faults form when rocks are brittle, and folds are found when rocks are plastic.

Sediments close to the surface are often so soft that they behave plastically, as do rocks at depths greater than 15–20 km (9–12 miles) where the continental crust is of sufficiently high temperature and pressure for slow rock flow to take place. Thus most continental faults are found between these levels. All major folds found in soft sediments apparently have a fault of some kind beneath them, and it is the failure of the fault to pass right through to the surface that creates the fold.

Folds are often extremely complicated and some geologists have tended to describe them in extraordinary detail, but in fact they are little more than brush strokes in the overall picture. Pre-existing faults beneath the folds tend to determine the folds' orientation. Once a continental fault has formed it provides a plane of weakness wherever the continental crust is subject to stress. Many faults around the Mediterranean Sea came into existence during a period of tension, and these are now being reactivated and produce the large earthquakes associated with the continuing collision of Africa with Europe.

At the end of all the complications and intricacies of continental collision, the final phase of mountain building—that involving uplift—remains perhaps the least understood. In the last two million years, for example, while man has been increasingly active on Earth, 2,500,000 sq km (almost 1,000,000 sq miles) of Tibet has risen 4,000 m (2 miles). But the origin of such gigantic and rapid movement lies within the Earth's mantle.

The highest mountains are the product of continental collisions. As the rocks are squeezed, folded and faulted, the original continental crust becomes shortened and thickened. Although the overall extent and height of mountain chains is controlled by mountain building, the whole range can only be viewed from a spacecraft. For the earthbound mountain visitor the familiar shapes of peaks and valleys are those formed by mountain destruction (1). Snow at high altitudes consolidates to form ice that moves slowly downhill in the form of glaciers. To wear away a mountain range at an average of 5 km (3 miles) above sea level requires the removal of more than 20 km (12 miles) of rock, as the thick continental crust that floats in the underlying mantle rises to compensate for the loss of surface mass. Half-eroded mountains (2), such as the Appalachians, pictured above, may linger on for tens of millions of years until, like large regions of the Canadian interior, the mountains are all eroded away and only the hard crystalline surface rocks that were once buried 20 km (12 miles) underground remain (3).

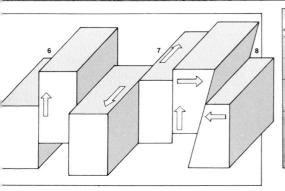

Rock Formation and History

All the rocks on Earth are interrelated through the rock cycle – a never-ending chain of processes that forms and modifies rocks and minerals on the Earth's surface, in its crust and in the mantle. These events are powered both by energy from the Sun and the heat of the Earth itself, and the processes include the forces of nature – from wind and water to the movements of the continents. This geological cycle of creation and destruction is one of the most distinctive features of our planet. Each feature of geological activity, each agent of landscape-making is but a stage of the continuing rock cycle.

CONSTANT CHANGE
The processes of formation and destruction of the three basic rock types—igneous, sedimentary and metamorphic—are linked in an interminable cycle of change. Igneous rocks are thrown up from inside the Earth, are eroded and eventually laid down as sediments. As accumulated sediments sink into the Earth, they are changed by heat and pressure—metamorphosed—before surfacing again in the processes of mountain building.

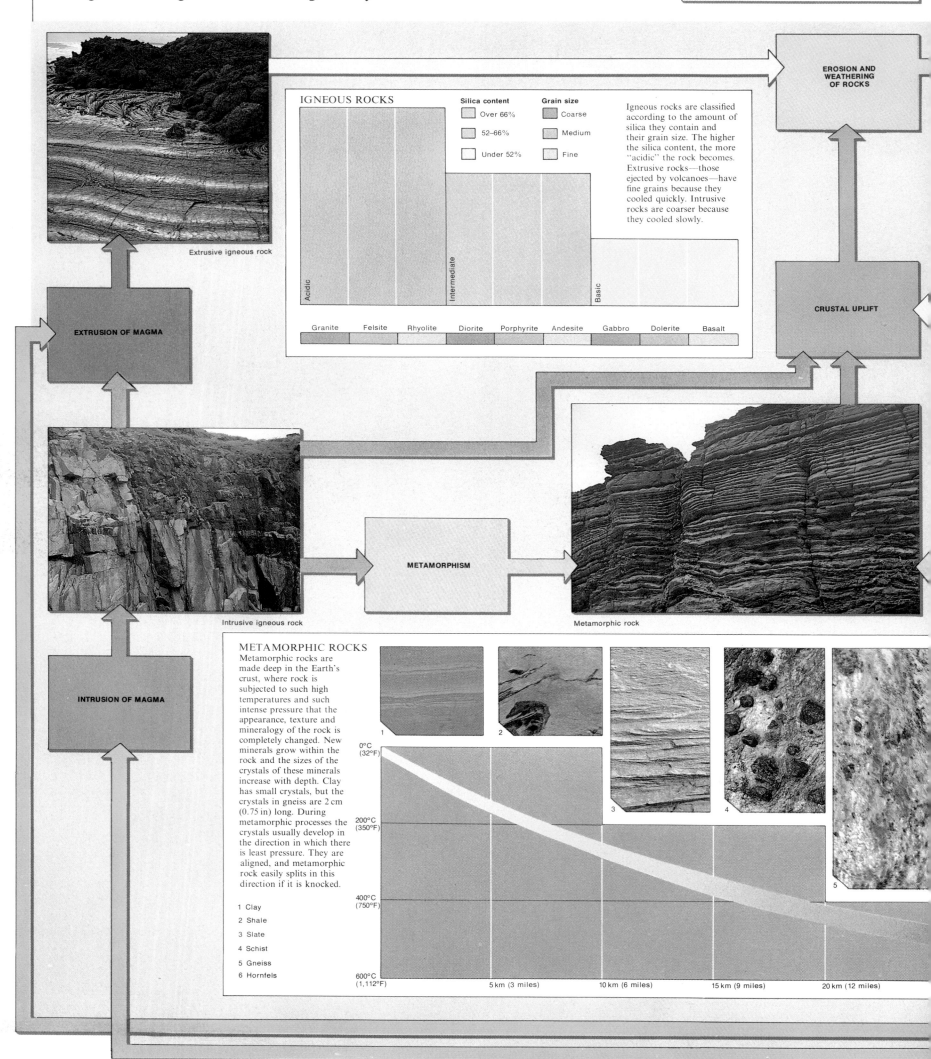

Extrusive igneous rock

EROSION AND WEATHERING OF ROCKS

EXTRUSION OF MAGMA

IGNEOUS ROCKS

Silica content
- Over 66%
- 52–66%
- Under 52%

Grain size
- Coarse
- Medium
- Fine

Igneous rocks are classified according to the amount of silica they contain and their grain size. The higher the silica content, the more "acidic" the rock becomes. Extrusive rocks—those ejected by volcanoes—have fine grains because they cooled quickly. Intrusive rocks are coarser because they cooled slowly.

Acidic   Intermediate   Basic

Granite   Felsite   Rhyolite   Diorite   Porphyrite   Andesite   Gabbro   Dolerite   Basalt

CRUSTAL UPLIFT

Intrusive igneous rock

METAMORPHISM

Metamorphic rock

INTRUSION OF MAGMA

METAMORPHIC ROCKS
Metamorphic rocks are made deep in the Earth's crust, where rock is subjected to such high temperatures and such intense pressure that the appearance, texture and mineralogy of the rock is completely changed. New minerals grow within the rock and the sizes of the crystals of these minerals increase with depth. Clay has small crystals, but the crystals in gneiss are 2 cm (0.75 in) long. During metamorphic processes the crystals usually develop in the direction in which there is least pressure. They are aligned, and metamorphic rock easily splits in this direction if it is knocked.

1 Clay
2 Shale
3 Slate
4 Schist
5 Gneiss
6 Hornfels

0°C (32°F)
200°C (350°F)
400°C (750°F)
600°C (1,112°F)

5 km (3 miles)   10 km (6 miles)   15 km (9 miles)   20 km (12 miles)

SEDIMENTARY ROCKS

Sediments can be turned into rock by means of three main processes. Cementation is the term used when water percolates between grains of sand. As it does so, any iron oxide, silica or calcium carbonate that were in solution are deposited in thin layers around the grains, thus cementing them into a hard sandstone (1). As more sediment is laid down, the increasing weight of the sediments on top exerts pressure on the underlying layers. Water is squeezed out and a dense rock is formed (2) by the process of compaction. This is the way clay becomes mudstone. Finally, during mountain-building processes forces are exerted on rock minerals that cause them to recrystallize into a solid mass of rock (3) that has no spaces between its mineral constituents.

TRANSPORTATION AND DEPOSITION OF SEDIMENTS

BURIAL AND FORMATION OF ROCK FROM SEDIMENTS (LITHIFICATION)

Sedimentary rock

METAMORPHISM

MELTING

25 km (15 miles)   30 km (18 miles)

All the rocks on Earth are formed at one stage or another in what is known as the rock cycle. All high ground on the continents suffers erosion; the eroded material is transported and deposited on lower ground; in time, these sediments may be elevated by mountain-building processes and so, in turn, become eroded. If, between their formation and destruction, sediments pass deep into the Earth's crust, they may be transformed by heat or pressure into metamorphic rock; or, at even greater depths, they may melt to form yet another kind of rock—igneous rock.

Materials at the bottom of a thick pile of sediments may be heated enough to melt. If this material then cools and solidifies underground, it is called plutonic rock. Sometimes, however, it escapes to the surface by means of a short cut—a volcano—to become part of the rock cycle. On the other hand, some sediments are lost off the edge of the continents on to the deep ocean floor, and they disappear into the mantle of the Earth by means of the downward movements of the oceanic crust. A measure of the difference between the input and the output of the continental rock cycle is a measure of how fast the continental crust is increasing or decreasing. Scientists believe it is increasing—at a rate of between 0.1 and 1.0 cu km a year.

Types of rock
The range of rock types found on the continents has been classified under three headings: sedimentary, igneous and metamorphic. Sedimentary rocks include all those formed at low temperatures on the Earth's surface; igneous rocks have all solidified from molten rock, or magma; and metamorphic rocks are sedimentary or igneous rocks that have changed their nature under conditions of high temperature and pressure.

There is a certain amount of difficulty in defining the boundaries between the different types. Ash formed from solidified magma falling out of the air after a volcanic eruption is igneous, but what if it should move downhill in a mudslide? If a metamorphic rock is deeply buried it may start to melt and form a "migmatite", which is part liquid and part solid. Is this igneous? And where does the boundary lie between a deeply buried sediment and a metamorphic rock? Coal seams that have been thoroughly metamorphosed from their original peat deposits are found as layers in unaltered sandstones. This classification does, however, provide a useful preliminary guide to understanding the nature of different types of rock.

Rock types are defined by studying their texture, the way they were formed, and their composition. There are interesting textural similarities between evaporites—salt deposits formed as an inland sea dries up—and some plutonic igneous rocks. Both have crystallized

directly from a liquid. There are similarities between sandstones and plutonic "cumulates", which form at the base of enormous magma reservoirs where strong magma currents deposit thick layers of crystals. So rock types must be defined in terms of more than just texture.

Rock formation
The simplest sedimentary rocks are those made up of whole fragments of eroded material. "Scree" deposits that accumulate at the base of a cliff or a steep valley side from angular rock fragments that have broken off the rock face above can make a sedimentary "breccia". A rock made from rounded stream pebbles is a "conglomerate". Further erosion reduces the rock into three components: dissolved ions (atoms with an electrical charge) such as those of calcium or magnesium; mineral grains (sand) that cannot be broken down chemically, such as quartz; and a variety of minerals containing sheet-like layers of silicate and alumina (silicon and aluminium oxides)—the minerals that are often the main constituents of clays.

A river carrying these minerals first deposits the sand, and then the clay, while the dissolved ions pass out into the sea, where some are absorbed by living organisms and used to construct protective shells and rigid skeletons. When the creatures die, the shells and bones again become part of the rock cycle, building up great thicknesses of limestone.

Igneous rocks are chemically far more complex than are sedimentary rocks, but are texturally simpler. The slower the magma cools, the larger are the crystals that form within it. If it cools too quickly it may not crystallize at all, forming instead a super-cooled liquid, or glass. A plutonic igneous rock—one cooled deep underground—is coarse-grained; a volcanic rock is fine-grained. A rock can, however, have both large and small crystals, testifying to a more complex history.

The most striking feature of Earth magmas is their uniformity. With few exceptions, they are all rich in silica. The greater the silica content, the higher their viscosity (resistance to flowing). Those rich in silica tend to solidify underground. The complex chemistry of magmas comes from the melting of the variety of minerals making up the mantle.

The chemistry of metamorphic rocks is like that of their igneous or sedimentary starting materials. As these become more deeply buried and heated, the constituent minerals grow larger. A mudstone metamorphoses to a slate, then to a schist and finally a gneiss. The "slatiness" or "schistosity" of these rocks is provided by micas and other sheet-shaped mineral grains. Such minerals require abundant alumina to form. If this is not present in the starting rock, it will be metamorphosed into more granular material.

A record in the rocks
Rocks contain an unwritten history of the Earth. Sedimentary rocks hold information about climates of the past and fossil relics of organisms that lived when the sediments were laid down. Igneous rocks record periods of crustal activity that relate to the movements of the continents; and metamorphic rocks indicate periods of uplift that exposed previously buried rock. From such information it is possible to construct a geological time-scale. Although fossils are a useful means of correlating one pile of sediment with another, good fossils go back only 600 million years. Earlier organisms are believed to have been soft-bodied and were not easily fossilized.

The only complete time-scale comes from the radioactive "clocks" in many igneous and metamorphic rocks. Certain forms of natural elements, or isotopes, are unstable and emit energy. By measuring the amount of "daughter" atoms that have been formed by the radioactive decay of a larger "parent" atom, it is possible to determine the age of a rock and events in the history of its formation. The dating of rocks from radioactive decay has thus enabled a true time-scale for the history of the Earth to be constructed.

Earth's Minerals

Minerals are the basic ingredients of the Earth, from crust to core. They make up not only the ores on which man has based much of his technology, and the gemstones which he values for their beauty or rarity, but also the components of rocks, pebbles and sands. Two million years ago minerals – in the form of stones – provided early man with his first tools. Today, man's use of minerals, such as uranium for nuclear power or silicon for microcomputers, is revolutionizing our lives.

Minerals, and the metals derived from them, have always had an inherent fascination for man, as well as providing the basis for his technology. Gold in particular, which was worked in Egypt as early as 5000 BC, still retains its mysterious attraction. Because of its chemical inactivity it is imperishable, immutable and nontarnishing, and has served as the basis of world trade for almost 2,000 years. Copper has been smelted since the early part of the third millennium BC, to be replaced eventually by harder alloys. Arsenical bronze, for instance, bridged the gap between the Copper and Bronze ages (bronze is an alloy of copper and tin). More complex technology was needed for the working of iron, which began c.1100 BC, whereas brass (an alloy of copper and zinc) did not appear until Roman times.

Although the steel-making process had its roots in antiquity, it was not until the nineteenth century that new techniques changed man's attitude to minerals. Before the modern age of plastics, the capacity to produce steel was the hallmark of industrial development, and together with coal it formed the linchpin of western industrial progress. Today minerals have come to assume their greatest importance as exploitable—but nonrenewable—resources.

Components of the Earth
The terms "mineral", "rock" and "stone" are often used interchangeably, but in fact all rocks are made up of minerals, which are natural and usually inorganic substances with a particular chemical make-up and crystal structure.

Certain stones have properties that satisfy basic human needs for beauty and colour. Some possess a flashing sparkle, others have special optical characteristics such as refraction and dispersion ("fire"), or contain inclusions that give rise to phenomena like the "asterism" found in opals and sapphires. About 100 such minerals are classified as gemstones and valued for their beauty, durability or rarity.

Most minerals occur as either pure (ore) deposits or mixed with other minerals in rocks—an economically important difference. Their exploitation has been vastly extended in recent decades through our greater understanding of the mineral-forming processes that take place in the Earth's crust. All mineral ores result from a separation process in which a mineral-rich solution separates into its various components according to the temperature, pressure and composition of the original mixture. Precipitation is the simplest kind of separation, as when calcium salts separate from circulating groundwater to yield stalactites and stalagmites in caves, in the form of calcite crystals.

Mineral formation
Most deposits of metallic ores originate in the intense physico-chemical activity that takes place at the boundaries between the Earth's huge crustal plates. Very high concentrations of minerals occur in association with warm solutions coming from springs in the sea bed, notably along the spreading zones in the southeastern Pacific Ocean, the Red Sea, the African Rift Valley and the Gulf of Aden. This process also occurs in shallow-water volcanic areas, as near the Mediterranean island of Thira and the submarine volcano of Bahu Wuhu, Indonesia. Cold seawater penetrates the crust and leaches out minerals from the basalts of these "hot spots", returning to the surface of the sea bed as hot springs. The minerals then precipitate in the cold, oxygen-rich seawater.

Mineral separation may also occur when part of the deep-seated magma forces its way into the upper layers of the Earth's crust and begins to cool. The great plugs of magma that form the

rock kimberlite, in which diamonds are found, must have come from a depth of at least 100 km (62 miles). If the magma reaches the surface through fissures as extrusive rocks, the pattern of minerals in the surrounding rocks is also changed by a process called contact metamorphism, with various bands or zones of minerals occurring at various distances from the contact boundary.

As rocks become weathered, mineral concentrations that resist weathering may be left. Alternatively, all the weathered materials may be transported by running water, becoming concentrated as they are sorted out according to their different densities. Gold is the best-known example of this alluvial type of mineral deposit—known as a placer deposit. If the minerals are washed into the sea, they may be distributed over deltas or over the sea floor, but when this happens the concentrations of minerals are usually very low.

Mineral energy
Fossil fuels such as coal and petroleum are major mineral sources of energy. But with the twentieth-century discovery of nuclear fission, uranium also became an important energy resource. The richest deposits occur, as with other minerals, as veins deposited in fractures by hot-water movements. These deposits, consisting of a uranium oxide called pitchblende, were the first to be mined, for example at Joachimstal (Czechoslovakia), Great Bear Lake (Canada) and Katanga (Zaire). Weathered products of such rocks, redeposited as sandstones, also contain uranium, as in Wyoming (USA) and in the Niger basin. In many respects uranium is similar to silver: both occur with similar geological abundance, their ores are enriched about 2,000 times during processing, and the metals are recovered by using chemicals to dissolve the metal selectively and then by "stripping" the metal from the solution.

MINERALS FROM THE OCEAN
Ocean sediments that originally came from land contain organic matter that absorbs the oxygen in the sediments. As a result, solutions of minerals such as manganese and iron are released, seeping upwards through the debris. When they come in contact with the oxygen in seawater they are precipitated, condensing into so-called "manganese" nodules in amounts that may eventually prove to be a valuable source of mineral wealth. Metallic elements also accumulate very slowly from the seawater itself.

METAL-RICH BRINES
Scientists have recently discovered deep hollows on the floor of the Red Sea and other similar enclosed basins connected with rift valleys. These prevent normal circulation of water and form undersea pools of hot, high-density brines. The brines contain sulphur and other minerals in very high concentrations, and overlie sediments rich in metals such as zinc, copper, lead, silver and gold. Hot springs in fissures below the pools escape into them, carrying up solutions of the metallic minerals which combine with sulphur to create a concentrated broth rich in metals.

METALS FROM THE INTERIOR
Rift zones on the bed of the Pacific Ocean, where the Earth's crustal plates are slowly separating, provide sensational visual evidence of metallic ores in the actual process of creation. Seawater percolates through the fractured surface to the molten rock below, where it leaches out the soluble metallic components, erupting in superheated hydrothermal springs to form geysers of mineral-rich water. Oxygen in the cold water of the sea floor causes the minerals to condense out, precipitating in plumes of dark powder. Continental drift, collision and sedimentation over millions of years will eventually incorporate these deposits into the landmasses.

Uranium, chromium and many other minerals are widely distributed through the Earth's crust, but they are valuable as a resource only if the technology exists to extract them economically. In mineral development, the high-grade ores are worked out first, followed by the poorer deposits if demand remains or increases. With uranium, the low-grade deposits contain far more of the total quantity of the mineral, but these are worth exploiting because of uranium's importance and because the technology exists. Chromium, on the other hand, is currently extracted only from high-grade ores. Large deposits of low-grade ores do exist, but technology for exploiting them economically has not yet been developed.

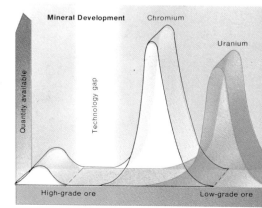

Mineral Development

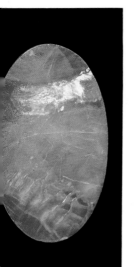

Sapphire gemstone (left), a form of the dull grey mineral carborundum (below), owes its colour to inclusions of titanium and iron. If cut with a rounded top it gives a starry effect known as asterism.

Opal (above), a silica mineral, often contains impurities which give it a range of colours. These flash and change according to the angle of vision, a result of the interference of light along minute internal cracks in the stone.

MINERALS IN THE SERVICE OF MAN

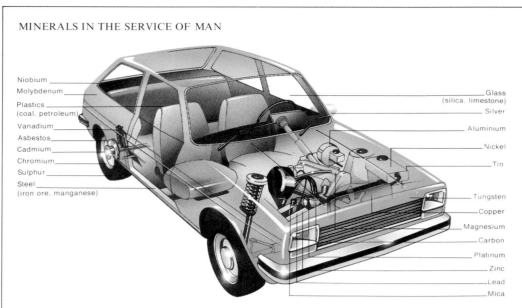

Niobium
Molybdenum
Plastics (coal, petroleum)
Vanadium
Asbestos
Cadmium
Chromium
Sulphur
Steel (iron ore, manganese)

Glass (silica, limestone)
Silver
Aluminium
Nickel
Tin
Tungsten
Copper
Magnesium
Carbon
Platinum
Zinc
Lead
Mica

The modern motorcar makes use of a whole alphabet of minerals in its composition, from aluminium to zinc. The importance of plastics, made from petroleum and coal, is constantly increasing, but the need for specialist metals is as great as ever. Cadmium, for example, is used in electro-plating; carbon goes into making electrodes and graphite seals; transistors and electric contact points require platinum; sulphur is present in vulcanizing rubber and lubricants; lamp filaments contain tungsten. Of basic metals, iron and steel still account for almost three-quarters of the total quantity of the metals used; lead for 1.19 per cent and copper for only 0.94 per cent. But the amount of useful metal is often a small fraction of the rock that has to be mined and processed. A copper ore, for instance, only yields about 0.7 per cent of metal, so to equip a single car's radiator with copper well over one and a half tonnes of rock will have to be excavated, of which 99.3 per cent will simply be discarded.

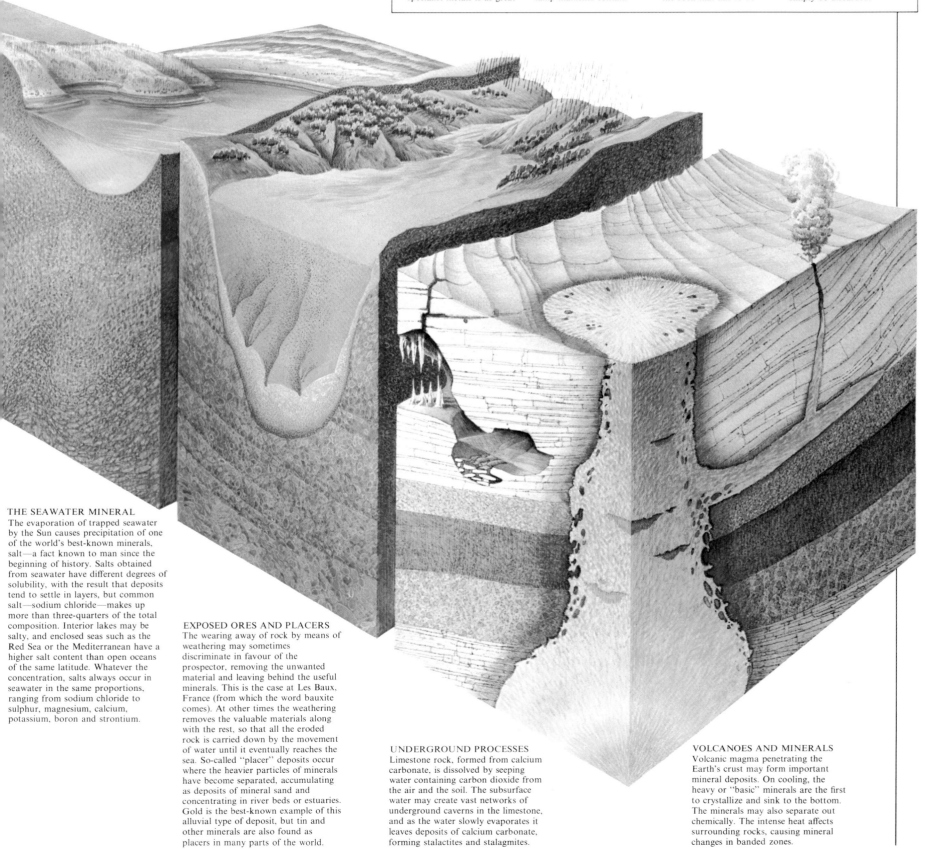

THE SEAWATER MINERAL
The evaporation of trapped seawater by the Sun causes precipitation of one of the world's best-known minerals, salt—a fact known to man since the beginning of history. Salts obtained from seawater have different degrees of solubility, with the result that deposits tend to settle in layers, but common salt—sodium chloride—makes up more than three-quarters of the total composition. Interior lakes may be salty, and enclosed seas such as the Red Sea or the Mediterranean have a higher salt content than open oceans of the same latitude. Whatever the concentration, salts always occur in seawater in the same proportions, ranging from sodium chloride to sulphur, magnesium, calcium, potassium, boron and strontium.

EXPOSED ORES AND PLACERS
The wearing away of rock by means of weathering may sometimes discriminate in favour of the prospector, removing the unwanted material and leaving behind the useful minerals. This is the case at Les Baux, France (from which the word bauxite comes). At other times the weathering removes the valuable materials along with the rest, so that all the eroded rock is carried down by the movement of water until it eventually reaches the sea. So-called "placer" deposits occur where the heavier particles of minerals have become separated, accumulating as deposits of mineral sand and concentrating in river beds or estuaries. Gold is the best-known example of this alluvial type of deposit, but tin and other minerals are also found as placers in many parts of the world.

UNDERGROUND PROCESSES
Limestone rock, formed from calcium carbonate, is dissolved by seeping water containing carbon dioxide from the air and the soil. The subsurface water may create vast networks of underground caverns in the limestone, and as the water slowly evaporates it leaves deposits of calcium carbonate, forming stalactites and stalagmites.

VOLCANOES AND MINERALS
Volcanic magma penetrating the Earth's crust may form important mineral deposits. On cooling, the heavy or "basic" minerals are the first to crystallize and sink to the bottom. The minerals may also separate out chemically. The intense heat affects surrounding rocks, causing mineral changes in banded zones.

Earthquakes and Volcanoes

Earthquakes and volcanic eruptions challenge man's faith in the stability of the world, but these violent releases of energy testify to our planet's ever-dynamic activity. Earthquakes are caused when the rigid crust is driven past or over itself by underlying movements that extend deep into the Earth's mantle. Stress builds up until it exceeds the strength of the rocks, when there follows a sudden movement. Volcanoes occur where molten rock, or magma, from the mantle forces its way to the surface through lines of weakness in the crust, often at the lithospheric plate boundaries.

MODIFIED MERCALLI SCALE

I Earthquake not felt, except by a few.

II Felt on upper floors by few at rest. Swinging of suspended objects.

III Quite noticeable indoors, especially on upper floors. Standing cars may sway.

IV Felt indoors. Dishes and windows rattle, standing cars rock. Like a heavy lorry hitting a building.

V Felt by nearly all, many wakened. Fragile objects broken, plaster cracked, trees and poles disturbed.

VI Felt by all, many run outdoors. Slight damage, heavy furniture moved, some fallen plaster.

VII People run outdoors. Average homes slightly damaged, substandard ones badly damaged. Noticed by car drivers.

VIII Well-built structures slightly damaged, others badly damaged. Chimneys and monuments collapse. Car drivers disturbed.

IX Well-designed buildings badly damaged, substantial ones greatly damaged, shifted off foundations. Conspicuous ground cracks open up.

X Well-built wood-structures destroyed, masonry structures destroyed. Rails bent, ground cracked, landslides. Rivers overflow.

XI Few masonry structures left standing. Bridges and underground pipes destroyed. Broad cracks in ground. Earth slumps.

XII Damage total. Ground waves seem like sea waves. Line of sight disturbed, objects thrown into the air.

The Earth's crust generally breaks along pre-existing planes of weakness, or faults. Such breakages give rise to an "explosive" release of stress that is familiar to surface dwellers as the vibrations of an earthquake.

Not all earthquakes, however, take place along pre-existing faults, otherwise no new faults would be generated. Many recent large earthquakes have been located immediately north of the Tonga Islands because a giant rent is developing through previously unbroken ocean crust. The crust to the south is being swallowed down into the mantle and that to the north continues at the surface to be subducted farther to the west. Once a fault has formed, however, it remains a plane of weakness even though the two sides tend to become partly resealed, so that when movement does occur there is a considerable release of energy.

Measuring earthquakes

Earthquakes are quantified in two ways. The actual energy release (magnitude) at the source of the earthquake (the focus) is measured on the Richter scale, a log scale where every unit of increase represents approximately 24 times the energy release. A magnitude 7 earthquake is roughly equivalent to the explosion of a one megaton nuclear bomb (one million tonnes of TNT). The strongest earthquake recorded this century was a magnitude 8.5 event in Alaska in 1964. Earthquakes as they are perceived are measured on the Modified Mercalli scale by their impact in terms of the amount of surface destruction. A medium-size earthquake under a town, such as that beneath Tangshan, China, in 1976 which killed more than a quarter of a million people, might record higher on the Mercalli scale than the Alaska event, which affected a large but sparsely populated region.

The magnitude of the earthquake depends on the frictional resistance that has to be overcome before movement can take place. This total frictional resistance, therefore, increases with the area of the fault plane. So the bigger the fault plane that moves, the bigger the earthquake. The largest earthquakes occur on wide fault planes that dip at a very shallow angle, and can pass through a great deal of relatively shallow crust that will not deform plastically.

Earthquakes are unlikely to occur where rocks are plastic and can flow to accommodate the build-up of stress. Some faults, such as the San Andreas Fault in the western United States, pass from brittle rocks into a plastic zone at depths of only a few kilometres. Therefore, the next San Francisco earthquake cannot be as great as the 1964 Alaskan one, although this may be of little comfort to the potential victims. Along some sections of the San Andreas Fault the plastic zone comes directly to the surface, and motion occurs without large earthquakes.

Earthquake prediction is still in its infancy, although it is recognized that a number of phenomena may occur before a major earthquake—the ground may swell, the electrical conductivity of groundwater may change, and the water height of wells may rapidly alter.

How volcanoes are formed

Volcanoes, although spectacular, are safer than earthquakes. While an average of 20,000 people are killed each year in earthquakes, only about 400 are killed by volcanoes; and many of the victims die from starvation due to crop failure after heavy ash-falls.

Volcanoes are formed when molten rock (magma) escapes through the Earth's crust to the Earth's surface. Most of this magma forms within the upper mantle between 30 and 100 km (20–60 miles) underground. The temperature increases with depth between 20° and 50°C per

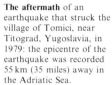

The aftermath of an earthquake that struck the village of Tomici, near Titograd, Yugoslavia, in 1979: the epicentre of the earthquake was recorded 55 km (35 miles) away in the Adriatic Sea.

Earthquakes occur when slabs of the Earth's crust move in relation to each other. The focus of the earthquake is the point where movement occurs (1), and the epicentre is the point on the surface directly above it (2). Blue lines represent zones of surface damage as measured on the Modified Mercalli scale.

km (35°–90°F per 3,250 ft) from the crust to the mantle, but even so the rocks are normally not hot enough to melt.

Basaltic magmas, found along mid-ocean spreading ridges and oceanic islands, are formed when hot, deep mantle rises and, on reduction of pressure, begins to melt. Such "basic" magmas generally have low silica and water content, a high temperature and flow easily—often, as in Hawaii, "quietly erupting" to form volcanoes with very gentle gradients known as shield volcanoes. Silica-rich magma forms under continental crust. Ocean crust sucks up water after it has formed at the oceanic spreading ridges and much of this water later becomes taken with the crust down a subduction zone, where it helps to lower the melting point of both mantle and ocean-crust rocks.

By the time these magmas reach the surface they are cooler and have a higher water content than basalts. These "intermediate" or andesite magmas are also more viscous (less willing to

flow) because they contain more silica. The eruptions are more explosive as the water and other gases dissolve out of the magma as it approaches the surface, and the lava remains close to the volcanic vent, building up the archetypal steep-sided conical stratified volcano, such as Mount Fujiyama in Japan. Sometimes the conical form may be destroyed in catastrophic eruptions, as has happened at Mount St Helens in the United States.

The most violent of all eruptions are found where magmas from the mantle have penetrated and melted a great thickness of continental rocks, so as to create highly viscous silica- and water-rich "acid" magmas. As such magmas approach the surface they may turn into a red-hot froth that blasts out from fissures to cover enormous areas in a volcanic material known as ignimbrite. The most extensive eruption known to have occurred in the past 2,000 years was probably on Mount Taupo, on North Island, New Zealand. In AD 150 it discharged some

THE VIOLENT EARTH

Large, destructive earthquakes occur somewhere in the world approximately every two weeks, but fortunately most take place under the sea, where they cause little harm. Most of the millions of small earthquakes that occur on Earth pass unnoticed. Volcanoes are the most impressive display of the Earth's dynamic activity, and are also responsible for forming the starting materials of the Earth's crust.

ASH FALLOUT

Some volcanic eruptions are so violent that ash is thrown high into the atmosphere to be carried away on the prevailing winds. Krakatoa in 1883 distributed ash around the world. The map shows the limits of airborne ash deposited by the eruption of Quizapu in Chile in 1932, the bulk of which fell within 10 km (6 miles).

Volcanoes are fed by magma, or molten rock, that wells up from deep in the Earth's mantle. The magma can either rise directly to the surface through fissures in the Earth's crust (1) and pour forth gently and continuously to form a shield volcano, or lava plateau, or be stored in a magma chamber (2) that swells up before erupting to the surface. To form the traditional cone-shaped stratified volcano, magma reaches the surface through a vent (3) and spews forth as gases, ash and lava (4, 5). Eventually the conical shape is made up of alternate layers of ash consolidated by lava. As rock and other debris build up around the main vent, and pressure increases, flank vents (6) open up other pathways to the surface, thereby creating parasitic cones (7).

When a volcano erupts violently the surrounding countryside can be devastated. The power of the blast flattens trees, poisonous gases kill all forms of wildlife, ash-falls damage property and crops and can create mudflows and avalanches, and lava pouring from the vent can dam rivers to create floods.

Other special features of a volcanic landscape include extinct craters, which sometimes fill with water to form lakes, and calderas (8). Calderas are created either by vast explosions or when the magma chamber and vent are emptied of magma and the volcano collapses in on itself. Magma may later force itself through the collapsed debris so as to form new active cones on the floor of the caldera.

In volcanic regions there are other forms of volcanic activity. Water may seep down to be heated by the hot magma and reach the surface some distance away as a geyser (9) or hot spring, or be mixed with soil and ejected as a mud volcano. Some vents emit gases and steam, and these are called fumaroles. Geysers are created when water is heated in underground passageways or caverns (10). Water is periodically converted to superheated steam, which builds up pressure until it is able to rush up a vent and throw steam and water great distances into the air.

Not all magma reaches the surface: some cools and solidifies underground to form volcanic intrusions. Dykes (11) are sheets of cooled magma that have cut through strata of overlying rock, sills (12) are magma sheets injected between strata, and laccoliths (13) are large lens-shaped pools of solidified magma. Years later, when weathering and erosion have removed the overlying rock, these intrusions become features of the landscape.

10 cu km (2½ cu miles) of ignimbrite in about 15 minutes—spreading across the landscape at more than 100 m (330 ft) per second.

Other more explosive eruptions, such as that of Krakatoa in 1883, or Santorini more than 3,000 years ago, can result in the collapse of the volcano into the underlying magma chamber after it has become partly emptied during an eruption to create a caldera. Many of the largest explosions are caused by the mixing of water with magma—at Krakatoa the cataclysm probably resulted from seawater breaking into the magma and flashing straight to steam, thereby allowing more seawater to enter until the chain reaction could set off more energy than the most powerful nuclear bomb.

Predicting at least the approximate time of an eruption is relatively easy. Small earthquakes indicate that a new batch of magma is rising towards the surface. Many volcanoes also swell prior to an eruption and release gases that indicate the arrival of new magma.

The Oceans

Earth is the water-planet. Of all the planets of the solar system only the Earth has abundant liquid water, and 97 per cent of this surface water is found in the seas and oceans. The water of the oceans appears to be passive and unchanging, whereas the rain and rivers seem active, but this is far from true. In reality the oceans are a turmoil of giant sluggish rivers – far larger than any of the land rivers – and of circulating surface currents that are driven by the prevailing winds.

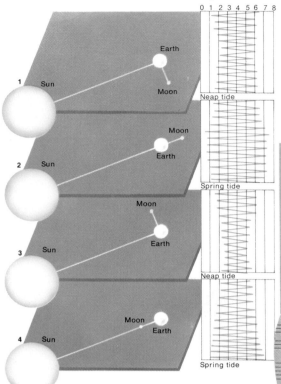

No topographic map of the Earth can be drawn unless there is some kind of base line from which to measure depths and heights. This base line has always been taken as the level of the sea, yet the sea is perpetually changing level. One can choose some kind of average to call "sea level", but even today different countries have defined that base line in different ways. The currents found within the sea itself can also give the water surface a slope—the calm Sargasso Sea off the northern coast of South America is, for example, about 1.5 m (5 ft) higher than the water to the west adjacent to the Gulf Stream.

Waves

The changes in the level of the sea, at its surface, provide the most familiar image of motion within the waters. Various changes take place over many different time periods, but the most rapid are those that we call waves.

Waves are produced by the wind moving over the water and catching on the surface. They can move at between 15 and 100 km/hr (10–60 mph) and wave crests may be separated by up to 300 m (1,000 ft) in the open ocean. In general, the greater the wavelength, the faster the wave's speed and the farther the distance travelled by the wave. Waves that have travelled a long way from the winds that created them are known as swell. Without the wind continually pushing them they become symmetrical and smooth. Wind waves produce spilling breakers more like the rapids of a mountain torrent, whereas swell produces giant plunging breakers.

A combination of strong winds and low atmospheric pressure associated with storms can cause yet another kind of wave, known as a storm surge. A storm surge is formed by the water being driven ahead of the wind, and rising as the atmospheric pressure weighing down on the water decreases. Where storms drive water into funnel-shaped coasts, the water can rise more than 10 m (33 ft) above normal sea level, flooding large areas of low-lying land at the head of the bay. Venice, the Netherlands and Bangladesh have been particularly subject to destructive storm surges. Other catastrophic changes in sea level have their origins in the sea bed. These are tsunamis (Japanese for "high-water in the harbour") and are generally triggered by underwater earthquakes that suddenly raise or lower large areas of the sea floor.

Tides

As the Earth orbits around the Sun the water in the oceans experiences a changing pull of gravity from both the Moon and the Sun. The Sun is overhead once a day, and because the Moon is itself orbiting the Earth, it is overhead once every 24 hours 50 minutes. The pull of gravity from the Sun is less than half that from the Moon, and so it is the Moon that sets the rhythm of the water movements we call tides. The variation in gravitational pull from the Moon is extremely small, however, and even if the whole of the Earth were covered with deep water a tide of only about 30 cm (12 in) would be produced, rushing around the world keeping pace with the circling Moon. Yet the tides in shallow coastal regions are often very much higher than this—for example, up to 18 m (60 ft) in the Bay of Fundy, Canada. The seas and bays with the highest tides are located where the whole mass of water is resonating—rebounding backwards and forwards like water in a bath, as the smaller tides in the outlying oceans push it twice each day.

The Bay of Fundy experiences a particularly high tidal range because it happens to have a resonant frequency—a range of movement— very close to the 12½-hour frequency between tides. Large enclosed seas such as the Mediterranean have very small tides because there is no outside push from an ocean to set them resonating. In contrast, where water movement associated with the tides passes through a narrow channel it can produce tidal currents of up to 30 km/hr (19 mph), such as the famous maelstrom of northern Norway.

After these relatively short-lived disturbances the sea returns to its normal, or at least to its average, level again. When the total volume of free water at the Earth's surface alters, or when the shapes of the ocean basins vary, the sea level itself may start to wander.

How does the volume of water vary? It can be buried in rocks—but the steam clouds above volcanoes return such water so it is normally recycled rather than lost. Some vapour can be broken down through radiation in the upper atmosphere and the hydrogen lost to outer space, but this is relatively insignificant. Or it can be frozen and stacked up on land in the form of ice—this is significant as we are still living in an ice age. The lowest ice-age sea levels produced beaches at about 130 m (430 ft) below present sea level, and the low-lying coastal regions of that period have now become flooded to form the continental shelves.

The salt content of the oceans

Average ocean water contains about 35 parts per 1,000 of salts which include 14 elements in concentrations greater than 1 part per million— the most abundant being sodium and chlorine. Where there is considerable surface evaporation, for example in enclosed seas such as the Dead Sea, the salt concentration builds up and the water becomes denser. Where the sea-surface is turning to ice the salt also becomes concentrated in the water.

The coldest, saltiest ocean water comes from the Antarctic. As it is also the densest it hugs the ocean bottom as it flows northwards, reaching as far as the latitudes of Spain. A similar current from the Arctic is slightly lighter and therefore rides above it—but travelling southwards, as far as the southern Atlantic. A second slightly lighter body of Antarctic water rides above the Arctic water—again travelling northwards. Where these water movements meet each other they rise up, bringing to the surface oxygenated water that can support a profusion of life in oceans that have been compared to a desert because of their lack of biological activity. Unlikely as it seems, it is the icy, stormy, polar waters that provide the lungs of the oceans.

Both the Sun and the Moon exert gravitational pull on the water in the oceans, but the pull of the Sun is less than half that of the Moon. It is the Moon, therefore, that sets the rhythm of the tides. Because the Moon orbits the Earth every 24 hours and 50 minutes, the time of high or low tide advances approximately an hour each day. When the Moon is in its first and last quarters (1, 3) it forms a right angle with the Earth and the Sun and the gravitational fields are opposed, thus causing only a small difference between high and low tide. These are called neap tides. When the Sun, Moon and Earth lie in a straight line (2, 4), at the full and the new Moon, then the high tides become higher and the low tides lower. These are the spring tides. The graph illustrates tidal range over a period of a month.

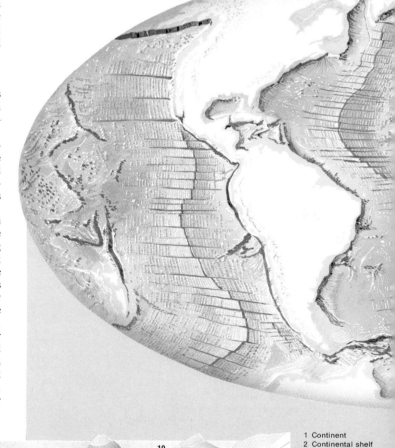

1 Continent
2 Continental shelf
3 Continental slope
4 Continental rise
5 Submarine canyon
6 Abyssal plain
7 Abyssal hills
8 Mid-ocean ridge
9 Oceanic trench
10 Island arc
11 Continental sea

THE CHANGING OCEANS

Nearly two-thirds of the Earth's surface is covered by the seas and oceans and this great expanse of water is continually in movement. The most familiar movements are waves formed by the wind and the rising and falling tides that respond to the position of the Moon. But even greater movements take place. Currents driven by prevailing winds form whirlpools an ocean in width, and below the surface flow great rivers of colder water. Sea level is also rising as ice melts from the polar caps.

Cl 55.0%
Na 30.6%
SO₄ 7.7%
Mg 3.7%
Ca 1.5%
K 1.5%

Seawater is about 96% pure water and the rest is made up of dissolved salts. Many elements are present in minute quantities, but only chlorine (Cl), sodium (Na), sulphate (SO₄), magnesium (Mg), calcium (Ca) and potassium (K) appear in concentrations of more than 1% of the total dissolved salts.

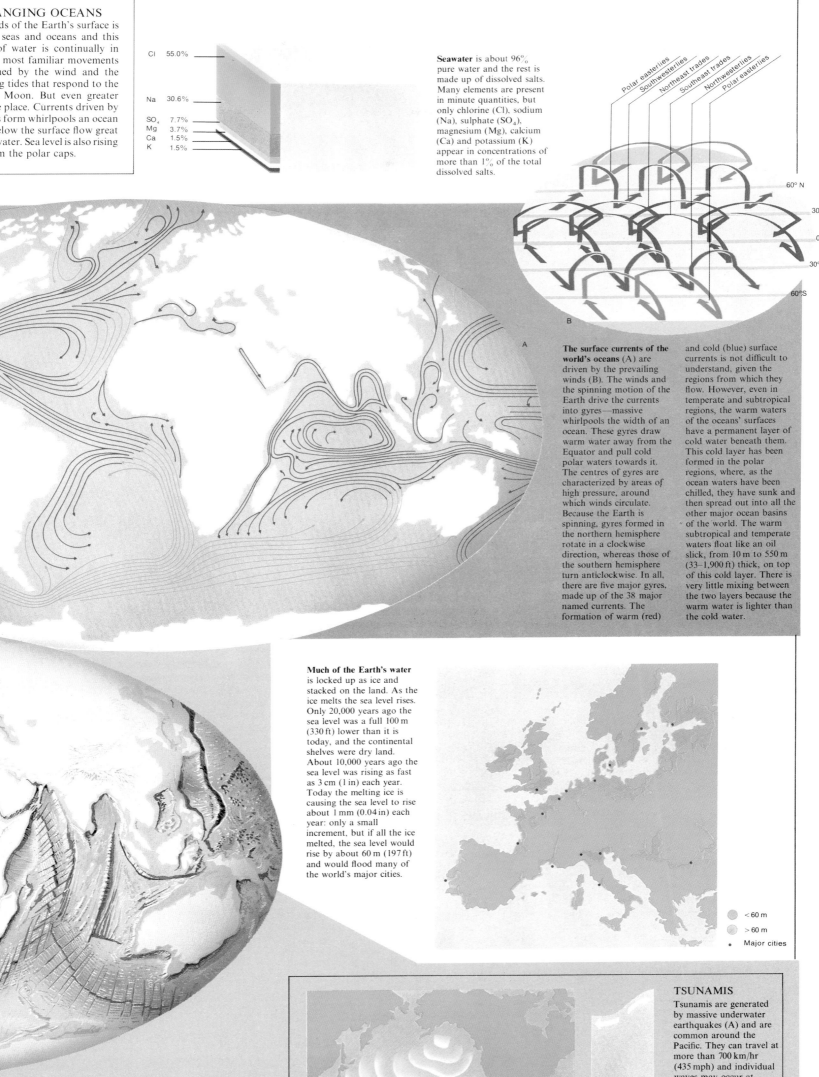

The surface currents of the world's oceans (A) are driven by the prevailing winds (B). The winds and the spinning motion of the Earth drive the currents into gyres—massive whirlpools the width of an ocean. These gyres draw warm water away from the Equator and pull cold polar waters towards it. The centres of gyres are characterized by areas of high pressure, around which winds circulate. Because the Earth is spinning, gyres formed in the northern hemisphere rotate in a clockwise direction, whereas those of the southern hemisphere turn anticlockwise. In all, there are five major gyres, made up of the 38 major named currents. The formation of warm (red) and cold (blue) surface currents is not difficult to understand, given the regions from which they flow. However, even in temperate and subtropical regions, the warm waters of the oceans' surfaces have a permanent layer of cold water beneath them. This cold layer has been formed in the polar regions, where, as the ocean waters have been chilled, they have sunk and then spread out into all the other major ocean basins of the world. The warm subtropical and temperate waters float like an oil slick, from 10 m to 550 m (33–1,900 ft) thick, on top of this cold layer. There is very little mixing between the two layers because the warm water is lighter than the cold water.

Much of the Earth's water is locked up as ice and stacked on the land. As the ice melts the sea level rises. Only 20,000 years ago the sea level was a full 100 m (330 ft) lower than it is today, and the continental shelves were dry land. About 10,000 years ago the sea level was rising as fast as 3 cm (1 in) each year. Today the melting ice is causing the sea level to rise about 1 mm (0.04 in) each year: only a small increment, but if all the ice melted, the sea level would rise by about 60 m (197 ft) and would flood many of the world's major cities.

< 60 m
> 60 m
• Major cities

The sea bed, more uniform than the land surface, also contains a landscape of underwater features that resemble the plains, valleys and mountains of the continents. Off the edge of continents lie the flat, shallow continental shelves, which are bounded by the steeper incline of the continental slope, which meets the true ocean floor at the continental rise.

Here deep submarine canyons may be found. These seem to be in a process of continual erosion from turbidity currents. River water pouring into major estuaries and carrying sediment can also scour out the slope—especially during periods of low sea level. The abyssal plain is rarely interrupted by volcanic hills and

mountains. The largest chains are at the mid-ocean ridge, where two crustal plates are moving apart and new ocean floor is being created. At some ocean margins deep trough-shaped valleys or trenches are the sites of ocean floor consumption at a subduction zone. The volcanic island arcs that form behind it sometimes isolate a continental sea.

TSUNAMIS

Tsunamis are generated by massive underwater earthquakes (A) and are common around the Pacific. They can travel at more than 700 km/hr (435 mph) and individual waves may occur at intervals of 15 minutes, or 200 km (125 miles). Low-lying atolls of the Pacific have extremely steep sides underwater, and are generally unharmed, but the gently shelving islands such as Hawaii slow down the tsunami and build it into a giant wave 30 m (100 ft) or more in height. This map plots the hourly position of a tsunami that originated south of Alaska.

Landscape-makers: Water

Of all the natural agents of erosion at work on the Earth's surface, water is probably the most powerful. Many of the finer details of the landscape, from the contouring of hills and valleys to the broad spread of plains, are the work of water. In recent years we have come to understand more fully the subtle factors at work in a river, for example, as it deepens mountain gorges or builds up sedimentary layers in its approach to the sea. The full force of a waterfall, the instability of a meandering stream, the multiple layering of river terraces – all are features of this most versatile landscape-maker.

Ninety-seven per cent of the world's water is in the oceans, another two per cent is locked up in the ice caps of Greenland and Antarctica, which leaves one per cent only on the surface of Earth, under the ground and in the air. The importance of this one per cent is, however, inestimable: most life forms could not exist without it, and yet at the same time many are threatened by it, in the form of flood and storm.

The Sun's energy "powers" the evaporation of water from the oceans. Water vapour then circulates in the atmosphere and is precipitated as rain or snow over land, from which it eventually drains back to the oceans. This is the vast, never-ending water cycle. Water in the air that falls as, for example, rain is replaced on average every 12 days. The total water supply remains constant and is believed to be exactly the same as it was 3,000 million years ago.

From raindrops to rivers

Rain falling on to the surface of the land has a great deal of energy: large drops may hit the ground with a terminal velocity of about 35 km/hr (20 mph). If the rain falls on bare soil, it splashes upwards, breaking off and transporting tiny fragments of soil, which come to rest downhill. Vegetation-covered soil breaks the impact and some of the rain may evaporate without ever reaching the ground.

Soil is rather like a sponge. If the holes or pores are very small, rain finds it difficult to penetrate and water runs over the surface of the soil. If the pores are large, rain infiltrates, filling up the pore spaces. Soils that are thin, have low infiltration rates, or already have a lot of water in them, are very susceptible to overland flow. The water may then concentrate into a channel called a gully, and this can have a dramatic effect upon the landscape. The creation of gullies, together with the splash effect, leads to soil erosion. The problem is particularly severe in semi-arid regions, where rainfall is sporadic but intense, vegetation is sparse and overgrazing is common. In extreme cases, badlands are formed and by this time recuperation of the land is impossible or is prohibitively expensive.

Where the infiltration rate is high, water percolates through the soil and eventually into the bedrock. There are two well-defined regions, the saturated and the unsaturated. The upper limit of the saturated zone is the water table. Beneath this, water moves at a rate of a few metres a day, but in rocks such as limestone it can move much more quickly along cracks and joints. In most rock types there are some soluble components which are removed as water continually flows through. In limestone regions, the dissolution of calcium salts results in spectacular cave formations.

Groundwater often provides a vital source for domestic consumption. In porous materials, especially chalk, water is stored in large quantities. Such strata are called aquifers and in some areas, notably North Africa, it is believed that water being pumped up now resulted from rainfall when the climate was wetter tens of thousands of years ago.

Water from a number of sources—from overland flow, soil seepage and springs draining aquifers—produces the flow in rivers. Groundwater appears days or even weeks after a heavy rainfall, but overland flow reaches the channel in hours, producing the sudden peak in flow that may cause flooding and occasionally great damage farther downstream. Flood waves usually rise quickly in mountain areas and the wave moves downstream as the river collects more and more water from its tributaries. Eventually, although the volume continues to increase downstream, the river channel becomes broader and flatter, so it moves more slowly and causes less damage. The most serious floods occur after intense rainfall on already saturated soils where upland rivers issue on to plains.

Rivers at work

The work of a river from its source to its mouth involves three processes, the first of which is erosion. This includes corrasion, or abrasion— the grinding of rocks and stones against the river's banks and bed—which produces both

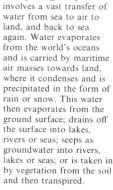
A RIVER SYSTEM

Rivers form by the accumulation of runoff water, groundwater and from springs and small streams. Few rivers reach the sea without gaining tributaries, thus forming a river system. Highland regions at source are called catchment areas and the total area drained by a river system is the drainage basin.

The course of a river from source to mouth includes distinctive stages and land forms. All rivers flow from high ground to lower ground. Many rise in an upland area where precipitation is heavy. The upper course is where vertical erosion is dominant and the resulting valley is narrow, deep and V-shaped. A gorge is formed if this downcutting is particularly rapid. If the river has a winding course, the valley walls project to produce interlocking spurs. In the middle course erosion is lateral rather than vertical and the valley takes a more open V-shape. The river may start to meander and bluffs are formed as interlocking spurs are eroded. In the lower course the river deposits much material as it meanders across an almost flat flood plain. The bed is sometimes higher than the plain and the river has raised banks, or levées, formed from material deposited when the river is in flood. Ox-bow lakes are common, as is a delta where the slow-flowing river enters the sea.

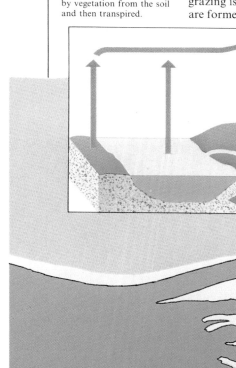

When a river reaches the sea, providing the coast is sheltered and the sea is shallow with no strong currents, its speed is checked and material is deposited (1). The river then forms distributaries (2) in order to continue its flow to the sea. A delta forms its characteristic fan shape (3) as it grows sideways and seawards. A river needs active erosion in its upper course in order to form a delta.

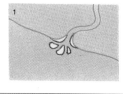
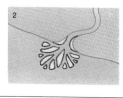
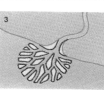

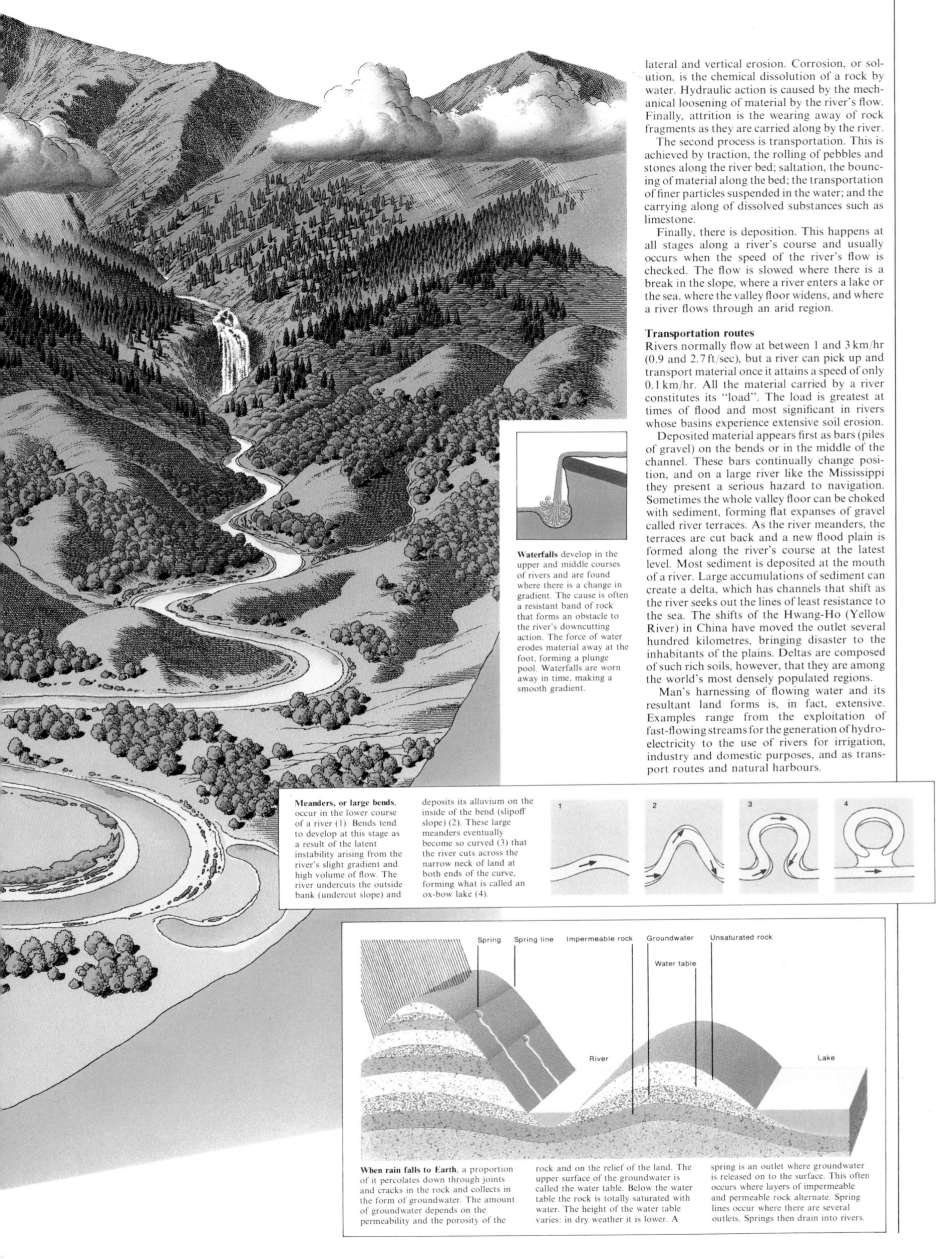

lateral and vertical erosion. Corrosion, or solution, is the chemical dissolution of a rock by water. Hydraulic action is caused by the mechanical loosening of material by the river's flow. Finally, attrition is the wearing away of rock fragments as they are carried along by the river.

The second process is transportation. This is achieved by traction, the rolling of pebbles and stones along the river bed; saltation, the bouncing of material along the bed; the transportation of finer particles suspended in the water; and the carrying along of dissolved substances such as limestone.

Finally, there is deposition. This happens at all stages along a river's course and usually occurs when the speed of the river's flow is checked. The flow is slowed where there is a break in the slope, where a river enters a lake or the sea, where the valley floor widens, and where a river flows through an arid region.

Transportation routes

Rivers normally flow at between 1 and 3 km/hr (0.9 and 2.7 ft/sec), but a river can pick up and transport material once it attains a speed of only 0.1 km/hr. All the material carried by a river constitutes its "load". The load is greatest at times of flood and most significant in rivers whose basins experience extensive soil erosion.

Deposited material appears first as bars (piles of gravel) on the bends or in the middle of the channel. These bars continually change position, and on a large river like the Mississippi they present a serious hazard to navigation. Sometimes the whole valley floor can be choked with sediment, forming flat expanses of gravel called river terraces. As the river meanders, the terraces are cut back and a new flood plain is formed along the river's course at the latest level. Most sediment is deposited at the mouth of a river. Large accumulations of sediment can create a delta, which has channels that shift as the river seeks out the lines of least resistance to the sea. The shifts of the Hwang-Ho (Yellow River) in China have moved the outlet several hundred kilometres, bringing disaster to the inhabitants of the plains. Deltas are composed of such rich soils, however, that they are among the world's most densely populated regions.

Man's harnessing of flowing water and its resultant land forms is, in fact, extensive. Examples range from the exploitation of fast-flowing streams for the generation of hydro-electricity to the use of rivers for irrigation, industry and domestic purposes, and as transport routes and natural harbours.

Waterfalls develop in the upper and middle courses of rivers and are found where there is a change in gradient. The cause is often a resistant band of rock that forms an obstacle to the river's downcutting action. The force of water erodes material away at the foot, forming a plunge pool. Waterfalls are worn away in time, making a smooth gradient.

Meanders, or large bends, occur in the lower course of a river (1). Bends tend to develop at this stage as a result of the latent instability arising from the river's slight gradient and high volume of flow. The river undercuts the outside bank (undercut slope) and deposits its alluvium on the inside of the bend (slipoff slope) (2). These large meanders eventually become so curved (3) that the river cuts across the narrow neck of land at both ends of the curve, forming what is called an ox-bow lake (4).

When rain falls to Earth, a proportion of it percolates down through joints and cracks in the rock and collects in the form of groundwater. The amount of groundwater depends on the permeability and the porosity of the rock and on the relief of the land. The upper surface of the groundwater is called the water table. Below the water table the rock is totally saturated with water. The height of the water table varies: in dry weather it is lower. A spring is an outlet where groundwater is released on to the surface. This often occurs where layers of impermeable and permeable rock alternate. Spring lines occur where there are several outlets. Springs then drain into rivers.

Landscape-makers: Ice and Snow

A series of glacial periods has punctuated the Earth's history for the last two million years. During the last glacial, the ice covered an area nearly three times larger than that covered by ice sheets and glaciers today. Its remnants are still found in the ice caps of the world: most present-day glacial ice is in Antarctica and Greenland in two great ice sheets which together contain about 97 per cent of all the Earth's ice. The rest is in glaciers in Iceland, the Alps and other high mountain chains.

During the Earth's major glacial periods, ice sheets almost as big as that of present-day Antarctica spread over the northern part of North America, reaching as far south as the Ohio River, and over northern Europe as far south as southern England, the Netherlands and southern Poland. Today glacial activity is more restricted, but the mechanisms by which it carves dramatic features of the Earth's landscape remain the same.

Types of glacier

There are six main types of ice mass: cirque glaciers, which occupy basin-shaped depressions in mountain areas; valley glaciers; piedmont glaciers, in which the ice spreads in a lobe over a lowland; floating ice tongues and ice shelves; mountain ice caps; and ice sheets. Climate and relief are responsible for these differences, but glaciers can also be classified according to their internal temperatures.

Cold glaciers are those in which the ice temperature is below freezing point and they are frozen to the rock beneath. This condition, which hinders the movement of glaciers, exists in many parts of Antarctica and Greenland, where air temperatures are low, as well as at high altitudes in some lower-latitude mountain regions. Temperate glaciers, on the other hand, show internal temperatures at or close to the melting point of ice. Unlike cold glaciers, they are not frozen to the rock beneath and can therefore slide over it. Ice melts on the surface of the glacier when the weather is warm, and underneath the glacier as it is warmed by geothermal heat from inside the Earth. Streams collecting meltwater may flow over, through or under the ice and emerge at the ice edge. In other glaciers cold ice may overlie temperate ice.

Glaciers are formed from snow that, as it accumulates year after year, becomes compacted, turning first into "névé" or "firn" and eventually, after several years or even decades, into glacial ice. This process of accumulation is offset by ablation, through which ice is lost by

melting, evaporation or, in glaciers that end in the sea or in lakes, by calving. If accumulation exceeds ablation, the glacier increases in size; conversely, if ablation is higher, the glacier shrinks and eventually disappears.

Glaciers move because of the force of gravity. The fastest-moving glaciers, for example those of coastal Greenland which descend steeply from areas of great accumulation, move at speeds of more than 20 m (65 ft) a day. A few metres a day is more common, however. Some glaciers move exceptionally quickly in surges, which usually last for a few weeks; rates of more than 100 m (330 ft) a day have been recorded. At the other extreme, some glaciers or parts of glaciers—the central zones of ice sheets and ice caps for example—are virtually motionless. When the ice in a glacier is subject to pressure or tension—as it flows down a valley, for example—it behaves rather like a plastic substance and changes its shape to fit the contours of the valley. Part or all of the movement of a glacier is accomplished by means of this internal deformation. In temperate glaciers, or glaciers whose lower layers are temperate, there is also basal sliding. Movement of a glacier produces cracks or crevasses in areas where stress exceeds the strength of the ice.

The work of glaciers

Glaciers and ice sheets can profoundly modify the landscape by both erosion and deposition. Measured rates of erosion of bedrock may be as much as several millimetres a year. Rock surfaces are scratched, or striated, and worn down by the constant grinding action (abrasion) of rock fragments embedded in the base of the ice. The extreme pressure of thick glacial ice on a basal boulder has been known to rupture solid bedrock beneath it.

The products of bedrock erosion range from fine clays and silts produced by abrasion, to large boulders picked up and transported by the ice. Some rocks have been carried hundreds of kilometres, from southern Scandinavia to

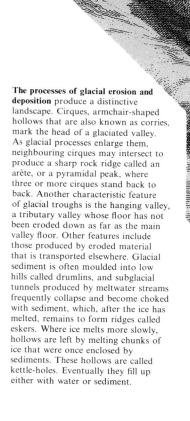

Pyramidal peak
Cirque
Arête
Névé
Medial moraine
Lateral moraine
Marginal crevasses

A U-shaped valley, such as Langdale (below) in the English Lake District, is a clear indication of a glaciated past. The floor is quite flat and the valley sides rise steeply from it.

A crevasse (below left) is created by stress within a glacier. Internally, the ice is rather like plastic but its surface is rigid and brittle. This causes tension and cracking on the surface.

This erratic (below right) is made of Silurian grit, yet it sits on a limestone perch. Ice left Yorkshire 20,000 years ago, since when the limestone surface has been lowered by solution.

1
2
3

Before the onset of glaciation a mountain region is often sculpted largely by the work of rivers and the processes of weathering. The hills are rounded and the valleys are V-shaped (1). During a period of glacial activity, valleys become filled with snow and eventually

glaciers and, after thousands of years, the region shows a typically glaciated landscape (2). When the ice has finally disappeared there remains a glacial trough (3) with hanging valleys, truncated spurs, waterfalls and all the landforms associated with deposition of material.

The processes of glacial erosion and deposition produce a distinctive landscape. Cirques, armchair-shaped hollows that are also known as corries, mark the head of a glaciated valley. As glacial processes enlarge them, neighbouring cirques may intersect to produce a sharp rock ridge called an arête, or a pyramidal peak, where three or more cirques stand back to back. Another characteristic feature of glacial troughs is the hanging valley, a tributary valley whose floor has not been eroded down as far as the main valley floor. Other features include those produced by eroded material that is transported elsewhere. Glacial sediment is often moulded into low hills called drumlins, and subglacial tunnels produced by meltwater streams frequently collapse and become choked with sediment, which, after the ice has melted, remains to form ridges called eskers. Where ice melts more slowly, hollows are left by melting chunks of ice that were once enclosed by sediments. These hollows are called kettle-holes. Eventually they fill up either with water or sediment.

eastern England, for example, and such far-
travelled rocks are termed erratics. The finer
sediments, compacted at the base of the glacier
by the weight of the overlying ice, form till or
boulder clay.

The surface of a glacier is often strewn with
rock debris, which either rests on the ice or is
within the glacier and revealed as the ice melts.
Lateral moraines consist of rock debris that has
accumulated along the sides of the glacier as a
result of rockfall from, and erosion of, the valley
sides. Where two glaciers join, the inner lateral
moraines merge to form a medial moraine. In
the ablation zone, the surface of the glacier
becomes increasingly laden with debris "melting out" so that the ice may become completely
buried. At the end of the glacier all rock debris is
dumped, forming a terminal moraine.

Meltwater streams pouring out from glaciers
or flowing in tunnels beneath them can be
powerful agents of erosion and can transport
large quantities of sediment. Bedrock surfaces
become potholed and carved by channels that
are eroded with great speed. As the streams
emerge from the edge of the ice, they carry with
them and deposit vast quantities of sand and
gravel which form flood plains (outwash
plains). Alternatively, meltwater streams may
deposit sediment between the edge of the glacier
and valley side, leaving a "kame terrace" when
the ice finally melts. Meltwater streams feeding
glacial lakes that are dammed by a glacier or
moraine, for example, construct deltas of sand
and gravel and lay down finer sediments (varved
clays) on the lake floor.

Snow processes
Snow plays a smaller part than glacial ice in
landform sculpture. Its most important role is in
avalanches, which, in mountain regions, regularly bring down thousands of tonnes of rock
debris. The mixture of snow, rock and other
debris forms avalanche boulder tongues on the
flat ground where the avalanche comes to rest
and the snow melts. Gullies (avalanche chutes)
on mountain slopes are swept clean of loose
debris several times a year and they are gradually enlarged. Snow patches that remain
stationary on more gentle slopes or in hollows
encourage rock weathering under and around
them. Such a process, termed nivation, may lead
to deepening and enlargement of hollows and
further snow accumulation. This is one way in
which new glaciers are formed.

A glaciated valley exhibits
a distinctive shape and
profile. A cross-section
shows a U-shape, while
longitudinally the valley
floor is marked by a series
of rocky steps and basins.
The zone of accumulation
is characterized by a
cirque, in which snow
collects to produce a firn
field. A bergschrund is a
type of crevasse that opens
up near the top of the firn
field where the head of the
glacier is pulled away from
the cirque walls. A rock
step is where the gradient
becomes much steeper. The
speed of the ice flow is
accelerated and consequent
tension within the ice
creates a number of deep
crevasses called an ice fall.
The zone of ablation has
large accumulations of
various kinds of rock debris.

Glacial erosion of rock
surfaces is typified by a
roche moutonnée, a
resistant rock hummock
that lies in the path of the
ice. The upstream side is
smooth as a result of
abrasion by rock debris
that is frozen into the base
of the glacier. This debris
scratches and scrapes rock,
producing striations. The
downstream side is rough
as a result of ice plucking.
Meltwater removes the
small blocks of rock.

A great variety of material
arrives at the terminus or
snout of a glacier—ranging
from large blocks of rock
and boulders to very finely
ground rock "flour". All
the material is dropped in
a haphazard way as the ice
melts. The mixture of clay
and boulders is termed
glacial till. If the ice
margin remains stationary,
till accumulates to form a
terminal moraine. If the
snout recedes continuously,
no ridge forms.

Landscape-makers: The Seas

The coastline is both the birthplace and the graveyard of the land. Over tens of thousands of years geological uplift of a continent, or a fall in sea level, may create an emerging fringe of new land, whereas a period of submergence drowns the coasts and floods the adjacent river valleys, destroying land but producing some of the most attractive coastal landscapes. More rapid are the changes brought about by the sea itself. Erosion of coastal rocks or beaches can cut back the coastline at a rate of several metres a year, whereas other coastlines are built up at a comparable rate from marine sediments.

Changing coastlines are apparent on a human time-scale. In temperate latitudes beaches tend to be combed down and narrowed by winter waves, only to be restored during the calmer weather of summer. They may be lost one week and replenished the next, demonstrating an invaluable ability to recover from the wounds of all but the most devastating storms. Cliffs are generally much less dynamic, particularly if composed of resistant rock, but any loss that they suffer is permanent because there is no process that is capable of rebuilding them.

Coasts vary greatly around the world. Tropical areas often have wide beaches made up of fine material which in many cases forms broad mangrove swamps that collect sediment and build up the coast. In more exposed tropical zones coral reefs are common, either fringing the shore or (particularly where the sea level is rising) separated from the shore by a lagoon to give a barrier reef. Continued submergence of a small island surrounded by such a reef may produce an atoll. In contrast, Arctic beaches are narrow and coarse, and may be ice-bound for up to 10 months each year. Recession of soft rock cliffs results more from melting of ice in the ground than from wave erosion.

Waves at work
Across great expanses of open ocean energy is transferred from the wind to the sea surface to produce waves, thus fuelling the machine that ultimately creates the coast. Originating as waves with heights of up to 20 or even 30 m (65–100 ft), they lose part of their energy quite rapidly as they travel, and once they have been reduced in height to the lower but more widely spaced ocean swell they continue to travel across enormous distances.

The coasts of western Europe receive waves produced almost 10,000 km (6,200 miles) away off Cape Horn, and swell reaching California has sometimes crossed more than 11,000 km

Cliffs are attacked by waves at the zone that lies between high tide (HT) and low tide (LT). The rate of erosion depends on the strength and jointing pattern of the rock and the angle at which the strata are presented to the sea. Erosion begins when water and rocks are hurled at the cliff and new fragments are broken off. The pressure of the water also compresses air in joints and cracks to shatter the rock face. As the base of the cliff is attacked, a notch (1) may be cut, and as this is made deeper the cliff above collapses. Eventually a wave-cut platform (2) is created, the top of which is exposed at low tide. The debris from the cliff is carried along the coast or deposited offshore (3). The shallow sea bed now slows down incoming waves: they attack the cliff (4), but their energy is reduced. In calm water, for example at the head of a bay (5), wave energy is diffused and light material such as sand is deposited as beaches.

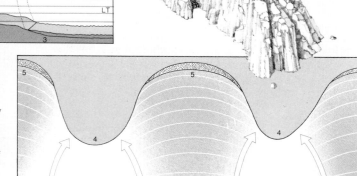

THE SEA COAST
The coastline is continually changing, whether day by day as the tides sift and sort the sand and shingle on the beaches, or over tens of thousands of years as the erosive power of waves carves out headlands and bays. And over millions of years the coastline is subjected to major changes of sea level, whether it is the land uplifting or sinking, or the sea itself rising or receding. Today, interference by man can damage the coast. Dam-building and river-channel engineering drastically reduce the amount of sediment reaching the coast; and sea walls built to protect the coast and groynes constructed to retard sand removal both pose a long-term threat to adjacent coasts, which become starved of the sediment that previously supplied their beaches.

When a headland has been created (below), wave erosion continues on both sides and a cave (1) may be formed. After many years of wave action the cave will break through to the other side and an arch (2) may be created.

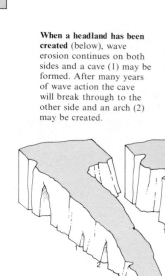

Light material such as mud, sand and shingle is carried by the sea. Waves tend to push the particles obliquely up a beach (right), but the backwash moves the material down again at right-angles to the shore. Thus the materials move in a zigzag fashion along the beach (1). This is known as longshore drift. When the load-carrying capacity of the waves is reduced for any reason, the material is deposited and forms a variety of features. The largest beaches (2) are found in the calmest waters such as in bays or at river mouths, with the finest grains sorted out nearest to the sea and larger pebbles stranded higher up. Spits (3) and bars (4) are sand ridges deposited across a bay or river mouth. When one end of the ridge is attached to the land it is called a spit. Spits are very often shaped like a hook as waves are refracted around the tip of land. Bars are formed where sand is deposited in shallow water offshore across the entrances to bays and run parallel to the coastline. Dunes, pictured above, are formed when sand on the beach is driven inland by onshore winds. Very often they isolate flooded land behind them to form coastal features such as salt marshes and mud flats.

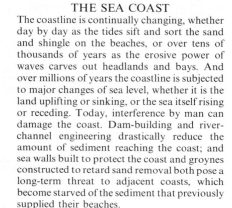

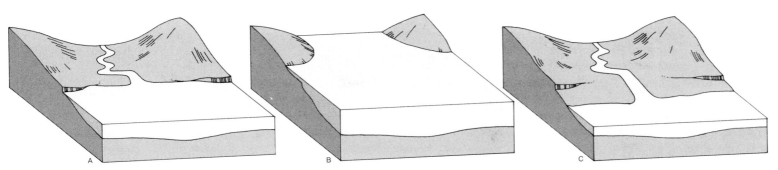

There are two major kinds of coastline—coastlines of submergence and coastlines of emergence. They are created by either a sinking or an uplift of the land, or by a change in sea level. A coastline with wave-cut cliffs and a river valley (A), for example, that experiences a rise in sea level will produce a new coastline (B) with a drowned estuary, coastal uplands isolated as islands, and a submerged coastal plain. The same coastline subjected to a drop in sea level (C) results in an extended river, abandoned cliffs far inland, and a raised beach that forms a new coastal plain.

(6,800 miles) of the Pacific from the storm belt south of New Zealand. The waves thus act as a giant conveyor for the energy that is finally used up in a few seconds of intense activity. Few other natural systems gather their energy so widely and then concentrate it so effectively.

A ball floating on the sea surface shows that, although a passing wave-form moves forward, the water (and ball) follow a near-circular path and end up almost where they started. Beneath the surface the water follows similar orbits, but the amount of movement becomes progressively less with depth, until it dies out altogether. The greater the wave-length (the distance between crests) the greater is the depth of disturbance.

Long-swell waves approaching a gentle shore start disturbing the sea bed far from the coast and these waves slow up, pack closer together and increase in height until they become unstable, thus producing the spilling white surf that carries much sediment to build up wide sandy beaches. Shorter local storm waves disturb the water to less depth, and thus reach much closer inshore before they interact with the sea bed. Such waves do not therefore break until they plunge directly down on to the beach, leading to severe erosion, which results in the production of steep pebble beaches.

Waves slow up in shallow water, and so an undulating sea bed causes their crests to bend and change their direction of approach. As a result, waves converge towards headlands (where their erosional attack is concentrated),

but they diverge as they enter bays, spreading out their energy and encouraging the deposition of the sediment they carry across the sea bed close inshore. The high-energy waves at the headlands remove any rock fragments that become detached and transport them to the beaches that form at the bayheads.

Erosional coasts
Much of the local variability of coastal scenery results from differing rates of erosion on different types of rock. Bays are cut back rapidly into soft rocks such as clay, sand or gravel. Headlands are evidence that the sea takes longer to remove higher areas of harder rock such as granite or limestone. Despite the enormous power of storm waves, erosion of resistant rocks is slow and relies on any weakness that the sea can exploit.

Joints, faults and bedding planes are etched out by the water and by rock fragments hurled against them by breaking waves. Air compressed into such crevices by water pressure widens and deepens them into cracks and then into caves. In this way a solid cliff face can be eroded to form the great variety of features.

Resistant rocks can form steep, simple cliffs of great height—more than 600 m (2,000 ft) in some places—and the sea may have to undercut them to produce collapse and retreat. Cliffs of weaker rocks rarely reach 100 m (330 ft) in height and are more rapidly eroded by atmospheric processes, by running water and by

landslips. There the role of the sea is largely confined to removing the rock debris from the foot of the cliff. Soft rock cliffs are gently sloping but complex in form.

Coasts of deposition
Although waves bend as they approach the shore, they rarely become completely parallel to the coastline. Wave crests drive sediment obliquely towards the beach, whereas the troughs carry it back directly offshore down the beach slope. In this way, sand and pebbles are transported in a zigzag motion, called longshore drift, away from the areas where they are produced. One such source of material is cliff erosion, but on average about 95 per cent of the material moving on to beaches was originally carried to the coast by rivers.

Beaches are built up wherever longshore drift is impeded (for example, by a headland) or where wave and current energy is reduced (as at the head of a bay). An abundant supply of sediment may build a sand bar across the mouth of a bay or in shallow water offshore. Where the coast changes direction, longshore drift may continue in its original direction and build a spit out from the land. Depositional features may become strengthened by vegetation. Plants may take root and bind together newly deposited sediments, but they constitute relatively delicate coasts that are vulnerable to erosion if for any reason they are not continually supplied with fresh deposits of sediment.

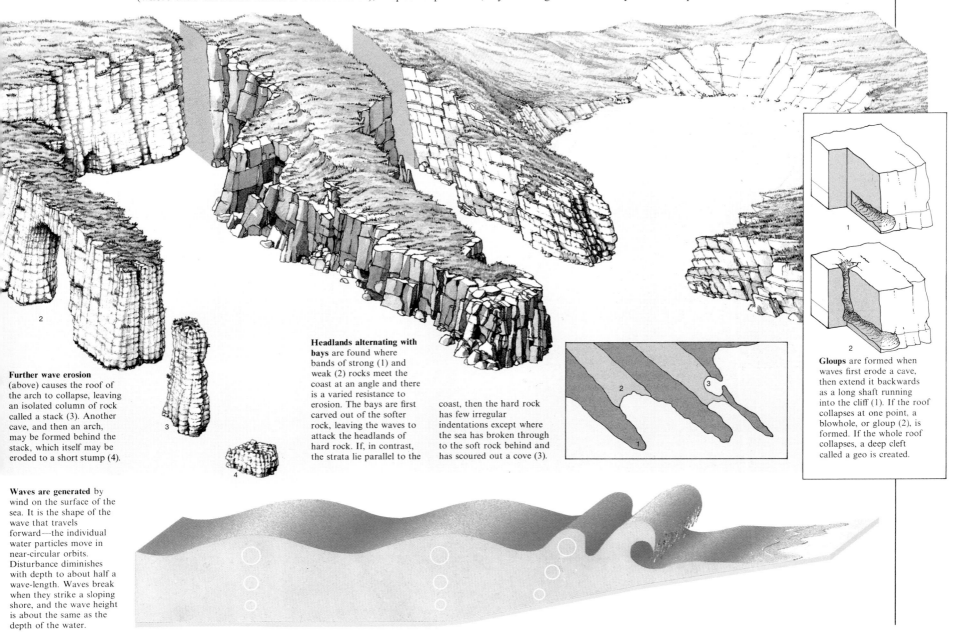

Further wave erosion (above) causes the roof of the arch to collapse, leaving an isolated column of rock called a stack (3). Another cave, and then an arch, may be formed behind the stack, which itself may be eroded to a short stump (4).

Headlands alternating with bays are found where bands of strong (1) and weak (2) rocks meet the coast at an angle and there is a varied resistance to erosion. The bays are first carved out of the softer rock, leaving the waves to attack the headlands of hard rock. If, in contrast, the strata lie parallel to the coast, then the hard rock has few irregular indentations except where the sea has broken through to the soft rock behind and has scoured out a cove (3).

Gloups are formed when waves first erode a cave, then extend it backwards as a long shaft running into the cliff (1). If the roof collapses at one point, a blowhole, or gloup (2), is formed. If the whole roof collapses, a deep cleft called a geo is created.

Waves are generated by wind on the surface of the sea. It is the shape of the wave that travels forward—the individual water particles move in near-circular orbits. Disturbance diminishes with depth to about half a wave-length. Waves break when they strike a sloping shore, and the wave height is about the same as the depth of the water.

Landscape-makers: Wind and Weathering

Winds are part of the global circulation of air and they can affect landforms wherever surface material is loose and unprotected by vegetation. The effects of a strong wind are a familiar sight – whether in the dust clouds that rise from a ploughed field after a dry spell, or in the sand swept along the beach on a windy day. Weathering is the disintegration and decomposition of rocks through their exposure to the atmosphere. It includes the changes that destroy the original structure of rocks, and few on the Earth's surface have not been weathered at one time or another in the history of our evolving landscape.

Active and fixed dunes in Africa and western Asia

Most sand seas today are being actively moulded by winds. The landscape has long been shaped by wind, and some dune fields produced in dry climates in the distant past may be "fossilized" now by soils and vegetation cover. Desertification often occurs where this vegetation is disturbed by man.

☐ Fixed sand dunes

⬚ Active sand dunes

Sand dunes cover only 20 per cent of the world's deserts, and tend to be concentrated in a small number of sand seas, or ergs, such as the Erg Bourharet in Algeria (above).

Longitudinal, or seif, dunes (below) are long, narrow ridges that lie parallel to the direction of prevailing winds. Surface heating and wind flow produce vertical spiralling motions of air.

Direction of wind

EROSION AND WEATHERING

Winds result from the differential heating of regions of the globe. They act indirectly as agents of erosion through water or waves, but they also directly affect the surface of the Earth, moulding landforms either by erosion or deposition. The nature of weathering processes and the rate at which they operate depend upon climate, the properties of the rock and the conditions of the biosphere. Both wind erosion and the various weathering processes are significant landscape-makers.

Many rocks are formed deep in the Earth, where they are in equilibrium with the forces that created them. If they become exposed at the surface, they are in disequilibrium with atmospheric forces. This brings about the changes —adjustments to atmospheric and organic agents—that we call weathering. Products of weathering are moved by agents of erosion, one of which is the wind. Where the surface is protected, for example by vegetation, the wind has little effect, but where strong winds attack loose surface material that is unprotected, erosion, abrasion and deposition may occur, producing characteristic landforms.

How wind shapes the surface

Strong winds occur in many places, but nowhere are they more effective in forming the surface of the land than in deserts, where their work is largely unhindered by vegetation. There the wind can pick up material and then, charged with sand particles, blast away at the ground, carrying away the debris and depositing it. Many notorious desert winds are associated with sand movement and dust storms—the harmattan of West Africa and the sirocco of the Middle East, for example.

Wind erosion occurs where winds charged with sand attack soils or rock. Dry soils may be broken up and the resulting debris, which includes soil nutrients, is carried away as dust. This poses a serious problem, especially when arid and semi-arid lands experience drought. Wind erosion involving the lifting and blowing away of loose material from the ground surface is called deflation.

Erosion by sand and rock fragments carried by winds is called abrasion. In this way winds erode individual surface pebbles into distinctive shapes known as ventifacts. They can also mould larger rock masses into aerodynamic shapes known as yardangs—features that often look rather like upturned rowing boats. Some of these features are so large that they have been identified only since satellite photographs have become available. Finally, winds erode by attrition, which involves the mutual wearing down of particles as they are carried along.

Winds can transport material in three different ways. They can lift loose, sand-sized particles into the air and carry them downwind along trajectories that resemble those of ballistic missiles: the particles rise steeply and descend along gentle flight paths. This produces a bouncing movement known as saltation in a layer extending approximately 1 m (3 ft) above the

in   Direction of wind   cm

Grain path   Rebound

Sand cloud

Surface creep

Loose sand surface

Sand particles move in a series of long jumps—a process called saltation. Particles describe a curved path (above), the height and length of which depends upon the mass of the grain, the wind velocity and the number of other particles moving around. Saltation only occurs in a layer extending up to approximately 1 m (3 ft) above the ground surface. Sand grains moving in this way are also responsible for the abraded base of features such as pedestal rocks (right). These landforms are weathered first—for example by the crystallization of salts—and are then eroded by the sand-laden winds.

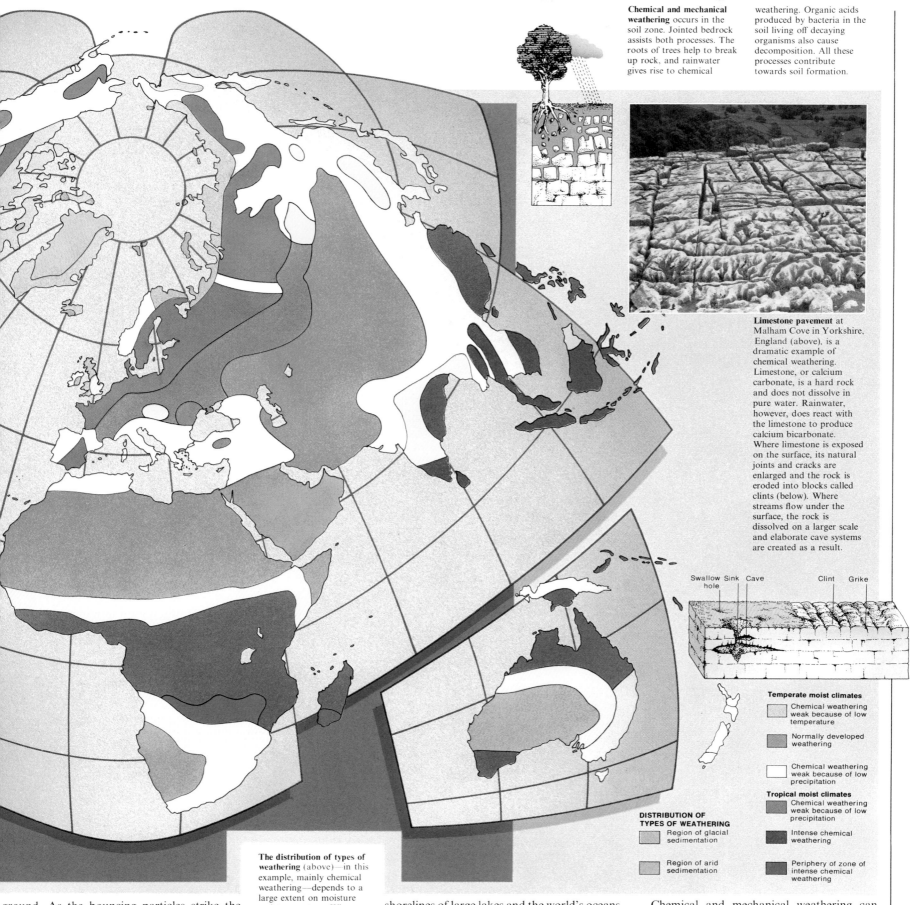

Chemical and mechanical weathering occurs in the soil zone. Jointed bedrock assists both processes. The roots of trees help to break up rock, and rainwater gives rise to chemical weathering. Organic acids produced by bacteria in the soil living off decaying organisms also cause decomposition. All these processes contribute towards soil formation.

Limestone pavement at Malham Cove in Yorkshire, England (above), is a dramatic example of chemical weathering. Limestone, or calcium carbonate, is a hard rock and does not dissolve in pure water. Rainwater, however, does react with the limestone to produce calcium bicarbonate. Where limestone is exposed on the surface, its natural joints and cracks are enlarged and the rock is eroded into blocks called clints (below). Where streams flow under the surface, the rock is dissolved on a larger scale and elaborate cave systems are created as a result.

Swallow Sink Cave   Clint Grike
hole

DISTRIBUTION OF
TYPES OF WEATHERING

Region of glacial sedimentation

Region of arid sedimentation

Temperate moist climates

Chemical weathering weak because of low temperature

Normally developed weathering

Chemical weathering weak because of low precipitation

Tropical moist climates

Chemical weathering weak because of low precipitation

Intense chemical weathering

Periphery of zone of intense chemical weathering

The distribution of types of weathering (above)—in this example, mainly chemical weathering—depends to a large extent on moisture and temperature. When classifying regions with different rates of chemical weathering in terms of climatic zones, many areas of the world can be placed into one of two principal categories: tropical moist climates and temperate moist climates. The white areas on the map are mountain ranges or regions of tectonic activity where there is no appreciable weathering mantle.

ground. As the bouncing particles strike the surface, they push other particles along the ground (creep or drift). Fine particles that are disturbed by saltation rise up into the airflow and are carried away as dust (suspension).

The materials eroded and transported by winds must eventually come to rest in features of deposition, the most extensive of which are sand dunes. Sand seas at first sight appear to be random and complex, rather like a choppy ocean, but their features generally fall into three size groups: small ripples, which have a wavelength of up to 3 m (10 ft) and a height of 20 cm (8 in); dunes, with a wavelength of 20–300 m (65–1,000 ft) and a height of up to 30 m (68 ft); and sand mountains or "draa", which have a wavelength of 1–3 km (0.6–1.5 miles) and rise to a height of up to 200 m (650 ft). Within each size group various forms can be explained in terms of the nature of the sand and the kinds of winds that blow over it. Where winds blow consistently from one direction, long linear dunes form parallel or transverse to the wind direction. Where sand supply is limited, horned "barchan" dunes may form. If winds blow from several directions during a year, then star-shaped dunes and other complex patterns appear. Sand dunes are also common along the

shorelines of large lakes and the world's oceans, where onshore winds can pile quite extensive areas of loose drifting sand.

Agents of weathering

Weathering takes two forms: mechanical weathering breaks up rock without altering its mineral constituents, whereas chemical weathering changes in some way the nature of mineral crystals. One agent of mechanical weathering is temperature change. It used to be thought that rocks disintegrated as a result of a huge daily range of temperature (thermal weathering). Despite travellers' tales of rocks splitting in the desert night with cracks like pistol shots, there is little evidence to support this view. In the presence of water, however, alternate heating and cooling of rocks does result in fracture. Frost is also an effective rock-breaker. The freezing of water and expansion of ice in the cracks and pores of rocks create disruptive pressures; alternate freezing and thawing eventually causes pieces of rock to break off in angular fragments. Finally, the roots of plants and trees grow into the joints of rock and widen them, thus loosening the structure of the rock. Animals burrowing through the soil can have a similar effect on rocks.

Chemical and mechanical weathering can work hand in hand. In arid regions, for example, the crystallization of salts results in the weathering of rock. As water evaporates from the rock surface, salt crystals grow (from minerals dissolved in the water) in small openings in the rock. In time these crystals bring to bear enough pressure to break off rock fragments from the parent block.

Chemical weathering is most effective in humid tropical climates, however, and it usually involves the decomposition of rocks as a result of their exposure to air and rainwater, which contains dissolved chemicals. Carbon dioxide from the air, for example, becomes dissolved in rainwater, making it into weak carbonic acid. This reacts with minerals such as calcite, which is found in many rocks. Similarly, rocks can be oxidized by oxygen in the air. This happens to rocks that contain iron, for example, if they are exposed on the surface: a reddish iron oxide is produced which causes the rocks to crumble.

Over many thousands, even millions, of years, the processes of mechanical and chemical weathering have affected many of the rocks on the Earth's surface. When rocks are weakened in such a way, they then fall prey to the agents of erosion—water, ice, winds and waves.

Landscape-makers: Man

Man has done much to reshape the face of the planet since his first appearance on Earth more than two million years ago. Early man did little to harm the environment but, with the rise of agriculture, the landscape began to change. An increasing population and the growth of urban settlements gradually created greater demands for agricultural land and living space. But industrialization during the last 200 years has had the biggest impact. Man's search for and exploitation of the Earth's resources has to a large extent transformed the natural landscape and at the same time created totally artificial man-made environments.

MAN THE GEOLOGICAL AGENT
In 1864 a conservationist named George Perkins Marsh introduced the thesis that "man in fact made the Earth" rather than the converse. The idea of man as a geological agent was further developed in the 1920s. Man modifies the landscape in many ways; sometimes he transforms the Earth completely—he even creates land where no land was before.

Man's major impact on the landscape has been through forest clearance. He made the first attack on natural forests about 8,000 years ago in Neolithic times in northern and western Europe, as revealed by the changing composition of tree pollen deposited in bogs. After Roman times, especially in the Mediterranean region, there was another spate of forest clearance, so that by the Middle Ages little original forest survived in the Old World. As population and emigration increased, it was the turn of trees in the New World and Africa to fall before the axe and plough. Man's present voracious appetite for timber and its products could, if unchecked, clear most of the Earth's great forests by the end of this century.

Forest clearance not only changes the appearance of the landscape but can alter the balance of nature within a region. The hydrological cycle may be affected, and soil erosion may be increased, which in turn chokes rivers with sediment and leads to the silting up of harbours and estuaries. The coastal area of Valencia in Spain, for example, has widened by nearly 4 km (2.5 miles) since Roman times, much of which can be accounted for by forest clearance, and subsequent soil erosion and the deposition of the material by rivers as they near the sea. Reafforestation of an area can reduce soil erosion and the threat of flooding. Landscape management can reduce wind speeds: for example, shelter belts in the Russian steppes have been planted over distances of more than 100 km (62 miles).

Water management
The second great impact of man has been on the waterways of the world. The most spectacular changes are caused by the construction of dams to make vast new lakes. Such projects have frequently had effects far beyond those originally anticipated. The Aswan High Dam on the River Nile was completed in 1970, creating Lake Nasser and making possible the irrigation of an additional 550,000 hectares (1,358,000 acres) in upper Egypt. But some would argue that the dam holds back silt from the rivers and stores it in the lake, a fact that has seriously reduced the rate of silting in the Nile delta. This has resulted in increased salinity and some loss of fertility of the soil, as well as changes to the delta's coastline. The storage of silt in Lake Nasser has caused increased erosion of the river bed downstream and the undermining of the foundations of bridges and barrages.

Other man-made changes to rivers include straightening and canalization, usually for

Massive power stations (left) symbolize man's modifications to the landscape in modern, industrialized society. Demand for energy and mineral resources has led to the creation of huge holes in the ground like this borax mine (below left) in the Mojave Desert in California. The open pit is 100 m (330 ft) deep, 1,460 m (4,800 ft) long and 915 m (3,000 ft) wide. In opening up resource areas in Brazil, the Trans-Amazonian highway has disturbed the forest (below).

Hong Kong's bustling waterfront (below) captures the true essence of urban man. If space is in short supply, he expands his world vertically and maximizes his use of every square metre. Central business districts in the world's major cities reflect this concern with space.

flood protection, but also to prevent the channel from shifting. As long ago as the third millennium BC, during the reign of Emperor Yao, a hydraulic engineer was apparently appointed to control the wandering course of the Hwang-Ho (Yellow River), and the system he devised survived for at least 1,500 years. Even so, over the centuries, the river has changed course radically, and today measures are still being taken to control the fine sediment that the river carries and the flooding caused by its deposition. The Missouri River in the United States is estimated to erode material from an area of about 3,680 hectares (9,000 acres) annually over a length of 1,220 km (758 miles). It is little wonder that engineers attempt to control rivers by means of realignment or try to "train" a river's flow by using concrete stays.

New land from old

The continuing pressure of population on food resources and the need to create new agricultural land illustrate still further the impact of man as a landscape-shaper. As part of irrigation projects land is often levelled and new waterways are created in the form of canals. Pakistan has one of the most extensive man-made irrigation systems in the world. It controls almost completely the flow of the Indus, Sutlej and Punjab rivers through some 640 km (400 miles) of linking canals.

A huge demand for rice in many parts of southeastern Asia has led to farmers terracing steep slopes on many mountainous islands. In the Netherlands, about one-third of the entire cultivated area of the country is land that has been reclaimed from the sea. In the future more grandiose schemes are likely. Any large-scale expansion of agricultural land in the Soviet Union will be mainly dependent on water supply. There have been plans since the 1930s to divert northward-flowing rivers to irrigated areas in the south and west. This idea, and it is believed that it might become a reality by the turn of the century, could have serious implications for the waters of the Arctic Ocean. If the amount of fresh water flowing into the ocean is reduced, salinity will increase, thus affecting the melting of ice floes and, consequently, sea level.

Man has also made his mark along the coastlines, from small-scale measures, such as

the construction of groynes—wooden piles that reduce the amount of sand that is transported along the beach by wave action—to large-scale man-made harbours.

Modern man, the urban dweller of the machine age, has brought great changes to the face of the landscape. The need for materials for the construction of the urban fabric has led to the creation of huge quarries, in which building stone and road-building materials are extracted from the ground. Demand for energy and minerals leads to extensive modification of the landscape, especially where mineral deposits are near the surface and can be extracted by open-cast mining. The largest holes on Earth (excluding ocean basins) are those that result from the extraction of fuel (coal) and minerals.

The side effects of mining can be detrimental to the environment. Land may subside and despoliation of the landscape by slag heaps, for example, is considerable. Escaping coal dust can suffocate vegetation in a mining area, and gases given off during some mining operations can also damage plant and animal life.

Reclamation of spoiled areas is obligatory in many countries. Old open-cast workings are often filled with water to be used for recreational facilities, and slag heaps are treated and planted with vegetation: research has produced certain strains of plants that will grow even in the most acidic soils.

The true impact of man

During the last hundred years or so man has become much more aware of his role as an agent of landscape creation and destruction. The significance of man the landscape-maker, in comparison with slow, natural changes, is the speed with which he effects transformation, the sheer amount of energy which he can apply to a relatively small area, and the selectiveness and determination with which he applies that energy. Man's increased impact has not been a smooth and continuous process: it has occurred at different rates in different places and at different times. While it can be argued that some landscapes have been constructed which themselves conserve and often beautify the natural environment, man's active role has primarily been destructive: he has transformed the Earth's surface, perhaps irreversibly.

THE DUTCH POLDERS

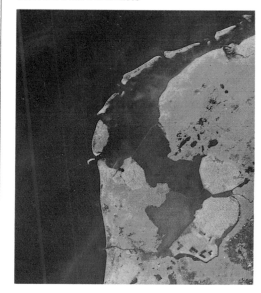

Reclamation of the Dutch polders from the North Sea is an example of man creating land. Many centuries ago a large part of what is now the western Netherlands was beneath the sea. From the 15th to the 17th centuries (A) dykes were constructed to enclose land and protect it against inundation from the sea, and enable it to be farmed. Later, windmills were used to drain away sea water. Further reclamation in the 19th and 20th centuries (B) has brought the total area to

165,000 hectares (408,000 acres). In 1932 a 40 km (25 mile) dam was completed, enclosing the Zuider Zee—which is now a freshwater lake that was renamed the IJsselmeer—and reducing Holland's vulnerable coastline by 320 km (200 miles). To create a polder, a dyke is built and the water pumped out. Reeds are grown to help dry out the soil. After a few years drains are put in to remove water remaining. Newly created polders (light blue) show up well on this satellite image (top).

Man-made environments have become increasingly complex and large scale. Highway construction—this vast interchange (left) is in Chicago—is typical of the extensive use of land for modern transport systems alone. The acreage of land use classified as urban continues to increase. Man's endeavours to make still more land available for his many purposes have extended to cultivating previously inhospitable desert lands (above). More than half the land in Israel is

naturally unproductive because of its aridity. By means of elaborate water carriage and storage schemes and scientifically researched irrigation projects, the desert has been totally transformed from a barren wasteland into intensively cultivated fields. Output from agriculture can also be increased by terracing. In densely populated areas, or mountainous regions, as in Luzon in the Philippines (right), man's skilful landscaping has completely reshaped the topography.

Part 3

THE EMERGENCE OF LIFE

How life on Earth began and developed
How life has evolved and spread over the planet
How man came to inherit the Earth

THE STAGES OF LIFE

Simple organic molecules, the precursors of life, could certainly have evolved in Earth's primitive atmosphere. Energy from the Sun, volcanoes and electric storms had the power to combine the basic chemicals into the amino acids and other molecules that are the constituents of living matter, forming droplets of "pre-life" in pools and on shorelines. Concentrations of droplets collected round some minerals, coagulating in a "soup" of long-chain polymers—proteins and nucleic acids which together form the living cell. Thus far have scientists re-created life's origins, but the combining of proteins and nucleic acids into a living unit remains to be achieved.

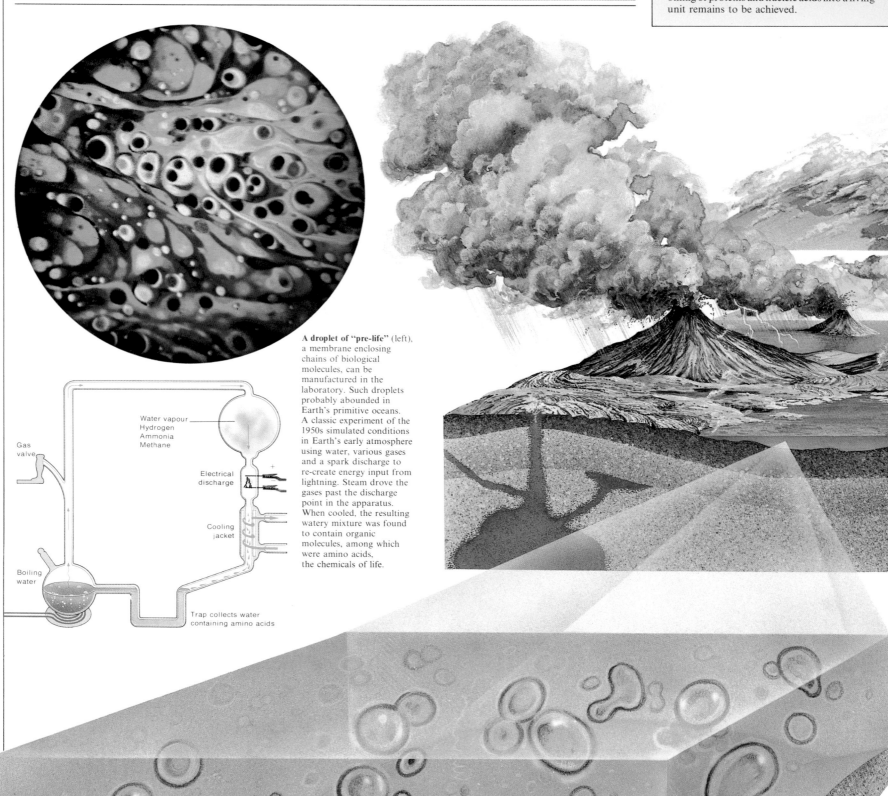

A droplet of "pre-life" (left), a membrane enclosing chains of biological molecules, can be manufactured in the laboratory. Such droplets probably abounded in Earth's primitive oceans. A classic experiment of the 1950s simulated conditions in Earth's early atmosphere using water, various gases and a spark discharge to re-create energy input from lightning. Steam drove the gases past the discharge point in the apparatus. When cooled, the resulting watery mixture was found to contain organic molecules, among which were amino acids, the chemicals of life.

Gas valve

Water vapour
Hydrogen
Ammonia
Methane

Electrical discharge

Cooling jacket

Boiling water

Trap collects water containing amino acids

LIFE BEGINS

A "primordial soup" of organic molecules, each separated from the water by a membrane, formed thick concentrations in Earth's shallow pools. From these evolved the long-chain polymers that form proteins and nucleic acids in every living cell.

The Source of Life

Life may have come to Earth from outer space – some meteorites contain life-like organic molecules – but the basic constituents of life, the biochemical structures called proteins and nucleic acids, could just as well have formed on Earth itself. By simulating possible primitive conditions on Earth, and applying a likely energy source, American scientists of the 1950s manufactured, from inorganic substances, the amino acids that form the sub-units of all living things.

Water played a key part in the creation of life on Earth. At first the temperature of the newly formed planet was far too high for water to exist in a liquid state. Instead, it formed a dense atmosphere of steam, which, as the Earth cooled, condensed into droplets of rain that poured down for perhaps thousands of years. This torrential, thundery rain eroded the land and dissolved the minerals, which collected in pools on the surface.

Earth's original atmosphere was also very different from today's. Most importantly, it contained no free oxygen, the gas which makes air-breathing life possible; the primitive atmosphere was composed of carbon monoxide, carbon dioxide, hydrogen and nitrogen. But the absence of oxygen created two conditions that are essential if life is to evolve. First, without oxygen the atmosphere could have no layer of ozone (an oxygen compound), which now acts as a barrier to most of the Sun's high-energy radiation (mainly ultraviolet light). Second, the absence of free oxygen meant that any complex chemicals that might be formed would not immediately break down again. Thus the molecules of life could form.

The chemistry of life

Life may be distinguished from nonlife in three ways: living organisms are able to increase the complexity of their parts through synthetic, self-building reactions; they obtain and use energy by breaking down chemical compounds; and they can make new copies of themselves.

It is the combined properties of the chemicals

of life that make them so special, not just the chemicals themselves. Experiments in the last few decades have given us a very good idea of how life could have arisen from the simple, non-living chemicals which compose it. In the early 1950s Harold Urey and Stanley Miller simulated the atmosphere of a primitive world by filling a flask with water, ammonia, methane and hydrogen. They supplied it with energy in the form of heat and an electric spark—to simulate lightning—and the experiment was left to run for a week.

Analysing the mixture formed, they found it contained many chemicals that are associated with living things, particularly nitrogen compounds called amino acids—the really important chemicals of life. Further experiments brought together other gas mixtures, including the one that is now thought to have covered the young Earth, and these gave similar results, as long as there was no free oxygen present. The resulting mixture of organic compounds in water came to be known as the "primordial

soup", and it is from this "soup" that life may have emerged.

Miller and Urey had shown that the basic substances of life can be derived from a primitive atmosphere. But there are still large gaps in our understanding of how these substances became more organized and self-regulating: in other words, how they became alive. More complex molecular structures somehow developed through the linking up of the basic units to form long, chain-like sequences of larger units, called polymers. But how this happened is still not fully understood.

The two most important classes of biological molecules are proteins and nucleic acids, both of which are polymers. Proteins are the building materials of living matter, the chief components of muscles, skin and hair. They also form enzymes—the chemicals that control biochemical reaction in living cells. Nucleic acids—DNA (deoxyribonucleic acid) and RNA (ribonucleic acid)—are so called because they are found in the central nuclei of cells. They are the cell's genetic material, the raw stuff of heredity. They act as the memories and the messengers of life, storing information in units called genes, and releasing that information to the cells when it is needed. Nucleic acids can reproduce themselves and, without this ability, life would not exist or continue.

The basic units that link together to form proteins are amino acids, and all proteins in living organisms are made up of just 20 different amino acids. In chemical terms, a protein molecule is a polymer consisting of a long chain of amino acid units joined together in a particular sequence, and the code to this sequence is held by DNA.

How living chemicals joined

Experiments with simulated primordial conditions have produced many amino acids other than the 20 commonly found in proteins. All amino acids (and other types of chemicals) tend to "stick" on to the surface of clay, but those 20 found in proteins stick particularly well to clays rich in the metal nickel. This suggests that the first proteins may have been formed in pools or on the fringes of seas, where the primordial soup was in contact with nickel-rich clays. There heat from the Sun or a volcano could have combined the amino acids to form a primitive protein.

The four classes of chemicals that form the basic components of nucleic acids have also, like the amino acids, been "cooked up" in a primordial soup, and they too will stick to clay to form long-chain polymers. And, just as nickel-rich clays are best at absorbing the amino acid constituents of protein, so clays rich in zinc absorb the building blocks of nucleic acids. This suggests that such clays could have been the birth-place of genes, which are the "messengers" of inheritance.

However, the coupling of proteins and nucleic acids, which together form the living cell, has yet to be explained, and it is improbable that proteins or nucleic acids alone could have provided the basis for life.

The Russian biochemist I. A. Oparin has shown that, in water, solutions of polymers (such as proteins) have a tendency to form droplets surrounded by an outer membrane very like that which encloses living cells. As these droplets grow by absorbing more polymers, some split in two when they become too large for stability. If such a droplet had protein enzymes to harness energy and make more polymers, and if it had nucleic acids with instructions for making those proteins, and if each new droplet received a complete copy of the nucleic acid instructions, the droplet would be alive—it would be a living cell.

THE RADIANT SUN
A dense atmosphere of water vapour and various gases—but not oxygen—formed round the cooling planet Earth after its creation 4,600 million years ago. Oxygen in the atmosphere would have prevented the evolution of life from nonliving organic matter by blocking the Sun's ultraviolet radiation (which may have provided energy for the forming of organic compounds), and free oxygen would also have destroyed such compounds as they began to accumulate.

THE PRIMITIVE ATMOSPHERE
Volcanic eruptions drove water vapour and gases into the atmosphere of the young Earth; lightning and other discharges of atmospheric electricity accompanied the torrential rain; dissolved minerals collected in the pools. These were some of the preconditions for life on Earth, whereby mixtures of organic compounds in water may have combined to form more complex units essential for life.

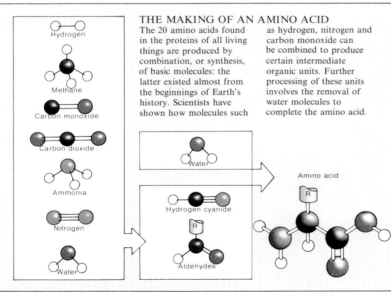

THE MAKING OF AN AMINO ACID
The 20 amino acids found in the proteins of all living things are produced by combination, or synthesis, of basic molecules: the latter existed almost from the beginnings of Earth's history. Scientists have shown how molecules such as hydrogen, nitrogen and carbon monoxide can be combined to produce certain intermediate organic units. Further processing of these units involves the removal of water molecules to complete the amino acid.

Hydrogen
Methane
Carbon monoxide
Carbon dioxide
Ammonia
Nitrogen
Water

Water
Hydrogen cyanide
Aldehydes
Amino acid

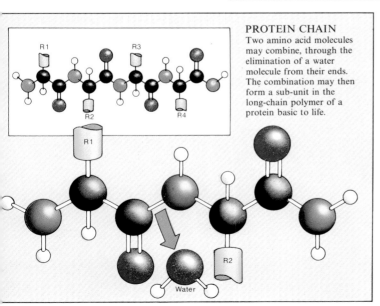

PROTEIN CHAIN
Two amino acid molecules may combine, through the elimination of a water molecule from their ends. The combination may then form a sub-unit in the long-chain polymer of a protein basic to life.

Water

The Structure of Life

All life forms stem from a single cell, and every cell contains in its nucleus instructions for the re-creation of the organism of which it forms a part. These are encoded in chromosomes, which contain the miraculous molecular substance of DNA, sectioned into units of heredity called genes. The genetic code determines in detail the physical characteristics of an individual creature, so that variations in DNA cause variations in the individual. Scientists believe that it is the interaction of the individual variation with the environment that ultimately leads to the evolution of the similar, interbreeding groups of creatures that are known as species.

THE HIDDEN SECRET
Dramatic discoveries in recent decades have revolutionized biology, the primary life science. Scientists can now trace parts of the genetic blueprint that lays down the pattern for every form of life, linking the large-scale unfolding of species that we know as evolution with the ultra-microscopic activity of the molecules within the nucleus of every cell. This may be the secret behind the rich diversity of life on Earth.

Deoxyribonucleic acid (DNA) consists of a "backbone" of alternating sugar and phosphate molecules, and to each sugar is attached one of four nitrogenous bases (adenine, guanine, thymine and cytostine, or A, G, T, C). A single gene might contain 2,000 of these bases, and in the body cell of a human being the 46 chromosomes (thread-like bodies of DNA and protein) run to 3,000 million bases. The sequence of these bases stores the information for making amino acids into proteins, just as the sequence of letters in this sentence stores the information for making a particular verbal structure. But the DNA alphabet has only four letters (A, G, T, C).

The thread of life

DNA is a double molecule, resembling a twisted ladder, its two main strands twining around each other to form the famous double helix. The strands are linked by pairs of bases—A and T, or G and C—whose shape is such that each pair fits together neatly, like pieces of a jigsaw, to form the rungs of the DNA ladder. As a result, the information on the strands can be duplicated by "unzipping" the double helix and making new strands by using the old ones as templates. DNA stores, duplicates and passes on the information that makes life alive.

Cells multiply by splitting in two, and each newly made cell thus gets instructions for its existence by the mechanism of heredity, the gene. But heredity is a word more often applied to the passing on of DNA from an organism to its offspring. In sexual reproduction the offspring gets some of the DNA, usually half, from one parent, and the rest from the other, ending up with a unique mix all of its own.

The laws of heredity

Man has long known that characteristics can be passed on from one generation to the next, for he has been selectively breeding crops and animals for thousands of years. However, it was not until the mid-nineteenth century that an obscure Austrian monk, Gregor Mendel (1822–84), discovered the laws that govern inheritance, and his work was ignored until the beginning of the twentieth century, when more powerful microscopes made possible the direct observation of the cell.

Mendel experimented with pea plants because they had easily recognizable traits, and because, although normally self-fertilizing, they could be cross-fertilized with pollen from a different plant. Mendel made many crosses between different pure-bred plants and found that in the offspring, or hybrids, some characters always prevailed over others: red flowers over white, tall plants over short, and so on. He called the prevailing characters dominant, and the non-prevailing characters recessive. He then let the first-generation hybrids self-fertilize, and found not only that the recessive traits reappeared in the hybrids' offspring, but also that they reappeared in a constant proportion of three dominant to one recessive; the second generation contained three times as many red-flowered peas as white-flowered peas.

To explain his results, Mendel proposed that each plant had two hereditary "factors"—today called alleles—for each character, and that the dominant factor suppressed the recessive factor. If a plant inherited both a dominant and a recessive factor, the dominant one would prevail. Only if both factors were recessive would the recessive character be apparent. Mendel found many other pairs of traits where one form was dominant and the other recessive. He established that permutations arising from the crossing of the two first-generation hybrids allows the dominant gene to be present in three out of four crosses in the second generation; but

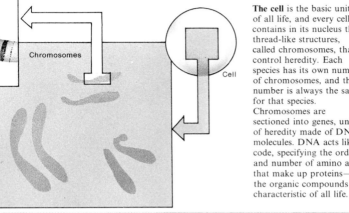

Genes

Chromosomes

Cell

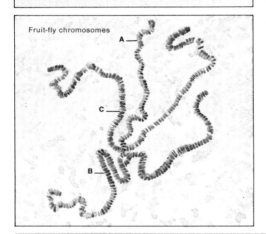

Protein (myoglobin)   Amino acids

Fruit-fly chromosomes

A

C

B

The cell is the basic unit of all life, and every cell contains in its nucleus the thread-like structures, called chromosomes, that control heredity. Each species has its own number of chromosomes, and the number is always the same for that species. Chromosomes are sectioned into genes, units of heredity made of DNA molecules. DNA acts like a code, specifying the order and number of amino acids that make up proteins—the organic compounds characteristic of all life.

Chromosomes (below left) of the fruit fly, much magnified, show bands of DNA arranged in sections that correspond exactly with specific genes, the chemical units of heredity. The proof of this correspondence came when the American geneticist Hermann Muller introduced the use of ionizing radiation to damage the fruit flies' chromosomes at ultra-microscopic points, causing precise point mutations in offspring of parents whose DNA had been damaged at the places indicated. Random mutations may occur in any organism, and not only as a result of radiation. A gradual accumulation of minor mutations may lead to evolutionary change.

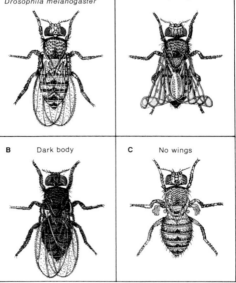

Fruit fly
Drosophila melanogaster

A   Curly wings

B   Dark body

C   No wings

in the fourth cross, only the two recessive alleles of the genes are present. So there is always a three-to-one ratio of dominant to recessive.

Theories of evolution

Mendel's work was of course unknown to his contemporaries, Charles Darwin and Alfred Russel Wallace, who even then were providing solutions to the major mystery of biology—the way that species evolve, change and develop over time. Evolution was not a new idea in Darwin's day. In 1809 the French naturalist Jean-Baptiste Lamarck had proposed a theory of the inheritance of acquired characteristics, suggesting that new habits learned by an organism in response to environmental change may become physically incorporated in the animal's descendants. For instance, the fact that the ancestral giraffe had to stretch its neck to reach food might give its offspring long necks to enable them to reach food more easily. Less satisfactory than the "natural selection" theory of Darwin and Wallace (who independently reached the same conclusion), Lamarckism founders on the fact that there is no genetic mechanism enabling acquired characters to pass on in this way.

Darwin's theory of natural selection has three key elements: all individuals vary, and some variations are passed on to the next generation; the gap between the potential and the actual number of offspring reproduced by organisms is very wide and implies that not all will survive; organisms best adapted to the environment will survive, their offspring will have been selected, and the favourable variation

will spread through the population, perhaps eventually changing it.

Genetic variation, the mainspring of natural selection, is reflected in variations of DNA, the material substance of heredity. Changes in the order of DNA's nitrogenous bases—called mutations—produce changes in the proteins which are usually, but not always, harmful. More important than these is the effect of genes recombining in sexually reproduced offspring.

Sexual reproduction provides the offspring with two sets of DNA, one from each parent. The processes that give rise to a half-set of chromosomes in a sperm or egg shuffle and recombine the genes on each chromosome to provide new combinations. Then, when sperm and egg fuse together at fertilization, the half-sets come together and even more combinations are produced. The world's enormous diversity of life can be explained in terms of a struggle that favours certain genetic combinations.

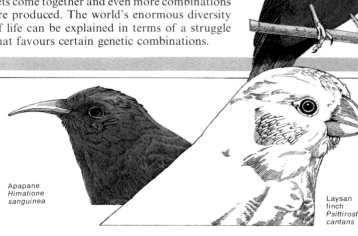

Iiwi
Vestiaria coccinea

Apapane
Himatione sanguinea

Laysan finch
Psittirostra cantans

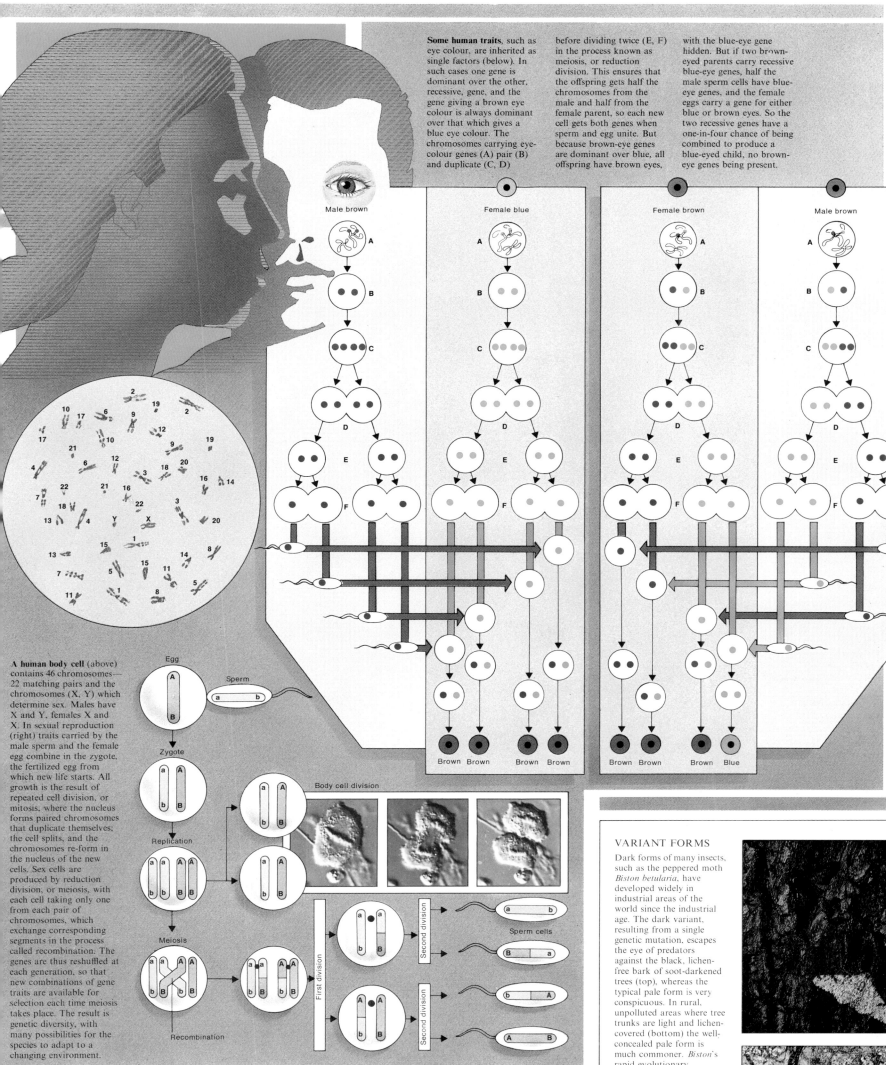

Some human traits, such as eye colour, are inherited as single factors (below). In such cases one gene is dominant over the other, recessive, gene, and the gene giving a brown eye colour is always dominant over that which gives a blue eye colour. The chromosomes carrying eye-colour genes (A) pair (B) and duplicate (C, D) before dividing twice (E, F) in the process known as meiosis, or reduction division. This ensures that the offspring gets half the chromosomes from the male and half from the female parent, so each new cell gets both genes when sperm and egg unite. But because brown-eye genes are dominant over blue, all offspring have brown eyes, with the blue-eye gene hidden. But if two brown-eyed parents carry recessive blue-eye genes, half the male sperm cells have blue-eye genes, and the female eggs carry a gene for either blue or brown eyes. So the two recessive genes have a one-in-four chance of being combined to produce a blue-eyed child, no brown-eye genes being present.

Male brown

Female blue

Female brown

Male brown

Brown Brown · Brown Brown · Brown Brown · Brown Blue

A human body cell (above) contains 46 chromosomes— 22 matching pairs and the chromosomes (X, Y) which determine sex. Males have X and Y, females X and X. In sexual reproduction (right) traits carried by the male sperm and the female egg combine in the zygote, the fertilized egg from which new life starts. All growth is the result of repeated cell division, or mitosis, where the nucleus forms paired chromosomes that duplicate themselves; the cell splits, and the chromosomes re-form in the nucleus of the new cells. Sex cells are produced by reduction division, or meiosis, with each cell taking only one from each pair of chromosomes, which exchange corresponding segments in the process called recombination. The genes are thus reshuffled at each generation, so that new combinations of gene traits are available for selection each time meiosis takes place. The result is genetic diversity, with many possibilities for the species to adapt to a changing environment.

Egg

Sperm

Zygote

Replication

Meiosis

Recombination

Body cell division

First division

Second division

Second division

Sperm cells

VARIANT FORMS

Dark forms of many insects, such as the peppered moth *Biston betularia*, have developed widely in industrial areas of the world since the industrial age. The dark variant, resulting from a single genetic mutation, escapes the eye of predators against the black, lichen-free bark of soot-darkened trees (top), whereas the typical pale form is very conspicuous. In rural, unpolluted areas where tree trunks are light and lichen-covered (bottom) the well-concealed pale form is much commoner. *Biston*'s rapid evolutionary response is remarkable: in 1849 only one dark example was recorded at Manchester, England, but by 1900 98% of the moths caught in the area were of the dark type. A similar change occurred in other industrial areas, during the period when the most coal was being burned and the population was most rapidly expanding. But with today's clean-air laws the number of pale moths in these areas is once again on the increase.

A diversity of forms (left) has stemmed from a single ancestor of the Hawaiian honeycreeper, which now numbers 14 species. These have adapted in their mid-Pacific isolation to fill niches usually taken by other birds, ranging from the nectar-feeding iiwi to the Laysan finch with its thick beak for cracking seeds, and the short-billed apapane, which includes insects in its diet. But the honeycreepers' success in divergence may have led to overspecialization, with at least eight species now extinct. The Australian marsupial mouse and the Indian spiny mouse (right) look very similar, due to the fact that they fill similar ecological niches, but they belong to groups evolving separately for almost 100 million years.

Indian spiny mouse *Mus platythrix*

Australian marsupial mouse *Sminthopsis murina*

Earliest Life Forms

Earth's original atmosphere lacked oxygen, without which there could be no survival for air-breathing creatures. This vital gas was supplied by life itself, in the form of microscopic organisms that flourished in the atmosphere of the time and emitted oxygen as "waste". In this way a breathable atmosphere built up; increasingly complex life forms were able to develop in the seas; early plants and insects gained a foothold on the shores; and, finally, larger animals could survive on land.

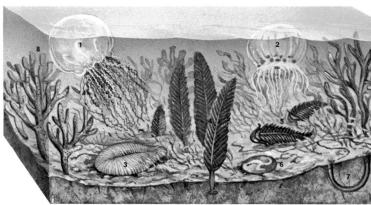

A BREATHABLE ATMOSPHERE

Without oxygen, life as we know it could not exist; yet Earth's original atmosphere contained practically none. The oxygenation of the atmosphere was the work of the planet's first life—primeval bacteria and algae. Of these, some released oxygen as waste while consuming carbon dioxide or nitrogen in photosynthesis. Colonies of algae forming stromatolites ("stony carpets") generated even more oxygen, but this was first taken up by ocean rocks, visible today as "banded iron formations". Once all the ocean rocks were oxidized, an oxygen-rich atmosphere could develop, with an ozone layer to filter out harmful radiation from the Sun.

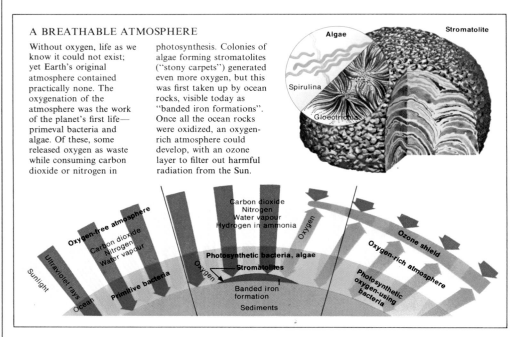

Scientists have identified bacteria-like microfossils in the rocks that were formed more than 3,500 million years ago. Some of these organisms appear to have been capable of photosynthesis—the process of utilizing sunlight, water and carbon dioxide for "food", with release of oxygen as the vitally important by-product. As a result, surplus oxygen very gradually accumulated in the Earth's atmosphere, forming an upper-atmosphere shield of ozone (which kept out damaging ultraviolet radiation from the Sun) and providing an oxygen-rich atmosphere in which breathing life could develop.

At least five types of microfossil have been found in ancient sediments of Western Australia, aged about 3,560 million years, and these provide the earliest evidence of life so far discovered. Other early proof of life comes from the so-called "stromatolites", some of which may date back as far as 3,400 million years. These curious columns, growing in warm, shallow waters, are formed of blue-green algae which have entrapped chalky sediments, bacteria and other microfossils. Their study is made easier by the fact that similar structures have developed at later geological times, and some are even being formed at the present day.

Living below the surface of the water and not initially reliant on oxygen for life, such bacteria and algae were shielded from the Sun's ultraviolet rays as they imperceptibly altered the Earth's atmosphere. For hundreds of millions of years life of this kind persisted, with few obvious developments or changes.

Breathing life

About 1,800 million years ago, the effects of these microscopic photosynthesizers became dramatically apparent in the "rusting" of the ocean sediments, when the red colour of the rocks being formed at that time indicates that there was enough free oxygen on Earth to bring about the process known as oxidation. Once the ocean rocks capable of absorbing oxygen had done so, forming the red "banded iron formations" known to geologists, oxygen could enter the atmosphere in ever greater quantities.

It has been estimated that a breathable atmosphere existed on Earth about 1,700 million years ago, and aerobic (oxygen-using) organisms first became abundant not very long afterwards. These organisms were single-celled, and it may have been almost 1,000 million years before multicellular animals evolved. The fossilized remains of animals alive 800 million years ago have been found in many parts of the world, but it is not yet known whether multicellular animals had a long history before these earliest known forms, or whether they had developed and radiated rapidly from a creature capable of feeding as well as photosynthesizing.

One of the earliest collections of animals of this type was discovered in the Ediacara Sandstones of the Flinders Range in Australia, where some 650 million years ago the rocks once formed part of an ancient beach. Here a spectacular collection of soft-bodied animals, similar to today's coelenterates (such as jellyfish) and worms, was washed ashore and preserved in silt from the nearby shallow sea. Comparable, mainly floating forms have been found in other parts of the world in rocks dating from between 650 and 580 million years ago.

The first vertebrates

One of the most important changes in animal life seems to have occurred about 580 million years ago. At that date many creatures evolved hard, protective shells, which also acted as areas of muscle attachment and as support for their bodies—in other words, as external skeletons. Hard shells were more easily preserved as fossils than the soft bodies of earlier animals, so rich collections have been recovered from rocks of the Cambrian Period, beginning 580 million years ago, as well as from later strata.

The first fish-like animals—the earliest true vertebrates—are found in rocks of the Ordovician Period, from about 500 million years ago, and these were in many ways very similar to the lampreys and hagfishes of today. But unlike them, these ancient creatures were heavily armoured with external bone. They must have been poor swimmers, living mainly on the sea bed and filtering edible particles from the sediments, which they sucked into their jawless mouths. From them arose true fishes, with backbones, jaws and teeth, and they came to replace the less efficient earlier forms.

During the Devonian Period, about 400 million years ago, the fishes diversified greatly, adapting to fit all kinds of aquatic environments. Some grew to a huge size, such as *Dunkleosteus*, which achieved a length of up to 9 m (29 ft 7 in), although it belonged to a group of fishes that retained heavy armour. Some of these curious creatures probably used their stilt-like pectoral fins to hitch themselves across the beds of the pools in which they lived.

From water to land

The fishes that teemed in the seas and fresh waters of the Devonian world found their way into difficult environments such as swamps and oasis pools, where there was a danger of drying out in the warmer weather. Many of these fishes had rudimentary lungs, and one group developed powerful jointed fins.

Such marginal habitats were not ideal for fishes, but they were nevertheless rich in species, and it is from them that the first land vertebrates developed. When the water dried up they survived, for their strong fins held them up so that they did not flop over helplessly.

They found themselves in a new, dry world, but one which was already inhabited, at least round the water's edges, with plants related to modern liverworts, mosses and club mosses. There were also numerous invertebrate animals such as millipedes, spiders and wingless insects. These plants and animals provided shelter and food, so that the environment was not wholly hostile to larger animals.

The first steps on land probably took the form of strong flexions of the body—desperate swimming movements which swung the fins forward, pegging the animal's position in the drying mud. But in a geologically very short time, animals had evolved in which the rays of the lobe fins had vanished, leaving stubby legs with which the animals—no longer fishes but amphibians—could haul themselves over land. But they still had to return to water to breed and lay eggs.

THE FIRST SHELLED CREATURES

These evolved (right) in the seas when conditions allowed soft-bodied life to form protective casings. In the fossil record of 550 million years ago, soft and shelled forms are found. The trilobites (1, 2, 3)—a now extinct order of woodlouse-like animals—dominated the scene, but other early arthropods (4) included a possible insect ancestor (5), and there may even have been an ancestor to fish (6). Sponges (7), crinoids (8), early moluscs (9), bristleworms (10) and lampshells (11) were plentiful, but other creatures (12) are bewilderingly strange.

THE FIRST AMPHIBIANS

Amphibians (1) emerged some 345 million years ago (right), inhabiting swampy environments with luxuriant vegetation—club mosses and ferns (2, 3) that made up the early coal forests. Lungfish (4) were well adapted to life in oxygen-poor waters, but the move to land was probably made by related fish with a passage linking nostrils to throat—*Eusthenopteron* (5). Land offered food (6, 7, 8) and suitably damp conditions for a possibly stranded aquatic animal.

Palaeozoic			Mesozoic		Cenozoic
500	400	300	200	100	0

Millions of years ago

A timescale of life on Earth emerges from the record of fossils embedded in rock strata. Major breaks in faunas (animal assemblages) separate eras coinciding roughly with periods of intense mountain-building activity. These eras are broken down into geological periods, which are separated by lesser faunal breaks and which are generally named from the area where rocks of that age were first discovered. The geological eras and periods do not imply particular rock types.

| 600 | Shelled/skeletal animals | **CAMBRIAN** | 550 | First fishes | ▶ORDOVICIAN |

THE AGE OF JELLYFISH

Jellyfish (left) and other soft-bodied animals flourished in the pre-Cambrian seas, more than 600 million years ago. The forms of one group, imprinted on sand, have been preserved as fossils in the Australian Ediacara Sandstones. They include varieties similar to modern jellyfish (1, 2); worm-like crawlers (3); sea pens (4) very like modern types; segmented worms (5); "three-legged" creatures like no known animal (6); and sand casts of burrowing worms (7).

LIFE ON SEA AND LAND

For more than half the Earth's existence, its atmosphere has been hostile to air-breathing life. Then, about 1,600 million years ago, the photosynthesizing action of minute organisms built up enough free oxygen in the atmosphere for more complex oxygen-dependent forms to develop. The first multicellular life led to the soft-bodied animals of the pre-Cambrian time—worms, jellyfish and sea pens. About 580 million years ago many animals developed hard parts, including shells. Over 1,200 new marine species date from this period, and the evolutionary explosion came to fill the Earth's seas with fishes. Some of these had powerful jointed fins and rudimentary lungs, and lived in swamps where primitive plants and insects had already made the move to land. As the pools dwindled the stranded animals could survive by breathing air.

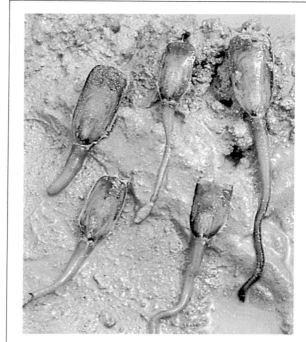
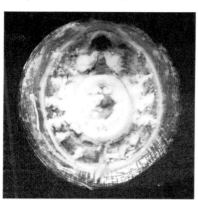

LIVING FOSSILS

Some life forms that emerged 570 million years ago have survived virtually unchanged to the present day. These "living fossils" include *Lingula* (left), today found in warm, brackish coastal waters, poor in oxygen and unsuited to most life, off the Pacific and Indian oceans. *Neopilina* (below), a primitive marine mollusc first found alive in 1952, has features unlike other molluscs but suggesting much closer affinities with the annelids (worms) and arthropods (insects, crabs, etc.).

THE AGE OF JELLYFISH
1 Jellyfish (*Ediacaria*)
2 Jellyfish (*Medusina*)
3 Flatworm (*Dickinsonia costata*)
4 Sea pens (*Rangea, Charnia*)
5 Segmented worms (*Spriggina floundersi*)
6 Unknown animal (*Tribrachidium*)
7 Burrowing worm (fossil casts)
8 Sponges and algae (hypothetical)

THE FIRST SHELLED CREATURES
1 Trilobites (*Waptia*)
2 Trilobites (*Marella splendens*)
3 Trilobite (*Olenoides serratus*)
4 Primitive arthropod (*Perspicaris dictynna*)
5 Primitive arthropod (*Aysheaia pedunculata*)
6 Ancestral lancelet fish (*Branchiostoma*)
7 Sponge (*Vauxia*)
8 Crinoids (*Echmatocrinus*)
9 Mollusc (*Wiwaxia*)
10 Bristleworm (*Nereis*)
11 Brachiopod (*Lingulella*)
12 Unknown animal (*Hallucigenia sparsa*)

THE AGE OF FISHES
1 Primitive plant (*Nematophyton*)
2 Psilophite plant (*Asteroxylon*)
3 Psilophite plant (*Rhynia*)
4 Primitive insect (*Rhyniella*)
5 Placoderm fish (*Bothriolepis*)
6 Placoderm fish (*Phyllolepis*)
7 Placoderm fish (*Dunkleosteus*)
8 Early shark (*Cladoselache*)
9 Lungfish (*Dipterus*)
10 Lobe-fin fish (*Osteolepis*)
11 Crustacean (*Montecaris*)

THE FIRST AMPHIBIANS
1 Amphibian (*Ichthyostega*)
2 Club moss (*Cyclostigma*)
3 Fern (*Pseudosporochnus*)
4 Lungfish (*Scaumenacia*)
5 Rhipidistian fish (*Eusthenopteron*)
6 Millipede (*Acantherpestes ornatus*)
7 Early scorpion (*Palaeophonus*)
8 Spider-like creature (*Palaeocharinoides*)
9 Small plant (*Sciadophyton*)

THE AGE OF FISHES

Fishes (left) filled the brackish Devonian waters, about 350 million years ago, while primitive plants and insects had pioneered the land. Giant weeds (1) grew above muddy waters, and vascular plants (2, 3) colonized the shores, sheltering early insects (4). Primitive fishes (5, 6, 7) remained, but ray-finned types (8)—ancestors of modern fish—were dominant. However, it was from the lobe-finned fishes (9, 10) that the first land vertebrates emerged.

The Age of Reptiles

When the Carboniferous Period began, the world was already populated with animals and plants of many kinds. The oceans were full of fishes, invertebrates and aquatic plants. The land, meanwhile, was producing dramatic new species: giant mosses and ferns, spiders and insects and, most important of all, the rapidly evolving amphibians. These creatures were taking the first evolutionary steps on a path that would lead to some of the most remarkable creatures ever to live – the dinosaurs.

The broad, low-lying, swampy plains of the late Carboniferous provided ideal conditions for the world's early plants. They spread and diversified, and some of them grew to enormous size. Giant club mosses, huge horsetails and luxuriant tree ferns took on the proportions of modern-day trees and formed the world's first forests. These new forests were full of animal life: primitive spiders and scorpions hunting their prey, giant dragonflies hovering over the marshy waters and other insects scavenging or hunting on the mossy forest floor or in the branches of the "trees". In the huge coal-forest swamps, the most advanced of all animals, the amphibians, were rapidly evolving. Some of these would ultimately return to life in the water. But others were developing stronger legs and were becoming better able to cope with an existence on dry land.

It was from this second group that the reptiles evolved—the first animals to be equipped with waterproof skins. Unlike their amphibian ancestors, they could stay out of the water indefinitely without losing their body fluids through their skins. They were no longer tied to the water's edge and the pattern of life was revolutionized. The world was soon inhabited by the first wave of land vertebrates—reptiles, which then rapidly diversified.

Included among these first reptiles were creatures known as sailbacks. They had a row of long, bony spines that supported a great fin running down from the back of their heads to the base of their tails. This whole apparatus functioned as a heat-exchange organ: the fin absorbed heat from the atmosphere in the early, cooler parts of the day, when the animal was cold, and blushed off warmth later, when it became overheated. Unlike the cold-blooded reptiles, sailbacked reptiles could, to a certain extent, regulate their body temperatures.

Mammal-like reptiles
It was only about 50 million years later, however, that animals skeletally identical to mammals were found throughout the world. Almost certainly these creatures had a degree of warm-bloodedness. But they were all rather small—the biggest was no larger than a domestic cat—and this may account for their decline. They were destined to be overshadowed for many millions of years by the dinosaurs.

The late Triassic Period, about 200 million years ago, is marked by a sudden decline in the

THE RULING REPTILES
Seymouria and other advanced amphibians evolved to form the first reptiles, such as *Scutosaurus*. From these a multitude of adaptations evolved. Some herbivores, such as *Corythosaurus*, developed 2,000 or more teeth, to help them consume tough, fibrous food plants. Another herbivorous group attained enormous size—*Brachiosaurus* weighed as much as 80 tonnes—and this may have been an adaptation to regulate body temperature (large objects lose and gain heat more slowly than small objects). Another adaptation, but one that developed mainly in the carnivores, was that of offensive weaponry: *Deinonychus* had a huge sickle-shaped claw on each hind foot and the later *Tyrannosaurus* combined a massive body with a jagged mouthful of 60 teeth. Armour plating was a defensive adaptation, produced by herbivores such as *Triceratops*, whereas speed of movement was developed both by some herbivores and by small carnivores such as *Struthiomimus*.

Corythosaurus

Seymouria

Scutosaurus

Deinonychus

Lystrosaurus

Dimetrodon

THE MAMMAL LINE
Sailbacks such as *Dimetrodon* mark the beginning of mammal history. These reptiles had developed the first method of regulating body temperature—each was equipped with a large fin on its back which acted as a heat-exchange organ, a living solar panel. From these strange creatures, para-mammals such as *Lystrosaurus* evolved, animals with many mammal-like features. Some of the later members of this group, such as *Thrinaxodon*, probably even had fur on their bodies. Then, about 200 million years ago, the first true warm-blooded mammals, such as *Morganucodon*, developed. But by this time the group as a whole was declining in response to reptilian competition. Mammals would have to wait 140 million years before becoming successful again.

Thrinaxodon

Morganucodon

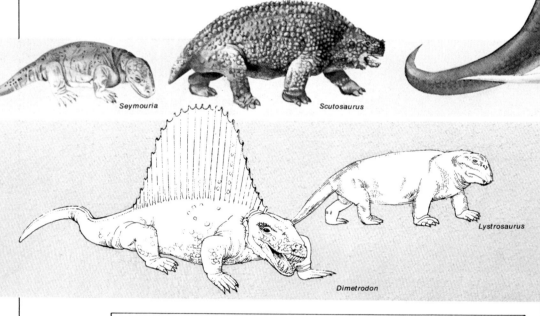

COAL FORMATION
Coal consists of carbon from plant remains and most of it was formed in the swamp-forests from which reptiles emerged. First, peat formed from rotted vegetation. Sea levels rose, ocean covered the peat bogs and marine sediments were laid down. The resulting pressure converted peat to coal. The cycle recurred and the deepest coal seams were compressed and hardened.

Coal-forming forest swamp
Peat layer
Lignite seam
Bituminous seam
Anthracite seam

Palaeozoic   Mesozoic   Cenozoic
500   400   300   200   100   0
Millions of years ago

Three geological eras mark the evolution of life on Earth. It was the Mesozoic era, beginning 230 million years ago, that spanned the age of reptiles. Until then, throughout the Palaeozoic era, life had been slowly evolving from the primitive organisms that appeared 400 million years earlier.

By the Mesozoic, the earliest reptiles had developed. Among their descendants were dinosaurs and early representatives of the mammalian line. Mammals, however, would have to wait another 165 million years, until the Cenozoic, before they achieved dominance.

The plant communities underwent as many developments in the course of the Mesozoic era as did the reptiles. The end of the Palaeozoic saw changes in climate—the Permian Period was much drier than the Carboniferous. Giant horsetails, ferns and club mosses that had formed the world's first forests gave way to other types of plant: early conifers and their relatives

(the gymnosperms) came to the fore. These new species, such as the Cycadales, had evolved a new, improved method of reproduction—using seeds not spores. By Jurassic times, the climate had changed again and the moist conditions supported dense forests of ferns and of conifers. The final major Mesozoic development took place in Cretaceous times, when the flowering plants evolved.

Cycadale

Gingko biloba

CARBONIFEROUS   300   Earliest reptiles **PERMIAN** Early conifers   250   First radiation of reptiles **TRIASSIC**   First mammals

EVOLUTION AND ADAPTATION

Once their amphibian ancestors had crawled from the swamps, reptiles rapidly evolved and developed a remarkable range of adaptations: they took to the air, invaded the seas and held dominion over the land. By early Jurassic times, they had firmly established their claim to the title Ruling Reptiles. Another group of early reptile descendants led to the mammals, and although these were long overshadowed by the dinosaurs, they were destined to rise to dominance.

Brachiosaurus

Tyrannosaurus rex

Struthiomimus

mammal-like reptiles and by the extraordinary evolutionary radiation of the so-called Archosaurs ("ruling reptiles"). These began to fill every available ecological niche. They evolved into carnivores, herbivores and omnivores. They included the Crocodilians, which adapted to a life in the water; the flying pterosaurs, which were the first vertebrates to fly, and, most important of all, the dinosaurs, whose evolutionary reign over the land was to endure for the next 140 million years.

Dinosaurs adapted well to life on the land. They developed "fully erect" limbs (not unlike those of the later higher mammals) rather than the splayed legs found in most other reptiles. The new position of their limbs, which gave them the necessary mobility on dry land, was also accompanied by a general increase in size. But the dinosaurs were not the only land reptiles of the time; many other forms, including tortoises, snakes and lizards, were also carving their niches during the Mesozoic era.

Similarly, the pterosaurs did not remain the only creatures of the sky. By 170 million years ago birds, in the form of claw-winged *Archaeopteryx*, had evolved, and these were to prove a serious challenge to the primitive winged reptiles which had poor flying abilities.

Aquatic reptiles

Just as the land and the air were rapidly inhabited by newly evolving forms, so the water produced many new developments. Several of the Mesozoic reptiles began to adapt to aquatic life in ways often parallel to present-day mammals: the long-necked, fish-eating plesiosaurs led a life much like that of seals; the larger

pliosaurs had a streamlined shape similar to that of certain whales; some mollusc-eating placodonts could be likened to the walrus; and the elegant icthyosaurs were in many ways like dolphins. Large invertebrates were also found in the seas. The most dramatic of these were the ammonites—shelled relatives of the octopus—some of which grew to more than 2 m (6 ft) in size. Among fishes a new type emerged, the Teleosts, and these were destined to become the dominant fishes of the modern world.

Wholesale extinction

At the end of the Cretaceous Period, the reptiles were flourishing. Then suddenly, 65 million years ago, a catastrophe occurred. Virtually every species, including all the large animals, were wiped out. Throughout the Mesozoic, a series of dinosaurs and other reptiles had been evolving and slowly becoming extinct, but they were always replaced by other species. This wholesale extinction was unprecedented.

The cause of the catastrophe is unknown, but since the nature of the Earth itself was unchanged, it seems likely that some outside phenomenon was responsible. One theory suggests that a large meteorite collided with the Earth, throwing enough dust into the atmosphere to blot out the sun for several years—long enough to kill almost all the green plants on land and in the sea. If this was the case, only small animals that fed on carrion, decaying vegetation, seeds or nuts could hope to survive. Whatever the cause, the reign of the reptiles was at an end, leaving the small, adaptable mammals and birds to recolonize the virtually empty planet during the Cenozoic era.

Rhamphorhynchus

Triceratops

Archaeopteryx

Plesiosaurus

Ichthyornis

Birds are relatives of the reptiles. The first bird, *Archaeopteryx*, evolving in Jurassic times, had many reptilian features—a long, bony tail, toothed mouth and clawed wings. By Cretaceous times, birds such as *Ichthyornis* had a more familiar form.

Plesiosaurs evolved at the same time as the dinosaurs and were as successful in their marine environment as were the dinosaurs on land. They were most common in Jurassic times.

Pterosaurs such as *Rhamphorhynchus* were the first vertebrates to take to the sky. They were not strong fliers and probably glided on air currents much of the time.

Norfolk Island pine
Araucaria heterophylla

Williamsonia

Common oak
Quercus robur

Fig tree
Ficus sp

Plane tree
Platanus sp

tion of reptiles JURASSIC First birds   150   CRETACEOUS First flowering plants   100 First modern fishes   Extinction of dinosaurs

41

The Age of Mammals

After the time of the great dying, 65 million years ago, reptiles never regained the importance they had achieved during the Mesozoic era. A new era, the Cenozoic, had begun. On the continental landmasses mammals and birds, newly released from 160 million years of reptilian domination, began to occupy their niches in the rich, empty habitats. They flourished and diversified, and the cold-blooded reptiles became second-class citizens in a world of warm-blooded animals.

While reptiles still dominated the world, during the late Mesozoic, a new group of mammals had arisen. These were the first creatures on Earth to give birth to fully formed, live young. Until this time, the most advanced of the mammals had been marsupials whose young were still virtually embryos at birth and had to develop in the mother's pouch, or marsupium. The new mammals had evolved a more sophisticated system—the mother retained the foetus safely inside her body until it was fully formed, nourishing it during this time through a special organ developed during pregnancy, the placenta. These mammals, the placentals, were destined to become the major mammalian group.

Although all the Mesozoic placentals were small, they had already evolved into a number of different forms that existed alongside the dinosaurs. Besides the insectivores, which were the ancestral type, they included early representatives of the Primates (precursors of modern monkeys and apes), the Carnivores, and the now extinct Condylarthrans (primitive hoofed mammals). When suddenly, 65 million years ago, there was no longer competition from the large land reptiles, these early groups rapidly evolved and extravagant forms developed.

But just as the first reptiles had passed through an early evolution, largely to be replaced by a second evolutionary wave, so the first large mammals were, in many cases, superseded by other, more successful lines. In the earliest part of the Cenozoic era, the different groups of placentals, although not closely related, all tended to be heavy limbed and heavy tailed and to walk on the whole length of their feet (as do modern bears) or on thick, stubby toes. These ungainly, thickset mammals soon died out. Some became extinct because their descendants, more efficiently adapted to their environment, overtook and replaced them. Others, such as the powerful taeniodonts and the large rodent-like tillodonts, seem to have been evolutionary blind alleys.

Spectacular developments

It was the Oligocene Period, 36 million years ago, that saw the end of most of these early essays in mammalian gigantism, but, in many parts of the world, they were replaced by others just as spectacular. In South America, the giant sloths and glyptodonts (massive relatives of the armadillos) survived until comparatively recently. The ground sloths, at least, were contemporaries of the first men on the continent.

As each group of early mammals evolved, during the early and middle part of the Cenozoic era, many of their developments closely reflected changes taking place in their environment. The first horse-like creature, for example, was *Hyracotherium*, also called *Eohippus* or "dawn horse". It lived 54 million years ago and was a small, multi-toed creature, well adapted to its densely forested habitat. The teeth of its descendants gradually changed in size and complexity, but it was not until the Miocene Period, nearly 20 million years later, that any radical alterations took place. This was the time when grasses (the Gramineae), until then a rare family of plants, came to the fore. The world's plains suddenly became clothed in a food plant very suitable for the attention of grazing creatures such as the early horses.

Animals of the grasslands

Horses and many other animals moved from the forests to make use of this new and abundant food supply. Once on the plains, different adaptations for survival were required: high-crowned teeth to deal with tough grasses; limbs enabling the animal to run tirelessly without extra, unwanted weight from supporting side toes (which were lost); large eyes capable of seeing for long distances and placed far back on the head for detecting predators approaching from any direction (as a result of which, however, the ability to judge distances ahead had to be sacrificed). Thus, the modern horses are plains-dwelling animals, perfectly adapted to their present way of life.

Mammals reached the climax of diversity during the Pliocene Period, 10 million years ago. But in the following period, the Pleistocene, ice sheets swept down from the polar regions and from the high mountains of the north, bringing massive and sudden changes to the ecology of virtually every region in the world. This dramatic disturbance to the environment brought extinction to an enormous number of species.

The survivors consisted mainly of the smaller species. Unfortunately for many of them, however, they included *Homo sapiens*. Man rose to success at the end of the Pleistocene and has, in the last 10,000 years, taken dominion over virtually every part of the world. During this time, he has proved far more destructive to other animal species than any natural force has ever been. More than 5,000 years ago, the giant sloths may have been a dying species, but there is no doubt that early human hunters hurried on their extinction. Since then, the list of species eliminated by man has grown ever longer. Today the human race is causing the extinction of both animals and plants at a rate comparable to that of 65 million years ago, when some dramatic natural catastrophe swept the dinosaurs from the face of the world. Unless man, the super-efficient species, can curb his numbers and his destructive activities, a new age of dying may soon be upon the world.

By early Cenozoic times, many forms had evolved from the insectivorous mammals of the Mesozoic Period. *Miacis*, *Hyaenodon* and *Oxyaena* were flesh-eaters. Plant-eating mammals, such as Taeniodonts, *Arsinoitherium* and *Phenacodus* (one of the first hoofed mammals), had also evolved, while other early forms, such as *Andrewsarchus*, were omnivorous. The early Primates, however, remained insect-eaters for millions of years.

EARLY STAGES

Miacis

Andrewsarchus

Hyaenodon

Diatryma

Euryapteryx

CENOZOIC BIRDS

Giant flightless birds came to the fore more than once during the Cenozoic era. *Diatryma*, a massive, flesh-eating bird, ruled the North American grasslands in early Cenozoic times, while mammals were still small, fairly primitive and easily dominated. *Euryapteryx* and its relatives (the moas) evolved in New Zealand, where, because there were no mammals, they filled an empty ecological niche.

The Carnivores diversified into two major types—the cats and their kin (Aeluroidea), and the dogs and their relatives (Arctoidea). During the Oligocene Period, about 36 million years ago, Aeluroidea gave rise not only to early relatives of modern cats, such as sabre-toothed *Hoplophoneus*, but also to two other families, the civets and the hyenas. At the same time, Arctoidea also diversified and produced the dogs, weasels, bears and racoons. It was a complex group, with many forms that were later to become extinct—the massive bear-dogs, such as *Daphoenus*, for example, which lived during the Miocene Period. Cats and dogs evolved to exploit different habitats. The cats adapted to life in forests, and learned to hide and then stalk and ambush their prey. Dogs evolved as plains animals, and used pack-hunting techniques to catch fleet-footed, grassland animals.

Perissodactyls and Artiodactyls were two important groups that evolved from the primitive hoofed mammals; Perissodactyls had an odd number of toes on each foot, Artiodactyls had an even number. These two groups suffered very different fortunes. Artiodactyls are still at the height of their success; the early stock produced the modern pig, camel, deer, giraffe, hippopotamus, antelope, sheep, goat and cow. Perissodactyls, however, are in decline and the only survivors are the horse, rhinoceros and tapir. But they were once important and many, now-extinct, kinds such as *Moropus* and *Brontotherium* existed alongside more familiar types such as *Hyracotherium*. Few remained after the Pliocene Period, however. This was when the Artiodactyls came to the fore. They, too, had had casualties—the pig-like *Archaeotherium* was by then extinct—but many other Artiodactyls, such as the early giraffe, *Palaeotragus*, were evolving. Most important, however, was small *Archaeomeryx*, for it had developed the key to Artiodactyl success—it was a ruminant and this enabled it to make the best possible use of the world's new grasslands.

Palaeozoic			Mesozoic		Cenozoic
500	400	300	200	100	0

Millions of years ago

Three geological eras mark the slow evolution of life on Earth. The Palaeozoic era, 570 million years ago, saw the appearance of the first primitive life forms. By the end of the era, 340 million years later, the reptiles had evolved and the following Mesozoic era was the age of reptilian domination. This reign over the land ended 65 million years ago as the Cenozoic era began. Then mammals came to the fore and the age of mammalian dominance of the world had dawned.

EARLY GRASSES

Grasses first appeared in the densely forested lands of 60 million years ago. Probably similar to the sedges (right) found in wet woodland areas today, they offered an attractive meal to many mammals. But it was not until the Miocene Period, when a change in climate reduced forest cover, that grasses became widespread. Then many forest creatures migrated to grassland areas.

Wood sedge
Carex sylvatica

THE MARSUPIALS

Thylacosmilus and mouse-like *Argyrolagus* were two of the many forms of marsupial mammal that evolved in Cenozoic times in South America. Almost everywhere else, the marsupials, unable to compete with their more efficient placental cousins, met with an early extinction. But in two remote regions—South America (then separate from North America) and Australia—there was no competition from placentals, and there the marsupials flourished.

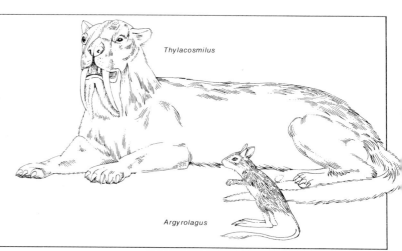

Thylacosmilus

Argyrolagus

TERTIARY	First radiation of mammals and birds		Forest horses			Second radiation of mammals
Palaeocene	60	**Eocene**	50		40	**Oligocene**

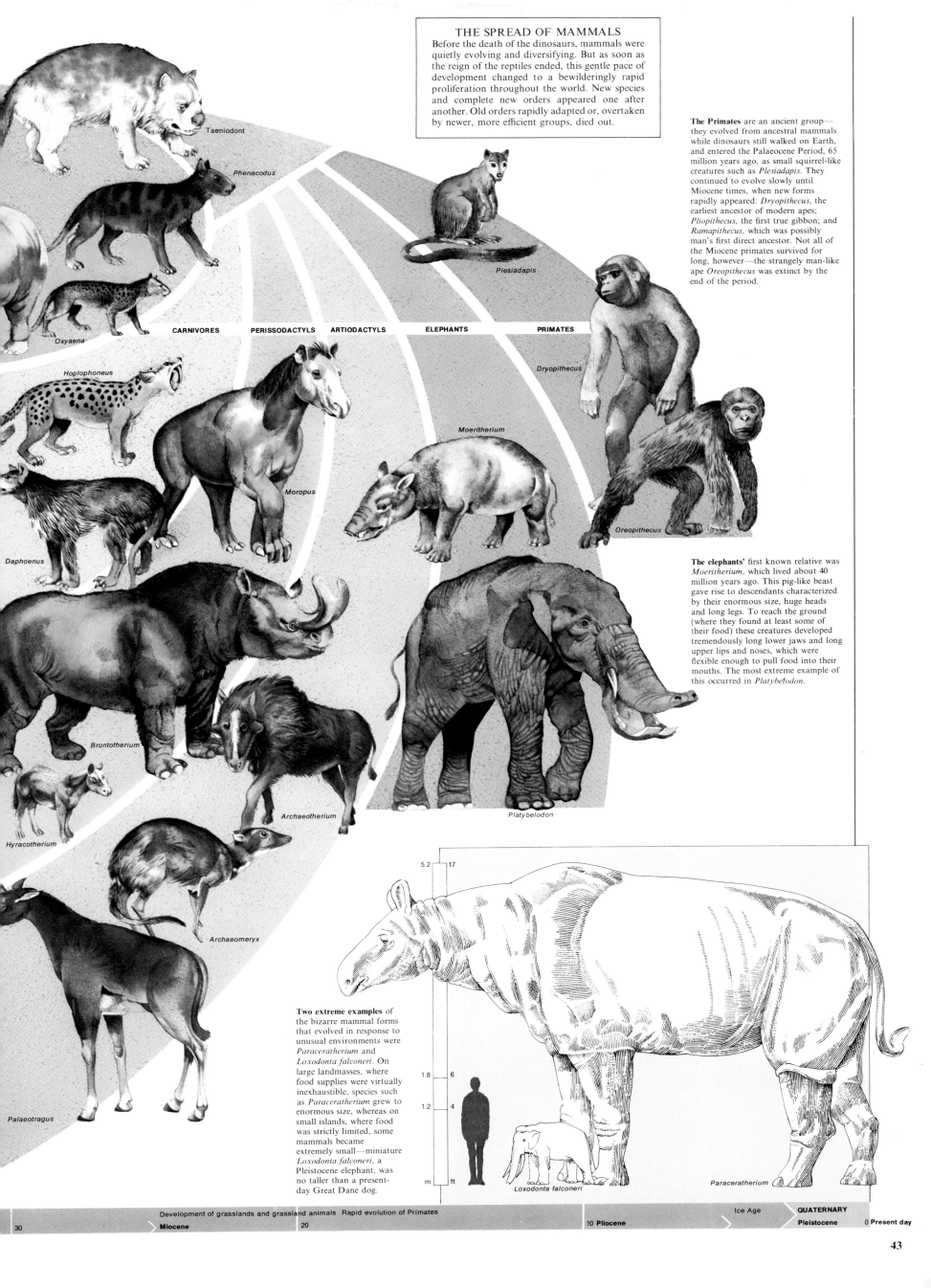

Before the death of the dinosaurs, mammals were quietly evolving and diversifying. But as soon as the reign of the reptiles ended, this gentle pace of development changed to a bewilderingly rapid proliferation throughout the world. New species and complete new orders appeared one after another. Old orders rapidly adapted or, overtaken by newer, more efficient groups, died out.

Taeniodont

Phenacodus

Oxyaena

Plesiadapis

The Primates are an ancient group—they evolved from ancestral mammals while dinosaurs still walked on Earth, and entered the Palaeocene Period, 65 million years ago, as small squirrel-like creatures such as *Plesiadapis*. They continued to evolve slowly until Miocene times, when new forms rapidly appeared: *Dryopithecus*, the earliest ancestor of modern apes; *Pliopithecus*, the first true gibbon; and *Ramapithecus*, which was possibly man's first direct ancestor. Not all of the Miocene primates survived for long, however—the strangely man-like ape *Oreopithecus* was extinct by the end of the period.

CARNIVORES   PERISSODACTYLS   ARTIODACTYLS   ELEPHANTS   PRIMATES

Hoplophoneus

Dryopithecus

Moropus

Moeritherium

Daphoenus

Oreopithecus

The elephants' first known relative was *Moeritherium*, which lived about 40 million years ago. This pig-like beast gave rise to descendants characterized by their enormous size, huge heads and long legs. To reach the ground (where they found at least some of their food) these creatures developed tremendously long lower jaws and long upper lips and noses, which were flexible enough to pull food into their mouths. The most extreme example of this occurred in *Platybelodon*.

Brontotherium

Hyracotherium

Archaeotherium

Platybelodon

Archaeomeryx

5.2   17

1.8   6

1.2   4

m   ft

Two extreme examples of the bizarre mammal forms that evolved in response to unusual environments were *Paraceratherium* and *Loxodonta falconeri*. On large landmasses, where food supplies were virtually inexhaustible, species such as *Paraceratherium* grew to enormous size, whereas on small islands, where food was strictly limited, some mammals became extremely small—miniature *Loxodonta falconeri*, a Pleistocene elephant, was no taller than a present-day Great Dane dog.

Palaeotragus

Loxodonta falconeri

Paraceratherium

Spread of Life

Different parts of the Earth have their own characteristic groups of animals, and this pattern of distribution caused nineteenth-century zoologists to divide the world into zoogeographical regions. Charles Darwin suggested how these assemblages of animals may have come about by the process of evolution. But we now know that movements of the Earth's land surfaces are also responsible for the present-day distribution of many of the world's animal species and groups.

The evolution of a major group of animals, such as the reptiles or the mammals, tends to follow a set pattern in five stages. First the original ancestral group spreads out, with each subgroup adapting to its environment. This process, called adaptive radiation, results in a variety of different kinds of animals, each suited to life in a particular niche or habitat—determined largely by food supply and environmental conditions. The different kinds then move into all of the areas they can reach in which the environment is right, producing the second stage of widespread distribution.

Competition for food or living space, or changes in climate may then cause some forms to decline and disappear from parts of the range, resulting in a third stage of discontinuous distribution. Any further reduction leads to isolated relict populations—the fourth stage—in which the animal exists only in one or two limited areas. The final stage is extinction.

In all distribution patterns, however, there is not only an ecological element but also a historical one, with past events determining where animals are and where they are not. There are thus two basic types of distribution: continuous, where the area is not interrupted by an insurmountable barrier (such as a mountain range), and discontinuous, where the area of distribution is subdivided and there is no way that members of one group can interchange with members of another.

One of these factors—the earliest and most important—is the (continuing) movement of the Earth's tectonic plates. This caused the supercontinent Pangaea to break up, probably in the Triassic Period (225–180 million years ago), and the continental masses to drift apart to their present positions. New oceans developed, separating the Americas from the Euro-African block and splitting both from Antarctica. Madagascar and Australia became islands, India moved north from Africa to join the Asian block, and mountain ranges such as the Alps, Andes, Rockies and Himalayas were thrown up. As a result, animal types that had already evolved on Pangaea or its fragments before they had significantly separated (i.e. all the major invertebrate groups and most of the earlier vertebrates) can be expected to exist on all the present-day continents.

Bridging the continents

Independently of these activities, ice ages occurred from time to time, resulting in the vast accumulations of ice at the poles and a consequent general lowering of the sea level by as much as 100 m (330 ft). This temporarily exposed the previously submerged continental shelves, providing additional land for colonization, and new corridors that linked existing areas, such as the land bridge that appeared between Alaska and Siberia.

Groups that had evolved after the break-up of Pangaea, e.g. the hare, squirrel and dog families, made use of land bridges as the climate allowed, and came to occupy more than one continent. Flying animals—birds and bats—also made intercontinental crossings and established themselves on both sides of oceans, although a surprising number of these have remained very restricted in distribution. But most animals have to stay where they are because of special dietary or environmental requirements, or because they are "trapped" on islands, such as Madagascar and Australia, and cannot get off. These areas have the most distinctive faunas in the world.

Barriers and corridors

The extent to which an expanding group can spread from its original area depends on whether there are barriers, such as mountain ranges, deserts or seas, or corridors that link major areas in which the animals can live. Different animals have different environmental requirements, and so a topographical feature that is a barrier for one may be a corridor for another.

The dispersal of many animals is achieved by "hopping" from lake to lake across a continent, or from island to island across a sea. Some, such as insects, are good at this, whereas others, such as land mammals, are bad. Thus a considerable range of weevils (Curculionidae) are found on islands from New Caledonia to the Marquesas, some 6,500 km (4,000 miles) across the southern Pacific Ocean, whereas the marsupials of the region are concentrated in Australia, Papua New Guinea and a few adjacent islands, with only one genus reaching the Celebes and none crossing Wallace's Line into Borneo.

An example of colonization by "hopping" is seen on the volcanic island of Krakatoa near Java, which exploded in 1883 destroying all life. Within 25 years there were 263 species of animals on the island. Most were insects, but there were three species of land snails, two species of reptiles and 16 of birds. In another 22 years, 46 species of vertebrates had arrived, including two species of rats.

The effect of man

Animal distribution cannot be considered merely as a natural phenomenon, because it has been greatly and increasingly modified by man's impact on the environment. Agricultural practice has made large sections of the land area unsuitable for many of the animals that originally lived there, notably through the clearing of forests and the draining of marshes.

Man has also introduced animals, either deliberately or accidentally, to regions where they were not endemic. The rabbit in Australia and the deer in New Zealand were both deliberately introduced, but rats, cockroaches and many other animals have been accidentally transported throughout the world on ships and aircraft. The enormous growth in human population has driven many animals from their natural homes and into more remote environments, such as mountains. Indeed, in the past century human interference has altered the pattern of animal distribution more drastically than any topographic or climatic change.

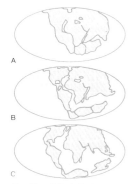

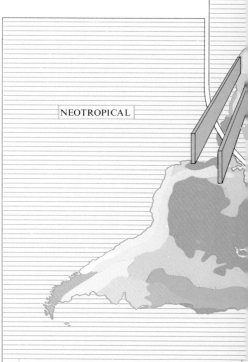

Earth's original single landmass, Pangaea (A), probably began to break up more than 200 million years ago. Species that had already evolved diversified on the Noah's Arks of the drifting supercontinents (B), called Laurasia and Gondwanaland. As the process continued (C), related animals flourished in the separated continents of the southern hemisphere.

PATTERNS OF ANIMALS

Over the ages the shape of the Earth has changed. Whole continents have moved; mountains and deserts have grown; land bridges between continents have opened and closed. These events, together with food supply, climate and other animals, account for the present natural pattern of life in the six zoogeographical regions, each containing a unique mix of animals. But man's activities have drastically affected this natural distribution in all parts of the world.

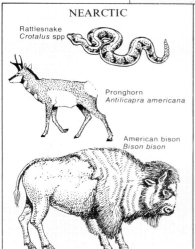

NEARCTIC

Rattlesnake
Crotalus spp

Pronghorn
Antilocapra americana

American bison
Bison bison

The Nearctic or "New North" region covers all of North America, from the highlands of Mexico in the south to Greenland and the Aleutian Islands in the north. Its climate and vegetation resemble that of the Palearctic region, and many of its mammals crossed over from the Palearctic via the Bering land bridge, which linked Siberia and Alaska when the sea level was lower. Animals unique to the Nearctic group include the pronghorn, an antelope-like mammal that inhabits the grasslands and plains of western and central America, and the bison, another large mammal that inhabits the prairies. Several species of rattlesnake also belong to the Nearctic group, although they are not exclusive to this region.

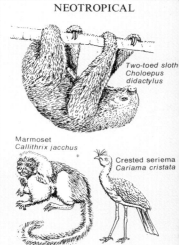

NEOTROPICAL

Two-toed sloth
Choloepus didactylus

Marmoset
Callithrix jacchus

Crested seriema
Cariama cristata

The Neotropical or "New Tropical" region consists of South America, the West Indies and most of Mexico. The climate and vegetation are mostly tropical—only the southern tip is in the temperate zone—and it is linked to the Nearctic by the Central American corridor. The Neotropical region has more distinctive families than any other. These include, among mammals, the sloth, which inhabits the tropical forests and has adapted to an upside-down existence. Among birds, the long-legged crested seriema is also unique to the region. Neotropical monkeys, such as the marmoset, have lateral-facing nostrils, which distinguish them from their downward-nosed relatives found in the Old World.

Land routes around the world have altered with the ages, sometimes allowing invaders to penetrate new lands, or closing to form natural sanctuaries for less efficient animals. The Central American isthmus (A) opened South America to placental mammals from the north. The Sahara desert closed most of Africa (B) to Eurasian species. Asia and Australia (C) share "island hoppers" in the transitional zones, but sea barriers have kept the regions separate.

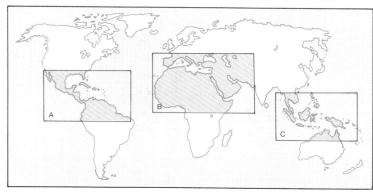

A land bridge between the Americas emerged about three million years ago, breaking the long isolation of the south. The primitive pouched mammals which had developed there were now threatened by more advanced mammals from the north, and many extinctions followed. Northern invaders included peccaries, raccoons and a llama-like camelid. But members of the armadillo and opossum families were successful in making their way to the northern region.

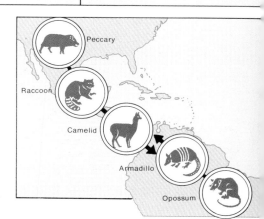

Peccary

Raccoon

Camelid

Armadillo

Opossum

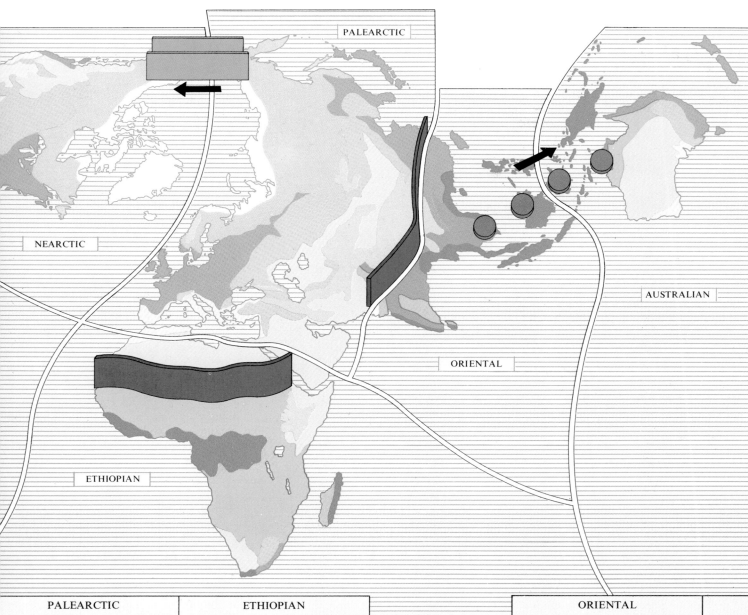

PALEARCTIC

NEARCTIC

ORIENTAL

AUSTRALIAN

ETHIOPIAN

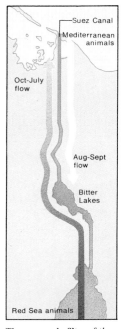

The man-made filter of the Suez Canal, cut in 1869, is an animal corridor between the Mediterranean and Red Sea. But movement is mainly from the latter, for the channel passes through the hot, salty Bitter Lakes, favouring animals adapted to these conditions, and the current flows northwards for 10 months of the year. However, not all the 130 invading species are likely to survive Mediterranean conditions.

PALEARCTIC

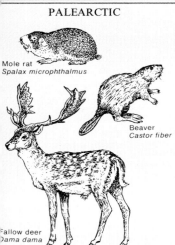

Mole rat
Spalax microphthalmus

Beaver
Castor fiber

Fallow deer
Dama dama

The Palearctic or "Old North" region covers the entire northerly part of the Old World, with seas to the north, east and west. To the south, the Sahara desert and the Himalaya mountains form barriers that separate the Palearctic from the Ethiopian and Oriental regions, although these regions are all part of the same landmass. One of the few species of mammals unique to the Palearctic is the Mediterranean mole rat, a thick-furred rodent. Another Palearctic rodent, the beaver, is shared with the Nearctic region. Fallow deer occur throughout Europe. They have been introduced by man into many other parts of the world, but their origin is almost certainly Mediterranean.

ETHIOPIAN

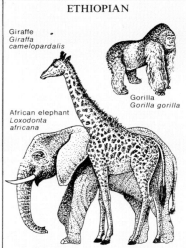

Giraffe
Giraffa camelopardalis

Gorilla
Gorilla gorilla

African elephant
Loxodonta africana

The Ethiopian region includes southern Arabia as well as all Africa south of the Sahara. It resembles in many ways the Neotropical region and is almost as rich in unique families. Its fauna also has much in common with the Oriental region. Unique mammals include the giraffe, at 5.5 m (18 ft) the tallest of living land animals, which inhabits the savanna. The region also supports two of the world's four great apes, the gorilla and the chimpanzee, which are found in the forests of western and central Africa. (The other great apes, the orang-utan and the gibbon, are Oriental.) The African elephant is distinguished from its Indian relative by its greater size and by its huge ears and massive tusks.

	Polar
	Tundra
	Taiga
	Mountain
	Temperate forest
	Temperate grassland
	Mediterranean
	Savanna
	Tropical rainforest
	Monsoon
	Desert
	Barrier
	Corridor
	Stepping stone
→	Prevailing movement

ORIENTAL

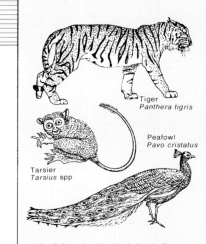

Tiger
Panthera tigris

Peafowl
Pavo cristatus

Tarsier
Tarsius spp

The Oriental region includes India, southern China, southeastern Asia and part of Malaysia. It is bounded to the north by the Himalayas and on either side by ocean, and is separated from the Australian region by a line known as Wallace's Line. It shares a quarter of its mammal families with Africa, but has more primates than any other region. The tarsier, a small relative of the monkey, is unique to southeastern Asia and represents an important early stage of primate evolution. The tiger was once widespread, but its natural habitats are steadily diminishing and the tiger itself is in danger of extinction by man. The peacock is one of the region's many brilliantly coloured birds.

AUSTRALIAN

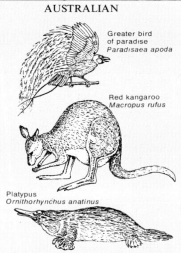

Greater bird of paradise
Paradisaea apoda

Red kangaroo
Macropus rufus

Platypus
Ornithorhynchus anatinus

The Australian region is unique in having no land connection with any other region. Its native fauna has developed in isolation from the rest of the world for at least 50 million years. Most of the mammals are marsupial—animals such as the kangaroo that carry their young in a pouch. Even more of a biological curiosity than the marsupials is the duckbilled platypus, a monotreme or egg-laying mammal. It lives along the banks of streams in Australia and Tasmania, and lays small, leathery eggs like those of snakes and turtles, but it is a true mammal and nurses its young with milk. Some 13 bird families are unique to the region, including the magnificent bird of paradise.

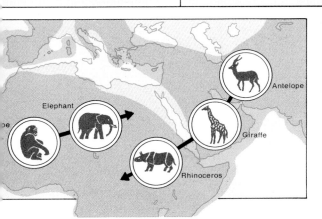

Elephant
Antelope
Giraffe
Rhinoceros

A desert barrier gradually began to form in northern Africa about nine million years ago, replacing the forest corridor between the Ethiopian and Palearctic regions. During the change, many animals typical of the African plains moved in from the north, including ancestors of today's antelopes, giraffes and rhinoceroses. But African animals also moved up north: early elephants and, much later, apes, which may have been precursors of modern man.

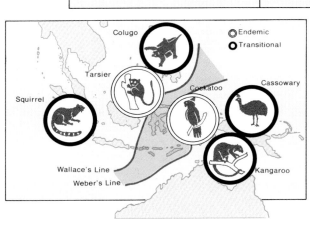

Colugo
Tarsier
Squirrel
Cockatoo
Cassowary
Kangaroo
Wallace's Line
Weber's Line

◎ Endemic
◯ Transitional

The transitional area of "Wallacea" contains animals from both the Oriental and Australian regions, bounded by Wallace's and Weber's Lines, but few have crossed to the other region. Some Oriental mammals, such as tarsiers, are found in Wallacea, but the gliding colugo and varieties of squirrel are not. The Australian cockatoo has reached the transition area, but the flightless cassowary and the tree kangaroo have not.

Spread of Man

Modern Man, *Homo sapiens sapiens*, has proved a highly successful animal since his emergence some 50,000 years ago: today more than 4,000 million members of this subspecies of the *Homo* (Man) group occupy the Earth, living in even the most inhospitable regions. But the fossil record shows that man's lineage goes back millions of years, with different stages of development leading to a greater control of the environment, and with climate itself helping man's ultimate domination of Earth.

Man's lineage may go back at least 14 million years to a small woodland creature known as *Ramapithecus* (Rama's ape). Since the first discoveries of *Ramapithecus* in the Indian subcontinent, its fossils have come to light in many parts of the world, including China, eastern Europe, Turkey and eastern Africa. Fossil remains show that it survived for several million years until, about eight million years ago, there is a tantalizing gap in the fossil record. Then, about four and a half million years later (according to recent discoveries in eastern Africa), we have solid evidence of an upright hominid—a member of man's zoological family. This is "Lucy", a fossil skeleton found in 1973 by Donald Johanson and Tom Gray, and subsequently classified with many other finds as *Australopithecus afarensis*.

This may be man's ancestral "rootstock", but a little later there existed two kinds of "apeman" (*Australopithecus*), and our own direct ancestor Handy Man (*Homo habilis*). Datable volcanic ash found with the fossils provides a time-scale and indicates that, about two million years ago, ape-man and "true" man lived side by side in the lush grassland that then covered the eastern African plains.

One and a half million years ago, according to the fossil evidence, there was again only one hominid species. The varieties of australopithecines had died out, and Handy Man (*Homo habilis*) had apparently evolved into Upright Man (*Homo erectus*). Remains of Upright Man have been found in many regions of the world, from various parts of Africa and Europe to China and Indonesia, although not in the Americas. But there is reason to believe that it was in Africa, well over one million years ago, that he evolved from his ancestor, and began a very gradual expansion out of the continent.

Upright Man had about one million years to spread across the Old World, adapting as he did so to local conditions, just as people of today are adapted in their various ways. He was a nomadic hunter-gatherer, socially organized in groups. His skills included the use of fire and cooking, as well as the making of quite large structures out of wood. Recent discoveries suggest that, during the million years of his existence, *Homo erectus* gradually evolved into the next stage of man – *Homo sapiens*.

The next step is revealed most clearly in fossils from more than 100,000 to less than 50,000 years ago. Called Neanderthal Man in Europe, Solo Man in Indonesia, and Rhodesian Man in southern Africa, these types of human being were all descendants of *Homo erectus*.

Variable in brain size, but with prominent eyebrow ridges and receding jaws, they may have been dead-ends on the evolutionary road; or some may have led to, or been incorporated in, Modern Man (*Homo sapiens sapiens*).

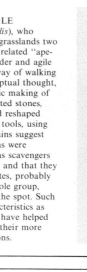

THE AFRICAN CRADLE
Handy Man (*Homo habilis*), who shared the East African grasslands two million years ago with a related "apeman" species, was a slender and agile creature with a human way of walking and a capacity for conceptual thought, as evidenced in systematic making of tools. Handy Man collected stones, often from far away, and reshaped them into purpose-made tools, using other stones. Fossil remains suggest that these earliest humans were efficient hunters as well as scavengers of larger predators' kills, and that they brought food to camp sites, probably sharing it among the whole group, rather than eating it on the spot. Such specifically human characteristics as the sharing of food may have helped our ancestors to survive their more primitive hominid relations.

MAN THE FIRE-BRINGER
Upright Man (*Homo erectus*) emerged about 1.5 million years ago, evolving from his predecessor, Handy Man. For one million years these people developed and adapted, spreading over most of the Old World and following a nomadic hunter-gatherer life style, assisted by a more sophisticated tool technology. The cooler climates of northern Asia and Europe may have encouraged their most impressive innovation—the use of fire for warmth, cooking and hunting game—and also their ability to construct quite elaborate shelters. It seems likely that they possessed language; and traces of ochre lumps at a camp site perhaps 400,000 years old suggest the possibility of ritual adornment or some kind of body-painting.

THE HUMANIZING OF MAN
Modern man's predecessor, although called Wise Man (*Homo sapiens*), was long regarded as more brutish than human. But widespread finds have now changed this image, as can be seen in an old and an updated reconstruction of the same Neanderthal skull (right). Many scientists believe that these people showed a human concern for each other, burying their dead with ceremonial reverence, and looking after disabled members of the group. In their Neanderthal form they inhabited Europe and the Middle East from about 100,000 to 40,000 years ago, and were perhaps adapted to ice-age conditions. *Homo sapiens* counterparts of Neanderthal Man also occur in Africa and southeastern Asia.

Updated reconstruction

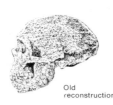
Old reconstruction

The burial of a Neanderthal man took place 60,000 years ago at Shanidar in the Iraq highlands. Fossil traces suggest that the body was laid on a bed of branches, and that flowers were brought to the grave and placed deliberately around the body. The flowers included many varieties still known locally for their medicinal properties. Ritual burials occur at many Neanderthal sites, from the Pyrenees to Soviet Asia, and indicate a sensitivity that contradicts Neanderthal Man's traditional image.

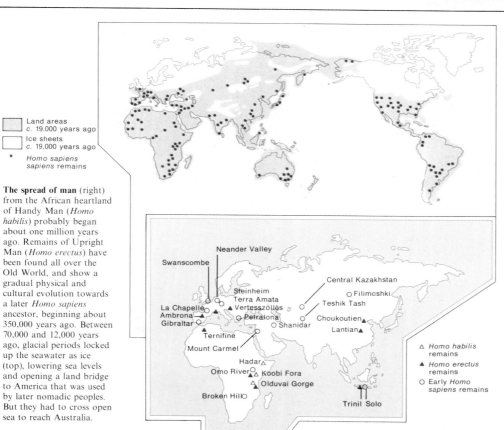

Land areas *c.* 19,000 years ago
Ice sheets *c.* 19,000 years ago
Homo sapiens sapiens remains

The spread of man (right) from the African heartland of Handy Man (*Homo habilis*) probably began about one million years ago. Remains of Upright Man (*Homo erectus*) have been found all over the Old World, and show a gradual physical and cultural evolution towards a later *Homo sapiens* ancestor, beginning about 350,000 years ago. Between 70,000 and 12,000 years ago, glacial periods locked up the seawater as ice (top), lowering sea levels and opening a land bridge to America that was used by later nomadic peoples. But they had to cross open sea to reach Australia.

Neander Valley
Swanscombe
Steinheim
Terra Amata
La Chapelle
Ambrona
Gibraltar
Vértesszöllös
Petralona
Ternifine
Mount Carmel
Hadar
Omo River
Koobi Fora
Olduvai Gorge
Broken Hill
Central Kazakhstan
Filimoshki
Teshik Tash
Choukoutien
Lantian
Shanidar
Trinil Solo

△ Homo habilis remains
▲ Homo erectus remains
○ Early Homo sapiens remains

THE AGE OF ART
Towards the end of the last Ice Age, from about 35,000 years ago, truly modern humans began to depict their world in wonderfully vivid terms. The age of art may have reached its peak at Lascaux, France, some 15,000 years ago, but less well-preserved cave paintings from Africa show that the artistic impulse was equally present elsewhere. Called Cro-Magnon Man in Europe, these people spread to all parts of the world, crossing to the Americas by way of the Bering land bridge (when ice locked up the water of the straits), and even venturing over the seas to Australia. Physically these people were just like present-day humans. They led a nomadic, hunter-gathering life, living in large, organized groups, hunting such animals as mammoths, reindeer, bison and horses, and using a technology, as well as an artistry, far in advance of anything previously developed.

Fossils almost four million years old, found since 1973, may mark the ancestral "rootstock" of humanity, but the earliest form of true man is thought to be *Homo habilis*, who shared his African habitat with "apeman" relatives some two million years ago. His successor, *Homo erectus*, spread over Asia and Europe, evolving gradually into modern man's predecessors, creatures whose large brow ridges belie many typically human characteristics. These were replaced by Modern Man.

Australopithecus afarensis
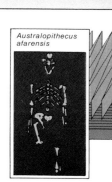

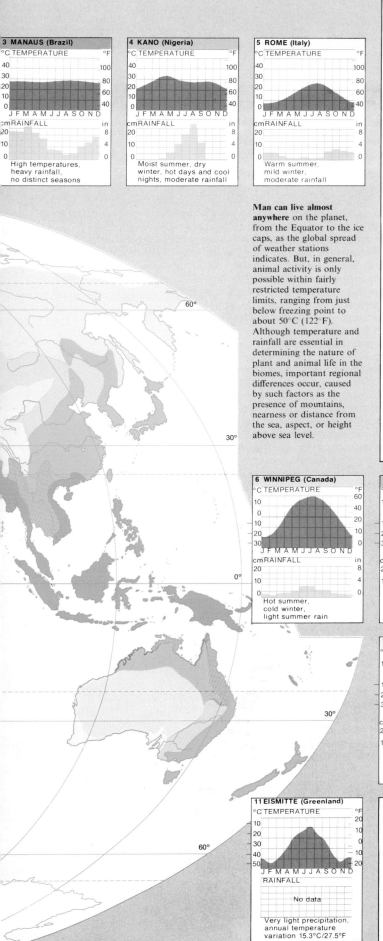

3 MANAUS (Brazil)
°C TEMPERATURE °F
High temperatures, heavy rainfall, no distinct seasons

4 KANO (Nigeria)
°C TEMPERATURE °F
Moist summer, dry winter, hot days and cool nights, moderate rainfall

5 ROME (Italy)
°C TEMPERATURE °F
Warm summer, mild winter, moderate rainfall

Man can live almost anywhere on the planet, from the Equator to the ice caps, as the global spread of weather stations indicates. But, in general, animal activity is only possible within fairly restricted temperature limits, ranging from just below freezing point to about 50°C (122°F). Although temperature and rainfall are essential in determining the nature of plant and animal life in the biomes, important regional differences occur, caused by such factors as the presence of mountains, nearness or distance from the sea, aspect, or height above sea level.

6 WINNIPEG (Canada)
°C TEMPERATURE °F
Hot summer, cold winter, light summer rain

7 BORDEAUX (France)
°C TEMPERATURE °F
Warm summer, mild winter, four distinct seasons

8 PIKE'S PEAK (USA)
°C TEMPERATURE °F
4,300 m (14,111ft) Temperature decreases with increasing altitude

9 ARKHANGELSK (USSR)
°C TEMPERATURE °F
Short summer, long and cold winter, light summer rain

10 BARROW (Alaska)
°C TEMPERATURE °F
Brief summer, very long and cold winter, very light rainfall

11 EISMITTE (Greenland)
°C TEMPERATURE °F
No data
Very light precipitation, annual temperature variation 15.3°C/27.5°F

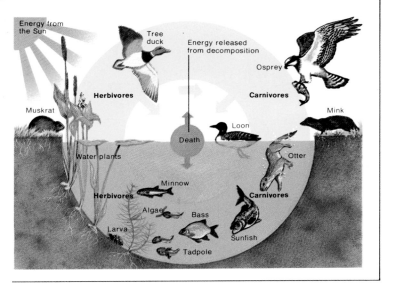

Energy from the Sun
Tree duck
Energy released from decomposition
Osprey
Herbivores
Carnivores
Muskrat
Mink
Death
Loon
Water plants
Otter
Minnow
Herbivores
Carnivores
Algae
Bass
Larva
Sunfish
Tadpole

Earth's Natural Regions

Geographers have long looked for ways of classifying conditions such as climate, soil and vegetation to describe the general similarities and differences from area to area throughout the world. By identifying distinctive patterns of climate and vegetation they have provided a convenient global division into natural regions or biomes. And recent developments in ecology – the study of plants and animals in relation to their environments – have given such divisions a greater depth.

Divisions according to climate were first suggested by the Greek philosopher Aristotle, and his ideas were still in use until about 100 years ago. Aristotle posited a number of climatic zones—called torrid, temperate and frigid—defined by latitude. But with time it became increasingly apparent that the complex distribution of atmospheric pressure, winds, rainfall and temperature could not be related to such a simple frame. Nineteenth-century scientists divided the world into 35 climatic provinces. Then in 1900 the German meteorologist Wladimir Köppen produced a more sophisticated climatic classification based on temperature and moisture conditions related to the needs of plants. At about the same time other scientists studied the distribution of vegetation types throughout the world. These studies together provided the basis for much of the later work on climatic regions.

An important step forward was made in 1904 by the British geographer A. J. Herbertson. He argued that subdivision of physical environments should take into account the distribution of the various phenomena as they related to each other. He conceived the idea of *natural regions*, each with "a certain unity of configuration (relief), climate and vegetation". His final classification contained four groups or regions: Polar Types, Cool Temperate Types, Warm Temperate Types and Tropical Hot Lands. Herbertson's scheme, controversial at first, was later much used for teaching geography.

Ecology

Meanwhile the study of environmental problems had been advanced by the idea of *ecology*, the relationship of living things between each other and their surroundings. The term was first used in 1868 by Ernst Haeckel, the German biologist, but it was not until the end of the nineteenth century that scientists really began to study life forms in relation to their habitat. In addition to the central ideas of interdependence between the members of plant and animal communities and between the community and the physical environment, there now came the suggestion that communities develop in a sequence that leads to a "climax"—a final step of equilibrium or balance. Their climax stage depends on conditions of climate or soil.

Later the British botanist A. G. Tansley, a leading exponent of ecological thinking, introduced the term *ecosystem* to describe a group of living organisms and its effective environment. Tansley's definition of 1935 referred to the whole system, including "not only the organism complex, but also the whole complex of physical factors forming what we call the environment of the biome". The idea became very influential and has been used in the social sciences as well as in the natural ones. But it is difficult to apply in practice, partly because of the highly complex and often diverse interactions that take place in different parts of the ecosystem.

Ecologists have developed special methods and have given particular attention to the ways in which energy is transferred within the system. The term *biome* refers to the whole complex of organisms, both animals and plants, that live together naturally as a society. By *environment* is meant all the external conditions that affect the life and development of an organism.

Biomes

The biomes shown on the map are broadly drawn generalizations. They should be regarded as idealized regions, within which many local variations may exist—for example, of climate or soil conditions. On a larger scale such features as mountain ranges may cause variations at a regional level. Scientists have tried to work out "hierarchies" that include many levels or orders of scale leading to the major climatic-vegetation realms or biomes. These realms give a broad picture that is useful at the world level of scale, and which forms a starting point for further analysis. Any map of the biomes has to have lines to indicate the boundaries of each region, but these too are generalizations. Although climate and vegetation do sometimes change abruptly from place to place, more often there are transitional zones, and the boundaries on the maps give the broad locations of these.

Herbertson's concept of natural regions attempted also to take account of the influence of man as an important factor in the environment. But he was not totally successful in including man in his analysis, no doubt because of the complexity of the problems involved and because of the immense influence that man has had upon the natural vegetation of the world. The cutting of forests, the drainage and reclamation of land, the introduction, use and spread of cultivated plants, the domestication of animals, the development of sophisticated systems of agriculture and many other actions all create, over large areas of the biomes, landscapes that are more man-made than natural.

Resource systems

An idea that clarifies the study of the interrelations of societies and environments, and the ways in which these change with the passage of time, is that of the *resource system*. This is a model of a population of human beings and their social and economic characteristics, including their technical skills and resources, together with those aspects of the natural environment that affect them and which they influence. The model includes the sequences by which natural materials are obtained, transformed and used. It tries to show how societies are organized according to their natural resources, the effects of that use, and the ways in which natural conditions limit or expand the life and work of the society. But it is easier to apply such a model to societies that have direct relations with natural conditions, through farming, fishing or forestry, than to great urban–industrial complexes.

The sections that follow present a picture of the diversity of habitats from ice caps to equatorial forests, the principal ways man has modified the environment and the problems of maintaining healthy resource systems.

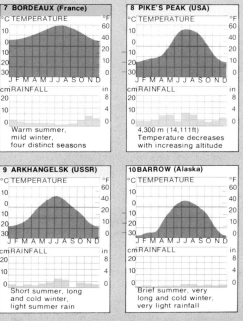

Climate and Weather

The pattern of world climates depends largely on great circulations of air in the atmosphere. These movements of air are driven by energy from the Sun, and they transfer surplus heat from the tropics to the polar regions. Over a long period of time – such as months, seasons or years – they create the climate. Over a short period – day by day, or week by week – they form the weather. Together, climate and weather are among the most significant natural components of the world's diverse environments.

The world's tropical zones receive more heat from the Sun than they re-emit into space, and so their land and sea surfaces become warm. The polar regions, on the other hand, emit more radiation than they receive, and so they become cold. Warm air is less dense than cold air, and this means that atmospheric pressure becomes low at the Equator and high at the poles. As a result, a circulation of air—both vertical and horizontal—is set up. But because of the Earth's rotation and the distribution of land and sea there is not a simple air circulation pattern in each hemisphere; winds are deflected to the right in the northern hemisphere and to the left in the southern hemisphere, a phenomenon known as the Coriolis effect.

A climatic patchwork

When warm air rises it expands and cools and the water vapour it is carrying condenses to form clouds. For this reason heavy, showery rain is frequent in the belt of rising air near the Equator. In the subtropical zones (where the air is sinking), clouds evaporate and the weather is fine. Air moves out of the subtropical high-pressure belts in the lower atmosphere. Some of it flows towards the poles and meets colder air, flowing out of the polar high-pressure region, in a narrow zone called the polar front. This convergence of air is concentrated around low-pressure systems known as depressions.

The pattern of climates does not remain constant throughout the year because of seasonal changes in the amount of radiation from the Sun—the "fuel" of the atmospheric engine. In June, when the northern hemisphere is tilted towards the Sun, the radiation is at a maximum at latitude 23°N and all the climatic belts shift northwards. In December it is summer in the southern hemisphere and all the belts move southwards.

Climate is also affected by the distribution of land and sea across the globe. The temperature of the land changes more quickly than that of

TYPES OF WEATHER

There is a constant flow of air between the world's polar and tropical regions, and this has a prime effect on the weather in other regions. In the high and middle latitudes cold and warm fronts succeed each other, and along coasts sea fogs often form. In temperate and tropical regions thunderstorms are frequent, and the tropics are characterized by the turbulent storms known as hurricanes in the Caribbean area and typhoons in the Pacific.

POLAR WEATHER

Weather in high latitudes is marked by consistently low temperatures—on the ice caps temperatures are nearly always below freezing. At the poles the sun never rises for six months of the year and for the remaining six months it never sets. Even in summer it stays low on the horizon and its rays are so slanted that they bring very little warmth. On the tundra the temperature rises above freezing for a few months in summer, but severe frosts are likely to occur at any time. As well as being bitterly cold, polar weather is predominantly dry. The lower the temperature the less moisture the air can contain. Clouds, when they form, are high, thin sheets of cirrostratus. Composed of ice crystals, they often produce a halo effect around the sun. Snow, when it falls, is usually dry and powdery.

DEPRESSIONS

Low-pressure weather systems, or depressions, form when polar and subtropical air masses converge. Cloud and rain usually occur at the boundary, or front, of the different air masses. Seen in cross-section, a fully developed depression shows both warm (A) and cold (B) fronts. As the wave of warm air rises over the cold, its moisture condenses into the "layered" clouds that usually precede a warm front. Behind the warm front, cold air forces under the warm air, producing the wedge-shaped cold front.

FOG

Fogs form as a result of the condensation of water vapour in the air; they may occur when warm, moist air is cooled by its passage over a cold surface. Off the coast of California, for example, air near the surface of the sea is cooled by the cold California Current and sea fog is frequent. The air at higher levels is still warm and acts like a lid over the fog, and mountains prevent the fog from dispersing in an easterly direction. Fumes and smoke are trapped by this temperature inversion, creating the notorious Los Angeles smog.

THUNDERSTORMS

These develop when air is unstable to a great height. Particularly violent storms occur when cold, dry air masses meet warm, moist air, causing the latter to rise rapidly. As the warm air surges upwards it cools and its moisture condenses into cumulonimbus, or thunder, clouds. Flat cloud-tops mark the level where stable air occurs again. Quickly moving raindrops and hail in the clouds become electrically charged and cause lightning, and the explosion of heated air along the path of the flash creates the sound wave that is heard as thunder.

HURRICANES

These are tropical storms on a vast scale that build up over warm oceans. Their core is an area of low pressure around which large quantities of warm, moist air are carried to the high atmosphere at great speed. The Earth's rotation is responsible for the huge swirling movement: in the northern hemisphere the movement is anticlockwise, in the southern hemisphere it is clockwise. Towering bands of clouds produce torrential rain. The central region, or "eye", of a hurricane, however, has light winds, clear skies and no rainfall.

THE WORLD'S CLIMATIC REGIONS

Climate is the characteristic weather of a region over a long period of time. It is often described in terms of average monthly and yearly temperatures and rainfall. These in turn depend largely on latitude, which determines whether a region is basically hot or cold and whether it has pronounced seasonal changes. Climate is also influenced by prevailing winds, by ocean currents and by geographical features such as the distribution of land and water. Highland climates are influenced by altitude and are always cooler than those of nearby lowland regions. Tropical climates are always warm. Near the Equator rain falls for most of the year, but towards the subtropics the wet and dry seasons are more marked. Temperate climates reflect the conflict between warm and cold air masses. They range from the Mediterranean type with hot, dry summers and mild, moist winters to the cooler, wetter climates of higher latitudes. The subarctic is mainly cold and humid; polar climates are always cold and mainly dry.

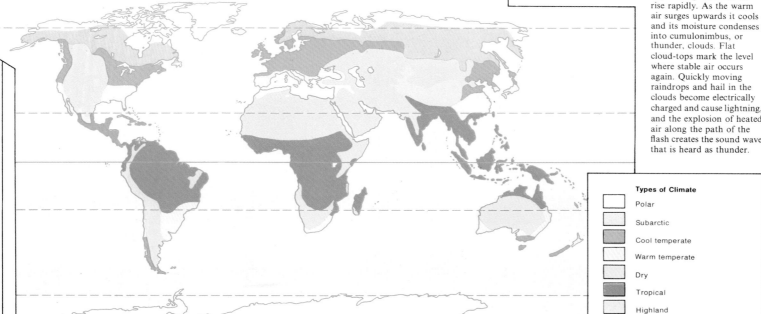

Types of Climate

- Polar
- Subarctic
- Cool temperate
- Warm temperate
- Dry
- Tropical
- Highland

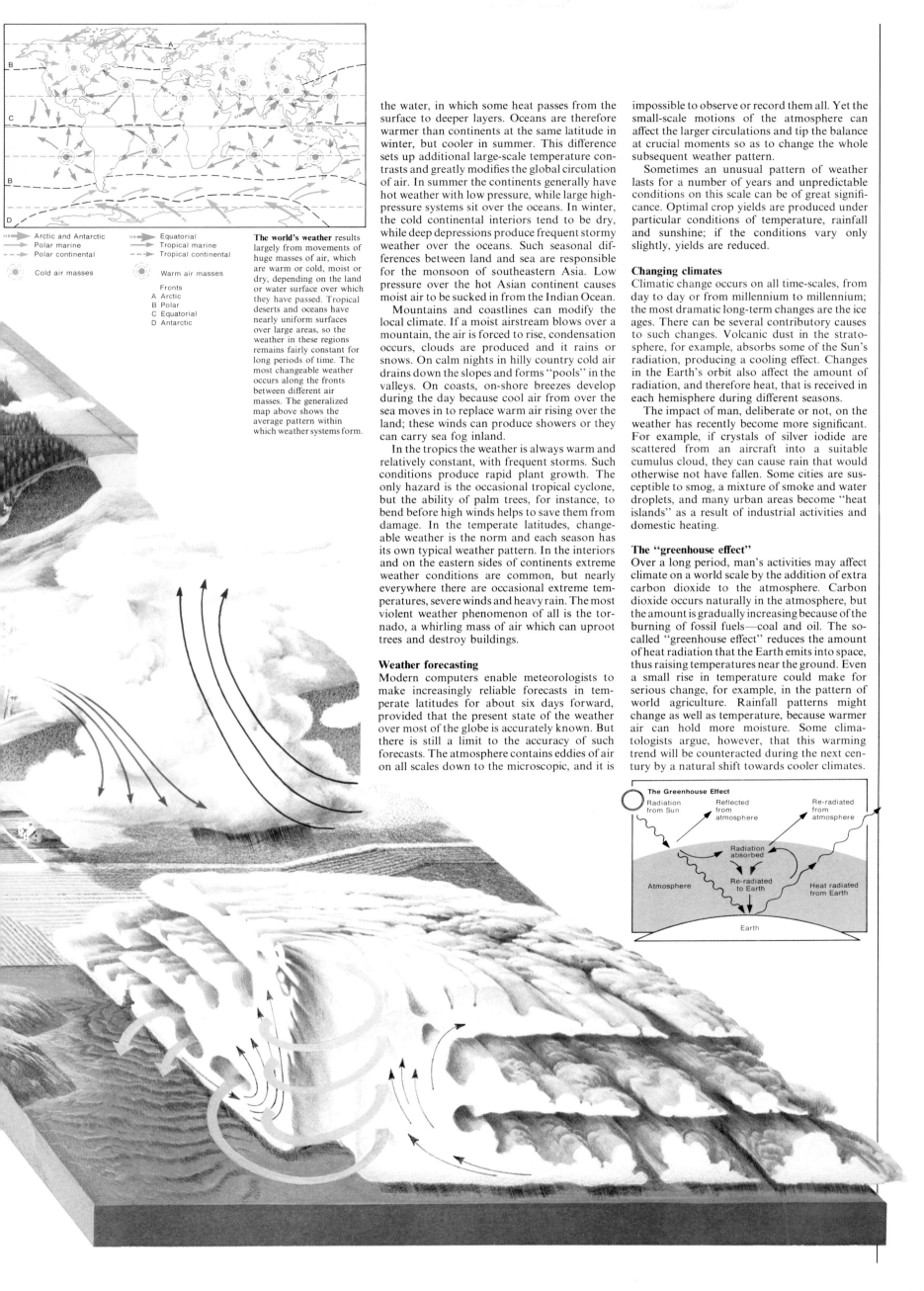

Arctic and Antarctic   Equatorial
Polar marine   Tropical marine
Polar continental   Tropical continental

Cold air masses   Warm air masses

Fronts
A Arctic
B Polar
C Equatorial
D Antarctic

The world's weather results largely from movements of huge masses of air, which are warm or cold, moist or dry, depending on the land or water surface over which they have passed. Tropical deserts and oceans have nearly uniform surfaces over large areas, so the weather in these regions remains fairly constant for long periods of time. The most changeable weather occurs along the fronts between different air masses. The generalized map above shows the average pattern within which weather systems form.

the water, in which some heat passes from the surface to deeper layers. Oceans are therefore warmer than continents at the same latitude in winter, but cooler in summer. This difference sets up additional large-scale temperature contrasts and greatly modifies the global circulation of air. In summer the continents generally have hot weather with low pressure, while large high-pressure systems sit over the oceans. In winter, the cold continental interiors tend to be dry, while deep depressions produce frequent stormy weather over the oceans. Such seasonal differences between land and sea are responsible for the monsoon of southeastern Asia. Low pressure over the hot Asian continent causes moist air to be sucked in from the Indian Ocean.

Mountains and coastlines can modify the local climate. If a moist airstream blows over a mountain, the air is forced to rise, condensation occurs, clouds are produced and it rains or snows. On calm nights in hilly country cold air drains down the slopes and forms "pools" in the valleys. On coasts, on-shore breezes develop during the day because cool air from over the sea moves in to replace warm air rising over the land; these winds can produce showers or they can carry sea fog inland.

In the tropics the weather is always warm and relatively constant, with frequent storms. Such conditions produce rapid plant growth. The only hazard is the occasional tropical cyclone, but the ability of palm trees, for instance, to bend before high winds helps to save them from damage. In the temperate latitudes, change-able weather is the norm and each season has its own typical weather pattern. In the interiors and on the eastern sides of continents extreme weather conditions are common, but nearly everywhere there are occasional extreme temperatures, severe winds and heavy rain. The most violent weather phenomenon of all is the tornado, a whirling mass of air which can uproot trees and destroy buildings.

Weather forecasting
Modern computers enable meteorologists to make increasingly reliable forecasts in temperate latitudes for about six days forward, provided that the present state of the weather over most of the globe is accurately known. But there is still a limit to the accuracy of such forecasts. The atmosphere contains eddies of air on all scales down to the microscopic, and it is

impossible to observe or record them all. Yet the small-scale motions of the atmosphere can affect the larger circulations and tip the balance at crucial moments so as to change the whole subsequent weather pattern.

Sometimes an unusual pattern of weather lasts for a number of years and unpredictable conditions on this scale can be of great significance. Optimal crop yields are produced under particular conditions of temperature, rainfall and sunshine; if the conditions vary only slightly, yields are reduced.

Changing climates
Climatic change occurs on all time-scales, from day to day or from millennium to millennium; the most dramatic long-term changes are the ice ages. There can be several contributory causes to such changes. Volcanic dust in the stratosphere, for example, absorbs some of the Sun's radiation, producing a cooling effect. Changes in the Earth's orbit also affect the amount of radiation, and therefore heat, that is received in each hemisphere during different seasons.

The impact of man, deliberate or not, on the weather has recently become more significant. For example, if crystals of silver iodide are scattered from an aircraft into a suitable cumulus cloud, they can cause rain that would otherwise not have fallen. Some cities are susceptible to smog, a mixture of smoke and water droplets, and many urban areas become "heat islands" as a result of industrial activities and domestic heating.

The "greenhouse effect"
Over a long period, man's activities may affect climate on a world scale by the addition of extra carbon dioxide to the atmosphere. Carbon dioxide occurs naturally in the atmosphere, but the amount is gradually increasing because of the burning of fossil fuels—coal and oil. The so-called "greenhouse effect" reduces the amount of heat radiation that the Earth emits into space, thus raising temperatures near the ground. Even a small rise in temperature could make for serious change, for example, in the pattern of world agriculture. Rainfall patterns might change as well as temperature, because warmer air can hold more moisture. Some climatologists argue, however, that this warming trend will be counteracted during the next century by a natural shift towards cooler climates.

The Greenhouse Effect
Radiation from Sun / Reflected from atmosphere / Re-radiated from atmosphere

Radiation absorbed

Atmosphere / Re-radiated to Earth / Heat radiated from Earth

Earth

Resources and Energy

Resources, it has been said, comprise mankind's varying needs from generation to generation and are valued because of the uses societies can make of them. They represent human appraisals and are the products of man's ingenuity and experience. While natural resources remain vitally important in themselves, they must always be regarded as the rewards of human skill in locating, extracting and exploiting them. The development of resources depends on many factors, including the existence of a demand, adequate transport facilities, the availability of capital and the accessibility, quality and quantity of the resource itself.

The world's extraction of its resources highlights the inequality of their distribution. Each resource shown on the map is attributed to the three countries with the largest production percentages of that commodity. So, in 1976, the three leading bauxite producers were Australia (26.69%), Jamaica (14.19%) and Rep. of Guinea (13.9%). Usually, the larger and more wealthy a state the greater its monopoly of resources—although the tiny Pacific island of New Caledonia produces more than 14% of the world's nickel. China is reputed to mine 75% of the world's tungsten and to be increasing its oil supply rapidly. Energy consumption figures are for the year 1976, since when there have been some outstanding changes to patterns of availability, perhaps most noticeably in Britain's new-found oil and gas surplus. Bahrain and Tobago, too small to be shown on this map, also have surpluses of energy production.

A dictionary defines the term "resource" as "a means of aid or support", implying anything that lends support to life or activity. Man has always assessed nature with an eye to his own needs, and it is these varying needs that endow resources with their usefulness. Fossil fuels such as oil have lain long in the Earth, but it was not until about 1900 that the large-scale needs fostered by the rising demands of motor vehicles led to the development of new techniques for locating and extracting this raw material. Today oil has also become precious in the manufacture of a wide variety of industrial products, which themselves are resources that are much used by other industries.

The nature of resources

Resources can be most usefully classified in two groups: "renewable" and "nonrenewable". The latter is composed of materials found at or near the Earth's surface, which are sometimes known as "physical" resources. They include such essential minerals as uranium, iron, copper, nickel, bauxite, gold, silver, lead, mercury and tungsten. Oil, coal and natural gas are the principal nonrenewable fuel and energy resources, but after they have been used for producing heat or power their utility is lost and part of the geological capital of 325 million years of history is gone for ever. Some minerals such as iron and its product, steel, can be recycled and renewed, however. "Renewable" resources are basically biological, being the food and other vegetable matter which life needs to sustain human needs. Provided soil quality is maintained, their productivity may even be increased as better strains of plants and breeds of animals are developed.

Work has long been in progress to improve renewable resources, and has moved forward to manufacturing vegetable-flavoured protein (VFP) from soya beans as a meat substitute and to viable experiments to extract protein from leaves. In Brazil, many cars have been converted to run successfully on alcohol extracted from sugar. One renewable resource—the tree—can be closely related to other resources: some conservationists are alarmed at the overuse of firewood as a source of fuel and energy in the semi-arid areas of Africa. This may be an important factor in increasing the tendency for the deserts to spread in that continent, and in such a situation there is a new realization of the concept of closely managing resources such as soil, timber and fisheries. This is partly because we have a clearer understanding of the ecology of vegetation and the important interdependence of climate, soil, plants and animal life. Much, however, remains to be done.

The politics of nonrenewable resources

Today we are naturally troubled about the availability of natural resources. Oil is a prime cause for concern. Although many believe that production will grow until the mid-2020s and that new oil reserves will be discovered, oil's scarcity, based on a growing rate of demand and increasingly wasteful use, is now widely accepted. Because, like many resources, it is unevenly distributed, those countries with large and accessible supplies—such as the members of OPEC—have used their political power on a number of occasions to raise oil's price, with adverse effects on the economies of most importers. Ironically, these substantial price rises have had the effect of stimulating exploration and development in many new areas; there are already signs of increased production in China.

Other nonrenewable resources are also distributed unevenly, but have not been mined on any scale comparable with their availability; vast reserves of coal in the USSR and China have not been worked on any scale resembling their known extent.

New energy sources

As resources such as oil become less available and more expensive, the renewable resources of power such as water, wind, waves and solar energy, all of which are currently under study or development, will receive new injections of capital. Attention will also have to be paid to more widespread nuclear energy production. Energy has been called "the ultimate resource", and it is imperative that we make wise provisions for its future availability.

Future resources

It has been calculated that within four years of the launch of Sputnik I, more than 3,000 products resulting from space research were put into commercial production. These included new alloys, ceramics, plastics, fabrics and chemical compounds. Satellite developments have meant that land use can now be measured quickly and potential mineral sources closely identified. A satellite capable of converting solar power to electricity and contributing to the Earth's energy deficit has been widely discussed, while the Moon and planets have been mooted as future possible sources of minerals.

Conclusions

Resources are, in the main, the products of man's skill, ingenuity and expertise, and their widespread use, as in the case of timber and iron for shipbuilding, became apparent only as man's needs for them became clear. Our forebears were once concerned about the availability of flint, seaweed, charcoal and natural rubber; countries even went to war over supplies of spices. Today our requirements are slightly different—we no longer depend only on local sites for resources, and improved transport facilities and appropriate technologies have lowered the costs of obtaining materials for manufacture.

Nevertheless, the principles remain the same. A continual search for new resources capable of exploitation and wide application must be maintained, together with a close regard for the value of the renewable resources such as animal and vegetable products required to support man in his search for new resources. Perhaps the most vital consideration is the need for wise policies of conservation relating to the proven reserves of nonrenewable resources still in the ground, and the careful future use of such valuable deposits known or thought to exist.

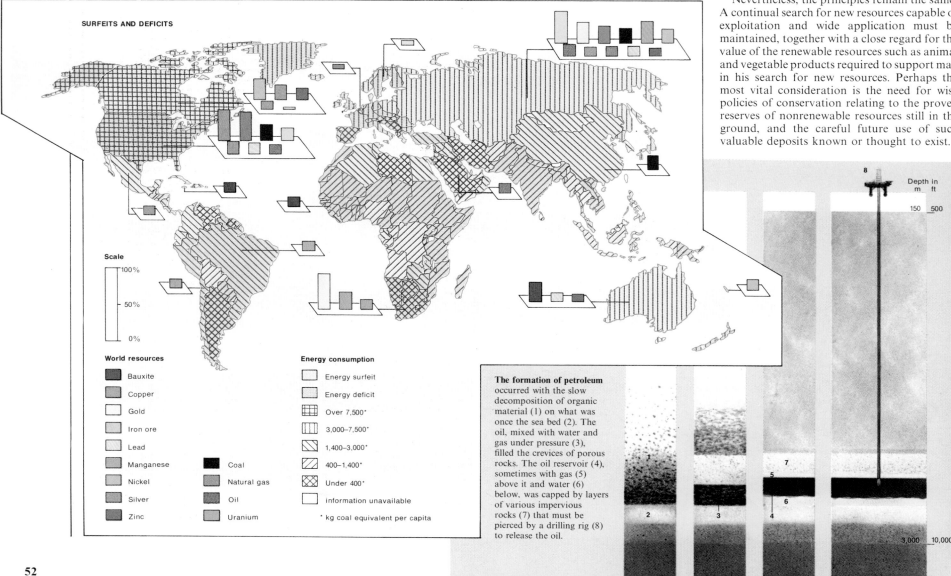

SURFEITS AND DEFICITS

Scale
100%
50%
0%

World resources
- Bauxite
- Copper
- Gold
- Iron ore
- Lead
- Manganese
- Nickel
- Silver
- Zinc
- Coal
- Natural gas
- Oil
- Uranium

Energy consumption
- Energy surfeit
- Energy deficit
- Over 7,500*
- 3,000–7,500*
- 1,400–3,000*
- 400–1,400*
- Under 400*
- information unavailable

* kg coal equivalent per capita

The formation of petroleum occurred with the slow decomposition of organic material (1) on what was once the sea bed (2). The oil, mixed with water and gas under pressure (3), filled the crevices of porous rocks. The oil reservoir (4), sometimes with gas (5) above it and water (6) below, was capped by layers of various impervious rocks (7) that must be pierced by a drilling rig (8) to release the oil.

Depth in m / ft
150 / 500
3,000 / 10,000

MAN'S ENDURING INGENUITY

A continuing search for new energy supplies has led man to explore potential oil sources in the offshore waters of the main continental land-masses. A firmly anchored production platform exemplifies the many new sites from which oil is being extracted, in an attempt to reduce reliance on the monopoly of reserves held by powerful organizations such as OPEC.

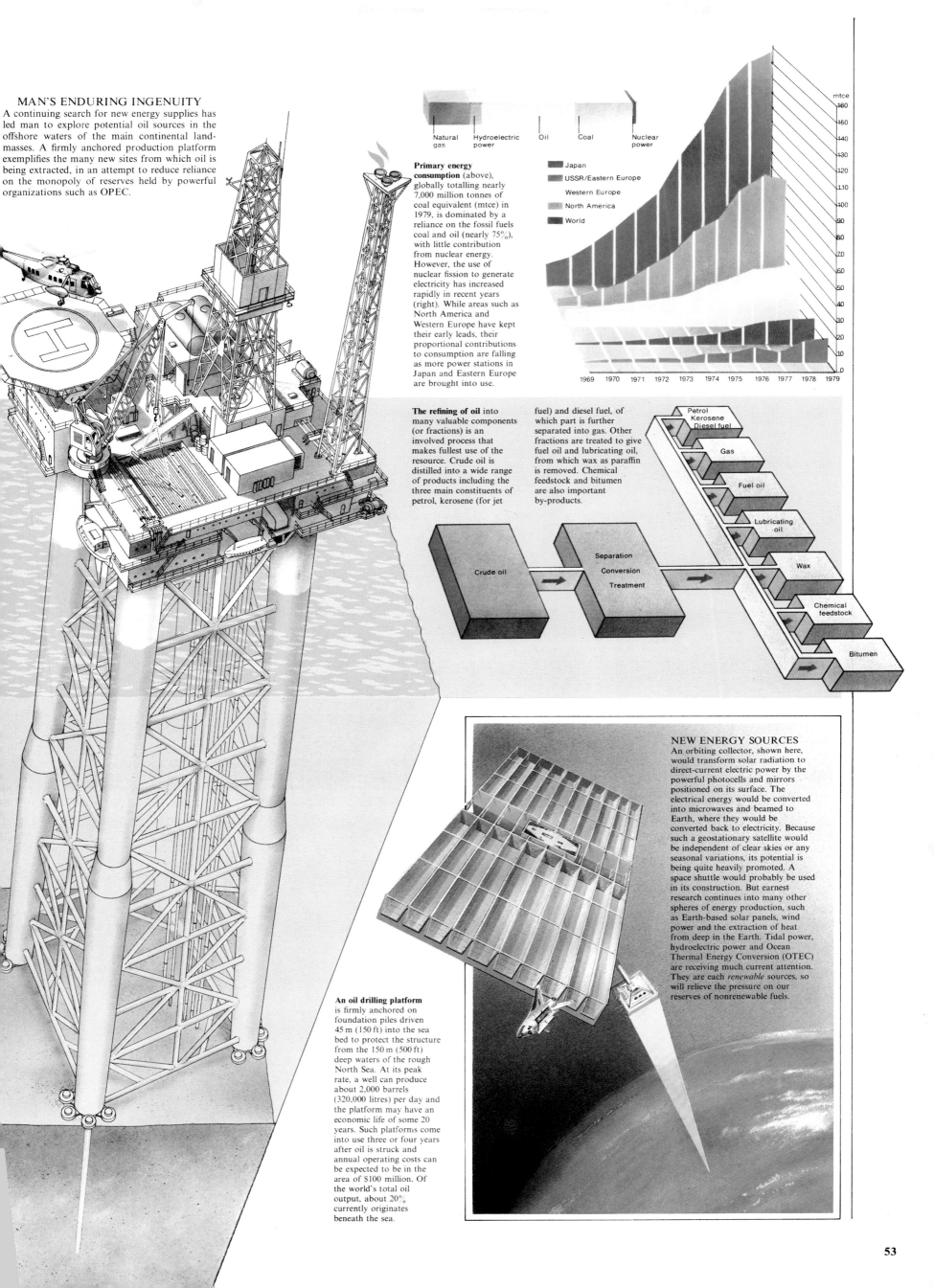

Natural gas   Hydroelectric power   Oil   Coal   Nuclear power

Japan
USSR/Eastern Europe
Western Europe
North America
World

Primary energy consumption (above), globally totalling nearly 7,000 million tonnes of coal equivalent (mtce) in 1979, is dominated by a reliance on the fossil fuels coal and oil (nearly 75%), with little contribution from nuclear energy. However, the use of nuclear fission to generate electricity has increased rapidly in recent years (right). While areas such as North America and Western Europe have kept their early leads, their proportional contributions to consumption are falling as more power stations in Japan and Eastern Europe are brought into use.

mtce: 160 150 140 130 120 110 100 90 80 70 60 50 40 30 20 10 0

1969 1970 1971 1972 1973 1974 1975 1976 1977 1978 1979

The refining of oil into many valuable components (or fractions) is an involved process that makes fullest use of the resource. Crude oil is distilled into a wide range of products including the three main constituents of petrol, kerosene (for jet fuel) and diesel fuel, of which part is further separated into gas. Other fractions are treated to give fuel oil and lubricating oil, from which wax as paraffin is removed. Chemical feedstock and bitumen are also important by-products.

Crude oil → Separation Conversion Treatment → Petrol Kerosene Diesel fuel / Gas / Fuel oil / Lubricating oil / Wax / Chemical feedstock / Bitumen

An oil drilling platform is firmly anchored on foundation piles driven 45 m (150 ft) into the sea bed to protect the structure from the 150 m (500 ft) deep waters of the rough North Sea. At its peak rate, a well can produce about 2,000 barrels (320,000 litres) per day and the platform may have an economic life of some 20 years. Such platforms come into use three or four years after oil is struck and annual operating costs can be expected to be in the area of $100 million. Of the world's total oil output, about 20% currently originates beneath the sea.

NEW ENERGY SOURCES

An orbiting collector, shown here, would transform solar radiation to direct-current electric power by the powerful photocells and mirrors positioned on its surface. The electrical energy would be converted into microwaves and beamed to Earth, where they would be converted back to electricity. Because such a geostationary satellite would be independent of clear skies or any seasonal variations, its potential is being quite heavily promoted. A space shuttle would probably be used in its construction. But earnest research continues into many other spheres of energy production, such as Earth-based solar panels, wind power and the extraction of heat from deep in the Earth. Tidal power, hydroelectric power and Ocean Thermal Energy Conversion (OTEC) are receiving much current attention. They are each *renewable* sources, so will relieve the pressure on our reserves of nonrenewable fuels.

Population Growth

Every minute of every day, more than 250 children are born into the world. The Earth's population now stands at about 4,300 million and is continuing to grow extremely rapidly. The problems associated with such growth are enormous – already, about two-thirds of the world's people are underfed, according to United Nations' recommended standards of nutrition. And an even greater number live in very poor housing conditions, have inadequate access to medical facilities, receive little or no education and, at present, have no hope of improving their lot. As yet, there are no simple or immediate solutions.

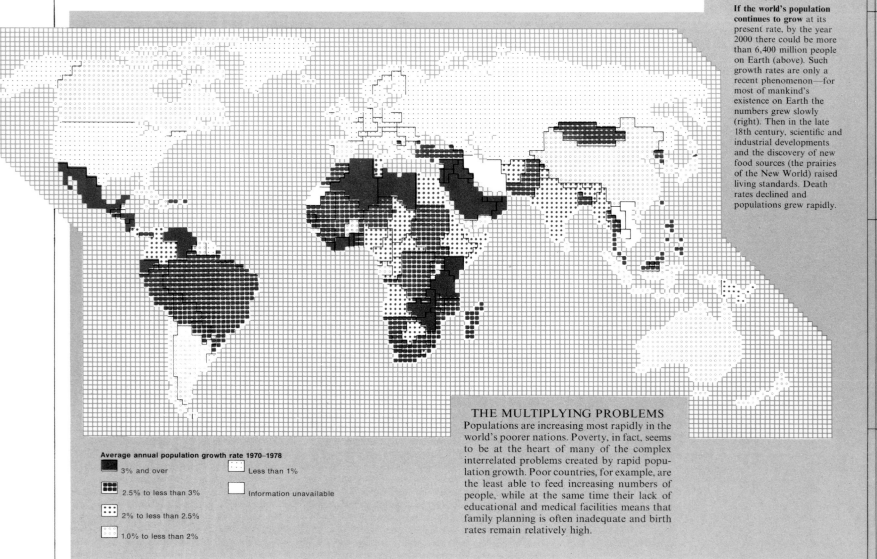

World population (millions)

If the world's population continues to grow at its present rate, by the year 2000 there could be more than 6,400 million people on Earth (above). Such growth rates are only a recent phenomenon—for most of mankind's existence on Earth the numbers grew slowly (right). Then in the late 18th century, scientific and industrial developments and the discovery of new food sources (the prairies of the New World) raised living standards. Death rates declined and populations grew rapidly.

Average annual population growth rate 1970–1978

- 3% and over
- 2.5% to less than 3%
- 2% to less than 2.5%
- 1.0% to less than 2%
- Less than 1%
- Information unavailable

THE MULTIPLYING PROBLEMS

Populations are increasing most rapidly in the world's poorer nations. Poverty, in fact, seems to be at the heart of many of the complex interrelated problems created by rapid population growth. Poor countries, for example, are the least able to feed increasing numbers of people, while at the same time their lack of educational and medical facilities means that family planning is often inadequate and birth rates remain relatively high.

In 1830, there were only about 1,000 million people on Earth. By 1930, this figure had doubled. And by 1975, it had doubled again. If the present rate of increase continues, it will have doubled again by the year 2020.

This may not happen—it is extremely difficult to predict how world population will behave. What is certain is that it will continue to increase and, moreover, that this increase will not be evenly distributed. Since more than 50 per cent of the human race lives in Asia, it is inevitable that the largest population increases will take place there. In fact, by the year 2000, the population of Asia may well have grown from about 2,000 million to more than 3,600 million. Substantial increases, of 400 million or more, will probably also occur in Africa, and Latin America is growing equally quickly.

In more prosperous North America and Europe, however, population growth seems to be stabilizing as women have fewer children and families become smaller—several countries, such as West Germany, now record a zero population growth rate. The poorer countries, the so-called Third World, are therefore gaining, and will probably continue to gain, an increasing share of the world's people. In 1930, about 64 per cent of the human race lived in the poor countries of Asia, Africa and Latin America. By 1980, this proportion had increased to more than 75 per cent. Population growth in these regions is creating enormous problems. It is estimated that there are now

more than 800 million people living in absolute poverty in the developing world, and these numbers can but increase as populations swell.

An obvious solution is to reduce birth rates, but this cannot be achieved quickly. In much of Africa and Asia, a very high proportion of the population is made up of young people who are, or soon will be, of child-bearing age. Population increases are therefore inevitable. This will probably change as family planning becomes more widespread and women have fewer children, but such relief lies in the future and is likely to affect the poorest countries last. The most pressing problem for the growing numbers of impoverished people today is that of hunger.

Food – the fundamental problem

In theory, no food supply problem should exist—already enough food is produced in the world to feed a population of 5,500 million people. In fact, however, two-thirds of this food is consumed by the rich industrialized nations, and supplies are not reaching many of those in need. The developed nations dominate world food markets because developing nations, and people within those nations, are too poor to buy food, and are themselves unable to produce sufficient quantities to feed their growing populations. The answer to under-nutrition and malnutrition lies largely in raising the incomes of poor peoples and improving distribution of supplies of food.

At a local level, food produced or imported

by developing countries must reach those in need at a price they can afford. One way of doing this is to encourage the rural poor to produce their own food. Small-scale, intensively farmed plots often prove to be the most efficient form of agriculture in areas where labour is plentiful. At present, many of the rural poor are either without land, or hold plots on extremely unfavourable terms of tenancy. By providing land, appropriate technology (small-scale, inexpensive farming equipment such as windpumps to draw water for irrigation), financial aid and information and education, small farmers could be helped to farm their land as effectively and efficiently as possible.

At a national level, too, developing countries must become more self-sufficient in food. This has already been achieved in some countries. India, although at one time heavily dependent upon imports of one of its staple foodstuffs— rice—has now increased production on such a scale that imports are no longer necessary. Unfortunately, for many developing countries this is not the case. Zaire, for example, was once an exporter of food. Today the country can no longer produce enough to keep pace with the demands of its own expanding population. At a world level, food production must be maintained as well, for unless production is kept high, prices are unstable and at times of bad harvests the poorer nations cannot afford to import essential supplies.

Food alone, however, is not enough to solve

FEEDING THE WORLD

How are the growing numbers of people on Earth to be fed when millions are already undernourished? In the short term, the food problem could be solved by improving distribution of supplies that are already available. But the world can also be made to produce more food. Fertilizers and pest control can make land more productive and genetic engineering could produce higher-yielding and more nutritious crops.

The world will have to produce more food than it does today (below) if future populations are to be fed. At present, large areas of the Earth's land surface cannot be farmed—they are either too cold, dry, marshy, mountainous or forested. Cultivatable areas could be extended, given the necessary investment.

THE HEALTH OF NATIONS

Many developing nations are severely short of medical and welfare facilities for their growing populations. Yet these are the very countries with high incidences of disease—mainly because of malnutrition, lack of clean water supplies, and inadequate and overcrowded housing. Furthermore, without health services family planning facilities are not widely available, and expanding populations continue to strain existing resources.

Birth and Death Rates
- High birth rate/ High death rate
- High birth rate/ Moderate or low death rate
- Low birth rate/ Low death rate
- Information unavailable

THE NON-PRODUCTIVE LANDS

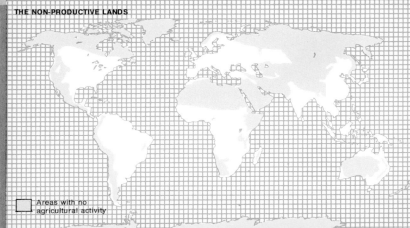

Areas with no agricultural activity

PATTERNS OF POPULATION GROWTH

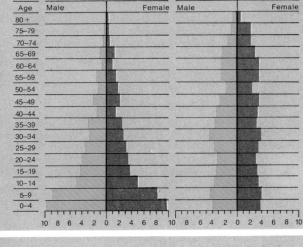

FOOD CONSUMPTION

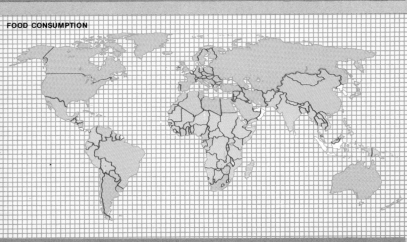

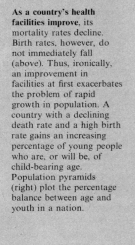

As a country's health facilities improve, its mortality rates decline. Birth rates, however, do not immediately fall (above). Thus, ironically, an improvement in facilities at first exacerbates the problem of rapid growth in population. A country with a declining death rate and a high birth rate gains an increasing percentage of young people who are, or will be, of child-bearing age. Population pyramids (right) plot the percentage balance between age and youth in a nation.

Calories per capita
- Less than 95% of needs
- 95% to 115% of needs
- More than 115% of needs
- Information unavailable

Malnutrition is widespread throughout the developing nations of Africa, Asia and South America. The problem is made worse by the fact that populations in these countries are growing more rapidly than anywhere else in the world.

the problems created by population growth. Broadly based economic development, such as in manufacturing and industry, is essential if developing countries are to have the income and other resources to enable them to cope with their evergrowing numbers of people.

INCOME

When the income level of a population is raised sufficiently, it seems that birth rates ultimately decline. This has been the pattern that has emerged in the Western world. If this is the case, then economic development of the Third World countries could eventually help to stabilize world population growth, as well as providing nations with the means to cope with, and provide for, their growing numbers.

POVERTY AND WEALTH

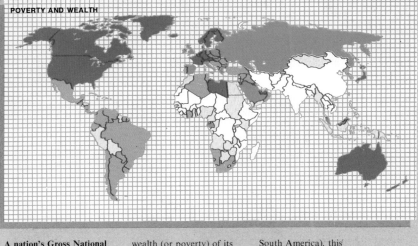

Economic growth

To achieve economic development, certain obstacles must be overcome. First, the Third World needs energy supplies at a price it can afford, for, with the exception of Nigeria and the now-rich Middle East, most developing regions are woefully short of the energy resources needed to fuel growth. Second, for sustained economic development a skilled labour force is required, as are educational facilities to provide the necessary skills from within the nations themselves. Third, investment is required to enable developing nations to exploit the resources they do have—minerals, for example. And this investment must be on terms that are as beneficial to the developing nations as they are to powerful multinational organizations that frequently fund such projects. Finally, and most important, more enlightened social and political outlooks are needed within many countries if their growing populations of impoverished people are to benefit from any economic development and consequent increase in national wealth.

It has been said that wealth is the best method of contraception and, judging by the history of population growth in the rich industrialized nations, this seems to be the case. If it s, economic development of the Third World may well alleviate many of the problems created y population growth.

Gross National Product per capita 1978 ($US)
- Less than $300
- $300 to $699
- $700 to $2,999
- $3,000 to $6,999
- $7,000 and over
- Information unavailable

A nation's Gross National Product (GNP), when divided by the number of its population, gives some indication of the relative wealth (or poverty) of its people. But because national wealth is not evenly distributed in many countries (particularly in South America), this figure can conceal the extreme poverty of very large numbers of a nation's people.

EDUCATIONAL RESOURCES

Education is essential if the people of the developing world are to be equipped to improve their lot. Basic education on health and hygiene could dramatically reduce the incidence of disease; education about birth control would help lower birth rates; agricultural advice could help the rural poor to produce more food. Finally, general schooling is required to provide skilled labour.

ILLITERACY

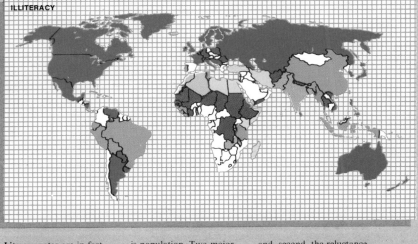

Illiteracy rate
- 80% and over
- 60% to less than 80%
- 40% to less than 60%
- 20% to less than 40%
- Less than 20%
- Information unavailable

Literacy rates are in fact improving in developing countries and national expenditure on schools is growing more quickly than is population. Two major problems are, first, the social traditions that severely restrict the number of girls attending school and, second, the reluctance of many rural poor to send to school children who provide valuable manual labour on the land.

55

Human Settlement

Man is naturally a gregarious animal. As an agriculturist he first settled in small communities, but it was not long before the emergence of towns and cities. Now nearly half the world's people live in these larger settlements, and by the year 2000, for the first time in history, more people will live in cities than in the countryside. Cities have grown up for various reasons, and are unevenly distributed across the world; but it is in the developing countries that the most rapid rates of urban growth are today taking place.

City life has a long and varied history going back to the early population centres of the Tigris–Euphrates, Indus and Nile valleys. Administrative and political needs led to the development of capital cities. Some, like London and Paris, evolved on conveniently located river crossings; others, such as Canberra, Islamabad and Brasilia, have locations that were deliberately planned.

Types of towns and cities
Market towns were established to exchange produce and, as trade expanded, hierarchies of service centres became established. These ranged from small "central places" that supplied rural areas with simple goods and services from elsewhere, to large cities that provided highly specialized services. Through such centrally placed systems, rural areas became connected with major industrialized areas. Mining towns such as Johannesburg, South Africa, and Broken Hill, Australia, sprang up as man began to exploit the Earth's mineral resources, their locations determined by the presence of rich ore deposits. Fishing ports and settlements dependent on forestry fall into the same group.

Increasing specialization, exemplified by the Black Country, England, and the Ruhr, West Germany, was a feature of European industrial development in the eighteenth and nineteenth centuries, and was based on the availability of capital investment and the presence of sources of fuel and power, especially water and steam power. Such industrialized cities relied on newly developed forms of transport to bring in new materials and to carry away manufactured products. Chicago is a good example of the relationship between the development of rail and water routes and the growth of a city as a market, agricultural processing and manufacturing centre. As transport developed, further specialized centres concentrated on locomotive, ship or aircraft construction.

Uneven settlement patterns
Across the world, density and distribution of population are uneven. The land surface of the Earth as a whole has a density of 28 people per sq km (73 per sq mile) although Manhattan, for example, has 26,000 per sq km (63,340 per sq mile) and Australia has only 1.5 per sq km (4 per sq mile). In Brazil, towns and cities are mostly sited in the rich southeast, in contrast to a sparseness of settlement in its interior. Contrasts also occur between Mediterranean North Africa and the deserted Sahara to the south; or Canada of the St Lawrence and the Canadian Shield to the north. Here the causes are not hard to find: extremes of climate, terrain and vegetation form effective barriers to settlement. Geographers estimate that two-thirds of the world's population lives within 500 km (310 miles) of the sea.

Any true consideration of human settlements must, however, be placed within the context of the economic, political and social systems in which they have evolved. Physical considerations alone cannot fully explain the urban concentrations of Western Europe, Japan or the northeastern USA, or the comparative absence of cities elsewhere. Only 5 per cent of Malawi's and 4.7 per cent of New Guinea's populations live in towns; in Belgium the percentage is 87, in Australia 86, in the UK 78 and in the USA 73.5. The figure for Norway is only 42 per cent. Urbanization is a varied phenomenon and cities grow for many reasons.

The attractions of the city
Cities have always acted as magnets to poor or unemployed rural populations, and migrations from the countryside have assisted high rates of city growth. Very large cities—Tokyo, New York and Los Angeles—are still found in the northern world, but many cities with far faster growth rates are sited in the Third World, especially in Asia. There the total number of inhabitants living in towns and cities is still much lower than in Europe, but centres such as Shanghai, Karachi, Bandung, New Delhi, Seoul, Jakarta and Manila are among the world's most rapidly expanding urban centres. Perhaps as many as a third of these city dwellers in Asia, Africa and Latin America put up with makeshift housing in shanty towns that present enormous problems of health, sanitation, education and unemployment: city growth in the developing world is a daunting prospect.

People on the move
In the past, one solution to population pressure on the land could be found in the migrations which occurred on a large scale from Asia into Europe, from Europe to the Americas and Australasia, and from China into southeastern Asia. But as claims are being made on almost every habitable area of the Earth, mass migrations have largely declined in importance. Many nations restrict movement to or from their countries. Australia has strict immigration quotas; Vietnam and the USSR restrict emigration for largely ideological reasons. Large movements of labour still take place, however, from the poorer regions of the Mediterranean to the industrial cities of France and Germany. Migrant workers from neighbouring countries in Africa also play an essential part in the mining economy of South Africa.

New trends in urbanization
In many industrialized countries, a strong process of decentralization is leading to reductions in the populations of cities and corresponding increases in those of the suburbs and beyond. In 1951 the geographer Jean Gottman showed how groups of city regions tend to form chains of functionally linked cities, to which he gave the term "megalopolis". His prime example was Megalopolis, USA, stretching from north of Boston to south of Washington DC. Similar settlements occur in the Tokyo–Yokohama–Osaka area of Japan and the Ruhr megalopolis of northwestern Europe. Ultimately, equally drastic and large-scale patterns are likely to emerge in the already overcrowded human settlements of the Third World.

THE DISTRIBUTION OF POPULATION
Human settlement is highly uneven because it is related to many social and topographical factors. At first, man was tied to the sites of his crops and the grazing land of his cattle; life in non-rural centres only became a typical feature of population development as specialized services came into demand and towns and cities arose to support these needs. But during the 20th century there has been a vast increase in urban populations, particularly in Third World countries.

Oil and gas deposits
Iron ore deposits
Farming
• Towns
⊙ Hydroelectric projects
+++ Iron ore railways
═══ Current oil and gas pipelines

Ciudad Guayana
Ciudad Bolivar
VENEZUELA
GUYANA

Expanding settlements (above) and new lines of communication are being developed in the poorly populated eastern lowlands of Venezuela in order fully to exploit the resources being discovered there. Huge deposits of iron ore and large supplies of oil and gas have been located, and Ciudad Bolivar and Ciudad Guayana have become steel-making and service centres. To feed the people of these new settlements, agriculture has been greatly expanded.

Immigration to the United States (below) from Europe was partly responsible for the growth of the vast Washington–Boston urban mass known as "Megalopolis". Since World War II, more immigrants have come from Puerto Rico and Mexico.

Boston
New York City
Philadelphia
Baltimore
Washington DC
Richmond

Immigrants in 000s
Year: 1840, 1860, 1880, 1900, 1920, 1940, 1960, 1980
(estimated)

Migrating refugees, the world total of which increases on average by 2,000–3,000 every day, can affect settlement patterns. The Ugandan children (below) fled to the northern province of Karamoja in the wake of the 1979 war with Tanzania and the resultant famine that occurred in much of Uganda.

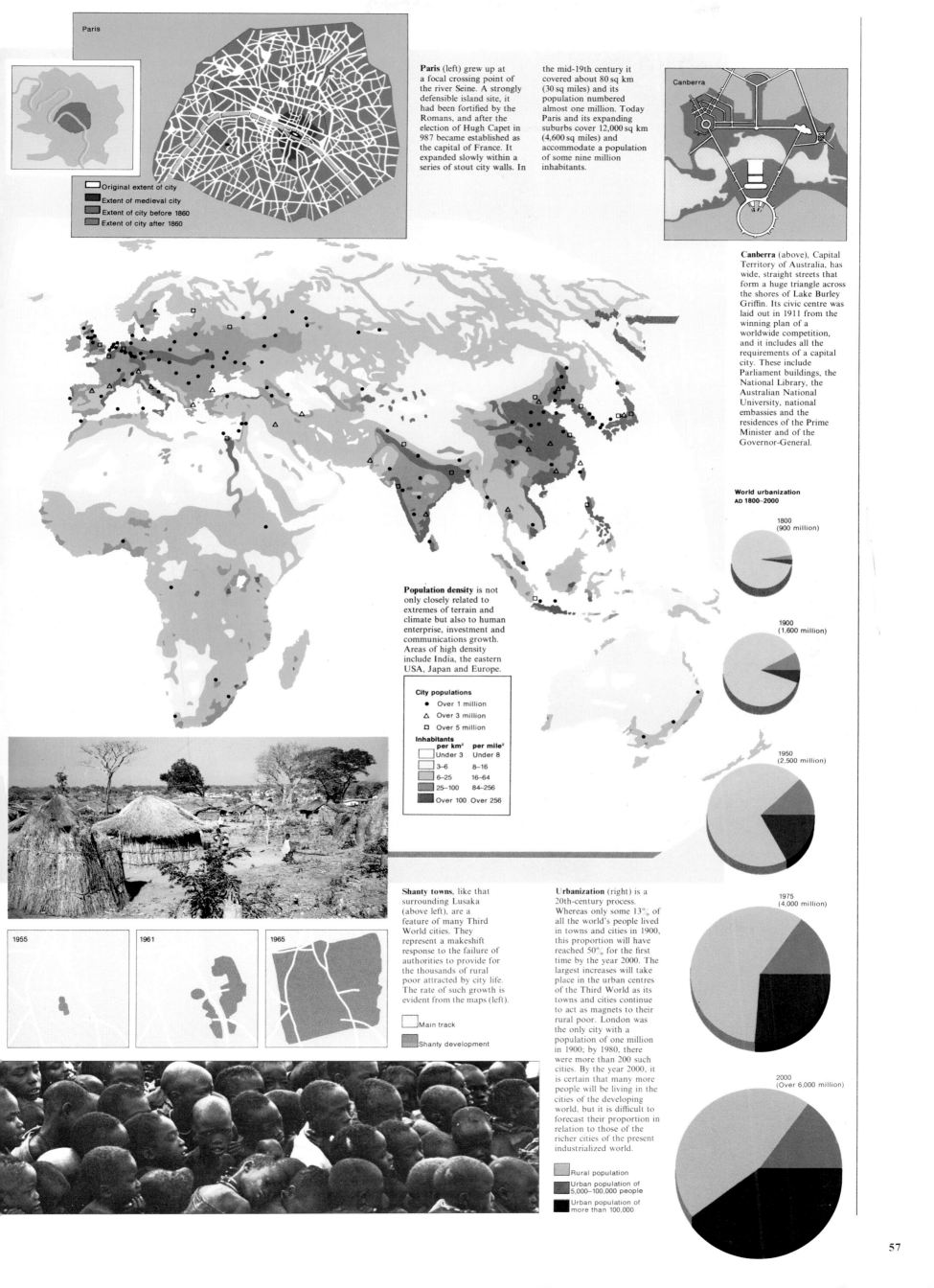

Paris

Paris (left) grew up at a focal crossing point of the river Seine. A strongly defensible island site, it had been fortified by the Romans, and after the election of Hugh Capet in 987 became established as the capital of France. It expanded slowly within a series of stout city walls. In the mid-19th century it covered about 80 sq km (30 sq miles) and its population numbered almost one million. Today Paris and its expanding suburbs cover 12,000 sq km (4,600 sq miles) and accommodate a population of some nine million inhabitants.

☐ Original extent of city
■ Extent of medieval city
▨ Extent of city before 1860
▨ Extent of city after 1860

Canberra

Canberra (above), Capital Territory of Australia, has wide, straight streets that form a huge triangle across the shores of Lake Burley Griffin. Its civic centre was laid out in 1911 from the winning plan of a worldwide competition, and it includes all the requirements of a capital city. These include Parliament buildings, the National Library, the Australian National University, national embassies and the residences of the Prime Minister and of the Governor-General.

Population density is not only closely related to extremes of terrain and climate but also to human enterprise, investment and communications growth. Areas of high density include India, the eastern USA, Japan and Europe.

City populations
- ● Over 1 million
- △ Over 3 million
- ☐ Over 5 million

Inhabitants

	per km²	per mile²
☐	Under 3	Under 8
	3–6	8–16
	6–25	16–64
	25–100	84–256
	Over 100	Over 256

World urbanization
AD 1800–2000

1800
(900 million)

1900
(1,600 million)

1950
(2,500 million)

1975
(4,000 million)

2000
(Over 6,000 million)

Shanty towns, like that surrounding Lusaka (above left), are a feature of many Third World cities. They represent a makeshift response to the failure of authorities to provide for the thousands of rural poor attracted by city life. The rate of such growth is evident from the maps (left).

1955

1961

1965

☐ Main track
▨ Shanty development

Urbanization (right) is a 20th-century process. Whereas only some 13% of all the world's people lived in towns and cities in 1900, this proportion will have reached 50% for the first time by the year 2000. The largest increases will take place in the urban centres of the Third World as its towns and cities continue to act as magnets to their rural poor. London was the only city with a population of one million in 1900; by 1980, there were more than 200 such cities. By the year 2000, it is certain that many more people will be living in the cities of the developing world, but it is difficult to forecast their proportion in relation to those of the richer cities of the present industrialized world.

☐ Rural population
▨ Urban population of 5,000–100,000 people
■ Urban population of more than 100,000

Trade and Transport

It is a commonplace that we live in a "shrinking" world. During the last century the development of communications has been so rapid that man appears almost to have conquered the challenge of distance; but such a concept depends on the kind of area to be covered and the cost of transporting goods in relation to their value, bulk and perishability. People, goods and services become accessible by trade. Transport makes trade possible: trade's demands lead to improvements in transport.

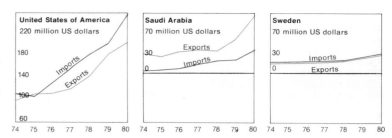

Exports in millions of US dollars (A)

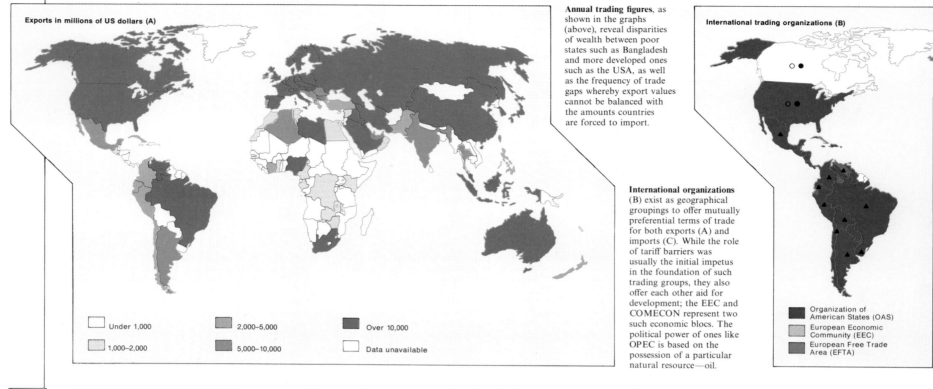

Under 1,000	2,000–5,000	Over 10,000
1,000–2,000	5,000–10,000	Data unavailable

International trading organizations (B)

Organization of American States (OAS)

European Economic Community (EEC)

European Free Trade Area (EFTA)

Annual trading figures, as shown in the graphs (above), reveal disparities of wealth between poor states such as Bangladesh and more developed ones such as the USA, as well as the frequency of trade gaps whereby export values cannot be balanced with the amounts countries are forced to import.

International organizations (B) exist as geographical groupings to offer mutually preferential terms of trade for both exports (A) and imports (C). While the role of tariff barriers was usually the initial impetus in the foundation of such trading groups, they also offer each other aid for development; the EEC and COMECON represent two such economic blocs. The political power of ones like OPEC is based on the possession of a particular natural resource—oil.

Japanese export of electronic products (1979)

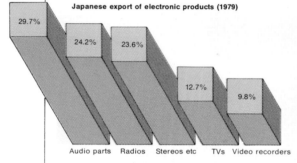

29.7% | 24.2% | 23.6% | 12.7% | 9.8%

Audio parts | Radios | Stereos etc | TVs | Video recorders

Electronic products comprise only one-sixth of Japanese exports (left); their high export value and reputation for quality make their sales abroad vital to Japan's economy. Trading links (below) with industrialized countries are very well established; now Japan is mounting new export drives to sell its products to much less traditional markets.

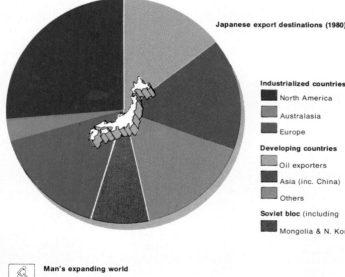

Japanese export destinations (1980)

Industrialized countries
North America
Australasia
Europe

Developing countries
Oil exporters
Asia (inc. China)
Others

Soviet bloc (including
Mongolia & N. Korea)

It is only a little more than two centuries since navigators completed the mapping of the world's major landmasses and much less since the mapping of the continental interiors was completed—even today some gaps still remain. Canals like the Suez (1869) and Panama (1915) reduced the extent of long sea voyages—the Suez Canal shortened the distance from northwestern Europe to India by 15,000 km (9,300 miles)—so that in transport terms, the various parts of the world became more accessible, especially as steamships and motor vessels replaced sailing ships, and time distances were reduced still further by the aeroplane.

Locational advantages

Inland waterways, roads and railways opened up new areas for mining or specialized agriculture, and created opportunities for the manufacture of goods and for the distribution of the finished products. The contrast, however, between locations such as London, Tokyo or Chicago (which are accessible to all forms of transport) and parts of South America where modern transport hardly penetrates, has become much more marked over the years. New transport developments tend to connect major centres first of all, and thus increase their already high locational status.

Such developments must nevertheless be seen in the light of the demand for communications and trade between different points, the nature of the goods being carried and the actual cost of transport. Transport improvements have allowed different parts of the world to share ideas

and products; ironically, they have also made such places more dissimilar, since each area of the Earth has had the chance to specialize in the services it can provide most efficiently.

Specialization of area

Before the widespread development of canals and railways, road transport was expensive and towns and villages tended to be more self-sufficient. Railways played a vital role in reducing transport costs in relation to distance and in providing an opportunity for different areas to specialize. After the emergence of railroad networks in North America, specialized areas of agricultural production quickly developed because they were well adjusted to the climatic conditions needed for growing maize (corn), cotton, fruit and fresh vegetables for the new urban markets. In the southern hemisphere, steamships and the introduction of refrigeration enabled meat, butter and cheese to be kept fresh on their journeys to the north.

This concept of specialization of area is basic to world trading patterns, since regions tend to concentrate on commodities and services that they can exchange for other specialized goods and products from other regional or world markets. Countries and areas do best when they concentrate on products for which they have comparative cost advantages in terms of the presence of natural resources, the availability of the skills to develop them, and a demand for the products. Enterprise in adapting natural conditions for the production of goods at competitive price levels is also important. Settlers in New

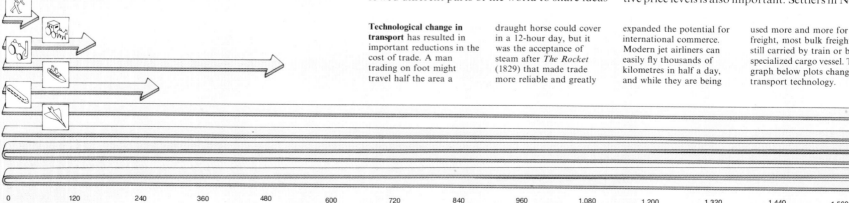

Man's expanding world

Technological change in transport has resulted in important reductions in the cost of trade. A man trading on foot might travel half the area a

draught horse could cover in a 12-hour day, but it was the acceptance of steam after *The Rocket* (1829) that made trade more reliable and greatly

expanded the potential for international commerce. Modern jet airliners can easily fly thousands of kilometres in half a day, and while they are being

used more and more for freight, most bulk freight is still carried by train or by specialized cargo vessel. The graph below plots changing transport technology.

| 0 | 120 | 240 | 360 | 480 | 600 | 720 | 840 | 960 | 1,080 | 1,200 | 1,320 | 1,440 | 1,560 |

Kilometres travelled in 12 hours

Economists measure a country's richness in terms of Gross National Product (GNP), the value of the goods and services available for consumption and for adding to its wealth. The difference in value between its exported and imported goods is often an important aspect of a nation's economy, and effective systems to transport such goods must play a major role in overseas trade. The 1980 Brandt Report highlighted the huge gap between the income of the rich world and the poverty of many developing states, but solutions to such problems of inequality will be difficult to obtain.

Poland — 8 million US dollars — Imports, Exports — 74 75 76 77 78 79 80
Ghana — 8 million US dollars — Imports, Exports — 74 75 76 77 78 79 80
Bangladesh — 8 million US dollars — Imports, Exports — 74 75 76 77 78 79 80
Colombia — 8 million US dollars — Imports, Exports — 74 75 76 77 78 79 80
Philippines — 8 million US dollars — Imports, Exports — 74 75 76 77 78 79 80

Imports in millions of US dollars (C)

Council for Mutual Economic Aid (COMECON)
Organization of Petroleum Exporting Countries (OPEC)
Association of South-East Asian Nations (ASEAN)
Organization for African Unity (OAU)
▲ Latin American Free Trade Association (LAFTA)
■ Arab League (AL)
○ Colombo Plan
● Organization for Economic Cooperation and Development (OECD)

Under 1,000
1,000–2,000
2,000–5,000
5,000–10,000
Over 10,000
Data unavailable

Zealand, for example, had little hesitation in clearing the prevailing tussock grass to create a new pastoral environment for their large-scale production of sheep and dairy products.

In the real world, however, there are many impediments to the operation of a free market system, and it is unwise for states like New Zealand to assume that they will always dominate Commonwealth dairy trade.

Impediments to free markets
Countries erect protectionist tariff barriers to assist their home industries and/or to obtain extra revenue. Import or export quotas may be imposed, and trade agreements with other countries give special preference to certain commodities. Problems arise from the exchange of currencies and their fluctuations in value. Tariff barriers may be erected for political, welfare or defence reasons. Sometimes special measures may be adopted to encourage the internal production of certain goods rather than obtaining them more cheaply from abroad, and such methods may be economically important to a country that has always relied on the export of raw materials for its income but now wishes domestically to manufacture previously imported goods.

Political ties are vital to the groupings of certain countries. For reasons of international politics, countries such as those of the Soviet bloc trade with each other rather than with the outside world; and historical links, as between the UK and the Commonwealth, France and her ex-colonies, and Spain and Portugal with Latin America, are also influential. The European Economic Community (EEC) is composed of countries that have formed a strong bloc among the developed countries.

Rich man, poor man
The developed countries of "the North" have more than 80 per cent of the world's manufacturing income but only a quarter of its population, whereas the poorer peoples of "the South" number 3,000 million and receive only a fifth of world income. Attempts have been made to obtain a better economic balance. The 1948 General Agreement on Tariffs and Trade (GATT) and the United Nations Conference on Trade and Development (UNCTAD) provided mechanisms for multinational trade negotiations, and the World Bank and the International Monetary Fund (IMF) together with the 1960 International Development Association (IDA) have all provided easier loans for less developed states.

The widening gap between rich and poor countries has led to understandable demands for a new international order calling for basic changes in the structure of world production, aid and trade, and the transfer of resources. The 1980 Independent Commission on International Development Issues (The Brandt Commission) advocated just such a transfer to the Third World. But during a major world recession there seems little sign of any international political will strong enough to take action on the scale needed to solve the problems that contrasts in wealth and poverty involve.

Land over 1,000 metres
Trans-African highways
Major railways
Copper belt

The weakness of African communications (above) results from the severe obstacles presented by its terrain and also from its very short period of economic development. Northern Zambia (below right) has copper which comprises some 90% of its exports and is much sought after by the industrialized world. But recent history has severely hampered its economic routes out of Africa; even though Zimbabwe and Mozambique no longer present export barriers, Zambia badly needs to invest in new track and rolling stock.

1,800   1,920   2,040   2,160   2,280   2,400   2,520   2,640   2,760   2,880   3,000   3,120   3,240   3,360

Polar Regions

Sunless in winter, and capped with permanent land ice and shifting sea ice, the world's polar regions present an image of intense and everlasting cold. But permanent ice caps have been the exception rather than the rule in the 4,600 million years of Earth's history. The most recent intensification of the present ice age (which began at least two million years ago) reached its maximum about 20,000 years ago and still continues to fluctuate. Polar conditions preclude all but the toughest life forms on land, but the plankton-rich waters attract many animals, and man is beginning to exploit the polar regions' potential.

There have been about a dozen ice ages since the world began. During the intervening periods there was still a zonal pattern of world temperatures, with hot equatorial regions and cooler poles. But the ice caps, which are both chilling and self-sustaining, were absent altogether—the poles being cold-temperate rather than icebound. The shiny ice surfaces of today's poles reflect more than 90 per cent of the solar radiation which reaches them from the low-angled summer sun, while in winter the sun never rises at all. Thus the regions are now permanently ice-capped.

Antarctica, the great southern polar continent, lies under an ice mantle 14 million sq km (5.4 million sq miles) in area, and sometimes more than 4,000 m (13,000 ft) thick. Many of its neighbouring islands also carry permanent ice. In the Arctic, the three islands of Greenland lie under a pall of ice of subcontinental size, more than 1.8 million sq km (700,000 sq miles) in area and up to 3,000 m (9,800 ft) thick.

The ice cover of polar seas varies. The central core of the Arctic Ocean carries a mass of permanent pack ice, slowly circulating within the polar basin, which is added to each winter by a belt of ice forming over the open sea. Currents and winds break this up to form pack ice that also circulates, gradually melting in summer or drifting south. Antarctica too is surrounded by fast ice, which breaks up in spring to form a broad belt of persistent pack ice. Circulating slowly about the continent, the pack ice forms huge gyres spreading far to the north, dotted with tabular bergs that have broken away from the continental ice sheet.

The frozen land

In the present glacial phase, the ice caps reached their farthest spread about 20,000 years ago, and then began the retreat which brought them, some 10,000 to 12,000 years ago, to their current position and size. Since then the climate of the polar regions has been both warmer and colder than it is at the present time.

The fluctuating nature of the polar climates creates very difficult conditions for plants and animals. Very little will grow on the terrestrial ice caps, but water scarcity rather than cold is the most important factor inhibiting plant growth: the small patches of lichens, algae and mosses that occur on rock faces and nunataks (points of rock jutting above the land ice) are usually in the path of a snowmelt runnel. Vegetation patches sometimes contain tiny populations of insects and mites, which may be active for only a few days each year when the sun warms them from a state of dormancy.

However, these tiny scattered plant communities appear all over Antarctica wherever rock surfaces break through the ice cap, and have been seen less than 300 km (190 miles) from the South Pole, and on peaks 2,000 m (6,600 ft) above sea level. Insects and mites occur within 600 km (380 miles) of the Pole itself. In specially favoured positions on the Antarctic Peninsula and the offshore islands, carpets of moss and grasses may be seen. Conditions around the northern terrestrial ice cap are similar, with aridity, strong winds and cold discouraging all but the hardiest plants and the smallest, toughest animal colonies.

The frozen seas

The marine ice caps, by contrast, are relatively lively places, especially during summer, when days are long and the sea ice is patchy. Water-lanes between floes are often rich in microscopic algae and the minute zooplanktonic animals that feed on them. These animals in turn attract fish, sea birds and seals in their thousands, as well as whales—including the largest baleen species. Some of the richest patches of sea are close to islands where strong currents stir the water and bring nutrients to the surface, and these attract semipermanent populations of seals and birds. The birds breed on the island cliffs and feed in the sheltered waters among the ice; the seals may breed on the ice itself, producing their pups on a floating nursery where food is close at hand.

Different species of seals are found on inshore and offshore ice environments. In the Arctic, bearded and ringed seals, which produce their young in spring as the inshore ice begins to break up, are often preyed upon by floe-riding polar bears; Eskimos too prize both species for their meat, blubber and skins. Farther out on the offshore pack ice live hooded and harp seals, where their pups are safe from all but the shipborne commercial hunters. In the Antarctic, Weddell seals are the inshore species, whereas crabeater and Ross seals prefer the distant pack ice. Crabeaters, which feed largely on planktonic krill (once thought to be crab larvae), are probably the most numerous of all seal species, with a population estimated at 10 to 15 million.

Sea ice in the north provides a precarious platform on which coastal human populations of the Arctic, such as Eskimos, can extend their winter hunting range. When the land is snowbound and animals are scarce, the sea may still provide food for hunters skilled in fishing, and in stalking seals to their breathing holes.

Nonindigenous inhabitants of the ice caps have greatly increased in recent years, following the discovery and exploitation of oil in the north, as well as other valuable minerals in both the regions. Scientists and technicians today occupy bases and weather stations which in some cases, such as the Amundsen-Scott at the South Pole, are several decades old and have to be maintained by means of aircraft.

The coldness of the poles is caused by the tilt of the Earth's axis, which prevents sunlight from reaching them at all in the winter. Even in summer, little heat is received from the sun because of the low angle at which its rays reach the surface; much even of this is reflected away by the ice.

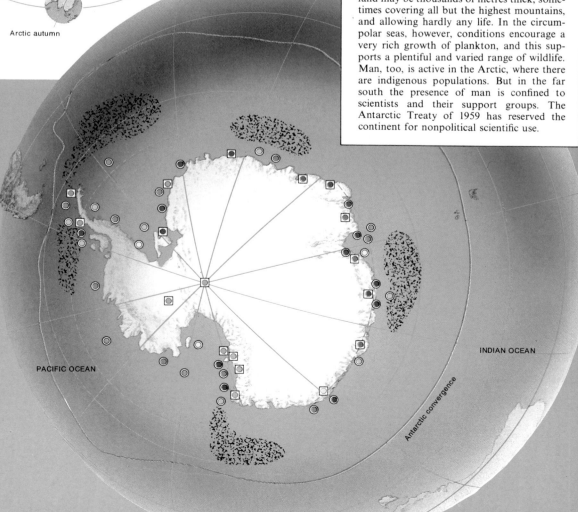

Arctic summer

Arctic spring

Arctic winter

Arctic autumn

ATLANTIC OCEAN

PACIFIC OCEAN

INDIAN OCEAN

Antarctic convergence

EARTH'S FROZEN LIMITS

The permanent ice around Earth's poles covers whole oceans, as well as landmasses of immense size. These ice sheets fluctuate, and on land may be thousands of metres thick, sometimes covering all but the highest mountains, and allowing hardly any life. In the circumpolar seas, however, conditions encourage a very rich growth of plankton, and this supports a plentiful and varied range of wildlife. Man, too, is active in the Arctic, where there are indigenous populations. But in the far south the presence of man is confined to scientists and their support groups. The Antarctic Treaty of 1959 has reserved the continent for nonpolitical scientific use.

THE FAR SOUTH

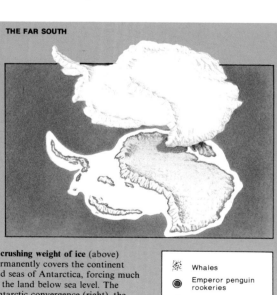

A crushing weight of ice (above) permanently covers the continent and seas of Antarctica, forcing much of the land below sea level. The Antarctic convergence (right), the line at which northern and southern water masses meet, marks a sharp change in temperature and marine life. Especially in areas of upwelling, nutrients make these waters rich in plankton. This feeds a multitude of shrimp-like krill that provide food for a huge number of other animals—fish, penguins, flying birds, seals and whales. The Antarctic landmass allows little natural life, but since the 1959 Antarctic Treaty it has proved to be an area of international scientific co-operation.

- Whales
- Emperor penguin rookeries
- Adélie penguins
- Antarctic terns and petrels
- Ross and crabeater seals
- Leopard seals

Scientific research stations

- United Kingdom
- USSR
- Japan
- Australia
- USA
- Chile
- France
- New Zealand
- Argentina

Pleistocene ice sheet | Iceberg tracks | Limit of pack ice
Iceberg source | Approx. iceberg limit

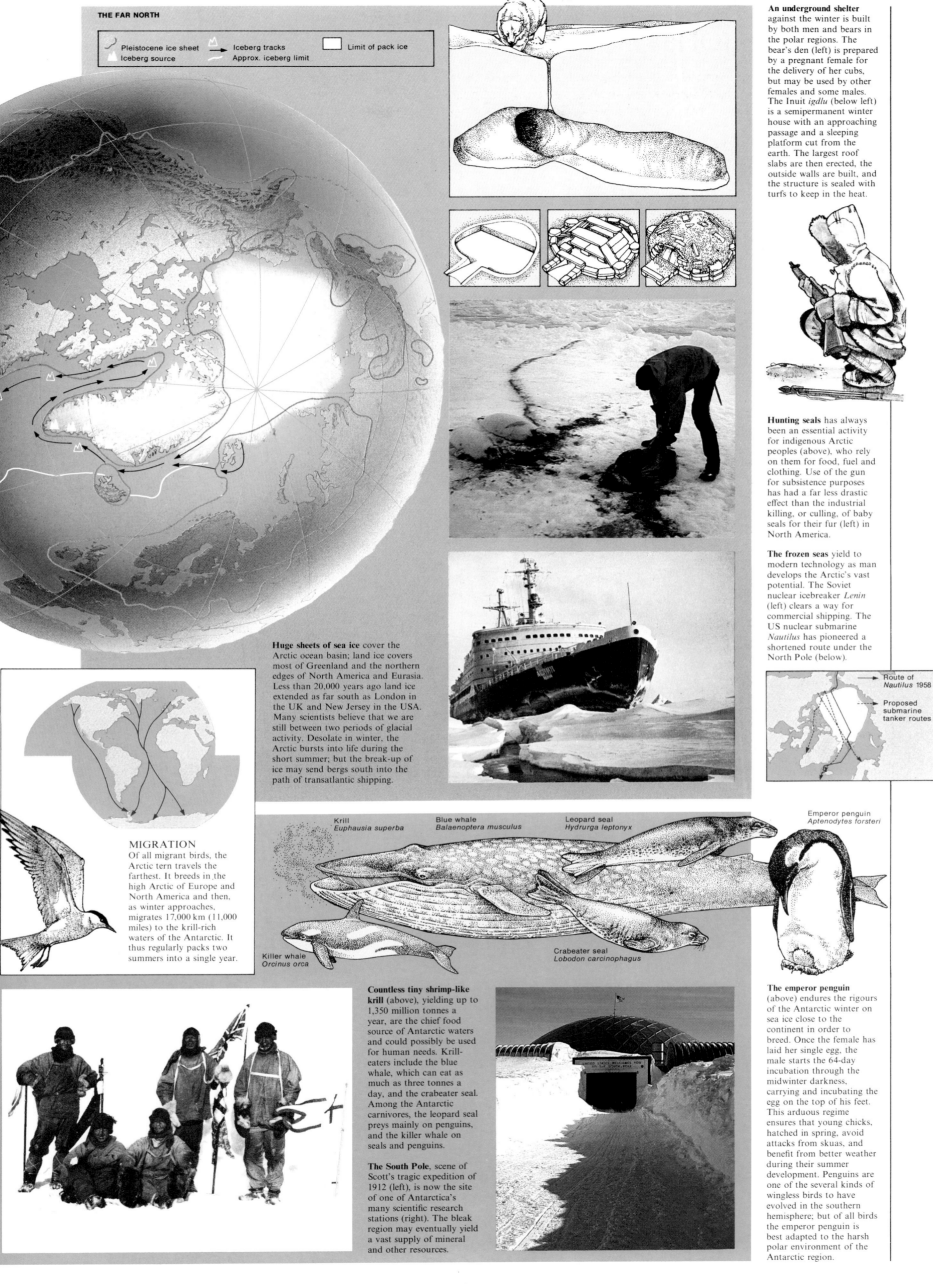

An underground shelter against the winter is built by both men and bears in the polar regions. The bear's den (left) is prepared by a pregnant female for the delivery of her cubs, but may be used by other females and some males. The Inuit *igdlu* (below left) is a semipermanent winter house with an approaching passage and a sleeping platform cut from the earth. The largest roof slabs are then erected, the outside walls are built, and the structure is sealed with turfs to keep in the heat.

Hunting seals has always been an essential activity for indigenous Arctic peoples (above), who rely on them for food, fuel and clothing. Use of the gun for subsistence purposes has had a far less drastic effect than the industrial killing, or culling, of baby seals for their fur (left) in North America.

The frozen seas yield to modern technology as man develops the Arctic's vast potential. The Soviet nuclear icebreaker *Lenin* (left) clears a way for commercial shipping. The US nuclear submarine *Nautilus* has pioneered a shortened route under the North Pole (below).

→ Route of *Nautilus* 1958
--→ Proposed submarine tanker routes

Huge sheets of sea ice cover the Arctic ocean basin; land ice covers most of Greenland and the northern edges of North America and Eurasia. Less than 20,000 years ago land ice extended as far south as London in the UK and New Jersey in the USA. Many scientists believe that we are still between two periods of glacial activity. Desolate in winter, the Arctic bursts into life during the short summer; but the break-up of ice may send bergs south into the path of transatlantic shipping.

MIGRATION
Of all migrant birds, the Arctic tern travels the farthest. It breeds in the high Arctic of Europe and North America and then, as winter approaches, migrates 17,000 km (11,000 miles) to the krill-rich waters of the Antarctic. It thus regularly packs two summers into a single year.

Krill
Euphausia superba

Blue whale
Balaenoptera musculus

Leopard seal
Hydrurga leptonyx

Emperor penguin
Aptenodytes forsteri

Killer whale
Orcinus orca

Crabeater seal
Lobodon carcinophagus

Countless tiny shrimp-like krill (above), yielding up to 1,350 million tonnes a year, are the chief food source of Antarctic waters and could possibly be used for human needs. Krill-eaters include the blue whale, which can eat as much as three tonnes a day, and the crabeater seal. Among the Antarctic carnivores, the leopard seal preys mainly on penguins, and the killer whale on seals and penguins.

The South Pole, scene of Scott's tragic expedition of 1912 (left), is now the site of one of Antarctica's many scientific research stations (right). The bleak region may eventually yield a vast supply of mineral and other resources.

The emperor penguin (above) endures the rigours of the Antarctic winter on sea ice close to the continent in order to breed. Once the female has laid her single egg, the male starts the 64-day incubation through the midwinter darkness, carrying and incubating the egg on the top of his feet. This arduous regime ensures that young chicks, hatched in spring, avoid attacks from skuas, and benefit from better weather during their summer development. Penguins are one of the several kinds of wingless birds to have evolved in the southern hemisphere; but of all birds the emperor penguin is best adapted to the harsh polar environment of the Antarctic region.

Tundra and Taiga

Tundra is land that has been exposed for only about 8,000 years, since the retreat of the ice caps, and only relatively recently occupied by plants. In consequence, few plants and animals have yet had time to adapt to the virtually soilless and treeless environment. The less rigorous conditions of neighbouring taiga forest allow a longer growing season and a somewhat wider range of species. The delicately balanced ecology of both areas is being increasingly threatened, however, by the activities of man.

"Tundra", from a Lapp word meaning "rolling, treeless plain", defines the narrow band of open, low ground that surrounds the Arctic Ocean. It lies north of the line beyond which the temperature of the warmest month usually fails to reach 10°C (50°F). North of this trees do not generally grow well, so the line forms a natural frontier between tundra and the broad band of coniferous forest that circles the northern hemisphere to its south between about 60°N and 48°N. This forest, forming the world's largest and most uninterrupted area of vegetation, is usually referred to by its Russian name of "taiga".

Cheerless landscapes

The tundra presents a desolate and restrictive environment for most of the year: in winter there are several months of semi-darkness. While there is considerable variation in the climates of places at the same latitude, temperatures average only −5°C (23°F) and are well below freezing for many months of the year. Frost-free days are restricted to a few weeks in midsummer and even then, although days are warmer, the sun is never high in the sky. Nearly all tundra has been free from ice for only a few thousand years. As a result, it either has no soil at all or has developed only a thin covering of

sandy, muddy or peaty soil, successfully colonized by only a few types of plants.

Trimmed by such grazing animals as hares, musk oxen and reindeer or caribou, and by strong winds carrying abrasive rock dust and ice particles, typical tundra vegetation forms a low, patchy mat a few centimetres deep. Much of it grows on permafrost — ground that thaws superficially in summer but remains perennially frozen beneath the surface. Here drainage is poor, shallow ponds are frequent and the scanty soils tend to be waterlogged and acidic. Nevertheless, a small number of grasses, sedges, mosses and marsh plants may grow well and the summer tundra in flower can be an impressive sight. Knee-high forests of dwarf birch, willow and alder grow in valleys sheltered from the strong and biting wind.

The taiga also is a dark and monotonous habitat. Again, while there is a good deal of variation in climatic conditions, on average the region has somewhat milder summers than the tundra with mean average temperatures of 2–6°C (34–42°F), less wind and a slightly longer growing season. The taiga is mostly older than the tundra, and its soils have had longer to mature. They support a small number of tree species, with coniferous spruce, pine, fir and

larch predominating. Short-season broadleaves such as willows, alders, birches and poplars tend to occur on the better soils of river valleys and the edges of forest lakes.

Animals of the far north

The number of animal species supported throughout the year by tundra and taiga is also comparatively small, with interdependent populations that may fluctuate wildly from season to season. In winter both tundra and taiga are silent, although far from deserted. Mice, voles and lemmings remain active, living in tunnels under the snow, which keeps them well insulated from the wind and sub-zero temperatures. Above the snow Arctic hares forage; they tend to gather in snow-free areas where food can still be found. Arctic foxes are mainly tundra animals and the musk oxen, too, winter on high, exposed tundra where their dense, shaggy coats protect them from the worst

The circumpolar north that surrounds the permanently frozen ice cap is dominated by tundra—open plain that remains snowfree for only several months in the summer—and taiga, the vast coniferous forest stretching right round the northern hemisphere. The Siberian taiga, for example, is one-third larger than the entire United States.

Tundra   Taiga

Producers
USSR
USA

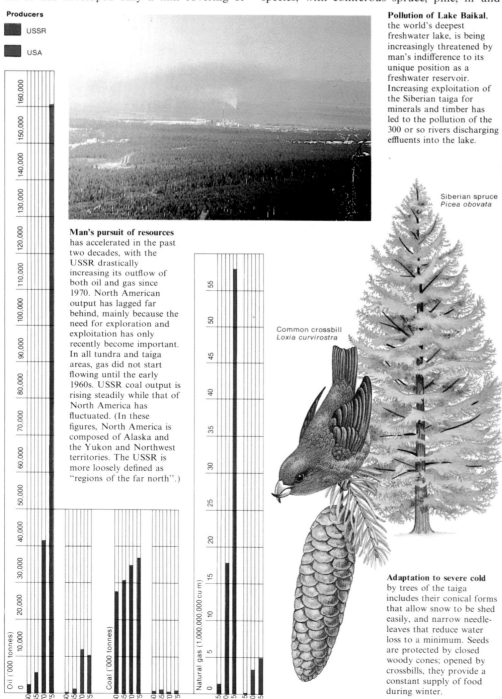

Pollution of Lake Baikal, the world's deepest freshwater lake, is being increasingly threatened by man's indifference to its unique position as a freshwater reservoir. Increasing exploitation of the Siberian taiga for minerals and timber has led to the pollution of the 300 or so rivers discharging effluents into the lake.

Man's pursuit of resources has accelerated in the past two decades, with the USSR drastically increasing its outflow of both oil and gas since 1970. North American output has lagged far behind, mainly because the need for exploration and exploitation has only recently become important. In all tundra and taiga areas, gas did not start flowing until the early 1960s. USSR coal output is rising steadily while that of North America has fluctuated. (In these figures, North America is composed of Alaska and the Yukon and Northwest territories. The USSR is more loosely defined as "regions of the far north".)

Siberian spruce
Picea obovata

Common crossbill
Loxia curvirostra

Adaptation to severe cold by trees of the taiga includes their conical forms that allow snow to be shed easily, and narrow needle-leaves that reduce water loss to a minimum. Seeds are protected by closed woody cones; opened by crossbills, they provide a constant supply of food during winter.

Reindeer or caribou
Rangifer tarandus

Raven
Corvus corax

January

February

March

April

May

June

Arctic fox
Alopex lagopus

Capercaillie
Tetrao urogallus

Snowy owl
Nyctea scandiaca

Brown lemming
Lemmus lemmus

Arctic Skua
Stercorarius parasiticus

Movement in these regions takes many directions. The capercaillie spends all winter in the taiga, where it thrives on the abundant conifer needles, buds and shoots. Some move southward into deciduous woods during the summer months. The Arctic skua breeds on the tundra but moves to the warmer oceans in winter, while the tundra movements of the all-scavenging raven and the snowy owl are governed by those of their

prey. The raven picks clean the carcasses left by other predators; the snowy owl feeds on small rodents such as mice and lemmings, as does the Arctic fox. Lemmings remain static and inconspicuous in normal years but some populations expand rapidly every third or fourth year, leading to mass local migration in every direction, possibly caused by an abundance of vegetation that encourages more frequent breeding.

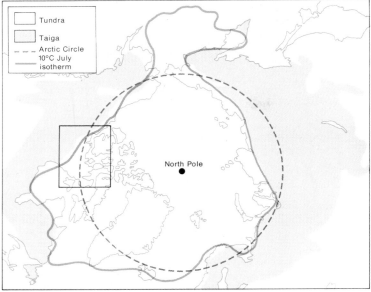

Tundra
Taiga
Arctic Circle
10°C July isotherm

North Pole

The rough boundary between the tundra and taiga—the tree line—approximates to the 10°C July isotherm, the climatic point north of which trees fail to grow successfully. Seasonal caribou migration in the Canadian barren grounds (boxed) is shown in the main diagram (below). Such migration is also undertaken by reindeer in northern Eurasia.

weather. Bears, badgers, beavers and squirrels are common taiga mammals. Elk and reindeer in North America, moose and caribou) winter in the shelter of the taiga; wolves are mostly woodland animals in winter, following their prey to the open tundra in spring. Red foxes, coyotes, mink and wolverines also move to the tundra in summer.

Snow buntings, ptarmigans and snowy owls live on the tundra throughout the coldest months and are fully adapted to life there. Crossbills and capercaillies are among taiga residents, equipped to live on its abundant conifer buds, seeds and needles. Enormous populations of migrant birds, especially water birds and waders, fly north to both tundra and taiga with the spring thaw. Waxwings, brambings, siskins and redpolls leave their temperate latitudes to feed on the lush and fast-growing vegetation and the profusion of insects that appear as soon as the snows begin to melt.

Man in the northlands
These circumpolar regions act as a strategic buffer between the USA and the USSR. Situated between the world's greatest centres of population, they are now criss-crossed with air routes. A total population of about nine million people currently inhabits the tundra and taiga. Numbers have been increased by the immigration of technicians and administrators during the last few decades; oil prospecting and mining, forest exploitation and other activities of these newcomers is altering the semi-nomadic lives of the million or so aboriginal peoples such as the Khanty (Ostyaks) and Nentsy (Samoyeds) of the USSR, the Samer (Lapps) of Scandinavia and the Soviet Union, and the Inuit (formerly Eskimos) of North America. New roads, exploitation of minerals and forests, and pipeline construction have disrupted the migration of their reindeer (caribou) and their land has been appropriated for hydroelectric schemes.

In the taiga, the Soviets are constructing railways and towns and extracting huge amounts of timber; they have prospected widely and successfully for gold, nickel, iron, tin, mica, diamonds and tungsten, and have discovered vast reserves of oil and natural gas in western Siberia. Alaskan oil, discovered in 1968, now flows across the state at 54–62°C (130–145°F), and to protect the permafrost from this heat the pipeline has had to be elevated for half its 1,300 km (800 mile) length. The pipe's route to the ice-free port of Valdez has interfered with the migration of caribou; hunting and other pressures have led to a drop in their population from three million to some 200,000 in about 30 years. Only official protection has saved the musk ox from a similar fate. These bleak areas are so vast and inhospitable that living space there will never be threatened. However, if only on a local scale, their ecologies are under increasing pressure from man.

The summer tundra—seen here in Swedish Lapland—provides a wide cover of low plants including "reindeer mosses" and other lichens. Grazing reindeer return minerals to the soil. Shallow ponds form as the frozen ground above the permafrost thaws for a few months in summer. Mountains stay partly snow-covered in the warmest weather and are a prominent physical feature of the tundra.

Many Norwegian Lapps (or Samer) derive their income from reindeer, which they domesticated many centuries ago to provide meat, milk and skins. Now they follow them through the seasons along well-worn and familiar routes. Such nomadic life styles are becoming rarer as Samer settle down.

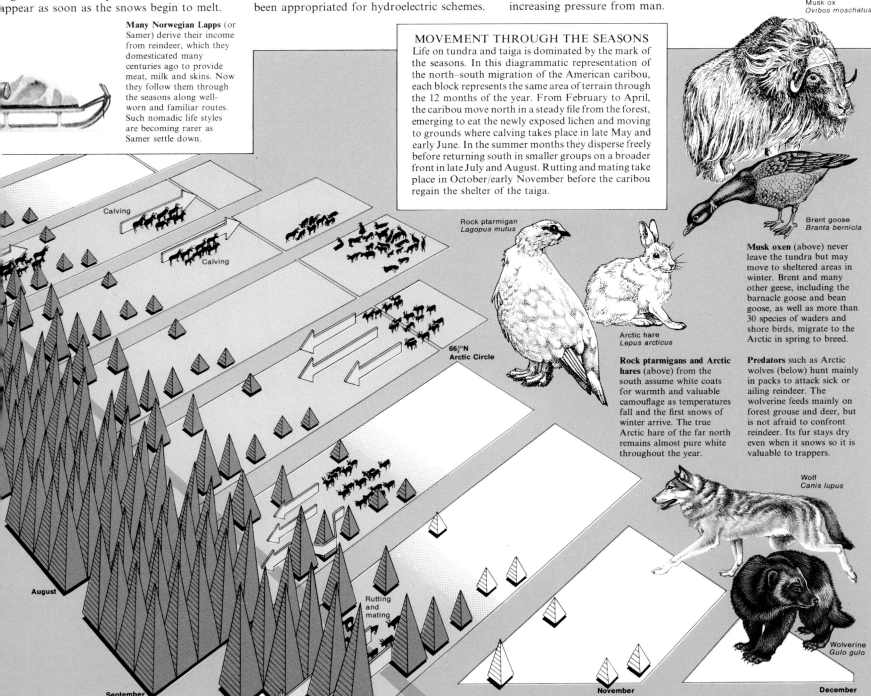

MOVEMENT THROUGH THE SEASONS
Life on tundra and taiga is dominated by the mark of the seasons. In this diagrammatic representation of the north–south migration of the American caribou, each block represents the same area of terrain through the 12 months of the year. From February to April, the caribou move north in a steady file from the forest, emerging to eat the newly exposed lichen and moving to grounds where calving takes place in late May and early June. In the summer months they disperse freely before returning south in smaller groups on a broader front in late July and August. Rutting and mating take place in October/early November before the caribou regain the shelter of the taiga.

Musk ox
Ovibos moschatus

Rock ptarmigan
Lagopus mutus

Arctic hare
Lepus arcticus

Brent goose
Branta bernicla

Wolf
Canis lupus

Wolverine
Gulo gulo

Calving

Calving

66½°N
Arctic Circle

August

September

October

Rutting and mating

62°N Approximate tree line

November

December

Musk oxen (above) never leave the tundra but may move to sheltered areas in winter. Brent and many other geese, including the barnacle goose and bean goose, as well as more than 30 species of waders and shore birds, migrate to the Arctic in spring to breed.

Rock ptarmigans and Arctic hares (above) from the south assume white coats for warmth and valuable camouflage as temperatures fall and the first snows of winter arrive. The true Arctic hare of the far north remains almost pure white throughout the year.

Predators such as Arctic wolves (below) hunt mainly in packs to attack sick or ailing reindeer. The wolverine feeds mainly on forest grouse and deer, but is not afraid to confront reindeer. Its fur stays dry even when it snows so it is valuable to trappers.

Temperate Forests

At one time, dense, primeval forests blanketed large areas of North America, Europe and eastern Asia. Almost all of the trees that flourished in these temperate regions were deciduous – they shed their leaves in autumn, stood bare-branched through winter and produced new foliage every spring. Little of this forest now exists. The few remaining pockets, however, still provide habitats for a large range of shade-loving plants: lichens and fungi, tree-hugging mosses, scrambling creepers and shrubs. And this vegetation in turn provides sanctuary for a surprisingly wide variety of forest creatures.

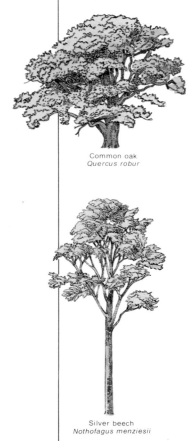

Common oak
Quercus robur

Silver beech
Nothofagus menziesii

Deciduous trees such as the oak (top) make up the temperate forests in cooler temperate regions. In milder, wetter climates, where the seasons are less distinct, evergreens such as southern beech (above) are typical temperate species.

The greater part of the temperate forest zone lies in the northern hemisphere, where winter soil temperatures reduce the ability of plants to absorb water. Hence the trees tend to shed their leaves, which use up moisture through evaporation. In the southern hemisphere, however, the temperate latitudes encourage a type of rainforest in such areas as southern Chile, Tasmania, New Zealand and parts of southeastern Australia. Here the climate is maritime, often with high rainfall and frequent fogs, and evergreen rather than deciduous types of trees grow. Temperate rainforests also occur in the northern hemisphere, in China and in northwestern and northeastern North America.

Deciduous forest consists of a mixture of trees, sometimes with one variety predominant. In central Europe, beech is the leading—and sometimes the only—tree species, whereas oaks mixed with other species made up the forest farther west and east. In North America, beech and maple were once extensive.

The climate in temperate forest zones varies sharply according to seasons—summers tend to be warm, winters moderately cold, and rainfall fairly regular. In fact, the seasonal rhythm is a central feature of temperate forests, and it affects the entire ecosystem—the whole community of plants and animals found there. Soils are generally of the fertile "brown earth" type: the leaf litter of deciduous forests in particular breaks down easily, and is quickly worked into the soil by burrowing animals such as earthworms. In wetter or rockier regions, the soil is more "podsolic"—bleached, sandy and less fertile than the true brown earths.

After the ice

Two million years ago, a series of ice sheets began to extend into the temperate latitudes. In Europe, species moving south before the advancing cold were cut off from the warmer climates by the east–west run of mountains. As a result, many varieties of plants and animals

Natural distribution: in the northern hemisphere's temperate zone deciduous forests occur in the cooler areas—in eastern USA, northeastern China, Korea, the northern parts of Japan's Honshu island and western Europe. These forests only give way to evergreens in the warmer and wetter parts of the zone. In the southern hemisphere, the climate is generally rather milder throughout the temperate zone and so there are virtually no deciduous forests. Evergreen forests, however, can be found in southeastern South Africa, Chile, New Zealand, Australia and Tasmania.

Deciduous forest · Warm-temperate rainforest · Cold-temperate rainforest

were killed off. Species were reduced still further in islands such as Britain, where the newly formed barriers of the English Channel, Irish Sea and North Sea made recolonization even more difficult after the ice had retreated.

Eastern Asia was one of the few areas in the world that escaped the extreme climatic changes of the ice ages and therefore its temperate forests, unlike those of Europe, still contain an enormous variety of tree species. North America also fared better than Europe, for although glaciers at one time extended deep into the continent, the north–south direction of the mountain ranges allowed relatively easy migration of trees southwards as the climate worsened. Hence most species survived and were able to reoccupy their former territories when the ice retreated. As a result, some 40 species of deciduous trees occur in the North American forests, and contribute to the spectacular display of colour during the autumn, notably in

the eastern USA. But a combination of climatic change and, more recently and importantly, of intense human activity, has meant that the remnants of temperate forest seen today differ greatly from the original forest in both composition and form. Only in remote regions such as the southern Appalachian Mountains do substantial areas of the original forest survive. Elsewhere, regrowth has occurred, but much of this is essentially scrub woodland.

The forest structure

Mature temperate deciduous forest is made up of distinct horizontal layers, particularly where the dominant tree is the oak, which allows enough light for a rich shrub layer to grow beneath it. The largest trees, such as oak, maple or ash, may be 25–50 m (80–160 ft) tall, and beneath them grows a prominent layer of smaller trees such as hazel, hornbeam or yew. Lower down again, a varied ground cover of perennial herbs, ferns, lichens and mosses flourishes in the comparative dampness of the forest floor. Because the trees are bare of leaves in winter, many of the plants growing on the forest floor take advantage of the warmth and light of spring to flower early in the year before the main trees come into full leaf and prevent the sun from reaching them. Various woody climbers, such as ivy and honeysuckle, are also present, growing over the trees and shrubs.

Much of the food supply in temperate forests is locked up in the trees themselves, but the annual fall of leaves in the deciduous forests produces a soil rich in nourishment. This supports a vast quantity of life, ranging in size from earthworms and insects to microscopic bacteria of the soil. The death of individual trees and branches also releases the food supply back to the earth. In shady, damp locations, insects, fungi, bacteria and other decomposing agents break down the leaves and other plant and animal debris more quickly, returning them to the soil as food for new plants.

Creatures of the forest

Temperate forests once contained many varieties of animal life, including several species of large animals. Herbivores such as wild oxen, wood bison, elk and moose ate grass and leaves; scavengers such as wild pigs rooted in the forest floor; predators such as wolves preyed on the other animals. Most of these have now been hunted to extinction by man or are extremely rare. Smaller animals still survive in comparatively large numbers, and include squirrels, chipmunks and raccoons, hedgehogs, wood mice, badgers and foxes.

The bird life of temperate forests is very diverse. Some species are insect-eaters, exploring the bark and crevices for insects and grubs. Others, such as the wood-pigeon, concentrate on seeds. Yet others, like the tawny owl, are predators. Complex interactions between predators and prey have developed at all levels of the forest, from the high canopy to the rotting ground litter, with each group evolving more efficient techniques of capture or escape in a kind of evolutionary race for survival.

The invertebrate insect life is also extremely varied and numerous, and forms a key component of the ecosystem. Oaks are particularly rich in insect life, and more than 100 species of moths feed on their leaves.

The plant and animal life of the temperate forest is remarkably rich and plentiful. And yet it is only a fraction of what once existed. Ever since man has occupied these regions he has found them so suited to his needs that he has long since cleared most of the original tree cover, replaced it with "civilization" and, in the process, destroyed innumerable species of forest wildlife.

THE SEASONAL CYCLE

It is the cycle of the four seasons that gives the temperate deciduous forest its distinctive character. All animals and plants have adapted their ways of life to cope with the seasonal changes in heat, light, moisture and food. The yearly shedding and regrowth of the forest's leaves is one of the most striking and important of adaptations to the seasonal cycle and one that affects all other life in the forest. In summer the leafy canopy of the trees blocks out the sunlight from the forest floor and creates unsuitable conditions for many other plants to flourish. When the leaves fall they form a layer over the soil and provide winter protection for the plant roots and hibernating animals beneath the ground. Finally, once the dead leaves have been broken down, they give fertility to the soil and provide food for future generations of plants.

SPRING

Between February and April, the low spring sun climbs steadily higher in the sky and, streaming through the still leafless branches of the trees, falls more directly on the forest floor, warming the soil and melting the last frosts. As soon as the days become warmer the sluggish sap in the trees begins to flow more quickly, carrying nutrients to the branches, where leaf buds start to form.

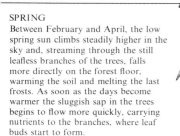

Bluebell
Endymion non-scriptus

Hepatica
Hepatica nobilis

Small emperor moth
Saturnia pavonia

Small plants of the forest floor, such as European bluebells and hepaticas taking advantage of the warm soil and plentiful light, flower in spring.

Forest insects emerge in spring, some, such as the emperor moth, from their winter cocoons, some from hibernation and some newly hatched from eggs.

European blackbird *Turdus merula*

Birds building nests in early spring make use of the forest's winter litter—broken twigs, dead leaves and dried grasses all serve as construction materials.

Woodchuck *Marmota monax*

Western European hedgehog *Erinaceus europaeus*

White-tailed deer *Odocoileus virginianus*

New plant growth and the increase in insects provide food for such animals as the North American woodchuck and the European hedgehog that wake thin and hungry from months of hibernation. Deer and other non-hibernating animals are also weak and thin—indeed many may have died during the harsh weather. The spring birth of young, however, soon restores their numbers.

SUMMER

By early summer the leaves of the trees are fully grown. They form a dense canopy, blocking out the sun and cooling the soil of the forest floor. Most of the small ground plants have long since finished flowering, but their leaves remain green and they continue actively storing food in their roots ready for their rapid spring growth.

Cranberry *Vaccinium oxycoccus*

Bramble
Rubus spp

Shrubs and bushes, such as bramble and cranberry, form tangled flowering masses wherever sunlight manages to filter through the forest's gloomy canopy.

Hordes of insects inhabit the forest in summer, living off the vast supply of food plants. The European stag beetle feeds on the sap of chestnut and oak trees.

Stag beetle
Lucanus cervus

Willow warbler
Phylloscopus trochilus

The North American pewee and the willow warbler are two of the forest's many summer visitors that feed on the insect population. Some seed-eating birds, finches for example, also take advantage of this summer food supply.

Eastern wood pewee *Contopus virens*

Hazel mouse *Muscardinus avellanarius*

The hazel mouse protects its young by raising them in a summer nest, which it builds in a tree: almost every creature in the forest is viewed as a source of food by some other animal and the young litters are particularly at risk.

AUTUMN

As the autumn days grow shorter and cooler the forest foliage begins to turn colour; the trees are responding to the drop in temperature and are cutting off the food supply to their leaves, which lose their green colour and fall to the ground, forming a thick carpet on the forest's floor. Rain, frost, insects, earthworms and fungi then break down the leaves, making them part of the fertile forest soil.

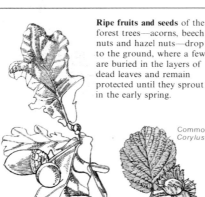

Ripe fruits and seeds of the forest trees—acorns, beech nuts and hazel nuts—drop to the ground, where a few are buried in the layers of dead leaves and remain protected until they sprout in the early spring.

Common hazel
Corylus avellana

Oak
Quercus spp

Preparing for winter, the acorn woodpecker stores seeds in holes that it drills in tree trunks. Chipmunks hide supplies of nuts in their winter nests.

Acorn woodpecker *Melanerpes formicivorus*

American black bear *Ursus americanus*

Eastern chipmunk *Tamias striatus*

The black bear of North America, like other winter hibernators, consumes vast quantities of food during autumn to build up its winter stores of food in the form of body fat.

WINTER

By winter, only evergreen shrubs and a few small hardy plants remain green. Many of the plants of the forest floor lose their green leaves during the first deep frost. The leaves of the trees still lie rotting on the bare ground, but within the soil, beneath the protective layers of leaf litter, plants are growing and spring flowers are developing buds.

Late-fruiting plants, such as holly, mistletoe and dog rose, provide food for winter residents of the temperate forest such as the European hawfinch.

Hawfinch
Coccothraustes coccothraustes

Holly
Ilex spp

Owls and foxes remain fairly active in winter, regularly leaving their nests or lairs to catch small animals or birds that are also in search of food.

North American screech owl *Otus asio*

European woodcock *Scolopax rusticola*

Woodcocks are insect-eaters. They can survive winter by prising insects from the soil with their long beaks, providing that the ground is not too deeply frozen.

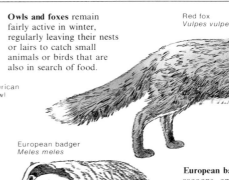

Red fox
Vulpes vulpes

European badger *Meles meles*

European badgers, like racoons, opossums, bears and skunks, are "shallow" hibernators. On mild winter days they wake and go to search for food.

THE EVERGREEN TEMPERATE RAINFORESTS

There are two main kinds of temperate rainforest, the warm-temperate, such as can still be found on North Island, New Zealand (left), and the cold-temperate, such as that of the Chilean coast. Both of these kinds of forest have one major feature in common: they have enough water for even the most moisture-greedy plants, such as mosses and ferns, to grow throughout the year. The animal life of the forest is also affected by the abundance of rain, so that snails, slugs, frogs and other water-loving creatures flourish. Most temperate rainforest is of the warm-temperate kind, normally found on the edges of subtropical regions, and the vegetation, with palms, lianas,

bamboos, as well as ferns and mosses, is similar to, although less rich than, the tropical rainforest's vegetation. The cold-temperate rainforests grow in cooler regions but their coastal position means that the climate is milder and wetter than inland (where deciduous trees dominate). Their vegetation is less lush and less varied than the warm-temperate forests, but mosses and ferns grow in abundance. Broad-leaved evergreens, such as New Zealand's southern beech, are the most common trees of these forests, although on the northwestern coast of North America Douglas firs and other conifers outnumber the broad-leaved evergreen species.

Man and the Temperate Forests

Temperate forests have suffered enormously at the hands of man. For the great civilizations of China, Europe and, later, North America the forests not only yielded cropland for expanding populations but also contributed materials and fuel for early technologies. More recently the demands of industry have reduced the forests still further. But today, scientists believe that this depleted resource could again play an important role in providing energy, food and materials for future generations.

PREHISTORIC FORESTS
Hunter-gatherers made clearings in the forest when they cut brushwood for building shelters and for fuel (1): human impact on the temperate forest was small. But 7,000 years ago in Europe, 6,000 years ago in eastern Asia and 1,000 years ago in eastern North America, the first farming communities of the temperate forest (2) began to clear larger pockets of forest to provide land for crops and timber for houses and tools.

PERMANENT SETTLEMENT
The Bronze Age and, later, the Iron Age laid the foundations of Chinese and Western civilizations. The forest shrank as permanent settlements grew (3) and, with the use of metals and improved technology, agricultural land was extended (4). But the forest was recognized as an important resource and areas were protected. Management techniques were introduced that, especially in medieval Europe, changed dense forest to coppiced woods (5).

EARLY INDUSTRIAL TIMES
Sources of cropland and timber had been discovered in the New World, but in the Far East and Europe forests were drastically reduced. Virtually no Chinese forest remained, and in Europe nations began importing timber to serve growing industrial needs (6). To help solve shortages, plantations were established on country estates (7), which were often landscaped into parkland and planted with introduced species of trees (8).

The aurochs, or wild ox, was one of the many forest animals that provided food for early hunter-gatherers. Once man began to farm the land, he domesticated some of these animals—the wild boar, the aurochs and the wild turkey.

The dwellings of the late Neolithic Chinese were relatively sophisticated, reflecting an increasingly settled way of life that was soon to alter the landscape as forests were felled to provide building materials and land to plant crops.

The fortified villages and the farms of the Eastern Woodland Indians were set in semipermanent clearings cut in the North American forest. Before European settlement, however, human populations were small and deforestation was negligible.

Grain harvesting is depicted in a Chinese tomb image. By the 1st century AD, China contained nearly 60 million people, and agriculture, along with stock raising and metal mining, was drastically depleting the tree cover.

Coppicing and pollarding allowed continual cropping of forests. Branches were cut from trees, the bases of which were left to regrow shoots. This technique reduced the density of tree cover, encouraging a richer growth of ground plants.

Coppicing

Pollarding

Production of charcoal (below), which was a basic raw material for smelting in early industrial times, was responsible for much deforestation of the land.

Human interference with the forests goes back deep into prehistory. There is evidence that fire was used to stampede hunted animals in southern Europe as long as 400,000 years ago. Human populations, while they remained small, had only a slight effect on the vast stretches of primeval forest. Even so, hunting practices and the use of fire to clear land reduced some of the forests of Europe and Asia even before the invention of agriculture. In the New World, too, Eastern Woodland Indians had already affected the North American forests, and early Maori hunters had burned much of the tree cover of New Zealand by the time Europeans arrived.

Nevertheless it was the development of agriculture in Neolithic (New Stone Age) times that had the first really destructive effect on the temperate forests. Clearings were made for crops and the felled trees provided fuel and building material for the new communities. Large forest animals suffered as well, some (such as deer) being hunted for food and others (such as wolves) because they threatened grazing animals. But it was the population increase resulting from the new, settled way of life that caused the extension of man-made cropland deep into former forests.

With man's development of metals, more forests were destroyed: wood and charcoal were used for smelting and the new iron tools made tree clearance easier and more thorough. Firing of forests was also a familiar military ploy, used by such warriors as the Romans.

Medieval woodlands
By medieval times, large tracts of forest had been cleared in Europe and in the Far East, although in the former area there remained extensive royal hunting forest reserves. Local woodlands were carefully managed to serve the needs of the community; the techniques used included pollarding and coppicing.

Pollarding involved the cropping of main branches at a certain height above ground. In coppicing, the "coppice with standards" method was used to harvest the smaller species, such as hazel and hornbeam, whereas the standards (such as oaks) were cut on a longer rotation of 100 years or so. Alternatively, the oak itself could be part of the coppice crop, its stems being cut near ground level so that shoots arose from the stump, to be cut 10 to 20 years later. For local communities, industries and cities, forests provided a variety of materials for building, tanning and fencing, as well as dye-stuffs, charcoal and domestic fuel.

The growth of the iron and shipbuilding industries in the sixteenth century devastated so much woodland and forest that in many regions good timber became scarce and had to be imported from considerable distances. The pressure on woodland continued until the production of coke and cheap coal brought some relaxation, but by the early twentieth century the coppice system had broken down and management of Europe's woodlands had largely been abandoned. In Europe the poor state of the deciduous forests was further worsened by two world wars. Many countries have since set up organizations with the specific task of building reserves of timber. Economic pressures, however, have led to the planting mainly of quick-growing conifers, rather than typical trees of the temperate deciduous forest.

New World forests
The migrants who settled in the New World were the descendants of the people who had largely destroyed the forests of Europe. Confronted by the temperate deciduous forests of eastern North America, they virtually continued where they had left off. Tracts were cleared to create arable and range land and to provide the massive amounts of timber needed for the colonization, industrialization and urbanization of North America. With the opening of the prairie lands for agriculture, however,

Disturbance to the natural vegetation has occurred throughout the temperate forest zone. Exploitation of this biome's greatest resource, its agricultural potential, has been one of the major causes of deforestation. The only forests that have escaped major disturbance are in remote areas, too rocky or too steep for cultivation. Today, intensive farming is still a major economic activity of the temperate forest regions. But farmland is not the only important resource to have disturbed the forests. Mining for key minerals such as copper, iron and coal, all of which made possible the development of Western and Chinese civilization, has also contributed to destruction of the forest cover. For centuries the forests provided man with food, fuel and materials, but, ironically, it has been the removal of the forest that has enabled man to exploit the most important of these regions' resources.

THE CHANGING LANDSCAPE

Mankind has been occupying the temperate forest regions for many thousands of years, at first with little effect on the natural forest ecology. But during the last 2,000 years human activity has destroyed the original tree cover at an accelerating pace. As populations increased and economies developed —at different rates in the three major regions— forests disappeared to be replaced by farms, cities, industries and communications networks. Today, scarcely any of the original forest cover remains.

THE 19TH CENTURY

The Industrial Revolution developed in Europe and the New World, large towns and cities sprang up (9), pushing back the woodlands and forests still farther. This process was aided by the spreading network of railways (10). Coke, iron and other minerals were replacing timber products as raw materials for growing industries (11), but demands were still made on the forests to provide, for example, railway sleepers and mine pit-props.

FORESTS TODAY

The 20th century has seen an increasing trend towards urbanization in areas that were once temperate forest. Housing complexes (12) and new factory sites (13) cover large areas, while roadbuilding (14), industrial agriculture (15) and opencast mining (16) destroy remaining woodland. Leisure areas (17) and nature reserves protect some woods, but plantations of exotic conifers (18) do not always provide suitable wildlife habitats.

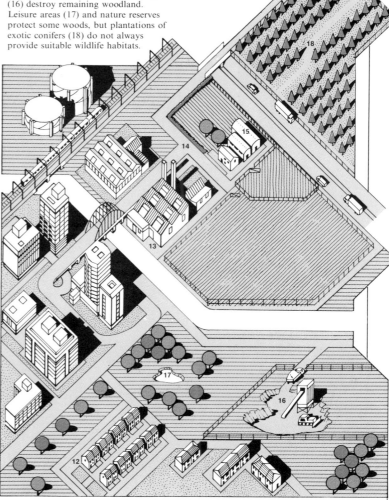

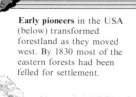

Early pioneers in the USA (below) transformed forestland as they moved west. By 1830 most of the eastern forests had been felled for settlement.

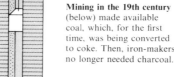

Mining in the 19th century (below) made available coal, which, for the first time, was being converted to coke. Then, iron-makers no longer needed charcoal.

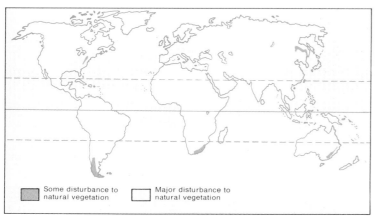

Large department stores appeared in 19th-century Chicago, a town that, within 100 years, had been transformed from a remote fort to a city. This rapid growth reflected the huge population increase in many 19th-century towns.

A reafforestation scheme (below) was set up in China in 1950 to replant areas that lost their original forest cover many centuries ago. Similar projects are under way in many other temperate forest regions.

The European wood bison has escaped extinction because one herd of the animals has lived, for centuries, in a royal hunting reserve. Today, wildlife parks throughout temperate regions protect endangered forest species.

Some disturbance to natural vegetation	Major disturbance to natural vegetation

the pressures shifted, some of the east coast deciduous forest grew up again, and it is possible that parts of the eastern USA may have nearly as much forest cover now as when the settlers first arrived. Nevertheless, other areas of forestland have been destroyed in recent decades by strip mining and the creation of a vast road and rail network. In the southern hemisphere, especially in the last 200 years, the temperate rainforests of Australia and New Zealand have been subjected to much the same pattern of events, although on a smaller and somewhat less devastating scale.

Conservation

Today the general need to preserve and extend the woodlands is clearly recognized, but great uncertainty exists about their future. The demand for hardwoods for veneers, quality papermaking and furniture still exceeds supply. Oak is still the preferred material for some types of boatbuilding and, particularly in Europe, for joinery work. But one of the major difficulties with forestry as a land use is forecasting future trends within the industry, largely as a result of the long-term nature of the crop—hardwood trees planted today will not yield their timber until well into the next century. Government tax policies can be all-important in deciding whether the majority of woodlands are, or will

continue to be, sound economic investments.

Temperate forests and woodlands still exist in sizeable quantities in central Europe and the USA, but many of today's plots, particularly in western Europe, are far too small for efficient conservation of plant and animal life, and are isolated from other woods. As a result, successful breeding and exchange of genetic material is very difficult, especially when modern agriculture is rapidly destroying the linking corridors of hedgerows. The use of woodlands for recreation is also presenting considerable problems. Controlling agencies have been formed to cope with leisure demands, and a start has been made in the multiple use of forests for recreation, conservation and timber felling, but progress still needs to be made in harmonizing these potentially conflicting interests. Meanwhile, natural expanses of woodland and forest are still being lost to agricultural and urban expansion and to plantations of non-native conifers.

Temperate forests are a biologically efficient form of land use. In terms of biomass—the amount of living material (animal and plant) in any one area—they could still play an important role in the provision of food, materials and even renewable energy. Thus on scientific, economic and aesthetic grounds a strong case can be made for immediate conservation measures.

Mediterranean Regions

Forests of evergreen trees once covered much of the Mediterranean regions. They flourished in spite of the hot, rainless summer months – as the original plant life, they had evolved to survive such harsh conditions. Man, however, has proved to be a greater threat than the climate. He introduced domestic animals and cleared the land to grow crops; the natural vegetation was burned, browsed and ploughed into nonexistence. Man's activities left behind tracts of impoverished soil which rapidly became scrubland. Today, scrub is the most typical vegetation in all the Mediterranean climate zones throughout the world.

CONVERGENCE
Isolated from each other by enormous areas of land and ocean, regions with a Mediterranean type of climate rarely have any plant species in common. But, by a process known as "convergent evolution", the plant communities in each of these areas have produced remarkably similar responses to their similar environments. This can be seen in the conifer communities, the broad-leaved evergreen trees, and in the various hardy shrubs and ground plants typical of each of the regions.

Monterey pine
Pinus radiata

California's Monterey pine and other Mediterranean conifers—South African podocarps and Chile pines, for example—have needle-shaped leaves that prevent rapid loss of water from such trees during drought.

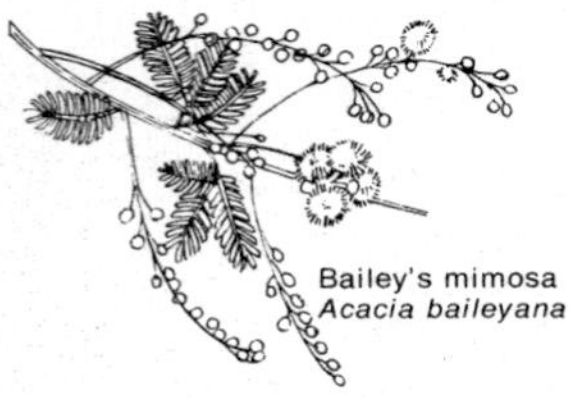
Bailey's mimosa
Acacia baileyana

Non-coniferous evergreens such as Australia's acacias and eucalypts, Chile's *quillajas* and California's evergreen oaks are typical Mediterranean trees. Their leathery leaves limit summer moisture loss.

Giant protea
Protea cynaroides

Shrubs and ground plants show various adaptations to drought. South African proteas and Europe's laurel have thick evergreen leaves. Narrow leaves and water-storing roots are other common adaptations.

Long, hot, dry summers and warm, moist winters form the seasonal rhythm of the "Mediterranean" year. This climatic pattern can be found in small areas of nearly every continent in the world, typically on the western side of landmasses and in the mild, temperate latitudes. North America's "Mediterranean" is in California, South America's occurs in Chile and Africa's lies at the southern tip of Cape Province. Australia has two small "Mediterranean" areas, one on the southern coast and one on the western. Europe's Mediterranean region, which has given its name to this climate, covers much of the southern part of the continent, and extends into northern Africa.

Wherever Mediterranean conditions prevail, the native plant life has adapted to survive the scanty annual rainfall and the long summer droughts. Some species have developed deep root systems that can tap low summer water tables, and many of the ground plants—such as bulbs and aromatic herbs—grow vigorously only in early summer while rain still moistens the soil. But it is the broad-leaved evergreens with their drought-resistant leaves that are the most typical of the Mediterranean areas.

This natural pattern of vegetation has been drastically altered by man. In southern Europe in particular, almost all the original evergreen forests have long since been destroyed and thickets of fast-growing, tough scrub plants have grown up in their place. This scrub, which once probably covered only small areas, is now so widespread that it is considered the most typically Mediterranean of all kinds of vegetation. It is the *maquis* of France, the *macchia* of Italy and the *mattoral* of Spain. A similar type of vegetation (although containing different species) can also be found in South Africa's fynbos, in California's chapparal, and in Australia's tracts of natural mallee scrub.

Classical land use

Southern Europe, with its long history of human settlement, farming and pastoralism, is the most altered of all the Mediterranean regions. Over the centuries vast tracts of original vegetation have been removed, either by farmers (for crop growing) or by grazing animals. And, particularly on the steep slopes and rocky outcrops, this has resulted in extensive deterioration and erosion of the soil. Agriculture generally has less serious effects upon the vegetation than has animal grazing. Mankind has learned, over many hundreds of years, which are the most suitable crops for the various soils, terrain and climatic conditions of the region. The Mediterranean "triad" of wheat on the lowlands and olives and vines on the hills has been a successful combination since Classical times.

Pastoral plundering of the land, however, has more serious consequences. The virtually omnivorous goat is particularly damaging and can strip a whole forest of its foliage, bark, shrubs, ground plants and grass. After such an assault the vegetation rarely returns to its former condition; normally a scrubby growth of kermes oak and shrubs springs up to form a typical maquis-type vegetation.

The rise and fall of each great Mediterranean civilization has seen forests destroyed in one area after another. The Greek colonization of southern Italy was provoked by deforestation and soil erosion in Attica. The Romans extended clearance north to the Po valley and into eastern Tunisia. From the seventh century onwards, Muslims made great inroads into the forests of North Africa as well as southern and eastern Spain; and in the north of Spain and southern France, medieval monks cleared forested valleys. During the seventeenth and eighteenth centuries large areas of Provence and Italy were cleared to plant vines and this process continued in the 1800s, when the great wine-producing areas of Languedoc and Algeria were established. During this time the iron industries of Spain and northern Italy, with their growing need for charcoal, were adding to the destruction. Recent reafforestation efforts have been puny compared to past degradation.

Protected species

But throughout this history of forest removal some tree species have been protected. These have been the natural tree crops that have, at times, supported complete peasant economies. The chestnut forests of Corsica, for example, sustained a large rural population until this century; the chestnuts provided flour for bread and fodder for pigs. In Portugal and Sardinia the cork-oak forests are still important today.

It is the olive, however, symbol of peace and of New Testament landscapes, that is the Mediterranean's most characteristic tree crop. Of all the Mediterranean plants, it is the most perfectly adapted to its environment, with its deep roots to search out scarce water and its hard, shiny leaves to conserve what it finds. In fact, the summer drought is essential to olive growers for it encourages the build-up of oil in the fruit. Paradoxically, however, the olive—like the vine, the fig and many other "Mediterranean" crops—did not originate in the Mediterranean but was introduced from Asia Minor.

In spite of massive destruction of the natural landscape, mankind has learned many valuable lessons during his occupation of this region. Ideas that were to become important in laying the foundations of sound land management policy were developed in the Mediterranean area. Hillside terracing, irrigation, crop rotation and manuring were all, from necessity, practised from early times. The flourishing agricultural industries of the world's other Mediterranean regions—the wine industry of California, the vast soft-fruit plantations of Australia and the citrus industry of South Africa—all owe a considerable debt to the generations of farmers who learned to exploit the red soils of the Mediterranean basin.

The Mediterranean regions occur between the latitudes 30° and 40°, on the western and southwestern sides of the continents. These areas are affected in summer by the high-pressure systems of nearby desert regions, and in winter by wet, low-pressure systems brought in from the oceans and over the land by the prevailing Westerlies. This distinct seasonal shifting of major influences on the climate produces the hot, waterless summers and warm, moist, sometimes stormy winters typical of the Mediterranean climate.

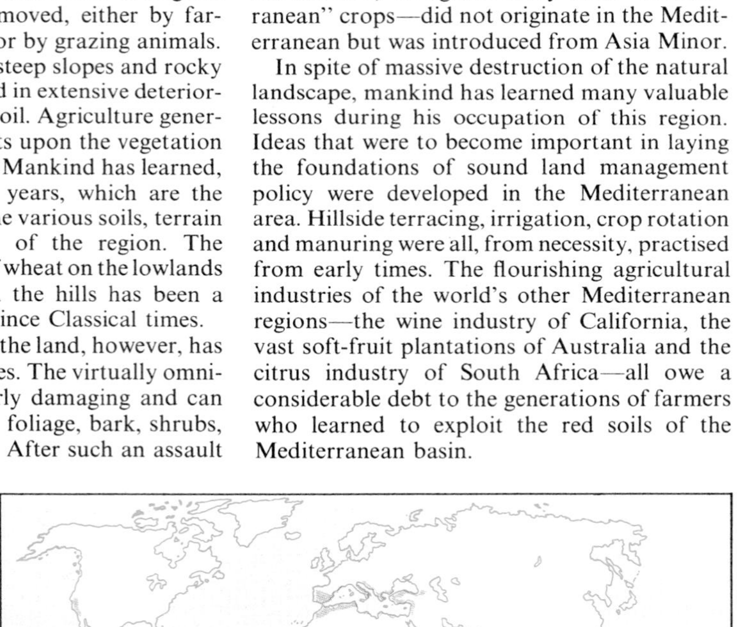
Mediterranean climate regions

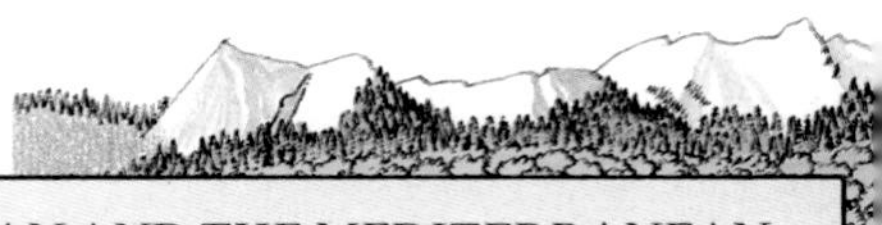

MAN AND THE MEDITERRANEAN
Even by Classical times, the once-forested lands fringing the Mediterranean Sea were suffering from massive deforestation and soil erosion. In the 5th century BC, Plato described the bare, dry hills of Attica, recently stripped of their woodlands. "What now remains," he wrote, "is like the skeleton of a sick man, all the fat and soft earth having been wasted away." By the end of the Classical period, irreparable damage had been done. At the same time, however, mankind was gradually learning through the mistakes he had already made. Suitable patterns of land use, better farming practices and improved land management techniques were slowly being adopted and were enabling man to make better use of the much-altered Mediterranean landscape.

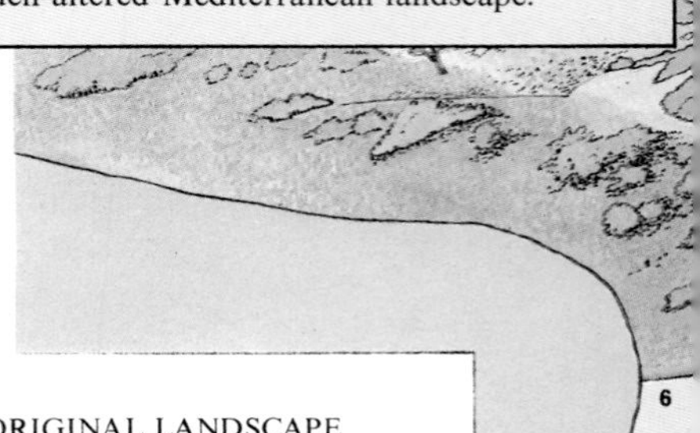
6

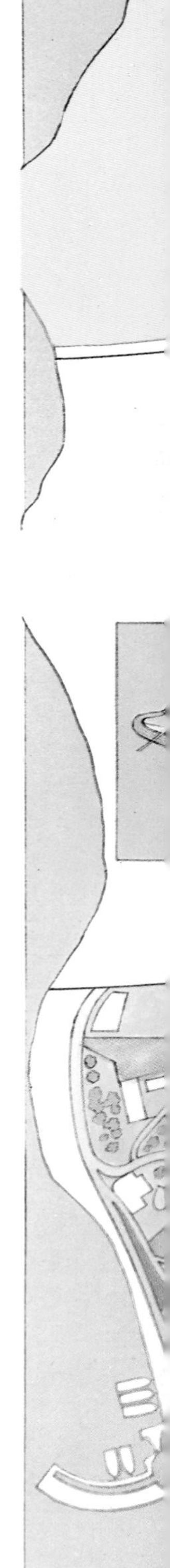

THE ORIGINAL LANDSCAPE
The landscape, unaltered by man, held a rich variety of vegetation. On high mountains, conifers such as black pine and cedar grew. On the lower slopes, these gave way to warmth-tolerant deciduous trees such as Turkey oak. In the foothills and valleys, forests of holm oaks, strawberry trees and other broad-leaved evergreens flourished. Limestone outcrops, common in the area, supported a poorer vegetation. Here, stunted Aleppo pines mixed with herbs such as lavender. Over sandstone, scrubby olives and cork oaks grew and by the sea stood isolated, wind-bent maritime pines.

THE CLASSICAL AGE
Civilizations followed one after another, each taking its toll of the environment. In the mountains, forests were felled, the tall, straight conifers sought after by shipbuilders such as the Phoenicians, and deciduous hardwood timber in demand for charcoal to fuel growing industries. Some replanting did take place, especially as groves of crop trees such as chestnuts. Below in the foothills, agriculture and the grazing of animals had destroyed vast areas of natural forest. Terracing techniques, however, helped to stop soil erosion, and irrigation reached the height of its Classical art with Roman aqueducts and canals. Tree crops, such as olives, were found best suited to the thin hill soils. On the plains, especially where alluvial soils had been deposited, cereals were grown. Meanwhile, towns sprang up and the coastline became densely populated as ships and ports were built and sea trade grew. Exotic food plants, such as pomegranate trees, citron trees and vines, were brought into the region by merchant seamen.

THE MEDITERRANEAN TODAY
The region today bears the scars of many centuries of human activity. The once-forested mountains will never return to their former state, although some regrowth and some replanting (mostly with introduced tree species) has occurred. As in Classical times, hillsides are terraced and planted with vines and fruit trees. But with modern irrigation and fertilizing, land is less readily exhausted and abandoned now. On the plains, native shrubs, such as lavender, are commercially cultivated and grain is widely grown, particularly durum wheat used for making pasta. Cork oaks are planted, especially over dry sandstone areas, but indigenous vegetation has not suffered by this—scrubby woodland is more widespread than ever and can be found throughout the landscape. Perhaps the single most important part of the Mediterranean basin today is the coastline, for this has produced the region's major modern industry—tourism.

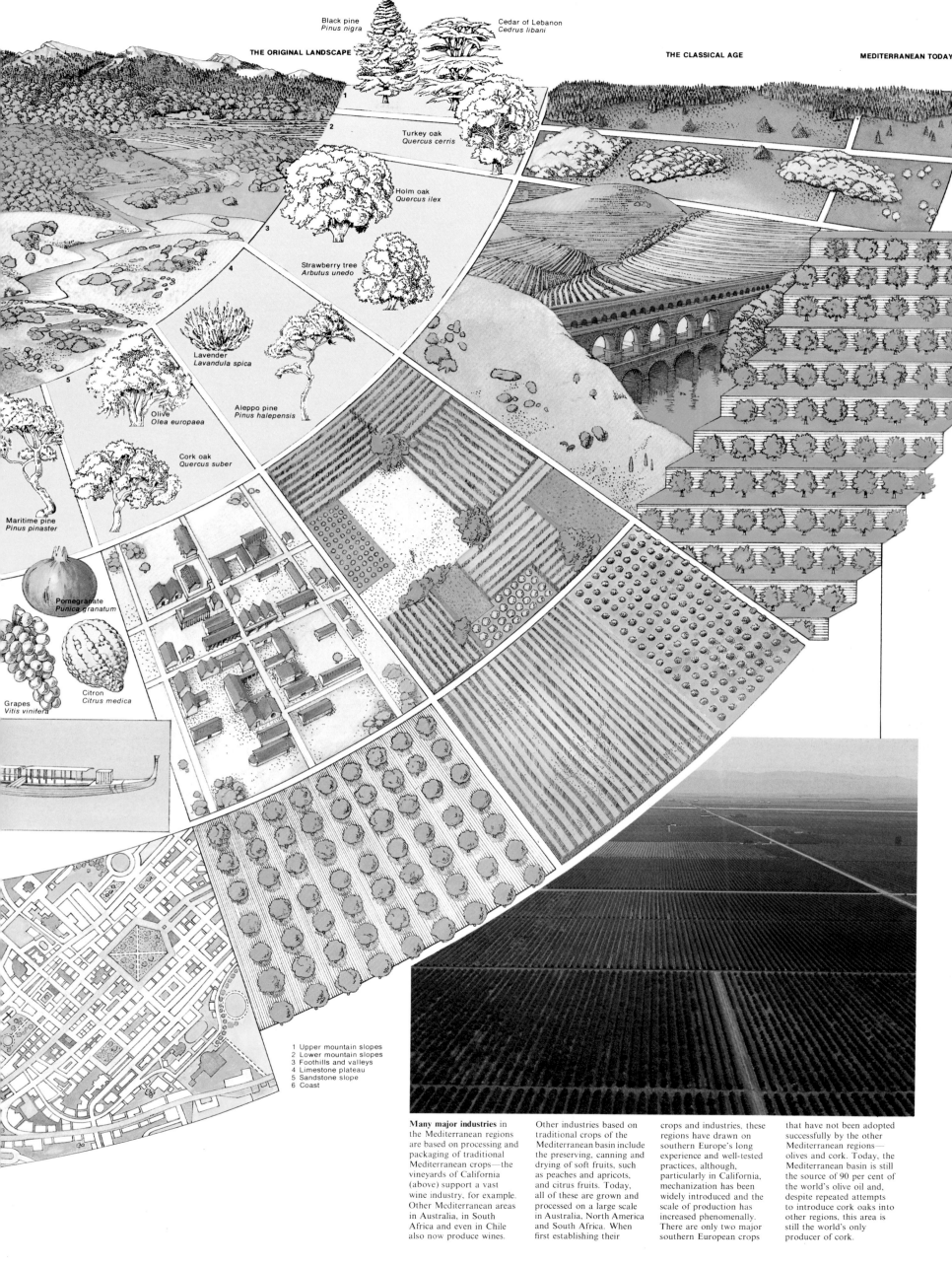

Black pine
Pinus nigra

Cedar of Lebanon
Cedrus libani

Turkey oak
Quercus cerris

Holm oak
Quercus ilex

Strawberry tree
Arbutus unedo

Lavender
Lavandula spica

Aleppo pine
Pinus halepensis

Olive
Olea europaea

Cork oak
Quercus suber

Maritime pine
Pinus pinaster

Pomegranate
Punica granatum

Citron
Citrus medica

Grapes
Vitis vinifera

1 Upper mountain slopes
2 Lower mountain slopes
3 Foothills and valleys
4 Limestone plateau
5 Sandstone slope
6 Coast

Many major industries in the Mediterranean regions are based on processing and packaging of traditional Mediterranean crops—the vineyards of California (above) support a vast wine industry, for example. Other Mediterranean areas in Australia, in South Africa and even in Chile also now produce wines.

Other industries based on traditional crops of the Mediterranean basin include the preserving, canning and drying of soft fruits, such as peaches and apricots, and citrus fruits. Today, all of these are grown and processed on a large scale in Australia, North America and South Africa. When first establishing their

crops and industries, these regions have drawn on southern Europe's long experience and well-tested practices, although, particularly in California, mechanization has been widely introduced and the scale of production has increased phenomenally. There are only two major southern European crops

that have not been adopted successfully by the other Mediterranean regions— olives and cork. Today, the Mediterranean basin is still the source of 90 per cent of the world's olive oil and, despite repeated attempts to introduce cork oaks into other regions, this area is still the world's only producer of cork.

Temperate Grasslands

Compared with other flowering plants, grasses are newcomers to the Earth. They appeared only 60 million years ago, but since then they have proved to be an extremely successful family of plants. Today, the grasses dominate large areas of the world's natural vegetation and play a vital part in the intricate balance of plant and animal life in these regions. In spite of the inroads made by man, vast stretches of original grassland still cover the interiors of the North American and Eurasian landmasses.

The prairies of North America and the steppes of Eurasia extend far into the interiors of the northern continents. These are the best known and the most extensive of the world's temperate grasslands. The southern hemisphere, however, has examples in the veld of South Africa and the pampas of South America. Extensive grasslands also occur in southern Australia, although these are sometimes described as semi-arid scrub because of the high average temperatures and the prolonged droughts in the region.

Temperate grasslands probably developed wherever the rainfall was too low to support forest and too high to result in semi-arid regions, conditions found typically in the interiors of large continents. Continental interiors tend to be somewhat drier than coastal regions, but they are also characterized by extreme changes in temperature from one season to the next. In the North American grasslands, for example, winter temperatures may fall well below freezing whereas summer temperatures of 38°C (100°F) are not unusual. And these sharp fluctuations in seasonal temperature greatly influence how much of the rainfall is made available to plants. In summer particularly, when most of the rain falls, high temperatures, strong winds and lack of protective tree cover cause much of the moisture to evaporate before it can be absorbed into the soil.

Climatic conditions are not the only factor responsible for the distribution and form of the temperate grasslands. There are many pointers that indicate the importance of fire in determining their continuing existence and their extent. Natural fires, caused by lightning and fuelled by the dry summer grasses, have always been a feature of these regions, but more recently, man-made fires have been crucial in fixing the boundary between forest and grassland.

Trees and shrubs frequently invade the margins of grasslands, but whenever there is a fire few of them survive. Grasses, however, have certain characteristics that enable them to withstand the potentially destructive impact of fire. The growing point of grasses is at the base of the leaves, close to the ground, and so destruction of the leaves above this point does not interrupt growth—in fact it may stimulate it. These same characteristics also serve to protect grasses from destruction by grazing animals. The large animals of these lands, such as the North American bison and the Eurasian horse, are able to crop the grasses without permanently damaging their food supply.

Grazers and predators

Large migrating herbivores with a strong herd instinct characterize one of the major types of temperate grassland animal. In the North American grasslands the bison (which may have numbered 60 million before being virtually exterminated by settlers) and the antelope-like pronghorn were the major examples of large herbivores. In Eurasia large herds of saiga antelopes, wild horses and asses at one time roamed the steppes, although they too have suffered from human activities, as has South America's largest grassland herd animal, the pampas deer. As these herds of grazing animals have been reduced, so have the carnivorous animals of the grasslands that preyed upon them. At one time, however, these predators played an important part in protecting the grasslands by continually keeping the numbers of grazing herd animals in check.

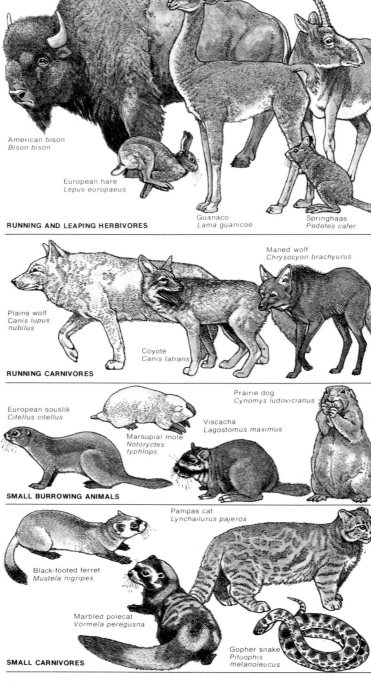

RUNNING AND LEAPING HERBIVORES

Saiga
Saiga tatarica

American bison
Bison bison

European hare
Lepus europaeus

Guanaco
Lama guanicoe

Springhaas
Pedetes cafer

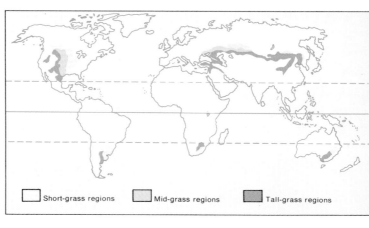

RUNNING CARNIVORES

Maned wolf
Chrysocyon brachyurus

Plains wolf
Canis lupus nubilus

Coyote
Canis latrans

SMALL BURROWING ANIMALS

European souslik
Citellus citellus

Marsupial mole
Notoryctes typhlops

Prairie dog
Cynomys ludovicianus

Viscacha
Lagostomus maximus

SMALL CARNIVORES

Black-footed ferret
Mustela nigripes

Marbled polecat
Vormela peregusna

Pampas cat
Lynchailurus pajeros

Gopher snake
Pituophis melanoleucus

The dominant native species of grass varies from area to area. In the undisturbed prairies, for example, tall bluestem and Indian grass grow in the east and in wet central lowlands, and mix with switch grass in drier parts. Farther west and on high land in the east little bluestem and also western wheatgrass grow. June grass grows in the north, and buffalo grass and blue grama grow farthest west.

Many flowering herbs grow in the grasslands and have developed resistance to summer droughts: Russian tarragon has narrow leaves to help prevent moisture evaporation; rhizomes and bulbs, such as Eurasia's iris and anemone, store water in their specialized "root" systems.

Russian tarragon
Artemisia dracunculoides

Iris
Iris sibirica

Anemone
Anemone patens

Indian grass
Sorgastrum nutans

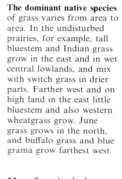

Little bluestem
Andropogon scoparius

Blue grama grass
Bouteloua gracilis

The natural distribution of the temperate grasslands is dictated mainly by rainfall: most occur in continental interiors where there is too little rain for forest but enough to prevent desert from forming. Between these limits the large range in rainfall allows three main types of grassland: tall grass in wetter areas, mid-grass, and short grass in drier parts. The largest grasslands exist in North America, Eurasia, South America, in Australia's Murray–Darling river basin and on the South African plateau.

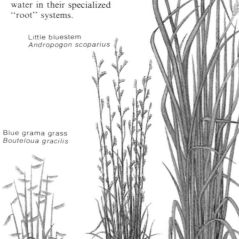

Short-grass regions
Mid-grass regions
Tall-grass regions

Short-grass prairies

Mid-grass prairies

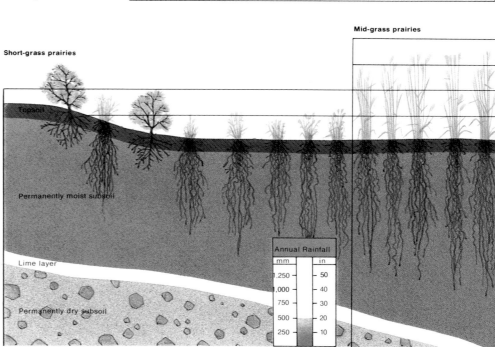

Topsoil

Permanently moist subsoil

Lime layer

Permanently dry subsoil

Annual Rainfall	
mm	in
1,250	50
1,000	40
750	30
500	20
250	10

GRASSLAND ADAPTATION

Animals of these regions have had to adapt to a difficult environment: vast, treeless expanses of grass offer little protection from harsh weather or predators. Different animals have found various answers to the problem and a clearly defined pattern of these adaptations can be traced throughout the grasslands.

Running and leaping herbivores survive because of their ability to move faster than a pursuer. The larger animals such as the Eurasian saiga, North America's bison and pronghorn and the guanaco of South America are runners. The leaping herbivores are usually smaller creatures that escape danger by bounding away to bolt-holes. They include the European hare and the African springhaas.

Running carnivores follow, and prey on, running and leaping herbivores. These animals, such as the coyote and the now extinct plains wolf of North America, and South America's maned wolf, also depend on speed—to enable them to catch their prey.

Small burrowing animals hide from predators by digging under the ground. Some, such as Australia's marsupial mole, spend most of their lives below ground. Others, such as the European souslik, South America's viscacha and North America's prairie dog, live and sleep under the ground but come to the surface to find food.

Small carnivores concentrate on the burrowers as their main source of food. They either, like the pampas cat, rely on surprise attack of their prey, or, like Eurasia's marbled polecat and the grasslands' many kinds of snake, depend on their long, lithe shape to follow creatures into their burrows.

Two distinctive types of grassland bird can be distinguished: the sky birds, which spend long periods of time on the wing, and the ground birds.

Birds of the sky include songbirds such as the skylark which, having no perch from which to proclaim its territory, sings in the sky, and birds of prey such as Eurasia's tawny eagle and North America's red-tailed hawk and prairie falcon, which ride the thermals scanning the ground for their prey.

Ground birds rarely take to the wing, although none has actually lost the ability to fly when necessary. They include birds such as the New World sage grouse and burrowing owl (which lives below ground in abandoned prairie dog burrows), the black grouse of Eurasia and songbirds such as North America's meadowlark.

Insects and other invertebrates have developed many different survival techniques. Some use camouflage: the praying mantis resembles a leafbud and the tumble bug is the colour of the dark grassland soil. Grasshoppers are miniature leaping herbivores and earthworms are small-scale versions of the grassland burrowers.

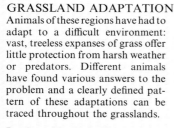

Skylark
Alauda arvensis

Tawny eagle
Aquila rapax

Red-tailed hawk
Buteo jamaicensis

Prairie falcon
Falco mexicanus

BIRDS OF THE SKY

Burrowing owl
Speotyto cunicularia

Western meadowlark
Sturnella neglecta

Sage grouse
Centrocercus urophasianus

Black grouse
Lyurus tetrix

GROUND BIRDS

Lubber grasshopper
Romalea microptera

Tumble bug
Canthonlaevis drury

Common earthworm
Lumbricus terrestris

Praying mantis
Mantis religiosa

INSECTS AND OTHER INVERTEBRATES

A typical cross-section, based on the North American prairies, shows temperate grasslands in relation to rainfall. Annual rainfall determines the depth of the permanently moist subsoil, which in turn dictates the length to which grass roots can grow. Tall grasses have deep root systems and need a considerable depth of moist subsoil. As the rainfall decreases, they gradually give way to shorter grass species. Short grasses require less water and their shallower roots are well suited to drier regions. On dry margins, desert plants start to dominate, and on the wet margins, trees appear.

Tall-grass prairies

cm	ft
215	7
180	6
150	5
120	4
90	3
60	2
30	1
0	0

Annual Rainfall	
mm	in
1,250	50
1,000	40
750	30
500	20
250	10

Annual Rainfall	
mm	in
1,250	50
1,000	40
750	30
500	20
250	10

Another major type of animal found in the temperate grasslands, and one that is better adapted to survive man's activities, is the small, burrowing animal, for example the prairie dog and the gopher of North America, the viscacha of South America and the little ground squirrel known as the souslik in Eurasia.

Unlike the large herd animals, these creatures tend not to migrate. Many of them live together in complex, permanent, underground communities. The colonial "townships" of the prairie dog, for example, may house more than one million individuals, which each year excavate vast quantities of the grassland soil. This has considerable effect upon the structure of the soil. By bringing up earth from lower layers to the surface, these animals are responsible for changing the mineral content of certain areas of topsoil. This then encourages isolated pockets of different plant species to flourish.

A third group of grassland animals, consisting of insects and other invertebrates such as earthworms, has an even more important effect upon the soil. They live in or on the soil and play a vital role in maintaining grassland fertility. These creatures may be herbivores, carnivores or primary (first-stage) decomposers (which break down such material as dead grass and animal remains). These three types of activity allow a complete range of organic matter to be processed and incorporated into the earth, where it is further broken down by the second-stage decomposers, the countless millions of soil bacteria. In this way nutrients continuously flow back to the earth and restore its fertility.

Fertile black earths

The topsoil of temperate grassland regions, therefore, contains large amounts of organic material, which is produced every year and is quickly incorporated into the soil. The low and intermittent rainfall and the protective cover of grasses mean that the topsoil undergoes little chemical leaching, a process in which minerals are removed and carried down to lower layers by rainfall percolating through the earth. The soils are thus dark in colour, generally fertile and of the "black earth" type ("chernozem" in Russian) which is, at least at first, capable of producing high yields of crops.

The most suitable and most widely grown crops are, predictably, the cultivated grasses, and it is these grasses that provide more food for mankind (either directly as grain or indirectly as animal fodder) than any other source. The temperate grassland biome is therefore an important agricultural resource. Undisturbed natural grasslands, however, are also valuable resources. They need to be preserved both for the information that they can provide about how complex communities of wildlife function efficiently, and because, as a rich source of genetic material, they hold many of the answers to the major agricultural problems that probably lie ahead for the human race.

Fire plays a major part in fixing and maintaining the natural boundaries of the temperate grasslands, where tree saplings and shrubs are continually attempting to invade (A). Man-made fires are recent phenomena, natural fires have always occurred. In summer, low-pressure systems build up in continental interiors, causing violent electrical storms. The dry sward of summer grass is easily ignited by lightning and fire is quickly spread by wind. Shrubs and saplings are killed or badly damaged by fire, but grasses, with their growing points close to the soil, remain unharmed (B). They may even benefit from this "pruning" and grow more quickly. Some species grow new buds from their underground shoots. Removal of the main shoot may encourage growth of "tillers" (shoots growing out sideways), which then increase the spread of the grasses as they begin to invade the area left vacant by the dead, or slowly recuperating, shrubs (C).

Man and the Temperate Grasslands

The vast areas of temperate grassland lay virtually empty until the end of the eighteenth century. Over the next 125 years they were occupied by millions of people, most of them migrants from overcrowded Europe. By 1914, the grasslands had become the granaries and the stockyards of the world. Today, they are still the most important food-producing regions on Earth and their riches, properly distributed, are the world's first reserve against the possibility of a hungry future for the human race.

The great nineteenth-century migration to the grasslands proved of immense significance to the human race. It meant that, within a single century, the area of productive land available was suddenly enlarged by thousands of millions of hectares. In all of mankind's history, such a thing had never happened before.

But before the grasslands could be occupied a number of major problems had to be solved. First, in order to reach these regions it was almost always necessary to travel deep into the continental interiors, and there were few navigable rivers and no mechanized forms of transportation for early pioneers. Second, with virtually no indigenous population, newcomers had to learn by their mistakes how best to exploit the new and unfamiliar environment. Third, even if settlers succeeded in using the land, they still had to find markets for their produce.

A number of technological developments, however, that took place in the nineteenth century provided the right combination of circumstances for the opening up of the grasslands. The Industrial Revolution in Europe produced the steamship and the railway locomotive, which created both a means of travel to and from these distant parts and an internal transport system for moving produce to ports and markets. It also produced the kind of machinery needed to plough and farm the great new open spaces; it made it possible for one family to cultivate an area 50 times as large as that which most farmers had known in Europe. Industrialization also threw thousands of Europeans out of work, and therefore provided a large supply of eager migrants. And it crowded further thousands into cities, thus creating vast markets for the settlers' produce.

It was the coming together of these various circumstances that acted as the catalyst and converted, for example, the Russian penetration of the Eurasian steppes in the late eighteenth

THE CRADLE OF AGRICULTURE

Stands of wild einkorn (A), emmer wheat (B) and wild barleys can be seen today in the grassy foothills that flank the Taurus and the Zagros mountains, and the uplands of northern Israel. It was in this region 10,000 years ago that the world's earliest farmers gathered seeds from these species and sowed the first crops. Wild einkorn is probably the oldest of all wheats and the parent of every modern variety—including the most important and most widely grown kind of grain in the world today, common bread wheat (C).

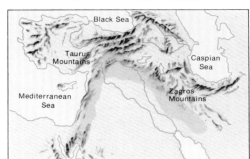

GRASSLAND EXPLOITATION

Today, temperate grasslands provide mankind with a superabundance of food. But the vast potential of these regions was not exploited until the mid-19th century, when mass migration by Europeans, combined with new technology, allowed full-scale development and settlement.

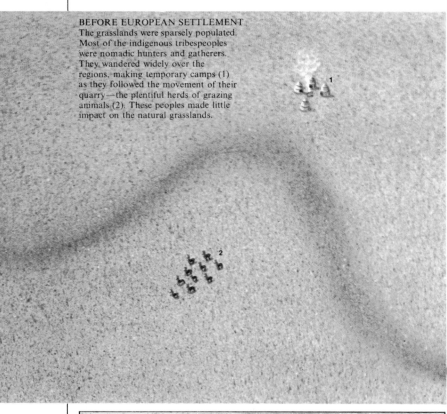

BEFORE EUROPEAN SETTLEMENT
The grasslands were sparsely populated. Most of the indigenous tribespeoples were nomadic hunters and gatherers. They wandered widely over the regions, making temporary camps (1) as they followed the movement of their quarry—the plentiful herds of grazing animals (2). These peoples made little impact on the natural grasslands.

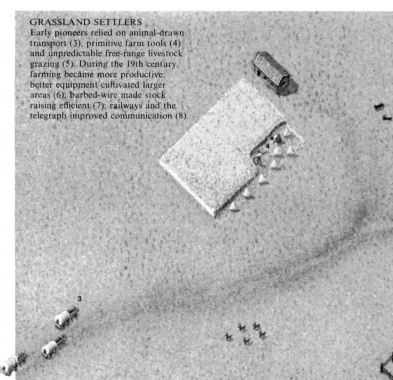

GRASSLAND SETTLERS
Early pioneers relied on animal-drawn transport (3), primitive farm tools (4) and unpredictable free-range livestock grazing (5). During the 19th century, farming became more productive: better equipment cultivated larger areas (6); barbed-wire made stock raising efficient (7); railways and the telegraph improved communication (8).

Tehuelche Indians (above) adopted horses for hunting from early Spanish settlers to the pampas. In South Africa and North America, too, the introduced horse became a valued asset for grassland hunters. For people of the Eurasian steppes, for example the Mongols (right), native horses have always been culturally important.

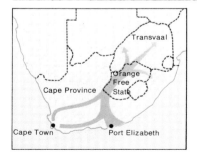

The **South African veld** was first settled by Europeans after 1836 (left). Dutch farmers (Boers), rejecting British rule of the Cape Colony, trekked north in search of new land. Moving into the Transvaal they discovered rich grassland, recently emptied of its original inhabitants, who had fled to escape the aggressive attentions of neighbouring Zulus.

Vaqueros were the original cowboys (left). Tending herds of cattle for the missionaries in 18th-century California, they developed techniques and traditions that served hundreds of later cowboys working the prairie ranges. In other grassland regions, as free-range stock raising became important, similar "cowboy" professions evolved—the Australian stockman and the gaucho of South America.

century into the explosive movement of hundreds of thousands of settlers a few years later. In the USA, too, by the year 1850, settlement had reached and then rapidly crossed the Mississippi. In the Argentine, genuine colonization of the pampas had begun, in South Africa, the Boers had reached the high veld, and in Australia pioneer settlers were moving outwards from the various areas of coastal settlement into the scrub grasslands of the interior.

Farmers or ranchers?

The fundamental question posed for these settlers was whether their newly found land should be used for crops or for livestock. Most grasslands have a dry edge and a wet edge, and it was therefore sensible to use the drier parts for stock raising and the wetter parts for cultivation. But the question was complicated by the fact that most of the newcomers were cultivators, and also that the line dividing dry from wet was vague—worse, it shifted from year to year.

Early attempts to define the dividing line tended to be ignored by the settlers themselves, and they pushed the limit of cultivation into areas where ploughing the soil led to its destruction. Several generations of farmers had to learn this bitter lesson, and they learned only slowly: the worst disasters on the American grasslands occurred in the 1930s and created the infamous

Dust Bowl region in the dry grasslands of the Mid-West. Similarly, the Soviet Virgin Lands Programme for growing cereals on the dry steppes was established in 1954 and is still experiencing difficulties.

Special methods are required both for farming and for ranching the grasslands successfully. Farming has to take account of the open, treeless surface, the scanty and variable rainfall and the comparatively shallow topsoil. To minimize the risk of soil erosion, farmers plant windbreaks, plough fields along the contour, and protect the soil with a covering of the previous year's stubble and by planting cover crops in rotation with cereals. Ranchers, too, have learned to live with variable rainfall. They build stock ponds, irrigate areas of fodder crops to be used as a reserve in dry years and avoid overstocking and consequent overgrazing, which destroys the quality of the grass.

Food for the world

Today, the world's principal trading supplies of cereals and meat flow from these lands, over the networks of railway which link the grasslands to mill towns, slaughter yards and ports of shipment such as Adelaide in Australia, Buenos Aires in Argentina and Montreal in Canada. Without these links to large towns, the grasslands would be of little value, for even

today their populations are sparse and the local markets are relatively insignificant.

Throughout most of the world, however, the human population continues to soar and it remains to be seen whether the grasslands can continue to supply these growing numbers with food. Undoubtedly, the output of cereals and meat can be increased, although at considerable cost in fertilizers, new crop strains, more irrigation and more machines. On the other hand, the problem at present is not mainly one of production, nor will it be in the near future. The land can produce more, but there is no point in doing so unless the yields can be made available where they are most needed.

The world's hungry people live in other regions, many of them in countries that are unable to afford imported food supplies, particularly during those years when prices are high. The major importers of temperate grassland produce are the rich industrialized nations, such as those of western Europe. Furthermore, much of the grain imported by these countries is not consumed by humans but used to feed stalled, beef-producing cattle—a highly inefficient way of using these supplies. Consequently, unless producer nations and wealthy importing nations can create a system for produce to reach those in need of it, extra output from the grasslands will be irrelevant.

9

MODERN-DAY FARMING
Livestock feed on carefully selected grasses, which are sown and fertilized by aircraft (9). Fodder crops are grown as reserve animal feed (10), and stock ponds ensure against drought (11). Feedlots (12) fatten stock on grain (13). Cereal farms (14) are highly mechanized, and road and rail serve even the remotest regions (15).

The steam-driven plough (below) went through many developments to reduce its unwieldiness and heaviness. The version produced in 1858 used a traction engine and pulley wheel system. The plough was drawn back and forth between these by a power-driven cable. This design was, however, superseded by the steam tractor, which, although unsuited to small European fields, was ideal for drawing multi-furrow ploughs across the grasslands.

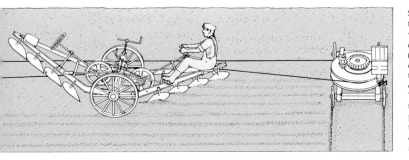

Sand-smothered farms in the heart of the Dust Bowl were rapidly abandoned during the 1930s and 40s (above). This was one costly lesson that man had to learn in the process of developing the grasslands. Traditionally grazing land, the western part of the prairies was first ploughed this century. Years of drought arrived, crops died and the desert encroached.

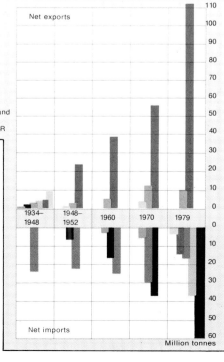

World grain-trading regions

Africa

North America

South America

Asia

Western Europe

Australia and New Zealand

Eastern Europe and USSR

World cereal supplies flow from temperate grasslands (right). North America is the most important producing region, for although almost all nations produce grain, few can grow enough to feed their populations and even fewer have any surplus to export or hold in reserve against poor harvests. But North America, with its prairie cornfields and its small population, exports many millions of tonnes.

Net exports

110
100
90
80
70
60
50
40
30
20
10
0

1934–1948   1948–1952   1960   1970   1979

0
10
20
30
40
50
60

Net imports   Million tonnes

Deserts

Much of the Earth's land surface is so short of water that it is defined as desert. Not all deserts are hot, sandy wastelands; some are cold, some are rocky, but all lack moisture for most of the year. Even so, a surprising variety of plants and animals have adapted to these hostile environments. Plants have developed ingenious ways of surviving long periods of drought, and many desert animals shelter during the intense heat of the day, emerging only at night to feed.

LIFE IN THE DESERT
The overriding need to obtain and conserve water dictates the pattern of desert life. Many plants close their pores during the day and most daytime creatures limit their activity to early morning and late afternoon. At night the temperature drops sharply and dew provides welcome moisture. Some plants bloom at night, and the desert is alive with insects, night-hunting birds, reptiles and small mammals.

DESERTS BY DAY

Many birds are at home in the desert. The lanner falcon of Africa and Asia gets all the moisture it needs from its diet of small birds and rodents. Sandgrouse live in the open deserts of Eurasia and North Africa; mainly seed-eaters, they must make long flights each day to find water. Roadrunners, in American deserts, hunt insects, lizards and small rattlesnakes.

Lanner falcon
Falco biarmicus

Pallas's sandgrouse
Syrrhaptes paradoxus

Roadrunner
Geococcyx californianus

Large mammals are nomadic and obtain most of the moisture they need from plants. Camels can go for long periods without food or water because their humped back stores fat which can be drawn on when food is scarce, and water stored in their body tissues prevents dehydration. Addax antelopes survive entirely on plants. They roam remote parts of the Sahara, their broad hooves enabling them to travel easily over soft sand. Gazelles rely on speed. Small and fleet-footed, they are able to disperse quickly over great distances to find food and water.

Arabian camel
Camelus dromedarius

Asian camel
Camelus bactrianus

Addax antelope
Addax nasomaculatus

Dorcas gazelle
Gazella dorcas

Insects and reptiles are well adapted to desert life. Desert locusts, when overpopulation threatens their food supply, change from a solitary to a swarming migratory form. Harvester ants store seeds against times of drought; desert tortoises withstand drought by becoming torpid. Lizards are cold-blooded and need the sun to warm them, but must shelter from the intense heat of midday. The thorny devil, a small Australian ant-eating lizard, is protected from potential predators by its prickly scales.

Desert locust
Schistocerca gregaria

swarming adult

solitary hopper

Harvester ants
Pogonomyrmex sp

Desert tortoise
Gopherus polyphemus

Gridiron-tailed lizard
Callisaurus draconoides

Thorny devil
Moloch horridus

Desert plants have evolved various ways of coping successfully with drought. The ocotillo of southwestern America sheds its leaves, reducing its need for water. Euphorbias, and cacti such as the prickly pear, store water in their stems. Blue kleinia, a South African succulent, has a waxy coating that limits water loss. Agaves mature very slowly, building up reserves of food and water in their leaves before they flower. Esparto, a needlegrass, is typical of many desert grasses.

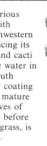

Ocotillo
Fouquieria splendens

Euphorbia
Euphorbia obesa

Prickly pear
Opuntia ficus-indica

Blue kleinia
Senecio articulatus

Agave
Agave americana

Deserts occur where rainfall is low and infrequent and where any moisture quickly evaporates or disappears instantly into the parched ground. In the driest deserts, rainfall rarely exceeds 100 mm (4 in) a year, and is so unreliable that some places may have no rain for 10 years or more. These are deserts in the truest sense of the word: harsh wildernesses that are almost totally without life. Regions with less than 255 mm (10 in) of rain a year are generally classified as arid and those with less than 380 mm (15 in) as semi-arid.

Hot deserts have very high daytime temperatures in summer, although they drop sharply at night, and the winters are relatively mild. In the so-called cold deserts the summers are hot but the winters are so cold that temperatures may fall as low as −30°C (−22°F).

Desert climates and landscapes
In the subtropical latitudes, swept by hot, drying winds, high-pressure weather systems prevent rain clouds from forming. In these regions, rain comes only from local storms or follows low-pressure weather systems (often seasonal) when they move in across the desert. Large areas of central Asia have become desert because they are so far from the sea that clouds have shed all their rain before they reach them. Other deserts occur because mountains cut them off from moisture-bearing winds. The Andes, for example, shelter the drylands of Argentina, and a high sierra stops rain from reaching the Mojave and Great Basin deserts of North America. Rain is also rare on the western sides of continents where cold ocean currents flow from the polar regions towards the Equator.

Desert climates vary not only from place to place but also with time. Over short periods rainfall is much less predictable than it is in temperate regions and droughts are frequent. Some droughts, such as those that occur along the southern fringe of the Sahara, are so severe that it may seem that the climate has changed permanently. But most droughts are short-lived and are followed by years of normal (although sparse) rainfall. Over longer periods of time, however, desert climates do change. Prehistoric cave drawings in the Saharan highlands, for example, show that elephants, rhinoceroses and even hippopotamuses—animals that are at home in wetter climates—lived in these now dry, barren uplands in a more moist period between 7,000 and 4,000 years ago.

Desert landscapes also vary enormously. They are as contrasted as the Colorado canyon country of the United States and the sandy wastes of the Middle East, but most include one or more of several basic features: steep, rocky mountain slopes, broad plains, basin floors dominated by dry lake beds or sand seas, and canyon-like valleys. In low-lying areas, evaporation sometimes leaves a glistening residue of salt. Where there is soil, it is often sandy or consists of little more than fragmented rock, and because plant life is usually sparse there is little or no humus to enrich the ground.

Where water is life
Plant growth depends on water, and desert plants are usually widely spaced to reduce competition for what little moisture is available. Many plants rely on short, sharp rainstorms; others make use of dew and grow in locations, such as crevices in rocks, where water can accumulate. Some complete their life cycle in a single wet season, producing seeds that lie dormant during the following drought and germinate only when enough moisture is available for them to grow. These are the ephemerals that carpet the desert with a brief but brilliant display of flowers shortly after rain has fallen.

Most desert plants, however, are able to tolerate or resist drought. These are the xerophytes ("dry plants") and phreatophytes ("deep-water plants"). Xerophytic trees and shrubs have a wide-spreading network of shallow roots that take in water from a large area of ground. Many xerophytes also limit the amount of water

Esparto grass
Stipa tenacissima

Adaptations to desert life: kangaroo rats, jerboas and gerbils (A) make prodigious leaps with their long back legs to escape predators, and some desert lizards (B) run at high speed on their hind legs when pursued, using their tail for balance. Spadefoot toads have scoop-like hind feet with which they dig burrows to avoid the intense heat of day. Skinks use flattened toes fringed with scales to "swim" through the sand. Fan-toed geckos have toes that spread into fans at the tips, enabling them to walk easily on sand dunes, and the Namib palmate gecko has webbed feet that support it on loose sand.

The saguaro dominates the desert landscapes of Mexico and southern America. Immensely slow growing, it can take 200 years to reach its full height, and more than four-fifths of its weight may be water stored in its stem to be used in times of drought. To minimize water loss, it opens its pores only at night to absorb carbon dioxide and to help radiate heat accumulated by day.

Five great arid regions are bordered by semi-arid steppe and scrub. Cold deserts—the Gobi in central Asia, the Great Basin in North America and the Patagonian Desert in South America—lie in the higher latitudes. Cold ocean currents also affect climate, causing fogs to form over coastal deserts in southwest Africa, South America and Baja California, Mexico.

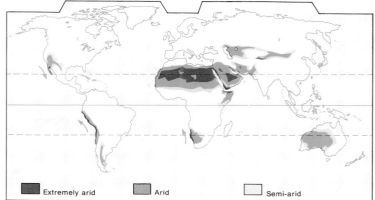

Extremely arid   Arid   Semi-arid

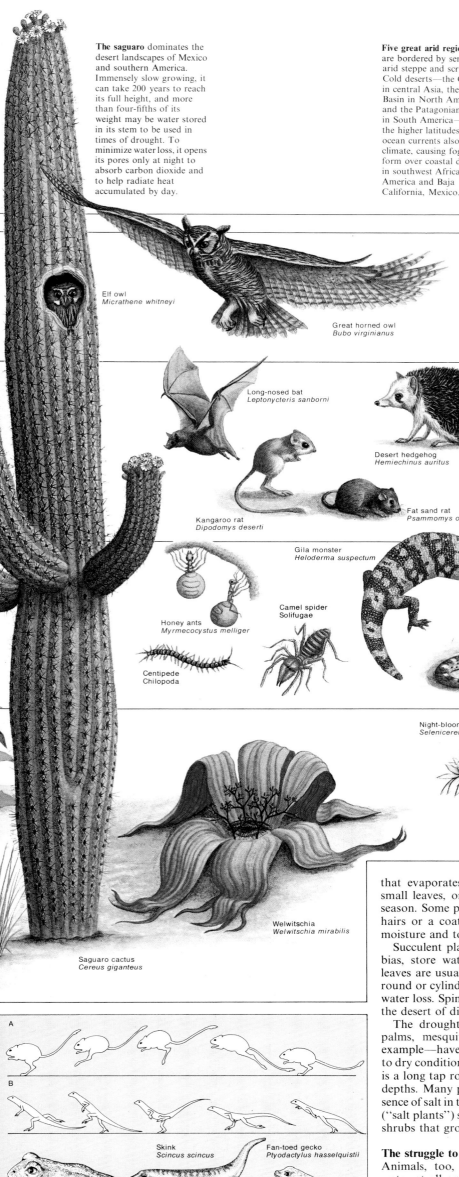

White-throated poorwill
Phalaenoptilus nuttallii

Elf owl
Micrathene whitneyi

Great horned owl
Bubo virginianus

Owls and nightjars hunt under cover of darkness. Elf owls shelter by day, emerging at dusk to catch insects, and great horned owls often come into the desert at night to hunt. The poorwill, a small desert nightjar, is known to American Indians as "the sleeper". An insect-eater, it sometimes survives the rigours of winter, when food is scarce, by hibernating.

Long-nosed bat
Leptonycteris sanborni

Desert hedgehog
Hemiechinus auritus

Kangaroo rat
Dipodomys deserti

Fat sand rat
Psammomys obesus

Fennec fox
Fennecus zerda

Most small animals are active at night. Nectar-eating bats visit plants that blossom at night, pollinating the flowers while they feed. American kangaroo rats obtain water from a dry diet of seeds, and conserve moisture by producing very concentrated urine. The sand rat of North Africa feeds on salty succulents and excretes great quantities of extremely salty urine. Hedgehogs are mainly insect-eaters; the long ears of desert species help to disperse body heat. The Saharan fennec, the smallest type of desert fox, hunts lizards, rodents and locusts.

Gila monster
Heloderma suspectum

Scorpion
Buthus occitanus

Honey ants
Myrmecocystus melliger

Camel spider
Solifugae

Centipede
Chilopoda

Sidewinder rattlesnake
Crotalus cerastes

Darkling beetle
Tenebrionidae

Among insects and other invertebrates the hunt for food intensifies at night. Honey ants gather nectar; centipedes and camel spiders hunt insects. The gila monster, a poisonous American lizard, eats centipedes, eggs and sometimes other lizards, and uses its tail to store fat. The sidewinder, a small rattlesnake, is active mainly at night, leaving its distinctive parallel tracks in the sand. Scorpions emerge from their burrows to stalk insects and spiders, and darkling beetles feed on dry, decomposing vegetation.

Night-blooming cereus
Selenicereus spp

Some desert plants are nocturnal, in the sense that they bloom only at night or make use of the dew that forms when the temperature falls. The welwitschia, unique to the Namib Desert in southwest Africa, has broad, sprawling leaves on which moisture condenses at night. The night-blooming cereus of the American deserts flowers for a single night in summer. Like other nocturnal plants, its flowers are luminously pale and strongly scented to attract pollinating night insects.

Welwitschia
Welwitschia mirabilis

Saguaro cactus
Cereus giganteus

A

B

Skink
Scincus scincus

Fan-toed gecko
Ptyodactylus hasselquistii

Palmate gecko
Palmatogecko rangei

Spadefoot toad
Scaphiopus couchi

that evaporates from their leaves by having small leaves, or by shedding them in the dry season. Some produce a protective covering of hairs or a coating of wax to prevent loss of moisture and to help withstand heat.

Succulent plants, such as cacti and euphorbias, store water in their thick stems. Their leaves are usually reduced to spines, and their round or cylindrical shape also helps to reduce water loss. Spines have the added advantage in the desert of discouraging foraging animals.

The drought-resisting phreatophytes—date palms, mesquite and cottonwood trees, for example—have a similar variety of adaptations to dry conditions, but their most typical feature is a long tap root that draws water from great depths. Many plants can also tolerate the presence of salt in the soil. These are the halophytes ("salt plants") such as saltbush and other small shrubs that grow in and around salt pans.

The struggle to survive
Animals, too, need to obtain and conserve water at all costs and to be able to adjust to extremes of temperature. Most are small enough to shelter under stones or in burrows during the intense heat of day; others survive adverse conditions by becoming dormant or by migrating. For most desert creatures it is also an advantage to be inconspicuous, and many are

pale in colour so that they are hard to see against their light background of sand or stones.

Many animals, especially those that are active by day, show adaptations that are strikingly similar to those of desert plants. Frogs and toads are activated by rain, emerging from dormancy to feed and mate in temporary pools and then quickly burying themselves until the next rain falls. Mammals have hairy coats that reduce water loss and also help to keep their body temperature at a tolerable level. Most desert insects have a waxy coating that serves much the same purpose.

Some geckos and other lizards store food, in the form of fat, in their tails, and camels store fat in their humped backs to sustain them when food is scarce. Honey ants force-feed nectar to some members of the colony, creating living "honey pots" for the rest of the community to feed from in times of drought. Many creatures are able to survive on the moisture contained in their food, and rarely need to drink. Most desert-dwellers also have extremely efficient kidneys that produce very concentrated urine, so that little or no moisture is lost in the process.

Man enjoys no such advantages. Nevertheless, he still seeks to live in deserts, as he has for thousands of years, and the pressures he exerts on the environment may well have irrevocably changed much of the world's desert landscapes.

Man and the Deserts

Water is the key to man's survival in deserts: where water has been available, great civilizations have flourished, and man's dream of making the desert bloom has become a reality. More recently, discoveries of great mineral wealth have spurred the opening up of some of Earth's most inhospitable regions. But while man's ingenuity has made many deserts both habitable and productive, the human tendency to increase the extent of deserts has become a problem of international proportions.

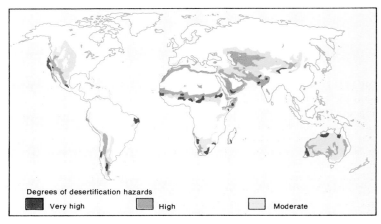

Degrees of desertification hazards

Very high   High   Moderate

Given water, much is possible, and not surprisingly man has tended to settle where water is most readily available: along the courses of rivers (such as the Nile) that rise outside the desert, and around oases fed by springs or by wells that tap groundwater supplies. But desert rainfall is so unreliable that often runoff and spring flow are uncertain in quantity and timing. Much groundwater is either also unreliable or it is fossil water that has accumulated in the geological past and is not being replenished by today's rainfall. Thus in areas such as southern Libya and some of the oasis settlements of the Arabian Gulf, and in America's arid west, groundwater is a non-renewable resource that is being rapidly depleted.

Making water go farther
Man has also used great ingenuity to secure water supplies and to transport them to where they are needed. Runoff from flash floods that follow rare desert storms may be collected in channels and distributed to crops in nearby fields, and terracing slopes to trap runoff is a traditional way of obtaining the maximum benefit from limited rainfall. Reservoirs, ranging from the small night tanks of the southern Atacama desert in Chile to the massive artificial lakes along the Colorado River in the United States, store seasonally or perennially unreliable runoff. Also, surface runoff may be increased by reducing the permeability of runoff surfaces, a

solution engineered by the Nabataeans in the Negev Desert more than 2,000 years ago and being re-employed by the Israelis today.

The transport of water is a fundamental desert activity. Open canals are typical, usually carrying water to irrigated fields—a practice used throughout the fertile crescent of Mesopotamia more than 8,000 years ago and still widespread today. A striking alternative are the ancient qanats, which limit the evaporation of water while it is in transit. Qanats are still found in the Middle East, although today pipelines are increasingly used.

Ultimately, the conversion of salt water to fresh water may ensure plentiful supplies for many desert regions. The process is expensive, but large-scale desalination has already become a reality in some affluent communities such as oil-rich Saudi Arabia and Kuwait. Increasing emphasis is also being placed on more efficient use of existing freshwater supplies: in Egypt and Israel, waste water from towns is being purified and recycled for use in agriculture.

Cultivating the desert
The successful control of water has enabled large areas of otherwise arid and semi-arid land to be made productive. The Egyptian civilization along the Nile depended, and still depends, on the management of seasonal floodwaters. In North America, the large-scale, long-distance piping of water has made central

Desertification—the advance of desert areas across the Earth—now affects more than 30 million sq km (12 million sq miles) and deserts are continuing to expand at an alarming rate. In recent years, on the southern edge

of the Sahara alone, as much as 650,000 sq km (250,900 sq miles) of land that was once productive have been lost, and in places there is little left to show where the Sahara ends and the Sahel–Sudan region begins. Intense and

often inappropriate human pressures are major causes, frequently aggravated by drought: overcultivating vulnerable land, chopping down trees for firewood and grazing too many livestock, especially on the margins of arid lands.

THE SHIFTING SANDS
Recent decades have seen unprecedented changes in the world's deserts. Increasing pressure on the environment, especially from pastoralists and farmers, has caused extensive damage and a rapid expansion of barren land. In many desert regions, nomadism has long been the only way in which man could survive, except in oases. Today, even these traditional ways of life are changing as the exploitation of oil and other mineral resources, and the introduction of new agricultural techniques, are drawing many of the deserts into a spectacular new age of development.

The traditional pastoral response to limited water supplies and forage in desert regions is nomadic livestock herding, still practised by the Tuareg of the northern Sahara (right) and by tribal groupings in Mongolia (left). The nomadic way of life has, however, become severely restricted in recent years. Long-distance migrations are often incompatible with the requirements of the modern state, and the poor rewards no longer match the incentives to settle in towns and cities.

Oases have provided welcome refuges in deserts since ancient times. Secure water supplies from wells or springs make settled life possible in the midst of the most arid landscapes. Many oases are intensively cultivated with three tiers of vegetation: tall date palms shade orchards of citrus fruits, apricots, peaches, pomegranates and figs, and both palms and orchard trees shade the ground crops of vegetables and cereals. Irrigation channels distribute water to the desert soils, which are frequently rich in plant foods although they lack humus. Windbreaks help to protect cultivated land from erosion and from migrating dunes, although many oases are losing the battle with encroaching sands and the oasis people are leaving to find work in the oil fields.

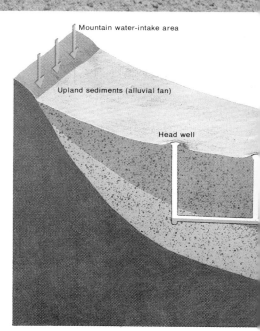

Mountain water-intake area

Upland sediments (alluvial fan)

Head well

California the most productive agricultural region in the world. But while irrigation can bring enormous benefits, it can also create problems. Too much water causes waterlogging of the land, and where water evaporates in the dry desert air concentrations of dissolved salts build up in the soil.

Farming without irrigation is possible only where rainfall, although meagre, is sufficient to sustain crops with a short growing season. Soil moisture is conserved by using dry surface mulches, by fallowing and crop rotation, by planting seeds sparsely and by controlling weeds. Geneticists are also producing new varieties of cereal crops that can survive for weeks without water. Dry farming, however, is precarious. Especially at times of drought it can cause serious problems of soil erosion, chiefly by the action of wind.

Man the desert maker

The extension of dry farming into unsuitable regions, and waterlogging and the accumulation of salts in irrigated areas, are major causes of desertification—the spread of deserts into formerly habitable land. Other major causes are the overgrazing of livestock on land with too little forage, and the removal of trees and shrubs for firewood by communities that have no alternative fuel supply. A sequence of drier than normal years does the rest.

Many scientists believe that desertification can be reversed, provided the pressures on the land are reduced sufficiently to allow vegetation to recover. But desertification affects such huge areas, often straddling national frontiers, that broad-scale, international co-operation is needed to co-ordinate reductions in population and livestock pressures and to improve understanding of drought.

In some countries the battle against desertification has already begun. In China, extensive

planting of drought-tolerant trees has created windbreaks to control sand movement and to protect farmland. In Algeria a broad belt of trees has been planted to keep the Sahara at bay, and in Iran advancing dunes have been halted by spraying them with petroleum residue: when the spray dries it forms a mulch that retains moisture and allows vegetation to grow, and much desert land has been reclaimed.

The deserts' riches

The exploitation of resources has also led to an "opening up" of many deserts. The rushes for precious metals in Arizona, Australia and South Africa started man's development of these regions in the nineteenth century. Some minerals, such as the evaporite deposits of Searles Basin in California and the nitrates of the Atacama desert in Chile, are actually products of the arid environment.

A resource that deserts also possess in abundance is solar power, and in many hot, dry regions the heat of the sun is used to evaporate mineral-rich solutions of salts, as well as being harnessed as a source of energy. Sunshine and the dry, clear air are also drawing ever-increasing numbers of tourists to the "sun cities" of the western United States and to Saharan oases, which were, until recently, only remote desert outposts.

No resource, however, has created as much attention or wealth as has oil. Oil has transformed the fortunes of several desert nations and provided an economic boom that has led to rapid industrialization and spectacular urban growth. The benefits of such growth in terms of affluence are substantial. The problems—the weakening of traditional desert societies, the submerging of traditional cities in the concrete labyrinths of modern complexes, and the precariousness of prosperity that is based on finite resources—are also clear.

Mineral wealth provides a powerful incentive for man's development of arid lands, and today the flow of oil rather than water is often a measure of a desert nation's prosperity. In some of the world's most desolate regions, flares signal the presence of modern "oases" where fossil fuels are being extracted—products, like the fossil waters that are sometimes trapped in the same sedimentary rocks, of the desert's geological past. Uranium, another mineral "fuel", also often lies beneath desert sands. Arid environments may also provide a rich harvest of other minerals: potash, phosphates and nitrates, valuable sources of commercial fertilizers; gypsum, manganese and salt; and borax, source of the element boron, used in nuclear reactors.

A "plastic" revolution has helped transform much of Israel's desert hinterland into productive farmland. Plastic cloches, plastic mulches and greenhouses trap moisture and reduce evaporation, and water trickled through thin plastic tubes irrigates the plants' roots with a minimum of wastage. Such innovative agricultural techniques enable Israel to produce most of its own food requirements, and fruit and vegetables grown in the relatively mild desert winters are also exported to Europe, where they command high prices.

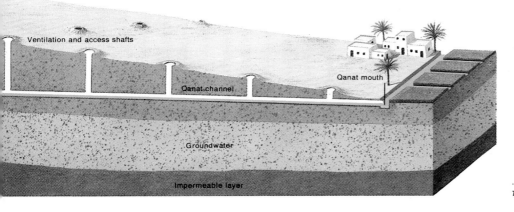

One of the most ingenious ways man has devised of bringing water to desert regions is by the ancient underground system known as the qanat. Invented by the Persians in the first millennium BC, qanats tap groundwater in upland sediments and carry it by gravity to the surface on lower land. The head well is dug first, sometimes to a depth of 100 m (330 ft), until water is reached. A line of shafts is then sunk to provide ventilation and to give access to the channel being tunnelled below. Work begins at the mouth end, and a typical channel is 10–20 km (6–12 miles) long when completed, depending on the depth of the head well and the slope of the land. Its slight gradient ensures that water flows freely but gently down to ground level. Surface canals then divert the water to where it is needed. Thousands of such qanats are still in use, their routes marked by mounds of excavated debris.

Ventilation and access shafts

Qanat mouth

Qanat channel

Groundwater

Impermeable layer

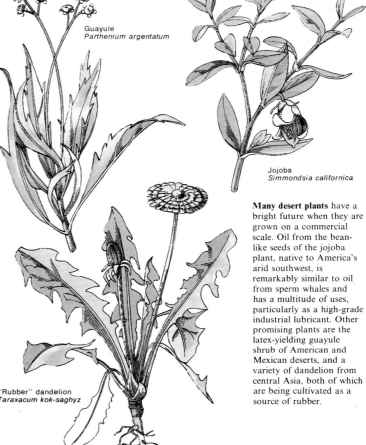

Guayule
Parthenium argentatum

Jojoba
Simmondsia californica

"Rubber" dandelion
Taraxacum kok-saghyz

Many desert plants have a bright future when they are grown on a commercial scale. Oil from the bean-like seeds of the jojoba plant, native to America's arid southwest, is remarkably similar to oil from sperm whales and has a multitude of uses, particularly as a high-grade industrial lubricant. Other promising plants are the latex-yielding guayule shrub of American and Mexican deserts, and a variety of dandelion from central Asia, both of which are being cultivated as a source of rubber.

Savannas

Between the tropical rainforest and desert regions lie large stretches of savanna, which are characterized by seasonal rainfall and long periods of drought. Those nearest to the forests usually take the form of open woodland, whereas those nearest the deserts consist of widely scattered thorn scrub or tufts of grass. Unlike temperate grasslands, where the summers are hot but the winters are cold, savanna regions are always warm and in the wet season rain falls in heavy tropical downpours.

The most extensive areas of savanna are in Africa, north and south of the rainforest, and in South America, where the two main regions are the *llanos* of Venezuela, north of the Amazon rainforest, and the *campos* of Brazil in the south. Smaller areas of savanna also occur in Australia, India and southeastern Asia.

Savannas range from thickly wooded grasslands to almost treeless plains. Some are the result of man's destruction of the forest, and most are maintained in their present state by the high incidence of fire, both natural and man-made. The grasses tend to be taller and coarser than their temperate counterparts and they grow in tufts rather than as a uniform ground cover. In areas of high rainfall some grasses grow up to 4.5 m (15 ft) tall. Trees and bushes are usually widely spaced so that they do not compete with each other for water in the dry season. Humid, or moist, savannas experience 3 to 5 dry months a year, dry savannas 6 to 7 months, and thornbush savannas 8 to 10 months. Rainfall also varies widely, from more than 1,200 mm (47 in) a year in humid savannas to as little as 200 mm (8 in) where the savanna merges into desert.

Types of savannas

Humid woodland savanna presents an abrupt contrast to the rainforest. Trees tend to be scattered and some are so low-growing that they are dwarfed by the tall grass that springs up during the summer rains. In the dry season the grass fuels fierce fires, which destroy all except thick-barked, large-leaved deciduous trees. Consequently, the proportion of fire-resistant trees and shrubs is large, and the grass quickly regenerates with the coming of the next rains.

In Africa this type of savanna is known as Guinea savanna north of the rainforest and as miombo savanna south of the rainforest. In South America it is known as *campo cerrado*, from the Portuguese words meaning field (*campo*) and dense. (*Campos sujos* are *campos* in which stretches of open grassland predominate and *campos limpos* are grasslands from which trees are entirely absent.) The *llanos*, or plains, of northern South America are grasslands interspersed with forests and swamps.

North of the Guinea savanna in Africa lies a belt known as Sudan savanna. The annual rainfall is in the range 500 to 1,000 mm (20–40 in) and the dry season lasts from October to April. This is typical dry savanna. Tall grasses between 1 and 1.5 m (3–5 ft) form an almost continuous ground cover and acacias and other thorny trees dot the landscape, together with branching dôm palms and massive water-storing baobab trees. Because of the interrupted tree cover the old name given to many savannas of this type was orchard steppe, and this description gives a good idea of the countryside. Like the humid woodland savannas it is maintained by regular burning of the grass in the dry season, and there is a delicate

balance and interaction between climate, soil, vegetation, animals and fire. On the desert margins the grasses grow in short tufts and the scattered acacias are seldom more than 3 m (10 ft) tall. The scrub and grasses are too widely dispersed for fires to spread, and this type of savanna is modified not by fire but by aridity and blistering heat.

Thorn-scrub and thorn-forest savannas frequently form transitional zones between tropical forests and grasslands. The *caatinga*, or "light forest", of northeastern Brazil is a typical thorn-forest savanna. Long, hot, dry seasons alternate with erratic downpours of rain, and the rate of evaporation is high. Drought-resisting trees and thorny shrubs mix with bromeliads, cacti and palm trees.

Abundance of life

No other environment supports animals so spectacular in size and so immense in numbers as do the African savannas. In spite of the concentration of animal life, however, competition for food is not severe. Each species has its own preferences and feeds from different levels of the vegetation. Giraffes and elephants can easily reach the upper branches of trees, antelopes feed on bushes at different heights from the ground, zebras and impalas eat the grasses and warthogs root for the underground parts of plants. With the onset of the dry season, massed herds assemble for the great migrations that are a major part of savanna life, moving to areas where rain has recently fallen and new grass is plentiful.

Following the grazing animals are the large predators: the lions, leopards and cheetahs. Wild dogs hunt in packs, and the scavengers—jackals, hyenas and vultures—move in to dispose of the remains of the kill.

The savannas of South America and Australia are much poorer in animal species. The only mammal of any size on the South American savanna is the elusive, nocturnal maned wolf, which eats almost anything from small animals to wild fruit. On the Australian savanna the largest inhabitant is the kangaroo, and the prime predator—apart from man—is the dingo, or native dog.

Many of the resident savanna birds are ground-living species such as the ostrich in Africa and its counterparts, the rhea in South America and the emu in Australia. The warm African climate attracts large numbers of visiting birds, which migrate each year across the Sahara to escape from the severe winter of the northern hemisphere.

For many thousands of years man has lived in harmony with the savanna. Within the last century, however, and in recent decades in particular, the savanna has come under increasing pressure. Inevitably, there is competition between the needs of the environment and those of the human population, and the future of the savanna is very much in the balance.

On each side of the Equator are broad tracts of tropical grassland known as savannas. In these regions there are distinct wet and dry seasons and temperatures are high all the year round, seldom falling below 21°C (70°F). Rain falls mainly in the hottest months, whereas the cooler months are generally dry. Thorn-scrub and thorn-forest savannas occur where the rainfall is more erratic; they have relatively little grass cover, and trees and bushes can tolerate long periods of drought.

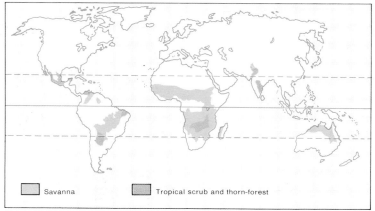

Savanna | Tropical scrub and thorn-forest

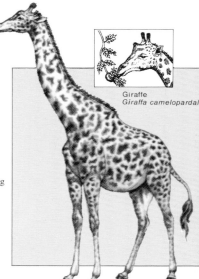

Giraffe
Giraffa camelopardalis

THE PLANT-EATERS
Most plant-eaters have adapted to feeding at a particular level of the vegetation. Giraffes browse on acacia tips that other animals cannot reach and elephants use their trunks to tear down succulent branches and leaves, although both feed on low-growing vegetation when it is easily available. Elephants will also uproot trees to gather leaves that are otherwise out of reach. The black rhinoceros plucks low-growing twigs and leaves by grasping them with its upper lip (the white rhinoceros has a broad, square mouth for grazing on grass). Eland often use their horns to collect twigs by twisting and breaking them. Zebra, wildebeest, topi and gazelle all graze on the same grasses, but at different stages of the plants' growth.

HUNTERS OF THE PLAINS
The plant-eaters provide rich hunting for the carnivores. Lions kill the largest prey and hunt in family groups; the lioness usually makes the kill but the male is the first to eat. The leopard is a solitary hunter. It lies in ambush or stalks its prey, mainly at night, in brush country where it has ground cover. Cheetahs are the swiftest of all the hunters. They usually hunt in pairs in open grassland, stalking their prey and then charging in a lightning-fast sprint. Hunting dogs travel in well organized packs. They exhaust their quarry by chasing it to a standstill and attacking as a team. Whereas lions, leopards and cheetahs usually kill by leaping for the neck or throat, packs of hunting dogs characteristically attack from the rear.

Lion
Panthera leo

THE SCAVENGERS
When the hunters have eaten, the scavengers move in. Jackals, small and quick, make darting runs to snatch tit-bits while packs of hyenas use their powerful bone-crushing jaws to demolish the bulk of the carcass. Hyenas are the most voracious of the carnivores, often driving the primary predator from its kill. Vultures are frequently the first to see a kill as they circle high in the sky, but must await their turn to feed on the skin and scraps because their descent attracts the more aggressive scavengers. Carrion beetles, carrion flies and the larvae of the horn-boring moth dispose of what is left. Most of the large scavengers, particularly the hyenas, also do their own hunting, singling out prey that is small, weak or sickly.

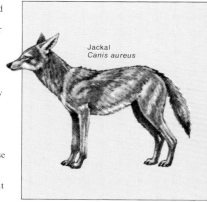

Jackal
Canis aureus

Plants in the savanna are remarkably well adapted to withstand drought, fire and the onslaughts of the animals that eat them. Acacias tolerate both drought and fire, and are armed with sharp thorns—although many animals do feed on them, thorns and all. Red oat grass survives fire because its seeds twist deep into the ground. Bermuda, or saw-tooth, grass is a favourite food of many grazers, but it recovers quickly from close cropping because its growing point lies too flat against the ground to be eaten.

Acacia
Acacia sp

Red oat grass
Themeda triandra

Bermuda grass
Cynodon dactylon

Zebras

Wildebeest and topi

Gazelles

SAVANNA SWAMPS, LAKES AND MARSHES

Swamps, lakes and marshes are especially characteristic of the African savanna. Many are fringed with papyrus, the paper reed, *Cyperus papyrus* (1) which grows to a height of 3.5 m (12 ft) or more, and most are rich in microscopic organisms that play the same role in the water as grass does on the plains, supporting large numbers of birds and animals. Swamps and marshes also act as natural reservoirs, which collect and hold excess water during the rainy season, and provide welcome dry-season grazing for plains animals when other savanna productivity is at its lowest. The lakes of the Great Rift Valley, which form a chain down the northeastern side of the continent, are also rich with life. Many provide a refuge for crocodiles, their numbers seriously depleted by systematic hunting, and for multitudes of birds, including huge flocks of flamingos.

Many birds and animals have adapted to a semi-aquatic way of life. The shoebill stork *Balaeniceps rex* (2) uses its feet and the hooked tip of its beak to stir up mud and dislodge the frogs, fish and soft-shelled turtles that form the bulk of its diet. The goliath heron *Ardea goliath* (3) is a shallow-water fisher. The sitatunga *Tragelaphus speki* (4) has long, splayed hooves that support its weight on soft mud. It hides by day among reeds on the edge of the swamp and moves to dry ground at night to feed. The jacana, or lily-trotter, *Actophilornis africana* (5) relies on long toes and constant motion to walk on floating plants. The hippopotamus *Hippopotamus amphibius* (6) wallows in the water for most of the day and leaves the swamp at dusk to graze. It helps to fertilize the swamp with the enormous amounts of waste matter it excretes.

Elephant
Loxodonta africana

Black rhinoceros
Diceros bicornis

Eland
Taurotragus oryx

Wildebeest
Connochaetes taurinus

Grant's zebra
Equus quagga boehmi

Topi
Damaliscus lunatus topi

Thomson's gazelle
Gazella thomsoni

Cheetah
Acinonyx jubatus

Leopard
Panthera pardus

Cape hunting dog
Lycaon pictus

White-backed vulture
Pseudogyps africanus

Carrion beetle

Carrion fly

Spotted hyena
Crocuta crocuta

Horn-boring moth larva

Ostrich
Struthio camelus

Secretary bird
Sagittarius serpentarius

LONG-LEGGED BIRDS

The ostrich, up to 2.4 m (8 ft) tall, can see for great distances across the plains and can outrun most of its enemies. Its territory is often shared with grazing animals, such as wildebeest, which take advantage of the ostrich's keen sight to alert them to danger. The secretary bird (so-called because of its quill-like crest) strides through the grass hunting small mammals, insects and snakes; it kills snakes by battering them with its powerful, long-clawed feet.

Large termite mounds
are a distinctive feature of many savanna landscapes. The mounds, or termitaria, are made of soil excavated by the termites and bound with their saliva. Thick walls help to keep the interior at a constant temperature, and some species of termite cultivate fungus "gardens" as a source of food. The royal chamber deep inside the mound is occupied by the colony's queen, grossly distended with eggs, and her consort. Predators include the aardwolf and the aardvark. The aardwolf is related to the hyena but is smaller and has weak jaws; it digs the termites out of their mound and scoops them up with its long sticky tongue. The aardvark, distantly related to the elephant, uses its powerful hoof-like claws to break into termite nests.

Aardwolf
Proteles cristatus

Aardvark
Orycteropus afer

Man and the Savannas

In their natural state, savannas are among the most strikingly productive of all Earth's regions. Before the coming of man they supported a wealth of animal life that has seldom been surpassed. As yet they are relatively undeveloped, but many of them lie in areas where the pressures of population growth are becoming increasingly acute. Wisely used, they offer great hope for the future, both as cattle lands and for the cultivation of food crops. But without proper management savannas can rapidly turn into wasteland, and man will be the poorer for the loss of such a great natural resource.

Throughout much of the savannas the climate is semi-arid and the soils tend to be poor: stripped of their plant cover, they bake hard and crack during the long months of hot sunshine, and during the wet season they often become waterlogged or are washed away by the rains. Man's indiscriminate use of fire, unwise agricultural methods and the unrestricted grazing of domestic animals have already led to much soil loss, and erosion is widespread in tropical Africa, Asia, South America and Australia.

Systematic burning has long been practised by the people of the savannas. Large areas are burned each year to clear land for agriculture or to remove dead grass and encourage a fresh growth to feed livestock. The resulting ash provides much-needed nutrients for crops, and the grasses rapidly produce new green shoots that provide a rich pasture for domestic herds. But although the short-term effects may be beneficial, repeated burning is harmful to the vegetation, the animals and the soil.

Trees are always more or less damaged by fire. Their trunks become twisted and gnarled, fresh shoots are killed and young trees are prevented from growing. Constant burning can destroy some species altogether, and when they disappear so too does the wildlife that depends on them for food and shelter.

Grasses, on the other hand, may be encouraged by burning, and the lush new growth that springs up when the first rains break the long dry season provides welcome nourishment for domestic herds and game animals alike. But whereas game animals move freely over the range, cropping grasses at various stages of growth, cattle tend to feed on grass only in the neighbourhood of wells and other sources of drinking water. They may trample the soil and continue to graze the same area until the grass is completely suppressed.

The hazards of large projects

Cultivation in marginal areas that are unsuited to intensive agriculture also contributes to the impoverishment of the savanna. The Sahel and Sudan savannas on the fringes of the Sahara are particularly vulnerable to large-scale development projects that fail to take account of local climate and soil. Mechanized agriculture in fragile areas bordering the desert may well lead to soil erosion and dustbowl conditions, and large-scale irrigation schemes often result in waterlogging and an accumulation of salts in the soil. Cultivation in the savannas requires understanding and care. Many smaller schemes are safer—and usually more productive—than a few large ones, but not all planners yet realize that agricultural methods that are effective in temperate regions seldom come up to expectations in tropical climates.

Man first inhabited the savannas, as he did many other regions of the world, as a hunter and gatherer. He took from the land only what he needed from day to day, and although he used fire as a hunting tool his impact was little more than that of any other savanna inhabitant. In East Africa, groups of nomadic Hadza (left) still hunt game and collect roots, fruit and the honey of wild bees, building grass huts as temporary shelters.

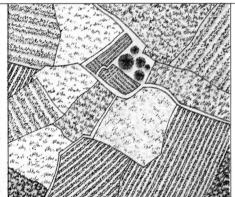

Small farms are scattered over much of the savannas. Plots close to houses are farmed continuously; beyond them lie the main fields, where periods of cultivation are usually followed by periods of fallow. Maize, millet and groundnuts are the main food crops, and early and late crops are sometimes sown on the same plot to extend the growing season. Most of the work is done by hand, and any surplus to a family's needs is sold.

THE VULNERABLE WILDERNESS

Nowhere has man's impact on the tropical grasslands been felt more keenly than in Africa, although much of what is happening in Africa is happening also in savannas elsewhere. The majority of the people still live on the land, where the determining factor is the length and severity of the annual dry season. In the moister savannas the people are primarily cultivators, while in savannas that are too dry to sustain agriculture the main occupation is raising livestock. Most of the savannas are as yet sparsely settled, but competition is inevitably growing between man and wildlife, particularly in Africa, for the remaining tracts of relatively untouched wilderness.

The development of mineral resources and industries has led to an increasing movement of people—mainly young adults—from rural areas to towns and mining centres, attracted by opportunities for work—often at the expense of agriculture, since the heavy work of farming is left to the women, old people and children. Mining enterprises such as those in the Zambian Copper Belt (above), may recruit large labour forces from the surrounding countryside. Mining also dramatically alters the landscape, especially where the bedrock containing the ore reaches the surface and is quarried in huge terraces. The need for electricity to power mining and other industries leads, in turn, to the development of hydro-electric schemes, many of which entail resettling people whose villages are flooded by the creation of large artificial lakes.

Large areas of savanna have been set aside in East and Central Africa, and to a lesser extent in South America and Australia, as national parks and reserves where the landscape is kept intact and animals can be studied in their natural habitats. In Africa, observation platforms are frequently built close to waterholes where animals congregate to drink, and wardens use light aircraft to patrol the vast areas involved. Camel units are also used to patrol near-desert regions where much of the wildlife flourishes. Animals, such as elephants, whose numbers can grow out of control in the protected environment of the reserves are culled by licensed hunters to prevent the vegetation being destroyed. Culling maintains the health of the community as a whole, and is also an economic source of meat in many countries where the people are short of protein foods.

Similarly, the introduction of European breeds of cattle into the savannas has not been an unqualified success. Not only are these breeds more susceptible to tropical pests and diseases than are the local varieties, but they are also adversely affected by the hot climate and their productivity is greatly reduced. In Africa and Brazil, native breeds are replacing more recent importations, and their productivity is being enhanced by selective breeding. In Australia, where most of the cattle are of British stock, tropical zebu, or humped cattle, are being introduced into the herds.

In the future, much more of the savanna may be developed as ranch lands, because the temperate grasslands will become less able to support enough animals to satisfy the world demand for meat. The *llanos* of Venezuela, the *campos* of Brazil and the tropical grasslands of Argentina and Australia already carry large herds of beef cattle. Throughout the savannas, however, ranching is still hampered by lack of water, poor natural pasture and remoteness from markets. In Africa, where herding is mainly nomadic, the sinking of wells by government organizations is changing the traditional ways of life, and cattle raising on a commercial scale is likely to become increasingly important. In Africa, too, the conservation and controlled cropping of game animals could become one of the most productive—and constructive—forms of land use.

Game as a resource
The value of game animals as a source of food is considerable. Buffaloes, for example, and kangaroos in Australia, can thrive on natural grasses that will not even maintain the weight of domestic stock, and they show greater gains in weight than African and European cattle on most forms of vegetation, while several species of antelopes can survive on a water ration that is wholly inadequate for cattle.

In recent years attention has been directed towards the economics of controlled cropping of wild game, and of ranching animals such as eland, which can be kept as if they were domesticated stock and can convert poor pasture into excellent meat. Game animals are also more resistant than cattle to the tsetse fly, which infests large areas of Africa and transmits the disease trypanosomiasis (known as nagana in cattle and as sleeping sickness in man).

But for the most part game animals are still considered to be a nuisance by man, and it is perhaps fortunate that by denying much of the savanna to domestic animals—and to man—the tsetse fly has preserved these regions from exploitation at the expense of the game. Many countries have also set aside large tracts of savanna as national parks and game reserves, where the natural environment is preserved and the wildlife can thrive.

Safeguarding the savanna
At a time when the pressure of the expanding human population calls for the development of areas hitherto uninhabited or only sparsely populated, it may seem paradoxical to maintain that the development of national parks and nature reserves is essential to the welfare of mankind. The aim of game conservation, however, is not simply to preserve rare or unusual animals for the enjoyment of posterity, or even for their scientific interest. It is to ensure that the land is put to its most economic and efficient use. The next few decades will show whether the savannas of the world will be developed into major sources of food and revenue for the countries that own them, or whether they will be misused and degraded into desert.

Commercial agriculture is important to the economies of many savanna countries. Cotton and coffee are major cash crops in Africa and Brazil, together with maize, tobacco, sisal and groundnuts—crops that need a cycle of wet and dry seasons and year-round warmth. But large-scale cultivation of one crop tends to attract pests and diseases, and dependence on a single crop makes the economy vulnerable to fluctuating world prices.

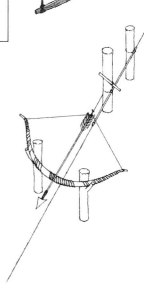

Cattle rearing takes the place of cultivation in areas that are too dry to be cropped successfully. In Africa, people such as the Masai are nomadic herders, moving their cattle long distances in search of pasture. Wealth is counted in terms of the numbers rather than the quality of the cattle they own, but improved management of their herds and better control of animal diseases are now making their cattle much more productive.

SAVANNA FIRES
Fires have been sweeping the savannas for thousands of years. Hunters set fires to flush game from cover, farmers use fire to clear land for crops, and cattle owners burn off parched, unpalatable grasses to make way for a fresh new growth for their stock. At the end of the dry season, when fires are particularly fierce, large areas of savanna lie under a thin haze of smoke.

Poaching, together with the takeover of wildlife ranges by farms and livestock, has led many animals to near-extinction in areas where they were once plentiful. Poisoned arrows are capable of killing even the biggest African game: sometimes they are set as traps and are triggered by the animal itself walking into a trip line. More sophisticated poachers use machine-guns and high-powered assault rifles, and airlift their illicit cargos of skins, ivory and rhinoceros horn. Illegal hunting for meat, which is dried and sold, has also become a large, highly organized and very profitable business in many areas.

Game animals also provide the spectacular displays that attract tourists and make tourism an important source of income for many developing nations. Today, most tourists pursue game with cameras instead of guns. The hunting that led to the wholesale slaughter of wildlife in previous years is banned, and so is the traffic in trophies, although even in the sanctuary provided by parks and reserves animals still fall prey to poachers.

Animals are frequently transferred from areas where they are at risk to safer areas such as game parks and reserves. In Kenya, helicopters came to the rescue of a herd of rare antelopes when their range was threatened by a proposed irrigation scheme and moved them to Tsavo National Park. Animals are also moved to introduce new blood to small, isolated herds or to re-stock areas from which they have been lost.

Tropical Rainforests

Tropical rainforests, extremely rich in both plant and animal life, consist of a series of layered or stratified habitats. These range from the dark and humid forest floor through a layer of shrubs to the emerging tops of the scattered giant trees towering above the dense main canopy of the forest. Each layer of vegetation is a miniature life zone containing a wide selection of animal species. These can be divided into a number of ecological groups according to their various ways of life, and many have evolved special adaptations to enable them to make maximum use of the plentiful food supply surrounding them.

Crested tree swift
Hemiprocne longipennis

Crowned eagle
Stephanoaetus coronatus

Tropical rainforests occur only in the regions close to the Equator; they have a heavy rainfall and a uniformly hot and moist climate. There are slightly more of these forests in the northern half of the world than in the southern half and they occur at altitudes of up to 1,500 m (5,000 ft). Temperatures are normally between 24°C and 30°C (77°–86°F) and rarely fall below 21°C (70°F) or rise above 32°C (90°F). The skies are often cloudy and the rain falls more or less evenly throughout the year. Rainfall is usually more than 2,000 mm (78 in) a year and is never less than 1,500 mm (59 in). A distinctive feature of this tropical, humid climate is that the average daily temperature range is much greater than the range between the hottest and coolest months.

A stratified habitat

There are usually three to five overlapping layers in the mature tropical rainforest. The tallest trees (called "emergents") rise above a closed, dense canopy formed by the crowns of less tall trees, which nevertheless can reach more than 40 m (130 ft) tall. Below this canopy is a third or middle layer of trees—the understorey; their crowns do not meet but they still form a dense layer of growth about 5–20 m (16–65 ft) tall. The fourth layer consists of woody shrubs of varying heights between 1–5 m (3–16 ft). The bottom layer comprises decomposers (fungi) that rarely reach 50 cm (20 in) in height.

Although the trees are so tall, few of them have really thick trunks. Nearly all are evergreens, shedding their dark, leathery leaves and growing new ones continuously. Many of the larger species grow buttresses—thin, triangular slabs of hard wood that spread out from the bases of their trunks. These support the trees, so removing the need for a heavy outlay of energy and resources on deep root systems. Hanging lianas (vines), thin and strong as rope, vanish like cables into the mass of foliage. They are especially abundant on river banks, where the canopy of trees is thinner; their leaves and flowers appear only among the treetops.

Epiphytes—plants that grow on other plants but do not take their nourishment from them—festoon the trunks and branches of trees, and up to 80 may grow on a single tree. They include many kinds of orchid and bromeliad. Their aerial roots make use of a humus substitute derived from the remains of other plants, often

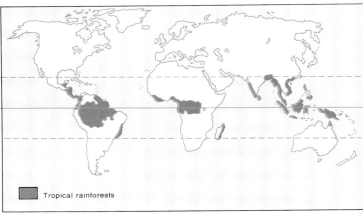

Tropical rainforests are located in the hot and wet equatorial lands of Latin America, West Africa, Madagascar and Asia. These areas have consistently high temperatures throughout the year and receive high rainfall from the moist and unstable winds blowing in from the oceans.

Tropical rainforests

The hummingbird numbers about 300 species, most of which are confined to the forests of South America. It is renowned for its ability to hover while gathering nectar, a feat achieved by the almost 180° rotations of its wings, which beat rapidly more than 80 times per second.

Moth orchid
Phalaenopsis sanderana

brought together by ants. The bases of their leaves may be broad and bowl-shaped and collect and hold water; they also provide homes for a variety of insects and reptiles.

Rainforest soils are not as fertile as might be supposed by the luxuriance of their vegetation. On the contrary, the silicates and compounds necessary for plant growth are leached away by the rain to leave red or yellow soils of poor quality. This process, known as laterization, is widespread in the humid tropics. Humus is rapidly broken down by bacteria, fungi and termites, while earthworms, which in more temperate regions normally contribute to the mixing of humus with mineral particles, are usually absent.

In rainforests there are often up to 25 different tree species on a single hectare of land (60 species to the acre). Most temperate forests have only a fifth of this number, with nothing like the abundance of plants that grow in the tropics. This incredible variety supports—directly or indirectly—a corresponding variety of animal species which has an abundant food supply because the forest never ceases to be productive. This is why most mammals do not move far; they stay where their food grows.

Life in the canopy

The dense leaves and branches of the canopy provide the most food and so support the greatest number of species. Macaws and toucans (from the American tropics) and parrots and trogons (which live in forests throughout the tropics) eat the fruit growing in the

THE LAYERS OF THE FOREST

Stratification—the existence of distinct layers of forest vegetation—is especially pronounced in the tropics, where there are usually five main storeys. These can overlap greatly and may vary in height from area to area. The large differences between the layers present many varied habitats and ecological niches for a very wide range of animals.

CANOPY LAYER

This dense storey exerts a powerful influence on the levels below since its trees, which grow between 20 m (65 ft) and 40 m (130 ft) tall, form such a thick layer of vegetation that they cut off sunlight from the forest below. The canopy is noted for the diversity of its fauna. Many birds and animals are adapted to running along branches to get the flowers, fruits or nuts that form their diets. The pointed tips of canopy leaves encourage rapid drainage.

Sacred langur
Presbytis ente...

Tree shrew
Tupaia glis

MIDDLE LAYER

This understorey comprises trees from 5 m (16 ft) to 20 m (65 ft) tall whose long, narrow crowns do not become quite so dense as those of the canopy. There is very often no clear distinction, however, between this level and the canopy. Middle-layer trees are strong enough to bear large animals such as leopards that spend part of their lives on the ground. Epiphytes are plentiful in this layer.

Leopard
Panthera pard...

Pouched tree frog
Gastrotheca ovifera

Orang-utan
Pongo pygmaeus

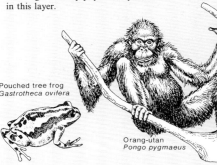

SHRUB LAYER

The vegetation of this level is sparse in comparison with that above it and consists of treelets and woody shrubs that rarely reach 5 m (16 ft). These grow up in any available space between the abundant boles of large trees. Life in this storey exists equally well at ground level.

Four-striped squirrel
Funisciurus lemniscatus

Oriental civet
Viverra tangalunga

Tree pangolin
Manis tricusp...

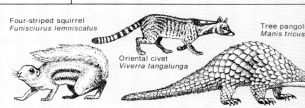

Flowering plants of the forest include epiphytes such as bromeliads and orchids like the species of *Phalaenopsis* illustrated here. Epiphytes grow on other plants such as trees where they can receive sunlight and are nourished by humus in the bark. Many epiphytic orchids have swellings in their roots or at the bases of their leaves where water can be stored. Seventy species of *Phalaenopsis* grow in southeast Asian forests and *P. sanderana*, one of the most beautiful, was first discovered in the Philippines in 1882.

GROUND LAYER

Shade-tolerant herbs, ferns and tree seedlings represent the only flora at ground level; there is no grass there. Light is less than one per cent of full daylight so that many mammals are well camouflaged in the gloom, whereas others have compact bodies to facilitate movement through the undergrowth. Ants and termites are well adapted to the high humidity and darkness of the forest floor. Fungi and a host of invertebrates quickly break down the litter of rotting leaves, fruit and fallen branches to provide vital nutrients for the fast-growing trees of the tropical rainforest.

Okapi
Okapia johnstoni

Forest buffalo
Syncerus caffer nanus

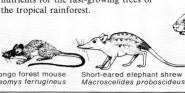

Congo forest mouse
Deomys ferrugineus

Short-eared elephant shrew
Macroscelides proboscideus

Orange-rumped agouti
Dasyprocta aguti

Mandrill
Mandrillus sphinx

Indian tiger
Panthera tigris tigris

Malayan tapir
Tapirus indicus

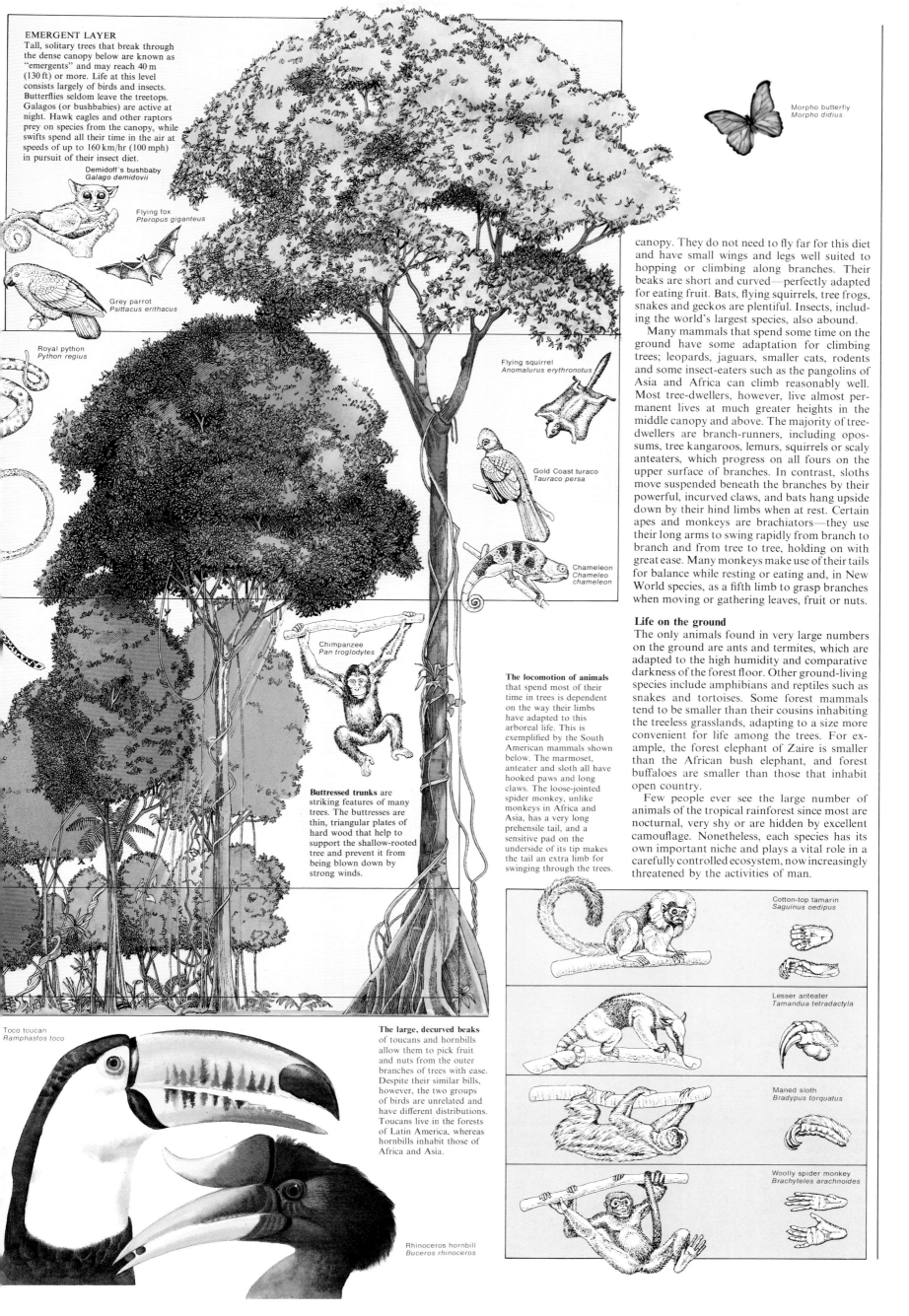

EMERGENT LAYER
Tall, solitary trees that break through the dense canopy below are known as "emergents" and may reach 40 m (130 ft) or more. Life at this level consists largely of birds and insects. Butterflies seldom leave the treetops. Galagos (or bushbabies) are active at night. Hawk eagles and other raptors prey on species from the canopy, while swifts spend all their time in the air at speeds of up to 160 km/hr (100 mph) in pursuit of their insect diet.

Demidoff's bushbaby
Galago demidovii

Flying fox
Pteropus giganteus

Grey parrot
Psittacus erithacus

Royal python
Python regius

Morpho butterfly
Morpho didius

Flying squirrel
Anomalurus erythronotus

Gold Coast turaco
Tauraco persa

Chameleon
Chameleo chameleon

Chimpanzee
Pan troglodytes

Buttressed trunks are striking features of many trees. The buttresses are thin, triangular plates of hard wood that help to support the shallow-rooted tree and prevent it from being blown down by strong winds.

canopy. They do not need to fly far for this diet and have small wings and legs well suited to hopping or climbing along branches. Their beaks are short and curved—perfectly adapted for eating fruit. Bats, flying squirrels, tree frogs, snakes and geckos are plentiful. Insects, including the world's largest species, also abound.

Many mammals that spend some time on the ground have some adaptation for climbing trees; leopards, jaguars, smaller cats, rodents and some insect-eaters such as the pangolins of Asia and Africa can climb reasonably well. Most tree-dwellers, however, live almost permanent lives at much greater heights in the middle canopy and above. The majority of tree-dwellers are branch-runners, including opossums, tree kangaroos, lemurs, squirrels or scaly anteaters, which progress on all fours on the upper surface of branches. In contrast, sloths move suspended beneath the branches by their powerful, incurved claws, and bats hang upside down by their hind limbs when at rest. Certain apes and monkeys are brachiators—they use their long arms to swing rapidly from branch to branch and from tree to tree, holding on with great ease. Many monkeys make use of their tails for balance while resting or eating and, in New World species, as a fifth limb to grasp branches when moving or gathering leaves, fruit or nuts.

Life on the ground
The only animals found in very large numbers on the ground are ants and termites, which are adapted to the high humidity and comparative darkness of the forest floor. Other ground-living species include amphibians and reptiles such as snakes and tortoises. Some forest mammals tend to be smaller than their cousins inhabiting the treeless grasslands, adapting to a size more convenient for life among the trees. For example, the forest elephant of Zaire is smaller than the African bush elephant, and forest buffaloes are smaller than those that inhabit open country.

Few people ever see the large number of animals of the tropical rainforest since most are nocturnal, very shy or are hidden by excellent camouflage. Nonetheless, each species has its own important niche and plays a vital role in a carefully controlled ecosystem, now increasingly threatened by the activities of man.

The locomotion of animals that spend most of their time in trees is dependent on the way their limbs have adapted to this arboreal life. This is exemplified by the South American mammals shown below. The marmoset, anteater and sloth all have hooked paws and long claws. The loose-jointed spider monkey, unlike monkeys in Africa and Asia, has a very long prehensile tail, and a sensitive pad on the underside of its tip makes the tail an extra limb for swinging through the trees.

Toco toucan
Ramphastos toco

The large, decurved beaks of toucans and hornbills allow them to pick fruit and nuts from the outer branches of trees with ease. Despite their similar bills, however, the two groups of birds are unrelated and have different distributions. Toucans live in the forests of Latin America, whereas hornbills inhabit those of Africa and Asia.

Rhinoceros hornbill
Buceros rhinoceros

Cotton-top tamarin
Saguinus oedipus

Lesser anteater
Tamandua tetradactyla

Maned sloth
Bradypus torquatus

Woolly spider monkey
Brachyteles arachnoides

Man and the Tropical Rainforests

Every three seconds a portion of original rainforest the size of a football field disappears as man fells the trees and extends his cultivation. Although tropical conditions allow rapid regrowth of secondary forest, the loss of primary forest is destroying thousands of plant and animal species that will never again be seen on Earth. Even by conservative estimates, it is likely that all the world's primary tropical forest will have disappeared within 85 years unless the trend is reversed.

The activities of man have only recently begun to threaten the tropical rainforest. Since pre-historic times, forests have offered shelter to people who, lacking any knowledge of agriculture, have existed as hunters and gatherers. They used only stone and wooden weapons such as bows and arrows to kill their animal prey, and collected berries, fruit and honey from their surroundings. Their influence on the forest environment was minimal and today a few races such as African pygmies and the Punans of Borneo still live in such a simple state of balance with nature. The Punans, for example, have no permanent homes, but use leaves and branches to construct temporary shelters that are used for only a few weeks before being abandoned. The pygmies build similar homes.

Shifting agriculture

Most forest-dwellers, however, live in more permanent settlements and grow most of their food in forest clearings they have made. Such people are expert at chopping down trees in order to set fire to them, and this "slash-and-burn" farming results in small areas littered with charred logs and stumps whose ashes enrich the ground. Crops such as wild tapioca (cassava or manioc) are widely grown, but after a year or two the soil loses the little fertility it once had so that a new tract of forest has to be cleared and burned. Such shifting agriculture provides food for more than 200 million inhabitants of the Third World. As a farming system it has been used throughout the world for more than 2,000 years. When there were few farmers per kilometre the land was allowed to lie fallow for at least 10 years so that the soil could recover. Today, however, population pressures are so great that fallow periods have been drastically reduced and a swift repetition of slash-and-burn degrades and removes nutrients from the soil.

Effects on world climate

Tropical forest floors seldom have deep layers of humus so that, once trees are removed, the shallow topsoil is exposed and soon becomes eroded. In turn, this reduces the capacity of the ground to retain moisture, and without this sponge-like effect runoff can become very erratic and lead to floods, such as those that frequently occur in India and Bangladesh. Estuary sedimentation is often greatly increased

A DIMINISHING RESOURCE

This idealized tract of rainforest includes many of the activities of man that are daily endangering the survival of the forest. Shifting "slash-and-burn" cultivation and excessive logging present the greatest threats. Antidotes such as reafforestation have so far made very little headway.

Living in harmony with the forest are small groups of hunter-gatherers who mainly live on a flesh diet, killing their prey with bows and arrows. Nuts and berries supplement this diet and leaves gathered from the immediate jungle cover their temporary dome-shaped shelters. These are abandoned as an area becomes exhausted and the tribe moves on. Twenty or so pygmies need about 500 sq km (200 sq miles) to support themselves.

Selective logging by gangs of men seeking out the straightest and most valuable hardwood species has been the most common form of tree extraction, even though 75 per cent of the canopy might have to be destroyed to remove just a few important trees. Today heavy axes are being replaced by power saws that have no difficulty in cutting down the large buttresses that were once left behind.

Plantation forestry has made increasing inroads into the forests over the decades. The commercial advantage of products that can be cropped several times during the hardwoods' maturation period is becoming increasingly apparent to farmers in the regions. Many rubber plantations in southeastern Asia consist of smallholdings that have tended to encroach upon the forest, and intercropping now takes place between the long-established trees.

Shifting cultivation converts thousands of square kilometres of primary forest to substandard cultivation every year. Forest is cleared by slash-and-burn, the resulting fertile clearing is cropped with staples such as manioc, and then left to degrade to secondary forest once the ash-strewn ground has lost its poor fertility. Inevitably, the ground becomes permanently degraded. One encouraging antidote to the futility of such shifting agriculture is the recent strategy of agroforestry (as used by countries such as Nigeria and Thailand), which encourages the planting of fast-growing trees at the same time as the farmer's normal crops. Such intercropping offers considerable financial incentives to the small itinerant farmer.

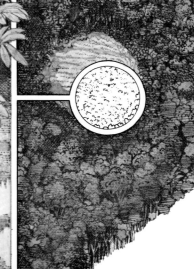

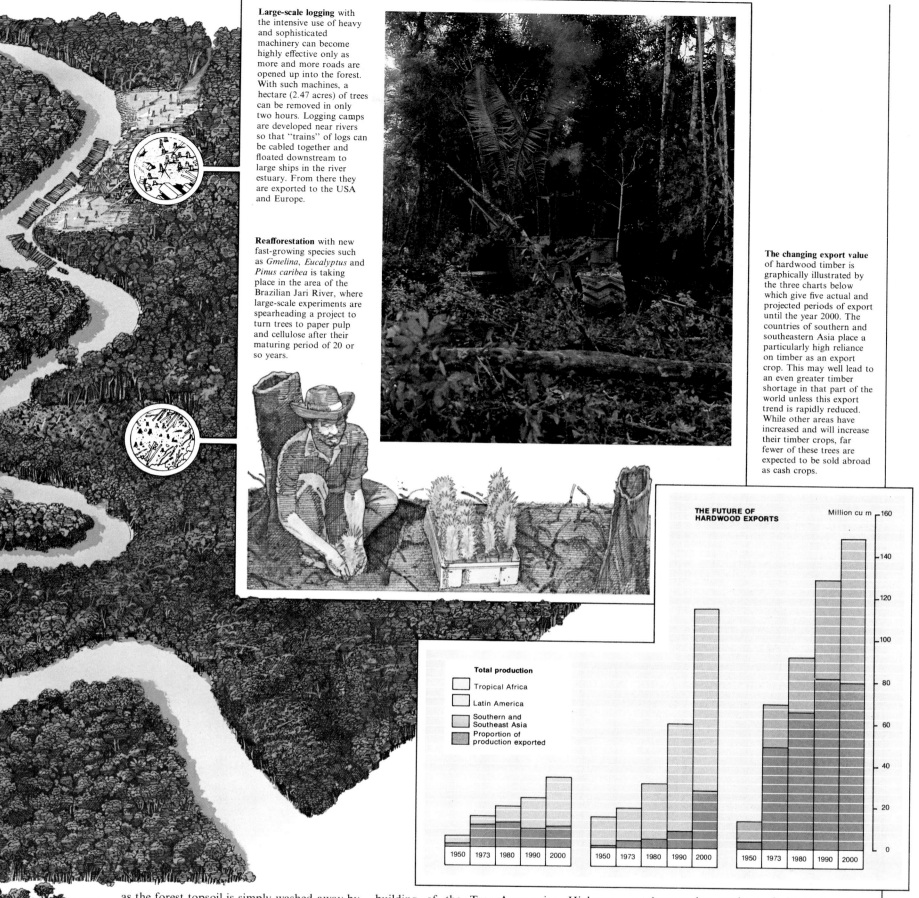

Large-scale logging with the intensive use of heavy and sophisticated machinery can become highly effective only as more and more roads are opened up into the forest. With such machines, a hectare (2.47 acres) of trees can be removed in only two hours. Logging camps are developed near rivers so that "trains" of logs can be cabled together and floated downstream to large ships in the river estuary. From there they are exported to the USA and Europe.

Reafforestation with new fast-growing species such as *Gmelina, Eucalyptus* and *Pinus caribea* is taking place in the area of the Brazilian Jari River, where large-scale experiments are spearheading a project to turn trees to paper pulp and cellulose after their maturing period of 20 or so years.

The changing export value of hardwood timber is graphically illustrated by the three charts below which give five actual and projected periods of export until the year 2000. The countries of southern and southeastern Asia place a particularly high reliance on timber as an export crop. This may well lead to an even greater timber shortage in that part of the world unless this export trend is rapidly reduced. While other areas have increased and will increase their timber crops, far fewer of these trees are expected to be sold abroad as cash crops.

THE FUTURE OF HARDWOOD EXPORTS
Million cu m

Total production
- Tropical Africa
- Latin America
- Southern and Southeast Asia
- Proportion of production exported

1950 1973 1980 1990 2000

as the forest topsoil is simply washed away by torrential rain. In parts of Asia, deforestation has caused changes in water flow that have interfered with the production of new high-yield rice crops.

Tropical forests contain an enormous store of carbon and some authorities believe that its release into the air (as carbon dioxide) when the forest is burned down may be as great in volume as that released by the rest of the world's fossil fuels. The higher proportion of carbon dioxide in the atmosphere may lead to an increase in global temperatures, especially at the poles. Trees also release oxygen into the air through photosynthesis, and some scientists have estimated that half of the world's oxygen is derived from this source. Others estimate that half of the rainfall of the Amazon basin is generated by the forest itself, so that any great reduction in tree cover would turn Amazonia into a much drier region.

Threats to Amazonia
Much attention has been paid to the situation of Amazonia, covering as it does some 6.5 million sq km (2½ million sq miles). In an attempt to give better access to timber and mineral reserves, the Brazilian government's building of the TransAmazonian Highway (3,000 km or 1,860 miles long) has opened the way to deforestation, and settlers have been encouraged to make smallholdings on the cleared forest beside the road. Between 1966 and 1978, the government calculated that farmers and big business interests had turned 80,000 sq km (31,000 sq miles) of forest into grazing land for 6 million cattle intended for hamburgers. However, like the wholesale extraction of timber, this has proved to be of doubtful economic value. Because costs rise steeply as less accessible areas are tapped, expenses tend to eliminate logging profits.

Threats in Africa
Even greater threats to tropical forest land have come from less cautious and realistic governments, such as that of Ivory Coast. There neither shifting agriculture nor excessive logging for valuable export sales appear to be under any sort of control. Accordingly, between 1966 and 1974, the area of forest declined from 156,000 sq km (60,000 sq miles) to 54,000 sq km (20,000 sq miles), much of the latter being secondary forest that can never be returned to its original status. Like many other developing countries, Ivory Coast has been more keen to cut down and export its profitable timbers than to think about protecting its invaluable forest environment. Inevitably, forest farmers move into cleared areas and often establish plantation cash crops such as coffee, cocoa and rubber, while the establishment of national parks to curtail depletion has often had very little profitable effect. The Malaysian rainforest is also disappearing rapidly, through widescale logging and opencast mining for bauxite (aluminium ore).

A large proportion of the world's rainforest occurs in tropical countries faced with severe problems of population control. It is therefore inevitable that the pressures on such forests will be great. Human interference does more than merely destroy the primary forest, to be replaced in time by secondary growth; more importantly, the wholesale removal of trees also drastically reduces the vast genetic reservoir contained in the number of plant and animal species the forests harbour. This in itself is a sound ecological argument for preserving forests and for reversing current trends towards monoculture in the tropics. All the warnings about forest depletion appear to be clear, yet there seems little hope that man will heed them until it is too late.

Monsoon Regions

The word monsoon often conjures up the image of torrential rain and steaming tropical jungles. Yet such a view is misleading, for very great contrasts occur in the regions of the tropical world with a monsoon climate. What distinguishes monsoon regions is not so much the amount of rainfall or the permanently high temperatures, but the dramatic contrast between seasons, with an extended dry season as an essential feature. And in fact the word monsoon derives from the Arabic word for season.

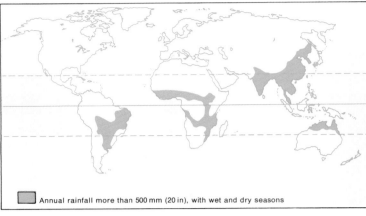

THE SEASON OF RAIN
Life in the monsoon regions balances on the expectation of seasonal heavy rain. In much of India, for instance, 85 per cent of the annual rainfall occurs during the limited monsoon periods, and humans as well as plants and animals depend on it wholly. About half the world's people live in these regions, in communities whose rhythm of life necessarily reflects the rains' seasonal nature.

This contrast between wet and dry seasons reflects the reversals of winds over sea and land, which in the northern hemisphere blow from the northeast in the dry winter season, and from the southwest in the wet summer periods.

The monsoon regions occur most widely in southern, southeastern and eastern Asia to the south of latitude 25°N, and in western and central Africa north of the Equator, but there are also smaller regions with a characteristically monsoon climate in eastern Africa, northern Australia and central America. Despite the similar overall climatic pattern, however, the monsoon regions are otherwise very diverse.

Before human settlement the original vegetation of the monsoon regions reflected the dominance of an extended dry season followed by a period of violent rainfall. Typical forest cover was provided by the sal (*Shorea robusta*) deciduous forest, which adjusts to extended periods of moisture deficiency by shedding its leaves. However, within the monsoon region rainfall varies from 200 mm (8 in) a year to more than 20,000 mm (800 in), and the rainy periods may vary between three and nine months.

The range of vegetation found in the monsoon regions reflects this diversity. Where tropical rainforest alters to monsoon forest, as in eastern Java, there is a sharp fall in the total number of plant and animal species, and species adapted to endure seasonal drought begin to be seen. At the other extreme of rainfall the forest thins and shades into semidesert vegetation in India's northwest. But if there is a "type" of monsoon vegetation it is tropical deciduous forest, with sal as the dominant species.

As well as contrasts in climate, the monsoon regions also exhibit pronounced changes in temperature and vegetation as a result of variations in altitude. The Western Ghats of India and the foothills of the Himalayas in Assam both rise to more than 2,500 m (8,200 ft). Temperatures decrease sharply at such altitudes with corresponding changes in vegetation. In southern India on the Nilgiri Hills a wet temperate forest is characteristic, with an intermingling of temperate and tropical species. Magnolias, planes and elms all grow there.

Agriculture in monsoon regions
Despite its extensive area there is no part of the monsoon world that is untouched by man and by man's activities. In southern Asia, agricultural activity can be traced back at least 5,000 years, and there have been agricultural settlements throughout the monsoon regions for at least 1,500 years. Man's activity and the grazing of domesticated animals have interfered with, and progressively modified, the natural vegetation. The range of species indicates that, in the whole of the monsoon biome, there is now virtually no primary forest left. The pace of man's interference has speeded up considerably over the last 100 years. As a result less than 10 per cent of the land in southern Asia is now forested, and other parts of the monsoon

Many parts of the world experience "monsoon" winds, blowing from sea to land in summer, and from land to sea in winter; but typical monsoon vegetation is most clearly seen in the regions of southeastern Asia and the Indian subcontinent. In climatic terms, however, the monsoon circulation of seasonal wind reversals, with wetter summers and dry winters, also affects considerable areas of Africa, South America and northern Australia.

Annual rainfall more than 500 mm (20 in), with wet and dry seasons

regions are similarly losing their forest cover.

Many of today's farming methods incorporate traditional cultivation practices, but there have also been very significant changes in recent decades. Traditional agriculture in the monsoon regions has been developed to take into account the seasonal nature of its rainfall pattern and the total rainfall received. The fundamental role of water throughout the region and the absence of low temperatures have placed great importance on either cultivating crops that can tolerate the seasonal rainfall pattern, or on providing irrigation.

Through most of southern Asia, overwhelmingly the most populous of the monsoon regions, the most important single crop is rice, which covers about one-third of the total cultivated area. Rice needs a great deal of water and for this reason is grown mainly in areas of high irrigation, such as the delta lands of the southern and eastern coasts of India, and in areas where rainfall is more than 1,500 mm (59 in) a year. Its cultivation creates a very distinctive landscape as a result of the fact that rice must spend much of its growing period with a few centimetres of water over the soil.

Rice cultivation gives the monsoon regions their characteristic pattern of paddy fields, but other cereal crops such as wheat, the millets and sorghum are also very important. These can tolerate far drier conditions than can rice, and occur in areas such as central India or upland Thailand, where uncertain and less abundant rainfall puts a premium on drought tolerance.

Even with traditional crops man has often interfered extensively with the environment in order to increase yields and attempt to guarantee successful cropping. Traditional irrigation schemes range from diverting rivers at times of flood, in order to lead water to dry land, to digging wells and building small reservoirs. But recent technological developments have brought a new dimension to agricultural activity in the monsoon regions. Large-scale dam and irrigation canal schemes have become important in Africa as well as in monsoon Asia. The introduction and speed of electric or diesel "pumpsets" have transformed well irrigation in regions with extensive groundwater. The

Heat differences in the atmosphere cause the seasonal wind reversals (left) characteristic of monsoon circulation. In January the northern hemisphere is tilted away from the sun, and cold, dry winds blow from the central Asian landmass towards the Equator. Here they change direction (an effect of the Earth's rotation), converge with other winds, and drop their rain. In July the situation is reversed when the heated Asian landmass attracts a flow of cooler air from the equatorial oceans, which moves northwards with the sun. The moist air condenses on reaching land, and the monsoon rains descend.

reliable water supply that irrigation can give has brought in its train the opportunity for farmers to adopt a wide range of new farming practices. Chemical fertilizers and new strains of seed have made possible great increases in the productivity of the land in many parts of the monsoon regions, but their use is generally restricted to areas of reliable water supply.

Subsistence cultivation over thousands of years has been by far the most important element in the transformation of the landscape and vegetation of the monsoon world, but the introduction of plantation cultivation during the last centuries has also had a major effect. Tea plantations, for instance, have led to the almost total replacement of natural vegetation in the hills of southern India and Sri Lanka.

Populations in all the countries of the monsoon regions are rapidly increasing, and demands for economic development are constantly growing, placing increasing pressures on the environment, pressures which to date have seemed almost irresistible.

DISAPPEARING ANIMALS
The dwindling wildlife of southeastern Asia includes species that may be regarded locally as pests—a fact that makes their protection difficult outside game reserves. Animals such as the tiger and the wild pig are doubly threatened as human cultivation spreads into the natural habitat: their hunting and foraging grounds are reduced, and their destruction of crops or livestock provides villagers with an obvious incentive for killing them in order to protect their own livelihoods.

Tiger
Panthera tigris

Wild pig
Sus scrofa

SELF-SUFFICIENCY IN CHINA
Local materials are turned into saleable products at a ratan factory in southern China. This factory is not owned by the state but by the village-sized brigade responsible for the manufacturing. The brigade functions as a smaller economic unit within the Ting Chow people's commune of 20 to 30 villages, but is encouraged to act independently, owning what it creates. The commune takes care of such matters as waterways—it contains 82 km (51 miles) of canals.

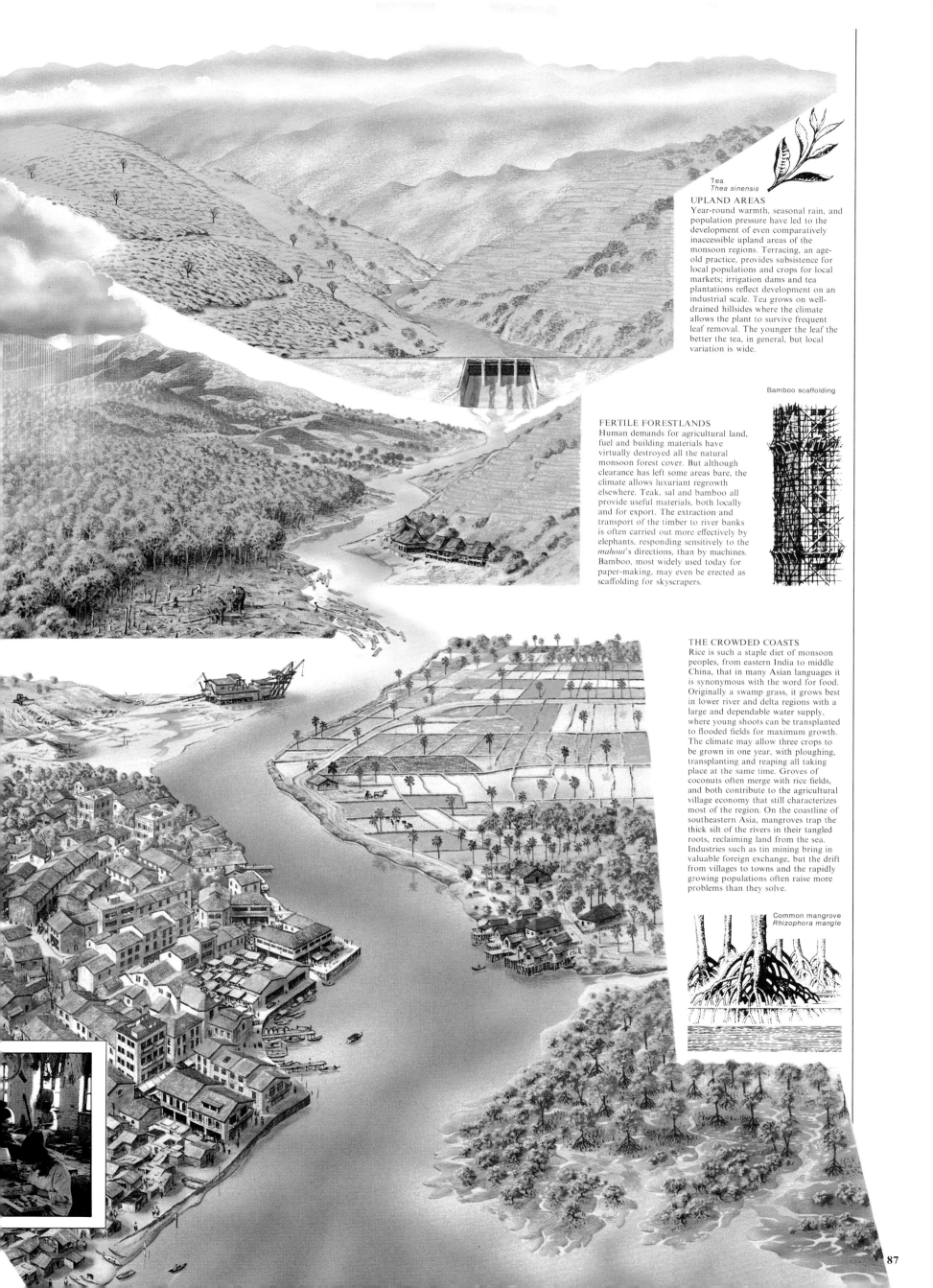

Tea
Thea sinensis

UPLAND AREAS
Year-round warmth, seasonal rain, and population pressure have led to the development of even comparatively inaccessible upland areas of the monsoon regions. Terracing, an age-old practice, provides subsistence for local populations and crops for local markets; irrigation dams and tea plantations reflect development on an industrial scale. Tea grows on well-drained hillsides where the climate allows the plant to survive frequent leaf removal. The younger the leaf the better the tea, in general, but local variation is wide.

Bamboo scaffolding

FERTILE FORESTLANDS
Human demands for agricultural land, fuel and building materials have virtually destroyed all the natural monsoon forest cover. But although clearance has left some areas bare, the climate allows luxuriant regrowth elsewhere. Teak, sal and bamboo all provide useful materials, both locally and for export. The extraction and transport of the timber to river banks is often carried out more effectively by elephants, responding sensitively to the *mahout*'s directions, than by machines. Bamboo, most widely used today for paper-making, may even be erected as scaffolding for skyscrapers.

THE CROWDED COASTS
Rice is such a staple diet of monsoon peoples, from eastern India to middle China, that in many Asian languages it is synonymous with the word for food. Originally a swamp grass, it grows best in lower river and delta regions with a large and dependable water supply, where young shoots can be transplanted to flooded fields for maximum growth. The climate may allow three crops to be grown in one year, with ploughing, transplanting and reaping all taking place at the same time. Groves of coconuts often merge with rice fields, and both contribute to the agricultural village economy that still characterizes most of the region. On the coastline of southeastern Asia, mangroves trap the thick silt of the rivers in their tangled roots, reclaiming land from the sea. Industries such as tin mining bring in valuable foreign exchange, but the drift from villages to towns and the rapidly growing populations often raise more problems than they solve.

Common mangrove
Rhizophora mangle

87

Mountain Regions

A quarter of Earth's land surface lies at heights of 1,000 m (3,300 ft) or more above sea level. But the highland regions are thinly populated by man, who is, generally speaking, a lowland dweller (most major population centres are less than 100 m (330 ft) above sea level). Some formerly lowland animals have fled from man to the harsh refuge of the mountains, joining with specially adapted plants and wildlife, but today man himself is finding the highland regions increasingly useful and desirable.

The world's highest mountain peaks rise to almost 9.6 km (6 miles) above sea level, but these heights are small compared to the total diameter of the Earth. The rough surface of an orange would have mountains higher than the Himalayas if scaled up to world size. But mountain environments, although they vary enormously from system to system, all tend to demand remarkable endurance and adaptability from the plants and animals that inhabit them.

Altitude rather than geological variation determines conditions of life on mountains. The temperature falls by 2°C with every 300 m (3.4°F every 1,000 ft)—hence the snow-capped beauty of the heights—and life forms must be adapted to increasingly harsh conditions as height increases. As a result, zones of different life occur at different levels, from tropical forests (at the base of low-latitude mountains) to arctic-type life in the zone of ice and snow at the summit. The latitude of the mountain affects the heights to which these zones extend: trees occur at 2,300 m (7,500 ft) in the southern Alps, whereas farther north, in central Sweden, trees cannot survive above 1,000 m (3,300 ft).

Life at the top
The specially adapted plant and animal life of the mountains occurs above the tree line, for here the variations in living conditions reach their greatest extremes. A plant that has found a foothold on a bare rock face may have to endure intense heat, even where the average temperature is low, when the summer sun blazing through the clear air warms the slabs to tropical temperatures. But when that part of the mountain falls into shadow, the temperature decreases very rapidly, often assisted by the high winds that blow almost constantly throughout the year in many mountain areas.

Soil necessary for plant life develops with the breakdown of the rock through the agency of water, frost and ice. Lichens, whose acids may aid in this destruction, can survive at very high levels, and as they die may add some humus to the newly forming soil. This may first accumulate in sheltered places where plants requiring high humidity, such as mosses and filmy ferns, are found. Flowering plants follow where a greater depth of soil has formed, although some grow in cracks between rocks.

Flowering plants of the mountains all tend to be small (to avoid harsh, drying winds), deep rooted (to anchor the plant firmly), and abundantly flowering (to benefit from the short growing season). Many unrelated species have independently developed a similar cushion form. This enables them to shed excess rainwater easily, and to retain heat better in a tight tangle of stems and leaves, where the temperature may be more than 10°C (18°F) higher than that of the outside air. Insects sheltering there are well placed to perform the vital task of pollination. But pollinating insects are relatively rare at high altitudes, and some mountain plants are wind pollinated. The brilliant colour of many others may be to increase their attractiveness for the insects. Nearly all upland plants are very slow-growing perennials, and many are evergreen, with leaves that exploit all available light.

Some large animals, such as the ibex or the Rocky Mountain goat, are adapted to spend their lives among the rocks and slopes. These stocky creatures, with hooves that act rather like suction cups, produce their summer young in the security of the heights, although in winter they descend to the shelter of the upper forests. Among smaller mammals, most of which are rodents, some dig burrows in which they hibernate through the winter. Others have very thick insulating coats, and may stay awake through the coldest weather in burrows under the snow.

Refugees from the lowlands
Some mountain animals, particularly carnivorous mammals and birds, have been driven by human persecution into remote mountain fastnesses. Many birds of prey, which could otherwise survive well in lowland areas, have their last strongholds among the mountains. They survive by feeding on small rodents, many of which are extremely wary. Some upland birds feed on insects or on seeds, but their number is comparatively small. The Alpine chough is one of the most interesting of mountain birds, for it has learned to find food among the scraps provided by climbers and skiers, whom it often follows to very high altitudes.

Insects and other small invertebrates, like their Arctic counterparts, may take several years to mature. Some are wingless, and many tend to fly low in order not to be blown away from their home range. Jumping spiders have been seen at heights of 6,700 m (22,000 ft) on the slopes of Mount Everest, where they exist on small flies and springtails, but even above this level springtails and glacier "fleas" occur where there are no plants, apparently surviving on wind-blown insects and pollen grains.

Man and the mountains
The remote beauty of the mountains has led many peoples to identify them as the abode of the gods, but man himself prefers to live in the more convenient lowlands. The rarefied atmosphere of the heights makes physical work difficult, although some mountain-dwelling peoples have developed adaptations of the blood system to enable them to carry scarce oxygen more efficiently. The short growing season prevents cultivation of all but the hardiest cereal crops, and most uplanders rely on their livestock—cattle, sheep, llamas or yaks—for their existence. The animals are often driven to high pasture during the summer, descending to the valleys in the winter.

Modern, urbanized man finds the beauty and freshness of mountains increasingly attractive. Climbers have invaded most of the world's mountain regions, and in winter hosts of skiers flock to the resorts. Many important wildlife sanctuaries and national parks, particularly in the United States, are in mountain areas.

Lowland populations often rely on the pure mountain streams for both water and energy. Whole upland valleys are sometimes flooded to store water for distant conurbations. And the forceful flow of the water as it descends from the snow-fed heights is frequently harnessed to produce electricity for entire regions hundreds of kilometres away. The clear mountain air also offers the best conditions for astronomical observation, and most observatories today are built in dry, cloudless mountain areas.

LIFE ON THE HEIGHTS
Mountain climates become colder the higher one goes. This change in conditions creates distinctive horizontal zones of plant and animal life, although the pattern may vary according to the latitude and aspect of a mountain. Some life forms manage to eke out a precarious existence even on the roof of the world. Lower down, the brief growing season encourages a short burst of plant and animal activity above the timber line, conspicuous for the brightly coloured summer flowers. Man mainly inhabits the lower slopes and valleys. He exploits mountain resources but rarely lives on the inhospitable heights.

Many peoples have believed that the gods have their abodes in the high places of the world. Tibet (above), one of the highest and most mountainous of all countries, has a large number of religious sites. Modern man also finds the clear, dry air suitable for the study of heavenly bodies: most modern observatories, such as Kitt Peak, USA (right), are built on mountain sites far from cities.

Activity in Earth's crust has produced mountains in every continent (left). Some thrust up sharply, while older mountains have been eroded to rounded shapes. The Scottish Highlands were made by mountain-building forces 400 million years ago (170 million years before the Appalachians and the Urals). The Rockies are 70 million years old and the Alps 15 million years old.

Ancient mountains (Caledonian orogenesis)
Intermediate mountains (Hercynian orogenesis)
Recent mountains (Alpine orogenesis)

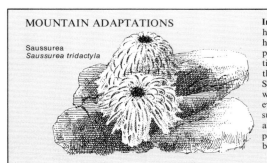

MOUNTAIN ADAPTATIONS

Saussurea
Saussurea tridactyla

Ingenious adaptations to harsh mountain conditions have been evolved by many plants, most of which have tiny cells with thick sap that does not freeze easily. Saussurea masks itself with white hair to reduce evaporation from the leaf surface. Alpine soldanellas are active even under snow, pushing up their flowers before the thaw.

Alpine soldanella
Soldanella alpina

SNOW-BOUND PEAKS
Perpetual snow, violent winds and atmospheric dryness impose harsh conditions on life in the high Himalayas. But wind-blown organic debris from the plains does support some life forms—springtails, flies and jumping spiders—where the air is too dry to allow even lichens to survive. Lower down, a cushion plant may take root in a rock-base niche, but there is little other vegetation. Among birds, the Alpine chough is a scavenger that has followed Everest expeditions to heights of 7,900 m (26,000 ft).

Jumping spider
Salticus scenicus

Alpine chough
Pyrrhocorax graculus

Cushion pink
Parrya lanuginosa

Fly
Diptera sp

Primula
Primula rosea

Royle's pika
Ochotona roylei

Blue sheep
Pseudois nayaur

Himalayan blue poppy
Meconopsis horridula

Domestic yak
Bos grunniens

Snow leopard
Panthera uncia

MOUNTAIN MEADOWS
Between the snow line and the zone of coniferous trees, the Himalayan slopes exhibit a glorious variety of flowering plants during summer. Small and slow-growing, these often have bright flowers which attract pollinating insects such as fly-like *Diptera*. The pika and other small, thick-furred rodents are the most common animals, although larger creatures, such as blue (bharal) sheep and yaks, also find summer pasturage at these heights. Snow leopards tend to inhabit the coniferous forests, but they travel up to higher parts to prey on the grazing herds. Few people live within the zone, but some Sherpas take their yak herds as high as 4,600 m (15,000 ft) for summer grazing, and even grow crops of potatoes at this height. Their permanent villages, however, are on the lower alpine slopes.

FORESTED SLOPES
Isolated birches mark the tree line— the transition from meadow to coniferous and rhododendron forest. In the upper parts of the forest, trees are dwarfed by cold and lack of moisture, and are twisted and bent from the wind. These low and tangled masses provide shelter for animals such as the Asian black bear and the red panda. Below the conifers lies a zone of broad-leaved evergreens, and in the foothills these in turn give way to tropical monsoon forests of sal trees (*Shorea robusta*) and thickets of bamboo. The raucous flocks of hill mynahs represent just one of the many kinds of birds found in this zone, which has the widest range of wildlife of all the kinds of mountain vegetation. Unfortunately, many species are in danger of extinction, for here man has settled, cut down forests and terraced hillsides to grow crops.

Rhododendron
Rhododendron sp

Asiatic black bear
Selenarctos thibetanus

Red panda
Ailurus fulgens

Hill mynah bird
Gracula religiosa

7,600 m
25,000 ft

4,900 m
16,000 ft

4,300 m
14,000 ft

3,700 m
12,000 ft

3,000 m
10,000 ft

2,400 m
8,000 ft

1,800 m
6,000 ft

1,200 m
4,000 ft

☐ Permanent snow

☐ Alpine meadows

☐ Isolated birches

☐ Coniferous forest

☐ Rhododendron groves

☐ Broad-leaved evergreen forest

☒ Bamboo

☐ Tropical monsoon forest

Rocky Mountain goat
Oreamnos americanus

Animals and humans adapt to mountain conditions in many ways. The Rocky Mountain goat (left) has evolved a fleecy undercoat and hooves with concave pads to grip on any surface. Comparison of the blood counts (right) of a lowlander (A) and an Andean (B) shows how the latter has a higher total content and more red cells.

litres pints

The golden eagle *Aquila chrysaetos* (left) epitomizes the grandeur of the heights. Although it lives and nests in remote regions, it could equally well find its food in the lowlands were it not for human competition. An eagle's territory may cover 130 sq km (50 sq miles): it preys on small mammals and even (it is believed) on young deer and lambs. It mates for life and returns each year to the same nest.

Freshwater Environments

Broad, muddy rivers, fast-running streams, miniature ponds and deep, ancient lakes all provide their own distinctive environments for populations of animals and colonies of aquatic plants. And in spite of the fact that these, the world's freshwater systems, contain only a minute proportion of the Earth's total supplies of water, the remarkable variety and richness of the wildlife they support make them among the most valuable and significant of all the world's natural habitats.

Freshwater is never really pure for, like seawater, and indeed like all other natural waters, it contains various dissolved minerals. Freshwater differs from seawater only in the relatively low concentrations of the minerals it contains. But these mineral traces are extremely important; they provide essential nutrients without which freshwater plants could not exist. And without plant life, there would be virtually no animal life either.

Not all parts of every freshwater system are rich in both plants and animals. Large, deep lakes are very similar to oceans—no light can penetrate their gloomy depths, and few plants can live in these conditions. The surface waters, on the other hand, where light is plentiful, teem with microscopic floating plants, mainly single-celled algae such as desmids and diatoms. The edges of lakes provide a different set of conditions again, for here the water is shallow and light can penetrate right through it. Plants can take root in the silt on the bottom, grow up through the water and thrust their leaves out into the light and air. Edges of lakes and, for the same reasons, the waters of small ponds are usually full of such plant life, which in turn supports many freshwater animals.

Running waters
Just as the still waters of lakes and ponds offer a variety of habitats, so the running waters of rivers support many different forms of life, each adapted to the particular conditions of its environment. In the upper reaches, where rivers are scarcely more than upland streams, water is fast-flowing and clear of silt. Few plants, except close-clinging mosses, can gain a hold on the bare stony bottom and most of the fish are well muscled and strong-bodied to enable them to withstand the constant tug of the current. As a river swells to form a mature lowland water course, however, it becomes slower moving and the water is warmer and richer in nutrients. Plants grow readily in these lower reaches and provide a supply of food for aquatic animals.

With such a wide range of conditions, freshwater environments support an enormous variety of animal life—insects, fishes, amphibians, reptiles, mammals and birds. In some ways insects are the most important of all these creatures: freshwater systems contain more insects and other invertebrates, representing a greater variety of species, than any other kind of animal. Furthermore, these, the smallest representatives of the freshwater animal world, provide one of the most important links in the complex freshwater food chain.

Insects may be the most numerous, but fishes are probably the most familiar of all freshwater creatures, and they certainly show some of the greatest varieties of adaptations to the many different habitats. Their sizes vary from the tiny, 14 mm ($\frac{1}{2}$ in) of the virtually transparent dwarf goby fish found in small streams and lakes in the Philippines to the 4 m (14 ft) of the arapaima found in deep rivers in tropical South America. Their feeding habits vary from those of the ferocious carnivorous piranha of South America to those of the North American paddle fish which, although more than three times the size of the largest piranha, feed solely on microscopic organisms which they filter from the water with their specially adapted throats.

The breeding habits of freshwater fish also vary widely, from the carefully maternal instincts of the African mouthbreeding cichlids—these retain the developing eggs safely in their mouths until the offspring hatch—to the rather more common ejection of eggs into the water, where their fertilization and survival is simply left to chance. Other adaptations include the ability to breathe air (as does the African lungfish), to leap waterfalls (a common practice among migrating salmon) and to emit an electric shock of up to 600 volts (an adaptation of the South American electric eel).

Creatures of the water's edge
Of all the other major groups of animals, amphibians (such as frogs and toads) are probably the most reliant on freshwater systems. Because their skins must not dry out and they have to lay their eggs in water, few amphibians can venture far from the water's edge. And because they cannot tolerate the salt in seawater (it causes them to lose their body fluids through their skins) they are totally dependent upon freshwater for their existence. Reptiles, rather less typical of freshwater environments, range in size from miniature North American terrapins to the giant crocodiles that live along the banks of the Nile. Freshwater mammals, on the other hand, with the considerable exception of the hippopotamus, all tend to be rather small creatures such as otters, beavers, coypus, aquatic moles and water shrews.

Birds are another important group of freshwater creatures. Although few birds are truly aquatic an enormous number of species live in or near freshwater systems and take advantage of the various food supplies: the plants and fish within the waters; the bankside vegetation and small animal life; and the many forms of freshwater insects. Marshes and swamps, for example, provide some of the richest bird habitats in the world.

Also numbered among the species dependent on Earth's freshwater systems is man. And although strictly a nonaquatic, land-living animal, man uses more freshwater than any other creature. His needs seem to be inexhaustible as he harnesses, channels, diverts and often pollutes freshwater systems throughout the world. Unfortunately, the vast requirements of the human race are not always compatible with the rather more humble needs of all other species that depend upon freshwater.

Volume of Lakes in cu km (cu miles)

Huron, North America
3,447 (827)

Nyasa, Africa
8,373 (2,009)

Superior, North America
12,153 (2,916)

Tanganyika, Africa
19,418 (4,659)

Baikal, Asia
23,260 (5,581)

Discharge of Rivers in cu m (cu ft) per second

Ganges, Asia
18,689 (660,000)

Brahmaputra, Asia
19,822 (700,000)

Yangtze, Asia
21,804 (770,000)

Congo, Africa
39,644 (1,400,000)

Amazon, South America
212,376 (7,500,000)

The five largest lakes in the world hold more than 53% of all freshwater that flows over the land. The rest of the world's lakes account for another 45%.

The world's largest river, the Amazon, discharges more than one-fifth of all freshwater that flows from the mouths of the world's rivers into the oceans.

THE UPPER REACHES
Here, water flows rapidly. Tumbling over bare rocks and stones, it is chilly, oxygen-rich and free of silt. Bird life attracted to these reaches includes the sure-footed dipper, which walks the stream bed hunting for caddis larvae. Slightly farther downstream, but where the river is still narrow and easily dammed, beavers are found. Few plants can live within the water, but river crowfoot has feathery underwater leaves that remain intact where most other plants would be shredded by the current. Many fish, such as trout, have streamlined bodies to offer the least resistance to the stream's pull, while others survive on the bottom by bracing against the rocks—the bullhead, for example. Insects have various means of anchoring themselves to the stream bed—blackfly larvae have hooks to fix themselves to pebbles.

Dipper
Cinclus cinclus

Beaver
Castor fiber

River crowfoot
Ranunculus fluitans

Brown trout
Salmo trutta

Blackfly larvae
Simulium spp

Bullhead
Cottus bairdi

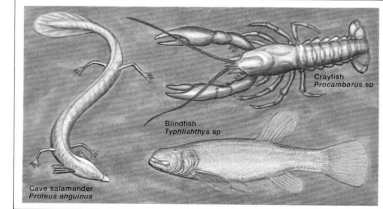

Crayfish
Procambarus sp

Blindfish
Typhlichthys sp

Cave salamander
Proteus anguinus

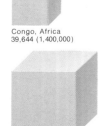

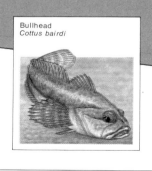

THE LIFE OF A RIVER

As a river makes its way from its upland source to the sea, it gradually changes its character. And at every stage in its progress, the animals and plants that inhabit the river banks and waters reflect these changes by their adaptations to their environments. Most distinctive and dramatic are those adaptations produced in the wildlife of the upper and lower river reaches.

African spoonbill
Platalea alba

Southern painted turtle
Chrysemys picta dorsalis

THE LOWER REACHES

The slowly flowing river and its muddy banks are rich in animals and plants. Many birds live along the water's edge; spoonbills wade in the shallows, filtering food from the water with their beaks. The banks, fringed with reedmaces and other plants, provide habitats for many reptiles, such as the American painted turtle, and mammals, such as the platypus. Plants also grow on the water—they range from large waterlilies to tiny algae that are food for river fishes: Africa's upside-down-feeding catfish, for example. In these waters, mammals as well as fish are to be found—Amazonian manatees live entirely aquatic lives. The plentiful river plants, such as curled pondweed, provide food for water snails and other herbivores, and cover for predators such as pike. Crustacea and insects living in the silt of the river bed are food for bottom-feeding fish such as the strange-looking North American paddle fish.

LAKES: CHANGE AND EVOLUTION

No two lakes are alike: each is virtually a self-contained world for its population of aquatic animals and plants. Furthermore, no individual lake remains the same for long: in every lake, slow, inexorable changes in conditions are gradually but constantly changing the balance of species inhabiting the lake bed, the bankside and the water.

Changing conditions may be caused by one of several processes. Accumulating sediments, one of the most common of these processes, may eliminate a lake altogether. The water becomes shallower as sediments thicken (1) and these sediments are then added to and consolidated by water plants taking root. Ultimately, land plants (2) invade the area.

Lakes develop their own peculiar species when the aquatic wildlife that evolves within them has no means of migrating to other freshwater systems to interbreed. The world's only existing species of freshwater seal, for example, is found in just one lake—isolated Lake Baikal in Asia.

Baikal seal
Phoca sibirica

Reedmace
Typha sp

Platypus
Ornithorhynchus anatinus

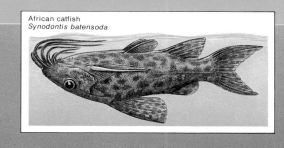

Waterlily
Nymphaea sp

African catfish
Synodontis batensoda

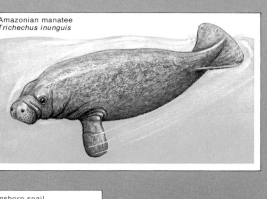

Amazonian manatee
Trichechus inunguis

Curled pondweed
Potamogeton crispus

White ramshorn snail
Planorbis albus

Pike
Esox lucius

DARK WATERS

Underground rivers that flow through many of the world's cave systems support surprising numbers of creatures that have adapted to the permanent darkness. Many of these, such as the American cave crayfish, have lost the coloration of their surface-living kin. Some, such as Kentucky blind fishes, no longer possess eyes. Some salamanders are sighted and black when born, but become blind and colourless by adulthood.

Paddle fish
Polydon spathula

Spectacled caiman
Caiman crocodilus

African lungfish
Protopterus annectens

Mosquito
Aedes impiger

WETLANDS

Marshes and swamps are the richest of freshwater habitats. Wading birds, such as Asia's painted stork *Ibis leucocephalus* (above), are particularly common. Reptiles include caimans, which lay their eggs in swamps' warm, rotting vegetation. Of the many insects, mosquitoes are probably the most numerous, and of the many fishes, African lungfish are perhaps best adapted to life in wetlands. They survive drought, when marshes dry up, by their ability to breathe air.

Man and the Freshwater Environments

From earliest times, man has been finding new uses for and making new demands upon the world's freshwater resources. Today, the whole of modern society depends upon a vast supply to serve its agricultural, industrial, domestic and other needs. To meet the ever-growing demand for water, man has performed remarkable engineering feats: altering the courses of rivers, creating and destroying lakes, drowning valleys and tapping water sources that lie deep within the Earth.

Water is essential to human life. Simply to remain alive, an active adult living in a temperate climate needs a liquid intake of about two litres ($3\frac{1}{2}$ pints) every day. In warmer climates, the body's fluid requirements are even greater. Consequently, man has always been tied to reliable sources of drinking water—rivers, springs, lakes and ponds—and the availability of these, until very recently, has dictated the routes of all his wanderings and determined the sites of all his settlements.

From the time of the earliest human settlements, however, man has looked upon freshwater systems not simply as a source of drinking water but also as an increasingly useful resource for a multitude of other purposes. Today, water enters into virtually every aspect of modern life, and enormous quantities are used in agriculture, in industry, in the home, in the production of energy, for transport and for recreation.

The farmer's resource

Of all the major activities that rely on freshwater, agriculture is by far the world's largest consumer. In much of Europe and North America, rainfall is usually plentiful and lack of sufficient water for crops is rarely a problem. But in other parts of the world the climate simply does not produce enough rainfall and water shortages are a perennial problem. There, irrigation is not just a sophisticated technique to improve the yields and increase the varieties of crops grown; it is, and always has been, an essential element of agriculture.

Methods of irrigation range from small-scale devices—such as miniature windpumps—used in many developing countries simply to lift water from rivers for bankside crops, to vast dams, reservoirs and canal systems such as the Indus River project in Pakistan, which irrigates 10 million hectares (25 million acres) of land.

Traditional irrigation techniques usually involve using open channels or furrows for conducting water to fields. But one of the major problems with these, particularly in hot climates, is that much of the water evaporates and is lost before it can be used. Several new techniques, such as sprinklers and drip-feed systems, have recently been developed, however, to help make more efficient use of available supplies.

Although the most severe water deficiencies are experienced in the dry subtropical and tropical regions of the world, the temperate regions of North America and Europe, in spite of their relatively wet climates, do suffer shortages. Large towns and cities rarely have enough locally available rainfall or river flow to satisfy both domestic demand and the insatiable needs of industry. In the developed nations, industry consumes more water than any other activity.

Industrial demands

Freshwater is not only an integral part of almost every manufacturing process, it has several other important industrial uses. As a source of power, it has been used since the early days of civilization—water wheels were one of man's first industrial inventions. Today, these simple devices are rarely seen in industrial societies, but water power is more important than ever before. Giant dams allow enormous volumes of water to be controlled and the power harnessed to drive turbines and generate electricity.

Freshwater systems have also, for centuries, provided industry with an important means of transporting its goods, and canal systems are still an essential part of industrial infrastructure in many countries of the world: the Europa Canal, when completed, will link three of Europe's major rivers, the Rhine, Main and Danube, and so form a continuous waterway running east–west across the breadth of Europe.

THE VERSATILE RESOURCE
Every day, more than seven billion litres (12 billion pints) of water are removed from the world's freshwater systems. Almost all of this water is then directed to one of four destinations—some is destined for industry, a certain amount is piped to towns and cities for use in public services and in homes, some is fed to agricultural regions, and the rest is stored in reservoirs for future use.

INDUSTRY 19.5%

DOMESTIC 4.4%

AGRICULTURE 73.8%

RESERVOIRS 2.3%

Man obtains freshwater by trapping it as it passes through one of the stages in the hydrological cycle—the never-ending circulation of Earth's waters from the ocean, to the atmosphere, to land. This cycle can be traced from the point at which water evaporates from the sea. The water vapour is blown across the land and falls as rain, hail or snow. Some then evaporates, but the rest completes the cycle by flowing over the land or through the soil or rocks back to the sea. It is at this point in its journey that man obtains his water supplies—from lakes (1), boreholes and wells (2) and dammed rivers (3). These supplies are then either used locally, or are transported by pipe or canal (4) to reservoirs (5) where they are stored ready for distribution.

→ Movement of water in the hydrological cycle

▨ Water-bearing rock

Already, the finished sections of the canal are carrying oil, chemicals, fertilizers, coal, coke and building materials to and from some of Europe's major industrial regions.

Many of Europe's waterways date back to the great canal-building days of the Industrial Revolution. Although a few of these are still used for commerce, many are today considered too narrow to transport economical quantities of goods. Some, however, are now finding a role to play in one of the world's fastest-growing new industries—the leisure market. Today, canals provide a wide range of aquatic activities for holiday-makers, tourists and sportsmen.

Recreation and sport

Freshwater systems throughout the world, in fact, are rapidly being recognized and developed as major recreational resources. Lakes and reservoirs are stocked with fish for anglers, silted waterways are dredged to provide sailing and swimming facilities, and old quarries and opencast workings are landscaped and flooded to provide entirely new freshwater systems purely for leisure pursuits. The projects not only help to rejuvenate previously misused land, they also provide significant incomes to otherwise underdeveloped areas, especially highland regions that are too remote to attract other industries, and are unsuitable for farming.

Unfortunately, however, few of the world's freshwater systems can continue indefinitely to absorb the ever-growing demands that are being made upon them. Overuse of water resources is already a problem and has led to the pollution and destruction of many water systems—in some places over-tapping has lowered water tables so drastically that rivers and lakes have been permanently destroyed. Although steps have been taken to protect certain waterways, legislation to guard against misuse and overuse is costly, time-consuming and, inevitably, comes up against vested interests. Nevertheless, stringent conservation measures are becoming increasingly necessary if society is to maintain one of its most precious resources.

RESERVOIRS

About 70 billion litres (15 billion gallons) of freshwater are held in storage during any one year. Reservoirs ensure a continuous supply of water in spite of the inevitable seasonal fluctuations in demand and in the natural supply from rivers and rainfall. And where reservoirs are formed by damming rivers, there are additional benefits—the vast quantities of water held can be controlled and the power used to generate electricity. The Kariba Dam in Zimbabwe (right) has the potential for producing 8,500 million kilowatt hours of electrical power every year.

1% of world's annual water consumption

In the developed nations of North America and Europe, industry is now the single largest user of freshwater. Water is not only one of the raw materials in many products (food and drink, for example), it is also used indirectly in the course of many manufacturing processes, and in power production. Freshwater canals and rivers also still provide an important means of transporting bulky industrial materials and goods.

The St Lawrence Seaway (left) is one of the busiest waterways in the world. An essential link between North America's east coast and the giant industrial towns of the Great Lakes region, the Seaway carries more than 65 million tonnes of cargo every year. The two-way traffic of cargo vessels takes iron ore west to US steel mills and carries coal and grain east to ports on the coast ready for world export.

Quantity of water to produce 1 tonne

	(cu m)
0 20 40 60 80 100 120 140	(cu m)
0 1,000 2,000 3,000 4,000 5,000	(cu ft)

Finished steel   Cement
Paper and textiles   Petroleum

Most industrial products require water for their manufacture (above), even though as finished articles they may contain none.

Industry, in fact, uses water mainly for cooling purposes (this accounts for the huge amounts required for producing a single tonne of steel). Other processes needing water include the washing of products and flushing away waste materials.

Clean water — Diatom, Perch, Stonefly nymph, Caddisfly larva

Polluted zone — Mosquito, Rat-tailed maggot, Tubifex worm, Sewage fungus

Recovery zone — Carp, Midge larva, Blackfly larvae

Clean water — Stonefly nymph, Caddisfly larva, Diatom, Perch

Industrial pollution of rivers and lakes is now a widespread problem and organic waste (from food factories, for example) is a particularly common form of pollutant. If, however, quantities of such waste are limited, a river may cleanse itself naturally. At first, bacteria that feed on the effluent will multiply, use up all of the water's oxygen, and so kill all life forms except such creatures as mosquito larvae that use surface oxygen. But once the waste is consumed, oxygen levels recover and the waters are then recolonized. Other forms of pollution are more damaging, however— mineral tailings leaking from mineworkings into rivers can permanently destroy wildlife, and oil spillage in rivers and lakes not only kills animal and plant communities, it can turn a waterway into a serious fire hazard.

DOMESTIC

Today, the majority of households in North America and Europe are linked to a mains water supply. This, along with rises in living standards, has created phenomenal increases in domestic water consumption. In the USA, demand averages more than 455 litres (100 gallons) per person per day. About 78% of this is used for washing, bathing and toilet flushing.

AGRICULTURE

More water is used for agriculture than for any other purpose. Irrigation schemes account for almost all of agriculture's consumption, although the extent of irrigated land varies considerably from country to country: in dry subtropical countries, such as Egypt, all farmland depends on irrigation, whereas in Britain more water is used for stock raising.

Quantity of water to produce 1 tonne

0 5 10 15 20 25 30 35	(1,000 cu m)
0 25 50 75 100 125 130	(1,000 cu ft)

Beef   Rice
Milk   Wheat

Agricultural products vary widely in the amounts of water they require (above).

Most kinds of rice need, literally, to be submerged in water while they grow, whereas wheat is a native of relatively dry climates. The water requirements for beef and milk production are mainly due to moisture needed for fodder crops.

Crop irrigation (left) was probably one of mankind's first farming practices. The earliest mechanical method, however, the noria (top left), was not invented until about 2,000 years ago. Developed in the Mediterranean region, it involved using a basic paddle wheel with jars attached which, driven around by the current of a river, lifted water and tipped it into a man-made channel. Such simple mechanisms are still in use in some parts of the world. For large-scale agriculture, however, especially in developed countries, irrigation techniques have become extremely sophisticated. Automatic spray devices (left), for example, are now widely used in North America and in parts of Europe.

Disappearing wetlands: Florida's swamp-forests (below), along with many others of the world's wetland areas, are slowly being destroyed. The fertile soils so often found beneath swamps and marshes have encouraged widespread draining and dredging. Now, man's development of these areas is posing a serious threat to the many plant and animal species inhabiting marshes, swamps and bogs.

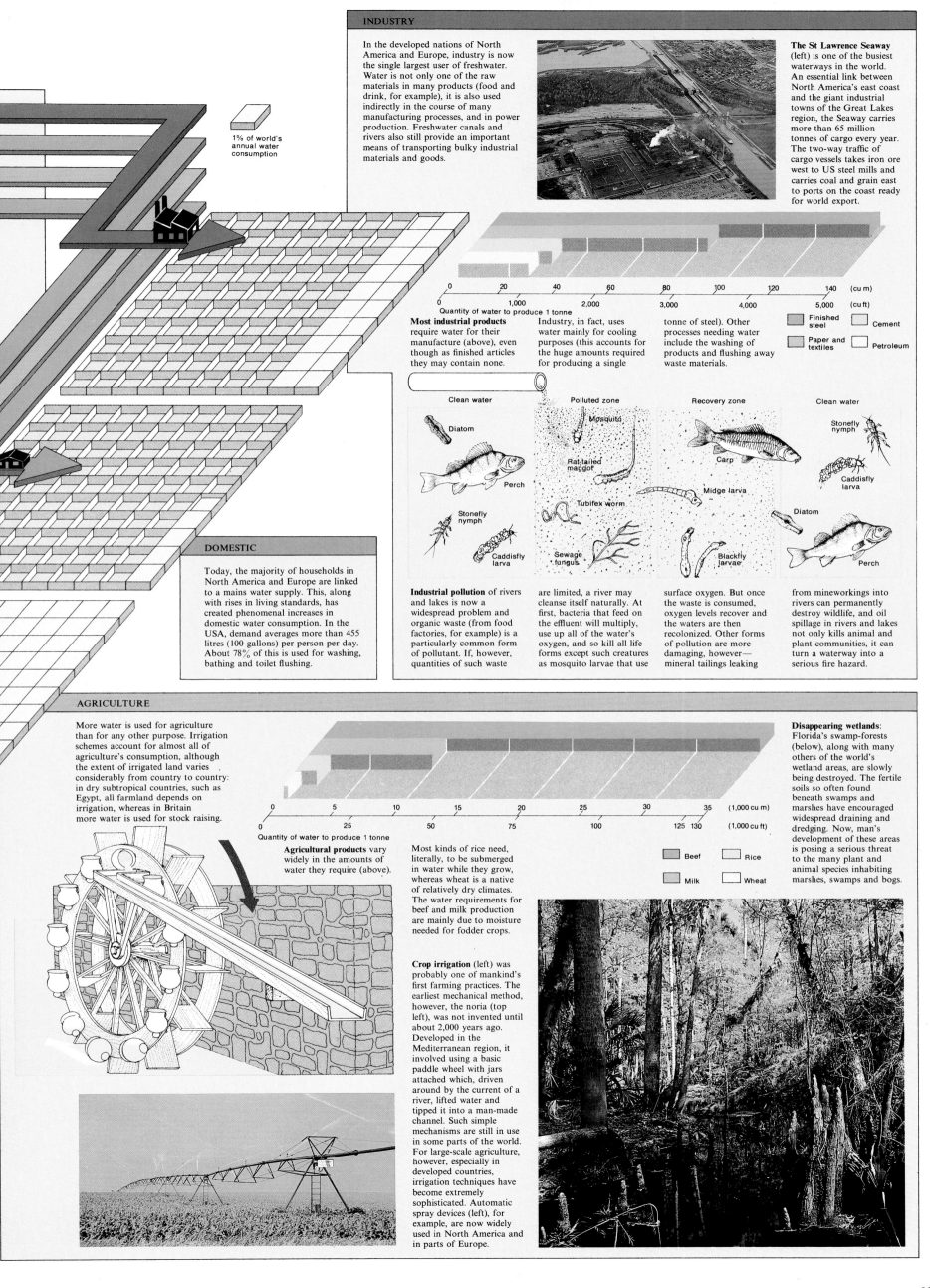

Seawater Environments

The oceans form by far the largest of the world's habitable environments, covering almost three-quarters of the Earth's surface at an average depth of more than 3,500 m (11,500 ft). Little more than a century ago, scientists believed that the deep sea's low temperatures, perpetual darkness and immense pressures made life in these regions completely untenable. But we now know that animals live at all depths in the ocean, even at the bottom of trenches more than 11,000 m (36,000 ft) deep.

THE PATTERN OF MARINE LIFE
The distribution of life in the seas is like an inverted pyramid whose broad base is formed by billions of minute single-celled plants—the phytoplankton. Plants need sunlight and nutrient salts, so phytoplankton occurs only in the upper, sunlit layers and where salts are present. Elsewhere, the distribution of marine life thins out rapidly.

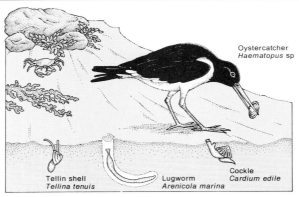

Shore life belongs to both land and sea, and thus has to cope with a wide range of conditions. Seaweeds get all their food from the sea and are quite unlike land plants. Many animals take refuge below the surface: tellin shell molluscs sift food particles through special "lips"; lugworms swallow sand, digesting any organic matter; cockles take in food and eject waste through two siphons. Some birds have bills adapted for opening bivalve molluscs.

Oystercatcher *Haematopus* sp
Tellin shell *Tellina tenuis*
Lugworm *Arenicola marina*
Cockle *Cardium edile*

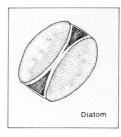
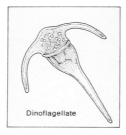
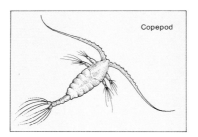

Marine plant life consists largely of diatoms—minute single-celled specks, each enclosed in a lidded box of silicon. Dinoflagellates, classed as plants but able to swim, dominate warmer waters. Both are food for copepods, the flea-sized grazers whose total weight, in the North Sea alone, is some seven million tonnes.

Diatom
Dinoflagellate
Copepod

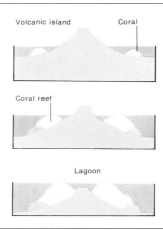

A coral atoll, forming in warm shallow water round an extinct volcano, makes up a living aquarium for thousands of tropical marine life forms. Countless billions of tiny polyps, each secreting a hard, calcareous skeleton, form the first layer of the reef, but die as the volcano gradually sinks. Their skeletons provide a base for further layers of corals, which enclose the sinking island to create a shallow, salt-water lagoon. Different coral species in the same reef provide homes for a great variety of life.

Volcanic island   Coral
Coral reef
Lagoon

Life is by no means evenly distributed throughout the oceans, either vertically or horizontally. The great majority of marine creatures are concentrated in the upper few hundred metres, for the biological organization of life in the seas, as on land, depends on photosynthesis (the process by which plants use the Sun's energy to combine carbon dioxide and water to produce more complex compounds). This near-surface layer is the euphotic ("well-lighted") zone.

Some of the Sun's rays are reflected from the surface of the sea, and those that penetrate are scattered and absorbed as they pass through the water, so that even in the clearest oceanic water there is insufficient light to support photosynthesis at depths greater than about 100 m (330 ft). In turbid inshore regions, where the water is less clear, this near-surface layer may be reduced to a very few metres. So the large seaweeds that anchor themselves to the sea bed are restricted to the small areas of the sea where the water is sufficiently shallow to allow them to photosynthesize. Of much greater importance over most of the oceans are the tiny floating plants of the phytoplankton, which live suspended in the sunlit surface layers.

Pastures of the sea
Phytoplankton, like all plant life, requires not only sunlight for survival but also adequate supplies of nutrient salts and chemical trace elements. River waters carry down considerable quantities of dissolved mineral salts and other matter, so that high levels of phytoplankton production may occur locally around major estuaries. But a far more important source of nutrient supply to the euphotic zone is the recycling of salts that have sunk into the deeper layers, locked up in the bodies of plants and animals or in their faecal pellets.

In those areas of the oceans that overlie the continental shelves (about six per cent of the total), the depth is nowhere more than about 200 m (650 ft), and the nutrient-rich bottom water is fairly readily brought back to the surface by currents and the stirring effect of storms. This stirring can reach much greater depths in near-polar latitudes, where the "water column" is not layered by temperature but remains more or less uniformly cold from top to bottom. In the Antarctic, cold (and therefore heavy) surface water sinks and is replaced by nutrient-rich water that may surface from depths of 1,000 m (3,300 ft).

In subtropical and tropical regions of the open ocean, where the warm surface layer is only a few tens of metres deep, the temperature falls rapidly with depth. There is little exchange between deep and shallow layers, and the euphotic zone receives an adequate supply of nutrient salts only in certain areas. These occur between westward-flowing and eastward-flowing currents in each of the major oceans. The Earth's rotation causes these currents to diverge so as to create an upwelling of nutrient-rich water along their common boundaries.

Finally, in restricted coastal regions of the tropics and subtropics the local climatic conditions cause an offshore movement of surface water, which is again replaced by upwelling nutrient-rich deep water. The central oceanic regions, including the deep blue subtropical waters, are in effect the deserts of the sea.

Sea grazers and carnivores
The abundance of animals in the oceans closely follows that of the plants. But very few of the larger marine animals can feed directly on the phytoplankton because the individual plants are so small—often only a fraction of a millimetre across. Instead, the phytoplankton supports an amazingly diverse community of planktonic animals, which also spend their lives in mid-water and are swept along by the ocean currents. This community, the zooplankton, includes many different protozoans (single-celled animals), crustaceans, worms and molluscs, and also the juvenile stages of fishes and of many invertebrate animals that live as adults on the sea bed. Most members of the zooplankton are very small and many of them graze on the phytoplankton. But some planktonic animals, particularly among the jellyfish and salps, may be a metre or more across and are voracious carnivores feeding on their planktonic neighbours. In turn, the zooplankton provides food for many of the active swimmers such as the fishes and baleen whales, while at the top of the food chain are larger carnivores including

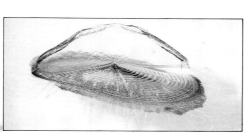

The by-the-wind sailor, *Velella*, is a so-called colonial animal, consisting of a whole collection of animals that function as a single individual. The gas-filled float of its body carries a vertical sail to catch the wind, and below dangle a group of modified polyps specialized for particular roles such as deterrence, reproduction, feeding and digesting.

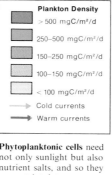

Plankton Density

▓	> 500 mgC/m²/d
▓	250–500 mgC/m²/d
▒	150–250 mgC/m²/d
░	100–150 mgC/m²/d
□	< 100 mgC/m²/d
→	Cold currents
→	Warm currents

Phytoplanktonic cells need not only sunlight but also nutrient salts, and so they are restricted to areas where these are available: coastal regions, high latitudes (particularly the Antarctic), narrow tongues extending across the tropical regions of the main ocean basins, and a number of subtropical upwelling regions.

Zones of life (below) extend from the teeming euphotic ("well-lighted") layer to the sparsely populated bathypelagic ("deep-sea") depths, while benthic ("bottom") life occurs at all sea-bed levels. Phytoplankton (plant life) (1) dictates the pattern of the rest, flourishing where surface conditions allow nutrient salts to well up from lower depths. Herbivores such as minute zooplankton (2) provide food for a host of surface-layer life, which in turn feeds larger predators. Dead animals and faecal pellets fall to lower levels, where they sustain life, but in far smaller quantity.

1 Phytoplankton
2 Zooplankton
3 Blue whale *Balaenoptera musculus*
4 Herring *Clupea harengus*
5 Grey seal *Halichoerus grypus*
6 Bluefin tuna *Thunnus thynnus*
7 Bottlenosed dolphin *Tursiops truncatus*
8 Mackerel *Scomber scomber*
9 Common squid *Loligo* spp
10 White shark *Carcharadon carcharias*
11 Hatchet fish *Argyropelecus hemigymnus*
12 Giant squid *Architeuthis* spp
13 Sea anemone *Cerianthus orientalis*
14 Tripod fish *Benthosaurus grallator*
15 Scarlet prawn *Notostomus longirostris*
16 Angler fish *Linophryne bicornis*
17 Brittle star *Ophiothrix fragilis*
18 Sea cucumber class Holothuroidea

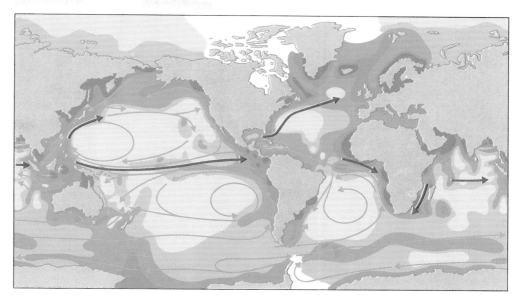

Bizarre life forms new to science live in the sunless depths, where plumes of hot mineral-rich water gush through deep-sea vents in the Earth's crust. These oases of life support huge, gutless tubeworms more than 1.5 m (5 ft) long, which appear to take food particles from the hot vents through blood-red tentacles. Other creatures include blind crabs and large white clams.

sharks, tuna-like fishes and toothed whales.

Beneath the euphotic zone, of course, there can be no herbivores at all, although some animals that spend the daylight hours in the deeper layers move upwards at night to feed in the plankton-rich surface waters. All of the permanent members of the deep-living communities are dependent for food upon material that sinks or is carried downwards from the euphotic zone. Many of them feed on dead animal remains and faecal material as it sinks through the water column or after it reaches the sea bed. These detritus eaters in turn support the predatory carnivores that feed upon the detritivores or upon each other.

In shallow areas the food material that reaches the bottom supports complex communities, notably the rich and varied groups of invertebrates and fishes associated with coral reefs. In the deep sea, however, where the euphotic zone is separated from the sea bed by several kilometres of water, much of the sinking material is recycled within the water column and relatively little reaches the bottom. Life on the deep-sea floor therefore becomes more and more sparse with increasing depth, but in recent years scientists have discovered that this community includes a surprising number of fishes, some many metres in length. So far man's knowledge of these deep-sea communities is relatively meagre, but with our increasing use of the deep oceans we may need to know much more about the life in this environment.

Man and the Seawater Environments

For thousands of years man has used the oceans as a source of food and other materials, and as a repository for wastes. But only in the last 100 years have technological advances and fast-growing human populations had a significant effect, to a point where overfishing and pollution are becoming a cause for concern. Harvesting of krill and seaweeds may ease the pressure on traditional seafoods, but legal restrictions on dumping of wastes or on overfishing are notoriously hard to enforce.

Until about the middle of the nineteenth century the seas had always seemed to be a boundless source of food and of income for fishermen who were brave enough to face the elements with their relatively small sailing ships and primitive gear. But once fishing vessels began to be fitted with steam engines in the 1880s they became relatively independent of the weather, while improvements in the fishing gear itself, such as steam-powered winches in trawling and harpoon guns in whaling, made the whole business of fishing much more efficient.

At first these advances resulted in enormous increases in catches, but in many fisheries this was rapidly followed by a distressing fall in the catch per unit of effort—that is, it was becoming more and more difficult in successive years to catch the same amount of fish as before. In most fisheries the initial response to this situation was to increase the size and number of fishing vessels and to search for new fishing grounds. But as the fishing pressure on the stocks increased, with smaller fish being captured, often before they were able to reproduce, the catch per unit of effort frequently continued to fall.

In many cases attempts were made to counter the effects of overfishing by introducing regulations to control the mesh size of the nets, so allowing the small fish to escape; by establishing closed seasons or quotas of fish which might legitimately be taken from a particular fishing ground in any one year; or even, as in the case of the British herring fishery in the late 1970s, by imposing a complete ban on fishing. Moral questions also sometimes intervene, as in whaling operations, which, many conservationists believe, have driven some species close to extinction despite attempts to rationalize the fisheries.

Fisheries in decline
The North Sea trawl fishery, the first to be affected by the new technology in the nineteenth century, has been declining in terms of catch per unit of effort since the early decades of this century. Dramatic but short-lived improvements after the "closed seasons" of the two world wars proved that fishing pressure had a serious effect on stocks, but by the 1970s many North Sea fishing ports had become almost deserted. This decline put pressure on more distant fishing grounds used by European fishermen, and recent decades have been marked by a series of fishing disputes, with nations fighting for the continued existence of their fisheries despite clear evidence that there are not enough catchable fish to satisfy everyone.

A similar story of declining catches during the present century could be told of many of the old-established fisheries around the world, but at the same time the demand for fish in a protein-hungry world has increased. To satisfy this demand the total annual world catch increased by about seven per cent from the end of World War II until the early 1970s, by this time reaching a figure of around 60–70 million tonnes. But this increase was achieved only by exploiting previously unfished stocks or new geographical areas. Such an increase cannot go on indefinitely, for we are rapidly running out of "new" areas and some of the new fisheries have already shown the same symptoms of overfishing as the older ones—and sometimes even more dramatically.

New foods from the sea
The indications are that the present total catch is close to the maximum that can be obtained from relatively conventional fisheries even with careful management, and that, to increase the total, or even to sustain it, we must look to completely new sources such as krill, the shrimp-like food of the whalebone whales.

Estimates of the sustainable annual catch of krill in the Antarctic range from about 50 to 500 million tonnes, that is up to about seven times as much as the current total from all other fisheries put together. Of course, the use of such an enormous quantity of small crustaceans would present considerable problems. Part of it might be converted into a protein-rich paste for human consumption, but much would be used indirectly as a feed for farm animals.

Many larger seaweeds are already cropped in several parts of the world, particularly in Japan, and are used not only for human food but also for animal food and in many industrial processes. About one million tonnes of seaweed are taken each year, but because seaweeds grow naturally only in relatively shallow areas of the oceans this figure could probably not be significantly increased using natural populations. However, seaweeds can be grown artificially on frames floating over deep water. Experiments suggest that, by enriching the surface layers through artificial upwelling of nutrient-rich deep water, each square kilometre of such a floating seaweed farm could produce enough food to feed 1,000–2,000 people, and enough energy and other products to satisfy the needs of a further 1,000. With an estimated 260 million sq km (100 million sq miles) of "arable" surface, the seas might thus support up to 10 times the present world population.

Polluted waters
Of course, the present century has seen an increase not only in what man takes out of the sea but also in the harmful substances that he throws into it. Not only oil but many other substances are dumped into the seas accidentally or intentionally, usually either in the discharged effluent from industrial plant or as a result of agricultural chemicals being leached into rivers and thence into the ocean. In many cases the amounts are very small compared with the amounts present in the oceans as a whole; the problem is that they are usually released, and accumulate, in restricted inshore areas near which we live and from which we obtain most of our sea-caught food.

Since the 1930s there have been both national and international attempts to control pollution by legislation, and since 1958 a series of United Nations conferences has sought agreement on many aspects of international maritime law, including pollution. Despite many prophecies of imminent doom, it does not seem that marine pollution yet poses any general threat to humanity. Nevertheless, with ever-increasing industrialization and the production of more and more toxic materials, including radioactive wastes, it is essential that we monitor the effects of man's activities on the ocean.

The ocean is home to the **Bajau** (above), the "sea gypsies" of southeastern Asia, who inhabit a tract of sea and islands stretching more than 6,500 km (4,000 miles).

Each group has its own clan pattern, blazoned on the sails of their *praus*. The Bajau may live on the open sea in clusters of boats, or in stilt-house villages built over estuaries.

Drilling derrick

Hydrophones

Sonar beacons

Core sample tube

Drilling head

THE MARINE RESOURCES
Modern technology has enabled man to expand his age-old exploitation of the seas to the limit in some areas, and a need for the careful management of our marine resource is imperative. But in some fields, such as energy and the extraction of fresh water, the seas may yield inexhaustible riches.

The deep-sea drilling ship *Glomar Challenger* (above) plays an important role in surveying and prospecting the oceans. It can drill in water depths of 7,000 m (23,000 ft) and obtain core samples 1,200 m (4,000 ft) below the ocean bed. The ship is positioned over the drill hole through signals from a sonar beacon to hydrophones in the hull.

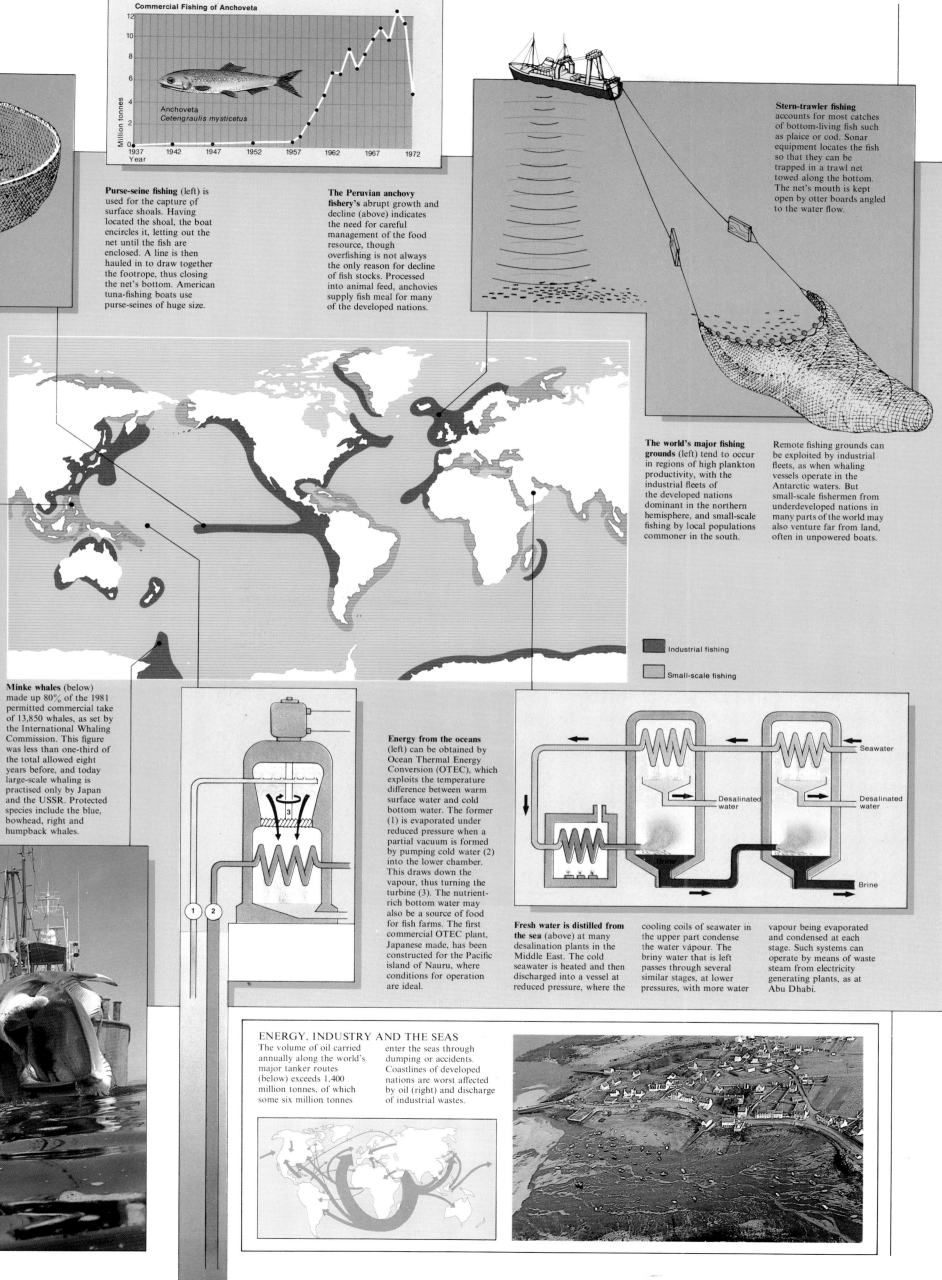

Commercial Fishing of Anchoveta

Anchoveta
Cetengraulis mysticetus

Purse-seine fishing (left) is used for the capture of surface shoals. Having located the shoal, the boat encircles it, letting out the net until the fish are enclosed. A line is then hauled in to draw together the footrope, thus closing the net's bottom. American tuna-fishing boats use purse-seines of huge size.

The Peruvian anchovy fishery's abrupt growth and decline (above) indicates the need for careful management of the food resource, though overfishing is not always the only reason for decline of fish stocks. Processed into animal feed, anchovies supply fish meal for many of the developed nations.

Stern-trawler fishing accounts for most catches of bottom-living fish such as plaice or cod. Sonar equipment locates the fish so that they can be trapped in a trawl net towed along the bottom. The net's mouth is kept open by otter boards angled to the water flow.

The world's major fishing grounds (left) tend to occur in regions of high plankton productivity, with the industrial fleets of the developed nations dominant in the northern hemisphere, and small-scale fishing by local populations commoner in the south.

Remote fishing grounds can be exploited by industrial fleets, as when whaling vessels operate in the Antarctic waters. But small-scale fishermen from underdeveloped nations in many parts of the world may also venture far from land, often in unpowered boats.

Industrial fishing

Small-scale fishing

Minke whales (below) made up 80% of the 1981 permitted commercial take of 13,850 whales, as set by the International Whaling Commission. This figure was less than one-third of the total allowed eight years before, and today large-scale whaling is practised only by Japan and the USSR. Protected species include the blue, bowhead, right and humpback whales.

Energy from the oceans (left) can be obtained by Ocean Thermal Energy Conversion (OTEC), which exploits the temperature difference between warm surface water and cold bottom water. The former (1) is evaporated under reduced pressure when a partial vacuum is formed by pumping cold water (2) into the lower chamber. This draws down the vapour, thus turning the turbine (3). The nutrient-rich bottom water may also be a source of food for fish farms. The first commercial OTEC plant, Japanese made, has been constructed for the Pacific island of Nauru, where conditions for operation are ideal.

Seawater

Desalinated water

Desalinated water

Brine

Brine

Fresh water is distilled from the sea (above) at many desalination plants in the Middle East. The cold seawater is heated and then discharged into a vessel at reduced pressure, where the cooling coils of seawater in the upper part condense the water vapour. The briny water that is left passes through several similar stages, at lower pressures, with more water vapour being evaporated and condensed at each stage. Such systems can operate by means of waste steam from electricity generating plants, as at Abu Dhabi.

ENERGY, INDUSTRY AND THE SEAS

The volume of oil carried annually along the world's major tanker routes (below) exceeds 1,400 million tonnes, of which some six million tonnes enter the seas through dumping or accidents. Coastlines of developed nations are worst affected by oil (right) and discharge of industrial wastes.

Part 5

UNDERSTANDING MAPS

What maps are and how they are made
New horizons and latest developments in maps and map-making
How to read the language of maps

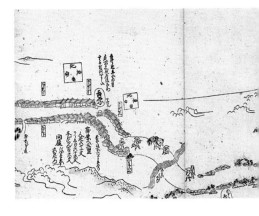

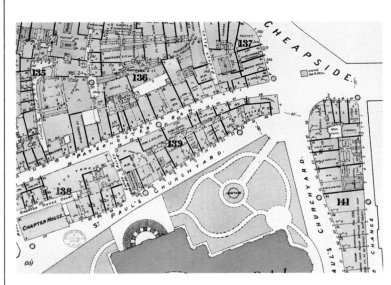

Elegant road maps with pictorial and geographical features have been produced by many different cultures. The woodcut map of the Tōkaidō (detail above), the great Japanese highway, 555 km (345 miles) long, between Edo (Tokyo) and Kyoto, was drawn as a panorama by the famous artist Moronobu in 1690. Its pictorial details do not prevent it being an accurate representation of the road's track. A Mexican map of the Tepetlaoztoc valley (right) drawn in 1583 marks roads with footprints between parallel lines, and hill ranges with wavy lines. Symbols in panels represent place-names.

Maps defining territory and ownership are almost as old as the human territorial instinct itself. The rock-carving maps of the Val Camonica, Italy (above), dating from the second and first millennia BC, show stippled square fields, paths, river-lines, houses, and even humans and animals. It is uncertain whether their purpose was legal, but the need to establish ownership is a basic function of many maps, as seen in a detail from Goad's 19th-century insurance map of London (left), where every occupation is recorded.

America first appears as a separate continent (below) in an inset to Martin Waldseemüller's world map of 1507, with the two hemispheres facing each other. Presiding over the Old World is Claudius Ptolemy, the 2nd-century geographer whose remarkably scientific maps, copied and re-copied over a thousand years, were revised and emended by Waldseemüller to show some of the results of Portuguese exploration. His New World counterpart is the Italian Amerigo Vespucci, one of the early explorers of the continent, after whom it was named. This is the first map to show the Pacific (not yet named) as an ocean between America and Asia. The west coast of South America, still to be explored by Europeans, seems to be inspired guesswork. The island between the landmasses is Cipango (Japan) known from Marco Polo.

The earliest surviving Chinese globe (above) was made in 1623 by two Jesuit missionaries, probably for the emperor of China. The long legend in Chinese expresses terms and ideas derived from early Chinese cosmology. It describes the Earth as "floating in the Heavens like the yolk of an egg . . . with all objects having mass tending towards its centre"— one of the first known references to gravity.

1 2

High-altitude photography (left) allows accurate updating of topographic maps (right), while data-gathering by satellites (above) expands the range. Landsat satellites carry electronic remote-sensing equipment that detects the energy emitted by surface materials and translates it into images. Healthy plants may show as bright red, sparse vegetation as pink, barren lands as light grey, and urban areas as green or dark grey. The folded shape of the Appalachians (1) is clearly seen; the Canada–US border (2) is revealed by land-use patterns; silt from the Mississippi (3) builds up the delta. Sudan irrigation (4) shows up as brilliant red.

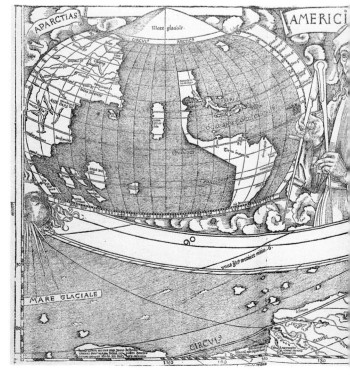

Mapping, Old and New

Map-making must have its origins in the earliest ages of human history, since people of pre-literate as well as literate cultures possess an innate skill in map-drawing. This innate capacity is further indicated by the ease with which almost anyone can sketch in the sand or on paper simple directions for showing the way. But maps may also define territory and express man's idea of the world in graphic representation. Today, modern technology has vastly extended the scope of cartography.

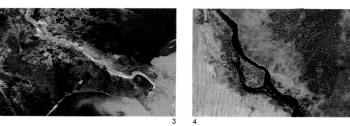

3   4

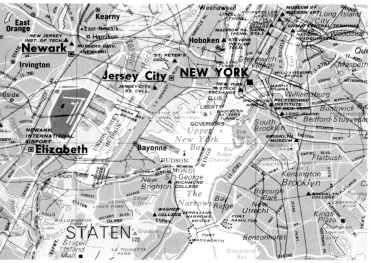

Many non-European cultures developed ingenious route-map techniques: the North American Indians, for example, made sketch maps of routes on birch bark. These were diagrammatic maps in which directions and distances were not accurate but relationships were true, as in London Underground or New York Subway maps. The people of the Marshall Islands in the western Pacific made route maps over the seas, depicting the direction of the main seasonal wave swells in relation to the islands.

Although maps of routes are the simplest type of map in concept, they developed complex forms as cartography progressed. A road map of the whole Roman Empire, drawn about AD 280, survives today in a thirteenth-century copy known as the Peutinger Table. Hernando Cortes, the Spanish conqueror, made his way across Mexico in the 1520s with the help of pre-conquest Mexican maps painted on cloth. These showed roads with double lines or coloured bands marked with footprints. Another type of map is the strip map depicting a single road along its entire length. Pictorial maps of the Tōkaidō highway from Edo to Kyoto in Japan, made from a survey of 1651, were popular in the Edo period of Japanese history.

Nautical charts evolved as a special type of direction-finding map to meet the needs of seamen. Those of the late Middle Ages came to be known as "portolan" charts, from the word "portolani", or sailing directions. They showed the sea and adjacent coasts superimposed on a network of radiating compass lines.

Territorial maps

Another basic type of map derives from man's sense of territorial possession. The earliest example of a "cadastral" plan (a map showing land parcels and property boundaries) appears to be that preserved as rock carvings at Bedolina in Val Camonica in northern Italy. However, in the ancient civilizations of Mesopotamia and Egypt, land surveying had become an established profession by 2000 BC. An idea of what Egyptian surveyors' plans of 1000 BC were like can be seen from the "Fields of the Dead" representing the Egyptians' idea of life after death. These show plots of land surrounded by water and intersected by canals. The Romans used cadastral surveys to determine land ownership and assess tax liability.

Another form of map showing territorial demarcations is the map of administrative units. The Chinese in the thirteenth century AD were making official district maps to help in the organization of grain supplies and the collection of taxes. Many of their gazetteers (*fang chih*), written in the form of local geographies and

histories from the eleventh century onwards, were illustrated with maps. Political maps showing the boundaries of states were increasingly significant in European cartography from the sixteenth century onwards.

A third major class of map is the general or topographical map expressing man's perception of the world, its regions and its place in the universe. A Babylonian world map of the seventh century BC is drawn on a clay tablet and shows the Earth as a circular disc surrounded by the Earthly Ocean. With the ancient Greeks, geography developed on scientific principles. The treatise on map-making by Claudius Ptolemy (AD 87–150), later known as the *Geographia*, was the most famous cartographic text of the period. It influenced the Arabic geographers of the Middle Ages, notably Muhammad Ibn Muhammad, Al-Idrisi (1099–1164), and with the revival of Ptolemy in fifteenth-century Europe became one of the major works of the Renaissance. Published, with engraved maps, at Bologna in 1477, the *Geographia* ranks as the first printed atlas in the western world. The invention of techniques of engraving in wood and copper facilitated a wide diffusion of geographical knowledge through the map-publishing trade. The first atlas made up of modern maps to a uniform design was Abraham Ortelius's *Theatrum Orbis Terrarum* published at Antwerp in 1570. From 1492, when Martin Behaim made his "Erdapfel" at Nürnberg, globes also became popular, and globe-makers vied with each other to make larger and more elaborate ones to keep pace with the growth of knowledge about the world.

Over the last two hundred years cartography has made rapid and remarkable advances. Observatories built in Paris in 1671 and at Greenwich in 1675 enabled the location of places to be established more exactly with the use of astronomical tables. Improvements in surveying instruments facilitated more accurate and rapid land survey. France was the pioneer in establishing (from 1679 onwards) a national survey on a geometrical basis of triangulation. By the end of the eighteenth century national surveys on small and medium scales had been begun by most European countries. In the United States the Geological Survey was set up in 1879 to undertake the topographical and geological mapping of the country.

Mapping today

Since World War II cartographic techniques have undergone a revolution. The use of air survey and photogrammetry has made it possible to map most of the Earth's surface. Electronic distance measurement by laser or light beams in surveying, and digital computers in mapping, are among the most recent advances in methods. Mosaics or air photography are used to produce orthophoto maps which can supplement or substitute for the conventional topographic map. Artificial satellites and manned space craft make it possible to provide a world-wide framework of geodetic networks.

Earth Resource Technology Satellites (ERTS) imagery has made it possible to map mountain ranges in Africa and features on the surface of Antarctica that were hitherto unknown. The imagery is made available by means of remote-sensing instruments, carried by the satellites, that are sensitive to invisible portions of the electromagnetic spectrum—longer and shorter wavelengths than can be sensed by the human eye. Remote-sensing instruments usually work in the infra-red bands. They can also pick up the energy emitted by all types of surface material—rocks, soils, vegetation, water and man-made structures—and produce photographs or images from it.

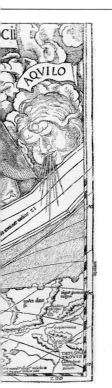

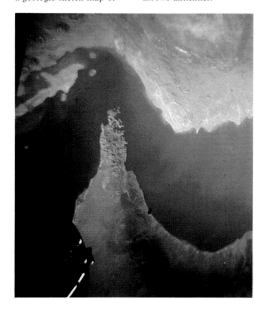

Space technology helps cartographers to map even interior details of the planet: its geology and mineral wealth. A photo (below) taken from Gemini 12 at an altitude of 272 km (168 miles) forms the basis of a geologic sketch map of SW Asia (below right), showing the oil-rich area around the region between the Persian Gulf and the Gulf of Oman. The symbol S on the map indicates salt plugs; diamonds show fold trends; double-headed arrows anticlines.

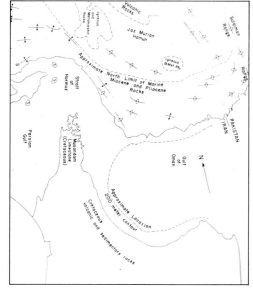

The Language of Maps

Map-makers for more than 4,000 years have tried to find the best way to represent the shape and features of the three-dimensional Earth on two-dimensional paper, parchment and cloth. The measurement of distance and direction is a basic requirement for accurate surveys, but until about 1800 theoretical understanding of the method was well in advance of the technical equipment available. Today the use of lasers and light beams sometimes takes the place of direct measurement on the ground.

A reference system must be used to show distance and direction correctly in the construction of maps. The simplest type is the rectangular or square grid. The Chinese map-maker Pei Xin made a map with a grid in about AD 270, and this system remained in continuous use in China until modern times. The Roman system of centuriation, a form of division of public lands on a square or rectangular basis, was also a "co-ordinate" system starting from a point of origin at the intersection of two perpendicular axes. Roman surveyors' maps, dating from the first century AD, are the earliest known European maps based on a grid system.

Latitude and longitude

Makers of small-scale regional maps and of world maps in early times also had to take account of the fact that the Earth is a sphere. The Greeks derived from the Babylonians the idea of dividing a circle into 360 degrees. In the second century BC the Greek geographer Eratosthenes (c. 276–194 BC) was the first to calculate the circumference of the globe and was reported to have made a world map based on the concept of the Earth's sphericity. From this the Greeks went on to develop the system of spherical co-ordinates which remains in use today. The poles at each end of the Earth's axis provide reference points for the Earth in its rotation in relation to the celestial sphere. Parallel circles around the Earth are degrees of latitude and express the idea of distance north or south of the Equator. Lines of longitude running north and south through the poles express east–west distances. One meridian is chosen as the meridian of origin, known as the prime meridian.

Whereas latitude from early times could be observed from the height of the Sun or (in the northern hemisphere) from the position of the Pole Star at night, accurate observations of longitude were not possible until the middle of the eighteenth century, when the chronometer was invented and more accurate astronomical tables were provided. In 1884 most countries agreed, at an international conference in Washington DC, to adopt the prime meridian through the Royal Greenwich Observatory in England and to calculate longitude to 180 degrees east and west of Greenwich.

Projection and distortion

The mathematical system by which the spherical surface of the Earth is transferred to the plane surface of a map is called a map projection. The Greek geographer Ptolemy gave instructions in his geographical treatise of AD 150 for the construction of two projections. When the *Geographia* was revised in Europe in the fifteenth century, and navigators began sailing across the oceans, map-makers devised new projections more appropriate to the expanding geographical knowledge of the world. The Dutch geographer Gerard Mercator invented the projection named after him, applying it to his world chart of 1569. This cylindrical projection, in which all points are at true compass courses from each other, was of great benefit to navigators and is still one of the most commonly used projections. Another advance was made when Johann Heinrich Lambert of Alsace (1728–1777) invented the azimuthal equal-area projection, in which the sizes of all areas are represented on the projection in correct proportion to one another, and the conformal projection, in which at any point on the map the scale is constant in all directions.

Since all projections involve deformation of the geometry of the globe, the cartographer has to choose the one that best suits the purpose of his map. "Conformal" or "orthomorphic" projections, in which angular relations (or shape) are preserved, are widely used for the construction of topographical maps. "Equivalent" or "equal-area" projections retain relative sizes and are particularly useful for general reference maps displaying economic, historical, political and other geographical phenomena.

Since the mid-fifteenth century, European map-makers have generally arranged their maps with north at the top of the sheet. Earlier maps, however, were not standardized in this way. The circular world maps of the Middle Ages were orientated with east at the top, because this was where the terrestrial paradise was traditionally sited. Indeed, the word "orientation" originally meant the arrangement of something so as to face east.

Map scale

Scale is another basic property of a map. The scale of a map is the ratio of the distance on the map to the actual distance represented. Whereas the Babylonians, Egyptians, Greeks and Romans drew surveys to scale, in medieval Europe map-makers used customary methods of estimating. The earliest known local map since Roman times which is drawn to scale (it displays a scale-bar) is a plan of Vienna, 1422.

Projection, grid, orientation and scale form the framework of a map. The language of maps in concept and content is much more complex. To represent the surface of the Earth on a map, the cartographer must select and generalize from a vast quantity of material, using symbols and conventional signs as codes.

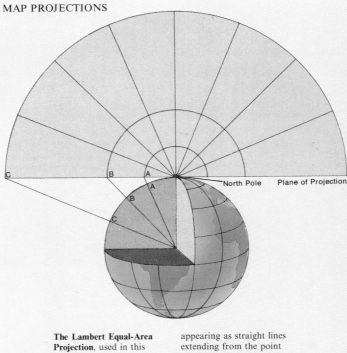

MAP PROJECTIONS

The Lambert Equal-Area Projection, used in this atlas, may be visualized as a flat plane placed at a tangent to the globe, with the lines of longitude appearing as straight lines extending from the point of tangency, the North Pole (above). Deformation increases away from this point (below).

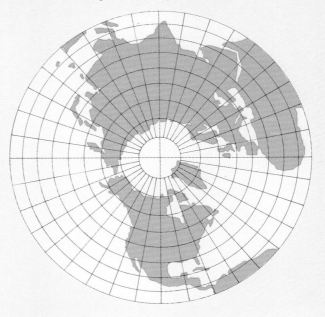

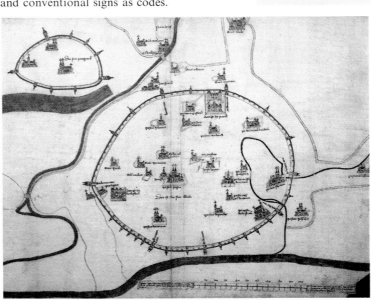

Map scales express the relationship between a distance measured on the map and the true distance on the ground. A plan of Vienna (left), originally made in 1422, is drawn in the bird's-eye-view style typical of early medieval town plans. But the scale-bar at its foot shows that it has been explicitly drawn to scale, indicating that the concept of a uniform scale had been grasped in medieval Europe.

Direction and distance are concepts used in the relative location of two or more points (below). These concepts are organized according to a general frame of reference, with direction following the grid system of co-ordinates. Thus places shown in (A) can be precisely located in terms of longitude and of latitude (B), with the degrees further subdivided into one-sixtieths of minutes.

Denver Colorado   Tokyo Japan

A

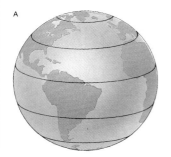 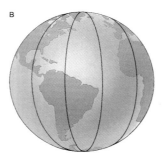 

A   B   C

Superimposed on the globe (left), lines of latitude (A) and longitude (B) allow every place to be exactly located in terms of a co-ordinate system (C). The parallels of latitude measure distance from 0° to 90° north and south of the Equator. The meridians of longitude measure distance from 0° to 180° east and west of a "prime meridian" at Greenwich.

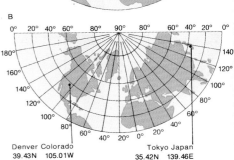

B

Denver Colorado
39.43N 105.01W

Tokyo Japan
35.42N 139.46E

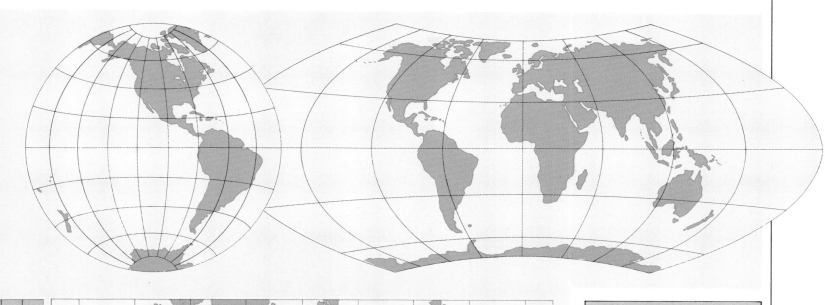

The Hammer Projection (far right), developed from the Lambert Projection of one hemisphere (right), is designed to show the whole world in a single view, and is used in this atlas in a version modified by Wagner and known as the Hammer-Wagner Projection. The Earth appears as an ellipse because the lines of longitude are plotted at twice their horizontal distance from the centre line, and numbered at twice their previous values. The central meridian is half the length of the Equator.

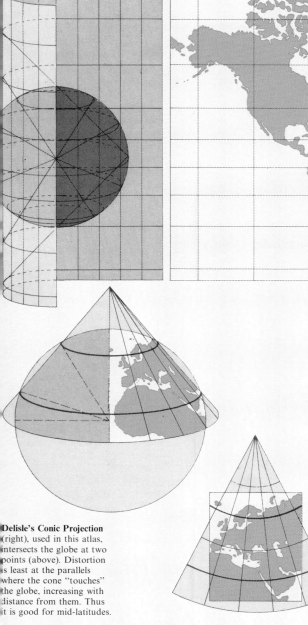

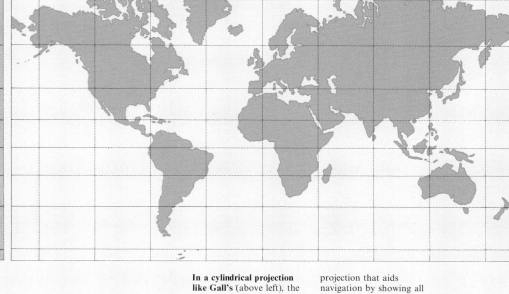

Delisle's Conic Projection (right), used in this atlas, intersects the globe at two points (above). Distortion is least at the parallels where the cone "touches" the globe, increasing with distance from them. Thus it is good for mid-latitudes.

In a cylindrical projection like Gall's (above left), the sphere is "unwrapped" on to a cylinder, making a complete transformation to a flat surface. Mercator's Projection (above), devised in 1569, is a cylindrical projection that aids navigation by showing all compass directions as straight lines. A projection (below), based on Peters', distorts shape to show land surface area ratios, emphasizing the Third World.

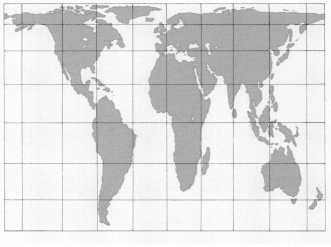

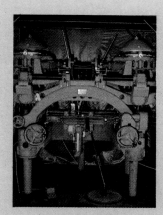

Photogrammetric plotting instruments (above) are now used in the preparation of large-scale accurate topographic maps. These are sophisticated machines that provide very precise measurements, plotting the map data in orthogonal projection.

The theodolite (above), a basic surveying instrument dating back to the 16th century, can measure angles and directions horizontally and vertically. A swivel telescope with cross-hairs inside it permits accurate alignment, and it may be used in the field.

EARTH MEASUREMENT THROUGH THE AGES

Surveying—the technique of making accurate measurements of the Earth's surface—is as old as civilization and has been an essential element in mankind's development of his environment. The need to establish land boundaries arose at least 3,500 years ago in the fertile valleys of the Nile, Tigris and Euphrates rivers. Man's urge to explore and to describe the world also led to the development of instruments determining position, distance and direction. The astrolabe, sometimes called the world's oldest scientific instrument, may date to the 3rd century BC. Today's techniques make increasing use of computers.

An Egyptian wall-painting (left) from the middle of the second millennium BC shows what appears to be the measurement of a grain field by means of a rope with knots at regular intervals on its length.

The astrolabe (right), used in classical times to observe the positions of celestial bodies, became a navigational instrument in the Middle Ages, when it was developed to permit establishment of latitude.

How to Use Maps

Today maps play a role more important than ever before in increasing our knowledge of the Earth, its regions and peoples. How maps communicate knowledge is now a subject of scientific study. The process comprises the collection and mapping of the data and the reading of the map. In this final stage the map-user is all-important. Through him the map is transformed into an image in the mind, and the effectiveness of the map depends on the reader being able to understand it.

The cartographer's map has to convey an objective picture of reality. To compile the map the cartographer selects and generalizes information, taking into account the purpose of his map. If he is making a topographical reference map, he has to reduce the three-dimensional landforms of the Earth on to the flat surface of the map. He adds cultural detail such as towns, roads and railways, and features not apparent to the eye, such as administrative boundaries. On the topographical base map he adds appropriate place-names, using typefaces which reflect their class and significance. All this requires the classification of phenomena, with emphasis to direct the reader's attention.

Themes and symbolization

The cartographer who seeks not merely to represent visible features but to convey geographical ideas about specific phenomena uses the techniques of thematic cartography, where the emphasis is on one or two elements, or themes. Maps today provide one of the most effective means of communicating many kinds of data and ideas relating to the world and its peoples. Their extensive use makes them an important force in education, planning, recreation, and in many other human affairs.

The map is designed in code, with symbols to represent features, and a legend, or key, to explain them. There are three types of symbol: point, line and area. Point symbols usually denote places, which may be distinguished into classes by the shape, colour and size of the symbol. Line symbols express connections, such as roads or traffic flow, and they may also define and distinguish areas. Area symbols in which variations of colour are often combined with patterns of lines or dots are used to depict spatial phenomena, such as types of soil, vegetation and density of population.

How much detail can be shown on a map will depend on its scale, which controls the process of generalization. Scale expresses the relationship of the distance on the map to the distance on the Earth, with the distance on the map always given as the unit 1. It is denoted in various ways: as a representative fraction such as 1:1,000,000; as a written statement; or by means of a graph or bar. Some map scales have become widely used and are generally familiar to map-users. The scale 1:25,000 is ideal for walkers and relief can be shown in detail. That of 1:50,000 is a typical medium scale for national surveys. The publication of an international map of the world on a scale of one to

one million (1:1,000,000) has been in progress since 1909. On this scale 1 mm represents 1 km on the ground. The regional maps of countries in this atlas are drawn on scales of 1:6,000,000, 1:3,000,000 and 1:1,500,000; those of the continents are at 1:30,000,000 and 1:15,000,000. The Map Section index maps show the arrangement.

Terrain depiction

Since the early days of map-making in ancient Chinese and classical Greek and Roman civilizations, map-makers have been concerned to show the configuration of the land. For many centuries they symbolized mountains and hills by pictorial features often looking like caterpillars or sugar loaves. As topographical mapping developed in Europe from the seventeenth century onwards, new techniques were devised to improve the visual impression of the features and to depict them accurately in terms of height and location. The system of hachuring (shading with fine parallel or crossed lines), first used in 1674, gives a good idea of relief but not of height. The use of contours, which became general from the nineteenth century onwards, is more exact in representing actual elevation, but for many regions, especially those of irregular relief, the appearance of the land is lost.

The addition of hypsometric tints (tints between contours which show elevation) helps clarify the elevation. Applying shadows to the form of the land through the process called hill shading or relief shading creates a visual impression of the configuration of the land surface. Hypsometric tints combined with hill shading gives both elevation information and surface form of the area being depicted, leading to an almost three-dimensional effect.

Maps are classed (right) as either general (A) or thematic (B,C). The purpose of a general reference map is to provide locational information, showing how the positions of various geographical phenomena relate to each other. Thematic maps concentrate on a particular type of information, or theme, such as the distribution of people (B) or rainfall (C), and are generally based on statistical data.

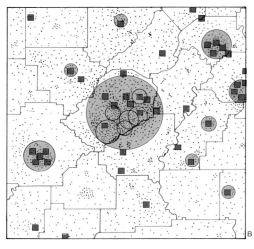

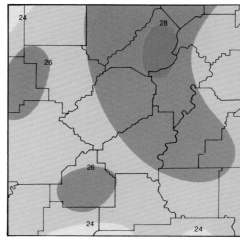

The ratio between a map's dimensions and those of the physical world is defined by the map scale (left and below), with the map distance always given as the unit 1. The larger the reduction, the smaller the scale, so that a scale of 1:6,000,000—1 mm (.04 in) to 6 km (3.74 miles)—is twice that of 1:12,000,000 (.04 in to 7.5 miles). The size of the scale reflects the amount of detail that needs to be shown. The projections are Lambert's Equivalent Azimuthal (left) and Delisle's Equidistant Conical (below).

Scale 1:12,000,000

Scale 1:6,000,000

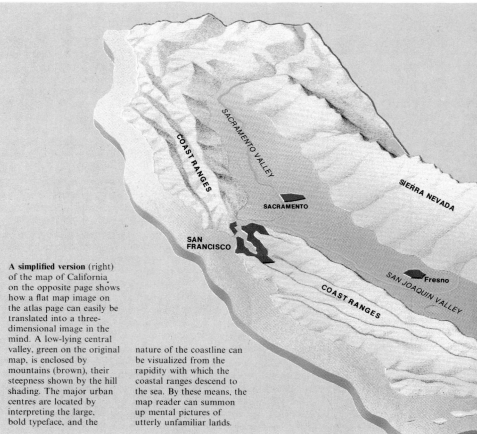

A simplified version (right) of the map of California on the opposite page shows how a flat map image on the atlas page can easily be translated into a three-dimensional image in the mind. A low-lying central valley, green on the original map, is enclosed by mountains (brown), their steepness shown by the hill shading. The major urban centres are located by interpreting the large, bold typeface, and the nature of the coastline can be visualized from the rapidity with which the coastal ranges descend to the sea. By these means, the map reader can summon up mental pictures of utterly unfamiliar lands.

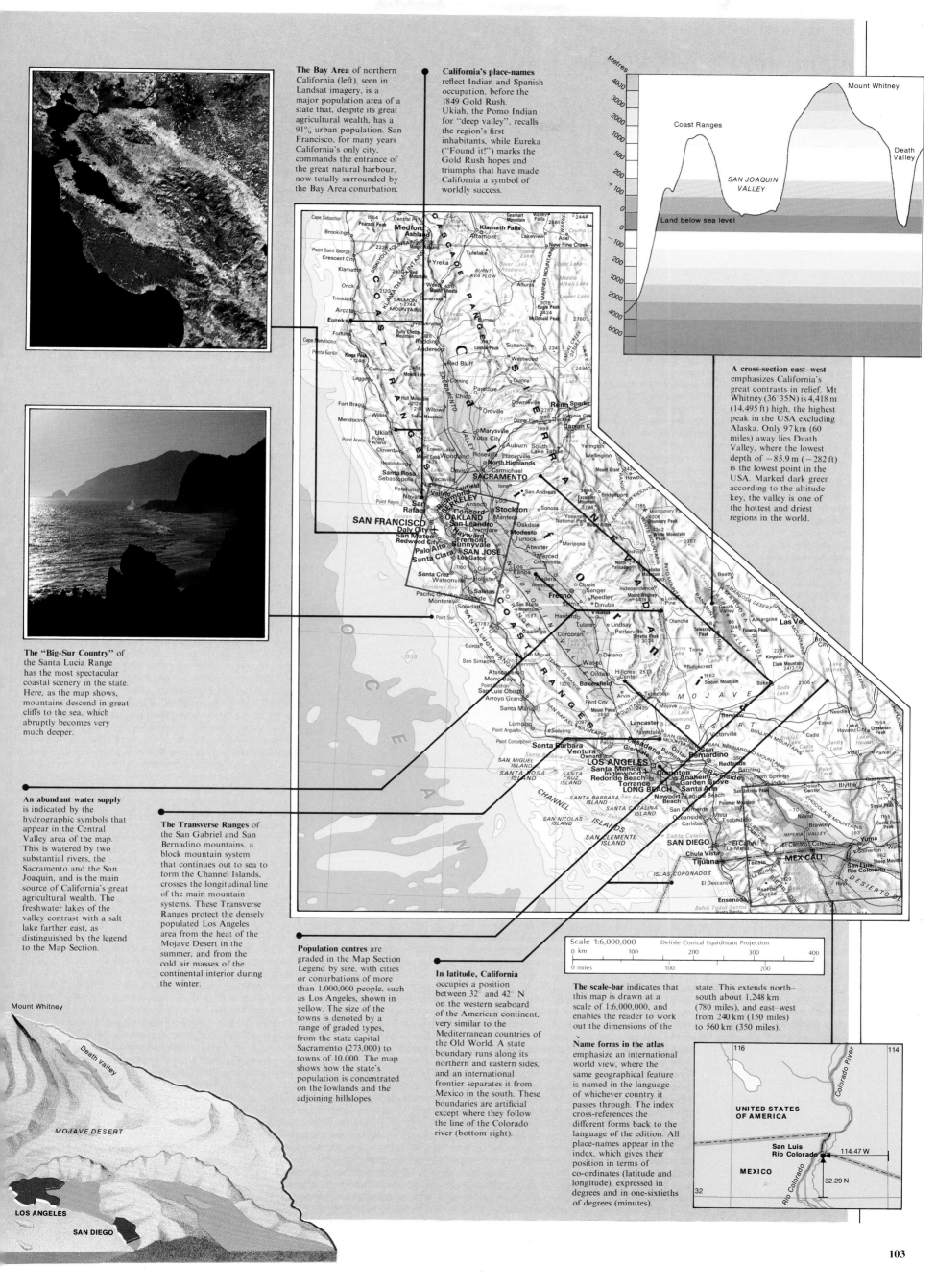

The Bay Area of northern California (left), seen in Landsat imagery, is a major population area of a state that, despite its great agricultural wealth, has a 91% urban population. San Francisco, for many years California's only city, commands the entrance of the great natural harbour, now totally surrounded by the Bay Area conurbation.

California's place-names reflect Indian and Spanish occupation, before the 1849 Gold Rush. Ukiah, the Pomo Indian for "deep valley", recalls the region's first inhabitants, while Eureka ("Found it!") marks the Gold Rush hopes and triumphs that have made California a symbol of worldly success.

A cross-section east–west emphasizes California's great contrasts in relief. Mt Whitney (36°35'N) is 4,418 m (14,495 ft) high, the highest peak in the USA excluding Alaska. Only 97 km (60 miles) away lies Death Valley, where the lowest depth of −85.9 m (−282 ft) is the lowest point in the USA. Marked dark green according to the altitude key, the valley is one of the hottest and driest regions in the world.

The "Big-Sur Country" of the Santa Lucia Range has the most spectacular coastal scenery in the state. Here, as the map shows, mountains descend in great cliffs to the sea, which abruptly becomes very much deeper.

An abundant water supply is indicated by the hydrographic symbols that appear in the Central Valley area of the map. This is watered by two substantial rivers, the Sacramento and the San Joaquin, and is the main source of California's great agricultural wealth. The freshwater lakes of the valley contrast with a salt lake farther east, as distinguished by the legend to the Map Section.

The Transverse Ranges of the San Gabriel and San Bernadino mountains, a block mountain system that continues out to sea to form the Channel Islands, crosses the longitudinal line of the main mountain systems. These Transverse Ranges protect the densely populated Los Angeles area from the heat of the Mojave Desert in the summer, and from the cold air masses of the continental interior during the winter.

Population centres are graded in the Map Section Legend by size, with cities or conurbations of more than 1,000,000 people, such as Los Angeles, shown in yellow. The size of the towns is denoted by a range of graded types, from the state capital Sacramento (273,000) to towns of 10,000. The map shows how the state's population is concentrated on the lowlands and the adjoining hillslopes.

In latitude, California occupies a position between 32° and 42° N on the western seaboard of the American continent, very similar to the Mediterranean countries of the Old World. A state boundary runs along its northern and eastern sides, and an international frontier separates it from Mexico in the south. These boundaries are artificial except where they follow the line of the Colorado river (bottom right).

The scale-bar indicates that this map is drawn at a scale of 1:6,000,000, and enables the reader to work out the dimensions of the state. This extends north–south about 1,248 km (780 miles), and east–west from 240 km (150 miles) to 560 km (350 miles).

Name forms in the atlas emphasize an international world view, where the same geographical feature is named in the language of whichever country it passes through. The index cross-references the different forms back to the language of the edition. All place-names appear in the index, which gives their position in terms of co-ordinates (latitude and longitude), expressed in degrees and in one-sixtieths of degrees (minutes).

Scale 1:6,000,000   Delisle Conical Equidistant Projection

ACKNOWLEDGMENTS

Senior Executive Art Editor
Michael McGuinness

Executive Editor
James Hughes

Co-ordinating Editor
Dian Taylor

Editors
Lesley Ellis
Judy Garlick
Ken Hewis

Art Editor
Mike Brown

Designers
Sue Rawkins
Lisa Tai

Picture Researcher
Flavia Howard

Researchers
Nicholas Law
Nigel Morrison
Alicia Smith

Editorial Assistant
Barbara Gish

Proof-reader
Kathie Gill

Indexers
Hilary and Richard Bird

Production Controller
Barry Baker

Typesetting by Servis Filmsetting
Limited, Manchester, England

Reproduction by Gilchrist
Brothers Limited, Leeds, England

CONTRIBUTORS AND CONSULTANTS

GENERAL CONSULTANT
Professor Michael Wise, CBE, MC, BA, PhD, D.Univ, Professor of
Geography, London School of Economics and Political Science

EDITORIAL CONSULTANT
John Clark

Frances Atkinson, BSc

British Museum (Natural History), Botany Library

Robert W. Bradnock, MA, PhD, Lecturer in Geography with special
reference to South Asia at the School of Oriental and African
Studies, University of London

Michael J. Bradshaw, MA, Principal Lecturer in Geography, College
of St Mark and St John, Plymouth

Dr J. M. Chapman, BSc, ARCS, PhD, MIBiol, Lecturer in Biology,
Queen Elizabeth College, University of London

Dr Jeremy Cherfas, Departmental Demonstrator in Zoology, Oxford
University

Dr M. J. Clark, Senior Lecturer in Geomorphology, Geography
Department, Southampton University

J. L. Cloudsley-Thompson, MA, PhD(Cantab), DSc(Lond),
Hon DSc(Khartoum), Professor of Zoology, Birkbeck College,
University of London

Professor R. U. Cooke, Department of Geography, University
College, London

Professor Clifford Embleton, MA, PhD, Department of Geography,
King's College, University of London

Dr John Gribbin, Physics Consultant to *New Scientist* magazine

Dr John M. Hellawell, BSc, PhD, FIBiol, MIWES, Principal,
Environmental Aspects, Severn Trent Water Authority, Birmingham

Dr Garry E. Hunt, BSc, PhD, DSc, FRAS, FRMetS, FIMA, MBCS,
Head of Atmospheric Physics, Imperial College, London

David K. C. Jones, Lecturer in Geography, London School of
Economics and Political Science

Dr Russell King, Department of Geography, University of Leicester

Dr D. McNally, Assistant Director, University of London
Observatory

Meteorological Office, Berkshire

Dr Robert Muir Wood, PhD

Dr B. O'Connor, Department of Geography, University of London

J. H. Paterson, MA, Professor of Geography in the University of
Leicester

Dr Nigel Pears, Department of Geography, University of Leicester

Joyce Pope, BA

Dr A. L. Rice, Institute of Oceanographic Sciences, Wormley, Surrey

Ian Ridpath, science writer and broadcaster

Royal Geographical Society

Helen Scoging, BSc, Department of Geography, London School of
Economics and Political Science

Bernard Stonehouse, DPhil, MA, BSc, Chairman, Post-Graduate
School of Environmental Science, University of Bradford

Dr Christopher B. Stringer, PhD, Senior Scientific Officer,
Palaeontology Department, British Museum (Natural History)

J. B. Thornes, Professor of Physical Geography and Head of
Department, Bedford College, University of London

UN Information Office and Library

Professor J. E. Webb, DSc, *Emeritus*, Department of Zoology,
Westfield College, University of London

Peter B. Wright, BSc, MPhil

UNDERSTANDING MAPS
Helen Wallis, MA, DPhil, FSA, The Map Librarian, British Library

A great many other individuals, organizations and institutions have
given invaluable advice and assistance during the preparation of this
Encyclopaedia Section and the publishers wish to extend their
thanks to them all.

ILLUSTRATION CREDITS

Maps in the Encyclopaedia Section by Creative Cartography
Limited unless otherwise specified. Map of the world's climatic
regions, page 50, adapted from *An Introduction to Climate* 4th
edition by Trewartha/*Elements of Geography* by G. T. Trewartha,
A. H. Robinson and E. H. Hammond © McGraw-Hill Book Co.,
N.Y., 1967. Used with permission of McGraw-Hill Book Co.
Map diagram page 101 (bottom) courtesy Doctor Arno Peters.

2–3 *Exploding universe* Product Support (Graphics); *others* Quill.
4–5 Bob Chapman. **6–7** Bob Chapman. **8–9** Mick Saunders;
Landsat diagrams Gary Marsh; *biowindows* Chris Forsey. **10–11**
Mick Saunders. **12–13** Bob Chapman. **14–15** *Diagrams* Chris Forsey;
mountain sequence Donald Myall. **16–17** Colin Salmon. **18–19** Peter
Morter; *graph* Mick Saunders; *car* Peter Owen. **20–21** Bob
Chapman; *diagram* Chris Forsey; *map* Colin Salmon. **22–23** Chris
Forsey (*including maps*). **24–25** Brian Delf. **26–27** Brian Delf.
28–29 Dave Etchell/John Ridyard. **30–31** Creative Cartography Ltd.
32–33 Mick Saunders. **34–35** Chris Forsey; *experiment* Gary Hincks;
others Mick Saunders. **36–37** Chris Forsey; *fruit flies, birds and mice*
Donald Myall. **38–39** Chris Forsey; *time-scale* Mick Saunders;
stromatolite and diagram Garry Hincks. **40–41** Donald Myall;
time-scale Mick Saunders. **42–43** Donald Myall; *time-scale* Mick
Saunders. **44–45** Creative Cartography Ltd. **46–47** Donald Myall;
diagram Kai Choi; *skulls* Jim Robins. **48–49** Creative Cartography
Ltd. **50–51** Peter Morter; *diagram* Marilyn Clark. **52–53** Kai Choi.
54–55 Creative Cartography Ltd. **56–57** Creative Cartography Ltd.
58–59 Creative Cartography Ltd. **60–61** Creative Cartography Ltd;
illustrations Jim Robins. **62–63** *Migration diagram and graph* Kai
Choi; *illustrations* Coral Mula. **64–65** Donald Myall. **66–67**
Landscape diagram Bill le Fever; *illustrations* Russell Barnett. **68–69**
Donald Myall. **70–71** Jim Robins; *plants, bottom left* Andrew
Macdonald. **72–73** Rory Kee; *bottom left* Russell Barnett; *plough*
Kai Choi; *grains and graph* Creative Cartography Ltd. **74–75** Bob
Bampton/The Garden Studio; *qanat* Bob Chapman. **78–79** David Ashby.
80–81 David Ashby. **82–83** Coral Mula; *trees, orchid, toucan and
hornbill* Donald Myall. **84–85** Jim Robins. **86–87** Creative
Cartography Ltd. **88–89** Brian Delf; *blood counts diagram* Colin
Salmon. **90–91** Bob Chapman; *animals and plants* Rod Sutterby.
92–93 Kai Choi; *hydrological cycle* Bob Chapman. **94–95** Andy
Farmer; *shore and plant life* Russell Barnett; *coral atoll* Colin
Salmon. **96–97** Creative Cartography Ltd. **98–99** *Topographic maps*
Rand McNally; *sketch map* Space Frontiers Ltd. **100–101** *Diagrams*
Creative Cartography Ltd. **102–103** *Maps* Istituto Geografico De
Agostini; Rand McNally; *diagrams* Creative Cartography Ltd.

PICTURE CREDITS

Credits read from top to bottom and from left to right on each page. Images that extend over two pages are credited to the left-hand page only.

2 US Naval Observatory; California Institute of Technology and Carnegie Institution of Washington. **3** Both pictures from Royal Observatory, Edinburgh. **8** All pictures from NASA. **9** All pictures from NASA except top and top right, courtesy of Garry Hunt, Laboratory of Planetary Atmospheres, University College, London. **14–15** Maurice and Sally Landre/Colorific! **16–17** All pictures courtesy of Dr Basil Booth, Geoscience Features. **18** Institute of Geological Sciences. **19** Paul Brierley; Institute of Geological Sciences. **20** Camera Press, London. **26** Barnaby's Picture Library; Barnaby's Picture Library; Institute of Geological Sciences. **28** Dr Alan Beaumont. **30** Tom Sheppard/Robert Harding Picture Library; Professor Ronald Cooke. **31** Institute of Geological Sciences. **32** Stuart Windsor; Sefton Photo Library, Manchester; Rio Tinto Zinc; Douglas Botting; Aspect Picture Library. **33** NASA; Mireille Vautier; Explorer/Vision International. **34** Paul Brierley. **37** Paediatric Research Unit, Guy's Hospital Medical School; Dr Laurence Cook, Zoology Department, University of Manchester. **39** Both pictures from British Museum (Natural History). **46** Colophoto Hans Hinz. **47** Dr P. G. Bahn, School of Archaeology and Oriental Studies, University of Liverpool/Musée des Antiquités Nationales, St. Germain-en-Laye. **56** UNICEF (Photo no. 8675 by H. Dalrymple). **57** Dr A. M. O'Connor, Department of Geography, University College, London. **61** International Fund for Animal Welfare; K. Kunov/Novosti Press Agency; Popperfoto; Charles Swithinbank. **62** Alan Robson. **63** Gösta Hakansson/Frank Lane Agency. **65** G. R. Roberts. **67** Anglo-Chinese Educational Trust; Aerofilms. **69** Ted Streshinsky. **72** Engraving from *At Home with the Patagonians.* **73** The Mansell Collection. **76** J. Bitsch/Zefa; Penny Tweedie/Colorific! **77** Alan Hutchison Library; Bill Holden/Zefa. **80** Syndication International; Gerald Cubitt/Bruce Coleman Ltd; Bruce Coleman Ltd. **81** Alan Hutchison Library; R. and M. Borland/Bruce Coleman Ltd; M. P. Kahl/Bruce Coleman Ltd; Jan and Des Bartlett/Bruce Coleman Ltd. **84** J. von Puttkamer/Alan Hutchison Library. **85** Marion Morrison. **86–87** Richard and Sally Greenhill. **88** Alan Hutchison Library; The Association of Universities for Research in Astronomy, Inc. **89** Gunter Ziesler/Bruce Coleman Ltd. **91** Mike Price/Bruce Coleman Ltd. **92** Ian Murphy. **93** Paolo Koch/Vision International; J. Allan Cash; M. Timothy O'Keefe/Bruce Coleman Ltd. **94** Heather Angel. **95** Institute of Oceanographic Sciences. **96** Fritz Prenzel/Bruce Coleman Ltd; Gordon Williamson/Bruce Coleman Ltd. **97** Martin Rogers/Susan Griggs Agency. **98** British Library; British Museum; Centro Camuno di Studi Preistorici; British Library; NASA; NASA; Rand McNally; British Museum; British Museum. **99** British Museum; NASA; NASA; Rand McNally; Space Frontiers Ltd; Paul G. Lowman/NASA Goddard SFC/Space Frontiers Ltd. **100** Historisches Museum, Vienna. **101** Hunting Surveys Ltd; Michael Holford/Science Museum, London; Michael Holford; Michael Holford/Science Museum, London. **103** Space Frontiers Ltd; F. Damm/Zefa.

Page numbers in *italic* refer to the illustrations and their captions.

A

aardvark, *79*
aardwolf, *79*
aborigines, 47
Abu Dhabi, *97*
Acacia, 78; *78–9*; *A. baileyana, 68*
Acantherpestes ornatus, 39
Acinonyx jubatus, 79
Actophilornis africanus, 79
Addax nasomaculatus, 74
Adelaide, 73
Aden, Gulf of, 18
Adriatic Sea, *20*
Aedes impiger, 91
Aegean Sea, 15
Aeluroidea, 42
Africa: aquifers, 24; cities, 56; climate, 68; continental drift, 15, 44; *12–13;* deforestation, 32; *30, 75;* early man, 46–7; *46;* energy sources, 52; mapping, 99; monsoon regions, 86; *86;* mountain building, *14;* population growth, 54; *55;* savannas, 78, 80, 81; *78–81;* spread of mammals to, *44;* transport, *59;* tropical rainforests, 83, 84–5; *82–3, 85*
African Rift Valley, 18
Agave americana, 74
agouti, orange-rumped, *82*
agriculture, 44, 58–9; and climate, 51; grasslands, 72–3; *72–3;* improvements, *55;* irrigation, 25, 32, 33, 68, 76–7, 80, 86, 92; *76–7, 93;* land reclamation, 33; *33;* Mediterranean regions, 68; *68–9;* monsoon regions, 86; *87;* prehistoric, *47;* satellite monitoring, 8; *9;* savannas, 80–1; *80–1;* and temperate forests, 66–7; *66–7;* Third World, 54; tropical rainforests, 84; *84;* use of water, 92; *92–3*
Ailurus fulgens, 89
air pressure, 7
air surveys, maps, 99
aircraft, *58*
Akimiski Island, *9*
Al-Idrisi, 99
Alaska, 13, 20, 44, 63; *44, 62*
Alauda arvensis, 71
Aldebaran, *2*
aldehydes, *35*
alder, 62
Aleutian Islands, *44*
algae, 38, 60, 90; *38–9*
Algeria, 68, 77; *30*
Allahabad, *48*
alluvial deposits, 18; *19*
Alopex lagopus, 62
Alpine-Himalayan Mountain Belt, 13
Alpine soldanella, *88*
Alps, 15, 26, 44, 88; *27, 88*
alumina, 17

aluminium, *10*
aluminium oxide, 17
Amazon river, *90*
Amazonia, 85; *32*
Ambrona, *46*
amino acids, 35, 36; *34–5*
ammonia, 6; *35*
ammonites, 41
amphibians, 38, 40, 83, 90; *38–40*
Amundsen-Scott base, 60
anchovy, *97*
Andes, 15, 44, 74
andesite, 15, 20; *16*
Andrewsarchus, 42
Andromeda Galaxy (M31), *3*
Andropogon scoparius, 70
Anemone patens, 70
angler fish, *95*
animals, *see* mammals
annelids, *39*
Anomalurus erythronotus, 83
Antarctic Treaty (1959), 60
Antarctica: glaciers, 26; ice, 24, 26, 60; krill, 60, 96; *60–1;* mapping, 99; ocean, 94; *95;* ocean currents, 22; plate tectonics, 13, 44; *12–13;* whaling, 97
Antares, *2*
anteater, lesser, *83;* scaly, 83
antelope, 81; *42, 45, 81;* Addax, *74*
anticlines, *14, 99*
Antilicapra americana, 44
ants, 82, 83; harvester, *74;* honey, 75; *75*
apapane, *36–7*
apes, 83; *45*
Appalachian Mountains, 64; *14–15, 88, 98*
Aptenodytes forsteri, 61
aquifers, 24
Aquila chrysaetos, 89; A. rapax, 71
Arabia, 15; *45*
Arabs, 99
arapaima, 90
Araucaria heterophylla, 41
Arbutus unedo, 69
Archaeomeryx, 42–3
Archaeopteryx, 41; 41
Archaeotherium, 42–3
Architeuthis spp., *95*
Archosaurs, 41
Arctic, 22, 28, 60; *60–1*
Arctic Ocean, 33, 60, 62; *61*
Arctoidea, 42
Ardea goliath, 79
Arenicola marina, 94
arêtes, 26
Argentina, 73, 74, 81; *60*
argon, 6
Argyrolagus, 42
Argyropelecus hemigymnus, 95
Aristotle, 49
Arizona, 77
Arkhangelsk, 49
armadillos, 42; *44*
arsenical bronze, 18
Arsinoitherium, 42
art, prehistoric, *46*
Artemisia dracunculoides, 70
arthropods, *38–9*
Artiodactyls, *41–2*
ash fallout, volcanoes, *21*
ash trees, 64

Asia: climate, 51; continental drift, 15, 44; *13;* deserts, 74; early man, 47; *46;* monsoon regions, 86; *86–7;* mountain formation, 15; population growth, 54; *55;* satellite mapping, 99; savanna, 78, 80; spread of animals to, *44–5;* temperate forests, 64, 66; *64, 66–7;* tropical rainforests, 85; *82–5;* urbanization, 56
Asia Minor, 68
Assam, 86
Association of South-East Asian Nations (ASEAN), *59*
asterism, 18; *19*
asteroids, 4, 11; *5*
Asteroxylon, 39
asthenosphere, 11
astrolabes, *101*
Astronomical Units (AU), *5*
astronomy, 3–5; *88*
Aswan High Dam, 32
Atacama desert, 76, 77
Atlantic Ocean: currents, 22; plate tectonics, 15; *13, 14;* satellite observations, *9*
atmosphere: and the climate, 50–1; and creation of life, 35; *35;* creation of oxygen in, 38; *38;* and destruction of rainforests, 85; Earth's, 6–7; *6–7;* hydrological cycle, 24; pressure, 7; structure, 7; *6–7*
atomic clocks, 4
Attica, 68; *68*
auroras, 7
auroch, 66
Australia: and Antarctica, 60; climate, 68; continental drift, 44; *13;* early man, 47; fossils, 38; *39;* grasslands, 70, 73; *70, 73;* marsupials, 44; *42, 45;* minerals, 77; monsoon regions, 86; population density, 56; *57;* rainforest, 64; savanna, 78, 80, 81; *80;* spread of animals to, *44;* temperate forests, 64, 67; *64;* wine, *69*
Australian zoogeographical region, *45*
Australopithecus afarensis, 46; 46; A. africanus, 47; A. boisei, 47
autumn equinox, *5*
avalanches, 27
Aysheaia pedunculata, 39

B

Babylonians, 99, 100
Bacon, Francis, *12*
bacteria, 38, 64, 71, 82; *31, 38*
badgers, 63, 64; *65*
badlands, 24
Bahu Wuhu, 18
Baikal, Lake, 62, *90–1*
Bailey's mimosa, 68
Baja California, 75
Bajau, 96
Balaeniceps rex, 79
Balaenoptera musculus, 61, 95
Baltimore, *9, 56*

bamboo, *65, 87*
Bandung, 56
Bangladesh, 22, 84
baobab tree, 78
Barrow, Alaska, *49*
basalt, 13, 18, 20; *16*
batholiths, 15
bats, 44, 83; long-nosed, *75*
Les Baux, *19*
bauxite, 52, 85; *19, 52*
beaches, 28, 29; *28*
bear-dogs, *42–3*
bears, 42, 63; *42*; Asiatic
   black, *89*; North American
   black, *65*; polar, 60; *61*
beaver, 63, 90; *45, 90*
Bedolina, *99*
beech, 64; silver, *64*;
   southern, *65*
Behaim, Martin, *99*
Belgium, 56
Benthosaurus grallator, 95
bergschrund, *27*
Bering land bridge, 47; *44*
Bermuda grass, *79*
bharal sheep, *89*
"Big Bang" theory, universe,
   3; *2*
biomes, 49; *48–9*
birch, *62*
bird of paradise, *45*
birds: deserts, *74–5*; evolution,
   41, 42; *41*; flightless, *42*;
   freshwater environment, 90;
   90–1; migration, *61*;
   mountains, 88; *89*; natural
   selection, *36–7*; polar
   regions, 60; *60–1*; savanna,
   78; *79*; spread of, 44; *45*;
   temperate forests, 64; *65*;
   temperate grasslands, *71*;
   tropical rainforests, *82–3*;
   tundra and taiga, 63; *63–4*
birth control, 54, 55; *55*
bison, 70; *44, 70–1*; European
   wood, 64; *67*
Bison bison, 44, 70
Biston betularia, 37
Bitter Lakes, *45*
bitumen, *53*
Black Country, England, 56
black holes, 3; *3*
blackbird, *65*
blackfly, 90, *93*
blindfish, *90*
blue grama grass, *70*
blue-green algae, 38
blue kleinia, *74*
bluebells, *65*
bluefin, tuna, *95*
Boers, 73; *72*
borax, *32, 77*
Bordeaux, *49*
Borneo, 44, 84
boron, *19*
Bos grunniens, 89
Boston, 56; *56*
Bothriolepis, 39
boulder clay, *27*
Bouteloua gracilis, 70
brachiopods, *39*
Brachiosaurus, 40–1
Brachyteles arachnoides, 83
Bradypus torquatus, 83
Brahmaputra river, *90*
brambles, *65*
brambling, *63*

Branchiostoma, 39
Brandt Commission, 59; *59*
Branta bernicla, 63
Brasilia, 56
brass, 18
Brazil, 8, 52, 56, 78, 81, 85;
   32, 81, 85
breccia, *17*
brines, metal-rich, *18*
bristleworms, *38–9*
Britain, 26, 27, 56, 59, 64, 96;
   9, 93
brittle star, *95*
Broken Hill, 56
bromeliads, 78, 82; *82*
Brontotherium, 42–3
bronze, 18
Bronze Age, 18; *66*
Bubo virginianus, 75
Buceros rhinoceros, 83
Buenos Aires, 73
buffalo, 81; forest, 83; *82*
buffalo grass, *70*
bullhead, *90*
bunting, snow, *63*
Burley Griffin, Lake, *57*
Buteo jamaicensis, 71
Buthus occitanus, 75
by-the-wind sailor, *95*

C

cacti, 75, 78; *75*
caddisfly, *93*
cadastral plans, *99*
cadmium, *19*
Caiman crocodilus, 91
calcite, 18, 31
calcium, 17; *19, 23*
calcium carbonate, *17, 19*
calcium salts, 18, 24
calderas, 21; *21*
Caledonian mountains, *14*
calendar, 4
California, 13, 28–9, 68, 77;
   13, 32, 50, 69, 72, 102–3
California Current, *50*
Callisaurus draconoides, 74
Callithrix jacchus, 44
Cambrian Period, 38
camelids, *44*
camels, 75; *42, 74*
Camelus bactrianus, 74;
   C. dromedarius, 74
Canada: grasslands, 73;
   mountain building, 15; *15*;
   population density, 56;
   satellites, 8; *9, 98*; tides, 22;
   tundra, *63*; uranium
   deposits, 18; *see also* North
   America
canals, 32–3, 76, 92; *93*
Canberra, 56; *57*
Canis aureus, 78; C. latrans,
   70; C. lupus, 63; C.l.
   nubilus, 70
Canthonlaevis drury, 71
Cape Horn, 28
Cape Province, 68
capercaillie, 63; *62*
Capet, Hugh, King of
   France, *57*
carbon, *19*
carbon dioxide: in amino
   acids, 35; in atmosphere, 6,
   85; *6, 19*; "greenhouse
   effect", 6, 51; *51*

carbon monoxide, 35
carbonic acid, 31
Carboniferous Period, 40; *40*
carborundum, *19*
Carcharadon carcharias, 95
Cardium edile, 94
Carex sylvatica, 42
Caribbean, 50
caribou, 62, 63; *62*
Carmel, Mount, 46
carnivores, 41, 42, 70; *40–1,*
   42, 70–1
carp, *93*
carrion beetle, *78–9*
carrion fly, *78–9*
cartography, 99–100, 102;
   98–103
cassowary, 45
cat family, *42–3*
catfish, African, *91*
cattle, 81, 88; *42–3, 81*
caves, 18, 24; *19, 90–1*
cedar of Lebanon, *68–9*
Cedrus libani, 69
Celebes, 44
cells, 35, 36; *36–7*
cementation, *17*
Cenozoic era, 41, 42; *42*
centipedes, 75
Central America, 47, 86; *44*
Centrocercus urophasianus, 71
Cereus giganteus, 75
Cerianthus orientalis, 95
Cetengraulis mysticetus, 97
chalk, 24
Chameleo chameleon, 83
chameleon, *83*
La Chapelle, 46
charcoal, 66, 68; *66, 68*
Charnia, 39
cheetah, 78; *78–9*
chemical weathering, 31; *31*
chernozem soils, 71; *48*
chestnut, 68; *68*
Chicago, 56, 58; *32–3, 67*
Chile, 64, 68, 76, 77; *21, 60,*
   64–5, 68–9
Chilopoda, 75
chimpanzee, *45, 83*
China, 45; communes, *86*;
   deforestation, *66–7*; deserts,
   77; early man, 46;
   earthquakes, *98*; mapping,
   8, 99, 100, 102; *98*; oil, 52;
   population movements, 56;
   rivers, 25, 33; temperate
   forests, 64; *64*
chipmunk, 64; eastern, *65*
chlorine, 22; *23*
Choloepus didactylus, 44
chough, Alpine, 88; *89*
Choukoutien, 46
chromium, *18, 19*
chromosomes, 36; *36–7*
chronometers, 100
Chrysemys picta dorsalis, 91
cichlids, 90
Cinclus cinclus, 90
cirques, 26; *26–7*
Citellus citellus, 70
cities, 56; *32, 57, 67*
citron, *68–9*
Citrus medica, 69
Ciudad Bolivar, 56
Ciudad Guayana, 56

civet, *42*; oriental, *82*
Cladoselache, 39
clams, *95*
clay, 27, 29, 35; *16–17, 27*
cliffs, 28, 29; *28–9*
climate, 49–51; *48–51*; deserts,
   74; *75*; grasslands, 70; *70–1*;
   Mediterranean, 68; *68*;
   monsoon, 86; *86–7*;
   mountains, 88; polar, 60;
   satellite monitoring, 8; *9*;
   savanna, 78, 80; *78*; and the
   spread of man, 47; taiga,
   62; tropical rainforests, 82;
   82; tundra, 62
clouds, 8, 50; *50–1*
club mosses, 38, 40; *38–40*
Clupea harengus, 95
coal, 6, 17, 18, 52, 66; *40,*
   52–3, 62, 67
coal forests, 40; *38*
coastlines, 28–9, 33; *28–9, 33*
Coccothraustes coccothraustes,
   65
cockatoo, *45*
cockle, *94*
cockroaches, 44
cocoa, 85
coconuts, *87*
coelenterates, 38
coffee, 85; *81*
Colombia, 59
Colombo Plan, 59
Colorado, 74
Colorado river, 76; *103*
colugo, 45
comets, 4
Commonwealth, 59
compaction, rock
   formation, *17*
compass navigation, 100; *101*
computers, mapping, 99; *101*
Condylarthrans, 42
conformal projections, 100
"conglomerates", rocks, *17*
Congo river, *90*
conic projections, *101*
conifers, 62, 66; *40, 62, 65, 68*
Connochaetes taurinus, 79
contact metamorphism, 18
continental drift, 12–13, 15,
   18, 44; *12–13*
continental shelf, 15, 22, 44,
   94; *23*
continental slope, *22–3*
continents, mountain
   formation, 15; *14–15*
Contopus virens, 65
contours, maps, 102
convergent evolution, 68
copepod, *94*
copper, 18, 52; *18–19, 52, 59*
Copper Age, 18
coppicing trees, 66; *66*
coral reefs, 28, 95; *94*
core, Earth's, 11; *10*
Coriolis effect, 50
corries, 26
Corsica, 68
Cortes, Hernando, 99
Corvus corax, 62
Corylus avellana, 65
Corythosaurus, 40
"cosmic microwave"
   radiation, 3
cosmic years, 3
cotton, *81*

cotton-top tamarin, *83*
cottonwood tree, 75
Cottus bairdi, 90
Council for Mutual Economic
   Aid (COMECON), *58–9*
cowboys, *72*
coyote, 63; *70–1*
coypu, 90
crabs, *39, 95*
cranberry, *65*
crayfish, *90*
crested seriema, *44*
Cretaceous Period, 41; *40–1*
crevasses, *26–7*
crinoids, *38–9*
crocodiles, 90; *79, 91*
Crocodilians, 41
Crocuta crocuta, 79
Cro-Magnon Man, *46–7*
crossbills, 63; *62*
Crotalus spp., *44;*
   C. cerastes, 75
crowfoot, river, *90*
crust, Earth's, 11, 13; *10,*
   12–13
crustaceans, 94; *39*
crystals, rocks, *16*
"cumulates", rocks, *17*
Curculionidae, 44
currents, oceans, 22; *23*
cushion pink, *89*
Cycadales, *40*
cyclones, 51
Cyclostigma, 39
Cynodon dactylon, 79
Cynomys ludovicianus, 70
Cyperus papyrus, 79
Czechoslovakia, 18

D

Dama dama, 45
Damaliscus lunatus topi, 79
dandelion, *77*
Danube, river, 92
Daphoenus, 42–3
darkling beetle, *75*
Darwin, Charles, 36, 44
Dasyprocta aguti, 82
"dawn horse", 42
Dead Sea, 22
Death Valley, *103*
deciduous trees, 64; *64–5*
deer, 44, 66; *42, 45, 62–3*;
   pampas, 70; white-tailed, *65*
deforestation, 8, 32, 52, 66–7;
   66–7
Deimos, 4
Deinonychus, 40
deltas, 25; *24*
Demidoff's bushbaby, *83*
Deomys ferrugineus, 82
deoxyribonucleic acid,
   see DNA
depressions, weather, 50; *50*
desalination, 76
deserts, 30, 52, 74–7; *30, 74–7*
desmids, 90
Devonian Period, 38; *38–9*
diamonds, 18, 63
diatoms, 90; *93, 94*
Diatryma, 42
Diceros bicornis, 79
Dickinsonia costata, 39
diesel fuel, *53*
Dimetrodon, 40
dingo, 78

Dinka, 47
dinoflagellates, *94*
dinosaurs, 40–1; *40–1*
diorite, 16
Dipodomys deserti, 75
dipper, 90
Diptera sp., *89*
Dipterus, 39
disease, 55
DNA (deoxyribonucleic acid), 35, 36; *36*
dogs, 44; *42*; Cape hunting, *78–9*; wild, 78
dolerite, 16
dolphin, bottlenosed, *95*
Dorcas gazelle, *74*
dragonflies, 40
Drosophila melanogaster, 36
drumlins, 26
dry farming, 77
Dryopithecus, 43
Dunkleosteus, 38; 39
dykes, volcanic, *21*

E

eagle, crowned, *82*; golden, *89*; hawk, *83*; tawny, *71*
Earth: crust, 13, 15; *12–13, 14*; latitude and longitude, 100; *100–1*; as a planet, 6–7; *6–7*; satellite observations, 8; *8–9*; in the Solar System, 4; *4–5*; structure of, 11; *10–11*
Earth Resource Technology Satellites (ERTS), 8, 99
earthquakes: causes, 20; *20*; plate tectonics, 12, 13, 15; *12*; and the structure of the Earth, 11; *10*; tsunamis, 22; *23*
earthworms, 64, 71, 82; *71*
Eastern Woodland Indians, 66; *66*
Echmatocrinus, 39
eclipses, *4*
ecology, 49
economic development, 55
ecosystems, 49; *48–9*
Ediacara Sandstones, 38; *39*
Edo, 99; *98*
education, 55
Egypt, 18, 76, 99, 100; *93, 101*
Einstein, Albert, 3
Eismitte, 49
eland, 81; *78–9*
electric eel, 90
elephants, 78; *43, 45, 78, 80, 87*; forest, 83
elk, 63, 64
elm, 86
emu, 78
Endymion non-scriptus, 65
energy: fossil fuels, 8, 18, 52; *53*; nuclear power, 18, 52; *53*; from the oceans, *53, 97*; sources, 52; *52–3*; in the Sun, 4; in the Third World, 55; water power, 25, 63, 88, 92; *53, 92*
England, *see* Britain
English Channel, 64
environment, 49
Environmental Science Services Administration (ESSA), 8

enzymes, 35
Eohippus, 42
epicentre, earthquakes, *20*
epiphytes, 82; *82*
Epsilon Eridani, *2*
Equal-Area Projection, 100
equivalent projections, 100
equinox, *5*
Equus quagga boehmi, 79
Eratosthenes, 100
Erg Bourharet, *30*
Erie, Lake, 9
Erinaceus europaeus, 65
erosion, 17; by ice, 26–7; *26–7*; mountains, *15*; by the sea, 28–9; *28–9*; soil, 24, 32, 68, 73, 77, 80; *68*; by water, 24–5; *24–5*; by wind, 30–1; *30–1*
erratics, 27; *26*
eskers, 26
Eskimos, 47, 60, 63; *47, 61*
Esox lucius, 91
esparto grass, 74
Ethiopian zoogeographical region, 45
Eucalyptus, 85
Euphausia superba, 61
Euphorbia obesa, 74
euphorbias, 75; *74*
Euphrates, river, 56; *101*
Eurasia, 70–1, 72–3; *13, 61, 70, 72*
Europa Canal, 92
Europe: coasts, 28; continental drift, 15, 44; early man, 46; *46*; energy, *53*; ice ages, 26; population, 54, 56; *57*; temperate forests, 64, 66, 67; *64, 66–7*; water, 92; *93*
European Economic Community (EEC), 59; *58*
European Free Trade Area (EFTA), 58
Euryapteryx, 42
Eusthenopteron, 38–9
evaporites, 17
Everest, Mount, 88
evergreen trees, 64, 68, 82; *64–5, 68*
evolution, theory of, 36, 44
exosphere, 7
extrusive rocks, 18; *16*
eyes, genetics, *37*

F

Falco biarmicus, 74; *F. mexicanus, 71*
fallow deer, 45
faults: in the Earth's crust, 15; *14–15*; and earthquakes, 20; plate tectonics, 13; *12*
felsite, 16
Fennecus zerda, 75
ferns, 40, 64, 88; *38–40, 65*
ferralitic soils, *48*
ferret, black-footed, 70
ferruginous soils, *48*
fertilizers, 86; *68, 77*
Ficus sp., *41*
fig tree, 68; *41*
Filimoshki, 46
finch, Laysan, *36–7*
fir, 62; Douglas, *65*
fire: savannas, 78, 80; *81*;

temperate grasslands, 70; *71*
firn ice, 26; *27*
fish, 38, 41, 90, 94–5, 96; *39, 90–1, 94–5, 96–7*
fishing, 96; *9, 96–7*
flamingo, 79
Flinders Range, 38
flood plains, 25, 27; *24–5*
floods, 22, 24, 33
Florida, *93*
flowering plants, 40
flying fox, *83*
flying squirrels, 83
fog, *50–1*
folds, in the Earth's crust, 15; *14, 99*
food, 52, 54, 73; *55*
forests: deforestation, 8, 32, 52, 66–7; rainforests, 64, 82–5; *48, 65, 82–5*; satellite observations, 8; *9*; taiga, 62–3; *62–3*; temperate, 64, 66–7; *48, 64–7*
fossil fuels, 8, 18, 52; *53*
fossils, 17, 38, 46
Fourquieria splendens, 74
foxes, 63, 64; *65*; Arctic, 62; *62*; fennec, *75*
France, 9, 56, 59, 68, 99; *19, 46–7, 57, 60*
freshwater environments, 8, 32–3, 90, 92; *90–3*
frogs, 75, 90; *65*; pouched tree, *82*; tree, 83
frost, weathering, 31
fruit flies, 36
fuels, *see* energy
Fujiyama, Mount, 20
fumaroles, *21*
Fundy, Bay of, 22
fungi, 64, 82
Funisciurus lemniscatus, 82

G

gabbro, *16*
galago, 83
Galago demidovii, 83
galaxies, 3; *3*
game animals, 80, 81; *81*
gamma rays, *7*
Ganges river, 90
Ganymede, *4*
gas, natural, 52, 63; *52–3, 62*
gases, in the universe, 3, 4, 6; *2*
Gastrotheca ovifera, 82
Gazella dorcas, 74; *G. thomsonii, 79*
gazelle, 78; Thomson's, *79*
gazetteers, 99
geckos, 75, 83; fan-toed, *74–5*; palmate, *74–5*
Gemini, 99
gemstones, 18; *19*
General Agreement of Tariffs and Trade (GATT), 59
genes, 35, 36; *37*
genetics, 35, 36; *36–7*
Geococcyx californianus, 74
geology: minerals, 18; *18–19*; mountains, *15*; plate tectonics, 13; rock formation, 17; *16–17*; satellite monitoring, 8; *9, 99*

gerbil, *74–5*
Germany, West, 54, 56
geysers, 18; *21*
Ghana, 59
gibbons, *43, 45*
Gibraltar, *46*
Gila monster, *75*
Gingko biloba, 40
Giraffa camelopardalis, 45, 78
giraffes, 78; *42, 45, 78*
glacial periods, *see* ice ages
glacial till, 27; *27*
glacial troughs, 26
glaciers, 26–7; *15, 26–7*
glass, natural, 17
gley, *48*
globes, cartographical, 99; *98*
Gloeotrichia, 38
gloups, 29
glyptodonts, 42
Gmelina, 85
gneiss, 17; *16*
Goad, 98
goats, 68; *42*; Rocky Mountain, 88; *89*
Gobi desert, 75
goby fish, dwarf, 90
gold, 18, 52, 63; *18, 19, 52*
goliath heron, 79
Gondwanaland, *13, 44*
goose, 63; Brent, *63*
gopher, 71
gopher snake, 70
Gopherus polyphemus, 74
gorges, 24
Gorilla gorilla, 45
gorillas, 45
Gottman, Jean, 56
Gracula religiosa, 89
Gramineae, 42
granite, 29; *10, 16*
grasses, 42, 62, 70–1; *42, 70–1*; savannas, 78, 80; *79*
grasshoppers, *71*
grasslands, 42; *42, 48*; savannas, 78–81; *78–81*; temperate, 70–3; *70–3*
gravity, 98; deep-ocean trenches, 13; effects on Earth's atmosphere, 7; and the tides, 22; *22*
Gray, Tom, 46
Great Basin desert, 74; *75*
Great Bear lake, 18
Great Nebula of Orion, *3*
Great Rift Valley, 79
Greece, ancient, 68, 99, 100, 102
"greenhouse effect", 6–7, 51
Greenland, 11, 24, 26, 60; *13, 44, 61*
Greenwich Observatory, 99, 100; *100*
grey-brown forest soils, *48*
grid system in mapping, 100; *100*
groundwater, 24, 76; *25, 76*
grouse, 63; black, *71*; sage, *71*
guanaco, *70–1*
guayule, 77
Gulf Stream, 22; *9*
gullies, 24, 27
Gulo gulo, 63
Gutenberg discontinuity, 11
gymnosperms, 40
gyres, 60; *23*

H

hachuring, maps, 102
Hadar, *46*
Hadza, *80*
Haeckel, Ernst, 49
Haematopus sp., *94*
hagfish, 38
Halichoerus grypus, 95
Hallucigenia sparsa, 39
halophytes, 75
Hammer-Wagner Projection, *101*
Handy Man, 46; *46–7*
hanging valleys, 26
hares, 44; *70–1*; Arctic, 62; *63*
harmattan, 30
hatchet fish, *95*
Hawaii, 11, 20; *23*
Hawaiian honeycreeper, *37*
hawfinch, *65*
hazel, 64, 66; *65*
headlands, 29; *28–9*
heat capacity mapping, *9*
hedgehog, 64; *65*; desert, *75*
helium, 3
Heloderma suspectum, 75
Hemiechinus auritus, 75
Hemiprocne longipennis, 82
Hepatica nobilis, 65
hepaticas, 65
Herbertson, A.J., 49
herbivores, 41, 70; *40–1, 70–1*
heredity, 36; *36–7*
herring, 96; *95*
hill mynah bird, *89*
hill shading, maps, 102
Himalayas, 15, 44, 86, 88; *14, 45*
Himatione sanguinea, 36
hippopotamus, 90; *42, 79*
Hippopotamus amphibius, 79
holly, 65
Holothuroidea, *95*
Homo erectus, 46–7; 46–7; H. habilis, 46; 46–7; H. sapiens, 42, 46; H.s. neanderthalensis 47; H.s. rhodesiensis, 47; H.s. sapiens, 47; H.s. soloensis, 47
honeysuckle, 64
Hong Kong, *32–3*
Honshu, 64
Hoplophoneus, 42–3
hornbeam, 64, 66
hornbill, rhinoceros, *83*
horn-boring moth, *78–9*
horses, 42, 70; *42–3, 72*
horsetails, 40; *40*
hot springs, *21*
Hubble, *3*
Hudson Bay, *9*
hummingbirds, 82
Huron, Lake, 90
hurricanes, *50–1*
Hwang-Ho, 25, 33
Hyaenodon, 42
hydroelectric power, 25, 63, 88, 92; *53, 92*
hydrogen, 3; *2*
hydrogen cyanide, 35
hydrological cycle, 24, 32; *24, 92*
hydrothermal springs, *18*
Hydrurga leptonyx, 61
hyena, 78; *42–3, 78–9*
hypsometric tints, maps, 102
Hyracotherium, 42; 42–3

I

ibex, 88
Ibis leucocephalus, 91
ice, *23*; effects on landscape, 26–7; *26–7*; polar, 60; *60–1*; satellite monitoring, 8; sheets, 26; shelves, 26
ice ages, 4, 22, 26, 42, 44, 47, 51, 60, 64
ice falls, 27
icebergs, 60; *61*
Iceland, 11, 26
Ichthyornis, 41
Ichthyostega, 39
icthyosaurs, 41
igneous rocks, 17; *16*
ignimbrite, 20–1
iiwi, *36–7*
IJsselmeer, *33*
Ilex spp., *65*
impala, 78
India, 44, 54, 78, 84, 86; *13, 45, 57*
Indian grass, 70
Indian Ocean, 13, 51; *13, 39*
Indians, North American, 66, 99; *66, 103*
Indo-Australian plate, *12*
Indonesia, 18, 46
Indus river, 33, 56, 92
Industrial Revolution, 18, 56, 72, 92; *67*
industry, 66, 92; *66–7, 93*
infra-red radiation, 99; *7*
insectivores, 42; *42*
insects: in deserts, 75; *74–5*; evolution, 38, 40; *39*; freshwater environments, 90; genetics, *36–7*; mountain regions, 88; *89*; polar regions, 60; spread of, 44; temperate forest regions, 64; *65*; temperate grassland regions, 71; *71*; tropical rainforest, 83
International Development Association (IDA), 59
International Monetary Fund (IMF), 59
International Whaling Commission, 97
intrusive rocks, *16*
Inuit, 63; *61*
invertebrates, 38, 41; *71, 75*
ionosphere, 7; *7*
Iran, 15, 77
Iraq, 46
Ireland, *9*
Iris sibirica, 70
iron, 11, 18, 52, 63; *10, 18–19, 52, 67*
Iron Age, 66
iron industry, 66, 68
iron oxide, *17*
irrigation, 25, 32, 33, 68, 76–7, 80, 86, 92; *76–7, 93*
Islamabad, 56
island arcs, *12, 23*
isostasy, 15; *14*
isostatic rebound, 15
isotopes, 17
Israel, 76; *33, 77*
Italy, 68, 99; *98*
Ivory Coast, 85
ivy, 64

J

jacana, *79*
jackal, 78; *78*
jaguar, 83
Jakarta, 56
Japan: and the Antarctic, *60*; energy sources, 53, 97; maps, 99; *98*; seaweed, 96; temperate forests, *64*; trade, 58; urbanization, 56; *57*; volcanoes, 20; whaling, 97
Japan, Sea of, 15
Jari river, 85
Java, 44, 86
jellyfish, 38, 94; *39*
jerboa, *74–5*
Jesuits, 98
Joachimstal, 18
Johannesburg, 56
Johanson, Donald, 46
jojoba, 77
June grass, 70
Jupiter, 4; *4–5*
Jurassic, *40–1*

K

kame terraces, 27
kangaroo, 78, 81; *45*; tree, 83
Kano, 49
Karachi, 56
Karamoja, 56
Kariba Dam, 92
Katanga, 18
Kazakhstan, 46
Kenya, 81
kerosene, 53
kettle-holes, *26–7*
Khanty, 63
kimberlite, 18
Kitt Peak, 88
Koobi Fora, 46
Köppen, Wladimir, 49
Krakatoa, 21, 44; *21*
krill, 60, 96; *60–1*
Kuwait, 76
Kyoto, 99; *98*

L

laccoliths, *20–1*
Lagopus mutus, 63
Lagostomus maximus, 70
Lake District (England), 26
lakes, 32, 90, 92; *21, 79, 90–1, 93*
Lama guanicoe, 70
Lamarck, Jean-Baptiste, 36
Lambert Equal-Area Projection, *100–1*
Lambert, Johann Heinrich, 100; *100–1*
lampreys, 38
lampshells, *38*
lancelet fish, *39*
land reclamation, 33; *33*
land surveys, 99, 100; *101*
Landsat, 8; *8–9, 98, 103*
landscape: effects of ice and snow, 26–7; *26–7*; influence of the sea, 28–9; *28–9*; man's influence on, 32–3; *32–3*; water erosion, 24–5; *24–5*; weathering, 30–1; *30–1*; wind erosion, 30–1

Langdale, *26*
Languedoc, 68
langur, sacred, *82*
lanner falcon, *74*
Lantian, *46*
Lapland, *63*
Lapps, 63; *63*
larch, 62
Lascaux, *46*
lateral moraine, 27; *26*
Latin America, 54, 56, 59; *82–3*
Latin American Free Trade Association (LAFTA), 59
latitude, 100; *100*
Laurasia, 13, 44
lava, 6, 13, 20–1; *21*
lava plateaus, *20–1*
Lavandula spica, 69
lavender, 69
lead, 52; *18–19, 52*
leap years, 4
lemmings, 62; *62*
Lemmus lemmus, 62
lemur, 83
Lenin (nuclear icebreaker), *61*
leopard, 78, 83; *78–9, 82*; snow, 89
Leptonycteris sanborni, 75
Lepus arcticus, 63; *L. europaeus, 70*
lianas, 82; *65*
Libya, 76
lichen, 60, 64, 88; *63*
life: earliest forms, 38–9; *38–9*; evolution of, 4, 6, 7; origins of, 35; *34–5*; structure of, 36; *36–7*
light waves, 7
lily-trotter, *79*
limestone, 17, 24, 25, 29; *19, 26, 31, 68*
limestone pavements, *31*
Lingula, 39
Lingulella, 39
Linophryne bicornis, 95
lions, 78; *78*
literacy, 55
lithosphere, 11, 12, 13; *12*
little bluestem, *70*
liverworts, 38
"living fossils", *39*
lizards, 41, 75; *74–5*; gridiron-tailed, *74*
llamas, 88
lobe-fin fish, *39*
Lobodon carcinophagus, 61
locusts, *74*
Loligo spp., *95*
London, 56, 58; *57, 61, 98*
longitude, 100; *100–1*
longshore drift, 29
Los Angeles, 56; *50, 103*
Loxia curvirostra, 62
Loxodonta africana, 45, 79; *L. falconeri, 43*
Lucanus cervus, 65
lugworm, 94
Lumbricus terrestris, 71
lunar eclipses, 4
lungfish, 90; *38–9, 91*
Lusaka, 57
Luzon, *33*
Lycaon pictus, 79
Lynchailurus pajeros, 70
Lystrosaurus, 40
Lyurus tetrix, 71

M

M32 (galaxy), *3*
M82 (galaxy), *3*
macaw, 82–3
mackerel, 95
Macropus rufus, 45
Macroscelides proboscideus, 82
Madagascar, 44; *13, 82*
magma, 11, 15, 17, 20; *12, 19, 21*
magma plugs, 18
magnesium, 11, 17; *10, 19, 23*
magnetic field, Earth's, 7
magnetism, Earth's, 11, 13; *10–13*
magnetite, 13
magnetopause, 7
magnetosphere, 7; *7*
magnolia, 86
Main, river, 92
Malawi, 56
Malaysia, 85; *45*
Malham Cove, 31
malnutrition, 54, 55
mammals: in deserts, 75; *74–5*; evolution, 40, 41, 42, 44; *40*; *42–3*; monsoon regions, 86; mountain regions, 88; 89; in oceans, 94; savanna, 78; *78–9*; spread of, 44; *44–5*; temperate forests, 64; *65*; temperate grasslands, 70–1; *70*; tropical rainforest, 83; *83–4*
man: chromosomes, *37*; and the deserts, 76–7; *76–7*; effect on environment, 32–3, 44, 49; *32–3*; evolution, 42; *43*; and freshwater environments, 92; *92–3*; influence on grasslands, 72–3; *72–3*; influence on landscape, 32–3; *32–3*; influence on savannas, 80–1; *80–1*; influence on temperate forests, 66–7; *66–7*; influence on weather, 51; and mountain regions, 88; and the oceans, 96; *96–7*; population distribution, 56–7; *56–7*; population growth, 54; *54–5*; spread of, 46–7; *46–7*; and tropical rainforests, 84–5; *84–5*
manatee, Amazonian, 91
Manaus, 49
mandrill, *82*
Mandrillus sphinx, 82
manganese, *18, 52*
manganese nodules, *18*
mangroves, 28; *87*
Manhattan, 56
Manila, 56
Manis tricuspis, 82
Mantis religiosa, 71
mantle, Earth's, 11, 12–13; *10, 12*
Maoris, 66
map projections, 100; *100–1*
maps; making, 99–100; *98–101*; by satellite, 8, 99; *8, 98–9*; using, 102; *102–3*
maples, 64
Marella splendens, 39
market towns, 56
marmoset, *44, 83*

Marmota monax, 65
Marquesas Islands, 44
Mars, 4, 6; *4–5*
Marsh, George Perkins, *32*
Marshall Islands, 99
marshes, 90; *79, 91, 93*
marshlands, *48–9*
marsupial mole, *70–1*
marsupials, 42, 44; *42, 44–5*
Masai, *81*
Massawa, 48
Matthews, Drummond, 13
meadowlark, 71
mechanical weathering, 31; *31*
Meconopsis horridula, 89
medial moraine, 27
Mediterranean regions, 68; *68–9*; continental faults, 15; deforestation, 32, 68; *68–9*; irrigation, 93; mineral deposits, 18; spread of animals, 45
Mediterranean Sea: continental drift, *13*; population migration, 56; salt, *19*; spread of animals, 45; tides, 22
Medusina, 39
megalopolis, 56; *56*
Melanerpes formicivorus, 65
Meles meles, 65
Mendel, Gregor, 36
Mercator, Gerard, 100
Mercator projection, 100; *101*
mercury, 52
Mercury, 4, 7; *4*
mesopause, 6
Mesopotamia, 76, 99
mesosphere, 7; *6*
Mesozoic era, 41, 42; *40, 42*
mesquite, 75
metals, 18, 52; *18–19, 52*
metamorphic rocks, 17; *16*
meteorites, 4, 11, 35, 41; *7*
meteors, 4; *7*
Meteosat, 8
methane, 6; *35*
Mexico, 99; *44, 56, 75, 77, 98*
Miacis, 42
mica, 17, 63
mice, 62; *62*; Congo forest, *82*; hazel, *65*; Indian spiny, *37*; marsupial, *37*; wood, 64
Michigan, *9*
Micrathene whitneyi, 75
microcomputers, 18
microfossils, 38
mid-ocean ridges, 11, 13, 20; *12, 23*
Middle East, 30, 55, 74, 76; *46–7, 97*
midges, *93*
migmatite, 17
migration, 56; *56*
Milky Way, 3; *3*
Miller, Stanley, 35
millipedes, 38; *39*
minerals, 18; *18–19*
mining, 33; *66–7, 80*
mink, 63
Miocene Period, 42; *42–3*
Mississippi river, 25, 73; *98*
Missouri river, 33
mites, 60
moas, 42
Modified Mercalli scale, 20; *20*

Moeritherium, 43
Mohorovičić discontinuity, 11
Mojave desert, 74; *32, 103*
mole, aquatic, 90; marsupial, *70–1*
mole rats, *45*
molluscs, 94; *38–9*
Moloch horridus, 74
Mongolia, *76–7*
Mongols, *72*
monkeys, 83; woolly spider, *83*
monoclines, *14*
monsoon, 51, 86; *86–7*
Montecaris, 39
Montreal, 73
Moon, 4, 22; *4–5, 22*
moose, 63, 64
moraine, 27; *27*
Morganucodon, 40
Moronobu, *98*
Moropus, *42–3*
Morpho butterfly, *83*
Morpho didius, *83*
mosquitos, 91, *93*
mosses, 38, 60, 62, 64, 88; *65*
moths, 64; peppered, *37*; small emperor, *65*
motorcars, metals, 52; *19*
mountain regions, 88; *88–9*; avalanches, 27; and deserts, 74; formation, 15; *14–15*; ice caps, 26; and climate, 51
Mozambique, *59*
mud volcanoes, *21*
Muller, Hermann, *36*
Murray-Darling river, *70*
Mus platythrix, 37
Muscardinus avellanarius, *65*
musk ox, 62–3; *63*
Muslims, 68
Mustela nigripes, *70*
mutations, genetic, 36; *36*
Myrmecocystus melliger, *75*

N

Nabataeans, *76*
Namib Desert, *75*
nappes, 15; *14*
Nasser, Lake, *32*
National Oceanic and Atmospheric Administration (NOAA), 8
natural selection, 36
Nauru, *97*
Nautilus, *61*
navigation charts, 99, 100; *101*
Neander Valley, *46*
Neanderthal Man, 46; *46*
neap tides, *22*
Nearctic zoogeographical region, *44*
Negev Desert, *76*
Nematophyton, 39
Nentsy, *63*
Neolithic, 32, 66; *66*
Neopilina, 39
Neotropical zoogeographical region, *44*
Neptune, 4; *5*
Nereis, 39
Netherlands, 22, 26, 33; *33*
névé ice, 26
New Caledonia, 44
New Delhi, 56
New Guinea, 56

New Jersey, *61*
New York City, 56; *9, 56*
New Zealand, 20–1, 29, 44, 59, 64, 66, 67; *42, 60, 64–5*
Newfoundland, *14*
NGC 205 (galaxy), *3*
Nice, *47*
nickel, 11, 35, 52, 63; *10, 52*
Niger basin, 18
Nigeria, 55; *84*
night-blooming cereus, *75*
nightjar, *75*
Nile, river, 32, 56, 76, 90; *101*
Nile delta, 32; *9*
Nilgiri Hills, 86
nitrates, 77
nitrogen, 6; *6, 35*
nivation, 27
nomads, *72, 76*
Norfolk Island pine, *41*
North Africa, 24, 56, 68
North America: climate, 68; *50*; continental drift, 44; *13*; deforestation, 32; *67*; deserts, 74; early man, 47; energy, *53*; fish, 90; flightless birds, *42*; temperate grasslands, 70–1, 72–3; *70, 72–3*; ice ages, 26; mapping, *98*; mountain building, 15; *14*; polar regions, *61*; population growth, 54; prairies, 70–1; *70*; satellite observations, *9*; temperate forests, 64, 66–7; *65–7*; transport, 58; tundra and taiga, 63; *62*; water resources, 92; *93*
North Sea, 64, 96; *53, 94*
northern lights, 7
Norway, 22, 56; *14, 63*
Nothofagus menziesii, 64
Notoryctes typhlops, 70
Notostomus longirostris, 95
nuclear energy, 18, 52; *53*
nuclear reactions, in the Sun, 4
nucleic acids, 35; *34*
Nyasa, Lake, 90
Nyctea scandiaca, 62
Nymphaea spp., *91*

O

oaks, 64, 66, 67; *64–5*; common, *41*; cork, 68; *68–9*; holm, *68–9*; kermes, 68; Turkey, *68–9*
oases, 76; *76*
observatories, 99; *88*
Ocean Thermal Energy Conversion (OTEC), *53, 97*
oceans, 94–6; *94–7*; charts, 99, 100; *101*; currents, 22, 94; *23*; desalination plants, 76; in the hydrological cycle, 24; influence on climate, 50–1; influence on landscape, 28–9, *28–9*; mid-ocean ridges, 11, 13, 20; *12, 23*; mineral content of seawater, *23*; mineral deposits, 18; *18*; plate tectonics, 13; polar, 60; salt content, 22; *19*; sea-bed, 11; *23*; sedimentary deposits, 17; tides, 22; *22*; trenches, 13, 23; *23*; waves, 22, 28–9

Ochotona roylei, 89
ocotillo, 74
Odocoileus virginianus, 65
Ohio river, 26
oil, 52, 60, 63, 77; *52–3, 62, 77, 97, 99*
okapi, 82
Okapia johnstoni, 82
Olea europaea, 69
Olduvai Gorge, 46
Olenoides serratus, 39
Oligocene Period, 42
olive, 68; *68–9*
Oman, Gulf of, 99
omnivores, 41
Omo river, *46*
Ontario, Lake, *9*
opals, 18; *19*
Oparin, I.A., 35
Ophiothrix fragilis, 95
Opuntia ficus-indica, 74
orang-utan, 45, 82
orchids, 82; *82*; moth, 82
Orcinus orca, 60
Ordovician Period, 38
Oreamnos americanus, 89
Oreopithecus, 43
Organization for African Unity (OAU), 59
Organization for Economic Cooperation and Development (OECD), 59
Organization of American States (OAS), 58
Organization of Petroleum Exporting Countries (OPEC), 52; *53, 58–9*
Oriental zoogeographical region, 45
Orion, Great Nebula, *3*
Ornithorhynchus anatinus, 45, *91*
Ortelius, Abraham, *Theatrum Orbis Terrarum*, 99
orthogonal projection, *101*
orthomorphic projection, 100
orthophoto maps, 99
Orycteropus afer, 79
Osaka, 56
Osteolepis, 39
ostrich, 78; *79*
Ostyaks, 63
Otus asio, 65
outwash plains, 27
overthrust folds, *14*
Ovibos moschatus, 63
owl, burrowing, *71*; elf, *75*; great horned, *75*; North American screech, *65*; snowy, 63; *62*; tawny, 64
ox, musk, *63*; wild, 64; *66*
ox-bow lakes, *24–5*
Oxyaena, *42–3*
oxygen: in atmosphere, 6, 7, 85; *6*; and creation of life, 35, 38; *35, 38*
oystercatcher, 94
ozone layer, 7, 35, 38; *6, 38*

P

Pacific Ocean: charts, 99; *98*; "living fossils", *39*; mineral deposits, 18; *18*; ocean swell, 29; plate tectonics, 13, 15; *12–13*; spread of life

across, 44; tsunamis, *23*; typhoons, *50*
pack ice, 60
paddle fish, 90; *91*
Pakistan, 33, 92
Palaeocene Period, *43*
Palaeocharinoides, 39
palaeomagnetism, *10*
Palaeophonus, 39
Palaeotragus, *42–3*
Palaeozoic era, 40, 42
Palearctic zoogeographical region, *44–5*
Pallas's sandgrouse, *74*
palm trees, 51, 78; *65*; date palm, 76; dôm palm, 78
Palmatogecko rangei, 75
pampas cat, *70–1*
Pan troglodytes, 83
Panama Canal, 58
panda, red, 89
Pangaea, 44; *13, 44*
pangolin, 83; *82*
Panthalassa Ocean, *13*
Panthera leo, 78; *P. pardus*, 79, *82*; *P. tigris*, 45, *86*; *P.t. tigris*, *82*; *P. uncia*, 89
Papua New Guinea, 44
papyrus, 79
Paraceratherium, 43
Paradisaea apoda, 45
paraffin, 53
Paris, 56, 99; *57*
parrots, 82–3; grey, *83*
Parrya lanuginosa, 89
Parthenium argentatum, 77
Patagonian Desert, 75
Pavo cristatus, 45
peafowl, 45
peccary, 44
pedestal rocks, 30
Pedetes cafer, 70
Pei Xin, 100
penguin, Emperor, *60–1*
Pennsylvania, *9*
Penzias, Arno, 3
perch, *93*
Perissodactyls, 42
permafrost, 62; *48, 63*
Permian Period, *40*
Persian Gulf, 99
Persians, 77
Perspicaris dictynna, 39
Peru, 97
Peters' projection, *101*
Petralona, *46*
petrels, 60
petroleum, *see* oil
Peutinger Table, 99
pewee, Eastern wood, 65
Phalaenopsis spp., *82*; *P. sanderana*, 82
Phalaenoptilus nuttalli, 75
Phenacodus, *42–3*
Philadelphia, 9, 56
Philippines, 90; *33, 59, 82*
Phoca sibirica, 91
phosphates, 77
photogrammetry, 99; *101*
photosynthesis, 38, 85, 94; *38*
phreatophytes, 74, 75
Phyllolepis, 39
Phylloscopus trochilus, 65
phytoplankton, 94; *95*
Picea obovata, 62
piedmont glaciers, 26
pigs, 64; *42*; wild, 86

pike, *91*
Pikes Peak, 49
pine, 62; Aleppo, *68–9*; black, *68–9*; Chile, 68; maritime, *68–9*; Monterey, 68
Pinus caribea, 85; *P. halepensis*, 69; *P. nigra*, 69; *P. pinaster*, 69; *P. radiata*, 68
piranha, 90
pitchblende, 18
Pituophis melanoleucus, 70
place-names, *103*
placental mammals, 42
placer deposits, 18; *19*
placoderm fish, 39
placodonts, 41
plane tree, 86; *41*
planets: atmospheres, 6–7; origins of, 3, 4; *2*; statistics, *4–5*
plankton, 60, 94–5; *60, 95, 97*
plants, *see* vegetation
Planorbis albus, 91
Platalea alba, 91
Platanus spp., *41*
plate tectonics, 15, 18, 44; *12–13*
platinum, *19*
Plato, 68
Platybelodon, 43
platypus, 45, *91*
Pleistocene Period, 42
Plesiadapis, 43
plesiosaurs, 41; *41*
Plesiosaurus, 41
Pliocene Period, 42
Pliopithecus, 43
pliosaurs, 41
Pluto, 4; *5*
plutonic rock, 17
Po Valley, 68
poaching, *81*
podocarps, 68
podsols, 64; *48*
Pogonomyrmex spp., 74
Poland, 26; *59*
polar regions, 8, 22, 50, 60; *23, 50, 60–1*
polders, *33*
polecat, marbled, *70–1*
pollarding trees, 66; *66*
pollution, 92, 96; *9, 62, 93, 97*
Polo, Marco, *98*
Polydon spathula, 91
polymers, 35; *34–5*
polyps, 94–5
pomegranate, 69
pondweed, curled, *91*
Pongo pygmaeus, 82
poplars, 62
poppy, Himalayan blue, 89
population distribution, 56–7; *56–7*
population growth, 54; *54–5*
porphyrite, *16*
portolan charts, 99
Portugal, 59, 68
Potamogeton crispus, 91
potash, 77
potassium, *19, 23*
poverty, 54; *54–5*
prairie dog, 71; *70–1*
prairie falcon, *71*
prawn, scarlet, 95
praying mantis, *71*
precious stones, 18

Presbytis entellus, 82
prickly pear, *74*
Primates, 42; *42, 43*
"primordial soup", 35; *34*
Primula rosea, 89
Procambarus spp., *90*
pronghorn, 70; *44, 71*
protea, giant, 68
Protea cynaroides, 68
proteins, 35, 52; *34–5*
Proteles cristatus, 79
Proteus anguinus, 90
Protopterus annectens, 91
protozoans, 94
Provence, 68
Psammomys obesus, 75
Pseudogyps africanus, 79
Pseudois nayaur, 89
Pseudosporochnus, 39
psilophites, 39
Psittacus erithacus, 83
Psittirostra cantans, 36
ptarmigan, 63; rock, *63*
Pteropus giganteus, 83
pterosaurs, 41
Ptolemy, Claudius,
    Geographia, 99, 100; *98*
Ptyodactylus hasselquistii, 75
Puerto Rico, 56
Punans, 84
Punica granatum, 69
Punjab river, 33
purse-seine fishing, *96–7*
pygmies, 84
pyramidal peaks, *26*
Pyrrhocorax graculus, 89
python, royal, *82–3*
Python regius, 83

Q

qanats, 76; *76–7*
quartz, 17
Quercus spp., *65*; *Q. cerris*, 69;
    Q. ilex, 69; *Q. robur*, 41,
    64; *Q. suber*, 69
quillajas, 68
Quizapu, *21*

R

rabbits, 44
raccoons, 64; *42, 44*
radar sensing, 8
radiation, infra-red, 99; *7*;
    ultraviolet, 7, 35, 38
radio astronomy, 3
radio waves, *7*
radioactive "clocks", 17
railways, 58, 72; *67*
rainfall, 24, 51, 70, 74, 82, 86;
    24–5, 48, 50, 64, 68, 70–1
rainforests, 64, 82–3, 84–5; *65,
    82–3, 84–5*
Ramapithecus, 46; *43*
Rangea, 39
Rangifer tarandus, 62
Ranunculus fluitans, 90
rats; fat sand, *75*;
    kangaroo, *74–5*
rat-tailed maggot, *93*
rattlesnakes, *44*
raven, *62*
recreation, 92
recumbent folds, *14*
red giants, stars, *2*
red oat grass, *79*

Red Sea, 13, 18; *18–19, 45*
red-tailed hawk, *71*
redpolls, 63
reedmace, *91*
reindeer, 62, 63; *63*
relativity, theory of, 3
relief shading, maps, 102
reptiles, 40–1, 44, 90; *40–1*
reservoirs, 76, 86, 92; *92*
resource systems, 49
resources, 52
Rhamphastos toco, 83
Rhamphorhynchus, 41
rhea, 78
Rhine, river, 92
rhinoceros, 42, 45, 78–9
rhipidistian fish, 39
Rhizophora mangle, 87
Rhodesian Man, 46
rhododendron, 89
Rhynia, 39
Rhyniella, 39
rhyolite, *16*
ribonucleic acid, *see* RNA
rice, 33, 85, 86; *87, 93*
Richmond, Virginia, *56*
Richter scale, 20
rift valleys, 13; *18*
Rigel, *2*
river terraces, 25
rivers, 17, 24–5, 32–3, 90;
    24–5, 90–1, 93
RNA (ribonucleic acid), 35
road maps, 98
roadrunner, *74*
roche moutonée, *27*
rock cycle, 17
rocks: dating, 17; earthquakes,
    20; erosion by ice, 26–7;
    26–7; formation, 17; *16–17*;
    minerals, 18; *18–19*;
    weathering, 18, 30–1; *19,
    30–1*
Rocky Mountains, 15, 44; *88*
Romalea microptera, *71*
Roman Empire, 18, 66, 68,
    99, 100, 102; *57, 68*
Rome, *49*
Royle's pika, *89*
rubber, 85; *84*
"rubber" dandelion, *77*
Rubus sp., 65
Ruhr, 56
ruminants, *42*

S

Sacramento, *103*
Sacramento river, *103*
Sagittarius serpentarius, 79
Saguaro cactus, 75
Saguinus oedipus, 83
Sahara, 56, 74, 77, 78, 80;
    44–5, 76
Sahel, 80; *76*
saiga, 70; *70–1*
Saiga tatarica, 70
sailbacks, 40; *40*
St Helens, Mount, 20
St Lawrence river, 56
St Lawrence Seaway, *93*
sal, 86; *87, 89*
salamander, cave, 90
Salmo trutta, 90
salmon, 90
salps, 94
salt, 22, 77

salt deposits, 15, 17; *19, 99*
saltation, 30; *30*
saltbush, 75
Salticus scenicus, 89
Salyut, 8
Samer, 63; *63*
Samoyeds, 63
San Andreas Fault, 13, 20; *13*
San Bernadino mountains,
    103
San Francisco, 20; *103*
San Gabriel mountains, *103*
San Joachim river, *103*
sand, 17, 29, 30; *17, 28, 30*
sand dunes, 30–1; *30*
sandstone, 17, 18; *17, 68*
Santa Lucia Range, *103*
Santorini, 21
sapphire, 18; *19*
Sardinia, 68
Sargasso Sea, 22
satellites, 8, 52; *8–9, 53*;
    mapping, 99; *98–9*
Saturn, 4; *5*
Saturnia pavonia, 65
Saudi Arabia, 76; *58*
Saussurea tridactyla, 88
savannas, 78, 80–1; *48, 78–81*
scale, maps, 100, 102; *100,
    102–3*
Scandinavia, 26, 63; *27*
Scaphiopus couchi, 75
Scaumenacia, 39
schist, 17; *16*
Schistocera gregaria, 74
Sciadophyton, 39
Scincus scincus, 74–5
Scolopax rusticola, 65
Scomber scomber, 95
scorpions, 40; *39, 75*
Scotland, *14, 88*
Scott, Captain, *61*
Scottish Highlands, *88*
screes, 17
scrubland, 68
Scutosaurus, 40
seas, *see* oceans
sea anemone, 95
sea cucumber, 95
sea level, 22, 33; *23*
sea pens, *39*
seals, 60; *61*; Baikal, *91*;
    crabeater, 60; *60–1*; grey,
    95; leopard, *60–1*; Ross,
    60; *60*
Searles Basin, 77
Seasat, 8
seasons, 4; *5*
seawater environments, *see*
    oceans
seaweed, 94, 96; *94*
secretary bird, 79
sedges, 62; *42*
sedimentary basins, 15; *14*
sedimentary rocks, 17
sediments: deposited by the
    sea, 29; folds, 15; glacial,
    27; *26*; river deposits, 25,
    32; *24–5*; rock formation,
    17; *17*
Seine, river, *57*
Selenarctos thibetanus, 89
Selenicereus spp., 75
Senecio articulatus, 74
Seoul, 56
sewage fungus, *93*
sexual reproduction, 36; *37*

Seymouria, 40
shading, maps, 102
shale, *16*
Shanghai, 56
Shanidar, *46*
sharks, 95; *39*; white, *95*
sheep, 88; *42*; blue
    (bharal), 89
shield volcanoes, 20; *21*
shipbuilding, 68
shoebill stork, 79
Shorea robusta, 86; *89*
shrew, short-eared elephant,
    82; tree, *82*; water, 90
sial, 11; *10*
Siberia, 44, 47, 63; *44, 47, 62*
sidewinder rattlesnake, *75*
Sierra Nevada, *102–3*
silica, 17, 20; *16–17*
silicates, 17
silicon, 11, 18; *10*
silicon oxide, 17
sills, *21*
Silurian grit, *26*
silver, 18, 52; *18, 52*
sima, 11; *10*
Simmondsia californica, 77
Simulium spp., *90*
sirocco, 30
siskin, 63
sitatunga, 79
skink, *74–5*
skuas, *61*; Arctic, *62*
Skylab, 8
skylark, *71*
"slash-and-burn" agriculture,
    84; *84*
slate, 17; *16*
sloths, 42, 83; *44*; maned, *83*
slugs, 65
Sminthopsis murina, 37
smog, 51; *50*
snails, 65; white ramshorn, *91*
snakes, 41, 83
snow, 24, 26, 27; *24*
snow line, *27*
sodium, 22; *23*
sodium chloride, *see* salt
soil: erosion, 24, 30, 32, 68,
    73, 77, 80; *68*; mountains,
    88; savannas, 80; temperate
    forests, 64; temperate
    grasslands, 71; *70–1*;
    tropical rainforests, 82,
    84–5; types, 48
Solar System, 3, 4; *2, 4–5*
solar wind, 7
Soldanella alpina, 88
Solifugae, 75
Solo Man, 46; *46*
solstice, 5
Sorgastrum nutans, 70
souslik, 71; *70*
South Africa, 56, 68, 70, 73,
    77; *64, 69, 70, 72*
South America: climate, 68;
    continental drift, 44; *13*;
    deserts, 75; early mammals,
    42; early man, 47; fish, 90;
    grasslands, 70–1; *70, 72*;
    mapping, 98; marsupials, 42;
    population growth, 55;
    savannas, 78, 80; *80*; spread
    of mammals to, *44*;
    transport, 58; tropical
    rainforests, *82–3*
South Pole, 60; *61*

southern lights, 7
soya beans, 52
space-time, Einstein's theory
    of, 3
Spain, 22, 32, 59, 68
Spalax microphthalmus, 45
spectacled caiman, *91*
Speotyto cunicularia, 71
spiders, 38, 40; *39*; camel, *75*;
    jumping, 88; *89*
spiral galaxies, *3*
spirulina, 38
sponges, *38–9*
spoonbill, *91*
Sprigina floundersi, 39
spring equinox, *5*
spring tides, *22*
springhaas, *70–1*
springs, 25
spruce, 62; Siberian, *62*
squid, 95
squirrels, 44, 63, 64; *45*;
    flying, *83*; four-striped, *82*
Sri Lanka, 86
stag beetle, 65
stalactites, 18; *19*
stalagmites, 18; *19*
stars, 3; *2–3*
steel, 18, 52; *19, 93*
Steinheim, *46*
Stephanoaetus coronatus, 82
Stercorarius parasiticus, 62
Stipa tenacissima, 74
stonefly, *93*
stork, painted, *91*
storm surges, 22
storms, 51; *50–1*
stratopause, 6
stratosphere, 7; *6*
strawberry tree, *68–9*
streams, glacial, 26, 27
striations, 26; *27*
strike-slip faults, *14–15*
stromatolites, 38; *38*
strontium, *19*
Struthio camelus, 79
Struthiomimus, *40–1*
Sturnella neglecta, 71
subarctic climate, 50
subduction zones, 13, 15, 20;
    12, 23
subtropical zones, 50; *50*
Sudan, 47, 78, 80; *76, 98*
Suez Canal, 58; *45*
sugar cane, 52
sulphate, *23*
sulphur, 6; *18–19*
summer solstice, 5
Sun, 3; *2–3*; and creation of
    life, 35; eclipses, *4*; effect on
    Earth's atmosphere, 7;
    energy, 4; evaporation of
    water from oceans, 24;
    gravitational pull on
    oceans, 22; *22*; influence on
    climate, 50; and the oceans,
    94; radiation, *7*; solar
    power, 52, 77; *53*
Superior, Lake, 90
supernovae, *3*
surveying, 99, 100; *101*
Sus scrofa, 86
Sutlej river, 33
swamps, 28, 90; *79, 91, 93*
Swanscombe, *46*
Sweden, 88; *58, 63*
swift, crested tree, *82*

switch grass, 70
symbols, maps, 102; *103*
Syncerus caffer nanus, 82
Synodontis batensoda, 91
Syrrhaptes paradoxus, 74

T

taeniodonts, 42; *42–3*
taiga, 62–3; *48, 62–3*
Tamandua tetradactyla, 83
Tamias striatus, 65
Tanganyika, Lake, 90
Tangshan, 20
Tansley, A.G., 49
Tanzania, *56*
tapioca, 84
tapir, 42; Malayan, *82*
Tapirus indicus, 82
Taraxacum kok-saghyz, 77
tarragon, Russian, 70
tarsier, *45*
Tarsius spp., *45*
Tasmania, 64; *45, 64*
Taupo, Mount, 20–1
Tauraco persa, 83
Taurotragus oryx, 79
tea, 86; *87*
Tehuelche Indians, *72*
Teleosts, 41
tellin shell, *94*
Tellina tenuis, 94
temperate forests, 64, 66–7; *64–7*
temperate grasslands, 70–3; *70–3*
temperate zones, 50
Tenebrionidae, 75
Tepetlaoztoc, *98*
terminal moraine, 27; *27*
termites, 82, 83; *79*
tern, Antarctic, *60*; Arctic, *61*
Ternifine, *46*
Terra Amata, 46
terraces, 33, 76; *33, 87*; river, 25
terrapins, 90
territorial maps, 99
Teshik Tash, *46*
Tethys Sea, *13*
Tetrao urogallus, 62
Thailand, 86; *84*
thematic cartography, 102; *102*
Themeda triandra, 79
theodolites, *101*
thermal imagery, *9*
thermosphere, *6–7*
Thira, 18
Third World, 59; energy, 55; urbanization, 56; *57*
thorny devil, *74*
three-dimensional maps, *102–3*
Thrinaxodon, 40
thrust faults, *14–15*
thunderstorms, *50–1*
Thunnus thynnus, 95
Thylacosmilus, 42
Tibet, 15; *88*
tidal power, 52; *53*
tides, 22; *22*
tiger, *45, 82, 86*
Tigris-Euphrates, 56; *101*
tillodonts, 42
time, 4; Einstein's theory of space-time, 3
Timor Strait, 47

tin, 18, 63; *19, 87*
Ting Chow, 86
Tiros, 8; *9*
titanium, *19*
Titograd, 20
toads, 75, 90; spadefoot, *74–5*
Toco toucan, *83*
Tokaido highway, 99; *98*
Tokyo, 56, 58
Tomici, 20
Tonga Islands, 20; *12*
topi, *79*
topographical maps, 99, 100, 102; *101*
tornados, 51
tortoises, 41, 83; desert, *74*
toucan, 82–3; *83*
tourism, 77, 92; *68, 81*
towns and cities, *see* cities
trace elements, in the atmosphere, *6*
trade, 58–9; *58–9*
Tragelaphus speki, 79
Trans-Amazonian highway, *32*
transcurrent faults, *12*
transform faults, *12*
transport 56, 58–9, 72; *58–9*
Transvaal, *72*
Trapezium, *3*
tree ferns, 40
tree kangaroo, *45*
trees: as fuel, 52; savannas, 78, 80; *see also* forests
trenches, oceanic, 13, 23; *23*
Triassic Period, 40–1, 44
Tribrachidium, 39
Triceratops, 40–1
Trichechus inunguis, 91
trilobites, *38–9*
Trinil, 46
tripod fish, *95*
trogons, 82–3
tropical rainforest, 82–5; *82–5*
tropical regions, 28, 50, 51; *50*
tropopause, *6*
troposphere, 7; *6*
trout, brown, *90*
trypanosomiasis, 81
Tsavo National Park, *81*
tsetse fly, 81
tsunamis, 22; *23*
Tuareg, *76*
tubeworms, *95*
tubifex worm, *93*
tumble bug, *71*
tundra, 62–3; *48, 50, 62–3*
tungsten, 52, 63; *19*
Tunisia, 68
Tupaia glis, 82
turaco, Gold Coast, *83*
Turdus merula, 65
Turkey, 46
Tursiops truncatus, 95
turtle, southern painted, *91*
Typha spp., *91*
Typhlichthys spp., *90*
typhoons, *50*
Tyrannosaurus, 40–1

U

Uganda, *56*
ultraviolet radiation, 7, 35, 38; *35*
United Nations, 54, 96
United Nations Conference

on Trade and Development (UNCTAD), 59
United States of America: and Antarctica, *60*; deserts, 74; earthquake zones, 20; Geological Survey, 99; immigration, *56*; mountain regions, 88; population distribution, 56; *57*; prairies, 73; river management, 33; satellites, 8; temperate forests, *64*; trade, *58*; uranium deposits, 18; volcanoes, 20; water, 76–7; *93*; *see also* North America
universe: measurement of space, *5*; origins of, 2–3
Upright Man, 46–7; *46–7*
Urals, 15; *88*
uranium, 18, 52; *18, 52, 77*
Uranus, 4; *5*
urbanization, 56; *57*
Ursus americanus, 65
USSR: and Antarctica, *60*; coal, 52; emigration restrictions, 56; river management, 33; satellites, 8; steppes, 32, 72–3; trade, 59; tundra and taiga, 63; *62*; whaling, 97

V

Vaccinium oxycoccus, 65
Val Camonica, 99; *98*
Valdez, 63
Valencia, 32
valley glaciers, 26
valleys: glaciated, 26–7; hanging, 26; river, *24*
Van Allen Belts, 7
varved clays, 27
Vauxia, 39
vegetation: deserts, 74–5; *74–5*; evolution, *40*; freshwater environments, 90; *90–1*; Mediterranean regions, 68; monsoon regions, 86; mountains, 88; *88–9*; polar regions, 60; savannas, *79*; satellite mapping, *98*; temperate grasslands, 70; *70–1*; tropical rainforests, 82; *82–3*; tundra, 62; zones, 49; *48–9*
Velella, 95
Venezuela, 78, 81; *56*
Venice, 22
Venus, 4, 6; *4*
vertebrates, 38, 40–1; *39*
Vertesszöllös, 46
Vespucci, Amerigo, *98*
Vestiaria coccinea, 36
Vienna, 100; *100*
Vietnam, 56
Vine, Fred, 13
vines, grape 68; *68–9*
viscacha, 71; *70–1*
Vitis vinifera, 69
Viverra tangalunga, 82
volcanoes, 6; coral reefs, *94*; formation, 20–1; *21*; influence on climate, 51; intrusions, *21*; mineral deposits, 18; *19*; mountain

formation, 15; plate tectonics, 12; *12*; and the primitive atmosphere, *35*; rock formation, 17; *16*
voles, 62
Vormela peregusna, 70
Vulpes vulpes, 65
vultures, 78; *78–9*

W

Wagner Projection, Hammer-, *101*
Waldseemüller, Martin, *98*
Wallace, Alfred Russel, 36
Wallace's Line, 44; *45*
Waptia, 39
warbler, willow, *65*
warthog, 78
Washington, 56; *56*
water: and the creation of life, 35; *35*; desalination, 97; in deserts, 76; *76–7*; effects on landscape, 24–5; *24–5*; as key to life, 7; map symbols, *103*; water cycle, 24, 32; *24, 92*; water power, 25, 63, 88, 92; *53, 92*; water table, 24; *25*; *see also* freshwater environments; marshes; oceans; rivers; swamps
water vapour, in atmosphere, 22, 24; *6*
waterfalls, 25–6
waterlily, *91*
waves, 22, 28–9; *23, 28–9*
waxwing, 63
weasels, *42*
weather, 50–1; *50–1*; forecasts, 8, 51; *9*
weathering, rocks, 18, 30–1; *19, 30–1*
Weber's Line, *45*
weevils, 44
Wegener, Alfred, 12, 13
Welwitschia mirabilis, 75
West Indies, 44
Western Ghats, 86
western wheatgrass, *70*
whales, 60, 94–5; *60*; blue, *60–1, 95, 97*; killer, *60–1*; minke, *96–7*
whaling, 96; *96–7*
wheat, 73; *68–9, 73–4, 93*
white-throated poorwill, *75*
Whitney, Mount, *103*
wildebeest, 78
Williamsonia, 41
willow, 62
Wilson, Robert, 3
winds: effects on landscape, 30–1; *30–1*; on oceans, 22
Winnipeg, *49*
winter solstice, *5*
Wiwaxia, 39
Wolf 359, *2*
wolverines, 63; *63*
wolves, 63, 64, 66; *63*; maned, 78; *70–1*; plains, *70–1*
wood-pigeon, 64
wood sedge, *42*
woodchuck, *65*
woodcock, *65*
woodpecker, acorn, *65*
World Bank, 59
worms, 38, 94; *39*
Wyoming, 18

X

X-rays, 7
xerophytes, 74–5
Xin, Pei, 100

Y

yak, 88; *89*
Yangtze river, 90
Yao, Emperor of China, 33
yardangs, 30
Yellow river, 25, 33
yew, 64
Yokohama, 56
Yorkshire, 26, 31
Yugoslavia, 20
Yukon, 62

Z

Zagros Mountains, 15
Zaire, 18, 54, 83
Zambia, 59, 80
zebra, 78; *78–9*; Grant's, *79*
zebu, 81
Zimbabwe, 59, 92
zinc, 18, 35; *18, 52*
zooplankton, 60, 94
Zulus, 72
Zuider Zee, *33*

INTERNATIONAL MAP SECTION CREDITS AND ACKNOWLEDGMENTS

Cartographic and Geographic Director
Giuseppe Motta

Geographic Research
G. Baselli
M. Colombo

Toponymy and Translation
C. Carpine
M. Colombo
H. R. Fischer
R. Nuñez de las Cuevas
Rand McNally Cartographic Research Staff
I. Straube

Computerized Data Organization
C. Bardesono
E. Ciano
G. Comoglio
E. Di Costanzo

Index
S. Osnaghi
T. Tomasini

Cartographic Editor
V. Castelli

Cartographic Compilation
G. Albera
L. Cairo
C. Camera
G. Conti
G. Fizzotti
G. Gambaro
M. Mochetti
O. Passarelli
M. Peretti
G. Rassiga
A. Saino
F. Valsecchi

Terrain Illustration
S. Andenna
E. Ferrari

Cartographic Production
F. Tosi
G. Capitini
A. Carnero

Filmsetting
S. Fiorini
P. L. Gatta
E. Geranio
G. Ghezzi
L. Lorena
R. Martelli
E. Morchio
M. Morganti
C. Pezzana
P. Uglietti
D. Varalli

Photographic Processing
G. Fracassina
G. Klaus
L. Mella

Co-ordination
S. Binda
L. Pasquali
G. Zanetta

The editors wish to thank the many organizations, institutions and individuals who have given their valuable help and advice during the preparation of this International Map Section. Special thanks are extended to the following:

Agenzia Novosti, Rome, Italy
D. Arnold, Acting Chief of Documentation and Terminology Section, United Nations, New York, USA
Australian Bureau of Statistics, Brisbane, Australia
J. Breu, United Nations Group of Experts on Geographical Names, Vienna, Austria
Bureau Hydrographique International, Monaco, Principality of Monaco
Canada Map Office, Ottawa, Canada
Cartactual, Budapest, Hungary
Census and Statistical Department, Tripoli, Libya
Central Bureau of Statistics, Accra, Ghana
Central Bureau of Statistics, Jerusalem, Israel
Central Bureau of Statistics, Ministry of Economic Planning and Development, Nairobi, Kenya
Central Department of Statistics, Riyadh, Saudi Arabia
Central Statistical Board of the USSR, Moscow, USSR
Central Statistical Office, London, UK
Centro de Informaçao e Documentaçao Estadística, Rio de Janeiro, Brazil
Committee for the Reform of Chinese Written Language, Peking, China
Danmark Statistik, Copenhagen, Denmark
Defense Mapping Agency, Distribution Office for Latin America, Miami, USA
Defense Mapping Agency, Washington DC, USA
Department of National Development and Energy, Division of National Mapping, Belconnen ACT, Australia
Department of State Coordinator for Maps and Publications, Washington DC, USA
Department of State Map Division, Sofia, Bulgaria
Department of Statistics, Wellington, New Zealand
Direcçao Nacional de Estadística, Maputo, Mozambique
Dirección de Cartografía Naciónal, Caracas, Venezuela
Dirección de Estadística y Censo de la Repubblica de Panama, Panama
Dirección General de Estadística, Mexico City, Mexico
Dirección General de Estadística y Censos, San Salvador, El Salvador
Direcţia Centrala de Statistică, Bucharest, Romania
Directorate of National Mapping, Kuala Lumpur, Malaysia
Directorate of Overseas Surveys, London, UK
Elaborazione Dati e Disegno Automatico, Torino, Italy
Federal Office of Statistics, Lagos, Nigeria
Federal Office of Statistics, Prague, Czechoslovakia
Geographical Research Institute, Hungarian Academy of Sciences, Budapest, Hungary
Geological Map Service, New York, USA
G. Gomez de Silva, Chief Conference Services Section, United Nations Environment Programme, New York, USA
Government of the People's Republic of Bangladesh, Statistics Division, Ministry of Planning, Dacca, Bangladesh
High Commissioner for Trinidad and Tobago, London, UK
L. Iarotski, World Health Organization, Geneva, Switzerland Information Division, Valletta, Malta
Institut für Angewandte Geodäsie, Frankfurt, West Germany
Institut Géographique, Abidjan, Ivory Coast
Institut Géographique du Zaïre, Kinshasa, Zaïre
Institut Géographique National, Brussels, Belgium
Institut Géographique National, Paris, France
Institut Haïtien de Statistique, Port-au-Prince, Haiti
Institut National de Géodésie et Cartographie, Antananarivo, Madagascar
Institut National de la Statistique, Tunis, Tunisia
Institute of Geography, Polish Academy of Sciences, Warsaw, Poland
Instituto Geográfico Militar, Buenos Aires, Argentina
Instituto Nacional de Estadística, La Paz, Bolivia
Instituto Nacional de Estadística, Madrid, Spain
Istituto Centrale di Statistica, Rome, Italy
Istituto Geografico Militare, Florence, Italy
Istituto Idrografico della Marina, Genoa, Italy
Landesverwaltung des Fürstentums, Vaduz, Liechtenstein
Ministère des Affaires Economiques, Brussels, Belgium
Ministère des Ressources Naturelles, des Mines et des Carrières, Kigali, Rwanda
Ministère des Travaux Publics, des Transports et de l'Urbanisme, Ouagadougou, Upper Volta
Ministry of Finance, Department of Statistics and Research, Nicosia, Cyprus

Ministry of Lands, Housing and Urban Development, Surveys and Mapping Division, Dar es Salaam, Tanzania
Ministry of the Interior, Jerusalem, Israel
National Census and Statistics Office, Manila, Philippines
National Central Bureau of Statistics, Stockholm, Sweden
National Geographic Society, Washington DC, USA
National Institute of Polar Research, Tokyo, Japan
National Ocean Survey, Riverdale, Maryland, USA
National Statistical Institute, Lisbon, Portugal
National Statistical Office, Zomba, Malawi
National Statistical Service of Greece, Athens, Greece
J. Novotny, Prague, Czechoslovakia
Office Nationale de la Recherche Scientifique et Technique, Yaoundé, Cameroon
Officina Comercial del Gobierno de Colombia, Rome, Italy
Ordnance Survey of Ireland, Dublin, Ireland
Österreichisches Statistisches Zentralamt, Vienna, Austria
Państwowe Przędsiebiorstwo Wydawnictw Kartograficznych, Warsaw, Poland
Scott Polar Research Institute, University of Cambridge, Cambridge, UK
Secrétariat d'Etat au Plan, Algiers, Algeria
Servicio Geografico Militar, Montevideo, Uruguay
Z. Shiying, Research Institute of Surveying and Mapping, Peking, China
Statistisches Bundesamt, Wiesbaden, West Germany
Statistisk Sentralbyrå, Oslo, Norway
Survey and National Mapping Department, Kuala Lumpur, Malaysia
Ufficio Turismo e Informazioni della Turchia, Rome, Italy
United States Board on Geographic Names, Washington DC, USA
M. C. Wu, Chinese Translation Service, United Nations, New York, USA
Z. Youguang, Committee for the Reform of Chinese Written Language, Peking, China

The editors are also grateful for the assistance provided by the following embassies, consulates and official state representatives:

Angolan Embassy, Rome
Australian Embassy, Rome
Austrian Embassy, Rome
Embassy of Bangladesh, Rome
Embassy of Botswana, Brussels
Brazilian Embassy, Rome
British Embassy, Rome
Burmese Embassy, Rome
Embassy of Cameroon, Rome
Embassy of Cape Verde, Lisbon
Consulate of Chad, Rome
Chilean Embassy, Rome
Embassy of the People's Republic of China in Italy, Rome
Danish Embassy, Rome
Embassy of El Salvador, Rome
Ethiopian Embassy, Rome
Finnish Embassy, Rome
Embassy of the German Democratic Republic, Rome
Greek Embassy, Rome
Honduras Republic Embassy, Rome
Hungarian Embassy, Rome
Consulate General of Iceland, Rome
Embassy of India, Rome
Embassy of the Republic of Indonesia, Rome
Embassy of the Islamic Republic of Iran, Rome

Irish Embassy, Rome
Embassy of Israel, Rome
Japanese Embassy, Rome
Korean Embassy, Rome
Luxembourg Embassy, Rome
Embassy of Malta, Rome
Mexican Embassy, Rome
Moroccan Embassy, Rome
Netherlands Embassy, Rome
Embassy of New Zealand, Rome
Embassy of Niger, Rome
Embassy of Pakistan, Rome
Peruvian Embassy, Rome
Philippine Embassy, Rome
Romanian Embassy, Rome
Somali Embassy, Rome
South African Embassy, Rome
Spanish Embassy, Rome
Consulate General of Switzerland, Milan
Royal Thai Embassy, Rome
Consulate of Upper Volta, Rome
Uruguay Embassy, Rome
Embassy of the Socialist Republic of Vietnam in Italy, Rome
Permanent Mission of Yemen to United Nations Educational, Scientific and Cultural Organization, Paris

INTERNATIONAL MAP SECTION

Hydrographic and Topographic Features
Symboles hydrographiques et morphologiques   Idrografia, Morfologia
Gewässer- und Geländeformen   Hidrografía y morfología

River, Stream
Cours d'eau permanent
Ständig wasserführender Fluß
Corso d'acqua perenne
Corriente de agua de régimen permanente

Lake
Lac d'eau douce
Süßwassersee
Lago d'acqua dolce
Lago de agua dulce

Rocks
Ecueils, Roches
Klippen, Felsriffe
Scogli, Rocce
Escollos, Rocas

Summer Limit of Pack Ice
Limite du pack en été
Packeisgrenze im Sommer
Limite estivo del pack ghiacciato
Límite estival de banco de hielo

Intermittent Stream
Cours d'eau intermittent
Zeitweilig wasserführender Fluß
Corso d'acqua periodico
Corriente de agua intermitente

Intermittent Lake
Lac d'eau douce temporaire
Zeitweiliger Süßwassersee
Lago d'acqua dolce periodico
Lago de agua dulce intermitente

Reef, Atoll
Barrière. Atoll
Riff, Atoll
Barriera, Atollo
Barrera de arrecifes

Winter Limit of Pack Ice
Limite du pack en hiver
Packeisgrenze im Winter
Limite invernale del pack ghiacciato
Límite invernal de banco de hielo

Disappearing Stream
Perte de cours d'eau
Versickernder Fluß
Corso d'acqua che si inabissa
Corriente de agua que desaparece

Salt Lake
Lac d'eau salée
Salzsee
Lago d'acqua salata
Lago de agua salada

Mangrove
Mangrove
Mangrove
Mangrovie
Manglar

Limit of Icebergs
Limite des glaces flottantes
Treibeisgrenze
Limite dei ghiacci alla deriva
Limite de hielo a la deriva

Undefined or Fluctuating River Course
Cours d'eau incertain
Fluß mit veränderlichem Lauf
Fiume dal corso incerto
Corriente de agua incerta

Intermittent Salt Lake
Lac d'eau salée temporaire
Zeitweiliger Salzsee
Lago d'acqua salata periodico
Lago de agua salada intermitente

Continental Ice-cap
Glacier continental
Inlandeis. Gletscher
Ghiacciaio continentale
Glaciar continental

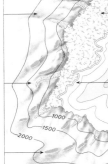
Ice Shelf
Banquise
Schelfeis oder Eisschelf
Banchisa polare (Ice-shelf)
Banquisa

Waterfall, Rapids, Cataract
Chute, Rapide, Cataracte
Wasserfall, Stromschnelle, Katarakt
Cascata, Rapida, Cateratta
Cascada, Rapido, Catarata

Dry Lake Bed
Lac asséché
Trockener Seeboden
Alveo di lago asciutto
Lecho de lago seco

Glacial Tongue
Langue glaciaire
Gletscherzunge
Lingua di ghiaccio
Lengua de glaciar

Limit of Ice Shelf
Limite de la banquise
Schelfeisgrenze
Limite della banchisa
Límite de la banquisa

Canal
Canal
Kanal
Canale
Canal

Lake Surface Elevation
Cote du lac au-dessus du niveau de la mer
Höhe des Seespiegels
Altitudine del lago
Elevación de lago sobre el nivel del mar

Rocky Areas (Antarctica)
Région de roches (Antarctique)
Eisfreie Gebiete, Gebirge (Antarktika)
Aree rocciose (Antartide)
Area rocosa (Antártida)

Contour Lines in Continental Ice
Courbes de niveau dans les régions glaciaires
Höhenlinien auf vergletschertem Gebiet
Curve altimetriche nelle aree ghiacciate
Curvas de nivel en areas heladas

Navigable Canal
Canal navigable
Schiffbarer Kanal
Canale navigabile
Canal navegable

Lake Depth
Profondeur du lac
Seetiefen
Profondità del lago
Profundidad del lago

Defined Shoreline
Trait de côte définie
Küsten- oder Uferlinie
Linea di costa definita
Línea de costa definida

Bathymetric Contour
Courbe bathymétrique
Tiefenlinie
Curva batimetrica
Curva batimétrica

Swamp
Marais
Sumpf
Palude d'acqua dolce
Pantano

Sand Area
Région de sable, Désert
Sandgebiet, Sandwüste
Area sabbiosa, Deserto
Zona arenosa, desierto

Undefined or Fluctuating Shoreline
Trait de côte indéfinie
Unbestimmte oder veränderliche Uferlinie
Linea di costa indefinita
Línea de costa indefinida

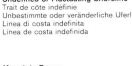
Depth of Water
Valeur de sonde
Tiefenzahl
Quota batimetrica
Cota batimétrica

Salt Marsh
Marais d'eau salée
Salzsumpf
Palude d'acqua salata
Pantano de agua salada

Sandbank, Sandbar
Banc de sable
Sandbank
Bassofondo sabbioso
Banco submarino de arena

Mountain Range
Chaîne de montagnes
Bergkette
Catena di monti
Cadena montañosa

Mountain
Mont
Berg, Bergmassiv
Monte
Monte

Salt Pan
Marais salant
Salzpfanne
Salina
Salina

Port Facilities
Installations portuaires
Hafenanlagen
Impianti portuali
Instalaciones portuarias

Elevation
Cote, Altitude
Höhenzahl
Quota altimetrica
Cota altimétrica

Mountain Pass, Gap
Passage, Col, Port
Paß, Joch, Sattel
Passo, Colle, Valico
Paso, Collado, Puerto de montaña

Key to Elevation and Depth Tints
Hypsométrie, Bathymétrie   Altimetria, Batimetria
Höhenstufen, Tiefenstufen   Altimetría, Batimetría

Scales in Metric and English Measures
Échelle des teintes hypsométriques et bathymétriques
Farbskala der Höhen- und Tiefenstufen
Scala delle tinte Altimetriche e Batimetriche
Escala de tintas hipsométricas y batimétricas

Land Elevation Below Sea Level
Dépression et cote au-dessous du niveau de la mer
Senke mit Tiefenzahl unter dem Meeresspiegel
Depressione e quota sotto il livello del mare
Depresión y elevación bajo el nivel del mar

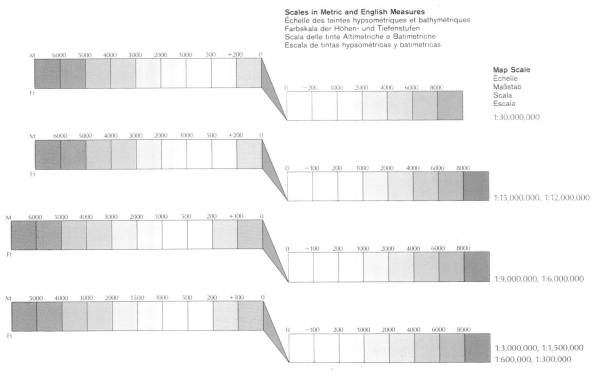

Map Scale
Échelle
Maßstab
Scala
Escala

1:30.000.000

1:15,000,000, 1:12,000,000

1:9,000,000, 1:6,000,000

1:3,000,000, 1:1,500,000
1:600,000, 1:300,000

The meanings of the symbols on the Legend pages are in English, French, German, Italian, and Spanish languages
to permit the interpretation of the maps by a broad readership.

Boundaries, Capitals
Frontières, Soulignements
Grenzen, Unterstreichungen
Confini, Sottolineature
Límites, Subrayados

Other Symbols
Symboles divers   Simboli vari
Sonstige Zeichen   Signos varios

Defined International Boundary
Frontière internationale définie
Staatsgrenze
Confine di Stato definito
Límite de Nación definido

Second-order Political Boundary
Frontière d'État fédéré, Région
Bundesstaats-, Regionsgrenze
Confine di Stato federato, Regione
Límite de Estado federado, Región

International Airport
Aéroport international
Internationaler Flughafen
Aeroporto internazionale
Aeropuerto internacional

Church, Monastery, Abbey
Monastère, Église, Abbaye
Kloster, Kirche, Abtei
Monastero, Chiesa, Abbazia
Monasterio, Iglesia, Abadía

International Boundary (Continent Maps)
Frontière internationale (Continents)
Staatsgrenze (Erdteilkarten)
Confine di Stato (Carte dei Continenti)
Límite de Nación (Continentes)

Third-order Political Boundary
Frontière de Province, Comté, Bezirk
Provinz-, Grafschafts-, Bezirksgrenze
Confine di Provincia, Contea, Bezirk
Límite de Provincia, Condado, Bezirk

Lighthouse
Phare
Leuchtturm
Faro
Faro

Castle
Château
Burg, Schloß
Castello
Castillo

Undefined International Boundary
Frontière internationale indéfinie
Nicht genau festgelegte Staatsgrenze
Confine di Stato indefinito
Límite de Nación indefinido

Administrative District Boundary (U.S.S.R.)
Frontière de Circonscription
Kreisgrenze
Confine di Circondario
Límite de Circunscripción administrativa

Dam
Barrage
Staudamm, Staumauer
Diga artificiale, Sbarramento
Presa

Ruin, Archeological Site
Ruine, Centre archéologique
Ruine, Archäologisches Zentrum
Rovina, Zona archeologica
Ruina, Zona arqueológica

International Ocean Floor Boundary Defined by Treaty or Bilateral Agreement
Frontière d'état en mer définie par traités et conventions bilatéraux
Durch Verträge festgelegte Staatsgrenze im Meeresgebiet
Confine di Stato nel mare definito da trattati e convenzioni bilaterali
Límite de Nación en el Mar definido por los tratados bilaterales

International Ocean Floor Boundary
Frontière d'état en mer
Staatsgrenze im Meeresgebiet
Confine di Stato nel mare
Límite de Nación en el mar

Undefined Ocean Floor Boundary
Frontière indéfinie d'état tracée en mer
Unbstimmte Staatsgrenze im Meeresgebiet
Confine di Stato indefinito nel mare
Límite indefinido de Nación en el mar

Section of a City
Faubourg
Stadt- oder Ortsteil
Sobborgo urbano
Suburbio

Monument, Historic Site, etc.
Monument
Denkmal
Monumento
Monumento

Uninhabited Locality, Hamlet
Ville inhabitée, Ferme, Hameau
Unbewohnte Stadt, Gehöft, Weiler
Città disabitata, Fattoria, Nucleo di case
Ciudad despoblada, Granja, Casar

Wall
Muraille
Wall, Mauer
Vallo, Muraglia
Muralla

National Capital
Capitale d'État
Hauptstadt eines unabhängigen Staates
Capitale di Stato
Capital de Nación

ROMA

Third - order Capital
Capitale de Province, Comté, Bezirk
Provinz-, Grafschafts-, Bezirkshauptstadt
Capoluogo di Provincia, Contea, Bezirk
Capital de Provincia, Condado, Bezirk

Kristiansand

Periodically Inhabited Oasis
Oasis habitées périodiquement
Zeitweilig bewohnte Oase
Oasi periodicamente abitate
Oasis periodicamente habitados

Point of Interest
Curiosité
Sehenswürdigkeit
Curiosità
Curiosidad

Dependency or Second-order Capital
Capitale d'État fédéré, Région
Bundesstaats-, Regionshauptstadt
Capitale di Stato federato, Regione
Capital de Estado federado, Región

RIGA

Administrative District Capital (U.S.S.R.)
Capitale de Circonscription
Kreishauptstadt
Capoluogo di Circondario
Capital de Circunscripción administrativa

Anadyr

Scientific Station
Base géophysique
Geophysikalische Beobachtungsstation
Base geofisica
Base geofísica

Cave
Grotte, Caverne
Höhle
Grotta, Caverna
Cueva, Gruta

Populated Places
Population   Popolazione
Bevölkerung   Población

Transportation
Communications   Comunicazioni
Verkehrsnetz   Comunicaciones

Continent Maps
Cartes des Continents   Carte dei Continenti
Erdteilkarten   Mapas de Continentes

o   < 25 000
   25 000-100 000
   100 000-250 000
   250 000-1 000 000
   > 1 000 000

Regional Maps
Cartes à plus grande échelle   Carte di sviluppo
Karten größeren Maßstabs   Mapas a gran escala

o   < 10 000
o   10 000-25 000
   25 000-100 000
   100 000-250 000
   250 000-1 000 000
   > 1 000 000

Symbols represent population of inhabited localities
Les symboles représentent le nombre d'habitants des localités
Die Signaturen entsprechen der Einwohnerzahl des Ortes
I simboli sono relativi al valore demografico dei centri abitati
Los símbolos son proporcionales a la población del lugar

Town area symbol represents the shape of the urban area
Le petit plan de la ville reproduit la configuration de l'aire urbaine
Die Plansignatur stellt die Gestalt des Stadtgebietes dar
La piantina della città rappresenta la configurazione dell'area urbana
El pequeño plano de la ciudad representa la forma del área urbana

Primary Railway
Chemin de fer principal
Hauptbahn
Ferrovia principale
Ferrocarril principal

Secondary Railway
Chemin de fer secondaire
Sonstige Bahn
Ferrovia secondaria
Ferrocarril secundario

Motorway, Expressway
Autoroute
Autobahn
Autostrada
Autopista

Road
Route de grande communication, Autres Routes
Fernverkehrsstraße, andere Straßen
Strada principale, Altre Strade
Carretera principal, Otras Carreteras

Trail, Caravan Route
Piste, Voie caravanière
Wüstenpiste, Karawanenweg
Pista nel deserto, Carovaniera
Pista en el desierto, Vía de Carabanas

Ferry, Shipping Lane
Bac, Ligne maritime
Fähre, Schiffahrtslinie
Traghetto, Linea di navigazione
Transbordador (Ferry), Línea de navegación

Type Styles
Caractères utilisés pour la toponymie
Zur Namenschreibung verwendete Schriftarten
Caratteri usati per la toponomastica
Caracteres utilizados para la toponimia

ITALY
Hessen RIBE

Political Units
Etat, Dépendance, Division administrative
Staat, abhängiges Gebiet, Verwaltungsgliederung
Stato, Dipendenza, Divisione amministrativa
Nación, Dependencia, División administrativa

Ankaratra   Monte Bianco
Tsiafajavona   Ngorongoro Crater
Nevado del Tolima   Kings Peak

Small Mountain Range, Mountain, Peak
Petit massif, Mont, Cime
Bergmassiv, Berg, Gipfel
Piccolo gruppo montuoso, Monte, Vetta
Macizo pequeño, Monte, Cima

LABRADOR SEA
Gulf of Alaska   Hudson Bay
Estrecho de Magallanes

Sea, Gulf, Bay, Strait
Mer, Golfe, Baie, Détroit
Meer, Golf, Bucht, Meeresstraße
Mare, Golfo, Baia, Stretto
Mar, Golfo, Bahía, Estrecho

SAXONY
THRACE SUSSEX

Historical or Cultural Region
Région historique ou culturelle
Historische oder Kulturlandschaft
Regione storico - culturale
Región histórica y cultural

Cabo de São Vicente   Land's End
Mizen Head   Point Conception
Col de la Perche   Passo della Cisa

Cape, Point, Pass
Cap, Pointe, Passe
Kap, Landspitze, Paß
Capo, Punta, Passo
Cabo, Punta, Paso

West Mariana Basin
Galapagos Fracture Zone
Mid-Atlantic Ridge

Undersea Features
Formes du relief sous-marin
Formen des Meeresbodens
Forme del rilievo sottomarino
Formas del relieve submarino

PATAGONIA
BASSIN DE RENNES
PENÍNSULA DE YUCATÁN

Physical Region (plain, peninsula)
Région physique (plaine, péninsule)
Landschaft (Ebene, Halbinsel)
Regione fisica (pianura, penisola)
Región natural (llanura, península)

MAHÉ   ALDABRA ISLANDS
CORSE CHANNEL ISLANDS
SULU ARCHIPELAGO

Island, Archipelago
Ile, Archipel
Insel, Archipel
Isola, Arcipelago
Isla, Archipiélago

Tarfaya

Tombouctou

Agadir

Nouakchott

BRAZZAVILLE

CASABLANCA

Size of type indicates relative importance of inhabited localities
La dimension des caractères indique l'importance d'une localité
Die Schriftgröße entspricht der Gesamtbedeutung des Ortes
La grandezza del carattere è proporzionale all'importanza della località
La dimensión de los caracteres de imprenta indica la importancia de la localidad

PYRENEES
CUMBRIAN MOUNTAINS
SIERRA DE GÁDOR   LA SILA

Mountain Range
Chaîne de montagnes
Bergkette, Gebirge
Catena di monti
Cadena montañosa

Thames Po Victoria Falls
Lotagipi Swamp   Göta kanal
Lago Maggiore

River, Waterfall, Cataract, Canal, Lake
Fleuve, Chute d'eau, Cataracte, Canal, Lac
Fluß, Wasserfall, Katarakt, Kanal, See
Fiume, Cascata, Cateratta, Canale, Lago
Río, Cascada, Catarata, Canal, Lago

INDEX MAPS

WORLD PHYSICAL AND POLITICAL MAPS

1/2   1:70,000,000

THE OCEANS

3   1:70,000,000

WORLD TRANSPORTATION AND TIME ZONES

4   1:90,000,000

PHYSICAL AND POLITICAL CONTINENT MAPS

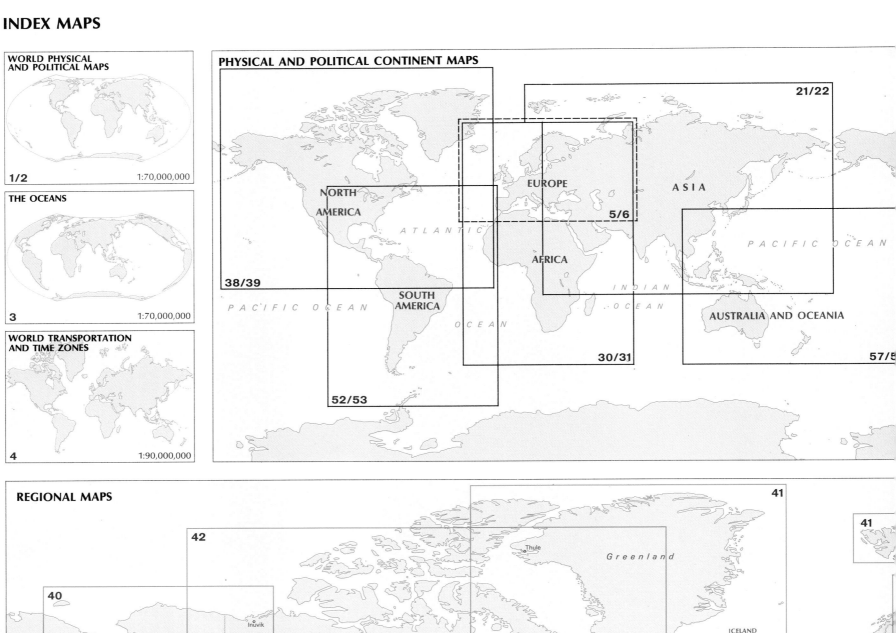

NORTH AMERICA

EUROPE   5/6

ASIA

21/22

AFRICA

ATLANTIC OCEAN

PACIFIC OCEAN

INDIAN OCEAN

SOUTH AMERICA

PACIFIC OCEAN

AUSTRALIA AND OCEANIA

38/39

52/53

30/31

57/5

REGIONAL MAPS

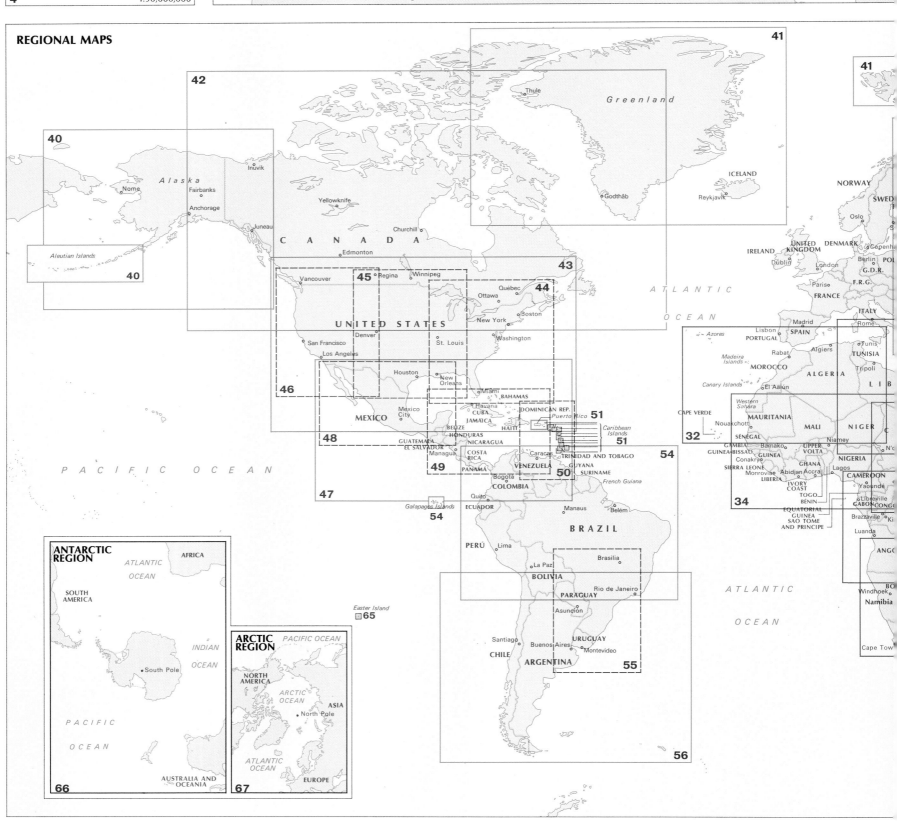

40   42   41

Alaska   Nome   Fairbanks   Anchorage   Juneau   Inuvik

Aleutian Islands   40

Yellowknife   Edmonton   CANADA   Churchill

Thule   Greenland   ICELAND   Godthåb   Reykjavik

41

NORWAY   SWED   Oslo

IRELAND   UNITED KINGDOM   DENMARK   Copenhe   Dublin   London   Berlin   POL   G.D.R.   Paris   F.R.G.   FRANCE

43   Vancouver   45   Regina   Winnipeg   Québec   Ottawa   44   Boston   New York

UNITED STATES   Denver   San Francisco   St. Louis   Washington   Los Angeles

ATLANTIC OCEAN

Azores   Lisbon   SPAIN   Madrid   Rome   ITALY   PORTUGAL   Tunis   Madeira Islands   Rabat   Algiers   TUNISIA   MOROCCO   Tripoli   Canary Islands   El Aaiún   ALGERIA   LIB

46   Houston   New Orleans   Miami   BAHAMAS

Western Sahara   CAPE VERDE   Nouakchott   MAURITANIA   MALI   NIGER   32   SENEGAL   Niamey

MEXICO   Mexico City   Havana   CUBA   DOMINICAN REP.   Puerto Rico   51   JAMAICA   HAITI   Caribbean Islands   51

48   BELIZE   HONDURAS   GUATEMALA   NICARAGUA   EL SALVADOR   Managua   COSTA RICA   49   PANAMA   Caracas   TRINIDAD AND TOBAGO   54   VENEZUELA   50   GUYANA   SURINAME

GAMBIA   Bamako   UPPER VOLTA   GUINEA-BISSAU   GUINEA   Conakry   NIGERIA   Lagos   SIERRA LEONE   GHANA   Monrovia   Abidjan   Accra   LIBERIA   IVORY COAST   TOGO   BENIN   CAMEROON   Yaoundé

47   Bogotá   COLOMBIA   French Guiana   34   EQUATORIAL GUINEA   Libreville   GABON   CONGO   SAO TOME AND PRINCIPE

PACIFIC OCEAN

Galapagos Islands   54   ECUADOR   Quito   Manaus   Belém   Brazzaville   Ki   Luanda

BRAZIL   PERÚ   Lima   ANG

ANTARCTIC REGION

AFRICA   ATLANTIC OCEAN   SOUTH AMERICA   INDIAN OCEAN   South Pole   PACIFIC OCEAN

66

Easter Island   65

Brasília   La Paz   BOLIVIA   Rio de Janeiro   PARAGUAY   Asunción   ATLANTIC OCEAN   Windhoek   Namibia   BO   Cape Tow

ARCTIC REGION

PACIFIC OCEAN   NORTH AMERICA   ARCTIC OCEAN   ASIA   North Pole   ATLANTIC OCEAN   AUSTRALIA AND OCEANIA   EUROPE

67

Santiago   Buenos Aires   URUGUAY   Montevideo   CHILE   ARGENTINA   55

56

GIONAL MAPS OF EUROPE

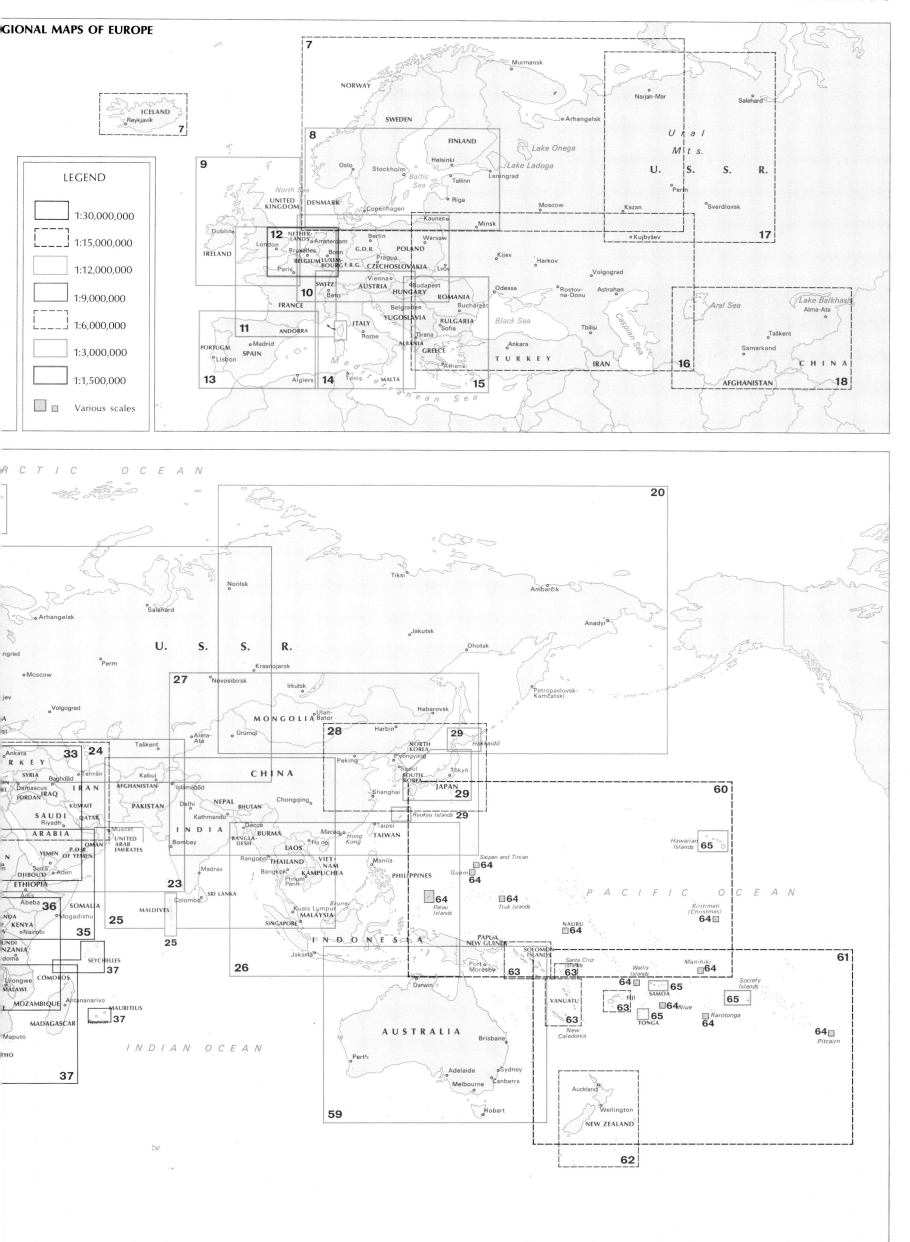

LEGEND

☐	1:30,000,000
☐	1:15,000,000
☐	1:12,000,000
☐	1:9,000,000
☐	1:6,000,000
☐	1:3,000,000
☐	1:1,500,000
▨ ☐	Various scales

Map 1 **WORLD, PHYSICAL**

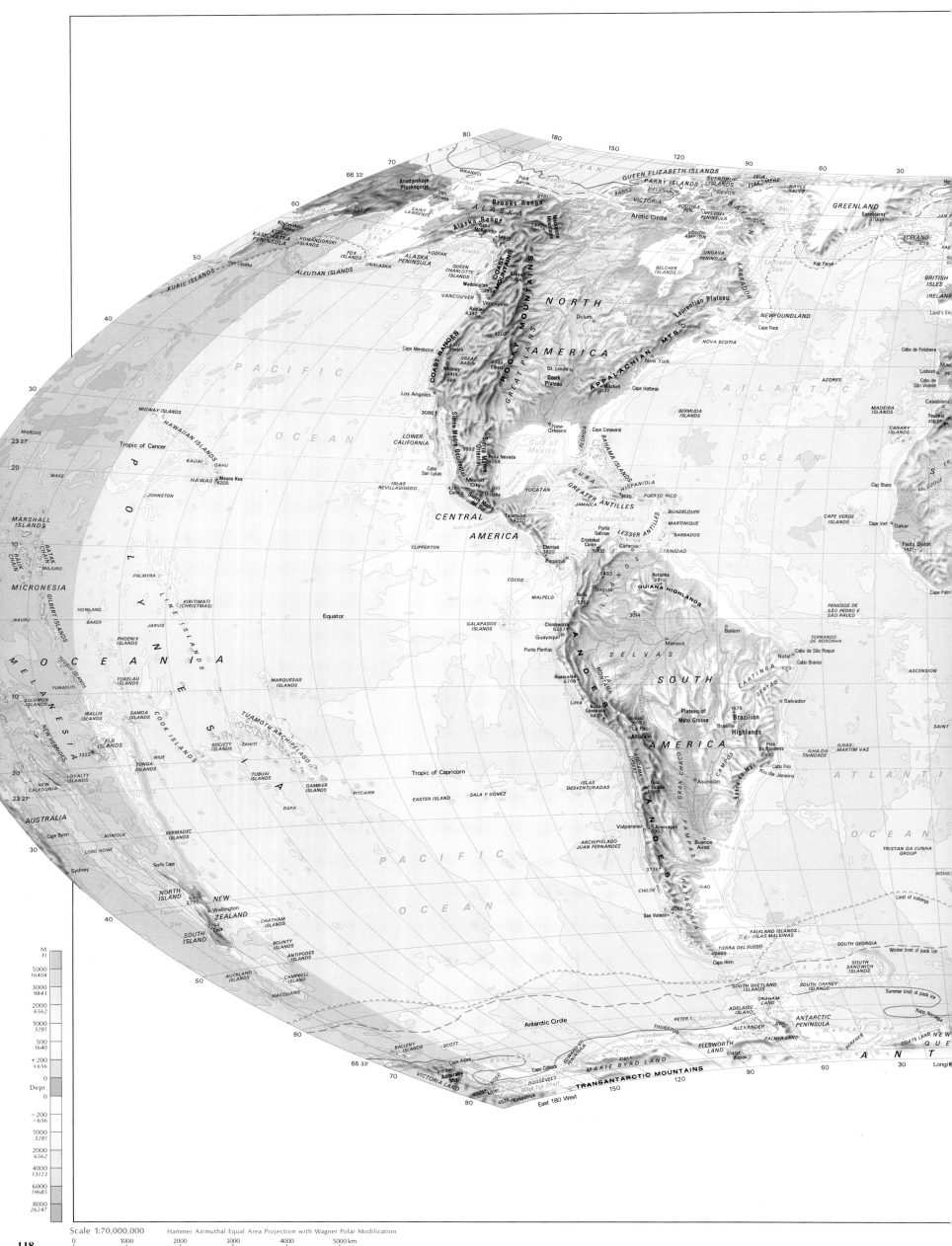

Scale 1:70,000,000   Hammer Azimuthal Equal-Area Projection with Wagner Polar Modification

Map 2 **WORLD, POLITICAL**

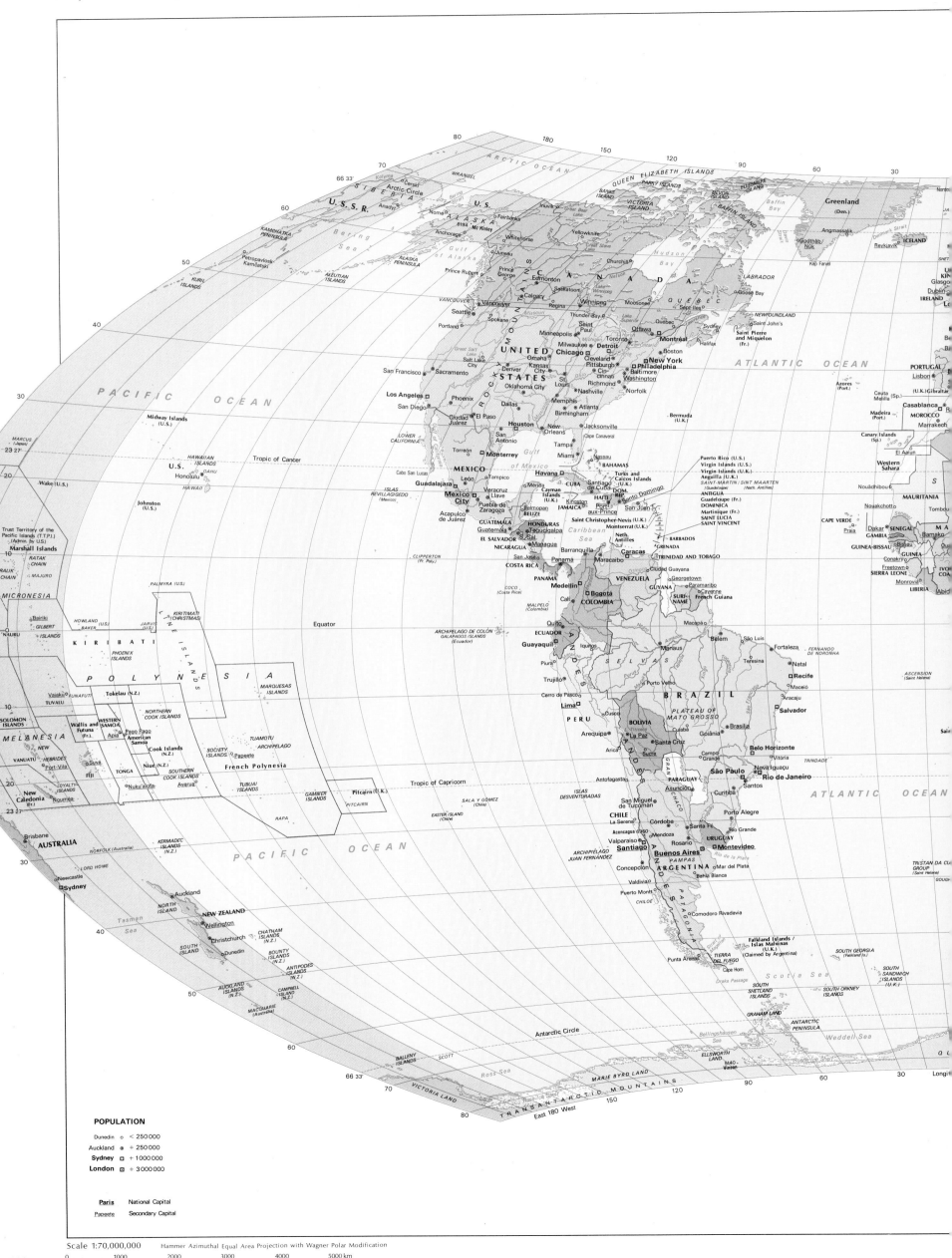

POPULATION

Dunedin ○	< 250 000
Auckland ◉	+ 250 000
Sydney ▫	+ 1 000 000
London ▣	+ 3 000 000

Paris	National Capital
Papeete	Secondary Capital

Scale 1:70 000 000   Hammer Azimuthal Equal Area Projection with Wagner Polar Modification

0   1000   2000   3000   4000   5000 km

0   1000   2000   3000 miles

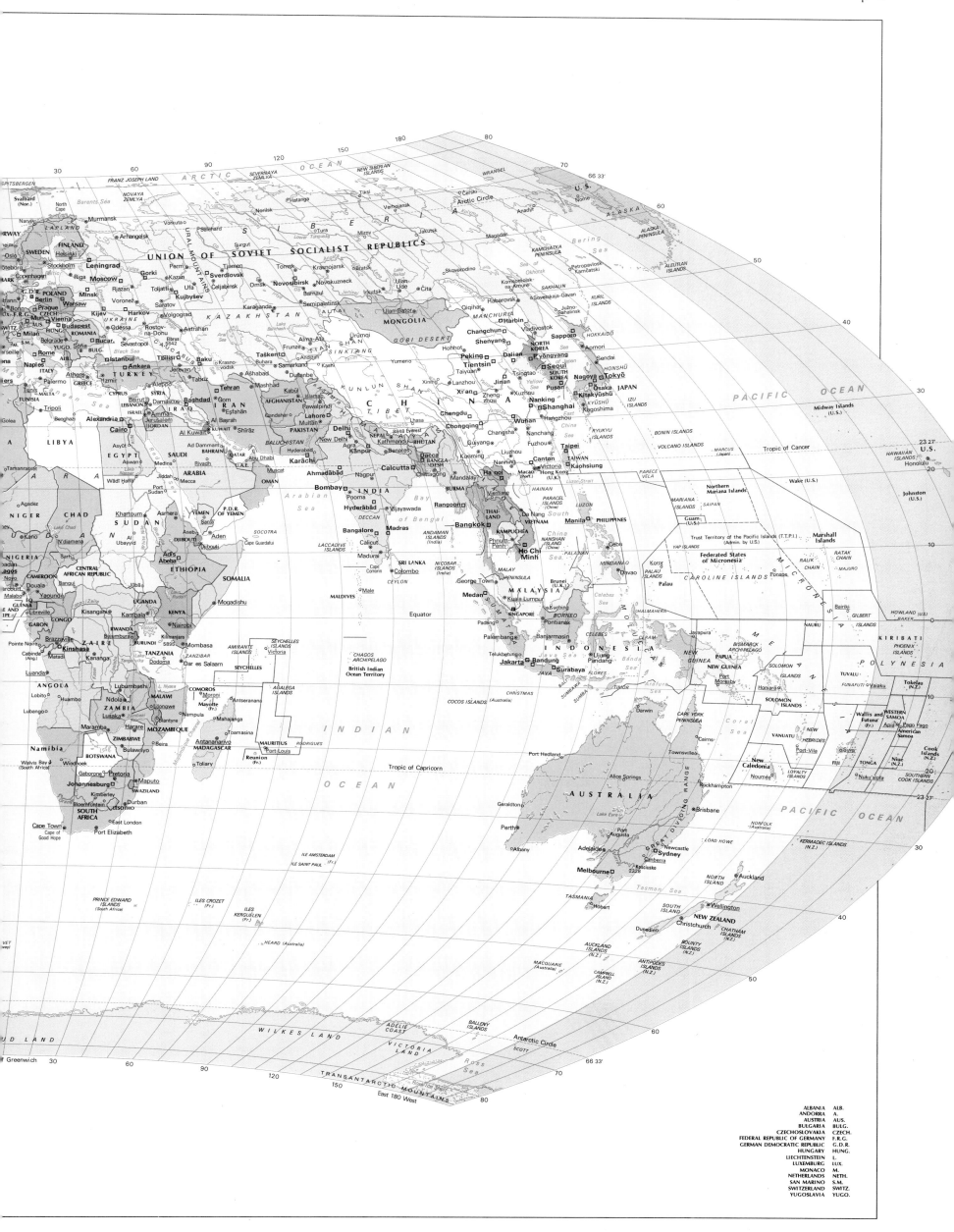

ALBANIA — ALB.
ANDORRA — A
AUSTRIA — AUS.
BULGARIA — BULG.
CZECHOSLOVAKIA — CZECH.
FEDERAL REPUBLIC OF GERMANY — F.R.G.
GERMAN DEMOCRATIC REPUBLIC — G.D.R.
HUNGARY — HUNG.
LIECHTENSTEIN — L.
LUXEMBURG — LUX.
MONACO — M.
NETHERLANDS — NETH.
SAN MARINO — S.M.
SWITZERLAND — SWITZ.
YUGOSLAVIA — YUGO.

Map 3 **THE OCEANS**

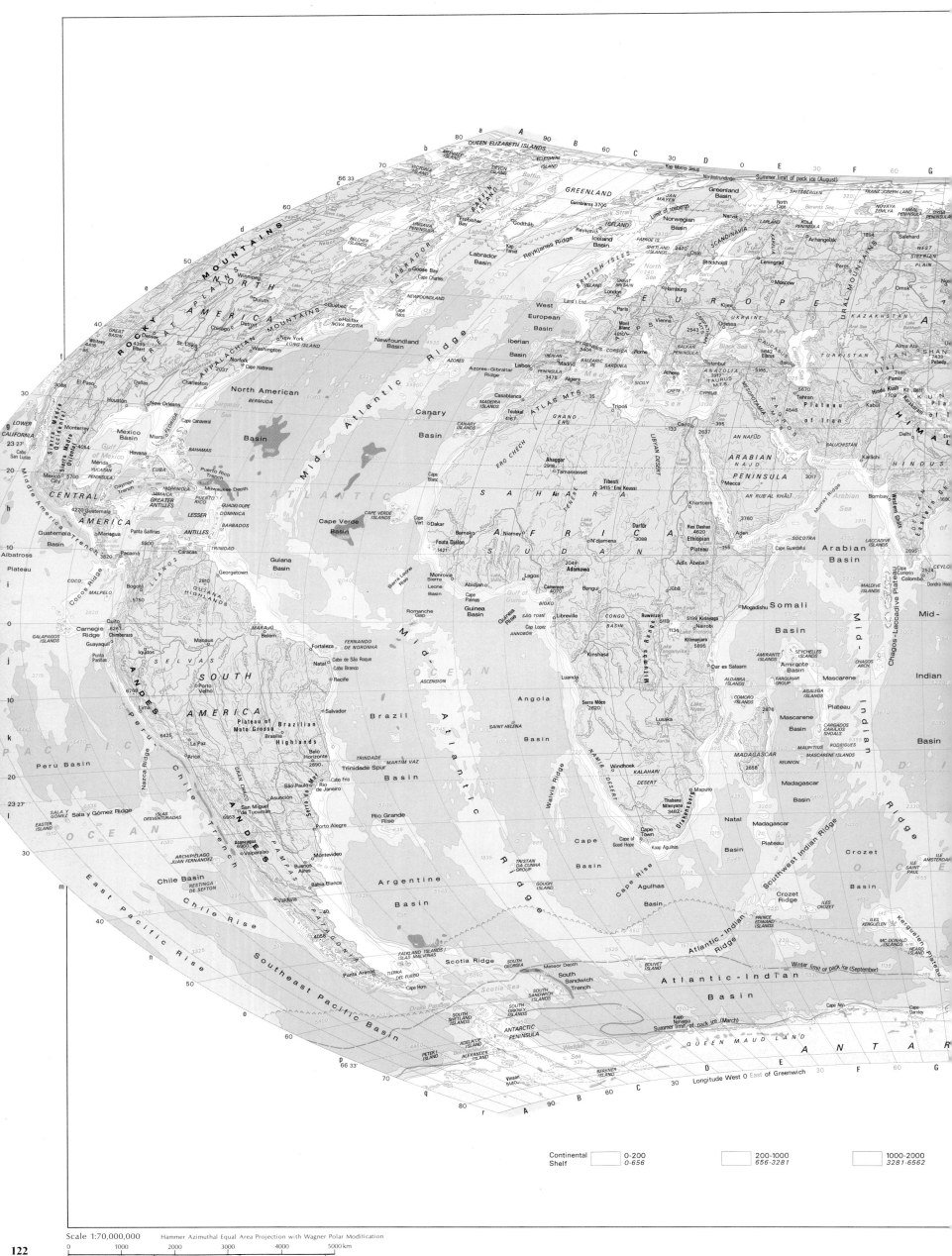

Continental Shelf | 0-200 / 0-656 | 200-1000 / 656-3281 | 1000-2000 / 3281-6562

Scale 1:70,000,000   Hammer Azimuthal Equal Area Projection with Wagner Polar Modification

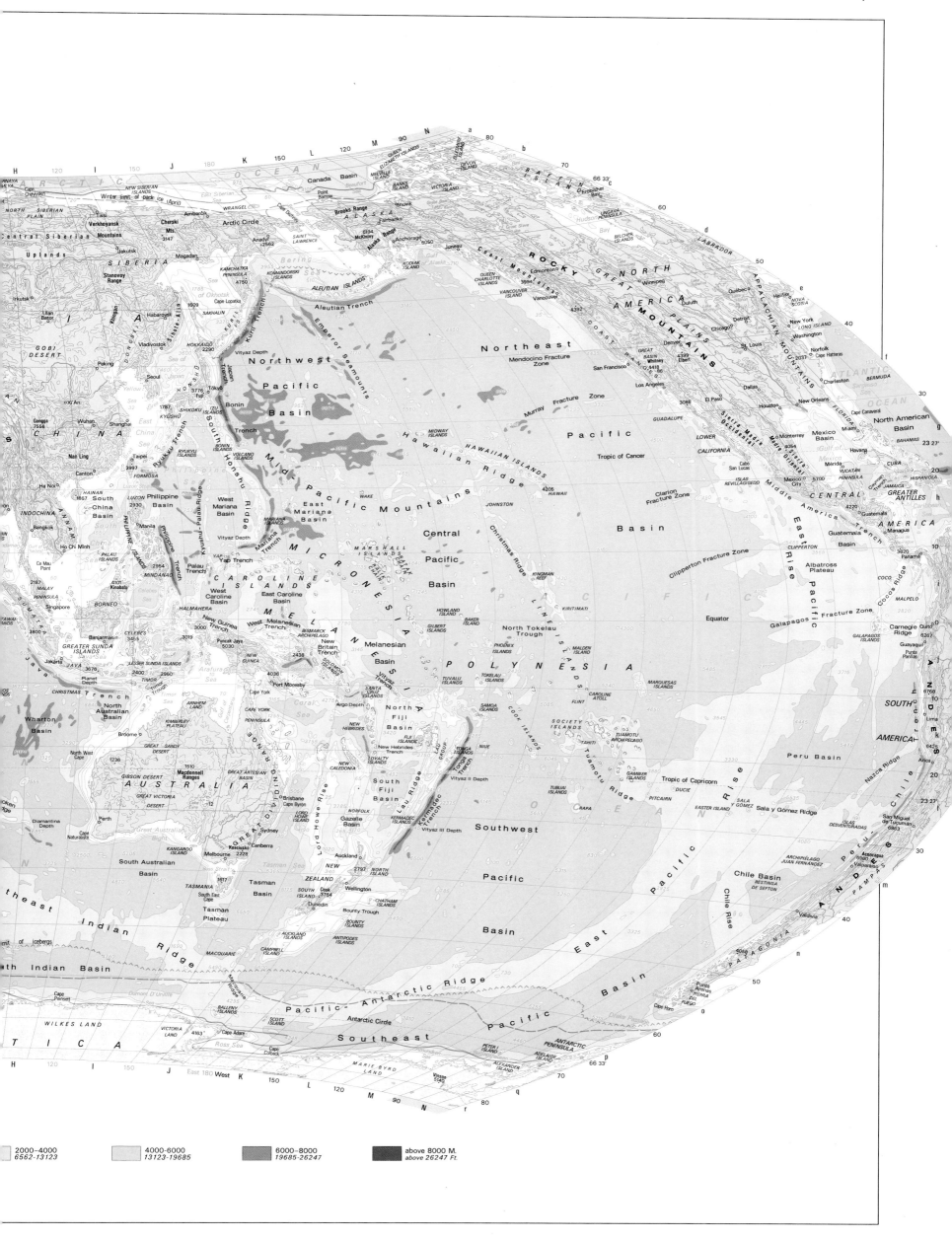

2000–4000 *6562–13123*	4000–6000 *13123–19685*	6000–8000 *19685–26247*	above 8000 M. *above 26247 Ft.*

Map 4 **WORLD TRANSPORTATION AND TIME ZONES**

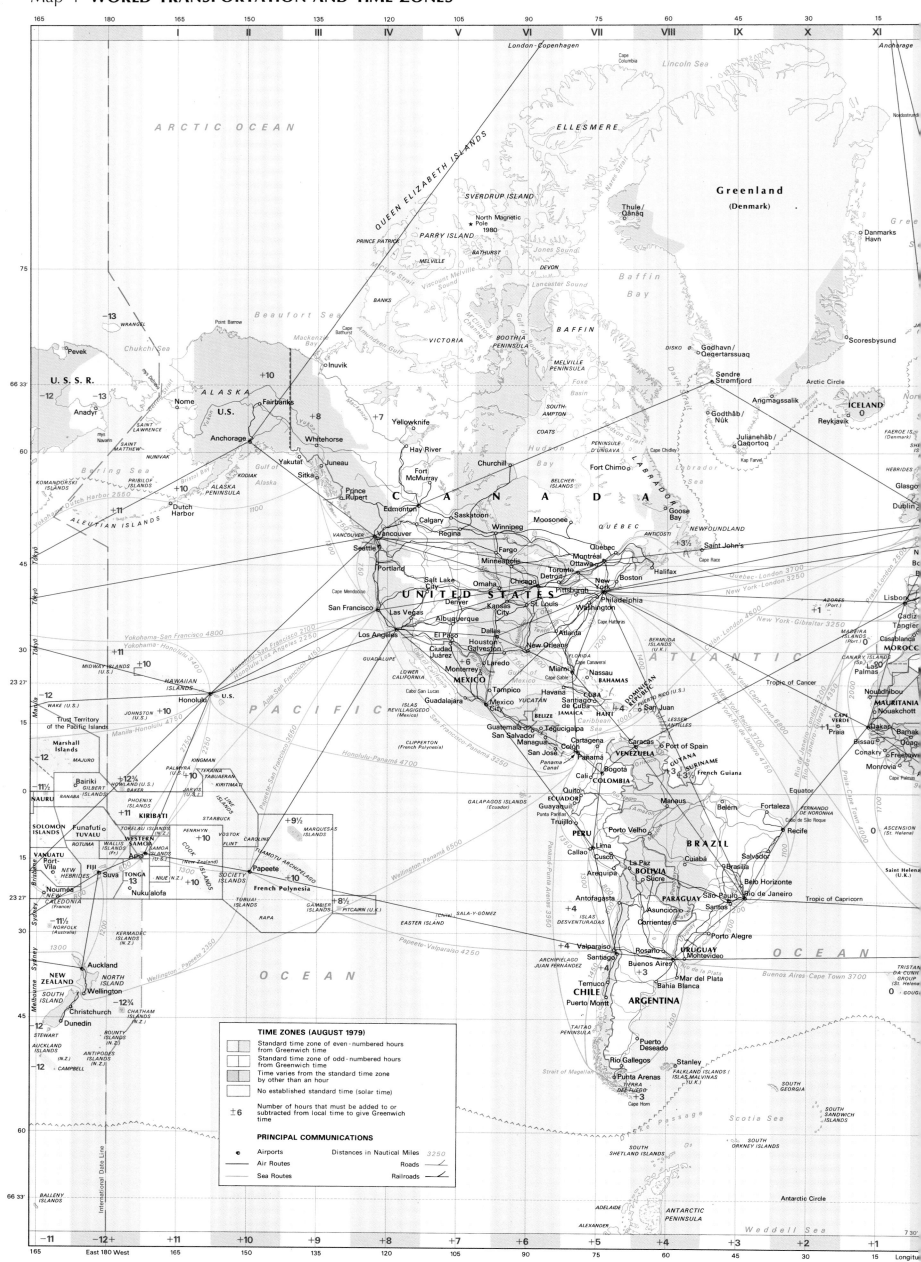

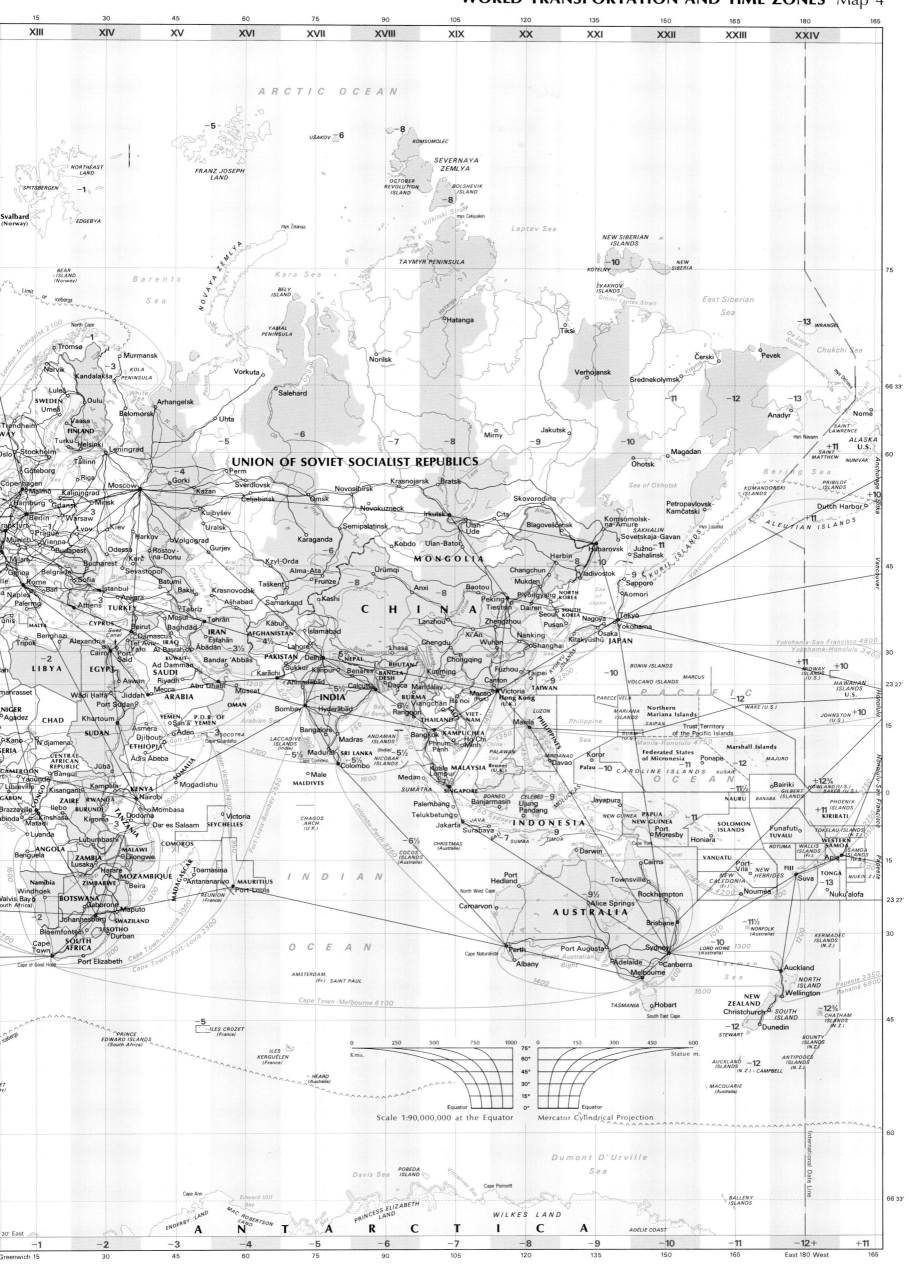

Scale 1:90,000,000 at the Equator   Mercator Cylindrical Projection

Map 5 **EUROPE, PHYSICAL**

Scale 1:15,000,000   Lambert Azimuthal Equal Area Projection

| 0 | 200 | 400 | 600 | 800 | 1000 km |

| 0 | 250 | 500 miles |

Longitude East 10 of Greenwich

Map 6 EUROPE, POLITICAL

Greenland (Den.)

KING FREDERIK VI COAST

KING CHRISTIAN IX LAND

Greenland Sea

Denmark Strait

JAN MAYEN (Norway)

ICELAND

Reykjavík

Arctic Circle

VATNAJÖKULL

Norwegian Sea

NORWAY

SWEDEN

Faeroe Islands (Den.)

SHETLAND ISLANDS

Oslo

Bergen

Stavanger

ORKNEY ISLANDS

HEBRIDES

North Sea

DENMARK

København Copenhagen

Malmö

Glasgow

Edinburgh

Newcastle upon Tyne

IRELAND

Galway

Belfast

Dublin

Manchester

Liverpool

UNITED KINGDOM

Leeds

Sheffield

Kingston-upon-Hull

Nottingham

Cork

Birmingham

Leicester

Norwich

Cardiff

Bristol

London

Amsterdam

's-Gravenhage Den Haag

Rotterdam

NETHERLANDS

Hamburg

Bremen

GERMAN FED. REP. OF GERMANY

Berlin

DEM. REP.

Magdeburg

Leipzig

Dresden

POLAND

Plymouth

English Channel

BELGIUM

Brussel Bruxelles

Köln Cologne

Bonn

Frankfurt

Essen

Düsseldorf

LUXEMBOURG

Wiesbaden

Mannheim

Karl-Marx-Stadt

Praha Prague

CZECHOSLOVAKIA

Le Havre

Rouen

Paris

Reims

Luxembourg

Saarbrücken

Stuttgart

Nürnberg

Brest

Rennes

Le Mans

Orléans

FRANCE

Strasbourg

München Munich

Wien Vienna

AUSTRIA

Nantes

Tours

Dijon

Zürich

SWITZERLAND

LIECHTENSTEIN

Salzburg

Graz

La Rochelle

Limoges

Clermont-Ferrand

Lyon

Genève Geneva

Milano Milan

Ljubljana

Zagreb

YUGOSLAVIA

Bordeaux

Toulouse

PYRENEES

Marseille

Nice

MONACO

Torino Turin

Genova Genoa

Verona

Venezia Venice

Trieste

La Coruña

Gijón

Oviedo

Santander

San Sebastián

Bilbao

Pamplona

ANDORRA

la Vella

Montpellier

Avignon

Toulon

CORSICA (Fr.)

Bologna

Firenze Florence

SAN MARINO

Ancona

Vigo

Braga

Porto

León

Valladolid

Burgos

Zaragoza Saragossa

Barcelona

Perpignan

Ligurian Sea

Livorno Leghorn

ITALY

VATICAN CITY

Roma Rome

PORTUGAL

Coimbra

Salamanca

Madrid

SPAIN

Castellón de la Plana

Tarragona

Balearic Islands

MINORCA

Palma

MAJORCA

SARDINIA

Napoli Naples

Salerno

Bari

Lisboa Lisbon

Setúbal

Toledo

Badajoz

Albacete

Valencia

IBIZA

Tyrrhenian Sea

Évora

Córdoba

Murcia

Alicante

Huelva

Sevilla

Granada

Cartagena

Cagliari

Palermo

Messina

Reggio di Calabria

Faro

Cádiz

Málaga

Almería

Gibraltar (U.K.)

SICILY

Mt. Etna

Catania

Siracusa Syracuse

MALTA

Valletta

Tanger Tangier

Ceuta (Spain)

Tétouan

Melilla (Spain)

Oran

Al Jazā'ir Algiers

Constantine

Tūnis Tunis

Tripoli

MADEIRA ISLANDS

Funchal

Madeira (Portugal)

Casablanca

Rabat

Meknès

Fès

Oujda

TUNISIA

Tarābulus Tripoli

Canary Islands (Spain)

Santa Cruz de Tenerife

TENERIFE

GRAN CANARIA

Las Palmas de Gran Canaria

MOROCCO

Marrakech

ATLAS MOUNTAINS

ALGERIA

LIBYA

Western Sahara

GRAND ERG OCCIDENTAL

GRAND ERG ORIENTAL

TRIPOLITANIA

MEDITERRANEAN SEA

ATLANTIC OCEAN

Azores (Portugal)

SÃO MIGUEL

SANTA MARIA

Scale 1:15,000,000   Lambert Azimuthal Equal Area Projection

Longitude East 10 of Greenwich

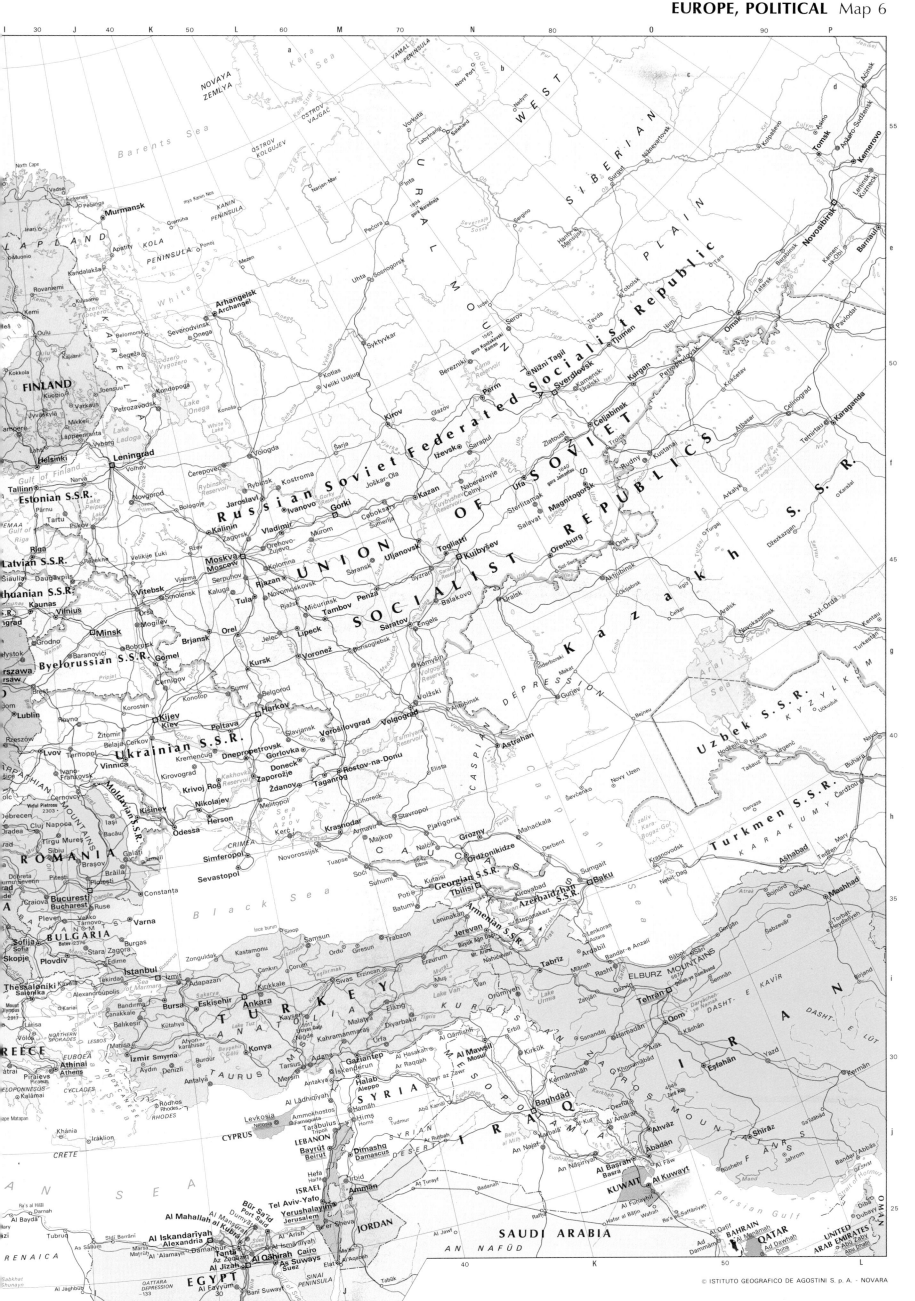

Map 7 **NORTHERN EUROPE**

ÍSLAND ICELAND

NORGE
NORWAY

SVERIGE
SWEDEN

SUOMI

FINLAND

DANMARK
DENMARK

COPENHAGEN KØBENHAVN

BUNDESREPUBLIK
DEUTSCHLAND
FEDERAL REPUBLIC
OF GERMANY

DEUTSCHE
DEMOKRATISCHE
REPUBLIK
GERMAN DEMOCRATIC
REPUBLIC

HAMBURG

BERLIN

POLSKA
POLAND

Eesti NSV
Estonian SSR

TALLINN

RIGA

Latvijas PSR
Latvian SSR

Lietuvos TSR
Lithuanian SSR

VILNIUS

KAUNAS

KALININGRAD

MINSK

Byelorussian

Belorusskaja

Scale 1:6,000,000   Delisle Conic Equidistant Projection

SOJUZ SOVETSKIH
SOCIALISTIČESKIH
RESPUBLIK (SSSR)

UNION OF SOVIET
SOCIALIST
REPUBLICS (USSR)

Rossijskaja Sovetskaja
Federativnaja
Socialističeskaja
Respublika (RSFSR)

Russian Soviet
Federated Socialist
Republic (RSFSR)

8 Arhangelskaja oblast
8A Nanecki nac. okrug
11 Brjanskaja oblast
14 Gorkovskaja oblast
15 Ivanovskaja oblast
17 Jaroslavskaja
oblast
18 Kaliningradskaja oblast
19 Kalininskaja oblast
20 Kalužskaja oblast
23 Kirovskaja oblast
24 Kostromskaja oblast
25 Kujbyševskaja oblast
28 Leningradskaja oblast
29 Lipeckaja oblast
31 Moskovskaja oblast
32 Murmanskaja
oblast
33 Novgorodskaja
oblast
36 Orenburgskaja oblast
37 Orlovskaja oblast
38 Penzenskaja oblast
39 Permskaja oblast
39A Komi-Permjacki nac.
okrug

40 Pskovskaja oblast
42 Rjazanskaja oblast
44 Saratovskaja oblast
45 Smolenskaja oblast
47 Tambovskaja oblast
48 Tjumenskaja oblast
48A Hanty-Mansijski
nac. okrug
50 Tulskaja oblast
51 Uljanovskaja oblast
52 Vladimirskaja oblast
54 Vologodskaja oblast

Belorusskaja SSR

Byelorussian SSR

3 Grodnenskaja oblast
4 Minskaja oblast
5 Mogilevskaja oblast
6 Vitebskaja oblast

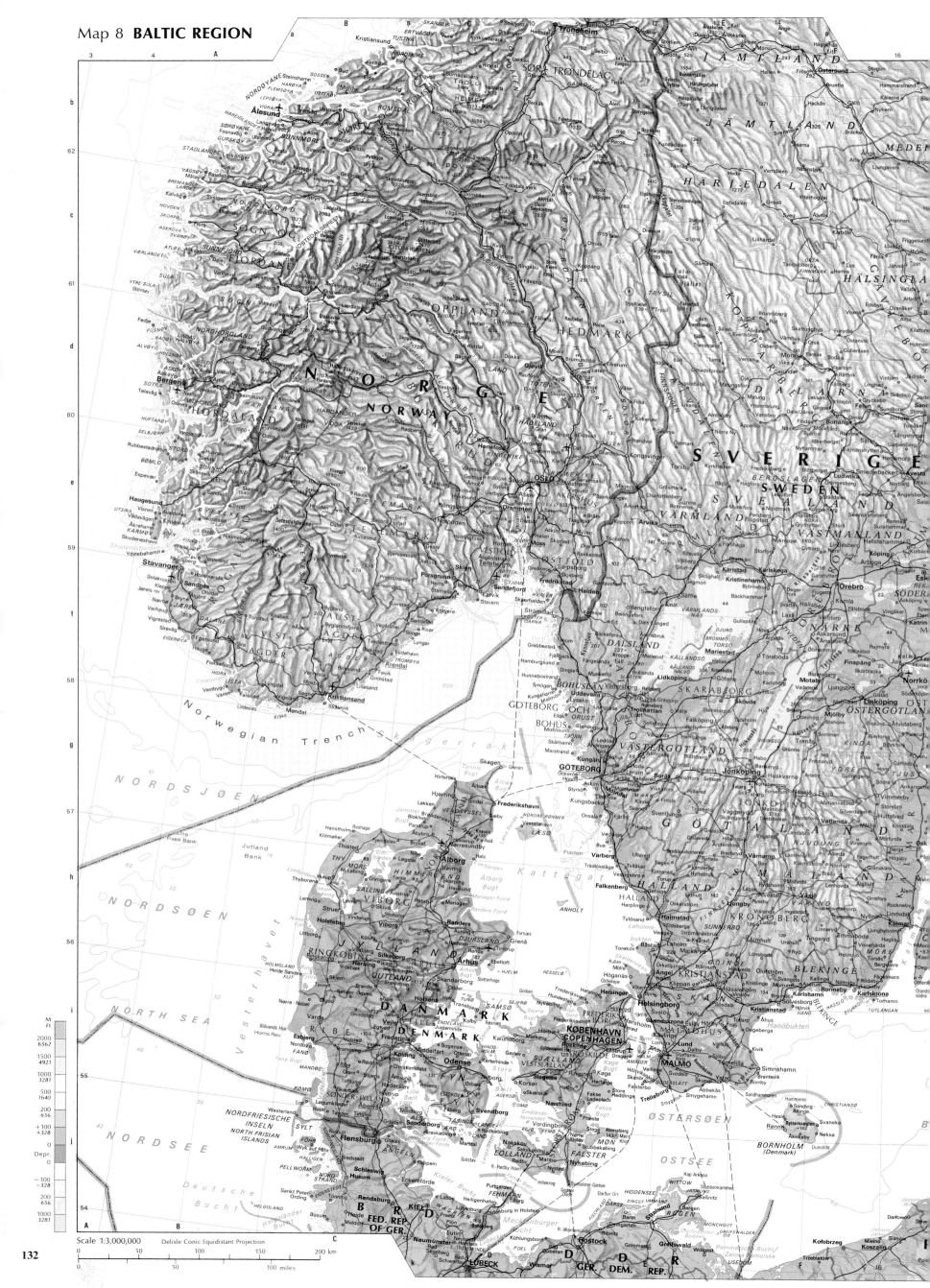

Map 8 BALTIC REGION

Scale 1:3,000,000   Delisle Conic Equidistant Projection

M Ft
2000 6562
1500 4921
1000 3281
500 1640
200 656
+100 +328
0
Depr.
0
- 100 -328
200 656
1000 3281

0   50   100   150   200 km

0   50   100 miles

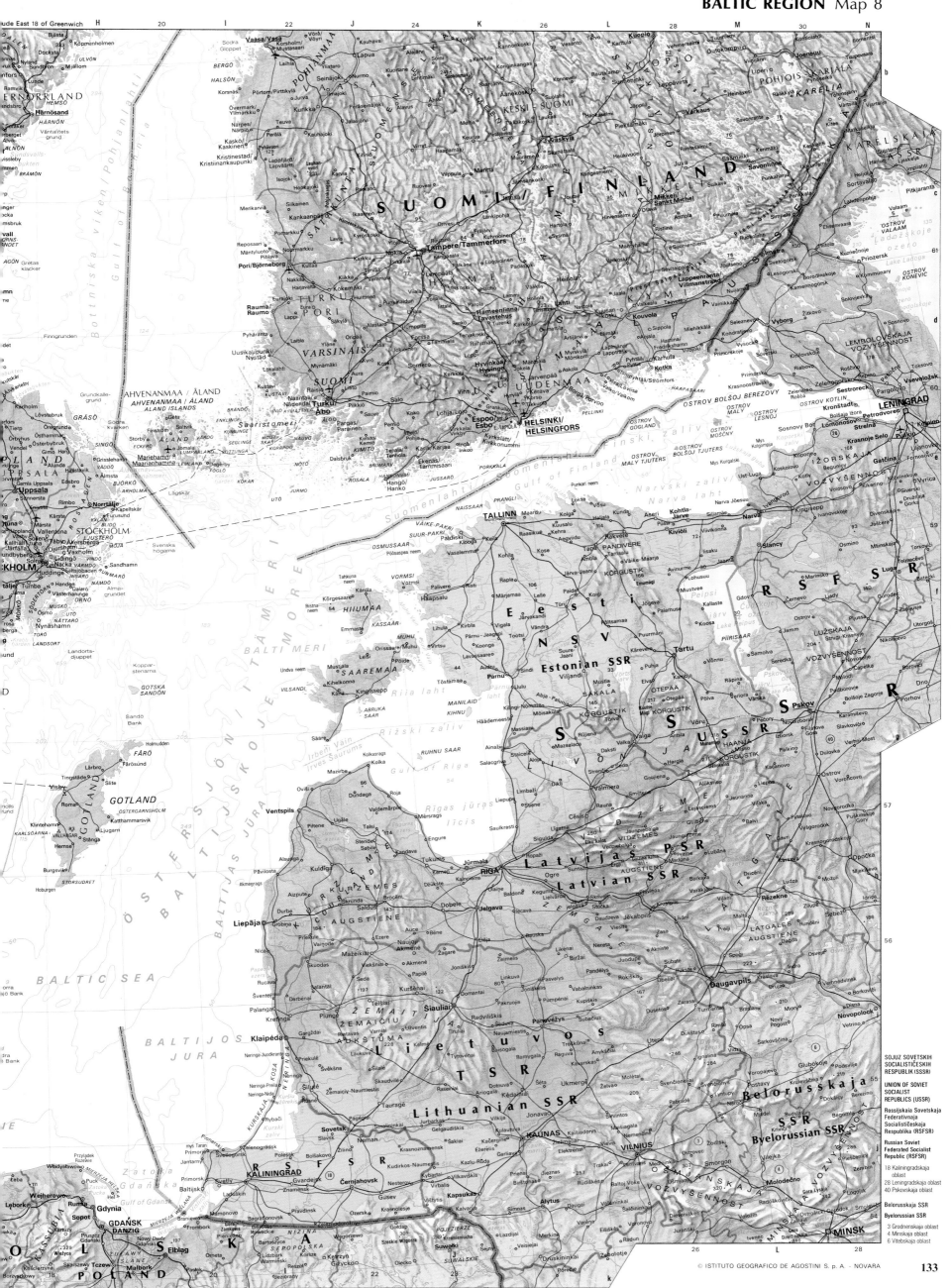

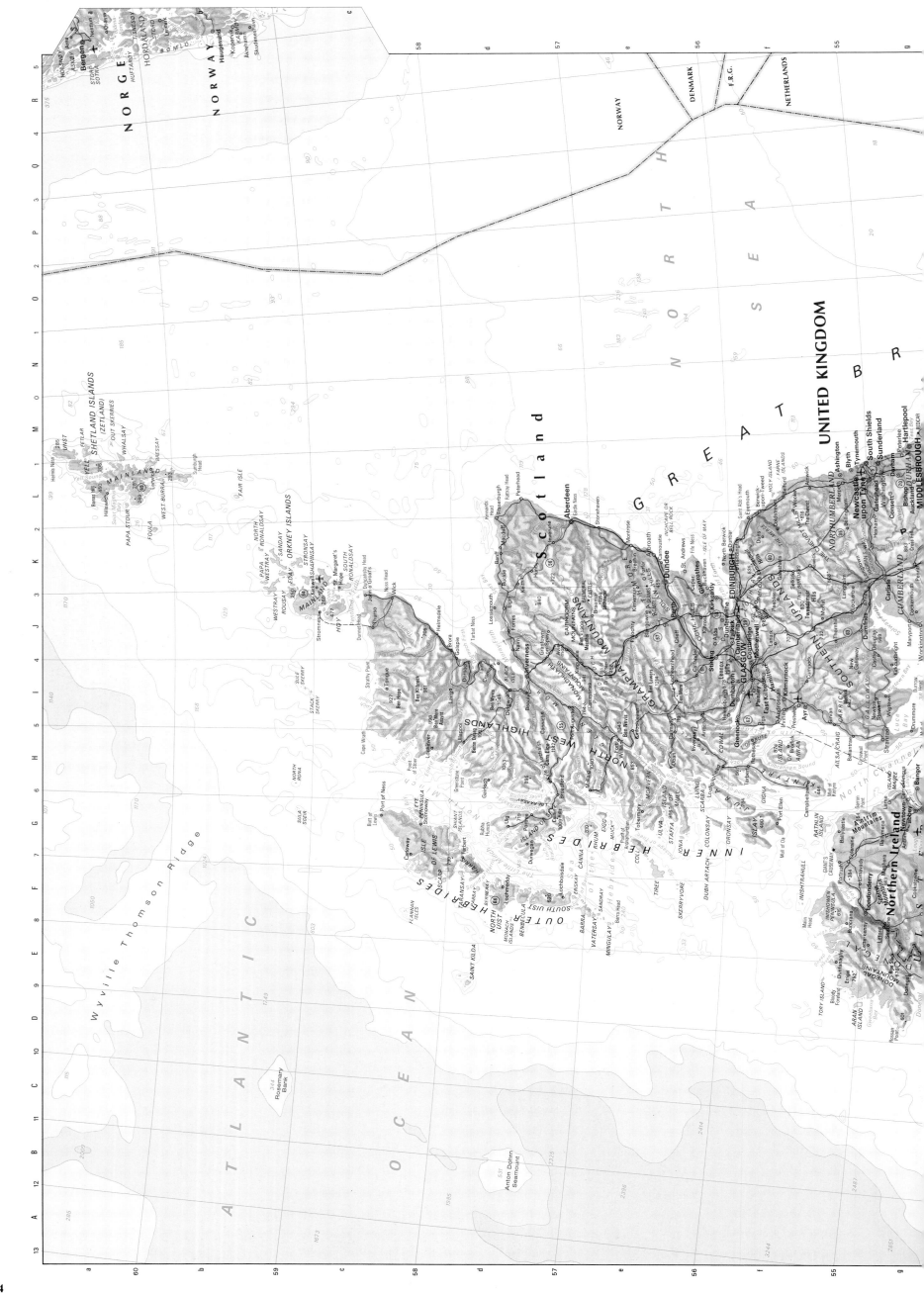

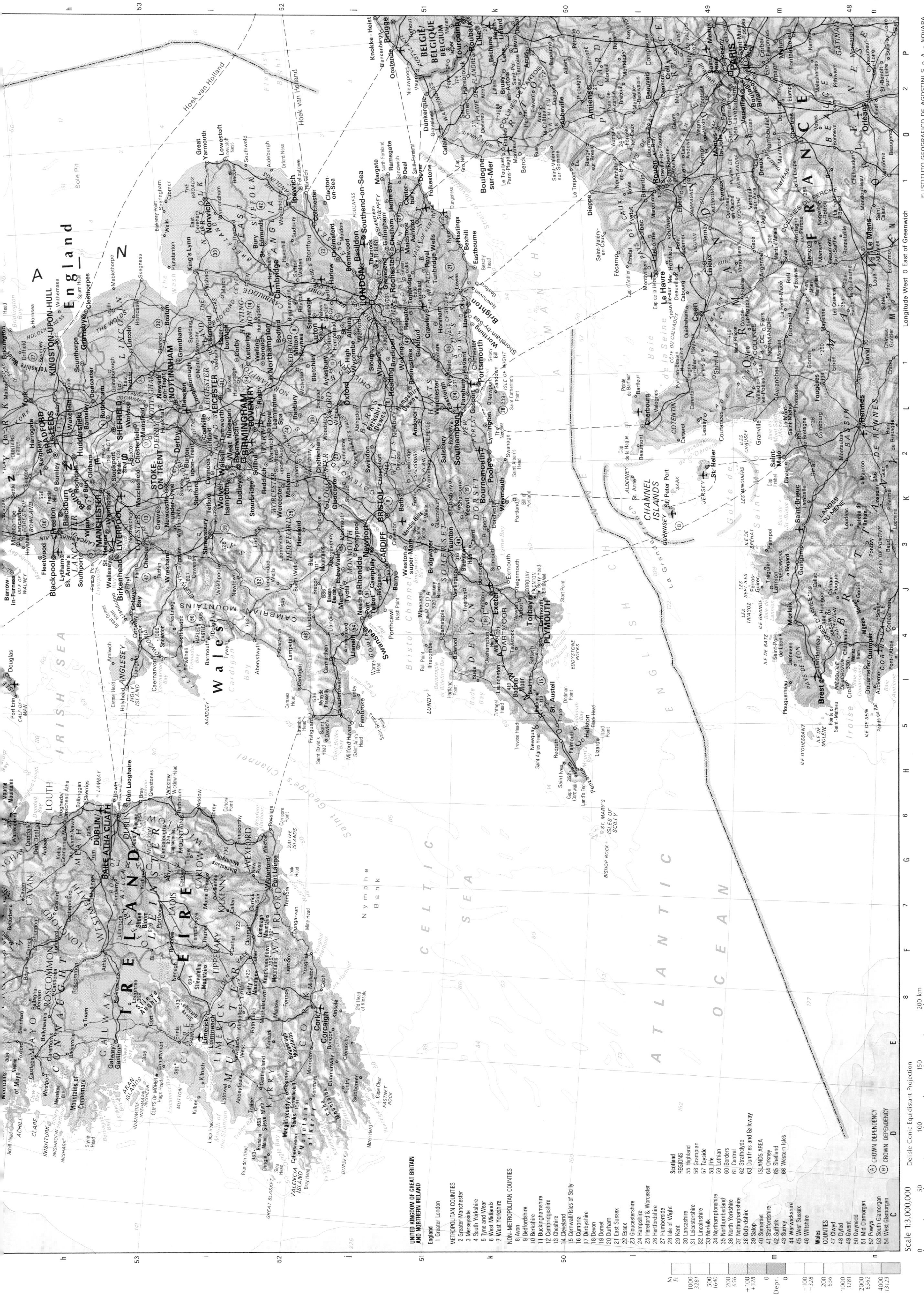

England

Wales

IRELAND / ÉIRE

DUBLIN / BAILE ÁTHA CLIATH

IRISH SEA

ATLANTIC OCEAN

CELTIC SEA

Saint George's Channel

Bristol Channel

ENGLISH CHANNEL / LA MANCHE

CHANNEL ISLANDS

FRANCE

BELGIË / BELGIQUE / BELGIEN

NORMANDIE

PICARDIE

BRETAGNE

PARIS

LONDON

Major places (selection): KINGSTON-UPON-HULL, LEEDS, BRADFORD, SHEFFIELD, MANCHESTER, LIVERPOOL, BIRKENHEAD, STOKE-ON-TRENT, NOTTINGHAM, LEICESTER, COVENTRY, BIRMINGHAM, WOLVERHAMPTON, DUDLEY, WEST BROMWICH, SOLIHULL, CARDIFF, BRISTOL, PLYMOUTH, EXETER, SOUTHAMPTON, PORTSMOUTH, BRIGHTON, SOUTHEND-ON-SEA, IPSWICH, NORWICH, CAMBRIDGE, BELFAST, DÚN LAOGHAIRE, CORCAIGH / CORK, LIMERICK / LUIMNEACH, GALWAY / GAILLIMH, DUNKERQUE, OOSTENDE / OSTENDE, BRUGGE / BRUGES, TOURCOING, ROUBAIX, AMIENS, BOULOGNE-sur-Mer, DIEPPE, ROUEN, LE HAVRE, CAEN, LE MANS, RENNES, BREST, QUIMPER, ST HELIER, St Peter Port

© ISTITUTO GEOGRAFICO DE AGOSTINI S.p.A. - NOVARA

Longitude West 0 East of Greenwich

UNITED KINGDOM OF GREAT BRITAIN AND NORTHERN IRELAND

England

METROPOLITAN COUNTIES
1 Greater London
2 Greater Manchester
3 Merseyside
4 South Yorkshire
5 Tyne and Wear
6 West Midlands
7 West Yorkshire

NON-METROPOLITAN COUNTIES
8 Avon
9 Bedfordshire
10 Berkshire
11 Buckinghamshire
12 Cambridgeshire
13 Cheshire
14 Cleveland
15 Cornwall/Isles of Scilly
16 Cumbria
17 Derbyshire
18 Devon
19 Dorset
20 Durham
21 East Sussex
22 Essex
23 Gloucestershire
24 Hampshire
25 Hereford & Worcester
26 Hertfordshire
27 Humberside
28 Isle of Wight
29 Kent
30 Lancashire
31 Leicestershire
32 Lincolnshire
33 Norfolk
34 Northamptonshire
35 Northumberland
36 North Yorkshire
37 Nottinghamshire
38 Oxfordshire
39 Shropshire
40 Somerset
41 Staffordshire
42 Suffolk
43 Surrey
44 Warwickshire
45 West Sussex
46 Wiltshire

Wales

COUNTIES
47 Clwyd
48 Dyfed
49 Gwent
50 Gwynedd
51 Mid Glamorgan
52 Powys
53 South Glamorgan
54 West Glamorgan

Scotland

REGIONS
55 Highland
56 Grampian
57 Tayside
58 Fife
59 Lothian
60 Central
61 Strathclyde
62 Borders
63 Dumfries and Galloway

ISLANDS AREA
64 Orkney
65 Shetland
66 Western Isles

(A) CROWN DEPENDENCY
(B) CROWN DEPENDENCY

Scale 1:3,000,000

Delisle Conic Equidistant Projection

0 50 100 150 200 km
0 50 100 miles

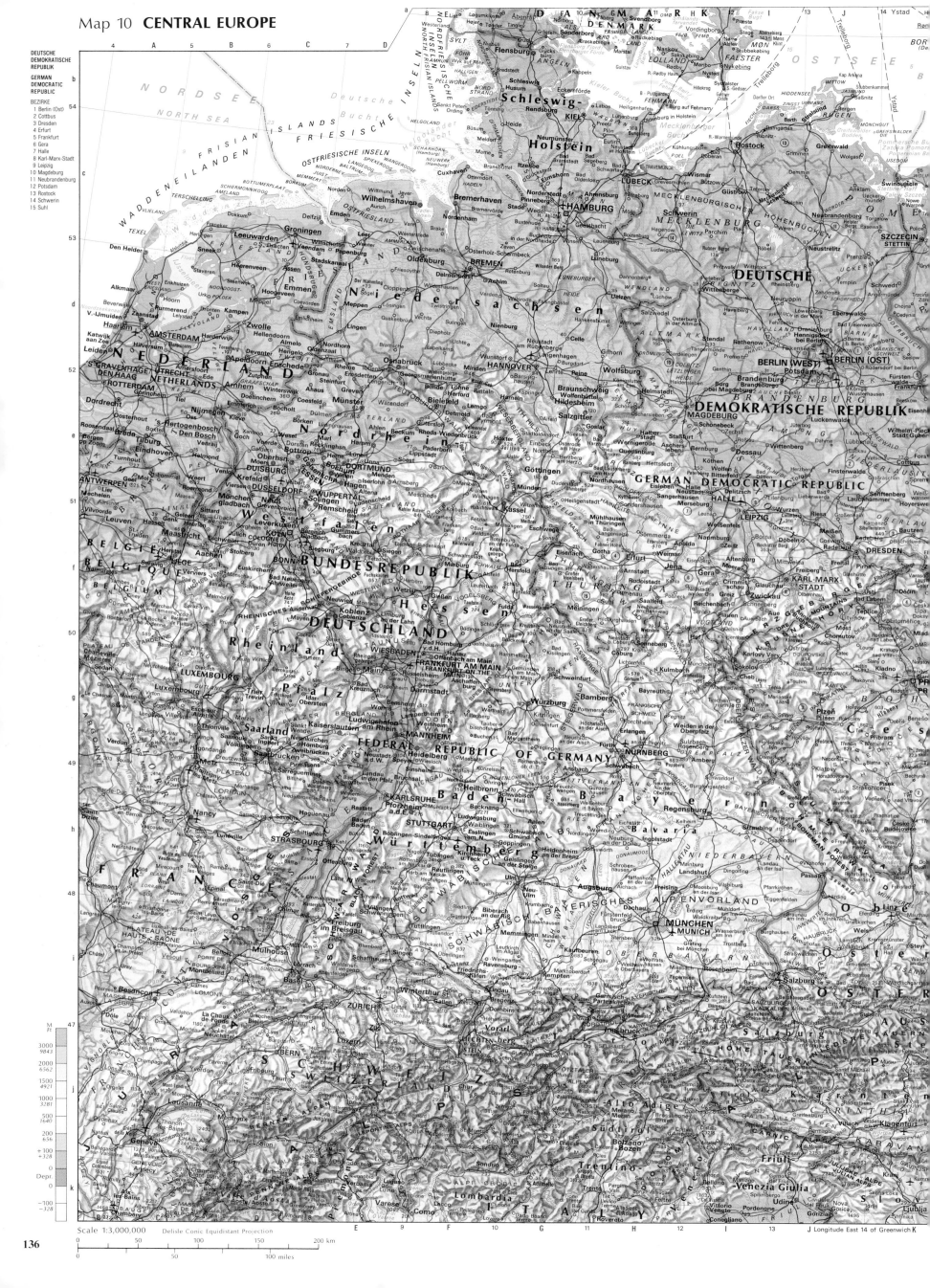

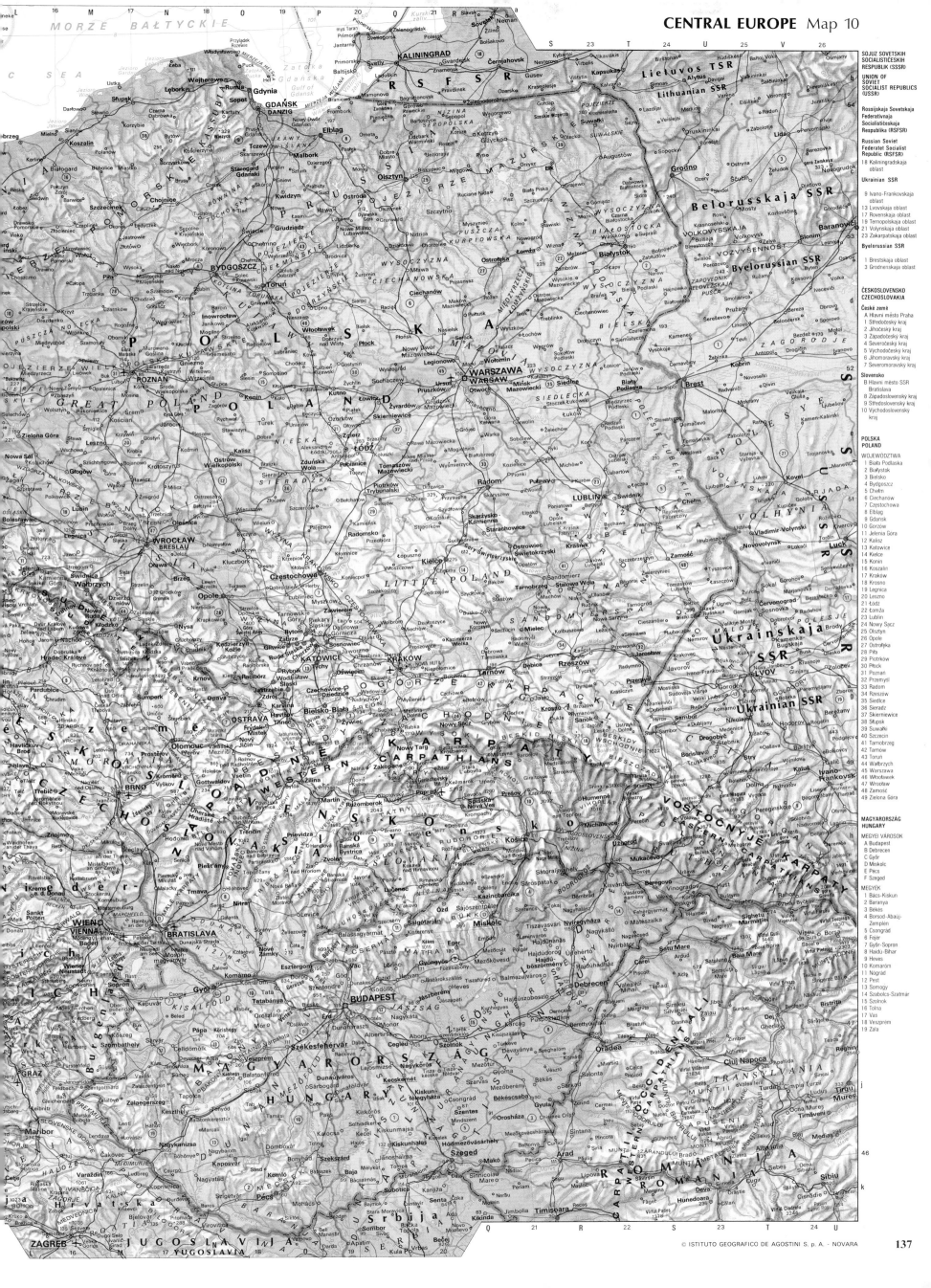

Map 11 **FRANCE AND BENELUX**

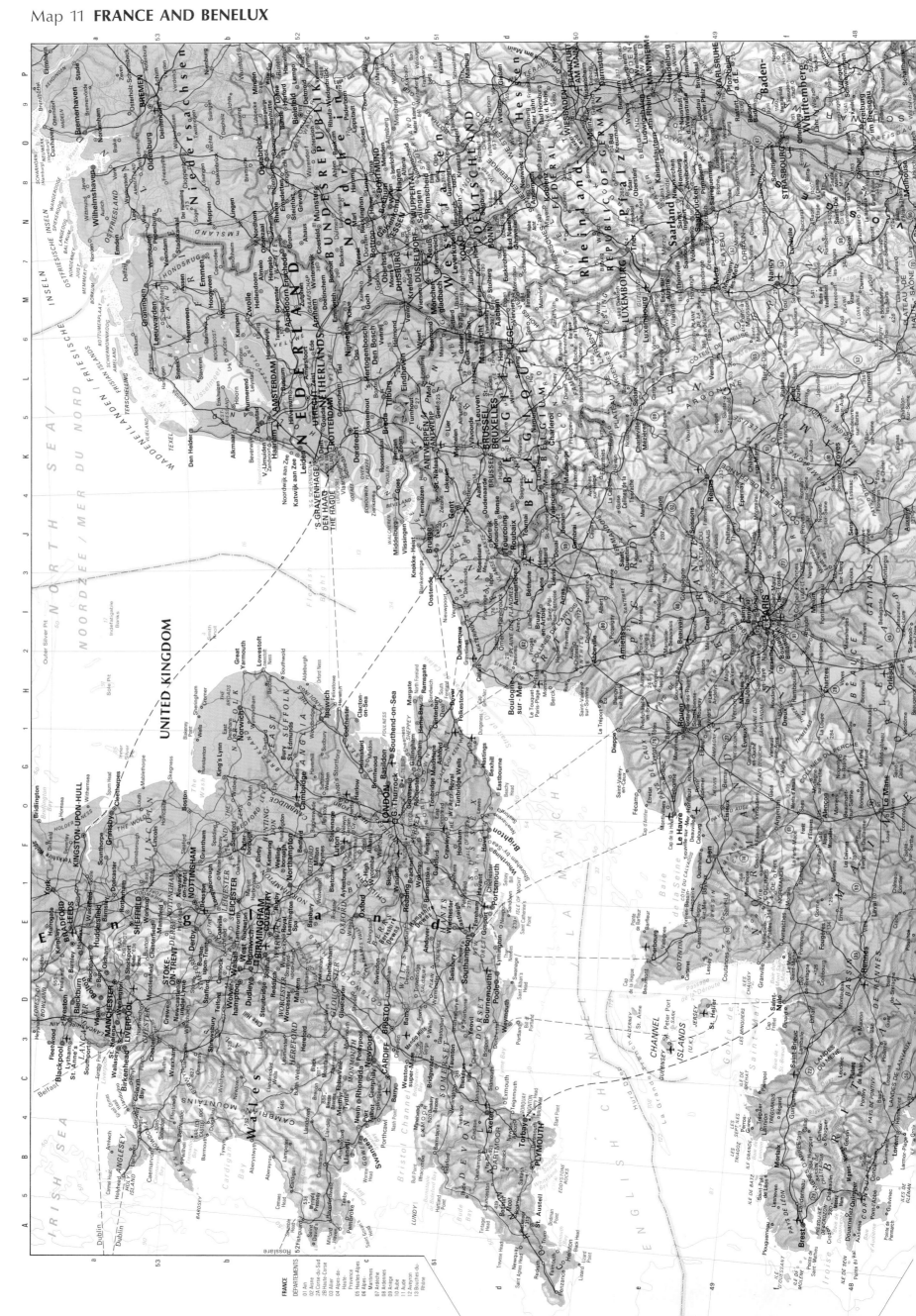

FRANCE
DÉPARTEMENTS
01 Ain
02 Aisne
2A Corse-du-Sud
2B Haute-Corse
04 Alpes-de-
Haute-
Provence
05 Hautes-Alpes
06 Alpes-
Maritimes
07 Ardèche
08 Ardennes
09 Ariège
10 Aube
11 Aude
12 Aveyron
13 Bouches-du-
Rhône

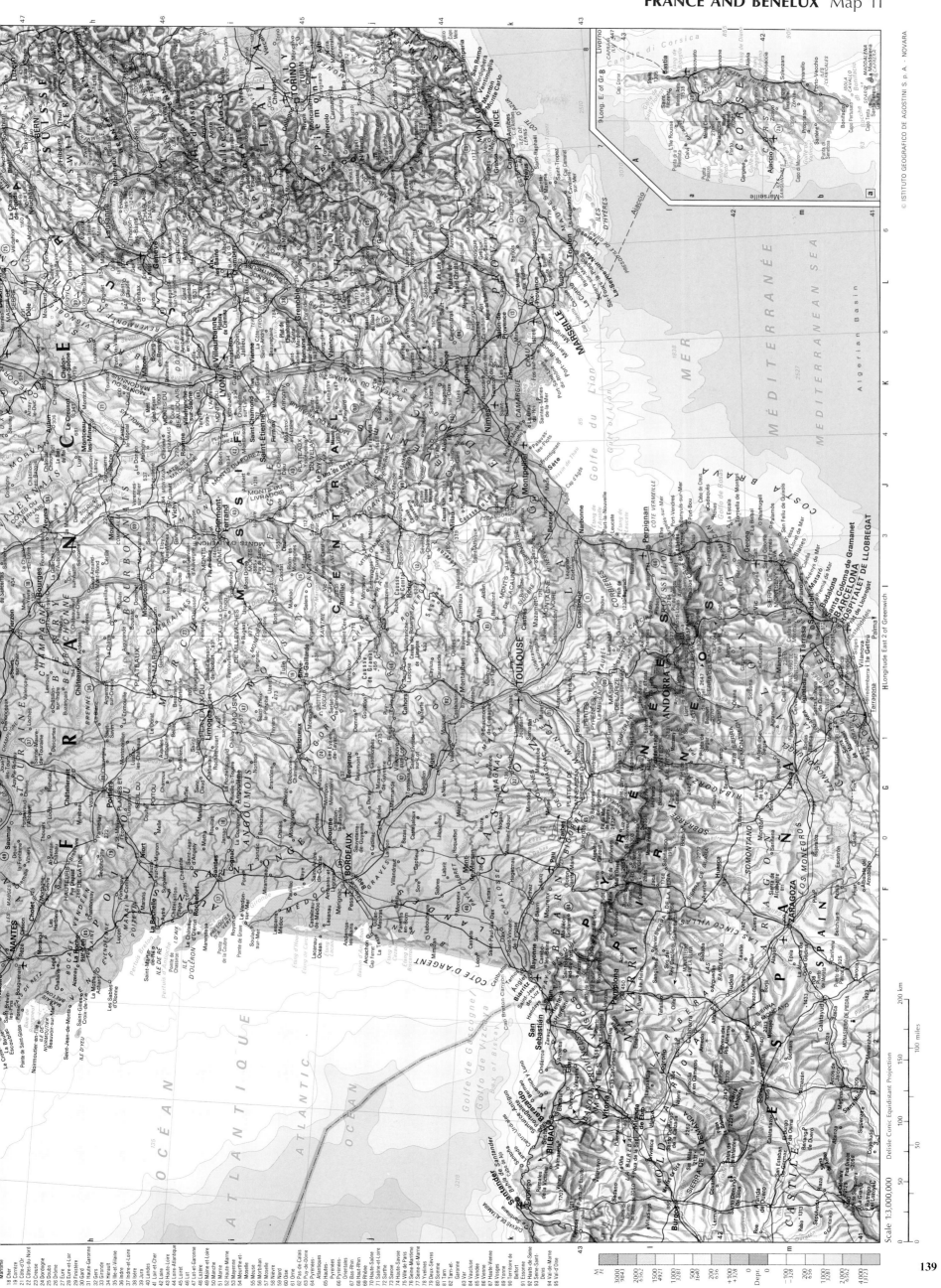

Scale 1:3,000,000

Delisle Conic Equidistant Projection

Map 12 BELGIUM, NETHERLANDS AND LUXEMBOURG

UNITED KINGDOM

NORTH SEA / NOORDZEE / MER DU NORD

ENGLISH CHANNEL / LA MANCHE

FRANCE

FRANCE
DÉPARTEMENTOS
75 Ville de Paris
92 Hauts-de-Seine
93 Seine-Saint-Denis
94 Val-de-Marne

M
Ft
500 1640
200 656
100 328
0
Depr.

Scale 1:1,500,000
Delisle Conic Equidistant Projection
0   25   50   75   100 km
0   25   50 miles

Map 12

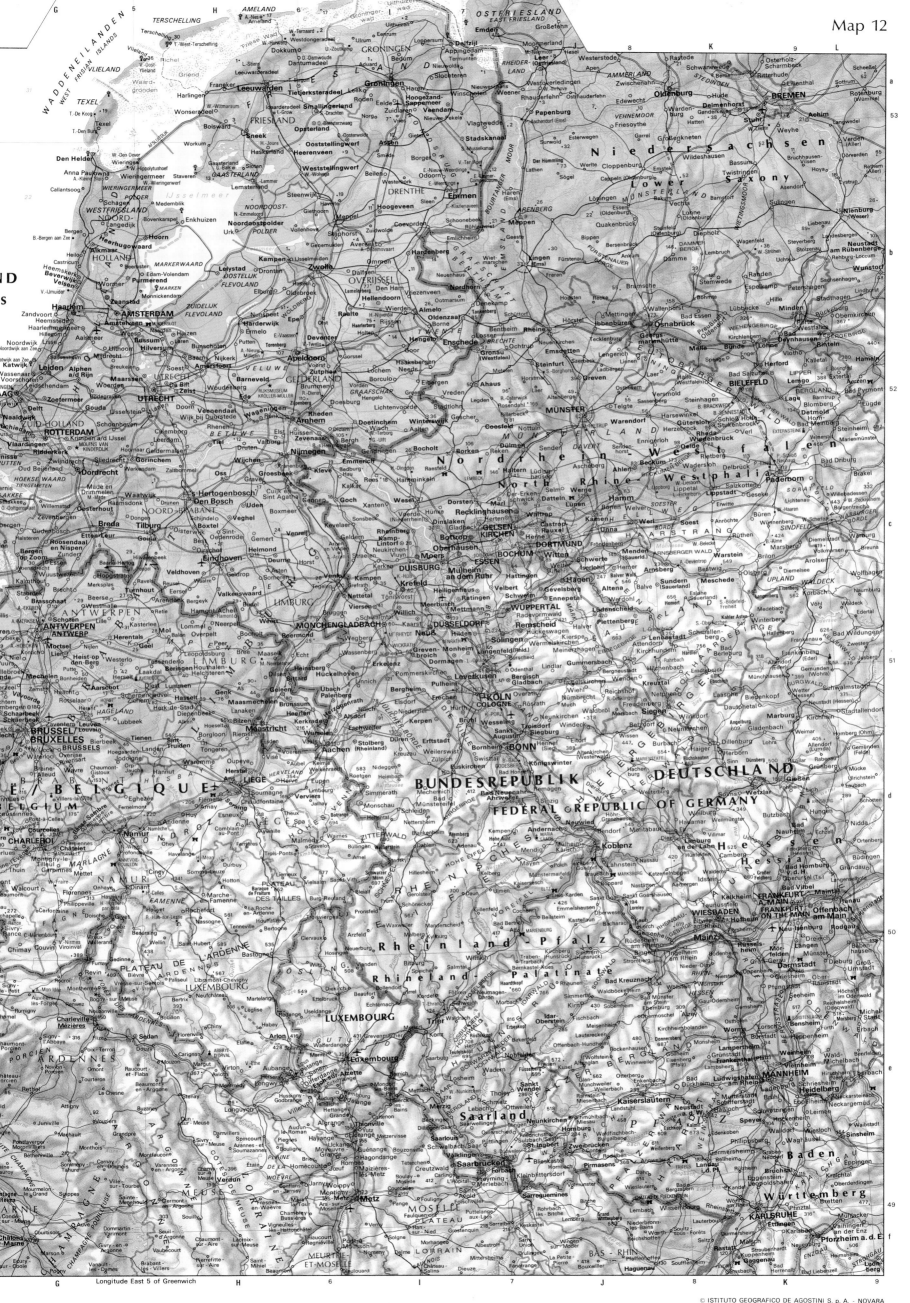

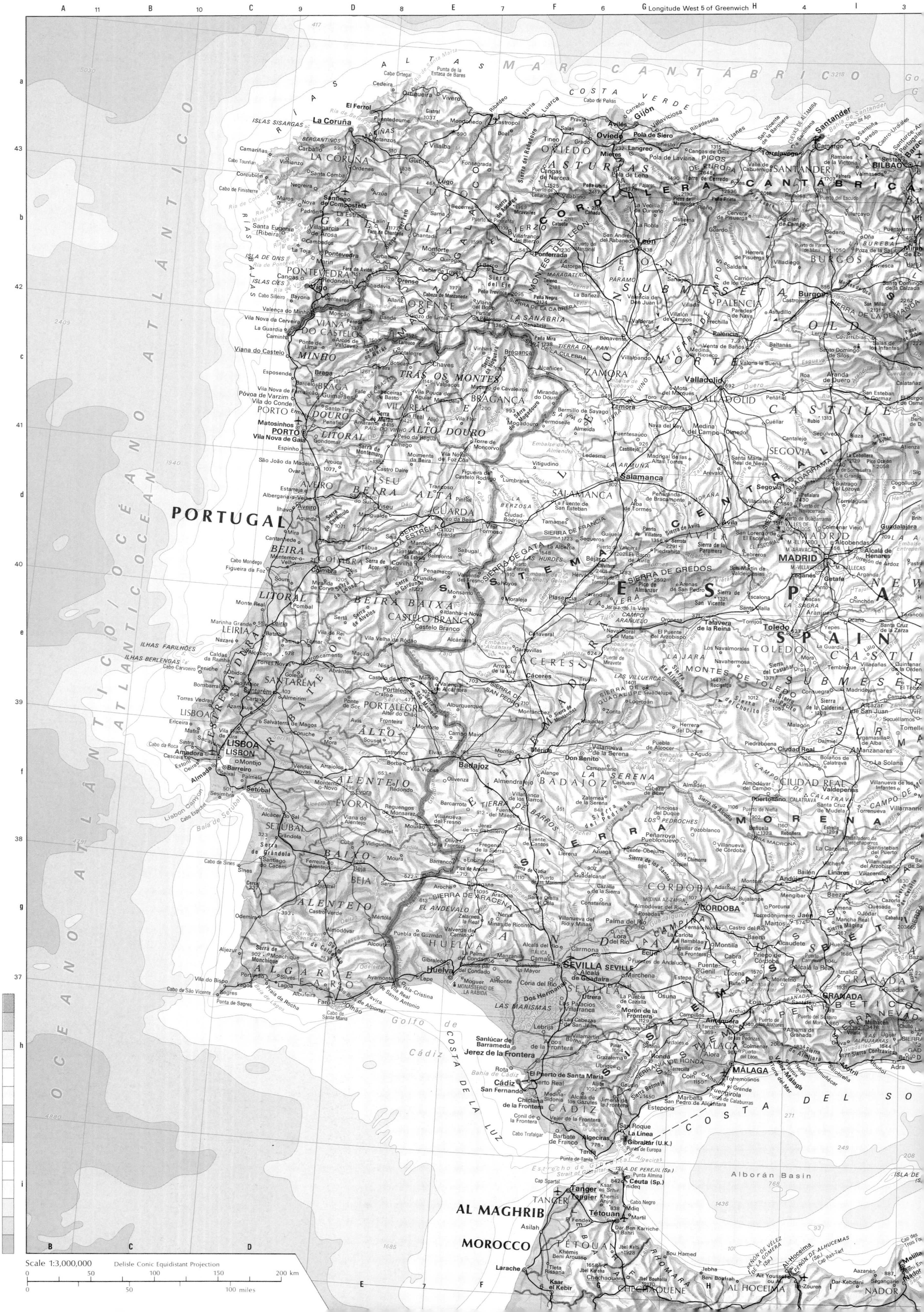

Map 13 **SPAIN AND PORTUGAL**

Longitude West 5 of Greenwich

MAR CANTÁBRICO

COSTA VERDE

OCÉANO ATLÂNTICO

OCÉANO ATLÂNTICO

PORTUGAL

SPAIN

MINHO
TRÁS-OS-MONTES
DOURO LITORAL
ALTO DOURO
BEIRA ALTA
BEIRA LITORAL
BEIRA BAIXA
ESTREMADURA
RIBATEJO
ALTO ALENTEJO
BAIXO ALENTEJO
ALENTEJO
ALGARVE

LISBOA · LISBON
PORTO
COIMBRA
LEIRIA
SANTARÉM
SETÚBAL
ÉVORA
BEJA
FARO
AVEIRO
VISEU
GUARDA
CASTELO BRANCO
PORTALEGRE
BRAGANÇA
VILA REAL
BRAGA

La Coruña
El Ferrol
Santiago de Compostela
Lugo
Oviedo
Gijón
Avilés
Santander
BILBAO
ASTURIAS
CORDILLERA CANTÁBRICA
PICOS DE EUROPA
LEÓN
Ponferrada
ZAMORA
VALLADOLID
PALENCIA
BURGOS
OLD CASTILE
SEGOVIA
SALAMANCA
ÁVILA
SIERRA DE GREDOS
SIERRA DE GUADARRAMA
CORDILLERA CENTRAL
MADRID
Alcalá de Henares
NEW CASTILE
GUADALAJARA
TOLEDO
Talavera de la Reina
CÁCERES
EXTREMADURA
BADAJOZ
Mérida
SIERRA MORENA
CIUDAD REAL
SUBMESETA SUR
MONTES DE TOLEDO
CÓRDOBA
SEVILLA · SEVILLE
HUELVA
CÁDIZ
Jerez de la Frontera
GRANADA
MÁLAGA
COSTA DEL SOL
SIERRA NEVADA
Gibraltar (U.K.)
Algeciras
La Línea
ANDALUCÍA

Golfo de Cádiz
Bahía de Cádiz
COSTA DE LA LUZ
Estrecho de Gibraltar · Strait of Gibraltar
Ceuta (Sp.)
Tánger · TANGER
Tétouan
AL MAGHRIB
MOROCCO
Alborán Basin

M
Ft
3000 9843
2000 6562
1500 4921
1000 3281
500 1640
200 656
+100 +328
0
−100 −328
200 656
1000 3281
2000 6562
4000 13123

Scale 1:3,000,000   Delisle Conic Equidistant Projection

0   50   100   150   200 km
0   50   100 miles

KILOMETERS

FRANCE

LANGUEDOC

PROVENCE

CÔTE D'ARGENT

LANDES

BÉARN

PYRÉNÉES

MONTS MALDITOS

ANDORRA

ROUSSILLON

TOULOUSE

Montpellier

Nîmes

Avignon

MARSEILLE

Toulon

ÎLES D'HYÈRES

Golfe du Lion

Gulf of Lion

Perpignan

COSTA BRAVA

GERONA

Gerona

Figueras

Golfo de Rosas

Genova

San Sebastián

Pamplona

NAVARRA
NAVARRA

HUESCA

Huesca

LÉRIDA

BARCELONA

Tarrasa

Sabadell

BARCELONA

HOSPITALET DE LLOBREGAT

Badalona

Santa Coloma de Gramanet

ZARAGOZA SARAGOSSA

ZARAGOZA

LOS MONEGROS

ARAGON

CATALUÑA

COSTA DORADA

TARRAGONA

Tarragona

Reus

Tortosa

Delta del Ebro

TERUEL

Teruel

CASTELLÓN

Castellón de la Plana

ISLAS COLUMBRETES

COSTA DEL AZAHAR

VALENCIA

VALENCIA

Sagunto

Golfo de Valencia

COSTA BLANCA

ALICANTE

Alicante

Elche

MURCIA

MURCIA

Cartagena

COSTA BLANCA

Cabo de Palos

Cabo de Gata

ISLAS BALEARES
BALEARIC ISLANDS

MENORCA MINORCA

Ciudadela

Mahón

MALLORCA MAJORCA

PALMA

Inca

BALEARES

ISLA CABRERA

IBIZA IVIZA

FORMENTERA

ISLA CONEJERA

San Antonio Abad

Santa Eulalia del Río

Algerian Basin

MEDITERRANEAN SEA

MER MÉDITERRANÉE

ALGERIA
AL JAZĀ'IR

ALGER
AL JAZĀ'IR
ALGIERS

ORAN

MOSTAGANEM

TIZI OUZOU

Béjaïa

GRANDE KABYLIE

PETITE KABYLIE

Sétif

ATLAS TELLIEN

TLEMCEN

MASCARA

SIDI BEL ABBES

TIARET

PLAINE DU HODNA

Map 14 **ITALY, AUSTRIA AND SWITZERLAND**

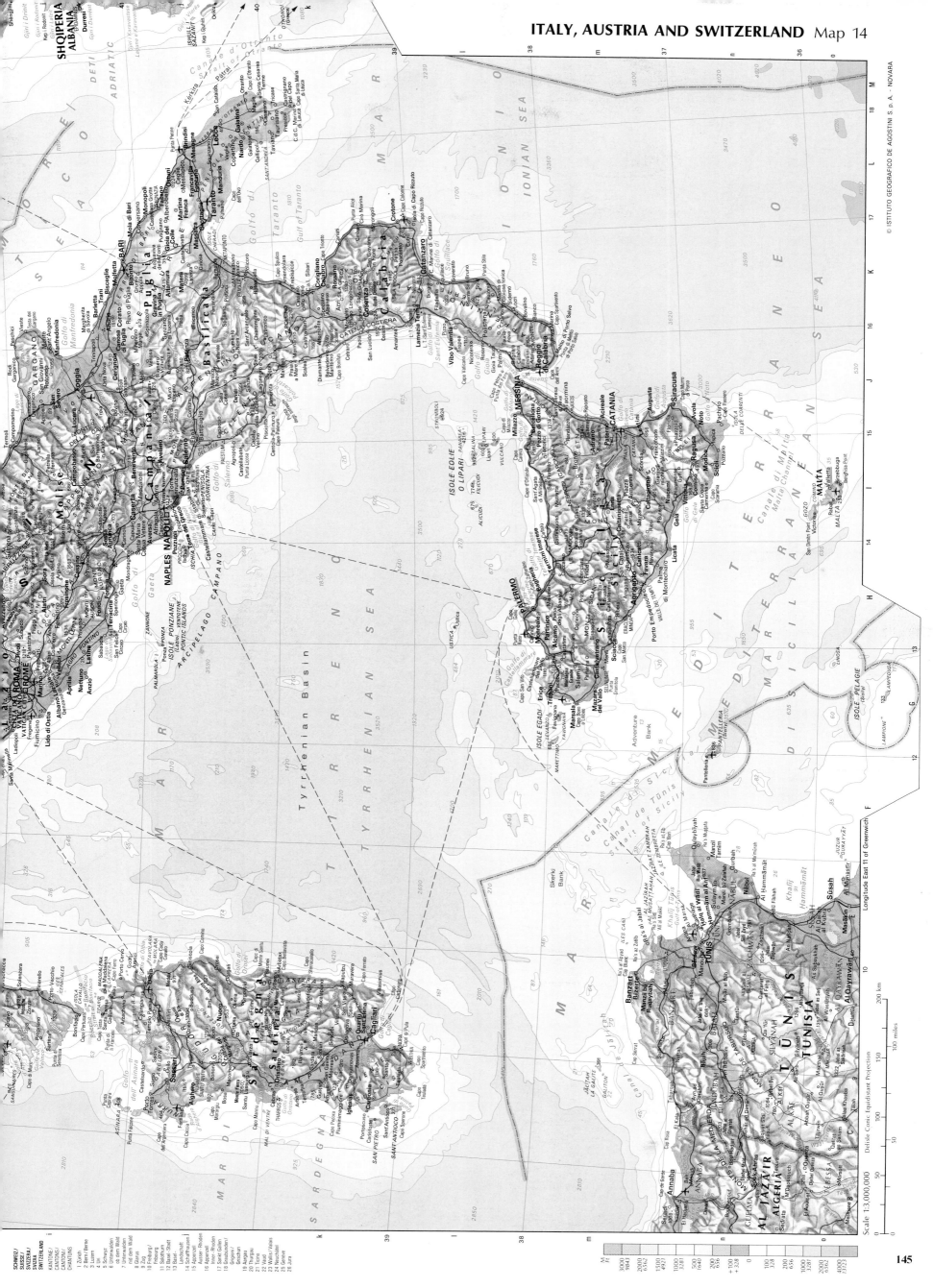

Longitude East 11 of Greenwich

Daldise Conic Equidistant Projection

Scale 1:3,000,000

Map 15 **SOUTHEASTERN EUROPE**

Map 15

© ISTITUTO GEOGRAFICO DE AGOSTINI S. p. A. - NOVARA

Scale 1:3,000,000

Delisle Conic Equidistant Projection

Map 16 **SOUTHWESTERN SOVIET UNION**

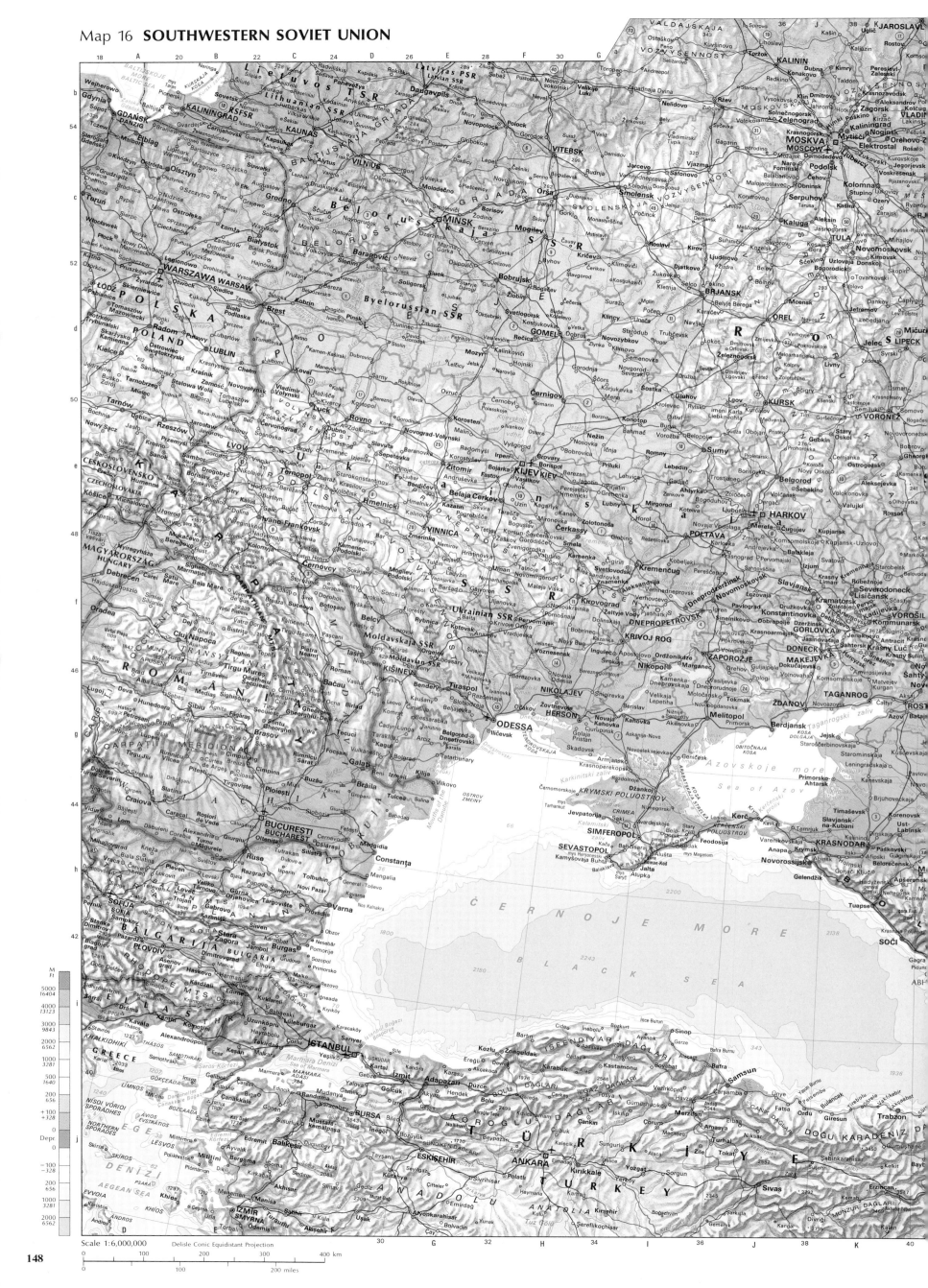

Scale 1:6,000,000   Delisle Conic Equidistant Projection

0   100   200   300   400 km

0   100   200 miles

SOJUZ SOVETSKIH
SOCIALISTIČESKIH
RESPUBLIK (SSSR)
UNION OF
SOVIET
SOCIALIST
REPUBLICS (USSR)

Rossijskaja Sovetskaja
Federativnaja
Socialističeskaja
Respublika (RSFSR)
Russian Soviet
Federated Socialist
Republic (RSFSR)

3 Krasnodarski kraj
3A Adygejskaja
    avtonomnaja oblast
6 Stavropolski kraj
6A Karačajevo-
    Čerkesskaja
    avtonomnaja oblast
9 Astrahanskaja oblast
10 Belgorodskaja oblast
11 Brjanskaja oblast
12 Čeljabinskaja oblast
14 Gorkovskaja oblast
15 Ivanovskaja oblast
17 Jaroslavskaja oblast
18 Kaliningradskaja
    oblast
19 Kalininskaja oblast
21 Kalužskaja oblast
23 Kirovskaja oblast
24 Kostromskaja oblast
26 Kurganskaja oblast
27 Kurskaja oblast
29 Lipeckaja oblast
31 Moskovskaja oblast
33 Novgorodskaja oblast
36 Orenburgskaja oblast
37 Orlovskaja oblast
39 Penzenskaja oblast
40 Pskovskaja oblast
42 Rostovskaja oblast
43 Rjazanskaja oblast
45 Saratovskaja oblast
47 Smolenskaja oblast
47 Tambovskaja oblast
50 Tulskaja oblast
51 Uljanovskaja oblast
52 Vladimirskaja oblast
53 Volgogradskaja oblast
55 Voronežskaja oblast

Ukrainskaja SSR
Ukrainian SSR

1 Čerkasskaja oblast
2 Černigovskaja oblast
3 Černovickaja oblast
4 Dnepropetrovskaja
  oblast
5 Doneckaja oblast
6 Harkovskaja oblast
7 Hersonskaja oblast
8 Hmelnickaja oblast
9 Ivano-Frankovskaja
  oblast
10 Kievskaja oblast
11 Kirovogradskaja oblast
12 Krymskaja oblast
13 Lvovskaja oblast
14 Nikolajevskaja oblast
15 Odesskaja oblast
16 Poltavskaja oblast
17 Rovenskaja oblast
18 Sumskaja oblast
19 Ternopolskaja oblast
20 Vinnickaja oblast
21 Volynskaja oblast
22 Vorošilovgradskaja
   oblast
23 Zakarpatskaja oblast
24 Zaporožskaja oblast
25 Žitomirskaja oblast

Belorusskaja SSR
Byelorussian SSR

1 Brestskaja oblast
2 Gomelskaja oblast
3 Grodnenskaja oblast
4 Minskaja oblast
5 Mogilevskaja oblast
6 Vitebskaja oblast

Kazahskaja SSR
Kazakh SSR

1 Aktjubinskaja oblast
7 Gurjevskaja oblast
9 Kzyl-Ordinskaja oblast
11 Kustanajskaja oblast
12 Mangyšlakskaja
   oblast
18 Uralskaja oblast

Gruzinskaja SSR
Georgian SSR

1 Jugo-Osetinskaja
  avtonomnaja oblast

Azerbajdžanskaja SSR
Azerbaidzhan SSR

1 Nagorno-Karabahskaja
  avtonomnaja oblast

Turkmenskaja SSR
Turkmen SSR

1 Ašhabadskaja oblast
3 Krasnovodskaja oblast
5 Tašauzskaja oblast

© ISTITUTO GEOGRAFICO
DE AGOSTINI S. p. A. - NOVARA

Map 17 THE URALS

Scale 1:6,000,000   Delisle Conic Equidistant Projection

Longitude East 60 of Greenwich

0   100   200   300   400 km

0   100   200 miles

150

© ISTITUTO GEOGRAFICO DE AGOSTINI S. p. A. - NOVARA

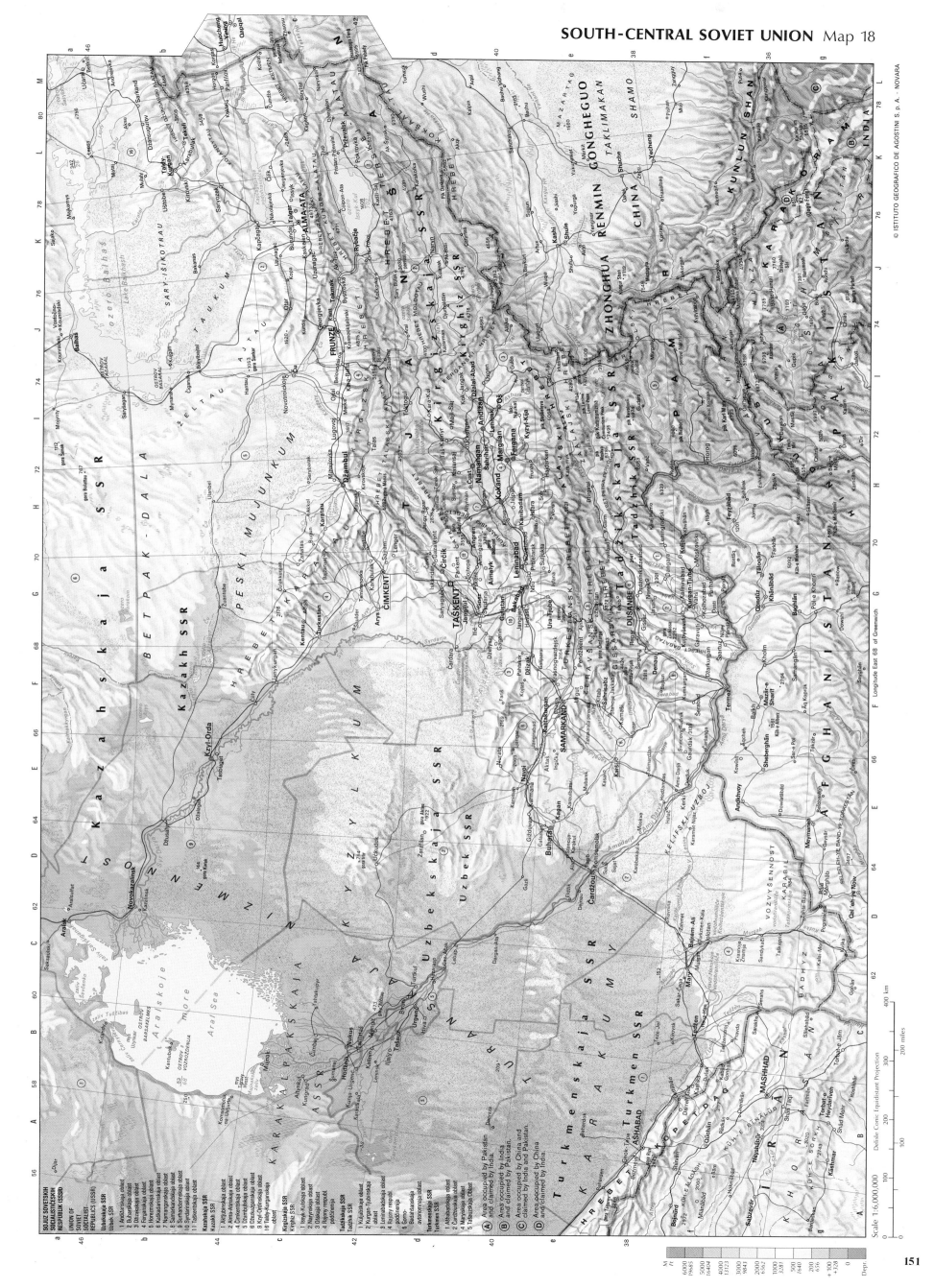

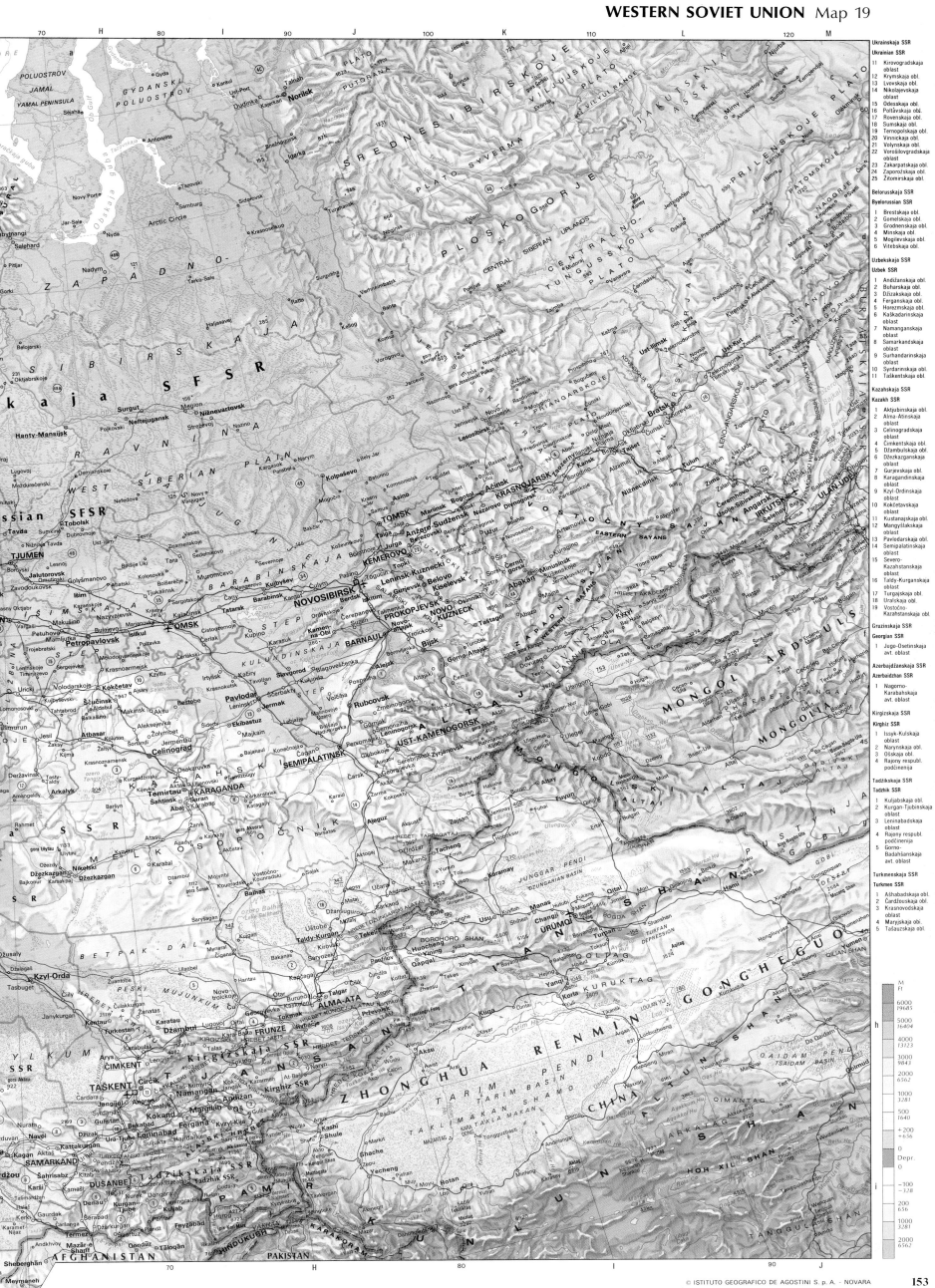

© ISTITUTO GEOGRAFICO DE AGOSTINI S.p.A. - NOVARA

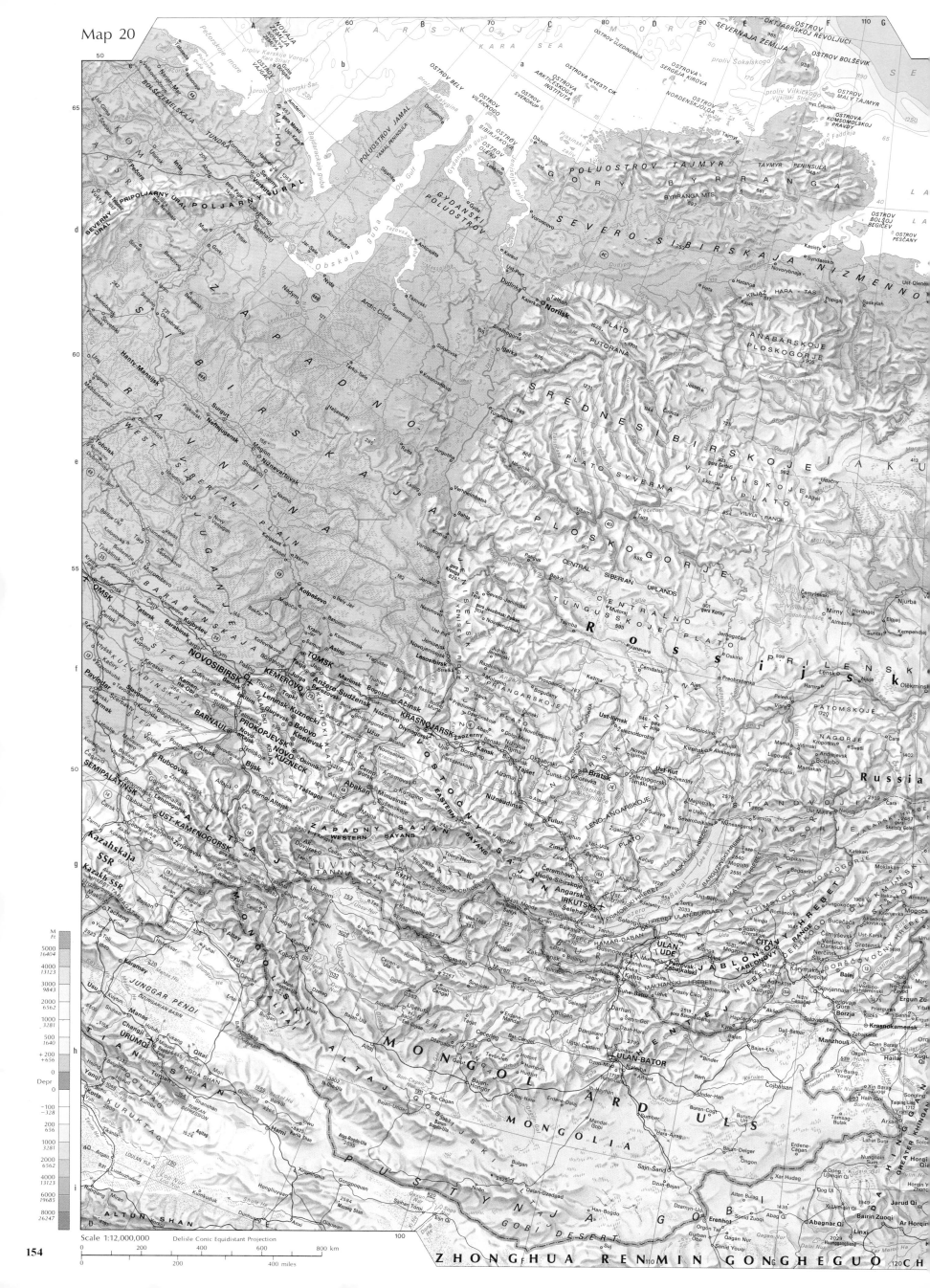

SOJUZ SOVETSKIH
SOCIALISTIČESKIH
RESPUBLIK (SSSR)

UNION OF
SOVIET SOCIALIST
REPUBLICS (USSR)

Rossijskaja Sovetskaja
Federativnaja
Socialističeskaja
Respublika (RSFSR)

Russian Soviet
Federated Socialist
Republic (RSFSR)

1 Altajski kraj
1A Gorno-Altajskaja
 avtonomnaja oblast
2 Habarovski kraj
2A Jevrejskaja
 avtonomnaja oblast
4 Krasnojarski kraj
4A Hakasskaja
 avtonomnaja oblast
4B Evenkijski nac.
 okrug
4C Tajmyrski (Dolgano-
 Neneckij) nac. okrug
5 Primorski kraj
7 Amurskaja oblast
8A Neneckí nac. okrug
13 Čitinskaja oblast
13A Aginski Burjatski
 nac. okrug
16 Irkutskaja oblast
16A Ust-Ordynski
 Burjatski nac. okrug
21 Kamčatskaja oblast
21A Korjakski nac.
 okrug
22 Kemerovskaja
 oblast
30 Magadanskaja
 oblast
30A Čukotski nac. okrug
34 Novosibirskaja
 oblast
35 Omskaja oblast
43 Sahalinskaja oblast
48 Tjumenskaja oblast
48A Hanty-Mansijski
 nac. okrug
48B Jamalo-Neneckí
 nac. okrug
49 Tomskaja oblast

Kazahskaja SSR

Kazakh SSR

13 Pavlodarskaja
 oblast
14 Semipalatinskaja
 oblast
19 Vostočno-
 Kazahstanskaja
 oblast

Map 21 **ASIA, PHYSICAL**

Map 22 **ASIA, POLITICAL**

Map 23 **SOUTHWESTERN ASIA**

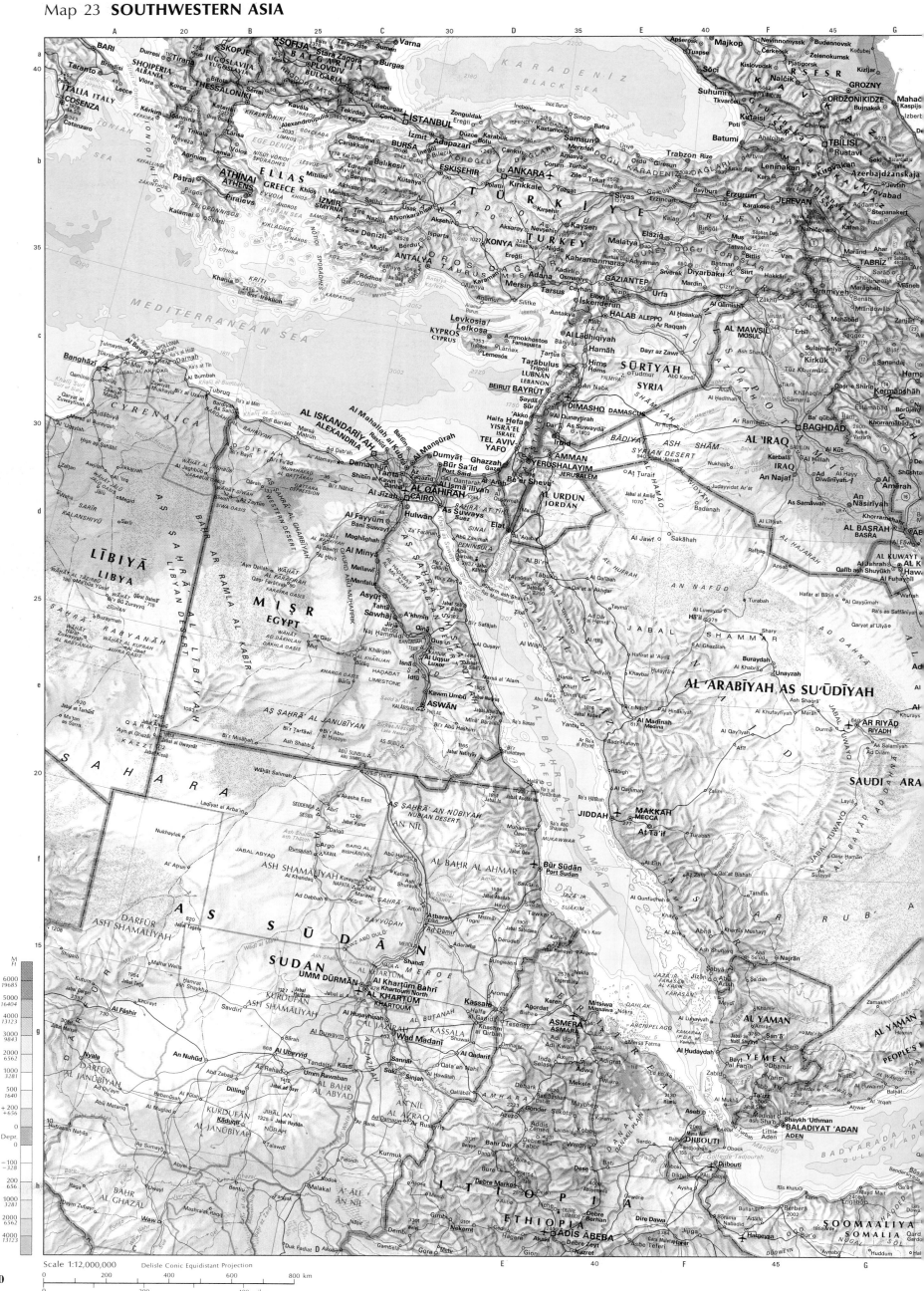

Scale 1:12,000,000   Delisle Conic Equidistant Projection

0   200   400   600   800 km

0   200   400 miles

AFGHANISTAN

VELĀYAT

1 Badakhshan
2 Bādghīsāt
3 Baghlān
4 Balkh
5 Bāmiān
6 Farāh
7 Fāryāb
8 Ghazni
9 Ghowr
10 Helmand
11 Herāt
12 Jowzjān
13 Kābul
14 Kāpīsā
15 Konarha
16 Laghmān
17 Lowgar
18 Nangarhār
19 Nīmrūz
20 Orūzgān
21 Paktiā
22 Parvān
23 Qandahār
24 Qondūz
25 Samangān
26 Takhār
27 Vardak
28 Zābol

ĪRĀN

OSTĀN

1 Āzarbāījān-e Gharbī
2 Āzarbāījān-e Sharqī
3 Bakhtīārī va Chahār Mahāll
4 Balūchestān va Sīstān
5 Boyer Ahmadī-ye Sardsīr va Kohkīlūyeh
6 Būshehr
7 Esfahān
8 Fārs
9 Gīlān
10 Hamadān
11 Īlām va Poshtkūh
12 Jazāyer va Banāder-e Khalīj-e Fārs va Daryā-ye 'Omān
13 Kermān
14 Kermānshāhān
15 Khorāsān
16 Khūzestān
17 Kordestān
18 Lorestān
19 Māzandarān
20 Semnān
21 Tehrān
22 Yazd
23 Zanjān

Ⓐ Area occupied by Pakistan and claimed by India.
Ⓑ Area occupied by India and claimed by Pakistan.
Ⓒ Area occupied by China and claimed by India and Pakistan.
Ⓓ Area occupied by China and claimed by India.

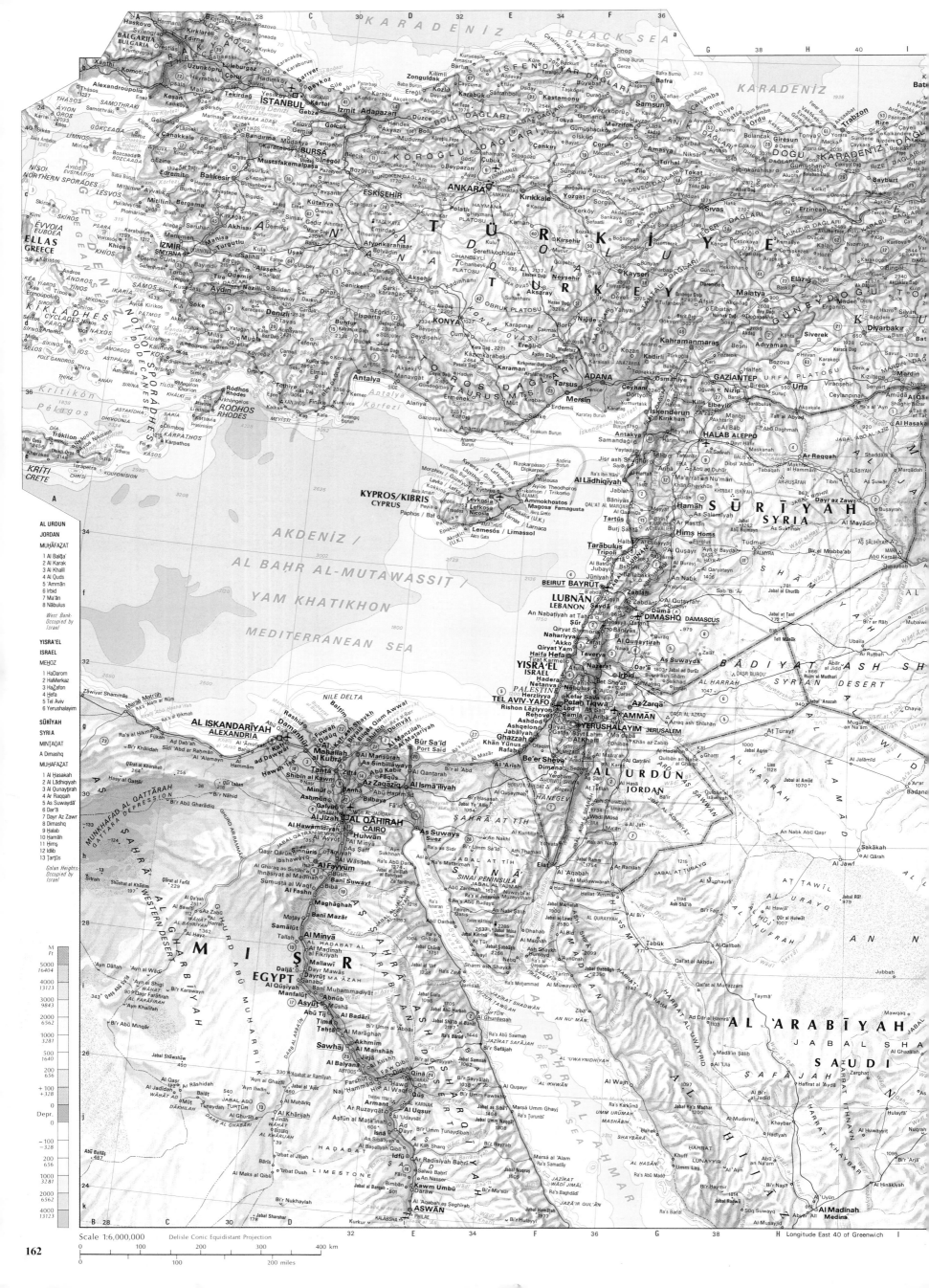

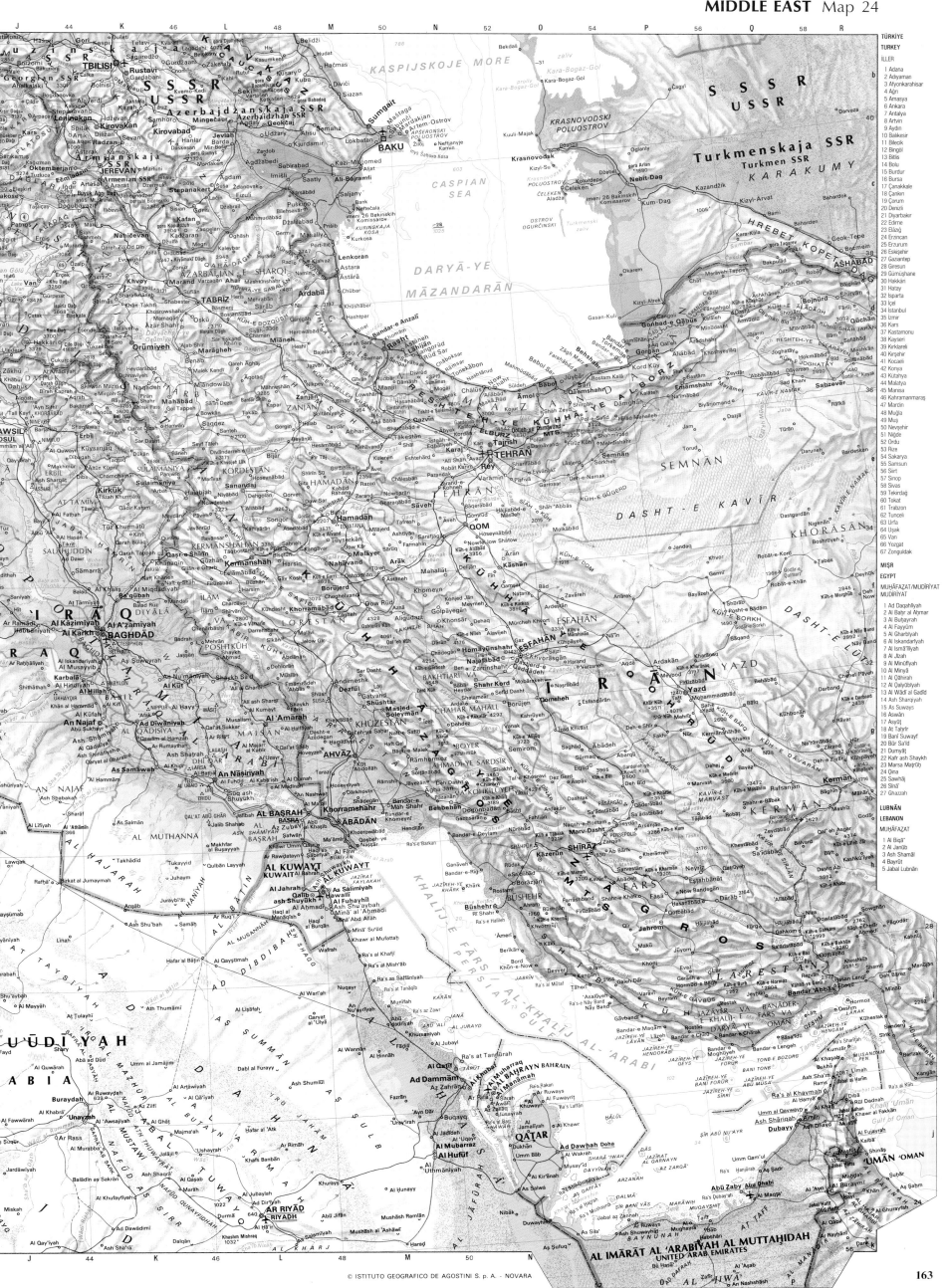

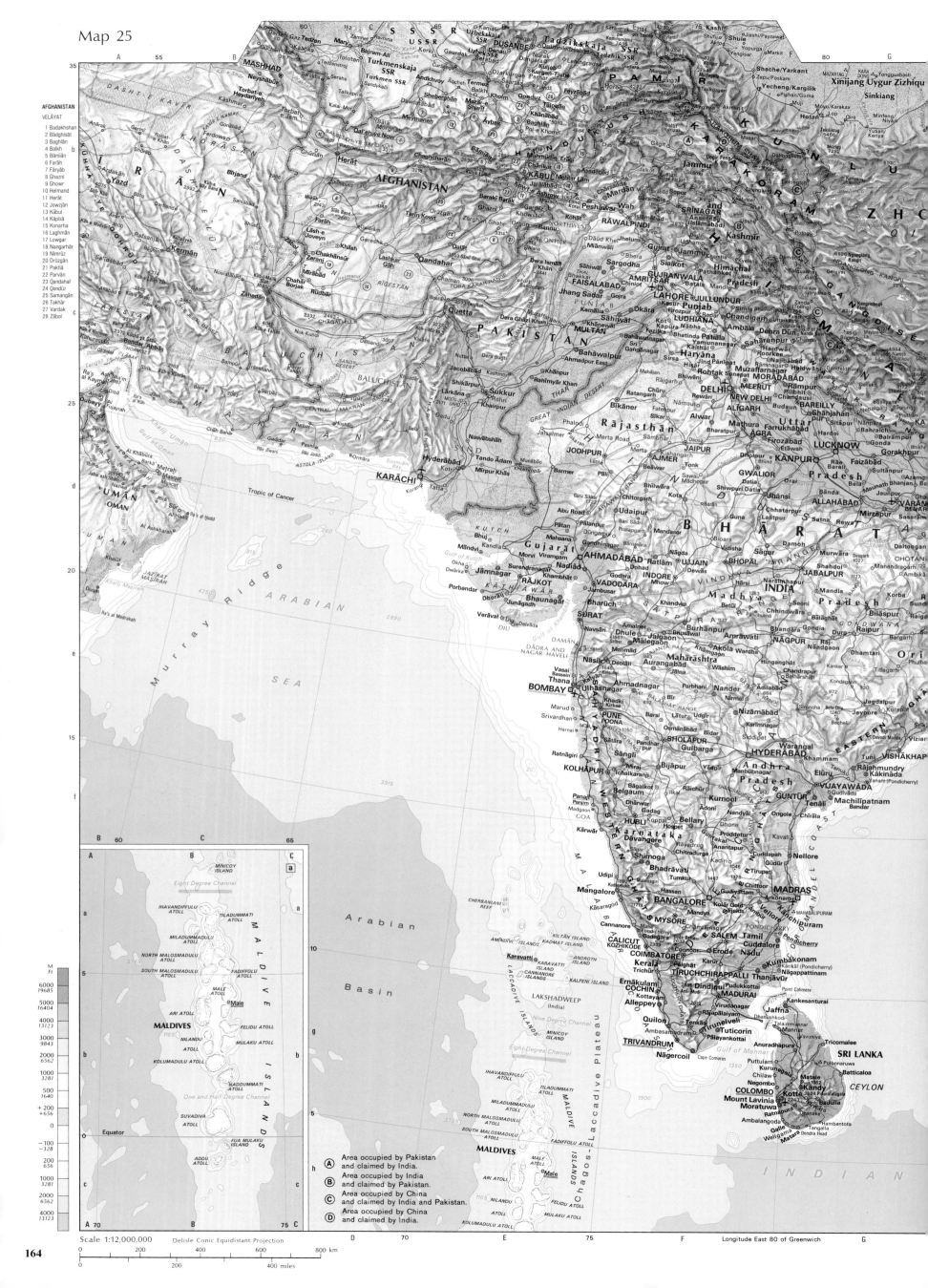

Map 25

Scale 1:12,000,000   Delisle Conic Equidistant Projection

Longitude East 80 of Greenwich

Map 26 **SOUTHEAST ASIA**

Scale 1:12,000,000 at the Equator

Mercator Cylindrical Projection

Longitude East 110 of Greenwich

Tropic of Cancer

PHILIPPINE SEA

Philippine Basin

West Mariana Basin

PACIFIC OCEAN

LUZON

Laoag
Banguei
Vigan
San Fernando
Baguio
Dagupan
Lingayen
Tarlac
Angeles
Olongapo
MANILA
QUEZON CITY
Lipa
Batangas
Calapan
MINDORO
Legazpi
Naga
Virac

PILIPINAS
PHILIPPINES

Roxas
PANAY
Iloilo
Bacolod
Cadiz
San Carlos
Toledo
CEBU
NEGROS
Dumaguete
Tagbilaran

Masbate
MASBATE
Calbayog
SAMAR
Catbalogan
Tacloban
Ormoc
LEYTE

Surigao
SIARGAO

Dipolog
Oroquieta
Ozamis
Pagadian
ZAMBOANGA
Cagayan de Oro
Iligan
Marawi
Cotabato
Davao
MINDANAO
Basilan City
Isabela
Jolo
General Santos
SULU ARCHIPELAGO

West Caroline Basin

CAROLINE ISLANDS

Trust Territory of the Pacific Islands
(Administered by the United States)

Sabah
Tawau
Sandakan

KEPULAUAN TALAUD
TALAUD ISLANDS

LAUT SULAWESI
Celebes Basin
CELEBES SEA

YAP ISLANDS
Colonia

Equator

Manado
Tondano
Gorontalo

HALMAHERA
Ternate

New Guinea Trench

Samarinda
Balikpapan
INDONESIA

SULAWESI
CELEBES

MOLUCCA SEA

MALUKU

SERAM CERAM
Ambon

Jayapura

PAPUA
NEW GUINEA

NEW GUINEA

UJUNG PANDANG
MAKASAR

PULAU IRIAN

LAUT BANDA
BANDA SEA

MALUKU

PULAU FLORES
Ende

TIMOR
NUSA TENGGARA TIMUR
Kupang

LAUT ARAFURA
ARAFURA SEA

TIMOR SEA

AUSTRALIA
Darwin

Map 27 **CHINA AND MONGOLIA**

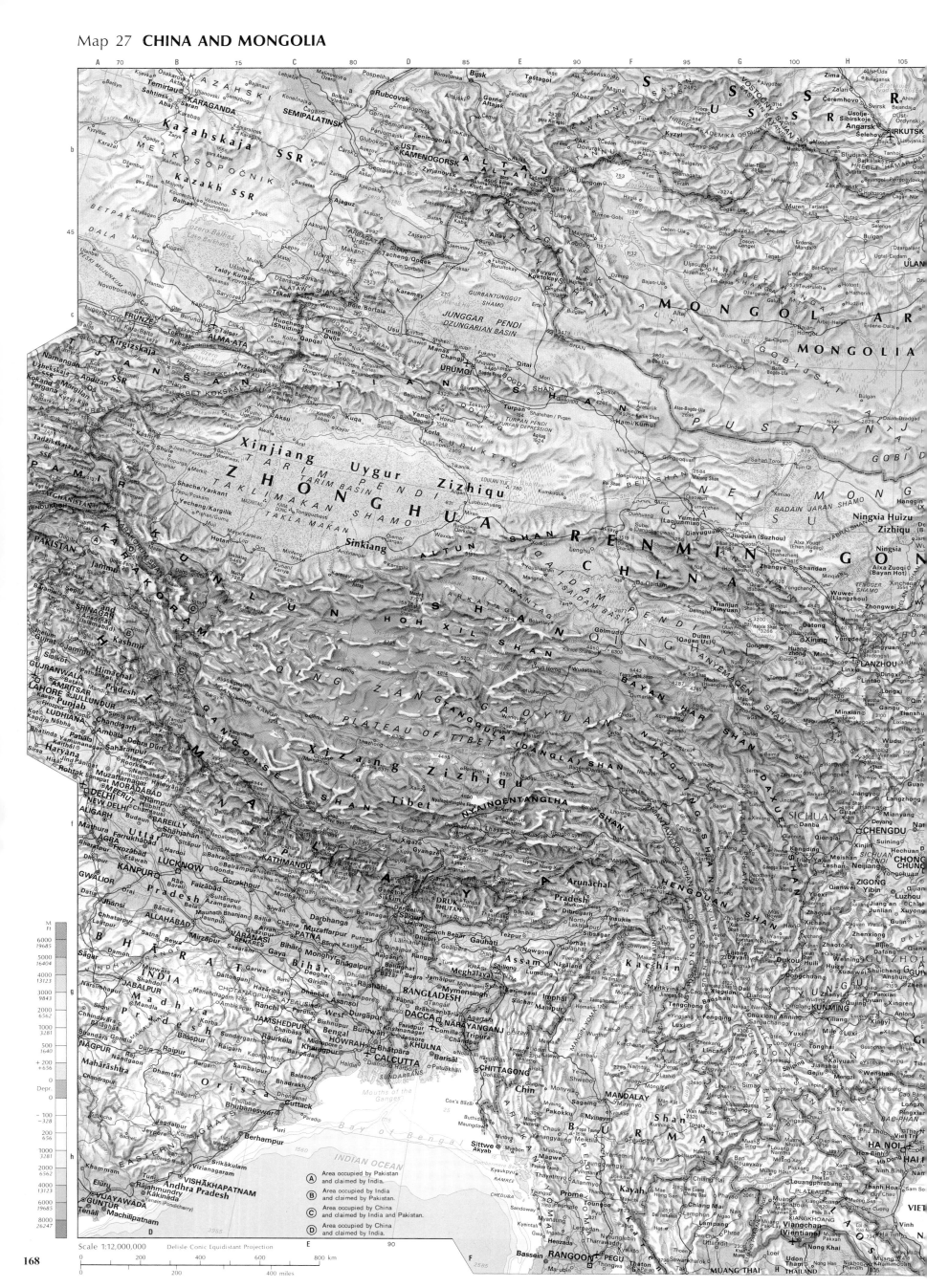

Scale 1:12,000,000

Delisle Conic Equidistant Projection

(A) Area occupied by Pakistan
and claimed by India.

(B) Area occupied by India
and claimed by Pakistan.

(C) Area occupied by China
and claimed by India and Pakistan.

(D) Area occupied by China
and claimed by India.

ZHONGHUA
RENMIN
GONGHEGUO

CHINA

1 Beijing Shi
2 Shanghai Shi
3 Tianjin Shi

Map 28   **NORTHEASTERN CHINA, KOREA AND JAPAN**

Scale 1:6,000,000   Delisle Conic Equidistant Projection

OHOTSKOJE MORE/
HOK-KAI

SEA OF OKHOTSK

KURILSKIJE OSTROVA
CHISHIMA-RETTŌ
KURIL ISLANDS
1845 (U.S.S.R.)

OSTROV ITURUP/
ETOROFU-TŌ

OSTROV SAHALIN/
SAKHALIN (U.S.S.R.)

OSTROV KUNAŠIR/
KUNASHIRI-TŌ

Japan Basin

JAPONSKOJE MORE/

TONG-HAE / NIPPON-KAI

Yamato Rise

SEA OF JAPAN

CHOSŎN M.I.K.

NORTH KOREA

NIPPON

JAPAN

TAEHAN-
MIN'GUK

SOUTH KOREA

HONSHŪ

HOKKAIDŌ

SAPPORO

HAKODATE

AOMORI

AKITA

SENDAI

NIIGATA

KŌRIYAMA

IWAKI

UTSUNOMIYA

MAEBASHI

NAGANO

TOYAMA

KANAZAWA

TOKYO

YOKOHAMA

KAWASAKI

CHIBA

URAWA

KYŌTO

NAGOYA

ŌSAKA

KOBE

NARA

HIMEJI

OKAYAMA

HIROSHIMA

KITAKYŪSHŪ

FUKUOKA

NAGASAKI

KUMAMOTO

KAGOSHIMA

MIYAZAKI

KŌCHI

MATSUYAMA

TAKAMATSU

TOKUSHIMA

WAKAYAMA

HAMAMATSU

TOYOHASHI

SHIZUOKA

GIFU

SHIKOKU

KYŪSHŪ

PACIFIC OCEAN

Shikoku Basin

Nankai Trench

TAIHÉIYŌ

Japan Trench

Bonin Trench

NIPPON
JAPAN
1 Hokkaidō Ken
2 Aomori Ken
3 Iwate Ken
4 Miyagi Ken
5 Akita Ken
6 Yamagata Ken
7 Fukushima Ken
8 Ibaraki Ken
9 Tochigi Ken
10 Gunma Ken
11 Saitama Ken
12 Chiba Ken
13 Tōkyō To
14 Kanagawa Ken
15 Niigata Ken
16 Toyama Ken
17 Ishikawa Ken
18 Fukui Ken
19 Yamanashi Ken
20 Nagano Ken
21 Gifu Ken
22 Shizuoka Ken
23 Aichi Ken
24 Mie Ken
25 Shiga Ken
26 Kyōto Fu
27 Ōsaka Fu
28 Hyōgo Ken
29 Nara Ken
30 Wakayama Ken
31 Tottori Ken
32 Shimane Ken
33 Okayama Ken
34 Hiroshima Ken
35 Yamaguchi Ken
36 Tokushima Ken
37 Kagawa Ken
38 Ehime Ken
39 Kōchi Ken
40 Fukuoka Ken
41 Saga Ken
42 Nagasaki Ken
43 Kumamoto Ken
44 Ōita Ken
45 Miyazaki Ken
46 Kagoshima Ken

CHOSŎN M.I.K.
NORTH KOREA
1 Chagang-Do
2 Ch'ŏngjin Si
3 Hamgyŏng-Namdo
4 Hamgyong-Pukto
5 Hwanghae-Namdo
6 Hwanghae-Pukto
7 Kaesŏng Si
8 Kangwŏn-Do
9 P'yŏngan-Namdo
10 P'yŏngan-Pukto
11 P'yŏngyang Si
12 Yanggang-Do

TAEHAN-MIN'GUK
SOUTH KOREA
1 Cheju-Do
2 Chŏlla-Namdo
3 Chŏlla-Pukto
4 Ch'ungch'ŏng-
   Namdo
5 Ch'ungch'ŏng-Pukto
6 Kangwŏn-Do
7 Kyŏngi-Do
8 Kyŏngsang-Namdo
9 Kyŏngsang-Pukto
10 Pusan Si
11 Sŏul Si

ZHONGHUA RENMIN
GONGHEGUO
CHINA
1 Beijing Shi
2 Shanghai Shi
3 Tianjin Shi

M
ft
3000
9843
2000
6562
1000
3281
500
1640
200
656
+100
+328
0
- 100
-328
200
656
1000
3281
2000
6562
4000
13123
6000
19685
8000
26247

Ⓐ Ostrov Kunašir, ostrov Iturup and
Malaja Kurilskaja Grjada, occupied by
the U.S.S.R. since 1945, are claimed by
Japan pending a final peace treaty.

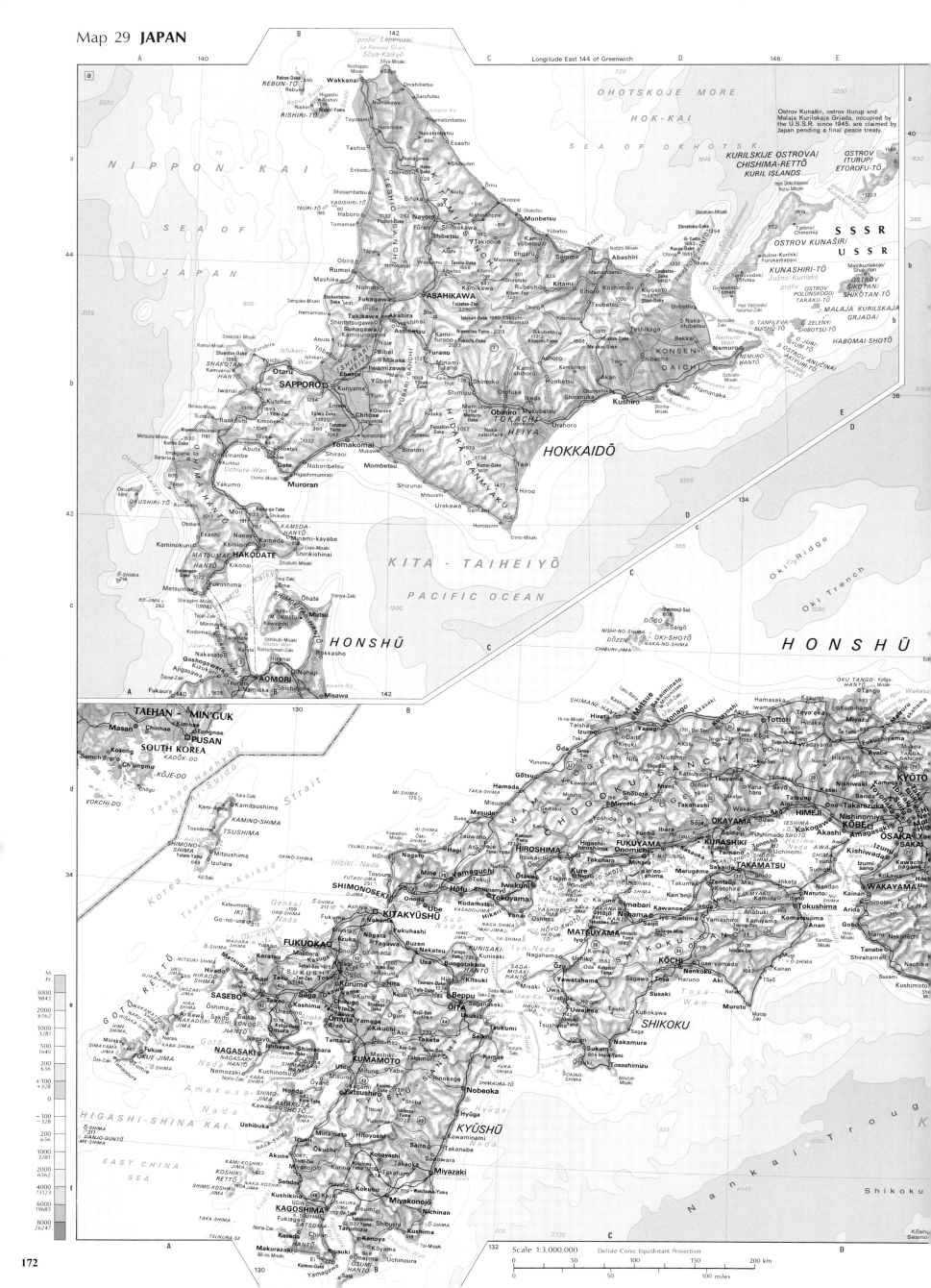

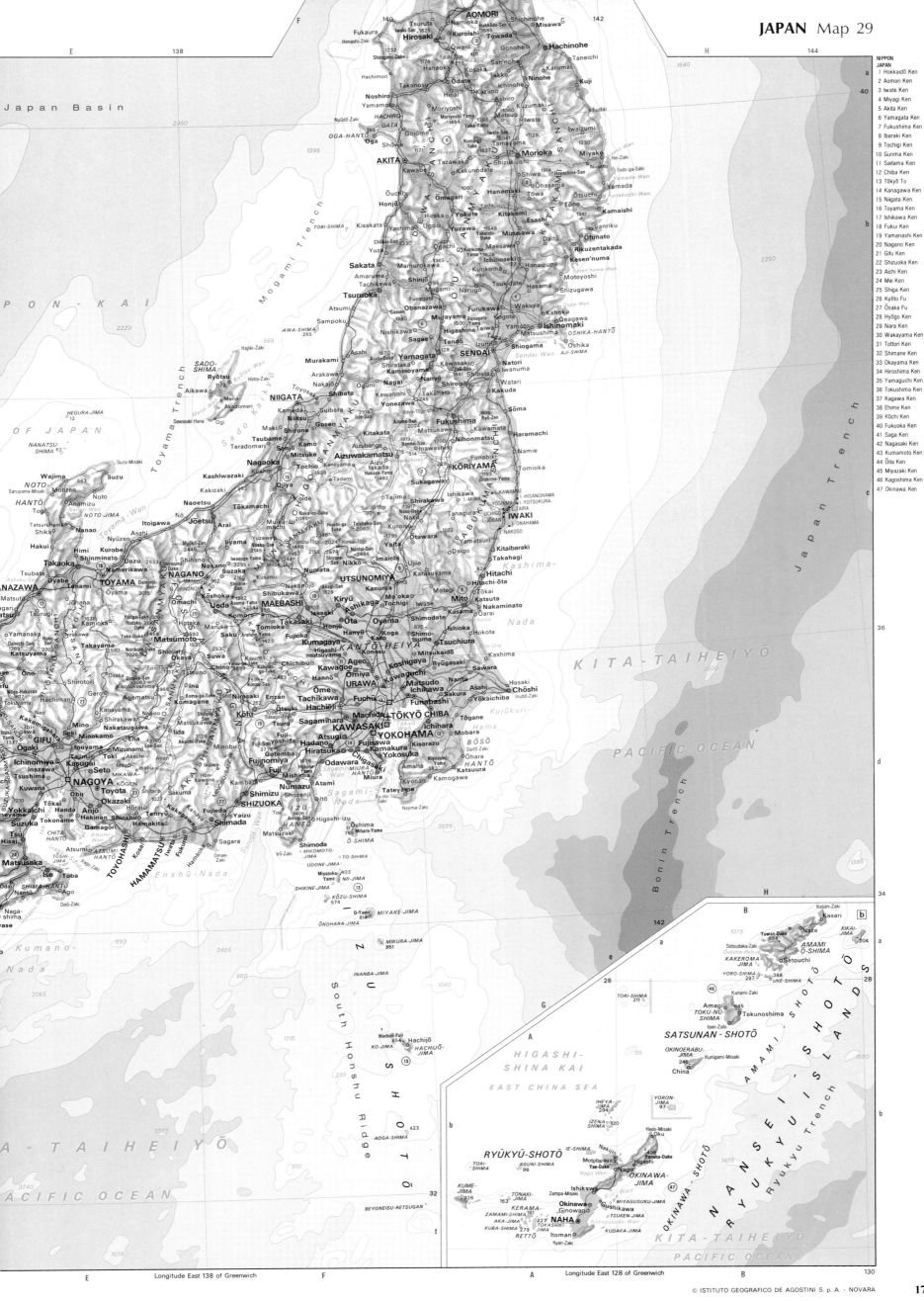

Map 30 **AFRICA, PHYSICAL**

Map 30

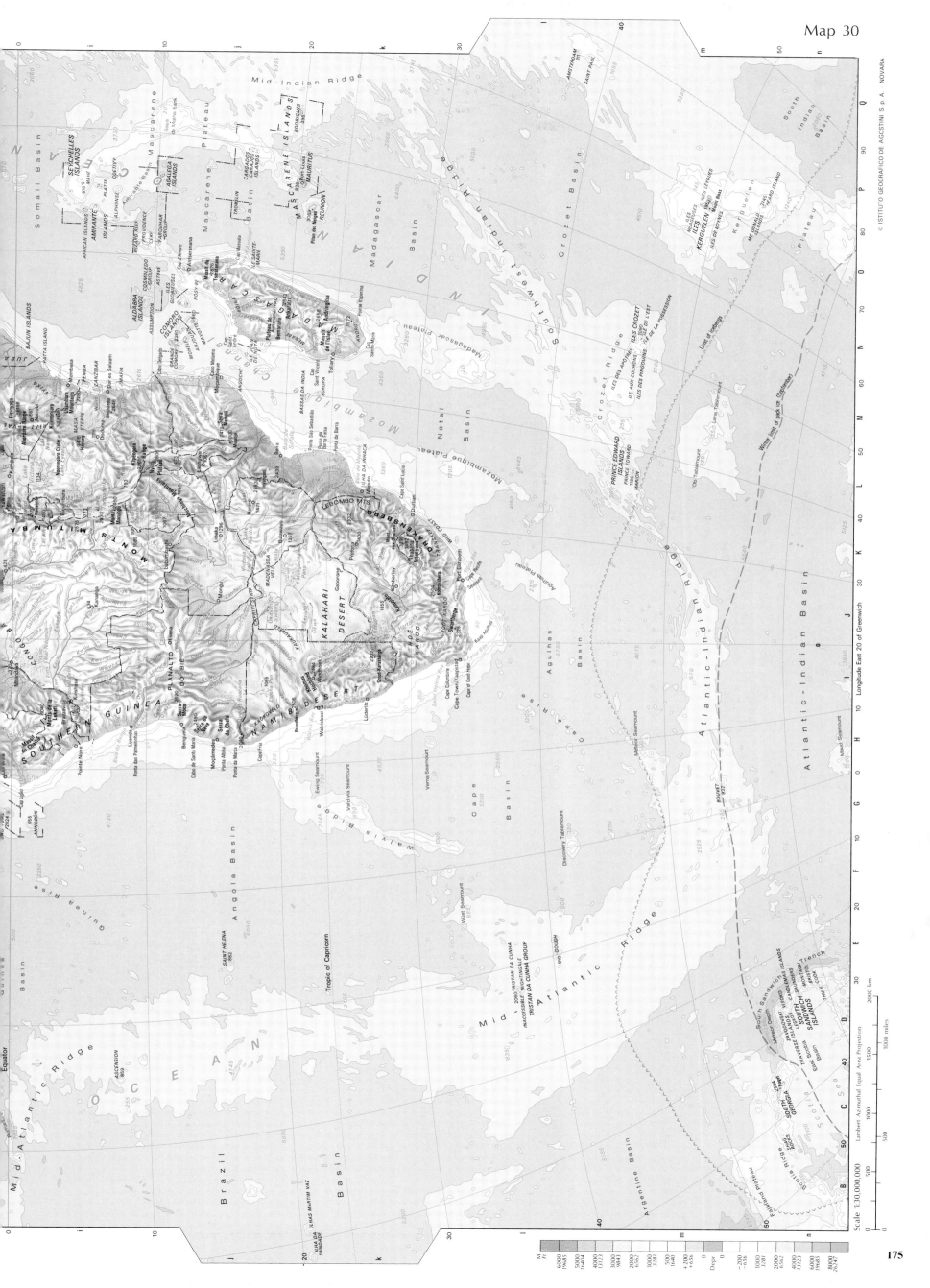

Map 31 **AFRICA, POLITICAL**

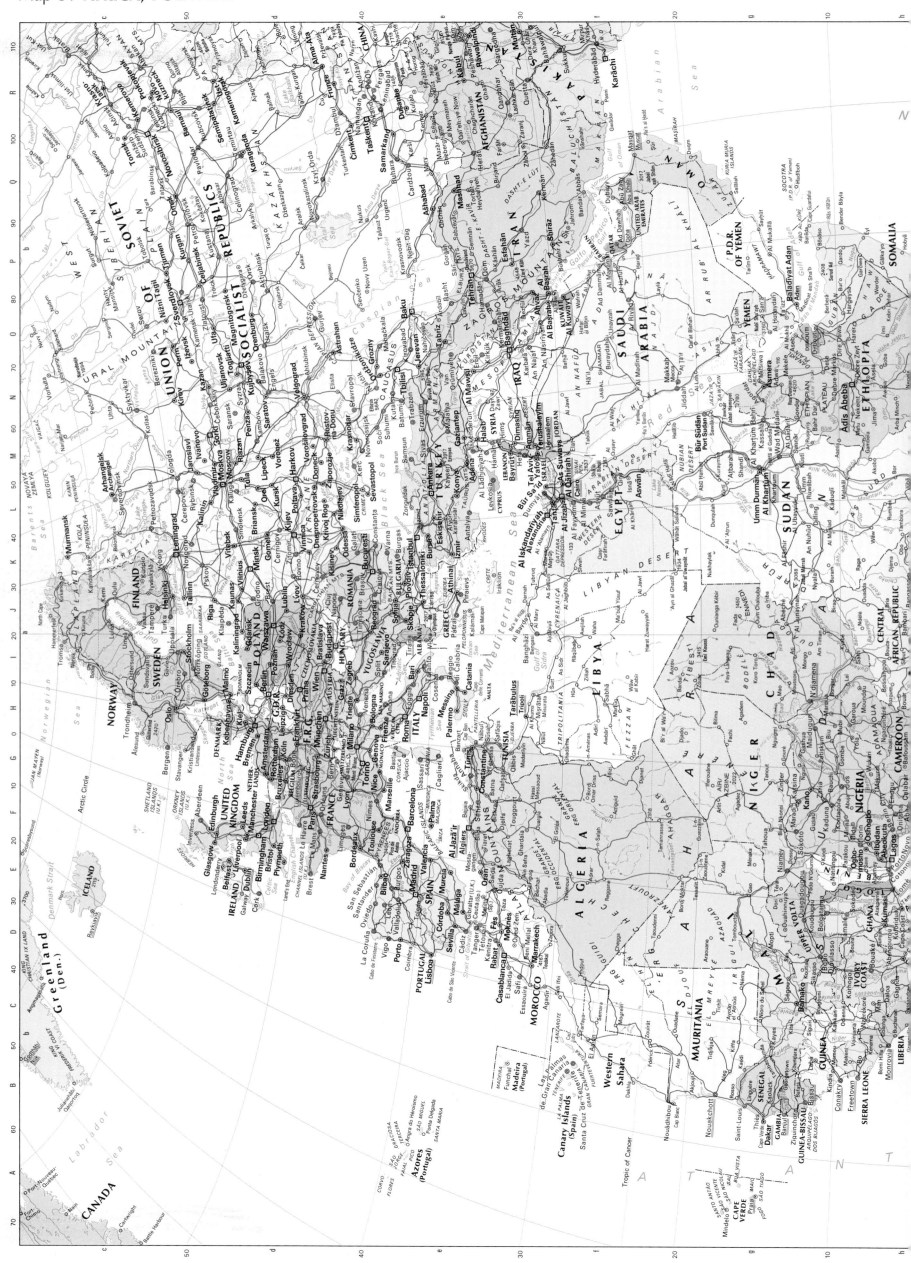

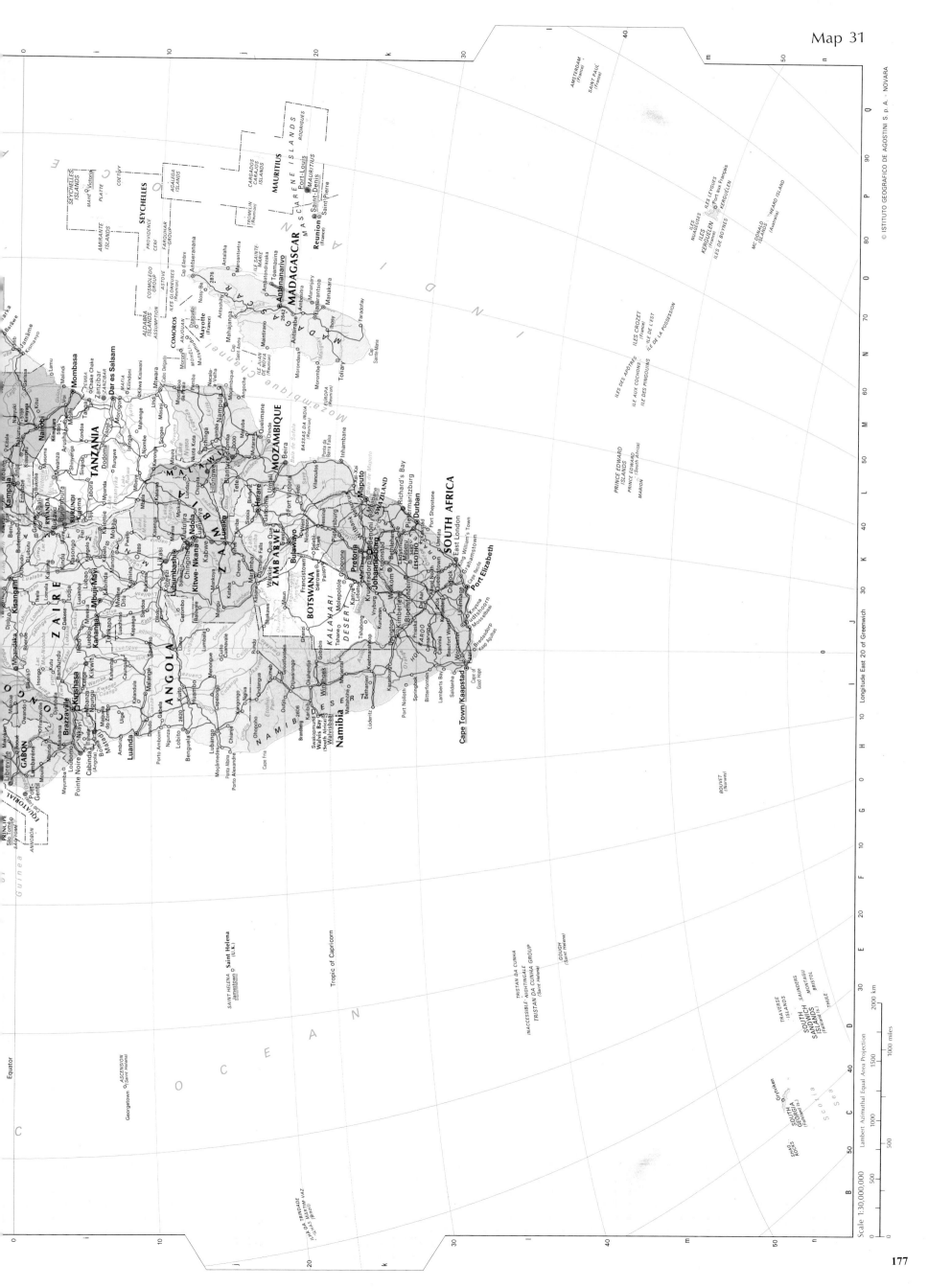

Map 31

Map 32

**AL JAZĀ'IR
ALGERIA**

WILĀYĀTE
1 Adrar
2 Al Jazā'ir
3 Annaba
4 Batna
5 Béchar
6 Bejaia
7 Biskra
8 Blida
9 Bouira
10 Cheliff
11 Constantine
12 Djelfa
13 Guelma
14 Jijel
15 Laghouat
16 Mascara
17 Médéa
18 Mostaganem
19 M'Sila
20 Oran
21 Ouargla
22 Oum el Bouaghi
23 Saida
24 Setif
25 Sidi Bel Abbes
26 Skikda
27 Tamanrasset
28 Tebessa
29 Tiaret
30 Tizi Ouzou
31 Tlemcen

**AL MAGHRIB
MOROCCO**

PRÉFECTURES
A Casablanca
B Rabat-Salé

PROVINCES
1 Agadir
2 Al Hoceima
3 Ar Rachidiya
4 Azilal
5 Beni Mellal
6 Boulemane
7 Chechaouene
8 El Jadida
9 El Kelaa des Srarhna
10 Essaouira
11 Fès
12 Figuig
13 Kenitra
14 Khemisset
15 Khenifra
16 Khouribga
17 Marrakech
18 Meknès
19 Nador
20 Ouarzazate
21 Oujda
22 Safi
23 Settat
24 Tanger
25 Tan Tan
26 Taounate
27 Tata
28 Taza
29 Tetouan
30 Tiznit

**TŪNIS
TUNISIA**

WILĀYĀTE
1 Al Kāf
2 Al Mahdīyah
3 Al Munastir
4 Al Qaṣrayn
5 Al Qayrawān
6 Bājah
7 Banzart
8 Jundubah
9 Madaniyin
10 Nābul
11 Qābis
12 Qafṣah
13 Qamūdah
14 Ṣafāqis
15 Silyānah
16 Sūsah
17 Tūnis
18 Zaghwān

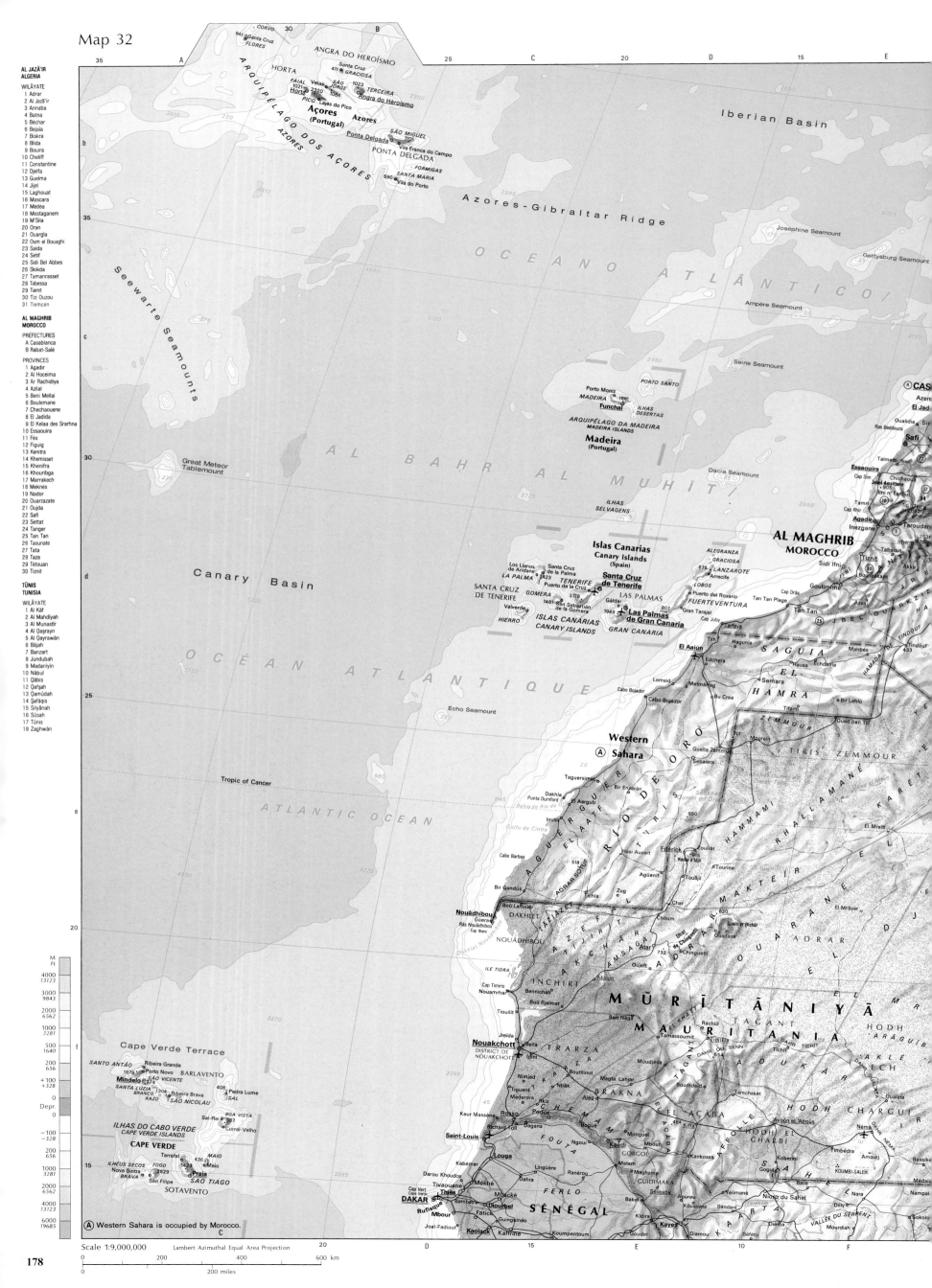

Ⓐ Western Sahara is occupied by Morocco.

Scale 1:9,000,000
Lambert Azimuthal Equal Area Projection

178

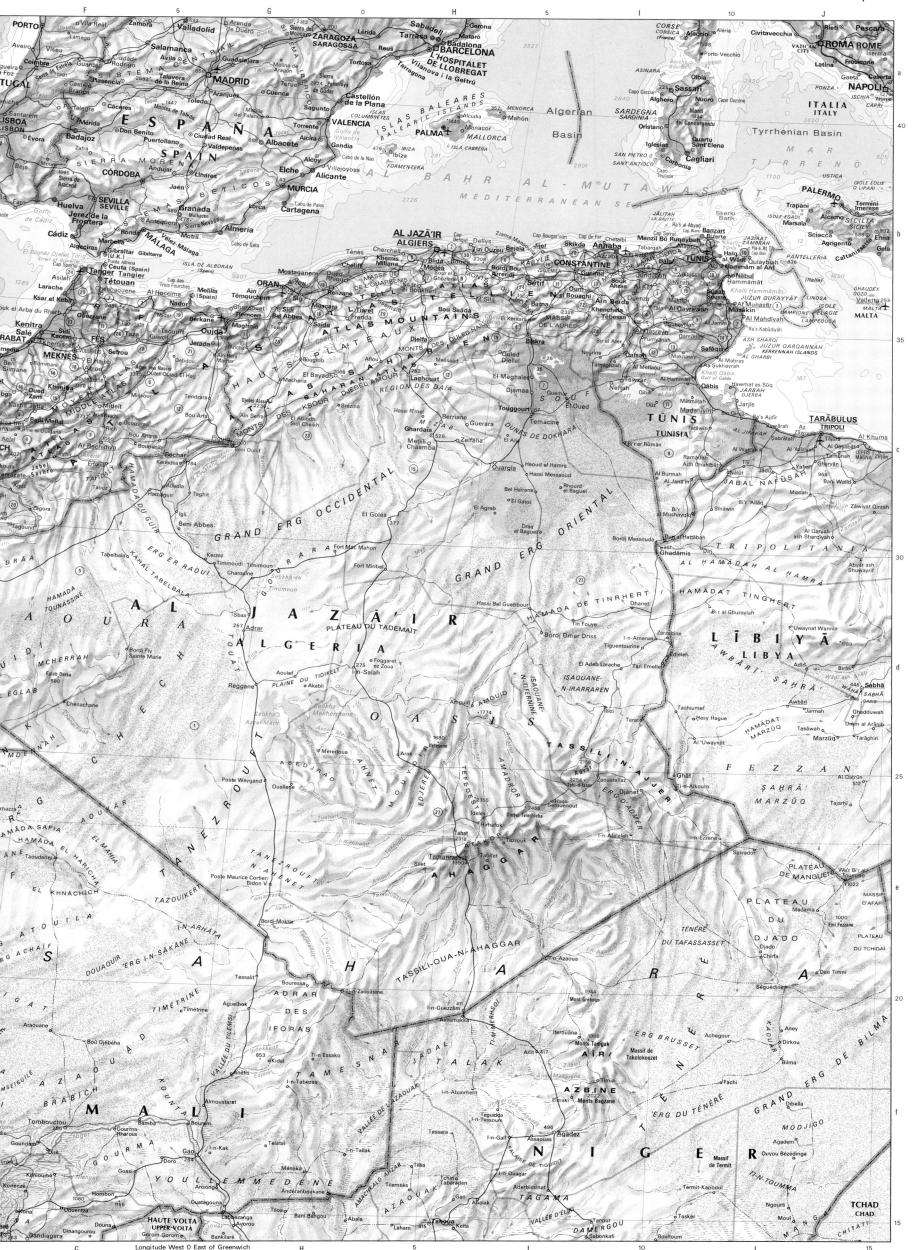

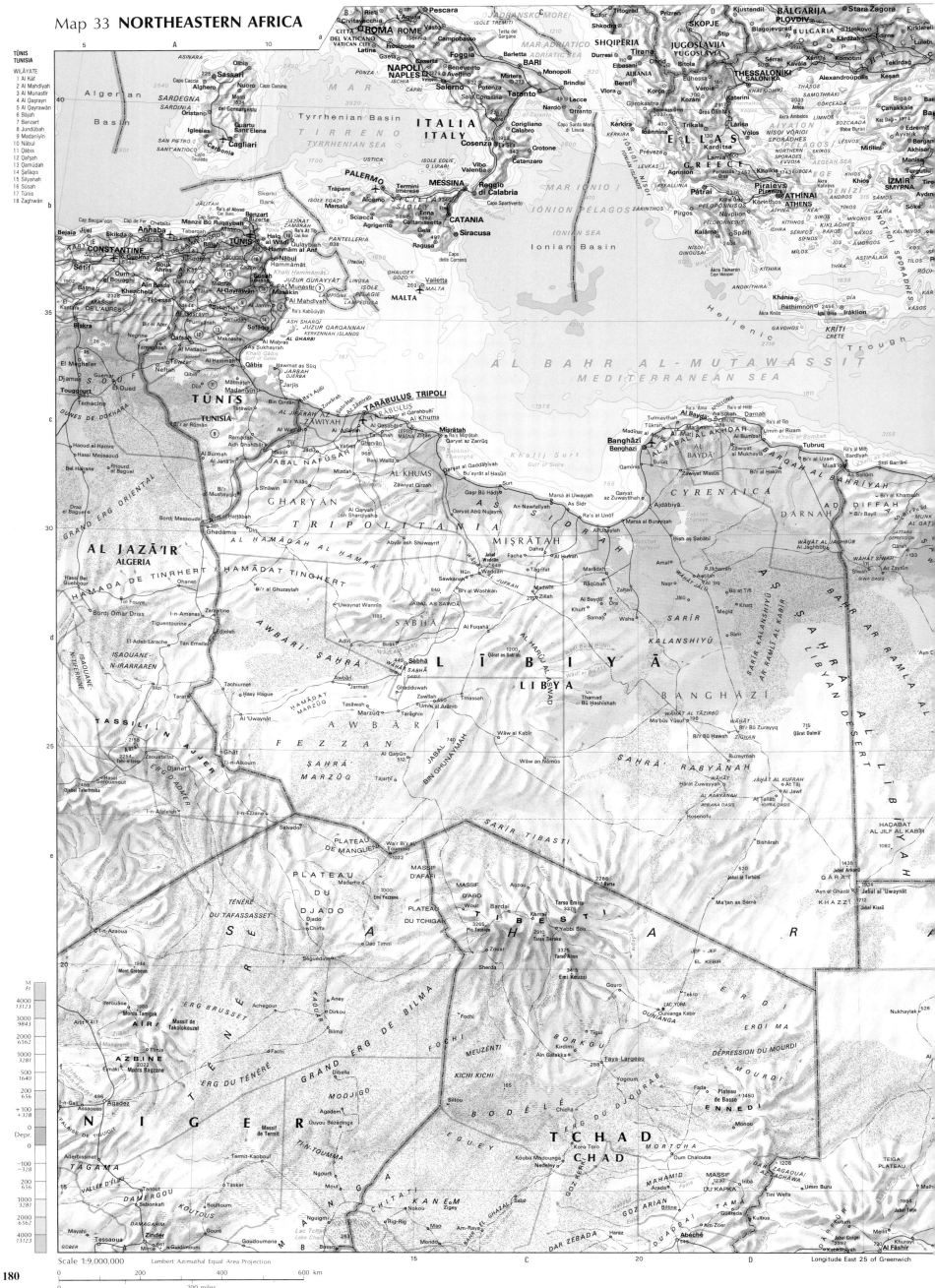

Map 33 NORTHEASTERN AFRICA

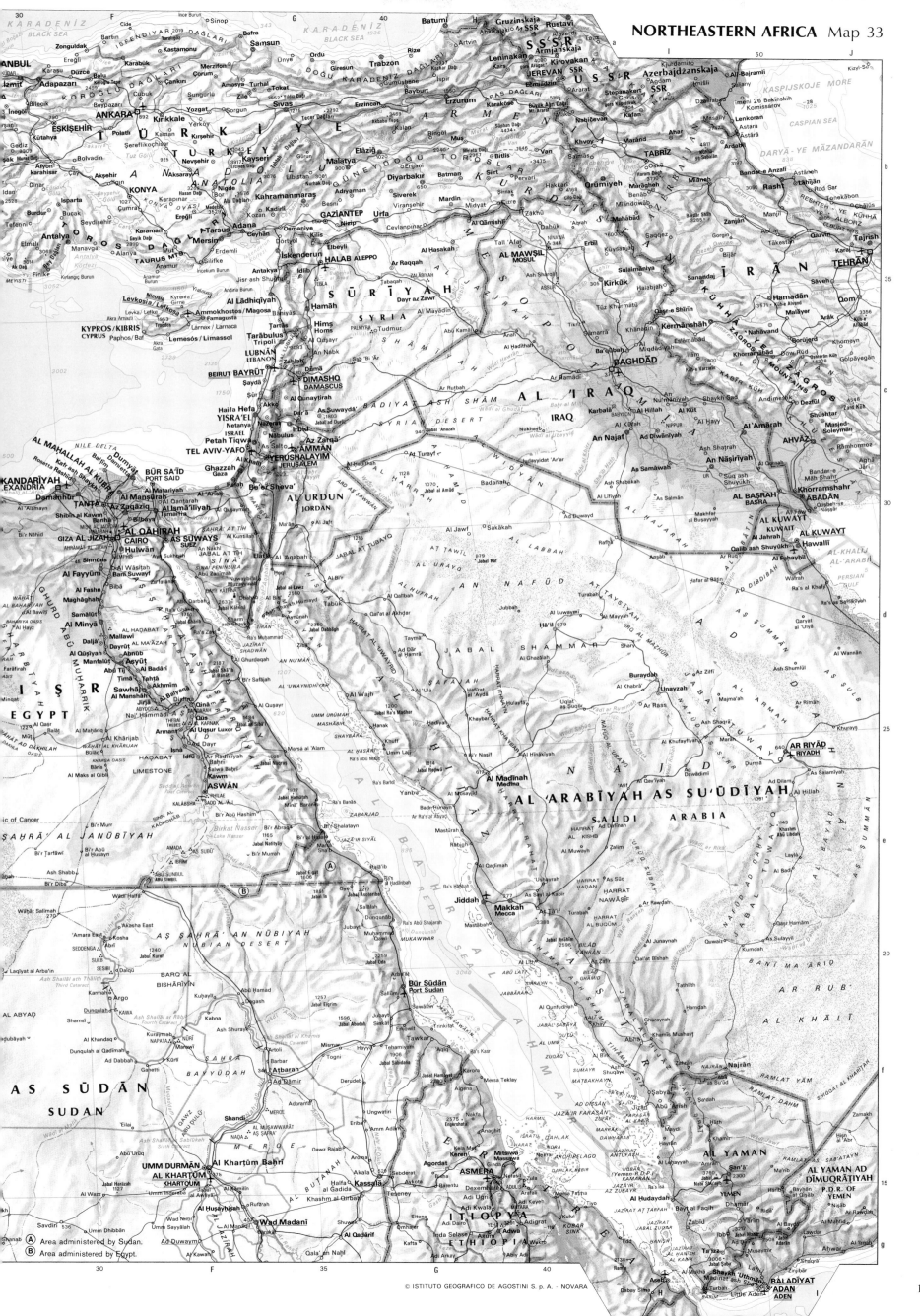

Ⓐ Area administered by Sudan.
Ⓑ Area administered by Egypt.

© ISTITUTO GEOGRAFICO DE AGOSTINI S.p.A. - NOVARA

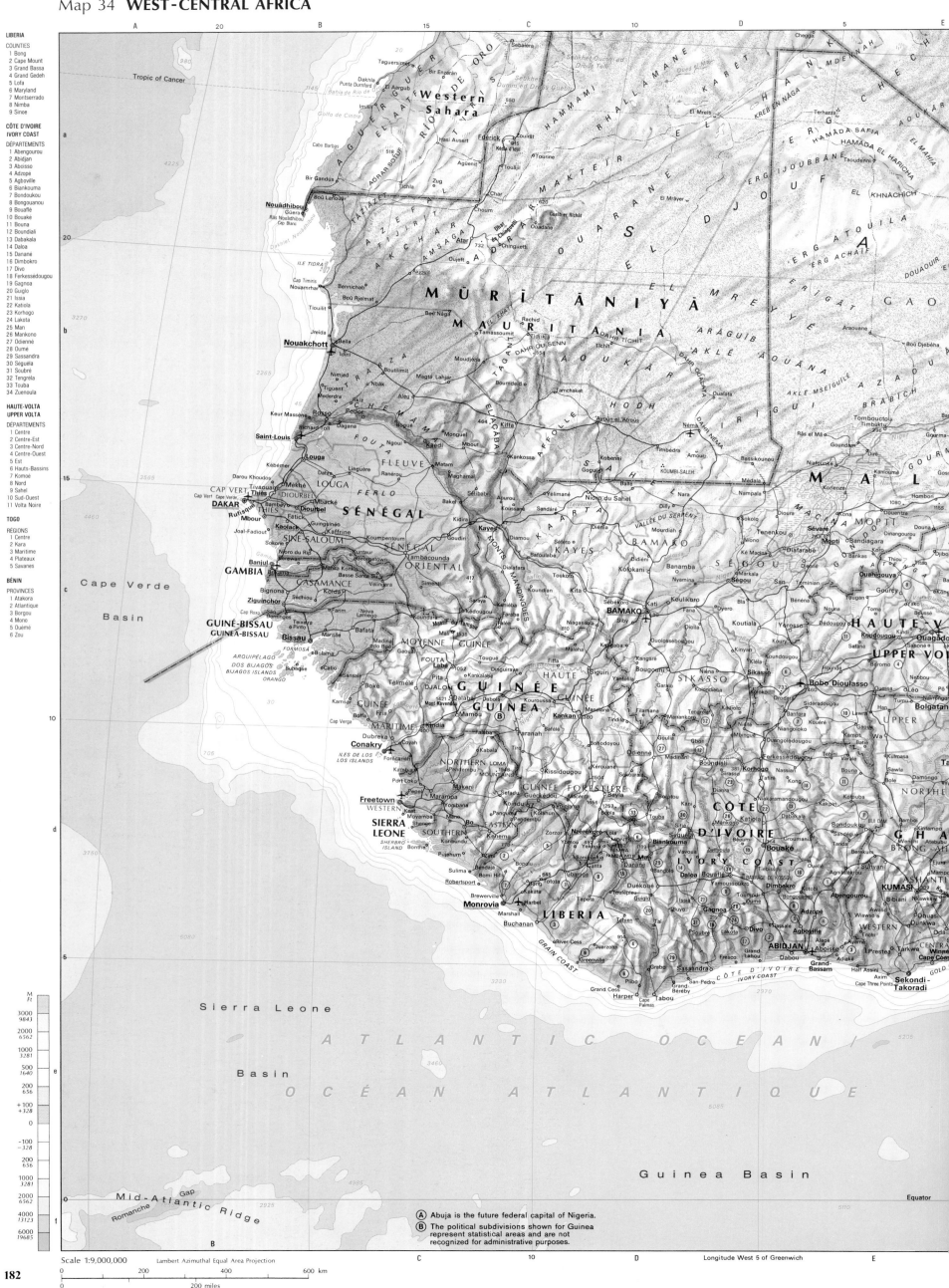

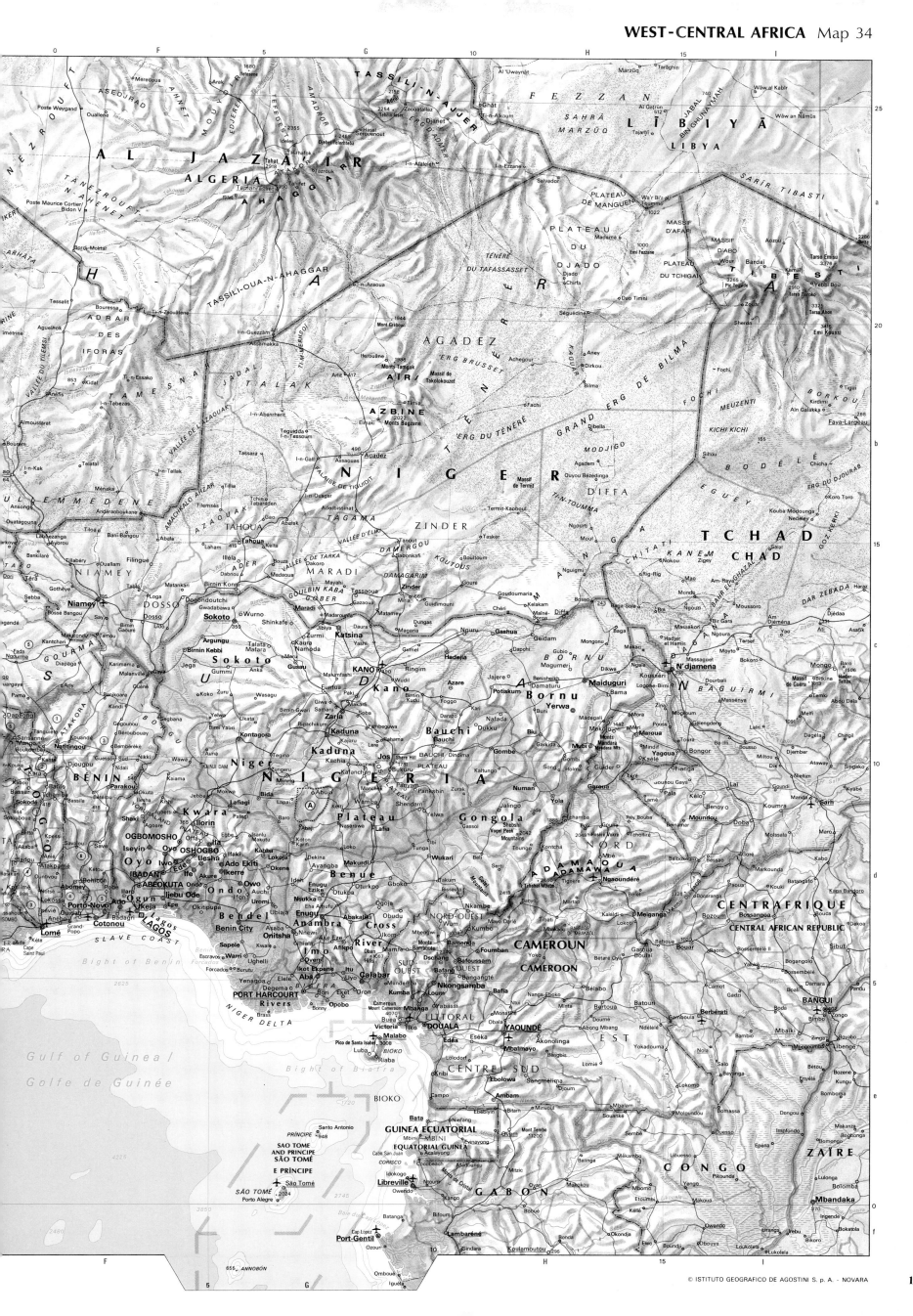

Map 35 **EAST-CENTRAL AFRICA**

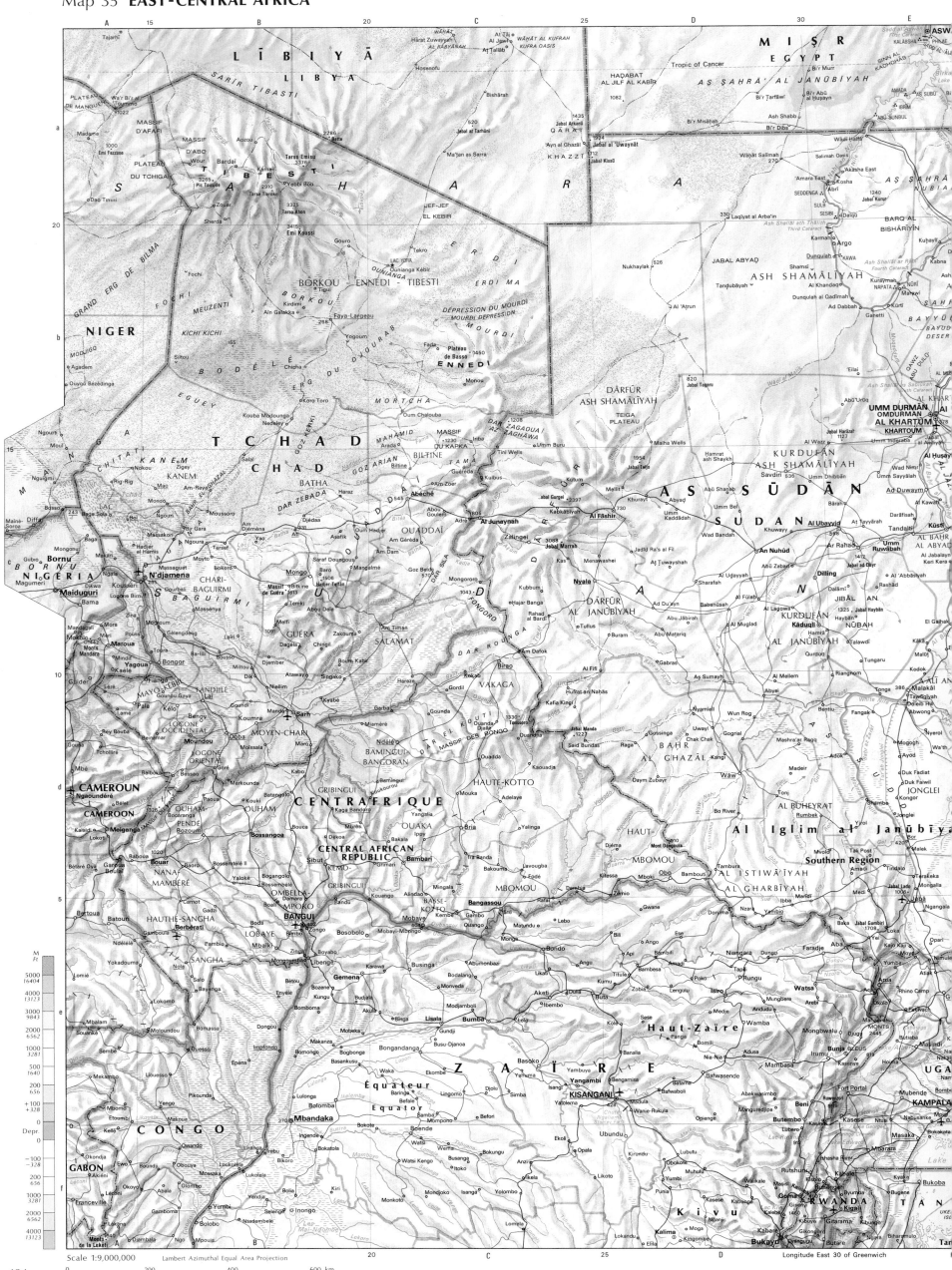

Scale 1:9,000,000

Lambert Azimuthal Equal Area Projection

Longitude East 30 of Greenwich

0   200   400   600 km

0   200 miles

AL IMĀRĀT
AL 'ARABĪYAH AL MUTTAHIDAH
Arādah • UNITED ARAB EMIRATES

AL 'ARABĪYAH AS SUŪDĪYAH
SAUDI ARABIA

Jiddah
Makkah
Mecca

'UMĀN
OMAN

Būr Sūdān
Port Sudan

ERITREA

ASMERA
Mitsiwa
Massawa

Kassala

AL YAMAN

AL YAMAN AD DIMUQRĀTĪYAH

Madanī

Al Qadārif

TIGRAY

YEMEN

P.D.R. OF YEMEN

Al Hudaydah

Al Mukallā

Ta'izz

GONDER

Mekele

Aseb

SUQUTRĀ SOCOTRA
(P.D.R. of Yemen)

Bahr Dar

DJIBOUTI

Gulf of Aden

GOJAM

Djibouti

SHEWA

Debre Markos

ĀDĪS ĀBEBA
ADDIS ABABA

Dire Dawa

Harer

Hargeysa

GUBAN

SANAAG

BARI
KARKĀR

WELEGA

Debre Berhan

NUGAAL

ITIOPYA

ARSI

TOG-DHEER

NUGAAL

ETHIOPIA

HARERGE

OGADEN

MUDUG

KEFA

BALE

SOOMAALIYA

SOMALIA

GAMO GOFA

SIDAMO

GAL GADUUD

HIIRAAN

BAKOOL

SHABEELLAHA
DHEXE

GEDO

Isha Baydabo

BAY

KENYA

JUBBADA DHEXE

MUQDISHO MOGADISHU
BANAADIR

SHABEELLAHA HOOSE
Marka

NAIROBI

JUBBADA
HOOSE

Kismaayo

Equator

Somali Basin

BAJUN ISLANDS

Ⓐ Area administered by Sudan
Ⓑ Area administered by Egypt

Map 36 **EQUATORIAL AFRICA**

Scale 1:9,000,000
Lambert Azimuthal Equal Area Projection

0   200   400   600 km

0   200 miles

Map 37 **SOUTHERN AFRICA**

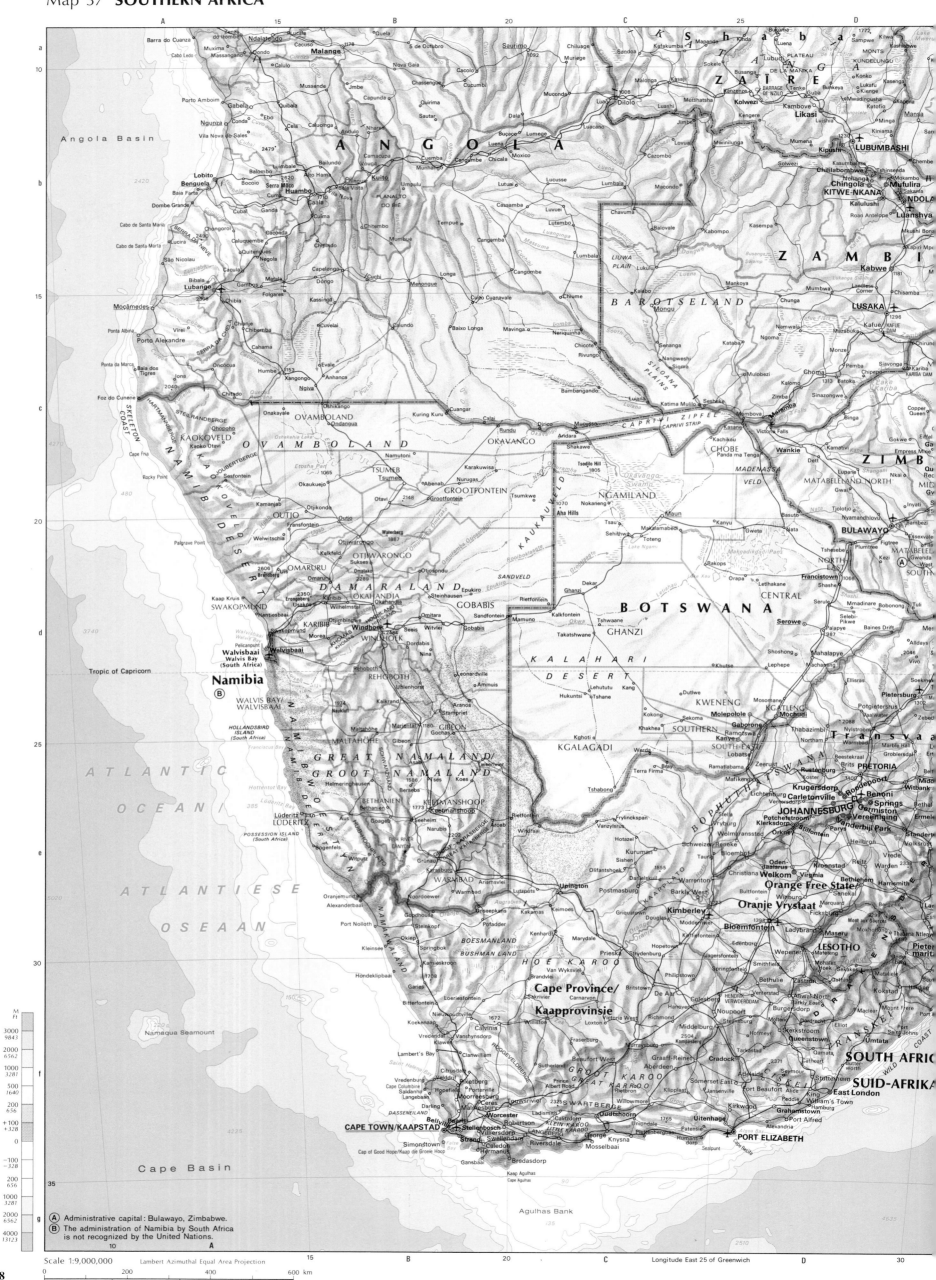

Scale 1:9,000,000   Lambert Azimuthal Equal Area Projection

Ⓐ Administrative capital: Bulawayo, Zimbabwe.
Ⓑ The administration of Namibia by South Africa is not recognized by the United Nations.

Map 38 **NORTH AMERICA, PHYSICAL**

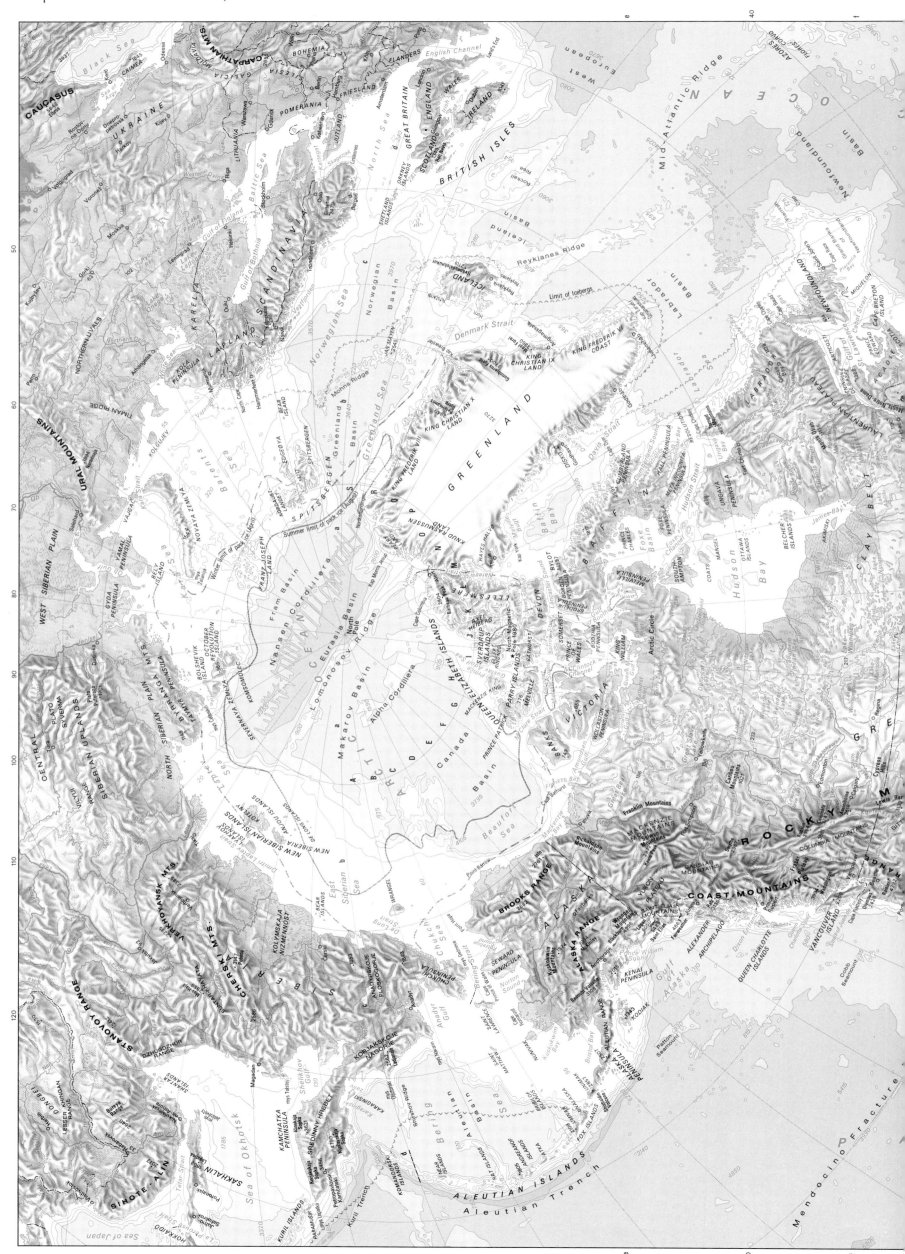

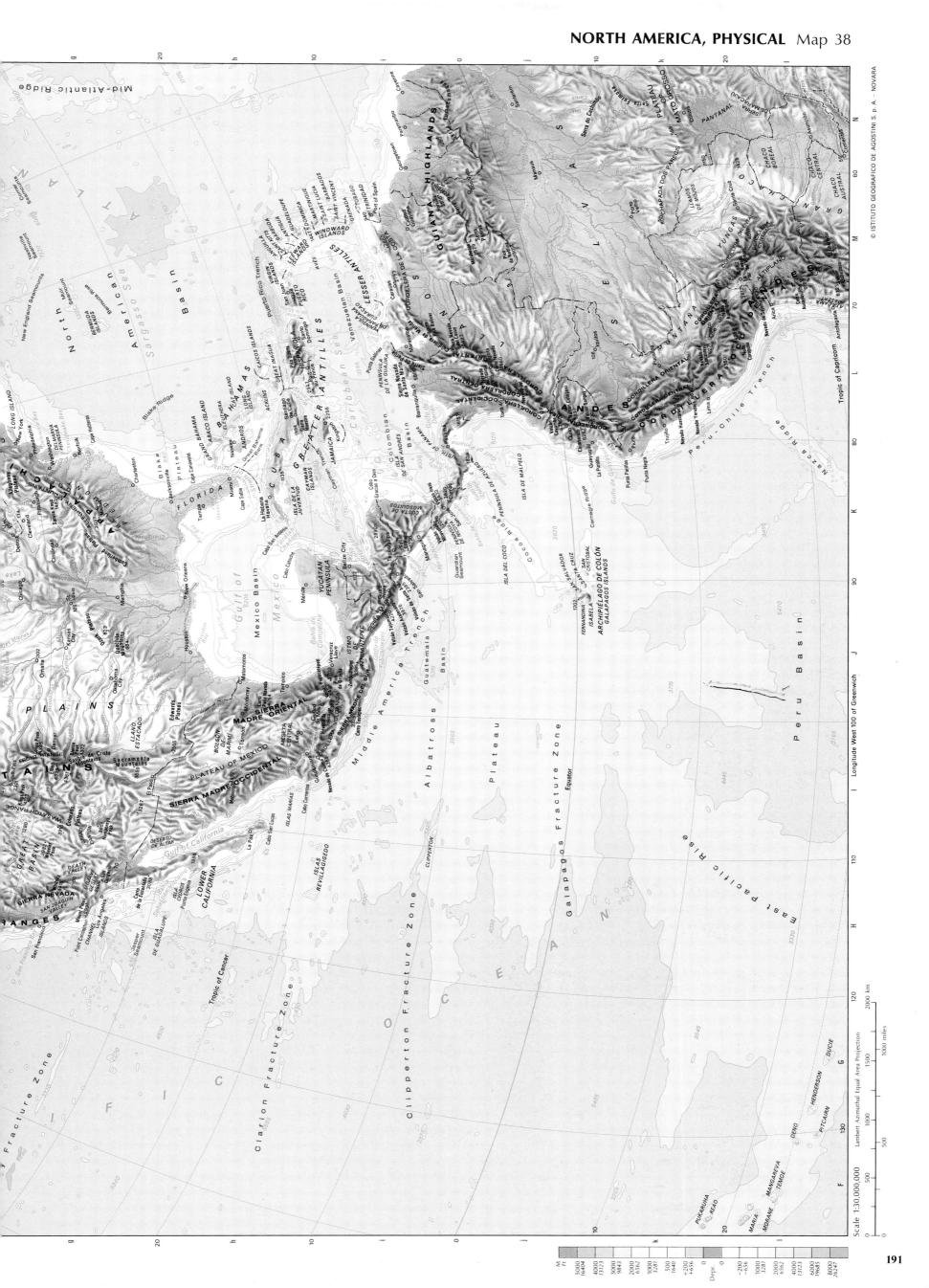

© ISTITUTO GEOGRAFICO DE AGOSTINI S. p. A. - NOVARA

Mid-Atlantic Ridge

North
American
Basin

Sargasso
Sea

A T L A N T I C

O C E A N

New England Seamounts
Bermuda Rise
BERMUDA ISLANDS

Blake Ridge

GUIANA HIGHLANDS

V E N E Z U E L A

LESSER ANTILLES
WINDWARD ISLANDS
LEEWARD ISLANDS
VIRGIN ISLANDS
ANTIGUA
GUADELOUPE
DOMINICA
MARTINIQUE
SAINT LUCIA
BARBADOS
SAINT VINCENT
GRENADA
TOBAGO
TRINIDAD
Port of Spain

Puerto Rico Trench
PUERTO RICO
San Juan
Santo Domingo
HISPANIOLA
HAITI

GREATER ANTILLES
GRAND BAHAMA ISLAND
ABACO ISLAND
ELEUTHERA
B A H A M A S
ANDROS
LONG ISLAND
CAT ISLAND
GREAT INAGUA
ACKLINS
CAICOS ISLANDS

C U B A
La Habana Havana
ISLA DE LA JUVENTUD
Santiago de Cuba
CAYMAN ISLANDS
JAMAICA
Kingston

Caribbean Sea

Venezuelan Basin
Aves

Barranquilla
Maracaibo
Caracas
PENINSULA DE LA GUAJIRA
Sierra Nevada de Santa Marta
CORDILLERA DE LA COSTA

Colombian Basin
ISLAS DE SAN ANDRES
Cabo Gracias a Dios

C O L O M B I A

CORDILLERA OCCIDENTAL
CORDILLERA CENTRAL
CORDILLERA ORIENTAL

A N D E S

MATO GROSSO PLATEAU
CHAPADA DOS PAREÇIS
PANTANAL
Serra de Carbiúna
CHACO BOREAL
CHACO CENTRAL
CHACO AUSTRAL
LLANOS DE MOJOS
ALTIPLANO
YUNGAS

CORDILLERA REAL
CORDILLERA ORIENTAL
CORDILLERA OCCIDENTAL

Peru-Chile Trench

Nazca Ridge

Tropic of Capricorn

B R A Z I L

B O L I V I A

P E R U

Lima

A P P A L A C H I A N   M O U N T A I N S
Allegheny Plateau
Cumberland Plateau
Washington
Philadelphia
New York
LONG ISLAND
DELMARVA PENINSULA
Chesapeake Bay
Cape Hatteras
Cleveland
Detroit
Cincinnati
Charleston
Jacksonville

F L O R I D A
Blake Plateau
Cape Canaveral
Miami
Tampa
Cape Sable

Gulf of Mexico
Mexico Basin

YUCATAN PENINSULA
Mérida
Bahía de Campeche
Belize City

Chicago
St. Louis
Memphis
New Orleans
Houston
Kansas City
Omaha
Oklahoma City
Des Moines

P L A I N S

Quachita Mountains

LLANO ESTACADO
Edwards Plateau

Monterrey
Matamoros
Tampico
Ciudad Victoria

SIERRA MADRE ORIENTAL
MESETA CENTRAL
PLATEAU OF MEXICO
BOLSÓN DE MAPIMÍ
Torreón

SIERRA MADRE OCCIDENTAL
Chihuahua
El Paso

ISTMO DE TEHUANTEPEC
Veracruz
SIERRA MADRE DEL SUR
Acapulco
GUATEMALA
Guatemala
SAN SALVADOR

Middle America Trench
Guatemala Basin

M E X I C O

COSTA DE MOSQUITOS

ISTMO DE PANAMÁ
Gulf of Panamá
PENÍNSULA DE AZUERO

Cabo San Antonio

Denver
Pikes Peak
Sangre de Cristo Mountains
Sacramento Mountains

R O C K Y   M O U N T A I N S
FRONT RANGE
GREAT BASIN
WASATCH RANGE
Salt Lake City
DEATH VALLEY
SIERRA NEVADA
SAN JOAQUIN VALLEY
COAST RANGES
San Francisco
Los Angeles
CHANNEL ISLANDS
San Diego

LOWER CALIFORNIA
Gulf of California
DESIERTO DE ALTAR
La Paz
Cabo San Lucas
ISLAS MARÍAS
ISLAS REVILLAGIGEDO
Cabo Corrientes

ISLA DE GUADALUPE
ISLA CEDROS
Point Conception

Tropic of Cancer

P A C I F I C   O C E A N

ISLA DE MALPELO
ISLA DEL COCO
Cocos Ridge
Carnegie Ridge
Malpelo Ridge

ARCHIPIÉLAGO DE COLÓN
GALAPAGOS ISLANDS
FERNANDINA
ISABELA
SAN CRISTÓBAL
SANTA CRUZ

Guardian Seamount

Albatross Plateau

Clipperton Fracture Zone
CLIPPERTON

Clarion Fracture Zone

Galapagos Fracture Zone

Equator

Longitude West 100 of Greenwich

Peru Basin

East Pacific Rise

Fracture Zone

PUKARUHA
REAO
DUCIE
HENDERSON
PITCAIRN
OENO
MORANE
MARIA
MANGAREVA
TEMOE

Lambert Azimuthal Equal Area Projection

Scale 1:30,000,000

0   500   1000   1500   2000 km

0   500   1000   miles

191

M ft
5000 16404
4000 13123
3000 9843
2000 6562
1000 3281
500 1640
+200 +656
Depr. 0
−200 −656
1000 3281
2000 6562
4000 13123
6000 19685
8000 26247

Map 39 **NORTH AMERICA, POLITICAL**

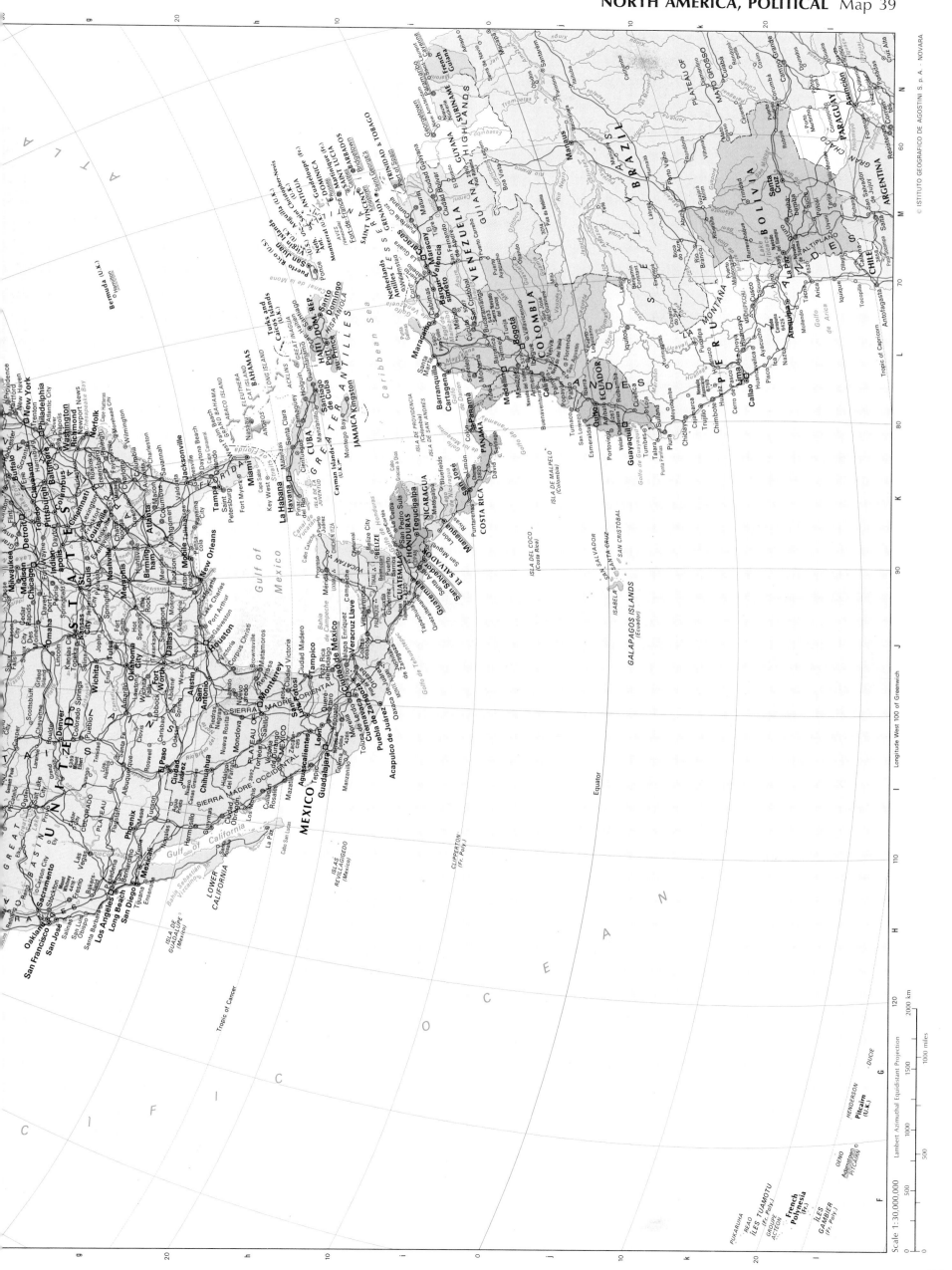

© ISTITUTO GEOGRAFICO DE AGOSTINI S. p. A. NOVARA

Scale 1:30,000,000

Lambert Azimuthal Equidistant Projection

Map 40 ALASKA

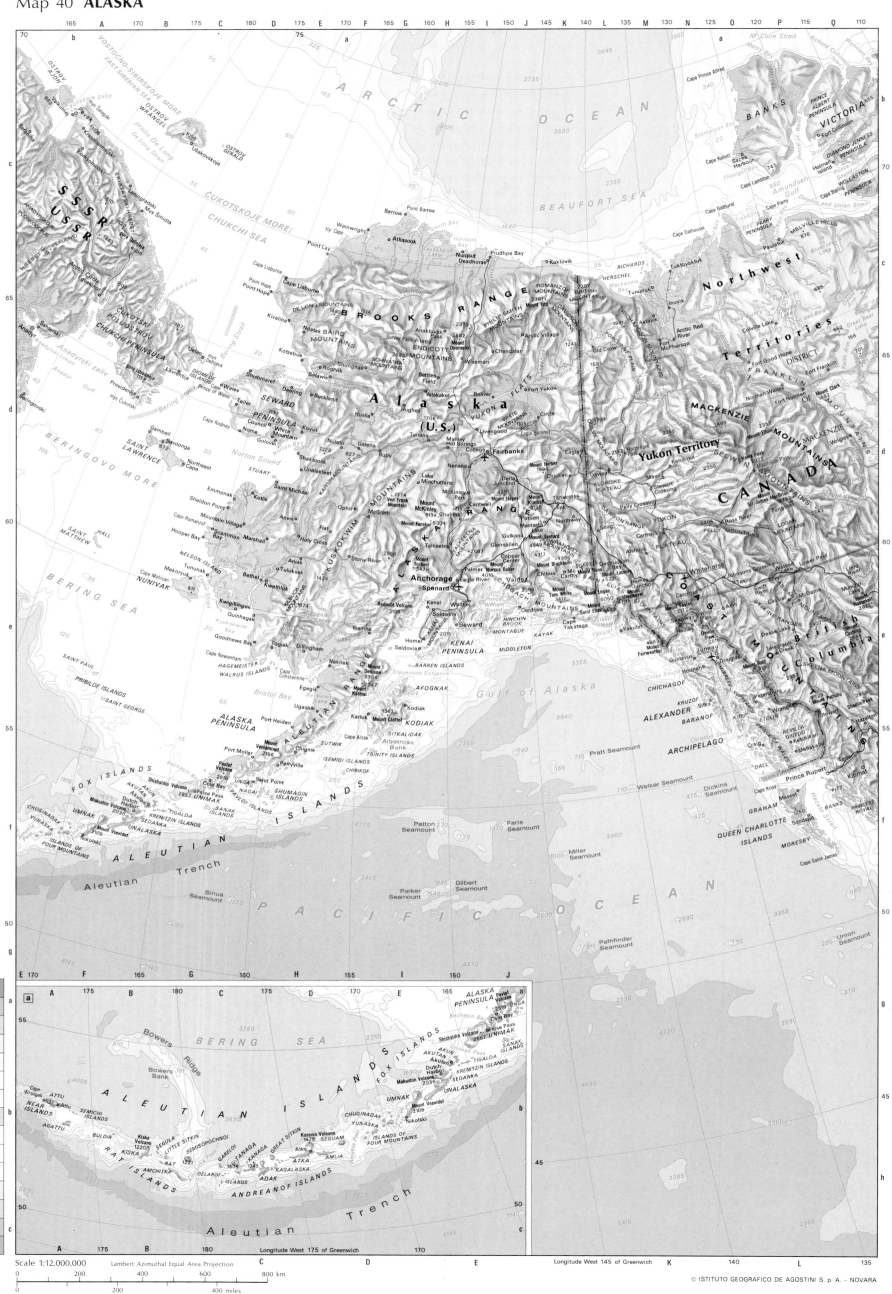

Scale 1:12,000,000   Lambert Azimuthal Equal Area Projection

© ISTITUTO GEOGRAFICO DE AGOSTINI S.p.A. - NOVARA

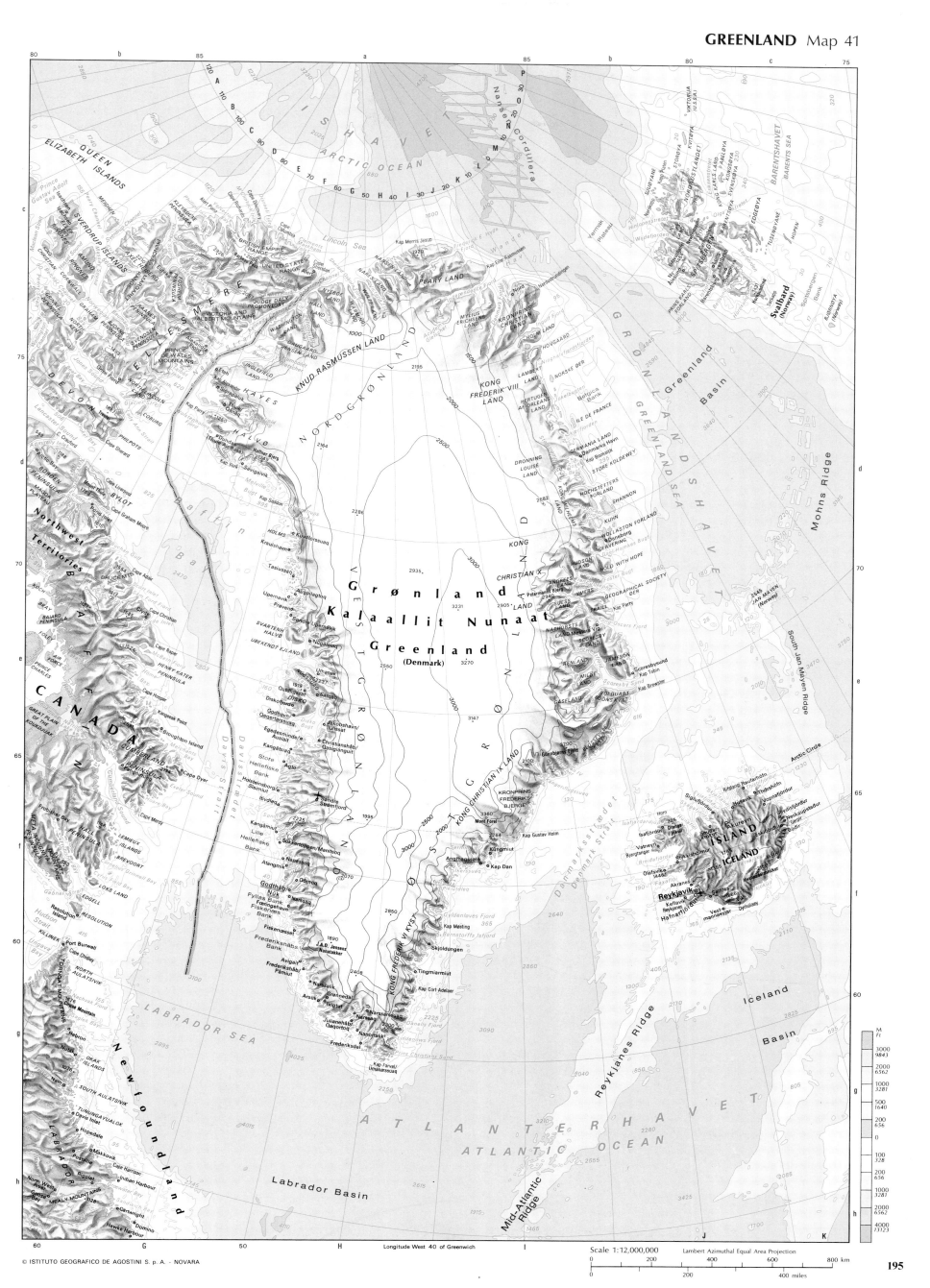

QUEEN ELIZABETH ISLANDS

SVERDRUP ISLANDS

ELLESMERE

DEVON

BYLOT

Northwest Territories

CANADA

BAFFIN

CUMBERLAND PENINSULA

HALL PENINSULA

Davis Strait

Baffin Bay

LABRADOR SEA

Newfoundland

LABRADOR

TORNGAT MOUNTAINS

Hudson Strait

Ungava Bay

ARCTIC OCEAN

IS HAVE

Nansen Cordillera

Lincoln Sea

PEARY LAND

KNUD RASMUSSEN LAND

HAYES HALVØ

NORDGRØNLAND

KONG FREDERIK VIII LAND

DRONNING LOUISE LAND

KONG WILHELMS LAND

KONG CHRISTIAN X LAND

Grønland
Kalaallit Nunaat
Greenland
(Denmark)

VESTGRØNLAND

INLANDSIS

ØSTGRØNLAND

Godthåb

Nûk

KONG FREDERIK VI KYST

KONG CHRISTIAN IX LAND

KRONPRINS FREDERIKS BJERGE

Mont Forel

Angmagssalik

Kap Farvel / Umanarssuaq

GRØNLANDSHAVET
GREENLAND SEA

Greenland Basin

Mohns Ridge

Svalbard (Norway)

BARENTSHAVET
BARENTS SEA

South Jan Mayen Ridge

Jan Mayen (Norway)

DANMARKSSTRÆDET
Denmark Strait

ISLAND
ICELAND

Reykjavík

Iceland Basin

Reykjanes Ridge

ATLANTERHAVET
ATLANTIC OCEAN

Labrador Basin

Mid-Atlantic Ridge

Arctic Circle

Scale 1:12,000,000   Lambert Azimuthal Equal Area Projection

0   200   400   600   800 km
0   200   400 miles

Longitude West 40 of Greenwich

M / Ft
3000 / 9843
2000 / 6562
1000 / 3281
500 / 1640
200 / 656
0
100 / 328
200 / 656
1000 / 3281
2000 / 6562
4000 / 13123

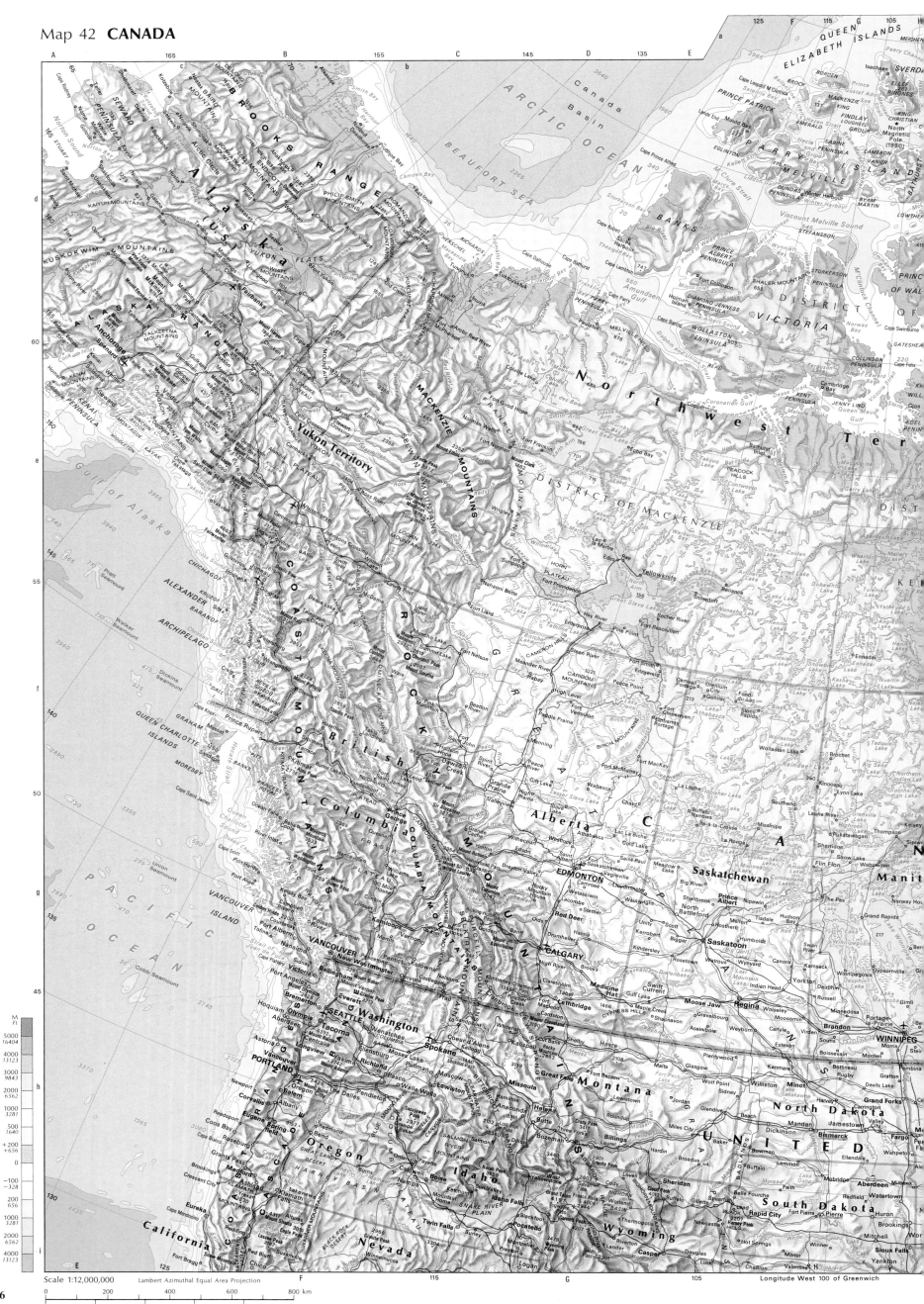

Map 42 **CANADA**

Scale 1:12,000,000   Lambert Azimuthal Equal Area Projection

Longitude West 100 of Greenwich

Map 43 **UNITED STATES**

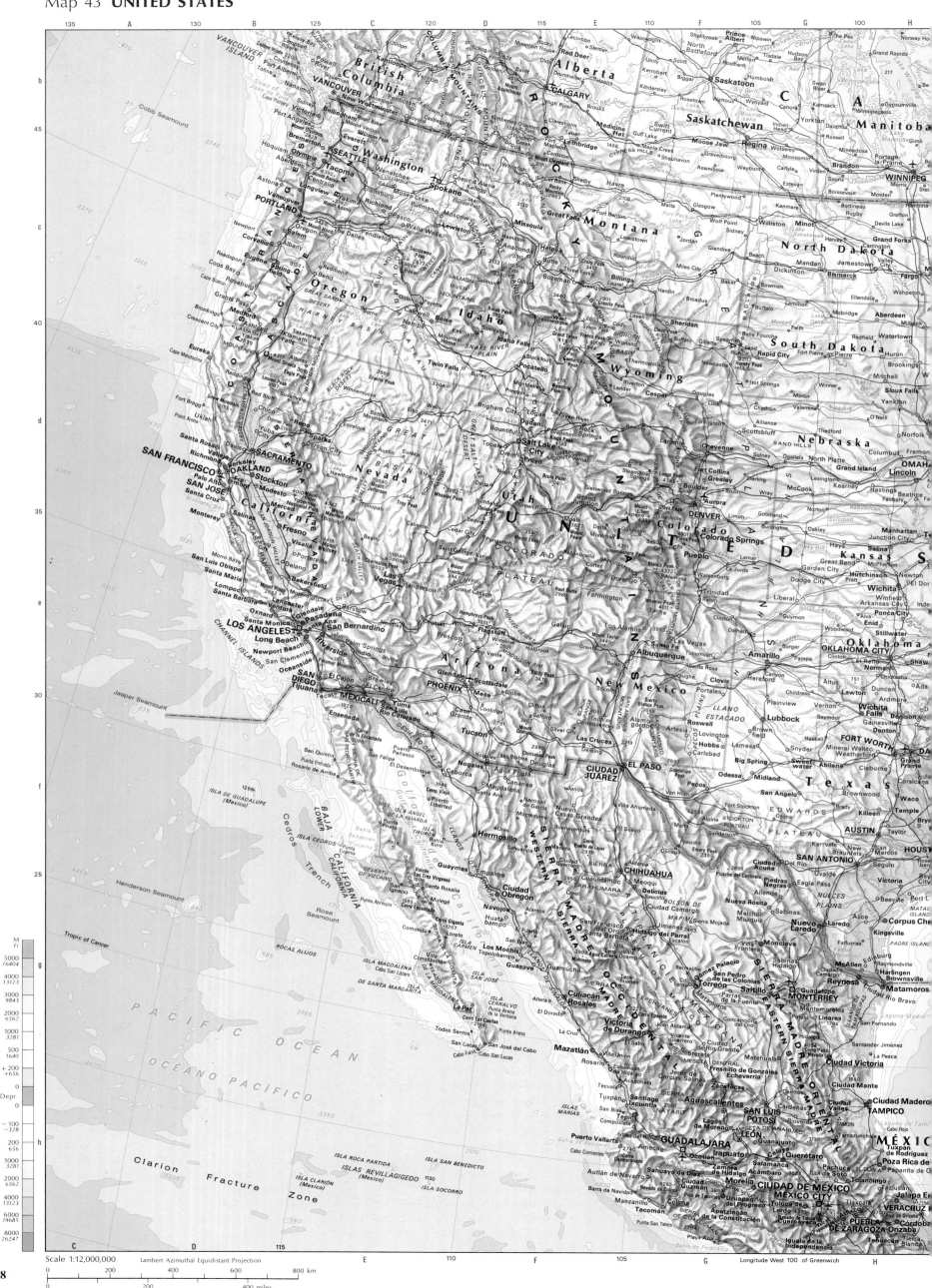

Scale 1:12,000,000
Lambert Azimuthal Equidistant Projection

Longitude West 100 of Greenwich

Map 44

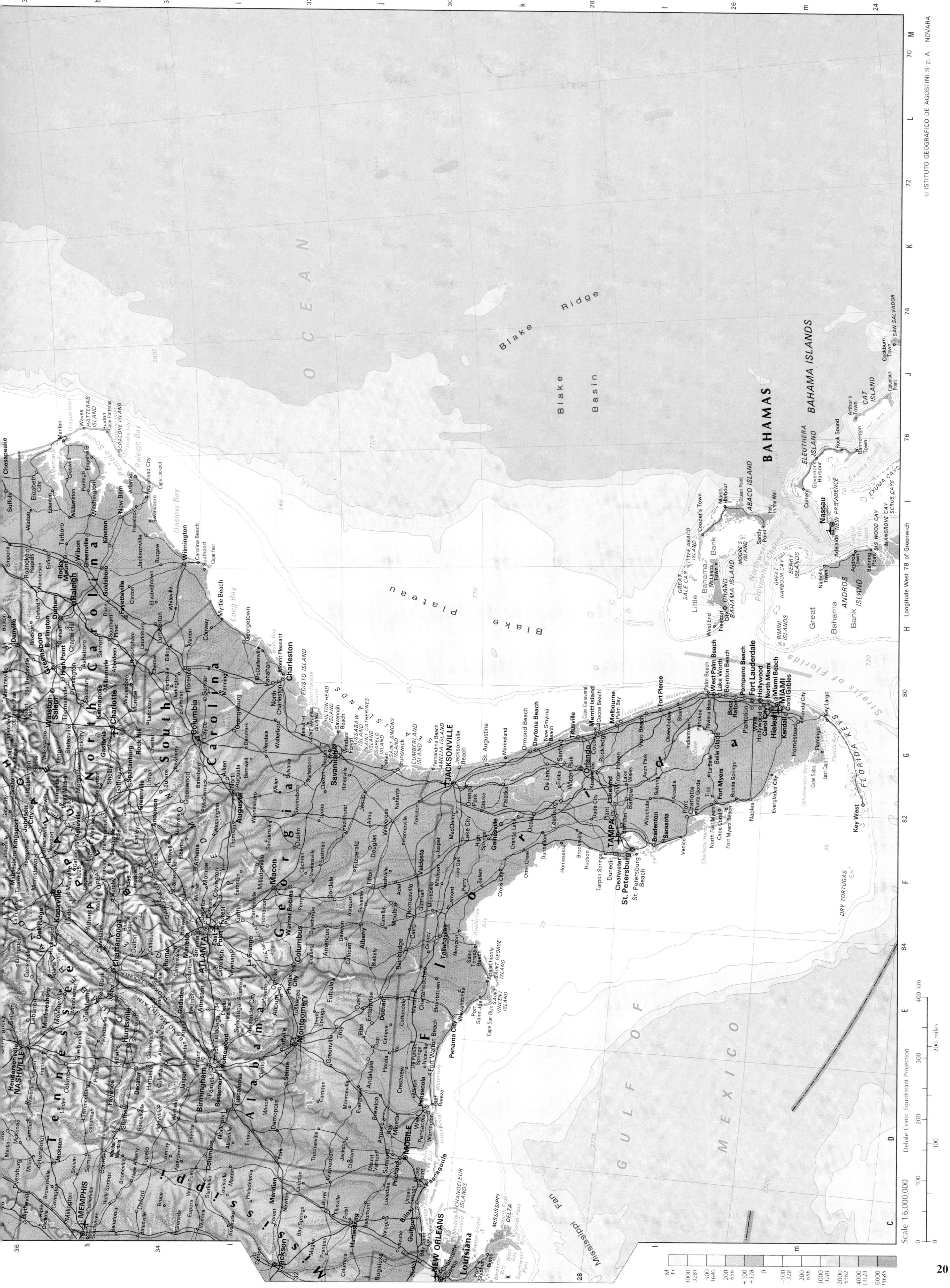

OCEAN

BAHAMAS

BAHAMA ISLANDS

Blake Ridge

Blake Basin

Blake Plateau

ELEUTHERA ISLAND

CAT ISLAND

SAN SALVADOR

ANDROS ISLAND

ABACO ISLAND

GRAND BAHAMA ISLAND

BERRY ISLANDS

BIMINI ISLANDS

Nassau

NEW PROVIDENCE

Straits of Florida

GULF OF MEXICO

MISSISSIPPI FAN

DRY TORTUGAS

FLORIDA KEYS

Key West

Miami

MIAMI

Fort Lauderdale

West Palm Beach

Pompano Beach

Boca Raton

Hialeah

Coral Gables

Hollywood

North Miami

Key Largo

Homestead

Naples

Fort Myers

Sarasota

Bradenton

St. Petersburg

TAMPA

Clearwater

Lakeland

Orlando

Winter Park

Daytona Beach

Ormond Beach

St. Augustine

JACKSONVILLE

Gainesville

Ocala

Tallahassee

Panama City

Pensacola

MOBILE

NEW ORLEANS

Gulfport

Biloxi

Jackson

MEMPHIS

NASHVILLE

Chattanooga

Knoxville

ATLANTA

Columbus

Macon

Warner Robins

Savannah

Augusta

Columbia

Charleston

Charlotte

Winston-Salem

Greensboro

Durham

Raleigh

Wilmington

Myrtle Beach

Greenville

Spartanburg

Asheville

Birmingham

Montgomery

Tuscaloosa

Huntsville

Tennessee

Alabama

Mississippi

Louisiana

Georgia

Florida

South Carolina

North Carolina

Chesapeake

Longitude West 78 of Greenwich

Delisle Conic Equidistant Projection

Scale 1:6,000,000

© ISTITUTO GEOGRAFICO DE AGOSTINI S.p.A. - NOVARA

201

Map 45

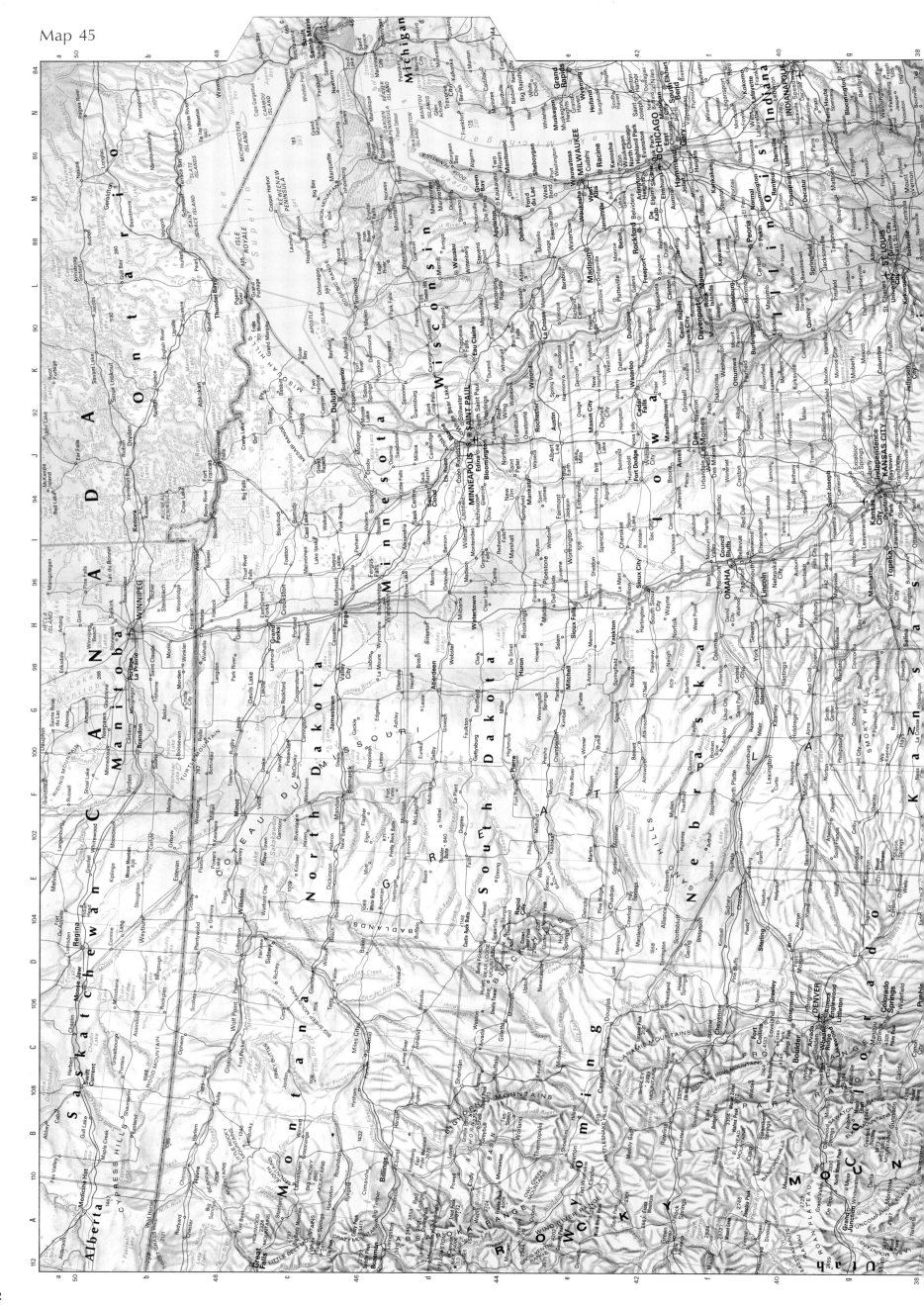

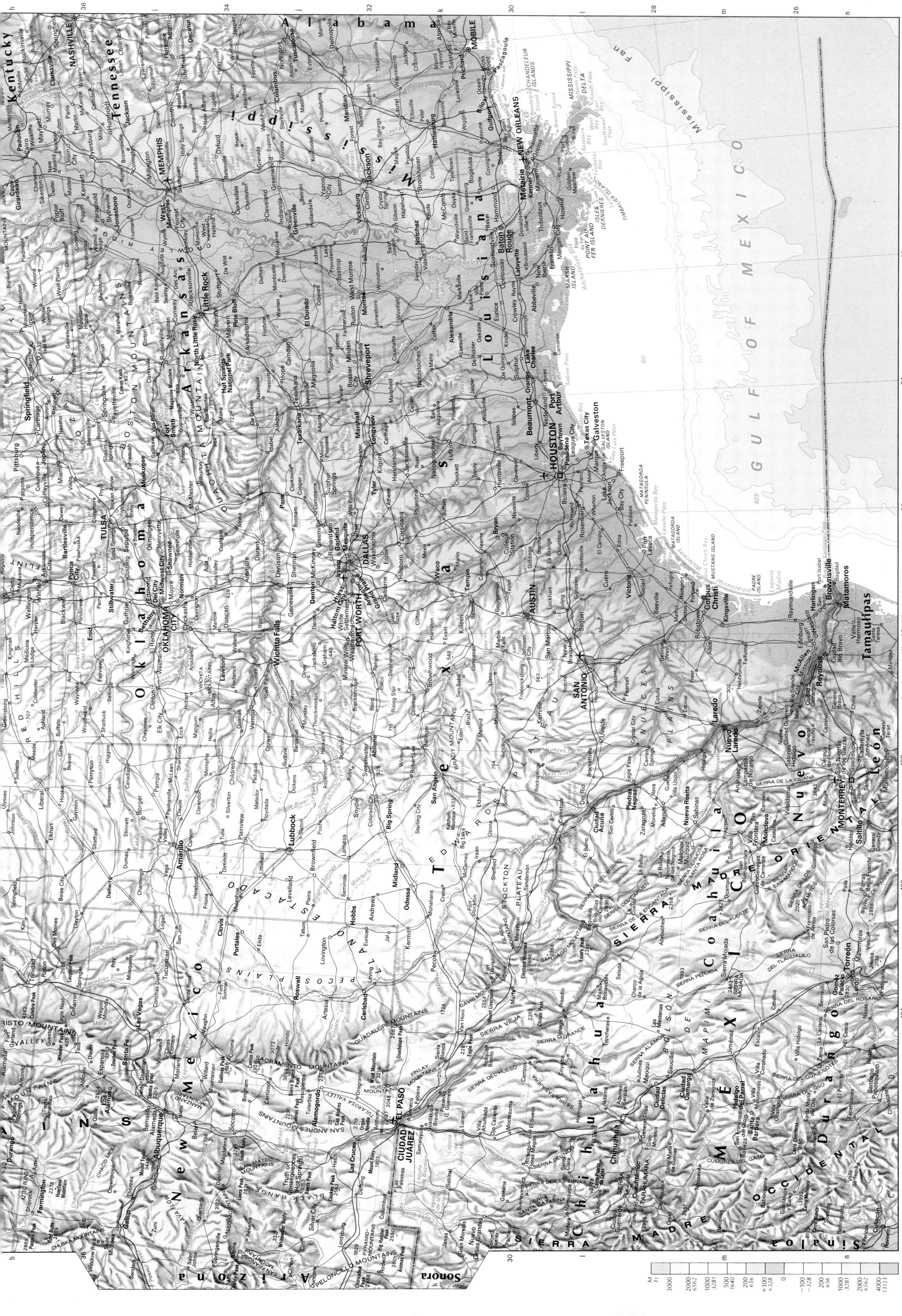

© ISTITUTO GEOGRAFICO DE AGOSTINI S. p. A. - NOVARA

GULF OF MEXICO

Kentucky
Tennessee
Alabama
Mississippi
Arkansas
Louisiana
Oklahoma
Texas
New Mexico
Sonora
Chihuahua
Coahuila
Nuevo León
Tamaulipas
Durango
Sinaloa

MEMPHIS
NASHVILLE
NEW ORLEANS
MOBILE
Baton Rouge
Shreveport
Little Rock
North Little Rock
Hot Springs National Park
Fort Smith
Springfield
TULSA
OKLAHOMA CITY
Wichita Falls
DALLAS
FORT WORTH
Denton
Waco
AUSTIN
HOUSTON
Beaumont
Port Arthur
Orange
Galveston
Corpus Christi
Brownsville
Matamoros
Laredo
Nuevo Laredo
SAN ANTONIO
Abilene
San Angelo
Lubbock
Amarillo
Big Spring
Midland
Odessa
Hobbs
Roswell
Carlsbad
EL PASO
CIUDAD JUÁREZ
Las Cruces
Alamogordo
Albuquerque
Santa Fe
MONTERREY
Saltillo
Torreón
Gómez Palacio
Reynosa

OUACHITA MOUNTAINS
BOSTON MOUNTAINS
OZARK
SIERRA MADRE ORIENTAL
SIERRA MADRE OCCIDENTAL
GUADALUPE MOUNTAINS
DAVIS MOUNTAINS
SACRAMENTO MOUNTAINS
SAN ANDRES MOUNTAINS
BRADY MOUNTAINS
EDWARDS PLATEAU
STOCKTON PLATEAU
LLANO ESTACADO
PECOS RIVER
RIO GRANDE
RED HILLS
BOLSÓN DE MAPIMÍ

Longitude West 98 of Greenwich
Delisle Conic Equidistant Projection
Scale 1:6,000,000

400 km
300
200
100
0

200 miles
100
0

Map 46 **WESTERN UNITED STATES**

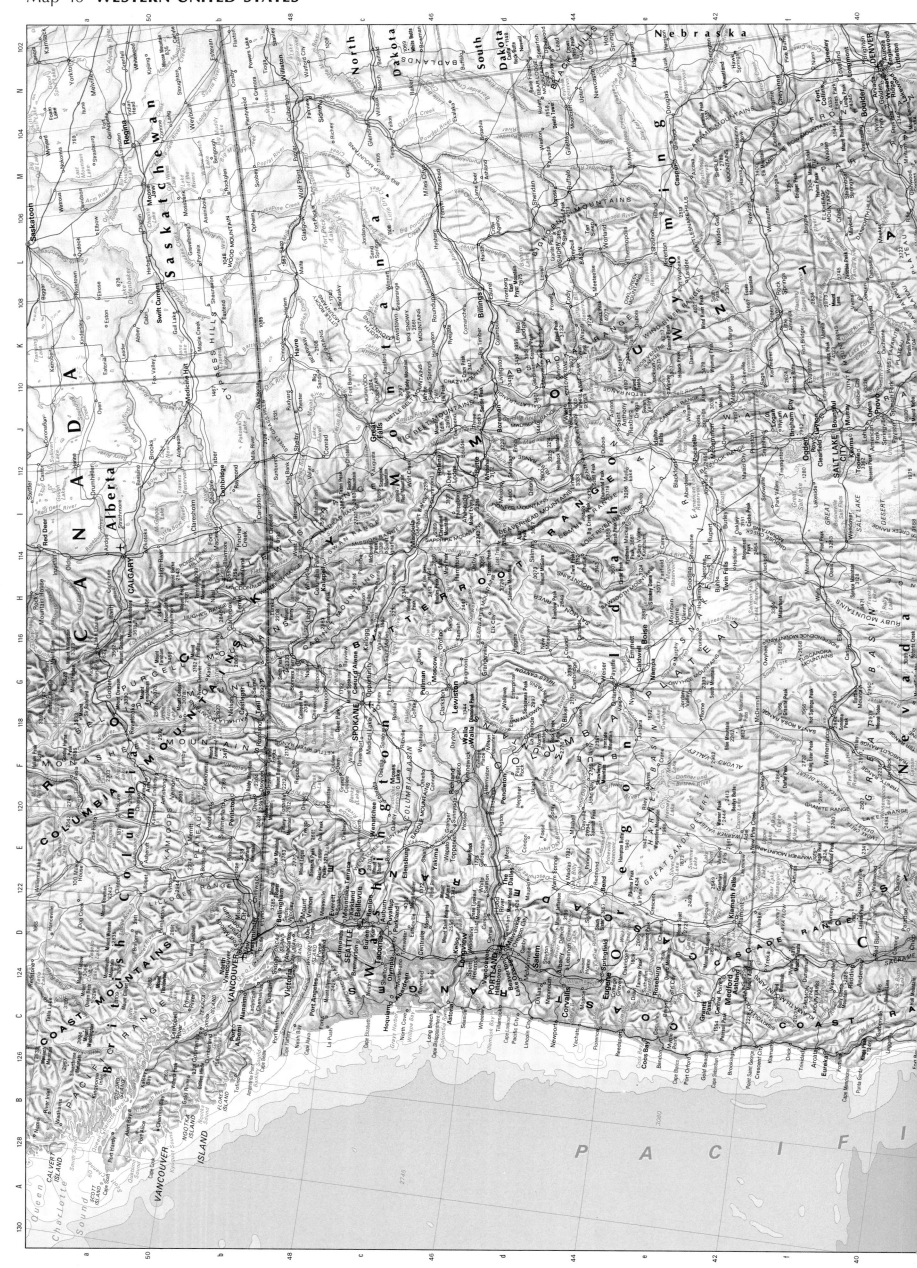

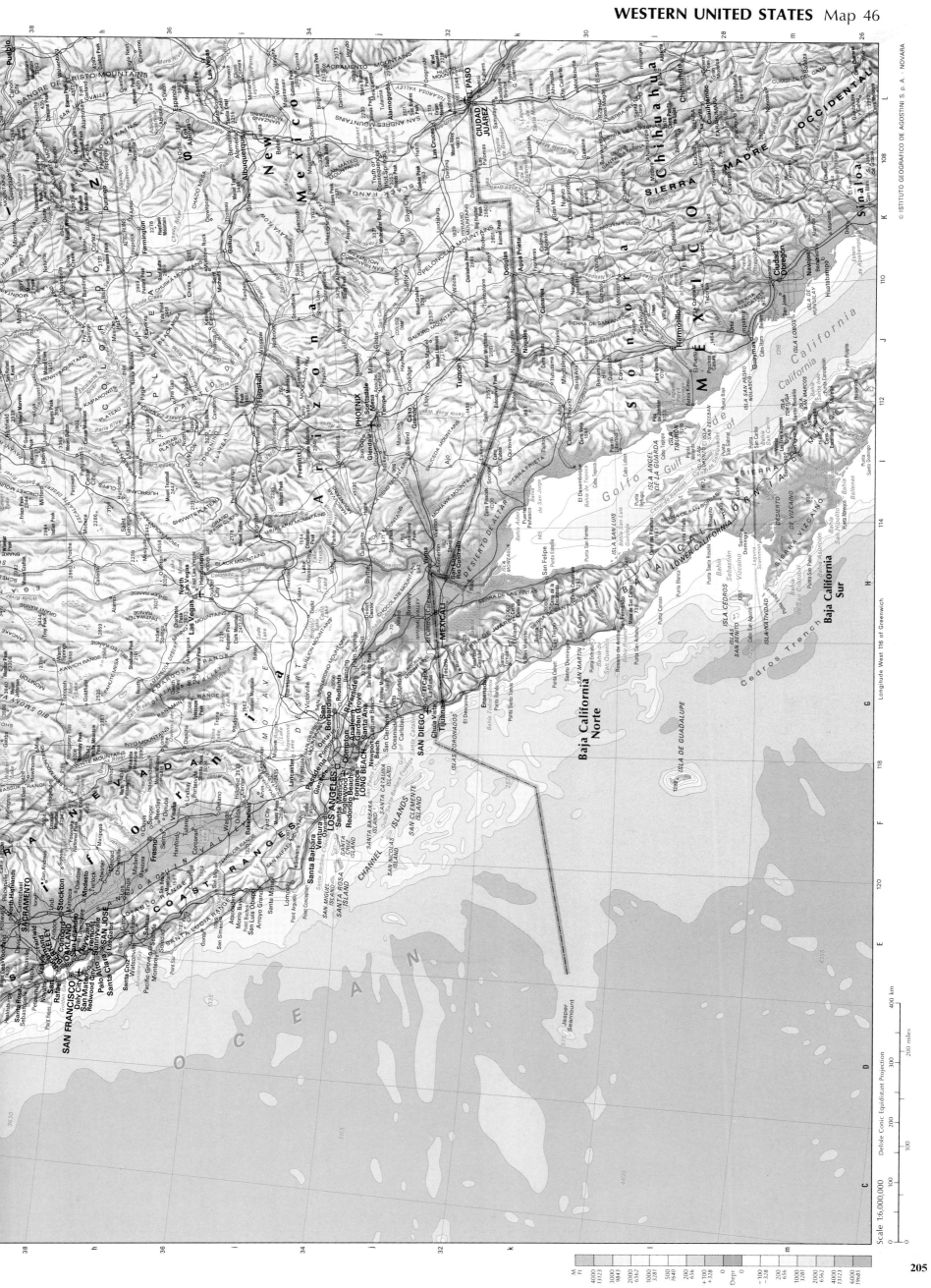

Scale 1:6,000,000

Delisle Conic Equidistant Projection

Longitude West 116 of Greenwich

Map 47 **MIDDLE AMERICA**

MÉXICO
ESTADOS
D.F. Distrito Federal
1 Aguascalientes
2 Baja California Norte
3 Baja California Sur
4 Campeche
5 Coahuila
6 Colima
7 Chiapas
8 Chihuahua
9 Durango
10 Guanajuato
11 Guerrero
12 Hidalgo
13 Jalisco
14 México
15 Michoacán
16 Morelos
17 Nayarit
18 Nuevo León
19 Oaxaca
20 Puebla
21 Querétaro
22 Quintana Roo
23 San Luis Potosí
24 Sinaloa
25 Sonora
26 Tabasco
27 Tamaulipas
28 Tlaxcala
29 Veracruz
30 Yucatan
31 Zacatecas

M
Ft
5000 16404
4000 13123
3000 9843
2000 6562
1000 3281
500 1640
+200 +656
0
Depr.
−100 −328
200 656
1000 3281
2000 6562
4000 13123
6000 19685
8000 26247

UNITED STATES
Kansas
Oklahoma
OKLAHOMA CITY
Missouri
Arkansas
MEMPHIS
Texas
New Mexico
Arizona
California
LOS ANGELES
SAN DIEGO
MEXICALI
Tijuana
PHOENIX
Tucson
El Paso
CIUDAD JUÁREZ
DALLAS
FORT WORTH
AUSTIN
SAN ANTONIO
HOUSTON
NEW ORLEANS
Mississippi
Louisiana
BATON ROUGE

BAJA CALIFORNIA
LOWER CALIFORNIA
Golfo de California
SIERRA MADRE OCCIDENTAL
SIERRA MADRE ORIENTAL
Hermosillo
Guaymas
Ciudad Obregón
Los Mochis
Culiacán
Mazatlán
CHIHUAHUA
Delicias
Torreón
Saltillo
MONTERREY
Nuevo Laredo
Matamoros
Reynosa
TAMPICO
Ciudad Victoria
Ciudad Madero
SAN LUIS POTOSÍ
GUADALAJARA
León
Querétaro
Morelia
CIUDAD DE MÉXICO
MEXICO CITY
D.F.
Toluca
Cuernavaca
PUEBLA DE ZARAGOZA
VERACRUZ LLAVE
Córdoba
Orizaba
Acapulco de Juárez
Chilpancingo
Oaxaca de Juárez
Coatzacoalcos
Minatitlán
Villahermosa
Tuxtla Gutiérrez
San Cristóbal de las Casas
MÉRIDA
Campeche
PENÍNSULA DE YUCATÁN
GUATEMALA
SAN SALVADOR

Gulf of Mexico/Golfo
Mexico Basin
Campeche Bay
Middle America Trench
OCÉANO PACÍFICO
PACIFIC OCEAN
Albatross Plateau
Guatemala Basin
Equator

Scale 1:12,000,000
Lambert Azimuthal Equal Area Projection
0 200 400 600 800 km
0 200 400 miles
Longitude West 90 of Greenwich

206

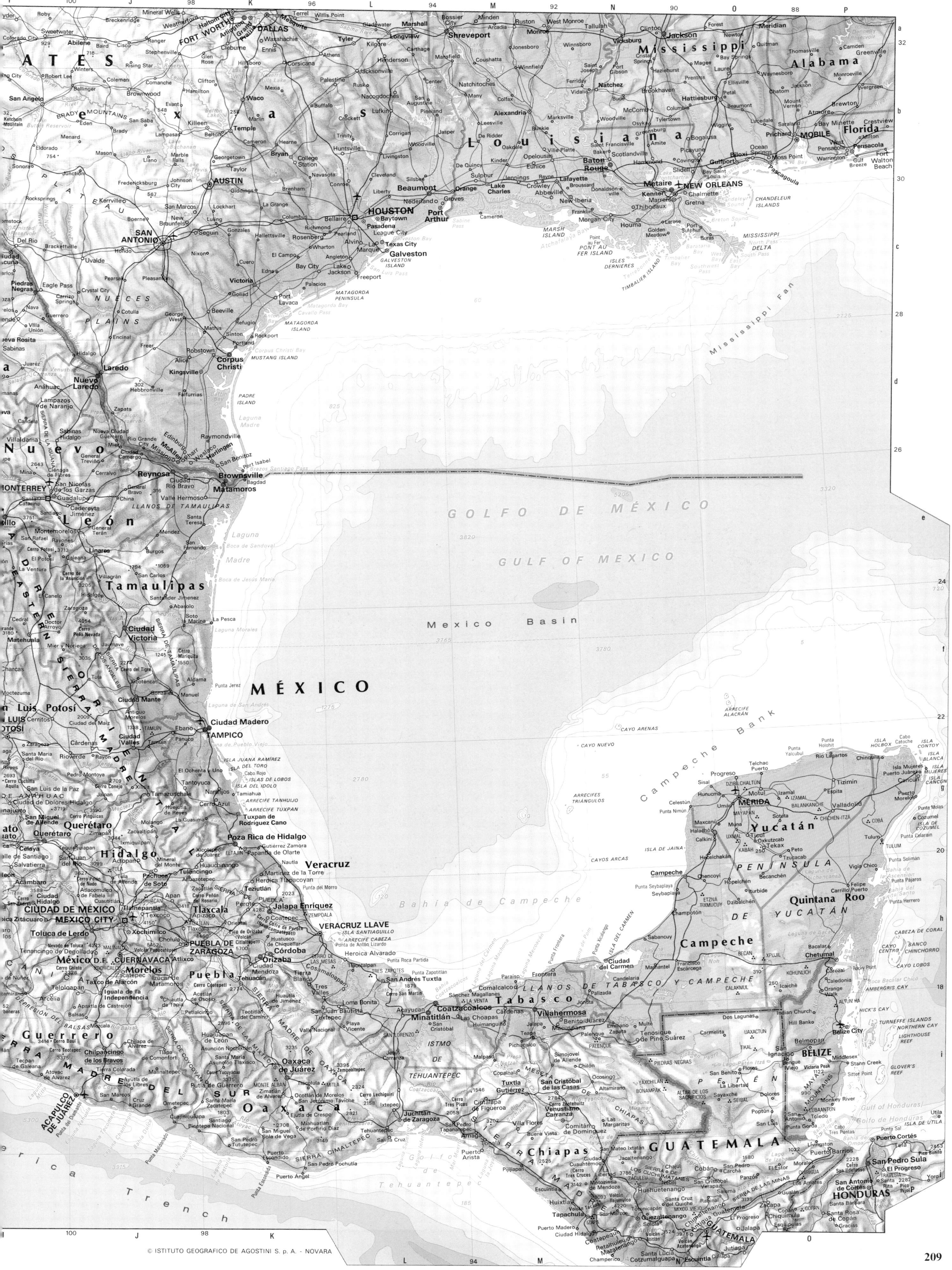

GOLFO DE MÉXICO

GULF OF MEXICO

Mexico Basin

MÉXICO

UNITED STATES

Texas

Louisiana

Mississippi

Alabama

Florida

Nuevo León

Tamaulipas

San Luis Potosí

Hidalgo

Querétaro

Ciudad de México / MEXICO CITY

Morelos

Puebla

Guerrero

Oaxaca

Veracruz

Tabasco

Chiapas

Campeche

Quintana Roo

Yucatán

PENÍNSULA DE YUCATÁN

Campeche Bank

Bahía de Campeche

GUATEMALA

HONDURAS

BELIZE

FORT WORTH, DALLAS, AUSTIN, SAN ANTONIO, HOUSTON, Galveston, Corpus Christi, Laredo, Nuevo Laredo, Brownsville, Matamoros, Reynosa, MONTERREY, Ciudad Victoria, TAMPICO, Ciudad Madero, Veracruz, Poza Rica de Hidalgo, Jalapa Enríquez, Orizaba, Córdoba, Tlaxcala, PUEBLA DE ZARAGOZA, CUERNAVACA, Toluca de Lerdo, Querétaro, San Luis Potosí, Ciudad Valles, Coatzacoalcos, Minatitlán, Villahermosa, Oaxaca de Juárez, Acapulco de Juárez, Chilpancingo de los Bravos, Tuxtla Gutiérrez, San Cristóbal de las Casas, Tapachula, Campeche, Ciudad del Carmen, Chetumal, MÉRIDA, Cancún, Valladolid, Belize City, Puerto Barrios, Puerto Cortés, San Pedro Sula

Shreveport, Baton Rouge, New Orleans, Mobile, Pensacola, Jackson

SIERRA MADRE ORIENTAL
SIERRA MADRE DEL SUR
ISTMO DE TEHUANTEPEC
Golfo de Tehuantepec
LLANOS DE TABASCO Y CAMPECHE
Laguna Madre
Padre Island

Map 49 **CENTRAL AMERICA AND WESTERN CARIBBEAN**

Scale 1:6,000,000   Delisle Conic Equidistant Projection

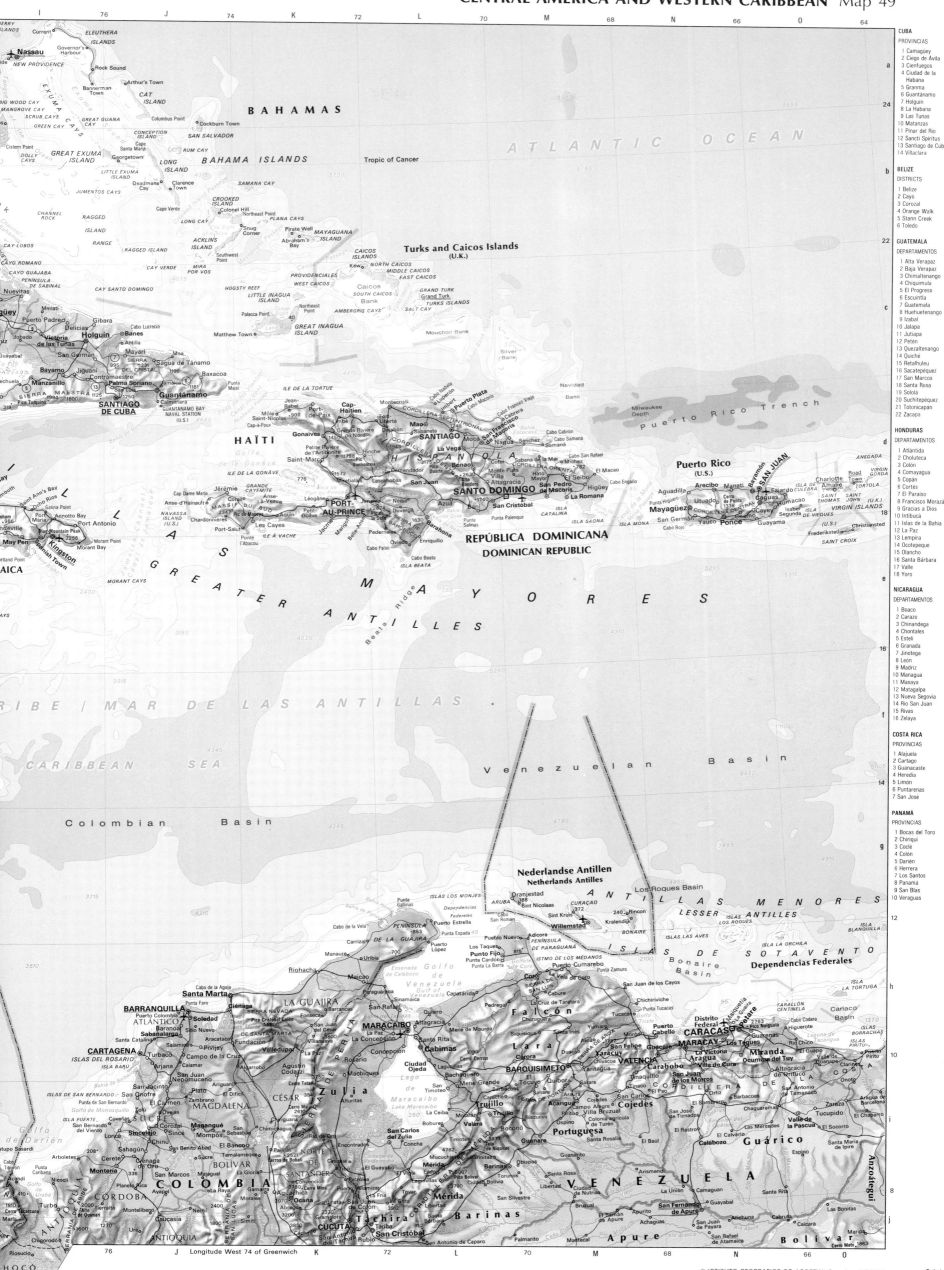

Map 50 **EASTERN CARIBBEAN**

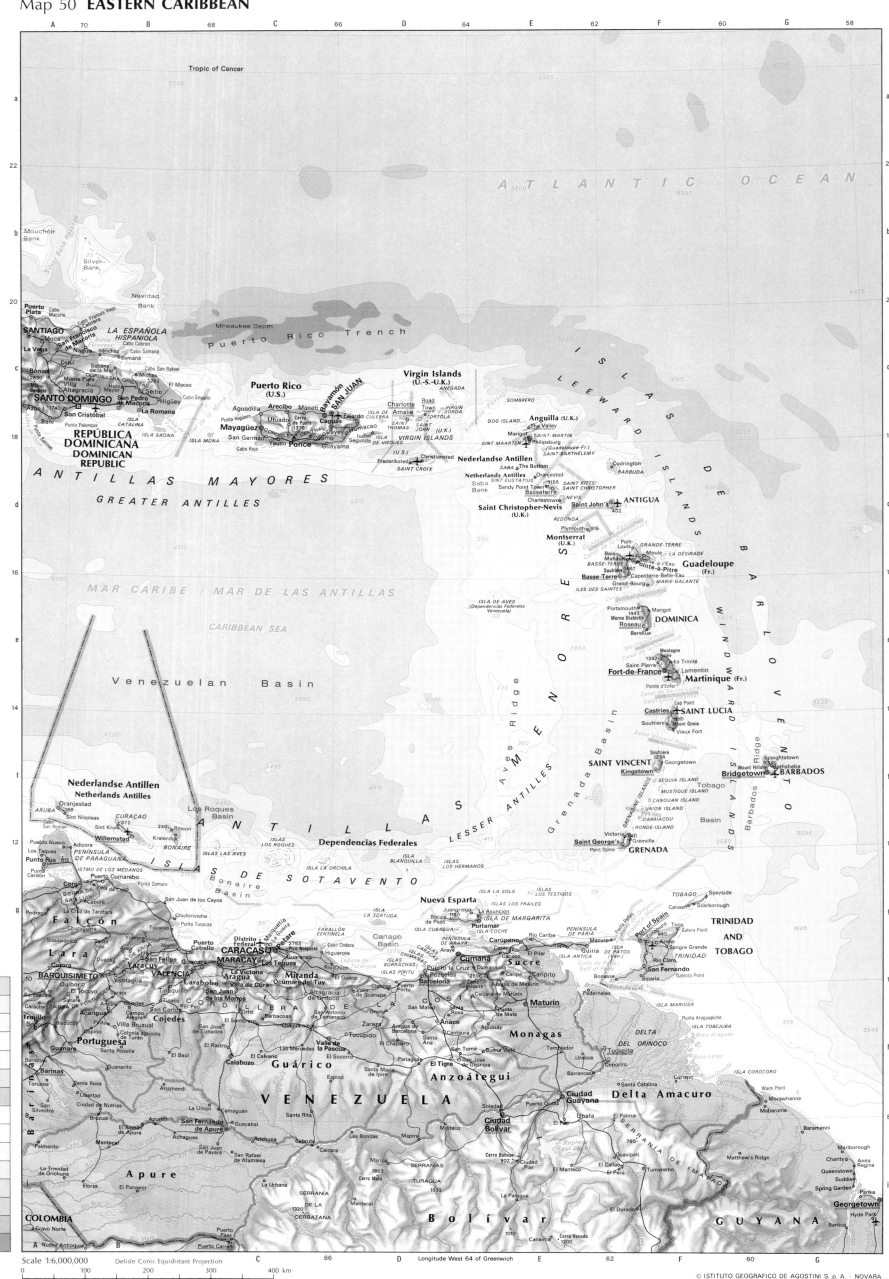

Scale 1:6,000,000

Delisle Conic Equidistant Projection

Longitude West 64 of Greenwich

© ISTITUTO GEOGRAFICO DE AGOSTINI S. p. A. - NOVARA

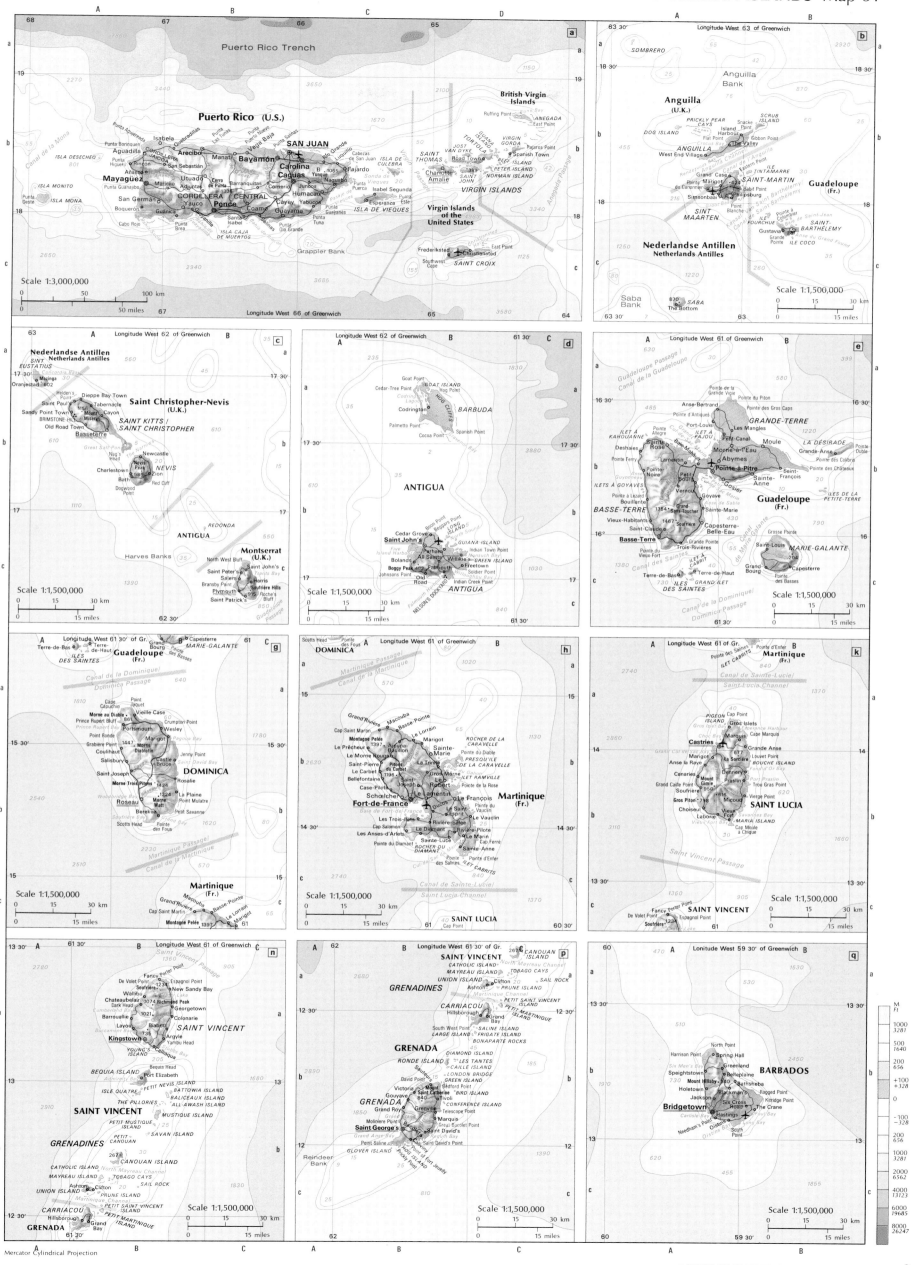

Map 52

SOUTH AMERICA, PHYSICAL

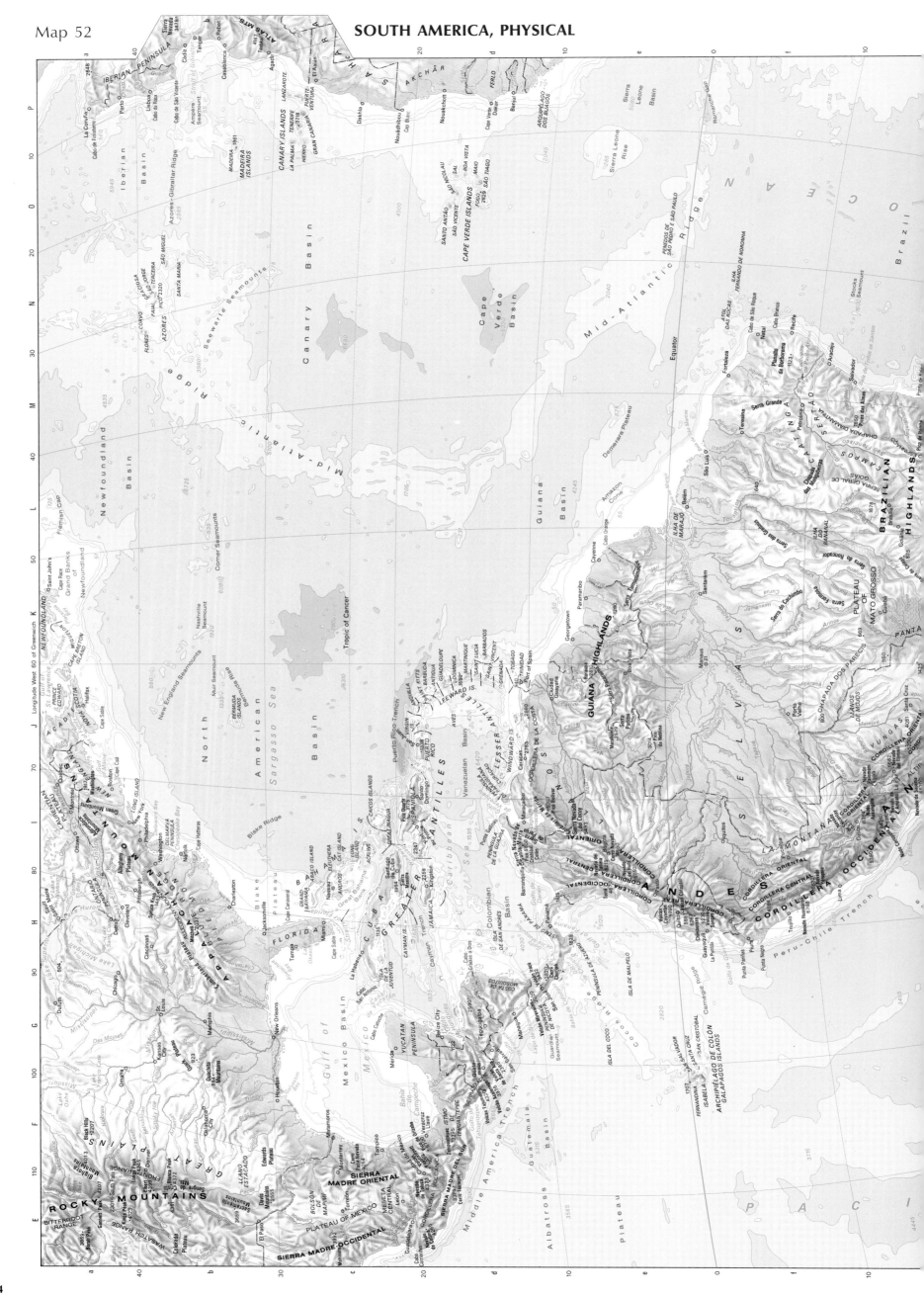

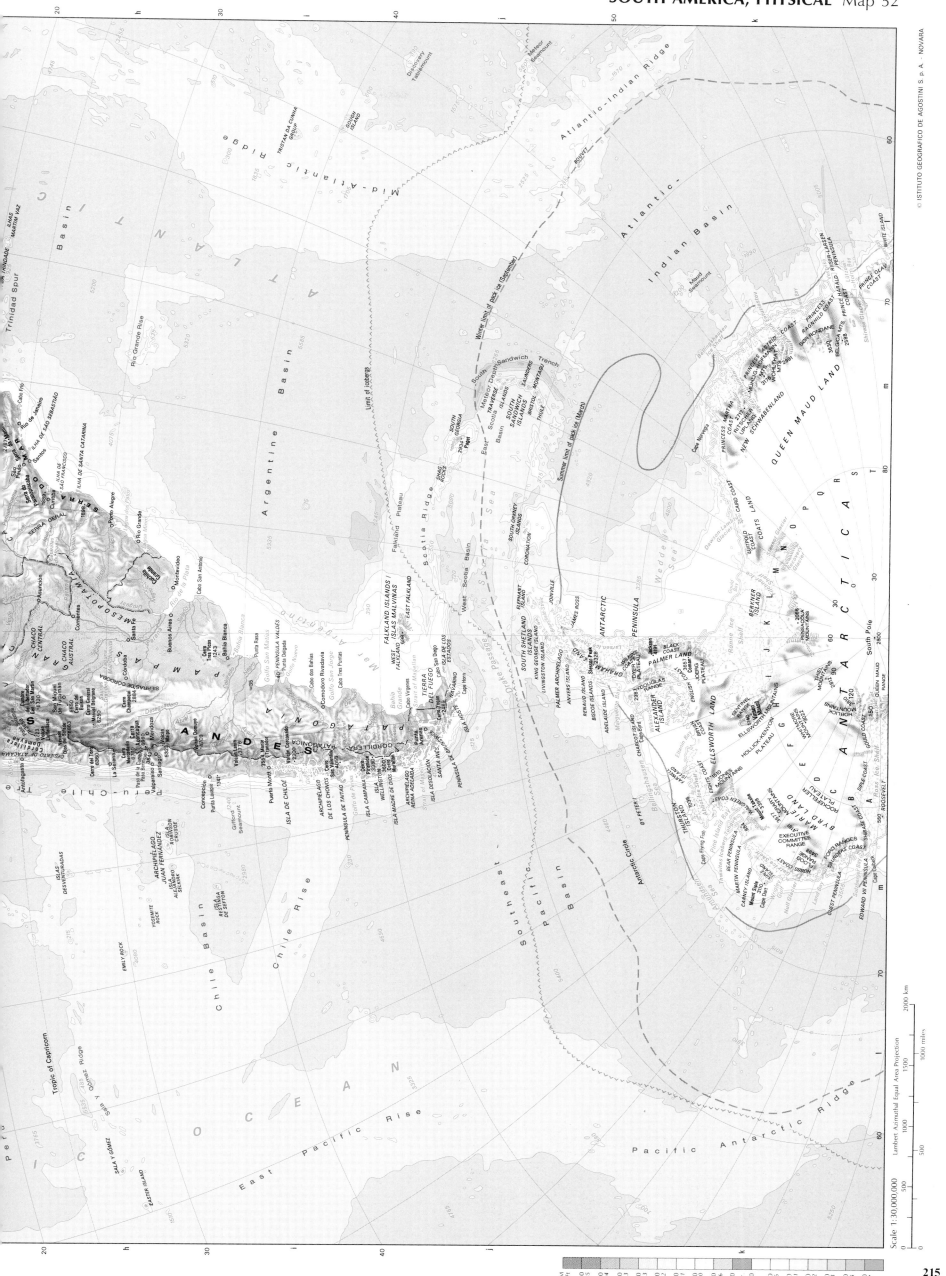

Scale 1:30,000,000

Lambert Azimuthal Equal Area Projection

M Ft		
6000 19685		
5000 16404		
4000 13123		
3000 9843		
2000 6562		
1000 3281		
500 1640		
+200 +656		
Depth 0		
-200 -656		
1000 3281		
2000 6562		
4000 13123		
6000 19685		
8000 26247		

Map 53

SOUTH AMERICA, POLITICAL

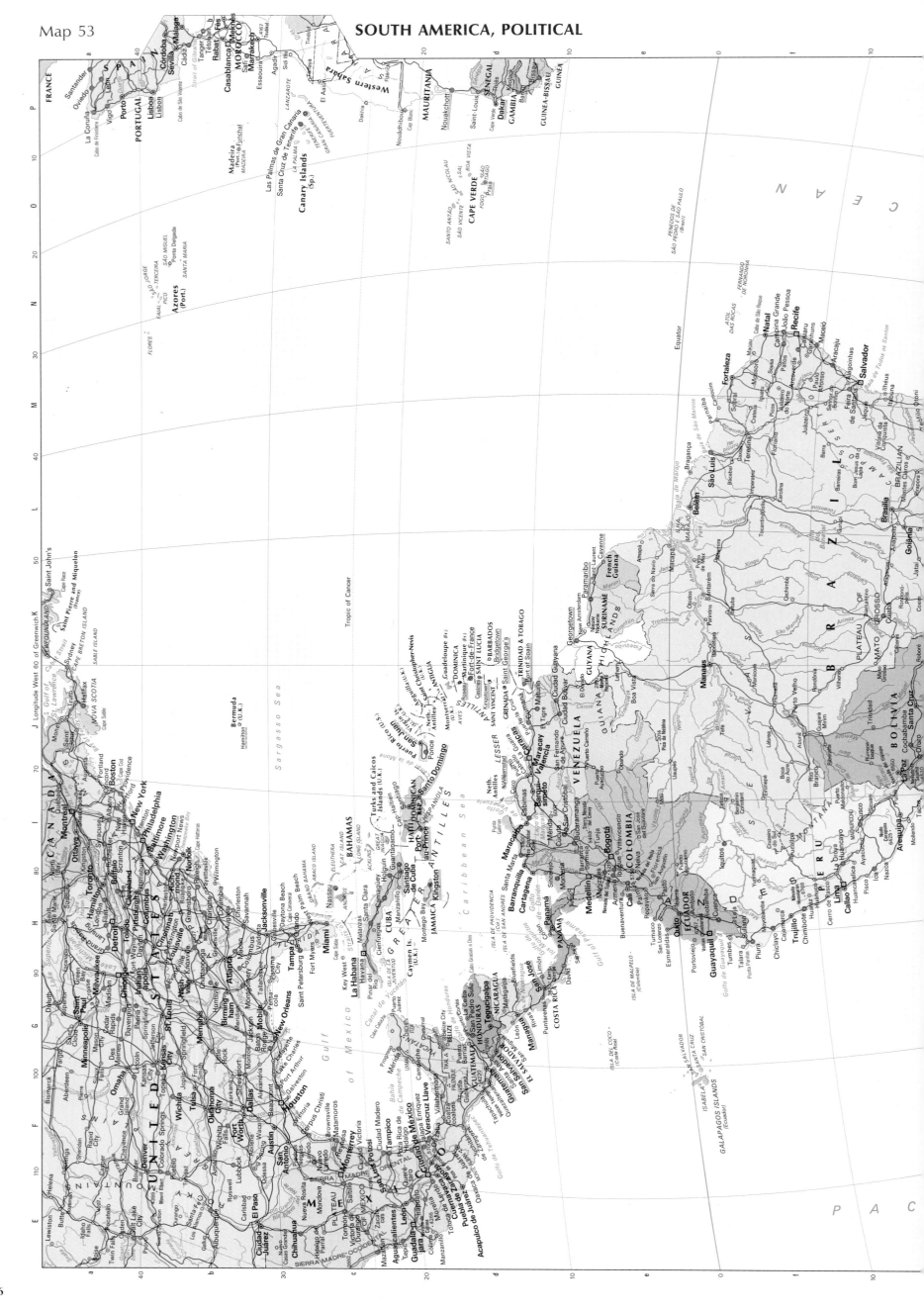

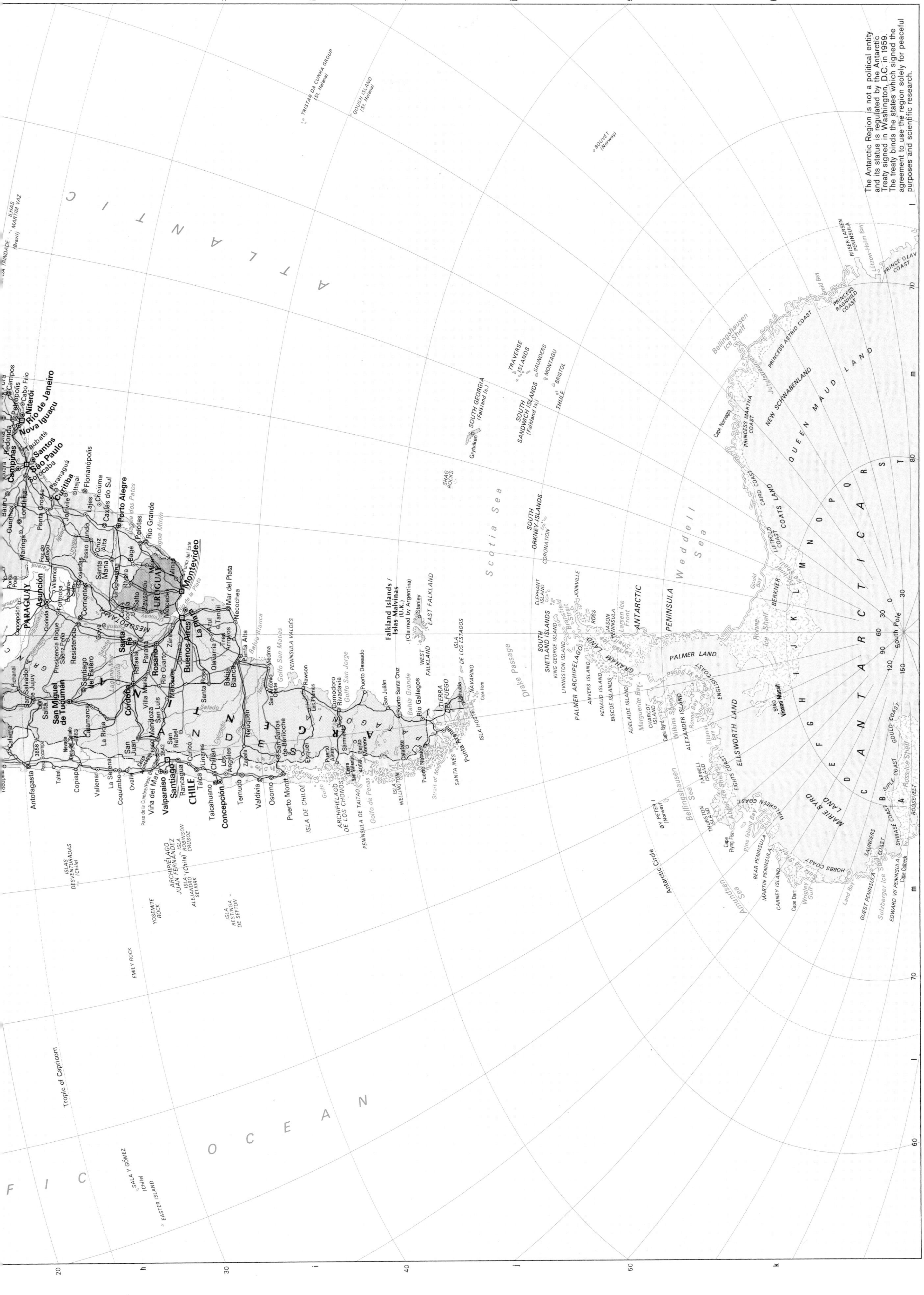

© ISTITUTO GEOGRAFICO DE AGOSTINI S. p. A. - NOVARA

The Antarctic Region is not a political entity
and its status is regulated by the Antarctic
Treaty signed in Washington, D.C. in 1959.
The treaty binds the states which signed the
agreement to use the region solely for peaceful
purposes and scientific research.

ATLANTIC

TRISTAN DA CUNHA GROUP
(St. Helena)

GOUGH ISLAND
(St. Helena)

BOUVET
(Norway)

ILHAS MARTIM VAZ (Brazil)

ILHA TRINDADE (Brazil)

Cabo Frio
Campos
Petrópolis
Rio de Janeiro
Niterói
Nova Iguaçu
Santos
São Paulo
Campinas
Curitiba
Florianópolis
Porto Alegre
Caxias do Sul
Rio Grande
Pelotas
Bagé

PARAGUAY
Asunción

URUGUAY
Montevideo
Mar del Plata
Necochea

Santiago del Estero
San Miguel de Tucumán
Salta
Catamarca
La Rioja
San Juan
Mendoza
San Luis
San Rafael
Córdoba
Rosario
Santa Fe
Paraná
Buenos Aires
La Plata
Bahía Blanca

CHILE
Valparaíso
Santiago
Rancagua
Talca
Chillán
Concepción
Talcahuano
Temuco
Valdivia
Osorno
Puerto Montt

ARCHIPIÉLAGO JUAN FERNÁNDEZ
ISLA (Chile) ROBINSON CRUSOE
ISLA ALEJANDRO SELKIRK

ISLAS DESVENTURADAS
ISLA (Chile)

EASTER ISLAND
SALA Y GÓMEZ (Chile)

YOSEMITE ROCK
EMILY ROCK

ISLA RESTINGA DE SEFTON

Antofagasta
Copiapó
Vallenar
Coquimbo
Ovalle

ISLA DE CHILOÉ
ARCHIPIÉLAGO DE LOS CHONOS
PENÍNSULA DE TAITAO
GOLFO DE PENAS
WELLINGTON I.

Comodoro Rivadavia
Puerto Deseado
Puerto Santa Cruz
Río Gallegos

TIERRA DEL FUEGO
Río Grande
Punta Arenas
Ushuaia
Cape Horn
ISLA DE LOS ESTADOS
ISLA NAVARINO
ISLA HOSTE
SANTA INÉS
Strait of Magellan

PENÍNSULA VALDÉS
GOLFO SAN MATIAS
GOLFO SAN JORGE

Falkland Islands /
Islas Malvinas
(U.K.)
(Claimed by Argentina)
Stanley
WEST FALKLAND
EAST FALKLAND

SHAG ROCKS

SOUTH GEORGIA
(Falkland Is.)
Grytviken

TRAVERSE ISLANDS
SAUNDERS
MONTAGU
BRISTOL
THULE
SOUTH SANDWICH ISLANDS
(Falkland Is.)

Scotia Sea

SOUTH ORKNEY ISLANDS
CORONATION

Drake Passage

SOUTH SHETLAND ISLANDS
KING GEORGE ISLAND
LIVINGSTON ISLAND
ELEPHANT ISLAND
PALMER ARCHIPELAGO
ANVERS ISLAND
RENAUD ISLAND
BISCOE ISLANDS
ADELAIDE ISLAND
ALEXANDER ISLAND
CHARCOT ISLAND

JOINVILLE
ROSS
GRAHAM LAND
PALMER LAND
ANTARCTIC PENINSULA
Larsen Ice Front
Larsen Ice Shelf

Weddell Sea
Ronne Ice Shelf
Filchner Ice Shelf
BERKNER
LUITPOLD COAST
COATS LAND
CAIRD COAST

RIISER-LARSEN PENINSULA
PRINCESS RAGNHILD COAST
PRINCESS ASTRID COAST
PRINCE OLAV COAST
QUEEN MAUD LAND
NEW SCHWABENLAND
PRINCESS MARTHA COAST
Lützow-Holm Bay

Bellingshausen Ice Shelf

ANTARCTICA
South Pole

ELLSWORTH LAND
Vinson Massif
SIPLE COAST
GOULD COAST

MARIE BYRD LAND

Ross Ice Shelf
ROOSEVELT
Ross Sea

Bellingshausen Sea
THURSTON ISLAND
PETER I (Norway)
BEAR PENINSULA
MARTIN PENINSULA
CARNEY ISLAND
GUEST PENINSULA
EDWARD VII PENINSULA
Sulzberger Ice Shelf

Amundsen Sea
Cape Dart
Cape Colbeck

HOBBS COAST
WALGREEN COAST
EIGHTS COAST
FARWELL COAST
BRYAN COAST
ENGLISH COAST

Antarctic Circle

Tropic of Capricorn

PACIFIC OCEAN

ATLANTIC OCEAN

Scale 1:30.000.000

Lambert Azimuthal Equal Area Projection

0   500   1000   1500   2000 km
0   500   1000 miles

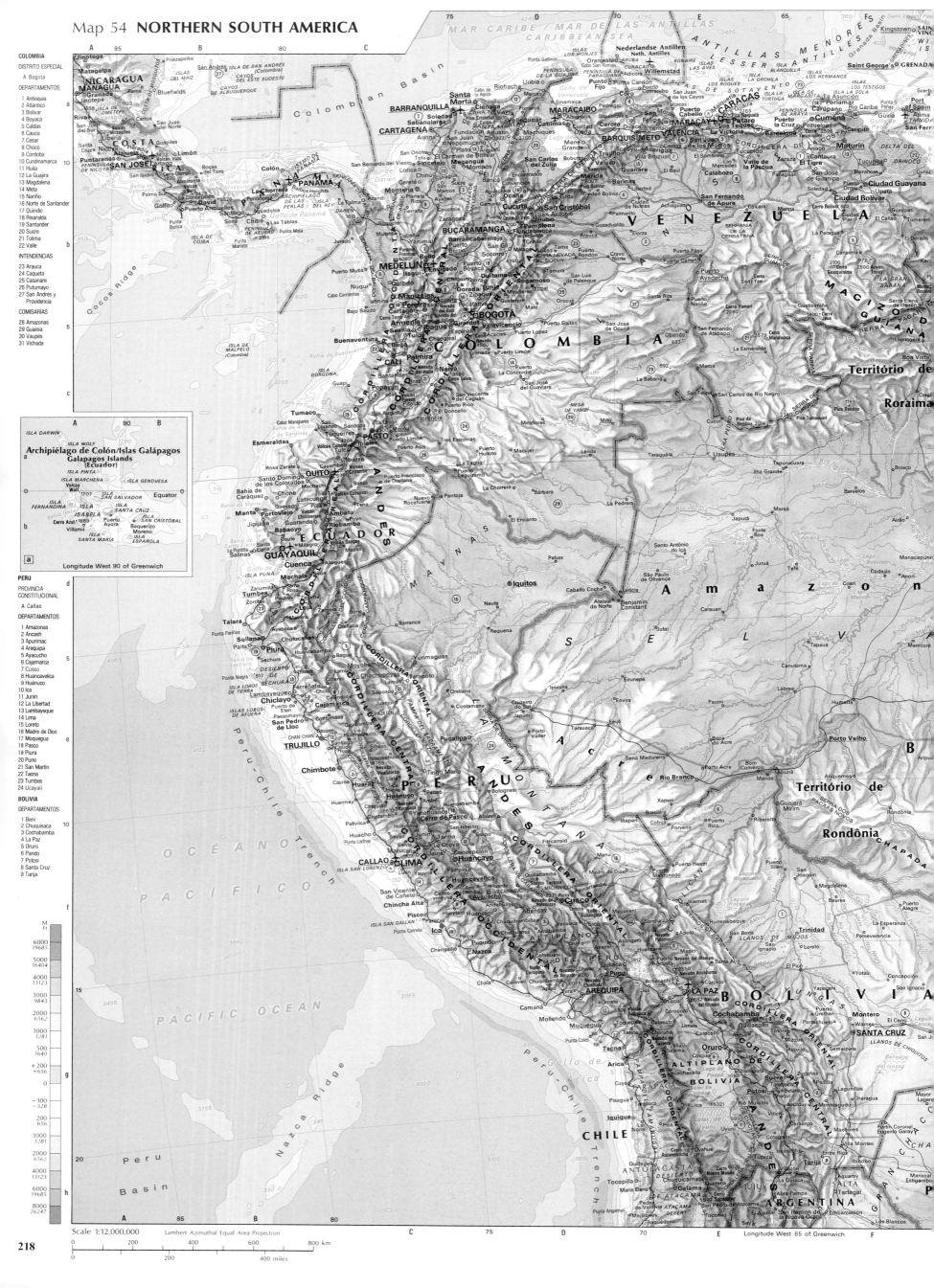

Map 55 **EAST-CENTRAL SOUTH AMERICA**

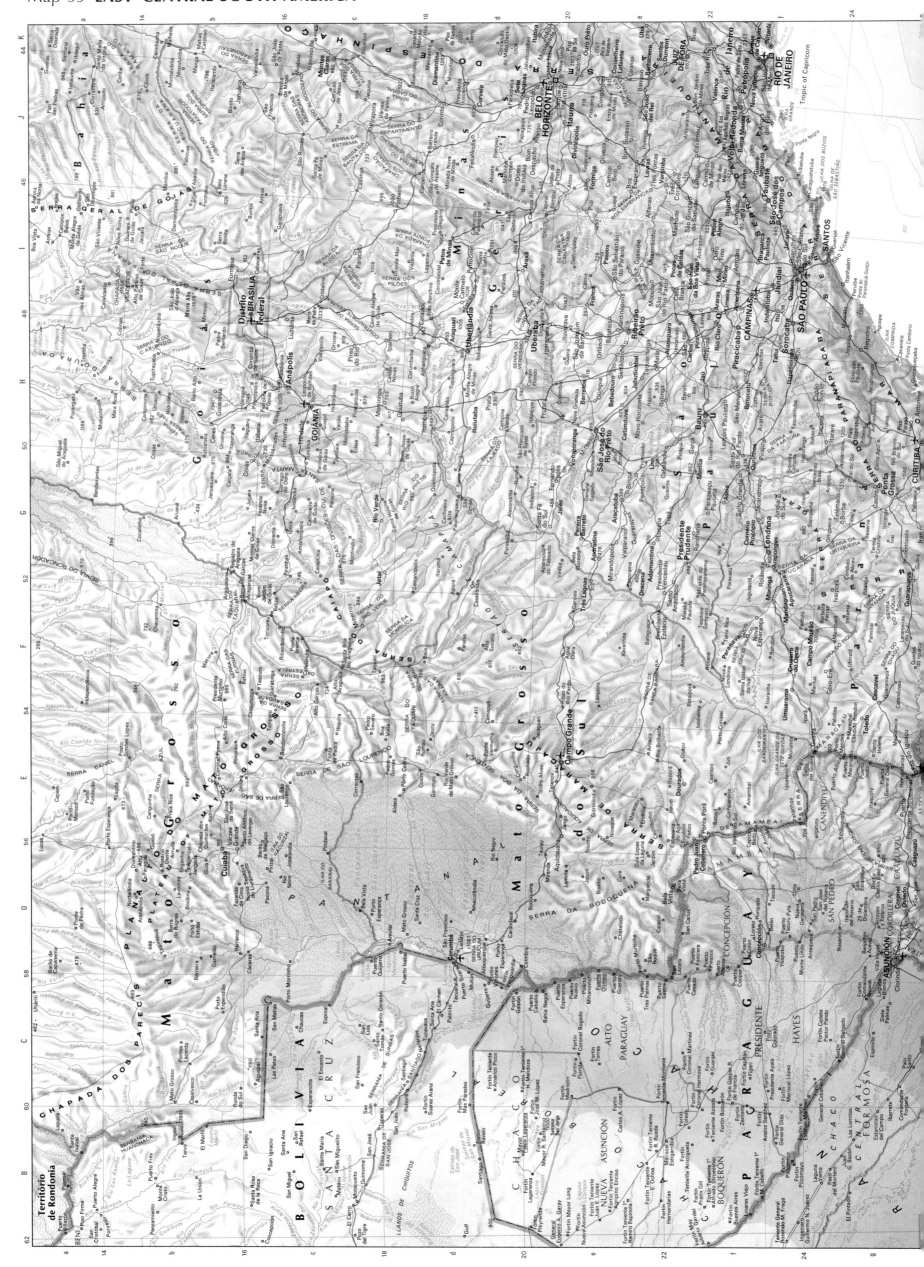

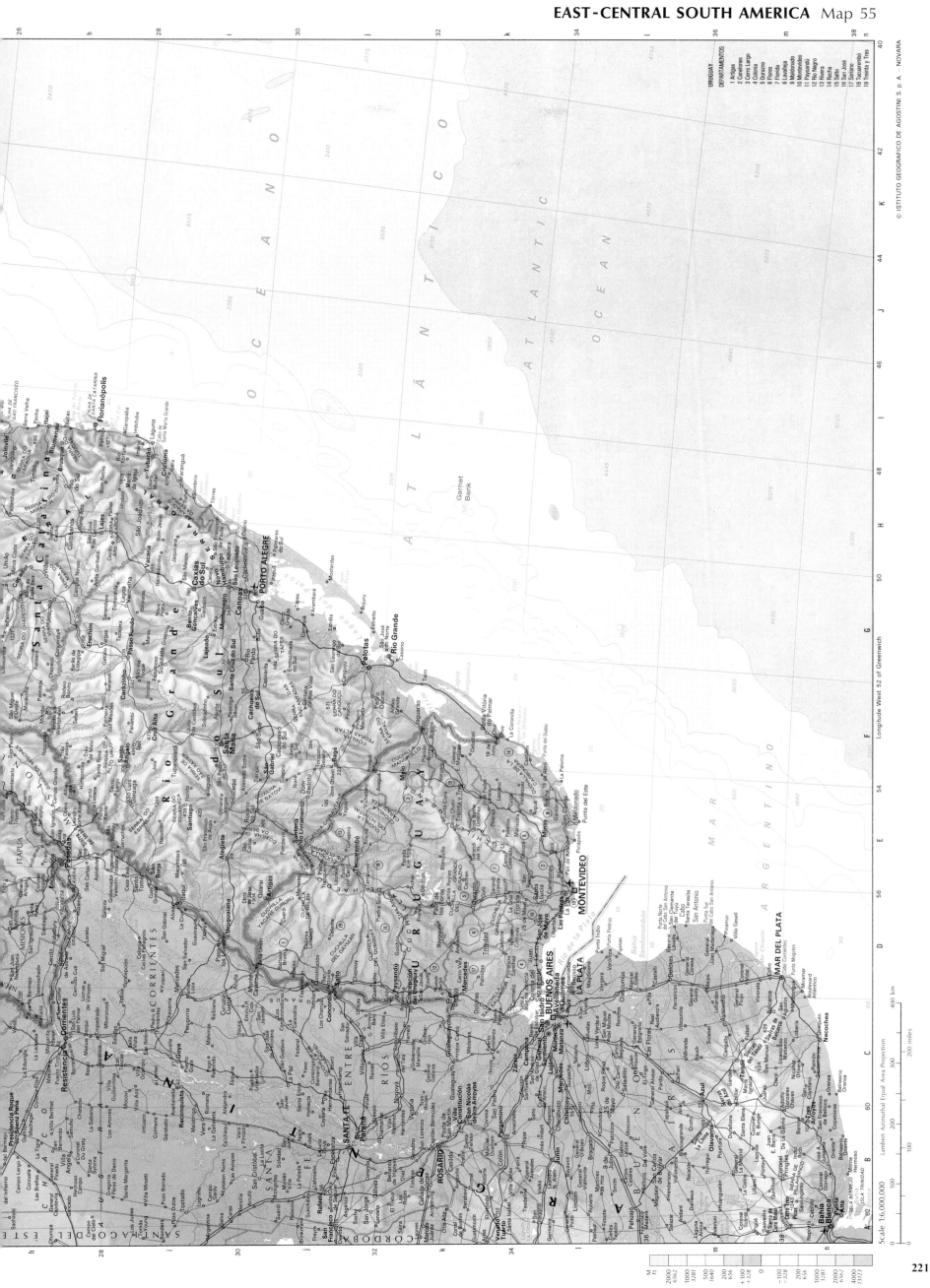

URIGUAY
DEPARTAMENTOS

1 Artigas
2 Canelones
3 Cerro Largo
4 Colonia
5 Durazno
6 Flores
7 Florida
8 Lavalleja
9 Maldonado
10 Montevideo
11 Paysandú
12 Río Negro
13 Rivera
14 Rocha
15 Salto
16 San José
17 Soriano
18 Tacuarembó
19 Treinta y Tres

Scale 1:6,000,000

Lambert Azimuthal Equal Area Projection

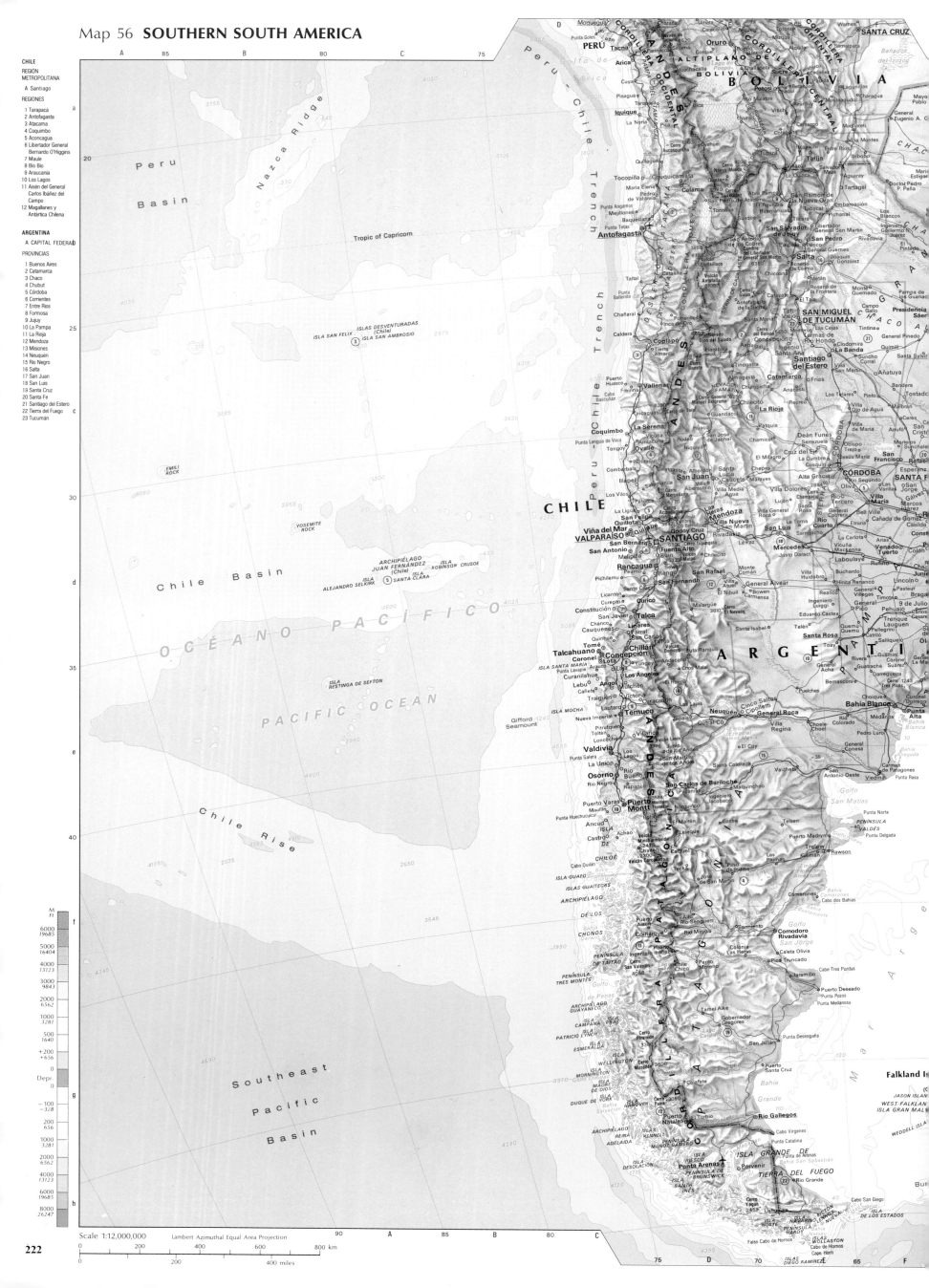

Map 56 **SOUTHERN SOUTH AMERICA**

CHILE
REGIÓN
METROPOLITANA
A Santiago

REGIONES
1 Tarapacá
2 Antofagasta
3 Atacama
4 Coquimbo
5 Aconcagua
6 Libertador General
  Bernardo O'Higgins
7 Maule
8 Bio Bio
9 Araucania
10 Los Lagos
11 Aisén del General
   Carlos Ibáñez del
   Campo
12 Magallanes y
   Antártica Chilena

ARGENTINA
A CAPITAL FEDERAL

PROVINCIAS
1 Buenos Aires
2 Catamarca
3 Chaco
4 Chubut
5 Córdoba
6 Corrientes
7 Entre Ríos
8 Formosa
9 Jujuy
10 La Pampa
11 La Rioja
12 Mendoza
13 Misiones
14 Neuquén
15 Rio Negro
16 Salta
17 San Juan
18 San Luis
19 Santa Cruz
20 Santa Fe
21 Santiago del Estero
22 Tierra del Fuego
23 Tucumán

M
Ft
6000 / 19685
5000 / 16404
4000 / 13123
3000 / 9843
2000 / 6562
1000 / 3281
500 / 1640
+200 / +656
Depr.
− 100 / −328
200 / 656
1000 / 3281
2000 / 6562
4000 / 13123
6000 / 19685
8000 / 26247

Scale 1:12,000,000   Lambert Azimuthal Equal Area Projection

0   200   400   600   800 km
0   200   400 miles

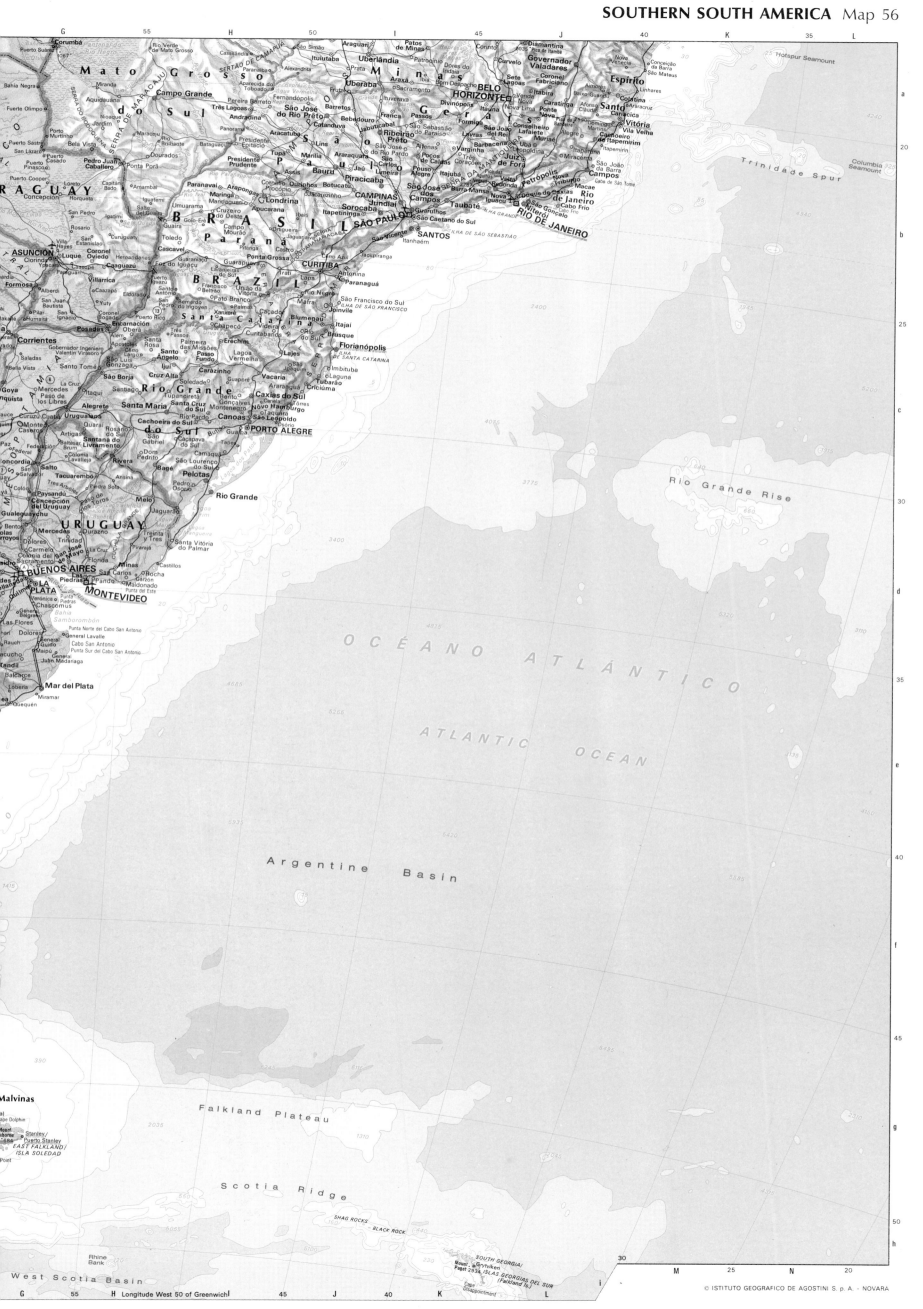

Map 57 **AUSTRALIA AND OCEANIA, PHYSICAL**

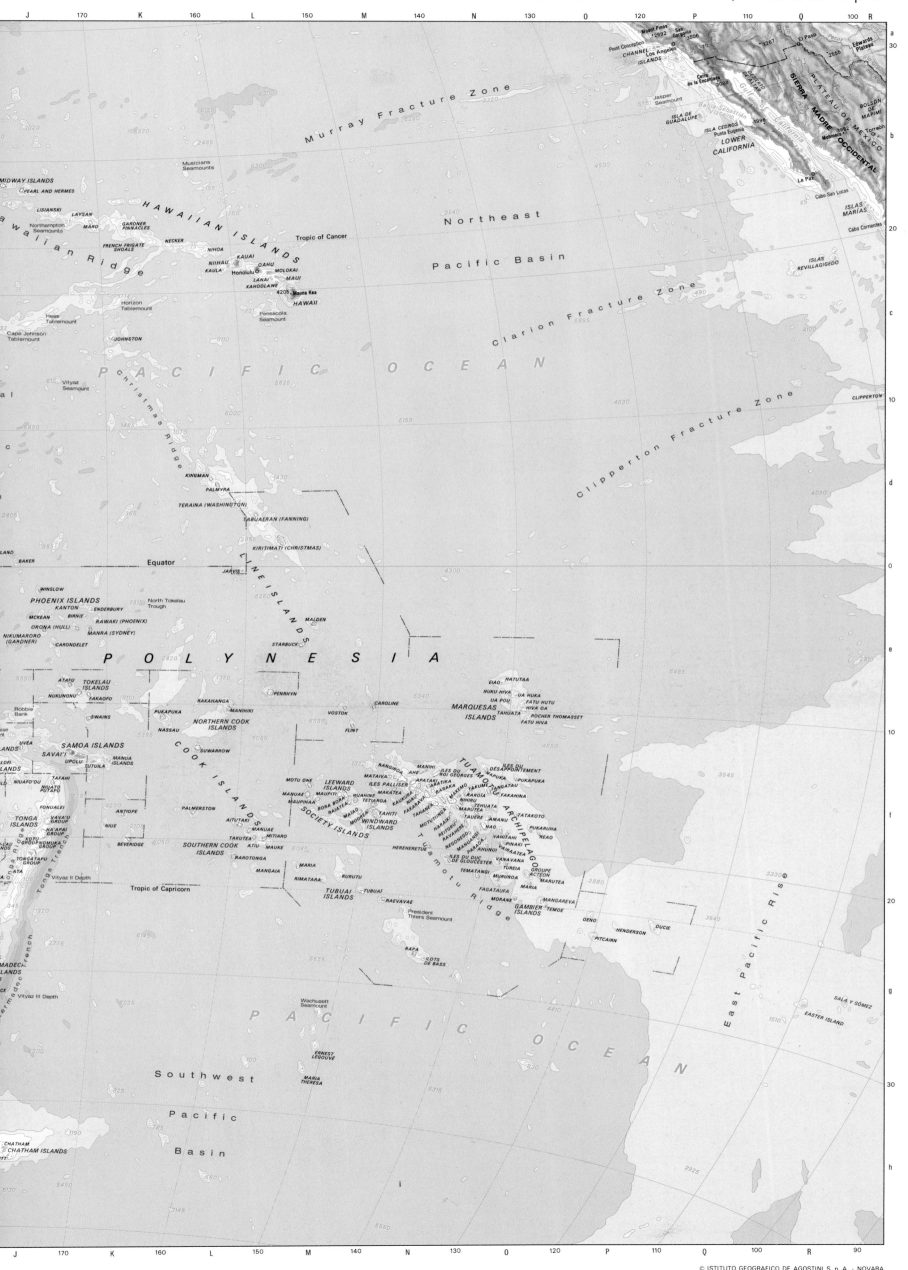

Map 58 **AUSTRALIA AND OCEANIA, POLITICAL**

Scale 1:30,000,000   Lambert Azimuthal Equal Area Projection   Longitude East 170 of Greenwich

PACIFIC OCEAN

UNITED STATES

San Luis
Obispo
Santa Barbara
Los Angeles
Long Beach
San Bernardino
San Diego
Tijuana
Ensenada

Bakersfield
Pasadena
Phoenix
Mesa
El Paso
Yuma
Mexicali
Nogales
Tucson

Ciudad
Juárez

ISLA DE
GUADALUPE
(Mexico)

LOWER
CALIFORNIA

Hermosillo
Ciudad
Obregón
Los Mochis
Culiacán
Rosales

Chihuahua

Nuevo
Rosita
Monclova
Torreón
Victoria
de
Durango

MEXICO

La Paz
Cabo San Lucas
Mazatlán

Tropic of Cancer

way Islands
(U.S.)
PEARL AND HERMES

LISIANSKI
LAYSAN
MARO
GARDNER
PINNACLES
FRENCH FRIGATE
SHOALS
NECKER
NIHOA
KAUAI
NIHAU
KAULA
OAHU
MOLOKAI
MAUI
LANAI
KAHOOLAWE
Hawi
Hilo
HAWAII

HAWAIIAN ISLANDS

Hawaii
(U.S.)
Honolulu

ISLAS
REVILLAGIGEDO
(Mexico)

Johnston
(U.S.)

CLIPPERTON
(French Polynesia)

KINGMAN
(U.S.)
PALMYRA
(U.S.)
TERAINA
(WASHINGTON)
TABUAERAN
(FANNING)
KIRITIMATI
(CHRISTMAS)

LINE ISLANDS

ND
BAKER
(U.S.)
JARVIS
(U.S.)

Equator

WINSLOW
PHOENIX ISLANDS
KANTON
MCKEAN
BIRNIE
ENDERBURY
RAWAKI
(PHOENIX)
ORONA
(HULL)
MANRA
(SYDNEY)
CARONDELET
NIKUMARORO
(GARDNER)

KIRIBATI

MALDEN
VOSTOK
STARBUCK
FLINT

POLYNESIA

EIAO
NUKU HIVA
UA HUKA
MARQUESAS
UA POU
HIVA OA
TAHUATA
FATU HIVA
ISLANDS

Tokelau (New Zealand)
ATAFU
TOKELAU
ISLANDS
NUKUNONU
FAKAOFO
SWAINS

WESTERN
SAMOA
SAMOA ISLANDS
SAVAI'I
Apia
UPOLU
Pago Pago
MANUA
TUTUILA
ISLANDS
American
Samoa
(U.S.)

a
Mata-Utu
WALLIS
UVEA
UNA
IFI

NIUAFO'OU
TAFAHI
NIUATO PUTAPU

TONGA

FONUALEI
VAVA'U
GROUP
HA'APAI GROUP
TONGA
ISLANDS
KOTU GROUP
NOMUKA GROUP
Nuku'alofa
TONGATAPU
GROUP
ATA
A REEFS

PUKAPUKA
NASSAU

NORTHERN
COOK ISLANDS

SUWARROW

RAKAHANGA
MANIHIKI
PENRHYN

Cook Islands
(New Zealand)

PALMERSTON
AITUTAKI
ANTIOPE
Alofi
Niue
(New Zealand)
MANUAE
TAKUTEA
MITIARO
ATIU
MAUKE
BEVERIDGE
SOUTHERN
COOK
ISLANDS
RAROTONGA
Avarua
MANGAIA

CAROLINE

CAROLINE

MOTU
ONE
LEEWARD
ISLANDS
ILES PALLISER
MAUPITI
MANUAE
MAUPIHAA
BORA-BORA
HUAHINE
RAIATEA
TAHAA
MOOREA
RANGIROA
MATAIVA
RANGIROA
MANIHI
ILES DU
ROI GEORGES
APATAKI
ARATIKA
KAUKURA
FAKARAVA
TAHANEA
Papeete
TETIAROA
Tahiti
MOTUTUNGA
WINDWARD ISLANDS
SOCIETY ISLANDS

ILES DU
DÉSAPPOINTEMENT
PUKAPUKA
TAKUME
FANGATAU
FAKAHINA
MAKEMO
MARUTEA
TATAKOTO
RAVAHERE
HAO
AMANU
KARUHA
VAHITAHI
REAO

TUAMOTU ARCHIPELAGO

HEREHERETUE
MARIA
RURUTU
RIMATARA
French
Polynesia
TEMATANGI
MANUANGI
AHUNUI
ILES DU DUC
DE GLOUCESTER
TUREIA
MURUROA
FAGATAUFA
GROUPE
ACTEON
MARIA
MARUTEA
MORANE
MANGAREVA
GAMBIER
TEMOE
ISLANDS
DENO
HENDERSON
DUCIE
RAEVAVAE
TUBUAI
ISLANDS
TUBUAI

Tropic of Capricorn

Adamstown
PITCAIRN
Pitcairn
(U.K.)

RAPA
ILOTS
DE BASS

OUL
ERMADEC
ISLANDS
(ew Zealand)
ANCE ROCK

SALA Y GÓMEZ
(Chile)
EASTER ISLAND
(Chile)

ERNEST
LEGOUVE

MARIA THERESA

CHATHAM ISLANDS
(New Zealand)

Map 59 **AUSTRALIA**

INDONESIA

JAWA — JAVA

LAUT JAWA — JAVA SEA

SEMARANG, SURABAYA, YOGYAKARTA, SURAKARTA, MALANG, Madiun, Magelang, Kediri, Kudus, Rembang, Tuban, Gresik, Bangkalan, Probolinggo, Bondowoso, Banjuwangi, Jember, Lumajang, Tulungagung, Pamekasan, Sumenep, Depasar, Mataram

PULAU MADURA, PULAU BAWEAN, PULAU BALI, PULAU LOMBOK, NUSA PENIDA, PULAU SUMBAWA, Sumbawa Besar, Raba, Gunung Tambora, PULAU MOYO, KEPULAUAN KANGEAN, KEPULAUAN TENGAH, KEPULAUAN LIUKANG TENGGAYA, BONE RATE

LAUT FLORES — FLORES SEA

PULAU FLORES, Larantuka, Ruteng, Ende, Maumere, KEPULAUAN SOLOR, KEPULAUAN ALOR, PULAU LOMBLEN, PULAU ALOR, PULAU WETAR, PULAU ROMANG, KEPULAUAN BARAT DAYA, KEPULAUAN LETI, KEPULAUAN SERMATA, KEPULAUAN BABAR, KEPULAUAN TANIMBAR, PULAU YAMDENA, PULAU SELARU, Saumlaki

LAUT SAWU — SAWU SEA

PULAU SUMBA, Waikabubak, Baing, Waingapu, KEPULAUAN SAWU, PULAU ROTI, PULAU TIMOR, Kupang, Soe, Atambua, Dili, Tata Mailau, Manatuto, Gunung Mutis

TIMOR SEA, Timor Trough, ARAFURU [Arafura Sea]

HIBERNIA REEF, ASHMORE ISLANDS, CARTIER ISLAND, SCOTT REEF, SERINGAPATAM REEF, BROWSE ISLAND, Holothuria Banks, D'Artagnan Bank, Corona Bank

INDIAN OCEAN

North Australian Basin, Java Trench, Planet Deep, Exmouth Plateau, Cuvier Basin, Diamantina Deep, Diamantina Trench, South Australian Basin

Tropic of Capricorn

KIMBERLEY PLATEAU, KING LEOPOLD RANGES, Derby, Broome, Fitzroy, Halls Creek, Wyndham, Kununurra, Gibb River, Mount Hann, Mount Ord, Mount Wells, Turkey Creek, Mount Parker, Mount Napier, DAMPIER LAND, BUCCANEER ARCHIPELAGO, BONAPARTE ARCHIPELAGO, Yampi Sound, Cape Leveque, ADELE ISLAND, LACEPEDE ISLANDS, Kuri Bay, Kalumburu Mission, Cape Londonderry, Cape Scott, Joseph Bonaparte Gulf, Christmas Creek, Cape Bossut, EIGHTY MILE BEACH, Roebuck Bay

Darwin, BATHURST ISLAND, MELVILLE ISLAND, Cape Van Diemen, Snake Bay, COBURG PENINSULA, CROKER ISLAND, Cape Croker, Rum Jungle, Batchelor, Adelaide River, Pine Creek, Katherine, Mataranka, ARNHEM LAND, Mount Evelyn

NORTHERN TERRITORY, TANAMI DESERT, Tanami, The Granites, Wave Hill, Top Springs, Victoria River Downs, Newcastle Waters, Elliott, Willeroo, Daly Waters, Birdum, Larrimah, Barrow Creek, Tea Tree, MACDONNELL RANGES, Mount Zeil, Mount Liebig, Mount Conway, Henbury, Erldunda, Kulgera, STUART BLUFF RANGE, GEORGE GILL RANGE, Mount Olga, Docker River, Mount Davies, MUSGRAVE RANGES, EVERARD RANGES, Mount Woodroffe, Mount Morris, Mount Leisler, BIRKSGATE RANGE

GREAT SANDY DESERT, PATERSON RANGE, Nullagine, Marble Bar, Port Hedland, Goldsworthy, Roy Hill, Larrey Point, Poissonnier Point, CANNING BASIN, Lake Mackay, Lake Disappointment, Lake Auld, Lake Gregory

Western Australia

GIBSON DESERT, GREAT VICTORIA DESERT, RAWLINSON RANGES, WARBURTON RANGE, Warburton Mission, Meteorological Station, Simpson Hill, Lake Carnegie, Lake Throssell, Lake Wells, Lake Macdonald, Lake Rason

HAMERSLEY RANGE, CHICHESTER RANGE, ROBERTSON RANGE, OPHTHALMIA RANGE, CARNARVON RANGE, Newman, Mundiwindi, Mount Bruce, Mount Meharry, Tom Price, Paraburdoo, Breckman, Dampier, Roebourne, Onslow, Exmouth, Learmonth, Point Cloates, DAMPIER ARCHIPELAGO, MONTE BELLO ISLANDS, BARROW ISLAND, MUIRON ISLANDS, North West Cape, Chabiawardoo Bay

BARLEE RANGE, ROBINSON RANGE, KENNEDY RANGE, Mount Augustus, Mount Vernon, Mount Egerton, Mount Essendon, Mount Hale, Carnarvon, Gascoyne Junction, Minilya, Geographe Channel, Cape Farquhar, BERNIER ISLAND, DORRE ISLAND, DIRK HARTOG ISLAND, Cape Inscription, Shark Bay (Denham), Useless Loop, Woorabee

WELD RANGE, NICHOLSON RANGE, Meekatharra, Wiluna, Cue, Sandstone, Agnew, Leonora, Laverton, Mount Shenton, Mount Redcliffe, Serpentine Lakes, Jubilee Lake

Murchison, Yalgoo, Mount Magnet, Mount Wysmandoo, Mullewa, Morawa, Mingenew, Dongara, Mount Singleton, Menzies, Kalgoorlie, Coolgardie, Kambalda, Southern Cross, Widgiemooltha, Norseman, Fraser Range, BALLADONIA, Zanthus, Rawlinna, NULLARBOR PLAIN, Forrest, Cook, Nullarbor, Eucla, Oldea, Colona, Penong, Maralinga

Geraldton, Northampton, Bluff Point, HOUTMAN ABROLHOS, Dongara, Carnamah, Three Springs, Watheroo, Moora, Gingin, Lancelin, Dalwallinu, Wongan Hills, Goomalling, Wyalkatchem, Mukinbudin, Bullfinch, Nungarin, Merredin, Kellerberrin, Bruce Rock, Koorda, Northam, York, Cunderdin, Quairading

PERTH, ROTTNEST ISLAND, FREMANTLE, Rockingham, Mandurah, Pinjarra, Waroona, Harvey, Bunbury, Collie, Donnybrook, Bridgetown, Manjimup, Pemberton, Nannup, Busselton, Margaret River, Augusta, Cape Naturaliste, Cape Leeuwin, Beverley, Brookton, Corrigin, Kondinin, Wickepin, Narrogin, Wagin, Kojonup, Katanning, Cranbrook, Mount Barker, Albany, Denmark, King George Sound, Point D'Entrecasteaux, Bald Head

Lake Grace, Nyabing, Gnowangerup, Ravensthorpe, Hopetoun, Esperance, Peak Charles, Lake King, Lake Cowan, Lake Lefroy, Lake Dundas, RUSSELL RANGE, Point Culver, Twilight Cove, Head of Bight, Fowlers Bay, Great Australian Bight, Cape Arid, ARCHIPELAGO OF THE RECHERCHE, Hood Point, Esperance Bay

South Australia

INDIAN OCEAN

Scale 1:12,000,000 Delisle Conic Equidistant Projection

0 200 400 600 800 km
0 200 400 miles

M Ft
4000 13123
3000 9843
2000 6562
1000 3281
500 1640
200 +656
0 Depr 0
-100 -328
200 656
1000 3281
2000 6562
4000 13123
6000 19685
8000 26247

PULAU IRIAN NEW GUINEA

PAPUA NEW GUINEA

NEW GUINEA

PAPUA

BISMARCK ARCHIPELAGO

NEW IRELAND ISLAND

NEW BRITAIN

BOUGAINVILLE ISLAND

SOLOMON ISLANDS

Solomon Basin

SOLOMON SEA

New Britian Trench

ONTONG JAVA

SANTA ISABEL ISLAND

NEW GEORGIA ISLANDS

CHOISEUL ISLAND

Honiara

MALAITA ISLAND

GUADALCANAL ISLAND

SAN CRISTÓBAL ISLAND

PULAU DOLAK

PULAU KOMORAN

HUON PENINSULA

Lae

Gulf of Papua

Port Moresby

OWEN STANLEY RANGE

D'ENTRECASTEAUX ISLANDS

TROBRIAND ISLANDS

WOODLARK ISLAND

NORMANBY ISLAND

LOUISIADE ARCHIPELAGO

CORAL SEA

Coral Sea Basin

POCKLINGTON REEF

INDISPENSABLE REEFS (Vanuatu)

Gulf of Carpentaria

Cape Wessel

WESSEL ISLANDS

GOVE PENINSULA

CAPE YORK PENINSULA

Cape York

Thursday Island

PRINCE OF WALES ISLAND

Weipa

Coral Sea Islands Territory

OSPREY REEF

HOLMES REEFS

WILLIS GROUP

HERALDS CAYS

MAGDELAINE CAYS

CORINGA ISLETS

FLINDERS REEFS

TREGROSSE ISLETS

LIHOU REEFS AND CAYS

MELLISH REEF

MORNINGTON ISLAND

WELLESLEY ISLANDS

SOUTH WELLESLEY ISLANDS

BENTINCK ISLAND

Normanton

Burketown

Karumba

GREAT DIVIDING RANGE

GREAT BARRIER REEF

Cairns

Cooktown

MARION REEFS

RECIFS ET ILES CHESTERFIELD

ILE DE SABLE

TABLELAND

Alexandria

Avon Downs

Camooweal

Mount Isa

SELWYN RANGE

Cloncurry

Duchess

Dajarra

Julia Creek

Richmond

Hughenden

Townsville

MAGNETIC ISLAND

Ayr

Bowen

HINCHINBROOK ISLAND

PALM ISLANDS

Ingham

Charters Towers

Mount Hogarth

Mount Gordon

Winton

Muttaburra

Aramac

Pentland

Torrens Creek

Mackay

CUMBERLAND ISLANDS

WHITSUNDAY ISLAND

Proserpine

Collinsville

NORTHUMBERLAND ISLANDS

Sarina

FREDERICK REEF

Queensland

Boulia

Bedourie

Diamantina Lakes

Longreach

Barcaldine

Isisford

Blackall

Jericho

Emerald

Clermont

PERCY ISLANDS

SWAIN REEFS

Cape Townshend

KENN REEF

Nouvelle-Calédonie New Caledonia (France)

Birdsville

Windorah

Stonehenge

Yaraka

Tambo

Springsure

Rockhampton

Gladstone

CAPRICORN GROUP

CURTIS ISLAND

BUNKER GROUP

WRECK REEF

CATO ISLAND

GREAT ARTESIAN BASIN

RECIFS BELLONA

Innamincka

Quilpie

Adavale

Augathella

Charleville

Mitchell

Morven

Roma

Taroom

Theodore

Biloela

Bundaberg

Maryborough

FRASER ISLAND

Hervey Bay

Sandy Cape

Tropic of Capricorn

Kelso Bank

STURT DESERT

Thargomindah

Eromanga

Wyandra

Bollon

Cunnamulla

Mitchell

Tara

Dalby

Toowoomba

Ipswich

BRISBANE

Gympie

Nambour

Maroochydore

Caloundra

MORETON ISLAND

NORTH STRADBROKE ISLAND

Kejpel Bank

Marree

Leigh Creek

Freeling Heights

Milparinka

Mount Shannon

Tibooburra

White Cliffs

Bourke

Brewarrina

Walgett

Dirranbandi

Goondiwindi

Warwick

Stanthorpe

Gold Coast

Beaudesert

Murwillumbah

Byron Bay

Cape Byron

Ballina

Woomera

Saint Mary Peak

Hawker

Quorn

Peterborough

Broken Hill

Wilcannia

Cobar

Nyngan

Narrabri

Moree

Mungindi

Tenterfield

Lismore

Grafton

Coffs Harbour

New South Wales

GREY RANGE

BARRIER RANGE

FLINDERS RANGES

Mount Remarkable

Whyalla

Port Pirie

Crystal Brook

Menindee

Ivanhoe

Louth

Tilpa

Coonamble

Coonabarabran

Gilgandra

Gunnedah

Barraba

Inverell

Glen Innes

Armidale

Tamworth

NANDEWAR RANGE

LIVERPOOL RANGE

WARRUMBUNGLE RANGE

Kempsey

Port Macquarie

Smoky Cape

ELIZABETH REEF (Australia)

MIDDLETON REEF (Australia)

Port Augusta

Whyalla

Cowell

ADELAIDE

Elizabeth

Port Pirie

Gawler

Barmera

Renmark

Wentworth

Mildura

Balranald

Hay

Booligal

Roto

Condobolin

Parkes

Forbes

Wellington

Dubbo

Mudgee

Gosford

The Entrance

Woy Woy

Newcastle

Maitland

Cessnock

Singleton

Taree

LORD HOWE ISLAND (Australia)

BALL'S PYRAMID

Spencer Gulf

KANGAROO ISLAND

Murray Bridge

Pinnaroo

Loxton

Swan Hill

Kerang

West Wyalong

Young

Cowra

Bathurst

Lithgow

Katoomba

SYDNEY

CAMPBELLTOWN

Wollongong

Shellharbour

RIVERINA

Griffith

Narrandera

Goulburn

Nowra

Beecroft Head

Cape Jaffa

Kingston South East

Keith

Bordertown

Naracoorte

Nhill

Dimboola

Horsham

Charlton

Donald

St Arnaud

Echuca

Shepparton

Wangaratta

Deniliquin

Wagga Wagga

Gundagai

Tumut

Yass

Queanbeyan

Canberra

Australian Capital Territory

Batemans Bay

Mount Gambier

Penola

Millicent

Portland

Hamilton

Ararat

Ballarat

Bendigo

Castlemaine

Seymour

Mount Macedon

Whittlesea

MELBOURNE

Geelong

Wodonga

Albury

Corryong

Mount Kosciuszko

Mount Bogong

Benalla

Mansfield

Wangaratta

Warragul

Sale

Bairnsdale

Lakes Entrance

Orbost

Cape Howe

Eden

Bombala

Cooma

GREAT DIVIDING RANGE

Victoria

Warrnambool

Camperdown

Colac

Cape Otway

Apollo Bay

Lorne

Wonthaggi

NINETY MILE BEACH

WILSONS PROMONTORY

South East Point

KENT GROUP

FLINDERS ISLAND

FURNEAUX GROUP

Cape Barren

CAPE BARREN ISLAND

KING ISLAND

Currie

Cape Grim

Stanley

Smithton

Burnie

Devonport

Ulverstone

Launceston

Scottsdale

Eddystone Point

Saint Helens

Saint Marys

Queenstown

Rosebery

Zeehan

Savage River

BASS STRAIT

TASMAN SEA

Tasman Basin

Tasmania

FREYCINET PENINSULA

MARIA ISLAND

Hobart

TASMAN PENINSULA

BRUNY ISLAND

South West Cape

South East Cape

Cape Pillar

PACIFIC OCEAN

© ISTITUTO GEOGRAFICO DE AGOSTINI S. p. A. - NOVARA

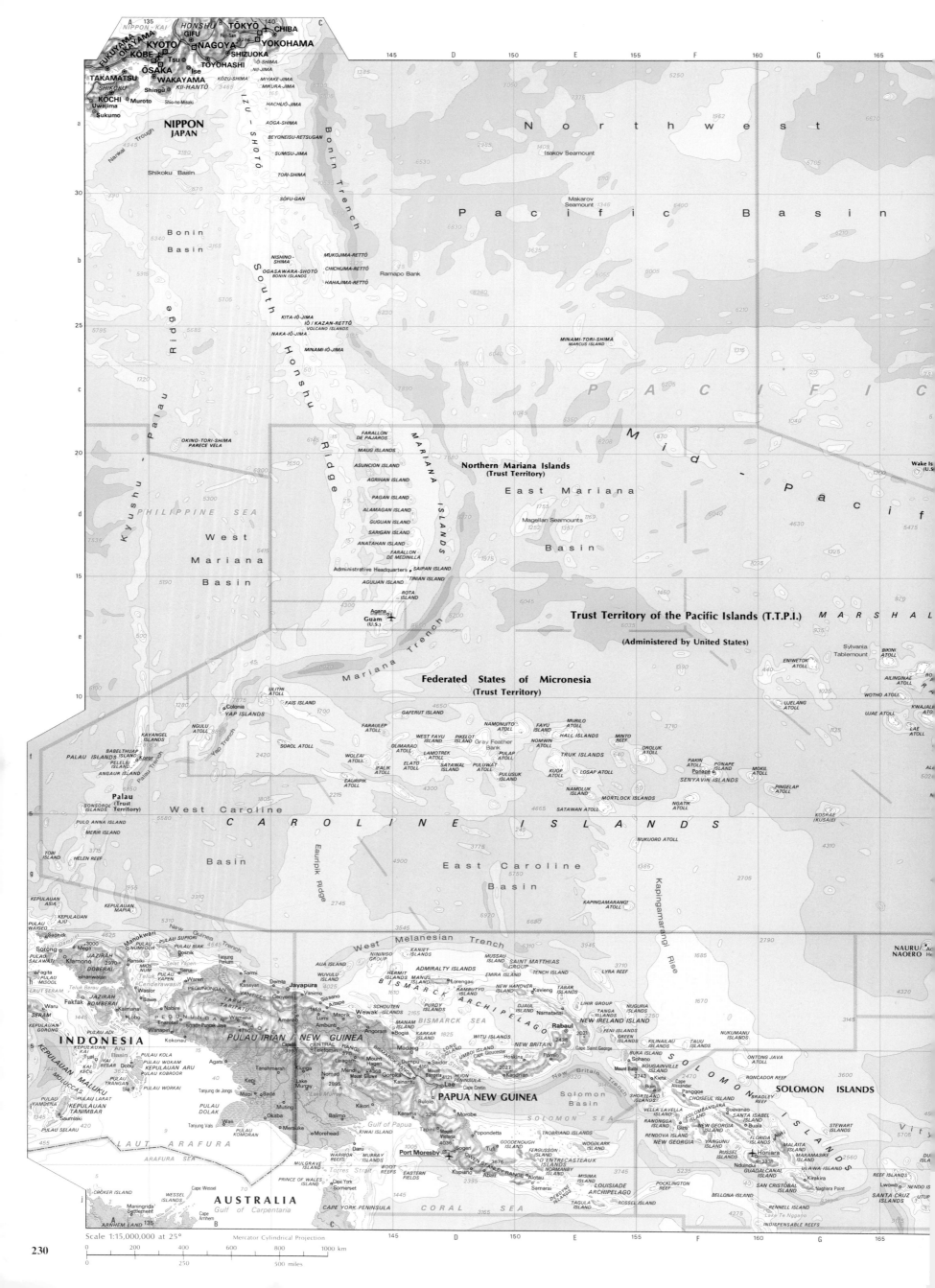

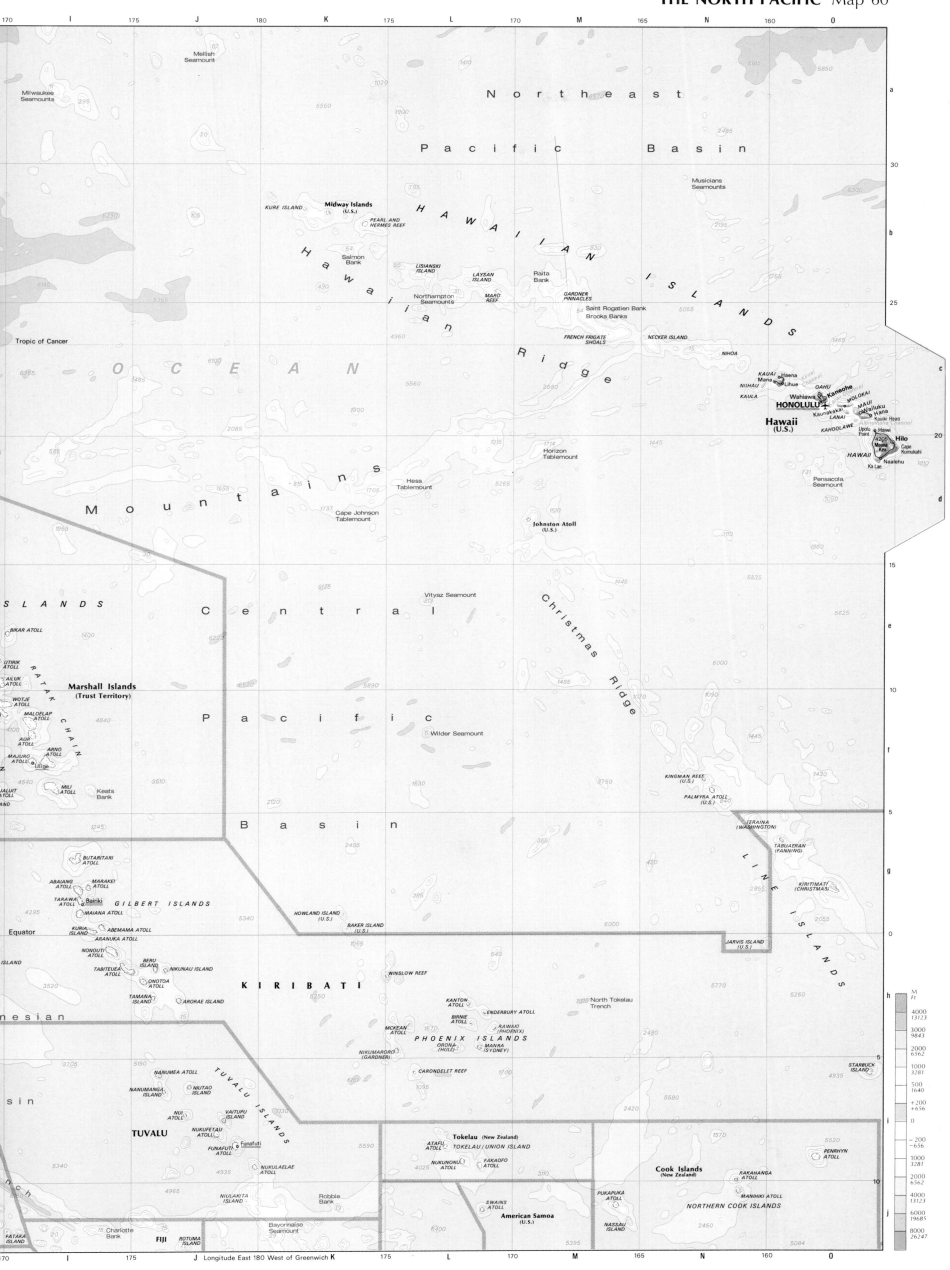

Milwaukee Seamounts
Meilish Seamount
Musicians Seamounts
Northeast Pacific Basin
Midway Islands (U.S.)
KURE ISLAND
PEARL AND HERMES REEF
Salmon Bank
LISIANSKI ISLAND
LAYSAN ISLAND
Raita Bank
HAWAIIAN ISLANDS
Northampton Seamounts
MARO REEF
GARDNER PINNACLES
Saint Rogatien Bank
Brooks Banks
Tropic of Cancer
FRENCH FRIGATE SHOALS
NECKER ISLAND
NIHOA
KAUAI Haena
Mana Lihue
OAHU Kaneohe
NIIHAU Wahiawa MOLOKAI
KAULA HONOLULU Kaunakakai MAUI Wailuku
Kamalo LANAI Hana
Hawaii Kauiki Head
(U.S.) KAHOOLAWE
HAWAIIAN Upolu
OCEAN Point Hawi
Mauna Kea Hilo
Ridge HAWAII Cape Kumukahi
Naalehu
Ka Lae
Horizon Tablemount
Hess Tablemount
Pensacola Seamount
Mountains
Cape Johnson Tablemount
Johnston Atoll (U.S.)
ISLANDS
BIKAR ATOLL
UTIRIK ATOLL
AILUK ATOLL
WOTJE ATOLL
Central
MALOELAP ATOLL
AUR ATOLL
ARNO ATOLL
MAJURO ATOLL
Ulige
Vityaz Seamount
Christmas Ridge
Marshall Islands (Trust Territory)
RATAK CHAIN
Pacific
JALUIT ATOLL
MILI ATOLL
Keats Bank
Wilder Seamount
Basin
KINGMAN REEF (U.S.)
PALMYRA ATOLL (U.S.)
TERAINA (WASHINGTON)
BUTARITARI ATOLL
TABUAERAN (FANNING)
ABAIANG ATOLL
MARAKEI ATOLL
TARAWA ATOLL Bairiki
GILBERT ISLANDS
MAIANA ATOLL
KIRITIMATI (CHRISTMAS)
LINE ISLANDS
Equator
KURIA ISLAND
ABEMAMA ATOLL
HOWLAND ISLAND (U.S.)
ARANUKA ATOLL
BAKER ISLAND (U.S.)
NONOUTI ATOLL
ISLAND
BERU ISLAND
NIKUNAU ISLAND
JARVIS ISLAND (U.S.)
TABITEUEA ATOLL
ONOTOA ATOLL
KIRIBATI
WINSLOW REEF
TAMANA ISLAND
ARORAE ISLAND
KANTON ATOLL
North Tokelau Trench
ENDERBURY ATOLL
BIRNIE ATOLL
MCKEAN ATOLL
RAWAKI (PHOENIX)
nesian
NIKUMARORO (GARDNER)
PHOENIX ISLANDS
ORONA (HULL)
MANRA (SYDNEY)
STARBUCK ISLAND
CARONDELET REEF
NANUMEA ATOLL
TUVALU ISLANDS
NANUMANGA ISLAND
NIUTAO ISLAND
NUI ATOLL
VAITUPU ISLAND
ATAFU ATOLL
Tokelau (New Zealand)
TOKELAU / UNION ISLAND
sin
TUVALU
NUKUFETAU ATOLL
FUNAFUTI ATOLL Funafuti
NUKUNONU ATOLL
FAKAOFO ATOLL
PENRHYN ATOLL
RAKAHANGA ATOLL
Cook Islands (New Zealand)
NIULAKITA ISLAND
NUKULAELAE ATOLL
Robbie Bank
MANIHIKI ATOLL
nch
FATAKA ISLAND
Charlotte Bank
FIJI
ROTUMA ISLAND
Bayonnaise Seamount
SWAINS ATOLL
American Samoa (U.S.)
PUKAPUKA ATOLL
NASSAU ISLAND
NORTHERN COOK ISLANDS

M Ft
4000 13123
3000 9843
2000 6562
1000 3281
500 1640
+200 +656
0
-200 -656
1000 3281
2000 6562
4000 13123
6000 19685
8000 26247

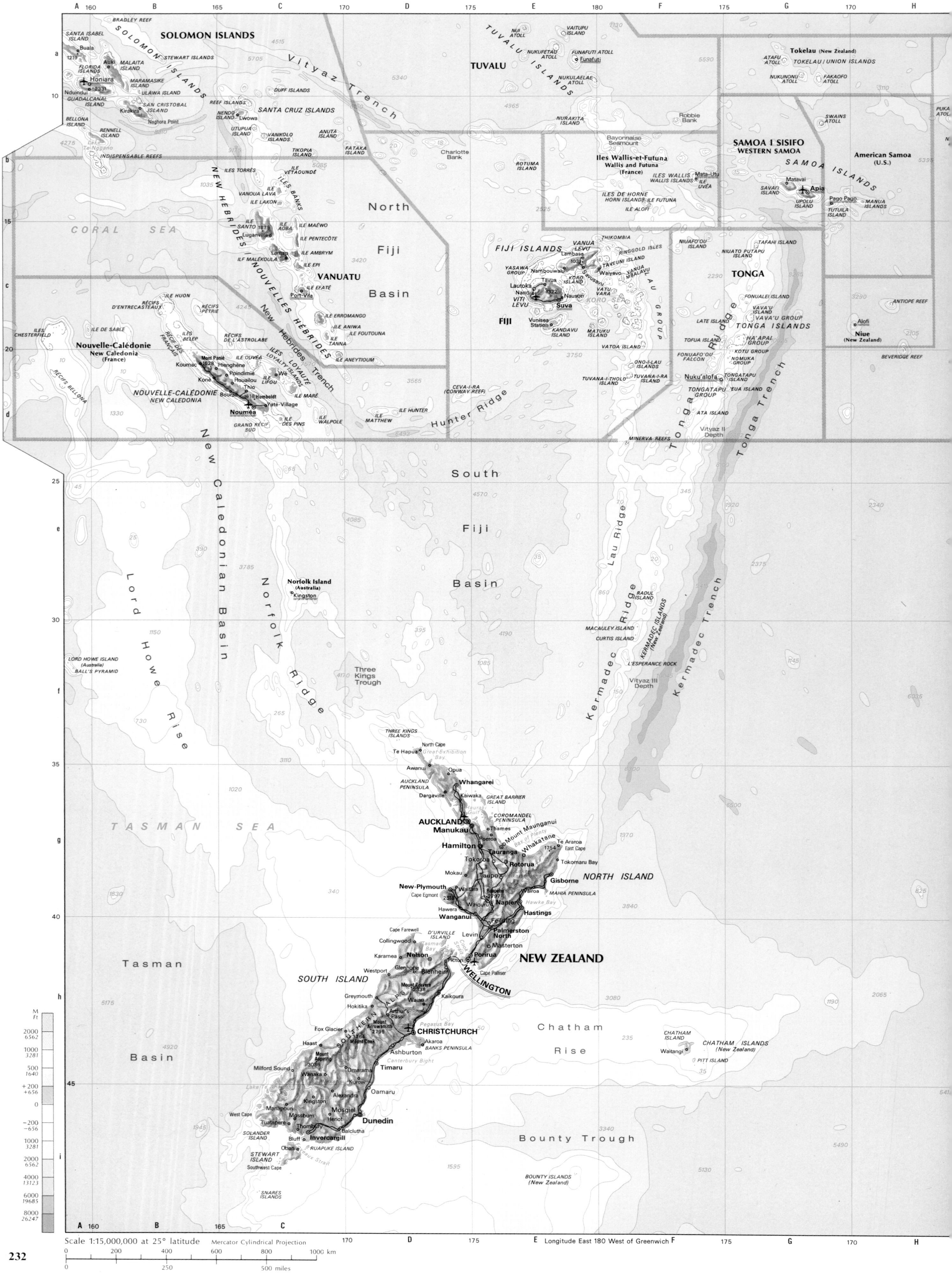

Map 61 **THE SOUTH PACIFIC**

SOLOMON ISLANDS

Santa Isabel Island
Buala
Florida Islands
Auki
MALAITA ISLAND
Honiara
GUADALCANAL ISLAND
Nduindui
Kirakira
San Cristobal Island
ULAWA ISLAND
BELLONA ISLAND
RENNELL ISLAND
Lake Te Nggano
Naghoa Point
INDISPENSABLE REEFS
MARAMASIKE ISLAND
STEWART ISLANDS
Vityaz Trench
REEF ISLANDS
DUFF ISLANDS
NENDO ISLAND
SANTA CRUZ ISLANDS
UTUPUA ISLAND
VANIKOLO ISLANDS
TIKOPIA ISLAND
ANUTA ISLAND
FATAKA ISLAND
Charlotte Bank

TUVALU

NUI ISLAND
VAITUPU ISLAND
NUKUFETAU ATOLL
FUNAFUTI ATOLL
Funafuti
TUVALU ISLANDS
NUKULAELAE ATOLL
NURAKITA ISLAND
Robbie Bank

Bayonnaise Seamount
ROTUMA ISLAND

Iles Wallis-et-Futuna
Wallis and Futuna (France)
ILES WALLIS
Mata-Utu
ILE UVÉA
ILES DE HORNE
HORN ISLANDS
ILE FUTUNA
ILE ALOFI

Tokelau (New Zealand)
ATAFU ISLAND
TOKELAU / UNION ISLANDS
NUKUNONU ATOLL
FAKAOFO ATOLL
SWAINS ATOLL
PUKA-PUKA ATOLL

SAMOA I SISIFO
WESTERN SAMOA
SAVAI'I ISLAND
Matavai
Apia
UPOLU ISLAND
American Samoa (U.S.)
MANUA ISLANDS
Pago Pago
TUTUILA ISLAND
SAMOA ISLANDS

NEW HEBRIDES
ILES TORRÈS
ILE VANUA LAVA
ILES BANKS
ILE LAKON
ILE VETAOUNDÉ
ILE AOBA
ILE SANTO
Luganville
Lamen
ILE MAÊWO
ILE PENTECÔTE
ILE MALÉKOULA
ILE AMBRYM
ILE EPI
ILE AMIWA
ILE EFATÉ
Port-Vila
ILE ERROMANGO
ILE TANNA
ILE FOUTOUNA
ILE ANEITYOUM

VANUATU

FIJI ISLANDS
VANUA LEVU
YASAWA GROUP
Lambasa
THIKOMBIA
RINGGOLD ISLES
TAVEUNI ISLAND
VANUA MBALAVU
Nambouwalu
Tavua
KORO ISLAND
Waiyevo
KORO SEA
Lautoka
Nandi
VITI LEVU
Suva
VATU VARA
LAU GROUP
FIJI
Vunisea Station
KANDAVU ISLAND
MATUKU ISLAND
VATOA ISLAND
ONO-I-LAU ISLANDS
CEVA-I-RA (CONWAY REEF)
TUVANA-I-THOLO ISLAND
TUVANA-I-RA ISLAND
MINERVA REEFS

TONGA
NIUAFO'OU ISLAND
TAFAHI ISLAND
NIUATO PUTAPU ISLAND
FONUALEI ISLAND
VAVA'U ISLAND
VAVA'U GROUP
LATE ISLAND
TONGA ISLANDS
TOFUA ISLAND
HA'APAI GROUP
FONUAFO'OU OR FALCON
KOTU GROUP
NOMUKA GROUP
Nuku'alofa
TONGATAPU GROUP
'EUA ISLAND
ATA ISLAND
Vityaz II Depth

ANTIOPE REEF
Alofi
Niue (New Zealand)
BEVERIDGE REEF

CORAL SEA

North Fiji Basin

South Fiji Basin

Nouvelle-Calédonie
New Caledonia (France)
RÉCIFS D'ENTRECASTEAUX
ILES CHESTERFIELD
RÉCIFS PÉTRIE
ILE HUON
ILES BELEP
Koumac
Mont Panié
Henghène
Poindimié
Pouailou
Thio
Koné
Bourail
Houmbolt
NOUVELLE-CALÉDONIE
NEW CALEDONIA
ILE OUVEA
LOYALTY ISLANDS
We
ILE LIFOU
Yate-Village
Nouméa
GRAND RÉCIF SUD
ILE DES PINS
ILE MARÉ
ILE WALPOLE
ILE HUNTER
ILE MATTHEW

RÉCIFS BELLONA
ILE DE SABLE

New Caledonian Basin
Norfolk Ridge
New Hebrides Trench
Loyalty Trench

Lord Howe Rise

Hunter Ridge

Norfolk Island (Australia)
Kingston

LORD HOWE ISLAND (Australia)
BALL'S PYRAMID

Lau Ridge
Kermadec Ridge
Kermadec Trench
Tonga Ridge
Tonga Trench

Three Kings Trough

Three Kings Islands

RAOUL ISLAND
MACAULEY ISLAND
KERMADEC ISLANDS (New Zealand)
CURTIS ISLAND
L'ESPERANCE ROCK
Vityaz III Depth

North Cape
Te Hapua
Great Exhibition Bay
Awanui
Opua
Whangarei
AUCKLAND PENINSULA
Kaiwaka
GREAT BARRIER ISLAND
Dargaville
Hauraki Gulf
COROMANDEL PENINSULA
AUCKLAND
Manukau
Thames
Hamilton
Paeroa
Tauranga
Mount Maunganui
BAY OF PLENTY
Whakatane
Rotorua
Te Araroa
East Cape
Tokoroa
Mokau
Taupo
Tokomaru Bay
New-Plymouth
Waitara
NORTH ISLAND
Gisborne
Cape Egmont
Wairoa
MAHIA PENINSULA
Hawera
Napier
Hawke Bay
Wanganui
Hastings
Feilding
Cape Farewell
D'URVILLE ISLAND
Levin
Palmerston North
Collingwood
Masterton
Karamea
Tasman Bay
Nelson
Picton
Porirua
Westport
Glenhope
Blenheim
WELLINGTON
Cape Palliser
NEW ZEALAND
SOUTH ISLAND
Greymouth
Mount Tapuae-o-Uenuku
Waiau
Hokitika
Kaikoura
Arthur's Pass
SOUTHERN ALPS
Fox Glacier
Mount Cook
Pegasus Bay
CHRISTCHURCH
Haast
Akaroa
BANKS PENINSULA
Ashburton
Mount Aspiring
Canterbury Bight
Milford Sound
Timaru
Wanaka
Omarama
Oamaru
Kurow
Manapouri
Alexandra
Mossburn
Kingston
Mosgiel
Heriot
West Cape
Tuatapere
Thornbury
Balclutha
Dunedin
SOLANDER ISLAND
Bluff
Invercargill
Oban
RUAPUKE ISLAND
Foveaux Strait
STEWART ISLAND
Southwest Cape
SNARES ISLANDS

CHATHAM ISLAND
Waitangi
CHATHAM ISLANDS (New Zealand)
PITT ISLAND

Chatham Rise

Bounty Trough

BOUNTY ISLANDS (New Zealand)

TASMAN SEA

Tasman Basin

Scale 1:15,000,000 at 25° latitude   Mercator Cylindrical Projection

0   200   400   600   800   1000 km
0   250   500 miles

Longitude East 180 West of Greenwich

M/Ft
2000/6562
1000/3281
500/1640
+200/+656
0
−200/−656
1000/3281
2000/6562
4000/13123
6000/19685
8000/26247

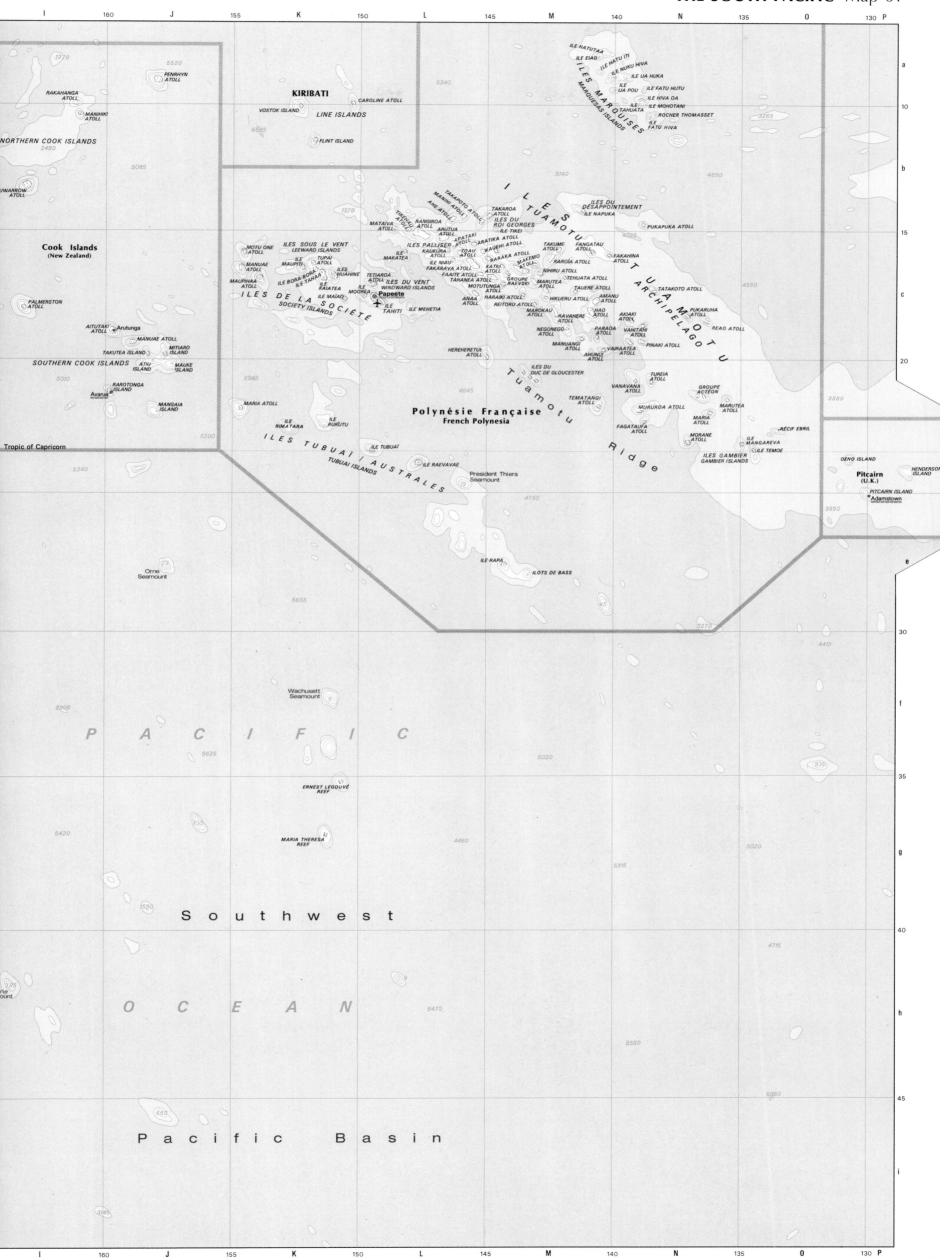

ILE HATUTAA
ILE EIAO
ILE HATU ITI
ILE NUKU HIVA
ILE
UA POU
ILE UA HUKA
ILE FATU HUTU
ILE HIVA OA
ILE MOHOTANI
ILE TAHUATA
ROCHER THOMASSET
ILE FATU HIVA

ILES MARQUISES
MARQUESAS ISLANDS

KIRIBATI
CAROLINE ATOLL
VOSTOK ISLAND
LINE ISLANDS
FLINT ISLAND

RAKAHANGA ATOLL
PENRHYN ATOLL
MANIHIKI ATOLL
NORTHERN COOK ISLANDS
SUWARROW ATOLL

Cook Islands
(New Zealand)

PALMERSTON ATOLL

AITUTAKI ATOLL Arutunga
MANUAE ATOLL
TAKUTEA ISLAND
MITIARO ISLAND
ATIU ISLAND
MAUKE ISLAND
SOUTHERN COOK ISLANDS
RAROTONGA ISLAND
Avarua
MANGAIA ISLAND

ILES DU DÉSAPPOINTEMENT
ILE NAPUKA
PUKAPUKA ATOLL

TAKAPOTO ATOLL
MANIHI ATOLL
AHE ATOLL
TIKEHAU ATOLL
RANGIROA ATOLL
ARUTUA ATOLL
MATAIVA ATOLL
ILES DU ROI GEORGES
ILE-TIKEI
TAKAROA ATOLL

I L E S   T U A M O T U

APATAKI ATOLL
ILES PALLISER
ILES SOUS LE VENT
LEEWARD ISLANDS
ARATIKA ATOLL
KAUKURA ATOLL
TOAU ATOLL
KAUEHI ATOLL
TAKUME ATOLL
FANGATAU ATOLL
FAKAHINA ATOLL
MOTU ONE ATOLL
ILE MAKATEA
KATIU ATOLL
KARAKA ATOLL
MAKEMO ATOLL
KAROIA ATOLL
MANUAE ATOLL
TUPAI ATOLL
ILE MAUPITI
ILE NIAU
FAKARAVA ATOLL
NIHIRU ATOLL
ILE HUAHINE
TEHUATA ATOLL
MAUPIHAA ATOLL
ILE BORA-BORA
ILE TAHAA
TETIAROA ATOLL
FAAITE ATOLL
GROUPE RAEVSKI
TAUERE ATOLL
ILE RAIATEA
ILES DU VENT
WINDWARD ISLANDS
TAHANEA ATOLL
MARUTEA ATOLL
TATAKOTO ATOLL
ILE MAIAO
ILE MOOREA
MOTUTUNGA ATOLL
ILES DE LA SOCIÉTÉ
Papeete
ANAA ATOLL
HARAIKI ATOLL
HIKUERU ATOLL
AMANU ATOLL
PUKARUHA ATOLL
SOCIETY ISLANDS
ILE TAHITI
REITORU ATOLL
AKIAKI ATOLL
REAO ATOLL
ILE MEHETIA
MAROKAU ATOLL
HAO ATOLL
RAVAHERE ATOLL
NEGONEGO ATOLL
PARAOA ATOLL
VAHITAHI ATOLL
HEREHERETUE ATOLL
MANUANGI ATOLL
AHUNUI ATOLL
PINAKI ATOLL
VAIRAATEA ATOLL

T U A M O T U   A R C H I P E L A G O

ILES DU DUC DE GLOUCESTER
TUREIA ATOLL
GROUPE ACTÉON
VANAVANA ATOLL
MARIA ATOLL
TEMATANGI ATOLL
MURUROA ATOLL
MARUTEA ATOLL
RÉCIF EBRIL
FAGATAUFA ATOLL
MORANE ATOLL
MARIA ATOLL
ILE MANGAREVA
ILES GAMBIER
GAMBIER ISLANDS
ILE TEMOE

Tuamotu Ridge

MARIA ATOLL
ILE RIMATARA
ILE RURUTU
Polynésie Française
French Polynesia

Tropic of Capricorn

ILES TUBUAI / AUSTRALES
TUBUAI ISLANDS
ILE TUBUAI
ILE RAEVAVAE
President Thiers Seamount
OENO ISLAND
HENDERSON ISLAND
Pitcairn
(U.K.)
PITCAIRN ISLAND
Adamstown

ILE RAPA
ILOTS DE BASS

Orne Seamount

Wachusett Seamount

P A C I F I C

ERNEST LEGOUVÉ REEF

MARIA THERESA REEF

S o u t h w e s t

O C E A N

P a c i f i c   B a s i n

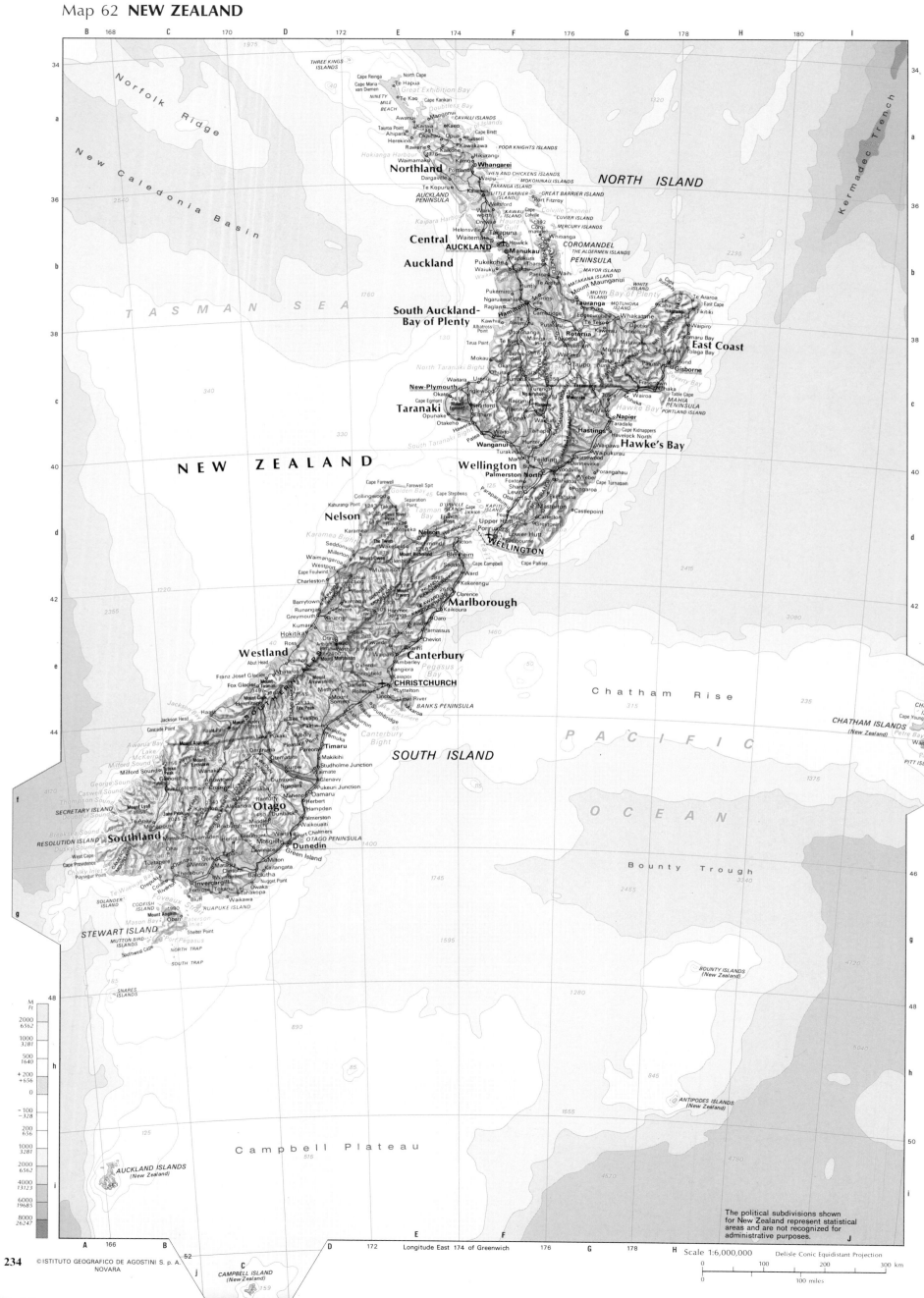

Map 62 NEW ZEALAND

NORTH ISLAND

NEW ZEALAND

Northland

Central Auckland

Auckland

South Auckland-
Bay of Plenty

East Coast

Taranaki

Hawke's Bay

Wanganui

Wellington

Nelson

Marlborough

Westland

Canterbury

SOUTH ISLAND

Otago

Southland

STEWART ISLAND

TASMAN SEA

Norfolk Ridge

New Caledonia Basin

Kermadec Trench

Chatham Rise

PACIFIC OCEAN

Bounty Trough

Campbell Plateau

CHATHAM ISLANDS
(New Zealand)

BOUNTY ISLANDS
(New Zealand)

ANTIPODES ISLANDS
(New Zealand)

AUCKLAND ISLANDS
(New Zealand)

CAMPBELL ISLAND
(New Zealand)

Longitude East 174 of Greenwich

The political subdivisions shown
for New Zealand represent statistical
areas and are not recognized for
administrative purposes.

Scale 1:6,000,000   Delisle Conic Equidistant Projection

0   100   200   300 km

0   100 miles

234 ©ISTITUTO GEOGRAFICO DE AGOSTINI S. p. A.
NOVARA

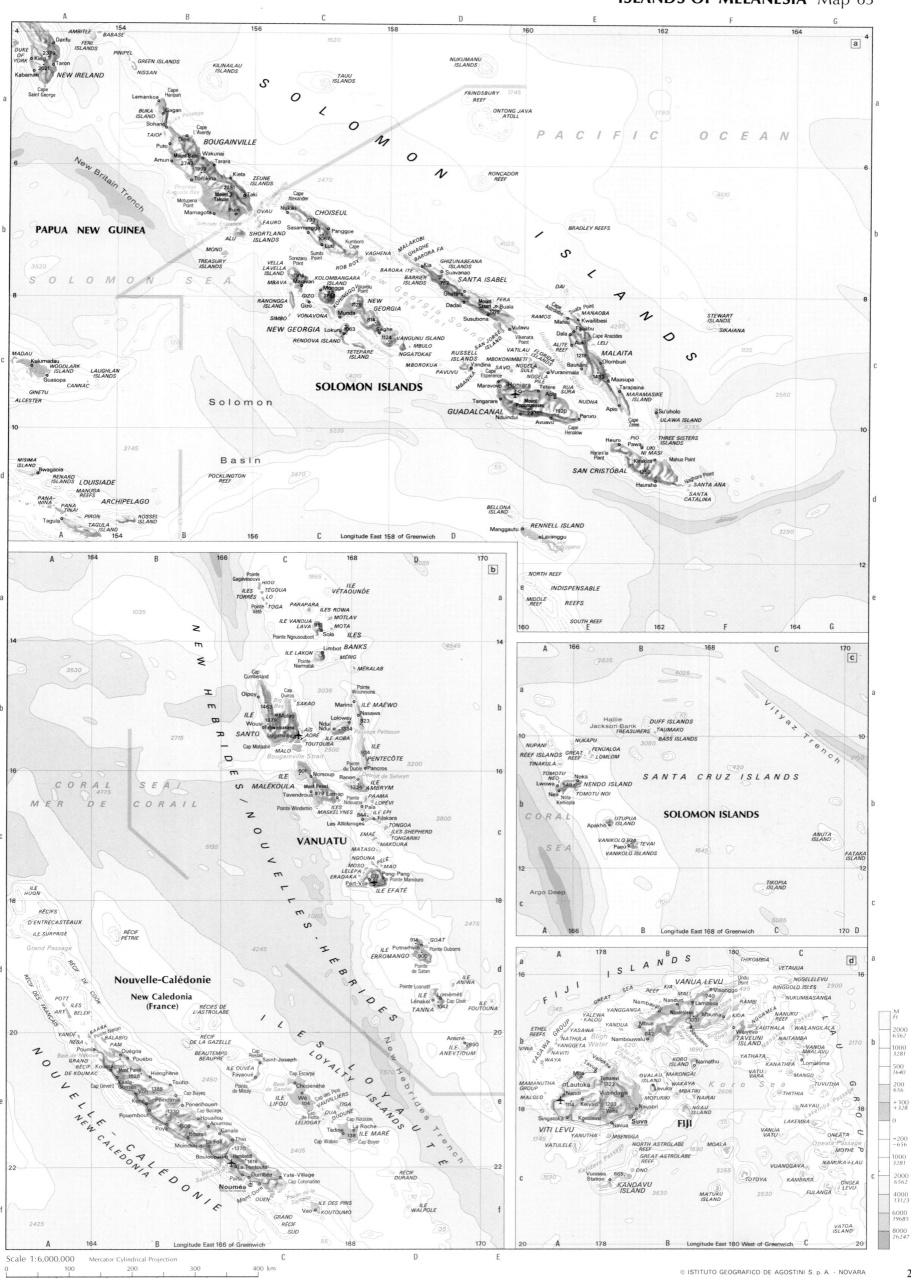

Map 64 ISLANDS OF MICRONESIA-POLYNESIA

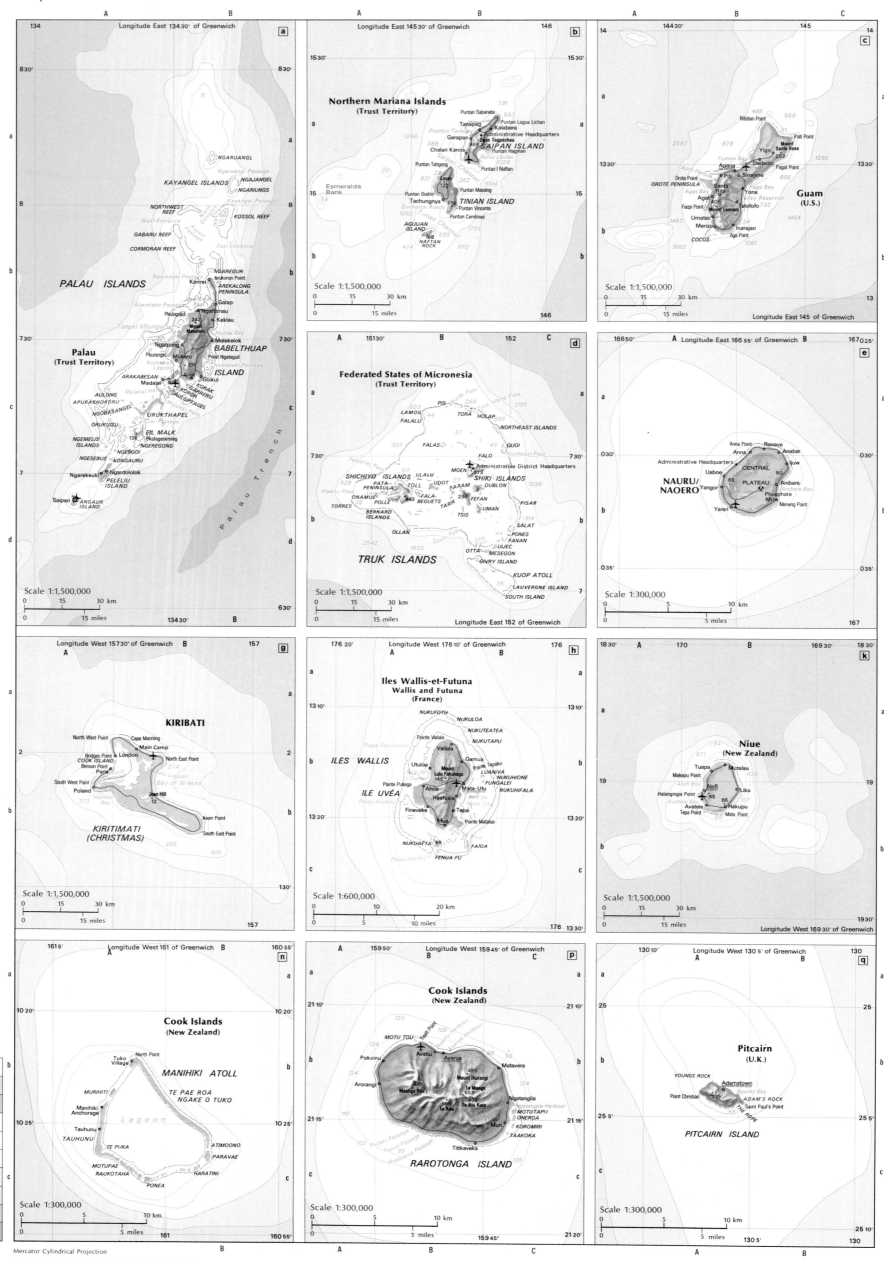

Mercator Cylindrical Projection

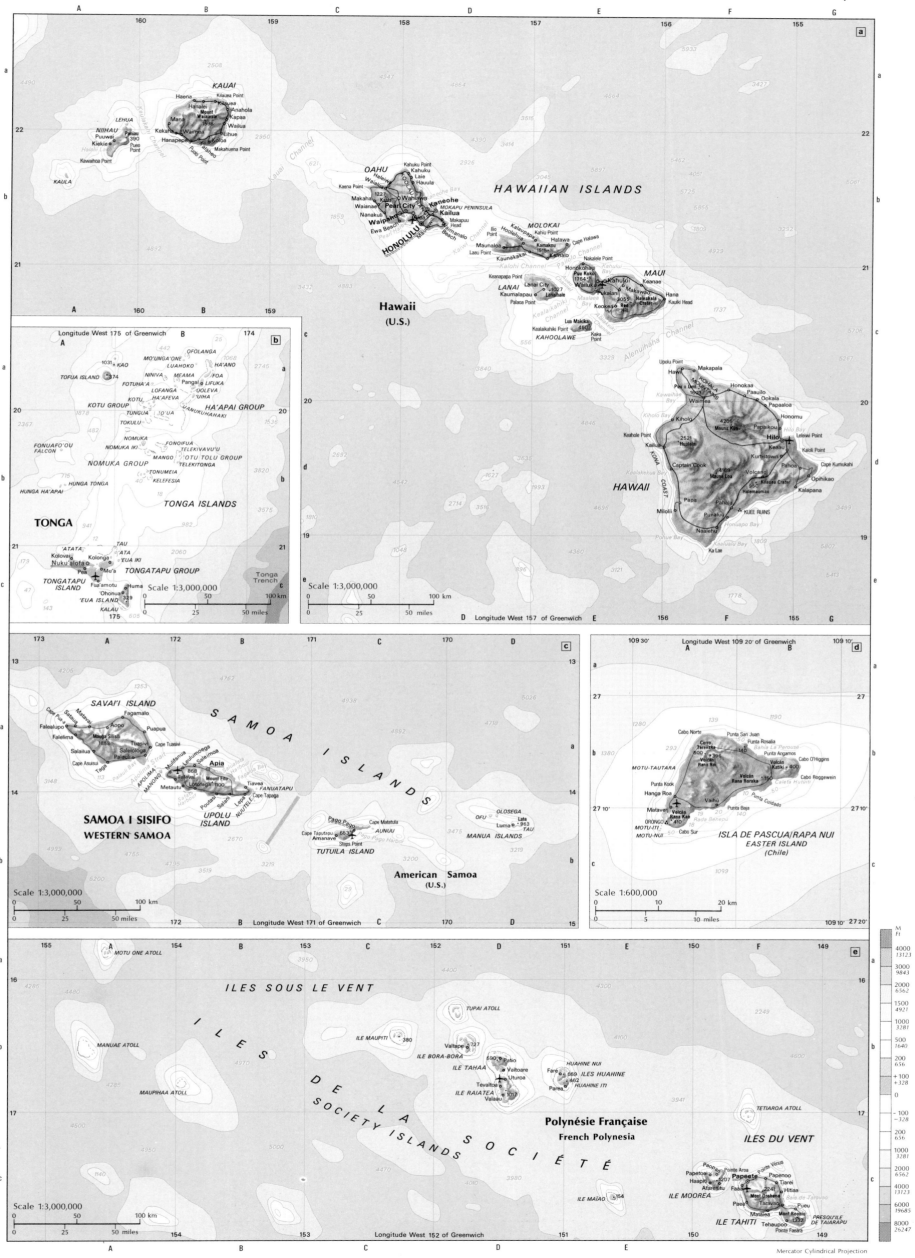

Map 66 **ANTARCTIC REGION**

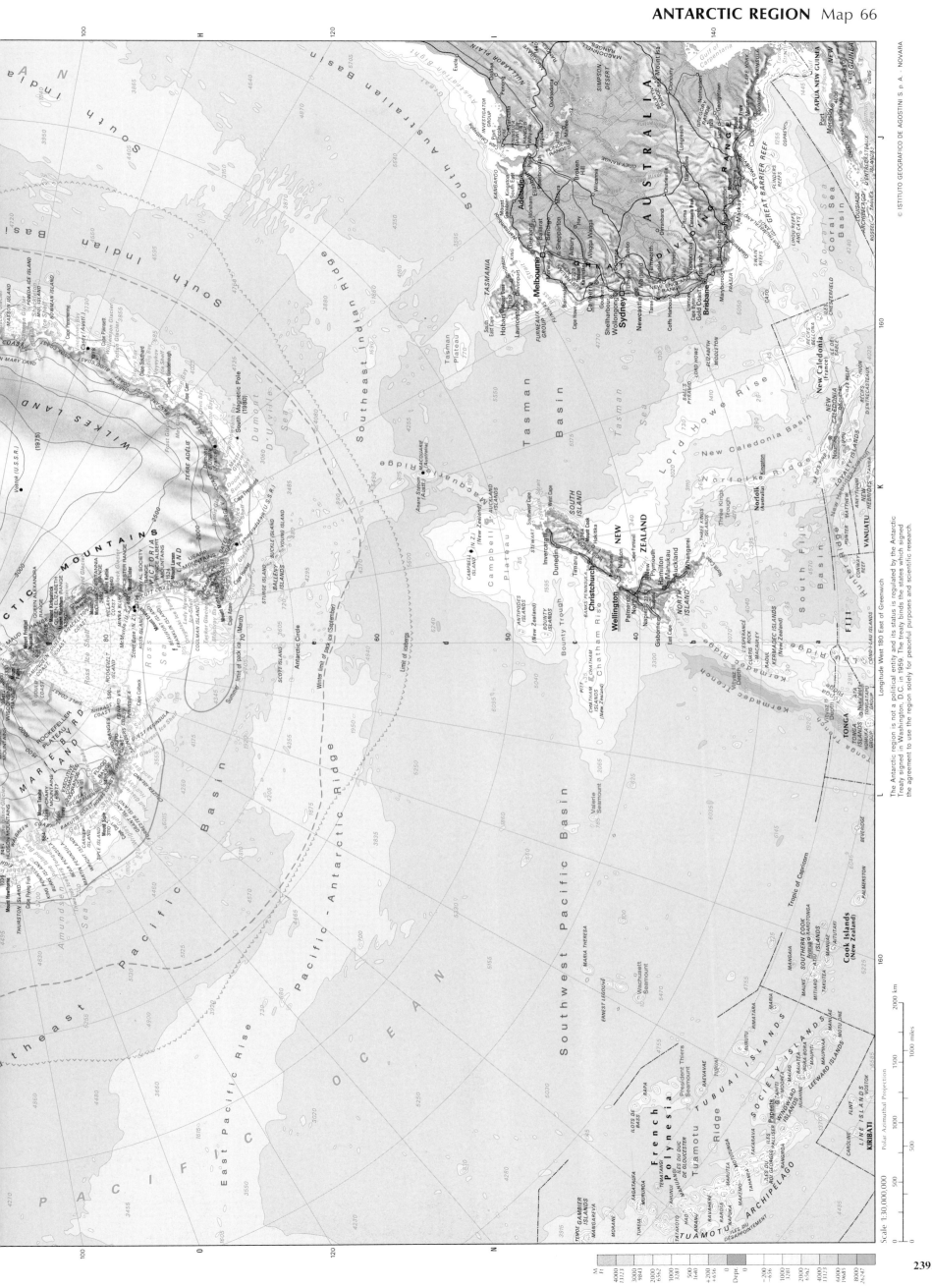

The Antarctic region is not a political entity and its status is regulated by the Antarctic Treaty signed in Washington, D.C. in 1959. The treaty binds the states which signed the agreement to use the region solely for peaceful purposes and scientific research.

Longitude West 180 East of Greenwich

Polar Azimuthal Projection

Scale 1:30,000,000

Map 67 **ARCTIC REGION**

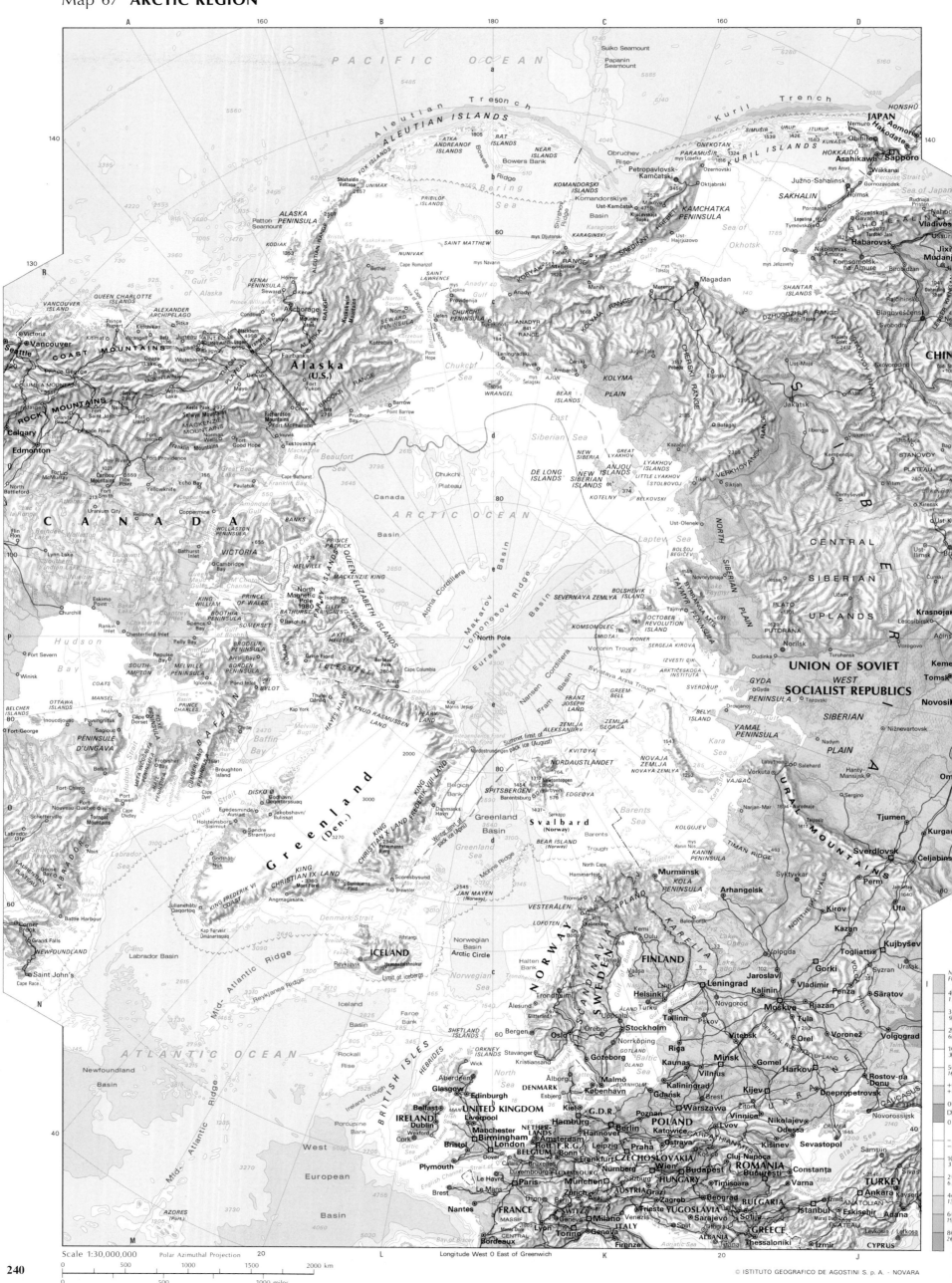

Scale 1:30,000,000 — Polar Azimuthal Projection

Longitude West 0 East of Greenwich

© ISTITUTO GEOGRAFICO DE AGOSTINI S. p. A. - NOVARA

UNITED KINGDOM AND IRELAND MAP SECTION

CONTENTS

242–243   ENGLAND AND WALES, SOUTH 1 : 1,000,000
          CHANNEL ISLANDS (inset)
          ISLES OF SCILLY (inset)

244–245   ENGLAND AND WALES, NORTH 1 : 1,000,000
          ISLE OF MAN
          (IRELAND)

246–247   SCOTLAND AND THE HEBRIDES 1 : 1,000,000
          ORKNEY ISLANDS
          SHETLAND ISLANDS (inset)

248–249   IRELAND 1 : 1,000,000
          NORTHERN IRELAND
          REPUBLIC OF IRELAND

250–256   UNITED KINGDOM AND IRELAND
          MAP INDEX

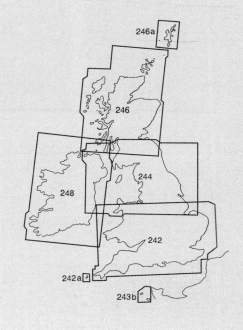

MAP LEGEND

Political Boundaries

━ ━ ━	International
━ ━	International (indefinite or undefined)
━━━	Country, Principality, Province (major divisions)
───	County, Region (minor divisions)

Capitals of Political Units

LONDON	Independent Nation
Douglas	Dependency
Belfast	Major Division
Carlisle	Minor Division
ISLE OF MAN (U.K)	Administering Country

Inhabited Localities

▭	Urban Area (area of continuous industrial, commercial, and residential development)
▭	Non Urban
Greenwich	Section of a City, Neighbourhood

The symbol represents the number of inhabitants within the locality

•	0—10,000	▫	100,000—250,000
○	10,000—25,000	▪	250,000—1,000,000
◉	25,000—100,000	■	>1,000,000

The size of type indicates the relative economic and political importance of the locality

Hilltown	**Dover**
Penzance	**Derby**
Pembroke	**LONDON**

Miscellaneous Cultural Features

RUNNYMEDE ▲	Point of Interest (battlefield, museum, historical site, etc.)
YORK MINSTER ⛪	Church, Monastery
STONEHENGE ∴	Ruins
WINDSOR CASTLE ⌷	Castle
⌇⌇⌇⌇	Wall

Transportation

(M-5)	Motorway
(A-303)	Major Road
———	Secondary Road
┼─┼─┼	Railways
LONDON (HEATHROW) AIRPORT ✈	Airport
SEVERN BRIDGE	Bridge
SEVERN TUNNEL	Tunnel
TO ABERDEEN	Ferry
Ulster Canal	Canal

Hydrographic Features

Loch Lomond	Lake, Reservoir
Thames	River, Stream
▭	Irrigation or Drainage Canal
\	Dam
NORTH SEA	Ocean or Sea
The Wash	Lakes, Channels, Bays, etc.
Severn	Rivers, Streams

Topographic Features

Elevation and depths are given in metres

348 △	Elevation Above Sea Level
(48)	Elevation of City or Town
Ben Nevis ▲ 1343	Highest Elevation in Country
Yanley ▼ 3	Lowest Elevation in Country
⋆	Rock (maritime)
PENNINES	Mountain Range
EXMOOR	Plateau, Valley, Upland, Forest, etc.

ENGLAND AND WALES, SOUTH

Kilometres

Statute Miles

Scale 1:1,000,000

One centimetre represents 10 kilometres.
One inch represents approximately 16 miles.

Lambert Conformal Conic Projection

NORTH SEA

Kilometres | 0 10 20 30 40 50 Km.
Statute Miles | 0 10 20 30 40 50 Mi.

Scale 1:1,000,000

One centimetre represents 10 kilometres.
One inch represents approximately 16 miles.

Lambert Conformal Conic Projection

SCOTLAND

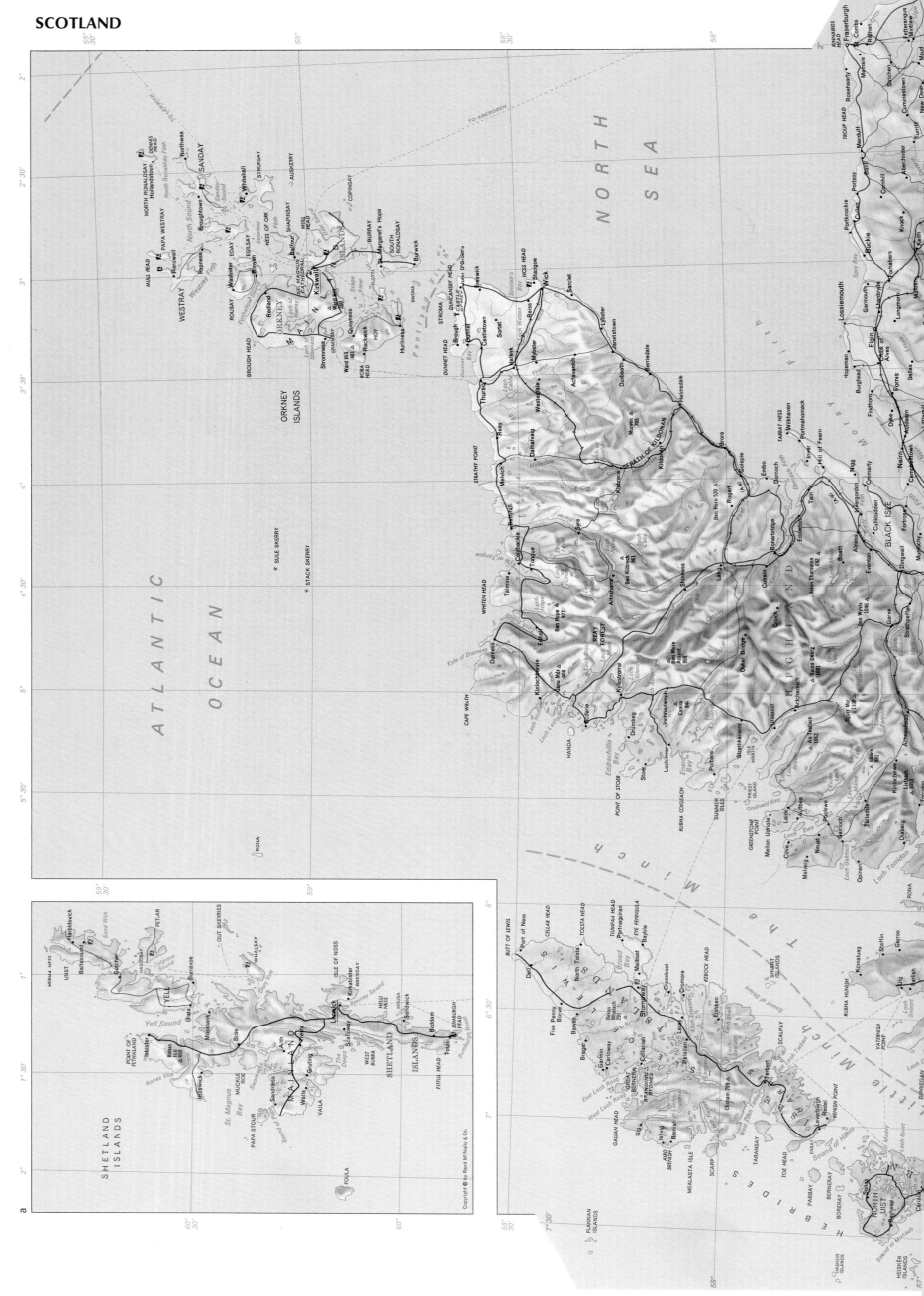

Copyright © by Rand McNally & Co.

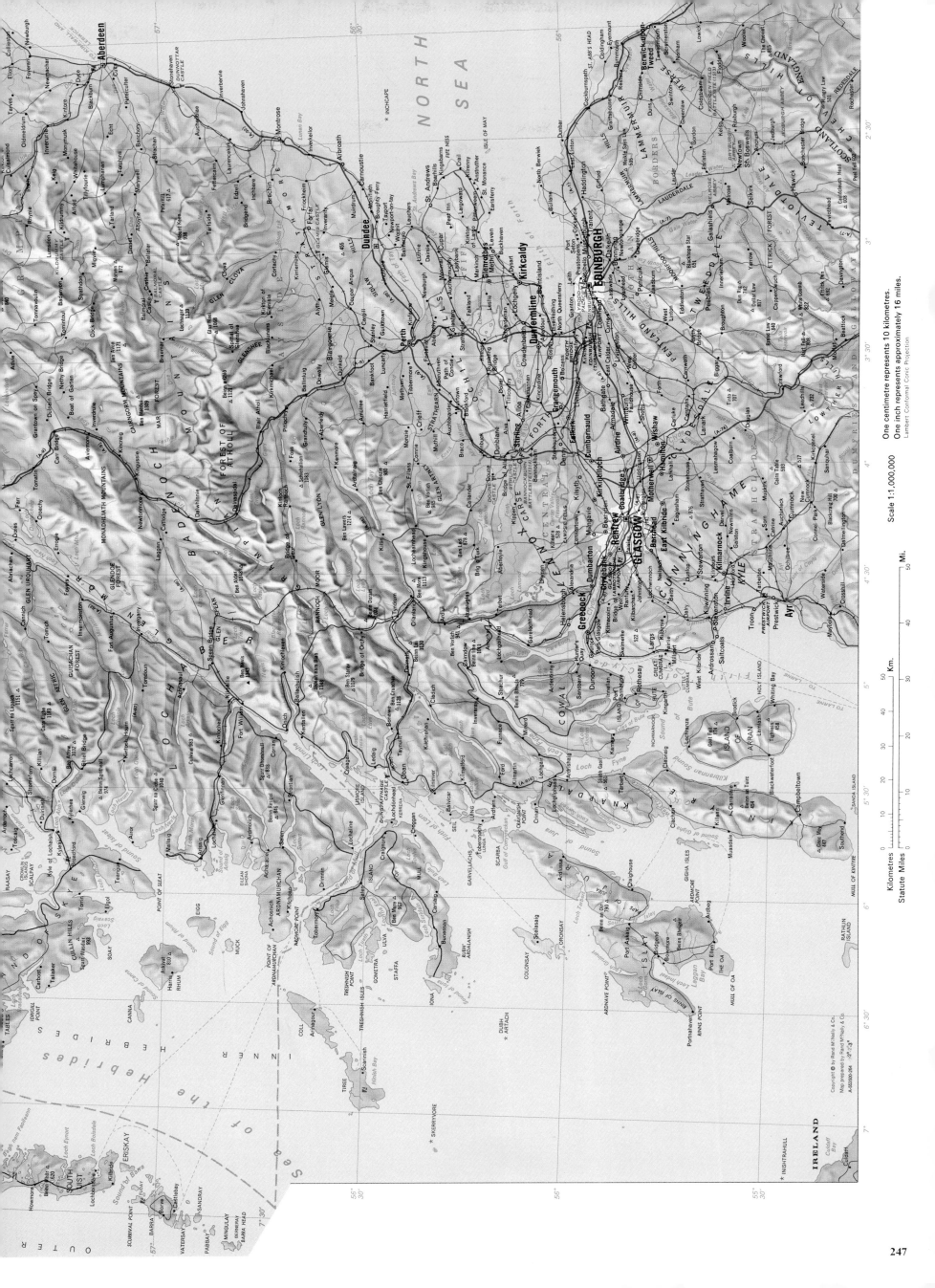

NORTH SEA

INNER HEBRIDES

Sea of the Hebrides

OUTER HEBRIDES

IRELAND

Aberdeen

Dundee

Perth

EDINBURGH

GLASGOW

Greenock

Renfrew

Kirkcaldy

Dunfermline

Stirling

Ayr

Kilmarnock

ARRAN ISLAND

ISLAY

JURA

MULL

SKYE

Scale 1:1,000,000

One centimetre represents 10 kilometres.
One inch represents approximately 16 miles.

Lambert Conformal Conic Projection

Kilometres

Statute Miles

Mi.

Km.

Copyright © by Rand McNally & Co.
Map prepared by Rand McNally & Co.
A-583000-264

247

IRELAND

248

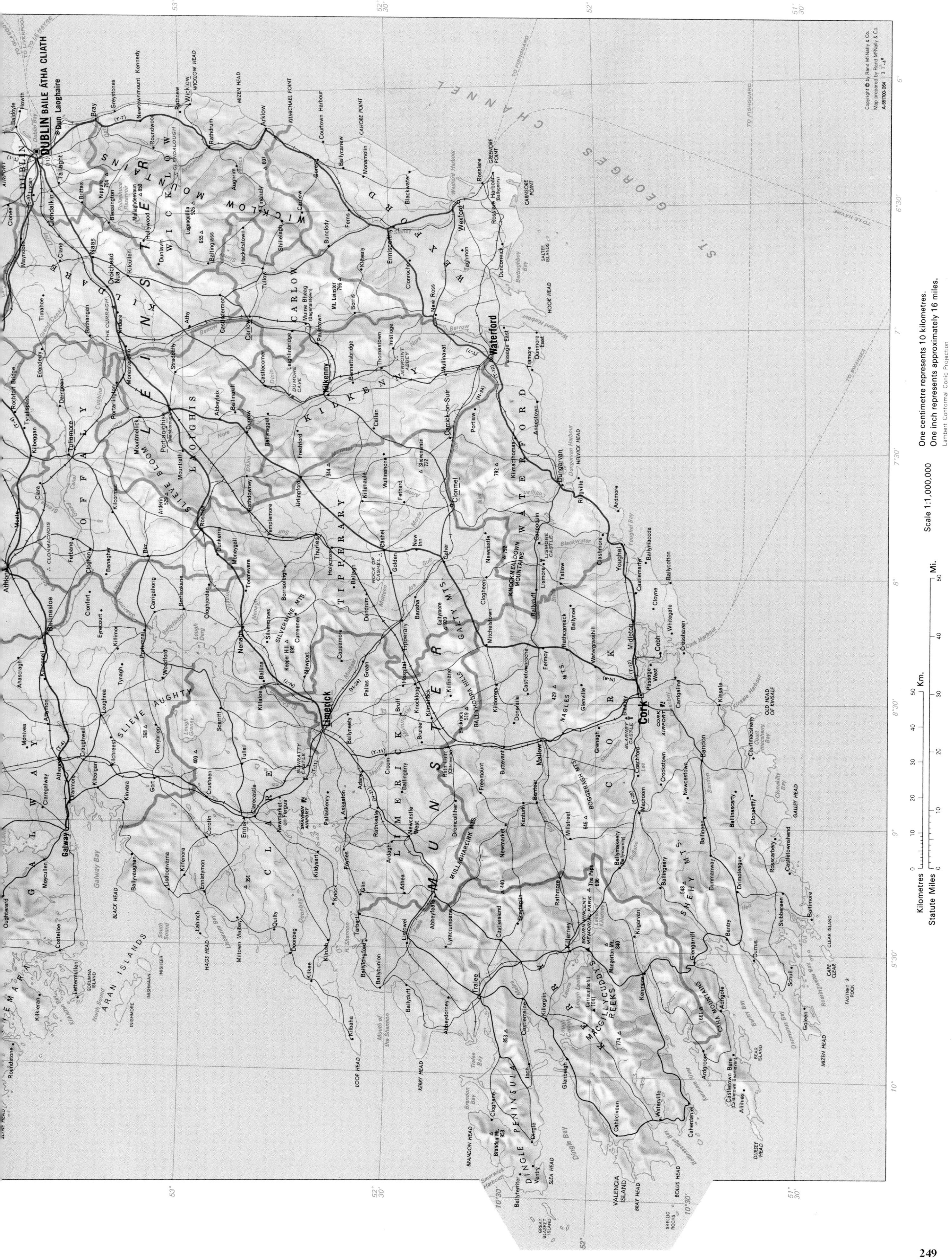

GEORGE'S CHANNEL

ST. GEORGE'S CHANNEL

TO LIVERPOOL
TO LE HAVRE
TO FISHGUARD
TO SWANSEA

Scale 1:1,000,000

One centimetre represents 10 kilometres.
One inch represents approximately 16 miles.

Lambert Conformal Conic Projection

Kilometres
Statute Miles
Km.
Mi.

DUBLIN BAILE ÁTHA CLIATH

Dun Laoghaire

Galway

Limerick

Cork

Waterford

Kilkenny

LEINSTER

MUNSTER

CONNAUGHT

GALWAY

CLARE

LIMERICK

KERRY

CORK

TIPPERARY

WATERFORD

KILKENNY

CARLOW

LAOIGHIS

OFFALY

KILDARE

WICKLOW

WEXFORD

WICKLOW MOUNTAINS

SLIEVE BLOOM MOUNTAINS

SLIEVE AUGHTY

GALTY MTS.

SILVERMINE MTS.

KNOCKMEALDOWN MOUNTAINS

COMERAGH MTS.

MACGILLYCUDDY'S REEKS

NAGLES MTS.

BOGGERAGH MTS.

MULLAGHAREIRK MTS.

SHEHY MTS.

CAHA MOUNTAINS

DINGLE PENINSULA

ARAN ISLANDS

VALENCIA ISLAND

Galway Bay

Tralee Bay

Dingle Bay

Kenmare River

Bantry Bay

Dunmanus Bay

Cork Harbour

Waterford Harbour

Wexford Harbour

Dublin Bay

Mouth of the Shannon

Lough Derg

249

United Kingdom and Ireland Map Index

The index includes in a single alphabetical list some 5,000 names appearing on the maps. Each name is followed by a page reference and by the location of the feature on the map. The map location is designated by latitude and longitude coordinates. If a page contains several maps, a lowercase letter identifies the inset map. The page reference for two-page maps is always to the left hand page.

The features indexed are of three types: *point*, *areal*, and *linear*. For *point* features (for example, cities, mountain peaks, dams), latitude and longitude coordinates give the location of the point on the map. For *areal* features (countries, mountain ranges, etc.), the coordinates generally indicate the approximate center of the feature. For *linear* features (rivers, canals, aqueducts), the coordinates locate a terminating point—for example, the mouth of a river, or the point at which a feature reaches the map margin.

ALPHABETIZATION Names are alphabetized in the order of the letters of the English alphabet. Diacritical marks are disregarded in alphabetization.

The names of physical features may appear inverted, since they are always alphabetized under the proper, not the generic, part of the name, thus: "Clyde, Firth of C^{1}". Otherwise every entry, whether consisting of one word or more, is alphabetized as a single continuous entity. "Blackford," for example, appears after "Black Devon" and before "Black Head." Names beginning with articles are not inverted. Names beginning "Mc" are alphabetized as though spelled "Mac," and names beginning "St." and "Sainte" as though spelled "Saint."

In the case of identical names, towns are listed first, then political divisions, then physical features. Entries that are completely identical (including symbols, discussed below) are distinguished by abbreviations of country or regional names. (See list of abbreviations below.)

ABBREVIATION AND CAPITALIZATION Abbreviation and styling have been standardized. A period is used after every abbreviation even when this may not be the local practice.

All names are written with an initial capital letter. Capitalization of noninitial words in a name generally follows local practice.

SYMBOL The symbols that appear in the index graphically represent the broad categories of the features named, for example, ⊜ for lake (Tay, Loch ⊜). Superior numbers following some symbols in the index indicate finer distinctions, for example, ⊜^{1} for (Pitsford Reservoir ⊜^{1}). A complete list of the symbols and those with superior numbers is given below. All cross references are indicated by the symbol →.

LIST OF ABBREVIATIONS

EIRE	Ireland	EUR.	Europe	N. IRE.	Northern Ireland	U.K.	United Kingdom
ENG.	England	I. OF MAN	Isle of Man	SCOT.	Scotland		

KEY TO SYMBOLS

- ∧ **Mountain**
- ∧^{2} Hill
- ⋀⋀ **Mountains**
- ⋀⋀^{1} Plateau
- ⋀⋀^{2} Hills
-)(**Pass**
- ∨ **Valley**
- ≃ **Plain**
- ≃^{1} Basin
- ≃^{2} Delta
- ≻ **Cape**
- ≻^{1} Peninsula
- ≻^{2} Spit, Sand Bar
- I **Island**
- I^{2} Rock
- II **Islands**
- II^{1} Rocks
- ⊕ **Other Topographic Features**
- ⊕^{1} Continent
- ⊕^{2} Coast, Beach
- ⊕^{3} Isthmus
- ⊕^{4} Cliff
- ⊕^{5} Cave, Caves
- ⊕^{6} Crater
- ⊕^{7} Depression
- ⊕^{8} Dunes
- ≃ **River**
- ≃^{1} River Channel
- ≅ **Canal**
- ≅^{1} Aqueduct
- ⌊ **Waterfall, Rapids**
- ⊔ **Strait**
- C **Bay, Gulf**
- C^{1} Estuary
- C^{3} Bight
- ⊜ **Lake, Lakes**
- ⊜^{1} Reservoir
- ⁞⁞ **Swamp**
- ⊤ **Other Hydrographic Features**
- ⊤^{1} Ocean
- ⊤^{2} Sea
- ⊤^{3} Anchorage
- ✣ **Submarine Features**
- ✣^{2} Reef, Shoal
- □ **Political Unit**
- □^{1} Independent Nation
- □^{2} Dependency
- □^{4} Region
- □^{6} County
- □^{7} City, Municipality
- □^{8} Miscellaneous
- □^{9} Historical
- ⊽ **Cultural Institution**
- ⊽^{1} Religious Institution
- ⊽^{2} Educational Institution
- ⊽^{3} Scientific, Industrial Facility
- ⊥ **Historical Site**
- ♠ **Recreational Site**
- ⊠ **Airport**
- ■ **Military Installation**
- ◆ **Miscellaneous**
- ◆^{1} Region
- ◆^{3} Forest, Moor
- ◆^{4} Reserve, Reservation
- ◆^{5} Transportation
- ◆^{6} Dam
- ◆^{7} Mine, Quarry
- ◆^{8} Neighborhood

Name	Page	Lat ° ′	Long ° ′
A			
Abbert ≃	248	53.26 N	9.54 W
Abbeydorney	248	52.19 N	9.41 W
Abbeyfeale	248	52.24 N	9.18 W
Abbey Head ≻	244	54.46 N	3.58 W
Abbeyleix	248	52.55 N	7.20 W
Abbey Town	244	54.50 N	3.17 W
Abbotsbury	242	50.40 N	2.36 W
Abbots Langley	242	51.43 N	0.25 W
Aberaman	242	51.42 N	3.25 W
Aberavon → Port Talbot	242	51.36 N	3.47 W
Aberayron	242	52.15 N	4.15 W
Abercarn	242	51.39 N	3.08 W
Aberchirder	246	57.33 N	2.38 W
Aberdare	242	51.43 N	3.27 W
Aberdaron	242	52.49 N	4.43 W
Aberdeen	246	57.10 N	2.04 W
Aberdour	246	56.03 N	3.19 W
Aberdovey	242	52.33 N	4.02 W
Aberdulais	242	51.41 N	3.48 W
Aberfeldy	246	56.37 N	3.54 W
Aberfoyle	246	56.11 N	4.23 W
Abergavenny	242	51.50 N	3.00 W
Abergele	244	53.17 N	3.34 W
Abergwynfi	242	51.40 N	3.35 W
Abergynolwyn	242	52.40 N	3.58 W
Aberlour	246	57.28 N	3.14 W
Abernethy	246	56.20 N	3.19 W
Aberporth	242	52.09 N	4.33 W
Abersoch	242	52.50 N	4.29 W
Abersychan	242	51.44 N	3.04 W
Abertillery	242	51.45 N	3.09 W
Aberuthven	246	56.19 N	3.39 W
Aberystwyth	242	52.25 N	4.05 W
Abingdon	242	51.41 N	1.17 W
Aboyne	246	57.05 N	2.50 W
Abriachan	246	57.22 N	4.24 W
Accrington	244	53.46 N	2.21 W
Acharacle	246	56.44 N	5.47 W
Achavanich	246	58.22 N	3.24 W
Achill Head ≻	248	53.59 N	10.13 W
Achill Island I	248	54.00 N	10.00 W
Achill Sound	248	53.55 N	9.58 W
Achnasaul	246	56.58 N	4.59 W
Achnasheen	246	57.35 N	5.06 W
Achosnich	246	56.45 N	6.06 W
Acle	242	52.38 N	1.33 E
Acton Turville	242	51.32 N	2.17 W
Adare	248	52.34 N	8.48 W
Adderbury	242	52.00 N	1.17 W
Addingham	244	53.57 N	1.53 W
Adlington	244	53.37 N	2.36 W
Adrigole	248	51.40 N	9.42 W
Adur ≃	242	50.49 N	0.16 W
Advie	246	57.23 N	3.27 W
Adwick le Street	244	53.34 N	1.11 W
Ae, Water of ≃	244	55.08 N	3.27 W
Aeron ≃	242	52.14 N	4.16 W
Affric ≃	246	57.19 N	4.50 W
Affric, Glen ∨	246	57.17 N	4.56 W
Aghleam	248	54.08 N	10.07 W
Agnews Hill ∧^{2}	248	54.51 N	5.56 W
Ahascragh	248	53.24 N	8.20 W
Aide ≃	242	52.10 N	1.27 E
Ailsa Craig I	244	55.16 N	5.07 W
Ainsdale	244	53.36 N	3.02 W
Airdrie	246	55.52 N	3.59 W
Aire ≃	244	53.44 N	0.54 W
Airor	246	57.04 N	5.46 W
Aith	246	60.16 N	1.23 W
Alasdair, Sgurr ∧	246	57.12 N	6.14 W
Alaw ≃	244	53.18 N	4.32 W
Alaw, Llyn ⊜^{1}	244	53.20 N	4.22 W
Albrighton	242	52.38 N	2.16 W
Alcester	242	52.13 N	1.52 W
Alconbury Brook ≃	242	52.19 N	0.12 W
Aldbourne	242	51.31 N	1.37 W
Aldbrough	244	53.50 N	0.07 W
Aldbury	242	51.48 N	0.36 W
Alde ≃	242	52.03 N	1.28 E
Aldeburgh	242	52.09 N	1.35 E
Alder, Ben ∧	246	56.48 N	4.28 W
Alderley Edge	244	53.18 N	2.15 W
Aldermaston	242	51.23 N	1.09 W
Alderney I	243b	49.43 N	2.12 W
Aldershot	242	51.15 N	0.47 W
Aldridge	242	52.36 N	1.55 W
Aled ≃	244	53.14 N	3.34 W
Ale Water ≃	246	55.31 N	2.35 W
Alexandria	246	55.59 N	4.36 W
Alford, Eng., U.K.	244	53.16 N	0.10 E
Alford, Scot., U.K.	246	57.13 N	2.42 W
Alfriston	242	50.48 N	0.10 E
Allan Water ≃	246	56.08 N	3.56 W
Allen ≃	244	54.58 N	2.19 W
Allen, Lough ⊜	248	54.08 N	8.08 W
Allendale Town	244	54.54 N	2.15 W
Allestree	242	52.57 N	1.29 W
Allihies	248	51.38 N	10.03 W
Alloa	246	56.07 N	3.49 W
Allonby	244	54.46 N	3.25 W
Almond ≃, Scot., U.K.	246	56.25 N	3.27 W
Almond ≃, Scot., U.K.	246	55.58 N	3.18 W
Almondsbury	242	51.34 N	2.34 W
Aln ≃	244	55.23 N	1.37 W
Alne ≃	242	52.13 N	1.52 W
Alness	246	57.41 N	4.15 W
Alnmouth	244	55.23 N	1.36 W
Alnwick	244	55.25 N	1.42 W
Alphington	242	50.42 N	3.31 W
Alsh, Loch C	246	57.15 N	5.39 W
Alston	244	54.49 N	2.26 W
Alt ≃	244	53.32 N	3.03 W
Altarnun	242	50.37 N	4.30 W
Altnaharra	246	58.16 N	4.27 W
Alton	242	51.09 N	0.59 W
Altrincham	244	53.24 N	2.21 W
Alva	246	56.09 N	3.48 W
Alvechurch	242	52.21 N	1.57 W
Alveston	242	51.36 N	2.32 W
Alwen ≃	242	52.58 N	3.24 W
Alyth	246	56.37 N	3.13 W
Amber ≃	244	53.08 N	1.29 W
Amble	244	55.20 N	1.34 W
Amblecote	242	52.28 N	2.09 W
Ambleside	244	54.26 N	2.58 W
Amersham	242	51.40 N	0.38 W
Amesbury	242	51.10 N	1.45 W
Amlwch	244	53.25 N	4.20 W
Ammanford	242	51.45 N	0.35 W
Ampleforth	244	54.12 N	1.06 W
Ampthill	242	52.02 N	0.30 W
Amulree	246	56.30 N	3.47 W
Ancaster	242	52.59 N	0.32 W
Ancholme ≃	244	53.41 N	0.32 W
Ancrum	246	55.31 N	2.35 W
Andover	242	51.13 N	1.28 W
Angle	242	51.41 N	5.06 W
Anglesey I	244	53.17 N	4.22 W
Angmering	242	50.48 N	0.28 W
Anlaby	244	53.45 N	0.27 W
Annagassan	248	53.53 N	6.20 W
Annalee ≃	248	54.03 N	7.24 W
Annan	244	54.59 N	3.16 W
Annan ≃	244	54.59 N	3.16 W
Annandale ∨	244	55.10 N	3.25 W
Anner ≃	248	52.22 N	7.39 W
Annestown	248	52.07 N	7.16 W
Annet I	242a	49.54 N	6.21 W
Annfield Plain	244	54.51 N	1.45 W
Anstey	242	52.40 N	1.11 W
Anstruther	246	56.13 N	2.42 W
An Teallach ∧	246	57.48 N	5.14 W
Antrim	248	54.43 N	6.13 W
An Uaimh → Navan	248	53.39 N	6.41 W
Ape Dale ∨	242	52.30 N	2.45 W
Appleby	244	54.36 N	2.29 W
Applecross	246	57.25 N	5.49 W
Appledore	242	51.03 N	4.10 W
Ara ≃	248	52.24 N	7.56 W
Aran Fawddwy ∧	242	52.47 N	3.41 W
Aran Island I	248	54.58 N	8.33 W
Aran Islands II	248	53.07 N	9.43 W
Arbroath	246	56.34 N	2.35 W
Ard, Loch ⊜	246	56.11 N	4.28 W
Ardagh	248	52.28 N	9.04 W
Ardalanish, Rubh' ≻	246	56.17 N	6.18 W
Ardara	248	54.46 N	8.25 E
Ardarroch	246	57.25 N	5.38 W
Ardbeg	246	55.39 N	6.05 W
Ardcharnich	246	57.51 N	5.05 W
Ardee	248	53.52 N	6.33 W
Arden, Forest of ◆^{3}	242	52.23 N	1.42 W
Ardentinny	246	56.03 N	4.55 W
Arderin ∧^{2}	248	53.02 N	7.40 W
Ardfern	246	56.10 N	5.32 W
Ardglass	248	54.16 N	5.36 W
Ardgroom	248	51.42 N	9.52 W
Ardlui	246	56.18 N	4.43 W
Ardlussa	246	56.02 N	5.47 W
Ardmolich	246	56.49 N	5.41 W
Ardmore	248	51.57 N	7.43 W
Ardmore Point ≻, Scot., U.K.	246	55.42 N	6.01 W
Ardmore Point ≻, Scot., U.K.	246	56.39 N	6.07 W
Ardnamurchan ≻^{1}	246	56.43 N	6.00 W
Ardnamurchan, Point of ≻	246	56.44 N	6.13 W
Ardnaree	248	54.06 N	9.08 W
Ardnave Point ≻	246	55.44 N	6.20 W
Ardrishaig	246	56.01 N	5.27 W
Ardrossan	246	55.39 N	4.49 W
Ardsley	244	53.32 N	1.28 W
Ardtalnaig	246	56.31 N	4.06 W
Arennig Fawr ∧	242	52.55 N	3.45 W
Arinagour	246	56.37 N	6.31 W
Arisaig	246	56.51 N	5.51 W
Arisaig, Sound of C	246	56.51 N	5.51 W
Arkaig, Loch ⊜	246	56.58 N	5.08 W
Arklow	248	52.48 N	6.09 W
Armadale	246	55.54 N	3.42 W
Armagh	248	54.21 N	6.39 W
Armthorpe	244	53.32 N	1.03 W
Arney ≃	248	54.16 N	7.37 W
Arnold	244	53.00 N	1.08 W
Arran, Island of I	246	55.36 N	5.15 W
Arrochar	246	56.12 N	4.44 W
Arrow ≃, Eng., U.K.	242	52.12 N	2.43 W
Arrow ≃, Eng., U.K.	242	52.09 N	1.53 W
Arrow, Lough ⊜	248	54.04 N	8.21 W
Artney, Glen ∨	246	56.20 N	4.04 W
Arun ≃	242	50.48 N	0.33 W
Arundel	242	50.51 N	0.34 W
Arvagh	248	53.55 N	7.34 W
Ascot	242	51.25 N	0.41 W
Ash, Eng., U.K.	242	51.17 N	1.16 E
Ash, Eng., U.K.	242	51.15 N	0.44 W
Ash ≃	242	51.48 N	0.02 W
Ashbourne, Eire	248	53.31 N	6.24 W
Ashbourne, Eng., U.K.	244	53.02 N	1.44 W
Ashburton	242	50.31 N	3.45 W
Ashby-de-la-Zouch	242	52.46 N	1.28 W
Ashdown Forest ◆^{3}	242	51.04 N	0.03 E
Ashford	242	51.08 N	0.53 E
Ashford Airport ⊠	242	51.04 N	1.01 E
Ashington	244	55.12 N	1.35 W
Ashtead	242	51.19 N	0.18 W
Ashton-in-Makerfield	244	53.29 N	2.39 W
Ashton-under-Lyne	244	53.29 N	2.06 W
Ashwater	242	50.44 N	4.16 W
Askeaton	248	52.36 N	8.58 W
Askern	244	53.37 N	1.09 W
Askival ∧	246	56.59 N	6.17 W
Askrigg	244	54.19 N	2.04 W
Aspatria	244	54.46 N	3.20 W
Assynt, Loch ⊜	246	58.11 N	5.06 W
Aston Clinton	242	51.48 N	0.44 W
Athboy	248	53.37 N	6.55 W
Athea	248	52.28 N	9.17 W
Athenry	248	53.18 N	8.45 W
Atherstone	242	52.35 N	1.31 W
Atherton	244	53.31 N	2.31 W
Athleague	248	53.34 N	8.15 W
Athlone	248	53.25 N	7.56 W
Áth Luain → Athlone	248	53.25 N	7.56 W
Atholl, Forest of ◆^{3}	246	56.50 N	4.00 W
Athy	248	53.00 N	7.00 W
Attleborough	242	52.31 N	1.01 E
Attow, Ben ∧	246	57.13 N	5.18 W
Attymon	248	53.19 N	8.35 W
Auchenblae	246	56.54 N	2.26 W
Auchencairn	244	54.51 N	3.53 W
Auchinleck	244	55.28 N	4.17 W
Auchterarder	246	56.18 N	3.43 W
Auchterderran	246	56.09 N	3.16 W
Auchtermuchty	246	56.17 N	3.15 W
Augher	248	54.26 N	7.09 W
Aughnacloy	248	54.25 N	6.58 W
Aughrim	248	52.51 N	6.17 W
Aughty, Slieve ⋀⋀	248	53.05 N	8.35 W
Auldearn	246	57.34 N	3.49 W
Aultbea	246	57.50 N	5.35 W
Aurigny → Alderney I	243b	49.43 N	2.12 W
Auskerry I	246	59.02 N	2.34 W
Avan ≃	242	51.35 N	3.48 W
Avebury	242	51.27 N	1.51 W
Avebury Stone Circle ⊥	242	51.28 N	1.51 W
Avich, Loch ⊜	246	56.16 N	5.20 W
Aviemore	246	57.12 N	3.50 W
Avoca ≃	248	52.48 N	6.09 W
Avon □^{6}	242	51.30 N	2.40 W
Avon ≃, Eng., U.K.	242	51.30 N	2.43 W
Avon ≃, Eng., U.K.	242	50.17 N	3.52 W
Avon ≃, Eng., U.K.	242	50.43 N	1.46 W
Avon ≃, Eng., U.K.	242	52.25 N	1.31 W
Avon ≃, Eng., U.K.	242	51.59 N	2.10 W
Avon ≃, Scot., U.K.	246	57.25 N	3.23 W
Avon ≃, Scot., U.K.	246	56.00 N	3.40 W
Avon, Ben ∧	246	57.05 N	3.27 W
Avonmore ≃	248	52.50 N	6.13 W
Avonmouth	242	51.31 N	2.42 W
Avon Water ≃	246	55.47 N	4.01 W
Awe, Loch ⊜	246	56.15 N	5.17 W
Axbridge	242	51.18 N	2.49 W
Axe ≃, Eng., U.K.	242	51.19 N	2.59 W
Axe ≃, Eng., U.K.	242	50.42 N	3.03 W
Axminster	242	50.47 N	3.00 W
Axmouth	242	50.42 N	3.02 W
Aylesbury	242	51.50 N	0.50 W
Aylesford	242	51.18 N	0.29 E
Aylesham	242	51.13 N	1.13 E
Aylsham	242	52.49 N	1.15 E
Ayr	244	55.28 N	4.38 W
Ayr ≃	244	55.29 N	4.28 W
Ayre, Point of ≻	244	54.26 N	4.22 W
Aysgarth	244	54.17 N	2.00 W
B			
Ba, Loch ⊜	246	56.36 N	4.44 W
Babbacombe Bay C	242	50.30 N	3.25 W
Bacton	242	52.52 N	1.28 E
Bacup	244	53.43 N	2.12 W
Badenoch ◆^{1}	246	56.57 N	4.19 W
Badenyon	246	57.15 N	3.05 W
Baggy Point ≻	242	51.09 N	4.16 W
Bagshot	242	51.22 N	0.42 W
Baildon	244	53.52 N	1.46 W
Baile Átha Cliath → Dublin	248	53.20 N	6.15 W
Bailieborough	248	53.54 N	6.59 W
Bain ≃	244	53.05 N	0.12 W
Bakewell	244	53.13 N	1.40 W
Bala	242	52.54 N	3.35 W
Balallan	246	58.05 N	6.35 W
Balbriggan	248	53.37 N	6.11 W
Balcombe	242	51.04 N	0.08 W
Baldock	242	51.59 N	0.12 W
Baldoyle	248	53.24 N	6.08 W
Baleshare I	246	57.31 N	7.22 W
Balfour	246	59.01 N	2.55 W
Balfron	246	56.04 N	4.20 W
Balla	248	53.48 N	9.09 W
Ballachulish	246	56.40 N	5.10 W
Ballagh	248	52.35 N	7.59 W
Ballaghaderreen	248	53.55 N	8.36 W
Ballantrae	244	55.06 N	5.00 W
Ballater	246	57.03 N	3.03 W
Ballaugh	244	54.20 N	4.32 W
Ballina	248	52.49 N	8.26 W
Ballinakill	248	52.53 N	7.18 W
Ballinalack	248	53.37 N	7.28 W
Ballinascarty	248	51.40 N	8.51 W
Ballinasloe	248	53.20 N	8.13 W
Ballindine	248	53.39 N	8.59 W
Ballineen	248	51.44 N	8.56 W
Ballingarry	248	52.29 N	8.52 W
Ballingeary	248	51.49 N	9.13 W
Ballinluig	246	56.38 N	3.39 W
Ballinrobe	248	53.37 N	9.13 W
Ballinskelligs Bay C	248	51.50 N	10.15 W
Ballintoy	248	55.14 N	6.21 W
Ballintra	248	54.35 N	8.08 W
Balloch	246	57.29 N	4.07 W
Ballybay	248	54.08 N	6.54 W
Ballybofey	248	54.48 N	7.47 W
Ballybogy	248	55.07 N	6.34 W
Ballybunion	248	52.31 N	9.40 W
Ballycanew	248	52.36 N	6.19 W
Ballycastle, Eire	248	54.16 N	9.23 W
Ballycastle, N. Ire., U.K.	248	55.12 N	6.15 W
Ballyclare	248	54.46 N	6.01 W
Ballyconneely	248	53.26 N	10.02 W
Ballyconnell	248	54.07 N	7.35 W
Ballycotton	248	51.50 N	8.01 W
Ballycroy	248	54.01 N	9.51 W
Ballyduff, Eire	248	52.27 N	9.40 W
Ballyduff, Eire	248	52.09 N	8.03 W
Ballyferriter	248	52.09 N	10.26 W
Ballyfinboy ≃	248	53.02 N	8.15 W
Ballygar	248	53.32 N	8.20 W
Ballygawley	248	54.28 N	7.02 W
Ballygorman	248	55.22 N	7.21 W
Ballyhaise	248	54.03 N	7.19 W
Ballyhalbert	248	54.30 N	5.28 W
Ballyhaunis	248	53.46 N	8.46 W
Ballyhoura Hills ⋀⋀^{2}	248	52.20 N	8.35 W
Ballyjamesduff	248	53.52 N	7.12 W
Ballylongford	248	52.33 N	9.28 W
Ballymacoda	248	51.57 N	7.54 W
Ballymahon	248	53.34 N	7.45 W
Ballymakeery (Ballyvourney)	248	51.55 N	9.09 W
Ballymena	248	54.52 N	6.17 W
Ballymoe	248	53.42 N	8.29 W
Ballymoney	248	55.04 N	6.31 W
Ballymote	248	54.06 N	8.31 W
Ballymurray	248	53.35 N	8.08 W
Ballynahinch	248	54.24 N	5.54 W
Ballyneety	248	52.35 N	8.33 W
Ballynoe	248	52.03 N	8.05 W
Ballyquintin Point ≻	248	54.20 N	5.29 W
Ballyragget	248	52.47 N	7.20 W
Ballysadare	248	54.13 N	8.31 W
Ballyshannon	248	54.30 N	8.11 W
Ballyvaughan	248	53.07 N	9.07 W
Ballyvoy	248	55.12 N	6.11 W
Ballywalter	248	54.33 N	5.30 W
Balmerino	246	56.24 N	3.02 W
Balmoral Castle	246	57.02 N	3.13 W
Balmoral Castle ⊥	246	57.02 N	3.14 W
Balnacra	246	57.28 N	5.23 W
Balsham	242	52.08 N	0.20 E
Baltasound	246a	60.45 N	0.52 W
Baltimore	248	51.29 N	9.22 W
Baltinglass	248	52.55 N	6.41 W

Symbols in the index entries are identified on page 250.

Name	Page	Lat	Long
Balvicar	246	56.14 N	5.38 W
Bamburgh	244	55.36 N	1.42 W
Bampton, Eng., U.K.	242	51.00 N	3.29 W
Bampton, Eng., U.K.	242	51.44 N	1.33 W
Banagher	248	53.11 N	7.59 W
Banbridge	248	54.21 N	6.16 W
Banbury	242	52.04 N	1.20 W
Banchory	246	57.30 N	2.30 W
Bandon	248	51.45 N	8.45 W
Bandon ≃	248	51.42 N	8.30 W
Banff	246	57.40 N	2.33 W
Bangor	244	53.13 N	4.08 W
Bangor Erris	248	54.09 N	9.45 W
Bankfoot	246	56.30 N	3.30 W
Bann ≃	248	55.10 N	6.45 W
Bannockburn	246	56.06 N	3.55 W
Bannockburn Battlesite (1314) ⊥	246	56.06 N	3.54 W
Bansha	248	52.28 N	8.04 W
Banstead	242	51.19 N	0.12 W
Banteer	248	52.07 N	8.54 W
Bantry	248	51.41 N	9.27 W
Bantry Bay C	248	51.38 N	9.48 W
Banwell	242	51.20 N	2.52 W
Banwy ≃	242	52.42 N	3.16 W
Bardney	244	53.12 N	0.21 W
Bardsey Island I	242	52.45 N	4.45 W
Bardsey Sound ᴗ	242	52.47 N	4.45 W
Bargoed	242	51.43 N	3.15 W
Barking ⁸	242	51.33 N	0.06 E
Barlby	242	53.48 N	1.03 W
Barmouth	242	52.43 N	4.03 W
Barmouth Bay C	242	52.42 N	4.08 W
Barnard Castle	244	54.33 N	1.55 W
Barnet ⁸	242	51.40 N	0.13 W
Barnetby le Wold	244	53.35 N	0.25 W
Barnoldswick	244	53.55 N	2.11 W
Barnsley	244	53.34 N	1.28 W
Barnstaple	242	51.05 N	4.04 W
Barnstaple Bay C	242	51.05 N	4.20 W
Barnt Green	242	52.22 N	1.59 W
Barra I	246	56.58 N	7.29 W
Barra, Sound of ᴗ	246	57.05 N	7.25 W
Barra Head ⊁	246	56.46 N	7.38 W
Barrhead	246	55.48 N	4.24 W
Barrhill	246	55.07 N	4.46 W
Barrow ≃	248	52.15 N	7.00 W
Barrowford	242	52.15 N	2.13 W
Barrow-in-Furness	244	54.07 N	3.14 W
Barry	242	51.23 N	3.18 W
Barton Mills	242	52.20 N	0.31 E
Barton-under-Needwood	242	52.45 N	1.43 W
Barton-upon-Humber	244	53.41 N	0.27 W
Barvas	246	58.22 N	6.32 W
Barwell	242	52.32 N	1.21 W
Basildon	242	51.35 N	0.25 E
Basingstoke	242	51.15 N	1.05 W
Baslow	244	53.15 N	1.38 W
Bassenthwaite	244	54.41 N	3.12 W
Bassenthwaite Lake ⊜	244	54.38 N	3.13 W
Bath	242	51.23 N	2.22 W
Bathgate	246	55.55 N	3.39 W
Batley	244	53.44 N	1.37 W
Battle	242	50.55 N	0.29 E
Bawdeswell	242	52.45 N	1.01 E
Bawtry	244	53.26 N	1.01 W
Bayhead	246	57.33 N	7.24 W
Beachy Head ⊁	242	50.44 N	0.16 E
Beacon Hill ∧²	242	52.23 N	3.12 W
Beaconsfield	242	51.37 N	0.39 W
Beagh, Slieve ∧²	248	54.21 N	7.12 W
Beaminster	242	50.49 N	2.45 W
Bear Island I	248	51.40 N	9.48 W
Bearsden	246	55.56 N	4.20 W
Beattock	244	55.18 N	3.28 W
Beaulieu	242	50.49 N	1.27 W
Beauly	246	57.29 N	4.29 W
Beauly ≃	246	57.28 N	4.28 W
Beauly Firth C¹	246	57.30 N	4.23 W
Beaumaris	244	53.16 N	4.05 W
Bebington	244	53.23 N	3.00 W
Beccles	242	52.28 N	1.34 E
Beckington	242	51.16 N	2.18 W
Bedale	244	54.17 N	1.35 W
Beddgelert	244	53.01 N	4.06 W
Bedford	242	52.08 N	0.29 W
Bedford Level ≃	242	52.27 N	0.02 W
Bedfordshire □⁶	242	52.05 N	0.30 W
Bedwas	242	51.35 N	3.13 W
Bedworth	242	52.28 N	1.29 W
Beela ≃	244	54.13 N	2.47 W
Beeston	242	52.56 N	1.12 W
Beith	246	55.45 N	4.38 W
Belcoo	248	54.17 N	7.52 W
Belfast	248	54.35 N	5.55 W
Belfast Lough C	248	54.40 N	5.36 W
Belford	244	55.36 N	1.49 W
Bellahy	248	53.58 N	8.48 W
Bell Crags ∧²	244	54.33 N	2.22 W
Belleek	248	54.28 N	8.06 W
Bellingham	244	55.09 N	2.16 W
Belmullet	248	54.14 N	10.00 W
Beltra	248	54.13 N	8.37 W
Belturbet	248	54.06 N	7.28 W
Belvoir, Vale of ᴠ	242	52.57 N	0.53 W
Bembridge	242	50.41 N	1.05 W
Benbane Head ⊁	248	55.15 N	6.28 W
Benbecula I	246	57.26 N	7.21 W
Beneraird ∧²	246	55.04 N	4.57 W
Benllech	244	53.19 N	4.13 W
Bennettsbridge	248	52.36 N	7.12 W
Benson	242	51.38 N	1.05 W
Bentley	244	53.33 N	1.09 W
Benwee ∧	248	54.20 N	9.50 W
Benwee Head ∧	248	54.20 N	9.50 W
Bere Alston	242	50.29 N	4.11 W
Bere Regis	242	50.46 N	2.14 W
Berkeley	242	51.42 N	2.27 W
Berkeley, Vale of ᴠ	242	51.43 N	2.25 W
Berkhamsted	242	51.46 N	0.35 W
Berkshire □⁶	242	51.30 N	1.20 W
Berkshire Downs ∧¹	242	51.33 N	1.24 W
Berneray I	246	57.43 N	7.12 W
Bernisdale	246	57.27 N	6.22 W
Berriedale	246	58.11 N	3.29 W
Berry Head ⊁	242	50.24 N	3.29 W
Bertraghboy Bay C	248	53.23 N	9.52 W
Berwick-upon-Tweed	244	55.46 N	2.00 W
Berwyn ∧¹	242	52.55 N	3.24 W
Bethersden	242	51.08 N	0.48 E
Bethesda	244	53.11 N	4.03 W
Bettyhill	246	58.32 N	4.14 W
Betws-y-Coed	244	53.05 N	3.48 W
Beult ≃	242	51.14 N	0.25 E
Beverley	244	53.52 N	0.26 W
Beverley Minster †	244	53.50 N	0.27 W
Bewdley	242	52.22 N	2.19 W
Bexhill on Sea	242	50.50 N	0.29 E
Bexley ⁸	242	51.26 N	0.10 E
Bheigeir, Beinn ∧²	246	55.44 N	6.05 W
Bheula, Beinn ∧²	246	56.08 N	4.58 W
Bian, Bidean nam ∧	246	56.38 N	5.02 W
Bicester	242	51.54 N	1.09 W
Bicknender	242	51.07 N	0.39 E
Biddulph	244	53.08 N	2.10 W
Bideford	242	51.01 N	4.13 W
Bidford-on-Avon	242	52.10 N	1.51 W
Bigbury Bay C	242	50.16 N	3.48 W
Biggar	246	55.38 N	3.32 W
Biggin Hill ⁸	242	51.18 N	0.04 E
Biggleswade	242	52.05 N	0.17 W
Billericay	242	51.38 N	0.25 E
Billesdon	242	52.37 N	0.55 W
Billingham	244	54.36 N	1.17 W
Billingshurst	242	51.01 N	0.28 W
Bilston	242	52.34 N	2.04 W
Bingham	242	52.57 N	0.57 W
Bingley	244	53.51 N	1.50 W
Birchington	242	51.23 N	1.19 E
Birkenhead	244	53.24 N	3.02 W
Birmingham	242	52.30 N	1.50 W
Birmingham Airport ⊠	242	52.27 N	1.45 W
Birstall	242	53.05 N	7.54 W
Birtley	244	54.54 N	1.34 W
Bishop Auckland	244	54.40 N	1.40 W
Bishop's Castle	242	52.29 N	3.00 W
Bishop's Cleeve	242	51.57 N	2.04 W
Bishops Frome	242	52.08 N	2.29 W
Bishops Lydeard	242	51.04 N	3.12 W
Bishop's Stortford	242	51.53 N	0.09 E
Bishopsteignton	242	50.34 N	3.31 W
Bishopstoke	242	50.59 N	1.19 W
Bishop's Waltham	242	50.58 N	1.12 W
Bisley	242	51.45 N	2.08 W
Blackadder Water ≃	246	55.46 N	2.15 W
Blackburn, Eng., U.K.	244	53.45 N	2.29 W
Blackburn, Scot., U.K.	246	57.12 N	2.18 W
Blackcraig Hill ∧	244	55.20 N	4.08 W
Black Devon ≃	246	56.06 N	3.47 W
Black Down Hills ∧²	242	50.57 N	3.09 W
Black Esk ≃	242	51.52 N	5.10 W
Blackford	246	56.15 N	3.46 W
Blackhall Colliery	244	54.44 N	1.14 W
Black Head ⊁, Eire	248	53.08 N	9.17 W
Black Head ⊁, Eng., U.K.	242	50.01 N	5.06 W
Blackhope Star ∧	246	55.44 N	3.05 W
Black Isle ⊁¹	246	57.35 N	4.15 W
Blacklunans	246	56.44 N	3.22 W
Blackmoor ∧²	242	50.24 N	4.46 W
Blackmoor Vale ᴠ	242	50.56 N	2.25 W
Black Mountain ∧	242	51.52 N	3.46 W
Black Mountains ∧²	242	51.57 N	3.08 W
Blackpool	244	53.50 N	3.03 W
Blackrock ∧²	248	52.18 N	8.32 W
Black Rock I²	248	54.05 N	10.22 W
Blacksod Bay C	248	54.08 N	10.00 W
Blackwater	246	56.29 N	6.21 W
Blackwater ≃, Eire	248	51.51 N	7.50 W
Blackwater ≃, Eng., U.K.	242	51.45 N	1.00 E
Blackwaterfoot	246	55.30 N	5.19 W
Blackwater Reservoir ⊜¹	246	56.41 N	4.46 W
Bladnoch ≃	244	54.51 N	4.25 W
Blaenau Ffestiniog	242	52.59 N	3.56 W
Blaenavon	242	51.48 N	3.05 W
Blagdon	242	51.20 N	2.43 W
Blaina	242	51.46 N	3.10 W
Blair Atholl	246	56.46 N	3.51 W
Blairgowrie	246	56.36 N	3.21 W
Blakeney, Eng., U.K.	242	52.58 N	1.00 E
Blakeney, Eng., U.K.	242	51.46 N	2.29 W
Blandford Forum	242	50.52 N	2.11 W
Blarney	248	51.56 N	8.34 W
Blarney Castle ⊥	248	51.56 N	8.34 W
Blaydon	244	54.58 N	1.42 W
Blean	242	51.19 N	1.02 E
Blenheim Palace ⊥	242	51.47 N	1.21 W
Blessington	248	53.10 N	6.32 W
Bletchley	242	52.00 N	0.46 W
Blithe ≃	242	52.45 N	1.50 W
Blithfield Reservoir ⊜¹	242	52.48 N	1.53 W
Blockley	242	52.01 N	1.45 W
Bloody Foreland ⊁	248	55.09 N	8.17 W
Bloom, Slieve ∧	248	53.05 N	7.35 W
Bloxham	242	52.02 N	1.22 W
Blue Stack Mountains ∧¹	248	54.45 N	8.05 W
Blyth	244	55.07 N	1.30 W
Blyth ≃, Eng., U.K.	244	55.08 N	1.31 W
Blyth ≃, Eng., U.K.	242	52.18 N	1.40 E
Blyth Bridge	244	55.42 N	3.24 W
Blythe ≃	242	52.31 N	1.42 W
Boarhills	246	56.19 N	2.42 W
Boath	246	57.44 N	4.23 W
Boat of Garten	246	57.20 N	3.44 W
Boddam	246	59.55 N	1.17 W
Boder, Lough ⊜			
Bodiam	242	51.00 N	0.33 E
Bodmin	242	50.29 N	4.43 W
Bodmin Moor ᴧ	242	50.33 N	4.33 W
Boggeragh Mountains ∧¹	248	52.03 N	8.55 W
Bognor Regis	242	50.47 N	0.41 W
Bogrie Hill ∧²	244	55.08 N	3.55 W
Boisdale, Loch C	246	57.08 N	7.19 W
Boldon	244	54.57 N	1.27 W
Bollin ≃	244	53.23 N	2.28 W
Bollington	244	53.18 N	2.06 W
Bolsover	244	53.14 N	1.18 W
Bolton	244	53.35 N	2.26 W
Bolton Abbey	244	53.59 N	1.53 W
Bolton Abbey ⊥			
Bolton Bridge	244	53.59 N	1.54 W
Bolton-le-Sands	244	53.58 N	1.57 W
Bolton upon Dearne	244	53.31 N	1.19 W
Bolus Head ⊁	248	51.46 N	10.21 W
Bonawe	246	56.26 N	5.13 W
Bo'ness	246	56.01 N	3.37 W
Bonnybridge	246	55.52 N	3.08 W
Bonnyrigg	246	55.52 N	3.08 W
Boot	244	54.24 N	3.17 W
Bootle	244	53.28 N	3.01 W
Borders □⁴	246	55.35 N	2.50 W
Boreham Wood	242	51.40 N	0.15 W
Boreray I	246	57.42 N	7.18 W
Borough Green	242	51.17 N	0.19 E
Borris	248	52.35 N	6.56 W
Borrisokane	248	52.59 N	8.07 W
Borrisoleigh	248	52.45 N	7.57 W
Borrowdale	244	54.31 N	3.10 W
Borth	242	52.29 N	4.03 W
Borthwick Water ≃	244	55.24 N	2.50 W
Borve	246	56.58 N	7.32 W
Boscastle	242	50.41 N	4.42 W
Boston	242	52.59 N	0.01 W
Bosworth Field (1485) ⊥	242	52.36 N	1.25 W
Botley	242	50.56 N	1.18 W
Bottesford	242	52.56 N	0.48 W
Boughton Street	242	51.18 N	0.59 E
Boulsworth Hill ∧	244	53.48 N	2.06 W
Bourne	242	52.46 N	0.23 W
Bourne ≃	242	51.02 N	1.47 W
Bournemouth	242	50.43 N	1.54 W
Bourn Vincent Memorial Park ⁴	248	52.01 N	9.30 W
Bourton-on-the-Water	242	51.53 N	1.45 W
Bovey ≃	242	50.34 N	3.37 W
Bovey Tracey	242	50.36 N	3.40 W
Bovingdon	242	51.44 N	0.32 W
Bow Brook ≃	242	52.04 N	2.07 W
Bowgreave	244	53.52 N	2.45 W
Bowland, Forest of ⁴³	244	53.58 N	2.32 W
Bowmont Water ≃			
Bowmore	246	55.34 N	2.09 W
Bowness-on-Windermere	246	55.45 N	6.17 W
Box	242	54.22 N	2.55 W
Boyle	248	51.26 N	2.15 W
Boyne ≃	248	53.58 N	8.18 W
Boyne Battlesite ⊥	248	53.43 N	6.15 W
Braan ≃	246	56.33 N	3.35 W
Bracadale, Loch C	246	57.19 N	6.30 W
Bracebridge Heath	244	53.13 N	0.33 W
Brackley	242	52.02 N	1.09 W
Bracknell	242	51.26 N	0.45 W
Braco	246	56.15 N	3.53 W
Bradford	244	53.48 N	1.45 W
Bradford-on-Avon	242	51.20 N	2.15 W
Brading	242	50.41 N	1.09 W
Bradwell-on-Sea	242	51.44 N	0.54 E
Bradworthy	242	50.54 N	4.22 W
Brae	246a	60.23 N	1.21 W
Braemar	246	57.01 N	3.23 W
Bragar	246	58.24 N	6.40 W
Braich-y-Pwll ⊁	242	52.48 N	4.36 W
Brain ≃	242	51.48 N	0.39 E
Braint ≃	242	53.08 N	4.19 W
Braintree	242	51.53 N	0.32 E
Bramford	242	52.04 N	1.06 E
Brampton, Eng., U.K.	242	52.19 N	0.14 W
Brampton, Eng., U.K.	244	54.57 N	2.43 W
Brancaster	242	52.58 N	0.39 E
Brandon, Eng., U.K.	242	52.27 N	0.37 E
Brandon, Eng., U.K.	244	54.46 N	1.39 W
Brandon Bay C	248	52.15 N	10.05 W
Brandon Head ⊁			
Brandon Mountain ∧	248	52.16 N	10.14 W
Brant ≃	244	53.10 N	0.35 W
Braunton	242	51.07 N	4.10 W
Bray	248	53.12 N	6.06 W
Bray ≃	242	50.59 N	3.53 W
Bray Head ⊁	248	51.53 N	10.26 W
Breamish ≃	244	55.31 N	1.56 W
Bream's Eaves	242	51.45 N	2.34 W
Brechfa	242	51.54 N	4.36 W
Brechin	246	56.44 N	2.40 W
Breckland ⁺¹	242	52.28 N	0.37 E
Brecknock → Brecon			
Brecon	242	51.57 N	3.24 W
Brecon Beacons ∧	242	51.57 N	3.24 W
Brecon Beacons National Park ⁴	242	51.53 N	3.31 W
Bredon Hill ∧²	242	51.52 N	3.25 W
Breedoge ≃	242	52.06 N	2.03 W
Brendon Hills ∧²	248	53.55 N	8.27 W
Brenish	242	51.07 N	3.25 W
Brenish, Aird ⊁	246	58.08 N	7.08 W
Brent ⁸	246	58.08 N	7.08 W
Brent ≃	242	51.34 N	0.17 W
Brentwood	242	51.28 N	0.18 W
Bressay I	242	51.38 N	0.18 E
Bressay Sound ᴗ	246a	60.08 N	1.05 W
Brett ≃	246a	60.07 N	1.09 W
Brewood	242	51.58 N	0.58 E
Bri Chualann → Bray	242	52.41 N	2.10 W
Bride ≃	248	53.12 N	6.06 W
Bride ≃	244	54.22 N	4.22 W
Bridgend, Scot., U.K.	242	52.04 N	7.52 W
Bridgend, Scot., U.K.	246	56.48 N	2.45 W
Bridgend, Wales, U.K.	246	55.48 N	6.16 W
Bridge of Allan	242	51.31 N	3.35 W
Bridge of Gaur	246	56.09 N	3.57 W
Bridge of Orchy	246	56.41 N	4.27 W
Bridge of Weir	246	56.30 N	4.46 W
Bridgnorth	246	55.52 N	4.35 W
Bridgwater	242	52.33 N	2.25 W
Bridgwater Bay C	242	51.08 N	3.00 W
Bridlington	244	54.05 N	0.12 W
Bridlington Bay C	244	54.04 N	0.08 W
Bridport	242	50.44 N	2.46 W
Brierfield	242	53.50 N	2.14 W
Brierley Hill	242	52.29 N	2.07 W
Brigg	244	53.34 N	0.30 W
Brighouse	244	53.42 N	1.47 W
Brighstone	242	50.38 N	1.24 W
Brightlingsea	242	51.49 N	1.02 E
Brighton	242	50.50 N	0.08 W
Brig o' Turk	246	56.13 N	4.22 W
Brill	242	51.49 N	1.03 W
Brimfield	242	52.18 N	2.42 W
Brimington	244	53.16 N	1.23 W
Brinyan	246	59.07 N	2.59 W
Bristol	242	51.27 N	2.35 W
Bristol (Lulsgate) Airport ⊠	242	51.23 N	2.43 W
Bristol Channel ᴗ	242	51.20 N	4.00 W
Briton Ferry	242	51.38 N	3.49 W
Brittas	248	53.14 N	6.27 W
Brixham	242	50.23 N	3.30 W
Brixworth	242	52.20 N	0.54 W
Broad Bay C	246	58.15 N	6.15 W
Broad Chalke	242	51.02 N	1.57 W
Broad Clyst	242	50.46 N	3.26 W
Broadford	246	57.14 N	5.54 W
Broad Haven C	248	54.18 N	9.55 W
Broad Law ∧	244	55.30 N	3.22 W
Broadstairs	242	51.22 N	1.27 E
Broadway	242	52.02 N	1.51 W
Broadwindsor	242	50.49 N	2.48 W
Brochel	246	57.26 N	6.01 W
Brock ≃	244	53.52 N	2.47 W
Brockenhurst	242	50.49 N	1.34 W
Brockworth	242	51.50 N	2.09 W
Brodick	246	55.35 N	5.09 W
Bromborough	244	53.20 N	2.59 W
Bromley ⁸	242	51.24 N	0.02 E
Brompton	242	54.22 N	1.25 W
Bromsgrove	242	52.20 N	2.03 W
Bromyard	242	52.11 N	2.30 W
Bronllys	242	52.01 N	3.16 W
Brookeborough	248	54.19 N	7.24 W
Brookland	242	50.59 N	0.50 E
Broom, Little Loch C	246	57.54 N	5.22 W
Broom, Loch C	246	57.52 N	5.08 W
Brora	246	58.01 N	3.51 W
Brora ≃	246	58.01 N	3.52 W
Broseley	242	52.36 N	2.29 W
Brosna ≃	248	53.13 N	7.58 W
Brotton	244	54.34 N	0.56 W
Brough, Eng., U.K.	244	54.32 N	2.19 W
Brough, Eng., U.K.	244	53.44 N	0.35 W
Brough, Scot. ⁺	246	58.39 N	3.20 W
Brough Head ⊁	246	59.08 N	3.17 W
Broughshane	248	54.54 N	6.12 W
Broughton, Eng., U.K.	242	52.23 N	0.46 W
Broughton, Scot., U.K.	246	55.37 N	3.25 W
Broughton in Furness	244	54.17 N	3.12 W
Broughtown	246	59.15 N	2.36 W
Broughty Ferry	246	56.28 N	2.53 W
Brown Clee Hill ∧²	242	52.28 N	2.35 W
Brownhills	242	52.39 N	1.55 W
Brown Willy ∧²	242	50.35 N	4.36 W
Brue ≃	242	51.13 N	3.00 W
Bruff	248	52.29 N	8.33 W
Brures	248	52.26 N	8.36 W
Bruton	242	51.07 N	2.27 W
Bryher I	242a	49.57 N	6.20 W
Brynamman	242	51.49 N	3.52 W
Bryn Brawd ∧²	242	52.09 N	3.54 W
Bryncethin	242	51.33 N	3.34 W
Brynmawr	242	51.49 N	3.11 W
Buckden, Eng., U.K.	242	52.17 N	0.16 W
Buckden, Eng., U.K.	244	54.12 N	2.05 W
Buckfastleigh	242	50.29 N	3.46 W
Buckhaven	246	56.11 N	3.03 W
Buckie	242	57.40 N	2.58 W
Buckingham	242	52.00 N	1.00 W
Buckinghamshire □⁶	242	51.45 N	0.48 W
Buckland Brewer	242	50.57 N	4.14 W
Buckley	244	53.09 N	3.04 W
Bude	242	50.50 N	4.33 W
Bude Bay C	242	50.50 N	4.37 W
Budleigh Salterton	242	50.38 N	3.20 W
Bugle	242	50.24 N	4.47 W
Buie, Loch C	246	56.20 N	5.52 W
Builth Wells	242	52.09 N	3.24 W
Bulkington	242	52.29 N	1.25 W
Bunclody	248	52.38 N	6.40 W
Buncrana	248	55.08 N	7.27 W
Bundoran	248	54.28 N	8.17 W
Bunessan	246	56.19 N	6.14 W
Bungay	242	52.28 N	1.26 E
Bunnahowen	248	54.11 N	9.54 W
Bunratty Castle ⊥			
Buntingford	242	51.57 N	0.01 W
Burbage	242	52.31 N	1.20 W
Bure ≃	242	52.31 N	1.43 E
Burford	242	51.49 N	1.38 W
Burgess Hill	242	50.57 N	0.07 W
Burghead	242	57.42 N	3.30 W
Burley	244	54.12 N	1.38 W
Burnham	242	51.33 N	0.39 W
Burnham Market	242	52.57 N	0.44 E
Burnham-on-Crouch	242	51.38 N	0.49 E
Burnham-on-Sea	242	51.15 N	3.00 W
Burnley	244	53.48 N	2.14 W
Burnmouth	246	55.50 N	2.04 W
Burntisland	246	56.03 N	3.15 W
Burravoe	246a	60.32 N	1.28 W
Burray I	246	58.50 N	2.54 W
Burrow Head ⊁	244	54.41 N	4.24 W
Burry Holms I	242	51.37 N	4.18 W
Burry Port	242	51.42 N	4.15 W
Burscough	244	53.35 N	2.51 W
Burton Fleming	244	54.08 N	0.20 W
Burton Latimer	242	52.23 N	0.41 W
Burton-upon-Trent	242	52.49 N	1.36 W
Burwell	242	52.16 N	0.19 E
Burwick	246	58.44 N	2.57 W
Bury, Eng., U.K.	244	53.36 N	2.17 W
Bury, Eng., U.K.	242	50.54 N	0.34 W
Bury Saint Edmunds	242	52.15 N	0.43 E
Bushey	242	51.39 N	0.22 W
Bushmills	248	55.12 N	6.32 W
Bute, Island of I			
Bute, Kyles of ᴗ	246	55.50 N	5.06 W
Bute, Sound of ᴗ	246	55.53 N	5.13 W
Butlers Bridge	246	55.44 N	5.12 W
Buttermere	244	54.02 N	7.22 W
Butterwick	244	54.33 N	3.17 W
Buttevant	242	52.59 N	0.05 E
Buxton	248	52.14 N	8.40 W
Bwlch	244	53.15 N	1.55 W
Byfield	242	51.54 N	3.15 W
Byfleet	242	52.11 N	1.14 W
	242	51.20 N	0.29 W
C			
Cader Bronwy ∧	242	52.54 N	3.22 W
Cader Idris ∧	242	52.42 N	3.54 W
Cadnam	242	50.55 N	1.35 W
Caergwrle	244	53.07 N	3.03 W
Caerleon	242	51.37 N	2.57 W
Caernarvon	242	53.08 N	4.16 W
Caernarvon Bay C	244	53.05 N	4.30 W
Caernarvon Castle ⊥	244	53.08 N	4.16 W
Caerphilly	242	51.35 N	3.14 W
Caerphilly Castle ⊥	242	51.34 N	3.14 W
Caersws	242	52.31 N	3.25 W
Caha Mountains ∧⁶	248	51.45 N	9.45 W
Caher	248	52.21 N	7.56 W
Caherdaniel	248	51.45 N	10.05 W
Cahirciveen	248	51.57 N	10.14 W
Cahore Point ⊁	248	52.34 N	6.11 W
Cain ≃	242	52.46 N	3.08 W
Cairndow	246	56.15 N	4.56 W
Cairngorm Mountains ∧	246	57.04 N	3.50 W
Cairnryan	244	54.58 N	5.02 W
Cairnsmore of Carsphairn ∧	246		
Cairnsmore of Fleet ∧	244	55.15 N	4.12 W
Cairn Table ∧	244	55.29 N	4.20 W
Cairn Water ≃	244	55.07 N	3.45 W
Caister-on-Sea	242	52.39 N	1.44 E
Caistor	244	53.30 N	0.20 W
Calder ≃	244	53.44 N	1.21 W
Calder, Loch C	246	58.31 N	3.36 W
Calder Bridge	244	54.27 N	3.29 W
Caldew ≃	244	54.54 N	2.56 W
Caldey Island I	242	51.38 N	4.41 W
Caldicot	242	51.36 N	2.45 W
Cale ≃	242	50.59 N	2.20 W
Caledonian Canal ꟾ	246	56.50 N	5.06 W
Calf of Man I	244	54.03 N	4.48 W
Callan	248	52.33 N	7.23 W
Callander	246	56.15 N	4.13 W
Callanish	246	58.12 N	6.43 W
Callington	242	50.30 N	4.18 W
Calne	242	51.27 N	2.00 W
Calshot	242	50.49 N	1.19 W
Calstock	242	50.30 N	4.12 W
Caltra	248	53.26 N	8.25 W
Camberley	242	51.21 N	0.45 W
Cambo	244	55.10 N	1.57 W
Cambois	244	55.10 N	1.31 W
Camborne	242	50.12 N	5.19 W
Cambrian Mountains ∧	242	52.35 N	3.35 W
Cambridge	242	52.13 N	0.08 E
Cambridgeshire □⁶			
Camden ⁸	242	52.20 N	0.05 E
Camel ≃	242	51.33 N	0.10 W
Camelford	242	50.37 N	4.41 W
Camlad ≃	242	50.37 N	4.41 W
Camowen ≃	248	54.36 N	7.18 W
Campbeltown	246	55.26 N	5.36 W
Campsie Fells ∧²	246	56.02 N	4.12 W
Camrose	242	51.51 N	5.01 W
Can ≃	242	51.48 N	0.25 E
Canisp ∧	246	58.07 N	5.03 W
Canna I	246	57.04 N	6.34 W
Canna, Sound of ᴗ			
Cannich	246	56.59 N	6.40 W
Cannich ≃	246	57.21 N	4.46 W
Cannock	246	57.21 N	4.44 W
Cannock Chase ⁺⁴	242	51.09 N	3.04 W
Canonbie	242	52.42 N	2.00 W
Canterbury	244	55.05 N	2.57 W
Canterbury Cathedral ⊐¹	242	51.17 N	1.05 E
Canvey	242	51.32 N	0.36 E
Canvey Island	242	51.33 N	0.34 E
Caolisport, Loch C	246	55.54 N	5.37 W
Cappamore	248	52.37 N	8.20 W
Cappercleuch	244	55.29 N	3.12 W
Cappoquin	248	52.08 N	7.50 W
Car, Slieve ∧	248	54.03 N	9.40 W
Caragh, Lough C			
Carbost	246	57.18 N	6.22 W
Cardiff	242	51.29 N	3.13 W
Cardigan	242	52.06 N	4.40 W
Cardigan Bay C	242	52.30 N	4.20 W
Cardigan Island I	242	52.08 N	4.41 W
Cargill	246	56.30 N	3.22 W
Carinish	246	57.31 N	7.18 W
Carisbrooke	242	50.41 N	1.19 W
Carlisle	244	54.54 N	2.55 W
Carlow	248	52.50 N	6.55 W
Carlow □⁶	248	58.17 N	6.48 W
Carloway	246	52.58 N	1.05 W
Carlton	242	55.45 N	3.51 W
Carluke	246	51.52 N	4.19 W
Carmarthen	242		
Carmarthen Bay C	242	51.40 N	4.30 W
Carmel Head ⊁	244	53.24 N	4.34 W
Carnarvon → Caernarvon	244	53.08 N	4.16 W
Carncastle	248	54.54 N	5.53 W
Carndonagh	248	55.15 N	7.15 W
Carned Llewelyn ∧			
Carnedd Wen ∧	244	53.10 N	3.58 W
Carnew	242	52.41 N	3.35 W
Carnforth	242	52.43 N	6.30 W
Carnlough	244	54.08 N	2.46 W
Carno	244	54.59 N	5.59 W
Carnoustie	242	52.33 N	3.31 W
Carnwath	246	56.30 N	2.44 W
Carra, Lough ⊜	248	52.10 N	6.22 W
Carradale	246	55.43 N	3.38 W
Carrantoohil ∧	246	53.42 N	9.16 W
Carrbridge	246	55.35 N	5.28 W
Carrick □⁹	242	52.00 N	9.45 W
Carrick-a-rede ⊥	246	57.17 N	3.49 W
Carrickfergus	246	55.12 N	4.38 W
Carrickmacross	246	55.10 N	7.47 W
Carrick-on-Shannon	244	54.43 N	5.49 W
Carrick-on-Suir	248	53.58 N	6.43 W
Carriganorig	248	53.57 N	8.05 W
Carrigaline	248	52.21 N	7.25 W
Carrigallen	248	53.04 N	8.09 W
Carron ≃, Scot., U.K.	248	51.48 N	8.24 W
Carron ≃, Scot., U.K.	248	53.32 N	7.39 W
Carron ≃, Scot., U.K.	246	57.53 N	4.21 W
Carron, Loch C	246	56.02 N	3.44 W
Carronbridge	246	57.25 N	5.27 W
Carron Valley Reservoir ⊜¹	244	55.16 N	3.48 W
Carrowmore Lake ⊜	246	56.02 N	4.05 W
Carsaig	248	54.12 N	9.47 W
Carstairs	246	56.17 N	6.00 W
Cary ≃	246	55.42 N	3.42 W
Cashel, Eire	242	51.09 N	2.59 W
Cashel, Eire	248	53.25 N	9.48 W
Cashel, Eire	248	52.31 N	7.53 W
Cassley ≃	248	57.58 N	4.35 W
Castel	243b	49.28 N	2.34 W
Castlebar	248	53.52 N	9.17 W
Castlebay	246	56.57 N	7.28 W
Castlebellingham	248	53.54 N	6.23 W
Castleblayney	248	54.07 N	6.44 W
Castle Cary	242	51.06 N	2.31 W
Castlecomer	248	52.48 N	7.12 W
Castledermot	248	52.55 N	6.50 W
Castle Donington	242	52.51 N	1.19 W
Castle Douglas	244	54.57 N	3.56 W
Castleford	244	53.44 N	1.21 W
Castleisland	248	52.14 N	9.27 W
Castlemaine	248	52.10 N	9.43 W
Castlemartyr	248	51.55 N	8.03 W
Castlepollard	248	53.40 N	7.17 W
Castlerea	248	53.46 N	8.29 W
Castlereagh	248	54.33 N	5.48 W
Castleside	244	54.50 N	1.52 W
Castleton, Eng., U.K.	244	54.28 N	0.56 W
Castleton, Eng., U.K.	244	53.20 N	1.46 W
Castletown, Eire	248	53.26 N	7.38 W
Castletown, I. of Man	244	54.04 N	4.40 W
Castletown, Scot., U.K.	246	58.35 N	3.23 W
Castletown Bere (Castletown Bearhaven)	248	51.39 N	9.55 W
Castletownroche	248	52.10 N	8.28 W
Castletownshend	248	51.32 N	9.11 W
Castlewellan	248	54.16 N	5.57 W
Caterham	242	51.16 N	0.04 W
Catskill, Eire	248	52.46 N	7.22 W
Catterick	244	54.23 N	1.38 W
Catterick Camp	244	54.22 N	1.43 W
Catton	244	54.55 N	2.15 W
Cauldcleuch Head ∧	244	55.18 N	2.51 W
Caulkerbush	244	54.56 N	3.40 W
Cavan	248	53.59 N	7.21 W
Cavan □⁶	248	53.55 N	7.30 W
Cawdor	246	57.31 N	3.56 W
Cawood	244	53.50 N	1.07 W
Cawston	242	52.46 N	1.10 E
Ceanannus Mór	248	53.44 N	6.53 W
Ceatharlach → Carlow			
Cefni ≃	244	53.12 N	4.23 W
Ceiriog ≃	242	52.56 N	3.02 W
Cellar Head ⊁	246	58.22 N	6.11 W
Cemaes Head ⊁	242	52.08 N	4.44 W
Central □⁴	246	56.05 N	4.10 W
Ceri ≃	242	52.43 N	3.09 W
Cerne Abbas	242	50.49 N	2.29 W
Cerrigydrudion	244	53.01 N	3.33 W
Chacewater	242	50.15 N	5.10 W
Chadderton	244	53.33 N	2.08 W
Chalfont Saint Peter	242	51.37 N	0.33 W
Chalford	242	51.43 N	2.09 W
Chandler's Ford	242	50.59 N	1.23 W
Chapel-en-le-Frith	244	53.20 N	1.54 W
Chapelfell Top ∧	244	54.41 N	2.13 W
Chapel Point ⊁	242	50.16 N	4.46 W
Char ≃	242	50.44 N	2.53 W
Chard	242	50.53 N	2.58 W
Charing	242	51.13 N	0.48 E
Charlbury	242	51.53 N	1.29 W
Charlestown	248	53.57 N	8.49 W
Charlton Kings	242	51.53 N	2.03 W
Charminster	242	50.43 N	2.28 W
Charmouth	242	50.45 N	2.55 W
Charnwood Forest ⁺³	242	52.43 N	1.15 W
Chasetown	242	52.41 N	1.56 W
Chatham	242	51.23 N	0.32 E
Chatteris	242	52.27 N	0.03 E
Chatton	244	55.33 N	1.55 W
Cheadle, Eng., U.K.	242	52.59 N	1.59 W
Cheadle, Eng., U.K.	244	53.24 N	2.13 W
Cheadle Hulme	244	53.22 N	2.12 W
Cheddar	242	51.17 N	2.46 W
Chellaston	242	52.53 N	1.27 W
Chelmer ≃	242	51.48 N	0.40 E
Chelmsford	242	51.44 N	0.28 E
Cheltenham	242	51.54 N	2.04 W
Chepstow	242	51.39 N	2.41 W
Chertsey	242	51.24 N	0.30 W
Cherwell ≃	242	51.44 N	1.15 W
Chesham	242	51.43 N	0.38 W
Cheshire □⁶	244	53.23 N	2.30 W
Cheshire Plain ≃	244	53.17 N	2.40 W
Cheshunt	242	51.43 N	0.02 W
Chesil Beach ₂²	242	50.38 N	2.33 W
Chester	244	53.12 N	2.54 W
Chesterfield	244	53.15 N	1.25 W
Chester-le-Street	244	54.52 N	1.34 W
Chet ≃	242	52.33 N	1.32 E
Chevington Drift	244	55.17 N	1.36 W
Chew Magna	242	51.22 N	2.35 W
Chichester	242	50.50 N	0.48 W
Chickerell	242	50.37 N	2.30 W
Chieveley	242	51.27 N	1.19 W
Chigwell	242	51.38 N	0.05 E
Chilham	242	51.15 N	0.57 E
Chiltern Hills ∧²	242	51.42 N	0.48 W
Chinnor	242	51.43 N	0.56 W
Chippenham	242	51.28 N	2.07 W
Chipping Campden	242	52.03 N	1.46 W
Chipping Norton	242	51.56 N	1.32 W
Chipping Ongar	242	51.43 N	0.15 E
Chipping Sodbury	242	51.33 N	2.24 W
Chirk	242	52.56 N	3.03 W
Chirnside	246	55.48 N	2.13 W
Chiseldon	242	51.31 N	1.44 W
Cholsey	242	51.34 N	1.10 W
Chonzie, Ben ∧	246	56.27 N	3.59 W
Chorley	244	53.39 N	2.39 W
Christchurch	242	50.44 N	1.45 W
Chudleigh	242	50.36 N	3.38 W
Chulmleigh	242	50.55 N	3.52 W
Churchdown	242	51.53 N	2.10 W
Church Stretton	242	52.32 N	2.49 W
Churn ≃	242	51.38 N	1.53 W
Churnet ≃	242	52.55 N	1.50 W
Chwefru ≃	242	52.09 N	3.25 W
Ciche, Sgurr na ∧	246	57.01 N	5.27 W
Cill Airne → Killarney	248	52.03 N	9.30 W
Cill Choinnigh → Kilkenny	248	52.39 N	7.15 W
Cinderford	242	51.50 N	2.29 W
Cirencester	242	51.44 N	1.59 W
Clachan	246	55.45 N	5.34 W
Clackmannan	246	56.06 N	3.46 W
Clacton-on-Sea	242	51.48 N	1.09 E
Cladich	246	56.21 N	5.05 W
Claerwen ≃	242	52.44 N	3.37 W
Claerwen Reservoir ⊜¹	242	52.17 N	3.43 W
Clane	248	53.18 N	6.41 W
Claonaig	246	55.46 N	5.22 W
Clàr, Loch nan ⊜	246	58.17 N	4.08 W
Clara	248	53.20 N	7.36 W
Clare	242	52.05 N	0.35 E
Clare □⁶	248	52.50 N	9.03 W
Clare ≃	248	53.20 N	9.03 W
Clarecastle	248	52.49 N	8.57 W
Claregalway	248	53.21 N	8.57 W
Clare Island I	248	53.48 N	10.00 W
Claremorris	248	53.44 N	9.00 W
Clatteringshaws Lake ⊜	244	55.05 N	4.17 W
Claughton	244	54.06 N	2.40 W
Clay Cross	244	53.10 N	1.24 W
Claydon	242	52.06 N	1.07 E
Clayton	242	53.47 N	1.52 W
Clayton-le-Moors	244	53.47 N	2.23 W
Clear, Cape ⊁	248	51.24 N	9.30 W
Clear Island I	248	51.26 N	9.30 W
Cleator Moor	244	54.31 N	3.30 W
Clee Hills ∧²	242	52.24 N	2.35 W
Cleethorpes	244	53.34 N	0.02 W
Cleeve Cloud ∧²	242	51.54 N	2.01 W
Cleggan	248	53.33 N	10.09 W
Clehonger	242	52.03 N	2.45 W
Cleobury Mortimer	242	52.23 N	2.29 W
Clevedon	242	51.27 N	2.51 W
Cleveland □⁶	244	54.35 N	1.15 W
Cleveland Hills ∧²	244	54.23 N	1.05 W
Cleveleys	244	53.53 N	3.03 W
Clew Bay C	248	53.50 N	9.50 W
Cley next the Sea	242	52.58 N	1.03 E
Clifden	248	53.29 N	10.01 W
Clifden Bay C	248	53.28 N	10.05 W
Cliffe	242	51.28 N	0.30 E
Clifton Gorge ∧²			
Clisham ∧	246	57.58 N	6.49 W
Clitheroe	244	53.53 N	2.23 W
Cloghan, Eire	248	54.51 N	7.56 W
Cloghan, Eire	248	53.13 N	7.53 W
Cloghane	248	52.10 N	10.12 W
Clogheen	248	52.16 N	8.00 W
Clogher	248	54.25 N	7.12 W
Clogher Head ⊁	248	53.48 N	6.12 W
Cloghjordan	248	52.57 N	8.02 W
Clonakilty	248	51.37 N	8.54 W
Clonakilty Bay C			
Clonard	248	53.27 N	7.00 W
Clondalkin	248	53.19 N	6.24 W
Clones	248	54.11 N	7.15 W
Clonfert	248	53.14 N	8.03 W
Clonmacnois ⊥	248	53.20 N	7.59 W
Clonmany	248	55.16 N	7.25 W
Clonmel	248	52.21 N	7.42 W
Clonmellon	248	53.39 N	7.01 W
Clonmore	248	52.49 N	6.35 W
Clonroche	248	52.27 N	6.43 W
Cloone	248	53.57 N	7.46 W
Clova, Glen ᴠ	246	56.49 N	3.04 W
Clovelly	242	51.00 N	4.24 W
Clowne	244	53.16 N	1.16 W
Cluain Meala → Clonmel	248	52.21 N	7.42 W
Cluanie, Loch ⊜			
Clun	242	52.25 N	3.02 W
Clun ≃	242	52.26 N	2.55 W
Clunbury	242	52.25 N	2.54 W
Clunie Water ≃	246	57.00 N	3.24 W
Clwyd □⁶	244	53.05 N	3.20 W
Clwyd ≃	244	53.20 N	3.30 W
Clwyd, Vale of ᴠ	244	53.12 N	3.24 W
Clwydian Range ∧			
Clydach	242	51.43 N	3.54 W
Clyde ≃	242	52.59 N	3.50 W
Clyde ≃	246	55.44 N	4.55 W

Name	Page	Lat °'	Long °'
Clyde, Firth of C¹	246	55.40 N	5.00 W
Clydebank	246	55.54 N	4.24 W
Clydesdale V	246	55.42 N	3.50 W
Clynnog-fawr	244	53.01 N	4.23 W
Clywedog ≈	242	52.27 N	3.32 W
Cnoc Moy ∧²	246	55.23 N	5.46 W
Coachford	248	51.53 N	8.48 W
Coalbrookdale	242	52.38 N	2.30 W
Coalburn	246	55.36 N	3.54 W
Coalisland	248	54.32 N	6.42 W
Coalpit Heath	242	51.32 N	2.28 W
Coalville	242	52.44 S	1.20 W
Coatbridge	246	55.52 N	4.01 W
Cobh	248	51.51 N	8.17 W
Cobham	246	51.20 N	0.25 W
Cock Bridge	246	57.09 N	3.14 W
Cockburnspath	246	55.56 N	2.21 W
Cockenzie	246	55.58 N	2.58 W
Cockerham	242	53.59 N	2.50 W
Cockermouth	244	54.40 N	3.21 W
Cod ≈	246	54.10 N	1.22 W
Coddenham	242	52.09 N	1.07 E
Codsall	242	52.38 N	2.12 W
Coggeshall	242	51.52 N	0.41 E
Coigeach, Rubha ⊁	246	58.06 N	5.26 W
Coire, Loch ⊜	246	58.13 N	4.21 W
Colchester	246	51.54 N	0.54 E
Coldbackie	246	58.31 N	4.23 W
Cold Fell ∧	244	54.54 N	2.36 W
Coldingham	246	55.53 N	2.10 W
Coldstream	246	55.39 N	2.15 W
Cole ≈, Eng., U.K.	242	52.28 N	1.44 W
Cole ≈, Eng., U.K.	242	51.42 N	1.42 W
Coleraine	248	55.08 N	6.40 W
Coleshill	242	52.30 N	1.42 W
Colgrave Sound U	246	60.37 N	0.58 W
Coll I	246	56.38 N	6.34 W
Collier Law ∧²	246	54.46 N	1.58 W
Collieston	246	57.21 N	1.56 W
Colligan ≈	248	52.06 N	7.38 W
Collingbourne Kingston	242	51.18 N	1.13 W
Collon	242	53.47 N	6.29 W
Collooney	248	54.11 N	8.29 W
Colmonell	244	55.08 N	4.55 W
Coln ≈	242	51.42 N	1.42 W
Colne	244	53.52 N	2.09 W
Colne ≈	242	51.48 N	1.01 E
Colonsay I	246	56.04 N	6.13 W
Colsterworth	242	52.48 N	0.37 W
Coltishall	242	52.44 N	1.22 E
Colwell	246	55.04 N	2.04 W
Colwyn Bay	244	53.18 N	3.43 W
Colyton	244	50.44 N	3.04 W
Combe Martin	244	51.13 N	4.02 W
Comber	248	54.33 N	5.45 W
Comberton	242	52.11 N	0.02 E
Comrie	246	56.22 N	4.00 W
Cona ≈	246	56.46 N	5.14 W
Cong	246	53.32 N	9.19 W
Congleton	244	53.10 N	2.13 W
Congresbury	244	51.23 N	2.48 W
Coningsby	242	53.07 N	0.10 W
Coisbrough	244	53.29 N	1.13 W
Coniston	244	54.22 N	3.05 W
Coniston Water ⊜	244	54.20 N	3.04 W
Conn, Lough ⊜	248	54.04 N	9.20 W
Connah's Quay	244	53.13 N	3.03 W
Connaught □⁹	248	53.45 N	9.00 W
Connel Park	246	55.23 N	4.12 W
Connemara ◦¹	248	53.25 N	9.45 W
Conon ≈	246	57.34 N	6.26 W
Consett	244	54.51 N	1.49 W
Conway	244	53.17 N	3.50 W
Conway ≈	244	53.17 N	3.50 W
Conway, Vale of V	246	53.12 N	3.48 W
Conway Bay C	246	53.18 N	3.55 W
Cookham	242	51.34 N	0.43 W
Cookstown	246	54.39 N	6.45 W
Coolaney	248	54.11 N	8.29 W
Cootehill	248	54.04 N	7.05 W
Copinsay I	246	58.54 N	2.40 W
Copplestone	242	50.49 N	3.45 W
Coquet ≈	246	55.22 N	1.37 W
Coquet Dale V	246	55.16 N	1.50 W
Corbiere Point ⊁	243b	49.11 N	2.15 W
Corby	242	52.29 N	0.40 W
Corcaigh → Cork			
Corfe Castle	242	50.38 N	2.04 W
Cork	248	51.54 N	8.28 W
Cork □⁶	248	51.54 N	8.28 W
Cork Airport ⊠	248	51.51 N	8.29 W
Cork Harbour C	248	51.45 N	8.15 W
Cornforth	244	54.42 N	1.31 W
Cornhill	244	57.36 N	2.42 W
Cornwall □⁶	242	50.30 N	4.40 W
Corofin	248	52.56 N	9.03 W
Corran	246	56.43 N	5.14 W
Corraun Peninsula ⊁¹	248	54.54 N	9.53 W
Corrib, Lough	248	53.05 N	9.10 W
Corryvreckan, Gulf of U	246	56.09 N	5.44 W
Corserine ∧	246	55.09 N	4.22 W
Corsham	242	51.26 N	2.11 W
Corsock	246	55.04 N	3.57 W
Cortachy	246	56.43 N	2.58 W
Corton	242	52.32 N	1.44 E
Corve ≈	242	52.22 N	2.43 W
Corve Dale V	242	52.30 N	2.40 W
Corwen	242	52.59 N	3.22 W
Cosby	242	52.33 N	1.11 W
Coseley	242	52.33 N	2.06 W
Costelloe	248	53.17 N	9.32 W
Costessey	242	52.40 N	1.11 E
Cothi ≈	242	51.52 N	4.10 W
Cotswold Hills ∧²	242	51.45 N	2.10 W
Cottenham	242	52.18 N	0.09 E
Cottingham (Haltemprice)	244	53.47 N	0.24 W
Coupar Angus	246	56.33 N	3.17 W
Courtmacsherry	248	51.38 N	8.43 W
Courtmacsherry Bay C	248	51.35 N	8.40 W
Courtown Harbour	248	52.38 N	6.13 W
Cove	246	57.51 N	5.42 W
Coventry	242	52.25 N	1.30 W
Coventry Cathedral ⊽¹	242	52.25 N	1.30 W
Cover ≈	242	54.17 N	1.46 W
Cowal ⊁¹	246	56.05 N	5.08 W
Cowbridge	242	51.28 N	3.27 W
Cowdenbeath	246	56.07 N	3.21 W
Cowes	242	50.45 N	1.18 W
Cow Green Reservoir ⊜	244	54.40 N	2.18 W
Cowie Water ≈	246	56.58 N	2.12 W
Cowley	242	51.43 N	1.12 W
Cowplain	242	50.54 N	1.01 W
Coyle, Water of ≈	244	55.28 N	4.32 W
Craighouse	246	55.51 N	5.57 W
Craignish Point ⊁	246	56.07 N	5.37 W
Craignure	246	56.28 N	5.42 W
Crail	246	56.16 N	2.38 W
Crake ≈	244	54.14 N	3.03 W
Cramlington	244	55.05 N	1.36 W
Cranborne Chase ⊼³	242	50.55 N	2.05 W
Cranbrook	242	51.06 N	0.33 E
Cranfield	242	52.05 N	0.35 W
Cranleigh	242	51.09 N	0.30 W
Crathie	246	57.02 N	3.12 W
Craughwell	248	53.13 N	8.43 W
Craven Arms	242	52.26 N	2.50 W
Crawford	246	55.28 N	3.40 W
Crawley	242	51.07 N	0.12 W
Cray	242	51.55 N	3.36 W
Creagan	246	56.33 N	5.17 W
Creagorry	246	57.26 N	7.19 W
Crediton	244	50.47 N	3.39 W
Cree ≈	244	54.52 N	4.20 W
Creetown	244	54.54 N	4.23 W
Cregganbaun	248	53.42 N	9.51 W
Creran, Loch C	246	56.31 N	5.20 W
Creswell	244	53.16 N	1.12 W
Crewkerne	242	50.53 N	2.48 W
Crianlarich	246	56.23 N	4.36 W
Criccieth	242	52.55 N	4.14 W
Crick	242	52.21 N	1.07 W
Crickhowell	242	51.53 N	3.07 W
Cricklade	242	51.39 N	1.51 W
Crieff	246	56.23 N	3.52 W
Criffel ∧	244	54.57 N	3.38 W
Crinan	246	56.05 N	5.35 W
Croachy	246	57.19 N	4.14 W
Crocketford	244	55.02 N	3.50 W
Croggan	246	56.22 N	5.42 W
Croglin	244	54.49 N	2.39 W
Croick	246	57.53 N	4.35 W
Cromarty	246	57.40 N	4.02 W
Cromarty Firth C¹	246	57.41 N	4.07 W
Cromer	242	52.56 N	1.18 E
Cromore	246	58.09 N	6.29 W
Crook	244	54.43 N	1.44 W
Crook of Alves	246	57.38 N	3.27 W
Crookstown	246	51.50 N	8.50 W
Croom	248	52.31 N	8.42 W
Crosby	244	53.30 N	3.02 W
Crossbost	246	58.08 N	6.23 W
Cross Fell ∧	244	54.42 N	2.29 W
Crossgar	248	54.24 N	5.45 W
Crosshaven	248	51.48 N	8.17 W
Crosshill	246	55.19 N	4.39 W
Crossmaglen	248	54.05 N	6.37 W
Crossmolina	248	54.06 N	9.20 W
Crouch ≈	242	51.37 N	0.52 E
Crowborough	242	51.03 N	0.09 E
Crowland	242	52.41 N	0.11 W
Crowle	244	53.37 N	0.49 W
Crowlin Islands II	246	57.20 N	5.44 W
Crowthorne	242	51.23 N	0.49 W
Croxley Green	242	51.39 N	0.27 W
Croy	242	57.31 N	4.02 W
Croyde	242	51.07 N	4.13 W
Croydon ◦⁸	242	51.23 N	0.06 W
Cruachan, Ben ∧	246	56.25 N	5.08 W
Cruden Bay	246	57.25 N	1.50 W
Crudgington	242	52.46 N	2.33 W
Crumlin	248	54.37 N	6.14 W
Crummock Water ⊜	244	54.34 N	3.18 W
Crusheen	248	52.58 N	8.53 W
Crymmych	242	51.59 N	4.40 W
Cuckfield	242	51.00 N	0.09 W
Cuckney	244	53.15 N	1.08 W
Cudworth	244	53.35 N	1.25 W
Cuffley	242	51.47 N	0.07 W
Cuilcagh ∧	248	54.10 N	7.48 W
Cúil Raithin → Coleraine			
Culdaff Bay C	246	55.17 N	7.10 W
Cullen	246	57.41 N	2.49 W
Cullicudden	246	57.39 N	4.13 W
Cullin, Lough	248	53.57 N	9.12 W
Cullin Hills ∧²	246	57.15 N	6.15 W
Culloden Battlesite ⊥	246	57.28 N	4.05 W
Cullompton	242	50.52 N	3.24 W
Culm ≈	242	50.46 N	3.31 W
Culrain	246	57.55 N	4.24 W
Cults	246	57.07 N	2.10 W
Culvain ∧	246	56.56 N	5.17 W
Cumbernauld	246	55.58 N	3.59 W
Cumbria □⁶	244	54.30 N	3.00 W
Cumbrian Mountains ∧	244	54.30 N	3.05 W
Cuminestown	246	57.32 N	2.20 W
Cumnock	246	55.27 N	4.16 W
Cumnor	242	51.44 N	1.20 W
Cumwhinton	244	54.52 N	2.51 W
Cunningham □⁹	246	55.40 N	4.30 W
Cupar	246	56.19 N	3.01 W
Curreeney	248	52.43 N	8.08 W
Currie	246	55.54 N	3.20 W
Curry Rivel	242	51.02 N	2.52 W
Cushendall	248	55.06 N	6.04 W
Cushendun	248	55.07 N	6.02 W
Cushina	248	53.11 N	7.05 W
Cwmbran	242	51.39 N	3.00 W
Cynin ≈	242	51.48 N	4.29 W
Cynwyl Elfed	242	51.55 N	4.22 W
D			
Daingean	248	53.18 N	7.17 W
Dairsie	248	56.20 N	2.56 W
Dairy	246	55.43 N	4.43 W
Dalbeattie	244	54.56 N	3.49 W
Dalch ≈	242	50.52 N	3.47 W
Dale	246	51.43 N	5.11 W
Dalhalvaig	246	58.28 N	3.54 W
Dalkeith	246	55.54 N	3.04 W
Dallas	246	57.33 N	3.26 W
Dalmally	246	56.24 N	4.58 W
Dalmellington	246	55.19 N	4.14 W
Dalnaspidal	246	56.50 N	4.14 W
Dalry, Scot., U.K.	246	55.07 N	4.10 W
Dalry, Scot., U.K.	246	55.43 N	4.44 W
Dalton-in-Furness	244	54.09 N	3.11 W
Dalwhinnie	246	56.56 N	4.14 W
Damerham	242	50.57 N	1.52 W
Danbury	242	51.44 N	0.33 E
Dane ≈	242	53.15 N	2.31 W
Darenth	242	51.28 N	0.13 E
Dargle ≈	248	53.11 N	6.04 W
Darlaston	242	52.34 N	2.02 W
Darlington	244	54.31 N	1.34 W
Dart ≈	242	50.20 N	3.33 W
Dartford	242	51.27 N	0.14 E
Dartington	242	50.35 N	4.00 W
Dartmoor National Park ⊼	242	50.37 N	3.52 W
Dartmouth	242	50.33 N	3.35 W
Darton	242	53.36 N	1.32 W
Darvel	246	55.37 N	4.18 W
Darwen	242	53.42 N	2.28 W
Darwen ≈	242	53.45 N	2.41 W
Daventry	242	52.16 N	1.09 W
Davington	242	55.18 N	3.12 W
Daviot	246	57.25 N	4.08 W
Dawley	242	52.40 N	2.28 W
Dawlish	242	50.34 N	3.28 W
Deal	242	51.14 N	1.24 E
Dean ≈	242	53.20 N	2.14 W
Dean, Forest of ⊢³	242	51.48 N	2.30 W
Dearg, Beinn ∧	246	57.47 N	4.56 W
Dearne ≈	244	53.30 N	1.16 W
Dear Reservoir ⊜	246	55.20 N	3.37 W
Deben ≈	242	51.58 N	1.24 E
Debenham	242	52.13 N	1.11 E
Deddington	242	51.59 N	1.19 W
Dee ≈, Eng., U.K.	244	53.52 N	3.12 W
Dee ≈, Scot., U.K.	244	54.50 N	4.03 W
Dee ≈, Scot., U.K.	246	57.09 N	2.07 W
Dee, Loch ⊜	244	55.05 N	4.24 W
Deeping Fen ⊞	242	52.46 N	0.13 W
Deer Sound U	246	58.58 N	2.48 W
Degawny	246	53.18 N	3.47 W
Delabole	242	50.37 N	4.44 W
Delamere Forest ⊢³	244	53.14 N	2.38 W
Dell	246	58.30 N	6.20 W
Delvin	248	53.36 N	7.05 W
Denbigh	244	53.11 N	3.25 W
Denby Dale	244	53.35 N	1.38 W
Denge Marsh ⊞	242	50.57 N	0.55 E
Dennis Head ⊁	246	59.23 N	2.23 W
Denny	246	56.02 N	3.55 W
Denton	244	53.27 N	2.07 W
Derby	244	52.55 N	1.29 W
Derbyshire □⁶	244	53.00 N	1.33 W
Derg ≈	248	54.44 N	7.25 W
Derg, Lough ⊜, Eire	248	53.00 N	8.20 W
Derg, Lough ⊜, Eire	248	54.36 N	7.53 W
Derravaragh, Lough	248	53.40 N	7.24 W
Derry → Londonderry	248	55.00 N	7.19 W
Derrybrien	248	53.04 N	8.36 W
Derrykeevan	248	55.08 N	6.29 W
Derryveagh Mountains ⋏	248	55.00 N	8.05 W
Dersingham	242	52.51 N	0.30 E
Derwent ≈, Eng., U.K.	242	52.50 N	1.15 W
Derwent ≈, Eng., U.K.	244	53.45 N	0.57 W
Derwent ≈, Eng., U.K.	244	54.57 N	1.41 W
Derwent ≈, Eng., U.K.	244	54.38 N	3.34 W
Derwent Reservoir ⊜	244	54.50 N	2.00 W
Derwent Water ⊜	244	54.34 N	3.08 W
Desborough	242	52.27 N	0.49 W
Desford	242	52.39 N	1.17 W
Deveron ≈	246	57.40 N	2.31 W
Devil's Bridge	242	52.23 N	3.51 W
Devil's Water ≈	244	54.58 N	2.02 W
Devizes	242	51.22 N	1.59 W
Devon □	242	50.45 N	3.50 W
Devon ≈	246	56.07 N	3.51 W
Devonport	242	50.22 N	4.10 W
Dewsbury	244	53.42 N	1.37 W
Dherue, Loch an ⊜	246	58.25 N	4.27 W
Dhomhnuill, Sgurr ∧	246	56.45 N	5.27 W
Diabaig	246	57.34 N	5.40 W
Didcot	242	51.37 N	1.15 W
Dinas	242	52.00 N	4.54 W
Dinas Head ⊁	242	52.02 N	4.55 W
Dinas Powis	246	51.26 N	3.14 W
Dingle	248	52.08 N	10.15 W
Dingle Bay C	248	52.05 N	10.15 W
Dingle Peninsula ⊁¹	248	52.12 N	10.05 W
Dingwall	246	57.35 N	4.29 W
Dinin ≈	248	52.43 N	7.18 W
Dinnet	246	57.03 N	2.54 W
Dinnington	244	53.22 N	1.12 W
Diss	242	52.23 N	1.07 E
Distington	244	54.36 N	3.32 W
Dizzard Point ⊁	242	52.30 N	2.35 W
Dochart ≈	242	50.45 N	4.38 W
Docking	242	56.28 N	4.20 W
Dodman Point ⊁	242	52.55 N	0.38 E
Dolanog	242	50.13 N	4.48 W
Dolgarrog	244	53.11 N	3.51 W
Dolgellau	244	52.44 N	3.53 W
Dollar	246	56.09 N	3.40 W
Dollar Law ∧	246	55.33 N	3.17 W
Dolton	242	50.53 N	4.01 W
Don ≈, Eng., U.K.	244	53.39 N	0.59 W
Don ≈, Scot., U.K.	246	57.08 N	2.05 W
Donaghadee	248	54.39 N	5.33 W
Donaghmore	248	54.32 N	6.49 W
Donard, Slieve ∧	248	54.11 N	5.55 W
Doncaster	244	53.32 N	1.07 W
Donegal	248	54.39 N	8.07 W
Donegal □⁶	248	54.50 N	8.00 W
Donegal Bay C	248	54.30 N	8.30 W
Doneraile	248	52.13 N	8.35 W
Donington	242	52.55 N	0.12 W
Donoughmore	248	51.57 N	8.45 W
Dooagh	248	53.59 N	10.09 W
Doon ≈	246	55.26 N	4.38 W
Doon, Loch	246	55.15 N	4.22 W
Doonbeg	248	52.44 N	9.32 W
Doonbeg ≈	248	52.44 N	9.34 W
Dorain, Beinn ∧	246	56.30 N	4.42 W
Dorback Burn ≈	246	57.31 N	3.40 W
Dorchester, Eng., U.K.	242	51.39 N	1.10 W
Dorchester, Eng., U.K.	242	50.43 N	2.26 W
Dordon	242	52.36 N	1.37 W
Dore ≈	242	51.57 N	2.52 W
Dores	242	57.22 N	4.15 W
Dorking	242	51.14 N	0.20 W
Dornie	246	57.17 N	5.31 W
Dornoch	246	57.52 N	4.02 W
Dornoch Firth C¹	246	57.53 N	4.00 W
Dorridge	242	52.22 N	1.45 W
Dorset □⁶	242	50.47 N	2.20 W
Douglas, I. of Man	244	54.09 N	4.28 W
Douglas, Scot., U.K.	246	55.33 N	3.51 W
Douglas ≈	244	53.43 N	2.50 W
Douglas Water ≈	246	55.38 N	3.46 W
Doune	246	56.12 N	4.05 W
Doune Castle ⊥	246	56.11 N	4.03 W
Dove ≈	242	52.50 N	1.35 W
Dovenby	244	51.08 N	1.19 E
Dover	242	51.08 N	1.19 E
Dover, Strait of U	242	51.00 N	1.30 W
Dovercourt	242	51.56 N	1.16 E
Dovey Valley V	242	52.35 N	3.50 W
Dowally	242	56.36 N	3.37 W
Downham	242	52.26 N	0.15 E
Downham Market	242	52.36 N	0.23 E
Downpatrick	248	54.20 N	5.43 W
Downpatrick Head ⊁	248	54.20 N	9.20 W
Downton	242	51.00 N	1.44 W
Draperstown	248	54.48 N	6.46 W
Driffield	244	54.00 N	0.27 W
Drimnin	246	56.36 N	6.00 W
Drimoleague	248	51.38 N	9.14 W
Drogheda	248	53.43 N	6.21 W
Droichead Átha → Drogheda	248	53.43 N	6.21 W
Droichead Nua	248	53.11 N	6.48 W
Droitwich	242	52.16 N	2.09 W
Dromahair	248	54.14 N	8.19 W
Dromcollier	248	52.20 N	8.54 W
Dromod	248	53.51 N	7.55 W
Dromore West	248	54.25 N	6.09 W
Drumbeg	248	54.15 N	8.53 W
Drumcliffe	248	54.14 N	5.12 W
Drumlish	248	53.50 N	8.30 W
Drummore	242	53.48 N	7.46 W
Drumquin	248	54.37 N	7.30 W
Drumshanbo	248	54.02 N	8.02 W
Dryburgh Abbey ⊽¹	246	55.34 N	2.40 W
Dryfe Water ≈	246	55.08 N	3.26 W
Drymen	246	56.04 N	4.27 W
Dubh Artach ⊠	246	56.08 N	6.40 W
Dublin (Baile Átha Cliath)	248	53.20 N	6.15 W
Dublin □⁶	248	53.20 N	6.15 W
Dublin Bay C	248	53.20 N	6.06 W
Duddington	242	52.36 N	0.32 W
Duddon ≈	244	54.15 N	3.13 W
Dudley	242	52.30 N	2.05 W
Dufftown	246	57.26 N	3.08 W
Duich, Loch C	246	57.14 N	5.30 W
Duirinish	246	57.19 N	5.41 W
Dulais ≈	242	51.41 N	3.47 W
Dulas ≈, Wales, U.K.	242	52.36 N	3.50 W
Dulas ≈, Wales, U.K.	242	52.16 N	3.22 W
Dulas Bay C	244	53.23 N	4.15 W
Duleek	248	53.39 N	6.25 W
Dulnain Bridge	246	57.16 N	3.41 W
Dulnan ≈	246	57.18 N	3.40 W
Dulverton	242	51.03 N	3.33 W
Dumbarton	246	55.57 N	4.35 W
Dumfries	246	55.04 N	3.37 W
Dumfries and Galloway □⁴	246	55.00 N	4.00 W
Dunaff Head ⊁	248	55.17 N	7.33 W
Dunbar	246	56.00 N	2.31 W
Dunbeath	246	58.15 N	3.25 W
Dunblane	246	56.12 N	3.59 W
Duncansby Head ⊁	246	58.39 N	3.02 W
Dunchurch	242	52.20 N	1.16 W
Duncormick	248	52.14 N	6.39 W
Dundalk	248	54.01 N	6.25 W
Dundalk Bay C	248	53.57 N	6.17 W
Dún Dealgan → Dundalk	248	54.01 N	6.25 W
Dundee	248	56.28 N	3.00 W
Dundrum, N. Ire., U.K.	248	54.16 N	5.51 W
Dundrum Bay C	248	54.14 N	5.45 W
Duneaton Water ≈	246	55.32 N	3.42 W
Dunfanaghy	248	55.11 N	7.59 W
Dunfermline	246	56.04 N	3.29 W
Dungannon	246	54.31 N	6.46 W
Dungarvan	248	52.05 N	7.37 W
Dungarvan Harbour C	248	52.10 N	7.35 W
Dungeness ⊁	242	50.55 N	0.58 E
Dungiven	248	54.55 N	6.55 W
Dungloe	248	54.57 N	8.22 W
Dunheved → Launceston	246	50.38 N	4.21 W
Dunkeld	246	56.34 N	3.35 W
Dunkellin ≈	248	53.12 N	8.54 W
Dunkerrin	248	52.55 N	7.55 W
Dunkery Hill ∧²	242	51.11 N	3.35 W
Dunkineely	248	54.38 N	8.23 W
Dún Laoghaire	248	53.17 N	6.08 W
Dunlavin	248	53.02 N	6.41 W
Dunleary → Dún Laoghaire	248	53.17 N	6.08 W
Dunleer	248	53.50 N	6.24 W
Dunlop	246	55.43 N	4.32 W
Dunloy	248	55.01 N	6.25 W
Dunmanus Bay C	248	51.35 N	9.45 W
Dunmanway	248	51.43 N	9.06 W
Dunmore	248	53.36 N	8.46 W
Dunmore Cave ⌁⁵	248	52.44 N	7.15 W
Dunmore East	248	52.09 N	7.00 W
Dunmurry	248	54.33 N	6.01 W
Dunnamanagh	248	54.52 N	7.18 W
Dunnet	246	58.31 N	3.20 W
Dunnet Bay C	246	58.37 N	3.24 W
Dunnet Head ⊁	246	58.40 N	3.24 W
Dunnottar Castle ⊥	246	56.57 N	2.11 W
Dunoon	246	55.57 N	4.56 W
Dun Rig ∧	246	55.34 N	3.10 W
Duns	246	55.47 N	2.20 W
Dunsford	242	50.41 N	3.40 W
Dunstable	242	51.53 N	0.32 W
Dunstaffnage Castle ⊥	246	56.26 N	5.32 W
Dunster	246	51.12 N	3.27 W
Duntelchaig, Loch ⊜	246	57.20 N	4.18 W
Dunton Green	242	51.18 N	0.11 E
Dunvegan	246	57.26 N	6.35 W
Dunvegan, Loch C	246	57.28 N	6.40 W
Dunvegan Castle ⊥	246	57.26 N	6.35 W
Dunvegan Head ⊁	246	57.31 N	6.43 W
Durham	244	54.47 N	1.34 W
Durham □⁶	244	54.45 N	1.45 W
Durham Cathedral ⊽¹	244	54.46 N	1.36 W
Durness	246	58.33 N	4.45 W
Durness, Kyle of C	246	58.34 N	4.49 W
Durrington	242	51.13 N	1.45 W
Durris	246	55.36 N	9.31 W
Durrow	248	52.50 N	7.22 W
Dursey Head ⊁	248	51.35 N	10.14 W
Dursley	242	51.42 N	2.21 W
Dury Voe C	246a	60.20 N	1.08 W
Duston	242	52.14 N	0.56 W
Dwyfor ≈	242	52.55 N	4.17 W
Dyce	246	57.12 N	2.11 W
Dyfed □⁶	242	52.00 N	4.30 W
Dyfi ≈	242	52.32 N	4.03 W
Dyke	246	57.36 N	3.41 W
Dymchurch	242	51.02 N	1.00 E
Dymock	242	51.59 N	2.26 W
Dysart	246	56.08 N	3.08 W
Dysynni ≈	242	52.36 N	4.05 W
E			
Eaglesfield	244	55.03 N	3.12 W
Eaglesham	246	55.44 N	4.18 W
Ealing ◦⁸	242	51.31 N	0.20 W
Eamont ≈	244	54.40 N	2.39 W
Earby	244	53.56 N	2.08 W
Eardisley	242	52.08 N	2.59 W
Earlish	246	57.34 N	6.23 W
Earls Colne	242	51.56 N	0.42 E
Earl Shilton	242	52.35 N	1.20 W
Earl Soham	242	52.14 N	1.16 E
Earlston	246	55.39 N	2.40 W
Earn ≈	246	56.21 N	3.19 W
Earn, Loch	246	56.23 N	4.14 W
Earsdon	244	55.04 N	1.29 W
Easingwold	244	54.07 N	1.11 W
Eask, Lough	248	54.41 N	8.03 W
Easky	248	54.18 N	8.58 W
East Aberthaw	242	51.23 N	3.22 W
East Allen ≈	244	54.55 N	2.19 W
Eastbourne	242	50.46 N	0.17 E
East Calder	246	55.53 N	3.27 W
Eastchurch	242	51.25 N	0.52 E
East Cleddau ≈	242	51.46 N	4.52 W
East Dereham	242	52.41 N	0.56 E
Eastern Isles II	242a	49.57 N	6.15 W
East Grinstead	242	51.08 N	0.01 W
East Harling	242	52.26 N	0.56 E
East Hoathly	242	50.55 N	0.10 E
East Ilsley	242	51.32 N	1.17 W
East Kilbride	246	55.46 N	4.10 W
Eastleigh	242	50.58 N	1.22 W
East Linton	246	55.59 N	2.39 W
East Loch Roag C	246	58.14 N	6.48 W
East Loch Tarbert C	246	57.52 N	6.45 W
East Looe	244	50.22 N	4.27 W
East Markham	244	53.15 N	0.54 W
East Midlands Airport ⊠	242	52.50 N	1.20 W
Easton	242	50.32 N	2.26 W
East Peckham	242	51.15 N	0.23 E
East Retford	244	53.19 N	0.56 W
Eastry	242	51.15 N	1.18 E
East Stour ≈	242	51.08 N	0.53 E
East Wittering	242	50.46 N	0.53 W
Eastwood	244	53.01 N	1.18 W
Eaton Socon	242	52.13 N	0.18 W
Eau ≈	244	53.31 N	0.44 W
Ebbw ≈	242	51.33 N	2.59 W
Ebbw Vale	242	51.47 N	3.12 W
Ecclefechan	244	55.03 N	3.17 W
Eccles	244	53.29 N	2.21 W
Ecclesfield	244	53.27 N	1.27 W
Eccleshall	242	52.52 N	2.15 W
Echt	246	57.08 N	2.26 W
Eck, Loch	246	56.05 N	5.00 W
Eckington	246	53.19 N	1.21 W
Eday I	246	59.11 N	2.47 W
Edderton	246	57.50 N	4.10 W
Eddleston	246	55.43 N	3.13 W
Eddrachillis Bay C	246	58.18 N	5.15 W
Eddystone Rocks II	242	50.12 N	4.15 W
Eden ≈, Eng., U.K.	242	51.10 N	0.11 E
Eden ≈, Eng., U.K.	244	54.57 N	3.01 W
Eden ≈, Scot., U.K.	246	56.22 N	2.50 W
Edenbridge	242	51.12 N	0.04 E
Edenderry	248	53.21 N	7.35 W
Edenside V	244	54.40 N	2.35 W
Ederny	248	54.32 N	7.39 W
Edge Hill ∧²	242	52.08 N	1.27 W
Edgeworthstown	248	53.42 N	7.36 W
Edinburgh	246	55.57 N	3.13 W
Edinburgh (Turnhouse) Airport ⊠	246	55.57 N	3.13 W
Edinburgh Castle ⊥	246	55.56 N	3.14 W
Edmondbyers	244	54.51 N	1.58 W
Edwinstowe	244	53.12 N	1.04 W
Edzell	246	56.48 N	2.39 W
Egglestone Abbey ⊽¹	244	54.32 N	1.54 W
Egham	242	51.26 N	0.34 W
Egilsay I	246	59.09 N	2.56 W
Eglinton	248	55.01 N	7.11 W
Egloskerry	242	50.39 N	4.27 W
Egremont	244	54.29 N	3.33 W
Egton	244	54.26 N	0.45 W
Ehen ≈	244	54.25 N	3.30 W
Eigg I	246	56.54 N	6.10 W
Eigg, Sound of U	246	56.51 N	6.13 W
Eighe, Càrn ∧	246	57.17 N	5.07 W
Eishken	246	58.01 N	6.32 W
Eishort, Loch C	246	57.10 N	5.59 W
Eithon ≈	242	52.12 N	3.27 W
Elgin	246	57.39 N	3.20 W
Elgol	246	57.09 N	6.06 W
Elham	242	51.10 N	1.07 E
Elie	246	56.11 N	2.50 W
Elland	244	53.41 N	1.50 W
Ellen ≈	244	54.43 N	3.30 W
Ellesmere	242	52.54 N	2.54 W
Ellesmere Port	244	53.17 N	2.54 W
Ellington	244	55.13 N	1.34 W
Ellon	246	57.22 N	2.05 W
Elm	242	52.38 N	0.12 E
Elmswell	242	52.15 N	0.53 E
Elphin	246	58.05 N	4.19 W
Elstead	242	51.11 N	0.43 W
Elstree	242	51.39 N	0.16 W
Elwy ≈	242	53.16 N	3.26 W
Ely	242	52.24 N	0.16 E
Ely, Isle of ◦¹	242	52.24 N	0.10 E
Ely Cathedral ⊽¹	242	52.24 N	0.10 E
Embleton	244	55.30 N	1.37 W
Embo	246	57.54 N	3.59 W
Emneth	242	52.38 N	0.11 E
Emsworth	242	50.51 N	0.56 W
Emyvale	248	54.20 N	6.59 W
Enard Bay C	246	58.05 N	5.20 W
Enborne ≈	242	51.24 N	1.06 W
Enderby	242	52.36 N	1.12 W
Enfield ◦⁸	242	51.40 N	0.05 W
England □⁸, U.K.	242	52.30 N	1.30 W
England □⁸, U.K.	244	54.00 N	1.30 W
English Channel U	242	50.20 N	1.00 W
Ennell, Lough	248	53.28 N	7.24 W
Ennerdale Water ⊜	244	54.31 N	3.23 W
Ennis	248	52.50 N	8.59 W
Enniscorthy	248	52.30 N	6.34 W
Enniskillen	248	54.21 N	7.38 W
Ennistymon	248	52.57 N	9.15 W
Ensay I	246	57.46 N	7.05 W
Eport, Loch C	246	57.33 N	7.11 W
Epping	242	51.43 N	0.07 E
Epping Forest ⊢³	242	51.40 N	0.03 E
Epsom	242	51.20 N	0.16 W
Epworth	244	53.32 N	0.49 W
Eriboll	246	58.28 N	4.41 W
Eriboll, Loch C	246	58.31 N	4.41 W
Ericht, Loch ⊜	246	56.48 N	4.24 W
Eriskay I	246	57.04 N	7.18 W
Erisort, Loch C	246	58.07 N	6.24 W
Erkina ≈	248	52.56 N	7.23 W
Erne, Lower Lough	248	54.30 N	8.16 W
Erne, Upper Lough	248	54.26 N	7.46 W
Erne ≈	248	54.30 N	8.16 W
Errigal ∧	248	55.02 N	8.07 W
Erris Head ⊁	248	54.19 N	10.00 W
Errochty, Loch ⊜	246	56.45 N	4.12 W
Errogie	246	57.16 N	4.22 W
Escrick	244	53.53 N	1.02 W
Esher	242	51.23 N	0.22 W
Esk ≈, U.K.	246	55.56 N	3.04 W
Esk ≈, Eng., U.K.	244	54.29 N	0.37 W
Esk ≈, Eng., U.K.	244	54.21 N	3.23 W
Esk ≈, Scot., U.K.	246	55.57 N	3.03 W
Eskdale V	246	55.12 N	3.09 W
Essex □⁶	242	51.48 N	0.40 E
Eston	244	54.34 N	1.07 W
Etive, Loch C	246	56.29 N	5.09 W
Eton	242	51.31 N	0.37 W
Ettrick Forest ⊢³	246	55.30 N	3.00 W
Ettrick Pen ∧	244	55.23 N	3.16 W
Ettrick Water ≈	246	55.31 N	2.55 W
Evanton	246	57.40 N	4.20 W
Evenlode ≈	242	51.47 N	1.21 W
Evercreech	242	51.09 N	2.30 W
Evesham	242	52.06 N	1.56 W
Evesham, Vale of V	242	52.06 N	1.50 W
Ewe, Loch C	246	57.48 N	5.40 W
Ewe Water ≈	244	55.08 N	3.00 W
Exe ≈	242	50.37 N	3.25 W
Exeter	242	50.43 N	3.31 W
Exford	242	51.08 N	3.39 W
Exminster	242	50.41 N	3.29 W
Exmoor ∧	242	51.10 N	3.45 W
Exmoor National Park ⊼	242	51.12 N	3.45 W
Exmouth	242	50.37 N	3.25 W
Eyam	244	53.17 N	1.40 W
Eye, Eng., U.K.	242	52.19 N	0.10 W
Eye, Eng., U.K.	242	52.35 N	1.09 E
Eyemouth	246	55.52 N	2.06 W
Eye Peninsula ⊁¹	246	58.13 N	6.13 W
Eye Water ≈	246	55.53 N	2.06 W
Eynhallow Sound U	246	59.08 N	3.06 W
Eynort, Loch C	246	57.13 N	7.16 W
Eynsham	242	51.48 N	1.22 W
Eyrecourt	248	53.18 N	8.07 W
Eythorne	242	51.11 N	1.17 E
F			
Fada, Lochan ⊜	246	57.41 N	5.18 W
Fahan	248	55.05 N	7.28 W
Failsworth	244	53.31 N	2.09 W
Fairbourne	242	52.41 N	4.03 W
Fairford	242	51.44 N	1.47 W
Fair Head ⊁	248	55.13 N	6.09 W
Fair Isle I	246	59.32 N	1.39 W
Fairlie	246	55.46 N	4.51 W
Fairlight	242	50.53 N	0.40 E
Fairy Water ≈	248	54.37 N	7.20 W
Fakenham	242	52.50 N	0.51 E
Fal ≈	242	50.08 N	5.02 W
Falkirk	246	56.00 N	3.48 W
Falkland	246	56.15 N	3.12 W
Falmouth	242	50.08 N	5.04 W
Falmouth Bay C	242	50.07 N	3.36 W
Falstone	244	55.11 N	2.25 W
Fanad Head ⊁	248	55.16 N	7.38 W
Fane ≈	248	53.56 N	6.23 W
Fannich, Loch ⊜	246	57.38 N	5.00 W
Faoileann, Bàgh nam C	246	56.23 N	7.17 W
Fareham	242	50.51 N	1.10 W
Faringdon	242	51.40 N	1.35 W
Farnborough	242	51.17 N	0.46 W
Farne Islands II	244	55.38 N	1.38 W
Farnham	244	51.13 N	0.49 W
Farnworth	244	53.33 N	2.24 W
Farr	246	57.21 N	4.12 W
Farrar ≈	246	57.24 N	4.50 W
Fastnet Rock I²	248	51.24 N	9.35 W
Fauldhouse	246	55.50 N	3.37 W
Faversham	242	51.20 N	0.53 E
Fawley	242	50.49 N	1.20 W
Fazeley	242	52.28 N	9.40 W
Featherstone	244	53.41 N	1.21 W
Feeagh, Lough	248	53.55 N	9.36 W
Felixstowe	242	51.58 N	1.20 E
Felling	244	54.57 N	1.33 W
Felpham	242	50.47 N	0.39 W
Fen Ditton	242	52.13 N	0.10 E
Fenny Compton	242	52.09 N	1.20 W
Fenny Stratford	242	52.00 N	0.43 W
Ferbane	248	53.15 N	7.49 W
Ferndown	242	50.48 N	1.55 W
Ferns	248	52.35 N	6.31 W
Ferryhill	244	54.41 N	1.33 W
Feshie ≈	246	57.08 N	3.55 W
Fetcham	242	51.17 N	0.22 W
Fethaland, Point of ⊁	246a	60.38 N	1.18 W
Fethard	246a	52.11 N	7.41 W
Fetlar I	246a	60.37 N	0.52 W
Fetteresso	246	56.51 N	2.34 W
Fettercairn	246	56.51 N	2.34 W
Ffestiniog	242	52.58 N	3.55 W
Fforest Fawr ∧¹	242	51.52 N	3.36 W
Fife □⁴	246	56.13 N	3.02 W
Fife Ness ⊁	246	56.17 N	2.36 W
Filey	244	54.12 N	0.17 W
Filey Bay C	244	54.12 N	0.16 W
Filton	242	51.31 N	2.35 W
Finlas, Loch ⊜	246	56.37 N	3.05 W
Fincham	242	52.35 N	0.30 E
Finchingfield	242	51.58 N	0.27 E
Findhorn	246	57.39 N	3.36 W
Findhorn ≈	246	57.38 N	3.38 W
Findochty	246	57.42 N	2.54 W
Findon	242	50.54 N	0.24 W
Finedon	242	52.20 N	0.39 W
Finn ≈	248	54.50 N	7.28 W
Finstown	246	59.00 N	3.07 W
Fintona	248	54.30 N	7.19 W
Fintry	246	56.04 N	4.13 W
Finvoy	248	55.00 N	6.30 W
Fionn Loch ⊜	246	57.46 N	5.29 W
Fishbourne	242	50.44 N	1.12 W
Fishguard	242	51.59 N	4.59 W
Fitful Head ⊁	246a	59.54 N	1.23 W
Fivemiletown	248	54.23 N	7.18 W
Five Penny Borve	246	58.25 N	6.25 W
Flamborough Head ⊁	244	54.07 N	0.04 W
Flannan Islands II	246	58.18 N	7.36 W
Flat Holm I	242	51.23 N	3.08 W
Fleet	242	51.16 N	0.50 W
Fleet ≈	244	54.57 N	4.05 W
Fleetwood	244	53.56 N	3.01 W
Flimby	244	54.41 N	3.31 W
Flint	244	53.15 N	3.07 W
Flitwick	242	52.00 N	0.29 W
Flodden Field Battlesite (1513) ⊥	244	55.38 N	2.13 W
Flotta I	246	58.50 N	3.07 W
Fochabers	246	57.37 N	3.05 W
Folkestone	242	51.05 N	1.11 E
Folkingham	242	52.54 N	0.24 W
Font ≈	244	55.10 N	1.44 W
Ford	246	56.10 N	5.26 W
Forden	242	52.36 N	3.08 W
Fordingbridge	242	50.56 N	1.47 W
Foreland Point ⊁	242	51.16 N	3.47 W
Forest Row	242	51.06 N	0.02 E
Forfar	246	56.38 N	2.54 W
Formby	244	53.34 N	3.05 W
Formby Point ⊁	244	53.33 N	3.06 W
Forres	246	57.37 N	3.38 W
Fort Augustus	246	57.09 N	4.41 W
Fortevoit	246	56.20 N	3.32 W
Forth	246	55.47 N	3.41 W
Forth, Carse of ≈	246	56.03 N	3.44 W
Forth, Firth of C¹	246	56.10 N	2.45 W
Forth Bridge ◦⁵	246	56.00 N	3.25 W
Fortrose	246	57.34 N	4.09 W
Fort William	246	56.49 N	5.07 W
Forty Foot Drain ≈	242	52.30 N	0.05 W
Foss	246	56.41 N	3.58 W
Foss ≈	246	53.57 N	1.06 W
Fothergill	244	54.38 N	3.30 W
Foula I	246a	60.08 N	2.05 W
Foulden	244	55.47 N	2.11 W
Foulness Island I	242	51.36 N	0.55 E
Foulness Point ⊁	242	51.38 N	0.57 E
Fountains Abbey ⊽¹	244	54.07 N	1.34 W
Foveran	246	57.18 N	2.02 W
Fowey	242	50.20 N	4.38 W
Fowey ≈	242	50.33 N	9.08 W
Foxholes	244	54.08 N	0.28 W
Foyers	246	57.15 N	4.29 W
Foyle ≈, Eur.	248	55.04 N	7.15 W
Foyle, Lough C	248	55.06 N	7.08 W
Foynes	246	52.37 N	9.06 W
Framlingham	242	52.13 N	1.21 E
Frampton on Severn	242	51.46 N	2.22 W
Fraserburgh	246	57.42 N	2.00 W
Freemount	242	52.16 N	6.53 W
Fremington	244	51.04 N	4.07 W
Frenchpark	248	53.52 N	8.26 W
Freshwater	242	52.43 N	7.24 W
Freswick	246	58.35 N	3.05 W
Fridaythorpe	244	54.01 N	0.40 W
Frinton-on-Sea	242	51.50 N	1.14 E
Friockheim	246	56.38 N	2.38 W
Frisa, Loch ⊜	246	56.34 N	6.05 W
Frizington	244	54.32 N	3.30 W
Frodsham	244	53.18 N	2.44 W
Frome	242	51.14 N	2.20 W

Symbols in the index entries are identified on page 250.

Name	Page	Lat °'	Long °'
Frome ≃, Eng., U.K.	242	52.03 N	2.38 W
Frome ≃, Eng., U.K.	242	50.41 N	2.04 W
Fuday ▌	248	57.03 N	7.23 W
Fulwood	244	53.47 N	2.41 W
Funshinagh, Lough	248	53.31 N	8.07 W
Furnace	246	56.09 N	5.10 W
Furness Abbey ♣¹	244	54.07 N	3.12 W
Furness Fells ♣¹	244	54.18 N	3.07 W
Fyfield	242	51.45 N	0.16 E
Fylde ▸¹	244	53.47 N	2.56 W
Fyne, Loch C	246	55.56 N	5.24 W
Fyvie	246	57.25 N	2.23 W

G

Name	Page	Lat °'	Long °'
Gaerwen	244	53.13 N	4.16 W
Gainford	244	54.32 N	1.44 W
Gainsborough	244	53.24 N	0.46 W
Gairloch	246	57.42 N	5.40 W
Gairloch, Loch C	246	57.44 N	5.44 W
Gairn ≃	246	57.03 N	3.05 W
Galashiels	246	55.37 N	2.49 W
Gala Water ≃	246	55.37 N	2.47 W
Galgate	244	54.00 N	2.47 W
Gallan Head ⟩	246	58.14 N	7.03 W
Galley Head ⟩	248	51.30 N	8.57 W
Gallimh → Galway	248	53.16 N	9.03 W
Galloway □⁹	244	55.00 N	4.25 W
Galloway, Mull of ⟩	244	54.38 N	4.50 W
Galston	246	55.36 N	4.24 W
Galtymore ⋀	248	52.22 N	8.10 W
Galty Mountains ⋀⁸	248	52.25 N	8.10 W
Galway	248	53.16 N	9.03 W
Galway □⁶	248	53.20 N	9.00 W
Galway Bay C	248	53.10 N	9.15 W
Gamph, Slieve ⋀⁸	248	54.05 N	9.00 W
Ganu Mór ⋀	246	58.25 N	4.53 W
Gara, Lough ⊜	248	53.55 N	8.25 W
Garboldisham	242	52.24 N	0.56 E
Gare Loch C	246	56.01 N	4.48 W
Garelochhead	246	56.05 N	4.50 W
Garforth	244	53.48 N	1.22 W
Gargrave	244	53.59 N	2.06 W
Garinin	244	58.21 N	6.50 W
Garlieston	244	54.48 N	4.22 W
Garmouth	246	57.40 N	3.07 W
Garnock ≃	246	55.38 N	4.42 W
Garrison	248	54.25 N	8.05 W
Garron Point ⟩	248	55.03 N	5.55 W
Garros	246	57.37 N	6.11 W
Garry ≃	246	56.43 N	3.47 W
Garsdale Head ⟩	244	54.19 N	2.20 W
Garstang	244	53.55 N	2.47 W
Garve	246	57.37 N	4.42 W
Garvellachs ▌▌	246	56.14 N	5.47 W
Gatehouse of Fleet	244	54.53 N	4.11 W
Gateshead	244	54.58 N	1.37 W
Gaunless ≃	244	54.40 N	1.41 W
Gayton	242	52.45 N	0.34 E
Gaywood	242	52.46 N	0.26 E
Gelt ≃	244	54.55 N	2.43 W
Ghló, Beinn a ⋀	246	56.50 N	3.43 W
Gibraltar Point ⟩	244	53.05 N	0.19 E
Gifford	246	55.54 N	2.45 W
Giggleswick	244	54.04 N	2.17 W
Gigha, Sound of U	246	55.41 N	5.42 W
Gigha Isles ▌▌	246	55.41 N	5.46 W
Gilford	246	54.23 N	6.22 W
Gill, Lough ⊜	248	54.16 N	8.24 W
Gillingham, Eng., U.K.	242	51.24 N	0.33 E
Gillingham, Eng., U.K.	242	51.02 N	2.17 W
Gilwern	242	51.51 N	3.06 W
Gipping ≃	242	52.04 N	1.10 E
Girvan	244	55.15 N	4.51 W
Girvan, Water of ≃	244	55.15 N	4.51 W
Glamis	246	56.36 N	3.00 W
Glamis Castle	246	56.37 N	3.00 W
Glanaman	242	51.48 N	3.54 W
Glascarnoch, Loch ⊜	246	57.40 N	4.50 W
Glasgow	246	55.53 N	4.15 W
Glasgow (Abbotsinch) Airport ⊠	246	55.52 N	4.26 W
Glaslyn ≃	246	52.56 N	4.06 W
Glas Maol ⋀	246	56.52 N	3.22 W
Glass, Loch ⊜	246	57.43 N	4.30 W
Glasson	246	53.28 N	7.52 W
Glastonbury	242	51.06 N	2.43 W
Glaven ≃	242	52.58 N	1.03 E
Glemsford	242	52.06 N	0.41 E
Glen ≃, Eire	248	54.38 N	8.40 W
Glen ≃, Eng., U.K.	242	52.51 N	0.06 W
Glenamaddy	248	53.37 N	8.35 W
Glenamoy	248	54.14 N	9.42 W
Glenarm	248	54.58 N	5.57 W
Glenavy	248	54.35 N	6.13 W
Glenbeigh	248	52.02 N	9.58 W
Glencolumbkille	248	54.43 N	8.45 E
Glencoul, Loch C	246	58.02 N	4.59 W
Glendalough ⌁	248	53.01 N	6.26 W
Glendoe Forest ⋀³	246	57.06 N	4.37 W
Glendowan	248	54.58 N	7.57 W
Glenelg	246	57.13 N	5.38 W
Glenelly ≃	248	54.44 N	7.18 W
Glenfarg	246	56.16 N	3.24 W
Glenfarne	248	54.17 N	7.59 W
Glenfield	242	52.39 N	1.12 W
Glenfinnan	246	56.52 N	5.27 W
Glengarriff	248	51.45 N	9.33 W
Glenluce	244	54.53 N	4.49 W
Glenluce Abbey ♣¹	244	54.53 N	4.58 W
Glenrothes	246	56.12 N	3.10 W
Glenshee ↓	246	56.48 N	3.30 W
Glenties	248	54.47 N	8.17 W
Glenville	248	52.03 N	8.26 W
Glin	248	52.34 N	9.17 W
Glossop	244	53.27 N	1.57 W
Gloucester	242	51.53 N	2.14 W
Gloucester, Vale of V	242	51.55 N	2.10 W
Gloucestershire □⁶	242	51.47 N	2.15 W
Glyde ≃	248	53.52 N	6.21 W
Glyme ≃	242	51.49 N	1.22 W
Glynneath	242	51.46 N	3.38 W
Goat Fell ⋀	246	55.39 N	5.11 W
Goathland	244	54.23 N	0.44 W
Godalming	242	51.11 N	0.37 W
Godmanchester	242	52.19 N	0.11 W
Godshill	242	50.38 N	1.14 W
Godstone	242	51.15 N	0.04 W
Goil, Loch C	246	56.08 N	4.54 W
Goili ▌	248	55.05 N	8.22 W
Golden	248	52.29 N	7.58 W
Golden Valley V			
Goleen	248	51.28 N	9.43 W
Golspie	246	57.58 N	3.58 W
Gometra ▌	246	56.29 N	6.17 W
Goodwick	242	52.00 N	5.00 W
Goole	244	53.42 N	0.52 W
Gordon	246	55.41 N	2.34 W
Gorebridge	246	55.51 N	3.02 W
Gorey, Eire	248	52.40 N	6.18 W
Gorey, Jersey	243b	49.12 N	2.02 W
Goring	242	51.32 N	1.08 W
Goring-by-Sea	242	50.49 N	0.25 W
Goring Gap V	242	51.32 N	1.08 W
Gorleston on Sea	242	52.36 N	1.43 E
Gorm, Loch ⊜	246	55.48 N	6.25 W
Gorseinon	242	51.40 N	4.02 W
Gort	248	53.04 N	8.50 W
Gortahork	248	55.08 N	8.09 W
Gorumna Island	248	53.14 N	9.40 W
Gosforth, Eng., U.K.	244	54.26 N	3.27 W
Gosforth, Eng., U.K.	244	55.01 N	1.37 W
Gosport	242	50.48 N	1.08 W
Goudhurst	242	51.07 N	0.28 E
Gourock	246	55.58 N	4.49 W
Gower ⟩¹	242	51.36 N	4.10 W
Gowerton	242	51.39 N	4.01 W
Gowna, Lough ⊜	248	53.51 N	7.34 W
Gowy ≃	244	53.17 N	2.51 W
Graemsay ▌	246	58.56 N	3.17 W
Grafham Water ⊜	242	52.17 N	0.20 W
Grain ≃	242	51.28 N	0.43 E
Grain, Isle of ▌	242	51.27 N	0.41 E
Grampian □⁴	246	57.15 N	2.45 W
Grampian Mountains ⋀⁸	246	56.55 N	4.00 W
Granard	248	53.47 N	7.30 W
Grand Canal ⊟	248	53.21 N	6.14 W
Grandtully	246	56.39 N	3.46 W
Graney, Lough ⊜	248	52.59 N	8.40 W
Grangemouth	246	56.02 N	3.45 W
Grange-over-Sands	244	54.12 N	2.55 W
Gramoch, Loch ≃	244	55.00 N	4.17 W
Granta ≃	242	52.10 N	0.06 E
Grantham	242	52.55 N	0.39 W
Granton	246	55.59 N	3.14 W
Grantown on Spey	246	57.20 N	3.58 W
Granthouse	246	55.53 N	2.19 W
Grasmere	244	54.28 N	3.02 W
Grassington	244	54.04 N	1.59 W
Gravesend	242	51.27 N	0.24 E
Grayshott	242	51.11 N	0.45 W
Grays Thurrock	242	51.29 N	0.20 E
Great Baddow	242	51.43 N	0.29 E
Great Bernera ▌	246	58.13 N	6.49 W
Great Blasket Island ▌	248	52.05 N	10.32 W
Great Clifton	244	54.31 N	3.29 W
Great Cumbrae I	244	55.46 N	4.57 W
Great Cumbrae Island ▌	244	55.46 N	4.55 W
Great Dunmow	242	51.53 N	0.22 E
Great Eau ≃	244	53.25 N	0.13 E
Greater London □⁶	242	51.30 N	0.10 W
Greater Manchester □⁶	244	53.30 N	2.20 W
Great Gable ⋀	244	54.28 N	3.12 W
Great Grimsby → Grimsby	244	53.35 N	0.05 W
Great Harwood	244	53.48 N	2.24 W
Great Malvern (Malvern)	242	52.07 N	2.19 W
Great Massingham	242	52.46 N	0.40 E
Great Missenden	242	51.43 N	0.43 W
Great Mis Tor ⋀	242	50.34 N	4.01 W
Great Ormes Head ⟩	244	53.21 N	3.52 W
Great Ouse ≃	242	52.47 N	0.22 E
Great Shelford	242	52.09 N	0.09 E
Great Stour ≃	242	51.19 N	1.15 E
Great Torrington	242	50.57 N	4.08 W
Great Whernside ⋀	244	54.09 N	1.59 W
Great Yarmouth	242	52.37 N	1.44 E
Greencastle	248	55.12 N	6.59 W
Greenfield	244	53.18 N	3.13 W
Greenisland	248	54.42 N	5.52 W
Greenlaw	246	55.43 N	2.28 W
Greenock	246	55.57 N	4.45 W
Greenodd	244	54.14 N	3.04 W
Greenore Point ⟩	248	52.15 N	6.18 W
Greenstone Point ⟩	246	57.55 N	5.38 W
Grenagh	248	52.00 N	8.37 W
Grenoside	244	53.27 N	1.30 W
Greta ≃, Eng., U.K.	244	54.32 N	1.53 W
Greta ≃, Eng., U.K.	244	54.36 N	3.10 W
Gretna Green	244	54.59 N	3.04 W
Greyabbey	244	54.32 N	5.30 W
Greystoke	244	54.40 N	2.52 W
Greystones	248	53.09 N	6.04 W
Gribbin Head ⟩	242	50.19 N	4.40 W
Grimsby	244	53.35 N	0.05 W
Grosnez Point ⟩	243b	49.16 N	2.15 W
Grovely Ridge ⋀⁹	242	51.08 N	2.04 W
Gruinard Bay C	246	57.53 N	5.31 W
Gruinart, Loch C	246	55.52 N	6.20 W
Grunavat, Loch ⊜	246	58.14 N	6.55 W
Gruting	246	60.14 N	1.30 W
Guernsey □²	243b	49.28 N	2.35 W
Guildford	242	51.14 N	0.35 W
Guildtown	246	56.28 N	3.24 W
Guilsfield	242	52.42 N	3.09 W
Guisachan Forest ⋀³	246	57.17 N	4.55 W
Guisborough	244	54.32 N	1.04 W
Guiseley	244	53.53 N	1.42 W
Gulland Rock ▌▌	242	50.34 N	4.59 W
Gullane	246	56.02 N	2.50 W
Gullion, Slieve ⋀	248	54.08 N	6.26 W
Gunnislake	242	50.31 N	4.12 W
Gutcher	246	60.40 N	1.00 W
Gwalchmai	244	53.15 N	4.25 W
Gwash ≃	242	52.39 N	0.27 W
Gwaun ≃	242	52.00 N	4.58 W
Gweebarra ≃	248	54.50 N	8.20 W
Gweebarra Bay C	248	54.08 N	8.20 W
Gweedore	248	55.03 N	8.14 W
Gweesalia	248	54.07 N	9.54 W
Gwendraeth Fâch ≃	242	51.44 N	4.18 W
Gwendraeth Fawr ≃	242	51.43 N	4.18 W
Gwent □⁶	242	51.43 N	2.57 W
Gwynedd □⁶	244	53.00 N	4.00 W
Gypsey Race ≃	244	54.05 N	0.12 W

H

Name	Page	Lat °'	Long °'
Hacketstown	248	52.52 N	6.33 W
Hackney ♦⁸	242	51.33 N	0.03 W
Haddenham, Eng., U.K.	242	52.22 N	0.09 E
Haddenham, Eng., U.K.	242	51.46 N	0.56 W
Haddington	246	55.58 N	2.47 W
Hadleigh	242	52.03 N	0.58 E
Hadlow	242	51.14 N	0.20 E
Hadrian's Wall ⌁	244	54.59 N	2.26 W
Hagley	242	52.26 N	2.08 W
Hags Head ⟩	248	52.57 N	9.30 W
Hailsham	242	50.52 N	0.16 E
Halberton	242	50.55 N	3.25 E
Halesowen	242	52.27 N	2.03 W
Halesworth	242	52.21 N	1.30 E
Halifax	244	53.44 N	1.52 W
Halkirk	246	58.30 N	3.30 W
Halladale ≃	246	58.33 N	3.55 W
Halstead	242	51.57 N	0.38 E
Haltwhistle	244	54.58 N	2.27 W
Halwell	242	50.22 N	3.43 W
Hamble	242	50.52 N	1.19 W
Hambledon	242	50.56 N	1.04 W
Hambleton Hills ⋀²	244	54.16 N	1.12 W
Hamilton	246	55.47 N	4.03 W
Hammersmith ♦⁸	242	51.30 N	0.14 W
Hampshire □⁶	242	51.05 N	1.15 W
Hampshire Downs ⋀⁸	242	51.15 N	1.17 W
Hampton Court Palace ⌁	242	51.24 N	0.20 W
Handa ▌	246	58.22 N	5.12 W
Hangingstone Hill ⋀	242	50.39 N	3.57 W
Haringey ♦⁸	242	51.35 N	0.07 W
Harlech	242	52.52 N	4.07 W
Harleston	242	52.24 N	1.18 E
Harlow	242	51.47 N	0.08 E
Haroldswick	246a	60.41 N	0.50 W
Harpenden	242	51.49 N	0.22 W
Harper Town	244	54.55 N	2.31 W
Harray, Loch of ⊜	246	59.01 N	3.13 W
Harrietfield	246	56.25 N	3.39 W
Harrietsham	242	51.15 N	0.41 E
Harrington	244	54.37 N	3.34 W
Harris ⟩¹	246	56.59 N	6.20 W
Harris ⟩¹	246	57.55 N	6.50 W
Harris, Sound of U	246	57.45 N	7.10 W
Harrogate	244	54.00 N	1.33 W
Harrow ♦⁸	242	51.35 N	0.21 W
Hart Fell ⋀	244	55.25 N	3.25 W
Hartland	242	50.59 N	4.29 W
Hartland Point ⟩	242	51.02 N	4.31 W
Hartlepool	244	54.42 N	1.11 W
Hartshill	242	52.37 N	1.32 W
Harwell	242	51.37 N	1.18 W
Harwich	242	51.57 N	1.17 E
Hascosay ▌	246	60.37 N	0.59 W
Haskeir Islands ▌▌	246	57.42 N	7.41 W
Haslemere	242	51.06 N	0.43 W
Haslingden	244	53.43 N	2.18 W
Haslington	244	53.06 N	2.24 W
Hastings	242	50.51 N	0.36 E
Hastings Battlesite (1066) ⌁	242	50.53 N	0.31 E
Hatfield	242	51.46 N	0.13 W
Hatfield Peverel	242	51.47 N	0.35 E
Hatherleigh	242	50.49 N	4.04 W
Hathersage	242	53.19 N	1.38 W
Hatton	246	57.25 N	1.54 W
Haugh of Urr	244	54.58 N	3.52 W
Havant	242	50.51 N	0.59 W
Haverfordwest	242	51.49 N	4.58 W
Haverhill	242	52.05 N	0.26 E
Haverigg	244	54.11 N	3.17 W
Havering ♦⁸	242	51.34 N	0.14 E
Hawarden	244	53.11 N	3.02 W
Hawes	244	54.18 N	2.12 W
Haweswater Reservoir ⊜	244	54.32 N	2.48 W
Hawick	244	55.25 N	2.47 W
Hawkhurst	242	51.02 N	0.30 E
Haydock	244	53.28 N	2.39 W
Haydon Bridge	244	54.58 N	2.14 W
Haydon Wye	242	52.04 N	3.07 W
Haywards Heath	242	51.00 N	0.06 W
Hazel Grove	244	53.23 N	2.08 W
Heacham	242	52.55 N	0.30 E
Headcorn	242	51.11 N	0.37 E
Headford	248	53.28 N	9.05 W
Headington	242	51.45 N	1.13 W
Headley	242	51.07 N	0.50 W
Heanor	244	53.01 N	1.22 W
Heath End	242	51.22 N	1.09 W
Heathfield	242	50.59 N	0.17 E
Hebburn	244	54.59 N	1.30 W
Hebden Bridge	244	53.45 N	2.00 W
Hebrides ▌▌	246	57.00 N	6.30 W
Hebrides, Sea of the ⊽²	246	57.07 N	6.55 W
Heckington	242	52.59 N	0.18 W
Hednesford	242	52.43 N	2.00 W
Hedon	244	53.44 N	0.12 W
Heisker Islands ▌▌	246	57.31 N	7.40 W
Helensburgh	246	56.01 N	4.44 W
Hellifield	244	54.01 N	2.12 W
Helli Ness ⟩	246	60.02 N	1.10 W
Helmsdale	246	58.07 N	3.40 W
Helmsdale ≃	246	58.07 N	3.40 W
Helmsley	244	54.14 N	1.04 W
Helsby	244	53.16 N	2.46 W
Helston	242	50.05 N	5.16 W
Helvellyn ⋀	244	54.31 N	3.01 W
Helvick Head ⟩	248	52.03 N	7.33 W
Hemel Hempstead	242	51.46 N	0.28 W
Hempnall	242	52.30 N	1.19 E
Hemsworth	244	53.38 N	1.21 W
Hendy	242	51.43 N	4.04 W
Henfield	242	50.56 N	0.17 W
Hengoed	242	51.39 N	3.10 W
Henley-in-Arden	242	52.17 N	1.46 W
Henley-on-Thames	242	51.32 N	0.56 W
Henlow	242	52.02 N	0.18 W
Henstridge	242	50.59 N	2.24 W
Hereford	242	52.04 N	2.43 W
Hereford and Worcester □⁶	242	52.10 N	2.30 W
Hereford Cathedral ⌁	242	52.04 N	2.43 W
Herma Ness ⟩	246a	60.50 N	0.55 W
Herne Bay	242	51.23 N	1.08 E
Hersham	242	51.22 N	0.23 W
Herstmonceux	242	50.53 N	0.20 E
Hertford	242	51.48 N	0.05 W
Hertfordshire □⁶	242	51.50 N	0.10 W
Hessle	244	53.44 N	0.26 W
Heswall	244	53.20 N	3.06 W
Hetton-le-Hole	244	54.50 N	1.27 W
Hexham	244	54.58 N	2.06 W
Heysham	244	54.02 N	2.54 W
Heywood	244	53.36 N	2.13 W
Hibaldstow	244	53.31 N	0.32 W
Higham Ferrers	242	52.18 N	0.36 W
Higham Upshire	242	51.26 N	0.28 E
High Bentham	244	54.08 N	2.30 W
Highbridge	242	51.13 N	2.49 W
High Force ↳	244	54.38 N	2.13 W
Highland □⁴	246	57.40 N	5.00 W
High Peak ⋀	244	53.22 N	1.50 W
High Seat ⋀	244	54.24 N	2.18 W
High Street ⋀	244	54.29 N	2.52 W
High Willhays ⋀	242	50.41 N	3.59 W
Highworth	242	51.38 N	1.43 W
High Wycombe	242	51.38 N	0.45 W
Hillingdon ♦⁸	242	51.32 N	0.27 W
Hill of Fearn	246	57.45 N	3.56 W
Hillsborough	248	54.28 N	6.05 W
Hillswick	246	60.28 N	1.30 W
Hilltown	248	54.12 N	6.08 W
Hilpsford Point ⟩	244	54.03 N	3.12 W
Hinckley	242	52.33 N	1.21 W
Hindhead	242	51.07 N	0.44 W
Hindley	244	53.32 N	2.35 W
Hindon	242	51.06 N	2.08 W
Hinish Bay C	246	56.28 N	6.50 W
Hirwaun	242	51.45 N	3.30 W
Histon	242	52.15 N	0.06 E
Hitchin	242	51.57 N	0.17 W
Hockley	242	51.37 N	0.40 E
Hoddesdon	242	51.46 N	0.01 W
Hodder ≃	244	53.50 N	2.35 W
Hodnet	242	52.51 N	2.35 W
Hog's Back ⋀⁴	242	51.13 N	0.38 W
Holbeach	242	52.49 N	0.01 E
Holbeach Marsh ⋿	242	52.52 N	0.05 E
Holderness ⟩¹	244	53.47 N	0.10 W
Holland-on-Sea	242	51.48 N	1.13 E
Hollandstoun	246	59.21 N	2.16 W
Hollywood	248	53.06 N	6.35 W
Holme ≃	244	53.41 N	1.43 W
Holmfirth	244	53.35 N	1.46 W
Holsworthy	242	50.49 N	4.21 W
Holycross	248	52.38 N	7.52 W
Holyhead	246	53.19 N	4.38 W
Holyhead Bay C	244	55.23 N	4.37 W
Holy Island ▌, Eng., U.K.	244	55.41 N	1.48 W
Holy Island ▌, Scot., U.K.	246	55.32 N	5.05 W
Holy Island ▌, Wales, U.K.	244	53.18 N	4.37 W
Holyrood Palace ⌁	246	55.56 N	3.12 W
Holywell	244	53.17 N	3.13 W
Holywood	244	54.38 N	5.49 W
Honddu ≃, Wales, U.K.	242	51.54 N	2.58 W
Honddu ≃, Wales, U.K.	242	51.57 N	3.23 W
Honiton	242	50.48 N	3.13 W
Hook	242	51.17 N	0.58 W
Hook Head ⟩	248	52.07 N	6.55 W
Hope, Ben ⋀	246	58.24 N	4.37 W
Hope, Loch C	246	58.27 N	4.39 W
Hopeman	246	57.42 N	3.25 W
Horden	244	54.46 N	1.18 W
Horley	242	51.11 N	0.11 W
Horn, Ben ⋀²	246	58.01 N	4.02 W
Horncastle	244	53.13 N	0.07 W
Horndean	242	50.55 N	1.00 W
Horn Head ⟩	248	55.14 N	7.59 W
Hornsea	244	53.55 N	0.10 W
Horrabridge	242	50.31 N	4.05 W
Horsforth	244	53.51 N	1.39 W
Horsham	242	51.04 N	0.21 W
Horsham Saint Faith	242	52.41 N	1.16 E
Horsted Keynes	242	51.02 N	0.01 W
Horton in Ribblesdale	244	54.09 N	2.17 W
Horwich	244	53.37 N	2.33 W
Hospital	248	52.29 N	8.25 W
Houghton-le-Spring	244	54.51 N	1.28 W
Houghton Regis	242	51.55 N	0.31 W
Hounslow ♦⁸	242	51.29 N	0.22 W
Hourn, Loch C	246	57.08 N	5.36 W
Hove	242	50.49 N	0.10 W
Howardian Hills ⋀²	244	54.07 N	1.00 W
Howden	244	53.45 N	0.52 W
Howmore	246	57.18 N	7.23 W
Howth	248	53.23 N	6.04 W
Hoy ▌	246	58.51 N	3.18 W
Hoylake	244	53.23 N	3.11 W
Hucclecote	242	51.51 N	2.11 W
Huddersfield	244	53.39 N	1.47 W
Hugh Town	242a	49.55 N	6.17 W
Hull → Kingston upon Hull	244	53.45 N	0.20 W
Hull ≃	244	53.44 N	0.19 W
Hullavington	242	51.33 N	2.09 W
Hullbridge	242	51.37 N	0.38 E
Humber ≃	244	53.40 N	0.10 W
Humber, Mouth of the ≃	244	53.32 N	0.08 E
Humberside □⁶	244	53.55 N	0.40 W
Hungerford	242	51.26 N	1.30 W
Hungry Law ⋀	244	55.21 N	2.24 W
Hunish, Rubha ⟩	246	57.41 N	6.21 W
Hunstanton	242	52.57 N	0.30 E
Hunter's Quay	246	55.58 N	4.55 W
Huntingdon	242	52.20 N	0.12 W
Huntington	244	54.01 N	1.04 W
Huntly	246	57.27 N	2.47 W
Hurlford	246	55.36 N	4.28 W
Hurliness	246	58.47 N	3.15 W
Hursley	242	51.01 N	1.24 W
Hurstbourne Tarrant	242	51.17 N	1.23 W
Hurstpierpoint	242	50.56 N	0.11 W
Huthwaite	244	53.09 N	1.17 W
Huyton-with-Roby	244	53.25 N	2.52 W
Hyde	244	53.27 N	2.04 W
Hythe, Eng., U.K.	242	51.05 N	1.05 E
Hythe, Eng., U.K.	242	50.51 N	1.24 W

I

Name	Page	Lat °'	Long °'
Ibstock	242	52.42 N	1.23 W
Idrigill Point ⟩	246	57.20 N	6.35 W
Ilchester	242	51.01 N	2.41 W
Ilen ≃	248	51.33 N	9.18 W
Ilfracombe	242	51.13 N	4.08 W
Ilkeston	242	52.59 N	1.18 W
Ilkley	244	53.55 N	1.50 W
Illminster	242	50.56 N	2.55 W
Ime, Beinn ⋀	246	56.14 N	4.49 W
Immingham Dock	244	53.37 N	0.12 W
Inch	248	52.08 N	9.59 W
Inchard, Loch C	246	58.27 N	5.04 W
Inchbare	246	56.47 N	2.38 W
Inchcape ▌²	246	56.55 N	2.50 W
Inchmarnock ▌	246	55.46 N	5.10 W
Inchnadamph	246	58.09 N	4.59 W
Inchture	246	56.26 N	3.10 W
Indaal, Loch C	246	55.45 N	6.21 W
Ingatestone	242	51.41 N	0.22 E
Ingleborough ⋀	244	54.11 N	2.23 W
Ingleton	244	54.10 N	2.27 W
Inglewood Forest ⋀³	244	54.45 N	2.50 W
Inishbofin ▌, Eire	248	53.37 N	10.15 W
Inishbofin ▌, Eire	248	55.09 N	8.11 W
Inisheer ▌	248	53.02 N	9.26 W
Inishmaan ▌	248	53.05 N	9.32 W
Inishmore ▌	248	53.07 N	9.45 W
Inishowen Peninsula ⟩¹	248	55.12 N	7.20 W
Inishowen Point ⟩	248	55.14 N	6.56 W
Inishshark ▌	248	53.37 N	10.18 W
Inishtrahull ▌	248	55.26 N	7.14 W
Inishturk ▌	248	53.42 N	10.07 W
Inistioge	248	52.29 N	7.04 W
Innellan	246	55.54 N	4.57 W
Inner Hebrides ▌▌	246	56.30 N	6.00 W
Inner Sound U	246	57.25 N	5.56 W
Inniscrone	248	54.12 N	9.06 W
Inny ≃, Eire	248	53.30 N	7.48 W
Inny ≃, Eng., U.K.	242	50.35 N	4.17 W
Inver	246	57.49 N	3.37 W
Inveraray	246	56.13 N	5.04 W
Inverbervie	246	56.51 N	2.17 W
Invergarry	246	57.02 N	4.47 W
Invergordon	246	57.42 N	4.10 W
Inverkeilor	246	56.38 N	2.32 W
Inverkeithing	246	56.02 N	3.25 W
Invermoriston	246	57.13 N	4.38 W
Inverness	246	57.27 N	4.15 W
Inverurie	246	57.17 N	2.23 W
Iona ▌	246	56.19 N	6.25 W
Iona, Sound of U	246	56.19 N	6.24 W
Ipswich	242	52.04 N	1.10 E
Ireland □¹	248	53.00 N	8.00 W
Irish Sea ⊽²	246	53.30 N	5.20 W
Irlam	244	53.28 N	2.25 W
Iron Bridge	242	52.38 N	2.29 W
Irt ≃	244	54.25 N	3.25 W
Irthing ≃	244	54.55 N	2.50 W
Irthlingborough	242	52.20 N	0.37 W
Irvine	246	55.37 N	4.40 W
Irvine ≃	246	55.37 N	4.41 W
Irvinestown	248	54.28 N	7.38 W
Irwell ≃	244	53.27 N	2.17 W
Isbister	246	60.36 N	1.19 W
Isla ≃	246	57.30 N	2.47 W
Islay ▌	246	55.48 N	6.12 W
Islay, Sound of U	246	55.50 N	6.01 W
Isle ≃	242	50.59 N	2.53 W
Isleat, Sound of U	246	57.05 N	5.52 W
Isle of Man □²	244	54.15 N	4.30 W
Isle of Wight □⁶	242	50.40 N	1.20 W
Islington ♦⁸	242	51.34 N	0.06 W
Islip	242	51.50 N	1.14 W
Islivig	246	58.05 N	7.11 W
Ivybridge	242	50.23 N	3.56 W
Ixworth	242	52.18 N	0.50 E

J

Name	Page	Lat °'	Long °'
Jamestown	248	53.55 N	8.02 W
Janetstown	246	58.16 N	3.20 W
Jarrow	244	54.59 N	1.29 W
Jaywick	242	51.47 N	1.08 E
Jedburgh	246	55.29 N	2.34 W
Jedburgh Abbey ♣¹	244	55.27 N	2.34 W
Jed Water ≃	246	55.32 N	2.33 W
Jerpoint Abbey ♣¹	248	53.29 N	7.08 W
Jersey □²	243b	49.15 N	2.10 W
Jervaulx Abbey ♣¹	244	54.16 N	1.43 W
John O' Groats	246	58.38 N	3.05 W
Johnshaven	246	56.47 N	2.20 W
Johnston	242	51.46 N	5.00 W
Johnstone	246	55.50 N	4.31 W
Jura ▌	246	56.00 N	5.54 W
Jura, Sound of U	246	55.57 N	5.48 W

K

Name	Page	Lat °'	Long °'
Kale Water ≃	246	55.32 N	2.28 W
Kames	246	55.54 N	5.15 W
Kanturk	248	52.10 N	8.55 W
Katesbridge	248	54.17 N	6.08 W
Katrine, Loch ⊜	246	56.15 N	4.31 W
Keady	248	54.15 N	6.42 W
Keal, Loch na C	246	56.28 N	6.04 W
Kebock Head ⟩	246	58.01 N	6.20 W
Keen, Mount ⋀	246	56.58 N	2.54 W
Keeper Hill ⋀	248	52.45 N	8.16 W
Kegworth	242	52.50 N	1.16 W
Keighley	246	53.52 N	1.54 W
Keith	246	57.32 N	2.57 W
Kells → Ceanannus Mór	248	53.44 N	6.53 W
Kelsall	244	53.13 N	2.43 W
Kelsey Head ⟩	242	50.24 N	5.08 W
Kelso	246	55.36 N	2.25 W
Kelvedon	242	51.51 N	0.42 E
Kempston	242	52.07 N	0.30 W
Ken, Loch ⊜	244	55.02 N	4.02 W
Ken, Water of ≃	244	55.04 N	4.08 W
Kendal	244	54.20 N	2.45 W
Kenilworth	242	52.21 N	1.34 W
Kenilworth Castle ⌁	242	52.21 N	1.34 W
Kenmare	248	51.53 N	9.35 W
Kenmare River ≃	248	51.45 N	10.00 W
Kenmore	246	56.34 N	3.59 W
Kennet ≃, Eng., U.K.	242	51.28 N	0.57 W
Kennet ≃, Eng., U.K.	242	52.26 N	0.28 E
Kent □⁶	242	51.10 N	0.54 E
Kent ≃	244	54.15 N	0.40 E
Kent, Vale of V	242	51.10 N	0.30 E
Kentallen	246	56.39 N	5.13 W
Kenton	246	50.38 N	3.28 W
Kerrera ▌	246	56.23 N	5.34 W
Kerry	242	52.30 N	3.16 W
Kerry □⁶	248	52.10 N	9.30 W
Kerry Head ⟩	248	52.25 N	9.57 W
Kesh	248	54.32 N	7.43 W
Kessingland	242	52.25 N	1.42 E
Keswick	244	54.37 N	3.08 W
Kettering	242	52.24 N	0.44 W
Kettlewell	244	54.09 N	2.02 W
Keymer	242	50.55 N	0.08 W
Keynsham	242	51.26 N	2.30 W
Kidderminster	242	52.23 N	2.14 W
Kidlington	242	51.50 N	1.17 W
Kidsgrove	244	53.06 N	2.15 W
Kidwelly	242	51.45 N	4.18 W
Kielder	244	55.14 N	2.35 W
Kilbaha	248	52.33 N	9.52 W
Kilbarchan	246	55.50 N	4.33 W
Kilbeggan	248	53.22 N	7.29 W
Kilbirnie	246	55.46 N	4.41 W
Kilbrannan Sound U	246	55.40 N	5.25 W
Kilbride	246	57.05 N	7.27 W
Kilcar	246	54.38 N	8.35 W
Kilchoan	246	56.42 N	6.06 W
Kilchreest	248	53.10 N	8.38 W
Kilchrenan	246	56.21 N	5.11 W
Kilcolgan	248	53.13 N	8.52 W
Kilconnell	248	53.20 N	8.25 W
Kilcormac	248	53.10 N	7.43 W
Kilcullen	248	53.08 N	6.45 W
Kildare	248	53.10 N	6.55 W
Kildare □⁶	248	53.10 N	6.50 W
Kildonan, Strath ✗	246	58.10 N	3.51 W
Kildorrery	248	52.15 N	8.26 W
Kildrummy	246	57.14 N	2.52 W
Kildrummy Castle ⌁	246	57.14 N	2.52 W
Kildysart	248	52.41 N	9.06 W
Kilfenora	248	52.59 N	9.13 W
Kilfinane	248	52.21 N	8.28 W
Kilgarvan	248	51.54 N	9.26 W
Kilham	244	54.04 N	0.23 W
Kilkee	248	52.41 N	9.38 W
Kilkeel	248	54.04 N	6.00 W
Kilkelly	248	53.53 N	8.51 W
Kilkenny	248	52.39 N	7.15 W
Kilkenny □⁶	248	52.35 N	7.15 W
Kilkerrin	248	53.33 N	8.34 W
Kilkhampton	242	50.53 N	4.29 W
Kilkieran	248	53.19 N	9.43 W
Kilkieran Bay C	248	53.15 N	9.45 W
Killadoon	248	53.42 N	9.56 W
Killala	248	54.13 N	9.13 W
Killala Bay C	248	54.15 N	9.10 W
Killaloe	248	52.48 N	8.27 W
Killamarsh	244	53.19 N	1.19 W
Killarney	248	52.03 N	9.30 W
Killarney, Lakes of ⊜	248	52.00 N	9.32 W
Killashandra	248	54.00 N	7.32 W
Killavally	248	53.45 N	9.23 W
Killenaule	248	52.34 N	7.40 W
Killimor	248	53.10 N	8.17 W
Killin	246	56.28 N	4.19 W
Killorglin	248	52.06 N	9.47 W
Killough	248	54.16 N	5.39 W
Killybegs	248	54.38 N	8.27 W
Killyleagh	248	54.24 N	5.39 W
Kilmacolm	246	55.54 N	4.38 W
Kilmacthomas	248	52.12 N	7.25 W
Kilmaganny	248	52.27 N	7.19 W
Kilmaine	248	53.33 N	9.08 W
Kilmallock	248	52.23 N	8.34 W
Kilmaluag	246	57.41 N	6.17 W
Kilmarnock	246	55.36 N	4.30 W
Kilmartin	246	56.07 N	5.29 W
Kilmar Tor ⋀²	242	50.33 N	4.28 W
Kilmaurs	246	55.39 N	4.32 W
Kilmelford	246	56.16 N	5.29 W
Kilnaleck	248	53.52 N	7.19 W
Kilninver	246	56.20 N	5.29 W
Kilrenny	246	56.14 N	2.41 W
Kilrush	248	52.39 N	9.30 W
Kilsyth	246	55.59 N	4.04 W
Kiltealy	248	52.34 N	6.45 W
Kiltimagh	248	53.51 N	9.01 W
Kiltoom	248	53.28 N	8.01 W
Kimbolton	242	52.18 N	0.24 W
Kinbrace	246	58.15 N	3.56 W
Kinbuck	246	56.13 N	3.57 W
Kincardine	246	56.04 N	3.44 W
Kincraig	246	57.08 N	3.55 W
Kinder Scout ⋀	244	53.23 N	1.52 W
Kineton	242	52.10 N	1.30 W
Kinfauns	246	56.23 N	3.21 W
Kingarth	246	55.45 N	5.03 W
Kingsbarns	246	56.18 N	2.39 W
Kingsbridge	242	50.17 N	3.46 W
Kingsbury	242	52.35 N	1.40 W
Kingsclere	242	51.20 N	1.14 W
Kingscourt	248	53.53 N	6.48 W
Kingsdown	242	51.11 N	1.25 E
Kingshouse	246	56.21 N	4.19 W
Kingskerswell	242	50.30 N	3.33 W
Kingsland	242	52.15 N	2.47 W
Kings Langley	242	51.43 N	0.28 W
King's Lynn	242	52.45 N	0.24 E
King's Sutton	242	52.01 N	1.16 W
Kingsteignton	242	50.33 N	3.35 W
Kingston upon Hull (Hull)	244	53.45 N	0.20 W
Kingstown → Dún Laoghaire	248	53.17 N	6.08 W
Kingswear	242	50.21 N	3.34 W
Kingswinford	242	52.29 N	2.10 W
Kingswood	242	51.27 N	2.22 W
King's Worthy	242	51.06 N	1.18 W
Kington	242	52.12 N	3.01 W
Kingussie	246	57.05 N	4.03 W
Kinlochleven	246	56.42 N	4.58 W
Kinlochbervie	246	58.28 N	5.03 W
Kinlocheil	246	57.56 N	5.20 W
Kinlochewe	246	57.36 N	5.20 W
Kinloch Hourn	246	57.06 N	5.22 W
Kinloch Rannoch	246	56.42 N	4.11 W
Kinnairds Head ⟩	246	57.42 N	2.00 W
Kinnegad	246	53.26 N	7.05 W
Kinneil Water ≃	242	52.47 N	2.59 W
Kinross	246	56.13 N	3.27 W
Kinsale	248	51.42 N	8.32 W
Kinsale, Old Head of ⟩	248	51.36 N	8.32 W
Kinsale Harbour C	248	51.41 N	8.30 W
Kintore	246	57.13 N	2.21 W
Kintyre ⟩¹	246	55.35 N	5.35 W
Kintyre, Mull of ⟩	244	55.17 N	5.55 W
Kinvara	248	53.08 N	8.55 W
Kinver	242	52.27 N	2.14 W
Kippure ⋀	248	53.11 N	6.18 W
Kirbymoorside	244	54.16 N	0.55 W
Kirby Muxloe	242	52.38 N	1.13 W
Kircubbin	248	54.29 N	5.28 W
Kirkabister	246	60.07 N	1.08 W
Kirkbride	244	54.54 N	3.12 W
Kirkburton	242	53.37 N	1.42 W
Kirkby	244	53.29 N	2.54 W
Kirkby Lonsdale	244	54.13 N	2.36 W
Kirkby Malzeard	244	54.11 N	1.38 W
Kirkby Stephen	244	54.28 N	2.20 W
Kirkcaldy	246	56.07 N	3.10 W
Kirkcolm	244	54.58 N	5.05 W
Kirkconnel	244	55.23 N	4.00 W
Kirkcudbright	244	54.50 N	4.03 W
Kirkcudbright Bay C	244	54.48 N	4.04 W
Kirkham	244	53.47 N	2.53 W
Kirkhill	244	57.28 N	4.26 W
Kirkintilloch	246	55.57 N	4.10 W
Kirkliston	246	55.58 N	3.25 W
Kirkmichael	246	56.43 N	3.29 W
Kirkstile	244	55.12 N	3.00 W
Kirkton of Culsalmond	246	57.23 N	2.34 W
Kirkton of Glenisla	246	56.44 N	3.17 W
Kirktown of Auchterless	246	57.27 N	2.28 W
Kirkwall	246	58.59 N	2.58 W
Kirriemuir	246	56.41 N	3.01 W
Kirtle Water ≃	244	55.00 N	3.12 W
Kirton	242	52.56 N	0.04 W
Kirton of Largo	246	56.13 N	2.55 W
Kishorn, Loch C	246	57.21 N	5.41 W
Klibreck, Ben ⋀	246	58.14 N	4.24 W
Knaik ≃	246	56.14 N	3.52 W
Knapdale ▸¹	246	55.55 N	5.30 W
Knaresborough	244	54.00 N	1.27 W
Knighton	242	52.21 N	3.03 W
Knoc ≃	248	52.38 N	9.20 W
Knock	246	57.33 N	2.45 W
Knocklong	248	52.26 N	8.24 W
Knockmealdown Mountains ⋀⁸	248	52.10 N	8.00 W
Knottingley	244	53.43 N	1.14 W
Knowle	242	52.23 N	1.44 W
Knutsford	244	53.19 N	2.22 W
Kyle □⁹	246	55.32 N	4.25 W
Kyleakin	246	57.16 N	5.44 W
Kyle of Lochalsh	246	57.17 N	5.43 W
Kylerhea	246	57.14 N	5.41 W
Kylestrome	246	58.16 N	5.02 W
Kym ≃	242	52.14 N	0.17 W

L

Name	Page	Lat °'	Long °'
Lack	248	54.33 N	7.35 W
Ladybank	246	56.16 N	3.08 W
Ladybower Reservoir ⊜	244	53.23 N	1.45 W
Laggan	246	57.02 N	4.16 W
Laggan, Loch ⊜	246	56.57 N	4.28 W
Laggan Bay C	246	55.41 N	6.19 W
Laghy	248	54.37 N	8.03 W
Laide	246	57.52 N	5.32 W
Laindon	242	51.34 N	0.26 E
Lairg	246	58.01 N	4.24 W
Lake District ♣¹	244	54.30 N	3.10 W
Lake District National Park ♣¹	244	54.30 N	3.05 W
Lakenheath	242	52.25 N	0.31 E
Lambay Island ▌	248	53.29 N	6.01 W
Lambeth ♦⁸	242	51.30 N	0.07 W
Lambourn	242	51.31 N	1.31 W
Lambourne ≃	242	51.28 N	1.20 W
Lamlash	246	55.32 N	5.08 W
Lammermuir Hills ⋀⁸	246	55.50 N	2.44 W
Lampeter	242	52.07 N	4.05 W
Lanark	246	55.41 N	3.46 W
Lancashire □⁶	244	53.45 N	2.40 W
Lancashire Plain ≅	244	53.40 N	2.45 W
Lancaster	244	54.03 N	2.48 W
Lancing	242	50.50 N	0.19 W

Name	Page	Lat	Long
Langavat, Loch ⊜	246	58.04 N	6.48 W
Langholm	244	55.09 N	3.00 W
Langport	244	51.02 N	2.50 W
Laoighis □6	242	53.00 N	7.30 W
Lapaich, Sgurr na ᴧ	246	57.21 N	5.04 W
Lapford	242	50.55 N	3.47 W
Largoward	246	56.15 N	2.51 W
Largs	246	55.48 N	4.52 W
Larkhall	244	55.45 N	3.59 W
Larkhill	242	51.12 N	1.50 W
Larne	244	54.51 N	5.49 W
Lasham	242	51.11 N	1.03 W
Lasswade	246	55.53 N	3.08 W
Lauder	246	55.43 N	2.45 W
Lauderdale V	246	55.43 N	2.42 W
Laugharne	242	51.47 N	4.28 W
Launceston	242	50.38 N	4.21 W
Laune ≈	248	52.07 N	9.48 W
Laurencekirk	246	56.50 N	2.29 W
Lavagh More ᴧ	248	54.45 N	8.05 W
Lavendon	242	52.11 N	0.40 W
Lavenham	242	52.06 N	0.47 E
Laver ≈	244	54.08 N	1.30 W
Lawers, Ben ᴧ	246	56.34 N	4.13 W
Laxay	246	58.09 N	6.35 W
Laxey	244	54.14 N	4.23 W
Laxford, Loch C	246	58.23 N	5.06 W
Lea ≈	242	51.30 N	0.01 E
Leach ≈	242	51.41 N	1.39 W
Leadburn	244	55.47 N	3.14 W
Leadgate	244	54.52 N	1.48 W
Leadhills	244	55.25 N	3.47 W
Leadon ≈	242	51.53 N	2.16 W
League ᴧ	248	54.39 N	8.44 W
Leam ≈	242	52.17 N	1.14 W
Leamington Spa → Royal Leamington Spa	242	52.18 N	1.31 W
Leane, Lough ⊜	248	52.05 N	9.35 W
Leannan ≈	246	55.02 N	7.38 W
Leatherhead	242	51.18 N	0.20 W
Lechlade	242	51.43 N	1.41 W
Ledaig	246	56.30 N	5.23 W
Ledbury	242	52.02 N	2.25 W
Ledi, Ben ᴧ	246	56.15 N	4.19 W
Lee ≈	248	51.54 N	8.22 W
Leeds	244	53.50 N	1.35 W
Leeds and Bradford (Yeadon) Airport ⊠	244	53.52 N	1.38 W
Leedstown	242	50.10 N	5.22 W
Leek	244	53.06 N	2.01 W
Leen ≈	242	52.57 N	1.11 W
Leenaun	246	53.36 N	9.45 W
Lee-on-the-Solent	242	50.47 N	1.12 W
Leicester	242	52.38 N	1.05 W
Leicestershire □6	242	52.40 N	1.10 W
Leigh	244	53.30 N	2.33 W
Leighlinbridge	248	52.44 N	6.59 W
Leigh-on-Sea	242	51.33 N	0.38 E
Leighton Buzzard	242	51.55 N	0.40 W
Leinster □9	246	55.05 N	7.00 W
Leinster, Mount ᴧ	248	52.37 N	6.44 W
Leintwardine	242	52.23 N	2.51 W
Leith	246	55.59 N	3.10 W
Leith, Water of ≈	246	55.59 N	3.11 W
Leith Hill ᴧ2	242	51.11 N	0.23 W
Leitrim	248	54.00 N	8.04 W
Leitrim □6	248	54.20 N	8.20 W
Lelant	242	50.11 N	5.26 W
Lennox □9	246	56.02 N	4.15 W
Lennoxtown	246	55.59 N	4.12 W
Leominster	242	52.14 N	2.45 W
Leri ≈	242	52.32 N	4.02 W
Lerwick	246a	60.09 N	1.09 W
Lesbury	246	55.24 N	1.36 W
Leslie	246	56.12 N	3.13 W
Lesmahagow	246	55.39 N	3.55 W
Letchworth	242	51.58 N	0.14 W
Letterfrack	248	53.33 N	10.00 W
Letterkenny	248	54.57 N	7.44 W
Lettermullen	248	53.13 N	9.42 W
Letterston	242	51.56 N	5.00 W
Leuchars	246	56.23 N	2.53 W
Leven	246	56.12 N	3.00 W
Leven ≈, Eng., U.K.	244	54.31 N	1.21 W
Leven ≈, Eng., U.K.	244	54.14 N	3.01 W
Leven, Loch ⊜, Scot., U.K.	246	56.41 N	5.07 W
Leven, Loch ⊜, Scot., U.K.	246	56.12 N	3.22 W
Leverburgh	246	57.45 N	7.00 W
Lewes	242	50.52 N	0.01 E
Lewis, Butt of ⊁	246	58.31 N	6.16 W
Lewis, Isle of I	246	58.20 N	6.35 W
Lewisham ⇻8	242	51.27 N	0.01 E
Leyburn	244	54.19 N	1.49 W
Leyland	244	53.42 N	2.42 W
Leysdown-on-Sea	242	51.24 N	0.55 E
Lhanbryde	246	57.37 N	3.13 W
Liathach ᴧ	246	57.35 N	5.29 W
Lichfield	242	52.42 N	1.48 W
Liddel Water ≈	244	55.04 N	2.57 W
Liddesdale V	244	55.12 N	2.46 W
Lifford	248	54.50 N	7.29 W
Lifton	242	50.39 N	4.17 W
Lilleshall	242	52.44 N	2.21 W
Limavady	248	55.03 N	6.57 W
Limerick	248	52.40 N	8.38 W
Limerick □6	248	52.30 N	9.00 W
Limpsfield	242	51.16 N	0.01 E
Lincluden	246	55.05 N	3.38 W
Lincoln	244	53.14 N	0.33 W
Lincoln Cathedral ⛪1	244	53.14 N	0.33 W
Lincoln Heath ᴧ2	244	53.10 N	0.32 W
Lincoln Marsh ≋	242	53.17 N	0.12 E
Lincolnshire □6	242	52.55 N	0.22 W
Lincolnshire Wolds ᴧ2	242	53.20 N	0.10 W
Lindfield	242	51.01 N	0.05 W
Ling ≈	242	51.19 N	5.27 W
Lingfield	242	51.11 N	0.01 W
Linlithgow	246	55.59 N	3.37 W
Linney Head ⊁	242	51.38 N	5.04 W
Linnhe, Loch C	246	56.39 N	5.21 W
Linslade	242	51.55 N	0.41 W
Linton	242	52.06 N	0.17 E
Liphook	242	51.05 N	0.49 W
Lisburn	248	54.31 N	6.03 W
Liscannor Bay C	248	52.55 N	9.25 W
Liscarney	248	53.43 N	9.35 W
Lisdoonvarna	248	53.01 N	9.15 W
Liskeard	242	50.28 N	4.28 W
Lismore	248	52.08 N	7.55 W
Lismore Castle ⏣	248	52.08 N	7.52 W
Lismore Island I	248	56.29 N	5.33 W
Lisnaskea	248	54.15 N	7.27 W
Liss	242	51.03 N	0.55 W
Listowel	248	52.27 N	9.29 W
Litcham	242	52.44 N	0.47 E
Litherland	244	53.28 N	2.59 W
Little Avon ≈	242	51.42 N	2.28 W
Littleborough	244	53.39 N	2.05 W
Little Brosna ≈	248	53.10 N	8.05 W
Little Cumbrae Island I	246	55.43 N	4.57 W
Little Dart ≈	242	50.54 N	3.51 W
Littlehampton	242	50.48 N	0.33 W
Littlemill	246	57.32 N	3.49 W
Little Minch ∪	246	57.35 N	6.55 W
Little Ouse ≈	242	52.30 N	0.22 E
Littleport	242	52.28 N	0.19 E
Little Stour ≈	242	51.19 N	1.15 E
Little Walsingham	242	52.54 N	0.51 E
Liverpool	244	53.25 N	2.55 W
Liverpool (Speke) Airport ⊠	244	53.21 N	2.52 W
Liverpool Bay C	244	53.30 N	3.16 W
Livingston	246	55.53 N	3.32 W
Lizard	242	49.58 N	5.12 W
Lizard Point ⊁	242	49.56 N	5.13 W
Llanaber	242	52.45 N	4.05 W
Llanaelhaiarn	242	52.59 N	4.24 W
Llanarth	242	52.12 N	4.18 W
Llanarthney	242	51.52 N	4.09 W
Llanbedrog	242	52.52 N	4.29 W
Llanbister	242	52.21 N	3.27 W
Llanboidy	242	51.54 N	4.36 W
Llanbrynmair	242	52.37 N	3.57 W
Llanbyther	242	52.04 N	4.09 W
Llandaff	242	51.30 N	3.14 W
Llandaff Cathedral ⛪1	242	51.29 N	3.15 W
Llanddewi Brefi	242	52.10 N	3.57 W
Llandeilo	242	51.52 N	3.59 W
Llandinam	242	52.29 N	3.26 W
Llandissilio	242	51.53 N	4.14 W
Llandovery	242	51.59 N	3.48 W
Llandrindod Wells	242	52.15 N	3.23 W
Llandudno	244	53.19 N	3.49 W
Llandybie	242	51.50 N	4.00 W
Llandyssul	242	52.02 N	4.19 W
Llanelli	242	51.42 N	4.10 W
Llanelltyd	242	52.45 N	3.54 W
Llanenddwyn	242	52.49 N	4.06 W
Llanerchymedd	244	53.20 N	4.22 W
Llanfaethlu	244	53.21 N	4.32 W
Llanfair Caereinion	242	52.39 N	3.20 W
Llanfairfechan	242	53.15 N	3.58 W
Llanfair-pwllgwyngyll	244	53.13 N	4.12 W
Llanfrynach	242	51.56 N	3.21 W
Llanfyllin	242	52.46 N	3.17 W
Llanfynydd	242	52.06 N	4.06 W
Llanfyrnach	242	51.57 N	4.35 W
Llangadog	242	51.56 N	3.53 W
Llangefni	244	53.16 N	4.18 W
Llangennech	242	51.41 N	4.04 W
Llangollen	242	52.58 N	3.10 W
Llangranog	242	52.09 N	4.29 W
Llangurig	242	52.25 N	3.36 W
Llangwyrfon	242	52.19 N	4.03 W
Llangynog	242	52.50 N	3.25 W
Llanharan	242	51.33 N	3.25 W
Llanidloes	242	52.27 N	3.32 W
Llanilar	242	52.21 N	4.01 W
Llanon	242	52.17 N	4.10 W
Llanpumsaint	242	51.56 N	4.18 W
Llanrhaeadr-ym-Mochnant	242	52.51 N	3.17 W
Llanrhidian	242	51.37 N	4.11 W
Llanrhystyd	242	52.18 N	4.09 W
Llanrwst	244	53.08 N	3.48 W
Llansantffraid-ym-Mechain	242	52.47 N	3.08 W
Llansawel	242	52.01 N	4.00 W
Llantrisant	242	51.33 N	3.23 W
Llantwit Major	242	51.25 N	3.30 W
Llanuwchllyn	242	52.52 N	3.41 W
Llanwenog	242	52.06 N	4.12 W
Llanwrda	242	51.58 N	3.53 W
Llanwrtyd Wells	242	52.07 N	3.38 W
Lleyn Peninsula ⊁1	242	52.54 N	4.30 W
Llyswen	242	52.02 N	3.17 W
Loanhead	246	55.53 N	3.09 W
Lochaber ⇻1	246	56.57 N	5.06 W
Lochailort	246	56.53 N	5.40 W
Lochaline	246	56.32 N	5.47 W
Lochar Water ≈	244	54.59 N	3.27 W
Lochboisdale	246	57.09 N	7.19 W
Lochcarron	246	57.24 N	5.30 W
Lochearnhead	246	56.26 N	4.41 W
Lochenbreck	246	56.23 N	4.17 W
Lochgair	246	56.03 N	5.20 W
Loch Garman → Wexford	248	52.20 N	6.27 W
Lochgelly	246	56.08 N	3.19 W
Lochgilphead	246	56.03 N	5.26 W
Lochgoilhead	246	56.10 N	4.54 W
Lochinchorb ⊜	246	57.24 N	3.43 W
Lochinver	246	58.09 N	5.15 W
Lochmaben	244	55.08 N	3.27 W
Lochmaddy	246	57.36 N	7.10 W
Lochnagar ᴧ	246	56.57 N	3.16 W
Lochranza	246	55.42 N	5.18 W
Lochwinnoch	246	55.48 N	4.39 W
Lochy, Loch ⊜	246	56.57 N	4.53 W
Lockerbie	244	55.07 N	3.22 W
Loddon	242	52.32 N	1.29 E
Loddon ≈	242	51.30 N	0.53 W
Loftus	244	54.33 N	0.53 W
Lomond, Loch ⊜	246	56.05 N	4.36 W
London	242	51.30 N	0.10 W
London (Stansted) Airport ⊠, Eng., U.K.	242	51.40 N	0.15 E
London (Heathrow) Airport ⊠, Eng., U.K.	242	51.27 N	0.28 W
London (Gatwick) Airport ⊠, Eng., U.K.	242	51.09 N	0.11 W
Londonderry	248	55.00 N	7.19 W
Longbenton	244	55.02 N	1.35 W
Long Buckby	242	52.19 N	1.04 W
Long Crendon	242	51.47 N	1.01 W
Long Eaton	242	52.54 N	1.15 W
Longford	248	53.44 N	7.47 W
Longford □6	248	53.40 N	7.40 W
Longframlington	244	55.18 N	1.47 W
Longhorsley	244	55.15 N	1.46 W
Longhoughton	244	55.26 N	1.36 W
Longleat ⏣	242	51.12 N	2.17 W
Long Melford	242	52.05 N	0.43 E
Longmorn	246	57.36 N	3.17 W
Long Mountain ᴧ2	242	52.39 N	3.09 W
Long Preston	244	54.02 N	2.15 W
Longridge	244	53.51 N	2.36 W
Long Sutton	242	52.47 N	0.08 E
Longtown	244	55.01 N	2.58 W
Loop Head ⊁	248	52.34 N	9.56 W
Lorn, Firth of C1	246	56.20 N	5.45 W
Lossie ≈	246	57.43 N	3.16 W
Lossiemouth	246	57.43 N	3.18 W
Lostwithiel	242	50.25 N	4.40 W
Lothian □4	246	55.55 N	3.05 W
Lothian Region □4	246		
Loughborough	242	52.47 N	1.11 W
Loughor	242	51.40 N	4.04 W
Loughor ≈	242	51.40 N	4.04 W
Loughrea	248	53.12 N	8.34 W
Loughros More Bay C	248	54.48 N	8.35 W
Louisburgh	248	53.46 N	9.51 W
Louth, Eire	248	53.57 N	6.33 W
Louth, Eng., U.K.	244	53.22 N	0.01 W
Louth □6	248	53.55 N	6.30 W
Lowestoft	242	52.29 N	1.45 E
Lowick, Eng., U.K.	244		
Lowther ≈	244	55.38 N	2.44 W
Lowther Hills ᴧ2	244	55.19 N	3.38 W
Loyal, Loch ⊜	246	58.23 N	4.22 W
Loyne, Loch ⊜	246	57.06 N	5.00 W
Lucan	248	53.22 N	6.27 W
Luce, Water of ≈	244		
Luce Bay C	244	54.52 N	4.48 W
Ludgershall	242	51.16 N	1.37 W
Ludlow	242	52.22 N	2.43 W
Lugg ≈	242	52.02 N	2.38 W
Lugnaquillia ᴧ	248	52.58 N	6.27 W
Lui, Beinn ᴧ	246	56.24 N	4.49 W
Luichart, Loch ⊜	246	57.37 N	4.46 W
Luimneach → Limerick	248	52.40 N	8.38 W
Luing I	246	56.13 N	5.40 W
Lumphanan	246	57.07 N	2.41 W
Lumsden	246	57.15 N	2.52 W
Lunan Bay C	246	56.39 N	2.28 W
Luncarty	246	56.27 N	3.28 W
Lundy I	242	51.10 N	4.40 W
Lune ≈	244	54.02 N	2.50 W
Lunga I	246	56.13 N	5.42 W
Lurgan	248	54.28 N	6.20 W
Lusk	248	53.32 N	6.10 W
Luthrie	246	56.21 N	3.05 W
Luton	242	51.53 N	0.25 W
Lutterworth	242	52.28 N	1.10 W
Lybster	246	58.18 N	3.13 W
Lydd	242	50.57 N	0.55 E
Lydden V	242	50.50 N	2.22 W
Lydford	242	50.39 N	4.06 W
Lydham	242	52.31 N	2.58 W
Lydney	242	51.44 N	2.32 W
Lyme Bay C	242	50.38 N	3.00 W
Lyme Regis	242	50.44 N	2.57 W
Lyminge	242	51.08 N	1.05 E
Lymington	242	50.46 N	1.33 W
Lympne	242	51.05 N	1.02 E
Lyndhurst	242	50.52 N	1.34 W
Lyne ≈	244	54.58 N	3.10 W
Lyneham	242	51.31 N	1.58 W
Lynemouth	244	55.12 N	1.31 W
Lyne Water ≈	244	54.39 N	3.16 W
Lynher ≈	242	50.28 N	4.12 W
Lynmouth	242	51.15 N	3.50 W
Lynton	242	51.15 N	3.50 W
Lyon ≈	246	56.37 N	4.01 W
Lyon, Glen V	246	56.35 N	4.20 W
Lyon, Loch ⊜	246	56.32 N	4.36 W
Lyracrumpane	248	52.20 N	9.30 W
Lytham Saint Anne's	244	53.45 N	2.57 W
M			
Maam Cross	248	53.27 N	9.31 W
Maas	248	54.50 N	8.22 W
Maberry, Loch ⊜	244	55.02 N	4.41 W
Mablethorpe	244	53.21 N	0.15 E
Macaterick, Loch ⊜	246	55.12 N	4.26 W
Macclesfield	244	53.16 N	2.07 W
Macduff	246	57.40 N	2.29 W
Macdui, Ben ᴧ	246	57.05 N	3.38 W
Macgillycuddy's Reeks ᴧ	248	51.55 N	9.45 W
Machynlleth	242	52.35 N	3.51 W
Macroom	248	51.54 N	8.57 W
Maddy, Loch C	246	57.36 N	7.08 W
Madeley, Eng., U.K.	242	52.59 N	2.20 W
Madeley, Eng., U.K.	242	52.39 N	2.28 W
Maenclochog	242	51.54 N	4.48 W
Maesteg	242	51.37 N	3.40 W
Magee, Island ⊁	248	54.49 N	5.42 W
Maghera	248	54.51 N	6.40 W
Magherafelt	248	54.45 N	6.36 W
Maghull	244	53.32 N	2.57 W
Maidenhead	242	51.32 N	0.44 W
Maiden Newton	242	50.46 N	2.35 W
Maidstone	242	51.17 N	0.32 E
Maine ≈	248	52.09 N	9.45 W
Mainland I, Scot., U.K.	246	59.00 N	3.10 W
Mainland I, Scot., U.K.	246a	60.16 N	1.16 W
Malahide	248	53.27 N	6.09 W
Maldon	242	51.45 N	0.40 E
Malham	244	54.04 N	2.09 W
Malin	248	55.18 N	7.15 W
Malin Beg	248	54.40 N	8.48 E
Malin Head ⊁	248	55.23 N	7.24 W
Mallaig	246	57.00 N	5.50 W
Mallaranny	248	53.54 N	9.49 W
Mallow	248	52.08 N	8.39 W
Malmesbury	242	51.36 N	2.06 W
Malmesbury, Vale of V	242	51.22 N	2.10 W
Maltby	244	53.26 N	1.11 W
Malton	244	54.08 N	0.48 W
Malvern Hills ᴧ2	242	52.05 N	2.21 W
Malvern Link	242	52.08 N	2.18 W
Manacle Point ⊁	242	50.03 N	5.03 W
Manchester	244	53.30 N	2.15 W
Manchester Airport ⊠	244	53.21 N	2.15 W
Manea	242	52.30 N	0.11 E
Mangerton Mountain ᴧ	248	51.59 N	9.29 W
Mangotsfield	242	51.28 N	2.28 W
Manifold ≈	242	53.03 N	1.47 W
Manningtree	242	51.57 N	1.04 E
Manorbier	242	51.39 N	4.48 W
Manorhamilton	248	54.18 N	8.10 W
Mansfield	244	53.09 N	1.11 W
Mansfield Woodhouse	244	53.11 N	1.12 W
Manulla ≈	248	53.57 N	9.12 W
March	242	52.33 N	0.06 E
Maree, Loch ⊜	246	57.42 N	5.30 W
Marfleet	244	53.45 N	0.17 W
Mar Forest ⁻3	246	57.00 N	3.35 W
Margam	242	51.33 N	3.44 W
Margate	242	51.24 N	1.24 E
Market Bosworth	242	52.37 N	1.24 W
Market Deeping	242	52.41 N	0.19 W
Market Drayton	242	52.54 N	2.29 W
Market Harborough	242	52.29 N	0.55 W
Market Lavington	242	51.18 N	1.59 W
Market Rasen	244	53.24 N	0.21 W
Market Weighton	244	53.52 N	0.40 W
Markinch	246	56.12 N	3.08 W
Marlborough	242	51.25 N	1.43 W
Marlborough Downs ᴧ1	242	51.30 N	1.45 W
Marlow	242	51.35 N	0.48 W
Marnhull	242	50.58 N	2.18 W
Marple	244	53.24 N	2.03 W
Marshfield	242	51.28 N	2.19 W
Marske-by-the-Sea	244	54.36 N	1.01 W
Marston Moor ≈	244	53.57 N	1.17 W
Marston Moor Battlesite (1644) ⚔	244	53.57 N	1.17 W
Marteg ≈	242	52.20 N	3.33 W
Martin, Isle I	246	57.55 N	5.14 W
Martock	242	50.59 N	2.46 W
Maryborough → Portlaoighise	248	53.02 N	7.17 W
Maryport	248	55.12 N	3.55 W
Marywell	246	57.02 N	2.42 W
Masham	244	54.13 N	1.40 W
Mask, Lough ⊜	248	53.35 N	9.20 W
Mathry	242	51.57 N	5.05 W
Matlock	244	53.08 N	1.32 W
Mauchline	246	55.31 N	4.24 W
Maud	246	57.31 N	2.06 W
Mawgan	242	50.06 N	5.06 W
Maxwelltown	244	55.03 N	3.38 W
May, Isle of I	246	56.11 N	2.34 W
Maybole	246	55.21 N	4.41 W
Maynooth	248	53.23 N	6.35 W
Mayo □6	248	53.50 N	9.30 W
Meadie, Loch ⊜	246	58.19 N	4.35 W
Mealasta Isle I	246	58.05 N	7.08 W
Measham	242	52.43 N	1.30 W
Meath □9	248	53.35 N	6.40 W
Meath □9	248	53.36 N	6.54 W
Medina ≈	242	50.44 N	1.18 W
Medway ≈	242	51.27 N	0.44 E
Meese ≈	242	52.46 N	2.39 W
Meig ≈	246	57.34 N	4.41 W
Meigle	246	56.35 N	3.09 W
Meikle Millyea ᴧ	246	55.07 N	4.19 W
Meikle Says Law ᴧ	246	55.55 N	2.40 W
Melbost	246	58.15 N	6.22 W
Melbourn	242	52.05 N	0.01 E
Melbourne	242	52.49 N	1.25 W
Melby House	246	60.18 N	1.39 W
Melcombe Regis	242	50.38 N	2.28 W
Melfort, Loch C	246	56.15 N	5.31 W
Melksham	242	51.23 N	2.09 W
Mellon Udrigle	246	57.55 N	5.39 W
Melmerby	244	54.44 N	2.35 W
Melrose	246	55.36 N	2.44 W
Melrose Abbey ⛪1	246	55.37 N	2.45 W
Melton Constable	242	52.53 N	1.01 E
Melton Mowbray	242	52.46 N	0.53 W
Melvaig	246	57.48 N	5.49 W
Melvich	246	58.33 N	3.55 W
Melvin, Lough ⊜	248	54.26 N	8.10 W
Memsie	246	57.39 N	2.02 W
Menai Bridge	244	53.14 N	4.10 W
Menai Strait ∪	242	53.12 N	4.12 W
Mendip Hills ᴧ2	242	51.15 N	2.40 W
Mendlesham	242	52.16 N	1.05 E
Meon ≈	242	50.48 N	1.15 W
Mepal	242	52.24 N	0.07 E
Mere	242	51.06 N	2.16 W
Meriden	242	52.26 N	1.37 W
Merrick ᴧ	246	55.08 N	4.29 W
Merriott	242	50.54 N	2.48 W
Merse V	246	55.39 N	2.15 W
Mersea Island I	242	51.47 N	0.55 E
Mersey ≈	244	53.25 N	3.00 W
Merseyside □6	244	53.25 N	2.50 W
Merthyr Tydfil	242	51.46 N	3.23 W
Merton ⇻8	242	51.25 N	0.12 W
Methil	246	56.10 N	3.01 W
Methlick	246	57.25 N	2.14 W
Methwold	242	52.31 N	0.33 E
Methven	246	56.25 N	3.34 W
Mevagissey	242	50.16 N	4.48 W
Mexborough	244	53.30 N	1.17 W
Mey, Castle of ⏣	246	58.38 N	3.14 W
Mholach, Beinn ᴧ2	246	56.45 N	4.18 W
Mhòr, Beinn ᴧ	246	57.17 N	7.19 W
Mhòr, Loch ⊜	246	57.14 N	4.26 W
Micheldever	242	51.09 N	1.15 W
Mickle Fell ᴧ2	244	54.38 N	2.18 W
Mickleover	242	52.55 N	1.34 W
Middleham	244	54.17 N	1.49 W
Middle Level Main Drain ≊	242	52.43 N	0.22 E
Middlesbrough	244	54.35 N	1.14 W
Middleton, Eng., U.K.	244	53.33 N	2.13 W
Middleton, Eng., U.K.	244	53.45 N	1.32 W
Middleton in Teesdale	244	54.38 N	2.04 W
Middleton-on-the-Wolds	244	53.56 N	0.33 W
Middletown	246	54.18 N	6.50 W
Middlewich	244	53.11 N	2.27 W
Mid Glamorgan □6	242	51.40 N	3.30 W
Midhurst	242	50.59 N	0.45 W
Midleton	248	51.55 N	8.10 W
Midsomer Norton	242	51.18 N	2.28 W
Migvie	246	57.08 N	2.56 W
Milborne Port	242	50.58 N	2.27 W
Mildenhall	242	52.21 N	0.30 E
Milford, Eng., U.K.	242	55.11 N	1.38 W
Milford Haven	242	51.40 N	5.02 W
Milford Haven C	242	51.42 N	5.03 W
Milford-on-Sea	242	50.44 N	1.36 W
Milk Hill ᴧ2	242	51.23 N	1.51 W
Millbrook	242	50.20 N	4.13 W
Milleur Point ⊁	244	55.01 N	5.06 W
Millford	242	51.36 N	2.06 W
Millom	244	54.13 N	3.18 W
Millport	246	55.46 N	4.55 W
Millstreet	248	52.03 N	9.04 W
Milngavie	246	55.57 N	4.20 W
Milnrow	244	53.37 N	2.06 W
Milnthorpe	244	54.14 N	2.46 W
Milton Abbot	242	50.35 N	4.15 W
Miltown Malbay	248	52.50 N	9.23 W
Milverton	242	51.02 N	3.16 W
Minard	246	56.07 N	5.15 W
Minchinhampton	242	51.42 N	2.10 W
Minehead	242	51.13 N	3.29 W
Mingulay I	246	56.49 N	7.38 W
Minnigaff	244	54.58 N	4.30 W
Minnoch, Water of ≈	244	55.02 N	4.33 W
Minster, Eng., U.K.	242	51.20 N	0.49 E
Minster, Eng., U.K.	242	51.26 N	1.19 E
Minsterley	242	52.39 N	2.55 W
Mintlaw	246	57.31 N	2.00 W
Mirfield	244	53.40 N	1.41 W
Misterton, Eng., U.K.	244	53.27 N	0.51 W
Misterton, Eng., U.K.	242	50.52 N	2.47 W
Mitcheldean	242	51.51 N	2.30 W
Mitchelstown	248	52.16 N	8.16 W
Mizen Head ⊁, Eire	248	52.51 N	6.01 W
Mizen Head ⊁, Eire	248	51.27 N	9.49 W
Mmanford	242	51.48 N	3.59 W
Moate	248	53.24 N	7.58 W
Modbury	242	50.21 N	3.53 W
Moel Fferna ᴧ	242	52.57 N	3.18 W
Moffat	246	55.20 N	3.27 W
Moffat Water ≈	246	55.18 N	3.25 W
Mohill	248	53.54 N	7.52 W
Moira	248	54.30 N	6.17 W
Mold	244	53.10 N	3.08 W
Mole ≈, Eng., U.K.	242	51.24 N	0.21 W
Mole ≈, Eng., U.K.	242	50.57 N	3.54 W
Monach, Sound of ∪	246	57.34 N	7.35 W
Monadhliath Mountains ᴧ	246	57.10 N	4.00 W
Monaghan	248	54.15 N	6.58 W
Monaghan □6	248	54.10 N	7.00 W
Monar, Loch ⊜	246	57.25 N	5.06 W
Monasterevin	248	53.07 N	7.02 W
Moneygall	248	52.53 N	7.57 W
Moneymore	248	54.42 N	6.41 W
Monifieth	246	56.29 N	2.49 W
Monikie	246	56.18 N	3.08 W
Monivea	248	53.18 N	8.43 W
Monmouth	242	51.50 N	2.43 W
Monnow ≈	242	51.48 N	2.42 W
Montgomery	242	52.33 N	3.03 W
Montrose	246	56.43 N	2.28 W
Monymusk	246	57.13 N	2.31 W
Monzie	246	56.24 N	3.48 W
Moorfoot Hills ᴧ2	246	55.45 N	3.02 W
Mòr, Ben ᴧ	246	57.10 N	4.40 W
Mòr, Sgurr ᴧ	246	57.42 N	5.03 W
Moràr, Loch ⊜	246	56.57 N	5.43 W
Moray Firth C1	246	57.45 N	3.30 W
More, Ben ᴧ, Scot., U.K.	246	56.25 N	6.01 W
More, Ben ᴧ, Scot., U.K.	246	56.21 N	4.35 W
More, Loch ⊜	246	58.17 N	4.52 W
More Assynt, Ben ᴧ	246	58.08 N	4.53 W
Morecambe	244	54.04 N	2.53 W
Morecambe Bay C	244	54.07 N	3.00 W
Moretonhampstead	242	50.40 N	3.45 W
Moreton-in-Marsh	242	51.59 N	1.42 W
Morfa Nefyn	242	52.56 N	4.33 W
Morie, Loch ⊜	246	57.44 N	4.28 W
Moriston ≈	246	57.12 N	4.36 W
Morley	244	53.46 N	1.36 W
Morningstar ≈	248	52.27 N	8.41 W
Morpeth	244	55.10 N	1.41 W
Morte Point ⊁	242	51.11 N	4.13 W
Morven ᴧ, Scot., U.K.	246	57.07 N	3.02 W
Morven ᴧ, Scot., U.K.	246	58.14 N	3.42 W
Morwenstow	242	50.54 N	4.33 W
Mossbank	246	60.27 N	1.12 W
Mossley	244	53.32 N	2.02 W
Mostyn	244	53.19 N	3.16 W
Motherwell	246	55.48 N	4.00 W
Mottisfont	242	51.02 N	1.32 W
Mountain Ash	242	51.42 N	3.24 W
Mount Bellew Bridge	248	53.28 N	8.29 W
Mountmellick	248	53.07 N	7.20 W
Mountrath	248	53.00 N	7.27 W
Mount's Bay C	242	50.03 N	5.25 W
Mountsorrel	242	52.44 N	1.07 W
Mourne ≈	248	54.49 N	7.28 W
Mourne Mountains ᴧ	248	54.10 N	6.05 W
Mousa I	246	60.00 N	1.11 W
Moville	248	55.11 N	7.03 W
Moy	246	54.27 N	6.42 W
Moy ≈	248	54.12 N	9.08 W
Moycullen	248	53.21 N	9.09 W
Moyle □6	248	55.12 N	6.05 W
Muasdale	246	55.36 N	5.41 W
Much Dewchurch	242	51.59 N	2.46 W
Much Wenlock	242	52.36 N	2.34 W
Muck I	246	56.50 N	6.15 W
Muckle Roe I	246a	60.22 N	1.27 W
Muick, Loch ⊜	246	56.55 N	3.10 W
Muine Bheag	248	52.41 N	6.58 W
Muirdrum	246	56.31 N	2.42 W
Muirkirk	246	55.31 N	4.04 W
Muir of Ord	246	57.31 N	4.27 W
Muirtown	246	56.16 N	3.45 W
Mulben	246	57.33 N	3.06 W
Mulkear ≈	248	52.40 N	8.33 W
Mull, Island of I	246	56.25 N	5.54 W
Mull, Sound of ∪	246	56.32 N	5.50 W
Mullagh	246	53.49 N	6.57 W
Mullaghareirk Mountains ᴧ	248	52.20 N	9.10 W
Mullaghcleevaun ᴧ	248	53.06 N	6.23 W
Mullaghmore	248	54.28 N	8.27 W
Mullet Peninsula ⊁1	248	54.12 N	10.00 W
Mull Head ⊁, Scot., U.K.	246	58.58 N	2.43 W
Mull Head ⊁, Scot., U.K.	246	59.23 N	2.54 W
Mullinahone	248	52.30 N	7.30 W
Mullinavat	248	52.21 N	7.10 W
Mullingar	248	53.32 N	7.20 W
Mullion	242	50.01 N	5.15 W
Multeen ≈	248	52.31 N	8.01 W
Mumbles Head ⊁	242	51.35 N	3.59 W
Mundesley	242	52.53 N	1.26 E
Munlochy	246	57.32 N	4.15 W
Munster □9	248	52.25 N	8.20 W
Murton	244	54.49 N	1.24 W
Musselburgh	246	55.57 N	3.04 W
Muthill	246	56.19 N	3.50 W
Mweelrea ᴧ	248	53.38 N	9.50 W
Mybster	246	58.27 N	3.25 W
Mynydd Bach ᴧ2	242	52.15 N	4.05 W
Mynydd Eppynt ᴧ2	242	52.05 N	3.30 W
Mynydd Pencarreg ᴧ2	242	52.04 N	4.04 W
Mynydd Prescelly ᴧ	242	51.58 N	4.42 W
N			
Naas	248	53.13 N	6.39 W
Nadder ≈	242	51.03 N	1.48 W
Nagles Mountains ᴧ	248	52.05 N	8.30 W
Nailsea	242	51.26 N	2.43 W
Nailsworth	242	51.42 N	2.14 W
Nairn	246	57.35 N	3.53 W
Nairn ≈	246	57.35 N	3.52 W
Nant Bran ≈	242	51.57 N	3.35 W
Nant-y-moch Reservoir ⊜1	242	52.27 N	3.50 W
Napton on the Hill	242	52.15 N	1.24 W
Nar ≈	242	52.45 N	0.24 E
Narberth	242	51.48 N	4.45 W
Naseby	242	52.25 N	0.58 W
Naust	246	57.47 N	5.39 W
Navan	248	53.39 N	6.41 W
Naver ≈	246	58.32 N	4.15 W
Naver, Loch ⊜	246	58.17 N	4.23 W
Nayland	242	51.59 N	0.52 E
Neagh, Lough ⊜	248	54.37 N	6.25 W
Neath	248	51.40 N	3.48 W
Neath ≈	244	51.37 N	3.50 W
Needham Market	242	52.09 N	1.03 E
Nefyn	242	52.57 N	4.31 W
Neilston	246	55.47 N	4.27 W
Nelson	244	53.51 N	2.13 W
Nenagh	248	52.52 N	8.12 W
Nenagh ≈	248	52.56 N	8.17 W
Nene ≈	242	52.48 N	0.13 E
Nephin ᴧ	248	54.01 N	9.22 W
Nephin Beg Range ᴧ	248	54.00 N	9.35 W
Ness, Loch ⊜	246	57.18 N	4.27 W
Neston	244	53.18 N	3.04 W
Nethan ≈	246	55.42 N	3.52 W
Nethy Bridge	246	57.16 N	3.38 W
Netley Marsh	242	50.53 N	1.31 W
Nettlebed	242	51.35 N	1.00 W
Nevis ≈	246	56.50 N	5.00 W
Nevis, Ben ᴧ	246	56.48 N	4.59 W
Nevis, Loch C	246	57.00 N	5.43 W
New Abbey	244	54.59 N	3.38 W
New Alresford	242	51.06 N	1.10 W
New Bedford ≈	242	52.35 N	0.20 E
Newbiggin-by-the-Sea	244	55.11 N	1.30 W
Newbridge → Droichead Nua	248	53.11 N	6.48 W
Newbridge on Wye	242	52.13 N	3.27 W
Newburgh, Scot., U.K.	246	57.18 N	2.00 W
Newburgh, Scot., U.K.	246	56.21 N	3.15 W
Newburn	244	54.59 N	1.43 W
Newbury	242	51.24 N	1.19 W
Newby Bridge	244	54.16 N	2.58 W
Newcastle, Eire	248	52.27 N	9.03 W
Newcastle, Eng., U.K.	242	52.16 N	7.48 W
Newcastle, N. Ire., U.K.	248	54.12 N	5.54 W
Newcastle (Ouston) Airport ⊠	244	55.01 N	1.54 W
Newcastle Emlyn	242	52.02 N	4.28 W
Newcastletown	244	55.11 N	2.49 W
Newcastle-under-Lyme	244	53.00 N	2.14 W
Newcastle upon Tyne	244	54.59 N	1.35 W
Newcastle West	248	52.27 N	9.03 W
Newcestown	248	51.47 N	8.51 W
Newchurch	242	52.09 N	3.08 W
New Cumnock	244	55.24 N	4.12 W
New Deer	246	57.30 N	2.12 W
Newent	242	51.56 N	2.24 W
New Forest ⁻3	242	50.51 N	1.35 W
New Galloway	244	55.05 N	4.10 W
Newhall	242	51.32 N	1.34 W
Newham ⇻8	242	51.32 N	0.03 E
Newhaven	242	50.47 N	0.03 E
New Holland	244	53.42 N	0.22 W
Newington	242	51.21 N	1.08 E
New Inn	248	52.26 N	7.53 W
Newlyn East	242	50.22 N	5.03 W
Newmachar	246	57.16 N	2.11 W
Newmarket, Eire	248	52.13 N	9.00 W
Newmarket, Eng., U.K.	242	52.15 N	0.25 E
Newmarket-on-Fergus	248	52.45 N	8.53 W
New Mills	244	53.23 N	2.00 W
New Milton	242	50.44 N	1.40 W
Newnham	242	51.49 N	2.27 W
Newport, Eire	248	52.42 N	8.24 W
Newport, Eire	248	53.53 N	9.34 W
Newport, Eng., U.K.	242	50.42 N	1.18 W
Newport, Wales, U.K.	242	52.01 N	4.51 W
Newport, Wales, U.K.	242	51.35 N	3.00 W
Newport-on-Tay	246	56.26 N	2.55 W
Newport Pagnell	242	52.05 N	0.44 W
Newquay, Eng., U.K.	242	50.25 N	5.05 W
New Romney	242	50.59 N	0.57 E
New Ross	248	52.24 N	6.56 W
New Rossington	244	53.29 N	1.04 W
Newry	248	54.11 N	6.20 W
New Sarum → Salisbury	242	51.05 N	1.48 W
Newton	244	53.57 N	2.27 W
Newton Abbot	242	50.32 N	3.36 W
Newton Arlosh	244	54.53 N	3.15 W
Newton Aycliffe	244	54.36 N	1.32 W
Newton Ferrers	242	50.18 N	4.02 W
Newton Flotman	242	52.32 N	1.16 E
Newtongrange	246	55.52 N	3.04 W
Newton-le-Willows	244	53.28 N	2.37 W
Newtonmore	246	57.04 N	4.08 W
Newton Stewart	244	54.57 N	4.29 W
Newtown	242	52.32 N	3.19 W
Newtownabbey	248	54.40 N	5.54 W
Newtownards	248	54.36 N	5.41 W
Newtownbutler	248	54.12 N	7.23 W
Newtown Crommelin	248	54.59 N	6.13 W
Newtown Forbes	248	53.46 N	7.50 W
Newtownhamilton	248	54.11 N	6.35 W
Newtown Saint Boswells	246	55.34 N	2.40 W
Newtownstewart	248	54.43 N	7.24 W
New Tredegar	242	51.43 N	3.14 W
New Windsor → Windsor	242	51.29 N	0.38 W
Neyland	242	51.43 N	4.57 W
Nidd ≈	244	54.01 N	1.12 W
Nier ≈	248	52.17 N	7.48 W
Nigg	246	57.43 N	4.00 W
Ninfield	242	50.55 N	0.35 W
Nith ≈	244	55.00 N	3.35 W
Nithsdale V	244	55.14 N	3.46 W
Niton	242	50.35 N	1.16 W
Nore ≈	248	52.25 N	6.58 W
Norfolk □6	242	52.35 N	1.00 E
Norfolk Broads ⁻	242	52.43 N	1.30 E
Norham	244	55.43 N	2.10 W
Normanton	244	53.41 N	1.27 W
Northallerton	244	54.20 N	1.26 W
Northam	242	51.02 N	4.12 W
Northamptonshire	242	52.14 N	0.54 W
Northamptonshire □6	242	52.16 N	0.50 W
North Berwick	246	56.04 N	2.44 W
North Channel ∪	244	55.10 N	5.40 W
North Dorset Downs ᴧ1	242	50.47 N	2.30 W
North Downs ᴧ1	242	51.17 N	0.10 E
Northern Ireland □3	248	54.40 N	6.45 W
North Esk ≈, Scot., U.K.	246	55.54 N	3.04 W
North Esk ≈, Scot., U.K.	246	56.44 N	2.28 W
Northfleet	242	51.27 N	0.21 E
North Foreland ⊁	242	51.23 N	1.27 E
North Hill	242	50.34 N	4.25 W
North Hinksey	242	51.45 N	1.16 W
Northleach	242	51.50 N	1.50 W
North Petherton	242	51.06 N	3.01 W
North Queensferry	246	56.01 N	3.25 W
North Ronaldsay	246		
North Ronaldsay Firth ∪	246	59.20 N	2.25 W
North Sea ⁻2	246	56.00 N	3.00 E
North Seaton Colliery	244	55.11 N	1.32 W
North Somercotes	244	53.28 N	0.08 E
North Sound ∪, Eire	248	53.11 N	9.43 W
North Sound ∪, Scot., U.K.	246	59.18 N	2.46 W
North Sunderland	244	55.35 N	1.39 W
North Tawton	242	50.48 N	3.53 W
North Tidworth	242	51.15 N	1.40 W
North Tolsta	246	58.20 N	6.13 W
North Tyne ≈	244	54.59 N	2.08 W
North Uist I	246	57.36 N	7.18 W
Northumberland □6	244	55.15 N	2.05 W
Northumberland National Park	244	55.15 N	2.20 W
Northwaa	246	59.20 N	2.17 W
North Walsham	242	52.50 N	1.24 E
Northwest Bassett	244	53.16 N	0.10 E
Northwich	244	53.16 N	2.32 W
Northwold	242	52.33 N	0.35 E
North York Moors ᴧ1	244	54.24 N	0.53 W
North York Moors National Park	244	54.23 N	0.50 W
North Yorkshire □6	244	54.15 N	1.30 W
Norton	244	54.09 N	0.47 W
Norton Canes	242	52.41 N	1.59 W
Norton Fitzwarren	242	51.02 N	3.09 W
Norwich	242	52.38 N	1.18 E
Norwich Airport ⊠	242	52.41 N	1.15 E
Noss ≈	246a	60.09 N	1.01 W
Noss Head ⊁	246	58.29 N	3.04 W
Nottingham	244	52.58 N	1.10 W
Nottinghamshire □6	244	53.10 N	1.00 W
Nuneaton	242	52.32 N	1.28 W
Nyfer ≈	242	52.02 N	4.50 W
O			
Oa, Mull of ⊁	246	55.35 N	6.19 W
Oadby	242	52.36 N	1.04 W
Oakengates	242	52.42 N	2.28 W
Oakham	242	52.40 N	0.43 W
Oban	246	56.25 N	5.29 W
Ochil Hills ᴧ2	246	56.16 N	3.25 W
Ochiltree	246	55.38 N	4.23 W
Ock ≈	242	51.39 N	1.17 W
Odiham	242	51.15 N	0.57 W
Offaly □6	248	53.20 N	7.30 W
O'Flynn, Lough ⊜	248	53.46 N	8.40 W

Symbols in the index entries are identified on page 250.

Name	Page	Lat ° ′	Long ° ′
Ogmore ≃	242	51.28 N	3.38 W
Ogmore Vale	242	51.38 N	3.31 W
Oir, Beinn an ▲	246	55.54 N	6.00 W
Okehampton	242	50.44 N	4.00 W
Okement ≃	242	50.50 N	4.01 W
Old Bedford ≃	242	52.35 N	0.20 E
Oldbury	242	52.30 N	2.00 W
Oldcastle	248	53.46 N	7.10 W
Old Colwyn	244	53.18 N	3.43 W
Old Fletton	242	52.33 N	0.15 W
Oldham	244	53.33 N	2.07 W
Old Howe ≃	244	53.57 N	0.21 W
Oldmeldrum	246	57.20 N	2.20 W
Old Nene ≃	242	52.40 N	0.10 E
Ollatrim ≃	248	52.52 N	8.13 W
Ollerton	244	53.12 N	1.00 W
Olney	242	52.09 N	0.42 W
Omagh	248	54.36 N	7.18 W
Ombersley	242	52.17 N	2.13 W
Onich	246	56.42 N	5.13 W
Onny ≃	242	52.23 N	2.45 W
Opinan	246	57.43 N	5.47 W
Oranmore	248	53.16 N	8.54 W
Ore ≃	246	56.10 N	3.15 W
Orford Ness ❯	242	52.05 N	1.34 E
Ork, Ness of ❯	246	59.05 N	2.48 W
Orkney Islands □4	246	59.00 N	3.00 W
Orkney Islands II	246	59.00 N	3.00 W
Ormesby	244	54.33 N	1.11 W
Ormesby Saint Margaret	242	52.40 N	1.42 E
Ormskirk	244	53.35 N	2.54 W
Oronsay ▮	246	56.01 N	6.16 W
Orrin, Glen ∨	246	57.30 N	4.46 W
Orrin, Loch ◎	246	57.30 N	4.45 W
Orwell ≃	242	51.57 N	1.17 E
Osmington	242	50.38 N	2.22 W
Ossett	244	53.41 N	1.35 W
Ossian, Loch ◎	246	56.46 N	4.38 W
Oswaldtwistle	244	53.43 N	2.26 W
Oswestry	242	52.52 N	3.04 W
Otford	242	51.19 N	0.12 E
Othery	242	51.05 N	2.53 W
Otley	244	53.54 N	1.41 W
Otter ≃	242	50.46 N	3.17 W
Otterburn	244	55.14 N	2.10 W
Ottery ≃	242	50.39 N	4.20 W
Ottery Saint Mary	242	50.45 N	3.17 W
Oughter, Lough ◎	248	54.00 N	7.30 W
Oughterard	248	53.25 N	9.17 W
Oulton Broad	242	52.31 N	1.42 E
Oundle	242	52.29 N	0.29 W
Ouse ≃, Eng., U.K.	242	50.47 N	0.03 E
Ouse ≃, Eng., U.K.	244	53.42 N	0.41 W
Outer Hebrides II	246	57.45 N	7.00 W
Out Skerries II	246a	60.25 N	0.42 W
Outwell	242	52.37 N	0.14 E
Outwood	244	53.42 N	1.30 W
Overseal	242	52.44 N	1.34 W
Overstrand	242	52.56 N	1.20 E
Overton	242	51.15 N	1.15 W
Over Wallop	242	51.09 N	1.35 W
Owel, Lough ◎	248	53.34 N	7.25 W
Owenboy ≃	248	51.48 N	8.18 W
Owenea ≃	248	54.47 N	8.26 W
Owenkillew ≃	248	54.44 N	7.18 W
Owenmore ≃	248	54.07 N	9.50 W
Oxford	242	51.46 N	1.15 W
Oxfordshire □6	242	51.50 N	1.15 W
Oxted	242	51.16 N	0.01 W
Oykel ≃	246	57.56 N	4.25 W
Oykel Bridge	246	57.58 N	4.43 W
P			
Pabbay ▮, Scot., U.K.	246	56.51 N	7.35 W
Pabbay ▮, Scot., U.K.	246	57.46 N	7.15 W
Paddock Wood	242	51.11 N	0.23 E
Padiham	244	53.49 N	2.19 W
Padstow	242	50.33 N	4.56 W
Paignton	242	50.26 N	3.34 W
Painscastle	242	52.07 N	3.12 W
Painswick	242	51.48 N	2.11 W
Paisley	246	55.50 N	4.26 W
Pallas Grean	248	52.33 N	8.22 W
Pallaskenry	248	52.39 N	8.52 W
Pangbourne	242	51.29 N	1.05 W
Papa, Sound of ⋃	246a	60.18 N	1.41 W
Papa Stour ▮	246a	60.20 N	1.42 W
Papa Westray ▮	246	59.21 N	2.54 W
Paps of Jura ▲	246	55.55 N	6.00 W
Par	242	50.21 N	4.43 W
Parrett ≃	242	51.13 N	3.01 W
Parton	244	54.34 N	3.35 W
Partree	248	53.41 N	9.19 W
Passage East	248	52.13 N	6.59 W
Passage West	248	51.52 N	8.20 W
Patcham	242	50.52 N	0.08 W
Patchway	242	51.32 N	2.34 W
Pateley Bridge	244	54.05 N	1.45 W
Path of Condie	246	56.15 N	3.30 W
Patrington	244	53.41 N	0.02 W
Patterdale	244	54.32 N	2.56 W
Paulstown	248	52.41 N	7.01 W
Peacehaven	242	50.47 N	0.01 E
Peak District National Park ♣	244	53.17 N	1.45 W
Peat Inn	246	56.17 N	2.53 W
Peebles	246	55.39 N	3.12 W
Peel	244	54.13 N	4.40 W
Peel Fell ▲	244	55.17 N	2.35 W
Pegswood	244	55.11 N	1.38 W
Pegwell Bay C	242	51.18 N	1.26 E
Pembrey	242	51.42 N	4.16 W
Pembroke	242	51.41 N	4.55 W
Pembroke Castle ⊥	242	51.41 N	4.56 W
Pembroke Dock	242	51.42 N	4.56 W
Pembrokeshire Coast National Park ♣	242	51.47 N	5.06 W
Pembury	242	51.09 N	0.20 E
Penarth	242	51.27 N	3.11 W
Pencader	242	52.01 N	4.16 W
Pencoed	242	51.32 N	3.30 W
Pendle Hill ▲2	244	53.52 N	2.17 W
Penicuik	246	55.50 N	3.14 W
Penistone	244	53.32 N	1.37 W
Penmaenmawr	244	53.16 N	3.54 W
Pennines ⋀	244	54.10 N	2.05 W
Penrhyn Bay	244	53.19 N	3.45 W
Penrhyn-deudraeth	242	52.56 N	4.04 W
Penrith	244	54.40 N	2.44 W
Penryn	242	50.09 N	5.06 W
Penshaw	244	54.53 N	1.29 W
Pentire Point ❯	242	50.36 N	4.55 W
Pentland Firth ⋃	246	58.44 N	3.07 W
Pentland Hills ⋀2	246	55.46 N	3.25 W
Pentraeth	244	53.17 N	4.12 W
Pen-y-Ghent ▲	244	54.09 N	2.14 W
Penygroes, Wales, U.K.	242	51.49 N	4.02 W
Penygroes, Wales, U.K.	244	53.04 N	4.17 W
Penzance	242	50.07 N	5.33 W
Perranporth	242	50.20 N	5.09 W
Pershore	242	52.07 N	2.05 W
Perth	246	56.24 N	3.28 W
Peterborough	242	52.35 N	0.15 W
Peterculter	246	57.05 N	2.16 W
Peter Hill ▲	246	56.58 N	2.42 W
Peterlee	244	54.46 N	1.19 W
Petersfield	242	51.00 N	0.56 W
Petteril ≃	244	54.54 N	2.55 W
Pettigo	248	54.33 N	7.50 W
Petworth	242	50.59 N	0.38 W
Pevensey	242	50.49 N	0.20 E
Pevensey Levels ≡	242	50.50 N	0.20 E
Pewsey	242	51.21 N	1.46 W
Pewsey, Vale of ∨	242	51.20 N	1.48 W
Pickering	244	54.14 N	0.46 W
Pickering, Vale of ∨	244	54.12 N	0.45 W
Piddle ≃	242	50.42 N	2.04 W
Piddletrenthide	242	50.48 N	2.25 W
Pierowall	246	59.20 N	2.59 W
Pinhoe	242	50.44 N	3.27 W
Pinwherry	244	55.09 N	4.50 W
Pitlochry	246	56.43 N	3.45 W
Pitsford Reservoir ◎1	242	52.20 N	0.52 W
Pittenweem	246	56.12 N	2.44 W
Plumbridge	248	54.46 N	7.15 W
Plym ≃	242	50.12 N	4.07 W
Plymouth	242	50.23 N	4.10 W
Plympton	242	50.23 N	4.03 W
Plymstock	242	50.22 N	4.04 W
Plynlimon ▲	242	52.28 N	3.47 W
Pocklington	244	53.56 N	0.46 W
Polbain	246	58.02 N	5.23 W
Polden Hills ⋀2	242	51.08 N	2.50 W
Polegate	242	50.49 N	0.15 E
Polesworth	242	52.37 N	1.36 W
Pollaphuca Reservoir ◎1	248	53.08 N	6.31 W
Polperro	242	50.19 N	4.31 W
Polruan	242	50.19 N	4.36 W
Pomeroy	248	54.36 N	6.56 W
Pontardawe	242	51.44 N	3.51 W
Pontardulais	242	51.43 N	4.03 W
Pontefract	244	53.42 N	1.18 W
Ponteland	244	55.03 N	1.44 W
Ponterwyd	242	52.25 N	3.50 W
Pontesbury	242	52.39 N	2.54 W
Pontrhydfendigaid	242	52.17 N	3.51 W
Pontyberem	242	51.17 N	4.09 W
Pontycymmer	242	51.37 N	3.34 W
Pontypool	242	51.43 N	3.02 W
Pontypridd	242	51.37 N	3.22 W
Poole	242	50.43 N	1.59 W
Poole Bay C	242	50.42 N	1.52 W
Poolewe	246	57.45 N	5.37 W
Porlock	242	51.14 N	3.36 W
Portacloy	248	54.19 N	9.48 W
Portadown	248	54.26 N	6.27 W
Portaferry	248	54.23 N	5.33 W
Portarlington	248	53.10 N	7.11 W
Port Askaig	246	55.51 N	6.07 W
Port Bannatyne	246	55.52 N	5.05 W
Port Ellen	246	55.39 N	6.12 W
Port Erin	244	54.06 N	4.44 W
Porteynon	242	51.33 N	4.13 W
Porteynon Point ❯	242	51.32 N	4.12 W
Port Glasgow	246	55.57 N	4.41 W
Portglenone	248	54.53 N	6.27 W
Porth	242	51.38 N	3.25 W
Porthcawl	242	51.29 N	3.43 W
Porth Neigwl C	242	52.48 N	4.34 W
Port Isaac	242	50.35 N	4.49 W
Portishead	242	51.30 N	2.46 W
Portknockie	246	57.41 N	2.51 W
Port Lairghe → Waterford	248	52.15 N	7.06 W
Portland, Bill of ❯	242	50.31 N	2.27 W
Portland, Isle of ▮	242	50.33 N	2.27 W
Portlaoighise	248	53.02 N	7.17 W
Portlaw	248	52.17 N	7.19 W
Port Logan	244	54.43 N	4.56 W
Portmadoc	242	52.55 N	4.08 W
Portmahomack	246	57.49 N	3.50 W
Portnaguiran	246	58.17 N	6.13 W
Portnahaven	246	55.41 N	6.31 W
Portobello	246	55.58 N	3.07 W
Port of Ness	246	58.29 N	6.13 W
Portpatrick	244	54.51 N	5.07 W
Portree	246	57.24 N	6.12 W
Portrush	248	55.12 N	6.40 W
Portsalon	248	55.13 N	7.37 W
Port Seton	246	55.58 N	2.57 W
Portslade	242	50.50 N	0.11 W
Portsmouth	242	50.48 N	1.05 W
Portsoy	246	57.41 N	2.41 W
Portstewart	248	55.11 N	6.43 W
Port Talbot	242	51.36 N	3.47 W
Portumna	248	53.06 N	8.13 W
Port William	244	54.46 N	4.35 W
Potter Heigham	242	52.44 N	1.33 E
Potters Bar	242	51.42 N	0.11 W
Potter Street	242	51.46 N	0.08 E
Potton	242	52.08 N	0.14 W
Poulton-le-Fylde	244	53.51 N	2.59 W
Poundstock	242	50.46 N	4.33 W
Powis, Vale of ∨	242	52.38 N	3.08 W
Powys □6	242	52.17 N	3.20 W
Poyntzpass	248	54.18 N	6.23 W
Prawle Point ❯	242	50.13 N	3.42 W
Prescot	244	53.26 N	2.48 W
Prestatyn	244	53.20 N	3.24 W
Presteigne	242	52.17 N	3.00 W
Preston, Eng., U.K.	244	53.46 N	0.12 W
Preston, Eng., U.K.	244	53.46 N	2.42 W
Prestonpans	246	55.57 N	3.00 W
Prestwich	244	53.32 N	2.17 W
Prestwick	244	55.30 N	4.37 W
Prestwick Airport ⊠	246	55.30 N	4.36 W
Priest Island ▮	246	57.58 N	5.30 W
Princes Risborough	242	51.44 N	0.51 W
Princetown	242	50.33 N	4.00 W
Probus	242	50.17 N	4.57 W
Prudhoe	244	54.58 N	1.51 W
Prysor ≃	242	52.56 N	4.00 W
Puddletown	242	50.45 N	2.21 W
Pudsey	244	53.48 N	1.40 W
Pulborough	242	50.58 N	0.30 W
Pulham Market	242	52.26 N	1.14 E
Pumpsaint	242	52.03 N	3.58 W
Purbeck, Isle of ▮	242	50.38 N	2.00 W
Purfleet	242	51.29 N	0.15 E
Purton	242	51.36 N	1.52 W
Pwllheli	242	52.53 N	4.25 W
Pyle	242	51.32 N	3.42 W
Q			
Quantock Hills ⋀2	242	51.07 N	3.10 W
Queenborough	242	51.26 N	0.45 E
Queensbury	244	53.46 N	1.50 W
Queensferry, Scot., U.K.	246	55.59 N	3.25 W
Queensferry, Wales, U.K.	244	53.12 N	3.01 W
Queenstown → Cobh	248	51.51 N	8.17 W
Quilty	248	52.47 N	9.26 W
Quoich, Loch ◎	246	57.04 N	5.17 W
Quorndon	242	52.45 N	1.09 W
Quoyness	246	58.54 N	3.18 W
R			
Raasay ▮	246	57.23 N	6.04 W
Raasay, Sound of ⋃	246	57.27 N	6.06 W
Rackwick	246	58.52 N	3.23 W
Radcliffe	244	53.34 N	2.20 W
Radcliffe-on-Trent	242	52.57 N	1.03 W
Radlett	242	51.42 N	0.20 W
Radnor Forest ⋀	242	52.18 N	3.10 W
Radstock	242	51.18 N	2.28 W
Raglan	242	51.47 N	2.51 W
Rainford	244	53.30 N	2.48 W
Rainham	242	51.23 N	0.36 E
Rainham ◆8	242	51.31 N	0.11 E
Rainhill	244	53.26 N	2.46 W
Rainworth	244	53.07 N	1.08 W
Ramasaig	246	57.24 N	6.44 W
Rame Head ❯	242	50.19 N	4.13 W
Ramor, Lough ◎	248	53.49 N	7.05 W
Rampside	244	54.05 N	3.10 W
Ramsbottom	244	53.40 N	2.19 W
Ramsey, I. of Man	244	54.20 N	4.21 W
Ramsey, Eng., U.K.	242	51.56 N	1.14 E
Ramsey, Eng., U.K.	242	52.27 N	0.07 W
Ramsey Island ▮	242	51.52 N	5.10 W
Ramsgate	242	51.20 N	1.25 E
Randalstown	248	54.45 N	6.18 W
Ranfurly	246	55.52 N	4.33 W
Rannoch, Loch ◎1	246	56.41 N	4.18 W
Rannoch Moor ◆3	246	56.38 N	4.40 W
Raphoe	248	54.52 N	7.36 W
Rapness	246	59.14 N	2.51 W
Rathangan	248	53.12 N	6.59 W
Rathcormack	248	52.54 N	8.17 W
Rathdowney	248	52.50 N	7.34 W
Rathdrum	248	52.56 N	6.13 W
Rathen	246	57.38 N	2.02 W
Rathfriland	248	54.14 N	6.10 W
Rathkeale	248	52.32 N	8.56 W
Rathlin Island ▮	248	55.18 N	6.13 W
Rathlin Sound ⋃	248	55.16 N	6.17 W
Rath Luirc	248	52.21 N	8.41 W
Rathmelton	248	55.02 N	7.38 W
Rathmore	248	52.03 N	9.13 W
Rathmullen	248	55.06 N	7.33 W
Rathnew	248	53.00 N	6.05 W
Rathowen	248	53.40 N	7.31 W
Raunds	242	52.21 N	0.33 W
Ravenglass	244	54.21 N	3.24 W
Ravensthorpe	244	53.42 N	1.35 W
Rawmarsh	244	53.27 N	1.21 W
Rawtenstall	244	53.42 N	2.18 W
Ray ≃, Eng., U.K.	242	51.48 N	1.15 W
Ray ≃, Eng., U.K.	242	51.38 N	1.49 W
Rayleigh	242	51.36 N	0.36 E
Rea ≃, Eng., U.K.	242	52.18 N	2.32 W
Rea ≃, Eng., U.K.	242	52.30 N	1.51 W
Reading	242	51.28 N	0.59 W
Reay	246	58.33 N	3.47 W
Reay Forest ◆3	246	58.19 N	4.47 W
Redbourn	242	51.48 N	0.24 W
Redbridge ◆8	242	51.34 N	0.05 E
Redcar	244	54.37 N	1.04 W
Red Dial	244	54.48 N	3.10 W
Redditch	242	52.19 N	1.56 W
Rede ≃	244	55.08 N	2.13 W
Redesdale ∨	244	55.17 N	2.16 W
Redhill	242	51.14 N	0.11 W
Redland	246	59.05 N	3.05 W
Redruth	242	50.13 N	5.14 W
Red Wharf Bay C	244	53.18 N	4.10 W
Ree, Lough ◎	248	53.35 N	8.00 W
Reepham	242	52.46 N	1.07 E
Reigate	242	51.14 N	0.13 W
Reiss	246	58.28 N	3.10 W
Renfrew	246	55.53 N	4.24 W
Renish Point ❯	246	57.44 N	6.59 W
Resipol, Beinn ▲	246	56.43 N	5.39 W
Resolven	242	51.42 N	3.42 W
Resort, Loch C	246	58.03 N	7.06 W
Reston	246	55.51 N	2.11 W
Rhayader	242	52.18 N	3.30 W
Rheidol ≃	242	52.25 N	4.05 W
Rhinns of Kells ⋀	244	55.07 N	4.22 W
Rhiw ≃	242	52.36 N	3.11 W
Rhondda	242	51.40 N	3.27 W
Rhosneigr	244	53.14 N	4.31 W
Rhos-on-Sea	244	53.19 N	3.45 W
Rhossilli	242	51.34 N	4.17 W
Rhuddlan	244	53.18 N	3.27 W
Rhum ▮	246	57.00 N	6.20 W
Rhum, Sound of ⋃	246	56.56 N	6.14 W
Rhyl	244	53.19 N	3.29 W
Rhymney	242	51.46 N	3.17 W
Rhymney ≃	242	51.28 N	3.10 W
Rhynie	246	57.19 N	2.50 W
Rib ≃	242	51.48 N	0.04 W
Ribble ≃	244	53.44 N	2.50 W
Riccall	244	53.50 N	1.04 W
Richmond	244	54.24 N	1.44 W
Richmond ◆8	242	51.28 N	0.18 W
Rickmansworth	242	51.39 N	0.29 W
Riddon, Loch C	246	55.58 N	5.12 W
Riecawr, Loch ◎	244	55.13 N	4.27 W
Rillington	244	54.09 N	0.42 W
Rindown Castle ⊥	248	53.32 N	7.59 W
Ringford	244	54.54 N	4.03 W
Ringmer	242	50.53 N	0.04 E
Ringville	248	52.02 N	7.34 W
Ringwood	242	50.51 N	1.47 W
Rinnes, Ben ▲	246	57.23 N	3.15 W
Rinns of Islay ⋀	246	55.45 N	6.25 W
Rinns Point ❯	246	55.41 N	6.30 W
Ripon	244	54.08 N	1.31 W
Ripponden	244	53.41 N	1.57 W
Risca	242	51.37 N	3.07 W
Roadhead	244	55.04 N	2.46 W
Roan Fell ▲	244	55.13 N	2.52 W
Roaringwater Bay C	248	51.25 N	9.35 W
Robe ≃	248	53.37 N	9.16 W
Robertsbridge	242	50.59 N	0.29 E
Robertstown	248	53.15 N	6.59 W
Robin Hood's Bay	244	54.25 N	0.33 W
Roch ≃	244	53.34 N	2.18 W
Rochdale	244	53.38 N	2.09 W
Roche	242	50.24 N	4.50 W
Rochester, Eng., U.K.	242	51.24 N	0.30 E
Rochester, Eng., U.K.	244	55.16 N	2.16 W
Rochford	242	51.36 N	0.43 E
Rochfort Bridge	248	53.23 N	7.17 W
Rockcorry	248	54.07 N	7.01 W
Rockingham Forest ◆3	242	52.30 N	0.37 W
Rock of Cashel ⊥	248	52.31 N	7.53 W
Rodel	246	57.41 N	7.05 W
Roden ≃	242	52.43 N	2.36 W
Roding ≃	242	51.31 N	0.06 E
Rogan's Seat ▲	244	54.25 N	2.07 W
Rogart	246	58.00 N	4.09 W
Roman ≃	242	51.51 N	0.57 E
Romney Marsh ≡	242	51.03 N	0.55 E
Romsey	242	50.59 N	1.30 W
Rona ▮, Scot., U.K.	246	57.34 N	5.59 W
Rona ▮, Scot., U.K.	246	59.07 N	5.48 W
Ronas Hill ▲2	246a	60.31 N	1.28 W
Ronas Voe C	246	60.32 N	1.29 W
Ronay ▮	246	57.29 N	7.11 W
Rora Head ❯	246	58.52 N	3.25 W
Roscommon	248	53.38 N	8.11 W
Roscommon □6	248	53.40 N	8.30 W
Roscrea	248	52.57 N	7.47 W
Rosehearty	246	57.42 N	2.07 W
Ros Mhic Treoin → New Ross	248	52.24 N	6.56 W
Rossan Point ❯	248	54.42 N	8.48 W
Rosscarbery	248	51.35 N	9.01 W
Rossendale ∨	244	53.45 N	2.47 W
Rosses Bay C	248	55.10 N	8.27 W
Rosses Point	248	54.18 N	8.33 W
Rosslare	248	52.17 N	6.23 W
Rosslare Harbour	248	52.15 N	6.22 W
Rosslea	248	54.14 N	7.11 W
Ross-on-Wye	242	51.55 N	2.35 W
Rosstrevor	248	54.06 N	6.12 W
Rosyth	246	56.03 N	3.26 W
Rothbury	244	55.19 N	1.55 W
Rothbury Forest ◆3	244	55.18 N	1.54 W
Rother ≃	242	50.57 N	0.32 W
Rotherham	244	53.26 N	1.20 W
Rothes	246	57.31 N	3.13 W
Rothesay	246	55.51 N	5.03 W
Rothwell, Eng., U.K.	242	52.25 N	0.48 W
Rothwell, Eng., U.K.	244	53.46 N	1.29 W
Rottingdean	242	50.48 N	0.04 W
Roundstone	248	53.23 N	9.53 W
Roundwood	248	53.04 N	6.13 W
Rousay ▮	246	59.10 N	3.02 W
Rowlands Gill	244	54.54 N	1.45 W
Rowley Regis	242	52.29 N	2.03 W
Roxburgh	246	55.34 N	2.30 W
Royal Canal ⊠	248	53.21 N	6.15 W
Royal Leamington Spa	242	52.18 N	1.31 W
Royal Tunbridge Wells → Tunbridge Wells	242	51.08 N	0.16 E
Roydon	242	51.46 N	0.03 E
Royston, Eng., U.K.	242	52.03 N	0.01 W
Royston, Eng., U.K.	244	53.37 N	1.27 W
Royton	244	53.34 N	2.08 W
Rozel	243b	49.14 N	2.03 W
Ruabon	242	52.59 N	3.02 W
Ruathair, Lochan ◎	246	58.18 N	3.56 W
Rubery	242	52.24 N	2.00 W
Rugby	242	52.23 N	1.15 W
Rugeley	242	52.46 N	1.55 W
Rumbling Bridge	246	56.10 N	3.35 W
Rumney	242	51.31 N	3.07 W
Runcorn	244	53.20 N	2.44 W
Runnymede ⊥	242	51.26 N	0.34 W
Rush	248	53.32 N	6.06 W
Rushden	242	52.17 N	0.36 W
Rustington	242	50.48 N	0.31 W
Rutherglen	246	55.50 N	4.12 W
Ruthin	244	53.07 N	3.18 W
Ruyton-Eleven-Towns	242	52.48 N	2.54 W
Ryan, Loch C	244	54.58 N	5.02 W
Ryde	242	50.44 N	1.10 W
Ryder's Hill ⋀2	242	50.31 N	3.53 W
Rye	242	50.57 N	0.44 E
Rye ≃	244	54.10 N	0.45 W
Ryhope	244	54.52 N	1.21 W
Ryton	244	54.59 N	1.46 W
Ryton ≃	244	53.25 N	1.00 W
Ryton-on-Dunsmore	242	52.22 N	1.26 W
S			
Saddleback ▲	244	54.38 N	3.03 W
Saddleworth	244	53.33 N	1.59 W
Saffron Walden	242	52.01 N	0.15 E
Saint Abb's Head ❯	246	55.54 N	2.09 W
Saint Agnes	242	50.18 N	5.13 W
Saint Agnes ▮	242a	49.54 N	6.20 W
Saint Albans	242	51.46 N	0.21 W
Saint Aldhelm's Head ❯	242	50.34 N	2.04 W
Saint Andrews	246	56.20 N	2.48 W
Saint Andrews Bay C	246	56.22 N	2.50 W
Saint Anne	243b	49.42 N	2.12 W
Saint Anne's	244	53.45 N	3.02 W
Saint Ann's Head ❯	242	51.41 N	5.10 W
Saint Arvans	242	51.40 N	2.41 W
Saint Asaph	244	53.16 N	3.26 W
Saint Athan	242	51.24 N	3.25 W
Saint Aubin	243b	49.11 N	2.10 W
Saint Austell	242	50.20 N	4.48 W
Saint Bees Head ❯	244	54.32 N	3.38 W
Saint Blazey	242	50.22 N	4.43 W
Saint Brides Bay C	242	51.48 N	5.15 W
Saint Bride's Major	242	51.28 N	3.38 W
Saint Catherine's Point ❯	242	50.34 N	1.15 W
Saint Clears	242	51.50 N	4.30 W
Saint Columb Major	242	50.26 N	5.03 W
Saint Combs	246	57.39 N	1.54 W
Saint David's	242	51.54 N	5.16 W
Saint David's Cathedral ✝1	242	51.54 N	5.16 W
Saint David's Head ❯	242	51.55 N	5.19 W
Saint Dennis	242	50.23 N	4.53 W
Saint Dogmaels	242	52.05 N	4.40 W
Saintfield	248	54.28 N	5.47 W
Saint Fillans	246	56.23 N	4.07 W
Saint George's Channel ⋃	248	52.00 N	6.15 W
Saint Germans	242	50.24 N	4.18 W
Saint Govan's Head ❯	242	51.36 N	4.55 W
Saint Helens, Eng., U.K.	242	50.42 N	1.06 W
Saint Helens, Eng., U.K.	244	53.28 N	2.44 W
Saint Helier	243b	49.12 N	2.37 W
Saint Ives, Eng., U.K.	242	50.12 N	5.29 W
Saint Ives, Eng., U.K.	242	52.20 N	0.05 W
Saint Ives Bay C	242	50.14 N	5.26 W
Saint John	243b	49.15 N	2.08 W
Saint Just	242	50.07 N	5.42 W
Saint Keverne	242	50.03 N	5.06 W
Saint Kilda ▮	246	57.49 N	8.36 W
Saint Leonards	242	50.51 N	0.34 E
Saint Magnus Bay C	246a	60.24 N	1.34 W
Saint Magnus Cathedral ✝1	246	58.58 N	2.57 W
Saint Margaret's at Cliffe	242	51.09 N	1.24 E
Saint Margaret's Hope	246	58.49 N	2.57 W
Saint Martin's ▮	242a	49.58 N	6.20 W
Saint Mary Bourne	242	51.16 N	1.24 W
Saint Mary's ▮	242a	49.55 N	6.18 W
Saint Mary's Bay C	242	51.00 N	0.58 E
Saint Mawes	242	50.09 N	5.01 W
Saint Mawgan	242	50.28 N	4.58 W
Saint Merryn	242	50.31 N	4.58 W
Saint Monance	246	56.12 N	2.46 W
Saint Neots	242	52.14 N	0.17 W
Saint Peter Port	243b	49.27 N	2.32 W
Saint Sampson	243b	49.29 N	2.31 W
Saint Saviour	243b	49.11 N	2.06 W
Saint Tudy	242	50.33 N	4.43 W
Salcombe	242	50.13 N	3.47 W
Sale	244	53.26 N	2.19 W
Salen, Scot., U.K.	246	56.43 N	5.47 W
Salen, Scot., U.K.	246	56.31 N	5.57 W
Salford	244	53.28 N	2.18 W
Salisbury	242	51.05 N	1.48 W
Salisbury Cathedral ✝1	242	51.05 N	1.48 W
Salisbury Plain ≡	242	51.12 N	1.55 W
Salop □6	242	52.40 N	2.40 W
Saltash	242	50.24 N	4.12 W
Saltburn-by-the-Sea	244	54.35 N	0.58 W
Saltcoats	246	55.38 N	4.47 W
Saltee Islands II	248	52.07 N	6.36 W
Sampford Peverell	242	50.56 N	3.22 W
Samson ▮	242a	49.56 N	6.22 W
Sanda Island ▮	244	55.18 N	5.34 W
Sanday ▮	246	59.15 N	2.35 W
Sanday Sound C	246	59.11 N	2.31 W
Sandbach	244	53.09 N	2.22 W
Sandbank	246	55.59 N	4.58 W
Sandgate	242	51.05 N	1.08 E
Sandhead	244	54.48 N	4.58 W
Sandhurst	242	51.19 N	0.48 W
Sandness	246a	60.17 N	1.38 W
Sandown	242	50.39 N	1.09 W
Sandray ▮	246	56.53 N	7.30 W
Sandringham	242	52.50 N	0.30 E
Sandringham House ⊥	242	52.50 N	0.30 E
Sandwich	242	51.17 N	1.20 E
Sandwick	246a	60.00 N	1.15 W
Sand Wick C	246	60.42 N	0.52 W
Sandy	242	52.08 N	0.18 W
Sanquhar	244	55.22 N	3.56 W
Sarclet	246	58.22 N	3.07 W
Sark ▮	243b	49.26 N	2.21 W
Sark ≃	244	54.58 N	3.04 W
Saundersfoot	242	51.43 N	4.43 W
Savernake Forest ◆3	242	51.24 N	1.38 W
Sawbridgeworth	242	51.50 N	0.09 E
Sawel Mountain ▲	248	54.49 N	7.02 W
Sawston	242	52.07 N	0.10 E
Sawtry	242	52.27 N	0.17 W
Saxilby	244	53.17 N	0.40 W
Saxmundham	242	52.13 N	1.29 E
Scafell Pikes ▲	244	54.27 N	3.12 W
Scalasaig	246	56.04 N	6.11 W
Scalby	244	54.18 N	0.27 W
Scalloway	246a	60.08 N	1.18 W
Scalpay ▮, Scot., U.K.	246	57.52 N	6.40 W
Scalpay ▮, Scot., U.K.	246	57.17 N	5.59 W
Scapa Flow C	246	58.55 N	3.06 W
Scarba ▮	246	56.11 N	5.43 W
Scarborough	244	54.17 N	0.24 W
Scardroy	246	57.31 N	4.59 W
Scarinish	246	56.29 N	6.48 W
Scarp ▮	246	58.02 N	7.08 W
Scarriff	248	52.55 N	8.31 W
Scartaglin	248	52.10 N	9.26 W
Scavaig, Loch C	246	57.09 N	6.10 W
Schiehallion ▲	246	56.40 N	4.06 W
Schull	248	51.32 N	9.33 W
Scilly, Isles of II	242a	49.55 N	6.20 W
Scole	242	52.22 N	1.10 E
Scolt Head ❯	242	52.58 N	0.42 E
Scotland □8, U.K.	244	55.15 N	3.30 W
Scotland □8, U.K.	246	57.00 N	4.00 W
Scour ≃	244	55.13 N	3.46 W
Scourie	246	58.20 N	5.08 W
Scridain, Loch C	246	56.21 N	6.07 W
Scrooby	244	53.25 N	1.01 W
Scunthorpe	244	53.36 N	0.38 W
Scurrival Point ❯	246	57.04 N	7.31 W
Seaford	242	50.46 N	0.06 E
Seaforth, Loch C	246	57.54 N	6.40 W
Seaham	244	54.52 N	1.21 W
Seahouses	244	55.35 N	1.38 W
Seascale	244	54.24 N	3.29 W
Seaton, Eng., U.K.	242	50.43 N	3.05 W
Seaton, Eng., U.K.	244	54.41 N	3.33 W
Seaton, Eng., U.K.	244	53.54 N	0.14 W
Seaton ≃	242	50.22 N	4.22 W
Seaton Delaval	244	55.04 N	1.31 W
Sedbergh	244	54.20 N	2.31 W
Sedgefield	244	54.39 N	1.26 W
Sedgley	242	52.33 N	2.08 W
Seil ▮	246	56.18 N	5.39 W
Selborne	242	51.06 N	0.56 W
Selby	244	53.48 N	1.04 W
Selkirk	246	55.33 N	2.50 W
Selly Oak ◆8	242	52.25 N	1.52 W
Selsey	242	50.44 N	0.48 W
Selsey Bill ❯	242	50.43 N	0.48 W
Senghenydd	242	51.36 N	3.16 W
Sennybridge	242	51.57 N	3.34 W
Serqo → Sark ▮	243b	49.26 N	2.21 W
Settle	244	54.04 N	2.16 W
Seven ≃	244	54.11 N	0.52 W
Sevenoaks	242	51.16 N	0.12 E
Seven Sisters	242	51.46 N	3.43 W
Severn ≃	242	51.35 N	2.40 W
Severn, Mouth of the ⋃	242	51.25 N	3.00 W
Severn Bridge ◆5	242	51.39 N	2.42 W
Severn Tunnel ◆5	242	51.35 N	2.44 W
Sgritheall, Beinn ▲	246	57.08 N	5.35 W
Shaftesbury	242	51.01 N	2.12 W
Shanklin	242	50.38 N	1.10 W
Shannon ≃	248	52.36 N	9.41 W
Shannon, Mouth of the ≃1	248	52.30 N	9.50 W
Shannon Airport ⊠	248	52.41 N	8.55 W
Shap	244	54.32 N	2.41 W
Shapinsay ▮	246	59.03 N	2.53 W
Shawbury	242	52.47 N	2.39 W
Sheaf ≃	244	53.23 N	1.26 W
Shedfield	242	50.55 N	1.12 W
Sheelin, Lough ◎	248	53.48 N	7.22 W
Sheep Haven C	248	55.10 N	7.52 W
Sheerness	242	51.27 N	0.45 E
Sheffield	244	53.23 N	1.30 W
Shefford	242	52.02 N	0.20 W
Shehy Mountains ⋀	248	51.48 N	9.15 W
Shell, Loch C	246	58.00 N	6.30 W
Sheppey, Isle of ▮	242	51.24 N	0.50 E
Shepshed	242	52.47 N	1.18 W
Shepton Mallet	242	51.12 N	2.33 W
Sherborne	242	50.57 N	2.31 W
Sherborne Saint John	242	51.18 N	1.07 W
Shercock	248	54.00 N	6.54 W
Sheringham	242	52.57 N	1.12 E
Sherwood Forest ◆3	244	53.08 N	1.08 W
Shetland Islands □4	246a	60.30 N	0.15 W
Shetland Islands II	246a	60.30 N	1.00 W
Shiant, Sound of ⋃	246	57.55 N	6.25 W
Shiant Islands II	246	57.53 N	6.21 W
Shiel, Loch ◎	246	56.47 N	5.35 W
Shiel Bridge	246	57.12 N	5.25 W
Shieldaig	246	57.31 N	5.39 W
Shifnal	242	52.40 N	2.21 W
Shilbottle	244	55.23 N	1.42 W
Shildon	244	54.38 N	1.39 W
Shillelagh	248	52.45 N	6.32 W
Shillingstone	242	50.54 N	2.14 W
Shin, Loch ◎	246	58.06 N	4.34 W
Shinnel Water ≃	244	55.13 N	3.49 W
Shinness	246	58.05 N	4.28 W
Shipdham	242	52.37 N	0.53 E
Shipley	244	53.50 N	1.47 W
Shipston-on-Stour	242	52.04 N	1.37 W
Shirebrook	244	53.12 N	1.13 W
Shirrell Heath	242	50.55 N	1.12 W
Shoeburyness	242	51.32 N	0.48 E
Shona, Eilean ▮	246	56.47 N	5.52 W
Shoreham-by-Sea	242	50.49 N	0.16 W
Shotley Gate	242	51.58 N	1.15 E
Shotton Colliery	244	54.44 N	1.20 W
Shotts	246	55.49 N	3.48 W
Shournagh ≃	248	51.53 N	8.35 W
Shrewsbury	242	52.43 N	2.45 W
Shrewton	242	51.12 N	1.55 W
Shrivenham	242	51.36 N	1.39 W
Shrule	248	53.30 N	9.08 W
Sible Hedingham	242	51.58 N	0.35 E
Sidlaw Hills ⋀2	246	56.30 N	3.10 W
Sidmouth	242	50.41 N	3.15 W
Sighty Crag ▲	244	55.07 N	2.37 W
Silloth	244	54.52 N	3.23 W
Silsden	244	53.55 N	1.55 W
Silvermine Mountains ⋀	248	52.45 N	8.15 W
Silvermines	248	52.47 N	8.13 W
Silverstone	242	52.05 N	1.02 W
Silverton	242	50.48 N	3.28 W
Simonsbath	242	51.09 N	3.45 W
Sinclair's Bay C	246	58.30 N	3.07 W
Singleton	242	50.55 N	0.46 W
Sinking ≃	248	53.37 N	8.52 W
Sionascaig, Loch ◎	246	58.04 N	5.11 W
Sittingbourne	242	51.21 N	0.44 E
Sixmilecross	248	54.34 N	7.08 W
Skegness	244	53.10 N	0.21 E
Skellig Rocks II1	248	51.48 N	10.31 W
Skelmersdale	244	53.33 N	2.48 W
Skelmorlie	246	55.51 N	4.53 W
Skelton, Eng., U.K.	244	54.33 N	0.59 W
Skelton, Eng., U.K.	244	54.43 N	2.51 W
Skerne ≃	244	54.29 N	1.34 W
Skerryvore II1	246	56.19 N	7.07 W
Skewen	242	51.40 N	3.51 W
Skibbereen	248	51.33 N	9.15 W
Skiddaw ▲	244	54.38 N	3.08 W
Skipton	244	53.58 N	2.01 W
Skirfare ≃	244	54.07 N	2.01 W
Skokholm Island ▮	242	51.42 N	5.16 W
Skomer Island ▮	242	51.44 N	5.17 W
Skreen	248	54.15 N	8.45 W
Skye ▮	246	57.15 N	6.10 W
Skye, Island of ▮	246	57.18 N	6.15 W
Slaney ≃	248	52.21 N	6.30 W
Slea Head ❯	248	52.06 N	10.27 W
Sleat, Point of ❯	246	57.01 N	6.02 W
Sleat, Sound of ⋃	246	57.06 N	5.49 W
Sledmere	244	54.04 N	0.35 W
Sliabh Gaoil ▲	246	55.55 N	5.28 W
Slievenaman ▲	248	52.25 N	7.34 W
Sligeach → Sligo	248	54.17 N	8.28 W
Sligo	248	54.17 N	8.28 W
Sligo □6	248	54.10 N	8.40 W
Sligo Bay C	248	54.20 N	8.40 W
Slioch ▲	246	57.41 N	5.22 W
Slough	242	51.31 N	0.36 W
Slyne Head ❯	248	53.24 N	10.13 W
Smerwick Harbour C	248	52.12 N	10.24 W
Smethwick (Warley)	242	52.30 N	1.58 W
Smite ≃	242	52.57 N	0.53 W
Smithfield	244	54.59 N	2.52 W
Snaefell ▲	244	54.16 N	4.27 W
Snettisham	242	52.53 N	0.30 E
Snizort, Loch C	246	57.34 N	6.28 W
Snodland	242	51.20 N	0.27 E
Snowdon ▲	244	53.04 N	4.05 W
Snowdonia National Park ♣	244	53.09 N	3.57 W
Soay ▮	246	57.08 N	6.14 W
Soham	242	52.20 N	0.20 E
Solihull	242	52.25 N	1.45 W
Sollas	246	57.39 N	7.21 W
Solva	242	51.52 N	5.11 W
Solva ≃	242	51.52 N	5.17 W
Solway Firth C1	244	54.50 N	3.35 W
Somerset □6	242	51.08 N	3.00 W
Somersham	242	52.23 N	0.01 E
Somerton	242	51.03 N	2.44 W
Sonning	242	51.29 N	0.55 W
Sorbie	244	54.48 N	4.26 W
Sorel Point ❯	243b	49.16 N	2.10 W
Sorn	246	55.30 N	4.18 W
Sortat	246	58.33 N	3.13 W
Southam	242	52.15 N	1.23 W
Southampton	242	50.55 N	1.25 W
Southampton (Eastleigh) Airport ⊠	242	50.57 N	1.21 W
South Barrule ⋀2	244	54.12 N	4.40 W
South Benfleet	242	51.33 N	0.34 E
Southborough	242	51.10 N	0.15 E
South Brent	242	50.25 N	3.50 W
South Cave	244	53.46 N	0.35 W
South Dorset Downs ⋀1	242	50.40 N	2.25 W
South Downs ⋀1	242	50.55 N	0.25 W
Southend	246	55.20 N	5.38 W
Southend Municipal Airport ⊠	242	51.34 N	0.41 E
Southend-on-Sea	242	51.33 N	0.43 E
Southery	242	52.32 N	0.23 E
South Esk ≃, Scot., U.K.	246	55.53 N	3.04 W
South Esk ≃, Scot., U.K.	246	56.42 N	2.32 W
South Foreland ❯	242	51.09 N	1.23 E
South Forty Foot Drain ≃	242	52.56 N	0.15 W
South Glamorgan □6	242	51.30 N	3.25 W
South Hams ≡	242	50.22 N	3.50 W
South Hayling	242	50.47 N	0.59 W
South Kirkby	244	53.34 N	1.20 W
Southminster	242	51.40 N	0.50 E
South Molton	242	51.01 N	3.50 W
South Ockendon	242	51.32 N	0.18 E
South Petherton	242	50.58 N	2.49 W
Southport	244	53.39 N	3.01 W
South Ronaldsay ▮	246	58.46 N	2.58 W
South Shields	244	55.00 N	1.25 W
South Sound ⋃	248	53.02 N	9.28 W
South Tyne ≃	244	54.59 N	2.08 W
South Uist ▮	246	57.15 N	7.21 W
Southwark ◆8	242	51.30 N	0.06 W
Southwick	242	50.50 N	0.13 W
Southwold	242	52.20 N	1.40 E
South Woodham Ferrers	242	51.39 N	0.37 E
South Yorkshire □6	244	53.30 N	1.15 W
South Zeal	242	50.44 N	3.54 W
Sow ≃	242	52.48 N	2.00 W
Sowerby	244	54.13 N	1.21 W
Sowerby Bridge	244	53.43 N	1.54 W
Spalding	242	52.47 N	0.10 W
Sparkford	242	51.02 N	2.34 W
Spean, Glen ∨	246	56.53 N	4.45 W
Spean Bridge	246	56.53 N	4.54 W
Spelve, Loch C	246	56.22 N	5.46 W
Spennymoor	244	54.42 N	1.35 W
Sperrin Mountains ⋀	248	54.50 N	7.05 W
Spey ≃	246	57.40 N	3.06 W
Spey Bay C	246	57.41 N	3.00 W
Spithead ⋃	242	50.45 N	1.05 W
Spittal of Glenshee	246	56.48 N	3.28 W
Spondon	242	52.54 N	1.25 W

Symbols in the index entries are identified on page 250.

Name	Page	Lat °'	Long °'
Sprint	244	54.22 N	2.45 W
Spurn Head	244	53.34 N	0.07 E
Stack, Loch	246	58.20 N	4.55 W
Stackpoie Head	242	51.37 N	4.54 W
Stack Skerry	246	59.01 N	4.31 W
Staffa	246	56.25 N	6.20 W
Staffin	246	57.37 N	6.12 W
Stafford	242	52.48 N	2.07 W
Staffordshire	242	52.50 N	2.00 W
Staines	242	51.26 N	0.31 W
Stainforth	244	53.36 N	1.01 W
Stainmore Forest	244	54.30 N	2.10 W
Stalbridge	242	50.58 N	2.23 W
Stalham	242	52.47 N	1.31 E
Stamford	242	52.39 N	0.29 W
Stamford Bridge	244	53.59 N	0.55 W
Standing Stones	246	58.12 N	6.48 W
Standish	244	53.36 N	2.41 W
Standon	242	51.53 N	0.02 E
Stanford le Hope	242	51.31 N	0.26 E
Stanhope	244	54.45 N	2.01 W
Stanley, Eng., U.K.	244	54.52 N	1.42 W
Stanley, Scot., U.K.	246	56.28 N	3.27 W
Stanlow	244	53.17 N	2.52 W
Stannington	244	55.06 N	1.40 W
Stanstead Abbots	242	51.47 N	0.01 E
Stansted Mountfitchet	242	51.54 N	0.12 E
Stanton	242	52.19 N	0.53 E
Stanwix	244	54.54 N	2.55 W
Stapleford	242	52.56 N	1.16 W
Staplehurst	242	51.10 N	0.33 E
Starav, Ben	246	56.32 N	5.03 W
Starcross	242	50.38 N	3.27 W
Start Bay	242	50.17 N	3.36 W
Start Point	242	50.13 N	3.38 W
Staveley	244	53.16 N	1.20 W
Staxigoe	246	58.28 N	3.04 W
Steep Holm	242	51.21 N	3.07 W
Steeping	244	53.06 N	0.18 E
Stenhousemuir	246	56.02 N	3.48 W
Stenness, Loch of	246	59.00 N	3.15 W
Stevenage	242	51.55 N	0.14 W
Stevenston	246	55.39 N	4.45 W
Stewarton	246	55.41 N	4.31 W
Stewartstown	248	54.35 N	6.41 W
Steyning	242	50.53 N	0.20 W
Stinchar	244	55.06 N	5.00 W
Stiperstones	242	52.35 N	2.56 W
Stirling	246	56.07 N	3.57 W
Stirling Castle	246	56.07 N	3.57 W
Stockbridge	242	51.07 N	1.29 W
Stockport	244	53.25 N	2.10 W
Stocksbridge	244	53.27 N	1.34 W
Stockton-on-Tees	244	54.34 N	1.19 W
Stoer	246	58.12 N	5.20 W
Stoer, Point of	246	58.15 N	5.21 W
Stoke Golding	242	52.34 N	1.24 W
Stokenchurch	242	51.40 N	0.55 W
Stoke-on-Trent	244	53.00 N	2.10 W
Stokesley	244	54.28 N	1.11 W
Stone	242	52.54 N	2.10 W
Stonehaven	246	56.38 N	2.13 W
Stonehenge	242	51.11 N	1.49 W
Stonehouse, Eng., U.K.	242	51.45 N	2.17 W
Stonehouse, Scot., U.K.	246	55.43 N	4.00 W
Stoneleigh	242	52.21 N	1.31 W
Stony Stratford	242	52.04 N	0.52 W
Stornoway	246	58.12 N	6.23 W
Storrington	242	50.55 N	0.28 W
Stotfold	242	52.01 N	0.14 W
Stour, Eng., U.K.	242	51.18 N	1.22 E
Stour, Eng., U.K.	242	50.43 N	1.46 W
Stour, Eng., U.K.	242	52.20 N	2.15 W
Stour, Eng., U.K.	242	51.52 N	1.16 E
Stourbridge	242	52.27 N	2.09 W
Stourport-on-Severn	242	52.21 N	2.16 W
Stowmarket	242	52.11 N	1.00 E
Stow-on-the-Wold	242	51.56 N	1.44 W
Strabane	248	54.49 N	7.27 W
Strachan	246	57.01 N	2.32 W
Strachur	246	56.10 N	5.04 W
Stradbally	248	53.00 N	7.08 W
Stradbroke	242	52.19 N	1.16 E
Stradone	248	53.58 N	7.14 W
Strandhill	248	54.17 N	8.36 W
Strangford	248	54.22 N	5.34 W
Strangford Lough	248	54.30 N	5.36 W
Stranorlar	248	54.48 N	7.46 W
Stranraer	244	54.55 N	5.02 W
Strata Florida Abbey	242	52.16 N	3.51 W
Stratford-upon-Avon	242	52.12 N	1.41 W
Strathaven	246	55.40 N	4.04 W
Strathclyde	246	56.00 N	5.15 W
Strathdearn	246	57.15 N	4.05 W
Strathdon	246	57.11 N	3.02 W
Strathearn	246	56.18 N	3.45 W
Strathkanaird	246	57.59 N	5.11 W
Strathminglo	246	56.16 N	3.16 W
Strathmore	246	56.39 N	3.00 W
Strathpeffer	246	57.35 N	4.33 W
Strathy	246	58.34 N	4.00 W
Strathy Point	246	58.35 N	4.02 W
Stratton	242	50.50 N	4.31 W
Stratton Saint Margaret	242	51.35 N	1.45 W
Street	242	51.07 N	2.42 W
Stretford	244	53.27 N	2.19 W
Stretton, Eng., U.K.	242	52.44 N	0.35 W
Stretton, Eng., U.K.	244	53.21 N	2.35 W
Strichen	246	57.34 N	2.05 W
Striven, Loch	246	55.58 N	5.09 W
Strokestown	248	53.47 N	8.08 W
Stroma	246	58.41 N	3.08 W
Stromeferry	246	57.21 N	5.34 W
Stromness	246	58.57 N	3.18 W
Stronsay	246	59.07 N	2.37 W
Stronsay Firth	246	59.02 N	2.41 W
Strontian	246	56.41 N	5.44 W
Strood	242	51.24 N	0.28 E
Stroud	242	51.45 N	2.12 W
Strule	248	54.43 N	7.25 W
Strumble Head	242	52.02 N	5.04 W
Struy	246	57.24 N	4.39 W
Studland	242	50.39 N	1.58 W
Studley	242	52.16 N	1.52 W
Sturminster Newton	242	50.50 N	2.19 W
Sturry	242	51.18 N	1.07 E
Suck	248	53.16 N	8.03 W
Sudbury	242	52.02 N	0.44 E
Suffolk	242	52.10 N	1.20 E
Suir	248	52.15 N	7.00 W
Sule Skerry	246	59.05 N	4.26 W
Sullane	248	51.53 N	8.56 W
Sumburgh Head	246a	59.53 N	1.20 W
Sumburgh Roost	246	59.49 N	1.19 W
Summer Bridge	244	54.03 N	1.41 W
Summerhill	248	53.29 N	6.44 W
Summer Isles	246	58.02 N	5.28 W
Sunart, Loch	246	56.41 N	5.43 W
Sunderland	244	54.55 N	1.23 W
Sunninghill	242	51.25 N	0.40 W
Surrey	242	51.10 N	0.20 W
Sussex, East	242	50.55 N	0.15 E
Sussex, Vale of	242	50.57 N	0.17 W
Sutton	242	52.23 N	0.07 E
Sutton	242	51.22 N	0.12 W
Sutton Bridge	242	52.46 N	0.12 E
Sutton Coldfield	242	52.34 N	1.48 W
Sutton Courtenay	242	51.39 N	1.17 W
Sutton-in-Ashfield	244	53.08 N	1.15 W
Sutton-on-Sea	244	53.19 N	0.17 E
Sutton on Trent	244	53.10 N	0.49 W
Sutton Scotney	242	51.10 N	1.21 W
Sutton Valence	242	51.12 N	0.36 E
Sutton Veny	242	51.11 N	2.08 W
Swadlincote	242	52.47 N	1.33 W
Swaffham	242	52.39 N	0.41 E
Swale	244	54.06 N	1.20 W
Swaledale	244	54.25 N	1.47 W
Swanage	242	50.37 N	1.58 W
Swanley	242	51.24 N	0.12 E
Swanlinbar	248	54.10 N	7.42 W
Swansea	242	51.38 N	3.57 W
Swansea Bay	242	51.35 N	3.52 W
Sway	242	50.47 N	1.37 W
Sweetheart Abbey	244	54.59 N	3.38 W
Swift	242	52.23 N	1.16 W
Swilly	248	54.57 N	7.42 W
Swilly, Lough	248	55.10 N	7.38 W
Swindon	242	51.34 N	1.47 W
Swinford	248	53.57 N	8.57 W
Swinton, Eng., U.K.	244	53.28 N	1.20 W
Swinton, Scot., U.K.	246	55.43 N	2.15 W
Swona	246	58.45 N	3.03 W
Swords	248	53.28 N	6.13 W
Syre	246	58.22 N	4.14 W
Syston	242	52.42 N	1.04 W

T

Name	Page	Lat °'	Long °'
Tadcaster	244	53.53 N	1.16 W
Tadley	242	51.21 N	1.08 W
Tadworth	242	51.17 N	0.14 W
Taff	242	51.27 N	3.09 W
Taghmon	248	52.18 N	6.39 W
Tain	246	57.48 N	4.04 W
Talgarreg	242	52.08 N	4.18 W
Talgarth	242	52.00 N	3.15 W
Talisker	246	57.17 N	6.27 W
Talladale	246	57.42 N	5.29 W
Tallaght	248	53.26 N	6.21 W
Tallow	248	52.05 N	8.00 W
Talmine	246	58.31 N	4.26 W
Talsarnau	242	52.54 N	4.03 W
Talybont	242	52.29 N	3.59 W
Tamar	242	50.22 N	4.10 W
Tame	242	52.44 N	1.43 W
Tamerton Foliot	242	50.26 N	4.08 W
Tanat	242	52.46 N	3.07 W
Tandragee	248	54.21 N	6.25 W
Tanworth-in-Arden	242	52.39 N	1.40 W
Taransay	246	57.54 N	7.01 W
Tarbat Ness	246	57.51 N	3.47 W
Tarbert, Eire	248	52.32 N	9.23 W
Tarbert, Scot., U.K.	246	57.54 N	6.49 W
Tarbert, Scot., U.K.	246	55.52 N	5.26 W
Tarbert, Loch	246	55.57 N	6.00 W
Tarbet	246	56.12 N	4.43 W
Tarbolton	246	55.31 N	4.29 W
Tarfside	246	56.54 N	2.50 W
Tarf Water	244	54.55 N	4.35 W
Tarland	246	57.08 N	2.52 W
Tarleton	244	53.41 N	2.50 W
Tarporley	244	53.09 N	2.40 W
Tarrant Hinton	242	50.53 N	2.05 W
Tarves	246	57.22 N	2.13 W
Tas	242	52.36 N	1.18 E
Taunton	242	51.01 N	3.06 W
Taunton, Vale of	242	51.02 N	3.08 W
Tavistock	242	50.33 N	4.08 W
Tavy	242	50.16 N	4.10 W
Taw	242	51.04 N	4.11 W
Tawe	242	51.37 N	3.55 W
Tay	246	56.22 N	3.21 W
Tay, Firth of	246	56.26 N	3.00 W
Tay, Loch	246	56.31 N	4.10 W
Taynuilt	246	56.25 N	5.14 W
Tayport	246	57.27 N	2.53 W
Tayside	246	56.30 N	3.30 W
Teangue	246	57.07 N	5.50 W
Tebay	244	54.26 N	2.35 W
Tees	244	54.34 N	1.16 W
Tees Bay	244	54.39 N	1.07 W
Teesdale	244	54.38 N	2.07 W
Teesside → Middlesbrough	244	54.35 N	1.14 W
Teesside (Saint George) Airport	244	54.31 N	1.25 W
Tegid, Llyn	242	52.53 N	3.36 W
Teifi	242	52.07 N	4.42 W
Teifiside	242	52.02 N	4.22 W
Teign	242	50.33 N	3.29 W
Teignmouth	242	50.33 N	3.30 W
Teith	246	56.08 N	3.59 W
Teme	242	52.09 N	2.18 W
Templecombe	242	51.00 N	2.25 W
Temple Ewell	242	51.09 N	1.16 E
Templemore	248	52.48 N	7.50 W
Temple Sowerby	244	54.39 N	2.35 W
Tenbury Wells	242	52.19 N	2.35 W
Tenby	242	51.41 N	4.43 W
Tenterden	242	51.05 N	0.42 E
Ter	242	51.50 N	0.36 E
Tern	242	52.47 N	2.32 W
Terrington Saint Clement	242	52.45 N	0.18 E
Test	242	50.55 N	1.29 W
Tetbury	242	51.39 N	2.10 W
Tettenhall	242	52.36 N	2.09 W
Teviot	246	55.35 N	2.26 W
Teviotdale	244	55.25 N	2.50 W
Teviothead	244	55.21 N	2.56 W
Tewkesbury	242	51.59 N	2.09 W
Teynham	242	51.20 N	0.50 E
Thame	242	51.45 N	0.59 W
Thames	242	51.28 N	0.43 E
Thanet, Isle of	242	51.22 N	1.20 E
Tharsuinn, Beinn	246	57.47 N	4.21 W
Thatcham	242	51.25 N	1.15 W
Thaxted	242	51.57 N	0.20 E
Theale	242	51.27 N	1.04 W
The Cheviot	244	55.28 N	2.09 W
The Curragh	248	53.10 N	6.52 W
The Deeps	246a	60.09 N	1.23 W
The Downs	242	51.13 N	1.27 E
The Fens	242	52.38 N	0.02 E
The Glenkens	244	55.10 N	4.15 W
The Long Mynd	242	52.35 N	2.48 W
The Machars	244	54.50 N	4.30 W
The Machars	244	55.20 N	4.33 W
The Minch	246	58.10 N	5.50 W
The Moors	244	54.56 N	4.40 W
The Mumbles	242	51.34 N	4.00 W
The Naze	242	51.53 N	1.16 E
The Needles	242	50.39 N	1.34 W
The Oa	246	55.37 N	6.16 W
The Paps	248	52.00 N	9.17 W
The Rhins	244	54.50 N	5.00 W
The Road	242a	49.56 N	6.20 W
The Solent	242	50.46 N	1.20 W
The Storr	246	57.31 N	6.12 W
The Swale	242	51.22 N	0.56 E
Thet	242	52.27 N	0.33 E
Thetford	242	52.25 N	0.45 E
The Twelve Pins	248	53.31 N	9.50 W
The Wash	242	52.55 N	0.15 E
The Weald	242	51.05 N	0.05 E
The Wrekin	242	52.41 N	2.34 W
Thirlmere	244	54.33 N	3.04 W
Thirsk	244	54.14 N	1.20 W
Thomastown	248	52.31 N	7.08 W
Thormanby	244	54.10 N	1.14 W
Thornaby-on-Tees	244	54.34 N	1.18 W
Thornbury	242	51.37 N	2.32 W
Thorndon	242	52.17 N	1.08 E
Thorne	244	53.37 N	0.58 W
Thorney	242	52.37 N	0.07 W
Thornhill	244	55.15 N	3.46 W
Thornton	244	53.53 N	3.02 W
Thornton Dale	244	54.14 N	0.43 W
Thorpe-le-Soken	242	51.52 N	1.10 E
Thorpe Saint Andrew	242	52.38 N	1.20 E
Thrapston	242	52.24 N	0.32 W
Three Bridges	242	51.07 N	0.09 W
Threlkeld	244	54.38 N	3.03 W
Throckley	244	54.59 N	1.45 W
Thrushel	242	50.39 N	4.15 W
Thurles	248	52.41 N	7.49 W
Thurnscoe	244	53.31 N	1.19 W
Thursby	244	54.51 N	3.03 W
Thurso	246	58.35 N	3.32 W
Thurso	246	58.36 N	3.30 W
Tibbermore	246	56.22 N	3.32 W
Ticehurst	242	51.03 N	0.25 E
Tickhill	244	53.26 N	1.06 W
Tighvein	246	55.30 N	5.10 W
Tilbury	242	51.28 N	0.23 E
Till, Eng., U.K.	244	55.41 N	2.12 W
Till, Eng., U.K.	244	53.16 N	0.37 W
Tillicoultry	246	56.09 N	3.45 W
Tillyfourie	246	57.11 N	2.35 W
Tilt	246	56.46 N	3.50 W
Tinahely	248	52.47 N	7.26 W
Tintagel	242	50.40 N	4.45 W
Tintagel Head	242	50.41 N	4.46 W
Tintern Abbey	242	51.41 N	2.40 W
Tintern Parva	242	51.42 N	2.40 W
Tinto	246	55.36 N	3.39 W
Tipperary	248	52.29 N	8.10 W
Tipperary	248	52.40 N	8.20 W
Tipton	242	52.32 N	2.05 W
Tiptree	242	51.49 N	0.45 E
Tiree	246	56.30 N	6.55 W
Tirry	246	58.02 N	4.26 W
Tisbury	242	51.04 N	2.03 W
Titchfield	242	50.51 N	1.13 W
Titterstone Clee Hill	242	52.23 N	2.35 W
Tiumpan Head	246	58.16 N	6.09 W
Tiverton	242	50.55 N	3.29 W
Tobercurry	248	54.03 N	8.43 W
Tobermory	246	56.37 N	6.05 W
Toberonochy	246	56.13 N	5.38 W
Toddington	242	51.57 N	0.32 W
Todmorden	244	53.43 N	2.05 W
Toe Head	246	57.50 N	7.08 W
Tollesbury	242	51.46 N	0.50 E
Tolob	246a	59.53 N	1.19 W
Tolpuddle	242	50.45 N	2.18 W
Tolsta Head	246	58.20 N	6.10 W
Tomatin	246	57.20 N	3.59 W
Tomdoun	246	57.04 N	5.03 W
Tomich	246	57.18 N	4.48 W
Tomintoul	246	57.14 N	3.22 W
Tomnavoulin	246	57.18 N	3.19 W
Tonbridge	242	51.12 N	0.16 E
Tongue	246	58.28 N	4.25 W
Tongue, Kyle of	246	58.30 N	4.26 W
Tonyrefail	242	51.36 N	3.25 W
Toomebridge	248	54.45 N	6.27 W
Toomevara	248	52.50 N	8.02 W
Toormakeady	248	53.39 N	9.24 W
Topsham	242	50.41 N	3.27 W
Torbay → Torquay	242	50.28 N	3.30 W
Tor Bay	242	50.25 N	3.30 W
Torne	244	53.36 N	0.44 W
Torphins	246	57.06 N	2.37 W
Torpoint	242	50.22 N	4.11 W
Torquay (Torbay)	242	50.28 N	3.30 W
Torridge	242	51.03 N	4.11 W
Torridon	246	57.33 N	5.31 W
Torridon, Loch	246	57.35 N	5.46 W
Torrin	246	57.12 N	6.02 W
Torteval	243b	49.27 N	2.38 W
Tory Island	248	55.16 N	8.14 W
Tory Sound	248	55.14 N	8.14 W
Toscaig	246	57.24 N	5.50 W
Totnes	242	50.25 N	3.41 W
Tottington	244	53.37 N	2.20 W
Totton	242	50.56 N	1.29 W
Tove	242	52.05 N	0.38 W
Towan Head	242	50.25 N	5.07 W
Towcester	242	52.08 N	1.00 W
Tower Hamlets	242	51.32 N	0.03 W
Tow Law	244	54.44 N	1.49 W
Traighli → Tralee	248	52.16 N	9.42 W
Tralee	248	52.16 N	9.42 W
Tralee Bay	248	52.15 N	9.59 W
Tramore	248	52.10 N	7.10 W
Tranent	246	55.57 N	2.58 W
Trannon	242	52.31 N	3.25 W
Trawbreaga Bay	248	55.17 N	7.18 W
Trawsfynydd	242	52.54 N	3.55 W
Tredegar	242	51.47 N	3.16 W
Tregaron	242	52.13 N	3.55 W
Treharris	242	51.41 N	3.16 W
Treig, Loch	246	56.50 N	4.44 W
Tremadoc	242	52.56 N	4.09 W
Tremadoc Bay	242	52.52 N	4.15 W
Trent	244	53.42 N	0.41 W
Trent, Vale of	242	52.44 N	1.50 W
Tresco	242a	49.57 N	6.19 W
Treshnish Isles	246	56.30 N	6.24 W
Treshnish Point	246	56.33 N	6.21 W
Tresta	246	60.14 N	1.21 W
Trevose Head	242	50.33 N	5.01 W
Trillick	248	54.27 N	7.30 W
Trim	248	53.34 N	6.47 W
Tring	242	51.48 N	0.40 W
Troon	246	55.32 N	4.40 W
Trostan	248	55.03 N	6.10 W
Troup Head	246	57.41 N	2.18 W
Trowbridge	242	51.20 N	2.13 W
Truim	246	57.02 N	4.10 W
Truro	242	50.16 N	5.03 W
Trwyn Cilan	242	52.46 N	4.30 W
Tryweryn	242	52.24 N	3.35 W
Tuam	248	53.31 N	8.50 W
Tuath, Loch	246	56.30 N	6.12 W
Tud	242	52.38 N	1.15 E
Tudweiliog	242	52.54 N	4.35 W
Tuirc, Beinn an	246	55.34 N	5.34 W
Tulla	248	52.52 N	8.45 W
Tullamore	248	53.16 N	7.30 W
Tullow	248	52.48 N	6.44 W
Tulsk	248	53.47 N	8.16 W
Tummel	246	56.38 N	3.40 W
Tunbridge Wells	242	51.08 N	0.16 E
Turriff	246	57.32 N	2.28 W
Tusker Rock	242	51.27 N	3.40 W
Tweed	244	55.46 N	2.00 W
Tweeddale	246	55.37 N	2.55 W
Twrch, Wales, U.K.	242	52.42 N	3.29 W
Twrch, Wales, U.K.	242	51.46 N	3.46 W
Twyford, Eng., U.K.	242	51.01 N	1.19 W
Twyford, Eng., U.K.	242	51.29 N	0.53 W
Twymyn	242	52.38 N	3.44 W
Tyldesley	244	53.31 N	2.28 W
Tynagh	248	53.09 N	8.22 W
Tyndrum	246	56.27 N	4.44 W
Tyne, Eng., U.K.	244	55.01 N	1.26 W
Tyne, Scot., U.K.	246	56.01 N	2.37 W
Tyne and Wear	244	54.55 N	1.35 W
Tynemouth	244	55.01 N	1.24 W
Tyrrellspass	248	53.23 N	7.22 W
Tywardreath	242	50.22 N	4.41 W
Tywi	242	51.46 N	4.22 W
Tywyn	242	52.35 N	4.05 W

U

Name	Page	Lat °'	Long °'
Uckfield	242	50.58 N	0.06 E
Uddingston	246	55.50 N	4.06 W
Uffculme	242	50.54 N	3.20 W
Ugie	246	57.30 N	1.47 W
Uig, Scot., U.K.	246	58.12 N	7.00 W
Uig, Scot., U.K.	246	57.35 N	6.22 W
Ullapool	246	57.54 N	5.10 W
Ullswater	244	54.34 N	2.54 W
Ulsta	246	60.30 N	1.09 W
Ulster	248	54.37 N	7.15 W
Ulster Canal	248	54.08 N	7.22 W
Ulva	246	56.29 N	6.14 W
Ulverston	244	54.12 N	3.06 W
United Kingdom, Eur.	244	54.00 N	2.00 W
United Kingdom, Eur.	248	54.40 N	6.45 W
Unst	246a	60.45 N	0.53 W
Upavon	242	51.18 N	1.49 W
Up Holland	244	53.33 N	2.44 W
Upper Tean	242	52.57 N	1.58 W
Uppingham	242	52.35 N	0.43 W
Upton	244	53.13 N	2.52 W
Upton upon Severn	242	52.04 N	2.13 W
Upwell	242	52.36 N	0.12 E
Ure	244	54.01 N	1.12 W
Urie	246	57.19 N	2.30 W
Urlingford	248	52.42 N	7.35 W
Urmston	244	53.27 N	2.21 W
Urquhart, Glen	246	57.20 N	4.35 W
Urr Water	244	54.53 N	3.49 W
Usk	242	51.43 N	2.54 W
Usk	242	51.36 N	2.58 W
Uttoxeter	242	52.54 N	1.51 W

V

Name	Page	Lat °'	Long °'
Vaich, Loch	246	57.43 N	4.46 W
Vaila	246a	60.12 N	1.37 W
Vale	243b	49.29 N	2.31 W
Valencia Island	248	51.52 N	10.20 W
Valle Crucis Abby	242	52.59 N	3.12 W
Vaternish Point	246	57.36 N	6.38 W
Vatersay	246	56.55 N	7.32 W
Veil, Loch	246	56.20 N	4.25 W
Venachar, Loch	246	56.13 N	4.19 W
Ventnor	242	50.36 N	1.11 W
Ventry	248	52.08 N	10.22 W
Ver	242	51.42 N	0.20 W
Verulamium	242	51.45 N	0.22 W
Verwood	242	50.53 N	1.52 W
Veryan	242	50.13 N	4.54 W
Vickie	246	59.53 N	1.18 W
Virginia	248	53.49 N	7.04 W
Vorlich, Ben	246	56.20 N	4.14 W
Vyrnwy, Lake	242	52.47 N	3.30 W

W

Name	Page	Lat °'	Long °'
Waddesdon	242	51.51 N	0.56 W
Waddingham	244	53.27 N	0.31 W
Wadebridge	242	50.32 N	4.50 W
Wadhurst	242	51.04 N	0.21 E
Wainfleet All Saints	244	53.07 N	0.14 E
Wakefield	244	53.42 N	1.29 W
Walberswick	242	52.19 N	1.39 E
Walbury Hill	242	51.21 N	1.30 W
Waldon	242	50.22 N	4.14 W
Wales	242	52.30 N	3.30 W
Walkden	244	53.32 N	2.24 W
Wallasey	244	53.26 N	3.03 W
Wallingford	242	51.37 N	1.08 W
Walls	246a	60.14 N	1.35 W
Wallsend	244	55.00 N	1.31 W
Walmer	242	51.13 N	1.24 E
Walney, Isle of	244	54.07 N	3.15 W
Walpole Saint Peter	242	52.42 N	0.15 E
Walsall	242	52.35 N	1.58 W
Walsoken	242	52.41 N	0.12 E
Waltham Abbey	242	51.42 N	0.01 E
Waltham Forest	242	51.35 N	0.01 W
Waltham on the Wolds	242	52.49 N	0.49 W
Walton, Eng., U.K.	242	51.58 N	1.21 E
Walton, Eng., U.K.	242	51.24 N	0.25 W
Walton-le-Dale	244	53.45 N	2.39 W
Walton-on-the-Naze	242	51.51 N	1.16 E
Wampool	244	54.54 N	3.14 W
Wanborough	242	51.33 N	1.42 W
Wandsworth	242	51.27 N	0.11 W
Wansbeck	244	55.10 N	1.34 W
Wantage	242	51.36 N	1.25 W
Ward Hill, Scot., U.K.	246	58.57 N	3.09 W
Ward Hill, Scot., U.K.	246	58.54 N	3.20 W
Wardle	244	53.39 N	2.08 W
Wardour, Vale of	242	51.05 N	2.00 W
Ward's Stone	244	54.02 N	2.38 W
Ware	242	51.49 N	0.02 W
Wareham	242	50.41 N	2.07 W
Warks Burn	244	55.03 N	2.08 W
Warkworth	244	55.21 N	1.36 W
Warley → Smethwick	242	52.30 N	1.58 W
Warlingham	242	51.19 N	0.04 W
Warlington	242	51.39 N	1.01 W
Warmington	242	52.08 N	1.24 W
Warminster	242	51.13 N	2.12 W
Warrenpoint	248	54.06 N	6.15 W
Warrington	244	53.24 N	2.37 W
Warsop	244	53.13 N	1.09 W
Warton	244	54.09 N	2.47 W
Warwick	242	52.17 N	1.34 W
Warwick Castle	242	52.17 N	1.34 W
Warwickshire	242	52.13 N	1.37 W
Wasbister	246	59.10 N	3.07 W
Washington	244	54.55 N	1.30 W
Washurn	244	53.54 N	1.39 W
Wast Water	244	54.26 N	3.18 W
Watchet	242	51.12 N	3.20 W
Waterbeach	242	52.16 N	0.11 E
Waterford	248	52.15 N	7.06 W
Waterford	248	52.10 N	7.40 W
Waterford Harbour	248	52.10 N	6.55 W
Watergate Bay	242	50.27 N	5.05 W
Watergrasshill	248	52.01 N	8.21 W
Waterloo	244	53.28 N	3.02 W
Waterlooville	242	50.53 N	1.02 W
Waterside	244	55.21 N	4.28 W
Waterville	248	51.49 N	10.13 W
Watford	242	51.40 N	0.25 W
Wath upon Dearne	244	53.29 N	1.20 W
Watlington	242	51.37 N	1.00 W
Watten, Loch	246	58.29 N	3.19 W
Watton	242	52.35 N	0.48 E
Waveney	242	52.28 N	1.45 E
Waver	244	54.52 N	3.17 W
Wear	244	54.55 N	1.22 W
Wearhead	244	54.45 N	2.13 W
Weaver	244	53.19 N	2.44 W
Weaverham	244	53.16 N	2.35 W
Wedmore	242	51.14 N	2.49 W
Wednesbury	242	52.34 N	2.00 W
Wednesfield	242	52.36 N	2.04 W
Weedon Beck	242	52.14 N	1.05 W
Welland	242	52.53 N	0.02 E
Wellesbourne	242	52.12 N	1.35 W
Wellingborough	242	52.19 N	0.42 W
Wellington, Eng., U.K.	242	52.43 N	2.31 W
Wellington, Eng., U.K.	242	50.59 N	3.14 W
Wells	242	51.13 N	2.39 W
Wells Cathedral	242	51.13 N	2.39 W
Wells-next-the-Sea	242	52.58 N	0.51 E
Welney	242	52.31 N	0.15 E
Welshpool	242	52.40 N	3.09 W
Welwyn Garden City	242	51.50 N	0.13 W
Wem	242	52.51 N	2.44 W
Wendover	242	51.46 N	0.46 W
Wenlock Edge	242	52.30 N	2.40 W
Wenning	244	54.07 N	2.39 W
Wensleydale	244	54.19 N	2.00 W
Wensum	242	52.37 N	1.19 E
Went	244	53.39 N	0.59 W
Weobley	242	52.09 N	2.51 W
West Allen	244	54.55 N	2.19 W
West Auckland	244	54.38 N	1.43 W
West Bergholt	242	51.55 N	0.51 E
West Bridgford	242	52.56 N	1.08 W
West Bromwich	242	52.31 N	1.56 W
West Burra	246a	60.05 N	1.21 W
Westbury, Eng., U.K.	242	51.16 N	2.11 W
Westbury, Eng., U.K.	242	52.41 N	2.57 W
Westbury-on-Severn	242	51.50 N	2.24 W
West Calder	246	55.52 N	3.35 W
West Cleddau	242	51.46 N	4.54 W
Westerdale	246	58.27 N	3.30 W
Westerham	242	51.16 N	0.05 E
Western Isles Islands	246	57.40 N	7.00 W
Westfield	242	50.55 N	0.35 E
Westgate-on-Sea	242	51.23 N	1.21 E
West Glamorgan	242	51.35 N	3.35 W
West Kilbride	246	55.42 N	4.51 W
West Kingsdown	242	51.21 N	0.17 E
West Kirby	244	53.22 N	3.10 W
West Linton	246	55.46 N	3.22 W
West Loch Roag	246	58.13 N	6.53 W
West Loch Tarbert, Scot., U.K.	246	55.48 N	5.32 W
West Loch Tarbert, Scot., U.K.	246	57.55 N	6.54 W
West Looe	242	50.21 N	4.28 W
West Lulworth	242	50.38 N	2.15 W
West Malling	242	51.18 N	0.25 E
Westmeath	248	53.30 N	7.30 W
West Meon	242	51.01 N	1.05 W
West Mersea	242	51.47 N	0.55 E
West Midlands	242	52.30 N	2.00 W
West Moors	242	50.49 N	1.55 W
Weston-super-Mare	242	51.21 N	2.59 W
Weston upon Trent	242	52.45 N	2.02 W
Westport	248	53.48 N	9.32 W
Westray	246	59.18 N	3.00 W
Westray Firth	246	59.12 N	2.55 W
West Sussex	242	50.55 N	0.35 W
Westward H9o	242	51.02 N	4.15 W
West Water	246	56.47 N	2.38 W
West Wellow	242	50.58 N	1.35 W
West Wycombe	242	51.39 N	0.49 W
West Yorkshire	244	53.45 N	1.40 W
Wetherby	244	53.56 N	1.23 W
Wetwang	244	54.01 N	0.34 W
Wexford	248	52.20 N	6.27 W
Wexford	248	52.20 N	6.40 W
Wexford Harbour	248	52.20 N	6.55 W
Wey	242	51.23 N	0.28 W
Weybridge	242	51.23 N	0.28 W
Weymouth	242	50.36 N	2.28 W
Whaley Bridge	244	53.20 N	1.59 W
Whalley	244	53.50 N	2.24 W
Whalsay	246a	60.20 N	0.59 W
Whaplode	242	52.48 N	0.02 W
Wharfe	244	53.51 N	1.07 W
Wharfedale	244	54.01 N	1.56 W
Whauphill	244	54.49 N	4.29 W
Wheathampstead	242	51.49 N	0.17 W
Wheatley Hill	244	54.45 N	1.23 W
Wheelock	244	53.12 N	2.26 W
Whernside	244	54.14 N	2.23 W
Whiddon Down	242	50.43 N	3.51 W
Whiston	244	53.25 N	2.50 W
Whitburn	246	55.52 N	3.42 W
Whitby	244	54.29 N	0.37 W
Whitby Abbey	244	54.28 N	0.38 W
Whitchurch, Eng., U.K.	242	51.53 N	0.51 W
Whitchurch, Eng., U.K.	242	51.14 N	1.20 W
Whitchurch, Eng., U.K.	242	52.58 N	2.41 W
Whitchurch, Eng., U.K.	242	51.52 N	2.39 W
Whitchurch, Wales, U.K.	242	51.33 N	3.14 W
White Coomb	244	55.26 N	3.20 W
White Esk	244	55.12 N	3.10 W
Whitegate	248	51.50 N	8.14 W
Whitehall	246	59.07 N	2.37 W
Whitehaven	244	54.33 N	3.35 W
Whitehead	248	54.46 N	5.43 W
White Horse, Vale of	242	51.37 N	1.37 W
Whitehorse Hill	242	51.34 N	1.34 W
Whitehouse	246	57.13 N	2.37 W
Whiten Head	246	58.34 N	4.36 W
Whitford Point	242	51.38 N	4.14 W
Whithorn	244	54.44 N	4.25 W
Whiting Bay	244	55.29 N	5.06 W
Whitland	242	51.50 N	4.37 W
Whitley Bay	244	55.03 N	1.25 W
Whitstable	242	51.22 N	1.02 E
Whittingham	244	55.24 N	1.54 W
Whittington	242	52.52 N	3.00 W
Whittlesey	242	52.34 N	0.08 W
Whitwick	242	52.44 N	1.21 W
Whitworth	244	53.40 N	2.10 W
Wiay	246	57.23 N	7.13 W
Wick	246	58.26 N	3.06 W
Wick	246	58.27 N	3.05 W
Wickford	242	51.38 N	0.31 E
Wickham	242	50.54 N	1.10 W
Wickham Market	242	52.09 N	1.22 E
Wicklow	248	52.59 N	6.03 W
Wicklow	248	53.00 N	6.30 W
Wicklow Head	248	52.58 N	6.00 W
Wicklow Mountains	248	53.02 N	6.24 W
Widecombe in the Moor	242	50.35 N	3.48 W
Widemouth Bay	242	50.47 N	4.32 W
Widnes	244	53.22 N	2.44 W
Wigan	244	53.33 N	2.38 W
Wigglesworth	244	54.01 N	2.17 W
Wight, Isle of	242	50.40 N	1.20 W
Wigmore	242	52.19 N	2.51 W
Wigston Magna	242	52.36 N	1.05 W
Wigton	244	54.49 N	3.09 W
Wigtown	244	54.52 N	4.26 W
Wigtown Bay	244	54.46 N	4.15 W
Wilkhaven	246	57.52 N	3.45 W
Willenhall	242	52.36 N	2.02 W
Willerby	244	53.46 N	0.27 W
Willingdon	242	50.47 N	0.15 E
Willingham	242	52.19 N	0.04 E
Willington	244	54.43 N	1.41 W
Williton	242	51.10 N	3.20 W
Willow Brook	242	52.32 N	0.24 W
Wilmslow	244	53.20 N	2.15 W
Wilshamstead	242	52.05 N	0.27 W
Wilton	242	51.05 N	1.52 W
Wiltshire	242	51.15 N	1.50 W
Wimborne Minster	242	50.48 N	1.59 W
Wincanton	242	51.04 N	2.25 W
Winchcombe	242	51.57 N	1.58 W
Winchelsea	242	50.55 N	0.42 E
Winchester	242	51.04 N	1.19 W
Winchester Cathedral	242	51.04 N	1.19 W
Windermere	244	54.23 N	2.54 W
Windermere	244	54.22 N	2.56 W
Windrush	242	51.42 N	1.25 W
Windsor	242	51.29 N	0.38 W
Windsor Castle	242	51.29 N	0.36 W
Windsor Forest	242	51.27 N	0.43 W
Wingham	242	51.17 N	1.13 E
Winsford, Eng., U.K.	242	51.06 N	3.33 W
Winsford, Eng., U.K.	244	53.12 N	2.32 W
Winshill	242	52.48 N	1.36 W
Winslow	242	51.57 N	0.54 W
Winterbourne Abbas	242	50.43 N	2.34 W
Winterton-on-Sea	242	52.43 N	1.42 E
Wisbech	242	52.40 N	0.10 E
Wishaw	246	55.47 N	3.56 W
Wissey	242	52.33 N	0.21 E
Witham	242	51.48 N	0.38 E
Witham	244	53.06 N	0.13 W
Witheridge	242	50.55 N	3.42 W
Withernsea	244	53.44 N	0.02 E
Witley	242	51.09 N	0.38 W
Witney	242	51.48 N	1.29 W
Wiveliscombe	242	51.03 N	3.19 W
Wivenhoe	242	51.52 N	0.58 E
Wnion	242	52.45 N	3.54 W
Woburn Sands	242	52.01 N	0.39 W
Woking	242	51.20 N	0.34 W
Wokingham	242	51.25 N	0.51 W
Wolf's Castle	242	51.54 N	4.58 W
Wolsingham	244	54.44 N	1.52 W
Wolverhampton	242	52.36 N	2.08 W
Wolverton	242	52.04 N	0.50 W
Wombwell	244	53.31 N	1.24 W
Woodbridge	242	52.06 N	1.19 E
Woodbury	242	50.41 N	3.24 W
Woodchurch	242	51.05 N	0.46 E
Woodford	248	53.03 N	8.23 W
Woodford Halse	242	52.10 N	1.12 W
Woodley	242	51.28 N	0.54 W
Woodmansey	244	53.50 N	0.29 W
Woodplumpton	244	53.48 N	2.47 W
Woodstock	242	51.52 N	1.21 W
Wool	242	50.41 N	2.14 W
Woolacombe	242	51.10 N	4.13 W
Wooler	244	55.33 N	2.01 W
Woolpit	242	52.13 N	0.54 E
Wootton Bassett	242	51.33 N	1.54 W
Wootton Wawen	242	52.16 N	1.47 W
Worcester	242	52.11 N	2.13 W
Workington	244	54.39 N	3.35 W
Worksop	244	53.18 N	1.07 W
Wormit	246	56.25 N	2.59 W
Worms Head	242	51.34 N	4.20 W
Worthen	242	52.38 N	3.00 W
Worthing	242	50.48 N	0.23 W
Wotton-under-Edge	242	51.39 N	2.21 W
Wragby	244	53.18 N	0.19 W
Wrath, Cape	246	58.37 N	5.01 W
Wrentham	242	52.23 N	1.40 E
Wrexham	244	53.03 N	3.00 W
Writtle	242	51.44 N	0.26 E
Wrotham	242	51.19 N	0.19 E
Wroughton	242	51.31 N	1.46 W
Wroxham	242	52.42 N	1.24 E
Wye	242	51.11 N	0.56 E
Wye, Eng., U.K.	242	51.37 N	2.39 W
Wye, Eng., U.K.	244	53.12 N	1.37 W
Wyke Regis	242	50.36 N	2.29 W
Wylye	242	51.04 N	1.52 W
Wymondham	242	52.34 N	1.07 E
Wyre	244	53.55 N	3.00 W
Wyre Forest	242	52.23 N	2.23 W
Wyvis, Ben	246	57.42 N	4.35 W

Y

Name	Page	Lat °'	Long °'
Yarcombe	242	50.52 N	3.05 W
Yare	242	52.35 N	1.44 E
Yarmouth, Eng., U.K.	242	50.42 N	1.29 W
Yarmouth → Great Yarmouth, Eng., U.K.	242	52.37 N	1.44 E
Yarrow	246	55.32 N	3.01 W
Yarty	242	50.47 N	3.01 W
Yate	242	51.32 N	2.25 W
Yatton	242	51.24 N	2.49 W
Yaxley	242	52.31 N	0.16 W
Yeadon	244	53.52 N	1.41 W
Yealm	242	50.18 N	4.03 W
Yealmpton	242	50.21 N	3.59 W
Yell	246a	60.36 N	1.06 W
Yell Sound	246a	60.32 N	1.15 W
Yelverton	242	50.30 N	4.05 W
Yeo	242	51.02 N	2.49 W
Yeovil	242	50.57 N	2.39 W
Yes Tor	242	50.42 N	4.00 W
Yetminster	242	50.53 N	2.33 W
York	244	53.58 N	1.05 W
York, Vale of	244	54.10 N	1.20 W
York Minster	244	53.57 N	1.04 W
Yorkshire Dales National Park	244	54.13 N	2.10 W
Yorkshire Wolds	244	54.00 N	0.40 W
Youghal	248	51.51 N	7.50 W
Youghal Bay	248	51.52 N	7.50 W
Ysbyty Ystwyth	242	52.20 N	3.48 W
Yscir	242	51.57 N	3.27 W
Ystalyfera	242	51.47 N	3.47 W
Ystrad	244	53.13 N	3.20 W
Ystrad Aeron	242	52.11 N	4.11 W
Ystradfellte	242	51.48 N	3.34 W
Ystradgynlais	242	51.47 N	3.45 W
Ystwyth	242	52.24 N	4.05 W
Ythan	246	57.18 N	2.00 W

Z

Name	Page	Lat °'	Long °'
Zone Point	242	50.08 N	5.00 W

Symbols in the index entries are identified on page 250.

GEOGRAPHICAL INFORMATION AND INTERNATIONAL MAP INDEX

A·2–A·7	WORLD INFORMATION TABLE
A·8–A·10	WORLD GEOGRAPHICAL TABLES
A·11	MAJOR METROPOLITAN AREAS OF THE WORLD
A·12–A·13	POPULATIONS OF MAJOR CITIES
A·14–A·15	SOURCES
A·16	TRANSLITERATION SYSTEMS
A·17–A·24	GEOGRAPHICAL GLOSSARY
A·25–A·144	INTERNATIONAL MAP INDEX

World Nations

This table gives the area, population, population density, form of government, capital and location of every country in the world.

Area figures include inland water.

The populations are estimates made by Rand McNally and Company on the basis of official data, United Nations estimates and other available information.

Besides specifying the form of government for all political areas, the table classifies them into five groups according to their political status. Units labeled A are independent sovereign nations. (Several of these are designated as members of the British Commonwealth of Nations.) Units labeled B are independent as regards internal affairs, but for purposes of foreign affairs they are under the protection of another country. Units labeled C are colonies, overseas territories, dependencies, etc. of other countries. Units labeled D are states, provinces or other major administrative subdivisions of important countries. Units in the table with no letter designation are regions, islands or other areas that do not constitute separate political units by themselves.

Map Plate numbers refer to the International Map section of the Atlas.

Country, Division, or Region English (Conventional)	Local Name	Area km²	Area sq mi	Population 1/1/82	Pop. Density per km²	Pop. Density per sq mi	Form of Government and Political Status	Capital	Continent and Map Plate
Afars and Issas, *see* Djibouti	. . .	. . .	. . .			. . .			. . . .
†AFGHANISTAN	Afghanistan	647,497	250,000	13,220,000	20	53	Socialist Republic	A Kābul	Asia 23
AFRICA	. . .	30,323,000	11,708,000	490,300,000	16	42			Africa . . . 30–31
Alabama, U.S.	Alabama	133,667	51,609	3,975,000	30	77	State (U.S.)	D Montgomery	N. Amer.. 44
Alaska, U.S.	Alaska	1,527,470	589,759	415,000	0.3	0.7	State (U.S.)	D Juneau	N. Amer.. 40
†ALBANIA	Shqiperia	28,748	11,100	2,820,000	98	254	Socialist Republic	A Tirana	Europe . . 15
Alberta, Can.	Alberta	661,185	255,285	2,190,000	3.3	8.6	Province (Canada)	D Edmonton	N. Amer.. 42
†ALGERIA	Al Jazā'ir	2,381,741	919,595	19,270,000	8.1	21	Socialist Republic	A Algiers (Al Jazā'ir)	Africa . . . 32
American Samoa (U.S.)	American Samoa	197	76	34,000	173	447	Unincorporated Territory (U.S.)	C Pago Pago	Oceania.. 65
Andaman and Nicobar Islands, India	Andaman and Nicobar	8,293	3,202	195,000	24	61	Territory of India	D Port Blair	Asia 25
ANDORRA	Andorra	453	175	40,000	88	229	Co-Principality (Spanish and French protection)	B Andorra la Vella	Europe . . 13
†ANGOLA	Angola	1,246,700	481,353	7,335,000	5.9	15	Socialist Republic	A Luanda	Africa . . . 36
ANGUILLA	Anguilla	90	34	7,900	90	232	Associated State (U.K.)	B The Valley	N. Amer.. 51
Anhwei, China	Anhui	139,859	54,000	49,055,000	351	908	Province (China)	D Hefei	Asia 28
ANTARCTICA	. . .	14,000,000	5,405,000	. . .(1)					Ant. 66
†ANTIGUA (incl. Barbuda)	Antigua	440	170	77,000	175	453	Parliamentary State (Comm. of Nations) .	A Saint John's	N. Amer.. 51
Arabian Peninsula	. . .	3,003,200	1,159,500	21,050,000	7.0	18			Asia 23
†ARGENTINA	Argentina	2,776,889	1,068,301	28,420,000	10	27	Federal Republic	A Buenos Aires	S. Amer.. 56
Arizona, U.S.	Arizona	295,024	113,909	2,795,000	9.5	25	State (U.S.)	D Phoenix	N. Amer.. 46
Arkansas, U.S.	Arkansas	137,539	53,104	2,335,000	17	44	State (U.S.)	D Little Rock	N. Amer.. 45
Armenian S.S.R., U.S.S.R.	Armjanskaja S.S.R.	29,800	11,506	3,115,000	105	271	Soviet Socialist Republic (U.S.S.R.)	D Jerevan	Asia 16
Aruba (Neth. Ant.)	Aruba	193	75	67,000	347	893	Division of Netherlands Antilles	Oranjestad	N. Amer.. 49
Ascension (U.K.)	Ascension	88	34	1,000	11	29	Dependency of St. Helena (U.K.)	C Georgetown	Africa . . 30–31
ASIA	. . .	44,798,000	17,297,000	2,724,900,000	61	158			Asia 21–22
†AUSTRALIA	Australia	7,686,850	2,967,909	14,910,000	1.9	5.0	Parliamentary State (Federal) (Comm. of Nations)	A Canberra	Oceania.. 59
Australian Capital Territory, Austl.	Australian Capital Territory	2,432	939	235,000	97	250	Territory (Australia)	D Canberra	Oceania.. 59
†AUSTRIA	Österreich	83,850	32,375	7,510,000	90	232	Federal Republic	A Vienna (Wien)	Europe . . 14
Azerbaidzhan S.S.R., U.S.S.R.	Azerbajdžanskaja S.S.R.	86,600	33,436	6,210,000	72	186	Soviet Socialist Republic (U.S.S.R.)	D Baku	Asia 16
Azores (Port.)	Açores	2,335	902	235,000	101	261	Part of Portugal (3 districts)		Africa . . . 32
†BAHAMAS	Bahamas	13,939	5,382	235,000	17	44	Parliamentary State (Comm. of Nations)	A Nassau	N. Amer.. 47
†BAHRAIN	Al Baḥrayn	662	256	400,000	604	1,563	Constitutional Monarchy	A Al Manāmah	Asia 24
Balearic Islands, Spain	Islas Baleares	5,014	1,936	730,000	146	377	Province of Spain (Baleares)	D Palma	Europe . . 13
Baltic Republics (U.S.S.R.)	. . .	174,000	67,182	7,555,000	43	112	Part of U.S.S.R. (3 republics)		Europe . . 8
†BANGLADESH	Bangladesh	143,998	55,598	91,860,000	638	1,652	Republic (Comm. of Nations)	A Dacca	Asia 25
†BARBADOS	Barbados	430	166	260,000	605	1,566	Parliamentary State (Comm. of Nations)	A Bridgetown	N. Amer.. 51
†BELGIUM	Belgique (French) Belgïe (Flemish)	30,513	11,781	9,880,000	324	839	Constitutional Monarchy	A Brussels (Bruxelles)	Europe . . 12
†BELIZE	Belize	22,963	8,866	160,000	7.0	18	Parliamentary State (Comm. of Nations) .	A Belmopan	N. Amer.. 49
Benelux	. . .	74,259	28,672	24,535,000	330	856	Economic Union		Europe . . 12
†BENIN	Bénin	112,622	43,484	3,715,000	33	85	Socialist Republic	A Porto-Novo	Africa . . . 34
Bermuda (U.K.)	Bermuda	53	21	69,000	1,302	3,286	Colony (U.K.)	C Hamilton	N. Amer.. 47
†BHUTAN	Druk	47,000	18,147	1,345,000	29	74	Monarchy (Indian protection)	B Thimphu	Asia 25
Bioko, Equat. Gui.	Bioko	2,034	785	94,000	46	120	Province of Equatorial Guinea	D Malabo	Africa . . . 34
†BOLIVIA	Bolivia	1,098,581	424,164	5,845,000	5.3	14	Republic	A Sucre and La Paz	S. Amer.. 54
Borneo, Indonesian	Kalimantan	539,460	208,287	6,815,000	13	33	Part of Indonesia (4 provinces)		Asia 26
†BOTSWANA	Botswana	600,372	231,805	875,000	1.5	3.8	Republic (Comm. of Nations)	A Gaborone	Africa . . . 37
†BRAZIL	Brasil	8,511,965	3,286,487	124,760,000	15	38	Federal Republic	A Brasília	S. Amer. . 54–56
British Columbia, Can.	British Columbia	948,596	366,255	2,725,000	2.9	7.4	Province (Canada)	D Victoria	N. Amer.. 42
British Honduras, *see* Belize	. . .	. . .	. . .	. . .		. . .			. . . .
British Indian Ocean Territory (U.K.)	British Indian Ocean Territory	60	23	. . .(1)	. . .	. . .	Colony (U.K.)	C	Africa . . . 22
British Solomon Islands, *see* Solomon Islands		. . .	. . .						
BRUNEI	Brunei	5,765	2,226	245,000	42	110	Constitutional Monarchy (U.K. protection)	B Bandar Seri Begawan	Asia 26
†BULGARIA	Balgarija	110,912	42,823	8,915,000	80	208	Socialist Republic	A Sofia (Sofija)	Europe . . 15
†BURMA	Burma	676,577	261,228	35,710,000	53	137	Socialist Republic	A Rangoon	Asia 25
†BURUNDI	Burundi	27,834	10,747	4,705,000	169	438	Republic	A Bujumbura	Africa . . . 36
†Byelorussian S.S.R., U.S.S.R.	Belorusskaja S.S.R.	207,600	80,155	9,755,000	47	122	Soviet Socialist Republic (U.S.S.R.)	D Minsk	Europe . . 16
California, U.S.	California	411,015	158,694	24,155,000	59	152	State (U.S.)	D Sacramento	N. Amer.. 46
Cambodia, *see* Kampuchea	. . .	. . .	. . .	. . .		. . .			. . . .
†CAMEROON	Cameroun	475,442	183,569	8,860,000	19	48	Republic	A Yaoundé	Africa . . . 34
†CANADA	Canada	9,922,330	3,831,033	24,335,000	2.5	6.4	Parliamentary State (Federal) (Comm. of Nations)	A Ottawa	N. Amer.. 42
Canary Islands (Sp.)	. . .	7,273	2,808	1,685,000	232	600	Part of Spain (2 provinces)		Africa . . . 32
†CAPE VERDE	Cabo Verde	4,033	1,557	330,000	82	212	Republic	A Praia	Africa . . . 32
Cayman Islands (U.K.)	Cayman Islands	259	100	18,000	69	180	Colony (U.K.)	C Georgetown	N. Amer.. 49
Celebes (Indonesia)	Sulawesi	189,216	73,057	10,755,000	57	147	Part of Indonesia (4 provinces)		Asia 26
†CENTRAL AFRICAN REPUBLIC	Centrafrique	622,984	240,535	2,300,000	3.7	9.6	Republic	A Bangui	Africa . . . 35
Central America	. . .	523,000	202,000	23,970,000	46	119			N. Amer.. 49
Central Asia, Soviet (U.S.S.R.)	. . .	1,277,100	493,090	26,495,000	21	54	Part of U.S.S.R. (4 republics)		Asia 19
Ceylon, *see* Sri Lanka	. . .	. . .	. . .	. . .		. . .			. . . .

Country, Division, or Region English (Conventional)	Local Name	Area km²	Area sq mi	Population 1/1/82	Population Density per km²	Population Density per sq mi	Form of Government and Political Status		Capital	Continent and Map Plate	
†CHAD	Tchad	1,284,000	495,755	4,675,000	3.6	9.4	Republic	A	N'djamena	Africa . . .	35
Channel Islands (U.K.)	Channel Islands	195	75	133,000	682	1,773				Europe . .	9
Chekiang, China	Zhejiang	101,787	39,300	38,115,000	374	970	Province (China)	D	Hangzhou	Asia	27
†CHILE	Chile	756,626	292,135	11,375,000	15	39	Republic	A	Santiago	S. Amer. .	56
†CHINA (excl. Taiwan)	Zhonghua Renmin Gongheguo	9,560,939	3,691,500	995,000,000	104	270	Socialist Republic	A	Peking (Beijing)	Asia	27
China (Nationalist), see Taiwan	. . .	. . .	. . .	. . .	. . .	. . .				. . . .	. . .
Christmas Island (Austl.)	Christmas Island	140	54	3,200	23	60	External Territory (Australia)	C	Flying Fish Cove	Oceania. .	26
Cocos (Keeling) Islands (Austl.)	Cocos (Keeling) Islands	14	5.4	400	29	74	External Territory (Australia)	C	. . .	Oceania. .	22
†COLOMBIA	Colombia	1,138,914	439,737	28,185,000	25	64	Republic	A	Bogotá	S. Amer. .	54
Colorado, U.S.	Colorado	270,000	104,248	2,960,000	11	28	State (U.S.)	D	Denver	N. Amer. .	45
Commonwealth of Nations	. . .	27,629,000	10,667,000	1,106,308,000	40	104	Political Union			. . . .	. . .
†COMOROS	Comores	2,171	838	380,000	175	453	Republic	A	Moroni	Africa . . .	37
†CONGO	Congo	342,000	132,047	1,595,000	4.7	12	Socialist Republic	A	Brazzaville	Africa . . .	36
Connecticut, U.S.	Connecticut	12,973	5,009	3,165,000	244	632	State (U.S.)	D	Hartford	N. Amer. .	44
†COOK ISLANDS	Cook Islands	236	91	18,000	76	198	Self-governing Territory (New Zealand protection)	B	Avarua	Oceania. .	61
Corsica (Fr.)	Corse	8,681	3,352	184,000	21	55	Part of France (2 departments)		. . .	Europe . .	11
†COSTA RICA	Costa Rica	51,100	19,730	2,340,000	46	119	Republic	A	San José	N. Amer. .	49
†CUBA	Cuba	114,524	44,218	9,805,000	86	222	Socialist Republic	A	Havana (La Habana)	N. Amer. .	49
Curaçao (Neth. Ant.)	Curaçao	444	171	170,000	383	994	Division of Netherlands Antilles	. . .	Willemstad	N. Amer. .	49
†CYPRUS	Kypros (Greek) Kıbrıs (Turkish)	9,251	3,572	650,000	70	182	Republic (Comm. of Nations)	A	Nicosia (Levkosia)	Asia	24
†CZECHOSLOVAKIA	Československo	127,877	49,374	15,345,000	120	311	Socialist Republic	A	Prague (Praha)	Europe . .	10
Dahomey, see Benin	. . .	. . .	. . .	. . .	. . .	. . .				. . . .	. . .
Delaware, U.S.	Delaware	5,328	2,057	600,000	113	292	State (U.S.)	D	Dover	N. Amer. .	44
†DENMARK	Danmark	43,080	16,633	5,150,000	120	310	Constitutional Monarchy	A	Copenhagen (København)	Europe . .	8
Denmark and Possessions	. . .	2,220,079	857,177	5,246,000	2.4	6.1			Copenhagen (København)	. . . .	. . .
District of Columbia, U.S.	District of Columbia	174	67	640,000	3,678	9,552	District (U.S.)	D	Washington	N. Amer. .	44
†DJIBOUTI	Djibouti	23,000	8,880	124,000	5.4	14	Republic	A	Djibouti	Africa . . .	35
†DOMINICA	Dominica	752	290	75,000	100	259	Republic (Comm. of Nations)	A	Roseau	N. Amer. .	51
†DOMINICAN REPUBLIC	República Dominicana	48,442	18,704	5,660,000	117	303	Republic	A	Santo Domingo	N. Amer. .	49
†ECUADOR	Ecuador	283,561	109,483	8,725,000	31	80	Republic	A	Quito	S. Amer. .	54
†EGYPT	Mişr	1,001,400	386,643	43,565,000	44	113	Socialist Republic	A	Cairo (Al Qāhirah)	Africa . . .	33
Ellice Islands, see Tuvalu	. . .	. . .	. . .	. . .	. . .	. . .				. . . .	. . .
†EL SALVADOR	El Salvador	21,041	8,124	5,270,000	250	649	Republic	A	San Salvador	N. Amer. .	49
England, U.K.	England	130,439	50,362	46,575,000	357	925	Administrative division of U.K.	D	London	Europe . .	9
†EQUATORIAL GUINEA	Guinea Ecuatorial	28,051	10,831	375,000	13	35	Republic	A	Malabo	Africa . . .	36
Estonian S.S.R., U.S.S.R.	Eest: N.S.V.	45,100	17,413	1,505,000	33	86	Soviet Socialist Republic (U.S.S.R.)	D	Tallinn	Europe . .	8
†ETHIOPIA	Itiopya	1,223,600	472,434	30,370,000	25	64	Monarchy.	A	Ādīs Ābeba	Africa . . .	35
Eurasia	. . .	54,730,000	21,132,000	3,291,300,000	60	156	. . . .		. . .		. . .
EUROPE	. . .	9,932,000	3,835,000	666,400,000	67	174				Europe . .	5–6
FAEROE ISLANDS	Føroyar (Faeroese) Færøerne (Danish)	1,399	540	45,000	32	83	Part of Danish Realm	B	Tórshavn	Europe . .	6
Falkland Islands (Islas Malvinas) (excl. Dependencies) (U.K.)[3]	Falkland Islands	12,173	4,700	1,900	0.2	0.4	Colony (U.K.)	C	Stanley	S. Amer. .	56
†FIJI	Fiji	18,272	7,055	645,000	35	91	Parliamentary State (Comm. of Nations)	A	Suva	Oceania. .	63
†FINLAND	Suomi (Finnish) Finland (Swedish)	337,032	130,129	4,805,000	14	37	Republic	A	Helsinki (Helsingfors)	Europe . .	7
Florida, U.S.	Florida	151,670	58,560	10,215,000	67	174	State (U.S.)	D	Tallahassee	N. Amer. .	44
†FRANCE	France	547,026	211,208	54,045,000	99	256	Republic	A	Paris	Europe . .	11
France and Possessions	. . .	675,114	260,661	55,618,000	82	213		. . . .	Paris	. . . .	. . .
Franklin (Can.)	Franklin	1,422,559	549,253	8,000	0.01	0.01	District of Northwest Territories (Canada)			N. Amer. .	42
French Guiana (Fr.)	Guyane Française	91,000	35,135	66,000	0.7	1.9	Overseas Department (France)	D	Cayenne	S. Amer. .	54
French Polynesia (Fr.)	Polynésie Française	4,000	1,544	150,000	38	97	Overseas Territory (France)	C	Papeete	Oceania. .	61
French West Indies	. . .	2,879	1,112	620,000	215	558				N. Amer. .	50
Fukien, China	Fujian	123,024	47,500	22,490,000	183	474	Province (China)	D	Fuzhou	Asia	27
†GABON	Gabon	267,667	103,347	560,000	2.1	5.4	Republic	A	Libreville	Africa . . .	36
Galapagos Islands, Ecuador	Archipiélago de Colón	7,964	3,075	6,100	0.8	2.0	Province of Ecuador (Galápagos)	D	Baquerizo Moreno	S. Amer. .	54
†GAMBIA	Gambia	11,295	4,361	625,000	55	143	Republic (Comm. of Nations)	A	Banjul	Africa . . .	34
Georgia, U.S.	Georgia	152,489	58,876	5,570,000	37	95	State (U.S.)	D	Atlanta	N. Amer. .	44
Georgian S.S.R., U.S.S.R.	Gruzinskaja S.S.R.	69,700	26,911	5,135,000	74	191	Soviet Socialist Republic (U.S.S.R.)	D	Tbilisi	Asia	16
†GERMAN DEMOCRATIC REPUBLIC	Deutsche Demokratische Republik	108,179	41,768	16,750,000	155	401	Socialist Republic	A	East Berlin (Ost-Berlin)	Europe . .	10
†GERMANY, FEDERAL REPUBLIC OF (incl. West Berlin)	Bundesrepublik Deutschland	248,650	96,004	61,680,000	248	642	Federal Republic	A	Bonn	Europe . .	10
Germany (Entire)	Deutschland	356,829	137,772	78,430,000	220	569				Europe . .	10
†GHANA	Ghana	238,537	92,100	11,730,000	49	127	Republic (Comm. of Nations)	A	Accra	Africa . . .	34
Gibraltar (U.K.)	Gibraltar	6.0	2.3	30,000	5,000	13,043	Colony (U.K.)	C	Gibraltar	Europe . .	13
Gilbert Islands, see Kiribati	. . .	. . .	. . .	. . .	. . .	. . .				. . . .	. . .
Great Britain, see United Kingdom	. . .	. . .	. . .	. . .	. . .	. . .				. . . .	. . .
†GREECE	Ellas	131,944	50,944	9,840,000	75	193	Republic	A	Athens (Athínai)	Europe . .	15
GREENLAND	Grønland (Danish) Kalaallit Nunaat (Eskimo)	2,175,600	840,003	51,000	0.02	0.06	Part of Danish Realm	B	Godthåb	N. Amer. .	41
†GRENADA	Grenada	344	133	112,000	326	842	Parliamentary State (Comm. of Nations)	A	Saint George's	N. Amer. .	51
Guadeloupe (incl. Dependencies) (Fr.)	Guadeloupe	1,779	687	320,000	180	466	Overseas Department (France)	D	Basse-Terre	N. Amer. .	51
Guam (U.S.)	Guam	549	212	110,000	200	519	Unincorporated Territory (U.S.)	C	Agana	Oceania. .	64
†GUATEMALA	Guatemala	108,889	42,042	7,375,000	68	175	Republic	A	Guatemala	N. Amer. .	49
Guernsey (incl. Dependencies) (U.K.)	Guernsey	77	30	55,000	714	1,833	Bailiwick (U.K.)	C	St. Peter Port	Europe . .	9
†GUINEA	Guinée	245,857	94,926	5,200,000	21	55	Republic	A	Conakry	Africa . . .	34
†GUINEA-BISSAU	Guiné-Bissau	36,125	13,948	820,000	23	59	Republic	A	Bissau	Africa . . .	34
†GUYANA	Guyana	214,969	83,000	925,000	4.3	11	Republic (Comm. of Nations)	A	Georgetown	S. Amer. .	54
†HAITI	Haïti	27,750	10,714	5,145,000	185	480	Republic	A	Port-au-Prince	N. Amer. .	49
Hawaii, U.S.	Hawaii	16,706	6,450	995,000	60	154	State (U.S.)	D	Honolulu	N. Amer. .	60
Heilungkiang, China	Heilongjiang	705,254	272,300	31,340,000	44	115	Province (China)	D	Harbin	Asia	27
Hispaniola	La Española	76,192	29,418	10,805,000	142	367				N. Amer. .	49
Holland, see Netherlands	. . .	. . .	. . .	. . .	. . .	. . .				. . . .	. . .

Country, Division, or Region English (Conventional)	Local Name	Area km²	Area sq mi	Population 1/1/82	Pop. Density per km²	Pop. Density per sq mi	Form of Government and Political Status		Capital	Continent and Map Plate	
Honan, China	Henan	166,795	64,400	71,840,000	431	1,116	Province (China)	D	Chengchow (Zhengzhou)	Asia	27
†HONDURAS	Honduras	112,088	43,277	3,880,000	35	90	Republic	A	Tegucigalpa	N. Amer.	49
Hong Kong (U.K.)	Hong Kong	1,061	410	5,375,000	5,066	13,110	Colony (U.K.)	C	Victoria	Asia	27
Hopeh, China	Hebei	192,954	74,500	59,925,000	311	804	Province (China)	D	Shijiazhuang	Asia	28
Hunan, China	Hunan	210,566	81,300	52,435,000	249	645	Province (China)	D	Changsha	Asia	27
†HUNGARY	Magyarország	93,036	35,921	10,715,000	115	298	Socialist Republic	A	Budapest	Europe	10
Hupeh, China	Hubei	187,515	72,400	46,665,000	249	645	Province (China)	D	Wuhan	Asia	27
†ICELAND	Ísland	103,000	39,769	230,000	2.2	5.8	Republic	A	Reykjavík	Europe	7
Idaho, U.S.	Idaho	216,413	83,557	975,000	4.5	12	State (U.S.)	D	Boise	N. Amer.	46
Illinois, U.S.	Illinois	150,028	57,926	11,650,000	78	201	State (U.S.)	D	Springfield	N. Amer.	45
†INDIA (incl. part of Jammu and Kashmir)	Bhārat	3,203,975	1,237,061	695,230,000	217	562	Federal Socialist Republic (Comm. of Nations)	A	New Delhi	Asia	25
Indiana, U.S.	Indiana	94,585	36,519	5,595,000	59	153	State (U.S.)	D	Indianapolis	N. Amer.	44
†INDONESIA	Indonesia	1,919,270	741,034	151,500,000	79	204	Republic	A	Jakarta	Asia	26
Inner Mongolia, China	Nei Mongol	424,499	163,900	8,555,000	20	52	Autonomous Region (China)	D	Hohhot	Asia	27
Iowa, U.S.	Iowa	145,791	56,290	2,980,000	20	53	State (U.S.)	D	Des Moines	N. Amer .	45
†IRAN	Īrān	1,648,000	636,296	38,565,000	23	61	Republic	A	Tehrān	Asia	23
†IRAQ	Al 'Irāq	434,924	167,925	13,465,000	31	80	Socialist Republic	A	Baghdād	Asia	24
†IRELAND	Eire	70,283	27,136	3,495,000	50	129	Republic	A	Dublin (Baile Átha Cliath)	Europe	9
ISLE OF MAN	Isle of Man	588	227	66,000	112	291	Self-governing Territory (U.K. protection)	B	Douglas	Europe	9
†ISRAEL	Yisra'el	20,325	7,848	3,980,000	196	507	Republic	A	Jerusalem (Yerushalayim)	Asia	24
Israeli Occupied Areas	. . .	7,000	2,703	1,235,000	176	457				Asia	24
†ITALY	Italia	301,262	116,318	57,270,000	190	492	Republic	A	Rome (Roma)	Europe	14
†IVORY COAST	Côte d'Ivoire	320,763	123,847	8,145,000	25	66	Republic	A	Abidjan	Africa	34
†JAMAICA	Jamaica	10,991	4,244	2,235,000	203	527	Parliamentary State (Comm. of Nations)	A	Kingston	N. Amer.	49
†JAPAN	Nippon	372,313	143,751	118,650,000	319	825	Constitutional Monarchy	A	Tōkyō	Asia	29
Java (incl. Madura) (Indon.)	Jawa	132,187	51,038	93,780,000	709	1,837	Part of Indonesia (5 provinces)			Asia	26
Jersey (U.K.)	Jersey	117	45	78,000	667	1,733	Bailiwick (U.K.)	C	St. Helier	Europe	9
†JORDAN	Al Urdun	91,000	35,135	2,300,000	25	65	Constitutional Monarchy	A	'Ammān	Asia	24
†KAMPUCHEA	Kampuchea Prăcheathipâtéyy	181,035	69,898	6,965,000	38	100	Socialist Republic	A	Phnum Pénh	Asia	26
Kansas, U.S.	Kansas	213,064	82,264	2,405,000	11	29	State (U.S.)	D	Topeka	N. Amer.	45
Kansu, China	Gansu	720,276	278,100	20,895,000	29	75	Province (China)	D	Lanzhou	Asia	27
Kashmir, Jammu and	Jammu and Kashmīr	222,802	86,024	9,920,000	45	115	In dispute (India and Pakistan)	. . .	Srīnagar and Jammu	Asia	25
Kazakh S.S.R., U.S.S.R.	Kazahskaja S.S.R.	2,717,300	1,049,155	15,105,000	5.6	14	Soviet Socialist Republic (U.S.S.R.)	D	Alma-Ata	Asia	19
Keewatin (Can.)	Keewatin	590,932	228,160	5,000	0.01	0.02	District of Northwest Territories (Canada)			N. Amer.	42
Kentucky, U.S.	Kentucky	104,623	40,395	3,745,000	36	93	State (U.S.)	D	Frankfort	N. Amer.	44
†KENYA	Kenya	582,646	224,961	17,790,000	31	79	Republic (Comm. of Nations)	A	Nairobi	Africa	36
Kerguelen Islands (Fr.)	Iles Kerguèlen	6,993	2,700	90	0.01	0.03	Part of French Southern and Antarctic Territory (France)	C	. . .	S. Amer.	30–31
Kiangsi, China	Jiangxi	164,723	63,600	28,260,000	172	444	Province (China)	D	Nanchang	Asia	27
Kiangsu, China	Jiangsu	92,981	35,900	67,105,000	722	1,869	Province (China)	D	Nanjing	Asia	28
Kirghiz S.S.R., U.S.S.R.	Kirgizskaja S.S.R.	198,500	76,641	3,655,000	18	48	Soviet Socialist Republic (U.S.S.R.)	D	Frunze	Asia	18
KIRIBATI	Kiribati	754	291	59,000	78	203	Republic (Comm. of Nations)	A	Bairiki	Oceania	60
Kirin, China	Jilin	271,690	104,900	22,385,000	82	213	Province (China)	D	Changchun	Asia	27
KOREA, NORTH	Chosŏn Minjujuŭi In'min Konghwaguk	120,538[4]	46,540[4]	18,540,000	154	398	Socialist Republic	A	P'yŏngyang	Asia	28
KOREA, SOUTH	Taehan-Min'guk	98,484[4]	38,025[4]	40,755,000	414	1,072	Republic	A	Seoul (Sŏul)	Asia	28
Korea (Entire)	Chosŏn	220,284	85,052	59,295,000	269	697				Asia	28
†KUWAIT	Al Kuwayt	17,818	6,880	1,480,000	83	215	Constitutional Monarchy	A	Al Kuwayt	Asia	24
Kwangsi, China	Guangxi	240,092	92,700	32,040,000	133	346	Province (China)	D	Nanning	Asia	27
Kwangtung, China	Guangdong	211,602	81,700	54,725,000	259	670	Province (China)	D	Canton (Guangzhou)	Asia	27
Kweichow, China	Guizhou	174,047	67,200	26,565,000	153	395	Province (China)	D	Guiyang	Asia	27
Labrador (Can.)	Labrador	292,218	112,826	35,000	0.1	0.3	Part of Newfoundland Province (Canada)			N. Amer.	42
†LAOS	Laos	236,800	91,429	3,850,000	16	42	Socialist Republic	A	Viangchan	Asia	26
Latin America	. . .	20,561,900	7,938,600	571,655,000	18	47				N.A., S.A.	52–53
Latvian S.S.R., U.S.S.R.	Latvijas P.S.R.	63,700	24,595	2,580,000	41	105	Soviet Socialist Republic (U.S.S.R.)	D	Rīga	Europe	8
†LEBANON	Lubnān	10,400	4,015	3,275,000	315	816	Republic	A	Beirut (Bayrūt)	Asia	24
†LESOTHO	Lesotho	30,355	11,720	1,385,000	46	118	Monarchy (Comm. of Nations)	A	Maseru	Africa	37
Liaoning, China	Liaoning	229,473	88,600	45,970,000	200	519	Province (China)	D	Mukden (Shenyang)	Asia	28
†LIBERIA	Liberia	111,369	43,000	1,975,000	18	46	Republic	A	Monrovia	Africa	34
†LIBYA	Lībiyā	1,759,540	679,362	3,155,000	1.8	4.6	Socialist Republic	A	Tripoli (Tarābulus)	Africa	33
LIECHTENSTEIN	Liechtenstein	169	62	27,000	169	435	Constitutional Monarchy	A	Vaduz	Europe	14
Lithuanian S.S.R., U.S.S.R.	Lietuvos T.S.R.	65,200	25,174	3,470,000	53	138	Soviet Socialist Republic (U.S.S.R.)	D	Vilnius	Europe	8
Louisiana, U.S.	Louisiana	125,675	48,523	4,300,000	34	89	State (U.S.)	D	Baton Rouge	N. Amer.	45
†LUXEMBOURG	Luxembourg	2,586	999	355,000	137	355	Constitutional Monarchy	A	Luxembourg	Europe	12
Macao (Port.)	Macau	16	6.0	275,000	17,188	45,833	Overseas Province (Portugal)	D	Macau	Asia	27
Macias Nguema Biyogo, see Bioko	. . .	. . .	. . .	. . .	. . .					. . .	
†Mackenzie (Can.)	Mackenzie	1,366,193	527,490	36,000	0.03	0.07	District of Northwest Territories (Canada)		. . .	N. Amer.	42
†MADAGASCAR	Madagasikara	587,041	226,658	9,085,000	15	40	Republic	A	Antananarivo	Africa	37
Madeira Islands, Port.	Arquipélago da Madeira	796	307	265,000	333	863	District of Portugal (Madeira)	D	Funchal	Africa	32
Maine, U.S.	Maine	86,027	33,215	1,115,000	13	34	State (U.S.)	D	Augusta	N. Amer.	44
Malagasy Republic, see Madagascar	. . .	. . .	. . .	. . .						. . .	
†MALAWI	Malawi	118,484	45,747	6,200,000	52	136	Republic (Comm. of Nations)	A	Lilongwe	Africa	36
Malaya	Malaya	131,312	50,700	12,235,000	93	241	Part of Malaysia (11 States)			Asia	26
†MALAYSIA	Malaysia	332,632	128,430	14,495,000	44	113	Constitutional Monarchy (Comm. of Nations)	A	Kuala Lumpur	Asia	26
†MALDIVES	Maldives	298	115	155,000	520	1,348	Republic	A	Male	Asia	25
†MALI	Mali	1,240,000	478,766	7,175,000	5.8	15	Republic	A	Bamako	Africa	34
†MALTA	Malta	316	122	360,000	1,139	2,951	Republic (Comm. of Nations)	A	Valletta	Europe	14
Manitoba, Can.	Manitoba	650,087	251,000	1,045,000	1.6	4.2	Province (Canada)	D	Winnipeg	N. Amer .	42
Maritime Provinces (excl. Newfoundland) (Can.)	Maritime Provinces	134,584	51,963	1,677,000	12	32	Part of Canada (3 provinces)			N. Amer.	42
Marshall Islands (T.T.P.I.)	Marshall Islands	181	70	31,000	171	443	Part of Trust Territory of the Pacific Islands (U.S. administration)	C	Uliga	Oceania	60

A • 4

Country, Division, or Region English (Conventional)	Local Name	Area km²	Area sq mi	Population 1/1/82	Pop. Density per km²	Pop. Density per sq mi	Form of Government and Political Status		Capital	Continent and Map Plate	
Martinique (Fr.)	Martinique	1,100	425	300,000	273	706	Overseas Department (France)	D	Fort-de-France	N. Amer. .	51
Maryland, U.S.	Maryland	27,394	10,577	4,300,000	157	407	State (U.S.)	D	Annapolis	N. Amer. .	44
Massachusetts, U.S.	Massachusetts	21,386	8,257	5,800,000	271	702	State (U.S.)	D	Boston	N. Amer. .	44
†MAURITANIA	Mūrītāniyā	1,030,700	397,955	1,730,000	1.7	4.3	Republic	A	Nouakchott	Africa . . .	32
†MAURITIUS (incl. Dependencies)	Mauritius	2,045	790	985,000	482	1,247	Parliamentary State (Comm. of Nations)	A	Port-Louis	Africa . . .	37
Mayotte (Fr.)	Mayotte	374	144	54,000	144	375	Overseas Department (France)	D	Dzaoudzi	Africa . . .	37
†MEXICO	México	1,972,547	761,604	70,515,000	36	93	Federal Republic	A	Mexico (Ciudad de México)	N. Amer. .	48
Michigan, U.S.	Michigan	250,687	96,791	9,455,000	38	98	State (U.S.)	D	Lansing	N. Amer. .	44
Micronesia, Federated States of (T.T.P.I.)	Federated States of Micronesia	694	268	71,000			Part of Trust Territory of the Pacific Islands (U.S. administration)	C	Ponape	Oceania. .	60
Middle America	. . .	2,703,900	1,055,600	123,855,000	46	117			. . .	N. Amer. .	47
Midway Islands (U.S.)	Midway Islands	5.2	2.0	1,500	288	750	Unincorporated Territory (U.S.)	C	. . .	Oceania. .	60
Minnesota, U.S.	Minnesota	223,465	86,280	4,160,000	19	48	State (U.S.)	D	St. Paul	N. Amer. .	45
Mississippi, U.S.	Mississippi	123,584	47,716	2,565,000	21	54	State (U.S.)	D	Jackson	N. Amer. .	45
Missouri, U.S.	Missouri	180,487	69,686	5,015,000	28	72	State (U.S.)	D	Jefferson City	N. Amer. .	45
Moldavian S.S.R., U.S.S.R.	Moldavskaja S.S.R.	33,700	13,012	4,030,000	120	310	Soviet Socialist Republic (U.S.S.R.)	D	Kišinev	Europe . .	16
MONACO	Monaco	1.5	0.6	27,000	18,000	45,000	Constitutional Monarchy	A	Monaco	Europe . .	11
†MONGOLIA	Mongol Ard Uls	1,565,000	604,250	1,750,000	1.1	2.9	Socialist Republic	A	Ulan-Bator	Asia	27
Montana, U.S.	Montana	381,087	147,138	810,000	2.1	5.5	State (U.S.)	D	Helena	N. Amer. .	46
Montserrat (U.K.)	Montserrat	103	40	12,000	117	300	Colony (U.K.)	C	Plymouth	N. Amer. .	51
†MOROCCO (excl. Western Sahara)	Al Maghrib	446,550	172,414	21,795,000	49	126	Constitutional Monarchy	A	Rabat	Africa . . .	32
†MOZAMBIQUE	Moçambique	783,030	302,329	12,385,000	16	41	Socialist Republic	A	Maputo	Africa . . .	37
Muscat and Oman, see Oman	. . .	. . .	. . .	. . .	. . .	. . .				. . . .	
Namibia (excl. Walvis Bay) (S. Afr.)(5)	Namibia	824,292	318,261	1,070,000	1.3	3.4	Under South African Administration	C	Windhoek	Africa . . .	37
NAURU	Nauru (English) Naoero (Nauruan)	21	8.2	7,900	376	963	Republic (Comm. of Nations)	A	Domaneab	Oceania. .	64
Nebraska, U.S.	Nebraska	200,018	77,227	1,595,000	8.0	21	State (U.S.)	D	Lincoln	N. Amer. .	45
†NEPAL	Nepal	140,797	54,362	15,520,000	110	285	Constitutional Monarchy	A	Kathmandu	Asia	25
†NETHERLANDS	Nederland	41,160	15,892	14,300,000	347	900	Constitutional Monarchy	A	Amsterdam	Europe . .	12
Netherlands Guiana, see Suriname	. . .	. . .	. . .	. . .	. . .	. . .				. . . .	
NETHERLANDS ANTILLES	Nederlandse Antillen	993	383	260,000	262	679	Self-governing Territory (Netherlands protection)	B	Willemstad	N. Amer. .	50
Nevada, U.S.	Nevada	286,299	110,541	855,000	3.0	7.7	State (U.S.)	D	Carson City	N. Amer. .	46
New Brunswick, Can.	New Brunswick	73,436	28,354	705,000	9.6	25	Province (Canada)	D	Fredericton	N. Amer. .	42
New Caledonia (incl. Dependencies) (Fr.)	Nouvelle-Calédonie	19,058	7,358	140,000	7.3	19	Overseas Territory (France)	C	Nouméa	Oceania. .	63
New England (U.S.)	New England	172,514	66,608	12,550,000	73	188	Part of U.S. (6 states)		. . .	N. Amer. .	43
Newfoundland, Can.	Newfoundland	404,517	156,185	585,000	1.4	3.7	Province (Canada)	D	St. John's	N. Amer. .	42
Newfoundland (excl. Labrador) (Can.)	Newfoundland	112,299	43,359	550,000	4.9	13	Part of Newfoundland Province, Canada		. . .	N. Amer. .	42
New Hampshire, U.S.	New Hampshire	24,097	9,304	950,000	39	102	State (U.S.)	D	Concord	N. Amer. .	44
New Hebrides, see Vanuatu	. . .	. . .	. . .	. . .	. . .	. . .				. . . .	
New Jersey, U.S.	New Jersey	20,295	7,836	7,515,000	370	959	State (U.S.)	D	Trenton	N. Amer. .	44
New Mexico, U.S.	New Mexico	315,115	121,667	1,350,000	4.3	11	State (U.S.)	D	Santa Fe	N. Amer. .	45
New South Wales, Austl.	New South Wales	801,428	309,433	5,245,000	6.5	17	State (Australia)	D	Sydney	Oceania. .	59
New York, U.S.	New York	137,795	53,203	17,680,000	128	332	State (U.S.)	D	Albany	N. Amer. .	44
†NEW ZEALAND	New Zealand	269,057	103,883	3,195,000	12	31	Parliamentary State (Comm. of Nations)	A	Wellington	Oceania. .	62
†NICARAGUA	Nicaragua	130,000	50,193	3,035,000	23	60	Republic	A	Managua	N. Amer. .	49
†NIGER	Niger	1,267,000	489,191	5,538,000	4.4	11	Republic	A	Niamey	Africa . . .	34
†NIGERIA	Nigeria	923,768	356,669	80,765,000	87	226	Federal Republic (Comm. of Nations)	A	Lagos	Africa . . .	34
Ningsia, China	Ningxia	66,304	25,600	2,985,000	45	117	Autonomous Region (China)	D	Yinchuan	Asia	27
NIUE	Niue	263	102	3,000	11	29	Self-governing Territory (New Zealand)	B	Alofi	Oceania. .	64
Norfolk Island (Austl.)	Norfolk Island	36	14	2,300	64	164	External Territory (Australia)	C	Kingston	Oceania. .	61
NORTH AMERICA	. . .	24,360,000	9,406,000	379,400,000	16	40			. . . .	N. Amer. .	38–39
North Borneo, see Sabah	. . .	. . .	. . .	. . .	. . .	. . .				. . . .	
North Carolina, U.S.	North Carolina	136,198	52,586	5,985,000	44	114	State (U.S.)	D	Raleigh	N. Amer. .	44
North Dakota, U.S.	North Dakota	183,022	70,665	670,000	3.7	9.5	State (U.S.)	D	Bismarck	N. Amer. .	45
Northern Ireland, U.K.	Northern Ireland	14,120	5,452	1,545,000	109	283	Administrative division of United Kingdom	D	Belfast	Europe . .	9
Northern Mariana Islands (T.T.P.I.)	Northern Mariana Islands	474	183	18,000	38	98	Part of Trust Territory of the Pacific Islands (U.S. administration)	C	Saipan (island)	Oceania. .	60
Northern Territory, Austl.	Northern Territory	1,375,519	520,280	125,000	0.09	0.2	Territory (Australia)	D	Darwin	Oceania. .	59
Northwest Territories, Can.	Northwest Territories	3,379,684	1,304,903	49,000	0.01	0.04	Territory (Canada)	D	Yellowknife	N. Amer. .	42
†NORWAY (incl. Svalbard and Jan Mayen)	Norge	386,317	149,158	4,115,000	13	33	Constitutional Monarchy	A	Oslo	Europe . .	7
Nova Scotia, Can.	Nova Scotia	55,491	21,425	850,000	15	40	Province (Canada)	D	Halifax	N. Amer. .	42
OCEANIA (incl. Australia)	. . .	8,513,000	3,287,000	23,200,000	2.7	7.1			. . .	Oceania. .	57–58
Ohio, U.S.	Ohio	115,719	44,679	11,025,000	95	247	State (U.S.)	D	Columbus	N. Amer. .	44
Oklahoma, U.S.	Oklahoma	181,090	69,919	3,100,000	17	44	State (U.S.)	D	Oklahoma City	N. Amer. .	45
†OMAN	'Umān	212,457	82,030	930,000	4.4	11	Monarchy	D	Muscat (Masqaṭ)	Asia	23
Ontario, Can.	Ontario	1,068,582	412,582	8,665,000	8.1	21	Province (Canada)	D	Toronto	N. Amer. .	42
Oregon, U.S.	Oregon	251,181	96,981	2,680,000	11	28	State (U.S.)	D	Salem	N. Amer. .	46
Orkney Islands (U.K.)	Orkney Islands	974	376	19,000	20	51	Part of Scotland, U.K. (Orkney Island Area)		. . . Kirkwall	Europe . .	9
†PAKISTAN (incl. part of Jammu and Kashmir)	Pākistān	828,453	319,867	92,070,000	111	288	Federal Republic	A	Islāmābād	Asia	25
Palau (T.T.P.I.)	Palau	461	178	14,000	. . .	. . .	Part of Trust Territory of the Pacific Islands (U.S. administration)	C	Koror	Oceania. .	60
†PANAMA	Panamá	77,082	29,762	1,910,000	25	64	Republic	A	Panamá	N. Amer. .	49
†PAPUA NEW GUINEA	Papua New Guinea	462,840	178,703	3,115,000	6.7	17	Parliamentary State (Comm. of Nations)	A	Port Moresby	Oceania. .	60
†PARAGUAY	Paraguay	406,752	157,048	3,205,000	7.9	20	Republic	A	Asunción	S. Amer. .	56
Peking, China	Beijing	17,094	6,600	8,000,000	468	1,212	Autonomous City (China)	D	Beijing	Asia	28
Pennsylvania, U.S.	Pennsylvania	119,316	46,068	11,995,000	101	260	State (U.S.)	D	Harrisburg	N. Amer. .	44

A • 5

Country, Division, or Region English (Conventional)	Local Name	Area km²	Area sq mi	Population 1/1/82	Population Density per km²	Population Density per sq mi	Form of Government and Political Status		Capital	Continent and Map Plate	
Persia, *see* Iran	. . .	. . .	. . .	. . .	. . .	. . .	. . .			. . . . . .	. .
†PERU	Peru	1,285,216	496,224	18,510,000	14	37	Republic	A	Lima	S. Amer. .	54
†PHILIPPINES	Pilipinas	300,000	115,831	50,960,000	170	440	Republic	A	Manila	Asia	26
Pitcairn (excl. Dependencies) (U.K.)	Pitcairn	4.7	1.8	65	14	36	Colony (U.K.)	C	Adamstown	Oceania. .	61
†POLAND	Polska	312,683	120,728	36,035,000	115	298	Socialist Republic	A	Warsaw (Warszawa)	Europe . .	10
†PORTUGAL	Portugal	88,940	34,340	10,050,000	113	293	Republic	A	Lisbon (Lisboa)	Europe . .	13
Portuguese Guinea, *see* Guinea-Bissau											
Prairie Provinces (Can.)	Prairie Provinces	1,963,172	757,985	4,235,000	2.2	5.6	Part of Canada (3 provinces)			N. Amer. .	42
Prince Edward Island, Can.	Prince Edward Island	5,657	2,184	122,000	22	56	Province (Canada)	D	Charlottetown	N. Amer. .	42
PUERTO RICO	Puerto Rico	8,897	3,435	3,270,000	368	952	Commonwealth (U.S. protection)	B	San Juan	N. Amer. .	51
†QATAR	Qaṭar	11,000	4,247	235,000	21	55	Monarchy.	A	Ad Dawḥah (Doha)	Asia	24
Quebec, Can.	Québec	1,540,680	594,860	6,375,000	4.1	11	Province (Canada)	D	Québec	N. Amer. .	42
Queensland, Austl.	Queensland	1,727,522	667,000	2,310,000	1.3	3.5	State (Australia).	D	Brisbane	Oceania. .	59
Reunion (Fr.)	Réunion	2,510	969	525,000	209	542	Overseas Department (France)	D	Saint-Denis	Africa . . .	37
Rhode Island, U.S.	Rhode Island	3,144	1,214	950,000	302	783	State (U.S.).	D	Providence	N. Amer. .	44
Rhodesia, *see* Zimbabwe	. . .	. . .	. . .	. . .	. . .	. . .	. . .			. . . . . .	. .
Rodrigues (Maur.)	Rodrigues	109	42	32,000	294	762	Part of Mauritius			Africa . . .	30–31
†ROMANIA	România	237,500	91,699	22,445,000	95	245	Socialist Republic	A	Bucharest (Bucureşti)	Europe . .	15
Russian Soviet Federated Socialist Republic, U.S.S.R.	Rossijskaja S.F.S.R.	17,075,400	6,592,846	140,580,000	8.2	21	Soviet Federated Socialist Republic (U.S.S.R.).	D	Moscow (Moskva)	Eur./Asia .	19–20
†RWANDA	Rwanda	26,338	10,169	5,175,000	196	509	Republic	A	Kigali	Africa . . .	36
Sabah, Malaysia	Sabah	76,115	29,388	915,000	12	31	State of Malaysia.	D	Kota Kinabalu	Asia	26
St. Christopher-Nevis	St. Christopher-Nevis	269	104	41,000	152	394	Associated State (U.K.)	B	Basseterre	N. Amer. .	51
St. Helena (incl. Dependencies) (U.K.)	St. Helena	419	162	6,600	16	41	Colony (U.K.)	C	Jamestown	Africa . . .	31
†SAINT LUCIA	Saint Lucia	616	238	124,000	201	521	Parliamentary State (Comm. of Nations)	A	Castries	N. Amer. .	51
St. Pierre and Miquelon (Fr.)	St.-Pierre et Miquelon	242	93	6,700	28	72	Overseas Department (France)	D	Saint-Pierre	N. Amer. .	42
†ST. VINCENT	St. Vincent	389	150	128,000	329	853	Parliamentary State (Comm. of Nations).	A	Kingstown	N. Amer. .	50
Samoa (entire)	Samoa Islands	3,039	1,173	189,000	62	161				Oceania. .	65
SAN MARINO	San Marino	61	24	24,000	393	1,000	Republic	A	San Marino	Europe . .	14
†SAO TOME AND PRINCIPE	São Tomé e Príncipe	964	372	89,000	92	239	Republic	A	São Tomé	Africa . . .	34
Sarawak, Malaysia	Sarawak	125,205	48,342	1,345,000	11	28	State of Malaysia.	D	Kuching	Asia	26
Sardinia	Sardegna	24,090	9,301	1,605,000	67	173	Part of Italy (Sardegna Autonomous Region).	D	Cagliari	Europe . .	14
Saskatchewan, Can.	Saskatchewan	651,900	251,700	1,000,000	1.5	4.0	Province (Canada)	D	Regina	N. Amer. .	42
†SAUDI ARABIA	Al 'Arabīyah as Sa'ūdīyah	2,149,690	830,000	8,755,000	4.1	11	Monarchy.	A	Riyadh (Ar Riyāḍ)	Asia	23
Scandinavia (incl. Finland and Iceland)	. . .	1,320,900	510,000	22,680,000	17	44				Europe . .	7
Scotland, U.K.	Scotland	78,775	30,416	5,135,000	65	169	Administrative division of U.K.	D	Edinburgh	Europe . .	9
†SENEGAL	Sénégal	196,722	75,955	5,880,000	30	77	Republic	A	Dakar	Africa . . .	34
Senegambia	Senegambia	208,067	80,316	6,505,000	31	81	Economic Union			Africa . . .	34
†SEYCHELLES	Seychelles	443	171	68,000	153	398	Republic (Comm. of Nations)	A	Victoria	Africa . . .	37
Shanghai, China	Shanghai	5,698	2,200	11,300,000	1,893	5,136	Autonomous City (China)	D	Shanghai	Asia	28
Shansi, China	Shanxi	157,212	60,700	24,575,000	156	405	Province (China)	D	Taiyuan	Asia	27
Shantung, China	Shandong	153,586	59,300	83,380,000	543	1,406	Province (China)	D	Jinan	Asia	28
Shensi, China	Shaanxi	195,803	75,600	29,650,000	151	392	Province (China)	D	Xi'an	Asia	27
Shetland Islands (U.K.)	Shetland Islands	1,427	551	24,000	17	44	Part of Scotland, U.K. (Shetland Island Area).	. . .	Lerwick	Europe . .	9
Siam, *see* Thailand	. . .	. . .	. . .	. . .	. . .	. . .				. . . . . .	. .
Sicily	Sicilia	25,708	9,926	5,040,000	196	508	Part of Italy (Sicilia Autonomous Region).	D	Palermo	Europe . .	14
†SIERRA LEONE	Sierra Leone	72,325	27,925	3,615,000	50	129	Republic (Comm. of Nations)	A	Freetown	Africa . . .	34
†SINGAPORE	Singapore (English) Singapura (Malay)	581	224	2,860,000	4,923	12,768	Republic (Comm. of Nations)	A	Singapore	Asia	26
Sinkiang, China	Xinjiang	1,646,714	635,800	9,550,000	5.8	15	Autonomous Region (China).	D	Ürümqi	Asia	27
†SOLOMON ISLANDS	Solomon Islands	29,800	11,500	235,000	7.9	20	Parliamentary State (Comm. of Nations).	A	Honiara	Oceania. .	63
†SOMALIA	Soomaaliya	637,657	246,200	5,100,000	8.0	21	Socialist Republic	A	Mogadishu (Muqdisho)	Africa . . .	35
†SOUTH AFRICA (incl. Walvis Bay)	South Africa (English) Suid-Afrika (Afrikaans)	1,221,042	471,447	30,495,000	25	65	Republic	A	Pretoria and Cape Town	Africa . . .	37
SOUTH AMERICA	. . .	17,828,000	6,883,000	247,800,000	14	36				S. Amer. .	52–53
South Australia, Austl.	South Australia	984,377	380,070	1,315,000	1.3	3.5	State (Australia).	D	Adelaide	Oceania. .	59
South Carolina, U.S.	South Carolina	80,432	31,055	3,190,000	40	103	State (U.S.).	D	Columbia	N. Amer. .	44
South Dakota, U.S.	South Dakota	199,552	77,047	695,000	3.5	9.0	State (U.S.).	D	Pierre	N. Amer. .	45
Southern Yemen, *see* Yemen, People's Democratic Republic of	. . .	. . .	. . .	. . .	. . .	. . .				. . . . . .	. .
South Georgia (incl. Dependencies) (U.K.)(3)	South Georgia	4,092	1,580	20	.005	0.01	Dependency of Falkland Islands (U.K.).	C	. . .	S. Amer. .	56
South West Africa, *see* Namibia	. . .	. . .	. . .	. . .	. . .	. . .				. . . . . .	. .
Soviet Union, *see* Union of Soviet Socialist Republics	. . .	. . .									
†SPAIN	España	504,741	194,882	37,865,000	75	194	Constitutional Monarchy	A	Madrid	Europe . .	13
Spanish North Africa (Sp.)(2)	Plazas de Soberanía en el Norte de África	32	12	127,000	3,969	10,583	Five Possessions (No Central Government)	C		Africa . . .	13
Spanish Sahara, *see* Western Sahara	. . .	. . .	. . .	. . .	. . .	. . .				. . . . . .	. .
†SRI LANKA	Sri Lanka	65,000	25,097	15,605,000	240	622	Socialist Republic (Comm. of Nations).	A	Colombo	Asia	25
†SUDAN	As Sūdān	2,505,813	967,500	20,180,000	8.1	21	Republic	A	Khartoum (Al Kharṭūm)	Africa . . .	35
Sumatra	Sumatera	473,606	182,860	23,785,000	50	130	Part of Indonesia (7 provinces).			Asia	26
†SURINAME	Suriname	163,265	63,037	365,000	2.2	5.8	Republic	A	Paramaribo	S. Amer. .	54
†SWAZILAND	Swaziland	17,364	6,704	580,000	33	87	Monarchy (Comm. of Nations)	A	Mbabane	Africa . . .	37
†SWEDEN	Sverige	450,089	173,780	8,335,000	19	48	Constitutional Monarchy	A	Stockholm	Europe . .	7
SWITZERLAND	Schweiz (German) Suisse (French) Svizzera (Italian)	41,293	15,943	6,315,000	153	396	Federal Republic	A	Bern (Berne)	Europe . .	14
†SYRIA	Sūrīyah	185,180	71,498	9,475,000	51	133	Socialist Republic	A	Damascus (Dimashq)	Asia	24
Szechwan, China	Sichuan	569,020	219,700	106,765,000	188	486	Province (China)	D	Chengdu	Asia	27
Tadzhik S.S.R., U.S.S.R.	Tadžikskaja S.S.R.	143,100	55,251	3,950,000	28	71	Soviet Socialist Republic (U.S.S.R.). . . .	D	Dušanbe	Asia	18

| Country, Division, or Region | | Area | | Population | Population Density per | | Form of Government | | | Continent |
English (Conventional)	Local Name	km²	sq mi	1/1/82	km²	sq mi	and Political Status		Capital	and Map Plate
TAIWAN	Taiwan	35,989	13,895	18,365,000	510	1,322	Republic	A	Taipei	Asia 27
†TANZANIA	Tanzania	945,087	364,900	19,115,000	20	52	Republic (Comm. of Nations)	A	Dodoma	Africa . . . 36
Tasmania, Austl.	Tasmania	68,332	26,383	430,000	6.3	16	State (Australia)	D	Hobart	Oceania . . 59
Tennessee, U.S.	Tennessee	109,412	42,244	4,690,000	43	111	State (U.S.)	D	Nashville	N. Amer. . 44
Texas, U.S.	Texas	692,405	267,339	14,520,000	21	54	State (U.S.)	D	Austin	N. Amer. . 45
†THAILAND	Muang Thai	513,113	198,114	48,860,000	95	247	Constitutional Monarchy	A	Bangkok (Krung Thep)	Asia 26
Tibet, China	Xizang	1,221,697	471,700	1,690,000	1.4	3.6	Autonomous Region (China)	D	Lhasa	Asia 27
Tientsin, China	Tianjin	4,144	1,600	7,000,000	1,689	4,375	Autonomous City (China)	D	Tianjin	Asia 28
†TOGO	Togo	56,785	21,925	2,730,000	48	125	Republic	A	Lomé	Africa . . . 34
Tokelau (N.Z.)	Tokelau	10	3.9	1,600	160	410	Island Territory (New Zealand)	C	. . .	Oceania . . 61
TONGA	Tonga	699	270	101,000	144	374	Constitutional Monarchy (Comm. of Nations)	A	Nuku'alofa	Oceania . . 61
Transcaucasia (U.S.S.R.)	. . .	186,100	71,853	14,460,000	78	201	Part of U.S.S.R. (3 republics)		. . .	Asia 16
†TRINIDAD AND TOBAGO	Trinidad and Tobago	5,128	1,980	1,165,000	227	588	Republic (Comm. of Nations)	A	Port of Spain	N. Amer. . 50
Tristan da Cunha (U.K.)	Tristan da Cunha	104	40	300	2.9	7.5	Dependency of St. Helena (U.K.)	C	Edinburgh	Africa . . . 30–31
Trucial States, see United Arab Emirates		. . .	. . .	. . .		. . .				. . . .
Trust Territory of the Pacific Islands	Trust Territory of the Pacific Islands	1,810	699	140,000	77	200	U.N. Trusteeship administered by U.S. . . .	C	Saipan (island)	Oceania . . 60
Tsinghai, China	Qinghai	721,053	278,400	3,880,000	5.4	14	Province (China)	D	Xining	Asia 27
†TUNISIA	Tūnis	163,610	63,170	6,585,000	40	104	Republic	A	Tūnis	Africa . . . 32
†TURKEY	Türkiye	779,452	300,948	46,435,000	60	154	Republic	A	Ankara	Eur./As.. . 24
Turkey in Europe	. . .	23,764	9,175	4,005,000	169	437	Part of Turkey.		. . .	Europe . . 24
Turkmen S.S.R., U.S.S.R.	Turkmenskaja S.S.R.	488,100	188,456	2,875,000	5.9	15	Soviet Socialist Republic (U.S.S.R.)	D	Ašhabad	Asia 19
Turks and Caicos Islands (U.K.)	Turks and Caicos Islands	430	166	7,700	18	46	Colony (U.K.)	C	Grand Turk	N. Amer. . 49
TUVALU	Tuvalu	26	10	8,100	312	810	Parliamentary State (Comm. of Nations).	A	Funafuti	Oceania . . 60
†UGANDA	Uganda	236,036	91,134	13,440,000	57	147	Republic (Comm. of Nations)	A	Kampala	Africa . . . 36
†Ukrainian S.S.R., U.S.S.R.	Ukrainskaja S.S.R.	603,700	233,090	50,760,000	84	218	Soviet Socialist Republic (U.S.S.R)	D	Kiev (Kijev)	Europe . . 16
†UNION OF SOVIET SOCIALIST REPUBLICS	Sojuz Sovetskih Socialističeskih Respublik	22,274,900	8,600,383	268,740,000	12	31	Federal Socialist Republic	A	Moscow (Moskva)	Eur./Asia . 19–20
U.S.S.R. in Europe	. . .	4,974,818	1,920,789	174,790,000	35	91	Part of U.S.S.R..		. . .	Europe . . 19
†UNITED ARAB EMIRATES	Al Imārāt al 'Arabīyah al Muttahidah	83,600	32,278	1,050,000	13	33	Federation of Monarchs.	A	Abū Ẓaby	Asia 23
United Arab Republic, see Egypt	. . .	. . .	. . .	. . .		. . .			. . .	. . . .
†UNITED KINGDOM	United Kingdom	244,102	94,249	56,035,000	230	595	Constitutional Monarchy (Comm. of Nations)	A	London	Europe . . 9
United Kingdom and Possessions	. . .	294,415	113,676	62,049,000	211	546	. . . .		London	. . . .
†UNITED STATES	United States	9,528,318	3,678,896	231,160,000	24	63	Federal Republic	A	Washington, D.C.	N. Amer. . 43
United States and Possessions	. . .	9,540,129	3,683,456	234,817,000	25	64	. . . .		Washington	. . . .
†UPPER VOLTA	Haute-Volta	274,200	105,869	7,180,000	26	68	Republic	A	Ouagadougou	Africa . . . 34
†URUGUAY	Uruguay	176,215	68,037	2,930,000	17	43	Republic	A	Montevideo	S. Amer. . 55
Utah, U.S.	Utah	219,932	84,916	1,510,000	6.9	18	State (U.S.)	D	Salt Lake City	N. Amer. . 46
Uzbek S.S.R., U.S.S.R.	Uzbekskaja S.S.R.	447,400	172,742	16,015,000	36	93	Soviet Socialist Republic (U.S.S.R.)	D	Taškent	Asia 19
†VANUATU	Vanuatu	14,800	5,714	120,000	8.1	21	Parliamentary State (Comm. of Nations).	A	Port-Vila	Oceania . . 63
VATICAN CITY	Città del Vaticano	0.4	0.2	1,000	2,500	5,000	Ecclesiastical State.	A	Vatican City (Città del Vaticano)	Europe . . 14
†VENEZUELA	Venezuela	912,050	352,144	14,515,000	16	41	Federal Republic	A	Caracas	S. Amer. . 54
Vermont, U.S.	Vermont	24,887	9,609	530,000	21	55	State (U.S.)	D	Montpelier	N. Amer. . 44
Victoria, Austl.	Victoria	227,619	87,884	3,955,000	17	45	State (Australia).	D	Melbourne	Oceania . . 59
†VIETNAM	Viet-nam Dan-chu Cong-hoa	329,556	127,242	55,455,000	168	436	Socialist Republic	A	Hanoi	Asia 26
Virginia, U.S.	Virginia	105,716	40,817	5,455,000	52	134	State (U.S.)	D	Richmond	N. Amer. . 44
Virgin Islands (U.S.)	Virgin Islands	344	133	101,000	294	759	Unincorporated Territory (U.S.)	C	Charlotte Amalie	N. Amer. . 51
Virgin Islands, British (U.K.)	British Virgin Islands	153	59	11,000	72	186	Colony (U.K.)	C	Road Town	N. Amer. . 51
Wake Island (U.S.)	Wake Island	7.8	3.0	200	26	67	Unincorporated Territory (U.S.)	C	. . .	Oceania . . 60
Wales, U.K.	Wales	20,768	8,019	2,780,000	134	347	Administrative division of U.K.	D	Cardiff	Europe . . 9
Wallis and Futuna (Fr.)	Iles Wallis-et-Futuna	255	98	11,000	43	112	Overseas Territory (France)	C	Mata-Utu	Oceania . . 61
Washington, U.S.	Washington	176,617	68,192	4,205,000	24	62	State (U.S.)	D	Olympia	N. Amer. . 46
Western Australia, Austl.	Western Australia	2,527,621	975,920	1,295,000	0.5	1.3	State (Australia).	D	Perth	Oceania . . 59
Western Sahara	. . .	266,000	102,703	120,000	0.5	1.2	Occupied by Morocco.	C	El Aaiún	Africa . . . 32
†WESTERN SAMOA	Samoa i Sisifo	2,842	1,097	155,000	55	141	Constitutional Monarchy (Comm. of Nations)	A	Apia	Oceania . . 65
West Indies	West Indies (English) Indias Occidentales (Spanish)	238,200	92,000	29,370,000	123	319	. . . .		. . .	N. Amer. . 47
West Virginia, U.S.	West Virginia	62,629	24,181	1,990,000	32	82	State (U.S.)	D	Charleston	N. Amer. . 44
White Russia, see Byelorussian S.S.R.	. . .	. . .	. . .	. . .		. . .				. . . .
Wisconsin, U.S.	Wisconsin	171,499	66,216	4,810,000	28	73	State (U.S.)	D	Madison	N. Amer. . 45
Wyoming, U.S.	Wyoming	253,597	97,914	485,000	1.9	5.0	State (U.S.)	D	Cheyenne	N. Amer. . 46
†YEMEN	Al Yaman	195,000	75,290	6,140,000	31	82	Republic	A	Şan'ā'	Asia 23
†YEMEN, PEOPLE'S DEMOCRATIC REPUBLIC OF	Al Yaman ad Dīmuqrāţīyah	332,968	128,560	2,060,000	6.2	16	Socialist Republic	A	Aden (Baladiyat 'Adan)	Asia 23
†YUGOSLAVIA	Jugoslavija	255,804	98,766	22,635,000	88	229	Federal Socialist Republic	A	Belgrade (Beograd)	Europe . . 14–15
Yukon Territory, Can.	Yukon Territory	482,515	186,300	24,000	0.05	0.1	Territory (Canada)	D	Whitehorse	N. Amer. . 42
Yunnan, China	Yunnan	436,154	168,400	27,860,000	64	165	Province (China)	D	Kunming	Asia 27
†ZAIRE	Zaïre	2,345,409	905,567	29,060,000	12	32	Republic	A	Kinshasa (Léopoldville)	Africa . . . 36
†ZAMBIA	Zambia	752,614	290,586	5,905,000	7.8	20	Republic (Comm. of Nations)	A	Lusaka	Africa . . . 36
Zanzibar	Zanzibar	2,461	950	520,000	211	547	Part of Tanzania	D	Zanzibar	Africa . . . 36
†ZIMBABWE	Zimbabwe	390,580	150,804	7,700,000	20	51	Republic (Comm. of Nations)	A	Harare	Africa . . . 37
WORLD	. . .	149,754,000	57,821,000	4,532,000,000	30	78	. . . .		. . . .	 1–2

† Member of the United Nations (1981).
. . .None, or not applicable.
[1] No permanent population.
[2] Comprises Ceuta, Melilla, and several small islands.
[3] Claimed by Argentina.
[4] The 1,262 km² or 487 sq mi of the demilitarized zone are not included in either North or South Korea.
[5] In October 1966 the United Nations terminated the South African mandate over Namibia, a decision which South Africa did not accept.

World Geographical Tables

The Earth: Land and Water

	Total Area		Area of Land			Area of Oceans and Seas		
	km²	sq mi	km²	sq mi	%	km²	sq mi	%
Earth	510,100,000	197,000,000	149,400,000	57,700,000	29.3	360,700,000	139,300,000	70.7
N. Hemisphere	255,050,000	98,500,000	106,045,650	40,950,000	41.6	149,004,350	57,550,000	58.4
S. Hemisphere	255,050,000	98,500,000	43,354,350	16,750,000	17.0	211,695,650	81,750,000	83.0

The Continents

Continent	Area km² sq mi	Population Estimate (1/1/82)	Population per km² sq mi	Mean Elevation m ft *	Highest Elevation m/ft	Lowest Elevation m/ft (below sea level)	Highest Recorded Temperature °C/°F	Lowest Recorded Temperature °C/°F
Europe	9,932,000 3,835,000	666,400,000	67 174	340 1,000	Mt. Elbrus, U.S.S.R. 5,642/18,510	Caspian Sea, U.S.S.R.-Iran −28/−92	Sevilla, Spain 50°/122°	Ust-Ščugor, U.S.S.R. −55°/−67°
Asia	44,798,000 17,297,000	2,724,900,000	61 158	960 3,150	Mt. Everest, China-Nepal 8,848/29,029	Dead Sea, Israel-Jordan −395/−1,296	Tirat Zevi, Israel 54°/129°	Ojmjakon, U.S.S.R.; Verkhoyansk U.S.S.R. −68°/−90°
Africa	30,323,000 11,708,000	490,300,000	16 42	750 2,450	Kilimanjaro, Tanzania 5,895/19,341	Lac Assal, Djibouti −155/−509	Al 'Azīzīyah, Libya 58°/136°	Ifrane, Morocco −24°/−11°
North America	24,360,000 9,406,000	379,400,000	16 40	720 2,350	Mt. McKinley, United States 6,194/20,320	Death Valley, United States −86/−282	Death Valley, United States 57°/134°	Northice, Greenland −66°/−87°
South America	17,828,000 6,883,000	247,800,000	14 36	590 1,940	Aconcagua, Argentina 6,960/22,835	Salinas Chicas, Argentina −42/−138	Rivadavia, Argentina 49°/120°	Sarmiento, Argentina −33°/−27°
Oceania, incl. Australia	8,513,000 3,287,000	23,200,000	3 7	....	Mt. Wilhelm, Papua N. Gui. 4,509/14,793	Lake Eyre, Australia −12/−39	Cloncurry, Australia 53°/128°	Charlotte Pass, Australia −22°/−8°
Australia	7,686,850 2,967,909	14,910,000	2 5	340 1,100	Mt. Kosciusko, Australia 2,228/7,310	Lake Eyre, Australia −12/−39	Cloncurry, Australia 53°/128°	Charlotte Pass, Australia −22°/−8°
Antarctica	14,000,000 5,405,000	....	... ...	2,600 8,550	Vinson Massif 5,140/16,864	unknown	Esperanza 14°/58°	Vostok −90°/−127°
World	149,754,000 57,821,000	4,532,000,000	30 78	840 2,750	Mt. Everest, China-Nepal 8,848/29,029	Dead Sea, Israel-Jordan −395/−1,296	Al 'Azīzīyah, Libya 58°/136°	Vostok −90°/−127°

All temperatures are rounded to the nearest degree. * Elevations in feet are converted from metric equivalents and rounded.

Principal Mountains

Mountain	Country	Height M	Ft
Europe			
Elbrus, Mount	U.S.S.R.	5,642	18,510
Dyhtau	U.S.S.R.	5,203	17,070
Blanc, Mont	△France-△Italy	4,810	15,781
Rosa, Monte	Italy-△Switzerland	4,633	15,200
Matterhorn	Italy-Switzerland	4,478	14,692
Jungfrau	Switzerland	4,158	13,642
Grossglockner	△Austria	3,797	12,457
Teide, Pico de	△Spain (Canary Is.)	3,718	12,198
Mulhacén	Spain	3,478	11,411
Aneto, Pico de	Spain	3,404	11,168
Etna, Mount	Italy	3,340	10,958
Corno Grande	Italy	2,914	9,560
Gerlachovský štít	△Czechoslovakia	2,655	8,711
Glittertind	△Norway	2,470	8,104
Narodnaja, gora	U.S.S.R.	1,894	6,214
Nevis, Ben	△United Kingdom	1,343	4,406
Snowdon	United Kingdom	1,085	3,560
Asia			
Everest, Mount	△China-△Nepal	8,848	29,029
K2 (Godwin Austen)	China-△Pakistan	8,611	28,251
Kānchenjunga	△India-Nepal	8,598	28,207
Dhaulagiri	Nepal	8,172	26,811
Annapurna	Nepal	8,078	26,503
Muztag	China	7,723	25,338
Tirich Mīr	Pakistan	7,690	25,230
Communism Peak (pik Kommunizma)	△U.S.S.R.	7,495	24,590
Pobeda Peak (pik Pobedy)	China-U.S.S.R.	7,439	24,406
Demavend, Mount (Qolleh-ye Damāvand)	△Iran	5,670	18,602
Ararat, Mount (Büyük Ağrı Dağı)	△Turkey	5,165	16,946
Jaya, Puncak	△Indonesia	5,030	16,503
Klyuchevskaya Sopka (vulkan Ključevskaja Sopka)	U.S.S.R.	4,750	15,584
Kinabalu, Gunong	△Malaysia	4,101	13,455
Yu Shan	△Taiwan	3,997	13,114
Kerinci, Gunong	Indonesia	3,800	12,467
Fuji-San	△Japan	3,776	12,388
Nabī Shu'ayb, Jabal an	△Yemen	3,760	12,336
Sauda, Qurnet es	△Lebanon	3,083	10,115
Shām, Jabal ash	△Oman	3,017	9,898
Apo, Mount	△Philippines	2,954	9,692
Hermon, Mount	Lebanon-△Syria	2,814	9,232
Mayon, Mount	Philippines	2,462	8,077

Mountain	Country	Height M	Ft
Africa			
Kilimanjaro	△Tanzania	5,895	19,341
Kirinyaga (Mount Kenya)	△Kenya	5,199	17,057
Margherita Peak (Ruwenzori Range)	△Uganda-△Zaire	5,119	16,795
Ras Dashen	△Ethiopia	4,620	15,157
Toubkal, Jebel	△Morocco	4,167	13,671
Cameroun, Mont	△Cameroon	4,070	13,353
North America			
McKinley, Mount	△U.S.	6,194	20,320
Logan, Mount	△Canada	6,050	19,849
Orizaba, Pico de (Volcán Citlaltépetl)	△Mexico	5,700	18,701
Popocatépetl, Volcán	Mexico	5,452	17,887
Whitney, Mount	U.S.	4,418	14,494
Elbert, Mount	U.S.	4,399	14,433
Rainier, Mount	U.S.	4,392	14,410
Shasta, Mount	U.S.	4,317	14,162
Pikes Peak	U.S.	4,301	14,410
Tajumulco, Volcán	△Guatemala	4,220	13,845
Kea, Mauna	U.S.	4,205	13,796
Grand Teton	U.S.	4,197	13,770
Waddington, Mount	Canada	3,994	13,104
Chirripó, Cerro	△Costa Rica	3,820	12,533
Hood, Mount	U.S.	3,426	11,239
Duarte, Pico	△Dominican Republic	3,175	10,417
Mitchell, Mount	U.S.	2,037	6,684
Clingmans Dome	U.S.	2,025	6,643
Washington, Mount	U.S.	1,917	6,288
South America			
Aconcagua, Cerro	△Argentina	6,960	22,835
Ojos del Salado, Nevado	Argentina-△Chile	6,863	22,516
Huascarán, Nevado	△Peru	6,768	22,205
Chimborazo, Volcán	△Ecuador	6,267	20,561
Cristóbal Colón, Pico	△Colombia	5,800	19,029
Bolívar, Pico	△Venezuela	5,007	16,427
Neblina, Pico da	△Brazil	3,014	9,888
Oceania			
Wilhelm, Mount	△Papua New Guinea	4,509	14,793
Cook, Mount	△New Zealand	3,764	12,349
Kosciusko, Mount	△Australia	2,228	7,310
Antarctica			
Vinson Massif	△Antarctica	5,140	16,864
Jackson, Mount	Antarctica	4,191	13,750

△Highest mountain in country.

Oceans, Seas, and Gulfs

Name	Area km²	Area sq mi	Greatest Depth m	Greatest Depth ft
Pacific Ocean	165,200,000	63,800,000	11,022	36,161
Atlantic Ocean	82,400,000	31,800,000	9,220	30,249
Indian Ocean	74,900,000	28,900,000	7,450	24,442
Arctic Ocean	14,000,000	5,400,000	5,450	17,881
Arabian Sea	3,863,000	1,492,000	5,800	19,029
South China Sea	3,447,000	1,331,000	5,560	18,241
Caribbean Sea	2,754,000	1,063,000	7,680	25,197
Mediterranean Sea	2,505,000	967,000	5,020	16,470
Bering Sea	2,270,000	876,000	4,191	13,750
Bengal, Bay of	2,172,000	839,000	5,258	17,251
Okhotsk, Sea of	1,580,000	610,000	3,372	11,063
Norwegian Sea	1,547,000	597,000	4,020	13,189
Mexico, Gulf of	1,544,000	596,000	4,380	14,370
Hudson Bay	1,230,000	475,000	259	850
Greenland Sea	1,205,000	465,000	4,846	15,899

Waterfalls

Waterfall	Country	River	Height m	Height ft
Angel	Venezuela	Churún	972	3,189
Tugela	South Africa	Tugela	948	3,110
Yosemite	United States	Yosemite Creek	739	2,425
Sutherland	New Zealand	Arthur	579	1,900
Gavarnie	France	Gave de Pau	421	1,381
Lofoi	Zaire	Lofoi	384	1,260
Krimml	Austria	Krimml	381	1,250
Takakkaw	Canada	Yoho	380	1,248
Staubbach	Switzerland	Staubbach	305	1,001
Mardalsfoss	Norway	. . .	297	974
Gersoppa	India	Sharavati	253	830
Kaieteur	Guyana	Potaro	247	810

Principal Rivers

River	Location	Length km	Length mi
Nile-Kagera	Africa	6,671	4,145
Yangtze (Chang Jiang)	China	6,300	3,915
Amazon-Ucayali	Brazil-Peru	6,280	3,902
Mississippi-Missouri-Red Rock	U.S.	6,019	3,741
Yellow (Huang He)	China	5,464	3,395
Ob-Irtysh	China-U.S.S.R.	5,410	3,362
Río de la Plata-Paraná	South America	4,700	2,920
Mekong	Asia	4,500	2,796
Paraná	South America	4,500	2,796
Amur	China-U.S.S.R.	4,416	2,744
Lena	U.S.S.R.	4,400	2,734
Mackenzie	Canada	4,241	2,635
Congo (Zaire)	Africa	4,200	2,610
Niger	Africa	4,160	2,585
Yenisey (Jenisej)	U.S.S.R.	4,092	2,543
Mississippi	U.S.	3,778	2,348
Missouri	U.S.	3,725	2,315
Ob	U.S.S.R.	3,680	2,287
Volga	U.S.S.R.	3,531	2,194
Murray-Darling	Australia	3,490	2,169
Madeira-Mamoré	Bolivia-Brazil	3,200	1,988
Purus	Brazil-Peru	3,200	1,988
Yukon	Canada-U.S.	3,185	1,979
Indus	Asia	3,180	1,976
Rio Grande	Mexico-U.S.	3,033	1,885
Syr Darya (Syrdarja)	U.S.S.R.	2,991	1,859
Brahmaputra	Asia	2,900	1,802
São Francisco	Brazil	2,900	1,802
Danube	Europe	2,860	1,777
Salween	Asia	2,849	1,770
Euphrates	Asia	2,760	1,715
Orinoco	Colombia-Venezuela	2,736	1,700
Darling	Australia	2,720	1,690
Ganges	Bangladesh-India	2,700	1,678
Saskatchewan	Canada	2,672	1,660
Zambezi	Africa	2,660	1,653
Tocantins	Brazil	2,640	1,640
Amu Darya (Amudarja)	Afghanistan-U.S.S.R.	2,600	1,616
Murray	Australia	2,589	1,609
Kolyma	U.S.S.R.	2,575	1,600
Paraguay	South America	2,549	1,584
Ural	U.S.S.R.	2,428	1,509
Arkansas	U.S.	2,333	1,450
Colorado	Mexico-U.S.	2,333	1,450
Irrawaddy	Burma	2,293	1,425
Dnepr	U.S.S.R.	2,201	1,368
Araguaia	Brazil	2,199	1,367
Kasai	Angola-Zaire	2,153	1,338
Tarim	China	2,137	1,328
Brazos	U.S.	2,106	1,309

Principal Islands

Island	Area km²	Area sq mi	Name	Highest Point m	Highest Point ft
Greenland (Grønland)	2,175,600	840,004	Gunnbjørns Fjeld	3,700	12,139
New Guinea	785,000	303,090	Puncak Jaya	5,030	16,503
Borneo	746,545	288,243	Gunong Kinabalu	4,101	13,455
Madagascar	587,041	226,658	Maromokotro	2,876	9,436
Baffin	476,065	183,810	unnamed	2,147	7,045
Sumatra (Sumatera)	473,606	182,860	Kerinci	3,800	12,467
Great Britain	227,581	87,870	Ben Nevis	1,343	4,406
Honshū	227,414	87,805	Fuji	3,776	12,388
Ellesmere	212,687	82,119	Barbeau Peak	2,604	8,543
Victoria	212,198	81,930	unnamed	655	2,150
Celebes (Sulawesi)	189,216	73,057	Rantekombola	3,455	11,335
South Island	150,461	58,093	Cook	3,764	12,349
Java (Jawa)	132,187	51,038	Semeru	3,676	12,060
North Island	114,728	44,297	Ruapehu	2,797	9,177
Cuba	114,524	44,218	Pico Turquino	1,994	6,542
Newfoundland	112,299	43,359	Lewis Hills	814	2,671
Luzon	104,687	40,420	Pulog	2,930	9,613
Iceland (Ísland)	103,000	39,769	Hvannadalshnúkur	2,119	6,952
Mindanao	94,630	36,537	Apo	2,954	9,692
Ireland	84,403	32,588	Carrantuohill	1,041	3,415
Hokkaidō	78,073	30,144	Daisetzu-Zan	2,290	7,513
Sakhalin (Sahalin)	76,400	29,498	Lopatina	1,609	5,279
Hispaniola	76,192	29,418	Pico Duarte	3,175	10,417
Banks	70,028	27,038	Durham	747	2,450
Tasmania	68,332	26,383	Ossa	1,617	5,305
Sri Lanka (Ceylon)	65,000	25,097	Pidurutalagala	2,524	8,281
Devon	55,247	21,331	Treuter	1,887	6,191
Novaya Zemlya (N. part)	48,904	18,882	unnamed	1,547	5,075
Tierra del Fuego	48,174	18,600	Yogan	2,469	8,100
Kyūshū	41,997	16,215	Kuju-San	1,787	5,863

Major Lakes

Lake	Country	Area km²	Area sq mi	Depth m	Depth ft
Caspian Sea	Iran-U.S.S.R	371,000	143,200	1,025	3,363
Superior	Canada-U.S.	82,414	31,820	406	1,333
Victoria	Africa	68,100	26,293	80	262
Aral Sea (Aral'skoje more)	U.S.S.R.	66,500	25,676	68	223
Huron	Canada-U.S.	59,596	23,010	229	750
Michigan	U.S.	58,016	22,400	281	923
Tanganyika	Africa	32,893	12,700	1,436	4,711
Baikal (ozero Bajkal)	U.S.S.R.	31,500	12,162	1,620	5,315
Great Bear	Canada	31,328	12,096	413	1,356
Nyasa	Africa	30,800	11,892	678	2,224
Great Slave	Canada	28,570	11,031	559	1,834
Erie	Canada-U.S.	25,745	9,940	64	210
Winnipeg	Canada	24,390	9,417	18	60
Ontario	Canada-U.S.	19,529	7,540	244	802
Ladoga (Ladožskoje ozero)	U.S.S.R.	18,400	7,104	225	738
Balkhash (ozero Balhaš)	U.S.S.R.	18,200	7,027	26	85
Chad (Lac Tchad)	Africa	16,300	6,293	4	13
Onega (Onežskoje ozero)	U.S.S.R.	9,610	3,710	120	393
Eyre	Australia	9,583	3,700	1	4
Rudolf	Ethiopia-Kenya	8,600	3,320	61	200
Nicaragua	Nicaragua	8,430	3,255	43	141
Titicaca	Bolivia-Peru	8,300	3,205	272	892
Athabasca	Canada	7,936	3,064	124	407
Gairdner	Australia	7,700	2,973	☆	☆
Reindeer	Canada	6,651	2,568	219	720
Issyk-Kul	U.S.S.R.	6,280	2,425	702	2,303
Urmia (Daryācheh-ye Orūmīyeh)	Iran	5,800	2,239	15	49
Torrens	Australia	5,776	2,230	☆	☆
Vänern	Sweden	5,585	2,156	100	328
Winnipegosis	Canada	5,374	2,075	12	38

☆Intermittently dry lake

Drainage Basins

Name	Continent	Area km²	Area sq mi
Amazon-Ucayali	South America	7,050,000	2,722,000
Congo (Zaire)	Africa	3,690,000	1,425,000
Mississippi-Missouri	North America	3,221,000	1,243,700
Río de la Plata-Paraná	South America	3,140,000	1,212,000
Ob	Asia	2,975,000	1,149,000
Nile	Africa	2,867,000	1,107,000
Yenisey (Jenisej)	Asia	2,580,000	996,000
Lena	Asia	2,490,000	961,000
Niger	Africa	2,092,000	808,000
Amur	Asia	1,855,000	716,000
Yangtze (Chang Jiang)	Asia	1,807,000	698,000
Mackenzie	North America	1,760,000	680,000
Saint Lawrence-Great Lakes	North America	1,463,000	565,000
Volga	Europe	1,360,000	525,000

World Geographical Tables

Historical Population of the World

AREA	1650	1750	1800	1850	1900	1914	1920	1939	1950	1982*
Europe	*100,000,000*	*140,000,000*	*190,000,000*	265,000,000	*400,000,000*	*470,000,000*	*453,000,000*	526,000,000	530,000,000	666,400,000
Asia	*335,000,000*	*476,000,000*	*593,000,000*	754,000,000	*932,000,000*	*1,006,000,000*	*1,000,000,000*	1,247,000,000	1,418,000,000	2,724,900,000
Africa	*100,000,000*	*95,000,000*	*90,000,000*	95,000,000	*118,000,000*	*130,000,000*	*140,000,000*	170,000,000	199,000,000	490,300,000
North America	*5,000,000*	*5,000,000*	*13,000,000*	39,000,000	*106,000,000*	*141,000,000*	*147,000,000*	186,000,000	219,000,000	379,400,000
South America	*8,000,000*	*7,000,000*	*12,000,000*	20,000,000	*38,000,000*	*55,000,000*	*61,000,000*	90,000,000	111,000,000	247,800,000
Oceania, incl. Australia	*2,000,000*	*2,000,000*	*2,000,000*	*2,000,000*	*6,000,000*	*8,000,000*	*9,000,000*	11,000,000	13,000,000	23,200,000
Australia					*4,000,000*	*5,000,000*	*6,000,000*	7,000,000	8,000,000	14,910,000
World	*550,000,000*	*725,000,000*	*900,000,000*	1,175,000,000	*1,600,000,000*	*1,810,000,000*	*1,810,000,000*	2,230,000,000	2,490,000,000	4,532,000,000

* Figures prior to 1982 are rounded to the nearest million.   Figures in italics represent very rough estimates.

Largest Countries: Population

	Country	Population 1/1/82
1.	China	995,000,000
2.	India	695,230,000
3.	U.S.S.R	268,740,000
4.	United States	231,160,000
5.	Indonesia	151,500,000
6.	Brazil	124,760,000
7.	Japan	118,650,000
8.	Pakistan	92,070,000
9.	Bangladesh	91,860,000
10.	Nigeria	80,765,000
11.	Mexico	70,515,000
12.	Germany, Fed. Rep.	61,680,000
13.	Italy	57,270,000
14.	United Kingdom	56,035,000
15.	Vietnam	55,455,000
16.	France	54,045,000
17.	Philippines	50,960,000
18.	Thailand	48,860,000
19.	Turkey	46,435,000
20.	Egypt	43,565,000
21.	Korea, South	40,755,000
22.	Iran	38,565,000
23.	Spain	37,865,000
24.	Poland	36,035,000
25.	Burma	35,710,000
26.	South Africa	30,495,000
27.	Ethiopia	30,370,000
28.	Zaire	29,060,000
29.	Argentina	28,420,000
30.	Colombia	28,185,000
31.	Canada	24,335,000
32.	Yugoslavia	22,635,000
33.	Romania	22,445,000
34.	Morocco	21,795,000
35.	Sudan	20,180,000
36.	Algeria	19,270,000
37.	Tanzania	19,115,000
38.	Korea, North	18,540,000
39.	Peru	18,510,000
40.	Taiwan	18,365,000
41.	Kenya	17,790,000
42.	German Dem. Rep.	16,750,000
43.	Sri Lanka	15,605,000
44.	Nepal	15,520,000
45.	Czechoslovakia	15,345,000

Largest Countries: Area

	Country	km²	sq mi
1.	U.S.S.R	22,274,900	8,600,383
2.	Canada	9,922,330	3,831,033
3.	China	9,560,939	3,691,500
4.	United States	9,528,318	3,678,896
5.	Brazil	8,511,965	3,286,487
6.	Australia	7,686,850	2,967,909
7.	India	3,203,975	1,237,061
8.	Argentina	2,766,889	1,068,301
9.	Sudan	2,505,813	967,500
10.	Algeria	2,381,741	919,595
11.	Zaire	2,345,409	905,567
12.	Greenland	2,175,600	840,004
13.	Saudi Arabia	2,149,690	830,000
14.	Mexico	1,972,547	761,604
15.	Indonesia	1,919,270	741,034
16.	Libya	1,759,540	679,362
17.	Iran	1,648,000	636,296
18.	Mongolia	1,565,000	604,250
19.	Peru	1,285,216	496,224
20.	Chad	1,284,000	495,755
21.	Niger	1,267,000	489,191
22.	Angola	1,246,700	481,353
23.	Mali	1,240,000	478,766
24.	Ethiopia	1,223,600	472,434
25.	South Africa	1,221,042	471,447
26.	Colombia	1,138,914	439,737
27.	Bolivia	1,098,581	424,164
28.	Mauritania	1,030,700	397,955
29.	Egypt	1,001,400	386,643
30.	Tanzania	945,087	364,900
31.	Nigeria	923,768	356,669
32.	Venezuela	912,050	352,144
33.	Pakistan	828,453	319,867
34.	Mozambique	783,030	302,329
35.	Turkey	779,452	300,948
36.	Chile	756,626	292,135
37.	Zambia	752,614	290,586
38.	Burma	676,577	261,228
39.	Afghanistan	647,497	250,000
40.	Somalia	637,657	246,200
41.	Central African Republic	622,984	240,535
42.	Botswana	600,372	231,805
43.	Madagascar	587,041	226,658
44.	Kenya	582,646	224,961
45.	France	547,026	211,208

Smallest Countries: Population

	Country	Population 1/1/82
1.	Vatican City	1,000
2.	Niue	3,000
3.	Anguilla	7,900
	Nauru	7,900
4.	Tuvalu	8,100
5.	Cook Islands	18,000
6.	San Marino	24,000
7.	Liechtenstein	27,000
	Monaco	27,000
8.	Andorra	40,000
9.	St. Kitts-Nevis	41,000
10.	Faeroe Islands	45,000
11.	Greenland	51,000
12.	Kiribati	59,000
13.	Isle of Man	66,000
14.	Seychelles	68,000
15.	Dominica	75,000
16.	Antigua	77,000
17.	Sao Tome and Principe	89,000
18.	Tonga	101,000
19.	Grenada	112,000
20.	Vanuatu	120,000
21.	Djibouti	124,000
	Saint Lucia	124,000
22.	St. Vincent	128,000
23.	Maldives	155,000
	Western Samoa	155,000
24.	Belize	160,000
25.	Iceland	230,000
26.	Bahamas	235,000
	Qatar	235,000
	Solomon Is.	235,000
27.	Brunei	245,000
28.	Barbados	260,000
	Netherlands Antilles	260,000
29.	Cape Verde	330,000
30.	Luxembourg	355,000
31.	Malta	360,000
32.	Suriname	365,000
33.	Equatorial Guinea	375,000
34.	Comoros	380,000
35.	Bahrain	400,000
36.	Gabon	560,000
37.	Swaziland	580,000
38.	Gambia	625,000

Smallest Countries: Area

	Country	km²	sq mi
1.	Vatican City	0.4	0.2
2.	Monaco	1.5	0.6
3.	Nauru	21	8.2
4.	Tuvalu	26	10
5.	San Marino	61	24
6.	Anguilla	88	34
7.	Liechtenstein	160	62
8.	Cook Islands	236	91
9.	Niue	263	102
10.	St. Kitts-Nevis	269	104
11.	Maldives	298	115
12.	Malta	316	122
13.	Grenada	344	133
14.	St. Vincent	389	150
15.	Barbados	430	166
16.	Antigua	440	170
17.	Seychelles	443	171
18.	Andorra	453	175
19.	Singapore	581	224
20.	Isle of Man	588	227
21.	Saint Lucia	616	238
22.	Bahrain	662	256
23.	Tonga	699	270
24.	Dominica	752	290
25.	Kiribati	754	291
26.	Sao Tome and Principe	964	372
27.	Netherlands Antilles	993	383
28.	Faeroe Islands	1,399	540
29.	Mauritius	2,045	790
30.	Comoros	2,171	838
31.	Luxembourg	2,586	999
32.	Western Samoa	2,842	1,097
33.	Cape Verde	4,033	1,557
34.	Trinidad and Tobago	5,128	1,980
35.	Brunei	5,765	2,226
36.	Puerto Rico	8,897	3,435
37.	Cyprus	9,251	3,572
38.	Lebanon	10,400	4,015
39.	Jamaica	10,991	4,244
40.	Qatar	11,000	4,247
41.	Gambia	11,295	4,361
42.	Bahamas	13,939	5,382
43.	Vanuatu	14,800	5,714
44.	Swaziland	17,364	6,704
45.	Kuwait	17,818	6,880

Highest Population Densities

	Country	Density per km²	sq mi		Country	Density per km²	sq mi
1.	Monaco	18,000	45,000	16.	St. Vincent	329	853
2.	Singapore	4,923	12,768	17.	Grenada	326	842
3.	Vatican City	2,500	5,000	18.	Belgium	324	839
4.	Malta	1,139	2,951	19.	Japan	319	825
5.	Bangladesh	638	1,652	20.	Lebanon	315	816
6.	Barbados	605	1,566	21.	Tuvalu	312	810
7.	Bahrain	604	1,563	22.	Netherlands Antilles	262	679
8.	Maldives	520	1,348	23.	El Salvador	250	649
9.	Taiwan	510	1,322	24.	Germany, Fed. Rep. of	248	642
10.	Mauritius	482	1,247	25.	Sri Lanka	240	622
11.	Korea, South	414	1,072	26.	United Kingdom	230	595
12.	San Marino	393	1,000	27.	Trinidad and Tobago	227	588
13.	Nauru	376	963	28.	India	217	562
14.	Puerto Rico	368	952	29.	Jamaica	203	527
15.	Netherlands	347	900	30.	Saint Lucia	201	521

Lowest Population Densities

	Country	Density per km²	sq mi		Country	Density per km²	sq mi
1.	Greenland	0.02	0.06		Oman	4.4	11
2.	Mongolia	1.1	2.9	15.	Congo	4.7	12
3.	Botswana	1.5	3.8	16.	Bolivia	5.3	14
4.	Mauritania	1.7	4.3	17.	Djibouti	5.4	14
5.	Libya	1.8	4.6	18.	Mali	5.8	15
6.	Australia	1.9	5.0	19.	Angola	5.9	15
7.	Gabon	2.1	5.4	20.	Yemen, P.D.R. of	6.2	16
8.	Iceland	2.2	5.8	21.	Papua New Guinea	6.7	17
	Suriname	2.2	5.8	22.	Belize	7.0	18
9.	Canada	2.5	6.4	23.	Zambia	7.8	20
10.	Chad	3.6	9.4	24.	Paraguay	7.9	20
11.	Central African Republic	3.7	9.6		Solomon Islands	7.9	20
12.	Saudi Arabia	4.1	11	25.	Somalia	8.0	21
13.	Guyana	4.3	11	26.	Algeria	8.1	21
14.	Niger	4.4	11		Vanuatu	8.1	21

Major Metropolitan Areas of the World

This table lists the major metropolitan areas of the world according to their estimated population on January 1, 1982. For convenience in reference, the areas are grouped by major region, and the number of areas in each region and size group is given.

There are 29 areas with more than 5,000,000 population each; these are listed in rank order of estimated population, with the world rank given in parentheses following the name. For example, New York's 1982 rank is second. Below the 5,000,000 level, the metropolitan areas are listed alphabetically within region, not in order of size.

For ease of comparison, each metropolitan area has been defined by Rand McNally & Company according to consistent rules. A metropolitan area includes a central city, surrounding communities linked to it by continuous built-up areas and more distant communities if the bulk of their population is supported by commuters to the central city. Some metropolitan areas have more than one central city, for example Tōkyō–Yokohama or San Francisco–Oakland–San Jose.

POPULATION CLASSIFICATION	UNITED STATES and CANADA	LATIN AMERICA	EUROPE (excl. U.S.S.R.)	U.S.S.R	ASIA	AFRICA-OCEANIA
Over 15,000,000 (4)	New York, U.S. (2)	Mexico City, Mex. (3)			Tōkyō-Yokohama, Jap. (1) Ōsaka-Kōbe-Kyōto, Jap. (4)	
10,000,000–15,000,000 (8)	Los Angeles, U.S. (12)	São Paulo, Braz. (5) Buenos Aires, Arg. (9)	London, U.K. (10)	Moscow (6)	Seoul, Kor. (7) Calcutta, India (8) Bombay, India (11)	
5,000,000–10,000,000 (17)	Chicago, U.S. (16) Philadelphia–Trenton–Wilmington, U.S. (26)	Rio de Janeiro, Braz. (15)	Paris, Fr. (13) Essen–Dortmund–Duisburg (The Ruhr), Ger., Fed. Rep. of (27) İstanbul, Tur. (29)	Leningrad (23)	Shanghai, China, (17) Delhi–New Delhi, India (18) Manila, Phil. (19) Jakarta, Indon. (20) Peking (Beijing), China (21), Tehrān, Iran (22) Bangkok, Thai. (24) Karāchi, Pak. (25) Tientsin (Tianjin), China (28)	Cairo, Eg. (14)
3,000,000–5,000,000 (32)	Boston, U.S. Detroit, U.S.–Windsor, Can. Montréal, Can. San Francisco–Oakland–San Jose, U.S. Toronto, Can. Washington, U.S.	Bogotá, Col. Caracas, Ven. Lima, Peru Santiago, Chile	Athens, Greece Barcelona, Sp. Berlin, Ger. Madrid, Sp. Milan, It. Rome, It.		Baghdād, Iraq Bangalore, India Chungking (Chongqing), China Dacca, Bngl. Lahore, Pak. Madras, India Mukden (Shenyang), China Nagoya, Jap. Pusan, Kor. Rangoon, Bur. Taipei, Taiwan Victoria, Hong Kong Wuhan, China	Alexandria, Eg. Johannesburg, S. Afr. Sydney, Austl.
2,000,000–3,000,000 (46)	Atlanta, U.S. Cleveland, U.S. Dallas–Fort Worth, U.S. Houston, U.S. Miami–Fort Lauderdale, U.S. Minneapolis–St. Paul, U.S. Pittsburgh, U.S. St. Louis, U.S. San Diego, U.S.–Tijuana, Mex. Seattle–Tacoma, U.S.	Belo Horizonte, Braz. Guadalajara, Mex. Havana, Cuba Medellín, Col. Monterrey, Mex. Porto Alegre, Braz. Recife, Braz.	Birmingham, U.K. Brussels, Bel. Bucharest, Rom. Budapest, Hung. Hamburg, Ger., Fed. Rep. of Katowice–Bytom–Gliwice, Pol. Lisbon, Port. Manchester, U.K. Naples, It. Warsaw, Pol.	Donetsk–Makeyevka Kiev Tashkent	Ahmadābād, India Ankara, Tur. Canton (Guangzhou), China Chengtu (Chendu), China Hanoi, Viet. Harbin, China Ho Chi Minh City (Saigon), Viet. Hyderābād, India Sian (Xi'an) China Singapore, Singapore Surabaya, Indon.	Algiers, Alg. Casablanca, Mor. Kinshasa, Zaire Lagos, Nig. Melbourne, Austl.
1,500,000–2,000,000 (37)	Baltimore, U.S. Phoenix, U.S.	Fortaleza, Braz. Salvador, Braz. San Juan, P.R.	Amsterdam, Neth. Cologne, Ger., Fed. Rep. of Copenhagen, Den. Frankfurt am Main, Ger., Fed. Rep. of Glasgow, U.K. Leeds–Bradford, U.K. Liverpool, U.K. Munich, Ger., Fed. Rep. of Stuttgart, Ger., Fed. Rep. of Turin, It. Vienna, Aus.	Baku Dnepropetrovsk Gorki Kharkov Novosibirsk	Bandung, Indon. Chittagong, Bngl. Colombo, Sri Lanka Damascus, Syria Fukuoka, Jap. Hiroshima–Kure, Jap. Kānpur, India Kaohsiung, Taiwan Kitakyūshū–Shimonoseki, Jap. Medan, Indon. Nanking (Nanjing), China Pune, India Sapporo, Jap. Taegu, Kor.	Cape Town, S. Afr. Durban, S. Afr.
1,000,000–1,500,000 (90)	Buffalo–Niagara Falls, U.S.–St. Catharines–Niagara Falls, Can. Cincinnati, U.S. Denver, U.S. El Paso, U.S.–Ciudad Juárez, Mex. Hartford–New Britain, U.S. Indianapolis, U.S. Kansas City, U.S. Milwaukee, U.S. New Orleans, U.S. Portland, U.S. San Antonio, U.S. Vancouver, Can.	Barranquilla, Col. Belém, Braz. Brasília, Braz. Cali, Col. Córdoba, Arg. Curitiba, Braz. Guatemala, Guat. Guayaquil, Ec. Montevideo, Ur. Rosario, Arg. Santo Domingo, Dom. Rep.	Antwerp, Bel. Belgrade, Yugo. Bilbao, Sp. Dublin, Ire. Düsseldorf, Ger., Fed. Rep. of Hannover, Ger., Fed. Rep. of Lille, Fr. Łódź, Pol. Lyon, Fr. Mannheim, Ger., Fed. Rep. of Marseille, Fr. Newcastle–Sunderland, U.K. Nürnberg, Ger., Fed. Rep. of Porto, Port. Prague, Czech. Rotterdam, Neth. Sofia, Bul. Stockholm, Swe. Valencia, Sp.	Alma–Ata Chelyabinsk Kazan Kuybyshev Minsk Odessa Omsk Perm Rostov-na-Donu Saratov Sverdlovsk Tbilisi Ufa Volgograd Yerevan	Anshan, China Asansol, India Beirut, Leb. Changchun, China Chengchou (Zhengzhou), China Faisalabad (Lyallpur), Pak. Fushun, China İzmir, Tur. Jaipur, India Kābul, Afg. Kuala Lumpur, Mala. Kunming, China Kuwait, Kuw. Lanchou (Lanzhou), China Lucknow, India Lūta (Dairen), China Nāgpur, India Patna, India P'yŏngyang, Kor. Rāwalpindi–Islāmābād, Pak. Riyadh, Sau. Ar. Semarang, Indon. Shihchiachuang (Shijiazhuang), China Surat, India Taiyuan, China Tel Aviv-Yafo, Isr. Tsinan (Jinan), China Tsingtao (Qingdao), China	Abidjan, I.C. Addis Ababa, Eth. Brisbane, Austl. Khartoum, Sud. Tunis, Tun.
Total by Region (234)	34	29	50	25	80	16

Populations of Major Cities

The largest and most important of the world's major cities are listed in the following table. Also included are some smaller cities because of their regional significance.

Local official name forms have been used throughout the table. When a commonly used "conventional" name form exists, it has been featured, with the official name following, within parentheses. Former names are identified by italics. Each city name is followed by the English name of its country. Whenever two well-known cities of the same name are in the same country, the state or province name has been added for identification.

Many cities have population figures within parentheses following the country name. These are metropolitan populations, comprising the central city and its suburbs. When a city is within the metropolitan area of another city the name of the metropolitan central city is specified in parentheses preceded by an (*). The symbol (†) identifies a political district population which includes some rural population. For these cities the estimated city population has been based upon the district figure.

The population of each city has been dated for ease of comparison. The date is followed by a letter designating: Census (C); Official Estimate (E); and in a few instances Unofficial Estimates (UE).

City and Country	Population	Date
Aachen, Fed. Rep. of Ger. (540,000)	242,971	79E
Abidjan, Ivory Coast	1,100,000	78E
Acapulco [de Juárez], Mexico	421,000	78E
Accra, Ghana (738,498)	633,880	70C
Adelaide, Australia (933,300)	13,400	79E
Aden (Baladīyat 'Adan), People's Dem. Rep. of Yemen	271,600	77E
Addis Ababa (Ādīs Ābeba), Ethiopia	1,125,340	78E
Āgra, India (770,352)	723,676	81C
Ahmadābād, India (2,400,000)	2,024,917	81C
Aleppo (Halab), Syria	878,000	78E
Alexandria (Al Iskandarīyah), Egypt (2,850,000)	2,409,000	78E
Algiers (Al Jazā'ir), Algeria (1,800,000)	1,503,720	74E
Allahābād, India (642,420)	609,232	81C
Alma-Ata, U.S.S.R. (970,000)	928,000	80E
'Ammān, Jordan	648,587	79E
Amritsar, India	589,227	81C
Amsterdam, Netherlands (1,810,000)	716,919	80E
Ankara, Turkey (2,290,000)	2,203,729	80C
Anshan, China	1,050,000	75UE
Antananarivo, Madagascar	484,000	77E
Antwerp, (Antwerpen, Anvers), Belgium (1,105,000)	194,073	80E
Asansol, India (1,050,000)	187,039	81C
Asunción, Paraguay (655,000)	463,700	78E
Athens (Athínai), Greece (2,540,241)	867,023	71C
Atlanta, U.S. (1,950,600)	425,022	80C
Auckland, New Zealand (775,000)	147,600	79E
Augsburg, Fed. Rep. of Ger. (390,000)	245,940	79E
Austin, U.S. (422,700)	345,496	80C
Baghdād, Iraq (2,183,800)	1,300,000	70E
Baku, U.S.S.R. (1,800,000)	1,030,000	80E
Baltimore, U.S. (1,883,100)	786,775	80C
Bamako, Mali	404,022	76C
Bandung, Indonesia (1,525,000)	1,462,637	80C
Bangalore, India (2,950,000)	2,482,507	81C
Bangkok (Krung Thep), Thailand (3,375,000)	3,133,834	72E
Barcelona, Spain (3,975,000)	1,902,713	78E
Barranquilla, Colombia (950,000)	859,000	73C
Basel, Switzerland (580,000)	182,143	80C
Basra (Al Baṣrah), Iraq	370,900	70E
Beirut (Bayrūt), Lebanon (1,010,000)	474,870	70E
Belém, Brazil (660,000)	565,097	70C
Belfast, U.K. (710,000)	354,400	78E
Belgrade (Beograd), Yugoslavia (1,150,000)	770,140	71C
Belo Horizonte, Brazil (2,450,000)	1,814,990	80C
Berlin, East (Ost), Ger. Dem. Rep. (*Berlin)	1,128,983	78E
Berlin, West, Fed. Rep. of Ger. (3,775,000)	1,902,250	79E
Bern, Switzerland (286,903)	145,254	80C
Bhopāl, India	672,329	81C
Bielefeld, Fed. Rep. of Ger. (525,000)	312,357	79E
Bilbao, Spain (995,000)	452,921	78E
Birmingham, U.K. (2,660,000)	1,033,900	79E
Birmingham, U.S. (697,900)	284,413	80C
Bogotá, Colombia (4,150,000)	4,067,000	79E
Bologna, Italy (550,000)	471,554	79E
Bombay, India (9,950,000)	8,227,332	81C
Bonn, Fed. Rep. of Ger. (555,000)	286,184	79E
Bordeaux, France (612,456)	223,131	75C
Boston, U.S. (3,738,800)	562,994	80C
Brasília, Brazil	1,202,683	80C
Brazzaville, Congo	175,000	70C
Bremen, Fed. Rep. of Ger. (800,000)	556,128	79E
Bremerhaven, Fed. Rep. of Ger. (190,000)	138,987	79E
Brisbane, Australia (1,014,700)	702,000	79E
Bristol, U.K. (635,000)	408,000	79E

City and Country	Population	Date
Brussels (Bruxelles, Brussel), Belgium (2,400,000)	143,957	80E
Bucharest (Bucureşti), Romania (2,050,000)	1,858,418	78E
Budapest, Hungary (2,600,000)	2,060,000	80C
Buenos Aires, Argentina (10,700,000)	2,908,001	80C
Buffalo, U.S. (1,154,600)	357,870	80C
Bursa, Turkey	466,178	80C
Cairo (Al Qāhirah), Egypt (8,500,000)	5,278,000	78E
Calcutta, India (11,100,000)	3,291,655	81C
Cali, Colombia (1,340,000)	1,293,000	79E
Canberra, Australia (241,500)	221,000	79E
Canton (Guangzhou), China	2,500,000	75UE
Cape Town (Kaapstad), South Africa (1,125,000)	697,514	70C
Caracas, Venezuela (2,475,000)	1,658,500	71C
Cardiff, U.K. (625,000)	282,000	79E
Casablanca (Dar-el-Beida), Morocco (1,575,000)	1,506,373	71C
Catania, Italy (515,000)	398,426	79E
Cebu, Philippines (500,000)	413,025	75C
Changchun, China	1,300,000	75UE
Changsha, China	840,000	75UE
Charleroi, Belgium (495,000)	221,911	80E
Chelyabinsk (Čeljabinsk), U.S.S.R. (1,215,000)	1,042,000	80E
Chengchou (Zhengzhou), China	1,100,000	75UE
Chengtu, (Chendu), China	1,800,000	75UE
Chicago, U.S. (7,803,800)	3,005,072	80C
Chittagong, Bangladesh (1,388,476)	980,000	81C
Chungking (Chongqing), China	2,900,000	75UE
Cincinnati, U.S. (1,476,600)	385,457	80C
Ciudad Juárez, Mexico (*El Paso, U.S.)	597,100	78E
Cleveland, U.S. (2,218,300)	573,822	80C
Cochin, India (552,408)	513,081	81C
Coimbatore, India (965,000)	700,923	81C
Cologne, (Köln), Fed. Rep. of Ger. (1,815,000)	976,136	79E
Colombo, Sri Lanka (1,540,000)	616,000	77E
Columbus, Ohio, U.S. (943,300)	564,871	80C
Copenhagen, (København), Denmark (1,470,000)	498,850	80E
Córdoba, Argentina (1,070,000)	1,052,147	80C
Coventry, U.K. (655,000)	339,300	79E
Curitiba, Brazil (1,300,000)	1,052,147	80C
Dacca, Bangladesh (3,458,602)	1,850,000	81C
Dakar, Senegal	798,792	76C
Dallas, U.S. (2,811,800)	904,078	80C
Damascus (Dimashq), Syria (1,550,000)	1,156,000	79E
Dar es Salaam, Tanzania	870,000	78C
Dayton, U.S. (898,000)	203,588	80C
Delhi, India (7,200,000)	4,865,077	81C
Denver, U.S. (1,414,200)	491,396	80C
Detroit, U.S. (4,399,000)	1,203,339	80C
Dnepropetrovsk, U.S.S.R. (1,460,000)	1,083,000	80E
Donetsk (Doneck), U.S.S.R. (2,075,000)	1,032,000	80E
Dortmund, Fed. Rep. of Ger. (*Essen)	609,954	79E
Douala, Cameroon	458,246	76C
Dresden, Ger. Dem. Rep. (640,000)	514,508	78E
Dublin (Baile Atha Cliath), Ireland (1,110,000)	544,586	79C
Duisburg, Fed. Rep. of Ger. (*Essen)	559,066	79E
Durban, South Africa (1,040,000)	736,852	70C
Düsseldorf, Fed. Rep. of Ger. (1,225,000)	594,770	79E
Edinburgh, U.K. (635,000)	455,126	79E
Edmonton, Canada (554,228)	461,361	76C
El Paso, U.S. (1,122,300)	425,259	80C
Essen, Fed. Rep. of Ger. (5,125,000)	652,501	79E

City and Country	Population	Date
Faisalabad, (Lyallpur), Pakistan	823,343	72C
Florence (Firenze), Italy (660,000)	462,690	79E
Fortaleza, Brazil (1,490,000)	1,338,733	80C
Frankfurt am Main, Fed. Rep. of Ger. (1,880,000)	628,203	79E
Freetown, Sierra Leone (335,000)	274,000	74C
Frunze, U.S.S.R.	543,000	80E
Fukuoka, Japan (1,575,000)	1,088,617	80C
Fushun, China	1,150,000	75UE
Gdańsk (Danzig), Poland (820,000)	449,200	79E
Geneva (Genève), Switzerland (435,000)	156,505	80C
Genoa (Genova), Italy (855,000)	782,476	79E
Gent, Belgium (470,000)	241,695	80E
Giza (Al Jizah), Egypt (*Cairo)	1,246,713	76C
Glasgow, U.K. (1,830,000)	794,316	79E
Gorki, U.S.S.R. (1,900,000)	1,358,000	80E
Göteborg, Sweden (665,000)	434,699	79E
Graz, Austria (275,000)	250,900	76E
Guadalajara, Mexico (2,350,000)	1,813,100	78E
Guatemala, Guatemala (945,000)	717,322	73C
Guayaquil, Ecuador	1,022,010	78E
Haifa (Hefa), Israel (415,000)	229,300	79E
Hamburg, Fed. Rep. of Ger. (2,260,000)	1,653,043	79E
Hangchou (Hangzhou), China	900,000	75UE
Hannover, Fed. Rep. of Ger. (1,005,000)	535,854	79E
Hanoi, Vietnam	1,600,000	71E
Harare (Salisbury), Zimbabwe (633,000)	118,500	79E
Harbin, China	2,400,000	75UE
Hartford, U.S. (1,055,700)	136,392	80C
Havana (La Habana), Cuba (2,000,000)	1,961,674	76C
Helsinki, Finland (885,000)	484,879	78E
Hiroshima, Japan (1,525,000)	899,394	80C
Ho Chi Minh City (Saigon), Vietnam (2,750,000)	1,804,900	71E
Honolulu, U.S. (762,900)	324,871	80C
Houston, U.S. (2,689,200)	1,594,086	80C
Hyderābād, India (2,750,000)	2,142,087	81C
Hyderābād, Pakistan (660,000)	600,796	72C
Ibadan, Nigeria	847,000	75E
Inch'ŏn, South Korea (*Seoul)	1,084,730	80C
Indianapolis, U.S. (1,104,200)	700,807	80C
Innsbruck, Austria (150,000)	120,400	76E
Irkutsk, U.S.S.R.	561,000	80E
İstanbul, Turkey (4,765,000)	2,853,539	80C
İzmir, Turkey (1,190,000)	753,749	80C
Jacksonville, Florida, U.S. (615,300)	540,898	80C
Jaipur, India (1,025,000)	966,677	81C
Jakarta, Indonesia (6,700,000)	6,503,449	80C
Jerusalem (Yerushalayim), Israel (420,000)	398,200	79E
Jiddah, Saudi Arabia	561,104	74C
Johannesburg, South Africa (2,550,000)	654,232	70C
Kābul, Afghanistan	749,000	75E
Kananga, Zaire	601,000	74E
Kano, Nigeria	399,000	75E
Kānpur, India (1,875,000)	1,531,345	81C
Kansas City, Missouri, U.S. (1,254,600)	448,159	80C
Kaohsiung, Taiwan (1,480,000)	1,172,977	77E
Karāchi, Pakistan (4,500,000)	2,800,000	75E
Karaganda, U.S.S.R.	577,000	80E
Kathmandu, Nepal (215,000)	150,402	71C
Katowice, Poland (2,590,000)	351,300	79E
Kawasaki, Japan (*Tōkyō)	1,040,698	80C
Kazan', U.S.S.R. (1,050,000)	1,002,000	80E
Khabarovsk (Habarovsk), U.S.S.R.	538,000	80E
Khar'kov (Harkov), U.S.S.R. (1,750,000)	1,464,000	80E

City and Country	Population	Date
Khartoum (Al Kharṭūm), Sudan (790,000)	333,921	73C
Kiel, Fed. Rep. of Ger. (335,000)	250,750	79E
Kiev, (Kijev), U.S.S.R. (2,430,000)	2,192,000	80E
Kingston, Jamaica	665,050	78E
Kinshasa, Zaire	2,202,000	75E
Kishinev (Kišinev), U.S.S.R.	519,000	80E
Kitakyūshū, Japan (1,515,000)	1,065,084	80C
Kōbe, Japan (*Ōsaka)	1,367,392	80C
Kowloon, Hong Kong (*Victoria)	749,600	76C
Kraków, Poland (708,000)	706,100	79E
Krasnoyarsk (Krasnojarsk), U.S.S.R.	807,000	80E
Kuala Lumpur, Malaysia (750,000)	451,728	70C
Kueiyang (Guiyang), China	800,000	75UE
Kunming, China	1,225,000	75UE
Kuwait (Al Kuwayt), Kuwait (780,000)	78,116	75C
Kuybyshev (Kujbyšev), U.S.S.R. (1,440,000)	1,226,000	80E
Kwangju, South Korea	727,627	80C
Kyōto, Japan (*Ōsaka)	1,472,993	80C
Lagos, Nigeria (1,450,000)	1,060,800	75E
Lahore, Pakistan (2,200,000)	2,022,577	72C
Lanchou (Lanzhou), China	950,000	75UE
La Paz, Bolivia	654,713	76C
Leeds, U.K. (1,540,000)	724,300	79E
Leipzig, Ger. Dem. Rep. (710,000)	563,980	78E
Leningrad, U.S.S.R. (5,360,000)	4,119,000	80E
León, Mexico	590,000	78E
Liège, Belgium (765,000)	220,183	78E
Lille, France (1,015,000)	172,280	75C
Lima, Peru (3,350,000)	340,339	72C
Linz, Austria (290,000)	208,000)	76E
Lisbon, (Lisboa), Portugal (1,950,000)	829,900	75E
Liverpool, U.K. (1,535,000)	520,200	79E
Łódź, Poland (1,025,000)	830,800	79E
Lomas de Zamora, Argentina (*Buenos Aires)	508,620	80C
London, U.K. (11,050,000)	6,877,100	79E
Los Angeles, U.S. (9,840,200)	2,966,763	80C
Louisville, U.S. (881,100)	298,451	80C
Luanda, Angola	475,328	70C
Lubumbashi, Zaire	404,000	74E
Lucknow, India (1,060,000)	895,947	81C
Ludhiāna, India	606,250	81C
Lusaka, Zambia	641,000	80E
Lüta *(Dairen)*, China (1,700,000†)	1,100,000	75UE
Lvov, U.S.S.R.	676,000	80E
Lyon, France (1,170,660)	456,716	75C
Madras, India (4,475,000)	3,266,034	81C
Madrid, Spain (4,415,000)	3,367,438	78E
Madurai, India (960,000)	817,562	80C
Managua, Nicaragua	552,900	78E
Manchester, U.K. (2,800,000)	479,100	79E
Mandalay, Burma	458,000	77E
Manila, Philippines (5,500,000)	1,479,116	75C
Mannheim, Fed. Rep. of Ger. (1,395,000)	303,247	79E
Maputo *(Lourenço Marques)*, Mozambique	341,922	70C
Maracaibo, Venezuela	651,574	71C
Marseille, France (1,070,912)	908,600	75C
Mecca (Makkah), Saudi Arabia	366,801	74C
Medan, Indonesia (1,450,000)	1,378,955	80C
Medellín, Colombia (2,025,000)	1,477,000	79E
Melbourne, Australia (2,739,700)	65,800	79E
Memphis, U.S. (843,200)	646,356	80C
Mexico City (Ciudad de México), Mexico (14,400,000)	8,988,200	78E
Miami, U.S. (2,689,100)	346,931	80C
Milan (Milano), Italy (3,800,000)	1,677,109	79E
Milwaukee, U.S. (1,358,600)	636,212	80C
Minneapolis, U.S. (1,978,000)	370,951	80C
Minsk, U.S.S.R. (1,330,000)	1,295,000	80E
Mombasa, Kenya	342,000	79C
Monrovia, Liberia	204,210	74C
Monterrey, Mexico (1,925,000)	1,054,000	78E
Montevideo, Uruguay (1,350,000)	1,229,748	75C
Montréal, Canada (2,802,485)	1,080,546	76C
Morón, Argentina (*Buenos Aires)	596,769	80C
Moscow (Moskva), U.S.S.R. (11,950,000)	7,915,000	80E
Mukden (Shenyang), China	3,300,000	75UE
Multān, Pakistan (538,000)	504,365	72C
Munich (München), Fed. Rep. of Ger. (1,940,000)	1,299,693	79E
Mysore, India (476,446)	439,185	80C
Nagoya, Japan (3,700,000)	2,087,884	80C
Nāgpur, India (1,325,000)	1,215,425	81C
Nairobi, Kenya	835,000	79C
Nanking (Nanjing), China	1,800,000	75UE
Nantes, France (453,500)	256,693	75C
Naples (Napoli), Italy (2,740,000)	1,223,228	79E
Nashville, U.S. (608,400)	455,651	80C
Newcastle upon Tyne, U.K. (1,295,000)	287,300	79E
New Delhi, India (*Delhi)	271,990	81C
New Kowloon, Hong Kong (*Victoria)	1,628,880	76C
New Orleans, U.S. (1,175,800)	557,482	80C
New York, U.S. (16,573,600)	7,071,030	80C
Niamey, Niger	225,300	77E
Norfolk, U.S. (795,600)	219,214	80C
Nottingham, U.K. (645,000)	278,600	79E
Novokuznetsk (Novokuzneck), U.S.S.R.	545,000	80E
Novosibirsk, U.S.S.R. (1,460,000)	1,328,000	80E
Nürnberg, Fed. Rep. of Ger. (1,025,000)	484,184	79E
Odessa, U.S.S.R. (1,120,000)	1,057,000	80E
Okayama, Japan	545,737	80C
Oklahoma City, U.S. (742,000)	403,213	80C
Omaha, U.S. (548,400)	311,681	80C
Omsk, U.S.S.R. (1,040,000)	1,028,000	80E
Orlando, U.S. (568,300)	128,394	80C
Ōsaka, Japan (15,200,000)	2,648,158	80C
Oslo, Norway (725,000)	454,819	80E
Ostrava, Czechoslovakia (745,000)	325,473	79E
Ottawa, Canada (693,288)	304,462	76C
Palermo, Italy	693,949	79E
Panamá, Panama (645,000)	439,800	78E
Paris, France (9,450,000)	2,050,500	80E
Patna, India (1,025,000)	773,720	81C
Peking (Beijing), China (8,500,000†)	5,700,000	78E
Perm, U.S.S.R. (1,075,000)	1,008,000	80E
Perth, Australia (883,600)	88,850	79E
Philadelphia, U.S. (5,153,400)	1,688,210	80C
Phnom Penh (Phnum Pénh), Kampuchea	393,995	62C
Phoenix, U.S. (1,483,500)	764,911	80C
Pittsburgh, U.S. (2,165,100)	423,938	80C
Port-au-Prince, Haiti (800,000)	745,700	78E
Portland, Oregon, U.S. (1,220,000)	366,383	80C
Porto, Portugal (1,150,000)	335,700	75E
Porto Alegre, Brazil (2,225,000)	1,158,709	80C
Portsmouth, U.K. (490,000)	191,000	79E
Poznań, Poland (610,000)	545,600	79E
Prague (Praha), Czechoslovakia (1,275,000)	1,193,345	79E
Pretoria, South Africa (575,000)	545,450	70C
Providence, U.S. (897,000)	156,804	80C
Puebla [de Zaragoza], Mexico	678,000	78E
Pune, India (1,775,000)	1,202,848	81C
Pusan, South Korea	3,160,276	80C
P'yŏngyang, North Korea	840,000	67E
Québec, Canada (542,158)	177,082	76C
Quezon City, Philippines (*Manila)	956,864	75C
Quito, Ecuador	742,858	78E
Rabat, Morocco (540,000)	367,620	71C
Rangoon, Burma (3,000,000)	2,276,000	77E
Rāwalpindi, Pakistan (725,000)	372,919	72C
Recife *(Pernambuco)*, Brazil (2,300,000)	1,240,897	80C
Richmond, Virginia, U.S. (548,100)	219,214	80C
Rīga, U.S.S.R. (920,000)	843,000	80E
Rio de Janerio, Brazil (8,975,000)	5,184,292	80C
Riyadh (Ar Riyāḍ), Saudi Arabia	666,840	74C
Rochester, New York, U.S. (809,500)	241,741	80C
Rome (Roma), Italy (3,195,000)	2,911,671	79E
Rosario, Argentina (1,045,000)	935,471	80C
Rostov-na-Donu, U.S.S.R. (1,075,000)	946,000	80E
Rotterdam, Netherlands (1,085,000)	579,194	80E
Saarbrücken, Fed. Rep. of Ger. (390,000)	194,452	79E
Sacramento, U.S. (848,800)	275,741	80C
St. Louis, U.S. (2,216,100)	453,085	80C
St. Paul, U.S. (*Minneapolis)	270,230	80C
St. Petersburg, U.S. (699,800)	236,893	80C
Sakai, Japan (*Ōsaka)	810,120	80C
Salt Lake City, U.S. (686,200)	163,033	80C
Salvador, Brazil (1,725,000)	1,525,831	80C
Samarkand, U.S.S.R.	481,000	80E
San Antonio, U.S. (1,012,300)	785,410	80C
San Bernardino, U.S. (715,300)	118,057	80C
San Diego, U.S. (1,597,000)	875,504	80C
San Francisco, U.S. (4,665,500)	678,974	80C
San José, Costa Rica (519,400)	239,800	78E
San Juan, Puerto Rico (1,535,000)	422,701	80C
San Justo, Argentina (*Buenos Aires)	946,715	80C
San Salvador, El Salvador (720,000)	397,100	77E
Santiago, Chile (2,925,000)	517,473	70C
Santo Domingo, Dominican Rep.	979,608	76E
Santos, Brazil (610,000)	341,317	70C
São Paulo, Brazil (12,525,000)	8,584,896	80C
Sapporo, Japan (1,450,000)	1,401,758	80C
Saragossa (Zaragoza), Spain	563,375	78E
Saratov, U.S.S.R. (1,090,000)	864,000	80E
Seattle, U.S. (2,077,100)	493,846	80C
Semarang, Indonesia (1,050,000)	1,026,671	80C
Sendai, Japan (925,000)	664,799	80C
Seoul (Sŏul), South Korea (11,200,000)	8,366,756	80C
Sevilla, Spain (740,000)	630,329	78E
Shanghai, China (10,980,000†)	8,100,000	78E
Sheffield, U.K. (705,000)	544,200	79E
Shihchiachuang (Shijiazhuang), China	940,000	75UE
Sian (Xi'an), China	1,900,000	75UE
Singapore (Singapura), Singapore (2,600,000)	2,390,800	80E
Sofia (Sofija), Bulgaria (1,133,733)	1,047,920	79E
Southampton, U.K. (410,000)	207,800	79E
Stockholm, Sweden (1,384,310)	649,384	79E
Stuttgart, Fed. Rep. of Ger. (1,935,000)	581,989	79E
Suchow (Xuzhou), China	800,000	75UE
Suez (As Suways), Egypt	204,000	78E
Surabaya, Indonesia (2,150,000)	2,027,913	80C
Surat, India (960,000)	775,711	81C
Sverdlovsk, U.S.S.R. (1,450,000)	1,225,000	80E
Sydney, Australia (3,193,300)	49,750	79E
Taegu, South Korea	1,607,458	80C
Taichung, Taiwan	585,205	77E
Tainan, Taiwan	572,590	77E
Taipei, Taiwan (3,825,000)	2,196,237	77E
Taiyuan, China	1,350,000	75UE
Tallinn, U.S.S.R.	436,000	80E
Tampa, U.S. (573,100)	271,523	80C
Tashkent (Taškent), U.S.S.R. (2,015,000)	1,816,000	80E
Tbilisi, U.S.S.R. (1,240,000)	1,080,000	80E
Tegucigalpa, Honduras	316,800	77E
Tehrān, Iran (4,700,000)	4,496,159	76C
Tel Aviv-Yafo, Israel (1,350,000)	336,300	79E
The Hague ('s-Gravenhage), Netherlands (775,000)	456,886	80E
Thessaloníki *(Salonika)*, Greece (557,360)	345,799	71C
Tientsin (Tianjin), China (7,210,000†)	4,650,000	78E
Tirana, Albania	192,300	76E
Tōkyō, Japan (25,800,000)	8,349,209	80C
Toledo, U.S. (571,200)	354,635	80C
Toronto, Canada (2,803,101)	633,318	76C
Tripoli (Tarābulus), Libya	264,000	70E
Tsinan (Jinan), China	1,125,000	75UE
Tsingtao (Qingdao), China	1,200,000	75UE
Tsitsihar (Qiqihar), China	850,000	75UE
Tucson, U.S. (495,200)	330,537	80C
Tula, U.S.S.R. (615,000)	518,000	80E
Tulsa, U.S. (569,100)	360,919	80C
Tūnis, Tunisia (915,000)	550,404	75C
Turin (Torino), Italy (1,670,000)	1,160,686	79E
Ufa, U.S.S.R. (1,000,000)	986,000	80E
Ujung Pandang *(Makasar)*, Indonesia	709,038	80C
Ulan-Bator, Mongolia	287,000	70E
Vadodara, India (744,043)	733,656	81C
Valencia, Spain (1,140,000)	750,994	78E
Valparaiso, Chile (530,000)	250,358	70C
Vancouver, Canada (1,166,348)	410,188	76C
Vārānasi *(Benares)*, India (925,000)	704,772	81C
Venice (Venezia), Italy (445,000)	355,865	79E
Victoria, Hong Kong (3,975,000)	1,026,870	76C
Vienna (Wien), Austria (1,925,000)	1,572,300	79E
Vladivostok, U.S.S.R.	558,000	80E
Volgograd *(Stalingrad)*, U.S.S.R. (1,230,000)	939,000	80E
Voronezh (Voronež), U.S.S.R.	796,000	80E
Warsaw (Warszawa), Poland (2,080,000)	1,576,600	79E
Washington, U.S. (3,220,700)	637,651	80C
Wellington, New Zealand (349,900)	137,600	79E
Wiesbaden, Fed. Rep. of Ger. (795,000)	273,267	79E
Winnipeg, Canada (578,217)	560,874	76C
Wrocław *(Breslau)*, Poland	609,100	79E
Wuhan, China	3,000,000	75UE
Wuppertal, Fed. Rep. of Ger. (870,000)	394,605	79E
Yaoundé, Cameroon	313,706	76C
Yerevan, (Jerevan), U.S.S.R. (1,155,000)	1,036,000	80E
Yokohama, Japan (*Tōkyō)	2,773,322	80C
Zagreb, Yugoslavia	566,084	71C
Zaporozhye (Zaporožje), U.S.S.R.	799,000	80E
Zhdanov (Ždanov), U.S.S.R.	507,000	80E
Zürich, Switzerland (780,000)	369,522	80C

Metropolitan area populations are shown in parentheses.
* City is located within the metropolitan area of another city; for example, Kyōto, Japan (*Ōsaka).
† Population of entire municipality or district, including rural area.

C Census
E Official Estimate
UE Unofficial Estimate

Sources

The maps in the Atlas have been compiled from diverse source materials, which are cited in the following lists. The citations are organized by continent and region or country. Within each regional or country group, atlases are listed alphabetically by title and then followed by maps, which are listed according to scale, from the smallest to the largest. Other sources, listed alphabetically by title, follow the map listings.

GENERAL SOURCES

Atlante dei confini sottomarini, *A. Giuffrè Editore, Milano 1979*
Atlante Internazionale del Touring Club Italiano, *TCI, Milano 1977*
Atlas Mira, *G.U.G.K. Moskva 1967*
Atlas Okeanov-Atlantičeski i Indijski Okeany, *Ministerstvo Oborony SSSR-Vojenno-Morskoj Flot, Moskva 1977*
Atlas Okeanov-Tihi Okean, *Ministerstvo Oborony SSSR-Vojenno-Morskoj Flot, Moska 1974*
Atlas of the World, *National Geographic Society (N.G.S.), Washington 1981*
Atlas zur Ozeanographie, *Bibliographisches Institut, Mannheim 1971*
Bertelsmann Atlas International, *C. Bertelsmann Verlag GmbH, München 1963*
Grande Atlante degli Oceani, *Instituto Geografico De Agostini (I.G.D.A.), Novara 1978*
Meyers Neuer Geographischer Handatlas, *Bibliographisches Institut, Mannheim 1966*
The New International Atlas, *Rand McNally & Company, Chicago 1980*
The Odyssey World Atlas, *Western Publishing Company Inc., New York 1966*
The Times Atlas of the World, *John Bartholomew & Son Ltd, Edinburgh 1980*
The World Book Atlas, *World Book Encyclopedia Inc, 1979*
The World Shipping Scene, *Weststadt-Verlag, München 1963*
Weltatlas Erdöl und Erdgas, *George Westermann Verlag, Braunschweig 1976*
Pacific Ocean Floor 1:36,432,000, *N.G.S., Washington 1969*
Atlantic Ocean Floor 1:30,580,000, *N.G.S., Washington 1973*
Indian Ocean 1:25,720,000, *N.G.S. Washington 1967*
Deutsche Meereskarte 1:25,000,000, *Kartographisches Institut Meyer*
Carte générale du Monde 1:10,000,000, *Institut Géographique National (I.G.N.), Paris*
Artic Ocean Floor 1:9,757,000, *N.G.S., Washington 1971*
Carte du Monde 1:5,000,000, *I.G.N., Paris*
Karta Mira 1:2,500,000, *G.U.G.K., Moskva*
Carte Internationale du Monde 1:1,000,000, *Geographical Survey Institute*
Carte Aéronautique du Monde 1:1,000,000, *I.G.N., Paris*
Calendario Atlante, *I.G.D.A., Novara 1982*
Cartactual, *Cartographia, Budapest*
Demographic Yearbook, *United Nations, New York, 1978*
Duden Wörterbuch Geographischer Namen, *Bibliographisches Institut, Mannheim 1966*
Gazetteers (Various), *U.S. Board on Geographical Names, Washington*
Meyers Enzyklopädisches Lexikon, *Bibliographisches Institut, Mannheim 1972–81*
Schtag nach!-Die Staaten der Erde, *Bibliographisches Institut, Mannheim 1977*
Statistical Yearbook, *United Nations, New York, 1978*
Statistik des Auslandes-Länderkurzberichte, *Statistisches Bundesamt, Wiesbaden*
The Columbia Lippincott Gazetteer of the World, *Columbia University Press, New York 1961*
The Europa Year Book 1981, *Europa Publication Ltd., London*
The Statesman's Yearbook 1981–82, *The Macmillan Press Ltd., London*
Webster's New Geographical Dictionary, *G & C Merriam Co, Springfield 1972*

EUROPE

ALBANIA

Shqiperia-Hartë Fizike 1:500,000, *MMS "Hamid Shijaku", Tirana 1970*
Shqiperia Politiko Administrative 1:500,000, *MMS "Hamid Shijaku", Tirana 1969*
Gjeografia e Shqiperise per shkollat e mesme, *Shtëpia Botuese e Librit Shkollor, Tirana 1970*

AUSTRIA

Neuer Schulatlas, *Freytag-Berndt und Artaria KG, Wien 1971*
Generalkarte Österreich 1:200,000, *Mairs Geographischer Verlag, Stuttgart 1974*
Gemeindeverzeichnis von Österreich, *Österreichischen Statistischen Zentralamt, Wien 1970*
Geographisches Namenbuch Österreichs, *Verlag der Österreichischen Akademie der Wissenschaften, Wien 1975*
Statistisches Handbuch für die Republik Österreich, *Österreichischen Statistischen Zentralamt, Wien 1978*

BELGIUM

Atlas de Belgique-Atlas van België, *Comité National de Géographie, Bruxelles 1974*
België, Luxemburg, Belgien 1:350,000, *Pneu. Michelin, Bruxelles 1976*
Belgique, Grand-Duché de Luxembourg, *Pneu. Michelin, Paris 1978*
Lista Alphabetique des Communes-fusion de 1963 à 1977, *Institut National de Statistique, Bruxelles*
Statistique Demographiques 1980, *Institut National de Statistique, Bruxelles*

BULGARIA

Atlas Narodna Republika Bulgarija, *Glavno Upravlenie po Geodezija i Kartografija, Sofija 1973*
Bulgaria 1:1,000,000, *PPWK, Warszawa 1977*
Statističeski Godišnik na Narodna Republika Bălgarija 1973, *Ministerstvo na Informacijata i Săobšenijata, Sofija*

CZECHOSLOVAKIA

Atlas ČSSR, *Kartografie, Praha 1972*
Školní Zeměpisný Atlas Československé Socialistické Republiky, *Kartografické* Nakladatelství, Praha 1970
Auto Atlas Č.S.S.R., *Kartografie, Praha 1971*
Č.S.S.R.-Fyzická Mapa 1:500,000, *Ustřední Správa Geodezie a Kartografie, Praha 1963*
Statistická Ročenka Č.S.S.R., *Federální Statistický Úřad, Praha 1980*

DENMARK

Haases Atlas, *P. Haase & Søns Forlag, København 1972*
Opgivne og Tilplantede Landbrugsarealer i Jylland, *Det Kongelige Danske Geografiske Selskab, København 1976*
Danmark 1:300,000, *Geodætisk Institut, København 1972*
Statistisk Årbog Danmark 1980, *Danmarks Statistik, København*

FINLAND

Oppikoulun Kartasto, *Werner Söderström Osakeyhtiö, Porvoo 1972*
Suomi-Finland 1:1,000,000, *Naanmittaushallituksen Kivipaino, Helsinki 1972*
Finland-Suomi 1:1,000,000, *Kümmerly & Frey, Bern 1981*
Suomen Tilastollinen Vuosikirja 1975, *Tilastokeskus, Helsinki*

FRANCE

Atlas Général Larousse, *Librairie Larousse, Paris 1976*
Atlas Général Bordas, *Bordas, Paris 1972*
Atlas Géographique Alpha, *I.G.D.A., Novara 1972*
Atlas Moderne Larousse, *Librairie Larousse-I.G.D.A., Paris 1976*
Carte Administrative de la France 1:1,400,000, *I.G.N., Paris 1977*
Carte de la France 1:1,000,000, *I.G.N., Paris 1971*
France: Routes-Autoroutes 1:1,000,000, *I.G.N., Paris 1978*
Carte Touristique 1:250,000, *I.G.N., Paris 1978*
France 1:200,000, *Pneu. Michelin, Paris*
Carte Touristique 1:100,000, *I.G.N., Paris*
Michelin 1977-France, *Pneu. Michelin, Paris*
Population de la France-Recensement 1975, *Institut National de la Statistique et des Études Économiques, Paris*

GERMAN DEMOCRATIC REPUBLIC

Haack Weltatlas, *V.E.B. Hermann Haack Geographisch-Kartographische Anstalt, Gotha-Leipzig 1972*
Weltatlas-Die Staaten der Erde und ihre Wirtschaft, *V.E.B. Hermann Haack Geographisch-Kartographische Anstalt, Gotha-Leipzig 1972*
Autokarte der D.D.R. 1:600,000, *V.E.B. Landkartenverlag, Berlin 1972*
Statistisches Jahrbuch der Deutschen Demokratischen Republik 1981, *Staatsverlag der D.D.R., Berlin*

GERMANY, FEDERAL REPUBLIC OF

Diercke Weltatlas, *Westermann Verlag, Braunschweig 1977*
Der Grosse Shell Atlas, *Mairs Geographischer Verlag, Stuttgart 1981–82*
Der Neue Weltatlas, *I.G.D.A., Novara 1977*
Deutschland-Strassenkarte 1:1,000,000, *Kümmerly & Frey, Bern 1981*
Bundesrepublik Deutschland-Übersichtskarte 1:500,000, *Institut für Angewandte Geodäsie, Frankfurt 1978*
Topographische Übersichtskarte 1:200,000, *Institut für Angewandte Geodäsie, Frankfurt*
Bevölkerung der Gemeinden, *Statistisches Bundesamt, Wiesbaden 1979*
Statistisches Jahrbuch für die B.R.D. 1980, *Statistisches Bundesamt, Wiesbaden*

GREECE

Greece-Autokarte 1:1,000,000, *Kümmerly & Frey, Bern*
Greece-Autokarte 1:650,000, *Freytag & Berndt, Wien*
Genikos Chartis tis Hellados 1:400,000, *Geografiki Hypiresia Stratoy, Athínai*
Etniki Statistiki Hypiresia tis Hellados 1:200,000, *E.S.Y.E., Athínai*
Statistiki Epetiris tis Hellados 1979, *E.S.Y.E., Athínai*

HUNGARY

Földrajzi Atlas a Középiskolák Számára, *Kartográfiai Vallalat, Budapest 1980*
A Magyar Népköztársaság 1:400,000, *Kartográfiai Vallalat, Budapest 1974*
Magyarorszag Domborzata és Vizei 1:350,000, *Kartográfiai Vallalat, Budapest 1961*
Megye Terképe, *Cartographia, Budapest 1979–80*
A Magyar Népköztársaság Helységnévtára 1973, *Statisztikai Kiadó Vállalat, Budapest*
Statistical Pocket Book of Hungary 1980, *Statistical Publishing House, Budapest*

ICELAND

Landabréfabok, *Ríkisutgáfa Námsbóka, Reykjavik 1970*
Iceland-Road Guide, *Örn & Örlygur H.F., Reykjavik 1975*

IRELAND

Irish Student's Atlas, *Educational Company of Ireland, Dublin-Cork 1971*
Ireland 1:575,000, *Ordnance Survey Office, Dublin 1979*
Ireland 1:250,000, *Ordnance Survey Office, Dublin 1962*
Census of Population of Ireland 1979, *The Stationery Office, Dublin*

ITALY

Atlante Metodico, *I.G.D.A., Novara 1981*
Atlante Stradale d'Italia 1:200,000, *Touring Club Italiano, Milano*
Carta d'Italia 1:1,250,000, *Istituto Geografico Militare, Firenze 1972*
Carte batimetriche, *Istituto Idrografico della Marina, Genova*
Carta Generale d'Italia 1:500,000, *Touring Club Italiano, Milano 1979*
Carta Generale d'Italia 1:200,000, *I.G.M., Firenze*
Enciclopedia Italiana, *Istituto della Enciclopedia Italiana G. Treccani, Roma*
Il Mare, *I.G.D.A., Novara*
La Montagna, *I.G.D.A., Novara*
XI Censimento Generale della Popolazione 24 ottobre 1971, *Istituto Centrale di Statistica, Roma*
XII Censimento Generale della Popolazione 25 ottobre 1981, *Istituto Centrale di Statistica, Roma*

LUXEMBOURG

Grand-Duché de Luxembourg 1:100,000, *I.G.N., Paris 1970*
Annuaire Statistique-Luxembourg 1981–82, *Service Central de la Statistique et des Études Économiques, Paris*

NETHERLANDS

Atlas van Nederland, *Staatsdrukkerij-en Uitgeverijbedrijf,'s-Gravenhage*
De Grote Vara Gezinsatlas, *Vara Omroepvereniging, Hilversum 1975*
Der Kleine Bosatlas, *Wolter-Noordhoff, Groningen 1974*
Pays-Bas/Nederland 1:400,000, *Pneu. Michelin, Paris 1981*
Gegevens per Gemeente Betreffende de Loop der Bevolking in het Jaar 1980, *Centraal Bureau voor der Statistik, Amsterdam*

NORWAY

Atlas-Større Utgave for Gymnaset, *J. W. Cappelens Forlag A.S., Oslo 1969*
Bilkart Bok Road Atlas, *J. W. Cappelens Forlag A.S., Oslo 1967*
Norge-Bit-Og Turistkart 1:400,000, *J. W. Cappelens Forlag A.S., Oslo 1965*
Folketallet i Kommunene 1972–73, *Statistik Sentralbyraå, Oslo*
Statistisk Årbok 1981, *Statistik Sentralbyrå, Oslo*

POLAND

Atlas Geograficzny, *PPWK, Warszawa 1979*
Narodowy Atlas Polski, *Polska Akademia Nauk, Warszawa 1978*
Polska Kontynenty Świat, *P.P.W.K., Warszawa 1977*
Powszechny Atlas Świat, *P.P.W.K. Warszawa 1981*
Polska Rzeczpospolito. Ludowa-Mapa Administracyjna 1:500,000, *P.P.W.K., Warszawa 1980*
Rocznik Statystyczny 1978, *Glówny Urzad Statystyczny, Warszawa*

PORTUGAL

Portugal 1:1,500,000, *Pneu. Michelin, Paris 1981*
Mapa do Estado das Estradas de Portugal 1:550,000, *Automovel Club de Portugal, Lisboa 1979*
Carto. Corográfica de Portugal 1:400,000, *Instituto Geografico e Cadastral, Lisboa 1968*
Anuário Estatístico-Portugal 1974, *Instituto Nacional de Estatística, Lisboa*

ROMANIA

Atlas Geografic General, *Editura Didactica si Pedagogica, București 1974*
Atlasul Republicii Socialiste România, *Institutul de Geologie si Geofizica, București*
Rumanien-Bulgarien 1:1,000,000, *Freytag-Berndt und Artaria K.G., Wien*
Anuarul Statistic al Republicii Socialiste România 1980, *Direcția Centrala de Statistică, București*

SPAIN

Atlas Bachillerato Universal y de España, *Aguilar, Madrid 1968*
Atlas Básico Universal, *I.G.D.A. Teide, Novara 1969*
Gran Atlas Aguilar, *Aguilar, Madrid 1969*
Peninsula Iberica, Baleares y Canarias 1:1,000,000, *Instituto Geografico y Catastral, Madrid 1966*
Mapa Militar de España 1:800,000, *Servicio Geografico del Ejercito, Madrid 1971*
España 1:500,000, *Firestone Hispania, Madrid*
España-Mapa Oficial de Carreteras 1:400,000 *Ministerio de Obras Publica, Madrid*
España-Anuario Estadistico 1979, *Instituto Nacional de Estadistica, Madrid*

SWEDEN

Atlas Över Välden, *Generalstabens Litografiska Anstalt, Stockholm 1972*
Atlas Över Välden, *Natur Miljö Befolkning, Stockholm 1974*
Kak Bil Atlas, *Generalstabens Litografiska Anstalt, Stockholm 1973*
Sverige-Bilkarta 1:625,000, *A.B. Kartlitografen, Stockholm 1972*
Statistisk Årsbok 1980, *Statistiska Centralbyrån, Stockholm*

SWITZERLAND

Atlas der Schweiz, *Verlag des Bundesamtes fur Landestopographie, Wabern-Bern*
Schweizerischer Mittelschulatlas, *Konferenz der Kantonalen Erziehungsdirektoren, Zürich 1976*
Switzerland 1:300,000, *Kümmerly & Frey, Bern 1979*
Carte Nazionale de la Suisse 1:200,000, *Service Topographique Federale, Wabern-Bern*

U.S.S.R.

Atlas Avtomobilnyh Dorog, *G.U.G.K., Moskva 1976*
Atlas Obrazovanie i Razvitie Sojuza S.S.R., *G.U.G.K., Moskva 1972*
Malyi Atlas S.S.S.R., *G.U.G.K., Moskva 1973*
SSSR 1:8,000,000, *G.U.G.K., Moskva 1980*
SSSR 1:4,000,000, *G.U.G.K., Moskva 1972*
Latvijskaja SSR 1:600,000, *G.U.G.K., Moskva 1967*
Litovskaja SSR 1:600,000, *G.U.G.K., Moskva 1969*
S.S.S.R. Administrativno-Territorialnoje Delenie Sojuznyh Respublik, *Prezidium Verhovnogo Soveta Sojuza Sovetskih Socialističeskih Respublik Moskva 1971*

UNITED KINGDOM

Philips' Modern School Economic Atlas, *George Philip & Son Ltd, London 1981*
Roads Atlas of Great Britain and Ireland, *George Philip & Son Ltd, London 1971*
The Atlas of Britain and Northern Ireland, *Clarendon Press, Oxford 1963*
Route Planning Map 1:625,000, *Ordnance Survey, Southampton 1973*
Cartes 1:400,000, *Michelin Tyre Co. Ltd., London 1981*

YUGOSLAVIA

Atlas, *Izrađenou u Oour Kartografiji Tlos "Učila", Zagreb 1980*
Jugoslavija-Auto Atlas, *Jugoslavenski Leksikografski Zavod, Zagreb 1972*
Školki Atlas, *Izrađenou u Oour Kartografiji Tlos "Učila", Zagreb 1975*
Jugoslavija 1:1,000,000, *Grafički Zavod Hrvatske, Zagreb 1980*
Statistički Godišnjak Jugoslavije 1975, *Savezni Zavod za Statistiku, Beograd*

ASIA

ARABIAN PENINSULA

The Oxford Map of Saudi Arabia 1:2,600,000, *GEO-projects, Beirut 1981*
Arabian Peninsula 1:2,000,000, *United States Geological Survey, Washington 1963*
Arabische Republik Jemen 1:1,000,000, *Deutsch-Jemenitische Gesellschaft e V, Schwaig 1976*
The United Arab Emirates 1:750,000, *GEO-projects, Beirut 1981*

MIDDLE EAST

Atlas of Iran, *"Sahab" Geographic & Drafting Institute, Tehrān 1971*
Modern Büyük Atlas, *Arkin Kitabevi-I.G.D.A., Istanbul 1981*
The New Israel Atlas-Zev Vilnay, *Israel Universities Press, Yerushalaym 1968*
Iran 1:2,500,000, *Imperial Government of Iran, Tehrān 1968*
Guide Map of Iran 1:2,250,000, *Gita Shenassi Co. Ltd, Tehrān*
Guide Map of Iraq 1:2,000,000, *"Sahab" Geographic & Drafting Institute, Tehrān 1971*
Türkiye 1:2,000,000, *Ravenstein Verlag GmbH, Frankfurt 1975*
Iran 1:1,500,000, *Imperial Government of Iran, Tehrān 1968*
Iraq Tourist Map 1:1,500,000, *Summer Resorts and Tourism Service, Baghdād 1967*
The Oxford Map of Syria 1:1,000,000, *GEO-projects, Beirut 1980*
Turkey-Road Map 1:1,000,000, *Kümmerly & Frey, Bern 1980*
Türkei und Naher Osten 1:800,000, *Reis und Verkehrsverlag, Berlin-Stuttgart 1977*
Israel und Angrenzende Länder-Strassenkarte 1:750,000, *Kümmerly & Frey, Bern 1981*
The Oxford Map of Jordan 1:730,000, *GEO-projects, Beirut 1979*
Map of Israel 1:500,000, *Survey of Israel, Yerushalaym 1979*
The Oxford Map of Kuwait 1:500,000, *GEO-projects, Beirut 1980*
The Oxford Map of Qatar 1:270,000, *GEO-projects, Beirut 1980*
Israel Map of the Cease-Fire Lines 1:250,000, *Survey of Israel, Yerushalaym 1973*
Qatar-Visitor's Map 1:250,000, *Ministry of Information, Doha 1979*
Carte Générale du Liban 1:200,000, *Ministère de la Défense Nationale, Beirut 1967*
Qatar 1:200,000, *Hunting Surveys Ltd., Borchamwood 1975*
Bahrain Islands 1:63,360, *Public Works Department, Al Manāmah 1968*
The Oxford Map of Bahrain 1:57,750, *GEO-projects, Beirut 1980*
Bahrain—A Map for Visitors 1:50,000, *Ministry of Information, Al Manāmah 1976*
Annual Abstract of Statistics 1978, *Central Statistical Organization, Baghdād*
Genel Nüfus Sayımı 12 ekim 1980, *Başbakanlik Devlet İstatistik Enstitüsü, Ankara*
Kuwait—Annual Statistical Abstract, *Central Statistical Office-Ministry of Planning, Al Kuwayt 1976*
List of Localities—Geographical Information and Population 1948–1961–1972–1975, *Central Bureau of Statistics, Yerushalaym*
Recueil de Statistiques Libanaises No. 8-1972, *Direction Centrale de la Statistique, Bayrūt*
Republic of Cyprus—Statistical Abstract 1973, *The Statistics and Research Department, Levkosia*
Statistical Abstract—Syrian Arab Republic 1973, *Central Bureau of Statistics, Dimashq*
Statistical Abstract of Israel 1979, *Central Bureau of Statistics, Yerushalaym*
The Hashemite Kingdom of Jordan, Statistical Yearbook 1976, *Department of Statistics, Ammān*
Türkiye İstatistik Yıllığı 1975, *Başbakanlik Devlet İstatistik Enstitüsü, Ankara*

SOUTH ASIA

National Atlas of India, *National Atlas & Thematic Mapping Organization, Calcutta*
Oxford School Atlas for Pakistan, *Oxford University Press—Pakistan Branch, Karachi 1973*
Tourist Atlas of India, *National Atlas Organization, Calcutta*
Physical Map of India 1:4,500,000, *Survey of India, Calcutta 1974*
Political Map of India 1:4,500,000, *Survey of India, Calcutta 1972*
Railway Map of India 1:3,500,000, *Government of India, Calcutta 1971*
Pākistān 1:3,168,000, *Survey of Pākistān, Rāwalpindi 1966*
Bangladesh 1:2,800,000, *Survey of Bangladesh, Dacca 1979*
Burma 1:2,000,000, *Army Map Service, Washington 1963*
Physical and Political Map of Afghanistan 1:1,500,000, *Afghan Cartographic Institute, Kabul 1968*
Ceylon Physical 1:1,000,000, *Survey Department, Colombo 1973*
New Map of Afghanistan 1:1,000,000, *"Sahab" Geographic & Drafting Institute, Tehrān*
Pākistān 1:1,000,000, *Survey of Pākistān, Rāwalpindi 1968*
Motor Map of Ceylon 1:506,880, *Survey Department, Colombo 1973*
Nepal 1:506,880, *Ministry of Defence, London 1967*
Nepal 1:408,000, *Kümmerly & Frey, Bern 1980*
Bangladesh Population Census Report 1974, *Statistics Division-Ministry of Planning, Dacca*
Geomedical Monograph Series—Afghanistan, *Springer-Verlag, Berlin 1968*
Pakistan Statistical Yearbook 1978, *Statistics Division, Karachi*
Statistical Pocket Book of the Democratic Socialist Republic of Sri Lanka 1979, *Department of Census and Statistics, Colombo*

SOUTHEAST ASIA

Atlas Indonesia, *Yayasan Dwidjendra, Denpasar-Jakarta 1977*
Atlas of Thailand, *Royal Thai Survey Department, Bangkok 1974*
Secondary Atlas for Malaysia and Singapore, *Niugini Press Pty. Ltd., Port Moresby 1975*
Secondary School Atlas for Malaysia, *McGraw-Hill Far Eastern Publishers Ltd., Singapore 1970*
Hành Chính Viet Nam 1:2,500,000, *Hô Chí Minh 1976*
Maluku dan Irian Jaya 1:2,250,000, *Pembina, Jakarta 1975–76*
Bàu-dô Viet Nam 1:2,000,000, *Saigon 1972*
Laos Administratif 1:2,000,000, *Service Géographique National du Laos, Vientiane 1968*
Malaysia 1:2,000,000, *Jabatanarah Pemetaan Negara, 1976*
Map of Thailand and Bangkok 1:2,000,000, *The Shell Company of Thailand Ltd., Bangkok*
Vietnam 1:2,000,000, *G.U.G.K., Moskva 1972*
Kalimantan 1:1,500,000, *Pembina, Jakarta 1975–76*
Philippines 1:1,500,000, *Philippine Coast and Geodetic Survey, Manila 1968*
Cambodia & South Vietnam—Southeast Asia 1:1,250,000, *Army Map Service, Washington 1966*
Carte Générale du Laos, *Service Géographique National du Laos, Vientiane 1968*
Sumatera 1:790,000, *Pembina, Jakarta 1975–76*
Malaysia Barat—West Malaysia 1:760,000, *Jabatanarah Pemetaan Negara, 1968*
Jawa Barat & D.K.I. Jakarta 1:500,000, *Pembina, Jakarta 1974–75*
Jawa Tengah & D.I. Yogyakarta 1:500,000, *Pembina, Jakarta 1974–75*
Jawa Timur 1:500,000, *Pembina, Jakarta 1974–75*

Sabah 1:500,000, *Jabatanarah Pemetaan Negara, 1976*
Nusa Tenggara Barat & Nusa Tenggara Timur 1:330,000, *Pembina, Jakarta 1975*
Jawa Madura 1:225,000, *Pembina, Jakarta 1975–76*
Sulawesi 1:220,000, *Pembina, Jakarta 1975–76*
Gulongan Masharakat-Banchi Pendudok dan Perumahan Malaysia 1970, *Jabatan Perangkaan, Kuala Lumpur*
Sensus Penduluk 1971, *Biro Pusat Statistik, Jakarta*
Statistical Summary of Thailand 1978, *Statistical Reports Division, Bangkok*
Statistik Indonesia 1974–75, *Biro Pusat Statistik, Jakarta*

CHINA, MONGOLIA
Zhonghua Renmin Gongheguo Fen Sheng Dituji, *Ditu Chubanshe, Beijing 1977*
Zhonghua Renmin Gongheguo Ditu 1:6,000,000, *Ditu Chubanshe, Beijing 1980*
China 1:5,500,000, *Cartographia, Budapest 1967*
Zhonghua Renmin Gongheguo Ditu 1:4,000,000, *Ditu Chubanshe, Beijing 1980*
Mongolskaja Narodnaja Respublika 1:3,000,000, *G.U.G.K., Moskva 1972*
Taiwan/Formosa 1:500,000, *Army Map Service, Washington 1964*
China's Changing Map, *Methuen & Co., London 1972*

JAPAN, KOREA
Japan—The Pocket Atlas, *Heibonsha Ltd., Tōkyō 1970*
The National Atlas of Japan, *Geographical Survey Institute, Tōkyō 1977*
Teikoku's Complete Atlas of Japan, *Teikoku Shoin Company Ltd., Tōkyō 1977*
Tourist Map of Japan 1:5,300,000, *Japan National Tourist Organisation, Tōkyō 1974*
Republic of Korea 1:1,000,000, *Chungang Map & Chart Service, Sŏul 1973*
Northern Korea—Road Map of Korea, *Republic of Korea Army Map Service, Sŏul 1971*
Southern Korea 1:700,000, *Republic of Korea Army Map Service, Sŏul 1977*

AFRICA

The Atlas of Africa, *Editions Jeune Afrique, Paris 1973*
Africa 1:14,000,000, *N.G.S., Washington 1980*
Africa 1:9,000,000, *V.E.B. Hermann Haack, Gotha-Leipzig 1977*
Afrique/Africa 1:4,000,000, *Pneu. Michelin, Paris-London*
Africa 1:2,000,000, *Army Map Service, Washington*

NORTH WEST AFRICA
Atlas International de l'Ouest Africain 1:2,500,000, *Organisation de l'Unité Africaine, Dakar 1971*
Mauritanie 1:2,500,000, *I.G.N., Paris 1978*
Algérie-Tunisie 1:1,000,000, *Pneu. Michelin, Paris 1975*
Maroc 1:1,000,000, *Pneu. Michelin, Paris 1975*
Generalkarte Gran Canaria-Tenerife 1:150,000, *Mairs Geographischer Verlag, Stuttgart 1979*
Annuaire Statistique du Maroc, *Direction de la Statistique, Rabat 1976*
Code Géographique National—Code des Communes, *Secretariat d'État au Plan, Alger 1975*
Recensement Général de la Population et des Logements 1975, *Institut National de la Statistique, Tūnis*

NORTH EAST AFRICA
Egypte 1:750,000, *Kummerly & Frey, Bern 1977*
Population Census 1973, *Census and Statistical Department, Tarābulus*

WEST AFRICA
Atlas de Côte d'Ivoire, *Institut de Géographie Tropicale-Université d'Abidjan, Abidjan 1971*
Atlas de Haute-Volta, *Centre Voltaïque de la Recherche Scientifique, Ouagadougou 1969*
Atlas du Cameroun, *Institut de Recherches Scientifiques du Cameroun, Yaoundé*
Atlas for the United Republic of Cameroon, *Collins-Longman, Glasgow 1977*
Ghana Junior Atlas, *E. A. Boateng-Thomas Nelson and Sons Ltd., London 1965*
Liberia in Maps, *Stefan von Gnielinski, Hamburg 1972*
Oxford Atlas for Nigeria, *Oxford University Press, London-Ibadan 1971*
School Atlas for Sierra Leone, *Collins-Longman, Glasgow 1975*
République du Mali 1:2,500,000, *I.G.N., Paris 1971*
Ghana-Administrative 1:2,000,000, *Survey of Ghana, Accra 1968*
Road Map of Nigeria 1:585,000, *Federal Surveys, Lagos 1969*
République Unie du Cameroun 1:1,000,000, *I.G.N., Paris 1972*
République de Haute-Volta-Carte Routière 1:1,000,000, *I.G.N., Paris 1968*
Philips' School Room Map of Ghana 1:1,000,000, *George Philip & Son Ltd., London 1963*
Sénégal 1:1,000,000, *I.G.N., Paris 1974*
Sénégal-Carte Administrative 1:1,000,000, *I.G.N., Paris 1966*
Physical Map of Nigeria 1:1,000,000, *Federal Surveys, Lagos 1965*
République du Côte d'Ivoire 1:1,000,000, *I.G.N., Paris 1970*
Côte d'Ivoire 1:800,000, *Pneu. Michelin, Paris 1978*
Mapa da Guiné 1:650,000, *J. R. Silva, Lisboa 1969*
République du Dahomey-Carte Routière et Touristique 1:500,000, *I.G.N., Paris 1968*
Road Map of Ghana 1:500,000, *Survey of Ghana, Accra 1970*
The Gambia Road Map 1:500,000, *Survey Department The Gambia, Banjul 1973*
Nigeria-Digest of Statistics 1973, *Federal Office of Statistics, Lagos*

EAST AND CENTRAL AFRICA
Atlas Pratique du Tchad, *Institut Tchadien pour les Sciences Humaines, Paris 1972*
Sudan Roads 1:4,000,000, *Sudan Survey Department, Khartoum 1976*
Äthiopie/Ethiopia 1:4,000,000, *Medizinische Länderkunde/Geomedical Monograph Series, Berlin 1972*
Carte de l'Afrique Centrale 1:2,500,000, *I.G.N., Paris 1968*
Highway Map of Ethiopia 1:2,000,000, *Imperial Ethiopian Government, Addis Ababa 1961*
République du Tchad-Carte Routière 1:1,500,000, *I.G.N., Paris 1968*
République Centrafricaine-Carte Routière 1:1,500,000, *I.G.N., Paris 1969*
Territoire Française des Afars et des Issas 1:400,000, *Office Developpement du Tourisme, Djibouti 1970*
Ethiopia-Statistical Abstract 1976, *Central Statistical Office, Addis Ababa*

EQUATORIAL AFRICA
Atlas du Congo, *Office de la Recherche Scientifique et Techique Outre-Mer, Brazzaville 1969*
Atlas for Malawi, *Collins-Longman, Glasgow 1969*
Atlas of Uganda, *Department of Lands and Surveys, Kampala 1967*
Malawi in Maps, *University of London Press Ltd., London 1972*
Tanzania in Maps, *University of London Press, Ltd., London 1975*
The First Kenya Atlas, *George Philip & Son Ltd., London 1973*
Carte de l'Afrique Centrale 1:2,500,000, *I.G.N., Paris 1968*
Carta Rodoviária de Angola 1:2,000,000, *Lello S.A.R.L., Luanda 1974*
Republic of Zambia 1:1,500,000, *Surveyor General, Ministry of Lands and Natural Resources, Lusaka 1972*
Tanzania 1:1,250,000, *Shell & B.P. Tanzania Ltd., Dar es Salaam 1973*
Malawi 1:1,000,000, *Malawi Government, Blantyre 1971*
Road Map of Kenya 1:1,000,000, *George Philip & Son Ltd., London 1972*
République Populaire du Congo 1:1,000,000, *I.G.N., Paris 1973*
Gabon 1:1,000,000, *I.G.N., Paris 1975*
Statistical Abstract 1979, *Central Bureau of Statistics, Nairobi*

SOUTHERN AFRICA
Large Print Atlas for Southern Africa, *George Philip & Son Ltd., London 1976*
Atlas de Madagascar, *Association des Géographes de Madagascar, Antananarivo 1971*
Atlas for Mauritius, *Macmillan Education Ltd., London 1971*
Ontwikkelingsatlas-Development Atlas, *Republic of South Africa-Department of Planning, Pretoria 1966*
Botswana Road Map and Climate Chart 1:6,000,000, *Department of Surveys and Lands, Gaborone 1980*
Madagascar et Comores 1:4,000,000, *I.G.N., Paris 1970*
Suidelike Afrika/Southern Africa 1:2,500,000, *The Government Printer, Pretoria 1973*
Roads of Zimbabwe 1:2,100,000, *Shell Zimbabwe Ltd., Salisbury, 1980*
Carta de Moçambique 1:2,000,000, *Ministerio do Ultramar, Lisboa 1971*
Mapa Rodoviário de Maçambique 1:2,000,000, *J.A.E.M. 1972*
The Black Homelands of South Africa 1:1,900,000, *Perskor Boeke Tekenkantoor, Johannesburg*
Road Map of Zimbabwe 1:1,800,000, *A.A. of Zimbabwe, Salisbury 1980*
Zimbabwe-Mobil 1:1,470,000, *M.O. Collins Ltd., Salisbury 1976*
Rhodesia Relief 1:1,000,000, *Surveyor General, Salisbury 1973*
Lafatsche La Botsvana/Republic of Botswana 1:1,000,000, *Department of Surveys and Lands, Gaborone 1970*
Suid Afrika/South Africa 1:500,000, *The Government Printer, Pretoria*
Lesotho, 1:250,000, *Government Overseas Surveys, Maseru 1969*

Île Maurice-Carte Touristique 1:100,000, *I.G.N., Paris 1978*
La Réunion-Carte Touristique 1:100,000, *I.G.N., Paris 1978*
Annual Statistical Bulletin 1973, *The Bureau of Statistics, Maseru*
Bi-Annual Digest of Statistics 1976, *Central Statistical Office, Port Louis*
Population Census 1970, *Department of Statistics, Pretoria*
Population de Madagascar au Ier Janvier 1972, *Direction Général du Gouvernement, Antananarivo*
South Africa 1980–81-Official Yearbook, *Chris van Rensburg Publications Ltd., Johannesburg*

NORTH AMERICA

CANADA
Atlas Larousse Canadien, *Les Editions Françaises Inc., Québec - Montréal 1971*
Oxford Regional Economic Atlas - United States & Canada, *Clarendon Press, Oxford 1967*
Road Atlas United States - Canada - Mexico, *Rand McNally & Co., Chicago 1981*
The National Atlas of Canada, *Department of Energy, Mines and Resources, Ottawa 1972*
Northwest Territories - Yukon Territory 1:4,000,000, *Department of Energy, Mines and Resources, Ottawa 1974*
Quebec and Newfoundland 1:3,700,000, *N.G.S., Washington 1980*
British Columbia, Alberta and the Yukon Territory 1:3,500,000, *N.G.S., Washington 1978*
Ontario 1:3,000,000, *N.G.S., Washington 1980*
Saskatchewan and Manitoba 1:2,600,000, *N.G.S., Washington 1979*
Canada Year Book 1978-79, *Minister of Industry, Trade and Commerce, Ottawa*

UNITED STATES
Oxford Regional Economic Atlas - United States & Canada, *Clarendon Press, Oxford 1967*
Road Atlas United States - Canada - Mexico, *Rand McNally & Co., Chicago 1981*
Transportation Map of the United States, *U.S. Department of Transportation, Washington 1976*
National Energy Transportation System 7,500,000, *U.S. Geological Survey, Reston, Virginia 1977*
Close-up: Alaska 1:3,295,000, *N.G.S., Washington 1975*
Close-up: The Southwest 1:2,124,000, *N.G.S., Washington 1977*
Close-up: The Northwest 1:2,000,000, *N.G.S., Washington 1973*
Close-up: The Southeast 1:1,780,000, *N.G.S., Washington 1975*
Close-up: California and Nevada 1:1,700,000, *N.G.S., Washington 1978*
Close-up: Florida 1:1,331,000, *N.G.S., Washington 1973*
Close-up: Illinois, Indiana, Ohio and Kentucky 1:1,267,000, *N.G.S., Washington 1977*
Close-up: The Northeast 1:1,215,000, *N.G.S., Washington 1978*
Close-up: The Mid-Atlantic States 1:886,000, *N.G.S., Washington 1973*
Topographic Maps 1:500,000, *U.S. Geological Survey, Washington*
Topographic Maps 1:250,000, *U.S. Geological Survey, Washington*
Topographic Maps 1:24,000, *U.S. Geological Survey, Washington*
Census of Population and Housing 1980, *Bureau of the Census, Washington*

MEXICO
Atlas of Mexico, *Bureau of Business Research, University of Texas, Austin 1975*
Road Atlas United States - Canada - Mexico, *Rand McNally & Co., Chicago 1981*
Mapas de los Estados-Serie Patria, *Libreria Patria S.A., México*
Carta Geografica de México 1:2,500,000, *Asociación Nacional Automovilística, Ciudad de México 1976*
Archeological Map of Middle America 1:2,250,000, *N.G.S., Washington 1968*

CENTRAL AMERICA AND THE CARIBBEAN
Atlas for Barbados, Windwards and Leewards, *Macmillan Education Ltd., London 1974*
Atlas for Guyana & Trinidad & Tobago, *Macmillan Education Ltd, London 1973*
Atlas for the Eastern Caribbean, *Collins-Longman, London 1977*
Atlas Nacional de Cuba, *Academia de Ciencias de Cuba, La Habana 1970*
Atlas of the Commonwealth of the Bahamas, *Kingston Publishers Ltd.-Ministry of Education, Kingston-Nassau 1976*
Jamaica in Maps, *University of London Press Ltd., London 1974*
West Indies and Central Amerika 1:4,500,000, *N.G.S., Washington 1981*
Mapa General-República de Honduras 1:1,000,000, *Instituto Geográfico Nacional, Tegucigalpa 1980*
Mapa Oficial de la República de Panamá 1:1,000,000, *Instituto Geográfico Nacional, Panamá 1979*
Mapa Preliminar de la República de Guatemala 1:1,000,000, *Instituto Geográfico Nacional, Guatemala 1976*
República de Nicaragua 1:1,000,000, *Instituto Geográfico Nacional, Managua 1975*
Belize 1:800,000, *Directorate of Overseas Surveys, London 1974*
Mapa de la República Dominicana 1:600,000, *Instituto Geográfico Universitario, Santo Domingo 1979*
Costa Rica - Mapa Fisico-Politico 1:500,000, *Instituto Geográfico de Costa Rica, San José 1974*
El Salvador 1:500,000, *Ministerio de Obras Públicas, San Salvador 1978*
Mapa Hipsométrico de la República de Guatemala 1:500,000, *Instituto Geográfico Nacional, Guatemala 1979*
Jamaica 1:280,000, *Fairey Surveys Ltd., Maidenhead 1974*
Mapa de Carreteras Estatales de Puerto Rico 1:250,000, *Autoridad de Carreteras Estatales, San Juan 1972*
Nicaragua-Costa Rica 1:250,000, *Instituto Geográfico Nacional, Managua 1972*
Puerto Rico e Islas Limitrofes 1:240,000, *U.S. Geological Survey, Washington 1970*
Turks & Caicos Islands 1:200,000, *Directorate of Overseas Surveys, London 1971*
Cayman Islands 1:150,000, *Directorate of Overseas Surveys, London 1972*
Trinidad 1:150,000, *Director of Surveys-Ministry of Defense, London 1970*
Guadeloupe-Carte Touristique 1:100,000, *I.G.N., Paris 1978*
Martinique-Carte Touristique 1:100,000, *I.G.N., Paris 1977*
Lesser Antilles-Antigua 1:50,000, *Directorate of Overseas Surveys, London 1973*
Tourist Map of Tobago 1:50,000, *Lands & Surveys Department, Port of Spain 1969*
Dominica 1:25,000, *Directorate of Overseas Surveys, London 1978*
Lesser Antilles-Barbuda 1:25,000, *Directorate of Overseas Surveys, London 1970*
Annuario Estadístico de Costa Rica 1977, *Direción General de Estadística, San José*
Annuario Estadístico de Cuba 1973, *Direción Central de Estadística, La Habana*
Caribbean Year Book 1978-80, *Caribook Ltd., Toronto*
Fact Sheets on the Commonwealth-Antigua, *British Information Services, London 1974*
Fact Sheets on the Commonwealth-Belize, *British Information Services, London 1976*
Guatemala-III Censo de Habitación 26 de marzo de 1973, *Direción General de Estadística, Guatemala*
Honduras-Annuario Estadístico 1978, *Direción General de Estadística, Censos, Tegucigalpa*
Nicaragua-Annuario Estadístico 1975, *Oficina Ejecutiva de Encuestas y Censos, Managua*
Statistical Yearbook for Latin America, *United Nations, New York 1976*
Zentralamerika-Karten zur Bevölkerungs und Wirtschaftsstruktur 1975, *H. Nuhn, P. Krieg & W. Schlick, Hamburg*

SOUTH AMERICA

NORTHERN SOUTH AMERICA
Atlas Basico de Colombia, *Instituto Geográfico Agustin Codazzi, Bogotá 1970*
Atlas de Colombia, *Instituto Geográfico Agustin Codazzi, Bogotá 1979*
Atlas de Venezuela, *Ministerio de Obras Públicas, Caracas 1970*
Atlas for Guyana, Trinidad & Tobago, *Macmillan Education Ltd., London 1973*
Atlas Histórico Geográfico y de Paisajes Peruanos, *Instituto Nacional de Planificación, Lima 1970*
Atlas Nacional do Brasil, *Instituto Brasileiro de Geografia*
Atlas Universal y del Perú, *Thomas Nelson & Sons Ltd., Sunbury on Thames 1968*
Brasil-Didáctico, Rodoviário, Turístico 1:5,000,000, *Gr. Editôra e Publicidade Ltda., Rio de Janeiro*
Mapa de la República de Bolivia 1:4,000,000, *Instituto Geográfico Militar, La Paz 1974*
Mapa Politico del Perú 1:2,400,000, *Editorial "Navarrete", Lima 1975*
Mapa de Carreteras del Perú 1:2,200,000, *Instituto Geográfico Militar, Lima 1979*
Mapa Fisico-Politico 1:2,000,000, *Instituto Geográfico Militar, Lima 1970*
Mapa Fisico de la República de Venezuela 1:2,000,000, *Ministerio de Obras Públicas, Bogotá 1975*
Brasil-Mapa Rodoviário 1:2,000,000, *Ministério dos Transportes, 1971*

Carte de la Guyane Française 1:1,500,000, *I.G.N., Paris 1973*
República de Colombia 1:1,500,000, *Ministerio de Hacienda y Credito Público, Bogotá 1979*
Ecuador 1:1,000,000, *Instituto Geográfico Militar, Quito 1971*
Kaart van Suriname 1:1,000,000, *C. Kersten & Co. N.V., Paramaribo*
Mapa de Bolivia 1:1,000,000, *Instituto Geográfico Militar, La Paz 1973*
Mapa Vial 1:1,000,000, *Ministerio de Obras Públicas, Caracas 1970*
República del Perú-Mapa Fisico-Politico, 1:1,000,000, *Instituto Geográfico Militar, Lima 1978*
Carte de la Guyane Française 1:500,000, *I.G.N., Paris 1976*
Suriname 1:500,000, *Uitgave Centraal Bureau Luchtkartering, 1969*
Guyana 1:500,000, *Ordnance Survey, Georgetown 1972*
Annuário Estatístico do Brasil 1978, *Fundacão Instituto Brasileiro de Geografia e Estatística, Rio de Janeiro*
Boletín Mensual de Estadística-agosto 1977, *D.A.N.E., Bogotá*
Dicionário Geográfico Brasileiro, *Editora Globo, Pôrto Alegre 1972*
Discover Bolivia, *Los Amigos del Libro, La Paz 1972*
Venezuela-Annuário Estadístico 1976, *Oficina Central de Estadística e Informatica, Caracas*

SOUTHERN SOUTH AMERICA
Atlas de la República Argentina, *Instituto Geográfico Militar, Buenos Aires 1972*
Atlas de la República Argentina, *Instituto Geográfico Militar, Santiago 1976*
Atlas de la República de Chile, *Instituto Geográfico Militar, Santiago 1970*
Atlas Escolar de Chile, *Instituto Geográfico Militar, Santiago 1978*
Atlas Universal y de la República Argentina, *Aguilar Argentina S.A. de Ediciones, Buenos Aires 1972*
Mapa de la República Argentina 1:5,000,000, *Instituto Geográfico Militar, Buenos Aires 1973*
Paraguay 1:1,000,000, *Instituto Geográfico Militar, Asuncíon 1974*
República Oriental del Uruguay 1:500,000, *Servicio Geográfico Militar, Montevideo 1961*
Uruguay-Moyennes et Petites Villes 1972, *Institut des Hautes Etudes de l'Amerique Latine, Paris*

AUSTRALIA AND OCEANIA

Atlas of Australian Resources, *Division of National Mapping, Canberra 1980*
New Zealand-Mobil Travel Map, *Mobil Oil New Zealand Ltd., Wellington 1973*
New Zealand Atlas, *A.R. Shearer Government Printer, Wellington 1976*
The Jacaranda Atlas, *Jacaranda Press Pty. Ltd., 1971*
The Jacaranda Atlas For New Zealand, *Jacaranda Press Pty. Ltd., 1971*
Australia-Geographic Map 1:2,500,000, *Minister for National Development, Canberra 1967*
Territory of Papua and New Guinea 1:2,500,000, *Division of National Mapping, Canberra 1970*
Carte de l'Oceanie Française 1:2,000,000, *I.G.N., Paris 1971*
Îles Tuamotu-Îles Marquises 1:2,000,000, *I.G.N., Paris 1969*
New Zealand-Map Guide 1:1,900,000, *New Zealand Tourist and Publicity Department, Wellington 1978*
Mobil New Zealand Road Map, *Mobil Oil New Zealand Ltd., Wellington 1973*
Fiji Islands-World Aeronautical Chart 1:1,000,000, *Ordnance Survey, Southampton 1970*
Close-up: Hawaii 1:675,000, *N.G.S., Washington 1978*
Archipel des Nouvelles-Hébrides 1:500,000, *I.G.N., Paris 1976*
New Zealand 1:500,000, *Department of Lands and Survey, Wellington 1976*
Nouvelle Calédonie 1:500,000, *I.G.N., Paris 1978*
Palau Islands 1:165,000, *Defense Mapping Agency Hydrographic Center, Washington 1973*
General Map of Tokelau Islands 1:100,000, *Department of Lands & Survey, Wellington 1969*
Tahiti-Carte Touristique 1:100,000, *I.G.N., Paris 1977*
Christmas Islands - Gilbert and Ellice Islands Colony 1:50,000, *Directorate of Overseas Survey, London 1970*
Tuvalu, *Government of Tuvalu 1979*
Annual Statistical Abstract-Fiji 1970-71, *Bureau of Statistics, Suva*
Australia - Population and Dwellings in Local Government Areas and Urban Centres 1976, *Australian Bureau of Statistics, Canberra*
Fact Sheet - Pitcairn Islands Group, *British Information Services, London 1974*
Fact Sheet - The Gilbert Islands, *British Information Services, London 1977*
Fact Sheet - The New Hebrides, *British Information Services, London 1976*
Fact Sheet - The Solomon Islands, *British Information Services, London 1976*
Fact Sheet - Tuvalu, *British Information Services, London 1977*
New Zealand Pocket Digest of Statistics 1979, *Department of Statistics, Wellington*
New Zealand Official Yearbook 1978, *Department of Statistics, Wellington*

POLAR REGIONS

Antarctica 1:11,250,000, *U.S. Naval Oceanographic Office, Washington 1965*
Antarctica 1:10,000,000, *American Geographical Society, New York 1970*
Antarctica 1:10,000,000, *Division of National Mapping, Canberra 1979*
Antarctica 1:5,000,000, *American Geographical Society, New York 1970*
Map of the Artic Region 1:5,000,000, *American Geographical Society, New York 1975*

Transliteration Systems

Toponymy: Criteria Used for the Writing of Names on the Maps

The language of geography is a language which defines geographic features in universally recognized terms. In creating this language, toponymy experts and cartographers have confronted complex problems in finding terms which are universally acceptable. So that the reader can fully understand the maps in this atlas, here is a brief explanation of how the toponyms (place-names for geographic features) have been written, particularly those relating to regions or countries where the Roman alphabet is not used. Among these are the Slavic-speaking nations such as the Soviet Union, Yugoslavia and Bulgaria; and China and Japan, which use ideographic characters. Of the European countries, Greece has its own alphabet, which is totally different from the Roman alphabet. Many of the Islamic countries use Arabic, with variations derived from local dialects.

There are two basic systems for Romanizing writing. The first is by phonetic transcription, using combinations of different alphabetical signs for each language when the phonetic sound in other languages should be maintained. For example, the Italian sound "sc" (which must be followed by an "e" or "i" to remain soft) in French is "ch," in English is "sh," and in German is "sch."

The second system is transliteration, in which the words, letters or characters of one language are represented or spelled in the letters or characters of another language.

Chinese, Japanese and Arabic Languages

Various Asian and African countries use non-Roman forms in their writing. For example, the Chinese and Japanese languages use ideographic characters instead of an alphabet, and these ideographic characters are transformed into the Roman alphabet through phonetic transcription. Until recently, one of the methods used for transforming Chinese was the Wade-Giles system, named for its English authors. Used in this atlas is the Pinyin system, which was approved by the Chinese government in 1958 and has been incorporated into the official maps of the People's Republic of China. The Pinyin system also has been adopted by the United States Board on Geographic Names and is used in official United Nations documents. The Pinyin names, however, often are accompanied by the Wade-Giles form, as the latter was widely known.

In Japan, ideographic characters are used, although the Roman alphabet is used in many Japanese scientific works. Japan uses two principal systems for standardizing names. They are the Kunreisiki, used by the government in official publications, and the Hepburn method. Adopted for this atlas is the Hepburn method, the system used in international English-language publications and by the United States Board on Geographic Names.

Romanization of the Arabic alphabet, which is used in many Islamic countries, is by transliteration. Since English and French are still used as an international language in many Arab countries, the name forms proposed by the major English and French sources have been taken into consideration. Generally, the systems proposed by the United States Board on Geographic Names and the Permanent Committee on Geographical Names have been used for most Asian countries and Arab-speaking countries.

Greek, Russian and Other Slavic Languages

Practically all written languages in Europe use the Roman alphabet. The differences in phonetics and grammar are shown by the use of diacritical marks and by groupings of consonants, vocals and syllables which give meaning to the various tones in the language. According to a centuries-old tradition, each written language maintains its formal characters, using the translated form rather than the phonetic transcription when a geographical term must be given in another language. This system, therefore, makes it more a translation than a transliteration.

In the Aegean area, Greek and the Greek alphabet are particularly significant because of historical links to the beginning of European civilization. The 1962 United States Board on Geographic Names and the Permanent Committee on Geographical Names systems, based on modern Greek pronunciation, have been used in transcribing toponyms from official sources for these maps. (The table that follows has an example indicating essential norms for Romanizing the modern Greek alphabet.)

A different situation arises in countries using the Cyrillic alphabet. Six principal Slavic languages using this alphabet are Russian, Byelorussian, Ukrainian, Bulgarian, Serbian, and Macedonian. The Cyrillic alphabet also is used by the non-Slavic people of the central Soviet Union. The nomenclature of these regions has been transliterated in accordance with the system proposed by the International Organization for Standardization, taking into consideration sounds and letters and uses of the diacritical marks normal in Slavic languages. The International Organization for Standardization method is accepted and used in bibliographical works and international documents. (The table which follows gives the relationship between the letters of the Cyrillic and Roman alphabets for the above six languages.) An exception to this transliteration is made by the Soviet Balkan republics of Estonia, Latvia and Lithuania. Here the name forms deriving from the national languages have been adopted, using the Roman alphabet.

Special Cases: Conventional Forms and Multilinguals

Cartographic nomenclature generally derives from the official nomenclature of the sovereign and nonsovereign countries, although a number of cases need an explanation.

In numerous situations, English conventional forms are used along with the local or conventional name in referring to a geographical entity used outside the official language area. For example, Vienna, Prague, Copenhagen and Moscow are English forms for Wien, Praha, København and Moskva, respectively. There have been cases, however, where the conventional or historical form commonly used in English cartography has been applied with the same meaning. Thus, Peking and Nanking are the English conventional forms for Beijing and Nanjing, while Tsinan, Tientsin and Mukden are the former conventional spellings or names for Jinan, Tianjin and Shenyang, respectively. Other examples are Saigon, the former name for Ho Chi Minh, Vietnam; and Bangkok, the name for Krung Thep, which is used in Thailand.

The lack of reliable data for countries, especially ex-colonies without a firm national cartographic tradition, has made it necessary to utilize mapping skills of former colonist nations such as France, the United Kingdom and Belgium. A lack of data has led to the adoption of French and British forms in many areas, as these two languages are widely used for official purposes.

Another special case is that of the multilingual areas. Many countries and areas officially recognize two or more written and spoken languages; therefore, all of the principal written forms appear on the maps. This is true, for example, of Belgium where the official languages are French and Dutch (e.g. Bruxelles/Brussel) and of Italian regions such as Valle d'Aosta and Alto Adige, where French, German and Italian are used (e.g. Aosta/Aoste) (Bolzano/Bozen).

In preparing this atlas, each of these special cases has been taken into full consideration within the limits of the scale, space and readability of the maps.

Transliteration of the Cyrillic Alphabet
(International System—ISO)

Cyrillic Letter		Roman Letter		Cyrillic Letter		Roman Letter	
А	а	a		О	о	o	
Б	б	b		П	п	p	
В	в	v		Р	р	r	
Г	г	g		С	с	s	
Д	д	d		Т	т	t	
Е	е	e	initially, after a vowel or after the mute sign "Ъ", becomes "je"	У	у	u	
				Ф	ф	f	
				Х	х	h	
Ё	ё	ë		Ц	ц	c	
Ж	ж	ž		Ч	ч	č	
З	з	z		Ш	ш	š	
И	и	i		Щ	щ	šč	
Й	й	j	not written if preceded by "И" or "Ы"	Ъ	ъ	—	not written
				Ы	ы	y	
К	к	k		Ь	ь	—	not written
Л	л	l		Э	э	e	
М	м	m		Ю	ю	ju	
Н	н	n		Я	я	ja	

Transcription of Modern Greek
(U.S. B. G. N./P.C.G.N.)

Greek Letter (or combination)		Roman Letter (or combination)		Greek Letter (or combination)		Roman Letter (or combination)	
Α	α	a			μπ	b	beginning a word
	αι	ai				mb	within a word
	αυ	av		Ν	ν	n	
Β	β	v			ντ	d	beginning a word
Γ	γ	g				nd	within a word
	γγ	ng		Ξ	ξ	x	
	γκ	g	beginning a word	Ο	ο	o	
					οι	oi	
		ng	within a word		ου	ou	
Δ	δ	d		Π	π	p	
Ε	ε	e		Ρ	ρ	r	
	ει	i		Σ	σ	s	
	ευ	ev			ς	s	ending a word
Ζ	ζ	z		Τ	τ	t	
Η	η	i			τζ	tz	
	ηυ	iv		Υ	υ	i	
Θ	θ	th			υι	i	
Ι	ι	i		Φ	φ	f	
Κ	κ	k		Χ	χ	kh	
Λ	λ	l		Ψ	ψ	ps	
Μ	μ	m		Ω	ω	o	

The "Geographical Glossary" lists the principal geographical terms used on the maps. All of these terms, including abbreviations, prefixes and suffixes, appear in the cartographic table as they appear on the maps. Terms are listed in accordance with the English alphabet, without consideration of diacritical marks on letters or of particular groups of letters.

Prefixes and suffixes relating to principal names or forming part of geographical toponyms are followed or preceded by a dash and the language to which they refer: e.g. Chi-/*Dan*. (Chi, a Danish prefix, means large) ; -bor/*Slvn*. (-bor, a Slovakian suffix, means city). Suffixes can also appear as words in themselves. In this case, the suffix and primary word are coupled together: e.g. Berg, -berg (Berg, which means mountain, can be used alone or as part of another word, such as Hapsberg).

Certain terms are followed or preceded by their abbreviation used on the maps. Both instances are listed: e.g. Fjord, Fj. and Fj., Fjord.

All geographical terms are identified by the language or languages to which each belongs. The language or languages in italics follows the term: e.g. Abbey/*Eng*.; -bad/*Nor., Dut., Swed., Germ*. Each term is translated into a corresponding English term or terms.

Below is a table identifying the abbreviations of various language names used on the maps. Note that certain abbreviations represent a group of languages, instead of one language: e.g. Ural. is the abbreviation for Uralic, a group word for Udmurt, Komi, and Nenets.

Alt. = Altaic (Turkmen, Tatar, Bashkir, Kazakh, Karalpak, Nogai, Kirghiz, Uzbek, Uigur, Altaic, Yakut, Khakass)

Ban. = Bantu (KiSwahili, ChiLuba, Lingala, KiKongo)

Cauc. = Caucasian (Chechen, Ingush, Kalmuck, Georgian)
Iran. = Iranian (Baluchi, Tagus)
Mel. = Melanesian (Fijian, New Caledonian, Micronesian, Nauruan)
Mong. = Mongolian (Buryat, Khalka Mongol)
Poly. = Polynesian (Maori, Samoan, Tongan, Tahitian, Hawaiian)
Sah. = Saharan (Kanuri, Tubu)
Som. = Somalian (Somali, Galla)
Sud. = Sudanese (Peul, Ehoué, Mossi, Yoruba, Ibo)
Ural. = Uralic (Udmurt, Komi, Nenets).

Because of their technical application to geography, some geographical terms may not fully correspond with the meaning given for them in some dictionaries.

Abbreviations of Language Names

Abbreviations in English	English	Abbreviations in English	English	Abbreviations in English	English	Abbreviations in English	English	Abbreviations in English	English	Abbreviations in English	English
Afr.	Afrikaans	Bulg.	Bulgarian	Fr.	French	Khm.	Khmer	Pers.	Persian	Som.	Somalian
A.I.	American Indian	Burm.	Burmese	Gae.	Gaelic	Kor.	Korean	Pol.	Polish	Sp.	Spanish
		Cat.	Catalan	Georg.	Georgian	K.S.	Khoi-San	Poly.	Polynesian	Sud.	Sudanese
Alb.	Albanian	Cauc.	Caucasian	Germ.	German	Laot.	Laotian	Port.	Portuguese	Swa.	Swahili
Alt.	Altaic	Chin.	Chinese	Gr.	Greek	Lapp.	Lappish	Prov.	Provençal	Swed.	Swedish
Amh.	Amharic	Cz.	Czech	Hebr.	Hebrew	Latv.	Latvian	Rmsh.	Romansh	Tam.	Tamil
Ar.	Arabic	Dan.	Danish	Hin.	Hindi	Lith.	Lithuanian	Rom.	Romanian	Thai	Thai
Arm.	Armenian	Dut.	Dutch	Icel.	Icelandic	Mal.	Malay	Rus.	Russian	Tib.	Tibetan
Az.	Azerbaidzhani	Eng.	English	Indon.	Indonesian	Malag.	Malagasy	Sah.	Saharan	Tur.	Turkish
Ban.	Bantu	Esk.	Eskimo	Ir.	Irish	Mel.	Melanesian	S.C.	Serbo-Croatian	Ural.	Uralic
Bas.	Basque	Est.	Estonian	Iran.	Iranian	Mong.	Mongolian			Urdu	Urdu
Beng.	Bengali	Far.	Faroese	It.	Italian	Nep.	Nepalese	Sin.	Sinhalese	Viet.	Vietnamese
Ber.	Berber	Finn.	Finnish	Jap.	Japanese	Nor.	Norwegian	Slvk.	Slovak	Wall.	Walloon
Br.	Breton	Fle.	Flemish			Pash.	Pashto	Slvn.	Slovene	Wel.	Welsh

Glossary of Geographical Terms

Local Form	English	Local Form	English	Local Form	English	Local Form	English
A		Ait / *Ar.; Ber.*	sons	Ard- / *Gae.*	high	Badwëynta / *Som.*	ocean
		Aivi, -aivi / *Lapp.*	mountain	Areg / *Ar.*	dune	Badyarada / *Som.*	gulf
A- / *Ban.*	people	Ak / *Tur.*	white	Areia / *Port.*	beach	Baeg / *Kor.*	white
A' / *Icel.*	river	'Aklé / *Ar.*	dunes	Arena / *Sp.*	beach	Bæk / *Dan.*	brook
Å / *Dan.; Nor.; Swed.*	stream	Akmeņs / *Latv.*	stone	Argent / *Fr.*	silver	Bælt / *Dan.*	strait
a., an / *Germ.*	on	Ákra / *Gr.*	point	Arhipelag / *Rus.*	archipelago	Bagni / *It.*	thermal springs
Aa / *Germ.*	stream	Akti / *Gr.*	coast	Arkhaios / *Gr.*	old, antique	Baharu / *Mal.*	new
Aache / *Germ.*	stream	Ala / *Malag.*	forest	Arm / *Eng.; Germ.*	branch	Bahia / *Port.*	bay
Aaiún / *Ar.*	springs	Ala / *Finn.*	low, lower	Arquipélago / *Port.*	archipelago	Bahia / *Sp.*	bay
Aan / *Dut.; Fle.*	on	Alan / *Tur.*	field	Arr., Arroyo / *Sp.*	stream	Bahir / *Ar.*	river, lake, sea
Āb / *Pers.*	stream	Alb / *Rom.*	white	Arrecife / *Sp.*	reef	Bahnhof / *Germ.*	railway station
Ābād / *Pers.*	city, town	Albo / *Sp.*	white	Arroio / *Port.*	stream	Bahr / *Ar.*	wadi
Abad, -abad / *Pers.*	city, town	Albufera / *Sp.*	lagoon	Art / *Tur.*	pass, watershed	Baḥr / *Ar.*	river, lake, sea
Ābār / *Ar.*	spring	Alcalá / *Sp.*	castle	Aru / *Sin.; Tam.*	river	Baḥrat / *Ar.*	lake
Abbadia / *It.*	abbey	Alcázar / *Sp.*	castle	Ås / *Dan.; Nor.; Swed.*	hills	Bahri / *Ar.*	north, northern
Abbaye / *Fr.*	abbey	Aldea / *Sp.*	village	Asfar / *Ar.*	yellow	Baḥrī / *Ar.*	north
Abbazia / *It.*	abbey	Alföld / *Hung.*	lowland	Asif / *Ber.*	river	Baḥrīyah / *Ar.*	northern
Abbi / *Amh.*	great	Ali / *Amh.*	mountain	Asky / *Alt.*	lower	Bai / *Chin.*	white
Abd / *Ar.*	servant	Alia / *Poly.*	stream	Áspros / *Gr.*	white	Bāi / *Rom.*	thermal springs
Abeba / *Amh.*	flower	Alin / *Mong.*	range	Assa / *Ber.*	wadi	Baia / *Port.*	bay
Aber / *Br.; Wel.*	estuary	Alm / *Germ.*	mountain	Atalaya / *Sp.*	frontier	Baie / *Fr.*	bay
Abhang / *Germ.*	slope		pasture	Áth / *Gae.*	ford	Baigne / *Fr.*	seaside resort
Abū / *Ar.*	father, master	Alor / *Mal.*	river	Átha / *Gae.*	ford	Baile / *Gae.*	city, town
Abyad / *Ar.*	white	Alp / *Germ.*	mountain	Atol / *Port.*	atoll	Bains / *Fr.*	thermal springs
Abyaḍ / *Ar.*	white		pasture	Au / *Germ.*	meadow	Bains / *Fr.*	thermal springs
Abyār / *Ar.*	well	Alpe / *Germ.; Fr.; It.*	mountain	Aue / *Germ.*	irrigated field	Baixo / *Port.*	low, lower
Abyss / *Eng.*	ocean depth, deep		pasture	Aust / *Nor.*	east	Bajan / *Mong.*	rich
Ach / *Germ.*	stream	Alps / *Eng.*	mountains	Austur / *Icel.*	east	Bajo / *Sp.*	low
Achaïf / *Ar.*	dunes	Alsó / *Hung.*	low, lower	Ava / *Poly.*	canal	Bajrak / *Alb.*	tribe
Ache / *Germ.*	stream	Alt / *Germ.*	old	Aven / *Fr.*	doline, sink	Bakhtiyārī / *Pers.*	western
Achter / *Afr.; Dut.; Fle.*	back	Altin / *Tur.*	lower	Awa / *Poly.*	bay	Bakki / *Icel.*	hill
Acqua / *It.*	water	Altiplano / *Sp.*	plateau	Àyios / *Gr.*	saint	Bālā / *Pers.*	high
Açu / *A.I.*	great	Alto / *Sp.; It.; Port.*	high	'Ayn / *Ar.*	spring, well	Bald / *Eng.*	peak
Açude / *Port.*	reservoir, dam	Altopiano / *It.*	plateau	'Ayoún / *Ar.*	springs, wells	Balka / *Rus.*	gorge
Ada / *Tur.*	island	Älv / *Swed.*	river	'Ayoûn / *Ar.*	spring	Balkan / *Bulg.; Tur.*	mountain range
Adalar / *Tur.*	archipelago	Am / *Kor.*	mountain, peak	Aza / *Ber.*	wadi	Ballin / *Gae.*	mouth
Adasr / *Tur.*	island	Amane / *Ber.*	water	Azraq / *Ar.*	light blue	Ballon / *Fr.*	dome
Addis / *Amh.*	new	Amba / *Amh.*	mountain	Azul / *Port.; Sp.*	light blue	Bally / *Gae.*	city, town
Adi / *Amh.*	village	Ambato / *Malag.*	rock	Azur / *Fr.*	light blue	Balta / *Rom.*	marsh
Adrar / *Ber.*	mount, mountains	An / *Gae.*	of			Báltos / *Gr.*	marsh
		An, a. / *Germ.*	on			Ban / *Laot.*	village
Aéroport / *Fr.*	airport	Ana / *Poly.*	grotto	**B**		Bana / *Jap.*	promontory
Aeroporto / *It.; Port.*	airport	Anatolikós / *Gr.*	eastern			Baňa / *Slvk.*	mine
Aeropuerto / *Sp.*	airport	Äng / *Swed.*	meadow	B., Bay / *Eng.*	bay	Bañados / *Sp.*	marsh
Af / *Som.*	mouth, gorge	Angra / *Port.*	bay, anchorage	b., bei / *Germ.*	by	Banc / *Fr.*	bank
Afsluitdijk / *Dut.*	dam	Ani- / *Malag.*	center	B., Bucht / *Germ.*	bay	Banco / *It.; Sp.*	bank
Agadir / *Ber.*	castle	Áno / *Gr.*	upper	Ba / *Sud.*	river	Band / *Pers.*	dam, mountain range
Agiz / *Tur.*	mouth	Ánou / *Ber.*	well	Ba- / *Ban.*	people		
Agro / *Sp.; It.*	plain	Anse / *Fr.*	inlet	Ba / *Mel.*	hill, mountain	Bandao / *Chin.*	peninsula
Agua / *Sp.*	water	Ant- / *Malag.*	center	Baai / *Afr.*	bay	Bandar / *Ar.; Mal.; Pers.*	port, market
Aguja / *Sp.*	needle	Ao / *Chin.; Khm.; Thai*	gulf	Bab / *Ar.*	gate	Bang / *Indon.; Mal.*	stream
Agulha / *Port.*	needle, promontory	'Âouâna / *Ar.*	well	Bac / *Viet.*	north	Bangou / *Sah.*	well
Ahal / *Georg.*	new	Apă / *Rom.*	water	Bach / *Germ.*	brook, torrent	Banhado / *Port.*	marsh
Aḥmar / *Ar.*	red	'Aqabat / *Ar.*	pass	Bacino / *It.*	reservoir	Bani / *Ar.*	sons
Ahrāmāt / *Ar.*	pyramids	Aqueduc / *Fr.*	aqueduct	Back / *Eng.*	ridge	Banja / *Bulg.; S.C.; Slvn.*	thermal springs
Ahzar / *Ber.*	wadi	Ar / *Mong.*	north	Back / *Swed.*	brook	Banjaran / *Mal.*	mountain range
Aigialós / *Gr.*	coast	Ar / *Sin.; Tam.*	river	Bäck / *Swed.*	brook	Banka / *Rus.*	sandbank
Aigue / *Prov.*	water	'Arâguib / *Ar.*	hills	Backe / *Swed.*	hill	Banke / *Dan.*	bank
Aiguille / *Fr.*	needle	Arba / *Amh.*	mount	Bad, -bad / *Dan.; Germ.; Nor.; Swed.*	thermal springs	Baño / *Sp.*	thermal springs
Ain / *Ar.*	spring	Arbore / *Rom.*	tree	Baden, -baden / *Germ.*	thermal springs	Bansky / *Cz.*	upper
		Archipiélago / *Sp.*	archipelago	Bâdiyat / *Ar.*	desert	Bánya / *Hung.*	mine
		Arcipelago / *It.*	archipelago			Bar / *Gae.*	peak
		Arḍ / *Ar.*	region			Bar / *Eng.*	sandbar

Geographical Glossary

Local Form	English
Bar / Hin.	great
Bāra / Hin.	great
Bara / S.C.	pond
Barā / Urdu	great
Barajı / Tur.	dam
Barat / Indon.; Mal.	west, western
Barkas / Lith.	castle, city, town
Barlovento / Sp.	windward
Barq / Ar.	hill
Barra / Port.; Sp.	bar, bank
Barrage / Fr.	dam
Barragem / Port.	reservoir
Barranca / Sp.	gorge
Barranco / Port.; Sp.	gorge
Barre / Fr.	bar
Barun / Mong.	western
Bas / Fr.	low
-bas / Rus.	reservoir
Bassa / Port.	flat
Bassejn / Rus.	reservoir
Bassin / Fr.	basin
Bassure / Fr.	flat
Bassurelle / Fr.	flat
Bašta / S.C.	garden
Bataille / Fr.	battle
Batalha / Port.	battle
Batang / Indon.; Mal.	river
Batha / Sah.	stream
Baţin / Ar.	depression
Bāţlāq / Pers.	marsh
Batu / Mal.	rock
Bayan / Mong.	rich
Bayır / Tur.	mountain, slope
Bayou / Fr.	branch, stream
Bayt / Ar.	house
Bazar / Pers.	market
Be / Malag.	great
Beau / Fr.	beautiful
Becken / Germ.	basin
Bed / Eng.	river bed
Beek / Dut.	creek
Be'er / Hebr.	spring
Bei / Chin.	north
Bei, b. / Germ.	by
Beida / Ar.	white
Beinn / Gae.	mount
Bel / Ar.	son
Bel / Bulg.	white
Bel / Tur.	pass
Beled / Ar.	village
Belen / Tur.	mount
Belet / Ar.	village
Beli / S.C.; Slvn.	white
Beli / Tur.	pass
Bellah / Sah.	well
Belogorje / Rus.	mountains
Belt / Dan.; Germ.	strait
Bely / Rus.	white
Bělý / Cz.	white
Ben / Ar.	son
Ben / Gae.	mount
Bender / Pers.	port, market
Bendi / Tur.	dam
Beni / Ar.	son
Beo / S.C.	white
Bereg / Rus.	bank
Berg, -berg / Afr.; Dut.; Fle.; Germ.; Nor.; Swed.	mount
Berge / Afr.	mountain
Bergen / Dut.; Fle.	dunes
Bergland / Germ.	upland
Bermejo / Sp.	red
Besar / Mal.	great
Betsu / Jap.	river
Betta / Tam.	mountain
Bhani / Hin.	community
Bharu / Mal.	new
Bheag / Gae.	little
Bīābān / Pers.	desert
Biały / Pol.	white
Bianco / It.	white
Bien / Viet.	lake
Bight / Eng.	bay
Bijeli / S.C.	white
Bill / Eng.	promontory
Bilo / S.C.	range
Bilý / Cz.	white
Binnen / Dut.; Fle.; Germ.	inner
Biqā' / Ar.	valley
Bir / Ar.	well
Bi'r / Ar.	well
Birkat / Ar.	pond
Bistrica / Bulg.; S.C.; Slvn.	stream
Bjarg / Icel.	rock
Bjerg / Dan.	mount
Bjeshkët / Alb.	mountain pasture
Blaauw / Afr.	blue
Blanc / Fr.	white
Blanco / Sp.	white
Blau / Germ.	blue
Bleu / Fr.	blue
Bluff / Eng.	cliff
Bo- / Ban.	people
Bo / Chin.	white
Bo / Swed.	habitation
Boca / Sp.	gap, mouth
Bôca / Port.	gap, mouth
Bocage / Fr.	forest
Bocca / It.	gap, pass
Bocchetta / It.	gap, pass
Bodden / Germ.	bay, lagoon
Boden / Germ.	soil
Bœng / Khm.	lake, marsh
Bog / Eng.	marsh
Bogaz / Alt.; Az.; Tur.	strait
Bogāzi / Tur.	strait
Bogdo / Mong.	high
Bogen / Nor.	bay
Bois / Fr.	forest
Boka / S.C.	channel
Boloto / Rus.	marsh
Bolšoj / Rus.	great
Bolsón / Sp.	basin
Bom / Port.	good
Bong / Kor.	peak
Bongo / Malag.	upland
Bor / Cz.; Rus.	coniferous forest
Bór / Pol.	forest
-bor / Slvn.	city, town
Bóras / Gr.	north
Börde / Germ.	fertile plain
Bordj / Ar.	fort
Bóreios / Gr.	northern
Borg, -borg / Dan.; Nor.; Swed.	castle
Borgo / It.	village
Born / Germ.	spring
Bory / Pol.	forest
Bosch / Dut.; Fle.	forest
Bosco / It.	wood
Bosque / Sp.	forest
Bosse / Fr.	hill
Botn / Nor.	bay
Bou / Ar.	father, master
Bouche / Fr.	mouth
Boula / Sud.	well
Bourg / Fr.	city, town
Bourne, - bourne / Eng.	frontier
Boven / Afr.	upper
Boz / Tur.	grey
Bozorg / Pers.	great
Brána / Cz.	gate
Braña / Sp.	mountain pasture
Branche / Fr.	branch
Branco / Port.	white
Braţul / Rom.	branch
Bravo / Sp.	wild
Brazo / Sp.	branch
Brdo / Cz.; S.C.	hill
Bre / Nor.	glacier
Bredning / Dan.	bay
Breg / Alb.; Bulg.; S.C.	hill, coast
Brjag / Bulg.	bank
Bro / Dan.; Nor.; Swed.	bridge
Brod / Bulg.; Cz.; Rus.; S.C.; Slvk.; Slvn.	ford
Bród / Pol.	ford
Bron / Afr.	spring
Bronn / Germ.	spring
Bru / Nor.	bridge
Bruch / Germ.	peat-bog
Bruchzone / Germ.	fracture zone
Bruck, -bruck / Germ.	bridge
Brücke / Germ.	bridge
Brug / Dut.; Fle.	bridge
Brugge / Dut.; Fle.	bridge
Bruk / Nor.	factory
Brunn / Swed.	spring
-brunn / Germ.	spring
Brunnen / Germ.	spring
Brygg / Swed.	bridge
Brzeg / Pol.	coast
Bü / Ar.	father, master
Bucht, B. / Germ.	bay
Bugt / Dan.	bay
Buhayrat / Ar.	lake, lagoon
Bühel / Germ.	hill
Bühl / Germ.	hill
Buhta / Rus.	bay
Bukit / Mal.	mountain, peak
Bukt / Nor.; Swed.	bay
Buku / Indon.	hill, mountain
Bulag / Mong.; Tur.	spring
Bulak / Mong.; Tur.	spring
Būlāq / Tur.	spring
Bult / Afr.	hill
Bulu / Indon.	mountain
Bur / Som.	mount
Būr / Ar.	port
Burg, - burg / Afr.; Ar.; Dut.; Eng.; Germ.	castle
Burgh / Eng.	city, town
Burgo / Sp.	village
Burha / Hin.	old
Buri / Thai	city, town
Burj / Ar.	village
Burn / Eng.	stream
Burnu / Tur.	promontory
Burqat / Ar.	mount, marsh
Burun / Tur.	cape
Busen / Germ.	bay
Busu / Ban.	land
Būtat / Ar.	lake, pond
Butte / Eng.; Fr.	flat-topped hill
Büyük / Tur.	great
By / Eng.	near
By, -by / Dan.; Nor.; Swed.	city, town
Bystrica / Cz.; Slvk.	stream
Bystrzyca / Pol.	stream

C

Local Form	English
C., Cap / Cat.; Fr.; Rom.	cape
C., Cape / Eng.	cape
C., Colle / It.	pass
Caatinga / A.I.	forest
Cabeça / Port.	peak
Cabeço / Port.	peak
Cabeza / Sp.	peak
Cabezo / Sp.	peak, mountain
Cabo / Port.; Sp.	cape
Cachoeira / Port.	waterfall, rapids
Cachopo / Port.	reef
Cadena / Sp.	range
Caer / Wel.	castle
Cagan / Cauc.; Mong.	white
Cairn / Gae.	hill
Čāj / Az.; Tur.	river
Cajdam / Mong.	salt marsh
Caka / Chin.	lake
Cala / Sp.; It.	inlet
Calar / Sp.	plateau
Caldas / Sp.; Port.	thermal springs
Caleta / Sp.	inlet
Camp / Cat.; Fr.; Eng.	field
Campagna / It.	plain
Campagne / Fr.	plain
Campo / Sp.; It.; Port.	field
Cañada / Sp.	gorge, ravine
Canale / It.	canal, channel
Caño / Sp.	branch
Cañón / Sp.	gorge
Canyon / Eng.	gorge
Cao / Viet.	mountain
Cap, C. / Cat.; Fr.; Rom.	cape
Car / Gae.	castle
Càrn / Gae.	peak
Carrera / Sp.	road
Carrick / Gae.	rock
Casale / It.	hamlet
Cascada / Sp.	waterfall
Cascata / It.	waterfall
Castel / It.	castle
Castell / Cat.	castle
Castello / It.	castle
Castelo / Port.	castle
Castillo / Sp.	castle
Castro / Sp.; It.	village
Catarata / Sp.	cataract
Catena / It.	mountain range
Catinga / Port.	degraded forest
Cauce / Sp.	river bed
Causse / Fr.	highland
Cava / It.	stone quarry
Çay / Tur.	river
Cay / Eng.	islet, island
Caye / Fr.	island
Cayo / Sp.	islet, island
Ceann / Gae.	promontory
Centralny / Rus.	middle
Čeren / Alb.	black
Černi / Bulg.	black
Černý / Cz.	black
Cërny / Rus.	black
Cerrillo / Sp.	hill
Cerrito / Sp.	hill
Cerro / Sp.; Port.	hill, mountain
Cêrro / Port.	hill, mountain
Červen / Bulg.	red
Červony / Rus.	red
Cetate / Rom.	city, town
Chaco / Sp.	scrubland
Chāh / Pers.	well
Chaïf / Ar.	dunes
Chaîne / Fr.	mountain range
Champ / Fr.	field
Chang / Chin.	highland
Chapada / Port.	highland
Chapadão / Port.	highland
Château / Fr.	castle
Châtel / Fr.	castle
Chāy / Tur.	river
Chedo / Kor.	archipelago
Chenal / Fr.	canal
Cheng / Chin.	city, town, wall
Cheon / Kor.	city, river
Chergui / Ar.	eastern
Cherry, -cherry / Hin.; Tam.	city, town
Chew / Amh.	salt mine, salt
Chhâk / Khm.	bay
Chhotla / Hin.	little
Chi- / Ban.	great
Chi / Chin.	marsh, lake
Chi / Kor.	lake, pond
Chi- / Swa.	land
Chiang / Thai	city, town
Chico / Sp.	little
Chine / Eng.	ridge
Ch'on / Kor.	station
Ch'ŏn / Kor.	river
Chŏsuji / Kor.	reservoir
Chott / Ar.	salt marsh
Chu / Chin.; Viet.	mountain, hill
Chuôr phnum / Khm.	mountain range
Chute / Fr.	waterfall
Chutes / Fr.	waterfalls
Cidade / Port.	city, town
Ciems / Latv.	village
Čierny / Slvk.	black
Cime / Fr.	peak
Cîmp / Rom.	field
Cîmpie / Rom.	plain
Cinco / Sp.; Port.	five
Citeli / Georg.	red
Città / It.	city, town
Ciudad / Sp.	city, town
Ckali / Georg.	water
Ckaro / Georg.	spring
Co / Chin.	lake
Col / Cat.; Fr.	pass
Colina / Port.; Sp.	hill
Coll / Cat.	hill
Collado / Sp.	pass
Colle, C. / It.	pass
Collina / It.	hill
Colline / Fr.	hill
Colonia / Sp.; It.	colony
Coma / Sp.	hill country
Comb / Eng.	basin
Comba / Sp.	basin
Combe / Fr.	basin
Comté / Fr.	county, shire
Con / Viet.	island
Conca / It.	depression
Condado / Sp.	county, shire
Cone / Eng.	volcanic cone
Cône / Fr.	volcanic cone
Contraforte / Port.	front range
Cordal / Sp.	crest
Cordilheira / Port.	mountain range
Cordillera / Sp.	mountain range
Coring / Chin.	lake
Corixa / A.I.	stream
Corno / It.	peak
Cornone / It.	peak
Corrente / It.; Port.	stream
Corriente / Sp.	stream
Costa / Sp.; It.; Port.	coast
Côte / Fr.	coast
Coteau / Fr.	height, slope
Coxilha / Port.	ridge
Craig / Gae.	rock
Cratère / Fr.	crater
Cresta / Sp.; It.	crest
Crêt / Fr.	crest
Crête / Fr.	crest
Crkva / S.C.	church
Crni / S.C.; Slvn.	black
Crven / S.C.	red
Csatorna / Hung.	canal
Cuchilla / Sp.	ridge
Cuenca / Sp.	basin
Cuesta / Sp.	escarpment
Cueva / Sp.	cave
Čuka / Bulg.; S.C.	peak
Çukur / Tur.	well
Cu Lao / Viet.	island
Cumbre / Sp.	peak
Cun / Chin.	village
Cura / A.I.	stone
Curr / Alb.	rock
Cy., City / Eng.	city, town
Czarny / Pol.	black

D

Local Form	English
Da / Chin.	great
Da / Viet.	mountain, peak
Daal / Dut.; Fle.	valley
Daba / Mong.	pass
Daba / Som.	hill
Daban / Chin.; Mong.	pass
Dae / Kor.	great
Dağ / Tur.	mountain
Dağ., Daği / Tur.	mountain
Dāgh / Pers.; Tur.	mountain
Dağı, Dağ. / Tur.	mountain
Dağları / Tur.	mountain range
Dahar / Ar.	hill
Dahr / Ar.	plateau, escarpment
Dai / Chin.; Jap.	great
Daiet / Ar.	marsh
Dak / Viet.	stream
Dake / Jap.	mountain
Dakhla / Ar.	depression
Dakhlet / Ar.	depression, bay
Dal, -dal / Afr.; Dan.; Dut.; Fle.; Nor.; Swed.	valley
Dala / Alt.	steppe, plain
Dalaj / Mong.	lake, sea
Dalan / Mong.	wall
Dallol / Sud.	valley, torrent
Dalur / Icel.	valley
Damm / Germ.	dam
Dan / Kor.	point

Local Form	English
Danau / *Indon.*	lake
Danda / *Nep.*	mountains
Dao / *Chin.*	island, peninsula
Dao / *Viet.*	island
Dar / *Ar.*	house, region
Dar / *Swa.*	port
Dara / *Tur.*	torrent, valley
Darb / *Ar.*	track
Darja / *Alt.*	river, sea
Darya, Daryā / *Pers.*	river, sea
Daryācheh / *Pers.*	lake, sea
Daš / *Alt.; Az.*	rock
Dasht / *Pers.*	desert, plain
Dawḥat / *Ar.*	bay
Dayr / *Ar.*	convent
De / *Sp.; Fr.*	of
Deal / *Rom.*	hill
Dearg / *Gae.*	red
Debre / *Amh.*	hill, monastery
Dega / *Som.*	stone
Deh / *Pers.*	village
Dēḥ / *Som.*	stream
Deich / *Germ.*	dike
Dél / *Hung.*	south
Delft / *Dut.; Fle.*	deep
Delger / *Mong.*	wide, market
-den / *Eng.*	city, town
Deniz / *Tur.*	sea
Denizi / *Tur.*	sea
Dent / *Fr.*	peak
Deo / *Laot.; Viet.*	pass
Dépression / *Fr.*	depression
Depressione / *It.*	depression
Der / *Som.*	high
Dera / *Hin.; Urdu*	temple
Derbent / *Tur.*	gorge, pass
Dere / *Tur.*	river, valley
Désert / *Fr.*	desert
Desfiladero / *Sp.*	pass
Desh / *Hin.*	land, country
Desierto / *Sp.*	desert
Det / *Alb.*	sea
Détroit / *Fr.*	strait
Deux / *Fr.*	two
Dezh / *Pers.*	castle
Dhar / *Ar.*	heights, hills
Dhār / *Hin.; Urdu*	mountain
Dhitikós / *Gr.*	western
Dien / *Khm.; Viet.*	rice-field
Diep / *Dut.; Fle.*	deep, strait
Dijk, -dijk / *Dut.; Fle.*	dam
Ding / *Chin.*	mountain, peak
Dique / *Sp.*	dam
Di Sopra / *It.*	upper
Di Sotto / *It.*	lower
Distrito / *Sp.; Port.*	district
Diu / *Hin.*	island
Diz / *Pers.*	castle
Djebel / *Ar.*	mountain
Dji / *Ban.*	water
Djup / *Swed.*	deep
Do / *Kor.*	Island
Do / *S.C.*	valley
Dō / *Jap.*	island, administrative division
Dōho / *Som.*	valley
Doi / *Thai*	mountain, peak
Dol / *Bulg.; Cz.; Rus.; S.C.*	valley
Dol / *Pol.*	valley
Dolen / *Bulg.*	low
Dolgi / *Rus.*	long
Dolina / *Bulg.; Cz.; Pol.; Rus.; S.C.; Slvn.*	valley
Dolni / *Bulg.*	low
Dolni / *Pol.*	lower
Dolny / *Pol.*	lower
Domb / *Hung.*	hill
Dôme / *Fr.*	dome
Dong / *Chin.; Viet.*	east
Dong / *Kor.*	city, town
Dong / *Thai*	mountain
Dong / *Viet.*	marsh, plain
Donji / *S.C.*	low, lower
Dorf, -dorf / *Germ.*	village
Doroga / *Rus.*	road
Dorp, -dorp / *Afr.; Dut.; Fle.*	village
Dos / *Rom.*	ridge
Dos / *Sp.*	two
Douarn / *Br.*	land
Dougou / *Sud.*	settlement
Doukou / *Sud.*	settlement
Down / *Eng.*	hill
Drâa / *Ar.*	dunes, hills
Dracht / *Germ.*	sandbank
Draw / *Eng.*	ravine, valley
Drif / *Afr.*	ford
Drift / *Afr.*	ford
Droichead / *Gae.*	bridge
Droûs / *Ar.*	crest
Dry / *Pash.*	river
Dubh / *Gae.*	black
Dugi / *S.C.*	long
Dugu / *Sud.*	settlement
Dun / *Gae.*	castle
Duna / *Sp.; It.*	dune
Düne / *Germ.*	dune
Dungar / *Hin.*	mountain
Düngar / *Hin.*	mountain
Duong / *Viet.*	stream
Durchbruch / *Germ.*	gorge
Ḍurg / *Hin.*	castle
-durga / *Hin.*	castle
Duży / *Pol.*	great
Dvor / *Cz.*	court
Dvorec / *Rus.*	castle
Dvůr / *Cz.*	castle
Dwór / *Pol.*	court
Džebel / *Bulg.*	mountain
Dzong / *Tib.*	fort, monastery

E

Local Form	English
Ea / *Thai*	river
Eau / *Fr.*	water
Ebe / *Ban.*	forest
Ebene / *Germ.*	plain
Eck / *Germ.*	point
Eclusa / *Sp.*	lock
Écluse / *Fr.*	lock
Écueil / *Fr.*	cliff
Edeien / *Ber.*	sand desert
Edjérir / *Ber.*	wadi
Egg / *Germ.; Nor.*	crest, point
Eglab / *Ar.*	hills
Ehi / *Sah.*	mountain
Eid / *Nor.*	isthmus
Eiland / *Afr.*	island
Eisen / *Germ.*	iron
Eisenerz / *Germ.*	iron ore
El / *Amh.*	well
Elv, -elv / *Nor.*	river
Embalse / *Sp.*	reservoir
Embouchure / *Fr.*	mouth
Emi / *Sah.*	mountain
En / *Fr.*	in
Ende / *Germ.*	end
Enneri / *Sah.*	stream
Ennis / *Gae.*	island
Enseada / *Port.*	Bay, inlet
Ensenada / *Sp.*	bay, inlet
Ér / *Hung.*	stream
Erdö / *Hung.*	forest
Erg / *Ar.*	sand desert
Erz / *Germ.*	ore
Espigão / *Port.*	plateau
Estān / *Pers.*	land
Este / *Sp.*	east
Estero / *Sp.*	estuary, marsh
Estrecho / *Sp.*	strait
Estreito / *Port.*	strait
Estuaire / *Fr.*	estuary
Estuário / *Port.*	estuary
Estuario / *Sp.; It.*	estuary
Észak / *Hung.*	north
Étang / *Fr.*	pond
Ewaso / *Ban.*	river
Ey / *Icel.*	island
Eyja / *Icel.*	island
Eyjar / *Icel.*	islands
Eylandt / *Dut.*	island
Ežeras / *Lith.*	lake
Ezers / *Latv.*	lake

F

Local Form	English
Fa / *Mel.*	stream
Falaise / *Fr.*	cliff
Fall, -fall / *Germ.; Eng.; Swed.*	waterfall
Falls / *Eng.*	waterfall
Falu / *Hung.*	village
-falva / *Hung.*	village
Fan / *Sah.*	village
Faraglione / *It.*	cliff
Farallón / *Sp.*	cliff
Faro / *Sp.; It.*	lighthouse
Farvand / *Dan.*	strait
Fehér / *Hung.*	white
Fehn / *Germ.*	peat fen, peat-bog
Fekete / *Hung.*	black
Feld / *Dan.; Germ.*	field
Fell / *Eng.*	upland moor
Fell / *Icel.*	mountain
Fels / *Germ.*	rock
Fen / *Eng.*	marsh, peat-bog
Feng / *Chin.*	mountain, peak
Feste / *Germ.*	fort
Festung / *Germ.*	fort
Fier / *Rom.*	iron
Firn / *Germ.*	snow-field
Firth / *Eng.*	estuary, fjord
Fiume / *It.*	river
Fjäll / *Swed.*	mountain
Fjärd / *Swed.*	fjord
Fjell / *Nor.*	mountain
Fjöll / *Icel.*	mountain
Fjord, Fj. / *Dan.; Nor.; Swed.*	fjord
Fjörður / *Icel.*	fjord, bay
Fleuve / *Fr.*	river
Fließ / *Germ.*	torrent
Fljót / *Icel.*	river
Flói / *Icel.*	bay, gulf
Floresta / *Sp.; Port.*	forest
Flow / *Eng.*	strait
Flughafen / *Germ.*	airport
Fluß / *Germ.*	river
Fo / *Mel.*	stream
Foa / *Mel.*	stream
Foa / *Poly.*	cove
Foce / *It.*	mouth
Föld / *Hung.*	plain
Fonn / *Nor.*	glacier
Fontaine / *Fr.*	fountain
Fonte / *It.; Port.*	spring
Fontein / *Afr.; Dut.*	spring
Foort / *Afr.; Dut.*	ford
Forca / *It.*	pass
Forcella / *It.*	defile
Ford / *Rus.*	fjord
Förde / *Germ.*	fjord, gulf
Foreland / *Eng.*	promontory
Foresta / *It.*	forest
Forêt / *Fr.*	forest
Fors / *Swed.*	rapids, waterfall
Forst / *Germ.; Dut.*	forest
Forte / *It.; Port.*	fort
Fortin / *Sp.*	fort
Fosa / *Sp.*	trench
Foss / *Icel.; Nor.*	rapids, waterfall
Fossé / *Fr.*	trench
Foum / *Ar.*	pass
Fourche / *Fr.*	pass
Foz / *Sp.; Port.*	mouth
Frei / *Germ.*	free
Fronteira / *Port.*	frontier
Frontera / *Sp.*	frontier
Frontón / *Sp.*	promontory
Fuente / *Sp.*	spring
Fuerte / *Sp.*	fort
Fuji / *Jap.*	mountain
Fülat / *Ar.*	marsh
Furt / *Germ.*	ford
Fushë / *Alb.*	plain

G

Local Form	English
G., Gora / *Bulg.; Rus.; S.C.*	mountain, hill
G., Gunung / *Indon.*	mountain
Ga / *Jap.*	bay
Ga / *Mel.*	mountain, peak
Gabel / *Germ.*	pass
Gaissa / *Lapp.*	mountain
Gala / *Sin.; Tam.*	mountain
Gam / *Hin.; Urdu*	village
Gamle / *Nor.; Swed.*	old
Gana / *Sud.*	little
Gang / *Germ.*	passage
Gang / *Chin.*	port, bay
Gang / *Kor.*	stream, bay
Gang / *Tib.*	glacier
Ganga / *Hin.*	river
Ganj / *Hin.; Urdu*	market
-gaon / *Hin.*	city, town
Gaoyuan / *Chin.*	plateau
Gap / *Kor.*	point
Gar / *Hin.*	house
Gara / *Bulg.*	station
Gara / *Ar.*	hills, range
Gară / *Rom.*	station
Garaet / *Ar.*	marsh, intermittent lake
Garam / *Beng.; Hin.; Urdu*	village
-gard / *Pol.*	city, town
Gård, -gård / *Dan.; Nor.; Swed.*	farmhouse
Gardaneh / *Pers.*	pass
Gare / *Fr.*	railway station
Garet / *Ar.*	hill
Garh, -garh / *Hin.; Urdu*	castle
Garhi / *Hin.; Nep.; Urdu*	fort
Garten / *Germ.*	garden
Gat / *Dan.; Fle.; Dut.*	strait
Gata / *Jap.*	bay, lake
Gau, -gau / *Germ.*	district
Gäu, -gäu / *Germ.*	district
Gavan / *Rus.*	port
Gave / *Bas.*	torrent
Gawa / *Jap.*	river
Geb., Gebirge / *Germ.*	mountain range
Gebergte / *Afr.; Dut.*	mountain range
Gebirge, Geb. / *Germ.*	mountain range
Geç., Geçit / *Tur.*	pass
Geçidi / *Tur.*	pass
Geçit, Geç. / *Tur.*	pass
Geysir / *Icel.*	geyser
Ghar / *Hin.; Urdu*	house
Ghar / *Pash.*	mountain, mountain range
Gharbīyah / *Ar.*	western
Ghat / *Hin.; Nep.; Urdu*	pass
Ghubbat / *Ar.*	bay
Ghurd / *Ar.*	dune
Gi / *Kor.*	peninsula
Giang / *Viet.*	stream
Giri / *Hin.; Urdu*	mountain, hill
Girlo / *Rus.*	branch
Gjebel / *Ar.*	mountain
Gji / *Alb.*	bay
Glace / *Fr.*	ice
Glaciar / *Sp.*	glacier
Glacier / *Eng.; Fr.*	glacier
Glen / *Gae.*	valley
Gletscher / *Germ.*	glacier
Gobi / *Mong.*	desert
Godār / *Pers.*	ford
Gok / *Kor.*	river
Gök / *Tur.*	blue
Gol / *Cauc.; Mong.*	river
Göl / *Tur.*	lake
Gola / *It.*	gorge
Gold / *Germ.; Eng.*	gold
Golet / *S.C.*	mountain
Golf / *Germ.*	gulf
Golfe / *Fr.*	gulf
Golfete / *Sp.*	inlet
Golfo / *Sp.; It.; Port.*	gulf
Goljam / *Bulg.*	great
Gölü / *Tur.*	lake
Gong / *Tib.*	high
Gonggar / *Tib.*	mountain
Gongo / *Ban.*	mountain
Góra / *Pol.*	mountain
Gora, G. / *Bulg.; Rus.; S.C.*	mountain, hill
Gorica / *S.C.; Slvn.*	hill
Gorje / *S.C.*	mountain range
Gorlo / *Rus.*	gorge
Gorm / *Gae.*	blue
Gorni / *Bulg.; S.C.; Slvn.*	upper
Gornji / *S.C.; Slvn.*	upper
Górny / *Pol.*	high
Gorod / *Rus.*	city, town
Gorodok / *Rus.*	village
Gorski / *Bulg.*	upper
Gory / *Rus.*	mountains
-gou / *Chin.*	river
Goulbi / *Sud.*	river, lake
Goulbin / *Sud.*	wadi
Goulet / *Fr.*	gap
Gour / *Ar.*	hills, range
Gourou / *Sud.*	wadi
Goz / *Sah.*	dune
Graafschap / *Dut.*	county, shire
Graben / *Germ.*	ditch, canal
Gracht / *Dut.*	canal
Grad, -grad / *Bulg.; Rus.; S.C.; Slvn.*	city, town, castle
Gradac / *S.C.*	castle
Gradec / *Bulg.*	village
Gradec / *Slvn.*	castle
Græn / *Icel.*	green
Gran / *Sp.; It.*	great
Grande / *Sp.; It.; Port.*	great
Grao / *Cat.; Sp.*	gap
Grat / *Germ.*	crest
Grève / *Fr.*	beach
Grind / *Germ.*	peak
Grjada / *Rus.*	range
Gród, -gród / *Pol.*	castle, city, town
Grön / *Icel.*	green
Grond / *Afr.*	soil
Gronden / *Dut.; Fle.*	flat
Groot / *Afr.; Dut.; Fle.*	great
Groß / *Germ.*	great
Grotta / *It.*	grotto
Grotte / *Fr.; Germ.*	grotto
Grube / *Germ.*	mine
Grün / *Germ.*	green
Grunn / *Nor.*	ground
Gruppe / *Germ.*	mountain system
Gruppo / *It.*	mountain system
Gua / *Mal.*	cave
Guaçu / *A.I.*	great
Guan / *Chin.*	pass
Guazú / *A.I.*	great
Guba / *Rus.*	bay
Guchi / *Jap.*	strait
Guelb / *Ar.*	hill, mountain
Guelta / *Ar.*	well
Guic / *Br.*	village
Güney / *Tur.*	south, southern
Gunong / *Mal.*	mountain
Guntō / *Jap.*	archipelago
Gunung, G. / *Indon.*	mountain
Guo / *Chin.*	state, land
Gur / *Rom.*	mountain
Guri / *Jap.*	cliff
Gurud / *Ar.*	hills, dunes
Gyár / *Hung.*	factory

H

Local Form	English
Haag / *Dut.; Fle.*	hedge
-håb / *Dan.*	port
Haḍabat / *Ar.*	highland
Hadd / *Ar.*	point
Hadjer / *Ar.*	hill, mountain
Hae / *Kor.*	bay, sea
Haehyeop / *Kor.*	strait

Geographical Glossary

Local Form	English
Haf / Icel.	sea
Ḥafar / Ar.	well
Hafen / Germ.	port
Haff / Germ.	lagoon
Hafir / Ar.	spring, ditch
Hafnar / Icel.	port
Häfün / Som.	bay
Hage / Dan.	point
Hage / Dut.; Fle.	hedge
Hågna / Swed.	peak
Hai / Chin.	sea, lake, bay
Hain / Germ.	forest
Haixia / Chin.	strait
Ḥajar / Ar.	hill, mountain
Hajar / Ar.	hill country
Halbinsel / Germ.	peninsula
Halma / Hung.	hill
Halom / Hung.	hill
Halq / Ar.	gap
Hals / Nor.	peninsula
Halvø / Dan.	peninsula
Halvøy / Nor.	peninsula
Hama / Jap.	beach
Hamāda / Ar.	rocky desert
Ḥamādah / Ar.	plateau
Ḥamādat / Ar.	plateau
Hammam / Ar.	thermal springs
Ḥammām / Ar.	well
Hamn / Nor.; Swed.	port
Hamrä' / Ar.	red
Hāmün / Jap.	salt lake
Hana / Jap.	cape
Hana / Poly.	bay
Hane / Tur.	house
Hang / Kor.	port
Hank / Ar.	escarpment, plateau
Hantō / Jap.	peninsula
Har / Hebr.	mountain
Hara / Mong.	black
Harar / Swa.	well
Ḥarrah / Ar.	lava field
Ḥarrat / Ar.	lava field
Hasi / Ar.	well
Ḥasi / Ar.	well
Hassi / Ar.	well
Ḥasy / Ar.	well
Haug / Nor.	hill
Haupt- / Germ.	principal
Haure / Lapp.	lake
Haus / Germ.	house
Hausen / Germ.	village
Haut / Fr.	high
Hauteur / Fr.	hill
Hauts Plateaux / Fr.	highlands
Hauz / Pers.	reservoir
Hav / Dan.; Nor.; Swed.	sea, gulf
Haven / Eng.; Fle.; Dut.	port
Havn / Dan.; Nor.	port
Havre / Fr.	port
Hawr / Ar.	lake, marsh
Ház / Hung.	house
-háza / Hung.	house
Hazm / Ar.	height, mountain range
He / Chin.	river
Head / Eng.	headland
Hed / Dan.; Swed.	heath
Hegy / Hung.	mountain
Hegység / Hung.	mountain
Hei / Nor.	heath
Heide / Germ.	heath
Heijde / Dut.; Fle.	heath
Heilig / Germ.	saint
Heim, -heim / Germ.; Nor.	house
Heiya / Jap.	plain
-hely / Hung.	locality
Hem / Swed.	home
Hen / Br.	old
Higashi / Jap.	east, eastern
Hima / Hin.	ice
Himal / Nep.	peak
Hisar / Tur.	castle
Ho / Chin.	reservoir, river
Ho / Kor.	river, reservoir
Hō / Jap.	mountain
Hoch / Germ.	high, upper
Hochland / Germ.	highland
Hochplato / Afr.	highland
Hodna / Ar.	highland
Hoek / Dut.; Fle.	cape
Hof / Dut.; Germ.	court
Höfn / Icel.	port
Høg / Nor.	peak
Hög / Swed.	mountain
Hogna / Nor.	peak
Höhe / Germ.	peak
Høj / Dan.	hill
Hoj / Ural.	mountain range
Hok / Jap.	north
Hoku / Jap.	north, northern
Holm / Dan.; Nor.; Swed.	island
Holz / Germ.	forest
Hon / Viet.	island, point
Hong / Chin.; Viet.	red
Hono / Poly.	bay, anchorage
Hoog / Afr.; Dut.; Fle.	high
Hook / Eng.	point
Hoorn / Afr.; Dut.; Fle.	cape, point
Hora / Cz.; Slvk.	point
Horn / Eng.; Germ.; Icel.; Nor.; Swed.	point
Horni / Cz.	high
Horný / Slvk.	upper
Horst / Germ.	mountain
Horvot / Hebr.	ruins
Hory / Cz.; Slvk.	mountain range
Hout / Dut.; Fle.	forest
Hovd, -hovd / Dan.; Nor.	cape
Ḥowz / Pers.	basin
Hrad / Cz.; Slvk.	castle, city, town
Hradiště / Cz.	citadel
Hřeben / Cz.	crest
Hrebet / Rus.	mountain range
Hu / Rmsh.	lake
Huang / Chin.	yellow
Hude / Germ.	pasture
Huerta / Sp.	market garden
Hügel / Germ.	hill
Hügelland / Germ.	hill country
Huis, -huis / Afr.; Dut.; Fle.	house
Huisie / Afr.	house
Huizen, -huizen / Dut.	houses
Huk / Afr.; Dan.; Swed.	cape
Hum / S.C.	hill
Hurst / Eng.	grove
Hus / Dut.; Nor.; Swed.	house
Huta / Pol.; Slvk.	hut
Hütte / Germ.	hut
Hver / Icel.	crater
Hvit / Icel.	white
Hvost / Rus.	spit

I

Local Form	English
I., Island / Eng.	island
Ierós / Gr.	holy
Igarapé / A.I.	river
Ighazer / Ber.	torrent
Ighil / Ber.	hill
Iguidi / Ber.	dunes
Ih / Mong.	great
Ike / Jap.	pond
Ile / Fr.	island
Ilha / Port.	island
Iller / Tur.	administrative division
Ilot / Fr.	islet
Imi / Ar.	spring
I-n / Ber.	well
Inch / Gae.	island
Inder / Dan.; Nor.	inner
Indre / Nor.	inner
Inferiore / It.	lower
Inish / Gae.	island
Insel / Germ.	island
Insulă / Rom.	island
Inver / Gae.	mouth
Irhazér / Ber.	wadi
Irmak / Tur.	river
'Irq / Ar.	dunes
Is / Nor.	glacier
Ís / Icel.	ice
Isblink / Dan.	glacier
Ishi / Jap.	rock
Iske / Alt.	old
Isla / Sp.	island
Iso / Finn.	great
Iso / Jap.	cliff
Isola / It.	island
Isthmós / Gr.	isthmus
Istmo / Sp.; It.	isthmus
Ita / A.I.	stone
Itä / Finn.	east
Itivdleq / Esk.	isthmus
Iwa / Jap.	rock, cliff
Iztočni / Bulg.	eastern
Izvor / Bulg.; Rom.; S.C.; Slvn.	spring

J

Local Form	English
J., Jazīrat / Ar.	island
J., Jiang / Chin.	river
Jabal / Ar.	mountain
Jaha / Ural.	river
Jam / Ural.	lake, river
Jama / Rus.	cave
Jan / Alt.	great
Janga / Tur.	north
Jangi / Alt.; Iran.	new
Janūbīyah / Ar.	southern
Jar / Rus.	bank
Järv / Est.	lake
Järve / Finn.	lake
Järvi / Finn.	lake
Jasirēd / Som.	island
Jaun / Latv.	new
Jaur / Lapp.	lake
Jaure / Lapp.	lake
Javr / Lapp.	lake
Javrre / Lapp.	lake
Jazā'ir / Ar.	islands
Jazīrat, J. / Ar.	island
Jazovir / Bulg.	reservoir
Jbel / Ar.	mountain
Jebel / Ar.	mountain
Jedid / Ar.	new
Jedo / Kor.	archipelago
Jezero / S.C.; Slvn.	lake
Jezioro / Pol.	lake
Jhil / Hin.; Urdu	lake
Jian / Chin.	mountain
Jiang, J. / Chin.	river
Jiao / Chin.	cape, cliff
Jibāl / Ar.	mountain
Jih / Cz.	south
Jima / Jap.	island
Jin / Kor.	cove
Jing / Chin.	spring
Jisr / Ar.	bridge
Joch / Germ.	pass
Jōgi / Est.	river
Jøkel / Nor.	glacier
Joki / Finn.	river
Jokka / Lapp.	river
Jökull / Icel.	glacier
Jord, -jord / Nor.	earth
Ju / Ural.	river
Judeṭ / Rom.	district
Jugan / Ural.	river
Jura / Lith.	sea
Jūra / Latv.	sea
Jūras Līcis / Latv.	bay
Jürmala / Latv.	beach
Jurt / Cauc.	village
Južni / Bulg.; S.C.; Slvn.	southern
Južny / Rus.	southern
Juzur / Ar.	islands

K

Local Form	English
Ka / Poly.	lake
Kaap / Afr.	cape
Kabīr / Ar.	great
Kae / Kor.	inlet
Kāf / Ar.	peak, mountain
Kafr / Ar.	village
Kaga / Ban.	hills, mountain range
Kahal / Ar.	plateau, escarpment
Kai / Jap.	sea
Kaikyō / Jap.	strait
Kaise / Lapp.	mountain
Kal / Pers.	stream
Kala / Az.; Kor.	fort
Kala / Finn.	river
Kala / Hin.	black
Kala / Tur.	castle
Kalaa / Ar.	castle
Kalaki / Georg.	city, town
Kale / Tur.	castle
Kali / Hin.	black
Kali / Indon.; Mal.	bay, river
Kallio / Finn.	rock
Kaln / Latv.	mountain
Kalós / Gr.	beautiful, good
Kamen / Bulg.; Rus.; S.C.; Slvn.	mountain, peak
Kámen / Cz.	rock
Kameň / Slvk.	rock
Kami / Jap.	upper
Kamień / Pol.	rock
Kamm / Germ.	crest
Kamp / Germ.	field
Kâmpóng / Khm.	village
Kámpos / Gr.	field
Kampung / Indon.; Mal.	village
Kan.; Kanal / Alb.; Dan.; Germ.; Nor.; Rus.; S.C.; Slvn.; Swed.; Tur.	canal, channel
Kanaal / Dut.; Fle.	canal
Kanał / Pol.	canal
Kanal, Kan. / Alb.; Dan.; Germ.; Nor.; Rus.; S.C.; Slvn.; Swed.; Tur.	canal, channel
Kand, -kand / Pers.; Tur.	city, town
Kang / Chin.; Kor.	bay, river
Kangas / Fle.	heath
Kange / Esk.	east
Kangri / Tib.	snow-capped mountain
Kantara / Ar.	bridge
Kaöh / Khm.	island
Kap / Dan.; Germ.	cape
Kapija / S.C.	gate, gorge
Kapp / Nor.	cape
Kar / Tib.	white
Kar / Ural.	city, town
Kara / Tur.	black
Karang / Indon.; Mal.	sandbank, cliff
Kari / Finn.	cliff
Kariba / Ban.	gorge
Kariet / Ar.	village
Karki / Finn.	peninsula
Kastel / Germ.	castle
Kástron / Gr.	fort, city, town
Káto / Gr.	lower
Kaupstadur / Icel.	city, town
Kaupunki / Finn.	city, town
Kavir / Pers.	salt desert
Kawa / Jap.	river
Kawm / Ar.	hill
Kebir / Ar.	great
Kedi / Georg.	mountain range
Kédia / Ar.	mountain, plateau
Kedim / Ar.	old
Kef / Ar.	mountain
Kefála / Gr.	mountain, peak
Kefar / Hebr.	village
Kei / Jap.	river
Kelet / Hung.	east
Ken / Gae.	cape
Kent / Alt.; Iran.; Tur.	city, town
Kenya / Swa.	fog
Kep / Alb.	cape
Kep., Kepulauan / Mal.	archipelago
Kepulauan, Kep. / Mal.	archipelago
Kereszt / Hung.	cross
Kerk / Dut.; Fle.	church
Keski / Finn.	middle
Kette / Germ.	mountain range
Keur / Sud.	village
Key / Eng.	coral island
Kha / Tib.	valley
Khal / Hin.	canal
Khalīj / Ar.	gulf
Khand / Hin.	district
Khao / Thai	hill, mountain
Kharābeh / Pers.	ruins
Khashm / Ar.	promontory
Khatt / Ar.	wadi
Khawr / Ar.	mouth, bay
Khazzān / Ar.	dam
Khemis / Ar.	fifth
Khersónisos / Gr.	peninsula
Khirbat / Ar.	ruins
Khlong / Thai	stream, mouth
Khokhok / Thai	isthmus
Khor / Ar.	mouth, bay
Khóra / Gr.	land
Khorion / Gr.	village
Khowr / Pers.	bay
Khrisós / Gr.	gold
Ki- / Ban.	little
Kibali / Sud.	river
Kil / Gae.	church
Kilde / Dan.	spring
Kilima / Swa.	mountain
Kill / Gae.	strait
Kilwa / Ban.	lake
Kin / Gae.	cape
Kinn / Nor.	cape, point
Kirche / Germ.	church
Kirk / Eng.	church
Kis / Hung.	little
Kisiwa / Swa.	island
Kita / Jap.	north, northern
Kızıl / Tur.	red
Klein / Afr.; Dut.; Germ.	little
Kliff / Germ.	cliff
Klint / Dan.	reef
Klip / Afr.; Dut.	rock, cliff
Klit / Dan.	dune
Kloof / Afr.; Dut.	gorge
Kloster / Dan.; Germ.; Nor.; Swed.	convent
Knob / Eng.	mountain
Knock / Gae.	mountain, hill
Ko / Jap.	bay, lake, little
Ko / Sud.	stream
Ko / Thai	island, point
Købing / Dan.	town
Kogel / Germ.	dome
Kōgen / Jap.	plateau
Koh / Hin.; Pers.	mountain, mountain range
Kol / Alt.	river, valley
Kol / Alt.; Tur.	lake
Koll / Nor.	peak
Kólpos / Gr.	gulf
Kong / Dan.; Nor.; Swed.	king
Kong / Indon.; Mal.	mountain
Kong / Viet.	mountain, hill
Konge / Ban.	river
König / Germ.	king
Koog / Germ.	polder
Kop / Afr.	hill
Kopec / Cz.; Slvk.	hill
Kopf / Germ.	peak
Köping / Swed.	town
Köprü / Tur.	bridge
Körfezi / Tur.	gulf
Korfi / Gr.	rock
Koro / Mel.	mountain, island
Koro / Sud.	old
Koru / Finn.	forest
Kosa / Rus.	spit
Koška / Rus.	cliff
Koski / Finn.	rapids
Kosui / Jap.	lake
Kot / Urdu	castle
Kota / Mal.	city, town
Kotal / Pash.; Pers.	pass
Kotar / S.C.	cultivated area
Kotlina / Pol.	basin

Local Form	English
Kotlovina / Rus.	basin, plain
Kou / Chin.	mouth, pass
Kourou / Sud.	well
Kowr / Pers.	river
Kowtal / Pers.	pass
Koy / Tur.	bay
Köy / Tur.	village
Kraal / Afr.	village
Kraina / Pol.	land
Kraj / Rus.; S.C.	land
Kraj / Rus.	administrative division
Krajina / S.C.	land
Krak / Ar.	hill, castle
Krans / Afr.	mountain
Kras / S.C.; Slvn.	karst landscape
Krasny / Rus.	red
Kreb / Ar.	hills, mountain range
Kriaž / Ar.	mountain range
Krš / S.C.	karst area, limestone area
Krung / Thai	city, town
Ksar / Ar.	castle
Ksour / Ar.	fortified village
Ku- / Ban.	river branch
Kuala / Mal.	river, mouth
Kubra / Ar.	bridge
Küçük / Tur.	little
Kuduk / Tur.	spring
Küh / Pers.	mountain
Kühhā / Pers.	mountain range
Kul / Alt.; Iran.; Tur.	lake
Kulam, -kulam / Hin.; Tam.	pond
Kulle / Swed.	hill
Kulm / Germ.	peak
Kultuk / Rus.	bay
Kum / Tur.	dunes, sand desert
Kuppe / Germ.	dome, seamount
Kurayb / Ar.	hill
Kurgan / Alt.	hill
Kurgan / Tur.	fort
Kuro / Jap.	black
Kurort / Bulg.; Germ.; Rus.	spa
Kust / Dut.; Fle.	coast
Kust- / Swed.	coast
Küste / Germ.	coast
Kút / Hung.	spring
Kuyu / Tur.	spring
Kvemo / Georg.	low, lower
Kwa / Ban.	village
Kylä / Finn.	village
Kyle / Gae.	strait, channel
Kyō / Jap.	strait
Kyrka / Swed.	church
Kyst / Dan.; Nor.	coast
Kyun / Burm.	island
Kyūryō / Jap.	hills, mountains
Kyzyl / Tur.	red
Kzyl / Tur.	red

L

Local Form	English
L., Lake, Lago / Eng.; It.; Port.; Sp.	lake
La / Tib.	pass
Laagte / Afr.	stream, valley
Labuan / Indon.; Mal.	bay, port
Lac / Fr.	lake
Lach / Som.	stream, wadi
Lacul / Rom.	lake
Lae / Poly.	cape, point
Laem / Thai	bay, port
Låg / Nor.; Swed.	low, lower
Lag / Swed.	stream, wadi
Läge / Swed.	beach
Lagh / Som.	stream, wadi
Lago, L. / It.; Port.; Sp.	lake
Lagoa / Port.	lagoon
Laguna / Alb.; It.; Rus.; Sp.	lagoon, lake
Lagune / Fr.	lagoon
Laht / Est.	bay
Lahti / Finn.	bay, gulf
Laks / Mal.	bay
Lalla / Ar.	saint
Lampi / Finn.	pond
Lande / Fr.	heath
Lang / Afr.; Dut.; Germ.	long
Lang / Viet.	village
Lao / Chin.	old
Lapa / Poly.	mountain range, peak
Largo / Port.; Sp.	basin
Las / Pol.	forest
Las, Läs / Som.	well
Laut / Mal.	sea
Law / Gae.	hill, mountain
Lázně / Cz.	thermal springs
Lednik / Rus.	glacier
Leite / Germ.	coast
Lekh / Nep.	mountain range

Local Form	English
Les / Bulg.; Cz.; Rus.; Slvk.	forest
Leso / Rus.	forested
Levante / It.; Sp.	eastern
Levkós / Gr.	white
Levy / Rus.	left
Lha / Tib.	temple
Lhari / Hin.; Nep.	mountain
Lho / Tib.	south
Lido / It.	sandbar
Liedao / Chin.	archipelago
Liehtao / Chin.	archipelago
Liels / Latv.	great
Lilla / Swed.	little
Lille / Dan.; Nor.	little
Liman / Alb.; Rus.; Tur.	lagoon, bay
Liman / Tur.	bay, port
Limin / Gr.	port
Limni / Gr.	lake
Ling / Chin.	mountain range, peak
Linna / Finn.	castle
Liqen / Alb.	lake
Lithos / Gr.	stone
Litoral / Port.; Sp.	littoral
Litorale / It.	littoral
Llan / Wel.	church
Llano / Sp.	plain
Llanura / Sp.	plain
Lo- / Ban.	river
Loch / Gae.	lake, inlet
Loch / Germ.	grotto
Loka / Slvn.	forest
Loma / Sp.	hill
Long / Indon.	stream
Loo / Dut.; Fle.	clearing
Lough / Gae.	lake
Loutrá / Gr.	thermal springs
Ložbina / Rus.	depression
Lu- / Ban.	river
Lua / Ban.	river
Lua / Mel.	island, reef
Lua / Poly.	crater
Luang / Thai	yellow
Luch / Germ.	peat-bog
Lücke / Germ.	pass
Lug / Rus.	meadow
Luka / S.C.; Slvn.	port
Lule / Lapp.	east, eastern
Lum / Alb.	river
Lund / Dan.; Swed.	forest
Lung / Rom.	long
Lung / Tib.	valley
Luoto / Finn.	shoal
Lurg / Pers.	salt flat
Lut / Pers.	desert

M

Local Form	English
M., Monte / It.; Port.; Sp.	mountain
Ma / Ar.	water
Ma- / Ban.	people
Maa / Est.; Finn.	island, land
Ma'arrat / Ar.	height
Machi / Jap.	district
Macizo / Sp.	massif
Madhya / Hin.	central
Madīnah / Ar.	city, town
Mado / Swa.	well
Madu / Tam.	pond
Mae / Thai	stream
Mae nam / Thai	stream, mouth
Magh / Gae.	plain
Mägi / Est.	mountain
Măgura / Rom.	height
Mahā / Hin.	great
Mahal / Hin.; Urdu	palace
Mai / Amh.; Ban.	stream
Majdan / S.C.	quarry
Mäki / Finn.	mountain, hill
Makrós / Gr.	long
Mala / Hin.; Tam.	mountain
Malai / Hin.; Tam.	mountain
Malal / A.I.	fence
Malhão / Port.	dome
Mali / Alb.	mountain
Mali / S.C.; Slvn.	little
Malki / Bulg.	little
Malla / Tam.	mountain
Maly / Rus.	little
Malý / Cz.; Slvk.	little
Mały / Pol.	little
Man / Kor.	bay
Manastir / Bulg.; S.C.	monastery
Manche / Fr.	channel
Mar / It.; Port.; Sp.	sea
Mar / Tib.	red
Mar / Ural.	city, town
Marais / Fr.	marsh
Marché / Fr.	market
Mare / Fr.	pond
Mare / It.; Rom.	sea
Mare / Rom.	great
Marea / Rom.	sea
Marécage / Fr.	marsh
Marios / Lith.	reservoir

Local Form	English
Marisma / Sp.	marsh
Mark / Dan.; Nor.; Swed.	land
Markt / Germ.	market
Marsa / Ar.	anchorage, bay
Marsch / Germ.	marsh
Maru / Jap.	mountain
Mas / Prov.	farmhouse
Maşabb / Ar.	mouth
Mashra' / Ar.	landing, pier
Masivul / Rom.	massif
Massiv / Germ.; Rus.	massif
Mata / Poly.	point
Mata / Port.; Sp.	forest
Mata / Som.	waterfall
Mato / Port.; Sp.	forest
Matsu / Jap.	point
Mauna / Poly.	mountain
Mávros / Gr.	black
Mayo / Sud.	river
Maza / Lith.	little
Mazar / Pers.; Tur.	sanctuary
Mazs / Latv.	little
Me / Khm.	river
Me / Mel.	hill, mountain
Me / Thai	great
Medina / Ar.	city, town
Medjez / Ar.	ford
Meer / Dut.; Fle.	lake
Meer / Germ.	lake, sea
Megálos / Gr.	great
Mégas / Gr.	great
Megye / Hung.	district
Mélas / Gr.	black
Melkosopočnik / Rus.	hill country
Mellan / Swed.	central
Men / Chin.	gate, channel
Ménez / Br.	mountain
Menzel / Ar.	bivouac
Meos / Indon.	island
Mer / Fr.	sea
Mercato / It.	market
Merdja / Ar.	lagoon, marsh
Meri / Est.; Finn.	sea
Meridional / Rom.; Sp.	southern
Merin / A.I.	little
Merja / Ar.	lagoon, marsh
Mers / Ar.	port
Mersa / Ar.	port
Mesa / Sp.	mesa, tableland
Meseta / Sp.	plateau
Mésos / Gr.	central
Mesto / Bulg.; S.C.; Slvk.; Slvn.	city, town
Město / Cz.	city, town
Mestre / Port.	principal
Meydan / Tur.	square
Mezad / Hebr.	castle
Mező / Hung.	field
Mgne., Montagne / Fr.	mountain
Mgnes., Montagnes / Fr.	mountains
Miao / Chin.	temple
Miasto / Pol.	city, town
Mic / Rom.	little
Middel / Afr.; Dut.; Fle.	middle
Midi / Fr.	noon, south
Między / Pol.	central
Miedzyrzecze / Pol.	interfluve
Mierzeja / Pol.	sand spit
Mifraz / Hebr.	bay, gulf
Miftah / Ar.	gorge
Mikrós / Gr.	little
Mina / Port.; Sp.	mine
Mīnā' / Ar.	port
Minami / Jap.	south, southern
Minamoto / Jap.	spring
Minato / Jap.	port
Mine / Jap.	peak
Mirim / A.I.	little
Misaki / Jap.	cape
Mittel- / Germ.	middle
Mo / Chin.	sand desert
Mo / Nor.; Swed.	heath
Moana / Poly.	lake
Mogila / Bulg.; Rus.	hill
Moku / Poly.	island
Mølle / Dan.	mill
Monasterio / Sp.	monastery
Mond / Afr.; Dut.; Fle.	mouth
Mong / Burm.; Thai; Viet.	city, town
Moni / Gr.	monastery
Mont / Cat.; Fr.	mountain
Montagna / It.	mountain
Montagne, Mgne. / Fr.	mountain
Montagnes, Mgnes. / Fr.	mountains
Montaña / Sp.	mountain
Monte, M. / It.; Port.; Sp.	mountain
Monts, Mts. / Fr.	mountains
Moos / Germ.	moor
Mór / Gae.	great
More / Bulg.; Rus.; S.C.	sea
More / Gae.	great
Mori / Jap.	mountain, forest
Morne / Fr.	mountain
Moron / Mong.	river
Morro / Port.; Germ.	hill, peak
Morrón / Sp.	mountain
Morze / Pol.	sea

Local Form	English
Most / Bulg.; Cz.; Pol.; Rus.; S.C.; Slvn.	bridge
Moto / Jap.	spring
Motte / Fr.	hill
Motu / Mel.; Poly.	island, rock
Moutier / Fr.	monastery
Movilă / Rom.	hill
Moyen / Fr.	central
Mta / Georg.	mountain
Mts., Monts, Mountains / Eng.; Fr.	mountains
Muang / Laot.; Thai	city, town, land
Muara / Indon.; Mal.	mouth
Muela / Sp.	mountain
Mühle / Germ.	mill
Mui / Mel.	point
Mui / Viet.	point, cape
Muiden / Dut.; Fle.	mouth
Muir / Gae.	sea
Mukh / Hin.	mouth
Mull / Gae.	promontory
Münde / Germ.	mouth
Mündung / Germ.	mouth
Municipiul / Rom.	commune
Munkhafaḍ / Ar.	depression
Münster / Germ.	monastery
Munte / Rom.	mountain
Muntelé / Rom.	mountain
Munţii / Rom.	mountain range
Muren / Mong.	river
Mushāsh / Ar.	spring
Muz / Tur.	ice
Muztagh / Tur.	snow-capped mountain
Mwambo / Ban.	rock, cliff
Myit / Burm.	stream
Mynydd / Wel.	mountain
Myo / Burm.	city, town
Mýri / Icel.	marsh
Mys / Rus.	cape

N

Local Form	English
Na / Cz.; Pol.; Rus.; S.C.; Slvn.	on
Nab / Ar.	spring
Nad / Cz.; Pol.; Rus.	on
Nada / Jap.	bay, sea
Nadi, -nadi / Hin.; Urdu	river
Næs / Dan.	point
Nafūd / Ar.	dunes
Nag / Tib.	black
Nagar, -nagar / Hin.; Tib.	city, town
Nagaram / Hin.; Tam.	city, town
Nagorje / Rus.	plateau, mountains
Nagy / Hung.	great
Nahr / Ar.	river
Naikai / Jap.	sea
Naka / Jap.	central
Nakhon / Thai	city, town
Nam / Burm.; Laot.; Thai	river
Nam / Kor.	south
Namakzar / Pers.	salt desert
Nan / Chin.	south
Narrows / Eng.	strait
Narssaq / Esk.	plain, valley
Näs / Swed.	cape
Nationalpark / Swed.; Germ.	national park
Nau / Lith.	new
Nauja / Lith.	new
Navolok / Rus.	cape, promontory
Ne / Jap.	cliff
Neder / Flę.; Dut.	low
Neem / Est.	cape
Negro / Port.; Sp.	black
Negru / Rom.	black
Nehir / Tur.	river
Nei / Chin.	inner
Nene, -nene / Ban.	great
Néos / Gr.	new
Nero / It.	black
Nes / Icel.; Nor.	cape
Ness / Gae.	promontory
Neu / Germ.	new
Neuf / Fr.	new
Nevado / Sp.	snow-capped mountain
Nez / Fr.	cape
Ngok / Viet.	mountain, peak
Ngolo / Ber.	great
Ni / Kor.	village
Niecka / Pol.	basin
Niemi / Finn.	peninsula
Nieuw / Fle.; Dut.	new
Nij / Dut.	new
Nīl / Hin.	blue
Nishi / Jap.	west
Niski / Pol.	lower
Nisko / S.C.	low
Nisoi / Gr.	islands
Nisos / Gr.	island
Nizina / Pol.	lowland
Nížina / Cz.	depression
Nízký / Cz.	low, lower

Geographical Glossary

Local Form	English	Local Form	English	Local Form	English	Local Form	English
Nizmennost / *Rus.*	lowland, depression	Ostrov / *Rus.*	island	Petit / *Fr.*	little	Priehradni nàdrž / *Cz.*	reservoir
Nižni / *Rus.*	low, lower	Ostrovul / *Rom.*	island	Pétra / *Gr.*	rock	Pripoljarny / *Rus.*	subpolar
Nižný / *Slvk.*	low, lower	Ostrów / *Pol.*	island	Phanom / *Thai; Khm.*	mountain range, mountain	Pristan / *Rus.*	port
No / *Mel.*	stream	Ostrvo / *S.C.*	island	Phau / *Laot.*	mountain	Prohod / *Bulg.*	pass
Nock / *Gae.*	ridge	Otok / *S.C.; Slvn.*	island	Phnum / *Khm.*	hill, mountain	Proliv / *Rus.*	strait
Noir / *Fr.*	black	Otrog / *Rus.*	front range (mountains)	Phu / *Viet.*	mountain, hill	Promontoire / *Fr.*	promontory
Non / *Thai*	hill	Oua / *Mel.*	stream	Phum / *Thai*	forest	Prúchod / *Cz.*	pass
Nong / *Thai*	lake, marsh	Ouar / *Ar.*	rocky desert	Phumĭ / *Khm.*	village	Przedgorze / *Pol.*	front range (mountains)
Noord / *Afr.; Fle.; Dut.*	north	Oud / *Fle.; Dut.*	old	Pi / *Chin.*	cape		
Noordoost / *Afr.; Fle.; Dut.*	northeast	Oued / *Ar.*	wadi	Piana, Pianura / *It.*	plain	Przełęcz / *Pol.*	pass
Nor / *Arm.*	new	Ouest / *Fr.*	west	Piano / *It.*	plain	Przemysł / *Pol.*	industry
Nord / *Fr.; It.; Germ.*	north	Ouled / *Ar.*	son	Piatră / *Rom.*	stone	Przylądek / *Pol.*	cape
Nördlich / *Germ.*	northern	Oum / *Ar.*	mother	Pic / *Cat.; Fr.*	peak	Pua / *Mel.*	hill
Nørdre / *Dan.; Nor.*	northern	Ouro / *Port.*	gold	Picacho / *Sp.*	peak	Puebla / *Sp.*	village
Norra / *Swed.*	northern	Outu / *Poly.*	cape	Piccolo / *It.*	little	Puente / *Sp.*	bridge
Nørre / *Dan.*	northern	Ova / *Ban.*	people	Pico / *Port.; Sp.*	peak	Puerto / *Sp.*	port, pass
Norte / *Sp.*	north	Ova / *Tur.*	plain	Piedra / *Sp.*	rock, cliff	Puig / *Cat.*	peak
Nos / *Bulg.; Rus.; S.C.; Slvn.*	cape	Ovasi / *Tur.*	plain	Pietra / *It.*	stone	Puits / *Fr.*	well
Nosy / *Malag.*	island	Øver / *Nor.*	over	Pieve / *It.*	parish	Pul / *Pash.*	bridge
Nótios / *Gr.*	southern	Över / *Swed.*	over	Pik / *Rus.*	peak	Pulau, P. / *Mal.; Indon.*	island
Nou / *Rom.*	new	Övre / *Swed.*	over	Pils / *Latv.*	city, town	Pulau Pulau / *Mal.*	islands
Novi / *Bulg.; S.C.; Slvn.*	new	Øy / *Dan.; Nor.*	island	Pinar / *Sp.*	pine forest	Pulo / *Mal.; Indon.*	island
Novo / *Port.*	new	oz., Ozero / *Rus.*	lake	Pingyuan / *Chin.*	plain	Puna / *A.I.*	upland
Novy / *Rus.*	new	Ozek / *Alt.*	hollow	Pioda / *It.*	crest	Puncak / *Indon.*	mountain
Nový / *Cz.; Slvk.*	new	Ozera / *Rus.*	lakes	Pirgos / *Gr.*	tower, peak	Punjung / *Mal.; Indon.*	mountain
Now / *Pers.*	new	Ozero, oz. / *Rus.*	lake	Piš / *Pers.*	anterior, before	Punt / *Afr.*	point
Nowy / *Pol.*	new			Pitkä / *Finn.*	great	Punta / *It.; Sp.*	point
Nudo / *Sp.*	mountain			Piton / *Fr.*	mountain, peak	Pur, -pur / *Hin.; Urdu*	city, town
Nuevo / *Sp.*	new			Piz / *Rmsh.*	peak	-pura / *Hin.; Urdu*	city, town
Nui / *Viet.*	mountain	**P**		Pizzo / *It.*	peak	Pura / *Indon.*	city, town, temple
Numa / *Jap.*	marsh, lake			Pjasăci / *Bulg.*	beach		
Nummi / *Finn.*	heath	P., Pulau / *Mal.; Indon.*	island	Plaat / *Fle.; Dut.*	sandbank	Puri, -puri / *Hin.; Urdu*	city, town
Nunatak / *Esk.*	peak	Pää / *Finn.*	principal	Plage / *Fr.*	beach	Pus / *Alb.*	spring
Nuovo / *It.*	new	Pad / *Rus.*	valley	Plaine / *Fr.*	plain	Pušča / *Rus.*	forest
Nur / *Chin.*	lake	Padang / *Indon.*	plain	Plan / *Fr.*	plain	Pustynja / *Rus.*	desert
Nusa / *Mal.*	island	Padiş / *Rom.*	upland	Planalto / *Port.*	plateau	Puszcza / *Pol.*	heath
Nut, -nut / *Nor.*	peak	Padół / *Pol.*	valley	Planina / *Bulg.*	mountain	Puszta / *Hung.*	lowland
Nuwara / *Sin.; Tam.*	city, town	Pădure / *Rom.*	forest	Plano / *Sp.*	plain	Put / *Afr.*	well
Nuwe / *Afr.*	new	Pahorek / *Cz.*	hill	Plas / *Dut.; Fle.*	lake, marsh	Put / *Rus.; S.C.*	road
Nyanza / *Ban.*	water, river, lake	Pahorkatina / *Cz.*	plateau, hills	Plato / *Bulg.; Rus.*	plateau	Putra, -putra / *Hin.*	son
Nyasa / *Ban.*	lake	Pais / *Port.; Sp.*	land, country	Platosu / *Tur.*	plateau	Puu / *Poly.*	mountain, volcano
Nyeong / *Kor.*	pass	Pak / *Thai*	mouth	Platte / *Germ.*	plain, plateau	Puy / *Fr.*	peak
Nyika / *Ban.*	upland	Pala / *It.*	peak	Plav / *S.C.*	blue	Pwell / *Wel.*	pond
Nyöng / *Kor.*	mount, pass	Palaiós / *Gr.*	old	Plavnja / *Rus.*	marsh	Pyeong / *Kor.*	plain
Nyugat / *Hung.*	west	Palanka / *S.C.*	village	Playa / *Sp.*	beach	Pyhä / *Finn.*	saint
		Pali / *Poly.*	cliff	Ploskogorje / *Rus.*	plateau		
		-palli / *Hin.*	village	Plou / *Br.*	church		
O		Pampa / *Sp.*	plain, prairie	Po / *Kor.*	port	**Q**	
		Panda / *Swa.*	junction	Po / *Chin.*	lake, white		
Ō / *Jap.*	great	Panev / *Cz.*	basin	P'o / *Kor.*	bay, lake	Qagan / *Mong.*	white
Ó / *Hung.*	old	Pantanal / *Sp.*	swamp	Poa / *Mel.*	hill	Qala / *Pash.*	fortified town
Ö / *Swed.*	island	Pantano / *Sp.*	swamp, lake	Poarta / *Rom.*	pass	Qal'at / *Ar.*	castle
Ø, -ø / *Dan.; Nor.*	island	Pao / *Mel.*	hill	Poartă / *Rom.*	gate	Qalb / *Ar.*	hill
Öar / *Swed.*	islands	Pará / *A.I.*	river	Pobla / *Cat.*	village	Qalib / *Ar.*	spring
Ober / *Germ.*	upper	Paramera / *Sp.*	desert highland	Pobrzeże / *Pol.*	littoral, coast	Qaliq / *Ar.*	spring
Oblast / *Rus.*	province	Páramo / *Sp.*	moor	Poço / *Port.*	well	Qanăt / *Ar.*	canal
Obo / *Mong.*	mountain, hill	Paraná / *A.I.*	river	Poço / *Port.*	point	Qantara / *Ar.*	bridge
Occidental / *Fr.; Rom.; Sp.*	western	Parbat / *Hin.; Urdu*	mountain	Pod / *Cz.; Pol.; Rus.; S.C.; Slvn.*	bridge	Qaqortoq / *Esk.*	white
Océan / *Fr.*	ocean	Parc / *Fr.*	park			Qar / *Som.*	mountain
Océano / *Sp.*	ocean	Parco / *It.*	park	Podkamenny / *Rus.*	stony	Qara / *Pers.*	black
Oceano / *It.; Port.*	ocean	Parco Nazionale / *It.*	national park	Poggio / *It.*	hill	Qarah / *Tur.*	black
Ocnă / *Rom.*	salt mine	Pardo / *Port.*	grey	Pohja / *Finn.*	north, northern	Qārat / *Ar.*	height, mountain
Odde / *Dan.; Nor.*	promontory	Parque / *Sp.*	park	Pohjois- / *Finn.*	north		
Oeste / *Port.; Sp.*	west	Parque Nacional / *Sp.; Port.*	national park	Pojezierze / *Pol.*	lake region	Qāret / *Ar.*	village, hill
Oever / *Fle.; Dut.*	bank	Pas / *Fr.; Rom.*	pass, strait	Pol / *Pers.*	bridge	Qaryah / *Ar.*	village
Oewer / *Afr.*	bank	Pasaje / *Sp.*	passage	Pol, -pol / *Rus.*	city, town	Qaryat / *Ar.*	village
Oie / *Germ.*	islet	Pasir / *Mal.*	sand, beach	Pola / *Port.; Sp.*	village	Qasr / *Ar.*	castle
Ojos / *Sp.*	spring	Paso / *Sp.*	pass	Polder / *Fle.; Dut.*	reclaimed land	Qawz / *Ar.*	dunes
Oka / *Jap.*	coast	Passàgem / *Port.*	passage	Pole / *Pol.*	field	Qeqertarssuaq / *Esk.*	peninsula
Oke / *Sud.*	height	Passe / *Fr.*	pass	Pólis / *Gr.*	city, town	Qezel / *Tur.*	red
Okean / *Rus.*	ocean	Passo / *It.; Port.*	pass	Poljana / *Bulg.; Rus.; S.C.; Slvn.*	field, terrace	Qi / *Chin.*	river
Oki / *Jap.*	bay	Pasul / *Rom.*	pass			Qing / *Chin.*	blue, green
Okrug / *Rus.*	district	Patak / *Hung.*	stream	Poljarny / *Rus.*	polar	Qiryat / *Hebr.*	city, town
Ola / *Alt.*	city, town	Patam, -patam / *Hin.*	city, town	Polje / *S.C.; Slvn.*	valley, field, basin	Qolleh / *Pers.*	mountain, peak
Omuramba / *K.S.*	stream	Patnă / *Hin.*	city, town			Qu / *Chin.*	river, canal
Onder / *Afr.*	under	Patnam, -patnam / *Hin.*	city, town	Poluostrov / *Rus.*	peninsula	Quan dao / *Viet.*	islands
Oni / *Malag.*	river	Pattinam, -pattinam / *Hin.*	city, town	Pomorije / *Bulg.*	littoral	Quebracho / *Sp.*	stream
Oos / *Afr.*	east	Pays / *Fr.*	land, country	Pomorze / *Pol.*	littoral	Quebrada / *Sp.*	gorge, stream
Oost / *Fle.; Dut.*	east	Pazar / *Tur.*	market	Ponente / *It.*	western	Quedas / *Port.*	waterfalls
Oostelijk / *Dut.*	eastern	Pea / *Est.*	cape	Pont / *Cat.; Fr.*	bridge	Qulbān / *Ar.*	well
Opatija / *Slvn.*	abbey	Pech / *Cat.*	hill	Ponta / *Port.*	point	Qundao / *Chin.*	archipelago
Or / *Fr.*	gold	Pedhiás / *Gr.*	plain	Ponte / *It.; Port.*	bridge	Qūr / *Ar.*	height, hill
Oraş / *Rom.*	city, town	Pedra / *Port.*	rock, mountain	Póntos / *Gr.*	sea	Qytet / *Alb.*	city, town
Óri / *Gr.*	mountains	Peg., Pegunungan / *Mal.; Indon.*	mountain range	Poort / *Afr.; Fle.; Dut.*	pass	Qyteti / *Alb.*	city, town
Oriental / *Fr.; Port.; Rom.; Sp.*	eastern	Pegunungan, Peg. / *Mal.; Indon.*	mountain range	Pore, -pore / *Hin.; Urdu*	city, town		
				Porog / *Rus.*	rapids		
Orientale / *It.*	eastern	Pélagos / *Gr.*	sea	Porte / *Fr.*	gate	**R**	
Orilla / *Sp.*	bank	Pele / *Poly.*	peak, hill	Portile / *Rom.*	gorge		
Órmos / *Gr.*	bay	Pen / *Br.*	principal	Portillo / *Sp.*	pass	R., Rio, River / *Eng.; Sp.*	river
Óros / *Gr.*	mountain	Pen / *Br.; Gae.*	cape, mountain	Portiţa / *Rom.*	small gate	Rada / *It.; Sp.*	anchorage
Ország / *Hung.*	land	Peña / *Sp.*	peak	Porto / *It.*	port	Rade / *Fr.*	anchorage
Ort / *Germ.*	cape	Pendi / *Chin.*	basin	Pôrto / *Port.*	port	Rags / *Latv.*	cape
Orta / *Tur.*	central	Pendiente / *Sp.*	slope	Posht / *Pers.*	back, posterior	Rahad / *Ar.*	lake, pond
Orto / *Alt.*	central	Penha / *Port.*	peak	Potjo / *Indon.*	peak	Rajon / *Rus.*	district
Oseaan / *Afr.*	ocean	Peninsula / *Port.; Sp.*	peninsula	Potok / *Bulg.; Cz.; Pol.; Rus.; S.C.; Slvn.*	stream	Rak / *Fle.; Dut.*	strait
Ōshima / *Jap.*	large island	Péninsule / *Fr.*	peninsula			Rakai / *Poly.*	reef
Ost / *Dan.; Germ.*	east	Penisola / *It.*	peninsula	Póvoa / *Port.*	village	Ramla / *Ar.*	sand
Öst / *Swed.*	east	Peñon / *Sp.*	rock, island	Pozo / *Sp.*	well	Rancho / *Port.; Sp.*	farm, ranch
Ostän, -ostän / *Pers.*	province	Pente / *Fr.*	slope	Pozzo / *It.*	well	Rand / *Afr.; Germ.*	escarpment
Øster / *Dan.; Nor.*	east, eastern	Perekóp / *Rus.*	channel	Pradesh / *Hin.*	region, state	Range / *Eng.*	mountain range
Öster / *Swed.*	east, eastern	Pereval / *Rus.*	pass	Prado / *Sp.*	meadow	Rann / *Urdu*	marsh
Östlich / *Germ.*	eastern	Perevoz / *Rus.*	ford	Praia / *Port.*	beach	Rano / *Malag.*	water
Ostrog / *Rus.*	castle	Pertuis / *Fr.*	strait	Prato / *It.*	meadow	Ranta / *Finn.*	bank, beach
		Pešcara / *S.C.*	sandy soil	Pré / *Fr.*	meadow	Rapide / *Fr.*	rapids
		Peski / *Rus.*	sand desert	Prealpi / *It.*	prealps	Ras / *Amh.*	peak
				Presa / *Sp.*	reservoir	Rãs / *Ar.*	point, cape
				Presqu'île / *Fr.*	peninsula		
				Prêto / *Port.*	black		

Local Form	English
Ras, Ràs / Ar.	promontory, peak
Ràsiga / Som.	promontory
Rass / Ar.	promontory, peak
Rassa / Lapp.	mountain
Ráth / Gae.	castle
Raunina / Bulg.; Rus.	plain
Raz / Fr.	strait
Razliv / Rus.	flood plain
Récif / Fr.	reef
Recife / Port.	reef
Reede / Germ.; Dut.; Slvn.	anchorage
Reek / Afr.; Gae.	mountain range
Reg / Pash.	dunes
Région / Fr.	region
Rei / Port.	king
Reka / Bulg.; Rus.; S.C.; Slvn.	river
Řeka / Cz.	river
Réma / Gr.	torrent
Renne / Dan.; Nor.	deep
Reprêsa / Port.	dam, reservoir
Represa / Sp.	dam, reservoir
República / Port.; Sp.	republic
République / Fr.	republic
Rés., Réservoir / Fr.	reservoir
Res., Reservoir / Eng.	reservoir
Réservoir, Rés. / Fr.	reservoir
Reshteh / Pers.	mountain range
Respublika / Rus.	republic
Restinga / Port.	cliff, sandbank
Retsugan / Jap.	reef
Rettō / Jap.	archipelago
Rev / Dan.; Nor.; Swed.	reef
Rey / Sp.	king
Ri / Tib.	mountain
Ria / Sp.	estuary
Riacho / Port.	stream
Rialto / It.	plateau
Rialto / It.	rise
Riba / Port.	bank
Ribeira / Port.	river
Ribeirão / Port.	stream
Ribeiro / Port.	stream
Ribera / Sp.	coast
Ribnik / Slvn.	pond
Rid / Bulg.	mountain range
Rif / Icel.	cliff
Riff / Germ.	reef
Rīg / Pash.	dunes
Rijeka / S.C.	river
Rimāl / Ar.	sand desert
Rincón / Sp.	peninsula between two rivers
Ring / Tib.	long
Rinne / Germ.	trench
Rio / Port.	river
Rio, R. / Sp.	river
Riu / Rom.	river
Riva / It.	bank
Rive / Fr.	bank
Rivera / Sp.	brook, stream
Rivier, -rivier / Afr.; Dut.; Fle.	river
Riviera / It.	coast
Rivière / Fr.	river
Roads / Eng.	anchorage
Roc / Fr.	rock
Roca / Port.; Sp.	rock
Rocca / It.	castle
Roche / Fr.	rock
Rocher / Fr.	rock
Rock / Eng.	rock
Rod / Pash.	river
Rode / Germ.	tilled soil
Rodnik / Rus.	spring
Rog / Rus.; S.C.; Slvn.	peak
Roi / Fr.	king
Rojo / Sp.	red
Roque / Sp.	rock
Rot / Germ.	red
Roto / Poly.	lake
Rouge / Fr.	red
Równina / Pol.	plain
Rt / S.C.; Slvn.	cape
Ru / Tib.	mountain
Ruck / Germ.	ridge
Rücken / Germ.	ridge
Rud / Pers.	river
Ruda / Cz.; Slvk.	mine
Ruda / Pol.	ore
Rūdbār / Pers.	river
Rudha / Gae.	point
Rudnik / Rus.; S.C.; Slvn.	mine
Rug / Fle.; Dut.	ridge
Ruggen / Afr.	ridge
Ruina / Sp.	ruins
Ruine / Fr.; Dut.; Germ.	ruins
Rujm / Ar.	hill
Run / Eng.	stream

S

Local Form	English
S., See / Germ.	lake, sea
Saar / Est.	island
Saari / Finn.	island
Sabbia / It.	sand
Sabkhat / Ar.	salt flat, salt marsh
Sable / Fr.; Eng.	beach
Sacca / It.	anchorage
Saco / Port.	bay
Sad / Cz.; Slvk.	park
Sad / Pers.	wall
Sadd / Ar.; Pers.	cataract, dam
Safid / Pash.; Urdu; Hin.	white
Şafrā' / Ar.	desert
Sāgar / Hin.	reservoir
Saguia / Ar.	irrigation canal
Sahara / Ar.	desert
Sahel / Ar.	plain, coast
Sahr / Iran.	city, town
Şaḥrā' / Ar.	desert
Said / Ar.	sweet
Saj / Alt.	stream, valley
Saki / Jap.	point
Sala / Latv.; Lith.	island
Saladillo / Sp.	salt desert
Salar / Sp.	salt lake
Sale / Ural.	village
Salina / It.; Sp.	salt flat, salt marsh
Saline / Dut.; Fr.; Germ.	salt flat, salt marsh
Salmi / Finn.	strait
Salseleh-ye Kūh / Pers.	mountain range
Salto / Port.; Sp.	waterfall, rapids
Salz / Germ.	salt
Samudera / Indon.	ocean
Samudra / Hin.	lake
Samut / Thai	sea
San / Jap.; Kor.	mountain
San / It.; Sp.	saint
Sanchi / Jap.	mountain range
Sand / Dan.; Eng.; Nor.; Swed.; Germ.	beach
Šand / Mong.	spring
Sandur / Icel.	sand
Sank / Pers.	rock
Sankt, St. / Germ.; Swed.	saint
Sanmaeg / Kor.	mountain range
Sanmyaku / Jap.	mountain range
Sansanné / Sud.	campsite
Santo / It.; Port.; Sp.	saint
Santuario / It.	sanctuary
São / Port.	saint
Sar / Pers.	cape; peak
Šar / Rus.; Tur.	strait
Saraf / Ar.	well
Sari / Finn.	island
Sari / Tur.	yellow
Sarīr / Ar.	rocky desert
Sary / Tur.	yellow
Sasso / It.	stone
Sat / Rom.	village
Sattel / Germ.	pass
Saurum / Latv.	strait
Schleuse / Germ.	lock
Schloß / Germ.	castle
Schlucht / Germ.	gorge
Schnee / Germ.	snow
Schwarz / Germ.	black
Scoglio / It.	cliff
Se / Jap.	bank, shoal
Sebkha / Ar.	salt flat
Sebkhet / Ar.	salt flat
Sed / Ar.	dam
Seda / Ural.	mountain
See, S. / Germ.	lake, sea
Sefra / Ar.	yellow
Segara / Indon.	lagoon
Şehir / Tur.	city, town
Seki / Jap.	dam
Selat / Mal.; Indon.	strait
Selatan / Indon.	southern
Selkä / Finn.	ridge, lake
Sella / It.	pass
Selo / Bulg.; Rus.; S.C.; Slvn.	village
Selsela Kohe / Pers.	mountain range
Selva / It.; Sp.	forest
Semenanjung / Mal.	peninsula
Sen / Jap.	mountain
Seong / Kor.	castle
Sep / Alt.	canal
Serīr / Ar.	rocky desert
Serra / Cat.; Port.	mountain range
Serra / It.	mountain
Serrania / Sp.	mountain range
Sertão / Port.	steppe
Seto / Jap.	strait
Sett., Settentrionale / It.	northern
Settentrionale, Sett. / It.	northern
Seuil / Fr.	sill
Sev / Arm.	black
Sever / Rus.	north
Severny / Rus.	northern
Sfint / Rom.	saint
Sfintu / Rom.	saint
Sgeir / Gae.	cliff
Sha'b / Ar.	cliff
Shahr / Pers.; Hin.	city, town
Sha'īb / Ar.	stream
Shallāl / Ar.	cataract
Shām / Ar.	north; northern
Shamo / Chin.	sand desert
Shan / Chin.	mountain, mountain range
Shan / Gae.	old
Shand / Mong.	spring
Shankou / Chin.	pass
Shaqq / Ar.	wadi
Sharm / Ar.	bay
Sharqī / Ar.	east, eastern
Sharqīyah / Ar.	eastern
Shatt / Ar.	river, salt lake
Shatt / Tur.	stream
Shēn / Alb.	saint
Sheng / Chin.	province
Shi / Chin.	city, town
Shibīn / Ar.	village
Shih / Chin.	rock
Shima / Jap.	island
Shimo / Jap.	lower
Shin / Jap.	new
Shō / Jap.	island
Shotō / Jap.	archipelago
Shū / Jap.	administrative division
Shui / Chin.	river
Shuiku / Chin.	reservoir
Shur / Pers.	salt
Sidhiros / Gr.	iron
Sidi / Ar.	master
Sieben / Germ.	seven
Sierra / Sp.	mountain range
Sikt / Ural.	village
Sillon / Fr.	furrow
Šine / Mong.	new
Sink / Eng.	depression
Sinn / Ar.	point
Sint / Dut.; Fle.	saint
Sirt / Tur.	mountain range
Sirtlar / Tur.	mountain range
Sistema / It.; Sp.	mountain system
Sīyāh / Pers.	black
Sjø / Nor.	lake
Sjö / Swed.	lake, sea
Skag / Icel.	peninsula
Skala / Bulg.; Rus.	rock
Skála / Slvk.	rock
Skar / Nor.	pass
Skär / Swed.	cliff
Skeir / Gae.	cliff
Skerry / Gae.	cliff
Skog / Nor.; Swed.	forest
Skóg / Icel.	forest
Skov / Dan.; Nor.	forest
Slatina / S.C.; Slvn.	mineral water
Slätt / Swed.	plain
Slieve / Gae.	mountain
Slot / Dut.; Fle.	castle
Slott / Nor.; Swed.	castle
Slough / Eng.	creek, pond, marsh
Sluis / Dut.; Fle.	sluice
Små / Swed.	little
Sne / Nor.	snow
Sneeuw / Afr.; Dut.	snow
Snežny / Rus.	snowy
Snø / Nor.	snow
So / Kor.	little
Sø / Dan.; Nor.	lake; sea
So / Ural.	passage
Söder / Swed.	south
Södra / Swed.	southern
Solončak / Rus.	salt flat
Sommet / Fr.	peak
Son / Viet.	mountain
Sønder / Dan.; Nor.	southern
Søndre / Dan.	southern
Sone / Jap.	bank
Song / Viet.	river
Sopka / Rus.	volcano
Sopočnik / Rus.	mountain system
Soprana / It.	upper
Šor, Sor / Alt.	salt marsh
Sos / Sp.	upon
Sotavento / Sp.	leeward
Sotoviento / Sp.	leeward
Sottana / It.	lower
Souk / Ar.	market
Souq / Ar.	market
Sour / Ar.	rampart
Source / Eng.; Fr.	spring
Souto / Port.	forest
Spitze / Germ.	peak
Spruit / Afr.	current
Sreden / Bulg.	central
Sredni / Rus.	central
Średni / Pol.	central
Srednji / S.C.; Slvn.	central
St., Saint, Sankt / Eng.; Fr.; Germ.; Swed.	saint
Stadhur / Icel.	city, town
Stadt, -stadt / Germ.	city, town
Stag / Eng.	city, town
Stagno / It.	pond
-stan / Hin.; Pers.; Urdu	land
Star / Bulg.	old
Stari / S.C.; Slvn.	old
Starý / Pol.; Rus.	old
Starý / Cz.; Slvk.	old
Stat / Afr.; Dan.; Fle.; Nor.; Dut.; Swed.	city, town
Stathmós / Gr.	railway station
Stausee / Germ.	reservoir
Stavrós / Gr.	cross
Sted / Dan.; Nor.	place
Stedt / Germ.	place
Stein, -stein / Nor.; Germ.	stone
Sten / Nor.; Swed.	stone
Stena / S.C.; Slvn.	rock
Stěna / Cz.	mountain range
Stenón / Gr.	strait, pass
Step / Rus.	steppe
-sthān / Hin.; Pers.; Urdu	land
Stift / Germ.	foundation
Štít / Cz.; Slvk.	peak
Stock / Germ.	massif
Stok / Pol.	slope
Stor / Dan.; Nor.; Swed.	great
Store / Dan.	great
Stræde / Dan.	strait
Strana / Rus.	land
Strand / Germ.; Nor.; Swed.; Afr.; Dan.	beach
Straße / Germ.	street, road
Strath / Gae.	valley
Straum / Nor.; Swed.	stream
Střední / Cz.	central
Středný / Slvk.	central
Strelka / Rus.	spit
Stret / Nor.	strait
Stretto / It.	strait
Strom / Germ.	stream
Strøm / Nor.	stream
Ström / Swed.	stream
Stroom / Dut.	stream
Su / Jap.	sandbank
Su / Tur.	river
Suando / Finn.	pond
Suid / Afr.	south
Suidō / Jap.	strait
Sul / Port.	south
Sund / Dan.; Nor.; Swed.; Germ.	strait
Sungai / Mal.	river
Sunn / Nor.	south
Sūq / Ar.	market
Sur / Fr.	on
Sur / Sp.	south
Surkh / Pers.	red
Suu / Finn.	mouth, river mouth
Suur / Cat.	great
Svart / Nor.; Swed.	black
Sveti / S.C.; Slvn.	saint
Swa / Ban.	great
Swart / Afr.	black
Świety / Pol.	saint
Syrt / Alt.	ridge
Szállás / Hung.	village
Szczyt / Pol.	peak
Szeg / Hung.	bend
Székes / Hung.	residence
Szent / Hung.	saint
Sziget / Hung.	river island

T

Local Form	English
Tadi / Ban.	rock, cliff
Tae / Kor.	great
Tafua / Poly.	mountain
Tag / Alt.; Tur.	mountain
Tahta / Ar.	lower
Tahti / Ar.	lower
Tai / Chin.; Jap.	great
Taipale / Finn.	isthmus
Tajga / Rus.	forest
Take / Jap.	mountain
Tal / Germ.	valley
Tala / Mong.	plain, steppe
Tala / Ber.	spring
Tall / Ar.	hill
Talsperre / Germ.	dam
Tam / Viet.	stream
Tamgout / Ber.	peak
Tan / Chin.; Kor.	sandbank
Tana / Malag.	city, town
Tanana / It.	city, town
Tandjung / Mal.	cape, point
Tanezrouft / Ber.	desert
Tang / It.	upland
Tangeh / Pers.	strait
Tanjong / Mal.	cape, point
Tanjung, Tg. / Indon.	cape, point
Tanout / Ber.	well
Tao / Chin.	island
Taourirt / Ber.	peak
Targ / Pol.	market
Tărg / Bulg.	market
Tarn / Eng.	glacial lake
Tarso / Sah.	crater
Taš / Alt.	stone

Geographical Glossary

Local Form	English
Tassili / *Ber.*	upland
Tau / *Tur.*	mountain
Taung / *Burm.*	mountain
Ṭawīl / *Ar.*	hill
Tégi / *Sah.*	hill
Teguidda / *Ber.*	well
Tehi / *Ber.*	pass, mountain
Teich / *Germ.*	pond
Tell / *Tur.*	hill
Telok / *Mal.*	bay, port
Teluk / *Mal.*	bay, port
Tempio / *It.*	temple
Ténéré / *Ber.*	rocky desert
Tengah / *Indon.; Mal.*	central
Tepe / *Tur.*	hill
Tepesi / *Tur.*	hill
Termas / *Sp.*	thermal springs
Terme / *It.*	thermal springs
Terra / *It.; Dut.*	land, earth
Terrazzo / *It.*	guyot, tablemount
Terre / *Fr.*	land, earth
Teso / *Cat.*	hill
Téssa / *Ber.*	wadi, depression
Testa / *It.*	point
Téte / *Fr.*	peak
Tetri / *Georg.*	white
Teu / *Poly.*	reef
Teze / *Alt.*	new
Tg., Tanjung / *Indon.*	cape, point
Thaba / *Ban.*	mountain
Thabana / *Ban.*	mountain
Thal / *Germ.*	valley
Thálassa / *Gr.*	sea
Thale / *Thai*	lagoon
Thamad / *Ar.*	well
Theós / *Gr.*	god
Thermes / *Fr.*	thermal springs
Thog / *Tib.*	high, upper
Tian / *Chin.*	field
Tiefe / *Germ.*	deep
Tierra / *Sp.*	land, earth
Timur / *Indon.; Mal.*	eastern
Tind / *Nor.*	mountain
Tinto / *Sp.*	black
Tirg / *Rom.*	market
Tis / *Amh.*	new
Tizgui / *Ber.*	forest
Tizi / *Ber.*	pass
Tjåkko / *Lapp.*	mountain
Tjärn / *Swed.*	tarn, glacial lake
Tji / *Mal.*	stream
To / *Kor.*	island
To / *Mel.*	stream
Tō / *Jap.*	island
Tó / *Hung.*	lake
To / *Ural.*	lake
Tobe / *Tur.*	hill
Tofua / *Poly.*	mountain
Tog / *Som.*	valley
Tōge / *Jap.*	pass
Tokoj / *Alt.*	forest
Tônle / *Khm.*	stream, lake
Tope / *Dut.*	peak
Toplice / *S.C.; Slvn.*	thermal springs
Topp / *Nor.*	peak
Tor / *Gae.*	rock
Tor / *Germ.*	gate
Torbat / *Pers.*	tomb
Törl / *Germ.*	pass
Torp / *Swed.*	hut
Torre / *Cat.; It.; Sp.; Port.*	tower
Torrente / *It.; Sp.*	torrent, stream
Tossa / *Cat.*	mountain, peak
Tota / *Sin.*	port
Tour / *Fr.*	tower
Traforo / *It.*	tunnel
Träsk / *Swed.*	lake
Trg / *S.C.*	market
Trog / *Germ.*	trough, trench
Trois / *Fr.*	three
Trung / *Viet.*	central
Tse / *Tib.*	peak, point
Tsi / *Chin.*	pond
Tskali / *Georg.*	river
Tsu / *Jap.*	bay
Tulül / *Ar.*	hills
Tünel / *Pers.*	tunnel
Tunturi / *Lapp.*	mountain, tundra
Tur'ah / *Ar.*	irrigation canal
Turm / *Germ.*	tower
Turn / *Rom.*	tower
Turó / *Cat.*	dome
Tuz / *Tur.*	salt
Týn / *Cz.*	fortress

U

Local Form	English
U., Unter-, Upon / *Eng.; Germ.*	under, lower
Uaimh / *Gae.*	cave
Uchi / *Jap.*	bay
Udde / *Swed.*	cape
Údolní nádrž / *Cz.*	reservoir
Uebi / *Som.*	river
Új- / *Hung.*	new
Ujście / *Pol.*	mouth
Ujung / *Indon.*	point, cape
Ul / *Chin.; Mong.*	mountain, mountain range
Ula / *Mong.*	mountain range
Ulan / *Mong.*	red
Uls / *Mong.*	state
Umi / *Jap.*	bay
Umm / *Ar.*	mother, spring
Umne / *Mong.*	south
Under / *Mong.*	mountain, peak
Ungur / *Alt.*	cave
Unter-, U. / *Germ.*	under, lower
Upar / *Hin.*	river
'Uqlat / *Ar.*	well
Ür / *Tam.*	city, town
Ura / *Jap.*	bay, coast
Ura / *Alt.*	depression
Urd / *Mong.*	south
Uru / *Tam.*	city, town
Ušće / *S.C.*	mouth
Uske / *Alt.*	upper
Ust / *Rus.*	mouth
Ústí / *Cz.*	mouth
Ustup / *Rus.*	terrace
Utan / *Indon.; Mal.*	forest
Utara / *Indon.*	north, northern
Uusi / *Finn.*	new
Uval / *Rus.*	height
Úval / *Cz.*	mountain
'Uwaynāt / *Ar.*	well
Uzboj / *Alt.*	river bed
Uzun / *Tur.*	long
Užurekis / *Lith.*	gulf

V

Local Form	English
Va / *Alb.*	ford
Va / *Ural.*	water, river
Vaara / *Finn.*	mountain
Väärti / *Finn.*	bay
Vad / *Rom.*	ford
Vær / *Nor.*	port
Våg / *Nor.*	bay
Vähä / *Finn.*	little
Väike / *Est.*	little
Väin / *Est.*	strait
Val / *Fr.; It.*	valley
Val / *Rom.; Rus.*	wall
Valico / *It.*	pass
Vall / *Cat.*	valley
Vall / *Swed.*	pasture
Valle / *It.; Sp.*	valley
Vallée / *Fr.*	valley
Vallei / *Afr.*	valley
Vallo / *It.*	wall
Valta / *Finn.*	cape
Váltos / *Gr.*	marsh
Valul / *Rom.*	wall
Vann / *Dan.; Nor.*	water, lake
Vanua / *Mel.*	land
Vár / *Hung.*	fort
Vara / *Finn.*	mountain
Varoš / *S.C.*	city, town
Város / *Hung.*	city, town
Varre / *Lapp.*	mountain
Vary / *Fr.*	spring
Vas / *S.C.; Slvn.*	village
Vásár / *Hung.*	market
Väst / *Swed.*	west
Väster / *Swed.*	western
Vatn / *Icel.; Nor.*	lake
Vatten / *Swed.*	water, lake
Vatu / *Mel.; Poly.*	island, reef
Vdhr., Vodohranilišče / *Rus.*	reservoir
Vechiu / *Rom.*	old
Vecs / *Latv.*	old
Veen / *Dut.; Fle.*	moor
Vega / *Sp.*	irrigated crops
Veld / *Afr.; Dut.; Fle.*	field
Veli / *S.C.; Slvn.*	great
Velik / *Bulg.*	great
Veliki / *Rus.; S.C.; Slvn.*	great
Veliký / *Cz.*	great
Velký / *Cz.*	great
Vel'ky / *Slvk.*	great
Vella / *Cat.*	old
Ver / *Ural.*	forest
Verde / *It.; Sp.*	green
Verh / *Rus.*	peak
Verhni / *Rus.*	upper
Verk / *Swed.*	factory
Vermelho / *Port.*	red
Vert / *Fr.*	green
Ves / *Cz.*	village
Vesi / *Finn.*	water, lake
Vest / *Dan.; Nor.*	west
Vester / *Dan.; Nor.*	western
Vestur / *Icel.*	west
Vetta / *It.*	summit
Viaduc / *Fr.*	viaduct
Vidda / *Nor.*	upland
Vidde / *Nor.*	upland
Viejo / *Sp.*	old
Vier / *Germ.*	four
Viertel / *Germ.*	quarter
Vieux / *Fr.*	old
Vig / *Dan.*	bay
Vík / *Icel.; Nor.; Swed.*	gulf, bay
Vila / *Port.*	city, town
Villa / *Sp.*	city, town
Ville, -ville / *Eng.; Fr.*	city, town
Vinh / *Viet.*	bay
Virful / *Rom.*	peak, mountain
Virta / *Finn.*	river
Višni / *Rus.*	high
Visok / *S.C.*	high
Viz / *Hung.*	water
Víztároló / *Hung.*	reservoir
Vlakte / *Dut.; Fle.*	plain
Vlei / *Afr.*	pond
Vliet / *Dut.; Fle.*	river
Vloer / *Afr.*	depression
Voda / *Bulg.; Cz.; Rus.; S.C.; Slvn.*	water
Vodny put / *Rus.*	stream, canal
Vodohranilišče, vdhr. / *Rus.*	reservoir
Vodopad / *Rus.*	waterfall
Volcan / *Fr.*	volcano
Volcán / *Sp.*	volcano
Voll / *Nor.*	meadow
Vórios / *Gr.*	northern
Vorota / *Rus.*	gate
Vorrás / *Hung.*	north
Vostočny / *Rus.*	eastern
Vostok / *Rus.*	east
Võtn / *Icel.*	lake, water
Vož / *Ural.*	mouth
Vozvyšennost / *Rus.*	upland
Vpadina / *Rus.*	depression
Vrah / *Bulg.*	peak
Vrata / *Bulg.; S.C.; Slvn.*	pass
Vrch / *Cz.; Slvk.*	mountain
Vrch / *S.C.; Slvn.*	peak
Vrchni / *Cz.*	upper
Vrchovina / *Cz.*	upland
Vulcan / *Rom.; Rus.*	volcano
Vulcano / *It.*	volcano
Vulkan / *Germ.; Rus.*	volcano
Vuopio / *Lapp.*	bend
Vuori / *Finn.*	rock
Východný / *Cz.*	eastern
Vyšný / *Slvk.*	upper
Vysoki / *Rus.*	high
Vysoky / *Cz.; Slvk.*	high
Vyšši / *Cz.*	high

W

Local Form	English
W., Wādī / *Ar.*	wadi
Wa / *Ban.*	people
Wabe / *Amh.*	stream
Wad / *Ar.*	wadi
Wad / *Dut.*	tidal flat
Wādī, W. / *Ar.*	wadi
Wāḥāt / *Ar.*	oasis
Wai / *Mel.; Poly.*	stream
Wal / *Afr.*	wall
Wala / *Hin.*	mountain range
Wald / *Germ.*	forest
Wan / *Burm.*	village
Wan / *Chin.; Jap.*	bay
Wand / *Germ.*	bluff
War / *Som.*	pond
Wār / *Ar.*	desert
-waram / *Hin.; Tam.*	village
Wasser / *Germ.*	water
Wat / *Pol.*	wall
Wat / *Thai*	church
Waterval / *Afr.; Dut.*	waterfall
Watt / *Germ.*	tidal flat
Wāw / *Ar.*	oasis
Weald / *Eng.*	wooded country
Webi / *Som.*	stream
Weg / *Germ.*	way, road
Wei / *Chin.*	cape, point
Weide / *Germ.*	pasture
Weiler / *Germ.*	village
Weiß / *Germ.*	white
Weon / *Kor.*	field
Wer / *Som.*	pond
Werder / *Germ.*	river island
Werk / *Germ.*	factory
Wes / *Afr.*	west
Westlich / *Germ.*	western
Westr- / *Sca.*	western
Wēyn / *Som.*	great
Wēyne / *Som.*	great
Wick / *Eng.*	village
Wiek / *Germ.*	bay
Wielki / *Pol.*	great
Wieś / *Pol.*	village
Wijk / *Dut.; Fle.*	quarter, district
-willer / *Germ.*	village
Woda / *Pol.*	water
Woestyn / *Afr.*	desert
Wold / *Dut.; Fle.; Eng.*	forest
Wörth / *Germ.*	river island
Woud / *Dut.; Fle.*	forest
Wschodni / *Pol.*	eastern
Wysoczyzna / *Pol.*	upland
Wysoki / *Pol.*	upper
Wyspa / *Pol.*	island
Wyżyna / *Pol.*	highland
Wzgórze / *Pol.*	hill

X

Local Form	English
Xi / *Chin.*	west
Xia / *Chin.*	gorge, strait
Xian / *Chin.*	county, shire
Xiang / *Chin.*	village
Xiao / *Chin.*	little
Xin / *Chin.*	new
Xu / *Chin.*	island

Y

Local Form	English
Yam / *Hebr.*	lake, sea
Yama / *Jap.*	mountain
Yan / *Chin.*	mountain
Yang / *Chin.*	strait, ocean
Yani / *Tur.*	new
Yar / *Tur.*	gorge
Yarimada / *Tur.*	peninsula
Yazı / *Tur.*	plain
Yegge / *Sah.*	well
Yeni / *Tur.*	new
Yeon / *Kor.*	sea
Yeong / *Kor.*	mountain
Yeşil / *Tur.*	green
Ylä / *Finn.*	upper
Yli- / *Finn.*	upper
Yō / *Jap.*	ocean
Yobe / *Sud.*	great
Yōm / *Kor.*	island
Yoma / *Burm.*	mountain range
Yŏn / *Kor.*	lake, pond
Yŏng / *Kor.*	mountain, peak
Ytter / *Nor.; Swed.*	outer
Yttre / *Swed.*	outer
Yu / *Chin.*	old
Yu / *Chin.*	island
Yu / *Jap.*	thermal spring
Yüan / *Chin.*	spring, river
Yunhe / *Chin.*	canal

Z

Local Form	English
Zāb / *Ar.*	river
Zachodni / *Pol.*	western
Zaki / *Jap.*	cape
Zalew / *Pol.*	gulf
Zaliv / *Bulg.; Rus.; S.C.; Slvn.*	gulf
Zaljev / *Slvn.*	bay
Zámek / *Cz.*	castle
Zan / *Jap.*	mountain
Zand / *Dut.; Fle.*	sand
Zandt / *Dut.; Fle.*	sand
Zangbo / *Chin.*	river
Zapad / *Rus.*	west
Zapaden / *Bulg.*	western
Zapadni / *S.C.; Slvn.*	western
Západní / *Cz.*	western
Zapadny / *Rus.*	western
Zapovednik / *Rus.*	reserve
Zatoka / *Pol.*	gulf
Zavod / *Rus.*	roadstead
Zāwiyat / *Ar.*	monastery
Zdrój / *Pol.*	thermal springs
Ze / *Jap.*	islet
Zee / *Dut.; Fle.*	sea
Zelëny / *Rus.*	green
Žem / *Lith.*	land, country
Zemé / *Cz.; Slvk.*	land, country
Zemlja / *Rus.*	land
Zen / *Jap.*	mountain
Zhan / *Chin.*	mountain
Zhen / *Chin.*	market
Zhong / *Chin.*	central
Zhou / *Chin.*	quarter, district
Zhuang / *Chin.*	village
Ziemia / *Pol.*	land
Zigos / *Gr.*	pass
Zipfel / *Germ.*	tip, point
Ziwa / *Swa.*	marsh
Zizhiqu / *Chin.*	autonomous region
Zlato / *Bulg.*	gold
Zuid / *Dut.; Fle.*	south
Zuidelijk / *Dut.*	southern
Żuława / *Pol.*	marsh
Zun / *Mong.*	east
Zwart / *Dut.*	black
Zwei / *Germ.*	two

International Map Index

All of the toponyms (place-names) which appear on the maps are listed in the International Map Index. Each entry includes the following: Place-name and, where applicable, other forms by which it is written or known; a symbol, where applicable, indicating what kind of feature it is; the number of the map on which it appears; and the map-reference letters and geographical coordinates indicating its location on the map.

Toponyms

Each toponym, or place-name, is written in full, with accents and diacritical marks. Since many countries have more than one official language, many of these forms are included on the maps. For example, many Belgian place-names are listed as follows: Bruxelles/Brussel; Antwerpen/Anvers, and vice versa, Brussel/Bruxelles; Anvers/Antwerpen. In Italy, certain regions have a special status—they are largely autonomous and officially bilingual. As a result, Index listings appear as follows: Aosta/Aoste; Alto Adige/Sud Tirol, and vice versa. One name, however, may be the only name on the map.

In China, the written forms of commonly used regional languages have been taken into account. These forms are enclosed in parenthesis following the official name: e.g. Xiangshan (Dancheng). However, when the regional is listed first, it is linked to the official name with an→: e.g. Dancheng→Xiangshan. The same style is used for former or historical name forms: e.g. Rhodesia→Zimbabwe and Zimbabwe (Rhodesia).

Place-names for major features (countries, major cities, and large physical features), where applicable, include the English conventional form identified by (EN) and linked in the local name or names with an = sign: e.g. Italia=Italy (EN), and vice versa, Italy (EN)=Italia. Former English names are linked in the Index to the conventional form by an→.

Symbols

The last component with the place-name is a symbol, where applicable, specifying the broad category of the feature named. A table preceding the Index lists all of the symbols used and their meanings; this information also appears as a footnote on each page of the Index. Place-names without symbols are cities and towns.

Alphabetization

Place-names are listed in English alphabetical order—26 letters, from A to Z—because of its international usage. Names including two or more words are listed alphabetically according to the first letter of the word: e.g. De Ruyter is listed under D; Le Havre is listed under L. Names with the prefix Mc are listed as if spelled Mac. The generic portion of a name (lake, sierra, mountain, etc.) is placed after the name: e.g. Lake Erie is listed as Erie, Lake; Sierra Morena is listed as Morena, Sierra. In Spanish, "ch" and "ll" groups and the letter "ñ" are included respectively under C, L, and N, without any distinction.

The same place-name sometimes is listed in the Index several times. It may because of the various translations of a name, or it may be that several places have the same name.

Various translations of a name appear as follows:

Danube (EN)=Dunav	Danube (EN)=Donau
Danube (EN)=Dunărea	Danube (EN)=Dunaj

Several places with the same name appear as follows; however, only in these cases is the location—abbreviated and enclosed in brackets—included. A table of these abbreviations precedes the Index.

Abbeville [U.S.]	Aberdeen [Scot.-U.K.]
Abbeville [Fr.]	Aberdeen [N.C.-U.S.]
Aberdeen [S. Afr.]	

Map Number

Each map in the atlas is identified by a number. Where multiple maps are on one page, each map is additionally identified by a boxed letter in the upper-right-hand corner of the map. In the Index listing following the place-name and its variations in language and spelling, where applicable, is the number of the map on which it appears. If the map is one of several on a page, the Index listing includes the map number and letter.

Although a place-name may appear on one or more maps, it is indexed to only one map. Most places are indexed to the regional maps. However, if a place-name appears on either the physical or political continental maps, it is indexed to one of the two types of map. For example, a river or mountain would be indexed to a physical continental map; a city or state would be indexed to a political continental map.

Map-Reference Letters and Geographical Coordinates

The next elements in the Index listing are the map-reference letters and the geographical coordinates, respectively, locating the place on the map.

Map-reference letters consist of a capital and a lowercase letter. Capital letters are across the top and bottom of the maps; lowercase letters are down the sides. The map-reference letters assigned to each place-name refer to the location of the name within the area formed by grid lines connecting the geographical coordinates on either sides of the letters.

Geographical coordinates are the latitude (N for North, S for South) and longitude (E for East, W for West) expressed in degrees and minutes and based on the prime meridian, Greenwich.

Map-reference letters and coordinates for extensive geographical features, such as mountain ranges and countries, are given for the approximate central point of the area. Those for waterways, such as canals and rivers, are given for the mouth of the river, the point where it enters another river or where the feature reaches the map margin. On this page are sample maps showing points to which features are indexed according to map-reference letters and coordinates.

On most maps there is not enough space to place all of the names of administrative subdivisions. In these cases the location of the place is shown on the map by a circled letter or number and the place-name and circled letter or number are listed in the map margin. The map-reference numbers and coordinates for these places refer to the location of the circled letter or number on the map.

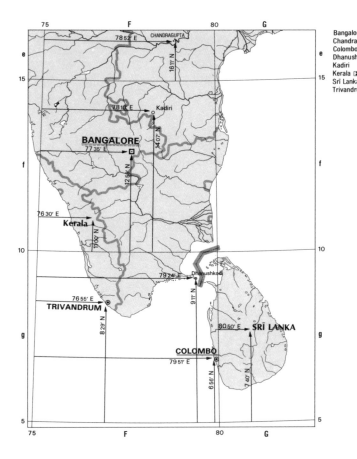

Bangalore	25	Ff	12°59'N 77°35'E
Chandragupta ⊡	35	Fe	16°11'N 78°52'E
Colombo	25	Fg	6°56'N 79°51'E
Dhanushkodi	25	Fg	9°11'N 79°24'E
Kadiri	25	Ff	14°07'N 78°10'E
Kerala ⊡	25	Ff	11°00'N 76°30'E
Sri Lanka ⊡	25	Gg	7°40'N 80°50'E
Trivandrum	25	Fg	8°29'N 76°55'E

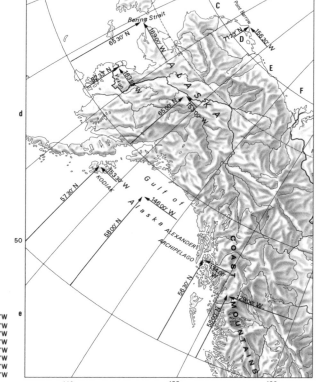

Alaska ⊡	38	Dc	65°00'N 153°00'W
Alaska, Gulf of- ⊡	38	Ed	58°00'N 146°00'W
Alexander Archipelago ⊡	38	Fd	56°30'N 134°00'W
Barrow, Point- ⊡	38	Db	71°23'N 156°30'W
Bering Strait ⊡	38	Cc	65°30'N 169°00'W
Coast Mountains ⊡	38	Gd	55°00'N 129°00'W
Kodiak ⊡	38	Dd	57°30'N 153°30'W
Yukon ⊡	38	Cc	62°33'N 163°59'W

List of Abbreviations

Abz.-U.S.S.R. Azerbaidzhan S.S.R., U.S.S.R.
Afg. Afghanistan
Afr. Africa
Agl. Anguilla
Ak.-U.S. Alaska, U.S.
Al.-U.S. Alabama, U.S.
Alb. Albania
Alg. Algeria
Alta.-Can. Alberta, Canada
Am. Sam. American Samoa
And. Andorra
Ang. Angola
Ant. Antarctica
Ar.-U.S. Arkansas, U.S.
Arg. Argentina
Arm.-U.S.S.R. Armenian S.S.R., U.S.S.R.
Asia Asia
Atg. Antigua
Aus. Austria
Austl. Australia
Az.-U.S. Arizona, U.S.
Azr. Azores
Bah. Bahamas
Bar. Barbados
B.A.T. British Antarctic Territory
B.C.-Can. British Columbia, Canada
Bel. Belgium
Ben. Benin
Ber. Bermuda
Bhr. Bahrain
Bhu. Bhutan
Blz. Belize
Bnd. Burundi
Bngl. Bangladesh
Bol. Bolivia
Bots. Botswana
Braz. Brazil
Bru. Brunei
Bul. Bulgaria
Bur. Burma
B.V.I. British Virgin Islands
Bye.-U.S.S.R. Byelorussian S.S.R., U.S.S.R.
Ca.-U.S. California, U.S.
Cam. Cameroon
C. Amer. Central America
Can. Canada
Can. Is. Canary Islands
C.A.R. Central African Republic
Cay. Is. Cayman Islands
Chad Chad
Chan. Is. Channel Islands
Chile Chile
China China
Co.-U.S. Colorado, U.S.
Cocos Is. Cocos Islands
Col. Colombia
Con. Congo
Cook Cook Islands
Cor. Sea Is. Coral Sea Islands
C.R. Costa Rica
Ct.-U.S. Connecticut, U.S.
Cuba Cuba
C.V. Cape Verde
Cyp. Cyprus

Czech. Czechoslovakia
D.C.-U.S. District of Columbia, U.S.
De.-U.S. Delaware, U.S.
Den. Denmark
Dji. Djibouti
Dom. Dominica
Dom. Rep. Dominican Republic
Ec. Ecuador
Eg. Egypt
El Sal. El Salvador
Eng.-U.K. England, U.K.
Eq. Gui. Equatorial Guinea
Est.-U.S.S.R. Estonian S.S.R., U.S.S.R.
Eth. Ethiopia
Eur. Europe
Falk. Is. Falkland Islands
Far. Is. Faeroe Islands
Fiji Fiji
Fin. Finland
Fl.-U.S. Florida, U.S.
Fr. France
F.R.G. Federal Republic of Germany
Fr. Gui. French Guiana
Fr. Poly. French Polynesia
F.S.M. Federated States of Micronesia
Ga.-U.S. Georgia, U.S.
Gabon Gabon
Gam. Gambia
G.D.R. German Democratic Republic
Geo.-U.S.S.R. Georgian S.S.R., U.S.S.R.
Ghana Ghana
Gib. Gibraltar
Grc. Greece
Gren. Grenada
Grld. Greenland
Guad. Guadeloupe
Guam Guam
Guat. Guatemala
Gui. Guinea
Gui. Bis. Guinea Bissau
Guy. Guyana
Haiti Haiti
Hi.-U.S. Hawaii, U.S.
H.K. Hong Kong
Hond. Honduras
Hun. Hungary
Ia.-U.S. Iowa, U.S.
I.C. Ivory Coast
Ice. Iceland
Id.-U.S. Idaho, U.S.
Il.-U.S. Illinois, U.S.
In.-U.S. Indiana, U.S.
India India
Indon. Indonesia
I. of M. Isle of Man
Iran Iran
Iraq Iraq
Ire. Ireland
Isr. Israel
It. Italy
Jam. Jamaica
Jap. Japan
Jor. Jordan
Kam. Kampuchea

Kaz.-U.S.S.R. Kazakh S.S.R., U.S.S.R.
Kenya Kenya
Ker. Is. Kermadec Islands
Kir. Kiribati
Kirg.-U.S.S.R. Kirghiz S.S.R., U.S.S.R.
Ks.-U.S. Kansas, U.S.
Kuw. Kuwait
Ky.-U.S. Kentucky, U.S.
La.-U.S. Louisiana, U.S.
Laos Laos
Lat.-U.S.S.R. Latvian S.S.R., U.S.S.R.
Lbr. Liberia
Leb. Lebanon
Les. Lesotho
Lib. Libya
Liech. Liechtenstein
Lith.-U.S.S.R. Lithuanian S.S.R., U.S.S.R.
Lux. Luxembourg
Ma.-U.S. Massachusetts, U.S.
Mac. Macao
Mad. Madagascar
Mala. Malaysia
Mald. Maldives
Mali Mali
Malta Malta
Man.-Can. Manitoba, Canada
Mar. Is. Marshall Islands
Mart. Martinique
Maur. Mauritius
May. Mayotte
Mco. Monaco
Md.-U.S. Maryland, U.S.
Me.-U.S. Maine, U.S.
Mex. Mexico
Mi.-U.S. Michigan, U.S.
Mid. Is. Midway Islands
Mn.-U.S. Minnesota, U.S.
Mo.-U.S. Missouri, U.S.
Mold.-U.S.S.R. Moldavian S.S.R., U.S.S.R.
Mong. Mongolia
Mont. Montserrat
Mor. Morocco
Moz. Mozambique
Ms.-U.S. Mississippi, U.S.
Mt.-U.S. Montana, U.S.
Mtna. Mauritania
Mwi. Malawi
Nam. Namibia
N. Amer. North America
Nauru Nauru
N.B.-Can. New Brunswick, Canada
Nb.-U.S. Nebraska, U.S.
N.C.-U.S. North Carolina, U.S.
N. Cal. New Caledonia
N.D.-U.S. North Dakota, U.S.
Nep. Nepal
Neth. Netherlands
Neth. Ant. Netherlands Antilles
Newf.-Can. Newfoundland, Canada
N.H.-U.S. New Hampshire, U.S.

Nic. Nicaragua
Nig. Nigeria
Niger Niger
N. Ire.-U.K. Northern Ireland, U.K.
N.J.-U.S. New Jersey, U.S.
N. Kor. North Korea
N.M.-U.S. New Mexico, U.S.
N.M. Is. Northern Mariana Islands
Nor. Norway
Nor. I. Norfolk Island
N.S.-Can. Nova Scotia, Canada
Nv.-U.S. Nevada, U.S.
N.W.T.-Can. Northwest Territories, Canada
N.Y.-U.S. New York, U.S.
N.Z. New Zealand
Ocn. Oceania
Oh.-U.S. Ohio, U.S.
Ok.-U.S. Oklahoma, U.S.
Oman Oman
Ont.-Can. Ontario, Canada
Or.-U.S. Oregon, U.S.
Pa.-U.S. Pennsylvania, U.S.
Pak. Pakistan
Pal. Palau
Pan. Panama
Pap. N. Gui. Papua New Guinea
Par. Paraguay
Pas. Pascua
P.D.R.Y. People's Democratic Republic of Yemen
P.E.I.-Can. Prince Edward Island, Canada
Peru Peru
Phil. Philippines
Pit. Pitcairn
Pol. Poland
Port. Portugal
P.R. Puerto Rico
Qatar Qatar
Que.-Can. Quebec, Canada
Reu. Reunion
R.I.-U.S. Rhode Island, U.S.
Rom. Romania
R.S.F.S.R.-U.S.S.R. Russian Soviet Federated Socialist Republic, U.S.S.R.
Rwn. Rwanda
S. Afr. South Africa
S. Amer. South America
Sao T.P. Sao Tome and Principe
Sask.-Can. Saskatchewan, Canada
Sau. Ar. Saudi Arabia
S.C.-U.S. South Carolina, U.S.
Scot.-U.K. Scotland, U.K.
S.D.-U.S. South Dakota, U.S.
Sen. Senegal
Sey. Seychelles
Sing. Singapore
S. Kor. South Korea
S.L. Sierra Leone
S. Lan. Sri Lanka
S.M. San Marino
S.N.A. Spanish North Africa

Sol. Is. Solomon Islands
Som. Somalia
Sp. Spain
St. C.N. Saint Christopher-Nevis
St. Hel. Saint Helena
St. Luc. Saint Lucia
St. P.M. Saint Pierre and Miquelon
St. Vin. Saint Vincent
Sud. Sudan
Sur. Suriname
Sval. Svalbard
Swe. Sweden
Switz. Switzerland
Syr. Syria
Tad.-U.S.S.R. Tadzhik S.S.R., U.S.S.R.
Tai. Taiwan
Tan. Tanzania
T.C. Is. Turks and Caicos Islands
Thai. Thailand
Tn.-U.S. Tennessee, U.S.
Togo Togo
Ton. Tonga
Trin. Trinidad and Tobago
T.T.P.I. Trust Territory of the Pacific Islands
Tun. Tunisia
Tur. Turkey
Tur.-U.S.S.R. Turkman S.S.R., U.S.S.R.
Tuv. Tuvalu
Tx.-U.S. Texas, U.S.
U.A.E. United Arab Emirates
Ug. Uganda
U.K. United Kingdom
Ukr.-U.S.S.R. Ukrainian S.S.R., U.S.S.R.
Ur. Uruguay
U.S. United States
U.S.S.R. Union of Soviet Socialist Republics
Ut.-U.S. Utah, U.S.
U.V. Upper Volta
Uzb.-U.S.S.R. Uzbek S.S.R., U.S.S.R.
Va.-U.S. Virginia, U.S.
Van. Vanuatu
V.C. Vatican City
Ven. Venezuela
Viet. Vietnam
V.I.U.S. Virgin Islands of the U.S.
Vt.-U.S. Vermont, U.S.
Wa.-U.S. Washington, U.S.
Wake Wake Island
Wales-U.K. Wales, U.K.
W.F. Wallis and Futuna
Wi.-U.S. Wisconsin, U.S.
W. Sah. Western Sahara
W. Sam. Western Samoa
W.V.-U.S. West Virginia, U.S.
Wy.-U.S. Wyoming, U.S.
Yem. Yemen
Yugo. Yugoslavia
Yuk.-Can. Yukon, Canada
Zaire Zaire
Zam. Zambia
Zimb. Zimbabwe

List of Symbols

Plains and Associated Features
- Plain, Basin, Lowland
- Delta
- Salt Flat

Valleys and Depressions
- Valley, Gorge, Ravine, Canyon
- Cave, Crater, Quarry
- Karst Features
- Depression
- Polder, Reclaimed Marsh

Vegetational Features
- Desert, Dunes
- Forest, Woods
- Heath, Steppe, Tundra, Moor
- Oasis

Political/Administrative Units
1. Independent Nation
2. State, Canton, Region
3. Province, Department, County, Territory, District
4. Municipality
5. Colony, Dependency, Administered Territory

Geographical Regions
- Continent
- Physical Region
- Historical or Cultural Region

Mountain Features
- Mount, Mountain, Peak
- Volcano
- Hill
- Mountains, Mountain Range
- Hills, Escarpment
- Plateau, Highland, Upland
- Pass, Gap

Coastal Features
- Cape, Point
- Coast, Beach
- Cliff
- Peninsula, Promontory
- Isthmus
- Sandbank, Tombolo, Sandbar

Islands Rocks, Reefs
- Island
- Atoll
- Rock, Reef
- Islands, Archipelago
- Rocks, Reefs
- Coral Reef

Hydrographic Features
- Well, Spring
- Geyser, Fumarole
- River, Stream, Brook
- Waterfall, Rapids, Cataract
- River Mouth, Estuary
- Lake
- Salt Lake
- Intermittent Lake, Dry Lake Bed
- Reservoir, Artificial Lake
- Swamp, Marsh, Pond
- Irrigation Canal, Navigable Canal, Ditch, Aqueduct

Ice Features
- Glacier, Snowfield
- Ice Shelf, Pack Ice

Marine Features
- Ocean
- Sea
- Gulf, Bay
- Strait, Fjord, Sea Channel
- Lagoon, Anchorage

Submarine Features
- Bank, Shoal
- Seamount
- Rise, Plateau, Tablemount
- Seamount Chain, Ridge
- Platform, Shelf
- Basin, Depression
- Escarpment, Slope, Sea Scarp
- Fracture
- Trench, Abyss, Valley, Canyon

Other Features
- National Park, Nature Reserve
- Scenic Area, Point of Interest
- Recreation Site, Sports Arena
- Cave, Cavern
- Historic Site, Memorial, Mausoleum, Museum
- Ruins
- Wall, Walls, Tower, Castle, Fortress
- Church, Abbey, Cathedral, Sanctuary
- Temple, Synagogue, Mosque
- Research or Scientific Station
- Airport, Heliport
- Port, Dock
- Lighthouse
- Mine
- Tunnel
- Dam, Bridge

A

Å 7 Cc 67.53N 12.59 E
Aa [Eur.] 12 Ic 51.50N 6.25 E
Aa [Fr.] 11 Ic 51.01N 2.06 E
Aa [Fr.] 12 Dd 50.44N 2.18 E
Aa [F.R.G.] 12 Kb 52.07N 8.41 E
Aa [F.R.G.] 12 Jb 52.15N 7.18 E
Aachen 10 Cf 50.46N 6.06 E
Aalen 10 Gh 48.50N 10.06 E
A'ālī an Nīl [3] 35 Ed 9.15N 33.00 E
Aalsmeer 12 Gb 52.15N 4.45 E
Aalst/Alost 11 Kd 50.56N 4.02 E
Aalten 12 Ic 51.55N 6.35 E
Aalter 12 Fc 51.05N 3.27 E
Äänekoski 7 Fe 62.36N 25.44 E
Aa of Weerijs 12 Gc 51.35N 4.46 E
Aar 12 Kd 50.23N 8.00 E
Aarau 14 Cc 47.25N 8.02 E
Aarbergen 12 Kd 50.13N 8.03 E
Aare 14 Cc 47.37N 8.13 E
Aargau [2] 14 Cc 47.30N 8.10 E
Aarlen/Arlon 11 Le 49.41N 5.49 E
Aarschot 11 Kd 50.59N 4.50 E
Aat/Ath 11 Jd 50.38N 3.47 E
Aazanèn 13 Ii 35.06N 3.02W
Āb 24 Md 36.00N 48.05 E
Aba [Nig.] 31 Hh 5.07N 7.22 E
Aba [Zaire] 31 Hk 3.52N 30.14 E
Aba/Ngawa 27 He 32.55N 101.45 E
Abā ad Dūd 24 Ki 27.02N 44.04 E
Abā as Su'ūd 23 Ff 17.28N 44.06 E
Abacaxis, Rio- 54 Gd 3.54 S 58.50W
Abaco Island 38 Lg 26.25N 77.10W
Abacou, Pointe l'- 49 Kd 18.03N 73.47W
Abadab. Jabal- 35 Fb 18.53N 35.59 E
Ābādān 22 Gf 30.10N 48.50 E
Ābādeh [Iran] 23 Hc 31.10N 52.37 E
Ābādeh [Iran] 24 Oh 29.08N 52.52 E
Abadiânia 55 Hc 16.06 S 48.48W
Abadla 31 Ge 31.01N 2.43W
Abaeté 55 Jd 19.09 S 45.27W
Abaeté, Rio- 55 Jd 18.02 S 45.12W
Abaetetuba 54 Id 1.42 S 48.54W
Abagnar Qi (Xilin Hot) 22 Ne 43.58N 116.08 E
Abag Qi (Xin Hot) 27 Jc 44.01N 114.59 E
Abai 55 Eh 26.01 S 55.57W
Abaiang Atoll 57 Id 1.51N 172.58 E
Abaj 19 Hf 49.38N 72.50 E
Abaji 34 Gd 8.28N 6.57 E
Abajo Mountains 46 Kh 37.50N 109.25W
Abakaliki 34 Gd 6.20N 8.03 E
Abakan 20 Ef 53.43N 91.30 E
Abakan 22 Ld 53.43N 91.26 E
Abakwasimbo 36 Eb 0.36N 28.43 E
Abala [Con.] 36 Cc 1.21 S 15.30 E
Abala [Niger] 34 Fc 14.56N 3.26 E
Abalak 34 Gb 15.27N 6.17 E
Aban 20 Ee 56.40N 96.10 E
Abancay 54 Df 13.35 S 72.55W
Abancourt 12 De 49.42N 1.46 E
Abanga 36 Bb 0.13N 10.28 E
Abano Terme 14 Fe 45.21N 11.47 E
Ābār al Jidd 24 Hf 32.50N 39.50 E
Abarqū 23 Hc 31.08N 53.17 E
Abarqu, Kavīr-e- 24 Og 31.00N 53.50 E
Abashiri 27 Pc 44.01N 144.17 E
Abashiri-Gawa 29a Db 43.56N 144.09 E
Abashiri-Ko 29a Da 44.00N 144.10 E
Abashiri-Wan 29a Da 44.00N 144.35 E
Abasolo 48 Je 24.04N 98.22W
Abatski 19 Hd 56.18N 70.28 E
Abau 60 Dj 10.11 S 148.42 E
Abava 7 Eh 57.06N 21.54 E
Abay=Blue Nile (EN) 30 Kg 15.38N 32.31 E
Abaya, Lake- 30 Kh 6.20N 37.55 E
Abaza 20 Ef 52.39N 90.06 E
Abbadia San Salvatore 14 Fh 42.53N 11.41 E
Abbah Quşūr 14 Co 35.57N 8.50 E
Āb Bārīk 24 Oh 29.45N 52.37 E
'Abbāsābād 24 Qd 36.20N 56.25 E
Abbekås 8 Ei 55.24N 13.36 E
Abberton Reservoir 12 Cc 51.50N 0.55 E
Abbeville [Fr.] 11 Hd 50.06N 1.50 E
Abbeville [La.-U.S.] 45 Jl 29.58N 92.08W
Abbeville [S.C.-U.S.] 44 Fh 34.10N 82.23W
Abbey 46 Ka 50.43N 108.45W
Abbeyfeale/Mainistir na Féile 9 Di 52.24N 9.18W
Abbiategrasso 14 Ce 45.24N 8.54 E
Abbot, Mount- 59 Jd 20.03 S 147.45 E
Abbot Ice Shelf 66 Pf 72.45 S 96.00W
'Abd Al 'Azīz, Jabal- 24 Id 36.25N 40.20 E
'Abd al Kurī 21 Hh 12.12N 52.13 E
Ābdānān 24 Lf 32.57N 47.26 E
Abdul Ghadir 35 Gc 10.42N 42.59 E
Abdulino 19 Fe 53.42N 53.38 E
Abe, Lake- 35 Gc 11.10N 41.45 E
Abéché 31 Jg 13.49N 20.49 E
Abeek 12 Hc 51.15N 6.00 E
Abe-Gawa 29 Fd 34.55N 138.22 E
Abeløya 41 Pc 79.00N 30.15 E
Abelvær 7 Cd 64.44N 11.11 E
Abemama Atoll 57 Id 0.21N 173.51 E
Abenab 37 Bc 19.12 S 18.06 E
Abengourou [3] 34 Ed 6.35N 3.25W
Abengourou 31 Gh 6.44N 3.29W
Åbenrå 7 Bi 55.02N 9.26 E
Åbenrå Fjord 8 Ci 55.05N 9.35 E
Abeokuta 31 Hh 7.09N 3.21 E
Āb-e-Pany 23 If 37.06N 68.20 E
Aberayron 9 Ii 52.15N 4.15W
Aberdare Range 30 Ki 0.25 S 36.38 E
Aberdeen [Id.-U.S.] 46 Ie 42.57N 112.50W
Aberdeen [Md.-U.S.] 44 If 39.30N 76.14W
Aberdeen [Ms.-U.S.] 45 Lj 33.49N 88.33W
Aberdeen [N.C.-U.S.] 44 Hh 35.08N 79.26W
Aberdeen [S.Afr.] 37 Cf 32.29 S 24.03 E
Aberdeen [Scot.-U.K.] 6 Fd 57.10N 2.04W
Aberdeen [S.D.-U.S.] 39 Je 45.28N 98.29W
Aberdeen [Wa.-U.S.] 43 Cb 46.59N 123.50W
Aberdeen Lake 42 Hd 64.28N 99.00W
Abergavenny 9 Kj 51.50N 3.00W
Aberystwyth 9 Ii 52.25N 4.05W
Abetone 14 Ef 44.08N 10.40 E
Abez 19 Gb 66.32N 61.46 E
Abhā 22 Gh 18.13N 42.30 E
Abhainn an Chláir/Clare 9 Dh 53.20N 9.03W
Abhainn an Lagáin/Lagan 9 Hg 54.37N 5.53W
Abhainn na Bandan/Bandon 9 Ej 51.40N 8.30W
Abhainn na Deirge/Derg 9 Fg 54.40N 7.25W
Abhar 24 Md 36.02N 49.45 E
Abhar 23 Gb 36.09N 49.13 E
Abhazskaja ASSR [3] 19 Eg 43.00N 41.10 E
Abibe, Serrania de- 54 Cb 8.00N 76.30W
Abidjan 31 Gh 5.19N 4.02W
Abidjan [3] 34 Ed 5.30N 4.30W
Abilene [Ks.-U.S.] 45 Hg 38.55N 97.13W
Abilene [Tx.-U.S.] 39 Jf 32.27N 99.44W
Abingdon 9 Lj 51.41N 1.17W
Abinsk 16 Kg 44.52N 38.10 E
Abiquiu 45 Ch 36.12N 106.19W
Abiquiu Reservoir 45 Ch 36.18N 106.32W
Abisko 7 Eb 68.20N 18.51 E
Abitibi 42 Jf 51.04N 80.55W
Abitibi, Lake- 38 Le 48.42N 79.45W
Abiy Adi 35 Fc 13.37N 39.01 E
Abiyata, Lake- 35 Fd 7.38N 38.36 E
Abja-Paluoja 8 Kf 58.02N 25.14 E
Abnūb 33 Fd 27.16N 31.09 E
Åbo/Turku 6 Ic 60.27N 22.17 E
Abo, Massif d'- 35 Ba 21.41N 16.08 E
Abóboras, Serra das- 55 Jc 16.12 S 44.35W
Abodo 35 Ed 7.50N 34.25 E
Aboisso [3] 34 Ed 5.28N 3.02W
Aboisso 34 Ed 5.28N 3.12W
Abomey 31 Hh 7.11N 1.59 E
Abong Mbang 34 He 3.59N 13.11 E
Abony 10 Pi 47.11N 20.00 E
Aborigen, Pik- 20 Jd 62.05N 149.10 E
Aborlar 26 Ge 9.26N 118.33 E
Aborrebierg 8 Ej 54.59N 12.32 E
Abou Deïa 35 Bc 11.27N 19.17 E
Abou Goulem 35 Cc 13.37N 21.38 E
Abovjan 16 Ni 40.14N 44.37 E
Abrād, Wādī- 23 Gf 15.51N 46.05 E
Abraham's Bay 49 Kb 22.21N 72.55W
Abramovski Bereg 7 Kc 66.25N 43.05 E
Abrántes 13 De 39.28N 8.12W
Abra Pampa 56 Gb 22.43 S 65.42W
Abrego 49 Ki 8.04N 73.14W
Abreojos, Punta- 47 Bc 26.42N 113.35W
'Abrī 35 Ea 20.48N 30.20 E
Abrolhos, Arquipélago dos- 54 Kg 18.00 S 38.40W
Abrud 15 Gc 46.16N 23.04 E
Abruka, Ostrov-/Abruka Saar 8 Jf 58.08N 22.25 E
Abruka Saar/Abruka, Ostrov- 8 Jf 58.08N 22.25 E
Abruzzi [2] 14 Hh 42.20N 13.45 E
Absaroka Range 43 Fc 44.45N 109.50W
Abtenau 14 Hc 47.33N 13.21 E
Abū, Ḩād, Wādī- 24 Ei 27.46N 33.30 E
Abū ad Duhūr 24 Ge 35.44N 37.02 E
Abū 'Alī 24 Mi 27.20N 49.33 E
Abū al Khaşīb 24 Lg 30.27N 47.59 E
Abū an Na'am 24 Hj 25.14N 38.49 E
Abū 'Arīsh 23 Ff 16.58N 42.50 E
Abū Ballaş 33 Ee 24.26N 27.39 E
Abū Daghmah 24 Hd 36.25N 38.15 E
Abū Darbah 33 Fd 28.29N 33.20 E
Abu Dhabi (EN)=Abū Z̧aby 22 Hg 24.28N 54.22 E
Abū Ḩadrīyah 24 Mi 27.20N 48.58 E
Abū Ḩamad 31 Kg 19.32N 33.19 E
Abū Ḩammād 24 Dg 30.32N 31.40 E
Abū Ḩarbah, Jabal- 24 Ei 27.17N 33.13 E
Abū Ḩashā'ifah, Khalīj- 24 Bg 31.16N 27.25 E
Abuja 31 Hh 9.10N 7.11 E
Abu Jābirah 35 Dc 11.04N 26.51 E
Abū Jifān 24 Lj 24.31N 47.43 E
Abū Kabīr 24 Dg 30.44N 31.40 E
Abū Kamāl 23 Fc 34.27N 40.55 E
Abukuma-Gawa 29 Gb 38.06N 140.52 E
Abukuma-Sanchi 29 Gc 37.20N 140.45 E
Abū Latt 33 Hf 19.58N 40.08 E
Abū Libdah, Khashm- 33 Ie 22.58N 46.13 E
Abū Maţāriq 35 Dc 10.58N 26.17 E
Abu Mendi 35 Fc 11.47N 35.42 E
Abumonbazi 36 Db 3.42N 22.10 E
Abū Muḩarrik, Ghurd- 33 Ed 27.00N 30.00 E
Abū Musā, Jazīreh-ye- 23 Id 25.52N 55.03 E
Abunã 53 Jf 9.42 S 65.23W
Abuná, Río- 52 Jf 9.41 S 65.23W
Abune Yosef 35 Fc 12.09N 39.12 E
Abū Qīr 24 Dg 31.19N 30.04 E
Abū Qīr, Khalīj- 24 Dg 31.20N 30.15 E
Abū Qumayyis, Ra's- 24 Nj 24.34N 51.30 E
Abu Road 25 Ed 24.29N 72.47 E
Abū Sawmah, Ra's- 24 Ei 26.51N 33.59 E
Abū Shanab 35 Dc 13.57N 27.47 E
Abu Simbel (EN)=Abū Sumbul 33 Fe 22.22N 31.38 E
Abū Şukhayr 24 Kg 31.52N 44.27 E
Abū Sumbul=Abu Simbel (EN) 33 Fe 22.22N 31.38 E
Abuta 28 Pc 42.31N 140.46 E
Abut Head 62 De 43.06 S 170.15 E
Abū Tij 33 Fd 27.02N 31.19 E
Abū Ţurţūr, Jabal- 24 Cj 25.20N 30.00 E
Abū'Urūq 35 Eb 15.54N 30.27 E
Abuyemeda 35 Fc 10.38N 39.43 E
Abū Zabad 35 Dc 12.21N 29.15 E
Abū Z̧aby=Abu Dhabi (EN) 22 Hg 24.28N 54.22 E
Abū Zanīmah 33 Fd 29.03N 33.06 E
Abwong 35 Ed 9.07N 32.12 E
Åby 8 Gf 58.40N 16.11 E
Abyaḑ 35 Dc 13.46N 26.28 E
Abyaḑ, Al Baḩr al-=White Nile (EN) 30 Kg 15.38N 32.31 E
Abyaḑ, Al Baḩr al-=White Nile (EN) [3] 35 Ec 12.40N 32.30 E
Abyaḑ, Ar Ra's al- 23 Ee 23.32N 38.32 E
Abyaḑ, Jabal- 35 Db 18.55N 28.40 E
Abyaḑ, Ra's al-=Blanc, Cape- (EN) 30 He 37.20N 9.50 E
Abyār Alī 24 Hj 24.25N 39.33 E
Abyār ash Shuwayrif 33 Bd 29.59N 14.16 E
Åbybro 7 Bh 57.09N 9.45 E
Abydos 33 Fd 26.11N 31.55 E
Abyei 35 Dd 9.36N 28.26 E
Ābyek 24 Nd 36.02N 50.31 E
Abymes 51e Ab 16.16N 61.31W
Acacias 54 Dc 3.59N 73.47W
Academy Gletscher 41 Ib 81.45N 33.35W
Acadie 38 Me 46.00N 65.00W
Acaill/Achill 9 Dh 54.00N 10.00W
Acajutla 49 Cg 13.36N 89.50W
Acalayong 34 Ge 1.05N 9.40 E
Acámbaro 47 Dd 20.02N 100.44W
Acandí 54 Cb 8.31N 77.17W
Acaponeta 47 Cd 22.30N 105.22W
Acaponeta, Río- 48 Gf 22.20N 105.37W
Acapulco de Juárez 39 Jh 16.51N 99.55W
Acará 54 Id 1.57 S 48.11W
Acarai, Serra- 54 Gc 1.50N 57.40W
Acaraú 54 Jd 2.53 S 40.07W
Acaray, Río- 55 Eg 25.29 S 54.42W
Acari, Rio- [Braz.] 54 Ge 5.18 S 59.42W
Acari, Rio- [Braz.] 55 Jb 16.00 S 45.03W
Acarigua 54 Eb 9.33N 69.12W
Acatenango, Volcán- 38 Jh 14.30N 91.40W
Acatlán de Osorio 48 Jh 18.12N 98.03W
Acayucan 47 Fe 17.57N 94.55W
Accéglio 14 Af 44.28N 7.00 E
Aččitau, Gora- 18 Cc 42.07N 60.31 E
Accomac 44 Jg 37.43N 75.40W
Accra 31 Gh 5.33N 0.13W
Acebal 55 Bk 33.14 S 60.50W
Acebuches 48 Hc 28.15N 102.43W
Aceguá [Braz.] 55 Ej 31.52 S 54.09W
Aceguá [Ur.] 55 Ej 31.52 S 54.12W
Aceh [3] 26 Cf 4.10N 96.50 E
Acerenza 14 Jj 40.48N 15.56 E
Acerra 14 Ij 40.57N 14.22 E
Achacachi 54 Eg 16.03 S 68.43W
Achaguas 54 Eb 7.46N 68.14W
Achaïf, 'Erg- 34 Ea 20.49N 4.34W
Achao 56 Ff 42.28 S 73.30W
Achegour 34 Hb 19.03N 11.53 E
Acheng 27 Mb 45.32N 126.56 E
Acheux-en-Amiénois 12 Ed 50.04N 2.32 E
Achiet-le-Grand 12 Ed 50.08N 2.47 E
Achill/Acaill 9 Dh 54.00N 10.00W
Achílleion 15 Cj 39.34N 19.55 E
Achill Head/Ceann Acla 9 Ch 53.59N 10.13W
Achim 10 Fc 53.02N 9.01 E
Achim 35 Bb 15.53N 19.31 E
Achterwasser 10 Jb 54.00N 13.57 E
Acı Gölü 24 Cd 37.50N 29.54 E
Ačinsk 22 Ld 56.17N 90.30 E
Acıpayam 24 Cd 37.25N 29.22 E
Acireale 14 Jm 37.37N 15.10 E
Acîş 15 Fb 47.32N 22.47 E
Ačisaj 18 Gc 43.33N 68.53 E
Ačit 17 Hh 56.48N 57.54 E
Ačit-Nur 27 Fb 49.30N 90.30 E
Acklins 38 Lg 22.25N 74.00W
Acklins, The Bight of- 49 Jb 22.30N 74.15W
Acle 12 Db 52.38N 1.33 E
Acobamba 54 Df 12.48 S 74.34W
Acolin 11 Jh 46.49N 3.23 E
Aconcagua [2] 56 Fd 32.15 S 70.50W
Aconcagua, Cerro- 52 Ji 32.39 S 70.00W
Açor, Serra de- 13 Ed 40.13N 7.48W
Açores=Azores (EN) [5] 31 Ee 38.30N 28.00W
Açores, Arquipélago dos-=Azores (EN) 30 Ee 38.30N 28.00W
Acorizal 55 Db 15.12 S 56.22W
Acoyapa 49 Eh 11.58N 85.10W
Acquapendente 14 Fh 42.44N 11.52 E
Acquasanta Terme 14 Hh 42.46N 13.24 E
Acquasparta 14 Gh 42.41N 12.33 E
Acquaviva delle Fonti 14 Kj 40.54N 16.50 E
Acqui Terme 14 Cf 44.41N 8.28 E
Acraman, Lake- 59 Hf 32.05 S 135.25 E
Acre [2] 54 Ee 9.00 S 70.00W
Acre, Rio- 52 Jf 8.45 S 67.22W
Acri 14 Kk 39.29N 16.23 E
Actéon, Groupe- 57 Ng 21.20 S 136.30W
Actopan 48 Jg 20.16N 98.56W
Açu 54 Ke 5.34 S 36.54W
Acuña 55 Di 29.55 S 57.58W
Ada [Ghana] 34 Fd 5.47N 0.38 E
Ada [Ok.-U.S.] 43 He 34.46N 96.41W
Ada [Yugo.] 15 Dd 45.48N 20.08 E
Adaba 35 Fd 7.03N 39.31 E
'Adād 35 Hb 8.23N 46.48 E
'Adādle 35 Gd 9.45N 44.41 E
Adair, Bahía- 48 Cb 31.30N 113.50W
Adair, Cape - 42 Kb 71.31N 71.24W
Adaja 13 Hc 41.32N 4.52W
Adak 40a Cb 51.45N 176.40W
Adalar 15 Mi 40.52N 29.07 E
'Adale 35 He 2.46N 46.20 E
Ådalen 8 Ga 63.20N 17.30 E
Adalselv 8 Dd 60.04N 10.11 E
Adam, Mount- 56 Hh 51.34 S 60.04W
Adamantina 55 Ge 21.42 S 51.04W
Adamaoua=Adamawa (EN) 30 Ih 7.00N 15.00 E
Adamawa (EN)=Adamaoua 30 Ih 7.00N 15.00 E
Adamello 14 Ed 46.09N 10.30 E
Adamovka 16 Ud 51.32N 59.59 E
Adams 45 Le 43.58N 89.49W
Adams, Mount- 43 Cb 46.12N 121.28W
Adams Lake 46 Fa 51.13N 119.33W
Adams River 42 Ff 50.54N 119.33W
Adam's Rock 64q Ab 25.04 S 130.05W
Adamstown 58 Ng 25.04 S 130.05W
Adamuz 13 Hf 38.02N 4.31W
Adana 22 Ff 37.01N 35.18 E
Adapazarı 24 Db 40.46N 30.24 E
Adarama 35 Eb 17.05N 34.54 E
Adarān, Jabal- 33 Ig 13.46N 45.08 E
Adare, Cape- 66 Kf 71.17 S 170.14 E
Adavale 59 Ie 25.55 S 144.36 E
Adda [It.] 5 Gf 45.08N 9.53 E
Adda [Sud.] 35 Cd 9.51N 24.50 E
Aḑ Ḑab'ah 33 Ec 31.02N 28.26 E
Ad Dabbah 35 Eb 18.03N 30.57 E
Ad Dafinah 33 He 23.18N 41.58 E
Aḑ Ḑafrah 24 Ok 23.25N 53.25 E
Ad Dahnā' 21 Gg 24.30N 48.10 E
Addala-Šuhgelmeer, Gora- 16 Oh 42.20N 46.15 E
Aḑ Ḑālī' 33 Hg 13.42N 44.44 E
Ad Damazin 35 Ec 11.49N 34.23 E
Ad 'Dāmir 35 Eb 17.35N 33.58 E
Ad Dammām 22 Hg 26.26N 50.07 E
Ad Dār al Ḩamrā' 23 Ed 27.19N 37.44 E
Ad Dawādimī 23 Fe 24.28N 44.18 E
Ad Dawḩah=Doha (EN) 22 Hg 25.17N 51.32 E
Ad Dawr 24 Je 34.27N 43.47 E
Ad Dayr 33 Fd 25.20N 32.35 E
Ad Dibdibah 24 Lh 28.00N 46.30 E
Aḑ Ḑiffah 33 Ec 30.30N 25.30 E
Ad Dikākah 35 Ib 19.25N 51.30 E
Ad Dilam 23 Ge 23.59N 47.10 E
Ad Dindar 35 Ec 13.20N 34.05 E
Ad Dir'īyah 24 Lj 24.48N 46.32 E
Ad Dissān 33 Hf 16.56N 41.41 E
Addis Zemen 35 Fc 12.05N 37.44 E
Ad Dīwānīya 23 Fc 31.59N 44.56 E
Addu Atoll 21 Jj 0.25 S 73.10 E
Ad Du'ayn 35 Dc 11.26N 26.09 E
Ad Duwayd 24 Jg 30.13N 42.18 E
Ad Duwaym 35 Ec 14.00N 32.19 E
Adel [Ga.-U.S.] 44 Fj 31.18N 83.25W
Adel [Or.-U.S.] 46 Fe 42.11N 119.54W
Adelaide [Austl.] 58 Eh 34.56 S 138.36 E
Adelaide [Bah.] 44 Im 25.00N 77.31W
Adelaide [S.Afr.] 37 Df 32.42 S 26.20 E
Adelaide Island 66 Qe 67.15 S 68.30W
Adelaide Peninsula 42 Hc 68.05N 97.50W
Adelaide River 58 Ef 13.15 S 131.06 E
Adelaye 35 Cd 7.07N 22.49 E
Adelboden 14 Bd 46.30N 7.33 E
Adèle Island 59 Ec 15.30 S 123.10 E
Adélie, Terre- 66 Ie 67.00 S 139.00 E
Ademuz 13 Kd 40.04N 1.17W
Aden (EN)=Baladiyat 'Adan 22 Gh 12.46N 45.01 E
Aden, Gulf of- 30 Lg 12.00N 48.00 E
Aden, Gulf of- (EN)='Admēd, Badyarada- 30 Lg 12.00N 48.00 E
Adenau 12 Id 50.23N 6.56 E
Ader 30 Hg 14.10N 5.05 E
Aderbissinat 34 Gb 15.37N 7.52 E
Adhan, Jabal- 24 Qj 25.27N 56.13 E
Adh Dhahībāt 32 Jc 32.01N 10.42 E
Adh Dhayd 24 Pj 25.17N 55.53 E
Adhélfi 15 Gj 39.08N 23.59 E
Adhelfoi 15 Jm 36.25N 26.37 E
'Adhırīyāt, Jıbāl- al- 24 Gg 30.25N 36.48 E
Adi, Pulau- 26 Jg 4.18 S 133.26 E
Adiaké 34 Ed 5.16N 3.17W
Adi Arkay 35 Fc 13.31N 38.00 E
Adícora 54 Ea 11.57N 69.48W
Adi Dairo 35 Fc 14.21N 38.12 E
Adigala 35 Gc 10.24N 42.18 E
Adige/Etsch 5 Hf 45.10N 12.20 E
Adigrat 35 Fc 14.16N 39.28 E
Adi Keyeh 35 Fc 14.48N 39.23 E
Adi Kwala 35 Fc 14.37N 38.51 E
Ādilābād 25 Fe 19.40N 78.32 E
Adīrī 31 If 27.30N 13.16 E
Adirondack Mountains 38 Le 44.00N 74.00W
Adis Abeba 31 Kh 9.01N 38.46 E
Adis Alem 35 Fd 9.03N 38.24 E
Adi Ugri 35 Fc 14.53N 38.49 E
Adiyaman 23 Eb 37.46N 38.17 E
Adjud 15 Kc 46.06N 27.10 E
Adjuntas 51a Bb 18.09N 66.43W
'Admēd, Badyarada-=Aden, Gulf of- (EN) 30 Lg 12.00N 48.00 E
Admer, Erg d'- 32 Ie 24.12N 9.10 E
Admiralty 40 Me 57.50N 134.30W
Admiralty Bay 51n Ba 13.00N 61.16W
Admiralty Gulf 59 Fb 14.20 S 125.50 E
Admiralty Inlet 42 Ib 72.30N 86.00W
Admiralty Islands 57 Fe 2.10 S 147.00 E
Admiralty Mountains 66 Kf 71.45 S 168.30 E
Admont 14 Ic 47.34N 14.27 E
Ado 34 Fd 6.36N 2.56 E
Ado Ekiti 34 Gd 7.38N 5.13 E
Adok 35 Ed 8.11N 30.19 E
Adolfo Gonzales Chaves 55 Bn 38.02 S 60.06W
Adolfo López Mateos, Presa- 48 Fe 25.05N 107.20W
Adonara, Pulau- 26 Hh 8.20 S 123.10 E
Ādoni 25 Fe 15.38N 77.17 E
Adra 13 Ih 36.44N 3.01W
Adrano 14 Im 37.40N 14.50 E
Adrar 30 Ff 20.30N 13.30W
Adrar 31 Gf 27.54N 0.17W
Adrar 30 Hf 25.12N 8.10 E
Adrar [Alg.] [3] 32 Gd 27.00N 1.00W
Adrar [Mtna.] [3] 32 Ee 21.00N 11.00W
Adré 35 Cc 13.28N 22.12 E
Adria 14 Ge 45.03N 12.03 E
Adrian 44 Ee 41.54N 84.02W
Adrianópolis 55 Hg 24.41 S 48.50W
Adriatic, Deti-=Adriatic Sea (EN) 5 Hg 43.00N 16.00 E
Adriatico, Mar-=Adriatic Sea (EN) 5 Hg 43.00N 16.00 E
Adriatic Sea (EN)=Adriatic, Deti- 5 Hg 43.00N 16.00 E
Adriatic Sea (EN)=Adriatico, Mar- 5 Hg 43.00N 16.00 E
Adriatic Sea (EN)=Jadransko More 5 Hg 43.00N 16.00 E
Aduard 12 Ia 53.15N 6.25 E
Adula 14 Dd 46.30N 9.05 E
Adulis 35 Fb 15.15N 39.37 E
Adur 12 Bd 50.49N 0.16W
Adusa 36 Eb 1.23N 28.01 E
Adventure Bank (EN) 14 Gm 37.20N 12.10 E
Adwa 31 Kg 14.10N 38.55 E
Adyča 21 Pc 68.13N 135.03 E
Adygalah 20 Jd 62.57N 146.25 E
Adygejskaja Avt. Oblast [3] 19 Eg 44.30N 40.05 E
Adžarskaja ASSR [3] 19 Eg 41.40N 42.10 E
Adzopé [3] 34 Ed 6.15N 3.45W
Adzopé 34 Ed 6.06N 3.52W
Adzva 17 Ic 66.36N 59.28 E
Aegean Sea (EN)=Aiyaíon Pélagos 5 Ih 39.00N 25.00 E
Aegean Sea (EN)=Ege Denizi 5 Ih 39.00N 25.00 E
Aegina (EN) = Aíyina 15 Gl 37.40N 23.30 E
Aegviidu 8 Ke 59.17N 25.37 E
Aeon Point 64g Bb 1.46N 157.11W
Aerfort na Sionainne/Shannon 9 Ei 52.42N 8.57W
Ærø 8 Dj 54.55N 10.20 E
Ærøskøbing 8 Dj 54.53N 10.25 E
Aerzen 12 Lb 52.02N 9.16 E
Afafi, Massif d'- 34 Ha 22.15N 15.00 E
'Afak 24 Kf 32.04N 45.15 E
Afanasjevo 7 Mg 58.54N 53.16 E
Afareaitu 65e Fc 17.33 S 149.47W
Afars and Issas → Djibouti [1] 31 Lg 11.30N 43.00 E
Aff 11 Dg 47.43N 2.07W
Affollé 30 Fg 16.55N 10.25W
Affrica, Scoglio d'- 14 Eh 42.20N 10.05 E
Afghanistan [1] 22 If 33.00N 65.00 E
Afgōye 35 He 2.09N 45.07 E
'Afif 23 Fe 23.55N 42.56 E
Afikpo 34 Gd 5.53N 7.55 E
Afipski 16 Kg 44.52N 38.50 E
Aflou 32 Hc 34.07N 2.06 E
Afmadōw 35 Ge 0.29N 42.06 E
Afognak 40 Ie 58.15N 152.30W
Afonso Cláudio 54 Jh 20.05 S 41.08W
Afon Teifi 9 Ii 52.06N 4.43W
Afon Tywi 9 Ij 51.40N 4.15W
Afragola 14 Ij 40.55N 14.18 E
Afrērā, Lake- 35 Gc 13.20N 41.03 E
Africa 30 Jh 10.00N 22.00 E
African Islands 30 Mi 4.53 S 43.24 E
Afşin 24 Gc 38.36N 36.55 E
Afsluitdijk 11 La 53.00N 5.15 E
Afton 46 Je 42.44N 110.56W
Afuá 54 Hd 0.10 S 50.23W
'Afula 24 Ff 32.36N 35.17 E
Afyonkarahisar 22 Ff 38.45N 30.40 E
Agadem 31 Ig 16.50N 13.17 E
Agadez 31 Hg 16.58N 7.59 E
Agadez [2] 34 Hb 19.45N 10.15 E
Agadir 31 Ge 30.25N 9.37W
Agadir [3] 32 Fc 30.00N 9.00W
Agadyr 19 Hf 48.17N 72.53 E
Agalega Islands 30 Mj 10.24 S 56.30 E
Agalta, Sierra de- 47 Ge 15.00N 85.53W
Agan 19 Hc 61.23N 74.35 E
Agana 58 Fc 13.28N 144.45 E
Agano-Gawa 28 Of 37.57N 139.07 E
Aga Point 64c Bb 13.14N 144.43 E
Agapovka 17 Ij 53.18N 59.10 E
Agaro 35 Fd 7.53N 36.36 E
Agartala 22 Lg 23.49N 91.16 E
Agassiz Pool 45 Ib 48.20N 95.58W
Agat 64c Bb 13.23N 144.39 E
Agat Bay 64c Bb 13.24N 144.39 E
Agats 58 Ee 5.33 S 138.08 E
Agattu 40a Ab 52.25N 173.35 E
Agawa Bay 44 Eb 47.22N 84.33W
Agawa Bay 44 Eb 47.20N 84.42W
Agboville 34 Ed 5.56N 4.13W
Agboville [3] 34 Ed 6.00N 4.15W
Agdam 19 Eh 39.58N 46.57 E
Agdaš 16 Oi 40.38N 47.29 E
Agde 11 Jk 43.19N 3.28 E
Agde, Cap d'- 11 Jk 43.16N 3.30 E
Agder 8 Cf 58.25N 8.15 E
Agdz 32 Fc 30.27N 7.56W
Agdžabedi 16 Oi 40.03N 47.28 E
Agematsu 29 Ed 35.47N 137.41 E
Agen 11 Gj 44.12N 0.38 E
Ageo 29 Fd 35.58N 139.35 E
Agepsta, Gora- 16 Lh 43.32N 40.30 E
Ager 14 Hb 48.05N 13.51 E
Agere Mariam 35 Fd 5.39N 38.15 E
Agersø 8 Di 55.10N 11.10 E
Agger 12 Jd 50.48N 7.11 E
Āghā Jārī 23 Gc 30.42N 49.50 E
Aghireşu 15 Gc 46.53N 23.15 E
Agiabampo, Estero de- 48 Ed 26.15N 109.15W
Ağın 24 Hc 38.57N 38.43 E

Index Symbols

[1] Independent Nation
[2] State, Region
[3] District, County
[4] Municipality
[5] Colony, Dependency
Continent
Physical Region
Historical or Cultural Region
Mount, Mountain
Volcano
Hill
Mountains, Mountain Range
Hills, Escarpment
Plateau, Upland
Pass, Gap
Plain, Lowland
Delta
Salt Flat
Valley, Canyon
Crater, Cave
Karst Features
Depression
Polder
Desert, Dunes
Forest, Woods
Heath, Steppe
Oasis
Cape, Point
Coast, Beach
Cliff
Peninsula
Isthmus
Sandbank
Island
Atoll
Rock, Reef
Islands, Archipelago
Rocks, Reefs
Coral Reef
Well, Spring
Geyser
River, Stream
Waterfall Rapids
River Mouth, Estuary
Lake
Salt Lake
Intermittent Lake
Reservoir
Swamp, Pond
Canal
Glacier
Ice Shelf, Pack Ice
Ocean
Sea
Gulf, Bay
Strait, Fjord
Lagoon
Bank
Seamount
Tablemount
Ridge
Shelf
Basin
Escarpment, Sea Scarp
Fracture
Trench, Abyss
National Park, Reserve
Point of Interest
Recreation Site
Cave, Cavern
Historic Site
Ruins
Wall, Walls
Church, Abbey
Temple
Scientific Station
Airport
Port
Lighthouse
Mine
Tunnel
Dam, Bridge

Aginski Burjatski Nacionalny Okrug [3] 20 Gf 51.00N 114.30 E
Aginskoje 20 Gf 51.03N 114.33 E
Agnew 59 Ee 28.01S 120.30 E
Agnibilékrou 34 Ed 7.08N 3.12W
Agnita 15 Hd 45.58N 24.37 E
Agno 14 Fe 45.32N 11.21 E
Agnone 14 Ii 41.48N 14.22 E
Ago 29 Ed 34.19N 136.50 E
Agoare 34 Fd 8.30N 3.25 E
Agogna 14 Ce 45.04N 8.54 E
Agön 8 Gc 61.35N 17.25 E
Agordat 31 Kg 15.32N 37.53 E
Agordo 14 Gd 46.17N 12.02 E
Agout 11 Hk 43.47N 1.41 E
Āgra 22 Jg 27.11N 78.01 E
Agrahanski Poluostrov 16 Oh 43.45N 47.35 E
Agramunt 13 Nc 41.47N 1.06 E
Agreda 13 Kc 41.51N 1.56W
Agri 14 Kj 40.13N 16.44 E
Agričaj 16 Oi 41.17N 46.43 E
Agrigento 6 Hh 37.19N 13.34 E
Agrihan Island 57 Fc 18.46N 145.40 E
Agrij 15 Gb 47.15N 23.16 E
Agrinion 15 Ek 38.38N 21.25 E
Agropoli 14 Ij 40.21N 14.59 E
Agro Pontino 14 Gi 41.25N 12.55 E
Agryz 7 Mh 56.31N 53.01 E
Agto 41 Ge 67.37N 53.49W
Agua Brava, Laguna- 48 Gf 22.10N 105.32W
Agua Caliente, Cerro- 47 Cc 26.27N 106.12W
Aguachica 54 Db 8.18N 73.38W
Agua Clara 55 Fe 20.27S 52.52W
Aguada de Pasajeros 49 Gb 22.23N 80.51W
Aguadez, Irhazer Oua-n- 34 Gb 17.28N 6.26 E
Aguadilla 49 Nd 18.26N 67.09W
Aguadulce 49 Gi 8.15N 80.33W
Agua Fria River 46 Ij 33.23N 112.21W
Agua Limpa, Rio- 55 Gb 14.58S 51.20W
Aguán, Rio- 49 Ef 15.57N 85.44W
Aguanaval, Rio- 48 Hf 25.28N 102.53W
Aguapei 55 Cc 16.12S 59.43W
Aguapei, Rio- 56 Jb 21.03S 51.47W
Aguapei, Rio- 55 Cb 15.53S 58.25W
Agua Prieta 39 If 31.18N 109.34W
Aguaray 56 Hb 22.16S 63.44W
Aguaray Guazú, Río- [Par.] 55 Dg 24.05S 56.40W
Aguaray Guazú, Río- [Par.] 55 Dg 24.47S 57.19W
Aguasay 50 Eh 9.25N 63.44W
Aguascalientes 39 Ig 21.53N 102.18W
Aguascalientes [2] 47 Dd 22.00N 102.30W
Aguasvivas 13 Lc 41.20N 0.25W
Água Verde, Rio- 55 Da 13.42S 56.43W
Agua Vermelha, Represa- 56 Ja 19.53S 50.17W
Agudo [Braz.] 55 Fi 29.38S 53.15W
Agudo [Sp.] 13 Hf 38.59N 4.52W
Agueda 13 Fc 41.02N 6.56W
Águeda 13 Dd 40.34N 8.27W
Aguelhok 34 Fb 19.28N 0.51 E
Aguenit 32 Ee 22.11N 13.08W
Aguerguer 30 Ff 23.09N 16.01W
Aguijan Island 57 Fc 14.51N 145.34 E
Aguilar de Campóo 13 Hb 42.48N 4.16W
Aguilar de la Frontera 13 Hg 37.31N 4.39W
Aguilas 13 Kg 37.24N 1.35W
Aguililla 48 Hh 18.44N 102.44W
Aguirre, Rio- 50 Fh 8.28N 61.02W
Aguja, Cabo de la- 54 Da 11.21N 73.59W
Agujereada, Punta- 51a Ab 18.31N 67.08W
Agul 20 Ee 55.40N 95.45 E
Agulhas, Cape-(EN)= Agulhas, Kaap- 30 Jl 34.50S 20.00 E
Agulhas, Kaap-=Agulhas, Cape-(EN) 30 Jl 34.50S 20.00 E
Agulhas Bank (EN) 37 Cg 35.30S 21.00 E
Agulhas Basin (EN) 3 En 47.00S 20.00 E
Agulhas Negras, Pico das- 52 Lh 22.23S 44.38W
Agulhas Plateau (EN) 30 Jm 40.00S 26.00 E
Agung, Gunung- 26 Gh 8.21S 115.30 E
Aguni-Shima 27 Mf 26.35N 127.15 E
Agupey, Rio- 55 Di 29.07S 56.36W
Agustin Codazzi 54 Da 10.02N 73.15W
Ağva 24 Cb 41.05N 29.50 E
Ahaggar 30 Hf 23.10N 5.50 E
Ahaggar, Tassili-oua-n- 30 Hf 20.30N 5.00 E
Aha Hills 37 Cc 19.45S 21.10 E
Ahalcihe 19 Eg 41.38N 42.59 E
Ahalkalaki 19 Eg 41.25N 43.29 E
Ahangaran 18 Gd 40.57N 69.37 E
Ahar 23 Gb 38.28N 47.04 E
Ahat 15 Mk 38.39N 29.47 E
Ahaus 10 Cd 52.04N 7.00 E
Ahe Atoll 57 Mf 14.30S 146.18W
Ahenet, Tanezrouft-n- 32 He 22.00N 1.00 E
Ahini 20 Ff 53.18N 105.01 E
Ahipara 62 Ea 35.10S 173.09 E
Ahja Jõgi 8 Lf 58.19N 27.15 E
Ahlat 24 Jc 38.45N 42.29 E
Ahlen 10 De 51.45N 7.55 E
Ahmadābād 22 Jg 23.02N 72.37 E
Aḥmadī 24 Qi 27.56N 56.42 E
Ahmadnagar 25 Ee 19.05N 74.44 E
Ahmadpur East 25 Ec 29.09N 71.16 E
Ahmar 30 Lh 9.23N 41.13 E
Aḥmar, Al Baḥr al-=Red Sea (EN) 30 Kf 25.00N 38.00 E
Ahmeta 16 Nh 42.02N 45.11 E
Ahmetli 15 Kk 38.31N 27.57 E
Ahnet 32 He 24.35N 3.15 E
Ahoa 64h Ab 13.17S 176.12W
Ahome 48 Ee 25.55N 109.11W
Ahon, Tarso- 35 Ba 20.23N 18.18 E
Ahr 10 Df 50.33N 7.17 E
Ahram 24 Nh 28.52N 51.16 E
Ahrāmāt al Jīzah 33 Fd 29.55N 31.05 E
Ahrensburg 10 Gc 53.41N 10.15 E
Ahrgebirge 12 Id 50.31N 6.54 E
Ahse 12 Jc 51.42N 7.51 E
Ahsu 16 Pi 40.35N 48.26 E
Ähtäri 7 Ee 62.02N 21.20 E
Ähtärinjärvi 8 Kb 62.40N 24.05 E
Ähtävänjoki 7 Fe 63.38N 22.48 E
Ahtopol 15 Kg 42.06N 27.57 E
Ahtuba 5 Kf 46.42N 48.00 E
Ahtubinsk 6 Kf 48.14N 46.14 E
Ahtyrka 19 De 50.19N 34.55 E
Ahuacapán 49 Cg 13.55N 89.51W
Ahuazotepec 48 Jg 20.03N 98.09W
Ahunui Atoll 57 Mf 19.35S 140.28W
Åhus 7 Di 55.55N 14.17 E
Ahvāz 22 Gf 31.19N 48.42 E
Ahvenanmaa/Åland [2] 7 Ef 60.15N 20.00 E
Ahvenanmaa/Åland=Aland Islands (EN) 5 Hc 60.15N 20.00 E
Ahvenanmeri 8 Hd 60.00N 19.30 E
Aḥwar 23 Gg 13.31N 46.42 E
Aibag Gol 28 Ad 41.42N 110.24 E
Aibetsu 29a Cb 43.55N 142.33 E
Aichach 10 Hh 48.28N 11.08 E
Aichi Ken [2] 28 Ng 35.00N 137.07 E
Aiea 65a Db 21.23N 157.56W
Aigle 14 Ad 46.20N 6.59 E
Aigoual, Mont- 11 Jj 44.07N 3.35 E
Aiguá 55 El 34.12S 54.45W
Aigues 11 Kj 44.07N 4.43 E
Aigues-Mortes 11 Kk 43.34N 4.11 E
Aiguilles 11 Mj 44.47N 6.52 E
Aiguillon 11 Gj 44.18N 0.21 E
Aigurande 11 Hh 46.26N 1.50 E
Ai He 28 Hd 40.13N 124.30 E
Aihui (Heihe) 22 Od 50.13N 127.26 E
Aikawa 29 Fb 38.02N 138.14 E
Aiken 43 Ke 33.34N 81.44W
Ailao Shan 27 Hg 23.15N 102.20 E
Ailette 12 Fe 49.35N 3.10 E
Ailinginae Atoll 57 Hc 11.08N 166.24 E
Aillte an Mhothair/Moher, Cliffs of- 9 Di 52.58N 9.27W
Ailly-le-Haut-Clocher 12 Dd 50.05N 1.59 E
Ailly-sur-Noye 12 Ee 49.45N 2.22 E
Ailsa Craig 9 Hf 55.16N 5.07W
Ailuk Atoll 57 Hc 10.20N 169.56 E
Aim 20 Ie 58.48N 134.12 E
Aimogasta 56 Gc 28.33S 66.49W
Aimorés 54 Jg 19.30S 41.04W
Ain [3] 11 Lh 46.10N 5.20 E
Ain 11 Li 45.48N 5.10 E
Ainazi/Ajnazi 7 Fh 57.52N 24.25 E
Aïn Beida 32 Ib 35.48N 7.24 E
Aïn Beni Mathar 32 Gc 34.01N 2.01W
Aïn Bessem 13 Ph 36.18N 3.40 E
Aïn Boucif 13 Pi 35.53N 3.09 E
Aïn Defla 13 Nh 36.16N 1.58 E
Aïn el Berd 13 Li 35.21N 0.31W
Aïn el Hammam 13 Qh 36.34N 4.19 E
Aïn el Turck 13 Li 35.44N 0.46W
Aïn Galakka 35 Bb 18.05N 18.31 E
Ainos Óros 15 Dk 38.07N 20.40 E
Aïn Oulmene 13 Ri 35.55N 5.18 E
Aïn Oussera 13 Oi 35.27N 2.54 E
Aïn Sefra 31 Ge 32.45N 0.35W
Ainsworth 45 Ge 42.33N 99.52W
Aïn Taghrout 13 Rh 36.08N 5.05 E
Aïn Tedeles 13 Mh 36.00N 0.18 E
Aïn Témouchent 32 Gb 35.18N 1.08W
Aïn Tolba 13 Ki 35.15N 1.15W
Aioi 29 Dd 34.49N 134.28 E
Aiquile 54 Eg 18.10S 65.10W
Air/Azbine 30 Hg 18.00N 8.30 E
Airabu, Pulau- 26 Ef 2.46N 106.14 E
Airai 64a Bc 7.21N 134.34 E
Airaines 12 De 49.58N 1.57 E
Airão 54 Fd 1.56S 61.22W
Airbangis 26 Cf 0.12N 99.23 E
Airdrie 46 Ha 51.18N 114.02W
Aire 11 Id 50.38N 2.24 E
Aire [Eng.-U.K.] 9 Mh 53.44N 0.54W
Aire [Fr.] 11 Ke 49.19N 4.49 E
Aire, Canal d'- 11 Id 50.38N 2.25 E
Aire, Isla del- 13 Qe 39.47N 4.16 E
Aire-sur-l'Adour 11 Fk 43.42N 0.16W
Air Force 42 Kc 67.55N 74.05W
Airolo 14 Cd 46.33N 8.35 E
Aïs 63b Cb 15.26S 167.15 E
Aisch 10 Hg 49.46N 11.01 E
Aisén del General Carlos Ibáñez del Campo [2] 56 Fg 46.00S 73.00W
Aishihik 42 Dd 61.34N 137.30W
Ai-Shima 29 Bd 34.30N 131.18 E
Aisne [3] 11 Je 49.30N 3.30 E
Aisne 11 Ie 49.26N 2.50 E
Aisne à la Marne, Canal de l'- 11 Je 49.24N 3.55 E
Aïssa, Djebel- 32 Gc 32.51N 0.30W
Aitana, Pico- 13 Lf 38.39N 0.16W
Aitape 60 Ch 3.08S 142.21 E
Aitolikón 15 Ek 38.26N 21.21 E
Aitutaki Atoll 57 Lf 18.52S 159.45W
Ait Youssef ou Ali 13 Ii 35.09N 3.55W
Aiud 15 Gc 46.18N 23.43 E
Aiviekste 7 Fh 56.36N 25.44 E
Aiviekste/Ajviekste 7 Fh 56.36N 25.44 E
Aiwokako Passage 64a Bb 7.39N 134.33 E
Aix, Ile d'- 11 Eh 46.01N 1.10W
Aix-en-Provence 11 Lk 43.32N 5.26 E
Aixe-sur-Vienne 11 Hi 45.48N 1.08 E
Aix-les-Bains 11 Li 45.42N 5.55 E
Aiyaíon Pélagos=Aegean Sea (EN) 5 Ih 39.00N 25.00 E
Aiyina 15 Gl 37.45N 23.26 E
Aiyina = Aegina (EN) 15 Gl 37.40N 23.30 E
Aiyinion 15 Fi 40.30N 22.33 E
Aiyion 15 Fk 38.15N 22.05 E
Aizawl 25 Id 23.44N 92.43 E
Aizenay 11 Eh 46.44N 1.37W
Aizpute/Ajzpute 7 Eh 56.45N 21.39 E
Aizubange 29 Fc 37.34N 139.49 E
Aizutakada 29 Fc 37.29N 139.48 E
Aizuwakamatsu 28 Of 37.30N 139.56 E
Ajā', Jabal- 24 Ii 27.30N 41.30 E
'Ajab Shīr 24 Kd 37.28N 45.54 E
Ajaccio 6 Gg 41.55N 8.44 E
Ajaccio, Golfe d'- 11a Ab 41.50N 8.41 E
Ajaguz 22 Ke 47.58N 80.27 E
Ajakli 20 Eb 70.13N 95.55 E
Ajan [R.S.F.S.R.] 20 Fe 59.38N 106.45 E
Ajan [R.S.F.S.R.] 20 Ie 56.27N 138.10 E
Ajanka 20 Ld 63.40N 167.30 E
Ajanta Range 25 Fd 20.30N 76.00 E
Ajat 17 Kj 52.54N 62.50 E
Ajax Peak 46 Id 45.20N 113.40W
Ajdābiyā 31 Je 30.46N 20.14 E
Ajdabul 19 Ge 52.42N 69.01 E
Ajdar 16 Ke 48.42N 39.13 E
Ajdar, Solončak- 18 Fd 40.50N 66.50 E
Ajdovščina 14 He 45.53N 13.53 E
Ajdyrlinski 17 Ij 52.03N 59.50 E
Ajhal 20 Gc 66.00N 111.32 E
Ajigasawa 28 Pd 40.47N 140.12 E
Aji-Shima 29 Gb 38.15N 141.30 E
Ajjer, Tassili-n- 30 Hf 25.30N 9.00 E
Ajka 10 Ni 47.06N 17.34 E
Ajke, Ozero- 16 Vd 50.55N 61.35 E
Ajkino 17 De 62.15N 49.56 E
'Ajlūn 24 Ff 32.20N 35.45 E
'Ajmah, Jabal al- 24 Fh 29.12N 34.02 E
'Ajmān 23 Id 25.25N 55.27 E
Ajmer 22 Jg 26.27N 74.38 E
Ajnaži/Ainazi 7 Fh 57.52N 24.25 E
Ajni 18 Ge 39.23N 68.36 E
Ajo 43 Ee 32.22N 112.52W
Ajo, Cabo de- 13 Ia 43.31N 3.35W
Ajon, Ostrov- 21 Sc 69.50N 168.40 E
Ajoupa-Bouillon 51h Ab 14.50N 61.08W
Ajsary 19 He 53.05N 71.00 E
Ajtos 15 Kg 42.42N 27.15 E
Aju, Kepulauan- 26 Jf 0.28N 131.03 E
'Ajūz, Jabal al- 24 Dj 25.49N 30.43 E
Ajviekste 7 Fh 56.36N 25.44 E
Ajviekste/Aiviekste 7 Fh 56.36N 25.44 E
Ajzpute/Aizpute 7 Eh 56.45N 21.39 E
Akaba 34 Fd 7.57N 1.03 E
Akabira 28 Qc 43.30N 142.04 E
Akabli 32 Hd 26.42N 1.22 E
Akademika Obručeva, Hrebet- 20 Ef 51.30N 96.45 E
Akadomari 29 Fc 37.54N 138.24 E
Aka-Gawa 29 Fb 38.54N 139.50 E
Akagi-San 29 Fc 36.33N 139.11 E
Akaishi-Dake 29 Fd 35.27N 138.09 E
Akaishi-Sanmyaku 29 Fd 35.25N 138.10 E
Akajaure 7 Dc 67.42N 17.30 E
Aka-Jima 29b Ab 26.14N 127.17 E
Akaki 35 Fd 8.51N 38.48 E
Akala 35 Fb 15.38N 36.12 E
Akan 29a Db 43.08N 144.07 E
Akan-Gawa 29a Db 43.00N 144.16 E
Akanthou 24 Ee 35.22N 33.45 E
Akar 24 Dc 38.38N 31.06 E
Akarnaniká Óri 15 Dk 38.45N 21.00 E
Akaroa 61 Dh 43.48S 172.59 E
Akasaki 29 Cd 35.31N 133.38 E
'Akasha East 35 Ea 21.05N 30.43 E
Akashi 28 Mg 34.38N 134.59 E
Akbaba Tepe 24 Hc 39.32N 39.33 E
Akbajtal, Pereval- 19 Hh 38.31N 73.41 E
Akbou 13 Qh 36.28N 4.32 E
Akbulak 19 Fe 51.03N 55.37 E
Akbura 18 Id 40.34N 72.45 E
Akçaabat 24 Hb 40.59N 39.34 E
Akçadağ 24 Gc 38.21N 37.59 E
Akçakale 24 Hd 36.41N 38.56 E
Akçakara Dağı 24 Ic 38.40N 40.52 E
Akçakoca 24 Db 41.05N 31.09 E
Akçaova [Tur.] 15 Mh 41.03N 29.57 E
Akçaova [Tur.] 15 Ll 37.30N 28.02 E
Akčatau 19 Hf 47.59N 74.02 E
Akçay 15 Ll 37.50N 28.15 E
Akçay 15 Mm 36.36N 29.45 E
Akchār 30 Ff 20.20N 14.28W
Ak Dağ [Tur.] 24 Ib 40.35N 41.46 E
Ak Dağ [Tur.] 23 Cb 36.32N 29.34 E
Akdağ [Tur.] 24 Gd 37.53N 37.56 E
Akdağ [Tur.] 24 Fb 40.57N 35.55 E
Akdağ [Tur.] 24 Cc 39.15N 28.49 E
Akdağ [Tur.] 15 Ll 37.42N 28.56 E
Akdağ [Tur.] 15 Mk 38.18N 29.58 E
Akdağ [Tur.] 15 Jk 38.33N 26.30 E
Ak Dağlar 24 Gc 39.30N 36.00 E
Ak Dağları 24 Ic 38.40N 40.12 E
Akdağmadeni 24 Fc 39.40N 35.54 E
Akdeniz=Mediterranean Sea (EN) 5 Hh 35.00N 20.00 E
Ak-Dovurak 20 Ef 51.10N 90.40 E
Akechi 29 Ed 35.18N 137.22 E
Ake Eze 34 Gd 5.55N 7.40 E
Akera 16 Oj 39.09N 46.48 E
Åkersberga 8 He 59.29N 18.18 E
Akershus [2] 7 Cf 60.00N 11.10 E
Aketi 31 Jh 2.44N 23.46 E
Akharnai 15 Gk 38.05N 23.44 E
Akhdar, al Jabal al- 21 Hg 23.30N 57.00 E
Akhḍar, al Jabal al- 30 Je 32.30N 21.30 E
Akhḍar, Wādī al- 24 Gh 28.35N 36.35 E
Akhelóös 15 Ej 38.18N 21.10 E
Akhisar 23 Cb 38.55N 27.51 E
Akhmīm 33 Fd 26.34N 31.44 E
Akhtarin 24 Gd 36.31N 37.20 E
Aki 29 Ce 33.30N 133.53 E
Akiaki Atoll 61 Nc 18.30S 139.12W
Akiéni 36 Bc 1.11S 13.53 E
Akimiski 38 Kd 53.00N 81.20W
Akimovka 16 If 46.42N 35.09 E
Aki-Nada 29 Cd 34.05N 132.40 E
Åkirkeby 8 Fi 55.04N 14.56 E
Akita 22 Qf 39.43N 140.07 E
Akita Ken [2] 28 Pe 39.45N 140.20 E
Akjoujt 31 Fg 19.44N 14.22W
Akka 32 Fd 29.25N 8.15W
Akkanburluk 17 Mj 52.46N 66.35 E
'Akko 23 Ec 32.55N 35.05 E
Akkol 18 Hc 43.25N 70.47 E
Akköy 24 Bd 37.29N 27.15 E
Akkystau 19 Ff 47.17N 51.03 E
Aklavik 42 Dc 68.14N 135.02W
Aklé Mseiguilé 34 Eb 16.20N 4.45W
Akmenė/Akmene 8 Jh 56.14N 22.43 E
Akmene/Akmenė 8 Jh 56.14N 22.43 E
Akmenrags/Akmeņrags 8 Ih 56.54N 20.55 E
Akmeņrags/Akmenrags 8 Ih 56.54N 20.55 E
Akmeqit 27 Cd 37.05N 76.55 E
Akniste 8 Kh 56.10N 25.54 E
Akō 29 Dd 34.45N 134.23 E
Akobo 30 Kh 7.48N 33.03 E
Akobo 31 Kh 7.47N 33.01 E
Akola 22 Jg 20.44N 77.00 E
Akonolinga 34 He 3.46N 12.15 E
Akosombo Dam 34 Fd 6.16N 0.03 E
Akpatok 42 Kd 60.24N 68.05W
Akqi 27 Cc 40.50N 78.01 E
Ákra Ámbelos 15 Gj 39.56N 23.56 E
Ákra Kambanós 15 Hl 37.59N 24.45 E
Akranes 7a Ab 64.19N 22.06W
Ákra Spathi 15 Gl 37.27N 23.31 E
Åkrehamn 7 Ag 59.16N 5.11 E
Akritas, Ákra-=Akritas, Cape- (EN) 15 Em 36.43N 21.53 E
Akritas Cape- (EN) = Akritas, Ákra- 15 Em 36.43N 21.53 E
Akron [Co.-U.S.] 45 Ef 40.10N 103.13W
Akron [Oh.-U.S.] 43 Kc 41.04N 81.31W
Akrotiri 24 Ee 34.36N 32.57 E
Akša 20 Gf 50.17N 113.17 E
Aksaj 16 Oh 43.32N 46.55 E
Aksaj [Kaz.-U.S.S.R.] 16 Fe 51.13N 53.01 E
Aksaj [R.S.F.S.R.] 16 Kf 47.15N 39.52 E
Aksakal 15 Li 40.09N 28.07 E
Aksakovo 17 Gi 54.02N 54.09 E
Aksaray 23 Db 38.23N 34.03 E
Aksay 27 Fd 39.28N 94.15 E
Akşehir 23 Db 38.21N 31.25 E
Akşehir Gölü 24 Dc 38.30N 31.28 E
Akseki 24 Dd 37.02N 31.48 E
Aksenovo-Zilovskoje 20 Gf 53.00N 117.35 E
'Aks-e Rostam 24 Ph 28.23N 54.52 E
Aksoran, Gora 19 Hf 48.25N 75.30 E
Akstafa 16 Ni 41.13N 45.27 E
Akstafa 16 Ni 41.06N 45.28 E
Aksu [China] 22 Ke 41.09N 80.15 E
Aksu [Kaz.-U.S.S.R.] 19 He 52.28N 71.59 E
Aksu [Kaz.-U.S.S.R.] 18 Lb 45.34N 79.30 E
Aksu [Kaz.-U.S.S.R.] 19 Hf 46.20N 78.15 E
Aksu [Tur.] 15 Ll 37.56N 28.56 E
Aksu [Tur.] 24 Dd 36.51N 30.54 E
Aksuat 19 If 47.48N 82.50 E
Aksubajevo 7 Mi 54.52N 50.50 E
Aksu He 21 Ke 40.28N 80.52 E
Aksum 35 Fc 14.07N 38.44 E
Ak-Šyjrak 18 Ld 41.49N 78.44 E
Aktag 27 Dd 36.45N 84.40 E
Aktaš [R.S.F.S.R.] 20 Df 50.18N 87.44 E
Aktaš [Uzb.-U.S.S.R.] 19 Gh 39.55N 65.53 E
Aktau 19 He 50.16N 73.07 E
Aktau, Gora- 19 Gg 41.45N 64.30 E
Aktjubinsk 6 Le 50.17N 57.10 E
Aktjubinskaja Oblast [3] 19 Ff 48.00N 58.00 E
Ak-Tjuz 18 Kc 42.50N 76.07 E
Akto 27 Cd 39.05N 76.02 E
Aktogaj 19 Hf 47.01N 79.40 E
Akula 36 Db 2.22N 20.11 E
Akun 40a Eb 54.12N 165.35W
Akune 28 Kh 32.01N 130.11 E
Akure 34 Gd 7.15N 5.12 E
Akureyri 6 Eb 65.40N 18.06W
Akuseki-Jima 28 Jj 29.28N 129.33 E
Akutan 40a Eb 54.10N 165.55W
Akutan 40a Eb 54.08N 165.46W
Akyab→Sittwe 22 Lg 20.09N 92.54 E
Akyazı 24 Db 40.41N 30.37 E
Akžajkyn, Ozero- 18 Fb 44.55N 67.45 E
Akzāl 19 If 49.13N 81.30 E
Ål 8 Cd 60.38N 8.34 E
Alà, Monti di- 14 Dj 40.35N 9.16 E
Alabama 38 Kf 31.08N 87.57W
Alabama [2] 43 Je 32.50N 87.30W
Al'Abbāsīyah 35 Ec 12.10N 31.18 E
Alaca 24 Fb 40.10N 34.51 E
Alaçam Dağları 15 Lj 39.20N 28.32 E
Alaçam 24 Fb 41.37N 35.37 E
Alaçati 15 Jk 38.16N 26.23 E
Aladağ 24 Jc 43.35N 39.20 E
Ala Dağ [Tur.] 24 Jb 40.11N 42.49 E
Ala Dağ [Tur.] 24 Ed 37.58N 32.04 E
Alādāgh, Kūh-e- 24 Qd 37.13N 57.30 E
Ala Dağları 24 Fd 37.55N 35.13 E
Aladža 16 Rj 39.21N 53.12 E
Aladža Manastir 15 Lf 43.17N 28.01 E
Alagir 16 Nh 43.01N 44.12 E
Alagna Valsesia 14 Be 45.51N 7.56 E
Alagnon 11 Ji 45.27N 3.19 E
Alagoas [2] 54 Ke 9.30S 36.30W
Alagoinhas 53 Mg 12.07S 38.26W
Alagón 13 Kc 41.46N 1.07W
Alagón 13 Fe 39.44N 6.53W
Ala Gou 27 Ec 42.42N 89.12 E
Alahanpanjang 26 Dg 1.05S 100.47 E
Alahärmä 7 Fe 63.14N 22.51 E
Al Aḥmadī 24 Mh 29.05N 48.04 E
Alaid, Vulkan 20 Kf 50.50N 155.33 E
Alajärvi 7 Fe 63.00N 23.49 E
Alajku 19 Hg 40.18N 74.29 E
Alajski Hrebet 21 Jf 39.45N 72.30 E
Alajuela [3] 49 Eh 10.30N 84.30W
Alajuela 47 Hf 10.01N 84.13W
Alajuela, Lago- 49 Hi 9.05N 79.24W
Alakol, Ozero- 21 Ke 46.05N 81.50 E
Alakurtti 7 Hc 66.59N 30.20 E
Alalakeiki Channel 65a Ec 20.35N 156.30W
Al 'Alamayn 31 Je 30.49N 28.57 E
Alalau, Rio- 54 Fd 0.30S 61.10W
Al Amādīyah 24 Jd 37.06N 43.29 E
Alamagan Island 57 Fc 17.36N 145.50 E
Al 'Amārah 23 Gc 31.50N 47.09 E
'Alam ar Rūm, Ra's- 24 Bg 31.22N 27.21 E
Alāmarvdasht 24 Oi 27.52N 52.34 E
Alamashindo 35 Ge 4.51N 42.04 E
Alamata 35 Fc 12.25N 39.37 E
Alameda 45 Ci 35.11N 106.37W
Alaminos 26 Gc 16.10N 119.59 E
Al 'Āmirīyah 24 Cg 31.01N 29.48 E
Alamito Creek 45 Dl 29.31N 104.17W
Alamitos, Sierra de los- 48 Hd 26.20N 102.15W
'Alāmo 35 Ge 4.23N 43.09 E
Alamo 46 Hh 37.22N 115.10W
Alamogordo 43 Fe 32.54N 105.57W
Alamos 47 Cc 27.01N 108.56W
Alamos, Sierra- 48 Gc 28.25N 105.00W
Alamosa 43 Fd 37.28N 105.52W
Al Anbār [3] 24 If 34.00N 42.00 E
Åland/Ahvenanmaa [2] 7 Ef 60.15N 20.00 E
Åland/Ahvenanmaa=Aland Islands (EN) 5 Hc 60.15N 20.00 E
Aland Islands (EN)= Ahvenanmaa/Åland 5 Hc 60.15N 20.00 E
Aland Islands (EN)=Åland/ Ahvenanmaa 5 Hc 60.15N 20.00 E
Ålandsbro 8 Gb 62.40N 17.50 E
Ålandshav 8 Hd 60.00N 19.30 E
Alange 13 Ff 38.47N 6.15W
Alanje 49 Fi 8.24N 82.33W
Alanya 23 Db 36.33N 32.01 E
Alaotra, Lac- 37 Hc 17.30S 48.30 E
Alapaha River 44 Fj 30.26N 83.06W
Alapajevsk 19 Gd 57.52N 61.42 E
Alaplı 24 Db 41.08N 31.25 E
Al 'Aqabah=Aqaba (EN) 23 Dd 29.31N 35.00 E
Al 'Aqabah aş Şaghīrah 24 Ej 24.14N 32.53 E
Al 'Arabīyah As-Su'ūdīyah= Saudi Arabia (EN) [1] 22 Gg 25.00N 45.00 E
Alarcón, Embalse de- 13 Je 39.45N 2.20W
Al 'Arish 33 Fc 31.08N 33.48 E
Al 'Armah 24 Lj 25.30N 46.30 E
Al Arṭāwīyah 24 Ki 26.30N 45.20 E
Alas, Selat- 26 Gh 8.40S 116.40 E
Al 'Aşab 24 Pk 23.20N 54.10 E
Alaşehir 24 Cc 38.21N 28.32 E
Al Ashkharah 23 Ie 21.47N 59.30 E
Al 'Āshūrīyah 24 Jg 31.02N 43.05 E
Alaska [2] 40 Ic 65.00N 153.00W
Alaska 38 Dc 65.00N 153.00W
Alaska, Gulf of- 38 Ed 58.00N 146.00W
Alaska Peninsula 38 Dd 57.00N 158.00W
Alaska Range 38 Ec 62.30N 150.00W
Alassio 14 Cf 44.00N 8.10 E
Alastaro 8 Jd 60.57N 22.51 E
Alat 18 De 39.26N 63.48 E
Alataw Shan 27 Cb 45.00N 80.00 E
Alataw Shankou= Dzungarian Gate (EN) 21 Ke 45.25N 82.25 E
Al 'Athāmīn 24 Jg 30.35N 43.40 E
Alatri 14 Hi 41.43N 13.21 E
Al 'Aṭrun 31 Jg 18.11N 26.36 E
Alatyr 7 Li 54.52N 46.36 E
Alatyr 19 Ee 54.50N 46.36 E
Álava [3] 13 Jb 42.50N 2.45W
Alava, Cape- 46 Cb 48.10N 124.43W
Alaverdi 19 Eg 41.08N 44.37 E
Alavijeh 24 Nf 33.03N 51.05 E
Alavo/Alavus 7 Fe 62.35N 23.37 E
Alavus/Alavo 7 Fe 62.35N 23.37 E
Al 'Awāliq 23 Gg 14.15N 46.30 E
Al 'Awāriq 35 Ha 20.25N 48.40 E
Al 'Awsajīyah 24 Ki 26.04N 44.08 E
'Ālayh 24 Ff 33.48N 35.36 E
Al 'Ayn [Sau.Ar.] 24 Hj 25.04N 38.06 E
Al 'Ayn [U.A.E.] 24 Pj 24.13N 55.45 E
Alayor 13 Qe 39.56N 4.08 E
Al 'Ayyāţ 24 Dh 29.37N 31.15 E
Al A'ẓamīyah 24 Kf 33.23N 44.22 E
Alazani 16 Oi 41.03N 46.40 E
Alazeja 20 Kb 70.55N 153.40 E
Al'Azīzīyah 33 Bc 32.32N 13.01 E
Alazores, Puerto de los- 13 Hg 37.05N 4.15W
Alb [Eur.] 10 Ei 47.35N 8.08 E
Alb [F.R.G.] 12 Ke 49.04N 8.20 E
Alba [2] 15 Gc 46.08N 23.30 E
Alba 14 Cf 44.42N 8.02 E
Alba Adriatica 14 Hh 42.50N 13.56 E
Al Bāb 24 Gd 36.22N 37.31 E
Albac 15 Fc 46.27N 22.58 E
Albacete 6 Fh 38.59N 1.51W
Albacete [3] 13 Kf 38.50N 2.00W
Al Badārī 33 Fd 26.59N 31.25 E
Alba de Tormes 13 Gd 40.49N 5.31W
Al Badi 33 Ie 22.02N 46.34 E
Al Bādi 24 Ie 35.56N 41.32 E
Albæk 8 Dg 57.36N 10.25 E
Albæk Bugt 8 Dg 57.35N 10.30 E
Al Bahrah 24 Lh 29.40N 47.52 E
Al Baḥr al Aḥmar [3] 35 Fb 19.50N 35.30 E
Al Baḥrayn 21 Hg 26.00N 50.30 E

Index Symbols

[1] Independent Nation
[2] State, Region
[3] District, County
[4] Municipality
[5] Colony, Dependency
Continent
Physical Region
Historical or Cultural Region
Mount, Mountain
Volcano
Hill
Mountains, Mountain Range
Hills, Escarpment
Plateau, Upland
Pass, Gap
Plain, Lowland
Delta
Salt Flat
Valley, Canyon
Crater, Cave
Karst Features
Depression
Polder
Desert, Dunes
Forest, Woods
Heath, Steppe
Oasis
Cape, Point
Coast, Beach
Cliff
Peninsula
Isthmus
Sandbank
Island
Atoll
Rock, Reef
Islands, Archipelago
Rocks, Reefs
Coral Reef
Well, Spring
Geyser
River, Stream
Waterfall Rapids
River Mouth, Estuary
Lake
Salt Lake
Intermittent Lake
Reservoir
Swamp, Pond
Canal
Glacier
Ice Shelf, Pack Ice
Ocean
Sea
Gulf, Bay
Strait, Fjord
Lagoon
Bank
Seamount
Tablemount
Ridge
Shelf
Basin
Escarpment, Sea Scarp
Fracture
Trench, Abyss
National Park, Reserve
Point of Interest
Recreation Site
Cave, Cavern
Historic Site
Ruins
Wall, Walls
Church, Abbey
Temple
Scientific Station
Airport
Port
Lighthouse
Mine
Tunnel
Dam, Bridge

Al Baḩrayn=Bahrain (EN) [1] 22 Hg 26.00N 50.29 E
Albaida 13 Lf 38.51N 0.31W
Alba Iulia 15 Gc 46.04N 23.35 E
Albalate del Arzobispo 13 Lc 41.07N 0.31W
Al Balyanā 33 Fd 26.14N 32.00 E
Alban 11 Ik 43.54N 2.28 E
Albanel, Lac- 42 Kf 51.05N 73.05W
Albani, Colli- 14 Gi 41.45N 12.45 E
Albania (EN)=Shqipëria [1] 6 Hg 41.00N 20.00 E
Albano, Lago- 14 Gi 41.45N 12.40 E
Albano Laziale 14 Gi 41.44N 12.39 E
Albany 38 Kd 52.17N 81.31W
Albany [Austl.] 58 Ch 35.02S 117.53 E
Albany [Ga.-U.S.] 43 Ke 31.35N 84.10W
Albany [Ky.-U.S.] 44 Eg 36.42N 85.08W
Albany [N.Y.-U.S.] 39 Le 42.39N 73.45W
Albany [Or.-U.S.] 43 Cc 44.38N 123.06W
Alba Posse 55 Eh 27.33S 54.42W
Albarche 13 He 39.58N 4.46W
Albardón 56 Gd 31.26S 68.32W
Albarracín 13 Kd 40.25N 1.26W
Albarracín, Sierra de- 13 Kd 40.30N 1.30W
Al Başalīyah Qiblī 24 Ej 25.06N 32.47 E
Al Başrah [3] 24 Lg 30.30N 47.27 E
Al Başrah=Basra (EN) 22 Gf 30.30N 47.47 E
Al Baţḩā' 24 Kg 31.07N 45.54 E
Al Bāţin 24 Lh 29.00N 46.35 E
Al Bāţinah 21 Hg 23.45N 57.20 E
Albatross Bank (EN) 40 Ie 56.10N 152.20W
Albatross Bay 59 Ib 12.45S 141.43 E
Albatross Plateau (EN) 3 Mi 10.00N 103.00W
Albatross Point 62 Fc 38.07S 174.40 E
Al Batrūn 24 Fe 34.15N 35.39 E
Al Bawīţī 33 Ed 28.21N 28.52 E
Al Bayāḑ 21 Gg 22.00N 47.00 E
Al Bayḑā' [3] 33 Dc 32.00N 21.30 E
Al Bayḑā' 33 Cd 28.21N 18.58 E
Al Bayḑā' 31 Je 32.46N 21.43 E
Al Bayḑā' 33 Ig 13.58N 45.35 E
Albegna 14 Fh 42.30N 11.11 E
Albemarle 44 Gh 35.21N 80.12W
Albemarle Sound 43 Ld 36.03N 76.12W
Albenga 14 Cf 44.03N 8.13 E
Alberdi 56 Ic 26.10S 58.09W
Albères, Chaîne des- 11 Il 42.28N 2.56 E
Albères, Montes-/Les Alberes 11 Il 42.28N 2.56 E
Albergaria-a-Velha 13 Dd 40.42N 8.29W
Alberique 13 Le 39.07N 0.31W
Alberobello 14 Lj 40.47N 17.16 E
Albert 11 Id 50.00N 2.39 E
Albert, Canal-/Albert Kanaal =Albert Canal (EN) 11 Ld 50.39N 5.37 E
Albert, Lake- [Afr.] 30 Kh 1.40N 31.00 E
Albert, Lake- [Or.-U.S.] 46 Ee 42.38N 120.13W
Albert, Lake- (EN)=Mobuto Sese Seko, Lac- 30 Kh 1.40N 31.00 E
Alberta [3] 42 Gf 55.00N 115.00W
Albert Canal (EN)=Albert, Canal-/Albert Kanaal 11 Ld 50.39N 5.37 E
Albert Canal (EN)=Albert Kanaal/Albert, Canal- 11 Ld 50.39N 5.37 E
Albert Edward, Mount- 59 Ja 8.23S 147.27 E
Albert Edward Bay 42 Hc 69.35N 103.10W
Alberti 56 He 35.02S 60.16W
Albertirsa 10 Pi 47.15N 19.37 E
Albert Kanaal/Albert, Canal- =Albert Canal (EN) 11 Ld 50.39N 5.37 E
Albert Lea 43 Ic 43.39N 93.22W
Albert Nile 30 Kh 3.36N 32.02 E
Albertville [Al.-U.S.] 44 Dh 34.16N 86.12W
Albertville [Fr.] 11 Mi 45.41N 6.23 E
Albestroff 12 If 48.56N 6.51 E
Albi 11 Ik 43.56N 2.09 E
Albia 45 Jf 41.02N 92.48W
Al Bid' 24 Fh 28.28N 35.01 E
Albina 54 Hb 5.30N 54.03W
Albina, Ponta- 30 Ij 15.51S 11.44 E
Albino 14 De 45.46N 9.47 E
Albion [Mi.-U.S.] 44 Ed 42.15N 84.45W
Albion [Nb.-U.S.] 45 Hf 41.42N 98.00W
Albion [N.Y.-U.S.] 44 Hd 43.15N 78.12W
Al Biqa' 24 Ge 34.10N 36.10 E
Al Bi'r 23 Ed 28.51N 36.15 E
Al Bi'r al Jadīd 23 Ed 26.01N 38.29 E
Al Birk 23 Ff 18.13N 41.33 E
Albis 14 Cc 47.20N 8.30 E
Albo, Monte- 14 Dj 40.32N 9.35 E
Albocàcer/Albocasser 13 Md 40.21N 0.02 E
Albocasser/Albocàcer 13 Md 40.21N 0.02 E
Alborán, Isla de- 5 Fh 35.58N 3.02W
Alboran Basin (EN) 13 Ii 36.00N 4.00W
Ålborg 6 Gd 57.03N 9.56 E
Ålborg Bugt 7 Ch 56.45N 10.30 E
Alborz, Reshteh-ye Kūhhā-ye-=Elburz Mountains (EN) 21 Hf 36.00N 53.00 E
Albox 13 Jg 37.23N 2.08W
Albret, Pays d'- 11 Fj 44.10N 0.20W
Ālbū 'Alī 24 Je 34.49N 43.35 E
Albufeira 13 Dg 37.05N 8.15W
Albū Gharz, Sabkhat- 24 Ie 34.45N 41.15 E
Al Buheyrat [3] 35 Dd 7.00N 29.30 E
Al Bumbah 33 Dc 32.13N 23.00 E
Albuñol 13 Ih 36.47N 3.12W
Albuquerque [Braz.] 55 Dd 19.23S 57.26W
Albuquerque [N.M.-U.S.] 39 If 35.05N 106.40W
Albuquerque, Cayos de- 47 Hf 12.10N 81.50W
Al Burayj 24 Ge 34.15N 36.46 E
Al Buraymī 23 Ie 24.15N 55.45 E
Al Burmah 32 Ic 31.45N 9.02 E
Alburquerque 13 Fe 39.13N 7.00W
Albury [Austl.] 58 Fh 36.05S 146.55 E
Albury [N.Z.] 62 Df 44.14S 170.53 E
Al Buţanah 30 Kg 15.00N 35.00 E
Al Buţayn 24 Kj 25.52N 45.50 E
Alby 8 Fb 62.30N 15.28 E
Alcácer do Sal 13 Df 38.22N 8.30W
Alcaçovar 13 Df 38.25N 8.13W
Alcalá de Chivert 13 Md 40.18N 0.14 E
Alcalá de Guadaira 13 Gg 37.20N 5.50W
Alcalá de Henares 13 Id 40.29N 3.22W
Alcalá del Júcar 13 Ke 39.12N 1.26W
Alcalá de los Gazules 13 Gh 36.28N 5.44W
Alcalá del Río 13 Gg 37.31N 5.59W
Alcalá la Real 13 Ig 37.28N 3.56W
Alcamo 14 Gm 37.59N 12.58 E
Alcanadre 13 Mc 41.37N 0.12 E
Alcañices 13 Fc 41.42N 6.21W
Alcañiz 13 Lc 41.03N 0.08W
Alcántara 13 Fe 39.43N 6.53W
Alcântara 54 Jd 2.24S 44.24W
Alcantara 14 Jm 37.49N 15.16 E
Alcántara, Embalse de- 13 Fe 39.45N 6.48W
Alcantarilla 13 Kg 37.58N 1.13W
Alcaraz 13 Jf 38.40N 2.29W
Alcaraz, Sierra de- 13 Jf 38.35N 2.25W
Alcaudete 13 Hg 37.36N 4.05W
Alcázar de San Juan 13 Ie 39.24N 3.12W
Alcester 63a Ac 9.33S 152.25 E
Alcira/Alzira 13 Le 39.09N 0.26W
Alcobaça [Braz.] 54 Kg 17.30S 39.13W
Alcobaça [Port.] 13 De 39.33N 8.59W
Alcobendas 13 Id 40.32N 3.38W
Alcoi/Alcoy 13 Lf 38.42N 0.28W
Alcolea del Pinar 13 Jc 41.02N 2.28W
Alcorta 55 Bk 33.32S 61.07W
Alcoutim 13 Eg 37.28N 7.28W
Alcova 46 Le 42.37N 106.36W
Alcoy/Alcoi 13 Lf 38.42N 0.28W
Alcubierre, Sierra de- 13 Lc 41.44N 0.29W
Alcudia 13 Pe 39.52N 3.07 E
Alcúdia, Badia d'-/Alcudia, Bahia de- 13 Pe 39.48N 3.13 E
Alcudia, Bahia de-/Alcúdia, Badia d'- 13 Pe 39.48N 3.13 E
Alcudia, Sierra de- 13 Hf 38.35N 4.35W
Aldabra Group 37b Ab 9.25S 46.22 E
Aldabra Islands 30 Li 9.25S 46.22 E
Aldama [Mex.] 48 Jf 22.55N 98.04W
Aldama [Mex.] 47 Cc 28.51N 105.54W
Aldan 22 Od 58.37N 125.24 E
Aldan [R.S.F.S.R.] 20 Hd 63.20N 129.25 E
Aldan [U.S.S.R.] 21 Oc 63.28N 129.35 E
Aldan Plateau (EN)=Aldanskoje Nagorje 21 Od 57.30N 127.30 E
Aldanskoje Nagorje=Aldan Plateau (EN) 21 Od 57.30N 127.30 E
Aldarhan 27 Gb 47.42N 96.36 E
Alde 12 Db 52.10N 1.32 E
Aldeburgh 9 Oi 52.09N 1.35 E
Aldeia 55 Ed 18.12S 55.10W
Aldeia, Serra da- 55 Ic 17.00S 46.50W
Alderney 9 Kl 49.43N 2.12W
Aldershot 12 Bc 51.15N 0.46W
Alderson 46 Ja 50.18N 111.26W
Aledo 45 Kf 41.12N 90.45W
Aleg 31 Fg 17.03N 13.53W
Alegranza 32 Ed 29.23N 13.30W
Alegre 54 Jh 20.46S 41.32W
Alegre, Rio- 55 Cb 15.14S 59.58W
Alegrete 56 Ic 29.46S 55.46W
Alej 20 Df 52.50N 83.25 E
Alejandra 55 Ci 29.54S 59.50W
Alejandro Selkirk, Isla- 52 Hi 33.45S 80.46W
Alejsk 20 Df 52.28N 82.45 E
Aleksandrija 16 He 48.40N 33.07 E
Aleksandrov 19 Dd 56.25N 38.42 E
Aleksandrov Gaj 19 Ee 50.08N 48.32 E
Aleksandrovka 16 He 48.59N 32.13 E
Aleksandrovsk 17 Hg 59.10N 57.35 E
Aleksandrovskoje 16 Mg 44.39N 43.00 E
Aleksandrovsk-Sahalinsk 22 Qd 50.54N 142.10 E
Aleksandrów Kujawski 10 Od 52.52N 18.42 E
Aleksandrów Łódzki 10 Pe 51.49N 19.19 E
Aleksandry, Zemlja- 21 Ga 80.45N 46.00 E
Aleksejevka [Kaz.-U.S.S.R.] 19 If 48.26N 85.40 E
Aleksejevka [Kaz.-U.S.S.R.] 19 He 51.58N 70.59 E
Aleksejevka [Kaz.-U.S.S.R.] 17 Nj 53.31N 69.28 E
Aleksejevka [R.S.F.S.R.] 19 De 50.39N 38.42 E
Aleksejevsk 20 Fe 57.50N 108.23 E
Aleksejevskoje 7 Mi 55.19N 50.03 E
Aleksin 16 Jb 54.31N 37.07 E
Aleksinac 15 Ef 43.32N 21.43 E
Alem 56 Ic 27.31S 55.15W
Ålem 7 Dh 56.57N 16.23 E
Alem Maya 35 Gd 9.27N 41.58 E
Ålen 8 Db 62.51N 11.17 E
Alençon 11 Gf 48.26N 0.05 E
Alenquer 54 Hd 1.56S 54.46W
Alenuihaha Channel 60 Oc 20.26N 156.00W
Alépé 34 Ed 5.30N 3.39W
Aleppo (EN)=Ḩalab 22 Ff 36.12N 37.10 E
Aléria 11a Ba 42.06N 9.31 E
Aléria, Plaine d'- 11a Ba 42.05N 9.30 E
Alert 39 Ma 82.30N 62.00W
Alert Bay 46 Ba 50.35N 126.55W
Alès 11 Kj 44.08N 4.05 E
Aleşd 15 Fb 47.04N 22.25 E
Alessandria 14 Cf 44.54N 8.37 E
Ålestrup 8 Ch 56.42N 9.30 E
Ålesund 6 Gc 62.28N 6.09 E
Aleutian Basin (EN) 38 Ad 57.00N 177.00 E
Aleutian Islands 38 Bd 52.00N 176.00W
Aleutian Range 38 Dd 59.00N 155.00W
Aleutian Trench (EN) 3 Je 51.00N 179.00 E
Alexander, Cape- 60 Fi 6.35S 156.30 E
Alexander, Kap- 41 Ec 78.10N 72.45W
Alexander Archipelago 38 Fd 56.30N 134.00W
Alexanderbaai 37 Be 28.40S 16.30 E
Alexander City 43 Je 32.56N 85.57W
Alexander Island 66 Qe 71.00S 70.00W
Alexandra 61 Ci 45.15S 169.24 E
Alexandra Fiord 42 Ka 79.17N 75.00W
Alexandretta (EN)=İskenderun 22 Ff 36.37N 36.07 E
Alexandretta, Gulf of- (EN) =İskenderun Körfezi 23 Eb 36.30N 35.40 E
Alexándria 15 Fi 40.38N 22.27 E
Alexandria [Austl.] 59 Hc 19.05S 136.40 E
Alexandria [La.-U.S.] 39 Jf 31.18N 92.27W
Alexandria [Mn.-U.S.] 43 Hb 45.53N 95.22W
Alexandria [Rom.] 15 If 43.59N 25.20 E
Alexandria [S.Afr.] 37 Df 33.39S 26.24 E
Alexandria [Va.-U.S.] 44 If 38.49N 77.06W
Alexandria (EN)=Al Iskandarīyah [Eg.] 31 Je 31.12N 29.54 E
Alexandria Bay 44 Jc 44.20N 75.55W
Alexandrina, Lake- 59 Hg 35.25S 139.10 E
Alexandrita 54 Hg 19.42S 50.27W
Alexandroúpolis 6 Ig 40.51N 25.52 E
'Aleyak, Godār-e- 24 Qd 36.30N 57.45 E
Alf 10 Df 50.03N 7.07 E
Alfabia, Sierra de- 13 Oe 39.45N 2.48 E
Alfambra 13 Kd 40.21N 1.07W
Al Fardah 35 Hc 14.51N 48.26 E
Alfaro 13 Kb 42.11N 1.45W
Al Fāshir 31 Jg 13.38N 25.21 E
Al Fashn 33 Fd 28.49N 30.54 E
Alfatar 15 Kf 43.57N 27.17 E
Al Fathah 24 Je 35.04N 43.34 E
Al Fāw 23 Gd 29.58N 48.29 E
Al Fawwārah 24 Ji 26.03N 43.05 E
Al Fayyūm 31 Kf 29.19N 30.50 E
Alfbach 12 Jd 50.03N 7.08 E
Alfeld 10 Fe 51.59N 9.50 E
Alfenas 54 Ih 21.26S 45.57W
Al Fifi 35 Dc 10.03N 25.01 E
Alfiós 15 El 37.37N 21.27 E
Alföld 5 If 47.15N 20.25 E
Alfonsine 14 Gf 44.30N 12.03 E
Alford 12 Ca 53.15N 0.11 E
Ålfotbreen 8 Ac 61.45N 5.40 E
Alfreton 12 Aa 53.06N 1.23W
Alfta 7 Df 61.21N 16.05 E
Al Fuḩayḩīl 23 Gd 29.05N 48.08 E
Al Fuhūd 24 Lg 30.58N 46.43 E
Al Fujayrah 23 Id 25.06N 56.21 E
Al Fūlah 35 Dc 11.48N 28.24 E
Al Fuqahā' 33 Cd 27.50N 16.21 E
Al Furāt=Euphrates (EN) 21 Gf 31.00N 47.25 E
Al Fuwayriţ 24 Ni 26.02N 51.22 E
Alga 19 Ff 49.55N 57.20 E
Algador 13 Ie 39.55N 3.53W
Al Gārah 24 Ih 29.52N 40.15 E
Algarås 8 Ff 58.48N 14.14 E
Ålgård 8 Af 58.46N 5.51 E
Algarrobo 49 Jh 10.12N 74.04W
Algarve 13 Dg 37.10N 8.15W
Algarve 5 Fh 37.10N 8.15W
Algeciras 6 Fh 36.08N 5.30W
Algeciras, Bahía de- 13 Gh 36.09N 5.25W
Algena 35 Fb 17.20N 38.34 E
Algeria (EN)=Al Jazā'ir [1] 31 Hf 28.00N 3.00 E
Algerian Basin (EN) 5 Gh 39.00N 5.00 E
Al Gharaq as Sulţānī 24 Dh 29.08N 30.42 E
Al Gharbī 32 Jc 34.40N 11.13 E
Al Ghāţ 24 Ki 26.00N 45.03 E
Al Ghaydah 23 Hf 16.12N 52.15 E
Alghero 14 Cj 40.33N 8.19 E
Alghero, Rada d'- 14 Cj 40.35N 8.20 E
Älghult 8 Fg 57.01N 15.34 E
Al Ghurāb 24 Dj 25.20N 30.20 E
Al Ghurayfah 24 Qk 23.59N 56.29 E
Al Ghurdaqah 33 Fd 27.14N 33.50 E
Algiers (EN)=Al Jazā'ir 31 He 36.47N 3.03 E
Algiers (EN)=Al Jazā'ir [3] 32 Hb 36.35N 3.00 E
Algoa Bay 30 Jl 33.50S 25.50 E
Algodoeiro, Serra do- 35 Jc 16.30S 44.45W
Algoma 45 Md 44.36N 87.27W
Algoma Uplands 44 Fb 47.00N 83.35W
Algona 45 Ie 43.04N 94.14W
Algonquin Park 44 Hc 45.27N 78.26W
Algrange 12 Ie 49.21N 6.03 E
Al Ḩabakah 24 Jh 29.51N 42.16 E
Al Ḩadd 23 Ie 22.29N 59.58 E
Al Ḩadīdah 23 Ia 21.31N 50.28 E
Al Ḩadīthah 23 Fc 34.07N 42.23 E
Al Ḩadīthah 24 Gg 31.28N 37.08 E
Al Ḩaḑr 24 Je 35.35N 42.44 E
Al Haffah 24 Ge 35.35N 36.02 E
Al Ḩahjarah 23 Fc 30.25N 44.30 E
Al Ḩā'ir 24 Lj 24.23N 46.50 E
Al Ḩajar 35 Hb 16.08N 47.50 E
Al Hajar 23 Ie 23.15N 57.30 E
Al Halfāyah 24 Lg 31.49N 47.26 E
Alhama 13 Kb 42.11N 1.45W
Al Ḩamād 21 Ff 32.00N 39.30 E
Alhama de Granada 13 Ih 37.00N 3.59W
Alhama de Murcia 13 Kg 37.51N 1.25W
Alhamilla, Sierra- 13 Jh 36.58N 2.20W
Al Ḩammāh 32 Ic 33.54N 9.48 E
Al Ḩammām [Eg.] 24 Cg 30.50N 29.23 E
Al Ḩammām [Iraq] 24 Kg 31.08N 44.04 E
Al Ḩamrā 24 Pj 25.42N 55.47 E
Al Hanīyah 24 Kh 29.10N 45.50 E
Al Ḩarrah 24 Ch 28.20N 29.07 E
Al Ḩarrah 24 Hg 31.00N 38.40 E
Al Harūj al Aswad 30 If 27.00N 17.10 E
Al Ḩasā 24 Fg 30.49N 35.59 E
Al Hasā' 21 Gg 26.35N 48.10 E
Al Ḩasakah 23 Fb 36.29N 40.45 E
Al Ḩasan 24 Je 34.39N 43.43 E
Al Ḩasānī 24 Gj 24.58N 37.05 E
Alhaurín el Grande 13 Hh 36.38N 4.41W
Al Hawāmidīyah 24 Dh 29.54N 31.15 E
Al Ḩawātah 35 Ec 13.25N 34.38 E
Al Ḩawjā' 24 Hh 28.59N 38.34 E
Al Ḩawrah 35 Hc 13.49N 47.35 E
Al Ḩayy 23 Gc 32.10N 46.03 E
Al Ḩayz 33 Ed 28.02N 28.39 E
Al Hibāk 23 He 20.20N 53.10 E
Al Ḩijāz 21 Fg 24.30N 38.30 E
Al Ḩillah 33 Ie 23.50N 46.51 E
Al Ḩillah 23 Fc 32.29N 44.25 E
Al Ḩinākīyah 23 Fe 24.51N 40.31 E
Al Hindīyah 24 Kf 32.32N 44.13 E
Al Ḩinnāh 24 Mi 26.56N 48.45 E
Al Hirmil 24 Ge 34.23N 36.23 E
Al Hoceima 32 Gb 35.15N 3.55W
Al Hoceima [3] 32 Gb 35.00N 4.15W
Alhucemas, Peñón de- 13 Ii 35.13N 3.53W
Al Ḩudaydah 22 Gh 14.48N 42.57 E
Al Ḩufrah 33 Cd 29.30N 17.55 E
Al Ḩufrah 23 Ed 28.49N 38.15 E
Al Hufūf 22 Gg 25.22N 49.34 E
Al Hūj 24 Hh 29.00N 38.25 E
Al Ḩunayy 24 Mj 24.48N 48.45 E
Al Ḩuşayḩişah 35 Ec 14.44N 33.18 E
Al Ḩuwaimī 23 Fg 13.58N 47.40 E
Al Ḩuwayyiţ 24 Ij 25.36N 40.23 E
Al Ḩyyānīyah 24 Jh 28.42N 42.18 E
'Alīābād [Iran] 23 Id 28.37N 55.51 E
'Alīābād [Iran] 24 Le 35.04N 46.58 E
'Alīābād [Iran] 24 Nd 36.37N 51.33 E
Aliābād 24 Pd 36.56N 54.50 E
Alīābād, Kūh-e- 23 Hc 34.13N 50.46 E
Aliaga 13 Ld 40.40N 0.42W
Aliağa 24 Bc 38.48N 26.59 E
Aliákmon 15 Fi 40.30N 22.40 E
'Alī al Gharbī 24 Lf 32.27N 46.41 E
'Alī ash Sharqī 24 Lf 32.07N 46.44 E
Ali-Bajramly 19 Eh 39.55N 48.57 E
Alibej, Ozero- 15 Nd 45.50N 30.00 E
Alibey Adasi 15 Jj 39.20N 26.38 E
Alibo 35 Fd 9.53N 37.05 E
Alibori 34 Fc 11.56N 3.17 E
Alibunar 15 Dd 45.04N 20.58 E
Alicante 6 Fh 38.21N 0.29W
Alicante [3] 13 Lf 38.30N 0.30W
Alicante, Golfo de- 13 Lf 38.20N 0.15W
Alice [S.Afr.] 37 Df 32.47S 26.50 E
Alice [Tx.-U.S.] 43 Hf 27.45N 98.04W
Alice, Punta- 14 Lk 39.12N 17.09 E
Alice Springs 58 Eg 23.42S 133.53 E
Aliceville 44 Ci 33.08N 88.09W
Alicudi 14 Il 38.30N 14.20 E
Aligarh 22 Jg 28.02N 78.17 E
Alīgūdarz 24 Mf 33.24N 49.41 E
Alihe→Oroqen Zizhiqi 27 La 50.35N 123.42 E
Alijó 13 Ec 41.16N 7.28W
Alijos, Rocas- 47 Ad 24.57N 115.44W
'Alī Jūq, Kūh-e- 24 Ng 31.30N 51.45 E
Al Ikhwan 21 Hh 12.08N 53.10 E
Al Ikhwān 24 Fi 26.19N 34.52 E
Alima 30 Ii 1.36S 16.36 E
Al Imārāt al 'Arabīyah al Muttaḩidah=United Arab Emirates (EN) [1] 22 Hg 24.00N 54.00 E
Alimiá 15 Km 36.16N 27.43 E
Alindao 35 Cd 5.02N 21.13 E
Alinglapalap Atoll 57 Hd 7.08N 168.16 E
Alingsås 7 Ch 57.56N 12.31 E
Aliquippa 44 Ge 40.38N 80.16W
Al 'Irāq=Iraq (EN) [1] 22 Gf 33.00N 44.00 E
Al'Irq 33 Dd 29.01N 21.31 E
Al 'Irqah 23 Gg 13.40N 47.18 E
Ali-Sabjeh 35 Gc 11.08N 42.43 E
'Alī Shāh 'Avaz 24 Ne 35.39N 51.04 E
Al Iskandarīyah [Eg.] = Alexandria (EN) 31 Je 31.12N 29.54 E
Al Iskandarīyah [Iraq] 24 Kf 32.53N 44.21 E
Aliskerovo 20 Lc 67.52N 167.40 E
Al Ismā'īlīyah=Ismailia (EN) 33 Fc 30.35N 32.16 E
Al Istiwā'īyah al Gharbīyah [3] 35 Dd 5.20N 28.30 E
Al Istiwā'īyah al Sharkīyah [3] 35 Ed 5.20N 33.50 E
Alistráti 15 Gh 41.04N 23.58 E
Alitak, Cape- 40 Ie 56.51N 154.21W
Alite Reef 63a Ec 8.53S 160.38 E
Alitus/Alytus 19 Ce 54.25N 24.08 E
Alivérion 15 Hk 38.25N 24.02 E
Aliwal North 31 Jl 30.44S 26.40 E
Al Jabalayn 35 Ec 12.36N 32.48 E
Al Jadīdah [Eg.] 24 Cj 25.34N 28.51 E
Al Jadīdah [Sau.Ar.] 24 Mj 25.39N 49.32 E
Al Jafr 24 Gg 30.18N 36.13 E
Al Jāfūrah 35 Ia 23.25N 50.17 E
Al Jāfūrah 24 Nj 25.00N 50.15 E
Al Jaghbūb 31 Jf 29.45N 24.31 E
Al Jahrah 23 Gc 29.20N 47.40 E
Al Jalāmīd 24 Ig 31.17N 40.06 E
Al Jamalīyah 24 Nj 25.37N 51.05 E
Al Jamm 32 Jb 35.18N 10.43 E
Al Jana'in 32 Jc 31.44N 10.09 E
Aljat 16 Pj 39.58N 49.27 E
Al Jawf [Lib.] 31 Jf 24.12N 23.18 E
Al Jawf [Sau.Ar.] 22 Fg 29.50N 39.52 E
Al Jazā'ir=Algeria (EN) [1] 31 Hf 28.00N 3.00 E
Al Jazā'ir=Algiers (EN) [3] 32 Hb 36.35N 3.00 E
Al Jazā'ir=Algiers (EN) 31 He 36.47N 3.03 E
Al Jazā'ir-El Harrach 13 Ph 36.43N 3.08 E
Al Jazīrah [3] 35 Ec 14.40N 33.30 E
Al Jazīrah [Asia] 21 Gf 35.10N 42.00 E
Al Jazīrah [Sud.] 30 Kg 14.25N 33.00 E
Aljezur 13 Dg 37.19N 8.48W
Aljibe 13 Gh 36.31N 5.37W
Al Jifārah 30 Ie 32.30N 11.45 E
Al Jiwā' 23 He 23.00N 54.00 E
Al Jīzah=Giza (EN) 31 Ke 30.01N 31.13 E
Al Jubayl 23 Gd 27.01N 49.40 E
Al Jubaylah 24 Lj 24.54N 46.27 E
Al Junaynah [Sau.Ar.] 33 He 20.17N 42.48 E
Al Junaynah [Sud.] 31 Jg 13.27N 22.27 E
Al Juraid 24 Mi 27.11N 49.52 E
Aljustrel 13 Dg 37.52N 8.10W
Alka 40a Db 52.15N 174.30W
Al Kaba'ish 24 Lg 30.58N 47.00 E
Al Kāf [3] 32 Ib 36.00N 9.00 E
Al Kāf 32 Ib 36.11N 8.43 E
Alkali Lake 46 Ff 41.42N 119.50W
Al Kamāsin 23 Fe 20.25N 44.48 E
Al Kāmilīn 35 Eb 15.05N 33.11 E
Al Karak 24 Fg 31.11N 35.42 E
Al Karkh 24 Kf 33.20N 44.20 E
Al Karnak 33 Fd 25.43N 32.39 E
Al Kawah 35 Ec 13.44N 32.30 E
Al Kāẓimīyah 24 Kf 33.22N 44.20 E
Alken 12 Hd 50.52N 5.18 E
Al Khabrā' 23 Fd 26.04N 43.33 E
Al Khābūra 23 Ie 23.50N 57.18 E
Al-Khalīj al- 'Arabi=Persian Gulf (EN) 21 Hg 27.00N 51.00 E
Al Khalīl 24 Fg 31.32N 35.06 E
Al Khālis 24 Kf 33.51N 44.32 E
Al Khandaq 35 Eb 18.36N 30.34 E
Al Khārijah 31 Kf 25.26N 30.33 E
Al Kharj 24 Lj 24.10N 47.30 E
Al Kharţūm=Khartoum (EN) [3] 35 Eb 15.50N 33.00 E
Al Kharţūm=Khartoum (EN) 31 Kg 15.36N 32.32 E
Al Kharţūm Baḩrī= Khartoum North (EN) 31 Kg 15.38N 32.33 E
Al Khaşab 24 Qi 26.12N 56.15 E
Al Khaţţ 24 Qk 25.37N 56.01 E
Al Khawr 23 Hd 25.40N 51.30 E
Al Khidr 24 Kg 31.12N 45.33 E
Al Khubar 23 Hd 26.17N 50.12 E
Al Khufayfīyah 24 Fe 24.55N 44.42 E
Al Khums [3] 33 Bc 31.20N 14.10 E
Al Khums 31 Ie 32.39N 14.16 E
Al Khunn 35 Ha 23.18N 49.15 E
Al Khuwayr 24 Ni 26.04N 51.05 E
Al Kidn 35 Ia 22.30N 54.00 E
Al Kilḩ Sharq 24 Ej 25.03N 32.52 E
Alkionidhon, Kólpos- 15 Fk 38.05N 23.00 E
Al Kir'ānah 24 Nj 25.00N 51.03 E
Alkmaar 11 Kb 52.37N 4.44 E
Al Kūfah 24 Kf 32.02N 44.24 E
Al Kumayt 24 Lf 32.02N 46.52 E
Al Kuntillah 33 Fc 30.00N 34.41 E
Al Kushḩ 24 Ei 26.14N 32.05 E
Al Kut 23 Gc 32.30N 45.49 E
Al Kuwayt=Kuwait (EN) [1] 22 Gg 29.30N 47.45 E
Al Kuwayt=Kuwait (EN) 22 Gg 29.20N 47.59 E
Al Labbah 24 Ih 29.20N 41.30 E
Al Lādhiqīyah=Latakia (EN) 22 Ff 35.31N 35.07 E
Allagash River 44 Mb 47.05N 69.20W
Al Lagowa 35 Dc 11.24N 29.08 E
Allahābād 22 Kg 25.27N 81.51 E
Allah-Jun 20 Id 60.27N 134.57 E
Allah-Jun 20 Id 61.08N 137.59 E
Allahüekber DaGı 24 Jb 40.35N 42.32 E
Allakaket 40 Ic 66.34N 152.41W
Allanmyo 25 Je 19.22N 95.13 E
Allariz 13 Eb 42.11N 7.48W
All-Awash Island 51n Bb 12.55N 61.10W
Alldays 37 Dd 22.41S 29.06 E
Ålleberg 8 Ef 58.08N 13.36 E
Allegan 44 Ed 42.32N 85.51W
Allegheny Mountains 38 Lf 38.30N 80.00W
Allegheny Plateau 38 Le 41.30N 78.00W
Allegheny Reservoir 44 He 42.00N 78.56W
Allegheny River 43 Lc 40.27N 80.00W
Allègre, Pointe- 51e Ab 16.22N 61.45W
Allen 26 Hd 12.30N 124.17 E
Allen, Bog of- 9 Gh 53.20N 7.00W
Allen, Lough-/Loch Aillionn 9 Eg 54.08N 8.08W
Allendale 44 Gi 33.01N 81.19W
Allende 47 Dc 28.20N 100.51W
Allendorf (Eder) 12 Kc 51.02N 8.40 E
Allendorf (Lumda) 12 Kd 50.41N 8.50 E
Allentown 43 Lc 40.37N 75.30W
Alleppey 22 Ji 9.29N 76.19 E
Aller 10 Fd 52.57N 9.11 E
Allevard 11 Mi 45.24N 6.04 E
Allgäuer Alpen 10 Gi 47.20N 10.25 E
Alliance [Nb.-U.S.] 43 Gc 42.06N 102.52W
Alliance [Oh.-U.S.] 44 Ge 40.56N 81.06W
Allier [3] 11 Ih 46.30N 3.00 E
Allier 5 Gf 46.57N 3.05 E
Al Lifīyah 23 Fc 30.35N 43.09 E
Al Lişāfah 24 Li 27.37N 46.52 E
Alliston 44 Hc 44.09N 79.52W
Al Līth 23 Fe 20.09N 40.16 E
Alloa 9 Je 56.07N 3.49W
Allonnes 11 Gg 47.58N 0.09 E
Allos 11 Mj 44.14N 6.38 E
All Saints 51d Bb 17.03N 61.48W
Al Luḩayyah 23 Ff 15.43N 42.42 E
Al Luwaymī 23 Fd 27.54N 42.22 E
Alm 14 Hb 48.05N 13.55 E
Alma [Ga.-U.S.] 44 Fj 31.33N 82.28W
Alma [Mi.-U.S.] 44 Ed 43.23N 84.39W
Alma [Nb.-U.S.] 45 Gf 40.06N 99.22W
Alma [Que.-Can.] 42 Kg 48.32N 71.40W
Alma-Ata 22 Je 43.15N 76.57 E
Alma-Atinskaja Oblast [3] 19 Hg 44.00N 77.00 E
Almada 13 Cf 38.41N 9.09W
Almadén 13 Hf 38.46N 4.50W
Al Madīnah [Iraq] 24 Lg 30.57N 47.16 E
Al Madīnah [Sau.Ar.] = Medina (EN) 22 Fg 24.28N 39.36 E
Al Madīnah al Fikrīyah 24 Di 27.56N 30.49 E
'Al Madōw 35 Hc 10.59N 48.42 E
Al Mafraq 24 Gf 32.21N 36.12 E
Al Maghrib=Morocco (EN) [1] 31 Ge 32.00N 5.50W
Almagro 13 If 38.53N 3.43W
Almagrundet 8 He 59.06N 19.00 E

Index Symbols

[1] Independent Nation
[2] State, Region
[3] District, County
[4] Municipality
[5] Colony, Dependency
Continent
Physical Region
Historical or Cultural Region
Mount, Mountain
Volcano
Hill
Mountains, Mountain Range
Hills, Escarpment
Plateau, Upland
Pass, Gap
Plain, Lowland
Delta
Salt Flat
Valley, Canyon
Crater, Cave
Karst Features
Depression
Polder
Desert, Dunes
Forest, Woods
Heath, Steppe
Oasis
Cape, Point
Coast, Beach
Cliff
Peninsula
Isthmus
Sandbank
Island
Atoll
Rock, Reef
Islands, Archipelago
Rocks, Reefs
Coral Reef
Well, Spring
Geyser
River, Stream
Waterfall Rapids
River Mouth, Estuary
Lake
Salt Lake
Intermittent Lake
Reservoir
Swamp, Pond
Canal
Glacier
Ice Shelf, Pack Ice
Ocean
Sea
Gulf, Bay
Strait, Fjord
Lagoon
Bank
Seamount
Tablemount
Ridge
Shelf
Basin
Escarpment, Sea Scarp
Fracture
Trench, Abyss
National Park, Reserve
Point of Interest
Recreation Site
Cave, Cavern
Historic Site
Ruins
Wall, Walls
Church, Abbey
Temple
Scientific Station
Airport
Port
Lighthouse
Mine
Tunnel
Dam, Bridge

Al Maḩallah al Kubrá 33 Fc 30.58N 31.10 E
Al Maḩāriq 33 Fd 25.37N 30.39 E
Al Mahdīyah 32 Jb 35.30N 11.04 E
Al Mahdīyah [3] 32 Jb 35.35N 11.00 E
Al Maḩfid 33 Ig 14.03N 46.55 E
Al Mahrah 23 Hf 16.56N 52.15 E
Al Maḩras 32 Jc 34.32N 10.30 E
Al Majarr al Kabīr 24 Lg 31.34N 47.10 E
Almajului, Munţii- 15 Fe 44.43N 22.12 E
Al Maks al Qiblī 33 Fe 24.35N 30.38 E
Almalyk 19 Gg 40.49N 69.38 E
Al Manādir 24 Pk 23.10N 55.10 E
Al Manāmah=Manama (EN) 22 Hg 26.13N 50.35 E
Al Manāqil 35 Ec 14.15N 32.59 E
Almanor, Lake- 46 Ef 40.15N 121.08W
Almansa 13 Kf 38.52N 1.05W
Almansa, Puerto de- 13 Lf 38.49N 0.58W
Al Manshāh 33 Fd 26.28N 31.48 E
Almansor 13 Df 38.56N 8.54W
Al Manşūrah 33 Fc 31.03N 31.23 E
Al Manzilah 24 Dg 31.09N 31.56 E
Almanzor, Pico de- 13 Gd 40.15N 5.18W
Almanzora 13 Jg 37.21N 2.08W
Al Ma'qil 24 Lg 30.33N 47.48 E
Al Maqnah 24 Fh 28.24N 34.45 E
Al Maqta' 24 Pj 24.25N 54.29 E
Almar 13 Gd 40.54N 5.29W
Al Marāghah 24 Di 26.42N 31.36 E
Al Marsá 14 En 36.53N 10.20 E
Al Mary 31 Je 32.30N 20.54 E
Almaş 15 Gb 47.14N 23.19 E
Almas, Picos de- 52 Lg 13.33S 41.56W
Almas, Rio das- 54 If 14.35S 49.02W
'Al Maskād 35 Hc 11.18N 49.41 E
Al Maţarīyah 33 Fc 31.11N 32.02 E
Al Mawşil=Mosul (EN) 22 Gf 36.20N 43.08 E
Al Mayādīn 24 Ie 35.01N 40.27 E
Al Mayyāh 24 Ji 27.51N 42.47 E
Almazán 13 Jc 41.29N 2.32W
Al Mazār 24 Eg 31.23N 33.23 E
Almazny 20 Gd 62.19N 114.04 E
Almazora 13 Le 39.57N 0.03W
Al Mazra'ah 24 Fg 31.16N 35.31 E
Alme, Brilon- 12 Kc 51.27N 8.37 E
Almeida 13 Fc 41.16N 6.04W
Almeirim [Braz.] 54 Hd 1.32S 52.34W
Almeirim [Port.] 13 De 39.12N 8.38W
Al Mellem 35 Dd 9.49N 28.45 E
Almelo 11 Mb 52.21N 6.39 E
Almenara, Sierra de la- 13 Kg 37.35N 1.31W
Almendra, Embalse de- 13 Fc 41.13N 6.10W
Almendralejo 13 Ff 38.41N 6.24W
Almeria [3] 13 Jg 37.10N 2.20W
Almería 6 Fh 36.50N 2.27W
Almería, Golfo de- 13 Jh 36.46N 2.30W
Almetjevsk 19 Fe 54.54N 52.20 E
Al Metlaoui 32 Ic 34.20N 8.24 E
Älmhult 7 Dh 56.33N 14.08 E
Almijara, Sierra de- 13 Ih 36.55N 3.55W
Almina, Punta- 13 Gi 35.54N 5.17W
Al Minyā [Eg.] 24 Dh 29.45N 31.18 E
Al Minyā [Eg.] 31 Kf 28.06N 30.45 E
Al Miqdādīyah 24 Kf 33.59N 44.56 E
Almirante 49 Fi 9.18N 82.24W
Almirante Brown 66 Qe 64.53S 62.53W
Almirós 15 Fj 39.11N 22.46 E
Almiroú, Órmos- 15 Hn 35.23N 24.20 E
Almodôvar 13 Dg 37.31N 8.04W
Almodóvar del Campo 13 Hf 38.43N 4.10W
Almodóvar del Río 13 Gg 37.48N 5.01W
Almonte 13 Fg 37.15N 6.31W
Almonte 13 Fe 39.42N 6.28W
Almora 25 Fc 29.37N 79.40 E
Almoustarat 34 Fb 17.22N 0.07 E
Älmsta 8 He 59.58N 18.48 E
Al Mubarraz 23 Gd 25.25N 49.35 E
Al Mudawwarah 24 Fh 29.19N 35.59 E
Al Mudhari, Rujm- 24 Hf 32.45N 39.08 E
Al Mughayrā' [Sau.Ar.] 24 Gh 29.17N 37.41 E
Al Mughayrā' [U.A.E.] 24 Oj 24.05N 53.32 E
Al Muglad 31 Jg 11.02N 27.44 E
Al Muḩarraq 24 Ni 26.16N 50.37 E
Al Mukallā 22 Gh 14.32N 49.08 E
Al Mukhā 23 Fg 13.19N 43.15 E
Al Munastīr [3] 32 Jb 35.40N 10.50 E
Al Munastīr 32 Jb 35.47N 10.50 E
Almuñécar 13 Ih 36.43N 3.41W
Al Murabba' 24 Kj 25.43N 44.18 E
Almus 24 Gb 40.23N 36.55 E
Al Musannāh 24 Lh 29.02N 47.12 E
Al Muşawwarāt aş Şafra' 35 Eb 16.25N 33.22 E
Al Musayjīd 24 Hj 24.05N 39.06 E
Al Musayyib 24 Kf 32.47N 44.18 E
Al Mustawī 24 Kj 25.55N 44.40 E
Al Muthanna [3] 24 Kg 30.50N 45.20 E
Al Muwayh 33 He 22.45N 41.35 E
Al Muwaylih 24 Fi 27.41N 35.28 E
Alnön 8 Gb 62.25N 17.25 E
Alnwick 9 Lf 55.25N 1.42W
Ålö 8 Jd 60.20N 22.15 E
Aloândia 55 Hc 17.43S 49.29W
Alofi 58 Kf 19.03S 169.56W
Alofi, Ile- 57 Jf 14.19S 178.02W
Alofi Bay 64k Bb 19.01S 169.56W
Aloja 7 Fh 57.44N 24.59 E
Along 25 Ic 28.10N 94.46 E
Alónnisos 15 Gj 39.13N 23.55 E
Alonsa 45 Ga 50.47N 99.00W
Alonso, Rio- 55 Gg 24.05S 51.35W
Alor, Kepulauan- 26 Hh 8.15S 124.30 E
Alor, Pulau- 21 Oj 8.15S 124.45 E
Alora 13 Hh 36.48N 4.42W
Alor Setar 22 Mi 6.07N 100.22 E
Alost/Aalst 11 Kd 50.56N 4.02 E
Alotau 60 Ej 10.31S 150.43 E
Aloysius, Mount- 59 Fe 26.00S 128.34 E
Alpen = Alps (EN) 5 Gf 46.25N 10.00 E
Alpena 43 Kb 45.04N 83.26W
Alpera 13 Kf 38.58N 1.13W
Alpes=Alps (EN) 5 Gf 46.25N 10.00 E
Alpes Bernoises/Berner Alpen=Bernese Alps (EN) 14 Bd 46.25N 7.30 E
Alpes Cottiennes 14 Af 44.45N 7.00 E
Alpes de Haute-Provence [3] 11 Lj 44.10N 6.00 E
Alpes Grées/Alpi Graie 14 Be 45.30N 7.10 E
Alpes Mancelles 11 Ff 48.25N 0.10W
Alpes Maritimes 14 Bf 44.15N 7.10 E
Alpes-Maritimes [3] 11 Nk 44.00N 7.10 E
Alpes Pennines/Alpi Pennine 14 Bd 46.05N 7.50 E
Alpes Valaisannes/Walliser Alpen 14 Bd 46.10N 7.30 E
Alpha Cordillera (EN) 67 Re 85.30N 125.00W
Alphen aan der Rijn 12 Gb 52.08N 4.42 E
Alphonse Island 30 Mi 7.00S 52.45 E
Alpi=Alps (EN) 5 Gf 46.25N 10.00 E
Alpi Apuane 14 Ef 44.05N 10.20 E
Alpi Aurine 10 Hi 47.00N 11.55 E
Alpi Carniche 14 Gd 46.40N 13.00 E
Alpi Cozie 14 Af 44.45N 7.00 E
Alpi Graie/Alpes Grées 14 Be 45.30N 7.10 E
Alpi Lepontine 14 Cd 46.25N 8.40 E
Alpi Liguri 14 Cf 44.10N 8.05 E
Alpi Marittime 14 Bf 44.15N 7.10 E
Alpine [Az.-U.S.] 46 Kj 33.51N 109.09W
Alpine [Tx.-U.S.] 43 Ge 30.22N 103.40W
Alpine [Wy.-U.S.] 46 Je 43.15N 110.59W
Alpi Orobie 14 Dd 46.00N 10.00 E
Alpi Pennine/Alpes Pennines 14 Bd 46.05N 7.50 E
Alpi Retiche=Rhaetian Alps (EN) 14 Dd 46.30N 10.00 E
Alpi Ticinesi 14 Cd 46.20N 8.45 E
Alpi Venoste 10 Gj 46.45N 10.55 E
Alprech, Cap d'- 12 Dd 50.42N 1.34 E
Alps (EN) = Alpen 5 Gf 46.25N 10.00 E
Alps (EN)=Alpes 5 Gf 46.25N 10.00 E
Alps (EN)=Alpi 5 Gf 46.25N 10.00 E
Al qa 'Āmiyāt 35 Hb 18.50N 48.30 E
Al Qābil 24 Pk 23.56N 55.49 E
Al Qaḑārif 31 Kg 14.02N 35.24 E
Al Qaḑīmah 23 Ee 22.21N 39.09 E
Al Qādisīya [3] 24 Kg 31.50N 45.00 E
Al Qādisīya 24 Kg 31.42N 44.28 E
Al Qadmūs 24 Ge 35.05N 36.10 E
Al Qaffāy 24 Nj 24.35N 51.44 E
Al Qāhirah=Cairo (EN) 31 Ke 30.03N 31.15 E
Al Qāhirah-Imbabah 33 Fc 30.05N 31.13 E
Al Qāhirah-Mişr al Jadīdah 33 Fc 30.06N 31.20 E
Al Qā'īyah 24 Ki 26.27N 45.35 E
Al Qal'ah al Kubrá 14 Eo 35.52N 10.32 E
Al Qalībah 23 Ed 28.24N 37.42 E
Al Qāmishlī 23 Fb 37.02N 41.14 E
Al Qanţarah 33 Fc 30.52N 32.19 E
Al Qaryah ash Sharqīyah 33 Bc 30.24N 13.36 E
Al Qaryatayn 24 Ge 34.14N 37.14 E
Al Qaşab 24 Kj 25.18N 45.30 E
Al Qaşabāt 33 Bc 32.35N 14.03 E
Al Qa'şah 24 Ch 28.25N 28.56 E
Al Qash 35 Fb 16.48N 35.51 E
Al Qaşr 33 Ed 25.42N 28.53 E
Al Qaşrayn 32 Ib 35.11N 8.48 E
Al Qaşrayn [3] 32 Ib 35.15N 9.00 E
Al Qaţīf 24 Mi 26.33N 50.00 E
Al Qaţrānī 24 Gg 31.15N 36.03 E
Al Qaţrūn 33 Be 24.56N 14.38 E
Al Qay'īyah 23 Fe 24.18N 43.30 E
Al Qayrawān 32 Jb 35.41N 10.07 E
Al Qayrawān [3] 32 Ib 35.30N 10.00 E
Al Qayşūmah [Sau.Ar.] 24 Jh 29.11N 42.58 E
Al Qayşūmah [Sau.Ar.] 23 Gd 28.16N 46.03 E
Alqōsh 24 Jd 36.44N 43.06 E
Al Qubayyāt 24 Ge 34.34N 36.17 E
Al Qunayţirah 23 Ec 33.07N 35.49 E
Al Qunfudhah 23 Ff 19.08N 41.05 E
Al Qurayyah 24 Gh 28.45N 36.12 E
Al Qurnah 24 Lg 31.00N 47.26 E
Al Quşaymah 33 Fc 30.40N 34.22 E
Al Quşayr [Eg.] 31 Kf 26.06N 34.17 E
Al Quşayr [Syr.] 24 Ge 34.31N 36.35 E
Al Qūşīyah 33 Fd 27.26N 30.49 E
Al Quşūr 14 Co 35.54N 8.53 E
Al Quţayfah 24 Gf 33.44N 36.36 E
Al Quwārah 24 Ji 26.47N 43.28 E
Al Quwayr 24 Jd 36.03N 43.30 E
Al Quzah 35 Hb 15.06N 49.08 E
Als 8 Ci 55.00N 9.55 E
Alsace 11 Nf 48.30N 7.30 E
Alsace, Ballon d'- 11 Mg 47.50N 6.51 E
Alsasua 13 Jb 42.54N 2.10W
Alsdorf 12 Id 50.53N 6.10 E
Alsea River 46 Cd 44.26N 124.05W
Alsenz 12 Je 49.49N 7.51 E
Alsfeld 10 Ff 50.45N 9.16 E
Alsina, Laguna- 55 Am 36.52S 62.07W
Alsten 7 Cd 65.57N 12.36 E
Alsterån 8 Gh 56.55N 16.26 E
Alsunga 8 Ig 57.02N 21.28 E
Alta 7 Fb 69.58N 23.14 E
Altaelva 7 Fb 69.58N 23.23 E
Altafjorden 7 Fa 70.12N 23.06 E
Altagracia 54 Da 10.07N 71.14W
Alta Gracia 56 Hd 31.40S 64.26W
Altagracia de Orituco 50 Ch 9.52N 66.23W
Altai (EN)= Altay Shan 21 Le 46.30N 93.00 E
Altaj 22 Le 46.20N 96.17 E
Altaj 21 Kd 51.30N 90.00 E
Altajskij 20 Df 51.58N 85.30 E
Altajskij Kraj [3] 20 Df 52.00N 82.30 E
Altamaha River 43 Ke 31.19N 81.17W
Altamira 53 Kf 3.12S 52.12W
Altamira, Cuevas de- 13 Ha 43.23N 4.05W
Altamira, Sierra de- 13 Ge 39.35N 5.10W
Altamirano 48 Mi 16.53N 92.09W
Altamont 46 Ee 42.12N 121.44W
Altamura 14 Kj 40.49N 16.33 E
Altamura, Isla de- 48 Ee 25.00N 108.10W
Altan Bulag 27 Jc 44.19N 113.28 E
Altan-Emel → Xin Barag Youqi 27 Kb 48.41N 116.47 E
Altan Xiret → Ejin Horo Qi 27 Id 39.31N 109.45 E
Altar 48 Db 30.43N 111.44W
Altar, Desierto de- 38 Hf 31.50N 114.15W
Altar, Rio- 48 Db 30.39N 111.55W
Altar de los Sacrificios 49 Be 16.28N 90.32W
Altata 47 Cd 24.38N 107.55W
Alta Verapaz [3] 49 Bf 15.40N 90.00W
Altavista 44 Hg 37.07N 79.18W
Altay 22 Ke 47.52N 88.07 E
Altay Shan=Altai (EN) 21 Le 46.30N 93.00 E
Altdorf 14 Cd 46.53N 8.40 E
Altea 13 Lf 38.36N 0.03W
Altena 12 Jc 51.18N 7.40 E
Altenberge 12 Jb 52.03N 7.28 E
Altenburg 10 If 50.59N 12.27 E
Altenglan 12 Je 49.33N 7.28 E
Altenkirchen (Westerwald) 12 Jd 50.42N 7.39 E
Alter do Chão 13 Ee 39.12N 7.40W
Altevatnet 7 Eb 68.32N 19.30 E
Altındağ 24 Ec 39.56N 32.52 E
Altınoluk 15 Jj 39.34N 26.44 E
Altınova 15 Jj 39.13N 26.47 E
Altıntaş 24 Dc 39.04N 30.07 E
Altınyayla 15 Mm 36.59N 29.33 E
Altkirch 11 Ng 47.37N 7.15 E
Altmark 10 Hd 52.40N 11.20 E
Altmühl 10 Hh 48.55N 11.52 E
Alto, Morro- 55 Ib 13.46S 46.50W
Alto, Pico- 54 Kd 4.20S 39.00W
Alto Alentejo 13 Ef 38.50N 7.40W
Alto Araguaia 54 Hg 17.19S 53.12W
Alto Coité 55 Eb 15.47S 54.20W
Alto Garças 55 Fc 16.56S 53.32W
Alto Hama 36 Ce 12.14S 15.34 E
Alto Longá 54 Je 5.15S 42.12W
Alto Molócuè 37 Fc 15.38S 37.42 E
Altomonte 14 Kk 39.42N 16.08 E
Alton [Eng.-U.K.] 12 Bc 51.08N 0.59W
Alton [Il.-U.S.] 43 Id 38.54N 90.10W
Altona, Hamburg- 10 Fc 53.33N 9.57 E
Altoona 43 Lc 40.32N 78.23W
Alto Paraguai 54 Gf 14.30S 56.31W
Alto Paraguay [3] 55 Ce 21.00S 59.00W
Alto Paraíso de Goiás 55 Ib 14.12S 47.38W
Alto Paraná [3] 55 Eg 25.00S 54.50W
Alto Parnaíba 54 Ie 9.06S 45.57W
Alto Purús, Rio- 54 De 9.34S 70.36W
Alto Rio Senguerr 56 Fg 45.02S 70.50W
Altos 54 Jd 5.03S 42.28W
Alto Sucuriú 55 Fd 19.19S 52.47W
Altötting 10 Ih 48.14N 12.41 E
Alto Uruguai, Serra do- 55 Fh 27.35S 53.40W
Altun Ha 49 Ce 17.50N 88.20W
Āltūn Kūprī 24 Ke 35.45N 44.09 E
Altun Shan 21 Kf 38.00N 88.00 E
Alturas 43 Cc 41.29N 120.32W
Alturitas 49 Ki 9.45N 72.25W
Altus 43 He 34.38N 99.20W
Altynkan 18 Hd 41.03N 70.43 E
Altynkul 18 Bc 43.07N 58.55 E
Alu 63a Bb 7.05S 155.47 E
Al 'Ubaylah 35 Ia 21.59N 50.57 E
Al Ubayyiḑ 31 Kg 13.11N 30.13 E
Alucra 24 Hb 40.20N 38.46 E
Al 'Udaysāt 24 Ej 25.35N 32.29 E
Al Uḑayyah 35 Dc 12.03N 28.17 E
Alūksne/Aluksne 7 Gh 57.26N 27.01 E
Aluksne/Alūksne 7 Gh 57.26N 27.01 E
Aluksne Ozero 8 Lg 57.22N 27.10 E
Aluksne Ozero/Alūksnes Ezers 8 Lg 57.22N 27.10 E
Alūksnes Ezers/Aluksne Ozero 8 Lg 57.22N 27.10 E
'Alūla 35 Ic 11.58N 50.48 E
Al 'Ulá 23 Ed 26.37N 37.52 E
Al Umm 33 Hf 18.18N 40.45 E
Alunda 8 Hd 60.04N 18.05 E
Alupka 19 Dg 44.24N 34.03 E
Al'Uqaylah 33 Cc 30.16N 19.12 E
Al 'Uqaylāt 24 Ii 26.43N 41.43 E
Al 'Uqayr 24 Nj 25.39N 50.13 E
Al Uqşur=Luxor (EN) 33 Fd 25.41N 32.39 E
Al Urayq 24 Hh 29.00N 39.10 E
Al Urdun=Jordan (EN) 22 Ff 31.00N 36.00 E
Al 'Urūq al Mu'Tariḑah 35 Ia 21.00N 54.00 E
Ālūs 24 Je 34.02N 42.26 E
Aluşta 19 Dg 44.42N 34.20 E
Al 'Uthmānīyah 24 Mj 25.15N 49.22 E
Al'Uwaynāt 33 Bd 25.48N 10.33 E
Al 'Uwaynidhīyah 24 Gi 26.38N 36.05 E
Al 'Uwayqīlah 24 Jg 30.21N 42.14 E
Al 'Uyūn 24 Hj 24.33N 39.35 E
Al Uzayin 24 Ke 34.02N 44.20 E
Al 'Uzayr 24 Lg 31.19N 47.25 E
Alva 43 Hd 36.48N 98.40W
Alva 13 Dd 40.18N 8.15W
Alvand, Kūh-e- 24 Me 34.41N 48.28 E
Älvängen 8 Eg 57.56N 12.09 E
Alvaro Obregón, Presa 48 Ed 28.00N 109.45W
Alvdal 7 Ce 62.07N 10.39 E
Älvdalen 8 Ed 60.30N 13.00 E
Älvdalen 7 Df 61.14N 14.02 E
Alvear 55 Di 29.06S 56.33W
Alvelos, Serra de- 13 De 39.55N 8.01W
Alvesta 7 Dh 56.54N 14.33 E
Alvik 8 Gb 62.25N 17.24 E
Älvik 7 Bf 60.26N 6.26 E
Alvin 45 Il 29.25N 95.15W
Älvkarleby 7 Df 60.34N 17.27 E
Alvord Valley 46 Fe 42.45N 118.25W
Alvøy 8 Ad 60.35N 4.50 E
Älvros 8 Fb 62.03N 14.39 E
Älvsborg [2] 7 Cg 58.00N 12.30 E
Älvsbyn 7 Ed 65.40N 21.00 E
Al Wāḩidī 23 Gg 14.20N 47.50 E
Al Wajh 22 Fg 26.14N 36.28 E
Al Wakrah 24 Nj 25.10N 51.36 E
Al Wannān 24 Mi 26.55N 48.24 E
Alwar 25 Fc 27.34N 76.36 E
Al Warī'ah 24 Li 27.50N 47.29 E
Al Wāsiţah 33 Fd 29.20N 31.12 E
Al Waslātīyah 14 Do 35.51N 9.35 E
Al Waţī'ah 33 Bc 32.28N 11.46 E
Al Wazz 35 Eb 15.01N 30.10 E
Al Widyān 21 Gf 31.10N 40.45 E
Alxa Youqi (Ehen Hudag) 27 Hd 39.12N 101.40 E
Alxa Zuoqi (Bayan Hot) 27 Id 38.50N 105.32 E
Al Yaman=Yemen (EN) [1] 22 Gh 15.00N 44.00 E
Al Yaman ad Dīmuqrāţīyah =Yemen, People's Democratic Republic of-(EN) [1] 22 Gh 14.00N 46.00 E
Alyangula 59 Hb 13.50S 136.25 E
Alygdžer 20 Ef 53.38N 98.16 E
Alymka 17 Ng 59.01N 68.40 E
Alytus/Alitus 19 Ce 54.25N 24.08 E
Alz 10 Ih 48.10N 12.48 E
Alzamaj 20 Ee 55.33N 98.39 E
Alzey 10 Eg 49.45N 8.07 E
Alzira/Alcira 13 Le 39.09N 0.26W
Amachkalo Ahzar 34 Fb 15.30N 3.20 E
Amacuro, Rio- 54 Fb 8.32N 60.28W
Amada 33 Fe 22.45N 32.10 E
Amadeus, Lake- 57 Eg 24.50S 130.45 E
Amadi [Sud.] 35 Ed 5.31N 30.20 E
Amadi [Zaire] 36 Eb 3.35N 26.47 E
Amadjuak Lake 42 Kd 64.55N 71.00W
Amadora 13 Cf 38.45N 9.14W
Amadror 32 Ie 24.50N 6.25 E
Amadror 32 Id 26.00N 5.21W
Amagasaki 29 Dd 34.42N 135.25 E
Amager 8 Ei 55.35N 12.35 E
Amagi [Jap.] 29 Be 33.26N 130.39 E
Amagi [Jap.] 29b Bb 27.47N 128.52 E
Amagi-San 29 Fd 34.51N 139.00 E
Amaha 29 Fd 35.13N 139.51 E
Amahai 26 Ig 3.20S 128.55 E
Amain, Monts d'- 11 Gf 48.39N 0.20 E
Amajac, Rio- 48 Jg 21.15N 98.46W
Amakusa-Nada 28 Jh 32.25N 129.40 E
Amakusa-Shotō 28 Kh 32.22N 130.12 E
Amal 33 Dd 29.25N 21.10 E
Åmål 7 Cg 59.03N 12.42 E
Amalfi 14 Ij 40.38N 14.36 E
Amaliás 15 El 37.48N 21.21 E
Amalner 25 Fd 21.03N 75.04 E
Amambai 54 Gh 23.05S 55.13W
Amambai, Rio- 55 Ff 23.22S 53.56W
Amambai, Serra de- 55 Ef 23.10S 55.30W
Amambay [3] 55 Df 23.00S 56.00W
Amami Islands (EN)= Amami-Shotō 21 Og 28.16N 129.21 E
Amami-Ō-Shima 27 Mf 28.15N 129.20 E
Amami-Shotō=Amami Islands (EN) 21 Og 28.16N 129.21 E
Amån 8 Fc 61.12N 14.45 E
Amanā, Lago- 54 Fd 2.35S 64.40W
Amana, Rio- 50 Eh 9.45N 62.39W
Amanave 65c Cb 14.19S 170.49W
Amangeldy 19 Ge 50.10N 65.13 E
Amankaragaj 17 Lj 52.27N 64.08 E
Amantea 14 Kk 39.07N 16.08 E
Amanu Atoll 57 Mf 17.48S 140.46W
Amanzimtoti 37 Ef 30.05S 30.53 E
Amapá 53 Ke 2.03N 50.48W
Amapá, Territorio do- [2] 54 Hc 1.30N 52.00W
Amapala 49 Dg 13.17N 87.40W
Amara 15 Ke 44.37N 27.19 E
Amara 30 Kg 11.30N 37.45 E
Amaradia 15 Ge 44.22N 23.43 E
'Amara East 35 Ea 20.48N 30.23 E
Amarante [Braz.] 54 Je 6.14S 42.50W
Amarante [Port.] 13 Dc 41.16N 8.05W
Amaranth 45 Ga 50.36N 98.43W
Amargosa 46 Gh 36.18N 116.25W
Amargosa Desert 46 Gh 36.40N 116.30W
Amargosa Range 46 Gh 36.30N 116.45W
Amargosa River 46 Gh 36.13N 116.48W
Amarillo 39 If 35.13N 101.49W
Amário 15 Hn 35.14N 24.39 E
Amarume 29 Fb 38.50N 139.54 E
Amasra 24 Eb 41.45N 32.34 E
Amasya 23 Ea 40.39N 35.51 E
Amathus 24 Ee 34.42N 33.08 E
Amatique, Bahía de- 49 Cf 15.55N 88.45W
Amatlán de Cañas 48 Gg 20.52N 104.27W
Amatrice 14 Hh 42.38N 13.17 E
Amaurilandia 55 Ff 22.10S 52.38W
Amay 12 Hd 50.33N 5.19 E
Amazar 20 Hf 53.54N 120.57 E
Amazon (EN)=Amazonas, Rio- (Solimões) 52 Lf 0.10S 49.00W
Amazon, Mouths of the- (EN) 52 Le 0.10S 49.00W
Amazonas [Braz.] [2] 54 Fd 5.00S 63.00W
Amazonas [Col.] [2] 54 Dd 1.00N 72.00W
Amazonas [Peru] [2] 54 Ce 5.00S 77.00W
Amazonas [Ven.] [2] 54 Ec 3.30N 66.00W
Amazonas, Rio-=Amazon (EN) 52 Lf 0.10S 49.00W
Amazonas, Rio- (Solimões) =Amazon (EN) 52 Lf 0.10S 49.00W
Amazon Cone (EN) 52 Ke 4.30N 52.00W
Amba Ferit 35 Fc 10.55N 38.55 E
Ambāla 25 Fb 30.21N 76.50 E
Ambalangoda 25 Gg 6.14N 80.03 E
Ambalavao 37 Hd 21.50S 46.57 E
Ambam 34 He 2.23N 11.17 E
Ambanja 37 Hb 13.39S 48.27 E
Ambarčik 22 Sc 69.39N 162.20 E
Ambarès-et-Lagrave 11 Fj 44.55N 0.29W
Ambargasta, Salinas de- 56 Hc 29.20S 64.30W
Ambarny 19 Db 65.54N 33.41 E
Ambasamudram 25 Fg 8.42N 77.28 E
Ambato 53 If 1.15S 78.37W
Ambato-Boéni 37 Hc 16.28S 46.40 E
Ambatofinandrahana 37 Hd 20.33S 46.47 E
Ambatolampy 37 Hc 19.23S 47.25 E
Ambatondrazaka 31 Lj 17.48S 48.26 E
Ambatosoratra 37 Hc 17.36S 48.32 E
Ambelau, Pulau- 26 Ig 3.51S 127.12 E
Amberg 10 Hg 49.27N 11.52 E
Ambergris Cay 49 Dd 18.03N 87.56W
Ambergris Cays 49 Lc 21.18N 71.37W
Ambérieu-en-Bugey 11 Li 45.57N 5.21 E
Amberley [Eng.-U.K.] 12 Bd 50.55N 0.32W
Amberley [N.Z.] 62 Ee 43.09S 172.45 E
Ambert 11 Ji 45.33N 3.45 E
Ambikāpur 25 Gd 23.07N 83.12 E
Ambila 37 Hd 21.58S 47.59 E
Ambilobe 37 Hb 13.11S 49.03 E
Ambitle 63a Aa 4.05S 153.40 E
Ambjörby 8 Ed 60.30N 13.10 E
Ambla 8 Ke 59.10N 25.44 E
Amblève 11 Ld 50.28N 5.36 E
Amblève/Amel 12 Id 50.21N 6.09 E
Ambo 54 Cf 10.07S 76.10W
Amboasary Sud 37 He 25.01S 46.23 E
Ambodifototra 37 Hc 16.58S 49.52 E
Ambohimahasoa 37 Hd 21.08S 47.12 E
Ambohimanarina 37 Hc 18.52S 47.29 E
Ambohitralanana 37 Ic 15.15S 50.28 E
Amboise 11 Gg 47.25N 0.59 E
Ambon 58 De 3.43S 128.12 E
Ambon, Pulau- 26 Ig 3.40S 128.10 E
Ambongo 37 Gc 16.50S 45.00 E
Amboseli, Lake- 36 Gc 2.37S 37.08 E
Ambositra 31 Lk 20.30S 47.14 E
Ambovombe 37 He 25.09S 46.06 E
Ambre, Cap d'-=Ambre, Cape d'-(EN) 30 Lj 11.57S 49.17 E
Ambre, Cape d'-(EN)= Ambre, Cap d'- 30 Lj 11.57S 49.17 E
Ambre, Montagne d'- 37 Hb 12.30S 49.10 E
Ambriz 31 Ii 7.50S 13.08 E
Ambrolauri 16 Mh 42.31N 43.05 E
Ambrym, Ile- 57 Hf 16.15S 168.07 E
Ambunti 60 Ch 4.14S 142.50 E
Āmbūr 25 Ff 12.47N 78.42 E
Amchitka 40a Bb 51.30N 179.00 E
Amchitka Pass 40a Cb 51.30N 179.30W
Am Dafok 35 Cc 10.28N 23.17 E
Am Dam 35 Cc 12.46N 20.29 E
Amded 32 He 22.10N 3.15 E
Amderma 19 Gb 69.45N 61.39 E
Am Djéména 35 Bc 13.06N 17.19 E
Amdo 27 Fe 32.29N 91.47 E
Ameca 47 Dd 20.33N 104.02W
Ameca, Rio- 48 Gg 20.41N 105.18W
Amel/Amblève 12 Id 50.21N 6.09 E
Ameland 12 Ha 53.26N 5.48 E
Ameland 11 La 53.25N 5.45 E
Ameland- Nes 12 Ha 53.26N 5.48 E
Amelia Island 44 Gj 30.37N 81.27W
Amélie-les-Bains-Palaloa 11 Il 42.28N 2.40 E
Amendola 14 Hh 42.59N 13.21 E
Amendolara 14 Kk 39.57N 16.35 E
'Āmerī 24 Nh 28.30N 51.05 E
Americana 55 If 22.45S 47.20W
American Falls 46 Ie 42.47N 112.51W
American Falls Reservoir 46 Ie 43.00N 113.00W
American Fork 46 Jf 40.23N 111.48W
American Highland 66 Ff 72.30S 78.00 E
American Samoa [5] 58 Kf 14.50S 170.00W
Americus 43 Ke 32.04N 84.14W
Amersfoort 11 Lb 52.09N 5.24 E
Amery Ice Shelf 66 Fe 69.30S 72.00 E
Ames 43 Ic 42.02N 93.37W
Amfilokhia 15 Ek 38.52N 21.10 E
Ámfissa 15 Fk 38.32N 22.23 E
Amfreville-la-Campagne 12 Ce 49.13N 0.57 E
Amga 20 Id 60.52N 131.50 E
Amga 21 Pc 62.40N 134.59 E
Amgalang → Xin Barag Zuoqi 27 Kb 48.13N 118.14 E
Am Géréda 35 Cc 12.52N 21.10 E
Amgu 28 Nb 45.51N 137.41 E
Amguema 20 Nc 68.03N 177.55W
Amguid 32 Id 26.30N 5.36 E
Amguid 31 Hf 26.26N 5.22 E
Amgun 21 Pd 52.56N 139.40 E
Amherst 42 Lg 45.49N 64.14W
Amherst, Mount- 59 Fc 18.11S 126.59 E
Amherst Island 44 Ic 44.12N 76.42W
Amiata, Monte- 14 Fh 42.53N 11.37 E
Amiens 6 Gf 49.54N 2.18 E
Āmij, Wādī- 24 If 33.48N 41.46 E
Amik Gölü 24 Gd 36.22N 36.17 E
Amīk Oölü 24 Gd 36.15N 36.12 E
Amili 25 Jc 28.26N 95.52 E
Amīndīvi Islands 25 Ef 11.23N 72.23 E
Aminuis 37 Bd 23.43S 19.21 E
'Āmir, Ra's- 30 Je 32.57N 21.43 E
Amirante Islands 30 Mi 6.00S 53.10 E
Amirante Trench (EN) 37 Bb 6.00S 52.30 E
Amisk Lake 42 Hf 54.35N 102.15W
Amistad, Presa de la- 45 Fl 28.34N 101.15W
Amistad Reservoir 43 Gf 28.34N 101.15W
Amite 45 Kk 30.44N 90.30W
Amlekhganj 25 Gc 27.17N 84.59 E
Amlia 40a Db 52.06N 173.30W
Amlwch 9 Ih 53.25N 4.20W

Index Symbols

[1] Independent Nation
[2] State, Region
[3] District, County
[4] Municipality
[5] Colony, Dependency
Continent
Physical Region
Historical or Cultural Region
Mount, Mountain
Volcano
Hill
Mountains, Mountain Range
Hills, Escarpment
Plateau, Upland
Pass, Gap
Plain, Lowland
Delta
Salt Flat
Valley, Canyon
Crater, Cave
Karst Features
Depression
Polder
Desert, Dunes
Forest, Woods
Heath, Steppe
Oasis
Cape, Point
Coast, Beach
Cliff
Peninsula
Isthmus
Sandbank
Island
Atoll
Rock, Reef
Islands, Archipelago
Rocks, Reefs
Coral Reef
Well, Spring
Geyser
River, Stream
Waterfall Rapids
River Mouth, Estuary
Lake
Salt Lake
Intermittent Lake
Reservoir
Swamp, Pond
Canal
Glacier
Ice Shelf, Pack Ice
Ocean
Sea
Gulf, Bay
Strait, Fjord
Lagoon
Bank
Seamount
Tablemount
Ridge
Shelf
Basin
Escarpment, Sea Scarp
Fracture
Trench, Abyss
National Park, Reserve
Point of Interest
Recreation Site
Cave, Cavern
Historic Site
Ruins
Wall, Walls
Church, Abbey
Temple
Scientific Station
Airport
Port
Lighthouse
Mine
Tunnel
Dam, Bridge

'Amm Adām	35	Fb	16.22N	36.09 E
'Ammān	22	Ff	31.57N	35.56 E
Ammanford	9	Jj	51.48N	3.59W
Ammarnäs	7	Dd	65.58N	16.12 E
Åmmeberg	8	Ff	58.52N	15.00 E
Ammer	10	Hi	47.57N	11.08 E
Ammerån	8	Ga	63.09N	16.13 E
Ammerland	10	Dc	53.15N	8.00 E
Ammersee	10	Hi	48.00N	11.08 E
Ammi-Moussa	13	Ni	35.52N	1.07 E
Ammóchostos = Famagusta (EN)	23	Dc	35.07N	33.57 E
Amnja	17	Me	63.45N	67.07 E
Amnok-kang	27	Ld	39.55N	124.20 E
Āmol	23	Hb	36.23N	52.20 E
Amolar	55	Dd	18.01 S	57.30W
Amorgós	15	Im	36.50N	25.53 E
Amorgós	15	Im	36.50N	25.59 E
Amorinópolis	55	Gc	16.36 S	51.08W
Amory	45	Lj	33.59N	88.29W
Amos	42	Jg	48.34N	78.07W
Åmot [Nor.]	8	Be	59.35N	8.00 E
Åmot [Nor.]	7	Bg	59.54N	9.54 E
Åmotfors	8	Ee	59.46N	12.22 E
Amoucha	13	Rh	36.23N	5.25 E
Amouliani	15	Gi	40.20N	23.55 E
Amour, Djebel-	32	Hc	33.45N	1.45 E
Amourj	32	Ff	16.10N	7.35W
Ampanihy	37	Gd	24.40 S	44.45 E
Amparafaravola	37	Hc	17.36 S	48.12 E
Amparo	55	If	22.42 S	46.47W
Amper	10	Hh	48.10N	11.50 E
Ampère Seamount (EN)	5	Eh	35.05N	12.13W
Amphitrite Point	46	Cb	48.56N	125.35W
Amposta	13	Md	40.43N	0.35 E
Ampthill	12	Bb	52.02N	0.29W
Ampurdán/L'Empordà	13	Ob	42.12N	2.45 E
Ampurias	13	Pb	42.10N	3.05 E
Amqui	44	Na	48.28N	67.26W
'Amrān	23	Ff	15.41N	43.55 E
Amrāvati	22	Jg	20.56N	77.45 E
Am-Raya	35	Bc	14.05N	16.30 E
Amritsar	22	Jf	31.35N	74.53 E
Amrum	8	Cj	54.40N	8.20 E
Amsaga	32	Ee	20.07N	14.10W
Amsittene, Jebel-	32	Fc	31.11N	9.40W
Amstel	12	Gb	52.22N	4.56 E
Amstelveen	12	Gb	52.18N	4.53 E
Amsterdam	30	Ol	37.57 S	77.40 E
Amsterdam [Neth.]	6	Ge	52.22N	4.54 E
Amsterdam [N.Y.-U.S.]	44	Jd	42.56N	74.12W
Amsterdam-Rijnkanaal	12	Hc	51.57N	5.25 E
Amstetten	14	Ib	48.07N	14.52 E
Am Timan	31	Jg	11.02N	20.17 E
Amūd, Jabal al-	23	Ec	30.59N	39.20 E
Āmūdā	24	Id	37.05N	40.54 E
Amu-Darja	18	Ef	37.57N	65.15 E
Amudarja = Amu Darya (EN)	21	He	43.40N	59.01 E
Āmū Daryā = Amu Darya (EN)	21	He	43.40N	59.01 E
Amu Darya (EN) = Amudarja	21	He	43.40N	59.01 E
Amu Darya (EN) = Āmū Daryā	21	He	43.40N	59.01 E
Amudat	36	Fb	1.58N	34.56 E
Amukta Pass	40a	Db	52.25N	172.00W
Amun	63a	Ba	5.57 S	154.45 E
Amund Ringnes	42	Ha	78.15N	97.00W
Amundsen Bay	66	Ee	66.55 S	50.00 E
Amundsen Coast	66	Mg	85.30 S	159.00W
Amundsen Glacier	66	Mg	85.35 S	159.00W
Amundsen Gulf	38	Gb	71.00N	124.00W
Amundsen-Scott Station	66	Bg	90.00 S	0.00
Amundsen Sea (EN)	66	Of	72.30 S	112.00W
Amungen	8	Fc	61.10N	15.40 E
Amuntai	22	Nj	2.26 S	115.15 E
Amur	21	Od	52.56N	141.10 E
'Amūr, Wādī	35	Eb	18.56N	33.34 E
Amurang	26	Hf	1.11N	124.35 E
Amursk	20	If	50.16N	136.55 E
Amurskaja Oblast	20	Hf	54.00N	128.00 E
Amurzet	20	Ig	47.41N	131.07 E
Amvrakia, Gulf of- (EN) = Amvrakikós Kólpos	15	Dk	39.00N	21.00 E
Amvrakikós Kólpos = Amvrakia, Gulf of- (EN)	15	Dk	39.00N	21.00 E
Amvrosijevka	16	Kf	47.44N	38.31 E
Am Zoer	35	Cc	14.13N	21.23 E
Anaa Atoll	61	Lc	17.25 S	145.30W
Anabar	64e	Ba	0.29 S	166.57 E
Anabar	21	Nb	73.08N	113.36 E
Anabarskoje Ploskogorje	21	Mc	70.00N	108.00 E
An Abhainn Dubh/Blackwater	9	Gh	53.39N	6.43W
An Abhainn Mhór/Blackwater [Ire.]	9	Fj	51.51N	7.50W
An Abhainn Mhór/Blackwater [N.Ire.-U.K.]	9	Gg	54.30N	6.35W
Anabuki	29	Dd	34.02N	134.11 E
Anacasti	56	Gc	28.49 S	65.30W
Anaco	54	Fb	9.27N	64.28W
Anaconda	43	Eb	46.08N	112.57W
Anacortes	46	Db	48.30N	122.37W
Anadarko	45	Gi	35.04N	98.15W
Anadolu = Anatolia (EN)	21	Ff	39.00N	35.00 E
Anadyr	21	Tc	64.55N	176.05 E
Anadyr	22	Tc	64.45N	177.29 E
Anadyr Gulf (EN) = Anadyrski Zaliv	21	Uc	64.00N	179.00W
Anadyr Range (EN) = Anadyrskoje Ploskogorje	21	Tc	67.00N	174.00 E
Anadyrski Liman	20	Md	64.30N	178.00 E
Anadyrski Zaliv = Anadyr Gulf (EN)	21	Uc	64.00N	179.00W
Anadyrskoje Ploskogorje = Anadyr Range (EN)	21	Tc	67.00N	174.00 E
Anáfi	15	Im	36.22N	25.47 E
Anaghit	35	Fb	16.20N	38.39 E
Anagni	14	Hi	41.44N	13.09 E
'Ānah	23	Fc	34.28N	41.56 E
Anaheim	46	Gj	33.51N	117.57W
Anahola	65a	Ba	22.09N	159.19W
Anáhuac	48	Id	27.14N	100.09W
Anahuac, Meseta de-	47	Dd	21.30N	101.00W
An Aird/Ards Peninsula	9	Hg	54.30N	5.30W
Anaj Mudi	21	Jh	10.10N	77.04 E
Anaktuvuk Pass	40	Ic	68.10N	151.50W
Analalava	37	Hb	14.38 S	47.45 E
Analavelona	37	Gd	22.37 S	44.10 E
Ana María, Golfo de-	49	Hc	21.25N	78.40W
Anambas, Kepulauan- = Anambas Islands (EN)	21	Mi	3.00N	106.00 E
Anambas Islands (EN) = Anambas, Kepulauan-	21	Mi	3.00N	106.00 E
Anambra	34	Gd	6.30N	7.30 E
Anamé	63b	De	20.08 S	169.49 E
Anamizu	28	Nf	37.14N	136.54 E
Anamur	23	Db	36.06N	32.50 E
Anamur Burun	23	Db	36.03N	32.48 E
Anan [Jap.]	28	Mh	33.55N	134.39 E
Anan [Jap.]	29	Ed	35.19N	137.48 E
Anane, Djebel-	13	Mi	35.12N	0.47 E
Anánes	15	Hm	36.31N	24.08 E
Ananjev	16	Ff	47.43N	29.59 E
Anankwin	25	Je	15.41N	97.59 E
Anantapur	25	Ff	14.41N	77.36 E
Anantnāg (Islāmābād)	25	Fb	33.44N	75.09 E
Anapa	19	Dg	44.53N	37.19 E
Anapo	14	Jm	37.03N	15.16 E
Anápolis	53	Lg	16.20 S	48.58W
Anapu, Rio-	54	Hd	2.15 S	51.30W
Anār	23	Ic	30.53N	55.18 E
Anārak	23	Hc	33.20N	53.42 E
Anare Station	66	Jd	54.30 S	158.55 E
Anaro, Río-	49	Lj	7.48N	70.12W
Añasco	51a	Ab	18.17N	67.10W
Anatahan Island	57	Fc	16.22N	145.40 E
Anatolia (EN) = Anadolu	21	Ff	39.00N	35.00 E
Anatoliki Rodhópi	15	Ih	41.44N	25.31 E
Añatuya	56	Hc	28.28 S	62.50W
Anauá, Rio-	54	Fc	0.58N	61.21W
Anazarba	24	Fd	37.15N	35.45 E
An Baile Meánach/Ballymena	9	Gg	54.52N	6.17W
An Bhanna/Bann	9	Gf	55.10N	6.46W
An Bhearú/Barrow	9	Gi	52.10N	7.00W
An Bhinn Bhuí/Benwee Head	9	Dg	54.21N	9.48W
An Bhograch/Boggeragh Mountains	9	Ei	52.05N	9.00W
An Bhóinn/Boyne	9	Gh	53.43N	6.15W
An Bhrosnach/Brosna	9	Fh	53.13N	7.58W
An Blascaod Mór/Great Blasket	9	Ci	52.05N	10.32W
Anbyŏn	28	Ie	39.02N	127.32 E
An Cabhán/Cavan	9	Fh	53.55N	7.30W
An Cabhán/Cavan	9	Fg	54.00N	7.21W
An Caisleán Nua/Newcastle	9	Hg	54.12N	5.54W
An Caisleán Nua/Newcastle West	9	Di	52.27N	9.03W
An Caisleán Riabhach/Castlerea	9	Eh	53.46N	8.29W
An Caoláire Rua/Killary Harbour	9	Dh	53.38N	9.55W
Ancares, Sierra de-	13	Fb	42.46N	6.54W
Ancash	54	Ce	9.30 S	77.45W
Ancenis	11	Eg	47.22N	1.10W
An Chathair/Caher	9	Fi	52.22N	7.55W
An Cheacha/Caha Mountains	9	Dj	51.45N	9.45W
Anchorage	39	Ec	61.13N	149.53W
An Chorr Chríochach/Cookstown	9	Gg	54.39N	6.45W
Anci (Langfang)	27	Kd	39.29N	116.40 E
An Clár/Clare	9	Ei	52.50N	9.00W
An Cóbh/Cóbh	9	Ej	51.51N	8.17W
Ancohuma, Nevado-	54	Eg	15.51 S	68.36W
Ancona	6	Hg	43.38N	13.30 E
Ancón de Sardinas, Bahía de-	54	Cc	1.30N	79.50W
Ancre	11	Ie	49.54N	2.28 E
Ancuabe	37	Fb	12.58 S	39.51 E
Ancud	56	Ff	41.52 S	73.50W
Ancud, Golfo de-	56	Ff	42.05 S	73.00W
Anda	27	Mb	46.24N	125.20 E
Anda (Sartu)	28	Ha	46.35N	125.00 E
Andacollo [Arg.]	56	Fe	37.11 S	70.41W
Andacollo [Chile]	56	Fd	30.14 S	71.06W
Andahuaylas	54	Df	13.39 S	73.23W
An Daingean/Dingle	9	Ci	52.08N	10.15W
Andalgalá	56	Gc	27.36 S	66.19W
Åndalsnes	7	Be	62.34N	7.42 E
Andalucía = Andalusia (EN)	13	Hg	37.30N	4.30W
Andalucía = Andalusia (EN)	5	Fh	37.30N	4.30W
Andalusia	43	Je	31.19N	86.29W
Andalusia (EN) = Andalucía	13	Hg	37.30N	4.30W
Andalusia (EN) = Andalucía	5	Fh	37.30N	4.30W
Andaman and Nicobar	25	If	12.30N	92.45 E
Andaman Basin (EN)	21	Lh	10.00N	94.00 E
Andaman Islands	21	Lh	12.30N	92.43 E
Andaman Sea (EN)	21	Lh	10.00N	95.00 E
Andamooka	59	Hf	30.27 S	137.12 E
'Andān, Wādī-	23	Ie	21.05N	58.23 E
Andant	55	Am	36.34 S	62.07W
Andapa	37	Hb	14.38 S	49.33 E
Andara	37	Cc	18.03 S	21.27 E
Andelle	12	De	49.19N	1.14 E
Andenes	7	Db	69.19N	16.08 E
Andenne	12	Hd	50.29N	5.06 E
Andenne-Namêche	12	Hd	50.28N	5.00 E
Andéranboukane	34	Fb	15.26N	3.02 E
Anderlecht	12	Gd	50.50N	4.18 E
Anderlues	12	Gd	50.24N	4.16 E
Andermatt	14	Cd	46.38N	8.37 E
Andernach	10	Df	50.26N	7.24 E
Andernos-les-Bains	11	Ej	44.44N	1.06W
Anderson	42	Ec	69.42N	129.01W
Anderson [Ca.-U.S.]	46	Df	40.27N	122.18W
Anderson [In.-U.S.]	43	Jc	40.10N	85.41W
Anderson [S.C.-U.S.]	43	Ke	34.30N	82.39W
Anderstorp	8	Eg	57.17N	13.38 E
Andes (EN) = Andes, Cordillera de los-	52	Jh	20.00 S	67.00W
Andes, Cordillera de los- = Andes (EN)	52	Jh	20.00 S	67.00W
Andevoranto	37	Hc	18.48 S	49.02 E
Andfjorden	7	Db	69.10N	16.20 E
Andhra Pradesh	25	Fe	16.00N	79.00 E
Andía, Sierra de-	13	Kb	42.45N	2.00W
Andikhásia Óri	15	Ej	39.47N	21.55 E
Andikira	15	Fk	38.23N	22.38 E
Andikíthira = Andikithira (EN)	15	Gn	35.52N	23.18 E
Andikithira (EN) = Andikíthira	15	Gn	35.52N	23.18 E
Andikithíron, Stenón-	15	Gn	35.45N	23.25 E
Andilamena	37	Hc	17.01 S	48.32 E
Andilanatoby	37	Hc	17.56 S	48.14 E
Andīmeshk	24	Mf	32.27N	48.21 E
Andímilos	15	Hm	36.47N	24.14 E
Andíparos	15	Il	37.00N	25.03 E
Andípaxoi	15	Dj	39.08N	20.14 E
Andípsara	15	Ik	38.33N	25.24 E
Andir He	27	Dd	38.00N	83.36 E
Andiria Burun	24	Fe	35.42N	34.35 E
Andırın	24	Gd	37.34N	36.20 E
Andirlangar	27	Dd	37.36N	83.50 E
Andírrion	15	Ek	38.20N	21.46 E
Andítilos	15	Km	36.22N	27.28 E
Andižan	22	Je	40.45N	72.22 E
Andižanskaja Oblast	19	Hg	40.45N	72.20 E
Andkhvoy	23	Kb	36.56N	65.08 E
Andŏng	27	Md	36.36N	128.44 E
Andorra (Valls d'Andorra)	6	Gg	42.30N	1.30 E
Andorra la Vella	6	Gg	42.31N	1.31 E
Andover	9	Lj	51.13N	1.28W
Andøya	7	Db	69.08N	15.54 E
Andradas	55	If	22.05 S	46.35W
Andradina	56	Jb	20.54 S	51.23W
Andraitx	13	Oe	39.35N	2.25 E
Andreanof Islands	38	Bd	52.00N	176.00W
Andreapol	7	Hh	56.39N	32.16 E
Andrées Land	41	Jd	73.20N	26.30W
Andrejevka [Kaz.-U.S.S.R.]	19	If	45.47N	80.35 E
Andrejevka [Ukr.-U.S.S.R.]	16	Je	49.32N	36.40 E
Andrejevo-Ivanovka	15	Nb	47.31N	30.21 E
Andrejevsk	20	Ge	58.10N	114.15 E
Andrelândia	55	Je	21.44 S	44.18W
Andrešito	55	Dk	33.08 S	57.09W
Andrespol	10	Pe	51.43N	19.40 E
Andrews	45	Ej	32.19N	102.33W
Andria	14	Ki	41.13N	16.17 E
Andriamena	37	Hc	17.28 S	47.29 E
Andriba	37	Hc	17.36 S	46.53 E
Andrijevica	15	Cg	42.44N	19.48 E
Andringitra	30	Lk	22.20 S	46.55 E
Andrítsaina	15	El	37.29N	21.54 E
Androka	37	Gd	24.59 S	44.04 E
Androna, Plateau de l'-	37	Hc	15.30 S	48.20 E
Ándros	5	Ih	37.50N	24.50 E
Andros	38	Lg	24.25N	78.00W
Ándros	15	Hl	37.50N	24.56 E
Androscoggin River	44	Md	43.55N	69.55W
Androssan	9	If	55.40N	4.55W
Andros Town	47	Id	24.43N	77.47W
Androth Island	25	Ef	10.50N	73.41 E
Androy	30	Lk	25.00 S	45.40 E
Andruševka	16	Fe	49.59N	29.01 E
Andrychów	10	Pg	49.52N	19.21 E
Andselv	7	Eb	69.04N	18.30 E
Andudu	36	Eb	2.29N	28.41 E
Andújar	13	Hf	38.03N	4.04W
Andulo	36	Ce	11.28 S	16.43 E
Andu Tan	26	Fe	7.35N	114.15 E
Anduze	11	Jj	44.03N	3.59 E
An Ea agail/Errigal	9	Ef	55.02N	8.07W
Aneby	8	Fg	57.50N	14.48 E
Anéfis	34	Fb	18.03N	0.36 E
Anegada	47	Le	18.45N	64.20W
Anegada, Bahía-	56	Hf	40.15 S	62.15W
Anegada Passage	47	Le	18.30N	63.40W
Aného	34	Fd	6.14N	1.36 E
An Éirne/Erne	9	Eg	54.30N	8.15W
An Eithne/Inny	9	Fh	53.35N	7.50W
An Eoghanach/Annalee	9	Fg	54.02N	7.25W
Anet	12	Df	48.51N	1.26 E
Aneto, Pico de-	5	Gg	42.38N	0.40 E
Aney	34	Hb	19.24N	12.56 E
Aneytioum, Ile-	57	Hg	20.12 S	169.49 E
An Feabhal	9	Ff	55.04N	7.15W
An Fhéil/Feale	9	Di	52.28N	9.40W
An Fheoir/Nore	9	Gi	52.25N	6.58W
Angamos, Punta- [Chile]	56	Fb	23.01 S	70.32W
Angamos, Punta- [Pas.]	65d	Bb	27.04 S	109.17W
Angara	21	Ld	58.06N	93.00 E
Angarsk	22	Md	52.34N	103.54 E
Angarski, Pereval-	16	Ig	44.47N	34.25 E
Angarski Krjaž	20	Fe	57.30N	103.00 E
Angathonisi	15	Jl	37.28N	27.00 E
Angaur Island	57	Ed	6.54N	134.09 E
Ånge	7	De	62.31N	15.37 E
Änge	8	Fa	63.27N	14.03 E
An Gearran/Garron Point	9	Hf	55.05N	5.58W
Ángel, Cerro-	48	Hf	22.49N	102.34W
Ángel, Salto- = Angel Falls (EN)	52	Je	5.57N	62.30W
Angelburg	12	Kd	50.47N	8.25 E
Angel de la Guarda, Isla-	47	Bc	29.20N	113.25W
Angeles	26	Hc	15.09N	120.35 E
Angeles, Sierra de los-	48	Jf	23.10N	99.20W
Angel Falls (EN) = Ángel, Salto-	52	Je	5.57N	62.30W
Angel Falls (EN) = Churún Merú	52	Je	5.57N	62.30W
Ängelholm	7	Ch	56.15N	12.51 E
Angélica	55	Bj	31.33 S	61.33W
Angeln	10	Fb	54.40N	9.45 E
Ängelsberg	8	Ge	59.58N	16.02 E
Anger	35	Fd	9.40N	36.06 E
Angereb	35	Fc	13.44N	36.28 E
Ångermanälven	5	Hc	62.48N	17.56 E
Angermünde	10	Jc	53.02N	14.00 E
Angers	6	Ff	47.28N	0.33W
Angkor	25	Kf	13.26N	103.52 E
Angikuni Lake	42	Hd	62.10N	99.55W
Angistrion	15	Gl	37.40N	23.20 E
Anglem, Mount-	62	Bg	46.44 S	167.54 E
Anglès	13	Oc	41.57N	2.39 E
Anglesey	5	Fe	53.18N	4.20W
Anglet	11	Ek	43.29N	1.32W
Angleton	45	Il	29.10N	95.26W
Anglin	11	Gh	46.42N	0.52 E
Anglona	14	Cj	40.45N	8.45 E
Angmagssalik	67	Mc	65.45N	37.30W
Ango	36	Eb	4.02N	25.52 E
Angoche	31	Kj	16.12 S	39.54 E
Angoche, Ilha-	30	Kj	16.20 S	39.51 E
Angol	56	Fe	37.48 S	72.43W
Angola	31	Ij	12.30 S	18.30 E
Angola	44	Ee	41.38N	85.00W
Angola Basin (EN)	3	Ek	15.00 S	3.00 E
Angoram	60	Ch	4.04 S	144.04 E
Angostura	48	Ee	25.22N	108.11W
Angostura, Presa de la-	48	Mi	16.30N	92.30W
Angostura, Salto-	54	Dc	2.43N	70.57W
Angostura Reservoir	45	Ee	43.18N	103.27W
Angoulême	11	Gi	45.39N	0.09 E
Angoumois	11	Fi	45.30N	0.10W
Angra do Heroísmo	32	Bb	38.42N	27.15W
Angra do Héroísmo	31	Ee	38.39N	27.13W
Angra dos Reis	55	Jf	23.00 S	44.18W
Angren	19	Hg	41.03N	70.10 E
Angu	36	Db	3.33N	24.28 E
Anguang	28	Gb	45.36N	123.48 E
Anguilla	39	Mh	18.15N	63.05W
Anguilla	38	Mh	18.15N	63.05W
Anguilla, Canal de l'- = Anguilla Channel (EN)	51b	Ab	18.09N	63.04W
Anguilla Bank (EN)	51b	Ab	18.30N	63.03W
Anguilla Cays	49	Hb	23.31N	78.33W
Anguilla Channel (EN) = Anguilla, Canal de l'-	51b	Ab	18.09N	63.04W
Anguli Nur	28	Cd	41.23N	114.30 E
Anguo	28	Ce	38.25N	115.20 E
Anhanca	36	Cf	16.47 S	15.33 E
Anhanguera	55	Hd	18.21 S	48.17W
An Hoa	25	Le	15.46N	108.03 E
Anholt	7	Ch	56.40N	11.35 E
Anhua (Dongping)	27	Jf	28.27N	111.15 E
Anhui Sheng (An-hui Sheng) = Anhwei (EN)	27	Ke	32.00N	117.00 E
An-hui Sheng → Anhui Sheng = Anhwei (EN)	27	Ke	32.00N	117.00 E
Anhwei (EN) = Anhui Sheng (An-hui Sheng)	27	Ke	32.00N	117.00 E
Anhwei (EN) = An-hui Sheng → Anhui Sheng	27	Ke	32.00N	117.00 E
Ani	29	Gb	39.59N	140.25 E
Aniak	40	Hd	61.34N	159.30W
An Iarmhí/Westmeath	9	Fh	53.30N	7.30W
Anibare	64e	Bb	0.32 S	166.57 E
Anibare Bay	64e	Bb	0.32 S	166.57 E
Aniche	12	Fd	50.20N	3.15 E
Ánidros	15	Im	36.37N	25.41 E
Anié	34	Fd	7.45N	1.12 E
Anie, Pic d'-	11	Fl	42.57N	0.43W
Aniene	14	Gi	41.56N	12.30 E
Anijangying → Luanping	28	Dd	40.55N	117.19 E
Anikščjaj/Anykščiai	7	Fi	55.31N	25.08 E
Animas Peak	45	Bk	31.35N	108.47W
Anina	15	Ed	45.05N	21.51 E
Anita Garibaldi	55	Gh	27.37 S	51.05W
Anittepe	15	Kh	41.21N	27.42 E
Aniva	20	Jg	46.41N	142.35 E
Aniva, Zaliv-	20	Jg	46.20N	142.40 E
Anivorano Nord	37	Hb	12.43 S	49.12 E
Aniwa, Ile-	57	Hf	19.16 S	169.35 E
Anizy-le-Château	12	Fe	49.30N	3.27 E
Anjala	7	Gf	60.41N	26.50 E
Anji	28	Ei	30.39N	119.41 E
Anjiang → Qianyang	27	Jf	27.19N	110.13 E
Anjō	29	Ed	34.57N	137.05 E
Anjou	11	Fg	47.20N	0.30W
Anjou, Ostrova- = Anjou Islands (EN)	21	Qb	75.30N	143.00 E
Anjouan/Nzwani	30	Lj	12.15 S	44.25 E
Anjou Islands (EN) = Anjou, Ostrova-	21	Qb	75.30N	143.00 E
Anjozorobe	37	Hc	18.24 S	47.52 E
Anju	27	Md	39.37N	125.40 E
Anjuj	20	Ig	49.20N	136.20 E
Anjujski Hrebet	20	Lc	67.20N	166.00 E
Anjuou, Val d'-	11	Fg	47.25N	0.15W
Anka	34	Gc	12.07N	5.55 E
Ankang (Xing'an)	22	Mf	32.37N	109.03 E
Ankara	22	Ff	39.56N	32.52 E
Ankaratra	30	Lj	19.25 S	47.12 E
Ankarsrum	7	Dh	57.42N	16.19 E
Ankavandra	37	Hc	18.45 S	45.18 E
Ankazoabo	37	Gd	22.16 S	44.30 E
Ankazobe	37	Hc	18.17 S	47.05 E
Ankeny	45	Jf	41.44N	93.36W
'Ankhor	35	Hc	10.47N	46.18 E
Anklam	10	Jc	53.52N	13.42 E
Ankober	35	Fd	9.40N	39.44 E
Ankoro	36	Ed	6.45 S	26.57 E
Ankum	12	Jb	52.33N	7.53 E
An Laoi/Lee	9	Ej	51.55N	8.30W
Anlong	27	If	25.02N	105.30 E
An Longfort/Longford	9	Fh	53.40N	7.40W
An Longfort/Longfort	9	Fh	53.44N	7.47W
An Lorgain/Lurgan	9	Gg	54.28N	6.20W
Anlu	27	Je	31.12N	113.46 E
An Mhí/Meath	9	Gh	53.35N	6.40W
An Mhuaidh/Moy	9	Dg	54.12N	9.08W
An Mhuir Cheilteach = Celtic Sea (EN)	5	Fe	51.00N	7.00W
An Muileann gCearr/Mullingar	9	Fh	53.32N	7.20W
An Muirthead/Mullet Peninsula	9	Cg	54.15N	10.04W
Ånn	7	Ce	63.15N	12.35 E
Ånn	8	Ea	63.19N	12.33 E
Ann, Cape- [Ant.]	66	Ee	66.10 S	51.22 E
Ann, Cape- [Ma.-U.S.]	44	Ld	42.39N	70.38W
Anna [Il.-U.S.]	45	Lh	37.28N	89.15W
Anna [Nauru]	64e	Ba	0.29 S	166.56 E
Anna [R.S.F.S.R.]	19	Ee	51.29N	40.26 E
Annaba	31	He	36.54N	7.46 E
Annaba	32	Ib	35.35N	8.00 E
An Nabaţīyah at Taḩtā	24	Gf	33.23N	35.29 E
Annaberg-Buchholz	10	If	50.34N	13.00 E
An Nabī Şāliḩ	24	Eh	28.38N	33.59 E
An Nabk	23	Ec	34.01N	36.44 E
An Nabk Abū Gaşr	24	Hg	30.21N	38.34 E
An Nafīdah	14	En	36.08N	10.23 E
An Nafūd	21	Gg	28.30N	41.00 E
An Najaf	22	Gf	31.59N	44.20 E
An Najaf	24	Kg	31.20N	44.07 E
An Nakhl	33	Fd	29.55N	33.45 E
Annalee/An Eoghanach	9	Fg	54.02N	7.25W
Annam (EN) = Trung Phan	21	Me	15.00N	108.00 E
Annamitique, Chaîne-	25	Le	17.00N	106.00 E
Annan	9	Jg	54.59N	3.16W
Annan	9	Jg	55.00N	3.16W
Anna Paulowna	12	Gb	52.52N	4.52 E
Anna Paulowna-Kleine Sluis	12	Gb	52.52N	4.52 E
Anna Point	64e	Ba	0.29 S	166.56 E
Annapolis	39	Lf	38.59N	76.30W
Annapolis Royal	44	Oc	44.45N	65.31W
Annapurna	21	Kg	28.34N	83.50 E
Ann Arbor	43	Kc	42.18N	83.45W
Anna Regina	50	Gi	7.16N	58.30W
An Nás/Naas	9	Gh	53.13N	6.39W
An Nashshāsh	24	Pk	23.05N	54.02 E
An Nashwah	24	Lg	30.49N	47.36 E
An Nāşirīyah	23	Gc	31.02N	46.16 E
An Nasser	24	Ej	24.36N	32.58 E
An Nawfalīyah	33	Cc	30.47N	17.50 E
Annecy	11	Mi	45.54N	6.07 E
Annecy, Lac d'-	11	Mi	45.51N	6.11 E
Annemasse	11	Mh	46.12N	6.15 E
Annevoie-Rouillon	12	Gd	50.21N	4.50 E
An Nīl	35	Ea	20.10N	33.00 E
An Nīl al Azraq	35	Ed	12.20N	34.15 E
Anning	27	Hg	24.58N	102.29 E
Anniston	43	Je	33.40N	85.50W
Annobón	30	Hi	1.32 S	5.38 E
Annonay	11	Ki	45.14N	4.40 E
Annotto Bay	49	Id	18.16N	76.46W
An Nu'ayrīyah	24	Mi	27.28N	48.27 E
An Nuhūd	31	Jg	12.42N	28.26 E
An Nu' Mān	24	Fi	27.06N	35.46 E
An Nu'mānīyah	24	Kf	32.32N	45.25 E
Annweiler am Trifels	12	Je	49.12N	7.58 E
Anoia/Noya	13	Nc	41.28N	1.56 E
Anoka	45	Jd	45.11N	93.23W
An Ómaigh/Omagh	9	Fg	54.36N	7.18W
Anori	54	Fd	3.47 S	61.38W
Anosyennes, Chaînes-	37	Hd	24.20 S	47.00 E
Ânou Makarene	34	Gb	18.07N	7.35 E
Áno Viánnos	15	In	35.03N	25.25 E
Anóyia	15	Hn	35.15N	24.54 E
Anping [China]	28	Ce	38.13N	115.32 E
Anping [China]	28	Gd	41.10N	123.25 E
An Pointe/Warrenpoint	9	Gg	54.06N	6.15W
Anpu	27	Ig	21.30N	110.00 E
Anpu Gang	27	Ig	21.25N	109.40 E
Anqing	22	Nf	30.32N	116.59 E
Anqiu	28	Ef	36.25N	119.12 E
An Ráth/Ráth Luirc	9	Ei	52.21N	8.41W
An Ribhéar/Kenmare River	9	Dj	51.50N	9.50W
Anröchte	12	Kc	51.34N	8.20 E
Ans	12	Hd	50.39N	5.32 E
Anşāb	23	Fd	29.11N	44.43 E
Ansauvillers	12	Ee	49.34N	2.24 E
Ansbach	10	Gg	49.18N	10.35 E
An Sciobairín/Skibbereen	9	Dj	51.33N	9.15W
An Seancheann/Kinsale, Old Head of-	9	Ej	51.36N	8.32W
Anse-à-Veau	49	Kd	18.30N	73.19W
Anse-Bertrand	51e	Ab	16.29N	61.31W
Anse-d'Hainault	49	Jd	18.30N	74.27W
Anse la Raye	51k	Ab	13.57N	61.03W
Anshan	22	Oe	41.08N	122.59 E
Anshun	22	Mg	26.15N	105.58 E
Ansina	56	Id	31.54 S	55.28W
Ansley	45	Gf	41.18N	99.23W
Anson Bay	59	Gb	13.20 S	130.05 E
Ansongo	34	Fb	15.40N	0.31 E
An Srath Bán/Strabane	9	Fg	54.49N	7.27W
Anta	54	Df	13.29 S	72.09W

Index Symbols

- 1 Independent Nation
- 2 State, Region
- 3 District, County
- 4 Municipality
- 5 Colony, Dependency
- Continent
- Physical Region
- Historical or Cultural Region
- Mount, Mountain
- Volcano
- Hill
- Mountains, Mountain Range
- Hills, Escarpment
- Plateau, Upland
- Pass, Gap
- Plain, Lowland
- Delta
- Salt Flat
- Valley, Canyon
- Crater, Cave
- Karst Features
- Depression
- Polder
- Desert, Dunes
- Forest, Woods
- Heath, Steppe
- Oasis
- Cape, Point
- Coast, Beach
- Cliff
- Peninsula
- Isthmus
- Sandbank
- Island
- Atoll
- Rock, Reef
- Islands, Archipelago
- Rocks, Reefs
- Coral Reef
- Well, Spring
- Geyser
- River, Stream
- Waterfall Rapids
- River Mouth, Estuary
- Lake
- Salt Lake
- Intermittent Lake
- Reservoir
- Swamp, Pond
- Canal
- Glacier
- Ice Shelf, Pack Ice
- Ocean
- Sea
- Gulf, Bay
- Strait, Fjord
- Lagoon
- Bank
- Seamount
- Tablemount
- Ridge
- Shelf
- Basin
- Escarpment, Sea Scarp
- Fracture
- Trench, Abyss
- National Park, Reserve
- Point of Interest
- Recreation Site
- Cave, Cavern
- Historic Site
- Ruins
- Wall, Walls
- Church, Abbey
- Temple
- Scientific Station
- Airport
- Port
- Lighthouse
- Mine
- Tunnel
- Dam, Bridge

Antabamba 54 Df 14.19S 72.55W
Antakya=Antioch (EN) 23 Eb 36.14N 36.07 E
Antalaha 31 Mj 14.55S 50.15 E
Antalya 22 Ff 36.53N 30.42 E
Antalya, Gulf of- (EN)=Antalya Körfezi 23 Db 36.30N 31.00 E
Antalya Körfezi=Antalya, Gulf of- (EN) 23 Db 36.30N 31.00 E
An Tan 25 Le 15.26N 108.39 E
Antananarivo 31 Lj 18.55S 47.30 E
Antananarivo [3] 37 Hc 19.00S 46.40 E
Antanimora 37 Hd 24.48S 45.39 E
An tAonach/Nenagh 9 Ei 52.52N 8.12W
Antarctica (EN) 66 Bg 90.00S 0.00
Antarctic Peninsula (EN) 66 Qe 69.30S 65.00W
Antas, Cachoeira das- 55 Ha 13.06S 48.09W
Antas, Rio das- 55 Gi 29.04S 51.21W
An Teampall Mór/Templemore 9 Fi 52.48N 7.50W
Antela, Laguna de- 13 Eb 42.07N 7.41W
Antelao 14 Gd 46.27N 12.16 E
Antelope Creek 46 Me 43.29N 105.23W
Anten 8 Ef 58.03N 12.30 E
Antequera [Par.] 55 Dg 24.08S 57.07W
Antequera [Sp.] 13 Hg 37.01N 4.33W
Anthony 45 Cj 32.00N 106.34W
Anti-Atlas 30 Ge 30.00N 8.30W
Antibes 11 Nk 43.35N 7.07 E
Antibes, Cap d'- 11 Nk 43.32N 7.07 E
Antica, Isla- 50 Eg 10.24N 62.43W
Anticosti, Île d'- 38 Me 49.30N 63.00W
Antigo 45 Ld 45.09N 89.09W
Antigonish 42 Lg 45.37N 61.58W
Antigua 38 Mh 17.03N 61.48W
Antigua [1] 39 Mh 17.03N 61.48W
Antigua Guatemala 47 Ff 14.34N 90.44W
Antiguo Cauce del Rio Bermejo 56 Hc 25.39S 60.11W
Antiguo Morelos 48 Jf 22.30N 99.05W
Antilla 49 Jc 20.50N 75.45W
Antillas, Mar de las-/Caribe, Mar-=Caribbean Sea (EN) 38 Lh 15.00N 73.00W
Antillas Mayores=Greater Antilles (EN) 38 Lh 20.00N 74.00W
Antillas Menores=Lesser Antilles (EN) 38 Mh 15.00N 61.00W
Antilles, Mer des-/Caraïbe, Mer-=Caribbean Sea (EN) 38 Lh 15.00N 73.00W
An tInbhear Mór/Arklow 9 Gi 52.48N 6.09W
Antioch 46 Eg 38.00N 121.49W
Antioch (EN)=Antakya 23 Eb 36.14N 36.07 E
Antioche, Pertuis d'- 11 Eh 46.05N 1.20W
Antiope Reef 57 Kf 18.18S 168.40W
Antioquia [2] 54 Cb 7.00N 75.30W
Antipajëta 20 Cc 69.09N 77.00 E
Antipodes Islands 57 Ii 49.40S 178.50 E
Antiques, Pointe d'- 51e Ab 16.26N 61.33W
An t-Iúr/Newry 9 Gg 54.11N 6.20W
Antler River 45 Fb 49.08N 101.00W
Antlers 45 Ii 34.14N 95.37W
Antofagasta [2] 56 Gb 23.30S 69.00W
Antofagasta 53 Ih 23.39S 70.24W
Antofagasta de la Sierra 56 Gc 26.04S 67.25W
Antofalla, Salar de- 56 Gc 25.44S 67.45W
Antofalla, Volcán- 56 Gc 25.34S 67.55W
Antoing 12 Fd 50.34N 3.27 E
Antón 49 Gi 8.24N 80.16W
Anton Dohrn Seamount (EN) 9 Cd 57.30N 11.00W
Antongil, Baie d'- 30 Lj 15.45S 49.50 E
Antonina 56 Kc 25.27S 48.43W
Antônio João 55 Ef 23.15S 55.31W
Antonito 45 Dh 37.05N 106.00W
Antón Lizardo, Punta de- 48 Lh 19.03N 95.58W
Antony 12 Ef 48.45N 2.18 E
Antopol 10 Ud 52.12N 24.53 E
Antracit 16 Ke 48.06N 39.06 E
Antreff 12 Ld 50.52N 9.15 E
Antrim/Aontroim 9 Gg 54.43N 6.13W
Antrim Mountains 9 Gf 55.00N 6.10W
Antrodoco 14 Hh 42.25N 13.05 E
Antsakabary 37 Hc 15.03S 48.56 E
Antsalova 37 Gc 18.42S 44.33 E
Antseranana [3] 37 Hb 13.40S 49.15 E
Antseranana 31 Lj 12.17S 49.17 E
An tSionainn/Shannon 5 Fe 52.36N 9.41W
Antsirabe 31 Lj 19.51S 47.01 E
An tSiúir/Suir 9 Gi 52.15N 7.00W
Antsla 7 Gh 57.52N 26.33 E
An tSláine/Slaney 9 Gi 52.21N 6.30W
Antsohihy 31 Lj 14.52S 47.58 E
An tSuca/Suck 9 Eh 53.16N 8.03W
Anttola 8 Lc 61.35N 27.39 E
Antu (Songjiang) 28 Jc 42.33N 128.20 E
An Tuc 25 Lf 13.57N 108.39 E
Antufash, Jazīrat- 33 Hf 15.42N 42.25 E
An Tulach/Tullow 9 Gi 52.48N 6.44W
An Tulach Mhór/Tullamore 9 Fh 53.16N 7.30W
Antwerp (EN)=Antwerpen/Anvers 6 Ge 50.38N 5.34 E
Antwerp (EN)=Anvers/Antwerpen 6 Ge 50.38N 5.34 E
Antwerpen [3] 12 Gc 51.10N 4.30 E
Antwerpen/Anvers=Antwerp (EN) 6 Ge 50.38N 5.34 E
Antwerpen-Ekeren 11 Kc 51.17N 4.25 E
Antwerpen-Hoboken 12 Gc 51.10N 4.21 E
Antwerpen-Merksem 12 Gc 51.15N 4.27 E
Antykan 20 If 54.55N 135.13 E
An Uaimh/Navan 9 Gh 53.39N 6.41W
Anuradhapura 25 Gg 8.21N 80.23 E
Anuta Island 57 Hf 11.38S 169.50 E
Anvers/Antwerpen=Antwerp (EN) 6 Ge 50.38N 5.34 E
Anvers Island 66 Qe 64.33S 63.35W
Anvik 40 Gd 62.40N 160.12W
Anxi 22 Le 40.30N 96.00 E
Anxiang 27 Jf 29.26N 112.11 E
Anxin 28 Ce 38.55N 115.56 E
Anxious Bay 59 Gf 33.25S 134.35 E
Anyang (Zhangde) 22 Nf 36.01N 114.25 E
A'nyêmaqen Shan 21 Lf 34.30N 100.00 E
Anyi 28 Cj 28.50N 115.31 E
Anykščiai/Anikščjaj 7 Fi 55.31N 25.08 E
Anyva, Mys- 20 Jg 46.00N 143.25 E
Anza 14 Ce 46.00N 8.17 E
Anze 28 Bf 36.09N 112.14 E
Anzegem 12 Fd 50.50N 3.28 E
Anžero-Sudžensk 22 Kd 56.07N 86.00 E
Anzi 36 Dc 0.52S 23.24 E
Anzio 14 Gi 41.27N 12.37 E
Anzoátegui [2] 54 Fb 9.00N 64.30W
Anzob, Pereval- 18 Ge 39.07N 68.53 E
Aoba, Ile- 61 Cc 15.25S 167.50 E
Ao Ban Don 25 Jg 9.20N 99.25 E
Aoga-Shima 27 Oe 32.30N 139.50 E
Aohan Qi (Xinhui) 28 Ec 42.18N 119.53 E
Aoiz 13 Kb 42.47N 1.22W
Aoji 28 Kc 42.31N 130.24 E
Aola 63a Ec 9.32S 160.29 E
Aomen/Macau=Macao (EN) [5] 22 Ng 22.10N 113.33 E
Aomen/Macau=Macao (EN) 27 Jg 22.12N 113.33 E
Aomori 22 Qe 40.49N 140.45 E
Aomori Ken [2] 28 Pd 40.40N 140.40 E
Aono-Yama 29 Bd 34.27N 131.48 E
Aontroim/Antrim 9 Gg 54.43N 6.13W
Aopo 65c Aa 13.29S 172.30W
Aôral, Phnum- 25 Kf 12.02N 104.10 E
Aoré 63b Cb 15.35S 167.10 E
Aosta / Aoste 14 Be 45.44N 7.20 E
Aosta, Val d'- 14 Be 45.45N 7.20 E
Aoste / Aosta 14 Be 45.44N 7.20 E
Aouk, Bahr- 30 Ih 8.51N 18.53 E
Aoukalé 35 Cd 9.10N 20.30 E
Aoukâr [Afr.] 32 Ge 24.00N 2.30W
Aoukâr [Mtna.] 30 Gg 17.30N 9.30W
Aoulef 32 Hd 26.58N 1.05 E
Aoumou 63b Be 21.24S 165.49 E
Aourou 34 Cc 14.28N 11.34W
Aoya 29 Cd 35.32N 133.59 E
Aozou 31 If 21.49N 17.25 E
Apa, Rio- 56 Ib 22.06S 58.00W
Apača 20 Kf 52.50N 157.10 E
Apache 46 Kk 31.44N 109.07W
Apache Junction 46 Jj 33.26N 111.32W
Apahida 15 Gc 46.49N 23.45 E
Apakho 63c Bb 11.25S 166.32 E
Apalachee Bay 38 Kg 29.30N 84.00W
Apalachicola 44 Ek 29.44N 84.59W
Apalachicola River 44 Ek 29.44N 84.59W
Apan 48 Jh 19.43N 98.25W
Apaporis, Río- 52 Jf 1.23S 69.25W
Aparecida do Taboado 54 Hg 20.05S 51.05W
Aparri 22 Oh 18.22N 121.39 E
Apataki Atoll 57 Mf 15.26S 146.20W
Apatin 15 Bd 45.40N 18.59 E
Apatity 6 Jb 67.34N 33.18 E
Apatzingán de la Constitucion 47 De 19.05N 102.21W
Apaxtla de Castrejón 48 Jh 18.09N 99.52W
Ape 7 Gh 57.32N 26.42 E
Apeldoorn 11 Lb 52.13N 5.58 E
Apeldoorn-Nieuw Milligen 12 Hb 52.14N 5.45 E
Apen 12 Ja 53.13N 7.48 E
Apennines (EN) = Appennini 5 Hg 43.00N 13.00 E
Apere, Río- 54 Ef 13.44S 65.18W
Aphrodisias 24 Cd 37.45N 28.40 E
Api 21 Kf 30.00N 80.57 E
Api 36 Eb 3.40N 25.26 E
Apia 58 Jf 13.50S 171.44W
Apiacás, Serra dos- 54 Gf 10.15S 57.15W
Apio 63a Ec 9.39S 161.23 E
Apipé Grande, Isla- 55 Di 27.30S 56.54W
Apizaco 48 Jh 19.25N 98.09W
Aplao 54 Dc 16.05S 72.31W
Apo, Mount- 21 Oi 6.59N 125.16 E
Apodi 54 Ke 5.39S 37.48W
Apolda 10 He 51.01N 11.30 E
Apolima 65c Aa 13.49S 172.07W
Apolima Strait 65c Aa 13.50S 172.10W
Apollo Bay 59 Ig 38.45S 143.40 E
Apollonia [Alb.] 15 Ci 40.43N 19.27 E
Apollonia [Lib.] 33 Dc 32.54N 21.58 E
Apolo 54 Ef 14.43S 68.31W
Apón, Río- 49 Kh 10.06N 72.23W
Apopka, Lake- 44 Gk 28.37N 81.38W
Aporé 55 Fd 18.58S 52.01W
Aporé, Rio- 52 Kg 19.27S 50.57W
Apostle Islands 43 Ib 46.50N 90.30W
Apostoles 56 Ic 27.55S 55.46W
Apostolovo 16 Hf 47.39N 33.43 E
Apoteri 54 Gc 4.02N 58.34W
Apôtres, Iles des- 30 Mm 45.40S 50.20 E
Appalachia 44 Fg 36.54N 82.48W
Appalachian Mountains 38 Lc 41.00N 77.00W
Äppelbo 8 Ed 60.30N 14.00 E
Appennini = Apennines (EN) 5 Hg 43.00N 13.00 E
Appennino Abruzzese 14 Hh 42.00N 13.55 E
Appennino Calabro 14 Kl 39.00N 16.30 E
Appennino Campano 14 Ii 40.50N 14.45 E
Appennino Ligure 14 Cf 44.30N 9.00 E
Appennino Lucano 14 Jj 40.30N 16.00 E
Appennino Tosco-Emiliano 14 Fg 44.00N 11.30 E
Appennino Umbro-Marchigiano 14 Gg 43.20N 12.55 E
Appenzell 14 Dc 47.20N 9.25 E
Appenzell Ausser-Rhoden [2] 14 Dc 47.20N 9.20 E
Appenzell Inner-Rhoden [2] 14 Dc 47.15N 9.25 E
Appingedam 12 Ia 53.19N 6.52 E
Appleby 9 Kg 54.36N 2.29W
Appleton 43 Jc 44.16N 88.25W
Appomattox 44 Hg 37.21N 78.51W
Apra Harbor 64c Bb 13.27N 144.38 E
Apricena 14 Ji 41.47N 15.27 E
Aprilia 14 Gi 41.36N 12.39 E
Apšeronsk 19 Dg 44.27N 39.44 E
Apšeronski Poluostrov=Apsheron Peninsula (EN) 5 Lg 41.00N 50.50 E
Apsheron Peninsula (EN)=Apšeronski Poluostrov 5 Lg 41.00N 50.50 E
Apt 11 Lk 43.53N 5.24 E
Apucarana 56 Jb 23.33S 51.29W
Apuoarana, Serra da- 55 Gf 23.50S 51.20W
Apuka 20 Ld 60.23N 169.45 E
Apuka 20 Ld 60.25N 169.35 E
Apulia (EN) = Puglia [2] 14 Ki 41.15N 16.15 E
Apurashokoru 64a Ac 7.17N 134.18 E
Apure [2] 54 Eb 7.10N 68.50W
Apure, Río- 52 Je 7.37N 66.25W
Apurímac [2] 54 Df 14.00S 73.00W
Apurímac, Río- 52 Ig 12.17S 73.56W
Apurito 50 Bi 7.56N 68.27W
Apuseni, Munţii-=Apuseni Mountains (EN) 5 If 46.30N 22.30 E
Apuseni Mountains (EN)=Apuseni, Munţii- 5 If 46.30N 22.30 E
Āq 24 Kc 38.59N 45.27 E
Āqā 24 Me 35.00N 47.00 E
Aqaba (EN)=Al 'Aqabah 23 Dd 29.31N 35.00 E
Aqaba, Gulf of- (EN)='Aqabah, Khalīj al- 30 Kf 29.00N 34.40 E
Āqā Bāba 24 Md 36.20N 49.46 E
'Aqabah, Khalīj al-=Aqaba, Gulf of- (EN) 30 Kf 29.00N 34.40 E
Āqcheh 23 Kb 36.56N 66.11 E
'Aqdā 24 Of 32.26N 53.37 E
'Aqīq 35 Fb 18.14N 38.12 E
Aqitag 27 Fc 41.49N 90.38 E
Āqotāq 24 Ld 37.10N 47.05 E
Āq Qal'eh 24 Pd 37.01N 54.30 E
Aqqikkol Hu 27 Ed 37.00N 88.20 E
'Aqrah 24 Jd 36.45N 43.54 E
Aqrin, Jabal- 24 Hg 31.32N 38.18 E
Āq Şū 24 Ke 34.35N 44.31 E
Aquidabã, Rio- 55 De 20.58S 57.50W
Aquidabán, Río- 55 Df 23.11S 57.32W
Aquidauana 54 Gh 20.28S 55.48W
Aquidauana, Rio- 54 Gg 19.44S 56.50W
Aquidauana, Serra de- 55 Ee 20.50S 55.30W
Aquiles Serdán 48 Gc 28.36N 105.53W
Aquin 49 Kd 18.16N 73.24W
Aquitaine, Bassin d'-=Aquitaine Basin (EN) 5 Fg 44.00N 0.10W
Aquitaine Basin (EN)=Aquitaine, Bassin d'- 5 Fg 44.00N 0.10W
Ara 13 Mb 42.25N 0.09 E
'Arab, Baḩr al- 30 Jh 9.02N 29.28 E
'Arab, Khalīj al- 33 Ec 30.55N 29.05 E
'Arab, Shaţţ al- 21 Gf 30.28N 47.59 E
'Arabah, Wādī- 24 Eh 29.07N 32.39 E
'Arabah, Wādī al- 24 Fg 30.58N 32.24 E
Arabatskaja Strelka, Kosa- 16 Ig 45.40N 35.05 E
'Arabestān 24 Mg 30.30N 50.00 E
Arabian Basin (EN) 3 Gh 11.30N 65.00 E
Arabian Desert (EN)=Sharqīyah, Aş Şaḩrā' ash- 30 Kf 28.00N 32.00 E
Arabian Peninsula (EN) 21 Gg 25.00N 45.00 E
Arabian Sea (EN) 21 Ih 15.00N 65.00 E
Araç 24 Eb 41.15N 33.21 E
Aracá, Rio- 54 Fd 0.25S 62.55W
Aracaju 53 Mg 10.55S 37.04W
Aracataca 49 Jh 10.35N 74.13W
Aracati 54 Kd 4.34S 37.46W
Araçatuba 53 Kh 21.12S 50.25W
Aracena 13 Fg 37.53N 6.33W
Aracena, Sierra de- 13 Fg 37.56N 6.50W
Aracides, Cape- 63a Ec 8.39S 161.01 E
Aracruz 54 Jg 19.49S 40.16W
Araçuai 54 Jg 16.52S 42.04W
Arad 6 If 46.11N 21.19 E
'Arad 24 Fg 31.15N 35.13 E
Arad [2] 15 Ec 46.11N 21.25 E
Arada 35 Cb 15.01N 20.40 E
'Arādah 35 Ia 22.59N 53.26 E
Arafali 35 Fb 15.04N 39.45 E
Ara Fana 35 Gd 6.01N 41.11 E
Arafune-Yama 29 Fc 36.12N 138.38 E
Arafura, Laut-=Arafura Sea (EN) 57 Ee 9.00S 133.00 E
Arafura Sea (EN)=Arafura, Laut- 57 Ee 9.00S 133.00 E
Aragac, Gora- 5 Kg 40.31N 44.10 E
Aragarças 53 Kg 15.55S 52.15W
Aragón 13 Kb 42.13N 1.44W
Aragón 5 Fg 41.00N 1.00W
Aragón 13 Lc 41.00N 1.00W
Aragona 14 Hm 37.24N 13.37 E
Aragua [2] 54 Eb 10.00N 67.10W
Araguacema 54 Ie 8.50S 49.34W
Aragua de Barcelona 50 Dh 9.28N 64.49W
Aragua de Maturín 50 Eh 9.58N 63.29W
Araguaia, Rio- 52 Lf 5.21S 48.41W
Araguaiana 55 Gb 16.49S 53.05W
Araguaina 54 Ie 7.12S 48.12W
Araguao, Boca- 54 Fb 9.17N 60.48W
Araguao, Caño- 50 Fh 9.15N 60.50W
Araguapiche, Punta- 50 Fh 9.29N 60.56W
Araguari 54 Ig 18.38S 48.11W
Araguari, Rio- [Braz.] 52 Le 1.15N 49.55W
Araguari, Rio- [Braz.] 55 Hd 18.21S 48.40W
Araguatins 54 Ie 5.38S 48.07W
'Arāguīb 32 Ff 18.50N 7.45W
Aragvi 16 Ni 41.50N 44.43 E
Arai 28 Of 37.09N 138.06 E
Árainn/Inishmore 9 Dh 53.07N 9.45W
Árainn Mhór/Aran Island 9 Ef 55.00N 8.30W
Araioses 54 Jd 2.53S 41.55W
Arāk 22 Gf 34.05N 49.41 E
Arak 32 Hd 25.18N 3.45 E
Arakabesan 64a Ac 7.21N 134.27 E
Arakan [2] 25 Ie 19.00N 94.15 E
Arakan Yoma 21 Lh 19.00N 94.40 E
Arakawa 29 Fb 38.09N 139.25 E
Ara-Kawa [Jap.] 29 Fb 38.09N 139.23 E
Ara-Kawa [Jap.] 29 Fc 37.11N 138.15 E
Árakhthos 15 Ej 39.01N 21.03 E
Araks 21 Gf 39.56N 48.20 E
Aral [China] 27 Dc 40.38N 81.24 E
Aral [Kirg.-U.S.S.R.] 19 Hg 41.48N 74.25 E
Aral Sea (EN)=Aralskoje More 21 He 45.00N 60.00 E
Aralsk 22 Ie 46.48N 61.40 E
Aralskoje More=Aral Sea (EN) 21 He 45.00N 60.00 E
Aralsor, Ozero- 16 Pe 49.05N 48.15 E
Aralsulfat 19 Gf 46.50N 61.59 E
Aramac 59 Jd 22.59S 145.14 E
Arambaré 55 Gj 30.55S 51.29W
Ārān 24 Ne 34.03N 51.30 E
Aranda de Duero 13 Ic 41.41N 3.41W
Arandelovac 15 De 44.18N 20.35 E
Arandilla 13 Ic 41.40N 3.41W
Aran Island/Árainn Mhór 9 Dh 53.07N 9.43W
Aran Islands 9 Ef 55.00N 8.30W
Aranjunez 13 Id 40.02N 3.36W
Aranos 37 Bd 24.09S 19.09 E
Arañuelo, Campo- 13 Ge 39.55N 5.30W
Aranuka Atoll 57 Id 0.11N 173.36 E
Arao 29 Be 32.59N 130.27 E
Araouane 31 Gg 18.53N 3.35W
Arapahoe 45 Gf 40.18N 99.54W
Arapey Grande, Río- 55 Dj 30.55S 57.49W
Arapiraca 54 Ke 9.45S 36.39W
Arápis, Ákra- 15 Gi 40.27N 24.00 E
Arapkir 24 Hc 39.03N 38.30 E
Arapoim, Rio- 55 Kb 15.45S 43.39W
Arapongas 56 Jb 23.23S 51.27W
Arapoti 55 Hg 24.08S 49.50W
'Ar'ar 24 Ig 30.59N 41.02 E
'Ar'ar, Wādī 24 Jg 31.23N 42.26 E
Araranguá 56 Kc 28.56S 49.29W
Araraquara 53 Lh 21.47S 48.10W
Araras 55 If 22.22S 47.23W
Araras, Açude- 54 Jd 4.20S 40.30W
Araras, Serra das- 55 Fd 18.45S 53.30W
Ararat [Arm.-U.S.S.R.] 19 Eh 39.50N 44.43 E
Ararat [Austl.] 59 Ig 37.17S 142.56 E
Ararat, Mount- (EN)=Büyük Ağrı Dağı 21 Gf 39.40N 44.24 E
Arari 54 Jd 3.28S 44.47W
Arari, Lago- 54 Id 0.37S 49.07W
Aras 21 Gf 39.56N 48.20 E
Aras Dağları 24 Jc 40.00N 43.00 E
Aratika Atoll 57 Mf 15.32S 145.32W
Aratürük/Yiwu 27 Fc 43.15N 94.35 E
Arauca [2] 54 Db 6.30N 71.00W
Arauca 54 Db 7.03N 70.47W
Arauca, Río- 52 Je 7.24N 66.35W
Araucanía [2] 56 Fe 37.50S 73.15W
Arauco 56 Fe 37.15S 73.19W
Araure 50 Bh 9.38N 69.15W
Aravaca, Madrid- 13 Id 40.27N 3.47W
Aravis 11 Mi 45.53N 6.28 E
Arawalli Range 21 Jg 25.00N 73.30 E
Araxá 54 Ig 19.35S 46.55W
Áraxos, Ákra- 15 Ek 38.10N 21.23 E
Araya 50 Dg 10.34N 64.15W
Araya, Península de- 54 Fa 10.35N 64.00W
Arba 13 Kc 41.52N 1.18W
Arba'āt 35 Fb 19.50N 37.03 E
Arba'īn, Darb al- 24 Di 26.40N 30.50 E
Arbaj-Here 27 Hb 46.15N 102.48 E
Arba Minch 31 Kh 5.59N 37.38 E
'Arbat 24 Ke 35.25N 45.35 E
Arbatax 14 Dk 39.56N 9.42 E
Arboga 7 Dg 59.24N 15.50 E
Arbogaån 8 Ge 59.26N 16.04 E
Arbois 11 Lh 46.54N 5.46 E
Arboletes 49 Ii 8.52N 76.25W
Arbolito 55 Ek 32.39S 54.15W
Arbon 14 Dc 47.30N 9.25 E
Arbore 15 Ib 47.44N 25.56 E
Arborea 14 Ck 39.46N 8.35 E
Arborea 14 Ck 39.50N 8.50 E
Arborg 45 Ha 50.55N 97.15W
Arbrå 7 Dc 61.29N 16.23 E
Arbroath 9 Ke 56.34N 2.35W
Arbus 14 Ck 39.32N 8.36 E
Arc [Fr.] 11 Mi 45.34N 6.12 E
Arc [Fr.] 11 Lk 43.31N 5.07 E
Arcachon 11 Ej 44.39N 1.10W
Arcachon, Bassin d'- 11 Ej 44.42N 1.09W
Arcadia [Fl.-U.S.] 44 Gl 27.14N 81.52W
Arcadia [La.-U.S.] 45 Jj 32.33N 92.55W
Arcagly-Ajat 17 Jj 53.00N 61.50 E
Arcas, Cayos- 47 Fd 20.12N 91.58W
Arcata 46 Cf 40.52N 124.05W
Arcelia 48 Ih 18.17N 100.16W
Arcen, Areen en Velden- 12 Ic 51.28N 6.11 E
Arcevia 14 Gg 43.30N 12.56 E
Archangel (EN)=Arhangelsk 6 Kc 64.34N 40.32 E
Archaringa Creek 59 He 28.15S 135.15 E
Archer River 59 Ib 13.28S 141.41 E
Archer's Post 36 Gb 0.39N 37.41 E
Archidona 13 Hg 37.05N 4.23W
Arcidosso 14 Fh 42.52N 11.33 E
Arcipelago Campano 5 Hg 40.30N 13.20 E
Arcipelago Toscano=Tuscan Archipelago (EN) 5 Hg 42.45N 10.20 E
Arcis-sur-Aube 11 Kf 48.32N 4.08 E
Arciz 16 Fg 45.59N 29.27 E
Arco [Id.-U.S.] 46 Ie 43.38N 113.18W
Arco [It.] 14 Ee 45.55N 10.53 E
Arconce 11 Jh 46.27N 4.00 E
Arcos 55 Je 20.17S 45.32W
Arcos de Jalón 13 Jc 41.13N 2.16W
Arcos de la Frontera 13 Gh 36.45N 5.48W
Arcos de Valdevez 13 Dc 41.51N 8.25W
Arcoverde 53 Mf 8.25S 37.04W
Arctic Bay 39 Kb 73.02N 85.11W
Arctic Ocean 67 Be 85.00N 170.00 E
Arctic Ocean (EN)=Ishavet 67 Be 85.00N 170.00 E
Arctic Ocean (EN)=Severny Ledovity Okean 67 Be 85.00N 170.00 E
Arctic Red River 42 Ec 67.27N 133.45W
Arctic Red River 42 Ec 67.22N 133.30W
Arctic Village 40 Jc 68.08N 145.19W
Arda [Eur.] 15 Jh 41.39N 26.29 E
Arda [It.] 14 Ee 45.02N 10.02 E
Ardabīl [Iran] 22 Gf 38.15N 48.18 E
Ardabīl [Iraq] 24 Ie 34.24N 40.59 E
Ardahan 24 Jb 41.07N 42.41 E
Ardakāh 23 Hc 32.19N 53.59 E
Ardakān 24 Og 30.16N 52.01 E
Ardal 24 Ng 31.59N 50.39 E
Ardales 13 Hh 36.52N 4.51W
Ardalsfjorden 8 Bc 61.15N 7.30 E
Årdalstangen 7 Bf 61.14N 7.43 E
Ardanuç 24 Jb 41.08N 42.03 E
Ardatov [R.S.F.S.R.] 7 Ki 55.17N 43.12 E
Ardatov [R.S.F.S.R.] 7 Li 54.53N 46.13 E
'Arde 35 Hd 9.58N 46.04 E
Ardèche 11 Kj 44.16N 4.39 E
Ardèche [3] 11 Kj 44.40N 4.20 E
Ardee/Béal Átha Fhirdhia 9 Gh 53.52N 6.33W
Ardencaple Fjord 41 Jd 75.15N 20.10W
Ardenne, Plateau de l'-/Ardennen, Plateau van der-=Ardennes (EN) 5 Ge 50.10N 5.45 E
Ardennen, Plateau van der-/Ardenne, Plateau de l'-=Ardennes (EN) 5 Ge 50.10N 5.45 E
Ardennes [3] 11 Ke 49.40N 4.40 E
Ardennes (EN)=Ardenne, Plateau de l'-/Ardennen, Plateau van der- 5 Ge 50.10N 5.45 E
Ardennes (EN)=Ardennen, Plateau van der-/Ardenne, Plateau de l'- 5 Ge 50.10N 5.45 E
Ardennes, Canal des- 11 Ke 49.26N 4.02 E
Ardennes, Forêt des- 12 Ge 49.48N 4.50 E
Ardentes 11 Hh 46.45N 1.50 E
Ardeşen 24 Ib 41.12N 41.00 E
Ardestān 24 Of 33.22N 52.23 E
Árdhas 15 Jh 41.39N 26.29 E
Ardila 13 Ef 38.12N 7.28W
Ard Mhacha/Armagh 9 Gg 54.21N 6.39W
Ardmore 43 He 34.10N 97.08W
Ardnamurchan, Point of- 9 Ge 56.45N 6.30W
Ardon 16 Nh 43.07N 44.13 E
Ardooie 12 Fd 50.59N 3.12 E
Ardre 12 Fe 49.18N 3.40 E
Ardres 12 Dd 50.51N 1.59 E
Ards Peninsula/An Aird 9 Hg 54.30N 5.30W
Ar Dub'al Khālī 21 Hg 21.00N 51.00 E
Ardud 15 Fb 47.38N 22.53 E
Arebi 36 Eb 2.50N 29.38 E
Arecibo 47 Ke 18.28N 66.43W
Areen en Valden 12 Ic 51.28N 6.11 E
Areen en Velden-Arcen 12 Ic 51.28N 6.11 E
Arėgala/Ariogala 8 Ji 55.13N 23.30 E
Areia, Ribeirão da- 55 Jc 16.07S 45.52W
Areia Branca 54 Kd 4.57S 37.08W
Arekalong Peninsula 64a Bb 7.40N 134.38 E
Aremberg 12 Id 50.25N 6.49 E
Arena 26 He 9.14N 120.46 E
Arena, Point- 43 Cd 38.57N 123.44W
Arena, Punta- 47 Cd 23.30N 109.30W
Arena de la Ventana, Punta- 47 Cd 24.04N 109.52W
Arenápolis 54 Gf 14.26S 56.49W
Arenas, Cayo- 47 Fd 22.08N 91.24W
Arenas, Punta de- 56 Gh 53.09S 68.13W
Arenas de San Pedro 13 Gd 40.12N 5.05W
Arenberg 12 Jb 52.42N 7.20 E
Arendal 7 Bg 58.27N 8.48 E
Arendonk 12 Hc 51.19N 5.05 E
Arénys de Mar/Arenys de Mar 13 Oc 41.35N 2.33 E
Arenys de Mar/Arénys de Mar 13 Oc 41.35N 2.33 E
Areópolis 15 Fm 36.40N 22.23 E
Areq, Sebkha bou- 13 Ji 35.10N 2.45W
Arequipa 53 Ig 16.24S 71.33W
Arequipa [2] 54 Dg 16.00S 72.30W
Arequito 55 Bk 33.09S 61.28W
Arero 35 Fe 4.44N 38.50 E
Ares, Muela de- 13 Ld 40.28N 0.07W
Åreskutan 8 Ea 63.26N 13.06 E
Åreskutan 7 Ce 63.24N 13.06 E
Arévalo 13 Hc 41.04N 4.43W
Arezzo 14 Fg 43.25N 11.53 E
Arga 13 Kb 42.18N 1.47W
Argajas 17 Ji 55.31N 60.55 E
Argamasilla de Alba 13 Ie 39.07N 3.06W
Argan 27 Ec 40.09N 88.22 E
Arganda 13 Id 40.30N 3.26W
Arga-Sala 20 Gc 68.37N 112.05 E
Argelès-Gazost 11 Fk 43.01N 0.06W
Argelès-sur-Mer 11 Jl 42.33N 3.01 E
Argens 11 Mk 43.24N 6.44 E

Index Symbols

[1] Independent Nation
[2] State, Region
[3] District, County
[4] Municipality
[5] Colony, Dependency
Continent
Physical Region
Historical or Cultural Region
Mount, Mountain
Volcano
Hill
Mountains, Mountain Range
Hills, Escarpment
Plateau, Upland
Pass, Gap
Plain, Lowland
Delta
Salt Flat
Valley, Canyon
Crater, Cave
Karst Features
Depression
Polder
Desert, Dunes
Forest, Woods
Heath, Steppe
Oasis
Cape, Point
Coast, Beach
Cliff
Peninsula
Isthmus
Sandbank
Island
Atoll
Rock, Reef
Islands, Archipelago
Rocks, Reefs
Coral Reef
Well, Spring
Geyser
River, Stream
Waterfall Rapids
River Mouth, Estuary
Lake
Salt Lake
Intermittent Lake
Reservoir
Swamp, Pond
Canal
Glacier
Ice Shelf, Pack Ice
Ocean
Sea
Gulf, Bay
Strait, Fjord
Lagoon
Bank
Seamount
Tablemount
Ridge
Shelf
Basin
Escarpment, Sea Scarp
Fracture
Trench, Abyss
National Park, Reserve
Point of Interest
Recreation Site
Cave, Cavern
Historic Site
Ruins
Wall, Walls
Church, Abbey
Temple
Scientific Station
Airport
Port
Lighthouse
Mine
Tunnel
Dam, Bridge

Argent, Côte d'-	11	Ej	44.00N	1.30W
Argenta	14	Ff	44.37N	11.50 E
Argentan	11	Ff	48.45N	0.01W
Argentario, Monte-	14	Fh	42.24N	11.09 E
Argentat	11	Hi	45.06N	1.56 E
Argentera	14	Bf	44.10N	7.18 E
Argenteuil	11	If	48.57N	2.15 E
Argentiera, Capo dell'-	14	Cj	40.44N	8.08 E
Argentina	55	Ai	29.33S	62.17W
Argentina [1]	53	Ji	34.00S	64.00W
Argentine Basin (EN)	3	Cn	45.00S	45.00W
Argentino, Lago-	52	Ik	50.13S	72.25W
Argentino, Mar-	52	Kj	46.00S	59.40W
Argenton	11	Fg	47.05N	0.13W
Argenton-Château	11	Fh	46.59N	0.27W
Argenton-sur-Creuse	11	Hh	46.35N	1.31 E
Arges	15	Jd	44.04N	26.37 E
Arges [2]	15	Hd	45.00N	24.50 E
Arghandāb	23	Jc	31.27N	64.23 E
Argo	35	Eb	19.31N	30.25 E
Argo Depth (EN)	3	Jk	12.10S	165.40W
Argolikós Kólpos = Argolis, Gulf of- (EN)	15	Fl	37.20N	22.55 E
Argolis, Gulf of- (EN) = Argolikós Kólpos	15	Fl	37.20N	22.55 E
Argonne	12	He	49.30N	5.00 E
Argonne	11	Ke	49.30N	5.00 E
Árgos	15	Fl	37.38N	22.44 E
Árgos Orestikón	15	Ei	40.30N	21.16 E
Argostólion	15	Dk	38.11N	20.29 E
Arguedas	13	Kb	42.10N	1.36W
Argueil-Fry	12	De	49.37N	1.31 E
Arguello, Point-	46	Ei	34.35N	120.39W
Arguenon	11	Df	48.35N	2.13W
Argun	16	Nh	43.16N	45.52 E
Argun	21	Od	53.20N	121.28 E
Argungu	34	Fc	12.45N	4.31 E
Argyle	51n	Ba	13.10N	61.10W
Argyle, Lake-	57	Df	16.15S	128.40 E
Argyll	9	Ie	56.20N	5.00W
Arhangelsk = Archangel (EN)	6	Kc	64.34N	40.32 E
Arhangelskaja Oblast [3]	19	Ec	63.30N	43.00 E
Arhara	20	Ig	49.30N	130.09 E
Arhavi	24	Ib	41.22N	41.16 E
Arholma	8	He	59.50N	19.05 E
Ar Horqin Qi (Tianshan)	27	Lc	43.55N	120.05 E
Århus [2]	8	Dh	56.10N	10.15 E
Århus	6	Hd	56.09N	10.13 E
Århus Bugt	8	Dh	56.10N	10.20 E
Arhust	27	Ib	47.42N	107.50 E
Ariadnoje	20	Ig	45.08N	134.25 E
Ariake-Kai	28	Kh	32.55N	130.27 E
Ariamsvlei	37	Be	28.08S	19.50 E
Ariano Irpino	14	Ji	41.09N	15.05 E
Ariari, Río-	54	Dc	2.35N	72.47W
Arias	56	Hd	33.38S	62.25W
Ari Atoll	25a	Bb	3.30N	72.45 E
Aribinda	34	Ec	14.14N	0.52W
Arica	53	Ig	18.29S	70.20W
Arica, Golfo de-	52	Ig	18.30S	70.30W
Arichuna	50	Ci	7.42N	67.08W
Arid, Cape-	59	Ef	34.00S	123.09 E
Arida	28	Mg	34.05N	135.07 E
Arida-Gawa	29	Dd	34.05N	135.06 E
Aridhaia	15	Fi	40.59N	22.04 E
Ariège	11	Hk	43.31N	1.25 E
Ariège [3]	11	Hk	43.00N	1.30 E
Ariel	55	Cm	36.32S	59.54W
Arieş	15	Gc	46.26N	23.59 E
Ariguaní	54	Db	9.50N	74.01W
Ariguaní, Río-	49	Ki	9.35N	73.46W
Arīḩā [Jor.]	24	Fg	31.52N	35.27 E
Arīḩā [Syr.]	24	Ge	35.48N	36.36 E
Arikaree River	45	Ff	40.01N	101.56W
Arikawa	29	Ae	32.59N	129.07 E
Arilje	15	Df	43.45N	20.06 E
Arima	54	Fa	10.38N	61.17W
Arinos	55	Ib	15.55S	46.04W
Arinos, Rio-	52	Kg	10.25S	58.20W
Arinos Novo, Rio-	55	Db	14.14S	56.01W
Ariogala/Arēgala	8	Ji	55.13N	23.30 E
Aripuanã	54	Fe	9.10S	60.38W
Aripuanã, Rio-	52	Jf	5.07S	60.24W
Ariquemes	54	Fe	9.56S	63.04W
Arisa	35	Gc	11.11N	41.38 E
'Arish, Wādī al-	24	Eg	31.09N	33.49 E
Arismendi	49	Mi	8.29N	68.22W
Arita	29	Ae	33.11N	129.52 E
Aritzo	14	Dk	39.57N	9.12 E
Arixang/Wenquan	27	Dc	44.59N	81.04 E
Ariza	13	Jc	41.19N	2.03W
Arizaro, Salar de-	56	Gb	24.42S	67.45W
Arize, Massif de l'-	11	Hl	42.50N	1.30 E
Arizona [2]	43	Ee	34.00N	112.00W
Arizpe	48	Db	30.20N	110.10W
Årjäng	7	Cg	59.23N	12.08 E
Arjeplog	7	Dc	66.03N	17.54 E
Arjo	35	Fd	8.45N	36.30 E
Arjona	54	Ca	10.15N	75.21W
Arkadak	19	Ee	51.58N	43.28 E
Arkadelphia	43	Ie	34.07N	93.04W
Arkalyk	22	Id	50.13N	66.50 E
Arkansas	38	Jf	33.48N	91.04W
Arkansas [2]	43	Id	34.50N	93.40W
Arkansas City	43	Hd	37.04N	97.02W
Arkanū, Jabal-	33	De	22.15N	24.45 E
Arkatag	21	Kf	36.45N	89.10 E
Arkhángelos	15	Lm	36.12N	28.08 E
Árki	15	Jl	37.22N	26.45 E
Arklow/An tInbhear Mór	9	Gi	52.48N	6.09W
Arkona, Kap-	10	Jb	54.41N	13.26 E
Arkonam	25	Ff	13.06N	79.40 E
Arkösund	8	Gf	58.30N	16.56 E
Arkoúdhion	15	Dk	38.33N	20.43 E
Arktičeskoga Instituta, Ostrova- = Arkticheski Institut Islands (EN)	20	Da	75.20N	81.50 E
Arkticheski Institut Islands (EN) = Arktičeskoga Instituta, Ostrova-	20	Da	75.20N	81.50 E
Arlan, Gora-	16	Sj	39.43N	54.40 E
Arlanza	13	Hb	42.06N	4.09W
Arlanzón	13	Hb	42.03N	4.17W
Arlberg	14	Ec	47.08N	10.12 E
Arles	11	Kk	43.40N	4.38 E
Arlington [Or.-U.S.]	46	Ed	45.46N	120.13W
Arlington [Tx.-U.S.]	45	Hj	32.44N	97.07W
Arlington [Va.-U.S.]	43	Ld	38.52N	77.05W
Arlington Heights	45	Me	42.05N	87.59W
Arlit	31	Hg	19.00N	7.38 E
Arlon/Aarlen	11	Le	49.41N	5.49 E
Arlöv	8	Ei	55.39N	13.05 E
Arly	34	Fc	11.35N	1.28 E
Armagh/Ard Mhacha	9	Gg	54.21N	6.39W
Armagnac	11	Gk	43.45N	0.10 E
Armagnac, Collines de l'-	11	Gk	43.30N	0.30 E
Armah, Wādī-	23	Hf	18.12N	51.02 E
Arman	20	Ke	59.43N	150.12 E
Armançon	11	Jg	47.57N	3.30 E
Armandale, Perth-	59	Df	32.09S	116.00 E
Armant	33	Fd	25.37N	32.32 E
Armáthia	15	Jn	35.26N	26.52 E
Armavir	6	Kf	45.00N	41.08 E
Armenia	53	Ie	4.31N	75.41W
Armenia (EN) = Ermenistan	23	Fb	39.10N	43.00 E
Armenia (EN) = Ermenistan	21	Gf	39.10N	43.00 E
Armenian SSR (EN) = Armjanskaja SSR [2]	19	Eg	40.00N	45.00 E
Armentières	11	Id	50.41N	2.53 E
Armería	48	Gh	18.56N	103.58W
Armi, Capo dell'-	14	Jm	37.57N	15.41 E
Armidale	58	Gh	30.31S	151.39 E
Armisvesi	8	Lb	62.30N	26.35 E
Armjansk	16	Hf	46.05N	33.41 E
Armjanskaja Sovetskaja Socialističeskaja Respublika [2]	19	Eg	40.00N	45.00 E
Armjanskaja SSR/Haikakan Sovetakan Socialistakan Respublika [2]	19	Eg	40.00N	45.00 E
Armjanskaja SSR = Armenian SSR (EN) [2]	19	Eg	40.00N	45.00 E
Armoricain, Massif- = Armorican Massif (EN)	5	Ff	48.00N	3.00W
Armorican Massif (EN) = Armoricain, Massif-	5	Ff	48.00N	3.00W
Armour	45	Ge	43.19N	98.21W
Arm River	46	Ma	50.46N	105.00W
Armstrong [Arg.]	55	Bk	32.47S	61.36W
Armstrong [B.C.-Can.]	46	Fa	50.27N	119.12W
Armstrong [Ont.-Can.]	42	If	50.18N	89.02W
Ārmūdiū	24	Qd	37.15N	56.05 E
Armutçuk Dağ	15	Ki	40.05N	27.23 E
Armutlu	15	Li	40.31N	28.50 E
Armutova	15	Jj	39.23N	26.50 E
Arnaia	15	Gi	40.29N	23.36 E
Arnaud	42	Kd	60.00N	69.55W
Arnautis, Akrōtērion-	24	Ee	35.06N	32.17 E
Arnay-le-Duc	11	Kg	47.08N	4.29 E
Arnedo	13	Jb	42.13N	2.06W
Årnes	7	Cf	60.09N	11.28 E
Arnhem	11	Lc	51.59N	5.55 E
Arnhem, Cape-	57	Ef	12.21S	136.21 E
Arnhem Bay	59	Hb	12.20S	136.10 E
Arnhem Land	57	Ef	13.10S	134.30 E
Arno	5	Hg	43.41N	10.17 E
Arno Atoll	57	Id	7.05N	171.41 E
Arnold	12	Aa	53.00N	1.08W
Arnon	11	Ig	47.13N	2.01 E
Arnøy	7	Ea	70.08N	20.36 E
Arnprior	44	Ic	45.26N	76.21W
Arnsberg	10	Ee	51.23N	8.05 E
Arnsberger Wald	12	Kc	51.26N	8.10 E
Arnsberg-Oeventrop	12	Kc	51.24N	8.08 E
Arnsburg	12	Kd	50.29N	8.48 E
Arnstadt	10	Gf	50.50N	10.57 E
Aro, Río-	50	Di	8.01N	64.11W
Aroa	50	Bg	10.26N	68.54W
Aroa, Pointe-	65e	Fc	17.28S	149.46W
Aroa, Río-	50	Bg	10.41N	68.18W
Aroa, Sierra de-	50	Bg	10.15N	68.55W
Aroab	37	Be	26.47S	19.40 E
Aroánia Óri	15	Fl	37.57N	22.13 E
Aroche	13	Fg	37.57N	6.57W
Aroche, Pico de-	13	Ff	38.01N	6.56W
Aroeira	55	Ee	21.41S	54.25W
Arolsen	10	Ff	51.22N	9.01 E
Aroma	35	Fb	15.49N	36.08 E
Aron	11	Jh	46.50N	3.27 E
Arona	14	Ce	45.46N	8.34 E
Aroostook River	44	Nb	46.48N	67.45W
Arorae Island	57	Ie	2.38S	176.49 E
Arorangi	64p	Bb	21.13S	159.49W
Aros, Río-	48	Ec	29.30N	109.15W
Arosa	14	Dd	46.47N	9.40 E
Arosa, Ría de-	13	Db	42.28N	8.57W
Aros Papigochic, Río-	48	Ec	29.09N	108.35W
Årøsund	8	Ci	55.15N	9.43 E
Arouca	13	Dd	40.56N	8.15W
Arpaçay	24	Jb	40.45N	43.25 E
Arpajon	11	If	48.35N	2.15 E
Arpino	14	Hi	41.39N	13.36 E
Arquata Scrivia	14	Cf	44.41N	8.53 E
Arque	54	Eg	17.48S	66.23W
Arques-la-Bataille	12	De	49.53N	1.08 E
Ar Rachidiya	32	Gc	31.55N	4.40W
Ar Rachidiya [3]	32	Gc	31.00N	4.00W
Ar Radīsīyah Baḩrī	33	Fe	24.57N	32.53 E
Arrah	25	Gc	25.34N	84.40 E
Ar Rahad	35	Ec	12.43N	30.39 E
Ar Rahad	30	Kg	14.28N	33.31 E
Arraias	54	If	12.56S	46.57W
Arraias, Rio- [Braz.]	54	Hf	11.10S	53.35W
Arraias, Rio- [Braz.]	55	Ia	12.28S	47.18W
Arraiolos	13	Ef	38.43N	7.59W
Ar Ramādī	23	Fc	33.25N	43.17 E
Ar Ramlah	24	Fh	29.32N	35.57 E
Ar Ramlī al Kabīr	33	Dd	26.30N	22.10 E
Arran, Island of-	9	Hf	55.35N	5.15W
Ar Rank	35	Ec	11.45N	32.48 E
Ar Raqqah	23	Eb	35.56N	39.01 E
Arras	11	Id	50.17N	2.47 E
Ar Rāshidah	24	Cj	25.35N	28.56 E
Ar Rass	24	Jj	25.52N	43.28 E
Ar Rastān	24	Ge	34.55N	36.44 E
Arrats	11	Gj	44.06N	0.52 E
Ar Rawḑah [Sau.Ar.]	33	He	21.16N	42.50 E
Ar Rawḑah [Alg.]	13	Ki	35.23N	1.05W
Ar Rawḑah [P.D.R.Y.]	33	Ig	14.28N	47.17 E
Ar Rawḑatayn	24	Lh	29.53N	47.44 E
Ar Rayḩānī	24	Pk	23.37N	55.58 E
Arrecife	32	Ed	28.57N	13.32W
Arrecife Alacrán	47	Gd	22.24N	89.42W
Arrecifes	56	Hd	34.03S	60.07W
Arrecifes, Río-	55	Ck	33.46S	59.31W
Arrée, Montagnes d'-	11	Cf	48.26N	3.55W
Arresø	8	Ei	55.55N	12.05 E
Arriaga	48	Mi	16.14N	93.54W
Ar Rifā'ī	24	Lg	31.43N	46.07 E
Ar Rihāb	24	Kg	30.52N	45.30 E
Ar Rimāh	24	Lj	25.34N	47.09 E
Ar Rimāl	21	Hg	22.00N	52.50 E
Ar Riyāḑ = Riyadh (EN)	22	Gg	24.38N	46.43 E
Arrochar	9	Ie	56.12N	4.45W
Arroio Grande	55	Fk	32.14S	53.05W
Arrojado	55	Ja	13.29S	44.37W
Arrojado, Rio-	55	Ja	13.24S	44.20W
Arromanches-les-Bains	12	Be	49.20N	0.37W
Arros	11	Gk	43.40N	0.02 E
Arroscia	14	Cg	44.03N	8.11 E
Arroux	11	Jh	46.29N	3.58 E
Arrow, Lough-/Loch Arabhach	9	Eg	54.05N	8.20W
Arrowsmith, Mount-	61	Dh	43.21S	170.59 E
Arrowtown	62	Cf	44.56S	168.50 E
Arroyo Barú	55	Cj	31.52S	58.26W
Arroyo de la Luz	13	Fe	39.29N	6.35W
Arroyo Grande	46	Ei	35.07N	120.34W
Arroyos y Esteros	55	Dg	25.04S	57.06W
Arruda	55	Db	15.02S	56.07W
Arrufó	56	Hd	30.15S	61.45W
Ar Rumaythah	24	Kg	31.32N	45.12 E
Ar Ruq'ī	24	Lh	29.01N	46.33 E
Ar Rusāfah	24	He	35.02N	36.17 E
Ar Ruşayriş	31	Kg	11.51N	34.23 E
Ar Ruţbah	23	Fc	33.02N	40.17 E
Ar Ruwayḑah	24	Ki	26.23N	44.14 E
Ar Ruways [Qatar]	23	Hd	26.08N	51.13 E
Ar Ruways [U.A.E.]	23	He	24.08N	52.45 E
Ar Ruzayqāt	24	Ej	25.35N	32.28 E
Års	8	Ch	56.48N	9.32 E
Arsenjān	24	Oh	29.56N	53.18 E
Arsenjev	20	Ih	44.12N	133.20 E
Arsi [3]	35	Fd	7.10N	40.00 E
Arsk	7	Lh	56.07N	49.52 E
Årskogen	8	Gb	62.05N	17.20 E
Arslanköy	24	Fd	37.01N	34.17 E
Ars-sur-Moselle	12	Ie	49.05N	6.04 E
Arsuk	41	Hf	61.11N	48.30W
Årsunda	8	Gd	60.32N	16.44 E
Art	63b	Ad	19.43S	163.39 E
Artá	13	Pe	39.42N	3.21 E
Arta	35	Gc	11.31N	42.50 E
Árta	15	Dj	39.09N	20.59 E
Artá, Cuevas de-	13	Pe	39.40N	3.24 E
Artašat	16	Nj	39.59N	44.33 E
Arteaga	48	Hh	18.28N	102.25W
Artem	20	Ih	43.23N	132.10 E
Artemisa	47	Hd	22.49N	82.46W
Artemón	15	Hm	36.57N	24.43 E
Artem-Ostrov	19	Fg	40.28N	50.18 E
Artemovsk [R.S.F.S.R.]	20	Ef	54.23N	93.30 E
Artemovsk [Ukr.-U.S.S.R.]	16	Ke	48.33N	38.03 E
Artemovski	17	Jh	57.25N	61.58 E
Artesa de Segre	13	Nc	41.54N	1.03 E
Artesia	43	Ge	32.51N	104.24W
Arthur	45	Ff	41.35N	101.31W
Arthur Creek	59	Hd	23.00S	136.58 E
Arthur River	59	Ih	41.00S	144.55 E
Arthur's Pass	61	Dh	42.57S	171.34 E
Arthur's Pass	62	De	42.54S	171.34 E
Arthur's Town	49	Ja	24.38N	75.32W
Arti	17	Ih	56.26N	58.32 E
Artibonite, Rivière de l'-	49	Kd	19.15N	72.47W
Artigas	56	Id	30.42S	56.28W
Artigas [2]	55	Dj	30.35S	57.00W
Artijarvi/Artsjö	8	Ld	60.45N	26.05 E
Artik	16	Mi	40.36N	43.58 E
Artillery Lake	42	Gd	63.08N	107.45W
Artois	11	Id	50.10N	2.30 E
Artois, Collines de l'-	11	Id	50.30N	2.15 E
Artoli	35	Eb	18.19N	33.54 E
Artsjö/Artijarvi	8	Ld	60.45N	26.05 E
Artux	27	Cd	39.40N	76.10 E
Artvin	23	Fa	41.11N	41.49 E
Artyk	20	Jd	64.12N	145.15 E
Aru	36	Fb	2.52N	30.51 E
Aru, Kepulauan- = Aru Islands (EN)	57	Ee	6.00S	134.30 E
Arua	31	Kh	3.01N	30.55 E
Aruanã	55	Gb	14.54S	51.05W
Aruba	54	Ea	12.30N	70.00W
Aru Bassin (EN)	26	Jg	5.00S	134.00 E
Aru Islands (EN) = Aru, Kepulauan-	57	Ee	6.00S	134.30 E
Arukoron Point	64a	Bb	7.43N	134.38 E
Arun	9	Mk	50.48N	0.33W
Arunāchal Pradesh [3]	25	Ic	27.50N	94.50 E
Arundel	12	Bd	50.51N	0.33W
Arun He	27	Lb	47.36N	124.06 E
Arun Qi	27	Lb	48.09N	123.29 E
Arus, Tanjung-	26	Hf	1.24N	125.06 E
Arusha [3]	36	Gc	3.30S	36.00 E
Arusha	31	Ki	3.22S	36.41 E
Arutua Atoll	61	Lc	15.18S	146.44W
Arutunga	61	Jc	18.52S	159.46W
Aruwimi	30	Jh	1.13N	23.36 E
Arvada [Co.-U.S.]	45	Dg	39.50N	105.05W
Arvada [Wy.-U.S.]	46	Ld	44.40N	106.03W
Arve	11	Mh	46.12N	6.08 E
Arvert, Presqu'île d'-	11	Ei	45.45N	1.05W
Arvida	42	Kg	48.26N	71.11W
Arvidsjaur	7	Ed	65.35N	19.10 E
Arvika	7	Cg	59.39N	12.36 E
Årviksand	7	Ea	70.12N	20.32 E
Arvin	46	Fi	35.12N	118.50W
Aryānah	14	En	36.52N	10.11 E
Arys	18	Gc	42.48N	68.15 E
Arys	19	Gg	42.26N	68.48 E
Arys, Ozero-	18	Fb	45.50N	66.20 E
Arz	11	Dg	47.39N	2.06W
Arzachena	14	Di	41.05N	9.23 E
Arzamas	19	Ed	55.23N	43.50 E
Arzanah	24	Oj	24.47N	52.34 E
Aržano	14	Kg	43.35N	16.59 E
Arzew	32	Gb	35.51N	0.19W
Arzew, Golfe d'-	13	Li	35.50N	0.10W
Arzew, Salines d'-	13	Li	35.42N	0.18W
Arzfeld	12	Id	50.05N	6.16 E
Arzgir	19	Ef	45.22N	44.13 E
Arzúa	13	Db	42.56N	8.09W
As	12	Hc	51.01N	5.35 E
Ås	8	De	59.40N	10.48 E
Aš	10	If	50.13N	12.12 E
Aša	19	Fd	55.02N	57.18 E
Aså	8	Dg	57.09N	10.25 E
Asab	37	Be	25.29S	17.59 E
Asaba	34	Gd	6.11N	6.45 E
Asad, Buḩayrat al-	24	He	35.57N	38.10 E
Asadābād [Afg.]	23	Lc	34.52N	71.09 E
Asadābād [Iran]	24	Me	34.47N	48.07 E
Asafik	35	Bc	13.10N	19.26 E
Asahi [Jap.]	29	Fb	38.15N	139.30 E
Asahi [Jap.]	29a	Ca	44.08N	142.35 E
Asahi [Jap.]	29	Gd	35.43N	140.35 E
Asahi [Jap.]	29	Ec	36.57N	137.34 E
Asahi-Dake	29	Fb	38.16N	139.55 E
Asahi-Gawa	29	Cd	34.36N	133.58 E
Asahikawa	22	Qe	43.46N	142.22 E
Asaka-Drainage	29	Gc	37.30N	140.15 E
Asale, Lake-	35	Gc	14.00N	40.20 E
'Asalūyeh	24	Oi	27.28N	52.37 E
Asama-Yama	28	Of	36.27N	138.30 E
Asan-Man	28	If	36.56N	126.51 E
Asansol	22	Kg	23.41N	86.59 E
Asarna	7	De	62.39N	14.21 E
Asarum	8	Fh	56.12N	14.50 E
'Asäyr = Guardaful, Cape- (EN)	30	Mg	11.49N	51.15 E
Asayta	35	Gc	11.33N	41.27 E
Asbest	17	Jh	57.01N	61.31 E
Asbestos	44	Lc	45.46N	71.57W
Asbe Teferi	35	Gd	9.05N	40.51 E
Asbury Park	44	Je	40.14N	74.01W
Ascension	30	Fi	7.57S	14.22W
Ascensión, Bahía de la-	47	Ge	19.40N	87.30W
Ascensión, Bahía de la-	48	Ph	19.40N	87.30W
Ascensión, Laguna de la-	48	Fb	31.05N	107.55W
Aschaffenburg	10	Fg	49.59N	9.09 E
Ascheberg	12	Jc	51.47N	7.37 E
Aschendorf (Ems), Papenburg-	12	Ja	53.04N	7.22 E
Aschersleben	10	He	51.45N	11.28 E
Aščikol, Ozero-	18	Fb	45.05N	67.20 E
Aščiozek	16	Pe	49.12N	48.06 E
Ascoli Piceno	14	Hh	42.51N	13.34 E
Ascoli Satriano	14	Ji	41.12N	15.34 E
Ascot	12	Bc	51.24N	0.40W
Aseb	31	Lg	13.00N	42.44 E
Åseda	7	Dh	57.10N	15.20 E
Asedjrad	30	Hf	24.42N	1.40 E
Asekejevo	16	Rc	53.36N	52.51 E
Asela	31	Kh	7.58N	39.08 E
As Ela	35	Gc	11.06N	42.06 E
Åsele	7	Dd	64.10N	17.20 E
Åsen [Nor.]	7	Ce	63.36N	11.03 E
Åsen [Swe.]	7	Cf	61.17N	13.50 E
Asendabo	35	Fd	9.47N	37.36 E
Asendorf	12	Kb	52.46N	9.00 E
Asenovgrad	15	Hg	42.01N	24.52 E
Åsensbruk	8	Ef	58.48N	12.25 E
Åseral	8	Bf	58.37N	7.25 E
Aseri/Azeri	7	Gg	59.29N	26.51 E
Asfeld	12	Ge	49.28N	4.07 E
Aşfūn al Maţā'inah	24	Ej	25.23N	32.32 E
Åsgårdstrand	8	De	59.21N	10.28 E
Ašhabad	22	Hf	37.57N	58.23 E
Ašhabadskaja Oblast [3]	19	Fh	38.30N	59.00 E
Ashanti [3]	34	Ed	6.45N	1.30W
Ashburn	44	Fj	31.43N	83.39W
Ashburton	61	Dh	43.54S	171.45 E
Ashburton River	57	Cg	21.40S	114.56 E
Ashdod	24	Fg	31.49N	34.39 E
Ashdown	45	Ij	33.41N	94.08W
Asheboro	44	Hh	35.42N	79.49W
Asheroft	46	Ea	50.43N	121.17W
Asheville	43	Kd	35.34N	82.33W
Ashford	9	Nj	51.09N	0.53 E
Ashford Airport	12	Cc	51.10N	0.59 E
Ash Fork	46	Ii	35.13N	112.29W
Ashibetsu	28	Qc	43.31N	142.11 E
Ashikaga	29	Fc	36.21N	139.27 E
Ashington	9	Lf	55.11N	1.34W
Ashiro	29	Ga	40.06N	141.01 E
Ashiya	29	Be	33.53N	130.40 E
Ashizuri-Misaki	28	Lh	32.44N	133.01 E
Ashkal, Qar'at al-	14	Dm	37.10N	9.40 E
Āshkhāneh	24	Qd	37.28N	57.00 E
Ashland [Ks.-U.S.]	45	Gh	37.11N	99.46W
Ashland [Ky.-U.S.]	43	Kd	38.28N	82.38W
Ashland [Mt.-U.S.]	46	Ld	45.35N	106.16W
Ashland [Oh.-U.S.]	44	Fe	40.52N	82.19W
Ashland [Or.-U.S.]	43	Cc	42.12N	122.42W
Ashland [Wi.-U.S.]	43	Ib	46.35N	90.53W
Ashland, Mount-	46	De	42.05N	122.43W
Ashley	45	Gc	46.02N	99.22W
Ashmore Islands	57	Df	12.15S	123.05 E
Ashmūn	24	Dg	30.18N	30.58 E
Ashoro	29a	Cb	43.14N	143.31 E
Ashqelon	24	Fg	31.40N	34.35 E
Ash Shabakah	24	Jg	30.49N	43.39 E
Ash Shabb	33	Ee	22.19N	29.46 E
Ash Shā'ib	24	Gh	28.59N	37.07 E
Ash Sha'm	23	Id	26.02N	56.05 E
Ash Shamālīyah [3]	35	Db	18.40N	30.00 E
Ash 'Shāmīyah	24	Kg	31.57N	44.36 E
Ash Shāmīyah	24	Lg	30.15N	46.55 E
Ash Shaqq	24	Lh	28.20N	47.30 E
Ash Shaqrā'	23	Gd	25.15N	45.15 E
Ash Sha'rā'	24	Kj	24.16N	44.11 E
Ash Sharīqah	23	Id	25.22N	55.23 E
Ash Sharqāţ	23	Fb	35.27N	43.16 E
Ash Sharqī	32	Jc	34.45N	11.15 E
Ash Sharqī	24	Ge	34.00N	36.30 E
Ash Sharqīyah	23	Ie	22.15N	58.30 E
Ash Shatrah	24	Lg	31.25N	46.10 E
Ash Shawbak	24	Fg	30.32N	35.34 E
Ash Shaykh Ḩumayd	24	Fh	28.07N	34.34 E
Ash Shifā	24	Fh	28.30N	35.30 E
Ash Shiḩr	23	Gg	14.44N	49.35 E
Ash Shināfīyah	24	Kg	31.35N	44.39 E
Ash Shu'aybah [Kuw.]	24	Mh	29.03N	48.08 E
Ash Shu'aybah [Sau.Ar.]	24	Ji	27.53N	42.43 E
Ash Shu'bah	24	Kh	28.54N	44.44 E
Ash Shumlūl	24	Li	26.31N	47.20 E
Ash Shuqayq	23	Ff	17.44N	42.01 E
Ash Shurayk	35	Eb	18.48N	33.34 E
Ash Shuwayhāt	24	Oj	24.05N	52.28 E
Ash Shuwaykh	24	Lh	29.21N	47.55 E
Ashtabula	43	Kc	41.53N	80.47W
Ashtabula, Lake-	45	Hc	47.11N	97.58W
Ashtīyān	24	Me	34.30N	49.55 E
Ashton [Id.-U.S.]	46	Jd	44.04N	111.27W
Ashton [St.Vin.]	51n	Bb	12.36N	61.27W
Ashuanipi	42	Kf	52.55N	66.00W
Ashuanipi Lake	42	Kf	52.45N	66.10W
Asia	21	Ke	40.00N	85.00 E
Asia, Kepulauan-	26	Jf	1.03N	131.18 E
Asiago	14	Fe	45.52N	11.30 E
Asiago, Altopiano di-	14	Fe	45.54N	11.30 E
Asilah	32	Fb	35.28N	6.02W
Asinara	5	Gg	41.04N	8.15 E
Asinara, Golfo dell'-	14	Cj	41.00N	8.35 E
Asino	20	De	56.58N	86.09 E
'Asīr	23	Ff	19.00N	42.00 E
Aškadar	17	Hi	53.37N	56.01 E
Aşkale	24	Ic	39.55N	40.42 E
Askanija-Nova	16	Hf	46.27N	33.52 E
Asker	8	De	59.50N	10.26 E
Askersund	7	Dg	58.53N	14.54 E
Askī Al Mawşil	24	Jd	36.34N	42.42 E
Askim [Nor.]	8	De	59.35N	11.10 E
Askim [Swe.]	8	Dg	57.38N	11.56 E
Áskion Óros	15	Ei	40.22N	21.34 E
Askiz	20	Ef	53.08N	90.32 E
Askja	5	Eb	65.03N	16.48W
Askola	8	Kd	60.32N	25.36 E
Äsköping	8	Ge	59.09N	16.04 E
Askøy	8	Ad	60.30N	5.05 E
Askøy	8	Ad	60.24N	5.11 E
Askrova	8	Ac	61.30N	4.55 E
Askvoll	7	Af	61.21N	5.04 E
Asl	24	Eh	29.30N	32.43 E
Aslanapa	15	Mj	39.13N	29.52 E
Asmara (EN) = Asmera	31	Kg	15.19N	38.57 E
Asmera = Asmara (EN)	31	Kg	15.19N	38.57 E
Åsnen	8	Fh	56.40N	14.40 E
Asni	32	Fc	31.15N	7.59W
Asnières-sur-Seine	12	Ef	48.55N	2.17 E
Aso	14	Hg	43.06N	13.51 E
Aso	29	Be	32.58N	131.02 E
Asola	14	Ee	45.13N	10.24 E
Asosa	31	Kg	10.02N	34.32 E
Aso-San	29	Be	32.53N	131.06 E
Asoteriba, Jabal-	35	Fa	21.51N	36.30 E
Asouf Mellene	32	Hd	25.40N	2.08 E
Asō-Wan	29	Ad	34.20N	129.15 E
Āspās	24	Og	30.40N	52.24 E
Aspe	13	Lf	38.21N	0.46W
Aspen	43	Fd	39.11N	106.49W
Aspermont	45	Fj	33.08N	100.14W
Aspiring, Mount-	61	Ch	44.23S	168.44 E
Aspromonte	14	Jl	38.10N	16.00 E
Assa	32	Fd	28.37N	9.25W
Aş Şadr	23	He	24.40N	54.41 E
Aş Şaff	24	Dh	29.34N	31.17 E
Aş Şāfī	24	Fg	31.02N	35.28 E
As Safīrah	24	Gd	36.04N	37.22 E
Aş Şaḩm	24	Qj	24.10N	56.53 E
Assahoun	34	Fd	6.27N	0.55 E
Aş Şa'īd	30	Kf	26.00N	32.00 E
Assal, Lac-	35	Gc	11.40N	42.22 E
As Salamīyah [Sau.Ar.]	23	Ge	24.12N	47.23 E
As Salamīyah [Syr.]	24	Ge	35.01N	37.03 E
Aş Şāliḩīyah	24	Ie	34.44N	40.45 E
As Sallūm	31	Je	31.34N	25.09 E
As Salmān	24	Kg	30.26N	44.30 E
As Salt	24	Ff	32.03N	35.44 E
As Salwá	23	He	24.45N	50.49 E

Index Symbols

- [1] Independent Nation
- [2] State, Region
- [3] District, County
- [4] Municipality
- [5] Colony, Dependency
- Continent
- Physical Region
- Historical or Cultural Region
- Mount, Mountain
- Volcano
- Hill
- Mountains, Mountain Range
- Hills, Escarpment
- Plateau, Upland
- Pass, Gap
- Plain, Lowland
- Delta
- Salt Flat
- Valley, Canyon
- Crater, Cave
- Karst Features
- Depression
- Polder
- Desert, Dunes
- Forest, Woods
- Heath, Steppe
- Oasis
- Cape, Point
- Coast, Beach
- Cliff
- Peninsula
- Isthmus
- Sandbank
- Island
- Atoll
- Rock, Reef
- Islands, Archipelago
- Rocks, Reefs
- Coral Reef
- Well, Spring
- Geyser
- River, Stream
- Waterfall Rapids
- River Mouth, Estuary
- Lake
- Salt Lake
- Intermittent Lake
- Reservoir
- Swamp, Pond
- Canal
- Glacier
- Ice Shelf, Pack Ice
- Ocean
- Sea
- Gulf, Bay
- Strait, Fjord
- Lagoon
- Bank
- Seamount
- Tablemount
- Ridge
- Shelf
- Basin
- Escarpment, Sea Scarp
- Fracture
- Trench, Abyss
- National Park, Reserve
- Point of Interest
- Recreation Site
- Cave, Cavern
- Historic Site
- Ruins
- Wall, Walls
- Church, Abbey
- Temple
- Scientific Station
- Airport
- Port
- Lighthouse
- Mine
- Tunnel
- Dam, Bridge

Assam ⊡	21 Lg 26.50N 94.00 E	ʼAtata ⊕	65b Ac 21.03S 175.15W
Assam ③	25 Ic 26.00N 93.00 E	Atauat, Phou- ▲	25 Le 16.01N 107.23 E
Assamakka	34 Gb 19.21N 5.38 E	Atauro, Pulau- ⊕	26 Ih 8.13S 125.35 E
As Samawah	23 Gc 31.18N 45.17 E	Atáviros ▲	15 Km 36.12N 27.52 E
As Sanām ⊡	35 Ia 22.00N 51.10 E	Ataway	35 Bd 9.59N 18.38 E
Assaouas	34 Gb 16.52N 7.27 E	Atbara ⊠	35 Eh 17.40N 33.56 E
As Sars	14 Dn 36.05N 9.01 E	ʼAṭbarah ⊠	30 Kg 17.40N 33.56 E
As Sayl al Kabīr	33 He 21.38N 40.25 E	ʼAṭbarah	31 Kg 17.42N 33.59 E
Asse	12 Gd 50.56N 4.12 E	Atbasar	22 Id 51.48N 68.20 E
Asse ⊠	11 Lk 43.53N 5.53 E	At-Baši	19 Hg 41.08N 75.51 E
Assebroek, Brugge-	12 Fc 51.12N 3.16 E	Atça	15 Ll 37.53N 28.13 E
Assekkārai ⊠	34 Fb 15.50N 2.52 E	Atchafalaya Bay ◪	43 If 29.25N 91.20W
Assemini	14 Dk 39.17N 9.01 E	Atchison	43 Hd 39.34N 95.07W
Assen	11 Ma 53.00N 6.34 E	Atebubu	34 Ed 7.45N 0.59W
Assenede	12 Fc 51.14N 3.45 E	Ateca	13 Kc 41.20N 1.47W
Assens	8 Ci 55.16N 9.55 E	Aterno ⊠	14 Hh 42.11N 13.51 E
As Sibāʼīyah	24 Ej 25.11N 32.41 E	Atessa	14 Ih 42.04N 14.27 E
As Sidr	31 Ie 30.39N 18.22 E	Ath/Aat	11 Jd 50.38N 3.47 E
As Sidrah = Sirte Desert (EN) ⊡	30 Ie 30.30N 17.30 E	Athabasca ⊠	38 Hd 58.40N 110.50W
As Sila'	23 He 24.02N 51.46 E	Athabasca ⊠	42 Gf 54.43N 113.17W
As Simbillāwayn	24 Dg 30.53N 31.27 E	Athabasca, Lake- ◪	38 Id 59.07N 110.00W
Assiniboia	42 Gg 49.38N 105.59W	Athamánon, Óri-▲	15 Ej 39.27N 21.08 E
Assiniboine ⊠	38 Je 49.53N 97.08W	Athamánon Óri ▲	15 Ej 39.27N 21.08 E
Assiniboine, Mount-▲	38 Hd 50.52N 115.39W	Athens [Al.-U.S.]	44 Dh 34.48N 86.58W
Assis	56 Jb 22.40S 50.25W	Athens [Ga.-U.S.]	43 Ke 33.57N 83.23W
Assisi	14 Gg 43.04N 12.37 E	Athens [Oh.-U.S.]	44 Ff 39.20N 82.06W
Aßlar	12 Kd 50.36N 8.28 E	Athens [Tn.-U.S.]	44 Eh 35.28N 84.35W
Assos ⊠	15 Jj 39.31N 26.20 E	Athens [Tx.-U.S.]	45 Ij 32.12N 95.51W
As Sālimīyah	24 Mh 29.20N 48.04 E	Athens (EN) = Athínai	6 Ih 37.59N 23.44 E
As Subaykhah	14 Eo 35.56N 10.01 E	Athéras ▲	15 Jl 37.38N 26.15 E
As Subū' ⊡	33 Fe 22.45N 32.34 E	Atherton	59 Jc 17.16S 145.29 E
As Sudān = Sudan (EN) ⊡	31 Jg 15.00N 30.00 E	Athi ⊠	36 Gc 2.59S 38.31 E
As Sudd ⊡	30 Kh 8.00N 31.00 E	Athies-sous-Laon	12 Fe 49.34N 3.41 E
As Sufāl	35 Hc 14.06N 48.43 E	Athínai = Athens (EN)	6 Ih 37.59N 23.44 E
Aş Şufuq	24 Nk 23.52N 51.45 E	Athi River	36 Gc 1.27S 36.59 E
Aş Şukhayrah	32 Jc 34.17N 10.06 E	Athis-de-l'Orne	12 Bf 48.49N 0.30W
As Sukhnah	24 He 34.52N 38.52 E	Athlone/Baile Átha Luain	9 Fh 53.25N 7.56W
As Sulaymī	24 Ii 26.17N 41.21 E	Athol	44 Kd 42.36N 72.14W
As Sulayyil	23 Ge 20.27N 45.34 E	Áthos ▲	15 Hi 40.10N 24.20 E
Aş Şulb ⊡	24 Mj 25.42N 48.25 E	Athos, Mount- (EN) = Áyion Óros ②	15 Hi 40.15N 24.15 E
As Sumayḥ	35 Dd 9.49N 27.39 E	Ath Thamad	24 Fh 29.41N 34.18 E
Aş Şummān ⊡	33 Ie 23.00N 48.00 E	Ath Thumāmī	24 Ki 27.42N 44.59 E
Aş Şummān ⊡	24 Li 27.00N 47.00 E	Athus, Aubange-	12 He 49.34N 5.50 E
Assumption Island ⊕	30 Li 9.45S 46.30 E	Athy	9 Gi 53.00N 7.00W
As Sūq	33 He 21.54N 42.03 E	Ati	31 Ig 13.13N 18.20 E
Assur ⊡	24 Je 35.25N 43.16 E	Atiak	36 Fb 3.16N 32.07 E
Aş Şuwār	24 Ie 35.30N 40.39 E	Atiamuri	62 Gc 38.23S 176.02 E
Aş Şuwaydā'	23 Ec 32.42N 36.34 E	Atibaia, Rio- ⊠	55 If 22.42S 47.17W
Aş Şuwayrah	24 Kf 32.55N 44.47 E	Atienza	13 Jc 41.12N 2.52W
As Suways = Suez (EN)	31 Kf 29.58N 32.33 E	Atikokan	42 Ig 48.45N 91.37W
Astakídha ◪	15 Jn 35.53N 26.50 E	Atikonak Lake ◪	42 Lf 52.40N 64.35W
Astakós	15 Ek 38.32N 21.05 E	Atimoono ⊙	64n Bc 10.26S 160.58W
Āstāneh [Iran]	24 Md 37.17N 49.59 E	Atitlán, Lago de- ◪	49 If 14.42N 91.12W
Āstāneh [Iran]	24 Mf 33.53N 49.22 E	Atitlán, Volcán- ▲	47 Ff 14.35N 91.11W
Āstārā	23 Gb 38.26N 48.52 E	Atiu Island ⊕	57 Lg 20.02S 158.07W
Astara	6 Kh 38.28N 48.52 E	ʼAtk, Wādī al- ⊠	24 Li 26.03N 46.30 E
Aštarak	16 Ni 40.16N 44.18 E	Atka ⊕	38 Bd 52.15N 174.30W
Asten	12 Hc 51.24N 5.45 E	Atka [Ak.-U.S.]	40a Db 52.12N 174.12W
Asti	14 Cf 44.54N 8.12 E	Atka [R.S.F.S.R.]	20 Kd 60.49N 151.58 E
Astico ⊠	14 Fe 45.37N 11.37 E	Atka Iceport	66 Bf 70.35S 7.45W
Astipálaia	15 Jm 36.33N 26.21 E	Atkarsk	19 Ee 51.52N 44.59 E
Astipálaia ⊕	15 Jm 36.35N 26.20 E	Atkasook	40 Hb 70.28N 157.24W
Asto, Monte-▲	11a Ba 42.30N 9.15 E	Atkinson	45 Ge 42.32N 98.59W
Astola Island ⊕	25 Cc 25.07N 63.51 E	Atlacomulco de Fabela	48 Jh 19.48N 99.53W
Astorga	13 Fb 42.27N 6.03W	Atlanta [Ga.-U.S.]	39 Kf 33.45N 84.23W
Astoria	43 Cb 46.11N 123.50W	Atlanta [Mi.-U.S.]	44 Ec 45.00N 84.09W
Åstorp	8 Eh 56.08N 12.57 E	Atlanta [Tx.-U.S.]	45 Ij 33.07N 94.10W
Astrahan	6 Kf 46.21N 48.03 E	Atlanterhavet = Atlantic Ocean (EN) ⊠	3 Di 2.00N 25.00 E
Astrahanskaja Oblast ⊡	19 Ef 47.10N 47.30 E	Atlantic [Ia.-U.S.]	45 If 41.24N 95.01W
Astrolabe, Cape- ⊠	63a Ec 8.20S 160.34 E	Atlantic [N.C.-U.S.]	44 Ih 34.54N 76.20W
Astrolabe, Récifs de l'- ⊠	57 Hf 19.49S 165.35 E	Atlantic City	39 Lf 39.27N 74.35W
Astudillo	13 Hb 42.12N 4.18W	Atlantic Coastal Plain ⊡	38 Lf 34.00N 79.00W
Asturias ③	13 Ga 43.20N 6.00W	Atlantic-Indian Basin (EN) ⊠	3 Eo 60.00S 15.00 E
Asuisui, Cape- ⊠	65c Aa 13.47S 172.29W	Atlantic-Indian Ridge (EN) ⊠	3 Eo 52.00S 25.00 E
Asunción	53 Kh 25.16S 57.40W	Atlántico ②	54 Da 10.40N 75.00W
Asunción, Bahía- ◪	48 Bd 27.05N 114.10W	Atlántico, Océano- = Atlantic Ocean (EN) ⊠	3 Di 2.00N 25.00 E
Asunción, Cerro de la-▲	48 Je 24.15N 99.56W	Atlántico, Oceano- = Atlantic Ocean (EN) ⊠	3 Di 2.00N 25.00 E
Asuncion Island ⊕	57 Fc 19.40N 145.24 E	Atlántico, Oceano- = Atlantic Ocean (EN) ⊠	3 Di 2.00N 25.00 E
Asunción Mita	49 Cf 14.20N 89.43W	Atlantik, Océano- = Atlantic Ocean (EN) = Atlanterhavet ⊠	3 Di 2.00N 25.00 E
Asunción Nochixtlán	48 Ki 17.28N 97.14W	Atlantico, Oceano- = Atlantic Ocean (EN) ⊠	3 Di 2.00N 25.00 E
Asunden ◪	8 Eg 58.00N 15.50 E	Atlantique, Océan- = Atlantic Ocean (EN) ⊠	3 Di 2.00N 25.00 E
Åsunden ◪	8 Eg 57.44N 13.22 E	Atlantique, Océan- = Atlantic Ocean (EN) = Atlanterhavet ⊠	3 Di 2.00N 25.00 E
Aswa ⊠	36 Fb 3.43N 31.55 E	Atlantischer Ozean (EN) = Atlantic Ocean (EN) = Muhit, ⊠	3 Di 2.00N 25.00 E
Aswān	31 Kf 24.05N 32.53 E	Al Baḥr al- ⊠	3 Di ʼ2.00N 25.00 E
Aswān, Sadd al- = First Cataract (EN) ⊠	30 Kf 24.01N 32.52 E	Atlántida ③	49 Df 15.30N 87.00W
Asyūṭ	31 Kf 27.11N 31.11 E	Atlantische Oseaan = Atlantic Ocean (EN) ⊠	3 Di 2.00N 25.00W
Asyūṭī, Wādī al- ⊠	24 Di 27.10N 31.16 E	Atlantique ③	34 Fd 6.35N 2.15 E
Aszód	10 Fi 47.39N 19.30 E	Atlantique, Océan- = Atlantic Ocean (EN) ⊠	3 Di 2.00N 25.00W
ʼAta ⊕	65b Bc 21.03S 174.59W	Atlantshaf = Atlantic Ocean (EN) ⊠	
Atacama ②	56 Gc 27.30S 70.00W	Atlas = Atlas Mountains (EN) ▲	30 Ge 32.00N 2.00W
Atacama, Desierto de- = Atacama Desert (EN) ⊡	52 Jh 22.30S 69.15W	Atlas Mountains (EN) ▲	30 Ge 32.00N 2.00W
Atacama, Salar de- ⊠	52 Jh 23.30S 68.15W	Atlasova, Ostrov- ⊕	20 Kg 46.00N 152.05 E
Atacama Desert (EN) =	52 Jh 22.30S 69.15W	Atlas Saharien = Saharan Atlas (EN) ▲	30 He 34.00N 2.00 E
Atacama, Desierto de- ⊡	3 Nm 30.00S 73.00W	Atlas Tellien = Tell Atlas (EN) ▲	30 He 36.00N 2.00 E
Atacama Trench (EN) ⊠	57 Je 8.33S 172.30W	Atlin	42 Ee 59.35N 133.42W
Atafu Atoll ⊙	20 Ee 55.06N 99.25 E	Atlin Lake ◪	42 Ee 59.35N 133.43W
Atagaj	57 Jg 21.03S 175.00W	Atlixco	47 Ee 18.54N 98.26W
Ata Island ⊕	30 Hf 23.13N 5.40 E	Atløy ⊕	8 Ac 61.20N 4.55 E
Atakor ⊡	34 Fc 10.00N 1.35 E	Atmore	44 Dj 31.02N 87.29W
Atakora ③	34 Fc 10.45N 1.30 E	Atna ⊠	8 Dc 61.44N 10.49 E
Atakora ▲	31 Hh 7.32N 1.08 E	Atna Peak ▲	42 Ef 53.57N 128.04W
Atalaia do Norte	54 Bd 4.20S 70.12W	Atö	29 Bd 34.24N 131.43 E
Ataláia ▲	15 Fk 38.39N 23.00 E	Atoka	45 Ia 34.23N 96.08W
Atalayasa ▲	13 Nf 38.55N 1.15 E	Atokos ⊕	15 Dk 38.29N 20.49 E
Atambua	26 Hh 9.07S 124.54 E	Atotonilco el Alto	48 Jg 20.33N 102.31W
Atami	29 Fd 35.05N 139.02 E	Atoui, Khatt- ⊠	32 De 20.04N 15.58W
Atangmik	41 Gf 64.53N 52.00W	Atouila, ʼErg- ⊡	30 Gf 21.15N 3.20W
Aṭār	31 Ff 20.30N 13.03W	Atoyac, Rio- ⊠	48 Ki 16.30N 97.31W
Atas-Bogdo-Ula ▲	27 Gc 43.20N 96.30 E	Atoyac de Alvarez	48 Ii 17.12N 100.26W
Atascadero	46 Ei 35.29N 120.41W	Atrak ⊠	14 Hh 42.35N 13.59 E
Atasu	19 Hf 48.42N 71.38 E	Åtran ⊠	14 Ih 42.04N 14.27 E

Ayiá 15 Fj 39.43N 22.46 E
Ayia Marina 15 Jl 37.09N 26.52 E
Ayiásos 15 Jj 39.06N 26.22 E
Ayía Triás 15 Hn 35.04N 24.45 E
Ayina 36 Bb 1.48N 13.10 E
Áyion Óros 15 Hi 40.15N 24.15 E
Áyion Óros=Athos, Mount- (EN) [2] 15 Hi 40.15N 24.15 E
Áyios Evstrátios 15 Hj 39.31N 25.00 E
Áyios Ioánnis, Ákra- 15 In 35.20N 25.46 E
Áyios Kírikos 15 Jl 37.35N 26.14 E
Áyios Minás 15 Jl 37.36N 26.34 E
Áyios Nikólaos 15 In 35.11N 25.43 E
Áyios Yeóryios 15 Gl 37.28N 23.56 E
Aykota 35 Fb 15.10N 37.03 E
Aylesbury 9 Mj 51.50N 0.50W
Ayllón, Sierra de- 13 Ic 41.15N 3.25W
Aylmer Lake 42 Gd 64.05N 108.30W
Aylsham 12 Db 52.47N 1.15 E
Ayna 13 Jf 38.33N 2.05W
'Aynabo 35 Hd 8.57N 46.30 E
'Ayn ad Darāhim 14 Cn 36.47N 8.42 E
'Ayn al Baydā 24 Ge 34.32N 37.55 E
'Ayn al Ghazāl [Eg.] 24 Dj 25.46N 30.38 E
'Ayn al Ghazāl [Lib.] 31 Jf 21.50N 24.55 E
'Ayn al Shigi 24 Ci 27.01N 28.02 E
'Ayn al Wādī 24 Ci 27.23N 28.13 E
'Ayn Bū Sālim 14 Cn 36.37N 8.59 E
'Ayn Dāllah 33 Ed 27.19N 27.20 E
'Ayn Dār 24 Mj 25.58N 49.14 E
'Ayn Dīwār 24 Jd 37.17N 42.11 E
'Ayn Ilwān 24 Dj 25.44N 30.25 E
'Ayn Khalīfah 24 Bi 26.46N 27.47 E
'Ayn Sifnī 24 Jd 36.42N 43.21 E
'Ayn Sukhnah 33 Fd 29.30N 32.10 E
'Aynūnah 23 Ed 28.05N 35.08 E
Ayod 35 Ed 8.08N 31.24 E
Ayora 13 Ke 39.04N 1.03W
Ayorou 34 Fc 14.44N 0.55 E
'Ayoûn el 'Atroûs 31 Gg 16.38N 9.36W
Ayr 9 If 55.29N 4.28W
Ayr [Austl.] 59 Jc 19.35S 147.24 E
Ayr [Scot.-U.K.] 9 If 55.28N 4.38W
Ayre, Point of- 9 Ig 54.26N 4.22W
Ayrolle, Étang de l'- 11 Jk 43.16N 3.30 E
Aysha 35 Gc 10.45N 42.35 E
Aytré 11 Eh 46.08N 1.06W
Ayutla 48 Gg 20.07N 104.22W
Ayutla de los Libres 48 Ji 16.54N 99.13W
Ayvacık 24 Gb 41.00N 36.45 E
Ayvacik 15 Jj 39.36N 26.24 E
Ayvalık 23 Cb 39.18N 26.41 E
Aywaille 12 Hd 50.28N 5.40 E
Āzādshahr 24 Pd 37.05N 55.08 E
Azahar, Costa del- 13 Me 39.58N 0.01 E
Azaila 13 Lc 41.17N 0.29W
Azambuja 13 De 39.04N 8.52W
Azamgarh 25 Gc 26.04N 83.11 E
Azángaro 54 Df 14.55S 70.13W
Azannes-et-Soumazannes 12 He 49.18N 5.28 E
Azaouâd=Azaouad (EN) 30 Gg 19.00N 3.00W
Azaouad (EN)=Azaouâd 30 Gg 19.00N 3.00W
Azaouak 34 Fb 15.30N 3.18 E
Azaouak 30 Hg 15.20N 4.55 E
Azaouak, Vallée de l'- 30 Hg 17.30N 3.40 E
Azar 34 Fb 16.02N 4.04 E
Āzarbāījān-e Gharbī [3] 23 Fb 37.00N 45.00 E
Āzarbāījān-e Sharqī [3] 23 Gb 37.00N 47.00 E
Azarbaijčan Sovet Socialistik Respublicasy/Azerbajdžanskaja SSR [2] 19 Eg 40.30N 47.30 E
Azare 34 Hc 11.41N 10.12 E
Āzār Shahr 24 Kd 37.45N 45.59 E
Azay-le-Rideau 11 Gg 47.16N 0.28 E
A 'zāz 24 Gd 36.35N 37.03 E
Azazga 13 Qh 36.44N 4.22 E
Azbine/Aïr 30 Hg 18.00N 8.30 E
Azdaak, Gora- 16 Ni 40.13N 44.59 E
Azdavay 24 Eb 41.39N 33.18 E
Azefal 30 Ff 21.00N 14.45W
Azeffoun 13 Qh 36.53N 4.25 E
Azemmour 32 Fc 33.17N 8.21W
Azerbaidzhan (EN) 21 Gf 37.00N 46.00 E
Azerbaidzhan SSR (EN)=Azerbajdžanskaja SSR [2] 19 Eg 40.30N 47.30 E
Azerbajdžanskaja Sovetskaja Socialističeskaja Respublika [2] 19 Eg 40.30N 47.30 E
Azerbajdžanskaja SSR/Azarbaijčan Sovet Socialistik Respublicasy [2] 19 Eg 40.30N 47.30 E
Azerbajdžanskaja SSR=Azerbaidzhan SSR (EN) [2] 19 Eg 40.30N 47.30 E
Azeri/Aseri 7 Gg 59.29N 26.51 E
Azevedo Sodré 55 Ej 30.04S 54.36W
Azezo 35 Fc 12.33N 37.25 E
Azilal [3] 32 Fc 32.09N 6.05W
Azilal 32 Fc 31.58N 6.35W
Aznā 24 Mf 33.56N 49.24 E
Aznakajevo 7 Mi 54.56N 53.04 E
Azogues 54 Cd 2.44S 78.48W
Azores (EN)=Açores [5] 31 Ee 38.30N 28.00W
Azores (EN)=Açores, Arquipélago dos- 30 Ee 38.30N 28.00W
Azores-Gibraltar Ridge (EN) 3 Df 37.00N 16.00W
Azoum. Bahr- 30 Jg 10.53N 20.15 E
Azov 19 Df 47.05N 39.25 E
Azov, Sea of- (EN)=Azovskoje More 5 Jf 46.00N 36.00 E
Azovskoje More=Azov, Sea of- (EN) 5 Jf 46.00N 36.00 E
Azpeitia 13 Ja 43.11N 2.16W
Azrak, Bahr- 35 Bc 10.50N 19.50 E
Azraq, Al Baḩr al-=Blue Nile (EN) 30 Kg 15.38N 32.31 E
Azraq ash Shīshān 24 Gg 31.50N 36.49 E
Azrou 32 Fc 33.26N 5.13W
Aztec 45 Ch 36.49N 107.59W
Aztec Ruins 46 Kh 36.51N 108.10W
Azua 49 Ld 18.27N 70.44W
Azuaga 13 Gf 38.16N 5.41W
Azuar 13 Ie 39.08N 3.36W
Azuero, Peninsula de-=Azuero Peninsula (EN) 38 Ki 7.40N 80.30W
Azuero Peninsula (EN)=Azuero, Peninsula de- 38 Ki 7.40N 80.30W
Azul 53 Ki 36.45S 59.50W
Azul, Arroyo del- 55 Cm 36.15S 59.07W
Azul, Cerro- 54a Ab 0.54S 91.21W
Azul, Cordillera- 54 Ce 8.30S 76.00W
Azul, Rio- 48 Oi 17.54N 88.52W
Azul, Serra- 55 Eb 14.50S 54.50W
Azul, Sierras del- 55 Cm 37.02S 59.55W
Azūm 35 Cc 10.53N 20.15 E
Azuma-San 29 Gc 37.44N 140.08 E
Azur, Côte d'- 11 Mk 43.30N 7.00 E
Azurduy 54 Fg 19.59S 64.29W
Azzaba 32 Ib 36.44N 7.06 E
Az Zāb al Kabīr 23 Fb 36.00N 43.21 E
Az Zāb aş Şaghīr 23 Fb 35.12N 43.25 E
Az Zabdānī 24 Gf 33.43N 36.05 E
Az Zabū 24 Ch 28.22N 28.56 E
Az Zafīr 23 Ff 19.57N 41.30 E
Az Zaghāwa 35 Cb 15.15N 23.14 E
Az Zāhirah 24 Qk 23.30N 56.15 E
Az Zallāq 24 Ni 26.03N 50.29 E
Az Zaqāzīq 33 Fc 30.35N 31.31 E
Az Zarqā' 24 Oj 24.53N 53.04 E
Az Zarqā' 24 Gf 32.05N 36.06 E
Az Zāwiyah [3] 33 Bc 32.40N 12.10 E
Az Zāwiyah 33 Bc 32.45N 12.44 E
Az Zaytūn 33 Ed 29.09N 25.47 E
Azzel Matti, Sebkha- 30 Hf 26.00N 0.55 E
Az Zilfī 24 Ki 26.18N 44.48 E
Az Zubayr 24 Lg 30.23N 47.43 E

B

Baa 26 Hi 10.43S 123.03 E
Baaba 63b Ae 20.03S 163.58 E
Ba'ādwēyn 35 Hd 7.12N 47.24 E
Bá an Daingin/Dingle Bay 9 Ci 52.05N 10.15W
Baar 10 Ei 48.00N 8.30 E
Baarle-Hertog 12 Gc 51.27N 4.56 E
Baarn 12 Hb 52.14N 5.17 E
Baas, Bassure de- 12 Dd 50.30N 1.15 E
Bāb 24 Ok 23.55N 53.45 E
Baba 35 Bd 6.25N 17.07 E
Baba 15 Ei 40.55N 21.10 E
Baba Burun [Tur.] 24 Db 41.18N 31.26 E
Baba Burun [Tur.] 24 Bc 39.29N 26.04 E
Babadağ 15 Ll 37.48N 28.52 E
Baba Dağ 15 Mm 36.32N 29.10 E
Babadag 15 Le 44.54N 28.43 E
Babadag, Gora- 16 Pi 41.01N 48.29 E
Babaeski 24 Bb 41.26N 27.06 E
Bābā-Ḩeydar 24 Nf 32.20N 50.28 E
Babajevo 19 Dd 59.24N 35.55 E
Babajtag, Gora- 18 Hd 41.13N 70.16 E
Babajurt 16 Oh 43.35N 46.47 E
Bāb al Māndab=Bab el Mandeb (EN) 30 Lg 12.35N 43.25 E
Babanūsah 35 Dc 11.20N 27.48 E
Babao → Qilian 27 Hd 38.14N 100.15 E
Babaoyo 54 Cd 1.50S 79.30W
Babar, Kepulauan- 26 Ih 7.50S 129.45 E
Babar, Pulau- 57 De 7.55S 129.45 E
Babase 63a Aa 4.01S 153.42 E
Babatag, Hrebet- 18 Ge 38.00N 68.10 E
Babati 36 Gc 4.13S 35.45 E
Babbitt 45 Kc 47.43N 91.57W
B'abdā 24 Ff 33.50N 35.32 E
Bab el Mandeb (EN)=Bāb al Māndab 30 Lg 12.35N 43.25 E
Babelthuap Island 57 Ed 7.30N 134.36 E
Babenhausen [F.R.G.] 12 Ke 49.58N 8.57 E
Babenhausen [F.R.G.] 10 Gh 48.09N 10.15 E
Babeni 15 He 44.59N 24.15 E
Baberton 44 Ge 41.02N 81.38W
Bá Bheanntraí/Bantry Bay 9 Dj 51.38N 9.48W
Babian Jiang=Black River (EN) 21 Mg 20.17N 106.34 E
Babil [3] 24 Kf 32.40N 44.50 E
Babine Lake 42 Ef 54.45N 126.00W
Babino Polje 14 Lh 42.43N 17.33 E
Babit Point 51b Ab 18.03N 63.02W
Babo 26 Jg 2.33S 133.25 E
Bābol 23 Hb 36.34N 52.42 E
Babol Sar 24 Od 36.43N 52.39 E
Baboquivari Peak 46 Jk 31.46N 111.35W
Babor, Djebel- 13 Rh 36.32N 5.28 E
Baborigame 48 Fd 26.27N 107.16W
Baboua 35 Ad 5.48N 14.49 E
Babozero, Ozero- 7 Ic 66.30N 37.25 E
Babu → Hexian 27 Jg 24.28N 111.34 E
Babuna 15 Eh 41.30N 21.40 E
Babuyan 26 Hc 19.32N 121.57 E
Babuyan 26 Gd 10.01N 118.58 E
Babuyan Channel 26 Hc 18.44N 121.40 E
Babuyan Islands 21 Oh 19.15N 121.40 E
Babylon 23 Fc 32.32N 44.25 E
Bač 15 Cd 45.23N 19.14 E
Bacabachi 48 Ed 26.55N 109.24W
Bacabal 53 Lf 4.14S 44.47W
Ba-Cagan 27 Gb 45.40N 99.30 E
Bacajá, Rio- 54 Hd 3.25S 51.50W
Bacalar 48 Oh 18.43N 88.27W
Bacalar, Laguna de- 48 Oh 18.43N 88.22W
Bacalar Chico, Boca- 49 Dd 18.12N 87.53W
Bacan, Kepulauan- 26 Ig 0.35S 127.30 E
Bacan, Pulau- 26 Ig 0.35S 127.30 E
Bacău [2] 15 Jc 46.36N 27.00 E
Bacău 6 If 46.34N 26.54 E
Baccarat 11 Mf 48.27N 6.45 E
Bacchiglione 14 Ge 45.11N 12.14 E
Baceşti 15 Kc 46.51N 27.14 E
Bachaquero 49 Li 9.56N 71.08W
Bacharach 12 Jd 50.04N 7.46 E
Bacheli 25 Ge 18.40N 81.15 E
Bachiniva 48 Fc 28.45N 107.15W
Bachu/Maralwexi 27 Cd 39.46N 78.15 E
Back 38 Jd 67.15N 95.15W
Bačka 15 Cd 45.50N 19.30 E
Bac Kan 25 Ld 22.08N 105.49 E
Bačka Palanka 15 Cd 45.15N 19.22 E
Bačka Topola 15 Cd 45.49N 19.39 E
Bäckefors 8 Ef 58.48N 12.10 E
Bäckhammar 8 Fe 59.10N 14.11 E
Backnang 10 Fh 48.57N 9.26 E
Bačkovski Manastir 15 Hh 41.56N 24.51 E
Bac Lieu 25 Lg 9.17N 105.43 E
Bac Ninh 25 Ld 21.11N 106.03 E
Bacolet 51p Bb 12.02N 61.41W
Bacolod 22 Oh 10.40N 122.57 E
Bac-Phan=Tonkin (EN) 21 Mg 22.00N 105.00 E
Bacqueville, Lac- 42 Ke 58.00N 74.00W
Bacqueville-en Caux 12 Ce 49.47N 1.00 E
Bácsalmás 10 Pj 46.08N 19.20 E
Bács-Kiskun [2] 10 Pj 46.30N 19.25 E
Bacton 12 Db 52.51N 1.28 E
Bād 23 Hc 33.41N 52.01 E
Badagara 25 Ff 11.36N 75.35 E
Badagri 34 Fd 6.25N 2.53 E
Badain Jaran Shamo 21 Me 40.20N 101.40 E
Badajós, Lago- 54 Fd 3.15S 62.45W
Badajoz 6 Fh 38.53N 6.58W
Badajoz [3] 13 Ff 38.40N 6.10W
Badakhshan [3] 23 Lb 36.45N 72.00 E
Badalona 13 Oc 41.27N 2.15 E
Badanah 23 Fc 30.59N 41.02 E
Badaohao 28 Fd 41.50N 121.59 E
Badas, Kepulauan- 26 Ef 0.35N 107.06 E
Bad Aussee 14 Hc 47.36N 13.47 E
Bad Axe 44 Fd 43.48N 83.00W
Bad Bergzabern 10 Dg 49.06N 8.00 E
Bad Berleburg 12 Kc 51.04N 8.24 E
Bad Bertrich 12 Jd 50.03N 7.02 E
Bad Bramstedt 10 Fc 53.55N 9.53 E
Bad Brückenau 10 Ff 50.18N 9.45 E
Badda 35 Fd 7.55N 39.23 E
Baddo 25 Cc 27.59N 64.21 E
Bad Doberan 10 Hb 54.06N 11.54 E
Bad Driburg 12 Lc 51.44N 9.01 E
Bad Düben 10 Ie 51.36N 12.35 E
Bad Dürkheim 12 Ke 49.28N 8.12 E
Bade 26 Kh 7.10S 139.35 E
Bademli 15 Lk 38.04N 28.04 E
Baden [Aus.] 14 Kb 48.01N 16.14 E
Baden [Switz.] 14 Cc 47.28N 8.18 E
Baden-Baden 10 Eh 48.45N 8.15 E
Badenoch 9 Je 56.50N 4.00W
Baden-Württemberg [2] 10 Eh 48.30N 9.00 E
Bad Essen 12 Kb 52.19N 8.20 E
Bad Freienwalde 10 Kd 52.47N 14.02 E
Badgastein 14 Hc 47.07N 13.08 E
Bādghīsat [3] 23 Jc 35.00N 63.45 E
Bad Gleichenberg 14 Jd 46.52N 15.54 E
Bad Godesberg, Bonn- 10 Df 50.41N 7.09 E
Bad Hall 14 Ib 48.02N 14.12 E
Bad Harzburg 10 Ge 51.53N 10.34 E
Bad Herrenalb 12 Kf 48.48N 8.25 E
Bad Hersfeld 10 Ff 50.52N 9.42 E
Bad Homburg 10 Ef 50.13N 8.37 E
Bad Honnef 12 Jd 50.38N 7.12 E
Bá Dhún na nGall/Donegal Bay 5 Fe 54.30N 8.30W
Badhyz 18 Cg 35.50N 62.00 E
Badiraguato 48 Fe 25.22N 107.31W
Bad Ischl 14 Hc 47.43N 13.37 E
Bad Kissingen 10 Gf 50.12N 10.05 E
Bad Kreuznach 10 Dg 49.50N 7.52 E
Badlands [S.D.-U.S.] 45 Ee 43.30N 102.20W
Badlands [U.S.] 43 Gb 46.45N 103.30W
Bad Langensalza 10 Ge 51.06N 10.39 E
Bad Lautenberg am Harz 10 Ge 51.38N 10.28 E
Bad Liebenwerda 10 Je 51.31N 13.24 E
Bad Liebenzel 12 Kf 48.46N 8.44 E
Bad Mergentheim 10 Fg 49.29N 9.46 E
Bad Mondorf/Mondorf-les-Bains 12 Ie 49.30N 6.17 E
Bad Münster am Stein Ebernburg 12 Je 49.49N 7.51 E
Bad Münstereifel 12 Id 50.34N 6.45 E
Bad Muskau 10 Ke 51.33N 14.43 E
Bad Nauheim 12 Kd 50.22N 8.45 E
Bad Neuenahr-Ahweiler 10 Df 50.33N 7.08 E
Bad Neustadt an der Saale 10 Gf 50.20N 10.13 E
Bad Oeynhausen 12 Kb 52.12N 8.48 E
Bad Oldesloe 10 Gc 53.49N 10.23 E
Ba Don 25 Le 17.45N 106.27 E
Badou [China] 28 Df 36.27N 117.56 E
Badou [Togo] 34 Fd 7.35N 0.36 E
Bad Pyrmont 10 Fe 51.59N 9.15 E
Bad Ragaz 14 Dc 47.00N 9.30 E
Badrah 24 Kf 33.06N 45.58 E
Bad Reichenhall 10 Ii 47.44N 12.53 E
Badr Ḩunayn 23 Ee 23.44N 38.46 E
Bad River 45 Fd 44.22N 100.22W
Bad Salzuflen 12 Kb 52.05N 8.46 E
Bad Salzungen 10 Gf 50.49N 10.14 E
Bad Schwartau 10 Gc 53.55N 10.42 E
Bad Segeberg 10 Gc 53.56N 10.19 E
Bad Tölz 10 Hi 47.46N 11.34 E
Badulla 25 Gg 6.59N 81.03 E
Bad Wildungen 10 Fe 51.07N 9.07 E
Bad Wimpfen 10 Fg 49.14N 9.08 E
Baena 13 Hg 37.37N 4.19W
Baeza [Ec.] 54 Cd 0.28S 77.53W
Baeza [Sp.] 13 Ig 37.59N 3.28W
Baf/Paphos 24 Ee 34.50N 32.35 E
Bafang 34 Hd 5.09N 10.11 E
Bafatà 31 Fg 12.10N 14.40W
Bafélé 34 Cc 10.09N 10.08W
Baffin 38 Mc 68.00N 70.00W
Baffin Bay 38 Mb 73.00N 65.00W
Bafia 34 He 4.45N 11.14 E
Bafilo 34 Fd 9.21N 1.16 E
Bafing [Afr.] 30 Fg 13.49N 10.50W
Bafing [I.C.] 34 Dd 7.52N 7.07W
Bafoulabé 34 Cc 13.48N 10.50W
Bafoussam 31 Ih 5.28N 10.25 E
Bāfq 23 Ic 31.35N 55.24 E
Bāfq, Kūh-e- 24 Pg 31.20N 55.10 E
Bafra 23 Ea 41.34N 35.56 E
Bafra Burnu 24 Fb 41.44N 35.58 E
Bāft 24 Qh 29.14N 56.38 E
Bafwaboli 36 Eb 0.39N 26.10 E
Bafwasende 36 Eb 1.05N 27.16 E
Baga 34 Hc 13.06N 13.50 E
Bagaces 49 Eh 10.31N 85.15W
Bagagem, Rio- 55 Ha 13.58S 48.21W
Bagajevski 16 Lf 47.19N 40.25 E
Bāgalkot 25 Fe 16.11N 75.42 E
Bagamoyo 36 Gd 6.26S 38.54 E
Bagansiapi-Api 26 Df 2.09N 100.49 E
Bağarasi 15 Kl 37.42N 27.33 E
Baga Sola 35 Ac 13.32N 14.19 E
Bagata 36 Cc 3.44S 17.57 E
Bagdad 48 Ke 25.57N 97.09W
Bagdarin 20 Gf 54.30N 113.36 E
Bağdere 24 Ic 38.10N 40.45 E
Bagé 53 Ki 31.20S 54.06W
Bages et de Sigean, Étang de- 11 Jk 43.05N 3.01 E
Baggs 46 Lf 41.02N 107.39W
Bágh Baile na Sgealg/Ballinskelligs Bay 9 Cj 51.50N 10.15W
Baghdād [3] 24 Kf 33.18N 44.36 E
Baghdād 22 Gf 33.21N 44.23 E
Baghdādī, Ra's- 24 Fj 24.40N 35.06 E
Bāgh-e Chenār 24 Qh 28.11N 56.54 E
Bāgh-e-Malek 24 Mg 31.32N 49.55 E
Bagheria 14 Hl 38.05N 13.30 E
Bāghīn 23 Ic 30.12N 56.48 E
Baghlān [3] 23 Kb 35.45N 69.00 E
Baghlān 23 Kb 36.13N 68.46 E
Bāglung 25 Gc 28.16N 83.36 E
Bagn 8 Cd 60.49N 9.34 E
Bagnara Calabra 14 Jl 38.17N 15.48 E
Bagnères-de-Bigorre 11 Gk 43.04N 0.09 E
Bagnères-de-Luchon 11 Gl 42.47N 0.36 E
Bagni di Lucca 14 Ef 44.01N 10.35 E
Bagno di Romagna 14 Fg 43.50N 11.57 E
Bagnolo Mella 14 Ee 45.26N 10.10 E
Bagnols-sur-Cèze 11 Kj 44.10N 4.37 E
Bagoé 30 Gg 12.36N 6.34W
Bagolino 14 Ee 45.49N 10.28 E
Bagrationovsk 8 Ij 54.23N 20.40 E
Bagrax/Bohu 27 Ec 41.58N 86.29 E
Bagrax Hu/Bosten 21 Ke 42.00N 87.00 E
Bagua 54 Ce 5.40S 78.31W
Baguio 22 Oh 16.25N 120.36 E
Baguirmi 30 Ig 11.40N 16.20 E
Bagzane, Monts- 30 Hg 17.43N 8.45 E
Bahama Islands 38 Lg 24.15N 76.00W
Bahamas [1] 39 Lg 24.15N 76.00W
Bahamas, Canal Viejo de-=Old Bahama Channel (EN) 49 Ib 22.30N 78.05W
Bahār 24 Me 34.54N 48.26 E
Baharden 19 Fh 38.28N 57.28 E
Bahardok 19 Fh 38.51N 58.24 E
Baharīyah, Wāḩāt al- 33 Ed 28.10N 29.00 E
Baḩarīyah, Wāḩāt al-=Bahariya Oasis (EN) 33 Ed 28.15N 28.57 E
Bahariya Oasis (EN)=Baḩarīyah, Wāḩāt al- 33 Ed 28.15N 28.57 E
Bahaur 26 Fg 3.20N 114.00 E
Bahāwalnagar 25 Ec 29.59N 73.16 E
Bahāwalpur 22 Jg 29.24N 71.41 E
Bahčisaraj 16 Hg 44.45N 33.51 E
Bahę 24 Gd 37.14N 36.34 E
Bahi 36 Gd 5.39S 35.19 E
Bahia [2] 54 Jf 12.00S 42.00W
Bahia, Islas de la- 47 Ge 16.20N 86.30W
Bahía Blanca 53 Ji 38.44S 62.16W
Bahia de Caráquez 54 Bd 0.37S 80.25W
Bahia Kino 47 Bc 28.50N 111.55W
Bahia Negra 56 Ib 20.15S 58.12W
Bahías, Cabo dos- 52 Jj 44.55S 65.32W
Bahīj 24 Cg 30.56N 29.35 E
Bahinga 36 Ed 5.57S 27.06 E
Bahi Swamp 36 Gd 6.05S 35.10 E
Bahlui 15 Kb 47.08N 27.44 E
Bahmač 19 De 51.11N 32.50 E
Bahoruco, Sierra de- 49 Ld 18.10N 71.25W
Bahraich 25 Gc 27.35N 81.36 E
Bahrain (EN)=Al Baḩrayn [1] 22 Hg 26.00N 50.29 E
Baḩr al Ghazāl [3] 35 Dd 8.15N 26.50 E
Bahr ar Ramla al Kabīr 33 Ed 27.00N 26.00 E
Baḩrayn, Khalij al- 24 Nj 25.45N 50.40 E
Bahr Dar 31 Kg 11.36N 37.22 E
Bahta 20 Dd 62.20N 89.15 E
Bahuşi 15 Jc 46.43N 26.42 E
Baia 15 Le 44.43N 28.40 E
Baia de Aramă 15 Fe 45.00N 22.50 E
Baia de Fier 15 Gd 45.10N 23.46 E
Baia dos Tigres 36 Bf 16.35S 11.43 E
Baia Farta 36 Be 12.37S 13.26 E
Baia Mare 15 Gb 47.40N 23.35 E
Baião 54 Id 2.41S 49.41W
Baia Sprie 15 Gb 47.40N 23.42 E
Baibiene 55 Ci 29.36S 58.10W
Baïbokoum 35 Bd 7.45N 15.41 E
Baicheng 22 Oe 45.34N 122.49 E
Baicheng/Bay 27 Dc 41.46N 81.52 E
Băicoi 15 Id 45.02N 25.51 E
Băiculeşti 15 Hd 45.04N 24.42 E
Baïdou 35 Cd 5.52N 20.41 E
Baie-Comeau 39 Me 49.13N 68.10W
Baie-du-Poste 42 Kf 50.30N 74.00W
Baie-Mahault 50 Fd 16.16N 61.35W
Baie-Saint-Paul 42 Kg 47.27N 70.30W
Baie-Trinité 44 Na 49.24N 67.19W
Baie Verte 42 Lg 49.55N 56.11W
Baiguan → Shangyu 28 Fi 30.01N 120.53 E
Baihe 27 Je 32.46N 110.06 E
Bai He [China] 28 Bh 32.10N 112.20 E
Bai He [China] 28 Dd 40.43N 116.33 E
Baikal, Lake- (EN)=Bajkal, Ozero- 21 Md 53.00N 107.40 E
Baikal Range (EN)=Bajkalski Hrebet 21 Md 55.00N 108.40 E
Baile an Chaistil/Ballycastle 9 Gf 55.12N 6.15W
Baile an Róba/Ballinrobe 9 Dh 53.37N 9.13W
Baile Átha Cliath/Dublin [2] 9 Gh 53.20N 6.15W
Baile Átha Cliath/Dublin 6 Fe 53.20N 6.15W
Baile Átha Luain/Athlone 9 Fh 53.25N 7.56W
Baile Átha Troim/Trim 9 Gh 53.34N 6.47W
Băile Borşa 15 Hb 47.41N 24.43 E
Baile Brigín/Balbriggan 9 Gh 53.37N 6.11W
Băile Govora 15 Hd 45.05N 24.11 E
Baile Locha Riach/Loughrea 9 Eh 53.12N 8.34W
Baile Mhistéala/Mitchelstown 9 Ei 52.16N 8.16W
Bailén 13 If 38.06N 3.46W
Baile na Mainistreach/Newtownabbey 9 Hg 54.42N 5.54W
Baile Nua na hArda/Newtownards 9 Hg 54.36N 5.41W
Băile Olăneşti 15 Hd 45.12N 24.14 E
Băileşti 15 Ge 44.01N 23.21 E
Bailleul 12 Ce 49.12N 0.26 E
Bailleul 12 Ed 50.44N 2.44 E
Ba Illi 35 Bc 10.31N 16.29 E
Bailong Jiang 27 Ie 32.42N 105.15 E
Bailundo 36 Ce 12.10S 15.56 E
Baima 27 He 33.05N 100.29 E
Bain 12 Ba 53.04N 0.12W
Bainbridge 43 Ke 30.54N 84.34W
Bain-de-Bretagne 11 Eg 47.50N 1.41W
Baines Drift 37 Dd 22.30S 28.43 E
Baing 26 Hi 10.14S 120.34 E
Baingoin 27 Ee 31.36N 89.48 E
Baiquan 27 Mb 47.38N 126.04 E
Bā'ir 24 Gg 30.46N 36.41 E
Bā'ir, Wādī- 24 Gg 31.12N 37.31 E
Baird 45 Gj 32.24N 99.24W
Baird Inlet 40 Gd 60.45N 164.00W
Baird Mountains 40 Gc 67.35N 161.30W
Baird Peninsula 42 Jc 69.00N 75.15W
Bairiki 58 Id 1.20N 173.01 E
Bairin Youqi (Daban) 27 Kc 43.30N 118.37 E
Bairin Zuoqi (Lindong) 27 Kc 43.59N 119.22 E
Bairnsdale 58 Fh 37.50S 147.38 E
Bais 26 He 9.35N 123.07 E
Bai Shan 27 Fc 40.53N 93.48 E
Baisogala/Bajsogala 8 Ji 55.35N 23.44 E
Baitou Shan 21 Oe 42.00N 128.00 E
Baitoushan Tian Chi 28 Jc 42.00N 128.03 E
Baixiang 28 Cf 37.29N 114.44 E
Baixo Alentejo 13 Dg 37.55N 8.10W
Baixo Guandu 54 Jg 19.31S 41.01W
Baixo Longa 36 Cf 15.42S 18.38 E
Baiyanghe 27 Ec 43.12N 88.28 E
Baiyü 27 Ge 31.13N 98.51 E
Baja 10 Oj 46.11N 18.58 E
Baja, Punta- [Mex.] 48 Dc 28.25N 111.45W
Baja, Punta- [Pas.] 65d Ab 27.10S 109.22W
Baja California=Lower California (EN) 38 Hg 28.00N 112.00W
Baja California Norte [2] 47 Ac 30.00N 115.00W
Baja California Sur [2] 47 Bd 25.50N 111.50W
Bājah [3] 32 Ib 36.30N 9.30 E
Bājah 32 Ib 36.44N 9.11 E
Bajalān 24 Md 37.18N 48.47 E
Bajan 27 Jb 49.15N 111.58 E
Bajanaul 19 He 50.47N 75.42 E
Bajandaj 20 Ff 53.04N 105.30 E
Bajan-Delger 27 Jb 45.55N 112.15 E
Bajangol 20 Ff 50.40N 103.25 E
Bajan-Hongor 22 Me 46.20N 100.40 E
Bajan-Ula [Mong.] 27 Jb 49.07N 112.45 E
Bajan-Ula [Mong.] 27 Gb 47.05N 95.15 E
Bajan-Under 27 Gc 44.45N 98.45 E
Baja Verapaz [3] 49 Bf 15.05N 90.20W
Bajawa 26 Hh 8.47S 120.59 E
Bajčunas 16 Rf 47.17N 53.03 E
Bajdarackaja Guba 20 Bc 69.00N 67.30 E
Bajdarata 17 Nb 68.12N 68.18 E
Bajdrag Gol 27 Hb 45.10N 100.45 E
Bājgīrān 24 Rd 37.36N 58.24 E
Baj-Haak 20 Ef 51.07N 94.34 E
Bajiazi 28 Jc 42.41N 129.13 E
Bajina Bašta 15 Cf 43.58N 19.34 E
Bajkal 20 Ff 51.53N 104.47 E
Bajkal, Ozero-=Baikal, Lake- (EN) 21 Md 53.00N 107.40 E
Bajkalovo 17 Kh 57.24N 63.40 E
Bajkalsk 20 Ff 51.30N 104.05 E
Bajkalski Hrebet=Baikal Range (EN) 21 Md 55.00N 108.40 E
Bajkit 20 Ed 61.41N 96.25 E
Bajkonur 19 Gf 47.50N 66.07 E
Bajmak 19 Fe 52.36N 58.19 E
Bajmba, Mount- 59 Ke 29.20S 152.05 E
Bajmok 15 Cd 45.58N 19.26 E
Bajo Baudó 54 Cc 4.58N 77.22W

Index Symbols

[1] Independent Nation
[2] State, Region
[3] District, County
[4] Municipality
[5] Colony, Dependency
Continent
Physical Region
Historical or Cultural Region
Mount, Mountain
Volcano
Hill
Mountains, Mountain Range
Hills, Escarpment
Plateau, Upland
Pass, Gap
Plain, Lowland
Delta
Salt Flat
Valley, Canyon
Crater, Cave
Karst Features
Depression
Polder
Desert, Dunes
Forest, Woods
Heath, Steppe
Oasis
Cape, Point
Coast, Beach
Cliff
Peninsula
Isthmus
Sandbank
Island
Atoll
Rock, Reef
Islands, Archipelago
Rocks, Reefs
Coral Reef
Well, Spring
Geyser
River, Stream
Waterfall Rapids
River Mouth, Estuary
Lake
Salt Lake
Intermittent Lake
Reservoir
Swamp, Pond
Canal
Glacier
Ice Shelf, Pack Ice
Ocean
Sea
Gulf, Bay
Strait, Fjord
Lagoon
Bank
Seamount
Tablemount
Ridge
Shelf
Basin
Escarpment, Sea Scarp
Fracture
Trench, Abyss
National Park, Reserve
Point of Interest
Recreation Site
Cave, Cavern
Historic Site
Ruins
Wall, Walls
Church, Abbey
Temple
Scientific Station
Airport
Port
Lighthouse
Mine
Tunnel
Dam, Bridge

Bajo Boquete 49 Fi 8.46N 82.26W
Bajram-Ali 19 Gh 37.39N 62.12 E
Bajram Curri 15 Dg 42.21N 20.04 E
Bajsogala/Baisogala 8 Ji 55.35N 23.44 E
Bajsun 18 Fe 38.14N 67.12 E
Bajun Islands 30 Li 0.50S 42.15 E
Bajžansaj 18 Gc 43.13N 69.56 E
Baka 35 Ee 4.33N 30.05 E
Bakacak 15 Ki 40.12N 27.05 E
Bakadžicite 15 Jg 42.25N 26.43 E
Bakal 19 Fe 54.56N 58.48 E
Bakala 35 Cd 6.11N 20.22 E
Bakanas 19 Hg 44.48N 76.15 E
Bakar 14 Ie 45.18N 14.32 E
Bakčar 20 De 57.01N 82.10 E
Bake 26 Dg 3.03S 100.16 E
Bakel 34 Cc 14.54N 12.27W
Baker [Ca.-U.S.] 46 Gi 35.15N 116.02W
Baker [La.-U.S.] 45 Kk 30.35N 91.10W
Baker [Mt.-U.S.] 43 Gb 46.22N 104.17W
Baker [Or.-U.S.] 43 Dc 44.47N 117.50W
Baker, Mount- 43 Cb 48.47N 121.49W
Baker Island 57 Jd 0.15N 176.27W
Baker Lake 39 Jc 64.10N 95.30W
Baker Lake 38 Jc 64.10N 95.30W
Bakersfield 39 Hf 35.23N 119.01W
Bâ Kêv 25 Lf 13.42N 107.12 E
Bakhma 24 Kd 36.38N 44.17 E
Bakhtegān, Daryācheh-ye- 24 Ph 29.20N 54.05 E
Bakhtīārī va Chahār Mahāll [3] 23 Hc 32.00N 50.00 E
Bakhūn, Kūh-e- 23 Id 27.56N 56.18 E
Bakir 24 Bc 38.55N 27.00 E
Bakırköy, İstanbul 15 Li 40.59N 28.52 E
Baklan 15 Ml 37.58N 29.36 E
Bako 35 Fd 7.19N 35.08 E
Bako [Eth.] 35 Fd 9.05N 37.07 E
Bako [Eth.] 35 Fd 5.50N 36.37 E
Bakony = Bakony Mountains (EN) 5 Hf 47.15N 17.50 E
Bakony Mountains (EN) = Bakony 5 Hf 47.15N 17.50 E
Bakool [3] 35 Ge 4.10N 43.50 E
Bakouma 35 Cd 5.42N 22.47 E
Bakoye 34 Cc 13.49N 10.50W
Bakpulād 24 Qc 38.10N 57.00 E
Baksan 16 Mh 43.40N 43.28 E
Baksan 16 Nh 43.42N 44.03 E
Baku 6 Kg 40.23N 49.51 E
Bakum 12 Kb 52.44N 8.11 E
Bakungan 26 Cf 2.56N 97.30 E
Bakuriani 16 Mi 41.43N 43.31 E
Bakutis Coast 66 Of 74.45S 120.00W
Balâ 24 Ec 39.34N 33.08 E
Bala, Cerros de- 54 Ef 14.30S 67.40W
Balabac 26 Ge 7.59N 117.04 E
Balabac 26 Ge 7.57N 117.01 E
Balabac, Selat- = Balabac Strait (EN) 21 Ni 7.40N 117.00 E
Balabac Strait (EN) = Balabac, Selat- 21 Ni 7.40N 117.00 E
Ba'labakk 24 Ge 34.00N 36.12 E
Balabalangan, Kepulauan- 26 Gg 2.20S 117.25 E
Balaban DaGı 24 Hb 40.28N 39.15 E
Balabanovo 16 Jb 55.11N 36.40 E
Balabio 63b Be 20.07S 164.11 E
Balaci 15 He 44.21N 24.55 E
Bal'ad 35 He 2.22N 45.24 E
Balad 24 Ke 34.01N 44.01 E
Balādīn as Sakrān 24 Kj 25.12N 44.37 E
Baladiyat 'Adan = Aden (EN) 22 Gh 12.46N 45.01 E
Balad Rūz 24 Kf 33.42N 45.05 E
Balagannoje 20 Je 59.43N 149.15 E
Balagansk 20 Ff 53.58N 103.02 E
Bālāghāt 25 Gd 21.48N 80.11 E
Bālāghāt Range 25 Fe 18.45N 76.30 E
Balagne 11a Aa 42.35N 8.50 E
Balaguer 13 Mc 41.47N 0.49 E
Balahna 19 Ed 56.31N 43.37 E
Balahta 20 Ee 55.24N 91.37 E
Balaka 36 Fe 14.59S 34.57 E
Balaklava 16 Hg 44.31N 33.34 E
Balakleja 19 Df 49.27N 36.52 E
Balakovo 6 Ke 52.02N 47.45 E
Balama 37 Fb 13.16S 38.36 E
Balambangam, Pulau- 26 Ge 7.17N 116.55 E
Bālā Morghāb 23 Jb 35.35N 63.20 E
Balan Daği 15 Lm 36.52N 28.20 E
Balankanche 48 Og 20.45N 88.30W
Balasan 26 Hd 11.28N 123.05 E
Balasore 25 Hd 21.30N 86.56 E
Balašov 19 Ee 51.33N 43.10 E
Balassagyarmat 10 Ph 48.05N 19.18 E
Balāţ 33 Ed 25.33N 29.16 E
Balaton 5 Hf 46.50N 17.45 E
Balatonfüred 10 Nj 46.57N 17.53 E
Balatonkeresztúr 10 Nj 46.42N 17.23 E
Balaurin 26 Hh 8.15S 123.43 E
Bălăuşeri 15 Hc 46.24N 24.41 E
Balayan 26 Hd 13.57N 120.44 E
Balazote 13 Jf 38.53N 2.08W
Balbi, Mount- 60 Ei 5.55S 154.59 E
Balboa Heights 47 Ig 8.57N 79.33W
Balbriggan/Baile Brigin 9 Gh 53.37N 6.11W
Balby 8 Ei 55.40N 13.20 E
Balcarce 56 Ie 37.50S 58.15W
Balcarce, Sierras de- 55 Cm 37.50S 58.40W
Bălceşti 15 Ge 44.37N 23.57 E
Balčik 15 Lf 43.25N 28.10 E
Balclutha 61 Ci 46.14S 169.44 E
Bald Eagle Mountain 44 Ie 41.00N 77.45W
Bald Head 59 Dg 35.07S 118.01 E
Bald Knob 44 Hg 37.56N 79.51W
Bald Knob 45 Ki 35.19N 91.34W
Baldo, Monte- 14 Ee 45.40N 10.50 E
Baldock 12 Bc 51.59N 0.11W
Baldone 8 Kh 56.41N 24.22 E
Baldur 45 Gb 49.23N 99.15W
Baldwin 44 Ed 43.54N 85.51W
Baldy Peak 43 Fe 33.55N 109.35W
Bale [3] 35 Gd 6.00N 41.00 E
Bâle/Basel 6 Gf 47.30N 7.30 E
Baleares [3] 13 Oe 39.30N 3.00 E
Baleares, Islas-/Balears, Illes- = Balearic Islands (EN) 5 Gh 39.30N 3.00 E
Balearic Islands (EN) = Baleares, Islas-/Balears, Illes- 5 Gh 39.30N 3.00 E
Balearic Islands (EN) = Balears, Illes-/Baleares, Islas- 5 Gh 39.30N 3.00 E
Balears, Illes-/Baleares, Islas- = Balearic Islands (EN) 5 Gh 39.30N 3.00 E
Balease, Gunung- 26 Hg 2.24S 120.33 E
Baleia, Ponta de- 52 Mg 17.40S 36.07W
Baleine, Rivière à la- 42 Ke 58.15N 67.38W
Balej 20 Gf 51.35N 116.38 E
Balen 12 Hc 51.10N 5.09 E
Baler 26 Hc 15.46N 121.34 E
Balezino 19 Fd 57.59N 53.02 E
Balfate 49 Df 15.48N 86.25W
Bălgarija = Bulgaria (EN) [1] 6 Ig 43.00N 25.00 E
Balgazyn 20 Ef 50.58N 95.12 E
Balguntay 27 Ec 42.45N 86.18 E
Balḩāf 23 Fg 13.58N 48.11 E
Balhaš 22 Je 46.49N 74.59 E
Balhaš, Ozero- = Balkhash, Lake- (EN) 21 Je 46.00N 74.00 E
Balho 35 Gc 12.00N 42.10 E
Balholm 7 Bf 61.12N 6.33 E
Bali [3] 26 Gh 8.30S 115.00 E
Bali, Laut- = Bali Sea (EN) 21 Nj 7.45S 115.30 E
Bali, Pulau- 21 Nj 8.20S 115.00 E
Bali, Selat- = Bali Strait (EN) 26 Fh 8.18S 114.25 E
Baliceaux Island 51n Bb 12.57N 61.08W
Baliem 26 Kg 4.25S 138.59 E
Balige 26 Cf 2.20N 99.04 E
Balikesir 23 Cb 39.39N 27.53 E
Balık Gölü 24 Jc 39.45N 43.36 E
Balīkh, Nahr- 24 He 35.53N 39.10 E
Balikpapan 22 Nj 1.17S 116.50 E
Balimbing 26 Dh 5.55S 104.34 E
Balimo 60 Ci 8.03S 142.56 E
Balingen 10 Eh 48.17N 8.51 E
Balinqiao 28 Ec 43.16N 118.38 E
Balintang Channel 26 Hc 19.49N 121.40 E
Balīs 24 He 35.59N 38.06 E
Bali Sea (EN) = Bali, Laut- 21 Nj 7.45S 115.30 E
Bali Strait (EN) = Bali, Selat- 26 Fh 8.18S 114.25 E
Balitung, Palau- 21 Mj 2.50S 107.55 E
Baliza 55 Fc 16.15S 52.25W
Balk, Gaasterland- 12 Hb 52.54N 5.36 E
Balkan Mountains (EN) = Stara Planina 5 Ig 43.15N 25.00 E
Balkan Peninsula (EN) 5 Ig 41.30N 23.00 E
Balkašino 19 Ge 52.32N 68.46 E
Balkh 23 Kb 36.46N 66.54 E
Balkh [3] 23 Kb 36.30N 67.00 E
Balkhash, Lake- (EN) = Balhaš, Ozero- 21 Je 46.00N 74.00 E
Balladonia 59 Ef 32.27S 123.51 E
Ballagen 7 Db 68.20N 16.50 E
Ballaghaderreen/Bealach an Doirin 9 Eh 53.55N 8.35W
Ballantrae 9 If 55.06N 5.00W
Ballantyne Strait 42 Ga 77.30N 115.00W
Ballarat 58 Fh 37.34S 143.52 E
Ballard, Lake- 59 Ee 29.25S 120.55 E
Ballé 34 Db 15.20N 8.36W
Ballenas, Bahia- 48 Cd 26.45N 113.25W
Ballenas, Canal de- 48 Cc 29.10N 113.25W
Ballenero, Canal- 56 Fh 54.50S 71.00W
Ballenita, Punta- 56 Fc 25.46S 70.44W
Balleny Islands 66 Ke 66.35S 162.50 E
Balleroy 12 Be 49.11N 0.50W
Balleza 48 Fd 26.57N 106.21W
Balli 15 Ki 40.50N 27.03 E
Ballia 25 Gc 25.45N 84.10 E
Ballina 59 Ke 28.52S 153.33 E
Ballina/Béal an Átha 9 Dg 54.07N 9.09W
Ballinasloe/Béal Átha na Sluaighe 9 Eh 53.20N 8.13W
Ballinger 45 Gk 31.44N 99.57W
Ballinrobe/Baile an Róba 9 Dh 53.37N 9.13W
Ballinskelligs Bay/Bágh Baile na Sgealg 9 Cj 51.50N 10.15W
Ballshi 15 Ci 40.36N 19.44 E
Ball's Pyramid 57 Gh 31.45S 159.15 E
Ballycastle/Baile an Chaistil 9 Gf 55.12N 6.15W
Ballyhaunis/Béal Átha hAmhnais 9 Eh 53.46N 8.46W
Ballymena/An Baile Meánach 9 Gg 54.52N 6.17W
Ballyshannon/Béal Átha Seanaidh 9 Eg 54.30N 8.11W
Balmazújváros 10 Ri 47.37N 21.21 E
Balmoral Castle 9 Jd 57.02N 3.15W
Balneario Orense 55 Cn 38.49S 59.46W
Balneario Oriente 55 Bn 38.55S 60.32W
Balombo 36 Be 12.21S 14.43 E
Balonne River 57 Fg 28.47S 147.56 E
Balota, Vîrful- 15 Gd 45.18N 23.53 E
Balovale 31 Jj 13.33S 23.07 E
Balrāmpur 25 Gc 27.26N 82.11 E
Balranald 59 If 34.38S 143.33 E
Balş 15 He 44.21N 24.06 E
Balsas [Braz.] 54 Ie 7.31S 46.02W
Balsas [Mex.] 48 Jh 18.00N 99.47W
Balsas, Depresión del- 48 Ih 18.00N 100.10W
Balsas, Río- [Mex.] 38 Ih 17.55N 102.10W
Balsas, Río- [Pan.] 49 Ii 8.15N 77.59W
Balsas, Rio das- [Braz.] 54 Ie 9.58S 47.52W
Balsas, Rio das- [Braz.] 54 Je 7.14S 44.33W
Bålsta 8 Ge 59.35N 17.30 E
Balsthal 14 Bc 47.19N 7.42 E
Balta 16 Ff 47.57N 29.38 E
Baltanás 13 Hc 41.56N 4.15W
Baltasar Brum 56 Id 30.44S 57.19W
Baltaţi 15 Kb 47.13N 27.09 E
Baltic Sea (EN) = Baltijas Jūra 5 Hd 57.00N 19.00 E
Baltic Sea (EN) = Baltijos Jura 5 Hd 57.00N 19.00 E
Baltic Sea (EN) = Balti Meri 5 Hd 57.00N 19.00 E
Baltic Sea- (EN) = Baltiskoje More 5 Hd 57.00N 19.00 E
Baltic Sea (EN) = Bałtyckie, Morze- 5 Hd 57.00N 19.00 E
Baltic Sea (EN) = Itämeri 5 Hd 57.00N 19.00 E
Baltic Sea (EN) = Östersjön 5 Hd 57.00N 19.00 E
Baltic Sea (EN) = Østersøen 5 Hd 57.00N 19.00 E
Baltic Sea (EN) = Ostsee 5 Hd 57.00N 19.00 E
Baltijas Jūra = Baltic Sea (EN) 5 Hd 57.00N 19.00 E
Baltijos Jura = Baltic Sea (EN) 5 Hd 57.00N 19.00 E
Baltijsk 19 Be 54.40N 19.58 E
Baltijskaja Grjada 7 Fi 55.00N 25.00 E
Baltīm 33 Fc 31.33N 31.05 E
Balti Meri = Baltic Sea (EN) 5 Hd 57.00N 19.00 E
Baltimore 39 Lf 39.17N 76.37W
Baltiskoje More = Baltic Sea (EN) 5 Hd 57.00N 19.00 E
Baltit (Hunza) 25 Ea 36.20N 74.40 E
Baltoj Voke 8 Kj 54.24N 25.16 E
Baltrum 10 Dc 53.44N 7.23 E
Bałtyckie, Morze- = Baltic Sea (EN) 5 Hd 57.00N 19.00 E
Baluarte, Rio- 48 Ff 22.49N 106.02W
Balūchestān va Sīstān [3] 23 Jd 28.30N 60.30 E
Baluchistān = Baluchistan (EN) 21 Ig 28.00N 63.00 E
Baluchistān = Baluchistan (EN) [3] 25 Cc 28.00N 63.00 E
Baluchistan (EN) = Baluchistān [3] 25 Cc 28.00N 63.00 E
Baluchistan (EN) = Baluchistān 21 Ig 28.00N 63.00 E
Balupe 8 Lh 56.54N 27.02 E
Balurghat 25 Hc 25.13N 88.46 E
Balvard 24 Qh 29.25N 56.06 E
Balve 12 Jc 51.20N 7.52 E
Balver Wald 12 Jc 51.21N 7.51 E
Balvi/Balvy 7 Gh 57.08N 27.20 E
Balvy/Balvi 7 Gh 57.08N 27.20 E
Balya 24 Bc 39.45N 27.35 E
Balygyčan 20 Kd 64.00N 154.10 E
Balykši 16 Qf 47.02N 51.55 E
Bām 24 Qd 36.58N 57.59 E
Bam 23 Id 29.06N 58.21 E
Bama 34 Hc 11.31N 13.41 E
Bamaji Lake 45 Ka 51.09N 91.25W
Bamako 31 Gg 12.38N 8.00W
Bamako [3] 34 Dc 13.00N 8.00W
Bamba 34 Eb 17.02N 1.24W
Bambama 36 Bc 2.32S 13.33 E
Bambana, Río- 49 Fg 13.27N 83.50W
Bambangando 36 Df 16.59S 20.57 E
Bambari 31 Jh 5.45N 20.40 E
Bamberg 10 Gg 49.42N 10.52 E
Bambesa 36 Eb 3.28N 25.43 E
Bambesi 35 Ed 9.45N 34.44 E
Bambey 34 Bc 14.42N 16.28W
Bambezi 37 Dc 19.57S 28.55 E
Bambili 36 Eb 3.39N 26.07 E
Bambio 35 Be 3.54N 16.59 E
Bamboi 34 Ed 8.10N 2.02W
Bambouti 35 Dd 5.24N 27.12 E
Bambouto, Monts- 30 Ih 5.44N 10.04 E
Bambuí 55 Je 20.01S 45.58W
Bam Co 27 Fe 31.15N 90.32 E
Bamenda 34 Hd 5.56N 10.10 E
Bāmīān [3] 23 Kc 34.45N 67.15 E
Bāmīān 23 Kc 34.50N 67.50 E
Bamiancheng 28 Gc 43.15N 124.00 E
Bamiantong → Muling 28 Kb 44.55N 130.32 E
Bamingui 35 Cd 7.34N 20.11 E
Bamingui 30 Ih 8.33N 19.05 E
Bamingui-Bangoran [3] 35 Cd 7.50N 20.15 E
Bampūr 23 Jd 27.12N 60.27 E
Bampūr 23 Id 27.18N 59.06 E
Banaadir 30 Lh 1.00N 44.00 E
Banaadir [3] 35 He 2.00N 45.15 E
Banaba Island 57 He 0.52S 169.35 E
Banabuiú, Açude- 54 Ke 5.20S 39.00W
Banagi 36 Fc 2.16S 34.51 E
Banalia 36 Eb 1.33N 25.20 E
Banamba 34 Dc 13.32N 7.27W
Bananal, Ilha do- [Braz.] 52 Kg 11.30S 50.15W
Bananal, Ilha do- [Braz.] 55 Dc 17.05S 56.25W
Bananga 25 Ig 6.57N 93.54 E
Banarli 15 Kh 41.04N 27.20 E
Banās 25 Fc 25.54N 76.45 E
Banās, Ra's- 30 Kf 23.54N 35.48 E
Banat 5 If 45.30N 21.00 E
Banat 15 Dd 45.30N 21.00 E
Banaz 24 Cc 38.46N 29.46 E
Banaz 24 Cc 38.12N 29.14 E
Banbar 27 Fe 30.48N 94.52 E
Banbridge/Droichead na Banna 9 Gg 54.21N 6.16W
Banbury 9 Li 52.04N 1.20W
Banco, Punta- 49 Fi 8.23N 83.09W
Bancroft 44 Ic 45.03N 77.51W
Bānda 25 Gc 25.29N 80.20 E
Banda, Kepulauan- = Banda Islands (EN) 26 Ig 4.35S 129.55 E
Banda, Laut- = Banda Sea (EN) 57 De 5.00S 128.00 E
Banda, Punta- 48 Ab 31.45N 116.45W
Banda Aceh 22 Li 5.34N 95.20 E
Bandai-San 29 Gc 37.38N 140.04 E
Banda Islands (EN) = Banda, Kepulauan- 26 Ig 4.35S 129.55 E
Bandak 8 Ce 59.25N 8.15 E
Bandama 30 Gh 5.10N 4.58W
Bandama Blanc 34 Dd 6.54N 5.31W
Bandar → Machilipatnam 25 Ge 16.10N 81.08 E
Bandar 'Abbās 22 Hg 27.11N 56.17 E
Bandar-e Anzalī 23 Gb 37.28N 49.27 E
Bandar-e Chārak 24 Pi 26.43N 54.16 E
Bandar-e Chīrū 24 Oi 26.43N 53.43 E
Bandar-e Deylam 23 Hg 30.05N 50.07 E
Bandar-e-Gaz 24 Od 36.47N 53.59 E
Bandar-e-Khomeynī 24 Mg 30.25N 49.08 E
Bandar-e Lengeh 23 Hd 26.33N 54.53 E
Bandar-e Māh Shahr 23 Gc 30.33N 49.12 E
Bandar-e Maqām 23 Hd 26.56N 53.29 E
Bandar-e Moghūyeh 24 Pi 26.35N 54.31 E
Bandar-e-Rīg 24 Nh 29.29N 50.38 E
Bandar-e-Torkeman 23 Gf 30.45N 51.33 E
Bandar Seri Begawan 22 Ni 4.53N 114.56 E
Banda Sea (EN) = Banda, Laut- 57 De 5.00S 128.00 E
Bande 13 Eb 42.02N 7.58W
Bandeira, Pico da- 52 Lh 20.26S 41.47W
Bandeirantes 55 Ga 13.41S 50.48W
Bandeirantes, Ilha dos- 55 Ff 23.22S 53.50W
Bandera 56 Hc 28.54S 62.16W
Bandera, Alto- 49 Ld 18.49N 70.37W
Banderas, Bahía de- 47 Cd 20.40N 105.25W
Bandiagara 34 Ec 14.20N 3.37W
Bandiat 11 Gi 45.46N 0.20 E
Bandırma 23 Ca 40.20N 27.58 E
Bandirma Körfezi 15 Ki 40.25N 28.00 E
Bandol 11 Lk 43.08N 5.45 E
Bandon 46 Ce 43.07N 124.25W
Bandon/Abhainn na Bandan 9 Ej 51.40N 8.30W
Bandon/Droichead na Bandan 9 Ej 51.45N 8.45W
Ban Don, Ao- 25 Jg 9.20N 99.25 E
Bandundu [2] 36 Cc 5.00S 17.00 E
Bandundu 31 Ii 3.18S 17.20 E
Bandung 22 Mj 6.54S 107.36 E
Bāneh 24 Ke 35.59N 45.53 E
Banes 47 Id 20.58N 75.43W
Banff [Alta.-Can.] 42 Ff 51.10N 115.34W
Banff [Scot.-U.K.] 9 Kd 57.40N 2.31W
Banfora 34 Ec 10.38N 4.46W
Banga 36 Dd 5.57S 20.28 E
Bangalore 22 Jh 12.59N 77.35 E
Bangangté 34 Hd 5.09N 10.31 E
Bangar 26 Gf 4.43N 115.04 E
Bangassou 31 Jh 4.44N 22.49 E
Bangeta, Mount- 60 Di 6.16S 147.04 E
Banggai 26 Hg 1.34S 123.30 E
Banggai, Kepulauan- = Banggai Archipelago (EN) 26 Hg 1.30S 123.15 E
Banggai, Selat- 26 Hg 1.55S 124.00 E
Banggai Archipelago (EN) = Banggai, Kepulauan- 26 Hg 1.30S 123.15 E
Banggi, Pulau- 26 Ge 7.17N 117.12 E
Banghāzī = Benghazi (EN) 31 Je 32.07N 20.04 E
Banghāzī = Benghazi (EN) [3] 33 Dd 27.00N 20.30 E
Bangka, Pulau- [Indon.] 26 If 1.48N 125.09 E
Bangka, Pulau- [Indon.] 21 Mj 2.15S 106.00 E
Bangka, Selat- = Bangka Strait (EN) 26 Eg 2.20S 105.45 E
Bangkalan 26 Fh 7.02S 112.44 E
Bangka Strait (EN) = Bangka, Selat- 26 Eg 2.20S 105.45 E
Bangkinang 26 Df 0.21N 101.02 E
Bangko 26 Dg 2.05S 102.17 E
Bangkok (EN) = Krung Thep 22 Mh 13.45N 100.31 E
Bangladesh [1] 22 Kg 24.00N 90.00 E
Bangli 26 Gh 8.27S 115.21 E
Bangolo 34 Dd 7.01N 7.09W
Bangong Co 27 Ce 33.45N 79.15 E
Bangor [Me.-U.S.] 43 Nc 44.49N 68.47W
Bangor [Wales-U.K.] 9 Ih 53.13N 4.08W
Bangor/Beannchar 9 Hg 54.40N 5.40W
Bangoran 35 Bd 8.42N 19.06 E
Bangsund 7 Cd 64.24N 11.24 E
Bangu 36 Dd 9.05S 23.44 E
Bangued 26 Hc 17.36N 120.37 E
Bangui [C.A.R.] 31 Ih 4.22N 18.35 E
Bangui [Phil.] 26 Hc 18.32N 120.46 E
Bangweulu, Lake- 30 Jj 11.05S 29.45 E
Bangweulu Swamps 36 Fe 11.30S 30.15 E
Banhā 33 Fc 30.28N 31.11 E
Ban Houayxay 25 Kd 20.18N 100.26 E
Bani 30 Gg 14.30N 4.12W
Baní 47 Je 18.17N 70.20W
Bani, Jbel- 30 Gf 28.30N 9.00W
Bani Bangou 34 Fb 15.03N 2.42 E
Banie 10 Kc 53.08N 14.38 E
Banifing 34 Dc 12.43N 6.25W
Banī Forūr, Jazīreh-ye- 24 Pi 26.07N 54.28 E
Banihal Pass 25 Fb 33.15N 75.09 E
Banija 14 Ke 45.10N 16.10 E
Banikoara 34 Fc 11.18N 2.26 E
Banī ma 'Āriḑ 33 Ie 20.42N 47.42 E
Banī Mazār 33 Fd 28.30N 30.48 E
Banī Muḩammadīyāt 24 Di 27.17N 31.05 E
Banī Suwayf 33 Fd 29.05N 31.05 E
Banī Tonb 24 Pi 26.12N 54.56 E
Banī Walīd 33 Bc 31.46N 13.59 E
Bāniyās 23 Ec 33.15N 35.41 E
Banja 15 Hg 42.33N 24.50 E
Banja Koviljača 15 Ce 44.30N 19.11 E
Banja Luka 14 Lf 44.46N 17.10 E
Banjarmarsin 22 Nj 3.20S 114.35 E
Banjul 31 Fg 13.27N 16.35W
Bank 16 Pj 39.27N 49.14 E
Bankas 34 Ec 14.05N 3.31W
Bankeryd 8 Fg 57.51N 14.07 E
Banket 37 Ec 17.23S 30.24 E
Bankhead Lake 44 Di 33.30N 87.15W
Bankilaré 34 Fc 14.35N 0.44 E
Bankja 15 Gg 42.42N 23.08 E
Ban Kongmi 25 Lf 14.31N 106.55 E
Banks [Can.] 38 Gb 73.15N 121.30W
Banks [Can.] 42 Ef 53.25N 130.10W
Banks, Iles- = Banks Islands (EN) 57 Hf 13.50S 167.35 E
Banks Island 59 Ib 10.10S 142.15 E
Banks Islands (EN) = Banks, Iles- 57 Hf 13.50S 167.35 E
Banks Lake 46 Fc 47.45N 119.15W
Banks Peninsula 57 Ii 43.40S 172.40 E
Banks Strait 59 Jh 40.40S 148.10 E
Bann/An Bhanna 9 Gf 55.10N 6.46W
Ban Na San 25 Jg 8.53N 99.17 E
Bannerman Town 44 Im 24.09N 76.09W
Banning 46 Gj 33.56N 116.52W
Bannock Range 46 Ie 42.30N 112.20W
Bannu 25 Eb 32.59N 70.36 E
Bañolas/Banyoles 13 Ob 42.07N 2.46 E
Bánovce nad Bebravou 10 Oh 48.44N 18.15 E
Banqiao 27 Hf 25.28N 104.02 E
Banská Bystrica 10 Ph 48.44N 19.09 E
Banská Štiavnica 10 Oh 48.27N 18.55 E
Bansko 15 Gh 41.50N 23.29 E
Bānswāra 25 Ed 23.33N 74.27 E
Banta 35 Ge 1.13N 42.30 E
Bantenan, Tanjung- 26 Fh 8.47S 114.33 E
Bantry/Beanntraí 9 Dj 51.41N 9.27W
Bantry Bay/Bá Bheanntraí 9 Dj 51.38N 9.48W
Bañuela 13 Hf 38.24N 4.11W
Banyak, Kepulauan- = Banyak Islands (EN) 26 Cf 2.10N 97.15 E
Banyak Islands (EN) = Banyak, Kepulauan- 26 Cf 2.10N 97.15 E
Banyo 34 Hd 6.45N 11.49 E
Banyoles/Bañolas 13 Ob 42.07N 2.46 E
Banyuls-sur-Mer 11 Jl 42.29N 3.08 E
Banyuwangi 22 Nj 8.12S 114.21 E
Banzare Coast 66 Ie 67.00S 126.00 E
Banzare Seamounts (EN) 66 Df 58.50S 77.44 E
Banzart [3] 32 Ib 37.00N 9.30 E
Banzart = Bizerte (EN) 31 He 37.17N 9.52 E
Banzart, Buḩayrat- 14 Dm 37.11N 9.52 E
Bao'an 27 Jg 22.35N 114.10 E
Bao'an → Zhidan 27 Id 36.48N 108.46 E
Baochang → Taibus Qi 27 Kc 41.55N 115.22 E
Baode 27 Jd 38.59N 111.07 E
Baodi 28 De 39.43N 117.18 E
Baoding 22 Nf 38.47N 115.30 E
Baofeng [China] 27 Je 33.48N 113.14 E
Baofeng [China] 28 Bh 33.52N 113.04 E
Baoji 22 Mf 34.26N 107.12 E
Baokang 27 Je 31.49N 111.13 E
Baokang → Horqin Zuoyi Zhongqi 27 Lc 44.06N 123.19 E
Bao Loc 25 Lf 11.32N 107.48 E
Baoqing 27 Nb 46.20N 132.11 E
Baoro 35 Bd 5.40N 15.58 E
Baoshan 22 Lg 25.09N 99.12 E
Baotou 22 Me 40.38N 110.00 E
Baoulé [Afr.] 30 Gg 12.35N 6.34W
Baoulé [Mali] 30 Gg 13.33N 9.54W
Baoying 28 Eh 33.15N 119.18 E
Bapaume 11 Id 50.06N 2.51 E
Baqên (Dartang) 27 Fe 31.58N 94.00 E
Bāqerābād 24 Ne 34.56N 50.50 E
Ba'qūbah 23 Fc 33.45N 44.38 E
Baquedano 56 Gb 23.20S 69.51W
Bar 12 Ge 49.42N 4.50 E
Bar [Ukr.-U.S.S.R.] 16 Ee 49.02N 27.40 E
Bar [Yugo.] 15 Cg 42.05N 19.06 E
Barabai 26 Gg 2.35S 115.23 E
Barabevú 55 Bk 33.20S 61.52W
Barabinsk 22 Jd 55.21N 78.21 E
Barabinskaja Step 20 Ce 55.00N 79.00 E
Baraboo 45 Le 43.28N 89.45W
Baracaldo 13 Ja 43.18N 2.59W
Baracoa 47 Jd 20.21N 74.30W
Bărăganului, Cîmpia- 15 Ke 44.55N 27.15 E
Baragoi 36 Gb 1.47N 36.47 E
Bārah 35 Ec 13.42N 30.22 E
Barahona 47 Je 18.12N 71.06W
Barak 24 Gd 36.51N 37.59 E
Baraka 35 Fb 18.13N 37.35 E
Barakah 35 Fb 18.13N 37.35 E
Barakāt 35 Ec 14.20N 33.36 E
Barakī Barak 23 Kc 33.58N 68.58 E
Baram 26 Ff 4.36N 113.59 E
Baram 26 Ff 4.36N 113.58 E
Baramanni 50 Gi 7.50N 59.13W
Barama River 50 Gi 7.40N 59.15W
Barāmūla 25 Eb 34.12N 74.21 E
Bāran 25 Fc 25.06N 76.31 E
Baran 7 Hi 54.29N 30.19 E
Baraniha 20 Lc 68.31N 168.25 E
Baranja 14 Me 46.00N 18.30 E
Baranoa 49 Jh 10.49N 75.03W
Baranof 40 Le 57.00N 135.00W

Index Symbols

[1] Independent Nation
[2] State, Region
[3] District, County
[4] Municipality
[5] Colony, Dependency
Continent
Physical Region
Historical or Cultural Region
Mount, Mountain
Volcano
Hill
Mountains, Mountain Range
Hills, Escarpment
Plateau, Upland
Pass, Gap
Plain, Lowland
Delta
Salt Flat
Valley, Canyon
Crater, Cave
Karst Features
Depression
Polder
Desert, Dunes
Forest, Woods
Heath, Steppe
Oasis
Cape, Point
Coast, Beach
Cliff
Peninsula
Isthmus
Sandbank
Island
Atoll
Rock, Reef
Islands, Archipelago
Rocks, Reefs
Coral Reef
Well, Spring
Geyser
River, Stream
Waterfall Rapids
River Mouth, Estuary
Lake
Salt Lake
Intermittent Lake
Reservoir
Swamp, Pond
Canal
Glacier
Ice Shelf, Pack Ice
Ocean
Sea
Gulf, Bay
Strait, Fjord
Lagoon
Bank
Seamount
Tablemount
Ridge
Shelf
Basin
Escarpment, Sea Scarp
Fracture
Trench, Abyss
National Park, Reserve
Point of Interest
Recreation Site
Cave, Cavern
Historic Site
Ruins
Wall, Walls
Church, Abbey
Temple
Scientific Station
Airport
Port
Lighthouse
Mine
Tunnel
Dam, Bridge

Baranoviči	6	Ie	53.08N	26.02 E
Baranovka	16	Ed	50.18N	27.41 E
Baranya [2]	10	Oj	46.05N	18.15 E
Barão de Capanema	55	Da	13.19S	57.52W
Barão de Cotegipe	55	Fh	27.37S	52.23W
Barão de Grajaú	54	Je	6.45S	43.01W
Barão de Melgaço	54	Gg	16.13S	55.58W
Baraque de Fraiture	11	Ld	50.15N	5.45 E
Baratang	25	If	12.13N	92.45 E
Barataria Bay	45	Ll	29.22N	89.57W
Barat Daja, Kepulauan-	21	Oj	7.25S	128.00 E
Barāwe	31	Lh	1.09N	44.03 E
Barbacena	53	Lh	21.14S	43.46W
Barbacoas [Ven.]	49	Li	9.49N	70.03W
Barbacoas [Ven.]	50	Ch	9.29N	66.58W
Barbacoas, Bahia de-	49	Jh	10.10N	75.35W
Barbado, Rio-	55	Cb	15.12S	58.58W
Barbados [1]	39	Nh	13.10N	59.32W
Barbados	38	Nh	13.10N	59.32W
Barbados Ridge (EN)	50	Gf	12.45N	59.35W
Barbagia	14	Dj	40.10N	9.10 E
Barbar	35	Eb	18.01N	33.59 E
Bárbara	54	Dd	0.52S	72.30W
Barbaros	15	Ki	40.54N	27.27 E
Barbas, Cabo-	32	De	22.18N	16.41W
Barbastro	13	Mb	42.02N	0.08 E
Barbate de Franco	13	Gh	36.12N	5.55W
Barbeau Peak	38	La	81.54N	75.01W
Barbeton	37	Ee	25.48S	31.03 E
Barbezieux	11	Fi	45.28N	0.09W
Barbourville	44	Fg	36.52N	83.53W
Barboza Ferraz	55	Fg	24.04S	52.03W
Barbuda	38	Mh	17.38N	61.48W
Barcaldine	58	Fg	23.33S	145.17 E
Barcarrota	13	Ff	38.31N	6.51W
Barcău	15	Ec	46.59N	21.07 E
Barcellona Pozzo di Gotto	14	Jl	38.09N	15.13 E
Barcelona [3]	13	Nc	41.40N	2.00 E
Barcelona [Sp.]	6	Gg	41.23N	2.11 E
Barcelona [Ven.]	54	Fa	10.08N	64.42W
Barcelonnette	11	Mj	44.23N	6.39 E
Barcelos [Braz.]	54	Fd	0.58S	62.57W
Barcelos [Port.]	13	Dc	41.32N	8.37W
Barcin	10	Nd	52.52N	17.57 E
Barcoo River	59	Ie	25.30S	142.50 E
Barcs	10	Nk	45.58N	17.28 E
Barda	16	Oi	40.25N	47.05 E
Bardagé	35	Ba	22.06N	16.28 E
Bardaï	31	If	21.21N	16.59 E
Bardār Shāh	24	Ld	36.45N	47.15 E
Bārdaw	14	En	36.49N	10.08 E
Bardawīl, Sabkhat al-	24	Eg	31.10N	33.10 E
Bardejov	10	Rg	49.18N	21.16 E
Bārḏēre	31	Lh	2.20N	42.20 E
Bardeskan	24	Qe	35.12N	57.58 E
Bardīyah	33	Ed	31.46N	25.06 E
Bardonecchia	14	Ae	45.05N	6.42 E
Bardsey	9	Ii	52.45N	4.45W
Bardstown	44	Eg	37.49N	85.28W
Barēda	31	Mg	11.52N	51.03 E
Bareilly	22	Jg	28.25N	79.23 E
Barencevo More=Barents Sea (EN)	67	Jd	74.00N	36.00 E
Barentin	11	Ge	49.33N	0.57 E
Barentsburg	67	Kd	78.04N	14.14 E
Barentshav=Barents Sea (EN)	67	Jd	74.00N	36.00 E
Barentsøya	41	Oc	78.27N	21.15 E
Barents Sea (EN)= Barencevo More	67	Jd	74.00N	36.00 E
Barents Sea (EN)= Barentshav	67	Jd	74.00N	36.00 E
Barents Trough (EN)	5	Ia	73.00N	29.00 E
Barentu	35	Fb	15.06N	37.36 E
Barfleur	11	Ee	49.40N	1.15W
Barfleur, Pointe de-	11	Ee	49.42N	1.16W
Barga	22	Kf	30.48N	81.17 E
Bārgāl	35	Ic	11.18N	51.07 E
Bargarh	25	Gd	21.20N	83.37 E
Barguelonne	11	Gj	44.07N	0.50 E
Barguzin	20	Ff	53.27N	108.58 E
Barguzinski Hrebet	20	Ff	54.30N	110.00 E
Bar Harbor	44	Mc	44.23N	68.13W
Barhi	25	Hd	24.18N	85.25 E
Bari [3]	35	Hd	10.00N	50.00 E
Bari	6	Hg	41.08N	16.51 E
Bari, Terra di-	14	Kj	41.05N	16.50 E
Ba Ria	25	Lf	10.30N	107.10 E
Barīdī, Ra's-	24	Gj	24.17N	37.31 E
Barika	13	Ri	35.22N	5.05 E
Barīm	33	Hg	12.39N	43.25 E
Barima, Río-	50	Fh	8.35N	60.25W
Barima River	50	Fh	8.35N	60.25W
Barinas	54	Db	8.38N	70.12W
Barinas [2]	54	Eb	8.10N	70.00W
Baring, Cape-	42	Fb	70.01N	117.28W
Baringa	36	Db	0.45N	20.52 E
Barinitas	49	Li	8.45N	70.25W
Baripāda	25	Hd	21.56N	86.43 E
Bariri	55	Hf	22.04S	48.44W
Bariri, Reprêsa-	55	Hf	22.21S	48.39W
Bārīs	33	Fe	24.40N	30.36 E
Bari Sādri	25	Ed	24.25N	74.28 E
Barisāl	25	Id	22.42N	90.22 E
Barisan, Pegunungan-= Barisan Mountains (EN)	21	Mj	3.00S	102.15 E
Barisan Mountains (EN)= Barisan, Pegunungan-	21	Mj	3.00S	102.15 E
Barito	21	Nj	3.32S	114.29 E
Barjols	11	Lk	43.33N	6.00 E
Barkā'	23	Ie	23.35N	57.55 E
Barkam	27	He	31.45N	102.32 E
Barkan, Ra's-e-	24	Mg	30.01N	49.35 E
Barkava	8	Lh	56.40N	26.45 E
Barkley, Lake-	43	Jd	36.40N	87.55W
Barkley Sound	46	Cb	48.53N	125.20W
Barkly East	37	Df	30.58S	27.33 E
Barkly Tableland	57	Ef	19.00S	138.00 E
Barkly West	37	Ce	28.05S	24.31 E
Barkol	27	Fc	43.35N	92.51 E
Barkol Hu	27	Fc	43.40N	92.39 E
Barlavento [3]	32	Cf	16.10N	24.40W
Bar-le-Duc	11	Lf	48.47N	5.10 E
Barlee, Lake-	57	Cg	29.10S	119.30 E
Barlee Range	59	Dd	23.35S	116.00 E
Barletta	14	Ki	41.19N	16.17 E
Barlinek	10	Lc	53.00N	15.12 E
Barlovento, Islas de-= Windward Islands (EN)	38	Mh	15.00N	61.00W
Barma	26	Jg	1.54S	133.00 E
Barmer	25	Ec	25.45N	71.23 E
Barmera	59	If	34.15S	140.28 E
Barmouth	9	Ii	52.43N	4.03W
Barnard Castle	9	Lg	54.33N	1.55W
Barnaul	22	Kd	53.22N	83.45 E
Barnes Ice Cap	42	Kc	70.00N	73.30W
Barnesville [Ga.-U.S.]	44	Ei	33.04N	84.09W
Barnesville [Mn.-U.S.]	45	Hc	46.39N	96.25W
Barnet, London-	12	Bc	51.39N	0.12W
Barneveld	12	Hb	52.08N	5.34 E
Barnim	10	Jd	52.40N	13.45 E
Barnsley	9	Lh	53.34N	1.28W
Barnstaple	9	Ij	51.05N	4.04W
Barnstaple (Bideford Bay)	9	Ij	51.05N	4.20W
Barnstorf	12	Kb	52.43N	8.30 E
Barntrup	12	Lc	51.59N	9.07 E
Barnwell	44	Gi	33.14N	81.21W
Baro	30	Kh	8.26N	33.14 E
Baro [Chad]	35	Bc	12.12N	18.58 E
Baro [Nig.]	34	Gd	8.36N	6.25 E
Baronnies	11	Lj	44.15N	5.30 E
Barora Fa	63a	Db	7.30S	158.20 E
Barora Ite	63a	Db	7.36S	158.24 E
Barotseland	36	Df	15.05S	24.00 E
Barqah=Cyrenaica (EN)	33	Dc	31.00N	22.30 E
Barqah=Cyrenaica (EN)	30	Je	31.00N	23.00 E
Barqah, Jabal al-	24	Ej	24.24N	32.34 E
Barqah al Bahrīyah= Marmarica (EN)	30	Je	31.40N	24.30 E
Barqū, Jabal-	14	Dn	36.04N	9.37 E
Barques, Pointe aux-	44	Fc	44.04N	82.58W
Barquisimeto	53	Jd	10.04N	69.19W
Barr	11	Nf	48.24N	7.27 E
Barr, Ra's al-	24	Nj	25.47N	50.34 E
Barra	53	Lg	11.05S	43.10W
Barra	9	Fd	57.00N	7.30W
Barra, Ponta da-	30	Kk	23.47S	35.32 E
Barra, Sound of-	9	Fd	57.10N	7.20W
Barraba	59	Kf	30.22S	150.36 E
Barra Bonita, Reprêsa-	55	Hf	22.38S	48.20W
Barra de Navidad	47	De	19.12N	104.41W
Barra do Bugres	54	Gg	15.05S	57.11W
Barra do Corda	54	Ie	5.30S	45.15W
Barra do Cuanza	36	Bd	9.18S	13.09 E
Barra do Dande	36	Bd	8.28S	13.22 E
Barra do Garças	54	Hg	15.53S	52.15W
Barra Falsa, Ponta da-	30	Kk	22.55S	35.37 E
Barra Head	9	Fe	56.46N	7.36W
Barra Mansa	54	Jh	22.32S	44.11W
Barrāmīyah, Wādī al-	24	Ej	25.00N	33.23 E
Barranca	54	Cd	4.50S	76.42W
Barrancabermeja	53	Ie	7.03N	73.52W
Barrancas [Col.]	49	Kh	10.57N	72.50W
Barrancas [Ven.]	54	Fb	8.42N	62.11W
Barrancas, Arroyo-	55	Cj	30.19S	59.25W
Barranco	55	Db	15.56S	57.41W
Barrancos	13	Ff	38.08N	6.59W
Barranqueras	56	Ic	27.29S	58.56W
Barranquilla	53	Id	10.59N	74.48W
Barranquitas	51a	Bb	18.12N	66.23W
Barra Patuca	49	Ef	15.50N	84.17W
Barras	54	Jd	4.15S	42.18W
Barra Velha	55	Hh	26.39S	48.43W
Barre	44	Kc	44.12N	72.30W
Barreira	55	Db	15.24S	57.52W
Barreiras	53	Lg	12.08S	45.00W
Barreirinha	54	Gd	2.47S	57.03W
Barreirinhas	54	Jd	2.45S	42.50W
Barreiro	13	Cf	38.40N	9.04W
Barreiro, Rio-	55	Fb	15.43S	52.45W
Barreiro Grande	55	Jd	18.12S	45.10W
Barreiros	54	Ke	8.49S	35.12W
Barren	25	If	12.16N	93.51 E
Barren, Iles-	37	Gc	18.25S	43.40 E
Barren Islands	40	Ie	58.55N	152.15W
Barretos	56	Kb	20.33S	48.33W
Barrie	42	Jh	44.24N	79.40W
Barrier Bay	66	Ge	67.45S	81.10 E
Barrier Islands	63a	Db	7.44S	158.32 E
Barrington Tops	59	Kf	32.00S	151.28 E
Barro Alto	55	Hb	15.04S	48.58W
Barrois, Plateau du-	11	Kf	48.45N	5.00 E
Barros, Lagoa dos-	55	Gi	29.56S	50.23W
Barros, Tierra de-	13	Ff	38.40N	6.25W
Barroso	55	Ke	21.11S	43.58W
Barrouallie	51n	Ba	13.14N	61.17W
Barrow [Ak.-U.S.]	39	Db	71.17N	156.47W
Barrow [Arg.]	55	Bn	38.18S	60.14W
Barrow/An Bhearú	9	Gi	52.10N	7.00W
Barrow, Point-	38	Db	71.23N	156.30W
Barrow Creek	58	Eg	21.33S	133.53 E
Barrow-in-Furness	9	Jg	54.07N	3.14W
Barrow Island	57	Cg	20.50S	115.25 E
Barrow Range	59	Fe	26.05S	127.30 E
Barrow Strait	38	Jb	74.21N	94.10W
Barru	26	Gg	4.25S	119.37 E
Barry	9	Jj	51.24N	3.18W
Barrytown	62	De	42.14S	171.20 E
Barsakelmes, Ostrov-	18	Bb	45.40N	59.55 E
Barsalogo	34	Ec	13.25N	1.03W
Barsatas	19	Hf	48.13N	78.33 E
Baršć/Forst	10	Ke	51.44N	14.38 E
Bārsi	25	Fe	18.14N	75.42 E
Barsinghausen	10	Fd	52.18N	9.27 E
Barstow	43	De	34.54N	117.01W
Bar-sur-Aube	11	Kf	48.14N	4.43 E
Bar-sur-Seine	11	Kf	48.07N	4.22 E
Baršyn	19	Gf	49.45N	69.36 E
Bārta/Barta	8	Ih	56.57N	20.57 E
Barta/Bārta	8	Ih	56.57N	20.57 E
Barţallah	24	Jd	36.23N	43.25 E
Bartang	18	Hf	37.55N	71.33 E
Barth	10	Ib	54.22N	12.44 E
Bartholomew, Bayou-	45	Jj	32.43N	92.04W
Bartica	54	Gb	6.24N	58.37W
Bartın	24	Eb	41.38N	32.21 E
Bartle Frere, Mount-	57	Ff	17.23S	145.49 E
Bartlesville	43	Hd	36.45N	95.59W
Bartlett	45	Gf	41.53N	98.33W
Bartoszyce	10	Qb	54.16N	20.49 E
Bartow	44	Gl	27.54N	81.50W
Barú, Isla-	49	Jh	10.26N	75.35W
Barú, Volcán	47	Hg	8.48N	82.33W
Bārūd, Ra's-	24	Ei	26.47N	33.39 E
Barumini	14	Dk	39.42N	9.01 E
Barun-Bogdo-Ula	27	Hb	45.00N	100.20 E
Bāruni	25	Hc	25.29N	85.59 E
Barun-Šabartuj, Gora-	20	Fg	49.43N	109.58 E
Barun-Urt	27	Jb	46.40N	113.12 E
Barwice	10	Mc	53.45N	16.22 E
Barwon River	57	Fg	30.00S	148.05 E
Barycz	10	Me	51.42N	16.15 E
Baryš	7	Lj	53.40N	47.08 E
Baryš	7	Li	54.35N	46.47 E
Bāsa'īdū	24	Pi	26.39N	55.17 E
Basail	55	Ch	27.52S	59.18W
Basankusu	36	Cb	1.14N	19.48 E
Basaral, Ostrov-	18	Ib	45.25N	73.45 E
Basauri	13	Ja	43.13N	2.53W
Basavilbaso	55	Ck	32.22S	58.53W
Bas Champs	12	Dd	50.20N	1.41 E
Basco	26	Hb	20.27N	121.58 E
Bascuñán, Cabo-	56	Fc	28.51S	71.30W
Base	11	Gj	44.17N	0.18 E
Basel [2]	14	Bc	47.35N	7.40 E
Basel/Bâle	6	Gf	47.30N	7.30 E
Baselland [2]	14	Bc	47.30N	7.45 E
Basentello	14	Kj	40.40N	16.23 E
Basento	14	Kj	40.20N	16.49 E
Başeu	15	Kb	47.44N	27.15 E
Basey	26	Id	11.17N	125.04 E
Bashi Channel (EN)=Bashi Haixia	27	Lg	22.00N	121.00 E
Bashi Haixia=Bashi Channel (EN)	27	Lg	22.00N	121.00 E
Bāsht	24	Ng	30.21N	51.09 E
Ba Shui	28	Ci	30.25N	115.02 E
Basilan	21	Oi	6.34N	122.03 E
Basilan City (Isabela)	22	Oi	6.42N	121.58 E
Basilan Strait	26	He	6.49N	122.05 E
Basildon	9	Nj	51.34N	0.25 E
Basilicata [2]	14	Kj	40.30N	16.30 E
Basingstoke	9	Lj	51.16N	1.05W
Basjanovski	17	Jg	58.19N	60.44 E
Başkale	24	Jc	38.02N	44.00 E
Baskatong, Réservoir-	42	Jg	46.47N	75.50W
Baškaus	20	Df	51.09N	87.43 E
Baskil	24	Hc	38.35N	38.40 E
Baškirskaja ASSR [3]	19	Fe	55.00N	56.00 E
Baskunčak, Uzero-	16	Oe	48.10N	46.55 E
Bašmakovo	16	Mc	53.12N	43.03 E
Bāsmenj	24	Ld	37.59N	46.29 E
Basoko	36	Db	1.14N	23.36 E
Basongo	36	Dc	4.20S	20.24 E
Basque Provinces (EN)= Euzkadi/Vascongadas	13	Ja	43.00N	2.30W
Basque Provinces (EN)= Vascongadas/Euzkadi	13	Ja	43.00N	2.30W
Basra (EN)=Al Başrah	22	Gf	30.30N	47.47 E
Bas Rhin [3]	11	Nf	48.35N	7.40 E
Bass, Ilots de-	57	Mg	27.55S	143.26W
Bassano	46	Ia	50.47N	112.28W
Bassano del Grappa	14	Fe	45.46N	11.44 E
Bassar	34	Fd	9.15N	0.47 E
Bassas da India	30	Lk	21.25S	39.42 E
Bassein	22	Lh	16.47N	94.44 E
Bassein → Vasai	25	Ee	19.21N	72.48 E
Basse-Kotto [3]	35	Ce	5.00N	21.30 E
Basse-Pointe	51h	Ab	14.52N	61.07W
Basses, Pointe des-	51e	Bc	15.52N	61.17W
Basse-Sambre	12	Gd	50.27N	4.37 E
Basse Santa Su	34	Cc	13.19N	14.13W
Basse-Terre	50	Fd	16.10N	61.40W
Basse-Terre	47	Le	16.00N	61.44W
Basseterre	47	Le	17.18N	62.43W
Bassett	45	Ge	42.35N	99.32W
Bassigny	11	Lf	48.00N	5.30 E
Bassikounou	32	Ff	15.52N	5.58W
Bassila	34	Fd	9.01N	1.40 E
Bass Islands	63c	Ba	9.58S	167.17 E
Basso, Plateau de-	30	Jg	17.20N	22.40 E
Bass Strait	57	Fh	39.20S	145.30 E
Bassum	12	Kb	52.51N	8.44 E
Basswood Lake	45	Kb	48.05N	91.35W
Båstad	7	Ch	56.26N	12.51 E
Bastak	24	Pi	27.14N	54.22 E
Bastām	24	Pd	36.29N	55.04 E
Bastenaken/Bastogne	11	Le	50.00N	5.43 E
Bastia [Fr.]	6	Gg	42.42N	9.27 E
Bastia [It.]	14	Gg	43.04N	12.33 E
Bastogne/Bastenaken	11	Le	50.00N	5.43 E
Bastrop	45	Kj	32.47N	91.55W
Basudan Ula	27	Fe	33.05N	91.00 E
Basuo → Dongfang	27	Ih	19.14N	108.39 E
Basuto	37	Dc	19.52S	26.32 E
Bas-Zaïre [2]	36	Bd	5.30S	14.30 E
Bata	31	Hh	1.51N	9.45 E
Batabanó, Golfo de-	47	Hd	22.15N	82.30W
Batagaj	20	Ic	67.38N	134.38 E
Batagaj-Alyta	20	Ic	67.53N	130.31 E
Bataguaçu	54	Hh	21.42S	52.22W
Bataiporã	55	Ff	22.20S	53.17W
Batajnica	15	De	44.54N	20.17 E
Batajsk	19	Df	47.05N	39.46 E
Batak	15	Hh	41.57N	24.13 E
Bataklık Gölü	24	Ed	37.42N	33.07 E
Batala	25	Fb	31.48N	75.12 E
Batalha	13	De	39.39N	8.50W
Batama	36	Eb	0.56N	26.39 E
Batamaj	20	Hd	63.30N	129.25 E
Batamšinski	19	Fe	50.36N	58.17 E
Batan	26	Hb	20.30N	121.50 E
Batang	27	Ge	30.02N	99.10 E
Batanga	36	Ac	0.21S	9.18 E
Batangafo	35	Bd	7.18N	18.18 E
Batangas	22	Oh	13.45N	121.03 E
Batanghari	26	Mj	1.00S	104.00 E
Batan Islands	21	Og	20.30N	121.50 E
Batanta, Pulau-	26	Jg	0.50S	130.40 E
Bátaszék	10	Oj	46.11N	18.44 E
Batatais	55	Ie	20.53S	47.37W
Batavia	44	Hd	43.00N	78.11W
Bat-Cengel	27	Hb	47.47N	101.58 E
Batchawana	44	Eb	46.58N	84.34W
Batchelor	59	Gb	13.04S	131.01 E
Bătdâmbâng	22	Mh	13.06N	103.12 E
Batéké, Plateaux-	36	Cc	3.30S	15.45 E
Batel, Esteros del-	55	Ci	28.30S	58.20W
Batemans Bay	59	Kg	35.43S	150.11 E
Batesburg	44	Gi	33.56N	81.33W
Batesville [Ar.-U.S.]	45	Ki	35.46N	91.39W
Batesville [Ms.-U.S.]	45	Li	34.18N	90.00W
Bath [Eng.-U.K.]	9	Kj	51.23N	2.22W
Bath [Me.-U.S.]	44	Md	43.55N	69.49W
Bath [N.B.-Can.]	44	Nb	46.32N	67.33W
Bath [St.C.N.]	51c	Ab	17.08N	62.37W
Batha	30	Ig	12.47N	17.34 E
Batha [3]	35	Bc	14.00N	19.00 E
Bá Thrá Lí/Tralee Bay	9	Di	52.15N	9.59W
Bathsheba	50	Gf	13.13N	59.31W
Bá Thuath Reanna/ Liscannor Bay	9	Di	52.55N	9.25W
Bathurst	38	Ib	76.00N	100.30W
Bathurst [Austl.]	59	Jf	33.25S	149.35 E
Bathurst [N.B.-Can.]	39	Me	47.36N	65.39W
Bathurst, Cape-	38	Gb	70.35N	128.00W
Bathurst Inlet	38	Ic	68.10N	108.50W
Bathurst Inlet	39	Ic	66.50N	108.01W
Bathurst Island	57	Ef	11.35S	130.25 E
Bati	35	Gc	11.13N	40.01 E
Batié	34	Ed	9.53N	2.55W
Bāţin, Wādī al-	23	Gc	30.25N	47.35 E
Batman	23	Fb	37.52N	41.07 E
Batman	24	Id	37.45N	41.00 E
Batna [3]	32	Ib	35.10N	6.00 E
Batna	31	He	35.34N	6.11 E
Ba To	25	Lf	14.46N	108.44 E
Bato Bato	26	Ge	5.06N	119.50 E
Batoka	36	Ef	16.47S	27.15 E
Baton Rouge	39	Jf	30.23N	91.11W
Batopilas	48	Fd	27.01N	107.44W
Batouri	34	He	4.26N	14.22 E
Batovi	55	Fb	15.53S	53.24W
Batovi, Coxilha de-	55	Ej	30.33S	54.27W
Båtsfjord	7	Ga	70.38N	29.44 E
Bat-Sumber	27	Ib	48.25N	106.42 E
Batticaloa	25	Gg	7.43N	81.42 E
Batti Maly	25	Ig	8.50N	92.51 E
Battipaglia	14	Ij	40.37N	14.58 E
Battle	12	Cd	50.55N	0.30 E
Battle	42	Gf	52.42N	108.15W
Battle Creek	46	Kb	48.36N	109.11W
Battle Creek	43	Jc	42.19N	85.11W
Battle Harbour	39	Nd	52.17N	55.35W
Battle Mountain	43	Dc	40.38N	116.56W
Battonya	10	Rj	46.17N	21.01 E
Battowia Island	51n	Bb	12.58N	61.09W
Batu	35	Fd	6.59N	39.37 E
Batu, Kepulauan-=Batu Islands (EN)	21	Lj	0.18S	98.28 E
Batuasa	26	Jg	3.32S	130.08 E
Batuata, Pulau-	26	Hh	6.12S	122.42 E
Batudaka, Pulau-	26	Hg	0.28S	121.48 E
Batui	26	Hg	1.17S	122.33 E
Batu Islands (EN)=Batu, Kepulauan-	21	Lj	0.18S	98.28 E
Batumi	6	Kg	41.38N	41.38 E
Batu Pahat	26	Df	1.51N	102.56 E
Baturaja	26	Dg	4.08S	104.10 E
Baturino	20	De	57.45N	85.12 E
Baturité	54	Kd	4.20S	38.53W
Batz, Ile de-	11	Bf	48.45N	4.01W
Bau	26	Ff	1.25N	110.09 E
Baubau	22	Oj	5.28S	122.38 E
Baucau	26	Ih	8.27S	126.27 E
Bauchi	31	Hg	10.19N	9.50 E
Bauchi [2]	34	Hc	10.40N	10.00 E
Bauchi Plateau	34	Gc	10.00N	9.30 E
Baud	11	Cg	47.52N	3.01W
Baudette	45	Ib	48.43N	94.36W
Baudo, Serrania de-	54	Cb	6.00N	77.05W
Baudour, Saint-Ghislain-	12	Fd	50.29N	3.49 E
Baugé	11	Fg	47.33N	0.06W
Bauges	11	Mi	45.38N	6.10 E
Baúl, Cerro-	48	Ii	17.38N	100.19W
Baula	26	Hg	4.09S	121.41 E
Bauld, Cape-	38	Nd	51.38N	55.25W
Bauman Fiord	42	Ia	77.45N	86.00W
Baume-les-Dames	11	Mg	47.21N	6.22 E
Baunach	10	Gg	49.59N	10.51 E
Baunani	63a	Ec	9.08S	160.51 E
Baunei	14	Dj	40.02N	9.40 E
Baures	54	Ff	13.35S	63.35W
Bauru	53	Lh	22.19S	49.04W
Baús	55	Fd	18.19S	53.10W
Baús, Serra dos-	55	Fd	18.20S	53.25W
Bauska	7	Fh	56.24N	24.13 E
Bautzen/Budyšin	10	Ke	51.11N	14.26 E
Bavaria (EN)=Bayern [2]	10	Hg	49.00N	11.30 E
Bavaria (EN)=Bayern	5	Hf	49.00N	11.30 E
Bavarian Forest (EN)= Bayerischer Wald	10	Ig	49.00N	12.55 E
Bavay	12	Fd	50.18N	3.47 E
Båven	8	Ge	59.00N	16.55 E
Bavispe	48	Eb	30.24N	108.50W
Bavispe, Río de-	48	Ec	29.15N	109.11W
Bavly	7	Mi	54.26N	53.18 E
Bawah, Pulau-	26	Ef	2.31N	106.03 E
Bawal, Pulau-	26	Fg	2.44S	110.06 E
Bawe	58	Ee	2.59S	134.43 E
Bawean, Pulau-	26	Fh	5.46S	112.40 E
Bawku	34	Ec	11.03N	0.15W
Baxian	27	Kd	39.03N	116.24 E
Baxol	27	Ge	30.07N	96.56 E
Bay [3]	35	Ge	2.50N	43.30 E
Bay/Baicheng	27	Dc	41.46N	81.52 E
Bayamo	47	Id	20.23N	76.39W
Bayamón	49	Nd	18.24N	66.09W
Bayan	28	Ia	46.05N	127.24 E
Bayanbulak	27	Dc	43.05N	84.05 E
Bayanga	35	Be	2.53N	16.19 E
Bayan Gol	27	Gd	37.18N	96.50 E
Bayan Gol → Dengkou	22	Me	40.25N	106.59 E
Bayan Har Shan	21	Lf	34.20N	97.00 E
Bayan Har Shankou	27	Ge	34.06N	97.38 E
Bayan Hot → Alxa Zuoqi	27	Id	38.50N	105.32 E
Bayan Hure → Chen Barag Qi	27	Kb	49.21N	119.25 E
Bayan Huxu → Horqin Youyi Zhongqi	27	Lb	45.04N	121.27 E
Bayano, Lago de-	49	Hi	9.00N	78.30W
Bayan Obo	27	Ic	41.50N	109.58 E
Bayan Qagan	28	Ga	46.11N	123.59 E
Bayan Qagan → Qahar Youyi Houqi	28	Bd	41.28N	113.10 E
Bayan Ul Hot → Xi Ujimqin Qi	27	Kc	44.31N	117.33 E
Bayas	48	Gf	23.32N	104.50W
Bayat	24	Fb	40.39N	34.15 E
Bayauca	55	Bl	34.51S	61.18W
Bayawan	26	He	9.20N	123.00 E
Bayāz̄	24	Pg	30.42N	55.28 E
Bayāzeh	24	Pf	30.42N	55.28 E
Baybay	26	Hd	10.41N	124.48 E
Bayburt	23	Fa	40.16N	40.15 E
Bay City [Mi.-U.S.]	43	Kc	43.36N	83.53W
Bay City [Tx.-U.S.]	43	Hf	29.09N	95.39W
Bayerische Alpen	10	Hi	47.30N	11.30 E
Bayerischer Wald=Bavarian Forest (EN)	10	Ig	49.00N	12.55 E
Bayern=Bavaria (EN)	5	Hf	49.00N	11.30 E
Bayern=Bavaria (EN) [2]	10	Hg	49.00N	11.30 E
Bayes, Cap-	63b	Be	20.57S	165.25 E
Bayeux	11	Fe	49.16N	0.42W
Bayfield	45	Kc	46.49N	90.49W
Bay Fiord	42	Ja	79.00N	84.00W
Baygorria	55	Dk	32.52S	56.44W
Baygorria, Lago Artificial de-	55	Dk	33.05S	57.00W
Bayḩān al Qişāb	33	Ig	14.48N	45.44 E
Bayındır	24	Bc	38.13N	27.40 E
Bayjī	24	Je	34.56N	43.29 E
Bay Minette	44	Dj	30.53N	87.47W
Baynūnah	24	Ok	23.50N	52.50 E
Bayombong	26	Hc	16.29N	121.09 E
Bayona	13	Db	42.07N	8.51W
Bayonnaise Seamount (EN)	57	Jf	12.00S	179.30W
Bayonne	6	Fg	43.29N	1.29W
Bayou Bodcau Lake	45	Jj	32.58N	93.30W
Bayou D'Arbonne Lake	45	Jj	32.45N	92.27W
Bayramiç	15	Jj	39.48N	26.37 E
Bayreuth	10	Hg	49.57N	11.35 E
Bayrūt=Beirut (EN)	22	Ff	33.53N	35.30 E
Bay Saint Louis	45	Lk	30.19N	89.20W
Bay Springs	45	Lk	31.59N	89.17W
Bayt al Faqīh	23	Fg	14.31N	43.17 E
Baytik Shan	27	Fb	45.15N	90.50 E
Bayt Laḩm=Bethlehem (EN)	24	Fg	31.43N	35.12 E
Baytown	43	If	29.44N	94.58W
Bayuda Desert (EN)= Bayyūḑah, Şaḩrā'-	30	Kg	18.00N	33.00 E
Bayunglencir	26	Dg	2.03S	103.41 E
Bayview	46	Gc	48.00N	116.30W
Bay View	62	Gc	39.26S	176.52 E
Bayy al Kabīr	33	Cc	31.11N	15.53 E
Bayyūḑah, Şaḩrā'-=Bayuda Desert (EN)	30	Kg	18.00N	33.00 E
Baza	13	Jg	37.29N	2.46W
Baza, Sierra de-	13	Jg	37.15N	2.45W
Bazardjuzju, Gora-	5	Kg	41.13N	47.51 E
Bazaruto, Ilha do-	37	Fd	21.40S	35.25 E
Bazas	11	Fj	44.26N	0.13W
Bazhong	27	Ie	31.54N	106.42 E
Bazoches-sur-Vesle	12	Fe	49.19N	3.37 E
Baztán	13	Ka	43.09N	1.31W
Beach	43	Gb	46.55N	103.52W
Beachy Head	9	Nk	50.44N	0.16 E
Beacon	44	Ke	41.31N	73.59W
Beaconsfield [Austl.]	59	Jh	41.12S	146.48 E
Beaconsfield [Eng.-U.K.]	12	Bc	51.36N	0.38W
Beagle, Canal-	56	Gh	54.53S	68.10W
Beagle Gulf	59	Gb	12.00S	130.20 E
Bealach an Doirín/ Ballaghaderreen	9	Eh	53.55N	8.35W
Béalanana	37	Hb	14.33S	48.44 E
Béal an Átha/Ballina	9	Dg	54.07N	9.09W
Béal an Bheara/Gweebarra Bay	9	Eg	54.52N	8.20W
Béal Átha Fhirdhia/Ardee	9	Gh	53.52N	6.33W
Béal Átha hAmhnais/ Ballyhaunis	9	Eh	53.46N	8.46W

Index Symbols

[1] Independent Nation
[2] State, Region
[3] District, County
[4] Municipality
[5] Colony, Dependency
Continent
Physical Region
Historical or Cultural Region
Mount, Mountain
Volcano
Hill
Mountains, Mountain Range
Hills, Escarpment
Plateau, Upland
Pass, Gap
Plain, Lowland
Delta
Salt Flat
Valley, Canyon
Crater, Cave
Karst Features
Depression
Polder
Desert, Dunes
Forest, Woods
Heath, Steppe
Oasis
Cape, Point
Coast, Beach
Cliff
Peninsula
Isthmus
Sandbank
Island
Atoll
Rock, Reef
Islands, Archipelago
Rocks, Reefs
Coral Reef
Well, Spring
Geyser
River, Stream
Waterfall Rapids
River Mouth, Estuary
Lake
Salt Lake
Intermittent Lake
Reservoir
Swamp, Pond
Canal
Glacier
Ice Shelf, Pack Ice
Ocean
Sea
Gulf, Bay
Strait, Fjord
Lagoon
Bank
Seamount
Tablemount
Ridge
Shelf
Basin
Escarpment, Sea Scarp
Fracture
Trench, Abyss
National Park, Reserve
Point of Interest
Recreation Site
Cave, Cavern
Historic Site
Ruins
Wall, Walls
Church, Abbey
Temple
Scientific Station
Airport
Port
Lighthouse
Mine
Tunnel
Dam, Bridge

Béal Átha na Muice/Swinford	9	Eh	53.57N	8.57W
Béal Átha na Sluaighe/Ballinasloe	9	Eh	53.20N	8.13W
Béal Átha Seanaidh/Ballyshannon	9	Eg	54.30N	8.11W
Beale, Cape-	46	Cb	48.44N	125.20W
Béal Easa/Foxford	9	Dh	53.59N	9.07W
Béal Feirste/Belfast	6	Fe	54.35N	5.55W
Beal Range	59	Ie	25.30S	141.30 E
Béal Tairbirt/Belturbet	9	Fg	54.06N	7.26W
Beanna Boirche/Mourne Mountains	9	Gg	54.10N	6.04W
Beannchar/Bangor	9	Hg	54.40N	5.40W
Beanntraí/Bantry	9	Dj	51.41N	9.27W
Bear Bay	42	Ia	75.45N	86.30W
Beardmore	45	Mb	49.36N	87.57W
Beardstown	45	Kg	39.59N	90.26W
Bear Island (EN)=Björnöya	5	Ha	74.30N	19.00 E
Bear Islands (EN)=Medveži, Ostrova-	21	Sb	70.52N	161.26 E
Bear Lake	43	Ec	42.00N	111.20W
Bear Lodge Mountains	45	Dd	44.35N	104.15W
Béarn	11	Fk	43.20N	0.45W
Bearpaw Mountains	46	Kb	48.15N	109.30W
Bear Peninsula	66	Of	74.36S	110.50W
Bear River	46	If	41.30N	112.08W
Bearskin Lake	42	If	53.57N	90.59W
Beās	25	Eb	31.10N	74.59 E
Beas de Segura	13	Jf	38.15N	2.53W
Beata, Cabo-	47	Je	17.36N	71.25W
Beata, Isla-	49	Le	17.35N	71.31W
Beata Ridge (EN)	47	Je	16.00N	72.30W
Beatrice	43	Hc	40.16N	96.44W
Beatrice, Cape-	59	Hb	14.15S	137.00 E
Beatton	42	Fe	56.06N	120.22W
Beatton River	42	Fe	56.10N	120.25W
Beatty	43	Dd	36.54N	116.46W
Beattyville	44	Ia	48.52N	77.10W
Beatys Butte	46	Fe	42.23N	119.20W
Beau-Bassin	37a	Bb	20.13S	57.27 E
Beaucaire	11	Kk	43.48N	4.38 E
Beaucamps-le-Vieux	12	De	49.50N	1.47 E
Beaucanton	44	Ha	49.05N	79.15W
Beauce	11	Hf	48.22N	1.50 E
Beaudesert	59	Ke	27.59S	153.00 E
Beaufort [Mala.]	26	Ge	5.20N	115.45 E
Beaufort [S.C.-U.S.]	44	Gi	32.26N	80.40W
Beaufort/Befort	12	Ie	49.50N	6.18 E
Beaufort, Massif de-	11	Mi	45.50N	6.40 E
Beaufort Island	66	Kf	76.57S	166.56 E
Beaufort Sea	67	Eb	73.00N	140.00W
Beaufort West	31	Jl	32.20S	22.33 E
Beaugency	11	Hg	47.47N	1.38 E
Beaujolais, Monts du-	11	Kh	46.00N	4.22 E
Beauly	9	Id	57.29N	4.29W
Beaumesnil	12	Ce	49.01N	0.43 E
Beaumetz-lès-Loges	12	Ed	50.14N	2.39 E
Beaumont [Bel.]	12	Gd	50.14N	4.14 E
Beaumont [Fr.]	11	Gj	44.46N	0.46 E
Beaumont [Fr.]	11	Ee	49.40N	1.51W
Beaumont [Fr.]	12	Hf	48.51N	5.47 E
Beaumont [Ms.-U.S.]	45	Lk	31.11N	88.55W
Beaumont [N.Z.]	62	Cf	45.49S	169.32 E
Beaumont [Tx.-U.S.]	39	Jf	30.05N	94.06W
Beaumont-de-Lomagne	11	Gk	43.53N	0.59 E
Beaumont-en-Argonne	12	He	49.32N	5.03 E
Beaumont-le-Roger	12	Ce	49.05N	0.47 E
Beaumont-sur-Oise	12	Ee	49.08N	2.17 E
Beaumont-sur-Sarthe	11	Gf	48.13N	0.08 E
Beaune	11	Kg	47.02N	4.50 E
Beaupré	44	Lb	47.03N	70.53W
Beauraing	12	Gd	50.07N	4.48 E
Beaurepaire	11	Li	45.20N	5.03 E
Beausejour	42	Hf	50.04N	96.33W
Beautemps Beaupré	63b	Ce	20.25S	166.08 E
Beauvais	11	Ie	49.26N	2.05 E
Beauval	12	Ed	50.06N	2.20 E
Beauvoir-sur-Mer	11	Dh	46.55N	2.03W
Beaver [Ak.-U.S.]	40	Jc	66.22N	147.24W
Beaver [Ok.-U.S.]	45	Fh	36.48N	100.30W
Beaver [Ut.-U.S.]	43	Ed	38.17N	112.38W
Beaver Creek [Co.-U.S.]	45	Ef	40.20N	103.33W
Beaver Creek [U.S.]	45	Ec	47.20N	103.39W
Beaver Creek [U.S.]	45	Gf	40.04N	99.20W
Beaver Creek [U.S.]	45	Ee	43.25N	103.59W
Beaver Dam	45	Le	43.28N	88.50W
Beaver Falls	44	Ge	40.45N	80.21W
Beaverhead Mountains	46	Id	45.00N	113.20W
Beaver Island	44	Ec	45.40N	85.31W
Beaver Lake	45	Jh	36.20N	93.55W
Beaver River [U.S.]	45	Gh	36.10N	98.45W
Beaver River [Ut.-U.S.]	46	Ig	39.10N	112.57W
Beaverton	46	Dd	45.29N	122.48W
Beāwar	25	Ec	26.06N	74.19 E
Bebedouro	56	Kb	20.56S	48.28W
Becan	48	Oh	18.37N	89.35W
Becanchén	48	Oh	19.50N	89.22W
Beccles	9	Oi	52.28N	1.34 E
Bečej	15	Dd	45.37N	20.03 E
Beceni	15	Jd	45.23N	26.47 E
Becerreá	13	Eb	42.51N	7.10W
Becerro, Cayos-	49	Ff	15.57N	83.17W
Béchar	31	Ge	31.37N	2.13W
Béchar [3]	32	Gd	30.00N	2.00W
Becharof Lake	40	He	58.00N	156.30W
Bechet	15	Gf	43.46N	23.57 E
Bechevin Bay	40	Ge	55.00N	163.27W
Bechyně	10	Kg	49.18N	14.28 E
Beckingen	12	Ie	49.24N	6.42 E
Beckley	43	Kd	37.46N	81.12W
Beckum	10	Ee	51.45N	8.02 E
Beckumer Berge	12	Kc	51.43N	8.10 E
Beclean	15	Hb	47.11N	24.11 E
Bédarieux	11	Jk	43.37N	3.09 E
Bedburg-Hau	12	Ic	51.46N	6.11 E
Bedele	35	Fd	8.27N	36.22 E
Bedesa	35	Gd	8.53N	40.46 E
Bedford	9	Mi	52.10N	0.50W
Bedford [Eng.-U.K.]	9	Mi	52.08N	0.29W
Bedford [In.-U.S.]	44	Df	38.52N	86.29W
Bedford [Pa.-U.S.]	44	He	40.00N	78.31W
Bedford [Va.-U.S.]	44	Hg	37.20N	79.31W
Bedford Level	9	Ni	52.30N	0.05 E
Bedford Point	51p	Bb	12.13N	61.36W
Bedfordshire [3]	9	Mi	52.05N	0.20W
Bednja	14	Kd	46.18N	16.45 E
Bednodemjanovsk	16	Mc	53.55N	43.12 E
Bedourie	59	Hd	24.21S	139.28 E
Bedum	12	Ia	53.18N	6.39 E
Beech Grove	44	Df	39.43N	86.03W
Beecroft Head	59	Kg	35.01S	150.50 E
Beef Island	51a	Db	18.27N	64.31W
Beelitz	10	Id	52.14N	12.58 E
Beemster	12	Gb	52.34N	4.56 E
Beerfelden	12	Ke	49.34N	8.59 E
Beernem	12	Fc	51.09N	3.20 E
Beerse	12	Gc	51.19N	4.52 E
Beersel	12	Gd	50.46N	4.18 E
Beersheba (EN)=Be'er Shevà	23	Dc	31.14N	34.47 E
Be'er Shevà=Beersheba (EN)	23	Dc	31.14N	34.47 E
Beerze	12	Hc	51.36N	5.19 E
Beeskow	10	Kd	52.10N	14.14 E
Beestekraal	37	De	25.23S	27.38 E
Beeston	9	Li	52.56N	1.12W
Beethoven Peninsula	66	Qf	71.40S	73.45W
Beetsterzwaag, Opsterland-	12	Ia	53.03N	6.04 E
Beeville	43	Hf	28.24N	97.45W
Befale	36	Db	0.28N	20.58 E
Befandriana Nord	37	Hc	15.15S	48.32 E
Befandriana Sud	37	Gd	22.06S	43.54 E
Befori	36	Db	0.06N	22.17 E
Befort/Beaufort	12	Ie	49.50N	6.18 E
Bega	15	Dd	45.13N	20.19 E
Bega	58	Fh	36.40S	149.50 E
Bégard	11	Cf	48.38N	3.18W
Begejski kanal	15	Dd	45.27N	20.27 E
Beggars Point	51d	Bb	17.10N	61.48W
Bègle	11	Fj	44.48N	0.32W
Begna	7	Bf	60.35N	10.00 E
Begoml	8	Mj	54.46N	28.14 E
Begunicy	8	Me	59.31N	29.30 E
Behābād	24	Pg	31.52N	55.57 E
Behbehān	23	Hc	30.35N	50.14 E
Behring Point	49	Ia	24.27N	77.43W
Behshahr	23	Hb	36.43N	53.34 E
Bei'an	22	Oe	48.16N	126.29 E
Beibu Wan=Tonkin, Gulf of- (EN)	21	Mh	20.00N	108.00 E
Beida He	27	Gc	40.18N	99.01 E
Beihai	22	Mg	21.31N	109.07 E
Bei Hulsan Hu	27	Gd	36.55N	95.55 E
Bei Jiang	27	Jg	23.02N	112.58 E
Beijing=Peking (EN)	22	Nf	39.55N	116.23 E
Beijing Shi (Pei-ching Shih) [4]	27	Kc	40.15N	116.30 E
Beïla	32	Df	18.10N	15.53W
Beilen	12	Ib	52.52N	6.32 E
Beiliutang He	28	Eg	34.12N	119.33 E
Beilrstroom	12	Ib	52.41N	6.12 E
Beilsteim	12	Jd	50.07N	7.15 E
Beilu He	27	Fe	34.34N	94.00 E
Beinamar	35	Bd	8.40N	15.23 E
Beine-Nauroy	12	Ge	49.15N	4.13 E
Beipiao	27	Lc	41.49N	120.45 E
Beira	31	Kj	19.50S	34.52 E
Beira Alta	13	Ed	40.40N	7.35W
Beira Baixa	13	Ee	39.55N	7.30W
Beira Litoral	13	Dd	40.15N	8.25W
Beiru He	28	Bh	33.40N	113.35 E
Beirut (EN)=Bayrūt	22	Ff	33.53N	35.30 E
Bei Shan	21	Le	41.30N	96.00 E
Beitstad	7	Cd	64.05N	11.22 E
Beiuş	15	Fc	46.40N	22.21 E
Beiwei Tan	27	Kg	21.10N	116.10 E
Beizhen [China]	27	Kd	37.24N	117.59 E
Beizhen [China]	28	Fd	41.36N	121.47 E
Beja	13	Ef	38.01N	7.52W
Beja [2]	13	Eg	37.58N	7.50W
Bejaïa [3]	32	Ib	36.40N	5.10 E
Bejaïa	31	He	36.45N	5.05 E
Bejaia, Golfe de-	13	Rh	36.45N	5.20 E
Béjar	13	Gd	40.23N	5.46W
Beji	25	Dc	29.47N	67.58 E
Bejneu	19	Ff	45.15N	55.05 E
Bejsug	16	Kf	46.02N	38.35 E
Bejsugski Liman	16	Kf	46.05N	38.25 E
Bekabad	19	Gg	40.13N	69.14 E
Bekasi	26	Eh	6.14S	106.59 E
Bekdaš	19	Fg	41.31N	52.40 E
Békés	10	Rj	46.46N	21.08 E
Békés [2]	10	Qj	46.45N	21.00 E
Békéscsaba	10	Rj	46.41N	21.06 E
Bekilli	15	Mk	38.14N	29.26 E
Bekily	37	Hd	24.12S	45.18 E
Bekkai	29a	Db	43.25N	145.07 E
Bekoji	35	Fd	7.32N	39.15 E
Bekopaka	37	Gc	19.08S	44.45 E
Bekovo	16	Mc	52.29N	43.45 E
Bela [India]	25	Gc	25.56N	81.59 E
Bela [Pak.]	25	Dc	26.14N	66.19 E
Bélabo	34	He	4.52N	13.10 E
Bela Crkva	15	Ee	44.54N	21.26 E
Bela Dila	25	Ge	18.40N	80.55 E
Bela Floresta	55	Ge	20.36S	51.16W
Belaga	26	Ff	2.42N	113.47 E
Belaja [R.S.F.S.R.]	20	Mc	65.30N	173.15 E
Belaja [R.S.F.S.R.]	5	Ld	56.00N	54.32 E
Belaja [R.S.F.S.R.]	16	Kg	45.03N	39.25 E
Belaja Cerkov	6	Jf	49.49N	30.07 E
Belaja Gora	20	Jc	68.30N	146.15 E
Belaja Holunica	19	Fd	58.53N	50.50 E
Belaja Kalitva	19	Ef	48.09N	40.49 E
Bela Krajina	14	Je	45.35N	15.15 E
Bela Lorena	55	Ib	15.13S	46.01W
Belang	26	Hf	0.57N	124.47 E
Bela Palanka	15	Ff	43.13N	22.19 E
Belarbi	13	Li	35.09N	0.27W
Belaruskaja Sovetskaja Socialistyčnaja Respublika /Belorusskaja SSR [2]	19	Ce	53.50N	28.00 E
Belasica	15	Fh	41.21N	22.50 E
Bela Vista [Ang.]	36	Ce	12.33S	16.14 E
Bela Vista [Braz.]	54	Gh	22.06S	56.31W
Bela Vista [Braz.]	55	Dc	17.37S	57.01W
Bela Vista [Moz.]	37	Ee	26.20S	32.40 E
Belawan	26	Cf	3.47N	98.41 E
Běła Woda/Weißwasser	10	Ke	51.31N	14.38 E
Belayan	26	Gg	0.14S	116.36 E
Belbo	14	Cf	44.54N	8.31 E
Bełchatow	10	Pe	51.22N	19.21 E
Belcher Channel	42	Ia	77.20N	94.30W
Belcher Islands	38	Ld	56.20N	79.30W
Belchite	13	Lc	41.18N	0.45W
Belcy	19	Cf	47.46N	27.55 E
Bełczyna	10	Ne	51.25N	17.50 E
Belebej	19	Fe	54.10N	54.07 E
Belecke, Warstein-	12	Kc	51.29N	8.20 E
Beled	10	Ni	47.28N	17.06 E
Beled Wēyne	31	Lh	4.47N	45.12 E
Bélel	34	Hd	7.03N	14.26 E
Belém [Moz.]	37	Fb	14.08S	35.58 E
Belém [Braz.]	53	Lf	1.27S	48.29W
Belem [Mex.]	48	Dd	27.45N	110.28W
Belém de São Francisco	54	Ke	8.46S	38.58W
Belen	43	Fe	34.40N	106.46W
Belén [Arg.]	56	Gc	27.39S	67.02W
Belén [Nic.]	49	Eh	11.30N	85.53W
Belén [Par.]	55	Df	23.30S	57.06W
Belén [Ur.]	55	Dj	30.47S	57.47W
Belén, Cuchilla de-	55	Dj	30.55S	56.30W
Belén de Escobar	55	Cl	34.21S	58.47W
Belene	15	If	43.39N	25.07 E
Bélep, Iles-	57	Hf	19.45S	163.40 E
Beles	35	Fc	10.55N	35.10 E
Belev	16	Jc	53.50N	36.10 E
Beleye	35	Fc	11.24N	36.10 E
Belfast [Me.-U.S.]	44	Mc	44.27N	69.01W
Belfast [S.Afr.]	37	Ee	25.43S	30.03 E
Belfast/Béal Feirste	6	Fe	54.35N	5.55W
Belfast Lough/Loch Lao	9	Hg	54.40N	5.50W
Belfield	45	Ec	46.53N	103.12W
Belford	9	Lf	55.36N	1.49W
Belfort	11	Mg	47.45N	7.00 E
Belgaum	22	Jh	15.52N	74.30 E
Belgica Bank (EN)	67	Ld	78.28N	15.00W
Belgicafjella	66	Df	72.35S	31.10 E
België/Belgique=Belgium (EN) [1]	6	Ge	50.30N	4.30 E
Belgique/België=Belgium (EN) [1]	6	Ge	50.30N	4.30 E
Belgium (EN)=België/Belgique [1]	6	Ge	50.30N	4.30 E
Belgium (EN)=Belgique/België [1]	6	Ge	50.30N	4.30 E
Belgorod	6	Je	50.36N	36.35 E
Belgorod-Dnestrovski	19	Df	46.12N	30.17 E
Belgorodskaja Oblast [3]	19	De	50.45N	37.30 E
Belgrade (EN) = Beograd	6	Ig	44.50N	20.30 E
Bel Haïrane	32	Ic	31.17N	6.20 E
Beli	34	Hd	7.52N	10.58 E
Belice	14	Gm	37.35N	12.52 E
Beli Drim	15	Dg	42.05N	20.20 E
Belidži	16	Pi	41.53N	48.20 E
Beli Lom	15	If	43.41N	26.00 E
Beli Manastir	14	Me	45.46N	18.37 E
Belimbegovo	15	Eh	42.00N	21.35 E
Belin	11	Fj	44.30N	0.47W
Belinga	36	Bb	1.04N	13.12 E
Belinski	16	Mc	52.58N	43.29 E
Belinyu	26	Eg	1.38S	105.46 E
Beliş	15	Gc	46.39N	23.02 E
Beli Timok	15	Ff	43.55N	22.18 E
Belize [1]	39	Kh	17.15N	88.45W
Belize (British Honduras)	49	Ce	17.35N	88.35W
Belize City	39	Kh	17.30N	88.12W
Belize River	49	Ce	17.32N	88.14W
Beljajevka	16	Gf	46.29N	30.14 E
Beljanica	15	Ee	44.07N	21.43 E
Belka	8	Mg	57.40N	29.47 E
Belkovski, Ostrov-	20	Ia	75.30N	136.00 E
Bellac	11	Hh	46.07N	1.03 E
Bella Coola	42	Ef	52.22N	126.46W
Bellagio	14	De	45.59N	9.15 E
Bellaire [Oh.-U.S.]	44	Ge	40.02N	80.46W
Bellaire [Tx.-U.S.]	45	Il	29.43N	95.28W
Bellaria-Igea Marina	14	Gf	44.09N	12.28 E
Bellary	22	Jh	15.09N	76.56 E
Bella Unión	55	Dj	30.15S	57.35W
Bella Vista [Arg.]	56	Ic	28.30S	59.03W
Bella Vista [Par.]	55	Df	22.08S	56.31W
Bellavista, Capo-	14	Dk	39.56N	9.43 E
Bell Bay	42	Jb	71.10N	84.55W
Belle-Anse	49	Kd	18.14N	72.04W
Belledonne	11	Mi	45.18N	6.08 E
Bellefontaine [Mart.]	51h	Ab	14.40N	61.10W
Bellefontaine [Oh.-U.S.]	44	Fe	40.22N	83.45W
Belle Fourche	43	Gc	44.40N	103.51W
Belle Fourche River	45	Ed	44.26N	102.19W
Bellegarde	11	If	47.59N	2.26 E
Bellegarde-sur-Valserine	11	Lh	46.06N	5.49 E
Belle Glade	44	Gl	26.41N	80.40W
Belle Ile	5	Ff	47.19N	3.11W
Belle Isle	42	Lf	51.55N	55.20W
Belle Isle, Strait of-	38	Nd	51.35N	56.30W
Bellencombre	12	De	49.42N	1.14 E
Belleplaine	51q	Ab	13.15N	59.34W
Belleville [Fr.]	11	Kh	46.06N	4.45 E
Belleville [Il.-U.S.]	45	Lg	38.31N	90.00W
Belleville [Ks.-U.S.]	45	Hg	39.49N	97.38W
Belleville [Ont.-Can.]	42	Jh	44.10N	77.23W
Bellevue [Nb.-U.S.]	45	If	41.09N	95.54W
Bellevue [Wa.-U.S.]	46	Dc	47.37N	122.12W
Belley	11	Li	45.46N	5.41 E
Bellheim	12	Ke	49.12N	8.17 E
Bellin	39	Lc	60.00N	70.01W
Bellingham [Eng.-U.K.]	9	Kf	55.09N	2.16W
Bellingham [Wa.-U.S.]	39	Ge	48.46N	122.29W
Bellingsfors	8	Ef	58.59N	12.15 E
Bellingshausen	66	Re	62.12S	58.56W
Bellingshausen Ice Shelf	66	Ce	71.00S	89.00W
Bellingshausen Sea (EN)	66	Pf	71.00S	85.00W
Bellinzona	14	Dd	46.11N	9.02 E
Bello	54	Cb	6.19N	75.34W
Bellocq	55	Bl	35.55S	61.32W
Bellona, Récifs-	57	Gg	21.00S	159.00 E
Bellona Island	60	Fj	11.17S	159.47 E
Bellot Strait	42	Ib	72.00N	94.30W
Bellow Falls	44	Kd	43.08N	72.28W
Bell Peninsula	42	Jd	63.45N	81.30W
Bell River	42	Jg	49.49N	77.39W
Bell Rock→Inchcape	9	Ke	56.26N	2.24W
Bellsund	41	Nc	77.39N	14.15 E
Belluno	14	Gd	46.09N	12.13 E
Bell Ville	56	Hd	32.37S	62.42W
Bellville	37	Bf	33.53S	18.36 E
Belmond	45	Je	42.51N	93.37W
Belmont	44	Hd	42.14N	78.02W
Belmonte [Braz.]	54	Kg	15.51S	38.54W
Belmonte [Port.]	13	Ed	40.21N	7.21W
Belmonte [Sp.]	13	Je	39.34N	2.42W
Belmopan	39	Kh	17.15N	88.46W
Beloeil	12	Fd	50.35N	3.43 E
Belogorsk [R.S.F.S.R.]	22	Od	50.57N	128.25 E
Belogorsk [Ukr.-U.S.S.R.]	16	Ig	45.01N	34.33 E
Belogradčik	15	Ff	43.38N	22.41 E
Belogradčiški	15	Ff	43.38N	22.28 E
Belo Horizonte	53	Lg	19.55S	43.56W
Beloit [Ks.-U.S.]	45	Gg	39.28N	98.06W
Beloit [Wi.-U.S.]	43	Jc	42.31N	89.02W
Belojarovo	20	Hf	51.35N	128.55 E
Belojarski	19	Gc	63.40N	66.45 E
Beloje More=White Sea (EN)	5	Kb	66.00N	44.00 E
Beloje Ozero=White Lake (EN)	5	Jc	60.11N	37.35 E
Belokany	16	Oi	41.43N	46.28 E
Belomorsk	6	Jc	64.29N	34.43 E
Belomorsko-Baltijski Kanal =White Sea-Baltic Canal (EN)	5	Jc	63.30N	34.48 E
Belomorsko-Kulojskoje Plato	7	Jd	65.20N	41.50 E
Beloozersk	16	Dc	52.28N	25.13 E
Belopolje	19	De	51.09N	34.18 E
Belorečensk	16	Kg	44.43N	39.52 E
Beloreck	19	Fe	53.58N	58.24 E
Belorusskaja Grjada	16	Ec	53.50N	27.00 E
Belorusskaja Sovetskaja Socialističeskaja Respublika [2]	19	Ce	53.50N	28.00 E
Belorusskaja SSR/Belaruskaja Sovetskaja Socialistyčnaja Respublika [2]	19	Ce	53.50N	28.00 E
Belorusskaja SSR=Byelorussian SSR (EN) [2]	19	Ce	53.50N	28.00 E
Belo-sur-Mer	37	Gd	20.44S	44.00 E
Belo-sur-Tsiribihina	37	Gc	19.39S	44.32 E
Belot, Lac -	42	Ec	66.50N	126.20W
Belovo	20	Df	54.25N	86.18 E
Belovodsk	16	Ke	49.10N	39.33 E
Belovodskoe	18	Jc	42.47N	74.13 E
Belozersk	19	Dd	60.03N	37.48 E
Belper	12	Aa	53.02N	1.28W
Belted Range	46	Gh	37.25N	116.10W
Belton [Mo.-U.S.]	45	Ig	38.49N	94.32W
Belton [Tx.-U.S.]	45	Hk	31.04N	97.28W
Belton Lake	45	Hk	31.08N	97.32W
Belturbet/Béal Tairbirt	9	Fg	54.06N	7.26W
Beluha	21	Ke	49.48N	86.35 E
Belvedere Marittimo	14	Jk	39.37N	15.52 E
Belvidere	45	Le	42.15N	88.50W
Bely	7	Hi	55.50N	32.58 E
Bely, Ostrov-=Bely Island (EN)	21	Jb	73.10N	70.45 E
Belyando River	59	Jd	21.38S	146.50 E
Bely Čeremoš	15	Ia	48.06N	25.04 E
Bely Island (EN)=Bely, Ostrov-	21	Jb	73.10N	70.45 E
Bely Jar	20	De	58.26N	85.03 E
Belyje Berega	16	Ic	53.12N	34.42 E
Belz	16	Dd	50.23N	24.03 E
Bełżec	10	Tf	50.24N	23.26 E
Belzoni	45	Kj	33.11N	90.29W
Bełżyce	10	Se	51.11N	22.18 E
Bemaraha, Plateau de-	30	Lj	19.00S	45.15 E
Bembe	36	Bd	7.02S	14.18 E
Bembéréké	34	Fc	10.13N	2.40 E
Bembézar	13	Gg	37.45N	5.13W
Bembridge	12	Ad	50.41N	1.05W
Bemidji	43	Ib	47.29N	94.53W
Ben	24	Nf	32.32N	50.45 E
Benāb	23	Gb	37.18N	46.05 E
Benabarre/Benavarn	13	Mb	42.07N	0.29 E
Bena Dibele	36	Dc	4.07S	22.50 E
Bénaize	11	Hh	46.34N	1.04 E
Benalla	59	Jg	36.33S	145.59 E
Benares→Vārānasi	22	Kg	25.20N	83.00 E
Benasc/Benasque	13	Mb	42.36N	0.32 E
Benasque/Benasc	13	Mb	42.36N	0.32 E
Benavarn/Benabarre	13	Mb	42.07N	0.29 E
Benavente	13	Gc	42.00N	5.41W
Benbecula	9	Fd	57.27N	7.20W
Bencheng → Luannan	28	Ee	39.30N	118.42 E
Ben-Chicao, Col de-	13	Oh	36.12N	2.51 E
Bend	43	Cc	44.03N	121.19W
Bendaja	34	Cd	7.10N	11.15W
Bendel [2]	34	Gd	6.00N	5.50 E
Bendela	36	Cc	3.18S	17.36 E
Bender Bäyla	31	Mh	9.30N	50.30 E
Bendersiyada	35	Hc	11.14N	48.57 E
Bendery	19	Cf	46.48N	29.22 E
Bendigo	58	Fh	36.46S	144.17 E
Bendorf	12	Jd	50.26N	7.34 E
Bēne/Bene	8	Jh	56.28N	23.01 E
Bene/Bēne	8	Jh	56.28N	23.01 E
Bénéna	34	Ec	13.06N	4.22W
Benepú, Rada-	65d	Ac	27.10S	109.25W
Benešov	10	Kg	49.47N	14.40 E
Benevento	14	Ii	41.08N	14.45 E
Bengal	21	Kg	24.00N	90.00 E
Bengal, Bay of- (EN)	21	Kh	15.00N	90.00 E
Bengamisa	36	Eb	0.57N	25.10 E
Bengbis	34	He	3.27N	12.27 E
Bengbu	22	Nf	32.47N	117.23 E
Benghazi (EN)=Banghāzī	31	Je	32.07N	20.04 E
Benghazi (EN)=Banghāzī [3]	33	Dd	27.00N	20.30 E
Benghisa Point	14	Io	35.50N	14.35 E
Bengkalis	26	Df	1.28N	102.08 E
Bengkulu [3]	26	Dg	3.48S	102.16 E
Bengkulu	22	Mj	3.48S	102.16 E
Bengo, Baía do-	30	Ii	8.43S	13.21 E
Bengo He	28	Eg	35.04N	118.22 E
Bengough	46	Mb	49.24N	105.08W
Bengtsfors	7	Cg	59.02N	12.13 E
Benguela	31	Ij	12.35S	13.26 E
Benguela [3]	36	Be	12.00S	15.00 E
Benguerir	32	Fc	32.14N	7.57W
Benguérua, Ilha-	37	Fd	21.53S	35.26 E
Bengue Viejo	49	Ce	17.05N	89.08W
Bengut, Cap-	32	Hb	36.55N	3.54 E
Beni	31	Jh	0.30N	29.28 E
Beni [2]	54	Ef	14.00S	65.30W
Beni, Río-	52	Jg	10.23S	65.24W
Beni Abbes	32	Gc	30.08N	2.10W
Beni Baufrah	13	Hi	35.05N	4.18W
Benicarló	13	Md	40.25N	0.26 E
Benicasim	13	Md	40.03N	0.04 E
Beni Chougran, Monts des-	13	Mi	35.30N	0.15 E
Benidorm	13	Lf	38.32N	0.08W
Beni Enzar	13	Ji	35.14N	2.57W
Beni Haoua	13	Nh	36.32N	1.34 E
Beni Mellal	31	Ge	32.20N	6.21W
Beni Mellal [3]	32	Fc	32.30N	6.30W
Benin	34	Gd	5.45N	5.04 E
Bénin=Benin (EN) [1]	31	Hh	9.30N	2.15 E
Bénin (Dahomey) [1]	31	Hh	9.30N	2.15 E
Benin (EN)=Bénin [1]	31	Hh	9.30N	2.15 E
Benin, Bight of-	30	Hh	5.30N	4.00 E
Benin City	31	Hh	6.20N	5.38 E
Beni Ounif	32	Gc	32.03N	1.15W
Benisa	13	Mf	38.43N	0.03 E
Beni Saf	13	Ki	35.19N	1.23W
Benisheikh	34	Hc	11.48N	12.29 E
Benito Juárez	48	Mi	17.50N	92.32W
Benito Juárez, Presa-	48	Li	16.27N	95.30W
Benjamen Island	37b	Bb	5.27S	53.21 E
Benjamin	45	Gj	33.35N	99.48W
Benjamín Aceval	55	Dg	24.58S	57.34W
Benjamin Constant	53	If	4.22S	70.02W
Benjamin Hill	48	Db	30.10N	111.10W
Benkei-Misaki	29a	Bb	42.50N	140.11 E
Benkelman	45	Ff	40.03N	101.32W
Benkovac	14	Jf	44.02N	15.37 E
Ben Mehidi	14	Bn	36.46N	7.54 E
Bennett, Lake-	59	Gd	23.50S	131.00 E
Bennett, Ostrov-	20	Ja	76.45N	149.00 E
Benneydale	62	Fc	38.31S	175.21 E
Bennichab	32	Df	19.26N	15.21W
Bennington	44	Kd	42.53N	73.12W
Benom	26	Df	3.50N	102.06 E
Benoni	31	Jk	26.19S	28.27 E
Bénoué=Benue (EN)	30	Hh	7.48N	6.46 E
Benoy	35	Bd	8.59N	16.19 E
Benrath	12	Ic	51.10N	6.52 E
Bensekrane	13	Ki	35.04N	1.13W
Bensheim	10	Eg	49.41N	8.37 E
Ben Slimane	32	Fc	33.37N	7.07W
Benson [Az.-U.S.]	46	Jk	31.58N	110.18W
Benson [Mn.-U.S.]	45	Id	45.19N	95.36W
Benson Point	64g	Ab	1.56N	157.30W
Bent	23	Id	26.17N	59.31 E
Benteng [Indon.]	26	Hg	0.24S	121.59 E
Benteng [Indon.]	26	Hh	6.08N	120.27 E
Bentheim	10	Dd	52.19N	7.10 E
Bentiaba	36	Be	14.29S	12.50 E
Bentinck	25	Jf	11.45N	98.03 E
Bentinck Island	59	Hc	17.05S	139.30 E
Bentiu	35	Dd	9.14N	29.50 E
Bento Conçalves	56	Jc	29.10S	51.31W
Bento Gomes, Rio-	55	Dc	16.40S	57.12W
Benton [Ar.-U.S.]	45	Ji	34.34N	92.35W
Benton [Il.-U.S.]	45	Lg	38.01N	88.55W
Bentong	26	Df	3.32N	101.55 E
Benton Harbor	44	Dd	42.07N	86.27W
Bentonville	45	Ih	36.22N	94.13W
Benua, Pulau-	26	Ef	0.56N	107.27 E
Benue [2]	34	Gd	7.15N	8.20 E
Benue	30	Hh	7.48N	6.46 E
Benue (EN)=Bénoué	30	Hh	7.48N	6.46 E
Benwee Head/An Bhinn Bhuí	9	Dg	54.21N	9.48W
Benxi	22	Oe	41.16N	123.48 E
Beo	26	If	4.15N	126.48 E
Beograd = Belgrade (EN)	6	Ig	44.50N	20.30 E
Beograd-Krnjača	15	De	44.52N	20.28 E
Beograd-Zemun	15	De	44.53N	20.25 E
Béoumi	34	Dd	7.40N	5.34W

Index Symbols

- [1] Independent Nation
- [2] State, Region
- [3] District, County
- [4] Municipality
- [5] Colony, Dependency
- Continent
- Physical Region
- Historical or Cultural Region
- Mount, Mountain
- Volcano
- Hill
- Mountains, Mountain Range
- Hills, Escarpment
- Plateau, Upland
- Pass, Gap
- Plain, Lowland
- Delta
- Salt Flat
- Valley, Canyon
- Crater, Cave
- Karst Features
- Depression
- Polder
- Desert, Dunes
- Forest, Woods
- Heath, Steppe
- Oasis
- Cape, Point
- Coast, Beach
- Cliff
- Peninsula
- Isthmus
- Sandbank
- Island
- Atoll
- Rock, Reef
- Islands, Archipelago
- Rocks, Reefs
- Coral Reef
- Well, Spring
- Geyser
- River, Stream
- Waterfall Rapids
- River Mouth, Estuary
- Lake
- Salt Lake
- Intermittent Lake
- Reservoir
- Swamp, Pond
- Canal
- Glacier
- Ice Shelf, Pack Ice
- Ocean
- Sea
- Gulf, Bay
- Strait, Fjord
- Lagoon
- Bank
- Seamount
- Tablemount
- Ridge
- Shelf
- Basin
- Escarpment, Sea Scarp
- Fracture
- Trench, Abyss
- National Park, Reserve
- Point of Interest
- Recreation Site
- Cave, Cavern
- Historic Site
- Ruins
- Wall, Walls
- Church, Abbey
- Temple
- Scientific Station
- Airport
- Port
- Lighthouse
- Mine
- Tunnel
- Dam, Bridge

Beppu	27	Ne	33.17N	131.30 E
Beppu-Wan	29	Be	33.20N	131.35 E
Bequia Head	51n	Ba	13.03N	61.12W
Bequia Island	50	Ff	13.01N	61.13W
Beraketa	37	Hd	24.11S	45.42 E
Berati	15	Ci	40.42N	19.57 E
Beratus, Gunung-	26	Gg	1.02S	116.20 E
Berau, Teluk-=McCluer Gulf (EN)	26	Jg	2.30S	132.30 E
Berberä	31	Lg	10.25N	45.02 E
Berbérati	31	Ih	4.16N	15.47 E
Berberia, Cabo-	13	Nf	38.38N	1.23 E
Berbice River	54	Gb	6.17N	57.32W
Berca	15	Jd	45.17N	26.41 E
Berchères-sur-Vesgre	12	Df	48.51N	1.33 E
Berchtesgaden	10	Ii	47.38N	13.00 E
Berck [Fr.]	12	Dd	50.24N	1.36 E
Berck [Fr.]	11	Hd	50.24N	1.34 E
Berck- Berck Plage	12	Dd	50.24N	1.34 E
Berck-Plage, Berck-	12	Dd	50.24N	1.34 E
Berda	16	Jf	46.47N	36.52 E
Berdäle	35	Hd	7.04N	47.51 E
Berdičev	19	Cf	49.53N	28.36 E
Berdigestjah	20	Hd	62.03N	126.50 E
Berdjansk	19	Df	46.43N	36.48 E
Berdsk	20	Df	54.47N	83.05 E
Beregomet	15	Ia	48.10N	25.24 E
Beregovo	19	Cf	48.13N	22.41 E
Bereku	36	Gc	4.27S	35.44 E
Berekua	50	Fe	15.14N	61.19W
Berekum	34	Ed	7.27N	2.35W
Berens	42	Hf	52.21N	97.01W
Berens River	42	Hf	52.22N	97.02W
Beresford	45	He	43.05N	96.47W
Berestečko	10	Vf	50.16N	25.14 E
Bereşti	15	Kc	46.06N	27.53 E
Berettyó	15	Ec	46.59N	21.07 E
Berettyóújfalu	10	Ri	47.13N	21.33 E
Bereza	19	Ce	52.33N	24.58 E
Berezan	16	Gd	50.19N	31.31 E
Berežany	16	De	49.29N	25.00 E
Berezina [Bye.-U.S.S.R.]	16	Dc	53.48N	25.59 E
Berezina [U.S.S.R.]	5	Je	52.33N	30.14 E
Berezino [Bye.-U.S.S.R.]	16	Fc	53.51N	29.00 E
Berezino [Bye.-U.S.S.R.]	8	Mj	54.55N	28.16 E
Berezino [Ukr.-U.S.S.R.]	15	Mc	46.16N	29.11 E
Bereznegovatoje	16	Hf	47.20N	32.49 E
Bereznik	19	Ec	62.53N	42.42 E
Berezniki	6	Ld	59.24N	56.46 E
Berezno	16	Ed	51.01N	26.45 E
Berezovka [Bye.-U.S.S.R.]	10	Vc	53.40N	25.37 E
Berezovka [R.S.F.S.R.]	17	Hd	64.59N	56.29 E
Berezovka [Ukr.-U.S.S.R.]	19	Df	47.12N	30.56 E
Berezovka Višerka	17	Hf	60.55N	56.50 E
Berezovo	19	Gc	63.58N	65.00 E
Berezovski [R.S.F.S.R.]	17	Jh	56.55N	60.50 E
Berezovski [R.S.F.S.R.]	20	De	55.39N	86.16 E
Berezovy	20	If	51.41N	135.52 E
Berga [Sp.]	13	Nb	42.06N	1.51 E
Berga [Swe.]	8	Gg	57.13N	16.02 E
Bergama	23	Cb	39.07N	27.10 E
Bergamo	14	De	45.41N	9.43 E
Bergantiños	13	Da	43.20N	8.45W
Bergby	7	Df	60.56N	17.02 E
Bergen [G.D.R.]	10	Jb	54.25N	13.26 E
Bergen [Neth.]	12	Gb	52.40N	4.42 E
Bergen [Nor.]	6	Gc	60.23N	5.20 E
Bergen/Mons	11	Jd	50.27N	3.56 E
Bergen aan Zee, Bergen-	12	Gb	52.40N	4.38 E
Bergen-Bergen aan Zee	12	Gb	52.40N	4.38 E
Bergen op Zoom	11	Kc	51.30N	4.17 E
Bergerac	11	Gj	44.51N	0.29 E
Bergeyk	12	Hc	51.19N	5.22 E
Bergh	12	Ic	51.53N	6.16 E
Bergheim	10	Cf	50.58N	6.39 E
Bergh-s'Heerenberg	12	Ic	51.53N	6.16 E
Bergisches Land	10	De	51.07N	7.10 E
Bergisch Gladbach	10	Df	50.59N	7.08 E
Bergkvara	8	Gh	56.23N	16.05 E
Bergneustadt	12	Jc	51.02N	7.39 E
Bergö	8	Ib	62.55N	21.10 E
Bergsjö	7	Df	61.59N	17.04 E
Bergslagen	8	Fd	60.05N	14.30 E
Bergstraße	12	Ke	49.40N	8.40 E
Bergues	12	Ed	50.58N	2.26 E
Bergum, Tietjerksteradeel-	12	Ha	53.12N	6.00 E
Bergviken	8	Gc	61.10N	16.45 E
Bergville	37	De	28.52S	29.18 E
Berh	27	Jb	47.45N	111.07 E
Berhala, Selat-	26	Dg	0.48S	104.25 E
Berhampore	25	Hd	24.06N	88.15 E
Berhampur	22	Kh	19.19N	84.47 E
Berici, Monti-	14	Fe	45.26N	11.31 E
Berīkān	24	Nh	28.17N	51.14 E
Berikulski	20	De	55.32N	88.08 E
Beringa, Ostrov-=Bering Island (EN)	20	Lf	55.00N	166.10 E
Beringen	12	Hc	51.03N	5.13 E
Bering Glacier	40	Kd	60.15N	143.30W
Bering Island (EN)= Beringa, Ostrov-	20	Lf	55.00N	166.10 E
Beringovo More=Bering Sea (EN)	38	Bd	60.00N	175.00W
Beringovski	22	Tc	63.07N	179.19 E
Bering Proliv=Bering Strait (EN)	38	Cc	65.30N	169.00W
Bering Sea	38	Bd	60.00N	175.00W
Bering Sea (EN)=Beringovo More	38	Bd	60.00N	175.00W
Bering Strait	38	Cc	65.30N	169.00W
Bering Strait (EN)=Bering Proliv	38	Cc	65.30N	169.00W
Berislav	16	Hf	46.51N	33.29 E
Berisso	55	Dl	34.52S	57.53W
Berit Dağı	24	Gc	38.01N	36.52 E
Berīzak	24	Qi	26.06N	57.15 E
Berja	13	Jh	36.51N	2.57W
Berkåk	7	Be	62.50N	10.00 E
Berkane	32	Gc	34.56N	2.20W
Berkel	10	Cd	52.09N	6.12 E
Berkeley	43	Cd	37.57N	122.18W
Berkhamsted	12	Bc	51.45N	0.33W
Berkner Island	66	Rf	79.30S	49.30W
Berkovica	15	Gf	43.14N	23.07 E
Berks	9	Lj	51.15N	1.20W
Berkshire [3]	9	Lj	51.30N	1.10W
Berkshire Downs	9	Lj	51.35N	1.25W
Berkshire Hills	44	Kd	42.20N	73.10W
Berlaimont	12	Fd	50.12N	3.49 E
Berlanga de Duero	13	Jc	41.28N	2.51W
Berlengas, Ilhas-	13	Ce	39.25N	9.30W
Berlevåg	7	Ga	70.51N	29.06 E
Berlin	43	Mc	44.29N	71.10W
Berlin (Ost)=East Berlin (EN) [2]	10	Jd	52.30N	13.25 E
Berlin (Ost)=East Berlin (EN)	6	He	52.31N	13.24 E
Berlin (West)=West Berlin (EN)	6	He	52.31N	13.24 E
Berlin-Pankow	10	Jd	52.34N	13.24 E
Bermeja, Sierra-	13	Gh	36.30N	5.15W
Bermejillo	47	Dc	25.53N	103.37W
Bermejito, Río-	55	Bg	25.39S	60.11W
Bermejo, Isla-	55	An	39.01S	62.01W
Bermejo, Paso-/Cumbre, Paso de la-	52	Ii	32.50S	70.05W
Bermejo, Río- [Arg.]	52	Ji	31.52S	67.22W
Bermejo, Río- [S.Amer.]	52	Kh	26.52S	58.23W
Bermen, lac-	42	Kf	53.35N	68.55W
Bermeo	13	Ja	43.26N	2.43W
Bermillo de Sayago	13	Fc	41.22N	6.06W
Bermuda [5]	39	Mf	32.20N	64.45W
Bermuda Islands	39	Mf	32.20N	64.45W
Bermuda Rise (EN)	38	Mf	32.30N	65.00W
Bern [2]	14	Bd	46.55N	7.40 E
Bern/Berne	6	Gf	46.55N	7.30 E
Bernalda	14	Kj	40.24N	16.41 E
Bernalillo	45	Ci	35.18N	106.33W
Bernard Islands	64d	Bb	7.18N	151.32 E
Bernardo de Irigoyen	55	Bk	32.10S	61.09W
Bernardo do Irigoyen	56	Jc	26.15S	53.39W
Bernasconi	56	He	37.54S	63.43W
Bernau bei Berlin	10	Jd	52.40N	13.35 E
Bernaville	12	Ed	50.08N	2.10 E
Bernay	11	Ge	49.06N	0.36 E
Bernburg	10	He	51.48N	11.44 E
Berndorf	14	Kc	47.57N	16.06 E
Berne [F.R.G.]	12	Ka	53.11N	8.29 E
Berne [In.-U.S.]	44	Ee	40.39N	84.57W
Berne/Bern	6	Gf	46.55N	7.30 E
Berner Alpen/Alpes Bernoises=Bernese Alps (EN)	14	Bd	46.25N	7.30 E
Berneray	9	Fd	57.43N	7.15W
Bernese Alps (EN)=Alpes Bernoises/Berner Alpen	14	Bd	46.25N	7.30 E
Bernese Alps (EN)=Berner Alpen/Alpes Bernoises	14	Bd	46.25N	7.30 E
Bernesga	13	Gb	42.28N	5.31W
Bernesq	12	Be	49.16N	0.56W
Bernier Bay	42	Ib	71.08N	88.00W
Bernier Island	59	Cd	24.50S	113.10 E
Bernina	14	Ed	46.25N	10.01 E
Bernina	5	Gf	46.22N	9.50 E
Berninapaß	14	Ed	46.25N	10.01 E
Bernissart	12	Fd	50.28N	3.38 E
Bernkastel-Kues	10	Dg	49.55N	7.04 E
Bernstorffs Isfjord	41	Hf	63.10N	40.45W
Berón de Astrada	55	Dh	27.33S	57.32W
Beroroha	37	Hd	21.39S	45.10 E
Béroubouay	34	Fc	10.32N	2.44 E
Beroun	10	Kg	49.58N	14.04 E
Berounka	10	Kg	50.00N	14.24 E
Berovo	15	Fh	41.43N	22.51 E
Berre, Étang de-	11	Lk	43.27N	5.08 E
Berriane	32	Hc	32.50N	3.46 E
Berrouaghia	13	Oh	36.08N	2.55 E
Berry	11	Hh	47.00N	2.00 E
Berry-au-Bac	12	Fe	49.24N	3.54 E
Berryessa, Lake-	46	Dg	38.37N	122.16W
Berry Head	9	Jk	50.24N	3.29W
Berry Islands	47	Ic	25.34N	77.45W
Berry River	46	Ja	50.50N	111.36W
Beršad	19	Cf	48.23N	29.33 E
Berseba	37	Be	26.01S	17.41 E
Bersenbrück	12	Jb	52.33N	7.56 E
Berthierville	44	Kb	46.05N	73.11W
Bertincourt	12	Ed	50.05N	2.59 E
Bertogne	12	Hd	50.05N	5.40 E
Bertolinia	54	Je	7.38S	43.57W
Bertoua	31	Ih	4.35N	13.41 E
Bertraghboy Bay	9	Dh	53.23N	9.50W
Bertrix	12	He	49.51N	5.15 E
Beru Island	57	Ie	1.20S	176.00 E
Berwick-upon-Tweed	9	Lf	55.46N	2.00W
Berwyn	9	Ji	52.53N	3.24W
Besalampy	37	Gc	16.44S	44.24 E
Besançon	6	Gf	47.15N	6.02 E
Besar, Gunung-	26	Gg	1.25S	115.39 E
Besbre	11	Jh	46.33N	3.44 E
Besed	16	Gc	52.38N	31.11 E
Besikama	26	Hh	9.36S	124.57 E
Beskid Mountains (EN)	5	Hf	49.40N	20.00 E
Beskid Niski	10	Rg	49.20N	21.30 E
Beskid Średni	10	Pg	49.45N	19.20 E
Beskid Wysoki	10	Pg	49.32N	20.00 E
Beskidy Wschodnie	10	Sg	49.20N	22.30 E
Beskidy Zachodnie	10	Pg	49.30N	19.30 E
Beskol	18	Ma	46.06N	81.01 E
Beslan	19	Eg	43.10N	44.35 E
Besna Kobila	15	Fg	42.32N	22.14 E
Besni	24	Gd	37.41N	37.52 E
Besparmak Dağ	15	Kl	37.30N	27.35 E
Bessao	35	Bd	7.53N	15.59 E
Bessarabia (EN)=Bessarabija	15	Lb	47.00N	28.30 E
Bessarabija=Bessarabia (EN)	15	Lb	47.00N	28.30 E
Bessarabka	16	Ff	46.20N	28.59 E
Bességes	11	Kj	44.17N	4.06 E
Bessemer	43	Je	33.25N	86.57W
Bessin	11	Fe	49.10N	1.00W
Bessines-sur-Gartempe	11	Hh	46.06N	1.22 E
Bessoki, Gora-	16	Rh	43.57N	52.30 E
Best	12	Hc	51.30N	5.24 E
Bestjah [R.S.F.S.R.]	20	Hc	66.00N	123.35 E
Bestjah [R.S.F.S.R.]	20	Hd	61.17N	128.50 E
Bestobe	19	He	52.30N	73.05 E
Bestwig	12	Kc	51.22N	8.24 E
Betafo	37	Hc	19.49S	46.50 E
Betanzos [Bol.]	54	Eg	19.34S	65.27W
Betanzos [Sp.]	13	Da	43.17N	8.12W
Betanzos, Ría de-	13	Da	43.23N	8.15W
Bétaré Oya	34	Hd	5.36N	14.05 E
Bétérou	34	Fd	9.12N	2.16 E
Beteta	13	Jd	40.34N	2.04W
Bethal	37	De	26.27S	29.28 E
Bethanien [3]	37	Be	26.30S	17.00 E
Bethanien	31	Ik	26.32S	17.11 E
Bethany [Mo.-U.S.]	45	If	40.16N	94.02W
Bethany [Ok.-U.S.]	45	Hi	35.31N	97.38W
Bethel	39	Cc	60.48N	161.46W
Bétheniville	12	Ge	49.18N	4.22 E
Bethlehem [Pa.-U.S.]	44	Je	40.36N	75.22W
Bethlehem [S.Afr.]	31	Jk	28.15S	28.15 E
Bethlehem (EN)=Bayt Laḩm	24	Fg	31.43N	35.12 E
Bethulie	37	Df	30.32S	25.59 E
Béthune	11	Id	50.32N	2.38 E
Béthune	11	He	49.53N	1.09 E
Betioky	37	Gd	23.42S	44.22 E
Betong	25	Kg	5.45N	101.05 E
Betor	35	Fc	11.37N	39.00 E
Bétou	36	Cb	3.03N	18.31 E
Betpak-Dala	21	Ie	46.00N	70.00 E
Betroka	37	Hd	23.15S	46.05 E
Bet She'an	24	Ff	32.30N	35.30 E
Betsiamites, Rivière-	42	Kg	48.56N	68.38W
Betsiboka	30	Lj	16.03S	46.36 E
Bette	30	If	22.00N	19.12 E
Bettembourg/Bettemburg	12	Ie	49.31N	6.06 E
Bettemburg/Bettembourg	12	Ie	49.31N	6.06 E
Bettendorf	45	Kf	41.32N	90.30W
Bettles Field	40	Ic	66.53N	151.51W
Bettna	8	Gf	58.55N	16.38 E
Bettola	14	Df	44.47N	9.36 E
Betūl	25	Fd	21.55N	77.54 E
Betuwe	11	Lc	51.55N	5.30 E
Betwa	25	Hc	25.55N	80.12 E
Betz	12	Ee	49.09N	2.57 E
Betzdorf	10	Df	50.47N	7.53 E
Beulah	44	Dc	44.38N	86.06W
Beult	12	Cc	51.13N	0.26 E
Beuvron	11	Hg	47.29N	1.15 E
Beuzeville	12	Ce	49.20N	0.21 E
Beveland	11	Jc	51.30N	3.40 E
Beveren	12	Gc	51.13N	4.15 E
Beveridge Reef	57	Kg	20.00S	168.00W
Beverley [Austl.]	59	Df	32.06S	116.56 E
Beverley [Eng.-U.K.]	9	Mh	53.51N	0.26W
Beverwijk	11	Kb	52.28N	4.40 E
Bewsher, Mount-	66	Ff	70.54S	65.28 E
Bexhill	9	Nk	50.50N	0.29 E
Bexley, London-	12	Cc	51.26N	0.09 E
Beyağaç	15	Ll	37.13N	28.57 E
Beyānlū	24	Ld	36.02N	47.53 E
Bey Dağı	24	Hc	38.15N	38.22 E
Bey Dağlari	23	Db	36.40N	30.15 E
Beykoz	24	Cb	41.08N	29.05 E
Beyla	34	Dd	8.41N	8.38W
Beyoğlu, İstanbul	15	Lh	41.02N	28.59 E
Beyoneisu-Retsugan	27	Oe	31.55N	139.55 E
Beypazari	24	Db	40.10N	31.55 E
Beyra	35	Hd	6.57N	47.19 E
Beyram	24	Oi	27.26N	53.31 E
Beyşehir	24	Dd	37.41N	31.43 E
Beyşehir Gölü	23	Db	37.40N	31.30 E
Bezaha	37	Gd	23.29S	44.30 E
Bežanickaja Vozvyšennost	7	Gh	56.45N	29.30 E
Bežanicy	7	Gh	56.58N	29.57 E
Bezdan	15	Bd	45.51N	18.56 E
Bezděz	10	Kf	50.32N	14.43 E
Bezdež	10	Vd	52.18N	25.20 E
Bežeck	19	Dd	57.50N	36.41 E
Bezenčuk	7	Lj	53.01N	49.24 E
Bezerra, Rio-	55	Ia	13.16S	47.31W
Bezerros	54	Ke	8.14S	35.45W
Beziers	11	Jk	43.21N	3.15 E
Bezmein	19	Fh	38.05N	58.12 E
Bežta	19	Eg	42.08N	46.08 E
Bhadrakh	25	Hd	21.04N	86.30 E
Bhadrāvati	25	Ff	13.52N	75.43 E
Bhāgalpur	22	Kg	25.15N	87.00 E
Bhairawa	25	Gc	27.31N	83.24 E
Bhaironghati	25	Fb	31.01N	78.53 E
Bhakkar	25	Eb	31.38N	71.04 E
Bhamo	25	Jd	24.16N	97.14 E
Bhandāra	25	Fd	21.10N	79.39 E
Bhanjan	25	Gc	25.47N	83.36 E
Bhārat Juktarashtra=India (EN) [1]	22	Jh	20.00N	77.00 E
Bharatpur	25	Fc	27.13N	77.29 E
Bharūch	25	Ed	21.46N	72.54 E
Bhatinda	25	Eb	30.12N	74.57 E
Bhātpāra	25	Hd	22.52N	88.24 E
Bhaunagar	22	Jg	21.46N	72.09 E
Bhera	25	Eb	32.29N	72.55 E
Bheri	25	Gc	28.44N	81.16 E
Bhīlwāra	25	Ec	25.21N	74.38 E
Bhīma	21	Jh	16.25N	77.17 E
Bhind	25	Fc	26.34N	78.48 E
Bhiwāni	25	Fc	28.47N	76.08 E
Bhopāl	22	Jg	23.16N	77.24 E
Bhubaneswar	22	Kg	20.14N	85.50 E
Bhuj	25	Dd	23.16N	69.40 E
Bhusāwal	25	Fd	21.03N	75.46 E
Bhutan (Druk-Yul) [1]	22	Lg	27.30N	90.30 E
Bia	34	Ed	5.21N	3.11W
Bia, Phou-	21	Mh	18.36N	103.01 E
Biá, Rio-	54	Ed	3.28S	67.23W
Bīābān, Kūh-e-	24	Qi	26.30N	57.25 E
Biabou	51n	Ba	13.12N	61.09W
Biafra	30	Hh	5.00N	7.30 E
Biafra, Bight of-	30	Hh	3.20N	9.20 E
Biak	26	Kg	1.10S	136.06 E
Biak, Pulau-	57	Ee	1.00S	136.00 E
Biała Piska	10	Sc	53.37N	22.04 E
Biała Podlaska [2]	10	Td	52.00N	23.05 E
Biała Podlaska	10	Td	52.02N	23.06 E
Białobrzegi	10	Qe	51.40N	20.57 E
Białogard	10	Lb	54.01N	16.00 E
Białostocka, Wysoczyzna-	10	Tc	53.23N	23.10 E
Białowieża	10	Td	52.41N	23.50 E
Białystok	6	Ie	53.09N	23.09 E
Białystok [2]	10	Tc	53.10N	23.10 E
Biancavilla	14	Im	37.38N	14.52 E
Bianco	14	Kl	38.05N	16.09 E
Bianco, Monte-	5	Gf	45.50N	6.52 E
Biankouma	34	Dd	7.44N	7.37W
Biankouma [3]	34	Dd	7.43N	7.40W
Bianzhuang → Cangshan	28	Eg	34.51N	118.03 E
Biaro, Pulau-	26	If	2.05N	125.20 E
Biarritz	11	Ek	43.29N	1.34W
Biasca	14	Cd	46.22N	8.57 E
Bibā	33	Fd	28.55N	30.59 E
Bibai	27	Pc	43.19N	141.52 E
Bibala	36	Be	14.50S	13.30 E
Biban, Chaine des-	13	Qh	36.12N	4.25 E
Bibbiena	14	Fg	43.42N	11.49 E
Biberach an der Riß	10	Fh	48.06N	9.48 E
Bibiani	34	Ed	6.28N	2.20W
Bic	44	Ma	48.22N	68.42W
Bicaj	15	Dh	41.59N	20.25 E
Bicas	55	Ke	21.43S	43.04W
Bicaz	15	Jc	46.55N	26.04 E
Bicaz, Pasul-	15	Ic	46.49N	25.52 E
Bičenekski, Pereval-	16	Nj	39.33N	45.48 E
Bicester	9	Lj	51.54N	1.09W
Bichena	35	Fc	10.21N	38.14 E
Bickerton Island	59	Hb	13.45S	136.10 E
Bicske	10	Oi	47.29N	18.38 E
Bičura	20	Ff	50.36N	107.35 E
Bīd	24	Qd	36.33N	57.35 E
Bida	31	Hh	9.05N	6.01 E
Bīdar	25	Fe	17.54N	77.33 E
Bidasoa	13	Ka	43.22N	1.47W
Biddeford	43	Mc	43.30N	70.26W
Bideford	9	Ij	51.01N	4.13W
Bideford Bay → Barnstaple	9	Ij	51.05N	4.20W
Bidon V/Poste Maurice Cortier	32	He	22.18N	1.05 E
Bié [3]	36	Ce	13.00S	17.30 E
Bié, Planalto do-	30	Ij	13.30S	17.02 E
Biebrza	10	Sc	53.13N	22.28 E
Biecz	10	Rg	49.44N	21.14 E
Biedenkopf	10	Ef	50.55N	8.32 E
Biei	29a	Cb	43.35N	142.28 E
Biel/Bienne	14	Bc	47.10N	7.15 E
Bielefeld	10	Ed	52.02N	8.32 E
Bielefeld-Brackwede	12	Kc	51.59N	8.31 E
Bielefeld-Sennestadt	12	Kc	51.57N	8.35 E
Biella	14	Ce	45.34N	8.03 E
Bielsk	10	Pd	52.40N	19.49 E
Bielska, Wysoczyzna-	10	Sd	52.35N	23.00 E
Bielsko [2]	10	Og	49.50N	19.00 E
Bielsko-Biała	10	Pg	49.49N	19.02 E
Bielsk Podlaski	10	Td	52.47N	23.12 E
Bien Dong=South China Sea (EN)	21	Ni	10.00N	113.00 E
Bien Hoa	25	Lf	10.57N	106.49 E
Bienne	11	Lh	46.20N	5.38 E
Bienne/Biel	14	Bc	47.10N	7.15 E
Bienvenida	13	Jd	40.30N	2.30W
Bienville, Lac -	42	Ke	55.20N	72.40W
Bierbeek	12	Gd	50.50N	4.46 E
Bieszczady	10	Sg	49.10N	22.35 E
Bièvre	12	He	49.56N	5.01 E
Biferno	14	Ji	41.59N	15.02 E
Bifoum	36	Bc	0.20S	10.23 E
Bifuka	28	Qb	44.29N	142.21 E
Biga	24	Bb	40.13N	27.14 E
Bigadiç	24	Cc	39.23N	28.08 E
Big Bald Mountain	44	Nb	47.37N	66.38W
Big Baldy Mountain	46	Jc	46.58N	110.37W
Big Bay [Mi.-U.S.]	44	Db	46.49N	87.44W
Big Bay [Van.]	63b	Cb	15.05S	166.54 E
Big Beaver House	42	If	52.58N	89.57W
Big Belt Mountains	46	Jc	46.40N	111.25W
Big Black River	45	Kj	32.00N	91.05W
Big Blue River	43	Hd	39.11N	96.32W
Big Creek Peak	46	Id	44.28N	113.32W
Big Dry Creek	46	Lc	47.30N	106.19W
Big Falls	45	Jb	48.11N	93.46W
Biggar	42	Gf	52.04N	108.00W
Biggenden	59	Ke	25.30S	152.00 E
Biggleswade	9	Mi	52.05N	0.17W
Big Hatchet Peak	45	Bk	31.37N	108.20W
Big Hole River	46	Id	45.34N	112.20W
Bighorn Basin	43	Fc	44.15N	108.10W
Bighorn Lake	46	Kd	45.08N	108.10W
Bighorn Mountains	38	Ie	44.00N	107.30W
Bighorn River	43	Fb	46.09N	107.28W
Bight, Head of-	59	Gf	31.30S	131.10 E
Big Island	42	Kd	62.43N	70.40W
Big Lake	44	Nc	45.10N	67.40W
Big Lake	45	Fk	31.12N	101.28W
Big Lost River	46	Ie	43.50N	112.44W
Big Muddy Creek	46	Mb	48.08N	104.36W
Big Muddy Lake	46	Mb	49.08N	104.54W
Bignona	34	Bc	12.49N	16.14W
Bigorre	11	Gk	43.06N	0.05 E
Big Porcupine Creek	46	Lc	46.17N	106.47W
Big Quill Lake	42	Hf	51.51N	104.18W
Big Rapids	44	Ed	43.42N	85.29W
Big River	42	Gf	53.50N	107.01W
Big River	42	Fb	72.50N	125.00W
Big Sand Lake	42	He	57.45N	99.45W
Big Sandy	46	Jb	48.11N	110.07W
Big Sandy Creek	45	Eg	38.06N	102.29W
Big Sandy River [Az.-U.S.]	46	Ii	34.19N	113.31W
Big Sandy River [Wy.-U.S.]	46	Kf	41.50N	109.48W
Big Sheep Mountains	46	Mc	47.03N	105.43W
Big Sioux River	43	Hc	42.30N	96.25W
Big Smoky Valley	43	Dd	38.30N	117.15W
Big Snowy Mountains	46	Kc	46.50N	109.30W
Big Spring	39	If	32.15N	101.28W
Big Spruce Knob	44	Gf	38.16N	80.12W
Big Stone Lake	45	Hd	45.25N	96.40W
Big Timber	46	Kd	45.50N	109.57W
Big Trout Lake	42	If	53.45N	90.00W
Biguglia, Étang de-	11a	Ba	42.36N	9.29 E
Big Wood Cay	49	Ia	24.21N	77.44W
Big Wood River	46	He	42.52N	114.55W
Bihać	14	Jf	44.49N	15.52 E
Bihār [3]	25	Hd	25.00N	86.00 E
Bihār	25	Hc	25.11N	85.31 E
Biharamulo	36	Fc	2.38S	31.20 E
Bihor [2]	15	Ec	47.00N	22.00 E
Bihoro	27	Pc	43.49N	144.07 E
Bihorului, Munţii-	15	Fc	46.40N	22.45 E
Bija	21	Kd	52.25N	85.05 E
Bijagós, Arquipélago dos-=Bijagos Islands (EN)	30	Fg	11.15N	16.05W
Bijagós Islands (EN)=Bijagós, Arquipélago dos-	30	Fg	11.15N	16.05W
Bijapur	25	Fe	16.50N	75.42 E
Bījār	23	Gb	35.52N	47.36 E
Bijeljina	14	Nf	44.45N	19.13 E
Bijelo Polje	15	Cf	43.02N	19.45 E
Bijiang (Zhiziluo)	27	Gf	26.39N	99.00 E
Bijie	27	If	27.15N	105.16 E
Bijlikol, Ozero-	18	Hc	43.05N	70.40 E
Bijou Creek	45	Ef	40.17N	103.52W
Bijoutier Island	37b	Bb	7.04S	52.45 E
Bijsk	22	Kd	52.34N	85.15 E
Bīkāner	22	Jg	28.01N	73.18 E
Bikar Atoll	57	Ic	12.15N	170.06 E
Bikeqi	28	Ad	40.45N	111.17 E
Bikin	20	Ig	46.43N	134.02 E
Bikin	20	Ig	46.51N	134.02 E
Bikini Atoll	57	Hc	11.35N	165.23 E
Bikoro	31	Ii	0.45S	18.07 E
Bilād Ghāmid	33	Hf	19.58N	41.38 E
Bilād Zahrān	33	He	20.15N	41.15 E
Bilāspur	22	Kg	22.03N	82.10 E
Bilate	35	Fd	6.34N	38.01 E
Bilauktaung Range	21	Lh	13.00N	99.00 E
Bilbao	6	Fg	43.15N	2.58W
Bilbays	33	Fc	30.25N	31.34 E
Bileća	14	Mh	42.53N	18.26 E
Bilecik	23	Ca	40.09N	29.59 E
Bīlehsavār	24	Mc	39.28N	48.20 E
Bilé Karpaty=White Carpathians (EN)	10	Nh	48.55N	17.50 E
Bilesha Plain	36	Hb	0.35N	40.45 E
Biłgoraj	10	Sf	50.34N	22.43 E
Bili	36	Db	4.50N	22.29 E
Bili	36	Eb	4.09N	25.10 E
Bilibino	22	Sc	68.03N	166.20 E
Biliran	26	Hd	11.35N	124.28 E
Bilishti	15	Di	40.37N	20.59 E
Biliu He	28	Ge	39.30N	122.36 E
Bill Baileys Bank (EN)	9	Ca	60.40N	10.20W
Billerbeck	12	Jc	51.58N	7.18 E
Billericay	12	Cc	51.37N	0.35 E
Billingen	8	Ef	58.24N	13.45 E
Billings	39	Jf	37.04N	93.33W
Billings, Reprêsa-	55	If	23.45S	46.40W
Billingshurst	12	Bc	51.01N	0.27W
Bill Williams River	46	Hi	34.17N	114.03W
Billy Chinook, Lake-	46	Ed	44.33N	121.20W
Bilma	31	Ig	18.41N	12.56 E
Biloela	59	Kd	24.24S	150.30 E
Bilo Gora	14	Le	45.50N	17.10 E
Biloku	54	Gc	1.46N	58.33W
Biloxi	43	Je	30.24N	88.53W
Bilqās Qism Awwal	24	Dg	31.13N	31.21 E
Bîlteni	15	Ge	44.52N	23.17 E
Biltine	35	Cc	14.32N	20.55 E
Biltine [3]	35	Cc	15.00N	21.00 E
Bilzen	12	Hd	50.51N	5.31 E
Bima	36	Eb	3.23N	25.09 E
Bimbān	24	Ej	24.26N	32.53 E
Bimberi Peak	59	Jg	35.40S	148.47 E
Bimbila	34	Fd	8.51N	0.04 E
Bimbo	35	Be	4.18N	18.33 E
Bimini Islands	47	Ic	25.44N	79.15W
Bināb	24	Md	36.35N	48.41 E
Binačka Morava	15	Eg	42.27N	21.47 E
Binaiya, Gunung-	26	Ig	3.11S	129.26 E
Binatang	26	Ff	2.10N	111.38 E
Bınboga Dağı	24	Gc	38.21N	36.32 E
Binche	12	Gd	50.24N	4.10 E
Binder	27	Jb	48.35N	110.36 E
Bindura	31	Kj	17.17S	31.20 E
Bine el Ouidane	32	Fc	32.08N	6.28W
Binéfar	13	Mc	41.51N	0.18 E
Binem	35	Bb	18.43N	19.40 E
Binga [Zaire]	36	Db	2.23N	20.30 E
Binga [Zimb.]	37	Dc	17.37S	27.20 E

Index Symbols

- [1] Independent Nation
- [2] State, Region
- [3] District, County
- [4] Municipality
- [5] Colony, Dependency
- Continent
- Physical Region
- Historical or Cultural Region
- Mount, Mountain
- Volcano
- Hill
- Mountains, Mountain Range
- Hills, Escarpment
- Plateau, Upland
- Pass, Gap
- Plain, Lowland
- Delta
- Salt Flat
- Valley, Canyon
- Crater, Cave
- Karst Features
- Depression
- Polder
- Desert, Dunes
- Forest, Woods
- Heath, Steppe
- Oasis
- Cape, Point
- Coast, Beach
- Cliff
- Peninsula
- Isthmus
- Sandbank
- Island
- Atoll
- Rock, Reef
- Islands, Archipelago
- Rocks, Reefs
- Coral Reef
- Well, Spring
- Geyser
- River, Stream
- Waterfall Rapids
- River Mouth, Estuary
- Lake
- Salt Lake
- Intermittent Lake
- Reservoir
- Swamp, Pond
- Canal
- Glacier
- Ice Shelf, Pack Ice
- Ocean
- Sea
- Gulf, Bay
- Strait, Fjord
- Lagoon
- Bank
- Seamount
- Tablemount
- Ridge
- Shelf
- Basin
- Escarpment, Sea Scarp
- Fracture
- Trench, Abyss
- National Park, Reserve
- Point of Interest
- Recreation Site
- Cave, Cavern
- Historic Site
- Ruins
- Wall, Walls
- Church, Abbey
- Temple
- Scientific Station
- Airport
- Port
- Lighthouse
- Mine
- Tunnel
- Dam, Bridge

Bingen	10	Dg	49.58N	7.54 E
Bingham [Me.-U.S.]	44	Mc	45.03N	69.53W
Bingham [N.M.-U.S.]	45	Cj	33.56N	106.17W
Binghamton	43	Lc	42.06N	75.55W
Bin Ghunaymah, Jabal-	30	If	25.00N	15.30 E
Bing Inlet	44	Gc	45.13N	80.30W
Bingöl	23	Fb	38.53N	40.29 E
Bingöl Dağları	24	Ic	39.20N	41.20 E
Binhai (Dongkan)	27	Ke	34.00N	119.52 E
Binjai	26	Cf	3.36N	98.30 E
Binkiliç	15	Lh	41.25N	28.11 E
Binongko, Pulau-	26	Hh	5.57S	124.02 E
Bin Qirdān	32	Jc	33.08N	11.13 E
Bintan, Pulau-	26	Df	1.05N	104.30 E
Bintuhan	26	Dg	4.48S	103.22 E
Bintulu	26	Ff	3.10N	113.02 E
Bin Walīd, Jabal-	14	En	36.52N	10.47 E
Binxian	28	Df	37.22N	117.57 E
Binxian (Binzhou) [China]	27	Mb	45.45N	127.27 E
Binxian (Binzhou) [China]	27	Id	35.02N	108.06 E
Binzhou → Binxian [China]	27	Id	35.02N	108.06 E
Binzhou → Binxian [China]	27	Mb	45.45N	127.27 E
Bioara	25	Fd	23.58N	76.55 E
Biobio	56	Fe	36.49S	73.10W
Bio Bio [2]	56	Fe	37.45S	72.00W
Biograd na Moru	14	Jg	43.57N	15.27 E
Bioko [3]	34	Ge	3.00N	8.40 E
Bioko	30	Hh	4.30N	9.30 E
Biokovo	14	Lg	43.18N	17.02 E
Biorra/Birr	9	Fh	53.05N	7.54W
Bippen	12	Jb	52.35N	7.44 E
Bīr	25	Fe	18.59N	75.46 E
Bira	20	Ig	49.03N	132.27 E
Bi'r Abraq	33	Fe	23.35N	34.48 E
Bi'r Abū al Ḩuşayn	33	Ee	22.53N	29.55 E
Bi'r Abū Gharādiq	24	Cg	30.06N	28.06 E
Bi'r Abū Hashim	33	Fe	23.42N	34.08 E
Bi'r Abū Minqat	33	Ed	26.30N	27.35 E
Bīrah Kaprah	24	Kd	36.52N	44.01 E
Birāk	33	Bd	27.39N	14.17 E
Birakan	20	Ig	49.02N	131.40 E
Bi'r al 'Abd	24	Eg	31.22N	32.58 E
Bi'r al Ghuzaylah	33	Bd	28.50N	10.45 E
Bi'r al Ḩakīm	33	Dc	31.36N	23.29 E
Bi'r al Hasa	35	Fa	22.58N	35.40 E
Bi'r al Khamsah	33	Ec	30.57N	25.46 E
Bi'r 'Allāq	33	Bc	31.10N	11.55 E
Bi'r al Mushayqīq	32	Jc	30.53N	10.18 E
Bi'r al Qurayyah	24	Ei	26.22N	33.01 E
Bi'r al Uzam	33	Dc	31.46N	23.59 E
Bi'r al Wa'r	31	Be	22.39N	14.10 E
Bi'r al Washkah	33	Cd	28.52N	15.35 E
Birao	31	Jg	10.17N	22.47 E
Bi'r 'Arjā'	24	Ij	25.17N	40.58 E
Bi'r ar Rāh	24	If	33.27N	40.25 E
Bi'r ar Rūmān	32	Ic	32.31N	8.21 E
Birātnagar	25	Hc	26.29N	87.17 E
Biratori	28	Qc	42.35N	142.12 E
Bi'r Baylī	33	Ec	30.32N	25.08 E
Bi'r Bayzaḩ	24	Fj	25.10N	34.05 E
Bi'r Bū Ḩawsh	33	Dd	24.34N	22.07 E
Bi'r Bū Zurayyq	33	Dd	24.32N	22.38 E
Bîrca	15	Gf	43.58N	23.37 E
Birch	42	Ge	58.28N	112.17W
Birch Mountains	42	Ge	57.20N	112.55W
Bird	42	Ie	56.30N	94.14W
Bi'r Dibs	33	Ee	22.12N	29.32 E
Bird Island [Gren.]	51p	Bb	12.12N	61.33W
Bird Island [Sey.]	37b	Ca	3.43S	55.12 E
Birdsville	59	He	25.54S	139.22 E
Birdum	59	Gc	15.39S	133.13 E
Birecik	24	Gd	37.02N	37.58 E
Bir El Ater	32	Ic	34.44N	8.03 E
Bīr el Mrabba'ab	24	He	34.30N	39.07 E
Bir Enzarán	32	Ee	23.53N	14.32W
Bireuen	26	Ce	5.12N	96.41 E
Bi'r Fajr	24	Gh	28.54N	37.54 E
Bi'r Fu'ād	33	Ec	30.27N	26.27 E
Bir Gandús	32	De	21.36N	16.30W
Bīrganj	25	Gc	27.00N	84.52 E
Bir Gara	35	Bc	13.11N	15.58 E
Bir-Ghbalou	13	Ph	36.16N	3.35 E
Birgi	15	Lk	38.15N	28.05 E
Bi'r Ḩasanah	24	Eg	30.28N	33.47 E
Bi'r Ḩaymir	24	Hj	24.41N	38.04 E
Bi'r Ḩulayyī	24	Fj	24.06N	34.32 E
Birigui	55	Ge	21.18S	50.19W
Biriliussy	20	Ee	57.07N	90.42 E
Bīrīn	24	Ge	35.01N	36.40 E
Birine	13	Pi	35.37N	3.13 E
Bīrjand	22	Hf	32.53N	59.13 E
Birjusa	21	Ld	57.43N	95.24 E
Birjusinsk	20	Ee	55.55N	97.55 E
Bi'r Karawayn	24	Ci	27.06N	28.32 E
Birkeland	7	Bg	58.20N	8.14 E
Birkenfeld	10	Dg	49.39N	7.11 E
Birkenhead	9	Jh	53.24N	3.02W
Birkerød	8	Ei	55.50N	12.26 E
Bi'r Khālidah	24	Bg	30.50N	27.15 E
Birksgate Range	59	Fe	27.10S	129.45 E
Bîrlad	15	Kc	46.14N	27.40 E
Bîrlad	15	Kc	45.36N	27.31 E
Bir Lehlú	32	Fd	26.21N	9.34W
Bi'r Ma'sūr	24	Fj	24.31N	34.12 E
Birmingham [Al.-U.S.]	39	Kf	33.31N	86.49W
Birmingham [Eng.-U.K.]	6	Fe	52.30N	1.50W
Bi'r Misāḩah	33	Ee	22.12N	27.57 E
Bi'r Murr	33	Fe	23.21N	30.05 E
Bi'r Murrah	33	Fe	22.32N	33.54 E
Bi'r Nāhid	33	Ec	30.13N	28.52 E
Bi'r Naşīf	23	Ee	24.51N	39.11 E
Birnie Atoll	57	Je	3.35S	171.31W
Birnin Gaouré	34	Fc	13.05N	2.54 E
Birnin Gwari	34	Gc	11.02N	6.47 E
Birnin Kebbi	34	Fc	12.28N	4.12 E
Birni Nkonni	31	Hg	13.48N	5.15 E
Birnin Kudu	34	Gc	11.27N	9.30 E
Birni Yauri	34	Fc	10.47N	4.49 E
Bi'r Nukhaylah	24	Dj	24.01N	30.52 E
Birobidžan	22	Pe	48.48N	132.57 E
Birr/Biorra	9	Fh	53.05N	7.54W
Birs	14	Bc	47.26N	7.33 E
Bi'r Safājah	33	Fd	26.50N	34.54 E
Bi'r Sayyālah	24	Ei	26.07N	33.56 E
Bi'r Shalatayn	33	Ge	23.08N	35.36 E
Birsk	19	Fd	55.25N	55.32 E
Birštonas	8	Kj	54.33N	24.07 E
Bi'r Ţarfāwī	33	Ee	22.55N	28.53 E
Biru	27	Fe	31.30N	93.50 E
Bi'r Umm al 'Abbās	24	Ei	26.57N	32.34 E
Bi'r Umm Fawākhīr	24	Ei	26.01N	33.38 E
Bi'r Umm Sa'īd	24	Eh	29.40N	33.34 E
Bi'r Umm Ţunayḑibah	24	Ej	25.16N	33.06 E
Biruni	19	Gg	41.42N	60.45 E
Biržai/Biržaj	19	Cd	56.12N	24.48 E
Biržaj/Biržai	19	Cd	56.12N	24.48 E
Bîrzava	15	Ec	46.07N	21.59 E
Bîrzava	15	Dd	45.16N	20.49 E
Birzebbuga	14	Io	35.49N	14.32 E
Bisa, Pulau-	26	Ig	1.15S	127.28 E
Bisaccia	14	Ji	41.01N	15.22 E
Bisacquino	14	Hm	37.42N	13.15 E
Bisbee	43	Fe	31.27N	109.55W
Biscarrosse, Étang de-	11	Ej	44.21N	1.10W
Biscay, Bay of- (EN) = Gascogne, Golfe de-	5	Fg	44.00N	4.00W
Bisceglie	14	Ki	41.14N	16.30 E
Bischofslofen	10	Jc	47.25N	13.13 E
Bischofswerda/Biskopicy	10	Ke	51.07N	14.11 E
Biscoe Islands	66	Qe	66.00S	66.30W
Biscotasi Lake	44	Fb	47.20N	82.05W
Biscucuy	50	Bh	9.22N	69.59W
Bisert	17	Hh	56.39N	57.59 E
Bisert	19	Fd	56.52N	59.03 E
Biševiski Kanal	14	Kg	43.00N	16.03 E
Biševo	14	Kh	42.59N	16.01 E
Bisha	35	Fb	15.28N	37.33 E
Bishārah	33	De	22.58N	22.39 E
Bishārīyīn, Barq al-	35	Eb	19.26N	32.22 E
Bishnupur	25	Hd	23.05N	87.19 E
Bishop	43	Dd	37.22N	118.24W
Bishop Auckland	9	Lg	54.40N	1.40W
Bishop Rock	9	Gl	49.53N	6.25W
Bishop's Falls	42	Lg	49.01N	55.30W
Bishop's Stortford	9	Nj	51.53N	0.09 E
Bishop's Waltham	12	Ad	50.57N	1.13W
Bishrī, Jabal-	24	He	35.20N	39.20 E
Bishui	27	La	52.07N	123.43 E
Biskopicy/Bischofswerda	10	Ke	51.07N	14.11 E
Biskra	31	He	34.51N	5.44 E
Biskra [3]	32	Ic	34.40N	6.00 E
Biskupiec	10	Qc	53.52N	20.27 E
Bislig	26	Ie	8.13N	126.19 E
Bismarck	39	Ie	46.48N	100.47W
Bismarck, Kap-	41	Kc	76.40N	18.40W
Bismarck Archipelago	57	Fe	5.00S	150.00 E
Bismarck Sea	60	Dh	4.00S	147.30 E
Bismark Range	60	Ci	5.30S	144.45 E
Bismil	24	Id	37.51N	40.40 E
Bison	45	Ed	45.31N	102.28W
Bīsotūn	24	Le	34.23N	47.26 E
Bispfors	8	Ga	63.02N	16.37 E
Bissau	31	Fg	11.51N	15.35W
Bissaula	34	Hd	7.01N	10.27 E
Bissett	44	Hb	46.13N	78.02W
Bisson, Banc du-	37	Hb	12.00S	46.25 E
Bistcho Lake	42	Fe	59.45N	118.50W
Bistineau, Lake-	45	Jj	32.25N	93.22W
Bistra	15	Fd	45.29N	22.11 E
Bistra	15	Dh	41.37N	20.44 E
Bistreţ	15	Gf	43.54N	23.30 E
Bistrica	15	Dg	42.09N	20.59 E
Bistrica	15	Cf	43.28N	19.42 E
Bistriţa	15	Hb	47.08N	24.29 E
Bistriţa [Rom.]	15	Jc	46.30N	26.57 E
Bistriţa [Rom.]	15	Hb	47.04N	24.25 E
Bistriţa-Năsăud [2]	15	Hb	47.05N	24.35 E
Bitam	36	Bb	2.05N	11.29 E
Bitam	13	Ri	35.15N	5.11 E
Bitburg	10	Cg	49.58N	6.32 E
Bitche	11	Ne	49.03N	7.26 E
Bitéa	35	Cc	13.11N	20.10 E
Bithia	14	Cl	38.55N	8.52 E
Bithynia	15	Mi	40.20N	29.30 E
Bitjug	16	Kd	50.37N	39.55 E
Bitkine	35	Bc	11.59N	18.13 E
Bitlis	23	Fb	38.22N	42.06 E
Bitola	6	Ig	41.02N	21.20 E
Bitonto	14	Ki	41.06N	16.41 E
Bitterfeld	10	Ie	51.37N	12.19 E
Bitterfontein	31	Il	31.00S	18.32 E
Bitterroot Range	38	He	47.06N	115.10W
Bitterroot River	46	Hc	46.52N	114.06W
Bitti	14	Dj	40.29N	9.23 E
Bitung	26	If	1.27N	125.11 E
Biu	31	Ig	10.37N	12.12 E
Bivolari	15	Kb	47.32N	27.26 E
Bivolu, Vîrful-	15	Ib	47.15N	25.56 E
Bivona	14	Hm	37.37N	13.26 E
Biwa-ko	28	Ng	35.13N	136.05 E
Bixad [Rom.]	15	Ic	46.06N	25.52 E
Bixad [Rom.]	15	Gb	47.56N	23.24 E
Bixby	45	Ii	35.57N	95.53W
Biyalā	24	Dg	31.10N	31.13 E
Biyang	27	Je	32.40N	113.21 E
Biyārjomand	24	Pd	36.06N	55.53 E
Bižbuljak	17	Gj	53.43N	54.16 E
Biže	18	Kb	45.10N	77.58 E
Bizen	28	Mg	34.44N	134.09 E
Bizerte (EN) = Banzart	31	He	37.17N	9.52 E
Bjala	15	If	43.27N	25.44 E
Bjala Slatina	15	Gf	43.28N	23.56 E
Bjargtangar	5	Db	65.30N	24.32W
Bjärna/Perniö	7	Ff	60.12N	23.08 E
Bjärnum	8	Eh	56.17N	13.42 E
Bjästa	8	Ha	63.12N	18.30 E
Bjelašnica [Yugo.]	14	Mg	43.43N	18.09 E
Bjelašnica [Yugo.]	14	Mh	42.51N	18.09 E
Bjelašnica [Yugo.]	14	Mg	43.09N	18.23 E
Bjelolasica	14	Ie	45.16N	14.58 E
Bjelovar	14	Ke	45.54N	16.51 E
Bjerkvik	7	Db	68.33N	17.34 E
Bjerringbro	8	Ch	56.23N	9.40 E
Bjervamoen	8	Ce	59.25N	9.04 E
Bjeshkët e Nemuna	15	Cg	42.30N	19.50 E
Björdo	8	Fd	60.28N	14.42 E
Bjørkelangen	8	De	59.53N	11.34 E
Björkfors	8	Ff	58.01N	15.54 E
Björklinge	8	Gd	60.02N	17.33 E
Björkö	7	Eg	59.55N	19.00 E
Björna	7	Ee	63.34N	18.33 E
Bjørnafjorden	8	Ad	60.05N	5.20 E
Björneborg	8	Fe	59.15N	14.15 E
Björneborg/Pori	6	Ic	61.29N	21.47 E
Bjorne Peninsula	42	Ia	77.30N	87.00W
Bjornesfjorden	8	Bd	60.10N	7.40 E
Bjørnevatn	7	Gb	69.40N	30.00 E
Bjørnøya	67	Kd	74.30N	19.00 E
Björnöya = Bear Island (EN)	5	Ha	74.30N	19.00 E
Bjurholm	7	Ee	63.56N	19.13 E
Bjuröklubb	7	Ed	64.28N	21.35 E
Bjuv	8	Eh	56.05N	12.54 E
Bla	34	Dc	12.56N	5.45W
Blace	15	Ef	43.18N	21.18 E
Blackall	58	Gf	24.25S	145.28 E
Black Bank (EN) = Zwarte Bank	12	Fa	53.15N	3.55 E
Black Bay	45	Lb	48.40N	88.30W
Blackburn	9	Kh	53.45N	2.29W
Blackburn, Mount-	38	Ec	61.44N	143.26W
Black Butte Lake	46	Dg	39.45N	122.20W
Black Coast	66	Qf	71.45S	62.00W
Blackdown Hills	9	Jk	50.57N	3.09W
Blackduck	45	Ic	47.44N	94.33W
Blackfoot	43	Ec	43.11N	112.20W
Blackfoot Reservoir	46	Je	42.55N	111.35W
Black Forest (EN) = Schwarzwald	5	Gf	48.00N	8.15 E
Black Head	9	Hk	50.01N	5.03W
Black Hills	38	Ie	44.00N	104.00W
Black Isle	9	Id	57.35N	4.20W
Black Lake	42	Ge	59.11N	105.20W
Blackman's	51q	Ab	13.11N	59.32W
Black Mesa	46	Jh	36.35N	110.20W
Blackmoor	9	Ik	50.23N	4.50W
Black Mountain	43	Kd	36.54N	82.54W
Black Mountains [U.S.]	46	Hi	35.30N	114.30W
Black Mountains [Wales-U.K.]	9	Jj	51.57N	3.08W
Blackpool	9	Jh	53.50N	3.03W
Black Range	43	Fe	33.20N	107.50W
Black River	49	Id	18.01N	77.51W
Black River [Az.-U.S.]	46	Jj	33.44N	110.13W
Black River [Mi.-U.S.]	44	Fd	43.00N	82.25W
Black River [N.Y.-U.S.]	44	Id	43.59N	76.04W
Black River [U.S.]	45	Ki	35.38N	91.19W
Black River [Wi.-U.S.]	45	Ke	43.57N	91.22W
Black River (EN) = Babian Jiang	21	Mg	20.17N	106.34 E
Black River (EN) = Da, Sông-	21	Mg	20.17N	106.34 E
Black River Falls	45	Kd	44.16N	90.52W
Black Rock	56	Lh	53.39S	41.48W
Black Rock [Ire.]	9	Cg	54.05N	10.20W
Black Rock [Phil.]	26	Ge	8.48N	119.50 E
Black Rock Desert	43	Dc	41.10N	119.00W
Blacksburg	44	Gg	37.15N	80.25W
Black Sea (EN) = Černoje More	5	Jg	43.00N	35.00 E
Black Sea (EN) = Černo More	5	Jg	43.00N	35.00 E
Black Sea (EN) = Karadeniz	5	Jg	43.00N	35.00 E
Black Sea (EN) = Neagră, Marea-	5	Jg	43.00N	35.00 E
Blacksod Bay/Cuan an Fhóid Duibh	9	Dg	54.08N	10.00W
Blackstairs Mountains/Na Staighrí Dubha	9	Gi	52.33N	6.49W
Blackstone	44	Hg	37.04N	78.01W
Blackville	44	Ob	46.47N	65.54W
Black Volta	30	Gh	8.38N	1.30W
Black Volta (EN) = Volta Noire	30	Gh	8.38N	1.30W
Black Volta (EN) = Volta Noire [3]	34	Ec	12.30N	4.00W
Blackwater	12	Cc	51.43N	0.28 E
Blackwater/An Abhainn Dubh	9	Gh	53.39N	6.43W
Blackwater/An Abhainn Mhór [Ire.]	9	Fj	51.51N	7.50W
Blackwater/An Abhainn Mhór [N.Ire.-U.K.]	9	Gg	54.30N	6.35W
Blackwell	45	Hh	36.48N	97.17W
Blackwood River	59	Df	34.35S	115.02 E
Blagnac	11	Hk	43.38N	1.24 E
Blagodarny	16	Mg	45.04N	43.24 E
Blagojevgrad	15	Gg	42.01N	23.06 E
Blagojevgrad [2]	15	Gh	41.45N	23.25 E
Blagoveščenka	20	Cf	52.50N	79.55 E
Blagoveščensk [R.S.F.S.R.]	19	Fd	55.01N	55.59 E
Blagoveščensk [R.S.F.S.R.]	22	Od	50.17N	127.32 E
Blåhø	8	Cb	62.45N	9.19 E
Blain	11	Eg	47.29N	1.45W
Blaine [Mn.-U.S.]	45	Jd	45.11N	93.14W
Blaine [Wa.-U.S.]	46	Db	48.59N	122.44W
Blair	45	Hf	41.33N	96.08W
Blair Athol	59	Jd	22.42S	147.33 E
Blairgowrie	9	Je	56.36N	3.21W
Blairmore	46	Hb	49.36N	114.26W
Blaise	11	Kf	48.38N	4.43 E
Blaj	15	Gc	46.11N	23.55 E
Blake Basin (EN)	43	Mf	29.00N	76.00W
Blakely	44	Ej	31.23N	84.56W
Blakeney Point	9	Ni	52.59N	1.00 E
Blake Plateau (EN)	38	Lf	31.00N	79.00W
Blake Ridge (EN)	38	Lg	29.00N	73.30W
Blakstad	7	Bg	58.30N	8.39 E
Blanc, Cape- (EN) = Abyaḑ, Ra's al-	30	He	37.20N	9.50 E
Blanc, Cape- (EN) = Nouâdhibou, Râs-	30	Ff	20.46N	17.03W
Blanc, Lac-	44	Kb	47.45N	73.12W
Blanc, Mont-	5	Gf	45.50N	6.52 E
Blanca, Bahía-	52	Ji	38.55S	62.10W
Blanca, Cerro-	49	Gi	8.40N	80.35W
Blanca, Cordillera-	54	Ce	9.10S	77.35W
Blanca, Costa-	13	Lg	37.38N	0.40W
Blanca, Isla-	48	Pg	21.24N	86.50W
Blanca, Punta-	48	Bc	29.05N	114.45W
Blancagrande	55	Bm	36.32S	60.53W
Blanca Peak [Co.-U.S.]	43	Fd	37.34N	105.29W
Blanca Peak [U.S.]	38	If	37.35N	105.29W
Blanche, Lake- [Austl.]	59	Ed	22.25S	123.15 E
Blanche, Lake- [Austl.]	59	He	29.15S	139.40 E
Blanche, Point-	51b	Ac	18.00N	63.03W
Blanche Channel	63a	Cc	8.30S	157.30 E
Blanc-Nez, Cap-	12	Dd	50.56N	1.42 E
Blanco, Cabo- [C.R.]	47	Gg	9.33N	85.06W
Blanco, Cabo- [Sp.]	13	Oe	39.22N	2.46 E
Blanco, Cape-	43	Cc	42.50N	124.34W
Blanco, Cerro-	48	Fe	25.43N	107.39W
Blanco, Río-	54	Ff	12.30S	64.18W
Blanco del Sur, Cayo-	49	Gb	22.02N	81.24W
Blanda	7a	Bb	65.39N	20.18W
Blanding	46	Kh	37.37N	109.29W
Blanes	13	Oc	41.41N	2.48 E
Blangy-le-Château	12	Ce	49.14N	0.17 E
Blangy-sur-Bresle	11	He	49.56N	1.38 E
Blanice [Czech.]	10	Kg	49.48N	14.58 E
Blanice [Czech.]	10	Kg	49.17N	14.09 E
Blankaholm	8	Gg	57.35N	16.31 E
Blankenberge	11	Jc	51.19N	3.08 E
Blankenheim	12	Id	50.26N	6.39 E
Blanquilla, Isla-	54	Fa	11.51N	64.37W
Blanquillo	55	Ek	32.55S	55.40W
Blansko	10	Mg	49.22N	16.39 E
Blantyre	31	Ki	15.47S	35.00 E
Blantyre-Limbe	36	Gf	15.49S	35.03 E
Blåskavlen	8	Bd	60.58N	7.18 E
Błaszki	10	Oe	51.39N	18.27 E
Blatná	10	Jg	49.26N	13.53 E
Blato	14	Kh	42.56N	16.48 E
Blåvands Huk	5	Gd	55.33N	8.05 E
Blavet [Fr.]	11	Cf	48.13N	3.10W
Blavet [Fr.]	11	Cg	47.46N	3.18W
Blaye	11	Fi	45.08N	0.40W
Blaye-les-Mines	11	Ij	44.01N	2.08 E
Bled	14	Id	46.22N	14.08 E
Blefjell	8	Ce	59.48N	9.10 E
Bleialf	12	Id	50.14N	6.17 E
Blekinge [2]	7	Dh	56.20N	15.20 E
Blenheim	58	Ii	41.31S	173.57 E
Bletchley	9	Mj	52.00N	0.46W
Bleus, Monts-	36	Fb	1.30N	30.30 E
Blhārshāh	25	Fe	19.50N	79.22 E
Blida [3]	32	Hb	36.35N	2.30 E
Blida	31	He	36.34N	2.55 E
Blidö	8	He	59.35N	18.55 E
Blidsberg	8	Eg	57.56N	13.29 E
Blies	12	Je	49.07N	7.04 E
Blieskastel	12	Je	49.14N	7.15 E
Bligh Water	63d	Ab	17.00S	178.00 E
Blind River	42	Jg	46.10N	82.58W
Blitar	26	Fh	8.06S	112.09 E
Blitta	34	Fd	8.19N	0.59 E
Block Island	44	Le	41.11N	71.35W
Bloemfontein	31	Jk	29.12S	26.07 E
Bloemhof	37	De	27.38S	25.32 E
Blois	11	Hg	47.35N	1.20 E
Blokhus	8	Cg	57.15N	9.35 E
Blomberg	12	Lc	51.56N	9.05 E
Blönduós	7a	Bb	65.40N	20.18W
Bloody Foreland/Cnoc Fola	9	Ef	55.09N	8.17W
Bloomfield [Ia.-U.S.]	45	Jf	40.45N	92.25W
Bloomfield [In.-U.S.]	44	Df	39.01N	86.56W
Bloomington [Il.-U.S.]	43	Jc	40.29N	88.59W
Bloomington [In.-U.S.]	43	Jd	39.10N	86.32W
Bloomington [Mn.-U.S.]	45	Jd	44.50N	93.17W
Bloomsburg	44	Ie	41.01N	76.27W
Blosseville Kyst	41	Je	68.45N	27.25W
Blötberget	8	Fd	60.07N	15.04 E
Blountstown	44	Ej	30.29N	85.03W
Bludenz	14	Dc	47.09N	9.49 E
Blue Earth	45	Ie	43.38N	94.06W
Bluefield	43	Kd	37.14N	81.17W
Bluefields	39	Kh	12.00N	83.45W
Bluefields, Bahía de-	49	Fg	12.02N	83.44W
Blue Mesa Reservoir	45	Cg	38.28N	107.15W
Blue Mountain	44	Ie	40.15N	77.30W
Blue Mountain [Or.-U.S.]	46	Ge	42.25N	117.50W
Blue Mountain [U.S.]	45	Ii	34.41N	94.03W
Blue Mountain Lake	44	Jd	43.53N	74.26W
Blue Mountain Pass	46	Ge	42.18N	117.45W
Blue Mountain Peak	47	Ie	18.03N	76.35W
Blue Mountains [Austl.]	59	Kf	33.35S	150.15 E
Blue Mountains [U.S.]	43	Ec	44.35N	118.25W
Blue Mud Bay	59	Hb	13.25S	135.55 E
Blue Nile (EN) = Abay	30	Kg	15.38N	32.31 E
Blue Nile (EN) = Azraq, Al Baḩr al-	30	Kg	15.38N	32.31 E
Bluenose Lake	42	Fc	68.00N	121.00W
Blue Ridge	44	Eh	34.52N	84.20W
Blue Ridge	38	Kf	37.00N	82.00W
Blue Stack/Na Cruacha	9	Eg	54.45N	8.06W
Bluestone Lake	44	Gg	37.30N	80.50W
Bluff [N.Z.]	61	Ci	46.36S	168.21 E
Bluff [Ut.-U.S.]	46	Kh	37.17N	109.33W
Bluff Point	59	Ce	27.50S	114.05 E
Bluffton	44	Ee	40.44N	85.11W
Blumberg	10	Ei	47.50N	8.32 E
Blumenau	56	Kc	26.56S	49.03W
Blyth	12	Db	52.19N	1.41 E
Blyth	9	Lf	55.07N	1.30W
Blythe	43	Ee	33.37N	114.36W
Blytheville	43	Jd	35.56N	89.55W
Bø	7	Bg	59.25N	9.04 E
Bo	31	Fh	7.58N	11.45W
Boa	34	Dd	8.26N	7.10W
Boac	26	Hd	12.28N	122.28 E
Boaco [3]	49	Eg	12.35N	85.25W
Boaco	49	Eg	12.28N	85.40W
Boa Esperança	55	Je	21.05S	45.34W
Boa Esperança, Reprêsa-	54	Je	6.50S	44.00W
Boa Esperançao, Serra da-	55	Je	20.57S	45.40W
Bo'ai	28	Bg	35.10N	113.03 E
Boal	13	Fa	43.26N	6.49W
Boali	35	Be	4.48N	18.07 E
Boano, Pulau-	26	Ig	2.56S	127.56 E
Boardman	46	Fd	45.51N	119.43W
Boa Sentença, Serra da-	55	Ed	19.13S	57.33W
Boa Vista	30	Eg	16.05N	22.50W
Boa Vista [Braz.]	55	Ec	17.51S	54.13W
Boa Vista [Braz.]	55	Ia	12.40S	46.51W
Boa Vista [Braz.]	53	Je	2.49N	60.40W
Bobai	27	Ig	22.15N	109.58 E
Bobali, Cerros de-	49	Ki	8.53N	73.28W
Bobalí, Cerros de-	49	Ki	8.53N	73.28W
Bobbio	14	Df	44.46N	9.23 E
Bobigny	11	If	48.54N	2.27 E
Bobo Dioulasso	31	Gg	11.12N	4.18W
Bobojod, Gora-	18	Hd	40.50N	70.20 E
Bobolice	10	Mc	53.57N	16.36 E
Bobonong	37	Dd	21.58S	28.25 E
Bobovdol	15	Fg	42.22N	23.00 E
Bóbr	10	Ld	52.04N	15.04 E
Bobrik	16	Ec	52.08N	26.48 E
Bobrinec	16	He	48.04N	32.09 E
Bobrka	10	Ug	49.34N	24.20 E
Bobrov	19	Ee	51.06N	40.01 E
Bobrovica	16	Gd	50.43N	31.28 E
Bobrowniki	10	Tc	53.08N	23.50 E
Bobrujsk	6	Ie	53.09N	29.15 E
Bobures	54	Db	9.15N	71.11W
Boby, Pic-	37	Hd	22.12S	46.55 E
Boca del Ric	48	Ee	25.20N	108.25W
Boca de Pozo	50	Dg	11.00N	64.23W
Boca do Acre	53	Jf	8.45S	67.23W
Bocage, Cap-	63b	Be	21.12S	165.37 E
Bocâina	55	Db	15.16S	56.45W
Bocaiúva	55	Kc	17.07S	43.49W
Bocajá	55	Ef	22.45S	55.13W
Bocaranga	35	Bd	6.59N	15.39 E
Boca Raton	43	Kf	26.21N	80.05W
Bocas del Toro	47	Hg	9.20N	82.15W
Bocas del Toro [3]	49	Fi	8.50N	82.10W
Bocas del Toro, Archipiélago de-	49	Fi	9.20N	82.10W
Bocay	49	Ef	14.19N	85.10W
Bochaine	11	Lj	44.20N	5.50 E
Bochnia	10	Qg	49.58N	20.26 E
Bocholt [Bel.]	12	Hc	51.10N	5.35 E
Bocholt [F.R.G.]	10	Ce	51.50N	6.36 E
Bochum	10	De	51.29N	7.13 E
Bocognano	11a	Ba	42.05N	9.04 E
Bocoio	36	Be	12.28S	14.08 E
Boconó	49	Li	9.15N	70.16W
Bocşa	15	Ed	45.23N	21.47 E
Boda	35	Be	4.19N	17.28 E
Boda	8	Fc	61.01N	15.13 E
Böda	8	Gg	57.15N	17.03 E
Bodafors	8	Fg	57.30N	14.42 E
Bodajbo	22	Nd	57.51N	114.10 E
Bodalangi	36	Db	3.14N	22.14 E
Bode	10	Hd	52.01N	11.12 E
Bödefeld-Freiheit, Schmallenberg-	12	Kc	51.15N	8.24 E
Bodegraven	12	Gb	52.06N	4.44 E
Bodélé	30	Ig	16.30N	17.30 E
Boden	6	Ib	65.50N	21.42 E
Bodenheim	12	Ke	49.56N	8.18 E
Bodensee = Constance, Lake- (EN)	5	Gf	47.35N	9.25 E
Boderg, Lough-	9	Fh	53.52N	8.00W
Bodmin	9	Ik	50.29N	4.43W
Bodmin Moor	9	Ik	50.35N	4.40W
Bodø	6	Hb	67.17N	14.23 E
Bodoquena	55	De	20.12S	56.48W
Bodoquena, Serra da-	54	Gh	21.00S	56.50W
Bodrog	10	Rh	48.07N	21.25 E
Bodrogköz	10	Rh	48.15N	21.45 E
Bodrum	23	Cb	37.02N	27.06 E
Bodrum Yarimadasi	15	Kl	37.05N	27.30 E
Bodva	10	Qh	48.12N	20.47 E
Boën	11	Ji	45.44N	4.00 E
Boende	31	Ji	0.13S	20.52 E
Boeo, Capo- (Lilibeo, Capo-)	14	Gm	37.34N	12.41 E
Boerne	45	Gl	29.47N	98.44W
Boesmanland = Bushmanland (EN)	37	Be	29.30S	19.00 E
Boffa	34	Cc	10.10N	14.02W
Boga	15	Cg	42.24N	19.38 E
Bogale	25	Je	16.17N	95.24 E
Bogalusa	45	Lk	30.47N	89.52W
Bogandé	34	Ec	12.59N	0.08W
Bogangolo	35	Bd	5.34N	18.15 E
Bogatić	15	Ce	44.51N	19.29 E
Bogatynia	10	Kf	50.55N	14.59 E
Boğazkale	24	Fb	40.01N	34.35 E
Boğazlıyan	24	Fc	39.12N	35.15 E
Bogbonga	36	Cb	1.35N	19.25 E

Index Symbols

- [1] Independent Nation
- [2] State, Region
- [3] District, County
- [4] Municipality
- [5] Colony, Dependency
- Continent
- Physical Region
- Historical or Cultural Region
- Mount, Mountain
- Volcano
- Hill
- Mountains, Mountain Range
- Hills, Escarpment
- Plateau, Upland
- Pass, Gap
- Plain, Lowland
- Delta
- Salt Flat
- Valley, Canyon
- Crater, Cave
- Karst Features
- Depression
- Polder
- Desert, Dunes
- Forest, Woods
- Heath, Steppe
- Oasis
- Cape, Point
- Coast, Beach
- Cliff
- Peninsula
- Isthmus
- Sandbank
- Island
- Atoll
- Rock, Reef
- Islands, Archipelago
- Rocks, Reefs
- Coral Reef
- Well, Spring
- Geyser
- River, Stream
- Waterfall Rapids
- River Mouth, Estuary
- Lake
- Salt Lake
- Intermittent Lake
- Reservoir
- Swamp, Pond
- Canal
- Glacier
- Ice Shelf, Pack Ice
- Ocean
- Sea
- Gulf, Bay
- Strait, Fjord
- Lagoon
- Bank
- Seamount
- Tablemount
- Ridge
- Shelf
- Basin
- Escarpment, Sea Scarp
- Fracture
- Trench, Abyss
- National Park, Reserve
- Point of Interest
- Recreation Site
- Cave, Cavern
- Historic Site
- Ruins
- Wall, Walls
- Church, Abbey
- Temple
- Scientific Station
- Airport
- Port
- Lighthouse
- Mine
- Tunnel
- Dam, Bridge

Bogcang Zangbo 27 Ee 31.56N 87.24 E
Bogda Feng 27 Ec 43.45N 88.32 E
Bogdan 15 Hg 42.37N 24.28 E
Bogdanovka 16 Mi 41.15N 43.36 E
Bogda Shan 21 Ke 43.35N 90.00 E
Bogen 7 Db 68.32N 17.00 E
Bogenfels 37 Be 27.23S 15.22 E
Bogense 8 Di 55.34N 10.06 E
Boggeragh Mountains/An Bhograch 9 Ei 52.05N 9.00W
Boggy Peak 51d Bb 17.03N 61.51W
Boghar 13 Oi 35.55N 2.43 E
Boghni 13 Ph 36.32N 3.57 E
Bogia 60 Ch 4.16S 144.58 E
Bognor Regis 12 Bd 50.47N 0.39W
Bogny-sur-Meuse 12 Ge 49.54N 4.43 E
Bogoduhov 16 Id 50.12N 35.31 E
Bogomila 15 Eh 41.36N 21.28 E
Bogor 22 Mj 6.35S 106.47 E
Bogoridick 19 De 53.50N 38.08 E
Bogorodčany 10 Uh 48.45N 24.40 E
Bogorodsk 7 Kh 56.09N 43.32 E
Bogorodskoje [R.S.F.S.R.] 7 Mh 57.51N 50.48 E
Bogorodskoje [R.S.F.S.R.] 20 Jf 52.22N 140.30 E
Bogotá 53 Ie 4.36N 74.05W
Bogotol 20 De 56.17N 89.43 E
Bogøy 7 Dc 67.54N 15.11 E
Bogra 25 Hd 24.51N 89.22 E
Bogučany 20 Ee 58.23N 97.39 E
Bogučar 16 Le 49.57N 40.33 E
Bogué 32 Ef 16.36N 14.15W
Boguševsk 7 Hi 54.50N 30.13 E
Boguslav 19 Df 49.33N 30.54 E
Bo Hai=Chihli, Gulf of- (EN) 21 Nf 38.30N 120.00 E
Bohai Haixia 27 Ld 38.00N 121.30 E
Bohain-en-Vermandois 12 Fe 49.59N 3.27 E
Bohemia (EN)=Čechy 5 Hf 50.00N 14.30 E
Bohemia (EN)=Čechy 10 Kf 50.00N 14.30 E
Bohemian Forest (EN)= Böhmerwald 5 Hf 49.00N 13.30 E
Bohemian Forest (EN)= Český Les 10 Ig 49.50N 12.30 E
Bohemian Forest (EN)= Oberpfälzer Wald 10 Ig 49.50N 12.30 E
Bohemian Forest (EN)= Šumava 5 Hf 49.00N 13.30 E
Bohicon 34 Fd 7.12N 2.04 E
Böhmerwald=Bohemian Forest (EN) 5 Hf 49.00N 13.30 E
Bohmte 12 Kb 52.22N 8.19 E
Bohodoyou 34 Dd 9.46N 9.04W
Bohol 21 Oi 9.50N 124.10 E
Böhönye 10 Nj 46.24N 17.24 E
Bohor 14 Jd 46.04N 15.26 E
Bohu/Bagrax 27 Ec 41.58N 86.29 E
Bohus 8 Eg 57.51N 12.01 E
Bohuslän 8 Df 58.15N 11.50 E
Boiaçu 54 Fd 0.27S 61.46W
Boiano 14 Ii 41.29N 14.29 E
Boina 30 Lj 16.00S 46.30 E
Bois, Lac des - 42 Ec 66.50N 125.15W
Bois, Rio dos- [Braz.] 55 Gd 18.35S 50.02W
Bois, Rio dos- [Braz.] 55 Ha 13.55S 49.51W
Bois Blanc Island 44 Ec 45.45N 84.28W
Boischaut 11 Hb 46.40N 1.45 E
Boise 39 He 43.37N 116.13W
Boise City 45 Eh 36.44N 102.31W
Boise River 46 Ge 43.49N 117.01W
Boissay 12 De 49.31N 1.21 E
Boissevain 42 Hg 49.14N 100.03W
Boizenburg 10 Gc 53.23N 10.43 E
Bojador, Cabo- 30 Ff 26.08N 14.30W
Bojana 15 Ch 41.52N 19.22 E
Bojanowo 10 Me 51.42N 16.44 E
Bojarka 19 De 50.19N 30.20 E
Bojčinovci 15 Gf 43.28N 23.20 E
Bojnürd 23 Ib 37.28N 57.19 E
Bojonegoro 26 Fh 7.09S 111.52 E
Bojuru 55 Gj 31.38S 51.26W
Bokatola 36 Cc 0.38S 18.46 E
Boké 34 Cc 10.56N 14.13W
Bokhara River 59 Je 29.55S 146.42 E
Bokn 8 Ae 59.15N 5.25 E
Boknafjorden 5 Gd 59.10N 5.35 E
Boko 36 Bc 4.47S 14.38 E
Bokol Mayo 35 Ge 4.31N 41.32 E
Bokoro 35 Bc 12.23N 17.03 E
Bokote 36 Dc 0.05S 20.08 E
Bokpyin 25 Jf 11.16N 98.46 E
Boksitogorsk 19 Dd 59.29N 33.52 E
Bokungu 36 Dc 0.41S 22.19 E
Bol [Chad] 35 Ac 13.30N 14.41 E
Bol [Yugo.] 14 Kg 43.16N 16.40 E
Bola, Bahr- 35 Bd 9.50N 18.59 E
Bolama 34 Bc 11.35N 15.28W
Bolands 51d Bb 17.02N 61.53W
Bolaños, Río- 48 Gg 21.14N 104.08W
Bolattau, Gora- 18 Ha 46.44N 71.54 E
Bolayir 15 Ji 40.31N 26.45 E
Bolbec 11 Ge 49.34N 0.29 E
Bolda 16 Pg 45.58N 48.35 E
Bole [Eth.] 35 Fd 6.37N 37.22 E
Bole [Ghana] 34 Ed 9.02N 2.29W
Bole/Bortala 27 Dc 44.59N 81.57 E
Bolehov 16 Ce 49.03N 23.50 E
Bolesławiec 10 Le 51.16N 15.34 E
Bolgatanga 31 Gg 10.47N 0.51W
Bolgrad 16 Fg 45.40N 28.38 E
Bolhov 19 De 53.30N 36.01 E
Boli 27 Nb 45.46N 130.31 E
Bolia 36 Cc 1.36S 18.23 E
Boliden 7 Ed 64.52N 20.23 E
Bolinao, Cape- 26 Gc 16.22N 119.50 E
Bolintin Vale 15 Ie 44.27N 25.46 E
Bolívar [Col.] [2] 54 Db 9.00N 74.40W
Bolivar [Mo.-U.S.] 45 Jh 37.37N 93.25W
Bolivar [Tn.-U.S.] 44 Ch 35.15N 88.59W
Bolívar [Ven.] [2] 54 Fb 6.20N 63.30W
Bolívar, Cerro- 54 Fb 7.28N 63.25W
Bolívar, Pico- 52 Ie 8.30N 71.02W
Bolivia [1] 53 Jg 17.00S 65.00W
Bolivia, Altiplano de- 52 Jg 18.00S 68.00W
Boljevac 15 Ef 43.50N 21.58 E
Bollendorf 12 Ie 49.51N 6.22 E
Bollène 11 Kj 44.17N 4.45 E
Bollnäs 7 Df 61.21N 16.25 E
Bollon 59 Je 28.02S 147.28 E
Bollstabruk 8 Ga 63.00N 17.41 E
Bollullos par del Condado 13 Fg 37.20N 6.32W
Bolmen 7 Ch 56.55N 13.40 E
Bolnisi 16 Ni 41.28N 44.31 E
Bolobo 36 Cc 2.10S 16.14 E
Bolodek 20 If 53.43N 133.09 E
Bologna 6 Hg 44.29N 11.20 E
Bolognesi 54 Df 10.01S 74.05W
Bologoje 6 Jd 57.54N 34.02 E
Bolohovo 16 Jb 54.05N 37.52 E
Bolomba 36 Cb 0.29N 19.12 E
Bolombo 36 Dc 3.59S 21.22 E
Bolon 20 Ig 49.58N 136.04 E
Bolotnoje 20 De 55.41N 84.33 E
Bolovens, Plateau des- 25 Le 15.20N 106.20 E
Bolšaja Balahnja 20 Fb 73.37N 107.05 E
Bolšaja Berestovica 10 Uc 53.09N 24.02 E
Bolšaja Černigovka 7 Mj 52.08N 50.48 E
Bolšaja Glušica 7 Mj 52.24N 50.29 E
Bolšaja Ižora 8 Me 59.55N 29.40 E
Bolšaja Kinel 7 Mj 53.14N 50.32 E
Bolšaja Koksaga 7 Lh 56.07N 47.48 E
Bolšaja Kuonamka 20 Gc 70.50N 113.20 E
Bolšaja Oju 17 Jb 69.42N 60.42 E
Bolšaja Rogovaja 17 Jc 66.30N 60.40 E
Bolšaja Synja 17 Id 65.58N 58.01 E
Bolšaja Tap 17 Lg 59.55N 65.42 E
Bolšaja Ussurka 20 Ig 46.00N 133.30 E
Bolšaja Vladimirovka 19 He 50.53N 79.30 E
Bolšakovo 8 Ij 54.50N 21.36 E
Bolsena 14 Fh 42.39N 11.59 E
Bolsena, Lago di- 14 Fh 42.35N 11.55 E
Bolšerečje 19 Hd 56.06N 74.38 E
Bolšereck 20 Kf 52.22N 156.24 E
Bolšeustikinskoje 17 Ii 55.57N 58.20 E
Bolševik 20 Jd 62.40N 147.30 E
Bolševik, Ostrov-=Bolshevik Island (EN) 21 Mb 78.40N 102.30 E
Bolšezemelskaja Tundra 19 Fb 67.30N 58.30 E
Bolshevik Island (EN)= Bolševik, Ostrov- 21 Mb 78.40N 102.30 E
Bolšije Uki 19 Hd 56.57N 72.37 E
Bolšoj Anjuj 20 Lc 68.30N 160.50 E
Bolšoj Begičev, Ostrov- 20 Gb 74.20N 112.30 E
Bolšoj Berezovy, Ostrov- 8 Md 60.15N 28.35 E
Bolšoj Boktybaj, Gora- [Kaz.-U.S.S.R.] 19 Ff 48.30N 58.20 E
Bolšoj Boktybaj, Gora- [U.S.S.R.] 16 Ue 48.30N 58.25 E
Bolšoj Bolvanski Nos, Mys- 17 Ia 70.27N 59.05 E
Bolšoj Čeremšan 7 Li 54.12N 49.40 E
Bolšoje Muraškino 7 Ki 55.47N 44.46 E
Bolšoje Vlasjevo 20 Jf 53.25N 140.55 E
Bolšoje Zagorje 8 Mg 57.47N 28.58 E
Bolšoj Gašun 16 Mf 47.22N 42.42 E
Bolšoj Ik 17 Hj 51.47N 56.20 E
Bolšoj Irgiz 19 Ee 52.01N 47.24 E
Bolšoj Jenisej 20 Ef 51.40N 94.26 E
Bolšoj Jugan 19 Hc 60.55N 73.40 E
Bolšoj Kamen 20 Ih 43.08N 132.28 E
Bolšoj Klimecki, Ostrov- 7 Ie 62.00N 35.15 E
Bolšoj Kujalnik 16 Gf 46.46N 30.38 E
Bolšoj Kumak 16 Ud 51.22N 58.55 E
Bolšoj Ljahovski, Ostrov- 20 Jb 73.35N 142.00 E
Bolšoj Murta 20 Ee 56.55N 93.10 E
Bolšoj Nimnyr 20 He 58.08N 125.45 E
Bolšoj Pit 20 Ee 59.02N 91.40 E
Bolšoj Tjuters, Ostrov- 8 Le 59.50N 27.10 E
Bolšoj Uluj 20 Ee 56.45N 90.46 E
Bolšoj Uvat, Ozero- 17 Oh 57.35N 70.30 E
Bolšoj Uzen 5 Kf 48.50N 49.40 E
Bolsón, Cerro del- 52 Jh 27.13S 66.06W
Bolšovcy 10 Ug 49.08N 24.47 E
Bolsward 12 Ha 53.04N 5.30 E
Boltaña 13 Mb 42.27N 0.04 E
Bolton 9 Kh 53.35N 2.26W
Bolu 23 Da 40.44N 31.37 E
Bolu Dağları 24 Eb 41.05N 32.05 E
Bolungarvik 7a Aa 66.09N 23.15W
Boluntay 27 Fd 36.29N 92.18 E
Bolva 16 Ic 53.17N 34.20 E
Bolvadin 24 Dc 38.42N 31.04 E
Bolzano/Bozen 6 Hf 46.31N 11.22 E
Bom, Rio- 55 Gf 23.56S 51.44W
Boma 31 Ii 5.51S 13.03 E
Bomassa 36 Cb 2.12N 16.12 E
Bombala 59 Jg 36.54S 149.14 E
Bombarral 13 Ce 39.16N 9.09W
Bombay 22 Jh 18.58N 72.50 E
Bomberai, Jazirah- 26 Jg 3.00S 133.00 E
Bombo 36 Fb 0.35N 32.32 E
Bomboma 36 Cb 2.26N 18.57 E
Bom Comércio 54 Ee 9.45S 65.54W
Bom Conselho 54 Ke 9.10S 36.41W
Bom Despacho 54 Ig 19.43S 45.15W
Bomdila 25 Ic 27.16N 92.23 E
Bomi/Bowo 27 Ge 30.02N 95.39 E
Bomi Hills 31 Fh 6.52N 10.45W
Bomili 36 Eb 1.40N 27.01 E
Bom Jardim de Goiás 55 Fc 16.17S 52.07W
Bom Jardim de Minas 55 Je 21.57S 44.11W
Bom Jesus 55 Gi 28.42S 50.24W
Bom Jesus da Lapa 53 Lg 13.15S 43.25W
Bom Jesus de Goiás 55 Hd 18.12S 49.37W
Bømlafjorden 8 Ae 59.40N 5.20 E
Bømlo 7 Ag 59.45N 5.10 E
Bomokandi 36 Eb 3.30N 26.08 E
Bomongo 36 Cb 1.22N 18.21 E
Bom Retiro 55 Hh 27.48S 49.31W
Bom Sucesso 55 Je 21.02S 44.46W
Bomu 30 Jh 4.08N 22.26 E
Bomu (EN)=Mbomou 30 Jh 4.08N 22.26 E
Bomu (EN)=Mbomou [3] 35 Cd 5.30N 23.30 E
Bon, Cape- (EN)=Ţīb, Ra's Aţ- 30 Ie 37.05N 11.03 E
Bona, Mount- 40 Kd 61.20N 141.50W
Bonaire 54 Ea 12.10N 68.15W
Bonaire Basin (EN) 50 Cg 11.25N 67.30W
Bonampak 48 Ni 16.43N 91.05W
Bonanza 49 Ef 14.01N 84.35W
Bonanza Peak 46 Eb 48.14N 120.52W
Bonao 49 Ld 18.56N 70.25W
Bonaparte, Mount- 46 Fb 48.45N 119.08W
Bonaparte Archipelago 57 Df 14.20S 125.20 E
Bonaparte Lake 46 Ea 51.16N 120.35W
Bonaparte Rocks 51p Cb 12.24N 61.30W
Bonasse 50 Fg 10.05N 61.52W
Bonavista 42 Mg 48.39N 53.07W
Bonavista Bay 42 Mg 49.00N 53.20W
Bon-Cagan-Nur 27 Gb 45.35N 99.15 E
Bondeno 14 Ff 44.53N 11.25 E
Bondo 31 Jh 3.49N 23.40 E
Bondoukou 34 Ed 8.02N 2.48W
Bondoukou [3] 34 Ed 8.20N 2.55W
Bondowoso 26 Fh 7.55S 113.49 E
Bone, Gulf of- (EN)=Bone, Teluk- 21 Oj 4.00S 120.40 E
Bone, Teluk-=Bone, Gulf of- (EN) 21 Oj 4.00S 120.40 E
Bone Bay 51a Db 18.45N 64.22W
Bonelohe 26 Hh 5.48S 120.27 E
Bönen 12 Jc 51.36N 7.46 E
Bone Rate, Kepulauan- 26 Hh 7.00S 121.00 E
Bone Rate, Pulau- 26 Hh 7.22S 121.08 E
Bonete, Cerro- 56 Gc 27.51S 68.47W
Bong 34 Cd 6.49N 10.19W
Bong [3] 34 Dd 7.00N 9.40W
Bonga 35 Fd 7.16N 36.14 E
Bongabong 26 Hd 12.45N 121.29 E
Bongandanga 36 Db 1.30N 21.03 E
Bongo, Massif des- 30 Jh 8.40N 22.25 E
Bongolava 37 Hc 18.35S 45.20 E
Bongor 31 Ig 10.17N 15.22 E
Bongouanou [3] 34 Ed 6.43N 4.12W
Bongouanou 34 Ed 6.39N 4.12W
Bonham 45 Hj 33.35N 96.11W
Bonheiden 12 Gc 51.02N 4.32 E
Bonhomme, Col du- 11 Nf 48.10N 7.06 E
Bonhomme, Pic- 49 Kd 19.05N 72.15W
Bonifacio 11a Bb 41.23N 9.09 E
Bonifacio, Bocche di-= Bonifacio, Strait of- (EN) 5 Gg 41.18N 9.15 E
Bonifacio, Strait of- (EN)= Bonifacio, Bocche di- 5 Gg 41.18N 9.15 E
Bonifati, Capo- 14 Jk 39.33N 15.52 E
Bonin Basin (EN) 60 Bb 29.00N 137.00 E
Bonin Islands (EN)= Ogasawara-Shotō 21 Qg 27.00N 142.10 E
Bonin Trench (EN) 3 If 30.00N 145.00 E
Bonita Springs 44 Gl 26.21N 81.47W
Bonito [Braz.] 55 Jb 15.20S 44.46W
Bonito [Braz.] 55 De 21.08S 56.28W
Bonito, Pico- 47 Ge 15.38N 86.55W
Bonito, Rio- [Braz.] 55 Hb 15.18S 49.36W
Bonito, Rio- [Braz.] 55 Gc 16.31S 51.23W
Bonn 6 Ge 50.44N 7.06 E
Bonn-Bad Godesberg 10 Df 50.41N 7.09 E
Bonnebosq 12 Ce 49.12N 0.05 E
Bonnechère River 44 Ic 45.31N 76.33W
Bonners Ferry 46 Gb 48.41N 116.18W
Bonnet, Lac du- 45 Ia 50.22N 95.55W
Bonnétable 11 Gf 48.11N 0.26 E
Bonnet Plume 42 Ec 65.53N 134.58W
Bonneval 11 Hf 48.11N 1.24 E
Bonneville 11 Mh 46.05N 6.25 E
Bonneville Salt Flats 46 If 40.45N 113.50W
Bonnières-sur-Seine 12 De 49.02N 1.35 E
Bonningues-lès-Ardres 12 Ed 50.47N 2.01 E
Bonny 34 Ge 4.25N 7.10 E
Bono 14 Dj 40.25N 9.02 E
Bō-no-Misaki 29 Bf 31.15N 130.13 E
Bonorva 14 Cj 40.25N 8.46 E
Bontang 26 Gf 0.08N 117.30 E
Bonthain 26 Gh 5.32S 119.56 E
Bonthe 34 Cd 7.32N 12.30W
Bontoc 26 Hc 17.05N 120.58 E
Bonyhád 10 Oj 46.18N 18.32 E
Boo, Kepulauan- 26 Ig 1.12S 129.24 E
Boola 34 Dd 8.22N 8.43W
Booligal 59 If 33.52S 144.53 E
Boone [Ia.-U.S.] 45 Je 42.04N 93.53W
Boone [N.C.-U.S.] 44 Gg 36.13N 81.41W
Booneville [Ar.-U.S.] 45 Ji 35.08N 93.55W
Booneville [Ms.-U.S.] 45 Li 34.39N 88.34W
Boon Point 51d Bb 17.10N 61.50W
Boonville [In.-U.S.] 44 Df 38.03N 87.16W
Boonville [Mo.-U.S.] 45 Jg 38.58N 92.44W
Boos 12 De 49.23N 1.12 E
Boothia, Gulf of- 38 Jb 71.00N 91.00W
Boothia Peninsula 38 Jb 70.30N 95.00W
Boot Reefs 60 Cj 10.00S 144.35 E
Booué 31 Ii 0.06S 11.56 E
Bophuthatswana 37 De 26.00S 25.30 E
Bopolu 34 Cd 7.04N 10.29W
Boppard 12 Jd 50.14N 7.36 E
Boquerón [3] 55 Bf 23.00S 61.00W
Boquerón 51a Ab 18.03N 67.09W
Boquilla, Presa de la- 48 Gd 27.30N 105.30W
Boquillas del Carmen 48 Hc 29.17N 102.53W
Bor [Czech.] 10 Ig 49.43N 12.47 E
Bor [R.S.F.S.R.] 19 Ed 56.23N 44.07 E
Bor [Sud.] 31 Kh 6.12N 31.33 E
Bor [Swe.] 8 Fg 57.07N 14.10 E
Bor [Tur.] 24 Fd 37.54N 34.34 E
Bor [Yugo.] 15 Fe 44.06N 22.06 E
Bora-Bora, Ile- 57 Lf 16.30S 151.45W
Borah Peak 38 He 44.08N 113.14W
Boraldaj 18 Gc 42.30N 69.05 E
Bora Marina 14 Jm 37.56N 15.55 E
Bōramo 35 Gd 9.58N 43.07 E
Borås 7 Ch 57.43N 12.55 E
Borāzjān 24 Nh 29.16N 51.12 E
Borba [Braz.] 54 Gd 4.24S 59.35W
Borba [Port.] 13 Ef 38.48N 7.27W
Borborema, Planalto da- 52 Mf 7.00S 37.00W
Borca 15 Ib 47.11N 25.46 E
Borcea 15 Ke 44.20N 27.45 E
Borcea, Braţul- 15 Ke 44.40N 27.53 E
Borchgrevink Coast 66 Kf 73.00S 171.00 E
Borçka 24 Ib 41.22N 41.40 E
Borculo 12 Ib 52.07N 6.31 E
Borda da Mata, Serra- 55 Ie 21.18S 47.06W
Bordeaux 6 Fg 44.50N 0.34W
Borden 42 Ga 78.30N 110.30W
Borden Peninsula 38 Kb 73.00N 83.00W
Borders [3] 9 Kf 55.35N 3.00W
Bordertown 58 Fh 36.19S 140.47 E
Bordighera 14 Bg 43.46N 7.39 E
Bordj Bou Arreridj 32 Hb 36.04N 4.46 E
Bordj el Emir Abdelkader 13 Oi 35.52N 2.16 E
Bordj Fly Sainte Marie 32 Gd 27.18N 2.59W
Bordj-Menaïel 13 Ph 36.44N 3.43 E
Bordj Messouda 32 Ic 30.12N 9.25 E
Bordj Moktar 31 Hf 21.20N 0.56 E
Bordj Omar Driss 31 Hf 28.09N 6.49 E
Bord Khūn-e Now 24 Nh 28.03N 51.28 E
Bordon Camp 12 Bc 51.07N 0.51W
Boreal, Chaco- 52 Kh 23.00S 60.00W
Boren 8 Ff 58.35N 15.10 E
Borensberg 8 Ff 58.34N 15.17 E
Borgå/Porvoo 7 Ff 60.24N 25.40 E
Borgarnes 7a Bb 64.32N 21.55W
Børgefjell 7 Cd 65.23N 13.50 E
Borgentreich 12 Lc 51.34N 9.15 E
Borger [Neth.] 12 Ib 52.55N 6.48 E
Borger [Tx.-U.S.] 43 Gd 35.39N 101.24W
Borgholm 7 Dh 56.53N 16.39 E
Borghorst, Steinfurt- 12 Jb 52.08N 7.25 E
Borgia 14 Kl 38.49N 16.30 E
Borgloon 12 Hd 50.48N 5.20 E
Borgomanero 14 Ce 45.42N 8.28 E
Borgorose 14 Hh 42.11N 13.15 E
Borgo San Dalmazzo 14 Bf 44.20N 7.30 E
Borgo San Lorenzo 14 Fg 43.57N 11.23 E
Borgosesia 14 Ce 45.43N 8.16 E
Borgou [3] 34 Fc 10.30N 2.50 E
Borgo Val di Taro 14 Df 44.29N 9.46 E
Borgo Valsugana 14 Fd 46.03N 11.27 E
Borgu 30 Hg 10.35N 3.40 E
Borgworm/Waremme 11 Ld 50.42N 5.15 E
Bori 34 Ge 4.42N 7.21 E
Borinquen, Punta- 51a Ab 18.30N 67.10W
Borislav 19 Cf 49.18N 23.27 E
Borisoglebsk 6 Ke 51.23N 42.06 E
Borisov 19 Ce 54.15N 28.30 E
Borisovka 16 Jd 50.36N 36.06 E
Borispol 19 De 50.23N 30.59 E
Bo River 35 Dd 6.48N 27.55 E
Borja 14 Lf 44.31N 17.44 E
Borja [Peru] 54 Cd 4.26S 77.33W
Borja [Sp.] 13 Kc 41.50N 1.32W
Borjas Blancas/Les Borges Blanques 13 Mc 41.31N 0.52 E
Borken 10 Ce 51.51N 6.52 E
Borkou 30 Ig 18.15N 18.50 E
Borkou-Ennedi-Tibesti [3] 35 Bb 18.00N 19.00 E
Borkoviči 8 Mi 55.38N 28.23 E
Borkum 10 Cc 53.35N 6.41 E
Borlänge 7 Df 60.29N 15.25 E
Borlu 24 Cc 38.44N 28.27 E
Bormida 14 Cf 44.56N 8.40 E
Bormio 14 Ed 46.28N 10.22 E
Born 11 Fj 44.30N 1.00W
Borna 10 Ie 51.07N 12.30 E
Borndiep 12 Ha 53.25N 5.35 E
Borne 12 Ib 52.18N 6.45 E
Borneo/Kalimantan 21 Ni 1.00N 114.00 E
Bornheim 12 Id 50.46N 7.00 E
Bornholm 5 Hd 55.10N 15.00 E
Bornholm [2] 8 Fi 55.10N 15.00 E
Bornos 13 Gh 36.48N 5.44W
Bornova, İzmir- 24 Bc 38.27N 27.14 E
Bornu [2] 34 Hc 12.00N 12.40 E
Bornu 30 Ig 12.30N 13.00 E
Boro 30 Jh 8.52N 26.11 E
Borodino [R.S.F.S.R.] 7 Ii 55.32N 35.49 E
Borodino [R.S.F.S.R.] 20 Ee 55.57N 95.03 E
Borodinskoje 8 Md 61.00N 29.29 E
Borogoncy 20 Id 62.39N 131.08 E
Borohoro Shan 21 Ke 42.00N 85.00 E
Boromo 34 Ec 11.45N 2.56W
Borongan 26 Id 11.37N 125.26 E
Borotou 34 Dd 8.44N 7.30W
Borovan 15 Gf 43.26N 23.45 E
Borovec 15 Gg 42.16N 23.35 E
Boroviči 19 Dd 58.24N 33.56 E
Borovici 8 Mg 57.58N 29.47 E
Borovljanka 20 Df 52.38N 84.35 E
Borovo 14 Me 45.24N 18.59 E
Borovski 19 Gd 57.03N 65.44 E
Borovskoj 19 Ge 53.48N 64.17 E
Borrachas, Islas- 50 Dg 10.18N 64.44W
Borrān 35 Hc 10.11N 48.53 E
Borrby 8 Fi 55.27N 14.10 E
Borroloola 58 Ef 16.04S 136.17 E
Borş 15 Eb 47.07N 21.49 E
Borşa 15 Hb 47.39N 24.40 E
Borščovočny Hrebet= Borshchovochny Range (EN) 20 Gf 52.00N 118.30 E
Borsec 15 Ic 46.57N 25.34 E
Borshchovochny Range (EN) =Borščovočny Hrebet 20 Gf 52.00N 118.30 E
Borsod-Abaúj-Zemplén [2] 10 Qh 48.15N 21.00 E
Bortala/Bole 27 Dc 44.59N 81.57 E
Bortala He 27 Dc 44.53N 82.45 E
Bort-les-Orgues 11 Ii 45.24N 2.30 E
Borūjen 24 Ng 31.59N 51.18 E
Borūjerd 23 Gc 33.54N 48.46 E
Borzja 22 Nd 50.24N 116.31 E
Borzna 16 Hd 51.15N 32.29 E
Boržomi 16 Mi 41.50N 43.25 E
Borzsöny 10 Oi 47.55N 19.00 E
Borzyszkowy 10 Nb 54.03N 17.22 E
Bosa 14 Cj 40.18N 8.30 E
Bosanska Dubica 14 Ke 45.11N 16.48 E
Bosanska Gradiška 14 Le 45.09N 17.15 E
Bosanska Krupa 14 Kf 44.53N 16.10 E
Bosanski Brod 14 Me 45.08N 18.01 E
Bosanski Novi 14 Ke 45.03N 16.22 E
Bosanski Petrovac 14 Kf 44.34N 16.21 E
Bosanski Šamac 14 Me 45.04N 18.28 E
Bosansko Grahovo 23 Ff 44.11N 16.22 E
Bōsāso 31 Lg 11.13N 49.08 E
Bosavi, Mount- 59 Ia 6.35S 142.50 E
Bosbeek 12 Hc 51.06N 5.48 E
Bose 22 Mg 24.01N 106.32 E
Boshan 27 Kd 36.30N 117.50 E
Boshrūyeh 24 Qf 33.53N 57.26 E
Bosilegrad 15 Fg 42.30N 22.28 E
Bosingfeld, Extertal- 12 Lb 52.04N 9.07 E
Bosna 14 Me 45.04N 18.28 E
Bosna 15 Kg 42.11N 27.27 E
Bosna=Bosnia (EN) 5 Hg 44.00N 18.00 E
Bosna = Bosnia (EN) 14 Lf 44.00N 18.00 E
Bosna i Hercegovina = Bosnia-Hercegovina (EN) [2] 14 Lf 44.15N 17.50 E
Bosnia (EN) = Bosna 14 Lf 44.00N 18.00 E
Bosnia (EN)=Bosna 5 Hg 44.00N 18.00 E
Bosnia-Hercegovina (EN) = Bosna i Hercegovina [2] 14 Lf 44.15N 17.50 E
Bosnik 26 Kg 1.10S 136.14 E
Bošnjakovo 20 Jg 49.41N 142.10 E
Bosobolo 36 Cb 4.11N 19.54 E
Bōsō-Hantō 28 Pg 35.20N 140.10 E
Bosporus (EN)=İstanbul Boğazi 5 Ig 41.00N 29.00 E
Bosque Bonito 48 Gb 30.42N 105.06W
Bossangoa 31 Ih 6.29N 17.27 E
Bossé Bangou 34 Fc 13.21N 1.18 E
Bossembélé 35 Bd 5.16N 17.39 E
Bossemtélé II 35 Bd 5.41N 16.38 E
Bossier City 43 Ie 32.31N 93.43W
Bosso 34 Hc 13.42N 13.19 E
Bosso, Dallol- 30 Hg 12.25N 2.50 E
Bossut, Cape- 59 Ec 18.43S 121.38 E
Bostān 25 Db 30.26N 67.02 E
Bostānābād 24 Ld 37.50N 46.50 E
Bosten/Bagrax Hu 21 Ke 42.00N 87.00 E
Boston [Eng.-U.K.] 9 Mi 52.59N 0.01W
Boston [Ma.-U.S.] 39 Le 42.21N 71.04W
Boston Bar 46 Eb 49.52N 121.26W
Boston Deeps 12 Ca 53.00N 0.15 E
Boston Mountains 43 Id 35.50N 93.20W
Botan 24 Id 37.44N 41.48 E
Botas, Ribeirão das- 55 Fe 20.26S 53.43W
Botesdale 12 Db 52.20N 1.01 E
Botev 5 Ig 42.43N 24.55 E
Botevgrad 15 Gg 42.54N 23.47 E
Bothnia, Gulf of- (EN)= Bottniska viken 5 Hc 63.00N 20.00 E
Bothnia, Gulf of- (EN)= Pohjanlahti 5 Hc 63.00N 20.00 E
Boticas 13 Ec 41.41N 7.40W
Botletle 37 Cd 21.07S 24.42 E
Botlih 16 Oh 42.41N 46.13 E
Botna 15 Mc 46.48N 29.30 E
Botoşani [2] 15 Jb 47.40N 26.43 E
Botoşani 15 Jb 47.45N 26.40 E
Botrange 11 Md 50.30N 6.08 E
Botswana [1] 31 Jk 22.00S 24.00 E
Botte Donato 14 Kk 39.17N 16.27 E
Bottineau 43 Gb 48.50N 100.27W
Bottniska viken=Bothnia, Gulf of- (EN) 5 Hc 63.00N 20.00 E
Bottrop 10 Ce 51.31N 6.55 E
Botucatu 56 Kb 22.52S 48.26W
Botucatu, Serra de- 55 Hf 23.00S 48.20W
Botwood 42 Lg 49.08N 55.21W
Bouaflé 34 Dd 6.59N 5.45W
Bouaflé [3] 34 Dd 7.03N 5.48W
Bouaké 31 Gh 7.41N 5.02W
Bouaké [3] 34 Dd 7.45N 5.02W
Bou Anane 32 Gc 32.02N 3.03W
Bouar 31 Ih 5.57N 15.36 E
Bou Arfa 32 Gc 32.32N 1.57W
Boubín 10 Jh 48.58N 13.50 E
Bouca 31 Ih 6.30N 18.17 E
Bouchain 12 Fd 50.17N 3.19 E
Bouchegouf 14 Bn 36.28N 7.44 E
Bouche Island 51k Bb 13.57N 60.53W
Bouches-du-Rhône [3] 11 Kk 43.30N 5.00 E
Boudenib 32 Gc 31.57N 3.36W
Boudeuse Cay 37b Bb 6.05S 52.51 E
Boû Djébéha 34 Eb 18.33N 2.45W
Bouenza [3] 36 Bc 3.00S 13.00 E
Boufarik 13 Oh 36.34N 2.55 E
Bougaa 13 Rh 36.20N 5.05 E
Bougainville Island 57 Ge 6.00S 155.00 E
Bougainville Reef 59 Jc 15.30S 147.05 E
Bougainville Strait [Ocn.] 63a Cb 6.40S 156.10 E
Bougainville Strait [Van.] 63b Cb 15.50S 167.10 E
Bougouni 31 Gg 11.25N 7.28W

Index Symbols

[1] Independent Nation
[2] State, Region
[3] District, County
[4] Municipality
[5] Colony, Dependency
Continent
Physical Region
Historical or Cultural Region
Mount, Mountain
Volcano
Hill
Mountains, Mountain Range
Hills, Escarpment
Plateau, Upland
Pass, Gap
Plain, Lowland
Delta
Salt Flat
Valley, Canyon
Crater, Cave
Karst Features
Depression
Polder
Desert, Dunes
Forest, Woods
Heath, Steppe
Oasis
Cape, Point
Coast, Beach
Cliff
Peninsula
Isthmus
Sandbank
Island
Atoll
Rock, Reef
Islands, Archipelago
Rocks, Reefs
Coral Reef
Well, Spring
Geyser
River, Stream
Waterfall Rapids
River Mouth, Estuary
Lake
Salt Lake
Intermittent Lake
Reservoir
Swamp, Pond
Canal
Glacier
Ice Shelf, Pack Ice
Ocean
Sea
Gulf, Bay
Strait, Fjord
Lagoon
Bank
Seamount
Tablemount
Ridge
Shelf
Basin
Escarpment, Sea Scarp
Fracture
Trench, Abyss
National Park, Reserve
Point of Interest
Recreation Site
Cave, Cavern
Historic Site
Ruins
Wall, Walls
Church, Abbey
Temple
Scientific Station
Airport
Port
Lighthouse
Mine
Tunnel
Dam, Bridge

Bougtob	32	Hc	34.02N	0.05 E
Bouguenais	11	Eg	47.11N	1.37W
Bougzoul	13	Oi	35.42N	2.51 E
Bou Hadjar	14	Cn	36.30N	8.06 E
Bouhalla, Jbel-	13	Gi	35.06N	5.07W
Bou Hamed	13	Hi	35.19N	4.58W
Bouillante	51e	Ab	16.08N	61.46W
Bouillon	11	Le	49.48N	5.04 E
Bouira	32	Hb	36.23N	3.54 E
Bouira [3]	32	Hb	36.15N	4.10 E
Bou Ismail	13	Oh	36.38N	2.41 E
Bou Izakarn	32	Fd	29.10N	9.44W
Bou Kadir	13	Nh	36.04N	1.07 E
Boukombé	34	Fc	10.11N	1.06 E
Boû Lanouâr	32	De	21.16N	16.30W
Boulay-Moselle	12	Ie	49.11N	6.30 E
Boulder [Co.-U.S.]	39	Ie	40.01N	105.17W
Boulder [Mt.-U.S.]	46	Ic	46.14N	112.07W
Boulder City	46	Hi	35.59N	114.50W
Boulemane	32	Gc	33.22N	4.45W
Boulemane [3]	32	Gc	33.02N	4.04W
Boulevard Atlántico	55	Dn	38.19S	57.59W
Boulia	59	Hd	22.54S	139.54 E
Bouligny	11	Le	49.17N	5.45 E
Boulogne	11	Eg	47.05N	1.40W
Boulogne-Billancourt	11	If	48.50N	2.15 E
Boulogne-sur-Mer	11	Hd	50.43N	1.37 E
Boulonnais	11	Hd	50.42N	1.40 E
Bouloupari	63b	Ce	21.52S	166.03 E
Boulsa	34	Ec	12.39N	0.34W
Boultoum	34	Hc	14.40N	10.18 E
Bou Maad, Djebel-	13	Oh	36.26N	2.08 E
Boumba	34	Ie	2.02N	15.12 E
Boumdeïd	32	Ef	17.26N	11.21W
Boum Kabir	35	Bc	10.11N	19.24 E
Boumort	13	Nb	42.14N	1.08 E
Bouna	31	Gh	9.16N	3.00W
Bouna [3]	34	Ed	9.15N	3.20W
Boû Nâga	32	Ef	19.00N	13.13W
Bou Nasser, Adrar-	32	Gc	33.35N	3.53W
Boundary Peak	46	Fh	37.51N	118.21W
Boundiali [3]	34	Dd	9.23N	6.32W
Boundiali	34	Dd	9.31N	6.29W
Boundji	36	Cc	1.03S	15.22 E
Boungou	35	Cd	6.45N	22.06 E
Bountiful	43	Ec	40.53N	111.53W
Bounty Bay	64q	Ab	25.03S	130.05W
Bounty Islands	57	Ii	47.45S	179.05 E
Bounty Trough (EN)	3	Jn	46.00S	178.00 E
Bourail	61	Cd	21.34S	165.30 E
Bourbon-Lancy	11	Jh	46.37N	3.47 E
Bourbonnais	11	Ih	46.30N	3.00 E
Bourbonne-les-Bains	11	Lg	47.57N	5.45 E
Bourbourg	12	Ed	50.57N	2.12 E
Bourbre	11	Li	45.47N	5.11 E
Bourem	34	Eb	16.58N	0.21W
Bouressa	34	Fa	20.01N	2.18 E
Bourg-Achard	12	Ce	49.21N	0.49 E
Bourganeuf	11	Hi	45.57N	1.45 E
Bourgar'oûn, Cap-	32	Ib	37.06N	6.28 E
Bourg-de-Péage	11	Li	45.02N	5.03 E
Bourg-en-Bresse	11	Lh	46.12N	5.13 E
Bourges	6	Gf	47.05N	2.24 E
Bourget, Lac du-	11	Li	45.44N	5.52 E
Bourgneuf, Baie de-	11	Dg	47.05N	2.13W
Bourgogne	12	Ge	49.21N	4.04 E
Bourgogne=Burgundy (EN)	5	Gf	47.00N	4.30 E
Bourgogne=Burgundy (EN)	11	Kg	47.00N	4.30 E
Bourgogne, Canal de-	11	Jg	47.58N	3.30 E
Bourgogne, Porte de-	11	Mg	47.38N	6.52 E
Bourgoin-Jallieu	11	Li	45.35N	5.17 E
Bourgtheroulde-Infreville	12	Ce	49.18N	0.53 E
Bourguébus	12	Be	49.07N	0.18W
Boû Rjeïmat	32	Df	19.04N	15.08W
Bourke	58	Fh	30.05S	145.56 E
Bourne	12	Bb	52.46N	0.23W
Bournemouth	9	Lk	50.43N	1.54W
Bourtanger Moor	12	Jb	52.50N	7.06 E
Bourth	12	Cf	48.46N	0.49 E
Bou Saâda	32	Hb	35.12N	4.11 E
Bou Sellam	13	Qh	36.26N	4.34 E
Boussac	11	Ih	46.21N	2.13 E
Boussé	34	Ec	12.39N	1.53W
Boussens	11	Gk	43.11N	0.58 E
Bousso	35	Bc	10.29N	16.43 E
Bouthaleb, Djebel-	13	Ri	35.48N	5.12 E
Boutilimit	32	Ef	17.33N	14.42W
Bou-Tlélis	13	Li	35.34N	0.54W
Boutonne	11	Fi	45.55N	0.49W
Bouvet	66	Cd	54.26S	3.24 E
Bouxwiller	12	Jf	48.49N	7.29 E
Bouza	34	Gc	14.25N	6.02 E
Bouzanne	11	Hh	46.38N	1.28 E
Bouzghaïa	13	Nh	36.20N	1.15 E
Bouzonville	12	Ie	49.18N	6.32 E
Bovalino	14	Kl	38.09N	16.11 E
Bovec	14	Hd	46.20N	13.33 E
Bovenkarspel	12	Hb	52.42N	5.17 E
Boves	12	Ee	49.51N	2.23 E
Bovino	14	Ji	41.15N	15.20 E
Bovril	55	Cj	31.21S	59.26W
Bowa → Muli	27	Hf	27.55N	101.13 E
Bowen [Arg.]	56	Ge	35.02S	67.31W
Bowen [Austl.]	58	Fg	20.01S	148.15 E
Bowers Bank (EN)	40a	Bb	54.00N	180.00
Bowers Ridge (EN)	40a	Bb	54.30N	180.00
Bowie	45	Hj	33.34N	97.51W
Bowkān	24	Ld	36.31N	46.12 E
Bowland, Forest of-	9	Kh	54.00N	2.35W
Bowling Green [Ky.-U.S.]	43	Jd	37.00N	86.27W
Bowling Green [Oh.-U.S.]	44	Fe	41.22N	83.40W
Bowman	43	Gb	46.11N	103.24W
Bowman Bay	42	Kc	65.33N	73.40W
Bowman Island	66	He	65.17S	103.08 E
Bowman, Mount-	46	Ea	51.10N	121.55W
Bowo/Bomi	27	Ge	30.02N	95.39 E
Bowokan, Kepulauan-	26	Hg	2.05S	123.35 E
Bowral	59	Kf	34.28S	150.25 E
Bow River	42	Gg	49.56N	111.42W
Box Elder Creek	46	Kc	46.57N	108.04W
Boxelder Creek	46	Nd	45.59N	103.57W
Boxholm	7	Dg	58.12N	15.03 E
Boxian	27	Ke	33.46N	115.44 E
Boxing	27	Kd	37.07N	118.04 E
Boxmeer	12	Hc	51.39N	5.57 E
Boxtel	11	Lc	51.35N	5.20 E
Boyabat	24	Fb	41.28N	34.47 E
Boyabo	36	Cb	3.43N	18.46 E
Boyacá [2]	54	Db	5.30N	72.50W
Boyang	27	Kf	29.00N	116.41 E
Boyer, Cap-	63b	De	21.37S	168.07 E
Boyer Ahmadī-ye Sardsīr va Kohkīlūyeh [3]	23	Hc	31.00N	50.30 E
Boyle/Mainistir na Búille	9	Eh	53.58N	8.18W
Boyne/An Bhóinn	9	Gh	53.43N	6.15W
Boyne City	44	Ec	45.13N	85.01W
Boynes, Iles de-	30	Nm	49.58S	69.59 E
Boynton Beach	44	Gl	26.32N	80.03W
Boysen Reservoir	46	Ke	43.19N	108.11W
Boz, Kūh-e-	24	Pi	27.46N	55.54 E
Bozburun	15	Li	40.32N	28.46 E
Bozburun	15	Lm	36.41N	28.04 E
Bozburun Dağı	24	Dd	37.18N	31.03 E
Bozcaada	24	Bc	39.50N	26.04 E
Bozcaada	24	Bc	39.49N	26.03 E
Bozdağ	15	Lk	38.20N	28.06 E
Boz Dağı [Tur.]	24	Cd	37.18N	29.12 E
Boz Dağı [Tur.]	24	Cc	38.19N	28.08 E
Boz Dağları	15	Kj	38.20N	27.45 E
Bozdoğan	15	Ll	37.40N	28.19 E
Bozeman	39	He	45.41N	111.02W
Bozen / Bolzano	6	Hf	46.31N	11.22 E
Bozene	36	Cb	2.56N	19.12 E
Bozhen	28	De	38.04N	116.34 E
Bozkol, Zaliv-	18	Cb	45.20N	61.45 E
Bozkurt	24	Fb	41.57N	34.01 E
Bozok Platosu	24	Fc	39.05N	35.05 E
Bozouls	11	Ij	44.28N	2.43 E
Bozoum	31	Ih	6.19N	16.23 E
Bozova	24	Hd	37.22N	38.31 E
Bozovici	15	Ee	44.56N	22.00 E
Bozqūsh, Kūh-e-	24	Ld	37.45N	47.40 E
Bra	14	Bf	44.42N	7.51 E
Braås	8	Fg	57.04N	15.03 E
Braathen, Cape-	66	Pf	71.48S	96.05W
Brabant	11	Lc	51.10N	5.05 E
Brabant [3]	12	Gd	50.45N	4.30 E
Brabant-les-Villers	12	Gf	48.51N	4.59 E
Brâbîch	34	Eb	17.30N	3.00W
Brač	14	Kg	43.19N	16.40 E
Bracadale, Loch-	9	Gd	57.20N	6.35W
Bracciano	14	Gh	42.06N	12.40 E
Bracciano, Lago di-	14	Gh	42.05N	12.15 E
Bräcke	7	De	62.43N	15.27 E
Brackettville	45	Fl	29.19N	100.24W
Bracki Kanal	14	Kg	43.24N	16.40 E
Brackley	12	Ab	52.02N	1.09W
Bracknell	9	Mj	51.26N	0.46W
Brackwede, Bielefeld-	12	Kc	51.59N	8.31 E
Brad	15	Fc	46.08N	22.47 E
Bradano	14	Kj	40.23N	16.51 E
Bradenton	43	Kf	27.29N	82.34W
Bradford [Eng.-U.K.]	9	Lh	53.48N	1.45W
Bradford [Pa.-U.S.]	44	He	41.57N	78.39W
Bradley Reef	60	Gi	6.52S	160.48 E
Brady	43	He	31.08N	99.20W
Brady Mountains	45	Gk	31.20N	99.40W
Brædstrup	8	Ci	55.58N	9.37 E
Braemar	9	Jd	57.01N	3.24W
Braga [2]	13	Dc	41.35N	8.25W
Braga	6	Fg	41.33N	8.26W
Bragadiru	15	If	43.46N	25.31 E
Bragado	56	He	35.08S	60.30W
Bragança [2]	13	Fc	41.30N	6.45W
Bragança [Braz.]	53	Lf	1.03S	46.46W
Bragança [Port.]	13	Fc	41.49N	6.45W
Bragança Paulista	55	If	22.57S	46.34W
Brahestad/Raahe	7	Fd	64.41N	24.29 E
Brahmanbāria	25	Id	23.59N	91.07 E
Brāhmani	21	Kg	20.39N	86.46 E
Brahmaputra	21	Lg	24.02N	90.59 E
Brăila [2]	15	Kd	45.13N	27.48 E
Brăila	6	If	45.16N	27.59 E
Brăilei, Balta-	15	Ke	45.00N	28.00 E
Braine	12	Fe	49.20N	3.32 E
Braine-l'Alleud/Eigenbrakel	12	Gd	50.41N	4.22 E
Brainerd	43	Ib	46.21N	94.12W
Braintree	12	Cc	51.53N	0.34 E
Braithwaite Point	59	Gb	11.58S	134.00 E
Brake	10	Ec	53.20N	8.29 E
Brakel [Bel.]	12	Fd	50.47N	3.45 E
Brakel [F.R.G.]	12	Lc	51.43N	9.11 E
Brakna [3]	32	Ef	17.30N	13.30W
Brålanda	8	Ef	58.34N	12.22 E
Bralorne	46	Da	50.47N	122.49W
Bramming	8	Ci	55.28N	8.42 E
Brämön	8	Gb	62.10N	17.40 E
Brampton	44	Hd	43.41N	79.46W
Bramsche	10	Dd	52.24N	7.59 E
Bran, Pasul-	15	Id	45.26N	25.17 E
Branco	32	Cf	16.39N	24.41W
Branco, Cabo-	52	Mf	7.09S	34.47W
Branco, Rio- [Braz.]	52	Jf	1.24S	61.51W
Branco, Rio- [Braz.]	55	De	21.00S	57.48W
Branco ou Cabixi, Rio-	55	Ba	13.55S	60.10W
Brandberg	30	Ik	21.08S	14.35 E
Brandbu	7	Cf	60.26N	10.28 E
Brande	7	Bi	55.57N	9.07 E
Brandenburg	10	Id	52.25N	12.33 E
Brandenburg	10	Jd	52.10N	13.30 E
Brändö	8	Id	60.25N	21.05 E
Brandon [Eng.-U.K.]	12	Cb	52.27N	0.37 E
Brandon [Fl.-U.S.]	44	Fl	27.56N	82.17W
Brandon [Man.-Can.]	39	Je	49.50N	99.57W
Brandon [Vt.-U.S.]	44	Kd	43.47N	73.05W
Brandon Head/Na Machairí	9	Ci	52.16N	10.15W
Brandon Mount/Cnoc Bréanainn	9	Ci	52.14N	10.15W
Brandval	8	Ed	60.19N	12.02 E
Brandvlei	37	Cf	30.25S	20.30 E
Brandýs nad Labem-Stará Boleslav	10	Kf	50.11N	14.40 E
Brăneşti	15	Je	44.27N	26.20 E
Braniewo	10	Pb	54.24N	19.50 E
Bransby Point	51c	Bc	16.43N	62.14W
Bransfield Strait	66	Re	63.00S	59.00W
Brańsk	10	Sd	52.45N	22.51 E
Branson	45	Jh	36.39N	93.13W
Brantevik	8	Fi	55.31N	14.21 E
Brantford	42	Jh	43.08N	80.16W
Brantôme	11	Gi	45.22N	0.39 E
Bras d'Or Lake	42	Lg	45.50N	60.50W
Brasil=Brazil (EN) [1]	53	Kf	9.00S	53.00W
Brasil, Planalto do- = Brazilian Highlands (EN)	52	Lg	17.00S	45.00W
Brasiléia	54	Ef	11.00S	68.44W
Brasília	53	Lg	15.47S	47.55W
Brasília de Minas	55	Jc	16.12S	44.26W
Brasla	8	Kg	57.08N	24.50 E
Braslav	7	Gi	55.37N	27.05 E
Braşov [2]	15	Id	45.40N	25.10 E
Braşov	6	If	45.38N	25.35 E
Brass	34	Ge	4.19N	6.14 E
Brassac	11	Ik	43.38N	2.30 E
Brasschaat	12	Gc	51.17N	4.27 E
Brasstown Bald	44	Fh	34.52N	83.48W
Brastavăţu	15	Hf	43.55N	24.24 E
Brataj	15	Ci	40.16N	19.40 E
Bråte	8	De	59.43N	11.27 E
Bratea	15	Fc	46.56N	22.37 E
Bratislava	6	Hf	48.09N	17.07 E
Bratsk	22	Md	56.05N	101.48 E
Bratskoje Vodohranilišče = Bratsk Reservoir (EN)	20	Fe	56.30N	102.00 E
Bratsk Reservoir (EN) = Bratskoje Vodohranilišče	20	Fe	56.30N	102.00 E
Brattleboro	43	Mc	42.51N	72.36W
Brattvåg	8	Bb	62.36N	6.27 E
Braubach	12	Jd	50.17N	7.40 E
Braunau am Inn	14	Hb	48.16N	13.02 E
Braunschweig	10	Gd	52.16N	10.32 E
Brava	30	Eg	14.52N	24.43W
Brava, Costa-	13	Pc	41.45N	3.04 E
Bråviken	8	Gf	58.40N	16.30 E
Bravo del Norte, Rio- = Grande, Rio- (EN)	38	Jg	25.57N	97.09W
Brawley	43	De	32.59N	115.34W
Bray	42	Jc	69.20N	77.00W
Bray	37	Ce	25.26S	23.38 E
Bray/Brè	9	Gh	53.12N	6.06W
Bray, Pays de-	11	He	49.46N	1.26 E
Bray-Dunes	12	Ec	51.05N	2.31 E
Braye	11	Gg	47.45N	0.42 E
Bray Head	9	Cj	51.53N	10.25W
Bray-sur-Somme	12	Ee	49.56N	2.43 E
Brazi	15	Je	44.52N	26.01 E
Brazil	44	Df	39.32N	87.08W
Brazil (EN)=Brasil [1]	53	Kf	9.00S	53.00W
Brazil Basin (EN)	3	Dk	15.00S	25.00W
Brazilian Highlands (EN) = Brasil, Planalto do-	52	Lg	17.00S	45.00W
Brazos	38	Jg	28.53N	95.23W
Brazos Santiago Pass	45	Hm	26.05N	97.16W
Brazzaville	31	Ii	4.16S	15.17 E
Brčko	14	Mf	44.52N	18.49 E
Brda	10	Oc	53.07N	18.08 E
Brdy	10	Jg	49.35N	13.50 E
Bré/Bray	9	Gh	53.12N	6.06W
Brea, Punta-	51a	Bc	17.54N	66.55W
Breaden, Lake-	59	Fe	25.45S	125.40 E
Breaksea Sound	62	Bf	45.35S	166.40 E
Breaza [Rom.]	15	Id	45.11N	25.40 E
Breaza [Rom.]	15	Ib	47.37N	25.20 E
Breaza, Vîrful-	15	Hb	47.22N	24.02 E
Brebes	26	Eh	6.53S	109.03 E
Brêche	12	Ee	49.16N	2.30 E
Brechin	9	Ke	56.44N	2.40W
Brecht	12	Gc	51.21N	4.38 E
Brechte	12	Jb	52.15N	7.10 E
Breckenridge [Mn.-U.S.]	45	Hc	46.16N	96.35W
Breckenridge [Tx.-U.S.]	45	Gj	32.45N	98.54W
Breckland	9	Ni	52.30N	0.35 E
Břeclav	10	Mh	48.46N	16.54 E
Brecon	9	Jj	51.57N	3.24W
Brecon Beacons	9	Jj	51.53N	3.31W
Breda	11	Kc	51.35N	4.46 E
Bredaryd	8	Eg	57.10N	13.44 E
Bredasdorp	31	Jl	34.32S	20.02 E
Brede	12	Cd	50.55N	0.43 E
Bredene	12	Ec	51.14N	2.58 E
Bredstedt	10	Eb	54.37N	8.59 E
Bredy	19	Ge	52.26N	60.21 E
Bree	12	Hc	51.08N	5.36 E
Breg	10	Ei	47.57N	8.31 E
Bregalnica	15	Eh	41.36N	21.56 E
Bregenz	14	Dc	47.30N	9.46 E
Bréhat, Ile de-	11	Df	48.51N	3.00W
Breiðafjörður	5	Db	65.15N	23.15W
Breimsvatnet	8	Bc	61.40N	6.25 E
Breisach am Rhein	10	Dh	48.02N	7.35 E
Breisund	8	Ab	62.30N	6.00 E
Breit Bridge	37	Dd	22.12S	29.59 E
Breivikbotn	7	Fa	70.37N	22.19 E
Brejão	55	Ia	12.59S	46.28W
Brekken	7	Ce	62.39N	11.53 E
Brekstad	7	Be	63.41N	9.41 E
Bremangerlandet	7	Af	61.50N	5.00 E
Brembana, Val-	14	De	45.55N	9.40 E
Brembo	14	De	45.35N	9.32 E
Bremen [2]	10	Ec	53.05N	8.50 E
Bremen [F.R.G.]	6	Ge	53.05N	8.48 E
Bremen [In.-U.S.]	44	De	41.27N	86.09W
Bremerhaven	6	Ge	53.33N	8.35 E
Bremerton	43	Cb	47.34N	122.38W
Bremervörde	10	Fc	53.29N	9.08 E
Brendel	46	Kg	38.57N	109.50W
Brenham	45	Hk	30.10N	96.24W
Brenne	11	Hh	46.44N	1.14 E
Brennero, Passo del-= Brenner Pass (EN)	5	Hf	47.00N	11.30 E
Brennerpaß=Brenner Pass (EN)	5	Hf	47.00N	11.30 E
Brenner Pass (EN)= Brennero, Passo del-	5	Hf	47.00N	11.30 E
Brenner Pass (EN)= Brennerpaß	5	Hf	47.00N	11.30 E
Brenta	14	Ge	45.11N	12.18 E
Brentwood	9	Nj	51.38N	0.18 E
Brescia	6	Hf	45.33N	10.15 E
Breskens	12	Fc	51.24N	3.33 E
Breslau (EN)=Wrocław	6	He	51.06N	17.00 E
Bresle	11	Hd	50.04N	1.22 E
Bressanone / Brixen	14	Fd	46.43N	11.39 E
Bressay	9	La	60.08N	1.05W
Bresse	11	Lh	46.30N	5.15 E
Bressuire	11	Fh	46.51N	0.29W
Brest [Bye.-U.S.S.R.]	6	Ie	52.06N	23.42 E
Brest [Fr.]	6	Ff	48.24N	4.29W
Brestova	14	Ie	45.08N	14.14 E
Brestskaja Oblast [3]	19	Ce	52.20N	25.30 E
Bretagne=Brittany (EN)	11	Df	48.00N	3.00W
Bretagne=Brittany (EN)	5	Ff	48.00N	3.00W
Breţcu	15	Jc	46.03N	26.18 E
Breteuil [Fr.]	12	Cf	48.50N	0.55 E
Breteuil [Fr.]	11	Ie	49.38N	2.18 E
Breton, Marais-	11	Eh	46.56N	2.00W
Breton, Pertuis-	11	Eh	46.16N	1.22W
Breton Sound	45	Ll	29.30N	89.30W
Brett	12	Cc	51.58N	0.57 E
Brett, Cape-	62	Fa	35.10S	174.20 E
Bretten	12	Ke	49.03N	8.42 E
Bretteville-sur-Laize	12	Be	49.03N	0.20W
Breueh, Pulau-	26	Be	5.41N	95.05 E
Breuil Cervinia	14	Be	45.56N	7.38 E
Breukelen	12	Db	52.10N	5.01 E
Breuna	12	Lc	51.25N	9.11 E
Breves	54	Hd	1.40S	50.29W
Brevik	7	Bg	59.04N	9.42 E
Brevoort	42	Ld	63.30N	64.20W
Brewarrina	59	Je	29.57S	146.52 E
Brewerville	34	Cd	6.25N	10.47W
Brewster	46	Fb	48.06N	119.47W
Brewster, Kap-	67	Md	70.10N	21.30W
Brewton	43	Je	31.07N	87.04W
Brežice	14	Je	45.54N	15.35 E
Brézina	32	Hc	33.05N	1.16 E
Březnice	10	Jg	49.33N	13.57 E
Breznik	15	Fg	42.44N	22.54 E
Brezno	10	Ph	48.49N	19.39 E
Brezoi	15	Hd	45.21N	24.15 E
Brezolles	12	Df	48.41N	1.04 E
Brezovo	15	Ig	42.21N	25.05 E
Bria	31	Jh	6.32N	21.59 E
Briance	11	Hi	45.47N	1.12 E
Briançon	11	Mj	44.54N	6.39 E
Brianza	14	De	45.45N	9.15 E
Briare, Canal de-	11	If	48.02N	2.43 E
Bribie Island	59	Ke	27.00S	153.05 E
Bričany	15	Ka	48.18N	27.04 E
Bride	9	Fi	52.05N	7.50W
Bridgend	9	Jj	51.31N	3.35W
Bridgeport [Ca.-U.S.]	46	Fg	38.10N	119.13W
Bridgeport [Ct.-U.S.]	43	Mc	41.11N	73.11W
Bridgeport [Nb.-U.S.]	45	Ef	41.40N	103.06W
Bridge River	46	Ea	50.45N	121.55W
Bridger Peak	46	Lf	41.12N	107.02W
Bridges Point	64g	Bb	1.58N	157.28W
Bridgeton	44	Jf	39.26N	75.14W
Bridgetown [Austl.]	59	Df	33.57S	116.08 E
Bridgetown [Bar.]	39	Nh	13.06N	59.37W
Bridgewater	42	Lh	44.23N	64.31W
Bridgwater	9	Kj	51.08N	3.00W
Bridgwater Bay	9	Jj	51.16N	3.12W
Bridlington	9	Mg	54.05N	0.12W
Bridlington Bay	9	Mg	54.04N	0.08W
Bridport	9	Kk	50.44N	2.46W
Brie	11	Jf	48.40N	3.30 E
Brielle	12	Gc	51.54N	4.10 E
Brienzer-See	14	Bd	46.45N	7.55 E
Briey	11	Le	49.15N	5.56 E
Brig	14	Bd	46.20N	8.00 E
Brigach	10	Ei	47.58N	8.30 E
Brigham City	43	Ec	41.31N	112.01W
Brighstone	12	Ad	50.38N	1.23W
Bright	59	Jg	36.44S	146.58 E
Brightlingsea	12	Dc	51.48N	1.02 E
Brighton [Co.-U.S.]	45	Dg	39.59N	104.49W
Brighton [Eng.-U.K.]	6	Fe	50.50N	0.10W
Brignoles	11	Mk	43.24N	6.04 E
Brihuega	13	Jd	40.45N	2.52W
Brijuni	14	Hf	44.55N	13.46 E
Brikama	34	Bc	13.16N	16.39W
Brilhante, Rio-	54	Hh	21.58S	54.18W
Brilon	12	Kc	51.24N	8.35 E
Brilon-Alme	12	Kc	51.27N	8.37 E
Brimstone Hill	51c	Ab	17.21N	62.49W
Brindisi	6	Hg	40.38N	17.56 E
Brinkley	45	Ki	34.53N	91.12W
Brinkmann	55	Aj	30.52S	62.02W
Brionne	12	Ce	49.12N	0.43 E
Brioude	11	Ji	45.18N	3.24 E
Brisbane	58	Gg	27.28S	153.02 E
Brisighella	14	Ff	44.13N	11.46 E
Bristol	66	Ad	59.02S	26.31W
Bristol [Eng.-U.K.]	6	Fe	51.27N	2.35W
Bristol [Tn.-U.S.]	44	Fg	36.36N	82.11W
Bristol Bay	38	Dd	58.00N	159.00W
Bristol Channel	5	Fe	51.20N	4.00W
Bristol Lake	46	Hi	34.28N	115.41W
Bristow	45	Hi	35.50N	96.23W
Britannia Range	66	Jf	80.00S	158.00 E
British Columbia [3]	42	Fe	55.00N	125.00W
British Honduras → Belize	49	Ce	17.35N	88.35W
British Indian Ocean Territory [5]	22	Jj	7.00S	72.00 E
British Isles	5	Fd	54.00N	4.00W
British Mountains	40	Kc	69.20N	140.20W
British Solomon Islands → Solomon Islands [1]	58	Ge	8.00S	159.00 E
British Virgin Islands [5]	39	Mh	18.20N	64.50W
Brits	37	De	25.40S	27.46 E
Britstown	37	Cf	30.37S	23.30 E
Britt	45	Je	43.06N	93.48W
Brittany (EN)=Bretagne	5	Ff	48.00N	3.00W
Brittany (EN)=Bretagne	11	Df	48.00N	3.00W
Britton	45	Hd	45.48N	97.45W
Brive-la-Gaillarde	11	Hi	45.09N	1.32 E
Briviesca	13	Ib	42.33N	3.19W
Brixen / Bressanone	14	Fd	46.43N	11.39 E
Brixham	9	Jk	50.24N	3.30W
Brjansk	6	Je	53.15N	34.22 E
Brjanskaja Oblast [3]	19	De	52.50N	33.20 E
Brjuhoveckaja	16	Kg	45.46N	39.01 E
Brjukoviči	10	Jg	49.52N	24.00 E
Brno	6	Hf	49.12N	16.37 E
Broa, Ensenada de la-	49	Fb	22.35N	82.00W
Broad Bay	9	Gc	58.15N	6.15W
Broadford	9	Hd	57.14N	5.54W
Broad Sound	59	Jd	22.10S	149.45 E
Broadstairs	12	Dc	51.22N	1.27 E
Broadus	43	Fb	45.27N	105.25W
Brocēni/Broceny	8	Jh	56.41N	22.30 E
Broceny/Brocēni	8	Jh	56.41N	22.30 E
Brochet	42	He	57.53N	101.40W
Brochu, Lac-	44	Ja	48.26N	74.15W
Brock	42	Ga	77.55N	114.30W
Brocken	10	Ge	51.48N	10.36 E
Brockman, Mount-	59	Dd	22.28S	117.18 E
Brockton	44	Ld	42.05N	71.01W
Brockville	42	Jh	44.35N	75.41W
Brod	15	Eh	41.31N	21.14 E
Brodarevo	15	Cf	43.14N	19.43 E
Broderick Falls	36	Fb	0.37N	34.46 E
Brodeur Peninsula	38	Kb	73.00N	88.00W
Brodick	9	Hf	55.35N	5.09W
Brodnica	10	Pc	53.16N	19.23 E
Brody	16	Dd	50.04N	25.12 E
Broglie	12	Ce	49.01N	0.32 E
Brok	10	Rd	52.43N	21.52 E
Brok	10	Rd	52.38N	21.55 E
Broken Arrow	45	Ih	36.03N	95.48W
Broken Bow	45	If	41.24N	99.38W
Broken Bow Lake	45	Ii	34.10N	94.40W
Broken Hill	58	Fh	31.57S	141.27 E
Broken Ridge (EN)	3	Hm	31.30S	95.00 E
Brokind	8	Ff	58.13N	15.40 E
Brokopondo	54	Hb	5.04N	55.00W
Bromarv	8	Je	59.55N	23.00 E
Bromley, London-	12	Cc	51.25N	0.01 E
Bromölla	7	Dh	56.04N	14.28 E
Brønderslev	8	Cg	57.16N	9.58 E
Brong-Ahafo [3]	34	Ed	7.45N	1.30W
Bronnikovo	17	Ng	58.29N	68.27 E
Brønnøysund	7	Cd	65.28N	12.13 E
Bronte	14	Im	37.47N	14.50 E
Brooke's Point	26	Ge	8.47N	117.50 E
Brookfield	45	Jg	39.47N	93.04W
Brookhaven	45	Kk	31.35N	90.26W
Brookings [Or.-U.S.]	43	Cc	42.03N	124.17W
Brookings [S.D.-U.S.]	43	Hc	44.19N	96.48W
Brooks	42	Gf	50.35N	111.53W
Brooks Banks (EN)	60	Mc	24.05N	166.50W
Brooks Range	38	Dc	68.00N	154.00W
Brookston	45	Jc	46.50N	92.32W
Brooksville	44	Fk	28.33N	82.23W
Brookton	59	Df	32.22S	117.01 E
Brookville [In.-U.S.]	44	Ef	39.25N	85.01W
Brookville [Pa.-U.S.]	44	He	41.10N	79.06W
Broom	9	Hd	57.45N	5.05W
Broom, Loch-	9	Hd	57.55N	5.15W
Broome	58	Df	17.58S	122.14 E
Brora	9	Jc	58.00N	3.50W
Brora	9	Jc	58.01N	3.51W
Brosna/An Bhrosnach	9	Fh	53.13N	7.58W
Broşteni	15	Ib	47.14N	25.42 E
Brou	11	Hf	48.13N	1.11 E
Brough	9	Kg	54.32N	2.19W
Broughton Island	39	Mc	67.35N	63.50W
Broussard	45	Kk	30.09N	91.58W
Brovary	16	Gd	50.32N	30.48 E
Brovst	8	Cg	57.06N	9.32 E
Brown Bank (EN)=Bruine Bank	12	Fb	52.35N	3.20 E
Brownfield	43	Ge	33.11N	102.16W
Browning	46	Ib	48.34N	113.01W
Browns Bank (EN)	42	Kh	42.40N	66.05W
Brownsville [Tn.-U.S.]	44	Ch	35.36N	89.15W
Brownsville [Tx.-U.S.]	39	Jg	25.54N	97.30W
Brownwood	43	He	31.43N	98.59W
Browse Island	59	Eb	14.05S	123.35 E
Broye	14	Bd	46.55N	7.02 E
Bruay-en-Artois	11	Id	50.29N	2.33 E
Bruay-sur-l'Escaut	12	Fd	50.23N	3.32 E
Bruce	45	Lj	33.59N	89.21W
Bruce, Mount-	57	Cg	22.36S	118.08 E
Bruce Crossing	44	Cb	46.32N	89.10W
Bruce Peninsula	42	Jh	44.59N	81.20W
Bruce Rock	59	Df	31.53S	118.09 E
Bruche	11	Nf	48.34N	7.43 E

Index Symbols

- [1] Independent Nation
- [2] State, Region
- [3] District, County
- [4] Municipality
- [5] Colony, Dependency
- Continent
- Physical Region
- Historical or Cultural Region
- Mount, Mountain
- Volcano
- Hill
- Mountains, Mountain Range
- Hills, Escarpment
- Plateau, Upland
- Pass, Gap
- Plain, Lowland
- Delta
- Salt Flat
- Valley, Canyon
- Crater, Cave
- Karst Features
- Depression
- Polder
- Desert, Dunes
- Forest, Woods
- Heath, Steppe
- Oasis
- Cape, Point
- Coast, Beach
- Cliff
- Peninsula
- Isthmus
- Sandbank
- Island
- Atoll
- Rock, Reef
- Islands, Archipelago
- Rocks, Reefs
- Coral Reef
- Well, Spring
- Geyser
- River, Stream
- Waterfall Rapids
- River Mouth, Estuary
- Lake
- Salt Lake
- Intermittent Lake
- Reservoir
- Swamp, Pond
- Canal
- Glacier
- Ice Shelf, Pack Ice
- Ocean
- Sea
- Gulf, Bay
- Strait, Fjord
- Lagoon
- Bank
- Seamount
- Tablemount
- Ridge
- Shelf
- Basin
- Escarpment, Sea Scarp
- Fracture
- Trench, Abyss
- National Park, Reserve
- Point of Interest
- Recreation Site
- Cave, Cavern
- Historic Site
- Ruins
- Wall, Walls
- Church, Abbey
- Temple
- Scientific Station
- Airport
- Port
- Lighthouse
- Mine
- Tunnel
- Dam, Bridge

Name	Page	Grid	Lat.	Long.
Bruchhausen Vilsen	12	Lb	52.50N	9.01 E
Bruchmühlbach Miesau	12	Je	49.23N	7.28 E
Bruchsal	10	Eg	49.08N	8.36 E
Bruck an der Leitha	14	Kb	48.01N	16.46 E
Bruck an der Mur	14	Jc	47.25N	15.17 E
Brue	9	Kj	51.13N	3.00W
Bruges/Brugge	11	Jc	51.13N	3.14 E
Brugg	14	Cc	47.29N	8.12 E
Brugge/Bruges	11	Jc	51.13N	3.14 E
Brugge-Assebroek	12	Fc	51.12N	3.16 E
Brüggen	12	Ic	51.15N	6.11 E
Brugge-Sint-Andries	12	Fc	51.12N	3.10 E
Brühl [F.R.G.]	12	Id	50.50N	6.54 E
Brühl [F.R.G.]	12	Ke	49.24N	8.32 E
Bruine Bank=Brown Bank (EN)	12	Fb	52.35N	3.20 E
Bruin Point	43	Ed	39.39N	110.22W
Brule River	44	Cc	45.57N	88.12W
Brumado	54	Jf	14.13S	41.40W
Brummen	12	Ib	52.06N	6.10 E
Brummo	8	Ef	58.50N	13.40 E
Brumunddal	7	Cf	60.53N	10.56 E
Bruna	14	Eh	42.45N	10.53 E
Brune	12	Fe	49.45N	3.47 E
Bruneau	46	He	42.53N	115.48W
Bruneau River	46	He	42.57N	115.58W
Bruneck / Brunico	14	Fd	46.48N	11.56 E
Brunehamel	12	Ge	49.46N	4.11 E
Brunei [5]	22	Ni	4.30N	114.40 E
Brunei, Teluk-	21	Ni	5.05N	115.18 E
Brunette Downs	59	Hc	18.38S	135.57 E
Brunflo	8	Fa	63.05N	14.49 E
Brunico / Bruneck	14	Fd	46.48N	11.56 E
Brunna	8	Ge	59.52N	17.25 E
Brunner	62	De	42.26S	171.19 E
Brunner, Lake-	62	De	42.35S	171.25 E
Brunnsberg	8	Ec	61.17N	13.55 E
Brunsbüttel	10	Fc	53.54N	9.07 E
Brunssum	12	Hd	50.57N	5.57 E
Brunswick [Ga.-U.S.]	43	Ke	31.10N	81.29W
Brunswick [Me.-U.S.]	43	Nc	43.55N	69.58W
Brunswick, Peninsula de-	52	Ik	53.30S	71.25W
Brunswick Lake	44	Fa	49.00N	83.23W
Bruntál	10	Ng	49.59N	17.28 E
Bruny Island	59	Jh	43.30S	147.05 E
Brus	15	Ef	43.23N	21.02 E
Brus, Laguna de-	49	Ef	15.50N	84.35W
Brush	43	Gc	40.15N	103.37W
Brus Laguna	49	Ef	15.47N	84.35W
Brusque	56	Kc	27.06S	48.56W
Brussel/Bruxelles=Brussels (EN)	6	Ge	50.50N	4.20 E
Brussels (EN)=Brussel/ Bruxelles	6	Ge	50.50N	4.20 E
Brussels (EN)=Bruxelles/ Brussel	6	Ge	50.50N	4.20 E
Brusset, 'Erg-	34	Hb	18.55N	10.30 E
Brusturi	15	Fb	47.09N	22.15 E
Brusy	10	Nc	53.53N	17.45 E
Bruxelles/Brussel=Brussels (EN)	6	Ge	50.50N	4.20 E
Bruzual	50	Bh	8.03N	69.19W
Bryan [Oh.-U.S.]	44	Ee	41.30N	84.34W
Bryan [Tx.-U.S.]	43	He	30.40N	96.22W
Bryan Coast	66	Pf	73.35S	84.00W
Bryne	7	Ag	58.44N	5.39 E
Brza Palanka	15	Fe	44.28N	22.27 E
Brzava kanal	15	Dd	45.16N	20.49 E
Brzeg	10	Nf	50.52N	17.27 E
Brzeg Dolny	10	Me	51.15N	16.40 E
Brzeziny	10	Pe	51.48N	19.46 E
Brzozów	10	Sg	49.42N	22.02 E
Bsharrī	24	Ge	34.15N	36.01 E
Bû	12	Df	48.48N	1.30 E
Bua	8	Eg	57.14N	12.07 E
Buada Lagoon	64e	Ab	0.32S	166.54 E
Buala	58	Ge	8.10S	159.35 E
Bū al Ḩīdān, Wādī-	33	Cd	27.25N	19.22 E
Buapinang	26	Hg	4.46S	121.34 E
Buatan	26	Df	0.44N	101.51 E
Bū aţ Tifl	33	Dd	28.54N	22.30 E
Bua Yai	25	Ke	15.34N	102.24 E
Bu'ayrāt al Ḩasūn	33	Cc	31.24N	15.44 E
Bubanza	36	Ec	3.06S	29.23 E
Bubaque	34	Bc	11.17N	15.50W
Būbīyan	24	Mh	29.45N	48.15 E
Bubu	36	Gd	6.03S	35.19 E
Bubye	37	Ed	22.20S	31.07 E
Buca	15	Kk	38.22N	27.11 E
Bučač	16	De	49.04N	25.23 E
Bucačača	20	Gf	52.59N	116.55 E
Buçaco	36	De	11.27S	20.12 E
Bucak	24	Dd	37.28N	30.36 E
Bucaramanga	53	Ie	7.08N	73.09W
Bucas Grande	26	Ie	9.40N	125.58 E
Buccament Bay	51n	Ba	13.12N	61.17W
Buccaneer Archipelago	59	Ec	16.17S	123.20 E
Bucecea	15	Jb	47.46N	26.26 E
Buchanan	31	Fh	5.53N	10.03W
Buchanan, Lake- [Austl.]	59	Jd	21.30S	145.50 E
Buchanan, Lake- [Tx.-U.S.]	45	Gk	30.48N	98.25W
Buchanan Bay	42	Ka	78.55N	75.00W
Buchan Gulf	42	Kb	71.48N	74.06W
Buchardo	56	Hd	34.43S	63.31W
Bucharest (EN)=Bucureşti	6	Ig	44.26N	26.06 E
Buchen	10	Fg	49.31N	9.20 E
Buchholz in der Nordheide	10	Fc	53.20N	9.52 E
Buchon, Point-	46	Ei	35.15N	120.54W
Buchs	14	Dc	47.10N	9.30 E
Buchy	12	De	49.35N	1.22 E
Bückeburg	12	Lb	52.16N	9.03 E
Buckeye	46	Ij	33.22N	112.35W
Buckhaven	9	Je	56.11N	3.03W
Buckie	9	Kd	57.40N	2.58W
Buckingham [Eng.-U.K.]	12	Bb	52.00N	0.59W
Buckingham [Que.-Can.]	44	Jc	45.35N	75.25W
Buckingham Bay	59	Hb	12.10S	135.46 E
Buckinghamshire [3]	9	Mj	51.50N	0.55W
Buckland	40	Gc	66.16N	161.20W
Buckle Island	66	Ke	66.47S	163.14 E
Buckley Bay	66	Je	68.16S	148.12 E
Bucks	9	Mj	51.50N	0.55W
Bucksport	44	Mc	44.34N	68.48W
Buco Zau	36	Bc	4.50S	12.33 E
Bu Craa	32	Ed	26.17N	12.46W
Bucureşti [2]	15	Je	44.30N	26.05 E
Bucureşti=Bucharest (EN)	6	Ig	44.26N	26.06 E
Bucy-lès-Pierrepont	12	Fe	49.39N	3.54 E
Bucyrus	44	Fe	40.47N	82.57W
Bud	7	Be	62.55N	6.55 E
Budacu, Vîrful-	15	Ib	47.07N	25.41 E
Buda-Koševelo	16	Gc	52.43N	30.39 E
Budapest [2]	10	Pi	47.30N	19.05 E
Budapest	6	Hf	47.30N	19.05 E
Búdardalur	7a	Bb	65.07N	21.46W
Budaun	25	Fc	28.03N	79.07 E
Budbud	35	He	4.13N	46.31 E
Budd Coast	66	He	66.30S	113.00 E
Buddusò	14	Di	40.35N	9.15 E
Bude [Eng.-U.K.]	9	Ik	50.50N	4.33W
Bude [Ms.-U.S.]	45	Kk	31.28N	90.51W
Bude Bay	9	Ik	50.50N	4.37W
Budel	12	Hc	51.16N	5.30 E
Budennovsk	19	Eg	44.45N	44.08 E
Budeşti	15	Je	44.14N	26.27 E
Budia	13	Jd	40.38N	2.45W
Büdingen	10	Ff	50.18N	9.07 E
Búdir	7a	Cb	64.56N	14.01W
Budjala	36	Cb	2.39N	19.42 E
Budkowiczanka	10	Nf	50.52N	17.33 E
Budogošč	7	Hg	59.19N	32.29 E
Budrio	14	Ff	44.32N	11.32 E
Budslav	8	Lj	54.49N	27.32 E
Budva	15	Bg	42.17N	18.51 E
Budyšin/Bautzen	10	Ke	51.11N	14.26 E
Budžjak	15	Lc	46.15N	28.45 E
Buea	34	Ge	4.09N	9.14 E
Buech	11	Lj	44.12N	5.57 E
Buenaventura [Col.]	53	Ie	3.53N	77.04W
Buenaventura [Mex.]	47	Cc	29.51N	107.29W
Buenaventura, Bahia de-	54	Cc	3.45N	77.15W
Buenavista	48	Ef	23.39N	109.42W
Buena Vista [Co.-U.S.]	45	Cg	38.50N	106.08W
Buena Vista [Mex.]	48	Mi	16.05N	93.00W
Buena Vista [Mex.]	48	Bb	31.10N	115.40W
Buena Vista [Ven.]	50	Eh	9.02N	63.49W
Buenavista, Bahía de-	49	Hb	22.30N	79.08W
Buendia, Embalse de-	13	Jd	40.25N	2.43W
Buenópolis	55	Jc	17.54S	44.11W
Buenos Aires [2]	56	Ie	36.00S	60.00W
Buenos Aires [Arg.]	53	Ki	34.36S	58.27W
Buenos Aires [C.R.]	49	Fi	10.04N	84.26W
Buenos Aires, Lago-	52	Ij	46.30S	72.00W
Buffalo	42	Fe	60.52N	115.03W
Buffalo [N.Y.-U.S.]	39	Le	42.54N	78.53W
Buffalo [Ok.-U.S.]	45	Gh	36.50N	99.38W
Buffalo [S.D.-U.S.]	43	Gb	45.35N	103.33W
Buffalo [Tx.-U.S.]	45	Hk	31.28N	96.04W
Buffalo [Wy.-U.S.]	43	Fc	44.21N	106.42W
Buffalo Bill Reservoir	46	Kd	44.29N	109.13W
Buffalo Lake	42	Fd	60.12N	115.25W
Buffalo Narrows	42	Ge	55.51N	108.30W
Buffalo Pound Lake	46	Ma	50.38N	105.20W
Buffels	37	Be	29.41S	17.04 E
Bū Fishah	14	En	36.18N	10.28 E
Buford	44	Fh	34.07N	84.00W
Buftea	15	Ie	44.34N	25.57 E
Bug	5	Ie	52.31N	21.05 E
Buga	54	Cc	3.55N	76.18W
Bugarach, Pech de-	11	Il	42.52N	2.23 E
Bugeat	11	Hi	45.36N	1.56 E
Bugene	36	Fc	1.35S	31.08 E
Bugey	11	Li	45.48N	5.30 E
Bugojno	23	Ff	44.03N	17.27 E
Bugøynes	7	Gb	69.58N	29.39 E
Bugrino	17	Db	68.48N	49.09 E
Bugsuk	26	Ge	8.15N	117.18 E
Bugt	27	Lb	48.47N	121.55 E
Bugulma	19	Fe	54.33N	52.48 E
Bugun	18	Hc	43.22N	70.10 E
Bugun	18	Gc	42.56N	68.36 E
Bügür/Luntai	27	Dc	41.46N	84.10 E
Buguruslan	19	Fe	53.39N	52.30 E
Buhara	22	If	39.49N	64.25 E
Buharskaja Oblast [3]	19	Gg	41.20N	64.20 E
Bū Ḩaşā'	24	Ok	23.20N	53.20 E
Buhera	37	Ec	19.18S	31.29 E
Buh He	27	Gd	36.58N	99.48 E
Buhl	46	He	42.36N	114.46W
Bühl	10	Eh	48.42N	8.09 E
Būhōdle	35	Hd	8.15N	46.20 E
Buhtarminskoje Vodohranilišče	19	If	49.10N	84.00 E
Bui Dam	34	Ed	8.22N	2.10W
Builth Wells	9	Ji	52.09N	3.24W
Buin [Chile]	56	Fd	33.44S	70.44W
Buin [Pap.N.Gui.]	60	Fi	6.50S	155.44 E
Buinsk	19	Ee	54.59N	48.17 E
Buir Nur	27	Kb	47.48N	117.42 E
Buitrago del Lozoya	13	Id	41.00N	3.38W
Buj	17	Gh	56.15N	54.12 E
Buj	19	Ed	58.29N	41.31 E
Bujalance	13	Hg	37.54N	4.22W
Bujanovac	15	Eg	42.28N	21.47 E
Bujaraloz	13	Lc	41.30N	0.09W
Buje	14	He	45.24N	13.40 E
Bujnaksk	19	Eg	42.49N	47.07 E
Bujukly	20	Jg	49.33N	142.55 E
Bujumbura	31	Ji	3.23S	29.22 E
Bujunda	20	Kd	62.00N	153.30 E
Buk	10	Md	52.22N	16.31 E
Bük	10	Mi	47.23N	16.45 E
Buk	10	Hb	54.10N	11.42 E
Buka Island	57	Ge	5.15S	154.35 E
Bukakata	36	Fc	0.18S	32.02 E
Bukama	31	Ji	9.12S	25.51 E
Buka Passage	63a	Ba	5.25S	154.41 E
Bukavu	31	Ji	2.30S	28.52 E
Bukene	36	Fc	4.14S	32.53 E
Bukhā	24	Qi	26.10N	56.09 E
Bukit Besi	26	Df	4.46N	103.12 E
Bukit Mertajam	26	De	5.22N	100.28 E
Bukittinggi	22	Mj	0.19S	100.22 E
Bükk	10	Qh	48.05N	20.30 E
Bukoba	31	Ki	1.20S	31.49 E
Bukovina	15	Ia	48.00N	25.30 E
Bukowiec	10	Ld	52.23N	15.20 E
Bukuru	34	Gd	9.48N	8.52 E
Būl, Kūh-e-	23	Hc	30.48N	52.45 E
Bulajevo	19	He	54.53N	70.26 E
Bulan	26	Hd	12.40N	123.52 E
Bulanaš	17	Kh	57.16N	62.02 E
Bulancak	24	Hb	40.57N	38.14 E
Bulanık	24	Jc	39.05N	42.15 E
Būlāq	33	Fd	25.12N	30.32 E
Bulawayo	31	Jk	20.09S	28.34 E
Buldan	24	Cc	38.03N	28.51 E
Buldir	40a	Bb	52.21N	175.54 E
Bulgan [Mong.]	27	Hc	44.05N	103.32 E
Bulgan [Mong.]	27	Hb	48.45N	103.34 E
Bulgan [Mong.]	27	Fb	46.05N	91.34 E
Bulgaria (EN)=Bălgarija [1]	6	Ig	43.00N	25.00 E
Buli	26	If	0.53N	128.18 E
Buli, Teluk-	26	If	0.45N	128.30 E
Buliluyan, Cape-	26	Ge	8.20N	117.11 E
Bulki	35	Fd	6.01N	36.36 E
Bullahār	35	Gc	10.23N	44.27 E
Bullange/Büllingen	12	Id	50.25N	6.16 E
Bullaque	13	Hf	38.59N	4.17W
Bulla Regia	14	Cn	36.33N	8.45 E
Bullas	13	Kf	38.03N	1.40W
Bulle	14	Bd	46.37N	7.04 E
Buller	62	Dd	41.44S	171.35 E
Bullfinch	59	Df	30.59S	119.06 E
Büllingen/Bullange	12	Id	50.25N	6.16 E
Bullion Mountains	46	Hi	34.25N	116.00W
Bulloo River	57	Fg	28.43S	142.30 E
Bull Point [Eng.-U.K.]	9	Ij	51.12N	4.10W
Bull Point [Falk.Is.]	56	Ih	52.19S	59.18W
Bulls	62	Fd	40.10S	175.23 E
Bulls Bay	44	Hi	32.59N	79.33W
Bull Shoals Lake	45	Jh	36.30N	92.50W
Bully Choop Mountain	46	Df	40.35N	122.45W
Bully-les-Mines	12	Ed	50.26N	2.43 E
Bulo Berde	35	He	3.52N	45.40 E
Bulolo	60	Di	7.12S	146.39 E
Bulqiza	15	Dh	41.30N	20.21 E
Bulter	45	Ig	38.16N	94.20W
Bultfontein	37	De	28.20S	26.05 E
Bulukumba	26	Hh	5.33S	120.11 E
Bulungu [Zaire]	36	Cc	4.33S	18.36 E
Bulungu [Zaire]	36	Dd	6.04S	21.54 E
Bumba	31	Jh	2.11N	22.28 E
Bumbah, Khalīj al-	33	Dc	32.25N	23.06 E
Buna	15	Ch	41.52N	19.22 E
Buna	36	Gb	2.47N	39.31 E
Bunbury	58	Ch	33.19S	115.38 E
Buncrana/Bun Cranncha	9	Ff	55.08N	7.27W
Bun Cranncha/Buncrana	9	Ff	55.08N	7.27W
Bunda	36	Fc	2.03S	33.52 E
Bundaberg	58	Gg	24.52S	152.21 E
Bünde	10	Ed	52.12N	8.35 E
Bundesrepublik Deutschland =Germany, Federal Republic of- (EN) [1]	6	Ge	51.00N	9.00 E
Bun Dobhráin/Bundoran	9	Eg	54.28N	8.17W
Bundoran/Bun Dobhráin	9	Eg	54.28N	8.17W
Bungay	12	Db	52.27N	1.27 E
Bungku	26	Hg	2.33S	121.58 E
Bungo	36	Cd	7.26S	15.24 E
Bungo Strait (EN)=Bungo-Suidō	28	Lh	32.40N	132.18 E
Bungo-Suidō=Bungo Strait (EN)	28	Lh	32.40N	132.18 E
Bungotakada	29	Be	33.33N	131.27 E
Bungsberg	10	Gb	54.12N	10.43 E
Bunguran, Kepulauan-= Natuna Islands (EN)	21	Mi	2.45N	109.00 E
Buni	34	Hc	11.12N	12.02 E
Bunja	31	Kh	1.34N	30.15 E
Bunji	25	Ea	35.40N	74.36 E
Bunker	45	Kh	37.27N	91.13W
Bunker Group	59	Kd	23.50S	152.20 E
Bunkeya	36	Ee	10.24S	26.58 E
Bunkie	45	Jk	30.57N	92.11W
Bunnerfjällen	8	Ea	63.10N	12.34 E
Buñol	13	Le	39.25N	0.47W
Bunschoten	12	Hb	52.14N	5.24 E
Buntingford	12	Bc	51.57N	0.01W
Buntok	26	Fg	1.42S	114.48 E
Bünyan	24	Fc	38.51N	35.52 E
Bunyu, Pulau-	26	Gf	3.30N	117.50 E
Buor-Haja, Guba-	20	Ib	71.00N	131.00 E
Buotama	20	Hd	61.17N	128.55 E
Buqayaq	23	Gd	25.56N	49.40 E
Buqda Kōsār	35	Ge	4.31N	44.49 E
Bur	20	Hb	71.40N	123.40 E
Bura	36	Gc	1.06S	39.57 E
Buram	31	Jg	10.49N	25.10 E
Buran	19	If	48.04N	85.15 E
Burang	27	De	30.18N	81.08 E
Burāq	24	Gf	33.10N	36.29 E
Buras	45	Ll	29.21N	89.32W
Buraydah	22	Gg	26.20N	43.59 E
Burbach	12	Kd	50.43N	8.03 E
Būrdab	35	Hd	9.05N	46.30 E
Burdekin River	59	Jc	19.39S	147.30 E
Burdēre	35	He	3.30N	45.37 E
Burdur	23	Db	37.43N	30.17 E
Burdur Gölü	24	Dd	37.44N	30.12 E
Burdwān	25	Ad	23.15N	87.51 E
Burdwood Bank (EN)	56	Ih	54.15S	59.00W
Bure	12	Db	52.38N	1.45 E
Bure [Eth.]	35	Fd	8.20N	35.08 E
Bure [Eth.]	35	Fc	10.43N	37.03 E
Bureå	7	Ed	64.37N	21.12 E
Bureinski Hrebet=Bureya Range (EN)	21	Pd	50.40N	134.00 E
Bureja	20	Hg	49.43N	129.51 E
Bureja	21	Oe	49.25N	129.35 E
Büren	10	Ee	51.33N	8.34 E
Buren-Cogt	27	Jb	46.45N	111.30 E
Bureya Range (EN)= Bureinski Hrebet	21	Pd	50.40N	134.00 E
Burfjord	7	Fb	69.56N	22.03 E
Būr Gābo	35	Gf	1.10S	41.50 E
Burgas	6	Ig	42.30N	27.28 E
Burgas [2]	15	Kg	42.30N	27.20 E
Burgas, Gulf of- (EN)= Burgaski Zaliv	15	Kg	42.30N	27.33 E
Burgaski Zaliv=Burgas, Gulf of- (EN)	15	Kg	42.30N	27.33 E
Burg auf Fehmarn	10	Hb	54.26N	11.12 E
Burg auf Fehmarn-Puttgarden	10	Hb	54.30N	11.13 E
Burgaw	44	Ih	34.33N	77.56W
Burgaz Daği	15	Mk	38.25N	29.46 E
Burg bei Magdeburg	10	Hd	52.16N	11.51 E
Burgdorf [F.R.G.]	10	Gd	52.27N	10.01 E
Burgdorf [Switz.]	14	Bc	47.04N	7.37 E
Burgenland [2]	14	Kc	47.30N	16.25 E
Burgersdorp	37	Df	31.00S	26.20 E
Burgess Hill	12	Bd	50.58N	0.08W
Burgfjället	7	Dd	64.56N	15.03 E
Burghausen	10	Ih	48.10N	12.50 E
Burghūth, Sabkhat al-	24	Ie	34.58N	41.06 E
Burglengenfeld	10	Ig	49.12N	12.02 E
Burgos [3]	13	Ib	42.20N	3.40W
Burgos [Mex.]	48	Je	24.57N	98.57W
Burgos [Sp.]	6	Fg	42.21N	3.42W
Burg-Reuland	12	Id	50.12N	6.09 E
Burgsvik	7	Eh	57.03N	18.16 E
Burgundy (EN)= Bourgogne	5	Gf	47.00N	4.30 E
Burgundy (EN)= Bourgogne	11	Kg	47.00N	4.30 E
Burgwald	12	Kd	50.57N	8.48 E
Būr Hakkaba	35	Ge	2.43N	44.10 E
Burhaniye	24	Bc	39.30N	26.58 E
Burhānpur	22	Jg	21.18N	76.14 E
Burias	26	Hd	12.57N	123.08 E
Buribaj	17	Ij	51.57N	58.11 E
Burica, Punta-	47	Hg	8.03N	82.53W
Burien	46	Dc	47.27N	122.21W
Burin Peninsula	42	Lg	47.00N	55.40W
Buriram	25	Kf	14.59N	103.08 E
Buriti, Rio-	55	Ca	12.50S	58.28W
Buriti Alegre	55	Hd	18.09S	49.03W
Buriti Bravo	54	Je	5.50S	43.50W
Buriti dos Lopes	54	Jd	3.10S	41.52W
Buritis	55	Ib	15.37S	46.26W
Burj al Ḩaţţābah	32	Ic	30.20N	9.30 E
Burjasot	13	Le	39.31N	0.25W
Burjatskaja ASSR [3]	20	Ff	53.00N	110.00 E
Burj Şāfītā	24	Ge	34.49N	36.07 E
Burkandja	20	Jd	63.27N	147.27 E
Burkburnett	45	Gi	34.06N	98.34W
Burke	45	Ge	43.11N	99.18W
Burke, Mount-	46	Ha	50.18N	114.30W
Burke Island	66	Of	73.08S	105.06W
Burke River	59	Hd	23.12S	139.33 E
Burkesville	44	Eg	36.48N	85.22W
Burketown	58	Ef	17.44S	139.22 E
Burley	43	Ec	42.32N	113.48W
Burli	16	Rd	51.28N	52.44 E
Burlingame	45	Ig	38.45N	95.50W
Burlington [Co.-U.S.]	43	Gd	39.18N	102.16W
Burlington [Ia.-U.S.]	43	Ic	40.49N	91.07W
Burlington [Ks.-U.S.]	45	Ig	38.12N	95.45W
Burlington [N.C.-U.S.]	44	Hg	36.06N	79.26W
Burlington [Ont.-Can.]	44	Hd	43.19N	79.43W
Burlington [Vt.-U.S.]	43	Mc	44.28N	73.14W
Burlington [Wi.-U.S.]	45	Le	42.41N	88.17W
Burma [1]	22	Lg	22.00N	98.00 E
Burma [1] (Myanma-Nainggan-Daw)	22	Lg	22.00N	98.00 E
Burnazului, Cîmpia-	15	Ie	44.10N	25.50 E
Burnett River	59	Kd	24.46S	152.25 E
Burney	46	Ef	40.53N	121.40W
Burnham Market	12	Cb	52.57N	0.44 E
Burnham-on-Crouch	12	Cc	51.37N	0.50 E
Burnie	59	Jh	41.04S	145.54 E
Burnley	9	Kh	53.48N	2.14W
Burns	43	Dc	43.35N	119.03W
Burnside	42	Gc	66.51N	108.04W
Burnside, Lake-	59	Ee	25.20S	123.10 E
Burns Lake	42	Ef	54.14N	125.46W
Burnsville	44	Fh	35.55N	82.18W
Burnt Lava Flow	46	Ef	41.35N	121.35W
Burnt River	44	Hc	44.35N	78.46W
Burntwood	42	He	56.08N	96.33W
Bur'o	31	Lh	9.30N	45.34 E
Burqin	27	Eb	47.43N	86.53 E
Burqin He	27	Eb	47.42N	86.50 E
Burqūm, Ḩarrat al-	33	He	20.54N	42.00 E
Burra	59	Hf	33.40S	138.56 E
Burragorang Lake	59	Kf	34.00S	150.25 E
Burreli	15	Ch	41.37N	20.00 E
Burrendong Reservoir	59	Jf	32.40S	149.10 E
Burriana	13	Le	39.53N	0.05W
Burro, Serranias del	48	Ic	28.50N	101.35W
Burrow Head	9	Ig	54.41N	4.24W
Bursa	22	Ee	40.11N	29.04 E
Būr Sa'īd=Port Said (EN)	31	Ke	31.16N	32.18 E
Burscheid	12	Jc	51.06N	7.07 E
Bürstadt	12	Ke	49.38N	8.27 E
Burštyn	16	De	49.16N	24.37 E
Būr Sūdān=Port Sudan (EN)	31	Kg	19.37N	37.14 E
Burt Lake	44	Ec	45.27N	84.40W
Burtnieku, Ozero-	8	Kg	57.35N	25.10 E
Burtnieku, Ozero-/Burtnieku Ezers	8	Kg	57.35N	25.10 E
Burtnieku Ezers	8	Kg	57.35N	25.10 E
Burtnieku Ezers/Burtnieku, Ozero-	8	Kg	57.35N	25.10 E
Burton	44	Fd	43.02N	83.36W
Burton Latimer	12	Bb	52.21N	0.40W
Burton-upon-Trent	9	Li	52.49N	1.36W
Burträsk	7	Ed	64.31N	20.39 E
Buru, Pulau-	57	De	3.24S	126.40 E
Burullus, Buḩayrat al-	24	Dg	31.30N	30.50 E
Burultokay/Fuhai	27	Eb	47.06N	87.23 E
Burum Gana	34	Hc	13.00N	11.57 E
Burūn, Ra's-	24	Eg	31.14N	33.04 E
Burundaj	19	Hg	43.20N	76.49 E
Burundi [1]	31	Ki	3.15S	30.00 E
Bururi	36	Ec	3.57S	29.37 E
Burutu	34	Gd	5.21N	5.31 E
Bury	9	Kh	53.36N	2.17W
Burylbajtal	18	Ib	44.56N	73.59 E
Buryn	16	Hd	51.13N	33.48 E
Bury Saint Edmunds	9	Ni	52.15N	0.43 E
Burzil Pass	25	Ff	34.54N	75.06 E
Busalla	14	Cf	44.34N	8.57 E
Busanga [Zaire]	36	Ee	10.12S	25.23 E
Busanga [Zaire]	36	Dc	0.51S	22.04 E
Busanga Swamp	36	Ee	14.10S	25.50 E
Buşayrah	24	Ie	35.09N	40.26 E
Būsh	24	Dh	29.09N	31.08 E
Būshehr [3]	23	Hd	28.00N	52.00 E
Būshehr	22	Hg	28.59N	50.50 E
Būshgān	24	Nh	28.48N	51.42 E
Bushimaie	29	Ji	6.02S	23.45 E
Bushmanland (EN) = Boesmanland	37	Be	29.30S	19.00 E
Busia	36	Fb	0.28N	34.06 E
Busigny	12	Fd	50.02N	3.28 E
Businga	36	Db	3.20N	20.53 E
Busira	30	Ii	0.15S	18.59 E
Busk	16	Dd	50.01N	24.37 E
Buskerud [2]	7	Bf	60.30N	9.10 E
Busko-Zdrój	10	Qf	50.28N	20.44 E
Busoga [3]	36	Fb	0.45N	33.30 E
Buşrá ash Shām	24	Gf	32.31N	36.29 E
Busselton	59	Df	33.39S	115.20 E
Bussum	11	Lb	52.16N	5.10 E
Bustamante, Bahía-	56	Gg	45.07S	66.27W
Buşteni	15	Id	45.24N	25.32 E
Busto Arsizio	14	Ce	45.37N	8.51 E
Buštyna	10	Th	48.03N	23.28 E
Busuanga	26	Hd	12.05N	120.05 E
Busu-Djanoa	36	Db	1.43N	21.23 E
Büsum	10	Eb	54.08N	8.51 E
Buta	31	Jh	2.48N	24.44 E
Butajira	35	Fd	8.08N	38.27 E
Buta Ranquil	56	Ge	37.03S	69.50W
Butare	36	Ec	2.36S	29.44 E
Butaritari Atoll	57	Id	3.03N	172.49 E
Bute, Island of-	9	Hf	55.50N	5.05W
Bute Inlet	46	Ca	50.37N	124.53W
Butembo	31	Jh	0.09N	29.17 E
Butera	14	Im	37.11N	14.11 E
Butere	36	Fb	0.13N	34.30 E
Butha Qi (Zalantum)	27	Lb	48.02N	122.42 E
Buthidaung	25	Id	20.52N	92.32 E
Butiá	56	Jd	30.07S	51.58W
Butiaba	36	Fb	1.49N	31.19 E
Butler	44	He	40.51N	79.55W
Butser Hill	12	Bd	50.57N	0.59W
Butte	39	He	46.00N	112.32W
Butterworth [Mala.]	26	Df	5.25N	100.24 E
Butterworth [S.Afr.]	37	Df	32.23S	28.04 E
Button Bay	42	Ie	58.45N	94.25W
Butuan	22	Oi	8.57N	125.33 E
Butung, Palau-	21	Oj	5.00S	122.55 E
Buturlinovka	16	Ld	50.48N	40.45 E
Butzbach	12	Kd	50.26N	8.41 E
Bützow	10	Hc	53.50N	11.59 E
Buxtehude	10	Fc	53.27N	9.42 E
Buxton [Eng.-U.K.]	9	Lh	53.15N	1.55W
Buxton [N.C.-U.S.]	44	Jh	35.16N	75.32W
Buyo	34	Dd	6.16N	7.03W
Büyük Ağri Daği=Ararat, Mount- (EN)	21	Gf	39.40N	44.24 E
Büyükanafarta	15	Ji	40.17N	26.22 E
Büyükçekmece	15	Lh	41.01N	28.34 E
Büyükkariştiran	15	Kh	41.18N	27.32 E
Büyük Kemikli Burun	15	Ji	40.18N	26.14 E
Büyük Mahya	15	Kh	41.47N	27.36 E
Büyük Menderes	23	Cb	37.57N	28.58 E
Büyükorhan	15	Lj	39.45N	28.55 E
Buyun Shan	27	Lc	40.06N	122.42 E
Buzači, Poluostrov-	19	Ff	45.00N	52.00 E
Buzan	16	Pf	46.18N	49.06 E
Buzançais	11	Hh	46.53N	1.25 E
Buzancy	12	Ge	49.25N	4.57 E
Buzău [2]	15	Jd	45.09N	26.50 E
Buzău	15	Jd	45.09N	26.50 E
Buzău	15	Kd	45.26N	27.44 E
Buzaymah	33	De	24.55N	22.02 E
Buzen	29	Be	33.37N	131.08 E
Buzet	14	He	45.24N	13.59 E
Būzhān	24	Le	34.09N	47.05 E
Búzi	37	Ec	19.51S	34.30 E
Búzi	37	Ec	19.52S	34.46 E
Buziaş	15	Ed	45.39N	21.36 E
Búzios, Ilha dos-	55	Jf	23.48S	45.08W
Bužora, Gora-	10	Th	48.24N	23.15 E
Buzuluk	19	Fe	52.46N	52.17 E
Buzuluk [R.S.F.S.R.]	16	Md	50.13N	42.12 E
Buzuluk [R.S.F.S.R.]	16	Rc	52.47N	52.16 E
Buzzards Bay	44	Le	41.33N	70.47W

Index Symbols

[1] Independent Nation
[2] State, Region
[3] District, County
[4] Municipality
[5] Colony, Dependency
Continent
Physical Region
Historical or Cultural Region
Mount, Mountain
Volcano
Hill
Mountains, Mountain Range
Hills, Escarpment
Plateau, Upland
Pass, Gap
Plain, Lowland
Delta
Salt Flat
Valley, Canyon
Crater, Cave
Karst Features
Depression
Polder
Desert, Dunes
Forest, Woods
Heath, Steppe
Oasis
Cape, Point
Coast, Beach
Cliff
Peninsula
Isthmus
Sandbank
Island
Atoll
Rock, Reef
Islands, Archipelago
Rocks, Reefs
Coral Reef
Well, Spring
Geyser
River, Stream
Waterfall Rapids
River Mouth, Estuary
Lake
Salt Lake
Intermittent Lake
Reservoir
Swamp, Pond
Canal
Glacier
Ice Shelf, Pack Ice
Ocean
Sea
Gulf, Bay
Strait, Fjord
Lagoon
Bank
Seamount
Tablemount
Ridge
Shelf
Basin
Escarpment, Sea Scarp
Fracture
Trench, Abyss
National Park, Reserve
Point of Interest
Recreation Site
Cave, Cavern
Historic Site
Ruins
Wall, Walls
Church, Abbey
Temple
Scientific Station
Airport
Port
Lighthouse
Mine
Tunnel
Dam, Bridge

Bwagaoia 63a Ad 10.42S 152.50 E
Byälven 8 Ee 59.06N 12.54 E
Byam Martin 42 Ha 75.15N 104.15W
Byam Martin Channel 42 Ha 76.00N 105.00W
Bychawa 10 Se 51.01N 22.32 E
Byczyna 10 Oe 51.07N 18.11 E
Bydgoszcz [2] 10 Nc 53.10N 18.00 E
Bydgoszcz 6 He 53.08N 18.00 E
Byelorussian SSR (EN)= Belorusskaja SSR [2] 19 Ce 53.50N 28.00 E
Bygdin 8 Cc 61.20N 8.35 E
Bygland [Nor.] 7 Bg 58.51N 7.51 E
Bygland [Nor.] 8 Bf 58.41N 7.48 E
Byglandsfjorden 8 Bf 58.50N 7.50 E
Byhov 19 De 53.31N 30.15 E
Byk 15 Mc 46.55N 29.25 E
Bykovec 15 Lb 47.12N 28.18 E
Bykovo 16 Ne 49.47N 45.25 E
Bykovski 20 Hb 71.56N 129.05 E
Bylot 38 Lb 73.13N 78.34W
Byrd, Cape- 66 Qe 69.38S 76.07W
Byrdbreen 66 Df 71.35S 26.00 E
Byrd Glacier 66 Jg 80.15S 160.20 E
Byron, Cape- 57 Gg 28.39S 153.38 E
Byron Bay 42 Gc 68.55N 108.25W
Byron Bay 59 Ke 28.39S 153.37 E
Byrranga Gory=Byrranga Mountains (EN) 21 Mb 75.00N 104.00 E
Byrranga Mountains (EN)= Byrranga Gory 21 Mb 75.00N 104.00 E
Bystraja 20 Kf 52.40N 156.10 E
Bystreyca 10 Se 51.40N 22.33 E
Bystřice 10 Lf 50.11N 15.30 E
Bystrovka 18 Jc 42.45N 75.43 E
Bystrzyca [Pol.] 10 Se 51.16N 22.45 E
Bystrzyca [Pol.] 10 Me 51.13N 16.54 E
Bystrzyca Kłodzka 10 Mf 50.19N 16.39 E
Bytantaj 20 Ic 68.40N 134.50 E
Bytča 10 Og 49.14N 18.35 E
Byten 10 Vd 52.49N 25.33 E
Bytom 10 Of 50.22N 18.54 E
Bytów 10 Nb 54.11N 17.30 E
Byumba 36 Fc 1.35S 30.04 E
Byxelkrok 7 Dh 57.20N 17.00 E
Bzura 10 Qd 52.23N 20.09 E
Bzyb 16 Lh 43.12N 40.15 E

C

Cà, Sông- 25 Le 18.40N 105.40 E
Caacupé 56 Ic 25.23S 57.09W
Čaadajevka 16 Nc 53.09N 45.56 E
Caaguazú 56 Ic 25.26S 56.02W
Caaguazú [3] 55 Eg 25.00S 55.45W
Caála 36 Ce 12.55S 15.35 E
Caapucú 55 Dh 26.13S 57.12W
Caarapó 55 Ef 22.38S 54.48W
Caatinga 54 Ig 17.10S 45.53W
Caatinga 52 Lf 9.00S 42.00W
Caatinga, Rio- 55 Jc 17.10S 45.52W
Caazapá [3] 55 Dh 26.10S 56.00W
Caazapá 56 Ic 26.09S 56.24W
Cabaçal, Rio- 55 Db 16.00S 57.42W
Cabadbaran 26 Ie 9.10N 125.38 E
Cabaiguán 49 Hb 22.05N 79.30W
Caballeria, Cabo de- 13 Qd 40.05N 4.05 E
Caballo Cocha 54 Dd 3.54S 70.32W
Caballo Reservoir 45 Cj 32.58N 107.18W
Cabañas 13 Jg 37.40N 3.00W
Cabanatuan 22 Oh 15.29N 120.58 E
Cabano 44 Mb 47.41N 68.54W
Čabar 14 Ie 45.36N 14.39 E
Cabeceira do Apa 55 Ef 22.01S 55.46W
Cabeceiras 55 Ib 15.48S 46.59W
Cabeceiras de Basto 13 Ec 41.31N 7.59W
Cabeza, Arrecife- 48 Lh 19.04N 95.50W
Cabeza de Buey 13 Gf 38.43N 5.13W
Cabildo 55 Bn 38.29S 61.54W
Cabimas 53 Id 10.23N 71.28W
Cabinda 31 Ii 5.35S 12.13 E
Cabinda [3] 36 Bd 5.00S 12.30 E
Cabinet Mountains 46 Hb 48.08N 115.46W
Cabo Bojador 32 Ed 26.08N 14.30W
Cabo Frio 53 Lh 22.53S 42.01W
Cabo Gracias a Dios 49 Ff 14.59N 83.10W
Cabonga, Réservoir- 42 Jg 47.20N 76.35W
Caboolture 59 Ke 27.05S 152.50 E
Cabora Bassa, Dique de- 37 Ec 15.34S 32.42 E
Cabora Bassa, Lago-= Cabora Bassa, Lake-(EN) 30 Kj 15.40S 31.40 E
Cabora Bassa, Lake-(EN)= Cabora Bassa, Lago- 30 Kj 15.40S 31.40 E
Caborca 47 Bb 30.37N 112.06W
Cabot Strait 38 Ne 47.20N 59.30W
Cabourg 11 Fe 49.17N 0.08W
Cabo Verde=Cape Verde (EN) [1] 31 Eg 16.00N 24.00W
Cabo Verde, Ilhas do-=Cape Verde Islands (EN) 30 Eg 16.00N 24.10W
Cabra 13 Hg 37.28N 4.27W
Cabral, Serra do- 55 Jc 17.45S 44.22W
Cabras 14 Ck 39.56N 8.32 E
Cabras, Stagno di- 14 Ck 39.55N 8.30 E
Cabreira 13 Dc 41.39N 8.04W
Cabrejas, Puerto de- 13 Jd 40.08N 2.25W
Cabrera 49 Md 19.38N 69.54W
Cabrera, Isla- 13 Oe 39.09N 2.56 E
Cabrera, Sierra de la- 13 Fb 42.10N 6.25W
Cabri 46 Ka 50.37N 108.28W
Cabriel 13 Ke 39.14N 1.03W
Cabrit, Ilet 'a- 51e Ac 15.53N 61.36W
Cabrits, Ilet- 51h Bc 14.23N 60.52W
Cabrón, Cabo- 49 Md 19.22N 69.12W
Cabruta 50 Ci 7.38N 66.15W
Čabulja 14 Lg 43.30N 17.35 E
Cabure 49 Mh 11.08N 69.38W
Cacacas, Islas- 50 Dg 10.22N 64.26W
Caçador 56 Jc 26.47S 51.00W
Čačak 15 Df 43.54N 20.21 E
Caçapava dó Sul 56 Jd 30.30S 53.30W
Caccamo 14 Hm 37.56N 13.40 E
Caccia, Capo- 14 Cj 40.34N 8.09 E
Cacequi 55 Ei 29.53S 54.49W
Cáceres [3] 13 Ge 39.40N 6.00W
Cáceres [Braz.] 53 Kg 16.04S 57.41W
Cáceres [Sp.] 13 Fe 39.29N 6.22W
Cáceres, Laguna- 55 Dd 18.56S 57.48W
Cachari 56 Ie 36.24S 59.32W
Cache Peak 46 Ie 42.11N 113.40W
Cacheu 34 Bc 12.10N 16.21W
Cachimbo 53 Kf 9.08S 55.10W
Cachimbo, Serra do- 52 Kf 8.30S 55.50W
Cachimo 36 Dd 8.20S 21.21 E
Cáchira 49 Kj 7.46N 73.03W
Cáchira, Rio- 49 Kj 7.52N 73.40W
Cachoeira 54 Kf 12.36S 38.58W
Cachoeira Alta 55 Gd 18.48S 50.58W
Cachoeira de Goiás 55 Gc 16.44S 50.38W
Cachoeira do Arari 54 Id 1.01S 48.58W
Cachoeira do Sul 56 Jc 29.58S 52.54W
Cachoeira Dourada, Represa de- 54 Ig 18.30S 49.00W
Cachoeirinha 55 Gi 29.57S 51.05W
Cachoeiro de Itapemirim 54 Jh 20.51S 41.06W
Cacinbinho 55 Ee 21.50S 55.43W
Căciulaţi 15 Je 44.38N 26.10 E
Cacolo 36 Ce 10.08S 19.18 E
Caconda 36 Ce 13.45S 15.05 E
Cacuaco 36 Bd 8.47S 13.21 E
Cacuchi 36 Ce 14.23S 16.59 E
Cacula 36 Be 14.29S 14.10 E
Caculé 54 Jf 14.30S 42.13W
Caculuvar 36 Bf 16.46S 14.56 E
Cacuso 36 Cd 9.26S 15.45 E
Čadan 20 Ef 51.17N 91.40 E
Cadaqués 13 Pb 42.17N 3.17 E
Čadca 10 Og 49.26N 18.48 E
Caddo Lake 45 Ij 32.42N 94.01W
Cadena Costero Catalana/ Serralada Litoral Catalana =Catalan Coastal Range (EN) 5 Gg 41.35N 1.40 E
Cadereyta Jiménez 48 Ie 25.36N 100.00W
Cadí, Serra del-/Cadí, Sierra del- 13 Nb 42.17N 1.42 E
Cadibarrawirracanna, Lake- 59 He 28.50S 135.25 E
Cadibona, Colle di- 14 Cf 44.20N 8.22 E
Cadillac [Fr.] 11 Fj 44.38N 0.19W
Cadillac [Mi.-U.S.] 43 Jc 44.15N 85.24W
Cadí,Sierra del/Cadí, Serra del- 13 Nb 42.17N 1.42 E
Cadiz 26 Hd 10.57N 123.18 E
Cádiz [3] 13 Gh 36.30N 5.45W
Cádiz 6 Fh 36.32N 6.18W
Cadiz [Ca.-U.S.] 46 Hi 34.30N 115.30W
Cadiz [Ky.-U.S.] 44 Dg 36.52N 87.50W
Cádiz, Bahía de- 13 Fh 36.32N 6.16W
Cádiz, Golfo de- 5 Fh 36.50N 7.10W
Cadiz Lake 46 Hi 34.18N 115.24W
Cadore 14 Gd 46.30N 12.20 E
Cadwell 43 Dc 43.40N 116.41W
Čadyr-Lunga 16 Ff 46.04N 28.52 E
Caen 6 Ff 49.11N 0.21W
Caen, Campagne de- 11 Fe 49.05N 0.20W
Caernarvon 9 Ih 53.08N 4.16W
Caernarvon Bay 9 Ih 53.05N 4.30W
Caerphilly 9 Jj 51.35N 3.14W
Caetité 54 Jf 14.04S 42.29W
Cafayate 56 Gc 26.05S 65.58W
Cafelândia [Braz.] 55 Fc 16.40S 53.25W
Cafelândia [Braz.] 55 Ie 21.49S 49.35W
Cafundó, Serra do- 55 Hb 14.40S 48.23W
Čagan 19 He 50.30N 79.10 E
Cagan-Aman 19 Ef 47.32N 46.43 E
Cagan-Nur [Mong.] 27 Eb 49.40N 89.55 E
Cagan-Nur [Mong.] 27 Ia 50.25N 105.15 E
Cagan-Ula 27 Gb 49.35N 98.25 E
Cagatá, Arroyo- 55 Df 23.26S 56.36W
Cagayan 26 Hc 18.22N 121.37 E
Cagayan de Oro 22 Oi 8.29N 124.39 E
Cagayan Islands 26 He 9.40N 121.16 E
Cagayan Sulu 26 Ge 7.01N 118.30 E
Čagda 20 Ie 58.42N 130.37 E
Cageri 16 Mh 42.39N 42.42 E
Çağış 15 Lj 39.30N 28.01 E
Cagli 14 Gg 43.33N 12.39 E
Cagliari 6 Gh 39.13N 9.07 E
Cagliari, Golfo di- 14 Dk 39.10N 9.10 E
Cagliari, Stagno di- 14 Dk 39.15N 9.05 E
Čaglinka 17 Nj 53.59N 69.47 E
Cagnes-sur-Mer 11 Nk 43.40N 7.09 E
Čagoda 7 Ig 59.12N 35.13 E
Čagodošča 7 Ig 58.58N 36.37 E
Caguas 47 Ke 18.14N 66.02W
Çagyl 19 Fg 40.43N 55.25 E
Cahama 36 Bf 16.16S 14.17 E
Caha Mountains/An Cheacha 9 Dj 51.45N 9.45W
Caher/An Chathair 9 Fi 52.22N 7.55W
Cahersiveen/Cathair Saidhbhin 9 Cj 51.57N 10.13W
Cahore Point/Rinn Chathóir 9 Gi 52.34N 6.11W
Cahors 11 Hj 44.26N 1.26 E
Cai, Rio- 55 Gi 29.56S 51.16W
Caia 37 Fc 17.49S 35.20 E
Caia 13 Ef 38.50N 7.05W
Caiabis, Serra dos- 54 Gf 11.40S 56.30W
Caiapó, Rio- 55 Gb 15.49S 51.53W
Caiapó, Serra do- 52 Kg 17.00S 52.00W
Caiapônia 55 Gc 16.57S 51.49W
Caibarién 47 Id 22.31N 79.28W
Caiçara 55 Gb 15.34S 50.12W
Caicara 54 Eb 7.37N 66.10W
Caicara de Maturín 50 Eh 9.49N 63.36W
Caicó 54 Ke 6.27S 37.06W
Caicos Bank (EN) 47 Jd 21.35N 71.55W
Caicos Islands 38 Lg 21.45N 71.35W
Caicos Passage 47 Jd 22.00N 72.30W
Caille Island 51p Bb 12.17N 61.35W
Caimanera 49 Jd 19.59N 75.09W
Caine, Rio- 54 Eg 18.23S 65.21W
Cai Nuoc 25 Lg 8.56N 105.01 E
Caird Coast 66 Af 76.00S 24.30W
Cairngorms Mountains 9 Jd 57.06N 3.30W
Cairns 58 Ff 16.55S 145.46 E
Cairo [Ga.-U.S.] 44 Ej 30.53N 84.12W
Cairo [Il.-U.S.] 43 Jd 37.00N 89.11W
Cairo (EN)=Al Qāhirah 31 Ke 30.03N 31.15 E
Cairo Montenotte 14 Cf 44.24N 8.16 E
Caiseal/Cashel 9 Fi 52.31N 7.53W
Caisleán an Bharraigh/ Castlebar 9 Dh 53.52N 9.17W
Caister-on-Sea 12 Db 52.40N 1.45 E
Caiundo 36 Cf 15.42S 17.27 E
Caiúva, Lagoa- 55 Fk 32.24S 52.30W
Caiyuanzhen → Shengsi 28 Gi 30.42N 122.29 E
Caizi Hu 28 Di 30.48N 117.05 E
Čaja 20 De 58.17N 82.45 E
Cajabamba 54 Ce 7.58S 77.59W
Caja de Muertos, Isla- 51a Bc 17.53N 66.31W
Cajamarca 53 If 7.10S 78.31W
Cajamarca [2] 54 Ce 6.15S 78.50W
Cajapió 54 Jd 2.58S 44.48W
Cajarc 11 Hj 44.29N 1.51 E
Cajatambo 54 Cf 10.29S 77.02W
Čajkovski 19 Fd 56.47N 54.09 E
Çakırgöl Dağ 24 Hb 40.34N 39.42 E
Çakmak 24 Fd 37.37N 34.19 E
Çakmak Dağı 24 Jc 39.46N 42.12 E
Čakor 15 Dg 42.40N 20.02 E
Čakovec 14 Kd 46.23N 16.26 E
Čakrani 15 Ci 40.36N 19.37 E
Çal 24 Cc 38.05N 29.24 E
Cal, Rio de la- 55 Cc 17.27S 58.15W
Calabar 31 Hh 4.57N 8.19 E
Calabozo 54 Eb 8.56N 67.26W
Calabozo, Ensenada de- 49 Lh 11.30N 71.45W
Calabria [2] 14 Kl 39.00N 16.30 E
Calaburras, Punta de- 13 Hh 36.30N 4.38W
Calacoto 54 Eg 17.18S 68.39W
Calacuccia 11a Ba 42.20N 9.01 E
Calaf 13 Nc 41.44N 1.31 E
Calafat 15 Ff 43.59N 22.56 E
Calafate 53 Ik 50.20S 72.16W
Cala Figuera, Cabo de- 13 Oe 39.27N 2.31 E
Calagua Islands 26 Hd 14.27N 122.55 E
Calahorra 13 Kb 42.18N 1.58W
Calai 36 Cf 17.50S 19.20 E
Calais [Fr.] 6 Ge 50.57N 1.50 E
Calais [Me.-U.S.] 44 Nc 45.11N 67.17W
Calais, Pas de-=Dover, Strait of- (EN) 5 Ge 51.00N 1.30 E
Calakmul 48 Oh 18.05N 89.55W
Calalaste, Sierra de- 56 Gc 25.30S 67.30W
Calama 53 Jh 22.28S 68.56W
Calamar 49 Jh 10.14N 74.56W
Calamian Group 21 Nh 12.00N 120.00 E
Calamocha 13 Kd 40.55N 1.18W
Călan 15 Fd 45.44N 22.59 E
Calanda 13 Ld 40.56N 0.14W
Calang 26 Cf 4.30N 95.40 E
Calangiánus 14 Dj 40.56N 9.11 E
Calapan 26 Hd 13.25N 121.10 E
Calar Alto 13 Jg 37.15N 2.25W
Călăraşi 15 Ke 44.12N 27.20 E
Cala Ratjada 13 Pe 39.42N 3.25 E
Calar del Mundo 13 Jf 38.31N 2.28W
Calatafimi 14 Gm 37.55N 12.52 E
Calatañazor 13 Jc 41.42N 2.49W
Calatayud 13 Kc 41.21N 1.38W
Calatrava 13 If 38.35N 3.48W
Calatrava, Campo de- 13 Hf 38.50N 4.15W
Calavà, Capo- 14 Il 38.10N 14.55 E
Calavon 11 Kk 43.51N 5.00 E
Calayan 26 Hc 19.20N 121.27 E
Calbayog 22 Oh 12.04N 124.36 E
Calchaquí 56 Hc 29.54S 60.18W
Calçoene 54 Hc 2.30N 50.57W
Calcutta 22 Kg 22.32N 88.22 E
Caldaro / Kaltern 14 Fd 46.25N 11.14 E
Caldas [2] 54 Cb 5.15N 75.30W
Caldas da Rainha 13 Ce 39.24N 9.08W
Caldas Novas 55 Hc 17.45S 48.38W
Caldeirão, Serra de- 13 Dg 37.19N 8.04W
Calder 9 Lh 53.44N 1.21W
Caldera 56 Fc 27.04S 70.50W
Calderina, Sierra de la- 13 Ie 39.19N 3.48W
Caldes de Mombúy 13 Oc 41.38N 2.10 E
Caldwell 44 Gf 39.44N 81.32W
Caledon 37 Bf 34.12S 19.23 E
Caledon 30 Jl 30.32S 26.05 E
Caledonia [Blz.] 47 Gd 18.14N 88.29W
Caledonia [Mn.-U.S.] 45 Ke 43.38N 91.29W
Caledonian Canal 9 Id 57.20N 4.30W
Calella 13 Oc 41.37N 2.40 E
Caleta Olivia 56 Gg 46.26S 67.32W
Calexico 46 Hj 32.40N 115.30W
Çalgal Dağı 24 Hc 39.06N 38.05 E
Calgary 39 Hd 51.03N 114.05W
Calhoun 44 Eh 34.30N 84.57W
Cali 53 Ie 3.27N 76.31W
Calicut (Kozhikode) 22 Jh 11.19N 75.46 E
Caliente 43 Ed 37.37N 114.31W
California [2] 43 Dd 37.30N 119.30W
California, Golfo de-= California, Gulf of- (EN) 38 Hg 28.00N 112.00W
California, Gulf of- (EN)= California, Golfo de- 38 Hg 28.00N 112.00W
Căliman, Munţii- 15 Ib 47.07N 25.03 E
Călimăneşti 15 Hd 45.14N 24.20 E
Calimere, Point- 25 Ff 10.18N 79.52 E
Calingasta 56 Gd 31.19S 69.25W
Calispell Peak 46 Gb 48.26N 117.30W
Calitri 14 Jj 40.54N 15.26 E
Calitzdorp 37 Cf 33.33S 21.42 E
Caliviny 51p Bb 12.01N 61.43W
Calixtlahuaca 48 Jh 19.15N 99.45W
Calka 16 Ni 41.35N 44.05 E
Calkini 48 Ng 20.22N 90.03W
Callabonna, Lake- 59 Ie 29.45S 140.05 E
Callac 11 Cf 48.24N 3.26W
Callaghan, Mount- 46 Gg 39.42N 116.57W
Callainn/Callan 9 Fi 52.33N 7.23W
Callan/Callainn 9 Fi 52.33N 7.23W
Callander [Ont.-Can.] 44 Hb 46.13N 79.23W
Callander [Scot.-U.K.] 9 Ie 56.15N 4.13W
Callantsoog 12 Gb 52.50N 4.41 E
Callao 53 Ig 12.02S 77.05W
Callao [2] 54 Cf 2.04S 77.09W
Calliaqua 51n Ba 13.08N 61.12W
Callosa de Ensarriá 13 Lf 38.39N 0.07W
Callosa de Segura 13 Lf 38.08N 0.52W
Calmalli 48 Cc 28.14N 113.33W
Călmăţui [Rom.] 15 If 43.46N 25.10 E
Călmăţui [Rom.] 15 Ke 44.50N 27.50 E
Calonne 12 Ce 49.17N 0.12 E
Calore 14 Ii 41.11N 14.28 E
Čalovo 10 Ni 47.52N 17.47 E
Calpe 13 Mf 38.39N 0.03 E
Caltabellotta 14 Hm 37.34N 13.13 E
Caltagirone 14 Im 37.14N 14.31 E
Caltanissetta 14 Im 37.29N 14.04 E
Caltılıbük 15 Lj 39.57N 28.36 E
Çaltyr 16 Kf 47.17N 39.29 E
Caluago 36 Cd 8.15S 19.38 E
Calucinga 36 Ce 11.19S 16.13 E
Călugareni 15 Ie 44.11N 25.59 E
Calulo 36 Bd 9.59S 14.54 E
Caluquembe 36 Be 13.46S 14.41 E
Calvados [3] 11 Fe 49.10N 0.30W
Calvados, Côte du- 11 Fe 49.22N 0.30W
Calvert Island 46 Ba 51.35N 128.00W
Calvert River 59 Hc 16.17S 137.44 E
Calvi 11a Aa 42.34N 8.45 E
Calvillo 48 Hg 21.51N 102.43W
Calvinia 31 Il 31.25S 19.45 E
Calvitero 13 Gd 40.20N 5.43W
Cam 9 Ni 52.21N 0.15 E
Camabatela 36 Cd 8.13S 15.23 E
Camacá 54 Kg 15.24S 39.30W
Camacupa 36 Ce 12.01S 17.22 E
Camagüán 50 Ch 8.06N 67.36W
Camagüey [3] 49 Ic 21.30N 78.10W
Camagüey 39 Lg 21.23N 77.55W
Camagüey, Archipiélago de- 47 Id 22.18N 78.00W
Camaiore 14 Eg 43.56N 10.18 E
Camajuaní 49 Hb 22.28N 79.44W
Camamu 54 Kf 13.57S 39.07W
Camaná 54 Dg 16.37S 72.42W
Camapuã 55 Ed 19.30S 54.05W
Camapuã, Sertão de- 52 Kg 19.00S 51.30W
Camaquã 56 Jd 30.51S 51.49W
Camaquã, Rio- 55 Gj 31.17S 51.47W
Camarat, Cap- 11 Mk 43.12N 6.41 E
Camargo [Bol.] 54 Eh 20.39S 65.13W
Camargo [Sp.] 13 Ia 43.24N 3.54W
Camargos, Represa- 55 Je 21.20S 44.30W
Camargue 11 Kk 43.31N 4.34 E
Camariñas 13 Ca 43.07N 9.10W
Camarón, Cabo- 47 He 16.00N 85.04W
Camarones 56 Gf 44.48S 65.42W
Camarones, Bahía- 56 Gf 44.45S 65.34W
Camas [Sp.] 13 Fg 37.24N 6.02W
Camas [Wa.-U.S.] 46 Dd 45.35N 122.24W
Camatagua, Embalse de- 50 Ch 9.48N 66.55W
Ca Mau, Mui-=Ca Mau Point (EN) 21 Mi 8.38N 104.44 E
Ca Mau Point (EN)=Ca Mau, Mui- 21 Mi 8.38N 104.44 E
Cambados 13 Db 42.30N 8.48W
Camberg 12 Kd 50.18N 8.16 E
Camberley 12 Bc 51.21N 0.44W
Cambo 36 Cd 7.40S 17.17 E
Cambodia→Kampuchea [1] 22 Mh 13.00N 105.00 E
Cambo-les-Bains 11 Ek 43.22N 1.24W
Camboriú, Ponta- 55 Ig 25.10S 47.55W
Cambrai 11 Jd 50.10N 3.14 E
Cambremer 12 Ce 49.09N 0.03 E
Cambrésis 12 Fd 50.15N 3.05 E
Cambrian Mountains 5 Fe 52.35N 3.35W
Cambridge 9 Ni 52.25N 0.10 E
Cambridge [Eng.-U.K.] 9 Ni 52.12N 0.07 E
Cambridge [Id.-U.S.] 46 Gd 44.34N 116.41W
Cambridge [Ma.-U.S.] 44 Ld 42.22N 71.06W
Cambridge [Md.-U.S.] 44 If 38.34N 76.04W
Cambridge [Mn.-U.S.] 45 Jd 45.31N 93.14W
Cambridge [N.Z.] 62 Fb 37.53S 175.28 E
Cambridge [Oh.-U.S.] 44 Ge 40.02N 81.36W
Cambridge Airport 12 Cb 52.10N 0.08 E
Cambridge Bay 39 Ic 69.03N 105.05W
Cambridge Gulf 59 Fb 14.55S 128.15 E
Cambridgeshire [3] 9 Mi 52.55N 0.05W
Cambutal, Cerro- 49 Gj 7.16N 80.36W
Camden [Al.-U.S.] 44 Dj 32.00N 87.17W
Camden [Ar.-U.S.] 43 Ie 33.35N 92.50W
Camden [N.J.-U.S.] 44 Jf 39.57N 75.07W
Camden [S.C.-U.S.] 44 Gh 34.16N 80.36W
Camden [Tn.-U.S.] 44 Cg 36.04N 88.06W
Camden Bay 40 Kb 70.00N 145.00W
Camdenton 45 Jg 38.00N 92.45W
Camel 9 Ik 50.33N 4.55W
Çameli 24 Cd 37.05N 29.20 E
Camerino 14 Hg 43.08N 13.04 E
Cameron 42 Ha 76.15N 104.00W
Cameron [Az.-U.S.] 46 Ji 35.51N 111.25W
Cameron [La.-U.S.] 45 Jl 29.48N 93.19W
Cameron [Mo.-U.S.] 45 Ig 39.44N 94.14W
Cameron [Tx.-U.S.] 45 Hk 30.51N 96.59W
Cameron [Wi.-U.S.] 45 Kd 45.25N 91.44W
Cameron Hills 42 Fe 60.00N 118.00W
Cameron Mountains 62 Bf 46.00S 166.55 E
Cameroon (EN)= Cameroun [1] 31 Ih 6.00N 12.00 E
Cameroon, Mount- (EN)= Cameroun 30 Hh 4.12N 9.11 E
Camerota 14 Jj 40.02N 15.22 E
Cameroun=Cameroon (EN) [1] 31 Ih 6.00N 12.00 E
Cameroun=Cameroon, Mount-(EN) 30 Hh 4.12N 9.11 E
Cametá 54 Id 2.15S 49.30W
Camiguin [Phil.] 26 He 9.11N 124.42 E
Camiguin [Phil.] 26 Hc 18.56N 121.55 E
Camiling 26 Hc 15.42N 120.24 E
Camilla 44 Ej 31.14N 84.12W
Caminha 13 Dc 41.52N 8.50W
Camoapa 49 Eg 12.23N 85.31W
Camocim 53 Lf 2.54S 40.50W
Camonica, Val- 14 Ed 46.00N 10.20 E
Camooweal 59 Hc 19.55S 138.07 E
Camopi 54 Hc 3.13N 52.28W
Camorta 25 Ig 8.08N 93.30 E
Campagne-lès-Hesdin 12 Dd 50.24N 1.52 E
Campana 55 Cl 34.10S 58.57W
Campana, Isla- 52 Ij 48.20S 75.15W
Campanario 53 Gf 38.52N 5.37W
Campanário 55 Ef 22.48S 55.03W
Campania [2] 14 Ii 41.00N 14.30 E
Campanquiz, Cerros- 54 Cd 4.30S 77.40W
Campbell, Cape- 62 Fd 41.44S 174.16 E
Campbell Island 62 Ci 52.30S 169.10 E
Campbell Plateau (EN) 57 Ij 51.00S 170.00 E
Campbell River 42 Ef 50.01N 125.15W
Campbellsville 44 Eg 37.21N 85.20W
Campbellton 42 Kg 48.00N 66.40W
Campbelltown, Sydney- 59 Kf 34.05S 150.49 E
Campbeltown 9 Hf 55.26N 5.36W
Campeche 39 Jh 19.51N 90.32W
Campeche [2] 47 Fe 19.00N 90.30W
Campeche, Bahía de-= Campeche, Gulf of- (EN) 38 Jg 20.00N 94.00W
Campeche, Gulf of- (EN)= Campeche, Bahía de- 38 Jg 20.00N 94.00W
Campeche Bank (EN) 47 Fd 22.00N 90.00W
Campechuela 49 Ic 20.14N 77.17W
Camperdown 59 Ig 38.14S 143.09 E
Campidano 14 Ck 39.30N 8.45 E
Campiglia Marittima 14 Eg 43.03N 10.37 E
Campillos 13 Hg 37.03N 4.51W
Campina Grande 53 Mf 7.13S 35.53W
Campinas 53 Lh 22.54S 47.05W
Campina Verde 55 Hd 19.31S 49.28W
Campine/Kempen 11 Lc 51.10N 5.20 E
Campinorte 55 Hb 14.20S 49.08W
Campione d'Italia 14 Ce 45.59N 8.59 E
Campo 34 Ge 2.22N 9.49 E
Campo Alegre 50 Bh 9.15N 68.25W
Campo Alegre de Goiás 55 Ic 17.36S 47.46W
Campobasso 14 Ii 41.34N 14.39 E
Campo Belo 55 Je 20.53S 45.16W
Campo de Criptana 13 Ie 39.24N 3.07W
Campo de la Cruz 49 Jh 10.23N 74.52W
Campo del Cielo 55 Bh 27.53S 61.49W
Campo Florido 55 Hd 19.46S 48.34W
Campo Formoso 54 Jf 10.31S 40.20W
Campo Gallo 56 Hc 26.35S 62.51W
Campo Garay 55 Bi 29.41S 61.37W
Campo Grande [Arg.] 55 Eh 27.13S 54.58W
Campo Grande [Braz.] 53 Kh 20.27S 54.37W
Campo Largo [Arg.] 55 Bh 26.48S 60.50W
Campo Largo [Braz.] 55 Hg 25.26S 49.32W
Campo Maior [Braz.] 54 Jd 4.49S 42.10W
Campo Maior [Port.] 13 Ee 39.01N 7.04W
Campomarino 14 Ji 41.57N 15.02 E
Campo Mourão 56 Jb 24.03S 52.22W
Campos 53 Lh 21.45S 41.18W
Campos [Braz.] 52 Lg 15.00S 44.30W
Campos [Braz.] 52 Kh 21.00S 51.00W
Campos, Laguna- 55 Be 20.50S 61.31W
Campos, Tierra de- 13 Hb 42.10N 4.50W
Campos Altos 55 Id 19.41S 46.10W
Campos Belos 55 Ia 13.03S 46.53W
Campos do Jordão 55 Jf 22.44S 45.35W
Campos Novos 55 Gh 27.24S 51.12W
Campos Sales 54 Je 7.04S 40.23W
Campos Tures / Sand in Taufers 14 Fd 46.55N 11.57 E
Camp Verde 43 Ee 34.34N 111.51W
Cam Ranh 25 Lf 11.54N 109.13 E
Camrose 42 Gf 53.01N 112.50W
Camseil 42 Fc 65.40N 118.07W
Camsell Portage 42 Ge 59.38N 109.42W
Çan 24 Bb 40.02N 27.03 E
Canaan [Ct.-U.S.] 44 Kd 42.02N 73.20W
Canaan [Trin.] 50 Fg 11.09N 60.49W
Canaan Mountain 46 Jh 37.45N 111.51W
Cana Brava, Ribeirão- 55 Ic 16.35S 46.34W
Cana Brava, Rio- [Braz.] 55 Ib 14.40S 47.07W
Cana Brava, Rio- [Braz.] 55 Ha 12.12S 48.40W
Cana Brava, Rio- [Braz.] 55 Ha 13.11S 48.11W
Canada [1] 39 Jc 60.00N 95.00W
Cañada 13 Fb 42.50N 6.05W
Canada Basin (EN) 67 Ad 80.00N 145.00W
Cañada de Gomez 56 Hd 32.49S 61.24W
Canadian 45 Fi 35.55N 100.23W
Canadian River 38 Jf 35.27N 95.03W
Canaguá, Río- 49 Mj 7.57N 69.36W
Canaima 54 Db 9.49N 70.56W

Index Symbols

[1] Independent Nation
[2] State, Region
[3] District, County
[4] Municipality
[5] Colony, Dependency
Continent
Physical Region
Historical or Cultural Region
Mount, Mountain
Volcano
Hill
Mountains, Mountain Range
Hills, Escarpment
Plateau, Upland
Pass, Gap
Plain, Lowland
Delta
Salt Flat
Valley, Canyon
Crater, Cave
Karst Features
Depression
Polder
Desert, Dunes
Forest, Woods
Heath, Steppe
Oasis
Cape, Point
Coast, Beach
Cliff
Peninsula
Isthmus
Sandbank
Island
Atoll
Rock, Reef
Islands, Archipelago
Rocks, Reefs
Coral Reef
Well, Spring
Geyser
River, Stream
Waterfall Rapids
River Mouth, Estuary
Lake
Salt Lake
Intermittent Lake
Reservoir
Swamp, Pond
Canal
Glacier
Ice Shelf, Pack Ice
Ocean
Sea
Gulf, Bay
Strait, Fjord
Lagoon
Bank
Seamount
Tablemount
Ridge
Shelf
Basin
Escarpment, Sea Scarp
Fracture
Trench, Abyss
National Park, Reserve
Point of Interest
Recreation Site
Cave, Cavern
Historic Site
Ruins
Wall, Walls
Church, Abbey
Temple
Scientific Station
Airport
Port
Lighthouse
Mine
Tunnel
Dam, Bridge

Çanakkale Boğazi = Dardanelles (EN) 5 Ig 40.15N 26.25 E
Canala 63b Be 21.32S 165.57 E
Canandaigua 44 Id 42.53N 77.19W
Cananea 47 Bb 30.57N 110.18W
Cananéia 55 Ig 25.01S 47.57W
Canapolis 55 Hd 18.44S 49.13W
Canarias, Islas- = Canary Islands (EN) [5] 31 Ff 28.00N 15.30W
Canarias, Islas- = Canary Islands (EN) 30 Ff 28.00N 15.30W
Canaries 51k Ab 13.55N 61.04W
Canaronero, Laguna- 48 Ff 23.00N 106.15W
Canarreos, Archipiélago de los- 47 Hd 21.50N 82.30W
Canary Basin (EN) 3 Dg 30.00N 25.00W
Canary Islands (EN) = Canarias, Islas- 30 Ff 28.00N 15.30W
Canary Islands (EN) = Canarias, Islas- [5] 31 Ff 28.00N 15.30W
Cañas [C.R.] 49 Eh 10.25N 85.07W
Cañas [Pan.] 49 Gj 7.27N 80.16W
Canastra, Serra da- 55 Ie 20.00S 46.20W
Canatlán 48 Ge 24.31N 104.47W
Cañaveral 13 Fe 39.47N 6.23W
Canaveral, Cape- 38 Kg 28.30N 80.35W
Canavese 14 Be 45.20N 7.40 E
Canavieiras 54 Kg 15.39S 38.57W
Canazei 14 Fd 46.28N 11.46 E
Canberra 58 Fh 35.17S 149.08 E
Canby [Mn.-U.S.] 45 Hd 44.43N 96.16W
Canby [Or.-U.S.] 46 Dd 45.16N 122.42W
Cance 11 Ki 45.12N 4.48 E
Canche 11 Hd 50.31N 1.39 E
Cancon 11 Gj 44.32N 0.37 E
Cancún 47 Gd 21.05N 86.46W
Cancún, Isla- 48 Pg 21.05N 86.46W
Çandarli 15 Jk 38.56N 26.56 E
Çandarli Körfezi 15 Jk 38.52N 26.55 E
Candé 11 Eg 47.34N 1.02W
Candela 48 Id 26.50N 100.40W
Candelaria 48 Nh 18.18N 91.21W
Candelaria, Cerro- 48 Hf 23.25N 103.43W
Candelaria, Río- [Bol.] 55 Cc 17.17S 58.39W
Candelaria, Río- [Mex.] 48 Nh 18.38N 91.15W
Candelaro 14 Ji 41.34N 15.53 E
Cândido de Abreu 55 Gg 24.35S 51.20W
Cândido Mendes 54 Id 1.27S 45.43W
Candlemas Islands 66 Ad 57.03S 26.40W
Candói 55 Fg 25.43S 52.11W
Čandyr 16 Jj 38.13N 55.44 E
Canela 56 Jc 29.22S 50.50W
Canelli 14 Cf 44.43N 8.17 E
Canelones [2] 55 El 34.35S 56.00W
Canelones 55 Dl 34.32S 56.17W
Canendiyu [3] 55 Eg 24.20S 55.00W
Cañete [Chile] 56 Fe 37.48S 73.24W
Cañete [Sp.] 13 Kd 40.03N 1.39W
Cangallo 55 Cm 37.13S 58.42W
Cangamba 36 Ce 13.44S 19.53 E
Cangas 13 Db 42.16N 8.47W
Cangas de Narcea 13 Fa 43.11N 6.33W
Cangas de Onís 13 Ga 43.21N 5.07W
Cangola 36 Cd 7.58S 15.53 E
Cangombe 36 Ce 14.24S 19.59 E
Cangshan (Bianzhuang) 28 Eg 34.51N 118.03 E
Canguçu 55 Fj 31.24S 52.41W
Canguçu, Serra do- 55 Fj 31.20S 52.40W
Canguinha 55 Eb 14.42S 55.40W
Cangumbe 36 Ce 12.00S 19.09 E
Cangyuan 27 Gg 23.10N 99.15 E
Cangzhou 27 Kd 38.14N 116.58 E
Cani, Iles- 14 Em 37.21N 10.07 E
Caniapiscau 38 Md 57.40N 69.30W
Caniapiscau, Lac- 42 Kf 54.00N 70.10W
Canicatti 14 Hm 37.21N 13.51 E
Canigou, Pic du- 11 Il 42.31N 2.27 E
Canik Dağlari 24 Gb 40.50N 37.10 E
Canim Lake 46 Ea 51.52N 120.45W
Canindé 54 Kd 4.22S 39.19W
Canindé, Rio- 54 Je 6.15S 42.52W
Cañitas de Felipe Pescador 48 Hf 23.36N 102.43W
Çankaya 24 Ec 39.56N 32.52 E
Çankiri 23 Da 40.36N 33.37 E
Canna 9 Gd 57.03N 6.33W
Cannac 63a Ac 9.15S 153.29 E
Çannakale 23 Ca 40.09N 26.24 E
Cannanore 25 Ff 11.51N 75.22 E
Cannanore Islands 25 Ef 10.05N 72.10 E
Cannes 11 Nk 43.33N 7.01 E
Cannich 9 Id 57.20N 4.45W
Canning Basin 59 Ed 20.10S 123.00 E
Cannobio 14 Cd 46.04N 8.42 E
Cannock 9 Ki 52.42N 2.01W
Cannonball River 45 Fc 46.26N 100.38W
Cann River 59 Jg 37.34S 149.10 E
Caño, Isla del- 49 Fi 8.44N 83.53W
Canoas 56 Jc 29.56S 51.11W
Canoas, Punta- 48 Bc 29.25N 115.10W
Canoas, Rio- 56 Jc 27.36S 51.25W
Canoeiros 54 Ig 18.02S 45.31W
Canoinhas 55 Gh 26.10S 50.24W
Canoinhas, Rio- 55 Gh 26.07S 50.22W
Cañoles 13 Le 39.02N 0.29W
Canon City 43 Fd 38.27N 105.14W
Canon Fiord 42 Ja 80.15N 83.00W
Canonnier, Pointe du- 51b Ab 18.04N 63.10W
Canora 42 Hf 51.37N 102.26W
Canosa di Puglia 14 Ki 41.13N 16.04 E
Canouan Island 50 Ff 12.43N 61.20W
Canourgue 11 Jj 44.25N 3.13 E
Canso, Strait of - 42 Lg 45.35N 61.23W
Canta 54 Cf 11.25S 76.38W
Cantabrian Mountains (EN) = Cantábrica, Cordillera- 5 Fg 43.00N 5.00W
Cantábrica, Cordillera- = Cantabrian Mountains (EN) 5 Fg 43.00N 5.00W
Cantal 5 Gf 45.10N 2.50 E
Cantal [3] 11 Ii 45.05N 2.40 E
Cantalejo 13 Ic 41.15N 3.55W
Cantanhede 13 Dd 40.21N 8.36W
Cantaura 54 Fb 9.19N 64.21W
Cantavieja 13 Ld 40.32N 0.24W
Cantavir 15 Cd 45.55N 19.46 E
Canterbury [2] 62 De 43.30S 171.50 E
Canterbury 9 Oj 51.17N 1.05 E
Canterbury Bight 57 Ii 44.10S 172.00 E
Can Tho 22 Mi 10.02N 105.47 E
Cantiles, Cayo- 49 Fc 21.36N 82.02W
Canto do Buriti 54 Je 8.07S 42.58W
Canton [Il.-U.S.] 45 Kf 40.33N 90.02W
Canton [Mo.-U.S.] 45 Kf 40.08N 91.32W
Canton [Ms.-U.S.] 45 Kj 32.37N 90.02W
Canton [N.Y.-U.S.] 44 Jc 44.37N 75.11W
Canton [Oh.-U.S.] 43 Kc 40.48N 81.23W
Canton [S.D.-U.S.] 45 He 43.18N 96.35W
Canton (EN) = Guangzhou 22 Ng 23.07N 113.18 E
Cantù 14 De 45.44N 9.08 E
Cantwell 40 Jd 63.23N 148.57W
Cañuelas 55 Cl 35.03S 58.44W
Canumã, Rio- 52 Kf 3.55S 59.10W
Canutama 54 Fe 6.32S 64.20W
Canvey 12 Cc 51.31N 0.36 E
Čany 20 Ce 55.19N 76.56 E
Čany, Ozero- 21 Jd 54.50N 77.30 E
Cany-Barville 12 Ce 49.47N 0.38 E
Canyon [Mn.-U.S.] 45 Jc 47.02N 92.29W
Canyon [Tx.-U.S.] 43 Ge 34.59N 101.55W
Canyon [Wy.-U.S.] 46 Jd 44.44N 110.30W
Canyon Lake 45 Gl 29.52N 98.16W
Canzar 36 Dd 7.36S 21.33 E
Cao Bang 25 Ld 22.40N 106.15 E
Caojiahe → Qichun 28 Ci 30.15N 115.26 E
Caojian 27 Gf 25.38N 99.07 E
Caombo 36 Cd 8.42S 16.33 E
Caorle 14 Ge 45.36N 12.53 E
Caoxian 28 Cg 34.49N 115.33 E
Caozhou → Heze 27 Kd 35.14N 115.28 E
Capaccio 14 Jj 40.25N 15.05 E
Čapajev 19 Fe 50.14N 51.08 E
Čapajevsk 19 Ee 53.01N 49.36 E
Capanaparo, Río- 54 Eb 7.01N 67.07W
Capanema [Braz.] 54 Id 1.12S 47.11W
Capanema [Braz.] 55 Fg 25.40S 53.48W
Capanema, Serra do- 55 Fh 26.05S 53.16W
Capão Alto 55 Gh 27.56S 50.30W
Capão Bonito 55 Hf 24.01S 48.20W
Capão Doce, Morro do- 55 Gh 26.43S 51.25W
Caparo, Rio- 49 Lj 7.46N 70.23W
Capatárida 49 Lh 11.11N 70.37W
Capbreton 11 Ek 43.38N 1.26W
Cap Breton Canyon (EN) 11 Ek 43.40N 1.50W
Čapčama, Pereval- 18 Hd 41.34N 70.50 E
Cap-Chat 44 Na 49.06N 66.42W
Capcir 11 Il 42.45N 2.10 E
Cap-de-la-Madeleine 42 Kg 46.22N 72.32W
Capdenac-Gare 11 Ij 44.34N 2.05 E
Cape Barren Island 59 Jh 40.25S 148.10 E
Cape Basin (EN) 3 Em 37.00S 7.00 E
Cape Breton Island 38 Me 46.00N 60.30W
Cape Charles 44 Jg 37.17N 76.00W
Cape Coast 31 Gh 5.06N 1.15W
Cape Cod Bay 44 Le 41.52N 70.22W
Cape Coral 44 Gl 26.33N 81.58W
Cape Dorset 39 Lc 64.14N 76.32W
Cape Dyer 39 Mc 66.30N 61.18W
Cape Fear River 44 Ii 33.53N 78.00W
Cape Girardeau 43 Jd 37.19N 89.32W
Cape Johnson Tablemount (EN) 57 Jc 17.08N 177.15W
Capel 12 Bc 51.08N 0.19W
Cape Lisburne 40 Fc 68.52N 166.05W
Capelka 8 Mf 58.02N 29.07 E
Capelongo 31 Ij 14.29S 16.18 E
Capem 55 Ea 13.14S 55.14W
Cape May 44 Jf 38.56N 74.54W
Cape Mount [3] 34 Cd 7.05N 10.50W
Cape Province/Kaapprovinsie [2] 37 Cf 32.00S 22.00 E
Cape Rise (EN) 3 En 42.00S 15.00 E
Cape Smith 42 Jd 60.44N 78.29W
Capesterre 51e Bc 15.54N 61.13W
Capesterre-Belle-Eau 50 Fd 16.03N 61.34W
Cape Town / Kaapstad 31 Il 33.55S 18.22 E
Cape Verde (EN) = Cabo Verde [1] 31 Eg 16.00N 24.00W
Cape Verde (EN) = Cap Vert [3] 34 Bc 14.45N 17.20W
Cape Verde Basin (EN) 3 Ch 15.00N 30.00W
Cape Verde Islands (EN) = Cabo Verde, Ilhas do- 30 Eg 16.00N 24.10W
Cape Yakataga 40 Kd 60.04N 142.26W
Cape York Peninsula 57 Ff 14.00S 142.30 E
Cap-Haïtien 39 Lh 19.45N 72.15W
Capiibary, Arroyo- 55 Dg 24.06S 56.26W
Capiibary, Rio- 55 Eg 25.30S 55.33W
Capim, Rio- 52 Lf 1.40S 47.47W
Capinópolis 55 Hd 18.41S 49.35W
Capira 49 Hi 8.45N 79.53W
Capital Federal [2] 56 Id 34.36S 58.27W
Capitán Arturo Prat 66 Re 62.29S 59.39W
Capitán Bado 56 Ib 23.16S 55.32W
Capitán Bermúdez 55 Bk 32.49S 60.43W
Capitán Sarmiento 55 Cl 34.10S 59.48W
Capitão Noronha, Rio- 55 Ea 13.19S 54.36W
Capivara, Represa da- 55 Gf 22.40S 50.57W
Capivari, Rio- 55 Dd 19.16S 57.10W
Capivarita 55 Fj 30.18S 52.19W
Cap Lopez, Baie du- 36 Ac 0.40S 9.00 E
Čaplygin 16 Kc 53.17N 39.59 E
Cappeln (Oldenburg) 12 Kb 52.49N 8.07 E
Cap Point 50 Fe 14.07N 60.57W
Capraia 14 Dg 43.05N 9.50 E
Caprara, Punta- 14 Ci 41.07N 8.19 E
Capreol 44 Gb 46.43N 80.56W
Caprera 14 Di 41.10N 9.30 E
Capri 14 Ij 40.35N 14.15 E
Capri 14 Ij 40.33N 14.14 E
Capricorn, Cape- 59 Kd 23.30S 151.15 E
Capricorn Channel 59 Kd 22.15S 151.30 E
Capricorn Group 57 Gg 23.30S 152.00 E
Caprivi Strip (EN) = Caprivi Zipfel 30 Jj 18.00S 23.00 E
Caprivi Zipfel = Caprivi Strip (EN) 30 Jj 18.00S 23.00 E
Captain Cook 65a Fd 19.30N 155.55W
Captains Flat 59 Jg 35.35S 149.27 E
Captieux 11 Fj 44.17N 0.15W
Capua 14 Ii 41.06N 14.12 E
Capuchin, Cape- 51g Ba 15.38N 61.28W
Capunda 36 Ce 10.41S 17.23 E
Cap Vert = Cape Verde (EN) [3] 34 Bc 14.45N 17.20W
Caquetá [2] 54 Dc 1.00N 74.00W
Čara 21 Oc 60.17N 120.40 E
Čara [R.S.F.S.R.] 20 Ge 56.58N 118.17 E
Čara [R.S.F.S.R.] 20 Ge 58.54N 118.12 E
Carabobo [2] 54 Ea 10.10N 68.05W
Caracal 15 He 44.07N 24.21 E
Caracaraí 54 Fc 1.50N 61.08W
Caracas 53 Jd 10.30N 66.56W
Carache 49 Li 9.38N 70.14W
Caracol 55 De 21.59S 57.02W
Caracol, Rio- 55 Df 22.13S 57.03W
Caracollo 54 Eg 17.39S 67.10W
Cara Droma Rúisc/Carrick-on-Shannon 9 Eh 53.57N 8.05W
Caraguatá, Cuchilla- 55 Ek 32.05S 54.54W
Caraguatatuba 55 Jf 23.37S 45.25W
Caraïbe, Mer-/Antilles, Mer des- = Caribbean Sea (EN) 38 Lh 15.00N 73.00W
Carajas, Serra dos- 54 He 6.00S 51.20W
Caramoan Peninsula 26 Hd 13.48N 123.40 E
Caramulo, Serra do- 13 Dd 40.34N 8.11W
Caraná, Rio- 55 Ca 13.20S 59.17W
Carandai 55 Ke 20.57S 43.48W
Carandazal 55 Dd 19.50S 57.09W
Caransebeş 15 Fd 45.25N 22.13 E
Carapá, Rio- 55 Eg 24.30S 54.20W
Carapelle 14 Ji 41.30N 15.55 E
Caraş 15 Ee 44.49N 21.20 E
Caraş Severin [2] 15 Ed 45.20N 22.00 E
Caratasca, Cayo- 49 Fe 16.02N 83.20W
Caratasca, Laguna de- 47 He 15.20N 83.50W
Caratinga 54 Jg 19.47S 42.08W
Carauari 54 Ed 4.52S 66.54W
Caraúbas 54 Ke 5.47S 37.34W
Caravaca 13 Kf 38.06N 1.51W
Caravelas 53 Mg 17.45S 39.15W
Caraveli 54 Dg 15.46S 73.22W
Caravelle, Presqu'île de la- 51h Bb 14.45N 60.55W
Caravelle, Rocher de la- 51h Bb 14.48N 60.53W
Carazinho 56 Jc 28.18S 52.48W
Carazo [3] 49 Dh 11.45N 86.15W
Carballino 13 Db 42.26N 8.04W
Carballo 13 Da 43.13N 8.41W
Carberry 45 Gb 49.52N 99.20W
Carbet, Pitons du- 51h Ab 14.42N 61.07W
Carbon, Cap- [Alg.] 13 Rh 36.47N 5.06 E
Carbon, Cap- [Alg.] 13 Li 35.54N 0.20W
Carbonara, Capo- 14 Dk 39.06N 9.31 E
Carbondale [Il.-U.S.] 43 Jd 37.44N 89.13W
Carbondale [Pa.-U.S.] 44 Je 41.35N 75.31W
Carbonera, Cuchilla de la- 55 El 34.10S 54.00W
Carboneras 13 Kh 36.59N 1.54W
Carboneras, Cerro- 48 Ih 18.10N 101.10W
Carbones 13 Gg 37.36N 5.39W
Carbonia 14 Ck 39.10N 8.31 E
Carcans, Étang de- 11 Ei 45.06N 1.07W
Carcar 26 Hd 10.06N 123.38 E
Carcaraña, Rio- 55 Bk 32.27S 60.48W
Carcassonne 11 Ik 43.13N 2.21 E
Carcross 42 Ed 60.10N 134.42W
Çardak [Tur.] 15 Ji 40.22N 26.43 E
Çardak [Tur.] 24 Cd 37.48N 29.40 E
Čardara 19 Gg 41.15N 68.01 E
Čardarinskoje Vodohranilišče 18 Gd 41.05N 68.15 E
Cárdenas [Cuba] 47 Hd 23.02N 81.12W
Cárdenas [Mex.] 47 Ed 22.00N 99.40W
Cárdenas [Mex.] 48 Mi 17.59N 93.22W
Cárdenas, Bahía de- 49 Gb 23.05N 81.10W
Cardener/Cardoner 13 Nc 41.41N 1.51 E
Cardiel, Lago- 56 Fg 48.55S 71.15W
Cardiff 6 Fe 51.30N 3.13W
Cardigan 9 Ii 52.06N 4.40W
Cardigan Bay 5 Fe 52.30N 4.20W
Cardona [Sp.] 13 Nc 41.55N 1.41 E
Cardona [Ur.] 55 Dk 33.54S 57.22W
Cardoner/Cardener 13 Nc 41.41N 1.51 E
Cardozo 55 Dk 32.38S 56.21W
Cardston 42 Gg 49.12N 113.18W
Čardžou 22 If 39.06N 63.34 E
Čardžouskaja Oblast [3] 19 Gh 39.00N 63.00 E
Carei 15 Fb 47.41N 22.28 E
Careiro 54 Gd 3.12S 59.45W
Carentan 11 Ee 49.18N 1.14W
Carey 46 Ie 43.20N 113.58W
Carey, Lake- 57 Dg 29.05S 122.15 E
Cargados Carajos Islands 30 Mj 16.35S 59.40 E
Cargese 11a Aa 42.08N 8.35 E
Carhaix-Plouguer 11 Cf 48.17N 3.35W
Cari 14 Hi 41.23N 13.50 E
Caria 15 Ll 37.30N 29.00 E
Cariacica 54 Jh 20.16S 40.25W
Cariaco 50 Eg 10.29N 63.33W
Cariaco, Golfo de- 50 Eg 10.30N 64.00W
Cariaco Basin (EN) 50 Dg 10.37N 65.10W
Cariati 14 Kk 39.30N 16.57 E
Caribana, Punta- 49 Ii 8.37N 76.52W
Caribbean Sea 38 Lh 15.00N 73.00W
Caribbean Sea (EN) = Antillas, Mar de las-/Caribe, Mar- 38 Lh 15.00N 73.00W
Caribbean Sea (EN) = Antilles, Mer des-/Caraïbe, Mer- 38 Lh 15.00N 73.00W
Caribbean Sea (EN) = Caribe, Mar-/Antillas, Mar de las- 38 Lh 15.00N 73.00W
Caribe, Mar-/Antillas, Mar de las- = Caribbean Sea (EN) 38 Lh 15.00N 73.00W
Cariboo Mountains 42 Ff 53.00N 121.00W
Caribou 42 Ie 59.20N 94.45W
Caribou 44 Mb 46.52N 68.01W
Caribou Island 44 Eb 47.27N 85.52W
Caribou Lake 45 La 50.25N 89.00W
Caribou Mountains 38 Hd 59.12N 115.40W
Caribou Range 46 Je 43.05N 111.15W
Caričin Grad 15 Eg 42.57N 21.45 E
Carignan 11 Le 49.38N 5.10 E
Carignano 14 Bf 44.55N 7.40 E
Cariñena 13 Kc 41.20N 1.13W
Carinhanha 54 Jf 14.08S 43.47W
Carinhanha, Rio- 55 Kb 14.20S 43.47W
Carini 14 Hl 38.08N 13.11 E
Carinola 14 Hi 41.11N 13.58 E
Carinthia (EN) = Kärnten [2] 14 Hd 46.45N 14.00 E
Carinthia (EN) = Kärnten 14 Hd 46.45N 14.00 E
Caripe 50 Eg 10.21N 63.29W
Caripito 54 Fa 10.08N 63.06W
Caris, Rio- 50 Eh 8.09N 63.46W
Carlet 13 Le 39.14N 0.31W
Carleton Place 44 Ic 45.07N 76.08W
Carletonville 37 De 26.23S 27.22 E
Carlin 46 Gf 40.43N 116.07W
Carling 12 Ie 49.10N 6.43 E
Carlingford Lough/Loch Cairlinn 9 Gg 54.05N 6.14W
Carlinville 45 Lg 39.17N 89.53W
Carlisle [Eng.-U.K.] 6 Fe 54.54N 2.55W
Carlisle [Pa.-U.S.] 44 Ie 40.12N 77.12W
Carlisle Bay 51q Ab 13.05N 59.37W
Carloforte 14 Ck 39.08N 8.18 E
Carlos Beguerie 55 Cl 35.29S 59.06W
Carlos Casares 56 He 35.38S 61.21W
Carlos Chagas 54 Jg 17.43S 40.45W
Carlos Reyles 55 Dk 33.03S 56.29W
Carlos Tejedor 55 Al 35.23S 62.25W
Carlow/Ceatharlach 9 Gi 52.50N 6.55W
Carlow/Ceatharlach [2] 9 Gi 52.50N 7.00W
Carloway 9 Gc 58.17N 6.47W
Carlsbad [Ca.-U.S.] 46 Gj 33.10N 117.21W
Carlsbad [N.M.-U.S.] 39 If 32.25N 104.14W
Carlyle 42 Hg 49.38N 102.16W
Carlyle Lake 45 Lg 38.40N 89.18W
Carmacks 42 Dd 62.05N 136.18W
Carmagnola 14 Bf 44.51N 7.43 E
Carmarthen 9 Ij 51.52N 4.19W
Carmarthen Bay 9 Ij 51.40N 4.30W
Carmaux 11 Ij 44.03N 2.09 E
Carmel Head 9 Ih 53.24N 4.34W
Carmelita 49 Be 17.21N 90.10W
Carmelo 56 Id 34.00S 58.17W
Carmen 55 Dk 33.15S 56.01W
Carmen, Isla- 47 Bc 25.57N 111.12W
Carmen, Isla del- 48 Nh 18.42N 91.40W
Carmen, Laguna del- 48 Mh 18.15N 93.50W
Carmen, Rio del- 48 Fb 30.42N 106.29W
Carmen, Sierra del- 48 Hc 29.00N 102.30W
Carmen de Patagones 56 Hf 40.48S 62.59W
Carmensa 56 Ge 35.08S 67.38W
Carmi 45 Lg 38.07N 88.10W
Carmichael 46 Eg 38.38N 121.19W
Carmo de Minas 55 Jf 22.07S 45.08W
Carmo do Paranaiba 55 Id 18.59S 46.21W
Carmona 13 Gg 37.28N 5.38W
Carnac 11 Cg 47.35N 3.05W
Carnamah 59 De 29.42S 115.53 E
Carnarvon [Austl.] 58 Cg 24.53S 113.40 E
Carnarvon [S.Afr.] 31 Jl 30.56S 22.08 E
Carnarvon Range 59 Ee 25.10S 121.00 E
Carnatic (EN) 21 Jh 10.30N 79.00 E
Carnegie, Lake- 57 Dg 26.10S 122.30 E
Carnegie Ridge (EN) 3 Nj 1.00S 85.00W
Carn Eige 9 Hd 57.30N 5.05W
Carney Island 66 Nf 73.57S 121.00W
Carnia 14 Gd 46.25N 13.00 E
Car Nicobar 25 Ig 9.10N 92.47 E
Carnot 35 Be 4.48N 16.03 E
Carnoustie 9 Ke 56.30N 2.44W
Carnsore Point/Ceann an Chairn 9 Gi 52.10N 6.22W
Carn Ui Néid/Mizen Head 5 Fe 51.27N 9.49W
Caro 44 Fd 43.29N 83.24W
Carol City 44 Gm 25.56N 80.16W
Carolina [Braz.] 53 Lf 7.20S 47.28W
Carolina [P.R.] 51a Cb 18.24N 65.57W
Carolina [S.Afr.] 37 Ee 26.05S 30.06 E
Carolina Beach 44 Ih 34.02N 77.54W
Carolinas, Puntan- 64b Bb 14.54N 145.38 E
Caroline Atoll 57 Le 9.58S 150.13W
Caroline Islands 57 Fd 8.00N 147.00 E
Carondelet Reef 57 Je 5.34S 173.51W
Caroni, Rio- 52 Je 8.21N 62.43W
Caronie → Nebrodi 14 Im 37.55N 14.35 E
Carora 54 Da 10.11N 70.05W
Carpathian Mountains (EN) 5 If 48.00N 24.00 E
Carpathian Mountains (EN) = Carpații Occidentali 15 Fc 46.30N 22.10 E
Carpathian Mountains (EN) = Carpații Orientali 15 Ib 47.30N 25.30 E
Carpații Meridionali = Transylvanian Alps (EN) 5 If 45.30N 22.10 E
Carpații Occidentali = Carpathian Mountains (EN) 15 Fc 46.30N 22.10 E
Carpații Orientali = Carpathian Mountains (EN) 15 Ib 47.30N 25.30 E
Carpen 15 Ge 44.20N 23.15 E
Carpentaria, Gulf of- 57 Ef 14.00S 139.00 E
Carpentras 11 Lj 44.03N 5.03 E
Carpi 14 Ef 44.47N 10.53 E
Carpina 54 Ke 7.51S 35.15W
Carr, Cape- 66 Ie 66.07S 130.51 E
Carraig Fhearghais/Carrickfergus 9 Hg 54.43N 5.44W
Carraig na Siúire/Carrick-on-Suir 9 Fi 52.21N 7.25W
Carrantuohill 5 Fe 52.00N 9.45W
Carrara 14 Ef 44.05N 10.06 E
Carreiro, Rio- 55 Gi 29.07S 51.43W
Carreño 13 Ga 43.35N 5.46W
Carreta, Punta- 54 Cf 14.13S 76.18W
Carretero, Puerto- 13 Ig 37.28N 3.40W
Carriacou 50 Ff 12.30N 61.27W
Carrick 9 If 55.15N 4.40W
Carrickfergus/Carraig Fhearghais 9 Hg 54.43N 5.44W
Carrick-on-Shannon/cara Droma Rúisc 9 Eh 53.57N 8.05W
Carrick-on-Suir/Carraig na Siúire 9 Fi 52.21N 7.25W
Carrington 43 Hb 47.27N 99.08W
Carrión 13 Hc 41.53N 4.32W
Carrión de los Condes 13 Hb 42.20N 4.36W
Carrizal 49 Kh 11.58N 72.12W
Carrizo Peak 45 Dj 33.20N 105.38W
Carrizos 46 Gc 29.58N 105.16W
Carrizo Springs 45 Gl 28.31N 99.52W
Carrizo Wash 46 Ki 34.36N 109.26W
Carrizozo 45 Dj 33.38N 105.53W
Carroll 45 Ie 42.04N 94.52W
Carroll Inlet 66 Qf 73.18S 78.30W
Carrollton [Ga.-U.S.] 44 Ei 33.35N 85.05W
Carrollton [Il.-U.S.] 45 Kg 39.18N 90.24W
Carrollton [Ky.-U.S.] 44 Ef 38.41N 85.11W
Carrollton [Mo.-U.S.] 45 Jg 39.22N 93.30W
Carron, Loch- 9 Hd 57.30N 5.40W
Carrot 42 Hf 53.50N 101.18W
Carrowmore Lough 9 Dg 54.12N 9.47W
Çarşamba 24 Gb 41.12N 36.44 E
Çarşamba 24 Ed 37.53N 32.37 E
Čaršanga 19 Gh 37.31N 66.03 E
Čarsk 19 If 49.35N 81.05 E
Carson 46 Ed 45.44N 121.49W
Carson City 39 Hf 39.10N 119.46W
Carson Lake 46 Fg 39.19N 118.43W
Carson Sink 46 Fg 39.45N 118.30W
Cartagena [Col.] 53 Id 10.25N 75.32W
Cartagena [Sp.] 6 Fh 37.36N 0.59W
Cartago [3] 49 Fi 9.50N 83.45W
Cartago [Col.] 54 Cc 4.46N 75.56W
Cartago [C.R.] 47 Hg 9.52N 83.55W
Cartaxo 13 De 39.09N 8.47W
Carter, Mount- 59 Ib 13.05S 143.15 E
Cartered 11 Ee 49.23N 1.47W
Cartersville 44 Eh 34.10N 85.05W
Carterton 62 Fd 41.01S 175.31 E
Carthage [Mo.-U.S.] 45 Ih 37.11N 94.19W
Carthage [Tx.-U.S.] 45 Ij 32.09N 94.20W
Cartier 44 Gb 46.42N 81.32W
Cartier Island 57 Df 12.30S 123.30 E
Caruaru 53 Mf 8.17S 35.58W
Carúpano 54 Fa 10.40N 63.14W
Carutapera 54 Id 1.13S 46.01W
Čarvak 18 Gd 41.38N 69.56 E
Carvin 12 Ed 50.29N 2.58 E
Carvoeiro, Cabo- 13 Ce 39.21N 9.24W
Čaryn 18 Lc 43.50N 79.12 E
Čaryš 20 Df 52.22N 83.45 E
Casablanca [2] 32 Fc 33.37N 7.35W
Casablanca 31 Ge 33.36N 7.37W
Casa Branca 55 Ie 21.46S 47.05W
Casa Grande 43 Ee 32.53N 111.45W
Casalbordino 14 Ih 42.09N 14.35 E
Casale Monferrato 14 Ce 45.08N 8.27 E
Casalmaggiore 14 Ef 44.59N 10.26 E
Casalvasco 55 Cb 15.19S 59.59W
Casal Velino 14 Jj 40.11N 15.06 E
Casamance 34 Bc 12.33N 16.46W
Casamance [3] 34 Bc 12.50N 15.00W
Casanare [2] 54 Db 5.20N 72.00W
Casanare, Rio- 54 Eb 6.02N 69.51W
Casanay 50 Eg 10.30N 63.25W
Casa Nova 54 Je 9.25S 41.08W
Casarano 14 Mj 40.00N 18.10 E
Casas Grandes, Rio- 48 Eb 30.22N 107.31W
Casas-Ibáñez 13 Ke 39.17N 1.28W
Casca, Rio da- 55 Eb 14.52S 55.52W
Cascade 46 Hd 44.31N 115.59W
Cascade Point 62 Cf 44.01S 168.22 E
Cascade Range 38 Ge 45.00N 121.30W
Cascais 13 Cf 38.42N 9.25W
Cascavel 56 Jb 24.57S 53.28W
Cascia 14 Hh 42.43N 13.01 E
Casciana Terme 14 Eg 43.32N 10.38 E
Cascina 14 Eg 43.41N 10.33 E
Casentino 14 Fg 43.40N 11.50 E

Index Symbols

[1] Independent Nation
[2] State, Region
[3] District, County
[4] Municipality
[5] Colony, Dependency
Continent
Physical Region
Historical or Cultural Region
Mount, Mountain
Volcano
Hill
Mountains, Mountain Range
Hills, Escarpment
Plateau, Upland
Pass, Gap
Plain, Lowland
Delta
Salt Flat
Valley, Canyon
Crater, Cave
Karst Features
Depression
Polder
Desert, Dunes
Forest, Woods
Heath, Steppe
Oasis
Cape, Point
Coast, Beach
Cliff
Peninsula
Isthmus
Sandbank
Island
Atoll
Rock, Reef
Islands, Archipelago
Rocks, Reefs
Coral Reef
Well, Spring
Geyser
River, Stream
Waterfall Rapids
River Mouth, Estuary
Lake
Salt Lake
Intermittent Lake
Reservoir
Swamp, Pond
Canal
Glacier
Ice Shelf, Pack Ice
Ocean
Sea
Gulf, Bay
Strait, Fjord
Lagoon
Bank
Seamount
Tablemount
Ridge
Shelf
Basin
Escarpment, Sea Scarp
Fracture
Trench, Abyss
National Park, Reserve
Point of Interest
Recreation Site
Cave, Cavern
Historic Site
Ruins
Wall, Walls
Church, Abbey
Temple
Scientific Station
Airport
Port
Lighthouse
Mine
Tunnel
Dam, Bridge

Case-Pilote	51h	Ab	14.38N	61.08W
Caserta	14	Ii	41.04N	14.20 E
Casey	66	He	66.17S	110.32 E
Casey Bay	66	Ee	67.00S	48.00 E
Cashel/Caiseal	9	Fi	52.31N	7.53W
Casigua	49	Ki	8.46N	72.30W
Casilda	56	Hd	33.03S	61.10W
Casimcea	15	Le	44.24N	28.33 E
Casino	59	Ke	28.52S	153.03 E
Casiquiare, Brazo-	54	Ec	2.01N	67.07W
Čáslav	10	Lg	49.55N	15.25 E
Casma	54	Ce	9.28S	78.19W
Časnačorr, Gora-	7	Hc	67.45N	33.29 E
Čašniki	7	Gi	54.52N	29.08 E
Casoli	14	Ih	42.07N	14.18 E
Casoria	14	Ij	40.54N	14.17 E
Caspe	13	Lc	41.14N	0.02W
Casper	39	Ie	42.51N	106.19W
Caspian Depression (EN)= Prikaspijskaja Nizmennost	5	Lf	48.00N	52.00 E
Caspian Sea (EN)= Kaspijskoje More	5	Lg	42.00N	50.30 E
Caspian Sea (EN)= Māzandarān, Daryā-ye-	5	Lg	42.00N	50.30 E
Cassai	30	Ii	3.02S	16.57 E
Cassamba	36	De	13.04S	20.25 E
Cassange, Rio-	55	Dc	17.06S	57.23W
Cassano allo Ionio	14	Kk	39.47N	16.19 E
Cass City	44	Fd	43.36N	83.10W
Cassel	12	Ed	50.47N	2.29 E
Casselton	45	Hc	46.54N	97.13W
Cássia	55	Ie	20.36S	46.56W
Cassiar	42	Ee	59.16N	129.40W
Cassiar Mountains	38	Gd	59.00N	129.00W
Cassilândia	54	Hg	19.09S	51.45W
Cassino [Braz.]	55	Fk	32.11S	52.10W
Cassino [It.]	14	Hi	41.30N	13.49 E
Cassis	11	Lk	43.13N	5.32 E
Cass Lake	45	Ic	47.23N	94.36W
Cass River	44	Fd	43.23N	83.59W
Cassununga	55	Fc	16.03S	53.38W
Castagneto Carducci	14	Eg	43.10N	10.36 E
Castagniccia	11a	Ba	42.25N	9.30 E
Castañar, Sierra del-	13	He	39.35N	4.10W
Castanhal	54	Id	1.18S	47.55W
Castaños	48	Id	26.47N	101.25W
Castelbuono	14	Im	37.56N	14.05 E
Castel di Sangro	14	Ii	41.47N	14.06 E
Castelfidardo	14	Hg	43.28N	13.33 E
Castelfranco Veneto	14	Fe	45.40N	11.55 E
Casteljaloux	11	Gj	44.19N	0.06 E
Castellabate	14	Ij	40.17N	14.57 E
Castellammare, Golfo di-	14	Gl	38.10N	12.55 E
Castellammare del Golfo	14	Gl	38.01N	12.53 E
Castellammare di Stabia	14	Ij	40.42N	14.29 E
Castellana Grotte	14	Lj	40.53N	17.10 E
Castellane	11	Mk	43.51N	6.31 E
Castellaneta	14	Kj	40.38N	16.56 E
Castelldefels	13	Nc	41.17N	1.58 E
Castelli [Arg.]	56	Hc	25.57S	60.37W
Castelli [Arg.]	55	Dm	36.06S	57.47W
Castelló de la Plana/ Castellón de la Plana	6	Fh	39.59N	0.02W
Castellón	13	Ld	40.10N	0.10W
Castellón de la Plana/ Castelló de la Plana	6	Fh	39.59N	0.02W
Castellón de la Plana-El Grao	13	Me	39.58N	0.01 E
Castellote	13	Ld	40.48N	0.19W
Castelnaudary	11	Hk	43.19N	1.57 E
Castelnau-de-Médoc	11	Fi	45.02N	0.48W
Castelnovo ne' Monti	14	Ef	44.26N	10.24 E
Castelo Branco	13	Ee	40.00N	7.30W
Castelo Branco	13	Ee	39.49N	7.30W
Castelo de Vide	13	Ee	39.25N	7.27W
Castelo do Piauí	54	Je	5.20S	41.33W
Castel San Giovanni	14	De	45.04N	9.26 E
Castelsardo	14	Cj	40.55N	8.43 E
Castelsarrasin	11	Hj	44.02N	1.06 E
Casteltermini	14	Hm	37.32N	13.39 E
Castelvetrano	14	Gm	37.41N	12.47 E
Castets	11	Ek	43.53N	1.09W
Castiglione del Lago	14	Gg	43.07N	12.03 E
Castiglione della Pescaia	14	Eh	42.46N	10.53 E
Castiglion Fiorentino	14	Fg	43.20N	11.55 E
Castilla la Nueva=New Castile (EN)	13	Id	40.00N	3.45W
Castilla la Vieja=Old Castile (EN)	13	Ic	41.30N	4.00W
Castillejo	13	Gc	41.14N	5.30W
Castillon-la-Bataille	11	Fj	44.51N	0.02W
Castillonnès	11	Gj	44.39N	0.36 E
Castillos	56	Jd	34.12S	53.50W
Castillos, Laguna de-	55	Fl	34.20S	53.54W
Castlebar/Caisleán an Bharraigh	9	Dh	53.52N	9.17W
Castle Bruce	51g	Bb	15.26N	61.16W
Castle Dome Peak	46	Hj	33.05N	114.08W
Castle Douglas	9	Jg	54.57N	3.56W
Castlegar	42	Fg	49.19N	117.40W
Castleisland/Oileán Ciarraí	9	Di	52.14N	9.27W
Castlemaine	59	Ig	37.04S	144.13 E
Castle Peak	46	Hd	44.03N	114.32W
Castlepoint	62	Gd	40.55S	176.13 E
Castlepollard	9	Fh	53.41N	7.17W
Castlerea/An Caisleán Riabhach	9	Eh	53.46N	8.29W
Castlereagh Bay	59	Hb	12.10S	135.10 E
Castle Rock Butte	45	Ed	45.00N	103.27W
Castle Rock Lake	45	Le	43.56N	89.58W
Častoozerje	17	Mi	55.34N	67.53 E
Castor	46	Ja	52.13N	111.53W
Castres	11	Ik	43.36N	2.15 E
Castricum	12	Gb	52.33N	4.42 E
Castries	39	Mh	14.01N	61.00W
Castrignano del Capo	14	Mk	39.50N	18.20 E
Castro [Braz.]	56	Jb	24.47S	50.03W
Castro [Chile]	56	Ff	42.29S	73.46W
Castro Alves	54	Kf	12.45S	39.26W
Castrocaro Terme e Terra del Sole	14	Ff	44.10N	11.57 E
Castro Daire	13	Ed	40.54N	7.56W
Castro del Rio	13	Hg	37.41N	4.28W
Castrojeriz	13	Hb	42.17N	4.08W
Castropol	13	Ea	43.32N	7.02W
Castrop-Rauxel	12	Jc	51.33N	7.19 E
Castro Urdiales	13	Ia	43.23N	3.13W
Castro Verde	13	Dg	37.42N	8.05W
Castrovillari	14	Kk	39.49N	16.12 E
Castrovirreyna	54	Cf	13.16S	75.19W
Castuera	13	Gf	38.43N	5.33W
Častyje	17	Gh	57.19N	54.59 E
Casupá	55	El	34.09S	55.38W
Caswell Sound	62	Bf	45.00S	167.10 E
Çat	24	Ic	39.40N	41.02 E
Čata	10	Oi	47.58N	18.40 E
Catacamas	49	Ef	14.54N	85.56W
Catahoula Lake	45	Jk	31.30N	92.06W
Çatak	24	Jc	38.01N	43.07 E
Çatak	24	Jd	37.53N	42.39 E
Catalan Coastal Range (EN) =Cadena Costero Catalana /Serralada Litoral Catalana	5	Gg	41.35N	1.40 E
Catalan Coastal Range (EN) =Serralada Litoral Catalana/Cadena Costero Catalana	5	Gg	41.35N	1.40 E
Catalão	54	Ig	18.10S	47.57W
Çatal Balkan	15	Jg	42.46N	27.00 E
Çatalca	15	Lh	41.09N	28.27 E
Çatal Dağ	15	Lj	39.51N	28.20 E
Catalina	56	Gc	25.13S	69.43W
Catalina, Isla-	49	Md	18.21N	69.00W
Catalina, Punta-	56	Gh	52.32S	68.47W
Catalonia (EN)=Cataluña/ Catalunya	5	Gg	42.00N	2.00 E
Catalonia (EN)=Cataluña/ Catalunya	13	Nc	42.00N	2.00 E
Catalonia (EN)=Catalunya/ Cataluña	5	Gg	42.00N	2.00 E
Catalonia (EN)=Catalunya/ Cataluña	13	Nc	42.00N	2.00 E
Cataluña/Catalunya= Catalonia (EN)	5	Gg	42.00N	2.00 E
Cataluña/Catalunya= Catalonia (EN)	13	Nc	42.00N	2.00 E
Catalunya/Cataluña= Catalonia (EN)	13	Nc	42.00N	2.00 E
Catalunya/Cataluña= Catalonia (EN)	5	Gg	42.00N	2.00 E
Çatalzeytin	24	Fb	41.57N	34.13 E
Catamarca	23	Jh	28.30S	65.45W
Catamarca	56	Gc	27.00S	67.00W
Catanduanes	21	Oh	13.45N	124.15 E
Catanduva	56	Kb	21.08S	48.58W
Catanduvas	55	Fg	25.12S	53.08W
Catania	6	Hh	37.30N	15.06 E
Catania, Golfo di-	14	Jm	37.25N	15.10 E
Catania, Piana di-	14	Im	37.25N	14.50 E
Catanzaro	6	Hh	38.54N	16.35 E
Catarman	26	Hd	12.30N	124.38 E
Catastrophe, Cape-	57	Eh	35.00S	136.00 E
Catatumbo, Río-	49	Li	9.21N	71.45W
Catbalogan	26	Hd	11.46N	124.53 E
Catemaco, Lago-	48	Lh	18.25N	95.05W
Catete	36	Bd	9.07S	13.41 E
Cathair na Mart/Westport	9	Dh	53.48N	9.32W
Cathair Saidhbhín/ Cahersiveen	9	Cj	51.57N	10.13W
Cathcart	37	Df	32.18S	27.09 E
Catherine, Mount-	46	Ig	39.05N	112.04W
Catholic Island	51n	Bb	12.40N	61.24W
Catio	34	Bc	11.17N	15.15W
Cat Island	38	Lg	24.30N	75.30W
Čatkal	18	Hd	41.36N	70.05 E
Čatkalskij Hrebet	19	Hg	41.30N	70.50 E
Cat Lake	42	If	51.40N	91.52W
Catoche, Cabo-	38	Kg	21.36N	87.07W
Cato Island	57	Gg	23.15S	155.35 E
Catolé do Rocha	54	Ke	6.21S	37.45W
Catoute	13	Fb	42.45N	6.20W
Catria	14	Gg	43.28N	12.42 E
Catriló	56	He	36.26S	63.24W
Catrimani, Rio-	54	Fc	0.28N	61.44W
Catskill Mountains	44	Jd	42.10N	74.30W
Cattenom	12	Ie	49.25N	6.15 E
Cattolica	14	Gg	43.58N	12.44 E
Catu	54	Kf	12.21S	38.23W
Catuane	37	Ee	26.48S	32.14 E
Catumbela	36	Be	12.27S	13.29 E
Catur	37	Fb	13.45S	35.37 E
Catwick, Iles-	25	Lg	10.00N	109.00 E
Catwright	39	Nd	53.50N	56.45W
Čatyrkël, Ozero-	18	Jd	40.35N	75.20 E
Čatyrtaš	18	Kd	40.52N	76.23 E
Cauca	54	Cc	2.30N	77.00W
Cauca, Rio-	52	Ie	8.54N	74.28W
Caucasia	54	Cb	7.59N	75.13W
Caucasus (EN)=Kavkaz, Bolšoj-	5	Kg	42.30N	45.00 E
Caucete	56	Gd	31.38S	68.16W
Caudebec-en-Caux	12	Ce	49.32N	0.44 E
Caudete	13	Lf	38.42N	0.59W
Caudry	11	Jd	50.08N	3.25 E
Caulonia	14	Kl	38.23N	16.24 E
Caumont-l'Eventé	12	Be	49.05N	0.48W
Caungula	31	Ii	8.26S	18.37 E
Čaunskaja Guba	20	Lc	69.30N	170.00 E
Caupolican	54	Ef	13.30S	68.30W
Cauquenes	56	Fe	35.58S	72.21W
Caura, Rio-	52	Je	7.38N	64.53W
Causapscal	44	Na	48.22N	67.14W
Caussade	11	Hj	44.10N	1.32 E
Čausy	16	Gc	53.50N	30.59 E
Cauterets	11	Fl	42.53N	0.07W
Cauto, Rio-	49	Ic	20.33N	77.15W
Cauvery	21	Jh	11.09N	78.52 E
Caux, Pays de-	11	Ge	49.40N	0.40 E
Cávado	13	Dc	41.32N	8.48W
Cavaillon	11	Lk	43.50N	5.02 E
Cavalcante	55	Ia	13.48S	47.30W
Cavalese	14	Fd	46.17N	11.27 E
Cavalli Islands	62	Ea	35.00S	173.55 E
Cavallo, Isola-	11a	Bb	41.22N	9.16 E
Cavallo Pass	45	Hl	28.25N	96.26W
Cavally	30	Gh	4.22N	7.32W
Cavan/An Cabhán	9	Fg	54.00N	7.21W
Cavan/An Cabhán	9	Fh	53.55N	7.30W
Cavarzere	14	Ge	45.08N	12.05 E
Çavdarhisar	15	Mj	39.12N	29.37 E
Çavdir	15	Ml	37.09N	29.42 E
Caviana, Ilha-	54	Hc	0.10N	50.05W
Cavili	26	He	9.17N	120.50 E
Cavour, Canale-	14	Be	45.11N	7.54 E
Cavtat	14	Mh	42.35N	18.13 E
Caxambu	55	Je	21.59S	44.56W
Caxias	53	Lf	4.50S	43.21W
Caxias do Sul	53	Kh	29.10S	51.11W
Caxito	36	Bd	8.34S	13.40 E
Çay	24	Dc	38.35N	31.02 E
Cayambe	54	Cc	0.05N	78.08W
Cayambe, Volcán-	52	Ie	0.02N	77.59W
Cayastá	55	Bj	31.12S	60.10W
Cayce	44	Gi	33.59N	81.04W
Çaycuma	24	Eb	41.25N	32.05 E
Çayeli	24	Ib	41.05N	40.44 E
Cayenne	53	Ke	4.56N	52.20W
Cayeux-Sur-Mer	12	Dd	50.11N	1.29 E
Cayey	49	Nd	18.07N	66.10W
Çayırlı	24	Ic	39.48N	40.01 E
Çaykara	24	Ib	40.45N	40.19 E
Caylus	11	Hj	44.14N	1.47 E
Cayman Brac	47	Ie	19.43N	79.49W
Cayman Islands	39	Kh	19.30N	80.30W
Cayman Islands	38	Kh	19.30N	80.30W
Cayman Ridge (EN)	47	He	19.30N	80.30W
Cayman Trench (EN)	3	Bh	19.00N	80.00W
Cayo	49	Ce	17.10N	88.50W
Cayon	51c	Ab	17.21N	62.43W
Cayones, Cayos-	49	Fe	16.05N	83.12W
Cay Sal Bank	47	Hd	23.45N	80.00W
Cayuga Lake	44	Id	42.45N	76.45W
Cazalla de la Sierra	13	Gg	37.56N	5.45W
Caza Pava	55	Di	28.17S	56.07W
Cazaux, Étang de-	11	Ej	44.29N	1.10W
Cazombo	31	Jj	11.54S	22.53 E
Cazorla	13	Jg	37.55N	3.00W
Cazorla, Sierra de-	13	Jf	37.55N	2.55W
Cea	13	Gb	42.00N	5.36W
Ceahlău	15	Ib	47.03N	25.58 E
Ceanannas Mór/Kells	9	Gh	53.44N	6.53W
Ceanna Caillighe/Hags Head	9	Di	52.57N	9.28W
Ceann Acla/Achill Head	9	Ch	53.59N	10.13W
Ceann an Chairn/Carnsore Point	9	Gi	52.10N	6.22W
Ceann Chill Mhantáin/ Wicklow Head	9	Hi	52.58N	6.00W
Ceann Góilaim/Slyne Head	9	Ch	53.24N	10.13W
Ceann Iorrais/Erris Head	5	Fe	54.19N	10.00W
Ceann Léime/Loop Head	9	Di	52.34N	9.56W
Ceann Ros Eoghain/Rossan Point	9	Eg	54.42N	8.48W
Ceann Sléibhe/Slea Head	9	Ci	52.06N	10.27W
Ceann Toirc/Kanturk	9	Ei	52.10N	8.55W
Ceará	54	Kd	5.00S	39.30W
Ceará-Mirim	54	Ke	5.38S	35.26W
Ceatharlach/Carlow	9	Gi	52.50N	7.00W
Ceatharlach/Carlow	9	Gi	52.50N	6.55W
Cébaco, Isla-	49	Gj	7.32N	81.09W
Ceballos	48	Gd	26.32N	104.09W
Čebarkul	17	Ji	54.58N	60.25 E
Čeboksary	6	Kd	56.09N	47.15 E
Cebollati	55	Fk	33.16S	53.47W
Cebollati, Rio-	55	Fk	33.09S	53.38W
Cebollera, Sierra-	13	Jc	42.00N	2.40W
Ceboruco, Volcán-	48	Gg	21.09N	104.30W
Cebreros	13	Hd	40.27N	4.28W
Cebrikovo	15	Nb	47.09N	30.02 E
Cebu	21	Oh	10.20N	123.45 E
Cebu	21	Oh	10.18N	123.54 E
Cece	10	Oj	46.46N	18.39 E
Čečen, Ostrov-	16	Og	44.00N	47.45 E
Čečeno-Ingušskaja ASSR	19	Eg	43.15N	45.30 E
Cecen-Ula	27	Gb	48.45N	95.55 E
Cecerleg	22	Me	47.30N	101.27 E
Čečersk	16	Gc	52.56N	30.58 E
Čechy=Bohemia (EN)	5	Hf	50.00N	14.30 E
Čechy=Bohemia (EN)	10	Kf	50.00N	14.30 E
Cecina	14	Eg	43.18N	10.29 E
Cecina	14	Eg	43.10N	10.31 E
Čečuisk	20	Fe	58.07N	108.32 E
Cedar City	39	Hf	37.41N	113.04W
Cedar Creek	45	Fc	46.07N	101.18W
Cedar Creek Reservoir	45	Hj	32.20N	96.10W
Cedar Falls	43	Ic	42.32N	92.27W
Cedar Grove	51d	Bb	17.10N	61.49W
Cedar Lake	42	Hf	53.25N	100.00W
Cedar Rapids	39	Je	41.59N	91.40W
Cedar River [Nb.-U.S.]	45	Hf	41.22N	97.57W
Cedar River [U.S.]	43	Ic	41.17N	91.20W
Cedartown	44	Eh	34.01N	85.15W
Cedar-Tree Point	51d	Ba	17.42N	61.53W
Cedeira	13	Da	43.39N	8.03W
Cedral	48	If	23.48N	100.44W
Cedrino	14	Dj	40.23N	9.44 E
Cedro	54	Ke	6.36S	39.03W
Cedrón	13	Ie	39.48N	3.33W
Cedros, Isla- [Mex.]	47	Ac	28.12N	115.15W
Cedros, Isla [Mex.]=Cedros Island (EN)	38	Hg	28.10N	115.15W
Cedros Island (EN)=Cedros, Isla [Mex.]	38	Hg	28.10N	115.15W
Cedros Trench (EN)	47	Ac	27.45N	115.45W
Ceduna	59	Gf	32.07S	133.40 E
Cedynia	10	Kd	52.50N	14.14 E
Cefalù	14	Il	38.02N	14.01 E
Cega	13	Hc	41.33N	4.46W
Čegdomyn	22	Pd	51.07N	133.05 E
Čegem	16	Mh	43.36N	43.48 E
Cegléd	10	Pi	47.10N	19.48 E
Ceglie Messapico	14	Lj	40.39N	17.31 E
Cehegin	13	Kf	38.06N	1.48W
Cehotina	15	Bf	43.31N	18.45 E
Čehov [R.S.F.S.R.]	7	Ii	55.11N	37.29 E
Čehov [R.S.F.S.R.]	20	Jg	47.24N	142.05 E
Ceica	15	Fc	46.51N	22.11 E
Çekerek	24	Fb	40.34N	35.46 E
Çekerek	24	Fb	40.04N	35.31 E
Čekmaguš	17	Gi	55.10N	54.40 E
Cela	36	Ce	11.25S	15.07 E
Celano	14	Hh	42.05N	13.33 E
Celaya	47	Dd	20.31N	100.37W
Čelbas	16	Kf	46.06N	38.59 E
Célé	11	Hj	44.28N	1.38 E
Celebes/Sulawesi	21	Oj	2.00S	121.10 E
Celebes Basin (EN)	26	Hf	4.00N	122.00 E
Celebes Sea (EN)= Sulawesi, Laut-	21	Oj	3.00N	122.00 E
Čeleken	19	Fh	39.27N	53.10 E
Čeleken, Poluostrov-	16	Rj	39.25N	53.35 E
Celendín	54	Ce	6.52S	78.09W
Celerain, Punta-	48	Pg	20.16N	86.59W
Celeste	55	Dj	31.18S	57.04W
Celestún	48	Ng	20.52N	90.24W
Celinograd	22	Jd	51.10N	71.30 E
Celinogradskaja Oblast	19	Gh	51.00N	70.00 E
Čeljabinsk	22	Id	55.10N	61.24 E
Čeljabinskaja Oblast	19	Ge	54.00N	61.00 E
Celje	14	Jd	46.14N	15.16 E
Čeljuskin, Mys-	21	Mb	77.45N	104.20 E
Čelkar	19	Ff	47.50N	59.29 E
Celldömölk	10	Ni	47.15N	17.09 E
Celle	10	Gd	52.37N	10.05 E
Celles	12	Fd	50.43N	3.27 E
Celles, Houyet-	12	Hd	50.19N	5.01 E
Cellina	14	Ge	46.02N	12.47 E
Celone	14	Ji	41.36N	15.41 E
Celorico da Beira	13	Ed	40.38N	7.23W
Celtic Sea	5	Fe	51.00N	7.00W
Celtic Sea (EN)=An Mhuir Cheilteach	5	Fe	51.00N	7.00W
Cemaes Head	9	Ii	52.07N	4.44W
Čemal	20	Df	51.25N	86.05 E
Čemdalsk	20	Fe	59.45N	103.18 E
Čemernica	14	Lf	44.30N	17.15 E
Čemerno	15	Df	43.36N	20.26 E
Çemişkezek	24	Hc	39.04N	38.55 E
Cenajo, Embalse de-	13	Kf	38.20N	1.55W
Cenderawasih, Teluk-	26	Kg	2.25S	135.10 E
Cengel	27	Eb	48.56N	89.10 E
Çengel Geçidi	24	Kc	39.45N	44.02 E
Ceno	14	Ef	44.41N	10.05 E
Centenary	37	Ec	16.44S	31.07 E
Centennial	46	Lf	41.51N	106.07W
Centennial Lake	44	Ic	45.15N	77.00W
Centennial Mountains	46	Jd	44.35N	111.55W
Center	45	Ik	31.48N	94.11W
Center Hill Lake	44	Eg	36.00N	85.45W
Centerville	45	Jf	40.43N	92.52W
Centinela, Farallón-	50	Cg	10.49N	66.05W
Centinela, Picacho del-	47	Dc	29.07N	102.27W
Cento	14	Ff	44.43N	11.17 E
Centrafrique=Central African Republic (EN)	31	Jh	7.00N	21.00 E
Central [Bots.]	37	Dd	21.30S	26.00 E
Central [Ghana]	34	Ed	5.30N	1.00W
Central [Kenya]	36	Gc	0.45S	37.00 E
Central [Mwi.]	36	Fe	13.30S	34.00 E
Central [Par.]	55	Dg	25.30S	57.30W
Central [Scot.-U.K.]	9	Ie	56.15N	4.10W
Central [Ug.]	36	Fb	0.10N	32.05 E
Central [Zam.]	36	Ee	15.00S	29.00 E
Central, Chaco-	52	Kh	25.00S	59.45W
Central, Cordillera- [Dom.Rep.]	47	Je	18.45N	70.30W
Central, Cordillera- [P.R.]	49	Nd	18.10N	66.35W
Central, Massif-	5	Gf	45.00N	3.10 E
Central, Meseta-	38	Ig	23.00N	103.00W
Central African Republic (EN)=Centrafrique	31	Jh	7.00N	21.00 E
Central Auckland	62	Fb	36.45S	174.40 E
Central Brāhui Range	25	Dc	29.20N	66.55 E
Central City	45	Hf	41.07N	98.00W
Centralia [Il.-U.S.]	45	Lg	38.31N	89.08W
Centralia [Wa.-U.S.]	43	Cb	46.43N	122.58W
Central Lowland	38	Ke	40.20N	90.00W
Central Makrān Range	21	Ig	26.40N	64.30 E
Centralno Tungusskoje Plato	20	Fd	61.15N	102.00 E
Centralny-Kospašski	17	Hg	59.03N	57.50 E
Central Pacific Basin (EN)	3	Ki	5.00N	175.00W
Central Plateau	64e	Bb	0.32S	166.56 E
Central Point	46	De	42.23N	122.57W
Central Range	57	Fe	5.00S	142.30 E
Central Russian Uplands (EN)=Srednerusskaja Vozvyšennost	5	Je	52.00N	38.00 E
Central Siberian Uplands (EN)=Srednesibirskoje Ploskogorje	21	Mc	65.00N	105.00 E
Central Urals (EN)=Sredni Ural	5	Ld	58.00N	59.00 E
Centre [Togo]	34	Fd	9.15N	1.00 E
Centre [U.V.]	34	Ec	12.00N	1.00W
Centre, Canal du-	11	Jh	46.28N	3.59 E
Centre-Est	34	Ec	11.30N	0.20W
Centre-Nord	34	Ec	13.20N	0.55W
Centre-Ouest	34	Ec	12.00N	2.20W
Centre-Sud	34	He	3.30N	11.50 E
Centro, Cayo-	48	Ph	18.35N	87.20W
Centuripe	14	Im	37.37N	14.44 E
Čepca	19	Fd	58.35N	50.05 E
Čepelare	15	Hh	41.44N	24.41 E
Cephalonia (EN)= Kefallinía	5	Ih	38.15N	20.35 E
Čepin	14	Me	45.32N	18.34 E
Ceplenița	15	Jb	47.23N	26.58 E
Cepu	26	Fh	7.09S	111.35 E
Cer	15	Ce	44.37N	19.28 E
Ceram Sea (EN)=Seram, Laut-	57	De	2.30S	128.00 E
Cerbatana, Serranía de la-	54	Eb	6.50N	66.15W
Cerbicales, Iles-	11a	Bb	41.33N	9.22 E
Cercal	13	Dg	37.47N	8.42W
Čerchov	10	Rg	49.10N	21.05 E
Čerdakly	7	Li	54.23N	48.51 E
Čerdyn	17	Hf	60.25N	56.29 E
Cère	11	Hj	44.55N	1.49 E
Čereha	7	Gh	57.47N	28.22 E
Čeremhovo	22	Md	53.09N	103.05 E
Čerepanovo	20	Df	54.13N	83.32 E
Čerepovec	6	Jd	59.08N	37.54 E
Ceres [Arg.]	56	Hc	29.53S	61.57W
Ceres [Braz.]	54	Ig	15.17S	49.35W
Ceres [S.Afr.]	37	Bf	33.21S	19.18 E
Céret	11	Il	42.29N	2.45 E
Cereté	54	Cb	8.53N	75.47W
Cerf Island	30	Mi	9.31S	51.01 E
Cerfontaine	12	Gd	50.10N	4.25 E
Cergy	12	Ee	49.02N	2.04 E
Cerignola	14	Ji	41.16N	15.54 E
Čerikov	16	Gc	53.35N	31.25 E
Cérilly	11	Ih	46.37N	2.50 E
Čerkasskaja Oblast	19	Df	49.15N	31.15 E
Čerkassy	19	Df	49.26N	32.04 E
Çerkeş	24	Eb	40.50N	32.54 E
Čerkessk	19	Eg	44.14N	42.04 E
Çerkezköy	15	Kh	41.17N	28.00 E
Čerlak	19	He	54.09N	74.58 E
Čerlakskij	19	He	53.47N	74.31 E
Čermasan	17	Gi	55.10N	55.20 E
Cermei	15	Ec	46.33N	21.51 E
Çermenika	15	Dh	41.03N	20.20 E
Čermoz	17	Hg	58.47N	56.10 E
Cerna [Rom.]	15	Ge	44.37N	23.57 E
Cerna [Rom.]	15	Fd	44.42N	22.25 E
Cerna [Rom.]	15	Fe	45.53N	22.58 E
Černaja	17	Hb	68.35N	56.31 E
Černaja [R.S.F.S.R.]	17	Hb	68.35N	56.30 E
Černaja [Ukr.-U.S.S.R.]	15	Mb	47.39N	29.11 E
Černa Skala, Prohod-	15	Fg	42.02N	22.47 E
Černatica	15	Hh	41.53N	24.33 E
Černavčicy	10	Td	52.11N	23.47 E
Cernavoda	15	Le	44.22N	28.01 E
Cernay	11	Ng	47.49N	7.10 E
Cernay-en-Dormois	12	Ge	49.13N	4.46 E
Černevo	8	Mf	58.35N	28.23 E
Černigov	6	Je	51.30N	31.18 E
Černigovskaja Oblast	19	De	51.20N	32.00 E
Černi Lom	15	If	43.33N	25.57 E
Černi vrăh	15	Gg	42.35N	23.15 E
Černjahovsk	19	Ce	54.38N	21.48 E
Černjanka	16	Jd	50.55N	37.49 E
Černobyl	19	De	51.17N	30.13 E
Černogorsk	20	Ef	53.45N	91.18 E
Černoje More=Black Sea (EN)	5	Jg	43.00N	35.00 E
Černo More=Black Sea (EN)	5	Jg	43.00N	35.00 E
Černomorskoje	16	Hg	45.31N	32.42 E
Černovcy	6	If	48.18N	25.56 E
Černovickaja Oblast	19	Cf	48.20N	26.10 E
Černuška	19	Fd	56.31N	56.03 E
Černy Jar	16	Oe	48.03N	46.05 E
Černyje Zemli	16	Nf	45.55N	46.00 E
Černyševa, Grjada-	17	Ic	66.20N	59.45 E
Černyševa, Zaliv-	18	Bb	45.50N	59.10 E
Černyševsk	20	Gf	52.35N	117.02 E
Černyševskij	20	Gd	62.58N	112.15 E
Černyškovski	16	Me	48.27N	42.14 E
Cérou	11	Hj	44.08N	1.52 E
Cerralvo	48	Jd	26.06N	99.37W
Cerralvo, Isla-	47	Cd	24.15N	109.55W
Cerredo, Torre de-	13	Ha	43.13N	4.50W
Cerriku	15	Ch	41.02N	19.57 E
Cerrito [Col.]	54	Db	6.51N	72.42W
Cerrito [Par.]	55	Dh	27.19S	57.40W
Cerritos	47	Dd	22.26N	100.17W
Cerro Azul	48	Kg	21.12N	97.44W
Cêrro Azul	56	Kb	24.50S	49.15W
Cerro Chato	55	Ek	33.06S	55.08W
Cerro Colorado	55	Ek	33.52S	55.33W
Cerro de las Mesas	48	Kh	18.47N	96.05W
Cerro de Pasco	53	Ig	10.41S	76.16W
Cerro Grande	55	Gj	30.36S	51.45W
Cerro Largo	56	Jc	28.09S	54.45W
Cerro Largo	55	Ek	32.20S	54.20W
Cerron, Cerro-	49	Lh	10.19N	70.39W
Cerro San Valentín	52	Ij	46.36S	73.20W
Cerros Colorados, Embalse-	56	Ge	38.35S	68.40W
Cerro Vera	55	Dk	33.11S	57.28W
Cerrudo Cué	55	Dh	27.34S	57.57W
Čerski	22	Sc	68.45N	161.45 E
Čerskogo, Hrebet- [R.S.F.S.R.]	20	Gf	52.00N	114.00 E
Čerskogo, Hrebet- [R.S.F.S.R.]=Cherski Mountains (EN)	21	Qc	65.00N	145.00 E

Index Symbols

Independent Nation
State, Region
District, County
Municipality
Colony, Dependency
Continent
Physical Region

Historical or Cultural Region
Mount, Mountain
Volcano
Hill
Mountains, Mountain Range
Hills, Escarpment
Plateau, Upland

Pass, Gap
Plain, Lowland
Delta
Salt Flat
Valley, Canyon
Crater, Cave
Karst Features

Depression
Polder
Desert, Dunes
Forest, Woods
Heath, Steppe
Oasis
Cape, Point

Coast, Beach
Cliff
Peninsula
Isthmus
Sandbank
Island
Atoll

Rock, Reef
Islands, Archipelago
Rocks, Reefs
Coral Reef
Well, Spring
Geyser
River, Stream

Waterfall Rapids
River Mouth, Estuary
Lake
Salt Lake
Intermittent Lake
Reservoir
Swamp, Pond

Canal
Glacier
Ice Shelf, Pack Ice
Ocean
Sea
Gulf, Bay
Strait, Fjord

Lagoon
Bank
Seamount
Tablemount
Ridge
Shelf
Basin

Escarpment, Sea Scarp
Fracture
Trench, Abyss
National Park, Reserve
Point of Interest
Recreation Site
Cave, Cavern

Historic Site
Ruins
Wall, Walls
Church, Abbey
Temple
Scientific Station
Airport

Port
Lighthouse
Mine
Tunnel
Dam, Bridge

Certaldo 14 Fg 43.33N 11.02 E
Čertkovo 16 Le 49.20N 40.12 E
Cervaro 14 Ji 41.30N 15.52 E
Cervati 14 Jj 40.17N 15.29 E
Červeh 15 Jf 43.37N 26.02 E
Červen 16 Fc 53.43N 28.29 E
Červen brjag 15 Hf 43.16N 24.06 E
Cervera 13 Nc 41.40N 1.17 E
Cervera del Río Alhama 13 Kb 42.01N 1.57W
Cervera de Pisuerga 13 Hb 42.52N 4.30W
Cerveteri 14 Gh 42.00N 12.06 E
Cervia 14 Gf 44.15N 12.22 E
Cervin/Cervino 14 Be 45.58N 7.39 E
Cervino/Cervin 14 Be 45.58N 7.39 E
Cervione 11a Ba 42.20N 9.29 E
Červonoarmejsk 10 Vf 50.03N 25.18 E
Červonoarmejskoje 15 Ld 45.50N 28.38 E
Červonograd 19 Ce 50.24N 24.12 E
Cesano 14 Hg 43.45N 13.10 E
Cesar [2] 54 Db 9.50N 73.30W
César, Rio- 49 Ki 9.00N 73.58W
Cesena 14 Gf 44.08N 12.15 E
Cesenatico 14 Gf 44.12N 12.24 E
Cēsis/Cesis 19 Cd 57.18N 25.18 E
Cesis/Cēsis 19 Cd 57.18N 25.18 E
Česká Lípa 10 Kf 50.42N 14.32 E
Česká Třebová 10 Mg 49.54N 16.27 E
České Budějovice 10 Kh 48.58N 14.29 E
České středohoří 10 Jf 50.35N 14.00 E
České země [2] 10 Kg 49.45N 15.00 E
Českomoravská Vrchovina = Moravian Upland (EN) 5 Hf 49.20N 15.30 E
Československá Socialistická Republika (ČSSR) [1] 6 Hf 49.30N 17.00 E
Československo = Czechoslovakia (EN) [1] 6 Hf 49.30N 17.00 E
Český Krumlov 10 Kh 48.49N 14.19 E
Český Les = Bohemian Forest (EN) 10 Ig 49.50N 12.30 E
Cesma 14 Kf 45.35N 16.29 E
Česma 17 Jj 53.50N 60.40 E
Çeşme 24 Bc 38.18N 26.19 E
Çeşme Yarimadasi 15 Jk 38.30N 26.30 E
Češskaja Guba = Chesha Bay (EN) 5 Kb 67.20N 46.30 E
Cessnock 59 Kf 32.50S 151.21 E
Cestos 30 Gh 5.27N 9.35W
Cesvaine/Cesvajne 8 Lh 56.55N 26.20 E
Cesvajne/Cesvaine 8 Lh 56.55N 26.20 E
Cetate 15 Ge 44.06N 23.03 E
Cetina 14 Kg 43.27N 16.42 E
Cetinje 15 Bg 42.24N 18.55 E
Çetinkaya 24 Gc 39.15N 37.38 E
Cetraro 14 Jk 39.31N 15.56 E
Cetynia 10 Sd 52.33N 22.26 E
Ceuta [5] 31 Ge 35.53N 5.19W
Ceva-i-Ra (Conway Reef) 57 Ig 21.45S 174.35 E
Cevedale/Zufallspitze 14 Ed 46.27N 10.37 E
Cévennes 5 Gg 44.40N 4.00 E
Ceyhan 23 Eb 36.45N 35.42 E
Ceyhan 23 Eb 37.04N 35.47 E
Ceylanpınar 24 Id 36.51N 40.02 E
Ceylon 21 Ki 7.30N 80.30 E
Ceylon → Srī Lanka [1] 22 Ki 7.40N 80.50 E
Cézallier 11 Ii 45.20N 3.00 E
Cèze 11 Kj 44.06N 4.42 E
Chaalis, Abbaye de- 12 Ee 49.10N 2.40 E
Cha-am 25 Jf 12.48N 99.58 E
Chabanais 11 Gi 45.52N 0.43 E
Chabjuwardoo Bay 59 Cd 22.55S 113.50 E
Chablais 11 Mh 46.20N 6.30 E
Chāboksar 24 Nd 36.58N 50.34 E
Chabówka 10 Pg 49.34N 19.58 E
Chacabuco 56 Hd 34.38S 60.29W
Chachan, Nevado- 54 Dg 16.12S 71.33W
Chachapoyas 54 Ce 6.13S 77.51W
Chachoengsao 25 Kf 13.41N 101.03 E
Chaco [2] 56 Hc 26.00S 60.30W
Chaco [3] 55 Bd 20.00S 60.30W
Chaco, Gran- 52 Jh 23.00S 60.00W
Chaco Mesa 45 Ci 35.50N 107.35W
Chaco River 45 Bh 36.46N 108.39W
Chad (EN) = Tchad [1] 31 Ig 15.00N 19.00 E
Chad, Lake- (EN) = Tchad, Lac- 30 Ig 13.20N 14.00 E
Chādegān 24 Nf 32.46N 50.38 E
Chadileuvú, Río- 56 Ee 38.49S 64.57W
Chadiza 36 Fe 14.04S 32.26 E
Chadron 43 Gc 42.50N 103.02W
Chaeryŏng 28 He 38.24N 125.37 E
Chafarinas, Islas- 13 Ji 35.11N 2.26W
Chāgai Hills 21 Ig 29.30N 64.15 E
Chagang-Do [2] 28 Ie 40.50N 126.30 E
Chaghcharān 22 If 34.31N 65.15 E
Chagny 11 Kh 46.55N 4.45 E
Chagos Archipelago 21 Jj 6.00S 72.00 E
Chagos-Laccadive Plateau (EN) 3 Gi 3.00N 73.00 E
Chagu, Serra do- 55 Fg 25.10S 52.40W
Chaguaramas 50 Ch 9.20N 66.16W
Chahār Borjak 23 Jc 30.17N 62.03 E
Chāh Bahār 23 Jd 25.18N 60.37 E
Chahbounia 13 Oi 35.33N 2.36 E
Ch'aho 28 Jd 40.12N 128.38 E
Chai Badan 25 Ke 15.05N 101.04 E
Chaibāsa 25 Hd 22.34N 85.49 E
Chaigoubu → Huai'an 28 Cd 40.40N 114.25 E
Chai He 28 Gc 42.20N 123.51 E
Chaillu, Massif du- 30 Ii 2.32S 11.10 E
Chainat 25 Ke 15.10N 100.10 E
Chaitén 56 Ff 42.55S 72.43W
Chaiyaphum 25 Ke 16.09N 102.02 E
Chajul 49 Bf 15.30N 91.02W
Chakari 37 Dc 18.09S 29.52 E
Chak Chak 35 Dd 8.40N 26.54 E
Chake Chake 31 Ki 5.15S 39.46 E
Chakhānsūr 23 Jc 31.10N 62.04 E
Chala 54 Dg 15.52S 74.16W
Chalais 11 Gi 45.17N 0.02 E
Chalaltenango 49 Cf 14.03N 88.56W
Chalan Kanoa 64b Ba 15.08N 145.43 E
Chālās 22 Gf 37.16N 49.36 E
Chalbi Desert 30 Kh 3.00N 37.20 E
Chalchuapa 49 Cg 13.59N 89.41W
Chalcidice (EN) = Khalkidhikí 5 Ig 40.25N 23.25 E
Chālesbān 24 Ne 35.18N 50.03 E
Chaleur Bay 42 Kg 47.50N 65.30W
Chalhuanca 54 Df 14.17S 73.15W
Chaling 27 Jf 26.47N 113.32 E
Chalky Inlet 62 Bg 46.05S 166.30 E
Challans 11 Eh 46.51N 1.53W
Challapata 54 Eg 18.54S 66.47W
Challis 46 Hd 44.30N 114.14W
Chalmette 45 Ll 29.56N 89.58W
Châlons-sur-Marne 11 Kf 48.57N 4.22 E
Chalon-sur-Saône 11 Kh 46.47N 4.51 E
Chaltubo 16 Mh 42.19N 42.34 E
Chālūs 23 Hb 36.38N 51.26 E
Châlus 11 Gi 45.39N 0.59 E
Cham 10 Ig 49.13N 12.40 E
Chama 36 Fe 11.12S 33.10 E
Chama, Rio- 45 Ch 36.03N 106.05W
Chama, Rio- 49 Li 9.03N 71.37W
Chaman 25 Db 30.55N 66.27 E
Chaman Bid 24 Qd 37.25N 56.38 E
Chamba [India] 25 Fb 32.34N 76.08 E
Chamba [Tan.] 36 Ge 11.35S 36.58 E
Chambal 21 Jg 26.29N 79.15 E
Chambaran, Plateau de- 11 Li 45.10N 5.20 E
Chambas 49 Hb 22.12N 78.55W
Chamberlain 45 Ge 43.49N 99.20W
Chamberlain Lake 44 Mb 46.17N 69.20W
Chamberlain River 59 Fc 15.35S 127.51 E
Chambersburg 44 If 39.57N 77.40W
Chambéry 11 Li 45.34N 5.56 E
Chambeshi 30 Jj 11.53S 29.48 E
Chambley-Bussières 12 He 49.03N 5.54 E
Chambly 12 Ee 49.10N 2.15 E
Chambois 12 Cf 48.48N 0.07 E
Chambon, Lac de- 11 Ih 45.35N 2.55 E
Chambord 11 Hg 47.37N 1.31 E
Chamchamal 24 Ke 35.32N 44.50 E
Chame, Punta- 49 Hi 8.39N 79.42W
Chamela 48 Gh 19.32N 105.05W
Chamela, Bahía- 48 Gh 19.30N 105.10W
Chamelecón, Río- 49 Df 15.51N 87.49W
Chamical 56 Gd 30.21S 66.19W
Chamiss Bay 46 Ba 50.07N 127.22W
Chamoli 25 Fb 30.24N 79.21 E
Chamonix-Mont-Blanc 11 Mi 45.55N 6.52 E
Chamouchouane, Rivière- 44 Ka 48.40N 72.20W
Champagne 5 Gf 49.00N 4.30 E
Champagne 11 Kf 49.00N 4.30 E
Champagne Berrichonne 11 Hh 47.00N 2.00 E
Champagne Humide 11 Kf 48.20N 4.30 E
Champagne Pouilleuse 11 Kf 48.40N 4.20 E
Champagnole 11 Lh 46.45N 5.55 E
Champaign 43 Jc 40.07N 88.14W
Champaquí, Cerro- 52 Ji 31.59S 64.56W
Champasak 25 Lf 14.53N 105.52 E
Champaubert 12 Ff 48.53N 3.47 E
Champdoré, Lac- 42 Ke 55.55N 65.45W
Champeigne 11 Gg 47.15N 0.50 E
Champerico 49 Bf 14.18N 91.55W
Champlain, Lake- 43 Mc 44.45N 73.15W
Champlitte-et-le-Prélot 11 Lg 47.37N 5.31 E
Champotón 47 Fe 19.21N 90.43W
Champsaur 11 Mj 44.45N 6.10 E
Chāmrājnagar 25 Ff 11.55N 76.57 E
Chañaral 56 Fc 26.21S 70.37W
Chança 13 Eg 37.33N 7.31W
Chan Chan 54 Ce 8.07S 79.02W
Chanco 56 Fe 35.44S 72.32W
Chandalar 40 Jc 66.36N 145.48W
Chandalar 40 Jc 67.30N 148.30W
Chandausi 25 Fc 28.27N 78.46 E
Chandeleur Islands 43 Jf 29.48N 88.51W
Chandeleur Sound 45 Ll 29.55N 89.10W
Chandīgarh 22 Jf 30.44N 76.55 E
Chandler 42 Lg 48.21N 64.41W
Chandless, Rio 54 Ee 9.08S 69.51W
Chāndpur 25 Id 23.13N 90.39 E
Chandragupta 25 Fe 16.11N 78.52 E
Chandrapur 22 Jh 19.57N 79.18 E
Chang, Ko- 25 Kf 12.00N 102.23 E
Changajn Nuruu → Hangaj, Hrebet- = Khangai Mountains (EN) 21 Le 47.30N 100.00 E
Chang'an → Rong'an 27 If 25.16N 109.23 E
Changane 30 Kk 24.43S 33.32 E
Changbai 28 Jd 41.25N 128.11 E
Changbai Shan 21 Oe 42.00N 128.00 E
Changchun 22 Oe 43.51N 125.20 E
Changdao(Sihou) 28 Ff 37.56N 120.42 E
Changde 22 Ng 29.04N 111.42 E
Ch'angdo 28 Ie 38.30N 127.45 E
Changfeng (Shuijiahu) 28 Dh 32.29N 117.10 E
Changge 28 Bg 34.12N 113.45 E
Changhang 28 If 36.01N 126.42 E
Chang He 28 Ei 31.21N 118.21 E
Changhowŏn 28 If 37.07N 127.38 E
Changhua 27 Lg 24.05N 120.32 E
Changhŭng 28 Ig 34.40N 126.54 E
Changji 27 Ec 44.01N 87.16 E
Chang Jiang 28 Dj 28.59N 116.42 E
Changjiang (Shiliu) 27 Ih 19.20N 109.03 E
Chang Jiang (Yangtze Kiang) 21 Of 31.48N 121.10 E
Changjiang Kou 27 Le 31.24N 121.59 E
Changjin-gang 28 Id 40.30N 127.12 E
Changjin-ho 28 Id 40.30N 127.12 E
Changjin-ŭp 27 Mc 40.23N 127.15 E
Changli 28 Ee 39.43N 119.10 E
Changling 27 Lc 44.15N 123.58 E
Changlung 25 Fb 34.56N 77.29 E
Changping 28 Dd 40.14N 116.13 E
Changsha 22 Ng 28.12N 113.02 E
Changshan 28 Ej 28.55N 118.31 E
Changshan Qundao 28 Ge 39.10N 122.34 E
Changshu 28 Fi 31.38N 120.44 E
Changsŏng 28 Ig 35.19N 126.48 E
Changting 28 Jb 44.27N 128.50 E
Changtu 28 Hc 42.47N 124.08 E
Changuillo 54 Cf 14.40S 75.12W
Changuinola 49 Fi 9.26N 82.31W
Changwu 27 Id 35.17N 107.52 E
Changxing 28 Ei 31.01N 119.55 E
Changxing Dao 28 Fe 39.35N 121.42 E
Changyi 28 Ef 36.52N 119.25 E
Changyŏn 27 Md 38.15N 125.05 E
Changyuan 28 Cg 35.12N 114.40 E
Changzhi 27 Jd 36.07N 113.10 E
Changzhou 28 Ei 31.46N 119.56 E
Channel Islands [5] 9 Kl 49.20N 2.20W
Channel Islands [Chan.Is.] 5 Ff 49.20N 2.20W
Channel Islands [U.S.] 38 Hf 34.00N 120.00W
Channel Port-aux-Basques 39 Ne 47.35N 59.11W
Channel Rock 49 Ib 23.00N 77.55W
Channing 45 Ei 35.41N 102.20W
Chantada 13 Eb 42.37N 7.46W
Chantengo, Laguna- 48 Ji 16.35N 99.10W
Chanthaburi 25 Kf 12.35N 102.06 E
Chantilly 11 Ie 49.12N 2.28 E
Chantonnay 11 Eh 46.41N 1.03W
Chantrey Inlet 38 Jc 67.48N 96.20W
Chanute 45 Ih 37.41N 95.27W
Chanza 13 Eg 37.33N 7.31W
Chao'an (Chaozhou) 27 Kg 23.41N 116.37 E
Chaobai Xinhe 28 De 39.07N 117.41 E
Chao He 28 Dd 40.36N 117.08 E
Chao Hu 28 Di 31.31N 117.33 E
Chao Phraya 21 Mh 13.32N 100.36 E
Chaor He 27 Lb 46.49N 123.45 E
Chaoxian 27 Ke 31.37N 117.49 E
Chaoyang [China] 22 Oe 41.35N 120.26 E
Chaoyang [China] 27 Kg 23.17N 116.37 E
Chaoyang → Huinan 28 Ic 42.41N 126.03 E
Chaoyang → Jiayin 27 Nb 48.52N 130.21 E
Chaoyangchuan 28 Jc 42.53N 129.23 E
Chaoyangcun 27 La 50.01N 124.22 E
Chaozhong 27 La 50.53N 121.23 E
Chaozhou → Chao'an 27 Kg 23.41N 116.37 E
Chapada dos Guimarães 54 Gg 15.26S 55.45W
Chapadinha 54 Jd 3.44S 43.21W
Chapais 44 Ja 49.47N 74.56W
Chapala 48 Hg 20.18N 103.12W
Chapala, Lago de- 38 Ig 20.15N 103.00W
Chaparral 54 Cc 3.43N 75.28W
Chapecó 56 Jc 27.06S 52.36W
Chapecó, Rio- 55 Fh 27.06S 53.01W
Chapecó, Serra do- 55 Gh 26.44S 51.54W
Chapel Hill 44 Hh 35.55N 79.04W
Chapicuy 55 Dj 31.40S 57.55W
Chapleau 42 Jg 47.50N 83.24W
Chaplin 46 La 50.28N 106.40W
Chaplin Lake 46 La 50.18N 106.35W
Chapman, Cape - 42 Ic 69.15N 89.27W
Chappell 45 Ef 41.06N 102.28W
Chāpra 25 Gc 25.46N 84.45 E
Chapultepec 48 Hf 23.27N 103.04W
Chaqui 54 Eg 19.36S 65.32W
Char 32 Ee 21.31N 12.51W
Charadai 55 Ch 27.38S 59.54W
Charagua 54 Fg 19.48S 63.13W
Charām 24 Ng 30.45N 50.44 E
Charaña 54 Eg 17.36S 69.28W
Charcas 48 If 23.08N 101.07W
Charco de la Aguja 48 Gc 28.25N 104.01W
Charcot Island 66 Qe 69.45S 75.15W
Chard [Alta.-Can.] 42 Ge 55.48N 111.10W
Chard [Eng.-U.K.] 9 Kk 50.53N 2.58W
Chardāvol 24 Lf 33.45N 46.38 E
Chardonnières 49 Jd 18.16N 74.10W
Charente [3] 11 Gi 45.40N 0.05 E
Charente 11 Ei 45.57N 1.05W
Charente-Maritime [3] 11 Fi 45.30N 0.45W
Charentonne 12 Ce 49.07N 0.44 E
Chari 30 Ig 12.58N 14.31 E
Chari-Baguirmi [3] 35 Bc 12.00N 17.00 E
Chārīkār 23 Kb 35.01N 69.11 E
Charing 12 Cc 51.12N 0.48 E
Chariton 45 Jf 41.00N 93.19W
Chariton River 45 Jg 39.19N 92.57W
Charity 54 Gb 7.24N 58.36W
Charleroi 11 Kd 50.25N 4.26 E
Charleroi-Jumet 11 Kd 50.27N 4.26 E
Charleroi-Marcinelle 12 Gd 50.25N 4.28 E
Charles 42 Kd 62.38N 74.15W
Charles, Cape- [Can.] 38 Nd 52.13N 55.40W
Charles, Cape- [Va.-U.S.] 43 Ld 37.08N 75.58W
Charles, Peak- 59 Ef 32.52S 121.11 E
Charlesbourg 44 Lb 46.52N 71.16W
Charles City 43 Ic 43.04N 92.40W
Charles de Gaulle, Aéroport- = Charles de Gaulle Airport (EN) 12 Ee 49.02N 2.35 E
Charles de Gaulle Airport (EN) = Charles de Gaulle, Aéroport- 12 Ee 49.02N 2.35 E
Charleston [Il.-U.S.] 45 Lg 39.30N 88.10W
Charleston [Mo.-U.S.] 45 Lh 36.55N 89.21W
Charleston [Ms.-U.S.] 45 Ki 34.01N 90.04W
Charleston [N.Z.] 62 Dd 41.54S 171.27 E
Charleston [S.C.-U.S.] 39 Lf 32.48N 79.57W
Charleston [W.V.-U.S.] 39 Kf 38.21N 81.38W
Charleston Peak 43 Dd 36.16N 115.42W
Charles Town 44 If 39.18N 77.52W
Charlestown 50 Ed 17.08N 62.35W
Charleval 12 De 49.22N 1.23 E
Charleville 58 Fg 26.24S 146.15 E
Charleville-Mézières 11 Ke 49.46N 4.43 E
Charleville Mézières-Mohon 12 Ge 49.46N 4.43 E
Charlevoix 44 Ec 45.19N 85.16W
Charlieu 11 Kh 46.09N 4.11 E
Charlotte [Mi.-U.S.] 44 Ed 42.36N 84.50W
Charlotte [N.C.-U.S.] 39 Kf 35.14N 80.50W
Charlotte Amalie 47 Le 18.21N 64.56W
Charlotte Bank (EN) 57 If 11.47S 173.13 E
Charlotte Harbor 44 Fl 26.45N 82.12W
Charlottenberg 8 Ee 59.53N 12.17 E
Charlottesville 43 Ld 38.02N 78.29W
Charlottetown 39 Me 46.14N 63.08W
Charlton 59 Ig 36.16S 143.21 E
Charlton 42 Jf 52.00N 79.26W
Charly 12 Ff 48.58N 3.17 E
Charmes 11 Mf 48.22N 6.17 E
Charnley River 59 Ec 16.20S 124.53 E
Charny-sur-Meuse 12 He 49.12N 5.22 E
Charollais 11 Kh 46.26N 4.16 E
Charouine 32 Gd 29.01N 0.16W
Charroux 11 Gh 46.09N 0.24 E
Chārsadda 25 Eb 34.09N 71.44 E
Charters Towers 58 Fg 20.05S 146.16 E
Chartres 11 Hf 48.27N 1.30 E
Charzykowskie, Jezioro- 10 Nc 53.47N 17.30 E
Chascomus 56 Ie 35.34S 58.01W
Chase 46 Fa 50.49N 119.41W
Chasŏng 28 Id 41.25N 126.35 E
Chassengue 36 Ce 10.26S 18.32 E
Chassezac 11 Kj 44.26N 4.19 E
Chassiron, Pointe de- 11 Eh 46.03N 1.24W
Chat 24 Pd 37.59N 55.16 E
Châtaigneraie 11 Ij 44.45N 2.20 E
Chātāl 24 Pd 37.40N 55.45 E
Château-Arnoux 11 Lj 44.06N 6.00 E
Chateaubelair 51n Ba 13.17N 61.15W
Châteaubriant 11 Eg 47.43N 1.23W
Château-Chinon 11 Jg 47.04N 3.56 E
Château-du-Loir 11 Gg 47.42N 0.25 E
Châteaudun 11 Hf 48.05N 1.20 E
Château-Gontier 11 Fg 47.50N 0.42W
Châteaulin 11 Bf 48.12N 4.05W
Châteaulin, Bassin de- 11 Cf 48.18N 3.50W
Châteaumeillant 11 Ih 46.34N 2.12 E
Châteauneuf-de-Randon 11 Jj 44.39N 3.04 E
Châteauneuf-sur-Cher 11 Ih 46.51N 2.19 E
Châteauneuf-sur-Loire 11 Ig 47.52N 2.14 E
Château-Porcien 12 Ge 49.32N 4.15 E
Châteaurenard 11 Kk 43.53N 4.51 E
Château-Renault 11 Gg 47.35N 0.54 E
Châteauroux 11 Hh 46.49N 1.42 E
Château-Salins 11 Mf 48.49N 6.30 E
Château-Thierry 11 Je 49.03N 3.24 E
Châteaux, Pointe des- 51e Bb 16.15N 61.11W
Châtelaillon-Plage 11 Eh 46.04N 1.05W
Châtelet 12 Gd 50.24N 4.31 E
Châtelguyon 11 Ji 45.55N 3.04 E
Châtellerault 11 Gh 46.48N 0.32 E
Chatelodo 55 De 21.19S 57.28W
Chatham [Eng.-U.K.] 9 Nj 51.23N 0.32 E
Chatham [N.B.-Can.] 42 Kg 47.02N 65.26W
Chatham [Ont.-Can.] 42 Jh 42.24N 82.11W
Chatham [Va.-U.S.] 44 Hg 36.49N 79.26W
Chatham Island 57 Ji 44.00S 176.30W
Chatham Islands 57 Ji 44.00S 176.30W
Chatham Rise (EN) 57 Ii 43.30S 180.00
Chatham Strait 40 Me 57.30N 134.45W
Châtillon-en-Bazois 11 Jg 47.03N 3.40 E
Châtillon-sur-Indre 11 Hh 46.59N 1.10 E
Châtillon-sur-Marne 12 Fe 49.06N 3.45 E
Châtillon-sur-Seine 11 Kg 47.51N 4.33 E
Chatom 44 Cj 31.28N 88.16W
Chatsworth 37 Ec 19.38S 30.50 E
Chattahoochee 44 Ej 30.42N 84.51W
Chattahoochee 38 Kf 30.52N 84.57W
Chattanooga 39 Kf 35.03N 85.19W
Chatteris 12 Cb 52.27N 0.03 E
Chaucas 55 Cc 16.46S 58.44W
Chaudfontaine 12 Hd 50.35N 5.38 E
Chaudière, Rivière- 44 Lb 46.43N 71.17W
Chauk 25 Id 20.53N 94.49 E
Chaulnes 12 Ee 49.49N 2.48 E
Chaumont 11 Lf 48.07N 5.08 E
Chaumont-en-Vexin 12 De 49.16N 1.53 E
Chaumont-Gistoux 12 Gd 50.41N 4.44 E
Chaumont-Porcien 12 Ge 49.39N 4.15 E
Chaumont-sur-Aire 12 Hf 48.56N 5.15 E
Chaumont-sur-Loire 12 Hg 47.29N 1.11 E
Chauny 11 Je 49.37N 3.13 E
Chau Phu 25 Lf 10.42N 105.07 E
Chausey, Iles- 11 Ef 48.53N 1.50W
Chauvigny 11 Gh 46.34N 0.39 E
Chavantina 54 Hf 14.40S 52.21W
Chavarría 55 Ci 28.57S 58.35W
Chaves [Braz.] 54 Id 0.10S 49.55W
Chaves [Port.] 13 Ec 41.44N 7.28W
Chavigny, Lac - 42 Je 58.00N 75.05W
Chavuma 36 De 13.05S 22.42 E
Chazelles-sur-Lyon 11 Ki 45.38N 4.23 E
Chbar 25 Lf 12.46N 107.10 E
Cheaha Mountain 44 Ei 33.30N 85.47W
Cheat River 44 Hf 39.45N 79.55W
Cheb 10 If 50.04N 12.23 E
Cheboygan 43 Kb 45.39N 84.29W
Chech, 'Erg- 30 Gf 25.00N 3.00W
Chechaouene [3] 32 Fb 35.00N 5.00W
Chechaouene 32 Fb 35.10N 5.16W
Checheng 27 Lg 22.05N 120.42 E
Che-Chiang Sheng → Zhejiang Sheng [2] 27 Kf 29.00N 120.00 E
Chech'ŏn 28 Jf 37.08N 128.12 E
Chęciny 10 Qf 50.48N 20.28 E
Cheddar Gorge 9 Kj 51.13N 2.47W
Cheduba 25 Ie 18.48N 93.38 E
Chée 12 Gf 48.45N 4.39 E
Cheektowaga 44 Hd 42.57N 78.38W
Chefu 37 Ed 22.27S 32.45 E
Chegga 31 Gf 25.22N 5.49W
Cheghelvandī 24 Mf 33.42N 48.25 E
Chehel Pāyeh 24 Qg 31.54N 57.14 E
Cheju 27 Me 33.31N 126.32 E
Cheju-Do 21 Of 33.25N 126.30 E
Cheju-Do [2] 28 Ih 33.25N 126.30 E
Cheju-Haehyŏp 28 Ih 33.40N 126.28 E
Chela, Serra da- 30 Ij 16.00S 13.10 E
Chelan 46 Ec 47.51N 120.01W
Chelan, Lake- 46 Eb 48.05N 120.30W
Chelforó, Arroyo- 55 Cm 36.55S 58.12W
Cheliff [3] 32 Hb 36.10N 1.45 E
Cheliff 30 He 36.02N 0.08 E
Cheliff 32 Hb 36.10N 1.20 E
Cheliff, Plaine du- 13 Mi 35.57N 0.45 E
Chellalat el Adhaouara 13 Pi 35.56N 3.25 E
Chelleh Khāneh, Kūh-e- 24 Md 36.52N 48.36 E
Chełm [2] 10 Te 51.10N 23.30 E
Chełm 10 Te 51.10N 23.28 E
Chelmer 12 Cc 51.44N 0.42 E
Chełmińskie, Pojezierze- 10 Oc 53.20N 19.00 E
Chełmno 10 Oc 53.22N 18.26 E
Chelmsford 9 Nj 51.44N 0.28 E
Chełmża 10 Oc 53.12N 18.37 E
Cheltenham 9 Kj 51.54N 2.04W
Chelva 13 Le 39.45N 0.59W
Chemainus 46 Db 48.55N 123.43W
Chemāma 32 Ef 16.50N 14.00 E
Chemba 37 Ec 17.09S 34.53 E
Chembe 36 Ee 11.58S 28.45 E
Chemillé 11 Fg 47.13N 0.43W
Chemult 46 Ee 43.13N 121.47W
Chenāb 21 Jg 29.13N 70.49 E
Chenachane 32 Gd 26.00N 4.15W
Chenachane 32 Gd 25.17N 3.10W
Chenārbāshi 24 Lf 33.20N 46.20 E
Chen Barag Qi (Bayan Hure) 27 Kb 49.21N 119.25 E
Chencha 35 Fd 6.17N 37.40 E
Chencoyi 48 Nh 19.48N 90.14W
Cheney 46 Gc 47.29N 117.34W
Cheney Reservoir 45 Hh 37.45N 97.50W
Cheng'an 28 Cf 36.27N 114.41 E
Chengde 27 Kc 41.00N 117.57 E
Chengdu 22 Mf 30.45N 104.04 E
Chengkou 27 Ie 31.54N 108.37 E
Chengmai 27 Ih 19.50N 109.59 E
Chengshan Jiao 27 Ld 37.24N 122.42 E
Chengxi Hu 28 Dh 32.22N 116.12 E
Chengzitan 27 Ld 39.31N 122.28 E
Cheniskcali 16 Mh 42.06N 42.16 E
Chenjiagang 28 Eg 34.22N 119.48 E
Chenonceaux 11 Hg 47.20N 1.04 E
Chenxi 27 Jf 28.02N 110.15 E
Chenxian 27 Jf 25.49N 113.05 E
Chenying → Wannian 28 Dj 28.42N 117.04 E
Chépénéhé 63b Ce 20.47S 167.09 E
Chepes 56 Gd 31.21S 66.36W
Chepo 49 Hi 9.10N 79.06W
Cher [3] 11 Ig 47.00N 2.30 E
Cher 5 Gf 47.21N 0.29 E
Cheradi, Isole- 14 Lj 40.25N 17.10 E
Cherangany Hills 36 Gb 1.15N 35.27 E
Cheraw 44 Hh 34.42N 79.53W
Cherbaniani Reef 25 Ef 12.18N 71.53 E
Cherbourg 6 Ff 49.39N 1.39W
Cherchell 32 Hb 36.36N 2.12 E
Chère 11 Eg 47.42N 1.50W
Chergui, Chott Ech- 30 He 34.21N 0.30 E
Chéri 34 Hc 13.26N 11.21 E
Cherlen → Kerulen 21 Ne 48.48N 117.00 E
Cherokee 45 Ie 42.45N 95.33W
Cherokees, Lake O' the- 45 Ih 36.39N 94.49W
Cherski Mountains (EN) = Čerskogo, Hrebet- [R.S.F.S.R.] 21 Qc 65.00N 145.00 E
Chersterfield Inlet 39 Jc 63.21N 90.42W
Chertsey 12 Bc 51.23N 0.30W
Cherwell 9 Lj 51.44N 1.15W
Chesapeake 44 Ig 36.45N 76.15W
Chesapeake Bay 38 Lf 38.40N 76.25W
Chesapeake Bay Bridge-Tunnel 44 Ig 37.00N 76.02W
Chesha Bay (EN) = Češskaja Guba 5 Kb 67.20N 46.30 E
Chesham 12 Bc 51.42N 0.36W
Cheshire [3] 9 Kh 53.15N 2.30W
Cheshire Plain 9 Kh 53.20N 2.40W
Cheshunt 12 Bc 51.42N 0.02W
Chester 9 Kh 53.10N 2.55W
Chester [Eng.-U.K.] 9 Kh 53.12N 2.54W
Chester [Il.-U.S.] 45 Lh 37.55N 89.49W
Chester [Mt.-U.S.] 46 Jb 48.31N 110.58W
Chester [Pa.-U.S.] 44 Jf 39.50N 75.23W
Chester [S.C.-U.S.] 44 Gh 34.40N 81.12W
Chesterfield 9 Lh 53.15N 1.25W
Chesterfield, Ile- 37 Gc 16.20S 43.58 E
Chesterfield, Récifs et Iles- = Chesterfield Reefs and Islands (EN) 57 Gf 20.00S 159.00 E
Chesterfield Inlet 38 Jc 63.25N 90.45W
Chesterfield Reefs and Islands (EN) = Chesterfield, Récifs et Iles- 57 Gf 20.00S 159.00 E
Chesterton Range 59 Je 25.30S 147.30 E
Chestnut Ridge 44 He 40.10N 79.25W
Chesuncook Lake 44 Mb 46.00N 69.20W
Chetaibi 32 Ib 37.04N 7.23 E
Chetumal 39 Kh 18.35N 88.07W
Chetumal, Bahía de 47 Ge 18.20N 88.05W
Cheviot 62 Ee 42.49S 173.16 E
Chew Bahir = Stefanie, Lake- (EN) 30 Kh 4.38N 36.50 E
Chewelah 46 Gb 48.17N 117.43W
Cheyenne [Ok.-U.S.] 45 Gi 35.37N 99.40W

Index Symbols

[1] Independent Nation
[2] State, Region
[3] District, County
[4] Municipality
[5] Colony, Dependency
Continent
Physical Region
Historical or Cultural Region
Mount, Mountain
Volcano
Hill
Mountains, Mountain Range
Hills, Escarpment
Plateau, Upland
Pass, Gap
Plain, Lowland
Delta
Salt Flat
Valley, Canyon
Crater, Cave
Karst Features
Depression
Polder
Desert, Dunes
Forest, Woods
Heath, Steppe
Oasis
Cape, Point
Coast, Beach
Cliff
Peninsula
Isthmus
Sandbank
Island
Atoll
Rock, Reef
Islands, Archipelago
Rocks, Reefs
Coral Reef
Well, Spring
Geyser
River, Stream
Waterfall Rapids
River Mouth, Estuary
Lake
Salt Lake
Intermittent Lake
Reservoir
Swamp, Pond
Canal
Glacier
Ice Shelf, Pack Ice
Ocean
Sea
Gulf, Bay
Strait, Fjord
Lagoon
Bank
Seamount
Tablemount
Ridge
Shelf
Basin
Escarpment, Sea Scarp
Fracture
Trench, Abyss
National Park, Reserve
Point of Interest
Recreation Site
Cave, Cavern
Historic Site
Ruins
Wall, Walls
Church, Abbey
Temple
Scientific Station
Airport
Port
Lighthouse
Mine
Tunnel
Dam, Bridge

Cheyenne [Wy.-U.S.] 39 Ie 41.08N 104.49W
Cheyenne River 43 Gc 44.40N 101.15W
Cheyenne Wells 45 Eg 38.51N 102.11W
Cheyne Bay 59 Df 34.35S 118.50 E
Chhatarpur 25 Fd 24.54N 79.36 E
Chhindwāra 25 Fd 22.04N 78.56 E
Chi 25 Ke 15.11N 104.43 E
Chiamboni, Rās- 35 Gf 1.38S 41.36 E
Chiana, Val di- 14 Fg 43.15N 11.50 E
Chianciano Terme 14 Fg 43.02N 11.49 E
Chiang-hsi Sheng → Jangxi Sheng = Kiangsi (EN) [2] 27 Kf 28.00N 116.00 E
Chiang Mai 22 Lh 18.46N 98.58 E
Chiang Rai 22 Lh 19.54N 99.50 E
Chiang-su Sheng → Jiangsu Sheng = Kiangsu (EN) [2] 27 Ke 33.00N 120.00 E
Chiani 14 Gh 42.44N 12.07 E
Chianje 31 Ij 15.45S 13.54 E
Chianti 14 Fg 43.30N 11.25 E
Chiapa, Rio- 48 Mj 16.30N 93.10W
Chiapas [2] 47 Fe 16.30N 92.30W
Chiapas, Meseta de- 47 Fe 16.30N 92.00W
Chiaramonte Gulfi 14 Im 37.02N 14.42 E
Chiaravalle 14 Hg 43.36N 13.19 E
Chiaromonte 14 Kj 40.07N 16.13 E
Chiautla de Tapia 48 Jh 18.17N 98.36W
Chiavari 14 Df 44.19N 9.19 E
Chiavenna 14 Dd 46.19N 9.24 E
Chiayi 27 Lg 23.29N 120.27 E
Chiba 27 Pd 35.36N 140.07 E
Chiba Ken [2] 28 Pg 35.40N 140.20 E
Chibemba 36 Bf 15.45S 14.06 E
Chibia 36 Bf 15.11S 13.41 E
Chibougamau 39 Le 49.53N 74.21W
Chibougamau, Lac- 44 Ja 49.50N 74.15W
Chibougamau, Rivière- 44 Ja 49.50N 74.25W
Chiburi-Jima 28 Lf 36.00N 133.02 E
Chibuto 37 Ed 24.42S 33.33 E
Chicago 39 Ke 41.53N 87.38W
Chicago Heights 45 Mf 41.30N 87.38W
Chicala 36 Ce 11.59S 19.30 E
Chicapa 30 Ji 6.25S 20.48 E
Chic-Chocs, Monts- 44 Na 48.55N 66.45W
Chicha 35 Bb 16.52N 18.33 E
Chichagof 40 Le 57.30N 135.30W
Chichancanab, Laguna de- 48 Oh 19.54N 88.46W
Chichaoua 32 Fc 31.32N 8.46W
Chichas, Cordillera de- 54 Eh 20.30S 66.30W
Chicheng 27 Kc 40.55N 115.47 E
Chichén Itzá 39 Kg 20.40N 88.35W
Chichester 9 Mk 50.50N 0.48W
Chichester Range 59 Dd 22.20S 119.20 E
Chichibu 28 Og 35.59N 139.05 E
Chichigalpa 49 Dg 12.34N 87.02W
Chichijma-Rettō 60 Cb 27.06N 142.12 E
Chichilla de Monte-Aragón 13 Kf 38.55N 1.43W
Chichiriviche 49 Mh 10.56N 68.16W
Chickasawhay River 45 Lk 31.00N 88.45W
Chickasha 43 Hd 35.02N 97.58W
Chicken 40 Kd 64.04N 141.56W
Chiclana de la Frontera 13 Fh 36.25N 6.08W
Chiclayo 53 If 6.46S 79.50W
Chico 43 Cd 39.44N 121.50W
Chico, Rio- [Arg.] 52 Jj 43.48S 66.25W
Chico, Rio- [Arg.] 52 Jj 49.56S 68.32W
Chicoana 56 Gc 25.06S 65.33W
Chicomo 37 Ed 24.31S 34.17 E
Chicoñono 37 Fb 12.57S 35.45 E
Chicopee 44 Kd 42.10N 72.36W
Chicote 36 Df 16.01S 21.48 E
Chicoutimi 39 Le 48.26N 71.04W
Chicoutimi Nord 44 La 48.29N 71.02W
Chicualacuala 37 Ed 22.05S 31.42 E
Chidenguele 37 Ed 24.55S 34.10 E
Chidley, Cape- 38 Mc 60.25N 64.30W
Chiemsee 10 Ii 47.54N 12.29 E
Chiengi 36 Ed 8.39S 29.10 E
Chienti 14 Hg 43.18N 13.45 E
Chieri 14 Be 45.01N 7.49 E
Chiers 12 He 49.39N 5.00 E
Chiese 14 Ee 45.08N 10.25 E
Chieti 14 Ih 42.21N 14.10 E
Chièvres 12 Fd 50.35N 3.48 E
Chifeng/Ulanhad 27 Kc 42.16N 118.57 E
Chifumage 36 De 12.10S 22.30 E
Chifwefwe 36 Fe 13.35S 29.35 E
Chigasaki 29 Fd 35.19N 139.24 E
Chignik 40 He 56.18N 158.23W
Chigombe 37 Ed 23.26S 33.19 E
Chigorodó 49 Ij 7.41N 76.41W
Chigubo 37 Ed 22.50S 33.31 E
Chigu Co 27 Ff 28.40N 91.50 E
Chi He 28 Dh 32.51N 117.59 E
Chihli, Gulf of- (EN) = Bo Hai 21 Nf 38.30N 120.00 E
Chihuahua [2] 47 Cc 28.30N 106.00W
Chihuahua 39 Ig 28.38N 106.05W
Chii-san 28 Ig 35.20N 127.44 E
Chikaskia River 45 Hh 36.37N 97.15W
Chikugo 29 Be 33.13N 130.30 E
Chikugo-Gawa 29 Be 33.10N 130.21 E
Chikuma-Gawa 29 Fc 37.00N 138.35 E
Chikwana 36 Ff 16.03S 34.48 E
Chilapa de Alvarez 48 Ji 17.36N 99.10W
Chilās 25 Ea 35.26N 74.05 E
Chilaw 25 Fg 7.34N 79.47 E
Chilcotin 42 Ff 51.46N 122.22W
Childers 59 Ke 25.14S 152.17 E
Childress 43 Ge 34.25N 100.13W
Chile [1] 53 Ii 30.00S 71.00W
Chile Basin (EN) 3 Mm 33.00S 90.00W
Chile Chico 56 Fg 46.33S 71.44W
Chilecito [Arg.] 56 Gd 33.53S 69.03W
Chilecito [Arg.] 56 Gc 29.10S 67.30W
Chile Rise (EN) 3 Mm 40.00S 90.00W
Chili 35 Cb 16.44N 20.53 E
Chilia, Braţul- 15 Md 45.13N 29.43 E
Chililabombwe 36 Ee 12.22S 27.50 E
Chi-lin Sheng → Jilin Sheng = Kirin (EN) [2] 27 Mc 43.00N 126.00 E
Chilko Lake 46 Ca 51.20N 124.05W
Chilko River 46 Da 52.00N 123.40W
Chillán 53 Ii 36.36S 72.07W
Chillar 56 Ie 37.18S 59.59W
Chillicothe [Il.-U.S.] 45 Lf 40.55N 89.29W
Chillicothe [Mo.-U.S.] 45 Jg 39.48N 93.33W
Chillicothe [Oh.-U.S.] 43 Kd 38.20N 82.59W
Chilliwack 46 Eb 49.10N 121.57W
Chiloé, Isla de- 52 Ij 42.30S 73.55W
Chilón 48 Mi 17.14N 92.25W
Chiloquin 46 Ee 42.35N 121.52W
Chilpancingo de los Bravos 47 Ee 17.33N 99.30W
Chiltern Hills 9 Mj 51.42N 0.48W
Chilton 45 Ld 44.02N 88.10W
Chiluage 36 Dd 9.31S 21.46 E
Chilumba 36 Fe 10.27S 34.16 E
Chilwa, Lake- 36 Fc 15.12S 35.50 E
Chimala 36 Fd 8.51S 34.01 E
Chimaltenango 49 Bf 14.39N 90.49W
Chimaltenango [3] 49 Bf 14.40N 90.55W
Chimán 49 Hi 8.42N 78.37W
Chimanas, Islas- 50 Dg 10.17N 64.38W
Chimay 12 Gd 50.03N 4.19 E
Chimborazo, Volcán- 52 If 1.28S 78.48W
Chimbote 53 If 9.05S 78.36W
Chimichagua 49 Ki 9.16N 73.49W
Chimoio 37 Ec 19.00S 33.23 E
Chimorra 13 Hf 38.18N 4.53W
Chin [2] 25 Id 22.00N 93.30 E
China [Jap.] 29b Bb 27.20N 128.36 E
China [Mex.] 48 Je 25.42N 99.14W
China (EN) = Zhonghua Renmin Gongheguo [1] 22 Mf 35.00N 105.00 E
Chinacates 48 Ge 25.00N 105.13W
China Lake 46 Gi 35.46N 117.39W
Chinandega 47 Gf 12.37N 87.09W
Chinandega [3] 49 Dg 12.45N 87.05W
Chinati Peak 45 Dl 29.57N 104.29W
Chincha Alta 54 Cf 13.27S 76.08W
Chinchaga 42 Fe 58.52N 118.19W
Chinchilla 59 Ke 26.45S 150.38 E
Chinchón 13 Id 40.08N 3.25W
Chinchorro, Banco- 47 Ge 18.35N 87.20W
Chincoteague 44 Jg 37.55N 75.23W
Chinde 31 Kj 18.34S 36.27 E
Chin-Do 28 Ig 34.25N 126.15 E
Chindu 27 Ge 33.30N 96.31 E
Chindwin 21 Lg 21.26N 95.15 E
Ch'ing-hai Sheng → Qinghai Sheng = Tsinghai (EN) [2] 27 Gd 36.00N 96.00 E
Chingil 35 Bc 10.33N 18.57 E
Chingola 31 Jj 12.32S 27.52 E
Chinguar 36 Ce 12.33S 16.22 E
Chinguetti 32 Ee 20.27N 12.21W
Chinguetti, Dahr de- 32 Ee 20.43N 12.20W
Chinhae 28 Jg 35.08N 128.40 E
Chiniot 25 Eb 31.43N 72.59 E
Chinipas 48 Ed 27.23N 108.32W
Chinju 27 Md 35.11N 128.05 E
Chinko 30 Jh 4.50N 23.53 E
Chinle 46 Kh 36.09N 109.33W
Chinle Creek 46 Kh 37.12N 109.43W
Chinmen 27 Kg 24.25N 118.25 E
Chino 29 Fd 36.00N 138.09 E
Chinon 11 Gg 47.10N 0.15 E
Chinook 46 Kb 48.35N 109.14W
Chinquila 48 Pg 21.30N 87.25W
Chinsali 36 Fe 10.33S 32.04 E
Chinteche 36 Fe 11.50S 34.10 E
Chinú 54 Cb 9.06N 75.24W
Chinvali 19 Eg 42.13N 43.57 E
Chiny 12 He 49.44N 5.20 E
Chinyŏng 28 Jg 35.18N 128.44 E
Chioco 37 Ec 16.25S 32.50 E
Chioggia 14 Ge 45.13N 12.17 E
Chios (EN) = Khios 5 Ih 38.22N 26.00 E
Chipata 31 Kj 13.39S 32.40 E
Chipepo 36 Ef 16.49S 27.50 E
Chipindo 36 Ce 13.48S 15.48 E
Chiping 28 Df 36.35N 116.16 E
Chipinga 37 Ed 20.12S 32.38 E
Chipman 44 Ob 46.11N 65.53W
Chippenham 9 Kj 51.28N 2.07W
Chippewa, Lake- 45 Kd 45.56N 91.13W
Chippewa Falls 43 Ic 44.56N 91.24W
Chippewa River [Wi.-U.S.] 45 Id 44.56N 95.44W
Chippewa River [U.S.] 45 Jd 44.25N 92.10W
Chipping Ongar 12 Cc 51.42N 0.15 E
Chiputneticook Lakes 44 Mc 45.45N 68.45W
Chiquián 54 Cf 10.09S 77.11W
Chiquimula [3] 49 Cf 14.40N 89.25W
Chiquimula 49 Cf 14.48N 89.33W
Chiquimulilla 49 Bf 14.05N 90.23W
Chiquinquirá 54 Db 5.37N 73.50W
Chiquitos, Llanos de- 54 Fg 18.00S 61.30W
Chirāla 25 Ge 15.49N 80.21 E
Chiran 29 Bf 31.22N 130.27 E
Chiredzi 31 Kk 21.03S 31.45 E
Chirfa 34 Ha 20.57N 12.21 E
Chirgua, Rio- 50 Bh 8.30N 68.01W
Chiricahua Peak 43 Fe 31.52N 109.20W
Chiriguaná 49 Ki 9.22N 73.37W
Chirikof 40 He 55.50N 155.35W
Chiriqui [3] 49 Fi 8.30N 82.00W
Chiriqui, Golfo de- 38 Ki 8.00N 82.20W
Chiriqui, Laguna de- 47 Hg 9.03N 82.00W
Chiriqui Grande 49 Fi 8.57N 82.07W
Chirnogi 15 Je 44.07N 26.34 E
Chiromo 37 Fc 16.33S 35.08 E
Chirripó, Cerro- 38 Ki 9.29N 83.29W
Chirripó, Rio- [C.R.] 49 Fh 10.03N 83.16W
Chirripó, Rio- [C.R.] 49 Fh 10.41N 83.41W
Chirundu 37 Dc 15.59S 28.54 E
Chisamba 36 Ee 14.59S 28.23 E
Chisāpāni Garhi 25 Hc 27.34N 85.08 E
Chisenga 36 Fd 9.56S 33.26 E
Chishui 27 If 28.30N 105.44 E
Chişineu Criş 15 Ec 46.32N 21.31 E
Chisone 14 Bf 44.49N 7.25 E
Chitado 36 Bf 17.18S 13.54 E
Chita-Hantō 29 Ed 34.50N 136.50 E
Chitati 35 Ac 14.40N 14.30 E
Chita-Wan 29 Ed 34.50N 136.55 E
Chitembo 36 Ce 13.31S 16.45 E
Chitina 40 Kd 61.31N 144.27W
Chitina 40 Kd 61.30N 144.28W
Chitipa 36 Fd 9.43S 33.16 E
Chitorgarh 25 Ed 24.53N 74.38 E
Chitose 28 Pc 42.49N 141.39 E
Chitradurga 25 Ff 14.14N 76.24 E
Chitrāl 25 Ea 35.51N 71.47 E
Chitré 47 Hg 7.58N 80.26W
Chittagong 22 Lg 22.20N 91.50 E
Chittoor 25 Ff 13.12N 79.07 E
Chiumbe 30 Ji 6.59S 21.12 E
Chiume 36 Df 15.08S 21.12 E
Chiusi 14 Fg 43.01N 11.57 E
Chiusi, Lago di- 14 Fg 43.05N 12.00 E
Chiva 13 Le 39.28N 0.43W
Chivacoa 50 Bg 10.10N 68.54W
Chivapuri, Rio- 50 Ci 6.25N 66.23W
Chivasso 14 Be 45.11N 7.53 E
Chivay 54 Dg 15.38S 71.36W
Chivilcoy 56 Hd 34.53S 60.01W
Chixoy o Negro, Rio- 49 Be 16.28N 90.33W
Chizou → Guichi 27 Ke 30.38N 117.30 E
Chizu 29 Dd 35.15N 134.14 E
Chôâm Khsant 25 Kf 14.13N 104.56 E
Choapa, Rio- 56 Fd 31.38S 71.34W
Chobe 30 Jj 17.47S 25.10 E
Chobe 37 Cc 18.30S 25.00 E
Choc Bay 51k Ba 14.03N 60.59W
Choch'iwŏn 28 If 36.36N 127.18 E
Chocó [2] 54 Cb 6.00N 77.00W
Chocolate Mountains 46 Hj 33.25N 114.10W
Chodecz 10 Pd 52.24N 19.01 E
Chodov 10 If 50.15N 12.45 E
Chodzież 10 Md 52.59N 16.56 E
Choele-Choel 56 Ge 39.16S 65.41W
Choique 56 He 38.28S 62.43W
Choiseul 51k Ab 13.47N 61.03W
Choiseul Island 57 Ge 7.00S 157.00 E
Choix 48 Ed 26.43N 108.17W
Chojna 10 Kd 52.58N 14.28 E
Chojnice 10 Nc 53.42N 17.34 E
Chojnów 10 Le 51.17N 15.56 E
Chōkai-San 21 Of 39.10N 140.02 E
Choke 30 Kg 10.45N 37.35 E
Chókué 37 Ed 24.27S 32.55 E
Cho La 27 Ge 31.52N 98.51 E
Cholet 11 Fg 47.04N 0.53W
Chŏlla-Namdo [2] 28 Ig 34.45N 127.00 E
Chŏlla-Pukto [2] 28 Ig 35.45N 127.15 E
Cholo 36 Gf 16.04S 35.08 E
Cholula 48 Jh 19.04N 98.19W
Choluteca 47 Gf 13.18N 87.12W
Choluteca [3] 49 Dg 13.20N 87.10W
Choluteca, Rio- 49 Dg 13.07N 87.19W
Choma 31 Jj 16.49S 26.59 E
Chomo/Yadong 27 Ef 27.38N 89.03 E
Chomo Lhari 27 Ef 27.50N 89.16 E
Chomutov 10 Jf 50.28N 13.25 E
Ch'ŏnan 27 Md 36.48N 127.09 E
Chon Buri 25 Kf 13.22N 100.59 E
Chone 54 Bd 0.42S 80.07W
Ch'ŏngch'ŏn-gang 28 He 39.35N 125.28 E
Ch'ŏngjin 22 Oe 41.46N 129.49 E
Ch'ŏngjin Si [2] 28 Jd 41.45N 129.45 E
Chŏngju 27 Md 39.51N 125.15 E
Ch'ŏngju 27 Md 36.38N 127.30 E
Chongli (Xiwanzi) 28 Cd 40.57N 115.12 E
Chongming 28 Fi 31.38N 121.24 E
Chongming Dao 28 Fi 31.36N 121.33 E
Chongoroi 36 Be 13.34S 13.55 E
Chongqing (Yuzhou) = Chungking (EN) 22 Mg 29.34N 106.27 E
Chongqing → Yuzhou = Chungking (EN) 22 Mg 29.34N 106.27 E
Ch'ŏngsan-Do 28 Ig 34.11N 126.54 E
Chŏngŭp 28 Ig 35.34N 126.51 E
Chongyang 28 Cj 29.32N 114.02 E
Chongzuo 27 Ig 22.29N 107.22 E
Chŏnju 27 Md 35.49N 127.09 E
Chonos, Archipiélago de los- 52 Ij 45.00S 74.00W
Chontaleña, Cordillera- 49 Eh 11.50N 85.00W
Chontales [3] 49 Eg 12.05N 85.10W
Chopim, Rio- 55 Fg 25.35S 53.05W
Chopinzinho 55 Fg 25.51S 52.30W
Chorito, Sierra del- 13 He 39.25N 4.25W
Choroszcz 10 Sc 53.09N 22.59 E
Chorreras, Cerro- 48 Fd 26.02N 106.21W
Ch'ŏrwŏn 27 Md 38.15N 127.13 E
Chorzele 10 Qc 53.16N 20.55 E
Chorzów 10 Of 50.19N 18.57 E
Ch'osan 28 Hd 40.45N 125.50 E
Choŝebuz/Cottbus 10 Ke 51.46N 14.20 E
Chōshi 28 Pg 35.44N 140.50 E
Chos Malal 56 Fe 37.23S 70.16W
Chosŏn M.I.K. = North Korea (EN) [1] 22 Oe 40.00N 127.30 E
Chosŏn Minjuju-Inmin-Konghwaguk = Chosŏn M.I.K. [1] 22 Oe 40.00N 127.30 E
Choszczno 10 Lc 53.10N 15.26 E
Chota 54 Ce 6.33S 78.39W
Chotanagpur Plateau 21 Kg 22.00N 86.00 E
Choteau 46 Ic 47.49N 112.11W
Chotla, Cerro de- 48 Ii 17.55N 101.31W
Choukchot, Djebel- 13 Qh 36.01N 4.11 E
Choum 32 Ee 21.18N 12.59W
Chovd → Kobdo 27 Fb 48.06N 92.11 E
Chövsgöl nuur → Hubsugul Nur 21 Md 51.00N 100.30 E
Chowchilla 46 Eh 37.07N 120.16W
Chowra 25 Ig 8.27N 93.02 E
Chréa 13 Oh 36.25N 2.53 E
Chřiby 10 Ng 49.10N 17.20 E
Christchurch 58 Ii 43.32S 172.37 E
Christian, Cape- 42 Kb 70.32N 68.18W
Christian, Point- 64q Ab 25.04S 130.07W
Christiana 37 De 27.52S 25.08 E
Christian IV Gletscher 41 Ie 68.40N 30.20W
Christiansburg 44 Gg 37.07N 80.26W
Christiansfeld 8 Ci 55.21N 9.29 E
Christianshåb/Qasigiánguit 41 Ge 68.45N 51.30W
Christiansø 8 Fi 55.20N 15.10 E
Christian Sound 40 Me 55.56N 134.40W
Christiansted 50 Dd 17.45N 64.40W
Christiansted Harbor 51a Dc 17.46N 64.42W
Christie Bay 42 Gd 62.45N 110.15W
Christmas → Kiritimati Atoll 57 Ld 1.52N 157.20W
Christmas Creek 59 Fc 18.29S 125.23 E
Christmas Creek 59 Fc 18.53S 125.55 E
Christmas Island [5] 22 Mk 10.30S 105.40 E
Christmas Ridge (EN) 3 Ki 10.00N 165.00W
Chrudim 10 Lg 49.57N 15.47 E
Chrzanów 10 Pf 50.09N 19.24 E
Chrząstowa 10 Mc 53.35N 16.58 E
Chuansha 28 Fi 31.11N 121.42 E
Chūbar 24 Mc 38.11N 48.51 E
Chubut [2] 56 Gf 44.00S 69.00W
Chubut, Rio- 52 Jj 43.20S 65.03W
Chucunaque, Rio- 49 Ii 8.09N 77.44W
Chugach Mountains 40 Jd 61.00N 145.00W
Chuginadak 40 Ef 52.49N 169.50W
Chugoku-Sanchi 21 Pf 35.15N 133.30 E
Chu He 28 Eh 32.15N 119.03 E
Chuhuichupa 48 Ec 29.38N 108.22W
Chui 55 Fk 33.41S 53.27W
Chuka 36 Gc 0.20S 37.39 E
Chukai 26 Df 4.15N 103.25 E
Chukchi Peninsula (EN) = Čukotski Poluostrov 21 Uc 66.00N 175.00W
Chukchi Plateau (EN) 67 Bd 78.00N 165.00W
Chukchi Sea 67 Bd 69.00N 171.00W
Chukchi Sea (EN) = Čukotskoje More 67 Bd 69.00N 171.00W
Chula Vista 46 Gj 32.39N 117.05W
Chulitna 40 Jd 62.55N 149.39W
Chullo 13 Jg 37.10N 2.57W
Chulucanas 54 Be 5.06S 80.10W
Chumbicha 56 Gc 28.52S 66.14W
Chumphon 25 Jf 10.32N 99.13 E
Chumunjin 28 Jf 37.53N 128.49 E
Ch'unch'ŏn 27 Md 37.52N 127.44 E
Chunga 36 Ef 15.03S 26.00 E
Ch'ungch'ŏng-Namdo [2] 28 If 36.30N 127.00 E
Ch'ungch'ŏng-Pukto [2] 28 Jf 36.45N 128.00 E
Ch'ungju 27 Md 36.58N 127.56 E
Chungking (EN) = Chongqing (Yuzhou) 22 Mg 29.34N 106.27 E
Chungking (EN) = Yuzhou → Chongqing 22 Mg 29.34N 106.27 E
Ch'ungmu 28 Jg 34.51N 128.26 E
Chunya 36 Fd 8.32S 33.25 E
Chuquibamba 54 Dg 15.50S 72.39W
Chuquibambilla 54 Df 14.07S 72.43W
Chuquicamata 56 Gb 22.19S 68.56W
Chuquisaca [2] 54 Fg 20.00S 64.20W
Chur/Cuera 14 Dd 46.50N 9.35 E
Churchill 39 Jd 58.46N 94.10W
Churchill [Can.] 38 Md 53.30N 60.10W
Churchill [Can.] 38 Jd 58.47N 94.12W
Churchill, Cape- 42 Ie 58.46N 93.12W
Churchill Falls 42 Lf 53.30N 64.10W
Churchill Lake 42 Ge 55.58N 108.15W
Churchill Peak 42 Ee 58.20N 125.02W
Churchill Range 66 Jg 81.30S 158.30 E
Chūru 25 Ec 28.18N 74.57 E
Churuguara 54 Ea 10.49N 69.32W
Churún Merú = Angel Falls (EN) 52 Je 5.57N 62.30W
Chuska Mountains 46 Kh 36.15N 108.50W
Chute-des Passes 42 Kg 49.50N 71.00W
Chuxian 27 Ke 32.16N 118.15 E
Chuxiong 27 Hf 25.02N 101.32 E
Chuy 55 Fk 33.41S 53.27W
Ciamis 26 Eh 7.20S 108.21 E
Cianjur 26 Eh 6.49S 107.08 E
Ciarraí/Kerry [2] 9 Di 52.10N 9.30W
Ćiatura 16 Mh 42.17N 43.15 E
Cibuta, Cerro- 48 Db 31.02N 110.58W
Ćićarija 14 He 45.28N 13.54 E
Ćićevac 15 Ef 43.43N 21.27 E
Cicicleja 15 Nb 47.23N 30.50 E
Cicolano 14 Hh 42.15N 13.10 E
Cidacos 13 Kb 42.19N 1.55W
Cide 24 Eb 41.54N 33.00 E
Cidlina 10 Lf 50.09N 15.12 E
Ciechanów 10 Qd 52.53N 20.38 E
Ciechanów [2] 10 Qd 52.55N 20.40 E
Ciechanowiec 10 Sd 52.42N 22.31 E
Ciechanowska, Wysoczyzna- 10 Qc 53.10N 20.30 E
Ciego de Ávila 47 Id 21.51N 78.46W
Ciego de Ávila [3] 49 Hb 22.00N 78.40W
Ciénaga 54 Da 11.00N 74.14W
Ciénaga de Flores 48 Ie 25.57N 100.11W
Ciénaga de Oro 49 Ji 8.53N 75.38W
Cieneguita 48 Fd 27.57N 106.59W
Cienfuegos [3] 49 Gb 22.15N 80.30W
Cienfuegos 39 Kg 22.09N 80.27W
Cies, Islas de- 13 Db 42.13N 8.54W
Cieszanów 10 Tf 50.16N 23.08 E
Cieza 13 Kf 38.14N 1.25W
Çifteler 24 Dc 39.22N 31.03 E
Cifuentes 13 Jd 40.47N 2.37W
Čiganak 19 Hf 45.05N 73.58 E
Čigirin 16 He 49.03N 32.42 E
Cigüela 13 Ie 39.08N 3.44W
Cihanbeyli 24 Ec 38.40N 32.56 E
Cihanbeyli Platosu 24 Ec 38.40N 32.45 E
Čiharesi 16 Mh 42.47N 43.02 E
Cihuatlán 48 Gh 19.14N 104.35W
Čiily 19 Gg 44.13N 66.46 E
Cijara, Embalse de- 13 He 39.18N 4.52W
Cijulang 26 Eh 7.44S 108.27 E
Čik 15 Dd 45.42N 20.04 E
Čikoj 20 Ff 51.02N 106.39 E
Cikurački, Vulkan- 20 Kf 50.15N 155.29 E
Cilacap 26 Eh 7.44S 109.00 E
Çıldır 24 Jb 41.08N 43.07 E
Çıldır Gölü 24 Jb 41.04N 43.15 E
Cilento 14 Jj 40.20N 15.20 E
Čilik 18 Lc 43.42N 78.14 E
Čilik 19 Hg 43.35N 78.12 E
Cill Airne/Killarney 9 Di 52.03N 9.30W
Cill Chainnigh/Kilkenny 9 Fi 52.39N 7.15W
Cill Chainnigh/Kilkenny [2] 9 Fi 52.40N 7.20W
Cill Chaoi/Kilkee 9 Di 52.41N 9.38W
Cill Dara/Kildare [2] 9 Gh 53.15N 6.45W
Cill Dara/Kildare 9 Gh 53.10N 6.55W
Cill Mhantáin/Wicklow 9 Gi 52.59N 6.03W
Cill Mhantáin/Wicklow [2] 9 Gi 53.00N 6.30W
Cill Mocheallóg/Kilmallock 9 Ei 52.25N 8.35W
Cill Rois/Kilrush 9 Di 52.39N 9.29W
Cilma 17 Fd 65.25N 52.05 E
Cilo Daği 24 Kd 37.30N 44.00 E
Cimaltepec, Sierra- 47 Ee 16.00N 96.40W
Cimarron 38 Jf 36.10N 96.17W
Cimarron 45 Dh 36.31N 104.55W
Čimbaj 19 Fg 42.59N 59.47 E
Cimini, Monti- 14 Gh 42.24N 12.12 E
Čimišlija 16 Ff 46.32N 28.46 E
Čimkent 22 Ie 42.18N 69.36 E
Čimkentskaja Oblast [3] 19 Gg 43.00N 68.40 E
Cimljansk 19 Ef 47.37N 42.04 E
Cimljanskoje Vodohranilišče = Tsimlyansk Reservoir (EN) 5 Kf 48.00N 43.00 E
Cimone 14 Ef 44.12N 10.40 E
Cîmpeni 15 Gc 46.22N 23.03 E
Cîmpia Turzii 15 Gc 46.33N 23.53 E
Cîmpina 15 Id 45.08N 25.44 E
Cîmpulung 15 Id 45.16N 25.03 E
Cîmpulung Moldovenesc 15 Ib 47.32N 25.34 E
Cîmtarga, Gora- 18 Ge 39.14N 68.12 E
Cina, Tanjung- 26 Dh 5.55S 104.35 E
Çınar 24 Id 37.39N 40.06 E
Çinarcik 15 Mi 40.39N 29.06 E
Cinaruco, Rio- 50 Ci 6.41N 67.07W
Cina Selatan, Laut- = South China Sea (EN) 21 Ni 10.00N 113.00 E
Cinaz 18 Gd 40.56N 68.45 E
Cinca 13 Mc 41.26N 0.21 E
Cincar 14 Lg 43.54N 17.04 E
Cincinnati 39 Kf 39.06N 84.31W
Cinco de Otubro 36 Cd 9.34S 17.50 E
Cinco Irmãos, Serra dos- 55 Ff 22.55S 52.50W
Cinco Saltos 56 Ge 38.49S 68.04W
Cindrelu, Virful- 15 Gd 45.35N 23.48 E
Çine 24 Cd 37.36N 28.04 E
Çine 15 Kl 37.46N 27.49 E
Ciney 11 Ld 50.18N 5.06 E
Čingirlau 19 Fe 51.07N 54.05 E
Cingoli 14 Hg 43.22N 13.13 E
Cintalapa de Figueroa 48 Mi 16.44N 93.43W
Cinto, Monte- 5 Gg 42.23N 8.56 E
Cintra, Golfo de- 32 De 23.00N 16.15W
Cinzas, Rio das- 55 Gf 22.56S 50.32W
Ciociaria 14 Hi 41.45N 13.15 E
Cionn Mhálanna/Malin Head 5 Fd 55.23N 7.24W
Cionn tSáile/Kinsale 9 Ej 51.42N 8.32W
Ciorani 15 Je 44.49N 26.25 E
Ciovo 14 Kg 43.30N 16.18 E
Cipa 20 Ge 55.20N 115.55 E
Cipikan 20 Gf 54.58N 113.21 E
Cipó 54 Kf 11.06S 38.31W
Cipolletti 56 Ge 38.56S 67.59W
Ciprovci 15 Ff 43.23N 22.53 E
Čir 16 Me 48.35N 42.55 E
Circeo, Capo- 14 Hi 41.14N 13.03 E
Čirčik 19 Gg 41.28N 69.35 E
Circle [Ak.-U.S.] 40 Kc 65.50N 144.04W
Circle [Mt.-U.S.] 46 Mc 47.25N 105.35W
Circleville 44 Ff 39.36N 82.57W
Cirebon 22 Mj 6.44S 108.34 E
Cirencester 9 Lj 51.44N 1.59W
Ciríé 14 Be 45.14N 7.36 E
Čirinda 20 Fc 67.30N 100.35 E
Čirip, Vulkan- 20 Jg 45.20N 147.58 E
Čirka-Kem 7 Hd 64.45N 32.10 E
Cirò 14 Lk 39.23N 17.04 E
Cirò Marina 14 Lk 39.22N 17.08 E
Ciron 11 Fj 44.36N 0.18W
Čirpan 15 Ig 42.12N 25.20 E
Cirque Mountain 42 Le 58.55N 63.33W
Cisa, Passo della- 14 Df 44.28N 9.55 E
Ciscaucasia (EN) 5 Kf 45.00N 43.00 E
Cisco 45 Gj 32.23N 98.59W
Ciskei 37 Df 31.30S 26.40 E
Čišmy 19 Fe 54.35N 55.25 E
Cisnădie 15 Hd 45.43N 24.09 E
Cisne, Islas del- 47 He 17.22N 83.51W
Cistern Point 49 Ib 24.40N 77.45W
Cisterna 13 Gb 42.48N 5.07W
Čistoozernoje 20 Cf 54.43N 76.43 E
Čistopol 19 Fd 55.23N 50.39 E
Čita 22 Nd 52.03N 113.30 E
Çitak 15 Mk 38.08N 29.39 E

Index Symbols

[1] Independent Nation
[2] State, Region
[3] District, County
[4] Municipality
[5] Colony, Dependency
Continent
Physical Region
Historical or Cultural Region
Mount, Mountain
Volcano
Hill
Mountains, Mountain Range
Hills, Escarpment
Plateau, Upland
Pass, Gap
Plain, Lowland
Delta
Salt Flat
Valley, Canyon
Crater, Cave
Karst Features
Depression
Polder
Desert, Dunes
Forest, Woods
Heath, Steppe
Oasis
Cape, Point
Coast, Beach
Cliff
Peninsula
Isthmus
Sandbank
Island
Atoll
Rock, Reef
Islands, Archipelago
Rocks, Reefs
Coral Reef
Well, Spring
Geyser
River, Stream
Waterfall Rapids
River Mouth, Estuary
Lake
Salt Lake
Intermittent Lake
Reservoir
Swamp, Pond
Canal
Glacier
Ice Shelf, Pack Ice
Ocean
Sea
Gulf, Bay
Strait, Fjord
Lagoon
Bank
Seamount
Tablemount
Ridge
Shelf
Basin
Escarpment, Sea Scarp
Fracture
Trench, Abyss
National Park, Reserve
Point of Interest
Recreation Site
Cave, Cavern
Historic Site
Ruins
Wall, Walls
Church, Abbey
Temple
Scientific Station
Airport
Port
Lighthouse
Mine
Tunnel
Dam, Bridge

Citeli-Ckaro 16 Oi 41.28N 46.06 E
Čitinskaja Oblast [3] 20 Gf 52.30N 117.30 E
Citlaltépetl, Volcán- → Orizaba, Pico de- 38 Jh 19.01N 97.16W
Citrusdale 37 Bf 32.36S 19.00 E
Città del Vaticano = Vatican City (EN) [1] 6 Hg 41.54N 12.27 E
Città di Castello 14 Gg 43.27N 12.14 E
Cittanova 14 Kl 38.21N 16.05 E
Ciucaşu, Vîrful- 15 Id 45.31N 25.55 E
Ciucea 15 Fd 46.57N 22.49 E
Ciudad 48 Gf 23.44N 105.44W
Ciudad Acuña 47 Dc 29.18N 100.55W
Ciudad Altamirano 48 Ih 18.20N 100.40W
Ciudad Bolívar 53 Je 8.08N 63.33W
Ciudad Bolivia 54 Db 8.21N 70.34W
Ciudad Camargo [Mex.] 47 Ec 26.19N 98.50W
Ciudad Camargo [Mex.] 47 Cc 27.40N 105.10W
Ciudad Cuauhtémoc 48 Mj 15.37N 92.00W
Ciudad Darío 49 Dg 12.43N 86.08W
Ciudad de Areco 55 Cl 34.18S 59.46W
Ciudad de Dolores Hidalgo 48 Ig 21.10N 100.56W
Ciudad de la Habana [3] 49 Fb 23.10N 82.10W
Ciudad del Carmen 48 Fe 18.38N 91.50W
Ciudad del Maíz 48 Jf 22.24N 99.36W
Ciudad de México = Mexico City (EN) 39 Jh 19.24N 99.09W
Ciudad de Nutrias 54 Eb 8.07N 69.19W
Ciudad de Río Grande 47 Dd 23.50N 103.02W
Ciudadela/Ciutadella 13 Pd 40.02N 3.50 E
Ciudad Guayana 53 Je 8.22N 62.40W
Ciudad Guerrero 47 Cc 28.33N 107.30W
Ciudad Guzmán 47 De 19.41N 103.29W
Ciudad Hidalgo [Mex.] 48 Mj 14.41N 92.09W
Ciudad Hidalgo [Mex.] 48 Ih 19.41N 100.34W
Ciudad Juárez 39 If 31.44N 106.29W
Ciudad Lerdo 47 Dc 25.32N 103.32W
Ciudad Madero 39 Jg 22.16N 97.50W
Ciudad Mante 47 Ed 22.44N 98.57W
Ciudad Mendoza 48 Kh 18.48N 97.11W
Ciudad Obregón 39 Ig 27.59N 109.56W
Ciudad Ojeda 54 Da 10.12N 71.19W
Ciudad Piar 54 Fb 7.27N 63.19W
Ciudad Real 13 If 38.59N 3.56W
Ciudad Real [3] 13 If 39.00N 4.00W
Ciudad Rio Bravo 47 Ec 25.59N 98.06W
Ciudad-Rodrigo 13 Fd 40.36N 6.32W
Ciudad Valles 47 Ed 21.59N 99.01W
Ciudad Victoria 39 Jg 23.44N 99.08W
Ciutadella/Ciudadela 13 Pd 40.02N 3.50 E
Civa Burnu 24 Gb 41.22N 36.35 E
Cividale del Friuli 14 Hd 46.06N 13.25 E
Civilsk 7 Li 55.53N 47.29 E
Civita Castellana 14 Gh 42.17N 12.25 E
Civitanova Marche 14 Hg 43.18N 13.44 E
Civitavecchia 14 Fh 42.06N 11.48 E
Civitella del Tronto 14 Hh 42.46N 13.40 E
Çivril 24 Cc 38.56N 35.29 E
Cixerri 14 Ck 39.17N 8.59 E
Cixi (Hushan) 28 Fi 30.10N 121.14 E
Cixian 28 Cf 36.22N 114.22 E
Čiža 19 Eb 67.06N 44.19 E
Cizre 23 Fb 37.20N 42.12 E
Cjurupinsk 16 Hf 46.37N 32.43 E
Čkalovsk 7 Kh 56.47N 43.17 E
Clacton-on-Sea 9 Oj 51.48N 1.09 E
Clain 11 Gh 46.47N 0.33 E
Claire, Côte- 66 Ie 66.30S 133.00 E
Claire, Lake- 42 Ge 58.30N 112.00W
Clair Engle Lake 46 Df 40.52N 122.43W
Claise 11 Gh 46.56N 0.42 E
Clamecy 11 Jg 47.27N 3.31 E
Clan Alpine Mountains 46 Gg 39.40N 117.55W
Clanton 44 Di 32.50N 86.38W
Clanwilliam 37 Bf 32.11S 18.54 E
Claraz 55 Cm 37.54S 59.17W
Clár Chlainne Mhuiris/ Claremorris 9 Eh 53.44N 9.00W
Clare [Austl.] 59 Hf 33.50S 138.36 E
Clare [Mi.-U.S.] 44 Ed 43.49N 84.46W
Clare/Abhainn an Chláir 9 Dh 53.20N 9.03W
Clare/An Clár [2] 9 Ei 52.50N 9.00W
Clare/Clíara 9 Dh 53.49N 10.00W
Claremont 44 Kd 43.23N 72.21W
Claremore 45 Ih 36.19N 95.36W
Claremorris/Clár Chlainne Mhuiris 9 Eh 53.44N 9.00W
Clarence 62 Ee 42.10S 173.57 E
Clarence 62 Ee 42.10S 173.56 E
Clarence, Cape- 42 Ib 73.55N 90.12W
Clarence Cannon Reservoir 45 Kg 39.31N 91.45W
Clarence Island 66 Re 61.12S 54.05W
Clarence River 59 Ke 29.25S 153.22 E
Clarence Strait [Ak.-U.S.] 40 Me 55.25N 132.00W
Clarence Strait [Austl.] 59 Gb 12.00S 131.00 E
Clarence Town 49 Jb 23.06N 74.59W
Clarendon 45 Fi 34.56N 100.53W
Clarenville 42 Mg 48.09N 53.58W
Claresholm 42 Gf 50.02N 113.35W
Clarinda 45 If 40.44N 95.02W
Clarines 50 Dh 9.56N 65.10W
Clarion, Isla- 47 Be 18.22N 114.44W
Clarion Fracture Zone (EN) 3 Lh 18.00N 130.00W
Clarion River 44 He 41.07N 79.41W
Clark 45 Hd 44.53N 97.44W
Clark, Lake- 40 Id 60.15N 154.15W
Clark, Mount- 42 Fd 64.25N 124.14W
Clarkdale 46 Ii 34.46N 112.03W
Clarke Range 59 Jd 20.50S 148.35 E
Clark Fork 38 He 48.09N 116.15W
Clark Hill Lake 44 Fi 33.50N 82.20W
Clark Mountain 46 Hi 35.32N 115.35W
Clarksburg 43 Kd 39.17N 80.21W
Clarksdale 43 Ie 34.12N 90.34W
Clarks Fork 46 Kd 45.39N 108.43W
Clark's Harbour 44 Od 43.26N 65.38W
Clarkston 46 Gc 46.30N 117.03W
Clarksville [Ar.-U.S.] 45 Ji 35.28N 93.28W
Clarksville [Tn.-U.S.] 43 Jd 36.32N 87.21W
Clarksville [Tx.-U.S.] 45 Ij 33.37N 95.03W
Claro, Rio- [Braz.] 54 Hg 19.08S 50.40W
Claro, Rio- [Braz.] 54 Hg 15.28S 51.45W
Clary 12 Fd 50.00N 3.24 E
Claude 45 Fi 35.07N 101.22W
Claustra/Klosters 14 Dd 46.52N 9.52 E
Clavering 41 Jd 74.20N 21.10W
Claxton 44 Gi 32.10N 81.55W
Clay Belt 38 Kd 51.50N 82.00W
Clay Center 45 Hg 39.23N 96.08W
Clay Cross 12 Aa 53.09N 1.25W
Claye Souilly 12 Ef 48.57N 2.42 E
Clayton 43 Gd 36.27N 103.11W
Clear, Cape- 9 Dj 51.26N 9.31W
Clear Boggy Creek 45 Ii 34.03N 95.47W
Clear Creek [Az.-U.S.] 46 Ji 34.59N 110.38W
Clear Creek [U.S.] 46 Ld 44.53N 106.04W
Clearfield [Pa.-U.S.] 44 He 41.02N 78.27W
Clearfield [Ut.-U.S.] 46 If 41.07N 112.01W
Clear Fork Brazos 45 Gj 33.01N 98.40W
Clear Lake 43 Cd 39.02N 122.50W
Clear Lake [Ia.-U.S.] 45 Je 43.08N 93.23W
Clear Lake [S.D.-U.S.] 45 Hd 44.45N 96.41W
Clear Lake Reservoir 46 Ef 41.52N 121.08W
Clearwater 42 Ge 56.45N 111.22W
Clearwater 43 Kf 27.58N 82.48W
Clearwater Mountains 43 Db 46.00N 115.30W
Clearwater River [Alta.-Can.] 46 Ha 52.23N 114.50W
Clearwater River [U.S.] 46 Gc 46.25N 117.02W
Cleburne 43 He 32.21N 97.23W
Clécy 12 Bf 48.55N 0.29W
Clee Hills 9 Ki 52.25N 2.35W
Cleethorpes 9 Mh 53.34N 0.02W
Clères 12 De 49.36N 1.07 E
Clerf/Clervaux 12 Id 50.03N 6.02 E
Clermont [Austl.] 59 Jd 22.49S 147.39 E
Clermont [Fr.] 11 Ie 49.23N 2.24 E
Clermont-en-Argonne 12 He 49.06N 5.04 E
Clermont-Ferrand 6 Gf 45.47N 3.05 E
Clermont-l'Hérault 11 Jk 43.37N 3.26 E
Clervaux/Clerf 12 Id 50.03N 6.02 E
Clervé 12 Ie 49.57N 6.01 E
Cles 14 Fd 46.22N 11.02 E
Clevedon 9 Kj 51.27N 2.51W
Cleveland 9 Lg 54.25N 1.05W
Cleveland [3] 9 Mg 54.40N 1.00W
Cleveland [Ms.-U.S.] 45 Kj 33.45N 90.50W
Cleveland [Oh.-U.S.] 39 Ke 41.30N 81.41W
Cleveland [Tn.-U.S.] 43 Kd 35.10N 84.53W
Cleveland [Tx.-U.S.] 45 Ik 30.21N 95.05W
Cleveland, Mount- 43 Eb 48.56N 113.51W
Cleveland Heights 44 Ge 41.30N 81.34W
Clevelândia 55 Fh 26.24S 52.21W
Cleveland Mountain 46 Ic 46.37N 113.47W
Clew Bay/Cuan Mó 9 Dh 53.50N 9.50W
Cliara/Clare 9 Dh 53.49N 10.00W
Cliff 45 Bj 32.59N 108.36W
Clifton [Az.-U.S.] 43 Fe 33.03N 109.18W
Clifton [St.Vin.] 51n Bb 12.36N 61.26W
Clifton [Tx.-U.S.] 45 Hk 31.47N 97.35W
Clinch River 44 Eh 35.53N 84.29W
Cline, Mount- 46 Ga 52.10N 116.40W
Clines Corners 45 Di 35.01N 105.34W
Clingmans Dome 44 Fh 35.35N 83.30W
Clinton [Ar.-U.S.] 45 Ji 35.36N 92.28W
Clinton [B.C.-Can.] 42 Ff 51.05N 121.35W
Clinton [Ia.-U.S.] 43 Ic 41.51N 90.12W
Clinton [Il.-U.S.] 45 Lf 40.09N 88.57W
Clinton [Mo.-U.S.] 45 Jg 38.22N 93.46W
Clinton [Ms.-U.S.] 45 Kj 32.20N 90.20W
Clinton [N.C.-U.S.] 44 Hh 34.59N 78.20W
Clinton [N.Z.] 62 Cg 46.13S 169.23 E
Clinton [Ok.-U.S.] 43 Hd 35.31N 98.59W
Clinton-Colden Lake 42 Gd 63.55N 107.30W
Clintonville 45 Ld 44.37N 88.46W
Clipperton 38 Ih 10.17N 109.13W
Clipperton, Fracture Zone (EN) 3 Mi 10.00N 115.00W
Clisson 11 Eg 47.05N 1.17W
Cloates, Point- 59 Cd 22.45S 113.40 E
Clochán an Aifir/ 9 Gf 55.15N 6.35W
Giant's Causeway 9 Gf 55.15N 6.35W
Clodomira 56 Hc 27.35S 64.08W
Cloich na Coillte/Clonakilty 9 Ej 51.37N 8.54W
Clonakilty/Cloich na Coillte 9 Ej 51.37N 8.54W
Cloncurry 58 Fg 20.42S 140.30 E
Clones/Cluan Eois 9 Fg 54.11N 7.14W
Clonmel/Cluain Meala 9 Fi 52.21N 7.42W
Cloppenburg 10 Ed 52.51N 8.02 E
Cloquet 43 Ib 46.43N 92.28W
Clorinda 53 Kh 25.20S 57.40W
Cloud Peak 43 Fc 44.25N 107.10W
Clouère 11 Gh 46.26N 0.17 E
Cloverdale 46 Dg 38.48N 123.01W
Clovis [Ca.-U.S.] 46 Fh 36.49N 119.42W
Clovis [N.M.-U.S.] 39 If 34.24N 103.12W
Cluain Meala/Clonmel 9 Fi 52.21N 7.42W
Cluan Eois/Clones 9 Fg 54.11N 7.14W
Cluj [2] 15 Gc 46.49N 23.35 E
Cluj Napoca 6 If 46.46N 23.36 E
Cluny 11 Kh 46.26N 4.39 E
Cluses 11 Mh 46.04N 6.36 E
Clusone 14 De 45.53N 9.57 E
Clutha 62 Cg 46.21S 169.48 E
Clwyd 9 Jh 53.20N 3.30W
Clwyd [3] 9 Jh 53.10N 3.15W
Clyde 9 If 55.56N 4.29W
Clyde [N.W.T.-Can.] 39 Mb 70.25N 68.30W
Clyde [N.Z.] 62 Cf 45.11S 169.19 E
Clyde, Firth of- 9 If 55.42N 5.00W
Clyde Inlet 42 Kb 70.20N 68.20W
Cna 5 Ke 54.32N 42.05 E
Cnoc Bréanainn/Brandon Mount 9 Ci 52.14N 10.15W
Cnoc Fola/Bloody Foreland 9 Ef 55.09N 8.17W
Cnoc Mhaoldonn/ Knockmealdown Mountains 9 Fi 52.15N 8.00W
Cnori 16 Ni 41.35N 45.59 E
Cnossus (EN) = Knosós 15 In 35.18N 25.10 E
Côa 13 Ec 41.05N 7.06W
Coachella Canal 46 Hj 33.34N 116.00W
Coahuayana 48 Hh 18.44N 103.41W
Coahuila [2] 47 Dc 27.20N 102.00W
Coalcomán, Sierra de- 47 De 18.30N 102.55W
Coalcomán de Matamoros 48 Hh 18.47N 103.09W
Coaldale 46 Ib 49.43N 112.37W
Coalgate 45 Hi 34.32N 96.13W
Coalinga 46 Eh 36.09N 120.21W
Coalville 9 Li 52.44N 1.20W
Coamo 49 Nd 18.05N 66.22W
Coari 54 Fd 4.05S 63.08W
Coari, Lago de- 54 Fd 4.15S 63.25W
Coari, Rio- 52 Jf 4.30S 63.33W
Coast [3] 36 Gc 3.00S 39.30 E
Coast Mountains 38 Gd 55.00N 129.00W
Coast Plain (EN) = Kustvlakte 11 Ic 51.00N 2.30 E
Coast Ranges 38 Ge 41.00N 123.30W
Coatbridge 9 If 55.52N 4.01W
Coatepec 48 Kh 19.27N 96.58W
Coatepel, Cerro- 48 Kh 18.25N 97.35W
Coatepeque 49 Bf 14.42N 91.52W
Coats 38 Kc 62.30N 83.00W
Coats Land (EN) 66 Af 77.00S 28.00W
Coatzacoalcos 39 Jh 18.09N 94.25W
Coatzacoalcos, Bahía- 48 Lh 18.10N 94.27W
Coatzacoalcos, Río- 48 Lh 18.09N 94.24W
Coba 47 Gd 20.36N 87.35W
Cobadin 15 Le 44.05N 28.13 E
Cobalt 42 Jg 47.24N 79.41W
Cobán 47 Fe 15.29N 90.19W
Cobar 59 Jf 31.30S 145.49 E
Cobb, Mount- 46 Dg 38.45N 122.40W
Cobb Seamount (EN) 38 Fe 46.46N 130.43W
Cóbh/An Cóbh 9 Ej 51.51N 8.17W
Cobija 54 Ef 11.02S 68.44W
Cobo 55 Dm 37.48S 57.38W
Cobourg 42 Jh 43.58N 78.10W
Cobourg Peninsula 59 Gb 11.20S 132.15 E
Cóbué 37 Eb 12.07S 34.52 E
Coburg 42 Ja 75.57N 79.00W
Coburn Mountain 44 Lc 45.28N 70.06W
Coca, Pizzo di- 14 Ed 46.04N 10.01 E
Cocalinho 55 Gb 14.22S 51.00W
Cocentaina 13 Lf 38.45N 0.26W
Cochabamba 54 Eg 17.30S 65.40W
Cochabamba 53 Jg 17.24S 66.09W
Coche, Isla- 50 Eg 10.47N 63.56W
Cochem 10 Df 50.08N 7.09 E
Cochin 22 Ji 9.58N 76.14 E
Cochin China (EN) = Nam Phan 21 Mg 11.00N 107.00 E
Cochinos, Bahía de- = Pigs, Bay of- (EN) 49 Gb 22.07N 81.10W
Cochons, Ile aux- 30 Mm 46.05S 50.08 E
Cochran 44 Fi 32.23N 83.21W
Cochrane 42 He 57.55N 101.32W
Cochrane [Alta.-Can.] 46 Ha 51.11N 114.28W
Cochrane [Ont.-Can.] 39 Ke 49.04N 81.01W
Cockburn, Canal- 56 Fh 54.20S 71.30W
Cockburn, Mount- 59 Gd 22.46S 130.36 E
Cockburn Bank 9 El 49.40N 8.50W
Cockburn Island 44 Fc 45.55N 83.22W
Cockburn Town 49 Ja 24.02N 74.31W
Cockermouth 9 Jg 54.40N 3.21W
Coclé [3] 49 Gi 8.30N 80.15W
Coco, Cayo- 49 Hb 22.30N 78.28W
Coco, Ile- 51b Bc 17.52N 62.49W
Coco, Isla del- 38 Ki 5.32N 87.04W
Coco, Río-o Segovia, Río- 38 Kh 15.00N 83.08W
Cocoa 43 Kf 28.21N 80.44W
Cocoa Beach 44 Gk 28.19N 80.36W
Cocoa Point 51d Ba 17.33N 61.46W
Cocobeach 36 Ab 0.59N 9.36 E
Coco Channel 25 If 14.00N 93.00 E
Coco Islands 25 If 14.05N 93.18 E
Coconino Plateau 46 Ii 35.50N 112.30W
Cocorocuma, Cayos- 49 Ff 15.45N 83.00W
Cocos 64c Bb 13.14N 144.39 E
Côcos 55 Jb 14.10S 44.33W
Cocos Islands (Keeling Islands) 21 Lk 12.10S 96.55 E
Cocos Islands (Keeling Islands) [5] 22 Lk 12.10S 96.55 E
Cocos Ridge (EN) 3 Ni 5.30N 86.00W
Cocula 48 Hg 20.23N 103.50W
Cocuzzo 14 Kk 39.13N 16.08 E
Cod, Cape- 44 Me 41.50N 70.00W
Cod, Cape- 38 Le 41.42N 70.15W
Coda Cavallo, Capo- 14 Dj 40.51N 9.43 E
Codăeşti 15 Kc 46.52N 27.45 E
Codajás 54 Fd 3.50S 62.05W
Codera, Cabo- 50 Cg 10.35N 66.04W
Codfish Island 62 Bg 46.45S 167.40 E
Codigoro 14 Gf 44.49N 12.08 E
Codlea 15 Id 45.42N 25.27 E
Codó 54 Jd 4.29S 43.53W
Codogno 14 De 45.09N 9.42 E
Codrington 50 Fd 17.38N 61.50W
Codrington Lagoon 51d Ba 17.39N 61.51W
Codrului, Munţii- 15 Fc 46.35N 22.10 E
Cody 43 Fc 44.32N 109.05W
Coen 58 Ff 13.56S 143.12 E
Coesfeld 10 De 51.56N 7.09 E
Coetivy Island 30 Mi 7.08S 56.16 E
Coeur d'Alene 43 Db 47.41N 116.46W
Coevorden 11 Mb 52.40N 6.45 E
Coffeyville 45 Ih 37.02N 95.37W
Coffs Harbour 58 Gh 30.18S 153.08 E
Cofre de Perote, Cerro- (Nauhcampatépetl) 48 Kh 19.29N 97.08W
Cofrentes 13 Ke 39.14N 1.04W
Coggeshall 12 Cc 51.52N 0.41 E
Coghinas 14 Cj 40.56N 8.48 E
Coghinas, Lago del- 14 Dj 40.45N 9.05 E
Coglians 14 Gd 46.37N 12.53 E
Cognac 11 Fi 45.42N 0.20W
Cogne 14 Be 45.37N 7.21 E
Cogolludo 13 Id 40.57N 3.05W
Čograjskoje Vodohranilišče 16 Ng 45.30N 44.30 E
Coiba, Isla de- 47 Hg 7.27N 81.45W
Coig, Río- (Coyle) 56 Gh 50.58S 69.11W
Coihaique 56 Fg 45.34S 72.04W
Coimbatore 22 Jh 11.00N 76.58 E
Coimbra [2] 13 Dd 40.12N 8.25W
Coimbra [Braz.] 55 Dd 19.55S 57.47W
Coimbra [Port.] 6 Fg 40.12N 8.25W
Coín 13 Hh 36.40N 4.45W
Coipasa, Salar de- 54 Eg 19.30S 68.10W
Čojbalsan 22 Ne 48.04N 114.30 E
Cojedes 50 Bh 9.37N 68.55W
Cojedes [2] 54 Eb 9.20N 68.20W
Cojedes, Río- 50 Bh 8.44N 68.15W
Cojutepeque 49 Cg 13.43N 88.56W
Čoka 15 Dd 45.56N 20.09 E
Cokeville 46 Je 42.05N 110.55W
Cokover River 59 Ed 20.40S 120.45 E
Čokurdah 20 Jb 70.38N 147.55 E
Colac [Austl.] 59 Ig 38.20S 143.35 E
Colac [N.Z.] 62 Bg 46.22S 167.53 E
Colatina 53 Lg 19.32S 40.37W
Colbeck, Cape- 66 Mf 77.06S 157.48W
Colbitz-Letzlinger Heide 10 Hd 52.27N 11.35 E
Colby 45 Fg 39.24N 101.03W
Colchester 9 Nj 51.54N 0.54 E
Cold Bay 40 Ge 55.11N 162.30W
Cold Lake 42 Gf 54.27N 110.10W
Coldstream 9 Kf 55.39N 2.15W
Coldwater [Ks.-U.S.] 45 Gh 37.16N 99.19W
Coldwater [Mi.-U.S.] 44 Ee 41.57N 85.00W
Colebrook 44 Lc 44.53N 71.30W
Coleman 45 Gk 31.50N 99.26W
Coleman River 59 Ic 15.06S 141.38 E
Coleraine/Cúil Raithin 9 Gf 55.08N 6.40W
Coleridge, Lake- 62 De 43.20S 171.30 E
Coles, Punta- 54 Dg 17.42S 71.23W
Colesberg 37 Df 30.45S 25.05 E
Colfax [La.-U.S.] 45 Jk 31.31N 92.42W
Colfax [Wa.-U.S.] 46 Gc 46.53N 117.22W
Colfontaine 12 Fd 50.25N 3.50 E
Colhué Huapi, Lago- 56 Gg 45.30S 68.48W
Colibaşi 15 He 44.56N 24.54 E
Colibris, Pointe des- 51e Bb 16.17N 61.06W
Colima [2] 47 De 19.10N 104.00W
Colima 39 Ih 19.14N 103.43W
Colima, Nevado de- 38 Ih 19.33N 103.38W
Colinas 55 Hb 14.12S 48.03W
Coll 9 Ge 56.40N 6.35W
Collado Bajo 13 Kd 40.14N 1.50W
Collarada 13 Lb 42.43N 0.29W
Colle di Val d'Elsa 14 Fg 43.25N 11.07 E
Colleferro 14 Gi 41.44N 12.59 E
College 40 Jd 64.51N 147.47W
College Place 46 Fc 46.03N 118.23W
College Station 45 Hk 30.37N 96.21W
Collegno 14 Be 45.05N 7.34 E
Collie 59 Df 33.21S 116.09 E
Collier Bay 59 Ec 16.10S 124.15 E
Collierville 44 Ch 35.03N 89.40W
Collingwood [N.Z.] 61 Dh 40.41S 172.41 E
Collingwood [Ont.-Can.] 44 Gc 44.29N 80.13W
Collinson Peninsula 42 Hb 70.00N 101.10W
Collinsville 59 Jd 20.34S 147.51 E
Collmberg 10 Je 51.15N 13.02 E
Colmar 11 Nf 48.05N 7.22 E
Colmena 55 Bi 28.45S 60.06W
Colmenar 13 Hh 36.54N 4.20W
Colmenar Viejo 13 Id 40.40N 3.46W
Colne 12 Cc 51.51N 0.59 E
Colne Point 12 Dc 51.46N 1.03 E
Colnett, Punta- 48 Ab 31.00N 116.20W
Cologne (EN) = Köln 6 Ge 50.56N 6.57 E
Colombia [2] 53 Ie 4.00N 72.00W
Colombia 55 He 20.10S 48.40W
Colombian Basin (EN) 38 Lh 13.00N 76.00W
Colombier, Pointe à- 51b Bc 17.55N 62.53W
Colombo 22 Ji 6.56N 79.51 E
Colón [Arg.] 56 Hd 33.53S 61.07W
Colón [Arg.] 56 Id 32.13S 58.08W
Colón [Cuba] 47 Hd 22.43N 80.54W
Colón [Hond.] [3] 49 Ef 15.20N 84.30W
Colón [Pan.] [3] 49 Hi 9.30N 79.15W
Colón [Pan.] 39 Li 9.22N 79.54W
Colón [Ur.] 55 Ek 33.53S 54.43W
Colon, Archipiélago de-/ Galápagos, Islas- = Galapagos Islands (EN) 52 Gf 0.30S 90.30W
Colón, Montañas de- 49 Ef 14.55N 84.45W
Colona 59 Gf 31.38S 132.05 E
Colonarie 51n Ba 13.14N 61.08W
Colonarie 51n Ba 13.14N 61.08W
Colonel Hill 49 Jb 22.52N 74.15W
Colonia [2] 55 Dl 34.10S 57.30W
Colonia 60 Bf 9.31N 138.08 E
Colonia agricola de Turén 50 Bh 9.15N 69.05W
Colonia Carlos Pellegrini 55 Di 28.32S 57.10W
Colonia del Sacramento 56 Id 34.28S 57.51W
Colonia Elisa 55 Ch 26.56S 59.32W
Colonia Juaréz 48 Eb 30.19N 108.05W
Colonia Las Heras 56 Gg 46.33S 68.57W
Colonia Lavalleja 56 Id 31.06S 57.01W
Colonial Heights 44 Ig 37.15N 77.25W
Colonia Morelos 48 Eb 30.50N 109.10W
Colonne, Capo- 14 Lk 39.02N 17.12 E
Colonsay 9 Ge 56.05N 6.10W
Colorado 49 Fh 10.46N 83.35W
Colorado [2] 43 Fd 39.30N 105.30W
Colorado, Cerro- 48 Bb 31.31N 115.31W
Colorado, Rio- [Arg.] 52 Ji 39.50S 62.08W
Colorado, Rio- [N.Amer.] 38 Hf 31.45N 114.40W
Colorado City 45 Fj 32.24N 100.52W
Colorado Plateau 38 Hf 36.30N 118.00W
Colorado River [N.Amer.] 38 Hf 31.45N 114.40W
Colorado River [U.S.] 38 Jg 28.36N 95.58W
Colorados, Archipiélago de los- 49 Eb 22.36N 84.20W
Colorado Springs 39 If 38.50N 104.49W
Colotlán 48 Hf 22.03N 103.16W
Colpon-Ata 18 Kc 42.39N 77.06 E
Coltishall 12 Db 52.44N 1.22 E
Colui 36 Cf 15.10S 16.40 E
Columbia 38 Ge 46.15N 124.05W
Columbia [Ky.-U.S.] 44 Eg 37.06N 85.18W
Columbia [Mo.-U.S.] 43 Id 38.57N 92.20W
Columbia [Ms.-U.S.] 45 Lk 31.15N 89.56W
Columbia [Pa.-U.S.] 44 Ie 40.02N 76.30W
Columbia [S.C.-U.S.] 39 Kf 34.00N 81.03W
Columbia [Tn.-U.S.] 44 Dh 35.37N 87.02W
Columbia, Cape- 38 La 83.08N 70.35W
Columbia, Mount- 38 Hd 57.00N 117.00W
Columbia Basin 43 Db 46.45N 119.05W
Columbia Falls 43 Hb 48.23N 114.11W
Columbia Mountains 38 Hd 52.00N 119.00W
Columbia Plateau 38 He 44.00N 117.30W
Columbia Seamount (EN) 54 Lh 20.40S 31.30W
Columbine, Cape- 30 Il 32.49S 17.51 E
Columbretes, Islas-/ Columbrets, Els- 13 Me 39.52N 0.40 E
Columbrets, Els-/ Columbretes, Islas- 13 Me 39.52N 0.40 E
Columbus [Ga.-U.S.] 39 Kf 32.29N 84.59W
Columbus [In.-U.S.] 43 Jd 39.13N 85.55W
Columbus [Ks.-U.S.] 45 Ih 37.10N 94.50W
Columbus [Ms.-U.S.] 43 Je 33.30N 88.25W
Columbus [Mt.-U.S.] 46 Kd 45.38N 109.15W
Columbus [Nb.-U.S.] 43 Hc 41.25N 97.22W
Columbus [N.M.-U.S.] 45 Ck 31.50N 107.38W
Columbus [Oh.-U.S.] 39 Kf 39.57N 83.00W
Columbus [Tx.-U.S.] 45 Hl 29.42N 96.33W
Columbus Point 49 Ja 24.08N 75.16W
Colville 38 Dc 70.25N 150.30W
Colville, Cape- 62 Fb 36.28S 175.21 E
Colville Channel 62 Fb 36.25S 175.30 E
Colville Lake 42 Ec 67.10N 126.00W
Colville Lake 42 Ec 67.06N 126.00W
Col Visentin 14 Gd 46.05N 12.20 E
Colwyn Bay 9 Jh 53.18N 3.43W
Coma 35 Fd 8.27N 36.55 E
Comacchio 14 Gf 44.42N 12.11 E
Comacchio, Valli di- 14 Gf 44.40N 12.05 E
Comai (Damxoi) 27 Ff 28.26N 91.32 E
Comala 48 Hh 19.19N 103.45W
Comalcalco 47 Fe 18.16N 93.13W
Coman, Mount- 66 Qf 73.49S 64.18W
Comanche [Mt.-U.S.] 46 Kc 46.02N 108.54W
Comanche [Tx.-U.S.] 45 Gk 31.54N 98.36W
Comandante Fontana 55 Cg 25.20S 59.41W
Comandău 15 Jd 45.46N 26.16 E
Comăneşti 15 Jc 46.25N 26.26 E
Comayagua 47 Gf 14.25N 87.37W
Comayagua [3] 49 Df 14.30N 87.40W
Combarbala 56 Fd 31.11S 71.02W
Combeaufontaine 11 Lg 47.43N 5.53 E
Combermere Bay 25 Ie 19.37N 93.34 E
Comblain-au-Pont 12 Hd 50.28N 5.35 E
Combles 12 Ed 50.01N 2.52 E
Combourg 11 Ef 48.25N 1.45W
Combraille 11 Ih 46.30N 3.10 E
Combrailles 11 Ih 46.15N 2.10 E
Comedero 48 Fe 24.37N 106.46W
Comendador 49 Ld 18.53N 71.42W
Comeragh Mountains/Na Comaraigh 9 Fi 52.13N 7.35W
Comerío 51a Bb 18.13N 66.16W
Comilla 25 Id 23.27N 91.12 E
Comines 12 Fd 50.46N 3.01 E
Comines/Komen 12 Ed 50.46N 2.59 E
Comino 14 In 36.00N 14.20 E
Comino, Capo- 14 Dj 40.32N 9.49 E
Comiso 14 In 36.56N 14.36 E
Comitán de Dominguez 47 Fe 16.15N 92.08W
Commentry 11 Ih 46.17N 2.45 E
Commerce 45 Ij 33.15N 95.54W
Commercy 11 Lf 48.45N 5.35 E
Commiges 11 Gk 43.15N 0.45 E
Committee Bay 38 Kc 68.30N 86.30W
Commonwealth Bay 66 Je 66.54S 142.40 E
Communism Peak (EN) = Kommunizma, Pik- 21 Jf 38.57N 72.08 E
Como [China] 27 Ee 33.26N 85.21 E
Como [It.] 14 De 45.47N 9.05 E
Como, Lago di- 14 Dd 46.00N 9.15 E
Comodoro 55 Bl 35.19S 60.31W
Comodoro Ravadavia 53 Jj 45.50S 67.30W
Comondú 47 Bc 26.03N 111.46W
Comores/Comoros [1] 31 Lj 12.10S 44.10 E
Comores, Archipel des- = Comoro Islands (EN) 30 Lj 12.10S 44.15 E
Comorin, Cape- 21 Ji 8.04N 77.34 E
Comoro Islands (EN) = Comores, Archipel des- 30 Lj 12.10S 44.15 E
Comoros/Comores [1] 31 Lj 12.10S 44.10 E
Comox 46 Cb 49.40N 124.55W
Compiègne 11 Ie 49.25N 2.50 E
Compostela 47 Dd 21.14N 104.55W
Comprida, Ilha- 55 Ig 24.50S 47.42W
Compton 46 Fj 33.54N 118.13W
Comstock 45 Fl 29.41N 101.11W
Comtal, Causse du- 11 Ij 44.26N 2.38 E

Index Symbols

[1] Independent Nation
[2] State, Region
[3] District, County
[4] Municipality
[5] Colony, Dependency
Continent
Physical Region
Historical or Cultural Region
Mount, Mountain
Volcano
Hill
Mountains, Mountain Range
Hills, Escarpment
Plateau, Upland
Pass, Gap
Plain, Lowland
Delta
Salt Flat
Valley, Canyon
Crater, Cave
Karst Features
Depression
Polder
Desert, Dunes
Forest, Woods
Heath, Steppe
Oasis
Cape, Point
Coast, Beach
Cliff
Peninsula
Isthmus
Sandbank
Island
Atoll
Rock, Reef
Islands, Archipelago
Rocks, Reefs
Coral Reef
Well, Spring
Geyser
River, Stream
Waterfall Rapids
River Mouth, Estuary
Lake
Salt Lake
Intermittent Lake
Reservoir
Swamp, Pond
Canal
Glacier
Ice Shelf, Pack Ice
Ocean
Sea
Gulf, Bay
Strait, Fjord
Lagoon
Bank
Seamount
Tablemount
Ridge
Shelf
Basin
Escarpment, Sea Scarp
Fracture
Trench, Abyss
National Park, Reserve
Point of Interest
Recreation Site
Cave, Cavern
Historic Site
Ruins
Wall, Walls
Church, Abbey
Temple
Scientific Station
Airport
Port
Lighthouse
Mine
Tunnel
Dam, Bridge

Čona	21	Mc	62.00N	110.00 E
Cona	27	Ff	28.01N	91.57 E
Co Nag	27	Fe	32.00N	91.25 E
Conakry	31	Fh	9.31N	13.43W
Conara Junction	59	Jh	41.50S	147.26 E
Concarneau	11	Cg	47.52N	3.55W
Conceição da Barra	54	Kg	18.35S	39.45W
Conceição do Araguaia	54	Ie	8.15S	49.17W
Conceição do Mato Dentro	55	Kd	19.01S	43.25W
Concepción [3]	55	Df	23.00S	57.00W
Concepción [Arg.]	56	Gc	27.20S	65.35W
Concepción [Arg.]	55	Di	28.23S	57.53W
Concepción [Bol.]	54	Fg	16.15S	62.04W
Concepción [Chile]	53	Ii	36.50S	73.03W
Concepción [Par.]	53	Kh	23.25S	57.17W
Concepción [Peru]	54	Cf	11.55S	75.17W
Concepción [Ven.]	49	Lh	10.25N	71.41W
Concepción, Bahía-	48	Dd	26.40N	111.48W
Concepción, Laguna-	54	Fg	17.30S	61.25W
Concepción, Punta-	48	Dd	26.50N	111.50W
Concepción, Río-	55	Ab	15.46S	62.10W
Concepción del Bermejo	55	Bh	26.36S	60.57W
Concepción del Oro	47	Dd	24.38N	101.25W
Concepción del Uruguay	56	Id	32.29S	58.14W
Conception, Point-	38	Gf	34.27N	120.27W
Conception Bay	42	Mg	48.00N	52.50W
Conception Island	49	Jb	23.52N	75.03W
Concha	49	Li	9.02N	71.45W
Conchas	55	Hf	23.01S	48.00W
Conchas Dam	45	Di	35.22N	104.11W
Conchas Lake	45	Di	35.25N	104.14W
Conches-en-Ouche	11	Gf	48.58N	0.56 E
Concho River	45	Gk	31.32N	99.43W
Conchos, Río-	38	Ig	29.35N	104.25W
Concoran	46	Fh	36.06N	119.33W
Concord [Ca.-U.S.]	46	Eh	37.59N	122.00W
Concord [N.H.-U.S.]	39	Le	43.12N	71.32W
Concordia [Arg.]	53	Ki	31.24S	58.02W
Concordia [Braz.]	55	Fh	27.14S	52.01W
Concordia [Ks.-U.S.]	45	Hg	39.34N	97.39W
Concordia [Mex.]	48	Ff	23.17N	106.04W
Concordia Baai	51c	Aa	17.31N	62.58W
Con Cuong	25	Ke	19.02N	104.54 E
Conda	36	Be	11.06S	14.20 E
Condamine River	59	Je	27.00S	149.50 E
Condat	11	Ii	45.22N	2.46 E
Conde	54	Kf	11.49S	37.37W
Condé-en-Brie	12	Fe	49.01N	3.33 E
Condega	49	Dg	13.21N	86.24W
Condé-sur-l'Escaut	12	Fd	50.27N	3.35 E
Condé-sur-Marne	12	Ge	49.03N	4.11 E
Condé-sur-Noireau	11	Ff	48.51N	0.33W
Condobolin	59	Jf	33.05S	147.09 E
Condom	11	Gk	43.58N	0.22 E
Condon	46	Ed	45.14N	120.11W
Condor, Cordillera del-	54	Cd	4.20S	78.30W
Condroz/Condruzisch Plateau	11	Kd	50.25N	5.00 E
Condruzisch Plateau/ Condroz	11	Kd	50.25N	5.00 E
Conecuh River	44	Dj	30.58N	87.14W
Conegliano	14	Ge	45.53N	12.18 E
Conejera, Isla- [Sp.]	13	Nf	38.59N	1.12 E
Conejera, Isla- [Sp.]	13	Oe	39.11N	2.57 E
Conejo	48	De	24.05N	111.00W
Conejo, Cerro-	48	Jg	21.24N	99.06W
Conero	14	Hg	43.33N	13.36 E
Conesa	55	Bk	33.36S	60.21W
Conference Island	51p	Bb	12.09N	61.35W
Conflans-en-Jarnisy	12	He	49.10N	5.51 E
Conflans-Sainte-Honorine	12	Ef	48.59N	2.06 E
Confolens	11	Gh	46.01N	0.40 E
Confuso, Río-	55	Dg	25.09S	57.34W
Conghua	27	Jg	23.31N	113.30 E
Congo [1]	31	Ii	1.00S	15.00 E
Congo	30	Ii	6.04S	12.24 E
Congo, Dem. Rep. of the- → Zaïre [1]	31	Ji	1.00S	25.00 E
Congo Basin (EN)	30	Ih	0.00	17.00 E
Congonhas	55	Ke	20.30S	43.52W
Conil de la Frontera	13	Fh	36.16N	6.05W
Coniston	44	Gb	46.29N	80.51W
Conn, Lough-/Loch Con	9	Dg	54.04N	9.20W
Connacht/Connaught	9	Eh	53.30N	9.00W
Connaught/Connacht	9	Eh	53.30N	9.00W
Conneaut	44	Ge	41.58N	80.34W
Connecticut [2]	43	Mc	41.45N	72.45W
Connecticut River	43	Mc	41.17N	72.21W
Connell	46	Fc	46.40N	118.52W
Connellsville	44	He	40.02N	79.38W
Connemara, Mountains of-	9	Dh	53.30N	9.45W
Connersville	44	Ef	39.39N	85.08W
Conn Lake	42	Kb	70.30N	73.30W
Connors Range	59	Jd	21.40S	149.10 E
Conon	9	Id	57.35N	4.30W
Conquista	55	Id	19.56S	47.33W
Conrad	46	Jb	48.10N	111.57W
Conroe	45	Ik	30.19N	95.27W
Conroe Lake	45	Ik	30.25N	95.37W
Conscripto Bernardi	55	Cj	31.03S	59.05W
Conselheiro Lafaiete	54	Jh	20.40S	43.48W
Conselice	14	Ff	44.31N	11.49 E
Consett	9	Lg	54.51N	1.49W
Consolación del Sur	49	Fb	22.30N	83.31W
Con Son	25	Lg	8.43N	106.36 E
Constance, Lake- (EN)= Bodensee	5	Gf	47.35N	9.25 E
Constanţa [2]	15	Le	44.30N	28.30 E
Constanţa	6	Ig	44.11N	28.39 E
Constantina	13	Gg	37.52N	5.37W
Constantine [3]	32	Ib	36.20N	6.35 E
Constantine	31	He	36.22N	6.37 E
Constantine, Cape-	40	He	58.25N	158.50W
Constitución [Chile]	56	Fe	35.20S	72.25W
Constitución [Ur.]	55	Dj	31.05S	57.50W
Consuegra	13	Ie	39.28N	3.36W
Consuelo Peak	57	Fg	24.58S	148.10 E
Contamana	54	De	7.15S	74.54W
Contas, Rio de-	52	Mg	14.17S	39.01W
Contoy, Isla-	48	Pg	21.30N	86.48W
Contraforte Central, Serra do-	55	Ic	17.15S	47.50W
Contramaestre	49	Ic	20.18N	76.15W
Contraviesa, Sierra-	13	Ih	36.50N	3.10W
Contreras, Embalse de-	13	Ke	39.32N	1.30W
Contreras, Islas-	49	Gj	7.50N	81.47W
Contreras, Puerto de-	13	Ke	39.32N	1.30W
Contres	11	Hg	47.25N	1.26 E
Contumazá	54	Ce	7.22S	78.49W
Contursi	14	Jj	40.39N	15.14 E
Contwig	12	Je	49.15N	7.26 E
Contwoyto Lake	42	Gc	65.40N	110.40W
Conty	12	Ee	49.44N	2.09 E
Convención	54	Db	8.28N	73.20W
Conversano	14	Lj	40.58N	17.07 E
Conway	9	Jh	53.17N	3.50W
Conway [Ar.-U.S.]	43	Id	35.05N	92.26W
Conway [N.H.-U.S.]	44	Ld	43.58N	71.07W
Conway [S.C.-U.S.]	44	Hi	33.51N	79.04W
Conway [Wales-U.K.]	9	Jh	53.17N	3.50W
Conway, Mount-	59	Gd	23.45S	133.25 E
Conway Reef → Ceva-i-Ra	57	Ig	21.45S	174.35 E
Conyers	44	Fi	33.40N	84.00W
Conza, Sella di-	14	Jj	40.50N	15.18 E
Coober Pedy	58	Eg	29.01S	134.43 E
Cooch Behār	25	Hc	26.19N	89.26 E
Cook	66	Ad	59.27S	27.10W
Cook	59	Gf	30.37S	130.25 E
Cook, Bahia-	56	Fi	55.10S	70.10W
Cook, Cap-	63b	Dd	19.32S	169.30 E
Cook, Cape-	46	Ba	50.08N	127.55W
Cook, Mount-	57	Hi	43.36S	170.09 E
Cook, Récif de-	63b	Ad	19.25S	163.50 E
Cooke, Mount-	59	Df	32.25S	116.18 E
Cookes Peak	45	Cj	32.32N	107.44W
Cookeville	44	Eg	36.10N	85.31W
Cook Ice Shelf	66	Je	68.40S	152.30 E
Cook Inlet	38	Dc	60.30N	152.00W
Cook Island	64g	Bb	1.57N	157.28W
Cook Islands [5]	58	Lf	20.00S	158.00W
Cookstown/An Chorr Chriochach	9	Gg	54.39N	6.45W
Cook Strait	57	Ii	41.20S	174.25 E
Cooktown	58	Ff	15.28S	145.15 E
Coolgardie	59	Ef	30.57S	121.10 E
Coolidge [Az.-U.S.]	43	Ee	32.59N	111.31W
Coolidge [Ks.-U.S.]	45	Fg	38.03N	101.59W
Coolidge Dam	46	Jj	33.12N	110.32W
Cooma	59	Jg	36.14S	149.08 E
Coonabarabran	59	Jf	31.16S	149.17 E
Coonamble	59	Jf	30.57S	148.23 E
Coonoor	25	Ff	11.21N	76.49 E
Coon Rapids	45	Jd	45.09N	93.18W
Cooper	45	Ij	33.23N	95.35W
Cooper, Mount-	46	Ga	50.13N	117.12W
Cooper Creek	57	Eg	28.29S	137.46 E
Cooper's Town	44	Il	26.51N	77.31W
Cooperstown [N.D.-U.S.]	45	Gc	47.27N	98.07W
Cooperstown [N.Y.-U.S.]	44	Jd	42.43N	74.56W
Coosa River	44	Di	32.30N	86.16W
Coos Bay	43	Cc	43.22N	124.13W
Coos Bay	46	Ce	43.23N	124.16W
Cootamundra	59	Jf	34.39S	148.02 E
Čop	16	Ce	48.26N	22.14 E
Copaiapó, Río-	56	Fc	27.19S	70.56W
Copainalá	48	Mi	17.05N	93.12W
Copán [3]	49	Cf	14.50N	89.00W
Copan	39	Kh	14.50N	89.09W
Copán	49	Cf	14.50N	89.12W
Copenhagen (EN)= København	6	Hi	55.40N	12.35 E
Copertino	14	Mj	40.16N	18.03 E
Copetonas	55	Bn	38.43N	60.27W
Copiapó	53	Ih	27.22S	70.20W
Çöpköy	15	Jh	41.13N	26.49 E
Coporito	50	Fh	8.56N	62.00W
Coporolo	36	Be	12.56S	13.00 E
Copparo	14	Ff	44.54N	11.49 E
Copper	40	Kd	60.30N	144.50W
Copperbelt [3]	36	Ee	13.00S	28.00 E
Copper Center	40	Jd	61.58N	145.19W
Copper Cliff	42	Jg	46.28N	81.04W
Copper Harbor	44	Db	47.27N	87.53W
Coppermine	39	Hc	67.50N	115.05W
Coppermine	38	Hc	67.49N	115.04W
Coppermine Point	44	Eb	46.59N	84.47W
Copper Queen	37	Dc	17.31S	29.20 E
Coqên (Maindong)	27	Ee	31.15N	85.13 E
Coquet	9	Lf	55.22N	1.37W
Coquetá, Río-	52	Jf	3.08S	64.46W
Coquille	46	Ce	43.11N	124.11W
Coquimbo [2]	56	Fd	31.00S	71.00W
Coquimbo	53	Ih	29.58S	71.21W
Corabia	15	Hf	43.47N	24.30 E
Coracão de Jesus	55	Jc	16.42S	44.22W
Coradi o Cheradi, Isole-	14	Lj	40.27N	17.09 E
Corail	49	Kd	18.34N	73.53W
Corail, Mer de-=Coral Sea (EN)	57	Gf	20.00S	158.00 E
Coral, Cabeza de-	48	Ph	18.47N	87.19W
Coral Gables	43	Kf	25.45N	80.16W
Coral Harbour	39	Kc	64.08N	83.10W
Coral Sea	57	Gf	20.00S	158.00 E
Coral Sea (EN)=Corail, Mer de-	57	Gf	20.00S	158.00 E
Coral Sea Basin (EN)	57	Gf	14.00S	152.00 E
Coral Sea Islands Territory	59	Lc	18.00S	158.00 E
Coralville	45	Kf	41.40N	91.35W
Coralville Lake	45	Kf	41.47N	91.48W
Corantijn River	52	Ke	5.55N	57.05W
Corato	14	Ki	41.09N	16.25 E
Corbara, Lago di-	14	Gh	42.45N	12.15 E
Corbeil-Essones	11	If	48.36N	2.29 E
Corbie	12	Ee	49.55N	2.30 E
Corbières	11	Il	42.55N	2.38 E
Corbigny	11	Jg	47.15N	3.40 E
Corby	9	Mi	52.29N	0.40W
Corcaigh/Cork [2]	9	Ej	52.00N	8.30W
Corcaigh/Cork	6	Fe	51.54N	8.28W
Corcoran	46	Gi	35.45N	117.23W
Corcovado, Cerro-	48	Bb	30.40N	114.55W
Corcovado, Golfo	56	Ff	43.30S	73.30W
Corcovado, Golfo-	52	Ij	43.30S	73.30W
Corcovado, Volcán-	52	Ij	43.12S	72.48W
Corcubión	13	Cb	42.57N	9.11W
Corcubión, Ria de-	13	Cb	42.54N	9.09W
Cordele	43	Ke	31.58N	83.47W
Cordes	11	Hj	44.04N	1.57 E
Cordevole	14	Gd	46.05N	12.04 E
Cordilheiras, Serra das-	54	Ie	7.30S	48.30W
Cordillera [3]	55	Dg	25.15S	57.00W
Cordillera Central [Phil.]	26	Hc	17.20N	120.57 E
Cordillera Central [S.Amer.]	52	If	8.00S	77.00W
Cordillera Occidental	52	Ig	14.00S	74.00W
Cordillera Oriental	52	If	7.00S	76.00W
Córdoba [3]	13	Hf	38.00N	4.50W
Córdoba [Arg.] [2]	56	Hd	32.00S	64.00W
Córdoba [Arg.]	53	Ji	31.25S	64.10W
Córdoba [Col.] [2]	54	Cb	8.20N	75.40W
Córdoba [Mex.]	47	Ee	18.53N	96.56W
Córdoba [Sp.]	6	Fh	37.53N	4.46W
Córdoba, Sierras de-	52	Ji	31.15S	64.00W
Cordova	39	Ec	60.33N	145.46W
Corfu (EN)=Kérkira	5	Hh	39.40N	19.45 E
Corfu, Strait of- (EN) = Kerkíras, Stenón-	15	Dj	39.35N	20.05 E
Corguinho	55	Ed	19.53S	54.52W
Coria	13	Fe	39.59N	6.32W
Coria del Río	13	Fg	37.16N	6.03W
Coribe	55	Ja	13.50S	44.28W
Coricudgy, Mount-	59	Kf	32.50S	150.22 E
Corigliano Calabro	14	Kk	39.36N	16.31 E
Coringa Islets	59	Jc	17.00S	150.00 E
Corinne	46	Ma	50.06N	104.32W
Corinth	43	Je	34.56N	88.31W
Corinth (EN) = Kórinthos	15	Fl	37.55N	22.53 E
Corinth, Gulf of- (EN)= Korinthiakós Kólpos	5	Ih	38.12N	22.30 E
Corinth Canal (EN) = Korinthou, Dhiórix-	15	Fl	37.57N	22.58 E
Corinto [Braz.]	54	Jg	18.21S	44.27W
Corinto [Nic.]	49	Dg	12.29N	87.10W
Corisco	34	Ge	0.55N	9.19 E
Cork/Corcaigh	6	Fe	51.54N	8.28W
Cork/Corcaigh [2]	9	Ej	52.00N	8.30W
Cork Harbour	9	Ej	51.45N	8.15W
Corleone	14	Hm	37.49N	13.18 E
Çorlu	23	Ca	41.09N	27.48 E
Çorlu	15	Kh	41.12N	27.28 E
Cormeilles	12	Ce	49.15N	0.23 E
Cormoran Reef	64a	Bb	7.50N	134.32 E
Cornelio	48	Dc	29.55N	111.08W
Cornélio Procopio	56	Jb	23.08S	50.39W
Cornelius Grinnel Bay	42	Ld	63.20N	64.50W
Corner Brook	39	Ne	48.57N	57.57W
Corner Seamounts (EN)	38	Nf	35.30N	51.30W
Cornia	14	Eh	42.57N	10.33 E
Corning [Ar.-U.S.]	45	Kh	36.24N	90.35W
Corning [Ca.-U.S.]	46	Dg	39.56N	122.11W
Corning [N.Y.-U.S.]	44	Id	42.10N	77.04W
Corno Grande	14	Hh	42.28N	13.34 E
Cornouaille	11	Cg	48.00N	4.00W
Cornwall [3]	9	Ik	50.30N	4.30W
Cornwall	42	Kg	45.02N	74.44W
Cornwall	42	Ia	73.30N	95.00W
Cornwall	9	Hk	50.20N	5.05W
Cornwall	5	Fe	50.30N	4.40W
Cornwall, Cape-	9	Hk	50.08N	5.43W
Cornwallis	42	Ia	75.15N	95.00W
Coro	53	Jd	11.25N	69.41W
Coro, Golfete de-	49	Mh	11.34N	69.53W
Corocoro	54	Eg	17.12S	68.28W
Corocoro, Isla-	50	Fh	8.31N	60.05W
Corod	15	Kd	45.54N	27.37 E
Čoroh	23	Fa	41.36N	41.35 E
Coroico	54	Eg	16.10S	67.44W
Coromandel [Braz.]	55	Id	18.28S	47.13W
Coromandel [N.Z.]	62	Fb	36.46S	175.30 E
Coromandel Coast	21	Kh	14.00N	80.10 E
Coromandel Peninsula	61	Eg	36.50S	175.35 E
Coromandel Range	62	Fb	37.00S	175.40 E
Coron	26	Hd	12.00N	120.12 E
Corona	45	Di	34.15N	105.36W
Corona Bank (EN)	59	Db	12.20S	118.30 E
Coronado, Bahía de-	38	Ki	9.00N	83.50W
Coronado, Isla-	48	Aa	32.25N	117.15W
Coronados, Isla-	48	Dd	26.07N	111.17W
Coronation	66	Re	60.37S	45.35W
Coronation	46	Ja	52.05N	111.27W
Coronation, Cap-	63b	Cf	22.15S	167.02 E
Coronation Gulf	38	Ic	68.25N	110.00W
Coronda	55	Bj	31.58S	60.55W
Coronda, Laguna-	55	Bk	32.06S	60.52W
Coronel	56	Fe	37.01S	73.08W
Coronel Bogado	56	Ic	27.11S	56.18W
Coronel Dorrego	56	He	38.42S	61.17W
Coronel du Graty	55	Bh	27.40S	60.56W
Coronel Fabriciano	54	Jg	19.31S	42.38W
Coronel Oviedo	56	Ic	25.25S	56.27W
Coronel Ponce	55	Eb	15.34S	55.01W
Coronel Pringles	56	He	37.58S	61.22W
Coronel Rodolfo Bunge	55	Bm	37.34S	60.08W
Coronel Suárez	56	He	37.28S	61.55W
Coronel Vidal	55	Dm	37.27S	57.43W
Coronel Vivida	55	Fg	25.58S	52.34W
Coropuna, Nudo-	52	Ig	15.30S	72.41W
Çorovoda	15	Di	40.30N	20.13 E
Corozal [Blz.]	49	Cd	18.24N	88.24W
Corozal [Blz.]	49	Cd	18.15N	88.17W
Corozal [Col.]	49	Ji	9.18N	75.17W
Corpus Christi	39	Jg	27.48N	97.24W
Corpus Christi, Lake-	45	Hl	28.10N	97.53W
Corpus Christi Bay	45	Hm	27.48N	97.20W
Corque	54	Eg	18.21S	67.42W
Corral de Bustos	55	Ak	33.17S	62.12W
Corrèggio	14	Ef	44.46N	10.47 E
Córrego do Ouro	55	Gc	16.18S	50.32W
Corrente	54	If	10.27S	45.10W
Corrente, Rio- [Braz.]	54	Hg	19.19S	50.50W
Corrente, Rio- [Braz.]	55	Ka	13.08S	43.28W
Corrente, Rio- [Braz.]	55	Ib	14.14S	46.58W
Correntes	55	Ec	17.37S	54.59W
Correntes, Rio-	55	Ec	17.38S	55.08W
Correnti, Capo delle-	5	Hh	36.40N	15.05 E
Correntina	54	Jf	13.20S	44.39W
Corrèze	11	Hi	45.10N	1.28 E
Corrèze [3]	11	Hi	45.15N	1.50 E
Corrib, Lough-/Loch Coirib	9	Dh	53.05N	9.10W
Corrientes [2]	56	Ic	29.00S	58.00W
Corrientes	53	Kh	27.30S	58.50W
Corrientes, Cabo- [Arg.]	55	Dn	38.01S	57.32W
Corrientes, Cabo- [Col.]	54	Cb	5.30N	77.34W
Corrientes, Cabo- [Cuba]	49	Ec	21.45N	84.31W
Corrientes, Cabo- [Mex.]	38	Ig	20.25N	105.42W
Corrientes, Ensenada de-	49	Ec	21.45N	84.31W
Corrientes, Río- [Arg.]	55	Cj	30.21S	59.33W
Corrientes, Río- [Peru]	54	Dd	3.43S	74.40W
Corrieyairack Pass	9	Id	57.05N	4.40W
Corrigan	45	Ik	31.00N	94.50W
Corrigin	59	Df	32.21S	117.52 E
Corry	44	He	41.56N	79.39W
Corryong	59	Jg	36.12S	147.54 E
Corse=Corsica (EN)	5	Gg	42.00N	9.00 E
Corse, Cap-	5	Gg	43.00N	9.23 E
Corse-du-Sud [3]	11a	Ab	41.50N	9.00 E
Corsewall Point	9	Hf	55.02N	5.05W
Corsica (EN)=Corse	5	Gg	42.00N	9.00 E
Corsica, Canale di-	14	Dh	42.45N	9.45 E
Corsicana	43	He	32.06N	96.28W
Cort Adelaer, Kap-	41	Hf	61.45N	42.00W
Corte	11a	Ba	42.18N	9.09 E
Cortegana	13	Fg	37.55N	6.49W
Cortés [3]	49	Cf	15.30N	88.00W
Cortes	13	Kc	41.55N	1.25W
Cortez	43	Fd	37.21N	108.35W
Cortina d'Ampezzo	14	Gd	46.32N	12.08 E
Čortkov	16	De	48.59N	25.50 E
Cortland	44	Id	42.36N	76.10W
Cortona	14	Fg	43.16N	11.59 E
Corubal	34	Bc	11.57N	15.06W
Coruche	13	Df	38.57N	8.31W
Çoruh	23	Fa	41.36N	41.35 E
Çorum	24	Fb	40.29N	35.36 E
Çorum	23	Da	40.33N	34.58 E
Corumbá	53	Kg	19.01S	57.39W
Corumbá, Rio-	54	Ig	18.19S	48.55W
Corumbá de Goiás	55	Hb	15.55S	48.48W
Corumbáiba	55	Hd	18.09S	48.34W
Corumo, Río-	50	Fi	6.49N	60.52W
Corvallis	43	Cc	44.34N	123.16W
Corvo	30	De	39.42N	31.06W
Corzuela	55	Bh	26.57S	60.58W
Cosalá	48	Fe	24.23N	106.41W
Cosamaloapan	48	Lh	18.22N	95.48W
Cosenza	6	Hh	39.18N	16.15 E
Coshocton	44	Ge	40.16N	81.53W
Cosigüina, Punta-	49	Dg	12.54N	87.41W
Cosmoledo Group	30	Li	9.43S	47.35 E
Cosne-sur-Loire	11	Ig	47.24N	2.55 E
Cosquín	56	Hd	31.15S	64.29W
Cossato	14	Ce	45.34N	8.10 E
Costa, Cordillera de la-	52	Je	9.50N	66.00W
Costa Rica [1]	39	Ki	10.00N	84.00W
Costa Verde	13	Ga	43.40N	5.40W
Costeşti	15	He	44.40N	24.53 E
Costiera, Catena-	14	Kk	39.25N	16.10 E
Coswig	10	Je	51.08N	13.35 E
Cotabato	26	He	7.13N	124.15 E
Cotagaita	54	Eh	20.50S	65.41W
Cotahuasi	54	Dg	15.12S	72.56W
Côte d'Ivoire=Ivory Coast (EN) [1]	31	Gh	8.00N	5.00W
Côte d'Or	11	Kg	47.10N	4.50 E
Côte-d'Or [3]	11	Kg	47.30N	4.50 E
Cotentin	5	Ff	49.30N	1.30W
Côtes-du-Nord [3]	11	Df	48.25N	2.40W
Cotiella	13	Mb	42.31N	0.19 E
Cotmeana	15	He	44.24N	24.45 E
Cotmeana	15	He	44.58N	24.37 E
Cotonou	31	Hh	6.21N	2.26 E
Cotopaxi, Volcán-	52	If	0.40S	78.26W
Cotswold Hills	9	Kj	51.45N	2.10W
Cottage Grove	46	De	43.48N	123.03W
Cottbus [2]	10	Je	51.45N	14.00 E
Cottbus/Chośebuz	10	Ke	51.46N	14.20 E
Cottenham	12	Cb	52.17N	0.08 E
Cottondale	44	Ej	30.48N	85.23W
Cottonwood Wash	46	Ji	35.05N	110.22W
Cotuí	49	Ld	19.03N	70.09W
Cotulla	45	Gl	28.26N	99.14W
Coubre, Pointe de la-	11	Ei	45.42N	1.14W
Couburg	10	Gf	50.15N	10.58 E
Coucy-le-Château-Auffrique	12	Fe	49.31N	3.19 E
Coudekerque-Branche	12	Ec	51.02N	2.24 E
Coudersport	44	He	41.46N	78.01W
Couedic, Cape du-	59	Hg	36.10S	136.40 E
Couesnon	11	Ef	48.37N	1.31W
Couhé	11	Gh	46.18N	0.11 E
Couilly-Pont-aux-Dames	12	Ef	48.53N	2.52 E
Coulee Dam	46	Fb	48.00N	118.59W
Coulihaut	51g	Bb	15.30N	61.29W
Coulman Island	66	Kf	73.28S	169.45 E
Coulogne	12	Dd	50.55N	1.53 E
Coulommiers	11	Jf	48.49N	3.05 E
Coulonge, Rivière-	44	Ic	45.51N	76.45W
Coulounieix-Chamiers	11	Gi	45.10N	0.42 E
Council	46	Gd	44.44N	116.26W
Council Bluffs	43	Hc	41.16N	95.52W
Courcelles	12	Gd	50.28N	4.22 E
Courcelles-Chaussy	12	Ie	49.07N	6.24 E
Courland (EN) =Kurzeme	5	Id	57.00N	20.30 E
Courmayeur	14	Ae	45.47N	6.58 E
Cours	11	Kh	46.06N	4.19 E
Courseulles-sur-Mer	12	Be	49.20N	0.27W
Courtenay	42	Fg	49.41N	125.00W
Courtisols	12	Gf	48.59N	4.31 E
Courtrai/Kortrijk	11	Jd	50.50N	3.16 E
Coushatta	45	Jj	32.00N	93.21W
Cousin	11	Kh	46.58N	4.15 E
Coutances	11	Ee	49.03N	1.26W
Couto de Magalhães, Rio-	55	Fa	13.37S	53.09W
Coutras	11	Fi	45.02N	0.08W
Couture, Lac -	42	Jd	60.05N	75.20W
Couvin	11	Kd	50.03N	4.20 E
Couvin-Mariembourg	12	Gd	50.06N	4.31 E
Covarrubias	13	Ib	42.04N	3.31W
Covasna [2]	15	Id	46.00N	26.00 E
Covasna	15	Jd	45.51N	26.11 E
Coveñas	49	Ji	9.25N	75.42W
Coventry	9	Li	52.25N	1.30W
Covilhã	13	Ed	40.17N	7.30W
Covington [Ga.-U.S.]	44	Fi	33.37N	83.51W
Covington [Ky.-U.S.]	43	Kd	39.05N	84.30W
Covington [La.-U.S.]	45	Kk	30.29N	90.06W
Covington [Tn.-U.S.]	44	Ch	35.34N	89.39W
Covington [Va.-U.S.]	44	Hg	37.48N	79.59W
Cowal	9	He	56.05N	5.10W
Cowan, Lake-	59	Ef	31.50S	121.50 E
Cowan Knob	45	Ji	35.52N	93.29W
Cowell	59	Hf	33.41S	136.55 E
Cowes	12	Ad	50.46N	1.18W
Cowichan Lake	46	Cb	48.54N	124.20W
Cowra	59	Jf	33.50S	148.41 E
Coxim	53	Kg	18.30S	54.45W
Coxim, Rio-	55	Ed	18.34S	54.46W
Cox's Bāzār	25	Id	21.26N	91.59 E
Coyah	34	Cd	9.43N	13.23W
Coyame	48	Gc	29.28N	105.06W
Coyanosa Draw	45	Ek	31.18N	103.06W
Coycoyan, Sierra de-	48	Ji	17.30N	98.20W
Coyle—Coig, Río-	56	Gh	50.58S	69.11W
Coyote, Río-	48	Cb	30.48N	112.35W
Coyotitán	48	Ff	23.47N	106.35W
Coyuca, Laguna de-	48	Ii	16.57N	100.05W
Cozia, Pasul-	15	Hd	45.15N	24.15 E
Cozumel	48	Pg	20.31N	86.55W
Cozumel, Isla de-	47	Gd	20.25N	86.55W
Cradock	31	Jl	32.08S	25.36 E
Craig [Ak.-U.S.]	40	Me	55.29N	133.09W
Craig [Co.-U.S.]	43	Fc	40.31N	107.33W
Craigmont	46	Gc	46.15N	116.28W
Craigs Range	59	Ke	26.40S	151.30 E
Crailsheim	10	Gg	49.09N	10.05 E
Craiova	6	Ig	44.19N	23.48 E
Cranbrook [Austl.]	59	Df	34.18S	117.32 E
Cranbrook [B.C.-Can.]	42	Fg	49.31N	115.46W
Cranbrook [Eng.-U.K.]	12	Cc	51.05N	0.32 E
Crandon	45	Ld	45.34N	88.54W
Crane [Or.-U.S.]	46	Fe	43.25N	118.35W
Crane [Tx.-U.S.]	45	Ek	31.24N	102.21W
Crane Lake	45	Jb	48.16N	92.28W
Crane Lake	46	Ka	50.06N	109.06W
Cranleigh	12	Bc	51.08N	0.29W
Craon	11	Fg	47.51N	0.57W
Craonne	12	Fe	49.26N	3.47 E
Crapaud, Puy-	11	Fh	46.40N	0.40W
Crary Mountains	66	Of	76.48S	117.40W
Crasna	15	Fa	48.09N	22.20 E
Crasna [Rom.]	15	Kc	46.31N	27.51 E
Crasna [Rom.]	15	Fb	47.10N	22.54 E
Crater Lake [Or.-U.S.]	43	Cc	42.56N	122.06W
Crater Lake [St.Vin.]	51n	Ba	13.19N	61.11W
Crateús	53	Lf	5.10S	40.40W
Crati	14	Kk	39.43N	16.31 E
Crato [Braz.]	54	Ke	7.14S	39.23W
Crato [Port.]	13	Ee	39.17N	7.39W
Crau	11	Kk	43.36N	4.50 E
Crauford, Cape -	42	Jb	73.44N	84.51W
Cravo Norte	54	Db	6.17N	70.12W
Crawford	45	Ee	42.41N	103.25W
Crawfordsville	44	De	40.02N	86.54W
Crawley	9	Mj	51.07N	0.12W
Crazy Mountains	46	Jc	46.08N	110.20W
Crazy Peak	43	Eb	46.01N	110.16W
Creciente, Isla-	48	De	24.23N	111.37W
Crécy-en-Ponthieu	12	Dd	50.15N	1.53 E
Crécy-la-Chapelle	12	Ef	48.51N	2.55 E
Crécy-sur-Serre	12	Fe	49.42N	3.37 E
Crediton	9	Jk	50.47N	3.39W
Cree [Sask.-Can.]	42	Ge	58.50N	105.40W
Cree [Scot.-U.K.]	9	Ig	54.52N	4.20W
Creede	45	Ch	37.51N	106.56W
Creel	47	Cc	27.45N	107.38W
Cree Lake	42	Ge	57.30N	106.30W
Creglingen	10	Gg	49.28N	10.02 E
Creil	11	Ie	49.16N	2.29 E
Crema	14	De	45.22N	9.41 E
Cremenea, Braţul-	15	Ke	44.57N	27.54 E
Crémieu, Plateau de-	11	Li	45.40N	5.30 E
Cremona	14	Ee	45.07N	10.02 E
Crepaja	15	Dd	45.01N	20.39 E
Crepori, Rio-	54	Ge	5.42S	57.08W
Crépy-en-Valois	11	Ie	49.14N	2.54 E
Cres [Yugo.]	14	If	44.40N	14.25 E
Cres [Yugo.]	14	If	44.58N	14.24 E
Crescent	46	Ee	43.29N	121.41W
Crescent City	43	Cc	41.45N	124.12W
Crescent Lake	44	Gk	29.28N	81.30W
Crespo	55	Bk	32.02S	60.19W

Index Symbols

- [1] Independent Nation
- [2] State, Region
- [3] District, County
- [4] Municipality
- [5] Colony, Dependency
- Continent
- Physical Region
- Historical or Cultural Region
- Mount, Mountain
- Volcano
- Hill
- Mountains, Mountain Range
- Hills, Escarpment
- Plateau, Upland
- Pass, Gap
- Plain, Lowland
- Delta
- Salt Flat
- Valley, Canyon
- Crater, Cave
- Karst Features
- Depression
- Polder
- Desert, Dunes
- Forest, Woods
- Heath, Steppe
- Oasis
- Cape, Point
- Coast, Beach
- Cliff
- Peninsula
- Isthmus
- Sandbank
- Island
- Atoll
- Rock, Reef
- Islands, Archipelago
- Rocks, Reefs
- Coral Reef
- Well, Spring
- Geyser
- River, Stream
- Waterfall Rapids
- River Mouth, Estuary
- Lake
- Salt Lake
- Intermittent Lake
- Reservoir
- Swamp, Pond
- Canal
- Glacier
- Ice Shelf, Pack Ice
- Ocean
- Sea
- Gulf, Bay
- Strait, Fjord
- Lagoon
- Bank
- Seamount
- Tablemount
- Ridge
- Shelf
- Basin
- Escarpment, Sea Scarp
- Fracture
- Trench, Abyss
- National Park, Reserve
- Point of Interest
- Recreation Site
- Cave, Cavern
- Historic Site
- Ruins
- Wall, Walls
- Church, Abbey
- Temple
- Scientific Station
- Airport
- Port
- Lighthouse
- Mine
- Tunnel
- Dam, Bridge

Crest 11 Lj 44.44N 5.02 E
Crested Butte 45 Cg 38.52N 106.59W
Creston [B.C.-Can.] 46 Gb 49.06N 116.31W
Creston [Ia.-U.S.] 43 Ic 41.04N 94.22W
Crestone Peak 45 Dh 37.58N 105.36W
Crestview 43 Jc 30.46N 86.34W
Creswell 44 Ih 35.52N 76.23W
Creswell Bay 42 Ib 72.40N 93.30W
Creswell Creek 59 Hc 18.10S 135.11 E
Crete 45 Hf 40.38N 96.58W
Crete (EN) = Kriti 5 Ih 35.15N 24.45 E
Crete (EN) = Kriti [2] 15 Hn 35.35N 25.00 E
Crete, Sea of- (EN) = Kritikón Pélagos 15 Hn 36.00N 25.00 E
Créteil 11 If 48.47N 2.28 E
Cretin, Cape- 60 Di 6.40S 147.52 E
Creus, Cabo de-/Creus, Cap de- 5 Gg 42.19N 3.19 E
Creus, Cap de-/Creus, Cabo de- 5 Gg 42.19N 3.19 E
Creuse [3] 11 Hh 46.05N 2.00 E
Creuse 11 Gg 47.00N 0.34 E
Creutzwald 11 Me 49.12N 6.41 E
Crevecoeur-en-Auge 12 Ce 49.07N 0.01 E
Crèvecoeur-le-Grand 12 Ee 49.36N 2.05 E
Crevillente 13 Lf 38.15N 0.48W
Crewe 9 Kh 53.05N 2.27W
Crézancy 12 Fe 49.03N 3.30 E
Criciúma 53 Lh 28.40S 49.23W
Cricket Mountains 46 Ig 38.50N 113.00W
Crieff 9 Je 56.23N 3.52W
Criel-sur-Mer 12 Dd 50.01N 1.19 E
Criel sur Mer-Mesnil Val 12 Dd 50.03N 1.20 E
Crikvenica 14 Ie 45.11N 14.42 E
Crillon 12 De 49.31N 1.56 E
Crimea (EN)=Krymski Poluostrov 5 Jf 45.00N 34.00 E
Crimean Mountains (EN)= Krymskije Gory 5 Jg 44.45N 34.30 E
Crimmitschau 10 If 50.49N 12.23 E
Criquetot-l'Esneval 12 Ce 49.39N 0.16 E
Crissolo 14 Bf 44.42N 7.09 E
Cristal, Monts de- 36 Bb 0.30N 10.30 E
Cristal, Sierra del- 49 Jc 20.33N 75.31W
Cristalândia 54 If 10.36S 49.11W
Cristalina 54 Ig 16.45S 47.36W
Cristalino, Rio- 54 Hf 12.40S 50.40W
Cristallo 14 Gd 46.34N 12.12 E
Cristóbal Colón, Pico 52 Id 10.50N 73.45W
Cristuru Secuiesc 15 Ic 46.35N 25.47 E
Crişu Alb 15 Ec 46.42N 21.16 E
Crişu Negru 15 Ec 46.42N 21.16 E
Crişu Repede 15 Dc 46.55N 20.59 E
Crixás 55 Hb 14.27S 49.58W
Crixás-Açu, Rio- 54 Hf 13.19S 50.36W
Crixás Mirim, Rio- 55 Ga 13.28S 50.36W
Crkvena Planina 15 Fg 42.48N 22.22 E
Crna Gora 15 Eg 42.16N 21.35 E
Crna Gora 15 Ce 44.05N 19.50 E
Crna Gora = Montenegro (EN) [2] 15 Cg 42.30N 19.18 E
Crna Gora=Montenegro (EN) 15 Cg 42.30N 19.18 E
Crna Reka 15 Ef 43.50N 21.55 E
Crna reka 15 Eh 41.33N 21.59 E
Crni Drim 15 Dg 42.05N 20.23 E
Crni Timok 15 Ff 43.55N 22.18 E
Črni Vrh 14 Jd 46.29N 15.14 E
Crni vrh 14 Kf 44.36N 16.30 E
Črnomelj 14 Je 45.34N 15.12 E
Croatia (EN) = Hrvatska [2] 14 Jf 45.00N 15.30 E
Croatia (EN) = Hrvatska 5 Hf 45.00N 15.30 E
Croatia (EN) = Hrvatska 14 Je 45.00N 15.30 E
Crocker, Banjaran- 26 Ge 5.40N 116.20 E
Crockett 45 Ik 31.19N 95.28W
Crocq 11 Ii 45.52N 2.22 E
Crocus Bay 51b Ab 18.13N 63.05W
Croisette, Cap- 11 Lk 43.13N 5.20 E
Croisic, Pointe du- 11 Dg 47.17N 2.33W
Croisilles 12 Ed 50.12N 2.53 E
Croissy-sur-Celle 12 Ee 49.42N 2.11 E
Croix, Lac la- 45 Jb 48.21N 92.05W
Croix-Haute, Col de la- 11 Lj 44.43N 5.40 E
Croker, Cape- 59 Gb 10.58S 132.35 E
Croker Bay 42 Jb 74.38N 83.15W
Croker Island 59 Gb 11.10S 132.30 E
Cromarty 9 Id 57.40N 4.02W
Cromer 9 Oi 52.56N 1.18 E
Cromwell 62 Cf 45.03S 169.14 E
Crooked Island 47 Jd 22.45N 74.13W
Crooked Island Passage 47 Jd 22.55N 74.35W
Crooked River 46 Ed 44.34N 121.16W
Crookston 43 Hb 47.47N 96.37W
Crosby [Mn.-U.S.] 45 Jc 46.28N 93.57W
Crosby [N.D.-U.S.] 45 Eb 48.55N 103.18W
Cross 34 Ge 4.55N 8.15 E
Cross City 44 Fk 29.32N 83.07W
Crossett 45 Kj 33.08N 91.58W
Cross Fell 9 Kg 54.42N 2.29W
Cross Lake 42 Hf 54.47N 97.22W
Crossman Peak 46 Hi 34.32N 114.07W
Cross River [2] 34 Gd 5.40N 8.10 E
Cross Sound 40 Le 58.10N 136.30W
Crotone 14 Lk 39.05N 17.08 E
Crotto 55 Bm 36.35S 60.10W
Crouch 12 Cc 51.37N 0.53 E
Crow Agency 46 Ld 45.36N 107.27W
Crowborough 12 Cc 51.03N 0.09 E
Crow Creek 45 Df 40.23N 104.29W
Crowell 45 Gj 33.59N 99.43W
Crow Lake 45 Jb 49.12N 93.57W
Crowley 45 Jk 30.13N 92.22W
Crowley, Lake- 46 Fh 37.37N 118.44W
Crowley Ridge 45 Ki 35.45N 90.45W
Crownpoint 45 Bi 35.42N 108.07W
Crown Prince Frederik 42 Ic 70.05N 86.40W
Crowsnest Pass 42 Gg 49.00N 114.30W
Crows Nest Peak 45 Ed 44.03N 103.58W
Croydon 59 Ic 18.12S 142.14 E
Croydon, London- 9 Mj 51.23N 0.07W
Crozet, Iles- 30 Mm 46.30S 51.00 E
Crozet Basin (EN) 3 Gm 39.00S 60.00 E
Crozet Ridge (EN) 3 Fn 45.00S 45.00 E
Crozon 11 Bf 48.15N 4.29W
Crozon, Presqu'île de- 11 Bf 48.15N 4.25W
Crucero, Cerro- 48 Gg 21.41N 104.25W
Cruces 49 Gb 22.21N 80.16W
Crump Lake 46 Fe 42.17N 119.50W
Crumpton Point 51g Ba 15.35N 61.19W
Cruz, Cabo- 47 Ie 19.51N 77.44W
Cruz Alta [Arg.] 55 Bk 33.01S 61.49W
Cruz Alta [Braz.] 53 Kh 28.39S 53.36W
Cruz del Eje 56 Hd 30.44S 64.48W
Cruzeiro do Oeste 56 Jb 23.46S 53.04W
Cruzeiro do Sul 53 If 7.38S 72.36W
Cruzen Island 66 Mf 74.47S 140.42W
Cruz Grande 48 Ji 16.44N 99.08W
Crvanj 14 Mg 43.25N 18.11 E
Crvenka 15 Cd 45.39N 19.28 E
Crystal Brook 59 Hf 33.21S 138.13 E
Crystal City [Man.-Can.] 45 Gb 49.08N 98.57W
Crystal City [Tx.-U.S.] 45 Gl 28.41N 99.50W
Crystal Falls 44 Cb 46.06N 88.20W
Crystal Springs 45 Kk 31.59N 90.21W
Csákvár 10 Oi 47.24N 18.27 E
Cserhat 10 Pi 47.55N 19.30 E
Csongrád [2] 10 Qj 46.25N 20.15 E
Csongrad 10 Qj 46.42N 20.09 E
Csorna 10 Ni 47.37N 17.15 E
ČSSR → Československá Socialistická Republika [1] 6 Hf 49.30N 17.00 E
Csurgó 10 Nj 46.16N 17.06 E
Ctesiphon 24 Kf 33.05N 44.35 E
Ču 21 Ie 45.00N 67.44 E
Ču 22 Je 43.33N 73.45 E
Cuajinicuilapa 48 Ji 16.28N 98.25W
Cuale 36 Cd 7.40S 17.01 E
Cuamba 31 Kj 14.49S 36.33 E
Cuan an Fhóid Duibh/ Blacksod Bay 9 Dg 54.08N 10.00W
Cuanavale 36 Cf 15.07S 19.14 E
Cuan Bhaile Átha Cliath/ Dublin Bay 9 Gh 53.20N 6.06W
Cuan Chill Ala/Killala Bay 9 Dg 54.15N 9.10W
Cuan Dhun Dealgan/ Dundalk Bay 9 Gh 53.57N 6.17W
Cuan Dhún Droma/Dundrum Bay 9 Hg 54.13N 5.45W
Cuando 30 Jj 18.27S 23.32 E
Cuando-Cubango [3] 36 Df 16.00S 20.30 E
Cuan Eochaille/Youghal Harbour 9 Fj 51.52N 7.50W
Cuangar 36 Cf 17.36S 18.37 E
Cuango 30 Ii 3.14S 17.22 E
Cuango [Ang.] 36 Cd 9.07S 18.05 E
Cuango [Ang.] 36 Cd 6.17S 16.41 E
Cuan Loch Garman/Wexford Harbour 9 Gi 52.20N 6.25W
Cuan Mó/Clew Bay 9 Dh 53.50N 9.50W
Cuan na Gaillimhe/Galway Bay 5 Fe 53.10N 9.15W
Cuan na gCaorach/Sheep Haven 9 Ff 55.10N 7.52W
Cuan Phort Láirge/ Waterford Harbour 9 Gi 52.10N 6.57W
Cuan Shligigh/Sligo Bay 9 Eg 54.20N 8.40W
Cuanza 30 Ii 9.19S 13.08 E
Cuanza Norte [3] 36 Bd 8.50S 14.30 E
Cuanza Sul [3] 36 Be 10.50S 14.50 E
Cuareim, Arroyo- 55 Dj 30.12S 57.36W
Cuaró 55 Dj 30.37S 56.54W
Cuaró Grande, Arroyo- 55 Dj 30.18S 57.12W
Cuarto, Rio- 56 Hd 33.25S 63.02W
Cuatir 36 Cf 17.01S 18.09 E
Cuatro Ciénegas de Carranza 48 Hd 26.59N 102.05W
Cuauhtémoc 47 Cc 28.25N 106.52W
Cuautitlán 48 Jh 19.40N 99.11W
Cuay Grande 55 Di 28.40S 56.17W
Cuba 38 Lg 21.30N 80.00W
Cuba [1] 39 Lg 21.30N 80.00W
Cuba [Mo.-U.S.] 45 Kg 38.04N 91.24W
Cuba [N.M.-U.S.] 45 Ch 36.01N 107.04W
Cuba [Port.] 13 Ef 38.10N 7.53W
Cubabi, Cerro- 48 Cb 31.42N 112.46W
Cubagua, Isla- 50 Dg 10.49N 64.11W
Cubal 36 Be 13.03S 14.15 E
Cubal [Ang.] 36 Be 11.29S 13.48 E
Cubal [Ang.] 36 Bf 15.22S 12.39 E
Cubango 30 Jj 18.53N 22.24 E
Çubuk 24 Eb 40.59N 32.05 E
Čubukulah, Gora- 20 Kc 66.23N 153.59 E
Cucalón, Sierra de- 13 Kd 40.59N 1.10W
Cuchi 36 Ce 14.40S 16.52 E
Cuchi 30 Ij 15.28S 17.21 E
Cuchibi 36 De 15.00S 20.45 E
Cuchilla Áquila, Cerro- 48 Ig 21.27N 101.03W
Cuchivero, Rio- 50 Di 7.40N 65.57W
Cuchumatanes, Sierra de los- 49 Bf 15.35N 91.25W
Cuckfield 12 Bd 51.01N 0.08W
Cuckmere 12 Cd 50.45N 0.09 E
Cucui 54 Ec 1.12N 66.50W
Cucumbi 36 Ce 10.17S 19.03 E
Cucurpe 48 Db 30.20N 110.43W
Cúcuta 53 Ie 7.54N 72.31W
Cudahy 45 Me 42.57N 87.52W
Cudalbi 15 Kd 45.47N 27.42 E
Cuddalore 22 Jh 11.45N 79.45 E
Cuddapah 25 Ff 14.28N 78.49 E
Čudovo 19 Dd 59.08N 31.41 E
Čudskoje Ozero=Peipus, Lake- (EN) 5 Id 58.45N 27.30 E
Cue 59 De 27.25S 117.54 E
Cuebe 36 Cf 15.48S 17.30 E
Cuelei 36 Cf 15.33S 17.21 E
Cuéllar 13 Hc 41.29N 4.19W
Cuemba 36 Ce 12.09S 18.07 E
Cuenca [3] 13 Ke 40.00N 2.00W
Cuenca [Ec.] 53 If 2.53S 78.59W
Cuenca [Sp.] 13 Jd 40.04N 2.08W
Cuenca, Serranía de- 5 Fg 40.10N 1.55W
Cuencamé de Ceniceros 48 He 24.53N 103.42W
Cuera/Chur 14 Dd 46.50N 9.35 E
Cuerda del Pozo, Embalse de la- 13 Jc 41.51N 2.44W
Cuernavaca 39 Jh 18.55N 99.15W
Cuero 45 Hl 29.06N 97.18W
Cuevas del Almanzora 13 Kg 37.18N 1.53W
Cugir 15 Gd 45.50N 23.22 E
Cugo 36 Cd 7.22S 17.06 E
Čugujev 16 Je 49.50N 36.41 E
Čugujevka 28 Mb 44.08N 133.53 E
Čuhloma 19 Ed 58.47N 42.41 E
Cuiabá 53 Kg 15.35S 56.05W
Cuiabá, Rio- 52 Kg 17.05S 56.36W
Cuiabá Mirim, Rio- 55 Ec 16.20S 55.55W
Cuidado, Punta- 65d Bb 27.08S 109.19W
Cuijk, Cuijk en Sint Agatha- 12 Hc 51.44N 5.52 E
Cuijk en Sint Agatha-Cuijk 12 Hc 51.44N 5.52 E
Cuilapa 49 Bf 14.17N 90.18W
Cuillin Hills 9 Gd 57.14N 6.15W
Cuilo 30 Ii 3.22S 17.22 E
Cúil Raithin/Coleraine 9 Gf 55.08N 6.40W
Cuiluan 27 Mb 47.39N 128.34 E
Cuima 36 Ce 13.14S 15.38 E
Cuito 30 Jj 18.01S 20.48 E
Cuito Cuanavale 31 Ij 15.13S 19.08 E
Cuitzeo, Lago de- 48 Ih 19.55N 101.05W
Cuiuni, Rio- 54 Fd 0.45S 63.07W
Cujmir 15 Fe 44.13N 22.56 E
Čukata 15 Ih 41.50N 25.15 E
Čukotski Nacionalny okrug [3] 20 Mc 66.00N 172.30 E
Čukotski Poluostrov= Chukchi Peninsula (EN) 21 Uc 66.00N 175.00W
Čukotskoje More=Chukchi Sea (EN) 67 Bd 69.00N 171.00W
Çukurca 24 Jd 37.15N 43.37 E
Çukurdağı 15 Ll 37.58N 28.44 E
Čulakkurgan 19 Gg 43.48N 69.12 E
Culan 11 Ih 46.33N 2.21 E
Cu Lao, Hon- 25 Lf 10.30N 109.13 E
Culasi 26 Hd 11.26N 122.03 E
Culbertson 46 Mb 48.09N 104.31W
Culebra, Isla de- 49 Od 18.19N 65.17W
Culebra, Sierra de la- 13 Fc 41.55N 6.20W
Culebra Peak 45 Dh 37.06N 105.10W
Culemborg 12 Hc 51.57N 5.14 E
Culiacán, Rio de- 48 Fe 24.31N 107.41W
Culiacán Rosales 39 Ig 24.48N 107.24W
Culion 26 Gd 11.50N 119.55 E
Culion 26 Hd 11.53N 120.01 E
Culiseu, Rio- 54 Hf 12.14S 53.17W
Cullera 13 Le 39.10N 0.15W
Cullman 43 Je 34.11N 86.51W
Čulman 22 Od 56.52N 124.52 E
Culpeper 44 Hf 38.28N 78.01W
Culuene, Rio- 52 Kg 12.56S 52.51W
Culukidze 16 Mh 42.18N 42.25 E
Culver, Point- 59 Ef 32.54S 124.43 E
Culverden 62 Ee 42.46S 172.51 E
Čulym 20 De 55.06N 80.58 E
Čulym 21 Kd 57.40N 83.50 E
Čulyšman 20 Df 51.20N 87.45 E
Cuma 36 Ce 12.52S 15.04 E
Cumaná 53 Jd 10.28N 64.10W
Cumanacoa 50 Eg 10.15N 63.55W
Cumaovası 15 Kk 38.15N 27.09 E
Cumbal, Volcán- 54 Cc 0.57N 77.52W
Cumberland 9 Kg 54.40N 2.50W
Cumberland 38 Kf 37.09N 88.25W
Cumberland [B.C.-Can.] 46 Cb 49.37N 125.01W
Cumberland [Md.-U.S.] 43 Ld 39.39N 78.46W
Cumberland [Va.-U.S.] 44 Hg 37.31N 78.16W
Cumberland, Cap- 63b Cb 14.39S 166.37 E
Cumberland, Lake- 44 Eg 36.57N 84.55W
Cumberland Bay 51n Ba 13.16N 61.17W
Cumberland Island 44 Gj 30.51N 81.27W
Cumberland Islands 59 Jd 20.40S 149.10 E
Cumberland Lake 42 Hf 54.00N 102.20W
Cumberland Peninsula 38 Mc 66.50N 64.00W
Cumberland Plateau 38 Kf 36.00N 85.00W
Cumberland Sound 38 Mc 65.10N 65.30W
Cumbernauld 9 Jf 55.58N 3.59W
Cumbre, Paso de la-/ Bermejo, Paso- 52 Ii 32.50S 70.05W
Cumbria [3] 9 Kg 54.35N 2.45W
Cumbrian Mountains 9 Jg 54.30N 3.05W
Čumerna 15 Ig 42.47N 25.58 E
Čumikan 20 If 54.42N 135.19 E
Cummins 59 Hf 34.16S 135.44 E
Cumnock 9 If 55.27N 4.16W
Cumpas 48 Eb 30.02N 109.48W
Çumra 24 Ed 37.34N 32.48 E
Čumyš 20 Df 53.30N 83.10 E
Čuna 21 Ld 57.42N 95.35 E
Cunagua 49 Hb 22.05N 78.20W
Cuñapirú 55 Ej 31.32S 55.35W
Cuñapirú, Arroyo- 55 Ej 31.12S 55.31W
Cuñapirú, Cuchilla de- 55 Ej 31.12S 55.36W
Cunaviche, Rio- 50 Ci 7.19N 67.11W
Cunderdin 59 Df 31.39S 117.15 E
Cundinamarca [2] 54 Db 5.00N 74.00W
Čundža 19 Hg 43.32N 79.28 E
Cunene [3] 36 Cf 16.30S 15.00 E
Cunene=Kunene (EN) 30 Ij 17.20S 11.50 E
Cuneo 14 Bf 44.23N 7.32 E
Čunja 21 Lc 61.30N 96.20 E
Cunnamulla 58 Fg 28.04S 145.41 E
Čunski [R.S.F.S.R.] 20 Ee 56.03N 99.48 E
Čunski [R.S.F.S.R.] 20 Ee 57.23N 97.40 E
Cuorgné 14 Be 45.23N 7.39 E
Čupa 19 Db 66.17N 33.01 E
Cupar 9 Je 56.19N 3.01W
Cupica, Golfo de- 54 Cb 6.35N 77.30W
Čuprija 15 Ef 43.56N 21.22 E
Cupula, Pico- 48 De 24.47N 110.50W
Čur 7 Mh 57.11N 53.01 E
Curaçá 54 Ke 8.59S 39.54W
Curacao 52 Jd 12.11N 69.00W
Curacautín 56 Fe 38.26S 71.53W
Cura Malal, Sierra de- 55 Am 37.44S 62.16W
Curanilahue 56 Fe 37.28S 73.21W
Čurapča 20 Id 61.56N 132.18 E
Curaray, Rio- 54 Dd 2.20S 74.05W
Curcúbata, Virful- 15 Fc 46.25N 22.35 E
Curdimurka 58 Eg 29.30S 137.10 E
Curé 55 De 21.25S 56.25W
Cure 11 Jg 47.40N 3.41 E
Curepipe 37a Bb 20.19S 57.31 E
Curepto 56 Fe 35.05S 72.01W
Curiapo 54 Fb 8.33N 61.00W
Curicó 53 Ii 34.59S 71.14W
Curicuriari, Rio- 54 Ed 0.14S 66.48W
Curitabanos 56 Jc 27.18S 50.36W
Curitiba 53 Lh 25.25S 49.15W
Curoca 36 Bf 15.43S 11.55 E
Currais Novos 54 Ke 6.15S 36.31W
Curralinho 54 Id 1.48S 49.47W
Curral-Velho 32 Cf 15.59N 22.48W
Current River 45 Kh 36.15N 90.57W
Currie 59 Ig 39.56S 143.52 E
Curtea de Argeş 15 Hd 45.08N 24.41 E
Curtici 15 Ec 46.21N 21.18 E
Curtis 45 Ff 40.38N 100.31W
Curtis Channel 59 Kd 23.55S 152.05 E
Curtis Island 57 Jh 30.35S 178.36W
Curtis Island [Austl.] 59 Kd 23.40S 151.10 E
Curuá, Rio- [Braz.] 55 Ga 13.26S 51.24W
Curuá, Rio- [Braz.] 54 Gd 1.55S 55.07W
Curuá, Rio- [Braz.] 52 Kf 5.23S 54.22W
Curuçá 54 Id 0.43S 47.50W
Curuçá, Rio- 54 Dd 4.27S 71.23W
Curuguaty 56 Ib 24.31S 55.42W
Curuguaty, Arroyo- 55 Dg 24.06S 56.02W
Curup 26 Dg 3.28S 102.32 E
Curupira, Sierra de- 54 Fc 1.25N 64.30W
Cururupu 54 Jd 1.50S 44.52W
Curuzú Cuatiá 56 Ic 29.47S 58.03W
Curvelo 54 Jg 18.45S 44.25W
Cusco 53 Ig 13.31S 71.59W
Cushing 45 Hi 35.59N 96.46W
Cushing, Mount- 42 Ee 57.36N 126.51W
Čusovaja 5 Ld 58.13N 56.30 E
Čusovoj 19 Fd 58.17N 57.50 E
Cusset 11 Jh 46.08N 3.28 E
Cusseta 44 Ei 32.18N 84.47W
Čust 18 Hd 41.00N 71.15 E
Custer 45 Ee 43.46N 103.36W
Cutato 36 Ce 10.33S 16.48 E
Cut Bank 43 Eb 48.38N 112.20W
Cutervo 54 Ce 6.22S 78.51W
Cuthbert 44 Ej 31.46N 84.48W
Cutral Có 56 Ge 38.56S 69.14W
Cutro 14 Kk 39.02N 16.59 E
Cuttack 22 Kg 20.30N 85.50 E
Čuvašskaja ASSR [3] 19 Ed 55.30N 47.10 E
Cuvelai 36 Cf 15.40S 15.47 E
Cuvette [3] 36 Cc 0.10S 15.30 E
Cuvier Basin (EN) 59 Cd 22.00S 111.00 E
Cuvier Island 62 Fb 36.25S 175.45 E
Cuvo ou Queve 30 Ij 10.50S 13.47 E
Cuxhaven 10 Ec 53.53N 8.42 E
Cuya 56 Fa 19.07S 70.08W
Cuyahoga Falls 44 Ge 41.08N 81.55W
Cuyo Islands 26 Hd 11.04N 120.57 E
Cuyubini, Rio- 50 Fh 8.20N 60.20W
Cuyuni, Rio- 52 Kf 6.23N 58.41W
Cuyuni River 52 Kf 6.23N 58.41W
Cuyutlán, Laguna- 48 Gh 19.00N 104.10W
Cuzco [2] 54 Df 13.00S 72.30W
Cuzna 13 Hf 38.04N 4.41W
Cvikov 10 Kf 50.48N 14.40 E
Čvrsnica 14 Lg 43.35N 17.35 E
Cyangugu 36 Ec 2.29S 28.54 E
Cybinka 10 Kd 52.12N 14.48 E
Cyclades (EN) = Kikládhes 5 Ih 37.00N 25.10 E
Čyjyrčyk, Pereval- 18 Id 40.15N 73.20 E
Cypress Hills 38 Ie 49.40N 109.30W
Cypress Lake 46 Kb 49.28N 109.29W
Cyprus (EN)=Kıbrıs/ Kypros 22 Ff 35.00N 33.00 E
Cyprus (EN)=Kıbrıs/ Kypros 21 Ff 35.00N 33.00 E
Cyprus (EN)=Kypros/ Kıbrıs [1] 22 Ff 35.00N 33.00 E
Cyprus (EN)=Kypros/ Kıbrıs 21 Ff 35.00N 33.00 E
Cyrenaica (EN)=Barqah 33 Dc 31.00N 22.30 E
Cyrenaica (EN)=Barqah 30 Je 31.00N 23.00 E
Cyrene 33 Dc 32.48N 21.59 E
Cyrus Field Bay 42 Ld 62.50N 65.00W
Cysoing 12 Fd 50.34N 3.13 E
Cythera (EN)=Kithira 15 Fm 36.09N 23.00 E
Czaplinek 10 Mc 53.34N 16.14 E
Czarna [Pol.] 10 Pe 51.12N 19.53 E
Czarna [Pol.] 10 Rf 50.30N 21.15 E
Czarna Białostocka 10 Tc 53.18N 23.19 E
Czarna Dąbrówka 10 Nb 54.20N 17.32 E
Czarna Hańcza 10 Tc 53.50N 23.47 E
Czarnków 10 Md 52.55N 16.34 E
Czchów 10 Qg 49.50N 20.39 E
Czechoslovakia (EN)= Československo [1] 6 Hf 49.30N 17.00 E
Czechowice-Dziedzice 10 Og 49.54N 19.00 E
Czeremcha 10 Td 52.32N 23.15 E
Czersk 10 Nc 53.48N 18.00 E
Częstochowa 6 He 50.49N 19.06 E
Częstochowa [2] 10 Pf 50.50N 19.05 E
Człopa 10 Mc 53.06N 16.08 E
Człuchów 10 Nc 53.41N 17.21 E

D

Da, Sông- = Black River (EN) 21 Mg 20.17N 106.34 E
Da'an (Dalai) 27 Lb 45.35N 124.16 E
Dabaga 36 Gd 8.07S 35.55 E
Dabakala 34 Ed 8.22N 4.26W
Dabakala [3] 34 Ed 8.27N 4.28W
Daban → Bairin Youqi 27 Kc 43.30N 118.37 E
Dabas 10 Pi 47.11N 19.19 E
Daba Shan 21 Mf 32.15N 109.00 E
Dabat 35 Fc 12.58N 37.45 E
Dabay Sima 35 Gc 12.43N 42.17 E
Dabba/Daocheng 27 Hf 29.01N 100.26 E
Dabbāgh, Jabal- 23 Ed 27.52N 35.45 E
Dabeiba 54 Cb 7.02N 76.16W
Dąbie 10 Od 52.06N 18.49 E
Dabie, Jezioro- 10 Kc 53.29N 14.40 E
Dabie Shan 21 Nf 31.15N 115.00 E
Dabl, Wādī- [Sau.Ar.] 24 Gh 28.35N 39.04 E
Dabl, Wādī- [Sau.Ar.] 24 Gh 29.05N 36.14 E
Dabnou 34 Gc 14.09N 5.22 E
Dabola 34 Cc 10.45N 11.07W
Daborow 35 Hd 6.11N 48.22 E
Dabou 34 Ed 5.19N 4.23W
Dabqig → Uxin Qi 27 Id 38.27N 109.08 E
Dabraš 15 Gh 41.40N 23.50 E
Dąbrowa Białostocka 10 Tc 53.40N 23.20 E
Dąbrowa Górnicza 10 Pf 50.20N 19.11 E
Dąbrowa Tarnowska 10 Qf 50.11N 21.00 E
Dabsan Hu 27 Fd 36.58N 95.00 E
Dăbuleni 15 Hf 43.48N 24.05 E
Dabus 35 Fc 10.38N 35.10 E
Dacata 35 Gd 7.16N 42.15 E
Dacca 22 Lg 23.43N 90.25 E
Dachangzhen 28 Eh 32.13N 118.44 E
Dachau 10 Hh 48.16N 11.26 E
Dachen Dao 28 Fj 28.29N 121.53 E
Dachstein 14 Hc 47.30N 13.36 E
Dacia Seamount (EN) 5 Ei 31.10N 13.42W
Dačice 10 Lg 49.05N 15.26 E
Dac Lac, Caonguyen- 25 Lf 12.50N 108.05 E
Đacovica 15 Dg 42.23N 20.26 E
Dadali 63a Dc 8.07S 159.06 E
Dadanawa 54 Gc 2.50N 59.30W
Daday 24 Eb 41.28N 33.28 E
Dade City 44 Fk 28.22N 82.12W
Dadou 11 Hk 43.44N 1.49 E
Dādra and Nagar Haveli [3] 25 Ed 20.20N 72.50 E
Dadu 25 Dc 26.44N 67.47 E
Dadu He 21 Mg 29.32N 103.44 E
Dadukou 28 Di 30.30N 117.03 E
Dăeni 15 Le 44.50N 28.07 E
Daet 26 Hd 14.05N 122.55 E
Dafang 27 If 27.06N 105.32 E
Dafeng (Dazhongji) 28 Fh 33.11N 120.27 E
Dagana 34 Bb 16.31N 15.30W
Dagana 35 Bc 13.05N 16.00 E
Daga Post 35 Ed 9.13N 33.58 E
Dağardi 15 Lj 39.26N 29.00 E
Dagash 35 Eb 19.22N 33.24 E
Dagda 8 Lh 56.04N 27.36 E
Dagdan-Daba 27 Gb 48.20N 96.50 E
Dagéla 35 Bc 10.40N 18.26 E
Dagestanskaja [3] 19 Eg 43.00N 47.00 E
Dagestanskije Ogni 19 Eg 42.06N 48.12 E
Dagezhen → Fengning 28 Dd 41.12N 116.39 E
Dagu 28 De 38.58N 117.40 E
Daguan 27 Hf 27.48N 103.54 E
Dagu He 28 Ff 37.34N 121.17 E
Daguokui Shan 28 Jb 45.19N 129.50 E
Dagupan 26 Hc 16.03N 120.20 E
Dagxoi → Yidun 27 Ge 30.25N 99.28 E
Dagzê 27 Ff 29.41N 91.24 E
Dagzê Co 27 Ee 31.54N 87.29 E
Daheiding Shan 27 Mb 47.58N 129.10 E
Dahei He 28 Ad 40.34N 111.05 E
Da Hinggan Ling=Greater Khingan Range (EN) 21 Oe 49.00N 122.00 E
Dahlak Archipelago 30 Lg 15.40N 40.30 E
Dahlak Kebir 35 Gb 15.38N 40.11 E
Daḩl al Furayy 24 Li 26.45N 47.03 E
Dahlem 12 Id 50.23N 6.33 E
Dahlonega Plateau 44 Fh 34.30N 83.45W
Dahm, Ramlat- 33 If 16.25N 45.45 E
Dahme 10 Je 51.52N 13.26 E
Dahmouni 13 Ni 35.25N 1.29 E
Dahn 12 Je 49.09N 7.47 E
Dahomey → Bénin [1] 31 Hh 9.30N 2.15 E
Dahongliutan 27 Cd 36.00N 79.12 E
Dahra 13 Mh 36.18N 0.55 E
Dahra [Lib.] 33 Cd 29.40N 17.40 E
Dahra [Sen.] 34 Bb 15.21N 15.29W
Dahra, Massif de- 13 Oh 36.30N 2.05 E
Dahūk [3] 24 Jd 36.57N 43.00 E
Dahūk 24 Jd 36.52N 43.00 E
Dahushan 28 Gd 41.37N 122.09 E
Dahy, Nafūd ad- 33 Ie 22.00N 45.25 E
Dai 63a Eb 7.53S 160.37 E
Daia 15 If 44.00N 25.59 E
Daïa, Région des- 32 Hc 33.30N 3.25 E
Daicheng 28 De 38.42N 116.37 E
Daigo 28 Pf 36.46N 140.21 E
Dai Hai 28 Bd 40.31N 113.43 E
Dailekh 25 Gc 28.50N 81.44 E
Daimanji-San 29 Cc 36.15N 133.19 E
Daimiel 13 Ie 39.04N 3.37W

Index Symbols

[1] Independent Nation
[2] State, Region
[3] District, County
[4] Municipality
[5] Colony, Dependency
Continent
Physical Region
Historical or Cultural Region
Mount, Mountain
Volcano
Hill
Mountains, Mountain Range
Hills, Escarpment
Plateau, Upland
Pass, Gap
Plain, Lowland
Delta
Salt Flat
Valley, Canyon
Crater, Cave
Karst Features
Depression
Polder
Desert, Dunes
Forest, Woods
Heath, Steppe
Oasis
Cape, Point
Coast, Beach
Cliff
Peninsula
Isthmus
Sandbank
Island
Atoll
Rock, Reef
Islands, Archipelago
Rocks, Reefs
Coral Reef
Well, Spring
Geyser
River, Stream
Waterfall Rapids
River Mouth, Estuary
Lake
Salt Lake
Intermittent Lake
Reservoir
Swamp, Pond
Canal
Glacier
Ice Shelf, Pack Ice
Ocean
Sea
Gulf, Bay
Strait, Fjord
Lagoon
Bank
Seamount
Tablemount
Ridge
Shelf
Basin
Escarpment, Sea Scarp
Fracture
Trench, Abyss
National Park, Reserve
Point of Interest
Recreation Site
Cave, Cavern
Historic Site
Ruins
Wall, Walls
Church, Abbey
Temple
Scientific Station
Airport
Port
Lighthouse
Mine
Tunnel
Dam, Bridge

Dainanji-San 29 Ec 36.36N 137.42 E
Dainichi-San 29 Ec 36.09N 136.30 E
Dainkog 27 Ge 32.31N 97.59 E
Daiō-Zaki 28 Ng 34.22N 136.53 E
Dairan (EN)=Dalian (Luda) 22 Of 38.55N 121.39 E
Dairan (EN) = Lüda→Dalian 22 Of 38.55N 121.39 E
Dairbhre/Valentia 9 Cj 51.55N 10.20W
Daireaux 55 Bm 36.36S 61.45W
Dai-Sen 29 Cd 35.24N 133.34 E
Daisengen-Dake 29a Bc 41.35N 140.09 E
Daishan (Gaotingzhen) 28 Gi 30.15N 122.13 E
Daitō [Jap.] 29 Cd 35.19N 132.58 E
Daitō [Jap.] 29 Gb 39.02N 141.22 E
Daito Islands (EN)=Daitō Shotō 21 Pg 25.00N 131.15 E
Daitō Shotō=Daito Islands (EN) 21 Pg 25.00N 131.15 E
Daitō-Zaki 29 Gd 35.18N 140.24 E
Daixian 28 Be 39.03N 112.57 E
Daiyue→Shanyin 28 Be 39.30N 112.48 E
Dajabón 49 Ld 19.33N 71.42W
Dajarra 58 Eg 21.42S 139.31 E
Dajtit, Mali i- 15 Ch 41.22N 19.55 E
Daka 34 Ed 8.19N 0.13W
Dakar 31 Fg 14.40N 17.26W
Dākhilah, Wāḩāt al-= Dakhla Oasis (EN) 30 Jf 25.30N 29.10 E
Dakhla Oasis (EN)= Dākhilah, Wāḩāt al- 30 Jf 25.30N 29.10 E
Dakhlet Nouâdhibou [3] 32 De 20.30N 16.00W
Dakla 31 Ff 23.42N 15.56W
Dakoro 34 Gc 14.30N 6.25 E
Đakovo 14 Me 45.19N 18.25 E
Daksti 8 Kg 57.38N 25.32 E
Dak To 25 Lf 14.42N 107.51 E
Dal 8 Dd 60.15N 11.12 E
Dal, Jökulsá á- 7a Cb 65.40N 14.20W
Đala 15 Dc 46.09N 20.07 E
Dala [Ang.] 36 De 11.03S 20.17 E
Dala [Sol.Is.] 63a c 8.36S 160.41 E
Dalaba 34 Cc 10.42N 12.15W
Dalai → Da'an 27 Lb 45.35N 124.16 E
Dalai Nur 27 Kc 43.18N 116.15 E
Dala-Järna 8 Fd 60.33N 14.21 E
Dalākī 24 Nh 29.19N 51.06 E
Dalälven 5 Hc 60.38N 17.27 E
Dalaman 24 Cd 36.40N 28.45 E
Dalaman 15 Lm 36.44N 28.49 E
Dalāmī 35 Ec 11.52N 30.28 E
Dalān 24 Kj 24.15N 45.47 E
Dalan-Dzadgad 22 Me 43.47N 104.29 E
Dalane 8 Bf 58.35N 6.20 E
Dalarna 8 Fd 61.00N 14.05 E
Dalarö 8 He 59.08N 18.24 E
Da Lat 22 Mh 11.56N 108.25 E
Dālbandin 25 Cc 28.53N 64.25 E
Dalbosjön 8 Ef 58.45N 12.50 E
Dalboslätten 8 Ef 58.35N 12.25 E
Dalby 59 Ke 27.11S 151.16 E
Dale [Nor.] 7 Af 60.35N 5.49 E
Dale [Nor.] 7 Af 61.22N 5.25 E
Dale Hollow Lake 44 Eg 36.36N 85.19W
Dalen 7 Bg 59.27N 8.00 E
Dalfsen 12 Ib 52.30N 6.14 E
Dalgaranger, Mount- 59 De 27.51S 117.06 E
Dălgopol 15 Kf 43.03N 27.21 E
Dalhart 43 Gd 36.04N 102.31W
Dalhousie 42 Kg 48.04N 66.23W
Dalhousie, Cape- 42 Eb 70.15N 129.41W
Dali [China] 22 Mg 25.43N 100.07 E
Dali [China] 27 Ie 34.55N 110.00 E
Dalian (Lüda) = Dairan (EN) 22 Of 38.55N 121.39 E
Dalias 13 Jh 36.49N 2.52W
Daling He 28 Fd 40.56N 121.44 E
Dalizi 27 Mc 41.45N 126.50 E
Dalj 14 Me 45.29N 18.59 E
Daljā' 33 Fd 27.39N 30.42 E
Dalkowskie, Wzgórza- 10 Le 51.35N 15.50 E
Dall [Ak.-U.S.] 40 Mf 54.50N 132.55W
Dall [Can.] 2 Ef 55.00N 133.00W
Dallas [Or.-U.S.] 46 Dd 44.55N 123.19W
Dallas [Tx.-U.S.] 39 Jf 32.47N 96.48W
Dalmā' 24 Oj 24.30N 52.20 E
Dalmā', Qārat- 33 Dd 25.32N 23.57 E
Dalmacija 14 Kg 43.00N 17.00 E
Dalmacija = Dalmatia (EN) 5 Hg 43.00N 17.00 E
Dalmaj, Hawr- 24 Kf 32.20N 45.28 E
Dalmally 9 Ie 56.24N 4.58W
Dalmatia (EN) = Dalmacija 5 Hg 43.00N 17.00 E
Dalmatovo 17 Kh 56.16N 63.00 E
Dalnegorsk 22 Pe 44.31N 135.31 E
Dalnerečensk 22 Pe 45.55N 133.45 E
Dalni [R.S.F.S.R.] 20 Fh 53.15N 157.30 E
Dalni [R.S.F.S.R.] 20 Ih 44.57N 135.03 E
Dalnjaja, Gora- 20 Mc 68.08N 179.53 E
Daloa [3] 34 Dd 6.58N 6.23W
Daloa 31 Gh 6.53N 6.27W
Dalou Shan 21 Mg 28.00N 106.40 E
Dalqū 35 Ea 20.07N 30.35 E
Dalrymple, Mount- 57 Fg 21.02S 148.38 E
Dalsbruk 8 Jd 60.02N 22.31 E
Dalsbruk/Taalintendas 8 Jd 60.02N 22.31 E
Dalsfjorden 8 Ac 61.20N 5.05 E
Dalsjöfors 8 Eg 57.43N 13.05 E
Dalsland 8 Ef 58.35N 12.55 E
Dalslands kanal 8 Ef 58.50N 12.25 E
Dals Långed 7 Cg 58.55N 12.18 E
Dalton 44 Eh 34.47N 84.58W
Daltonganj 25 Gd 24.02N 84.04 E
Dalul 35 Gc 14.22N 40.21 E
Daluo 27 Hg 21.38N 100.15 E
Dalupiri 26 Hc 19.05N 121.12 E
Dalvik 7a Bb 65.58N 18.32W
Dalwallinu 59 Df 30.17S 116.40 E
Dalyan 15 Lm 36.50N 28.39 E
Daly Bay 42 Id 64.00N 89.40W
Daly City 46 Dh 37.42N 122.29W
Daly River 57 Ef 13.20S 130.19 E
Daly Waters 59 Gc 16.15S 133.22 E
Damā, Wādī- 24 Fi 27.09N 35.47 E
Damagarim 34 Gc 13.42N 9.00 E
Damān [3] 25 Ed 20.10N 73.00 E
Damanhūr 33 Fc 31.02N 30.28 E
Damar, Pulau- 26 Ih 7.09S 128.40 E
Damara 35 Be 4.58N 18.42 E
Damaraland 37 Bd 21.00S 17.30 E
Damas Cays 49 Hb 23.58N 79.55W
Damascus (EN)=Dimashq 22 Ff 33.30N 36.15 E
Dāmāsh 24 Md 36.46N 49.46 E
Damaturu 34 Hc 11.45N 11.58 E
Damāvand 24 He 35.56N 52.08 E
Damāvand, Qolleh-ye- 21 Hf 35.56N 52.08 E
Damba 36 Cd 6.50S 15.07 E
Dambaslar 15 Kh 41.13N 27.14 E
Dame Marie, Cap- 47 Je 18.36N 74.26W
Damergou 30 Hg 15.00N 9.00 E
Dāmghān 24 Pd 36.09N 54.22 E
Damianópolis 55 Ib 14.33S 46.10W
Damiao 27 He 30.52N 104.38 E
Damietta (EN)=Dumyāṭ 31 Ke 31.25N 31.48 E
Daming 28 Cf 36.17N 115.09 E
Daming Shan 27 Ig 23.23N 108.30 E
Damīr Qābū 24 Id 36.54N 41.47 E
Dammartin en Goële 12 Ee 49.03N 2.41 E
Dammastock 14 Cd 46.38N 8.25 E
Damme [Bel.] 12 Fc 51.15N 3.17 E
Damme [F.R.G.] 12 Kb 52.31N 8.12 E
Dammer Berge 12 Kb 52.35N 8.17 E
Damoh 25 Fd 23.50N 79.27 E
Damongo 34 Ed 9.05N 1.49W
Damous 13 Nh 36.33N 1.42 E
Dampier 58 Cg 20.39S 116.45 E
Dampier, Selat-=Dampier Strait (EN) 26 Jg 0.40S 130.40 E
Dampier Archipelago 59 Dd 20.35S 116.35 E
Dampier Land 59 Ec 17.30S 122.55 E
Dampierre 12 Df 48.42N 1.59 E
Dampier Strait 59 Ja 5.36S 148.12 E
Dampier Strait (EN)= Dampier, Selat- 26 Jg 0.40S 130.40 E
Damqawt 23 Hf 16.34N 52.50 E
Damqog Kanbab/Maquan He 27 Df 29.36N 84.09 E
Dam Qu 27 Fe 33.56N 92.41 E
Damville 12 Df 48.52N 1.04 E
Damvillers 12 He 49.20N 5.24 E
Damwoude, Dantumadeel- 12 Ha 53.18N 5.59 E
Damxoi → Comai 27 Ff 28.26N 91.32 E
Damxung 27 Fe 30.34N 91.16 E
Danakil=Danakil Plain (EN) 30 Lg 12.25N 40.30 E
Danakil Plain (EN)= Danakil 30 Lg 12.25N 40.30 E
Danané [3] 34 Dd 7.25N 8.10W
Danané 34 Dd 7.16N 8.09W
Da Nang 22 Mh 16.04N 108.13 E
Danba/Rongzhag 27 He 30.48N 101.54 E
Danbury 44 Ke 41.23N 73.27W
Danby Lake 46 Hi 34.14N 115.07W
Dancheng 28 Ch 33.36N 115.14 E
Dancheng→Xiangshan 27 Lf 29.29N 121.52 E
Dandarah 33 Fd 26.10N 32.39 E
Dandeldhura 25 Gc 29.18N 80.35 E
Dandenong, Melbourne- 59 Jg 37.59S 145.12 E
Dandong 22 Oe 40.10N 124.15 E
Daneborg 41 Jd 74.25N 20.10W
Danells Fjord 41 Hf 60.45N 42.45W
Daneţi 15 Hf 43.59N 24.03 E
Danfeng (Longjuzhai) 27 Je 33.44N 110.22 E
Danforth Hills 45 Cf 40.15N 108.00W
Danfu 63a Aa 4.12S 153.04 E
Dangara 19 Gh 38.09N 69.22 E
Dangchengwan → Subei 27 Fd 39.36N 94.58 E
Dang He 27 Fc 40.30N 94.42 E
Dangjin Shankou 21 Lf 39.15N 94.30 E
Dangla 35 Fc 11.16N 36.50 E
Dangla Shan→Tanggula Shan 21 Lf 33.00N 92.00 E
Dangoura, Mount- 35 Dd 6.12N 26.27 E
Dangrek Range (EN)=Dong Rak, Phanom- 21 Mh 14.25N 104.30 E
Dangshan 27 Ke 34.22N 116.21 E
Dangtu 28 Ei 31.33N 118.30 E
Dangu 12 De 49.15N 1.42 E
Dangyang 28 Ai 30.49N 111.47 E
Dan He 28 Bg 35.05N 112.59 E
Daniel 46 Je 42.52N 110.04W
Daniel, Serra- 55 Ea 13.40S 54.55W
Danielskuil 37 Ce 28.11S 23.33 E
Danilov 19 Ed 58.12N 40.13 E
Danilovgrad 15 Cg 42.33N 19.07 E
Danilovka 16 Nd 50.21N 44.06 E
Daning 27 Jd 36.31N 110.45 E
Danjiang → Junxian 27 Je 32.31N 111.32 E
Danjiangkou Shuiku 27 Je 32.37N 111.30 E
Danjo-Guntō 27 Me 32.00N 128.20 E
Đank 24 Qk 23.33N 56.16 E
Dankov 16 Kc 53.16N 39.07 E
Danli 49 Df 14.00N 86.35W
Danmark=Denmark (EN) [1] 6 Gd 56.00N 10.00 E
Danmark Fjord 67 Me 81.10N 23.20W
Danmarks Havn 67 Ld 76.50N 18.30W
Danmarksstraedet= Denmark Strait (EN) 38 Oc 67.00N 25.00W
Dannenberg 10 Hc 53.06N 11.06 E
Dannevirke 62 Gd 40.12S 176.06 E
Danot 35 Hd 7.33N 45.17 E
Dantumadeel 12 Ha 53.18N 5.59 E
Dantumadeel-Damwoude 12 Ha 53.18N 5.59 E
Danube (EN)=Donau 5 If 45.20N 29.40 E
Danube (EN)=Duna 5 If 45.20N 29.40 E
Danube (EN)=Dunaj 5 If 45.20N 29.40 E
Danube (EN)=Dunărea 5 If 45.20N 29.40 E
Danube (EN)=Dunav 5 If 45.20N 29.40 E
Danube, Mouths of the- (EN) = Dunării, Delta- 5 If 45.30N 29.45 E
Danville [Ar.-U.S.] 45 Ji 35.03N 93.24W
Danville [Il.-U.S.] 43 Jc 40.08N 87.37W
Danville [In.-U.S.] 44 Df 39.46N 86.32W
Danville [Ky.-U.S.] 43 Kd 37.39N 84.46W
Danville [Va.-U.S.] 43 Ld 36.34N 79.25W
Danxian (Nada) 27 Ih 19.38N 109.32 E
Danyang 28 Eh 32.00N 119.33 E
Danzig (EN)=Gdańsk 6 He 54.23N 18.40 E
Dao 26 Hd 10.31N 121.57 E
Dão 13 Dd 40.20N 8.11W
Daocheng/Dabba 27 Hf 29.01N 100.26 E
Daokou → Huaxian 28 Cg 35.33N 114.30 E
Daosa 25 Fc 26.53N 76.20 E
Dao Shui 28 Ci 30.42N 114.40 E
Dao Timni 34 Ha 20.38N 13.39 E
Daoura 32 Gd 29.03N 4.33W
Daoxian 27 Jf 25.37N 111.36 E
Dapaong 34 Fc 10.52N 0.12 E
Dapchi 34 Hc 12.29N 11.29 E
Daqing Shan 28 Ad 41.00N 111.00 E
Daqin Tal→Naiman Qi 27 Lc 42.49N 120.38 E
Daquing Shan 28 Ed 40.30N 119.38 E
Dar'ā 23 Ec 32.37N 36.06 E
Dārāb 24 Ph 28.45N 54.34 E
Darabani 15 Ja 48.11N 26.35 E
Daraçya Yarimadasi 15 Lm 36.40N 28.10 E
Darāfisah 35 Ec 13.23N 31.59 E
Dārān 24 Nf 32.59N 50.24 E
Darasun 20 Gf 51.39N 113.59 E
Đaravica 15 Dg 42.32N 20.08 E
Darāw 24 Ej 24.25N 32.56 E
Darazo 34 Hc 11.00N 10.25 E
Darband 23 Ic 31.38N 57.02 E
Darband, Kūh-e- 24 Qg 31.34N 57.08 E
Darbandī Khān, Sad ad- 24 Ke 35.07N 45.50 E
Darbat Alī, Ra's- 23 Hf 16.43N 53.33 E
Darbénai/Darbenaj 8 Ih 56.02N 21.08 E
Dar Ben Karriche el Bahri 13 Gi 35.51N 5.21W
Darbhanga 25 Hc 26.10N 85.54 E
Dārboruk 35 Gd 9.44N 44.31 E
Darby 46 Hc 46.01N 114.11W
Darchan→Darhan 22 Me 49.33N 106.21 E
Darda 14 Me 45.38N 18.42 E
Dardanelle Lake 45 Ji 35.25N 93.20W
Dardanelles (EN)= Çanakkale Boğazi 5 Ig 40.15N 26.25 E
Dardo/Kangding 27 He 30.01N 101.58 E
Dar el Kouti 30 Jh 8.50N 21.50 E
Darende 24 Gc 38.34N 37.30 E
Dar es Salaam [3] 36 Gd 6.50S 39.02 E
Dar es Salaam 31 Ki 6.48S 39.17 E
Darfield 62 Ee 43.29S 172.07 E
Darfo Boario Terme 14 Ee 45.53N 10.11 E
Dārfūr 30 Jg 12.40N 24.20 E
Dārfūr al Janūbīyah [3] 35 Dc 11.30N 25.10 E
Dārfūr ash Shamālīyah [3] 35 Db 16.00N 25.30 E
Dargan-Ata 19 Gg 40.29N 62.12 E
Dargaville 61 Dg 35.56S 173.52 E
Darhan (Darchan) 22 Me 49.33N 106.21 E
Darhan Muminggan Lianheqi 27 Jc 41.45N 110.24 E
Darica [Tur.] 15 Kj 40.00N 27.50 E
Darica [Tur.] 15 Mi 40.45N 29.23 E
Darién 47 Ig 8.30N 77.30W
Darien 44 Gj 31.22N 81.26W
Darién [3] 49 Ii 8.10N 77.45W
Darién, Golfo de- 52 Ie 8.25N 76.53W
Darién, Serrania del- 47 Ig 8.30N 77.30W
Dariense, Cordillera- 49 Eg 12.55N 85.30W
Darja 18 Ee 38.13N 65.46 E
Darjalyk 18 Ac 42.00N 57.45 E
Darjeeling 25 Hc 27.02N 88.16 E
Dar-Kebdani 13 Ii 35.07N 3.21W
Dark Head 51n Ba 13.17N 61.17W
Dărkhovīn 24 Mg 30.45N 48.25 E
Darlag 27 Ge 33.49N 99.08 E
Darling 37 Bf 33.23S 18.23 E
Darling Downs 59 Ke 27.30S 150.30 E
Darling Range 57 Ch 32.00S 116.30 E
Darling River 57 Fh 34.07S 141.55 E
Darlington [Eng.-U.K.] 9 Lg 54.31N 1.34W
Darlington [S.C.-U.S.] 44 Hh 34.19N 79.53W
Darłowo 10 Mb 54.26N 16.23 E
Darmouth 9 Jk 50.21N 3.35W
Darmstadt 10 Eg 49.52N 8.39 E
Darnah 31 Je 32.46N 22.39 E
Darnah [3] 33 Dc 31.00N 23.40 E
Darnétal 12 De 49.27N 1.09 E
Darney 11 Mf 48.05N 6.03 E
Darnley, Cape- 66 Fe 67.43S 69.30 E
Darnley Bay 42 Fc 69.45N 123.45W
Daroca 13 Kc 41.07N 1.25W
Darou Khoudos 34 Bb 15.06N 16.50W
Darovskoj 7 Lg 58.47N 47.59 E
Darrah, Mount- 46 Hb 49.28N 114.35W
Darregueira 56 He 37.42S 63.10W
Darrehshahr 24 Lf 33.10N 47.18 E
D'Arros Island 37b Bb 5.24S 53.18 E
Dar Rounga 35 Cd 10.45N 22.20 E
Dar Sila 35 Cc 12.11N 21.21 E
Darss 10 Ib 54.25N 12.31 E
Darßer Ort 10 Ib 54.29N 12.31 E
Dart 9 Jk 50.20N 3.33W
Dart, Cape- 66 Nf 73.06S 126.20W
D'Artagnan Bank (EN) 59 Eb 13.00S 121.00 E
Dartang → Baqên 27 Fe 31.58N 94.00 E
Dartford 12 Cc 51.27N 0.13 E
Dartmoor 9 Jk 50.35N 4.00W
Dartmouth 42 Lh 44.40N 63.34W
Dartuch, Cabo- 13 Pe 39.56N 3.48 E
Daru 60 Ci 9.04S 143.12 E
Daruneh 24 Qe 35.10N 57.18 E
Daruvar 14 Le 45.35N 17.14 E
Darvaza 19 Fg 40.15N 58.24 E
Darvel, Teluk- 26 Gf 4.50N 118.30 E
Darwin 58 Ef 12.28S 130.50 E
Darwin, Bahía- 56 Fg 45.27S 74.40W
Darwin, Isla- 54a Aa 1.39N 92.00W
Darwin, Port- 59 Gb 12.20S 130.40 E
Dar Zagaoua 35 Cb 15.15N 23.14 E
Dar Zebada 35 Bc 13.45N 18.50 E
Dās 24 Oj 25.09N 52.53 E
Dašava 10 Ug 49.13N 24.05 E
Daš-Balbar 27 Jb 49.31N 114.21 E
Dasha He 28 Ce 38.27N 114.39 E
Dashengtang Shan 28 Dc 42.07N 117.12 E
Dashennongjia 27 Je 31.47N 114.12 E
Dashennongjia 27 Je 31.26N 110.18 E
Dashiqiao → Yingkou 28 Gd 40.39N 122.31 E
Dashitou 28 Jc 43.18N 128.29 E
Dasht 24 Qd 37.17N 56.04 E
Dasht Āb 24 Qh 28.59N 56.32 E
Dashtak 24 Og 30.23N 52.30 E
Dasht-e-Āzādegan 24 Mg 31.32N 48.10 E
Daškesan 16 Oi 40.30N 46.03 E
Dasseneiland 37 Bf 33.26S 18.05 E
Dastgardān 24 Qe 34.19N 56.51 E
Dastjerd-e Qaddādeh 24 Nf 32.44N 51.32 E
Datça 24 Bd 36.45N 27.40 E
Date 28 Pc 42.27N 140.51 E
Dāth, Sha'īb ad- 24 Jj 25.45N 43.10 E
Datia 25 Fc 25.40N 78.28 E
Datian Ding 27 Jg 22.17N 111.13 E
Datil 45 Ci 34.09N 107.47W
Datong [China] 27 Hd 36.56N 101.40 E
Datong [China] 22 Ne 40.09N 113.17 E
Datteln 12 Jc 51.40N 7.23 E
Datteln-Hamm Kanal 12 Jc 51.39N 7.21 E
Datu 21 Mi 2.05N 109.39 E
Datu, Teluk 21 Ni 2.00N 111.00 E
Datu Plang 26 He 6.58N 124.40 E
Dāūd Khel 25 Eb 32.53N 71.34 E
Daudzeva 8 Kh 56.28N 25.18 E
Daugaard-Jensen Land 41 Fb 80.10N 63.30W
Daugai/Daugaj 8 Kj 54.20N 24.28 E
Daugaj/Daugai 8 Kj 54.20N 24.28 E
Daugava→Dvina(EN) 19 Cd 57.04N 24.03 E
Daugavpils 6 Id 55.53N 26.32 E
Daule 54 Cd 1.50S 79.57W
Daun 10 Cf 50.12N 6.50 E
Daung Kyun 25 Jf 12.14N 98.05 E
Daunia, Monti della- 14 Ji 41.25N 15.05 E
Dauphin 42 Hf 51.09N 100.03W
Dauphiné 11 Lj 44.50N 6.00 E
Dauphin Lake 42 Hf 51.15N 99.45W
Daura 34 Gc 13.02N 8.18 E
Dautphetal 12 Kd 50.52N 8.33 E
Dāvangere 25 Ff 14.28N 75.55 E
Davao 22 Oi 7.04N 125.36 E
Davao Gulf 21 Oi 6.40N 125.55 E
Dāvarān, Kūh-e- 24 Qg 30.40N 56.15 E
Dāvar Panāh 23 Jd 27.21N 62.21 E
Dāvarzan 24 Qd 36.23N 56.50 E
Đavat 15 Eh 41.04N 21.06 E
Davenport [Ia.-U.S.] 39 Je 41.32N 90.41W
Davenport [Wa.-U.S.] 46 Fc 47.39N 118.09W
Davenport Range 59 Gd 20.45S 134.50 E
Daventry 12 Ab 52.15N 1.10W
Davert 12 Jc 51.51N 7.36 E
Davey, Port- 59 Jh 43.20S 145.55 E
David 39 Ki 8.25N 82.27W
David City 45 Hf 41.15N 97.08W
David-Gorodok 16 Ec 52.03N 27.13 E
David Point 51p Bb 12.14N 61.39W
Davidson 46 Ma 51.18N 105.59W
Davidson Mountains 40 Kc 68.45N 142.10W
Davies, Mount- 59 Fe 26.14S 129.16 E
Davis 43 Cd 38.33N 121.44W
Davis 66 Fe 68.35S 77.58 E
Davis, Cape- 66 Ee 66.24S 56.50 E
Davis, Mount- 44 Hf 39.47N 79.10W
Davis Bay 66 Ie 66.08S 134.05 E
Davis Inlet 42 Le 56.00N 61.30W
Davis Mountains 45 Ek 30.35N 104.00W
Davis Sea (EN) 66 Ge 66.00S 92.00 E
Davisstrædet = Davis, Strait (EN) 38 Nc 68.00N 58.00W
Davis Strait 38 Nc 68.00N 58.00W
Davis Strait (EN) = Davisstrædet 38 Nc 68.00N 58.00W
Davlekanovo 19 Fe 54.13N 55.03 E
Davo 34 Dd 5.00N 6.08W
Davos/Tavau 14 Dd 46.47N 9.50 E
Davutlar 15 Kl 37.43N 27.17 E
Dawa 28 Gd 40.58N 122.01 E
Dawanlē 35 Gc 11.06N 42.38 E
Dawāsir, Wādī ad- 21 Gg 20.24N 46.29 E
Dawen He 28 Dg 35.37N 116.23 E
Dawes Range 59 Kd 24.30S 151.10 E
Dawḩarab 33 Hf 16.17N 41.57 E
Dawson [Ga.-U.S.] 44 Ej 31.47N 84.26W
Dawson [Yuk.-Can.] 39 Fc 64.04N 139.25W
Dawson, Mount- 46 Ga 51.09N 117.25W
Dawson Creek 39 Gd 55.45N 120.07W
Dawson-Lambton Glacier 66 Af 76.15S 27.30W
Dawson Range 42 Dd 65.15N 137.45W
Dawson River 59 Jd 23.38S 149.46 E
Dawu 27 He 30.45N 101.11 E
Dawu (Erlangdian) 28 Ci 31.33N 114.07 E
Dawu→Maqên 27 He 34.29N 100.01 E
Dawukou → Shizuishan 27 Id 39.03N 106.24 E
Dax 11 Ek 43.43N 1.03W
Da Xi 27 Lf 28.10N 120.14 E
Daxian 27 Ie 31.15N 107.28 E
Daxin 27 Ig 22.52N 107.14 E
Daxing 28 De 39.45N 116.19 E
Daxinggou 28 Jc 43.23N 129.39 E
Daxue Shan 21 Mf 30.30N 101.30 E
Dayan→Lijiang 22 Mg 26.56N 100.15 E
Dayang He 28 Ge 39.52N 123.40 E
Dayao 27 Hf 25.49N 101.18 E
Daye 28 Ci 30.05N 114.58 E
Dayishan→Guanyun 28 Eg 34.18N 119.14 E
Daymán, Cuchilla del- 55 Dj 31.38S 57.10W
Daymán, Río- 55 Dj 31.40S 58.02W
Daym Zubayr 35 Dd 7.43N 26.13 E
Dayong 27 Jf 29.09N 110.30 E
Dayr, Jabal ad- 35 Ec 12.27N 30.45 E
Dayr az Zawr 22 Gf 35.20N 40.09 E
Dayr Hāfir 24 Gd 36.09N 37.42 E
Dayr Kātrīnā = Saint Catherine Monastery of- (EN) 33 Fd 28.31N 33.57 E
Dayr Mawās 24 Di 27.38N 30.51 E
Dayrūṭ 33 Fd 27.33N 30.49 E
Dayton [Oh.-U.S.] 39 Kf 39.45N 84.15W
Dayton [Wa.-U.S.] 46 Gc 46.19N 117.59W
Daytona Beach 39 Kg 29.12N 80.59W
Dayu 27 Jf 25.29N 114.22 E
Da Yunhe=Grand Canal (EN) 21 Nf 39.54N 116.44 E
Dayville 46 Fd 44.28N 119.32W
Dayyīnah 24 Oj 24.57N 52.24 E
Dazhongji → Dafeng 28 Fh 33.11N 120.27 E
Dazhu 27 Ie 30.42N 107.12 E
Dazjā 24 Pe 35.50N 55.46 E
Dazkırı 24 Cd 37.54N 29.42 E
De Aar 31 Jl 30.39S 24.00 E
Dead 9 Ei 52.40N 8.30W
Deadhorse 40 Jb 70.11N 148.27W
Deadmans Cay 49 Jb 23.14N 75.14W
Dead Sea (EN)=Mayyit, Al Baḩr al- 21 Ff 31.30N 35.30 E
Deadwood 45 Ed 44.23N 103.44W
Deal 12 Dc 51.13N 1.24 E
Dealu Mare 15 Jb 47.27N 26.40 E
De'an 28 Cj 29.18N 115.45 E
Deán Funes 56 Hd 30.26S 64.21W
Dearborn 44 Fd 42.18N 83.10W
Dearg, Beinn- 9 Id 57.48N 4.57W
Deary 46 Gc 46.52N 116.31W
Dease 42 Ee 59.55N 128.29W
Dease Arm 42 Fc 66.50N 120.00W
Dease Lake 59 Fd 58.35N 130.02W
Dease Strait 42 Gc 69.00N 107.00W
Death Valley 38 Hf 36.30N 117.00W
Death Valley 46 Gh 36.20N 116.50W
Deauville 11 Ge 49.22N 0.04 E
Debak 26 Ff 1.34N 111.25 E
Debalcevo 16 Ke 48.20N 38.29 E
Debao 27 Ig 23.17N 106.21 E
Debar 15 Dh 41.32N 20.32 E
Debark 35 Fc 13.08N 37.53 E
Debdou 32 Gc 33.59N 3.03W
Debed 16 Ni 41.22N 44.58 E
Deben 12 Db 52.01N 1.22 E
De Beque 45 Bg 39.20N 108.13W
Dębica 10 Rf 50.04N 21.24 E
De Bilt 12 Hb 52.06N 5.11 E
Debin 20 Kd 62.18N 150.47 E
Dęblin 10 Re 51.35N 21.50 E
Dębno 10 Kd 52.45N 14.40 E
Débo, Lac- 34 Eb 15.18N 4.09W
Deborah East, Lake- 59 Df 30.45S 119.10 E
Deborah West, Lake- 59 Df 30.45S 119.05 E
Deboyne Islands 57 Gf 10.43S 152.22 E
Debrc 15 Ce 44.37N 19.54 E
Debre Berhan 35 Fd 9.41N 39.33 E
Debrecen 6 If 47.32N 21.38 E
Debrecen [2] 10 Ri 47.31N 21.40 E
Debre Libanos 35 Fd 9.43N 38.52 E
Debre Markos 31 Kg 10.10N 37.36 E
Debre Sina 35 Fd 9.51N 39.46 E
Debre Tabor 35 Fc 11.51N 38.00 E
Debre Zeyt 31 Kh 8.47N 39.00 E
De-Buka, Glacier- 66 Nf 76.00S 131.00W
Decatur [Al.-U.S.] 43 Je 34.36N 86.59W
Decatur [Ga.-U.S.] 44 Ei 33.46N 84.18W
Decatur [Il.-U.S.] 43 Jd 39.51N 89.32W
Decatur [In.-U.S.] 44 Ee 40.50N 84.56W
Decatur [Tx.-U.S.] 45 Hj 33.14N 97.35W
Decazeville 11 Ij 44.33N 2.15 E
Deccan 21 Jh 14.00N 77.00 E
Decelles, Reservoir- 44 Hb 47.40N 78.08W
Deception Bay 59a Ia 7.07S 144.05 E
Dechang 27 Hf 27.22N 102.12 E
Děčín 10 Kf 50.47N 14.13 E
Decize 11 Jh 46.50N 3.28 E
Decorah 45 Ke 43.18N 91.48W
Deda 15 Hc 46.56N 24.54 E
Dededo 64c Ba 13.31N 144.49 E
Dedegöl Daği 24 Dd 37.39N 31.17 E
Dedemsvaart, Avereest- 12 Ib 52.37N 6.27 E
Dédougou 34 Ec 12.28N 3.28W
Dedoviči 7 Gh 57.33N 29.58 E
Dedza 36 Fe 14.22S 34.20 E
Dee [Eng.-U.K.] 9 Jh 53.19N 3.11W
Dee [Scot.-U.K.] 9 Kd 57.08N 2.04W
Dee [Scot.-U.K.] 9 Ig 54.50N 4.03W
Deep Creek Range 46 If 40.00N 113.57W
Deering 40 Gc 66.05N 162.43W
Deer Isle 44 Mc 44.13N 68.41W
Deer Lake [Newf.-Can.] 42 Lg 49.10N 57.25W
Deer Lake [Ont.-Can.] 42 If 52.40N 94.30W
Deer Park 46 Gc 47.57N 117.28W
Defiance 44 Ee 41.17N 84.21W
Defla 13 Qi 35.14N 4.26 E
De Funiak Springs 44 Dj 30.43N 86.07W
Dega Ahmedo 35 Gd 7.50N 42.53 E
Dêgê 27 Ge 31.52N 98.36 E
Degebe 13 Ef 38.13N 7.29W
Degeh Bur 35 Gd 8.13N 43.34 E
Degema 34 Ge 4.45N 6.46 E
Degerby 8 Id 60.02N 20.23 E
Degerfors 7 Dg 59.14N 14.26 E
Degerhamn 7 Dh 56.21N 16.24 E
Deggendorf 10 Ih 48.50N 12.58 E

Index Symbols

[1] Independent Nation
[2] State, Region
[3] District, County
[4] Municipality
[5] Colony, Dependency
Continent
Physical Region
Historical or Cultural Region
Mount, Mountain
Volcano
Hill
Mountains, Mountain Range
Hills, Escarpment
Plateau, Upland
Pass, Gap
Plain, Lowland
Delta
Salt Flat
Valley, Canyon
Crater, Cave
Karst Features
Depression
Polder
Desert, Dunes
Forest, Woods
Heath, Steppe
Oasis
Cape, Point
Coast, Beach
Cliff
Peninsula
Isthmus
Sandbank
Island
Atoll
Rock, Reef
Islands, Archipelago
Rocks, Reefs
Coral Reef
Well, Spring
Geyser
River, Stream
Waterfall Rapids
River Mouth, Estuary
Lake
Salt Lake
Intermittent Lake
Reservoir
Swamp, Pond
Canal
Glacier
Ice Shelf, Pack Ice
Ocean
Sea
Gulf, Bay
Strait, Fjord
Lagoon
Bank
Seamount
Tablemount
Ridge
Shelf
Basin
Escarpment, Sea Scarp
Fracture
Trench, Abyss
National Park, Reserve
Point of Interest
Recreation Site
Cave, Cavern
Historic Site
Ruins
Wall, Walls
Church, Abbey
Temple
Scientific Station
Airport
Port
Lighthouse
Mine
Tunnel
Dam, Bridge

Değirmendere	15	Kk	38.06N	27.09 E
De Gray Lake	45	Ji	34.15N	93.15W
De Grey River	59	Dd	20.12S	119.11 E
Degtarsk	17	Jh	56.42N	60.06 E
De Haan	12	Fc	51.16N	3.02 E
Dēh 'Ain	35	Hd	8.55N	46.15 E
Dehaj	24	Pg	30.42N	54.53 E
Dehaq	24	Nf	32.55N	50.57 E
Deh Bārez	24	Qi	27.26N	57.12 E
Deh Bīd	24	Og	30.38N	53.13 E
Deh Dasht	24	Ng	30.47N	50.34 E
Dehdez	24	Ng	31.43N	50.17 E
Deh-e-Namak	24	Oe	35.25N	52.50 E
Deh-e Shīr	24	Og	31.29N	53.45 E
Deh-e Ziyār	24	Qg	30.40N	57.00 E
Dehgolān	24	Le	35.17N	47.25 E
Dehlorān	24	Lf	32.41N	47.16 E
Deh Now	24	Qf	33.01N	57.41 E
Dehra Dūn	25	Fb	30.19N	78.02 E
Dehui	27	Mc	44.33N	125.38 E
Deinze	11	Jd	50.59N	3.32 E
Dej	15	Gb	47.09N	23.52 E
Deje	8	Ee	59.36N	13.28 E
Dejen	35	Fc	10.05N	38.11 E
Dejës, Mali i-	15	Dh	41.42N	20.10 E
Dejnau	19	Gh	39.18N	63.11 E
De Jongs, Tanjung-	26	Kh	6.56S	138.32 E
De Kalb	45	Lf	41.56N	88.45W
Dekar	37	Cd	21.30S	21.58 E
Dekese	31	Ji	3.27S	21.24 E
Dekina	34	Gd	7.42N	7.01 E
Dékoa	35	Bd	6.19N	19.04 E
De Koog, Texel-	12	Ga	53.07N	4.46 E
De La Garma	55	Bm	37.58S	60.25W
De Land	44	Gk	29.02N	81.18W
Delano	43	Dd	35.41N	119.15W
Delano Peak	43	Ed	38.22N	112.23W
Delārām	23	Jc	32.11N	63.25 E
Delarof Islands	40a	Cb	51.30N	178.45W
Delaware	44	Fe	40.18N	83.06W
Delaware	45	Ek	32.00N	104.00W
Delaware [2]	43	Ld	39.10N	75.30W
Delaware Bay	38	Lc	39.05N	75.15W
Delaware River	43	Ld	39.20N	75.25W
Delbrück	12	Kc	51.46N	8.34 E
Del Carril	55	Cl	35.31S	59.30W
Delčevo	15	Fh	41.58N	22.47 E
Del City	45	Hi	35.27N	97.27W
Delegate	59	Jg	37.03S	148.58 E
Delémont/Delsberg	14	Bc	47.22N	7.21 E
Delet/Teili	8	Id	60.15N	20.35 E
Delfinópolis	55	Ie	20.20S	46.51W
Delft	11	Kb	52.00N	4.21 E
Delfzijl	11	Ma	53.19N	6.56 E
Delgada, Punta-	52	Jj	42.46S	63.38W
Delgado, Cabo-=Delgado, Cape-(EN)	30	Lj	10.40S	40.38 E
Delgado, Cabo-=Delgado, Cape-(EN) [3]	37	Fb	12.30S	39.00 E
Delgado, Cape-(EN)=Delgado, Cabo-	30	Lj	10.40S	40.38 E
Delgado, Cape-(EN)=Delgado, Cabo- [3]	37	Fb	12.30S	39.00 E
Delger Muren	27	Hb	49.17N	100.40 E
Delhi [Co.-U.S.]	45	Eh	37.42N	103.58W
Delhi [India]	25	Jg	28.40N	77.13 E
Delhi [N.Y.-U.S.]	44	Jd	42.17N	74.57W
Deliblatska Peščara	15	Dd	45.00N	21.00 E
Delice	24	Fc	39.58N	34.02 E
Deliceırmak	24	Fb	40.28N	34.10 E
Delicias [Cuba]	49	Ic	21.11N	76.34W
Delicias [Mex.]	47	Cc	28.13N	105.28W
Delījān	24	Nf	33.59N	50.40 E
Delingha	27	Gd	37.26N	97.25 E
Dēliņkalns/Delinkalns, Gora-	8	Lg	57.30N	27.02 E
Delinkalns, Gora-/Dēliņkalns	8	Lg	57.30N	27.02 E
Delitzsch	10	Ie	51.32N	12.21 E
Deljatin	15	Ha	48.29N	24.45 E
Delle	11	Mg	47.30N	7.00 E
Dell Rapids	45	He	43.50N	96.43W
Dellys	32	Hb	36.55N	3.55 E
Delmarva Peninsula	38	Lf	38.50N	75.30W
Delme	12	Ka	53.05N	8.40 E
Delme	12	If	48.53N	6.24 E
Delmenhorst	10	Ec	53.03N	8.37 E
Delnice	14	Ie	45.24N	14.48 E
Delo	35	Fd	5.49N	37.57 E
De Long Strait (EN)=Longa, Proliv-	21	Tb	70.20N	178.00 E
De-Longa, Ostrova-=De Long Islands (EN)	21	Rb	76.30N	153.00 E
De Long Islands (EN)=De-Longa, Ostrova-	21	Rb	76.30N	153.00 E
De Long Mountains	40	Gc	68.20N	162.00W
Deloraine	59	Jh	41.31S	146.39 E
Delorme, Lac-	42	Kf	54.35N	69.55W
Delphi (EN) = Dhelfoí	15	Fk	38.29N	22.30 E
Del Rio	43	Gf	29.22N	100.54W
Delsberg/Delémont	14	Bc	47.22N	7.21 E
Delsbo	7	Dc	61.48N	16.35 E
Delta [Co.-U.S.]	43	Fd	38.44N	108.04W
Delta [Ut.-U.S.]	43	Ed	39.21N	112.35W
Delta Amacuro [2]	54	Fb	8.30N	61.30W
Delta Junction	40	Jd	64.02N	145.41W
Delvāda	25	Ed	20.46N	71.02 E
Del Valle	55	Bl	35.54S	60.43W
Delvina	15	Dj	39.57N	20.06 E
Dëma	17	Gi	54.42N	55.58 E
Demanda, Sierra de la-	13	Ib	42.15N	3.05W
Demba	36	Dd	5.30S	22.16 E
Dembi	35	Fd	8.05N	36.28 E
Dembia	35	Cd	5.07N	24.25 E
Dembi Dolo	35	Ed	8.32N	34.49 E
De Medinilla, Farallon-	57	Fc	16.01N	146.04 E
Demer	11	Kd	50.58N	4.45 E
Demerara Plateau (EN)	52	Le	4.30N	44.00W
Demerara River	50	Gi	6.48N	58.10W
Demidov	16	Gb	55.15N	31.29 E
Demidovka	10	Vf	50.20N	25.27 E
Deming	43	Fe	32.16N	107.45W
Demini, Rio-	54	Fd	0.46S	62.56W
Demirci	24	Cc	39.03N	28.40 E
Demir Kapija	15	Fh	41.25N	22.15 E
Demirköy	15	Kh	41.49N	27.15 E
Demirtaş	15	Mi	40.16N	29.06 E
Demjanka	19	Gd	59.34N	69.20 E
Demjansk	7	Hh	57.38N	32.29 E
Demjanskoje	19	Gd	59.36N	69.18 E
Demmin	10	Jc	53.54N	13.02 E
Demopolis	44	Di	32.31N	87.50W
Dempo, Gunung-	21	Mj	4.02S	103.09 E
Demta	26	Lg	2.20S	140.08 E
Denain	11	Jd	50.20N	3.23 E
Denan	35	Gd	6.30N	43.30 E
Denau	19	Gh	38.18N	67.55 E
Den Bosch/'s-Hertogenbosch	11	Lc	51.41N	5.19 E
Den Burg, Texel-	12	Ga	53.03N	4.47 E
Den Chai	25	Ke	17.59N	100.04 E
Dendang	26	Eg	3.05S	107.54 E
Dender/Dendre	11	Kc	51.02N	4.06 E
Dendermonde/Termonde	12	Gc	51.02N	4.07 E
Dendre/Dender	11	Kc	51.02N	4.06 E
Dendtler Island	66	Pf	72.58S	89.57W
Denekamp	12	Jb	52.23N	7.00 E
Denežkin Kamen, Gora-	19	Fc	60.25N	59.31 E
Dengarh	25	Hd	23.50N	81.42 E
Dêngkagoin→Têwo	27	He	34.03N	103.21 E
Dengkou (Bayan Gol)	22	Me	40.25N	106.59 E
Dêngqên	27	Ge	31.29N	95.32 E
Dengzhou→Penglai	27	Ld	37.44N	120.45 E
Den Haag/'s-Gravenhage=The Hague (EN)	6	Ge	52.06N	4.18 E
Den Ham	12	Ib	52.28N	6.32 E
Denham→Shak Bay	59	Ce	25.55S	113.32 E
Denham, Mount-	49	Id	18.13N	77.32W
Denham Range	59	Jd	21.55S	147.45 E
Denham Sound	59	Ce	25.40S	113.15 E
Den Helder	11	Kb	52.54N	4.45 E
Denia	13	Mf	38.51N	0.07 E
Deniliquin	59	Ig	35.32S	144.58 E
Denio	46	Ff	41.59N	118.39W
Denis Island	37b	Ca	3.48S	55.40 E
Denison [Ia.-U.S.]	43	Hc	42.01N	95.20W
Denison [Tx.-U.S.]	43	He	33.45N	96.33W
Denison, Mount-	40	Ie	58.25N	154.27W
Denizli	23	Cb	37.46N	29.06 E
Denklingen, Reichshoft-	12	Jd	50.55N	7.39 E
Denman Glacier	66	Ge	66.45S	99.25 E
Denmark [Austl.]	59	Df	34.57S	117.21 E
Denmark [S.C.-U.S.]	44	Gi	33.19N	81.09W
Denmark (EN)=Danmark [1]	6	Gd	56.00N	10.00 E
Denmark Strait (EN)=Danmarksstraedet	38	Qc	67.00N	25.00W
Dennery	51k	Bb	13.55N	60.54W
Den Oever, Wieringen-	12	Hb	52.56N	5.02 E
Denpasar	22	Nj	8.39S	115.13 E
Denton	43	He	33.13N	97.08W
D'Entrecasteaux, Point-	59	Df	34.50S	116.00 E
D'Entrecasteaux Islands	57	Ge	9.35S	150.40 E
Denver	39	If	39.43N	105.01W
Deoghar	25	Hd	24.29N	86.42 E
Deolāli	25	Ee	19.54N	73.50 E
De Pajaros, Farallon-	57	Fb	20.32N	144.54 E
De Panne/La Panne	12	Ec	51.06N	2.35 E
De Pere	45	Ld	44.27N	88.04W
Deputatski	20	Ic	69.13N	139.55 E
Dêqên	27	Gf	28.32N	98.50 E
Deqing	27	Jg	23.14N	111.42 E
De Queen	45	Ii	34.02N	94.21W
De Quincy	45	Jk	30.27N	93.26W
Dequing	28	Fi	30.34N	120.05 E
Dera, Lach-	35	Ge	0.15N	42.17 E
Dera, Lagh-	30	Lh	0.15N	42.17 E
Dera Bugti	25	Dc	29.02N	69.09 E
Dera Ghāzi Khan	22	Jf	30.03N	70.38 E
Dera Ismāil Khan	25	Eb	31.50N	70.54 E
Derbent [R.S.F.S.R.]	6	Kg	42.00N	48.18 E
Derbent [Tur.]	15	Lk	38.11N	28.33 E
Derby	9	Lh	53.05N	1.40W
Derby [Austl.]	58	Df	17.18S	123.38 E
Derby [Eng.-U.K.]	9	Li	52.55N	1.30W
Derby [Ks.-U.S.]	45	Hh	37.33N	97.16W
Derbyshire [3]	9	Lh	53.10N	1.35W
Đerdap	15	Fe	44.41N	22.10 E
Derecske	10	Ri	47.21N	21.34 E
Dereköy	15	Kh	41.56N	27.21 E
Dereli	24	Hb	40.45N	38.27 E
Derg/Abhainn na Deirge	9	Fg	54.40N	7.25W
Derg, Lough-/Loch Deirgeirt	9	Ei	53.00N	8.20W
Dergači [R.S.F.S.R.]	16	Pd	51.13N	48.46 E
Dergači [Ukr.-U.S.S.R.]	16	Jd	50.09N	36.09 E
Der Grabow	10	Ib	54.23N	12.50 E
De Ridder	45	Jk	30.51N	93.17W
Derik	24	Id	37.22N	40.17 E
Derkul	16	Qd	51.17N	51.15 E
Dermott	45	Kj	33.32N	91.26W
Dernieres, Isles-	45	Kl	29.02N	90.47W
Derong	27	Gf	28.44N	99.18 E
De Rose Hill	59	Ge	26.25S	133.15 E
Déroute, Passage de la-	11	Ee	49.12N	1.51W
Dersa, Eglab-	32	Gd	26.45N	4.26W
Dersca	15	Jb	47.59N	26.12 E
Dersingham	12	Cb	52.51N	0.30 E
Derudeb	35	Fb	17.32N	36.06 E
Derventa	14	Lf	44.59N	17.55 E
Derwent [Eng.-U.K.]	9	Mg	54.10N	0.40W
Derwent [Eng.-U.K.]	12	Ab	52.53N	1.17W
Derwent River	59	Jh	43.03S	147.22 E
Deržavinsk	19	Ge	51.03N	66.19 E
Desaguadero, Rio-	52	Ji	34.13S	66.47W
Désappointement, Iles du-	57	Mf	14.10S	141.20W
Des Arc	45	Ki	34.58N	91.30W
Desborough	12	Bb	52.26N	0.49W
Descalvado	55	Ie	21.54S	47.37W
Descartes	11	Gh	46.58N	0.45 E
Deschambault Lake	42	Hf	54.50N	103.30W
Deschutes River	43	Cb	45.38N	120.54W
Descoberto, Rio-	55	Hc	16.20S	48.19W
Dese	31	Kg	11.07N	39.38 E
Deseado, Rio-	52	Jj	47.45S	65.54W
Desecheo, Isla-	51a	Ab	18.25N	67.28W
Desengaño, Punta-	56	Gg	49.15S	67.37W
Desenzano del Garda	14	Ee	45.28N	10.32 E
Desert Center	46	Hj	33.42N	115.26W
Desert Peak	46	If	40.28N	112.38W
Deshaies [Guad.]	51e	Ab	16.18N	61.48W
Deshaies [Guad.]	51e	Ab	16.18N	61.47W
Desiderio, Rio-	55	Ja	12.20S	44.50W
Desmaraisville	44	Ia	49.31N	76.10W
De Smet	45	Hd	44.23N	97.33W
Desmochado	55	Ch	27.07S	58.06W
Des Moines	38	Je	40.22N	91.26W
Des Moines [Ia.-U.S.]	39	Je	41.35N	93.37W
Des Moines [N.M.-U.S.]	45	Eh	36.46N	103.50W
Desmoronado, Cerro-	47	Dd	20.21N	105.01W
Desna	5	Je	50.33N	30.32 E
Desnățui	15	Ge	43.53N	23.35 E
Desolación, Isla-	52	Ik	53.00S	74.10W
De Soto	45	Kg	38.08N	90.33W
Despeñaperros, Desfiladero de-	13	If	38.24N	3.30W
Des Roches, Ile-	37b	Bb	5.41S	53.41 E
Dessau	10	Ie	51.50N	12.15 E
Destruction Bay	42	Dd	61.20N	139.00W
Desventuradas, Islas-	52	Ih	26.45S	80.00W
Desvres	11	Hd	50.40N	1.50 E
Deta	15	Ed	45.24N	21.14 E
Detmold	10	Ee	51.56N	8.53 E
Detour, Point-	44	Dc	45.36N	86.37W
Detroit [Mi.-U.S.]	39	Ke	42.20N	83.03W
Detroit [Or.-U.S.]	46	Dd	44.42N	122.10W
Detroit Lakes	45	Ic	46.49N	95.51W
Dett	37	Dc	18.37S	26.51 E
Dettifoss	7a	Cb	65.49N	16.24W
Detva	10	Ph	48.34N	19.25 E
Deûle	12	Ed	50.44N	2.56 E
Deurdeur	13	Oh	36.14N	2.16 E
Deurne	12	Hc	51.28N	5.48 E
Deutsche Bucht	10	Db	54.30N	7.30 E
Deutsche Demokratische Republik=German Democratic Republic (EN) [1]	6	He	52.00N	12.30 E
Deutschlandsberg	14	Jd	46.49N	15.13 E
Deux-Bassins, Col des-	13	Ph	36.27N	3.18 E
Deux Sèvres [3]	11	Fh	46.30N	0.15W
Deva	15	Fd	45.53N	22.54 E
Dévaványa	10	Qi	47.02N	20.58 E
Deveci Dağları	24	Gb	40.05N	36.00 E
Devecser	10	Ni	47.06N	17.26 E
Develi	24	Fc	38.22N	35.06 E
Deventer	11	Mb	52.15N	6.10 E
Deverd, Cap-	63b	Be	20.46S	164.22 E
Deveron	9	Kd	57.40N	2.30W
Devès, Monts du-	11	Jj	44.57N	3.46 E
Devetak	14	Mg	43.58N	19.00 E
Devil River Peak	62	Ed	40.58S	172.39 E
Devil's Hole	9	Ne	56.38N	0.40 E
Devil's Island (EN)=Diable, Ile du-	54	Hb	5.17N	52.35W
Devils Lake	43	Hb	48.07N	98.59W
Devils Lake	45	Gb	48.01N	98.52W
Devils Paw	40	Me	58.44N	133.50W
Devils River	45	Fl	29.39N	100.58W
Devils Tower	46	Md	44.31N	104.57W
Devin	15	Hh	41.45N	24.24 E
Devizes	9	Lj	51.22N	1.59W
Devnja	15	Kf	43.13N	27.33 E
Devodi Munda	25	Ge	17.37N	82.57 E
De Volet Point	51n	Ba	13.22N	61.13W
Devolli	15	Ci	40.49N	19.51 E
Devolli	15	Di	40.30N	20.50 E
Dévoluy	11	Lj	44.39N	5.53 E
Devon [3]	9	Jk	50.50N	3.50W
Devon	9	Jk	50.50N	4.00W
Devon	38	Kb	75.00N	87.00W
Devon	12	Ba	53.04N	0.49W
Devonport	57	Fi	41.11S	146.21 E
Devoto	55	Aj	31.24S	62.19W
Devrek	24	Db	41.13N	31.57 E
Devrez	24	Fb	41.06N	34.25 E
Dewa	30	Lh	4.11N	42.06 E
Dewar Lakes	42	Kc	68.00N	73.00W
Dewās	25	Fd	22.58N	76.04 E
Dewa-Sanchi	29	Gb	39.30N	140.15 E
Dewey	45	Ih	36.48N	95.56W
De Witt	45	Ki	34.18N	91.20W
Dexemhare	35	Fb	15.04N	39.03 E
Dexing	28	Dj	28.55N	117.33 E
Dexter	45	Lh	36.48N	89.57W
Deyang	27	He	31.07N	104.25 E
Dey-Dey, Lake-	59	Ge	29.15S	131.05 E
Deyhūk	24	Qf	33.17N	57.30 E
Deyyer	23	Hd	27.50N	51.55 E
Dez	24	Mg	31.39N	48.52 E
Dezfūl	22	Gf	32.23N	48.24 E
Dez Gerd	24	Ng	30.45N	51.57 E
Dezhou	27	Kd	37.28N	116.18 E
Dežneva, Mys-	21	Uc	66.06N	169.45 E
Dháfni	15	Fl	37.46N	22.02 E
Dhahab	33	Fd	28.29N	34.32 E
Dhamār	23	Fg	14.37N	44.23 E
Dhamtari	25	Gd	20.41N	81.34 E
Dhānbād	25	Hd	23.48N	86.27 E
Dhanushkodi	25	Fg	9.11N	79.24 E
Dhārwār	25	Fe	15.43N	75.01 E
Dhaulagiri	21	Kg	28.44N	83.25 E
Dhekeleia	24	Ee	35.03N	33.40 E
Dhelfoí = Delphi (EN)	15	Fk	38.29N	22.30 E
Dhelvinákion	15	Dj	39.56N	20.28 E
Dhenkanal	25	Hd	20.40N	85.36 E
Dheskáti	15	Ej	39.55N	21.49 E
Dhespotikó	15	Hm	36.58N	25.00 E
Dhiapóndioi Nísoi	15	Cj	39.50N	19.25 E
Dhībān	24	Fg	31.30N	35.47 E
Dhidhimótikhon	15	Jh	41.21N	26.30 E
Dhíkti Óros	15	In	35.15N	25.30 E
Dhílos	15	Il	37.24N	25.16 E
Dhílos	15	Il	37.24N	25.16 E
Dhimitsána	15	Fl	37.36N	22.03 E
Dhionisiádhes, Nísoi-	15	Jn	35.21N	26.10 E
Dhiórix Potídhaia	15	Gi	40.10N	23.20 E
Dhī-Qar [3]	24	Lg	31.10N	46.10 E
Dhī-Qar	24	Kf	32.14N	44.22 E
Dhírfis Óros	15	Gk	38.38N	23.50 E
Dhísoron Óros	15	Fh	41.11N	22.57 E
Dhivounia	15	Jn	35.50N	26.28 E
Dhodhekánisos = Dodecanese (EN)	15	Jm	36.20N	27.00 E
Dhodhóni = Dodona (EN)	15	Dj	39.33N	20.46 E
Dholpur	25	Fc	26.42N	77.54 E
Dhomokós	15	Fj	39.08N	22.18 E
Dhone	25	Fe	15.25N	77.53 E
Dhonoúsa	15	Il	37.10N	25.50 E
Dhorāij	25	Ed	21.44N	70.27 E
Dhoxáton	15	Hh	41.06N	24.14 E
Dhragónisos	15	Il	37.27N	25.29 E
Dhubri	25	Hc	26.02N	89.58 E
Dhule	22	Jg	20.54N	74.47 E
Dhuliān	25	Hd	24.41N	87.58 E
Dia	15	In	35.27N	25.13 E
Diable, Ile du-=Devil's Island (EN)	54	Hb	5.17N	52.35W
Diable, Morne au-	51g	Ba	15.37N	61.27W
Diable, Pointe du- [Mart.]	51h	Bb	14.47N	60.54W
Diable, Pointe du- [Van.]	63b	Dc	16.01S	168.12 E
Diablo, Punta del-	55	Fl	34.22S	53.46W
Diablo, Puntan-	64b	Ba	15.00N	145.34 E
Diablo Range	46	Eh	36.45N	121.20W
Diafarabé	34	Ec	14.10N	5.00W
Dialafara	34	Cc	13.27N	11.23W
Diamant, Pointe du-	51h	Ac	14.27N	61.04W
Diamant, Rocher du-	51h	Ac	14.27N	61.03W
Diamante [Arg.]	56	Hd	32.04S	60.39W
Diamante [It.]	14	Jk	39.41N	15.49 E
Diamante, Punta del-	48	Ji	16.47N	99.52W
Diamantina	54	Jg	18.15S	43.36W
Diamantina, Chapada-	52	Lg	11.30S	41.10W
Diamantina, Rio-	55	Fc	16.42S	52.45W
Diamantina Depth (EN)	3	Hm	33.30S	102.00 E
Diamantina Lakes	59	Id	23.46S	141.09 E
Diamantina River	57	Eg	26.45S	139.10 E
Diamantina Trench (EN)	3	Hm	36.00S	104.00 E
Diamantino	53	Kg	14.25S	56.27W
Diamantino, Rio-	55	Fc	16.08S	52.28W
Diamond Harbour	25	Hd	22.12N	88.12 E
Diamond Island	51p	Bb	12.20N	61.35W
Diamond Jenness Peninsula	42	Fb	71.00N	117.00W
Diamond Peak [Nv.-U.S.]	46	Hg	39.40N	115.48W
Diamond Peak [Or.-U.S.]	46	De	43.33N	122.09W
Diamond Peak [U.S.]	46	Id	44.09N	113.05W
Diamond Peak [U.S.]	46	Gc	46.07N	117.32W
Diamou	34	Cc	14.05N	11.16W
Diana, Baie-	42	Kd	61.00N	70.00W
Dianbai	27	Jg	21.33N	110.58 E
Dianbu → Feidong	28	Di	31.53N	117.29 E
Diancang Shan	27	Hf	25.42N	100.02 E
Dian Chi	27	Hg	24.50N	102.45 E
Diane, Étang de-	11a	Ba	42.07N	9.32 E
Dianjiang	27	Ie	30.19N	107.25 E
Diano Marina	14	Cg	43.54N	8.05 E
Dianópolis	54	If	11.38S	46.50W
Dianra	34	Dd	8.45N	6.18W
Diapaga	34	Fc	12.04N	1.47 E
Diaz	55	Bk	32.22S	61.05W
Dibā, Dawḩat-	24	Qk	25.38N	56.18 E
Dībagah	24	Je	35.52N	43.49 E
Dibang	25	Jc	27.50N	95.32 E
Dibaya	36	Dd	6.30S	22.57 E
Dibaya-Lubue	36	Cc	4.09S	19.52 E
Dibella	34	Hb	17.31N	12.59 E
Dibrugarh	22	Lg	27.29N	94.54 E
Dibs	24	Ke	35.40N	44.04 E
Dibsī Afnān	24	Ee	35.55N	38.16 E
Dickens	45	Fj	33.37N	100.50W
Dickinson	43	Gb	46.53N	102.47W
Dickins Seamount (EN)	40	Lf	54.30N	137.00W
Dickson	44	Dg	36.05N	87.23W
Dicle	24	Ic	38.22N	40.04 E
Dicle=Tigris (EN)	21	Gf	31.00N	47.25 E
Didam	12	Ic	51.56N	6.09 E
Didao	28	Kb	45.22N	130.48 E
Didcot	12	Ac	51.36N	1.15W
Didesa	35	Fd	9.30N	35.32 E
Didiéni	34	Dc	13.23N	8.05W
Didyma	15	Kl	37.21N	27.13 E
Die	11	Lj	44.45N	5.22 E
Dieburg	10	Eg	49.54N	8.51 E
Diecinueve de Abril	55	El	34.22S	54.04W
Dieciocho de Julio	55	Fk	33.41S	53.33W
Diefenbaker Lake	42	Gf	51.00N	107.00W
Diège	11	Ii	45.36N	2.16 E
Diego Garcia	21	Jj	6.20S	72.20 E
Diego Ramírez, Islas	56	Gi	56.30S	68.44W
Diekirch	11	Me	49.53N	6.10 E
Die Lewitz	10	Hc	53.30N	11.30 E
Diéma	34	Dc	14.33N	9.11W
Diemel	10	Fe	51.39N	9.27 E
Diemelsee	12	Kc	51.19N	8.43 E
Diemelstadt	12	Lc	51.27N	9.01 E
Dien Bien Phu	25	Kd	21.23N	103.01 E
Diepenbeek	12	Hd	50.54N	5.24 E
Diepholz	10	Ed	52.36N	8.22 E
Dieppe	11	He	49.56N	1.05 E
Dieppe Bay Town	51c	Ab	17.25N	62.48W
Dierdorf	12	Jd	50.33N	7.40 E
Dieren, Rheden-	12	Ib	52.03N	6.08 E
Di'er Songhua Jiang	27	Lc	45.26N	124.39 E
Diest	12	Hd	50.59N	5.03 E
Dieulefit	11	Lj	44.31N	5.04 E
Dieulouard	12	If	48.51N	6.04 E
Dieuze	11	Mf	48.49N	6.43 E
Dieveniškes	8	Kj	54.10N	25.44 E
Die Ville	12	Id	50.40N	6.55 E
Diez	12	Kd	50.22N	8.01 E
Dif	36	Hb	0.59N	40.57 E
Diffa [2]	34	Hb	16.00N	13.30 E
Diffa	34	Hc	13.19N	12.37 E
Differdange/Differdingen	11	Le	49.32N	5.52 E
Differdingen/Differdange	11	Le	49.32N	5.52 E
Digby	42	Kh	44.40N	65.50W
Dighton	45	Fg	38.29N	100.28W
Digne	11	Mj	44.06N	6.14 E
Digoin	11	Jh	46.29N	3.59 E
Digora	16	Nh	43.07N	44.06 E
Digos	26	Ie	6.45N	125.20 E
Digranes	7a	Ca	66.02N	14.45W
Digul	26	Kh	7.07S	138.42 E
Dihāng	25	Jc	27.48N	95.30 E
Dijar	16	Tf	46.33N	56.05 E
Dijlah=Tigris (EN)	21	Gf	31.00N	47.25 E
Dijle	11	Kd	50.53N	4.42 E
Dijon	6	Gf	47.19N	5.01 E
Dik	35	Bd	9.58N	17.31 E
Dikanäs	7	Dd	65.14N	16.00 E
Dikhil	35	Gc	11.06N	42.22 E
Dikili	24	Bc	39.04N	26.53 E
Dikli	8	Kg	57.30N	25.00 E
Diksmuide/Dixmude	11	Ic	51.02N	2.52 E
Dikson	22	Kb	73.30N	80.35 E
Dikwa	34	Hc	12.02N	13.55 E
Dila	35	Fd	6.23N	38.19 E
Dilbeek	12	Gd	50.51N	4.16 E
Dili	22	Oj	8.33S	125.34 E
Di Linh	25	Lf	11.35N	108.04 E
Diližan	16	Ni	40.46N	44.55 E
Dilj	14	Me	45.16N	18.01 E
Dill	12	Kd	50.33N	8.29 E
Dillenburg	10	Ef	50.44N	8.17 E
Dillia	30	Ig	14.09N	12.50 E
Dilling	31	Jg	12.03N	29.39 E
Dillingen (Saar)	12	Ie	49.21N	6.44 E
Dillingham	39	Dd	59.02N	158.29W
Dillon [Mt.-U.S.]	43	Eb	45.13N	112.38W
Dillon [S.C.-U.S.]	44	Hh	34.25N	79.22W
Dilly	34	Dc	14.57N	7.43W
Dilolo	31	Jj	10.42S	22.20 E
Dilsen	12	Hc	51.02N	5.44 E
Dimashq=Damascus (EN)	22	Ff	33.30N	36.15 E
Dimbelenge	36	Dd	5.30S	23.53 E
Dimbokro [3]	34	Ed	6.50N	4.45W
Dimbokro	34	Ed	6.39N	4.42W
Dimboola	59	Ig	36.27S	142.02 E
Dîmbovița	15	Je	44.14N	26.27 E
Dîmbovița [2]	15	Ie	44.55N	25.30 E
Dîmbovnic	15	Ie	44.20N	25.40 E
Dimitrovgrad [Bul.]	15	Ig	42.03N	25.36 E
Dimitrovgrad [R.S.F.S.R.]	19	Ee	54.14N	49.42 E
Dimitrovgrad [Yugo.]	15	Fg	43.01N	22.47 E
Dimmitt	45	Ei	34.33N	102.19W
Dimona	24	Fg	31.04N	35.02 E
Dimovo	15	Ff	43.44N	22.44 E
Dinagat	26	Id	10.12N	125.35 E
Dinājpur	25	Hc	25.38N	88.38 E
Dinan	11	Df	48.27N	2.02W
Dinangourou	34	Ec	14.27N	2.14W
Dinant	11	Kd	50.16N	4.55 E
Dinar	24	Dc	38.04N	30.10 E
Dīnar, Kūh-e-	24	Ng	30.50N	51.35 E
Dinara	14	Kf	44.04N	16.23 E
Dinara=Dinaric Alps (EN)	5	Hg	43.50N	16.35 E
Dinard	11	Df	48.38N	2.04W
Dinaric Alps (EN)=Dinara	5	Hg	43.50N	16.35 E
Dindar, Nahr ad-	35	Ec	14.06N	33.40 E
Dinder	35	Ec	14.06N	33.40 E
Dindigul	25	Ff	10.21N	77.57 E
Dindima	34	Hc	10.14N	10.09 E
Dinga	36	Cd	5.19S	16.34 E
Dingbian	27	Id	37.35N	107.37 E
Dingden, Hamminkeln-	12	Ic	51.46N	6.37 E
Dinggyê	27	Ef	28.25N	87.45 E
Dinghai	27	Le	30.05N	122.07 E
Dingle	8	Df	58.32N	11.34 E
Dingle/An Daingean	9	Ci	52.08N	10.15W
Dingle Bay/Bá an Daingin	9	Ci	52.05N	10.15W
Dingolfing	10	Ih	48.38N	12.30 E
Dingshuzhen	28	Ei	31.16N	119.50 E
Dingtao	28	Cg	35.04N	115.35 E
Dinguiraye	34	Cc	11.18N	10.43W
Dingwall	9	Id	57.35N	4.26W
Dingxi	27	Hd	35.33N	104.32 E
Dingxian	27	Jd	39.29N	115.00 E
Dingxiang	28	Be	38.32N	112.59 E
Dingxing	27	Kd	39.11N	115.48 E
Dingyuan	28	Dh	32.32N	117.41 E
Dingzi Gang	28	Ff	36.33N	120.59 E
Dinh, Mui-	21	Mh	11.22N	109.01 E
Dinkel	12	Ib	52.30N	6.58 E
Dinosaur	45	Bf	40.15N	109.01W
Dinskaja	16	Kg	45.09N	39.12 E
Dinslaken	12	Ic	51.34N	6.44 E
Dīnsōr	35	Ge	2.23N	42.58 E
Dintel	12	Gc	51.39N	4.24 E
Dinuba	46	Fh	36.36N	119.27W

Index Symbols

- [1] Independent Nation
- [2] State, Region
- [3] District, County
- [4] Municipality
- [5] Colony, Dependency
- Continent
- Physical Region
- Historical or Cultural Region
- Mount, Mountain
- Volcano
- Hill
- Mountains, Mountain Range
- Hills, Escarpment
- Plateau, Upland
- Pass, Gap
- Plain, Lowland
- Delta
- Salt Flat
- Valley, Canyon
- Crater, Cave
- Karst Features
- Depression
- Polder
- Desert, Dunes
- Forest, Woods
- Heath, Steppe
- Oasis
- Cape, Point
- Coast, Beach
- Cliff
- Peninsula
- Isthmus
- Sandbank
- Island
- Atoll
- Rock, Reef
- Islands, Archipelago
- Rocks, Reefs
- Coral Reef
- Well, Spring
- Geyser
- River, Stream
- Waterfall Rapids
- River Mouth, Estuary
- Lake
- Salt Lake
- Intermittent Lake
- Reservoir
- Swamp, Pond
- Canal
- Glacier
- Ice Shelf, Pack Ice
- Ocean
- Sea
- Gulf, Bay
- Strait, Fjord
- Lagoon
- Bank
- Seamount
- Tablemount
- Ridge
- Shelf
- Basin
- Escarpment, Sea Scarp
- Fracture
- Trench, Abyss
- National Park, Reserve
- Point of Interest
- Recreation Site
- Cave, Cavern
- Historic Site
- Ruins
- Wall, Walls
- Church, Abbey
- Temple
- Scientific Station
- Airport
- Port
- Lighthouse
- Mine
- Tunnel
- Dam, Bridge

Dinwiddie	44	Ig	37.05N	77.35W
Dioïla	34	Dc	12.28N	6.47W
Diois, Massif du-	11	Lj	44.35N	5.20 E
Dion	34	Dc	10.12N	8.39W
Diorama	55	Gc	16.21S	51.14W
Dios	63a	Ba	5.33S	154.58 E
Diosig	15	Eb	47.18N	22.00 E
Dioura	34	Dc	14.51N	5.15W
Diourbel [3]	34	Bc	14.45N	16.10W
Diourbel	34	Bc	14.40N	16.15W
Dipkarpas/Rizokarpásso	24	Fe	35.36N	34.23 E
Dipolog	22	Oi	8.35N	123.20 E
Dīr	25	Ea	35.12N	71.53 E
Dira, Djebel-	13	Ph	36.05N	3.38 E
Diré	34	Eb	16.15N	3.24W
Dire Dawa	31	Lh	9.35N	41.53 E
Diriamba	49	Dh	11.51N	86.14W
Dirico	36	Df	17.58S	20.45 E
Dirj	33	Bc	30.09N	10.26 E
Dirk Hartog Island	59	Ce	25.45S	113.00 E
Dirkou	34	Hb	19.01N	12.53 E
Dirranbandi	58	Fg	28.35S	148.14 E
Dirty Devil River	46	Jh	37.53N	110.24W
Disappointment, Cape- [B.A.T.]	56	Mh	54.53S	36.07W
Disappointment, Cape- [U.S.]	46	Cc	46.18N	124.03W
Disappointment, Lake-	57	Dg	23.30S	122.50 E
Discovery Tablemount (EN)	30	Hm	42.00S	0.10 E
Dishna	33	Fd	26.07N	32.28 E
Disko	67	Nc	69.50N	53.30W
Disko Bay (EN)=Disko Bugt	67	Nc	69.15N	52.30W
Disko Bugt=Disko Bay (EN)	67	Nc	69.15N	52.30W
Diskofjord	41	Ge	69.39N	53.45W
Disna	7	Gi	55.33N	28.12 E
Disna	7	Gi	55.34N	28.12 E
Disnaj, Ozero-/Dysnų Ežeras	7	Gi	55.35N	26.32 E
Dispur	25	Ic	26.07N	91.48 E
Diss	12	Db	52.23N	1.07 E
District of Columbia [2]	43	Ld	38.54N	77.01W
Distrito Federal [Braz.] [2]	54	Ig	15.45S	47.45W
Distrito Federal [Mex.] [2]	47	Ee	19.15N	99.10W
Disūq	24	Dg	31.08N	30.39 E
Dithmarschen	10	Fb	54.10N	9.15 E
Ditrău	15	Ic	46.49N	25.31 E
Dittaino	14	Im	37.25N	15.00 E
Diu [3]	25	Ed	20.42N	70.59 E
Dīvāndarreh	24	Le	35.55N	47.02 E
Divénié	36	Bc	2.41S	12.05 E
Divenskaja	8	Ne	59.09N	30.09 E
Dives	11	Fe	49.19N	0.05W
Dives-sur-Mer	12	Be	49.17N	0.06W
Diviaka	15	Ci	41.00N	19.32 E
Diviči	16	Pi	42.10N	49.01 E
Divin	10	Ue	51.57N	24.09 E
Divinópolis	53	Lh	20.09S	44.54W
Divion	12	Ed	50.28N	2.30 E
Divisões, Serra das-	54	Hg	16.40S	50.50W
Divisor, Serra de	54	De	8.00S	73.50W
Divnogorsk	20	Ee	55.58N	92.32 E
Divnoje	19	Ef	45.53N	43.22 E
Divo [3]	34	Dd	5.57N	5.15W
Divo	34	Dd	5.50N	5.22W
Divoká Orlice	10	Mf	50.09N	16.06 E
Divor	13	Df	38.59N	8.29W
Divriği	24	Hc	39.23N	38.07 E
Dīvrūd	24	Nd	36.52N	49.34 E
Dixmude/Diksmuide	11	Ic	51.02N	2.52 E
Dixon [Il.-U.S.]	45	Lf	41.50N	89.29W
Dixon [N.M.-U.S.]	45	Dh	36.11N	105.53W
Dixon Entrance	38	Fd	54.25N	132.30W
Diyālā	21	Gf	33.14N	44.31 E
Diyālá [3]	24	Kf	34.00N	45.00 E
Diyarbakir	23	Fb	37.55N	40.14 E
Dizy	12	Fe	49.04N	3.58 E
Dizy-le-Gros	12	Ge	49.38N	4.01 E
Dja	30	Ih	2.02N	15.12 E
Djado	31	If	21.01N	12.18 E
Djado, Plateau du-	30	If	21.45N	12.50 E
Djakovo	10	Th	48.03N	23.01 E
Djamaa	32	Ic	33.32N	6.00 E
Djambala	31	Ii	2.33S	14.45 E
Djanet	31	Hf	24.34N	9.29 E
Djaret	32	Hd	26.35N	1.38 E
Djatkovo	19	De	53.36N	34.20 E
Djatlovo	16	Dc	53.31N	25.24 E
Djaul Island	60	Eh	2.56S	150.55 E
Djebel Ṭāriq, El Bōghāz-=Gibraltar, Strait of- (EN)	5	Fh	35.57N	5.36W
Djédaa	35	Bc	13.31N	18.34 E
Djedi	30	He	34.39N	5.55 E
Djedoug, Djebel-	13	Qi	35.53N	4.20 E
Djelfa	31	He	34.40N	3.15 E
Djelfa [3]	32	Hc	34.15N	3.30 E
Djéma	31	Jh	6.03N	25.19 E
Djember	35	Bc	10.25N	17.50 E
Djemila	32	Ib	36.19N	5.44 E
Djenane	13	Pi	35.43N	3.59 E
Djenné	34	Ec	13.55N	4.33W
Djerem	34	Hd	5.20N	13.24 E
Dji	35	Cd	6.47N	22.14 E
Djibo	34	Ec	14.06N	1.38W
Djibouti	31	Lg	11.35N	43.08 E
Djibouti (Afars and Issas) [1]	31	Lg	11.30N	43.00 E
Djokupunda	36	Dd	5.27S	20.58 E
Djolu	31	Jh	0.37N	22.21 E
Djoua	36	Bb	1.13N	13.12 E
Djougou	34	Fd	9.42N	1.40 E
Djoum	34	He	2.40N	12.40 E
Djourab, Erg du- [Chad]	35	Bb	17.00N	19.30 E
Djourab, Erg du- [Chad]	35	Bb	16.40N	18.50 E
Djugu	36	Fb	1.55N	30.30 E
Djultydag, Gora-	16	Oi	41.58N	46.56 E
Djup	8	Bd	60.50N	8.00 E
Djúpi vogur	7a	Cb	64.39N	14.17W
Djurbeldžin	18	Jd	41.10N	74.59 E
Djurdjura, Djebel-	13	Qh	36.27N	4.15 E
Djurmo	8	Fd	60.33N	15.10 E
Djurö	8	Ef	58.50N	13.30 E
Djursholm	8	He	59.24N	18.05 E
Djursland	8	Dh	56.20N	10.45 E
Djurtjuli	19	Fd	55.29N	54.55 E
Dmitrija Lapteva, Proliv-=Dmitri Laptev Strait (EN)	21	Qb	73.00N	142.00 E
Dmitrijev-Lgovski	16	Ic	52.08N	35.05 E
Dmitri Laptev Strait (EN)=Dmitrija Lapteva, Proliv-	21	Qb	73.00N	142.00 E
Dmitrov	7	Ih	56.26N	37.31 E
Dmitrovsk-Orlovski	16	Ic	52.31N	35.09 E
Dnepr	5	Jf	46.30N	32.18 E
Dneprodzeržinsk	19	Df	48.30N	34.37 E
Dneprodzeržinskoje Vodohranilišče	16	Ie	48.45N	34.10 E
Dnepropetrovsk	6	Jf	48.27N	34.59 E
Dnepropetrovskaja Oblast [3]	19	Df	48.15N	35.00 E
Dneprorudnoje	16	If	47.23N	35.01 E
Dneprovski Liman	16	Gf	46.35N	31.55 E
Dneprovsko-Bugski Kanal	16	Dc	52.03N	25.10 E
Dnepr Upland (EN)=Pridneprovskaja Vozvyšennost	5	Jf	49.00N	32.00 E
Dnestr [U.S.S.R.]	5	Jf	46.18N	30.17 E
Dnestrovsk	15	Mc	46.39N	29.48 E
Dnestrovski Liman	16	Gf	46.15N	30.15 E
Dno	19	Cd	57.49N	29.59 E
Doany	37	Hb	14.22S	49.30 E
Doba	35	Bd	8.39N	16.51 E
Dobbiaco / Toblach	14	Gd	46.44N	12.14 E
Dobele	7	Fh	56.39N	23.16 E
Döbeln	10	Je	51.07N	13.07 E
Doberah, Jazirah-	26	Jg	1.30S	132.30 E
Dobo	26	Jh	5.46S	134.13 E
Doboj	14	Mf	44.44N	18.05 E
Dobra	10	Oe	51.54N	18.37 E
Dobre Miasto	10	Qc	53.59N	20.25 E
Dobreta Turnu Severin	6	Ig	44.38N	22.40 E
Dobrinka	16	Lc	52.08N	40.29 E
Dobřiš	10	Kg	49.47N	14.10 E
Dobrjanka	19	Fd	58.29N	56.29 E
Dobrodzień	10	Of	50.44N	18.27 E
Dobrogea=Dobruja (EN)	15	Ke	44.00N	28.00 E
Dobrogea = Dobruja (EN)	5	Ig	44.00N	28.00 E
Dobrogean, Masivul-	15	Le	44.50N	28.30 E
Dobromil	10	Sg	49.34N	22.49 E
Dobropolje	16	Je	48.28N	37.02 E
Dobroteşti	15	He	44.17N	24.53 E
Dobrotvor	10	Uf	50.10N	24.27 E
Dobrudžansko Plato	15	Kf	43.32N	27.50 E
Dobruja (EN)=Dobrogea	15	Ke	44.00N	28.00 E
Dobruja (EN) = Dobrogea	5	Ig	44.00N	28.00 E
Dobruš	16	Gc	52.26N	31.19 E
Dobruška	10	Mf	50.18N	16.10 E
Dobrzyń nad Wisłą	10	Pd	52.38N	19.20 E
Dobrzyńskie, Pojezierze-	10	Pc	53.00N	19.20 E
Dobšiná	10	Qh	48.49N	20.22 E
Doce, Rio- [Braz.]	52	Mg	19.37S	39.49W
Doce, Rio- [Braz.]	55	Gd	18.28S	51.05W
Doce Leguas, Cayos de las-	49	Hc	20.55N	79.05W
Doce Leguas, Laberinto de las-	49	Hc	20.39N	78.35W
Docker River	59	Fd	24.58S	129.03 E
Docksta	8	Ha	63.03N	18.20 E
Doctor Arroyo	48	If	23.40N	100.11W
Doctor Cecilio Baez	55	Dg	25.03S	56.19W
Doctor Pedro P. Peña	56	Hb	22.26S	62.22W
Doctor Petru Groza	15	Fc	46.37N	22.25 E
Doda	25	Fb	33.08N	75.34 E
Doda Betta	25	Ff	11.24N	76.44 E
Dodecanese (EN) = Dhodhekánisos	15	Jm	36.20N	27.00 E
Dodecanese (EN)= Nótioi Sporádhes	5	Ih	36.00N	27.00 E
Dodge City	43	Gd	37.45N	100.00W
Dodgeville	45	Ke	42.58N	90.08W
Dodman Point	9	Ik	50.13N	4.48W
Dodoma [3]	36	Gd	6.00S	36.00 E
Dodoma	31	Ki	6.11S	35.45 E
Dodona (EN) = Dhodhóni	15	Dj	39.33N	20.46 E
Dodurga	15	Mj	39.48N	29.55 E
Doesburg	12	Ib	52.01N	6.08 E
Doetinchem	11	Mc	51.58N	6.17 E
Dofa	26	Ig	1.47S	125.22 E
Dogai Coring	27	Ee	34.30N	89.10 E
Doğanbey	15	Jk	38.04N	26.53 E
Doğanşehir	24	Gc	38.06N	37.53 E
Dog Creek	46	Da	51.35N	122.15W
Dogger Bank	5	Ge	55.00N	3.00 E
Dog Island	50	Ec	18.15N	63.13W
Dog Lake [Man.-Can.]	45	Ga	51.02N	98.30W
Dog Lake [Ont.-Can.]	44	Ea	48.18N	84.10W
Dog Lake [Ont.-Can.]	45	Lb	48.46N	89.32W
Dogliani	14	Bf	44.32N	7.56 E
Dōgo	28	Lf	36.15N	133.17 E
Dogonbadān	23	Hc	30.21N	50.48 E
Dogondoutchi	34	Fc	13.38N	4.02 E
Dōgo-San	29	Cd	35.04N	133.14 E
Dog Rocks	49	Ha	24.05N	79.51W
Doğubayazıt	24	Kc	39.32N	44.08 E
Dogwood Point	51c	Ab	17.06N	62.38W
Doha (EN)=Ad Dawḩah	22	Hg	25.17N	51.32 E
Dohad	25	Ed	22.50N	74.16 E
Dohāzāri	25	Id	22.10N	92.04 E
Doi Luang Chinag Dao	25	Je	19.23N	98.54 E
Doilungdêqên	27	Ff	29.47N	90.49 E
Doire/Londonderry	6	Fd	55.00N	7.19W
Doire Baltée/Dora Baltea	14	Ce	45.11N	8.03 E
Doische	12	Gd	50.08N	4.45 E
Dojransko jezero	15	Fh	41.13N	22.44 E
Doka	35	Fc	13.31N	35.46 E
Dokhara, Dunes de-	32	Ic	32.50N	6.00 E
Dokka	8	Dd	60.49N	10.05 E
Dokka	7	Cf	60.50N	10.05 E
Dokkum	11	La	53.19N	6.00 E
Dokšicy	7	Gi	54.56N	27.46 E
Doksy	10	Kf	50.34N	14.40 E
Dokučajevsk	16	Jf	47.43N	37.47 E
Dolak, Pulau-	57	Ee	7.50S	138.30 E
Dolbeau	42	Kg	48.52N	72.14W
Dol-de-Bretagne	11	Ef	48.33N	1.45W
Dôle	11	Lg	47.06N	5.30 E
Doleib Hill	35	Ed	9.22N	31.36 E
Dolenjsko	14	Je	45.50N	15.10 E
Dolgaja, Kosa-	16	Jf	46.40N	37.45 E
Dolgellau	9	Ji	52.44N	3.53W
Dolgi, Ostrov-	17	Ib	69.15N	59.05 E
Dolgi Most	20	Ee	56.45N	96.58 E
Dolianova	14	Dk	39.22N	9.10 E
Dolina	16	De	48.58N	24.01 E
Dolinsk	20	Jg	47.20N	142.50 E
Dolinskaja	19	Df	48.07N	32.44 E
Dolinskoje	15	Mb	47.33N	29.50 E
Dolj [2]	15	Ge	44.10N	23.40 E
Dollart	11	Na	53.17N	7.10 E
Dolly Cays	49	Ib	23.39N	77.22W
Dolni Dăbnik	15	Hf	43.24N	24.26 E
Dolní Dvořiště	10	Kh	48.39N	14.27 E
Dolnomoravský úval	10	Nh	49.00N	17.15 E
Dolnośląskie, Bory-	10	Le	51.25N	15.20 E
Dolný Kubín	10	Pg	49.12N	19.17 E
Dolo	31	Lh	4.11N	42.05 E
Dolomites (EN) = Dolomiti	5	Hf	46.23N	11.51 E
Dolomiti = Dolomites (EN)	5	Hf	46.23N	11.51 E
Dolon, Pereval-	18	Jd	41.48N	75.45 E
Dolonnur/Duolun	27	Kc	42.10N	116.30 E
Dolores [Arg.]	56	Ie	36.20S	57.40W
Dolores [Guat.]	49	Ce	16.31N	89.25W
Dolores [Ur.]	56	Id	33.33S	58.13W
Dolores River	46	Kg	38.49N	109.17W
Dolphin, Cape-	56	Ih	51.15S	58.58W
Dolphin and Union Strait	42	Gc	69.00N	115.00W
Dom, Kūh-e-	24	Of	33.52N	53.00 E
Domačevo	10	Te	51.46N	23.37 E
Domaniç	24	Cc	39.48N	29.37 E
Domantai/Domantaj	8	Ji	55.57N	23.19 E
Domantaj/Domantai	8	Ji	55.57N	23.19 E
Domart-en-Ponthieu	12	Ed	50.04N	2.07 E
Domasa, údolná nádrž-	10	Rg	49.05N	21.47 E
Domažlice	10	Ig	49.27N	12.56 E
Dombaj-Ulgen, Gora-	16	Lh	43.14N	41.46 E
Dombarovski	19	Fe	50.47N	59.34 E
Dombås	6	Gc	62.05N	9.08 E
Dombe Grande	36	Be	12.56S	13.07 E
Dombes	11	Lh	46.00N	5.03 E
Dombóvár	10	Oj	46.23N	18.07 E
Dombrád	10	Rh	48.14N	21.56 E
Domburg	12	Fc	51.34N	3.30 E
Dôme, Monts-	11	Ii	45.45N	2.55 E
Dôme, Puy de-	11	Ii	45.47N	2.58 E
Domérat	11	Ih	46.21N	2.32 E
Domeyko, Cordillera-	52	Jh	24.30S	69.00W
Domfront	11	Ff	48.36N	0.39W
Domingo M. Irala	55	Eg	25.54S	54.43W
Domingos Martins	54	Jh	20.22S	40.40W
Dominica [1]	39	Mh	15.30N	61.20W
Dominica	38	Mh	15.30N	61.20W
Dominical	49	Fi	9.13N	83.51W
Dominicana, República-=Dominican Republic (EN) [1]	39	Lh	19.00N	70.40W
Dominican Republic (EN)=Dominicana, República- [1]	39	Lh	19.00N	70.40W
Dominica Passage	50	Fe	15.10N	61.15W
Dominica Passage (EN)=Dominique, Canal de la-	50	Fe	15.10N	61.15W
Dominion, Cape -	42	Kc	66.10N	74.30W
Dominique, Canal de la-=Dominica Passage (EN)	50	Fe	15.10N	61.15W
Domino	42	Lf	53.28N	55.46W
Domiongo	36	Dc	4.37S	21.15 E
Dommartin-Varimont	12	Gf	48.59N	4.46 E
Domme	11	Hj	44.48N	1.13 E
Dommel	11	Lc	51.40N	5.20 E
Domneşti	15	Hd	45.12N	24.50 E
Domo	35	Hd	7.57N	46.51 E
Domodedovo	7	Ii	55.27N	37.47 E
Domodossola	14	Cd	46.07N	8.17 E
Domont	12	Ee	49.02N	2.20 E
Dom Pedrito	56	Jd	30.59S	54.40W
Dom Pedro	54	Jd	5.00S	44.27W
Dompierre-sur-Besbre	11	Jh	46.31N	3.41 E
Dompu	26	Gh	8.32S	118.28 E
Domusnovas	14	Ck	39.19N	8.39 E
Domuyo, Volcán-	52	Ii	36.38S	70.26W
Don	48	Ed	26.26N	109.02W
Don [Eng.-U.K.]	9	Mh	53.39N	0.59W
Don [Fr.]	11	Eg	47.40N	1.56W
Don [R.S.F.S.R.]	5	Jf	47.04N	39.18 E
Don [Scot.-U.K.]	9	Kd	57.10N	2.04W
Donaldsonville	45	Kk	30.06N	90.59W
Donau=Danube (EN)	5	If	45.20N	29.40 E
Donaueschingen	10	Ei	47.57N	8.30 E
Donaumoos	10	Hh	48.40N	11.15 E
Donauried	10	Gh	48.35N	10.40 E
Donauwörth	10	Gh	48.42N	10.48 E
Don Benito	13	Gf	38.57N	5.52W
Doncaster	9	Lh	53.32N	1.07W
Dondjušany	15	Ka	48.11N	27.31 E
Dondo [Ang.]	31	Ii	9.40S	14.26 E
Dondo [Moz.]	37	Ec	19.36S	34.44 E
Dondra Head	21	Ki	5.55N	80.35 E
Donec	5	Kf	47.40N	40.50 E
Doneck [R.S.F.S.R.]	16	Ke	48.21N	39.59 E
Doneck [Ukr.-U.S.S.R.]	6	Jf	48.00N	37.48 E
Doneckaja Oblast [3]	19	Df	48.00N	37.45 E
Donecki Krjaž=Donec Ridge (EN)	5	Kh	48.15N	38.45 E
Donec Ridge (EN)=Donecki Krjaž	5	Kh	48.15N	38.45 E
Donegal/Dún na nGall	9	Eg	54.39N	8.06W
Donegal/Dún na nGall [2]	9	Fg	54.50N	8.00W
Donegal Bay/Bá Dhún na nGall	5	Fe	54.30N	8.30W
Donegal Mountains	9	Eg	54.50N	8.10W
Donga	34	Hd	8.19N	10.01 E
Dongara	59	Ce	29.15S	114.56 E
Dongbei Pingyuan	28	Gc	44.00N	124.00 E
Dongchuan (Tangdan)	27	Hf	26.07N	103.05 E
Dongcun → Lanxian	28	Ae	38.17N	111.38 E
Dong Dao	27	Jc	16.45N	113.00 E
Donge	12	Gc	51.41N	4.49 E
Dong'e (Tongcheng)	28	Df	36.19N	116.14 E
Dongen	12	Gc	51.37N	4.57 E
Donges	11	Dg	47.18N	2.04W
Dongfang (Basuo)	27	Ih	19.14N	108.39 E
Dongfanghong	28	La	46.15N	133.07 E
Dongfeng	28	Hc	42.41N	125.33 E
Donggala	26	Gg	0.40S	119.44 E
Donggou	27	Ld	39.55N	124.08 E
Dongguang	28	Df	37.54N	116.32 E
Dong Hai=East China Sea (EN)	21	Og	29.00N	125.00 E
Donghai Dao	27	Jg	21.00N	110.25 E
Dong He	27	Hc	42.12N	101.10 E
Dong Hoi	25	Le	17.29N	106.36 E
Dong Jang	21	Ng	23.02N	113.31 E
Dongkala	26	Hh	5.18S	122.03 E
Dongkan → Binhai	27	Ke	34.00N	119.52 E
Donglan	27	Ig	24.35N	107.22 E
Dongliao He	28	Gc	43.24N	123.42 E
Dongming	28	Cg	35.17N	115.04 E
Dongnan Qiuling	27	Jg	24.00N	113.00 E
Dongo	36	Ce	14.36S	15.43 E
Dongola (EN)=Dunqulah	31	Kg	19.10N	30.29 E
Dongou	36	Cb	2.02N	18.04 E
Dongoun → Haiyang	28	Ff	36.46N	121.09 E
Dongping	27	Kd	35.51N	116.15 E
Dongping → Anhua	27	Jf	28.27N	111.15 E
Dong Rak, Phanom-=Dangrek Range (EN)	21	Mh	14.25N	104.30 E
Dongsha Dao	27	Kg	20.45N	116.45 E
Dongsha Qundao	21	Ng	20.42N	116.43 E
Dongsheng	27	Id	39.48N	110.00 E
Dongtai	27	Le	32.47N	120.18 E
Dong Taijnar Hu	27	Fd	37.25N	94.00 E
Dongtin Hu	21	Ng	29.18N	112.45 E
Dong Ujimqin Qi (Uliastai)	27	Kc	45.31N	116.58 E
Dongwe	36	De	13.56S	23.53 E
Dongxiang	27	Kf	28.15N	116.38 E
Dongyang	28	Fj	29.16N	120.14 E
Dongying	27	Kd	37.30N	118.30 E
Dongzhi (Yaodu)	28	Di	30.06N	117.01 E
Donington	12	Bb	52.54N	.0.12W
Doniphan	45	Kh	36.37N	90.50W
Donja Brela	14	Kg	43.23N	16.55 E
Donji Miholjac	14	Me	45.45N	18.10 E
Donji Vakuf	14	Lf	44.08N	17.24 E
Dønna	7	Cc	66.06N	12.35 E
Donnacona	44	Lb	46.40N	71.47W
Donner Pass	43	Cd	39.19N	120.20W
Donnersberg	12	Je	49.38N	7.55 E
Donner und Blitzen River	46	Fe	43.17N	118.49W
Donnybrook	59	Df	33.35S	115.49 E
Donskaja Grjada=Don Upland (EN)	5	Kf	49.10N	42.00 E
Donskoj	16	Kb	54.01N	38.20 E
Don Upland (EN)=Donskaja Grjada	5	Kf	49.10N	42.00 E
Donuzlav, Ozero-	16	Hg	45.25N	33.10 E
Doolette Bay	66	Je	67.55S	147.00 E
Doon	9	If	55.26N	4.38W
Doonerak, Mount-	40	Ic	67.56N	150.37W
Doorn	12	Hb	52.02N	5.19 E
Doornik/Tournai	11	Jd	50.36N	3.23 E
Door Peninsula	45	Md	44.55N	87.20W
Do Qu	27	He	31.48N	102.09 E
Dora, Lake-	59	Ed	22.05S	122.56 E
Dora Baltea/Doire Baltée	14	Ce	45.11N	8.03 E
Dorada, Costa-	13	Nc	41.08N	1.10 E
Dora Riparia	14	Be	45.05N	7.44 E
Dorbiljin/Emin	27	Db	46.32N	83.39 E
Dorchester	9	Kk	50.43N	2.26W
Dorchester, Cape -	42	Jc	65.28N	77.30W
Dordabis	37	Bd	22.52S	17.38 E
Dordogne	5	Ff	45.02N	0.35W
Dordogne [3]	11	Gi	45.10N	0.50 E
Dordrecht [Neth.]	12	Gc	51.48N	4.40 E
Dordrecht [Neth.]	11	Kc	51.49N	4.40 E
Dordrecht [S.Afr.]	37	Df	31.20S	27.03 E
Dore	11	Ji	46.00N	3.28 E
Dore, Monts-	5	Gf	45.30N	2.45 E
Doré Lake	42	Gf	54.45N	107.20W
Dores do Indaia	54	Ig	19.27S	45.36W
Dorgali	14	Dj	40.17N	9.35 E
Dori	31	Gg	14.02N	0.02W
Doring	30	Il	31.52S	18.39 E
Dorking	12	Bc	51.13N	0.20W
Dormagen	12	Ic	51.06N	6.50 E
Dormans	11	Je	49.04N	3.38 E
Dormidontovka	20	Ig	47.45N	134.58 E
Dornbirn	14	Dc	47.25N	9.44 E
Dornoch	9	Id	57.52N	4.02W
Dornoch Firth	9	Id	57.52N	4.02W
Doro	34	Eb	16.09N	0.51W
Dorog	10	Oi	47.43N	18.44 E
Dorogobuž	16	Hb	54.56N	33.15 E
Dorohoi	15	Jb	47.57N	26.24 E
Dorotea	7	Dd	64.16N	16.24 E
Dorre Island	59	Ce	25.10S	113.05 E
Dorrigo	59	Kf	30.20S	152.45 E
Dorset [3]	9	Kk	50.50N	2.10W
Dorset	9	Kk	50.55N	2.15W
Dorsten	10	Ce	51.40N	6.58 E
Dortmund	6	Ge	51.31N	7.27 E
Dortmund-Ems-Kanal	10	De	51.32N	7.27 E
Doruma	36	Eb	4.44N	27.42 E
Dörverden	12	Lb	52.51N	9.14 E
Doseo, Bar-	35	Bd	9.01N	19.38 E
Dos Hermanas	13	Gg	37.17N	5.55W
Dos Lagunas	49	Ce	17.42N	89.36W
Dospat	15	Hh	41.39N	24.10 E
Dospat	15	Hh	41.23N	24.05 E
Dosse	10	Ic	53.13N	12.20 E
Dosso	31	Hg	13.03N	3.12 E
Dosso [2]	34	Fc	13.30N	3.30 E
Dossor	19	Ff	47.32N	53.01 E
Dostluk	18	Ef	37.45N	65.22 E
Dothan	43	Je	31.13N	85.24W
Dotnuva	8	Ji	55.18N	23.55 E
Dötyol	24	Gd	36.52N	36.12 E
Douai	11	Jd	50.22N	3.04 E
Douala	31	Hh	4.03N	9.42 E
Douaouir	34	Ea	20.45N	2.30W
Douarnenez	11	Bf	48.06N	4.20W
Douarnenez, Baie de-	11	Bf	48.10N	4.25W
Double Mountain Fork Brazos	45	Gj	33.15N	100.00W
Doubrava	10	Lf	50.03N	15.20 E
Doubs	11	Lh	46.54N	5.02 E
Doubs [3]	11	Mg	47.10N	6.25 E
Doubtful Sound	62	Bf	45.15S	166.50 E
Doubtless Bay	62	Ea	34.55S	173.25 E
Douchy-les-Mines	12	Fd	50.18N	3.23 E
Doudeville	12	Ce	49.43N	0.48 E
Doué-la-Fontaine	11	Fg	47.12N	0.17W
Douentza	34	Eb	15.03N	2.57W
Douera	13	Oh	36.40N	2.57 E
Dougga	32	Ib	36.24N	9.13 E
Douglas [Ak.-U.S.]	40	Me	58.16N	134.26W
Douglas [Az.-U.S.]	43	Fe	31.21N	109.33W
Douglas [Ga.-U.S.]	44	Fj	31.31N	82.51W
Douglas [S.Afr.]	37	Ce	29.04S	23.46 E
Douglas [U.K.]	9	Ig	54.09N	4.28W
Douglas [Wy.-U.S.]	43	Fc	42.45N	105.24W
Douglas Lake	44	Fh	36.00N	83.22W
Douglas Range	66	Qf	70.00S	69.35W
Doullens	11	Id	50.09N	2.21 E
Doumé	34	He	4.14N	13.27 E
Douna	34	Ec	14.39N	1.43W
Doupovské hory	10	Jf	50.13N	13.08 E
Dour	12	Fd	50.24N	3.47 E
Dourada, Serra- [Braz.]	55	Gb	16.00S	50.05W
Dourada, Serra- [Braz.]	55	Ha	13.10S	48.45W
Dourados	53	Kh	22.13S	54.48W
Dourados, Rio- [Braz.]	55	Ee	21.58S	54.18W
Dourados, Rio- [Braz.]	55	Id	18.17S	47.36W
Dourbali	35	Bc	11.49N	15.52 E
Dourdan	11	If	48.32N	2.01 E
Douro	5	Fg	41.08N	8.40W
Douro Litoral	13	Dc	41.05N	8.20W
Doushi → Gong'an	27	Je	30.05N	112.12 E
Douve	11	Ee	49.19N	1.44W
Douvres-la-Delivrande	12	Be	49.17N	0.23W
Douze	11	Fk	43.54N	0.30W
Douzy	12	He	49.40N	5.03 E
Dove	9	Li	52.50N	1.35W
Dove Bugt	41	Jd	76.25N	21.00W
Dove Creek	45	Bh	37.46N	108.54W
Dover [De.-U.S.]	39	Lf	39.10N	75.32W
Dover [Eng.-U.K.]	6	Ge	51.08N	1.19 E
Dover [N.H.-U.S.]	44	Ld	43.12N	70.55W
Dover [Oh.-U.S.]	44	Ge	40.32N	81.30W
Dover, Strait of-	5	Ge	51.00N	1.30 E
Dover, Strait of- (EN)=Calais, Pas de-	5	Ge	51.00N	1.30 E
Dover Foxcroft	44	Mc	45.11N	69.13W
Dovey	9	Ji	52.34N	3.59W
Dovre	8	Cc	61.59N	9.15 E
Dovrefjell	5	Gc	62.10N	9.25 E
Dowa	36	Fe	13.39S	33.56 E
Dowagiac	44	De	41.59N	86.06W
Dowlatābād	24	Qh	28.20N	57.13 E
Downey	46	Ie	42.26N	112.07W
Downhan Market	12	Cb	52.36N	0.22 E
Downieville	46	Eg	39.34N	120.50W
Downpatrick / Dún Pádraig	9	Hg	54.20N	5.43W
Dow Rūd	23	Gc	33.28N	49.04 E
Dow Sar	24	Me	35.06N	48.02 E
Dōzen	29	Cc	36.05N	132.59 E
Dozois, Reservoir-	44	Ib	47.30N	77.00W
Dozulé	12	Be	49.14N	0.03W
Drâa	30	Ff	28.40N	11.07W
Drâa, Cap-	32	Ed	28.44N	11.05W
Drâa, Hamada du-	30	Gf	28.30N	7.30W
Draa el Baguel	32	Ic	30.17N	6.25 E
Draa el Mizan	13	Ph	36.32N	3.50 E
Drac	11	Li	45.13N	5.41 E
Dracena	55	Ge	21.32S	51.29W
Drach, Cuevas del-	13	Pe	39.32N	3.15 E
Dragalina	15	Kc	44.26N	27.19 E
Dragan	7	Dd	64.00N	15.21 E
Drăgăneşti-Olt	15	He	44.09N	24.42 E
Drăgăneşti-Vlaşca	15	Ie	44.06N	25.36 E
Drăgăşani	15	He	44.39N	24.16 E
Dragobia	15	Cg	42.26N	19.59 E
Dragón, Bocas del-/Dragon's Mouths	54	Fa	10.45N	61.46W
Dragonera, Isla-/Dragonera, Sa-	13	Oe	39.35N	2.19 E
Dragonera, Sa-/Dragonera, Isla-	13	Oe	39.35N	2.19 E

Index Symbols

[1] Independent Nation; [2] State, Region; [3] District, County; [4] Municipality; [5] Colony, Dependency; Continent; Physical Region; Historical or Cultural Region; Mount, Mountain; Volcano; Hill; Mountains, Mountain Range; Hills, Escarpment; Plateau, Upland; Pass, Gap; Plain, Lowland; Delta; Salt Flat; Valley, Canyon; Crater, Cave; Karst Features; Depression; Polder; Desert, Dunes; Forest, Woods; Heath, Steppe; Oasis; Cape, Point; Coast, Beach; Cliff; Peninsula; Isthmus; Sandbank; Island; Atoll; Rock, Reef; Islands, Archipelago; Rocks, Reefs; Coral Reef; Well, Spring; Geyser; River, Stream; Waterfall Rapids; River Mouth, Estuary; Lake; Salt Lake; Intermittent Lake; Reservoir; Swamp, Pond; Canal; Glacier; Ice Shelf, Pack Ice; Ocean; Sea; Gulf, Bay; Strait, Fjord; Lagoon; Bank; Seamount; Tablemount; Ridge; Shelf; Basin; Escarpment, Sea Scarp; Fracture; Trench, Abyss; National Park, Reserve; Point of Interest; Recreation Site; Cave, Cavern; Historic Site; Ruins; Wall, Walls; Church, Abbey; Temple; Scientific Station; Airport; Port; Lighthouse; Mine; Tunnel; Dam, Bridge

Dragon's Mouths/Dragón, Bocas del- 54 Fa 10.45N 61.46W
Dragør 8 Ei 55.36N 12.41 E
Draguignan 11 Mk 43.32N 6.28 E
Drahanska vrchovina 10 Mg 49.30N 16.45 E
Drain 46 De 43.40N 123.19W
Drake 45 Fc 47.55N 100.23W
Drake, Estrecho de-=Drake Passage (EN) 52 Jk 58.00S 70.00W
Drakensberg 30 Jk 29.00S 29.00 E
Drake Passage (EN)=Drake, Estrecho de- 52 Jk 58.00S 70.00W
Dráma 15 Hh 41.09N 24.09 E
Drammen 6 Hd 59.44N 10.15 E
Dramselva 8 De 59.44N 10.14 E
Drangajokull 7a Aa 66.09N 22.15W
Dranse 11 Mh 46.24N 6.30 E
Drau=Drava (EN) 5 Hf 45.33N 18.55 E
Dráva=Drava (EN) 5 Hf 45.33N 18.55 E
Drava (EN)=Drau 5 Hf 45.33N 18.55 E
Drava (EN)=Dráva 5 Hf 45.33N 18.55 E
Dravograd 14 Jd 46.35N 15.01 E
Drawa 10 Ld 52.52N 15.59 E
Drawno 10 Lc 53.13N 15.45 E
Drawsko, Jezioro- 10 Mc 53.33N 16.10 E
Drawsko Pomorskie 10 Lc 53.32N 15.48 E
Drayton Valley 42 Gf 53.13N 115.00W
Drean 14 Bn 36.41N 7.45 E
Dreieich 12 Ke 50.01N 8.43 E
Drenovci 14 Mf 44.55N 18.55 E
Drenthe 12 Ib 52.45N 6.30 E
Dresden 10 Je 51.10N 14.00 E
Dresden 6 He 51.03N 13.45 E
Dreux 11 Hf 48.44N 1.22 E
Drevsjø 7 Cf 61.54N 12.02 E
Drezdenko 10 Ld 52.51N 15.50 E
Dricēni/Driceni 8 Lh 56.39N 27.11 E
Driceni/Dricēni 8 Lh 56.39N 27.11 E
Driffield 9 Mg 54.01N 0.26W
Driggs 46 Je 43.44N 111.14W
Drina 5 Hg 44.53N 19.21 E
Drincea 15 Fe 44.07N 22.59 E
Drin Gulf (EN)=Drinit, Gjiri i- 15 Ch 41.45N 19.28 E
Drini 5 Hg 41.45N 19.34 E
Drini i Zi 15 Dg 42.05N 20.23 E
Drinit, Gjiri i-=Drin Gulf (EN) 15 Ch 41.45N 19.28 E
Drinjača 14 Nf 44.17N 19.10 E
Drinosi 15 Di 40.17N 20.02 E
Drissa 7 Gi 55.47N 27.57 E
Drisvjaty, Ozero-/Drūkšiu Ežeras 8 Lj 55.37N 26.45 E
Driva 8 Cb 62.40N 8.34 E
Drjanovo 15 Ig 42.58N 25.28 E
Drniš 14 Kg 43.52N 16.09 E
Drøbak 7 Cg 59.39N 10.39 E
Drocea, Vîrful- 15 Fc 46.12N 22.14 E
Drogheda/Droichead Átha 9 Gh 53.43N 6.21W
Drogičin 16 Dc 52.13N 25.10 E
Drogobyč 16 Ce 49.22N 23.33 E
Drohiczyn 10 Sd 52.24N 22.41 E
Droichead Átha/Drogheda 9 Gh 53.43N 6.21W
Droichead na Bandan/Bandon 9 Ej 51.45N 8.45W
Droichead na Banna/Banbridge 9 Gg 54.21N 6.16W
Drokija 16 Ee 48.01N 27.53 E
Drôme 12 Be 49.19N 0.45W
Drôme 11 Lj 44.35N 5.10 E
Drömling 10 Hd 52.29N 11.04 E
Dronero 14 Bf 44.28N 7.22 E
Dronne 11 Fi 45.02N 0.09W
Dronning Fabiola-Fjella 66 Df 71.30S 35.40 E
Dronning Louise Land 41 Jc 76.45N 24.00W
Dronten 11 Lb 52.31N 5.42 E
Dropt 11 Fj 44.35N 0.06W
Drovjanoj 20 Cb 72.25N 72.45 E
Drowning River 45 Na 50.55N 84.35W
Druja 7 Gi 55.47N 27.29 E
Drūkšiu Ežeras/Drisvjaty, Ozero- 8 Lj 55.37N 26.45 E
Druk-Yul→Bhutan 22 Lg 27.30N 90.30 E
Drulingen 12 Jf 48.52N 7.11 E
Drumheller 42 Gf 51.28N 112.42W
Drummond [Mt.-U.S.] 46 Ic 46.40N 113.09W
Drummond [Wi.-U.S.] 45 Kc 46.20N 91.15W
Drummond Island 44 Fb 46.00N 83.40W
Drummond Range 59 Jd 23.30S 147.15 E
Drummondville 42 Kg 45.50N 72.20W
Drummore 9 Ig 54.42N 4.54W
Drumochter, Pass of- 9 Ie 56.50N 4.12W
Drunen 12 Hc 51.41N 5.10 E
Druskininkai/Druskininkaj 7 Fi 54.04N 24.06 E
Druskininkaj/Druskininkai 7 Fi 54.04N 24.06 E
Drut 16 Gc 53.04N 30.35 E
Druten 12 Hc 51.54N 5.38 E
Družba 16 Hc 52.02N 33.59 E
Druzba 19 If 45.18N 82.29 E
Družkovka 16 Je 48.36N 37.33 E
Družnaja Gorka 8 Ne 59.11N 30.10 E
Družnino 17 Ih 56.48N 59.29 E
Drużno, Jezioro- 10 Pb 54.08N 19.30 E
Drvar 14 Kf 44.22N 16.23 E
Drvenik 14 Lg 43.09N 17.15 E
Drwęca 10 Oc 53.00N 18.42 E
Dryden 42 Ig 49.47N 92.50W
Dry Fork 46 Me 43.30N 105.24W
Drygalski Ice Tongue 66 Kf 75.24S 163.30 E
Drygalski Island 66 Ge 65.45S 92.30 E
Drysdale River 59 Fb 13.59S 126.51 E
Dry Tortugas 43 Kg 24.38N 82.55W
Drzewica 10 Qe 51.27N 20.28 E
Drzewiczka 10 Qe 51.33N 20.35 E
Dschang 34 Hd 5.27N 10.04 E
Dua 36 Db 3.20N 20.53 E
Duaca 54 Ea 10.18N 69.10W
Duancun→Wuxiang 28 Bf 36.50N 112.51 E
Duarte, Pico- 38 Lh 19.00N 71.00W
Duartina 55 Hf 22.24S 49.25W
Dubai=Dubayy 42 Hd 64.30N 100.06W
Dubawnt 38 Ic 63.08N 101.30W
Dubawnt Lake 24 Pj 24.20N 54.09 E
Ḑubay'ah, Ra's- 22 Hg 25.18N 55.18 E
Dubayy 58 Fh 32.15S 148.36 E
Dubbo 10 Ie 51.40N 12.40 E
Dübener Heide 16 Td 51.29N 56.38 E
Dubenski 9 Ge 56.08N 6.39W
Dubh Artach 14 Ke 45.13N 16.48 E
Dubica 43 Ke 32.32N 82.54W
Dublin 9 Gh 53.20N 6.15W
Dublin/Baile Átha Cliath 6 Fe 53.20N 6.15W
Dublin/Baile Átha Cliath
Dublin Bay/Cuan Bhaile Átha Cliath 9 Gh 53.20N 6.06W
Dubljany 10 Tg 49.26N 23.16 E
Dublon 64d Bb 7.23N 151.53 E
Dubna 8 Lh 56.20N 26.31 E
Dubna 19 Dd 56.47N 37.10 E
Dubnica nad Váhom 10 Oh 48.58N 18.10 E
Dubno 19 Ce 50.29N 25.46 E
Du Bois 44 He 41.06N 78.46W
Dubois [Id.-U.S.] 46 Id 44.10N 112.14W
Dubois [Wy.-U.S.] 46 Ke 43.33N 109.38W
Dubossary 16 Ff 47.17N 29.10 E
Dubovka 19 Ef 49.03N 44.50 E
Dubovoje 10 Ih 48.08N 23.59 E
Dubreka 34 Cd 9.48N 13.31W
Dubrovica 16 Ed 51.34N 26.34 E
Dubrovnik 6 Hg 42.39N 18.07 E
Dubrovno 7 Hi 54.33N 30.41 E
Dubrovnoje 19 Gd 57.58N 69.25 E
Dubuque 43 Ic 42.30N 90.41W
Dubysa 8 Ji 55.02N 23.27 E
Duc de Gloucester, Iles du-=Duke of Gloucester, Islands (En) 57 Mg 20.38S 143.20W
Duchang 28 Dj 29.16N 116.11 E
Duchesne 46 Jf 40.10N 110.24W
Duchess 59 Hd 21.22S 139.52 E
Ducie Atoll 57 Qg 24.40S 124.47W
Duck River 44 Dg 36.02N 87.52W
Duckwater Peak 46 Hg 38.58N 115.26W
Duclair 12 Ce 49.29N 0.53 E
Duc Lap 25 Lf 12.27N 107.38 E
Ducos 51h Bb 14.34N 60.58W
Dudelange/Düdelingen 12 Ie 49.28N 6.06 E
Duderstadt 10 Ge 51.31N 10.16 E
Dudinka 22 Kc 69.25N 86.15 E
Dudley 9 Ki 52.30N 2.05W
Ḑūdo 35 Id 9.20N 50.14 E
Dudub 35 Hd 6.55N 46.42 E
Dudune 63b Ce 21.21S 167.44 E
Dudvàh 10 Ni 47.58N 17.50 E
Dudweiler, Saarbrücken- 12 Je 49.17N 7.02 E
Düdwëyn 35 Gd 9.19N 44.53 E
Dudypta 20 Db 70.55N 89.50 E
Duékoué 34 Dd 6.45N 7.21W
Dueodde 8 Fj 54.59N 15.05 E
Duerna 13 Gb 42.19N 5.54W
Duero 5 Fg 41.08N 8.40W
Dufek Coast 66 Lg 84.30S 179.00W
Duffer Peak 46 Ff 41.40N 118.44W
Duff Islands 57 He 9.50S 167.10 E
Dugi Otok 14 Ii 44.00N 15.00 E
Dugo Selo 14 Ke 45.48N 16.15 E
Du Gué, Rivière- 42 Ke 57.20N 70.46W
Duhovnickoje 16 Pc 52.29N 48.15 E
Duijan Yan 27 He 31.01N 103.28 E
Duiru→Wuchuan 27 If 28.28N 107.57 E
Duisburg 10 Ce 51.26N 6.45 E
Duitama 54 Db 5.50N 73.02W
Dujūma 35 Ge 1.14N 42.34 E
Dukagjini 15 Cg 42.18N 19.45 E
Dūkān 24 Ke 35.56N 44.58 E
Dukan, Sad ad- 24 Kd 36.10N 44.56 E
Dukat 15 Fg 42.26N 22.21 E
Duke of Gloucester Islands (EN)=Duc de Gloucester, Iles du- 57 Mg 20.38S 143.20W
Duke of York 63a Aa 4.10S 152.28 E
Duke of York Bay 42 Jc 65.25N 84.50W
Duk Fadiat 35 Ed 7.45N 31.25 E
Duk Faiwil 35 Ed 7.30N 31.29 E
Dukhān 23 Hd 25.25N 50.48 E
Dukielska, Przełecz- 10 Rg 49.25N 21.42 E
Dukku 34 Hc 10.49N 10.46 E
Dukla 10 Rg 49.34N 21.41 E
Dukou 22 Mg 26.31N 101.44 E
Dūkštas/Dukštas 8 Li 55.32N 26.28 E
Dukštas/Dūkštas 8 Li 55.32N 26.28 E
Dulan (Qagan Us) 22 Lf 36.29N 98.29 E
Dulce, Bahia- 48 Ji 16.30N 98.50W
Dulce, Golfo- 47 Hg 8.36N 83.15W
Dulce, Rio- 52 Ji 30.31S 62.32W
Dulce Nombre de Culmi 49 Ef 15.09N 85.37W
Duldurga 20 Gf 50.38N 113.35 E
Dulgalah 21 Pc 67.30N 133.20 E
Dulia 36 Db 2.57N 24.08 E
Dülmen 10 De 51.50N 7.18 E
Dulovka 8 Mg 57.27N 28.29 E
Dulovo 15 Kf 43.49N 27.09 E
Duluth 39 Je 46.47N 92.06W
Dūmā 24 Gf 33.35N 36.24 E
Dumaguete 26 He 9.18N 123.18 E
Dumai 26 Df 1.41N 101.27 E
Dumaran 26 Gd 10.33N 119.51 E
Dumaresq River 59 Ke 28.40S 150.28 E
Dumas [Ar.-U.S.] 45 Kj 33.53N 91.29W
Dumas [Tx.-U.S.] 45 Fi 35.52N 101.58W
Dumayr 24 Gf 33.38N 36.40 E
Dumbarton 9 If 55.57N 4.35W
Dumbéa 63b Cf 22.09S 166.27 E
Dumbrăveni [Rom.] 15 Jb 47.39N 26.25 E
Dumbrăveni [Rom.] 15 Hc 46.14N 24.34 E
Dumfries 9 Jf 55.04N 3.37W
Dumfries and Galloway 9 Jf 55.10N 3.35W
Dumka 25 Hd 24.16N 87.15 E
Dumlupinar 15 Mk 38.52N 30.00 E
Dümmer 10 Ed 52.31N 8.19 E
Dumoine, Lac- 44 Ib 46.52N 77.52W
Dumoine, Rivière- 44 Ib 46.13N 77.50W
Dumont d'Urville 66 Je 66.40S 140.01 E
Dumont D'Urville Sea (EN) 66 Je 63.00S 140.00 E
Dumpu 58 Fe 5.52S 145.46 E
Dümrek 15 Lk 38.40N 28.24 E
Dumuhe 28 La 46.21N 133.33 E
Dumyāţ=Damietta (EN) 31 Ke 31.25N 31.48 E
Dumyāţ, Maşabb- 24 Dg 31.27N 31.51 E
Duna=Danube (EN) 5 If 45.20N 29.40 E
Dunaföldvár 10 Oi 46.48N 18.56 E
Dunaharaszti 10 Pi 47.21N 19.05 E
Dunaj 20 Ih 42.57N 132.20 E
Dunaj=Danube (EN) 5 If 45.20N 29.40 E
Dunajec 10 Qf 50.15N 20.44 E
Dunajevcy 16 Ee 48.51N 26.44 E
Dunajská Streda 10 Ni 47.01N 17.38 E
Dunakeszi 10 Pi 47.38N 19.08 E
Dunántúl 10 Nj 47.00N 18.00 E
Dunărea=Danube (EN) 5 If 45.20N 29.40 E
Dunărea Veche 15 Ld 45.17N 28.02 E
Dunării, Delta-=Danube, Mouths of the- (EN) 5 If 45.30N 29.45 E
Duna-Tisza Köze 10 Pj 46.45N 19.30 E
Dunaújváros 10 Oj 46.58N 18.56 E
Dunav=Danube (EN) 5 If 45.20N 29.40 E
Dunavăţu de Jos 15 Me 44.59N 29.13 E
Dunav-Tisa-Dunav kanal 15 Dd 45.10N 20.50 E
Dunback 62 Df 45.23S 170.38 E
Dunbar 9 Kf 56.00N 2.31W
Duncan [Az.-U.S.] 46 Kj 32.43N 109.06W
Duncan [B.C.-Can.] 46 Db 48.47N 123.42W
Duncan [Ok.-U.S.] 43 He 34.30N 97.57W
Duncan Passage 25 If 11.00N 92.00 E
Duncansby Head 5 Fd 58.39N 3.01W
Dundaga 8 Jg 57.31N 22.14 E
Dundalk 44 If 39.15N 76.31W
Dundalk/Dún Dealgan 9 Gg 54.01N 6.25W
Dundalk Bay/Cuan Dhun Dealgan 9 Gh 53.57N 6.17W
Dundas [Grld.] 41 Fc 76.30N 69.00W
Dundas [Ont.-Can.] 44 Hd 43.16N 79.58W
Dundas, Lake- 59 Ef 32.35S 121.50 E
Dundas Peninsula 42 Gb 74.40N 113.00W
Dundas Strait 59 Gb 11.20S 131.35 E
Dún Dealgan/Dundalk 9 Gg 54.01N 6.25W
Dundee [S.Afr.] 37 Ee 28.12S 30.16 E
Dundee [Scot.-U.K.] 6 Fd 56.28N 3.00W
Dund Hot→Zhenglan Qi 28 Cc 42.14N 115.59 E
Dundrum Bay/Cuan Dhún Droma 9 Hg 54.13N 5.45W
Dunedin [Fl.-U.S.] 44 Fk 28.02N 82.47W
Dunedin [N.Z.] 58 Ii 45.53S 170.31 E
Dunfanaghy 9 Ff 55.11N 7.59W
Dunfermline 9 Je 56.04N 3.29W
Dungannon/Dún Geanainn 9 Gg 54.31N 6.46W
Dún Garbhán/Dungarvan 9 Fi 52.05N 7.37W
Düngarpur 25 Ed 23.50N 73.43 E
Dungarvan/Dún Garbhán 9 Fi 52.05N 7.37W
Dungas 34 Gc 13.04N 9.20 E
Dungau 10 Ih 48.45N 12.30 E
Dún Geanainn/Dungannon 9 Gg 54.31N 6.46W
Dungeness 9 Nk 50.55N 0.58 E
Dungu 36 Eb 3.42N 28.40 E
Dungu 36 Eb 3.37N 28.34 E
Dunhua 27 Mc 43.22N 128.12 E
Dunhuang 27 Fc 40.10N 94.50 E
Dunkerque 11 Ic 51.03N 2.22 E
Dunkery Beacon 9 Jj 51.11N 3.35W
Dunkirk 43 Lc 42.29N 79.21W
Dunkwa 34 Ed 5.58N 1.47W
Dún Laoghaire 9 Gh 53.17N 6.08W
Dún Mánmhai/Dunmanway 9 Dj 51.43N 9.07W
Dunmanway/Dún Mánmhai 9 Dj 51.43N 9.07W
Dunn 44 Hh 35.19N 78.37W
Dún na nGall/Donegal 9 Fg 54.50N 8.00W
Dún na nGall/Donegal 9 Eg 54.39N 8.06W
Dunnellon 44 Fk 29.03N 82.28W
Dunnet Head 9 Jc 58.39N 3.23W
Dunning 45 Ff 41.50N 100.06W
Dún Pádraig/Downpatrick 9 Hg 54.20N 5.43W
Dunqulah=Dongola (EN) 31 Kg 19.10N 30.29 E
Dunqulah al Qadimah 35 Eb 18.13N 30.45 E
Dunqunāb 35 Fa 21.06N 37.05 E
Dunqunāb, Khalīj- 35 Fa 21.05N 37.08 E
Dunrankin 44 Fa 48.39N 83.04W
Duns 9 Kf 55.47N 2.20W
Dünsberg 12 Kd 50.39N 8.35 E
Dunsmuir 46 Df 41.13N 122.16W
Dunstable 12 Bc 51.53N 0.31W
Dunstan Mountains 62 Cf 44.55S 169.30 E
Dun-sur-Auron 11 Ih 46.53N 2.34 E
Dun-sur-Meuse 12 He 49.23N 5.11 E
Duntroon 62 Df 44.51S 170.41 E
Dunvegan 9 Gd 57.26N 6.35W
Duobukur 27 La 50.19N 124.57 E
Duolun/Dolonnur 27 Kc 42.10N 116.30 E
Duong Dong 25 Kf 10.13N 103.58 E
Dupree 45 Fd 45.03N 101.36W
Duqm 22 Hf 19.41N 57.32 E
Duque de Bragança, Quedas- 30 Ii 9.05S 16.10 E
Duque de Caxias 54 Jh 22.47S 43.18W
Duque de York, Isla- 56 Eh 50.40S 75.20W
Du Quoin 45 Lg 38.01N 89.14W
Durack Range 59 Fc 17.00S 128.00 E
Durack River 59 Fc 15.33S 127.52 E
Duragan 24 Fb 41.25N 35.04 E
Durance 5 Gg 43.55N 4.44 E
Durand 45 Kd 44.38N 91.58W
Durand, Récif- 63b Df 22.02S 168.39 E
Durango 47 Dd 24.50N 104.50W
Durango [Co.-U.S.] 39 If 37.16N 107.53W
Durango [Sp.] 13 Ja 43.10N 2.37W
Durañona 55 Bm 37.15S 60.31W
Durant 43 He 33.59N 96.23W
Duras 11 Gj 44.40N 0.11 E
Duratón 13 Hc 41.37N 4.07W
Durazno 56 Id 33.22S 56.31W
Durazno 55 Dk 33.05S 56.05W
Durazno, Cuchilla Grande del- 55 Dk 33.15S 56.15W
Durazzo (EN)=Durresi 15 Ch 41.19N 19.26 E
Durban 31 Kk 29.55S 30.56 E
Durbe 8 Ih 56.39N 21.14 E
Durbet-Daba, Pereval- 27 Eb 49.37N 89.25 E
Ḑurbo 35 Ic 11.30N 50.18 E
Durbuy 12 Hd 50.21N 5.28 E
Đurđevac 14 Ld 46.02N 17.04 E
Düren 10 Cf 50.48N 6.29 E
Durg 25 Gd 21.11N 81.17 E
Durgapūr 25 Hd 23.30N 87.15 E
Durgen-Nur 27 Fb 47.40N 93.30 E
Durham 9 Lg 54.45N 1.45W
Durham 9 Lg 54.45N 1.40W
Durham [Eng.-U.K.] 9 Lg 54.47N 1.34W
Durham [N.C.-U.S.] 43 Ld 35.59N 78.54W
Durkee 46 Gd 44.36N 117.28W
Durlas/Thurles 9 Fi 52.41N 7.49W
Ḑurmā 23 Ge 24.37N 46.08 E
Durmersheim 12 Kf 48.56N 8.16 E
Durmitor 5 Hg 43.09N 19.02 E
Durmford, Punta- 32 De 23.37N 16.00W
Durresi=Durazzo (EN) 15 Ch 41.19N 19.26 E
Durrësit, Gjiri- 15 Ch 41.16N 19.28 E
Dursey/Oiléan Baoi 9 Cj 51.36N 10.12W
Dursunbey 24 Cc 39.35N 28.38 E
Durtal 11 Fg 47.40N 0.15W
Duru→Wuchuan 27 If 28.28N 107.57 E
Duruksi 35 Hd 8.29N 45.38 E
Dursu Gölü 15 Lh 41.20N 28.38 E
Durūz, Jabal ad- 24 Gf 32.40N 36.44 E
D'Urville Island 61 Dh 40.50S 173.50 E
Dušak 18 Cf 37.15N 60.01 E
Dusa Mareb 35 Hd 5.31N 46.24 E
Dušanbe 22 If 38.35N 68.48 E
Dušeti 16 Nh 42.05N 44.42 E
Dusetos 8 Li 55.42N 26.02 E
Dushan 22 Mg 25.55N 107.36 E
Dushan Hu 28 Dg 35.06N 116.48 E
Dusios Ežeras/Dusja, Ozero- 8 Jj 54.15N 23.45 E
Dusja, Ozero-/Dusios Ežeras 8 Jj 54.15N 23.45 E
Dusky Sound 62 Bf 45.45S 166.30 E
Düsseldorf 6 Ge 51.13N 6.46 E
Dusti 18 Gf 37.22N 68.43 E
Dutch Harbor 40a Eb 53.53N 166.32W
Dutlwe 37 Cd 23.58S 23.54 E
Dutton, Mount- 46 Ig 38.01N 112.13W
Duved 8 Ea 63.24N 12.52 E
Duvergé 49 Ld 18.22N 71.31W
Düvertepe 15 Lj 39.14N 28.27 E
Duvno 14 Lg 43.43N 17.14 E
Duwayhin 23 He 24.16N 51.20 E
Duwayhin, Khawr- 24 Nj 24.20N 51.25 E
Duyfken Point 59 Ib 12.35S 141.40 E
Duyun 27 If 26.20N 107.28 E
Düz 32 Ic 33.28N 9.01 E
Dūzce 23 Da 40.50N 31.10 E
Dve Mogili 15 If 43.36N 25.52 E
Dvina (EN)=Daugava 19 Cd 57.04N 24.03 E
Dvina Gulf (EN)=Dvinskaja Guba 5 Jb 65.00N 39.45 E
Dvinskaja Guba=Dvina Gulf (EN) 5 Jb 65.00N 39.45 E
Dvor 14 Ke 45.04N 16.23 E
Dvuh Cirkov, Gora- 20 Lc 67.30N 168.20 E
Dvůr Králové nad Labem 10 Lf 50.26N 15.48 E
Dwārka 25 Dd 22.14N 68.58 E
Dworshak Reservoir 46 Hc 46.45N 116.00W
Dyer, Cape- 38 Mc 66.37N 61.18W
Dyero 34 Dc 12.50N 6.30W
Dyer Plateau 66 Qf 70.45S 65.30W
Dyersburg 43 Jd 36.03N 89.23W
Dyfed 9 Ji 52.05N 4.00W
Dyhtau, Gora- 16 Mh 43.05N 43.12 E
Dyje 10 Mh 48.37N 16.56 E
Dyjsko-Svratecký úval 10 Mh 48.56N 16.25 E
Dyle 12 Gd 50.57N 4.40 E
Dylewska Góra 10 Pc 53.34N 19.57 E
Dynów 10 Sg 49.49N 22.14 E
Dyr, Djebel- 14 Cn 36.13N 8.46 E
Dyrhólaey 5 Ec 63.24N 19.08W
Dysnų Ežeras/Disnaj, Ozero- 7 Gi 55.35N 26.32 E
Dytike Rodhópi 15 Hh 41.45N 24.05 E
Dzabhan 21 Le 48.54N 93.23 E
Džagdy, Hrebet- 20 If 53.40N 131.00 E
Džalagaš 19 Gf 45.05N 64.40 E
Džalal-Abad 18 Id 40.56N 73.05 E
Džalilabad 19 Eh 39.12N 48.31 E
Džalinda 20 Hf 53.31N 123.59 E
Džambejty 16 Rd 50.14N 52.38 E
Džambul [Kaz.-U.S.S.R.] 22 Je 42.54N 71.22 E
Džambul [Kaz.-U.S.S.R.] 19 Hf 47.17N 71.42 E
Džambulskaja Oblast 19 Hg 44.30N 72.30 E
Dzamyn-Ud 27 Jb 43.50N 111.45 E
Džanak 16 Si 40.30N 55.35 E
Džanga 19 Fg 40.01N 53.10 E
Džankoj 19 Df 45.42N 34.22 E
Džansugurov 19 Hf 45.23N 79.29 E
Džanybek 19 Ef 49.24N 46.50 E
Dzaoudzi 31 Lj 12.47S 45.17 E
Dzardžan 20 Hc 68.55N 124.05 E
Džargalant 27 Gb 47.20N 99.35 E
Dzargalant 27 Ib 48.35N 105.50 E
Džarkurgan 19 Gh 37.29N 67.25 E
Džava 16 Mh 42.24N 43.53 E
Džebariki-Haja 20 Id 62.23N 135.50 E
Džebel [Bul.] 15 Ih 41.30N 25.18 E
Džebel [Tur.-U.S.S.R.] 16 Sj 39.37N 54.18 E
Džebrail 16 Oj 39.23N 47.01 E
Dzereg 27 Fb 47.08N 92.50 E
Džergalan 18 Lc 42.33N 79.02 E
Dzermuk 16 Nj 39.48N 45.39 E
Dzeržinsk [Bye.-U.S.S.R.] 16 Ec 53.44N 27.08 E
Dzeržinsk [R.S.F.S.R.] 19 Ed 56.16N 43.32 E
Dzeržinsk [Ukr.-U.S.S.R.] 16 Je 48.22N 37.50 E
Dzeržinskaja, Gora- 8 Lk 53.53N 27.10 E
Dzeržinskoje 20 Ee 56.49N 95.18 E
Džetygara 22 Id 52.11N 61.12 E
Džetysaj 18 Gd 40.49N 68.20 E
Džezkazgan [Kaz.-U.S.S.R.] 19 Gf 47.53N 67.27 E
Džezkazgan [Kaz.-U.S.S.R.] 22 Ie 47.47N 67.46 E
Džezkazganskaja Oblast 19 Gf 47.30N 70.00 E
Dzhugdzhur Range (EN)=Džugdžur, Hrebet- 21 Pd 58.00N 136.00 E
Działdówka 10 Qd 52.58N 20.05 E
Działdowo 10 Qc 53.15N 20.10 E
Działoszyce 10 Qf 50.22N 20.21 E
Dzibalchén 48 Oh 19.31N 89.45W
Dzibilchaltún 48 Og 21.05N 89.36W
Dzierzgoń 10 Pc 53.56N 19.21 E
Dzierżoniów 10 Mf 50.44N 16.39 E
Džirgatal 18 He 39.13N 71.12 E
Džizak 19 Gg 40.07N 67.52 E
Džizakskaja Oblast 19 Gg 40.20N 67.40 E
Džugdžur, Hrebet-=Dzhugdzhur Range (EN) 21 Pd 58.00N 136.00 E
Džūkste/Džukste 8 Jh 56.45N 23.10 E
Džukste/Džūkste 8 Jh 56.45N 23.10 E
Džulfa 16 Nj 38.59N 45.35 E
Džuma 18 Fe 39.44N 66.39 E
Dzun-Bajan 27 Jc 44.26N 110.03 E
Dzungarian Basin (EN)=Junggar Pendi 21 Ke 45.00N 88.00 E
Dzungarian Gate (EN)=Alataw Shankou 21 Ke 45.25N 82.25 E
Dzungarian Gate (EN)=Džungarskije Vorota 21 Ke 45.25N 82.25 E
Džungarski Alatau, Hrebet- 21 Ke 45.00N 81.00 E
Džungarskije Vorota=Dzungarian Gate (EN) 21 Ke 45.25N 82.25 E
Dzun-Hara 27 Ib 48.40N 106.40 E
Dzun-Mod 27 Ib 47.50N 106.57 E
Džurak-Sal 16 Mf 47.18N 43.36 E
Džusaly 19 Gf 45.29N 64.05 E
Džvari 16 Mh 42.42N 42.02 E

E

Éadan Doire/Edenderry 9 Fh 53.21N 7.03W
Eads 45 Eg 38.29N 102.47W
Eagle 40 Kd 64.46N 141.16W
Eagle 42 Lf 53.35N 57.25W
Eagle Creek 46 La 52.22N 107.24W
Eagle Lake 44 Mb 47.02N 68.36W
Eagle Lake [Ca.-U.S.] 46 Ef 40.39N 120.44W
Eagle Lake [Me.-U.S.] 44 Mb 46.20N 69.20W
Eagle Lake [Ont.-Can.] 45 Jb 49.42N 93.13W
Eagle Mountain 45 Kc 47.54N 90.33W
Eagle Nest 45 Dh 36.35N 105.14W
Eagle Pass 43 Gf 28.43N 100.30W
Eagle Peak [Ca.-U.S.] 43 Cc 41.17N 120.12W
Eagle Peak [Tx.-U.S.] 45 Dk 30.56N 105.01W
Eagle River [Ak.-U.S.] 40 Jd 61.19N 149.34W
Eagle River [Wi.-U.S.] 45 Ld 45.55N 89.15W
Eagle Summit 40 Jc 65.30N 145.38W
Ealing, London- 12 Bc 51.30N 0.19W
Ear Falls 45 Ja 50.38N 93.13W
Earn 9 Je 56.25N 3.30W
Earn, Loch- 9 Ie 56.28N 4.10W
Earnslaw, Mount- 62 Cf 44.37S 168.25 E
Easley 44 Fh 34.50N 82.36W
East Alligator River 59 Gb 12.08S 132.42 E
East Anglia 9 Ni 52.25N 1.00 E
East Angus 44 Lc 45.29N 71.40W
East Bay [Can.] 42 Jd 64.05N 81.30W
East Bay [U.S.] 45 Ll 29.05N 89.15W
East Berlin (EN)=Berlin (Ost) 10 Jd 52.30N 13.25 E
East Berlin (EN)=Berlin (Ost) 6 He 52.31N 13.24 E
Eastbourne [Eng.-U.K.] 9 Nk 50.46N 0.17 E
Eastbourne [N.Z.] 62 Fd 41.17S 174.54 E
East Caicos 49 Lc 21.41N 71.30W
East Cape [Fl.-U.S.] 44 Gm 25.07N 81.05W
East Cape [N.Z.] 57 Ih 37.41S 178.33 E
East Caroline Basin (EN) 3 Ii 4.00N 146.45 E
East Chicago 44 De 41.38N 87.27W
East China Sea (EN)=Dong Hai 21 Og 29.00N 125.00 E
East China Sea (EN)=Higashi-Shina-Kai 21 Og 29.00N 125.00 E
East Coast 62 Gc 38.20S 177.50 E
East Dereham 9 Ni 52.41N 0.56 E
Eastend 46 Kb 49.31N 108.48W
East Entrance 64a Bb 7.50N 134.40 E
Easter Island (EN)=Pascua, Isla de-/Rapa Nui 57 Qg 27.07S 109.22W
Easter Island (EN)=Rapa Nui/Pascua, Isla de- 57 Qg 27.07S 109.22W
Eastern [Ghana] 34 Ed 6.30N 0.30W
Eastern [Kenya] 36 Gb 0.05N 38.00 E
Eastern [S.L.] 34 Cd 8.15N 11.00W
Eastern [Ug.] 36 Fb 1.30N 33.50 E
Eastern [Zam.] 36 Fe 13.00S 32.15 E
Eastern Fields 60 Dj 10.03S 145.22 E

Index Symbols

Independent Nation
State, Region
District, County
Municipality
Colony, Dependency
Continent
Physical Region
Historical or Cultural Region
Mount, Mountain
Volcano
Hill
Mountains, Mountain Range
Hills, Escarpment
Plateau, Upland
Pass, Gap
Plain, Lowland
Delta
Salt Flat
Valley, Canyon
Crater, Cave
Karst Features
Depression
Polder
Desert, Dunes
Forest, Woods
Heath, Steppe
Oasis
Cape, Point
Coast, Beach
Cliff
Peninsula
Isthmus
Sandbank
Island
Atoll
Rock, Reef
Islands, Archipelago
Rocks, Reefs
Coral Reef
Well, Spring
Geyser
River, Stream
Waterfall Rapids
River Mouth, Estuary
Lake
Salt Lake
Intermittent Lake
Reservoir
Swamp, Pond
Canal
Glacier
Ice Shelf, Pack Ice
Ocean
Sea
Gulf, Bay
Strait, Fjord
Lagoon
Bank
Seamount
Tablemount
Ridge
Shelf
Basin
Escarpment, Sea Scarp
Fracture
Trench, Abyss
National Park, Reserve
Point of Interest
Recreation Site
Cave, Cavern
Historic Site
Ruins
Wall, Walls
Church, Abbey
Temple
Scientific Station
Airport
Port
Lighthouse
Mine
Tunnel
Dam, Bridge

Eastern Ghats	21	Jh	14.00N	78.50 E
Eastern Point	51b	Ab	18.07N	63.01W
Eastern Sayans (EN)= Vostočny Sajan	21	Ld	53.00N	97.00 E
Eastern Siberia (EN)	21	Rc	65.00N	155.00 E
Eastern Sierra Madre (EN)= Madre Oriental, Sierra-	38	Jg	22.00N	99.30W
Eastern Turkistan (EN)	21	Jf	40.00N	80.00 E
East Falkland/Soledad, Isla-	52	Kk	51.45S	58.50W
East Fork	45	Ie	42.41N	94.12W
East Friesland (EN)= Ostfriesland	10	Dc	53.20N	7.40 E
East Frisian Islands (EN)= Ostfriesische Inseln	10	Dc	53.45N	7.25 E
East Grand Forks	45	Hc	47.56N	97.01W
East Grand Rapids	44	Ed	42.56N	85.35W
East Greenland (EN)= Østgrønland [2]	41	Id	72.00N	35.00W
East Grinstead	9	Mj	51.08N	0.01W
East Ilsley	12	Ac	51.32N	1.17W
East Kilbride	9	If	55.46N	4.10W
East Lansing	44	Ed	42.44N	84.29W
East Las Vegas	46	Hh	36.07N	115.01W
Eastleigh	9	Lk	50.58N	1.22W
East London	31	Jl	33.00S	27.55 E
East Lynn Lake	44	Ff	38.05N	82.20W
Eastmain	42	Jf	52.15N	78.34W
Eastmain	42	Jf	52.14N	78.31W
Eastman	44	Fi	32.12N	83.11W
East Mariana Basin (EN)	3	Jh	12.00N	153.00 E
East Midlands Airport	12	Ab	52.50N	1.20W
East Novaya Zemlya Trough (EN)	67	Hd	73.30N	61.00 E
Easton	44	Je	40.41N	75.13W
East Pacific Rise (EN)	3	Ml	20.00S	110.00W
East Point	44	Ei	33.40N	84.27W
East Point [B.V.I.]	51a	Db	18.43N	64.16W
East Point [V.I.U.S.]	51a	Dc	17.46N	64.33W
Eastport	44	Nc	44.54N	67.00W
East Pryor Mountain	46	Kd	45.14N	108.30W
East Retford	9	Mh	53.19N	0.56W
East Road	12	Cd	51.00N	1.02 E
East Schelde (EN)= Oosterschelde	11	Jc	51.30N	4.00 E
East Scotia Basin (EN)	52	Mk	57.00S	35.00W
East Siberian Sea (EN)= Vostočno Sibirskoje More	67	Cd	74.00N	166.00 E
East St. Louis	43	Id	38.38N	90.05W
East Sussex [3]	9	Nk	50.55N	0.15 E
East Tavaputs Plateau	46	Kg	39.45N	109.30W
East Wear Bay	12	Dc	51.08N	1.18 E
Eaton	44	Ef	39.44N	84.37W
Eatonia	46	Ka	51.13N	109.23W
Eatonton	44	Fi	33.20N	83.23W
Eatonville	46	Dc	46.51N	122.17W
Eau Claire	43	Ic	44.49N	91.31W
Eau-Claire, Lac à l' -	42	Ke	56.20N	74.00W
Eauripik Atoll	57	Fd	6.42N	143.03 E
Eauripik Ridge (EN)	60	Cg	3.00N	142.00 E
Eauze	11	Gk	43.52N	0.06 E
Ebano	48	Jf	22.13N	98.24W
Ebbegebirge	10	De	51.10N	7.45 E
Ebbw Vale	9	Jj	51.47N	3.12W
Ebebiyin	34	He	2.09N	11.20 E
Ebeltoft	8	Dh	56.12N	10.41 E
Ebensburg	44	He	40.28N	78.44W
Ebensee	14	Hc	47.48N	13.46 E
Eberbach	10	Eg	49.28N	8.59 E
Eber Gölü	24	Dc	38.38N	31.12 E
Ebersbach	10	Ke	51.01N	14.35 E
Eberswalde	10	Jd	52.50N	13.50 E
Ebetsu	28	Pc	43.07N	141.34 E
Ebino	28	Kh	32.02N	130.47 E
Ebinur Hu	21	Ke	44.55N	82.55 E
Ebla	23	Eb	35.42N	36.50 E
Ebo	36	Ce	11.02S	14.40 E
Ebola	36	Db	3.20N	20.57 E
Eboli	14	Jj	40.36N	15.04 E
Ebolowa	31	Ih	2.54N	11.09 E
Ebombo	36	Ed	5.42S	26.07 E
Ebon Atoll	57	Hd	4.38N	168.43 E
Ebre/Ebro	5	Gg	40.43N	0.54 E
Ebre, Delta de l'-/Ebro, Delta del-	13	Md	40.43N	0.54 E
Ebril, Récif-	61	Od	22.40S	133.30W
Ebro/Ebre	5	Gg	40.43N	0.54 E
Ebro, Delta del-/Ebre, Delta de l'-	13	Md	40.43N	0.54 E
Ebro, Embalse del-	13	Ia	43.00N	3.58W
Ebschlob	10	Ef	50.58N	8.15 E
Ecaussines	12	Gd	50.34N	4.10 E
Ecbatana	24	Me	34.48N	48.30 E
Eceabat	15	Ji	40.11N	26.21 E
Echdeiria	32	Ed	27.14N	10.27W
Echegarate, Puerto de-	13	Jb	42.57N	2.14W
Echeng [China]	28	Ci	30.24N	114.52 E
Echeng [China]	27	Kd	36.10N	116.03 E
Echez	11	Gk	43.28N	0.02 E
Echigo-Sanmyaku	29	Fc	37.30N	139.15 E
Echizen-Misaki	29	Dd	35.59N	135.57 E
Echo Bay	39	Hc	66.04N	118.00W
Echo Seamount (EN)	32	Dd	25.23N	19.25W
Echt	12	Hc	51.06N	5.52 E
Echternach	12	Ie	49.49N	6.25 E
Echuca	59	Ig	36.10S	144.45 E
Echzell	12	Kd	50.23N	8.52 E
Ecija	13	Gg	37.32N	5.05W
Eckernförde	10	Fb	54.28N	9.50 E
Eckerö	7	Ef	60.15N	19.35 E
Eclipse Sound	42	Jb	72.40N	79.30W
Ečmiadzin	19	Eg	40.09N	44.18 E
Ecommoy	11	Gg	47.50N	0.16 E
Ecos	12	De	49.10N	1.39 E
Ecouis	12	De	49.19N	1.26 E
Écouves, Forêt d'-	11	Gf	48.32N	0.04 E

Écrin, Barre des-	11	Mj	44.55N	6.22 E
Ecuador [2]	53	If	2.00S	77.30W
Ecury-sur-Coole	12	Gf	48.54N	4.20 E
Ed	7	Cf	58.54N	11.56 E
Edam-Volendam	12	Hb	52.30N	5.03 E
Edane	8	Ee	59.38N	12.49 E
Eday	9	Kb	59.11N	2.47W
Edchera	32	Ed	27.02N	13.04W
Eddrachillis Bay	9	Hc	58.19N	5.15W
Eddystone Point	59	Jh	41.00S	148.20 E
Eddystone Rocks	9	Ik	50.15N	4.10W
Eddyville	44	Cg	37.03N	88.04W
Ede [Neth.]	11	Lb	52.03N	5.40 E
Ede [Nig.]	34	Fd	7.44N	4.26 E
Edéa	31	Ih	3.48N	10.08 E
Ed Edd	35	Gc	13.56N	41.40 E
Edefors	7	Ec	66.13N	20.54 E
Edéia	55	Hc	17.18S	49.55W
Edelény	10	Qh	48.18N	20.44 E
Eden	9	Jg	54.57N	3.01W
Eden [Austl.]	59	Jg	37.04S	149.54 E
Eden [Tx.-U.S.]	45	Gk	31.13N	99.51W
Edenburg	37	De	29.45S	25.56 E
Edenderry/Éadan Doire	9	Fh	53.21N	7.03W
Edenkoben	12	Ke	49.17N	8.09 E
Edenton	44	Ig	36.04N	76.39W
Eder	10	Fe	51.13N	9.27 E
Edersee	12	Lc	51.11N	9.03 E
Edertal	12	Lc	51.09N	9.09 E
Edewecht	12	Ja	53.08N	7.59 E
Edgar Ranges	59	Ec	18.43S	123.25 E
Edgartown	44	Le	41.23N	70.31W
Edgecumbe	62	Gb	37.58S	176.50 E
Edgeley	45	Gc	46.22N	98.43W
Edgell	42	Ld	61.50N	65.00W
Edgemont	45	Ee	43.18N	103.50W
Edgeøya	67	Jd	77.45N	22.30 E
Édhessa	15	Fi	40.48N	22.03 E
Edina	45	Jd	44.55N	93.20W
Edinburg	43	Hf	26.18N	98.10W
Edinburgh	6	Fd	55.57N	3.13W
Edinburgh, Arrecife-	49	Ff	14.50N	82.39W
Edincik	24	Bb	40.20N	27.51 E
Edingen/Enghien	12	Gd	50.42N	4.02 E
Edirne	24	Bb	41.40N	26.34 E
Edisto Island	44	Gi	32.35N	80.10W
Edisto River	44	Gi	32.39N	80.24W
Edith, Mount-	46	Jc	46.26N	111.11W
Edith Ronne Land (EN)	66	Qf	78.30S	61.00W
Edjeleh	32	Id	27.42N	9.53 E
Edjereh	32	He	24.35N	4.30 E
Édjérir	34	Fb	18.06N	0.50 E
Edmond	45	Hi	35.39N	97.29W
Edmonds	46	Dc	47.48N	122.22W
Edmonton	39	Hd	53.33N	113.28W
Edmundston	42	Kg	47.22N	68.20W
Edna	45	Hl	28.42N	96.39W
Edremit	23	Cb	39.35N	27.01 E
Edremit, Gulf of- (EN)= Edremit Körfezi	24	Bc	39.30N	26.45 E
Edremit Körfezi=Edremit, Gulf of- (EN)	24	Bc	39.30N	26.45 E
Edsbro	7	Eg	59.54N	18.29 E
Edsbruk	8	Gf	58.02N	16.28 E
Edsbyn	8	Fc	61.23N	15.49 E
Edson	42	Ff	53.35N	116.26W
Edsvalla	8	Ee	59.26N	13.13 E
Eduardo Castex	56	He	35.54S	64.18W
Eduni, Mount-	42	Ed	64.08N	128.10W
Edward, Lake-	30	Ji	0.25S	29.30 E
Edward, Lake- (EN)= Rutanzige, Lac-	30	Ji	0.25S	29.30 E
Edwards Creek	59	He	28.21S	135.51 E
Edwards Plateau	38	If	31.20N	101.00W
Edward VIII Bay	66	Ee	66.50S	57.00 E
Edward VII Peninsula	66	Mf	77.40S	155.00W
Edzo	42	Fd	62.47N	116.08W
Eeklo	11	Jc	51.11N	3.34 E
Eelde	12	Ia	53.08N	6.33 E
Eel River	43	Cc	40.40N	124.20W
Eem	12	Hb	52.16N	5.20 E
Eems	11	Na	53.19N	7.03 E
Eemskanaal	12	Ia	53.19N	6.57 E
Eenrum	12	Ia	53.23N	6.25 E
Eersel	12	Hc	51.22N	5.19 E
Eesti Nõukogude Socialistlik Vabarijk/Estonskaja SSR [2]	19	Cd	59.00N	26.00 E
Eesti NSV=Estonian SSR (EN) [2]	19	Cd	59.00N	26.00 E
Efaté, Ile-	57	Hf	17.40S	168.25 E
Eferding	14	Ib	48.19N	14.01 E
Efes = Ephesus (EN)	15	Kl	37.55N	27.20 E
Effingham	45	Lg	39.07N	88.33W
Eflâni	24	Eb	41.26N	32.57 E
Eforie	15	Le	44.01N	28.38 E
Ega	13	Kb	42.19N	1.55W
Egadi, Isole-=Egadi Islands (EN)	5	Hh	38.00N	12.15 E
Egadi Islands (EN)=Egadi, Isole-	5	Hh	38.00N	12.15 E
Egan Range	46	Hg	39.00N	115.00W
Eganville	44	Ic	47.33N	77.06W
Egbe	34	Gd	8.13N	5.31 E
Ege Denizi=Aegean Sea (EN)	5	Ih	39.00N	25.00 E
Egedesminde/Ausiait	67	Nc	68.50N	52.45W
Egegik	40	He	58.13N	157.22W
Egentliga Finland/Varsinais-Suomi	8	Jd	60.40N	22.30 E
Eger	10	Kf	50.32N	14.08 E
Eger	10	Qi	47.54N	20.23 E
Egersund	7	Ag	58.27N	6.00 E
Egerton, Mount-	59	Dd	24.45S	117.45 E
Egeskov	8	Di	55.10N	10.30 E
Eggegebirge	10	Ee	51.40N	8.55 E
Eggenfelden	10	Ih	48.24N	12.46 E

Eggenstein Leopoldshafen	12	Ke	49.05N	8.23 E
Eggum	7	Cb	68.19N	13.42 E
Eghezée	12	Gd	50.36N	4.56 E
Egijn-Gol	27	Ha	49.24N	103.36 E
Egletons	11	Ii	45.24N	2.03 E
Eglinton	42	Fa	75.45N	118.50W
Egmont, Cape-	61	Dg	39.17S	173.45 E
Egmont, Mount-	62	Fc	39.18S	174.04 E
Egnazia	14	Lj	40.50N	17.25 E
Eğridir	24	Dd	37.52N	30.51 E
Eğridir Gölü	23	Db	38.02N	30.53 E
Eğrigöz Dağ	15	Mj	39.21N	29.07 E
Egtved	8	Ci	55.37N	9.18 E
Éguas ou Correntina, Rio das-	55	Ja	13.26S	44.14W
Eguey	30	Ig	16.10N	16.10 E
Egvekinot	22	Tc	66.19N	179.10 E
Egypt (EN)=Mişr [1]	31	Jf	27.00N	30.00 E
Eha Amufu	34	Gd	6.40N	7.46 E
Ehen Hudag → Alxa Youqi	27	Hd	39.12N	101.40 E
Ehime Ken [2]	28	Lh	33.35N	132.40 E
Ehingen	10	Fh	48.17N	9.44 E
Ehrang, Trier-	12	Ie	49.49N	6.41 E
Ehrwald	14	Ec	47.24N	10.55 E
Ei	29	Bf	31.13N	130.30 E
Eiao, Ile-	57	Me	8.00S	140.40W
Eibar	13	Ja	43.11N	2.28W
Eibergen	12	Ib	52.07N	6.40 E
Eichsfeld	10	Ge	51.25N	10.20 E
Eichstätt	10	Hh	48.53N	11.11 E
Eickelborn, Lippetal-	12	Kc	51.39N	8.13 E
Eide	8	Bb	62.55N	7.26 E
Eider	10	Eb	54.19N	8.58 E
Eiderstedt	10	Eb	54.22N	8.50 E
Eidet	7	Cd	64.27N	13.37 E
Eidfjord	7	Bf	60.28N	7.05 E
Eidfjorden	8	Bd	60.25N	6.45 E
Eidslandet	8	Ad	60.44N	5.45 E
Eidsvåg	7	Be	62.47N	8.03 E
Eidsvoll	7	Cf	60.19N	11.14 E
Eidsvollfiellet	41	Nc	79.00N	13.00 E
Eierlandse Gat	12	Ga	53.12N	4.52 E
Eifel	10	Cf	50.15N	6.45 E
Eiffel Flats	37	Dc	18.15S	29.59 E
Eigenbrakel/Braine-l'Alleud	12	Gd	50.41N	4.22 E
Eigerøya	8	Af	58.25N	5.55 E
Eigg	9	Ge	56.54N	6.10W
Eight Degree Channel	21	Ji	8.00N	73.00 E
Eights Coast	66	Pf	73.30S	96.00W
Eighty Mile Beach	59	Ec	19.45S	121.00 E
Eigrim, Jabal-	35	Fb	19.22N	35.18 E
Eijsden	12	Hd	50.46N	5.42 E
Eikeren	8	Ce	59.40N	10.00 E
Eikesdalsvatnet	8	Cb	62.35N	8.10 E
'Eilai	35	Eb	16.33N	30.54 E
Eildon, Lake-	59	Jg	37.10S	145.50 E
Eilenburg	10	Ie	51.28N	12.37 E
Eiler Rasmussen, Kap-	41	Kb	82.40N	20.00W
Eil Malk	64a	Ac	7.09N	134.22 E
Eina	8	Dd	60.38N	10.36 E
Einasleigh	59	Ic	18.31S	144.05 E
Einasleigh River	59	Ic	17.30S	142.17 E
Einbeck	10	Fe	51.49N	9.52 E
Eindhoven	11	Lc	51.26N	5.28 E
Einsiedeln	14	Cc	47.08N	8.45 E
Éire/Ireland [1]	6	Fe	53.00N	8.00W
Eiríksjökull	7a	Bb	64.46N	20.24W
Eirunepé	53	Jf	6.40S	69.52W
Eisack/Isarco	14	Fd	46.27N	11.18 E
Eisacktal/Isarco, Valle-	14	Fd	46.45N	11.35 E
Eisacktal/Valle Isarco	14	Fd	46.45N	11.35 E
Eisenach	10	Gf	50.59N	10.19 E
Eisenberg	10	Hf	50.58N	11.54 E
Eisenberg	12	Kc	51.15N	8.50 E
Eisenberg (Pfalz)	12	Ke	49.33N	8.06 E
Eisenerz	14	Ic	47.32N	14.53 E
Eisenerzer Alpen	14	Ic	47.30N	14.40 E
Eisenhüttenstadt	10	Kd	52.10N	14.42 E
Eisenstadt	14	Kc	47.51N	16.31 E
Eisenwurzen	14	Jc	47.56N	15.02 E
Eišiškės/Ejšiškes	7	Fi	54.14N	25.02 E
Eisleben	10	He	51.32N	11.33 E
Eitorf	12	Jd	50.46N	7.27 E
Eivissa/Ibiza=Iviza (EN)	5	Gh	39.00N	1.25 E
Eje, Sierra del-	13	Fb	42.20N	6.55W
Ejea de los Caballeros	13	Kb	42.08N	1.08W
Ejeda	37	Gd	24.19S	44.21 E
Ejido	54	Db	8.33N	71.14W
Ejido Insurgentes	48	De	25.12N	111.45W
Ejin Horo Qi (Altan Xiret)	27	Id	39.31N	109.45 E
Ejin Qi	22	Me	41.50N	100.50 E
Ejšiškes/Eišiškės	7	Fi	54.14N	25.02 E
Ejura	34	Ed	7.23N	1.22W
Ejutla de Crespo	47	Ee	16.34N	96.44W
Ekalaka	46	Md	45.53N	104.33W
Ekecek Dağı	24	Fc	38.39N	34.03 E
Ekenäs/Tammisaari	7	Fg	59.58N	23.26 E
Ekeren, Antwerpen-	11	Kc	51.17N	4.25 E
Eket	34	Ge	4.39N	7.56 E
Eketahuna	62	Fd	40.39S	175.44 E
Ekhinádhes Nísoi	15	Ek	38.25N	21.02 E
Ekiatapski Hrebet	20	Mc	68.40N	177.50 E
Ekibastuz	19	He	51.42N	75.22 E
Ekimčan	20	If	53.07N	133.02 E
Ekoli	36	Dc	0.23S	24.16 E
Ekoln	8	Ge	59.45N	17.35 E
Ekombe	36	Db	1.16N	21.36 E
Ekonda	20	Fc	65.47N	105.17 E
Eksjö	7	Dh	57.40N	14.57 E
Ekuma	37	Bc	18.10S	15.47 E
Ekwan	42	Jf	53.12N	82.15W
El Aaiún	31	Ff	27.10N	13.12W
El Aargub	32	De	23.37N	15.52W
El Aatf	32	De	23.30N	15.30W
El Abadia	13	Nh	36.13N	1.40 E
El-Abd	13	Mi	35.29N	0.42 E
El Abiodh Sidi Cheikh	32	Hc	32.53N	0.34 E

El 'Açâba [3]	32	Ef	16.30N	12.00W
El 'Açâba	30	Fg	16.49N	12.05W
El Adeb Larache	32	Id	27.22N	8.52 E
El Affroun	13	Oh	36.28N	2.37 E
Elafónisi Channel (EN) = Elafonísou, Stenón-	15	Fm	36.25N	23.00 E
Elafónisos	15	Fm	36.29N	22.58 E
Elafonísou Stenón-= Elafónisi Channel (EN)	15	Fm	36.25N	23.00 E
El Agreb	32	Ic	30.48N	5.30 E
El Aguilar	56	Gb	32.12S	65.42W
El Álamo	48	Ab	31.34N	116.02W
El Alia	32	Ic	32.42N	5.26 E
El-Amria	13	Ki	35.32N	1.01W
Elan	15	Lc	46.06N	28.04 E
El Andévalo	13	Fg	37.40N	7.00W
El Aouinet	14	Bo	35.52N	7.54 E
El Arahal	13	Gg	37.16N	5.33W
El Aricha	32	Gc	34.13N	1.16W
Elása	15	Jn	35.17N	26.20 E
Elassón	15	Fj	39.54N	22.11 E
Elat	22	Fg	29.33N	34.57 E
Eláti	15	Dk	38.43N	20.39 E
Elato Atoll	57	Fd	7.28N	146.10 E
El Attaf	13	Nh	36.13N	1.40 E
Elâzığ	23	Eb	38.41N	39.14 E
El Azúcar, Presa de-	48	Jd	26.15N	99.00W
Elba	44	Dj	31.25N	86.04W
Elba	5	Hg	42.45N	10.15 E
Elban	20	If	50.05N	136.30 E
El Banco	54	Db	9.01N	73.58W
El Barco de Ávila	13	Gd	40.21N	5.31W
El Barco de Valdeorras	13	Fb	42.25N	6.59W
Elbasani	15	Dh	41.06N	20.05 E
El Baúl	54	Eb	8.57N	68.17W
El Bayadh	32	Hc	33.41N	1.01 E
Elbe	5	Ge	53.50N	9.00 E
Elbe (EN)=Labe	5	Ge	53.50N	9.00 E
Elbe-Lübeck-Kanal	10	Gc	53.50N	10.36 E
Elbert, Mount-	38	If	39.07N	106.27W
Elberton	44	Fh	34.07N	82.52W
Elbe-Seitenkanal	10	Gd	52.22N	10.34 E
Elbeuf	11	Ge	49.17N	1.00 E
Elbeyl	23	Eb	36.41N	37.26 E
El Bierzo	13	Fb	42.40N	6.50W
Elbıstan	24	Gc	38.13N	37.12 E
Elbląg [2]	10	Pb	54.10N	19.25 E
Elbląg	6	He	54.10N	19.25 E
Elbląski, Kanał-	10	Pc	53.43N	19.53 E
El Bolsón	56	Ff	41.58S	71.31W
El Bonillo	13	Jf	38.57N	2.32W
Elbow	46	La	51.07N	106.35W
Elbow Cays	49	Gb	23.57N	80.29W
Elbow Lake	45	Id	46.00N	95.58W
Elbrus	5	Kg	43.21N	42.26 E
Elbsandsteingebirge	10	Kf	50.50N	14.12 E
'Ēlbūr	35	He	4.40N	46.40 E
Elburg	11	Lb	52.26N	5.50 E
El Burgo de Osma	13	Ic	41.35N	3.04W
Elburgon	36	Gc	.0.18S	35.49 E
El Burro	48	Ic	29.16N	101.55W
Elburz Mountains (EN)= Alborz, Reshteh-ye Kūhhā-ye-	21	Hf	36.00N	53.00 E
El Cajon	43	De	32.48N	116.58W
El Callao	54	Fb	7.21N	61.49W
El Calvario	50	Ch	8.59N	67.00W
El Campo	45	Hl	29.12N	96.16W
El Canelo	48	Ie	24.19N	100.23W
El Cármen	55	Cd	18.49S	58.33W
El Carmen de Bolívar	54	Cb	9.43N	75.07W
El Casco	48	Ge	25.34N	104.35W
El Castillo	49	Eh	11.01N	84.24W
El Centro	43	De	32.48N	115.34W
El Cerro	54	Fg	17.31S	61.34W
El Chaparro	50	Dh	9.10N	65.01W
Elche	13	Lf	38.15N	0.42W
Elcho Island	59	Hb	11.55S	135.45 E
El Cury	56	Ge	39.56S	68.20W
Elda	13	Lf	38.29N	0.47W
Ēldab	35	Hd	8.58N	46.38 E
Elde	10	Ic	53.17N	12.40 E
'Ēl Ḍēre	31	Lh	3.55N	47.10 E
El Dere	35	Gd	5.07N	43.12 E
El Descanso	48	Aa	32.12N	116.55W
El Desemboque	47	Bb	30.30N	112.59W
El Dificil	49	Ji	9.51N	74.14W
Eldikan	20	Id	60.38N	135.07 E
El Djouf	30	Gf	21.25N	6.40W
El Doncello	54	Cc	1.43N	75.17W
Eldorado	45	Fk	30.52N	100.36W
Eldorado	56	Jc	26.24S	54.38W
El Dorado [Ar.-U.S.]	43	Ie	33.13N	92.40W
El Dorado [Ks.-U.S.]	43	Hd	37.49N	96.52W
El Dorado [Mex.]	47	Cd	24.17N	107.31W
El Dorado [Ven.]	53	Je	6.44N	61.38W
Eldorado Paulista	55	Hg	24.32S	48.06W
El Dorado Springs	45	Ih	37.52N	94.01W
Eldoret	36	Gb	0.31N	35.17 E
Eldsberga	8	Eh	56.36N	12.59 E
'Ēl Ḍubbo	35	Ge	3.52N	44.45 E
Eldžik	18	De	39.25N	63.01 E
Elefantes, Rio dos-	37	Ed	24.03S	32.40 E
El Eglab	30	Gf	26.30N	5.00W
Elēja/Eleja	7	Fh	56.28N	23.41 E
Eleja/Elēja	7	Fh	56.28N	23.41 E
Elektrénai/Elektrenaj	8	Kj	54.46N	24.47 E
Elektrenaj/Elektrénai	8	Kj	54.46N	24.47 E
Elektrostal	19	Dd	55.48N	38.29 E
Elele	34	Gd	5.06N	6.49 E
Elena	15	Ig	42.56N	25.53 E
El Encanto [Bol.]	55	Cc	16.57S	59.24W
El Encanto [Col.]	54	Dd	1.37S	73.13W
Elephant Butte Reservoir	45	Cj	33.19N	107.10W
Elephant Island	66	Re	61.10S	55.14W
Elephant Mountain	45	Ek	30.02N	103.30W
Elesbão Veloso	54	Je	6.13S	42.08W

El Escorial	13	Hd	40.35N	4.10W
Eleşkirt	24	Jc	39.49N	42.40 E
El Estor	49	Cf	15.32N	89.21W
Eleuthera	38	Lg	25.15N	76.20W
Elevsís	15	Gk	38.02N	23.32 E
Elevtheroúpolis	15	Hi	40.55N	24.15 E
El Fendek	13	Gi	35.34N	5.35W
El Ferrol del Caudillo	13	Da	43.29N	8.14W
El Fud	35	Gd	7.15N	42.51 E
El Fuerte [Mex.]	48	Hf	23.50N	103.06W
El Fuerte [Mex.]	47	Cc	26.25N	108.39W
Elgåhogna	8	Eb	62.09N	12.04 E
'Ēl Gāl	35	Ic	11.23N	50.23 E
El Galhak	35	Ec	11.03N	32.42 E
El Gassi	32	Ic	30.55N	5.50 E
Elgen	20	Kd	62.45N	150.40 E
Elgepiggen	7	Ce	62.10N	11.22 E
El Ghomri	13	Mi	35.41N	0.12 E
Elgi	20	Jd	64.20N	142.05 E
Elgin [Il.-U.S.]	43	Jc	42.02N	88.17W
Elgin [N.D.-U.S.]	45	Fc	46.24N	101.51W
Elgin [Or.-U.S.]	46	Gd	45.34N	117.55W
Elgin [Scot.-U.K.]	9	Jd	57.39N	3.20W
Elginski	20	Jd	64.48N	141.50 E
Elgjaij	20	Gd	62.28N	117.37 E
El Goléa	31	He	30.34N	2.53 E
Elgon, Mont-	30	Kh	1.08N	34.33 E
Elgoran	35	Gd	5.04N	44.22 E
El Grao, Castellón de la Plana-	13	Me	39.58N	0.01 E
El Grao, Valencia-	13	Le	39.27N	0.20W
El Guapo	50	Dg	10.09N	65.58W
El Guayabo	49	Ki	8.37N	72.20W
El Hadjar	14	Bn	36.48N	7.45 E
El Hajeb	32	Fc	33.42N	5.22W
El-Ham	13	Qi	35.42N	4.52 E
El Hammam	13	Li	35.50N	0.15W
'Ēl Ḥamurre	35	Hd	7.11N	48.55 E
El Hank	30	Gf	24.00N	6.30W
El Harrach, Al Jazā'ir-	13	Ph	36.43N	3.08 E
Elhotovo	16	Nh	43.20N	44.13 E
Elhovo	15	Jg	42.10N	26.34 E
El Huecú	56	Fe	37.37S	70.36W
Elida	45	Ej	33.57N	103.39W
Èliki, Vallée d'-	34	Gc	14.45N	7.15 E
Elila	36	Ec	2.43S	25.53 E
Elila	30	Ji	2.45S	25.53 E
Elimäki	8	Ld	60.43N	26.28 E
Elin Pelin	15	Gg	42.40N	23.36 E
Elisejna	15	Gf	43.05N	23.29 E
Elisenvaara	8	Mc	61.19N	29.47 E
Elista	6	Kf	46.16N	44.14 E
Elizabeth [Austl.]	58	Eh	34.45S	138.39 E
Elizabeth [N.J.-U.S.]	44	Je	40.40N	74.13W
Elizabeth, Cape-	46	Cc	47.22N	124.22W
Elizabeth City	43	Ld	36.18N	76.14W
Elizabeth Reef	57	Gg	29.55S	159.05 E
Elizabethton	44	Fg	36.21N	82.13W
Elizabethtown [Ky.-U.S.]	44	Eg	37.42N	85.52W
Elizabethtown [N.C.-U.S.]	44	Hh	34.38N	78.37W
El Jadida [3]	32	Fc	32.54N	8.30W
El Jadida	31	Ge	33.15N	8.30W
El Jícaro	49	Dg	13.43N	86.08W
'Ēl Jilib	35	He	3.48N	47.07 E
Ełk	10	Sc	53.50N	22.22 E
Ełk	10	Sc	53.32N	22.47 E
El Kala	32	Ib	36.54N	8.27 E
El Kantara	32	Ib	35.13N	5.43 E
El-Karimia	13	Nh	36.07N	1.33 E
Elk City [Id.-U.S.]	46	Hd	45.51N	115.29W
Elk City [Ok.-U.S.]	45	Gi	35.25N	99.25W
El Kelaa des Srarhna [3]	32	Fc	32.03N	7.30W
El Kelaa des Srarhna	32	Fc	32.03N	7.24W
El Kere	35	Gd	5.51N	42.06 E
Elkhart [In.-U.S.]	43	Jc	41.41N	85.58W
Elkhart [Ks.-U.S.]	45	Fh	37.00N	101.54W
El Khatt	32	Ef	19.00N	12.25W
Elkhead Mountains	45	Cf	40.50N	107.05W
El Khnâchîch	34	Ea	21.20N	3.45W
Elkhorn River	45	Hf	41.07N	96.19W
Elkins	44	Hf	38.56N	79.53W
Elk Lake	44	Gb	47.42N	80.11W
Elk Mountain	46	Lf	41.38N	106.32W
Elk Mountains	45	Cg	38.55N	106.50W
Elko	39	He	40.50N	115.46W
Elk Peak	46	Jc	46.27N	110.46W
Elk River	44	Gf	38.21N	81.38W
Elk River	45	Jd	45.18N	93.35W
Elku Kalns	8	Kg	57.04N	25.23 E
Ell, Lake-	59	Fe	29.15S	127.45 E
Ellás=Greece (EN) [1]	6	Ih	39.00N	22.00 E
Ellé	11	Cg	47.52N	3.32W
Ellef Ringnes	38	Ib	78.30N	104.00W
Ellen, Mount-	43	Ed	38.07N	110.49W
Ellendale	43	Hb	46.06N	98.32W
Ellensburg	43	Cb	46.40N	120.32W
Ellenville	44	Je	41.43N	74.23W
Ellesmere	38	Kb	79.00N	82.00W
Ellesmere, Lake-	62	Ee	43.45S	172.30 E
Ellice	42	Hc	68.02N	103.25W
Ellice Islands → Tuvalu [1]	58	Ie	8.00S	178.00 E
Elliot [Austl.]	59	Gc	17.35S	133.35 E
Elliot [S.Afr.]	37	Df	31.18S	27.50 E
Elliot, Mount-	59	Jc	19.29S	146.58 E
Elliot Lake	42	Jg	46.23N	82.39W
Ellisras	37	Dd	23.40S	27.46 E
Elliston	59	Gf	33.39S	134.55 E
Ellisville	45	Lk	31.36N	89.12W
Ellmau	14	Gc	47.31N	12.18 E
Ellös	7	Cg	58.11N	11.27 E
Ellsworth [Ks.-U.S.]	45	Gg	38.44N	98.14W
Ellsworth [Me.-U.S.]	44	Mc	44.33N	68.26W
Ellsworth [Nb.-U.S.]	45	Ee	42.04N	102.15W
Ellsworth, Lake-	45	Gi	34.48N	98.20W
Ellsworth Land (EN)	66	Pf	75.30S	80.00W
Ellsworth Mountains	66	Pf	78.30S	85.00W
Ellwangen	10	Gh	48.57N	10.08 E

Index Symbols

[1] Independent Nation
[2] State, Region
[3] District, County
[5] Municipality
[6] Colony, Dependency
Continent
Physical Region

Historical or Cultural Region
Mount, Mountain
Volcano
Hill
Mountains, Mountain Range
Hills, Escarpment
Plateau, Upland

Pass, Gap
Plain, Lowland
Delta
Salt Flat
Valley, Canyon
Crater, Cave
Karst Features

Depression
Polder
Desert, Dunes
Forest, Woods
Heath, Steppe
Oasis
Cape, Point

Coast, Beach
Cliff
Peninsula
Isthmus
Sandbank
Island
Atoll

Rock, Reef
Islands, Archipelago
Rocks, Reefs
Coral Reef
Well, Spring
Geyser
River, Stream

Waterfall Rapids
River Mouth, Estuary
Lake
Salt Lake
Intermittent Lake
Reservoir
Swamp, Pond

Canal
Glacier
Ice Shelf, Pack Ice
Ocean
Sea
Gulf, Bay
Strait, Fjord

Lagoon
Bank
Seamount
Tablemount
Ridge
Shelf
Basin

Escarpment, Sea Scarp
Fracture
Trench, Abyss
National Park, Reserve
Point of Interest
Recreation Site
Cave, Cavern

Historic Site
Ruins
Wall, Walls
Church, Abbey
Temple
Scientific Station
Airport

Port
Lighthouse
Mine
Tunnel
Dam, Bridge

Name	Page	Grid	Lat.	Long.
Elm	10	Gd	52.09N	10.53 E
El Macao	49	Md	18.46N	68.33W
Elmadağ	24	Ec	39.55N	33.15 E
Elma Daği	15	Mk	38.46N	29.32 E
El Maestrat/El Maestrazgo	13	Ld	40.30N	0.10W
El Maestrazgo/El Maestrat	13	Ld	40.30N	0.10W
El Mahia	34	Ea	22.30N	2.30W
El Maitén	56	Ff	42.03S	71.10W
Elmaki	34	Gb	17.55N	8.20 E
El Malah	13	Ph	36.18N	3.14 E
Elmalı	24	Ic	39.25N	40.35 E
Elmali	24	Cd	36.44N	29.56 E
El Manteco	50	Ei	7.27N	62.32W
El Marfil	55	Bb	15.35S	60.19W
El Marsa	13	Mh	36.24N	0.55 E
El Medo	35	Gd	5.41N	41.46 E
El Meghaier	32	Ic	33.57N	5.56 E
Elmhurst	45	Mf	41.53N	87.56W
El Milagro	56	Gd	31.01S	65.59W
Elmira	43	Lc	42.06N	76.50W
El Mrâyer	32	Fe	21.30N	8.10W
El Mreïti	32	Fe	23.29N	7.52W
El Mreyyé	30	Gg	19.30N	7.00W
Elmshorn	10	Fc	53.45N	9.39 E
Elmstein	12	Je	49.22N	7.56 E
Elne	11	Il	42.36N	2.58 E
El Nevado, Cerro-	56	Ge	35.35S	68.30W
El Niabo	35	Fe	4.33N	39.59 E
El Nihuil	56	Gd	34.58S	68.40W
El Novillo	48	Ec	28.40N	109.30W
El Novillo, Presa-	48	Ec	29.05N	109.45W
El Ochenta y Uno	48	Kg	21.35N	97.57W
Elorn	11	Bf	48.27N	4.16W
Elortondo	55	Bk	33.42S	61.37W
Elorza	54	Eb	7.03N	69.31W
Elota, Rio-	48	Ff	23.52N	106.56W
El Oued	32	Ic	33.20N	6.53 E
Eloy	46	Jj	32.45N	111.33W
El Palmar	50	Fh	8.01N	61.53W
El Palmito	48	Ge	25.40N	104.59W
El Panadés/El Penedès	13	Nc	41.25N	1.30 E
El Pao [Ven.]	50	Eh	8.06N	62.33W
El Pao [Ven.]	50	Bh	9.38N	68.08W
El Paraiso [3]	49	Df	14.10N	86.30W
El Paraíso	49	Dg	13.51N	86.34W
El Páramo	13	Gb	42.25N	5.45W
El Pardo, Madrid-	13	Id	40.32N	3.46W
El Paso [Il.-U.S.]	45	Lf	40.44N	89.01W
El Paso [Tx.-U.S.]	39	If	31.45N	106.29W
El Penedès/El Panadés	13	Nc	41.25N	1.30 E
El Perú	50	Fi	7.19N	61.49W
El Pico	54	Fg	15.57S	64.42W
El Pilar	50	Eg	10.32N	63.09W
El Pintado	56	Hb	24.38S	61.27W
El Porvenir [Hond.]	49	Df	14.41N	87.11W
El Porvenir [Pan.]	49	Hi	9.12N	80.08W
El Porvenir [Ven.]	50	Bi	6.55N	68.42W
El Potosi	48	Ie	24.51N	100.19W
El Prat de Llobregat/Prat de Llobregat	13	Oc	41.20N	2.06 E
El Priorat/El Priorato	13	Mc	41.10N	1.00 E
El Priorato/El Priorat	13	Mc	41.10N	1.00 E
El Progreso [3]	49	Cf	14.50N	90.00W
El Progreso [Guat.]	49	Bf	14.51N	90.04W
El Progreso [Hond.]	47	Ge	15.21N	87.49W
El Puente del Arzobispo	13	Ge	39.48N	5.10W
El Puerto	48	Dc	28.45N	111.20W
El Puerto de Santa María	13	Fh	36.36N	6.13W
El Rastro	50	Ch	9.03N	67.27W
El Real de Santa María	49	Ii	8.08N	77.43W
El Reno	43	Hd	35.32N	97.57W
El Ribeiro	13	Db	42.25N	8.10W
Elrose	46	Ka	51.13N	108.01W
El Saler	13	Le	39.23N	0.20W
El Salto	47	Cd	23.47N	105.23W
El Salvador [1]	39	Kh	13.50N	88.55W
El Samán de Apure	50	Bi	7.55N	68.44W
El Sauce [Mex.]	48	De	24.34N	111.29W
El Sauce [Nic.]	49	Dg	12.53N	86.32W
El Sáuz	48	Fc	29.03N	106.15W
Elsberry	45	Kg	39.10N	90.47W
Elsdorf	12	Id	50.56N	6.34 E
Else	12	Kb	52.12N	8.40 E
El Seibo	49	Md	18.46N	68.52W
Elsen, Paderborn-	12	Kc	51.44N	8.41 E
Elsen Nur	27	Fd	35.08N	92.20 E
'Ēl Shāma	35	Ge	2.46N	41.03 E
El Socorro	50	Dh	8.59N	65.44W
El Sombrero	54	Eb	9.23N	67.03W
Elst	12	Hc	51.55N	5.52 E
Elsterwerda	10	Je	51.27N	13.32 E
El Sueco	47	Cc	29.54N	106.24W
El-Taht	13	Mi	35.27N	0.46 E
El Tajín	47	Ed	20.27N	97.23W
El Tala	56	Gc	26.07S	65.17W
Eltanin Bay	66	Pf	73.40S	82.00W
Eltham	62	Fc	39.26S	174.18 E
El Tigre	53	Je	8.55N	64.15W
El Tigre, Isla-	49	Dg	13.16N	87.38W
El Toboso	13	Je	39.31N	3.00W
El Tocuyo	54	Eb	9.47N	69.48W
Elton	16	Oe	49.08N	46.50 E
Elton, Ozero-	19	Ef	49.10N	46.40 E
El Torcal	13	Hh	36.55N	4.35W
El Trébol	55	Bk	32.12S	61.42W
El Trigo	55	Cl	35.52S	59.24W
El Triunfo [Hond.]	49	Dg	13.06N	87.00W
El Triunfo [Mex.]	47	Df	23.47N	110.08W
El Tuito	48	Gg	20.19N	105.22W
El Turbio	56	Fh	51.41S	72.05W
Eltville am Rhein	12	Kd	50.02N	8.07 E
Eltz	12	Jd	50.12N	7.18 E
Elūru	25	Ge	17.05N	82.15 E
Elva	7	Gg	58.13N	26.25 E
El Valle	49	Gi	8.31N	80.08W
El Valles/Valles	13	Oc	41.35N	2.15 E
Elvas	13	Ef	38.53N	7.10W
El Vejo, Cerro-	54	Db	7.30N	73.05W
El Venado, Isla-	49	Fh	11.57N	83.44W
El Vendrell/Vendrell	13	Nc	41.13N	1.32 E
Elverum	7	Cf	60.53N	11.34 E
El Viejo	49	Dg	12.40N	87.10W
El Viejo, Volcán	38	Kh	12.38N	87.11W
El Vigia	49	Li	8.38N	71.39W
El Vigía, Cerro-	48	Gg	21.25N	104.00W
El Wak	36	Hb	2.49N	40.56 E
Elwell, Lake-	46	Jb	48.22N	111.17W
Elwood	44	Ee	40.17N	85.50W
Ely [Eng.-U.K.]	9	Ni	52.24N	0.16 E
Ely [Mn.-U.S.]	43	Ib	47.54N	91.51W
Ely [Nv.-U.S.]	39	Hf	39.15N	114.53W
Elyria	44	Fe	41.22N	82.06W
El Yunque	51a	Cb	18.18N	65.47W
Elz	12	Kd	50.25N	8.02 E
Elzbach	12	Jd	50.12N	7.22 E
Emaé	63b	Dc	17.04S	168.22 E
Ema Jõgi/Emajygi	8	Lf	58.20N	27.15 E
Emajygi/Ema Jõgi	8	Lf	58.20N	27.15 E
Emali	36	Gc	2.05S	37.28 E
Emāmshahr [Iran]	23	Ib	36.25N	55.01 E
Emāmshahr [Iran]	22	Hf	36.50N	54.29 E
Emāmzādeh 'Abbās	24	Lf	32.25N	47.55 E
Emān	7	Dh	57.08N	16.30 E
Emba	19	Ff	48.50N	58.10 E
Emba	5	Lf	46.38N	53.04 E
Embaracai, Rio-	55	Ff	23.27S	53.58W
Embarcación	56	Hb	23.13S	64.06W
Embarras Portage	42	Ge	58.25N	111.27W
Embarras River	45	Mg	38.39N	87.37W
Embira, Rio-	54	De	7.19S	70.15W
Embrun	11	Mj	44.34N	6.30 E
Embu	36	Gc	0.32S	37.27 E
Emden	10	Dc	53.22N	7.13 E
Emeldžak	20	He	58.27N	126.57 E
Emerald	58	Fg	23.32S	148.10 E
Emerald	42	Ga	76.50N	114.00W
Emerson	45	Hb	49.00N	97.12W
Emet	24	Cc	39.20N	29.15 E
Emiliano Zapata	48	Ni	17.45N	91.46W
Emilia-Romagna [2]	14	Ef	44.45N	11.00 E
Emilio R. Coni	55	Cj	30.04S	58.16W
Emili Rock	52	Hh	29.40S	87.25W
Emin/Dorbiljin	27	Db	46.32N	83.39 E
Emine, Nos-	15	Kg	42.42N	27.54 E
Emira Island	60	Dh	1.40S	150.00 E
Emirdağ	24	Dc	39.01N	31.10 E
Emisu, Tarso-	30	If	21.13N	18.32 E
Emlichheim	10	Cd	52.37N	6.51 E
Emmaboda	7	Dh	56.38N	15.32 E
Emmaste	7	Fg	58.43N	22.36 E
Emme	14	Bd	47.10N	7.35 E
Emmeloord, Noordoostpolder-	12	Hb	52.42N	5.44 E
Emmelshausen	12	Jd	50.09N	7.34 E
Emmen	11	Mb	52.47N	6.55 E
Emmendingen	10	Dh	48.08N	7.51 E
Emmen-Emmer-Compascuum	12	Jb	52.49N	7.03 E
Emmen-Klazienaveen	12	Jb	52.44N	7.01 E
Emmen-Nieuw Weerdinge	12	Jb	52.52N	7.01 E
Emmental	14	Bd	46.55N	7.45 E
Emmen-Weerdinge	12	Ib	52.49N	6.57 E
Emmer	12	Lb	52.03N	9.23 E
Emmer-Compascuum, Emmen-	12	Jb	52.49N	7.03 E
Emmerich	10	Ce	51.50N	6.15 E
Emmet	59	Id	24.40S	144.28 E
Emmetsburg	45	Ie	43.07N	94.41W
Emmett	46	Ge	43.52N	116.30W
Emmonak	40	Gd	62.46N	164.30W
Emőd	10	Qi	47.56N	20.49 E
Emory	46	Jf	41.05N	111.16W
Emory Peak	43	Gf	29.13N	103.17W
Empalme	47	Bc	27.58N	110.51W
Empangeni	37	Ee	28.50S	31.48 E
Empedrado	56	Ic	27.57S	58.48W
Emperor Seamounts (EN)	3	Je	40.00N	171.00 E
Empoli	14	Eg	43.43N	10.57 E
Emporia [Ks.-U.S.]	43	Hd	38.24N	96.11W
Emporia [Va.-U.S.]	44	Ig	36.42N	77.33W
Emporium	44	He	41.31N	78.14W
Empress Augusta Bay	63a	Bb	6.25S	155.05 E
Empress Mine	37	Dc	18.27S	29.27 E
Ems	11	Na	53.19N	7.03 E
Emsbach	12	Kd	50.24N	8.06 E
Emsdetten	10	Dd	52.11N	7.32 E
Ems-Jade-Kanal	10	Dc	53.19N	7.10 E
Emsland	10	Dd	52.50N	7.20 E
Emstek	12	Kb	52.50N	8.09 E
Emumägi/Emumjagi	8	Lf	58.54N	26.23 E
Emumjagi/Emumägi	8	Lf	58.54N	26.23 E
Ena	29	Ed	35.27N	137.24 E
Enånger	7	Df	61.32N	17.00 E
Enaratoli	26	Kg	3.55S	136.21 E
Enard Bay	9	Hc	58.06N	5.20W
Ena-San	29	Ed	35.26N	137.36 E
Enbetsu	28	Pb	44.44N	141.47 E
Encantada, Cerro de la-	38	Hf	31.00N	115.29W
Encantada, Sierra de la-	48	Hc	28.30N	102.20W
Encantadas, Serra das	55	Fj	30.40S	53.00W
Encantado, Cerro-	47	Bc	27.03N	112.30W
Encarnación	53	Kh	27.20S	55.54W
Encarnación de Díaz	48	Hg	21.31N	102.14W
Enchi	34	Ed	5.49N	2.49W
Encinal	45	Gl	28.02N	99.21W
Encinasola	13	Ff	38.08N	6.52W
Encontrados	54	Db	8.46N	72.30W
Encounter Bay	59	Hg	35.35S	138.45 E
Encrucijada	49	Hb	22.37N	79.52W
Encruzilhada do Sul	55	Fj	30.32S	52.31W
Encs	10	Rh	48.20N	21.08 E
Ende	22	Oj	8.50S	121.39 E
Endeavour Strait	59	Ib	10.50S	142.15 E
Endelave	8	Di	55.45N	10.15 E
Enderbury Atoll	57	Je	3.08S	171.05W
Enderby	46	Fa	50.33N	119.08W
Enderby Land	66	Ee	67.30S	53.00 E
Endicott Mountains	40	Ic	67.50N	152.00W
Ené, Rio-	54	Df	11.09S	74.19W
Energetik	19	Fe	51.44N	58.48 E
Enez	24	Bb	40.44N	26.04 E
Enez Körfezi	15	Ii	40.45N	26.00 E
Enfer, Portes d'-	36	Ed	5.05S	27.30 E
Enfield	44	Ig	36.11N	77.47W
Enfield, London-	12	Bc	51.40N	0.04W
Engadin/Engiadin'ota/Engadina	14	Dd	46.35N	10.00 E
Engadina/Engadin/Engiadin'ota	14	Dd	46.35N	10.00 E
Engaño, Cabo-	47	Ke	18.37N	68.20W
Engaru	28	Qb	44.03N	143.31 E
Engelberg	14	Cd	46.50N	8.24 E
Engelhard	44	Jh	35.31N	76.00W
Engels	6	Ke	51.30N	46.07 E
Engelskirchen	12	Jd	50.59N	7.24 E
Engenho	55	Db	15.10S	56.25W
Enger	12	Kb	52.08N	8.34 E
Engeren	8	Ec	61.35N	12.05 E
Engershatu	35	Fb	16.34N	38.15 E
Enggano, Pulau-	21	Mj	5.24S	102.16 E
Enghien/Edingen	12	Gd	50.42N	4.02 E
Engiadin'ota/Engadina/Engadin	14	Dd	46.35N	10.00 E
England	5	Fe	52.30N	1.30W
England [2]	9	Li	52.30N	1.30W
Englehart	42	Jg	47.49N	79.52W
Englewood	45	Dg	39.39N	104.59W
English	44	Df	38.20N	86.28W
English Bāzār	25	Hc	25.00N	88.09 E
English Channel	5	Fe	50.20N	1.00W
English Coast	66	Qf	73.30S	73.00W
English River	45	Ia	50.12N	95.00W
English River	45	Kb	49.13N	90.58W
Engozero, Ozero-	7	Hd	65.45N	33.30 E
Enguera	13	Lf	38.59N	0.41W
Engure/Engures	8	Jg	57.09N	23.06 E
Engures/Engure	8	Jg	57.09N	23.06 E
Engures, Ozero-/Engures Ezers	8	Jg	57.15N	23.10 E
Engures Ezers/Engures, Ozero-	8	Jg	57.15N	23.10 E
Enh-Gajvan	27	Gb	48.05N	97.35 E
Enid	39	Jf	36.19N	97.48W
Enid Lake	45	Li	34.10N	89.50W
Eniwa	28	Pc	42.53N	141.14 E
Eniwa-Dake	29a	Bb	42.47N	141.17 E
Eniwetok Atoll	57	Hc	11.30N	162.15 E
Enkeldoorn	37	Ec	19.01S	30.53 E
Enkenbach Alsenborn	12	Je	49.29N	7.53 E
Enkhuizen	11	Lb	52.42N	5.17 E
Enklinge	8	Id	60.20N	20.45 E
Enköping	7	Dg	59.38N	17.04 E
Enna	14	Im	37.34N	14.16 E
Ennadai	42	Hd	61.10N	101.00W
Ennadei Lake	42	Hd	60.55N	101.20W
Enné	35	Bc	14.24N	18.45 E
Ennedi	30	Jg	17.15N	22.00 E
Ennell, Lough-/Loch Ainninn	9	Fh	53.28N	7.24W
Ennepetal	12	Jc	51.18N	7.21 E
Ennigerloh	12	Kc	51.50N	8.01 E
Enning	45	Ed	44.37N	102.31W
Ennis [Mt.-U.S.]	46	Jd	45.21N	111.44W
Ennis [Tx.-U.S.]	45	Hj	32.20N	96.38W
Ennis/Inis	9	Ei	52.50N	8.59W
Enniscorthy/Inis Córthaidh	9	Gi	52.30N	6.34W
Enniskillen/Inis Ceithleann	9	Fg	54.21N	7.38W
Ennistymon/Inis Diomáin	9	Di	52.57N	9.13W
Enns	14	Ib	48.12N	14.28 E
Enns	5	Hf	48.14N	14.30 E
Ennstaler Alpen	14	Ic	47.37N	14.35 E
Eno	7	He	62.48N	30.09 E
Enontekiö	7	Fb	68.23N	23.38 E
Enonvesi [Fin.]	8	Mb	62.10N	28.55 E
Enonvesi [Fin.]	8	Lc	61.20N	26.30 E
Enozero, Ozero-	7	Ib	68.10N	38.00 E
Enrekang	26	Gg	3.34S	119.47 E
Enrique Carbó	55	Ck	33.08S	59.14W
Enriquillo	49	Le	17.54N	71.14W
Enriquillo, Lago-	47	Je	18.27N	71.39W
Enschede	11	Mb	52.12N	6.53 E
Ensenada [Arg.]	55	Dl	34.51S	57.55W
Ensenada [Mex.]	39	Hf	31.52N	116.37W
Enshi	27	Ie	30.16N	109.26 E
Enshū-Nada	29	Ed	34.30N	138.00 E
Entebbe	31	Kh	0.04N	32.28 E
Entenbühl	10	Ig	49.46N	12.24 E
Enterprise [Al.-U.S.]	44	Ej	31.19N	85.51W
Enterprise [N.W.T.-Can.]	42	Fd	60.39N	116.08W
Enterprise [Or.-U.S.]	46	Gd	45.25N	117.17W
Entinas, Punta-	13	Jh	36.41N	2.46W
Entrada, Punta-	47	Ab	30.22N	115.59W
Entraygues-sur-Truyère	11	Ij	44.39N	2.34 E
Entrecasteaux, Récifs d'-	57	Hf	18.20S	163.00 E
Entrepeñas, Embalse de-	13	Jd	40.34N	2.42W
Entre Rios [2]	56	Id	32.00S	59.00W
Entre Rios	54	Fh	21.32S	64.12W
Entre Rios de Minas	55	Je	20.41S	44.04W
Entrevaux	11	Mk	43.57N	6.49 E
Entroncamento	13	De	39.28N	8.28W
Enugu	31	Hh	6.26N	7.29 E
Enugu Ezike	34	Gd	6.59N	7.27 E
Envermeu	12	De	49.54N	1.16 E
Envigado	54	Cb	6.08N	75.39W
Envira	54	De	7.18S	70.13W
Enyamba	36	Dc	3.40S	24.58 E
Enyélé	36	Cb	2.49N	18.06 E
Enz	10	Fh	49.00N	9.10 E
Enza	14	Ef	44.54N	10.31 E
Enzan	28	Og	34.52N	138.44 E
Enzgau	12	Kf	48.48N	8.37 E
Eo	13	Ea	43.28N	7.03W
Eochaill/Youghal	9	Fj	51.57N	7.50W
Eolie o Lipari, Isole-=Lipari Islands (EN)	5	Hh	38.35N	14.55 E
Epanomí	15	Fi	40.26N	22.56 E
Epazote, Cerro-	47	Cd	24.35N	105.07W
Epe [Neth.]	12	Hb	52.21N	5.59 E
Epe [Nig.]	34	Fd	6.35N	3.59 E
Epéna	36	Cb	1.22N	17.29 E
Épernay	11	Je	49.03N	3.57 E
Epe-Vaassen	12	Hb	52.17N	5.58 E
Ephesus (EN)=Efes	15	Kl	37.55N	27.20 E
Ephraim	46	Jg	39.22N	111.35W
Ephrata	46	Fc	47.19N	119.33W
Epi, Ile-	57	Hf	16.43S	168.15 E
Epidamnus	15	Ch	41.19N	19.26 E
Epidaurus (EN) = Epídhavros	15	Gl	37.38N	23.09 E
Epídhavros = Epidaurus (EN)	15	Gl	37.38N	23.09 E
Epila	13	Kc	41.36N	1.17W
Épinal	11	Mf	48.11N	6.27 E
Epirus (EN)=Ipiros	5	Ih	39.30N	20.40 E
Epirus (EN)=Ipiros	15	Dj	39.30N	20.40 E
Episkopi	24	Ee	34.40N	32.54 E
Epping	12	Cc	51.42N	0.07 E
Eppingen	12	Ke	49.08N	8.54 E
Epsom	9	Mj	51.20N	0.16W
Epte	11	He	49.04N	1.31 E
Epukiro	37	Bd	21.41S	19.08 E
Epukiro	37	Bd	21.28S	19.59 E
Epulu	36	Eb	1.15N	28.21 E
Eqlīd	23	Hc	30.55N	52.39 E
Équateur=Equator (EN) [2]	36	Eb	1.00N	20.00 E
Equator (EN)=Équateur [2]	36	Eb	1.00N	20.00 E
Equatorial Guinea (EN)= Guinea Ecuatorial [1]	1	Hh	2.00N	9.00 E
Equinox Mountain	44	Kd	43.15N	73.10W
Era [It.]	14	Eg	43.40N	10.38 E
Era [Sud.]	35	Dd	5.30N	29.50 E
Eraclea	14	Kj	40.15N	16.40 E
Eraclea Minoa	14	Hm	37.25N	13.18 E
Eradaka	63b	Dc	17.39S	168.08 E
Eräjärvi	8	Kc	61.35N	24.34 E
Eratiní	15	Fk	38.22N	22.14 E
Erbaa	24	Gb	40.42N	36.36 E
Erbach	10	Eg	49.39N	9.00 E
Erbeskopf	10	Dg	49.44N	7.05 E
Erbīl [3]	24	Je	36.10N	44.00 E
Erbīl	22	Gf	36.11N	44.01 E
Ercek	24	Jc	38.39N	43.36 E
Erçek Gölü	24	Jc	38.39N	43.32 E
Erciş	24	Jc	39.00N	43.19 E
Erciyas Daği	21	Ff	38.32N	35.28 E
Ercolano	14	Ij	40.48N	14.21 E
Ercsi	10	Oi	47.15N	18.54 E
Érd	10	Oi	47.22N	18.56 E
Erdaobaihe	27	Mc	42.28N	128.05 E
Erdao Jiang	28	Ic	42.35N	127.10 E
Erdek	24	Bb	40.24N	27.48 E
Erdek Körfezi	24	Bb	40.25N	27.45 E
Erdemli	24	Fd	36.37N	34.18 E
Erdene-Cagan	27	Kb	45.55N	115.30 E
Erdene-Dalaj	27	Hb	46.02N	104.55 E
Erdene-Mandal	27	Hb	48.30N	101.21 E
Erdi	30	Jg	19.05N	22.40 E
Erdi Ma	35	Cb	18.35N	23.30 E
Erding	10	Hh	48.18N	11.56 E
Erdinger Moos	10	Hh	48.20N	11.50 E
Erdre	11	Eg	47.13N	1.32W
Erebus, Mount-	66	Kf	77.32S	167.09 E
Erechim	56	Jc	27.38S	52.17W
Ereğli [Tur.]	23	Db	37.31N	34.04 E
Ereğli [Tur.]	23	Da	41.17N	31.25 E
Erei, Monti-	14	Im	37.35N	14.20 E
Ereke	26	Hg	4.45S	123.10 E
Eren	24	Dd	37.25N	30.05 E
Erenhot	22	Ne	43.35N	112.00 E
Erepecu, Lago do-	54	Gd	1.20S	56.35W
Eresma	13	Hc	41.26N	4.45W
Erétria	15	Gk	38.25N	23.48 E
Erfelek	24	Fb	41.55N	34.57 E
Erfengshan	28	Ag	35.50N	111.47 E
Erfoud	32	Gc	31.26N	4.14W
Erft	10	Ce	51.11N	6.44 E
Erftstadt	12	Id	50.48N	6.49 E
Erfurt	6	He	50.59N	11.02 E
Erfurt [2]	10	Gf	51.00N	11.00 E
Ergani	24	Hc	38.17N	39.46 E
Ergene	24	Bb	41.01N	26.22 E
Erges	13	Ee	39.40N	7.01W
Ergig, Bahr-	35	Bc	11.22N	15.24 E
Ērgļi/Ergli	7	Fh	56.55N	25.41 E
Ergli/Ērgļi	7	Fh	56.55N	25.41 E
Ergun He	21	Od	53.20N	121.28 E
Ergun Youqi (Labudalin)	27	La	50.16N	120.09 E
Ergun Zuoqi (Genhe)	22	Od	50.47N	121.32 E
Er Hai	27	Hf	25.45N	100.10 E
Eria	13	Gb	42.03N	5.44W
Eriba	35	Fb	16.37N	36.04 E
Eriboll, Loch-	9	Ic	58.30N	4.40W
Eric	42	Kf	51.52N	65.45W
Erice	14	Gl	38.02N	12.35 E
Ericeira	13	Cf	38.59N	9.25W
Erichsen Lake	42	Jb	70.38N	80.20W
Ericht, Loch-	9	Ie	56.50N	4.25W
Erick	45	Gi	35.13N	99.52W
Eridu [3]	24	Lg	36.00N	44.00 E
Erie	39	Ke	42.08N	80.04W
Erie, Lake-	38	Ke	42.15N	81.00W
'Erigābo	35	Hc	10.37N	47.24 E
Erîgât	30	Gg	19.40N	4.50W
Erikoússa	15	Cj	39.53N	19.35 E
Eriksdale	45	Ga	50.52N	98.06W
Eriksenstretet	41	Oc	79.00N	26.00 E
Erikub Atoll	57	Id	9.08N	170.02 E
Erímanthos Óros	15	El	37.58N	21.48 E
Erimo-Misaki	27	Pc	41.55N	143.15 E
Eriskay	9	Fd	57.04N	7.13W
Eritrea	30	Kg	15.00N	40.00 E
Eritrea [3]	35	Fb	15.00N	39.00 E
Eritrea	35	Fb	15.00N	40.00 E
Erjas	13	Ee	39.40N	7.01W
Erkelenz	12	Ic	51.05N	6.19 E
Erken	8	He	59.50N	18.35 E
Erkowit	35	Fb	18.46N	37.07 E
Erlangdian → Dawu	28	Ci	31.33N	114.07 E
Erlangen	10	Hg	49.36N	11.01 E
Erlang Shan	27	Hf	29.58N	102.20 E
Erlauf	14	Jb	48.12N	15.11 E
Erldunda	59	Ge	25.14S	133.12 E
Erlenbach	12	Ke	49.07N	8.11 E
Erlong Shan	27	Mc	43.30N	128.44 E
Ermelo [Neth.]	12	Hb	52.19N	5.37 E
Ermelo [S.Afr.]	37	De	26.34S	29.58 E
Ermenek	24	Ed	36.38N	32.54 E
Ermenistan=Armenia (EN)	23	Fb	39.10N	43.00 E
Ermenistan=Armenia (EN)	21	Gf	39.10N	43.00 E
Ermenonville	12	Ee	49.08N	2.42 E
Ermesinde	13	Dc	41.13N	8.33W
Ermoúpolis	15	Hl	37.27N	24.56 E
Ernākulam	25	Fg	9.59N	76.17 E
Erndtebrück	12	Kd	50.59N	8.16 E
Erne/An Éirne	9	Eg	54.30N	8.15W
Ernée	11	Ff	48.18N	0.56W
Ernest Legouvé Reef	57	Lh	35.12S	150.35W
Ernici, Monti-	14	Hi	41.50N	13.20 E
Erode	25	Ff	11.21N	77.44 E
Eromanga	59	Ie	26.40S	143.16 E
Erongoberg	37	Bd	21.40S	15.40 E
Erpengdianzi	28	Hd	41.12N	125.29 E
Errego	37	Fc	16.02S	37.10 E
Errigal/An Ea agail	9	Ef	55.02N	8.07W
Erris Head/Ceann Iorrais	5	Fe	54.19N	10.00W
Erromango, Ile-	57	Hf	18.48S	169.05 E
Erseka	15	Di	40.20N	20.41 E
Erstein	11	Nf	48.26N	7.40 E
Ertai	27	Fb	46.02N	90.10 E
Ertil	19	Ee	51.50N	40.51 E
Ertix He	21	Ke	47.52N	84.16 E
Erts	37	De	25.08S	29.55 E
Ertvågøy	8	Ca	63.15N	8.25 E
Eruh	24	Jd	37.46N	42.15 E
Ervânia	55	Ee	21.43S	55.32W
Erve	11	Fg	47.50N	0.20W
Ervy-le-Châtel	11	Jf	48.02N	3.55 E
Erwin	44	Fg	36.09N	82.25W
Erwitte	12	Kc	51.37N	8.21 E
Eryuan	27	Gf	26.09N	99.56 E
Erzeni	15	Ch	41.26N	19.27 E
Erzgebirge=Ore Mountains (EN)	5	He	50.30N	13.15 E
Erzin	20	Ef	50.17N	95.10 E
Erzincan	23	Eb	39.44N	39.29 E
Erzurum	22	Gf	39.55N	41.17 E
Esan-Misaki	28	Pd	41.48N	141.12 E
Esashi [Jap.]	28	Pd	41.52N	140.07 E
Esashi [Jap.]	28	Qb	44.56N	142.35 E
Esashi [Jap.]	28	Pe	39.12N	141.09 E
Esbjerg	6	Gd	55.28N	8.27 E
Esbo/Espoo	7	Ff	60.13N	24.40 E
Escalante	46	Jh	37.47N	111.36W
Escalante Desert	46	Ih	37.50N	113.30W
Escalante River	46	Jh	37.17N	110.53W
Escalaplano	14	Dk	39.37N	9.21 E
Escalón	47	Dc	26.45N	104.20W
Escalona	13	Hd	40.10N	4.24W
Escanaba	39	Ke	45.45N	87.04W
Escanaba River	44	Dc	45.47N	87.04W
Escandón, Puerto de-	13	Ld	40.17N	1.00W
Escandorgue	11	Jk	43.46N	3.14 E
Escarpada Point	21	Oh	18.31N	122.13 E
Escarpé, Cap-	63b		20.41S	167.13 E
Escatrón	13	Lc	41.17N	0.19W
Escaut=Schelde (EN)	11	Kc	51.22N	4.15 E
Esch an der Alzette/Esch-sur-Alzette	11	Le	49.30N	5.59 E
Eschkopf	12	Je	49.19N	7.51 E
Esch-sur-Alzette/Esch an der Alzette	11	Le	49.30N	5.59 E
Eschwege	10	Ge	51.11N	10.04 E
Eschweiler	10	Cf	50.49N	6.17 E
Escocesa, Bahia-	49	Md	19.25N	69.45W
Escondida, Punta-	48	Kj	15.49N	97.03W
Escondido	46	Gj	33.07N	117.05W
Escondido, Río-	49	Fg	12.04N	83.45W
Escravos	34	Gd	5.36N	5.11 E
Escudo, Puerto del-	13	Ia	43.05N	3.50W
Escudo de Veraguas, Isla-	49	Gi	9.06N	81.33W
Escuintla [3]	49	Bf	14.10N	91.00W
Escuintla [Guat.]	47	Ff	14.18N	90.47W
Escuintla [Mex.]	48	Mj	15.20N	92.38W
Escuro, Rio- [Braz.]	55	Ic	17.31S	46.39W
Escuro, Rio- [Braz.]	55	Ha	12.50S	49.28W
Ese	36	Eb	4.04N	26.40 E
Ese-Hajja	20	Ic	67.35N	134.55 E
Eséka	34	He	3.39N	10.46 E
Eşen	24	Cd	36.27N	29.16 E
Esendere	24	Kd	37.46N	44.40 E
Esera	13	Mb	42.06N	0.15 E
Esfahān [3]	23	Hc	32.50N	51.50 E
Eşfahān=Isfahan (EN)	22	Hf	32.40N	51.38 E
Esfandārān	24	Og	31.52N	52.32 E
Esfarāyen, Reshteh-ye-	24	Qd	36.46N	57.10 E
Esgueva	13	Hc	41.40N	4.43W

Index Symbols

- [1] Independent Nation
- [2] State, Region
- [3] District, County
- [4] Mónicipality
- [5] Colony, Dependency
- Continent
- Physical Region
- Historical or Cultural Region
- Mount, Mountain
- Volcano
- Hill
- Mountains, Mountain Range
- Hills, Escarpment
- Plateau, Upland
- Pass, Gap
- Plain, Lowland
- Delta
- Salt Flat
- Valley, Canyon
- Crater, Cave
- Karst Features
- Depression
- Polder
- Desert, Dunes
- Forest, Woods
- Heath, Steppe
- Oasis
- Cape, Point
- Coast, Beach
- Cliff
- Peninsula
- Isthmus
- Sandbank
- Island
- Atoll
- Rock, Reef
- Islands, Archipelago
- Rocks, Reefs
- Coral Reef
- Well, Spring
- Geyser
- River, Stream
- Waterfall Rapids
- River Mouth, Estuary
- Lake
- Salt Lake
- Intermittent Lake
- Reservoir
- Swamp, Pond
- Canal
- Glacier
- Ice Shelf, Pack Ice
- Ocean
- Sea
- Gulf, Bay
- Strait, Fjord
- Lagoon
- Bank
- Seamount
- Tablemount
- Ridge
- Shelf
- Basin
- Escarpment, Sea Scarp
- Fracture
- Trench, Abyss
- National Park, Reserve
- Point of Interest
- Recreation Site
- Cave, Cavern
- Historic Site
- Ruins
- Wall, Walls
- Church, Abbey
- Temple
- Scientific Station
- Airport
- Port
- Lighthouse
- Mine
- Tunnel
- Dam, Bridge

Name	Ref	Lat	Long
Eshowe	37 Ee	28.58 S	31.29 E
Eshtehärd	24 Ne	35.44 N	50.23 E
Esino �River	14 Hg	43.39 N	13.22 E
Esk �River	9 Jg	54.58 N	3.04 W
Eskifjördur	7a Cb	65.04 N	14.01 W
Eskilstuna	7 Dg	59.22 N	16.30 E
Eskimo Point	39 Jc	61.07 N	94.03 W
Eskişehir	22 Ff	39.46 N	30.32 E
Esla �River	13 Fc	41.29 N	6.03 W
Eslāmābād	23 Gc	34.11 N	46.35 E
Eşler Daği ⌷	15 Ml	37.24 N	29.43 E
Eslohe (Sauerland)	12 Kc	51.15 N	8.10 E
Eslöv	7 Ci	55.50 N	13.20 E
Eşme	24 Cc	38.24 N	28.59 E
Esmeralda [Braz.]	55 Gi	28.03 S	51.12 W
Esmeralda [Cuba]	49 Hc	21.51 N	78.07 W
Esmeralda, Isla- ⌷	56 Eg	48.57 S	75.25 W
Esmeralda Bank (EN) ⌷	65b Ab	14.57 N	145.15 E
Esmeraldas	53 Ie	0.59 N	79.42 W
Esnagami Lake ⌷	45 Ma	50.21 N	86.48 W
Esneux	12 Hd	50.32 N	5.34 E
Espada, Punta- ⌷	49 Lg	12.05 N	71.07 W
Espagnol Point ⌷	51n Ba	13.22 N	61.09 W
Espalion	11 Ij	44.31 N	2.46 E
Espalmador, Isla- ⌷	13 Nf	38.47 N	1.26 E
España = Spain (EN) ⌷	6 Fg	40.00 N	4.00 W
Espanola [N.M.-U.S.]	45 Ch	36.06 N	106.02 W
Espanola [Ont.-Can.]	44 Gb	46.15 N	81.46 W
Española, Isla- ⌷	54a Bb	1.25 S	89.42 W
Espardell, Isla- ⌷	13 Nf	38.47 N	1.27 E
Esparta	49 Ei	9.59 N	84.40 W
Espeland	8 Ad	60.23 N	5.28 E
Espelkamp	10 Ed	52.25 N	8.37 E
Esperance	58 Dh	33.51 S	121.53 E
Esperance, Cape- ⌷	63a Dc	9.15 S	159.43 E
Esperance Bay ⌷	59 Ef	33.50 S	121.55 E
Esperance Harbour ⌷	51k Ba	14.04 N	60.55 W
Esperancita	55 Bc	16.55 S	60.06 W
Esperantina	54 Jd	3.54 S	42.14 W
Esperanza ⌷	66 Re	63.26 S	57.00 W
Esperanza [Arg.]	56 Hd	31.27 S	60.56 W
Esperanza [Mex.]	48 Ed	27.35 N	109.56 W
Esperanza [P.R.]	51a Cb	18.06 N	65.29 W
Esperanza, Sierra la- ⌷	49 Ef	15.40 N	85.45 W
Espevær	7 Ag	59.36 N	5.10 E
Espichel, Cabo- ⌷	13 Cf	38.25 N	9.13 W
Espiel	13 Gf	38.12 N	5.01 W
Espigão Serra do- ⌷	55 Gh	26.55 S	50.25 W
Espinal [Bol.]	55 Cc	17.13 S	58.43 W
Espinal [Col.]	54 Dc	4.10 N	74.54 W
Espinazo del Diablo, Sierra- ⌷	48 Ff	24.00 N	106.00 W
Espinhaço, Serra do- ⌷	52 Lg	17.30 S	43.30 W
Espinho	13 Dc	41.01 N	8.38 W
Espinillo	55 Cg	24.58 S	58.34 W
Espino	50 Dh	8.34 N	66.01 W
Espinosa	54 Jf	14.56 S	42.50 W
Espinouse ⌷	11 Ik	43.32 N	2.46 E
Espírito Santo ⌷	54 Jg	20.00 S	40.30 W
Espíritu Santo, Bahía del- ⌷	48 Ph	19.20 N	87.35 W
Espíritu Santo, Isla- ⌷	48 De	24.30 N	110.22 W
Espita	48 Og	21.01 N	88.19 W
Esplanada	54 Kf	11.47 S	37.57 W
Espoo/Esbo	7 Ff	60.13 N	24.40 E
Espoo-Tapiola	8 Kd	60.11 N	24.49 E
Esposende	13 Dc	41.32 N	8.47 W
Espumoso	55 Fi	28.44 S	52.51 W
Espuña, Sierra de- ⌷	13 Kg	37.52 N	1.34 W
Espungabera	37 Ed	20.28 S	32.46 E
Esquel	53 Ij	42.55 S	71.20 W
Esquina	56 Id	30.01 S	59.32 W
Esquinapa de Hidalgo	47 Cd	22.51 N	105.48 W
Esquipular	49 Cf	14.34 N	89.21 W
Essandsjøen ⌷	3a Cc	63.05 N	12.00 E
Essaouira	31 Ge	31.31 N	9.46 W
Essaouira ⌷	32 Fc	31.04 N	9.03 W
Essen [Bel.]	12 Gc	51.28 N	4.28 E
Essen [F.R.G.]	6 Ge	51.27 N	7.01 E
Essen (Oldenburg)	12 Jb	52.42 N	7.55 E
Essendon, Mount- ⌷	59 Ed	24.59 S	120.28 E
Essequibo River ⌷	52 Ke	6.50 N	58.30 W
Essex	46 Hi	34.42 N	115.12 W
Essex ⌷	9 Nj	51.50 N	0.30 E
Essex [3]	9 Mj	51.50 N	0.35 E
Essex Mountain ⌷	46 Ke	42.02 N	109.13 W
Essexvale	37 Dd	20.18 S	28.56 E
Esslingen am Neckar	10 Fh	48.45 N	9.18 E
Esso	20 Ke	55.55 N	158.40 E
Essonne ⌷	11 If	48.37 N	2.29 E
Essonne [3]	11 If	48.36 N	2.20 E
Est [Cam.] [3]	34 He	4.00 N	14.00 E
Est [U.V.] [3]	34 Fc	12.00 N	1.00 E
Est, Canal de l'- ⌷	11 Lf	48.45 N	5.35 E
Est, Cap- ⌷	37 Ic	15.16 S	50.29 E
Est, Île de l'- ⌷	30 Mm	46.15 S	52.05 E
Est, Pointe de l'- ⌷	42 Lg	49.08 N	61.41 W
Estaca de Bares, Punta la- ⌷	5 Fg	43.46 N	7.42 W
Estados, Isla de los- = Staten Island (EN) ⌷	52 Jk	54.47 S	64.15 W
Estados Unidos Mexicanos ⌷	39 Ig	23.00 N	102.00 W
Eşţahbānāt	24 Ph	29.08 N	54.04 E
Estaimpuis	12 Fd	50.42 N	3.15 E
Estância	54 Kf	11.16 S	37.26 W
Estancias, Sierra de las- ⌷	13 Jg	37.35 N	2.20 W
Estanislao del Campo	55 Bg	25.03 S	60.06 W
Estarreja	13 Dd	40.45 N	8.34 W
Estats, Pica d'- ⌷	11 Hn	42.40 N	1.24 E
Estats, Pica d'-/Estats, Pico d'- ⌷	11 Hn	42.40 N	1.24 E
Estats, Pico d'- ⌷	11 Hn	42.40 N	1.24 E
Estats, Pico d'- ⌷	11 Hn	42.40 N	1.24 E
Estats, Pico d'-/Estats, Pica d'- ⌷	11 Hn	42.40 N	1.24 E
Estcourt	37 De	29.01 S	29.52 E
Este	14 Fe	45.14 N	11.39 E
Este, Punta- ⌷	51a Cb	18.08 N	65.16 W
Este, Punta del- ⌷	56 Jd	34.59 S	54.57 W
Esteban Rams	55 Bi	29.47 S	61.29 W
Esteli	47 Gf	13.05 N	86.23 W
Esteli [3]	49 Dg	13.10 N	86.20 W
Estella	13 Jb	42.40 N	2.02 W
Estepa	13 Hg	37.18 N	4.54 W
Estepona	13 Gh	36.26 N	5.08 W
Estérel ⌷	11 Mk	43.30 N	6.50 E
Esternay	12 Ff	48.44 N	3.34 E
Esterri d'Aneu/Esterri de Aneu	13 Nb	42.38 N	1.08 E
Esterri de Aneu/Esterri d'Aneu	13 Nb	42.38 N	1.08 E
Esterwegen	12 Jb	52.59 N	7.37 E
Estes Park	45 Df	40.23 N	105.31 W
Este Sudeste, Cayos del- ⌷	47 Hf	12.26 N	81.27 W
Estevan	42 Hg	49.07 N	103.05 W
Estherville	45 Ie	43.24 N	94.50 W
Estissac	11 Jf	48.16 N	3.49 E
Eston	46 Ka	51.10 N	108.46 W
Estonia (EN) ⌷	5 Id	59.00 N	26.00 E
Estonian SSR (EN) = Eesti NSV ⌷	19 Cd	59.00 N	26.00 E
Estonskaja Sovetskaja Socialisticeskaja Respublika ⌷	19 Cd	59.00 N	26.00 E
Estonskaja SSR/Eesti Nõukogude Socialistlik Vabarijk ⌷	19 Cd	59.00 N	26.00 E
Estoril	13 Cf	38.42 N	9.24 W
Estrées-Saint-Denis	12 Ee	49.26 N	2.39 E
Estreito	55 Gj	31.50 S	51.44 W
Estreito, Represa do- ⌷	55 Ie	20.15 S	47.09 W
Estrêla [Braz.]	55 Gi	29.29 S	51.58 W
Estrêla [Braz.]	55 Gj	31.15 S	21.45 W
Estrela, Arroyo- ⌷	55 Df	22.05 S	56.25 W
Estrela, Serra da- ⌷	55 Fc	16.27 S	53.24 W
Estrela, Serra da- ⌷	5 Fg	40.20 N	7.38 W
Estrêla do Sul	55 Id	18.21 S	47.49 W
Estrella ⌷	13 If	38.28 N	3.35 W
Estrella, Punta- ⌷	48 Bb	30.55 N	114.40 W
Estrema, Serra da- ⌷	55 Jc	16.50 S	45.07 W
Estremadura ⌷	13 Ce	39.15 N	9.10 W
Estremoz	13 Ef	38.51 N	7.35 W
Estrondo, Serra do- ⌷	54 Ie	9.00 S	48.45 W
Estry	12 Bf	48.54 N	0.44 W
Estuaire [3]	36 Ab	0.10 N	10.00 E
Esztergom	10 Oi	47.48 N	18.45 E
Etah	41 Ec	78.19 N	72.38 W
Étain	11 Le	49.13 N	5.38 E
Etajima	29 Cd	34.15 N	132.29 E
Etalle	12 He	49.41 N	5.36 E
Étampes	11 If	48.26 N	2.09 E
Étaples	11 Hd	50.31 N	1.39 E
Etāwah	25 Fc	26.46 N	79.02 E
Ethe, Virton-	12 He	49.35 N	5.35 E
Ethel Reefs ⌷	63d Ab	16.56 S	177.13 E
Ethiopia (EN) = Itiopya ⌷	31 Kh	9.00 N	39.00 E
Ethiopian Plateau (EN) ⌷	30 Kg	10.00 N	38.10 E
Etive, Loch- ⌷	9 He	56.35 N	5.15 W
Etna ⌷	3 Dd	60.50 N	10.03 E
Etna ⌷	5 Hh	37.50 N	14.55 E
Etne	8 Ae	59.40 N	5.56 E
Etoile Cay ⌷	37b Bb	5.53 S	53.01 E
Etolin Island ⌷	40 Me	56.08 N	132.26 W
Etolin Strait ⌷	40 Fd	60.20 N	165.15 W
Etomo-Misaki ⌷	29a Bb	42.20 N	140.55 E
Etosha Pan ⌷	30 Ij	18.50 S	16.20 E
Etoumbi	36 Bb	0.01 N	14.57 E
Étrépagny	12 De	49.18 N	1.37 E
Étretat	11 Ge	49.42 N	0.12 E
Étropole	15 Gg	42.50 N	24.00 E
Etruria	56 Hd	32.56 S	63.15 W
Etsch/Adige ⌷	5 Hf	45.10 N	12.20 E
Ettelbrück/Ettelbruck	12 Ie	49.51 N	6.07 E
Ettelbruck/Ettelbrück	12 Ie	49.51 N	6.07 E
Etten-Leur	12 Gc	51.35 N	4.39 E
Ettersberg ⌷	10 He	51.03 N	11.15 E
Ettlingen	12 Kf	48.57 N	8.24 E
Etzna Tixmucuy ⌷	48 Nh	19.35 N	90.13 W
Eu	11 Hd	50.03 N	1.25 E
'Eua Iki ⌷	65b Bc	21.07 S	174.59 W
Eua Island ⌷	61 Gd	21.22 S	174.56 W
Euboea (EN) = Évvoia ⌷	5 Ih	38.30 N	24.00 E
Eucla	58 Dh	31.43 S	128.52 E
Euclid	44 Gd	41.34 N	81.33 W
Euclides da Cunha	54 Kf	10.31 S	39.01 W
Eucumbene, Lake- ⌷	59 Jg	36.05 S	148.45 E
Eudora	45 Kj	33.07 N	91.16 W
Eufaula	44 Ej	31.54 N	85.09 W
Eufaula Lake ⌷	45 Jh	35.17 N	95.31 W
Eugene	14 Fe	45.19 N	11.40 E
Eugenia, Punta- ⌷	39 Ge	44.02 N	123.05 W
Eugênio Penzo	38 Hg	27.50 N	115.03 W
Eugmo ⌷	55 Ef	22.13 S	55.53 W
Eume ⌷	7 Fe	63.49 N	22.45 E
Eunice [La.-U.S.]	13 Da	43.25 N	8.08 W
Eunice [N.M.-U.S.]	45 Jk	30.30 N	92.26 W
Eupen	45 Ej	32.26 N	103.09 W
Euphrates (EN) = Al Furāt ⌷	11 Md	50.38 N	6.02 E
Euphrates (EN) = Firat ⌷	21 Gf	31.00 N	47.25 E
Eupora	45 Lj	33.32 N	89.16 W
Eura	7 Ff	61.08 N	22.08 E
Eurajoki	8 Ic	61.12 N	21.44 E
Eurasia Basin (EN) ⌷	67 Ge	87.00 N	80.00 E
Eure ⌷	11 He	49.18 N	1.12 E
Eure [3]	11 He	49.18 N	1.11 E
Eure-et-Loir [3]	11 Hf	48.30 N	1.30 E
Eureka [Ca.-U.S.]	39 Ge	40.47 N	124.09 W
Eureka [Ks.-U.S.]	45 Hh	37.49 N	96.17 W
Eureka [Mt.-U.S.]	46 Hh	48.53 N	115.03 W
Eureka [Nv.-U.S.]	43 Dd	39.31 N	115.58 W
Eureka [N.W.T.-Can.]	42 Ia	80.00 N	85.59 W
Eureka [S.D.-U.S.]	45 Gd	45.46 N	99.38 W
Eureka [Ut.-U.S.]	46 Ig	39.57 N	112.07 W
Eureka Sound ⌷	42 Ia	79.00 N	87.00 W
Europa ⌷	30 Lk	22.20 S	40.22 E
Europa, Picos de- ⌷	5 Fg	43.12 N	4.48 W
Europe ⌷	5 Ie	50.00 N	20.00 E
Europoort	11 Jc	51.58 N	4.00 E
Euskirchen	10 Cf	50.40 N	6.47 E
Eustis	44 Gk	28.51 N	81.41 W
Eutaw	44 Di	32.50 N	87.53 W
Eutin	10 Gb	54.08 N	10.37 E
Euzkadi/Vascongadas = Basque Provinces (EN) ⌷	13 Ja	43.00 N	2.30 W
Evale	36 Cf	16.33 S	15.44 E
Evans, Lac- ⌷	42 Jf	50.50 N	77.00 W
Evans, Mount- ⌷	46 Ic	46.05 N	113.07 W
Evans Strait ⌷	42 Jd	63.20 N	82.00 W
Evanston [Il.-U.S.]	45 Me	42.03 N	87.42 W
Evanston [Wy.-U.S.]	43 Ec	41.16 N	110.58 E
Evansville	39 Kf	37.58 N	87.35 W
Evant	45 Gk	31.29 N	98.09 W
Evart	44 Ed	43.54 N	85.14 W
Evaux-les-Bains	11 Ih	46.10 N	2.29 E
Evaz	24 Oi	27.46 N	53.59 E
EVciler [Tur.]	15 Jj	39.46 N	26.46 E
Evciler [Tur.]	15 Mk	38.03 N	29.54 E
Evelyn, Mount- ⌷	59 Gb	13.36 S	132.53 E
Evenkijski Nac. okrug [3]	20 Ed	65.00 N	98.00 E
Evensk	22 Rc	61.57 N	159.14 E
Everard, Lake- ⌷	59 Hf	31.25 S	135.05 E
Everard Ranges ⌷	59 Ge	27.05 S	132.30 E
Everest, Mount- (EN) = Qomolangma Feng ⌷	21 Kg	27.59 N	86.56 E
Everest, Mount- (EN) = Saragmatha ⌷	21 Kg	27.59 N	86.56 E
Everett	43 Cb	47.59 N	122.13 W
Everett Mountains ⌷	42 Kd	62.45 N	67.10 W
Evergem	12 Fc	51.07 N	3.42 E
Evergem-Sleidinge	12 Fc	51.08 N	3.41 E
Everglades City	44 Gm	25.52 N	81.23 W
Evergreen	44 Dj	31.26 N	86.57 W
Evertsberg	8 Ec	61.08 N	13.57 E
Evesham	9 Li	52.05 N	1.56 W
Evesham, Vale of- ⌷	9 Li	52.05 N	1.50 W
Evian-les-Bains	11 Mh	46.23 N	6.35 E
Evijärvi	7 Fe	63.22 N	23.29 E
Evinayong	34 He	1.27 N	10.34 E
Évinos ⌷	15 Ek	38.19 N	21.32 E
Evje	7 Bg	58.36 N	7.51 E
Évora	5 Fh	38.34 N	7.54 W
Évora [2]	13 Ef	38.35 N	7.50 W
Evoron	20 If	51.23 N	136.23 E
Evowghlï	24 Kc	38.43 N	45.13 E
Evre ⌷	11 Eg	47.22 N	1.02 W
Evrecy	12 Be	49.06 N	0.30 W
Evreux	11 He	49.01 N	1.09 E
Evron	11 Ff	48.10 N	0.24 W
Évros ⌷	15 Ji	40.52 N	26.12 E
Evrótas ⌷	15 Fm	36.48 N	22.41 E
Evry	11 If	48.38 N	2.27 E
Évvoia = Euboea (EN) ⌷	5 Ih	38.30 N	24.00 E
Évvoia, Gulf of- (EN) = Vórios Evvoïkós Kólpos ⌷	15 Gk	38.45 N	23.10 E
Evzonoi	15 Fh	41.06 N	22.33 E
Ewa Beach	65a Cb	21.19 N	158.00 W
Ewing Seamount (EN) ⌷	30 Hk	23.20 S	8.45 E
Ewo	36 Bc	0.55 S	14.49 E
Excelsior Mountain ⌷	46 Fg	38.02 N	119.18 W
Excelsior Mountains ⌷	46 Fg	38.10 N	118.30 W
Excelsior Springs	45 Ig	39.20 N	94.13 W
Exe ⌷	9 Jk	50.37 N	3.25 W
Executive Committee Range ⌷	66 Nf	76.50 S	126.00 W
Exeter [Eng.-U.K.]	6 Fe	50.43 N	3.31 W
Exeter [N.H.-U.S.]	44 Jd	42.59 N	70.56 W
Exeter Sound ⌷	42 Lc	66.10 N	62.00 W
Exmoor ⌷	9 Jj	51.10 N	3.45 W
Exmouth [Austl.]	59 Cd	21.55 S	114.07 E
Exmouth [Eng.-U.K.]	9 Jk	50.37 N	3.25 W
Exmouth Gulf ⌷	57 Cg	22.00 S	114.20 E
Exmouth Plateau (EN) ⌷	59 Cc	16.00 S	114.00 E
Expedition Range ⌷	59 Jd	24.30 S	149.05 E
Explorer Tablemount (EN) ⌷			
Externsteine ⌷	47 He	16.55 N	83.15 W
Extertal	12 Kc	51.52 N	8.55 E
Extertal-Bösingfeld	12 Lb	52.04 N	9.07 E
Extremadura ⌷	13 -Ge	39.00 N	6.00 W
Exuma Cays ⌷	49 Id	24.20 N	76.20 W
Exuma Cays ⌷	47 Id	24.20 N	76.40 W
Exuma Sound ⌷	49 Ia	24.15 N	76.00 W
Eyasi, Lake- ⌷	30 Ki	3.40 S	35.05 E
Eydehavn	8 Ce	58.31 N	8.53 E
Eye	12 Db	52.19 N	1.09 E
Eyemouth	9 Kf	55.52 N	2.06 W
Eye Peninsula ⌷	9 Gc	58.13 N	6.05 W
Eygurande	11 Ii	45.40 N	2.28 E
Eyjafjallajökull ⌷	7a Bc	63.38 N	19.36 W
Eyl	31 Lh	8.00 N	49.51 E
Eymoutiers	11 Hi	45.44 N	1.44 E
Eynesil	24 Hb	41.03 N	39.08 E
Eyrarbakki	7a Bc	63.52 N	21.09 W
Eyre	59 Ff	32.15 S	126.18 E
Eyre, Lake- ⌷	57 Eg	28.43 S	137.11 E
Eyre Creek ⌷	59 Gd	25.00 S	138.00 E
Eyre Mountains ⌷	62 Cf	45.20 S	168.20 E
Eyre North, Lake- ⌷	59 Ge	28.40 S	137.10 E
Eyre Peninsula ⌷	57 Ef	34.00 S	135.45 E
Eyre South, Lake- ⌷	59 He	29.30 S	137.20 E
Eyrieux ⌷	11 Kj	44.58 N	4.48 E
Eystrup	12 Lb	52.47 N	9.13 E
Eythorne	12 Dc	51.11 N	1.17 E
Eyvänakï	24 Oe	35.24 N	51.56 E
Ezequiel Ramos Mexia, Embalse- ⌷	56 Ge	39.30 S	69.00 W
Ezere	8 Jh	56.27 N	22.17 E
Ezerelis	8 Jj	54.50 N	23.38 E
Ezine	24 Bc	39.47 N	26.20 E
Eznas/Jieznas	8 Kj	54.34 N	24.17 E
Eżva	17 Ef	61.47 N	50.40 E

F

Name	Ref	Lat	Long
Faaa	65e Fc	17.33 S	149.36 W
Faaite Atoll ⌷	61 Lc	16.45 S	145.14 W
Fabens	45 Ck	31.30 N	106.10 W
Fåberg	8 Dc	61.10 N	10.24 E
Faber Lake ⌷	42 Fd	63.55 N	117.15 W
Fåborg	7 Ci	55.06 N	10.15 E
Fabriano	14 Gg	43.20 N	12.54 E
Făcăeni	15 Ke	44.34 N	27.54 E
Facatativá	54 Dc	4.49 N	74.22 W
Facha	33 Cd	29.30 N	17.20 E
Fachi	31 Ig	18.06 N	11.34 E
Facpi Point ⌷	64c Bb	13.20 N	144.38 E
Fada	31 Jg	17.14 N	21.33 E
Fada N'Gourma	31 Fg	12.04 N	0.21 E
Faddeja, Zaliv- ⌷	20 Fa	76.30 N	107.30 E
Faddejevski, Ostrov- ⌷	20 Ja	75.30 N	144.00 E
Fadiffolu Atoll ⌷	25a Ba	5.25 N	73.30 E
Făgăli	24 Mi	26.58 N	49.15 E
Faeara, Pointe- ⌷	65e Fc	17.52 S	149.11 W
Faenza	14 Ff	44.17 N	11.53 E
Færøe Bank (EN) ⌷	9 Ea	60.55 N	8.40 W
Faeroe-Iceland Ridge (EN) ⌷	5 Fc	64.00 N	10.00 W
Faeroe Islands (EN) = Færøerne/Føroyar ⌷	5 Fc	62.00 N	7.00 W
Faeroe Islands (EN) = Færøerne/Føroyar ⌷	6 Fc	62.00 N	7.00 W
Faeroe Islands (EN) = Føroyar/Færøerne [5]	5 Fc	62.00 N	7.00 W
Faeroe Islands (EN) = Føroyar/Færøerne ⌷	5 Fc	62.00 N	7.00 W
Færøerne/Føroyar = Faeroe Islands (EN) ⌷	5 Fc	62.00 N	7.00 W
Færøerne/Føroyar = Faeroe Islands (EN) [5]	6 Fc	62.00 N	7.00 W
Fafa	35 Bd	7.18 N	18.16 E
Fafe	13 Dc	41.27 N	8.10 W
Fafen ⌷	30 Lh	5.47 N	44.11 E
Faga ⌷	34 Fc	13.45 N	0.58 E
Fagaloa Bay ⌷	65c Ba	13.54 S	171.28 W
Fagamalo	65c Aa	13.25 S	172.21 W
Fâgăraş	15 Hd	45.51 N	24.58 E
Fâgarasului, Munţii- ⌷	15 Hd	45.35 N	25.00 E
Fagataufa Atoll ⌷	57 Ng	22.14 S	138.45 W
Fagelmara	8 Fh	56.15 N	15.57 E
Fagerhult	8 Fg	57.09 N	15.40 E
Fagernes	7 Bf	60.59 N	9.15 E
Fagersta	7 Df	60.00 N	15.47 E
Făget	15 Fd	45.51 N	22.11 E
Fagita	26 Jg	1.48 S	130.25 E
Fagnano, Lago- ⌷	56 Gh	54.38 S	68.00 W
Fagne ⌷	11 Kd	50.10 N	4.25 E
Faguibine, Lac- ⌷	30 Fg	16.45 N	3.54 W
Fahlián	24 Ng	30.12 N	51.28 E
Fahner Höhe ⌷	10 Ge	51.10 N	10.45 E
Faial	30 Ee	38.34 N	28.42 W
Fä'id	24 Eg	30.19 N	32.19 E
Faioa ⌷	64h Bc	13.23 S	176.08 W
Fairbairn Reservoir ⌷	59 Jd	23.40 S	148.00 E
Fairbanks	39 Ec	64.51 N	147.43 W
Fairborn	44 Ff	39.48 N	84.03 W
Fairbury	43 Hc	40.08 N	97.11 W
Fairchild	45 Kd	44.36 N	90.58 W
Fairfield [Al.-U.S.]	44 Di	33.29 N	86.55 W
Fairfield [Ca.-U.S.]	46 Dg	38.15 N	122.01 W
Fairfield [Id.-U.S.]	45 Kf	40.59 N	91.57 W
Fairfield [Il.-U.S.]	46 Hd	43.21 N	114.48 W
Fairfield [Il.-U.S.]	45 Lg	38.23 N	88.22 W
Fair Isle ⌷	9 Lb	59.30 N	1.40 W
Fairlie	62 Df	44.06 S	170.50 E
Fairmont [Mn.-U.S.]	43 Ic	43.39 N	94.28 W
Fairmont [W.V.-U.S.]	43 Hd	39.28 N	80.08 W
Fair Ness ⌷	42 Kd	63.24 N	72.05 W
Fairview [Mt.-U.S.]	46 Mc	47.51 N	104.03 W
Fairview [Ok.-U.S.]	45 Hh	36.16 N	98.29 W
Fairview Peak ⌷	46 De	43.35 N	122.39 W
Fairweather, Mount- ⌷	38 Fd	58.54 N	137.32 W
Fais Island ⌷	57 Fd	9.46 N	140.31 E
Faistós ⌷	15 Hn	35.03 N	24.48 E
Faizābād	25 Gc	26.47 N	82.08 E
Fajardo	49 Od	18.20 N	65.39 W
Fajou, Îlet 'a- ⌷	51e Ab	16.17 N	61.34 W
Fakahina Atoll ⌷	57 Mf	15.59 S	140.08 W
Fakaofo Atoll ⌷	57 Je	9.22 S	171.14 W
Fakarava Atoll ⌷	57 Mf	16.15 S	145.37 W
Fakaura	29 Fa	40.38 N	139.55 E
Fakel	17 Gh	57.40 N	53.05 E
Fakenham	12 Cb	52.50 N	0.50 E
Fakfak	57 Fe	2.55 S	132.18 E
Fakhr	24 Pg	31.25 N	54.01 E
Fakse Bugt ⌷	8 Ei	55.10 N	12.15 E
Faksefjell ⌷	8 Ec	61.20 N	12.52 E
Fakse Ladeplads	8 Ei	55.15 N	12.08 E
Faku	27 Mb	42.30 N	123.24 E
Falaba	34 Cd	9.51 N	11.19 W
Fala-Beguets ⌷	64b Bb	7.21 N	151.40 E
Falaise	11 Ff	48.54 N	0.12 W
Falaise de Tiguidit ⌷	34 Gb	16.22 N	7.45 E
Falakrón Óros ⌷	5 Hh	41.16 N	23.50 E
Falalu	64b Ba	7.38 N	151.41 E
Falam	25 Id	22.55 N	93.41 E
Falas ⌷	64b Ba	7.32 N	151.46 E
Fălciu	15 Lc	46.18 N	28.08 E
Falcón [2]	54 Ea	11.00 N	69.50 W
Falcon, Cap- ⌷	13 Li	35.46 N	0.48 W
Falcon, Presa- ⌷	45 Gm	26.37 N	99.11 W
Falconara Marittima	14 Hg	43.37 N	13.24 E
Falcone, Punta- ⌷	14 Cj	40.58 N	8.12 E
Falcon Reservoir ⌷	43 Hf	26.37 N	99.11 W
Faléa	34 Cc	12.16 N	11.15 W
Faleallej Pass ⌷	64d Bb	7.26 N	151.34 E
Falealupo	65c Aa	13.30 S	172.48 W
Falelima	65c Aa	13.32 S	172.41 W
Falémé ⌷	30 Fg	14.46 N	12.14 W
Falenki	7 Mg	58.23 N	51.36 E
Falerum	8 Gf	58.09 N	16.13 E
Faleşty	16 Ef	47.35 N	27.44 E
Falevai	65c Ba	13.55 S	171.59 W
Falfurrias	43 Hf	27.14 N	98.09 W
Falkenberg	7 Ch	56.54 N	12.28 E
Falkensee	10 Jd	52.34 N	13.05 E
Falkirk	9 Jf	56.00 N	3.48 W
Falkland Islands/Malvinas, Islas- [5]	53 Kk	51.45 S	59.00 W
Falkland Islands/Malvinas, Islas- ⌷	52 Kk	51.45 S	59.00 W
Falkland Plateau (EN) ⌷	52 Lk	51.00 S	50.00 W
Falkland Sound ⌷	56 Ih	51.45 S	59.25 W
Falkonéra ⌷	15 Gm	36.50 S	23.53 E
Falköping	7 Cg	58.10 N	13.31 E
Fallingbostel	10 Fd	52.52 N	9.42 E
Fallon [Mt.-U.S.]	46 Mc	46.48 N	105.00 W
Fallon [Nv.-U.S.]	46 Fg	39.28 N	118.47 W
Fall River	43 Mc	41.43 N	71.08 W
Falls City	43 Hc	40.03 N	95.36 W
Falmouth [Atg.]	51d Bb	17.01 N	61.46 W
Falmouth [Eng.-U.K.]	9 Hk	50.08 N	5.04 W
Falmouth [Jam.]	49 Id	18.30 N	77.39 W
Falmouth [Ky.-U.S.]	44 Ef	38.40 N	84.20 W
Falmouth Bay ⌷	9 Hk	50.10 N	5.05 W
Falmouth Harbour ⌷	51d Bb	17.01 N	61.46 W
Falo	64d Bb	7.29 N	151.53 E
False Bay ⌷	30 Il	34.15 S	18.35 E
False Pass	40 Gf	54.52 N	163.24 W
Falset	13 Mc	41.08 N	0.49 E
Falso, Cabo- [Dom.Rep.] ⌷	49 Le	17.47 N	71.41 W
Falso, Cabo- [Hond.] ⌷	49 Ff	15.12 N	83.20 W
Falso, Cabo- [Mex.] ⌷	47 Cd	22.52 N	109.58 W
Falso Cabo de Hornos ⌷	56 Gi	55.43 S	68.05 W
Falster ⌷	7 Ci	54.50 N	12.00 E
Falsterbo	8 Ei	55.24 N	12.50 E
Falterona ⌷	14 Fg	43.52 N	11.42 E
Fălticeni	15 Jc	47.27 N	26.18 E
Falun	6 Hc	60.36 N	15.38 E
Fama ⌷	35 Cb	15.22 N	20.34 E
Famagusta (EN) = Ammókhöstos	23 Dc	35.07 N	33.57 E
Famagusta (EN) = Magosa	23 Dc	35.07 N	33.57 E
Famatina, Nevados de- ⌷	56 Gc	29.00 S	67.51 W
Famenne ⌷	11 Ld	50.15 N	5.15 E
Fana	34 Dc	12.45 N	6.57 W
Fanan ⌷	64d Bb	7.11 N	151.59 E
Fanchang	27 Ke	31.00 N	118.11 E
Fancy	51n Ba	13.22 N	61.12 W
Fandriana	37 Hd	20.13 S	47.20 E
Fangak	35 Ed	9.04 N	30.53 E
Fangatau Atoll ⌷	57 Mf	15.50 S	140.52 W
Fangcheng	27 Je	33.09 N	113.05 E
Fangliao	27 Lg	22.22 N	120.25 E
Fangshan	28 Ce	39.43 N	115.58 E
Fangxian	27 Je	32.03 N	110.41 E
Fangzheng	27 Mb	45.50 N	128.49 E
Fangzi	28 Ef	36.36 N	119.08 E
Fanjiatun	28 Hc	43.42 N	125.05 E
Fanjing Shan ⌷	27 If	27.57 N	108.50 E
Fannärdxen ⌷	8 Bc	61.31 N	7.55 E
Fanning → Tabuaeran Atoll ⌷	57 Ld	3.52 N	159.20 W
Fano	14 Hg	43.50 N	13.01 E
Fano ⌷	8 Ci	55.25 N	8.25 E
Fano Bugt ⌷	8 Ci	55.25 N	8.10 E
Fanshi	28 Be	39.11 N	113.16 E
Fan Si Pan ⌷	21 Lg	22.15 N	103.50 E
Fan Si Pan ⌷	25 Kd	22.18 N	103.46 E
Fanuatapu ⌷	65c Ba	13.59 S	171.20 W
Fanxian	28 Dg	35.33 S	115.29 E
Farab	18 Ke	39.12 N	63.38 E
Faraba	34 Cc	12.52 N	11.23 W
Faraday ⌷	66 Qe	65.15 S	64.15 W
Faraday Seamounts (EN) ⌷	5 Df	49.30 N	28.30 W
Faradje	36 Eb	3.44 N	29.43 E
Farafangana	31 Lk	25.01 S	46.59 E
Farafangana	37 Hd	22.48 S	47.50 E
Farāfirah, Wāḩāt al- ⌷			
Farafra Oasis (EN) ⌷	30 Jf	27.15 N	28.10 E
Farafra Oasis (EN) = Farāfirah, Wāḩāt al- ⌷	30 Jf	27.15 N	28.10 E
Farāh	21 If	32.22 N	62.07 E
Farāh ⌷	21 If	33.29 N	61.24 E
Farāh [3]	23 Jc	33.00 N	62.30 E
Far'ah, Wādī al- ⌷	24 Od	36.47 N	53.06 E
Farahah	34 Cc	10.02 N	10.44 W
Farasan	23 If	16.42 N	42.00 E
Farasan, Jazā'ir- ⌷	21 Hh	16.48 N	41.54 E
Farasan al Kabir ⌷	33 Hf	16.42 N	42.00 E
Faraulep Atoll ⌷	57 Fd	8.36 N	144.33 E
Farciennes	12 Gd	50.26 N	4.33 E
Fardes ⌷	13 Ig	37.45 N	3.12 W
Fare	65e Db	16.42 S	151.01 W
Fareham	9 Lk	50.51 N	1.10 W
Farewell, Cape- ⌷	57 Ii	40.33 S	172.43 E
Farewell Spit ⌷	62 Dd	40.30 S	172.50 E
Färgelanda	8 Df	58.34 N	11.59 E
Fargo	39 Je	46.52 N	96.48 W
Faribault	45 Kd	44.18 N	93.16 W
Faribault, Lac- ⌷	42 Ke	58.00 N	72.00 W

Index Symbols

- [1] Independent Nation
- [2] State, Region
- [3] District, County
- [4] Municipality
- [5] Colony, Dependency
- ■ Continent
- [≡] Physical Region
- ◨ Historical or Cultural Region
- ▲ Mount, Mountain
- ⌷ Volcano
- ▣ Hill
- ▦ Mountains, Mountain Range
- ◪ Hills, Escarpment
- ⊟ Plateau, Upland
- ⌷ Pass, Gap
- ◫ Plain, Lowland
- ◨ Delta
- ▣ Salt Flat
- ◲ Valley, Canyon
- ◫ Crater, Cave
- ⊠ Karst Features
- ▦ Depression
- ◨ Polder
- ▣ Desert, Dunes
- ▦ Forest, Woods
- ◪ Heath, Steppe
- ▣ Oasis
- ◫ Cape, Point
- ▣ Coast, Beach
- ▣ Cliff
- ▦ Peninsula
- ◪ Isthmus
- ▣ Coral Reef
- ▣ Island
- ⊚ Atoll
- ▣ Rock, Reef
- ◨ Islands, Archipelago
- ▣ Rocks, Reefs
- ▣ Well, Spring
- ◫ Geyser
- ⊠ River, Stream
- ⊠ Waterfall Rapids
- ⊟ River Mouth, Estuary
- ⊟ Lake
- ⊟ Salt Lake
- ⊟ Intermittent Lake
- ⊟ Reservoir
- ⊠ Swamp, Pond
- ⊟ Canal
- ⊟ Glacier
- ⊟ Ice Shelf, Pack Ice
- ⊟ Ocean
- ⊟ Sea
- ⊟ Gulf, Bay
- ⊟ Strait, Fjord
- ⊟ Lagoon
- ⊟ Bank
- ⊟ Seamount
- ⊟ Tablemount
- ⊟ Ridge
- ⊟ Shelf
- ⊟ Basin
- ⊟ Escarpment, Sea Scarp
- ⊟ Fracture
- ⊟ Trench, Abyss
- ⊟ National Park, Reserve
- ⊟ Point of Interest
- ⊟ Recreation Site
- ⊟ Cave, Cavern
- ▣ Historic Site
- ▣ Ruins
- ▦ Wall, Walls
- ▣ Church, Abbey
- ▣ Temple
- ▣ Scientific Station
- ▣ Airport
- ▣ Port
- ▣ Lighthouse
- ▣ Mine
- ▣ Tunnel
- ▣ Dam, Bridge

Name	Pg	Grid	Lat	Long
Farīd, Qārat al-	24	Ch	28.43N	28.21 E
Faridpur	25	Hd	23.36N	89.50 E
Fårila	7	Df	61.48N	15.51 E
Farilhões, Ilhas-	13	Ce	39.28N	9.34W
Farim	34	Bc	12.29N	15.13W
Farini d'Olmo	14	Df	44.43N	9.34 E
Fāris	24	Ej	24.37N	32.54 E
Fariš	18	Fd	40.33N	66.52 E
Fāris	35	Ia	20.11N	50.56 E
Faris Seamount (EN)	40	Jf	54.30N	147.15W
Fårjestaden	7	Dh	56.39N	16.27 E
Farkadhón	45	Fj	39.36N	22.04 E
Farmakonísi	15	Kl	37.18N	27.08 E
Farmerville	45	Jj	32.47N	92.24W
Farmington [Me.-U.S.]	44	Lc	44.40N	70.09W
Farmington [Mo.-U.S.]	45	Kh	37.47N	90.25W
Farmington [N.M.-U.S.]	43	Fd	36.44N	108.12W
Farmville	44	Hg	37.17N	78.25W
Färnäs	8	Fc	61.00N	14.38 E
Farnborough	12	Bc	51.16N	0.44W
Farne Deep	9	Mf	55.30N	0.50W
Farne Islands	9	Lf	55.38N	1.38W
Farnham [Eng.-U.K.]	12	Bc	51.12N	0.48W
Farnham [Que.-Can.]	44	Kc	45.17N	72.59W
Farnham, Mount-	46	Ga	50.29N	116.30W
Fårö	7	Eh	57.55N	19.10 E
Faro	34	Hd	9.21N	12.55 E
Faro [2]	13	Dg	37.12N	8.10W
Faro	6	Ff	37.01N	7.56W
Faro, Punta-	49	Jh	11.07N	74.51W
Faro, Sierra del-	13	Cb	42.37N	7.55W
Faro de Avión	13	Db	42.18N	8.16W
Faro de Chantada	13	Cb	42.37N	7.55W
Farofa, Serra da-	55	Gh	28.00S	50.10W
Farosund	8	Hg	57.55N	19.05 E
Fårösund	7	Eh	57.52N	19.03 E
Farquhar, Cape-	59	Cd	23.35S	113.35 E
Farquhar Group	30	Mj	10.10S	51.10 E
Farrar	9	Id	57.27N	4.35W
Farråshband	24	Oh	28.53N	52.06 E
Farris	8	Ce	59.05N	10.00 E
Farruch, Cabo-	13	Pe	39.47N	3.21 E
Farrukhābād	25	Fc	27.24N	79.34 E
Fārs	21	Hg	29.00N	53.00 E
Fārs [3]	23	Hd	29.00N	53.00 E
Fårsabad	24	Mc	39.30N	48.05 E
Fársala	15	Fj	39.18N	22.23 E
Farshūţ	24	Ei	26.03N	32.09 E
Farsø	8	Ch	56.47N	9.21 E
Farsund	7	Bg	58.05N	6.48 E
Fartak, Ra's-	23	Hf	15.38N	52.15 E
Fartura, Rio-	55	Gc	16.29S	50.33W
Fartura, Serra da- [Braz.]	55	Hf	23.20S	49.25W
Fartura, Serra da- [Braz.]	55	Hf	26.21S	52.52W
Fārūj	24	Rd	37.14N	58.14 E
Farvel, Kap-/Ûmánarssuaq	67	Nb	59.50N	43.50W
Farwell Island	66	Pf	72.49S	91.10W
Fāryāb [3]	23	Jb	36.00N	65.00 E
Fasā	24	Oh	28.56N	53.42 E
Fasano	14	Lj	40.50N	17.22 E
Fastnet Rock	9	Dj	51.24N	9.35W
Fastov	19	De	50.06N	30.01 E
Fataka Island	57	If	11.55S	170.12 E
Fatala	34	Cc	10.13N	14.00W
Fatehpur	25	Ec	28.01N	74.58 E
Fatež	16	Ic	52.06N	35.52 E
Father Lake	44	Ja	49.24N	75.18W
Fatick	34	Bc	14.20N	16.25W
Fátima	13	De	39.37N	8.39W
Fatjrah, Wādī-	24	Ei	26.39N	32.58 E
Fatsa	24	Gd	40.59N	37.24 E
Fatu Hiva, Ile-	57	Nf	10.28S	138.38W
Fatu Hutu, Ile-	57	Ne	9.00S	138.50W
Fatumanini, Passe-	64h	Aa	13.14S	176.13W
Fatunda	36	Cc	4.08S	17.13 E
Fauabu	63a	Ec	8.34S	160.43 E
Faucigny	11	Mh	46.05N	6.35 E
Faucille, Col de la-	11	Mh	46.22N	6.02 E
Faulkton	45	Gd	45.02N	99.08W
Faulquemont	12	Ie	49.03N	6.36 E
Fauquembergues	12	Ed	50.36N	2.05 E
Fāurei	15	Kd	45.04N	27.14 E
Fauro	63a	Cb	6.55S	156.07 E
Fauske	7	Dc	67.15N	15.24 E
Fauville-en-Caux	12	Ce	49.39N	0.35 E
Faux-Lap	37	Me	25.32S	45.30 E
Fåvang	8	Dc	61.26N	10.13 E
Favara	14	Hm	37.19N	13.39 E
Faversham	12	Cc	51.19N	0.54 E
Favignana	14	Gm	37.55N	12.19 E
Favignana	14	Gm	37.56N	12.20 E
Favorite	12	Kf	48.49N	8.16 E
Fawley	12	Ad	50.49N	1.21W
Fawn	42	Ie	55.22N	88.20W
Fa'w Qiblī	24	Ei	26.07N	32.24 E
Faxaflói	5	Dc	64.24N	23.00W
Faxinal	55	Gf	23.59S	51.22W
Faya-Largeau	31	Ig	17.55N	19.07 E
Fayaoué	63a	Ce	20.39S	166.32 E
Fayd	24	Ji	27.07N	42.31 E
Fayette [Al.-U.S.]	44	Di	33.42N	87.50W
Fayette [Oh.-U.S.]	44	Ee	41.41N	84.20W
Fayetteville [Ar.-U.S.]	43	Id	36.04N	94.10W
Fayetteville [N.C.-U.S.]	39	Lf	35.03N	78.54W
Fayetteville [Tn.-U.S.]	44	Dh	35.09N	86.35W
Faylakah, Jazīrat-	24	Mh	29.27N	48.20 E
Faysh Khābūr	24	Jd	37.04N	42.22 E
Fayu Island	57	Gd	8.35N	151.22 E
Fazenda de Cima	55	Db	15.56S	56.37W
Fazenda Nova	55	Gc	16.11S	50.48W
Fázilka	25	Eb	30.24N	74.02 E
Fazrán	24	Mi	26.13N	49.12 E
Fazzán = Fezzan = Fezzān (EN)	33	Bd	25.30N	14.00 E
Fazzán = Fezzan = Fezzān (EN)	30	If	26.00N	14.00 E
Fdérick	31	Ff	22.39N	12.43W
Feale/An Fhéil	9	Di	52.28N	9.40W
Fear, Cape-	43	Le	33.50N	77.58W
Featherston	62	Fd	41.07S	175.19 E
Feathertop, Mount-	59	Jg	36.54S	147.08 E
Fécamp	11	Ge	49.45N	0.22 E
Fecht	11	Nf	48.11N	7.26 E
Federacion	56	Id	31.00S	57.54W
Federal	56	Id	30.55S	58.45W
Federated States of Micronesia [5]	58	Gd	6.30N	152.00 E
Federovka [Kaz.-U.S.S.R.]	19	Ge	53.38N	62.42 E
Federovka [R.S.F.S.R.]	19	Gf	53.10N	55.10 E
Federsee	10	Fh	48.05N	9.38 E
Fedje	7	Af	60.47N	4.42 E
Fedorovka	16	Qd	51.16N	52.00 E
Fefan	64d	Bb	7.21N	151.51 E
Fegen	8	Eg	57.11N	13.09 E
Fegen	8	Eg	57.06N	13.02 E
Fehérgyarmat	10	Si	47.59N	22.31 E
Fehmarn	10	Hb	54.30N	11.10 E
Fehmarnbelt	8	Dj	54.35N	11.15 E
Fehrbellin	10	Id	52.48N	12.46 E
Feicheng	28	Df	36.15N	116.46 E
Feidong (Dianbu)	28	Di	31.53N	117.29 E
Fei Huang He	28	Eg	34.15N	120.17 E
Feijó	54	De	8.09S	70.21W
Feilding	61	Eh	40.13S	175.35 E
Feira	36	Ff	15.37S	30.25 E
Feira de Santana	53	Mg	12.15S	38.57W
Feiran Oasis	24	Eh	28.42N	33.38 E
Feistritz	14	Kc	47.01N	16.08 E
Feixi (Shangpaihe)	28	Di	31.42N	117.09 E
Feixian	28	Dg	35.16N	117.59 E
Feixiang	28	Cf	36.32N	114.47 E
Fejão Prêto ou Furtado, Rio-	55	Dc	17.33S	57.23W
Fejér [2]	10	Oi	47.10N	18.35 E
Feje	8	Dj	54.55N	11.25 E
Fekete-viz	24	Fd	37.53N	35.58 E
Fekete-viz	10	Ok	45.47N	18.13 E
Felanitx	13	Pe	39.28N	3.08 E
Feldbach	14	Kc	46.57N	15.53 E
Feldioara	15	Id	45.49N	25.36 E
Feldkirch	14	Dc	47.14N	9.36 E
Feldkirchen	14	Id	46.43N	14.06 E
Feliciano, Arroyo-	55	Cj	31.06S	59.54W
Felidu Atoll	25a	Bb	3.30N	73.30 E
Felipe Carrillo Puerto	47	Ge	19.35N	88.03W
Felix, Cape-	42	Hc	69.55N	97.47W
Felixlándia	55	Jd	18.47S	44.55W
Felixstowe	9	Oj	51.58N	1.20 E
Felletin	11	Ii	45.53N	2.11 E
Feltre	14	Fd	46.01N	11.54 E
Femer Bælt	8	Dj	54.35N	11.15 E
Femø	8	Dj	54.55N	11.35 E
Femund	7	Ce	62.15N	11.50 E
Fena Valley Reservoir	64c	Bb	13.22N	144.45 E
Fener Burnu	24	Hb	41.07N	39.25 E
Fénérive	37	Hc	17.22S	49.25 E
Fenerwa	35	Fc	13.05N	39.01 E
Fénétrange	12	Jf	48.51N	7.01 E
Fengcheng [China]	27	Lc	40.28N	124.01 E
Fengcheng [China]	28	Ej	28.11N	115.47 E
Fengdu	28	Cj	29.40N	121.24 E
Fenghua	28	Fj	29.40N	121.24 E
Fengjie	27	He	31.06N	104.30 E
Fenglingdu	28	Jr	34.40N	110.19 E
Fengnan (Xugezhuang)	28	Ee	39.34N	118.05 E
Fengning (Dagezhen)	28	Dd	41.12N	116.39 E
Fengqing	27	Gg	24.41N	99.53 E
Fengqiu	28	Cg	35.02N	114.24 E
Fengrun	28	Ee	39.50N	118.09 E
Fengshui Shan	27	La	52.15N	123.30 E
Fengtai [China]	28	Dh	32.43N	116.43 E
Fengtai [China]	28	De	39.51N	116.17 E
Fengweiba → Zhenkang	27	Gg	23.54N	99.00 E
Fengxian (Nanqiao)	28	Fi	30.55N	121.27 E
Fengxian	27	Ie	34.32N	107.34 E
Fengxiang → Luobei	27	Nb	47.36N	130.58 E
Fengxin	28	Cj	28.42N	115.23 E
Fengyang	28	Dh	32.53N	117.33 E
Fengzhen	27	Jc	40.28N	113.09 E
Fen He [China]	27	Jd	35.36N	110.42 E
Fen He [China]	28	Ae	38.06N	111.52 E
Feni Islands	57	Ge	4.05S	153.42 E
Fennimore	45	Ke	42.59N	90.39W
Fensfjorden	8	Ad	60.50N	4.50 E
Fenton	44	Fd	42.48N	83.42W
Fenua Fu	64h	Ac	13.23S	176.11W
Fenualoa	63c	Bb	10.16S	166.15 E
Fenyang	27	Jd	37.17N	111.45 E
Feodosija	19	Gf	45.02N	35.23 E
Fer, Cap de-	32	Ib	37.05N	7.10 E
Feragen	8	Db	62.30N	11.55 E
Férai	15	Ji	40.54N	26.10 E
Ferdows	23	Ic	34.00N	58.09 E
Fère-Champenoise	11	Jf	48.45N	3.59 E
Fère-en-Tardenois	12	Fe	49.12N	3.31 E
Feren	8	Da	63.34N	11.50 E
Ferentino	14	Hi	41.42N	13.15 E
Ferfer [Eth.]	35	Hd	5.06N	45.09 E
Ferfer [Som.]	35	Hd	5.07N	45.07 E
Fergana	22	Je	40.23N	71.46 E
Fergana [3]	19	Hg	40.30N	71.00 E
Ferganskaja Oblast [3]	19	Hg	40.30N	71.20 E
Ferganski Hrebet	19	Hg	41.00N	74.00 E
Fergus Falls	43	He	46.17N	96.04W
Ferguson Lake	42	Hc	69.00N	105.00W
Fergusson Island	60	Ib	9.30S	150.40 E
Ferkéssédougou	34	Ed	9.20N	4.55W
Ferkéssédougou	34	Dd	9.36N	5.12W
Ferlo	30	Fg	15.00N	14.00W
Ferlo	30	Fg	15.42N	15.30W
Fermo	14	Hg	43.09N	13.43 E
Fermoselle	13	Fc	41.19N	6.23W
Fermoy/Mainistir Fhear Mai	9	Ei	52.08N	8.16W
Fernandina, Isla-	52	Gf	0.25S	91.30W
Fernandina Beach	44	Gj	30.40N	81.27W
Fernando de Noronha, Ilha-	52	Mf	3.51S	32.25W
Fernando de Noronha, Território de- [2]	54	Ld	3.50S	33.00W
Fernandópolis	56	Kb	20.16S	50.00W
Fernán-Núñez	13	Hg	37.40N	4.43W
Fernelmont	12	Hd	50.35N	5.02 E
Fernie	46	Hb	49.30N	115.03W
Ferrandina	14	Kj	40.29N	16.27 E
Ferrara	14	Ff	44.50N	11.35 E
Ferrat, Cap-	13	Ll	35.54N	0.23W
Ferrato, Capo-	14	Dk	39.18N	9.38 E
Ferré	55	Bl	34.08S	61.06W
Ferré, Cap-	51b	Bc	14.28N	60.49W
Ferreira do Alentejo	13	Df	38.03N	8.07W
Ferreñafe	54	Ce	6.38S	79.48W
Ferret, Cap-	11	Ej	44.37N	1.15W
Ferriday	45	Kk	31.38N	91.33W
Ferrières	12	Hd	50.24N	5.36 E
Ferro, Capo-	14	Di	41.09N	9.31 E
Ferro, Rio-	55	Ea	12.27S	54.31W
Ferru, Monte-	14	Cj	40.08N	8.36 E
Ferry, Pointe-	51e Ab		16.17N	61.40W
Fertilia	14	Cj	40.36N	8.17 E
Fertő → Neusiedler See	10	Mi	47.50N	16.45 E
Fès	31	Ge	34.02N	4.59W
Fès [3]	32	Gc	34.00N	5.00W
Feshi	36	Cd	6.07S	18.10 E
Fessenden	45	Gc	47.39N	99.38W
Festieux	12	Fe	49.31N	3.45 E
Festus	45	Kg	38.13N	90.24W
Fethesti	15	Ke	44.23N	27.50 E
Fethiye	23	Cb	36.37N	29.07 E
Fethiye Körfezi	24	Cb	36.40N	29.00 E
Fetlar	9	Ma	60.37N	0.52W
Fetsund	7	Cg	59.56N	11.10 E
Feuchtwangen	10	Gg	49.10N	10.20 E
Feuilles, Baie aux -	42	Ke	58.55N	69.15W
Feuilles, Rivière aux-	42	Ke	58.46N	70.05W
Feurs	11	Ki	45.45N	4.14 E
Fevik	8	Cf	58.23N	8.42 E
Feyzābād	22	Jf	37.06N	70.34 E
Fezzan (EN) = Fazzān	33	Bd	25.30N	14.00 E
Fezzan (EN) = Fazzān	30	If	26.00N	14.00 E
Fezzane, Emi-	34	Ha	21.42N	14.15 E
Ffestiniog	9	Ji	52.58N	3.55W
Fiambalá	56	Gc	27.41S	67.38W
Fianarantsoa	37	Lk	21.28S	47.05 E
Fianarantsoa [3]	37	Hd	21.30S	47.05 E
Fianga	35	Bd	9.55N	15.09 E
Fiche	35	Gd	9.48N	38.44 E
Fichtelgebirge	5	He	50.00N	12.00 E
Ficksburg	37	Ee	28.57S	27.50 E
Fidenza	14	Ef	44.52N	10.03 E
Fieni	15	Id	45.08N	25.25 E
Fier	11	Li	45.56N	5.50 E
Fieri	15	Ci	40.43N	19.34 E
Fife [3]	9	Je	56.05N	3.15W
Fife Ness	9	Ke	56.17N	2.36W
Fiffa	34	Dc	11.27N	9.52W
Fifth Cataract (EN) = Khāmis, Ash Shallāl al-	30	Kg	18.23N	33.47 E
Figalo, Cap-	13	Kl	35.35N	1.12W
Figeac	11	Ij	44.36N	2.02 E
Figeholm	8	Gg	57.22N	16.33 E
Figtree	37	Dd	20.22S	28.20 E
Figueira, Baía da-	16	Ol	16.33S	57.25W
Figueira da Foz	13	Dd	40.09N	8.52W
Figueira de Castelo Rodrigo	13	Fd	40.54N	6.58W
Figueras	13	Ob	42.16N	2.58 E
Figueres	13	Ob	42.16N	2.58 E
Figueres/Figueras	13	Ob	42.16N	2.58 E
Figuig [3]	32	Gc	33.00N	2.01W
Figuig	31	Ge	32.06N	1.14W
Fiherenana	37	Le	23.19S	43.37 E
Fijāj, Shatt al-	32	Ic	33.55N	9.10 E
Fiji [1]	58	If	18.00S	178.00 E
Fiji Islands	57	If	18.00S	178.00 E
Fik	35	Gd	8.08N	42.18 E
Filabres, Sierra de los-	13	Jg	37.15N	2.20W
Filadélfia [Arg.]	55	Ci	28.02S	59.15W
Filadélfia [Col.]	55	Dk	33.53S	57.24W
Filadélfia [C.R.]	49	Eh	10.26N	85.34W
Filadelfia [It.]	14	Kl	38.47N	16.17 E
Filákora	63b	Dc	16.49S	168.24 E
Filákovo	10	Ph	48.16N	19.50 E
Filamana	34	Dc	10.30N	7.57W
Filatova Gora	8	Mg	57.39N	28.21 E
Filchner Ice Shelf	66	Af	79.00S	40.00W
Filey	9	Mg	54.12N	0.17W
Filiaşi	15	Ge	44.33N	23.31 E
Filiátai	15	Dj	39.36N	20.49 E
Filiatrá	15	El	37.09N	21.35 E
Filicudi	14	Il	38.35N	14.35 E
Filingué	34	Fc	14.21N	3.19 E
Filiouri	15	Ji	40.57N	25.20 E
Filippiás	15	Dj	39.12N	20.53 E
Filippoi	15	Hh	41.02N	24.20 E
Filippoi → Philippi (EN)	15	Hh	41.02N	24.18 E
Filipstad	7	Dg	59.43N	14.10 E
Fillefjell	8	Cc	61.09N	8.15 E
Filliévres	12	Ed	50.19N	2.10 E
Fillmore	46	Ig	38.58N	112.20W
Fils	10	Fg	48.41N	9.36 E
Filtu	35	Gd	5.06N	40.40 E
Fimbul Isbrae	15	Jf	35.31N	26.26 E
Fimi	36	Cc	3.01S	16.58 E
Fin [Iran]	24	Pi	28.57N	55.55 E
Fin [Iran]	24	Nf	33.57N	51.24 E
Finale Emilia	14	Ff	44.50N	11.17 E
Finale Ligure	14	Df	44.10N	8.20 E
Findhorn	9	Jd	57.41N	3.32W
Findıklı	24	Ib	41.17N	41.09 E
Findlay	43	Kc	41.02N	83.40W
Findlay, Mount-	46	Ga	50.04N	116.28W
Findlay Group	42	Ha	77.15N	104.00W
Fineveke	64h	Ab	13.19S	176.12W
Fingoé	37	Ec	15.10S	31.53 E
Finike	24	Dd	36.18N	30.09 E
Finistère [3]	11	Cf	48.20N	4.00W
Finisterre, Cabo de-	5	Fg	42.53N	9.16W
Finisterre Range	59	Ja	5.50S	146.05 E
Finke	58	Eg	25.34S	134.35 E
Finke, Mount-	59	Gf	30.55S	134.02 E
Finke River	57	Eg	27.00S	136.10 E
Finland/Suomi [1]	6	Ic	64.00N	26.00 E
Finland, Gulf of- (EN) = Finski Zaliv	5	Ic	60.00N	27.00 E
Finland, Gulf of- (EN) = Soomenlaht	5	Ic	60.00N	27.00 E
Finland, Gulf of- (EN) = Suomenlaht	5	Ic	60.00N	27.00 E
Finlay	42	Fe	55.59N	123.50W
Finlay Mountains	45	Dk	31.30N	105.35W
Finne	10	He	51.13N	11.19 E
Finngrunden	8	Hc	61.00N	18.19 E
Finnigan, Mount-	59	Jc	15.50S	145.20 E
Finniss, Cape-	59	Gf	33.38S	134.51 E
Finnmark	7	Fb	71.00N	26.00 E
Finnmark [3]	7	Fb	69.50N	24.10 E
Finnmarksvidda	5	Ib	69.30N	24.20 E
Finney	8	Ae	59.10N	5.50 E
Finnskogen	8	Ed	60.40N	12.40 E
Finnsnes	7	Eb	69.14N	18.02 E
Finnveden	8	Eg	56.50N	13.40 E
Finote Selam	35	Fc	10.42N	37.12 E
Finschhafen	59	Ja	6.35S	147.50 E
Finse	8	Bd	60.36N	7.30 E
Finski Zaliv → Finland, Gulf of- (EN)	5	Ic	60.00N	27.00 E
Finspång	7	Dg	58.43N	15.47 E
Finstadå	8	Dc	61.47N	11.10 E
Finsteraarhorn	14	Cd	46.32N	8.08 E
Finsterwalde	10	Je	51.38N	13.43 E
Finström	8	Hd	60.16N	19.50 E
Fiora	14	Fh	42.20N	11.34 E
Fiorenzuola d'Arda	14	Ef	44.56N	9.55 E
Firat = Euphrates (EN)	21	Gd	31.00N	47.25 E
Firenze = Florence (EN)	6	Hg	43.46N	11.15 E
Firenzuola	14	Ff	44.07N	11.23 E
Firmat	55	Bk	33.27S	61.29W
Firminópolis	55	Gc	16.40S	50.19W
Firminy	11	Ki	45.23N	4.18 E
Firozābād	25	Fc	27.09N	78.25 E
Firozpur	25	Eb	30.55N	74.36 E
First Cataract (EN) = Aswān, Sadd al-	30	Kf	24.01N	32.52 E
Fīrūzābād	24	Pg	31.59N	54.20 E
Fīrūzābād	24	Le	34.09N	46.25 E
Fīrūz Kūh	24	Oe	35.45N	52.47 E
Fischbach	12	Je	49.44N	7.24 E
Fischbacher Alpen	14	Jc	47.25N	15.30 E
Fischland	10	Ib	54.22N	12.25 E
Fish [Nam.]	30	Ik	17.11S	28.08 E
Fish [S.Afr.]	37	Cf	31.14S	20.15 E
Fisher Glacier	66	Ef	73.15S	66.00 E
Fisher Peak	44	Gg	36.33N	80.50W
Fisher Strait	42	Jd	63.00N	84.00W
Fishguard	6	Fe	51.59N	4.59W
Fish River' Canyon	37	Bc	27.35S	17.35 E
Fiskárdhon	15	Dk	38.28N	20.35 E
Fiskenaes Bank (EN)	41	Gf	63.18N	52.10W
Fiskenaesset	41	Gf	63.10N	50.45W
Fismes	11	Je	49.18N	3.41 E
Fišt, Gora-	19	Gg	43.57N	39.55 E
Fitchburg	44	Ld	42.35N	71.48W
Fitjar	7	Ag	59.55N	5.20 E
Fito, Mount-	65c	Ba	13.55S	171.44W
Fitri, Lac-	35	Bc	12.50N	17.28 E
Fitzcarrald	54	Df	11.49S	71.48W
Fitzgerald [Alta.-Can.]	42	Gc	59.52N	111.40W
Fitzgerald [Ga.-U.S.]	44	Fj	31.43N	83.15W
Fitzroy Crossing	59	Fc	18.11S	125.35 E
Fitzroy River [Austl.]	59	Ec	23.32S	150.52 E
Fitzroy River [Austl.]	57	Df	17.31S	123.35 E
Fitzwilliam Island	44	Gc	45.30N	81.45W
Fiuggi	14	Hi	41.48N	13.13 E
Fiumicino	14	Gi	41.46N	12.14 E
Five Island Harbour	51d	Bb	17.06N	61.54W
Fivizzano	14	Ef	44.14N	10.08 E
Fizi	31	Ji	4.18S	28.57 E
Fizuli	19	Eh	39.35N	47.11 E
Fjällbacka	8	Df	58.36N	11.17 E
Fjäräs	8	Df	57.27N	12.09 E
Fjerritslev	7	Ch	57.05N	9.16 E
Fjöllum, Jökulsá á-	7a	Ca	66.02N	16.27W
Fjugesta	8	Fe	59.10N	14.52 E
Flacq	37a	Bb	20.12S	57.43 E
Flade Isblink	41	Kb	81.35N	16.00W
Flagler	45	Dg	39.17N	103.04W
Flagstaff	39	Hf	35.12N	111.39W
Flåm	7	Bf	60.50N	7.07 E
Flamborough Head	9	Mg	54.07N	0.04W
Fläming	10	Ie	52.00N	13.00 E
Flaming Gorge Reservoir	46	Kf	41.15N	109.30W
Flamingo	44	Gm	25.09N	80.56W
Flamingo, Teluk-	26	Kh	5.33S	138.00 E
Flanders (EN) = Flandres/Vlaanderen	5	Ge	51.00N	3.20 E
Flanders (EN) = Flandres/Vlaanderen	11	Jc	51.00N	3.20 E
Flanders Plain (EN) = Flandres, Plaine des-	11	Id	50.40N	2.50 E
Flanders Plain (EN) = Vlaamse Vlakte	11	Id	50.40N	2.50 E
Flandreau	45	Hd	44.03N	96.36W
Flandres/Vlaanderen = Flanders (EN)	11	Jc	51.00N	3.20 E
Flandres/Vlaanderen = Flanders (EN)	5	Ge	51.00N	3.20 E
Flandres, Plaine des- = Flanders Plain (EN)	11	Id	50.40N	2.50 E
Flannan Isles	9	Fc	58.20N	7.35W
Flåren	8	Fh	57.00N	14.05 E
Flasher	45	Fc	46.27N	101.14W
Fläsjön	7	Dd	64.06N	15.51 E
Flat	40	Hd	62.27N	158.01W
Flatey	7a	Ab	65.22N	22.56W
Flateyri	7a	Aa	66.03N	23.31W
Flathead Lake	43	Eb	47.52N	114.08W
Flathead Range	46	Ib	48.05N	113.28W
Flathead River	46	Hc	47.22N	114.47W
Flat Point	51b	Ab	18.15N	63.05W
Flat River	45	Kh	37.51N	90.31W
Flattery, Cape-	38	Ge	48.23N	124.43W
Flåvatnet	8	Ce	59.20N	8.50 E
Flaxton	45	Eb	48.54N	102.24W
Flaygreen Lake	42	Hf	53.50N	97.20W
Fleckenstein, Château de-	12	Je	49.05N	7.48 E
Fleet	12	Bc	51.16N	0.50W
Fleetwood	9	Jh	53.56N	3.01W
Flekkefjord	7	Bg	58.17N	6.41 E
Flémalle	12	Hd	50.36N	5.29 E
Flemish Bight [Eur.]	11	Dc	51.44N	2.30W
Flemish Bight [U.K.]	9	Pi	52.10N	2.50 E
Flemish Cap (EN)	38	Oe	47.00N	45.00W
Flemsøya	8	Bb	62.40N	6.20 E
Flen	7	Dg	59.04N	16.35 E
Flensborg Fjord	8	Cj	54.50N	9.45 E
Flensburg	6	Ge	54.47N	9.26 E
Flensburger Förde	8	Cj	54.50N	9.45 E
Flers	11	Ff	48.45N	0.34W
Flesberg	8	Ce	59.51N	9.27 E
Fleurance	11	Gk	43.50N	0.40 E
Fleury-sur-Andelle	12	De	49.22N	1.21 E
Flevoland	11	Lb	52.25N	5.30 E
Flian	8	Eh	58.27N	13.05 E
Flims	14	Dd	46.50N	9.16 E
Flinders Bay	59	Bf	34.25S	115.19 E
Flinders Island	57	Fi	40.00S	148.00 E
Flinders Passage	59	Jc	18.50S	149.00 E
Flinders Ranges	57	Eh	31.25S	138.45 E
Flinders Reefs	57	Ff	17.40S	148.30 E
Flinders River	57	Ff	17.36S	140.36 E
Flin Flon	39	Id	54.56N	101.53W
Flint [Mi.-U.S.]	39	Ke	43.01N	83.41W
Flint [Wales-U.K.]	9	Jh	53.15N	3.07W
Flint Hills	45	Hh	37.20N	96.35W
Flint Island	57	Lf	11.26S	151.48W
Flint River	43	Ke	30.52N	84.38W
Flisa	7	Cf	60.37N	12.04 E
Flisa	8	Ed	60.36N	12.01 E
Flisegga	8	Ce	59.20N	7.50 E
Flitwick	12	Bb	52.00N	0.29W
Flix	13	Mc	41.14N	0.33 E
Flixecourt	12	Ed	50.01N	2.05 E
Flize	12	Ge	49.42N	4.46 E
Flobecq/Vloesberg	12	Fd	50.44N	3.44 E
Floby	8	Ef	58.08N	13.20 E
Floda [Swe.]	8	Ee	60.26N	14.49 E
Floda [Swe.]	8	Eg	57.48N	12.22 E
Flood Range	66	Nf	76.03S	134.00W
Flora [Il.-U.S.]	45	Lg	38.40N	88.29W
Flora [Nor.]	7	Af	61.36N	5.00 E
Florac	11	Jj	44.19N	3.36 E
Florala	44	Dj	31.00N	86.20W
Florange	11	Ie	49.19N	6.07 E
Florence [Al.-U.S.]	43	Je	34.49N	87.40W
Florence [Ks.-U.S.]	45	Hg	38.15N	96.56W
Florence [Or.-U.S.]	46	Ef	44.01N	124.07W
Florence [S.C.-U.S.]	43	Le	34.12N	79.44W
Florence = Firenze	6	Hg	43.46N	11.15 E
Florencia [Arg.]	55	Ci	28.02S	59.15W
Florencia [Col.]	53	Ec	1.36N	75.36W
Florencio Sánchez	55	Dk	33.53S	57.24W
Florennes	12	Gd	50.15N	4.37 E
Florentino Ameghino, Embalse-	56	Gf	43.48S	66.25W
Florenville	11	Le	49.42N	5.18 E
Flores [2]	55	Dk	33.35S	56.50W
Flores	30	Oe	39.26N	31.13W
Flores [Guat.]	49	Fe	16.56N	89.53W
Flores [Guat.]	47	Fe	16.56N	89.53W
Flores, Arroyo de las-	55	Cl	35.36S	59.01W
Flores, Laut- = Flores Sea (EN)	21	Oj	8.00S	121.00 E
Flores, Pulau-	21	Oj	8.30S	121.00 E
Flores Island	46	Bb	49.20N	126.10W
Flores Sea (EN) = Flores, Laut-	21	Oj	8.00S	121.00 E
Floresti	16	Fe	47.55N	28.18 E
Floriano	53	Lf	6.47S	43.01W
Florianópolis	53	Lh	27.35S	48.34W
Florida [Braz.]	55	Di	25.59S	54.36W
Florida [Cuba]	47	Id	21.32N	78.14W
Florida [U.S.] [3]	43	Kf	28.00N	82.00W
Florida [Ur.]	56	Id	34.06S	56.13W
Florida, Estrecho de- = Florida, Straits of- (EN)	38	Kg	24.00N	81.00W
Florida, Straits of- (EN) = Florida, Estrecho de-	38	Kg	24.00N	81.00W
Florida Bay	44	Gm	25.00N	80.45W
Floridablanca	54	Db	7.04N	73.06W

Florida City 44 Gm 25.27N 80.29W
Florida Islands 60 Gi 9.00S 160.10 E
Florida Keys 43 Kg 24.45N 81.00W
Floridia 14 Jm 37.05N 15.09 E
Florido, Río- 48 Gd 27.43N 105.10W
Flórina 15 Ei 40.47N 21.24 E
Flörsheim 12 Kd 50.01N 8.26 E
Flotte, Cap de- 63b Ce 21.11S 167.24 E
Floydada 45 Fj 33.59N 101.20W
Fluessen 11 Lb 52.57N 5.30 E
Flumen 13 Lc 41.43N 0.09W
Flumendosa 14 Dk 39.26N 9.37 E
Fluminimaggiore 14 Ck 39.26N 8.30 E
Flumini Mannu 14 Ck 39.16N 9.00 E
Flums 14 Dc 47.05N 9.20 E
Fluvià 13 Pb 42.12N 3.07 E
Flying Fish, Cape- 66 Of 72.06S 102.29W
Fly River 57 Fe 8.00S 142.21 E
Fnideq 13 Gi 35.50N 5.22W
Fnjóská 7a Bb 65.54N 18.07W
Foa 65b Ba 19.45S 174.18W
Foam Lake 46 Na 51.39N 103.33W
Foça 15 Jk 38.39N 26.46 E
Foča 14 Mg 43.31N 18.47 E
Fochi 35 Bb 18.25N 15.40 E
Fochi 35 Bb 18.56N 15.57 E
Focşani 15 Kd 45.42N 27.11 E
Fodda 13 Nh 36.14N 1.33 E
Fodé 35 Cd 5.29N 23.18 E
Fœringehavn 41 Gf 63.45N 51.28W
Foga, Dallol- 34 Fc 12.05N 3.32 E
Foggaret ez Zoua 32 Hd 27.22N 2.50 E
Foggia 6 Hg 41.27N 15.34 E
Foggo 34 Gc 11.23N 9.57 E
Foglia 14 Gg 43.55N 12.54 E
Föglö 8 Ie 60.00N 20.25 E
Fogo [Can.] 42 Mg 49.40N 54.10W
Fogo [C.V.] 30 Eg 14.55N 24.25W
Fohnsdorf 14 Ic 47.12N 14.41 E
Föhr 10 Eb 54.45N 8.30 E
Föhren 12 Ie 49.51N 6.46 E
Foix 11 Hl 42.58N 1.36 E
Fojnica 23 Fg 43.58N 17.54 E
Fokino 16 Ic 53.27N 34.26 E
Folda 7 Dc 67.36N 14.50 E
Folégandros 15 Hm 36.38N 24.54 E
Foley 42 Kc 68.30N 75.00W
Foleyet 42 Jg 48.16N 82.30W
Folgares 36 Ce 14.54S 15.05 E
Folgefonni 7 Bf 60.00N 6.20 E
Foligno 14 Gh 42.57N 12.42 E
Folkestone 9 Oj 51.05N 1.11 E
Folkingham 12 Bb 52.52N 0.24W
Folkston 44 Fj 30.50N 82.01W
Folldals verk 7 Bb 62.08N 10.00 E
Follebu 7 Cf 61.14N 10.17 E
Föllinge 7 De 63.40N 14.37 E
Follo 8 De 59.55N 10.55 E
Follonica 14 Eh 42.55N 10.45 E
Follonica, Golfo di- 14 Eh 42.55N 10.40 E
Folschviller 12 Ie 49.04N 6.41 E
Fomboni 37 Gb 12.16S 43.45 E
Fomento 49 Hb 22.06N 79.43W
Fond d'Or Bay 51k Bb 13.56N 60.54W
Fond-du-Lac 42 Ge 59.19N 107.10W
Fond-du-Lac 42 Ge 59.17N 106.00W
Fond du Lac 43 Jc 43.47N 88.27W
Fondi 14 Hi 41.21N 13.25 E
Fongen 8 Da 63.11N 11.38 E
Fongoro 35 Cc 11.30N 22.25 E
Fonni 14 Dj 40.07N 9.15 E
Fonoifua 65b Bb 20.17S 174.38W
Fonsagrada 13 Ea 43.08N 7.04W
Fonseca 54 Da 10.53N 72.50W
Fonseca, Golfo de- 38 Kh 13.08N 87.40W
Fonsecas, Serra dos- 55 Jc 17.02S 44.13W
Fontaine-Bellenger 12 De 49.11N 1.16 E
Fontainebleau 11 If 48.24N 2.42 E
Fontaine-Henry, Château de- 12 Be 49.17N 0.27W
Fontaine-le-Dun 12 Ce 49.49N 0.51 E
Fontaine-l'Evêque 12 Gd 50.25N 4.19 E
Fontas 42 Fe 58.17N 121.46W
Fonte Boa 54 Ed 2.32S 66.01W
Fontenay-le-Comte 11 Fh 46.28N 0.49W
Fontenay Trésigny 12 Ef 48.42N 2.52 E
Fontenelle Reservoir 46 Je 42.05N 110.06W
Fontevraud-l'Abbaye 11 Gg 47.11N 0.03 E
Fontur 5 Eb 66.23N 14.32W
Fonuafo'ou Falcon 61 Fd 20.19S 175.25W
Fonualei Island 57 Jf 18.01S 174.19W
Fonyód 10 Nj 46.44N 17.33 E
Foraker, Mount- 40 Id 62.56N 151.26W
Forbach 11 Me 49.11N 6.54 E
Forbes 59 Jf 33.23S 148.01 E
Forbes, Mount- 46 Ga 51.52N 116.56W
Forcados 34 Gd 5.23N 5.19 E
Forcados 34 Gd 5.21N 5.25 E
Forcalquier 11 Lk 43.58N 5.47 E
Forchheim 10 Hg 49.43N 11.04 E
Ford City 46 Fi 35.09N 119.27W
Førde 7 Af 61.27N 5.52 E
Førdefjorden 8 Ac 61.30N 5.40 E
Ford Ranges 66 Mf 77.00S 145.00W
Fordyce 45 Jj 33.49N 92.25W
Forécariah 34 Cd 9.26N 13.06W
Forel, Mont- 67 Mc 67.05N 36.55W
Forelshogna 8 Db 62.41N 10.47 E
Forest 45 Lj 32.22N 89.28W
Forest Park 44 Ei 33.37N 84.22W
Forestville 44 Ma 48.45N 69.06W
Forez, Monts du- 11 Ji 45.35N 3.48 E
Forez, Plaine du- 11 Ki 45.50N 4.10 E
Forfar 9 Ke 56.38N 2.54W
Forges-les-Eaux 11 He 49.37N 1.33 E
Forggensee 10 Gi 47.36N 10.44 E
Forks 46 Cc 47.57N 124.23W
Forlì 14 Gf 44.13N 12.03 E
Forlì, Bocca di- 14 Ii 41.45N 14.10 E
Formby Point 9 Jh 53.33N 3.06W
Formentera 5 Gh 38.42N 1.28 E
Formentor, Cabo de-/Formentor, Cap de- 13 Pe 39.58N 3.12 E
Formentor, Cap de-/Formentor, Cabo de- 13 Pe 39.58N 3.12 E
Formerie 12 De 49.39N 1.44 E
Formia 14 Hi 41.15N 13.37 E
Formiga 54 Ih 20.27S 45.25W
Formigas 32 Cb 37.16N 24.47W
Formosa [2] 56 Ib 25.00S 60.00W
Formosa [Arg.] 53 Kh 26.10S 58.11W
Formosa [Braz.] 54 Ig 15.32S 47.20W
Formosa [Gui.Bis.] 34 Bc 11.45N 16.05W
Formosa [Tai.] 21 Og 23.30N 121.00 E
Formosa, Serra- 52 Kg 12.00S 55.00W
Formosa Bay 36 Hc 2.45S 40.20 E
Formosa Strait (EN) = Taiwan Haixia 21 Ng 24.00N 119.00 E
Formoso [Braz.] 55 Ib 14.57S 46.14W
Formoso [Braz.] 55 Ha 13.37S 48.54W
Formoso, Rio- [Braz.] 55 Ja 13.26S 44.14W
Formoso, Rio- [Braz.] 54 If 10.34S 49.59W
Formoso, Rio- [Braz.] 55 Fd 18.25S 52.28W
Fornæs 7 Ch 56.27N 10.58 E
Fornosovo 8 Ne 59.31N 30.45 E
Fornovo di Taro 14 Ef 44.42N 10.06 E
Föroyar/Færøerne = Faeroe Islands (EN) [5] 6 Fc 62.00N 7.00W
Föroyar/Færøerne = Faeroe Islands (EN) 5 Fc 62.00N 7.00W
Forres 9 Jd 57.37N 3.38W
Forrest 59 Ff 30.51S 128.06 E
Forrest City 45 Ki 35.01N 90.47W
Forrester Island 66 Nf 74.06S 132.00W
Forsayth 59 Ic 18.35S 143.36 E
Forsbacka 8 Gd 60.37N 16.53 E
Forserum 8 Fg 57.42N 14.28 E
Forshaga 7 Cg 59.32N 13.28 E
Forsnäs 7 Ec 66.14N 18.39 E
Forssa 7 Ff 60.49N 23.38 E
Forst/Baršć 10 Ke 51.44N 14.38 E
Forsyth 46 Lc 46.16N 106.41W
Fort Albany 39 Kd 52.15N 81.37W
Fortaleza 53 Mf 3.43S 38.30W
Fortaleza, Ribeirão- 55 Fd 19.50S 53.25W
Fort Augustus 9 Id 57.09N 4.41W
Fort Beaufort 37 Df 32.46S 26.40 E
Fort Benton 43 Eb 47.49N 110.40W
Fort Bragg 43 Cd 39.26N 123.48W
Fort Bridger 46 Jf 41.19N 110.23W
Fort-Carnot 37 Hd 21.53S 48.26 E
Fort Chimo 39 Md 58.10N 68.30W
Fort Chipewyan 42 Ge 58.42N 111.08W
Fort Cobb Reservoir 45 Gi 35.12N 98.29W
Fort Collins 43 Fc 40.35N 105.05W
Fort Collinson 42 Fb 71.37N 117.57W
Fort Coulonge 44 Ic 45.51N 76.44W
Fort Davis 45 Ek 30.35N 103.54W
Fort-de-France 39 Mh 14.36N 61.05W
Fort-de-France, Baie de- 51h Ab 14.34N 61.04W
Fort Dodge 43 Ic 42.30N 94.10W
Forte 55 Ib 14.16S 47.17W
Forte dei Marmi 14 Eg 43.57N 10.10 E
Fortescue River 57 Cg 21.00S 116.06 E
Fort Frances 39 Je 48.36N 93.24W
Fort Franklin 42 Fc 65.12N 123.26W
Fort Garland 45 Dh 37.26N 105.26W
Fort George 39 Ld 53.50N 79.00W
Fort Gibson Lake 45 Ih 36.00N 95.18W
Fort Good-Hope 39 Gc 66.15N 128.38W
Forth 9 Je 56.04N 3.42W
Forth, Firth of- 5 Fd 56.05N 2.55W
Fort Hall 36 Gc 0.43S 37.09 E
Fort Hope 42 If 51.32N 88.00W
Fortin Avalos Sanchez 55 Bf 23.28S 60.07W
Fortin Boquerón 55 Cf 22.47S 59.57W
Fortin Buenos Aires 55 Bf 22.57S 61.51W
Fortin Cadete Pastor Pando 55 Cg 24.20S 58.54W
Fortin Capitán Figari 55 Cf 23.12S 59.32W
Fortin Carlos A. Lopez 55 Ce 21.19S 59.44W
Fortin Comandante Nowak 55 Cg 24.51S 58.15W
Fortin Coronel Bogado 55 Ce 20.46S 59.09W
Fortin Coronel Eugenio Garay 56 Hb 20.31S 62.08W
Fortin Coronel Hermosa 55 Bf 22.33S 60.01W
Fortin Coronel Martinez 55 Cf 22.15S 59.09W
Fortin Florida 55 Ce 20.45S 59.17W
Fortin Galpón 55 Cd 19.51S 58.16W
Fortin Gaspar Rodriguez de Francia 55 Cf 23.01S 59.57W
Fortin General Caballero 55 Cg 24.08S 59.30W
Fortin General Delgado 55 Cg 24.28S 59.15W
Fortin General Diaz 56 Hb 23.31S 60.34W
Fortin Guarani 55 Cf 22.44S 59.30W
Fortin Hernandarias 55 Be 21.58S 61.30W
Fortin José M. López 55 Be 20.07S 60.15W
Fortin Lagerenza 55 Be 20.06S 61.03W
Fortin Madrejón 55 Ce 20.38S 59.52W
Fortin Mariscal López 55 Cf 23.39S 59.44W
Fortin Max Paredes 55 Cd 19.16S 59.58W
Fortin May Alberto Gardel 55 Af 22.46S 62.12W
Fortin Mayor Long 55 Ae 20.33S 62.01W
Fortin Mayor R. Santacruz 55 Be 20.15S 60.37W
Fortin Nueva Asunción 55 Be 20.42S 61.55W
Fortin Pikyrenda 55 Be 20.05S 61.48W
Fortin Pilcomayo [Par.] 55 Bf 23.44S 60.51W
Fortin Pilcomayo [Arg.] 55 Bf 23.52S 60.53W
Fortin Pratts Gill 55 Bf 22.41S 61.33W
Fortin Presidente Ayala 55 Cf 23.30S 59.46W
Fortin Ravelo 55 Bd 19.18S 60.35W
Fortin Suarez Arana 55 Bd 18.40S 60.09W
Fortin Teniente 1° Alfredo Stroessner 55 Bf 22.45S 61.32W
Fortin Teniente 1° H. Mendoza 55 Cd 19.54S 59.47W
Fortin Teniente 1° M. Cabello 55 Bf 23.28S 61.19W
Fortin Teniente 1° Ramiro Espinola 55 Be 21.28S 61.18W
Fortin Teniente Acosta 55 Bf 22.41S 60.32W
Fortin Teniente Agripino Enciso 55 Be 21.12S 61.34W
Fortin Teniente Américo Picco 55 Cd 19.35S 59.43W
Fortin Teniente Aristigueta 55 Bf 22.21S 60.38W
Fortin Teniente E. Ochoa 55 Be 21.42S 61.02W
Fortin Teniente Esteban Martinez 55 Cg 24.02S 59.51W
Fortin Teniente Juan E. López 55 Be 21.05S 61.48W
Fortin Teniente Montania 55 Cf 22.04S 59.57W
Fortin Teniente R. Rueda 55 Be 21.49S 60.49W
Fortin Toledo 55 Bf 22.20S 60.21W
Fortin Torres 55 Ce 21.01S 59.30W
Fortin Vanguardia 55 Cd 19.39S 58.10W
Fortin Vitiones 55 Cd 19.30S 58.06W
Fortin Zenteno 55 Cf 23.10S 59.59W
Fort Jeudy, Point of- 51p Bb 12.00N 61.42W
Fort Kent 44 Mb 47.15N 68.36W
Fort Knox 44 Eg 37.53N 85.55W
Fort Lamy → N'djamena 31 Ig 12.07N 15.03 E
Fort Lauderdale 43 Kf 26.07N 80.08W
Fort Liard 39 Gc 60.15N 123.28W
Fort-Liberté 49 Ld 19.38N 71.57W
Fort MacKay 42 Ge 57.08N 111.42W
Fort Macleod 42 Gg 49.43N 113.25W
Fort Mac Mahon 32 Hd 29.46N 1.37 E
Fort Madison 45 Kf 40.38N 91.21W
Fort-Mahon-Plage 12 Dd 50.21N 1.34 E
Fort McMurray 39 Hd 56.44N 111.23W
Fort McPherson 39 Fc 67.27N 134.53W
Fort Miribel 32 Hd 29.26N 3.00 E
Fort Morgan 45 Ef 40.15N 103.48W
Fort Myers 39 Kg 26.37N 81.54W
Fort Myers Beach 44 Gl 26.27N 81.57W
Fort Nelson 39 Gd 58.49N 122.39W
Fort Nelson 42 Fe 59.33N 124.01W
Fort Norman 42 Ed 64.56N 125.22W
Fortore 14 Ji 41.55N 15.17 E
Fort Payne 44 Eh 34.27N 85.43W
Fort Peck 46 Lb 48.01N 106.27W
Fort Peck Lake 43 Fb 47.45N 106.50W
Fort Pierce 43 Kf 27.27N 80.20W
Fort Pierre 43 Gc 44.21N 100.22W
Fort Portal 36 Fb 0.39N 30.17 E
Fort Providence 39 Hc 61.21N 117.39W
Fort Qu'Appelle 46 Na 50.56N 103.09W
Fort Resolution 42 Gd 61.10N 113.40W
Fortrose 62 Cg 46.34S 168.48 E
Fort Rupert 39 Ld 51.25N 78.45W
Fort Saint James 42 Ff 54.26N 124.15W
Fort Saint John 39 Gd 56.15N 120.51W
Fort Sandenam 25 Db 31.20N 69.27 E
Fort Saskatchewan 42 Gf 53.43N 113.13W
Fort Scott 45 Ih 37.50N 94.42W
Fort-Ševčenko 19 Fg 44.30N 50.14 E
Fort Severn 39 Kd 56.00N 87.38W
Fort Simpson 39 Gc 61.52N 121.23W
Fort Smith [Ar.-U.S.] 39 Jf 35.23N 94.25W
Fort Smith [N.W.T.-Can.] 39 Hd 60.00N 111.53W
Fort Stockton 43 Ge 30.53N 102.53W
Fort Sumner 45 Di 34.28N 104.15W
Fortuna 46 Cf 40.36N 124.09W
Fortuna, Rio de la- 55 Cc 16.36S 58.46W
Fortune Bay 42 Lg 47.15N 55.40W
Fort Vermilion 42 Fe 58.24N 116.00W
Fort Victoria 31 Kk 20.05S 30.50 E
Fort Walton Beach 43 Je 30.25N 86.36W
Fort Washakie 46 Ke 43.00N 108.53W
Fort Wayne 39 Ke 41.04N 85.09W
Fort William 9 He 56.49N 5.07W
Fort Worth 39 Jf 32.45N 97.20W
Fort Yates 45 Fc 46.05N 100.38W
Fort Yukon 39 Ec 66.34N 145.17W
Forūr, Jazīreh-ye- 24 Pi 26.17N 54.32 E
Foshan 22 Ng 22.59N 113.05 E
Fosheim Peninsula 42 Ja 80.00N 84.30W
Fosnavåg 8 Ab 62.21N 5.39 E
Fosnøy 8 Ad 60.45N 4.55 E
Fossacesia 14 Ih 42.15N 14.29 E
Fossano 14 Bf 44.33N 7.43 E
Fossato, Colle di- 14 Gg 43.20N 12.49 E
Fossberg 8 Cc 61.50N 8.34 E
Fossil 46 Ed 44.59N 120.13W
Fossil Bluff 66 Qf 71.20S 68.17W
Fossombrone 14 Gg 43.41N 12.48 E
Fosston 45 Ic 47.35N 95.45W
Fos-sur-Mer 11 Kk 43.26N 4.57 E
Foster 59 Jg 38.39S 146.12 E
Foster, Mount- 40 Le 59.48N 135.29W
Foster Bugt 41 Jd 73.40N 21.40W
Fostoria 44 Fe 41.10N 83.25W
Fotuha'a 65b Ba 19.49S 174.44W
Foucarmont 12 De 49.51N 1.34 E
Fougamou 36 Bc 1.13S 10.36 E
Fougères 11 Ef 48.21N 1.12W
Foul, Khalīj- 33 Ge 23.30N 35.40 E
Foula 9 Ka 60.10N 2.05W
Foul Bay 51q Bb 13.06N 59.27W
Fouligny 12 Ie 49.06N 6.30 E
Foulness 9 Nj 51.36N 0.55 E
Foulness Point 12 Cc 51.37N 0.57 E
Foulwind, Cape- 62 Dd 41.45S 171.28 E
Foumban 34 Hd 5.43N 10.55 E
Foumbouni 37 Gb 11.50S 43.30 E
Foum Zguid 32 Fc 30.05N 6.52W
Foundation Ice Stream 66 Qg 83.15S 60.00W
Fountains Abbey 9 Lg 54.07N 1.34W
Fouquet Island 37b Bb 5.25S 53.20 E
Fourchambault 11 Jg 47.01N 3.05 E
Fourchue, Ile- 51b Bc 17.57N 62.55W
Fourmies 11 Kd 50.00N 4.03 E
Four Mountains, Islands of the- 40a Db 52.50N 170.00W
Foúrnoi 15 Jl 37.34N 26.30 E
Fouron/Voeren 12 Hd 50.45N 5.48 E
Fours 11 Jh 46.49N 3.43 E
Fourth Cataract (EN) = Rabi', Ash Shallāl ar- 30 Kg 18.47N 32.03 E
Fous, Pointe des- 51g Bb 15.12N 61.20W
Fouta 34 Cb 16.18N 14.48W
Fouta Djalon 30 Fg 11.30N 12.30W
Foutouna, Ile- 57 If 19.32S 170.13 E
Foux, Cap-à- 49 Kd 19.45N 73.27W
Fouzon 11 Hg 47.16N 1.27 E
Foveaux Strait 57 Hi 46.40S 168.10 E
Fowler [Co.-U.S.] 45 Eg 38.08N 104.00W
Fowler [In.-U.S.] 44 De 40.37N 87.19W
Fowlers Bay 59 Gf 32.00S 132.25 E
Fowman 24 Md 37.13N 49.19 E
Foxe Basin 38 Lc 68.25N 77.00W
Foxe Channel 38 Lc 64.30N 80.00W
Foxen 8 De 59.25N 11.55 E
Foxe Peninsula 38 Lc 65.00N 76.00W
Foxford/Béal Easa 9 Dh 53.59N 9.07W
Fox Glacier 61 Ch 43.28S 170.00 E
Fox Islands 38 Cd 54.00N 168.00W
Fox Peak 62 De 43.50S 170.47 E
Fox River 45 Lf 41.21N 88.50W
Foxton 62 Fd 40.28S 175.17 E
Fox Valley 46 Ka 50.29N 109.28W
Foyle 9 Ff 55.04N 7.15W
Foyle, Lough-/Loch Feabhail 9 Ff 55.05N 7.10W
Foz do Cunene 36 Bf 17.15S 11.48 E
Foz do Iguaçu 53 Kh 25.33S 54.35W
Fraga 13 Mc 41.31N 0.21 E
Fragoso, Cayo 49 Hb 22.44N 79.30W
Fraire, Walcourt- 12 Gd 50.16N 4.30 E
Fram 55 Eh 27.06S 55.58W
Fram Basin (EN) 67 He 88.00N 80.00 E
Framlingham 12 Db 52.13N 1.20 E
Franca 56 Kb 20.32S 47.24W
Franca-Josifa, Zemlja- = Franz Joseph Land (EN) 21 Ha 81.00N 55.00 E
Francavilla al Mare 14 Ih 42.25N 14.17 E
Francavilla Fontana 14 Lj 40.32N 17.35 E
France [1] 6 Gf 46.00N 2.00 E
Frances 42 Ed 60.16N 129.11W
Francés, Punta- 49 Fc 21.38N 83.12W
Francesi, Punta di li- 14 Di 41.08N 9.02 E
Francés Viejo, Cabo- 49 Md 19.39N 69.55W
Franceville 31 Ii 1.38S 13.35 E
Franche-Comté 11 Lh 47.00N 6.00 E
Franches Montagnes/Freiberge 14 Ac 47.15N 7.00 E
Francia 55 Dk 32.34S 36.38W
Francia, Sierra de- 13 Fd 40.35N 6.05W
Francis Case, Lake- 38 Je 43.15N 99.00W
Francisco Beltrão 56 Jc 26.05S 53.04W
Francisco Escárcega 48 Nh 18.37N 90.43W
Francisco I. Madero 48 Ge 24.32N 104.22W
Francisco Madero 55 Al 35.52S 62.03W
Francisco Morazán [3] 49 Df 14.15N 87.15W
Francisco Sá 54 Jg 16.28S 43.30W
Franciscus Bay 37 Ae 25.00S 14.50 E
Francistown 31 Jk 21.09S 27.31 E
Francofonte 14 Im 37.14N 14.53 E
Franconian Jura (EN) = Fränkische Alb 5 Hf 49.00N 11.30 E
Francs Peak 43 Fc 43.58N 109.20W
Franeker 11 La 53.11N 5.32 E
Frankenau 12 Kc 51.06N 8.56 E
Frankenberg (Eder) 10 Ee 51.04N 8.40 E
Frankenhöhe 10 Gg 49.15N 10.15 E
Frankenthal (Pfalz) 12 Ke 49.32N 8.21 E
Frankenwald 10 Hf 50.18N 11.36 E
Frankfort [In.-U.S.] 44 De 40.17N 86.31W
Frankfort [Ky.-U.S.] 39 Kf 38.12N 84.52W
Frankfort [Mi.-U.S.] 44 Dc 44.38N 86.14W
Frankfort on the Main (EN) = Frankfurt am Main 6 Ge 50.07N 8.41 E
Frankfurt 10 Kd 52.21N 14.33 E
Frankfurt [2] 10 Kd 52.20N 14.30 E
Frankfurt am Main = Frankfort on the Main (EN) 6 Ge 50.07N 8.41 E
Fränkische Alb = Franconian Jura(EN) 5 Hf 49.00N 11.30 E
Fränkische Saale 10 Ff 50.03N 9.42 E
Fränkische Schweiz 10 Hg 49.45N 11.20 E
Franklin [In.-U.S.] 44 Df 39.29N 86.03W
Franklin [Ky.-U.S.] 44 Dg 36.43N 86.35W
Franklin [La.-U.S.] 45 Kl 29.48N 91.30W
Franklin [N.C.-U.S.] 44 Fh 35.11N 83.23W
Franklin [N.H.-U.S.] 44 Ld 43.27N 71.39W
Franklin [Pa.-U.S.] 44 He 41.24N 79.49W
Franklin [Tn.-U.S.] 44 Dh 35.55N 86.52W
Franklin, District of- [3] 42 Hb 72.00N 96.00W
Franklin Bay 38 Gc 68.45N 125.35W
Franklin Delano Roosevelt Lake 43 Db 48.20N 118.10W
Franklin Island 66 Kf 76.05S 168.11 E
Franklin Lake [Nv.-U.S.] 46 Hf 40.24N 115.12W
Franklin Lake [N.W.T.-Can.] 42 Hc 66.55N 96.05W
Franklin Mountains 38 Gc 63.15N 123.30W
Franklin Strait 42 Hb 71.30N 96.30W
Fransfontein 37 Bd 20.12S 15.01 E
Fränsta 8 Gb 62.30N 16.09 E
Franz Josef Glacier 62 De 43.23S 170.11 E
Franz Joseph Land (EN) = Franca-Josifa, Zemlja- 21 Ha 81.00N 55.00 E
Frascati 14 Gi 41.48N 12.41 E
Fraser [Can.] 38 Ge 49.09N 123.12W
Fraser [Newf.-Can.] 42 Le 56.39N 63.08W
Fraserburg 37 Cf 31.55S 21.30 E
Fraserburgh 9 Ld 57.42N 2.00W
Fraserdale 42 Jg 49.51N 81.38W
Fraser Island 57 Gg 25.15S 153.10 E
Fraser Plateau 38 Gd 51.30N 122.00W
Fraser Range 59 Ef 32.03S 122.48 E
Frasertown 62 Gc 38.58S 177.24 E
Frasnes-lez-Anvaing 12 Fd 50.40N 3.36 E
Frauenfeld 14 Cc 47.35N 8.54 E
Fray Bentos 56 Id 33.08S 58.18W
Frechen 12 Id 50.55N 6.49 E
Frechilla 13 Hb 42.08N 4.50W
Fredericia 7 Bi 55.35N 9.46 E
Frederick [Md.-U.S.] 44 If 39.25N 77.25W
Frederick [Ok.-U.S.] 45 Gi 34.23N 99.01W
Frederick E. Hyde Fjord 41 Jb 82.40N 25.45W
Frederick Reef 57 Gg 21.00S 154.25 E
Fredericksburg [Tx.-U.S.] 45 Gk 30.17N 98.52W
Fredericksburg [Va.-U.S.] 44 If 38.18N 77.30W
Fredericktown 45 Kh 37.33N 90.18W
Frederico Westphalen 55 Fh 27.22S 53.24W
Fredericton 39 Me 45.58N 66.39W
Frederiksborg [2] 8 Ei 55.55N 12.15 E
Frederiksdal 41 Hf 60.15N 45.30W
Frederikshåb/Påmiut 41 Hf 62.00N 49.45W
Frederikshåb Bank (EN) 41 Hf 62.16N 49.45W
Frederikshavn 6 Hd 57.26N 10.32 E
Frederikssund 8 Ei 55.50N 12.04 E
Frederiksted 50 Dd 17.42N 64.48W
Frederiksværk 8 Ei 55.58N 12.02 E
Fredonia 46 Ih 36.57N 112.32W
Fredrika 7 Ed 64.05N 18.24 E
Fredriksberg 7 Df 60.08N 14.23 E
Fredrikshamn/Hamina 7 Gf 60.34N 27.12 E
Fredrikstad 7 Cg 59.13N 10.57 E
Fredvang 7 Cb 68.05N 13.10 E
Freeling Heights 59 Hf 30.10S 139.25 E
Freels, Cape- 42 Mg 49.13N 53.29W
Freeport [Bah.] 47 Ic 26.30N 78.45W
Freeport [Il.-U.S.] 43 Jc 42.17N 89.36W
Freeport [N.Y.-U.S.] 44 Ke 40.40N 73.35W
Freeport [Tx.-U.S.] 43 Hf 28.55N 95.22W
Freer 45 Gm 27.53N 98.37W
Freetown [Atg.] 51d Bb 17.03N 61.42W
Freetown [S.L.] 31 Fh 8.30N 13.15W
Fregenal de la Sierra 13 Ff 38.10N 6.39W
Fregene 14 Gi 41.51N 12.12 E
Frei 8 Ba 63.01N 7.48 E
Freiberg 10 Jf 50.55N 13.22 E
Freiberge/Franches Montagnes 14 Ac 47.15N 7.00 E
Freiberger Mulde 10 Ie 51.10N 12.48 E
Freiburg/Fribourg 14 Bd 46.50N 7.10 E
Freiburg im Breisgau 6 Gf 48.00N 7.51 E
Freilassing 10 Ii 47.51N 12.59 E
Freirina 56 Fc 28.30S 71.06W
Freisen 12 Je 49.33N 7.15 E
Freising 10 Hh 48.24N 11.44 E
Freistadt 14 Ib 48.30N 14.30 E
Freital 10 Je 51.01N 13.39 E
Fréjus 11 Mk 43.26N 6.44 E
Fréjus, Col du- 11 Mi 45.07N 6.40 E
Fremantle, Perth- 59 Df 32.03S 115.45 E
Fremont [Ca.-U.S.] 43 Cd 37.34N 122.01W
Fremont [Nb.-U.S.] 43 Hc 41.26N 96.30W
Fremont [Oh.-U.S.] 44 Fe 41.21N 83.08W
Fremont River 46 Jg 38.24N 110.42W
French Frigate Shoals 57 Kb 23.45N 166.10W
French Guiana (EN) = Guyane Française [5] 53 Ke 4.00N 53.00W
French Lick 44 Df 38.33N 86.37W
Frenchman Creek 45 Ff 40.13N 100.50W
Frenchman River 43 Fb 48.24N 107.05W
French Pass 62 Ed 40.55S 173.50 E
French Plain (EN) 5 Gf 47.00N 1.00 E
French Polynesia (EN) = Polynésie Française [5] 58 Mf 16.00S 145.00W
French River 44 Gc 45.56N 80.54W
Frenda 32 Hb 35.04N 1.02 E
Frénel, Cap- 11 Df 48.42N 2.19W
Frentani, Monti dei- 14 Ii 41.55N 14.30 E
Freren 12 Jb 52.29N 7.33 E
Fresco 34 Dd 5.05N 5.34W
Fresco, Rio- 54 He 6.39S 52.00W
Freshfield, Cape- 66 Je 68.22S 151.05 E
Fresnes-en-Woëvre 12 He 49.06N 5.37 E
Fresnillo de Gonzales Echeverria 47 Dd 23.10N 102.53W
Fresno 39 Hf 36.45N 119.45W
Fresno, Portillo del- 13 Ib 42.35N 3.40W
Fresno River 46 Eh 37.05N 120.33W
Fresquel 11 Ik 43.14N 2.24 E
Fresvikbreen 8 Bc 61.02N 6.45 E
Freu, Cabo- 13 Pe 39.45N 3.27 E
Freudenberg 12 Jd 50.54N 7.52 E
Freudenstadt 10 Eh 48.26N 8.25 E
Frévent 11 Id 50.16N 2.17 E
Freycinet Estuary 59 Ce 26.25S 113.45 E
Freycinet Peninsula 59 Jh 42.15S 148.20 E
Freyming-Merlebach 12 Ie 49.09N 6.47 E
Freyre 55 Aj 31.10S 62.02W
Freyung 10 Jh 48.48N 13.33 E
Fri 15 Jn 35.25N 26.56 E
Fria 34 Cc 10.27N 13.32W
Fria, Cape- 30 Ij 18.27S 12.01 E
Frias 56 Gc 28.39S 65.09W
Fribourg [2] 14 Bd 46.40N 7.10 E
Fribourg/Freiburg 14 Bd 46.50N 7.10 E
Fridtjof Nansen, Mount- 66 Lg 85.21S 167.33W
Friedberg [Aus.] 14 Kc 47.26N 16.03 E
Friedberg [F.R.G.] 10 Ef 50.21N 8.46 E
Friedrichshafen 10 Fi 47.39N 9.29 E
Friedrichsthal 12 Je 49.19N 7.06 E
Friesach 14 Id 46.57N 14.24 E
Friese Gat 12 Ia 53.30N 6.05 E
Friese Wad 12 Ha 53.25N 5.50 E
Friese Wad 12 Ha 53.24N 5.45 E
Friesland [3] 12 Ha 53.03N 5.45 E
Friesland 11 La 53.05N 6.00 E
Friesland 5 Ge 53.05N 6.00 E

Index Symbols

[1] Independent Nation
[2] State, Region
[3] District, County
[4] Municipality
[5] Colony, Dependency
Continent
Physical Region
Historical or Cultural Region
Mount, Mountain
Volcano
Hill
Mountains, Mountain Range
Hills, Escarpment
Plateau, Upland
Pass, Gap
Plain, Lowland
Delta
Salt Flat
Valley, Canyon
Crater, Cave
Karst Features
Depression
Polder
Desert, Dunes
Forest, Woods
Heath, Steppe
Oasis
Cape, Point
Coast, Beach
Cliff
Peninsula
Isthmus
Sandbank
Island
Atoll
Rock, Reef
Islands, Archipelago
Rocks, Reefs
Coral Reef
Well, Spring
Geyser
River, Stream
Waterfall Rapids
River Mouth, Estuary
Lake
Salt Lake
Intermittent Lake
Reservoir
Swamp, Pond
Canal
Glacier
Ice Shelf, Pack Ice
Ocean
Sea
Gulf, Bay
Strait, Fjord
Lagoon
Bank
Seamount
Tablemount
Ridge
Shelf
Basin
Escarpment, Sea Scarp
Fracture
Trench, Abyss
National Park, Reserve
Point of Interest
Recreation Site
Cave, Cavern
Historic Site
Ruins
Wall, Walls
Church, Abbey
Temple
Scientific Station
Airport
Port
Lighthouse
Mine
Tunnel
Dam, Bridge

Friesoythe 10 Dc 53.01N 7.51 E
Frigate Island 51p Cb 12.25N 61.29W
Friggesund 8 Gc 61.54N 16.32 E
Frignano 14 Ef 44.20N 10.50 E
Frindsbury Reef 63a Da 5.00S 159.07 E
Frinnaryd 8 Fg 57.56N 14.49 E
Frinton-on-Sea 12 Dc 51.50N 1.15 E
Frio, Cabo- 52 Lh 22.53S 42.00W
Frio, Rio- 49 Eh 11.08N 84.46W
Frio Draw 45 Ei 34.50N 102.08W
Friona 45 Ei 34.38N 102.43W
Frio River 45 Gl 28.30N 98.10W
Frisco Peak 46 Ig 38.31N 113.14W
Frisian Islands (EN) 5 Ge 54.00N 7.00 E
Fristad 8 Eg 57.50N 13.01 E
Fritsla 8 Eg 57.33N 12.47 E
Fritzlar 10 Fe 51.08N 9.17 E
Friuli 14 Ge 46.00N 13.00 E
Friuli-Venezia Giulia [2] 14 Gd 46.00N 13.00 E
Frobisher Bay 39 Mc 63.44N 68.28W
Frobisher Bay 38 Mc 62.30N 66.00W
Frobisher Lake 42 Ge 56.20N 108.20W
Froidchapelle 12 Gd 50.09N 4.20 E
Froissy 12 Ee 49.34N 2.13 E
Frolovo 19 Ef 49.45N 43.39 E
Fromberg 46 Kd 45.23N 108.54W
Frombork 10 Pb 54.22N 19.41 E
Frome 9 Kj 51.14N 2.20W
Frome, Lake- 57 Eh 30.50S 139.50 E
Frondenberg 12 Jc 51.28N 7.46 E
Fronteira 13 Ee 39.03N 7.39W
Fronteiras 54 Je 7.05S 40.37W
Frontera 48 Mh 18.32N 92.38W
Frontera, Punta- 48 Mh 19.36N 92.42W
Fronteras 48 Eb 30.56N 109.31W
Frontignan 11 Jk 43.27N 3.45 E
Frontino, Paramo- 54 Cb 6.28N 76.04W
Front Range 38 If 39.45N 105.45W
Front Royal 44 Hf 38.56N 78.13W
Frosinone 14 Hi 41.38N 13.19 E
Frösö 8 Fa 63.11N 14.32 E
Frostburg 44 Hf 39.39N 78.56W
Frost Glacier 66 Ie 67.05S 129.00 E
Frövi 8 Fe 59.28N 15.22 E
Frøya 7 Be 63.43N 8.42 E
Frøysjøen 8 Ac 61.50N 5.05 E
Frozen Strait 42 Jc 65.50N 84.30W
Fruges 11 Id 50.31N 2.08 E
Frunze [Kirg.-U.S.S.R.] 18 Hd 40.06N 71.45 E
Frunze [Kirg.-U.S.S.R.] 22 Je 42.54N 74.36 E
Frunzovka 15 Mb 47.20N 29.37 E
Fruška Gora 15 Cd 45.10N 19.35 E
Frutal 54 Ih 20.02S 48.55W
Frutigen 14 Bd 46.35N 7.40 E
Fry Canyon 46 Jh 37.38N 110.08W
Frýdek Místek 10 Og 49.41N 18.22 E
Frylinckspan 37 Ce 26.46S 22.28 E
Ftéri 15 Ej 39.09N 21.33 E
Fua'amotu 65b Ac 21.15S 175.08W
Fua Mulaku Island 25a Bc 0.15S 73.30 E
Fu'an 27 Kf 27.10N 119.44 E
Fu-chien Sheng→Fujian Sheng=Fukien (EN) [2] 27 Kf 26.00N 118.00 E
Fuchskauten 10 Ef 50.40N 8.05 E
Fuchū [Jap.] 29 Cd 34.34N 133.14 E
Fuchū [Jap.] 29 Fd 35.41N 139.28 E
Fuchun Jiang 28 Fi 30.15N 120.15 E
Fuchunjiang-Shuiku 28 Ej 29.29N 119.31 E
Fucino, Conca del- 14 Hj 42.01N 13.31 E
Fudai 29 Ga 40.01N 141.52 E
Fuding 27 Lf 27.19N 120.08 E
Fuengirola 13 Hh 36.32N 4.37W
Fuente Alto 56 Fd 33.37S 70.35W
Fuente del Maestre 13 Ff 38.32N 6.27W
Fuente-Obejuna 13 Gf 38.16N 5.25W
Fuentesaúco 13 Gc 41.14N 5.30W
Fuentes de Andalucía 13 Gg 37.28N 5.21W
Fuentes de Cantos 13 Ff 38.15N 6.18W
Fuerte 47 Cc 25.54N 109.22W
Fuerte, Isla- 49 Ii 9.23N 76.11W
Fuerte, Sierra del- 48 Hd 27.30N 102.45W
Fuerte Olimpo 56 Ib 21.02S 57.54W
Fuerteventura 30 Ff 28.20N 14.00W
Fuga 26 Hc 18.52N 121.22 E
Fugong 27 Gf 27.03N 98.57 E
Fugou 28 Cg 34.04N 114.23 E
Fugu 27 Jd 39.02N 111.03 E
Fuguo→Zhanhua 28 Ef 37.42N 118.08 E
Fuhai/Burultokay 27 Eb 47.06N 87.23 E
Fuhayrī, Wādī- 23 Hf 16.04N 52.11 E
Fu He 28 Dj 28.36N 116.04 E
Fuji 28 Og 35.09N 138.38 E
Fujian Sheng (Fu-chien Sheng)=Fukien (EN) [2] 27 Kf 26.00N 118.00 E
Fujieda 29 Fd 34.51N 138.15 E
Fuji-Gawa 29 Fd 35.07N 138.38 E
Fujin 27 Nb 47.15N 132.01 E
Fujinomiya 29 Fd 35.12N 138.38 E
Fujioka 29 Fc 36.15N 139.03 E
Fuji-San 21 Pf 35.26N 138.43 E
Fujisawa 29 Fd 35.21N 139.27 E
Fuji-yoshida 29 Fd 35.29N 138.47 E
Fukagawa 27 Pc 43.43N 142.03 E
Fūkah 24 Bg 31.04N 27.55 E
Fukang 27 Ec 44.10N 87.59 E
Fuka-Shima 29 Be 32.43N 131.56 E
Fukiage 29 Bf 31.30N 130.20 E
Fukien (EN)=Fu-chien Sheng→Fujian Sheng [2] 27 Kf 26.00N 118.00 E
Fukien (EN)=Fujian Sheng (Fu-chien Sheng) [2] 27 Kf 26.00N 118.00 E
Fukuchiyama 28 Mg 35.18N 135.07 E
Fukue 28 Jh 32.41N 128.50 E
Fukueichiao 27 Lf 25.19N 121.34 E
Fukue-Jima 28 Jh 32.41N 128.48 E
Fukui 27 Od 36.04N 136.13 E
Fukui Ken [2] 28 Ng 36.00N 136.20 E
Fukuma 29 Be 33.47N 130.28 E
Fukuoka 22 Pf 33.35N 130.24 E
Fukuoka Ken [2] 28 Kh 33.28N 130.45 E
Fukuroi 29 Ed 34.45N 137.54 E
Fukushima [Jap.] 27 Pd 37.45N 140.28 E
Fukushima [Jap.] 27 Pc 41.29N 140.15 E
Fukushima Ken [2] 28 Pf 37.25N 140.10 E
Fukuyama 27 Ne 34.29N 133.22 E
Fūlādī, Kūh-e- 23 Kc 34.38N 67.32 E
Fūlād Mahalleh 24 Od 36.02N 53.44 E
Fulanga 63d Cc 19.08S 178.34W
Fulda 5 Ge 51.25N 9.39 E
Fulda 10 Ff 50.33N 9.40 E
Fuliji 28 Dh 33.47N 116.59 E
Fulin → Hanyuan 27 Hf 29.25N 102.12 E
Fuling 27 If 29.40N 107.21 E
Fullerton 45 Hf 41.22N 97.58W
Fulton [Arg.] 55 Cm 37.25S 58.48W
Fulton [Il.-U.S.] 45 Kf 41.52N 90.11W
Fulton [Ky.-U.S.] 44 Cg 36.30N 88.53W
Fulton [Mo.-U.S.] 45 Kg 38.52N 91.57W
Fulton [N.Y.-U.S.] 44 Id 43.20N 76.26W
Fulufjället 8 Ec 61.33N 12.43 E
Fumaiolo 14 Gg 43.47N 12.04 E
Fumay 11 Kd 50.00N 4.42 E
Fumel 11 Gj 44.30N 0.58 E
Funabasi 28 Og 35.42N 139.59 E
Funabiki 29 Gc 37.26N 140.35 E
Funafuti 58 Ie 8.01S 178.00 E
Funafuti Atoll 57 Ie 8.31S 179.08 E
Funagata 29 Gb 38.42N 140.18 E
Funagata-Yama 29 Gb 38.27N 140.37 E
Funakoshi-Wan 29 Hb 39.25N 142.00 E
Funan 28 Ch 32.38N 115.35 E
Funäsdalen 7 Ce 62.32N 12.33 E
Funchal 31 Fe 32.38N 16.54W
Fundación 54 Da 10.29N 74.12W
Fundão 13 Ed 40.08N 7.30W
Fundy, Bay of- 38 Me 45.00N 66.00W
Funeral Peak 46 Gh 36.08N 116.37W
Fungalei 64h Bb 13.17S 176.07W
Funhalouro 37 Ed 23.05S 34.24 E
Funing [China] 27 Ig 23.39N 105.33 E
Funing [China] 28 Eh 33.48N 119.47 E
Funing [China] 28 Ee 39.56N 119.15 E
Funiu Shan 27 Je 33.40N 112.10 E
Funtua 34 Gc 11.32N 7.19 E
Fuping 28 Ce 38.49N 114.15 E
Fuqing 27 Kf 25.47N 119.24 E
Furancungo 37 Eb 14.54S 33.37 E
Furano 28 Qc 43.21N 142.23 E
Füren 29a Ca 44.17N 142.25 E
Furenai 29a Cb 43.43N 142.15 E
Füren-Ko 29a Db 43.20N 145.20 E
Fürg 24 Ph 28.18N 55.13 E
Fur Jiang 28 Hc 42.37N 125.33 E
Furmanov 7 Jh 57.16N 41.07 E
Furnas, Represa de- 54 Ih 21.20S 45.50W
Furnas, Serra das- 55 Fb 15.45S 53.20W
Furneaux Group 57 Fi 40.10S 148.05 E
Furnes/Veurne 11 Ic 51.04N 2.40 E
Furqlus 24 Ge 34.36N 37.05 E
Furrīyānah 32 Ic 34.57N 8.34 E
Fürstenau 12 Jb 52.31N 7.43 E
Furstenauer Berge 12 Jb 52.35N 7.45 E
Fürstenfeld 14 Kc 47.03N 16.05 E
Fürstenfeldbruck 10 Hh 48.11N 11.15 E
Fürstenlager 12 Ke 49.42N 8.38 E
Fürstenwalde 10 Kd 52.22N 14.04 E
Fürth [F.R.G.] 10 Gg 49.28N 11.00 E
Fürth [F.R.G.] 12 Ke 49.39N 8.47 E
Furth im Wald 10 Ig 49.18N 12.51 E
Furubira 29a Bb 43.16N 140.39 E
Furudal 7 Df 61.10N 15.08 E
Furukawa 27 Pd 38.34N 140.58 E
Furusund 8 He 59.40N 18.55 E
Fury and Hecla Strait 42 Jc 69.55N 84.00W
Fushan [China] 28 Ff 37.30N 121.15 E
Fushan [China] 28 Ag 35.58N 111.51 E
Fushë-Arëzi 15 Dg 42.04N 20.02 E
Fushë-Lura 15 Dh 41.48N 20.13 E
Fu Shui 28 Cj 29.52N 115.26 E
Fushun 22 Oe 41.46N 123.56 E
Fusong 27 Mc 42.20N 127.17 E
Füsselberg 12 Je 49.32N 7.14 E
Füssen 10 Gi 47.34N 10.42 E
Futa, Passo della- 14 Ff 44.05N 11.17 E
Futago-Yama 29 Be 33.35N 131.38 E
Futaoi-Jima 29 Bd 34.06N 130.47 E
Futog 15 Cd 45.15N 19.42 E
Futuna, Ile- 57 Jf 14.17S 178.09W
Fuwah 24 Dg 31.12N 30.33 E
Fuxian (Wafangdian) 27 Ld 39.38N 121.59 E
Fuxian Hu 27 Hg 24.30N 102.55 E
Fuxin 22 Oe 41.59N 121.38 E
Fuxin Monggolzu Zizhixian 28 Fc 42.06N 121.46 E
Fuyang 27 Ke 32.47N 115.46 E
Fuyang He 28 Dg 38.14N 116.05 E
Fuyang Zhan 28 Ch 32.56N 115.53 E
Fuyu [China] 27 Lb 45.10N 124.52 E
Fuyu [China] 27 Lb 47.48N 124.26 E
Fuyuan [China] 27 Lc 42.44N 124.57 E
Fuyuan [China] 27 Nb 48.21N 134.18 E
Fuyuan [China] 27 Hf 25.43N 104.20 E
Fuyun/Koktokay 22 Ke 47.13N 89.39 E
Füzesabony 10 Qi 47.45N 20.25 E
Fuzhou [China] 22 Ng 26.10N 119.20 E
Fuzhou [China] 27 Kf 27.58N 116.20 E
Fuzhou He 28 Fe 39.36N 121.35 E
Fyllas Bank (EN) 41 Gf 64.00N 53.00W
Fyn 5 Hd 55.20N 10.30 E
Fyn [2] 8 Di 55.20N 10.30 E
Fyne, Loch- 9 He 56.10N 5.20W
Fyresdal 7 Bg 59.11N 8.06 E
Fyresvatn 8 Ce 59.05N 8.10 E
Fzåra, Garaʼet- 14 Bn 36.47N 7.30 E

G

Gaasbeek 12 Gd 50.48N 4.10 E
Gaasterland 12 Hb 52.54N 5.36 E
Gaasterland 12 Hb 52.53N 5.35 E
Gaasterland-Balk 12 Hb 52.54N 5.36 E
Gabaru Reef 64a Bb 7.53N 134.31 E
Gabas 11 Fk 43.46N 0.42W
Gabba' 35 Id 8.02N 50.08 E
Gabbs 46 Gg 38.52N 117.55W
Gabela 31 Ij 10.52S 14.23 E
Gabès, Gulf of-(EN)=Qābis, Khalīj- 30 Ie 34.00N 10.25 E
Gabon 36 Ab 0.25N 9.20 E
Gabon [1] 31 Ii 1.00S 11.45 E
Gaborone 31 Jk 24.40S 25.55 E
Gabras 35 Dc 10.16N 26.14 E
Gabriel Strait 42 Kd 61.50N 65.40W
Gabriel y Galán, Embalse de- 13 Fd 40.15N 6.15W
Gabrovo 15 Ig 42.52N 25.19 E
Gabrovo [2] 15 Ig 42.52N 25.19 E
Gacé 11 Gf 48.48N 0.18 E
Gachsārān 24 Ng 30.12N 50.47 E
Gackle 45 Gc 46.38N 99.09W
Gacko 14 Mg 43.10N 18.32 E
Gadag 25 Fe 15.25N 75.37 E
Gäddede 7 Dd 64.30N 14.09 E
Gadê 27 Ge 34.13N 99.29 E
Gadjač 16 Id 50.22N 34.01 E
Gádor, Sierra de- 13 Jh 36.55N 2.45W
Gadsden 43 Je 34.02N 86.02W
Gadūk, Gardaneh-ye- 24 Oe 35.55N 52.55 E
Gadzi 35 Be 4.47N 16.42 E
Gael Hamkes Bugt 41 Jd 74.00N 22.00W
Găeşti 15 Ie 44.43N 25.19 E
Gaeta 14 Hi 41.12N 13.35 E
Gaeta, Golfo di- 14 Hi 41.05N 13.30 E
Gaferut Island 57 Fd 9.14N 145.23 E
Gaffney 44 Gh 35.05N 81.39W
Gagan 63a Ba 5.14S 154.37 E
Gagarin [R.S.F.S.R.] 19 Dd 55.35N 35.01 E
Gagarin [Uzb.-U.S.S.R.] 18 Gd 40.40N 68.05 E
Gagévésouva, Pointe- 63b Ca 13.04S 166.32 E
Gaggenau 12 Kf 48.48N 8.20 E
Gagnef 7 Df 60.35N 15.04 E
Gagnoa 31 Gh 6.08N 5.56W
Gagnoa [3] 34 Dd 6.03N 6.00W
Gagnon 42 Kf 51.55N 68.10W
Gagra 19 Eg 43.17N 40.15 E
Gahkom 24 Ph 28.12N 55.50 E
Gahkom, Kūh-e- 24 Ph 28.10N 55.57 E
Gaiba, Laguna- 55 Dc 17.45S 57.43W
Gail 14 Hd 46.36N 13.53 E
Gaillac 11 Hk 43.54N 1.55 E
Gaillefontaine 12 De 49.39N 1.37 E
Gaillimh/Galway 6 Fe 53.16N 9.03W
Gaillimh/Galway [2] 9 Eh 53.20N 9.00W
Gaillon 12 De 49.10N 1.20 E
Gailtaler Alpen 14 Gd 46.40N 13.00 E
Gaiman 56 Gf 43.17S 65.29W
Găineşti 15 Ib 47.25N 25.55 E
Gainesville [Fl.-U.S.] 39 Kg 29.40N 82.20W
Gainesville [Ga.-U.S.] 43 Ke 34.18N 83.50W
Gainesville [Mo.-U.S.] 45 Jh 36.36N 92.26W
Gainesville [Tx.-U.S.] 43 He 33.37N 97.08W
Gainsborough 9 Mh 53.24N 0.46W
Gairdner, Lake- 57 Eh 31.35S 136.00 E
Gairloch 9 Hd 57.43N 5.40W
Gaizina Kalns/Gajzinkalns 8 Kh 56.50N 25.59 E
Gaj 19 Fe 51.31N 58.30 E
Gajny 19 Fc 60.20N 54.15 E
Gajsin 19 Cf 48.50N 29.27 E
Gajvoron 16 Fe 48.22N 29.52 E
Gajzinkalns/Gaizina Kalns 8 Kh 56.50N 25.59 E
Galaasija 18 Ee 39.52N 64.27 E
Gălăbovo 15 Ig 42.08N 25.51 E
Gala Gölü 15 Ji 40.45N 26.12 E
Galaico, Macizo- 13 Eb 42.30N 7.20W
Galán, Cerro- 56 Gc 25.55S 66.52W
Galana 30 Li 3.09S 40.08 E
Galanta 10 Nh 48.12N 17.44 E
Galap 64a Bb 7.38N 134.39 E
Galápagos, Islas-/Colón, Archipiélago de-=Galapagos Islands (EN) 52 Gf 0.30S 90.30W
Galapagos Fracture Zone (EN) 3 Mi 0.00 100.00W
Galapagos Islands (EN)=Colón, Archipiélago de-/Galápagos, Islas- 52 Gf 0.30S 90.30W
Galapagos Islands (EN)=Galápagos, Islas-/Colón, Archipiélago de- 52 Gf 0.30S 90.30W
Galarza 55 Di 28.06S 56.41W
Galashiels 9 Kf 55.37N 2.49W
Galaţi 6 If 45.27N 28.03 E
Galaţi [2] 15 Kd 45.33N 27.56 E
Galatina 14 Mj 40.10N 18.10 E
Galatone 14 Mj 40.09N 18.04 E
Galatzó 13 Oe 39.38N 2.29 E
Galdar 32 Dd 28.09N 15.39W
Galdhøpiggen 7 Bf 61.37N 8.17 E
Galeana [Mex.] 48 Fb 30.07N 107.38W
Galeana [Mex.] 48 Ie 24.50N 100.04W
Galeh Dār 24 Oi 27.38N 52.42 E
Galela 58 Dd 1.50N 127.50 E
Galena [Ak.-U.S.] 40 Hd 64.44N 156.57W
Galena [Il.-U.S.] 45 Ke 42.25N 90.26W
Galeota Point 50 Fg 10.08N 60.59W
Galera, Punta- 56 Fe 39.59S 73.43W
Galera, Rio- 55 Bb 14.25S 60.07W
Galera Point 50 Fg 10.49N 60.55W
Galesburg 43 Ic 40.57N 90.22W
Galga 10 Pi 47.33N 19.43 E
Gal Gaduud [3] 35 Hd 5.00N 47.00 E
Galheirão, Rio- 55 Ja 12.23S 45.05W
Galheiros 55 Ia 13.18S 46.25W
Gali 16 Lh 42.36N 41.42 E
Galič [R.S.F.S.R.] 19 Ed 58.23N 42.21 E
Galič [Ukr.-U.S.S.R.] 16 De 49.06N 24.43 E
Galicea Mare 15 Ge 44.06N 23.18 E
Galicia 5 Fg 43.00N 8.00W
Galicia 13 Eb 43.00N 8.00W
Galicia (EN)=Galicija 5 If 49.50N 21.00 E
Galicia (EN)=Galicija [Eur.] 10 Qg 49.50N 21.00 E
Galicia (EN)=Galicja 10 Qg 49.50N 21.00 E
Galicia (EN)=Galicja 5 If 49.50N 21.00 E
Galicija [Eur.]=Galicia (EN) 10 Qg 49.50N 21.00 E
Galicija [Ukr.-U.S.S.R.] 10 Jg 49.00N 24.00 E
Galicija=Galicia (EN) 5 If 49.50N 21.00 E
Galicja=Galicia (EN) 5 If 49.50N 21.00 E
Galicja=Galicia (EN) 10 Qg 49.50N 21.00 E
Galilee, Lake- 59 Jd 22.20S 145.55 E
Galimy 20 Kd 62.19N 156.00 E
Galina Point 49 Id 18.24N 76.53W
Galion 44 Fe 40.44N 82.46W
Galion, Baie du- 51h Bb 14.44N 60.57W
Galiton 14 Cm 37.30N 8.52 E
Galiuro Mountains 46 Jj 32.40N 110.20W
Gālka'yo 31 Lh 6.49N 47.23 E
Galkino 17 Ki 55.40N 62.55 E
Gallarate 14 Ce 45.40N 8.47 E
Gallatin 44 Dg 36.24N 86.27W
Gallatin Range 46 Jd 45.15N 111.05W
Gallatin River 46 Jd 45.56N 111.29W
Galle 22 Ki 6.02N 80.13 E
Gállego 13 Lc 41.39N 0.51W
Gallegos, Río- 52 Jk 51.36S 68.59W
Gallinas, Punta- 52 Id 12.25N 71.40W
Gallinas Peak 45 Di 34.15N 105.45W
Gallipoli 14 Lj 40.03N 17.58 E
Gallipoli Peninsula (EN)=Gelibolu Yarimadası 15 Ji 40.20N 26.30 E
Gallipolis 44 Ff 38.49N 82.14W
Gällivare 6 Ib 67.08N 20.42 E
Galljaaral 18 Fd 40.02N 67.35 E
Gallo 13 Jd 40.48N 2.09W
Gällö 7 De 62.55N 15.14 E
Gallo, Capo- 14 Hl 38.15N 13.19 E
Gallo Mountains 45 Bi 34.00N 108.15W
Galloway 9 If 55.00N 4.25W
Galloway, Mull of- 9 Ig 54.38N 4.50W
Gallup 39 If 35.32N 108.44W
Gallur 13 Kc 41.52N 1.19W
Gallura 14 Dj 41.00N 9.15 E
Galmaarden/Gammerages 12 Fd 50.45N 3.58 E
Galole 36 Hc 1.30S 40.02 E
Galt 44 Gd 43.22N 80.19W
Gal Tardo 35 He 3.37N 45.58 E
Galtasen 8 Eg 57.48N 13.30 E
Galty Mountains/Na Gaibhlte 9 Ei 52.23N 8.11W
Galut 27 Hb 46.43N 100.08 E
Galveston 39 Jg 29.18N 94.48W
Galveston Bay 38 Jg 29.36N 94.57W
Galveston Island 45 Il 29.13N 94.55W
Gálvez 56 Hd 32.02S 61.13W
Galway/Gaillimh [2] 9 Eh 53.20N 9.00W
Galway/Gaillimh 6 Fe 53.16N 9.03W
Galway Bay/Cuan na Gaillimhe 5 Fe 53.10N 9.15W
Gamaches 12 De 49.59N 1.33 E
Gamagōri 29 Ed 34.49N 137.13 E
Gamarra 54 Db 8.19N 73.44W
Gamba [China] 27 Ef 28.17N 88.31 E
Gamba [Gabon] 36 Ac 2.37S 10.00 E
Gambaga 34 Ec 10.32N 0.26W
Gambela 31 Kh 8.15N 34.36 E
Gambell 40 Ed 63.46N 171.46W
Gambia 30 Fg 13.28N 16.34W
Gambia [1] 31 Fg 13.25N 16.00W
Gambie 34 Bc 13.28N 16.34W
Gambier, Iles-=Gambier Islands (EN) 57 Ng 23.09S 134.58W
Gambier Islands (EN)=Gambier, Iles- 57 Ng 23.09S 134.58W
Gambo 35 Ce 4.39N 22.16 E
Gamboma 36 Cc 1.53S 15.51 E
Gambos 36 Be 14.45S 14.05 E
Gamboula 35 Be 4.08N 15.09 E
Gamda → Zamtang 27 He 32.23N 101.05 E
Gamelão 55 Db 15.29S 57.50W
Gamkonora, Gunung- 26 If 1.21N 127.31 E
Gamlakarleby/Kokkola 6 Ic 63.50N 23.07 E
Gamla Uppsala 8 Ge 59.54N 17.38 E
Gamleby 7 Dh 57.54N 16.24 E
Gamo Gofa [3] 35 Fd 5.45N 37.20 E
Gamua 64h Bb 13.15S 176.08W
Gamud 35 Fe 4.05N 38.06 E
Gamvik 7 Ga 71.03N 28.14 E
Ganāne, Webi-=Juba (EN) 30 Lh 0.15S 42.38 E
Gananoque 44 Ic 44.20N 76.10W
Ganāveh 24 Nh 29.32N 50.31 E
Gancedo 55 Bh 27.30S 61.42W
Gancevičí 16 Ec 52.45N 26.29 E
Gand/Gent=Ghent (EN) 11 Jc 51.03N 3.43 E
Ganda 36 Be 12.59S 14.40 E
Gandadiwata, Bulu- 26 Gg 2.42S 119.27 E
Gandajika 36 Dd 6.45S 23.57 E
Gandak 25 Hc 25.39N 85.13 E
Gander 39 Ne 48.57N 54.34W
Ganderkesee 12 Ka 53.04N 8.33 E
Gandesa 13 Mc 41.03N 0.26 E
Gandhinagar 22 Jg 23.21N 72.40 E
Gāndhi Sāgar 25 Fd 24.30N 75.30 E
Gandia 13 Lf 38.58N 0.11W
Gandía-Grao de Gandía 13 Lf 38.59N 0.09W
Gandisê Shan 21 Kf 31.00N 83.00 E
Gandu 54 Kf 13.45S 39.30W
Ganetti 35 Eb 17.58N 31.13 E
Ganga=Ganges (EN) 21 Lg 23.20N 90.30 E
Gangaw 25 Id 22.10N 94.08 E
Gangca (Shaliuhe) 27 Hd 37.30N 100.14 E
Ganges 11 Jk 43.56N 3.42 E
Ganges (EN)=Ganga 21 Lg 23.20N 90.30 E
Ganges, Mouths of the- (EN) 21 Lg 23.20N 90.30 E
Gangi 14 Im 37.48N 14.12 E
Gango 36 Cd 9.48S 15.40 E
Gangtok 22 Kg 27.20N 88.37 E
Gangu 27 Ie 34.45N 105.12 E
Gangziyao 28 Cf 36.17N 114.06 E
Gan He 27 Mb 49.12N 125.14 E
Ganhe 27 La 50.43N 123.00 E
Gani 26 Ig 0.47S 128.13 E
Ganjgah 24 Md 37.42N 48.16 E
Gan Jiang 21 Ng 29.12N 116.00 E
Ganjig→Horqin Zuoyi Houqi 27 Lc 42.57N 122.14 E
Gannan 27 Lb 47.53N 123.26 E
Gannat 11 Jh 46.06N 3.12 E
Gannett Peak 38 Ie 43.10N 109.40W
Gansbaai 37 Bf 34.35S 19.22 E
Gansu Sheng (Kan-su Sheng)=Kansu (EN) [2] 27 Hd 38.00N 102.00 E
Ganta 34 Dd 7.14N 8.59W
Gantang → Taiping 28 Ei 30.18N 118.07 E
Ganyu (Qingkou) 28 Eg 34.50N 119.07 E
Ganzhou 22 Ng 25.49N 114.56 E
Gao [3] 34 Eb 18.15N 1.00W
Gao [Mali] 31 Hg 16.15N 0.01 E
Gao [Niger] 34 Gb 15.25N 5.45 E
Gao'an 27 Kf 28.27N 115.24 E
Gaobeidian → Xincheng 28 Ce 39.20N 115.50 E
Gaocheng 28 Ce 38.02N 114.50 E
Gaolan (Shidongsi) 27 Hd 36.23N 103.55 E
Gaoliangjian → Hongze 27 Ke 33.10N 119.58 E
Gaoligong Shan 27 Gf 25.45N 98.45 E
Gaolou Ling 27 Ig 24.47N 106.48 E
Gaomi 28 Ef 36.23N 119.45 E
Gaoping 27 Jd 35.46N 112.55 E
Gaoqing (Tianzhen) 28 Df 37.10N 117.50 E
Gaotai 27 Gd 39.20N 99.58 E
Gaotingzhen→Daishan 28 Gi 30.15N 122.13 E
Gaoua 34 Ec 10.20N 3.11W
Gaoual 34 Cc 11.45N 13.12W
Gaoyang 28 Ce 38.42N 115.47 E
Gaoyi 28 Cf 37.37N 114.37 E
Gaoyou 28 Eh 32.46N 119.27 E
Gaoyou Hu 27 Ke 32.50N 119.15 E
Gaozhou 27 Jg 21.56N 110.47 E
Gap 11 Mj 44.34N 6.05 E
Gar 27 Ce 32.12N 79.57 E
Gara, Lough-/Loch Ui Ghadra 9 Eh 53.55N 8.30W
Gara'ad 35 Hd 6.54N 49.20 E
Garabato 55 Bi 28.56S 60.09W
Garachiné 49 Hi 8.04N 78.22W
Garachiné, Punta- 49 Hi 8.06N 78.25W
Gara Dragoman 15 Fg 42.55N 22.56 E
Ga'raet el Oubeïra 14 Cn 36.50N 8.23 E
Gara Kostenec 15 Gg 42.18N 23.52 E
Garalo 34 Dc 11.00N 7.26W
Gara Muleta 35 Gd 9.05N 41.43 E
Garanhuns 53 Mf 8.54S 36.29W
Garapan 64b Ba 15.12N 145.43 E
Garapuava 55 Ic 16.06S 46.33W
Garavuti 18 Gf 37.36N 68.29 E
Garba 35 Cd 9.12N 20.30 E
Garbahārrey 35 Ge 3.20N 42.17 E
Garberville 46 Df 40.06N 123.48W
Gārbosh, Kūh-e- 24 Nf 32.36N 50.04 E
Garça 55 Hf 22.14S 49.37W
Garças, Rio das- 55 Fb 15.54S 52.16W
Garcias 55 Fe 20.34S 52.13W
Gard [3] 11 Jj 44.00N 4.00 E
Gard 11 Kk 43.51N 4.37 E
Garda 14 Ee 45.34N 10.42 E
Garda, Lago di-=Garda, Lake- (EN) 5 Hf 45.35N 10.35 E
Garda, Lake- (EN)=Garda, Lago di- 5 Hf 45.35N 10.35 E
Gardabani 16 Ni 41.29N 45.05 E
Garde, Cap de- 14 Bn 36.58N 7.47 E
Gardelegen 10 Hd 52.32N 11.22 E
Garden City [Ga.-U.S.] 44 Gi 32.06N 81.09W
Garden City [Ks.-U.S.] 43 Gd 37.58N 100.53W
Garden Grove 46 Gj 33.46N 117.57W
Garden Peninsula 44 Dc 45.40N 86.35W
Gardermoen 8 Dd 60.13N 11.06 E
Gardey 55 Cm 37.17S 59.21W
Gardēz 23 Kc 33.37N 69.07 E
Gardiner 46 Jd 45.02N 110.42W
Gardiner Range 59 Fc 19.15S 128.50 E
Gardner→Nikumaroro Atoll 57 Je 4.40S 174.32W
Gardner Pinnacles 57 Kb 25.00N 167.55W
Gardno, Jezioro- 10 Nb 54.43N 17.05 E
Gardone Riviera 14 Ee 45.37N 10.34 E
Gardždai/Gargždaj 7 Ei 55.43N 21.24 E
Gareloi 40a Cb 51.47N 178.48W
Garessio 14 Cf 44.12N 8.02 E
Garfagnana 14 Ef 44.05N 10.30 E
Gargaliánoi 15 El 37.04N 21.38 E
Gargano 5 Hg 41.50N 16.00 E
Gargano, Testa del- 14 Ki 41.35N 16.12 E
Gargantua, Cape- 44 Eb 47.36N 85.02W
Gargždai/Gargždaj 7 Ei 55.43N 21.24 E
Gari 19 Gd 59.28N 62.25 E
Garibaldi 55 Gi 29.15S 51.32W
Garibaldi, Mount- 46 Db 49.51N 123.01W
Garies 37 Bf 30.30S 18.00 E
Garigliano 14 Hi 41.13N 13.45 E
Garimpo 55 Ed 18.41S 54.50W
Garissa 31 Ki 0.28S 39.38 E

Index Symbols

[1] Independent Nation
[2] State, Region
[3] District, County
[4] Municipality
[5] Colony, Dependency
Continent
Physical Region
Historical or Cultural Region
Mount, Mountain
Volcano
Hill
Mountains, Mountain Range
Hills, Escarpment
Plateau, Upland
Pass, Gap
Plain, Lowland
Delta
Salt Flat
Valley, Canyon
Crater, Cave
Karst Features
Depression
Polder
Desert, Dunes
Forest, Woods
Heath, Steppe
Oasis
Cape, Point
Coast, Beach
Cliff
Peninsula
Isthmus
Sandbank
Island
Atoll
Rock, Reef
Islands, Archipelago
Rocks, Reefs
Coral Reef
Well, Spring
Geyser
River, Stream
Waterfall Rapids
River Mouth, Estuary
Lake
Salt Lake
Intermittent Lake
Reservoir
Swamp, Pond
Canal
Glacier
Ice Shelf, Pack Ice
Ocean
Sea
Gulf, Bay
Strait, Fjord
Lagoon
Bank
Seamount
Tablemount
Ridge
Shelf
Basin
Escarpment, Sea Scarp
Fracture
Trench, Abyss
National Park, Reserve
Point of Interest
Recreation Site
Cave, Cavern
Historic Site
Ruins
Wall, Walls
Church, Abbey
Temple
Scientific Station
Airport
Port
Lighthouse
Mine
Tunnel
Dam, Bridge

Name	Page	Grid	Lat.	Long.
Garkida	34	Hc	10.25N	12.34 E
Garland	45	Hj	32.54N	96.39W
Garlasco	14	Ce	45.12N	8.55 E
Garliava/Garljava	8	Jj	54.46N	23.55 E
Garljava/Garliava	8	Jj	54.46N	23.55 E
Garm	18	He	39.02N	70.18 E
Garmisch-Partenkirchen	10	Hi	47.30N	11.06 E
Garmsar	24	Oe	35.20N	52.13 E
Garnet Bank (EN)	55	Hk	33.05S	49.25W
Garnet Range	46	Ic	46.45N	113.15W
Garnett	45	Ig	38.17N	95.14W
Garonne	5	Ff	45.02N	0.36W
Garonne, Canal latéral à la-	11	Fj	44.34N	0.09W
Garopâba	55	Hi	28.04S	48.40W
Garoua	31	Ih	9.18N	13.24 E
Garoua Boulaï	35	Ad	5.53N	14.33 E
Garoubi	34	Fc	13.07N	2.18 E
Garöwe	31	Lh	8.25N	48.33 E
Garpenberg	8	Gd	60.19N	16.12 E
Garphyttan	8	Fe	59.19N	14.56 E
Garrel	12	Kb	52.57N	8.01 E
Garreru	64a	Bc	7.20N	134.33 E
Garri, Kūh-e-	24	Mf	33.59N	48.25 E
Garrigues	11	Kj	44.10N	4.30 E
Garrison	45	Fc	47.40N	101.25W
Garron Point/An Gearran	9	Hf	55.05N	5.58W
Garrovillas	13	Fe	39.43N	6.33W
Garruchos	55	Ei	28.11S	55.39W
Garry	9	Je	56.45N	3.45W
Garry Bay	42	Ic	69.00N	85.10W
Garry Lake	38	Jc	66.00N	100.00W
Garsen	36	Hc	2.16S	40.07 E
Gartar/Qianning	27	He	30.27N	101.29 E
Gartempe	11	Gh	46.47N	0.50 E
Gartog → Markam	27	Gf	29.32N	98.33 E
Garut	26	Eh	7.13S	107.54 E
Garuva	55	Hh	26.01S	48.51W
Garvie Mountains	62	Cf	45.30S	168.50 E
Garwa	25	Gd	24.11N	83.49 E
Garwolin	10	Re	51.54N	21.37 E
Gary	43	Jc	41.36N	87.20W
Garyarsa	27	De	31.40N	80.26 E
Garzê	27	Ge	31.42N	99.58 E
Garzón [Col.]	54	Cc	2.13N	75.38W
Garzón [Ur.]	56	Jd	34.36S	54.33W
Gasan-Kuli	19	Fh	37.29N	53.59 E
Gascogne = Gascony (EN)	11	Gk	43.30N	0.10 E
Gasconade River	45	Kg	38.40N	91.33W
Gascony (EN) = Gascogne	11	Gk	43.30N	0.10 E
Gascoyne Junction	59	De	25.03S	115.12 E
Gascoyne River	57	Cg	24.52S	113.37 E
Gasefjord	41	Je	70.00N	27.30W
Gaseland	41	Jd	70.20N	29.00W
Gash	30	Kg	16.48N	35.51 E
Gas Hu	27	Fd	38.08N	90.45 E
Gashua	31	Ig	12.52N	11.03 E
Gaspar Strait (EN)=Kelasa, Selat-	26	Eg	2.40S	107.15 E
Gaspé	39	Me	48.50N	64.29W
Gaspé, Cap de-	42	Lg	48.45N	64.10W
Gaspé, Péninsule de-= Gaspe Peninsula (EN)	38	Me	48.30N	65.00W
Gaspe Peninsula (EN)= Gaspé, Péninsule de-	38	Me	48.30N	65.00W
Gassan	29	Gb	38.34N	140.01 E
Gassol	34	Hd	8.32N	10.28 E
Gaston, Lake-	44	Ig	36.35N	78.00W
Gastonia	43	Kd	35.16N	81.11W
Gastoúni	15	El	37.51N	21.15 E
Gastre	56	Gf	42.17S	69.14W
Gästrikland	8	Gd	60.30N	16.30 E
Gata, Akrotérion-	24	Ee	34.34N	33.02 E
Gata, Cabo de-	5	Fh	36.43N	2.12W
Gata, Sierra de-	13	Fd	40.15N	6.45W
Gătaia	15	Ed	45.26N	21.26 E
Gatčina	19	Dd	59.34N	30.09 E
Gate	45	Fh	36.51N	100.01W
Gate City	44	Fg	36.38N	82.37W
Gateshead	9	Lg	54.58N	1.37W
Gateshead	42	Hb	70.35N	100.15W
Gathemo	12	Bf	48.46N	0.58W
Gâtinais	11	If	48.00N	2.20 E
Gâtine, Hauteurs de-	11	Fh	46.38N	0.38W
Gatineau, Rivière-	42	Jg	45.27N	75.42W
Gatlinburg	44	Fh	35.43N	83.31W
Gato, Cumbres del-	48	Fd	27.00N	106.35W
Gatooma	31	Jj	18.21S	29.55 E
Gattinara	14	Ce	45.37N	8.22 E
Gatún	49	Hi	9.16N	79.55W
Gatún, Lago-=Gatun Lake (EN)	47	Ig	9.12N	79.55W
Gatun Lake (EN)=Gatún, Lago-	47	Ig	9.12N	79.55W
Gatvand	24	Mf	32.15N	48.50 E
Gatwick Airport	12	Bc	51.08N	0.12W
Gaucín	13	Gh	36.31N	5.19W
Gauhati	22	Lg	26.11N	91.44 E
Gauiena/Gaujiena	8	Lg	57.25N	26.28 E
Gauja	7	Fh	57.10N	24.16 E
Gaujiena/Gauiena	8	Lg	57.25N	26.28 E
Gaula [Nor.]	8	Da	63.21N	10.14 E
Gaula [Nor.]	8	Ac	61.22N	5.41 E
Gauldalen	8	Db	63.00N	11.00 E
Gauley River	44	Gf	38.10N	81.12W
Gau-Odernheim	12	Ke	49.46N	8.12 E
Gaurdak	19	Gh	37.49N	66.01 E
Gausdal	8	Cc	61.20N	9.55 E
Gausta	7	Bg	59.50N	8.39 E
Gāvbandī	24	Oi	27.12N	53.04 E
Gāvbūs, Kūh-e-	24	Oi	27.10N	54.00 E
Gavdhopoúla	15	Go	34.56N	24.00 E
Gávdhos	5	Ii	34.50N	24.05 E
Gāveh	24	Le	35.00N	46.58 E
Gavere	12	Fd	50.56N	3.40 E
Gavkhūnī, Bātlāq-e-	24	Of	32.06N	52.52 E
Gāv Kosh	24	Le	34.00N	48.00 E
Gävle	6	Hc	60.40N	17.10 E
Gävleborg [2]	7	Df	61.30N	16.15 E
Gävlebukten	8	Gd	60.40N	17.20 E
Gavorrano	14	Eh	42.55N	10.54 E
Gavri	8	Lh	56.49N	27.58 E
Gavrilov-Jam	7	Jh	57.19N	39.51 E
Gāw Koshi	23	Id	28.38N	57.12 E
Gawler	59	Hf	34.37S	138.44 E
Gawler Ranges	57	Eh	32.30S	136.00 E
Gaxun Nur	21	Me	42.25N	101.00 E
Gaya [India]	22	Kg	24.47N	85.00 E
Gaya [Niger]	34	Fc	11.53N	3.27 E
Gaya He	28	Jc	42.58N	129.52 E
Gaylord	44	Ec	45.02N	84.40W
Gayndah	59	Ke	25.37S	151.36 E
Gaz	24	Nf	32.48N	51.37 E
Gaza [3]	37	Ed	23.30S	33.00 E
Gaz-Ačak	19	Gg	41.11N	61.27 E
Gazalkent	18	Gd	41.33N	69.46 E
Gazaoua	34	Gc	13.32N	7.55 E
Gazelle, Récif de la-	63b	Be	20.11S	165.27 E
Gaziantep	22	Ff	37.05N	37.22 E
Gaziemir	15	Kk	38.19N	27.10 E
Gazimur	20	Hf	52.57N	120.22 E
Gazipaşa	24	Ed	36.17N	32.20 E
Gazli	19	Gg	40.09N	63.23 E
Gbarnga	31	Gh	7.00N	9.29W
Gboko	34	Gd	7.21N	8.58 E
Gbon	34	Dd	9.50N	6.27W
Gdańsk [2]	10	Ob	54.25N	18.40 E
Gdańsk=Danzig (EN)	6	He	54.23N	18.40 E
Gdansk, Gulf of- (EN)= Gdanska, Zatoka-	5	He	54.40N	19.15 E
Gdánska, Zatoka-=Gdansk, Gulf of- (EN)	5	He	54.40N	19.15 E
Gdov	7	Gg	58.47N	27.54 E
Gdynia	6	He	54.32N	18.33 E
Gearhart Mountain	46	Ee	42.30N	120.53W
Gêba	34	Bc	11.58N	15.00W
Gebe, Pulau-	26	Ig	0.05S	129.20 E
Gebze	24	Cb	40.48N	29.25 E
Gecha	35	Fd	7.29N	35.25 E
Gedi	36	Hc	3.18S	40.01 E
Gedinne	12	Ge	49.59N	4.56 E
Gediz	24	Cc	39.02N	29.25 E
Gedo	35	Ge	2.20N	41.20 E
Gedo [3]	35	Ge	3.00N	42.00 E
Gedo	35	Fd	9.00N	37.29 E
Gedser, Sydfalster-	7	Ci	54.35N	11.57 E
Gedser Odde	8	Dj	54.34N	11.59 E
Geel	11	Kc	51.10N	5.00 E
Geelong	58	Fh	38.08S	144.21 E
Geelvink Channel	59	Ce	28.30S	114.10 E
Geer	12	Hd	50.51N	5.42 E
Geeste	12	Jb	52.36N	7.16 E
Geesthacht	10	Gc	53.26N	10.22 E
Gê'gyai	27	De	32.29N	80.52 E
Ge Hu	28	Ei	31.36N	119.51 E
Geidam	34	Hc	12.53N	11.56 E
Geigar	35	Ec	11.59N	32.46 E
Geihoku	29	Cd	34.44N	132.17 E
Geikie	42	He	57.48N	103.46W
Geilo	7	Bf	60.31N	8.12 E
Geiranger	8	Bb	62.06N	7.12 E
Geisenheim	12	Je	49.59N	7.58 E
Geislingen an der Steige	10	Fh	48.37N	9.51 E
Geita	36	Fc	2.52S	32.10 E
Geithus	7	Bg	59.57N	9.59 E
Geiyo-Shotō	29	Cd	34.15N	132.45 E
Gejiu	22	Mg	23.22N	103.14 E
Gel [Sud.]	30	Jh	7.46N	29.36 E
Gel [Sud.]	35	Ed	6.08N	31.17 E
Gela	14	Im	37.04N	14.15 E
Gela, Golfo di-	14	Im	37.05N	14.10 E
Geladi	35	Hd	6.57N	46.25 E
Geldenaken/Jodoigne	12	Gd	50.43N	4.52 E
Gelderland [3]	12	Hb	52.10N	5.50 E
Geldermalsen	12	Hc	51.53N	5.19 E
Geldern	10	Ce	51.31N	6.20 E
Geldrop	12	Hc	51.25N	5.33 E
Geleen	11	Ld	50.58N	5.52 E
Gelembé	15	Kj	39.10N	27.50 E
Gelemso	35	Gd	8.48N	40.32 E
Gelendžik	19	Dg	44.33N	38.06 E
Gélengdeng	35	Bc	10.56N	15.32 E
Gelgaudiškis	8	Ji	55.02N	22.58 E
Gelibolu	24	Bb	40.24N	26.40 E
Gelibolu Yarimadası = Gallipoli Peninsula (EN)	15	Ji	40.20N	26.30 E
Gélise	11	Gj	44.11N	0.17 E
Gellinsör	35	Hd	6.24N	46.46 E
Gelnhausen	10	Ff	50.12N	9.11 E
Gelsenkirchen	10	De	51.31N	7.06 E
Gemena	31	Ih	3.15N	19.46 E
Gemerek	24	Gc	39.11N	36.05 E
Gemert	12	Hc	51.33N	5.41 E
Gemi, Jabal-	35	Ed	9.01N	34.09 E
Gemlik	24	Cb	40.26N	29.09 E
Gemlik Körfezi	24	Cb	40.25N	28.55 E
Gemona del Friuli	14	Hd	46.16N	13.09 E
Gemünden (Felda)	12	Ld	50.42N	9.03 E
Gemünden (Wohra)	12	Kd	50.58N	8.58 E
Gemünden am Main	10	Ff	50.03N	9.42 E
Genale	30	Lh	0.15S	42.38 E
Genç	24	Ic	38.46N	40.35 E
Gendringen	12	Ic	51.52N	6.23 E
Gendringen-Ulft	12	Ic	51.54N	6.24 E
Genemuiden	12	Ib	52.37N	6.02 E
General Acha	56	He	37.23S	64.36W
General Alvear [Arg.]	56	Gd	34.58S	67.42W
General Alvear [Arg.]	56	Ie	36.03S	60.01W
General Arenales	55	Bl	34.18S	61.18W
General Artigas	55	Dh	26.53S	56.17W
General Belgrano	56	Ie	35.46S	58.30W
General Belgrano Station	66	Af	77.50S	38.00W
General Bernardo O'Higgins	66	Re	63.19S	57.54W
General Bravo	48	Je	25.48N	99.10W
General Cabrera	56	Hd	32.48S	63.52W
General Capdevila	55	Bh	27.26S	61.28W
General Carneiro	55	Gh	26.28S	51.25W
General Carrera, Lago-	52	Ij	46.30S	72.00W
General Cepeda	48	Ie	25.23N	101.27W
General Conesa [Arg.]	55	Dm	36.30S	57.20W
General Conesa [Arg.]	56	Hf	40.06S	64.26W
General Enrique Martinez	55	Fk	33.12S	53.50W
General Galarza	55	Ck	32.43S	59.24W
General Güemes	56	Hb	24.40S	65.00W
General Guide	56	Ie	36.40S	57.46W
General José de San Martin	55	Ch	26.33S	59.21W
General Juan Madariaga	56	Ie	37.00S	57.09W
General La Madrid	56	He	37.16S	61.17W
General Lavalle	56	Ie	36.24S	56.58W
General Manuel Belgrano, Cerro-	52	Jh	29.01S	67.49W
General O'Brien	55	Bl	34.54S	60.45W
General Pico	56	He	35.40S	63.44W
General Pinedo	56	Hc	27.19S	61.17W
General Pinto	55	Bl	34.46S	61.53W
General Pirán	55	Dm	37.16S	57.45W
General Roca	56	Ge	39.02S	67.35W
General Salgado	55	Ge	20.39S	50.22W
General Santos	22	Oi	6.05N	125.10 E
General Sarmiento	55	Cl	34.33S	58.43W
General Terán	48	Je	25.16N	99.41W
General-Toševo	15	Lf	43.42N	28.02 E
General Treviño	48	Jd	26.14N	99.29W
General Trias	48	Fc	28.21N	106.22W
General Vargas	55	Ei	29.42S	54.40W
General Viamonte	55	Bl	35.01S	61.01W
General Villegas	56	He	35.02S	63.01W
Genesee River	44	Id	43.16N	77.36W
Geneseo	44	Id	42.46N	77.49W
Geneva [Al.-U.S.]	44	Ej	31.02N	85.52W
Geneva [Nb.-U.S.]	45	Hf	40.32N	97.36W
Geneva [N.Y.-U.S.]	44	Id	42.53N	76.59W
Geneva (EN) = Genève	6	Gf	46.10N	6.10 E
Geneva, Lake- (EN) = Léman, Lac-	5	Gf	46.25N	6.30 E
Genève [2]	14	Ad	46.10N	6.15 E
Genève = Geneva (EN)	6	Gf	46.10N	6.10 E
Genevois	11	Mh	46.00N	6.10 E
Genhe → Ergun Zuoqi	22	Od	50.47N	121.32 E
Geni	35	Ed	8.31N	33.10 E
Geničesk	19	Df	46.12N	34.48 E
Genil	13	Gg	37.42N	5.19W
Genk	11	Ld	50.58N	5.30 E
Genkai-Nada	29	Ae	33.45N	130.00 E
Gennargentu	14	Dj	40.00N	9.20 E
Gennep	12	Hc	51.42N	5.59 E
Genoa (EN) = Genova	6	Gg	44.25N	8.57 E
Genoa, Gulf of- (EN) = Genova, Golfo di-	5	Gg	44.10N	8.55 E
Genova = Genoa (EN)	6	Gg	44.25N	8.57 E
Genova, Golfo di- = Genoa, Gulf of- (EN)	5	Gg	44.10N	8.55 E
Genova-Nervi	14	Df	44.23N	9.02 E
Genova-Voltri	14	Cf	44.26N	8.45 E
Genovesa, Isla-	54a	Ba	0.20N	89.58W
Gent/Gand=Ghent (EN)	11	Jc	51.03N	3.43 E
Gentbrugge, Gent-	12	Fc	51.03N	3.45 E
Gent-Gentbrugge	12	Fc	51.03N	3.45 E
Genthin	10	Id	52.24N	12.10 E
Gent-Sint-Amandsberg	12	Fc	51.04N	3.45 E
Genū, Kūhhā-ye-	23	Id	27.25N	56.09 E
Genyem	26	Lg	2.46S	140.12 E
Genzano di Lucania	14	Kj	40.51N	16.02 E
Genzano di Roma	14	Fi	41.42N	11.41 E
Geographe Bay	57	Ch	33.35S	115.15 E
Geographe Channel	59	Cd	24.40S	113.20 E
Geographical Society Øer	41	Jd	72.40N	22.20W
Geokčaj	16	Oi	40.40N	47.42 E
Geok-Tepe	19	Fh	38.10N	57.58 E
Geomagnetic Pole (1975) (EN)	66	Hf	78.40S	109.33 E
Georga, Zemlja-	21	Ga	80.30N	49.00 E
George	38	Md	58.30N	66.00W
George	37	Cf	33.58S	22.24 E
George, Lake- [Austl.]	59	Jg	35.05S	149.25 E
George, Lake- [Fl.-U.S.]	44	Gk	29.17N	81.36W
George, Lake- [Ug.]	36	Fc	0.00	30.12 E
George, Lake- [U.S.]	44	Kd	43.35N	73.35W
George Gill Range	59	Gd	24.15S	131.35 E
Georges Bank (EN)	43	Nc	41.15N	67.30W
George Sound	62	Bf	44.50S	167.20 E
George Town	58	Fi	41.06S	146.50 E
Georgetown	45	Hk	30.38N	97.41W
George Town	22	Mi	5.25N	100.20 E
Georgetown [Austl.]	58	Ff	18.18S	143.33 E
Georgetown [Bah.]	49	Jb	23.30N	75.46W
Georgetown [Cay.Is.]	47	He	19.18N	81.23W
Georgetown [De.-U.S.]	44	Jf	38.42N	75.23W
Georgetown [Gam.]	31	Fg	13.32N	14.46W
Georgetown [Guy.]	53	Ke	6.48N	58.10W
Georgetown [Ky.-U.S.]	44	Ef	38.13N	84.33W
Georgetown [Oh.-U.S.]	44	Ff	38.52N	83.54W
Georgetown [S.C.-U.S.]	43	Le	33.23N	79.18W
Georgetown [St.Hel.]	31	Fi	7.56S	14.25W
Georgetown [St.Vin.]	50	Ff	13.16N	61.08W
George V Coast	66	Je	68.30S	147.30 E
George VI Sound	66	Qf	71.00S	68.00W
George West	45	Gl	28.20N	98.07W
Georgia [2]	43	Ke	32.50N	83.15W
Georgia (EN)	5	Kg	42.00N	44.00 E
Georgia, Strait of-	42	Fg	49.00N	123.20W
Georgia del Sur, Islas-/ South Georgia	66	Ad	54.15S	36.45W
Georgian Bay	38	Ke	45.15N	80.50W
Georgian SSR (EN)= Gruzinskaja SSR [2]	19	Eg	42.00N	44.00 E
Georgijevka [Kaz.-U.S.S.R.]	19	Hg	43.02N	74.43 E
Georgijevka [Kaz.-U.S.S.R.]	19	If	49.19N	81.35 E
Georgijevsk	16	Mg	44.09N	43.28 E
Georgina River	57	Eg	23.30S	139.47 E
Georgsmarienhütte	10	Ed	52.16N	8.02 E
Gera	10	Ge	51.08N	10.56 E
Gera	10	If	50.52N	12.05 E
Gera [2]	10	Hf	50.45N	11.55 E
Geraardsbergen/Grammont	12	Fd	50.46N	3.52 E
Gerais, Chapadão dos-	55	Jc	17.40S	45.35W
Geral, Serra- [Braz.]	55	Gi	29.10S	50.15W
Geral, Serra- [Braz.]	52	Kh	26.30S	50.30W
Geral, Serra- [Braz.]	55	Gf	23.54S	50.46W
Geral da Serra, Coxilha-	55	Ej	30.20S	55.15W
Geral de Goiás, Serra-	52	Lg	13.00S	46.15W
Geraldine	62	Df	44.05S	171.15 E
Geral do Paraná, Serra-	55	Ib	14.45S	47.30W
Geraldton [Austl.]	58	Cg	28.46S	114.36 E
Geraldton [Ont.-Can.]	42	Ig	49.44N	86.57W
Gérardmer	11	Mf	48.04N	6.53 E
Geräsh	24	Pi	27.40N	54.06 E
Gerbiči, Gora-	20	Fc	66.39N	105.02 E
Gerca	15	Ja	48.10N	26.17 E
Gercüş	24	Id	37.34N	41.23 E
Gerecse	10	Oi	47.41N	18.29 E
Gerede	24	Eb	40.52N	32.39 E
Gerede	24	Eb	40.48N	32.12 E
Gerês, Serra do-	13	Ec	41.48N	8.00W
Gereshk	23	Jc	31.48N	64.34 E
Gérgal	13	Jg	37.07N	2.33W
Gering	45	Ef	41.50N	103.40W
Gerlachovský štít	10	Qg	49.12N	20.09 E
Gerlogubi	35	Hd	6.56N	45.03 E
Gerlos	14	Gc	47.14N	12.02 E
Gerlovo	15	Kf	43.03N	27.35 E
German Democratic Republic (EN)=Deutsche Demokratische Republik [1]	6	He	52.00N	12.30 E
Germania	55	Al	34.34S	62.03W
Germania Land	41	Kc	76.50N	20.00W
Germany, Federal Republic of- (EN)=Bundesrepublik Deutschland [1]	6	Ge	51.00N	9.00 E
Germencik	15	Kl	37.51N	27.37 E
Germersheim	12	Ke	49.13N	8.22 E
Germī	23	Hc	33.32N	54.58 E
Germi	24	Mc	39.01N	48.03 E
Germiston	37	De	26.15S	28.05 E
Gernsbach	12	Kf	48.46N	8.19 E
Gernsheim	12	Ke	49.45N	8.29 E
Gero	28	Ng	35.48N	137.14 E
Gerolstein	12	Id	50.13N	6.40 E
Gerona [3]	13	Ob	42.10N	2.40 E
Gerona/Girona	13	Oc	41.59N	2.49 E
Gerpinnes	12	Gd	50.20N	4.31 E
Gers	11	Gj	44.09N	0.39 E
Gers [3]	11	Gk	43.40N	0.30 E
Gersprenz	12	Le	49.59N	9.04 E
Gêrzê	27	De	32.20N	84.04 E
Gerze	24	Fb	41.48N	35.12 E
Gescher	12	Jc	51.57N	7.00 E
Geseke	12	Kc	51.39N	8.31 E
Geser	26	Jg	3.53S	130.54 E
Gesunda	8	Fd	60.54N	14.32 E
Gesunden	8	Fa	63.10N	15.55 E
Geta	7	Ef	60.23N	19.50 E
Getafe	13	Id	40.18N	3.43W
Gete	11	Ld	50.55N	5.08 E
Getinge	7	Ch	56.49N	12.44 E
Gettysburg	45	Gd	45.01N	99.57W
Gettysburg Seamount (EN)	32	Eb	36.32N	11.37W
Getúlio Vargas	55	Fh	27.50S	52.16W
Getz Ice Shelf	66	Nf	74.15S	125.00W
Geul	12	Hd	50.40N	5.43 E
Gévaudan	11	Jj	44.27N	3.30 E
Gevelsberg	12	Jc	51.19N	7.20 E
Gevgelija	15	Fh	41.08N	22.31 E
Gévora	13	Ff	38.53N	6.57W
Gevsjön	8	Ea	63.25N	12.40 E
Gewane	35	Gc	10.10N	40.39 E
Gex	11	Mh	46.20N	6.04 E
Gexianzhuang → Qinghe	28	Cf	37.03N	115.39 E
Geyersberg	10	Fg	49.50N	9.30 E
Geyik Dağı	24	Ed	36.54N	32.10 E
Geyikli	15	Jj	39.48N	26.12 E
Geyser, Banc du-	37	Hb	12.25S	46.25 E
Geysir	5	Dc	64.19N	20.18W
Geyve	24	Db	40.30N	30.18 E
Ghabārī, Darb al-	24	Cj	25.10N	29.50 E
Ghadāmis	31	He	30.08N	9.30 E
Ghadduwah	33	Bd	26.26N	14.18 E
Ghaghara	21	Kg	24.52N	84.55 E
Ghaghe	63a	Db	7.23S	158.12 E
Ghallah, Wādī al-	30	Jg	10.25N	27.32 E
Ghamrah, Wādī al-	24	Hj	25.47N	38.45 E
Ghana [1]	31	Gh	8.00N	2.00W
Ghanzi	31	Jk	21.42S	21.38 E
Ghanzi [3]	37	Cd	22.00S	23.00 E
Ghār ad Dimā'	14	Cn	36.27N	8.26 E
Gharaqābād	24	Me	35.06N	49.50 E
Gharbī, Al Hajar al-	24	Qj	24.10N	56.15 E
Gharbīyah, Aş Şahrā' al-= Western Desert (EN)	30	Jf	27.30N	28.00 E
Ghardaïa	31	He	32.29N	3.40 E
Ghārib, Jabal-	33	Fd	28.07N	32.54 E
Gharrāf, Shaṭṭ al-	24	Kf	32.30N	45.48 E
Gharsah, Shaṭṭ al-	32	Ic	34.06N	7.50 E
Gharyān	33	Bc	32.10N	13.01 E
Gharyān [3]	33	Bc	30.35N	12.00 E
Ghāt	31	If	24.58N	10.11 E
Ghatere	63a	Db	7.58S	159.01 E
Ghaṭṭī	24	Gg	31.16N	37.31 E
Ghazāl, Baḥr al-	35	Ed	9.31N	30.25 E
Ghazal, Bahr el-	30	Ig	13.01N	15.28 E
Ghazal, Bahr el-	35	Bc	14.00N	16.30 E
Ghazaouet	32	Gb	35.06N	1.51W
Ghazipur	25	Gc	25.35N	83.34 E
Ghaznī	22	If	33.33N	68.26 E
Ghāznī [3]	23	Kc	33.00N	68.00 E
Ghent (EN)=Gand/Gent	11	Jc	51.03N	3.43 E
Ghent (EN)=Gent/Gand	11	Jc	51.03N	3.43 E
Gheorghe Gheorghiu-Dej	15	Jc	46.12N	26.46 E
Gheorghieni	15	Ic	46.43N	25.37 E
Gheorghiu-Dej	19	Dd	51.00N	39.31 E
Gherla	15	Gb	47.02N	23.55 E
Ghidigeni	15	Kc	46.03N	27.30 E
Ghidole (EN)=Gidole	35	Fd	5.37N	37.29 E
Ghilarza	14	Cj	40.07N	8.50 E
Ghimeş, Pasul-	15	Jc	46.33N	26.07 E
Ghisonaccia	11a	Ba	42.00N	9.24 E
Ghizunabeana Islands	63a	Db	7.33S	158.45 E
Ghowr [3]	23	Jc	34.00N	65.00 E
Ghriss	13	Mi	35.15N	0.10 E
Ghubbat al Qamar	21	Hh	16.00N	52.30 E
Ghudāf, Wādī al-	24	Jf	32.56N	43.30 E
Ghurāb, Jabal al-	24	Hf	34.00N	38.42 E
Ghurayrah	33	Hf	18.37N	42.41 E
Ghūriān	23	Jc	34.21N	61.30 E
Ghurrah, Jabal al-	14	Cn	36.36N	8.23 E
Ghuzayyil, Sabkhat-	33	Dd	29.50N	19.45 E
Giaginskaja	16	Lg	44.47N	40.05 E
Giala, Jabal-	24	Ei	27.20N	32.57 E
Gialo Oasis (EN)=Jālū, Wāḥāt-	30	Jf	29.00N	21.20 E
Gialoúsa	24	Fe	35.35N	34.15 E
Gia Nghia	25	Lf	11.59N	107.42 E
Giannutri	14	Fh	42.15N	11.05 E
Giant's Causeway/Clochán an Aifir	9	Gf	55.15N	6.35W
Giarre	14	Jm	37.43N	15.11 E
Gibara	49	Ic	21.07N	76.08W
Gibbon Point	51b	Bb	18.14N	63.00W
Gibb River	59	Fc	16.25S	126.25 E
Gibbs Islands	66	Re	61.30S	55.31W
Gibellina	14	Gm	37.47N	12.58 E
Gibeon [3]	37	Bd	25.00S	18.30 E
Gibeon	37	Be	25.09S	17.43 E
Gibostad	7	Db	69.21N	18.00 E
Gibraleón	13	Fg	37.23N	6.58W
Gibraltar	6	Fh	36.11N	5.22W
Gibraltar [5]	6	Fh	36.11N	5.22W
Gibraltar, Estrecho de-= Gibraltar, Strait of- (EN)	5	Fh	35.57N	5.36W
Gibraltar, Strait of- (EN)= Djebel Ṭāriq, El Bōghāz-	5	Fh	35.57N	5.36W
Gibraltar, Strait of- (EN)= Gibraltar, Estrecho de-	5	Fh	35.57N	5.36W
Gibson Desert	57	Dg	24.30S	126.00 E
Gidami	35	Ed	8.58N	34.40 E
Giddings	45	Hk	30.11N	96.56W
Gidigič	15	Lb	47.04N	28.38 E
Gidole=Ghidole (EN)	35	Fd	5.37N	37.29 E
Gien	11	Ig	47.42N	2.38 E
Giens, Presqu'île de-	11	Mk	43.02N	6.08 E
Gier	11	Ki	45.35N	4.46 E
Gießen	10	Ef	50.35N	8.39 E
Gieten	12	Ia	53.01N	6.48 E
Giethoorn	12	Ib	52.43N	6.07 E
Gifford	42	Jb	70.21N	83.05W
Gifford Seamount (EN)	52	Hi	39.00S	82.00W
Gifhorn	10	Gd	52.29N	10.33 E
Gift Lake	42	Fe	55.49N	115.57W
Gifu	22	Pf	35.25N	136.45 E
Gifu Ken [2]	28	Ng	35.50N	137.00 E
Gigant	16	Lf	46.29N	41.20 E
Giganta, Cerro-	47	Bc	26.07N	111.36W
Giganta, Sierra de la-	47	Bc	26.18N	111.39W
Gigante	54	Cc	2.24N	75.34W
Gigen	15	Hf	43.42N	24.29 E
Gigha	9	Hf	55.41N	5.44W
Giglio	14	Eh	42.20N	10.55 E
Gijón	6	Fg	43.32N	5.40W
Gikongoro	36	Ec	2.30S	29.35 E
Gila Bend	46	Ij	32.57N	112.43W
Gila Bend Mountains	46	Ij	33.10N	113.10W
Gilān [3]	23	Gb	37.00N	49.50 E
Gilān-e-Gharb	24	Ke	34.08N	45.55 E
Gila River	43	Ee	32.43N	114.33W
Gilbert, Mount-	46	Ca	50.51N	124.20W
Gilbert Islands	57	Ie	0.01S	174.00 E
Gilbert River	59	Ic	16.35S	141.15 E
Gilbert Seamount (EN)	40	If	52.50N	150.10W
Gilbués	54	Ie	9.50S	45.21W
Gilé	37	Fc	16.09S	38.19 E
Giles Meteorological Station	59	Fe	25.02S	128.18 E
Gilford Island	46	Ba	50.45N	126.25W
Gilgandra	59	Jf	31.42S	148.39 E
Gilğau	15	Gb	47.17N	23.43 E
Gilgil	36	Gc	0.30S	36.19 E
Gilgit	25	Ea	35.44N	74.38 E
Gilgit	22	Jf	35.55N	74.18 E
Giljuj	20	Hf	54.17N	127.05 E
Gillam	42	Ie	56.21N	94.43W
Gilleleje	8	Eh	56.07N	12.19 E
Gillen, Lake-	59	Ee	26.10S	124.40 E
Gillenfeld	12	Id	50.07N	6.54 E
Gillette	43	Fc	44.18N	105.30W
Gillian, Lake-	42	Jc	69.30N	75.30W
Gillingham	9	Nj	51.24N	0.33 E
Gilo	35	Ed	8.10N	33.15 E
Gilort	15	Ge	44.36N	23.27 E
Gilroy	46	Eh	37.00N	121.34W
Giluwe, Mount-	60	Ci	6.04S	143.53 E
Gilvān	24	Md	36.47N	49.08 E
Gimån	8	Gb	62.28N	16.20 E
Gimbi	35	Fd	9.10N	35.51 E
Gimie, Mount-	50	Ff	13.52N	61.01W
Gimli	42	Hf	50.39N	97.00W
Gimo	8	Hd	60.11N	18.11 E
Gimolskoje, Ozero-	7	He	63.00N	32.15 E
Gimone	11	Hk	44.00N	1.06 E
Ginda	35	Fb	15.27N	39.06 E
Ginetu	63a	Ac	9.30S	152.43 E

Index Symbols

[1] Independent Nation
[2] State, Region
[3] District, County
[4] Municipality
[5] Colony, Dependency
Continent
Physical Region
Historical or Cultural Region
Mount, Mountain
Volcano
Hill
Mountains, Mountain Range
Hills, Escarpment
Plateau, Upland
Pass, Gap
Plain, Lowland
Delta
Salt Flat
Valley, Canyon
Crater, Cave
Karst Features
Depression
Polder
Desert, Dunes
Forest, Woods
Heath, Steppe
Oasis
Cape, Point
Coast, Beach
Cliff
Peninsula
Isthmus
Sandbank
Island
Atoll
Rock, Reef
Islands, Archipelago
Rocks, Reefs
Coral Reef
Well, Spring
Geyser
River, Stream
Waterfall Rapids
River Mouth, Estuary
Lake
Salt Lake
Intermittent Lake
Reservoir
Swamp, Pond
Canal
Glacier
Ice Shelf, Pack Ice
Ocean
Sea
Gulf, Bay
Strait, Fjord
Lagoon
Bank
Seamount
Tablemount
Ridge
Shelf
Basin
Escarpment, Sea Scarp
Fracture
Trench, Abyss
National Park, Reserve
Point of Interest
Recreation Site
Cave, Cavern
Historic Site
Ruins
Wall, Walls
Church, Abbey
Temple
Scientific Station
Airport
Port
Lighthouse
Mine
Tunnel
Dam, Bridge

Gin Gin	59	Kd	25.00S	151.58 E
Gingin	59	Df	31.21S	115.42 E
Gingoog	26	Ie	8.50N	125.07 E
Ginir	35	Gd	7.08N	40.43 E
Ginosa	14	Kj	40.35N	16.45 E
Ginowan	29b	Ab	26.17N	127.45 E
Ginzo de Limia	13	Eb	42.03N	7.43W
Giofra Oasis (EN)=Jufrah, Wāḩāt al- ♣	30	If	29.10N	16.00 E
Gioia, Golfo di- ◧	14	Jl	38.30N	15.45 E
Gioia del Colle	14	Kj	40.48N	16.55 E
Gioia Tauro	14	Jl	38.25N	15.54 E
Gion	35	Fd	8.24N	37.55 E
Gióna Óros ⛰	15	Fk	38.35N	22.15 E
Giovi, Passo dei- ◡	14	Cf	44.33N	8.57 E
Giraltovce	10	Rg	49.07N	21.31 E
Girardot	54	Dc	4.18N	74.49W
Girdle Ness ▶	9	Kd	57.08N	2.02W
Giresun	23	Ea	40.55N	38.24 E
Giresun Dağları ⛰	24	Hb	40.40N	38.10 E
Giri ∿	36	Cb	0.28N	17.59 E
Giridih	25	Hd	24.11N	86.18 E
Giriftu	36	Gb	2.00N	39.45 E
Girne/Kyrenia	24	Ee	35.20N	33.19 E
Girón	54	Cd	3.10S	79.09W
Girona/Gerona	13	Oc	41.59N	2.49 E
Gironde [3]	11	Fj	44.55N	0.30W
Gironde ≈	5	Ff	45.35N	1.03W
Gironella	13	Nb	42.02N	1.53 E
Girou ∿	11	Hk	43.46N	1.23 E
Girvan	9	If	55.15N	4.51W
Girvas	7	He	62.31N	33.44 E
Gisborne	58	Ih	38.39S	178.01 E
Gisenyi	36	Ec	1.42S	29.15 E
Gislaved	8	Eg	57.18N	13.32 E
Gisors	11	He	49.17N	1.47 E
Gissar	18	Ge	38.31N	68.36 E
Gissarski Hrebet ⛰	18	Ge	39.00N	68.40 E
Gistad	8	Ff	58.27N	15.55 E
Gistel	12	Ec	51.10N	2.57 E
Gistral ▲	13	Ea	43.28N	7.35W
Gitarama	36	Ec	2.05S	29.16 E
Gitega	36	Ec	3.26S	29.56 E
Gitu	24	Me	35.20N	48.05 E
Giudicarie, Valli- ◡	14	Ed	46.00N	10.40 E
Giulianova	14	Hh	42.45N	13.57 E
Giumalău, Vîrful- ▲	15	Ib	47.26N	25.29 E
Giurgeni	15	Ke	44.35N	27.48 E
Giurgiu	15	If	43.53N	25.58 E
Give	8	Ci	55.51N	9.15 E
Givors	11	Ki	45.35N	4.46 E
Givry-en-Argonne	12	Gf	48.57N	4.53 E
Givry Island ◆	64d	Bb	7.07N	151.53 E
Giwa	34	Gc	11.18N	7.27 E
Giza (EN)=Al Jīzah	31	Ke	30.01N	31.13 E
Giždu van	19	Gg	40.06N	64.40 E
Gižiga	20	Ld	62.03N	160.30 E
Gižiginskaja Guba ◧	20	Kd	61.10N	158.30 E
Gizo ◆	63a	Cc	8.07S	156.50 E
Gizo	60	Fi	8.06S	156.51 E
Giżycko	10	Rb	54.03N	21.47 E
Gjalicës, Mali i- ▲	15	Dg	42.01N	20.28 E
Gjamyš, Gora- ▲	16	Oi	40.20N	46.25 E
Gjende ≈	8	Cc	61.30N	8.35 E
Gjerstad	8	Cf	58.52N	9.00 E
Gjevilvatn ≈	8	Cb	62.40N	9.25 E
Gjirokastra	15	Di	40.05N	20.10 E
Gjoa Haven	39	Jc	68.38N	95.57W
Gjøvik	6	Hc	60.48N	10.42 E
Gjuhës, Kep i- ▶	15	Ci	40.25N	19.18 E
Glace Bay	42	Lg	46.12N	59.57W
Glacier Bay ◧	40	Le	58.40N	136.00W
Glacier Peak ▲	43	Cb	48.07N	121.07W
Glacier Strait ═	42	Ja	76.15N	79.00W
Gladbeck	12	Ic	51.34N	6.59 E
Gladenbach	12	Kd	50.46N	8.34 E
Gladewater	45	Ij	32.33N	94.56W
Gladstone [Austl.]	58	Gg	23.51S	151.16 E
Gladstone [Man.-Can.]	45	Ga	50.15N	98.50W
Gladstone [Mi.-U.S.]	44	Dc	45.51N	87.03W
Gladstone [Mo.-U.S.]	45	Ig	39.13N	94.34W
Glafsfjorden ≈	8	Ee	59.35N	12.35 E
Glåma ∿	5	Hd	59.12N	10.57 E
Gláma ▲	7a	Ab	65.48N	23.00W
Glamis Castle	9	Ke	56.37N	3.00W
Glamoč	23	Ff	44.03N	16.51 E
Glan ≈	7	Dg	58.35N	15.55 E
Glan [Aus.] ∿	14	Id	46.36N	14.25 E
Glan [F.R.G.] ∿	10	Dg	49.47N	7.43 E
Glan-Münchweiler	12	Je	49.28N	7.26 E
Glarner Alpen ⛰	14	Cd	46.55N	9.00 E
Glärnisch ▲	14	Cd	47.00N	9.00 E
Glarus [2]	14	Dd	46.55N	9.05 E
Glarus	14	Dc	47.03N	9.04 E
Glasgow [Ky.-U.S.]	44	Eg	37.00N	85.55W
Glasgow [Mt.-U.S.]	43	Fb	48.12N	106.38W
Glasgow [Scot.-U.K.]	6	Fd	55.53N	4.15W
Glashütte	10	Jf	50.51N	13.47 E
Glass ∿	9	Id	57.25N	4.30W
Glassboro	44	Jf	39.42N	75.07W
Glass Mountains ⛰	45	Ek	30.25N	103.15W
Glastonbury	9	Kj	51.09N	2.43W
Glauchau	10	If	50.49N	12.32 E
Glava	8	Ee	59.33N	12.34 E
Glazov	6	Ld	58.09N	52.40 E
Gleann Dá Loch/Glendalough	9	Gh	53.00N	6.20W
Gledićske Planine ⛰	15	Df	43.49N	20.55 E
Gleinalpe ⛰	14	Jc	47.10N	15.05 E
Gleisdorf	14	Jc	47.06N	15.43 E
Glen ∿	12	Bb	52.50N	0.07W
Glénan, Iles de- ⁘	11	Cg	47.43N	4.00W
Glen Arbor	44	Ec	44.53N	85.58W
Glenavy	62	Df	44.55S	171.06 E
Glen Canyon	46	Jh	37.05N	111.41W
Glencoe [Mn.-U.S.]	45	Id	44.46N	94.09W
Glencoe [S.Afr.]	37	Ee	28.12S	30.07 E
Glendale [Az.-U.S.]	43	Ee	33.32N	112.11W
Glendale [Ca.-U.S.]	43	De	34.10N	118.17W
Glendalough/Gleann Dá Loch	9	Gh	53.00N	6.20W
Glendive	43	Gb	47.06N	104.43W
Glendo Reservoir ≈	46	Me	42.31N	104.58W
Glenhope	61	Dh	41.39S	172.39 E
Glen Innes	58	Gg	29.44S	151.44 E
Glennallen	40	Jd	62.07N	145.33W
Glenner ∿	14	Dd	46.46N	9.12 E
Glenns Ferry	46	He	42.57N	115.18W
Glenorchy	62	Cf	44.52S	168.24 E
Glenrock	46	Me	42.52N	105.52W
Glen Rose	45	Hj	32.14N	97.45W
Glenrothes	9	Je	56.12N	3.05W
Glens Falls	44	Kd	43.17N	73.41W
Glenville	44	Gf	38.57N	80.51W
Glenwood [Ia.-U.S.]	45	If	41.03N	95.45W
Glenwood [Mn.-U.S.]	45	Id	45.39N	95.23W
Glenwood Springs	43	Fd	39.32N	107.19W
Glibokaja	15	Ja	48.05N	26.00 E
Glina	14	Ke	45.20N	16.06 E
Glinjany	10	Ug	49.46N	24.33 E
Glittertind ▲	5	Gc	61.39N	8.33 E
Gliwice	10	Of	50.17N	18.40 E
Globe	43	Ee	33.24N	110.47W
Globino	16	He	49.24N	33.18 E
Głogów	10	Me	51.40N	16.05 E
Glomfjord	7	Cc	66.49N	13.58 E
Glommersträsk	7	Ed	65.16N	19.38 E
Glonn ∿	10	Hh	48.11N	11.45 E
Glorieuses, Iles- ◆	30	Lj	11.30S	47.20 E
Glottof, Mount- ▲	40	Ie	57.30N	153.30W
Gloucester ▣	9	Kj	51.55N	2.15W
Gloucester [Eng.-U.K.]	9	Kj	51.53N	2.14W
Gloucester [Ma.-U.S.]	44	Ld	42.41N	70.39W
Gloucester, Cape- ▶	60	Di	5.27S	148.25 E
Gloucestershire [3]	9	Lj	51.50N	1.55W
Glover Island ◆	51p	Bb	11.59N	61.47W
Glover's Reef ✳	49	De	16.49N	87.48W
Gloversville	44	Jd	43.03N	74.21W
Głowno	10	Pe	51.58N	19.44 E
Głubczyce	10	Nf	50.13N	17.49 E
Glubokoje [Bye.-U.S.S.R.]	19	Cd	55.08N	27.41 E
Glubokoje [Kaz.-U.S.S.R.]	19	Ie	50.06N	82.19 E
Glubokoje, Ozero- ≈	8	Md	60.30N	29.25 E
Głuchołazy	10	Nf	50.20N	17.22 E
Glücksburg	10	Fb	54.50N	9.33 E
Glückstadt	10	Fc	53.47N	9.25 E
Gluhov	19	De	51.43N	33.57 E
Gluša	16	Fc	53.06N	28.52 E
Glyngøre	8	Ch	56.46N	8.52 E
Gmünd [Aus.]	14	Hd	46.54N	13.32 E
Gmünd [Aus.]	14	Ib	48.46N	14.59 E
Gmunden	14	Hc	47.55N	13.48 E
Gnarp	7	De	62.03N	17.16 E
Gnesta	7	Dg	59.03N	17.18 E
Gniben ▶	8	Dh	56.01N	11.18 E
Gniew	10	Oc	53.51N	18.49 E
Gniewkowo	10	Od	52.54N	18.25 E
Gniezno	10	Nd	52.31N	17.37 E
Gnjilane	15	Eg	42.28N	21.29 E
Gnosjö	7	Ch	57.22N	13.44 E
Gnowangerup	59	Df	33.56S	117.50 E
Goa, Damān and Diu [3]	25	Ee	15.35N	74.00 E
Goageb	37	Be	26.44S	17.15 E
Goālpāra	25	Ic	26.10N	90.37 E
Goat ◆	63b	Dd	18.42S	169.17 E
Goat Island ◆	51d	Ba	17.44N	61.51W
Goat Point ▶	51d	Ba	17.44N	61.51W
Goba	31	Kh	7.01N	39.59 E
Gobabis	31	Ik	22.30S	18.58 E
Gobabis [3]	37	Bd	22.00S	19.00 E
Göbel	15	Lj	40.00N	28.09 E
Gober ⧗	34	Gc	13.48N	6.51 E
Gobernador Gregores	56	Fg	48.46S	70.15W
Gobernador Ingeniero Valentín Virasoro	56	Ic	28.03S	56.02W
Gobernador Mansilla	55	Ck	32.33S	59.22W
Gobi, Pustynja-=Gobi Desert (EN) ◢	21	Me	43.00N	106.00 E
Gobi Altai (EN)=Gobijski Altaj ⛰	21	Me	44.00N	102.00 E
Gobi Desert (EN)=Gobi, Pustynja- ◢	21	Me	43.00N	106.00 E
Gobijski Altaj=Gobi Altai (EN) ⛰	21	Me	44.00N	102.00 E
Gobō	28	Mh	33.53N	135.10 E
Göçbeyli	15	Kj	39.13N	27.25 E
Goceano ⧗	14	Dj	40.30N	9.15 E
Goceano, Catena del- ⛰	14	Cj	40.30N	9.00 E
Goce Delčev	15	Gh	41.33N	23.42 E
Goch	10	Ce	51.40N	6.10 E
Gochas	37	Bd	24.55S	18.55 E
Goczałkowickie, Jezioro- ≈	10	Og	49.53N	18.50 E
Göd	10	Pi	47.42N	19.08 E
Godafoss ∿	7a	Cb	65.41N	17.33W
Godalming	12	Bc	51.11N	0.36W
Godār	24	Qh	29.45N	57.30 E
Godār-e Shah ◡	24	Me	34.45N	48.10 E
Godāvari ∿	21	Kh	17.00N	81.45 E
Godbout, Rivière- ∿	44	Na	49.21N	67.42W
Gode	35	Gd	5.55N	43.40 E
Godeč	15	Gf	43.01N	23.03 E
Godelbukta Breidvika ◧	66	Df	70.15S	24.15 E
Goderich	44	Gd	43.45N	81.43W
Goderville	12	Ce	49.39N	0.22 E
Godhavn/Qeqertarssuaq	67	Nc	69.20N	53.35W
Godhra	25	Ed	22.45N	73.38 E
Godinlabe	35	Hd	5.54N	46.40 E
Gödöllő	10	Pi	47.36N	19.22 E
Godoy Cruz	56	Gd	32.55S	68.50W
Gods Lake	42	If	54.40N	94.09W
Gods Lake ≈	42	If	54.40N	94.20W
Gods Mercy, Bay of- ◧	42	Id	63.30N	86.10W
Gods River ∿	42	Ie	56.22N	92.52W
Godthåb/Nûk	67	Nc	64.15N	51.40W
Godthåbfjord ═	41	Gf	64.20N	51.30W
Godwin Austen (EN)=K2 ▲	21	Jf	35.53N	76.30 E
Godwin Austen (EN)=Qogir Feng ▲	21	Jf	35.53N	76.30 E
Goedereede	12	Fc	51.49N	3.58 E
Goéland, Lac au- ≈	42	Jg	49.45N	76.50W
Goélands, Lac aux- ≈	42	Le	55.30N	64.30W
Goële ⧗	12	Ee	49.10N	2.40 E
Goelette Island ◆	37b	Bc	10.13S	51.08 E
Goeree ◆	11	Jc	51.50N	3.55 E
Goes	11	Jc	51.30N	3.54 E
Gogama	42	Jg	47.40N	81.43W
Gō-Gawa ∿	29	Cd	35.01N	132.13 E
Gogebic Range ⛰	44	Cb	46.45N	89.25W
Gogland, Ostrov- ◆	7	Gf	60.05N	27.00 E
Gog Magog Hills ◠	12	Cb	52.09N	0.11 E
Gogounou	34	Fc	10.50N	2.50 E
Gogrial	35	Dd	8.32N	28.07 E
Gogu, Vîrful- ▲	15	Fd	45.12N	22.30 E
Gogui	34	Db	15.39N	9.21W
Goğu Karadeniz Dağları ⛰	24	Ib	40.40N	40.00 E
Gohelle ⧗	12	Ed	50.28N	2.45 E
Goiandira	54	Ig	18.08S	48.06W
Goianésia	54	Ig	15.19S	49.04W
Goiânia	53	Lg	16.40S	49.16W
Goianinha	54	Ke	6.16S	35.12W
Goiás [2]	54	If	12.00S	48.00W
Goiás	54	Hg	15.56S	50.08W
Goiatuba	54	Ig	18.01S	49.22W
Goikul	64a	Bc	7.22N	134.36 E
Göinge ⧗	8	Eh	56.20N	13.50 E
Goio-Erê	56	Jb	24.12S	53.01W
Goioxim	55	Gg	25.14S	52.01W
Goirle	12	Hc	51.34N	5.05 E
Góis	13	Dd	40.09N	8.07W
Goito	14	Ee	45.15N	10.40 E
Gojam [3]	35	Fc	10.33N	37.35 E
Gojō	29	Dd	34.21N	135.42 E
Gojōme	29	Gb	39.56N	140.07 E
Gojra	25	Eb	31.09N	72.41 E
Gojthski, Pereval- ◡	16	Kg	44.15N	39.18 E
Gokase-Gawa ∿	29	Be	32.35N	131.42 E
Gokasho-Wan ◧	29	Ed	34.20N	136.40 E
Gökbel Dağı ▲	15	Kl	37.28N	28.00 E
Gökçay ∿	24	Ed	36.36N	33.23 E
Gökçeada ◆	24	Ac	40.10N	25.50 E
Gökçeören	15	Lk	38.35N	28.32 E
Gökçeyazi	15	Kj	39.38N	27.39 E
Gökdere ∿	24	Ed	36.39N	33.35 E
Gökırmak ∿	24	Fb	41.24N	35.08 E
Göksu [Tur.] ∿	24	Fd	36.20N	34.05 E
Göksu [Tur.] ∿	24	Fd	37.37N	35.35 E
Göksu [Tur.] ∿	15	Mi	40.23N	29.58 E
Göksun	24	Gc	38.03N	36.30 E
Gök Tepe ▲	15	Mm	36.53N	29.17 E
Göktepe	15	Ll	37.16N	28.36 E
Gokwe	37	Dc	18.13S	28.55 E
Gol	7	Bf	60.42N	8.57 E
Golāghāt	25	Ic	26.31N	93.58 E
Golaja Pristan	16	Hf	46.29N	32.31 E
Gołańcz	10	Nd	52.57N	17.18 E
Golconda [Il.-U.S.]	45	Lh	37.22N	88.29W
Golconda [Nv.-U.S.]	46	Gf	40.57N	117.30W
Gölcük	24	Cb	40.44N	29.44 E
Golčův Jeníkov	10	Lg	49.49N	15.30 E
Gołdap	10	Sb	54.19N	22.19 E
Gold Beach	46	Ce	42.25N	124.25W
Gold Coast	58	Gg	27.58S	153.25 E
Gold Coast ▦	30	Gh	5.20N	0.45W
Golden [B.C.-Can.]	42	Ff	51.18N	116.58W
Golden [Co.-U.S.]	45	Dg	39.46N	105.13W
Golden Bay ◧	62	Ed	40.50S	172.50 E
Goldendale	46	Ed	45.49N	120.50W
Goldene Aue ◡	10	Ge	51.25N	11.00 E
Golden Gate ═	46	Dh	37.49N	122.29W
Golden Hinde ▲	42	Eg	49.39N	125.45W
Golden Meadow	45	Kl	29.23N	90.16W
Golden Vale/Machaire na Mumhan ⧗	9	Fi	52.30N	8.00W
Goldfield	46	Gh	37.42N	117.14W
Gold River	46	Bb	49.41N	126.08W
Goldsboro	43	Ld	35.23N	77.59W
Goldsworthy	59	Dd	20.20S	119.30 E
Göle	24	Jb	40.48N	42.36 E
Golegã	13	De	39.24N	8.29W
Goleniów	10	Kc	53.36N	14.50 E
Golešnica ▲	15	Eh	41.42N	21.33 E
Goleta, Cerro- ▲	48	Ih	18.38N	100.04W
Golfito	47	Hg	8.38N	83.11W
Golfo Aranci	14	Dj	41.00N	9.37 E
Gölgeli Dağları ⛰	15	Ml	37.15N	29.06 E
Gölhisar	15	Ml	37.08N	29.30 E
Goliad	45	Hl	28.40N	97.23W
Golija [Yugo.] ⛰	15	Df	43.19N	20.18 E
Golija [Yugo.] ⛰	15	Bf	43.02N	18.47 E
Goljak ⛰	15	Eg	42.44N	21.31 E
Goljama Kamčija ∿	15	Kf	43.03N	27.29 E
Goljama Sjutkja ▲	15	Hh	41.54N	24.01 E
Goljamo Konare	15	Hg	42.16N	24.33 E
Goljam Perelik ▲	15	Hh	41.36N	24.34 E
Goljam Persenk ▲	15	Hh	41.49N	24.33 E
Gölköy	24	Gb	40.15N	37.26 E
Gölkük	15	Kj	39.19N	27.59 E
Göllheim	12	Ke	49.35N	8.03 E
Gölmarmara	15	Kk	38.42N	27.56 E
Golmud He ∿	27	Gd	36.54N	95.11 E
Golo ∿	11a	Ba	42.31N	9.32 E
Goloby	10	Ve	51.06N	25.06 E
Gologory ⛰	10	Ug	49.35N	24.30 E
Gololcha	35	Gd	8.12N	40.05 E
Golovin	40	Gd	64.33N	163.02W
Golovnin Seamount (EN) ⊼	20	Kg	46.50N	157.00 E
Golpāyegān	23	Hc	33.27N	50.18 E
Gölpazarı	24	Db	40.17N	30.19 E
Golšanka ∿	10	Kb	54.00N	26.16 E
Golspie	9	Jd	57.58N	3.58W
Gol Tappeh	24	Kd	36.35N	45.45 E
Golubac	15	Ee	44.39N	21.38 E
Golub-Dobrzyń	10	Pc	53.08N	19.02 E
Golungo Alto	36	Bd	9.08S	14.47 E
Golyšmanovo	19	Gd	56.23N	68.23 E
Goma	31	Ji	1.37S	29.12 E
Gómara	13	Jc	41.37N	2.13W
Gombe	31	Ig	10.17N	11.10 E
Gombi	34	Hc	10.10N	12.44 E
Gomel	6	Je	52.25N	31.00 E
Gomelskaja Oblast [3]	19	Ce	52.20N	29.40 E
Gomera ◆	30	Ff	28.06N	17.08W
Gómez Farías	48	Ie	24.57N	101.02W
Gómez Palacio	47	Dc	25.34N	103.30W
Gomo Co ≈	27	Ee	33.45N	85.35 E
Goms ⧗	14	Cd	46.25N	8.10 E
Gonābād	23	Ic	34.20N	58.42 E
Gonaïves	47	Je	19.27N	72.43W
Gonam ∿	20	Ie	57.18N	131.20 E
Gonâve, Golfe de la- ◧	47	Je	19.00N	73.30W
Gonâve, Ile de la- ◆	47	Je	18.51N	73.03W
Gonbad-e Qābūs	23	Ib	37.15N	55.09 E
Gonda	25	Gc	27.08N	81.56 E
Gonder [3]	35	Fc	12.00N	38.00 E
Gonder	31	Kg	12.38N	37.27 E
Gondia	25	Gd	21.27N	80.12 E
Gondo ⧗	30	Gg	14.20N	3.10W
Gondomar	13	Dc	41.09N	8.32W
Gondwana ⧗	21	Kg	23.00N	81.00 E
Gönen	24	Bb	40.06N	27.39 E
Gönen ∿	24	Bb	40.06N	27.36 E
Gonfreville-l'Orcher	12	Ce	49.30N	0.14 E
Gong'an (Doushi)	27	Je	30.05N	112.12 E
Gongbo'gyamda	27	Ff	29.59N	93.25 E
Gonggar	27	Ff	29.17N	90.50 E
Gongga Shan ▲	21	Mg	29.34N	101.53 E
Gonghe	27	Hd	36.21N	100.47 E
Gongliu/Tokkuztara	27	Dc	43.30N	82.15 E
Gongola ∿	30	Ih	9.30N	12.04 E
Gongola [2]	34	Hd	8.40N	11.20 E
Gongpoquan	27	Gc	41.50N	97.00 E
Gongshan	27	Gf	27.39N	98.35 E
Gongxian ∿	27	Kf	26.05N	119.32 E
Gongxian (Xiaoyi)	28	Bg	34.46N	112.57 E
Gongzhuling → Huaide	27	Lc	43.30N	124.52 E
Goñi	55	Dk	33.31S	56.24W
Goniądz	10	Sc	53.30N	22.45 E
Gonīshān	24	Pd	37.04N	54.06 E
Gonjo	27	Ge	30.52N	98.20 E
Gonohe	29	Ga	40.31N	141.19 E
Go-no-ura	29	Ae	33.45N	129.41 E
Gönuk ∿	24	Ic	39.00N	40.41 E
Gonzales	45	Hl	29.30N	97.27W
Gonzáles, Riacho- ∿	55	Df	22.48S	57.54W
González	48	Jf	22.50N	98.27W
Goodenough, Cape- ▶	66	Ie	66.16S	126.10 E
Goodenough Bay ◧	59	Ja	9.55S	150.00 E
Goodenough Island ◆	60	Ei	9.22S	150.16 E
Good Hope, Cape of-/Groeie Hoop, Kaap die- ▶	30	Il	34.21S	18.28 E
Goodhouse	37	Be	28.57S	18.13 E
Gooding	46	He	42.56N	114.43W
Goodland	43	Gd	39.21N	101.43W
Goodnews Bay	40	Ge	59.07N	161.35W
Goodsir, Mount- ▲	46	Ga	51.12N	116.20W
Good Spirit Lake ≈	46	Na	51.34N	102.40W
Goodwin Sands ▦	12	Dc	51.15N	1.35 E
Goodyear	46	Ij	33.26N	112.21W
Goole	9	Mh	53.42N	0.52W
Goomalling	59	Df	31.19S	116.49 E
Goondiwindi	58	Gg	28.32S	150.19 E
Goonyella	59	Jd	21.43S	147.58 E
Goor	12	Ib	52.14N	6.37 E
Goose Bay	39	Md	53.19N	60.24W
Goose Lake ≈	43	Cc	41.57N	120.25W
Goose River ∿	45	Hc	47.28N	96.52W
Gopło, Jezioro- ≈	10	Od	52.35N	18.20 E
Göppingen	10	Fh	48.42N	9.40 E
Góra	10	Me	51.40N	16.33 E
Gora ⧗	15	Di	40.40N	20.30 E
Góra Kalwaria	10	Re	51.59N	21.12 E
Gorakhpur	22	Kg	26.45N	83.22 E
Goransko	15	Bf	43.07N	18.50 E
Gorata ⛰	15	Ih	41.45N	25.55 E
Goražde	14	Mg	43.40N	18.59 E
Gorda	46	Ei	35.55N	121.27W
Gorda, Cayo ✳	49	Ff	15.55N	82.15W
Gorda, Punta- [Ca.-U.S.] ▶	46	Cf	40.16N	124.20W
Gorda, Punta- [Cuba] ▶	49	Fb	22.24N	82.10W
Gorda, Punta- [Nic.] ▶	49	Ff	14.21N	83.12W
Gördes	15	Lk	38.54N	28.18 E
Gördes ∿	15	Kj	38.46N	27.58 E
Gordil	35	Cd	9.44N	21.35 E
Gordior ⁖	24	Ec	39.37N	32.00 E
Gordon [Nb.-U.S.]	45	Ee	42.48N	102.12W
Gordon [Wi.-U.S.]	45	Kc	46.15N	91.47W
Gordon, Lake- ≈	59	Jh	43.05S	146.05 E
Gordon Horne Peak ▲	46	Fa	51.46N	118.50W
Gordonvale	59	Jc	17.05S	145.47 E
Goré	35	Bd	7.55N	16.38 E
Gore [Eth.]	35	Fd	8.09N	35.34 E
Gore [N.Z.]	62	Cg	46.06S	168.56 E
Görele	24	Hb	41.02N	39.00 E
Görenez Dağı ▲	15	Lk	39.00N	28.01 E
Gorenjsko ⧗	14	Id	46.20N	14.10 E
Gorey/Guaire	9	Gi	52.40N	6.18W
Gorgān ∿	24	Pd	36.59N	54.05 E
Gorgān	24	Jf	33.21N	43.40 E
Gorgān, Khalīj-e- ◧	24	Od	36.40N	53.50 E
Gorgany ⛰	10	Jh	48.30N	24.15 E
Gorgin	24	Ld	36.15N	47.55 E
Gorgol [3]	32	Ef	15.45N	13.00W
Gorgol el Abiod ∿	32	Ef	16.14N	12.58W
Gorgona ◆	14	Dg	43.25N	9.55 E
Gorgona, Isla- ◆	54	Cc	2.59N	78.12W
Gorgora	35	Fc	12.14N	37.17 E
Gorham	44	Lc	44.23N	71.11W
Gori	19	Eg	42.00N	44.02 E
Gorinchem	11	Kc	51.50N	5.00 E
Goring	12	Ac	51.31N	1.08W
Goris	16	Oj	39.31N	46.22 E
Gorizia	14	He	45.57N	13.38 E
Gorj [2]	15	Gd	45.00N	23.20 E
Gorjačegorsk	20	De	55.24N	88.55 E
Gorjači Kljuc	16	Kg	44.36N	39.07 E
Gorjanci ⛰	14	Je	45.45N	15.20 E
Gorki [Bye.-U.S.S.R.]	16	Gb	54.17N	31.00 E
Gorki [R.S.F.S.R.]	6	Kd	57.38N	45.05 E
Gorki [R.S.F.S.R.]	20	Bc	65.05N	65.15 E
Gorko-Solenoje, Ozero- ≈	16	Oe	49.20N	46.05 E
Gorkovskaja Oblast [3]	19	Ed	56.15N	44.45 E
Gorkovskoje Vodohranilišče =Gorky Reservoir (EN) ≈	5	Kd	57.00N	43.10 E
Gorkum ▲	10	Hf	50.10N	11.08 E
Gorky Reservoir (EN)= Gorkovskoje Vodohr. ≈	5	Kd	57.00N	43.10 E
Gørlev	8	Di	55.32N	11.14 E
Gorlice	10	Rg	49.40N	21.10 E
Görlitz	10	Ke	51.10N	15.00 E
Gorlovka	6	Jf	48.18N	38.03 E
Gornalunga ∿	14	Jm	37.24N	15.03 E
Gorna Orjahovica	15	If	43.07N	25.41 E
Gornjak [R.S.F.S.R.]	20	Df	51.00N	81.29 E
Gornjak [Ukr.-U.S.S.R.]	10	Uf	50.16N	24.13 E
Gornji Milanovac	15	De	44.02N	20.27 E
Gornji Vakuf	23	Fg	43.56N	17.36 E
Gorno-Altajsk	22	Kd	51.58N	85.58 E
Gorno-Altajskaja Avtonomnaja Oblast [3]	20	Df	51.00N	87.00 E
Gorno-Badahšanskaja Avtonomnaja Oblast [3]	19	Hh	38.15N	73.00 E
Gorno-Čujski	20	Ge	57.40N	111.40 E
Gornozavodsk [R.S.F.S.R.]	20	Jg	46.30N	141.55 E
Gornozavodsk [R.S.F.S.R.]	17	Ig	58.25N	58.20 E
Gorny [R.S.F.S.R.]	20	Ih	44.50N	133.56 E
Gorny [R.S.F.S.R.]	16	Pd	51.45N	48.34 E
Gorny [R.S.F.S.R.]	20	If	50.48N	136.26 E
Gornyje Ključi	28	Lb	45.15N	133.30 E
Gorochan ▲	35	Fd	9.26N	37.05 E
Gorodec [R.S.F.S.R.]	19	Ed	56.40N	43.30 E
Gorodec [R.S.F.S.R.]	8	Mf	58.30N	29.55 E
Gorodenka	16	De	48.42N	25.32 E
Gorodišče [Bye.-U.S.S.R.]	10	Vc	53.16N	26.03 E
Gorodišče [R.S.F.S.R.]	16	Nc	53.16N	45.42 E
Gorodišče [Ukr.-U.S.S.R.]	16	Ge	49.17N	31.27 E
Gorodnica	16	Ed	50.49N	27.22 E
Gorodnja	16	Gd	51.55N	31.31 E
Gorodok [Bye.-U.S.S.R.]	19	Cd	55.26N	29.59 E
Gorodok [Ukr.-U.S.S.R.]	16	Ee	49.10N	26.31 E
Gorodok [Ukr.-U.S.S.R.]	16	Ce	49.47N	23.39 E
Gorodovikovsk	19	Ef	46.05N	41.59 E
Gorohov	10	Uf	50.28N	24.47 E
Gorohovec	7	Kh	56.12N	42.42 E
Goroka	58	Fe	6.02S	145.22 E
Gorom-Gorom	34	Ec	14.26N	0.14W
Gorong, Kepulauan- ⁘	26	Jg	4.05S	131.20 E
Gorongosa, Serra da- ⛰	37	Ec	18.24S	34.06 E
Gorontalo	22	Oi	0.33N	123.03 E
Goroual ∿	34	Fc	14.42N	0.53 E
Górowo Iławeckie	10	Qb	54.17N	20.30 E
Gorron	11	Ff	48.25N	0.49W
Goršečnoje	16	Kd	51.33N	38.09 E
Gorski Kotar ⧗	14	Ie	45.26N	14.40 E
Gorssel	12	Ib	52.12N	6.13 E
Gort	9	Eh	53.04N	8.50W
Goru, Vîrful- ▲	15	Jd	45.48N	26.25 E
Görükle	15	Li	40.14N	28.50 E
Goryn ∿	19	Ce	52.09N	27.17 E
Gorzów [2]	10	Ld	54.25N	15.15 E
Gorzów Wielkopolski	10	Ld	52.44N	15.15 E
Goschen Strait ═	59	Kb	10.09S	150.56 E
Gosen	28	Of	37.44N	139.11 E
Gosford	59	Kf	33.26S	151.21 E
Goshen	44	Ee	41.35N	85.50W
Goshogawara	28	Pd	40.48N	140.27 E
Gosier	51e	Bb	16.12N	61.30W
Goslar	10	Ge	51.54N	10.26 E
Gospić	14	Jf	44.33N	15.23 E
Gosport	9	Lk	50.48N	1.08W
Gossen ◆	8	Bb	62.50N	6.55 E
Gossi	34	Eb	15.47N	1.15W
Gossinga	35	Dd	8.39N	25.59 E
Gostivar	15	Dh	41.48N	20.54 E
Gostyń	10	Me	51.53N	17.00 E
Gostynin	10	Pd	52.26N	19.29 E
Gota älv ∿	5	Hd	57.42N	11.52 E
Göta Kanal ≡	5	Hd	58.50N	13.58 E
Götaland ⧗	5	Hd	57.30N	14.30 E
Götaland ▣	7	Dg	57.30N	14.30 E
Göteborg	6	Hd	57.43N	11.58 E
Göteborg och Bohus [2]	7	Cg	58.30N	11.30 E
Gotel Mountains ⛰	30	Ih	7.00N	11.40 E
Gotemba	29	Fd	35.18N	138.56 E
Götene	7	Cg	58.32N	13.29 E
Gotha	10	Gf	50.57N	10.43 E
Gothenburg	45	Ff	40.56N	100.09W
Gothèye	34	Fc	13.52N	1.34 E
Gotland [2]	7	Eh	57.30N	18.30 E
Gotland ◆	5	Hd	57.30N	18.30 E
Gotō-Nada ≋	29	Ae	32.45N	129.30 E
Gotō-Rettō ⁘	27	Me	32.50N	129.00 E
Gotowasi	26	If	0.38N	128.26 E
Gotska Sandön ◆	7	Eg	58.25N	19.15 E
Gōtsu	28	Lg	35.00N	132.14 E
Göttingen	10	Fe	51.32N	9.56 E
Gottwaldov	10	Ng	49.13N	17.39 E
Goubangzi	28	Fd	41.23N	121.48 E
Gouda	11	Kc	52.01N	4.43 E
Goudiri	34	Cc	14.11N	12.43W
Gouet ∿	11	Df	48.32N	2.45W
Gough Island ◆	30	Gm	40.20S	10.00W
Gough Lake ≈	46	Ia	52.02N	112.28W
Gouin, Réservoir- ≈	42	Kg	48.35N	74.50W
Goulbin Kaba ⧗	34	Gc	13.42N	6.19 E
Goulburn	58	Fh	34.45S	149.43 E

Index Symbols

- [1] Independent Nation
- [2] State, Region
- [3] District, County
- [4] Municipality
- [5] Colony, Dependency
- ■ Continent
- ⧗ Physical Region
- ▣ Historical or Cultural Region
- ▲ Mount, Mountain
- ⩘ Volcano
- ◠ Hill
- ⛰ Mountains, Mountain Range
- ◠ Hills, Escarpment
- ⌓ Plateau, Upland
- ◡ Pass, Gap
- ▭ Plain, Lowland
- ◣ Delta
- ▤ Salt Flat
- ◡ Valley, Canyon
- ◡ Crater, Cave
- ✲ Karst Features
- ◡ Depression
- ▭ Polder
- ◢ Desert, Dunes
- ♠ Forest, Woods
- ʬ Heath, Steppe
- ♣ Oasis
- ▶ Cape, Point
- ▦ Coast, Beach
- ◧ Cliff
- ▶ Peninsula
- ⧓ Isthmus
- ▤ Sandbank
- ◆ Island
- ⊙ Atoll
- ✳ Rock, Reef
- ⁘ Islands, Archipelago
- ✳ Rocks, Reefs
- ✳ Coral Reef
- ⊙ Well, Spring
- ⊤ Geyser
- ∿ River, Stream
- ∿ Waterfall Rapids
- ≈ River Mouth, Estuary
- ≈ Lake
- ≈ Salt Lake
- ◌ Intermittent Lake
- ≈ Reservoir
- ʬ Swamp, Pond
- ≡ Canal
- ◡ Glacier
- ◩ Ice Shelf, Pack Ice
- ≋ Ocean
- ≋ Sea
- ◧ Gulf, Bay
- ═ Strait, Fjord
- ◎ Lagoon
- ▦ Bank
- ⊼ Seamount
- ⊼ Tablemount
- ⛰ Ridge
- ▬ Shelf
- ◡ Basin
- ◥ Escarpment, Sea Scarp
- ≷ Fracture
- ▽ Trench, Abyss
- ◢ National Park, Reserve
- ▼ Point of Interest
- ⇑ Recreation Site
- ◓ Cave, Cavern
- ▲ Historic Site
- ⁖ Ruins
- ▥ Wall, Walls
- ⛪ Church, Abbey
- ⌂ Temple
- ⊠ Scientific Station
- ✈ Airport
- ⚓ Port
- ⚑ Lighthouse
- ⚒ Mine
- ⌒ Tunnel
- ⌿ Dam, Bridge

Goulburn Islands	59	Gb	11.50S	133.30 E
Gould Bay	66	Rf	78.10S	44.00W
Gould Coast	66	Mg	84.30S	150.00W
Goulia	34	Dc	10.01N	7.11W
Goulimine	32	Ed	28.59N	10.04W
Gouménissa	15	Fi	40.57N	22.27 E
Gouna	34	Hd	8.32N	13.34 E
Gounda	35	Cd	9.09N	21.15 E
Goundam	34	Eb	16.24N	3.38W
Goundi	35	Bd	9.22N	17.22 E
Goundoumaria	34	Hc	13.42N	11.10 E
Gounou Gaya	35	Bd	9.38N	15.31 E
Gourara	32	Hd	29.30N	0.40 E
Gouraya	13	Nh	36.34N	1.55 E
Gourcy	34	Ec	13.13N	2.21W
Gourdon	11	Hj	44.44N	1.23 E
Gouré	31	Ig	13.58N	10.18 E
Gourin	11	Cf	48.08N	3.36W
Gourma [Mali]	30	Gg	15.45N	2.00W
Gourma [U.V.]	30	Hg	12.20N	1.30 E
Gourma-Rharous	34	Eb	16.52N	1.55W
Gournay-en-Bray	11	He	49.29N	1.44 E
Gourniá	15	In	35.06N	25.48 E
Gouro	35	Bb	19.40N	19.28 E
Gourrama	32	Gc	32.20N	4.05W
Goussainville	12	Ee	49.01N	2.28 E
Gouyave	51p	Bb	12.10N	61.44W
Gouzeaucourt	12	Fd	50.03N	3.07 E
Gouzon	11	Ih	46.11N	2.14 E
Govena, Mys-	20	Le	59.47N	166.02 E
Gove Peninsula	59	Hb	13.02S	136.50 E
Goverla, Gora-	19	Cf	48.10N	24.32 E
Governador Valadares	53	Lg	18.51S	41.56W
Governor's Harbour	47	Ic	25.10N	76.14W
Gowanda	44	Hd	42.28N	78.57W
Gower	9	Ij	51.36N	4.10W
Gowganda	44	Gb	47.38N	80.46W
Goya	53	Kh	29.10S	59.20W
Goyave	51e	Ab	16.08N	61.34W
Goyaves, Ilets 'a-	51e	Ab	16.10N	61.48W
Goyder River	59	Hb	12.38S	135.05 E
Göynücek	24	Fb	40.24N	35.32 E
Göynük	15	Ni	40.20N	30.05 E
Göynük	24	Db	40.24N	30.47 E
Gozaisho-Yama	29	Ed	35.01N	136.24 E
Goz Arian	35	Bc	14.35N	20.00 E
Goz Beïda	35	Cc	12.13N	21.25 E
Gozha Co	27	De	34.59N	81.06 E
Goz Kerki	35	Bb	15.30N	18.50 E
Gözlü Baba Dağı	15	Lk	38.15N	28.28 E
Gozo	5	Hh	36.05N	14.15 E
Graaff-Reinet	37	Cf	32.14S	24.32 E
Graafschap	11	Mb	52.05N	6.30 E
Graben Neudorf	12	Ke	49.10N	8.28 E
Grabia	10	Oe	51.26N	18.56 E
Grabière Point	51g	Bb	15.30N	61.29W
Grabowa	10	Mb	54.26N	16.20 E
Gračac	14	Jf	44.18N	15.51 E
Gračanica	14	Mf	44.42N	18.18 E
Gračanica, Manastir-	15	Eg	42.36N	21.12 E
Gracias	49	Cf	14.35N	88.35W
Gracias a Dios [3]	49	Ef	15.20N	84.20W
Gracias a Dios, Cabo	38	Kh	15.00N	83.08W
Graciosa [Azr.]	30	Ee	39.04N	28.00W
Graciosa [Can.Is.]	32	Ed	29.15N	13.30W
Gradačac	14	Mf	44.53N	18.26 E
Gradaús, Serra dos-	52	Kf	8.00S	50.45W
Grado [It.]	14	He	45.40N	13.23 E
Grado [Sp.]	13	Fa	43.23N	6.04W
Grænalon	7a	Cb	64.10N	17.24W
Grænlandshaf=Greenland Sea (EN)	67	Ld	77.00N	1.00W
Grafenau	10	Jh	48.51N	13.24 E
Grafham Water	12	Bb	52.19N	0.10W
Grafing bei München	10	Hh	48.03N	11.58 E
Grafschaft Bentheim	12	Jb	52.30N	7.05 E
Grafton [Austl.]	59	Ke	29.41S	152.56 E
Grafton [N.D.-U.S.]	43	Hb	48.25N	97.25W
Grafton [W.V.-U.S.]	44	Hf	39.21N	80.00W
Grafton, Mount-	46	Hg	38.40N	114.45W
Graham	42	Ef	53.40N	132.30W
Graham [N.C.-U.S.]	44	Hg	36.05N	79.25W
Graham [Tx.-U.S.]	45	Gj	33.06N	98.35W
Graham, Mount-	43	Fe	32.42N	109.52W
Graham Land (EN)	66	Qe	66.00S	63.30W
Graham Moore, Cape -	42	Jb	72.51N	76.05W
Grahamstown	31	Jl	33.19S	26.31 E
Grain Coast	30	Gh	5.00N	9.00W
Graisivaudan	11	Li	45.15N	5.50 E
Grajaú	54	Ie	5.49S	46.08W
Grajaú, Rio-	54	Jd	3.41S	44.48W
Grajewo	10	Sc	53.39N	22.27 E
Gram	8	Ci	55.17N	9.04 E
Gramalote	49	Kj	7.54N	72.48W
Gramat	11	Hj	44.47N	1.43 E
Gramat, Causse de-	11	Hj	44.40N	1.50 E
Graminha, Represa da-	55	Ie	21.33S	46.38W
Grammerages/Galmaarden	12	Fd	50.45N	3.58 E
Grammichele	14	Im	37.13N	14.38 E
Grammont/Geraardsbergen	12	Fd	50.46N	3.52 E
Grámmos Óros	15	Di	40.20N	20.45 E
Grampian [3]	9	Kd	57.25N	2.35W
Grampian Mountains	5	Fd	56.45N	4.00W
Gramshi	15	Di	40.52N	20.11 E
Gran	8	Dd	60.22N	10.34 E
Granada [Col.]	54	Dc	3.33N	73.44W
Granada [Nic.] [3]	49	Eh	11.50N	86.00W
Granada [Nic.]	47	Gf	11.56N	85.57W
Granada [Sp.] [3]	13	Ig	37.15N	3.15W
Granada [Sp.]	6	Fh	37.13N	3.41W
Granada, Vega de-	13	Ig	37.15N	4.00W
Gránard/Granard	9	Fh	53.47N	7.30W
Granard/Gránard	9	Fh	53.47N	7.30W
Granby	42	Kg	45.24N	72.43W
Gran Canaria	30	Ff	28.00N	15.36W
Gran Chaco	52	Jh	23.00S	60.00W
Grand Anse Bay	51p	Bb	12.02N	61.45W
Grand Bahama	38	Lg	26.40N	78.20W
Grand Ballon	11	Ng	47.55N	7.08 E
Grand Bank	42	Lg	47.06N	55.47W
Grand Banks (EN)	38	Oe	45.00N	50.00W
Grand Bassa [3]	34	Dd	6.10N	9.40W
Grand-Bassam	31	Gh	5.12N	3.44W
Grand Bay	51g	Bb	15.14N	61.19W
Grand Bay	51p	Cb	12.29N	61.23W
Grand-Béréby	34	De	4.38N	6.55W
Grand-Bourg	50	Fe	15.53N	61.19W
Grand Cache	42	Ff	53.14N	119.00W
Grand Caille Point	51k	Ab	13.52N	61.05W
Grandcamp-Maisy	12	Ae	49.23N	1.02W
Grand Canal	9	Gh	53.21N	6.14W
Grand Canal (EN)=Da Yunhe	21	Nf	39.54N	116.44 E
Grand Canyon	43	Ed	36.03N	112.09W
Grand Canyon	38	Hc	36.10N	112.45W
Grand' Case	51b	Ab	18.06N	63.03W
Grand Cayman	47	He	19.20N	81.15W
Grand Cess	34	De	4.24N	8.13W
Grand Chartreuse	11	Li	45.22N	5.50 E
Grand Colombier	11	Li	45.54N	5.46 E
Grand Coulee	46	Fc	47.56N	119.00W
Grand-Couronne	12	De	49.21N	1.01 E
Grandcourt	12	De	49.55N	1.30 E
Grand Cul de Sac Bay	51k	Ab	13.59N	61.02W
Grand Cul-de-Sac Marin	51e	Ab	16.20N	61.35W
Grande, Arroyo-	55	Dm	37.32S	57.34W
Grande, Bahía-	52	Jk	50.45S	68.45W
Grande, Boca-	54	Fb	8.45N	60.35W
Grande, Cachoeira-	55	Gb	15.37S	51.48W
Grande, Cerro-	48	If	23.40N	100.40W
Grande, Ciénaga-	49	Ji	9.13N	75.46W
Grande, Corixa-	55	Cc	17.10S	58.20W
Grande, Cuchilla- [Arg.]	55	Cj	31.45S	58.35W
Grande, Cuchilla- [Ur.]	52	Ki	33.15S	55.07W
Grande, Ile-	11	Cf	48.48N	3.35W
Grande, Ilha	54	Jh	23.10S	44.10W
Grande, Rio- [Ven.]	54	Fb	8.39N	60.59W
Grande, Rio- [Braz.]	52	Lg	11.05S	43.09W
Grande, Rio- [N.Amer.]	38	Jg	25.57N	97.09W
Grande, Rio- (EN)=Bravo del Norte, Rio-	38	Jg	25.57N	97.09W
Grande, Rio- o Guapay, Rio-	52	Jg	15.51S	64.39W
Grande, Serra-	52	Lf	6.00S	40.52W
Grande, Sierra-	48	Gc	29.40N	104.55W
Grande-Anse	51e	Bb	16.18N	61.04W
Grande Anse	51k	Ba	14.01N	60.54W
Grande Briere	11	Dg	47.22N	2.15W
Grande Casse	11	Mi	45.24N	6.50 E
Grande Cayemite	49	Kd	18.37N	73.45W
Grande Comore/Njazidja	30	Lj	11.35S	43.20 E
Grande de Santa Marta, Ciénaga-	49	Jh	10.50N	74.25W
Grande de Santiago, Rio-	38	Ig	21.36N	105.26W
Grande do Gurupa, Ilha-	54	Hd	1.00S	51.30W
Grande Inferior, Cuchilla-	55	Dk	33.50S	56.10W
Grande Kabylie	13	Ph	36.45N	4.00 E
Grande ou Sete Quedas, Ilha-	55	Ef	23.45S	54.03W
Grande Pointe [Guad.]	51b	Bc	17.50N	62.50W
Grande Pointe [Guad.]	51e	Ac	15.59N	61.38W
Grande Prairie	39	Hd	55.10N	118.48W
Grand Erg de Bilma	30	Ig	18.30N	13.50 E
Grand Erg Occidental	30	He	30.20N	0.01 E
Grand Erg Oriental	30	He	30.00N	7.00 E
Grande Rio-	52	Kh	20.06S	51.04W
Grande Rivière à Goyaves	51e	Ab	16.18N	61.37W
Grande Rivière de la Baleine	38	Ld	55.15N	77.45W
Grande Rivière du Nord	49	Kd	19.35N	72.11W
Grande Ronde River	46	Gc	46.05N	116.59W
Grandes, Salinas-	52	Ji	30.05S	65.05W
Grande Sebkha d'Oran	13	Li	35.32N	0.48W
Grandes Rousse	11	Mi	45.06N	6.07 E
Grande-Synthe	12	Ec	51.01N	2.17 E
Grand Etang	51p	Bb	12.06N	61.42W
Grande-Terre	50	Fd	16.20N	61.25W
Grande Vigie, Pointe de la-	51e	Ba	16.31N	61.28W
Grand Falls [N.B.-Can.]	42	Kg	47.03N	67.44W
Grand Falls [Newf.-Can.]	39	Ne	48.56N	55.40W
Grand Forks [B.C.-Can.]	46	Fb	49.02N	118.27W
Grand Forks [N.D.-U.S.]	39	Je	47.55N	97.03W
Grand Found, Anse du-	51b	Bc	17.53N	62.49W
Grand Gedeh [3]	34	Dd	5.45N	8.05W
Grand Haven	44	Dd	43.04N	86.10W
Grand Ilet	51e	Ac	15.50N	61.36W
Grand Island	39	Je	40.55N	98.21W
Grand Junction	39	If	39.05N	108.33W
Grand-Lahou	34	Dd	5.08N	5.01W
Grand Lake [La.-U.S.]	45	Kl	29.55N	91.35W
Grand Lake [La.-U.S.]	45	Jl	29.55N	92.47W
Grand Lake [N.B.-Can.]	44	Nc	45.42N	66.05W
Grand Lake [Newf.-Can.]	42	Lg	49.00N	57.20W
Grand Lake [Oh.-U.S.]	44	Ee	40.30N	84.32W
Grand Lake Victoria	44	Ib	47.35N	77.33W
Grand Lieu, Lac de-	11	Eg	47.05N	1.40W
Grand Manan Channel	44	Nc	44.45N	66.52W
Grand Manan Island	42	Kh	44.40N	66.50W
Grand Marais [Mi.-U.S.]	44	Eb	46.40N	85.59W
Grand Marais [Mn.-U.S.]	45	Kc	47.45N	90.20W
Grand-Mère	44	Kb	46.37N	72.41W
Grand Morin	11	If	48.54N	2.50 E
Grândola	13	Df	38.10N	8.34W
Grândola, Serra de-	13	Df	38.06N	8.38W
Grand Passage	63b	Ad	18.45S	163.10 E
Grand-Popo	34	Fd	6.17N	1.50 E
Grand Portage	45	Lc	47.58N	89.41W
Grand Prairie	43	He	32.45N	96.59W
Grandpré	12	Ge	49.20N	4.52 E
Grand Rapids [Man.-Can.]	42	Hf	53.10N	99.17W
Grand Rapids [Mi.-U.S.]	39	Ke	42.58N	85.40W
Grand Rapids [Mn.-U.S.]	43	Ib	47.14N	93.31W
Grand Récif Sud	61	Cd	22.38S	167.00 E
Grand River [Mi.-U.S.]	44	Dd	43.04N	86.15W
Grand River [Mo.-U.S.]	45	Jg	39.23N	93.06W
Grand River [Ont.-Can.]	44	Hd	42.51N	79.34W
Grand River [S.D.-U.S.]	45	Fd	45.40N	100.32W
Grand'Rivière	51h	Ab	14.52N	61.11W
Grand Roy	51p	Bb	12.08N	61.45W
Grand-Sans-Toucher	51e	Ab	16.06N	61.41W
Grand Teton	43	Ec	43.44N	110.48W
Grand Traverse Bay	43	Jb	45.02N	85.30W
Grand Turk	49	Lc	21.30N	71.10W
Grand Turk	47	Jd	21.28N	71.09W
Grand Union Canal	12	Bc	51.30N	0.02W
Grand Valley	45	Bg	39.27N	108.03W
Grandview [Man.-Can.]	45	Fa	51.10N	100.45W
Grandview [Mo.-U.S.]	45	Ig	38.53N	94.32W
Grandvilliers	12	De	49.40N	1.56 E
Grand Wash Cliffs	46	Ii	35.45N	113.45W
Grand Wintersberg	11	Ne	48.59N	7.37 E
Granger	46	Ec	46.21N	120.11W
Grängesberg	8	Fd	60.05N	14.59 E
Grangeville	46	Gd	45.56N	116.07W
Gran Guardia	56	Ic	25.52S	58.53W
Granite City	45	Kg	38.42N	90.09W
Granite Falls	45	Id	44.49N	95.33W
Granite Pass	46	Ld	44.38N	107.30W
Granite Peak [Nv.-U.S.]	43	Dc	41.40N	117.35W
Granite Peak [U.S.]	43	Fb	45.10N	109.48W
Granite Range	46	Ff	41.00N	119.35W
Granitola, Punta-	14	Gm	37.34N	12.41 E
Grankulla/Kauniainen	8	Kd	60.13N	24.45 E
Granma [3]	49	Ic	20.30N	77.00W
Gran Malvina, Isla-/West Falkland	52	Kk	51.40S	60.00W
Gran Morelos [Mex.]	48	Eb	30.40N	108.35W
Gran Morelos [Mex.]	48	Fc	28.15N	106.30W
Gränna	8	Ff	58.01N	14.28 E
Granollers/Granollérs	13	Oc	41.37N	2.18 E
Granollérs/Granollers	13	Oc	41.37N	2.18 E
Gran Paradis/Gran Paradiso	14	Be	45.32N	7.16 E
Gran Paradiso/Gran Paradis	14	Be	45.32N	7.16 E
Gran Pilastro/Hochfeiler	14	Fd	46.58N	11.44 E
Gran San Bernardo	14	Be	45.50N	7.10 E
Gran Sasso d'Italia	5	Hg	42.25N	13.40 E
Grant	45	Ff	40.50N	101.56W
Grant, Mount-	46	Fg	38.34N	118.48W
Gran Tarajal	32	Ed	28.12N	14.01W
Grantham	9	Mi	52.54N	0.38W
Grant Island	66	Nf	74.24S	131.20W
Grantown-on-Spey	9	Jd	57.20N	3.38W
Grant Range	46	Hg	38.25N	115.30W
Grants	43	Fd	35.09N	107.52W
Grantsburg	45	Jd	45.47N	92.41W
Grants Pass	43	Cc	42.26N	123.19W
Granville	11	Ef	48.50N	1.36W
Granville Lake	42	He	56.00N	100.20W
Granvin	8	Bd	60.33N	6.43 E
Grao de Gandia, Gandia-	13	Lf	38.59N	0.09W
Grao de Sagunto, Sagunto-	13	Le	39.40N	0.16W
Grappa, Monte-	14	Fe	45.52N	11.48 E
Grappler Bank (EN)	51a	Cc	17.48N	65.55W
Graskop	37	Ed	24.58S	30.49 E
Gräsmark	8	Ee	59.57N	12.55 E
Gräsö	7	Ef	60.25N	18.25 E
Grasse	11	Mk	43.40N	6.55 E
Grasset,Lac-	44	Ha	49.58N	78.10W
Grassrange	46	Kc	47.01N	108.48W
Gråsten	7	Bi	54.55N	9.36 E
Grästorp	8	Ef	58.20N	12.40 E
Graubünden [2]	14	Dd	46.35N	9.35 E
Graulhet	11	Hk	43.46N	2.00 E
Graus	13	Mb	42.11N	0.20 E
Grave	12	Hc	51.45N	5.45 E
Grave, Pointe de-	11	Ei	45.34N	1.04W
Gravedona	14	Dd	46.09N	9.18 E
Gravelbourg	42	Gg	49.53N	106.34W
Gravelines	11	Id	50.59N	2.07 E
Gravenhurst	44	Hc	44.55N	79.22W
Gravenor Bay	51d	Ba	17.33N	61.45W
Graves	11	Fj	44.35N	0.30W
Gravesend	9	Nj	51.27N	0.24 E
Gravesend-Tilbury	9	Nj	51.28N	0.23 E
Gravina in Puglia	14	Kj	40.49N	16.25 E
Gravone	11a	Ab	41.55N	8.47 E
Gray	11	Lg	47.27N	5.35 E
Gray Feather Bank (EN)	60	Df	8.00N	148.40 E
Grayling	44	Ec	44.40N	84.43W
Grays Harbor	46	Cc	46.56N	124.05W
Grayson	44	Ff	38.20N	82.57W
Grays Peak	43	Fd	39.37N	105.45W
Graz	6	Hf	47.04N	15.27 E
Grazalema	13	Gh	36.46N	5.22W
Grdelica	15	Fg	42.54N	22.04 E
Greåker	8	De	59.16N	11.02 E
Great	51p	Bb	12.10N	61.38W
Great Artesian Basin	57	Fg	25.00S	143.00 E
Great Astrolabe Reef	63d	Bc	18.52S	178.31 E
Great Australian Bight	57	Eh	35.00S	130.00 E
Great Bacolet Point	51p	Bb	12.05N	61.37W
Great Bahama Bank (EN)	38	Lg	23.15N	78.00W
Great Bardfield	12	Cc	51.56N	0.29 E
Great Barrier Island	57	Ih	36.10S	175.25 E
Great Barrier Reef	57	Ff	19.10S	149.00 E
Great Basin	38	Hf	40.00N	117.00W
Great Bay	44	Jf	39.30N	74.23W
Great Bear	42	Ed	64.54N	125.35W
Great Bear Lake	38	Hc	66.00N	120.00W
Great Belt (EN)=Store Bælt	5	Hd	55.30N	11.00 E
Great Bend	43	Hd	38.22N	98.46W
Great Blasket/An Blascaod Mór	9	Ci	52.05N	10.32W
Great Britain	5	Fd	54.00N	3.00W
Great Central Lake	46	Cb	49.27N	125.12W
Great Channel	21	Li	6.00N	94.00 E
Great Chesterford	12	Cb	52.04N	0.12 E
Great Dismal Swamp	44	Ig	36.30N	76.30W
Great Dividing Range	57	Fg	25.00S	147.00 E
Great Dunmow	12	Cc	51.53N	0.22 E
Greater Accra [3]	34	Fd	5.45N	0.10 E
Greater Antilles (EN)= Antillas Mayores	38	Lh	20.00N	74.00W
Greater Khingan Range (EN) =Da Hinggan Ling	21	Oe	49.00N	122.00 E
Greater London [3]	9	Mj	51.35N	0.05W
Greater Manchester [3]	9	Kh	53.35N	2.10W
Greater Sunda Islands (EN)	21	Nj	3.52S	111.20 E
Great Exhibition Bay	61	Df	34.40S	173.00 E
Great Exuma Island	47	Id	23.32N	75.50W
Great Falls	39	He	47.30N	111.17W
Great Harbour Cay	44	Im	25.45N	77.52W
Great Inagua	38	Lg	21.02N	73.20W
Great Indian Desert/Thar	21	Ig	27.00N	70.00 E
Great Karasberge (EN)= Groot-Karasberge	30	Ik	27.20S	18.45 E
Great Karroo (EN)=Groot Karoo	30	Jl	33.00S	22.00 E
Great Lake	59	Jh	41.52S	146.45 E
Great Namaland/Groot Namaland	37	Be	26.00S	17.00 E
Great Nicobar	21	Li	7.00N	93.50 E
Great North East Channel	59	Ia	9.30S	143.25 E
Great Ormes Head	9	Jh	53.21N	3.52W
Great Ouse	9	Ni	52.44N	0.23 E
Great Plain of the Koukdjuak	42	Kc	66.25N	72.50W
Great Plains	38	Je	42.00N	100.00W
Great Reef	63c	Bb	10.14S	166.02 E
Great Ruaha	30	Ki	7.56S	37.52 E
Great Sacandaga Lake	44	Jd	43.08N	74.10W
Great Sale Cay	44	Hl	27.00N	78.12W
Great Salt Lake	38	He	41.10N	112.30W
Great Salt Lake Desert	43	Ec	40.40N	113.30W
Great Salt Plains Lake	45	Gh	36.44N	98.12W
Great Salt Pond	51c	Ab	17.15N	62.38W
Great Sandy Desert [Austl.]	57	Dg	21.30S	125.00 E
Great Sandy Desert [U.S.]	43	Cc	43.35N	120.15W
Great Sea Reef	63d	Bb	16.15S	178.33 E
Great Shelford	12	Cb	52.07N	0.08 E
Great Sitkin	40a	Cb	52.03N	176.07W
Great Slave Lake	38	Hd	61.30N	114.00W
Great Smoky Mountains	44	Fh	35.35N	83.30W
Great Stour	9	Oj	51.19N	1.15 E
Great Valley [U.S.]	44	Ie	40.15N	76.50W
Great Valley [U.S.]	43	Kd	36.30N	82.00W
Great Victoria Desert	57	Dg	28.30S	127.45 E
Great Yarmouth	9	Oi	52.37N	1.44 E
Grebbestad	7	Cg	58.42N	11.15 E
Grebenka	16	Hd	50.07N	32.25 E
Gréboun, Mont-	34	Gb	20.00N	8.35 E
Greci	15	Ld	45.11N	28.14 E
Gredos, Sierra de-	13	Gd	40.20N	5.05W
Greece (EN)=Ellás [1]	6	Ih	39.00N	22.00 E
Greeley [Co.-U.S.]	43	Gc	40.25N	104.42W
Greeley [Nb.-U.S.]	45	Gf	41.33N	98.32W
Greely Fiord	42	Ja	80.40N	85.00W
Greem-Bell	21	Ia	81.10N	64.00 E
Green	46	De	43.07N	123.28W
Green Bay	43	Jb	45.00N	87.30W
Green Bay	39	Ke	44.30N	88.01W
Greencastle	44	Df	39.38N	86.52W
Green Cay	49	Ia	24.02N	77.11W
Greeneville	44	Fg	36.10N	82.50W
Greenfield [In.-U.S.]	44	Ef	39.47N	85.46W
Greenfield [Ma.-U.S.]	44	Kd	42.36N	72.36W
Greenhorn Mountain	45	Dh	37.57N	105.00W
Green Island	62	Df	45.54S	170.26 E
Green Island [Atg.]	51d	Bb	17.03N	61.40W
Green Island [Gren.]	51p	Bb	12.14N	61.35W
Green Islands	57	Ge	4.30S	154.10 E
Greenland	51q	Ab	13.15N	59.34W
Greenland (EN)=Grønland/ Kalaallit Nunaat	38	Pb	70.00N	40.00W
Greenland (EN)=Grønland/ Kalaallit Nunaat [5]	39	Pb	70.00N	40.00W
Greenland (EN)=Kalaallit Nunaat/Grønland	38	Pb	70.00N	40.00W
Greenland (EN)=Kalaallit Nunaat/Grønland [5]	39	Pb	70.00N	40.00W
Greenland Basin (EN)	3	Gb	77.00N	0.00
Greenland Sea (EN)= Grænlandshaf	67	Ld	77.00N	1.00W
Greenland Sea (EN)= Grønlandshavet	67	Ld	77.00N	1.00W
Green Lookout Mountain	46	Dd	45.52N	122.08W
Green Mountains	38	Le	43.45N	72.45W
Greenock	9	If	55.57N	4.45W
Greenough River	59	Ce	28.51S	114.38 E
Green Peter Lake	46	Dd	44.28N	122.30W
Green River [U.S.]	44	Dg	37.55N	87.30W
Green River [U.S.]	38	If	38.11N	109.53W
Green River [Ut.-U.S.]	43	Ed	38.59N	110.10W
Green River [Wy.-U.S.]	43	Fc	41.32N	109.28W
Green River Lake	44	Eg	37.15N	85.15W
Greensboro	39	Lf	36.04N	79.47W
Greensburg [In.-U.S.]	44	Ef	39.20N	85.29W
Greensburg [Ks.-U.S.]	45	Gh	37.36N	99.18W
Greensburg [La.-U.S.]	45	Kk	30.51N	90.42W
Greenstone Point	9	Hd	57.55N	5.40W
Greenvale	59	Jc	18.55S	145.05 E
Greenville [Al.-U.S.]	44	Dj	31.50N	86.38W
Greenville [Il.-U.S.]	45	Lg	38.53N	89.25W
Greenville [Lbr.]	31	Gh	4.59N	9.02W
Greenville [Me.-U.S.]	44	Mc	45.28N	69.35W
Greenville [Ms.-U.S.]	43	Ie	33.25N	91.05W
Greenville [N.C.-U.S.]	43	Ld	35.37N	77.23W
Greenville [Oh.-U.S.]	44	Ee	40.06N	84.37W
Greenville [Pa.-U.S.]	44	Ge	41.24N	80.24W
Greenville [S.C.-U.S.]	39	Kf	34.51N	82.23W
Greenville [Tx.-U.S.]	43	He	33.08N	96.07W
Greenwich	44	Fe	41.02N	82.32W
Greenwich, London-	9	Mj	51.28N	0.00
Greenwood [Ms.-U.S.]	43	Ie	33.31N	90.11W
Greenwood [S.C.-U.S.]	44	Fh	34.12N	82.10W
Greenwood, Lake-	44	Gh	34.15N	82.00W
Greer	44	Fh	34.55N	82.14W
Greers Ferry Lake	45	Ji	35.30N	92.10W
Greeson, Lake-	45	Ji	34.10N	93.45W
Grefrath	12	Ic	51.18N	6.19 E
Gregoria Pérez de Denis	55	Bi	28.14S	61.32W
Gregorio, Rio-	54	De	6.50S	70.46W
Gregório, Rio-	55	Ha	13.42S	49.58W
Gregory, Lake-	59	He	28.55S	139.00 E
Gregory Lake	59	Fd	20.10S	127.20 E
Gregory Range	57	Ff	19.00S	143.00 E
Gregory River	59	Hc	17.53S	139.17 E
Greifenburg	14	Hd	46.45N	13.11 E
Greifswald	10	Jb	54.06N	13.23 E
Greifswalder Bodden	10	Jb	54.15N	13.35 E
Greifswalder Oie	10	Jb	54.14N	13.55 E
Grein	14	Ib	48.13N	14.51 E
Greiz	10	If	50.39N	12.12 E
Grëko, Akrōtērion-	24	Fe	34.56N	34.05 E
Gremiha	6	Jb	68.03N	39.29 E
Gremjačinsk	17	Hg	58.34N	57.51 E
Grenå	7	Ch	56.25N	10.53 E
Grenada [1]	39	Mh	12.07N	61.40W
Grenada	38	Mh	12.07N	61.40W
Grenada	45	Lj	33.47N	89.55W
Grenada Basin (EN)	47	Lf	13.30N	62.00W
Grenada Lake	45	Lj	33.50N	89.40W
Grenadines	47	Lf	12.40N	61.15W
Grenchen	14	Bc	47.11N	7.25 E
Grenen	5	Hd	57.44N	10.40 E
Grenfell	45	Ea	50.25N	102.56W
Grenoble	6	Gf	45.10N	5.43 E
Grenora	45	Eb	48.37N	103.56W
Grense-Jakobselv	7	Hb	69.47N	30.50 E
Grenville	50	Ff	12.07N	61.37W
Grenville, Cape-	59	Ib	12.00S	143.15 E
Gréoux-les-Bains	11	Lk	43.45N	5.53 E
Gresham	46	Dd	45.30N	122.26W
Gresik	26	Fh	7.09S	112.38 E
Gressoney-la-Trinité	14	Be	45.50N	7.49 E
Gretas Klackar	8	Gc	61.34N	17.50 E
Gretna	45	Kl	29.55N	90.03W
Grevelingen	12	Fc	51.45N	4.00 E
Greven	10	Dd	52.06N	7.37 E
Grevená	15	Ei	40.05N	21.25 E
Grevenbroich	10	Ce	51.05N	6.35 E
Grevenbrück, Lennestadt-	12	Kc	51.08N	8.01 E
Grevenmacher	12	Ie	49.41N	6.27 E
Grevesmühlen	10	Hc	53.52N	11.11 E
Grey	62	De	42.26S	171.11 E
Greybull	46	Kd	44.30N	108.03W
Greybull River	46	Kd	44.28N	108.03W
Grey Islands	42	Lf	50.50N	55.35W
Greymouth	61	Dh	42.27S	171.12 E
Grey Range	57	Fg	27.00S	143.35 E
Greystones/Ná Clocha Liatha	9	Gh	53.09N	6.04W
Greytown	37	Ee	29.07S	30.30 E
Greytown	62	Fd	41.05S	175.28 E
Gribanovski	16	Ld	51.29N	41.58 E
Gribb Bank (EN)	66	Ge	63.00S	90.30 E
Gribës, Mali i-	15	Ci	40.34N	19.34 E
Gribingui [3]	35	Bd	7.00N	19.30 E
Gribingui	35	Bd	8.33N	19.05 E
Griend	12	Ha	53.15N	5.20 E
Griesheim	12	Ke	49.52N	8.33 E
Grieskirchen	14	Hb	48.14N	13.50 E
Griffin	43	Ke	33.15N	84.16W
Griffith	59	Jf	34.17S	146.03 E
Grigoriopol	15	Mb	47.09N	29.13 E
Grijalva	38	Jh	18.36N	92.39W
Grim, Cape-	59	Ih	40.41S	144.41 E
Grimari	35	Cd	5.44N	20.03 E
Grimbergen	12	Gd	50.56N	4.23 E
Grimma	10	Ie	51.14N	12.43 E
Grimmen	10	Jb	54.06N	13.03 E
Grimsby	9	Mh	53.35N	0.05W
Grimsey	7a	Ca	66.33N	18.00W
Grimsstadir	7a	Cb	65.39N	16.07W
Grimstad	7	Bg	58.20N	8.36 E
Grimsvotn	7a	Cb	64.24N	17.22W
Grindavik	7a	Ac	63.50N	22.30W
Grindelwald	14	Cd	46.38N	8.03 E
Grindsted	7	Bi	55.45N	8.56 E
Grinnell	45	Jf	41.45N	92.43W
Grinnel Peninsula	42	Ia	76.40N	95.00W
Grintavec	14	Id	46.22N	14.32 E
Griquatown	37	Ce	28.49S	23.15 E
Grise Fiord	39	Kb	76.10N	83.15W
Gris-Nez, Cap-	11	Hd	50.52N	1.35 E
Grisslehamn	8	Hd	60.06N	18.50 E
Grjazi	19	De	52.29N	39.57 E
Grjazovec	19	Ed	58.53N	40.15 E
Grmeč	14	Kf	44.43N	16.15 E
Grobiņa/Grobinja	7	Eh	56.33N	21.11 E
Grobinja/Grobiņa	7	Eh	56.33N	21.11 E
Groblersdal	37	De	25.15S	29.25 E
Grocka	15	De	44.41N	20.43 E
Grodk/Spremberg	10	Ke	51.33N	14.22 E
Grodków	10	Nf	50.43N	17.22 E
Grodnenskaja Oblast [3]	19	Ce	53.45N	25.10 E
Grodno	6	Ie	53.42N	23.50 E
Grodzisk Mazowiecki	10	Qd	52.07N	20.37 E
Grodzjanka	16	Fc	53.34N	28.48 E
Groeie Hoop, Kaap die-/ Good Hope, Cape of-	30	Il	34.21S	18.28 E

Index Symbols

[1] Independent Nation
[2] State, Region
[3] District, County
[4] Municipality
[5] Colony, Dependency
Continent
Physical Region

Historical or Cultural Region
Mount, Mountain
Volcano
Hill
Mountains, Mountain Range
Hills, Escarpment
Plateau, Upland

Pass, Gap
Plain, Lowland
Delta
Salt Flat
Valley, Canyon
Crater, Cave
Karst Features

Depression
Polder
Desert, Dunes
Forest, Woods
Heath, Steppe
Oasis
Cape, Point

Coast, Beach
Cliff
Peninsula
Isthmus
Sandbank
Island
Atoll

Rock, Reef
Islands, Archipelago
Rocks, Reefs
Coral Reef
Well, Spring
Geyser
River, Stream

Waterfall Rapids
River Mouth, Estuary
Lake
Salt Lake
Intermittent Lake
Reservoir
Swamp, Pond

Canal
Glacier
Ice Shelf, Pack Ice
Ocean
Sea
Gulf, Bay
Strait, Fjord

Lagoon
Bank
Seamount
Tablemount
Ridge
Shelf
Basin

Escarpment, Sea Scarp
Fracture
Trench, Abyss
National Park, Reserve
Point of Interest
Recreation Site
Cave, Cavern

Historic Site
Ruins
Wall, Walls
Church, Abbey
Temple
Scientific Station
Airport

Port
Lighthouse
Mine
Tunnel
Dam, Bridge

Groenlo 12 Ib 52.04N 6.39 E
Groesbeek 12 Hc 51.47N 5.56 E
Grofa, Gora- 15 Ha 48.34N 24.03 E
Groix 11 Cg 47.38N 3.28W
Groix, Ile de- 11 Cg 47.38N 3.28W
Grójec 10 Qe 51.52N 20.52 E
Gröll Seamount (EN) 54 Lf 14.00S 32.00W
Gromnik 10 Nf 50.42N 17.07 E
Gronau (Westfalen) 10 Dd 52.12N 7.02 E
Grong 7 Cd 64.30N 12.27 E
Groningen [3] 12 Ia 53.13N 6.33 E
Groningen [Neth.] 6 Ge 53.13N 6.33 E
Groningen [Sur.] 54 Gb 5.48N 55.28W
Groninger-wad 12 Ia 53.27N 6.25 E
Groningerwad 12 Ia 53.25N 6.30 E
Grønland/Kalaallit Nunaat= Greenland (EN) 38 Pb 70.00N 40.00W
Grønland/Kalaallit Nunaat= Greenland (EN) [5] 67 Nd 70.00N 40.00W
Grønlandshavet=Greenland Sea (EN) 67 Ld 77.00N 1.00W
Grønnedal 41 Hf 61.20N 47.45W
Grönskara 8 Fg 57.05N 15.44 E
Groot 30 Jl 33.45S 24.58 E
Groot Baai 51b Ab 18.01N 63.04W
Groote Eylandt 57 Ef 14.00S 136.40 E
Grootfontein 31 Ij 19.32S 18.05 E
Grootfontein [3] 37 Bc 19.00S 19.00 E
Groot-Karasberge=Great Karasberge (EN) 30 Ik 27.20S 18.45 E
Groot Karoo=Great Karroo (EN) 30 Jl 33.00S 22.00 E
Grootlaagte 37 Cd 20.55S 21.27 E
Groot Namaland/Great Namaland 37 Be 26.00S 17.00 E
Grootvloer 37 Ce 30.00S 20.40 E
Gropeni 15 Kd 45.05N 27.54 E
Gros Caps, Pointe des- 51e Bb 16.28N 61.25W
Gros Islet Bay 51k Ba 14.05N 60.58W
Gros Islets 51k Ba 14.05N 60.58W
Gros-Morne 51h Ab 14.43N 61.01W
Gros-Morne 42 Lg 49.00N 57.22W
Grosne 11 Kh 46.42N 4.56 E
Gros Piton 51k Ab 13.49N 61.04W
Große Aa 12 Jb 52.25N 7.23 E
Große Aue 12 Kb 52.30N 8.38 E
Großefehn 12 Ja 53.24N 7.33 E
Große Laaber 10 Ih 48.50N 12.30 E
Großenhain 10 Je 51.17N 13.33 E
Großenkneten 12 Kb 52.57N 8.16 E
Grosse Pointe 51e Bb 16.01N 61.17W
Großer Arber 10 Jg 49.07N 13.07 E
Großer Gleichberg 10 Gf 50.23N 10.35 E
Großer Inselsberg 10 Gf 50.52N 10.28 E
Grosseto 14 Fh 42.46N 11.08 E
Grosseto, Formiche di- 14 Eh 42.40N 10.55 E
Groß-Gerau 10 Eg 49.55N 8.29 E
Großglockner 5 Hf 47.04N 12.42 E
Großräschen 10 Je 51.35N 14.00 E
Groß-Umstadt 12 Ke 49.52N 8.56 E
Großvenediger 14 Gc 47.06N 12.21 E
Grostenquin 12 If 48.59N 6.44 E
Gros Ventre Range 46 Je 43.30N 110.15W
Groswater Bay 38 Nd 54.20N 57.30W
Grøtavær 7 Db 68.58N 16.16 E
Grote Nete 12 Gc 51.07N 4.34 E
Grotli 7 Be 62.01N 7.40 E
Grottaglie 14 Lj 40.32N 17.26 E
Grottammare 14 Hh 42.59N 13.52 E
Groumania 34 Ed 7.55N 4.00W
Groundhog River 44 Ga 49.43N 81.58W
Grouse Creek Montains 46 If 41.55N 113.50W
Grove Mountains 66 Ff 72.53S 74.53 E
Groves 45 Jl 29.57N 93.55W
Grovfjord 7 Db 68.41N 17.09 E
Grow, Idaarderadeel- 12 Ha 53.06N 5.50 E
Grozny 6 Kg 43.20N 45.42 E
Grubišno Polje 14 Le 45.42N 17.10 E
Grudovo 15 Kg 42.21N 27.10 E
Grudziądz 10 Oc 53.29N 18.45 E
Grumento Nova 14 Jj 40.17N 15.53 E
Grumo Appula 14 Ki 41.01N 16.42 E
Grums 8 Ee 59.21N 13.06 E
Grünau 37 Be 27.47S 18.23 E
Grünberg 12 Kd 50.36N 8.57 E
Gründau 12 Ld 50.14N 9.05 E
Grundy 44 Fg 37.17N 82.06W
Gruñidera 48 Ie 24.15N 101.58W
Grünstadt 12 Ke 49.34N 8.10 E
Grunwald 10 Qc 53.30N 20.05 E
Gruppo di Brenta 14 Ed 46.10N 10.55 E
Gruyère 14 Bd 46.40N 7.10 E
Gruža 15 Df 43.54N 20.47 E
Gruzinskaja Sovetskaja Socialističeskaja Respublika [2] 19 Eg 42.00N 44.00 E
Gruzinskaja SSR/ Sakartvelos Sabčata Socialisturi Respublica [2] 19 Eg 42.00N 44.00 E
Gruzinskaja SSR=Georgian SSR (EN) [2] 19 Eg 42.00N 44.00 E
Grybów 10 Qg 49.38N 20.56 E
Grycksbo 8 Fd 60.41N 15.28 E
Gryfice 10 Lc 53.56N 15.12 E
Gryfino 10 Kc 53.15N 14.30 E
Grythyttan 8 Fe 59.42N 14.32 E
Grytviken 66 Ad 54.17S 36.31W
Gstaad 14 Bd 46.28N 7.17 E
Guacanayabo, Golfo de- 47 Id 20.28N 77.30W
Guacara 50 Cg 10.14N 67.53W
Guaçu 55 Ef 22.11S 54.31W
Guadaioz 13 Hg 37.50N 4.51W
Guadaira 13 Fg 37.20N 6.01W
Guadalajara [3] 13 Jd 40.50N 2.30W
Guadalajara [Mex.] 39 Ig 20.40N 103.20W
Guadalajara [Sp.] 13 Id 40.38N 3.10W
Guadalaviar 13 Kd 40.21N 1.08W
Guadalbullón 13 Ig 37.59N 3.47W
Guadalcanal 13 Gf 38.06N 5.49W
Guadalcanal Island 57 He 9.32S 160.12 E
Guadalén 13 If 38.05N 3.32W
Guadalentin o Sangonera 13 Kg 37.59N 1.04W
Guadalete 13 Fh 36.35N 6.13W
Guadalfeo 13 Ih 36.43N 3.35W
Guadalimar 13 Ig 37.59N 3.44W
Guadalmena 13 Jf 38.20N 2.55W
Guadalmez 13 Gf 38.46N 5.04W
Guadalope 13 Lc 41.15N 0.03W
Guadalquivir 5 Fh 36.47N 6.22W
Guadalupe [Mex.] 47 Dc 25.41N 100.15W
Guadalupe [Mex.] 48 Hf 22.45N 102.31W
Guadalupe [Mex.] 48 Id 26.12N 101.23W
Guadalupe [Sp.] 13 Ge 39.27N 5.19W
Guadalupe, Isla de- 38 Hg 29.00N 118.16W
Guadalupe, Sierra de- 13 Ge 39.25N 5.25W
Guadalupe Bravos 48 Fb 31.23N 106.07W
Guadalupe Mountains 45 Dj 32.20N 105.00W
Guadalupe Peak 43 Ge 31.50N 104.52W
Guadalupe River 45 Hl 28.30N 96.53W
Guadalupe Victoria, Presa- 48 Gf 23.50N 104.55W
Guadalupe y Calvo 48 Fd 26.06N 106.58W
Guadarrama 13 He 39.53N 4.10W
Guadarrama, Puerto de- 13 Hd 40.43N 4.10W
Guadarrama, Sierra de- 13 Id 40.55N 4.00W
Guadazaón 13 Ke 39.42N 1.36W
Guadeloupe 38 Mh 16.15N 61.35W
Guadeloupe [5] 39 Mh 16.15N 61.35W
Guadeloupe, Canal de la-= Guadeloupe Passage (EN) 47 Le 16.40N 61.50W
Guadeloupe Passage 50 Fd 16.40N 61.50W
Guadeloupe Passage (EN)= Guadeloupe, Canal de la- 47 Le 16.40N 61.50W
Guadiana 5 Fh 37.14N 7.22W
Guadiana, Canal del- 13 Ie 39.20N 3.20W
Guadiana, Ojos del- 13 Ie 39.08N 3.31W
Guadiana Menor 13 Ig 37.56N 3.15W
Guadiaro 13 Gh 36.17N 5.17W
Guadiela 13 Jd 40.22N 2.49W
Guadix 13 Ig 37.18N 3.08W
Guafo, Boca del- 56 Ff 43.40S 74.15W
Guafo, Isla- 56 Ff 43.36S 74.43W
Guaiba 56 Jd 30.06S 51.19W
Guaiba, Rio- 55 Gj 30.15S 51.12W
Guaimaca 49 Df 14.52N 86.51W
Guaimorato, Laguna de- 49 Ef 15.58N 85.55W
Guainía [2] 54 Ec 2.30N 69.00W
Guainia, Río- 52 Je 2.01N 67.07W
Guaiquinima, Cerro- 54 Fb 5.49N 63.40W
Guaira [3] 55 Dg 25.45S 56.30W
Guaira [Braz.] 56 Jb 24.04S 54.15W
Guaira [Braz.] 55 He 20.19S 48.18W
Guaira Falls (EN) = Sete Quedas, Saltos das- 56 Jb 24.02S 54.16W
Guairas 55 Ja 12.39S 44.16W
Guaire/Gorey 9 Gi 52.40N 6.18W
Guaitecas, Islas- 56 Ff 43.57S 73.50W
Guajaba, Cayo- 49 Ic 21.50N 77.30W
Guajará Mirim 53 Jg 10.48S 65.22W
Guajira, Peninsula de la- 52 Id 12.00N 71.30W
Guajolotes, Sierra del- 48 Ge 26.00N 105.15W
Guakolak, Tanjung- 26 Eh 6.50S 105.14 E
Gualaco 49 Df 15.06N 86.07W
Gualán 49 Cf 15.08N 89.22W
Gualdo Tadino 14 Gg 43.14N 12.47 E
Gualeguay 55 Ck 33.09S 59.20W
Gualeguay, Río- 55 Ck 33.19S 59.39W
Gualeguaychu 56 Id 33.01S 58.31W
Gualeguaychú, Río- 55 Ck 33.05S 58.25W
Gualicho, Salina del- 56 Gf 40.24S 65.15W
Guam [5] 58 Fc 13.28N 144.47 E
Guam 57 Fc 13.28N 144.47 E
Guaminí 56 He 37.02S 62.25W
Guampi, Sierra de- 54 Eb 6.00N 65.35W
Guamuchil 47 Cc 25.22N 108.22W
Gua Musang 26 Df 4.53N 101.58 E
Gu'an 28 De 39.24N 116.10 E
Guanabacoa 49 Fb 23.07N 82.18W
Guanabara, Baia de- 55 Kf 22.50S 43.10W
Guanacaste [3] 49 Eh 10.30N 85.15W
Guanacaste, Cordillera de- 49 Eh 10.45N 85.05W
Guanacevi 48 Ge 25.56N 105.57W
Guanahacabibes, Golfo de- 49 Eb 22.08N 84.35W
Guanahacabibes, Peninsula de- 49 Ec 21.57N 84.35W
Guana Island 51a Db 18.29N 64.34W
Guanaja 49 Ee 16.27N 85.54W
Guanaja, Isla de- 49 Ee 16.30N 85.55W
Guanajay 49 Fb 22.55N 82.42W
Guanajibo 51a Ab 18.10N 67.09W
Guanajibo, Punta- 51a Ab 18.12N 67.10W
Guanajuato 47 Dd 21.01N 101.15W
Guanajuato [2] 47 Dd 21.00N 101.00W
Guanambi 54 Jf 14.13S 42.47W
Guanare 54 Eb 9.03N 69.45W
Guanare, Río- 50 Ch 8.13N 67.46W
Guanare Viejo, Río- 49 Mi 8.19N 68.10W
Guanarito 50 Bh 8.42N 69.12W
Guandacol 56 Gc 29.31S 68.32W
Guandi Shan 27 Jd 38.09N 111.27 E
Guane 47 Hd 22.12N 84.05W
Guangde 27 Ke 30.51N 119.26 E
Guangdong Sheng (Kuang-tung Sheng)= Kwangtung (EN) [2] 27 Jg 23.00N 113.00 E
Guangfeng 28 Ej 28.27N 118.12 E
Guanghua 27 Je 32.18N 111.45 E
Guangji (Wuxue) 27 Kf 29.58N 115.32 E
Guangling 28 Ce 39.46N 114.16 E
Guangmao Shan 27 Hf 26.48N 100.56 E
Guangming Ding 28 Ei 30.09N 118.11 E
Guangnan 27 Ig 24.02N 105.04 E
Guangrao 28 Ef 37.03N 118.25 E
Guangshan 28 Ci 32.02N 114.53 E
Guangshui 28 Ci 31.37N 114.01 E
Guangxi Zhuangzu Zizhiqu (Kuang-hsi-chuang-tsu Tzu-chih-ch'ü)=Kwangsi Chuang (EN) [2] 27 Ig 24.00N 109.00 E
Guangyuan 22 Mf 32.27N 105.55 E
Guangzhou=Canton (EN) 22 Ng 23.07N 113.18 E
Guan He 28 Ch 32.18N 115.44 E
Guánica 51a Bc 17.59N 66.56W
Guanipa, Río- 50 Eh 9.56N 62.26W
Guannan (Xin'anzhen) 28 Eg 34.04N 119.21 E
Guantánamo [3] 49 Jc 20.10N 75.00W
Guantanamo 39 Lg 20.08N 75.12W
Guantánamo, Bahía de- 49 Jd 20.00N 75.10W
Guantánamo Bay 47 Id 20.00N 75.10W
Guantanamo Bay Naval Station 49 Jd 20.00N 75.08W
Guantao (Nanguantao) 28 Cf 36.33N 115.18 E
Guanting Shuiku 28 Cd 40.13N 115.36 E
Guanxian 22 Mf 31.00N 103.38 E
Guanyun (Dayishan) 28 Eg 34.18N 119.14 E
Guapé 55 Je 20.47S 45.55W
Guapí 54 Cc 2.35N 77.55W
Guápiles 49 Fh 10.13N 83.46W
Guapó 55 Hc 16.51S 49.33W
Guaporé 55 Gi 29.10S 51.54W
Guaporé 56 Jc 28.51S 51.54W
Guaporé, Rio- 52 Jg 11.55S 65.04W
Guaqui 54 Eg 16.35S 68.51W
Guará 55 Gg 25.23S 51.17W
Guara, Sierra de- 13 Lb 42.17N 0.10W
Guarabira 54 Ke 6.51S 35.29W
Guaranda 54 Cd 1.35S 78.59W
Guaraniacu 56 Jc 25.06S 52.52W
Guarani de Goiás 55 Ia 13.57S 46.28W
Guarapiche, Río- 50 Eh 9.57N 62.52W
Guarapuava 56 Jc 25.23S 51.27W
Guaraqueçaba 55 Hg 25.17S 48.21W
Guararapes 55 Ge 21.15S 50.38W
Guaratinguetá 55 Jf 22.49S 45.13W
Guaratuba 55 Hg 25.54S 48.34W
Guarayos, Río- 55 Bb 14.38S 62.11W
Guarda 13 Ed 40.32N 7.16W
Guarda [2] 13 Ed 40.40N 7.10W
Guardafui, Cape-(EN)= 'Asäyr 30 Mg 11.49N 51.15 E
Guardal 13 Jg 37.36N 2.45W
Guarda-Mor 55 Ic 17.47S 47.06W
Guardiagrele 14 Ih 42.11N 14.13 E
Guardian Seamount (EN) 38 Ki 9.32N 87.40W
Guardo 13 Hb 42.47N 4.50W
Guardunha, Serra da- 13 Ed 40.05N 7.31W
Guareí, Rio- 55 Ff 22.40S 53.34W
Guareña 13 Gc 41.29N 5.23W
Guarenas 50 Cg 10.28N 66.37W
Guaribas, Rio- 55 Jc 16.22S 45.03W
Guaribe, Río- 50 Dh 9.53N 65.11W
Guárico [2] 54 Eb 8.40N 66.35W
Guárico, Embalse del- 50 Ch 9.00N 67.20W
Guarico, Río- 54 Eb 7.55N 67.23W
Guariquito, Río- 50 Ci 7.40N 66.18W
Guarita, Rio- 55 Fh 27.11S 53.44W
Guaritico, Caño- 50 Bi 7.52N 68.53W
Guaritire, Río- 55 Ba 13.43S 60.38W
Guarujá 55 If 24.00S 46.16W
Guarulhos 56 Kb 23.28S 46.32W
Guasave 47 Cc 25.34N 108.27W
Guasdualito 54 Db 7.15N 70.44W
Guasipati 54 Fb 7.28N 61.54W
Guasopa 63a Ac 9.14S 152.55 E
Guastalla 14 Ef 44.55N 10.39 E
Guatemala 39 Jh 14.38N 90.31W
Guatemala [3] 49 Bf 14.40N 90.30W
Guatemala [1] 39 Jh 14.38N 90.31W
Guatemala Basin (EN) 3 Mh 11.00N 95.00W
Guateque [Col.] 54 Db 5.05N 73.30W
Guateque [Col.] 54 Db 5.00N 73.28W
Guatimozín 55 Ak 33.27S 62.27W
Guatisimiña 54 Fc 4.33N 63.57W
Guatraché 56 He 37.40S 63.32W
Guaviare, Río- 52 Je 4.03N 67.44W
Guaviravi 55 Di 29.22S 56.50W
Guaxupé 55 Ie 21.18S 46.42W
Guayabal [Cuba] 49 Ic 20.42N 77.36W
Guayabal [Ven.] 50 Ci 8.00N 67.24W
Guayabero, Río- 52 Je 4.03N 67.44W
Guayalejo, Río- 48 Kf 22.13N 97.52W
Guayama 49 Ne 17.59N 66.07W
Guayana, Macizo de la- = Guiana Highlands (EN) 52 Ke 5.00N 60.00W
Guayana Basin (EN) 3 Ci 10.00N 52.00W
Guayaneco, Archipiélago- 56 Eg 47.45S 75.10W
Guayanés, Punta- 51a Cb 18.04N 65.48W
Guayanilla 51a Bb 18.02N 66.47W
Guayanilla, Bahía de- 51a Bc 17.58N 66.45W
Guayape, Río- 49 Df 14.26N 86.02W
Guayaquil 53 If 2.10S 79.50W
Guayaquil, Golfo de- 52 Hf 3.00S 80.30W
Guaycurú, Río- 55 Ch 27.19S 58.45W
Guaymas 39 Hg 27.56N 110.54W
Guayquiraró, Río- 55 Cj 30.10S 58.34W
Guba [Eth.] 35 Fc 11.15N 35.20 E
Guba [Zaire] 36 Ee 10.38S 26.25 E
Guba Dolgaja 19 Fa 70.19N 58.45 E
Gubaha 19 Fd 58.52N 57.36 E
Guban 30 Lg 10.15N 44.26 E
Gubbio 14 Gg 43.21N 12.25 E
Gubdor 17 Hf 60.15N 56.35 E
Guber 10 Rb 54.13N 21.02 E
Gubin 10 Ke 51.56N 14.45 E
Gubio 34 Hc 12.30N 12.47 E
Gubkin 19 De 51.17N 37.33 E
Gúdar, Sierra de- 13 Ld 40.27N 0.42W
Gudara 19 Hh 38.23N 72.42 E
Gudauta 16 Lh 43.07N 40.37 E
Gudbrandsdalen 7 Bf 61.30N 10.00 E
Gudenå 8 Dh 56.29N 10.13 E
Gudermes 19 Eg 43.22N 46.08 E
Gudivāda 25 Ge 16.27N 80.59 E
Gudiyāttam 25 Ff 12.57N 78.52 E
Gudou Shan 27 Jg 22.12N 112.57 E
Güdül 24 Eb 40.13N 32.15 E
Gūdūr 25 Ff 14.08N 79.51 E
Gudvangen 8 Bd 60.52N 6.50 E
Guebwiller 11 Ng 47.55N 7.12 E
Guéckédou 34 Cd 8.33N 10.09W
Guelma [3] 32 Ib 36.15N 7.30 E
Guelma 32 Ib 36.28N 7.26 E
Guelph 42 Jh 43.33N 80.15W
Guelta Zemmur 32 Ed 25.08N 12.22W
Guemar 32 Ic 33.29N 6.48 E
Guéméné-Penfao 11 Eg 47.38N 1.50W
Guénange 12 Ie 49.18N 6.11 E
Guéné 34 Fc 11.44N 3.13 E
Guer 11 Dg 47.54N 2.07W
Guéra [3] 35 Bc 11.30N 18.30 E
Güera 32 De 20.52N 17.03W
Guéra, Massif de- 30 Ig 11.55N 18.12 E
Guérande 11 Dg 47.20N 2.26W
Guerara 32 Hc 32.48N 4.30 E
Guercif 32 Gc 34.14N 3.22W
Guerdjoumane, Djebel- 13 Oh 36.25N 2.51 E
Güere, Río- 50 Dh 9.50N 65.08W
Guéréda 35 Cc 14.31N 22.05 E
Guéret 11 Hh 46.10N 1.52 E
Guérin-Kouka 34 Fd 9.41N 0.37 E
Guernica y Luno 13 Ja 43.19N 2.41W
Guernsey 9 Kl 49.27N 2.35W
Guerrero [2] 47 De 17.40N 100.00W
Guerrero 48 Ic 28.20N 100.26W
Guessou-Sud 34 Fc 10.03N 2.38 E
Guest Peninsula 66 Mf 76.18S 148.00W
Guge 35 Fd 6.12N 37.30 E
Gügerd, Kūh-e- 24 Oe 34.50N 53.00 E
Guglionesi 14 Ii 41.55N 14.55 E
Guguan Island 57 Fc 17.19N 145.51 E
Guia 55 Db 15.22S 56.14W
Guia Lopes da Laguna 55 De 21.26S 56.07W
Guiana Highlands (EN) = Guayana, Macizo de la- 52 Ke 5.00N 60.00W
Guiana Island 51d Bb 17.06N 61.44W
Guichi (Chizhou) 27 Ke 30.38N 117.30 E
Guichón 55 Dk 32.21S 57.12W
Guide 27 Hd 36.00N 101.30 E
Guider 34 Hd 9.56N 13.57 E
Guidimaka [3] 32 Ef 15.30N 12.00W
Guidimouni 34 Gc 13.42N 9.30 E
Guiding 27 If 26.33N 107.16 E
Guidong 27 Jf 26.11N 113.58 E
Guiers 11 Li 45.37N 5.37 E
Guiglo 34 Dd 6.33N 7.29W
Guiglo [3] 34 Dd 6.30N 7.40W
Guijá 37 Ed 24.29S 33.00 E
Güija, Lago de- 49 Cf 14.13N 89.34W
Gui Jiang 21 Ng 23.28N 111.18 E
Guijk en Sint Agatha 12 Hc 51.44N 5.52 E
Guijuelo 13 Gd 40.33N 5.40W
Guil 11 Mj 44.40N 6.36 E
Guildford 9 Mj 51.14N 0.35W
Guiler Gol 28 Ga 46.03N 122.06 E
Guilin 22 Ng 25.21N 110.15 E
Guillaume Delisle, Lac- 42 Je 56.25N 76.00W
Guillestre 11 Mj 44.40N 6.39 E
Guilvinec 11 Bg 47.47N 4.17W
Guimarães [Braz.] 54 Jd 2.08S 44.36W
Guimarães [Port.] 13 Dc 41.27N 8.18W
Guimaras 26 Hd 10.35N 122.37 E
Guinchos Cay 49 Hb 22.45N 78.06W
Guinea (EN)=Guinée [1] 31 Fg 11.00N 10.00W
Guinea, Gulf of- 30 Hh 2.00N 2.30 E
Guinea, Gulf of- (EN)= Guinée, Golfe de- 30 Hh 2.00N 2.30 E
Guinea Basin (EN) 3 Di 0.00 5.00W
Guinea-Bissau (EN)=Guiné-Bissau [1] 31 Fg 12.00N 15.00W
Guinea Ecuatorial= Equatorial Guinea (EN) [1] 31 Hh 2.00N 9.00 E
Guinea Rise (EN) 3 Dj 4.00S 0.00
Guiné-Bissau=Guinea-Bissau (EN) [1] 31 Fg 12.00N 15.00W
Guinée=Guinea (EN) [1] 31 Fg 11.00N 10.00W
Guinée, Golfe de-=Guinea, Gulf of- (EN) 30 Hh 2.00N 2.30 E
Guinée Forestière [3] 34 Dd 8.40N 9.50W
Guinée Maritime [3] 34 Cc 10.00N 14.00W
Guînes 12 Dd 50.52N 1.52 E
Güines 47 Hd 22.50N 82.02W
Guingamp 11 Cf 48.33N 3.09W
Guinguinéo 34 Bc 14.16N 15.57W
Guiones, Punta- 49 Eh 9.54N 85.41W
Guiping 27 Ig 23.23N 110.00 E
Guipúzcoa [3] 13 Ja 43.10N 2.10W
Guir, Hamada du- 30 Ge 31.00N 3.20W
Güira de Melena 49 Fb 22.48N 82.30W
Guiratinga 54 Hg 16.21S 53.45W
Güiria 54 Fa 10.34N 62.18W
Guiscard 12 Fe 49.39N 3.03 E
Guise 11 Je 49.54N 3.38 E
Guitiriz 13 Ea 43.11N 7.54W
Guiuan 26 Id 11.02N 125.43 E
Guixi 27 Kf 28.18N 117.15 E
Guixian 27 Ig 23.10N 109.35 E
Guiyang 22 Mg 26.38N 106.43 E
Guizhou Sheng (Kuei-chou Sheng)=Kweichow (EN) [2] 27 If 27.00N 107.00 E
Gujan-Mestras 11 Ej 44.38N 1.04W
Gujarāt [3] 25 Ed 22.51N 71.30 E
Gujarāt 21 Jg 22.51N 71.30 E
Gujranwala 22 Jf 32.09N 74.11 E
Gujrāt 25 Eb 32.34N 74.05 E
Gukovo 16 Ke 48.04N 39.58 E
Gulang 27 Hd 37.30N 102.54 E
Gulbarga 22 Jh 17.20N 76.50 E
Gulbene 19 Cd 57.12N 26.49 E
Gulča 19 Hg 40.19N 73.33 E
Gulf 55 Ad 19.08S 62.01W
Gulf Breeze 44 Dj 30.22N 87.07W
Gulf Coastal Plain 38 Jf 31.00N 92.00W
Gulfport 43 Je 30.22N 89.06W
Gulian 27 La 52.58N 122.09 E
Gulin 27 If 28.02N 105.47 E
Gulistan 19 Gg 40.30N 68.45 E
Guliya Shan 27 Lb 49.48N 122.25 E
Gulja 20 Hf 54.43N 121.03 E
Gulja/Yining 27 Dc 43.54N 81.21 E
Guljajpole 16 Jf 47.37N 36.18 E
Gulkana 40 Jd 62.16N 145.23W
Gulkeviči 16 Lg 45.19N 40.44 E
Gull Bay 45 Lb 49.47N 89.02W
Gulleråsen 8 Fc 61.04N 15.11 E
Gullfoss 7a Bb 64.20N 20.08W
Gullkronafjärd 8 Jd 60.05N 22.15 E
Gull Lake 42 Gf 50.08N 108.27W
Gullringen 8 Fg 57.48N 15.42 E
Gull River 45 Lb 49.50N 89.04W
Gullspång 8 Ff 58.59N 14.06 E
Güllü 15 Mk 38.16N 29.07 E
Güllük 24 Bd 37.14N 27.36 E
Gülpinar 15 Jj 39.32N 26.07 E
Gülşehir 24 Fc 38.45N 34.38 E
Gulstav 8 Dj 54.43N 10.41 E
Gulu 31 Kh 2.47N 32.18 E
Guma /Pishan 27 Cd 37.38N 78.19 E
Gumbiri, Jabal- 35 Ee 4.18N 30.57 E
Gumel 34 Gc 12.38N 9.23 E
Gummersbach 10 De 51.02N 7.33 E
Gummi 34 Gc 12.09N 5.07 E
Gümüşçey 15 Ki 40.17N 27.17 E
Gümüşhacıköy 24 Fb 40.53N 35.14 E
Gümüşhane 23 Ea 40.27N 39.29 E
Gümüşsu 15 Nk 38.14N 30.01 E
Guna 35 Fc 11.44N 38.15 E
Guna 25 Fd 24.19N 77.19 E
Gundagai 59 Jg 35.04S 148.07 E
Gundji 36 Db 2.05N 21.27 E
Gündoğdu 15 Ki 40.15N 27.07 E
Gündoğmuş 24 Ed 36.48N 32.01 E
Güney 15 Mk 38.09N 29.05 E
Güneydoğu Toroslar 21 Gf 38.30N 41.00 E
Gungu 36 Cd 5.44S 19.19 E
Gunma Ken [2] 28 Of 36.20N 139.05 E
Gunnar 42 Ge 59.23N 108.53W
Gunnbjørns Fjeld 67 Mc 68.55N 29.20W
Gunnedah 59 Kf 30.59S 150.15 E
Gunnison 43 Fd 38.33N 106.56W
Gunt 18 Hf 37.30N 71.03 E
Guntakal 25 Fe 15.10N 77.23 E
Guntersville 44 Dh 34.21N 86.18W
Guntersville Lake 44 Dh 34.45N 86.03W
Guntūr 22 Kh 16.18N 80.27 E
Gunungapi, Pulau- 26 Ih 6.38S 126.40 E
Gunungsitoli 26 Cf 1.17N 97.37 E
Günz 10 Gh 48.27N 10.16 E
Günzburg 10 Gh 48.27N 10.16 E
Gunzenhausen 10 Gg 49.06N 10.45 E
Guo He 28 Dh 32.58N 117.13 E
Guojiadian 28 Hc 43.20N 124.37 E
Guoyang 28 Dh 33.31N 116.12 E
Guozhen 28 Bj 29.24N 113.09 E
Gurahonţ 15 Fc 46.16N 22.21 E
Gura Humorului 15 Ib 47.33N 25.54 E
Gurban Obo 27 Jc 43.06N 112.28 E
Gurbantünggüt Shamo 27 Eb 45.30N 87.30 E
Gurdžaani 16 Ni 41.43N 45.48 E
Güre 15 Mk 38.39N 29.10 E
Gurgei, Jabal- 35 Cc 13.50N 24.19 E
Gurghiului, Munţii- 15 Ic 46.41N 25.12 E
Gurgueia, Rio- 52 Lf 6.50S 43.24W
Guri — Raúl Leoni, Represa- 54 Fb 7.30N 63.00W
Gurjev 6 Lf 47.07N 51.56 E
Gurjevsk 20 Df 54.20N 86.00 E
Gurjevskaja Oblast [3] 19 Ff 47.30N 52.00 E
Gurk 14 Id 46.36N 14.31 E
Gurk 14 Id 46.52N 14.18 E
Gurktaler Alpen 14 Hd 46.55N 14.00 E
Guro 37 Ec 17.26S 33.20 E
Gürpınar 24 Jc 38.18N 43.25 E
Gurskoje 20 If 50.20N 138.05 E
Gurskøy 7 Ae 62.15N 5.40 E
Gürsu 15 Mi 40.13N 29.12 E
Gurué 37 Fc 15.28S 36.59 E
Gurumeti 36 Fc 2.05S 33.57 E
Gürün 24 Gc 38.43N 37.17 E
Gurupá 54 Hd 1.25S 51.39W
Gurupi 53 Lg 11.43S 49.04W
Gurupi, Rio- 52 Lf 1.13S 46.06W
Gurupi, Serra do- 54 Id 5.00S 47.30W
Guru Sikhar 25 Ed 24.39N 72.46 E
Gus 7 Ji 55.00N 41.12 E
Gusau 31 Hg 12.10N 6.40 E
Gusev 19 Ce 54.37N 22.12 E
Gushan 28 Ge 39.54N 123.36 E
Gushi 27 Ke 32.02N 115.39 E
Gushikawa 29b Ab 26.21N 127.52 E
Gūshk 24 Ph 28.13N 55.52 E
Gus-Hrustalny 7 Ji 55.38N 40.40 E
Gusinaja, Guba- 20 Kb 72.00N 150.00 E
Gusinaja Zemlja, Poluostrov- 19 Fa 71.50N 52.00 E
Gusinje 15 Cg 42.34N 19.50 E
Gusinoozersk 20 Ff 51.17N 106.30 E
Guspini 14 Ck 39.32N 8.37 E
Güssing 14 Kc 47.04N 16.20 E
Gustav Holm, Kap- 41 Ie 66.45N 34.00W
Gustavia 51b Bc 17.54N 62.52W

Index Symbols

[1] Independent Nation
[2] State, Region
[3] District, County
[4] Municipality
[5] Colony, Dependency
Continent
Physical Region
Historical or Cultural Region
Mount, Mountain
Volcano
Hill
Mountains, Mountain Range
Hills, Escarpment
Plateau, Upland
Pass, Gap
Plain, Lowland
Delta
Salt Flat
Valley, Canyon
Crater, Cave
Karst Features
Depression
Polder
Desert, Dunes
Forest, Woods
Heath, Steppe
Oasis
Cape, Point
Coast, Beach
Cliff
Peninsula
Isthmus
Sandbank
Island
Atoll
Rock, Reef
Islands, Archipelago
Rocks, Reefs
Coral Reef
Well, Spring
Geyser
River, Stream
Waterfall Rapids
River Mouth, Estuary
Lake
Salt Lake
Intermittent Lake
Reservoir
Swamp, Pond
Canal
Glacier
Ice Shelf, Pack Ice
Ocean
Sea
Gulf, Bay
Strait, Fjord
Lagoon
Bank
Seamount
Tablemount
Ridge
Shelf
Basin
Escarpment, Sea Scarp
Fracture
Trench, Abyss
National Park, Reserve
Point of Interest
Recreation Site
Cave, Cavern
Historic Site
Ruins
Wall, Walls
Church, Abbey
Temple
Scientific Station
Airport
Port
Lighthouse
Mine
Tunnel
Dam, Bridge

Gustavs/Kustavi 8 Id 60.30N 21.25 E
Gustavs/Kustavi 8 Id 60.33N 21.21 E
Gustavsfors 8 Ee 59.12N 12.06 E
Gustavus 40 Le 58.25N 135.44W
Güstrow 10 Ic 53.48N 12.10 E
Gusum 8 Gf 58.16N 16.29 E
Gütersloh 10 Ee 51.54N 8.23 E
Guthrie [Ok.-U.S.] 45 Hi 35.53N 97.25W
Guthrie [Tx.-U.S.] 45 Fj 33.37N 100.19W
Gutian 27 Kf 26.40N 118.42 E
Gutiérrez Zamora 48 Kg 20.27N 97.05W
Gutîi, Vîrful- 15 Gb 47.42N 23.52 E
Guting → Yutai 28 Dg 35.00N 116.40 E
Gutland 11 Me 49.40N 6.10 E
Gutu 37 Ec 19.39S 31.10 E
Guyana [1] 53 Ke 5.00N 59.00W
Guyane Française = French Guiana (EN) [5] 53 Ke 4.00N 53.00W
Guyang 27 Jc 41.02N 110.04 E
Guyenne 11 Gj 44.35N 1.00 E
Guymon 43 Gd 36.41N 101.29W
Guyonneau, Anse- 51e Ab 16.14N 61.47W
Guyuan 27 Id 36.01N 106.17 E
Guyuan (Pingdingbu) 28 Cd 41.40N 115.41 E
Guzar 18 Fe 38.37N 66.18 E
Güzelyurt/Mórphou 24 Ee 35.12N 32.59 E
Güzhān 24 Le 34.20N 46.57 E
Guzhen 28 Dh 33.20N 117.19 E
Guzhou → Rongjiang 27 If 25.58N 108.30 E
Guzmán, Laguna de- 48 Fb 31.20N 107.30W
Gvardejsk 7 Ei 54.40N 21.03 E
Gvardejskoje 16 Hg 45.06N 33.59 E
Gvary 8 Ce 59.23N 9.09 E
Gwa 25 Ie 17.36N 94.35 E
Gwadabawa 34 Gc 13.22N 5.14 E
Gwādar 22 Ig 25.07N 62.19 E
Gwai 30 Jj 17.59S 26.52 E
Gwai 37 Dc 19.17S 27.39 E
Gwalior 22 Jg 26.13N 78.10 E
Gwanda 37 Dd 20.56S 29.00 E
Gwane 36 Eb 4.43N 25.50 E
Gwda 10 Mc 53.04N 16.44 E
Gweebarra Bay/Béal an Bheara 9 Eg 54.52N 8.20W
Gwelo 31 Jj 19.27S 29.49 E
Gwent [3] 9 Kj 51.45N 2.55W
Gweta 37 Dd 20.13S 25.14 E
Gwydir River 59 Je 29.27S 149.48 E
Gwynedd [3] 9 Ji 52.50N 3.50W
Gyaca 27 Ff 29.09N 92.38 E
Gya'gya → Saga 27 Ef 29.22N 85.15 E
Gyai Qu 27 Fe 31.30N 94.40 E
Gyaisi/Jiulong 27 Hf 28.58N 101.33 E
Gya La 27 Gf 29.05N 98.41 E
Gyala Shankou 27 Gf 29.05N 98.41 E
Gyangzê 27 Ef 29.00N 89.38 E
Gyaring Co 27 Ee 31.10N 88.15 E
Gyaring Hu 27 Ge 34.55N 98.00 E
Gyda 20 Cb 70.52N 78.30 E
Gydanskaja Guba 20 Cb 71.20N 76.30 E
Gydanski Poluostrov = Gyda Peninsula (EN) 21 Jb 70.50N 79.00 E
Gyda Peninsula (EN) = Gydanski Poluostrov 21 Jb 70.50N 79.00 E
Gyigang → Zayü 27 Gf 28.43N 97.25 E
Gyirong (Zongga) 27 Ef 28.57N 85.12 E
Gyldenløves Fjord 41 Hf 64.10N 40.30W
Gyldenløves Høj 8 Di 55.33N 11.52 E
Gympie 58 Gg 26.11S 152.40 E
Gyoma 10 Qj 46.56N 20.50 E
Gyöngyös 10 Pi 47.47N 19.56 E
Győr 6 Hf 47.41N 17.38 E
Győr [2] 10 Ni 47.40N 17.39 E
Győr-Sopron [2] 10 Ni 47.40N 17.15 E
Gypsumville 42 Hf 51.45N 98.35W
Gysinge 8 Gd 60.17N 16.53 E
Gyttorp 8 Fe 59.31N 14.58 E
Gyula 10 Rj 46.39N 21.17 E

H

Haacht 12 Gd 50.59N 4.38 E
Häädemeeste/Hjademeste 8 Uf 58.00N 24.28 E
Ha'afeva 65b Ba 19.57S 174.43W
Haafusia 64h Bb 13.18S 176.09W
Haag, Mount- 66 Qf 77.40S 79.00W
Haaksbergen 12 Ib 52.09N 6.45 E
Haamstede, Westerschouwen- 12 Fc 51.42N 3.45 E
Haanja Kõrgustik 8 Lg 57.30N 27.30 E
Ha'ano 65b Ba 19.40S 174.17W
Ha'apai Group 57 Jf 19.47S 174.27W
Haapajärvi 7 Fe 63.45N 25.20 E
Haapamäki 8 Kb 62.15N 24.28 E
Haapasaari 8 Ld 60.15N 27.10 E
Haapaselkä [Fin.] 8 Mc 61.35N 28.15 E
Haapaselkä [Fin.] 8 Mb 62.10N 28.10 E
Haapiti 65e Fc 17.34S 149.52W
Haapsalu 19 Cd 58.57N 23.32 E
Ha'arava 24 Fg 30.58N 32.24 E
Haardt 10 Dg 49.15N 8.00 E
Haardtkopf 12 Je 49.51N 7.04 E
Haaren, Wünnenberg- 12 Kc 51.34N 8.44 E
Haarlem 11 Kb 52.23N 4.38 E
Haarlemmermeer 12 Gb 52.20N 4.41 E
Haarlerberg 12 Ib 52.20N 6.25 E
Haarstrang 12 Kc 51.30N 8.20 E
Haast 58 Hi 43.52S 169.01 E
Haast Pass 62 Cf 44.06S 169.21 E
Habahe/Kaba 27 Eb 47.53N 86.12 E
Habarovsk 22 Pe 48.27N 135.06 E
Habarovski Kraj [3] 20 If 53.00N 137.00 E
Habarūt 23 Hf 17.22N 52.42 E
Habashīyah, Jabal- 35 Ib 16.45N 50.05 E
Habaswein 36 Gb 1.01N 39.29 E
Habay [Alta.-Can.] 42 Fe 58.52N 118.45W
Habay [Bel.] 12 He 49.45N 5.38 E
Habay [Som.] 35 Ge 1.08N 43.46 E
Ḥabbān 35 Hc 14.21N 47.05 E
Ḥabbānīyah, Hawr al- 24 Jf 33.17N 43.29 E
Habibas, Iles- 13 Ki 35.44N 1.08W
Habichtswald 10 Fe 51.20N 9.25 E
Habo 8 Fg 57.55N 14.04 E
Haboro 27 Pc 44.22N 141.42 E
Ḥabshān 24 Ok 23.50N 53.37 E
Hache 10 Ec 53.05N 8.50 E
Hachenburg 12 Jd 50.39N 7.50 E
Hachijō 29 Fe 35.15N 139.45 E
Hachijō-Fuji 29 Fe 33.08N 139.46 E
Hachijō-Jima 27 Oe 33.05N 139.50 E
Hachiman 29 Ed 35.46N 136.57 E
Hachimori 29 Fa 40.22N 140.00 E
Hachinohe 22 Qe 40.30N 141.29 E
Hachiōji 29 Fd 35.39N 139.18 E
Hachiro-Gata 29 Fa 40.00N 140.00 E
Hacibey De 24 Kd 36.58N 44.18 E
Hackar Dağı 24 Ib 40.50N 41.10 E
Hackås 7 De 62.55N 14.31 E
Håckren 8 Ea 63.10N 13.35 E
Hačmas 19 Eg 41.25N 48.52 E
Hadagang 28 Kb 45.24N 131.12 E
Hadamar 12 Kd 50.27N 8.03 E
Ḥaḍan, Ḥarrat- 33 He 21.30N 41.23 E
Hadano 29 Fd 35.22N 139.14 E
Ḥadāribah, Ra's al- 35 Fa 22.04N 36.54 E
Ḥadd, Ra's al- 21 Hg 22.32N 59.59 E
Haddad 30 Ig 14.40N 18.46 E
Hadded 35 Hc 10.10N 48.28 E
Haddington 9 Kf 55.58N 2.47W
Haddummati Atoll 25a Bb 1.45N 73.30 E
Hadejia 34 Hc 12.27N 10.03 E
Hadejia 34 Hc 12.50N 10.51 E
Hadeland 8 Dd 60.25N 10.35 E
Hadeln 10 Ec 53.45N 8.45 E
Hadera 24 Ff 32.26N 34.55 E
Haderslev 7 Bi 55.15N 9.30 E
Hadībah 23 Hg 12.39N 54.02 E
Hadım 24 Ed 36.59N 32.28 E
Hadimköy 24 Cb 41.09N 28.37 E
Hadīyah 23 Ed 25.34N 38.41 E
Hadjer el Hamis 35 Ac 12.51N 14.50 E
Hadjout 13 Oh 36.31N 2.25 E
Hadleigh 12 Cb 52.03N 0.56 E
Hadley Bay 42 Gb 72.30N 108.30W
Ha Dong 25 Ld 20.58N 105.46 E
Ḥaḍramawt 23 Gf 15.00N 50.00 E
Hadrian's Wall 9 Kg 54.59N 2.26W
Hadsten 8 Dh 56.20N 10.03 E
Hadsund 8 Dh 56.43N 10.07 E
Hadytajaha 17 Nc 66.57N 69.12 E
Hadyžensk 16 Kg 44.25N 39.31 E
Hadzibeiski Liman 15 Nc 46.40N 30.30 E
Haedo, Cuchilla de- 55 Dj 31.40S 56.18W
Haeju 28 He 38.02N 125.42 E
Haena 60 Oc 22.13N 159.34W
Ḥafar al 'Atk 24 Lj 25.56N 46.47 E
Ḥafar al Bāṭin 23 Gd 28.27N 46.00 E
Haffner Bjerg 41 Fc 76.30N 63.00W
Ḥaffūz 14 Do 35.38N 9.40 E
Hafik 24 Gc 39.52N 37.24 E
Ḥafīrat al 'Aydā 23 Ed 26.26N 39.12 E
Ḥafit 24 Pk 23.59N 55.49 E
Ḥafit, Jabal- 24 Pj 24.03N 55.46 E
Hafnarfjördur 7a Bb 64.04N 21.57W
Haft Gel 24 Mg 31.27N 49.27 E
Hāfūn 35 Ic 10.10N 51.05 E
Hāfūn, Rās- = Hafun, Ras-(EN) 30 Mg 10.27N 51.24 E
Hafun, Ras-(EN) = Hāfūn, Rās- 30 Mg 10.27N 51.24 E
Hāfūn Bay North 35 Ic 10.37N 51.15 E
Hāfūn Bay South 35 Ic 10.15N 51.05 E
Hagadera 36 Hb 0.02N 40.17 E
Hagby 8 Gh 56.33N 16.10 E
Hageland 12 Gd 50.55N 4.45 E
Hagemeister 40 Ge 58.40N 161.00W
Hagen 10 De 51.21N 7.28 E
Hagenow 10 Hc 53.26N 11.12 E
Hagere Hiywet 35 Fd 8.58N 37.53 E
Hagerman 46 He 42.49N 114.54W
Hagerstown 43 Ld 39.39N 77.43W
Hagetmau 11 Fk 43.40N 0.35W
Hagfors 7 Cf 60.02N 13.42 E
Häggenås 8 Fa 63.24N 14.55 E
Hagi 28 Kg 34.24N 131.25 E
Ha Giang 25 Kd 22.50N 104.59 E
Hágios Theódóros 24 Fe 35.20N 34.01 E
Hagman, Puntan- 64b Ba 15.09N 145.48 E
Hagondange 11 Me 49.15N 6.10 E
Hags Head/Ceanna Cailligh 9 Di 52.57N 9.28W
Hague, Cap de la- 5 Ff 49.43N 1.57W
Haguenau 11 Nf 48.49N 7.47 E
Hagunia 32 Ed 27.26N 12.24W
Hahajima-Rettō 60 Cb 26.37N 142.10 E
Hahns Peak 45 Cf 40.50N 107.01W
Hahót 10 Mj 46.38N 16.56 E
Hai'an 28 Fh 32.33N 120.26 E
Haicheng 27 Lc 40.51N 122.43 E
Haidenaab 10 Ig 49.35N 12.08 E
Hai Duong 25 Ld 20.56N 106.19 E
Haifa (EN) = Hefa 22 Ff 32.50N 35.00 E
Haifeng 27 Kg 22.58N 115.21 E
Haiger 12 Kd 50.45N 8.13 E
Hai He 28 De 38.57N 117.43 E
Haikakan Sovetakan Socialistakan Respublika/Armjanskaja SSR [2] 19 Eg 40.00N 45.00 E
Haikang (Leizhou) 27 Jg 20.56N 110.06 E
Haikou 22 Ng 20.05N 110.20 E
Ḥā'il 22 Gg 27.33N 41.42 E
Hailang He 28 Jb 44.33N 129.33 E
Hailar 22 Ne 49.14N 119.42 E
Hailar He 21 Ne 49.30N 117.50 E
Hailin 27 Mc 44.35N 129.22 E
Hailong (Meihekou) 27 Mc 42.32N 125.37 E
Hailsham 12 Cd 50.52N 0.16 E
Hailun 27 Mb 47.29N 126.55 E
Hailuoto/Karlö 5 Ib 65.02N 24.42 E
Haima Tan 27 Kd 10.52N 116.53 E
Haimen [China] 28 Fi 31.53N 121.10 E
Haimen [China] 28 Fj 28.40N 121.27 E
Haina 12 Kc 51.03N 8.56 E
Hainan Dao 21 Mh 19.00N 109.00 E
Hainaut 11 Jd 50.20N 3.50 E
Hainaut [3] 12 Fd 50.30N 4.00 E
Hainburg an der Donau 14 Kb 48.09N 16.56 E
Haines 39 Fd 59.14N 135.27W
Haines Junction 42 Dd 60.45N 137.30W
Hainich 10 Ge 51.05N 10.27 E
Hainleite 10 Ge 51.20N 10.48 E
Hai Phong 22 Mg 20.52N 106.41 E
Haïti = Haiti (EN) [1] 39 Lh 19.00N 72.25W
Haiti (EN) = Haïti [1] 39 Lh 19.00N 72.25W
Haixing (Suji) 28 De 38.10N 117.29 E
Haixin Shan 27 Hd 37.00N 100.03 E
Haiyan (Sanjiaocheng) 27 Hd 36.58N 100.50 E
Haiyan (Wuyuanzhen) 28 Fi 30.31N 120.56 E
Haiyang (Dongcun) 28 Ff 36.46N 121.09 E
Haiyang Dao 28 Ge 39.03N 123.12 E
Haiyou → Sanmen 27 Lf 29.08N 121.22 E
Haiyuan 27 Id 36.35N 105.40 E
Haizhou 28 Eg 34.34N 119.08 E
Haizhou Wan 21 Nf 35.00N 119.30 E
Hajar Banga 35 Cc 11.30N 23.00 E
Hajdarken 19 Hh 39.55N 71.24 E
Hajdú-Bihar [2] 10 Ri 47.25N 21.30 E
Hajdúböszörmény 10 Ri 47.40N 21.31 E
Hajdúhadház 10 Ri 47.41N 21.40 E
Hajdúnánás 10 Ri 47.51N 21.26 E
Hajdúság 10 Ri 47.35N 21.30 E
Hajdúszoboszló 10 Ri 47.27N 21.24 E
Hajihi-Zaki 29 Fb 38.19N 138.31 E
Ḥājjīābād [Iran] 24 Ph 28.19N 55.55 E
Ḥājjīābād [Iran] 24 Ph 28.21N 54.27 E
Ḥājjīābād-e Māsīleh 24 Ne 34.49N 51.13 E
Hajnówka 10 Td 52.45N 23.36 E
Hajós 10 Pj 46.24N 19.07 E
Hajpudyrskaja Guba 17 Ib 68.40N 59.30 E
Haka 25 Id 22.39N 93.37 E
Hakase-Yama 29 Fc 37.22N 139.43 E
Hakasskaja Avtonomnaja Oblast [3] 20 Df 53.30N 90.00 E
Hakata-Wan 29 Be 33.40N 130.20 E
Hakefjord 8 Dg 57.41N 11.44 E
Hakkâri 23 Fb 37.34N 43.45 E
Hakken-Zan 29 Dd 34.10N 135.54 E
Hakkōda San 29 Ga 40.40N 140.53 E
Hako-Dake 29a Ca 44.40N 142.25 E
Hakodate 22 Qe 41.45N 140.43 E
Hakone-Yama 29 Fd 35.13N 139.00 E
Hakui 28 Nf 36.53N 136.47 E
Hakupu 64k Bb 19.06S 169.50W
Haku-San 29 Ec 36.09N 136.45 E
Hal/Halle 11 Kd 50.44N 4.14 E
Halab 24 Md 36.17N 48.03 E
Ḥalab = Aleppo (EN) 22 Ff 36.12N 37.10 E
Halabjah 24 Ke 35.10N 45.59 E
Halač 19 Gh 39.04N 64.53 E
Halachó 48 Ng 20.29N 90.05W
Halahei 28 Ga 46.11N 122.46 E
Ḥalā'ib 31 Kf 22.13N 36.38 E
Halalii Lake 65a Ab 21.52N 160.11W
Halangingie Point 64k Bb 19.03S 169.58W
Hålaveden 8 Ff 58.05N 14.45 E
Halawa 65a Eb 21.10N 156.44W
Halawa, Cape- 65a Eb 21.10N 156.43W
Ḥalbā 24 Ge 34.33N 36.05 E
Halberstadt 10 He 51.54N 11.03 E
Halcon, Mount- 26 Hd 13.16N 121.00 E
Haldean-Sogotyn-Daba 27 Gb 49.05N 97.55 E
Halden 7 Cg 59.09N 11.23 E
Haldensleben 10 Hd 52.18N 11.25 E
Haldia 25 Hd 22.08N 88.05 E
Haldwani 25 Fc 29.13N 79.31 E
Hale, Mount- 59 De 26.00S 117.10 E
Haleakala Crater 65a Ec 20.43N 156.12W
Haleiwa 65a Cb 21.36N 158.06W
Halemaumau 65a Fd 19.24N 155.17W
Hale River 59 Hd 24.56S 135.53 E
Halesworth 12 Db 52.21N 1.30 E
Haleyville 44 Dh 34.14N 87.37W
Halfā al Gadida 31 Kg 15.19N 35.34 E
Half Assini 34 Ed 5.03N 2.53W
Halfeti 24 Gd 37.15N 37.52 E
Halfway 42 Fe 56.13N 121.26W
Halh-Gol 27 Kb 48.01N 118.10 E
Haliburton 44 Hc 45.03N 78.33W
Halifax 39 Me 44.39N 63.36W
Halifax, Mount- 59 Jc 19.05S 146.20 E
Halifax Bay 59 Jc 18.50S 146.30 E
Hālil 23 Id 27.28N 58.44 E
Halīleh, Ra's-e- 24 Nh 28.46N 50.56 E
Halilovo 16 Ud 51.27N 58.10 E
Halin 35 Hd 9.08N 48.47 E
Haliut → Urad Zhonghou Lianheqi 27 Ic 41.34N 108.32 E
Haljala 8 Le 59.22N 26.09 E
Haljasavej 20 Cd 63.20N 78.30 E
Hall 40 Ed 60.40N 173.05W
Halladale 9 Jc 58.30N 3.50W
Hallam Peak 46 Fa 52.11N 118.46W
Halland 8 Eh 57.00N 12.45 E
Halland [2] 7 Ch 56.45N 13.00 E
Hallandsås 8 Eh 56.23N 13.00 E
Halla-san 28 Ih 33.22N 126.32 E
Ḥallat 'Ammār 24 Gh 29.08N 36.02 E
Hall Beach 42 Jc 68.10N 81.56W
Halle 10 He 51.30N 12.00 E
Halle [2] 10 He 51.30N 11.50 E
Halle/Hal 11 Kd 50.44N 4.14 E
Halle (Westfalen) 12 Kb 52.05N 8.22 E
Halleberg 8 Ef 58.23N 12.25 E
Hällefors 8 Fe 59.47N 14.30 E
Hälleforsnäs 8 Ge 59.10N 16.30 E
Halleim 14 Hc 47.41N 13.06 E
Hällekis 8 Ef 58.38N 13.25 E
Hallen 8 Fb 63.11N 14.05 E
Hallenberg 12 Kc 51.07N 8.38 E
Hallencourt 12 De 49.59N 1.53 E
Halle-Neustadt 10 He 51.31N 11.53 E
Hallertau 10 Hh 48.35N 11.50 E
Hallestad 8 Ff 58.44N 15.34 E
Hallettsville 45 Hl 29.27N 96.57W
Halley Bay 66 Af 75.31S 26.38W
Halli 8 Kc 61.52N 24.50 E
Hallie-Jackson Bank (EN) 63c Ba 9.45S 166.10 E
Halligen 10 Eb 54.35N 8.35 E
Hallingdal 7 Bf 60.40N 9.15 E
Hallingdalselva 8 Cd 60.23N 9.35 E
Hallingskarvet 5 Gc 60.37N 7.45 E
Hall Islands 57 Gd 8.37N 152.00 E
Halliste Jõgi 8 Kf 58.23N 24.25 E
Hall Lake 42 Jc 68.40N 82.20W
Hall Land 41 Fb 81.12N 61.10W
Hallock 45 Hb 48.47N 96.57W
Hall Peninsula 38 Mc 63.30N 66.00W
Hallsberg 7 Dg 59.04N 15.07 E
Halls Creek 58 Df 18.13S 127.40 E
Hallstahammar 7 Dg 59.37N 16.13 E
Hallstatt 14 Hb 47.33N 13.39 E
Hallstavik 7 Ef 60.03N 18.36 E
Halluin 12 Fd 50.47N 3.08 E
Halmahera 57 Dd 1.00N 128.00 E
Halmahera, Laut- = Halmahera Sea (EN) 57 De 1.00S 129.00 E
Halmahera Sea (EN) = Halmahera, Laut- 57 De 1.00S 129.00 E
Halmer-Ju 19 Gb 67.58N 64.40 E
Halmeu 15 Gb 48.00N 23.01 E
Halmstad 6 Hd 56.39N 12.50 E
Haloze 14 Jd 46.20N 15.50 E
Ḥalq al Wādī 32 Jb 36.49N 10.18 E
Hals 7 Cg 57.00N 10.19 E
Hälsingland 8 Gc 61.30N 17.00 E
Halsön 8 Ib 62.50N 21.10 E
Halstead 12 Cc 51.57N 0.38 E
Halsteren 12 Gc 51.32N 4.16 E
Haltang He 27 Fd 39.00N 94.40 E
Halten Bank (EN) 7 Bd 64.45N 8.45 E
Haltern 12 Jc 51.44N 7.11 E
Haltiatunturi 7 Eb 69.18N 21.16 E
Haltom City 45 Hj 32.48N 97.16W
Halturin 19 Ed 58.35N 48.55 E
Hālūl 24 Oj 25.40N 52.25 E
Halver 12 Jc 51.12N 7.29 E
Ham 11 Je 49.45N 3.04 E
Ham, Roches de- 12 Ae 49.02N 1.02W
Hamada 29 Cd 34.53N 132.03 E
Hamadān 22 Gf 34.48N 48.30 E
Hamadān [3] 23 Gb 35.00N 48.40 E
Hamadia 13 Ni 35.28N 1.52 E
Hamaguir 32 Gc 30.54N 3.02W
Hamāh 23 Eb 35.08N 36.45 E
Hamakita 29 Ed 34.49N 137.45 E
Hamamasu 29a Bb 43.36N 141.21 E
Hamamatsu 27 Oe 34.42N 137.44 E
Hamanaka 29a Db 43.05N 145.05 E
Hamanaka-Wan 29a Db 43.07N 145.10 E
Hamana-Ko 29 Ed 34.45N 137.34 E
Hamanen, Oued el- 32 Hd 25.52N 1.26 E
Hamaoka 29 Fd 34.39N 138.07 E
Hamar 6 Hc 60.48N 11.06 E
Hamar-Daran, Hrebet- 20 Ff 51.10N 105.00 E
Hamasaka 29 Dd 35.38N 134.27 E
Ḥamāṭah, Jabal- 33 Ge 24.12N 35.00 E
Hamatonbetsu 28 Qb 45.07N 142.23 E
Hambantota 25 Gg 6.10N 81.07 E
Hambre, Cayos del- 49 Fb 22.15N 82.47W
Hamburg [2] 10 Fc 53.35N 10.00 E
Hamburg [F.R.G.] 6 Ge 53.33N 10.00 E
Hamburg [S.Afr.] 37 Df 33.18S 27.28 E
Hamburg-Altona 10 Fc 53.33N 9.57 E
Hamburg-Harburg 10 Fc 53.28N 10.00 E
Hamburgsund 8 Df 58.33N 11.16 E
Ḥamḍah 33 Hf 19.02N 43.36 E
Ḥamḍh, Wādī al- 21 Fg 25.58N 36.42 E
Häme [2] 7 Ff 61.30N 24.30 E
Häme 8 Kc 61.30N 25.30 E
Hämeenkangas 8 Jc 61.45N 22.40 E
Hämeenlinna/Tavastehus 7 Ff 61.00N 24.27 E
Hämeenselkä 8 Kb 62.30N 25.00 E
Hamelin Pool 59 Ce 26.15S 114.05 E
Hameln 10 Fd 52.06N 9.21 E
Hamero Hadad 35 Gd 7.28N 42.13 E
Hamersley Range 59 Dd 21.55S 116.45 E
Hamgyŏng-Namdo [2] 28 Id 40.00N 127.30 E
Hamgyŏng-Pukto [2] 28 Jd 41.45N 129.50 E
Hamgyŏng-Sanmaek 28 Jd 41.00N 128.45 E
Hamhŭng 22 Of 39.54N 127.32 E
Hami/Kumul 22 Le 42.48N 93.27 E
Ḥamīdīyeh 24 Mg 31.29N 48.26 E
Hamilton [Austl.] 59 Ig 37.45S 142.02 E
Hamilton [Ber.] 39 Mf 32.17N 64.46W
Hamilton [Mt.-U.S.] 43 Eb 46.15N 114.09W
Hamilton [N.Z.] 58 Ih 37.47S 175.17 E
Hamilton [Oh.-U.S.] 43 Kd 39.23N 84.33W
Hamilton [Ont.-Can.] 39 Le 43.15N 79.51W
Hamilton [Scot.-U.K.] 9 If 55.47N 4.03W
Hamilton [Tx.-U.S.] 45 Gk 31.42N 98.07W
Hamilton, Lake- 45 Ji 34.30N 93.05W
Hamilton, Mount- 46 Hg 39.14N 115.32W
Hamilton River 59 Hd 23.30S 139.47 E
Ḥamīn, Wādī al- 33 Dc 30.28N 22.00 E
Hamina/Fredrikshamn 7 Gf 60.34N 27.12 E
Hamm 10 De 51.41N 7.48 E
Ḥammām al 'Alīl 24 Jd 36.10N 43.16 E
Ḥammām al Anf 32 Jb 36.44N 10.20 E
Ḥammāmāt 32 Jb 36.24N 10.37 E
Ḥammāmāt, Khalīj- 32 Jb 36.05N 10.40 E
Hammam Bou Hadjar 13 Li 35.23N 0.58W
Hammami 30 Ff 23.03N 11.30W
Hammam Righa 13 Oh 36.23N 2.24 E
Ḥammār, Hawr al- 23 Gc 30.50N 47.10 E
Hammarstrand 8 Ga 63.06N 16.21 E
Hamme 12 Gc 51.06N 4.08 E
Hammelburg 10 Ff 50.07N 9.54 E
Hammerdal 7 De 63.36N 15.21 E
Hammeren 8 Fi 55.18N 14.47 E
Hammerfest 6 Ia 70.40N 23.45 E
Hamminkeln 12 Ic 51.44N 6.35 E
Hamminkeln-Dingden 12 Ic 51.46N 6.37 E
Hammond [In.-U.S.] 44 De 41.36N 87.30W
Hammond [La.-U.S.] 43 Ie 30.30N 90.28W
Hammonton 44 Jf 39.38N 74.48W
Hamont, Hamont-Achel- 12 Hc 51.15N 5.33 E
Hamont-Achel 12 Hc 51.15N 5.33 E
Hamont-Achel-Hamont 12 Hc 51.15N 5.33 E
Hamoyet, Jabal- 30 Kg 17.33N 38.02 E
Hampden 62 Df 45.20S 170.49 E
Hampshire [3] 9 Lk 51.00N 1.10W
Hampshire Downs 9 Lj 51.15N 1.15W
Hampton [Ia.-U.S.] 45 Je 42.45N 93.12W
Hampton [Va.-U.S.] 44 Ig 37.02N 76.23W
Hampton Butte 46 Ee 43.46N 120.17W
Hamp'yong 28 Ig 35.04N 126.31 E
Ḥamrā' 35 Dc 10.54N 29.54 E
Hamra [R.S.F.S.R.] 20 Gd 60.17N 114.10 E
Hamra [Swe.] 8 Fc 61.39N 15.00 E
Ḥamrā', Al Ḥamādah al- 30 If 29.30N 12.00 E
Hamra, Saguia el- 30 Ff 27.24N 13.43W
Ḥamrān 24 Kd 36.22N 45.44 E
Ḥamrat ash Shaykh 35 Dc 14.35N 27.58 E
Ḥamrīn, Jabal- 24 Ke 34.30N 44.30 E
Hāmūn-e Hirmand, Daryācheh-ye- 23 Jc 31.30N 61.20 E
Han 34 Ec 10.41N 2.27W
Hana 60 Oc 20.45N 155.59W
Hanahan 44 Hi 32.55N 80.00W
Hanaizum 29 Gb 38.51N 141.12 E
Ḥanak 23 Ed 25.33N 36.56 E
Hanalei 65a Ba 22.13N 159.30W
Hanamaki 28 Pe 39.23N 141.07 E
Hanang 30 Ki 4.26S 35.24 E
Hanaoka 29 Ga 40.21N 140.34 E
Hanapepe 65a Bb 21.55N 159.35W
Hanau 10 Ef 50.08N 8.55 E
Han-Bogdo 27 Ic 43.12N 107.10 E
Hanceville 42 Ff 51.55N 123.02W
Hancheng 27 Jd 35.30N 110.25 E
Hanchuan 28 Bi 30.39N 113.46 E
Hancock 44 Cb 47.07N 88.35W
Handa 29 Ed 34.53N 136.56 E
Handan 22 Nf 36.35N 114.28 E
Handen 8 He 59.10N 18.08 E
Handeni 36 Gd 5.26S 38.01 E
Handlová 10 Oh 48.44N 18.46 E
Handöl 8 Ea 63.16N 12.26 E
Handyga 22 Pc 62.40N 135.36 E
Hănegev = Negev Desert (EN) 24 Fg 30.30N 34.55 E
Hanford 46 Fh 36.20N 119.39W
Hangaj, Hrebet- (Changajn Nuruu) = Khangai Mountains (EN) 21 Le 47.30N 100.00 E
Han-gang 27 Md 37.45N 126.11 E
Hanga Roa 65d Ab 27.09S 109.26W
Hang'bu He 28 Di 31.33N 117.05 E
Hanggin Houqi (Xamba) 27 Ic 40.59N 107.07 E
Hanggin Qi (Xin Zhen) 27 Id 39.54N 108.55 E
Hangö/Hanko 7 Fg 59.50N 22.57 E
Hangöudde/Hankoniemi 8 Je 59.50N 23.10 E
Hangu 28 De 39.16N 117.50 E
Hangzhou 22 Of 30.18N 120.11 E
Hangzhou Wan 28 Fi 30.25N 121.00 E
Ḥanish 33 Hg 13.45N 42.45 E
Ḥanish al Kabīr, Jazīrat al- 33 Hg 13.43N 42.45 E
Hanja, Vozvyšennost- 8 Lg 57.30N 27.30 E
Ḥanjūrah, Ra's- 24 Pj 24.44N 54.39 E
Hanka, Ozero- = Khanka Lake (EN) 21 Pe 45.00N 132.24 E
Hankasalmi 8 Lb 62.23N 26.26 E
Hankensbüttel 10 Gd 52.44N 10.36 E
Hanko/Hangö 7 Fg 59.50N 22.57 E
Hankoniemi/Hangöudde 8 Je 59.50N 23.10 E
Hankou, Wuhan- 28 Ci 30.35N 114.16 E
Hanksville 46 Jg 38.25N 110.10W
Hanlar 16 Oi 40.34N 46.20 E
Hanmej, Gora- 17 Lc 67.08N 66.00 E
Hanmer Springs 62 Ee 42.31S 172.50 E
Hann, Mount- 59 Fc 15.50S 125.50 E
Hanna [Alta.-Can.] 42 Gf 51.38N 111.54W
Hanna [Wy.-U.S.] 46 Lf 41.52N 106.34W
Hannah Bay 42 Jf 51.15N 79.50W
Hannibal 43 Id 39.42N 91.22W
Hanningfield Reservoir 12 Cc 51.37N 0.28 E
Hannō 29 Fd 35.51N 139.17 E
Hannover 6 Ge 52.22N 9.43 E
Hann River 59 Fc 17.10S 126.10 E
Hannuit/Hannut 12 Hd 50.40N 5.05 E
Hannut/Hannuit 12 Hd 50.40N 5.05 E
Hano 8 Fi 56.00N 14.50 E
Hanöbukten 8 Fi 55.45N 14.30 E
Ha Noi 22 Mg 21.02N 105.51 E
Hanover [N.H.-U.S.] 44 Kd 43.42N 72.17W
Hanover [Ont.-Can.] 44 Gc 44.09N 81.02W
Hanover [Pa.-U.S.] 44 If 39.47N 76.59W
Hanover [S.Afr.] 37 Cf 31.04S 24.29 E
Hanover, Isla- 56 Fh 51.00S 74.40W
Hanpan, Cape- 59 Ka 5.01S 154.37 E
Han Pijesak 14 Mf 44.05N 18.57 E

Index Symbols

[1] Independent Nation
[2] State, Region
[3] District, County
[4] Municipality
[5] Colony, Dependency
Continent
Physical Region
Historical or Cultural Region
Mount, Mountain
Volcano
Hill
Mountains, Mountain Range
Hills, Escarpment
Plateau, Upland
Pass, Gap
Plain, Lowland
Delta
Salt Flat
Valley, Canyon
Crater, Cave
Karst Features
Depression
Polder
Desert, Dunes
Forest, Woods
Heath, Steppe
Oasis
Cape, Point
Coast, Beach
Cliff
Peninsula
Isthmus
Sandbank
Island
Atoll
Rock, Reef
Islands, Archipelago
Rocks, Reefs
Coral Reef
Well, Spring
Geyser
River, Stream
Waterfall Rapids
River Mouth, Estuary
Lake
Salt Lake
Intermittent Lake
Reservoir
Swamp, Pond
Canal
Glacier
Ice Shelf, Pack Ice
Ocean
Sea
Gulf, Bay
Strait, Fjord
Lagoon
Bank
Seamount
Tablemount
Ridge
Shelf
Basin
Escarpment, Sea Scarp
Fracture
Trench, Abyss
National Park, Reserve
Point of Interest
Recreation Site
Cave, Cavern
Historic Site
Ruins
Wall, Walls
Church, Abbey
Temple
Scientific Station
Airport
Port
Lighthouse
Mine
Tunnel
Dam, Bridge

Hansen Mountains 66 Ee 68.16S 58.47 E
Hanshan 28 Ei 31.43N 118.07 E
Hanshou 28 Aj 28.55N 111.58 E
Han Shui 21 Nf 30.34N 114.17 E
Hanstholm 8 Cg 57.07N 8.38 E
Han Sum 28 Eb 44.33N 119.58 E
Han-sur-Lesse, Rochefort- 12 Hd 50.08N 5.11 E
Han-sur-Nied 12 If 48.59N 6.26 E
Hantajskoje, Ozero- 20 Ec 68.25N 91.00 E
Hantau 19 Hg 44.13N 73.48 E
Hantengri Feng 27 Dc 42.03N 80.11 E
Hants 9 Lj 51.10N 1.10W
Hanty-Mansijsk 22 Ic 61.00N 69.06 E
Hanty-Mansijski Nacionalny Okrug [3] 19 Hc 62.00N 72.30 E
Hantzsch 42 Kc 67.32N 72.26W
Hanušovice 10 Mf 50.05N 16.55 E
Hanwang 27 He 31.25N 104.13 E
Hanyang 28 Ci 30.34N 114.01 E
Hanyang, Wuhan- 28 Ci 30.33N 114.16 E
Hanyū 29 Fc 36.11N 139.32 E
Hanyuan (Fulin) 27 Hf 29.25N 102.12 E
Hanzhong [China] 22 Mf 32.59N 107.11 E
Hanzhong [China] 27 Ie 33.07N 107.00 E
Hanzhuang 28 Dg 34.38N 117.23 E
Hao Atoll 57 Mf 18.15S 140.54W
Haouach 30 Ig 16.30N 19.55 E
Haoud el Hamra 32 Ic 31.58N 5.59 E
Hao Xi 28 Ej 28.28N 119.56 E
Haoxue 28 Bi 30.02N 112.25 E
Haparanda 7 Fd 65.50N 24.10 E
Hapčeranga 20 Gg 49.42N 112.20 E
Hapsu 28 Jd 41.13N 128.51 E
Ḩaql 24 Fh 29.18N 34.57 E
Ḩaql al Barqan 24 Lh 28.55N 47.57 E
Ḩaql al Manāqīsh 24 Lh 29.02N 47.32 E
Ḩaql as Şābirīyah 24 Lh 29.48N 47.50 E
Hara, Zaliv-/Hara Laht 8 Ke 59.35N 25.30 E
Hara-Ajrag 27 Ib 45.50N 109.20 E
Harabali 19 Ef 47.25N 47.16 E
Ḩaraḑ 23 Ge 24.14N 49.11 E
Haraiki Atoll 57 Mf 17.28S 143.27W
Hara Laht/Hara, Zaliv- 8 Ke 59.35N 25.30 E
Haramachi 28 Pf 37.38N 140.58 E
Haram Dāgh 23 Gb 37.35N 46.43 E
Harami, Pereval- 16 Oh 42.48N 46.12 E
Harand 24 Of 32.34N 52.26 E
Harani'ia Point 63a Ed 10.21S 161.16 E
Hara Nur 27 Fb 48.05N 93.12 E
Ḩararḑēre 35 He 4.32N 47.53 E
Harare 31 Kj 17.50S 31.10 E
Harat 35 Fb 16.05N 39.28 E
Hara-Tas, Krjaž- 20 Fb 72.00N 107.00 E
Haratini 64n Bc 10.28S 160.58W
Ḩarat Zuwayyah 31 Jf 24.14N 21.59 E
Hara-Us-Nur 27 Fb 48.00N 92.10 E
Haraz 35 Bc 13.57N 19.26 E
Harāz 24 Od 36.40N 52.43 E
Harāzah, Jabal- 35 Eb 15.03N 30.27 E
Haraze 35 Cd 9.55N 20.48 E
Harbel 34 Cd 6.16N 10.21W
Harbin 22 Oe 45.45N 126.37 E
Harbor Beach 44 Fd 43.51N 82.39W
Harbour Breton 42 Lg 47.29N 55.50W
Harbour Grace 42 Mg 47.41N 53.15W
Harburg, Hamburg- 10 Fc 53.28N 10.00 E
Harcourt 44 Ob 46.30N 65.15W
Harcuvar Mountains 46 Ii 34.00N 113.30W
Harcyzsk 16 Kf 47.59N 38.11 E
Hardanger 8 Bd 60.20N 6.30 E
Hardangerfjorden 5 Gc 60.10N 6.00 E
Hardangerjøkulen 8 Bd 60.35N 7.25 E
Hardangervidda 7 Bf 60.20N 7.30 E
Hardelot Plage, Neufchâtel Hardelot- 12 Dd 50.38N 1.35 E
Hardenberg 12 Ib 52.34N 6.37 E
Harderwijk 11 Lb 52.21N 5.36 E
Hardin 43 Fb 45.44N 107.37W
Harding 37 Df 30.34S 29.58 E
Hardinsburg 44 Dg 37.47N 86.28W
Härdler 12 Kc 51.06N 8.14 E
Hardoi 25 Gc 27.25N 80.07 E
Hardy, Peninsula- 56 Gi 55.25S 68.30W
Hareid 8 Bb 62.22N 6.02 E
Hareidlandet 7 Ae 62.20N 5.55 E
Hare Indian 42 Ec 66.18N 128.38W
Harelbeke 12 Fd 50.51N 3.18 E
Haren 12 Ia 53.11N 6.38 E
Haren (Ems) 12 Jb 52.47N 7.14 E
Harer 31 Lh 9.18N 42.08 E
Harerge [3] 35 Gd 9.00N 41.30 E
Harēri Mālinwarfā 35 He 4.34N 47.21 E
Harewa 35 Gd 9.54N 41.58 E
Harfleur 12 Ce 49.30N 0.12 E
Harg 8 Hd 60.11N 18.24 E
Hargeysa 31 Lh 9.30N 44.03 E
Harghiţa [2] 15 Ic 46.25N 25.45 E
Harghita, Munţii- 15 Ic 46.31N 25.33 E
Harghita, Vîrful- 15 Ic 46.27N 25.35 E
Hargla 8 Lg 57.31N 26.25 E
Harhorin 27 Hb 47.13N 102.50 E
Har Hu 38.15N 97.40 E
Ḩarīb 23 Gg 14.56N 45.30 E
Haricha, Hamâda el- 34 Ea 22.36N 3.31W
Harihari 62 De 43.09S 170.34 E
Hari Kurk 8 Je 59.00N 22.50 E
Harim 24 Gd 36.12N 36.31 E
Harīm, Jabal al- 24 Qj 25.58N 56.14 E
Harima-Nada 29 Dd 34.30N 134.35 E
Haringey, London- 12 Bc 51.36N 0.06W
Harīrūd 21 If 37.24N 60.38 E
Härjångsfjallet 8 Ea 63.01N 12.35 E
Harjavalta 7 Ff 61.19N 22.08 E
Härjedalen 8 Eb 62.20N 13.05 E
Härjehågna 8 Ec 61.44N 12.08 E
Hårkan 8 Fa 63.20N 14.55 E
Harkov 6 Je 50.00N 36.15 E
Harkovskaja Oblast [3] 19 Df 49.40N 36.30 E
Harlan [Ia.-U.S.] 45 If 41.39N 95.19W
Harlan [Ky.-U.S.] 44 Fg 36.51N 83.19W
Harlan County Lake 45 Gf 40.04N 99.16W
Harlech Castle 9 Ii 52.52N 4.07W
Harlem 46 Kb 48.32N 108.47W
Harleston 12 Db 52.24N 1.18 E
Harlingen [Neth.] 11 La 53.10N 5.24 E
Harlingen [Tx.-U.S.] 43 Hf 26.11N 97.42W
Harlovka 7 Ib 68.47N 37.20 E
Harlovka 7 Ib 68.47N 37.15 E
Harlow 9 Nj 51.47N 0.08 E
Harlowton 46 Kc 46.26N 109.50W
Harlu 7 Hf 61.51N 30.54 E
Hărman 15 Id 45.43N 25.41 E
Harmancık 24 Cc 39.41N 29.10 E
Harmånger 7 Df 61.56N 17.13 E
Harmanli 15 Ih 41.56N 25.54 E
Harmil 35 Gb 16.30N 40.12 E
Harmony 45 Ke 43.33N 91.59W
Harnai 25 Ee 17.48N 73.06 E
Harney Basin 38 Ge 43.15N 120.40W
Harney Lake 43 Dc 43.14N 119.07W
Harney Peak 43 Gc 44.00N 103.30W
Härnön 8 Gb 62.35N 18.00 E
Härnösand 6 Hc 62.38N 17.56 E
Haro 13 Jb 42.35N 2.51W
Harovsk 19 Ed 59.59N 40.11 E
Harøya 8 Bb 62.45N 6.25 E
Harøyfjorden 8 Bb 62.45N 6.35 E
Harpenden 12 Bc 51.48N 0.21W
Harper [Ks.-U.S.] 45 Gh 37.17N 98.01W
Harper [Lbr.] 31 Gh 4.22N 7.43W
Harper, Mount- 40 Kd 64.14N 143.50W
Harper Pass 62 De 42.44S 171.53 E
Harplinge 8 Eh 56.45N 12.43 E
Harqin Qi (Jinshan) 28 Ed 41.57N 118.40 E
Harqin Zuoyi Monggolzu Zizhixian 28 Ed 41.05N 119.40 E
Ḩarrah 23 Hg 14.57N 50.19 E
Ḩarrat al 'Uwayrid 23 Ed 27.00N 37.30 E
Harricana 42 Jf 51.10N 79.47W
Harricana, Rivière- 44 Ha 51.10N 79.45W
Harrington-Harbour 42 Lf 50.26N 59.30W
Harris 9 Gd 57.53N 6.55W
Harris 51c Bc 16.28N 62.10W
Harris, Lake- 44 Gk 28.46N 81.49W
Harris, Sound of- 9 Fd 57.45N 7.08W
Harrisburg 39 Le 40.16N 76.52W
Harrismith 37 De 28.18S 29.03 E
Harrison [Ar.-U.S.] 45 Jh 36.14N 93.07W
Harrison [Mi.-U.S.] 44 Ec 44.01N 84.48W
Harrison [Nb.-U.S.] 45 Ee 42.41N 103.53W
Harrison, Cape - 42 Lf 54.56N 57.55W
Harrison Bay 40 Ib 70.30N 151.30W
Harrisonburg 44 Hf 38.27N 78.54W
Harrison Lake 46 Eb 49.31N 121.59W
Harrison Point 51q Ab 13.18N 59.38W
Harrisonville 45 Ig 38.39N 94.21W
Harrisville [Mi.-U.S.] 44 Fc 44.39N 83.17W
Harrisville [W.V.-U.S.] 44 Gf 39.13N 81.04W
Harrodsburg 44 Eg 37.46N 84.51W
Harrogate 9 Lh 54.00N 1.33W
Harrow, London- 12 Bc 51.36N 0.20W
Harry S. Truman Reservoir 45 Jg 38.00N 93.45W
Har Sai Shan 27 Gd 35.26N 97.41 E
Harsewinkel 12 Kc 51.58N 8.14 E
Harshō 35 Hc 11.17N 47.30 E
Harsim 24 Lf 33.48N 46.50 E
Harsīn 24 Le 34.16N 47.35 E
Harstad 7 Db 68.47N 16.30 E
Harsvik 7 Cd 64.03N 10.02 E
Hart 44 Dd 43.42N 86.22W
Hart 42 Dc 65.51N 136.22W
Hartao 28 Gc 42.30N 122.08 E
Hartbees 30 Jk 28.45S 20.33 E
Hartberg 14 Jc 47.17N 15.58 E
Hårteigen 8 Bd 60.12N 7.04 E
Hartford [Ct.-U.S.] 39 Le 41.46N 72.41W
Hartford [Ky.-U.S.] 44 Dg 37.27N 86.55W
Hartford City 44 Ee 40.29N 85.23W
Hartington 45 He 42.37N 97.16W
Hartland 44 Nb 46.18N 67.32W
Hartland Point 9 Ij 51.02N 4.31W
Hartlepool 9 Lg 54.42N 1.11W
Hartley 37 Ec 18.07S 30.08 E
Hartmannberge 37 Ac 17.30S 12.23 E
Hartola 7 Gf 61.35N 26.01 E
Harts 28.24S 24.18 E
Hartselle 44 Dh 34.27N 86.56W
Harts Range 59 Gd 23.05S 134.55 E
Hartsville 44 Gh 34.23N 80.04W
Hartwell 44 Fh 34.21N 82.56W
Hartwell Lake 44 Fh 34.30N 82.55W
Harun, Bukit- 26 Gf 4.06N 115.46 E
Haruno 29 Ce 33.30N 133.30 E
Harves Bank (EN) 51c Ac 16.52N 62.35W
Harvey [Austl.] 59 Df 33.05S 115.54 E
Harvey [N.D.-U.S.] 43 Hb 47.47N 99.56W
Harvey Bay 59 Kd 25.00S 153.00 E
Harwich 9 Oj 51.57N 1.17 E
Haryana [3] 25 Fc 29.30N 76.30 E
Harz 5 He 51.45N 10.30 E
Hasaki 29 Gd 35.44N 140.48 E
Hasama 29 Gb 38.42N 141.13 E
Hasan 20 Ih 42.26N 130.39 E
Ḩasanābād [Iran] 24 Ph 28.47N 54.19 E
Ḩasanābād [Iran] 24 Nd 36.28N 50.17 E
Hasan Dağı 23 Db 38.08N 34.12 E
Ḩasan Langī 24 Qi 27.22N 56.52 E
Hasavjurt 16 Oh 43.16N 46.35 E
Hāsbayyā 24 Ff 33.43N 33.52 E
Hasdo 25 Hd 21.44N 82.44 E
Hase 10 Dd 52.41N 7.18 E
Hasekijata 15 Kg 42.08N 27.30 E
Hasenkamp 55 Cj 31.31S 59.51W
Hashimoto 29 Dd 34.19N 135.37 E
Hashtpar 24 Md 37.48N 48.55 E
Hasi Hausert 32 Ee 22.35N 14.18W
Haskell 43 He 33.10N 99.44W
Haskerland 12 Hb 52.58N 5.47 E
Haskerland-Joure 12 Hb 52.58N 5.47 E
Haskovo 15 Ih 41.56N 25.33 E
Haskovo [2] 15 Ih 41.50N 25.55 E
Hasle 8 Fi 55.11N 14.43 E
Haslemere 9 Mj 51.06N 0.43W
Haslev 8 Di 55.20N 11.58 E
Hăşmaşu Mare, Vîrful- 15 Ic 46.30N 25.50 E
Haspengouws Plateau/Hesbaye 11 Ld 50.35N 5.10 E
Haspres 12 Fd 50.15N 3.25 E
Hassa 24 Gd 36.50N 36.29 E
Hassan 25 Ff 13.00N 76.05 E
Hassberge 10 Gf 50.12N 10.29 E
Hassela 7 De 62.07N 16.42 E
Hassel Sound 42 Ha 78.30N 99.00W
Hasselt 11 Ld 50.56N 5.20 E
Hassi Bel Guebbour 32 Id 28.30N 6.41 E
Hassi el Ghella 13 Ki 35.27N 1.03W
Hassi-Mamèche 13 Mi 35.51N 0.04 E
Hassi Messaoud 31 He 31.43N 6.03 E
Hassi R'mel 32 Hc 32.55N 3.16 E
Hassi Serouenout 32 Ie 24.00N 7.50 E
Hässleholm 7 Ch 56.09N 13.46 E
Hasslö 8 Fh 56.05N 15.25 E
Haßloch 12 Ke 49.23N 8.16 E
Hastière 12 Gd 50.13N 4.50 E
Hastière-Hastière par-delà 12 Gd 50.13N 4.50 E
Hastière-par-delà, Hastière- 12 Gd 50.13N 4.50 E
Hastings [Bar.] 51q Ab 13.04N 59.35W
Hastings [Eng.-U.K.] 9 Nk 50.51N 0.36 E
Hastings [Mi.-U.S.] 44 Ed 42.39N 85.17W
Hastings [Mn.-U.S.] 45 Jd 44.44N 92.51W
Hastings [Nb.-U.S.] 43 Hc 40.35N 98.23W
Hastings [N.Z.] 61 Eg 39.38S 176.50 E
Hästveda 8 Eh 56.16N 13.56 E
Hašuri 16 Mi 41.59N 43.33 E
Hasvik 7 Fa 70.29N 22.09 E
Ḩasy al Qaţţār 33 Ec 30.14N 27.11 E
Ḩasy Hague 33 Bd 26.17N 10.31 E
Hat'ae-Do 28 Hg 34.23N 125.17 E
Hatanga 22 Mb 71.58N 102.30 E
Hatanga 21 Mb 72.55N 106.00 E
Hatch 45 Cj 32.40N 107.09W
Hatches Creek 59 Hd 20.56S 135.12 E
Haţeg 15 Fd 45.37N 22.57 E
Hatgal 27 Ha 50.26N 100.09 E
Ḩaţībah, Ra's- 23 Ee 21.59N 38.55 E
Ha Tien 25 Kf 10.23N 104.29 E
Ha Tinh 25 Le 18.20N 105.54 E
Hato Mayor 49 Md 18.46N 69.15W
Ḩattá, Jabal- 24 Qj 24.45N 56.04 E
Hattem 12 Ib 52.28N 6.06 E
Hatten 12 Ka 53.03N 8.23 E
Hatteras, Cape- 38 Lf 35.13N 75.32W
Hatteras Inlet 44 Jh 35.00N 75.40W
Hatteras Island 43 Ld 35.25N 75.30W
Hattfjelldal 7 Cd 65.36N 14.00 E
Hattiesburg 43 Je 31.19N 89.16W
Hattingen 12 Jc 51.24N 7.10 E
Hatu Iti, Ile- 61 Ma 8.42S 140.43W
Hatutaa, Ile- 57 Me 7.30S 140.38W
Hatvan 10 Pi 47.40N 19.41 E
Hat Yai 25 Kg 7.01N 100.27 E
Hatyrka 20 Md 62.03N 175.05 E
Hau Bon 25 Lf 13.24N 108.27 E
Haubourdin 12 Ed 50.36N 2.59 E
Hauge 7 Bg 58.21N 6.17 E
Haugesund 6 Gd 59.25N 5.18 E
Hauho 8 Kc 61.10N 24.33 E
Hauhungaroa Range 62 Fc 38.40S 175.35 E
Haukeligrend 7 Bg 59.51N 7.11 E
Haukipudas 7 Fd 65.15N 25.28 E
Haukivesi 5 Ic 62.05N 28.30 E
Haukivuori 8 Lb 62.01N 27.13 E
Hauraha 63a Ed 10.49S 161.57 E
Hauraki Gulf 61 Eg 36.35S 175.00 E
Hauroko, Lake- 62 Bf 45.55S 167.20 E
Hausa 32 Ed 27.06N 11.01W
Hausruck 14 Hb 48.07N 13.35 E
Haut, Isle au- 44 Mc 44.03N 68.38W
Haut Atlas=High Atlas (EN) 30 Ge 32.00N 6.00W
Haute-Champagne 12 Ge 49.18N 4.15 E
Haute-Corse [3] 11a Aa 42.30N 9.00 E
Haute-Garonne [3] 11 Hk 43.25N 1.30 E
Haute-Guinée [3] 34 Dc 11.30N 10.00W
Haute-Kotto [3] 35 Cd 7.00N 23.00 E
Haute-Loire [3] 11 Ji 45.05N 4.00 E
Haute-Marne [3] 11 Lf 48.05N 5.10 E
Hauterive 44 Ma 49.11N 68.16W
Hautes-Alpes [3] 11 Mj 44.40N 6.30 E
Haute-Sangha [3] 35 Be 4.30N 16.00 E
Haute-Saône [3] 11 Mg 47.40N 6.10 E
Haute-Saône, Plateau de- 11 Lg 47.50N 6.00 E
Haute-Savoie [3] 11 Mi 46.00N 6.20 E
Hautes Fagnes/Hoge Venen 10 Bf 50.30N 6.00 E
Hautes-Pyrénées [3] 11 Gk 43.00N 0.10 E
Haute-Vienne [3] 11 Hi 45.50N 1.10 E
Haute-Volta=Upper Volta (EN) [1] 31 Gg 13.00N 2.00W
Haut-Mbomou [3] 35 Dd 6.00N 26.00 E
Hautmont 11 Jd 50.15N 3.56 E
Haut-Ogooué [3] 36 Bc 2.00S 14.00 E
Haut Rhin [3] 11 Ng 48.00N 7.20 E
Hauts-Bassins [3] 34 Ec 12.30N 4.30W
Hauts-de-Seine [3] 11 If 48.50N 2.11 E
Hauts-Plateaux 30 He 34.00N 0.01 E
Haut-Zaïre [2] 36 Eb 2.30N 25.30 E
Hauula 65a 21.36N 157.54W
Hauz-Han 18 Cf 37.16N 61.15 E
Hauz-Hanskoje Vodohr. 18 Cf 37.10N 61.20 E
Havana 45 Kf 40.18N 90.04W
Havana (EN)=La Habana 39 Kg 23.08N 82.22W
Havant 9 Mk 50.51N 0.59W
Havast 18 Gd 40.16N 68.51 E
Havasu, Lake- 46 Hi 34.30N 114.20W
Havel 10 Hd 52.53N 11.58 E
Havelange 12 Hd 50.23N 5.14 E
Havelange-Méan 12 Hd 50.22N 5.20 E
Havelberg 10 Id 52.49N 12.05 E
Havelland 10 Id 52.25N 12.45 E
Havelländisches Luch 10 Id 52.40N 12.40 E
Havelock [N.C.-U.S.] 44 Ih 34.53N 76.54W
Havelock [N.Z.] 62 Ed 41.17S 173.46 E
Havelock North 62 Gc 39.40S 176.53 E
Havelte 12 Ib 52.46N 6.16 E
Haverfordwest 9 Ij 51.49N 4.58W
Haverhill [Eng.-U.K.] 9 Ni 52.05N 0.26 E
Haverhill [Ma.-U.S.] 44 Ld 42.47N 71.05W
Havering, London- 12 Cc 51.36N 0.11 E
Havířov 10 Og 49.48N 18.27 E
Havlíčkův Brod 10 Lg 49.36N 15.34 E
Havøysund 7 Fa 71.03N 24.40 E
Havran 24 Bc 39.33N 27.06 E
Havre 39 Ie 48.33N 109.41W
Havre-Saint-Pierre 39 Md 50.15N 63.36W
Havsa 15 Jh 41.33N 26.49 E
Havza 24 Fb 41.05N 35.45 E
Hawaii [2] 58 Kb 24.00N 167.00W
Hawaiian Islands 57 Kb 24.00N 167.00W
Hawaiian Ridge (EN) 3 Kg 24.00N 165.00W
Hawaii Island 57 Lc 19.30N 155.30W
Ḩawallī 23 Gd 29.19N 48.02 E
Ḩawār 24 Nj 25.40N 50.45 E
Hawarden 62 Ee 42.56S 172.39 E
Ḩawashīyah, Wādī- 24 Eh 28.31N 32.58 E
Hawaymī, Sha'īb al- 24 Kg 30.58N 44.15 E
Hawd 30 Lh 7.40N 47.43 E
Ḩawḑ Al Waqf 24 Ei 26.03N 32.22 E
Hawea, Lake- 62 Cf 44.30S 169.20 E
Hawera 61 Dg 39.35S 174.17 E
Hawi 58 Lb 20.14N 155.50W
Hawick 9 Kf 55.25N 2.47W
Ḩawīzah, Hawr al- 24 Lg 31.35N 47.38 E
Hawkdun Range 62 Cf 44.50S 170.00 E
Hawke Bay 61 Eg 39.25S 177.20 E
Hawke Harbour 42 Lf 53.01N 55.50W
Hawker 59 Hf 31.53S 138.25 E
Hawkes, Mount- 66 Rg 83.55S 56.05W
Hawke's Bay [2] 62 Gc 39.30S 176.40 E
Hawkesbury 44 Jc 45.36N 74.37W
Hawkhurst 12 Cc 51.02N 0.30 E
Hawkinsville 44 Fi 32.17N 83.28W
Hawksbill 44 Hf 38.33N 78.23W
Hawk Springs 46 Mf 41.48N 104.09W
Ḩawmat as Sūq 32 Jc 33.53N 10.51 E
Hawng Tuk 25 Jd 20.28N 99.56 E
Ḩawrā' 35 Hb 15.43N 48.18 E
Hawrān, Wādī al- 23 Fc 33.58N 42.34 E
Ḩawsh 'Isá 24 Dg 30.55N 30.17 E
Hawthorne 43 Dd 38.32N 118.38W
Hawthorne, Mount- 66 Pf 72.10S 98.39W
Haxtun 45 Ef 40.39N 102.38W
Hay 58 Fh 34.30S 144.51 E
Hay 38 Hc 60.51N 115.44W
Hayachine-San 29 Gb 39.34N 141.29 E
Hayakita 29a Bb 42.45N 141.48 E
Hayange 11 Me 49.20N 6.03 E
Hayasui-no-Seto 28 Kh 33.20N 132.00 E
Hayato 29 Bf 31.45N 130.43 E
Haybān 35 Ec 11.13N 30.31 E
Haybān, Jabal- 35 Ec 11.15N 30.31 E
Hayden 46 Jj 33.00N 110.47W
Hayes [Man.-Can.] 42 Ie 57.00N 92.15W
Hayes [N.W.T.-Can.] 42 Hc 67.20N 95.02W
Hayes, Mount- 40 Jd 63.37N 146.43W
Hayes Halvø=Hayes Peninsula (EN) 67 Od 77.40N 64.30W
Hayes Peninsula (EN)=Hayes Halvø 67 Od 77.40N 64.30W
Ḩayl 24 Qj 24.33N 56.06 E
Hayl, Wādī al- 24 He 34.47N 39.18 E
Hayling Island 12 Bd 50.48N 0.58W
Haymana 24 Ec 39.27N 32.30 E
Haymana Platosu 24 Ec 39.25N 32.45 E
Haynin 23 Gf 15.50N 48.18 E
Hayrabolu 24 Bb 41.12N 27.06 E
Ḩayrān 33 Hf 16.02N 42.49 E
Hay River 59 Hd 25.00S 138.00 E
Hay River 39 Hc 60.51N 115.40W
Hayrūt 35 Ib 15.59N 52.09 E
Hays 43 Hd 38.53N 99.20W
Hay Springs 45 Ee 42.41N 102.41W
Haystack Peak 46 Ig 39.50N 113.55W
Hayward [Ca.-U.S.] 46 Dh 37.40N 122.05W
Hayward [Wi.-U.S.] 45 Kc 46.01N 91.29W
Haywards Heath 12 Bc 51.00N 0.06W
Hazar, Wādī- 35 Hb 17.50N 49.07 E
Hazarasp 18 Cd 41.19N 61.08 E
Hazard 44 Fg 37.15N 83.12W
Hazar Gölü 24 Hc 38.30N 39.25 E
Hazārībāgh 25 Hd 23.59N 85.21 E
Hazebrouck 11 Id 50.43N 2.32 E
Hazelton 42 Ee 55.15N 127.40W
Hazen 45 Fc 47.18N 101.38W
Hazen Strait 42 Ga 77.15N 110.00W
Ḩaẕeva 24 Fg 30.48N 35.15 E
Hazlehurst [Ga.-U.S.] 44 Fj 31.52N 82.36W
Hazlehurst [Ms.-U.S.] 45 Kk 31.52N 90.24W
Hazleton 44 Je 40.58N 76.00W
Hazlett, Lake- 59 Fd 21.30S 128.50 E
Hazrah, Ra's al- 24 Nj 24.22N 51.36 E
Hazro 24 Ic 38.15N 40.47 E
Heacham 12 Cb 52.55N 0.29 E
Headley 12 Bc 51.07N 0.49W
Healdsburg 46 Dg 38.37N 122.52W
Heanor 12 Aa 53.00N 1.18W
Heard Island 30 On 53.00S 73.35 E
Hearne 45 Hk 30.53N 96.36W
Hearst 42 Jg 49.41N 83.40W
Heart River 45 Fc 46.47N 100.51W
Heathrow Airport London 12 Bc 51.28N 0.30W
Hebbronville 45 Gm 27.18N 98.41W
Hebei Sheng (Ho-pei Sheng) =Hopeh (EN) [2] 27 Kd 39.00N 116.00 E
Heber City 46 Jf 40.30N 111.25W
Hebi 27 Jd 35.53N 114.09 E
Hebian 27 Jd 38.35N 113.06 E
Hebiji 28 Cf 36.00N 114.08 E
Hebrides 5 Fd 57.00N 6.30W
Hebrides, Sea of the- 9 Ge 57.00N 7.00W
Hebron [N.D.-U.S.] 45 Ec 46.54N 102.03W
Hebron [Newf.-Can.] 42 Le 58.15N 62.35W
Heby 8 Ge 59.56N 16.53 E
Hecate Strait 42 Ef 53.20N 131.00W
Hecelchakán 48 Ng 20.10N 90.08W
Hechi (Jnchengjiang) 27 Ig 24.44N 108.02 E
Hechingen 10 Eh 48.21N 8.59 E
Hechuan 27 Ie 30.07N 106.15 E
Hecla 45 Gd 45.43N 98.09W
Hecla and Griper Bay 42 Ga 76.00N 111.30W
Hecla Island 45 Ha 51.08N 96.45W
Heddalsvatnet 8 Ce 59.30N 9.15 E
Hede 7 Ce 62.25N 13.30 E
Hede → Sheyang 28 Fh 33.47N 120.15 E
Hedemarken 8 Dd 60.50N 11.20 E
Hedemora 7 Df 60.17N 15.59 E
Hedensted 8 Ci 55.46N 9.42 E
Hedesunda 7 Df 60.25N 17.00 E
Hedesunda fjärdarna 8 Gd 60.20N 17.00 E
Hedmark [2] 7 Cf 61.30N 11.45 E
Hedo-Misaki 29b Bb 26.52N 128.16 E
Heemskerk 12 Gb 52.30N 4.42 E
Heemstede 12 Gb 52.21N 4.37 E
Heerenveen 11 Lb 52.57N 5.55 E
Heerhugowaard 12 Gb 52.40N 4.50 E
Heerlen 11 Ld 50.54N 5.59 E
Hefa=Haifa (EN) 22 Ff 32.50N 35.00 E
Hefei 22 Nf 31.47N 117.15 E
Hefeng 27 Jf 29.49N 110.01 E
Hegang 22 Pe 47.20N 130.12 E
Hegau 10 Ei 47.50N 8.45 E
Hegura Jima 27 Od 37.50N 136.55 E
Heide 10 Fb 54.12N 9.06 E
Heidelberg 10 Eg 49.25N 8.42 E
Heidenheim an der Brenz 10 Gh 48.41N 10.09 E
Heidenreichstein 14 Jb 48.52N 15.07 E
Hei-Gawa 29 Gb 39.38N 141.58 E
Heigun-Tō 29 Ce 33.47N 132.15 E
Hei He 27 Hd 38.15N 100.15 E
Heihe → Aihui 22 Od 50.13N 127.26 E
Heilbron 37 De 27.21S 27.58 E
Heilbronn 10 Fg 49.08N 9.13 E
Heiligenblut 14 Gd 47.02N 12.50 E
Heiligenhafen 10 Gb 54.22N 10.59 E
Heiligenhaus 12 Ic 51.19N 6.58 E
Heiligenstadt 10 Ge 51.23N 10.08 E
Heilinzi 28 Ib 44.33N 126.41 E
Heilong Jiang 21 Qd 52.56N 141.10 E
Heilongjiang Sheng (Hei-lung-chiang Sheng)= Heilungkiang (EN) [2] 27 Mb 48.00N 128.00 E
Heiloo 12 Gb 52.36N 4.43 E
Hei-lung-chiang Sheng → Heilongjiang Sheng=Heilungkiang (EN) [2] 27 Mb 48.00N 128.00 E
Heilungkiang (EN)= Heilongjiang Sheng (Hei-lung-chiang Sheng) [2] 27 Mb 48.00N 128.00 E
Heilungkiang (EN)=Hei-lung-chiang Sheng → Heilongjiang Sheng [2] 27 Mb 48.00N 128.00 E
Heimæy 7a c 63.26N 20.17W
Heimbach 12 Id 50.38N 6.29 E
Heimdal 7 Ce 63.21N 10.22 E
Heimsheim 12 Kf 48.48N 8.51 E
Heinävesi 7 Ge 62.26N 28.36 E
Heinola 7 Gf 61.13N 26.02 E
Heinsberg 12 Ic 51.04N 6.05 E
Heishan 28 Gd 41.42N 122.07 E
Heishan Xia 27 Hd 37.18N 104.39 E
Heishui [China] 28 Ec 42.06N 119.22 E
Heishui [China] 27 He 32.03N 103.05 E
Heist, Knokke- 12 Fc 51.21N 3.15 E
Heist-op-den-Berg 12 Gc 51.05N 4.43 E
Hei-Zaki 29 Hb 39.39N 142.00 E
Hejgijaha 17 Pd 65.27N 72.50 E
Hejian 28 De 38.27N 116.05 E
Hejing 27 Ec 42.18N 86.18 E
Hejjaha 17 Kb 68.18N 62.32 E
Hekimhan 24 Gc 38.49N 37.56 E
Hekinan 29 Ed 34.52N 136.58 E
Hekla 5 Ec 64.00N 19.40W
Hekou 28 Ci 31.20N 114.25 E
Hekou → Yanshan 28 Dj 28.18N 117.41 E
Hel 10 Ob 54.37N 18.48 E
Helagsfjället 7 Ce 62.55N 12.27 E
Helan 27 Id 38.35N 106.16 E
Helan Shan 27 Id 39.00N 106.00 E
Helden's Point 51c Ab 17.24N 62.50W
Helena [Ar.-U.S.] 43 Ie 34.32N 90.35W
Helena [Guy.] 54 Gb 6.41N 57.55W
Helena [Mt.-U.S.] 39 He 46.36N 112.01W
Helen Glacier 66 Ge 66.40S 93.55 E
Helen Reef 57 Ed 2.53N 131.47 E
Helensburgh 9 Ie 56.01N 4.44W
Helensville 62 Fb 36.40S 174.27 E
Helgaå 8 Fi 55.53N 14.08 E
Helgasjön 8 Fh 56.55N 14.45 E
Helgeland 7 Cd 66.15N 13.05 E
Helgoland 10 Db 54.12N 7.53 E

Index Symbols

[1] Independent Nation
[2] State, Region
[3] District, County
[4] Municipality
[5] Colony, Dependency
Continent
Physical Region
Historical or Cultural Region
Mount, Mountain
Volcano
Hill
Mountains, Mountain Range
Hills, Escarpment
Plateau, Upland
Pass, Gap
Plain, Lowland
Delta
Salt Flat
Valley, Canyon
Crater, Cave
Karst Features
Depression
Polder
Desert, Dunes
Forest, Woods
Heath, Steppe
Oasis
Cape, Point
Coast, Beach
Cliff
Peninsula
Isthmus
Sandbank
Island
Atoll
Rock, Reef
Islands, Archipelago
Rocks, Reefs
Coral Reef
Well, Spring
Geyser
River, Stream
Waterfall Rapids
River Mouth, Estuary
Lake
Salt Lake
Intermittent Lake
Reservoir
Swamp, Pond
Canal
Glacier
Ice Shelf, Pack Ice
Ocean
Sea
Gulf, Bay
Strait, Fjord
Lagoon
Bank
Seamount
Tablemount
Ridge
Shelf
Basin
Escarpment, Sea Scarp
Fracture
Trench, Abyss
National Park, Reserve
Point of Interest
Recreation Site
Cave, Cavern
Historic Site
Ruins
Wall, Walls
Church, Abbey
Temple
Scientific Station
Airport
Port
Lighthouse
Mine
Tunnel
Dam, Bridge

Helgoländer Bucht 10 Eb 54.10N 8.04 E
Helikón Óros 15 Fk 38.20N 22.50 E
Helixi 28 Ei 30.39N 119.01 E
Heljulja 8 Nc 61.37N 30.38 E
Hella 7a Bc 63.50N 20.24W
Hellberge 10 Hd 52.34N 11.17 E
Hēlleh 24 Nh 29.10N 50.40 E
Hellendoorn 11 Mb 52.24N 6.26 E
Hellendoorn-Nijverdal 12 Ib 52.22N 6.27 E
Hellenic Trough (EN) 5 Ii 35.00N 24.00 E
Hellental 12 Id 50.29N 6.26 E
Hellesylt 7 Be 62.05N 6.54 E
Hellín 13 Kf 38.31N 1.41W
Hells Canyon 43 Db 45.20N 116.45W
Hellweg 12 Kc 51.40N 8.00 E
Helmand 21 If 31.12N 61.34 E
Helmand [3] 23 Jc 31.00N 64.00 E
Helme 10 He 51.20N 11.20 E
Helmeringhausen 37 Be 25.54S 16.57 E
Helmond 11 Lc 51.29N 5.40 E
Helmsdale 9 Jc 58.10N 3.40W
Helmsdale 9 Jc 58.07N 3.40W
Helmstedt 10 Gd 52.14N 11.00 E
Helong 27 Mc 42.32N 129.00 E
Helpe Majeure 12 Fd 50.11N 3.47 E
Helpringham 12 Bb 52.56N 0.18W
Helpter Berge 10 Jc 53.30N 13.36 E
Helsingborg 6 Hd 56.03N 12.42 E
Helsinge 8 Eh 56.01N 12.12 E
Helsingfors/Helsinki 6 Ic 60.10N 24.58 E
Helsingør 7 Ch 56.02N 12.37 E
Helsinki/Helsingfors 6 Ic 60.10N 24.58 E
Helska, Mierzeja- 10 Ob 54.45N 18.39 E
Helston 9 Hk 50.05N 5.16W
Helvecia 55 Bj 31.06S 60.05W
Helwān (EN)=Ḩulwān 33 Fd 29.51N 31.20 E
Ḩemār 24 Qg 31.42N 57.31 E
Hemčik 20 Ef 51.40N 92.10 E
Hemel Hempstead 9 Mj 51.46N 0.28W
Hemer 12 Jc 51.23N 7.46 E
Hemnesberget 7 Cc 66.14N 13.38 E
Hemsby 12 Db 52.41N 1.42 E
Hemse 8 Hg 57.14N 18.22 E
Hemsedal 8 Cd 60.50N 8.40 E
Hemsö 7 Ee 62.45N 18.05 E
Hen 8 Dd 60.13N 10.14 E
Henan 27 He 34.33N 101.55 E
Hen and Chickens Islands 62 Fa 35.55S 174.45 E
Henan Sheng (Ho-nan Sheng)=Honan (EN) [2] 27 Je 34.00N 114.00 E
Henares 13 Id 40.24N 3.30W
Henashi-Zaki 29 Fa 40.37N 139.51 E
Henbury 59 Gd 24.35S 133.15 E
Hendaye 11 Ek 43.22N 1.47W
Hendek 24 Db 40.48N 30.45 E
Henderson [Arg.] 55 Bm 36.18S 61.43W
Henderson [Ky.-U.S.] 44 Dg 37.50N 87.35W
Henderson [N.C.-U.S.] 44 Hg 36.20N 78.25W
Henderson [Nv.-U.S.] 43 Dd 36.02N 115.01W
Henderson [Tx.-U.S.] 45 Ij 32.09N 94.48W
Henderson Island 57 Og 24.22S 128.19W
Henderson Seamount (EN) 43 Df 25.34N 119.33W
Hendersonville [N.C.-U.S.] 44 Fh 35.19N 82.28W
Hendersonville [Tn.-U.S.] 44 Dg 36.18N 86.37W
Hendījān 24 Mg 30.14N 49.43 E
Hendorābī, Jazīreh-ye- 24 Oi 26.40N 53.37 E
Hendrik Verwderddam 30 Km 46.36S 37.55 E
Hengām, Jazīreh-ye- 24 Pi 26.39N 55.53 E
Hengduan Shan 21 Lg 27.30N 99.00 E
Hengelo [Neth.] 11 Mb 52.15N 6.45 E
Hengelo [Neth.] 12 Ib 52.03N 6.20 E
Heng Shan [China] 27 Jd 39.42N 113.45 E
Hengshan [China] 27 Jf 27.16N 112.51 E
Heng Shan [China] 27 Jf 27.18N 112.41 E
Hengshan [China] 27 Id 37.51N 109.20 E
Hengshan [China] 28 Kb 45.24N 131.01 E
Hengshui 27 Kd 37.39N 115.46 E
Hengxian 27 Ig 22.46N 109.15 E
Hengyang 22 Ng 26.56N 112.35 E
Henik Lakes 42 Hd 61.05N 97.20W
Hénin-Liétard 11 Id 50.25N 2.56 E
Henley-on-Thames 12 Bc 51.32N 0.54W
Hennan 8 Fb 62.05N 15.45 E
Hennan 7 De 62.02N 15.54 E
Hennebont 11 Cg 47.48N 3.17W
Hennef (Sieg) 12 Jd 50.47N 7.17 E
Hennigsdorf bei Berlin 10 Jd 52.38N 13.12 E
Henrietta Maria, Cape - 42 Je 55.09N 82.19W
Henrietty, Ostrov- 20 Ka 77.00N 157.00 E
Henry, Mount- 46 Hb 48.53N 115.31W
Henry Bay 66 Ie 66.40S 120.40 E
Henryetta 45 Ii 35.27N 95.59W
Henry Kater Peninsula 42 Kk 69.15N 67.30W
Henry Mountains 46 Jh 37.55N 110.50W
Henrys Fork River 46 Je 43.45N 111.56W
Henslow, Cape- 63a Ec 9.56S 160.38 E
Hentej 21 Me 48.50N 109.00 E
Hentiesbaai 37 Ad 22.08S 14.18 E
Henzada 22 Lh 17.38N 95.28 E
Heping → Yanhe 27 If 28.31N 108.28 E
Heppenheim (Bergstraße) 12 Ke 49.38N 8.39 E
Heppner 46 Fd 45.21N 119.33W
Hepu (Lianzhou) 27 Ig 21.40N 109.12 E
Hequ 27 Jd 39.22N 111.15 E
Herakol Dağı 24 Id 37.45N 42.35 E
Heralds Cays 59 Jc 16.55S 149.10 E
Herāt [3] 23 Jc 34.30N 62.00 E
Herāt 22 If 34.20N 62.12 E
Hérault [3] 11 Jk 43.40N 3.30 E
Hérault 11 Jk 43.17N 3.26 E
Herbert [N.Z.] 62 Df 45.13S 170.46 E
Herbert [Sask.-Can.] 46 La 50.26N 107.12W
Herberton 59 Jc 17.23S 145.23 E
Herbert River 59 Jc 18.32S 146.17 E
Herborn 10 Ef 50.41N 8.19 E
Herby 10 Of 50.45N 18.40 E
Hercegnovi 15 Bg 42.27N 18.32 E
Hercegovina 14 Lg 43.00N 17.50 E
Hercegovina 5 Hg 43.00N 17.50 E
Herdubreid 7a Cb 65.11N 16.21W
Heredia [3] 49 Fh 10.30N 84.00W
Heredia 47 Hf 10.00N 84.07W
Hereford 9 Ki 52.15N 2.50W
Hereford [Eng.-U.K.] 9 Ki 52.04N 2.43W
Hereford [Tx.-U.S.] 43 Ge 34.49N 102.24W
Hereford and Worcester [3] 9 Ki 52.10N 2.35W
Hereheretue Atoll 57 Mf 19.54S 144.58W
Hereke 15 Mi 40.48N 29.39 E
Herekino 62 Ea 35.16S 173.13 E
Herent 12 Gd 50.54N 4.40 E
Herentals 12 Gc 51.11N 4.50 E
Herfølge 8 Ei 55.25N 12.10 E
Herford 10 Ed 52.08N 8.41 E
Héricourt 11 Mg 47.35N 6.45 E
Herington 45 Hg 38.40N 96.57W
Heriot 61 Ci 45.51S 169.16 E
Herīs 24 Lc 38.14N 47.07 E
Herisau 14 Dc 47.24N 9.16 E
Herk 12 Hd 50.58N 5.07 E
Herk-de-Stad 12 Hd 50.56N 5.10 E
Herkimer 44 Jd 43.02N 74.59W
Herlen He 27 Kb 48.48N 117.00 E
Hermagor 14 Hd 46.37N 13.22 E
Hermanas 48 Id 27.14N 101.14W
Herma Ness 9 Ma 60.50N 0.54W
Hermano Peak 45 Bh 37.17N 108.48W
Hermansverk 8 Bc 61.11N 6.51 E
Hermanus 37 Bf 34.25S 19.16 E
Hermeskeil 12 Ie 49.39N 6.57 E
Hermiston 46 Fd 45.51N 119.17W
Hermitage 62 De 43.44S 170.05 E
Hermit Islands 57 Fe 1.32S 145.05 E
Hermosa de Santa Rosa, Sierra- 48 Id 28.00N 101.45W
Hermosillo 39 Hg 29.04N 110.58W
Hermoso Campo 55 Bh 27.36S 61.21W
Hérnad 10 Qh 48.00N 20.58 E
Hernandarias 56 Jc 25.22S 54.45W
Hernández [Arg.] 55 Bk 32.21S 60.02W
Hernández [Mex.] 48 Hf 23.02N 102.02W
Hernani 13 Ka 43.16N 1.58W
Herne 10 De 51.33N 7.13 E
Herne Bay 9 Oj 51.23N 1.08 E
Herning 6 Gd 56.08N 8.59 E
Heroica Alvarado 48 Lh 18.46N 95.46W
Heroica Tlapacoyan 48 Kh 19.58N 97.13W
Heroica Zitácuaro 48 Ih 19.24N 100.22W
Herouville-Saint-Clair 12 Be 49.12N 0.19W
Herowābād 24 Md 37.37N 48.32 E
Herradura 55 Ch 26.29S 58.18W
Herre 8 Ce 59.06N 9.34 E
Herrera 55 Ck 32.26S 58.38W
Herrera [3] 49 Gj 7.54N 80.38W
Herrera del Duque 13 Ge 39.10N 5.03W
Herrera de Pisuerga 13 Hb 42.36N 4.20W
Herrero, Punta- 48 Ph 19.10N 87.30W
Herrljunga 8 Ef 58.05N 13.02 E
Hers 11 Hk 43.47N 1.20 E
Herschel 42 Dc 69.35N 139.05W
Herselt 12 Gc 51.03N 4.53 E
Herserange 12 He 49.31N 5.47 E
Hershey 44 Ie 40.17N 76.39W
Hersilia 55 Bj 30.00S 61.51W
Herson 6 Jf 46.38N 32.35 E
Hersonesski, Mys- 16 Hg 44.33N 33.25 E
Hersonskaja Oblast [3] 19 Df 46.40N 33.30 E
Herstal 11 Ld 50.40N 5.38 E
Herten 12 Jc 51.36N 7.08 E
Hertford 9 Mj 51.50N 0.05W
Hertford 9 Mj 51.48N 0.05W
Hertfordshire [3] 9 Mj 51.45N 0.20W
Hertugen Af Orleans Land 41 Jc 78.15N 21.12W
Hervás 13 Gd 40.16N 5.51W
Herve 12 Hd 50.38N 5.48 E
Herve, Plateau van-/Herveland 12 Hd 50.40N 5.50 E
Herveland/Herve, Plateau van- 12 Hd 50.40N 5.50 E
Hervey Bay 59 Ke 25.15S 152.50 E
Herzberg 10 Je 51.41N 13.14 E
Herzberg am Harz 10 Ge 51.39N 10.20 E
Herzebrock 12 Kc 51.53N 8.15 E
Herzele 12 Fd 50.53N 3.53 E
Herzliyya 24 Ff 32.10N 34.51 E
Herzogenrath 12 Id 50.52N 6.06 E
Herzog-Ernst-Bucht (Vahsel Bay) 66 Af 77.48S 34.39W
Hesāmābād 24 Me 35.52N 48.25 E
Hesbaye/Haspengouws Plateau 11 Ld 50.35N 5.10 E
Hesdin 11 Id 50.22N 2.02 E
Hesel 12 Ja 53.18N 7.36 E
Heshī 24 Md 37.30N 48.15 E
Heshun 27 Jd 37.18N 113.32 E
Hesse (EN)=Hessen [2] 10 Ff 50.30N 9.15 E
Hesselberg 10 Gg 49.05N 10.35 E
Hesselø 8 Dh 56.10N 11.45 E
Hessen 12 Ke 49.47N 8.08 E
Hessen=Hesse (EN) [2] 10 Ff 50.30N 9.15 E
Hess Tablemount (EN) 57 Jc 17.50N 174.15W
Heta 21 Mb 71.54N 102.00 E
Heta 20 Eb 71.35N 99.45 E
Hettange-Grande 12 Ie 49.24N 6.09 E
Hettinger 45 Ec 46.00N 102.39W
Heuberg 10 Eh 48.06N 8.55 E
Heuchin 12 Ed 50.28N 2.16 E
Heuru 63a Ed 10.12S 161.25 E
Hève, Cap de la- 11 Fe 49.31N 0.04W
Heves 10 Qi 47.36N 20.17 E
Heves [2] 10 Qi 47.50N 20.15 E
Hexham 9 Kg 54.58N 2.06W
Hexi 27 Hf 27.44N 102.09 E
Hexian 28 Ei 31.43N 118.22 E
Hexian (Babu) 27 Jg 24.28N 111.34 E
Hexigten Qi (Jingfeng) 27 Kc 43.15N 117.31 E
Heydarābād 24 Kd 37.06N 45.27 E
Heysham 9 Kg 54.02N 2.54W
Heyuan 27 Jg 23.41N 114.43 E
Heywood 59 Ig 38.08S 141.38 E
Heze (Caozhou) 27 Kd 35.14N 115.28 E
Hezuo 27 Hd 35.02N 102.57 E
Hialeah 44 Gm 25.49N 80.17W
Hiawatha 45 Ig 39.51N 95.32W
Hibara-Ko 29 Gc 37.42N 140.03 E
Hibbing 43 Ib 47.25N 92.56W
Hibernia Reef 59 Eb 12.00S 123.25 E
Hibiki-Nada 29 Bd 34.15N 130.40 E
Hibiny 7 Hc 67.40N 33.35 E
Hiburi-Jima 29 Ce 33.10N 132.18 E
Hickman 44 Cg 36.34N 89.11W
Hickory 44 Gh 35.44N 81.21W
Hick's Cay 49 Ce 17.39N 88.08W
Hida-Gawa 29 Ed 35.25N 137.03 E
Hidaka [Jap.] 28 Qc 42.53N 142.28 E
Hidaka [Jap.] 29 Dd 35.28N 134.47 E
Hidaka-Gawa 29 De 33.53N 135.08 E
Hidaka Sanmyaku 28 Qc 42.25N 142.50 E
Hidalgo [2] 47 Ed 20.30N 99.00W
Hidalgo [Mex.] 47 Ed 24.15N 99.26W
Hidalgo [Mex.] 48 Jd 27.47N 99.52W
Hidalgo del Parral 39 Ig 26.56N 105.40W
Hida-Sanchi 29 Ec 36.20N 137.00 E
Hida-Sanmyaku 28 Nf 36.10N 137.30 E
Hiddensee 10 Jb 54.33N 13.07 E
Hidra 8 Bf 58.15N 6.35 E
Hidrolândia 55 Hc 16.58S 49.16W
Hidrolina 55 Hb 14.37S 49.25W
Hieflau 14 Ic 47.36N 14.44 E
Hiei-Zan 29 Dd 35.05N 135.50 E
Hienghène 61 Cd 20.35S 164.56 E
Hierro 30 Ff 27.45N 18.00W
Higashi 29b b 26.38N 128.08 E
Higashihiroshima 29 Cd 34.25N 132.43 E
Higashi-izu 29 Fd 34.48N 139.02 E
Higashi-matsuyama 29 Fc 36.02N 139.22 E
Higashimuroran 29a Bb 42.21N 141.02 E
Higashine 28 Pe 38.26N 140.24 E
Higashiōsaka 29 Dd 34.40N 135.37 E
Higashi Rishiri 29a Ba 45.16N 141.15 E
Higashi-Shina-Kai=East China Sea (EN) 21 Og 29.00N 125.00 E
Higgins 45 Fh 36.07N 100.02W
Higham Ferrers 12 Bb 52.18N 0.35W
High Atlas (EN)=Haut Atlas 30 Ge 32.00N 6.00W
Highland [3] 9 Id 57.30N 5.00W
Highland Park 45 Me 42.11N 87.48W
High Level 42 Fe 58.30N 117.05W
Highmore 45 Gd 44.31N 99.27W
High Plains 38 If 38.30N 103.00W
High Point 43 Ld 35.58N 79.59W
High Prairie 42 Fe 55.27N 116.30W
High River 42 Gf 50.35N 113.52W
Highrock Lake 42 He 55.49N 100.23W
High Springs 44 Fk 29.50N 82.36W
High Tatra (EN)=Vysoké Tatry 10 Pg 49.10N 20.00 E
High Willhays 9 Jk 50.41N 3.59W
Highwood Mountains 46 Jc 47.25N 110.30W
High Wycombe 9 Mj 51.38N 0.46W
Higuera de Zaragoza 48 Ee 25.59N 109.16W
Higüero, Punta- 49 Nd 18.22N 67.16W
Higuerote 50 Cg 10.29N 66.06W
Higüey 49 Md 18.37N 68.43W
Hiidenvesi 8 Kd 60.20N 24.10 E
Hii-Gawa 29 Cd 35.26N 132.52 E
Hiiraan [3] 35 He 4.00N 45.30 E
Hiitola 7 Gf 61.16N 29.42 E
Hiiumaa/Hiiuma 5 Id 58.50N 22.40 E
Hijar 13 Lc 41.10N 0.27W
Ḩijāz 23 Ee 24.30N 38.30 E
Hijāz, Jabal al- 33 Hf 19.45N 41.55 E
Hiji 29 Be 33.22N 131.32 E
Hiji-Gawa 29 Ce 33.36N 132.29 E
Hikami 29 Dd 35.11N 135.02 E
Hikari 28 Kh 33.58N 131.56 E
Hiketa 29 Dd 34.13N 134.24 E
Hikiä 8 Kd 60.45N 24.55 E
Hiki-Gawa 29 De 33.35N 135.26 E
Ḩikmah, Ra's al- 24 Bg 31.17N 27.44 E
Hikone 28 Ng 35.15N 136.15 E
Hiko-San 29 Be 33.29N 130.56 E
Hikueru Atoll 61 Mc 17.36S 142.37W
Hikurangi 62 Hb 37.55S 178.04 E
Hikurangi 62 Fa 35.36S 174.17 E
Hila 26 Ih 7.35S 127.24 E
Hilāl, Ra's al- 33 Dc 32.55N 22.11 E
Hiland 46 Le 43.08N 107.18W
Hilchenbach 12 Kc 51.00N 8.06 E
Hildburghausen 10 Gf 50.25N 10.45 E
Hilden 12 Ic 51.10N 6.56 E
Hildesheim 10 Fd 52.09N 9.58 E
Hillaby, Mount- 50 Gf 13.12N 59.35W
Hillared 8 Eg 57.38N 13.09 E
Hillary Coast 6 Kf 79.00S 161.00 E
Hill Bank 49 Ce 17.35N 88.42W
Hill City 45 Gg 39.22N 99.51W
Hillcrest Center 46 Fi 35.23N 118.57W
Hille 12 Kb 52.20N 8.45 E
Hillegom 12 Gb 52.18N 4.35 E
Hillekrog 8 Dj 54.36N 11.30 E
Hillerød 8 Ei 55.56N 12.19 E
Hillerstorp 8 Eg 57.19N 13.52 E
Hillesheim 12 Id 50.19N 6.41 E
Hillingdon, London- 12 Bc 51.31N 0.27W
Hillsboro [Il.-U.S.] 45 Lg 39.09N 89.29W
Hillsboro [N.D.-U.S.] 45 Hc 47.26N 97.03W
Hillsboro [Oh.-U.S.] 44 Ff 39.12N 83.37W
Hillsboro [Or.-U.S.] 46 Dd 45.31N 122.59W
Hillsboro [Tx.-U.S.] 45 Hj 32.01N 97.08W
Hillsborough 51p Cb 12.29N 61.26W
Hillsdale 44 Ee 41.55N 84.38W
Hillsville 44 Gg 36.46N 80.44W
Hillswich 9 La 60.28N 1.30W
Hilo 58 Lc 19.44N 155.05W
Hilo Bay 65a Fd 19.44N 155.05W
Hilok 21 Md 51.19N 106.59 E
Hilok 20 Gf 51.22N 110.30 E
Hilton Head Island 44 Gi 32.12N 80.45W
Hiltrup, Münster- 12 Jc 51.54N 7.38 E
Hilvan 24 Hd 37.30N 38.58 E
Hilvarenbeek 12 Hc 51.29N 5.08 E
Hilversum 11 Lb 52.14N 5.10 E
Himāchal Prādesh [3] 25 Fb 31.00N 78.00 E
Himalaya=Himalayas (EN) 21 Kg 29.00N 83.00 E
Himalayas (EN)=Himalaya 21 Kg 29.00N 83.00 E
Himara 15 Ci 40.07N 19.44 E
Himeji 27 Ne 34.49N 134.42 E
Hime-Jima 29 Be 33.43N 131.40 E
Hime-Kawa 29 Ec 37.02N 137.50 E
Hime-Shima 29 Ae 32.49N 128.41 E
Hime-Zaki 29 Fb 38.05N 138.34 E
Himi 28 Nf 36.51N 136.59 E
Himki 7 Ii 55.56N 37.28 E
Himmelbjerget 8 Ch 56.06N 9.42 E
Himmerfjärden 8 Ge 59.00N 17.43 E
Himmerland 8 Ch 56.50N 9.45 E
Himo 36 Gc 3.23S 37.33 E
Ḩimş=Homs (E) 22 Ff 34.44N 36.43 E
Hims, Bahrat- 24 Ge 34.39N 36.34 E
Hinai 29 Ga 40.13N 140.35 E
Hinca Renancó 56 Hd 34.50S 64.23W
Hinche 49 Kd 19.09N 72.01W
Hinchinbrook 40 Jd 60.22N 146.30W
Hinchinbrook Island 59 Jc 18.25S 146.15 E
Hinckley 12 Ab 52.32N 1.22W
Hindås 8 Eg 57.42N 12.27 E
Hindhead 12 Bc 51.06N 0.44W
Ḩindi, Badwēynta-=Indian Ocean (EN) 3 Gl 21.00S 82.00 E
Hindmarsh, Lake- 59 Ig 36.05S 141.55 E
Hinds 62 Df 44.00S 171.34 E
Hindsholm 8 Di 55.33N 10.40 E
Hindukush 21 Jf 35.00N 71.00 E
Hindustan 21 Jg 25.00N 79.00 E
Hinesville 44 Gj 31.51N 81.36W
Hinganghāt 25 Fd 20.34N 78.50 E
Hınıs 24 Ic 39.22N 41.44 E
Hınıs 24 Jc 39.18N 42.12 E
Hinlopenstretet 41 Oc 79.15N 21.00 E
Hinnøya 5 Hb 68.30N 16.00 E
Hino-Gawa 29 Cd 35.27N 133.22 E
Hinojosa del Duque 13 Gf 38.30N 5.09W
Hinokage 29 Be 32.39N 131.24 E
Hi-no-Misaki 29 Cd 35.26N 132.38 E
Hino-Misaki 29 De 33.53N 135.04 E
Hinterrhein 14 Dd 46.49N 9.25 E
Hinton 42 Ff 53.25N 117.34W
Hi-Numa 29 Gc 36.16N 140.30 E
Hınzır Burun 24 Fb 36.22N 35.45 E
Hiou 63b Ca 13.08S 166.33 E
Hipólito 48 Ie 25.41N 101.26W
Hippolytushoef, Wieringen- 12 Gb 52.54N 4.59 E
Hippone 14 Bn 36.52N 7.44 E
Hirado 28 Jh 33.22N 129.33 E
Hirado-Shima 28 Jh 33.19N 129.32 E
Hiraka 29 Gb 39.16N 140.29 E
Hirakata 29 Dd 34.48N 135.38 E
Hīrākud 25 Gd 21.15N 84.15 E
Hiraman 36 Gc 1.07S 39.55 E
Hiranai 29a Bc 40.54N 140.57 E
Hirara 27 Mg 24.48N 125.17 E
Hira-Shima 29 Ae 33.01N 129.15 E
Hirata 29 Cd 35.26N 132.49 E
Hiratsuka 29 Fd 35.19N 139.19 E
Hirfanlı barajı Gölü 24 Ec 39.10N 33.32 E
Hirgis 27 Fb 49.32N 93.48 E
Hirgis-Nur 21 Le 49.12N 93.24 E
Hirhafok 32 Ie 23.29N 5.45 E
Hîrlău 15 Jb 47.26N 26.54 E
Hiromi 29 Ce 33.15N 132.38 E
Hiroo 27 Pc 42.17N 143.19 E
Hirosaki 27 Pc 40.35N 140.28 E
Hiroshima 22 Pf 34.24N 132.27 E
Hiroshima Ken [2] 28 Lg 34.35N 132.50 E
Hiroshima-Wan 29 Cd 34.10N 132.20 E
Hirschhorn (Neckar) 12 Ke 49.27N 8.54 E
Hirson 11 Ke 49.55N 4.05 E
Hîrşova 15 Ke 44.41N 27.56 E
Hîrtibaciu 15 Hd 45.44N 24.14 E
Hirtshals 7 Bh 57.35N 9.58 E
Hirvensalmi 8 Lc 61.38N 26.48 E
Ḩīs 35 Hc 10.50N 46.54 E
Hisai 29 Ed 34.40N 136.28 E
Hisaka-Shima 29 Ae 32.48N 128.52 E
Hisar 15 Jg 42.35N 27.00 E
Hisar 25 Fc 29.10N 75.43 E
Hisarcik 15 Mj 39.15N 29.15 E
Hisarja 15 Hg 42.30N 24.42 E
Ḩismā 24 Fh 28.30N 35.50 E
Ḩişn al 'Abr 33 If 16.08N 47.14 E
Ḩişn aş Şaḩābī 33 Dc 30.01N 20.48 E
Hispaniola (EN)=La Española 38 Lh 19.00N 71.00W
Histon 12 Cb 52.15N 0.06 E
Histria 15 Le 44.30N 28.45 E
Hīt 24 Jf 33.38N 42.49 E
Hita 28 Kh 33.19N 130.56 E
Hitachi 28 Pf 36.36N 140.39 E
Hitachi-ōta 29 Gc 36.32N 140.31 E
Hitchin 12 Bc 51.57N 0.16W
Hitiaa 65e Fc 17.36S 149.18W
Hitotsuse-Gawa 29 Be 32.03N 131.31 E
Hitoyoshi 28 Kh 32.15N 130.45 E
Hitra 5 Gc 63.30N 8.45 E
Hiuchi-ga-Take 29 Fc 36.57N 139.17 E
Hiuchi-Nada 29 Cd 34.05N 133.15 E
Hiuma/Hiiumaa 5 Id 58.50N 22.40 E
Hiv 16 Oi 41.46N 47.57 E
Hiva 19 Gg 41.25N 60.23 E
Hiva Oa, Ile- 57 Ne 9.45S 139.00W
Hiw 24 Ei 26.01N 32.16 E
Hjademeste/Häädemeeste 8 Uf 58.00N 24.28 E
Hjallerup 8 Dg 57.10N 10.09 E
Hjälmare kanal 8 Fe 59.25N 15.55 E
Hjälmaren 5 Hd 59.15N 15.45 E
Hjelm 8 Dh 56.10N 10.50 E
Hjelmelandsvågen 7 Bg 59.15N 6.10 E
Hjelmsøya 7 Fa 71.05N 24.43 E
Hjerkinn 8 Cb 62.13N 9.32 E
Hjo 7 Dg 58.18N 14.17 E
Hjørring 7 Bh 57.28N 9.59 E
Hlatikulu 37 Ee 26.58S 31.19 E
Hlavní město Praha [3] 10 Kf 50.05N 14.25 E
Hlavní město SSR Bratislava [3] 10 Nh 48.10N 17.10 E
Hlinsko 10 Lg 49.46N 15.54 E
Hlohovec 10 Nh 48.25N 17.48 E
Hluhluwe 37 Ee 28.02S 32.17 E
Hmelnickaja Oblast [3] 19 Cf 49.30N 27.00 E
Hmelnicki 19 Cf 49.24N 26.57 E
Hmelnik 16 Ee 49.33N 27.59 E
Hnilec 10 Rh 48.53N 21.01 E
Ho 34 Fd 6.36N 0.28 E
Hoa Binh 25 Ld 20.50N 105.20 E
Hoai Nhon 25 Lf 14.26N 109.01 E
Hoanib 37 Ac 19.23S 13.06 E
Hoare Bay 42 Lc 65.30N 63.10W
Hoback Peak 46 Je 43.10N 110.33W
Hobart [Austl.] 58 Fi 42.53S 147.19 E
Hobart [Ok.-U.S.] 45 Gi 35.01N 99.06W
Hobbs 43 Ge 32.42N 103.08W
Hobbs Coast 66 Nf 74.50S 131.00W
Hobda 16 Sd 50.55N 54.38 E
Hoboken, Antwerpen- 12 Gc 51.10N 4.21 E
Hoboksar 27 Eb 46.47N 85.43 E
Hobq Shamo 27 Ic 40.30N 108.00 E
Hobro 7 Bh 56.38N 9.48 E
Hoburgen 7 Eh 56.55N 18.07 E
Hobyā 31 Lh 5.20N 48.38 E
Hocalar 15 Mk 38.37N 29.57 E
Hochalmspitze 14 Hc 47.01N 13.19 E
Hochfeiler/Gran Pilastro 14 Fd 46.58N 11.44 E
Hochgolling 14 Hc 47.16N 13.45 E
Ho Chi Minh (Saigon) 22 Mh 10.45N 106.40 E
Hochschwab 14 Jc 47.36N 15.05 E
Höchstadt an der Aisch 10 Gg 49.42N 10.44 E
Hochstetters Forland 41 Kc 75.45N 20.00W
Höchst im Odenwald 12 Ke 49.48N 9.00 E
Hochtor 14 Gc 47.05N 12.48 E
Hockenheim 12 Ke 49.19N 8.33 E
Hodaka-Dake 29 Ec 36.17N 137.39 E
Hodda 35 Ic 11.30N 50.45 E
Hoddesdon 12 Cc 51.45N 0.00
Hodgenville 44 Eg 37.34N 85.44W
Hodh 30 Gg 16.10N 8.40W
Hodh ech Chargui [3] 32 Ff 17.00N 7.15W
Hodh el Gharbi [3] 32 Ff 16.30N 10.00W
Hódmezővásárhely 10 Qj 46.25N 20.20 E
Hodna, Chott el- 32 Hb 35.25N 4.45 E
Hodna, Monts du- 32 Hb 35.50N 4.50 E
Hodna, Plaine du- 13 Qi 35.35N 4.35 E
Hodonín 10 Nh 48.52N 17.08 E
Hodorov 16 De 49.25N 24.18 E
Hodžambas 18 Ee 38.06N 65.01 E
Hodža-Pirjah, Gora- 18 Fe 38.47N 67.35 E
Hodžejli 19 Fg 42.23N 59.20 E
Hœdic, Ile de- 11 Dg 47.20N 2.52W
Hoegaarden 12 Gd 50.47N 4.53 E
Hoei/Huy 11 Ld 50.31N 5.14 E
Hoë Karoo 30 Jl 30.00S 21.30 E
Hoek van Holland 11 Kc 51.59N 4.09 E
Hoeselt 12 Hd 50.51N 5.29 E
Hof 10 Hf 50.19N 11.55 E
Höfdakaupstadur 7a Bb 65.50N 20.19W
Hofgeismar 10 Fe 51.29N 9.24 E
Hofheim 12 Kd 50.05N 8.27 E
Hofmeyr 37 Df 31.39S 25.50 E
Höfn 7a Cb 64.15N 15.13W
Hofsjökull 5 Ec 64.49N 18.48W
Hōfu 28 Kg 34.03N 131.34 E
Höganäs 8 Eh 56.12N 12.33 E
Hogarth, Mount- 59 Hd 21.48S 136.58 E
Hogback Mountain 46 Id 44.54N 112.07W
Hog Cliffs 51d Ba 17.38N 61.44W
Hoge Venen/Hautes Fagnes 10 Bf 50.30N 6.00 E
Högfors/Karkkila 7 Ff 60.32N 24.11 E
Hog Island 51p Bb 12.00N 61.44W
Hogne, Somme-Leuze- 12 Hd 50.15N 5.17 E
Hog Point 51d Ba 17.43N 61.48W
Högsby 7 Dh 57.10N 16.02 E
Høgste Breakulen 8 Bc 61.41N 7.02 E
Høgstegia 8 Db 62.23N 10.08 E
Hogsty Reef 49 Kc 21.41N 73.49W
Höhang-nyŏng 28 Jd 41.48N 128.20 E
Hohe Acht 10 Cf 50.23N 7.00 E
Hohe Eifel 12 Id 50.16N 6.50 E
Hohenau 55 Eh 27.05S 55.45W
Hohenems 14 Dc 47.22N 9.41 E
Hohenloher Ebene 10 Fg 49.20N 9.40 E
Hohes Venn 10 Bf 50.30N 6.00 E
Hohe Tauern 14 Gc 47.10N 12.30 E
Hohhot 22 Ne 40.51N 111.38 E
Hōhoku 29 Bd 34.17N 130.57 E
Höhr-Grenzhausen 12 Jd 50.26N 7.40 E
Höhtiäinen 8 Mb 62.50N 29.40 E
Hoh Xil Hu 27 Fd 35.35N 91.06 E
Hoh Xil Shan 21 Lf 35.20N 91.00 E
Hoi An 25 Le 15.52N 108.19 E

Index Symbols

- [1] Independent Nation
- [2] State, Region
- [3] District, County
- [4] Municipality
- [5] Colony, Dependency
- Continent
- Physical Region
- Historical or Cultural Region
- Mount, Mountain
- Volcano
- Hill
- Mountains, Mountain Range
- Hills, Escarpment
- Plateau, Upland
- Pass, Gap
- Plain, Lowland
- Delta
- Salt Flat
- Valley, Canyon
- Crater, Cave
- Karst Features
- Depression
- Polder
- Desert, Dunes
- Forest, Woods
- Heath, Steppe
- Oasis
- Cape, Point
- Coast, Beach
- Cliff
- Peninsula
- Isthmus
- Sandbank
- Island
- Atoll
- Rock, Reef
- Islands, Archipelago
- Rocks, Reefs
- Coral Reef
- Well, Spring
- Geyser
- River, Stream
- Waterfall Rapids
- River Mouth, Estuary
- Lake
- Salt Lake
- Intermittent Lake
- Reservoir
- Swamp, Pond
- Canal
- Glacier
- Ice Shelf, Pack Ice
- Ocean
- Sea
- Gulf, Bay
- Strait, Fjord
- Lagoon
- Bank
- Seamount
- Tablemount
- Ridge
- Shelf
- Basin
- Escarpment, Sea Scarp
- Fracture
- Trench, Abyss
- National Park, Reserve
- Point of Interest
- Recreation Site
- Cave, Cavern
- Historic Site
- Ruins
- Wall, Walls
- Church, Abbey
- Temple
- Scientific Station
- Airport
- Port
- Lighthouse
- Mine
- Tunnel
- Dam, Bridge

Name	Map	Grid	Lat.	Long.
Hoima	36	Fb	1.26N	31.21 E
Hoisington	45	Gg	38.31N	98.47W
Hoj, Vozvyšennost-	17	Ob	68.50N	71.30 E
Højer	8	Cj	54.58N	8.43 E
Hojniki	19	Ce	51.54N	29.56 E
Hōjō	28	Lh	33.58N	132.46 E
Hökensås	8	Ff	58.11N	14.08 E
Hokianga Harbour	62	Ea	35.30S	173.20 E
Hokitika	58	Ii	42.43S	170.58 E
Hok-Kai=Okhotsk, Sea of- (EN)	21	Qd	53.00N	150.00 E
Hokkaidō	21	Qe	43.00N	143.00 E
Hokkaidō Ken [2]	28	Qc	43.00N	143.00 E
Hokksund	7	Bg	59.47N	9.59 E
Hokmābād	24	Qd	36.37N	57.36 E
Hokota	29	Gc	36.10N	140.30 E
Hol	8	Cd	60.36N	8.22 E
Holap	64d	Ba	7.39N	151.54 E
Holbæk	8	Di	55.43N	11.43 E
Holbeach	12	Cb	52.48N	0.01 E
Holbeach Marsh	12	Cb	52.52N	0.02 E
Holbox, Isla-	48	Pg	21.33N	87.15W
Holbrook	43	Ee	34.54N	110.10W
Holdenville	45	Hi	35.05N	96.24W
Holderness	9	Mh	53.47N	0.10W
Holdrege	45	Gf	40.26N	99.22W
Hold With Hope	41	Jd	73.40N	21.45W
Hole in the Wall	44	Im	25.51N	77.12W
Hølen	8	De	59.32N	10.45 E
Holešov	10	Ng	49.20N	17.33 E
Holetown	51q	Ab	13.11N	59.39W
Holguin	39	Lg	20.53N	76.15W
Holguín [3]	49	Jc	20.40N	75.50W
Hol Hol	35	Gc	11.20N	42.50 E
Holitna	40	Hd	61.40N	157.12W
Höljes	7	Cf	60.54N	12.36 E
Hollabrunn	14	Kb	48.33N	16.05 E
Holland	44	Dd	42.47N	86.07W
Holland [Eng.-U.K.]	12	Bb	52.52N	0.10W
Holland [Neth.]	5	Ge	52.20N	4.45 E
Hollandale	45	Kj	33.10N	90.58W
Hollandsbird Island	37	Ad	24.45S	14.34 E
Hollands Diep	12	Gc	51.40N	4.30 E
Hollesley Bay	12	Db	52.04N	1.33 E
Hollick-Kenyon Plateau	66	Pf	79.00S	97.00W
Hollis	45	Gi	34.41N	99.55W
Hollister [Ca.-U.S.]	46	Eh	36.51N	121.24W
Hollister [Id.-U.S.]	46	He	42.23N	114.35W
Hollola	8	Kc	61.03N	25.26 E
Höllviksnäs	8	Ei	55.25N	12.57 E
Holly Springs	45	Li	34.41N	89.26W
Hollywood	43	Kf	26.00N	80.09W
Holm	7	Hh	57.09N	31.12 E
Holma	34	Hd	9.54N	13.03 E
Holman Island	42	Fb	70.40N	117.35W
Hólmavík	7a	Bb	65.43N	21.41W
Holmes Reefs	57	Ff	16.30S	148.00 E
Holmestrand	8	De	59.29N	10.18 E
Holm Land	41	Kb	80.16N	18.20W
Holms	41	Gd	74.30N	57.00W
Holmsjö	8	Fh	56.25N	15.32 E
Holmsjön [Swe.]	7	De	62.25N	15.20 E
Holmsjön [Swe.]	8	Gb	62.40N	16.35 E
Holmsk	20	Jg	47.00N	142.03 E
Holmski	16	Kg	44.50N	38.24 E
Holmsland Klit	8	Ch	56.00N	8.10 E
Holmsund	7	Ee	63.42N	20.21 E
Holmsveden	8	Gc	61.07N	16.43 E
Holmudden	8	Hg	57.57N	19.21 E
Holod	15	Fc	46.47N	22.08 E
Holohit, Punta-	48	Og	21.37N	88.08W
Holothuria Banks (EN)	59	Fb	13.25S	126.00 E
Holsnøy	8	Ad	60.35N	5.05 E
Holstebro	7	Bh	56.21N	8.38 E
Holsted	8	Ci	55.30N	8.55 E
Holstein	45	Ie	42.29N	95.33W
Holsteinsborg/Sisimiut	67	Nc	67.05N	53.45W
Holt	12	Db	52.54N	1.05 E
Holten	12	Ib	52.17N	6.27 E
Holton	45	Ig	39.28N	95.44W
Holtoson	20	Ff	50.18N	103.20 E
Holtyn-Daba	27	Ib	47.40N	107.20 E
Holwerd, Westdongeradeel-	12	Ha	53.22N	5.54 E
Holy Cross	40	Hd	62.12N	159.47W
Holyhead	9	Ih	53.20N	4.38W
Holy Island [Eng.-U.K.]	9	Lf	55.41N	1.48W
Holy Island [Wales-U.K.]	9	Ih	53.18N	4.37W
Holyoke [Co.-U.S.]	45	Ef	40.35N	102.18W
Holyoke [Ma.-U.S.]	44	Kd	42.12N	72.37W
Holýšov	10	Jg	49.36N	13.07 E
Homa Bay	36	Fc	0.31S	34.27 E
Homalin	25	Id	24.52N	94.55 E
Homāyūnshahr	23	Hc	32.42N	51.27 E
Homathko River	46	Ca	50.55N	124.50W
Homberg (Ohm)	12	Kd	50.44N	8.59 E
Hombori	34	Eb	15.17N	1.42W
Hombre Muerto, Salar del-	56	Gc	25.23S	67.06W
Homburg	10	Dg	49.19N	7.20 E
Home Bay	38	Mc	68.45N	67.10W
Homecourt	12	He	49.14N	5.59 E
Home Hill	59	Jc	19.40S	147.25 E
Homer [Ak.-U.S.]	39	Dd	59.39N	151.33W
Homer [La.-U.S.]	45	Jj	32.48N	93.04W
Homert	12	Kc	51.16N	8.06 E
Homerville	44	Fj	31.02N	82.45W
Homestead	44	Gm	25.29N	80.29W
Homewood	44	Di	33.29N	86.48W
Hommelstø	7	Cd	65.25N	12.30 E
Hommersåk	8	Af	58.55N	5.50 E
Homoine	37	Fd	23.52S	35.08 E
Homoljske Planina	15	Ee	44.20N	21.45 E
Homonhon	26	Id	10.44N	125.43 E
Homosassa	44	Fk	28.47N	82.37W
Homs (EN)=Ḩimş	22	Ff	34.44N	36.43 E
Honan (EN)=Henan Sheng (Ho-nan Sheng) [2]	27	Je	34.00N	114.00 E
Honan (EN)=Ho-nan Sheng → Henan Sheng [2]	27	Je	34.00N	114.00 E
Ho-nan Sheng → Henan Sheng=Honan (EN) [2]	27	Je	34.00N	114.00 E
Honaz	15	Ml	37.45N	29.17 E
Honaz Daği	15	Ml	37.41N	29.18 E
Honbetsu	28	Qc	43.18N	143.33 E
Honda	54	Db	5.13N	74.45W
Honda, Bahia-	49	Lg	12.21N	71.47W
Hondeklipbaai	37	Bf	30.20S	17.18 E
Hòn Diên, Núi-	25	Lf	11.33N	108.38 E
Hondo	47	Ge	18.29N	88.19W
Hondo [Jap.]	28	Kh	32.27N	130.12 E
Hondo [N.M.-U.S.]	45	Dj	33.23N	105.16W
Hondo [Tx.-U.S.]	45	Gl	29.21N	99.09W
Hondo, Rio-	45	Dj	33.22N	104.24W
Hondschoote	12	Ed	50.59N	2.35 E
Hondsrug	11	Mb	52.50N	6.50 E
Honduras [1]	39	Kh	15.00N	86.30W
Honduras, Cabo de-	49	De	16.01N	86.01W
Honduras, Golfo de-= Honduras, Gulf of- (EN)	38	Kh	16.10N	87.50W
Honduras, Gulf of-	38	Kh	16.10N	87.50W
Honduras, Gulf of- (EN)= Honduras, Golfo de-	38	Kh	16.10N	87.50W
Hønefoss	7	Cf	60.10N	10.18 E
Honey Lake	46	Ef	40.16N	120.19W
Honfleur	11	Ge	49.25N	0.14 E
Hông, Sông-=Red River (EN)	21	Mg	20.17N	106.34 E
Hong'an (Huang'an)	28	Ci	31.17N	114.37 E
Hongch'ŏn	28	If	37.41N	127.52 E
Hong-Do	28	Hg	34.41N	125.13 E
Hong He	28	Ch	32.24N	115.32 E
Honghton Lake	44	Ec	44.22N	84.43W
Hong Hu	27	Je	30.00N	113.25 E
Honghu (Xindi)	28	Bj	29.50N	113.28 E
Honghui	27	Id	36.46N	105.05 E
Hong Kong/Xianggang [5]	22	Ng	22.15N	114.10 E
Hongliuyuan	27	Gc	41.02N	95.24 E
Hongluoxian	28	Fd	41.01N	120.52 E
Hongning → Wulian	28	Eg	35.45N	119.13 E
Hongor	28	Bb	45.48N	112.45 E
Hongqizhen	27	Ih	18.48N	109.30 E
Hongshui He	21	Mg	23.47N	109.33 E
Hongsŏng	28	If	36.36N	126.40 E
Hongtong	28	Af	36.15N	111.41 E
Hongū	29	De	33.50N	135.46 E
Honguedo, Détroit d' -	42	Lg	49.30N	65.00W
Hongwansi → Sunan	27	Gd	38.59N	99.25 E
Hongwŏn	28	Id	40.02N	127.58 E
Hongyuan (Hurama)	27	He	32.45N	102.38 E
Hongze (Gaoliangjian)	27	Ke	33.10N	119.58 E
Hongze Hu	27	Ke	33.20N	118.40 E
Honiara	58	Ge	9.27S	159.57 E
Honikulu, Passe-	64h	Ac	13.23S	176.11W
Honiton	9	Jk	50.48N	3.13W
Honjō	28	Pe	39.23N	140.03 E
Honkajoki	8	Jb	61.59N	22.16 E
Hon-kawane	29	Fd	35.07N	138.06 E
Honningsvåg	7	Ga	70.59N	26.01 E
Hönö	8	Dg	57.42N	11.39 E
Honokaa	65a	Fc	20.05N	155.28W
Honokohau	65a	Eb	21.01N	156.37W
Honolulu	58	Lb	21.19N	157.52W
Honomu	65a	Fd	19.52N	155.07W
Honrubia	13	Je	39.37N	2.16W
Honshū	21	Pf	36.00N	136.00 E
Hontenisse	12	Gc	51.23N	4.00 E
Hontenisse-Kloosterzande	12	Gc	51.23N	4.00 E
Honuapo Bay	65a	Fd	19.05N	155.33W
Honuu	20	Jc	66.27N	143.06 E
Honyō	29	Fc	36.14N	139.10 E
Hood	42	Gc	67.25N	108.53W
Hood, Mount-	38	Ge	45.23N	121.41W
Hood Point	59	Df	34.23S	119.34 E
Hood River	46	Ed	45.43N	121.31W
Hoogeveen	11	Mb	52.43N	6.29 E
Hoogezand-Sappemeer	12	Ia	53.09N	6.48 E
Hooglede	12	Fd	50.59N	3.05 E
Hoogstraten	12	Gc	51.24N	4.46 E
Hooker	45	Fh	36.52N	101.13W
Hooker, Cape-	66	Kf	70.38S	166.45 E
Hook Head/Rinn Dúain	9	Gi	52.07N	6.55W
Hook Island	59	Jc	20.10S	148.55 E
Hoolehua	65a	Db	21.10N	157.05W
Hoonah	40	Le	58.07N	135.26W
Hooper, Cape -	42	Kc	68.24N	66.43W
Hooper Bay	40	Fd	61.31N	166.06W
Hoopeston	45	Mf	40.28N	87.40W
Höör	8	Ei	55.56N	13.32 E
Hoorn	11	Lb	52.38N	5.04 E
Hoornaar	12	Gc	51.53N	4.57 E
Hoover Dam	46	Hi	36.00N	114.27W
Hopa	24	Ib	41.25N	41.24 E
Hope [Ar.-U.S.]	45	Jj	33.40N	93.36W
Hope [Az.-U.S.]	46	Ij	33.44N	113.42W
Hope [B.C.-Can.]	46	Eb	49.23N	121.26W
Hope, Ben-	9	Ic	58.24N	4.36W
Hope, Lake-	59	Ef	32.50S	121.40 E
Hope, Point-	38	Cc	68.21N	166.50W
Hopedale	42	Le	55.50N	60.10W
Hopefield	37	Bf	33.04S	18.21 E
Hopeh (EN)=Hebei Sheng (Ho-pei Sheng) [2]	27	Kd	39.00N	116.00 E
Hopeh (EN)=Ho-pei Sheng → Hebei Sheng [2]	27	Kd	39.00N	116.00 E
Hopeh (EN)=Hu-pei Sheng → Hubei Sheng [2]	27	Je	31.00N	112.00 E
Ho-pei Sheng → Hebei Sheng =Hopeh (EN) [2]	27	Kd	39.00N	116.00 E
Hopelchén	48	Oh	19.46N	89.51W
Hopen	41	Oc	76.35N	25.10 E
Hopër	5	Kf	49.36N	42.19 E
Hopes Advance, Cap -	42	Kd	61.05N	69.33W
Hopetoun [Austl.]	59	Ig	35.44S	142.22 E
Hopetoun [Austl.]	58	Dh	33.57S	120.07 E
Hopetown	37	Ce	29.34S	24.03 E
Hopewell	44	Ig	37.17N	77.19W
Hopewell Islands	42	Je	58.20N	78.10W
Hopin	25	Jd	24.59N	96.31 E
Hopkins, Lake-	59	Fd	24.15S	128.50 E
Hopkinsville	43	Jd	36.52N	87.29W
Hopsten	12	Jb	52.23N	7.37 E
Hoptrup	8	Ci	55.11N	9.28 E
Hoquiam	43	Cb	46.59N	123.53W
Hor	20	Ig	47.48N	134.43 E
Hor	20	Ig	47.55N	135.01 E
Hōrai	29	Ed	34.55N	137.34 E
Hōrai-San	29	Dd	35.13N	135.53 E
Horasan	24	Jb	40.03N	42.11 E
Horaždovice	10	Jg	49.20N	13.42 E
Horb am Neckar	10	Eh	48.26N	8.41 E
Horconcitos	49	Fi	8.19N	82.10W
Hordaland [2]	7	Bf	60.15N	6.30 E
Hordogoj	20	Gd	62.32N	115.38 E
Horezmskaja Oblast [3]	19	Gg	41.30N	60.40 E
Horfors	7	Df	60.33N	16.17 E
Horgen	14	Cc	47.15N	8.36 E
Horgoš	15	Cc	46.09N	19.58 E
Horgos	19	Ig	44.10N	80.20 E
Hořice	10	Lf	50.22N	15.38 E
Horinger	28	Ad	40.24N	111.46 E
Horizon Tablemount (EN)	57	Kc	19.40N	168.30W
Horizontina	55	Eh	27.37S	54.19W
Horley	12	Bc	51.10N	0.10W
Horlick Mountains	66	Og	85.23S	121.00W
Hormigas	48	Gc	29.12N	105.45W
Hormoz [Iran]	24	Pi	27.32N	54.57 E
Hormoz [Iran]	23	Id	27.06N	56.28 E
Hormoz, Kūh-e-	23	Id	27.27N	55.10 E
Hormoz, Tangeh-ye-= Hormuz, Strait of- (EN)	21	Hg	26.34N	56.15 E
Hormūd-e Bāgh	24	Pi	27.30N	54.18 E
Hormuz, Strait of- (EN)= Hormoz, Tangeh-ye-	21	Hg	26.34N	56.15 E
Horn	42	Fd	61.30N	118.00W
Horn	5	Db	66.28N	22.30W
Horn [Aus.]	14	Jb	48.39N	15.39 E
Horn [Swe.]	8	Fg	57.54N	15.50 E
Horn, Cape- (EN)=Hornos, Cabo de-	52	Jk	55.59N	67.16W
Hornád	10	Qh	48.00N	20.58 E
Hornaday	42	Fc	69.22N	123.56W
Hornavan	7	Dc	66.14N	17.30 E
Hornbach	12	Je	49.12N	7.22 E
Horn-Bad Meinberg	12	Kc	51.54N	8.57 E
Hornby Bay	42	Fc	66.35N	117.50W
Horncastle	9	Mh	53.13N	0.07W
Horndal	8	Gd	60.18N	16.25 E
Horndean	12	Bd	50.55N	0.59W
Horne, Iles de-=Horn Islands (EN)	57	Jf	14.19S	178.05W
Hörnefors	7	Ee	63.38N	19.54 E
Hornell	44	Id	42.19N	77.39W
Hornepayne	42	Jg	49.13N	84.47W
Hornindalsvatn	8	Bc	61.55N	6.25 E
Hornisgrinde	10	Eh	48.36N	8.12 E
Horn Islands (EN)=Horne, Iles de-	57	Jf	14.19S	178.05W
Hörnli	14	Cc	47.23N	8.56 E
Hornomoravský úval	10	Ng	49.25N	17.20 E
Hornos, Cabo de-=Horn, Cape- (EN)	52	Jk	55.59S	67.16W
Hornoy-le-Bourg	12	De	49.51N	1.54 E
Horn Plateau	42	Fd	62.10N	119.30W
Hornsea	9	Mh	53.55N	0.10W
Hornslandet	8	Gc	61.40N	17.30 E
Horns Rev	8	Bi	55.30N	8.00 E
Horns Rev	8	Bi	55.30N	7.45 E
Hornsund	41	Nc	76.58N	15.28 E
Hornsundtind	41	Nc	76.55N	16.10 E
Horog	22	Jf	37.31N	71.33 E
Horokanai	29a	Ca	44.02N	142.09 E
Horol	16	He	49.29N	33.49 E
Horol [R.S.F.S.R.]	28	Lb	44.30N	132.03 E
Horol [Ukr.-U.S.S.R.]	16	He	49.47N	33.16 E
Horonobe	28	Pb	45.00N	141.51 E
Hořovice	10	Jg	49.50N	13.54 E
Horqin Youyi Qianqi (Ulan Hot)	22	Oe	46.04N	122.00 E
Horqin Youyi Zhongqi (Bayan Huxu)	27	Lb	45.04N	121.27 E
Horqin Zuoyi Houqi (Ganjig)	27	Lc	42.57N	122.14 E
Horqin Zuoyi Zhongqi (Baokang)	27	Lc	44.06N	123.19 E
Horqueta	56	Ib	23.24S	56.53W
Horred	8	Eg	57.21N	12.28 E
Horse Creek [Co.-U.S.]	45	Eg	38.05N	103.19W
Horse Creek [U.S.]	46	Nf	41.57N	103.58W
Horsehead Lake	45	Gc	47.02N	99.47W
Horsens	7	Bi	55.52N	9.52 E
Horsham [Austl.]	58	Fh	36.43S	142.13 E
Horsham [Eng.-U.K.]	9	Mj	51.04N	0.21W
Hørsholm	8	Ei	55.53N	12.30 E
Horšovský Týn	10	Ig	49.32N	12.57 E
Horst	12	Gd	50.56N	4.47 E
Horst	12	Ic	51.28N	6.03 E
Hörstel	12	Jb	52.19N	7.35 E
Horstmar	12	Jb	52.05N	7.19 E
Horsunlu	15	Ll	37.55N	28.36 E
Horta	32	Bb	38.32N	28.28W
Horta [3]	32	Bb	38.35N	28.40W
Horten	8	De	59.25N	10.30 E
Horton	42	Ec	70.01N	126.42W
Hörvik	8	Fh	56.03N	14.46 E
Ḥorvot 'Avedat	24	Fg	30.48N	34.46 E
Ḥorvot Meẕada	24	Fg	31.19N	35.21 E
Horwood Lake	44	Fa	48.03N	82.20W
Hosaina	35	Fd	7.33N	37.52 E
Hose Mountains	26	Ff	2.00N	114.10 E
Hosenofu	33	De	23.34N	21.15 E
Hoseynābād [Iran]	24	Ne	34.30N	50.59 E
Hoseynābād [Iran]	24	Le	35.33N	47.08 E
Hoseynīyeh	24	Mg	32.42N	48.14 E
Hoshāb	25	Cc	26.01N	63.56 E
Hosingen	12	Id	50.01N	6.05 E
Hoskins	60	Ei	5.30S	150.32 E
Hospet	25	Fe	15.16N	76.24 E
Hospital, Cuchilla del-	55	Ej	31.40S	54.53W
Hospitalet	13	Oc	41.22N	2.08 E
Hospitalet del Infante/ L'Hospitalet de l'Infant	13	Md	40.59N	0.56 E
Hoste, Isla-	52	Jk	55.15S	69.00W
Hot	25	Je	18.06N	98.35 E
Hotagen	7	De	63.53N	14.29 E
Hotaka	29	Ec	36.20N	137.53 E
Hotan	22	Jf	37.07N	79.55 E
Hotan He	21	Ke	40.30N	80.48 E
Hotazel	37	Ce	27.15S	23.00 E
Hotin	16	Ee	48.29N	26.29 E
Hoting	7	Dd	64.07N	16.10 E
Hotkovo	7	Ih	56.18N	38.00 E
Hotont	27	Hb	47.23N	102.30 E
Hot Springs	43	Gc	43.26N	103.29W
Hot Springs → Truth or Consequences	43	Fe	33.08N	107.15W
Hot Springs National Park	39	Jf	34.30N	93.03W
Hot Springs Peak	46	Gf	41.22N	117.26W
Hotspur Seamount (EN)	54	Kg	18.00S	36.00W
Hottah Lake	42	Fc	65.05N	118.36W
Hottentot Bay	37	Ae	26.07S	14.57 E
Hotton	12	Hd	50.16N	5.27 E
Hottstedt	10	He	51.39N	11.30 E
Houaïlou	61	Cd	21.17S	165.38 E
Houat, Ile de-	11	Dg	47.24N	2.58W
Houdan	11	Hf	48.47N	1.36 E
Houeillès	11	Gj	44.12N	0.02 E
Houffalize	12	Hd	50.08N	5.47 E
Houghton	43	Jb	47.06N	88.34W
Houillères, Canal des-	12	If	48.42N	6.55 E
Houji → Liangshan	28	Dg	35.48N	116.07 E
Houlgate	12	Be	49.18N	0.04W
Houlton	43	Nb	46.08N	67.51W
Houma [China]	27	Jd	35.36N	111.23 E
Houma [La.-U.S.]	43	If	29.36N	90.43W
Houndé	34	Ec	11.30N	3.31W
Hourtin, Étang d'-	11	Ei	45.10N	1.06W
House Range	46	Ig	39.30N	113.15W
Houston [Mo.-U.S.]	45	Kh	37.22N	91.58W
Houston [Tx.-U.S.]	39	Jg	29.46N	95.22W
Houthalen-Helchteren	12	Hc	51.02N	5.22 E
Houthulst	12	Ed	50.59N	2.57 E
Houthulst-Merkem	12	Ed	50.57N	2.51 E
Houtman Abrolhos	59	Ce	28.40S	113.50 E
Houtskär/Houtskari	8	Id	60.15N	21.20 E
Houtskari/Houtskär	8	Id	60.15N	21.20 E
Houyet	12	Hd	50.11N	5.01 E
Houyet-Celles	12	Hd	50.19N	5.01 E
Hov	8	Di	55.55N	10.16 E
Hova	8	Ff	58.52N	14.13 E
Hovden	8	Ac	61.40N	4.50 E
Hovden	8	Be	59.32N	7.21 E
Hove	9	Mk	50.49N	0.10W
Hoveyzeh	24	Mg	31.27N	48.04 E
Hovgaard	41	Kc	80.00N	18.45W
Hovmantorp	8	Fh	56.47N	15.08 E
Hovu-Aksy	20	Ef	51.01N	93.43 E
Howa	35	Db	17.30N	27.08 E
Howar	30	Jg	17.30N	27.08 E
Howard	45	Hd	44.01N	97.32W
Howe, Cape-	57	Fh	37.31S	149.59 E
Howell	44	Fd	42.36N	83.55W
Howick [N.Z.]	62	Fb	36.54S	174.56 E
Howick [S.Afr.]	37	Ee	29.28S	30.14 E
Howland	44	Mc	45.14N	68.40W
Howland Island	57	Jd	0.48N	176.38W
Howrah	22	Kg	22.35N	88.20 E
Howth	9	Gh	53.23N	6.04W
Ḥowẕ Soltān	24	Ne	35.06N	51.06 E
Hoxie	45	Fg	39.21N	100.26W
Höxter	10	Fe	51.46N	9.23 E
Hoxud	27	Ec	42.16N	86.51 E
Hoy	9	Jc	58.52N	3.18W
Hoya	12	Lb	52.48N	9.09 E
Høyanger	7	Bf	61.13N	6.05 E
Hoyerswerda/Wojerecy	10	Ke	51.26N	14.15 E
Hoyos	13	Fd	40.10N	6.43W
Hōyo-Shotō	29	Ce	33.50N	132.30 E
Hoytiäinen	7	Ge	62.48N	29.39 E
Hozat	24	Hc	39.07N	39.14 E
Hpunhpu	25	Jc	26.42N	97.17 E
Hradec Králové	10	Lf	50.13N	15.50 E
Hradiště	10	Jf	50.13N	13.08 E
Hrami	16	Ni	41.20N	45.07 E
Hrastnik	14	Jd	46.09N	15.06 E
Hřebeny	10	Kg	49.50N	14.10 E
Hristinovka	16	Fe	48.53N	29.56 E
Hroma	20	Jb	71.30N	144.49 E
Hromtau	19	Fe	50.18N	58.35 E
Hron	10	Oi	47.49N	18.45 E
Hrubieszów	10	Tf	50.49N	23.55 E
Hrubý-Jeseník	10	Nf	50.05N	17.10 E
Hrustalny	20	Ih	44.24N	135.06 E
Hrvatska = Croatia (EN) [2]	14	Jf	45.00N	15.30 E
Hrvatska = Croatia (EN)	14	Je	45.00N	15.30 E
Hrvatska = Croatia (EN)	5	Hf	45.00N	15.30 E
Ḥrvot Shivta	24	Fg	30.53N	34.38 E
Hsin-chiang-wei-wu-erh Tzu-chih-ch'ü → Xinjiang Uygur Zizhiqu=Sinkiang (EN) [2]	27	Ec	42.00N	86.00 E
Hsinchu	27	Lg	24.48N	120.58 E
Hsinying	27	Lg	23.25N	120.20 E
Hsipaw	25	Jd	22.37N	97.18 E
Hsi-tsang Tzu-chih-ch'ü → Xizang Zizhiqu [2]	27	Ee	32.00N	90.00 E
Hsuphāng	25	Jd	20.18N	98.42 E
Huab	37	Ad	20.49S	13.24 E
Huabei Pingyuan	21	Nf	37.00N	117.00 E
Huachacalla	54	Eg	18.45S	68.17W
Huachinera	48	Eb	30.15N	108.50W
Huacho	54	Cf	11.07S	77.37W
Huaco	56	Gd	30.09S	68.31W
Huacrachuco	54	Ce	8.39S	77.05W
Huade	27	Jc	41.50N	114.00 E
Huadian	27	Mc	42.59N	126.38 E
Hua Hin	25	Jf	12.34N	99.58 E
Huahine, Iles-	57	Lf	16.45S	151.00W
Huahine Iti	65e	Eb	16.45S	151.00W
Huahine Nui	65e	Eb	16.43S	151.00W
Huahuapán	48	Ge	24.31N	105.57W
Huai'an	28	Eh	33.30N	119.08 E
Huai'an (Chaigoubu)	28	Cd	40.40N	114.25 E
Huaibei	27	Ke	33.56N	116.48 E
Huaibin (Wulongji)	28	Ci	32.27N	115.23 E
Huaide (Gongzhuling)	27	Lc	43.30N	124.52 E
Huaidian → Shenqiu	27	Ke	33.27N	115.05 E
Huai He	21	Nf	33.12N	118.33 E
Huaiji	27	Jg	23.57N	112.12 E
Huailai (Shacheng)	27	Kc	40.29N	115.30 E
Huainan	22	Nf	32.32N	116.59 E
Huaining (Shipai)	28	Di	30.25N	116.39 E
Huairen	27	Jd	39.50N	113.07 E
Huairou	28	Dd	40.20N	116.37 E
Huaiyang	28	Ch	33.44N	114.52 E
Huaiyin (Wangying)	28	Eh	33.35N	119.02 E
Huaiyuan	28	Dh	32.58N	117.10 E
Huajuapan de León	47	Ee	17.48N	97.46W
Hualalai	65a	Fd	19.41N	155.52W
Hualapai Mountains	46	Ii	34.40N	113.45W
Hualien	27	Lg	23.58N	121.36 E
Huallaga, Río-	52	If	5.07S	75.30W
Huallanca	54	Ce	8.49S	77.52W
Huamachuco	54	Ce	7.48S	78.04W
Humahuaca	56	Gb	23.13S	65.23W
Huambo [3]	36	Ce	12.30S	15.40 E
Huambo	31	Ij	12.47S	15.43 E
Huanan	27	Nb	46.14N	130.33 E
Huancabamba [Peru]	54	Cf	10.21S	75.32W
Huancabamba [Peru]	54	Ce	5.14S	79.28W
Huancané	54	Eg	15.12S	69.46W
Huancapi	54	Df	13.41S	74.04W
Huancavelica [2]	54	Df	13.00S	75.00W
Huancavelica	53	Ig	12.46S	75.02W
Huancayo	53	Ig	12.04S	75.14W
Huanchaca, Serranía-	55	Bb	14.30S	60.39W
Huang'an → Hong'an	28	Ci	31.17N	114.37 E
Huangcaoba → Xingyi	27	Hf	25.03N	104.55 E
Huangchuan	27	Ke	32.00N	115.02 E
Huanggang	28	Ci	30.27N	114.53 E
Huanggangliang	27	Kc	43.33N	117.32 E
Huanggang Shan	27	Kf	27.50N	117.47 E
Huanggi Hai	28	Bd	40.51N	113.17 E
Huang Hai=Yellow Sea (EN)	21	Of	36.00N	124.00 E
Huang He=Yellow River (EN)	21	Nf	37.32N	118.19 E
Huanghe Kou	28	Ef	37.54N	118.48 E
Huangheyan → Madoi	22	Lf	35.00N	98.56 E
Huanghua	28	De	38.23N	117.21 E
Huanghuashi	28	Bj	28.14N	113.11 E
Huangliu	27	Ih	18.41N	108.46 E
Huangmao Jian	27	Kf	27.55N	119.11 E
Huangmei	28	Ci	30.05N	115.56 E
Huangnihe	28	Ic	43.33N	127.28 E
Huangpi	28	Ci	30.53N	114.22 E
Huangpu	27	Jg	23.05N	113.25 E
Huang Shan	27	Ke	30.10N	118.10 E
Huangshi	22	Nf	30.12N	115.00 E
Huang Shui	27	Hd	36.05N	103.20 E
Huangtu Gaoyuan	21	Mf	37.00N	108.00 E
Huanguelén	55	Bm	37.02S	61.57W
Huangxian	27	Ld	37.32N	120.30 E
Huangyan	27	Lf	28.39N	121.17 E
Huangyuan	27	Hd	36.40N	101.12 E
Huangzhai → Yangqu	28	Be	38.05N	112.37 E
Huangzhong	27	Hd	36.30N	101.30 E
Huanren	27	Mc	41.16N	125.22 E
Huan Shui	28	Ci	30.40N	114.21 E
Huanta	54	Df	12.56S	74.15W
Huantai (Suozhen)	28	Ef	36.57N	118.05 E
Huánuco [2]	54	Ce	9.30S	75.50W
Huánuco	53	If	9.55S	76.14W
Huanxian	27	Id	36.36N	107.06 E
Huaráz	53	If	9.32S	77.32W
Huarmey	54	Cf	10.04S	78.10W
Huarong	28	Bj	29.31N	112.33 E
Huascarán, Nevado-	52	If	9.07S	77.37W
Hua Shan	27	Je	34.27N	110.05 E
Huatabampo	47	Cc	26.50N	109.38W
Huatong	28	Fd	40.03N	121.56 E
Huatusco de Chiquellar	48	Kh	19.09N	96.57W
Huauchinango	48	Jg	20.11N	98.03W
Huautla de Jiménez	48	Kh	18.08N	96.51W
Huaxian (Daokou)	28	Cg	35.33N	114.30 E
Huayllay	54	Cf	11.01S	76.21W
Huaynamota, Río-	48	Gg	21.51N	104.42W
Huaytara	54	Cf	13.36S	75.22W
Hubbard Creek Lake	45	Gj	32.45N	99.00W
Hubbard Lake	44	Fc	44.49N	83.34W
Hubei Sheng (Hu-pei Sheng) =Hupeh (EN) [2]	27	Je	31.00N	112.00 E
Hubli	22	Jh	15.21N	75.10 E
Hubsugul Nur (Chövsgöl nuur)	21	Md	51.00N	100.30 E
Hückelhoven	12	Ic	51.03N	6.13 E
Hückeswagen	12	Jc	51.09N	7.21 E
Hucknall	9	Lh	53.02N	1.11W
Hucqueliers	12	Dd	55.03N	1.54 E
Huczwa	10	Tf	50.49N	23.59 E
Hudat [Abz.-U.S.S.R.]	16	Pi	41.34N	48.43 E
Hudat [Eth.]	35	Fe	4.45N	39.27 E
Huddersfield	9	Lh	53.39N	1.47W
Huddinge	8	Ge	59.14N	17.59 E
Ḥuddun	35	Hd	9.08N	47.32 E
Huddur Hadama	35	Ge	4.07N	43.55 E

Index Symbols

[1] Independent Nation
[2] State, Region
[3] District, County
[4] Municipality
[5] Colony, Dependency
Continent
Physical Region
Historical or Cultural Region
Mount, Mountain
Volcano
Hill
Mountains, Mountain Range
Hills, Escarpment
Plateau, Upland
Pass, Gap
Plain, Lowland
Delta
Salt Flat
Valley, Canyon
Crater, Cave
Karst Features
Depression
Polder
Desert, Dunes
Forest, Woods
Heath, Steppe
Oasis
Cape, Point
Coast, Beach
Cliff
Peninsula
Isthmus
Sandbank
Island
Atoll
Rock, Reef
Islands, Archipelago
Rocks, Reefs
Coral Reef
Well, Spring
Geyser
River, Stream
Waterfall Rapids
River Mouth, Estuary
Lake
Salt Lake
Intermittent Lake
Reservoir
Swamp, Pond
Canal
Glacier
Ice Shelf, Pack Ice
Ocean
Sea
Gulf, Bay
Strait, Fjord
Lagoon
Bank
Seamount
Tablemount
Ridge
Shelf
Basin
Escarpment, Sea Scarp
Fracture
Trench, Abyss
National Park, Reserve
Point of Interest
Recreation Site
Cave, Cavern
Historic Site
Ruins
Wall, Walls
Church, Abbey
Temple
Scientific Station
Airport
Port
Lighthouse
Mine
Tunnel
Dam, Bridge

Hude (Oldenburg) 12 Ka 53.07N 8.28 E
Huder 27 Lb 49.59N 121.30 E
Hudiksvall 6 Hc 61.44N 17.07 E
Hudson 38 Le 40.42N 74.02W
Hudson [Fl.-U.S.] 44 Fk 28.22N 82.42W
Hudson [N.Y.-U.S.] 44 Kd 42.15N 73.47W
Hudson, Lake- 45 Ih 36.20N 95.05W
Hudson Bay 42 Hf 52.52N 102.23W
Hudson Bay 38 Kd 60.00N 86.00W
Hudson Canyon (EN) 44 Kf 39.27N 72.12W
Hudson Hope 42 Fe 56.02N 121.55W
Hudson Land 41 Jd 73.45N 22.30W
Hudson Mountains 66 Pf 74.32S 99.20W
Hudson Strait 38 Lc 62.30N 72.00W
Hudžirt 27 Hb 47.05N 102.45 E
Hue 22 Mh 16.28N 107.36 E
Huebra 13 Fc 41.02N 6.48W
Huechucuicui, Punta- 56 Ff 41.47S 74.02W
Hueco Montains 45 Dj 32.05N 105.55W
Huedin 15 Gc 46.52N 23.03 E
Huehuetenango [3] 49 Bf 15.40N 91.35W
Huehuetenango 47 Fe 15.20N 91.28W
Huejutla de Reyes 48 Jg 21.08N 98.25W
Huelgoat 11 Cf 48.22N 3.45W
Huelma 13 Ig 37.39N 3.27W
Huelva [3] 13 Fg 37.40N 7.00W
Huelva 6 Fh 37.16N 6.57W
Huelva, Ribera de- 13 Gg 37.27N 6.00W
Huércal Overa 13 Kg 37.23N 1.57W
Huerfano Mountain 45 Bh 36.30N 108.10W
Huertas, Cabo de- 13 Lf 38.21N 0.24W
Huerva 13 Lc 41.39N 0.52W
Huesca 13 Lb 42.08N 0.25W
Huesca [3] 13 Lb 42.10N 0.10W
Huéscar 13 Jg 37.49N 2.32W
Hueso, Sierra del- 48 Gb 30.15N 105.20W
Huesos, Arroyo de los- 55 Cm 36.30S 59.09W
Huetamo de Núñez 48 Ih 18.35N 100.53W
Huete 13 Jd 40.08N 2.41W
Ḩufrat an Naḩās 35 Cd 9.45N 24.19 E
Huftarøy 8 Ad 60.05N 5.15 E
Hugh Butler Lake 45 Ff 40.22N 100.42W
Hughenden 58 Fg 20.51S 144.12 E
Hughes 40 Ic 66.03N 154.16W
Hughes Range 46 Hb 49.55N 115.28W
Hugo 45 Ii 34.01N 95.31W
Huguan 28 Bf 36.05N 113.12 E
Huhur He 28 Fc 43.55N 120.47 E
Hui'an 27 Kf 25.07N 118.47 E
Huiarau Range 62 Gc 38.35S 177.10 E
Huib-Hochplato 37 Be 27.10S 16.50 E
Huichang 27 Kf 25.33N 115.45 E
Huicheng → Shexian 28 Ej 29.53N 118.27 E
Huicholes, Sierra de los- 48 Gf 22.00N 104.00W
Huich'ŏn 27 Mc 40.10N 126.17 E
Huifa He 28 Ic 43.06N 126.53 E
Hui He [China] 27 Kb 48.51N 119.12 E
Hui He [China] 28 Be 39.21N 112.37 E
Huiji He 28 Ch 33.53N 115.37 E
Huila [2] 54 Cc 2.30N 75.45W
Huila [3] 36 Ce 15.00S 15.00 E
Huila, Nevado del- 52 Ie 3.00N 76.00W
Huilai 27 Kg 23.05N 116.18 E
Huili 27 Hf 26.37N 102.19 E
Huimanguillo 48 Mi 17.51N 93.23W
Huimin 27 Kd 37.29N 117.30 E
Huinan (Chaoyang) 28 Ic 42.41N 126.03 E
Huisne 11 Gg 47.59N 0.11 E
Huissen 12 Hc 51.56N 5.55 E
Huiten Nur 27 Fd 35.30N 91.55 E
Huittinen 8 Jc 61.11N 22.42 E
Huivulay, Isla de- 48 Dd 27.03N 110.01W
Huixian [China] 28 Bg 35.27N 113.47 E
Huixian [China] 27 Ie 33.46N 106.06 E
Huixtla 47 Fe 15.09N 92.28W
Huize 27 Hf 26.28N 103.18 E
Huizen 12 Hb 52.18N 5.16 E
Huizhou 27 Jg 23.02N 114.28 E
Hukou 28 Dj 29.44N 116.14 E
Hu Kou 31 Jd 36.09N 110.20 E
Hŭksan-Chedo 27 Me 34.30N 125.20 E
Hukuntsi 37 Cd 23.59S 21.44 E
Hulan 27 Mb 46.03N 126.36 E
Hulan He 27 Mb 45.54N 126.42 E
Ḩulayfā' 23 Fd 26.00N 40.47 E
Hulett 46 Md 44.41N 104.36W
Hulga 17 Jd 64.15N 60.58 E
Hulin 27 Nb 45.52N 132.58 E
Hulin He 28 Hb 45.19N 124.06 E
Hull 42 Jg 45.26N 75.43W
Hull → Kingston-upon-Hull 6 Fe 53.45N 0.20W
Hull → Orona Atoll 57 Je 4.29S 172.10W
Hull Bay 66 Nf 74.55S 137.40W
Hull Glacier 66 Nf 75.05S 137.15W
Hull Mountain 46 Dg 39.31N 122.59W
Hüls, Krefeld- 12 Ic 51.22N 6.31 E
Hultsfred 7 Dh 57.29N 15.50 E
Huludao 27 Lc 40.44N 120.59 E
Hulun Nur 21 Ne 49.00N 117.30 E
Ḩulwān=Helwân (EN) 33 Fd 29.51N 31.20 E
Hulwāt, Qūr al- 24 Hh 28.49N 38.50 E
Huma [China] 27 Ma 51.44N 126.36 E
Huma [Ton.] 65b Bc 21.19S 174.56W
Humacao 49 Od 18.09N 65.50W
Huma He 27 Ma 51.42N 126.42 E
Humaitá [Braz.] 53 Jf 7.31S 63.02W
Humaitá [Par.] 56 Ic 27.03S 58.33W
Humansdorp 37 Cf 34.02S 24.46 E
Humbe 36 Bf 16.42S 14.54 E
Humber 5 Fe 53.40N 0.10W
Humberside [3] 9 Mh 53.55N 0.30W
Humbolat River 38 He 40.02N 118.31W
Humboldt 61 Cd 21.53S 166.25 E
Humboldt [Ia.-U.S.] 45 Ie 42.43N 94.13W
Humboldt [Nb.-U.S.] 45 If 40.10N 95.57W
Humboldt [Sask.-Can.] 42 Gf 52.12N 105.07W
Humboldt [Tn.-U.S.] 44 Ch 35.49N 88.55W
Humboldt Gletscher 41 Fc 79.40N 63.45W
Humboldt Range 46 Ff 40.15N 118.10W
Hume, Lake- 59 Jg 36.05S 147.05 E
Humenné 10 Rh 48.56N 21.55 E
Hummelfjell 8 Db 62.27N 11.17 E
Hümmling, Der- 10 Dd 52.52N 7.31 E
Humphreys Peak 38 Hf 35.20N 111.40W
Humppila 7 Ff 60.56N 23.22 E
Humuya, Rio- 49 Df 15.13N 87.57W
Hün 31 If 29.07N 15.56 E
Húnaflói 5 Db 65.50N 20.50W
Hunan Sheng (Hu-nan Sheng) [3] 27 Jf 28.00N 112.00 E
Hu-nan Sheng → Hunan Sheng [3] 27 Jf 28.00N 112.00 E
Hunchun 28 Kc 42.52N 130.21 E
Hundested 8 Di 55.58N 11.52 E
Hunedoara [2] 15 Fd 45.45N 22.52 E
Hünfeld 10 Ff 50.40N 9.46 E
Hünfelden 12 Kd 50.19N 8.11 E
Hunga Ha'apai 65b Ab 20.33S 175.24W
Hungary (EN)= Magyarország [1] 6 Hf 47.00N 20.00 E
Hunga Tonga 65b Ab 20.32S 175.23W
Hungen 12 Kd 50.28N 8.54 E
Hüngnam 27 Md 39.50N 127.38 E
Hungry Horse Reservoir 46 Ib 48.15N 113.50W
Hun He [China] 28 Be 39.47N 113.15 E
Hun He [China] 28 Gd 40.41N 122.12 E
Hunhedoara 15 Fd 45.45N 22.54 E
Hunish, Rubha- 9 Gd 57.43N 6.20W
Hun Jiang 28 Hd 40.52N 125.42 E
Hunjiang 27 Mc 41.55N 126.27 E
Hunneberg 8 Ef 58.20N 12.27 E
Hunnebostrand 8 Df 58.27N 11.18 E
Hunsrück 10 Cg 49.50N 6.40 E
Hunstanton 9 Ni 52.57N 0.30 E
Hunte 10 Ed 52.30N 8.19 E
Hunter, Ile- 57 Ig 22.24S 172.03 E
Hunter Island 59 Ih 40.30S 144.45 E
Hunter Ridge (EN) 57 Ig 21.30S 174.30 E
Hunter River 59 Kf 32.50S 151.42 E
Hunterville 62 Fc 39.56S 175.34 E
Huntingdon 9 Mi 52.30N 0.10W
Huntingdon [Eng.-U.K.] 9 Mi 52.20N 0.12W
Huntingdon [Pa.-U.S.] 44 He 40.31N 78.02W
Huntingdon [Que.-Can.] 44 Jc 45.05N 74.08W
Huntington [In.-U.S.] 44 Ee 40.53N 85.30W
Huntington [W.V.-U.S.] 43 Kd 38.24N 82.26W
Huntly [N.Z.] 62 Fb 37.33S 175.10 E
Huntly [Scot.-U.K.] 9 Kd 57.27N 2.47W
Huntsville [Al.-U.S.] 39 Kf 34.44N 86.35W
Huntsville [Ont.-Can.] 42 Jg 45.20N 79.13W
Huntsville [Tx.-U.S.] 43 He 30.43N 95.33W
Hunucmá 48 Og 21.01N 89.52W
Hünxe 12 Ic 51.39N 6.47 E
Hunyani 37 Ec 15.37S 30.39 E
Hunyuan 27 Jd 39.38N 113.44 E
Hunza → Baltit 25 Ea 36.20N 74.40 E
Hunze 11 Ma 53.13N 6.40 E
Huocheng (Shuiding) 27 Dc 44.03N 80.49 E
Huojia 28 Bg 35.16N 113.39 E
Huolongmen 27 Mb 49.49N 125.49 E
Huolu 28 Ce 38.05N 114.18 E
Huon, Ile- 57 Hf 18.01S 162.57 E
Huon Gulf 59 Ja 7.10S 147.25 E
Huon Peninsula 60 Di 6.25S 147.30 E
Huonville 59 Jh 43.01S 147.02 E
Huoqin 28 Dh 32.21N 116.17 E
Huoshan 27 Ke 31.19N 116.20 E
Huo Shan [China] 27 Jd 37.00N 111.52 E
Huo Shan [China] 27 Ke 31.06N 116.12 E
Huoxian 27 Jd 36.39N 111.47 E
Hupeh (EN)=Hubei Sheng (Hu-pei Sheng) [2] 27 Je 31.00N 112.00 E
Hu-pei Sheng → Hubei Sheng=Hopeh (EN) [2] 27 Je 31.00N 112.00 E
Hür 24 Qg 30.50N 57.07 E
Hurama → Hongyuan 27 He 32.45N 102.38 E
Huränd 24 Lc 38.40N 47.20 E
Hurd, Cape- 44 Gc 45.13N 81.44W
Hurdalssjøen 8 Dd 60.20N 11.05 E
Hurd Deep=La Grande Trench (EN) 9 Kl 49.40N 3.00W
Hurdiyo 35 Ic 10.32N 51.08 E
Hurepoix 11 If 48.30N 2.10 E
Hure Qi 28 Fc 42.44N 121.44 E
Hurkett 45 Lb 48.50N 88.29W
Hurmuli 20 If 51.01N 136.56 E
Huroizumi 29a Cb 42.01N 143.07 E
Huron 43 Hc 44.22N 98.13W
Huron, Lake- 38 Ke 44.30N 82.15W
Huron Mountains 44 Db 46.45N 87.45W
Hurricane 46 Ih 37.11N 113.17W
Hurricane Cliffs 46 Ih 37.00N 113.05W
Hurrungane 8 Bc 61.27N 7.51 E
Hursley 12 Ac 51.01N 1.24W
Hurst 45 Hj 32.49N 97.09W
Hurstpierpoint 12 Bd 50.55N 0.10W
Hürth 10 Cf 50.52N 6.52 E
Hurum 8 De 59.35N 10.35 E
Hurunui 62 Ee 42.54S 173.18 E
Hurup 8 Ch 56.45N 8.25 E
Huş 15 Lc 46.41N 28.04 E
Húsavik 7a Ca 66.03N 17.21W
Hushan → Cixi 28 Fi 30.10N 121.14 E
Huskvarna 8 Fg 57.48N 14.16 E
Huslia 40 Hc 65.42N 156.25W
Husnes 8 Ae 59.52N 5.46 E
Husnesfjorden 8 Ae 59.50N 5.35 E
Hussigny-Godbrange 12 He 49.29N 5.52 E
Hust 16 Ce 48.10N 23.27 E
Hustadvika 8 Ba 63.00N 7.05 E
Husum [F.R.G.] 10 Fb 54.28N 9.03 E
Husum [Swe.] 7 Ee 63.20N 19.10 E
Hutag 27 Hb 49.23N 102.43 E
Hutchinson [Ks.-U.S.] 43 Hd 38.05N 97.56W
Hutchinson [Mn.-U.S.] 45 Id 44.54N 94.22W
Hutch Mountain 46 Ji 34.47N 111.22W
Ḩūth 33 Hf 16.14N 43.58 E
Hutou 27 Nb 46.00N 133.36 E
Hutte Sauvage, Lac de la- 42 Ke 55.57N 65.45W
Hutton, Mount- 59 Je 25.51S 148.20 E
Hutubi 27 Ec 44.07N 86.57 E
Hutuiti, Caleta- 65d Bb 27.07S 109.17W
Hutuo He 28 De 38.14N 116.05 E
Huvhojtun, Gora- 20 Le 57.44N 160.45 E
Huxley, Mount- 62 Cf 44.04S 169.41 E
Huy 10 Ge 51.55N 10.55 E
Huy/Hoei 11 Ld 50.31N 5.14 E
Huzhou → Wuxing 27 Le 30.47N 120.07 E
Hvaler 8 De 59.05N 11.00 E
Hvalynsk 19 Ee 52.30N 48.07 E
Hvammstangi 7a Bb 65.24N 20.57W
Hvannadalshnúkur 5 Ec 64.01N 16.41W
Hvar 14 Kg 43.07N 16.45 E
Hvar 14 Kg 43.11N 16.27 E
Hvarski kanal 14 Kg 43.15N 16.37 E
Hvatovka 16 Oc 52.21N 46.36 E
Hveragerdi 7a Bb 64.00N 21.12W
Hveravellir 7a Bb 64.54N 19.35W
Hvide Sande 8 Ci 55.59N 8.08 E
Hvitá [Ice.] 7a Bb 64.35N 21.46W
Hvitá [Ice.] 7a Bb 64.00N 20.58W
Hvittingfoss 8 De 59.29N 10.01 E
Hvojnaja 7 Ig 58.56N 34.31 E
Hwach'on-ni 28 Ie 38.58N 126.02 E
Hwang-Hae=Yellow Sea (EN) 21 Of 36.00N 124.00 E
Hwanghae-Namdo [2] 28 He 38.15N 125.30 E
Hwanghae-Pukto [2] 28 Ie 38.30N 126.25 E
Hwangju 28 He 38.40N 125.45 E
Hyannis [Ma.-U.S.] 44 Le 41.39N 70.17W
Hyannis [Nb.-U.S.] 45 Ff 42.00N 101.44W
Hybo 8 Gc 61.48N 16.12 E
Hyde Park 50 Gi 6.30N 58.16W
Hyderābād [India] 22 Jh 17.23N 78.28 E
Hyderābād [Pak.] 22 Ig 25.22N 68.22 E
Hyères 11 Mk 43.07N 6.07 E
Hyères, Iles d'- 11 Ml 43.00N 6.20 E
Hyesan 27 Mc 41.24N 128.10 E
Hyltebruk 7 Ch 57.00N 13.14 E
Hyndman Peak 46 He 43.50N 114.10W
Hyōgo Ken [2] 28 Mg 34.50N 134.48 E
Hyrov 10 Sg 49.32N 22.48 E
Hyrulä 8 Kd 60.24N 25.02 E
Hyrum 46 Jf 41.38N 111.51W
Hyrynsalmi 7 Gd 64.40N 28.32 E
Hysham 46 Lc 46.18N 107.14W
Hythe [Eng.-U.K.] 12 Ad 50.52N 1.24W
Hythe [Eng.-U.K.] 9 Oj 51.05N 1.05 E
Hyūga 28 Kh 32.25N 131.38 E
Hyūga-Nada 29 Be 32.25N 131.45 E
Hyvinge/Hyvinkää 7 Ff 60.38N 24.52 E
Hyvinkää/Hyvinge 7 Ff 60.38N 24.52 E

I

Iaco, Rio- 54 Ee 9.03S 68.35W
Iacobeni 15 Ib 47.26N 25.19 E
Iakora 37 Hd 23.08S 46.38 E
Ialomita [2] 15 Ke 44.30N 27.30 E
Ialomita 15 Kd 44.42N 27.51 E
Ialomiţei, Balta- 15 Ke 44.30N 28.00 E
Iapó, Rio- 55 Gg 24.30S 50.24W
Iaşi 6 If 47.10N 27.36 E
Iaşi [2] 15 Kb 47.07N 27.39 E
Iba 26 Gc 15.20N 119.58 E
Ibadan 31 Hh 7.23N 3.54 E
Ibague 53 Ie 4.27N 75.14W
Ibaiti 56 Jb 23.50S 50.10W
Iballja 15 Cg 42.11N 20.00 E
Ibans, Laguna de- 49 Ef 15.53N 84.52W
Ibar 15 Df 43.44N 20.45 E
Ibara 29 Cd 34.36N 133.28 E
Ibaraki 29 Dd 34.49N 135.34 E
Ibaraki Ken [2] 28 Pf 36.25N 140.30 E
Ibaré 55 Ej 30.49S 54.16W
Ibarra 53 Ie 0.21N 78.07W
Ibarreta 56 Ic 25.13S 59.51W
Ibb 22 Gh 13.58N 44.12 E
Ibba 35 De 4.48N 29.06 E
Ibba 35 Dd 7.09N 28.41 E
Ibbenbüren 10 Dd 52.16N 7.44 E
Ibdekkene 34 Fb 18.28N 0.38 E
Ibembo 36 Db 2.38N 23.37 E
Ibenga 36 Cb 2.20N 18.08 E
Iberá, Esteros del- 55 Di 28.05S 57.05W
Iberá, Laguna- 55 Di 28.30S 57.09W
Iberian Basin (EN) 3 De 40.00N 16.00W
Iberian Mountains (EN)= Sistema Ibérico 5 Fg 41.30N 2.30W
Iberian Peninsula (EN)= Península Ibérica 5 Fg 40.00N 4.00W
Iberville, Lac d'- 42 Ke 56.00N 73.10W
Ibestad 7 Db 68.48N 17.08 E
Ibi [Nig.] 34 Gd 8.11N 9.45 E
Ibi [Sp.] 13 Lf 38.38N 0.34W
Ibiá 54 Ig 19.29S 46.32W
Ibiagui 55 Ja 13.03S 44.12W
Ibiai 55 Jc 16.51S 44.55W
Ibibobo 54 Fh 21.35S 62.58W
Ibicaraí 54 Kf 14.51S 39.36W
Ibicuí, Rio- 52 Kh 29.25S 56.47W
Ibicuí da Armada, Rio- 55 Ej 30.16S 54.54W
Ibicuy 55 Ck 33.44S 59.10W
Ibicuy, Rio- 55 Ck 33.48S 59.10W
Ibigawa 29 Ed 35.29N 136.34 E
Ibipetuba 54 Jf 11.00S 44.32W
Ibiraiaras 55 Gi 28.22S 51.39W
Ibirama 55 Hh 27.04S 49.31W
Ibirapuitã, Rio- 55 Ei 29.22S 55.57W
Ibirocai, Arroio- 55 Di 29.26S 56.43W
Ibiruba 55 Fi 28.38S 53.06W
Ibitinga 55 He 21.45S 48.49W
Ibitinga, Represa- 55 He 21.41S 49.05W
Ibity 37 Hd 20.10S 46.58 E
Ibiza 13 Nf 38.54N 1.26 E
Ibiza/Eivissa=Iviza (EN) 5 Gh 39.00N 1.25 E
Iblei, Monti- 14 Im 37.10N 14.55 E
Ibn Hānī', Ra's- 24 Fe 35.35N 35.43 E
Ibn Qawrah 35 Ib 15.43N 50.32 E
Ibo 37 Gb 12.22S 40.36 E
Ibo-Gawa 29 Dd 34.46N 134.35 E
Iboundji, Mont- 36 Bc 1.08S 11.48 E
Ibrā' 23 Ie 22.38N 58.40 E
Ibrah 35 Dc 10.36N 25.20 E
Ibrāhīm, Jabal- 21 Gg 20.27N 41.09 E
Ibresi 7 Li 55.18N 47.05 E
'Ibrī 23 Ie 23.16N 56.32 E
Ibrim 33 Fe 22.39N 32.05 E
Ibshawāy 24 Dh 29.22N 30.41 E
Ibuki-Sanchi 29 Ed 35.35N 136.25 E
Ibuki-Yama 29 Ed 35.25N 136.24 E
Ibusuki 28 Ki 31.16N 130.39 E
Iča 20 Ke 55.28N 155.58 E
Ica [2] 54 Cf 14.20S 75.30W
Ica 53 Ig 14.04S 75.42W
Iça, Rio- 52 Jf 3.07S 67.58W
Icaiché 48 Oh 18.05N 89.10W
Icamaquã, Rio- 55 Ei 28.34S 56.00W
Icana, Rio- 54 Ec 0.26N 67.19W
Icara 55 Hi 28.42S 49.18W
Icaraima 55 Ff 23.23S 53.41W
Iceland (EN)=Island [1] 6 Eb 65.00N 18.00W
Iceland (EN)=Island 5 Eb 65.00N 18.00W
Iceland Basin (EN) 3 Dc 60.00N 20.00W
Ichalkaranji 25 Ee 16.42N 74.28 E
Ichibusa-Yama 29 Be 32.19N 131.06 E
Ichihara 28 Pg 35.31N 140.05 E
Ichi-Kawa 29 Dd 34.46N 134.43 E
Ichikawa 29 Fd 35.44N 139.55 E
Ichinohe 29 Pd 40.13N 141.17 E
Ichinomiya 28 Ng 35.18N 136.48 E
Ichinoseki 28 Pe 38.55N 141.08 E
Ich'ŏn [N.Kor.] 28 Ie 38.29N 126.53 E
Ich'ŏn [S.Kor.] 28 If 37.17N 127.27 E
Ichtegem 12 Fc 51.06N 3.00 E
Ičigemski Hrebet 20 Ld 63.30N 164.00 E
Ičinskaja Sopka, Vulkan- 21 Rd 55.39N 157.40 E
Ičnja 19 De 50.52N 32.25 E
Icó 54 Ke 6.24S 38.51W
Icy Cape 40 Gb 70.20N 161.52W
Idaarderadeel 12 Ha 53.06N 5.50 E
Idaarderadeel-Grow 12 Ha 53.06N 5.50 E
Idabel 45 Ij 33.54N 94.50W
Idah 34 Gd 7.06N 6.44 E
Idaho [2] 43 Ec 45.00N 115.00W
Idaho Falls 39 He 43.30N 112.02W
Idalia 45 Eg 39.43N 102.14W
Idân 35 Hd 6.03N 49.01 E
Idanha-a-Nova 13 Ee 39.55N 7.14W
Idar-Oberstein 10 Dg 49.42N 7.18 E
Idarwald 12 Je 49.50N 7.13 E
Idel 7 Id 64.08N 34.12 E
Ideles 32 Ie 23.49N 5.55 E
Ider 27 Hb 49.16N 100.41 E
Idfū 33 Fe 24.58N 32.52 E
Idhi Óros 5 Ih 35.15N 24.45 E
Idhra 15 Gl 37.20N 23.30 E
Idhra 15 Gl 37.21N 23.28 E
Idhras, Kólpos- 15 Gl 37.22N 23.22 E
Idice 14 Ff 44.35N 11.49 E
Idil 24 Id 37.21N 41.54 E
Idini 32 Df 17.58N 15.40W
Idiofa 36 Cc 4.59S 19.36 E
Idjil, Kédia d'- 32 Ee 22.38N 12.33W
Idkerberget 8 Fd 60.23N 15.14 E
Idle 9 Mh 53.27N 0.48W
Idlib 23 Eb 35.55N 36.38 E
Idokogo 36 Ab 0.35N 9.19 E
Idolo, Isla del- 48 Kg 21.25N 97.27W
Idre 8 Ec 61.52N 12.43 E
Idrica 8 Mh 56.18N 28.55 E
Idrija 14 Id 46.00N 14.02 E
Idro, Lago d'- 14 Ee 45.47N 10.30 E
Idstein 10 Ef 50.14N 8.16 E
Idževan 16 Ni 40.52N 45.04 E
Iecava 8 Jh 56.40N 23.40 E
Iecava 8 Kh 56.33N 24.11 E
Iepê 55 Gf 22.40S 51.05W
Ieper/Ypres 11 Id 50.51N 2.53 E
Ierápetra 15 In 35.01N 25.45 E
Ierisós 15 Gi 40.24N 23.53 E
Ierisoú, Kólpos- 15 Gi 40.26N 23.55 E
Iernut 15 Hc 46.27N 24.15 E
Ie-Shima 29b Ab 26.43N 127.47 E
Ieshima-Shotō 29 Dd 34.40N 134.30 E
Iesolo 14 Ge 45.32N 12.38 E
Iezerul, Virful- 15 Hd 45.28N 24.57 E
Ifakara 36 Gd 8.08S 36.41 E
Ifaki 34 Gd 7.48N 5.14 E
'Ifāl, Wādī al- 24 Fh 28.07N 35.02 E
Ifalik Atoll 57 Fd 7.15N 144.27 E
Ifanadiana 37 Hd 21.17S 47.35 E
Ife 34 Fd 7.28N 4.34 E
Iferouâne 31 Hg 19.04N 8.24 E
Ifetesene 32 Hd 25.30N 4.33 E
Ifni 32 Ed 29.15N 10.08W
Ifon 34 Gd 6.58N 5.55 E
Iforas, Adrar des- 30 Hg 19.00N 2.00 E
Iga 29 Ed 34.49N 136.12 E
Igal 10 Nj 46.32N 17.57 E
Iganga 36 Fb 0.37N 33.29 E
Igara Paraná, Rio- 54 Dd 2.09N 71.47W
Igarapava 55 Ie 20.03S 47.47W
Igarapé-Açu 54 Id 1.07S 47.37W
Igarapé-Miri 54 Id 1.59S 48.58W
Igarka 22 Kc 67.28N 86.35 E
Igatimi 56 Ib 24.05S 55.30W
Igawa 36 Fd 8.46S 34.23 E
Igbetti 34 Fd 8.45N 4.08 E
Iğdır 24 Kc 39.56N 44.02 E
Iggesund 7 Df 61.38N 17.04 E
Iglesias 14 Ck 39.19N 8.32 E
Iglesiente 14 Ck 39.20N 8.40 E
Igli 32 Gc 30.27N 2.18W
Iglim al Janūbīyah= Southern Region (EN) [2] 35 Dd 6.00N 30.00 E
Iglino 17 Hi 54.50N 56.28 E
Igloolik 39 Kc 69.24N 81.49W
Ignace 42 Ig 49.26N 91.41W
Ignalina 7 Gi 55.22N 26.13 E
Ignatovo 7 If 60.49N 37.48 E
Iğneada 24 Bb 41.50N 27.58 E
Iğneada Burun 15 Lh 41.54N 28.03 E
Igombe 36 Fc 4.25S 31.58 E
Igoumenitsa 15 Dj 39.30N 20.16 E
Igra 17 Fd 57.33N 53.10 E
Igreja, Morro de- 55 Hi 28.08S 49.30W
Igren 16 Ie 48.29N 35.13 E
Igrim 19 Gc 63.12N 64.29 E
Iguaçu, Rio- 52 Kh 25.36S 54.36W
Igualada 13 Nc 41.35N 1.38 E
Iguala de la Independencia 47 Ee 18.21N 99.32W
Iguana, Sierra de la- 48 Id 26.30N 100.15W
Iguape 55 Ig 24.43S 47.33W
Iguariaça, Serra do- 55 Ei 29.03S 55.15W
Iguassu Falls (EN)=Iguazú, Cataratas del- 52 Kh 25.41S 54.26W
Iguatemi 54 Hf 14.35S 49.02W
Iguatemi, Rio- 55 Ef 23.55S 54.10W
Iguatu 53 Mf 6.22S 39.18W
Iguazú, Cataratas del- = Iguassu Falls (EN) 52 Kh 25.41S 54.26W
Iguéla 36 Ac 1.55S 9.19 E
Iguidi, 'Erg- 30 Gf 27.00N 6.00W
Ihavandiffulu Atoll 25a Ba 7.00N 72.55 E
Iheya-Jima 29b Ab 27.03N 127.57 E
Ih-Hajrhan 27 Ib 46.56N 105.56 E
Ihiala 34 Gd 5.51N 6.51 E
Ihirene 32 He 20.28N 4.37 E
Ihnāsiyat al Madīnah 24 Dh 29.05N 30.56 E
Ih-Obo-Ula 27 Gc 44.55N 95.20 E
Ihosy 31 Lk 22.25S 46.07 E
Ihotry, Lac- 37 Gd 21.56S 43.41 E
Ihrhove, Westoverledingen- 12 Ja 53.10N 7.27 E
Ihsaniye 24 Dc 36.55N 34.46 E
Ihtiman 15 Gg 42.26N 23.49 E
Ih-Ula 27 Hb 49.27N 101.27 E
Ii 7 Fd 65.19N 25.27 E
Iida 28 Ng 35.31N 137.50 E
Iide-San 29 Fc 37.52N 139.41 E
Iijoki 7 Fd 65.20N 25.17 E
Iisaku/Isaku 8 Le 59.14N 27.41 E
Iisalmi 7 Ge 63.34N 27.11 E
Iisvesi 8 Lb 62.45N 26.50 E
Iittala 8 Kc 61.04N 24.10 E
Iivaara 7 Gd 65.47N 29.40 E
Iiyama 29 Fc 36.52N 138.20 E
Iizuka 29 Be 33.38N 130.41 E
Ija 20 Fe 55.02N 101.00 E
Ijebu Ode 34 Fd 6.49N 3.56 E
IJmuiden, Velsen- 12 Gb 52.28N 4.35 E
Ijoubbâne, 'Erg- 34 Da 22.30N 6.00W
IJssel 11 Lb 52.30N 6.00 E
IJsselmeer 11 Lb 52.45N 5.25 E
IJsselmuiden 12 Hb 52.34N 5.56 E
IJsselstein 12 Hb 52.01N 5.02 E
Ijuí 56 Jc 28.23S 53.55W
Ijuí, Rio- 55 Eh 27.58S 55.20W
Ijūin 29 Bf 31.37N 130.24 E
Ijuízinho, Rio- 55 Ei 28.20S 54.28W
Ijuw 64e Bb 0.31S 166.57 E
Ijzendijke 12 Fc 51.20N 3.37 E
IJzer 11 Ic 51.09N 2.43 E
Ik [R.S.F.S.R.] 5 Ld 55.55N 52.36 E
Ikaalinen 7 Ff 61.46N 23.03 E
Ikalamavony 37 Hd 21.10S 46.32 E
Ikamatua 62 De 42.17S 171.42 E
Ikaría 15 Jl 37.35N 26.10 E
Ikarion Pélagos 15 Jl 37.30N 26.35 E
Ikast 8 Ch 56.08N 9.10 E
Ikatski Hrebet 20 Gf 54.00N 111.15 E
Ikawa 29 Fd 35.13N 138.14 E
Ikeda [Jap.] 29 Cd 34.01N 133.48 E
Ikeda [Jap.] 27 Pc 42.55N 143.27 E
Ikeda-Ko 29 Bf 31.14N 130.34 E
Ikej 20 Ff 54.12N 100.04 E
Ikeja 34 Fd 6.36N 3.21 E
Ikela 31 Ji 1.11S 23.16 E
Ikelemba 36 Cb 0.07N 18.17 E
Ikerre 34 Gd 7.30N 5.14 E
Ikerssuaq 41 Ie 65.10N 39.45W
Iki 29 Ae 33.45N 129.45 E
Iki-Kaikyō 28 Jh 33.45N 129.50 E
Ikitsuki-Shima 29 Ae 33.25N 129.25 E
Ikizdere 24 Ib 40.47N 40.33 E
Ikom 34 Gd 5.58N 8.42 E
Ikongo 36 Gd 9.04S 36.51 E
Ikopa 37 Hc 16.50S 46.50 E
Ikot Ekpene 34 Gd 5.10N 7.43 E
Ikuno 29 Dd 35.10N 134.48 E
Ikurangi, Mount- 64p Bb 21.12S 159.45W
Ila 34 Fd 7.40N 4.40 E
Ilaferh 32 He 21.50N 1.20 E
Ilagan 22 Oh 17.10N 121.54 E
Ilām 23 Gc 33.38N 46.26 E
Ilam 25 Hc 26.55N 87.56 E
Ilām va Poshtkūh [3] 23 Gc 33.00N 47.00 E
Ilan 27 Lg 24.45N 121.44 E
Ilanski 20 Ee 56.10N 96.03 E
Ilaro 34 Fd 6.53N 3.01 E
Iława 10 Pc 53.37N 19.33 E

Index Symbols

[1] Independent Nation
[2] State, Region
[3] District, County
[4] Municipality
[5] Colony, Dependency
Continent
Physical Region
Historical or Cultural Region
Mount, Mountain
Volcano
Hill
Mountains, Mountain Range
Hills, Escarpment
Plateau, Upland
Pass, Gap
Plain, Lowland
Delta
Salt Flat
Valley, Canyon
Crater, Cave
Karst Features
Depression
Polder
Desert, Dunes
Forest, Woods
Heath, Steppe
Oasis
Cape, Point
Coast, Beach
Cliff
Peninsula
Isthmus
Sandbank
Island
Atoll
Rock, Reef
Islands, Archipelago
Rocks, Reefs
Coral Reef
Well, Spring
Geyser
River, Stream
Waterfall Rapids
River Mouth, Estuary
Lake
Salt Lake
Intermittent Lake
Reservoir
Swamp, Pond
Canal
Glacier
Ice Shelf, Pack Ice
Ocean
Sea
Gulf, Bay
Strait, Fjord
Lagoon
Bank
Seamount
Tablemount
Ridge
Shelf
Basin
Escarpment, Sea Scarp
Fracture
Trench, Abyss
National Park, Reserve
Point of Interest
Recreation Site
Cave, Cavern
Historic Site
Ruins
Wall, Walls
Church, Abbey
Temple
Scientific Station
Airport
Port
Lighthouse
Mine
Tunnel
Dam, Bridge

Ilbengja	20	Hd	62.55N	124.10 E
Ile-à-la-Crosse	42	Ge	55.27N	107.53W
Ilebo	31	Ji	4.44S	20.33 E
Ile de France	11	Ie	49.00N	2.20 E
Ile de France	41	Kc	77.45N	27.45W
Ile de France, Côte de l'-	11	Jf	48.55N	3.50 E
Ilek	19	Fe	51.32N	53.27 E
Ilek	5	Le	51.30N	53.20 E
Ileksa	7	Ie	62.30N	36.57 E
Ilerh	32	He	21.40N	2.22 E
Ileša	7	Le	62.37N	46.35 E
Ilesha [Nig.]	34	Fd	8.55N	3.25 E
Ilesha [Nig.]	34	Fd	7.37N	4.44 E
Ilet	7	Li	55.57N	48.14 E
Ilfov [2]	15	Je	44.30N	26.20 E
Ilfracombe	9	Ij	51.13N	4.08W
Ilgaz	24	Eb	40.56N	33.38 E
Ilgaz Dağları	24	Eb	41.00N	33.35 E
Ilgın	24	Dc	38.17N	31.55 E
Ilha Grande	54	Ed	0.27S	65.02W
Ilha Grande, Baia da-	55	Jf	23.09S	44.30W
Ilhas Desertas	32	Dc	32.30N	16.30W
Ilhavo	13	Dd	40.36N	8.40W
Ilhéus	53	Mg	14.49S	39.02W
Ili	21	Je	45.24N	74.08 E
Ilia	15	Fd	45.56N	22.39 E
Iliamna	40	Ie	59.45N	154.54W
Iliamna Lake	40	He	59.30N	155.00W
İliç	24	Hc	39.28N	38.34 E
Ilič	18	Gd	40.55N	68.29 E
Ilica	15	Kj	39.52N	27.46 E
Iličevsk [Abz.-U.S.S.R.]	16	Nj	39.33N	44.59 E
Iličevsk [Ukr.-U.S.S.R.]	19	Df	46.18N	30.37 E
Ilidža	14	Mg	43.50N	18.19 E
Iligan	22	Oi	8.14N	124.14 E
Iligan Bay	26	He	8.25N	124.05 E
Ilim	20	Fe	56.50N	103.25 E
Ilimskoje Vodohranilišče	20	Fe	57.20N	102.30 E
Ilinski [R.S.F.S.R.]	7	Hf	61.02N	32.42 E
Ilinski [R.S.F.S.R.]	20	Jg	47.59N	142.21 E
Ilinski [R.S.F.S.R.]	17	Gg	58.35N	55.41 E
Ilion	44	Jd	43.01N	75.04W
Ilio Point	65a	Db	21.13N	157.16W
Ilir	20	Fe	55.13N	100.45 E
Ilirska Bistrica	14	Ie	45.34N	14.16 E
Iljaly	18	Bd	41.53N	59.40 E
Ilkal	25	Fe	15.58N	76.08 E
Ilkeston	12	Ab	52.58N	1.18W
Ill	11	Nf	48.40N	7.53 E
Illampu, Nevado del-	54	Eg	15.50S	68.34W
Illana Bay	26	He	7.25N	123.45 E
Illapel	56	Fd	31.38S	71.10W
Illbillee, Mount-	59	Ge	27.02S	132.30 E
Ille	11	Ef	48.08N	1.40W
Ille-et-Vilaine [3]	11	Ef	48.10N	1.30W
Illéla	34	Gc	14.28N	5.15 E
Iller	10	Fh	48.23N	9.58 E
Illescas	13	Id	40.07N	3.50W
Ille-sur-Têt	11	Il	42.40N	2.37 E
Illi, Ba-	35	Bc	10.44N	16.21 E
Illimani, Nevado del-	52	Jg	16.39S	67.48W
Illingen	12	Je	49.22N	7.03 E
Illinois	38	Jf	38.58N	90.27W
Illinois [2]	43	Jd	40.00N	89.00W
Illinois Peak	46	Hc	47.02N	115.04W
Illizi	31	Hf	26.29N	8.28 E
Ilm	10	He	51.07N	11.40 E
Ilmajoki	8	Jb	62.44N	22.34 E
Ilmen, Ozero-	5	Jd	58.20N	31.20 E
Ilmenau	10	Gf	50.41N	10.54 E
Ilmenau	10	Gc	53.23N	10.10 E
Il Montello	14	Ge	45.49N	12.07 E
Ilo	54	Dg	17.38S	71.20W
Iloilo	22	Oh	10.42N	122.34 E
Ilok	14	Ne	45.13N	19.23 E
Ilomantsi	7	He	62.40N	30.55 E
Ilorin	31	Hh	8.30N	4.33 E
Iloron, Cerro-	48	Gg	20.57N	104.22W
Ilova	14	Ke	45.25N	16.45 E
Ilovik	14	If	44.27N	14.33 E
Ilovlja	16	Ne	49.18N	44.01 E
Ilovlja	16	Me	49.14N	43.54 E
Ilpyrski	20	Le	59.52N	164.12 E
Ilski	16	Kg	44.51N	38.32 E
Iltin	20	Nc	67.52N	178.48W
Ilubabor [3]	35	Ed	7.50N	35.00 E
Ilūkste/Ilukste	8	Li	55.58N	26.26 E
Ilukste/Ilūkste	8	Li	55.58N	26.26 E
Ilulissat/Jakobshavn	67	Nc	69.20N	50.50W
Ilwaki	26	Ih	7.56S	126.26 E
Ilyč	17	He	62.32N	56.40 E
Ilz	10	Jh	48.35N	13.30 E
Iłżanka	10	Re	51.14N	21.47 E
Imabari	28	Lg	34.03N	133.00 E
Imagane	28	Pc	42.26N	140.01 E
Imaichi	28	Of	36.43N	139.41 E
Imán, Sierra del-	55	Eh	27.42S	55.28W
Imanburluk	17	Mj	53.40N	67.15 E
Imandra, Ozero-	5	Jb	67.30N	33.00 E
Imano-Yama	29	Ce	32.51N	132.49 E
Imari	28	Jh	33.16N	129.53 E
Imarui	55	Hi	28.21S	48.49W
Imataca, Serranía de-	50	Fi	7.45N	61.00W
Imatra	7	Gf	61.10N	28.46 E
Imazu	29	Ed	35.24N	136.01 E
Imbabah, Al Qāhirah-	33	Fc	30.05N	31.13 E
Imba-Numa	29	Gd	35.45N	140.14 E
Imbert	49	Ld	19.45N	70.50W
Imbituba	56	Kc	28.14S	48.40W
Imeni 26 Bakinskih Komissarov [Abz.-U.S.S.R.]	19	Eh	39.19N	49.12 E
Imeni 26 Bakinskih Komissarov [Tur.-U.S.S.R.]	19	Fh	39.21N	54.12 E
Imeni Gastello	20	Jd	61.35N	147.59 E
Imeni Karla Liebknechta	16	Id	51.38N	35.29 E
Imeni Mariny Raskovoj	20	Jd	62.05N	146.30 E
Imeni Poliny Osipenko	20	If	52.23N	136.25 E
Imi	31	Lh	6.28N	42.11 E
Imilili	32	De	22.50N	15.54W
Imi n'Tanout	32	Fc	31.03N	8.08W
Imišli	19	Eh	39.53N	48.03 E
Imjin-gang	28	If	37.47N	126.40 E
Imlay	46	Ff	40.42N	118.07W
Immenstadt im Allgäu	10	Gi	47.34N	10.13 E
Imo [2]	34	Gd	5.30N	7.20 E
Imola	14	Ff	44.21N	11.42 E
Imotski	14	Lg	43.27N	17.13 E
Imperatriz	53	Lf	5.32S	47.29W
Imperia	14	Cg	43.53N	8.03 E
Imperial	45	Ff	40.31N	101.39W
Imperial de Aragón, Canal-	13	Kb	42.02N	1.33W
Imperial Valley	46	Hj	32.50N	115.30W
Impfondo	31	Ih	1.37N	18.04 E
Imphāl	22	Lg	24.49N	93.57 E
Imphy	11	Jh	46.56N	3.15 E
Impilanti	7	Hf	61.41N	31.12 E
Imrali Adasi	15	Li	40.32N	28.32 E
Imst	14	Ec	47.14N	10.44 E
Imtan	24	Gf	32.24N	36.49 E
Imuris	48	Db	30.47N	110.52W
Im-Zouren	13	Ii	35.04N	3.50W
Ina	28	Ng	35.50N	137.57 E
Ina	10	Kc	53.32N	14.38 E
I-n-Abanrherit	34	Gb	17.58N	6.05 E
Inabu	29	Ed	35.13N	137.30 E
Inaccessible Islands	66	Re	60.34S	46.44W
Inaccessible Island	30	Fi	37.17S	12.45W
I-n-Afaleleh	32	Ie	23.34N	9.12 E
I Naftan, Puntan-	64b	Ba	15.05N	145.45 E
Ina-Gawa	29	Fc	37.23N	139.18 E
I-n-Amenas	31	Hf	28.03N	9.33 E
Inami	29	De	33.48N	135.12 E
Inanba-Jima	29	Fe	33.39N	139.18 E
Inangahua Junction	62	Dd	41.52S	171.56 E
Inanwatan	26	Jg	2.08S	132.10 E
Iñapari	54	Ef	10.57S	69.35W
Inarajan	64c	Bb	13.16N	144.45 E
I-n-Arhâta	34	Ea	21.09N	0.18W
Inari	6	Ib	68.54N	27.01 E
Inari, Lake- (EN) = Inarijärvi	5	Ib	69.00N	28.00 E
Inarijärvi = Inari, Lake- (EN)	5	Ib	69.00N	28.00 E
Inawashiro	29	Gc	37.34N	140.05 E
Inawashiro-Ko	28	Pf	37.30N	140.03 E
I-n-Azaoua	34	Ga	20.47N	7.31 E
I-n-Azaoua	34	Ga	20.54N	7.28 E
Inazawa	29	Ed	35.15N	136.47 E
Inca	13	Oe	39.43N	2.54 E
Inca de Oro	56	Gc	26.45S	69.54W
Incaguasi	56	Fc	29.13S	71.03W
Ince Burun	15	Ki	40.28N	27.16 E
İnce Burun	23	Da	42.07N	34.56 E
İncekum Burun	24	Ed	36.13N	33.58 E
Inceler	15	Ml	37.42N	29.35 E
I-n-Chaouâg	34	Fb	16.23N	0.10 E
Inchcape (Bell Rock)	9	Ke	56.26N	2.24W
Inchiri [3]	32	Df	20.00N	15.00W
Inch'ŏn	22	Of	37.28N	126.38 E
Incirliova	15	Kl	37.50N	27.43 E
Incudine	11a	Bb	41.51N	9.12 E
Indaiá, Rio-	55	Jd	18.27S	45.22W
Indaia Grande, Ribeirão-	55	Fd	19.31S	52.29W
Indaiatuba	55	If	23.05S	47.14W
Indal	8	Gb	62.34N	17.06 E
Indalsälven	7	De	62.31N	17.27 E
Inda Selase	35	Fc	14.06N	38.17 E
Indawgyi	25	Jc	25.08N	96.20 E
Indefatigable Banks	9	Ph	53.35N	2.20 E
Independence [Ca.-U.S.]	46	Fh	36.48N	118.12W
Independence [Ia.-U.S.]	45	Ke	42.28N	91.54W
Independence [Ks.-U.S.]	43	Hd	37.13N	95.42W
Independence [Mo.-U.S.]	45	Ig	39.05N	94.04W
Independence [Va.-U.S.]	44	Gg	36.38N	81.11W
Independence Fjord	67	Me	82.00N	30.25W
Independence Mountains	46	Gf	41.15N	116.05W
Independência [Braz.]	54	Je	5.23S	40.19W
Independência [Braz.]	55	Fa	13.34S	53.57W
Independenta	15	Kd	45.29N	27.45 E
Inder → Jalaid Qi	27	Lb	46.41N	122.52 E
Inder, Ozero-	16	Qe	48.25N	51.55 E
Inderborski	16	Cf	48.32N	51.47 E
India (EN)	21	Jh	20.00N	77.00 E
India (EN) = Bhārat Juktarashtra [1]	22	Jh	20.00N	77.00 E
India Muerta, Arroyo de la-	55	Fk	33.40S	54.04W
Indiana [2]	43	Jc	40.00N	86.15W
Indiana	44	He	40.39N	79.11W
Indianapolis	39	Kf	39.46N	86.09W
Indian Church	49	Ce	17.45N	88.40W
Indian Creek Point	51d	Bb	17.00N	61.43W
Indian Harbour	42	Lf	54.27N	57.13W
Indian Head	42	Hf	50.32N	103.40W
Indian Ocean	3	Gl	21.00S	82.00 E
Indian Ocean (EN) = Ḥindi, Badwéynta-	3	Gl	21.00S	82.00 E
Indian Ocean (EN) = Indico, Oceano-	3	Gl	21.00S	82.00 E
Indian Ocean (EN) = Indien, Océan-	3	Gl	21.00S	82.00 E
Indian Ocean (EN) = Indiese Oseaan-	3	Gl	21.00S	82.00 E
Indian Ocean (EN) = Indonesia, Samudera-	3	Gl	21.00S	82.00 E
Indianola	45	Kj	33.27N	90.39W
Indianópolis	55	Id	19.02S	47.55W
Indian Peak	46	Ig	38.16N	113.53W
Indian Rock	46	Ec	46.01N	120.49W
Indian Springs	43	Dd	36.34N	115.40W
Indiantown	44	Gl	27.01N	80.28W
Indian Town Point	51d	Bb	17.06N	61.40W
Indiapora	55	Gd	19.57S	50.17W
Indias Occidentales = West Indies (EN)	47	Je	19.00N	70.00W
Indico, Oceano- = Indian Ocean (EN)	3	Gl	21.00S	82.00 E
Indien, Océan- = Indian Ocean (EN)	3	Gl	21.00S	82.00 E
Indiese, Oseaan- = Indian Ocean (EN)	3	Gl	21.00S	82.00 E
Indiga	19	Eb	67.41N	49.00 E
Indigirka	21	Qb	70.48N	148.54 E
Indigskaja Guba	17	Dc	67.45N	48.20 E
Inđija	15	Dd	45.03N	20.05 E
Indio	43	De	33.43N	116.13W
Indio, Rio-	49	Fh	10.57N	83.44W
Indio Rico	55	Bn	38.19S	60.53W
Indispensable Reefs	57	Hf	12.40S	160.25 E
Indispensable Strait	63a	Ec	9.00S	160.30 E
Indochina (EN)	21	Mh	16.00N	107.00 E
Indonesia [1]	22	Nj	5.00S	120.00 E
Indonesia, Samudera- = Indian Ocean (EN)	3	Gl	21.00S	82.00 E
Indore	22	Jg	22.43N	75.50 E
Indra	8	Li	55.53N	27.40 E
Indragiri	26	Dg	0.22S	103.26 E
Indramayu	26	Eh	6.20S	108.19 E
Indrāvati	25	Ge	18.44N	80.16 E
Indre	11	Gg	47.14N	0.11 E
Indre [3]	11	Hh	46.50N	1.40 E
Indre Arna	8	Ad	60.26N	5.30 E
Indre-et-Loire [3]	11	Gg	47.15N	0.45 E
Indus	21	Ig	24.20N	67.47 E
İnebolu	23	Da	41.58N	33.46 E
Inece	15	Kh	41.41N	27.04 E
Inecik	15	Ki	40.56N	27.16 E
İnegöl	23	Ca	40.05N	29.31 E
Inés Indart	55	Bl	34.24S	60.33W
Ineu	15	Ec	46.26N	21.51 E
Ineu, Vîrful-	15	Hb	47.32N	24.53 E
Inezgane	32	Fc	30.21N	9.32W
I-n-Ezzane	32	Je	23.29N	11.15 E
Inferior, Laguna-	48	Li	16.15N	94.45W
Infiernillo, Presa del-	47	De	18.35N	101.45W
Infiesto	13	Ga	43.21N	5.22W
Infreschi, Punta degli-	14	Jk	39.59N	15.25 E
Ingá	54	Ke	7.17S	35.36W
Inga	36	Bd	5.39S	13.39 E
Ingå/Inkoo	7	Ff	60.03N	24.01 E
Ingabu	25	Je	17.49N	95.16 E
Ingai, Rio-	55	Je	21.10S	44.52W
I-n-Gall	34	Gb	16.47N	6.56 E
Ingarö	8	He	59.15N	18.30 E
Ingavi	55	Bb	15.02S	60.29W
Ingelheim am Rhein	12	Ke	49.59N	8.02 E
Ingelmunster	12	Fd	50.55N	3.15 E
Ingelstad	8	Fh	56.45N	14.55 E
Ingende	36	Cc	0.15S	18.57 E
Ingeniero Guillermo N. Juarez	56	Hb	23.54S	61.51W
Ingeniero Jacobacci	56	Gf	41.18S	69.35W
Ingeniero Luiggi	56	He	35.25S	64.29W
Ingenio Santa Ana	56	Gc	27.28S	65.41W
Ingermanland (EN)	5	Id	59.00N	30.00 E
Ingham	58	Ff	18.39S	146.10 E
Ingička	18	Ee	39.47N	65.58 E
Inglefield Bredning	41	Fc	77.40N	65.00W
Inglefield Land	41	Fc	78.44N	68.20W
Inglewood [Austl.]	59	Ke	28.25S	151.05 E
Inglewood [Ca.-U.S.]	46	Fj	33.58N	118.21W
Inglewood [N.Z.]	62	Fc	39.09S	174.12 E
Ingolf Fjord	41	Kb	80.35N	17.35W
Ingólfshöfdi	7a	Cc	63.48N	16.39W
Ingolstadt	10	Hh	48.46N	11.26 E
Ingrid Christensen Kyst	66	Fe	69.30S	76.00 E
I-n-Guezzâm	31	Hg	19.32N	5.42 E
Ingul	16	Gf	47.02N	31.59 E
Ingulec	16	Hf	46.41N	32.48 E
Ingulec	19	Df	47.43N	33.10 E
Inguri	16	Lh	42.24N	41.32 E
Inhaca, Ilha da-	30	Kk	26.02S	32.58 E
Inhambane	31	Kk	23.52S	35.23 E
Inhambane [3]	37	Ed	23.00S	34.30 E
Inhambane, Baía de-	37	Fd	23.50S	35.20 E
Inhaminga	37	Fc	18.25S	35.01 E
Inhandui-Guaçu, Rio-	55	Fe	21.37S	52.59W
Inhanduizinho, Rio-	55	Fe	21.34S	53.36W
Inharrime	37	Fd	24.28S	35.01 E
Inhassoro	37	Fd	21.32S	35.12 E
Inhaúma	55	Ja	13.01S	44.39W
I-n-Hihaou	32	He	23.00N	2.00 E
Inhobi, Rio-	55	Ef	23.45S	54.40W
Inhumas	54	Ig	16.22S	49.30W
Iniö	8	Id	60.25N	21.25 E
Inirida, Rio-	52	Je	3.55N	67.52W
Inis/Ennis	9	Ei	52.50N	8.59W
Inis Airc/Inishark	9	Ch	53.37N	10.16W
Inis Bó Finne/Inishbofin	9	Ch	53.38N	10.12W
Inis Ceithleann/Enniskillen	9	Fg	54.21N	7.38W
Inis Córthaidh/Enniscorthy	9	Gi	52.30N	6.34W
Inis Diomáin/Ennistymon	9	Di	52.57N	9.13W
Inis Eoghain/Inishowen Peninsula	9	Ff	55.15N	7.20W
Inishark/Inis Airc	9	Ch	53.37N	10.16W
Inishbofin/Inis Bó Finne	9	Ch	53.38N	10.12W
Inisheer/Inis Oirr	9	Dh	53.03N	9.31W
Inishkea	9	Cg	54.08N	10.11W
Inishmaan/Inis Meáin	9	Dh	53.05N	9.35W
Inishmore/Árainn	9	Dh	53.07N	9.45W
Inishmurray/Inis Muirigh	9	Eg	54.26N	8.40W
Inishowen Peninsula/Inis Eoghain	9	Ff	55.15N	7.20W
Inishtranull	9	Ff	55.27N	7.14W
Inishturk/Inis Toirc	9	Ch	53.43N	10.05W
Inis Meáin/Inishmaan	9	Dh	53.05N	9.35W
Inis Muirigh/Inishmurray	9	Eg	54.26N	8.40W
Inis Oirr/Inisheer	9	Dh	53.03N	9.31W
Inis Toirc/Inishturk	9	Ch	53.43N	10.05W
Inja	20	Je	59.22N	144.50 E
Inja [R.S.F.S.R.]	20	Je	59.30N	144.48 E
Inja [R.S.F.S.R.]	20	Df	50.27N	86.42 E
Injeŭp	28	Je	38.04N	128.10 E
Injibara	35	Fc	10.55N	36.58 E
Injune	59	Je	25.51S	148.34 E
I-n-Kak	34	Fb	16.20N	0.17 E
Inkisi	36	Bc	4.46S	14.52 E
Inkoo/Ingå	7	Ff	60.03N	24.01 E
Inland Kaikoura Range	62	Ee	42.00S	173.35 E
Inland Sea (EN) = Setonaikai	21	Pf	34.10N	133.00 E
Inn	5	Hf	48.35N	13.28 E
Innamincka	59	Ie	27.45S	140.44 E
Inner Hebrides	9	Ge	57.00N	6.45W
Inner Mongolia (EN) = Nei Monggol Zizhiqu (Nei-meng-ku Tzu-chih-ch'ü) [2]	27	Jc	44.00N	112.00 E
Inner Silver Pit	9	Nh	53.30N	0.40 E
Inner Sound	9	Hd	57.30N	5.55W
Innerste	10	Fd	52.15N	9.50 E
Innisfail [Alta.-Can.]	46	Ia	52.02N	113.57W
Innisfail [Austl.]	59	Jc	17.32S	146.02 E
Innokentjevka	20	Ig	49.42N	136.55 E
Innokentjevski	20	Jg	48.38N	140.12 E
Innoko	40	Hd	62.14N	159.45W
Innsbruck	6	Hf	47.16N	11.24 E
Innuksuac	42	Je	58.27N	78.08W
Innviertel	14	Hb	48.15N	13.15 E
Innvikfjorden	8	Bc	61.50N	6.35 E
Inny/An Eithne	9	Fh	53.35N	7.50W
Ino	29	Ce	33.33N	133.26 E
Inobonto	26	Hf	0.52N	123.57 E
Inongo	31	Ii	1.57S	18.16 E
Inoni	36	Cc	3.04S	15.39 E
Inönü	15	Nj	39.48N	30.09 E
I-n-Ouagar	34	Gb	16.12N	6.54 E
Inoucdjauac	39	Ld	58.30N	78.15W
I-n-Ouzzal	32	He	21.34N	1.59 E
Inowrocław	10	Od	52.48N	18.15 E
I-n-Salah	31	Hf	27.13N	2.28 E
Insar	7	Ki	54.42N	45.18 E
Insar	7	Kj	53.52N	44.23 E
Inscription, Cape-	57	Cg	25.30S	112.59 E
Insjön	8	Fd	60.41N	15.05 E
Insko	10	Lc	53.27N	15.33 E
Instruč	8	Ij	54.39N	21.48 E
Insurăţei	15	Ke	44.55N	27.36 E
Inta	6	Mb	66.05N	60.08 E
I-n-Tabezas	34	Fb	17.54N	1.50 E
I-n-Tallak	34	Fb	16.19N	3.15 E
Intepe	15	Ji	40.00N	26.20 E
Interlaken	14	Bd	46.41N	7.52 E
International Falls	43	Ib	48.36N	93.25W
Interview	25	If	12.55N	92.43 E
Inthanon, Doi-	25	Je	18.35N	98.29 E
Intibucá [3]	49	Cf	14.20N	88.15W
Intiyaco	56	Hc	28.39S	60.05W
Intorsura Buzaului	15	Jd	45.41N	26.02 E
Intracoastal Waterway	45	Im	28.45N	95.40W
Inubō-Zaki	29	Gd	35.42N	140.52 E
Inutil, Bahia-	56	Fh	52.45S	71.24W
Inuvik	39	Fc	68.25N	133.30W
Inuyama	29	Ed	35.23N	136.56 E
Inva	17	Gg	58.59N	55.14 E
Inveraray	9	He	56.13N	5.05W
Invercargill	58	Hi	46.25S	168.21 E
Inverell	59	Ke	29.47S	151.07 E
Inverness	6	Fd	57.29N	4.15W
Inverurie	9	Kd	57.17N	2.23W
Investigator Group	57	Eh	33.45S	134.30 E
Investigator Strait	59	Hg	35.25S	137.10 E
Inyangani	30	Kj	18.18S	32.51 E
Inyangani	37	Ec	18.13S	32.46 E
Inyati	37	Dc	19.40S	28.51 E
Inyazura	37	Ec	18.43S	32.10 E
Inyo Mountains	46	Gh	36.50N	117.45W
Inza	19	Ee	53.53N	46.28 E
Inzá	54	Cc	2.33N	76.04W
Inžavino	16	Mc	52.19N	42.31 E
Inzer	17	Hi	54.30N	56.28 E
Inzer	17	Hi	54.14N	57.34 E
Inzia	36	Cc	3.45S	17.57 E
Iō/Kazan-Rettō = Volcano Islands (EN)	21	Qg	25.00N	141.00 E
Ioánnina	6	Ih	39.40N	20.50 E
Ioanninon, Limni-	15	Dj	39.40N	20.53 E
Iokanga	7	Jb	68.03N	39.40 E
Iola	45	Ih	37.55N	95.24W
Iolotan	19	Gh	37.18N	62.21 E
Iona	9	Ge	56.19N	6.25W
Iona	36	Bf	16.52S	12.34 E
Ionava/Jonava	7	Fi	55.05N	24.17 E
Ion Corvin	15	Ke	44.07N	27.48 E
Ione	46	Eg	38.21N	120.56W
Ionia	44	Ed	42.59N	85.04W
Ionian Basin (EN)	5	Hh	36.00N	20.00 E
Ionian Islands (EN) = Iónioi Nisoi	5	Ih	38.30N	20.30 E
Ionian Sea (EN) = Ionio, Mar-	5	Hh	39.00N	19.00 E
Ionian Sea (EN) = Iónion Pélagos	5	Hh	39.00N	19.00 E
Ionio, Mar- = Ionian Sea (EN)	5	Hh	39.00N	19.00 E
Iónioi Nisoi [2]	15	Dk	38.40N	20.10 E
Iónioi Nisoi = Ionian Islands (EN)	5	Ih	38.30N	20.30 E
Iónion Pélagos = Ionian Sea (EN)	5	Hh	39.00N	19.00 E
Ioniškelis/Joniškėlis	8	Ki	56.00N	24.14 E
Ioniškis/Joniškis	7	Fh	56.16N	23.37 E
Iony, Ostrov-	20	Je	56.15N	143.20 E
Iori	16	Oi	41.03N	46.27 E
Ios	15	Im	36.44N	25.18 E
Ios	15	Im	36.42N	25.20 E
Iō-Shima	28	Ki	31.51N	130.13 E
Iowa [2]	43	Ic	42.15N	93.15W
Iowa City	43	Ic	41.40N	91.32W
Iowa Falls	45	Je	42.31N	93.16W
Iowa Park	45	Gj	33.57N	98.40W
Iowa River	45	Kf	41.10N	91.02W
Iō-Yama	29a	Da	44.10N	145.10 E
Ipa	16	Fc	52.07N	29.12 E
Ipameri	54	Ig	17.43S	48.09W
Ipatovo	19	Ef	45.43N	42.53 E
Ipaumirim	54	Ke	6.47S	38.43W
Ipel'	10	Oi	47.49N	18.52 E
Ipiales	54	Cc	0.50N	77.37W
Ipiaú	54	Kf	14.08S	39.44W
Ipiranga	55	Gg	25.01S	50.35W
Ipiros [2]	15	Dj	39.30N	20.40 E
Ipiros = Epirus (EN)	15	Dj	39.30N	20.40 E
Ipiros = Epirus (EN)	5	Ih	39.30N	20.40 E
Ipixuma, Rio-	54	Fe	5.50S	63.00W
Ipixuna	54	De	7.34S	72.36W
Ipoh	22	Mi	4.35N	101.05 E
Ipoly	10	Oi	47.49N	18.52 E
Iporá	55	Ff	23.59S	53.37W
Iporá	54	Hg	16.28S	51.07W
Ippy	35	Cd	6.15N	21.12 E
Ipsala	24	Bb	40.55N	26.23 E
Ipsizonos Óros	15	Gi	40.28N	23.34 E
Ipswich [Austl.]	58	Gg	27.36S	152.46 E
Ipswich [Eng.-U.K.]	6	Ge	52.04N	1.10 E
Ipswich [S.D.-U.S.]	45	Gd	45.27N	99.02W
Ipu	54	Jd	4.20S	40.42W
Iput	16	Gc	52.26N	31.05 E
Iquique	53	Ih	20.13S	70.10W
Iquitos	53	If	3.50S	73.15W
Iraan	45	Fk	30.54N	101.54W
Ira Banda	35	Cd	5.57N	22.06 E
Irabu-Jima	27	Mg	24.50N	125.10 E
Iracoubo	54	Hb	5.29N	53.13W
Iraël	17	Gd	64.27N	55.08 E
Irago-Suidō	29	Ed	34.35N	136.55 E
Irago-Zaki	29	Ed	34.35N	137.01 E
Iráklia	15	Gh	41.10N	23.16 E
Iráklia	15	Im	36.50N	25.26 E
Iráklion	6	Ih	35.20N	25.08 E
Irān = Iran (EN) [1]	22	Hf	32.00N	53.00 E
Iran (EN) = Irān [1]	22	Hf	32.00N	53.00 E
Iran, Pegunungan- = Iran Mountains (EN)	21	Ni	2.05N	114.55 E
Iran, Plateau of- (EN)	21	Hf	32.00N	56.00 E
Irani, Serra do-	55	Fh	27.00S	52.12W
Iran Mountains (EN) = Iran, Pegunungan-	21	Ni	2.05N	114.55 E
Irānshahr	22	Ig	27.13N	60.41 E
Irapa	50	Eg	10.34N	62.35W
Irapuá, Arroio-	55	Fj	30.15S	53.10W
Irapuato	39	Ig	20.41N	101.28W
Iraq (EN) = Al 'Irāq [1]	22	Gf	33.00N	44.00 E
'Irāq al 'Arabi	24	Kg	31.50N	45.50 E
Irati	13	Kb	42.35N	1.16W
Irati	56	Jc	25.27S	50.39W
Irazú, Volcán-	38	Ki	9.59N	83.51W
Irbeni Väin	8	Ig	57.48N	22.05 E
Irbid	23	Ec	32.33N	35.51 E
Irbiktepe	15	Jh	41.00N	26.30 E
Irbit	17	Kh	57.42N	63.07 E
Irbit	19	Gd	57.41N	63.03 E
Irebu	36	Cc	0.37S	17.45 E
Irecê	54	Jf	11.18S	41.52W
Iregua	13	Jb	42.27N	2.24W
Ireland	5	Fe	53.00N	8.00W
Ireland/Éire [1]	6	Fe	53.00N	8.00W
Ireland Trough (EN)	5	Ed	55.00N	12.40W
Iren	17	Hh	57.27N	56.59 E
Ireng River	54	Gc	3.33N	59.51W
Irês Corações	54	Ih	21.42S	45.16W
Iretama	55	Fg	24.27S	52.02W
Irgiz	19	Gf	48.13N	62.08 E
Irgiz	19	Gf	48.36N	61.16 E
Irharhar [Alg.]	30	Hf	28.00N	6.15 E
Irharhar [Alg.]	32	Ie	21.01N	6.01 E
Irherm	32	Fc	30.04N	8.26W
Iri	28	Ig	35.56N	126.57 E
Iriba	31	Jg	15.07N	22.15 E
Iriguí	30	Gg	16.43N	5.30W
Iriklinski	16	Ud	51.39N	58.38 E
Iriklinskoje Vodohranilišče	16	Ud	51.45N	58.45 E
Iringa [3]	36	Gd	8.00S	35.30 E
Iringa	31	Ki	7.46S	35.42 E
Irinja, Gora-	20	Fe	58.20N	104.30 E
Iriomote Jima	27	Lg	24.20N	123.50 E
Iriona	49	Ef	15.57N	85.11W
Iriri, Rio-	52	Kf	3.52S	52.37W
Irish Sea	5	Fe	53.30N	5.20W
Irish Sea (EN) = Muir Eireann	5	Fe	53.30N	5.20W
Irituia	54	Id	1.46S	47.26W
Irkeštam	18	Ie	39.38N	73.55 E
Irkutsk	22	Md	52.16N	104.20 E
Irkutskaja Oblast [3]	20	Fe	56.00N	104.00 E
Irlir, Gora-	18	Dc	42.40N	63.30 E
Irminio	14	In	36.46N	14.36 E
Irnijärvi	7	Gd	65.36N	29.05 E
Iro, Lac-	35	Bc	10.06N	19.25 E
Iroise	11	Bf	48.15N	4.55W
Iron Gate (EN) = Portile de Fier	5	Ig	44.41N	22.31 E
Iron Knob	59	Hf	32.44S	137.08 E
Iron Mountain	43	Jb	45.49N	88.04W
Iron Mountains	9	Fg	54.15N	7.50W
Iron River [Mi.-U.S.]	43	Jb	46.05N	88.39W
Iron River [Wi.-U.S.]	45	Kc	46.34N	91.24W
Ironside Mountain	46	Fd	44.15N	118.08W
Ironton [Mo.-U.S.]	45	Kh	37.36N	90.38W
Ironton [Oh.-U.S.]	44	Ff	38.32N	82.40W
Ironwood	43	Ib	46.27N	90.10W
Iroquois Falls	42	Jg	48.46N	80.41W
Irō-Zaki	28	Og	34.35N	138.55 E

Index Symbols

[1] Independent Nation	Historical or Cultural Region	Pass, Gap	Depression	Coast, Beach	Rock, Reef	Waterfall Rapids	Canal	Lagoon	Escarpment, Sea Scarp	Historic Site	Port
[2] State, Region	Mount, Mountain	Plain, Lowland	Polder	Cliff	Islands, Archipelago	River Mouth, Estuary	Glacier	Bank	Fracture	Ruins	Lighthouse
[3] District, County	Volcano	Delta	Desert, Dunes	Peninsula	Rocks, Reefs	Lake	Ice Shelf, Pack Ice	Seamount	Trench, Abyss	Wall, Walls	Mine
[4] Municipality	Hill	Salt Flat	Forest, Woods	Isthmus	Coral Reef	Salt Lake	Ocean	Tablemount	National Park, Reserve	Church, Abbey	Tunnel
[5] Colony, Dependency	Mountains, Mountain Range	Valley, Canyon	Heath, Steppe	Sandbank	Well, Spring	Intermittent Lake	Sea	Ridge	Point of Interest	Temple	Dam, Bridge
Continent	Hills, Escarpment	Crater, Cave	Oasis	Island	Geyser	Reservoir	Gulf, Bay	Shelf	Recreation Site	Scientific Station	
Physical Region	Plateau, Upland	Karst Features	Cape, Point	Atoll	River, Stream	Swamp, Pond	Strait, Fjord	Basin	Cave, Cavern	Airport	

Irpen 19 De 50.31N 30.16 E
Irpinia 14 Ij 40.55N 15.00 E
Irrawaddy [3] 25 Ie 17.00N 95.00 E
Irrawaddy 21 Lh 15.50N 95.06 E
Irrawaddy, Mouths of the- (EN) 21 Lh 16.30N 95.00 E
Irrel 12 Ie 49.51N 6.28 E
Irsăva 10 Th 48.15N 23.05 E
Irsina 14 Kj 40.45N 16.14 E
Irtek 16 Rd 51.29N 52.42 E
Irthlingborough 12 Bb 52.19N 0.36W
Irtyš 21 Ic 61.04N 68.52 E
Irtyšsk 19 He 53.21N 75.27 E
Irumu 36 Eb 1.27N 29.52 E
Irún 13 Ka 43.21N 1.47W
Irurzun 13 Kb 42.55N 1.50W
Irves Šaurums 8 Ig 57.48N 22.05 E
Irvine 9 If 55.37N 4.40W
Irving 45 Hj 32.49N 96.56W
Is, Jabal- 35 Fa 21.49N 35.39 E
Isa, Ra's- 33 Hf 15.11N 42.39 E
Isabel 45 Fd 45.24N 101.26W
Isabel, Bahía- 54a Ab 0.38S 91.25W
Isabela 51a Ab 18.31N 67.07W
Isabela→Basilan City 26 He 6.42N 121.58 E
Isabela, Cabo- 49 Ld 19.56N 71.01W
Isabela, Isla- [Ec.] 52 Gf 0.30S 91.06W
Isabela, Isla- [Mex.] 48 Gg 21.51N 105.55W
Isabella, Cordillera- 47 Gf 13.30N 85.30W
Isabel Segunda 49 Od 18.09N 65.27W
Isabey 15 Ml 38.00N 29.24 E
Isaccea 15 Ld 45.16N 28.28 E
Isachsen 39 Ib 78.50N 103.30W
Isafjörour 6 Db 66.03N 23.09W
Isahaya 28 Jh 32.50N 130.03 E
Isakov, Seamount (EN) 57 Ga 31.35N 151.07 E
Isaku/Iisaku 8 Le 59.14N 27.41 E
Isana, Rio- 54 Ec 0.26N 67.19W
Isandja 36 Dc 2.59S 22.00 E
Isanga 36 Dc 1.26S 22.18 E
Isangi 36 Db 0.46N 24.15 E
Isanlu Makutu 34 Gd 8.16N 5.48 E
Isaouane-n-Irarraren 32 Id 27.15N 8.00 E
Isaouane-n-Tifernine 32 Id 27.00N 7.30 E
Isar 10 Ih 48.49N 12.58 E
Isarco/Eisack 14 Fd 46.27N 11.18 E
Isarco, Valle-/Eisacktal 14 Fd 46.45N 11.35 E
Isbergues 12 Ed 50.37N 2.27 E
Iscayachi 54 Eh 21.31S 65.03W
Ischgl 14 Ec 47.01N 10.17 E
Ischia 14 Hj 40.45N 13.55 E
Ischia 14 Hj 40.44N 13.57 E
Ise 27 Oe 34.29N 136.42 E
Isefjord 8 Di 55.50N 11.50 E
Isějevka 7 Li 54.28N 48.17 E
Isen 10 Ih 48.20N 12.45 E
Isenach 12 Ke 49.38N 8.28 E
Isen-Zaki 29b Bb 27.39N 128.55 E
Iseo, Lago d'- 14 Ee 45.45N 10.05 E
Iseran, Col de l'- 11 Ni 45.25N 7.02 E
Isère 11 Kj 44.59N 4.51 E
Isère [3] 11 Li 45.10N 5.50 E
Išerit, Gora- 17 If 61.08N 59.10 E
Iserlohn 10 De 51.22N 7.42 E
Isernia 14 Ii 41.36N 14.14 E
Isesaki 29 Fc 36.19N 139.12 E
Iset 21 Id 56.36N 66.24 E
Isetskoje 17 Lh 56.29N 65.21 E
Ise-Wan 28 Ng 34.40N 136.42 E
Iseyin 34 Fd 7.58N 3.36 E
Isfahan (EN)=Eşfahān 22 Hf 32.40N 51.38 E
Isfana 18 Ge 39.51N 69.32 E
Isfara 18 Hd 40.07N 70.38 E
Isfendiyar Dağları 23 Da 41.45N 34.10 E
Isfjorden 41 Nc 78.15N 15.00 E
Isha Baydabo 31 Lh 3.04N 43.48 E
Ishasha River 36 Ec 0.50S 29.40 E
Ishavet=Arctic Ocean (EN) 67 Be 85.00N 170.00 E
Isherton 54 Gc 2.19N 59.22W
Ishigaki 27 Lg 24.20N 124.09 E
Ishikari 29a Bb 43.13N 141.18 E
Ishikari-Dake 29a Cb 43.33N 143.00 E
Ishikari-Gawa 29a Bb 43.15N 141.20 E
Ishikari-Heiya 29a Bb 43.00N 141.40 E
Ishikari-Wan 27 Pc 43.25N 141.00 E
Ishikawa [Jap.] 27 Mf 26.27N 127.50 E
Ishikawa [Jap.] 29 Gc 37.09N 140.27 E
Ishikawa Ken [2] 28 Nf 36.35N 136.40 E
Ishim Steppe (EN)= Išimskaja Step 21 Id 55.00N 67.30 E
Ishinomaki 27 Pd 38.25N 141.18 E
Ishinomaki-Wan 29 Gb 38.20N 141.25 E
Ishioka 28 Pf 36.11N 140.16 E
Ishitate-San 29 De 33.44N 134.03 E
Ishizuchi-Yama 29 Ce 33.45N 133.05 E
Ishodnaja, Gora- 20 Nd 64.50N 173.26W
Ishpeming 44 Db 46.30N 87.40W
Isidro Alves 55 Ee 20.09S 55.12W
Isigny-sur-Mer 11 Ee 49.19N 1.06W
Isii 29 Dd 34.04N 134.26 E
Işıklar Dağı 24 Bb 40.50N 27.05 E
Işıklı 15 Mk 38.19N 29.51 E
Isikli Göl 15 Mk 38.14N 29.55 E
Isili 14 Dk 39.44N 9.06 E
Isilkul 19 He 54.55N 71.16 E
Išim 22 Id 56.09N 69.27 E
Išim 21 Jd 57.45N 71.12 E
Išimbaj 19 Fe 53.28N 56.02 E
Išimskaja Step=Ishim Steppe (EN) 21 Id 55.00N 67.30 E
Isinga 20 Gf 52.55N 112.00 E
Isiolo 36 Gb 0.21N 37.35 E
Isiro 31 Jh 2.48N 27.41 E
Isisford 59 Id 24.16S 144.26 E
Isjangulovo 17 Hj 52.12N 56.36 E
Iskandar 18 Gd 41.35N 69.43 E
Iskăr 15 Hf 43.44N 24.27 E
Iskăr, Jazovir- 15 Gg 42.25N 23.35 E
Iškašim 19 Hh 36.44N 71.39 E
İskenderun=Alexandretta (EN) 22 Ff 36.37N 36.07 E
İskenderun Körfezi= Alexandretta, Gulf of- (EN) 23 Eb 36.30N 35.40 E
Iskilip 24 Fb 40.45N 34.29 E
Iski-Naukat 18 Id 40.14N 72.41 E
Iskininski 16 Rf 47.13N 52.36 E
Iskitim 20 Df 54.38N 83.18 E
Iskushuban 35 Ic 10.13N 50.14 E
Iskut 42 Ee 56.45N 131.48W
Isla-Cristina 13 Eg 37.12N 7.19W
Íslâhiye 24 Gd 37.26N 36.41 E
Islāmābād 22 Jf 33.42N 73.10 E
Islāmābād→Anantnāg 25 Fb 33.44N 75.09 E
Isla Mujeres 48 Pg 21.12N 86.43W
Island=Iceland (EN) [1] 6 Eb 65.00N 18.00W
Island=Iceland (EN) 5 Eb 65.00N 18.00W
Island Harbour 51b Ab 18.16N 63.02W
Island Lagoon 59 Hf 31.30S 136.40 E
Island Lake 42 If 53.45N 94.30W
Island Lake 42 If 53.58N 94.46W
Island Pond 44 Lc 44.50N 71.53W
Islands, Bay of - [Can.] 42 Lg 49.10N 58.15W
Islands, Bay of- [N.Z.] 62 Fa 35.10S 174.10 E
Islao, Massif de l'- 30 Lk 22.30S 45.20 E
Islas de la Bahía [3] 49 De 16.20N 86.30W
Islay 5 Fd 55.46N 6.10W
Islaz 15 Hf 43.44N 24.45 E
Isle 11 Fj 44.55N 0.15W
Isle of Man [5] 9 Ig 54.15N 4.30W
Isle of Wight [3] 9 Lk 50.40N 1.15W
Isleta 45 Ci 34.55N 106.42W
Isle-Verte 44 Ma 48.01N 69.22W
Ismael Cortinas 55 Dk 33.56S 57.08W
Ismailia (EN)=Al Ismā'īlīyah 33 Fc 30.35N 32.16 E
Ismailly 16 Pi 40.47N 48.13 E
Ismantorps Borg 8 Gh 56.45N 16.40 E
Isnā 31 Kf 25.18N 32.33 E
Isny im Allgäu 10 Gi 47.42N 10.02 E
Isojärvi 8 Ic 61.45N 21.45 E
Isojoki 7 Ee 62.07N 21.58 E
Isojoki/Storå 7 Ee 62.07N 21.58 E
Isoka 36 Fe 10.08S 32.38 E
Isola del Liri 14 Hi 41.41N 13.34 E
Isola di Capo Rizzuto 14 Ll 38.58N 17.05 E
Isonzo 14 He 45.43N 13.33 E
Isonzo (EN)=Soča 14 He 45.43N 13.33 E
Isosyöte 7 Gd 65.37N 27.35 E
Isparta 23 Db 37.46N 30.33 E
Isperih 15 Jf 43.43N 26.50 E
Ispica 14 In 36.47N 14.55 E
İspir 24 Ib 40.29N 41.00 E
Ispiriz Dağı 24 Jc 38.03N 43.55 E
Israel (EN)=Yisra'el [1] 22 Ff 31.30N 35.00 E
Isratu 35 Fb 16.20N 39.55 E
Issa 8 Mh 56.55N 28.50 E
Issano 54 Gb 5.49N 59.25W
Issaran, Ra's- 24 Eh 28.50N 32.56 E
Issel 10 Cd 52.00N 6.10 E
Isser 13 Ph 36.51N 3.40 E
Issia [3] 34 Dd 6.30N 6.35W
Issia 34 Dd 6.29N 6.35W
Issoire 11 Ji 45.33N 3.15 E
Issoudun 11 Hh 46.57N 2.00 E
Issyk 18 Kc 43.20N 77.28 E
Issyk-Kul, Ozero- 21 Je 42.25N 77.15 E
Issyk-Kulskaja Oblast [3] 19 Hg 42.10N 78.00 E
Ist 14 If 44.17N 14.47 E
İstanbul 22 Ee 41.01N 28.58 E
İstanbul-Bakırköy 15 Li 40.59N 28.52 E
İstanbul-Beyoğlu 15 Lh 41.02N 28.59 E
İstanbul Boğazi=Bosporus (EN) 5 Ig 41.00N 29.00 E
İstanbul-Kadıköy 15 Mi 40.59N 29.01 E
Isteren 8 Db 62.00N 11.50 E
Istgāh-e Eqbālīyeh 24 Ne 35.50N 50.45 E
Isthilart 55 Dj 31.11S 57.58W
Istiaia 15 Gk 38.57N 23.09 E
Istisu 16 Nj 39.57N 46.00 E
Istmina 54 Cb 5.09N 76.42W
Isto, Mount- 38 Ec 69.12N 143.48W
Istok 15 Dg 42.47N 20.29 E
Istokpoga, Lake- 44 Gl 27.22N 81.17W
Istra=Istria (EN) 5 Hf 45.00N 14.00 E
Istres 11 Kk 43.31N 4.59 E
Istria 15 Le 44.34N 28.43 E
Istria (EN)=Istra 5 Hf 45.00N 14.00 E
Isulan 26 He 7.02N 124.29 E
Itabaiana 54 Kf 10.41S 37.26W
Itabaianinha 54 Kf 11.16S 37.47W
Itaberá 55 Hf 23.51S 49.09W
Itaberaba 54 Jf 12.32S 40.18W
Itaberai 54 Ig 16.02S 49.48W
Itabira 54 Jg 19.37S 43.13W
Itabirito 55 Ke 20.15S 43.48W
Itabuna 53 Mg 14.48S 39.16W
Itacaiúna, Rio- 54 Ie 5.21S 49.08W
Itacarambi 55 Jb 15.01S 44.03W
Itacoatiara 53 Kf 3.08S 58.25W
Itacolomi, Pico do- 55 Ke 20.26S 43.29W
Itacuaí, Rio- 54 Dd 4.20S 70.12W
Itacumbi 55 Ei 28.44S 55.08W
Itacurubí del Rosario 55 Dg 24.29S 56.41W
Itaguari, Rio- 55 Jb 14.11S 44.40W
Itaguaru 55 Hb 15.44S 49.37W
Itagüí 54 Cb 6.12N 75.40W
Itaimbézinho 55 Gi 28.38S 50.34W
Itaituba 53 Kf 4.17S 55.59W
Itajaí 53 Lh 26.53S 48.39W
Itajaí Açu, Rio- 55 Hh 26.54S 48.33W
Itajubá 54 Ih 22.26S 45.27W
Itajuípe 54 Kf 14.41S 39.22W
Itaka 20 Gf 53.54N 118.42 E
Italia=Italy (EN) [1] 6 Hg 42.50N 12.50 E
Itálica 13 Fg 37.25N 6.05W
Italy (EN)=Italia [1] 6 Hg 42.50N 12.50 E
Itambacuri 54 Jg 18.01S 41.42W
Itambé, Pico de- 52 Lg 18.23S 43.21W
Itämeri=Baltic, Sea (EN) 5 Hd 57.00N 19.00 E
Itampolo 37 Gd 24.41S 43.57 E
Itanagar 25 Ic 26.57N 93.15 E
Itanará, Rio- 55 Eh 24.00S 55.53W
Itanhaém 56 Kb 24.11S 46.47W
Itano 29 Dd 34.09N 134.28 E
Itapaci 55 Hb 14.57S 49.34W
Itapagé 54 Kd 3.41S 39.34W
Itapajipe 55 Hd 19.54S 49.22W
Itaparaná, Rio- 54 Fe 5.47S 63.03W
Itapebi 54 Kg 15.56S 39.32W
Itapecerica 55 Je 20.28S 45.07W
Itapecuru-Mirim 54 Jd 3.24S 44.20W
Itapemirim 54 Jh 21.01S 40.50W
Itaperina, Pointe- 30 Lk 24.59S 47.06 E
Itaperuna 54 Jh 21.12S 41.54W
Itapetinga 54 Jg 15.15S 40.15W
Itapetininga 56 Kb 23.36S 48.03W
Itapetininga, Rio- 55 Hf 23.35S 48.27W
Itapeva 55 Hf 23.58S 48.52W
Itapeva, Lagoa- 55 Hi 29.30S 49.55W
Itapicuru, Rio- [Braz.] 54 Kf 11.47S 37.32W
Itapicuru, Rio- [Braz.] 52 Lf 2.52S 44.12W
Itapipoca 54 Kd 3.31S 39.33W
Itapiranga [Braz.] 54 Gd 2.45S 58.01W
Itapiranga [Braz.] 55 Fh 27.08S 53.43W
Itapirapuã, Pico- 55 Hg 24.17S 49.12W
Itápolis 55 He 21.35S 48.46W
Itaporã 55 Ef 22.01S 54.54W
Itaporanga [Braz.] 55 Hf 23.42S 49.29W
Itaporanga [Braz.] 54 Ke 7.18S 38.10W
Itapúa [3] 55 Eh 26.50S 55.50W
Itapuã 55 Gj 30.16S 51.01W
Itapuranga 55 Ig 15.35S 49.59W
Itaqui 56 Ic 29.08S 56.33W
Itaquyry 55 Eg 24.56S 55.13W
Itararé 55 Hg 24.07S 49.20W
Itararé, Rio- 55 Hf 23.10S 49.42W
Itārsi 25 Fd 22.37N 77.45 E
Itarumã 55 Gd 18.42S 51.25W
Itati 55 Ch 27.16S 58.15W
Itatinga 55 Hf 23.07S 48.36W
Itatski 20 De 56.07N 89.20 E
Itaum 55 Ef 22.00S 55.20W
Itaúna 54 Jh 20.04S 44.34W
Itaya-Tōge 29 Gc 37.50N 140.13 E
Itbāy 30 Kf 22.00N 35.30 E
Itbayat 26 Hb 20.46N 121.50 E
Itchen 12 Ad 50.57N 1.22W
Ite 54 Dg 17.50S 70.58W
Itéa 15 Fk 38.26N 22.25 E
Ithaca 43 Lc 42.26N 76.30W
Ithaca (EN)=Itháki 15 Dk 38.24N 20.40 E
Itháki 15 Dk 38.22N 20.43 E
Itháki=Ithaca (EN) 15 Dk 38.24N 20.40 E
Ith Hils 10 Fd 52.05N 9.35 E
Ithnayn, Harrat- 24 Ii 26.40N 40.10 E
Itigi 36 Fd 5.42S 34.29 E
Itimbiri 30 Jh 2.02N 22.44 E
Itiopya=Ethiopia (EN) [1] 31 Kh 9.00N 39.00 E
Itiquira 54 Hg 17.05S 54.56W
Itiquira, Rio- 52 Kg 17.18S 56.44W
Itirapina 55 If 22.15S 47.49W
Itiúba 54 Kf 10.43S 39.51W
Itivdleq 41 Ge 66.38N 53.51W
Itō 28 Og 34.58N 139.05 E
Itoigawa 28 Nf 37.02N 137.51 E
Itoko 36 Dc 1.00S 21.45 E
Itoman 29b Ab 26.07N 127.40 E
Iton 11 Hf 49.09N 1.12 E
Itremo, Massif de l'- 37 Hd 20.45S 46.30 E
Itsā 24 Dh 29.15N 30.48 E
Itsukaichi 29 Cd 34.22N 132.22 E
Itsuki 29 Be 32.24N 130.50 E
Ittiri 14 Cj 40.36N 8.34 E
Itu [Braz.] 55 If 23.16S 47.19W
Itu [Nig.] 34 Gd 5.12N 7.59 E
Itu, Rio- 55 Ei 29.25S 55.51W
Itui, Rio- 54 Dd 4.38S 70.19W
Ituiutaba 54 Ig 18.58S 49.28W
Itula 36 Ec 3.29S 27.52 E
Itumbiara 54 Ig 18.25S 49.13W
Itumkale 16 Nh 42.43N 45.35 E
Ituna 46 Na 51.10N 103.30W
Itungi Port 36 Fd 9.35S 33.56 E
Itupiranga 54 Ie 5.09S 49.20W
Iturama 55 Gd 19.44S 50.11W
Iturbide 48 Oh 19.40N 89.37W
Ituri 30 Jh 1.40N 27.01 E
Iturregui 55 Bm 36.50S 61.08W
Iturup, Ostrov- 21 Qe 44.54N 147.30 E
Iturup, Ostrov-/Etorofu Tō 21 Qe 44.54N 147.30 E
Itutinga 55 Je 21.18S 44.40W
Ituverava 56 Kb 20.20S 47.47W
Ituxi, Rio- 52 Jf 7.18S 64.51W
Ituzaingó 55 Dh 27.36S 56.41W
Itz 10 Gg 49.58N 10.52 E
Itzehoe 10 Fc 53.55N 9.31 E
Ivacevići 16 Dc 52.43N 25.21 E
Ivaí 55 Gg 25.01S 50.52W
Ivaí, Rio- [Braz.] 55 Fi 29.08S 53.16W
Ivaí, Rio- [Braz.] 52 Kh 23.18S 53.42W
Ivaiporã 55 Gg 24.15S 51.45W
Ivajlovgrad 15 Jh 41.32N 26.08 E
Ivakoany, Massif de l'- 37 Hd 23.50S 46.25 E
Ivalojoki 7 Gc 68.43N 27.36 E
Ivančice 10 Mg 49.06N 16.22 E
Ivangorod 7 Gg 59.23N 28.20 E
Ivangrad 15 Cg 42.51N 19.52 E
Ivanhoe 58 Fh 32.54S 144.18 E
Ivanić-Grad 14 Ke 45.42N 16.24 E
Ivaniči 10 Uf 50.38N 24.24 E
Ivanjica 15 Df 43.35N 20.14 E
Ivanjska 14 Lf 44.55N 17.04 E
Ivankov 16 Fd 50.57N 29.58 E
Ivano-Frankovo 10 Tg 49.52N 23.46 E
Ivano-Frankovsk 6 If 48.55N 24.43 E
Ivano-Frankovskaja Oblast [3] 19 Cf 48.40N 24.40 E
Ivanovka [R.S.F.S.R.] 20 Hf 50.18N 127.59 E
Ivanovka [Ukr.-U.S.S.R.] 16 Gf 46.57N 30.28 E
Ivanovo [Bye.-U.S.S.R.] 16 Dc 52.10N 25.32 E
Ivanovo [R.S.F.S.R.] 6 Kd 57.00N 40.59 E
Ivanovskaja Oblast [3] 19 Ed 57.00N 41.50 E
Ivanovskoje 8 Me 59.12N 28.59 E
Ivanščica 14 Kd 46.11N 16.10 E
Ivdel 19 Gc 60.42N 60.28 E
Ivenec 8 Lk 53.55N 26.49 E
Ivigtut 41 Hf 61.15N 48.00W
Ivindo 30 Ii 0.09S 12.09 E
Ivinheima 55 Ff 22.10S 53.37W
Ivinheima, Rio- 54 Hh 23.14S 53.42W
Ivinski razliv 7 If 61.10N 35.00 E
Iviza (EN)=Eivissa/Ibiza 5 Gh 39.00N 1.25 E
Iviza (EN)=Ibiza/Eivissa 5 Gh 39.00N 1.25 E
Ivje 10 Vc 53.55N 25.51 E
Ivohibe 37 Hd 22.29S 46.52 E
Ivoire, Côte d'-=Ivory Coast (EN) 30 Gh 5.00N 5.00W
Ivolândia 55 Gc 16.34S 50.51W
Ivory Coast (EN)=Côte d'Ivoire [1] 31 Gh 8.00N 5.00W
Ivory Coast (EN)=Ivoire, Côte d'- 30 Gh 5.00N 5.00W
Ivösjön 8 Fh 56.05N 14.25 E
Ivrea 14 Be 45.28N 7.52 E
Ivrindi 15 Kj 39.34N 27.29 E
Ivry-la-Bataille 12 Df 48.53N 1.28 E
Ivry-sur-Seine 12 Ef 48.49N 2.23 E
Ivujivik 39 Lc 62.25N 77.54W
Iwai-Shima 29 Be 33.47N 131.58 E
Iwaizumi 28 Pe 39.50N 141.48 E
Iwaki 22 Qf 36.55N 140.48 E
Iwaki-Gawa 29 Ga 41.01N 140.22 E
Iwaki-Hisanohama 29 Gc 37.09N 140.59 E
Iwaki-Jōban 29 Gc 37.02N 140.50 E
Iwaki-Kawamae 29 Gc 37.12N 140.45 E
Iwaki-Miwa 29 Gc 37.09N 140.42 E
Iwaki-Nakoso 29 Gc 36.56N 140.48 E
Iwaki-Onahama 29 Gc 36.57N 140.53 E
Iwaki-San 29 Ga 40.40N 140.20 E
Iwaki-Taira 29 Gc 37.05N 140.55 E
Iwaki-Uchigō 29 Gc 37.04N 140.50 E
Iwaki-Yoshima 29 Gc 37.05N 140.50 E
Iwaki-Yotsukura 29 Gc 37.07N 140.58 E
Iwakuni 27 Ne 34.09N 132.11 E
Iwami 29 Dd 35.35N 134.20 E
Iwami-Kōgen 29 Cd 35.00N 132.30 E
Iwamizawa 27 Pc 43.12N 141.46 E
Iwanai 28 Pc 42.58N 140.30 E
Iwanuma 29 Gb 38.07N 140.52 E
Iwase 29 Gc 36.21N 140.06 E
Iwasuge-Yama 29 Fc 36.44N 138.32 E
Iwata 29 Ed 34.42N 137.48 E
Iwate 28 Pe 39.30N 141.30 E
Iwate Ken [2] 28 Pe 39.30N 141.15 E
Iwate San 28 Pe 39.49N 141.26 E
Iwo 34 Fd 7.38N 4.11 E
Iwŏn 27 Mc 40.19N 128.37 E
Iwuy 12 Fd 50.14N 3.19 E
Ixiamas 54 Ef 13.45S 68.09W
Ixmiquilpan 48 Jg 20.29N 99.14W
Ixopo 37 Ef 30.08S 30.00 E
Ixtapa, Punta- 48 Ii 17.39N 101.40W
Ixtepec 47 Ee 16.34N 95.06W
Ixtlahuacán del Rio 48 Hg 20.52N 103.15W
Ixtlán del Rio 47 Dd 21.02N 104.22W
Iyah 35 Hd 9.00N 49.38 E
Iyo 28 Lh 33.46N 132.42 E
Iyo-mishima 29 Ce 33.58N 133.33 E
Iyo-Nada 29 Ce 33.40N 132.15 E
Iž 7 Mh 56.00N 52.41 E
Iž 14 Jf 44.03N 15.06 E
Izabal [3] 49 Cf 15.30N 89.00W
Izabal, Lago de- 47 Ge 15.30N 89.10W
Izad Khvāst 24 Og 31.31N 52.07 E
Izamal 47 Gd 20.56N 89.01W
Izamal 48 Og 20.56N 89.01W
Izapa 47 Ff 14.55N 92.10W
'Izbat al Jājah 24 Dj 24.48N 30.35 E
'Izbat Dush 24 Dj 24.34N 30.42 E
Izberbaš 19 Eg 42.33N 47.52 E
Izbiceni 15 Hf 43.50N 24.39 E
Izborsk 8 Mg 57.39N 28.01 E
Izegem 12 Fd 50.55N 3.12 E
Izeh 24 Mg 31.50N 49.50 E
Izena-Shima 29b Ab 26.56N 127.56 E
Iževsk 6 Ld 56.51N 53.14 E
Izjaslav 16 Ed 50.09N 26.51 E
Izjum 19 Df 49.12N 37.17 E
Izkī 23 Ie 22.57N 57.49 E
Ižma 5 Lb 65.19N 52.54 E
Ižma 17 Fd 65.02N 53.55 E
Izmail 6 If 45.21N 28.50 E
İzmir=Smyrna (EN) 22 Ef 38.25N 27.09 E
İzmir, Gulf of- (EN)=İzmir Körfezi 24 Bc 38.30N 26.50 E
İzmir-Bornova 24 Bc 38.27N 27.14 E
İzmir Körfezi=Izmir, Gulf of- (EN) 24 Bc 38.30N 26.50 E
İzmit 22 Ee 40.46N 29.55 E
İzmit Körfezi 24 Cb 40.45N 29.35 E
İzmor 24 Ab 40.11N 25.55 E
Iznajar, Embalse de- 13 Hg 37.15N 4.30W
Iznalloz 13 Ig 37.23N 3.31W
İznik 24 Cb 40.26N 29.43 E
İznik Gölü 23 Ca 40.26N 29.30 E
Izobilny 16 Lg 45.19N 41.42 E
Izola 14 He 45.32N 13.40 E
Izōrskaja Vozvyšennost 8 Me 59.35N 29.30 E
Izozog, Bañados del- 54 Fg 18.50S 62.10W
Izra' 24 Gf 32.51N 36.15 E
Izsák 10 Pj 46.48N 19.22 E
Iztočni Rodopi 15 Ih 41.44N 25.31 E
Izúcar de Matamoros 48 Jh 18.36N 98.28W
Izu-Hantō 28 Og 34.55N 138.55 E
Izuhara 28 Jg 34.12N 129.17 E
Izu Islands (EN)=Izu-shotō 21 Pf 32.00N 140.00 E
Izumi [Jap.] 28 Kh 32.05N 130.22 E
Izumi [Jap.] 29 Dd 34.29N 135.26 E
Izumi [Jap.] 29 Gb 38.19N 140.51 E
Izumi-sano 29 Dd 34.24N 135.18 E
Izumo 28 Lg 35.22N 132.46 E
Izu-Shotō=Izu Islands (EN) 21 Pf 32.00N 140.00 E
Izvesti CIK, Ostrova-= Izvestiya Tsik Islands (EN) 20 Da 75.55N 82.30 E
Izvestiya Tsik Islands (EN)= Izvesti CIK, Ostrova- 20 Da 75.55N 82.30 E

J

Jaala 8 Lc 61.03N 26.29 E
Jaama/Jama 8 Lf 58.59N 27.45 E
Jääsjärvi 8 Lc 61.35N 26.05 E
Jaba 24 Qe 35.55N 56.35 E
Jabal, Bahr al-=Mountain Nile (EN) 30 Kh 9.30N 30.30 E
Jabal Abū Rujmayn 24 Ge 34.50N 37.56 E
Jabal al Awliyā' 35 Eb 15.14N 32.30 E
Jabal az Zannah 24 Oj 24.11N 52.38 E
Jabalón 13 Hf 38.53N 4.05W
Jabalpur 22 Jg 23.10N 79.57 E
Jabal Şabāyā 33 Hf 18.35N 41.03 E
Jabālyah 24 Fg 31.32N 34.29 E
Jabal Zuqar, Jazīrat- 33 Hg 14.00N 42.45 E
Jabbārah 33 Hf 19.27N 40.03 E
Jabbeke 12 Fc 51.11N 3.05 E
Jabjabah, Wādī- 35 Ea 22.37N 33.17 E
Jablah 24 Fe 35.21N 35.55 E
Jablanac 14 If 44.43N 14.53 E
Jablanica 15 Dh 41.15N 20.30 E
Jablanica [Bul.] 15 Hf 43.01N 24.06 E
Jablanica [Yugo.] 14 Lg 43.39N 17.45 E
Jabločny 20 Jg 47.09N 142.03 E
Jablonec nad Nisou 10 Lf 50.44N 15.10 E
Jablonicki, Pereval- 5 If 48.18N 24.28 E
Jablonovo 20 Gf 51.51N 112.50 E
Jablonovy Hrebet= Yablonovy Range (EN) 21 Nd 53.30N 115.00 E
Jablunkovský průsmyk 10 Og 49.31N 18.45 E
Jaboatão 54 Ke 8.07S 35.01W
Jaboti 55 De 20.48S 56.23W
Jabrīn 24 Ni 27.51N 51.26 E
Jabuka 14 Jg 43.05N 15.28 E
Jabung, Tanjung- 26 Dg 1.01S 104.22 E
Jabuticabal 56 Kb 21.16S 48.19W
Jabuticatubas 55 Kd 19.30S 43.45W
Jaca 13 Lb 42.34N 0.33W
Jacaltenango 49 Bf 15.40N 91.44W
Jacaré, Rio- 55 Je 21.03S 45.16W
Jacarei 55 Jf 23.19S 45.58W
Jacarezinho 56 Kb 23.09S 49.59W
Jáchal, Rio- 56 Jl 30.44S 68.08W
Jaciara [Braz.] 55 Ib 14.12S 46.41W
Jaciara [Braz.] 55 Eb 15.59S 54.57W
Jackman 44 Lc 45.38N 70.16W
Jack Mountain 46 Eb 48.47N 120.57W
Jackpot 46 Hf 41.59N 114.09W
Jacksboro 45 Gj 33.13N 98.10W
Jacks Mountain 44 Ie 40.45N 77.30W
Jackson [Al.-U.S.] 44 Dj 31.31N 87.53W
Jackson [Bar.] 51q Ab 13.10N 59.43W
Jackson [Ky.-U.S.] 44 Fg 37.33N 83.23W
Jackson [Mi.-U.S.] 43 Kc 42.15N 84.24W
Jackson [Mn.-U.S.] 45 Ie 43.37N 94.59W
Jackson [Mo.-U.S.] 45 Lh 37.23N 89.40W
Jackson [Ms.-U.S.] 39 Jf 32.18N 90.12W
Jackson [Oh.-U.S.] 44 Ff 39.03N 82.40W
Jackson [Tn.-U.S.] 43 Jd 35.37N 88.49W
Jackson [Wy.-U.S.] 46 Je 43.29N 110.38W
Jackson, Cape- 62 Fd 40.59S 174.19 E
Jackson, Mount- [Ant.] 66 Qf 71.23S 63.22W
Jackson, Mount- [Austl.] 59 Df 30.15S 119.16 E
Jackson Bay 62 Ce 43.55S 168.40 E
Jackson Head 62 Ce 43.58S 168.37 E
Jackson Lake 46 Je 43.55N 110.40W
Jacksonville [Ar.-U.S.] 45 Ji 34.52N 92.07W
Jacksonville [Fl.-U.S.] 39 Kf 30.20N 81.40W
Jacksonville [Il.-U.S.] 45 Kg 39.44N 90.14W
Jacksonville [N.C.-U.S.] 43 Le 34.45N 77.26W
Jacksonville [Tx.-U.S.] 43 He 31.58N 95.17W
Jacksonville Beach 43 Ke 30.18N 81.24W
Jacmel 47 Je 18.14N 72.32W
Jacobābād 25 Dc 28.17N 68.26 E
Jacobina 54 Jf 11.11S 40.31W
Jacob Lake 46 Ih 36.45N 112.13W
Jacobs 45 La 50.15N 89.46W
Jacona de Plancarte 48 Hh 19.57N 102.16W
Jacques-Cartier, Détroit de - 42 Lg 50.00N 63.30W
Jacques Cartier, Mont - 42 Kg 48.58N 65.57W
Jacuba, Rio- 55 Fd 18.25S 52.28W
Jacuí, Rio- 52 Ki 30.02S 51.15W
Jacuí-Mirim, Rio- 55 Fi 28.51S 53.07W
Jacundá 54 Id 4.33S 49.28W
Jacundá, Rio- 54 Hd 1.57S 50.26W
Jacupiranga 56 Kb 24.42S 48.00W
Jada 34 Hd 8.46N 12.09 E
Jadal 34 Fb 18.37N 5.00 E

Index Symbols

[1] Independent Nation
[2] State, Region
[3] District, County
[4] Municipality
[5] Colony, Dependency
Continent
Physical Region
Historical or Cultural Region
Mount, Mountain
Volcano
Hill
Mountains, Mountain Range
Hills, Escarpment
Plateau, Upland
Pass, Gap
Plain, Lowland
Delta
Salt Flat
Valley, Canyon
Crater, Cave
Karst Features
Depression
Polder
Desert, Dunes
Forest, Woods
Heath, Steppe
Oasis
Cape, Point
Coast, Beach
Cliff
Peninsula
Isthmus
Sandbank
Island
Atoll
Rock, Reef
Islands, Archipelago
Rocks, Reefs
Coral Reef
Well, Spring
Geyser
River, Stream
Waterfall Rapids
River Mouth, Estuary
Lake
Salt Lake
Intermittent Lake
Reservoir
Swamp, Pond
Canal
Glacier
Ice Shelf, Pack Ice
Ocean
Sea
Gulf, Bay
Strait, Fjord
Lagoon
Bank
Seamount
Tablemount
Ridge
Shelf
Basin
Escarpment, Sea Scarp
Fracture
Trench, Abyss
National Park, Reserve
Point of Interest
Recreation Site
Cave, Cavern
Historic Site
Ruins
Wall, Walls
Church, Abbey
Temple
Scientific Station
Airport
Port
Lighthouse
Mine
Tunnel
Dam, Bridge

Jadar [Yugo.] 15 Ce 44.38N 19.16 E
Jaddi, Rās- 25 Cc 25.14N 63.31 E
Jade 10 Ec 53.25N 8.05 E
Jadebusen 10 Ec 53.30N 8.10 E
Jadīd Ra's al Fīl 35 Dc 12.40N 25.43 E
Jadito Wash 46 Ji 35.22N 110.50W
J.A.D. Jensens Nunatakker 41 Hf 62.45N 48.20W
Jädraås 8 Gd 60.51N 16.28 E
Jadransko More=Adriatic Sea (EN) 5 Hg 43.00N 16.00 E
Jadrin 7 Li 55.57N 46.11 E
Jādū 33 Bc 31.57N 12.01 E
Ja'ēl 35 Ic 10.56N 51.09 E
Jaén [3] 13 If 38.00N 3.30W
Jaén 13 Ig 37.46N 3.47W
Jæren 8 Af 58.45N 5.45 E
Jærens rev 8 Af 58.45N 5.29 E
Jaffa, Cape- 59 Hg 36.58S 139.40 E
Jaffna 22 Ji 9.40N 80.00 E
Jafr, Qā' al- 24 Gg 30.17N 36.20 E
Jägala Jõgi 8 Ke 59.28N 25.04 E
Jagdalpur 22 Kh 19.04N 82.02 E
Jagdaqi 27 La 50.26N 124.02 E
Jaghbūb, Wāḥāt al-=Jarabub Oasis (EN) 30 Jf 29.41N 24.43 E
Jagotin 16 Gd 50.17N 31.47 E
Jagst 10 Fg 49.14N 9.11 E
Jaguapitã 55 Gf 23.07S 51.33W
Jaguaquara 54 Kf 13.32S 39.58W
Jaguarão 56 Jd 32.34S 53.23W
Jaguarão, Río- 55 Fk 32.39S 53.12W
Jaguarari 54 Jf 10.16S 40.12W
Jaguari 55 Ei 29.30S 54.41W
Jaguari, Rio- [Braz.] 55 Ei 29.42S 55.07W
Jaguari, Rio- [Braz.] 55 If 22.41S 47.17W
Jaguariaíva 56 Kb 24.15S 49.42W
Jaguaribe 54 Ke 5.53S 38.37W
Jaguaribe, Rio 52 Mf 4.25S 37.45W
Jaguaruana 54 Kd 4.50S 37.47W
Jagüey Grande 49 Gb 22.32N 81.08W
Jahadyjaha 17 Pc 67.03N 72.01 E
Jahām, 'Irq- 24 Li 26.12N 47.00 E
Jahorina 14 Mg 43.42N 18.35 E
Jahrom 23 Hd 28.31N 53.33 E
Jahroma 7 Ih 56.20N 37.29 E
Jaice 23 Ff 44.21N 17.17 E
Jaicoa, Cordillera- 51a Ab 18.25N 67.05W
Jaicós 54 Je 7.21S 41.08W
Jailolo 26 If 1.05N 127.30 E
Jailolo, Selat- 26 If 0.05N 129.05 E
Jaina, Isla de- 48 Ng 20.14N 90.40W
Jainca 27 Hd 35.57N 102.00 E
Jaipur 22 Jg 26.55N 75.49 E
Jaisalmer 25 Ec 26.55N 70.54 E
Jaja 20 De 56.12N 86.26 E
Jājarm 24 Qd 36.58N 56.27 E
Jajdúdorog 10 Ri 47.49N 21.30 E
Jajere 34 Hc 11.59N 11.26 E
Jajpan 18 Hd 40.23N 70.50 E
Jajsan 16 Td 50.51N 56.14 E
Jajva 19 Fd 59.20N 57.16 E
Jajva 17 Hg 59.16N 56.42 E
Jakarta 22 Mj 6.10S 106.46 E
Jakobshavn/Ilulissat 67 Nc 69.20N 50.50W
Jakobstad/Pietarsaari 7 Fe 63.40N 22.42 E
Jakoruda 15 Gg 42.02N 23.40 E
Jakupica 15 Eh 41.43N 21.26 E
Jakutsk 22 Oc 62.13N 129.49 E
Jakutskaja ASSR [3] 20 Hc 67.00N 130.00 E
Jal 45 Ej 32.07N 103.12W
Jalaid Qi (Inder) 27 Lb 46.41N 122.52 E
Jalājil 24 Kj 25.41N 45.28 E
Jalālābād 23 Lc 34.26N 70.28 E
Jalālah al Baḥrīyah, Jabal al- 24 Eh 29.20N 32.20 E
Jalālah al Qiblīyah, Jabal al- 24 Eh 28.42N 32.22 E
Jalán, Río- 49 Df 15.43N 86.34W
Jalapa [3] 49 Cf 14.35N 89.55W
Jalapa [Guat.] 47 Gf 14.38N 89.59W
Jalapa [Mex.] 48 Mi 17.43N 92.49W
Jalapa [Nic.] 47 Gf 13.55N 86.08W
Jalapa Enriquez 39 Jh 19.32N 96.55W
Jalasjarvi 7 Fe 62.30N 22.45 E
Jales 55 Ge 20.16S 50.33W
Jālgaon 25 Fd 21.01N 75.34 E
Jalhay 12 Hd 50.34N 5.58 E
Jalībah 24 Lg 30.35N 46.32 E
Jalib Shahab 24 Lg 30.23N 46.09 E
Jalingo 34 Hd 8.53N 11.22 E
Jalisco [2] 47 Dd 20.20N 103.40W
Jāliṭah=La Galite (EN) 30 He 37.32N 8.56 E
Jāliṭah, Canal de- 14 Cm 37.20N 9.00 E
Jallas 13 Cb 42.54N 9.08W
Jālna 25 Fe 19.50N 75.53 E
Jalón 13 Kc 41.47N 1.04W
Jalostotitlán 48 Hg 21.12N 102.28W
Jalpa 48 Hg 21.38N 102.58W
Jalpaiguri 25 Hc 26.31N 88.44 E
Jalpan 48 Jg 21.14N 99.29W
Jalpug, Ozero- 16 Fg 45.25N 28.40 E
Jalta 19 Dg 44.30N 34.10 E
Jaltepec, Río- 48 Li 17.26N 94.59W
Jālū 33 Dd 28.30N 21.05 E
Jālū, Wāḥāt-=Gialo Oasis (EN) 30 Jf 29.00N 21.20 E
Jaluit Atoll 57 Hd 6.00N 169.35 E
Jalūlā' 24 Ke 34.16N 45.10 E
Jalutorovsk 19 Gd 56.40N 66.18 E
Jam [Iran] 24 Pe 35.45N 55.02 E
Jam [Iran] 24 Oi 27.50N 52.22 E
Jama/Jaama 8 Lf 58.59N 27.45 E
Jamaari 30 Ig 12.06N 10.14 E
Jamaica 49 Jc 20.12N 75.09W
Jamaica 38 Lh 18.15N 77.30W
Jamaica [1] 39 Lh 18.15N 77.30W
Jamaica Channel 47 Ie 18.00N 75.30W
Jamaica Channel (EN)=Jamaïque, Canal de- 49 Jd 18.00N 75.30W
Jamaïque, Canal de-=Jamaica Channel (EN) 49 Jd 18.00N 75.30W
Jamal, Poluostrov-=Yamal Peninsula (EN) 21 Ib 70.00N 70.00 E
Jamalo-Nenecki Nacionalny okrug [3] 20 Cc 67.00N 75.00 E
Jamālpur 25 Hd 24.55N 89.56 E
Jamāme 31 Lh 0.04N 42.46 E
Jamantau, Gora- 5 Le 54.15N 58.06 E
Jamanxim, Rio- 52 Kf 4.43S 56.18W
Jamari, Rio- 54 Fe 8.27S 63.30W
Jamarovka 20 Gf 50.38N 110.16 E
Jambi 22 Oj 1.38S 123.42 E
Jambi [3] 26 Dg 1.36S 103.37 E
Jambol [2] 15 Jg 42.15N 26.35 E
Jambol 15 Jg 42.29N 26.30 E
Jambongan, Pulau- 26 Ge 6.41N 117.25 E
Jambuair, Tanjung- 26 Ce 5.16N 97.30 E
Jambusar 25 Ed 22.03N 72.48 E
James Bay 38 Kd 51.00N 80.30W
Jameson Land 41 Jd 70.45N 23.45W
James River [U.S.] 38 Je 42.52N 97.18W
James River [U.S.] 44 Ig 36.56N 76.27W
James Ross 66 Re 64.15S 57.45W
James Ross Strait 42 Hc 69.50N 96.30W
Jamestown [Austl.] 59 Hf 33.12S 138.36 E
Jamestown [N.D.-U.S.] 43 Hb 46.54N 98.42W
Jamestown [N.Y.-U.S.] 43 Lc 42.05N 79.15W
Jamestown [St.Hel.] 31 Gj 15.56S 5.43W
Jamestown Reservoir 45 Gc 47.15N 98.40W
Jamm 8 Mf 58.24N 28.15 E
Jammer Bugt 7 Bh 57.20N 9.30 E
Jammu 22 Jf 32.44N 74.52 E
Jammu and Kashmir [3] 25 Fb 34.00N 76.00 E
Jāmnagar 22 Jg 22.28N 70.04 E
Jamno, Jezioro- 10 Mb 54.15N 16.10 E
Jampol 16 Fe 48.16N 28.17 E
Jämsä 7 Ff 61.52N 25.12 E
Jamsah 24 Ei 27.38N 33.35 E
Jämsänkoski 8 Kc 61.55N 25.11 E
Jamshedpur 22 Kg 22.48N 86.11 E
Jamsk 20 Ke 59.37N 154.10 E
Jämtland [2] 7 De 63.00N 14.40 E
Jämtland 8 Fa 63.25N 14.05 E
Janā 24 Mi 27.22N 49.54 E
Jana 21 Pb 71.31N 136.32 E
Janakpur 25 Hc 26.42N 85.55 E
Janaucu, Ilha- 54 Hc 0.30N 50.10W
Janaul 17 Gh 56.16N 54.59 E
Janda, Laguna de la- 13 Gh 36.15N 5.51W
Jandaia 55 Gc 17.06S 50.07W
Jandaq 24 Pe 34.02N 54.26 E
Jandiatuba, Rio- 54 Ed 3.28S 68.42W
Jandowae 59 Ke 26.47S 151.06 E
Jandula 13 Hf 38.03N 4.06W
Jane Peak 62 Cf 45.20S 168.19 E
Janesville 43 Jc 42.41N 89.01W
Jangada 55 Db 15.14S 56.29W
Jangada, Rio- 55 Db 15.12S 56.24W
Jangao Shan 27 Gf 25.31N 98.08 E
Jange 27 Ie 31.59N 105.28 E
Jangijer 18 Gd 40.18N 68.50 E
Jangijul 19 Gg 41.07N 69.03 E
Jangirabad 18 Ed 40.03N 65.59 E
Jango 55 Ee 20.27S 55.29W
Jangxi Sheng (Chiang-hsi Sheng)=Kiangsi (EN) [2] 27 Kf 28.00N 116.00 E
Jangy-Bazar 18 Hd 41.40N 70.52 E
Janikowo 10 Od 52.45N 18.07 E
Janīn 24 Ff 32.28N 35.18 E
Janisjarvi, Ozero- 7 He 62.00N 31.00 E
Janja 14 Nf 44.40N 19.19 E
Jan Mayen 5 Fa 71.00N 8.30W
Jan Mayen Ridge (EN) 5 Fb 69.00N 8.00W
Jano-Indigirskaja Nizmennost 20 Ib 71.00N 139.30 E
Janos 47 Cb 30.56N 108.08W
Jánoshalma 10 Pj 46.18N 19.20 E
Jánosháza 10 Ni 47.07N 17.10 E
Janów Lubelski 10 Sf 50.43N 22.24 E
Janów Podlaski 10 Td 52.11N 23.11 E
Jansenville 37 Cf 32.56S 24.40 E
Jansha Jang 21 Mg 28.46N 104.38 E
Janski Zaliv 21 Pb 72.00N 136.00 E
Jantarny 8 Hj 54.53N 19.55 E
Jantra 15 If 43.38N 25.34 E
Januária 54 Jg 15.29S 44.22W
Janūbīyah, Aş Şaḥrā' al-=Southern Desert (EN) 30 Jf 24.00N 30.00 E
Janykurgan 19 Gg 43.55N 67.14 E
Janzhang Ansha 27 Ke 9.30N 116.59 E
Japan (EN) 21 Pf 35.00N 135.00 E
Japan (EN)=Nippon [1] 22 Pf 38.00N 137.00 E
Japan, Sea of- (EN)=Japonskoje More 21 Pf 40.00N 134.00 E
Japan, Sea of- (EN)=Nippon Kai 21 Pf 40.00N 134.00 E
Japan, Sea of- (EN)=Tong-Hae 21 Pf 40.00N 134.00 E
Japan Basin (EN) 27 Nc 40.00N 135.00 E
Japan Trench (EN) 3 If 37.00N 143.00 E
Japiim 54 De 7.37S 72.54W
Japonskoje More=Japan, Sea of- (EN) 21 Pf 40.00N 134.00 E
Jäppilä 8 Lb 62.23N 27.26 E
Japtiksale 17 Pb 69.25N 72.29 E
Japurá 54 Ed 1.24S 69.25W
Japurá, Rio- 52 Jf 3.08S 64.46W
Jaqué 49 Hj 7.31N 78.10W
Jaquet, Point- 51g Ba 15.38N 61.26W
Jaquirana 55 Gi 28.54S 50.23W
Jar 7 Mg 58.17N 52.06 E
Jarabub Oasis (EN)=Jaghbūb, Wāḥāt al- 30 Jf 29.41N 24.43 E
Jarābulus 24 Hd 36.49N 38.01 E
Jaraguá [Braz.] 55 Hb 15.45S 49.20W
Jaraguá [Braz.] 55 Hh 26.29S 49.04W
Jaraguá, Serra do- 55 Hh 26.40S 49.15W
Jaraguari 55 Ee 20.09S 54.25W
Jaraiz de la Vera 13 Gd 40.04N 5.45W
Jarama 13 Id 40.02N 3.39W
Jaramillo 56 Gg 47.11S 67.09W
Jarandilla 13 Gd 40.08N 5.39W
Jaransk 19 Ed 57.18N 47.55 E
Jarānwāla 25 Eb 31.20N 73.26 E
Jarash 24 Ff 32.17N 35.54 E
Jarau, Cêrro do- 55 Dj 30.18S 56.32W
Jarbah 30 Ie 33.48N 10.54 E
Järbo 7 Df 60.43N 16.36 E
Jarcevo [R.S.F.S.R.] 16 Hb 55.05N 32.45 E
Jarcevo [R.S.F.S.R.] 20 Ed 60.15N 90.10 E
Jardāwīyah 24 Jj 25.24N 42.42 E
Jardim 54 Gh 21.28S 56.09W
Jardine River 59 Ib 11.10S 142.30 E
Jardines de la Reina, Archipiélago de los- 47 Id 20.50N 78.55W
Jardinópolis 55 Ie 21.02S 47.46W
Jarega 17 Fe 63.27N 53.31 E
Jaremča 16 De 48.31N 24.33 E
Jarenga 7 Le 62.08N 49.03 E
Jarez de Garcías Salinas 47 Dd 22.39N 103.00W
Järfälla 8 Ge 59.24N 17.50 E
Jargava 15 Lc 46.27N 28.27 E
Jari, Rio- 52 Kf 1.09S 51.54W
Jarīd, Shaṭṭ al- 30 He 33.42N 8.26 E
Jarīr, Wādī- 24 Jj 25.38N 42.30 E
Jarjīs 32 Jc 33.30N 11.07 E
Jarkovo 17 Mh 57.26N 67.05 E
Jarmah 33 Bd 26.32N 13.04 E
Järna 8 Ge 59.06N 17.34 E
Jarnac 11 Fi 45.41N 0.10W
Järnlunden 8 Ff 58.10N 15.40 E
Jarny 11 Le 49.09N 5.53 E
Jarocin 10 Ne 51.59N 17.31 E
Jaroměř 10 Lf 50.21N 15.55 E
Jaroměřice nad Rokytnou 10 Lg 49.06N 15.54 E
Jaroslavl 6 Jd 57.37N 39.52 E
Jaroslavskaja Oblast [3] 19 Dd 57.45N 39.15 E
Jaroslavski 28 Lb 44.10N 132.13 E
Jarosław 10 Sf 50.02N 22.42 E
Järpen 8 Ea 63.21N 13.29 E
Jarrāḥī 24 Mg 30.44N 48.46 E
Jarroto, Ozero- 17 Oc 67.55N 71.40 E
Jar-Sale 20 Cc 66.50N 70.50 E
Jartai 27 Id 39.45N 105.46 E
Jartai Yanchi 27 Id 39.45N 105.40 E
Jarudej 17 Od 65.50N 71.50 E
Jarud Qi (Lubei) 27 Lc 44.30N 120.55 E
Järva-Jaani/Jarva-Jani 8 Ke 59.00N 25.49 E
Jarva-Jani/Järva-Jaani 8 Ke 59.00N 25.49 E
Jarvakanbdi/Järvakandi 8 Kf 58.45N 24.44 E
Järvakandi/Jarvakanbdi 8 Kf 58.45N 24.44 E
Järvenpää 7 Ff 60.28N 25.06 E
Jarvis Island 57 Ke 0.23S 160.01W
Järvsö 7 Df 61.43N 16.10 E
Jaščera 8 Ne 59.05N 30.00 E
Jaselda 16 Ec 52.07N 26.29 E
Jasień 10 Le 51.46N 15.01 E
Jasikan 34 Fd 7.24N 0.28 E
Jasinja 10 Uh 48.14N 24.31 E
Jasinovataja 16 Je 48.05N 37.57 E
Jasiołka 10 Rg 49.47N 21.30 E
Jasīra 35 He 1.57N 45.16 E
Jasīred Mayd 35 Hc 11.12N 47.13 E
Jāsk 23 Id 25.38N 57.46 E
Jaškul 16 Nf 46.17N 45.10 E
Jaškul 16 Nf 46.11N 45.17 E
Jasło 10 Rg 49.45N 21.29 E
Jasmund 10 Jb 54.32N 13.35 E
Jasnogorsk 16 Jb 54.29N 37.42 E
Jasny [R.S.F.S.R.] 19 Fe 51.01N 59.59 E
Jasny [R.S.F.S.R.] 20 Hf 53.18N 128.03 E
Jason Islands 56 Hh 51.00S 61.00W
Jasper [Alta.-Can.] 39 Hd 52.53N 118.05W
Jasper [Al.-U.S.] 43 Je 33.50N 87.17W
Jasper [Fl.-U.S.] 44 Fj 30.31N 82.57W
Jasper [In.-U.S.] 44 Df 38.24N 86.56W
Jasper [Tn.-U.S.] 44 Eh 35.04N 85.38W
Jasper [Tx.-U.S.] 45 Jk 30.55N 93.59W
Jasper Seamount (EN) 38 Gf 30.32N 122.42W
Jaşşān 24 Kf 32.58N 45.53 E
Jastrebarsko 14 Je 45.40N 15.39 E
Jastrowie 10 Mc 53.26N 16.49 E
Jastrzebie Zdrój 10 Og 49.58N 18.34 E
Jászapáti 10 Qi 47.31N 20.09 E
Jászárokszállás 10 Pi 47.38N 19.59 E
Jászberény 10 Pi 47.30N 19.55 E
Jászság 10 Pi 47.25N 20.00 E
Jat, Uad el- 30 Ff 26.47N 13.03W
Jataí 53 Kg 17.53S 51.43W
Jatapu, Rio- 54 Gd 2.30S 58.17W
Játiva/Xàtiva 13 Lf 38.59N 0.31W
Jatobá, Rio- 55 Ea 12.23S 54.07W
Jaú 56 Kb 22.18S 48.33W
Jaú, Rio- 54 Fd 1.55S 61.25W
Jaua, Cerro- 54 Fc 4.48N 64.26W
Jauaperi, Rio- 52 Jf 1.26S 61.35W
Jauja 54 Cf 11.48S 75.30W
Jaumave 48 Jf 23.25N 99.23W
Jaunanna 8 Lg 57.13N 27.10 E
Jaunelgava/Jaunjelgava 7 Fh 56.37N 25.06 E
Jaunfeld 14 Id 46.35N 14.45 E
Jaungulbene 8 Lh 57.00N 26.42 E
Jaunjelgava/Jaunelgava 7 Fh 56.37N 25.06 E
Jaunpiebalga 8 Lg 57.05N 26.03 E
Jaunpur 25 Gc 25.44N 82.41 E
Jauru 55 Ed 18.35S 54.17W
Jauru, Rio- [Braz.] 54 Hg 18.40S 54.36W
Jauru, Rio- [Braz.] 55 Dc 16.22S 57.46W
Java (EN)=Jawa 21 Mj 7.20S 110.00 E
Javalambre 13 Ld 40.06N 1.00W
Javalambre, Sierra de- 13 Ld 40.05N 1.00W
Javan 18 Ge 38.19N 69.01 E
Javānrūd 24 Le 34.48N 46.30 E
Javari, Rio- 52 If 4.21S 70.02W
Java Sea (EN)=Jawa, Laut- 21 Mj 5.00S 110.00 E
Java Trench (EN) 3 Hk 10.30S 110.00 E
Jávea 13 Mf 38.47N 0.10 E
Javier 13 Kb 42.36N 1.13W
Javor 14 Mf 44.07N 18.59 E
Javorie 10 Ph 48.27N 19.18 E
Javornik 10 Jh 48.10N 13.35 E
Javorníky 10 Og 49.20N 18.20 E
Javorov 16 Cd 50.00N 23.27 E
Javorová skála 10 Kg 49.31N 14.30 E
Jävre 7 Ed 65.09N 21.29 E
Jawa=Java (EN) 21 Mj 7.20S 110.00 E
Jawa, Laut-=Java Sea (EN) 21 Mj 5.00S 110.00 E
Jawa Barat [3] 26 Eh 7.00S 107.00 E
Jawa Tengah [3] 26 Eh 7.30S 110.00 E
Jawa Timur [3] 26 Fh 8.00S 113.00 E
Jawf, Wādī- 33 If 15.50N 45.30 E
Jawor 10 Me 51.03N 16.11 E
Jaworzno 10 Pf 50.13N 19.15 E
Jaya, Puncak- 57 Ee 4.10S 137.00 E
Jayapura 58 Fe 2.32S 140.42 E
Jayawijaya, Pegunungan- 26 Kg 4.30S 139.30 E
Jāyezān 24 Mg 30.50N 49.52 E
Jazāyer va Banāder-e Khalīj-e Fārs va Daryā-ye 'Omān [3] 23 Id 27.30N 56.00 E
Jaz Mūriān, Hāmūn-e- 23 Id 27.20N 58.55 E
Jazva 17 Hf 60.23N 56.50 E
Jazvān 24 Md 36.58N 48.40 E
Jazykovo 7 Li 54.20N 47.22 E
Jazzīn 24 Ff 33.32N 35.34 E
Jdiouia 13 Mi 35.56N 0.50 E
Jeannetty, Ostrov- 20 Ka 76.45N 158.25 E
Jean-Rabel 49 Kd 19.52N 73.11W
Jebala 13 Gi 35.25N 5.30W
Jebal Bārez, Kūh-e- 23 Id 28.30N 58.20 E
Jebba 34 Fd 9.08N 4.50 E
Jebel 15 Ed 45.33N 21.14 E
Jebha 13 Hi 35.13N 4.40W
Jedincy 16 Ee 48.06N 27.19 E
Jedisa 16 Nh 42.32N 44.14 E
Jędrzejów 10 Qf 50.39N 20.18 E
Jeetze 10 Hc 53.09N 11.04 E
Jefferson 45 Ie 42.01N 94.23W
Jefferson, Mount- [Nv.-U.S.] 43 Dd 38.46N 116.55W
Jefferson, Mount- [Or.-U.S.] 46 Ed 44.40N 121.47W
Jefferson City 39 Jf 38.34N 92.10W
Jefferson River 46 Jd 45.56N 111.30W
Jeffersonville 44 Ef 38.17N 85.44W
Jef-Jef el Kebir 35 Ca 20.30N 21.25 E
Jefremov 19 De 53.11N 38.07 E
Jega 34 Fc 12.13N 4.23 E
Jegersfontein 37 De 29.44S 25.29 E
Jegorjevsk 7 Ji 55.25N 39.07 E
Jegorlyk 16 Lf 46.32N 41.52 E
Jegorlykskaja 16 Lf 46.34N 40.44 E
Jehegnadzor 16 Nj 39.47N 45.18 E
Jeja 16 Kf 46.39N 38.36 E
Jejsk 19 Df 46.40N 38.15 E
Jejuí Guazú, Río- 55 Dg 24.13S 57.09W
Jēkabpils/Jekabpils 19 Cd 56.30N 25.59 E
Jekabpils/Jēkabpils 19 Cd 56.30N 25.59 E
Jekaterinovka 16 Nc 52.04N 44.30 E
Jekkevarre 7 Eb 69.28N 20.00 E
Jelabuga 19 Fd 55.48N 52.05 E
Jelai 26 Fg 2.59S 110.45 E
Jelan 16 Md 50.57N 43.43 E
Jelancy 20 Ff 52.44N 106.27 E
Jelanec 16 Gf 47.42N 31.50 E
Jelcz 10 Ne 51.01N 17.18 E
Jelec 6 Je 52.37N 38.30 E
Jeleckj 17 Lc 67.03N 64.15 E
Jelenia Góra 10 Lf 50.55N 15.46 E
Jelenia Góra [2] 10 Lf 50.55N 15.45 E
Jelgava 19 Cd 56.39N 23.41 E
Jelica 15 Df 43.47N 20.20 E
Jelin vrh 15 Cf 43.02N 19.27 E
Jelizavety, Mys- 5 Qd 54.30N 142.40 E
Jelizovo [Bye.-U.S.S.R.] 16 Fc 53.24N 29.00 E
Jelizovo [R.S.F.S.R.] 20 Kf 53.06N 158.20 E
Jelling 8 Ci 55.45N 9.26 E
Jelnja 16 Hb 54.35N 33.12 E
Jeloguj 20 Dd 63.10N 87.45 E
Jelow Gīr 24 Lf 32.58N 47.48 E
Jeløy 8 De 58.30N 10.40 E
Jelsk 16 Fd 51.49N 29.13 E
Jelva 17 Ee 63.05N 50.50 E
Jemaja, Pulau- 26 Ef 2.55N 105.45 E
Jemanželinsk 19 Ge 54.45N 61.20 E
Jember 26 Fh 8.10S 113.42 E
Jemca 7 Je 63.32N 41.56 E
Jemca 7 Je 63.04N 40.18 E
Jemeppe-sur-Sambre 12 Gd 50.28N 4.40 E
Jeminay 27 Eb 47.28N 85.48 E
Jemnice 10 Lg 49.01N 15.35 E
Jena 10 Hf 50.56N 11.35 E
Jenakijevo 16 Ke 48.12N 38.18 E
Jenašimski Polkan, Gora- 20 Ee 59.50N 92.45 E
Jendyr 17 Mf 61.38N 67.20 E
Jeneponto 26 Gh 5.41S 119.42 E
Jenisej = Yenisey (EN) 21 Kb 71.50N 82.40 E
Jenisejsk 20 Ee 58.27N 92.10 E
Jenisejski Krjaž=Yenisey Ridge (EN) 21 Ld 59.00N 92.30 E
Jenisejski Zaliv=Yenisey Bay (EN) 20 Db 72.00N 81.00 E
Jennersdorf 14 Kd 46.56N 16.08 E
Jennings 45 Jk 30.13N 92.39W
Jenny Lind 42 Hc 68.50N 101.30W
Jenny Point 51g Bb 15.28N 61.15W
Jensen 46 Kf 40.22N 109.17W
Jens Munk 42 Jc 69.40N 79.40W
Jequié 53 Lg 13.51S 40.05W
Jequitaí 55 Jc 17.15S 44.28W
Jequitaí, Rio 55 Jc 17.04S 44.50W
Jequitinhonha, Rio- 52 Mg 15.51S 38.53W
Jerada 32 Gc 34.19N 2.09W
Jeralijev 19 Fg 43.12N 51.43 E
Jerbogačën 20 Fd 61.15N 107.57 E
Jérémie 47 Je 18.39N 74.08W
Jeremoabo 54 Kf 10.04S 38.21W
Jerer 35 Gd 7.40N 43.48 E
Jerevan 6 Kg 40.11N 44.30 E
Jerez, Punta- 48 Kf 22.54N 97.46W
Jerez de la Frontera 13 Fh 36.41N 6.08W
Jerez de los Caballeros 13 Ff 38.19N 6.46W
Jergeni 5 Kf 47.00N 44.00 E
Jericho 59 Jd 23.36S 146.08 E
Jermak 19 He 52.02N 76.55 E
Jermakovskoje 20 Ef 53.16N 92.24 E
Jermentau 19 He 51.38N 73.10 E
Jermolajevo 17 Gj 52.43N 55.48 E
Jeroaquara 55 Gb 15.23S 50.25W
Jerofej Pavlovič 20 Hf 53.58N 121.57 E
Jerome 46 He 42.43N 114.31W
Jersa 17 Fc 66.19N 52.32 E
Jersey 9 Kl 49.15N 2.10W
Jersey City 43 Mc 40.44N 74.04W
Jerseyville 45 Kg 39.07N 90.20W
Jeršov 19 Ee 51.20N 48.17 E
Jertarski 17 Lh 56.47N 64.25 E
Jerte 13 Fe 39.58N 6.17W
Jerusalem (EN)=Yerushalayim 22 Ff 31.46N 35.14 E
Jeruslan 16 Od 50.20N 46.25 E
Jervis Bay 59 Kg 35.05S 150.44 E
Jerzu 14 Dk 39.47N 9.31 E
Jesberg 12 Lc 51.00N 9.09 E
Jesenice [Yugo.] 14 Jf 44.14N 15.34 E
Jesenice [Yugo.] 14 Id 46.27N 14.04 E
Jesenik 10 Nf 50.14N 17.12 E
Jesi 14 Hg 43.31N 13.14 E
Jesil 19 Ge 51.58N 66.24 E
Jeskianhor, Kanal- 18 Fe 39.15N 66.00 E
Jessej 20 Fc 68.29N 102.10 E
Jessentuki 16 Mg 44.03N 42.51 E
Jessheim 7 Cf 60.09N 11.11 E
Jessore 25 Hd 23.10N 89.13 E
Ještěd 10 Kf 50.42N 14.59 E
Jestro, Wabe- 30 Lh 4.11N 42.09 E
Jesup 43 Ke 31.36N 81.53W
Jesús Carranza 48 Li 17.26N 95.02W
Jesús María 56 Hd 30.59S 64.06W
Jesús María, Boca de- 48 Ke 24.29N 97.40W
Jesús María, Río- 48 Gg 21.55N 104.30W
Jetmore 45 Gg 38.03N 99.54W
Jever 10 Dc 53.35N 7.54 E
Jevgenjevka 18 Kc 43.27N 77.40 E
Jevišovka 10 Mh 48.52N 16.36 E
Jevlah 19 Eg 40.35N 47.10 E
Jevnaker 7 Cf 60.15N 10.28 E
Jevpatorija 19 Df 45.12N 33.18 E
Jevrejskaja Avtonomnaja Oblast [3] 20 Ig 48.30N 132.00 E
Jeyḥūn 24 Pi 27.16N 55.12 E
Jeypore 25 He 18.51N 82.35 E
Jezercës 5 Hg 42.26N 19.49 E
Jezero 14 Lf 44.21N 17.10 E
Jeziorak, Jezioro- 10 Pc 53.50N 19.35 E
Jeziorany 10 Qc 53.58N 20.46 E
Jeziorka 10 Rd 52.10N 21.06 E
Jhang Sadar 25 Eb 31.16N 72.19 E
Jhānsi 22 Jg 25.26N 78.35 E
Jhelum 25 Eb 32.56N 73.44 E
Jhelum 21 Jf 31.12N 72.08 E
Jiaji → Qionghai 27 Jh 19.25N 110.28 E
Jialing Jiang 21 Mg 29.34N 106.35 E
Jiamusi 22 Pe 46.49N 130.21 E
Ji'an [China] 27 Mc 41.08N 126.10 E
Ji'an [China] 22 Ng 27.12N 114.59 E
Jianchang 28 Ed 40.49N 119.46 E
Jianchuan 27 Gf 26.32N 99.53 E
Jiande (Baisha) 27 Kf 29.31N 119.17 E
Jiang'an 27 If 28.40N 105.07 E
Jiangao Shan 27 Gf 25.31N 98.08 E
Jiangbiancun 27 Kf 27.13N 115.57 E
Jiangcheng 27 Hg 22.37N 101.48 E
Jiangdu (Xiannümiao) 28 Eh 32.30N 119.33 E
Jianghua (Shuikou) 27 Jg 24.58N 111.56 E
Jiangjin 27 If 29.15N 106.18 E
Jiangle 27 Kf 26.48N 117.29 E
Jiangling (Jingzhou) 27 Je 30.21N 112.10 E
Jiangmen 27 Jg 22.35N 113.02 E
Jiangpu 28 Eh 32.03N 118.37 E
Jiangshan 28 Ej 28.45N 118.37 E
Jiangsu Sheng (Chiang-su Sheng)=Kiangsu (EN) [2] 27 Ke 33.00N 120.00 E
Jiangyou (Zhongba) 27 He 31.48N 104.39 E
Jianhu 28 Eh 33.28N 119.47 E
Jianli 27 Jf 29.50N 112.55 E
Jian'ou 27 Kf 27.08N 118.20 E
Jianping (Yebaishou) 27 Kc 41.55N 119.37 E
Jianshi 27 Ie 30.32N 109.43 E
Jianshui 27 Hg 23.39N 102.46 E
Jianyang 27 Kf 27.23N 118.03 E
Jiaocheng 27 Jd 37.32N 112.09 E
Jiaoding Shan 27 Lc 41.11N 120.01 E
Jiaohe [China] 27 Mc 43.43N 127.20 E
Jiaohe [China] 28 De 38.01N 116.17 E
Jiaolai He [China] 28 Ef 37.07N 119.35 E
Jiaolai He [China] 28 Fc 43.02N 120.48 E
Jiaoliu He 28 Gb 45.21N 122.48 E
Jiaonan (Wanggezhuang) 28 Eg 35.53N 119.58 E

Index Symbols

- [1] Independent Nation
- [2] State, Region
- [3] District, County
- Municipality
- Colony, Dependency
- Continent
- Physical Region
- Historical or Cultural Region
- Mount, Mountain
- Volcano
- Hill
- Mountains, Mountain Range
- Hills, Escarpment
- Plateau, Upland
- Pass, Gap
- Plain, Lowland
- Delta
- Salt Flat
- Valley, Canyon
- Crater, Cave
- Karst Features
- Depression
- Polder
- Desert, Dunes
- Forest, Woods
- Heath, Steppe
- Oasis
- Cape, Point
- Coast, Beach
- Cliff
- Peninsula
- Isthmus
- Sandbank
- Island
- Atoll
- Rock, Reef
- Islands, Archipelago
- Rocks, Reefs
- Coral Reef
- Well, Spring
- Geyser
- River, Stream
- Waterfall Rapids
- River Mouth, Estuary
- Lake
- Salt Lake
- Intermittent Lake
- Reservoir
- Swamp, Pond
- Canal
- Glacier
- Ice Shelf, Pack Ice
- Ocean
- Sea
- Gulf, Bay
- Strait, Fjord
- Lagoon
- Bank
- Seamount
- Tablemount
- Ridge
- Shelf
- Basin
- Escarpment, Sea Scarp
- Fracture
- Trench, Abyss
- National Park, Reserve
- Point of Interest
- Recreation Site
- Cave, Cavern
- Historic Site
- Ruins
- Wall, Walls
- Church, Abbey
- Temple
- Scientific Station
- Airport
- Port
- Lighthouse
- Mine
- Tunnel
- Dam, Bridge

Jiaoxian 27 Kd 36.20N 120.00 E
Jiaozhou-Wan 28 Ff 36.10N 120.15 E
Jiaozuo 22 Nf 35.15N 113.18 E
Jiashan 28 Fi 30.51N 120.54 E
Jiashan (Mingguang) 28 Dh 32.47N 118.00 E
Jiashi/Payzawat 27 Cd 39.29N 76.39 E
Jiawang 28 Dg 34.27N 117.26 E
Jiaxian 28 Bh 33.58N 113.13 E
Jiaxing 27 Le 30.44N 120.46 E
Jiayin (Chaoyang) 27 Nb 48.52N 130.21 E
Jiayu 27 Jf 30.00N 113.57 E
Jiayuguan 27 Gd 39.49N 98.18 E
Jibalei 35 Ic 10.07N 50.47 E
Jibão, Serra do- 55 Jb 14.48S 45.15W
Jibiya 34 Gc 13.06N 7.14 E
Jibou 15 Gb 47.16N 23.15 E
Jicarón, Isla- 49 Gj 7.16N 81.47W
Jičín 10 Lf 50.26N 15.22 E
Jiddah 22 Fg 21.29N 39.12 E
Jiddat al Ḩarāsīs 23 Ie 20.05N 56.00 E
Jiehu → Yinan 28 Eg 35.33N 118.27 E
Jieshou 28 Ch 33.17N 115.22 E
Jiesjavrre 7 Fb 69.40N 24.12 E
Jiexiu 27 Jd 37.00N 112.00 E
Jieyang 27 Kg 23.32N 116.25 E
Jieznas/Eznas 8 Kj 54.34N 24.17 E
Jifn, Wādī al- 24 Jj 25.48N 42.15 E
Jiftūn, Jazā'ir- 24 Ei 27.13N 33.56 E
Jigley 35 He 4.25N 45.22 E
Jiguaní 49 Ic 20.22N 76.26W
Jigüey, Bahía de- 49 Hb 22.08N 78.05W
Jigzhi 27 He 33.28N 101.29 E
Jihlava 10 Mh 48.55N 16.37 E
Jihlava 10 Lg 49.24N 15.34 E
Jihlavské vrchy 10 Lg 49.15N 15.20 E
Jihočeský kraj [3] 10 Kg 49.05N 14.30 E
Jihomoravský kraj [3] 10 Mg 49.10N 16.40 E
Jijel 32 Ib 36.48N 5.46 E
Jijel [3] 32 Ib 36.45N 5.45 E
Jijia 15 Lc 46.54N 28.05 E
Jijiga 35 Gd 9.21N 42.48 E
Jijona 13 Lf 38.32N 0.30W
Jikharrah 33 Dd 29.17N 21.38 E
Jilava 15 Je 44.20N 26.05 E
Jilf al Kabīr, Haḑabat al- 33 Ee 23.30N 26.00 E
Jilib 31 Lh 0.29N 42.47 E
Jilin 27 Mc 43.51N 126.33 E
Jilin Sheng (Chi-lin Sheng) =Kirin (EN) [2] 27 Mc 43.00N 126.00 E
Jiliu He 27 La 52.02N 120.41 E
Jiloca 13 Kc 41.21N 1.39W
Jima=Jimma (EN) 31 Kh 7.39N 36.49 E
Jimāl, Wādī- 24 Fj 24.40N 35.06 E
Jimani 49 Ld 18.28N 71.51W
Jimbe 36 De 11.05S 24.00 E
Jimbolia 15 Dd 45.48N 20.43 E
Jimena 13 Ig 37.50N 3.28W
Jimena de la Frontera 13 Gh 36.26N 5.27W
Jiménez 47 Dc 27.08N 104.55W
Jiménez del Teul 48 Gf 23.10N 104.05W
Jimma (EN)=Jima 31 Kh 7.39N 36.49 E
Jimo 28 Ff 36.24N 120.27 E
Jimsar 27 Ec 43.59N 89.04 E
Jimulco 48 He 25.20N 103.10W
Jināh 24 Dj 25.20N 30.31 E
Jinan=Tsinan (EN) 22 Nf 36.35N 117.00 E
Jincheng [China] 27 Jd 35.32N 112.53 E
Jincheng [China] 28 Fd 41.12N 121.25 E
Jinchuan /Quqên 27 He 31.02N 102.02 E
Jind 25 Fc 29.19N 76.19 E
Jindřichův Hradec 10 Kg 49.09N 15.00 E
Jinfo Shan 27 If 29.01N 107.14 E
Jing/Jinghe 27 Dc 44.39N 82.50 E
Jing'an 28 Cj 28.51N 115.21 E
Jingbian (Zhangjiapan) 27 Id 37.32N 108.45 E
Jingde 28 Ei 30.18N 118.30 E
Jingdezhen 22 Ng 29.18N 117.18 E
Jingfeng → Hexigten Qi 27 Kc 43.15N 117.31 E
Jinggang Shan 27 Jf 26.42N 114.07 E
Jinggu 27 Hg 23.28N 100.39 E
Jinghai 28 De 38.57N 116.56 E
Jinghe/Jing 27 Dc 44.39N 82.50 E
Jinghong (Yunjinghong) 27 Hg 21.59N 100.48 E
Jinghong Dao 27 Je 9.45N 114.28 E
Jingjiang 28 Fh 32.01N 120.15 E
Jingle 28 Ae 38.22N 111.56 E
Jingmen 27 Je 31.00N 112.11 E
Jingning 27 Id 35.30N 105.45 E
Jingping → Pinglu 28 Be 39.32N 112.14 E
Jingpo Hu 28 Jc 43.50N 128.53 E
Jingshan 28 Bi 31.04N 113.08 E
Jingtai 27 Hd 37.10N 104.08 E
Jingxian [China] 27 If 26.40N 109.37 E
Jingxian [China] 27 Ke 30.41N 118.29 E
Jingxing (Weishui) 28 Ce 38.03N 114.09 E
Jingyu 28 Ic 42.25N 126.48 E
Jingyuan 27 Hd 36.35N 104.40 E
Jingzhi 28 Ef 36.18N 119.22 E
Jingzhou → Jiangling 27 Je 30.21N 112.10 E
Jinhu (Licheng) 28 Eh 33.01N 119.01 E
Jinhua 27 Kf 29.09N 119.38 E
Jining [China] 22 Nf 37.26N 116.36 E
Jining [China] 22 Ne 41.02N 113.07 E
Jinja 31 Kh 0.26N 33.13 E
Jin Jiang 28 Cj 28.23N 115.48 E
Jinkou 28 Ci 30.20N 114.07 E
Jinotega [3] 49 Eg 14.00N 85.25W
Jinotega 47 Gf 13.06N 86.00W
Jinotepe 47 Gf 11.51N 86.12W
Jinping 27 Hg 22.45N 103.15 E
Jinsha 27 If 27.18N 106.16 E
Jinsha → Nantong 28 Fh 32.06N 120.52 E
Jinshan 28 Fi 30.54N 121.09 E
Jinshan → Harqin Qi 28 Ed 41.57N 118.40 E
Jinshi 28 Aj 29.03N 111.52 E
Jinta 27 Gc 40.00N 99.00 E
Jintan 28 Ei 31.45N 119.34 E
Jinxi 27 Lc 40.46N 120.50 E
Jinxian [China] 27 Ld 39.06N 121.44 E
Jinxian [China] 28 Dj 28.21N 116.16 E
Jinxiang 28 Dg 35.04N 116.19 E
Jinyang 27 Hf 27.39N 103.12 E
Jinyun 28 Fj 28.39N 120.05 E
Jinzhai (Meishan) 28 Ci 31.40N 115.52 E
Jinzhou 22 Oe 41.09N 121.08 E
Jinzū-Gawa 29 Ec 36.45N 137.13 E
Jiparaná, Rio- 52 Jf 8.03S 62.52W
Jipijapa 54 Bd 1.22S 80.34W
Jiquilisco 49 Cg 13.19N 88.35W
Jiquilisco, Bahía de- 49 Cg 13.10N 88.28W
Jirjā 33 Fd 26.20N 31.53 E
Jishou 27 If 28.18N 109.43 E
Jishu 28 Ib 44.16N 126.50 E
Jisr ash Shughur 24 Ge 35.48N 36.19 E
Jiu 15 Gd 43.47N 23.48 E
Jiucai Ling 27 Jf 25.33N 111.18 E
Jiucheng → Wucheng 28 Df 37.12N 116.04 E
Jiujiang 22 Ng 29.39N 116.00 E
Jiuling Shan 27 Jf 28.55N 114.50 E
Jiulong/Gyaisi 27 Hf 28.58N 101.33 E
Jiuquan (Suzhou) 22 Lf 39.46N 98.34 E
Jiurongcheng 28 Gf 37.22N 122.33 E
Jiutai 27 Mc 44.10N 125.50 E
Jiwani, Rās- 25 Cc 25.01N 61.44 E
Jixi [China] 28 Ei 30.04N 118.36 E
Jixi [China] 22 Pe 45.15N 130.55 E
Jixian [China] 28 Cg 35.23N 114.04 E
Jixian [China] 28 Cf 37.34N 115.34 E
Jixian [China] 28 Dd 40.03N 117.24 E
Jiyang 28 Df 36.59N 117.11 E
Jiyuan 28 Bg 35.06N 112.35 E
Jiyun He 28 De 39.05N 117.45 E
Jiz, Wādī al- 35 Ib 16.12N 52.14 E
Jizān 23 Gh 16.54N 42.32 E
Jize 28 Cf 36.54N 114.52 E
Jizera 10 Kf 50.10N 14.43 E
Jizerské Hory 10 Lf 50.50N 15.13 E
Jizl, Wādī al- 24 Hj 25.39N 38.25 E
Jizō-Zaki 28 Lg 35.33N 133.18 E
Jmbe 36 De 10.20S 16.40 E
Jnchengjiang → Hechi 27 Ig 24.44N 108.02 E
Joaçaba 55 Gh 27.10S 51.30W
Joal-Fadiout 34 Bc 14.10N 16.51W
João Câmara 54 Ke 5.32S 35.48W
João Monlevade 55 Kd 19.50S 43.06W
João Pessoa 53 Mf 7.07S 34.52W
João Pinheiro 54 Ig 17.45S 46.10W
Joaquín V. González 55 Hb 25.00S 64.11W
Jobado 49 Ic 20.54N 77.17W
Jódar 13 Ig 37.50N 3.21W
Jodhpur 22 Jg 26.17N 73.02 E
Jodoigne/Geldenaken 12 Gd 50.43N 4.52 E
Joensuu 6 Ic 62.36N 29.46 E
Joerg Plateau 66 Qf 75.00S 69.30W
Joes Hill 64g Bb 1.48N 157.19W
Jōetsu 27 Od 37.06N 138.15 E
Joeuf 12 Ie 49.14N 6.01 E
Jöf di Montasio 14 Hd 46.26N 13.26 E
Joffre, Mount- 46 Ha 50.32N 115.13W
Jogbani 25 Hc 26.25N 87.15 E
Jõgeva/Jygeva 7 Gg 58.46N 26.26 E
Joghatāy 24 Qd 36.36N 57.01 E
Joghatāy, Kūh-e- 24 Qd 36.30N 57.00 E
Jōhana 29 Ec 36.31N 136.54 E
Johannesburg 31 Jk 26.15S 28.00 E
Jōhen 29 Ce 32.57N 132.35 E
John Day 43 Dc 44.25N 118.57W
John Day River 43 Cb 45.44N 120.39W
John H. Kerr Reservoir 44 Hg 36.31N 78.18W
John Martin Reservoir 45 Eg 38.05N 103.02W
John o' Groat's 9 Jc 58.38N 3.05W
Johnson 45 Fh 37.34N 101.45W
Johnson, Pico de- 48 Cc 29.13N 112.07W
Johnson City [Tn.-U.S.] 43 Kd 36.19N 82.21W
Johnson City [Tx.-U.S.] 45 Gk 30.17N 98.25W
Johnsons Crossing 42 Ed 60.29N 133.17W
Johnsons Point 51d Bb 17.02N 61.53W
Johnstone, Lake- 59 Ef 32.20S 120.40 E
Johnstone Strait 46 Ca 50.25N 126.00W
Johnston Island 57 Kc 17.00N 168.30W
Johnston Island [5] 58 Kc 17.00N 168.30W
Johnstown [N.Y.-U.S.] 44 Jd 43.01N 74.22W
Johnstown [Pa.-U.S.] 43 Lc 40.20N 78.56W
Johor Baharu 22 Mi 1.28N 103.45 E
Joia 55 Ei 28.39S 54.08W
Joigny 11 Jg 47.59N 3.24 E
Joinvile 53 Lh 26.18S 48.50W
Joinville 11 Lf 48.27N 5.08 E
Joinville Island 66 Re 63.15S 55.45W
Jokau 35 Ed 8.24N 33.49 E
Jokela 8 Kd 60.33N 24.59 E
Jokelbugten 41 Kc 78.25N 19.00W
Jokioinen 8 Jd 60.49N 23.28 E
Jokkmokk 7 Ec 66.36N 19.51 E
Jøkuleggi 8 Cc 61.03N 8.12 E
Jolfā 24 Kc 38.57N 45.38 E
Joliet 43 Jc 41.32N 88.05W
Joliette 42 Kg 46.01N 73.26W
Jolo 26 He 6.00N 121.00 E
Jolo Group 21 Oi 6.00N 121.09 E
Jølstravatnet 8 Bc 61.30N 6.15 E
Jomala 8 Hd 60.09N 19.58 E
Jombang 26 Fh 7.33S 112.14 E
Jomda 27 Ge 31.37N 98.20 E
Jönåker 8 Gf 58.44N 16.40 E
Jonava/Ionava 7 Fi 55.05N 24.17 E
Jonē 27 He 34.35N 103.32 E
Jones Bank 9 Fl 49.50N 8.00W
Jonesboro [Ar.-U.S.] 43 Id 35.50N 90.42W
Jonesboro [La.-U.S.] 45 Jj 32.15N 92.43W
Jones Mountains 66 Pf 73.32S 94.00W
Jones Sound 38 Kb 76.00N 85.00W
Jonesville 44 Fg 36.41N 83.06W
Jonglei [3] 35 Ed 7.20N 32.00 E
Jonglei 35 Ed 6.50N 31.18 E
Jonglei, Tur'ah-=Jonglei Canal (EN) 35 Ed 9.22N 31.30 E
Jonglei Canal (EN)=Jonglei, Tur'ah- 35 Ed 9.22N 31.30 E
Joniškėlis/Ioniškelis 8 Ki 56.00N 24.14 E
Joniškis/Ioniškis 7 Fh 56.16N 23.37 E
Jönköping 6 Hd 57.47N 14.11 E
Jönköping [2] 7 Dh 57.30N 14.30 E
Jonquière 42 Kg 48.25N 71.15W
Jonuta 48 Mh 18.05N 92.08W
Jonzac 11 Fi 45.27N 0.26W
Joplin 39 Jf 37.06N 94.31W
Jordan 47 Fb 47.19N 106.55W
Jordan 23 Ec 31.46N 35.33 E
Jordan (EN)=Al Urdun [1] 22 Ff 31.00N 36.00 E
Jordan Valley 46 Ge 42.58N 117.03W
Jordão, Rio- 55 Fg 25.46S 52.07W
Jorhāt 22 Lg 26.45N 94.13 E
Jörn 7 Ed 65.04N 20.02 E
Joroinen 7 Ge 62.11N 27.50 E
Jørpeland 7 Bg 59.01N 6.03 E
Jos 31 Hh 9.55N 8.54 E
José A. Guisasola 55 Bn 38.40S 61.05W
José Battle y Ordóñez 55 Ek 33.28S 55.07W
José Bonifácio 55 He 21.03S 49.41W
José de San Martín 56 Ff 44.02S 70.29W
Joselandia 55 Dc 16.32S 56.12W
José Otávio 55 Ej 31.17S 54.07W
José Pedro Varela 55 Ek 33.27S 54.32W
Joseph, Lake- 44 Hc 45.14N 79.45W
Joseph Bonaparte Gulf 57 Df 14.55S 128.15 E
Josephine Seamount (EN) 5 Eh 36.52N 14.20W
Joseph Lake 42 Kf 52.48N 65.17W
Joshimath 25 Fb 30.34N 79.34 E
Joškar-Ola 6 Kd 56.40N 47.55 E
Jos Plateau 30 Hh 10.00N 9.30 E
Josselin 11 Dg 47.57N 2.33W
Jostedalen 8 Bc 61.35N 7.20 E
Jostedalsbreen 7 Bf 61.40N 7.00 E
Jostefonn 8 Bc 61.26N 6.33 E
Jost Van Dyke 51a Db 18.28N 64.45W
Jotunheimen 6 Gc 61.40N 8.20 E
Joubertberge 37 Ac 18.45S 13.55 E
Joué-lès-Tours 11 Gg 47.21N 0.40 E
Jouquara, Rio- 55 Db 15.06S 57.06W
Joure, Haskerland- 12 Hb 52.58N 5.47 E
Joutsa 7 Gf 61.44N 26.07 E
Joutseno 7 Gf 61.06N 28.30 E
Jovan, Deli- 15 Fe 44.15N 22.13 E
Jovellanos 49 Gb 22.48N 81.12W
Joviânia 55 Hc 17.49S 49.30W
Jowhar 31 Lh 2.46N 45.32 E
Jow Kār 24 Me 34.26N 48.42 E
Jowzjān [3] 23 Kb 36.30N 66.00 E
Joya, Laguna de la- 48 Mj 15.55N 93.40W
Jreïda 32 Df 18.10N 16.03W
Jrian Jaya [3] 26 Kg 3.55S 138.00 E
Juan Aldama 47 Dd 24.19N 103.21W
Juana Ramírez, Isla- 48 Kg 21.50N 97.40W
Juan Blanquier 55 Cl 35.46S 59.18W
Juancheng 28 Cg 35.33N 115.30 E
Juan de Fuca, Strait of- 38 Ge 48.20N 124.00W
Juan de Nova, Ile- 30 Lj 17.03S 42.45 E
Juan E. Barra 55 Bm 37.48S 60.29W
Juan Fernández, Archipielago-=Juan Fernández, Islands (EN) 52 Ii 33.00S 80.00W
Juan Fernandez Islands (EN)=Juan Fernández, Archipielago- 52 Ii 33.00S 80.00W
Juan G. Bazán 55 Bg 24.33S 60.50W
Juangriego 50 Eg 11.05N 63.57W
Juanjuy 54 Ce 7.11S 76.45W
Juan L. Lacaze 55 Dl 34.26S 57.27W
Juárez [Arg.] 56 Ie 37.40S 59.48W
Juárez [Mex.] 48 Id 27.37N 100.44W
Juárez, Sierra de- 48 Bb 32.00N 115.50W
Juarzohn 34 Dd 5.20N 8.58W
Juàzeirinho 54 Ke 7.04S 36.35W
Juàzeiro 53 Lf 9.25S 40.30W
Juàzeiro do Norte 53 Mf 7.12S 39.20W
Jūbā 31 Kh 4.51N 31.37 E
Juba (EN)=Ganāne, Webi- 30 Lh 0.15S 42.38 E
Juba, Rio- 55 Db 14.59S 57.44W
Jūbāl, Maḑīq- 24 Ei 27.40N 33.55 E
Jubaland (EN) 30 Lh 1.00N 42.00 E
Jubayl [Eg.] 24 Eh 28.12N 33.38 E
Jubayl [Leb.] 24 Fe 34.07N 35.39 E
Jubayt [Sud.] 35 Fb 18.57N 36.50 E
Jubayt [Sud.] 35 Fa 20.59N 36.18 E
Jubbada Dhexe [3] 35 Ge 1.15N 42.30 E
Jubbada Hoose [3] 35 Gf 0.30S 42.00 E
Jubbah 24 Ih 28.02N 40.56 E
Jubilee Lake 59 Fe 29.10S 126.40 E
Juby, Cap- 30 Ff 27.57N 12.55W
Júcar/Xúquer 5 Fh 39.09N 0.14W
Juçara 55 Gb 15.53S 50.51W
Jucaro 49 Hc 21.37N 78.51W
Jüchen 12 Ic 51.06N 6.30 E
Juchipila 48 Hg 21.25N 103.07W
Juchipila, Rio- 48 Hg 21.03N 103.25W
Juchitán de Zaragoza 39 Jh 16.26N 95.01W
Jučjugej 20 Jd 63.20N 142.15 E
Judas, Punta- 49 Ei 9.31N 84.32W
Judayyidat 'Ar'ar 23 Fc 31.22N 41.26 E
Judenburg 14 Ic 47.10N 14.40 E
Juding Shan 27 He 31.30N 104.00 E
Judith Mountains 46 Kc 47.12N 109.15W
Judith River 46 Kc 47.44N 109.38W
Judoma 20 Ie 59.08N 135.03 E
Judomski Hrebet 20 Jd 61.05N 141.30 E
Juegang → Rudong 28 Fh 32.19N 121.11 E
Juelsminde 8 Di 55.43N 10.01 E
Jufrah, Wāḩāt al-=Giofra Oasis (EN) 30 If 29.10N 16.00 E
Jug 5 Kc 60.45N 46.20 E
Jug 17 Hh 57.43N 56.12 E
Jugo-Osetinskaja Avtonomnaja Oblast [3] 19 Eg 42.20N 44.05 E
Jugorski Poluostrov 17 Kb 69.30N 62.30 E
Jugorski Šar, Proliv- 19 Gb 69.45N 60.35 E
Jugoslavija = Yugoslavia (EN) [1] 6 Hg 44.00N 19.00 E
Jugo-Tala 20 Kc 66.03N 151.05 E
Jugydjan 17 Gf 61.42N 54.58 E
Juhaym 24 Kh 29.36N 45.24 E
Juhnov 16 Ib 54.43N 35.12 E
Juhor 15 Ef 43.50N 21.15 E
Juhoslovenská nížina 10 Ph 48.10N 19.40 E
Juhua Dao 28 Fd 40.32N 120.48 E
Juigalpa 49 Eg 12.05N 85.24W
Juina, Rio- 55 Ca 12.36S 58.57W
Juine 11 If 48.32N 2.23 E
Juininha, Rio- 55 Ca 12.55S 59.13W
Juist 10 Cc 53.40N 7.00 E
Juiz de Fora 53 Lh 21.45S 43.20W
Jujuy [2] 56 Gb 23.00S 66.00W
Jukagirskoje Ploskogorje 20 Kc 66.00N 155.30 E
Jukonda 17 Mg 59.38N 67.20 E
Juksejevo 17 Gg 59.52N 54.16 E
Jula 7 Ke 63.48N 44.44 E
Juldybajevo 17 Hj 52.20N 57.52 E
Julesburg 45 Ef 40.59N 102.16W
Juli 54 Eg 16.13S 69.27W
Juliaca 54 Dg 15.30S 70.08W
Julia Creek 59 Id 20.39S 141.45 E
Julian Alps (EN)=Julijske Alpe 14 Hd 46.20N 13.45 E
Juliana Top 54 Gc 3.41N 56.32W
Julianehåb/Qaqortoq 67 Nc 60.50N 46.10W
Jülich 10 Cf 50.56N 6.22 E
Jülicher Borde 12 Id 50.50N 6.30 E
Julijske Alpe=Julian Alps (EN) 14 Hd 46.20N 13.45 E
Julimes 48 Gc 28.25N 105.27W
Júlio de Castilhos 55 Fi 29.14S 53.41W
Jullundur 22 Jf 31.19N 75.34 E
Julong/New Kowloon 22 Ng 22.20N 114.09 E
Julu 28 Cf 37.13N 115.02 E
Juma 7 Hd 65.05N 33.13 E
Juma He 28 De 39.31N 116.08 E
Jumet, Charleroi- 11 Kd 50.27N 4.26 E
Jumièges 12 Ce 49.26N 0.49 E
Jumilla 13 Kf 38.29N 1.17W
Jümme 12 Ja 53.13N 7.31 E
Junāgadh 25 Ed 21.31N 70.28 E
Junan (Shizilu) 28 Eg 35.10N 118.50 E
Junaynah, Ra's al- 24 Eh 29.01N 33.58 E
Juncal 48 De 24.50N 111.47W
Juncos 51a Cb 18.13N 65.55W
Junction [Tx.-U.S.] 45 Gk 30.29N 99.46W
Junction [Ut.-U.S.] 46 Ig 38.14N 112.13W
Junction City 43 Hd 39.02N 96.50W
Jundiaí 56 Kb 23.11S 46.52W
Jundiaí do Sul 55 Gf 23.27S 50.17W
Jundūbah 32 Ib 36.30N 8.45 E
Jundūbah [3] 32 Ib 36.28N 8.41 E
Juneau 39 Fd 57.20N 134.27W
Junee 59 Jf 34.52S 147.35 E
Jungar Qi (Shagedu) 27 Jd 39.37N 110.58 E
Jungfrau 14 Bd 46.32N 7.58 E
Junggar Pendi=Dzungarian Basin 21 Ke 45.00N 88.00 E
Junin [2] 54 Df 11.30S 75.00W
Junín [Arg.] 53 Ji 34.35S 60.57W
Junín [Peru] 54 Cf 11.10S 76.00W
Junín, Lago de- 54 Cf 11.02S 76.05W
Junín de los Andes 56 Fe 39.56S 71.05W
Juniville 12 Ge 49.24N 4.23 E
Jūniyah 24 Ff 33.59N 35.38 E
Junjaha 17 Jc 66.25N 62.00 E
Junlian 27 Hf 28.12N 104.34 E
Junsele 7 De 63.41N 16.54 E
Juntura 46 Fe 43.45N 118.05W
Junxian (Danjiang) 27 Je 32.31N 111.32 E
Juodupė 8 Kh 56.03N 25.44 E
Juojärvi 8 Mb 62.45N 28.35 E
Juoksengi 7 Fc 66.34N 23.51 E
Jupiá, Represa de- 56 Jb 20.47S 51.39W
Juquiá 55 Ig 24.19S 47.38W
Juquiá, Rio- 55 Ig 24.22S 47.49W
Juquiá, Serra do- 55 Gg 25.10S 52.00W
Jur 20 Ie 59.48N 137.29 E
Jur 30 Jh 8.39N 29.18 E
Jura [2] 14 Ac 47.25N 6.15 E
Jura 5 Gf 46.45N 6.30 E
Jura [3] 11 Lh 46.50N 5.50 E
Jura 9 Hf 56.00N 5.50W
Jūra/Jura 7 Fi 55.03N 22.10 E
Jura/Jūra 7 Fi 55.03N 22.10 E
Jura, Sound of- 9 Hf 55.55N 5.22W
Juradó 54 Cb 7.07N 77.46W
Juratiški 8 Kj 54.02N 26.00 E
Juraybī'āt 24 Lh 29.50N 46.03 E
Jurayby'āt 24 Kh 29.08N 45.30 E
Jurbarkas 7 Fi 55.08N 22.47 E
Jurdī, Wādī- 24 Ei 26.33N 32.44 E
Jurga 20 De 55.42N 84.55 E
Jurgamyš 17 Li 55.25N 64.28 E
Juribej 17 Nb 68.55N 69.05 E
Jurien Bay 59 Cf 30.15S 115.00 E
Jurigue, Rio- 55 Ec 16.29S 54.37W
Jurilovca 15 Le 44.46N 28.52 E
Jurja 7 Lg 59.03N 49.20 E
Jurjaha 17 Gc 66.42N 56.00 E
Jurjevec 7 Kh 57.22N 43.06 E
Jurjev-Polski 7 Jh 56.31N 39.44 E
Jurjuzan 17 Hi 55.43N 56.57 E
Jurjuzan 17 Ii 54.52N 58.28 E
Jurla 17 Gg 59.20N 54.16 E
Jurmala/Jūrmala 19 Cd 56.59N 23.38 E
Jūrmala/Jurmala 19 Cd 56.59N 23.38 E
Jurmo 8 Ie 59.50N 21.35 E
Jurong 28 Ei 31.56N 119.10 E
Juruá 54 Ed 3.27S 66.03W
Juruá, Rio- 52 Jf 2.37S 65.44W
Juruena, Rio- 52 Kf 7.20S 58.03W
Jurumirim, Represa de- 56 Kb 23.20S 49.00W
Juruti 54 Gd 2.09S 56.04W
Jurva 8 Ib 62.41N 21.59 E
Jusan-Kō 29a Bc 41.00N 140.20 E
Jusayrah 24 Nj 25.53N 50.36 E
Jusheng 27 Mb 48.44N 126.37 E
Ju Shui 28 Ci 31.09N 114.52 E
Juškozero 19 Dc 64.45N 32.08 E
Jussarö 8 Je 59.50N 23.35 E
Justo Daract 56 Gd 33.52S 65.11W
Jusva 17 Gg 58.59N 54.57 E
Jutai 54 Ee 5.11S 68.54W
Jutai, Rio- 52 Jf 2.43S 66.57W
Jüterbg 10 Je 51.59N 13.05 E
Juti 55 Ef 22.52S 54.37W
Jutiapa [3] 49 Bf 14.10N 89.50W
Jutiapa [Guat.] 47 Gf 14.17N 89.54W
Jutiapa [Hond.] 49 Df 15.46N 86.34W
Juticalpa 47 Gf 14.42N 86.15W
Jutland (EN)=Jylland 5 Gd 56.00N 9.15 E
Juuka 7 Ge 63.14N 29.15 E
Juva 7 Gf 61.54N 27.51 E
Juventud, Isla de la-=Pines, Isle of- (EN) 38 Kg 21.40N 82.50W
Juxian 27 Kd 35.33N 118.45 E
Jūybār 24 Od 36.38N 52.53 E
Juye 28 Dg 35.23N 116.05 E
Jüyom 24 Oh 28.10N 54.02 E
Juža 7 Kh 56.36N 42.01 E
Južnaja Keltma 17 Gf 60.30N 55.40 E
Južna Morava 15 Ef 43.41N 21.24 E
Južni Rodopi 15 Ih 41.15N 25.30 E
Južnoje 20 Jg 46.13N 143.27 E
Južno-Jenisejski 20 Ee 58.48N 94.45 E
Južno-Kurilsk 20 Jh 44.05N 145.52 E
Južno-Sahalinsk 22 Qe 46.58N 142.42 E
Južno-Uralsk 19 Ge 54.26N 61.15 E
Južny, Mys- 20 Ke 57.42N 156.55 E
Južny Bug 5 Jf 46.59N 31.58 E
Južny Ural=Southern Urals (EN) 5 Le 54.00N 58.30 E
Jygeva/Jõgeva 7 Gg 58.46N 26.26 E
Jylland=Jutland (EN) 5 Gd 56.00N 9.15 E
Jylland Bank 8 Bh 56.55N 7.20 E
Jyske Ås 8 Dg 57.15N 10.14 E
Jyväskylä 6 Ic 62.14N 25.44 E

K

K2=Godwin Austen (EN) 21 Jf 35.53N 76.30 E
Ka 34 Fc 11.39N 4.11 E
Kaabong 36 Fb 3.31N 34.09 E
Kaahka 19 Fh 37.21N 59.38 E
Kaala 65a Cb 21.31N 158.09W
Kaala-Gomén 63b Be 20.40S 164.24 E
Kaalualu Bay 65a Fe 18.58N 155.37W
Kaamanen 7 Gb 69.06N 27.12 E
Kaap Kruis 37 Ad 21.46S 13.58 E
Kaap Plateau (EN)=Kaapplato 30 Jk 27.30S 23.45 E
Kaapplato=Kaap Plateau (EN) 30 Jk 27.30S 23.45 E
Kaapprovinsie/Cape Province [2] 37 Cf 32.00S 22.00 E
Kaapstad / Cape Town 31 Il 33.55S 18.22 E
Kaarst 12 Ic 51.15N 6.37 E
Kaarta 34 Cc 14.35N 10.00W
Kaba/Habahe 27 Eb 47.53N 86.12 E
Kabaena, Pulau- 26 Hh 5.15S 121.55 E
Kabah 48 Og 20.07N 89.29W
Kabala 34 Cd 9.35N 11.33W
Kabale 36 Ec 1.15S 29.59 E
Kabalega Falls 36 Fb 2.17N 31.41 E
Kabalo 31 Ji 6.03S 26.55 E
Kabaman 63a Aa 4.38S 152.42 E
Kabambare 36 Ec 4.16S 27.07 E
Kabamet 36 Gb 0.30N 35.45 E
Kabanjahe 26 Cf 3.06N 98.30 E
Kabardino-Balkarskaja ASSR [3] 19 Eg 43.30N 43.30 E
Kabare 36 Ec 2.29S 28.48 E
Kabasalan 26 He 7.48N 122.45 E
Kaba-Shima [Jap.] 29 Ae 32.45N 129.00 E
Kaba-Shima [Jap.] 29 Ae 32.34N 129.47 E
Kabba 34 Gd 7.50N 6.04 E
Kåbdalis 7 Ec 66.09N 20.00 E
Kaberamaido 36 Fb 1.45N 33.10 E
Kabetogama Lake 45 Jb 48.28N 92.59W
Kabhegy 10 Ni 47.03N 17.39 E
Kabinakagami Lake 44 Ea 48.58N 84.25W
Kabinda 31 Ji 6.08S 24.29 E
Kabīr, Wādī al- 14 Dn 36.23N 9.52 E
Kabīr Kūh 24 Lf 33.25N 46.45 E
Kabkābīyah 35 Cc 13.39N 24.05 E
Kableškovo 15 Kg 42.39N 27.34 E
Kabna 35 Eb 19.10N 32.41 E
Kabo 35 Bd 7.35N 18.38 E
Kabompo 36 De 13.36S 24.12 E
Kabompo 30 Jj 14.11S 23.11 E
Kabondo Dianda 36 Ed 8.53S 25.40 E
Kabongo 36 Ed 7.19S 25.35 E
Kabou 34 Fd 9.27N 0.49 E
Kabūdiyāh, Ra's- 32 Jb 35.14N 11.10 E
Kabūd Rāhang 24 Me 35.12N 48.44 E
Kābul 22 If 34.31N 69.12 E
Kābul [3] 23 Kc 34.30N 69.00 E
Kābul 21 Jf 33.55N 72.14 E
Kabunda 36 Ee 12.13S 29.23 E

Index Symbols

[1] Independent Nation
[2] State, Region
[3] District, County
[4] Municipality
[5] Colony, Dependency
Continent
Physical Region
Historical or Cultural Region
Mount, Mountain
Volcano
Hill
Mountains, Mountain Range
Hills, Escarpment
Plateau, Upland
Pass, Gap
Plain, Lowland
Delta
Salt Flat
Valley, Canyon
Crater, Cave
Karst Features
Depression
Polder
Desert, Dunes
Forest, Woods
Heath, Steppe
Oasis
Cape, Point
Coast, Beach
Cliff
Peninsula
Isthmus
Sandbank
Island
Atoll
Rock, Reef
Islands, Archipelago
Rocks, Reefs
Coral Reef
Well, Spring
Geyser
River, Stream
Waterfall Rapids
River Mouth, Estuary
Lake
Salt Lake
Intermittent Lake
Reservoir
Swamp, Pond
Canal
Glacier
Ice Shelf, Pack Ice
Ocean
Sea
Gulf, Bay
Strait, Fjord
Lagoon
Bank
Seamount
Tablemount
Ridge
Shelf
Basin
Escarpment, Sea Scarp
Fracture
Trench, Abyss
National Park, Reserve
Point of Interest
Recreation Site
Cave, Cavern
Historic Site
Ruins
Wall, Walls
Church, Abbey
Temple
Scientific Station
Airport
Port
Lighthouse
Mine
Tunnel
Dam, Bridge

Kabunga	36	Ec	1.42S	28.08 E
Kaburuang, Pulau-	26	If	3.48N	126.48 E
Kabushi-ga-Take	29	Fd	35.54N	138.44 E
Kabwe	31	Jj	14.27S	28.27 E
Kabylie	32	Ib	36.15N	5.25 E
Kača	16	Hg	44.44N	33.32 E
Kačanik	15	Eg	42.14N	21.15 E
Kačanovo	8	Lg	57.24N	27.53 E
Kačergine	8	Jj	54.53N	23.49 E
Kachia	34	Gd	9.52N	7.57 E
Kachikau	37	Cc	18.09S	24.29 E
Kachin [2]	25	Jc	26.00N	97.30 E
Kačiry	19	He	53.04N	76.07 E
Kačkanar	19	Fd	58.42N	59.35 E
Kačug	20	Ff	54.00N	105.52 E
Kaczawa	10	Me	51.18N	16.27 E
Kadada	16	Oc	53.09N	46.01 E
Kadaň	10	Jf	50.23N	13.16 E
Kadan Kyun	25	Jf	12.30N	98.22 E
Kadeï	30	Ih	3.31N	16.03 E
Kadijevka	19	Df	48.32N	38.40 E
Kadiköy	24	Bb	40.51N	26.50 E
Kadıköy, İstanbul	15	Mi	40.59N	29.01 E
Kadina	59	Hf	33.58S	137.43 E
Kadınhanı	24	Ec	38.15N	32.14 E
Kadiolo	34	Dc	10.34N	5.45W
Kadiri	25	Ff	14.07N	78.10 E
Kadirli	23	Eb	37.23N	36.05 E
Kadja	35	Cc	12.02N	22.28 E
Kadmat Island	25	Ef	11.14N	72.47 E
Kadnikov	7	Jg	59.30N	40.24 E
Kadoka	45	Fe	43.50N	101.31W
Kaduj	7	Ig	59.14N	37.09 E
Kaduna [2]	34	Gc	11.00N	7.30 E
Kaduna	30	Hh	8.45N	5.48 E
Kaduna	31	Hg	10.31N	7.26 E
Kāduqlī	31	Jg	11.01N	29.43 E
Kadykčan	20	Jd	63.05N	146.58 E
Kadžaran	16	Oj	39.11N	46.10 E
Kadžerom	17	Gd	64.41N	55.54 E
Kadži-Saj	18	Kc	42.08N	77.10 E
Kaech'ŏn	28	He	39.42N	125.53 E
Kaédi	31	Fg	16.08N	13.31W
Kaélé	34	Hc	10.07N	14.27 E
Kaena Point	65a	Cb	21.35N	158.17W
Kaeo	62	Ea	35.06S	173.47 E
Kaesŏng	22	Of	37.58N	126.33 E
Kaesŏng Si [2]	28	Ie	38.05N	126.30 E
Kāf	24	Gg	31.24N	37.29 E
Kafakumba	36	Dd	9.41S	23.44 E
Kafan	19	Eh	39.12N	46.28 E
Kafanchan	34	Gd	9.35N	8.18 E
Kaffrine	34	Bc	14.06N	15.33W
Kafia Kingi	35	Cd	9.16N	24.25 E
Kafiréos, Dhiékplous-	15	Hl	38.00N	24.40 E
Kafirévs, Ákra-	15	Hk	38.10N	24.35 E
Kafr ad Dawwār	24	Dg	31.08N	30.07 E
Kafr ash Shaykh	33	Fc	31.07N	30.56 E
Kafta	35	Fc	13.54N	37.11 E
Kafu	36	Fb	1.39N	32.05 E
Kafue	30	Ef	15.56S	28.55 E
Kafue	31	Jj	15.47S	28.11 E
Kafue Dam	36	Ef	15.45S	28.28 E
Kafue Flats	36	Ef	15.40S	26.25 E
Kafufu	36	Fd	7.12S	31.31 E
Kaga	28	Nf	36.18N	136.18 E
Kaga Bandoro	35	Bd	7.02N	19.13 E
Kagalaska	40a	Cb	51.47N	176.23W
Kagalnik	16	Kf	47.04N	39.18 E
Kagami	29	Be	32.34N	130.40 E
Kagan	19	Gh	39.43N	64.32 E
Kagarlyk	16	Ge	49.53N	30.56 E
Kagawa Ken [2]	28	Mg	34.15N	134.15 E
Kagera	30	Ki	0.57S	31.47 E
Kağızman	24	Jb	40.09N	43.07 E
Kagoshima	22	Pf	31.36N	130.33 E
Kagoshima Bay (EN)=				
Kagoshima-Wan	28	Ki	31.27N	130.40 E
Kagoshima Ken [2]	28	Ki	31.45N	130.40 E
Kagoshima-Taniyama	29	Bf	31.31N	130.31 E
Kagoshima-Wan=				
Kagoshima Bay (EN)	28	Ki	31.27N	130.40 E
Kagul	15	Ld	45.32N	28.27 E
Kagul	19	Cf	45.53N	28.14 E
Kahal Tabelbala	32	Gd	28.45N	2.15W
Kahama	36	Fc	3.50S	32.36 E
Kahemba	31	Ii	7.17S	19.00 E
Kahi	16	Oi	41.23N	46.59 E
Kahiu Point	65a	Eb	21.13N	156.58W
Kahler Asten	10	Ee	51.11N	8.29 E
Kahnūj	24	Qi	27.58N	57.47 E
Kahoku	29	Gb	38.30N	141.20 E
Kahoku-Gata	29	Ec	36.40N	136.40 E
Kahoolawe Island	57	Lb	20.33N	156.35W
Kahouanne, Ilet à-	51e	Ab	16.22N	61.47W
Kahovka	19	Df	46.47N	33.32 E
Kahovskoje Vodohranilišče				
=Kakhovka Reservoir (EN)	5	Jf	47.25N	34.10 E
Kahramanmaraş	23	Eb	37.36N	36.55 E
Kahrūyeh	24	Ng	31.43N	51.48 E
Kâhta	24	Hd	37.46N	38.36 E
Kahuku	65a	Db	21.41N	157.57W
Kahuku Point	65a	Db	21.43N	157.59W
Kahului	65a	Ec	20.53N	156.27W
Kahului Bay	65a	Ec	20.55N	156.30W
Kahurangi Point	62	Ed	40.46S	172.13 E
Kai, Kepulauan-	57	Ee	5.35S	132.45 E
Kaiama	34	Fd	9.36N	3.57 E
Kaiapoi	62	Ee	43.23S	172.39 E
Kaibab Plateau	46	Ih	36.30N	112.15W
Kai Besar	26	Jh	5.35S	133.00 E
Kaidu He/Karaxabar He	27	Ec	41.55N	86.38 E
Kaieteur Falls	54	Gc	5.10N	59.28W
Kaifeng	22	Nf	34.45N	114.25 E
Kaihua	28	Ej	29.10N	118.24 E
Kai Kecil	26	Jh	5.45S	132.40 E
Kaikohe	62	Ea	35.24S	173.48 E
Kaikoura	61	Dh	42.25S	173.41 E
Kaili	27	If	26.35N	107.59 E
Kailu	27	Lc	43.37N	121.19 E
Kailua [Hi.-U.S.]	65a	Fd	19.39N	155.59W
Kailua [Hi.-U.S.]	65a	Db	21.23N	157.44W
Kaimana	26	Jg	3.39S	133.45 E
Kaimanawa Mountains	62	Fc	39.15S	176.00 E
Kaimon-Dake	29	Bf	31.10N	130.32 E
Kain, Tournai-	12	Fd	50.38N	3.22 E
Kainach	14	Jd	46.54N	15.31 E
Kainan [Jap.]	29	Dd	34.09N	135.12 E
Kainan [Jap.]	29	De	33.36N	134.22 E
Kainantu	60	Di	6.15S	145.53 E
Kainji Dam	34	Fd	9.55N	4.40 E
Kainji Reservoir	34	Fc	10.30N	4.35 E
Kaipara Harbour	62	Fb	36.25S	174.15 E
Kaiparowits Plateau	46	Jh	37.20N	111.15W
Kaiser Franz Josephs				
Fjord	41	Jd	73.30N	24.00W
Kaisersesch	12	Jd	50.14N	7.09 E
Kaiserslautern	10	Dg	49.27N	7.45 E
Kaiserstuhl	10	Dh	48.06N	7.40 E
Kaishantun	27	Mc	42.43N	129.37 E
Kaišiadorys/Kajšjadoris	7	Fi	54.53N	24.31 E
Kaita	29	Cd	34.20N	132.32 E
Kaitaia	62	Ea	35.07S	173.14 E
Kaitangata	62	Cg	46.17S	169.51 E
Kaithal	25	Fc	29.48N	76.23 E
Kaitong→Tongyu	27	Lc	44.47N	123.05 E
Kaituma River	50	Gh	8.11N	59.41W
Kaiwaka	61	Dg	36.10S	174.26 E
Kaiwi Channel	60	Oc	21.13N	157.30W
Kaixian	27	Ie	31.10N	108.25 E
Kaiyuan [China]	27	Lc	42.33N	124.04 E
Kaiyuan [China]	27	Hg	23.47N	103.15 E
Kaiyuh Mountains	40	Hd	64.00N	158.00W
Kaja	30	Jg	12.02N	22.28 E
Kajaani	6	Ic	64.14N	27.41 E
Kajaapu	26	Dh	5.26S	102.24 E
Kajabbi	58	Fg	20.02S	140.02 E
Kajak	20	Fb	71.30N	103.15 E
Kajang	26	Df	2.59N	101.47 E
Kajdak, Sor-	16	Rg	44.40N	53.30 E
Kajerkan	20	Dc	69.25N	87.30 E
Kajiado	36	Gc	1.51S	36.47 E
Kajiki	29	Bf	31.44N	130.40 E
Kajmakčalan	15	Ei	40.58N	21.48 E
Kajnar	15	Lb	47.50N	28.06 E
Kajo Kaji	35	Ee	3.53N	31.40 E
Kajrakkumskoje				
Vodohranilišče	18	Hd	40.20N	70.05 E
Kajrakty	19	Hf	48.31N	73.14 E
Kajšjadoris/Kaišiadorys	7	Fi	54.53N	24.31 E
Kajuru	34	Gc	10.19N	7.41 E
Kaka	35	Fd	7.28N	39.06 E
Kākā	35	Ec	10.36N	32.11 E
Kakagi Lake	45	Jb	49.13N	93.52W
Kakamas	37	Ce	28.45S	20.33 E
Kakamega	36	Fb	0.17N	34.45 E
Kakamigahara	29	Ed	35.25N	136.50 E
Kakanj	14	Mf	44.08N	18.05 E
Kaka Point	65a	Ec	20.32N	156.33W
Kakata	34	Cd	6.32N	10.21W
Kake	29	Cd	34.36N	132.19 E
Kakegawa	29	Ed	34.46N	138.00 E
Kakenge	36	Dc	4.51S	21.55 E
Kakeroma-Jima	29b	Ba	28.08N	129.15 E
Kakhovka Reservoir (EN)=				
Kahovskoje				
Vodohranilišče	5	Jf	47.25N	34.10 E
Kākī	24	Nh	28.19N	51.34 E
Kākināda	22	Kh	16.56N	82.13 E
Kakisa Lake	42	Fd	60.55N	117.40W
Kakizaki	29	Fc	37.16N	138.22 E
Kaklkan	24	Cd	36.15N	29.24 E
Kakogawa	29	Dd	34.46N	134.51 E
Kakpin	34	Ed	8.39N	3.48W
Kaktovik	40	Kb	70.08N	143.37W
Kakuda	29	Gc	37.58N	140.47 E
Kakuma	36	Fb	3.43N	34.52 E
Kakunodate	28	Pe	39.40N	140.32 E
Kakva	17	Jg	59.37N	60.50 E
Kakya	36	Gc	1.36S	39.02 E
Kalaa	13	Mi	35.35N	0.20 E
Kalaa Khasba	14	Co	35.38N	8.36 E
Kalaallit Nunaat/Grønland=				
Greenland (EN) [5]	39	Pb	70.00N	40.00W
Kalaallit Nunaat/Grønland=				
Greenland (EN)	38	Pb	70.00N	40.00W
Kalabahi	26	Hh	8.13S	124.31 E
Kalabáka	15	Ej	39.42N	21.38 E
Kalabera	64b	Ba	15.14N	145.48 E
Kalabo	36	De	14.58S	22.41 E
Kalâbsha	33	Fe	23.33N	32.50 E
Kalač	19	Ee	50.23N	41.01 E
Kalačinsk	19	Hd	55.03N	74.34 E
Kalač-na-Donu	19	Ef	48.43N	43.32 E
Kaladan	25	Id	20.09N	92.57 E
Ka Lae	60	Od	18.55N	155.41W
Kalahari Desert	30	Jk	23.00S	22.00 E
Kalaheo	65a	Bb	21.56N	159.32W
Kalai-Mor	19	Gh	35.37N	62.31 E
Kalaj Humo	18	He	38.25N	70.47 E
Kalajoki	7	Fd	64.15N	23.57 E
Kalakan	20	Ge	55.10N	116.45 E
Kalaldi	34	Hd	6.30N	14.04 E
Kalāleh	24	Pd	37.25N	55.40 E
Kalámai	6	Ih	37.02N	22.07 E
Kalamákion	15	Gl	37.55N	23.43 E
Kalamazoo	43	Jc	42.17N	85.32W
Kalambo Falls	36	Fd	8.36S	31.14 E
Kalamitski Zaliv	16	Hg	45.00N	33.25 E
Kálamos	15	Dk	38.37N	20.55 E
Kalamunda, Perth-	59	Df	31.57S	116.03 E
Kalan	23	Eb	39.07N	39.32 E
Kalandula	31	Ii	9.06S	15.58 E
Kalanshiyū, Sarīr-	30	Jf	27.00N	21.30 E
Kalao, Pulau-	26	Hh	7.18S	120.58 E
Kalaotoa, Pulau-	26	Hh	7.22S	121.47 E
Kalapana	65a	Gd	19.21N	154.59W
Kalaraš	16	Ff	47.16N	28.16 E
Kälarne	8	Gb	62.59N	16.05 E
Kalarski Hrebet	20	Ge	56.30N	118.50 E
Kalasin [Indon.]	26	Ff	0.12N	114.16 E
Kalasin [Thai.]	25	Ke	16.29N	103.31 E
Kalāt	25	Dc	29.02N	66.35 E
Kalāteh	24	Pd	36.29N	54.10 E
Kalau	65b	Bc	21.28S	174.57W
Kalaupapa	65a	Eb	21.12N	156.59W
Kalaus	16	Ng	45.43N	44.07 E
Kalavárdha	15	Km	36.20N	27.57 E
Kálavrita	15	Fk	38.02N	22.07 E
Kalbā'	24	Qj	25.03N	56.21 E
Kalbīyah, Sabkhat al-	14	Eo	35.51N	10.17 E
Kaldbakur	7a	Ab	65.49N	23.39W
Kaldygajty	16	Re	49.20N	52.38 E
Kale [Tur.]	24	Cd	37.26N	28.51 E
Kale [Tur.]	24	Cd	36.14N	29.59 E
Kalecik	24	Eb	40.06N	33.25 E
Kalehe	36	Ec	2.06S	28.55 E
Kalemie	31	Ji	5.56S	29.12 E
Kāl-e Shur	23	Jb	35.05N	60.59 E
Kalevala	19	Db	65.12N	31.10 E
Kalewa	25	Id	23.12N	94.18 E
Kaleybar	24	Lc	38.47N	47.02 E
Kalgoorlie	58	Dh	30.45S	121.28 E
Kaliakoúdha	15	Ek	38.48N	21.46 E
Kaliakra, Nos-	15	Lf	43.18N	28.30 E
Kalibo	26	Hd	11.43N	122.22 E
Kalí Limni	15	Kn	35.35N	27.08 E
Kalima	31	Ji	2.34S	26.37 E
Kalimantan/Borneo	21	Ni	1.00N	114.00 E
Kalimantan Barat [3]	26	Ff	0.01N	110.30 E
Kalimantan Selatan [3]	26	Gg	2.30S	115.30 E
Kalimantan Tengah [3]	26	Fg	2.00S	113.30 E
Kalimantan Timur [3]	26	Gf	1.30N	116.30 E
Kálimnos	15	Jm	36.57N	26.59 E
Kálimnos	15	Jl	37.00N	27.00 E
Kalinin [R.S.F.S.R.]	6	Jd	56.52N	35.55 E
Kalinin [Tur.-U.S.S.R.]	19	Fg	42.07N	59.40 E
Kalininabad	18	Gf	37.53N	68.57 E
Kaliningrad [R.S.F.S.R.]	6	Ie	54.43N	20.30 E
Kaliningrad [R.S.F.S.R.]	7	Ii	55.55N	37.57 E
Kaliningradskaja Oblast [3]	19	Ce	54.45N	21.20 E
Kalinino [Arm.-U.S.S.R.]	16	Ni	41.08N	44.14 E
Kalinino [R.S.F.S.R.]	16	Kg	45.05N	38.59 E
Kalininsk [Mold.-U.S.S.R.]	15	Ka	48.07N	27.16 E
Kalininsk [R.S.F.S.R.]	16	Nd	51.30N	44.30 E
Kalininskaja Oblast [3]	19	Dd	57.20N	34.40 E
Kalinkoviči	19	Ce	52.07N	29.23 E
Kalino	17	Hg	58.15N	57.35 E
Kalinovik	14	Mg	43.31N	18.26 E
Kalinovka	16	Fe	49.29N	28.32 E
Kaliro	36	Fb	0.54N	33.30 E
Kalispell	39	He	48.12N	114.19W
Kalisz [2]	10	Of	51.45N	18.05 E
Kalisz	10	Oe	51.46N	18.06 E
Kalisz Pomorski	10	Lc	53.19N	15.54 E
Kalitva	16	Le	48.10N	40.46 E
Kaliua	36	Fd	5.04S	31.48 E
Kalix	7	Fd	65.51N	23.08 E
Kalixälven	7	Fd	65.47N	23.13 E
Kalja	17	Jf	60.20N	60.01 E
Kaljazin	19	Dd	57.15N	37.55 E
Kalkandere	24	Ib	40.55N	40.28 E
Kalkar	12	Ic	51.44N	6.18 E
Kalkaska	44	Ec	44.44N	85.11W
Kalkfeld	37	Bd	20.53S	16.11 E
Kalkfontein	37	Cd	22.07S	20.54 E
Kalkim	15	Kj	39.48N	27.13 E
Kalkrand	37	Bd	24.03S	17.33 E
Kall	7	Ce	63.28N	13.15 E
Kållands Halvö	8	Ef	58.35N	13.05 E
Kållandsö	8	Ef	58.40N	13.10 E
Kallaste	7	Gg	58.41N	27.08 E
Kallavesi	5	Ic	62.50N	27.45 E
Kalletal	12	Kb	52.08N	8.57 E
Kallhäll	8	Ge	59.27N	17.48 E
Kallídhromon Óros	15	Fk	38.44N	22.34 E
Kallinge	7	Dh	56.14N	15.17 E
Kallonis, Kolpos-	15	Jj	39.07N	26.08 E
Kallsjön	7	Ce	63.35N	13.00 E
Kalmar	6	Hd	56.40N	16.22 E
Kalmar [2]	7	Dh	57.20N	16.00 E
Kalmarsund	7	Dh	56.40N	16.25 E
Kalmit	12	Ke	49.19N	8.05 E
Kalmius	16	Jf	47.03N	37.34 E
Kalmthout	12	Gc	51.23N	4.28 E
Kalmyckaja ASSR [3]	19	Ef	46.30N	45.30 E
Kalmykovo	16	Qe	49.05N	51.47 E
Kalnciems	8	Jh	56.48N	23.34 E
Kalnik	14	Kd	46.10N	16.30 E
Kalocsa	10	Oj	46.32N	19.00 E
Kalofer	15	Hg	42.37N	24.59 E
Kalohi Channel	65a	Ec	21.00N	156.56W
Kaloko	36	Ed	6.47S	25.47 E
Kalole	36	Ec	3.42S	27.22 E
Kaloli Point	65a	Gd	19.37N	154.57W
Kalomo	36	Ef	17.02S	26.30 E
Kalpa	25	Fb	31.37N	78.10 E
Kalpákion	15	Dj	39.53N	20.35 E
Kalpeni Island	25	Ef	10.05N	73.38 E
Kalpin	27	Cc	40.31N	79.03 E
Kalsūbai	21	Jh	19.36N	73.43 E
Kaltern/Caldaro	14	Fd	46.25N	11.14 E
Kaltungo	34	Hd	9.49N	11.19 E
Kaluga	6	Je	54.31N	36.16 E
Kalulushi	36	Ee	12.50S	28.05 E
Kalumburu Mission	59	Fb	14.18S	126.39 E
Kalundborg	7	Ci	55.41N	11.06 E
Kaluš	19	Cf	49.03N	24.23 E
Kałuszyn	10	Rd	52.13N	21.49 E
Kalužskaja Oblast [3]	19	De	54.20N	35.30 E
Kalvåg	8	Ac	61.46N	4.53 E
Kalvarija	7	Fi	54.27N	23.14 E
Kalya	36	Fd	6.28S	30.03 E
Kalyān	25	Ee	19.15N	73.09 E
Kám	10	Mi	47.06N	16.53 E
Kama	36	Ec	3.32S	27.07 E
Kama [R.S.F.S.R.]	17	Nf	60.27N	69.00 E
Kama [U.S.S.R.]	5	Ld	55.45N	52.00 E
Kamae	29	Be	32.48N	131.56 E
Kamaï	35	Ba	21.12N	17.30 E
Kamaing	25	Jc	25.31N	96.44 E
Kamaishi	28	Pe	39.16N	141.53 E
Kamakou	65a	Eb	21.07N	156.52W
Kamakura	29	Fd	35.19N	139.32 E
Kamālia	25	Eb	30.44N	72.39 E
Kamalo	65a	Eb	21.03N	156.53W
Kaman	24	Ec	39.25N	33.45 E
Kamand, Āb-e-	24	Mf	33.28N	49.04 E
Kamanjab	37	Ac	19.35S	14.51 E
Kamanyola	36	Ec	2.46S	29.00 E
Kamaran	23	Ff	15.12N	42.35 E
Kamarang	54	Fb	5.53N	60.35W
Kama Reservoir (EN)=				
Kamskoje				
Vodohranilišče	5	Ld	58.50N	56.15 E
Kamaši	19	Gh	38.48N	66.29 E
Kamativi	37	Dc	18.19S	27.03 E
Kambalda	59	Ef	31.10S	121.37 E
Kambalnaja Sopka, Vulkan-	20	Kf	51.17N	156.57 E
Kambara	29	Fd	35.07N	138.36 E
Kambara	63d	Cc	18.57S	178.57W
Kambarka	7	Nh	56.18N	54.14 E
Kambia	34	Cd	9.07N	12.55W
Kambja	8	Lf	58.11N	26.43 E
Kambove	36	Ee	10.52S	26.35 E
Kamčatka	20	Le	56.10N	162.30 E
Kamčatka, Poluostrov-=				
Kamchatka Peninsula (EN)	21	Rd	56.00N	160.00 E
Kamčatskaja Oblast [3]	20	Kf	54.50N	159.00 E
Kamčatski Zaliv	20	Le	55.30N	163.00 E
Kamchatka Peninsula (EN)				
=Kamčatka, Poluostrov-	21	Rd	56.00N	160.00 E
Kamčija	15	Kf	43.02N	27.53 E
Kamčijska Plato	15	Kg	42.56N	27.32 E
Kameda [Jap.]	29	Fc	37.52N	139.06 E
Kameda [Jap.]	29a	Bc	41.49N	140.46 E
Kameda-Hantō	29a	Bc	41.45N	141.00 E
Kámeiros	15	Km	36.18N	27.56 E
Kamelik	16	Pc	52.06N	49.30 E
Kamen	12	Jc	51.36N	7.40 E
Kaménai	15	Im	36.25N	25.25 E
Kamende	36	Dd	6.28S	24.33 E
Kamenec	10	Td	52.23N	23.49 E
Kamenec-Podolski	19	Cf	48.39N	26.33 E
Kamenijak, Rt-	14	Hf	44.46N	13.56 E
Kamenka [Kaz.-U.S.S.R.]	16	Qd	51.07N	50.20 E
Kamenka [Mold.-U.S.S.R.]	16	Fe	48.03N	28.45 E
Kamenka [R.S.F.S.R.]	16	Kd	50.43N	39.25 E
Kamenka [R.S.F.S.R.]	19	Ee	53.13N	44.03 E
Kamenka [R.S.F.S.R.]	7	Kd	65.54N	44.04 E
Kamenka [R.S.F.S.R.]	28	Nb	44.28N	136.01 E
Kamenka [Ukr.-U.S.S.R.]	19	Df	49.03N	32.06 E
Kamenka-Bugskaja	10	Uf	50.01N	24.25 E
Kamenka-Dneprovskaja	16	If	47.29N	34.29 E
Kamen-Kaširski	16	Dd	51.36N	24.59 E
Kamen-na-Obi	20	Df	53.47N	81.20 E
Kamennogorsk	7	Gf	60.59N	29.12 E
Kamennoje, Ozero-	7	Hd	64.30N	30.15 E
Kamennomostski	16	Lg	44.17N	40.12 E
Kamen-Rybolov	28	Kb	44.45N	132.04 E
Kamenskoje	20	Ld	62.30N	166.12 E
Kamensk-Šahtinski	16	Le	48.18N	40.16 E
Kamensk-Uralski	22	Id	56.28N	61.54 E
Kamenz/Kamjenc	10	Ke	51.16N	14.06 E
Kameoka	29	Dd	35.00N	135.35 E
Kameškovo	7	Jh	56.22N	41.01 E
Kamet	25	Fd	30.55N	79.35 E
Kameyama	29	Ed	34.51N	136.27 E
Kami-Agata	29	Ad	34.38N	129.25 E
Kamiah	46	Gc	46.14N	116.02W
Kamicharo	29a	Cb	43.11N	143.52 E
Kamienna	10	Re	51.06N	21.47 E
Kamienna Góra	10	Mf	50.47N	16.01 E
Kamień Pomorski	10	Kc	53.58N	14.46 E
Kamiénsk	10	Pe	51.12N	19.30 E
Kamieskroon	37	Bf	30.09S	17.56 E
Kami-furano	29a	Cb	43.29N	142.27 E
Kamiiso	28	Pd	41.49N	140.39 E
Kamiita	29	Dd	34.08N	134.24 E
Kamiji	36	Dd	6.39S	23.17 E
Kamikawa	29a	Cb	43.50N	142.47 E
Kami-Koshiki-Jima	29	Af	31.50N	129.55 E
Kamina	31	Ji	8.44S	24.59 E
Kaminak Lake	42	Id	62.13N	95.00W
Kaminokuni	29a	Bc	41.48N	140.05 E
Kamino-Shima	29	Ad	34.30N	129.25 E
Kaminoyama	28	Pe	38.09N	140.17 E
Kaminuriak Lake	42	Hd	63.00N	95.45W
Kamioka	28	Nf	36.16N	137.18 E
Kami-shihoro	29a	Cb	43.13N	143.16 E
Kamisunagawa	29a	Bb	43.28N	141.58 E
Kamitsushima	29	Ad	34.39N	129.28 E
Kamituga	36	Ec	3.04S	28.11 E
Kamiyama	29	De	33.58N	134.21 E
Kami-yūbetsu	29a	Ca	44.11N	143.34 E
Kamjenc/Kamenz	10	Ke	51.16N	14.06 E
Kamloops	39	Gd	50.40N	120.20W
Kamloops Plateau	46	Ea	50.10N	120.35W
Kamnik	14	Id	46.14N	14.37 E
Kamo [Arm.-U.S.S.R.]	16	Ni	40.22N	45.05 E
Kamo [Jap.]	29	Fc	37.39N	139.03 E
Kamo [N.Z.]	62	Fa	35.41S	174.17 E
Kamōda-Misaki	29	De	33.50N	134.45 E
Kamogawa	29	Gd	35.06N	140.05 E
Kamp	14	Jb	48.23N	15.48 E
Kampala	31	Kh	0.19N	32.35 E
Kampar	26	Df	4.18N	101.09 E
Kampar	26	Mi	0.32N	103.08 E
Kampen	11	Lb	52.33N	5.54 E
Kampene	36	Ec	3.36S	26.40 E
Kamphaeng Phet	25	Je	16.26N	99.33 E
Kamp-Lintford	12	Ic	51.30N	6.32 E
Kamp'o	28	Jg	35.48N	129.30 E
Kâmpóng Cham	22	Mh	12.00N	105.27 E
Kâmpóng Chhnâng	25	Kf	12.15N	104.40 E
Kâmpóng Saôm	22	Mh	10.38N	103.30 E
Kâmpóng Saôm, Chhâk-	25	Kf	10.50N	103.32 E
Kâmpóng Thum	25	Kf	12.42N	104.54 E
Kâmpôt	25	Kf	10.37N	104.11 E
Kampti	34	Ec	10.08N	3.27W
Kampuchea (Cambodia) [1]	22	Mh	13.00N	105.00 E
Kamrau, Teluk-	26	Jg	3.32S	133.37 E
Kamsack	42	Hf	51.34N	101.54W
Kamsar	34	Cc	10.40N	14.36W
Kamskoje Ustje	7	Li	55.14N	49.16 E
Kamskoje Vodohranilišče=				
Kama Reservoir (EN)	5	Ld	58.50N	56.15 E
Kam Summa	35	Ge	0.21N	42.44 E
Kamuenai	29a	Bb	43.08N	140.26 E
Kamui-Dake	29a	Cb	42.25N	142.52 E
Kamui-Misaki	27	Pc	43.20N	140.20 E
Kámuk, Cerro-	49	Fi	9.17N	83.04W
Kamvoúnia Óri	15	Ei	40.00N	21.52 E
Kāmyārān	24	Le	34.47N	46.56 E
Kamyšin	6	Ke	50.06N	45.24 E
Kamyšlov	19	Gd	56.52N	62.43 E
Kamyšovaja Buhta	16	Hg	44.31N	33.33 E
Kamysty-Ajat	17	Jj	53.01N	61.35 E
Kamyzjak	19	Ef	46.06N	48.05 E
Kan	24	Ne	35.45N	51.16 E
Kan	20	Ee	56.31N	93.47 E
Kana	37	Dc	18.32S	27.24 E
Kanaaupscow	42	Jf	54.01N	76.32W
Kanaaupscow	42	Jf	53.40N	77.08W
Kanab	43	Ed	37.03N	112.32W
Kanab Creek	46	Ih	36.24N	112.38W
Kanaga	40a	Cb	51.45N	177.10W
Kanagawa Ken [2]	28	Og	35.30N	139.10 E
Kanaliasem	26	Dg	1.44S	103.35 E
Kanami-Zaki	29b	Bb	27.53N	128.58 E
Kananga	31	Ji	5.54S	22.25 E
Kanariktok	42	Le	55.03N	60.10W
Kanaš	7	Li	55.31N	47.31 E
Kanathea	63d	Cb	17.16S	179.09W
Kanaya	29	Fd	34.48N	138.07 E
Kanayama	29	Ed	35.39N	137.09 E
Kanazawa	22	Pf	36.34N	136.39 E
Kanbalu	25	Jd	23.12N	95.31 E
Kanbe	25	Je	16.42N	96.01 E
Kanchanaburi	25	Jf	14.02N	99.33 E
Kānchenjunga	21	Kg	27.42N	88.08 E
Kānchipuram	25	Ff	12.50N	79.43 E
Kandalakša	6	Jb	67.09N	32.21 E
Kandalaksha, Gulf of- (EN)				
=Kandalakšski Zaliv	5	Jb	66.35N	32.45 E
Kandalakšski Zaliv=				
Kandalaksha, Gulf of- (EN)	5	Jb	66.35N	32.45 E
Kandangan	26	Gg	2.47S	115.16 E
Kándanos	15	Gn	35.20N	23.44 E
Kandava	7	Fh	57.03N	22.46 E
Kandavu Island	57	If	19.00S	178.13 E
Kandavu Passage	63d	Ac	18.45S	178.00 E
Kandel	12	Ke	49.05N	8.12 E
Kandel	10	Eh	48.04N	8.01 E
Kandhelioúsa	15	Jm	36.30N	26.58 E
Kandi	31	Hg	11.08N	2.56 E
Kandıra	24	Db	41.04N	30.09 E
Kandla	25	Ed	23.02N	70.14 E
Kando-Gawa	29	Cd	35.22N	132.40 E
Kandovān, Gardaneh-ye-	24	Nd	36.09N	51.18 E
Kandrian	60	Di	6.13S	149.33 E
Kandry	17	Gi	54.34N	54.10 E
Kandy	22	Ki	7.18N	80.38 E
Kane	44	He	41.40N	78.48W
Kane Bassin	67	Od	79.35N	67.00W
Kaneh	24	Pi	27.04N	54.18 E
Kanem [3]	35	Bc	15.00N	16.00 E
Kanem	30	Ig	14.45N	15.30 E
Kaneohe	60	Oc	21.25N	157.48W
Kaneohe Bay	65a	Db	21.28N	157.48W
Kánestron, Ákra-	15	Gj	39.56N	23.45 E
Kanev	16	Ge	49.42N	31.29 E
Kanevskaja	19	Df	46.06N	38.58 E
Kaneyama	29	Fc	37.27N	139.30 E
Kang	37	Cd	23.44S	22.50 E
Kangaba	34	Dc	11.56N	8.25W
Kangal	24	Gc	39.15N	37.24 E
Kangalassy	20	Hd	62.17N	129.58 E
Kangâmiut	41	Ge	65.39N	53.55W
Kangān [Iran]	24	Oi	27.50N	52.03 E
Kangān [Iran]	24	Qj	25.48N	57.28 E
Kangar	26	De	6.26N	100.12 E
Kangaré	34	Dc	11.37N	8.08W
Kangaroo Island	57	Eh	35.50S	137.05 E
Kangasala	8	Kc	61.28N	24.05 E
Kangasniemi	7	Gf	61.59N	26.38 E
Kangâtsiaq	41	Ge	68.20N	53.18W
Kangāvar	24	Le	34.30N	47.58 E
Kangbao	28	Cd	41.51N	114.37 E
Kangding/Dardo	27	He	30.01N	101.58 E
Kangean, Kepulauan-=				
Kangean Islands (EN)	26	Gh	6.55S	115.30 E
Kangean, Pulau-	26	Gh	6.54S	115.20 E
Kangean Islands (EN)=				
Kangean, Kepulauan-	26	Gh	6.55S	115.30 E
Kangeeak Point	42	Lc	68.01N	64.45W
Kangen	30	Kh	6.47N	33.09 E
Kangerdlugssuaq	41	Ie	68.20N	31.40W
Kangetet	36	Gb	1.58N	36.06 E

Index Symbols

[1] Independent Nation
[2] State, Region
[3] District, County
[4] Municipality
[5] Colony, Dependency
Continent
Physical Region
Historical or Cultural Region
Mount, Mountain
Volcano
Hill
Mountains, Mountain Range
Hills, Escarpment
Plateau, Upland
Pass, Gap
Plain, Lowland
Delta
Salt Flat
Valley, Canyon
Crater, Cave
Karst Features
Depression
Polder
Desert, Dunes
Forest, Woods
Heath, Steppe
Oasis
Cape, Point
Coast, Beach
Cliff
Peninsula
Isthmus
Sandbank
Island
Atoll
Rock, Reef
Islands, Archipelago
Rocks, Reefs
Coral Reef
Well, Spring
Geyser
River, Stream
Waterfall Rapids
River Mouth, Estuary
Lake
Salt Lake
Intermittent Lake
Reservoir
Swamp, Pond
Canal
Glacier
Ice Shelf, Pack Ice
Ocean
Sea
Gulf, Bay
Strait, Fjord
Lagoon
Bank
Seamount
Tablemount
Ridge
Shelf
Basin
Escarpment, Sea Scarp
Fracture
Trench, Abyss
National Park, Reserve
Point of Interest
Recreation Site
Cave, Cavern
Historic Site
Ruins
Wall, Walls
Church, Abbey
Temple
Scientific Station
Airport
Port
Lighthouse
Mine
Tunnel
Dam, Bridge

Kanggup'o	28	Id	41.07N	127.31 E
Kanggye	27	Mc	40.58N	126.36 E
Kangi	35	Dd	8.10N	27.39 E
Kangjin	28	Ig	34.38N	126.46 E
Kangmar	27	Ef	28.32N	89.43 E
Kangnŭng	27	Md	37.44N	128.54 E
Kango	36	Bb	0.09N	10.08 E
Kangondu	36	Gc	1.06S	37.42 E
Kangping	28	Gc	42.45N	123.20 E
Kangrinboqê Feng	27	De	31.04N	81.30 E
Kangto	25	Ic	27.52N	92.30 E
Kangwŏn-Do [N.Kor.] [2]	28	Ie	38.45N	127.35 E
Kangwŏn-Do [S.Kor.] [2]	28	Jf	37.45N	128.15 E
Kani	34	Dd	8.29N	6.36W
Kaniama	36	Dd	7.31S	24.11 E
Kanibadam	18	Hd	40.17N	70.25 E
Kaniet Islands	57	Fe	0.53S	145.30 E
Kanija	15	Lc	46.16N	28.13 E
Kanimeh	18	Ed	40.18N	65.09 E
Kanina	15	Ci	40.26N	19.31 E
Kanin Kamen	17	Bb	68.15N	45.15 E
Kanin Nos	19	Eb	68.39N	43.14 E
Kanin Nos, Mys-	5	Kb	68.39N	43.16 E
Kanin Peninsula (EN)= Kanin Poluostrov	5	Kb	68.00N	45.00 E
Kanin Poluostrov=Kanin Peninsula (EN)	5	Kb	68.00N	45.00 E
Kanioumé	34	Eb	15.46N	3.09W
Kanita	29a	Bc	41.02N	140.38 E
Kanjiža	15	Dc	46.04N	20.03 E
Kankaanpää	7	Ff	61.48N	22.25 E
Kankakee	43	Jc	41.07N	87.52W
Kankakee River	45	Lf	41.23N	88.16W
Kankalabé	34	Cc	11.00N	12.00W
Kankan	31	Gg	10.23N	9.18W
Kanker	25	Gd	20.17N	81.29 E
Kankesanturai	25	Gg	9.49N	80.02 E
Kankossa	32	Ef	15.55N	11.31W
Kankunski	20	He	57.39N	126.25 E
Kanla	10	Hf	50.48N	11.35 E
Kanmav Kyun	25	Jf	11.40N	98.28 E
Kanmon-Kaikyō	29	Bd	33.56N	130.57 E
Kanmuri-Yama	29	Cd	34.28N	132.05 E
Kannapolis	43	Kd	35.30N	80.37W
Kannone-Jima	28	Jj	28.51N	128.58 E
Kannonkoski	8	Kb	62.58N	25.15 E
Kannus	7	Fe	63.54N	23.54 E
Kano [2]	34	Gc	12.00N	9.00 E
Kano	31	Hg	12.00N	8.31 E
Kanona	36	Fe	13.04S	30.38 E
Kan'onji	28	Lg	34.07N	133.39 E
Kanoya	28	Ki	31.23N	130.51 E
Kanozero, Ozero-	7	Ic	67.00N	34.05 E
Kānpur	22	Kg	26.28N	80.21 E
Kansas	38	Jf	39.07N	94.36W
Kansas [2]	43	Hd	38.45N	98.15W
Kansas City [Ks.-U.S.]	39	Jf	39.07N	94.39W
Kansas City [Mo.-U.S.]	39	Jf	39.05N	94.35W
Kanshi	27	Kg	24.57N	116.52 E
Kansk	22	Ld	56.13N	95.41 E
Kansŏng	28	Je	38.22N	128.28 E
Kansu (EN)=Gansu Sheng (Kan-su Sheng) [2]	27	Hd	38.00N	102.00 E
Kansu (EN)=Kan-su Sheng→Gansu Sheng [2]	27	Hd	38.00N	102.00 E
Kan-su Sheng→Gansu Sheng=Kansu (EN) [2]	27	Hd	38.00N	102.00 E
Kansyat	26	Kg	2.15S	138.51 E
Kant	18	Jc	42.52N	74.50 E
Kantang	25	Jg	7.23N	99.32 E
Kantchari	34	Fc	12.29N	1.31 E
Kanté	34	Fd	9.57N	1.03 E
Kantemirovka	19	Df	49.45N	39.53 E
Kantō-Heiya	29	Fc	36.00N	139.30 E
Kanton Atoll	57	Je	2.50S	171.41W
Kantō-Sanchi	29	Fc	36.00N	138.45 E
Kantubek	18	Bb	45.06N	59.16 E
Kanturk/Ceann Toirc	9	Ei	52.10N	8.55W
Kanuma	29	Fc	36.34N	139.45 E
Kanye	31	Jk	24.58S	25.21 E
Kanyu	37	Cd	20.04S	24.36 E
Kanzenze	36	Ee	10.31S	25.12 E
Kao	65b	Aa	19.40S	175.01W
Kaohsiung	22	Og	22.38N	120.17 E
Kaôk Nhêk	25	Lf	13.05N	107.04 E
Kaoko Otavi	37	Ac	18.15S	13.37 E
Kaokoveld [3]	37	Ac	18.00S	13.00 E
Kaokoveld	30	Ij	19.30S	13.30 E
Kaolack	31	Fg	14.09N	16.04W
Kao Neua, Col de-	25	Le	18.23N	105.10 E
Kaouadja	35	Cd	8.00N	23.14 E
Kaouar	34	Hb	19.05N	12.52 E
Kapaa	65a	Ba	22.05N	159.19W
Kapanga	31	Ji	8.21S	22.35 E
Kapar	24	Ld	36.32N	47.30 E
Kapčagaj	19	Hg	43.52N	77.03 E
Kapčagajskoje Vodohranilišče	19	Hg	43.45N	78.00 E
Kapchorwa	36	Fb	1.24N	34.27 E
Kap Dan	41	Ie	65.32N	37.30W
Kapelle	12	Fc	51.39N	3.57 E
Kapellskär	8	He	59.43N	19.04 E
Kapena	36	Ee	10.47S	28.20 E
Kapenguria	36	Gb	1.14N	35.07 E
Kapfenberg	14	Jc	47.26N	15.18 E
Kapidaği Yarimadası	15	Ki	40.28N	27.50 E
Kapingamarangi Atoll	57	Gd	1.04N	154.46 E
Kapingamarangi Rise (EN)	57	Gd	1.00N	157.00 E
Kapiri Mposhi	36	Ee	13.58S	28.41 E
Kāpīsā [3]	23	Kc	34.45N	69.30 E
Kapit	26	Ff	2.01N	112.56 E
Kapiti Island	62	Fd	40.50S	174.55 E
Kapka, Massif du-	35	Cb	15.07N	21.45 E
Kapoeta	31	Kh	4.47N	33.35 E
Kapona	36	Ed	7.11S	29.09 E
Kapos	10	Oj	46.44N	18.29 E
Kaposvár	10	Nj	46.22N	17.48 E
Kapp	8	Dd	60.42N	10.52 E
Kappeln	10	Fb	54.40N	9.56 E
Kapša	7	Hg	59.52N	33.45 E
Kapsan	28	Jd	41.05N	128.18 E
Kapsukas	7	Fi	54.33N	23.23 E
Kapuas [Indon.]	26	Mj	0.25S	109.40 E
Kapuas [Indon.]	26	Fg	3.01S	114.20 E
Kapuas Hulu, Pegunungan- =Kapuas Mountains (EN)	26	Ff	1.25N	113.15 E
Kapuas Mountains (EN)= Kapuas Hulu, Pegunungan	26	Ff	1.25N	113.15 E
Kapugargin	15	Lm	36.40N	28.50 E
Kapušany	10	Rg	49.03N	21.21 E
Kapuskasing	39	Ke	49.25N	82.26W
Kapustin Jar	16	Ne	48.35N	45.45 E
Kapustoje	7	Ic	67.17N	34.12 E
Kaputdžuh, Gora-	16	Oj	39.12N	46.01 E
Kapuvár	10	Ni	47.36N	17.02 E
Kara	17	Lb	69.10N	64.45 E
Kara	34	Fd	9.33N	1.12 E
Kara [3]	34	Fd	9.35N	1.05 E
Kara Ada [Tur.]	15	Km	36.58N	27.28 E
Kara Ada [Tur.]	15	Jk	38.25N	26.20 E
Kara-Balta	19	Hg	42.49N	73.57 E
Karabas	19	Hf	49.30N	73.00 E
Karabaš	17	Ji	55.29N	60.13 E
Karabekaul	19	Gh	38.28N	64.10 E
Karabiga	15	Ki	40.24N	27.18 E
Karabil, Vozvyšennost-	18	Df	36.20N	63.30 E
Kara-Bogaz-Gol	19	Fg	41.01N	52.59 E
Kara-Bogaz-Gol, proliv-	16	Ri	41.04N	52.59 E
Kara-Bogaz-Gol, Zaliv-	5	Lg	41.00N	53.15 E
Karabuk	23	Da	41.12N	32.37 E
Karabulak [Kaz.-U.S.S.R.]	18	Lb	44.54N	78.29 E
Karabulak [Kaz.-U.S.S.R.]	19	Gg	42.31N	69.47 E
Kara Burun	15	Km	36.32N	27.58 E
Karaburun [Tur.]	24	Cb	41.21N	28.40 E
Karaburun [Tur.]	24	Bc	38.37N	26.31 E
Karabutak	19	Gf	49.57N	60.08 E
Karacabey	24	Cb	40.13N	28.21 E
Karaca Dağ	24	Hd	37.40N	39.50 E
Karačajevo-Čerkessakaja Avtonomnaja Oblast [3]	19	Eg	43.45N	41.45 E
Karačajevsk	16	Lh	43.44N	41.58 E
Karacaköy	24	Cb	41.22N	28.30 E
Karacaoğlan	15	Kh	41.32N	27.04 E
Karacasu	24	Cd	37.43N	28.37 E
Karačev	19	De	53.04N	34.59 E
Karāchi	22	Ig	24.52N	67.03 E
Kara Dağ [Tur.]	24	Jd	37.40N	43.42 E
Kara Dağ [Tur.]	24	Ed	37.23N	33.10 E
Karadah	16	Oh	42.29N	46.54 E
Karadeniz=Black Sea (EN)	5	Jg	43.00N	35.00 E
Kara Dong	27	Dd	38.26N	81.50 E
Karagajly	19	Hf	49.20N	75.48 E
Karaganda	22	Je	49.50N	73.10 E
Karagandinskaja Oblast [3]	19	Hf	50.00N	74.00 E
Karaginski, Ostrov-	21	Sd	58.48N	164.05 E
Karaginski Zaliv	21	Sd	58.50N	164.00 E
Kara Gölü	15	Mm	36.42N	29.50 E
Karagoš, Gora-	20	Df	51.44N	89.24 E
Karahalli	15	Mk	38.20N	29.32 E
Karaidelski	17	Hi	55.49N	57.05 E
Kara-Irtyš	21	Ke	47.52N	84.16 E
Karaisali	24	Fd	37.16N	35.03 E
Karaj	24	Ne	35.48N	50.59 E
Karaj	24	Ne	35.07N	51.35 E
Karak, Gora-	19	Gq	44.59N	63.05 E
Kara-Kala	19	Fh	38.28N	56.18 E
Karakalpak ASSR (EN)= Karakalpakskaja ASSR [3]	19	Fg	43.30N	59.00 E
Karakalpakskaja ASSR= Karakalpak ASSR (EN) [3]	19	Fg	43.30N	59.00 E
Karakax/Moyu	27	Cd	37.17N	79.42 E
Karakax He	27	Dd	38.06N	80.24 E
Karakeçi	24	Hd	37.26N	39.26 E
Karakelong, Pulau-	26	If	4.15N	126.48 E
Karakoçan	24	Ic	38.02N	40.07 E
Karakoin, Ozero-	18	Ga	46.10N	68.40 E
Karakojsu	16	Oh	42.30N	47.05 E
Karakolka	18	Kd	41.29N	77.24 E
Karakoram	21	Jf	34.00N	78.00 E
Karakoram Pass	21	Jf	35.30N	77.50 E
Karakore	35	Gc	10.25N	40.01 E
Karakoro	34	Cc	14.43N	12.03 E
Karakorum Shan	27	Cd	36.00N	76.00 E
Karakorum Shankou	27	Cd	35.30N	77.50 E
Karaköse	23	Fb	39.44N	43.03 E
Karaköy	24	Ic	39.04N	41.42 E
Kara-Kul	18	Id	41.34N	72.47 E
Karakul, Ozero-	19	Hh	39.05N	73.25 E
Karakumski kanal imeni V.I. Lenina	19	Gh	37.42N	64.20 E
Karakumy	21	Hf	39.00N	60.00 E
Karakuwisa	37	Bc	18.56S	19.40 E
Karam	20	Fe	55.09N	107.37 E
Karama	26	Gg	2.18S	119.06 E
Karaman	23	Db	37.11N	33.14 E
Karamanli	15	Ml	37.22N	29.49 E
Karamay	22	Ke	45.30N	84.55 E
Karamea	61	Dh	41.15S	172.06 E
Karamea Bight	62	Dd	41.25S	171.50 E
Karamet-Nijaz	19	Gh	37.43N	64.31 E
Karamiran He	27	Dd	37.50N	84.35 E
Karamiran Shankou	27	Ed	36.15N	87.05 E
Karamiševo	8	Mg	57.44N	28.50 E
Karamoja [3]	36	Fb	2.45N	34.15 E
Karamürsel	15	Mi	40.42N	29.36 E
Kara-myk	19	Hh	39.30N	71.51 E
Karamyš	16	Nd	51.18N	45.00 E
Karān	24	Mi	27.43N	49.49 E
Karaova	15	Kl	37.05N	27.40 E
Karapınar	24	Ed	37.43N	33.33 E
Kara-Saki	29	Ad	34.40N	129.29 E
Kara-Sal	16	Mf	47.18N	43.36 E
Karasay	27	Dd	36.48N	83.48 E
Karasburg	31	Ik	28.00S	18.43 E
Kara Sea (EN)=Karskoje More	67	Hd	76.00N	80.00 E
Karašica	14	Me	45.36N	18.36 E
Karasjok	7	Fb	69.27N	25.30 E
Kara Strait (EN)=Karskije Vorota, Proliv-	21	Hb	70.30N	58.00 E
Karasu	24	Db	41.04N	30.47 E
Karasu [Tur.]	21	Ff	38.52N	38.48 E
Karasu [Tur.]	24	Ic	38.49N	41.28 E
Karasu [Tur.]	24	Jc	38.32N	43.10 E
Karasu Dağları	24	Ic	39.30N	40.45 E
Karasuk	20	Cf	53.44N	78.08 E
Karasuk	20	Cf	53.35N	77.30 E
Karasuyama	29	Gc	36.39N	140.08 E
Karatá, Laguna-	49	Fg	13.56N	83.30W
Karatal	19	Hf	46.26N	77.10 E
Karataş [Tur.]	24	Fd	36.36N	35.21 E
Karataş [Tur.]	15	Lk	38.34N	28.17 E
Karataş Burun	24	Fb	36.35N	35.22 E
Karatau	19	Hg	43.10N	70.29 E
Karatau, Hrebet-	21	Ie	43.40N	69.00 E
Karatj	7	Ec	66.43N	18.33 E
Karatobe	16	Re	49.42N	53.33 E
Karaton	19	Ff	46.25N	53.34 E
Karatsu	28	Jh	33.26N	130.00 E
Karatsu-Wan	29	Be	33.30N	130.00 E
Kara-Turgaj	21	Ie	48.01N	62.45 E
Karaul [Kaz.-U.S.S.R.]	19	Hf	49.00N	79.20 E
Karaul [R.S.F.S.R.]	20	Db	70.10N	83.08 E
Karaulbazar	18	Ee	39.29N	64.47 E
Karaulkala	18	Bc	42.18N	58.41 E
Karáva	15	Ej	39.19N	21.36 E
Karavanke	14	Id	46.25N	14.25 E
Karavastase, Gjiri i-	15	Ci	40.55N	19.30 E
Karavastase, Laguna e-	15	Ci	40.55N	19.30 E
Karávi	15	Gm	36.45N	23.35 E
Karavonísia	15	Jn	35.59N	26.26 E
Karawa	36	Db	3.20N	20.18 E
Karaxabar He/Kaidu He	27	Ec	41.55N	86.38 E
Karažal	19	Hf	47.59N	70.53 E
Karbalā'	22	Gf	32.36N	44.02 E
Karbalā [3]	24	Jf	32.30N	43.45 E
Kårbole	7	Df	61.59N	15.19 E
Karcag	10	Qi	47.19N	20.56 E
Kardhámaina	15	Km	36.47N	27.09 E
Kardhámila	15	Jk	38.31N	26.06 E
Kardhíotissa	15	Im	36.38N	25.01 E
Kardhítsa	15	Ej	39.22N	21.55 E
Kärdla/Kjardla	7	Fg	59.01N	22.42 E
Kărdžali	15	Ih	41.39N	25.22 E
Kărdžali [2]	15	Ih	41.30N	25.30 E
Kareha, Jbel-	13	Gi	35.15N	5.30W
Karelia (EN)	5	Jc	64.00N	32.00 E
Karelskaja ASSR [3]	19	Dc	63.30N	33.30 E
Karema	36	Fd	6.49S	30.26 E
Karen [2]	25	Je	17.30N	97.45 E
Karen	25	If	12.51N	92.53 E
Karesuando	7	Fb	68.27N	22.29 E
Karêt	30	Gf	24.00N	7.30W
Kärevere/Kjarevere	8	Lf	58.23N	26.30 E
Kargala	16	Sd	51.59N	55.10 E
Kargapazarı Dağı	24	Ib	40.07N	41.35 E
Kargapolje	17	Li	55.57N	64.27 E
Kargasok	20	De	59.07N	81.01 E
Kargat	20	De	55.10N	80.17 E
Kargı	24	Fb	41.08N	34.30 E
Kargil	25	Fb	34.34N	76.06 E
Kargilik/Yecheng	22	Jf	37.54N	77.26 E
Kargopol	19	Dc	61.32N	38.58 E
Karhula	7	Gf	60.31N	26.57 E
Kari	34	Hc	11.14N	10.34 E
Kariaí	6	Ig	40.15N	24.15 E
Kariba	31	Jj	16.30S	28.45 E
Kariba, Lake-	30	Jj	17.00S	28.00 E
Kariba-Dake	29a	Ab	42.37N	139.56 E
Kariba Dam	37	Dc	16.30S	28.50 E
Karibib	31	Ik	21.58S	15.51 E
Karibib [3]	37	Bd	22.00S	16.00 E
Kariet-Arkmane	13	Ji	35.06N	2.45W
Karigasniemi	7	Fb	69.24N	25.50 E
Karijärvi	8	Jc	61.35N	22.30 E
Karikachi Tōge	29a	Cb	43.10N	142.40 E
Kārikāl	25	Ff	10.55N	79.50 E
Karikari, Cape-	62	Ea	34.47S	173.24 E
Karima (EN)=Kuraymah	31	Kg	18.33N	31.51 E
Karimama	34	Fc	12.04N	3.11 E
Karimata, Kepulauan-= Karimata Islands (EN)	26	Eg	1.25S	109.05 E
Karimata, Pulau-	26	Eg	1.36S	108.55 E
Karimata, Selat-=Karimata Strait (EN)	21	Mj	2.05S	108.40 E
Karimata Islands (EN)= Karimata, Kepulauan-	26	Eg	1.25S	109.05 E
Karimata Strait (EN)= Karimata, Selat-	21	Mj	2.05S	108.40 E
Karīmganj	25	Id	24.42N	92.33 E
Karīmnagar	25	Fe	18.26N	79.09 E
Karimunjawa, Kepulauan-= Karimunjawa Islands (EN)	26	Fh	5.50S	110.25 E
Karimunjawa Islands (EN)= Karimunjawa, Kepulauan-	26	Fh	5.50S	110.25 E
Karin [Som.]	35	Hc	10.59N	49.13 E
Karin [Som.]	35	Hc	10.51N	45.45 E
Karis/Karjaa	7	Ff	60.05N	23.40 E
Karisimbi	30	Ji	1.30S	29.27 E
Káristos	15	Hk	38.01N	24.25 E
Karjaa/Karis	7	Ff	60.05N	23.40 E
Karkār	35	Hd	9.57N	49.20 E
Karkaralinsk	19	Hf	49.23N	75.31 E
Karkar Island	57	Fe	4.40S	146.00 E
Karkas, Kūh-e	24	Nf	33.27N	51.48 E
Karkheh	23	Gc	31.31N	47.55 E
Karkinitski zaliv	5	Jf	45.55N	33.00 E
Karkkila/Högfors	7	Ff	60.32N	24.11 E
Karkku	8	Jc	61.25N	23.01 E
Kärkölä	8	Kd	60.55N	25.15 E
Kärla/Kjarla	8	Jf	58.16N	22.05 E
Karlholm	8	Gd	60.31N	17.37 E
Karlik Shan	21	Le	43.00N	94.30 E
Karlino	10	Lb	54.03N	15.51 E
Karliova	24	Ic	39.18N	41.01 E
Karl Marx, Pik-	19	Hh	37.08N	72.29 E
Karl-Marx-Stadt	6	He	50.50N	12.55 E
Karl-Marx-Stadt [2]	10	If	50.45N	12.50 E
Karlö/Hailuoto	5	Ib	65.02N	24.42 E
Karlobag	14	Jf	44.32N	15.05 E
Karlovac	14	Je	45.29N	15.33 E
Karlovka	16	Ie	49.28N	35.08 E
Karlovo	15	Hg	42.38N	24.48 E
Karlovy Vary	10	If	50.14N	12.52 E
Karlsbad	12	Kf	48.55N	8.35 E
Karlsborg	7	Df	58.32N	14.31 E
Karlshamn	7	Dh	56.10N	14.51 E
Karlskoga	7	Dg	59.20N	14.31 E
Karlskrona	6	Hd	56.10N	15.35 E
Karlsöarna	8	Gg	57.15N	18.00 E
Karlsruhe	10	Eg	49.01N	8.24 E
Karlstad [Mn.-U.S.]	45	Hb	48.35N	96.31W
Karlstad [Swe.]	6	Hd	59.22N	13.30 E
Karluk	40	Ie	57.34N	154.28W
Karmah=Kerma (EN)	35	Eb	19.38N	30.25 E
Karmana	18	Ed	40.09N	65.15 E
Karmøy	7	Ag	59.15N	5.15 E
Karnāli	25	Gc	28.45N	81.16 E
Karnataka (Mysore) [3]	25	Ff	13.30N	76.00 E
Karnobat	15	Jg	42.39N	26.59 E
Kärnten = Carinthia (EN) [2]	14	Hd	46.45N	14.00 E
Kärnten = Carinthia (EN)	14	Hd	46.45N	14.00 E
Karoi	37	Dc	16.50S	29.40 E
Karonga	31	Ki	9.56S	33.56 E
Karora	35	Fb	17.39N	38.22 E
Káros	15	Im	36.53N	25.39 E
Kárpathos	15	Kn	35.30N	27.14 E
Kárpathos=Karpathos (EN)	5	Ih	35.40N	27.10 E
Karpathos (EN)= Kárpathos	5	Ih	35.40N	27.10 E
Karpáthou, Stenón-	15	Kn	35.50N	27.30 E
Karpenísion	15	Ek	38.55N	21.47 E
Karpinsk	17	Jg	59.45N	60.01 E
Karpuzlu	15	Kl	37.33N	27.50 E
Kars	23	Fa	40.37N	43.05 E
Karsakpaj	19	Gf	47.48N	66.45 E
Kärsämäki	7	Fe	64.00N	25.46 E
Karsava/Kārsava	7	Gh	56.47N	27.42 E
Kārsava/Karsava	7	Gh	56.47N	27.42 E
Karši	22	If	38.53N	65.48 E
Karşiyaka	15	Ki	40.26N	28.00 E
Karsiyaka	15	Kk	38.27N	27.07 E
Karskije Vorota, Proliv-= Kara Strait (EN)	21	Hb	70.30N	58.00 E
Karskoje More=Kara Sea (EN)	67	Hd	76.00N	80.00 E
Kars Platosu	24	Jb	40.40N	43.07 E
Karst (EN)=Kras	5	Hf	45.48N	14.00 E
Kårsta	8	He	59.39N	18.14 E
Karstula	7	Fe	62.52N	24.47 E
Kartal	24	Cb	40.53N	29.10 E
Kartaly	19	Ge	53.03N	60.40 E
Kartaly-Ajat	17	Jj	53.01N	61.50 E
Karttula	8	Lb	62.53N	26.58 E
Kartuzy	10	Ob	54.20N	18.12 E
Karumai	29	Ga	40.20N	141.28 E
Karumba	59	Ic	17.29S	140.50 E
Karūn	21	Gf	30.25N	48.12 E
Karungi	7	Fc	66.03N	23.57 E
Karungu	36	Fc	0.51S	34.09 E
Karunki	7	Fc	66.02N	24.01 E
Karūr	25	Ff	10.57N	78.05 E
Karvia	7	Fe	62.08N	22.34 E
Karviná	10	Og	49.51N	18.32 E
Kārwār	25	Ef	14.48N	74.08 E
Karwendel Gebirge	14	Fc	47.28N	11.20 E
Karymskoje	20	Gf	51.37N	114.21 E
Kas	35	Cc	12.34N	24.14 E
Kaş	24	Cd	36.12N	29.38 E
Kasaba [Tur.]	15	Mm	36.18N	29.44 E
Kasaba [Zam.]	36	Ee	10.44S	29.43 E
Kasado-Shima	29	Be	33.57N	131.50 E
Kasah	16	Mi	40.03N	43.52 E
Kasai	29	Dd	34.56N	134.49 E
Kasai	30	Ii	3.02S	16.57 E
Kasai Occidental [2]	36	Dc	5.00S	21.30 E
Kasai Oriental [2]	36	Dc	3.00S	23.00 E
Kasaji	36	De	10.22S	23.27 E
Kasaku	36	Ec	1.55S	25.50 E
Kasama [Jap.]	29	Gc	36.22N	140.16 E
Kasama [Zam.]	31	Kj	10.13S	31.12 E
Kasan	18	Ee	39.01N	65.35 E
Kasane	31	Jj	17.48S	25.09 E
Kasanga	36	Fd	8.28S	31.09 E
Kasangulu	36	Bc	4.36S	15.10 E
Kasansaj	18	Hd	41.10N	71.32 E
Kasaoka	29	Cd	34.30N	133.29 E
Kāsaragod	25	Ef	12.30N	75.00 E
Kasari	29b	Ba	28.27N	129.41 E
Kašary	16	Le	49.02N	41.03 E
Kasatori-Yama	29	Ce	33.33N	132.55 E
Kasba Lake	42	Hd	60.20N	102.10W
Kasba Tatla	32	Fc	32.36N	6.16W
Kaseda	28	Ki	31.25N	130.19 E
Kasempa	36	Ee	13.27S	25.50 E
Kasenga	31	Jj	10.22S	28.37 E
Kasenye	36	Fb	1.24N	30.26 E
Kasese [Ug.]	36	Fb	0.10N	30.05 E
Kasese [Zaire]	36	Ec	1.38S	27.07 E
Kashaf	23	Jb	35.58N	61.07 E
Kāshān	22	Hf	33.59N	51.29 E
Kashi	22	Jf	39.29N	75.58 E
Kashihara	29	Dd	34.31N	135.47 E
Kashima [Jap.]	29	Cd	35.31N	132.59 E
Kashima [Jap.]	29	Gd	35.58N	140.38 E
Kashima [Jap.]	29	Be	33.07N	130.07 E
Kashima-Nada	29	Gc	36.30N	140.45 E
Kashiobwe	36	Ed	9.39S	28.37 E
Kashiwazaki	28	Of	37.25N	138.30 E
Kashkū'īyeh	24	Qh	28.58N	56.37 E
Kāshmar	23	Ib	35.12N	58.27 E
Kashmir	21	Jf	34.00N	76.00 E
Kashmor	25	Dc	28.26N	69.35 E
Kasimov	19	Ee	54.59N	41.28 E
Kašin	19	Dd	57.23N	37.37 E
Kasindi	36	Eb	0.02N	29.43 E
Kašira	7	Ji	54.52N	38.11 E
Kasiruta, Pulau-	26	Ig	0.25S	127.12 E
Kasisty	20	Fb	73.40N	109.45 E
Kaškadarinskaja Oblast [3]	19	Gh	38.50N	66.10 E
Kaškadarja	18	Ee	39.35N	64.38 E
Kaskaskia River	45	Lh	37.59N	89.56W
Kaskelen	19	Hg	43.09N	76.37 E
Kaskinen/Kaskö	7	Ee	62.23N	21.13 E
Kaskö/Kaskinen	7	Ee	62.23N	21.13 E
Kasli	17	Ji	55.53N	60.48 E
Kaslo	46	Gb	49.55N	116.55W
Kasongo	31	Ji	4.27S	26.40 E
Kasongo-Lunda	36	Cd	6.28S	16.49 E
Kásos	15	Jn	35.25N	26.55 E
Kásou, Stenón-	15	Jn	35.25N	26.35 E
Kaspi	16	Ni	41.58N	44.25 E
Kaspičan	15	Kf	43.18N	27.11 E
Kaspijsk	19	Eg	42.57N	47.35 E
Kaspijski	19	Ef	45.25N	47.22 E
Kaspijskoje More=Caspian Sea (EN)	5	Lg	42.00N	50.30 E
Kasplja	16	Gb	55.24N	30.43 E
Kasr, Ra's-	35	Fb	18.04N	38.33 E
Kassaar/Kassar	8	Jf	58.47N	22.40 E
Kassalā	31	Kg	15.28N	36.24 E
Kassalā [3]	35	Fc	14.40N	35.30 E
Kassándra	15	Gi	40.00N	23.30 E
Kassandra, Gulf of- (EN) = Kassándras, Kólpos-	15	Gi	40.05N	23.30 E
Kassándras, Ákra-	15	Gj	39.57N	23.21 E
Kassándras, Kólpos- = Kassandra, Gulf of- (EN)	15	Gi	40.05N	23.30 E
Kassar/Kassaar	8	Jf	58.47N	22.40 E
Kassel	10	Fe	51.19N	9.30 E
Kassinga	36	Cf	15.06S	16.06 E
Kassiópi	15	Cj	39.47N	19.55 E
Kastamonu	23	Da	41.22N	33.47 E
Kastanéai	15	Jh	41.39N	26.28 E
Kastellaun	12	Jd	50.04N	7.27 E
Kastéllion [Grc.]	15	In	35.12N	25.20 E
Kastéllion [Grc.]	15	Gn	35.30N	23.39 E
Kastéllos, Ákra-	15	Kn	35.23N	27.09 E
Kasterlee	12	Gc	51.15N	4.57 E
Kastlösa	8	Gh	56.28N	16.25 E
Kastoría	15	Ei	40.31N	21.16 E
Kastorías, Límni-	15	Ei	40.31N	21.18 E
Kastornoje	16	Kd	51.51N	38.07 E
Kastós	15	Dk	38.35N	20.55 E
Kasuga	29	Be	33.32N	130.27 E
Kasugai	29	Ed	35.14N	136.58 E
Kasulu	36	Fc	4.34S	30.06 E
Kasumbalesa	36	Ee	12.13S	27.48 E
Kasumi	29	Dd	35.38N	134.38 E
Kasumi-ga-Ura	28	Pf	36.00N	140.25 E
Kasumkent	16	Pi	41.42N	48.10 E
Kasungan	26	Fg	1.58S	113.24 E
Kasungu	36	Fe	13.02S	33.29 E
Kasupe	36	Gf	15.10S	35.18 E
Kasūr	25	Eb	31.07N	74.27 E
Kaszuby	10	Ob	54.10N	18.15 E
Kataba	31	Jj	16.05S	25.10 E
Katahdin, Mount-	43	Nb	45.55N	68.55W
Katajsk	17	Kh	56.18N	62.35 E
Katako-Kombe	36	Dc	3.24S	24.25 E
Katanga	36	Ed	10.00S	25.30 E
Katanga	20	Fd	60.10N	102.10 E
Katangli	20	Jf	51.43N	143.16 E
Katanning	59	Df	33.42S	117.33 E
Katav-Ivanovsk	17	Ii	54.47N	58.15 E
Katchall	25	Ig	7.57N	93.22 E
Katchi	32	Ef	17.00N	13.55W
Katende, Chutes de-	36	Dd	6.30S	22.10 E
Katerini	15	Fi	40.16N	22.30 E
Katesh	36	Gc	4.31S	35.23 E
Katete	36	Fe	14.06S	32.05 E
Katha	25	Jd	24.11N	96.21 E
Katherine	58	Ef	14.28S	132.16 E
Katherine River	59	Gb	14.39S	131.42 E
Kāthiāwār	21	Jg	21.58N	70.30 E
Kathmandu	22	Kg	27.43N	85.19 E
Kathua	36	Gc	1.17S	39.03 E
Kati	34	Dc	12.43N	8.05W
Katihār	25	Hc	25.32N	87.35 E
Katiki, Volcán-	65d	Bb	27.06S	109.16W
Katima Mulilo	36	Df	17.28S	24.14 E
Katiola	34	Dd	8.08N	5.06W
Katiola [3]	34	Dd	8.13N	5.02W
Katiu Atoll	61	Mc	16.26S	144.22W
Katla	7a	Bc	63.36N	18.58W
Katlabuh, Ozero-	15	Ld	45.25N	29.00 E
Katlanovo	15	Eh	41.54N	21.41 E
Katmai, Mount-	40	Ie	58.17N	154.56W
Káto Akhaia	15	Ek	38.09N	21.33 E
Katofio	36	Ee	11.02S	28.01 E
Katompi	36	Ed	6.11S	26.20 E
Katonga	36	Fb	0.10N	30.40 E
Katon-Karagaj	19	If	49.11N	85.37 E
Káto Ólimbos	15	Fj	39.55N	22.28 E
Katoomba	59	Kf	33.42S	150.18 E
Katopasa, Gunung-	26	Hg	1.14S	121.25 E

Index Symbols

[1] Independent Nation
[2] State, Region
[3] District, County
[4] Municipality
[5] Colony, Dependency
Continent
Physical Region
Historical or Cultural Region
Mount, Mountain
Volcano
Hill
Mountains, Mountain Range
Hills, Escarpment
Plateau, Upland
Pass, Gap
Plain, Lowland
Delta
Salt Flat
Valley, Canyon
Crater, Cave
Karst Features
Depression
Polder
Desert, Dunes
Forest, Woods
Heath, Steppe
Oasis
Cape, Point
Coast, Beach
Cliff
Peninsula
Isthmus
Sandbank
Island
Atoll
Rock, Reef
Islands, Archipelago
Rocks, Reefs
Coral Reef
Well, Spring
Geyser
River, Stream
Waterfall Rapids
River Mouth, Estuary
Lake
Salt Lake
Intermittent Lake
Reservoir
Swamp, Pond
Canal
Glacier
Ice Shelf, Pack Ice
Ocean
Sea
Gulf, Bay
Strait, Fjord
Lagoon
Bank
Seamount
Tablemount
Ridge
Shelf
Basin
Escarpment, Sea Scarp
Fracture
Trench, Abyss
National Park, Reserve
Point of Interest
Recreation Site
Cave, Cavern
Historic Site
Ruins
Wall, Walls
Church, Abbey
Temple
Scientific Station
Airport
Port
Lighthouse
Mine
Tunnel
Dam, Bridge

Name	Map	Grid	Lat.	Long.
Katowice [2]	10	Of	50.15N	19.00 E
Katowice	6	He	50.16N	19.00 E
Katrancık Dağı	24	Dd	37.27N	30.25 E
Kātrīnā, Jabal-	30	Kf	28.31N	33.57 E
Katrineholm	7	Dg	59.00N	16.12 E
Katsina	31	Hg	13.00N	7.36 E
Katsina Ala	34	Gd	7.48N	8.52 E
Katsumoto	28	Jh	33.51N	129.42 E
Katsuta	28	Pf	36.24N	140.32 E
Katsuura	28	Pg	35.08N	140.18 E
Katsuyama [Jap.]	28	Nf	36.03N	136.30 E
Katsuyama [Jap.]	29	Cd	35.06N	133.41 E
Kattakurgan	19	Gh	39.55N	66.15 E
Kattavía	15	Kn	35.57N	27.46 E
Kattegat	5	Hd	57.00N	11.00 E
Katthammarsvik	8	Hg	57.26N	18.50 E
Katulo, Lagh-	36	Hb	2.08N	40.56 E
Katumbi	36	Fe	10.49S	33.32 E
Katun	21	Kd	52.25N	85.05 E
Katwijk aan Zee	11	Kb	52.13N	4.24 E
Katwijk aan Zee, Katwijk-	12	Gb	52.12N	4.25 E
Katwijk-Katwijk aan Zee	12	Gb	52.12N	4.25 E
Katzenelnbogen	12	Jd	50.17N	7.57 E
Kau	26	If	1.11N	127.54 E
Kauai Channel	60	Oc	21.45N	158.50W
Kauai Island	57	Lb	22.03N	159.30W
Kaub	12	Jd	50.05N	7.46 E
Kauehi Atoll	61	Lc	15.51S	145.09W
Kaufbeuren	10	Gi	47.53N	10.37 E
Kauhajoki	7	Fe	62.26N	22.11 E
Kauhava	7	Fe	63.06N	23.05 E
Kauiki Head	60	Oc	20.46N	155.59W
Kaukauna	45	Ld	44.17N	88.17W
Kaukauveld	30	Jk	20.00S	21.50 E
Kaukonen	7	Fc	67.29N	24.54 E
Kaukura Atoll	57	Mf	15.45S	146.42W
Kaula Island	57	Kb	21.40N	160.32W
Kaulakahi Channel	65a	Ba	22.02N	159.53W
Kaumalapau	65a	Ec	20.47N	156.59W
Kaunakakai	60	Oc	21.05N	157.02W
Kaunas	6	Ie	54.54N	23.54 E
Kaunasskoje Vodohranilišče /Kauno Marios	8	Kj	54.50N	24.15 E
Kauniainen/Grankulla	8	Kd	60.13N	24.45 E
Kauno Marios/Kaunasskoje Vodohranilišče	8	Kj	54.50N	24.15 E
Kaunos	15	Lm	36.50N	28.35 E
Kaupanger	7	Bf	61.11N	7.14 E
Kau Paulatmada, Gunung-	26	Ig	3.15S	126.09 E
Kaura Namoda	34	Gc	12.36N	6.35 E
Kauriāla Ghāt	25	Gc	28.27N	80.59 E
Kaušany	16	Ff	46.39N	29.25 E
Kaustinen	7	Fe	63.32N	23.42 E
Kautokeino	7	Fb	68.59N	23.08 E
Kavacik	15	Lj	39.40N	28.30 E
Kavadarci	15	Fh	41.26N	22.01 E
Kavaja	15	Ch	41.11N	19.33 E
Kavak [Tur.]	15	Ji	40.36N	26.54 E
Kavak [Tur.]	24	Gb	41.05N	36.03 E
Kavaklidere	15	Ll	37.26N	28.22 E
Kavála	6	Ig	40.56N	24.25 E
Kaválas, Kólpos-	15	Hi	40.52N	24.25 E
Kavalerovo	20	Ih	44.19N	135.05 E
Kavali	25	Ff	14.55N	79.59 E
Kavār	24	Oh	29.11N	52.44 E
Kavaratti	22	Jh	10.33N	72.38 E
Kavaratti Island	25	Ef	10.33N	72.38 E
Kavarna	15	Lf	43.25N	28.20 E
Kavarskas/Kovarskas	8	Ki	55.24N	25.03 E
Kavendou, Mont-	30	Fg	10.41N	12.12W
Kavieng	60	Eh	2.34S	150.48 E
Kavīr, Dasht-e-	21	Hf	34.40N	54.30 E
Kavkaz	16	Jg	45.21N	36.12 E
Kavkaz, Bolšoj-=Caucasus (EN)	5	Kg	42.30N	45.00 E
Kävlinge	8	Ei	55.48N	13.06 E
Kävlingeån	8	Ei	55.47N	13.06 E
Kawa	35	Eb	19.10N	30.39 E
Kawabe	29	Gb	39.39N	140.15 E
Kawachi-nagano	29	Dd	34.27N	135.34 E
Kawagoe	29	Fd	35.55N	139.28 E
Kawaguchi	29	Fd	35.48N	139.42 E
Kawaihae Bay	65a	Fc	20.02N	155.51W
Kawaihoa Point	65a	Ab	21.47N	160.12W
Kawakawa	62	Fa	35.23S	174.04 E
Kawalusu, Pulau-	26	If	4.15N	125.19 E
Kawamata	29	Gc	37.40N	140.36 E
Kawambwa	36	Ed	9.47S	29.05 E
Kawaminami	29	Be	32.12N	131.32 E
Kawamoto	29	Cd	34.59N	132.29 E
Kawanishi	29	Gc	37.59N	140.03 E
Kawanoe	29	Cd	34.01N	133.34 E
Kawartha Lakes	44	Hc	44.32N	78.30W
Kawasaki [Jap.]	29	Gb	38.10N	140.38 E
Kawasaki [Jap.]	28	Og	35.32N	139.43 E
Kawashiri-Misaki	29	Bd	34.26N	130.58 E
Kawauchi	29a	Bc	41.12N	141.00 E
Kawau Island	62	Fb	36.25S	174.50 E
Kawaura	29	Be	32.21N	130.05 E
Kawerau	62	Gc	38.05S	176.42 E
Kawhia	62	Fc	38.04S	174.49 E
Kawich Range	46	Gh	37.40N	116.30W
Kawio, Kepulauan-	26	If	4.30N	125.30 E
Kawkareik	25	Je	16.33N	98.14 E
Kawm Umbū	33	Fe	24.28N	32.57 E
Kawthaung	25	Jg	9.59N	98.33 E
Kaxgar He	21	Jf	39.46N	78.15 E
Kax He	27	Dc	43.37N	81.48 E
Kaya	34	Ec	13.05N	1.05W
Kayah [2]	25	Je	19.15N	97.30 E
Kayak	40	Ke	59.52N	144.30W
Kayali Daği	15	Jj	39.58N	26.38 E
Kayan	21	Ni	2.55N	117.35 E
Kayanga	34	Bc	11.58N	15.00W
Kayangel Islands	57	Ed	8.04N	134.43 E
Kayangel Passage	64a	Ba	8.01N	134.42 E
Kaycee	46	Le	43.43N	106.38W
Kayenta	46	Jh	36.44N	110.17W
Kayes [3]	34	Cc	14.00N	11.00W
Kayes	31	Fg	14.26N	11.27W
Kayoa, Pulau-	26	Ig	0.05S	127.25 E
Kayseri	22	Ff	38.43N	35.30 E
Kayuagung	26	Dg	3.24S	104.50 E
Kayu Ara, Pulau-	26	Ef	1.31N	106.26 E
Kazačje	20	Ib	70.40N	136.13 E
Kazah	16	Ni	41.05N	45.22 E
Kazahskaja Sovetskaja Socialističeskaja Respublika [2]	19	Gf	48.00N	68.00 E
Kazahskaja SSR/Kazak Sovettik Socialistik Respublikasy [2]	19	Gf	48.00N	68.00 E
Kazahskaja SSR=Kazakh SSR (EN) [2]	19	Gf	48.00N	68.00 E
Kazahski Melkosopočnik=Kazakh Hills (EN)	21	Je	49.00N	73.00 E
Kazahski Zaliv	16	Rh	42.40N	52.25 E
Kazakh Hills (EN)=Kazahski Melkosopočnik	21	Je	49.00N	73.00 E
Kazakh SSR (EN)=Kazahskaja SSR [2]	19	Gf	48.00N	68.00 E
Kazakhstan (EN)	21	Hd	51.11N	52.52 E
Kazaklija	15	Lc	46.05N	28.38 E
Kazak Sovettik Socialistik Respublikasy [2]	19	Gf	48.00N	68.00 E
Kazalak	15	Ke	44.03N	27.24 E
Kazalinsk	19	Gf	45.46N	62.07 E
Kazan	6	Kd	55.45N	49.08 E
Kazan	38	Jc	64.02N	95.30W
Kazandžik	19	Fh	39.17N	55.34 E
Kazanka	7	Li	55.48N	49.05 E
Kazanka	16	Hf	47.50N	32.49 E
Kazanlăk	15	Ig	42.37N	25.24 E
Kazan-Rettō/Iō=Volcano Islands (EN)	21	Qg	25.00N	141.00 E
Kazanskoje	19	Gd	55.38N	69.14 E
Kazarman	19	Hg	41.20N	74.02 E
Kazatin	19	Cf	49.43N	28.50 E
Kazbek, Gora-	5	Kg	42.42N	44.31 E
Kaz Dağı	23	Cb	39.42N	26.50 E
Kaz Dağı	15	Mk	38.35N	29.15 E
Kāzerūn	22	Hg	29.37N	51.38 E
Kažim	17	Ef	60.20N	51.32 E
Kazi-Magomed	16	Pi	40.02N	48.56 E
Kazimierza Wielka	10	Qf	50.16N	20.30 E
Kâzımkarabekir	24	Ed	37.14N	32.59 E
Kazincbarcika	10	Qh	48.15N	20.38 E
Kazinga Channel	36	Ec	0.13S	29.53 E
Kazlų-Rūda/Kazlu-Ruda	8	Jj	54.42N	23.32 E
Kazlu-Ruda/Kazlų-Rūda	8	Jj	54.42N	23.32 E
Kazo	29	Fc	36.08N	139.36 E
Kaztalovka	16	Pe	49.46N	48.44 E
Kazumba	36	Dd	6.25S	22.02 E
Kazuno	28	Pd	40.14N	140.48 E
Kazym	19	Gc	63.54N	65.50 E
Kazyr	20	Ef	53.50N	92.53 E
Kcynia	10	Nd	53.00N	17.30 E
Kdyně	10	Jg	49.24N	13.02 E
Ké	35	Bb	18.32N	17.55 E
Kéa	15	Hl	37.37N	24.20 E
Kéa	15	Hl	37.39N	24.20 E
Keaau	65a	Fd	19.37N	155.03W
Keahole Point	65a	Ed	19.44N	156.04W
Kealaikahiki Channel	65a	Ec	20.37N	156.50W
Kealaikahiki Point	65a	Ec	20.32N	156.42W
Kealakekua Bay	65a	Fd	19.28N	155.56W
Keams Canyon	46	Ji	35.49N	110.12W
Keanae	65a	Ec	20.52N	156.09W
Keanapapa Point	65a	Dc	20.54N	157.04W
Kearney	43	Hc	40.42N	99.05W
Kearns	46	Jf	40.39N	111.59W
Kéas, Stenón-	15	Hl	37.40N	24.12 E
Keats Bank (EN)	57	Id	5.23N	173.28 E
Keb	8	Mg	57.44N	28.38 E
Keban Gölü	23	Eb	38.53N	39.00 E
Kébémer	34	Bb	15.22N	16.27W
Kebir, Oued el-	14	Bn	36.51N	7.57 E
Kebnekaise	5	Hb	67.53N	18.33 E
Kebri Dehar	31	Lh	6.45N	44.17 E
Kebumen	26	Eh	7.40S	109.39 E
Kecel	10	Pj	46.32N	19.16 E
Kechika	42	Ee	59.38N	127.09W
Kecskemét	10	Pj	46.54N	19.42 E
Kédainiai/Kedajnjaj	7	Fi	55.18N	23.59 E
Kedajnjaj/Kédainiai	7	Fi	55.18N	23.59 E
Kedgwick	44	Nb	47.39N	67.21W
Kediri	22	Nj	7.49S	112.01 E
Kédougou	34	Cc	12.33N	12.11W
Kedva	17	Fd	64.14N	53.30 E
Kędzierzyn-Koźle	10	Of	50.20N	18.10 E
Keele	42	Fd	64.24N	124.47W
Keele Peak	38	Fc	63.26N	130.19W
Keeling Islands → Cocos Islands	21	Lk	12.10S	96.55 E
Keeling Islands → Cocos Islands [5]	22	Lk	12.10S	96.55 E
Keelung	22	Og	25.08N	121.44 E
Keene	44	Kd	42.55N	72.17W
Keer-Weer, Cape-	59	Ib	13.58S	141.30 E
Keetmanshoop	31	Ik	26.36S	18.08 E
Keetmanshoop [3]	37	Be	26.30S	18.30 E
Keewatin	42	Ig	49.46N	94.34W
Keewatin, District of- [3]	42	Hd	64.00N	96.00W
Kefa [3]	35	Fd	7.00N	36.00 E
Kefallinía=Cephalonia (EN)	5	Ih	38.15N	20.35 E
Kefamenanu	26	Hh	9.27S	124.29 E
Kefar Sava	24	Ff	32.10N	34.54 E
Keffi	34	Gd	8.51N	7.52 E
Keflavik	7a	Ab	64.01N	22.34W
Kegen	19	Hg	42.58N	79.12 E
Kegums	8	Kh	56.41N	24.44 E
Kehdingen	10	Fc	53.45N	9.20 E
Kehl	10	Dh	48.35N	7.49 E
Kehra	7	Fg	59.19N	25.18 E
Keighley	9	Lh	53.52N	1.54W
Keila/Kejla	7	Fg	59.19N	24.27 E
Keila Jõgi/Kejla	8	Ke	59.25N	24.15 E
Keimoes	37	Ce	28.41S	21.00 E
Keipel Bank (EN)	59	Le	25.15S	159.30E
Keïta	34	Gc	14.46N	5.46 E
Kéita, Bahr-	35	Bd	9.14N	18.21 E
Keitele	5	Ic	62.55N	26.00 E
Keith [Austl.]	59	Ig	36.06S	140.21 E
Keith [Scot.-U.K.]	9	Kd	57.32N	2.57W
Keith Arm	42	Fc	65.20N	122.00W
Keiyasi	63d	Ab	17.53S	177.45 E
Kejla/Keila	7	Fg	59.19N	24.27 E
Kejla/Keila Jõgi	8	Ke	59.25N	24.15 E
Kejvy	7	Ic	67.30N	37.45 E
Kekaha	65a	Bb	21.58N	159.43W
Kekerengu	62	Ee	42.00S	174.00 E
Kékes	10	Qi	47.52N	20.01 E
Keklau	64a	Bb	7.35N	134.39 E
Kelafo	35	Gd	5.37N	44.13 E
Kelakam	34	Hc	13.35N	11.44 E
Kela Met	35	Fb	15.50N	38.23 E
Kelan	27	Jd	38.44N	111.34 E
Kelang	22	Mi	3.02N	101.27 E
Kelasa, Selat-=Gaspar Strait (EN)	26	Eg	2.40S	107.15 E
Kelberg	12	Id	50.18N	6.55 E
Këlcyra	15	Di	40.19N	20.11 E
Kelefesia	65b	Bb	20.30S	174.44W
Kelekçi	15	Ml	37.14N	29.28 E
Kelem	35	Fe	4.49N	35.59 E
Keles	15	Mj	39.55N	29.14 E
Keles	18	Gd	41.02N	68.37 E
Kelheim	10	Hh	48.55N	11.52 E
Kelifely, Causse du-	37	Hc	17.15S	45.30 E
Kelifski Uzboj	18	Ef	37.45N	64.40 E
Keli Hāji Ibrāhīm	24	Kd	36.42N	45.00 E
Kelkheim	12	Kd	50.08N	8.27 E
Kelkit	23	Ea	36.32N	40.46 E
Kelkit	24	Hb	40.08N	39.27 E
Kellé	36	Bc	0.06S	14.33 E
Kellerberrin	59	Df	31.38S	117.43 E
Kellerwald	10	Fe	51.03N	9.10 E
Kellett, Cape -	42	Eb	72.57N	125.27W
Kellett Strait	42	Fa	75.50N	117.40W
Kellog	20	Dd	62.27N	86.35 E
Kellogg	43	Db	47.32N	116.07W
Kelloselkä	7	Gc	66.56N	29.00 E
Kells/Ceanannas Mór	9	Gh	53.44N	6.53W
Kelmė/Kelme	7	Fi	55.39N	22.58 E
Kelme/Kelmė	7	Fi	55.39N	22.58 E
Kelmency	15	Ja	48.27N	26.47 E
Kelmis/La Calamine	12	Hd	50.43N	6.00 E
Kélo	35	Bd	9.15N	15.48 E
Kelowna	39	He	49.53N	119.29W
Kelsey	42	He	56.00N	97.00W
Kelsey Bay	42	Ef	50.24N	125.57W
Kelso	46	Dc	46.09N	122.54W
Kelso Bank	59	Ld	24.10S	159.10 E
Kelso Bank (EN)	59	Ld	24.10S	159.30 E
Kel Tepe [Tur.]	24	Eb	41.05N	32.27 E
Kel Tepe [Tur.]	15	Ni	40.39N	30.06 E
Keltie, Mount-	66	Jf	79.15S	159.00 E
Keluang	26	Df	2.02N	103.19 E
Kelvin Seamount (EN)	43	Od	38.50N	64.00W
Kelyeḥēd	35	Hd	8.44N	49.10 E
Kem	19	Dc	64.57N	34.31 E
Kema	7	If	60.19N	37.15 E
Ké Macina	34	Dc	13.57N	5.23W
Kemah	24	Hc	39.36N	39.02 E
Kemaliye	24	Hc	39.16N	38.29 E
Kemalpaşa	24	Cc	40.00N	28.20 E
Kemalpaşa	15	Kk	38.25N	27.26 E
Kembé	35	Ce	4.36N	21.54 E
Kemer [Tur.]	15	Mm	36.28N	29.21 E
Kemer [Tur.]	24	Dd	36.36N	30.34 E
Kemer Baraji	15	Ll	37.30N	28.35 E
Kemeri/Ķemeri	8	Jh	56.56N	23.25 E
Ķemeri/Kemeri	8	Jh	56.56N	23.25 E
Kemerovo	22	Kd	55.20N	86.05 E
Kemerovskaja Oblast [3]	20	De	55.00N	87.00 E
Kemi	6	Ib	65.44N	24.34 E
Kemijärvi	7	Gc	66.40N	27.25 E
Kemijärvi=Kenni, Lake- (EN)	7	Gc	66.36N	27.24 E
Kemijoki	5	Ib	65.47N	24.30 E
Kemiö	8	Jd	60.10N	22.40 E
Kemiö/Kimito	8	Jd	60.10N	22.40 E
Kemlja	7	Ki	54.43N	45.15 E
Kemmerer	46	Jf	41.48N	110.32W
Kémo-Gribingui [3]	35	Bd	6.00N	19.00 E
Kemp, Lake-	45	Gj	33.45N	99.13W
Kempaž	17	Jd	64.03N	61.02 E
Kempele	7	Fd	64.55N	25.30 E
Kempen	12	Ic	51.22N	6.25 E
Kempen/Campine	11	Lc	51.10N	5.20 E
Kempendjaj	20	Gd	62.02N	118.42 E
Kempenich	12	Jd	50.25N	7.08 E
Kemp Land	66	Ee	67.10S	58.00 E
Kemps Bay	49	Ia	24.02N	77.33W
Kempsey	59	Kf	31.05S	152.50 E
Kempston	12	Bb	52.06N	0.29W
Kempt, Lac-	42	Kg	47.25N	74.15W
Kempten	10	Gi	47.43N	10.19 E
Ken	25	Hc	25.46N	80.31 E
Ken, Loch-	9	If	55.02N	4.02W
Kena	7	Je	62.06N	39.05 E
Kenadsa	32	Gc	31.34N	2.26W
Kenai	39	Dc	60.33N	151.15W
Kenai Mountains	40	Ie	60.00N	150.00W
Kenai Peninsula	38	Ed	60.10N	150.00W
Kendal	9	Kg	54.20N	2.45W
Kendall	44	Gm	25.41N	80.19W
Kendall, Cape -	42	Id	63.36N	87.13W
Kendallville	44	Ee	41.27N	85.16W
Kendari	22	Oj	3.57S	122.35 E
Kendawangan	26	Fg	2.32S	110.12 E
Kenema	31	Fh	7.52N	11.12W
Kenge	31	Ii	4.52S	16.59 E
Kengere	36	Ee	11.10S	25.28 E
Keng Tung	25	Jd	21.17N	99.36 E
Kenhardt	37	Ce	29.19S	21.12 E
Kéniéba	34	Cc	12.50N	11.14W
Keningau	26	Ge	5.20N	116.10 E
Kenitra	31	Ge	34.16N	6.36W
Kenitra [3]	32	Fc	34.00N	6.00W
Kenli (Xishuanghe)	28	Ef	37.35N	118.30 E
Kenmare	43	Gb	48.40N	102.05W
Kenmare/Neidin	9	Dj	51.53N	9.35W
Kenmare River/An Ribhéar	9	Dj	51.50N	9.50W
Kennebunk	44	Ld	43.23N	70.33W
Kennedy Peak	25	Id	23.19N	93.46 E
Kennedy Range	59	Cd	24.30S	115.00 E
Kenner	45	Ki	29.59N	90.15W
Kennet	9	Mj	51.28N	0.57W
Kennett	45	Kh	36.14N	90.03W
Kennewick	46	Fc	46.12N	119.07W
Kenni, Lake- (EN)=Kemijärvi	7	Gc	66.36N	27.24 E
Kennington	12	Cc	51.09N	0.53 E
Kenn Reef	57	Gg	21.10S	155.50 E
Kénogami	44	La	48.26N	71.14W
Kénogami, Lac-	44	La	48.21N	71.28W
Kenogami River	42	Jf	51.06N	84.29W
Keno Hill	42	Dd	63.54N	135.18W
Kenora	39	Je	49.47N	94.29W
Kenosha	43	Jc	42.35N	87.49W
Kent	9	Nj	51.10N	0.55 E
Kent [3]	9	Nj	51.20N	0.55 E
Kent [S.L.]	34	Cd	8.10N	13.10W
Kent [Wa.-U.S.]	46	Dc	47.23N	122.14W
Kent, Vale of-	9	Nj	51.10N	0.30 E
Kentau	19	Gg	43.32N	68.33 E
Kent Group	59	Jg	39.30S	147.20 E
Kenton	44	Fe	40.38N	83.38W
Kent Peninsula	42	Gc	68.30N	107.00W
Kentucky [2]	43	Jd	37.30N	85.15W
Kentucky Lake	43	Jd	36.25N	88.05W
Kentucky River	44	Ef	38.41N	85.11W
Kenya [1]	31	Kh	1.00N	38.00 E
Kenya, Mount-/Kirinyaga	30	Ki	0.10S	37.20 E
Keokea	65a	Ec	20.42N	156.21W
Keokuk	43	Ic	40.24N	91.24W
Keonjhargarh	25	Hd	21.38N	85.35 E
Keowee, Lake-	44	Fh	34.55N	82.50W
Kepe	7	Hd	65.09N	32.08 E
Kepi	26	Kh	6.32S	139.19 E
Kępno	10	Ne	51.17N	17.59 E
Kepsut	24	Cc	39.41N	28.09 E
Kerala [3]	25	Ff	11.00N	76.30 E
Kerama-Rettō	29b	Ab	26.10N	127.15 E
Kerang	59	Ig	35.44S	143.55 E
Keratéa	15	Gl	37.48N	23.59 E
Kerava/Kervo	8	Kd	60.24N	25.07 E
Kerč	6	Jf	45.22N	36.27 E
Kerčenski Poluostrov	16	Ig	45.15N	36.00 E
Kerčenski Proliv	5	Jf	45.22N	36.38 E
Kerdhílion Óros	15	Gi	40.47N	23.39 E
Kerema	60	Di	7.58S	145.46 E
Keren	35	Fb	15.47N	38.27 E
Keret, Ozero-	7	Hd	65.50N	32.50 E
Kerewan	34	Bc	13.29N	16.06W
Kerguélen	30	Nm	49.20S	69.30 E
Kerguélen, Iles-	30	Nm	49.15S	69.10 E
Kerguelen Plateau (EN)	3	Go	55.00S	75.00 E
Kericho	36	Gc	0.22S	35.17 E
Keri Kera	35	Ec	12.21N	32.46 E
Kerimäki	8	Mc	61.55N	29.17 E
Kerinci, Gunung-	21	Mj	1.42S	101.16 E
Kerio	30	Kh	2.59N	36.07 E
Kerion	15	Dl	37.40N	20.49 E
Keriya/Yutian	22	Kf	36.52N	81.42 E
Keriya He	27	Dd	38.30N	82.10 E
Keriya Shankou	27	Dd	35.12N	81.44 E
Kerka	10	Mj	46.28N	16.36 E
Kerken	12	Ic	51.27N	6.26 E
Kerkennah Islands (EN)=Qarqannah, Juzur-	30	Ie	34.44N	11.12 E
Kerketevs Óros	15	Jl	37.44N	26.38 E
Kerki	19	Gh	37.50N	65.13 E
Kerkíni Óros	15	Fh	41.21N	22.50 E
Kérkira	15	Cj	39.36N	19.55 E
Kérkira=Corfu (EN)	5	Hh	39.40N	19.45 E
Kerkíras, Stenón- = Corfu, Strait of- (EN)	15	Dj	39.35N	20.05 E
Kerkrade	12	Id	50.52N	6.04 E
Kerma (EN)=Karmah	35	Eb	19.38N	30.25 E
Kermadec Islands	57	Jh	30.00S	178.30W
Kermadec Ridge (EN)	57	Jh	30.30S	178.30W
Kermadec Trench (EN)	3	Km	30.00S	177.00W
Kermajarvi	8	Mb	62.30N	28.40 E
Kermān [3]	23	Ic	30.50N	57.50 E
Kermān	22	Hf	30.17N	57.05 E
Kermānshāh	22	Gf	34.19N	47.04 E
Kermānshāhān [3]	23	Gc	34.15N	47.20 E
Kermānshāhān	24	Pg	31.17N	54.55 E
Kerme	15	Kl	37.02N	28.00 E
Kerme Körfezi	24	Bd	36.50N	28.00 E
Kermit	45	Ek	31.51N	103.06W
Kern River	46	Fi	35.13N	119.17W
Kérouané	34	Dd	9.16N	9.01W
Kerpen	12	Id	50.52N	6.41 E
Kerrobert	42	Gf	51.55N	109.08W
Kerrville	43	He	30.03N	99.08W
Kerry/Ciarraí [2]	9	Di	52.10N	9.30W
Kerry, Mountains of-	9	Dj	51.55N	9.50W
Kertamulya	26	Eg	0.23N	109.09 E
Kerteh	26	Df	4.31N	103.27 E
Kerteminde	8	Di	55.27N	10.40 E
Kerulen (Cherlen)	21	Ne	48.48N	117.00 E
Kervo/Kerava	8	Kd	60.24N	25.07 E
Kerzaz	32	Gd	29.27N	1.25W
Keržénec	7	Kh	56.04N	45.01 E
Kesagami Lake	42	Jf	50.23N	80.10W
Kesälahti	8	Mc	61.54N	29.50 E
Keşan	23	Ca	40.51N	26.37 E
Keşap	24	Hb	40.55N	38.31 E
Kesen'numa	28	Pe	38.54N	141.35 E
Kesen'numa-Wan	29	Gb	38.50N	141.35 E
Keshan	27	Mb	48.04N	125.51 E
Keskastel	12	Jf	48.58N	7.02 E
Keskin	24	Ec	39.41N	33.37 E
Keski-Suomi [2]	7	Fe	62.30N	25.30 E
Kestenga	7	Hd	65.53N	31.45 E
Keswick	9	Jg	54.37N	3.08W
Keszthely	10	Nj	46.46N	17.15 E
Ket	21	Kd	58.55N	81.32 E
Kéta	34	Fd	5.55N	0.59 E
Keta, Ozero-	20	Dc	68.45N	90.00 E
Ketanda	20	Jd	60.38N	141.30 E
Ketapang	22	Mj	1.52S	109.59 E
Ketchikan	39	Fd	55.21N	131.35W
Ketchum	43	Ec	43.41N	114.22W
Ketchum Mountain	45	Fk	31.15N	101.00W
Kete Krachi	34	Ed	7.46N	0.03W
Ketelmeer	12	Hb	52.35N	5.45 E
Ketli, Jbel-	13	Gi	35.22N	5.17W
Keţmen, Hrebet-	18	Lc	43.20N	80.00 E
Kétou	34	Fd	7.22N	2.36 E
Kętrzyn	10	Rb	54.06N	21.23 E
Kettering [Eng.-U.K.]	9	Mi	52.24N	0.44W
Kettering [Oh.-U.S.]	44	Ef	39.41N	84.10W
Kettle River	46	Fb	48.42N	118.07W
Kettle River Range	46	Fb	48.30N	118.40W
Keuka Lake	44	Id	42.27N	77.10W
Keur Massène	32	Df	16.33N	16.14W
Keuruu	7	Fe	62.16N	24.42 E
Keuruunselkä	8	Kb	62.10N	24.40 E
Kevelaer	12	Ic	51.35N	6.15 E
Kew	49	Kc	21.54N	72.02W
Kewanee	43	Jc	41.14N	89.56W
Keweenaw Bay	44	Cb	46.56N	88.23W
Keweenaw Peninsula	43	Jb	47.12N	88.25W
Key, Lough-/Loch Ce	9	Eg	54.00N	8.15W
Keya Paha River	45	Ge	42.54N	99.00W
Keyhole Reservoir	46	Md	44.21N	104.51W
Key Largo	44	Gm	25.04N	80.28W
Keypel Bank (EN)	59	Le	25.15S	159.30 E
Keystone Lake	45	Hh	36.15N	96.25W
Key West	39	Kg	24.33N	81.48W
Kez	7	Mh	57.56N	53.43 E
Kezi	37	Dd	20.55S	28.29 E
Kežma	20	Fe	59.02N	101.09 E
Kežmarok	10	Qg	49.08N	20.25 E
Kgalagadi [3]	37	Ce	25.00S	22.00 E
Kgatleng [3]	37	Dd	24.28S	26.05 E
Kghoti	37	Cd	24.55S	21.59 E
Khabr, Kūh-e-	23	Id	28.50N	56.26 E
Khābūr, Nahr al-	24	Ie	35.08N	40.26 E
Khadari, Wādī al-	35	Dc	10.29N	27.00 E
Khādim, Shūshat al-	24	Bh	28.35N	27.43 E
Khadki (Kirkee)	25	Ee	18.34N	73.52 E
Khadra	13	Mh	36.15N	0.35 E
Khafs Banbān	24	Lj	25.31N	46.27 E
Khairónia	15	Fk	38.30N	22.51 E
Khairpur	25	Dc	27.32N	68.46 E
Khāīz, Kūh-e-	24	Ng	30.27N	50.55 E
Khakhea	37	Cd	24.42S	23.30 E
Khalatse	25	Fb	34.20N	76.49 E
Khalīj-e Fārs=Persian Gulf (EN)	21	Hg	27.00N	51.00 E
Khálki	15	Km	36.13N	27.37 E
Khálki	15	Km	36.14N	27.36 E
Khalkidhikí=Chalcidice (EN)	5	Ig	40.25N	23.25 E
Khalkis	15	Gk	38.28N	23.36 E
Khaluf	23	Ie	20.29N	57.59 E
Khambhāt	25	Ed	22.18N	72.37 E
Khambhāt, Gulf of-	21	Jg	21.00N	72.30 E
Khāmgaon	25	Fd	20.41N	76.34 E
Khamili	15	Jn	35.52N	26.14 E
Khamir	23	Ff	15.59N	43.57 E
Khāmis, Ash Shallāl al-=Fifth Cataract (EN)	30	Kg	18.23N	33.47 E
Khamīs Mushayţ	23	Ff	18.18N	42.44 E
Khammam	25	Ge	17.15N	80.09 E
Khamseh	24	Md	36.40N	48.50 E
Khan	37	Ad	22.42S	14.54 E
Khān	24	Qj	24.13N	56.20 E
Khānābād	23	Kb	36.41N	69.07 E
Khān al Baghdādi	24	Jf	33.51N	42.33 E
Khān al Hammād	24	Kf	32.19N	44.17 E
Khānaqīn	23	Gc	34.21N	45.22 E
Khān az Zabīb	24	Gg	31.28N	36.06 E
Khandwa	25	Fd	21.50N	76.20 E
Khāneh Sorkh, Gardaneh-ye-	24	Qh	29.49N	56.06 E
Khānewāl	25	Eb	30.18N	71.56 E
Khangai Mountains (EN)=Changajn Nuruu → Hangaj, Hrebet-	21	Le	47.30N	100.00 E
Khangai Mountains (EN)=Hangaj, Hrebet- (Changajn Nuruu)	21	Le	47.30N	100.00 E
Khanh Hung	25	Lg	9.36N	105.58 E
Khánia	6	Ih	35.31N	24.02 E
Khanion, Kólpos-	15	Gn	35.35N	23.50 E
Khanka, Lake- (EN)=Hanka, Ozero-	21	Pe	45.00N	132.24 E
Khanka Lake (EN)=Xingkai Hu	21	Pe	45.00N	132.24 E
Khānpur	25	Ec	28.39N	70.39 E
Khān Shaykhūn	24	Ge	35.26N	36.38 E
Khan Takhtī	24	Kc	38.09N	44.55 E
Khān Yūnus	24	Fg	31.21N	34.19 E
Khānzīr, Rās-	35	Hc	10.50N	45.50 E

Index Symbols

[1] Independent Nation
[2] State, Region
[3] District, County
[4] Municipality
[5] Colony, Dependency
Continent
Physical Region
Historical or Cultural Region
Mount, Mountain
Volcano
Hill
Mountains, Mountain Range
Hills, Escarpment
Plateau, Upland
Pass, Gap
Plain, Lowland
Delta
Salt Flat
Valley, Canyon
Crater, Cave
Karst Features
Depression
Polder
Desert, Dunes
Forest, Woods
Heath, Steppe
Oasis
Cape, Point
Coast, Beach
Cliff
Peninsula
Isthmus
Sandbank
Island
Atoll
Rock, Reef
Islands, Archipelago
Rocks, Reefs
Coral Reef
Well, Spring
Geyser
River, Stream
Waterfall Rapids
River Mouth, Estuary
Lake
Salt Lake
Intermittent Lake
Reservoir
Swamp, Pond
Canal
Glacier
Ice Shelf, Pack Ice
Ocean
Sea
Gulf, Bay
Strait, Fjord
Lagoon
Bank
Seamount
Tablemount
Ridge
Shelf
Basin
Escarpment, Sea Scarp
Fracture
Trench, Abyss
National Park, Reserve
Point of Interest
Recreation Site
Cave, Cavern
Historic Site
Ruins
Wall, Walls
Church, Abbey
Temple
Scientific Station
Airport
Port
Lighthouse
Mine
Tunnel
Dam, Bridge

Name	Map	Grid	Lat.	Long.
Khao Laem	25	Kf	14.19N	101.11 E
Khao Miang	25	Ke	17.42N	101.01 E
Khao Mokochu	25	Je	15.56N	99.06 E
Khao Saming	25	Kf	12.16N	102.26 E
Khar	24	Me	35.53N	48.55 E
Kharagpur	22	Kg	22.20N	87.20 E
Khárakas	15	In	35.01N	25.07 E
Khārān	24	Qh	28.55N	57.09 E
Kharānaq	24	Pf	32.20N	54.39 E
Kharānaq, Kūh-e-	24	Pf	32.10N	54.39 E
Kharga Oasis (EN)= Khārijah, Wāḥāt al-	30	Kf	25.20N	30.35 E
Khārijah, Wāḥāt al-= Kharga Oasis (EN)	30	Kf	25.20N	30.35 E
Kharīt, Wādī al-	24	Ej	24.26N	33.03 E
Kharīṭah, Shiqqat al-	33	If	17.10N	47.50 E
Khārk	24	Nh	29.15N	50.20 E
Khārk, Jazīreh-ye-	23	Hd	29.15N	50.20 E
Khār Khū	24	Og	31.39N	53.46 E
Kharmān, Kūh-e-	23	Hd	29.13N	53.35 E
Kharshah, Qārat al-	24	Bg	30.35N	27.25 E
Khartoum (EN)=Al Kharṭūm [3]	35	Eb	15.50N	33.00 E
Khartoum (EN)=Al Kharṭūm	31	Kg	15.36N	32.32 E
Khartoum North (EN)=Al Kharṭūm Baḥrī	31	Kg	15.38N	32.33 E
Khāsh	23	Jc	31.31N	62.52 E
Khāsh	23	Jc	31.11N	62.05 E
Khashm al Qirbah	35	Fc	14.58N	35.55 E
Khāsi Jaintia	21	Lg	25.35N	91.38 E
Khatikhon, Yam-= Mediterranean Sea (EN)	5	Hh	35.00N	20.00 E
Khaṭṭ	33	Dd	28.40N	22.40 E
Khātūn, Kūh-e-	24	Og	30.25N	53.38 E
Khawr al Fakkān	24	Qk	25.21N	56.22 E
Khawr āl Juḥaysh	35	Ia	20.36N	50.59 E
Khawr al Mufattaḥ	24	Mh	28.40N	48.25 E
Khawr Umm Qasr	24	Lg	30.02N	47.56 E
Khay'	23	Ff	18.45N	41.24 E
Khaybar	23	Ed	25.42N	39.31 E
Khaybar, Ḥarrat-	24	Hj	25.30N	39.45 E
Khazzī, Qārat-	30	Jf	21.26N	24.30 E
Khemis	13	Qh	36.10N	4.04 E
Khemis Anjra	13	Gi	35.41N	5.32W
Khémis Beni Arouss	13	Gi	35.19N	5.38W
Khemis Miliana	32	Hb	36.16N	2.13 E
Khemissat	32	Fc	33.49N	6.04W
Khemisset [3]	32	Fc	33.49N	6.00W
Khemmarat	25	Ke	16.03N	105.11 E
Khenchela	32	Ib	35.26N	7.08 E
Khenifra	32	Fc	32.56N	5.40W
Khenifra [3]	32	Fc	33.00N	5.08W
Kherāmeh	24	Oh	29.32N	53.21 E
Khersan	24	Ng	31.33N	50.22 E
Khersónisos Akrotiri	15	Hn	35.35N	24.10 E
Kheyrābād [Iran]	24	Mg	31.49N	48.23 E
Kheyrābād [Iran]	24	Ph	29.26N	55.19 E
Khionótripa	15	Hh	41.18N	24.05 E
Khios	15	Jk	38.22N	26.08 E
Khios=Chios (EN)	5	Ih	38.22N	26.00 E
Khirbat Isrīyah	24	Ge	35.21N	37.46 E
Khirr, Nahr al-	24	Kf	33.17N	44.21 E
Khlomón Óros	15	Fk	38.36N	23.00 E
Khlong Yai	25	Kf	11.46N	102.53 E
Khokhropār	25	Ec	25.42N	70.12 E
Khok Kloi	25	Jg	8.17N	98.19 E
Khok Samrong	25	Ke	15.03N	100.44 E
Kholm	23	Kb	36.42N	67.41 E
Khomām	24	Md	37.22N	49.40 E
Khomas Highland (EN)= Khomas Hochland	30	Ik	22.40S	16.20 E
Khomas Hochland=Khomas Highland (EN)	30	Ik	22.40S	16.20 E
Khomeyn	24	Nf	33.38N	50.04 E
Khonj	24	Oi	27.52N	53.27 E
Khon Kaen	25	Ke	16.26N	102.50 E
Khonsār	24	Nf	33.21N	50.19 E
Khóra	15	El	37.03N	21.43 E
Khor Anghar	35	Gc	12.27N	43.18 E
Khorāsān	21	Hf	34.00N	56.00 E
Khorāsān [3]	23	Ic	35.00N	58.00 E
Khorāsānī, Godār-e	24	Qg	30.44N	57.03 E
Khóra Sfakion	15	Hn	35.12N	24.09 E
Khormūj, Kūh-e-	23	Hd	28.43N	51.22 E
Khorof Harar	36	Hb	2.14N	40.44 E
Khorramābād	23	Gc	33.30N	48.20 E
Khorramshahr	23	Gc	30.25N	48.11 E
Khorsābād	24	Jd	36.38N	43.17 E
Khoshyeylāq	24	Pd	36.53N	55.15 E
Khosrowābād	24	Mg	30.00N	48.25 E
Khosrowshah	24	Ld	37.57N	46.03 E
Khouribga [3]	32	Fc	32.56N	6.36W
Khouribga	32	Fc	32.53N	6.54W
Khowst	23	Kc	33.22N	69.57 E
Khrisí	15	Io	34.52N	25.42 E
Khrisoúpolis	15	Hi	40.59N	24.42 E
Khristianá	15	Im	36.14N	25.13 E
Khu Dağı	24	Jc	38.35N	43.40 E
Khuff [Lib.]	33	Cd	28.17N	18.20 E
Khuff [Sau.Ar.]	23	Ed	25.20N	37.20 E
Khulna	22	Kg	22.48N	89.33 E
Khūrān	24	Pi	26.50N	55.40 E
Khurayş	23	Gd	25.05N	48.02 E
Khurayt	35	Dc	13.57N	26.02 E
Khurīyā Murīyā, Jazā'ir-= Kuria Muria Islands (EN)	21	Hh	17.30N	56.00 E
Khurr, Wādī al-	24	Jg	30.52N	42.10 E
Khursanīyah	24	Mi	27.18N	49.16 E
Khūshābar	24	Md	37.59N	48.54 E
Khutse	37	Cd	23.20S	24.34 E
Khuwayy	35	Dc	13.05N	29.14 E
Khuzdār	25	Dc	27.48N	66.37 E
Khūzestān [3]	23	Gc	32.00N	48.30 E
Khūzestan	21	Gf	30.33N	50.00 E
Khvojeh Lāk, Kūh-e-	24	Le	35.43N	46.29 E
Khvor	24	Pf	33.47N	55.03 E
Khvorāsgān	24	Nf	32.39N	51.45 E
Khvormūj	24	Nh	28.39N	51.23 E
Khvoshkūh	24	Qi	27.37N	56.41 E
Khvoy	24	Kc	38.33N	44.58 E
Khyber Pass	25	Eb	34.05N	71.10 E
Kia	63a	Db	7.32S	158.26 E
Kia	63d	Bb	16.14S	179.05 E
Kiamba	26	He	5.59N	124.37 E
Kiambi	36	Ed	7.20S	28.01 E
Kiamichi River	45	Ij	33.57N	95.14W
Kiangarow, Mount-	59	Ke	26.49S	151.33 E
Kiangsi (EN)=Chiang-hsi Sheng→Jangxi Sheng [2]	27	Kf	28.00N	116.00 E
Kiangsi (EN)=Jangxi Sheng (Chiang-hsi Sheng) [2]	27	Kf	28.00N	116.00 E
Kiangsu (EN)=Chiang-su Sheng→Jiangsu Sheng [2]	27	Ke	33.00N	120.00 E
Kiangsu (EN)=Jiangsu Sheng (Chiang-su Sheng) [2]	27	Ke	33.00N	120.00 E
Kiantajärvi	7	Gd	65.03N	29.07 E
Kiáton	15	Fk	38.01N	22.45 E
Kibali	36	Eb	3.37N	28.34 E
Kibangou	36	Bc	3.27S	12.21 E
Kibartaj/Kybartai	8	Jj	54.38N	22.44 E
Kibasira Swamp	36	Gd	8.20S	36.18 E
Kibau	36	Gd	8.35S	35.17 E
Kibaya	36	Gd	5.18S	36.34 E
Kibbish	35	Fe	4.40N	35.53 E
Kiberg	7	Ha	70.17N	31.00 E
Kibikogen	29	Cd	34.45N	133.15 E
Kiboko	36	Gc	2.15S	37.42 E
Kibombo	36	Ec	3.54S	25.55 E
Kibondo	36	Fc	3.35S	30.42 E
Kibre Mengist	35	Fd	5.58N	39.00 E
Kıbrıs/Kypros=Cyprus (EN) [1]	22	Ff	35.00N	33.00 E
Kıbrıs/Kypros=Cyprus (EN)	21	Ff	35.00N	33.00 E
Kibungo	36	Fc	2.10S	30.32 E
Kibuye	36	Ec	2.03S	29.21 E
Kibwezi	36	Gc	2.25S	37.58 E
Kičevo	15	Dh	41.31N	20.58 E
Kichi Kichi	35	Bb	17.36N	17.19 E
Kicking Horse Pass	42	Ff	51.50N	116.30W
Kidal	31	Hg	18.26N	1.24 E
Kidapawan	26	Ie	7.01N	125.03 E
Kidatu	36	Gd	7.42S	36.57 E
Kidira	34	Cc	14.28N	12.13W
Kidnappers, Cape-	62	Gc	39.38S	177.06 E
Kiekie	65a	Ab	21.53N	160.13W
Kiel	6	He	54.20N	10.08 E
Kiel Canal (EN)=Nord-Ostsee Kanal	5	Ge	53.53N	9.08 E
Kielce	6	Ie	50.52N	20.37 E
Kielce [2]	10	Qf	50.50N	20.35 E
Kieler Bucht	10	Gb	54.35N	10.35 E
Kienge	36	Ee	10.33S	27.33 E
Kierspe	12	Jc	51.08N	7.35 E
Kieta	58	Ge	6.15S	155.37 E
Kietrz	10	Of	50.05N	18.01 E
Kiev (EN)=Kijev	6	Je	50.26N	30.31 E
Kiev Reservoir (EN)= Kijevskoje Vodohranilišče	5	Je	51.00N	30.25 E
Kiffa	31	Fg	16.36N	11.23W
Kifisiá	15	Gk	38.04N	23.49 E
Kifisós	15	Gk	38.26N	23.15 E
Kifrī	24	Ke	34.42N	44.58 E
Kigač	16	Pf	46.28N	49.08 E
Kigali	31	Ki	1.57S	30.04 E
Kiğı	24	Ic	39.19N	40.21 E
Kigille	35	Ed	8.40N	34.02 E
Kigoma	31	Ji	4.52S	29.38 E
Kigoma [3]	36	Fc	4.50S	30.05 E
Kigosi	36	Fc	4.40S	31.27 E
Kihelkonna	8	If	58.20N	21.54 E
Kihniö	8	Jb	62.12N	23.11 E
Kihnu	7	Fg	58.10N	24.00 E
Kiholo	65a	Fd	19.51N	155.55W
Kiholo Bay	65a	Fd	19.52N	155.56W
Kihti/Skiftet	8	Id	60.15N	21.05 E
Kii-Hantō	27	Oe	34.00N	135.45 E
Kiikka	8	Jc	61.20N	22.46 E
Kiil	16	Se	49.27N	54.50 E
Kiiminki	7	Fd	65.08N	25.44 E
Kii-Sanchi	29	Dd	34.15N	135.50 E
Kii-Suido	28	Mh	34.00N	134.55 E
Kija	20	De	56.52N	86.40 E
Kijev=Kiev (EN)	6	Je	50.26N	30.31 E
Kijevka	19	He	50.16N	71.34 E
Kijevskaja Oblast [3]	19	De	50.20N	30.45 E
Kijevskoje Vodohranilišče= Kiev Reservoir (EN)	5	Je	51.00N	30.25 E
Kijma	19	Ge	51.35N	67.34 E
Kikai-Jima	27	Mf	28.15N	130.00 E
Kikerino	8	Me	59.23N	29.38 E
Kikinda	15	Dd	45.50N	20.29 E
Kikládhes = Cyclades (EN)	5	Ih	37.00N	25.10 E
Kikonai	28	Pd	41.40N	140.26 E
Kikori	58	Fe	7.25S	144.13 E
Kikori River	57	Fe	7.23S	144.16 E
Kikuchi	29	Be	32.59N	130.49 E
Kikuma	29	Cd	34.03N	132.51 E
Kikvidze	16	Md	50.44N	43.03 E
Kikwit	31	Ii	5.02S	18.49 E
Kil [Nor.]	8	Cf	58.52N	9.19 E
Kil [Swe.]	7	Cg	59.30N	13.19 E
Kilafors	7	Df	61.15N	16.33 E
Kilambé, Cerro-	49	Eg	13.34N	85.42W
Kilauea	65a	Ba	22.13N	159.25W
Kilauea Crater	65a	Fd	19.24N	155.17W
Kilauea Point	65a	Ba	22.14N	159.24W
Kilbrannan Sound	9	Hf	55.40N	5.25W
Kilbuck Mountains	40	Hd	60.30N	159.45W
Kilchu	27	Mc	40.58N	129.20 E
Kilcoy	59	Ke	26.57S	152.33 E
Kildare/Cill Dara [2]	9	Gh	53.15N	6.45W
Kildare/Cill Dara	9	Gh	53.10N	6.55W
Kil'din, Ostrov-	7	Ib	69.20N	34.10 E
Kilembe	36	Cd	5.42S	19.55 E
Kilgore	45	Ij	32.23N	94.53W
Kilgoris	36	Fc	1.00S	34.53 E
Kiliao He	21	Oe	43.24N	123.42 E
Kiliç	15	Mi	40.40N	29.23 E
Kilifi	36	Gc	3.38S	39.51 E
Kili Island	57	Hd	5.39N	169.04 E
Kilija	19	Cf	45.27N	29.14 E
Kilijskoje girlo	15	Md	45.13N	29.43 E
Kilimanjaro [3]	36	Gc	4.00S	37.40 E
Kilimanjaro, Mount-	30	Ki	3.04S	37.22 E
Kilimli	24	Db	41.29N	31.50 E
Kilinailau Islands	60	Fh	4.45S	155.20 E
Kilindoni	31	Ki	7.55S	39.39 E
Kilingi-Nõmme/Kilingi-Nymme	7	Fg	58.08N	24.59 E
Kilingi-Nymme/Kilingi-Nõmme	7	Fg	58.08N	24.59 E
Kilis	23	Eb	36.44N	37.05 E
Kilitbahir	24	Bb	40.12N	26.20 E
Kilkee/Cill Chaoi	9	Di	52.41N	9.38W
Kilkenny/Cill Chainnigh	9	Fi	52.39N	7.15W
Kilkenny/Cill Chainnigh [2]	9	Fi	52.40N	7.20W
Kilkieran Bay	9	Dh	53.15N	9.45W
Kilkís	15	Fi	41.00N	22.52 E
Killala Bay/Cuan Chill Ala	9	Dg	54.15N	9.10W
Killarney/Cill Airne	9	Di	52.03N	9.30W
Killary Harbour/An Caoláire Rua	9	Dh	53.38N	9.55W
Killdeer	45	Ec	47.22N	102.45W
Killeen	43	He	31.08N	97.44W
Killinck	42	Ld	60.25N	64.40W
Killini	15	El	37.56N	21.09 E
Killini Óros	15	Fl	37.55N	22.26 E
Kilmallock/Cill Mocheallóg	9	Ei	52.25N	8.35W
Kilmarnock	9	If	55.37N	4.30W
Kilmez	7	Mh	56.58N	50.29 E
Kilmez	7	Mh	57.03N	51.24 E
Kilmore	59	Ig	37.18S	144.57 E
Kilombero	36	Gd	8.31S	37.22 E
Kilosa	31	Ki	6.50S	36.59 E
Kilpisjärvi	7	Eb	69.03N	20.48 E
Kilp-Javr	7	Hb	69.07N	32.28 E
Kilrush/Cill Rois	9	Di	52.39N	9.29W
Kilsbergen	8	Fe	59.20N	14.45 E
Kiltān Island	25	Ef	11.29N	73.00 E
Kilwa	36	Ed	9.17S	28.20 E
Kilwa Kisiwani	31	Ki	8.58S	39.30 E
Kilwa Kivinje	36	Gd	8.45S	39.24 E
Kilwa Masoko	36	Gd	8.56S	39.31 E
Kilyos→Kumköy	15	Mh	41.15N	29.02 E
Kim	45	Eh	37.15N	103.21W
Kimamba	36	Gd	6.47S	37.08 E
Kimba	59	Hf	33.09S	136.25 E
Kimball [Nb.-U.S.]	45	Ef	41.14N	103.40W
Kimball [S.D.-U.S.]	45	Ge	43.45N	98.57W
Kimball, Mount-	40	Kd	63.14N	144.39W
Kimbe	59	Ka	5.31S	150.12 E
Kimbe Bay	60	Ei	5.30S	150.30 E
Kimberley	57	Df	16.00S	126.00 E
Kimberley [B.C.-Can.]	42	Fg	49.41N	115.59W
Kimberley [S.Afr.]	31	Jk	28.43S	24.46 E
Kimberley Plateau	59	Fc	17.00S	127.00 E
Kimch'aek (Sŏngjin)	27	Mc	40.41N	129.12 E
Kimch'ŏn	27	Md	36.07N	128.07 E
Kimhandu	30	Ki	7.05S	37.35 E
Kimi	15	Hk	38.38N	24.06 E
Kimito	8	Jd	60.10N	22.40 E
Kimito/Kemiö	8	Jd	60.10N	22.40 E
Kimje	28	Ig	35.48N	126.53 E
Kimobetsu	29a	Bb	42.47N	140.56 E
Kímolos	15	Hm	36.48N	24.34 E
Kimongo	36	Bc	4.29S	12.58 E
Kimovsk	19	De	54.01N	38.36 E
Kimpu-San	29	Fd	35.52N	138.37 E
Kimry	19	Dd	56.52N	37.24 E
Kimvula	36	Cd	5.44S	15.58 E
Kinabalu, Gunong-	21	Ni	6.05N	116.33 E
Kinabatangan	26	Ge	5.42N	118.23 E
Kinango	36	Gc	4.08S	39.19 E
Kinaros	15	Jm	36.59N	26.17 E
Kincardine	42	Jh	44.11N	81.38W
Kind	8	Eg	57.35N	13.25 E
Kinda	36	Ed	9.18S	25.04 E
Kinda	8	Ff	58.05N	15.40 E
Kindamba	36	Bc	3.44S	14.31 E
Kinder	45	Jk	30.29N	92.51W
Kinder Scout	9	Lh	53.23N	1.52W
Kindersley	42	Gf	51.27N	109.10W
Kindi	34	Ec	12.26N	2.01W
Kindia	31	Fg	10.04N	12.51W
Kindu	31	Ji	2.57S	25.56 E
Kinel	7	Mj	53.14N	50.40 E
Kinesi	36	Fc	1.28S	33.52 E
Kinešma	19	Ed	57.28N	42.16 E
King	63a	Aa	4.24S	152.43 E
King, Cayos-	49	Fg	12.45N	83.20W
Kingaroy	59	Ke	26.33S	151.50 E
King Christian	42	Ha	77.45N	102.00W
King Christian IX Land (EN) = Kong Christian IX Land	67	Mc	68.00N	36.30W
King Christian X Land (EN) = Kong Christian X Land	67	Md	72.20N	32.30W
King City	43	Cd	36.13N	121.08W
King Edward River	59	Fb	14.14S	126.35 E
Kingfisher	45	Hi	35.52N	97.56W
King Frederik VI Coast (EN) =Kong Frederik VI Kyst	67	Nc	63.00N	43.30W
King Frederik VIII Land (EN) = Kong Frederik VIII Land	67	Md	78.30N	28.00W
King George Island	66	Re	62.00S	58.15W
King George Islands	42	Je	57.15N	78.30W
King George Sound	59	Dg	35.10S	118.10 E
Kingisepp	7	Gg	59.23N	28.37 E
Kingisepp/Kingissepp	19	Cd	58.17N	22.29 E
King Island	57	Fh	39.50S	144.00 E
Kingissepp/Kingisepp	19	Cd	58.17N	22.29 E
King Lear Peak	46	Ff	41.12N	118.34W
King Leopold Ranges	59	Fc	17.30S	125.45 E
Kingman [Az.-U.S.]	43	Ed	35.12N	114.04W
Kingman [Ks.-U.S.]	45	Gh	37.39N	98.07W
Kingman Reef	57	Kd	6.19N	162.28W
Kingombe [Zaire]	36	Ec	2.35S	26.37 E
Kingombe [Zaire]	36	Ec	3.52S	26.35 E
Kingoome Inlet	46	Ba	50.49N	126.13W
Kingoonya	58	Eh	30.54S	135.18 E
King Peninsula	66	Of	73.12S	101.00W
Kingsclere	12	Ac	51.19N	1.15W
Kingscote	59	Hg	35.40S	137.38 E
King's Lynn	9	Ni	52.45N	0.24 E
King Sound	57	Df	17.00S	123.30 E
Kings Peak [Ca.-U.S.]	46	Cf	40.10N	124.08W
Kings Peak [U.S.]	38	He	40.46N	110.22W
Kingsport	43	Kd	36.32N	82.33W
Kings River	46	Fh	36.03N	119.49W
Kingston [Jam.]	39	Lh	18.00N	76.50W
Kingston [Nor.I.]	58	Hg	29.04S	167.58 E
Kingston [N.Y.-U.S.]	43	Mc	41.55N	74.00W
Kingston [N.Z.]	61	Ci	45.20S	168.43 E
Kingston [Ont.-Can.]	39	Le	44.14N	76.30W
Kingston Peak	46	Hi	35.42N	115.52W
Kingston South East	58	Eh	36.50S	139.51 E
Kingston-upon-Hull (Hull)	6	Fe	53.45N	0.20W
Kingston-upon-Thames, London-	9	Mj	51.28N	0.19W
Kingstown	39	Mh	13.09N	61.14W
Kingsville	43	Hf	27.31N	97.52W
Kings Worthy	12	Ac	51.05N	1.18W
Kingussie	9	Id	57.05N	4.04W
King William	38	Jc	69.00N	97.30W
King William's Town	31	Jl	32.51S	27.22 E
Kiniama	36	Ee	11.26S	28.19 E
Kınık	24	Bc	39.05N	27.23 E
Kinkala	36	Bc	4.22S	14.46 E
Kinlochleven	9	Ie	56.43N	4.58W
Kinna	8	Eg	57.30N	12.41 E
Kinnairds Head	9	Ld	57.42N	2.00W
Kinnared	8	Eg	57.02N	13.06 E
Kinnekulle	8	Ef	58.35N	13.23 E
Kinneret, Yam-	24	Ff	32.48N	35.35 E
Kino-Kawa	29	Dd	34.13N	135.08 E
Kinomoto	29	Ed	35.31N	136.13 E
Kinoosao	42	He	57.06N	102.01W
Kinós Kefalai	15	Fj	39.25N	22.34 E
Kinross	9	Je	56.13N	3.27W
Kinsale/cionn tSáile	9	Ej	51.42N	8.32W
Kinsale, Old Head of-/An Seancheann	9	Ej	51.36N	8.32W
Kinsangire	36	Gd	7.26S	38.35 E
Kinsarvik	7	Bf	60.23N	6.43 E
Kinshasa [2]	36	Cc	4.00S	16.00 E
Kinshasa (Leopoldville)	31	Ii	4.18S	15.18 E
Kinsley	45	Gh	37.55N	99.25W
Kinston	43	Ld	35.16N	77.35W
Kintampo	34	Ed	8.03N	1.43W
Kintap	26	Gg	3.51S	115.13 E
Kintyre	9	Hf	55.32N	5.35W
Kintyre, Mull of-	9	Hf	55.17N	5.55W
Kin-Wan	29b	Ab	26.25N	127.54 E
Kinyan	34	Dc	11.51N	6.01W
Kinyeti	30	Kh	3.57N	32.54 E
Kinzig [Eur.]	10	Dh	48.37N	7.49 E
Kinzig [F.R.G.]	10	Ef	50.08N	8.54 E
Kioa	63d	Bb	16.39S	179.55 E
Kipaka	36	Ec	4.09S	26.30 E
Kiparissia	15	El	37.15N	21.40 E
Kiparissia, Gulf of- (EN) = Kiparissiakós Kólpos	15	El	37.30N	21.25 E
Kiparissiakós Kólpos = Kiparissia, Gulf of- (EN)	15	El	37.30N	21.25 E
Kipawa, Lac-	42	Jg	46.55N	79.00W
Kipembawe	36	Fd	7.39S	33.24 E
Kipengere Range	30	Ki	9.10S	34.15 E
Kiperčeny	15	Lb	47.32N	28.40 E
Kipili	36	Fd	7.26S	30.36 E
Kipini	36	Hc	2.32S	40.31 E
Kipling	45	Ea	50.10N	102.38W
Kippure	9	Gh	53.11N	6.20W
Kiprarenukk, Mys-/Undva Neem	8	If	58.25N	21.45 E
Kipushi	36	Ee	11.46S	27.14 E
Kirakira	58	Hf	10.27S	161.56 E
Kiraz	24	Cc	39.21N	27.25 E
Kirazlı	24	Bb	40.01N	26.40 E
Kirbla	8	Jf	58.42N	23.49 E
Kircasalih	15	Jh	41.23N	26.48 E
Kirchberg (Hunsrück)	12	Je	49.57N	7.24 E
Kirchhain	12	Kd	50.49N	8.58 E
Kirchheimbolanden	12	Ke	49.40N	8.01 E
Kirchheim unter Teck	10	Fh	48.39N	9.27 E
Kirchhundem	12	Kc	51.06N	8.06 E
Kirchhundem-Rahrbach	12	Jc	51.02N	7.59 E
Kirchlengern	12	Kb	52.12N	8.38 E
Kirdimi	35	Bb	18.11N	18.38 E
Kireç	15	Lj	39.33N	28.22 E
Kirenga	21	Md	57.47N	107.59 E
Kirensk	22	Md	57.46N	108.08 E
Kirghiz SSR (EN)= Kirgizskaja SSR [2]	19	Hg	41.30N	75.00 E
Kirghiz Steppe (EN)	5	Lf	49.30N	50.30 E
Kirgizskaja Sovetskaja Socialističeskaja Respublika [2]	19	Hg	41.30N	75.00 E
Kirgizskaja SSR/Kyrgyz Sovetik Socialistik Respublikasy [2]	19	Hg	41.30N	75.00 E
Kirgizskaja SSR=Kirghiz SSR (EN) [2]	19	Hg	41.30N	75.00 E
Kirgizskij Hrebet	19	Hg	42.30N	74.00 E
Kiri	36	Cc	1.27S	19.00 E
Kiribati [1]	58	Je	0.01S	174.00 E
Kirikhan	24	Gd	36.32N	36.19 E
Kırıkkale	23	Db	39.50N	33.31 E
Kirillov	7	Jg	59.54N	38.27 E
Kirillovskoje	8	Md	60.28N	29.28 E
Kirin (EN)=Chi-lin Sheng→Jilin Sheng [2]	27	Mc	43.00N	126.00 E
Kirin (EN)=Jilin Sheng (Chi-lin Sheng) [2]	27	Mc	43.00N	126.00 E
Kirinyaga/Kenya, Mount-	30	Ki	0.10S	37.20 E
Kirishima-Yama	29	Bf	31.56N	130.52 E
Kiriši	19	Dd	59.27N	32.02 E
Kiritimati Atoll (Christmas)	57	Ld	1.52N	157.20W
Kirja	7	Li	55.05N	46.52 E
Kırkağaç	24	Bc	39.06N	27.40 E
Kirkby Lonsdale	9	Kg	54.13N	2.36W
Kirkcaldy	9	Je	56.07N	3.10W
Kirkcudbright	9	Ig	54.50N	4.03W
Kirkee→Khadki	25	Ee	18.34N	73.52 E
Kirkenær	7	Cf	60.28N	12.03 E
Kirkenes	6	Jb	69.43N	30.03 E
Kirkjubæjarklaustur	7a	Bc	63.47N	18.04W
Kirkkonummi/Kyrkslätt	8	Kd	60.07N	24.26 E
Kirkland	46	Dc	47.41N	122.12W
Kirkland Lake	39	Ke	48.09N	80.02W
Kırklareli	23	Ca	41.44N	27.12 E
Kirkpatrick, Mont-	66	Kg	84.20S	166.19 E
Kırkpınar Dağı	24	Fd	37.14N	34.15 E
Kirksville	43	Ic	40.12N	92.35W
Kirkūk	22	Gf	35.28N	44.23 E
Kirkwall	9	Kc	58.59N	2.58W
Kirkwood [Mo.-U.S.]	45	Kg	38.35N	90.24W
Kirkwood [S.Afr.]	37	Df	33.22S	25.15 E
Kırlangıç Burun	24	Dd	36.13N	30.25 E
Kirn	10	Dg	49.47N	7.27 E
Kirobasi	24	Ed	36.43N	33.52 E
Kirov [R.S.F.S.R.]	19	De	54.03N	34.21 E
Kirov [R.S.F.S.R.]	6	Kd	58.33N	49.42 E
Kirova, Zaliv-	16	Pj	39.05N	49.05 E
Kirovabad	6	Kg	40.40N	46.22 E
Kirovakan	19	Eg	40.48N	44.28 E
Kirovgrad	17	Jh	57.26N	60.04 E
Kirovo	18	Hd	40.28N	70.34 E
Kirovo-Čepeck	19	Fd	58.35N	50.03 E
Kirovograd	6	Jf	48.30N	32.18 E
Kirovogradskaja Oblast [3]	19	Df	48.20N	31.50 E
Kirovsk [R.S.F.S.R.]	19	Db	67.37N	33.37 E
Kirovsk [R.S.F.S.R.]	7	Hg	59.53N	31.01 E
Kirovsk [Tur.-U.S.S.R.]	18	Cf	37.43N	60.24 E
Kirovskaja Oblast [3]	19	Ed	58.30N	50.00 E
Kirovski [Kaz.-U.S.S.R.]	19	Hg	44.53N	78.12 E
Kirovski [R.S.F.S.R.]	20	Ig	45.05N	133.27 E
Kirovski [R.S.F.S.R.]	16	Pg	45.48N	48.08 E
Kirovski [R.S.F.S.R.]	20	Kf	54.25N	155.37 E
Kirovski [R.S.F.S.R.]	20	Hf	54.26N	127.00 E
Kirovskoje	18	Hc	42.39N	71.35 E
Kirpilski Liman	16	Kg	45.50N	38.05 E
Kirriemuir	9	Je	56.41N	3.01W
Kirs	19	Fd	59.21N	52.18 E
Kirsanov	16	Mc	52.41N	42.45 E
Kırşehir	23	Db	39.09N	34.10 E
Kirthar Range	21	Ig	27.00N	67.20 E
Kirton	12	Bb	52.55N	0.03W
Kiruna	6	Ib	67.51N	20.13 E
Kirundu	36	Ec	0.44S	25.32 E
Kiryū	29	Fc	36.25N	139.20 E
Kiržač	7	Jh	56.11N	38.53 E
Kisa	7	Dh	57.59N	15.37 E
Kisabi	36	Ed	8.03S	29.11 E
Kisač	15	Cd	45.21N	19.44 E
Kisakata	29	Fb	39.14N	139.54 E
Kisaki	36	Gd	7.28S	37.36 E
Kisalföld	10	Mi	47.30N	17.00 E
Kisangani	31	Jh	0.25N	25.12 E
Kisarazu	29	Fd	35.23N	139.55 E
Kisbér	10	Oi	47.30N	18.02 E
Kiselevsk	20	Df	54.03N	86.49 E
Kiserawe	36	Gd	6.54S	39.05 E
Kishangarh	25	Ec	26.34N	74.52 E
Kishb, Ḥarrat al-	33	He	22.47N	41.30 E
Kishi	34	Fd	9.05N	3.51 E
Kishiwada	28	Mg	34.28N	135.22 E
Kisii	36	Fc	0.41S	34.46 E
Kisiju	36	Gd	7.24S	39.20 E
Kišinev	6	If	46.59N	28.52 E
Kısır Dağı	24	Jb	40.58N	43.04 E
Kiska	40a	Bb	52.00N	177.30 E
Kiska Volcano	40a	Bb	52.07N	177.36 E
Kisko	8	Jd	60.14N	23.29 E
Kiskörei Víztároló	10	Qi	47.44N	20.40 E
Kiskőrös	10	Pj	46.37N	19.18 E
Kiskunfélegyháza	10	Pj	46.33N	19.51 E
Kiskunhalas	10	Pj	46.26N	19.30 E
Kiskunmajsa	10	Pj	46.29N	19.45 E
Kiskunság	10	Pj	46.35N	19.15 E
Kislovodsk	19	Eg	43.54N	42.42 E
Kismayo	31	Li	0.22S	42.32 E
Kisofukushima	29	Ed	35.51N	137.41 E
Kiso-Gawa	28	Ng	35.05N	136.45 E
Kisoro	36	Ec	1.17S	29.41 E
Kiso-Sanmyaku	29	Ed	35.45N	137.45 E
Kisria, Daiet el-	13	Oi	35.44N	2.47 E
Kissámou, Kólpos-	15	Gn	35.35N	23.40 E
Kissidougou	34	Cd	9.11N	10.06W
Kissimmee	44	Gk	28.18N	81.24W
Kissimmee, Lake-	44	Gl	27.55N	81.16W
Kissū, Jabal-	35	Da	21.35N	25.09 E
Kistelek	10	Pj	46.28N	19.59 E
Kisterenye	10	Ph	48.01N	19.50 E

Index Symbols

[1] Independent Nation
[2] State, Region
[3] District, County
[4] Municipality
[5] Colony, Dependency
Continent
Physical Region
Historical or Cultural Region
Mount, Mountain
Volcano
Hill
Mountains, Mountain Range
Hills, Escarpment
Plateau, Upland
Pass, Gap
Plain, Lowland
Delta
Salt Flat
Valley, Canyon
Crater, Cave
Karst Features
Depression
Polder
Desert, Dunes
Forest, Woods
Heath, Steppe
Oasis
Cape, Point
Coast, Beach
Cliff
Peninsula
Isthmus
Sandbank
Island
Atoll
Rock, Reef
Islands, Archipelago
Rocks, Reefs
Coral Reef
Well, Spring
Geyser
River, Stream
Waterfall Rapids
River Mouth, Estuary
Lake
Salt Lake
Intermittent Lake
Reservoir
Swamp, Pond
Canal
Glacier
Ice Shelf, Pack Ice
Ocean
Sea
Gulf, Bay
Strait, Fjord
Lagoon
Bank
Seamount
Tablemount
Ridge
Shelf
Basin
Escarpment, Sea Scarp
Fracture
Trench, Abyss
National Park, Reserve
Point of Interest
Recreation Site
Cave, Cavern
Historic Site
Ruins
Wall, Walls
Church, Abbey
Temple
Scientific Station
Airport
Port
Lighthouse
Mine
Tunnel
Dam, Bridge

Name	Page	Grid	Lat.	Long.
Kisújszállás	10	Qi	47.13N	20.46 E
Kisuki	29	Cd	35.17N	132.54 E
Kisumu	31	Ki	0.06S	34.45 E
Kisvárda	10	Sh	48.13N	22.05 E
Kita	31	Gg	13.03N	9.30W
Kitab	19	Gh	39.08N	66.54 E
Kita-Daitō-Jima	27	Nf	25.55N	131.20 E
Kitaibaraki	28	Pf	36.48N	140.45 E
Kita-Iō-Jima	60	Cb	25.26N	141.17 E
Kitaj, Ozero-	15	Md	45.35N	29.15 E
Kitakami	27	Pd	39.30N	141.10 E
Kitakami-Gawa	29	Gb	38.25N	141.19 E
Kitakami-Sanchi	29	Gb	39.30N	141.30 E
Kitakata	28	Of	37.39N	139.52 E
Kitakyushū	22	Pf	33.53N	130.50 E
Kitale	31	Kh	1.01N	35.00 E
Kitamaiaioi	29a	Cb	43.33N	143.57 E
Kitami	27	Pc	43.48N	143.54 E
Kitami-Fuji	29a	Cb	43.42N	143.14 E
Kitami-Sanchi	28	Qb	44.30N	142.30 E
Kitami Tōge	29a	Cb	43.55N	142.55 E
Kitan-Kaikyō	29	Dd	34.15N	135.00 E
Kita-Taiheyō = Pacific Ocean (EN)	60	Ch	22.00N	167.00 E
Kita-Ura	29	Gc	36.00N	140.34 E
Kit Carson	45	Eg	38.46N	102.48W
Kitchener	42	Jh	43.27N	80.29W
Kitee	7	He	62.06N	30.09 E
Kitessa	35	Dd	5.22N	25.22 E
Kitgum	36	Fb	3.19N	32.53 E
Kíthira = Cythera (EN)	15	Fm	36.09N	23.00 E
Kíthira = Kythera (EN)	5	Ih	36.15N	23.00 E
Kithira Channel (EN) = Kithíron Dhiékplous	15	Fm	36.00N	23.00 E
Kithíron, Dhiékplous- = Kithira Channel (EN)	15	Fm	36.00N	23.00 E
Kíthnos	15	Hl	37.25N	24.26 E
Kíthnos	15	Hl	37.23N	24.25 E
Kithnou, Stenón-	15	Hl	37.25N	24.30 E
Kitimat	39	Gd	54.05N	128.38W
Kitimat Ranges	42	Ef	53.58N	128.39W
Kitoushi-Yama	29a	Cb	43.27N	143.25 E
Kitriani	15	Hm	36.54N	24.44 E
Kitridge Point	51q	Bb	13.09N	59.25W
Kítros	15	Fi	40.22N	22.35 E
Kitsuki	29	Be	33.25N	131.37 E
Kittanning	44	He	40.49N	79.31W
Kittery	44	Ld	43.05N	70.45W
Kittilä	7	Fc	67.40N	24.54 E
Kitui	31	Ki	1.22S	38.01 E
Kitunda	36	Fd	6.48S	33.13 E
Kitutu	36	Ec	3.17S	28.05 E
Kitwe-Nkana	31	Jj	12.49S	28.13 E
Kitzbühel	14	Gc	47.27N	12.23 E
Kitzbüheler Alpen	14	Gc	47.20N	12.20 E
Kitzingen	10	Gg	49.44N	10.10 E
Kiunga [Kenya]	36	Hc	1.45S	41.29 E
Kiunga [Pap.N.Gui.]	60	Ci	6.07S	141.18 E
Kiuruvesi	7	Ge	63.39N	26.37 E
Kivalina	40	Gc	67.59N	164.33W
Kivercy	16	Dd	50.50N	25.31 E
Kivijärvi [Fin.]	8	Ld	60.55N	27.40 E
Kivijärvi [Fin.]	7	Fe	63.10N	25.09 E
Kivik	7	Di	55.41N	14.15 E
Kiviõli/Kiviyli	7	Gg	59.23N	26.59 E
Kiviyli/Kiviõli	7	Gg	59.23N	26.59 E
Kivu [2]	36	Ec	2.30S	27.30 E
Kivu, Lac- = Kivu, Lake- (EN)	30	Ii	2.00S	29.10 E
Kivu, Lake- (EN) = Kivu, Lac-	30	Ii	2.00S	29.10 E
Kiwai Island	60	Ci	8.30S	143.25 E
Kīyāmakī Dāgh	24	Kc	38.47N	45.51 E
Kiyiköy	24	Cb	41.25N	28.01 E
Kiyosato	29a	Db	43.51N	144.35 E
Kizel	19	Fd	59.03N	57.40 E
Kizema	7	Kf	61.09N	44.46 E
Kizilcabölük	15	Ml	37.37N	29.01 E
Kızılca Dağı	24	Cd	36.55N	29.52 E
Kızılcahaman	24	Eb	40.28N	32.39 E
Kızıl Dağ	24	Ed	36.25N	32.42 E
Kizilhisar	15	Ml	37.33N	29.18 E
Kizilirmak	21	Fe	41.45N	35.59 E
Kızılırmak	24	Eb	40.22N	33.59 E
Kiziljurt	16	Oh	43.13N	46.55 E
Kizilskoje	17	Ij	52.44N	58.54 E
Kızıltepe	24	Id	37.12N	40.36 E
Kizimen, Vulkan-	20	Le	55.03N	160.27 E
Kižinga	20	Ff	51.51N	109.55 E
Kizir	20	Ef	54.10N	93.30 E
Kizljar	19	Eg	43.50N	46.42 E
Kizljarski Zaliv	16	Og	44.35N	46.55 E
Kizukuri	29a	Bc	40.48N	140.22 E
Kizyl-Arvat	19	Fh	39.01N	56.20 E
Kizyl-Atrek	19	Fh	37.38N	54.47 E
Kizyl-Su	19	Fh	39.46N	53.01 E
Kjahta	20	Ff	50.26N	106.25 E
Kjalvaz	16	Pj	38.38N	48.20 E
Kjardla/Kärdla	7	Fg	59.01N	22.42 E
Kjarevere/Kärevere	8	Lf	58.23N	26.30 E
Kjarla/Kärla	8	Jf	58.16N	22.05 E
Kjellerup	8	Ch	56.17N	9.26 E
Kjøllefjord	7	Ga	70.56N	27.27 E
Kjölur	7a	Bb	64.50N	19.25W
Kjøpsvik	7	Db	68.06N	16.21 E
Kjubjume	20	Jd	63.28N	140.30 E
Kjurdamir	19	Eg	40.20N	48.07 E
Kjusjur	20	Hb	70.35N	127.45 E
Kjustendil	15	Fg	42.17N	22.41 E
Kjustendil [2]	15	Fg	42.17N	22.41 E
Kjyosumi-Yama	29	Gd	35.10N	140.09 E
Klabat, Gunung-	26	If	1.28N	125.02 E
Kladanj	23	Gf	44.14N	18.42 E
Kladno	10	Kf	50.09N	14.07 E
Kladovo	15	Fe	44.37N	22.37 E
Klagenfurt	6	Hf	46.38N	14.18 E
Klaipėda/Klajpeda	6	Id	55.43N	21.07 E
Klajpeda/Klaipėda	6	Id	55.43N	21.07 E
Klamath	46	Cf	41.32N	124.02W
Klamath Falls	39	Ge	42.13N	121.46W
Klamath Mountains	43	Cc	41.40N	123.20W
Klamath River	46	Cf	41.33N	124.04W
Klamono	26	Jg	1.08S	131.30 E
Klarälven	5	Hd	59.23N	13.32 E
Klaten	26	Fh	7.42S	110.35 E
Klatovy	10	Jg	49.24N	13.19 E
Klavreström	8	Fg	57.08N	15.08 E
Klawer	37	Bf	31.44S	18.36 E
Klazienaveen, Emmen-	12	Jb	52.44N	7.01 E
Kleck	16	Ec	53.03N	26.40 E
Kłecko	10	Nd	52.38N	17.26 E
Kleinblittersdorf	12	Je	49.09N	7.02 E
Kleine Nete	12	Gc	51.08N	4.34 E
Kleine Sluis, Anna Paulowna-	12	Gb	52.52N	4.52 E
Klein-Karoo = Little Karroo (EN)	37	Cf	33.42S	21.20 E
Kleinsee	37	Be	29.40S	17.05 E
Klekovača	14	Kf	44.26N	16.31 E
Kléla	34	Dc	11.40N	5.40W
Kleppe	8	Af	58.46N	5.40 E
Klerksdorp	37	De	26.58S	26.39 E
Kletnja	19	De	53.27N	33.17 E
Kletski	16	Me	49.19N	43.04 E
Kleve	10	Ce	51.47N	6.09 E
Klibreck, Ben-	9	Ic	58.19N	4.30W
Klička	20	Gf	50.24N	118.01 E
Klimoviči	19	De	53.37N	32.01 E
Klimovo	16	Hc	52.23N	32.16 E
Klin	19	Dd	56.20N	36.42 E
Klina	15	Dg	42.37N	20.35 E
Klincy	19	De	52.46N	32.17 E
Klingbach	12	Ke	49.11N	8.24 E
Klingenthal	10	If	50.22N	12.28 E
Klínovec	10	If	50.24N	12.58 E
Klintehamn	7	Eh	57.24N	18.12 E
Klippan	8	Eh	56.08N	13.06 E
Kliplaat	37	Cf	33.02S	24.21 E
Kliškovcy	15	Ja	48.23N	26.13 E
Klisura	15	Hg	42.42N	24.27 E
Klitmøller	8	Cg	57.02N	8.31 E
Kljazma	5	Kd	56.10N	42.58 E
Ključevskaja Sopka, Vulkan-	21	Sd	56.04N	160.38 E
Kljuci	20	Le	56.14N	160.58 E
Kłobuck	10	Of	50.55N	18.57 E
Kłodawa	10	Od	52.16N	18.55 E
Kłodzka, Kotlina-	10	Mf	50.30N	16.35 E
Kłodzko	10	Mf	50.28N	16.40 E
Kløfta	8	Dd	60.04N	11.09 E
Kloga/Klooga	8	Ke	59.24N	24.10 E
Kłomnice	10	Pf	50.56N	19.21 E
Klondike Plateau	42	Dd	63.10N	139.55W
Klondike River	42	Dd	64.03N	139.26W
Klooga/Kloga	8	Ke	59.24N	24.10 E
Kloosteezande, Hontenisse-	12	Gc	51.23N	4.00 E
Klosi	15	Dh	41.29N	20.06 E
Klosterneuburg	14	Kb	48.18N	16.19 E
Klosters/Claustra	14	Dd	46.52N	9.52 E
Kloten	14	Cc	47.27N	8.35 E
Klotz, Lac -	42	Kd	60.40N	73.00W
Kluane Lake	42	Dd	61.15N	138.40W
Kluczbork	10	Of	50.59N	18.13 E
Knaben	8	Bf	58.39N	7.04 E
Knäred	8	Eh	56.32N	13.19 E
Kneža	15	Hf	43.30N	24.05 E
Knife River	45	Fc	47.20N	101.23W
Knin	14	Kf	44.02N	16.12 E
Knislinge	8	Fh	56.11N	14.05 E
Knittelfeld	14	Ic	47.13N	14.49 E
Knivsta	8	Ge	59.43N	17.48 E
Knjaževac	15	Ff	43.34N	22.15 E
Knobly Mountain	44	Hf	39.15N	79.05W
Knockmealdown Mountains/Cnoc Mhaoldonn	9	Fi	52.15N	8.00W
Knokke-Heist [Bel.]	12	Fc	51.21N	3.15 E
Knokke-Heist [Bel.]	11	Jc	51.21N	3.17 E
Knokke-Westkapelle	12	Fc	51.19N	3.18 E
Knolls grund	8	Gg	57.30N	17.30 E
Knøsen	8	Dg	57.12N	10.18 E
Knosós = Cnossus (EN)	15	In	35.18N	25.10 E
Knox, Cape -	42	Ef	54.11N	133.05W
Knox Coast	66	He	66.30S	105.00 E
Knoxville [Ia.-U.S.]	45	Jf	41.19N	93.06W
Knoxville [Tn.-U.S.]	39	Kf	35.58N	83.56W
Knud Rasmussen Land	67	Nd	80.00N	55.00W
Knüllgebirge	10	Ff	50.50N	9.30 E
Knutsholstind	8	Cc	61.26N	8.34 E
Knysna	31	Jl	34.02S	23.02 E
Ko, Kut	25	Kf	11.40N	102.35 E
Koartac	42	Kd	60.50N	69.30W
Koba	26	Eg	2.29S	106.24 E
Koba, Pulau-	26	Jh	6.25S	134.28 E
Kobar Sink	35	Gc	14.00N	40.30 E
Kobayashi	28	Ki	31.59N	130.59 E
Kobdo	22	Le	48.01N	91.38 E
Kobdo (Chovd)	27	Fb	48.06N	92.11 E
Kōbe	22	Pf	34.41N	135.10 E
Kobeljaki	16	Ie	49.08N	34.12 E
København [2]	8	Ei	55.40N	12.10 E
København = Copenhagen (EN)	6	Hi	55.40N	12.35 E
Kobenni	32	Ff	15.55N	9.05W
Kobern-Gondorf	12	Jd	50.19N	7.28 E
Kobjaj	20	Hd	63.30N	126.26 E
Koblenz	10	Df	50.21N	7.36 E
Kobo	35	Fc	12.09N	39.39 E
Koboldo	20	If	52.58N	132.42 E
Kobra	7	Mg	59.19N	50.54 E
Kobrin	19	Ce	52.13N	24.23 E
Kobrinskoje	8	Ne	59.22N	30.14 E
Kobroor, Pulau-	26	Jh	6.12S	134.32 E
Kobuk	38	Cc	66.45N	161.00W
Kobuleti	16	Li	41.47N	41.45 E
Koca	24	Eb	41.41N	32.15 E
Kocabaş	24	Bb	40.22N	27.19 E
Koca Çay	15	Lj	38.43N	28.30 E
Koca Çay [Tur.]	24	Bb	40.08N	27.57 E
Koca Çay [Tur.]	24	Cd	36.17N	29.16 E
Koca Çay/Orhaneli	15	Lj	39.56N	28.32 E
Kočani	15	Fh	41.55N	22.25 E
Kocasu	15	Mj	39.42N	29.31 E
Kočečum	20	Fd	64.17N	100.10 E
Kočetovka	16	Lc	53.01N	40.31 E
Kočevje	14	Ie	45.39N	14.51 E
Kočevski rog	14	Ie	45.41N	15.00 E
Koch	42	Jc	69.35N	78.20W
Kŏch'ang	28	Ig	35.41N	127.55 E
Ko Chang	25	Kf	12.00N	102.23 E
Kōchi	27	Ne	33.33N	133.33 E
Kōchi Ken [2]	28	Lh	33.20N	133.30 E
Kochisar Ovası	24	Ec	38.50N	33.30 E
Kock	10	Se	51.39N	22.27 E
Kočkorka	18	Jc	42.11N	75.45 E
Kočmar	15	Kf	43.41N	27.28 E
Kočubej	19	Eg	44.23N	46.31 E
Kočubejevskoje	16	Lg	44.41N	41.50 E
Kodiak	39	Dd	57.48N	152.23W
Kodiak	38	Dd	57.30N	153.30W
Kodino	7	Je	63.44N	39.40 E
Kodok	35	Ed	9.53N	32.07 E
Kodomari	29a	Bc	41.08N	140.18 E
Kodori	16	Lh	42.49N	41.10 E
Kodry	15	Lb	47.15N	28.15 E
Kodyma	16	Ge	48.01N	30.48 E
Kodža Balkan	15	Jg	42.50N	27.00 E
Koekenaap	37	Bf	31.29S	18.19 E
Koes	37	Be	25.59S	19.08 E
Kofa Mountains	46	Ij	33.20N	114.00W
Koţarli	15	Kl	37.45N	27.42 E
Kofąz	24	Bb	41.58N	27.12 E
Koffiefontein	37	Ce	29.30S	25.00 E
Kofiau, Pulau-	26	Ig	1.11S	129.50 E
Köflach	14	Jc	47.04N	15.05 E
Koforidua	31	Gh	6.05N	0.15W
Kōfu [Jap.]	29	Cd	35.18N	133.29 E
Kōfu [Jap.]	27	Od	35.39N	138.35 E
Koga	29	Fc	36.12N	139.42 E
Kogaluc	42	Je	59.38N	77.30W
Kōge	29	Dd	35.24N	134.15 E
Køge	7	Ci	55.27N	12.11 E
Køge Bugt	8	Ei	55.30N	12.20 E
Kogel	17	He	62.38N	57.07 E
Kogilnik	15	Md	45.51N	29.38 E
Kogilnik (Kunduk)	15	Md	45.51N	29.38 E
Kogon	34	Cc	11.09N	14.42W
Kogota	29	Gb	38.32N	141.01 E
Kohala Mountains	65a	Fc	20.05N	155.43W
Kohāt	25	Eb	33.35N	71.26 E
Kohila	8	Ke	59.11N	24.40 E
Kohima	25	Ic	25.40N	94.07 E
Koh-i Mārān	25	Dc	29.05N	66.50 E
Kohinggo	63a	Cc	8.13S	157.10 E
Kohma	7	Jh	56.57N	41.07 E
Kohtla-Jarve/Kohtla-Järve	19	Cd	59.25N	27.14 E
Kohtla-Järve/Kohtla-Jarve	19	Cd	59.25N	27.14 E
Kohu Daği	15	Mm	36.30N	29.50 E
Kohunlich	48	Oh	18.30N	88.55W
Koide	29	Fc	37.14N	138.57 E
Koigi/Kojgi	8	Kf	58.49N	25.40 E
Koin	17	Ee	63.10N	51.15 E
Koindu	34	Cd	8.28N	10.20W
Koitere	7	He	62.58N	30.45 E
Kojā	23	Jd	25:34N	61.13 E
Kojandytau	18	Lb	44.20N	78.45 E
Kojda	7	Kc	66.23N	42.31 E
Koje-Do	28	Jg	34.52N	128.37 E
Kojetín	10	Ng	49.21N	17.20 E
Kojgi/Koigi	8	Kf	58.49N	25.40 E
Ko-Jima [Jap.]	29	Fe	33.07N	139.40 E
Ko-Jima [Jap.]	28	Od	41.22N	139.47 E
Kojŏ	27	Md	38.57N	127.52 E
Kojonup	59	Df	33.50S	117.09 E
Kojtaš	18	Fd	40.14N	67.22 E
Kojtezek, Pereval-	18	If	37.29N	72.45 E
Kojur	24	Nd	36.23N	51.43 E
Kojva	17	Ig	58.15N	58.14 E
Kokab	35	Cc	10.03N	22.04 E
Kokai-Gawa	29	Gd	35.52N	140.08 E
Kokand	22	Je	40.33N	70.57 E
Kökar	7	Eg	59.55N	20.55 E
Kökarsfjärden	8	Ie	59.55N	20.45 E
Kokas	26	Jg	2.42S	132.26 E
Kokava nad Rimavicou	10	Ph	48.34N	19.50 E
Kokawa	29	Dd	34.17N	135.26 E
Kokčetav	22	Id	53.17N	69.25 E
Kokčetavskaja Oblast [3]	19	Ge	53.30N	70.00 E
Kokemäenjoki	8	Ic	61.33N	21.42 E
Kokemäki/Kumo	7	Ff	61.15N	22.21 E
Kok-Jangak	19	Hg	40.59N	73.15 E
Kokkina	24	Ee	35.10N	32.36 E
Kokkola/Gamlaklarleby	6	Ic	63.50N	23.07 E
Koko [Eth.]	35	Fc	10.20N	36.04 E
Koko [Nig.]	34	Fc	11.26N	4.30 E
Kokomo	43	Jc	40.29N	86.08W
Kokonau	26	Kg	4.43S	136.26 E
Kokong	37	Cd	24.27S	23.03 E
Koko Nor (EN) = Qinghai Hu	21	Mf	37.00N	100.20 E
Kokpekty	19	If	48.45N	82.24 E
Kokšaal-Tau, Hrebet-	19	Hg	41.00N	78.00 E
Kokšenga	7	Kf	61.27N	42.38 E
Koksijde	12	Ec	51.06N	2.39 E
Koksoak	42	Ke	58.31N	68.11W
Kokstad	31	Jl	30.32S	29.29 E
Koktal	18	Lb	44.05N	79.44 E
Koktokay/Fuyun	22	Ke	47.13N	89.39 E
Kokubu	28	Ki	31.44N	130.46 E
Kola	19	Db	68.53N	33.01 E
Kola, Pulau-	26	Jh	5.30S	134.35 E
Kolahun	34	Cd	8.17N	10.05W
Kolaka	26	Hg	4.03S	121.36 E
Kolamadulu Atoll	25a	Bb	2.25N	73.10 E
Kola Peninsula (EN) = Kolski Poluostrov	5	Jb	67.30N	37.00 E
Kolār Gold Fields	25	Ff	12.55N	78.17 E
Kolari	7	Fc	67.20N	23.48 E
Kólarovo	10	Ni	47.55N	18.00 E
Kolašin	15	Cg	42.49N	19.32 E
Kolbäck	8	Ge	59.34N	16.15 E
Kolbäcksån	8	Ge	59.32N	16.16 E
Kolbio	36	Hc	1.09S	41.12 E
Kolbuszowa	10	Rf	50.15N	21.47 E
Kolby	8	Di	55.48N	10.33 E
Kolčugino	7	Jh	56.16N	39.23 E
Kolda	34	Cc	12.53N	14.57W
Kolding	6	Gd	55.31N	9.29 E
Kole [Zaire]	36	Dc	3.31S	22.27 E
Kole [Zaire]	36	Eb	2.07N	25.26 E
Koléa	13	Oh	36.38N	2.46 E
Kolendo	20	Jf	53.43N	142.57 E
Kolente	34	Cd	8.55N	13.08W
Kolesnoje	15	Mc	46.04N	29.45 E
Kolga	8	Ke	59.28N	25.29 E
Kolga, Zaliv-/Kolga Laht	8	Ke	59.30N	25.15 E
Kolga Laht/Kolga, Zaliv-	8	Ke	59.30N	25.15 E
Kolgompja, Mys-	8	Me	59.44N	28.35 E
Kolgujev, Ostrov-	5	Kb	69.05N	49.15 E
Kolhāpur	22	Jh	16.42N	74.13 E
Kolhozabad	18	Gf	37.35N	68.39 E
Kolhozbentskoje, Vodohranilišče-	18	Df	37.10N	62.30 E
Koli	7	Ge	63.06N	29.53 E
Kolimbiné	34	Cc	14.45N	11.00 E
Kolín	10	Lf	50.02N	15.13 E
Kolito	35	Fd	7.25N	38.07 E
Koljučinskaja Guba	20	Nc	66.50N	174.30W
Kolka	8	Jg	57.44N	22.27 E
Kolkasrags	7	Fh	57.46N	22.37 E
Kolki	16	Dd	51.07N	25.42 E
Kollinai	15	Fl	37.17N	22.22 E
Kollumúli	7a	Cb	65.47N	14.21W
Kolmården	8	Gf	58.41N	16.35 E
Köln = Cologne (EN)	6	Ge	50.56N	6.57 E
Köln-Lövenich	12	Id	50.57N	6.50 E
Kolno	10	Rc	53.25N	21.56 E
Köln-Porz	10	Df	50.53N	7.03 E
Koło	10	Od	52.12N	18.38 E
Koloa	65a	Bb	21.54N	159.28W
Kołobrzeg	10	Lb	54.12N	15.33 E
Kolodnja	16	Hb	54.49N	32.11 E
Kologriv	7	Kg	58.51N	44.17 E
Kolokani	34	Dc	13.34N	8.03W
Koloko	34	Dc	11.05N	5.19W
Kolokolkova Guba	17	Fb	68.30N	52.30 E
Kololo	35	Gd	7.27N	41.59 E
Kolombangara Island	60	Fi	8.00S	157.05 E
Kolomna	6	Jd	55.05N	38.49 E
Kolomyja	19	Cf	48.32N	25.01 E
Kolondiéba	34	Dc	11.06N	6.53W
Kolonga	65b	Ac	21.08S	175.04W
Kolonodale	26	Hg	2.00S	121.19 E
Kolosovka	19	Hd	56.28N	73.36 E
Kolossa	34	Dc	13.52N	7.35W
Kolovai	65b	Ac	21.06S	175.20W
Kolozero, Ozero-	7	Hb	68.15N	33.15 E
Kolp	7	Ig	59.20N	36.50 E
Kolpaševo	22	Kd	58.20N	82.50 E
Kolpino	7	Hg	59.45N	30.33 E
Kolpny	16	Jc	52.16N	37.00 E
Kolski Poluostrov = Kola Peninsula (EN)	5	Jb	67.30N	37.00 E
Koltubanovski	16	Rc	52.57N	52.02 E
Kolubara	15	De	44.40N	20.15 E
Koluszki	10	Pe	51.44N	19.49 E
Koluton	19	Ge	51.42N	69.25 E
Kolva [R.S.F.S.R.]	19	Fb	65.55N	57.20 E
Kolva [R.S.F.S.R.]	17	Hf	60.22N	56.33 E
Kolvickoje, Ozero-	7	Hc	67.05N	33.30 E
Kölvrå	8	Ch	56.18N	9.08 E
Kolwezi	31	Jj	10.43S	25.28 E
Kolyma	21	Sc	69.30N	161.00 E
Kolyma Plain (EN) = Kolymskaja Nizmennost	21	Rc	68.30N	154.00 E
Kolyma Range (EN) = Kolymskoje Nagorje	21	Rc	62.30N	155.00 E
Kolymskaja Nizmennost = Kolyma Plain (EN)	21	Rc	68.30N	154.00 E
Kolymskoje Nagorje = Kolyma Range (EN)	21	Rc	62.30N	155.00 E
Kolyšlej	16	Nc	52.40N	44.31 E
Kolžat	19	Ig	43.29N	80.37 E
Kom	15	Gf	43.10N	23.03 E
Kom	36	Gb	1.05N	38.02 E
Komádi	10	Rj	47.00N	21.30 E
Komadugu Gana	34	Hc	13.05N	12.24 E
Komadugu Yobe	30	Ig	13.42N	13.24 E
Komagane	29	Ed	35.43N	137.54 E
Koma-ga-Take [Jap.]	29	Fd	35.45N	138.13 E
Koma-ga-Take [Jap.]	29	Gb	39.47N	140.50 E
Koma-ga-Take [Jap.]	29a	Bb	42.04N	140.40 E
Komandorski Islands (EN) = Komandorskije Ostrova	21	Sd	55.00N	167.00 E
Komandorskije Ostrova = Komandorski Islands (EN)	21	Sd	55.00N	167.00 E
Komandorskiye Basin (EN)	20	Le	57.00N	168.00 E
Komarin	16	Gd	51.27N	30.32 E
Komarno	10	Tg	49.34N	23.43 E
Komárno	10	Oi	47.46N	18.09 E
Komárom [2]	10	Oi	47.40N	18.15 E
Komárom	10	Oi	47.44N	18.07 E
Komatipoort	37	Ee	25.25S	31.55 E
Komatsu	27	Od	36.24N	136.37 E
Komatsujima	29	Dd	34.01N	134.35 E
Komba, Pulau-	26	Hh	7.47S	123.35 E
Kombissiri	34	Ec	12.04N	1.20W
Kombolcha	35	Fc	11.05N	39.45 E
Komebail Lagoon	64a	Ac	7.24N	134.27 E
Komen/Comines	12	Ed	50.46N	2.59 E
Komi ASSR [3]	19	Fc	64.00N	55.00 E
Komi-Permjacki Nacionalny Okrug [3]	19	Fd	60.00N	54.30 E
Komló	10	Oj	46.12N	18.16 E
Kommunarsk	16	Ke	48.27N	38.52 E
Kommunary	8	Nd	60.55N	30.10 E
Kommunizma, Pik- = Communism Peak (EN)	21	Jf	38.57N	72.08 E
Komodo, Pulau-	26	Gh	8.36S	119.30 E
Komoé	30	Gh	5.12N	3.44W
Komoé [3]	34	Ec	10.25N	4.20W
Komono	36	Bc	3.15S	13.14 E
Komoran, Pulau-	26	Kh	8.18S	138.45 E
Komoro	29	Fc	36.19N	138.24 E
Komotini	15	Ih	41.07N	25.24 E
Komovi	15	Cg	42.41N	19.39 E
Kompasberg	30	Jl	31.46S	24.32 E
Komrat	16	Ff	46.17N	28.38 E
Komsa	20	Dd	61.40N	89.25 E
Komsomolec	17	Kj	53.45N	62.02 E
Komsomolec, Ostrov-	21	La	80.30N	95.00 E
Komsomolec, Zaliv-	16	Rg	45.30N	52.45 E
Komsomolsk [R.S.F.S.R.]	7	Jh	57.02N	40.22 E
Komsomolsk [R.S.F.S.R.]	20	De	57.25N	86.02 E
Komsomolsk [Tur.-U.S.S.R.]	19	Gh	39.02N	63.36 E
Komsomolski [Kaz.-U.S.S.R.]	19	Ff	47.20N	53.44 E
Komsomolski [R.S.F.S.R.]	16	Og	45.22N	46.01 E
Komsomolski [R.S.F.S.R.]	7	Ki	54.27N	45.45 E
Komsomolski [R.S.F.S.R.]	19	Gb	67.35N	63.47 E
Komsomolski [R.S.F.S.R.]	17	Kf	61.20N	63.15 E
Komsomolski [R.S.F.S.R.]	20	Mc	69.12N	172.55 E
Komsomolsk-na-Amure	22	Pd	50.36N	137.02 E
Komsomolsk-na-Ustjurte	19	Fg	44.07N	58.17 E
Komsomolskoje [Ukr.-U.S.S.R.]	16	Je	49.36N	36.33 E
Komsomolskoje [Ukr.-U.S.S.R.]	16	Kf	47.37N	38.05 E
Komsomolskoj Pravdy, Ostrova-	20	Fa	77.15N	107.30 E
Kŏmun-Do	28	Ig	34.02N	127.19 E
Kömür Burun	15	Jk	38.39N	26.25 E
Komusan	27	Mc	42.07N	129.42 E
Kona	34	Ec	14.57N	3.53W
Kona Coast	65a	Fd	19.35N	155.56W
Konakovo	19	Dd	56.42N	36.46 E
Konar	23	Lc	34.25N	70.32 E
Konārak	25	Hh	19.54N	86.07 E
Konarha [3]	23	Lb	35.15N	71.00 E
Konda	19	Gc	60.40N	69.46 E
Kondagaon	25	Ge	19.36N	81.40 E
Kondinin	59	Df	32.30S	118.16 E
Kondinskoje	17	Mg	59.40N	67.25 E
Kondoa	31	Ki	4.54S	35.47 E
Kondopoga	6	Jc	62.13N	34.17 E
Kondratjevo	8	Md	60.36N	28.02 E
Kondrovo	19	De	54.49N	35.55 E
Kondurča	7	Mj	53.31N	50.24 E
Koné	61	Bd	21.04S	164.52 E
Konečnaja	19	He	50.45N	78.27 E
Konevic, Ostrov-	8	Nd	60.50N	30.45 E
Kong	34	Ed	9.09N	4.37W
Kŏng	25	Lf	13.32N	105.58 E
Kŏng, Kaôh-	25	Kf	11.20N	103.00 E
Konga/Koonga	8	Jf	58.34N	24.00 E
Kongauru	64a	Ac	7.04N	134.17 E
Kong Christian IX Land = King Christian IX Land (EN)	67	Mc	68.00N	36.30W
Kong Christian X Land = King Christian X Land (EN)	67	Md	72.20N	32.30W
Kongeå	8	Ci	55.23N	8.39 E
Kong Frederik VIII Land = King Frederik VIII Land (EN)	67	Md	78.30N	28.00W
Kong Frederik VI Kyst = King Frederik VI Coast (EN)	67	Nc	63.00N	43.30W
Konginkangas	8	Kb	62.46N	25.48 E
Kongju	28	If	36.27N	127.08 E
Kong Karls Land	41	Oc	78.50N	28.00 E
Kong Kong	35	Ed	7.26N	33.14 E
Kongolo	31	Ji	5.23S	27.00 E
Kongor	35	Ed	7.10N	31.21 E
Kong Oscars Fjord	67	Md	72.20N	23.00W
Kongoussi	34	Ec	13.19N	1.32W
Kongsberg	7	Bg	59.39N	9.39 E
Kongsøya	41	Oc	78.55N	28.40 E
Kongsvinger	7	Cf	60.12N	12.00 E
Kongur Shan	21	Jf	38.40N	75.21 E
Kongwa	36	Gd	6.12S	36.25 E
Kong Wilhelms Land	41	Jc	75.48N	23.15W
Koniecpol	10	Pf	50.48N	19.41 E
Königslutter am Elm	10	Gd	52.15N	10.49 E
Konigswinter	12	Jd	50.41N	7.11 E
Königs Wusterhausen	10	Jd	52.17N	13.37 E
Konin	10	Od	52.13N	18.16 E
Konin [2]	10	Od	52.15N	18.15 E
Konispoli	15	Dj	39.39N	20.10 E
Kónitsa	15	Di	40.03N	20.45 E
Konj	14	Kg	43.43N	16.55 E
Konjed Jān	24	Nf	33.30N	50.27 E
Konjic	14	Lg	43.39N	17.58 E
Konjuh	14	Mf	44.18N	18.33 E
Konkan	25	Ee	18.05N	73.25 E
Konkiep	37	Be	28.00S	17.23 E
Konko	36	Ed	10.12S	27.27 E
Konkouré	34	Cd	9.58N	13.42W
Konnevesi	8	Lb	62.40N	26.35 E
Konnevesi	8	Lb	62.37N	26.19 E
Konnivesi	8	Lc	61.10N	26.10 E
Konoša	6	Kc	60.58N	40.15 E

Index Symbols

[1] Independent Nation
[2] State, Region
[3] District, County
[4] Municipality
[5] Colony, Dependency
Continent
Physical Region
Historical or Cultural Region
Mount, Mountain
Volcano
Hill
Mountains, Mountain Range
Hills, Escarpment
Plateau, Upland
Pass, Gap
Plain, Lowland
Delta
Salt Flat
Valley, Canyon
Crater, Cave
Karst Features
Depression
Polder
Desert, Dunes
Forest, Woods
Heath, Steppe
Oasis
Cape, Point
Coast, Beach
Cliff
Peninsula
Isthmus
Sandbank
Island
Atoll
Rock, Reef
Islands, Archipelago
Rocks, Reefs
Coral Reef
Well, Spring
Geyser
River, Stream
Waterfall Rapids
River Mouth, Estuary
Lake
Salt Lake
Intermittent Lake
Reservoir
Swamp, Pond
Canal
Glacier
Ice Shelf, Pack Ice
Ocean
Sea
Gulf, Bay
Strait, Fjord
Lagoon
Bank
Seamount
Tablemount
Ridge
Shelf
Basin
Escarpment, Sea Scarp
Fracture
Trench, Abyss
National Park, Reserve
Point of Interest
Recreation Site
Cave, Cavern
Historic Site
Ruins
Wall, Walls
Church, Abbey
Temple
Scientific Station
Airport
Port
Lighthouse
Mine
Tunnel
Dam, Bridge

Kōnosu 29 Fc 36.04N 139.30 E
Konotop 6 Je 51.14N 33.12 E
Konqi He 21 Ke 41.48N 86.47 E
Konrei 64a Bb 7.43N 134.37 E
Konsei-Tōge 29 Fc 36.52N 139.22 E
Konsen-Daichi 29a Db 43.20N 144.50 E
Końskie 10 Qe 51.12N 20.26 E
Konstantinovka 16 Je 48.29N 37.43 E
Konstantinovsk 16 Lf 47.35N 41.05 E
Konstanz 10 Fi 47.40N 9.11 E
Kontagora 31 Hg 10.24N 5.29 E
Kontcha 34 Hd 7.58N 12.14 E
Kontich 12 Gc 51.08N 4.27 E
Kontiolahti 7 Ge 62.46N 29.51 E
Kontiomäki 7 Gd 64.21N 28.09 E
Kontum 25 Lf 14.21N 108.00 E
Kontum, Plateau de- 25 Lf 13.55N 108.05 E
Konusin, Mys- 7 Kc 67.10N 43.50 E
Konya 22 Ff 37.52N 32.31 E
Konya Ovası 24 Ed 37.30N 33.20 E
Konz 12 Ie 49.42N 6.35 E
Konza 36 Gc 1.45S 37.07 E
Konžakovski Kamen, Gora- 5 Ld 59.38N 59.08 E
Koocanusa, Lake- 46 Hb 48.45N 115.15W
Kook, Punta- 65d Ab 27.08S 109.26W
Koolau Range 65a Db 21.21N 157.47W
Koonga/Konga 8 Jf 58.34N 24.00 E
Koorda 59 Df 30.50S 117.29 E
Koosa 8 Lf 58.33N 27.07 E
Kootenay Lake 46 Gb 49.35N 116.50W
Kootenay River 38 He 49.15N 117.39W
Kopa 18 Jc 43.31N 75.48 E
Kopaonik 15 Df 43.15N 20.50 E
Kópasker 7a Ca 66.18N 16.27W
Kópavogur 7a Bb 64.06N 21.55W
Kopejsk 19 Gd 55.08N 61.39 E
Koper 14 He 45.33N 13.44 E
Kopervik 7 Ag 59.17N 5.18 E
Kopetdag, Hrebet- 21 Hf 37.45N 58.15 E
Kop Geçidi 24 Ib 40.01N 40.28 E
Ko Phangan 25 Jg 9.45N 100.00 E
Köping 7 Dg 59.31N 16.00 E
Köpingsvik 8 Gh 56.53N 16.43 E
Kopjevo 20 Df 54.59N 89.55 E
Kopliku 15 Cg 42.13N 19.26 E
Köpmanholmen 7 Ee 63.10N 18.34 E
Koporje 8 Me 59.40N 29.08 E
Koporski Zaliv 8 Me 59.45N 28.45 E
Koppal 25 Fe 15.21N 76.09 E
Koppang 7 Cf 61.34N 11.04 E
Koppány 10 Oj 46.35N 18.26 E
Kopparberg 8 Fe 59.52N 14.59 E
Kopparberg [2] 7 Df 61.00N 14.30 E
Kopparstenarna 8 Hf 58.32N 19.20 E
Koppom 8 Ee 59.43N 12.09 E
Koprivnica 14 Kd 46.10N 16.50 E
Kopru 24 Dd 36.49N 31.10 E
Köprüören 15 Mj 39.30N 29.47 E
Korab 5 Ig 41.44N 20.32 E
Korablino 7 Jj 53.57N 40.00 E
Korahe 35 Gd 6.36N 44.16 E
Korak 64a Bc 7.21N 134.34 E
Koralpe 14 Id 46.45N 15.00 E
Koramlik 27 Ed 37.32N 85.42 E
Korana 14 Je 45.30N 15.35 E
Korangi 25 Dd 24.47N 67.08 E
Koraput 25 Ge 18.49N 82.43 E
Korba 25 Gd 22.21N 82.41 E
Korbach 10 Ee 51.17N 8.52 E
Körby 8 Ei 55.51N 13.39 E
Korça 15 Di 40.37N 20.46 E
Korčula 14 Kh 42.57N 16.55 E
Korčula 14 Lh 42.58N 17.08 E
Korčulanski Kanal 14 Kg 43.03N 16.40 E
Kordān 24 Ne 35.56N 50.50 E
Kordel 12 Ie 49.50N 6.38 E
Kordestān [3] 23 Gb 35.30N 47.00 E
Kord Küy 23 Hb 36.48N 54.07 E
Kordun 14 Je 45.10N 15.35 E
Korea Bay (EN)=Sŏjosŏn-man 21 Of 39.15N 125.00 E
Korean Peninsula (EN) 21 Of 35.30N 125.30 E
Korea Strait (EN)=Taehan-Haehyŏp 21 Of 34.40N 129.00 E
Korea Strait (EN)=Tsushima-Kaikyō 21 Of 34.40N 129.00 E
Korec 16 Ed 50.37N 27.10 E
Korem 35 Fc 12.30N 39.32 E
Korenovsk 19 Df 45.28N 39.28 E
Korf 20 Ld 60.18N 166.01 E
Korfovski 20 Ig 48.11N 135.04 E
Korgen 7 Cc 66.05N 13.50 E
Kõrgesaare/Kyrgesare 8 Je 59.00N 22.25 E
Korhogo 31 Gh 9.27N 5.38W
Korhogo [3] 34 Dd 9.35N 5.55W
Koribundu 34 Cd 7.43N 11.42W
Korienzé 34 Eb 15.24N 3.47W
Korinthiakós Kólpos=Corinth, Gulf of- (EN) 5 Ih 38.12N 22.30 E
Kórinthos 15 Fl 37.55N 22.53 E
Kórinthos=Corinth (EN) 15 Fl 37.55N 22.53 E
Korinthou, Dhiórix-=Corinth Canal (EN) 15 Fl 37.57N 22.58 E
Koriolei 31 Lh 1.48N 44.30 E
Kőrishegy 10 Ni 47.12N 17.49 E
Koritnik 15 Dg 42.05N 20.34 E
Kōriyama 27 Pd 37.24N 140.23 E
Korjakskaja Sopka, Vulkan- 21 Rd 53.20N 158.47 E
Korjakski Nacionalny okrug [3] 20 Le 60.00N 163.00 E
Korjakskoje Nagorje=Koryak Range (EN) 21 Tc 62.30N 172.00 E
Korjažma 19 Ec 61.18N 47.07 E
Korjukovka 16 Hd 51.47N 32.17 E
Korkino 17 Ji 54.54N 61.25 E
Korkodon 20 Kd 64.43N 154.05 E
Korkuteli 24 Dd 37.04N 30.13 E
Korla 22 Ke 41.44N 86.09 E
Kormakiti Burun 24 Ee 35.24N 32.56 E
Körmend 10 Mi 47.01N 16.36 E
Kormy, Gora- 20 Fd 62.15N 106.08 E
Kornati 14 Jg 43.49N 15.20 E
Kornejevka 17 Ni 54.01N 68.27 E
Kornešty 15 Kb 47.23N 28.00 E
Korneuburg 14 Kb 48.21N 16.20 E
Kórnik 10 Nd 52.17N 17.04 E
Kornsjø 7 Cg 58.57N 11.39 E
Koro 34 Ec 14.05N 3.04W
Koroba 59 Ia 5.40S 142.45 E
Koroča 16 Jd 50.50N 37.13 E
Köroğlu Dağları 23 Da 40.40N 32.35 E
Köroğlu Tepe 24 Db 40.31N 31.53 E
Korogwe 36 Gd 5.09S 38.29 E
Koro Island 57 If 17.32S 179.42 E
Koroit 59 Ig 38.17S 142.22 E
Korolevo 10 Th 48.08N 23.07 E
Korolevu 63d Ac 18.12S 177.53 E
Korom, Bahr 35 Bc 10.35N 19.45 E
Koromiri 64p Cc 21.15S 159.43W
Koronadal 26 He 6.12N 125.01 E
Korónia, Limni- 15 Gi 40.40N 23.10 E
Koronowo 10 Nc 53.19N 17.57 E
Koronowski e, Jezioro- 10 Nc 53.22N 17.55 E
Koror 57 Ed 7.20N 134.30 E
Koror 58 Ed 7.20N 134.29 E
Körös 10 Qj 46.43N 20.12 E
Koro Sea 61 Ec 18.00S 180.00
Korosten 6 Ie 50.57N 28.39 E
Korostyšev 16 Fd 50.18N 29.05 E
Korotaiha 17 Jb 68.55N 60.55 E
Koro Toro 31 Ig 16.05N 18.30 E
Korovin Volcano 40a Db 52.22N 174.10W
Korpijärvi 8 Lc 61.15N 27.10 E
Korpilahti 7 Fe 62.01N 25.33 E
Korpo/Korppoo 8 Id 60.10N 21.35 E
Korppoo/Korpo 8 Id 60.10N 21.35 E
Korsakov 20 Jg 46.37N 142.51 E
Korshäs 7 Ee 62.47N 21.12 E
Korsholm/Mustasaari 8 Ia 63.05N 21.43 E
Korso 8 Kd 60.21N 25.06 E
Korsør 7 Ci 55.20N 11.09 E
Korsun-Ševčenkovski 16 Ge 49.26N 31.18 E
Korsze 10 Rb 54.10N 21.09 E
Kortemark 12 Fc 51.02N 3.02 E
Kortrijk/Courtrai 11 Jd 50.50N 3.16 E
Korucu 15 Kj 39.28N 27.22 E
Koru Dağ 15 Ji 40.42N 26.45 E
Koryak Range (EN)=Korjakskoje Nagorje 21 Tc 62.30N 172.00 E
Korzybie 10 Mb 54.18N 16.50 E
Kos 15 Km 36.53N 27.18 E
Kos 15 Km 36.50N 27.10 E
Kosa 17 Gg 59.56N 55.01 E
Kosa 17 Gf 60.11N 55.10 E
Kosai 29 Ed 34.43N 137.30 E
Kosaja Gora 16 Jb 54.09N 37.31 E
Kosaka 29 Ga 40.20N 140.44 E
Kō-Saki 29 Ad 34.05N 129.13 E
Ko Samui 25 Jg 9.30N 99.58 E
Kosan-ŭp 27 Md 38.51N 127.25 E
Kosčagyl 16 Rf 46.52N 53.47 E
Kościan 10 Md 52.06N 16.38 E
Kościerzyna 10 Nb 54.08N 18.00 E
Kosciusko 45 Lj 32.58N 89.35W
Kosciusko, Mount- 57 Fg 36.27S 148.16 E
Kose/Koze 8 Ke 59.11N 25.05 E
Köse Dağ 24 Gb 40.06N 37.58 E
Kosha 35 Ea 20.49N 30.32 E
Koshigaya 29 Fd 35.55N 139.45 E
Koshiji 29 Fc 37.24N 138.45 E
Koshiki-Kaikyō 29 Bf 31.45N 130.05 E
Koshiki Rettō 27 Me 31.45N 129.45 E
Koshimizu 29a Db 43.51N 144.25 E
Kōshoku 28 Of 36.38N 138.06 E
Kōshyū Seamount (EN) 29 Df 31.35N 135.50 E
Košice 6 If 48.43N 21.15 E
Kosjerić 15 Cf 44.00N 19.55 E
Kosju 17 Ic 66.18N 59.53 E
Kosju 17 Id 65.38N 58.59 E
Köşk 15 Ll 37.51N 28.03 E
Koski 8 Jd 60.39N 23.09 E
Koskolovo 8 Me 59.34N 28.30 E
Koslan 19 Ec 63.29N 48.52 E
Kosma 17 Dd 65.43N 49.50 E
Kosmaj 15 De 44.28N 20.33 E
Kosŏng 27 Md 38.40N 128.19 E
Kosov 15 Ia 48.15N 25.08 E
Kosovo 15 Eg 42.40N 21.05 E
Kosovo [3] 15 Dg 42.35N 21.00 E
Kosovska Mitrovica 15 Dg 42.53N 20.52 E
Kosrae (Kusaie) 57 Hd 5.19N 162.59 E
Kossol Passage 64a Bb 7.52N 134.36 E
Kossol Reef 64a Bb 7.57N 134.41 E
Kossou, Barrage de- 34 Dd 7.01N 5.29W
Kossovo 16 Dc 52.47N 25.10 E
Kostajnica 14 Ke 45.13N 16.33 E
Kostenec 15 Gg 42.16N 23.49 E
Koster 37 De 25.57S 26.42 E
Kosteröarna 8 Df 58.55N 11.05 E
Kostjukoviči 16 Hc 53.23N 32.06 E
Kostjukovka 16 Gc 52.32N 30.58 E
Kostolac 15 Ee 44.44N 21.12 E
Kostopol 16 Ed 50.53N 26.29 E
Kostriževka 15 Ia 48.31N 25.45 E
Kostroma 6 Kd 57.47N 40.59 E
Kostromskaja Oblast [3] 19 Ed 58.30N 44.00 E
Kostrzyń 10 Nd 52.25N 17.14 E
Kostrzyn 10 Kd 52.37N 14.39 E
Kosva 17 Hg 58.50N 56.45 E
Koszalin 10 Mb 54.12N 16.09 E
Koszalin [2] 10 Mb 54.10N 16.10 E
Kőszeg 10 Mi 47.23N 16.33 E
Kota 22 Jg 25.16N 75.55 E
Kotaagung 26 Dh 5.30S 104.38 E
Kota Baharu 22 Mi 6.08N 102.15 E
Kotabaru 26 Gg 3.14S 116.13 E
Kotabumi 22 Mj 4.50S 104.54 E
Kotadabok 26 Dg 0.30S 104.33 E
Kota Kinabalu 22 Ni 5.59N 116.04 E
Kotamobagu 26 Hf 0.46N 124.19 E
Ko Tao 25 Jf 10.05N 99.52 E
Kotari 14 Jf 44.05N 15.30 E
Ko Tarutau 25 Jg 6.35N 99.40 E
Kota Tinggi 26 Df 1.44N 103.54 E
Kotel 15 Jg 42.53N 26.27 E
Kotelnič 19 Ed 58.20N 48.20 E
Kotelnikovo 16 Mf 47.38N 43.09 E
Kotelny, Ostrov- 21 Pb 75.45N 138.44 E
Kotelva 16 Id 50.03N 34.45 E
Köthen 10 He 51.45N 11.58 E
Kotido 36 Fb 3.00N 34.09 E
Kotjužany 29 Gb 47.50N 28.27 E
Kotka 7 Gf 60.28N 26.55 E
Kot Kapūra 25 Eb 30.35N 74.54 E
Kotlas 6 Kc 61.16N 46.35 E
Kotlenik 15 Df 43.51N 20.42 E
Kotlenski prohod 15 Jg 42.53N 26.27 E
Kotlik 40 Gd 63.02N 163.33W
Kotlin, Ostrov- 8 Md 60.00N 29.45 E
Kotly 8 Me 59.30N 28.48 E
Kotobi 34 Ed 6.42N 4.08W
Kotohira 29 Cd 34.11N 133.48 E
Koton Karifi 34 Gd 8.06N 6.48 E
Kotor 15 Bg 42.25N 18.46 E
Kotorosl 7 Jh 57.38N 39.57 E
Kotorska, Boka- 15 Bg 42.25N 18.40 E
Kotor Varoš 14 Lf 44.37N 17.22 E
Kotouba 34 Ed 8.41N 3.12W
Kotovo 16 Ne 50.18N 44.48 E
Kotovsk [Mold.-U.S.S.R.] 16 Ff 46.49N 28.33 E
Kotovsk [R.S.F.S.R.] 19 Ee 52.35N 41.32 E
Kotovsk [Ukr.-U.S.S.R.] 19 Cf 47.43N 29.33 E
Kotra 10 Uc 53.32N 24.17 E
Kotri 25 Dc 25.22N 68.18 E
Kötschach 14 Gd 46.40N 13.00 E
Kottayam 25 Fg 9.35N 76.31 E
Kotte 25 Gg 6.54N 80.02 E
Kotto 30 Jh 4.14N 22.02 E
Kotton 35 Id 9.37N 50.32 E
Kotu 65b Ba 19.57S 174.48W
Kotu Group 57 Jg 20.00S 174.45W
Kotuj 21 Mb 71.55N 102.05 E
Kotujkan 20 Fb 70.40N 103.25 E
Koturdepe 16 Rj 39.26N 53.40 E
Kotzebue 39 Cc 66.53N 162.39W
Kotzebue Sound 38 Cc 66.20N 163.00W
Kouandé 34 Fc 10.20N 1.42 E
Kouango 35 Be 4.58N 19.59 E
Kouba Modounga 35 Bb 15.40N 18.15 E
Koudougou 31 Gg 11.44N 4.31W
Kouéré 34 Ec 10.27N 3.59W
Koufália 15 Fi 40.47N 22.35 E
Koufonision [Grc.] 15 Jo 34.56N 26.10 E
Koufonision [Grc.] 15 Im 36.55N 25.35 E
Koufonisiou, Stenón- 15 Jo 35.00N 26.10 E
Kouilou [3] 36 Bc 4.00S 12.00 E
Kouilou 30 Ii 4.28S 11.41 E
Koukdjuak 42 Kc 66.47N 73.10W
Kouki 35 Bd 7.10N 17.18 E
Koukourou 35 Cd 7.12N 20.02 E
Koulamoutou 36 Bc 1.08S 12.29 E
Koulikoro 34 Dc 12.51N 7.34W
Koulountou 34 Cc 13.15N 13.37W
Koumac 58 Hg 20.30S 164.12 E
Koumac, Grand Récif de- 63b Be 20.32S 164.04 E
Koumbi-Saleh 32 Ff 15.47N 7.58W
Koumi 29 Fc 36.05N 138.28 E
Koumpentoum 34 Cc 13.59N 14.34W
Koumra 35 Bd 8.55N 17.33 E
Koundara 31 Fg 12.29N 13.18W
Koundian 34 Cc 13.08N 10.42W
Kounoúpoi 15 Jm 36.32N 26.27 E
Kounradski 19 Hf 46.57N 75.01 E
Kounta 34 Eb 17.30N 0.40W
Koupéla 34 Ec 12.11N 0.21W
Kouqian → Yongji 28 Ic 43.40N 126.30 E
Kourou 54 Hb 5.09N 52.39W
Kouroussa 34 Dc 10.39N 9.53W
Koury 34 Ec 12.10N 4.48W
Koussané 34 Cc 14.52N 11.15W
Kousséri 34 Ic 12.05N 15.02 E
Koussi, Emi- 30 Ig 19.55N 18.30 E
Koutiala 31 Gg 12.23N 5.27W
Koutoumo 63b Cf 22.40S 167.32 E
Koutous 34 Hc 14.30N 10.00 E
Kouvola 7 Gf 60.52N 26.42 E
Kouyou 36 Cc 0.45S 16.38 E
Kova 20 Fe 58.20N 100.20 E
Kovač 15 Cf 43.31N 19.07 E
Kovačica 15 Dd 45.06N 20.38 E
Koval 10 Pd 52.31N 19.10 E
Kovalevka 15 Nc 46.42N 30.31 E
Kovarskas/Kavarskas 8 Ki 55.24N 25.03 E
Kovdor 19 Db 67.33N 30.25 E
Kovdozero, Ozero- 7 Hc 66.47N 32.00 E
Kovel 19 Ce 51.13N 24.43 E
Kovenskaja 17 Mf 61.24N 67.39 E
Kovin 15 De 44.45N 20.59 E
Kovinskaja Grjada 20 Fe 57.15N 101.00 E
Kovrov 19 Ed 56.24N 41.20 E
Kovylkino 7 Ki 54.02N 43.58 E
Kowŏn 27 Md 39.26N 127.15 E
Kowtal-e Do Rāh 23 Lb 36.07N 71.15 E
Kowt-e 'Ashrow 23 Kc 34.27N 68.48 E
Kōyama 29 Bf 31.19N 130.57 E
Köyceğiz 24 Cd 36.58N 28.43 E
Köycegiz Gölü 15 Lm 36.55N 28.40 E
Koyoshi-Gawa 29 Gb 39.24N 140.01 E
Koyuk 40 Gd 64.56N 161.08W
Koyukuk 38 Dc 64.56N 157.30W
Kozaklı 24 Fc 39.13N 34.49 E
Kozan 24 Fd 37.27N 35.49 E
Kozáni 15 Ei 40.18N 21.47 E
Kozara 14 Ke 45.00N 16.55 E
Kozawa 29a Bb 42.58N 140.40 E
Koze/Kose 8 Ke 59.11N 25.05 E
Kozelsk 19 De 54.01N 35.46 E
Koževnikovo 20 De 56.18N 84.00 E
Kozhikode → Calicut 22 Jh 11.19N 75.46 E
Kozienice 10 Re 51.35N 21.33 E
Kožim 17 Id 65.43N 59.31 E
Kožim 17 Id 65.45N 59.15 E
Kozima 14 He 45.37N 13.56 E
Kozjak 15 Eh 41.06N 21.54 E
Kozloduj 15 Gf 43.47N 23.44 E
Kozlovka 7 Li 55.52N 48.13 E
Kozlovščina 10 Vc 53.14N 25.20 E
Kozlu 24 Db 41.25N 31.46 E
Kozluk 24 Ic 38.11N 41.29 E
Koźmin 10 Ne 51.50N 17.28 E
Kozmodemjansk 7 Lh 56.20N 46.36 E
Kožozero, Ozero- 7 Je 63.05N 38.05 E
Kożuchów 10 Le 51.45N 15.35 E
Kožuf 15 Fh 41.09N 22.10 E
Kōzu-Shima 27 Oe 34.15N 139.10 E
Kožva 17 Hd 65.07N 56.57 E
Kožva 17 Hd 65.10N 57.00 E
Kozyrevsk 20 Ke 55.59N 159.59 E
Kpalimé 34 Fd 6.54N 0.38 E
Kpandu 34 Fd 7.00N 0.18 E
Kpessi 34 Fd 8.04N 1.16 E
Kra, Isthmus of- (EN)=Kra, Khokhok- 21 Lh 10.20N 99.00 E
Kra, Khokhok-=Kra, Isthmus of- (EN) 21 Lh 10.20N 99.00 E
Kraba 15 Ch 41.12N 19.59 E
Krabbfjärden 8 Gf 58.45N 17.40 E
Krabi 25 Jg 8.05N 98.53 E
Krabit, Mali i- 15 Cg 42.07N 19.59 E
Kra Buri 25 Jf 10.24N 98.47 E
Krâchéh 22 Mh 12.29N 106.01 E
Kragerø 7 Bg 58.52N 9.25 E
Kragujevac 15 De 44.01N 20.55 E
Kraichbach 12 Ke 49.22N 8.31 E
Kraichgau 10 Eg 49.10N 8.50 E
Kraichtal 12 Ke 49.07N 8.46 E
Krajina 14 Kf 44.45N 16.35 E
Krajina 15 Fe 44.10N 22.30 E
Krajište 15 Fg 42.35N 22.25 E
Krajnovka 16 Oh 43.57N 47.24 E
Kråka 8 Ca 63.28N 9.00 E
Krakatau, Gunung- 21 Mj 6.07S 105.24 E
Krak des Chevaliers 24 Ge 34.46N 36.19 E
Krakovec 10 Tg 49.56N 23.13 E
Kraków [2] 10 Pf 50.05N 20.00 E
Kraków 6 He 50.03N 19.58 E
Kraków-Nowa Huta 10 Qf 50.04N 20.05 E
Krakowsko-Częstochowska, Wyżyna- 10 Pf 50.50N 19.15 E
Kralendijk 50 Bf 12.10N 68.16W
Kraljevica 14 Ie 45.16N 14.34 E
Kraljevo 15 Df 43.44N 20.43 E
Kralupy nad Vltavou 10 Kf 50.14N 14.19 E
Kramatorsk 16 Je 48.43N 37.32 E
Kramfors 7 De 62.56N 17.47 E
Krammer 12 Gc 51.38N 4.15 E
Kranenburg 12 Ic 51.47N 6.01 E
Kranidhion 15 Gl 37.23N 23.09 E
Kranj 14 Id 46.14N 14.22 E
Krapina 14 Jd 46.10N 15.53 E
Krapkowice 10 Nf 50.29N 17.56 E
Kras=Karst (EN) 5 Hf 45.48N 14.00 E
Krasavino 19 Ec 60.59N 46.28 E
Krasiczyn 10 Sg 49.48N 22.39 E
Krasilov 16 Ee 49.37N 26.59 E
Kraskino 28 Kc 42.44N 130.48 E
Krāslava/Kraslava 7 Gi 55.54N 27.10 E
Kraslava/Krāslava 7 Gi 55.54N 27.10 E
Krasnaja Poljana 16 Lh 43.40N 40.12 E
Kraśnik 10 Sf 50.56N 22.13 E
Kraśnik Fabryczny, Kraśnik- 10 Sf 50.58N 22.12 E
Kraśnik-Kraśnik Fabryczny 10 Sf 50.58N 22.12 E
Krasnoarmejsk [Kaz.-U.S.S.R.] 19 Ge 53.57N 69.43 E
Krasnoarmejsk [R.S.F.S.R.] 19 Ee 51.02N 45.42 E
Krasnoarmejsk [Ukr.-U.S.S.R.] 16 Je 48.11N 37.12 E
Krasnoarmejski 20 Mc 69.37N 172.02 E
Krasnodar 6 Jf 45.02N 39.00 E
Krasnodarski Kraj [3] 19 Df 45.20N 39.30 E
Krasnodon 16 Ke 48.17N 39.44 E
Krasnogorodskoje 8 Mh 56.47N 28.18 E
Krasnogorsk [R.S.F.S.R.] 20 Jg 48.26N 142.10 E
Krasnogorsk [R.S.F.S.R.] 7 Ii 55.51N 37.20 E
Krasnogorski 17 Ji 54.36N 61.15 E
Krasnograd 19 Df 49.22N 35.27 E
Krasnogvardejsk 18 Fe 39.45N 67.16 E
Krasnogvardejskoje 16 Lg 45.49N 41.31 E
Krasnoholmski 17 Gh 56.02N 55.05 E
Krasnoilsk 15 Ia 48.02N 25.48 E
Krasnojarsk 22 Ld 56.01N 92.50 E
Krasnojarski 17 Ij 51.58N 59.57 E
Krasnojarski Kraj [3] 20 Ee 57.30N 95.00 E
Krasnojarskoje Vodohranilišče 20 Ee 55.05N 91.30 E
Krasnoje 10 Ug 49.49N 24.39 E
Krasnoje Selo 7 Hg 59.43N 30.03 E
Krasnoje Znamja 18 Df 36.50N 62.29 E
Krasnokamensk 20 Gf 50.00N 118.05 E
Krasnokamsk 19 Fd 58.04N 55.45 E
Krasnokutsk 19 He 52.59N 75.59 E
Krasnolesje 8 Jj 54.23N 22.25 E
Krasnolesny 16 Kd 51.52N 39.35 E
Krasnooktjabrski [Kirg.-U.S.S.R.] 18 Jc 42.45N 74.20 E
Krasnooktjabrski [R.S.F.S.R.] 7 Lh 56.43N 47.37 E
Krasnooskolskoje Vodohranilišče 16 Je 49.25N 37.35 E
Krasnoostrovski 8 Md 60.12N 28.39 E
Krasnoperekopsk 19 Df 45.57N 33.47 E
Krasnorečenski 28 Mb 44.38N 135.15 E
Krasnoščelje 7 Ic 67.23N 37.02 E
Krasnoselki 10 Uc 53.14N 24.30 E
Krasnoselkup 20 Dc 65.41N 82.28 E
Krasnoslobodsk [R.S.F.S.R.] 16 Ne 48.40N 44.31 E
Krasnoslobodsk [R.S.F.S.R.] 7 Ki 54.27N 43.47 E
Krasnoturinsk 19 Gd 59.46N 60.18 E
Krasnoufimsk 19 Fd 56.37N 57.46 E
Krasnouralsk 19 Gd 58.24N 60.03 E
Krasnousolski 19 Fe 53.54N 56.29 E
Krasnovišersk 19 Fc 60.23N 57.03 E
Krasnovodsk 22 He 40.00N 53.00 E
Krasnovodskaja Oblast [3] 19 Fh 39.50N 55.00 E
Krasnovodski Poluostrov 16 Rc 40.30N 53.15 E
Krasnovodski Zaliv 16 Rj 39.50N 53.15 E
Krasnozatonski 19 Fc 61.41N 51.01 E
Krasnozavodsk 7 Jh 56.29N 38.13 E
Krasnoznamensk [Kaz.-U.S.S.R.] 19 Ge 51.03N 69.30 E
Krasnoznamensk [R.S.F.S.R.] 8 Jj 54.52N 22.27 E
Krasny Čikoj 20 Ff 50.25N 108.45 E
Krasny Holm 7 Ig 58.04N 37.09 E
Krasny Jar [R.S.F.S.R.] 20 De 57.07N 84.40 E
Krasny Jar [R.S.F.S.R.] 19 Hd 55.14N 72.56 E
Krasnyje Barrikady 16 Of 46.13N 47.50 E
Krasnyje Okny 15 Mb 47.34N 29.23 E
Krasny Kut 19 Ee 50.58N 46.58 E
Krasny Liman 16 Je 48.59N 37.47 E
Krasny Luč 16 Ke 48.09N 38.57 E
Krasny Oktjabr 19 Gd 55.37N 64.48 E
Krasny Profintern 7 Jh 57.47N 40.29 E
Krasnystaw 10 Tf 50.59N 23.10 E
Krasny Sulin 16 Lf 47.53N 40.09 E
Kratovo 15 Fg 42.05N 22.12 E
Kraulshavn 41 Gd 74.10N 57.00W
Krâvanh, Chuŏr Phnum- 21 Mh 12.00N 103.15 E
Krawang 26 Eh 6.19S 107.17 E
Krefeld 10 Ce 51.20N 6.34 E
Krefeld-Hüls 12 Ic 51.22N 6.31 E
Kremastá, Limni- 15 Ek 38.50N 21.30 E
Kremenchug Reservoir (EN)=Kremenčugskoje Vodohranilišče 5 Jf 49.20N 32.30 E
Kremenčug 6 Jf 49.04N 33.25 E
Kremenčugskoje Vodohranilišče=Kremenchug Reservoir (EN) 5 Jf 49.20N 32.30 E
Kremenec 16 Dd 50.06N 25.43 E
Kremennaja 16 Ke 49.03N 38.14 E
Kremmling 45 Cf 40.03N 106.24W
Krems 14 Jb 48.25N 15.36 E
Krems an der Donau 14 Jb 48.25N 15.36 E
Kremsmünster 14 Ib 48.03N 14.08 E
Krenitzin Islands 40a Eb 54.08N 166.00W
Kresta, Zaliv- 20 Nc 65.30N 179.00W
Krestcy 7 Hg 58.15N 32.31 E
Krestovy, Pereval- 16 Nh 42.32N 44.30 E
Kretek 26 Fh 7.59S 110.19 E
Kretinga 7 Ei 55.55N 21.17 E
Kreuzau 12 Id 50.45N 6.29 E
Kreuzberg 10 Ff 50.22N 9.58 E
Kreuzlingen 14 Dc 47.39N 9.10 E
Kreuztal 10 Df 50.58N 7.59 E
Kría Vrísi 15 Fi 40.41N 22.18 E
Kribi 31 Hh 2.57N 9.55 E
Kričev 19 De 53.43N 31.43 E
Kričim 15 Hg 42.08N 24.31 E
Krim 14 Ie 45.56N 14.28 E
Krimml 14 Gc 47.13N 12.11 E
Krimpen aan den IJssel 12 Gc 51.55N 4.35 E
Kriós, Ákra- 5 Ih 35.14N 23.35 E
Krishna 21 Kh 15.57N 80.59 E
Krishnanagar 25 Hd 23.24N 88.30 E
Kristdala 8 Gg 57.24N 16.11 E
Kristiansand 6 Gd 58.10N 8.00 E
Kristianstad 7 Dh 56.02N 14.08 E
Kristianstad [2] 7 Ch 56.15N 14.00 E
Kristiansund 6 Gc 63.07N 7.45 E
Kristiinankaupunki/Kristinestad 7 Ee 62.17N 21.23 E
Kristineberg 7 Ed 65.04N 18.35 E
Kristinehamn 7 Dg 59.20N 14.07 E
Kristinestad/Kristiinankaupunki 7 Ee 62.17N 21.23 E
Kriti=Crete (EN) 5 Ih 35.15N 24.45 E
Kriti=Crete (EN) [2] 15 Hn 35.35N 25.00 E
Kritikón Pélagos=Crete, Sea of- (EN) 15 Hn 36.00N 25.00 E
Krivaja 14 Mf 44.27N 18.10 E
Kriva Palanka 15 Fg 42.12N 22.21 E
Kriviči 8 Lj 54.44N 27.20 E
Krivodol 15 Gf 43.23N 23.29 E
Krivoje Ozero 16 Gf 47.57N 30.21 E
Krivoj Rog 6 Jf 47.54N 33.21 E
Križevci 14 Kd 46.02N 16.32 E
Krk 14 Ie 45.05N 14.35 E
Krk 14 Ie 45.02N 14.35 E
Krka [Yugo.] 14 Jg 43.43N 15.51 E
Krka [Yugo.] 14 Je 45.53N 15.36 E
Krkonoše 10 Lf 50.46N 15.35 E
Krn 14 Hd 46.16N 13.40 E
Krndija 14 Le 45.27N 17.55 E
Krnjača, Beograd- 15 De 44.52N 20.28 E
Krnov 10 Nf 50.05N 17.41 E
Krobia 10 Me 51.47N 16.58 E
Krøderen 8 Cd 60.15N 9.40 E
Krokeai 15 Fm 36.53N 22.33 E
Krokek 8 Gf 58.40N 16.24 E
Kroken 7 Dd 65.22N 14.16 E

Index Symbols

[1] Independent Nation
[2] State, Region
[3] District, County
[4] Municipality
[5] Colony, Dependency
Continent
Physical Region
Historical or Cultural Region
Mount, Mountain
Volcano
Hill
Mountains, Mountain Range
Hills, Escarpment
Plateau, Upland
Pass, Gap
Plain, Lowland
Delta
Salt Flat
Valley, Canyon
Crater, Cave
Karst Features
Depression
Polder
Desert, Dunes
Forest, Woods
Heath, Steppe
Oasis
Cape, Point
Coast, Beach
Cliff
Peninsula
Isthmus
Sandbank
Island
Atoll
Rock, Reef
Islands, Archipelago
Rocks, Reefs
Coral Reef
Well, Spring
Geyser
River, Stream
Waterfall Rapids
River Mouth, Estuary
Lake
Salt Lake
Intermittent Lake
Reservoir
Swamp, Pond
Canal
Glacier
Ice Shelf, Pack Ice
Ocean
Sea
Gulf, Bay
Strait, Fjord
Lagoon
Bank
Seamount
Tablemount
Ridge
Shelf
Basin
Escarpment, Sea Scarp
Fracture
Trench, Abyss
National Park, Reserve
Point of Interest
Recreation Site
Cave, Cavern
Historic Site
Ruins
Wall, Walls
Church, Abbey
Temple
Scientific Station
Airport
Port
Lighthouse
Mine
Tunnel
Dam, Bridge

Name	Map	Grid	Lat.	Long.
Krokom	7	De	63.20N	14.28 E
Krolevec	16	Hd	51.32N	33.30 E
Kroměříž	10	Ng	49.18N	17.22 E
Krompachy	10	Qh	48.56N	20.52 E
Kronach	10	Hf	50.14N	11.19 E
Krŏng Kaôh Kŏng	25	Kf	11.37N	102.59 E
Kronoberg [2]	7	Dh	56.40N	14.40 E
Kronockaja Sopka, Vulkan- ◭	20	Lf	54.47N	160.35 E
Kronocki, Mys- ▸	20	Lf	54.43N	162.07 E
Kronocki Zaliv ◖	20	Lf	54.00N	161.00 E
Kronoki	20	Lf	54.33N	161.14 E
Kronprins Christian Land ◻	41	Jb	80.45N	22.00W
Kronprinsesse Mœrtha Kyst ▨	66	Bf	72.00S	7.30W
Kronprins Frederiks Bjerge ▨	41	Ie	67.20N	34.00W
Kronprins Olav Kyst ▨	66	Ee	68.30S	42.30 E
Kronstadt	19	Cc	60.01N	29.44 E
Kroonstad	31	Jk	27.46S	27.12 E
Kropotkin [R.S.F.S.R.]	19	Ef	45.06N	40.34 E
Kropotkin [R.S.F.S.R.]	20	Ge	58.36N	115.27 E
Kroppefjäll ◭	8	Ef	58.40N	12.13 E
Krośniewice	10	Pd	52.16N	19.10 E
Krosno	10	Rg	49.42N	21.46 E
Krosno [2]	10	Rg	49.40N	21.45 E
Krosno Odrzańskie	10	Ld	52.04N	15.05 E
Krossfjorden ▨	8	Ad	60.10N	5.05 E
Krotoszyn	10	Ne	51.42N	17.26 E
Kroviga, Gora- ◭	20	Gd	60.40N	91.30 E
Krško	14	Je	45.58N	15.28 E
Krstača ◭	15	Dg	42.58N	20.08 E
Krugersdorp	31	Jk	26.05S	27.35 E
Krui	26	Dh	5.11S	103.56 E
Kruibeke	12	Gc	50.10N	4.19 E
Kruiningen	12	Gc	51.27N	4.02 E
Kruja	15	Ch	41.30N	19.48 E
Kruleveščina	8	Li	55.03N	27.52 E
Krumbach	10	Gh	48.15N	10.22 E
Krumovgrad	15	Ih	41.28N	25.39 E
Krung Thep=Bangkok (EN)	22	Mh	13.45N	100.31 E
Krupanj	15	Ce	44.22N	19.22 E
Krupinica ◭	10	Oh	48.05N	18.54 E
Krupinská vrchovina ◭	10	Ph	48.20N	19.15 E
Kruša	8	Cj	54.50N	9.25 E
Kruševac	15	Cd	45.07N	19.57 E
Kruševac	15	Ef	43.35N	21.20 E
Kruševo	15	Eh	41.22N	21.15 E
Krušné Hory=Ore Mountains (EN) ◭	5	He	50.30N	13.15 E
Krustpils	8	Lh	56.29N	26.00 E
Kruzof ◈	40	Le	57.10N	135.40W
Krym	16	Jg	45.23N	36.36 E
Krymsk	19	Gd	44.54N	37.57 E
Krymskaja Oblast [3]	19	Dg	45.15N	34.20 E
Krymskije Gory=Crimean Mountains (EN) ◭	5	Jg	44.45N	34.30 E
Krymski Poluostrov=Crimea (EN) ◻	5	Jf	45.00N	34.00 E
Krynica	10	Qg	49.25N	20.56 E
Krzemieniucha ◭	10	Sb	54.12N	22.54 E
Krzepice	10	Of	50.58N	18.44 E
Krzna ◭	10	Td	52.08N	23.31 E
Krzywiń	10	Me	51.58N	16.49 E
Krzyż	10	Md	52.53N	16.01 E
Ksar el Boukhari	32	Hb	35.53N	2.45 E
Ksar el Kebir	32	Fc	35.00N	5.59W
Ksar es Srhir	13	Gi	35.51N	5.34W
Ksenjevka	20	Gf	53.34N	118.44 E
Kšenski	16	Jd	51.52N	37.44 E
Ksour, Monts des- ◭	32	Gc	32.45N	0.10W
Kstovo	7	Kh	56.12N	44.11 E
Kü', Wâdî al- ◭	35	Dc	12.12N	25.43 E
Kuai He ◭	28	Dh	33.09N	117.32 E
Kuala Belait	26	Ff	4.35N	114.11 E
Kuala Dungun	26	Df	4.47N	103.26 E
Kuala Kangsar	26	Df	4.46N	100.56 E
Kualakapuas	26	Fg	3.01S	114.21 E
Kuala Kerai	26	De	5.32N	102.12 E
Kualakurun	26	Fg	1.07S	113.53 E
Kualalangsa	26	Cf	4.32N	98.01 E
Kuala Lipis	26	Df	4.11N	102.03 E
Kuala Lumpur	22	Mi	3.10N	101.42 E
Kuala Pilah	26	Df	2.44N	102.15 E
Kuala Rompin	26	Df	2.49N	103.29 E
Kuala Terengganu	22	Mi	5.20N	103.08 E
Kuancheng	28	Ed	40.37N	118.31 E
Kuandang	26	Hf	0.52N	122.55 E
Kuandian	27	Lc	40.45N	124.48 E
Kuang-hsi-chuang-tsu Tzu-chih-ch'ü=Guangxi Zhuangzu Zizhiqu=Kwangsi Chuang (EN) [2]	27	Ig	24.00N	109.00 E
Kuang-tun Sheng=Guangdong Sheng=Kwangtung (EN) [2]	27	Jg	23.00N	113.00 E
Kuantan	26	Df	3.48N	103.20 E
Kuba	19	Eg	41.20N	48.35 E
Kuban ◭	5	Jf	45.20N	37.30 E
Kuba-Shima ◈	29b	Bb	26.10N	127.15 E
Kubaysah	24	Jf	33.35N	42.37 E
Kubbum	35	Cc	11.47N	23.47 E
Kubena ◭	7	Jg	59.37N	39.48 E
Kubenskoje, Ozero- ▨	7	Jg	59.40N	39.30 E
Kubnja ◭	7	Li	55.32N	48.28 E
Kubokawa	28	Lh	33.12N	133.08 E
Kubolta ◭	15	Lb	47.48N	28.03 E
Kubrat	15	Jf	43.48N	26.30 E
Kubumesaai	26	Gf	1.31N	115.06 E
Kučaj ◭	15	Ef	43.53N	21.44 E
Kučevo	15	Ee	44.20N	21.40 E
Kuching	22	Ni	1.33N	110.20 E
Kuchinoerabu-Shima ◈	28	Ki	30.28N	130.10 E
Kuchino-Shima ◈	27	Mf	29.55N	129.55 E
Kuchinotsu	29	Be	32.36N	130.12 E
Kuçukçekmece	15	Li	40.59N	28.46 E
Küçükkuyu	15	Jj	39.32N	26.36 E
Küçük Menderes ◭	15	Kl	37.57N	27.16 E
Kučurgan ◭	15	Mc	46.35N	29.55 E
Kudaka-Jima ◈	29b	Ab	26.10N	127.54 E
Kudamatsu	29	Bd	34.01N	131.53 E
Kudat	26	Ge	6.53N	116.50 E
Kudeb ◭	8	Mg	57.30N	28.16 E
Kudirkos-Naumestis	8	Jj	54.43N	22.49 E
Kudowa-Zdrój	10	Mf	50.27N	16.20 E
Kudremukh ◭	25	Ff	13.08N	75.16 E
Kudus	26	Fh	6.48S	110.50 E
Kudymkar	19	Fd	59.01N	54.37 E
Kuee Ruins ▨	65a	Fd	19.12N	155.23W
Kuei-chou Sheng→Guizhou Sheng=Kweichow (EN) [2]	27	If	27.00N	107.00 E
Kufi ◭	24	Cc	38.10N	29.43 E
Kufrah, Wâḩât al-=Kufra Oasis (EN) ▩	30	Jf	24.10N	23.15 E
Kufra Oasis (EN)=Kufrah, Wâḩât al- ▩	30	Jf	24.10N	23.15 E
Kufstein	14	Gc	47.35N	12.10 E
Kuganavolok	7	Ie	62.16N	36.55 E
Kugmallit Bay ◖	42	Ek	69.30N	133.20W
Kugoja ◭	16	Kf	46.33N	39.38 E
Kŭh, Ra's al- ▸	23	Id	25.48N	57.19 E
Kuḩayli	35	Eb	19.29N	32.49 E
Kühbonän	24	Qg	31.23N	56.19 E
Kühdasht	24	Lf	33.32N	47.36 E
Küh-e Bürh ◭	24	Pi	27.22N	54.40 E
Küh-e Gävbüs ◭	24	Oi	27.10N	54.00 E
Küh-e Karkas ◭	24	Nf	33.27N	51.48 E
Küh-e Kärün ◭	24	Ng	31.27N	50.18 E
Kühestak	24	Qi	26.47N	57.02 E
Kühin, Gardaneh-ye- ◭	24	Md	36.23N	49.37 E
Kühlungsborn	10	Hb	54.09N	11.43 E
Kuhmo	7	Gd	64.08N	29.31 E
Kuhmoinen	8	Kc	61.34N	25.11 E
Kuhn ◈	41	Kd	74.45N	19.45W
Kühpäyeh	23	Ic	30.35N	57.15 E
Kühpäyeh [Iran]	24	Of	32.43N	52.26 E
Kühpäyeh [Iran]	24	Qg	30.43N	57.30 E
Kührän, Küh-e- ◭	23	Id	26.46N	58.12 E
Kuhtuj ◭	20	Je	59.23N	143.10 E
Kuhva ◭	8	Mg	57.17N	28.17 E
Kuiseb ◭	37	Ad	23.00S	14.33 E
Kuishan Ding ◭	27	Ig	22.32N	109.52 E
Kuito	31	Ij	12.23S	16.56 E
Kuiu ◈	40	Me	57.45N	134.10W
Kuivaniemi	7	Fd	65.35N	25.11 E
Kujang	27	Md	39.52N	126.01 E
Kujawy ◻	10	Od	52.45N	18.30 E
Kujawy ◻	10	Od	52.45N	18.35 E
Kujbyšev	6	Le	53.12N	50.09 E
Kujbyšev [R.S.F.S.R.]	7	Li	55.01N	49.06 E
Kujbyšev [R.S.F.S.R.]	20	Cc	55.27N	78.29 E
Kujbyševskaja Oblast [3]	19	Fe	53.20N	50.30 E
Kujbyševski [Kaz.-U.S.S.R.]	19	Ge	53.15N	66.51 E
Kujbyševskij [Tadž.-U.S.S.R.]	18	Gf	37.53N	68.44 E
Kujbyševskoje Vodohranilišče=Kuybyshev Reservoir (EN) ▨	5	Ke	53.50N	49.00 E
Kujeda	17	Gh	56.26N	55.35 E
Kujgan	19	Hf	45.22N	74.10 E
Kuji	28	Pd	40.11N	141.46 E
Kuji-Gawa ◭	29	Gc	36.30N	140.37 E
Kujtun	20	Ff	54.21N	101.35 E
Kujūkuri-Hama ◭	29	Gd	35.40N	140.30 E
Kujū-San ◭	28	Kh	33.09N	131.15 E
Kūkalär, Küh-e- ◭	24	Ng	31.50N	50.53 E
Kukalaya, Rio- ◭	49	Fg	13.39N	83.37W
Kukësi	15	Dg	42.05N	20.24 E
Kukkia ▨	8	Kc	61.20N	24.40 E
Kukmor	7	Mh	56.13N	50.52 E
Kükürt Daği ◭	24	Ib	41.07N	41.27 E
Kula [Bul.]	15	Ff	43.53N	22.31 E
Kula [Tur.]	24	Cc	38.30N	28.40 E
Kula [Yugo.]	15	Cd	45.37N	19.32 E
Kulai	26	Df	1.40N	103.36 E
Kulanak	19	Jd	41.18N	75.34 E
Kulandy	19	Ff	46.08N	59.31 E
Kular	20	Ib	70.32N	134.26 E
Kular, Hrebet- ◭	20	Ic	69.00N	133.30 E
Kulata	15	Gh	41.23N	23.22 E
Kulautuva	8	Jj	54.55N	23.43 E
Kulbus	35	Cc	14.24N	22.31 E
Kuldiga/Kuldiga	8	Cd	56.59N	21.59 E
Kuldiga/Kuldiga	8	Cd	56.59N	21.59 E
Kuldur	20	Ig	49.10N	131.40 E
Kulebaki	7	Ki	55.26N	42.32 E
Kulen	24	Me	35.40N	49.30 E
Kulen Vakuf	14	Kf	44.33N	16.06 E
Kulikov	10	Ug	49.55N	24.06 E
Kulim	26	De	5.22N	100.34 E
Kuljab	19	Gh	37.55N	69.47 E
Kuljabskaja Oblast [3]	19	Gh	38.00N	69.40 E
Kullaa	8	Jc	61.28N	22.10 E
Kullen ▸	7	Ch	56.18N	12.26 E
Kulmasa	34	Ed	9.35N	2.27W
Kulmbach	10	Hf	50.06N	11.27 E
Kuloj	7	Kf	61.03N	42.30 E
Kuloj [R.S.F.S.R.] ◭	19	Eb	66.00N	43.30 E
Kuloj [R.S.F.S.R.] ◭	7	Kf	61.01N	42.12 E
Kuloj ◭	24	Ic	38.30N	41.02 E
Kulsary	19	Ff	46.57N	54.02 E
Kultuk	20	Ff	51.44N	103.42 E
Kulu [India]	25	Jb	31.58N	77.06 E
Kulu [Tur.]	24	Ec	39.06N	33.05 E
Kulunda	19	Ie	52.35N	78.57 E
Kulundinskaja Step ◻	20	Cf	52.45N	79.00 E
Kulundinskoje, Ozero- ▨	20	Cf	53.00N	79.30 E
Kum ◭	24	Bc	38.38N	27.32 E
Kum, Küh-e- ◭	24	Oh	29.55N	53.45 E
Kuma	29	Ce	33.39N	132.54 E
Kuma [R.S.F.S.R.] ◭	17	Mg	59.33N	66.40 E
Kuma [R.S.F.S.R.] ◭	7	Hc	66.15N	31.02 E
Kuma [U.S.S.R.] ◭	5	Kg	44.56N	47.00 E
Kumagaya	28	Of	36.08N	139.23 E
Kumai [Indon.]	26	Fg	2.44S	111.43 E
Kumai [Indon.]	26	Fg	3.23S	112.33 E
Kumaishi	29a	Ab	42.08N	139.59 E
Kumak	16	Vd	51.13N	60.08 E
Kumamoto	22	Pf	32.48N	130.43 E
Kumamoto Ken [2]	28	Kh	32.30N	130.50 E
Kumano	28	Nh	33.54N	136.05 E
Kumano-Gawa ◭	29	De	33.45N	135.59 E
Kumano-Nada ▨	29	Ee	34.00N	136.30 E
Kumanovo	15	Eg	42.08N	21.43 E
Kumara [N.Z.]	62	De	42.38S	171.11 E
Kumara [R.S.F.S.R.]	20	Hf	51.35N	126.45 E
Kumasi	31	Gh	6.41N	1.37W
Kumba	34	Ge	4.38N	9.25 E
Kumbakonam	25	Ff	10.58N	79.23 E
Kumbe	26	Lh	8.21S	140.13 E
Kumbo	34	Hd	6.12N	10.40 E
Kumboro Cape ▸	63a	Cb	7.18S	157.32 E
Kümch'ŏn	28	Ie	38.10N	126.30 E
Kum-Dag	19	Fh	39.13N	54.40 E
Kumdah	33	Ie	20.23N	45.05 E
Kume-Jima [Jap.] ◈	27	Mf	26.20N	126.45 E
Kumertau	19	Fe	52.46N	55.47 E
Kumhwa	28	Ie	38.17N	127.28 E
Kumihama	29	Dd	35.36N	134.54 E
Kuminski	19	Gd	58.40N	66.55 E
Kumköy (Kilyos)	15	Mh	41.15N	29.02 E
Kumkuduk	27	Fc	40.15N	91.55 E
Kumkurgan	18	Ff	37.50N	67.35 E
Kumla	7	Dg	59.08N	15.08 E
Kumlinge ◈	8	Id	60.15N	20.45 E
Kumluca	24	Dd	36.22N	30.18 E
Kummerower See ▨	10	Ic	53.49N	12.52 E
Kumo/Kokemäki ◭	7	Ff	61.15N	22.21 E
Kumo-Manyčski Kanal ◭	16	Ng	45.27N	44.38 E
Kumon Taung ◭	21	Lg	26.30N	96.50 E
Kumora	20	Ge	55.56N	111.13 E
Kumru	24	Gb	40.53N	37.17 E
Kumu	36	Eb	3.04N	25.09 E
Kumuh	16	Oh	42.11N	47.07 E
Kumukahi, Cape- ▸	60	Od	19.31N	154.49W
Kumul/Hami	22	Le	42.48N	93.27 E
Kümüx	27	Ec	42.15N	88.10 E
Kumzär	24	Qj	26.20N	56.25 E
Kunashiri-Tō/Kunašir, Ostrov- ◈	21	Qe	44.05N	145.51 E
Kunašir, Ostrov-/Kunashiri-Tō ◈	21	Qe	44.05N	145.51 E
Kunaširski Proliv=Nemuro Strait (EN) ▨	20	Jh	43.50N	145.30 E
Kunchaung	25	Jd	23.50N	96.35 E
Kunda	7	Gg	59.30N	26.30 E
Kunda Jögi ◭	8	Le	59.25N	26.27 E
Kundelungu, Monts- ◭	36	Ed	9.30S	28.00 E
Kundiawa	59	Ia	6.00S	145.00 E
Kunduchi	36	Gd	6.40S	39.13 E
Kunduk ◭	15	Md	45.39N	29.38 E
Kunduk→Kogilnik ◭	15	Md	45.51N	29.38 E
Kunduk→Sasyk, Ozero- ▨	16	Fg	45.45N	29.40 E
Kunene ◭	30	Ij	17.20S	11.50 E
Kunene (EN)=Cunene ◭	30	Ij	17.20S	11.50 E
Künes/Xinyuan	27	Dc	43.24N	83.18 E
Künes He ◭	27	Dc	43.32N	82.29 E
Kungäjv	7	Ch	57.52N	11.58 E
Kungej-Alatau, Hrebet- ◭	19	Hg	42.50N	77.15 E
Küngmiut	41	Ie	65.50N	36.45W
Kungrad	19	Fg	43.06N	58.54 E
Kungsbacka	7	Ch	57.29N	12.04 E
Kungsbackafjorden ◖	8	Eg	57.25N	12.04 E
Kungshamn	8	Df	58.21N	11.15 E
Kungsör	8	Ge	59.25N	16.05 E
Kungu	36	Cb	2.47N	19.12 E
Kungur	19	Fd	57.25N	56.57 E
Kunhegyes	10	Qi	47.22N	20.38 E
Kunhing	25	Jd	21.18N	98.26 E
Kunigami [2]	29b	Bb	26.45N	128.15 E
Kunigami-Misaki ▸	29b	Bb	27.26N	128.43 E
Kunimi-Dake ◭	28	Be	32.33N	131.01 E
Kunisaki	29	Be	33.34N	131.45 E
Kunisaki-Hantō ◻	29	Be	33.30N	131.40 E
Kunja-Urgenč	19	Fg	42.20N	59.12 E
Kunlong	25	Jd	23.25N	98.39 E
Kunlun Guan ◭	27	Jg	23.06N	108.40 E
Kunlun Shan ◭	21	Kf	36.00N	84.00 E
Kunlun Shankou ◭	27	Hd	35.40N	94.03 E
Kunming	22	Mg	25.08N	102.43 E
Kunnui	29a	Bb	42.26N	140.19 E
Kunovat ◭	17	Ld	64.59N	65.35 E
Kunsan	27	Md	35.59N	126.43 E
Kunshan	28	Fi	31.22N	120.57 E
Kuntaur	34	Cc	13.40N	14.53W
Kununurra	59	Fc	15.47S	128.44 E
Kunya	34	Gb	1.47N	35.03 E
Kunyu Shan ◭	28	Ff	37.15N	121.46 E
Künzelsau	10	Fg	49.17N	9.41 E
Kuohijärvi ▨	8	Kc	61.15N	24.55 E
Kuolimo ▨	8	Lc	61.15N	27.35 E
Kuop Atoll ◉	64d	Bb	7.03N	151.56 E
Kuopio	6	Jc	63.20N	27.35 E
Kuopio [2]	7	Gc	62.54N	27.41 E
Kuorboaivi ◭	7	Gb	69.41N	27.45 E
Kuortane	8	Jb	62.48N	23.30 E
Kupa ◭	14	Ke	45.28N	16.24 E
Kupang	22	Ok	10.10S	123.35 E
Kupiano	60	Dj	10.10S	148.02 E
Kupino	20	Cf	54.22N	77.18 E
Kupišķis	8	Ki	55.49N	25.01 E
Kupjansk	19	Df	49.42N	37.37 E
Kupjansk-Uzlovoj	16	Je	49.39N	37.45 E
Küplü [Tur.]	15	Jh	41.07N	26.21 E
Küplü [Tur.]	15	Mi	40.06N	30.00 E
Kuppenheim	12	Kf	48.50N	8.15 E
Kupreanof ◈	40	Me	56.50N	133.30W
Kuqa	22	Ke	41.43N	82.57 E
Kura [R.S.F.S.R.] ◭	16	Mh	44.05N	44.45 E
Kura [U.S.S.R.] ◭	5	Kh	39.20N	49.25 E
Kuragino	20	Ef	53.53N	92.40 E
Kurahashi-Jima ◈	29	Cd	34.08N	132.31 E
Kuraminski Hrebet ◭	18	Hd	40.50N	70.30 E
Kurashiki	28	Lg	34.35N	133.46 E
Kurashiki-Kojima	34	Cd	34.28N	133.48 E
Kurashiki-Tamashima	29	Cd	34.33N	133.40 E
Kura-Take ◭	29	Be	32.27N	130.20 E
Kuraymah=Karima (EN)	31	Kg	18.33N	31.51 E
Kurayoshi	28	Lg	35.28N	133.49 E
Kurbneshi	15	Dh	41.47N	20.05 E
Kurčatov	16	Id	51.41N	35.42 E
Kurdaj	18	Jc	43.18N	74.59 E
Kurdistan ◻	21	Gf	37.00N	44.00 E
Kurdistan ◻	23	Fb	37.00N	44.00 E
Kurdufän ◻	30	Jg	13.00N	30.00 E
Kurdufän al Janübiyah [3]	35	Dc	11.00N	29.30 E
Kurdufän ash Shamäliyah [3]	35	Dc	14.50N	29.40 E
Kure	28	Lg	34.14N	132.34 E
Küre	24	Eb	41.48N	33.43 E
Kure Island ◈	57	Jb	28.25N	178.25W
Kurejka ◭	21	Kc	66.25N	87.12 E
Kurgaldžinski	19	He	50.30N	70.03 E
Kurgalski, Mys- ▸	8	Me	59.39N	28.03 E
Kurgan	22	Id	55.26N	65.18 E
Kurganinsk	16	La	44.57N	40.35 E
Kurganskaja Oblast [3]	19	Gd	55.00N	65.00 E
Kurgan-Tjube	19	Gh	37.51N	68.46 E
Kurgan-Tjubinskaja Oblast [3]	19	Gh	37.30N	68.30 E
Kuria Island ◈	57	Id	0.14N	173.25 E
Kuria Muria Islands (EN)=Khurīyā Murīyā, Jazā'ir ◻	21	Hh	17.30N	56.00 E
Kuri Bay	59	Ec	15.35S	124.50 E
Kurikka	7	Fe	62.37N	22.25 E
Kurikoma	29	Gb	38.50N	140.59 E
Kurikoma-Yama ◭	29	Gb	38.57N	140.47 E
Kuril Basin (EN) ▨	20	Jg	47.00N	150.00 E
Kuril Islands (EN)=Kurilskije Ostrova ◻	21	Re	46.10N	152.00 E
Kurilsk	20	Jg	45.16N	147.58 E
Kurilskije Ostrova=Kuril Islands (EN) ◻	21	Re	46.10N	152.00 E
Kuril Trench (EN) ▨	3	Je	47.00N	155.00 E
Kuring Kuru	37	Bc	17.38S	18.33 E
Kurino	29	Bf	31.57N	130.43 E
Kurinskaja Kosa ◻	16	Pj	39.05N	49.10 E
Kurinwäs, Rio- ◭	49	Fg	12.49N	83.41W
Kuriyama	29a	Bb	43.03N	141.45 E
Kürkhüd, Küh-e- ◭	24	Qd	37.15N	56.30 E
Kurkosa ◈	16	Pj	38.59N	49.08 E
Kurkümä, Ra's- ▸	24	Gj	25.51N	36.39 E
Kurkur	24	Ek	23.54N	32.19 E
Kurlovski	7	Ji	55.29N	40.39 E
Kurmuk	35	Ec	10.33N	34.17 E
Kurnool	22	Jh	15.50N	78.03 E
Kurobe ◭	28	Nf	36.51N	137.26 E
Kurobe-Gawa ◭	29	Ec	36.55N	137.26 E
Kurogi	29	Be	33.14N	130.40 E
Kuroishi	28	Pd	40.38N	140.36 E
Kuroiso	28	Pf	36.58N	140.03 E
Kuromatsunai	28	Pc	42.40N	140.20 E
Kurono-Seto ▨	29	Be	32.05N	130.10 E
Kurort Družba	15	Kf	43.12N	28.00 E
Kurort Slánčev brjag	15	Kg	42.40N	27.42 E
Kurort Zlatni pjasäci	15	Lf	43.16N	28.02 E
Kuro-Shima ◈	29	Ji	31.52N	129.58 E
Kurovskoje	7	Ji	55.35N	38.59 E
Kurow	61	Dh	44.44S	170.28 E
Kurów	10	Se	51.25N	22.10 E
Kurpiowska, Puszcza- ▩	10	Rc	53.20N	21.30 E
Kuršėnai/Kuršenaj	19	Gd	56.03N	22.58 E
Kuršėnaj/Kuršėnai	19	Cd	56.03N	22.58 E
Kuršiu uzirekis ◖	8	Ic	55.05N	21.00 E
Kursk	6	Je	51.42N	36.12 E
Kurskaja Kosa ◻	7	Ei	55.18N	21.00 E
Kurskaja Oblast [3]	19	Ei	51.45N	36.15 E
Kurski zaliv ◖	7	Ei	55.05N	21.00 E
Kuršumlija	15	Ef	43.09N	21.16 E
Kurtalan	24	Jc	37.57N	41.42 E
Kurtamyš	19	Gd	54.55N	64.27 E
Kürti	31	Kg	18.07N	31.33 E
Kurtistown	65	Fd	19.36N	155.04W
Kurty ◭	18	Kb	44.19N	76.42 E
Kuru ◭	35	Dd	9.08N	26.57 E
Kurugsäle	24	Ee	41.30N	89.00 E
Kuruktag ◭	27	Ec	41.30N	89.00 E
Kuruman	30	Jk	26.56S	20.39 E
Kuruman ◭	31	Ik	27.28S	23.40 E
Kurume	28	Kh	33.19N	130.31 E
Kurunegala	25	Gg	7.29N	80.22 E
Kurur, Jabal- ◭	35	Ea	20.31N	31.32 E
Kurzeme=Courland (EN) ◻	8	Ih	56.50N	22.00 E
Kurzemes Augstiene/Kurzemskaja Vozvyšennost' ◭	8	Jh	56.45N	22.15 E
Kurzemskaja Vozvyšennost'/Kurzemes Augstiene ◭	8	Jh	56.45N	22.15 E
Kusa	17	Ii	55.20N	59.29 E
Kuşada Körfezi ▨	15	Kl	37.50N	27.08 E
Kusagaki-Guntö ◈	28	Ji	31.00N	129.00 E
Kusatsu [Jap.]	29	Fc	35.03N	135.59 E
Kusatsu [Jap.]	29	Fc	36.37N	138.35 E
Kuščinski	16	Kf	46.33N	39.37 E
Kusel	12	Je	49.33N	7.24 E
Kuş Gölü ▨	24	Bb	40.10N	27.59 E
Kushida-Gawa ◭	29	Ed	34.36N	136.34 E
Kushikino	28	Ki	31.44N	130.16 E
Kushima	28	Ki	31.29N	131.14 E
Kushimoto	28	Mh	33.28N	135.47 E
Kushiro	22	Qe	42.58N	144.23 E
Kushiro-Gawa ◭	29a	Dc	42.59N	144.23 E
Kushtia	25	Hd	23.55N	89.07 E
Kuška	18	Gi	35.16N	62.18 E
Kuskokwim ◭	38	Cc	60.17N	162.27W
Kuskokwim Bay ◖	38	Cd	59.45N	162.25W
Kuskokwim Mountains ◭	38	Dc	62.30N	156.00W
Kušmurun	19	Gd	52.27N	64.40 E
Kušmurun, Ozero- ▨	19	Ge	52.40N	64.45 E
Kušnarenkovo	17	Gi	55.06N	55.22 E
Kušnica	16	Ce	48.29N	23.20 E
Kusšharo Ko ▨	28	Rc	43.35N	144.15 E
Kustanaj	22	Id	53.10N	63.35 E
Kustanajskaja Oblast [3]	19	Ge	53.00N	64.00 E
Kustavi ◈	8	Id	60.30N	21.25 E
Kustavi ▸	8	Id	60.33N	21.21 E
Kustavi/Gustavs ◈	8	Id	60.30N	21.25 E
Küstenkanal ◭	10	Dd	52.57N	7.18 E
Küsti	31	Kg	13.10N	32.40 E
Kustvlakte=Coast Plain (EN) ◻	11	Ic	51.00N	2.30 E
Kusu	29	Be	33.16N	131.09 E
Kuşum ◭	16	Qd	51.06N	51.18 E
Kušva	19	Fd	58.18N	59.45 E
Kut, Ko- ◈	25	Kf	11.40N	102.35 E
Küt 'Abdollāh	24	Mg	31.13N	48.39 E
Kutacane	26	Cf	3.30N	97.48 E
Kutahya	23	De	39.25N	29.59 E
Kutaisi	6	Kg	42.15N	42.40 E
Kutch ◻	21	Jg	23.50N	70.30 E
Kutch, Gulf of- ◖	21	Ig	22.36N	69.30 E
Kutch, Rann of- ◻	21	Ed	24.05N	70.10 E
Kutchan	28	Pc	42.54N	140.45 E
Kutcharo-Ko	29a	Ca	45.10N	142.20 E
Kutina	14	Ke	45.29N	16.47 E
Kutkai	25	Jd	23.27N	97.56 E
Kutkašen	16	Oi	40.58N	47.52 E
Kutná Hora	10	Lg	49.57N	15.16 E
Kutno	10	Pd	52.15N	19.23 E
Kuttara-Ko ▨	29a	Bb	42.30N	141.10 E
Kutu	31	Ii	2.44S	18.09 E
Kutum	35	Cc	14.12N	24.40 E
Kúty	10	Nh	48.40N	17.01 E
Kuujja ◭	15	Ia	48.13N	25.15 E
Kuujja ◭	42	Fb	71.00N	115.15W
Kuuli-Majak	19	Fg	40.16N	52.45 E
Kuurne	12	Fd	50.51N	3.17 E
Kuusalu/Kusalu ◭	8	Ke	59.23N	25.25 E
Kuusamo	6	Jb	66.00N	29.11 E
Kuusankoski	8	Ld	60.54N	26.38 E
Kuutse Mägi/Kutse, Gora- ◭	8	Lg	57.58N	26.24 E
Kuvandyk	16	Td	51.29N	57.28 E
Kuvdlorssuaq	41	Gd	74.38N	56.40W
Kuvšinovo	7	Ih	57.03N	34.13 E
Kuwait (EN)=Al Kuwayt ◻	22	Gg	29.30N	47.45 E
Kuwait (EN)=Al Kuwayt	22	Gg	29.20N	47.59 E
Kuwana	29	Ee	35.04N	136.39 E
Kuybyshev Reservoir (EN)=Kujbyševskoje Vodohranilišče ▨	5	Ke	53.50N	49.00 E
Küysanjaq	24	Kd	36.05N	44.38 E
Kuytun	19	Dc	44.25N	84.58 E
Kuytun He ◭	27	Dc	44.50N	83.10 E
Kuyucak	15	Li	37.55N	28.28 E
Kuzneck	19	Ee	53.07N	46.36 E
Kuznecki Alatau ◭	21	Me	54.45N	88.00 E
Kuznečnoje	8	Mc	61.04N	29.58 E
Kuźnia Raciborska	10	Of	50.11N	18.15 E
Kuzomen	19	Db	66.18N	36.49 E
Kuzovatovo	7	Lj	53.33N	47.41 E
Kuzuryū-Gawa ◭	29	Ee	36.13N	136.08 E
Kvænangen ◭	7	Ea	70.05N	21.13 E
Kvaløy ▨	8	Eb	69.40N	18.30 E
Kvaløya ◈	7	Fa	70.37N	23.52 E
Kvalsund	7	Fa	70.30N	24.00 E
Kvam	6	Cc	61.40N	9.42 E
Kvareli	16	Ni	41.57N	45.47 E
Kvarken	17	Ij	52.05N	59.40 E
Kvarnbergsvattnet ▨	7	Dd	64.36N	14.03 E
Kvarner ◖	14	Jf	44.45N	14.15 E
Kvarnerić ◖	14	Jf	44.45N	14.35 E
Kvichak Bay ◖	40	He	58.48N	157.30W
Kvemo-Kedi	16	Oi	41.20N	46.31 E
Kvena ▸	8	Id	60.01N	7.56 E
Kvikne	6	Cc	62.35N	10.20 E
Kvikkjokk	7	Dc	66.57N	17.47 E
Kvina ◭	8	Bf	58.17N	6.56 E
Kvinesdal	7	Bg	58.19N	6.57 E
Kvisslebv	8	Gb	62.17N	17.21 E
Kvitegja ◭	8	Bb	62.05N	6.40 E
Kviteseid	8	Ce	59.24N	8.30 E
Kvitøya ◈	67	Je	80.08N	32.35 E
Kwa ◭	31	Ii	3.10S	16.11 E
Kwailibesi	63a	Ec	8.20S	160.40 E
Kwahu Plateau ◻	34	Ed	6.30N	1.00W
Kwajalein Atoll ◉	57	Hd	9.05N	167.20 E
Kwale [Kenya]	36	Gc	4.11S	39.27 E
Kwale [Nig.]	34	He	5.45N	6.26 E
Kwamouth	36	Cc	3.10S	16.12 E
Kwa Mtoro	36	Gd	5.14S	35.26 E
Kwando ◭	31	Jj	18.27S	23.32 E
Kwangdae-ri	27	Mc	40.34N	127.33 E
Kwangju	22	Qf	35.09N	126.55 E
Kwango ◭	30	Ii	3.14S	17.22 E

Index Symbols

[1] Independent Nation	Historical or Cultural Region	Pass, Gap	Depression
[2] State, Region	Mount, Mountain	Plain, Lowland	Polder
[3] District, County	Volcano	Delta	Desert, Dunes
[4] Municipality	Hill	Salt Flat	Forest, Woods
[5] Colony, Dependency	Mountains, Mountain Range	Valley, Canyon	Heath, Steppe
Continent	Hills, Escarpment	Crater, Cave	Oasis
Physical Region	Plateau, Upland	Karst Features	Cape, Point

Coast, Beach	Rock, Reef	Waterfall Rapids	Canal
Cliff	Islands, Archipelago	River Mouth, Estuary	Glacier
Peninsula	Rocks, Reefs	Lake	Ice Shelf, Pack Ice
Isthmus	Coral Reef	Salt Lake	Ocean
Sandbank	Well, Spring	Intermittent Lake	Sea
Island	Geyser	Reservoir	Gulf, Bay
Atoll	River, Stream	Swamp, Pond	Strait, Fjord

Lagoon	Escarpment, Sea Scarp	Historic Site	Port
Bank	Fracture	Ruins	Lighthouse
Seamount	Trench, Abyss	Wall, Walls	Mine
Tablemount	National Park, Reserve	Church, Abbey	Tunnel
Ridge	Point of Interest	Temple	Dam, Bridge
Shelf	Recreation Site	Scientific Station	
Basin	Cave, Cavern	Airport	

Name	Page	Grid	Lat.	Long.
Kwangsi Chuang (EN)= Guangxi Zhuangzu Zizhiqu (Kuang-hsi-chuang-tsu Tzu-chih-ch'ü) [2]	27	Ig	24.00N	109.00 E
Kwangsi Chuang (EN)= Kuang-hsi-chuang-tsu Tzu-chih-ch'ü → Guangxi Zhuangzu Zizhiqu [2]	27	Ig	24.00N	109.00 E
Kwangtung (EN)= Guangdong Sheng (Kuang-tung Sheng) [2]	27	Jg	23.00N	113.00 E
Kwangtung (EN)=Kuang-tun Sheng→ Guangdong Sheng [2]	27	Jg	23.00N	113.00 E
Kwanmo-bong	28	Jd	41.42N	129.13 E
Kwara [2]	34	Fd	8.30N	5.00 E
Kweichow (EN)=Guizhou Sheng (Kuei-chou Sheng) [2]	27	If	27.00N	107.00 E
Kweichow (EN)=Kuei-chou Sheng→Guizhou Sheng [2]	27	If	27.00N	107.00 E
Kweneng [3]	37	Cd	24.00S	24.00 E
Kwenge	30	Ii	4.50S	18.44 E
Kwethluk	40	Gd	60.49N	161.27W
Kwidzyn	10	Oc	53.45N	18.56 E
Kwigillingok	40	Ge	59.51N	163.08W
Kwilu	30	Ii	3.22S	17.22 E
Kwisa	10	Le	51.35N	15.25 E
Kwoka, Gunung-	26	Jg	0.31S	132.27 E
Kyabé	31	Ih	9.27N	18.57 E
Kyabram	59	Jg	36.19S	145.03 E
Kyaikkami	25	Je	16.04N	97.34 E
Kyaikto	25	Je	17.18N	97.01 E
Kyaka	36	Fc	1.16S	31.25 E
Kyancutta	58	Eh	33.08S	135.34 E
Kyan-Zaki	29b	Ab	26.05N	127.40 E
Kyaukpyu	25	Id	20.51N	92.58 E
Kyaukse	25	Jd	21.36N	96.08 E
Kybartai/Kibartaj	8	Jj	54.38N	22.44 E
Kyeintali	25	Ie	18.00N	94.29 E
Kyelang	25	Fb	32.35N	77.02 E
Kyffhauser	10	He	51.25N	11.10 E
Kyjov	10	Ng	49.01N	17.08 E
Kyle, Lake-	37	Ed	20.12S	31.00 E
Kyle of Lochalsh	9	Hd	57.17N	5.43W
Kyll	10	Cg	49.48N	6.42 E
Kyllburg	12	Id	50.02N	6.35 E
Kyma	7	Ld	64.48N	47.31 E
Kymi [2]	7	Gf	61.00N	28.00 E
Kymijoki	8	Ld	60.30N	26.52 E
Kyn	17	Ih	57.52N	58.32 E
Kynnefjäll	8	Df	58.42N	11.41 E
Kynsivesi	8	Lb	62.25N	26.10 E
Kyoga, Lake-	30	Kh	1.30N	33.00 E
Kyōga-Dake	29	Be	33.00N	130.05 E
Kyōga-Misaki	28	Mg	35.45N	135.11 E
Kyonan	29	Fd	35.07N	139.49 E
Kyŏnggi-Do [2]	28	If	37.30N	127.15 E
Kyŏnggi-man	28	Hf	37.25N	126.00 E
Kyŏngju	27	Md	35.50N	129.13 E
Kyŏngsang-Namdo [2]	28	Jg	35.15N	128.30 E
Kyŏngsang-Pukto [2]	28	Jf	36.20N	128.40 E
Kyŏngsŏng	28	Jd	41.40N	129.40 E
Kyōto	22	Pf	35.00N	135.45 E
Kyōto Fu [2]	28	Mg	35.25N	135.15 E
Kypros/Kıbrıs=Cyprus (EN) [1]	22	Ff	35.00N	33.00 E
Kypros/Kıbrıs=Cyprus (EN)	21	Ff	35.00N	33.00 E
Kyra	20	Gg	49.36N	111.58 E
Kyren	20	Ff	51.41N	102.10 E
Kyrenia/Girne	24	Ee	35.20N	33.19 E
Kyrgesare/Körgesaare	8	Je	59.00N	22.25 E
Kyrgyz Sovetik Socialistik Respublikasy/Kirgizskaja SSR [2]	19	Hg	41.30N	75.00 E
Kyritz	10	Id	52.57N	12.24 E
Kyrkheden	8	Ed	60.10N	13.29 E
Kyrksæterora	7	Be	63.17N	9.06 E
Kyrkslätt/Kirkkonummi	8	Kd	60.07N	24.26 E
Kyrö	8	Jd	60.42N	22.45 E
Kyrönjoki	8	Ia	63.14N	21.45 E
Kyrösjärvi	8	Jc	61.45N	23.10 E
Kyröskoski	8	Jc	61.40N	23.11 E
Kyštym	19	Gd	55.42N	60.34 E
Kysucké Nové Mesto	10	Og	49.18N	18.48 E
Kythera (EN)=Kíthira	15	Ih	36.15N	23.00 E
Kythraia	24	Ee	35.15N	33.29 E
Kyuquot Sound	46	Bb	49.55N	127.25W
Kyūshū	21	Pf	32.50N	131.00 E
Kyushu-Palau Ridge (EN)	3	Ih	20.00N	136.00 E
Kyushū-Sanchi	29	Be	32.40N	131.10 E
Kyyjärvi	7	Fe	63.02N	24.34 E
Kyyvesi	8	Lc	61.55N	27.05 E
Kyzikos	24	Bb	40.28N	27.47 E
Kyzyl	22	Ld	51.42N	94.27 E
Kyzylart, Pereval-	19	Hh	39.22N	73.20 E
Kyzyl-Kija	19	Hg	40.14N	72.12 E
Kyzylkum	21	Ie	42.00N	64.00 E
Kyzylrabot	19	Hh	37.28N	74.45 E
Kyzylsu [U.S.S.R.]	18	Gf	37.22N	69.22 E
Kyzylsu [U.S.S.R.]	18	He	39.17N	71.25 E
Kyzylžar	19	Gf	48.17N	69.49 E
Kzyl-Orda	22	Ie	44.48N	65.28 E
Kzyl-Ordinskaja Oblast [3]	19	Gf	45.00N	65.00 E
Kzyltu	19	He	53.41N	72.15 E
L				
Laa an der Thaya	14	Kb	48.43N	16.23 E
Laakdal	12	Gc	51.05N	4.59 E
La Alberca	13	Fd	40.29N	6.06W
La Alcarria	13	Jd	40.31N	2.45W
La Almunia de Doña Godina	13	Kc	41.29N	1.22W
La Ametlla de Mar	13	Md	40.54N	0.48 E
La Ardilla, Cerro-	48	Hf	22.15N	102.40W
La Armuña	13	Gc	41.05N	5.35W
Laasphe	12	Kd	50.56N	8.24 E
La Asunción	54	Fa	11.02N	63.53W
Laau Point	65a	Db	21.06N	157.16W
Laayoune	13	Ni	35.42N	2.00 E
Lab	15	Eg	42.45N	21.01 E
Laba	16	Kg	45.10N	39.40 E
La Babia	48	Hc	28.34N	102.04W
Laba Daği	15	Kl	37.22N	27.33 E
Labaddey	35	Ge	0.32N	42.45 E
Labadie Bank	9	Ek	50.30N	8.15W
La Banda	56	Hc	27.44S	64.15W
La Bañeza	13	Gb	42.18N	5.54W
La Barca	48	Hg	20.17N	102.34W
Labardén	55	Cm	36.57S	58.06W
La Barge	46	Je	42.16N	110.12W
La Barra, Punta-	49	Lh	11.30N	70.10W
La-Barre-en-Ouche	12	Cf	48.57N	0.40 E
La Baule-Escoublac	11	Dg	47.17N	2.24W
Labbezanga	34	Fc	14.59N	0.43 E
Labé	31	Fg	11.19N	12.17W
Labe=Elbe (EN)	5	Ge	53.50N	9.00 E
La Belle	44	Gl	26.46N	81.26W
Labelle	44	Jb	46.17N	74.45W
La Berzosa	13	Fd	40.35N	6.40W
Labin	14	Ie	45.05N	14.08 E
Labinsk	19	Eg	44.35N	40.44 E
Labis	26	Df	2.23N	103.02 E
La Bisbal/La Bisbal d'Empordà	13	Pc	41.57N	3.03 E
La Bisbal d'Empordà/La Bisbal	13	Pc	41.57N	3.03 E
La Blanca, Laguna-	55	Bj	30.14S	60.38W
Laboe	10	Gb	54.24N	10.13 E
Laborec	10	Rh	48.31N	21.54 E
Laborie	51k	Bb	13.45N	61.00W
Labota	26	Hg	2.52S	122.10 E
Labouheyre	11	Fj	44.13N	0.55W
Laboulaye	56	Hd	34.07S	63.24W
Labra, Peña-	13	Ha	43.03N	4.26W
Labrador	38	Md	55.00N	70.00W
Labrador, Coast of-	38	Me	56.00N	60.35W
Labrador Basin (EN)	3	Dd	53.00N	48.00W
Labrador City	39	Md	52.57N	66.54W
Labrador Sea	38	Nd	57.00N	53.00W
Labrang→Xiahe	27	Hd	35.18N	102.30 E
Lábrea	53	Jf	7.16S	64.46W
Labrieville	44	Ma	49.19N	69.34W
Labrit	11	Fj	44.06N	0.33W
Labuan, Pulau-	26	Ge	5.19N	115.13 E
Labudalin→Ergun Youqi	27	La	50.16N	120.09 E
Labuha	26	Ig	0.37S	127.29 E
Labuhan	26	Eh	6.22S	105.50 E
Labuhanbajo	26	Gh	8.29S	119.54 E
Labuhanbilik	26	Df	2.31N	100.10 E
Labuk, Teluk-	26	Ge	6.10N	117.50 E
La Bureba	13	Ib	42.36N	3.24W
Labutta	25	Ie	16.09N	94.46 E
Labytnangi	22	Ic	66.39N	66.21 E
Lac [3]	35	Ac	13.30N	14.20 E
Lača, Ozero-	7	Jf	61.20N	38.50 E
La Cadena	48	Ge	25.53N	104.12W
La Calamine/Kelmis	12	Hd	50.43N	6.00 E
La Calandria	55	Cj	30.48S	58.39W
Lac Allard	42	Lf	50.30N	63.30W
La Campiña	13	Hg	37.45N	4.45W
Lacanau	11	Ej	44.59N	1.05W
Lacanau, Étang de-	11	Ej	44.58N	1.07W
Lacanau-Océan	11	Ei	45.00N	1.12W
Lacantún, Río-	48	Ni	16.36N	90.39W
La-Capelle	11	Je	49.58N	3.55 E
Laćarak	15	Ce	45.00N	19.34 E
La Carlota [Arg.]	56	Hd	33.26S	63.18W
La Carlota [Phil.]	26	Hd	10.25N	122.55 E
La Carlota [Sp.]	13	Hg	37.40N	4.56W
La Carolina	13	If	38.15N	3.37W
Lacaune	11	Ik	43.43N	2.42 E
Lacaune, Monts de-	11	Ik	43.40N	2.36 E
Laccadive Islands	21	Jh	11.00N	72.00 E
Lac du Bonnet	45	Ha	50.35N	96.05W
La Ceiba [Hond.]	39	Kh	15.47N	86.50W
La Ceiba [Ven.]	49	Li	9.28N	71.04W
Lacepede Bay	59	Hg	36.45S	139.45 E
Lacepede Islands	59	Ec	16.50S	122.10 E
La Cerdaña/La Cerdanya	13	Nb	42.24N	1.40 E
La Cerdanya/La Cerdaña	13	Nb	42.24N	1.40 E
Lacey	46	Dc	47.07N	122.49W
Lac Giao	25	Lf	12.40N	108.03 E
La Chaise-Dieu	11	Ji	45.19N	3.42 E
La Charité-sur-Loire	11	Jg	47.11N	3.01 E
La Châtre	11	Hh	46.35N	1.59 E
La Chaux-de-Fonds	14	Ac	47.06N	6.50 E
Lachay, Punta-	54	Cf	11.18S	77.39W
La China, Sierra-	55	Bm	36.47S	60.34W
Lachine	44	Kc	45.26N	73.40W
Lachlan River	57	Fh	34.21S	143.57 E
La Chorrera [Col.]	54	Dd	0.45S	73.00W
La Chorrera [Pan.]	49	Ig	8.53N	79.47W
Laçi	15	Ch	41.38N	19.43 E
Lačin	16	Oj	39.39N	46.33 E
La Ciotat	11	Lk	43.10N	5.36 E
Łąck	10	Pd	52.28N	19.40 E
Lackawanna	44	Hd	42.49N	78.49W
Lac La Biche	42	Gf	54.46N	111.58W
Lac la Martre	42	Fd	63.21N	117.00W
Lac Mégantic	42	Kg	45.35N	70.53W
La Colina	55	Bm	37.20S	61.32W
La Coloma	49	Fb	22.15N	83.34W
La Colorada	48	Dc	28.41N	110.25W
Lacombe	42	Gf	52.28N	113.44W
Lacon	45	Lf	41.02N	89.24W
La Concepción [Pan.]	49	Fi	8.31N	82.37W
La Concepción [Ven.]	49	Lh	10.48N	71.46W
La Concha	48	Gg	21.46N	105.29W
Laconi	14	Dk	39.51N	9.03 E
Laconia	43	Mc	43.32N	71.29W
Laconia, Gulf of- (EN) = Lakonikós Kólpos	15	Fm	36.35N	22.40 E
La Coronilla	55	Fk	33.44S	53.31W
La Coruña	6	Fg	43.22N	8.23W
La Coruña [3]	13	Da	43.10N	8.25W
La Côte-Saint-André	11	Li	45.23N	5.15 E
La Couronne	11	Gi	45.37N	0.06 E
La Courtine-le-Trucq	11	Ii	45.42N	2.16 E
Lacq	11	Fk	43.25N	0.38W
Lacroix-sur-Meuse	12	Hf	48.58N	5.31 E
La Crosse [Ks.-U.S.]	45	Gg	38.32N	99.18W
La Crosse [Wi.-U.S.]	39	Je	43.49N	91.15W
La Cruz [Arg.]	56	Ic	29.10S	56.38W
La Cruz [C.R.]	49	Eh	11.04N	85.39W
La Cruz [Mex.]	47	Cd	23.55N	106.54W
La Cruz [Ur.]	56	Id	33.56S	56.15W
La Cruz de Rio Grande	49	Eg	13.06N	84.10W
La Cruz de Taratara	49	Mh	11.03N	69.44W
La Cuesta	48	Hc	28.45N	102.25W
La Cumbre	56	Hd	30.58S	64.30W
Lac Yora	35	Cb	19.08N	20.35 E
Ladário	55	Dd	19.01S	57.35W
Ladbergen	12	Jb	52.08N	7.45 E
Lądek-Zdrój	10	Mf	50.21N	16.50 E
Ladenburg	12	Ke	49.28N	8.37 E
La Désirade	50	Fd	16.19N	61.03W
La Digue Island	37b	Ca	4.21S	55.50 E
Lâdik	24	Fb	40.36N	36.45 E
Ladismith	37	Cf	33.30S	21.16 E
Ladispoli	14	Gi	41.56N	12.05 E
Lado, Jabal-	35	Ed	5.06N	31.35 E
Ladoga, Lake- (EN)= Ladožkoje Ozero	5	Jc	61.00N	31.00 E
Ladong	27	Ig	24.49N	109.34 E
La Dorada	54	Db	5.22N	74.42W
Ladožkoje Ozero=Ladoga, Lake (EN)	5	Jc	61.00N	31.00 E
Ladrones, Islas-	49	Fj	7.52N	82.26W
Laduškin	8	Ij	54.35N	20.10 E
Ladva-Vetka	7	If	61.20N	34.29 E
Lady Ann Strait	42	Ja	75.45N	80.00W
Ladybrand	37	De	29.19S	27.25 E
Lady Evelyn Lake	44	Gb	47.20N	80.10W
Lady Newnes Ice Shelf	66	Kf	73.40S	167.30 E
Ladysmith [B.C.-Can.]	46	Db	48.58N	123.49W
Ladysmith [S.Afr.]	31	Jk	28.34S	29.45 E
Ladysmith [Wi.-U.S.]	43	Ib	45.28N	91.07W
Ladyžin	16	Fe	48.40N	29.13 E
Lae	58	Fe	6.43S	147.01 E
Lae Atoll	57	Hd	8.56N	166.14 E
La Eduvigis	55	Ch	26.50S	59.05W
Laem, Khao-	25	Kf	14.19N	101.11 E
Laer [F.R.G.]	12	Kb	52.06N	8.05 E
Laer [F.R.G.]	12	Jb	52.04N	7.21 E
Lærdalsøyri	7	Bf	61.06N	7.29 E
La Escala/L'Escala	13	Pb	42.07N	3.08 E
La Esmeralda	54	Ec	3.10N	65.33W
Læsø	7	Bh	57.15N	10.00 E
Læsø Rende	8	Dg	57.15N	10.45 E
La Española=Hispaniola (EN)	38	Lh	19.00N	71.00W
La Esperanza [Bol.]	54	Ff	14.34S	62.10W
La Esperanza [Hond.]	49	Cf	14.20N	88.10W
La Estrada	13	Db	42.41N	8.29W
Lafayette [Al.-U.S.]	44	Ei	32.54N	85.24W
Lafayette [In.-U.S.]	43	Jc	40.25N	86.53W
Lafayette [La.-U.S.]	39	Jf	30.14N	92.01W
La Fère	12	Fe	49.40N	3.22 E
La Ferrière-sur-Risle	12	Cf	48.59N	0.48 E
La Ferté-Bernard	11	Gf	48.11N	0.40 E
La Ferté-Frênel	12	Cf	48.50N	0.30 E
La Ferté-Macé	11	Ff	48.36N	0.22W
La Ferté-Milon	12	Fe	49.10N	3.07 E
La Ferté-Saint-Aubin	11	Hg	47.43N	1.56 E
La Ferté-sous-Jouarre	11	Jf	48.57N	3.08 E
Laffān, Ra's-	24	Nj	25.54N	51.35 E
Lafia	34	Gd	8.29N	8.31 E
Lafiagi	34	Gd	8.52N	5.15 E
La Flèche	11	Fg	47.42N	0.05W
Lafnitz	14	Kd	46.57N	16.16 E
La Foa	63b	Be	21.43S	165.49 E
La Follette	44	Eg	36.23N	84.07W
La Fría	49	Ki	8.13N	72.15W
Laft	24	Pi	26.54N	55.46 E
La Fuente de San Esteban	13	Fd	40.48N	6.15W
Laga, Monti della-	14	Hh	42.45N	13.35 E
La Galite (EN)=Jālitah	30	He	37.32N	8.56 E
La Gallareta	55	Bi	29.34S	60.23W
Lagamar	55	Id	18.13S	46.48W
Lagan	8	Eh	56.33N	12.56 E
Lagan	8	Eh	56.55N	13.59 E
Lagan/Abhainn an Lagáin	9	Hg	54.37N	5.53W
Lagarina, Val-	14	Fe	45.50N	11.10 E
La Garita Mountains	45	Ch	38.00N	106.40W
Lagarto	54	Kf	10.54S	37.41W
Lagash	24	Lg	31.27N	46.13 E
Lagawe	26	Hc	16.49N	121.06 E
Lage	12	Kc	51.59N	8.48 E
Lågen	7	Cf	61.08N	10.25 E
Lagh Bogal	36	Gb	0.42N	40.55 E
Laghmān [3]	23	Lb	35.00N	70.15 E
Laghouat	31	He	33.48N	2.53 E
Laghouat [3]	32	Hc	33.30N	3.15 E
La Gloria	49	Ki	8.38N	73.48W
Lagny	11	If	48.52N	2.43 E
Lagoa	13	Dg	37.08N	8.27W
Lagoa	55	Eb	14.08S	55.20W
Lagoa da Prata	55	Je	20.01S	45.33W
Lagoa Vermelha	56	Jc	28.13S	51.32W
Lagodehi	16	Oi	41.50N	46.14 E
La Gomera	49	Bf	14.05N	91.03W
Lagonegro	14	Jj	40.07N	15.46 E
Lagonoy Gulf	26	Hd	13.35N	123.45 E
Lagoon	64n	Ab	10.23S	161.05W
Lagos	13	Dg	37.06N	8.40W
Lagos	31	Hh	6.27N	3.23 E
Lágos	15	Ih	41.01N	25.07 E
Lagos [2]	34	Fd	6.30N	3.30 E
Lagos, Baia de-	13	Dg	37.06N	8.39W
Lagosa	36	Ed	5.57S	29.53 E
Lagos de Moreno	47	Dd	21.21N	101.55W
La Grand-Combe	11	Kj	44.13N	4.02 E
La Grande	43	Db	45.20N	118.05W
La Grande Fosse	9	Kl	49.40N	3.00W
La Grande-Motte	11	Kk	43.34N	4.07 E
La Grande Rivière	38	Ld	53.50N	79.00W
La Grande Trench (EN)= Hurd Deep	9	Kl	49.40N	3.00W
La Grange	44	Ef	38.24N	85.23W
Lagrange	44	Ee	41.39N	85.25W
La Grange [Ga.-U.S.]	43	Je	33.02N	85.02W
La Grange [Tx.-U.S.]	45	Hl	29.54N	96.52W
La Gran Sabana	54	Fb	5.30N	61.30W
La Grita	54	Db	8.08N	71.59W
Lagskär	8	He	59.50N	20.00 E
La Guaira	53	Jd	10.36N	66.56W
La Guajira [2]	54	Da	11.30N	72.30W
Lagua Lichan, Puntan-	64b	Ba	15.16N	145.50 E
Laguardia	13	Jb	42.33N	2.35W
La Guardia [Sp.]	13	Dc	41.54N	8.53W
La Guardia [Sp.]	13	Ie	39.47N	3.29W
La Guasima	48	Kg	21.06N	97.49W
La Guerche-sur-l'Aubois	11	Ih	46.57N	2.57 E
Laguiole	11	Ij	44.41N	2.51 E
Laguna	56	Kc	28.29S	48.47W
Laguna Alsina	55	Am	36.49S	62.13W
Laguna Beach	46	Gj	33.33N	117.51W
Laguna Blanca	55	Cg	25.08S	58.15W
Laguna de Bay	26	Hd	14.23N	121.15 E
Laguna Limpia	55	Ch	26.29S	59.41W
Laguna Mountains	46	Gj	32.55N	116.25W
Laguna Paiva	56	Hd	31.19S	60.39W
Laguna Superior	47	Fe	16.20N	94.25W
Laguna Veneta	14	Ge	45.25N	12.20 E
Laguna Yema	55	Bg	24.15S	61.15W
Lagunillas [Bol.]	54	Fg	19.38S	63.43W
Lagunillas [Mex.]	48	Ii	17.50N	101.44W
Lagunillas [Ven.]	49	Lh	10.08N	71.16W
Lagunillas [Ven.]	49	Li	8.31N	71.24W
Laha	27	Lb	48.13N	124.36 E
La Habana [3]	49	Fb	22.45N	82.10W
La Habana=Havana (EN)	39	Kg	23.08N	82.22W
Lahad Datu	26	Ge	5.02N	118.19 E
Laham	34	Fc	14.54N	4.25 E
Lahat	26	Dg	3.48S	103.32 E
Lahdenpohja	7	Hf	61.33N	30.13 E
Lahewa	26	Cf	1.24N	97.11 E
Lahij	23	Fg	13.04N	44.53 E
Lāhījān	23	Hb	37.12N	50.01 E
Lahn	10	Df	50.18N	7.37 E
Lahnstein	12	Jd	50.20N	7.29 E
Laholm	7	Ch	56.31N	13.02 E
Laholmsbukten	8	Eh	56.35N	12.50 E
Lahore	22	Jf	31.35N	74.18 E
Lahr	10	Dh	48.20N	7.52 E
Lahti	6	Ic	60.58N	25.40 E
Laï	31	Ih	9.24N	16.18 E
Laiagam	60	Ci	5.31S	143.39 E
Lai'an	28	Eh	32.28N	118.26 E
Lai Chau	25	Kd	22.02N	103.10 E
Laich o'Moray	9	Jd	57.40N	3.30W
Laie	65a	Db	21.39N	157.56W
Laifeng	27	If	29.31N	109.23 E
Laighean/Leinster	9	Gh	53.00N	7.00W
L'Aigle	11	Gf	48.45N	0.38 E
Laignes	11	Kg	47.50N	4.22 E
Laihia	7	Fe	62.58N	22.01 E
Lainioälven	7	Fc	67.22N	22.39 E
Lairg	9	Ic	58.01N	4.25W
Lairi	35	Bc	10.49N	17.06 E
Lairi, Batha de-	35	Bc	12.28N	16.45 E
Lais	26	Dg	3.32S	102.03 E
La Isabela	49	Gb	22.57N	80.01W
Laisamis	36	Gb	1.36N	37.48 E
Laiševo	7	Li	55.26N	49.32 E
Laishui	28	Ce	39.23N	115.42 E
Laisvall	7	Dc	66.08N	17.10 E
Laitila	7	Ef	60.53N	21.41 E
Laiwu	28	Df	36.12N	117.40 E
Laiwui	26	Ig	1.22S	127.40 E
Laixi (Shuiji)	28	Ff	36.52N	120.31 E
Laiyang	27	Ld	36.59N	120.39 E
Laiyuan	27	Jd	39.19N	114.43 E
Laizhou Wan	28	Ef	37.30N	119.30 E
Laja	56	Fe	37.16S	72.42W
Laja	7	Hc	66.20N	56.16 E
La Jara	13	He	39.40N	4.55W
Lajeado	55	Gi	29.27S	51.58W
Lajeado, Serra do-	55	Hd	19.08S	49.56W
Lājerd	24	Oe	35.24N	53.04 E
Lajes [Braz.]	54	Ke	5.41S	36.14W
Lajes [Braz.]	53	Kh	27.48S	50.19W
Lajes do Pico	53	Bb	38.23N	28.16W
Lajosmizse	10	Pi	47.01N	19.33 E
La Junta [Co.-U.S.]	43	Gd	37.59N	103.33W
La Junta [Mex.]	48	Fc	28.28N	107.20W
Lak Bor	36	Hb	1.18N	40.40 E
Lake Cargelligo	59	Jf	33.18S	146.23 E
Lake Charles	39	Jf	30.12N	93.12W
Lake City	43	Ke	30.12N	82.38W
Lake District	9	Jg	54.30N	3.10W
Lake Fork Creek	46	Jf	40.13N	110.07W
Lake Geneva	45	Le	42.36N	88.26W
Lake George	44	Kd	43.25N	73.45W
Lake Grace	59	Df	33.06S	118.28 E
Lake Harbour	42	Kd	62.51N	69.53W
Lake Havasu City	46	Hi	34.27N	114.22W
Lake Itasca	45	Ic	46.51N	95.12W
Lake Jackson	45	Il	29.02N	95.27W
Lake King	59	Df	33.05S	119.40 E
Lakeland	43	Kf	28.03N	81.57W
Lake Louise	46	Ga	51.26N	116.11W
Lakemba	63d	Cc	18.13S	178.47W
Lakemba Passage	63d	Cb	17.53S	178.32W
Lake Mills	45	Je	43.25N	93.32W
Lake Minchumina	40	Ia	63.53N	152.19W
Lake Murray	60	Ci	6.54S	141.28 E
Lake Oswego	46	Dd	45.26N	122.39W
Lake Placid	44	Kc	44.18N	73.59W
Lake Providence	45	Kj	32.48N	91.11W
Lake Pukaki	62	Df	44.11S	170.08 E
Lake Range	46	Ff	40.15N	119.25W
Lake River	42	Jf	54.28N	82.30W
Lakes Entrance	59	Jg	37.53S	147.59 E
Lakeside	46	If	41.13N	112.57W
Lake Tekapo	62	Df	44.00S	170.29 E
Lakeview	43	Cc	42.11N	120.21W
Lakeville	45	Jd	44.39N	93.14W
Lake Wales	44	Gl	27.55N	81.35W
Lakewood [Co.-U.S.]	45	Dg	39.44N	105.06W
Lakewood [Oh.-U.S.]	44	Ge	41.29N	81.50W
Lake Worth	44	Gl	26.37N	80.03W
Lakhdar, Chergui Kef-	13	Pi	35.57N	3.16 E
Lakhdaria	13	Ph	36.34N	3.35 E
Lâki	15	Hh	41.50N	24.50 E
Lakin	45	Fh	37.58N	101.15W
Lakinsk	7	Jh	56.04N	39.58 E
Lákmos Óros	15	Ej	39.40N	21.07 E
Lakon, Ile-	57	Hf	14.17S	167.30 E
Lakonikós Kólpos = Laconia, Gulf of- (EN)	15	Fm	36.35N	22.40 E
Lakota [3]	34	Dd	5.53N	5.42W
Lakota [I.C.]	34	Dd	5.51N	5.41W
Lakota [N.D.-U.S.]	45	Gb	48.02N	98.21W
Laksefjorden	7	Ga	70.58N	27.00 E
Lakselv	7	Fa	70.03N	25.01 E
Lakshadweep [3]	25	Ef	11.00N	72.00 E
La Laguna	55	Bb	14.30S	61.06W
Lalanna	37	Hd	23.28S	45.05 E
Lalapaşa	15	Jh	41.50N	26.44 E
Lāleh Zār, Kūh-e-	24	Qh	29.24N	56.46 E
La Leonesa	55	Ch	27.03S	58.43W
Lālī	24	Mf	32.21N	49.06 E
Lalibela	35	Fc	12.00N	39.04 E
La Libertad [2]	54	Ce	8.00S	78.30W
La Libertad [ElSal.]	47	Gf	13.29N	89.16W
La Libertad [Guat.]	49	Be	16.47N	90.07W
La Libertad [Guat.]	49	Bf	15.30N	91.50W
La Libertad [Hond.]	49	Df	14.43N	87.36W
La Ligua	56	Fd	32.27S	71.14W
Lalín	13	Db	42.39N	8.07W
La Línea	13	Gh	36.10N	5.19W
Lalin He	28	Hb	45.28N	125.43 E
Lalitpur	25	Fd	24.41N	78.25 E
Lalla Khedidja	13	Qh	36.27N	4.14 E
Lālmanir Hāt	25	Hc	25.54N	89.27 E
La Loche	42	Ge	56.29N	109.27W
La Loupe	11	Hf	48.28N	1.01 E
La Louvière	11	Kd	50.29N	4.11 E
L'Alpe-d'Huez	11	Mi	45.06N	6.04 E
La Lucila	55	Bj	30.25S	61.01W
Lalzit, Gjiri i-	15	Ch	41.31N	19.29 E
La Machine	11	Jh	46.53N	3.28 E
La Maddalena	14	Di	41.13N	9.24 E
La Maiella	5	Hg	42.05N	14.07 E
La Maladeta/Malditos, Montes-	13	Mb	42.40N	0.50 E
La Malbaie	42	Kg	47.39N	70.10W
La Mancha	5	Fh	39.05N	3.00W
La Manche	5	Fe	50.20N	1.00W
Lamap	61	Cc	16.26S	167.43 E
Lamar	43	Gd	38.05N	102.37W
La Maragateria	13	Fb	42.25N	6.10W
La Marina	13	Lf	38.35N	0.05W
La Marmora	14	Dk	39.59N	9.20 E
La Marque	45	Il	29.22N	94.58W
Lamas	54	Ce	6.25S	76.35W
Lamastre	11	Kj	44.59N	4.35 E
Lamawan	28	Ad	40.05N	111.25 E
Lambach	14	Hb	48.05N	13.53 E
Lamballe	11	Df	48.28N	2.31W
Lambar, Rio-	55	Jd	19.30S	45.00W
Lambaréné	31	Ii	0.42S	10.13 E
Lambari	55	Je	21.58S	45.21W
Lambasa	61	Ec	16.26S	179.24 E
Lambay/Reachrainn	9	Gh	53.29N	6.01W
Lambayeque [2]	54	Ce	6.20S	80.00W
Lambayeque	54	Ce	6.42S	79.55W
Lambert Glacier	66	Ff	71.00S	70.00 E
Lambert Land	41	Jc	79.10N	21.00W
Lamberts Bay	31	Il	32.05S	18.17 E
Lambro	14	De	45.08N	9.32 E
Lambsheim	12	Ke	49.31N	8.17 E
Lambton, Cape-	42	Fb	71.04N	123.08W
Lamé	35	Ad	9.15N	14.32 E
Lame Deer	46	Ld	45.37N	106.40W
Lamego	13	Ec	41.06N	7.49W
Lamentin	51e	Ab	16.16N	61.38W
La Mesa	46	Gj	32.46N	117.01W
Lamesa	43	Ge	32.44N	101.57W
La Meta	14	Hj	41.41N	13.56 E
Lamezia Terme	14	Kl	38.59N	16.17 E
Lamia	15	Fk	38.54N	22.26 E
Lamina	55	De	20.34S	56.14W
Lamlam, Mount-	64c	Bb	13.20N	144.40 E
Lammermuir Hills	9	Kf	55.52N	2.40W
Lammhult	8	Fg	57.10N	14.35 E
Lammi	7	Ff	61.05N	25.01 E
Lamoil	64d	Ba	7.39N	151.41 E
Lamon Bay	21	Oh	14.25N	122.00 E
Lamone	14	Ff	44.29N	12.08 E
Lamoni	45	Jf	40.37N	93.56W
Lamont	44	Fj	30.21N	83.50W
La Montaña	52	If	10.00S	72.50W
La Moraña	13	Hd	40.45N	4.55W
La Mosquitia	49	Ef	15.00N	84.20W
La Mothe-Achard	11	Eh	46.37N	1.40W
Lamotrek Atoll	57	Fd	7.30N	146.20 E

Index Symbols

[1] Independent Nation
[2] State, Region
[3] District, County
[4] Municipality
[5] Colony, Dependency
Continent
Physical Region
Historical or Cultural Region
Mount, Mountain
Volcano
Hill
Mountains, Mountain Range
Hills, Escarpment
Plateau, Upland
Pass, Gap
Plain, Lowland
Delta
Salt Flat
Valley, Canyon
Crater, Cave
Karst Features
Depression
Polder
Desert, Dunes
Forest, Woods
Heath, Steppe
Oasis
Cape, Point
Coast, Beach
Cliff
Peninsula
Isthmus
Sandbank
Island
Atoll
Rock, Reef
Islands, Archipelago
Rocks, Reefs
Coral Reef
Well, Spring
Geyser
River, Stream
Waterfall Rapids
River Mouth, Estuary
Lake
Salt Lake
Intermittent Lake
Reservoir
Swamp, Pond
Canal
Glacier
Ice Shelf, Pack Ice
Ocean
Sea
Gulf, Bay
Strait, Fjord
Lagoon
Bank
Seamount
Tablemount
Ridge
Shelf
Basin
Escarpment, Sea Scarp
Fracture
Trench, Abyss
National Park, Reserve
Point of Interest
Recreation Site
Cave, Cavern
Historic Site
Ruins
Wall, Walls
Church, Abbey
Temple
Scientific Station
Airport
Port
Lighthouse
Mine
Tunnel
Dam, Bridge

Lamotte-Beuvron 11 Ig 47.36N 2.01 E
La Moure 45 Gc 46.21N 98.18W
Lampang 25 Je 18.16N 99.34 E
Lampasas 45 Gk 31.03N 98.12W
Lampazos de Naranjo 48 Id 27.01N 100.31W
Lampedusa 14 Go 35.30N 12.35 E
Lampertheim 10 Eg 49.36N 8.28 E
Lampeter 9 Ii 52.07N 4.05W
Lamphun 25 Je 18.35N 99.00 E
Lampione 14 Go 35.35N 12.20 E
Lampung [3] 26 Dg 5.00S 105.00 E
Lamu 31 Li 2.16S 40.54 E
Lamud 54 Ce 6.09S 77.55W
La Mure 11 Lj 44.54N 5.47 E
Lan 16 Ec 52.09N 27.18 E
Lana 14 Fd 46.37N 11.09 E
Lana, Rio de la- 48 Li 17.49N 95.09W
Lanai City 65a Ec 20.50N 156.55W
Lanaihale 65a Ec 20.49N 156.52W
Lanai Island 57 Lb 20.50N 156.55W
Lanaken 12 Hd 50.53N 5.39 E
Lanark 9 Jf 55.41N 3.48W
Lanbi Kyun 25 Jf 10.50N 98.15 E
Lancang (Menglangba) 27 Gg 22.37N 99.57 E
Lancang Jiang=Mekong (EN) 21 Mh 10.15N 105.55 E
Lancashire [3] 9 Kh 53.55N 2.40W
Lancashire Plain 9 Kh 53.40N 2.45W
Lancaster 9 Kh 53.45N 2.50W
Lancaster [Ca.-U.S.] 43 De 34.42N 118.08W
Lancaster [Eng.-U.K.] 9 Kg 54.03N 2.48W
Lancaster [Mo.-U.S.] 45 Jf 40.31N 92.32W
Lancaster [N.H.-U.S.] 44 Lc 44.29N 71.34W
Lancaster [Oh.-U.S.] 44 Ff 39.43N 82.37W
Lancaster [Ont.-Can.] 44 Jc 45.12N 74.30W
Lancaster [Pa.-U.S.] 43 Lc 40.01N 76.19W
Lancaster [S.C.-U.S.] 44 Gh 34.43N 80.47W
Lancaster Sound 38 Kb 74.13N 84.00W
Lançeiro 55 Fe 20.59S 53.43W
Lancelin 59 Df 31.01S 115.19 E
Lanciano 14 Ih 42.14N 14.23 E
Lančin 15 Ha 48.31N 24.49 E
Lancun 28 Ff 36.25N 120.11 E
Łańcut 10 Sf 50.05N 22.13 E
Land 8 Cd 60.45N 10.00 E
Lândana 36 Bd 5.15S 12.10 E
Landau an der Isar 10 Ih 48.41N 12.41 E
Landau in der Pfalz 10 Eg 49.12N 8.07 E
Land Bay 66 Mf 75.25S 141.45W
Landeck 14 Ec 47.08N 10.34 E
Landen 12 Hd 50.45N 5.05 E
Lander 43 Fc 42.50N 108.44W
Landerneau 11 Bf 48.27N 4.15W
Lander River 59 Gd 20.25S 132.00 E
Landeryd 8 Eg 57.05N 13.16 E
Landes 11 Fj 44.15N 1.00W
Landes [3] 11 Fj 44.00N 0.50W
Landesbergen 12 Lb 52.34N 9.08 E
Landeta 55 Ak 32.01S 62.04W
Landete 13 Ke 39.54N 1.22W
Landfallis 25 If 13.40N 93.02 E
Land Glacier 66 Mf 75.40S 141.45W
Landi Kotal 25 Eb 34.06N 71.09 E
Landless Corner 36 Ee 14.53S 28.04 E
Landrecies 12 Fd 50.08N 3.42 E
Landsberg am Lech 10 Gh 48.03N 10.52 E
Landsbro 8 Fg 57.22N 14.54 E
Land's End 5 Fe 50.03N 5.44W
Lands End 42 Fa 76.25N 122.45W
Landshut 10 Ih 48.32N 12.09 E
Landskrona 8 Ei 55.52N 12.50 E
Landsort 8 Gf 58.45N 17.50 E
Landsortsdjupet 8 Hf 58.40N 18.30 E
Landstuhl 12 Je 49.25N 7.34 E
Landusky 46 Kc 47.54N 108.37W
La Neuve-Lyre 12 Cf 48.54N 0.45 E
Lanfeng → Lankao 28 Cg 34.49N 114.48 E
Lang 46 Mb 49.56N 104.23W
La'nga Co 27 De 30.41N 81.17 E
Langadhás 15 Gi 40.45N 23.04 E
Langádhia 15 Fl 37.39N 22.03 E
Långan 7 De 63.19N 14.44 E
Langano, Lake- 35 Fd 7.36N 38.43 E
Langao 27 Ie 32.20N 108.53 E
Langara 26 Hg 4.02S 123.00 E
Langarfoss 7a Cb 65.35N 14.15W
Langasian 26 Ie 8.16N 125.39 E
Langdon 45 Gb 48.46N 98.22W
Langeac 11 Ji 45.06N 3.29 E
Langeais 11 Gg 47.20N 0.24 E
Langeb 35 Fb 17.46N 36.41 E
Langebaan 37 Bf 33.06S 18.02 E
Langeberg 37 Cf 33.56S 20.45 E
Langedijk 12 Gb 52.42N 4.48 E
Langeland 7 Ci 55.00N 10.50 E
Langelands Bælt 8 Dj 54.50N 10.55 E
Längelmävesi 8 Kc 61.30N 24.20 E
Langen 12 Ke 49.59N 8.40 E
Langenberg 12 Kc 51.17N 8.34 E
Langenburg 45 Fa 50.50N 101.43W
Langenfeld (Rheinland) 12 Ic 51.06N 6.57 E
Langenhagen 10 Fd 52.27N 9.45 E
Langenselbold 12 Ld 50.11N 9.02 E
Langenthal 14 Bc 47.13N 7.49 E
Langeoog 10 Dc 53.46N 7.32 E
Langeri 20 Jf 50.08N 143.20 E
Langesund 8 Ce 59.00N 9.45 E
Langesundsfjorden 8 Cf 59.00N 9.48 E
Langevåg 8 Bb 62.27N 6.12 E
Langfang → Anci 27 Kd 39.29N 116.40 E
Långfjället 8 Eb 62.10N 12.20 E
Langfjorden 8 Bb 62.45N 7.30 E
Langhe 14 Bf 44.30N 8.00 E
Langholm 9 Kf 55.09N 3.00W
Langjökull 5 Ec 64.39N 20.00W
Langkawi, Pulau- 26 Ce 6.22N 99.48 E
Langkon 26 Ge 6.32N 116.42 E
Langlade 44 Ja 48.12N 75.57W
Langnau im Emmental 14 Bd 46.56N 7.46 E
Langogne 11 Jj 44.43N 3.51 E
Langon 11 Fj 44.33N 0.15W
Langorüd 24 Md 37.11N 50.10 E
Langøya 7 Db 68.44N 14.50 E
Langreo 13 Ga 43.18N 5.41W
Langres 11 Lg 47.52N 5.20 E
Langres, Plateau de- 5 Gf 47.41N 5.03 E
Langrune-sur-Mer 12 Be 49.19N 0.22W
Langsa 22 Li 4.28N 97.58 E
Långsele 8 Ga 63.11N 17.04 E
Långshyttan 8 Gd 60.27N 16.01 E
Lang Son 25 Ld 21.50N 106.44 E
Lang Suan 25 Jg 9.55N 99.07 E
Languedoc 5 Gg 44.00N 4.00 E
Languedoc 11 Jj 44.00N 4.00 E
Langueyú, Arroyo- 55 Cm 36.39S 58.27W
Langwedel 12 Lb 52.58N 9.13 E
Langxi 28 Ei 31.08N 119.11 E
Langzhong 27 Ie 31.40N 106.04 E
Lan Hsu 27 Lg 22.00N 121.30 E
Laniel 44 Hb 47.06N 79.15W
Lanín, Volcán- 52 Ii 39.38S 71.30W
Lankao 27 Cd 35.12N 79.50 E
Lankao (Lanfeng) 27 Kg 21.00N 116.00 E
Lankao (Lanfeng) 28 Cg 34.49N 114.48 E
Länkipohja 8 Kc 61.44N 24.48 E
Lannemezan 11 Gk 43.08N 0.23 E
Lannemezan, Plateau de- 11 Gk 43.09N 0.27 E
Lannion 11 Cf 48.44N 3.28W
Lannion, Baie de- 11 Cf 48.43N 3.34W
La Noria 56 Gb 20.23S 69.53W
Lansdowne House 42 If 52.13N 87.53W
L'Anse 44 Cb 46.45N 88.27W
Lansing [Ia.-U.S.] 45 Ke 43.22N 91.13W
Lansing [Mi.-U.S.] 39 Ke 42.43N 84.34W
Lansjärv 7 Fc 66.39N 22.12 E
Łańskie, Jezioro- 10 Qc 53.33N 20.30 E
Lantar 20 Ie 56.05N 137.35 E
Lanta Yai, Ko- 25 Jg 7.35N 99.03 E
Lanteri 55 Ci 28.50S 59.39W
Lanterne 11 Mg 47.44N 6.03 E
Lanús 55 Cl 34.43S 58.24W
Lanusei 14 Dk 39.53N 9.32 E
Lanvaux, Landes de- 11 Dg 47.47N 2.36W
Lanxi [China] 28 Ej 29.13N 119.28 E
Lanxi [China] 28 Ha 46.15N 126.16 E
Lanxian (Dongcun) 28 Ae 38.17N 111.38 E
Lanyi He 28 Ae 38.40N 110.53 E
Lanzarote 30 Ff 29.00N 13.40W
Lanzhou 22 Mf 36.03N 103.41 E
Lanzo Torinese 14 Be 45.16N 7.28 E
Lao 14 Jk 39.47N 15.48 E
Laoag 22 Oh 18.12N 120.36 E
Laoang 26 Id 12.34N 125.00 E
Lao Cai 22 Mg 22.30N 103.57 E
Laocheng 28 Hc 42.37N 124.04 E
Laoha He 27 Lc 43.24N 120.39 E
Lao He 28 Cj 29.02N 115.47 E
Laohuanghe Kou 28 Ef 37.39N 119.02 E
Laois [2] 9 Fi 53.00N 7.30W
Laojunmiao → Yumen 22 Lf 39.50N 97.44 E
Laojun Shan 27 Je 33.45N 111.38 E
Lao Ling 28 Id 41.24N 126.10 E
Laon 11 Je 49.34N 3.37 E
Laona 45 Ld 45.34N 88.40W
Laonnois 12 Fe 49.35N 3.40 E
La Orchila, Isla- 54 Ea 11.48N 66.10W
La Oroya 53 Ig 11.32S 75.57W
Laos [1] 22 Mh 18.00N 105.00 E
Laoshan (Licun) 28 Ff 36.10N 120.25 E
Laotougou 28 Jc 42.54N 129.09 E
Laou 13 Gi 35.26N 5.05W
Laoye Ling 28 Kb 44.50N 130.10 E
Lapa 56 Kc 25.45S 49.42W
Lapai 34 Gd 9.03N 6.43 E
Lapalisse 11 Jh 46.15N 3.38 E
La Palma 30 Ff 28.40N 17.52W
La Palma [ElSal.] 49 Cf 14.19N 89.11W
La Palma [Pan.] 47 Ig 8.25N 78.09W
La Palma del Condado 13 Fg 37.23N 6.33W
La Paloma 55 El 34.40S 54.10W
La Pampa [2] 56 Ge 37.00S 66.00W
La Panne/De Panne 12 Ec 51.06N 2.35 E
La Paragua 54 Fb 6.50N 63.20W
La Partida, Isla- 48 De 24.30N 110.25W
La Paz [3] 49 Df 14.15N 87.50W
La Paz [2] 54 Eg 15.00S 68.00W
La Paz [Arg.] 56 Id 30.45S 59.39W
La Paz [Arg.] 56 Gd 33.28S 67.33W
La Paz [Bol.] 53 Jg 16.30S 68.09W
La Paz [Col.] 49 Kh 10.23N 73.10W
La Paz [Hond.] 47 Gf 14.16N 87.40W
La Paz [Mex.] 39 Hg 24.10N 110.18W
La Paz [Ur.] 55 Dl 34.46S 56.13W
La Paz [Ven.] 49 Lh 10.41N 72.00W
La Paz, Bahía de- 47 Bd 24.09N 110.25W
La Paz, Llano de- 48 De 24.00N 110.30W
La Paz Centro 49 Dg 12.20N 86.41W
La Pedrera 54 Ed 1.18S 69.40W
Lapeer 44 Fd 43.03N 83.19W
La Pelada 55 Bj 30.52S 60.59W
La Pérouse, Bahía- 65d Bb 27.04S 109.18W
La Perouse Strait (EN)= Laperuza, Proliv- 21 Qe 45.30N 142.00 E
La Perouse Strait (EN)= Sōya-Kaikyō 21 Qe 45.30N 142.00 E
Laperuza, Proliv-=La Perouse Strait (EN) 21 Qe 45.30N 142.00 E
La Pesca 47 Ed 23.47N 97.47W
Lápethos 24 Ee 35.20N 33.10 E
La Petite Pierre 12 Jf 48.52N 7.19 E
La Picasa, Laguna- 55 Al 34.20S 62.14W
La Piedad Cavadas 48 Hg 20.21N 102.00W
La Pine 46 Ee 43.40N 121.30W
Lapinjärvi/Lappträsk 8 Ld 60.36N 26.09 E
Lapinlahti 7 Ge 63.22N 27.30 E
La Plaine 51g Bb 15.20N 61.15W
La Plana 13 Ld 40.00N 0.05W
Lapland (EN)=Lappi 5 Ib 66.50N 22.00 E
Lapland (EN)=Lappland 5 Ib 66.50N 22.00 E
La Plant 45 Fd 45.10N 100.38W
La Plata 53 Ki 34.55S 57.57W
La Pobla de Lillet 13 Nb 42.15N 1.59 E
La Pobla de Segur/Pobla de Segur 13 Mb 42.15N 0.58 E
La Pocatièr 44 Lb 47.21N 70.02W
La Porte 44 Dd 41.36N 86.43W
Lapovo 15 Ee 44.11N 21.06 E
Lappajärvi 7 Fe 63.08N 23.40 E
Lappeenranta/Villmanstrand 6 Ic 61.04N 28.11 E
Lappfjärd/Lapväärtti 8 Ib 62.15N 21.32 E
Lappi [2] 7 Gc 67.40N 26.30 E
Lappi 8 Ic 61.06N 21.50 E
Lappi=Lapland (EN) 5 Ib 66.50N 22.00 E
Lappland=Lapland (EN) 5 Ib 66.50N 22.00 E
Lappo/Lapua 7 Fe 62.57N 23.00 E
Lappträsk/Lapinjärvi 8 Ld 60.36N 26.09 E
Lapri 20 He 55.45N 124.59 E
Laprida 56 He 37.33S 60.49W
Lâpseki 24 Bb 40.20N 26.41 E
Laptev Sea (EN)=Laptevyh, More- 67 Fd 76.00N 126.00 E
Laptevyh, More-=Laptev Sea (EN) 67 Fd 76.00N 126.00 E
Lapua/Lappo 7 Fe 62.57N 23.00 E
La Puebla 13 Pe 39.46N 3.01 E
La Puebla de Cazalla 13 Gg 37.14N 5.19W
Lapuna 55 Ba 13.19S 60.28W
La Puntilla 52 Hf 2.11S 81.01W
La Purísima 48 Cd 26.10N 112.04W
Lăpuş 15 Hb 47.30N 24.01 E
Lăpuş 15 Gb 47.39N 23.24 E
La Push 46 Cc 47.55N 124.38W
Lapväärtti/Lappfjärd 8 Ib 62.15N 21.32 E
Łapy 10 Sd 53.00N 22.53 E
Laqīyat al Arba'in 35 Da 20.03N 28.02 E
La Quemada 48 Hf 22.27N 102.45W
La Quiaca 56 Gb 22.06S 65.37W
L'Aquila 6 Hg 42.22N 13.22 E
Lar 23 Hd 27.41N 54.17 E
Lara [2] 54 Ea 10.10N 69.50W
Larache 32 Fb 35.12N 6.09W
Laragne-Montéglin 11 Lj 44.19N 5.49 E
Lārak 23 Id 26.52N 56.22 E
La Rambla 13 Hg 37.36N 4.44W
Laramie 39 Ie 41.19N 105.35W
Laramie Mountains 43 Fc 42.00N 105.40W
Laramie Peak 46 Me 42.17N 105.27W
Laramie River 46 Me 42.12N 104.32W
Laranjal, Rio- 55 Ff 23.12S 53.45W
Laranjeiras do Sul 56 Jc 25.25S 52.25W
Larantuka 26 Hh 8.21S 122.59 E
Larat 26 Jh 7.09S 131.45 E
Larat, Pulau- 26 Jh 7.10S 131.50 E
La Raya 49 Ji 8.20N 74.34W
L'Arba 13 Ph 36.34N 3.09 E
L'Arbaa-Naït-Irathen 13 Qh 36.38N 4.12 E
L'Arbresle 11 Ki 45.50N 4.37 E
Lärbro 7 Eh 57.47N 18.47 E
Larche, Col de- 11 Mj 44.25N 6.53 E
Larde 37 Fc 16.28S 39.43 E
Larderello 14 Eg 43.14N 10.53 E
La Réale 11 Fj 44.35N 0.02W
Laredo [Sp.] 13 Ia 43.24N 3.25W
Laredo [Tx.-U.S.] 39 Jg 27.31N 99.30W
Laren 12 Hb 52.16N 5.16 E
Lārestān 21 Hg 27.00N 55.30 E
Larestan 24 Pi 27.00N 55.30 E
Large Island 51p Cb 12.24N 61.30W
Largentière 11 Kj 44.32N 4.18 E
L'Argentière-la-Bessée 11 Mj 44.47N 6.33 E
Largo, Cayo- 49 Gc 21.38N 81.28W
Largs 9 If 55.48N 4.52W
La Ribagorça/Ribagorza 13 Mb 42.15N 0.30 E
La Ribera 13 Kb 42.30N 2.00W
Larimore 45 Hc 47.54N 97.38W
Larino 14 Ii 41.48N 14.54 E
La Rioja [2] 56 Gc 30.00S 67.30W
La Rioja [3] 13 Jb 42.20N 2.20W
La Rioja 53 Jh 29.25S 66.50W
Lárisa 6 Ih 39.38N 22.25 E
La Rivière-Thibouville, Nassandres- 12 Ce 49.07N 0.44 E
Lärkāna 25 Dc 27.33N 68.13 E
Larmor-Plage 11 Cg 47.42N 3.23W
Larnaka/Lárnax 23 Dc 34.55N 33.38 E
Lárnax/Larnaka 23 Dc 34.55N 33.38 E
Larne/Latharna 9 Hg 54.51N 5.49W
Larned 45 Gg 38.11N 99.06W
La Robla 13 Gb 42.48N 5.37W
La Roche 63b De 21.28S 168.02 E
La Roche-en-Ardenne 11 Ld 50.11N 5.35 E
La Rochefoucauld 11 Gi 45.44N 0.23 E
La Roche-Guyon 12 De 49.05N 1.38 E
La Rochelle 6 Ff 46.10N 1.09W
La Roche-sur-Yon 11 Eh 46.40N 1.26W
La Roda 13 Je 39.13N 2.09W
La Romana 47 Ke 18.25N 68.58W
La Ronge 42 Ge 55.06N 105.17W
La Ronge, Lac- 38 Id 55.05N 104.59W
Larose 45 Kl 29.35N 90.23W
La Rosita 48 Ic 28.24N 101.43W
Larouco 13 Ec 41.56N 7.40W
Larreynaga 49 Dg 12.40N 86.34W
Larrey Point 59 Dc 20.05S 119.10 E
Larrimah 58 Ef 15.35S 133.12 E
Larsa 24 Kg 31.16N 45.49 E
Lars Christensen Kyst 66 Fe 69.30S 68.00 E
Larsen, Mount- 66 Kf 74.51S 162.12 E
Larsen Ice Shelf 66 Qe 68.30S 62.30W
Lartijas Padomju Socialistiska Respublika/ Latvijskaja SSR [2] 19 Cd 57.00N 25.00 E
La Rumorosa 48 Aa 32.34N 116.06W
Laruns 11 Fk 43.00N 0.25W
Larvik 7 Bg 59.04N 10.00 E
La Sabana [Arg.] 55 Ch 27.52S 59.57W
La Sabana [Col.] 54 Ec 2.20N 68.32W
Las Adjuntas, Presa de- 48 Jf 23.55N 98.45W
La Sagra 13 Id 40.05N 4.00W
La Sagra 13 Jg 37.57N 2.34W
La Salle 45 Lf 41.20N 89.06W
La Salle, Pic- 47 Je 18.22N 71.59W
La Sal Mountains 46 Kg 38.30N 109.10W
Las Alpujarras 13 Ih 36.50N 3.25W
La Sanabria 13 Fb 42.08N 6.30W
Las Animas 45 Eg 38.04N 103.13W
Lās 'ānōd 35 Hd 8.26N 47.24 E
La Sarre 42 Jg 48.48N 79.12W
Las Aves, Islas- 54 Ea 11.58N 67.33W
Las Avispas 55 Bi 29.53S 61.18W
Las Bardenas 13 Kb 42.10N 1.25W
Las Bonitas 50 Di 7.52N 65.40W
Las Breñas 56 Hc 27.05S 61.05W
Las Cabezas de San Juan 13 Gh 36.59N 5.56W
Lascahobas 49 Ld 18.50N 71.56W
Lascano 55 Ek 33.40S 54.12W
Las Casitas, Cerro- 47 Cd 23.31N 109.53W
Lascaux, Grotte de- 11 Hi 45.03N 1.11 E
Las Cejas 56 Hc 26.53S 64.44W
Las Chilcas, Arroyo- 55 Cm 37.16S 58.26W
Las Choapas 47 Fe 17.55N 94.05W
Las Cinco Villas 13 Kb 42.05N 1.07W
Las Cruces 43 Fe 32.23N 106.29W
Läsdäred 35 Hc 10.10N 46.01 E
Las Dawa'o 35 Hc 10.22N 49.03 E
La Segarra 13 Nc 41.30N 1.10 E
La Selva 13 Oc 41.40N 2.50 E
La Serena 13 Gf 38.45N 5.30W
La Serena 53 Ih 29.54S 71.16W
La Seu d'Urgell/Seo de Urgel 13 Nb 42.21N 1.28 E
La-Seyne-sur-Mer 11 Lk 43.06N 5.53 E
Las Flores 56 Ie 36.03S 59.07W
Lāsh-e Joveyn 23 Jc 31.43N 61.37 E
Las Heras 56 Gd 32.51S 68.49W
Lashkar Gāh 22 If 31.35N 64.21 E
Las Hurdes 13 Fd 40.20N 6.20W
La Sila 5 Hh 39.15N 16.30 E
Łasin 10 Pc 53.32N 19.05 E
Łask 10 Pe 51.36N 19.07 E
Las Lajas 56 Fe 38.31S 70.22W
Las Lomitas 56 Hb 24.42S 60.36W
Las Margaritas 48 Ni 16.19N 91.59W
Las Mariñas 13 Da 43.20N 8.15W
Las Marismas 13 Fg 37.00N 6.15W
Las Mercedes 54 Eb 9.07N 66.24W
Las Mestenas 48 Gc 28.13N 104.35W
Las Minas, Cerro- 47 Gf 14.33N 88.39W
Las Minas, Sierra de- 47 Ge 15.05N 90.00W
Las Mixtecas, Sierra del- 48 Ki 17.45N 97.15W
La Sola, Isla- 54 Fa 11.20N 63.34W
La Solana 13 If 38.56N 3.14W
Lasolo 26 Hg 3.29S 122.04 E
La Sorcière 51k Bb 13.59N 60.56W
La Souterraine 11 Hh 46.14N 1.29 E
Las Palmas [3] 32 Ed 28.20N 14.20W
Las Palmas de Gran Canaria 31 Ff 28.06N 15.24W
Las Petas 55 Cc 16.23S 59.11W
La Spezia 6 Gg 44.07N 9.50 E
Las Piedras 56 Id 34.45S 56.13W
Las Plumas 53 Jj 43.40S 67.15W
Lās Qoray 35 Hc 11.15N 48.22 E
Las Rosas 55 Bk 32.28S 61.34W
Lassen Peak 43 Cc 40.29N 121.31W
Lassigny 12 Ee 49.35N 2.51 E
Laßnitz 14 Jd 46.46N 15.32 E
Lasso 64b Ba 15.02N 145.38 E
Las Tablas 49 Gj 7.46N 80.17W
Last Mountain Lake 42 Gf 51.10N 105.15W
Las Toscas 55 Ci 28.21S 59.17W
Lastoursville 36 Bc 0.49S 12.42 E
Lastovo 14 Kh 42.46N 16.55 E
Lastovo 14 Kh 42.45N 16.50 E
Lastovski kanal 14 Kh 42.50N 16.59 E
Las Tres Virgenes, Volcán- 47 Bc 27.27N 112.34W
Las Tunas [3] 49 Ic 21.00N 77.00W
Las Tunas, Punta- 51a Bb 18.30N 66.37W
Las Varillas 56 Hd 31.52S 62.43W
Las Vegas [N.M.-U.S.] 43 Fd 35.36N 105.13W
Las Vegas [Nv.-U.S.] 39 Hf 36.11N 115.08W
Las Villuercas 13 Ge 39.33N 5.27W
Łaszczów 10 Tf 50.32N 23.40 E
Lata 65c Db 14.14S 169.29W
Latacunga 54 Cd 0.55S 78.37W
La Tagua 54 Dd 0.03S 74.40W
Latakia (EN)=Al Lādhiqīyah 22 Ff 35.31N 35.07 E
Latarc, Causse du- 11 Jk 43.57N 3.11 E
Late Island 61 Gc 18.48S 174.39W
Laterza 14 Kj 40.37N 16.48 E
La Teste 11 Ej 44.38N 1.09W
Latgale 8 Lh 56.45N 27.30 E
Latgales Augstiene/ Latgalskaja Vozvyšennost 8 Lh 56.10N 27.30 E
Latgalskaja Vozvyšennost/ Latgales Augstiene 8 Lh 56.10N 27.30 E
Latharna/Larne 9 Hg 54.51N 5.49W
Lathen 12 Jb 52.52N 7.19 E
La Tigra 55 Bh 27.06S 60.34W
Latina 14 Gi 41.28N 12.52 E
Latisana 14 Ge 45.47N 13.00 E
Latium (EN) = Lazio [2] 14 Gh 42.02N 12.23 E
La Toja 13 Db 42.27N 8.50W
La Toma 56 Gd 33.03S 65.37W
La Tontouta 63b Ce 22.00S 166.15 E
Latorica 10 Rh 48.28N 21.50 E
La Tortuga, Isla- 54 Ea 10.56N 65.20W
La-Tour-du-Pin 11 Li 45.34N 5.27 E
La Trimouille 11 Hh 46.28N 1.03 E
La Trinidad 49 Dg 12.58N 86.14W
La Trinidad de Orichuna 50 Bi 7.07N 69.45W
La Trinité 50 Fe 14.44N 60.58W
Latronico 14 Kj 40.05N 16.01 E
Lattari, Monti- 14 Ij 40.40N 14.30 E
La Tuque 42 Kg 47.27N 72.47W
Lātūr 25 Fe 18.24N 76.35 E
Latvian SSR (EN)=Latvijas PSR [2] 19 Cd 57.00N 25.00 E
Latvijas PSR=Latvian SSR (EN) [2] 19 Cd 57.00N 25.00 E
Latvijskaja Sovetskaja Socialističeskaja Respublika [2] 19 Cd 57.00N 25.00 E
Latvijskaja SSR/Latvijas Padomju Socialistiska Respublika [2] 19 Cd 57.00N 25.00 E
Lau 30 Kh 6.56N 30.16 E
Laubach 12 Kd 50.33N 8.59 E
Lauchert 10 Fh 48.05N 9.15 E
Lauchhammer 10 Je 51.30N 13.48 E
Lauenburg 10 Gc 53.22N 10.34 E
Lauf an der Pegnitz 10 Hg 49.31N 11.17 E
Laughlan Islands 63a Ac 9.15S 153.40 E
Laughlin Peak 45 Dh 36.38N 104.12W
Lau Group 57 Jf 18.20S 178.30W
Lauhanvuori 8 Jb 62.10N 22.10 E
Laujar de Andarax 13 Jh 36.59N 2.51W
Laukaa 7 Fe 62.25N 25.57 E
Laukuva 8 Ji 55.35N 22.08 E
Laulau, Bahía- 64b Ba 15.08N 145.46 E
Launceston [Austl.] 58 Fi 41.26S 147.08 E
Launceston [Eng.-U.K.] 9 Ik 50.38N 4.21W
La Unión [Bol.] 55 Bb 15.18S 61.05W
La Unión [Chile] 56 Ff 40.17S 73.05W
La Unión [Col.] 54 Cc 1.37N 77.08W
La Unión [ElSal.] 47 Gf 13.20N 87.51W
La Unión [Mex.] 48 Ii 17.58N 101.49W
La Unión [Peru] 54 Ce 9.46S 76.48W
La Unión [Sp.] 13 Lg 37.37N 0.52W
La Unión [Ven.] 49 Ni 8.13N 67.46W
Laura 59 Ic 15.34S 144.28 E
La Urbana 50 Ci 7.08N 66.56W
Laurel [Ms.-U.S.] 43 Je 31.42N 89.08W
Laurel [Mt.-U.S.] 43 Fb 45.40N 108.46W
Laureles 55 Ej 31.23S 55.52W
Laurel Hill 44 He 40.02N 79.17W
Laurel Mountain 44 Hf 39.20N 79.50W
Laurens 44 Fh 34.30N 82.01W
Laurentian Plateau (EN)= Laurentien, Plateau- 38 Md 50.00N 70.00W
Laurentian Scarp 44 Ic 45.50N 76.15W
Laurentide Scarp 44 Kb 46.38N 73.00W
Laurentien, Plateau-= Laurentian Plateau (EN) 38 Md 50.00N 70.00W
Lauria 14 Jj 40.02N 15.50 E
Lau Ridge (EN) 3 Kl 25.00S 179.00 E
Laurie River 42 He 56.00N 100.58W
Laurinburg 44 Hh 34.47N 79.27W
Laurium 44 Cb 47.14N 88.26W
Lauro Muller 55 Hi 28.24S 49.23W
Lausanne 6 Gf 46.30N 6.40 E
Lausitzer Gebirge 10 Kf 50.48N 14.40 E
Lausitzer Neiße 10 Kd 52.04N 14.46 E
Laut, Pulau- 26 Ef 4.43N 107.59 E
Laut, Pulau- 21 Nj 3.40S 116.10 E
Lautaret, Col du- 11 Mi 45.02N 6.24 E
Lautaro 56 Fe 38.31S 72.27W
Lautém 26 Ih 8.22S 126.54 E
Lauter 10 Eg 48.58N 8.11 E
Lauterbach 10 Ff 50.38N 9.24 E
Lauterbourg 12 Kf 48.59N 8.11 E
Lauterecken 12 Je 49.39N 7.36 E
Lauthala 63d Cb 16.45S 179.41W
Laut Kecil, Kepulauan- 26 Gg 4.50S 115.45 E
Lautoka 61 Ec 17.37S 177.27 E
Lauvergne Island 64d Cb 7.00N 152.00 E
Lauwersmeer 12 Ia 53.25N 6.15 E
Lauzerte 11 Hj 44.15N 1.08 E
Lauzon 44 Lb 46.50N 71.10W
Lauzoue 11 Gj 44.03N 0.15 E
Lava 10 Rb 54.37N 21.14 E
Lava, Nosy- [Mad.] 37 Hb 12.49S 48.41 E
Lava, Nosy- [Mad.] 37 Hb 14.33S 47.36 E
Lavaca River 45 Hl 28.50N 96.36W
Lava Flow 45 Bi 34.45N 108.20W
Laval 11 Ff 48.01N 0.46W
Lavalle 55 Ci 29.01S 59.11W
Lavalleja [2] 55 El 34.00S 55.00W
Lāvān, Jazīreh-ye- 23 Hd 26.48N 53.00 E
Lavanggu 63a Ed 11.37S 160.15 E
Lavant 14 Id 46.38N 14.56 E
Lavapié, Punta- 52 Ii 37.09S 73.35W
Lāvar Meydān 24 Pg 30.20N 54.30 E
Lavassaare 8 Kf 58.29N 24.16 E
Lavaur 11 Hk 43.42N 1.49 E
La Vecilla 13 Gb 42.51N 5.24W
La Vega 47 Je 19.13N 70.31W
La Vela de Coro 49 Mh 11.27N 69.34W
Lavelanet 11 Hl 42.56N 1.51 E
Lavello 14 Ji 41.03N 15.48 E
La Venta 47 Fe 18.08N 94.03W
Laventie 12 Ed 50.38N 2.46 E
La Ventura 48 Ie 24.37N 100.54W
La Vera 13 Gd 40.05N 5.30W
L'Averdy, Cape- 63a Ba 5.33S 155.04 E
Laverton 59 Ee 28.38S 122.25 E
Lavia 7 Ff 61.36N 22.36 E
La Victoria 54 Ea 10.14N 67.20W
La Vila Jojosa/Villajoyosa 13 Lf 38.30N 0.14W
La Villita, Presa- 48 Hh 18.05N 102.05W
La Viña 54 Ce 6.54S 79.28W

Index Symbols

[1] Independent Nation
[2] State, Region
[3] District, County
[4] Municipality
[5] Colony, Dependency
Continent
Physical Region
Historical or Cultural Region
Mount, Mountain
Volcano
Hill
Mountains, Mountain Range
Hills, Escarpment
Plateau, Upland
Pass, Gap
Plain, Lowland
Delta
Salt Flat
Valley, Canyon
Crater, Cave
Karst Features
Depression
Polder
Desert, Dunes
Forest, Woods
Heath, Steppe
Oasis
Cape, Point
Coast, Beach
Cliff
Peninsula
Isthmus
Sandbank
Island
Atoll
Rock, Reef
Islands, Archipelago
Rocks, Reefs
Coral Reef
Well, Spring
Geyser
River, Stream
Waterfall Rapids
River Mouth, Estuary
Lake
Salt Lake
Intermittent Lake
Reservoir
Swamp, Pond
Canal
Glacier
Ice Shelf, Pack Ice
Ocean
Sea
Gulf, Bay
Strait, Fjord
Lagoon
Bank
Seamount
Tablemount
Ridge
Shelf
Basin
Escarpment, Sea Scarp
Fracture
Trench, Abyss
National Park, Reserve
Point of Interest
Recreation Site
Cave, Cavern
Historic Site
Ruins
Wall, Walls
Church, Abbey
Temple
Scientific Station
Airport
Port
Lighthouse
Mine
Tunnel
Dam, Bridge

La Vôge	11	Mf	48.05N	6.05 E
Lavoisier Island	66	Qe	66.12S	66.44W
Lavougba	35	Cd	5.37N	23.19 E
La Voulte-sur-Rhône	11	Kj	44.48N	4.47 E
Lavouras	55	Db	14.59S	56.47W
Lavras	54	Jh	21.14S	45.00W
Lavras do Sul	55	Fj	30.49S	53.55W
Lavrentija	20	Nc	65.33N	171.02W
Lávrion	15	Hl	37.43N	24.03 E
Lavumisa	37	Ee	27.15S	31.55 E
Lawas	26	Gf	4.51N	115.24 E
Lawdar	23	Gg	13.53N	45.52 E
Lawe	12	Ed	50.38N	2.42 E
Lawers, Ben-	9	Ie	56.33N	4.15W
Lawit, Gunong-	26	Ff	1.23N	112.55 E
Lawqah	24	Jh	29.49N	42.45 E
Lawra	34	Ec	10.39N	2.52W
Lawrence [Ks.-U.S.]	43	Hd	38.58N	95.14W
Lawrence [Ma.-U.S.]	43	Mc	42.42N	71.09W
Lawrence [N.Z.]	62	Cf	45.55S	169.42 E
Lawrenceburg [Ky.-U.S.]	44	Ef	38.02N	84.54W
Lawrenceburg [Tn.-U.S.]	44	Dh	35.15N	87.20W
Lawson, Mount-	59	Ja	7.44S	146.37 E
Lawton	39	Jf	34.37N	98.25W
Lawu, Gunung-	21	Nj	7.38S	111.11 E
Lawz, Jabal al-	24	Fh	28.41N	35.18 E
Laxå	7	Dg	58.59N	14.37 E
Lay	11	Eh	46.18N	1.17W
Laylá	23	Ge	22.17N	46.45 E
Layon	11	Fg	47.20N	0.45W
Layou	51g	Bb	15.23N	61.26W
Layou	51n	Ba	13.12N	61.17W
Laysan Island	57	Jb	25.50N	171.50W
Layton	46	Jf	41.04N	111.58W
La Zarca	48	Ge	25.50N	104.44W
Lazarev	20	Jf	52.13N	141.35 E
Lazarevac	15	De	44.23N	20.16 E
Lázaro Cárdenas, Presa-	48	Ge	25.35N	105.05W
Lazdijai/Lazdijaj	7	Fi	54.13N	23.33 E
Lazdijaj/Lazdijai	7	Fi	54.13N	23.33 E
Lāzeh	24	Oi	26.48N	53.22 E
Lazio = Latium (EN) [2]	14	Gh	42.02N	12.23 E
Lazo	28	Mc	43.25N	134.01 E
Lazovsk	16	Ff	47.38N	28.12 E
Łazy	10	Pf	50.27N	19.26 E
Lea	9	Nj	51.30N	0.01 E
Lead	43	Gc	44.21N	103.46W
Leader	46	Ka	50.53N	109.31W
Lead Hill	45	Jh	37.06N	92.38W
Leadville	43	Fd	39.15N	106.20W
Leaf River	45	Lk	31.00N	88.45W
League City	45	Il	29.31N	95.05W
Leamington	44	Fd	42.03N	82.36W
Leandro N. Alem	55	Bl	34.30S	61.24W
Leane, Lough-/Loch Léin	9	Di	52.05N	9.35W
Le'an Jiang	28	Dj	28.58N	116.41 E
Learmonth	59	Cd	22.13S	114.04 E
Leavenworth [Ks.-U.S.]	45	Ig	39.19N	94.55W
Leavenworth [Wa.-U.S.]	46	Ec	47.36N	120.40W
Łeba	10	Nb	54.47N	17.33 E
Łeba	10	Nb	54.43N	17.25 E
Lebach	12	Ie	49.24N	6.55 E
Lébamba	36	Bc	2.12S	11.30 E
Lebanon [In.-U.S.]	44	De	40.03N	86.28W
Lebanon [Ky.-U.S.]	44	Eg	37.34N	85.15W
Lebanon [Mo.-U.S.]	45	Jh	37.41N	92.40W
Lebanon [N.H.-U.S.]	44	Kd	43.38N	72.15W
Lebanon [Or.-U.S.]	46	Dd	44.32N	122.54W
Lebanon [Pa.-U.S.]	44	Ie	40.21N	76.25W
Lebanon [Tn.-U.S.]	44	Dg	36.12N	86.18W
Lebanon (EN) = Lubnān [1]	22	Ff	33.50N	35.50 E
Lebanon Mountains (EN) = Lubnān, Jabal-	23	Ec	34.00N	36.30 E
Lebap	18	Cd	41.02N	61.54 E
Le Bec-Hellouin	12	Ce	49.14N	0.43 E
Lebedin	19	De	50.36N	34.30 E
Lebediny	20	He	58.25N	125.58 E
Lebedjan	19	De	53.02N	39.07 E
Le Bény-Bocage	12	Bf	48.56N	0.50W
Lebjažje [Kaz.-U.S.S.R.]	19	He	51.28N	77.46 E
Lebjažje [R.S.F.S.R.]	17	Mi	55.16N	66.29 E
Le Blanc	11	Hh	46.38N	1.04 E
Lebo	36	Db	4.29N	23.57 E
Lebomboberge	30	Kk	26.15S	32.00 E
Lebombo Mountains	30	Kk	26.15S	32.00 E
Lębork	10	Nb	54.33N	17.44 E
Le Bourget	12	Ef	48.56N	2.25 E
Lebrija	13	Fh	36.55N	6.04W
Łebsko, Jezioro-	10	Nb	54.44N	17.24 E
Lebu	56	Fe	37.37S	73.39W
Le Carbet	51h	Ab	14.43N	61.11W
Le Cateau	12	Fd	50.06N	3.33 E
Le Catelet	12	Fd	50.01N	3.15 E
Lecce	6	Hg	40.23N	18.11 E
Lecco	14	De	45.51N	9.23 E
Lech	10	Gh	48.44N	10.56 E
Lech	14	Ec	47.12N	10.09 E
Le Champ du Feu	11	Nf	48.24N	7.15 E
Lechang	27	Jf	25.15N	113.25 E
Le Château-d'Oléron	11	Ei	45.54N	1.12W
Le Chesne	11	Ke	49.31N	4.46 E
Le Cheylard	11	Kj	44.54N	4.25 E
Lechfeld	10	Gh	48.10N	10.50 E
Lechiguiri, Cerro-	48	Li	16.43N	95.30W
Lechtaler Alpen	14	Ec	47.15N	10.30 E
Léconi	36	Bc	1.11S	13.16 E
Léconi	36	Bc	1.35S	14.14 E
Le Cornate	14	Eg	43.10N	10.58 E
Le Coudray-Saint-Germer	12	De	49.25N	1.50 E
Le Creusot	11	Kh	46.48N	4.26 E
Le Croisic	11	Dg	47.18N	2.30W
Le Crotoy	12	Dd	50.13N	1.37 E
Łęczna	10	Se	51.19N	22.52 E
Łęczyca	10	Pd	52.04N	19.13 E
Led	7	Ke	62.20N	43.00 E
Lede	12	Fd	50.57N	3.59 E
Ledesma	13	Gc	41.05N	6.00W
Le Diamant	51h	Ac	14.29N	61.02W
Ledjanaja, Gora- [R.S.F.S.R.]	21	Tc	61.45N	171.15 E
Ledjanaja, Gora- [R.S.F.S.R.]	21	Qe	49.28N	142.45 E
Lednik Entuziastov	66	Cf	70.30S	16.00 E
Lednik Mušketova	66	Cf	72.00S	14.00 E
Ledo, Cabo-	36	Bd	9.41S	13.12 E
Ledolom Tajmyrski	66	Ge	66.00S	83.00 E
Le Donjon	11	Jh	46.21N	3.48 E
Le Dorat	11	Hh	46.13N	1.05 E
Lędyczek	10	Mc	53.33N	16.58 E
Lee/An Laoi	9	Ej	51.55N	8.30W
Leech Lake	43	Ib	47.09N	94.23W
Leeds [Al.-U.S.]	44	Di	33.33N	86.33W
Leeds [Eng.-U.K.]	6	Fe	53.50N	1.35W
Leeds [N.D.-U.S.]	45	Gb	48.17N	99.27W
Leek	12	Ia	53.10N	6.24 E
Leer	10	Dc	53.14N	7.26 E
Leer (Ostfriesland)	10	Dc	53.14N	7.26 E
Leerdam	12	Hc	51.53N	5.06 E
Lées	11	Fk	43.38N	0.14W
Leesburg	43	Kf	29.49N	81.53W
Leeste, Weyhe-	12	Kb	52.59N	8.50 E
Leesville	45	Jk	31.08N	93.16W
Leeuwarden	11	La	53.12N	5.46 E
Leeuwarderadeel	12	Ha	53.16N	5.46 E
Leeuwarderadeel-Stiens	12	Ha	53.16N	5.46 E
Leeuwin, Cape-	59	Cf	34.25S	115.00 E
Leeward Islands	47	Le	17.00N	63.00W
Leeward Islands (EN) = Sous le Vent, Iles-	57	Lf	16.38S	151.30W
Léfini	36	Cc	2.57S	16.10 E
Lefka	15	Jh	41.52N	26.16 E
Lefke/Levka	24	Ee	35.07N	32.51 E
Lefkosa/Levkōsia = Nicosia (EN)	22	Ff	35.10N	33.22 E
Le François	51h	Bb	14.37N	60.54W
Lefroy, Lake-	59	Ef	31.15S	121.40 E
Łęg	10	Rf	50.38N	21.49 E
Leganés	13	Id	40.19N	3.45W
Legazpi	22	Oh	13.09N	123.44 E
Legden	12	Jb	52.02N	7.06 E
Legges Tor	59	Jh	41.32S	147.40 E
Leggett	46	Dg	39.52N	123.43W
Leghorn (EN) = Livorno	6	Hg	43.33N	10.19 E
Legionowo	10	Qd	52.25N	20.56 E
Léglise	12	He	49.48N	5.32 E
Legnago	14	Fe	45.11N	11.18 E
Legnano	14	Ce	45.36N	8.54 E
Legnica [2]	10	Me	51.15N	16.10 E
Legnica	10	Me	51.13N	16.09 E
Le Grand-Quevilly	12	De	49.25N	1.02 E
Le Grand Veymont	11	Lj	44.52N	5.32 E
Le Grau-du-Roi	11	Kk	43.32N	4.08 E
Léguer	11	Cf	48.44N	3.32W
Leh	25	Fb	34.10N	77.35 E
Le Havre	6	Gf	49.30N	0.08 E
Lehi	46	Jf	40.24N	111.51W
Lehmann	55	Bj	31.08S	61.27W
Le Hohneck	11	Nf	48.02N	7.01 E
Le Houlme	12	De	49.31N	1.02 E
Lehrte	10	Fd	52.23N	9.58 E
Lehtimäki	8	Jb	62.47N	23.55 E
Lehua Island	65a	Aa	22.01N	160.06W
Lehututu	37	Cd	23.53S	21.49 E
Leibnitz	14	Jd	46.46N	15.32 E
Leibo	27	Hf	28.13N	103.34 E
Leicester	6	Fe	52.38N	1.05W
Leicester	9	Mi	52.40N	1.00W
Leicestershire [3]	9	Mi	52.38N	1.00W
Leichhardt Range	59	Jd	20.40S	147.05 E
Leichhardt River	59	Hc	17.35S	139.48 E
Leiden	11	Kc	52.09N	4.30 E
Leidschendam	12	Gb	52.05N	4.26 E
Leie	11	Jc	51.03N	3.43 E
Leifear/Lifford	9	Fg	54.50N	7.29W
Leigh Creek	58	Eh	30.28S	138.25 E
Leighton Buzzard	12	Bc	51.55N	0.39W
Leigong Shan	27	If	26.23N	108.15 E
Leikanger	7	Ae	62.07N	5.20 E
Léim an Mhadaidh/Limavady	9	Gf	55.03N	6.57W
Leimen	12	Ke	49.21N	8.41 E
Leimus	49	Ef	14.44N	84.07W
Leine	10	Fd	52.40N	9.40 E
Leinster/Laighean	9	Gh	53.00N	7.00W
Leipzig	6	He	51.18N	12.20 E
Leipzig [2]	10	Ie	51.20N	12.20 E
Leira	8	Cd	60.58N	9.18 E
Leiria [2]	13	De	39.40N	8.50W
Leiria	13	De	39.45N	8.48W
Leirvik	7	Ag	59.47N	5.30 E
Leisi/Lejsi	8	Jf	58.33N	22.30 E
Leisler, Mount-	59	Fd	23.30S	129.20 E
Leiston	12	Db	52.12N	1.34 E
Leitariegos, Puerto de-	13	Fa	43.00N	6.25W
Leitha	14	Lc	47.52N	17.18 E
Leithagebirge	14	Kc	47.58N	16.40 E
Leitir Ceanainn/Letterkenny	9	Fg	54.57N	7.44W
Leitrim/Liatroim [2]	9	Eg	54.20N	8.20W
Leiva, Cerro-	54	Dc	2.54N	74.48W
Leiyang	27	Jf	26.30N	112.57 E
Leizhou → Haikang	27	Jg	20.56N	110.06 E
Leizhou Bandao	21	Ng	20.40N	110.05 E
Lejasciems	8	Lg	57.08N	26.36 E
Lejsi/Leisi	8	Jf	58.33N	22.30 E
Lek	11	Lc	52.00N	6.00 E
Leka	7	Cd	65.05N	11.37 E
Lékana	36	Cc	2.19S	14.36 E
Leketi, Monts de la-	30	Ii	2.34S	14.17 E
Lekhainá	15	El	37.56N	21.16 E
Lekhal	13	Ph	36.20N	3.51 E
Lekitobi	26	Hg	1.58S	124.33 E
Lekki Lagoon	34	Fd	6.30N	4.07 E
Leknes	7	Cb	68.10N	13.42 E
Łęknica	10	Ke	51.32N	14.48 E
Lékoumou [3]	36	Bc	3.00S	13.50 E
Leksand	7	Df	60.44N	15.01 E
Leksozero, Ozero-	7	He	63.45N	31.00 E
Leksula	26	Ig	3.46S	126.31 E
Leksvik	7	Ce	63.40N	10.37 E
Le Lamentin	50	Fe	14.37N	61.01W
Leland	45	Kj	33.24N	90.54W
Lelång	8	Ee	59.10N	12.10 E
Le Lavandou	11	Mk	43.08N	6.22 E
Lelčicy	16	Fd	51.49N	28.21 E
Leleiwi Point	65a	Gd	19.44N	155.00W
Lelepa	63b	Dc	17.36S	168.13 E
Leleque	56	Ff	42.23S	71.03W
Leli	63a	Ec	8.45S	161.02 E
Leli → Tianlin	27	Ig	24.22N	106.11 E
Lelija	14	Mg	43.26N	18.29 E
Leling	28	Df	37.44N	117.13 E
Léliogat	63b	Ce	21.18S	167.35 E
Lelle	7	Fg	58.53N	25.00 E
Le Locle	14	Ac	47.05N	6.45 E
Le Lorrain	51h	Ab	14.50N	61.04W
Lelystad	11	Lb	52.31N	5.27 E
Le Madonie	14	Hm	37.50N	14.00 E
Le Maire, Estrecho de-	56	Hh	54.50S	65.00W
Léman, Lac- = Geneva, Lake- (EN)	5	Gf	46.25N	6.30 E
Leman Bank	9	Oh	53.10N	1.58 E
Lemankoa	63a	Ba	5.03S	154.34 E
Le Mans	6	Gf	48.00N	0.12 E
Le Marin	51h	Bc	14.28N	60.52W
Le Mars	45	He	42.47N	96.10W
Le Mas-d'Azil	11	Hk	43.05N	1.22 E
Lembach	12	Je	49.00N	7.48 E
Lembeck	12	Ic	51.44N	6.59 E
Lemberg	12	Je	49.00N	7.23 E
Lembolovskaja Vozvyšennost	8	Md	60.50N	30.15 E
Lembruch	12	Kb	52.32N	8.21 E
Leme	55	If	22.12S	47.24W
Lemelerberg	12	Ib	52.29N	6.23 E
Lemesós/Limassol	23	Dc	34.40N	33.02 E
Lemgo	10	Ed	52.02N	8.54 E
Lemhi Range	46	Id	44.30N	113.25W
Lemieux Islands	42	Ld	64.00N	64.20W
Lemju	17	He	63.50N	56.57 E
Lemland	8	Id	60.05N	20.10 E
Lemmer, Lemsterland-	12	Hb	52.51N	5.42 E
Lemmon	43	Gb	45.56N	102.10W
Lemmon, Mount-	46	Jj	32.26N	110.47W
Lemnos (EN) = Límnos	5	Ih	39.55N	25.15 E
Le-Molay-Littry	12	Be	49.15N	0.53W
Le-Mont-Saint-Michel	11	Ef	48.38N	1.30W
Le Morne Rouge	51h	Ab	14.46N	61.08W
Lemotol Bay	64d	Bb	7.21N	151.35 E
Le Moyne, Lac -	42	Ke	57.00N	68.00W
Lempa, Río-	47	Gf	13.14N	88.49W
Lempäälä	8	Jc	61.19N	23.45 E
Lempira [3]	49	Cf	14.20N	88.40W
L'Empordà/Ampurdán	13	Ob	42.12N	2.45 E
Lemro	25	Id	20.25N	93.20 E
Lemsid	32	Ed	26.33N	13.51W
Lemsterland	12	Hb	52.51N	5.42 E
Lemsterland-Lemmer	12	Hb	52.51N	5.42 E
Le Murge	5	Hg	40.50N	16.40 E
Le Muy	11	Mk	43.28N	6.33 E
Lemvig	8	Ch	56.32N	8.18 E
Lemya	17	Jc	66.30N	62.00 E
Lena	21	Ob	72.25N	126.40 E
Lena, Mount-	46	Kf	40.50N	109.27W
Lénakel	63b	Dd	19.32S	169.16 E
Lena Mountains (EN) = Prilenskoje Plato	21	Oc	60.45N	125.00 E
Lena Tablemount (EN)	30	Ln	53.00S	45.00 E
Lençóis Paulista	55	Hf	22.36S	48.47W
Lendava	14	Kd	46.34N	16.27 E
Lendery	7	He	63.26N	31.12 E
Lendinara	14	Fe	45.05N	11.36 E
Le Neubourg	12	Ce	49.09N	0.55 E
Lenger	19	Gg	42.10N	69.55 E
Lengerich	10	Dd	52.11N	7.52 E
Lengoué	36	Cb	0.49N	15.47 E
Lengshuijiang	27	Jf	27.41N	111.28 E
Lengua de Vaca, Punta-	56	Fd	30.14S	71.38W
Lengulu	36	Eb	3.15N	26.30 E
Lenhovda	7	Dh	57.00N	15.17 E
Lenina, Pik- = Lenin Peak (EN)	21	Jf	39.19N	73.01 E
Leninabad	22	Ie	40.17N	69.37 E
Leninabadskaja Oblast [3]	19	Gh	40.00N	69.10 E
Leninakan	6	Kg	40.47N	43.50 E
Lenin Canal (EN) = Volgo-Donskoj sudohodny kanal imeni V. I. Lenina	5	Kf	48.40N	43.37 E
Leningrad	6	Jc	59.55N	30.15 E
Leningradskaja	66	Je	69.30S	159.23 E
Leningradskaja	16	Kf	46.17N	39.25 E
Leningradskaja Oblast [3]	19	Dd	60.00N	31.40 E
Leningradski [R.S.F.S.R.]	20	Mc	69.17N	178.10 E
Leningradski [Tad.-U.S.S.R.]	19	Hh	38.09N	70.01 E
Lenino	16	Ig	45.17N	35.44 E
Leninogorsk [Kaz.-U.S.S.R.]	22	Kd	50.27N	83.32 E
Leninogorsk [R.S.F.S.R.]	19	Fe	54.38N	52.30 E
Lenin Peak (EN) = Lenina, Pik-	21	Jf	39.19N	73.01 E
Leninsk [R.S.F.S.R.]	16	Ne	48.42N	45.11 E
Leninsk [Tur.-U.S.S.R.]	18	Bc	42.04N	59.24 E
Leninsk [Uzb.-U.S.S.R.]	18	Id	40.40N	72.20 E
Leninski [Kaz.-U.S.S.R.]	19	He	52.13N	76.50 E
Leninski [Mold.-U.S.S.R.]	15	Lb	47.50N	28.16 E
Leninski [R.S.F.S.R.]	20	He	58.32N	125.58 E
Leninsk-Kuznecki	22	Kd	54.38N	86.10 E
Leninskoje [Kaz.-U.S.S.R.]	19	Ge	54.05N	65.23 E
Leninskoje [R.S.F.S.R.]	7	Lg	58.21N	47.07 E
Leninskoje [R.S.F.S.R.]	20	Ig	47.59N	132.38 E
Leninváros	10	Ri	47.56N	21.05 E
Lenkoran	6	Kh	38.44N	48.50 E
Lenne	10	De	51.25N	7.30 E
Lenne	12	Jc	51.15N	7.50 E
Lennestadt	12	Kc	51.08N	8.01 E
Lennestadt-Grevenbrück	12	Kc	51.08N	8.01 E
Lennox Hills	9	Ie	56.05N	4.10W
Leno-Angarskoje Plato	20	Fe	55.00N	104.30 E
Lenoir	44	Gh	35.55N	81.32W
Le Nouvion-en-Thiérache	12	Fd	50.01N	3.47 E
Lens	11	Id	50.26N	2.50 E
Lensk	22	Nc	61.00N	114.50 E
Lenti	10	Mi	46.37N	16.33 E
Lentiira	7	Gd	64.21N	29.50 E
Lentini	14	Jm	37.17N	15.01 E
Lentua	7	Gd	64.14N	29.36 E
Lentvaris	8	Kj	54.38N	25.13 E
Léo	34	Ec	11.06N	2.06W
Leoben	14	Jc	47.23N	15.06 E
Léogâne	49	Kd	18.31N	72.38W
Leok	26	Hf	1.11N	121.26 E
Leola	45	Gd	45.43N	98.56W
Leominster	9	Ki	52.14N	2.45W
León	13	Gc	42.00N	6.00W
Léon	11	Ek	43.53N	1.18W
León [Mex.]	39	Ig	21.10N	101.42W
León [Nic.] [3]	49	Dg	12.35N	86.35W
León [Nic.]	39	Kh	12.26N	86.54W
León [Sp.]	6	Fg	42.36N	5.34W
León [Sp.] [3]	13	Gb	42.40N	6.00W
León, Montes de-	13	Fb	42.30N	6.20W
León, Puerto del-	13	Hh	36.50N	4.21W
Leonardville	37	Bd	23.29S	18.49 E
Leonberg	12	Kf	48.48N	9.01 E
Leone, Monte-	14	Cd	46.15N	8.10 E
Leones	55	Ak	32.39S	62.18W
Leonessa	14	Gh	42.34N	12.58 E
Leonforte	14	Im	37.38N	14.23 E
Leōnidhion	15	Fl	37.10N	22.52 E
Leonora	58	Dg	28.53S	121.20 E
Leon River	45	Hk	30.59N	97.24W
Leopold and Astrid Coast	66	Ge	67.10S	84.10 E
Leopoldina	54	Jh	21.32S	42.38W
Leopold McClintock, Cape -	42	Fa	77.38N	116.20W
Leopoldo de Bulhões	55	Hc	16.37S	48.46W
Leopoldsburg	12	Hc	51.07N	5.15 E
Leopoldville → Kinshasa	31	Ii	4.18S	15.18 E
Leovo	16	Ff	46.29N	28.15 E
Lepa	65c	Bb	14.01S	171.28W
Le Palais	11	Cg	47.21N	3.09W
Lepar, Pulau-	26	Eg	2.57S	106.50 E
Le Parcq	12	Ed	50.23N	2.06 E
Lepaterique	49	Df	14.02N	87.27W
Lepe	13	Eg	37.15N	7.12W
Lepel	19	Ce	54.53N	28.46 E
Lepenica	15	Ee	44.10N	21.08 E
Le Petit Caux	12	De	49.55N	1.20 E
Le Petit-Couronne	12	De	49.23N	1.01 E
Le Petit-Quevilly	12	De	49.26N	1.02 E
Lephepe	37	Dd	23.22S	25.52 E
Leping	27	Kf	28.59N	117.07 E
Lepini, Monti-	14	Gi	41.35N	13.00 E
Le Plessis-Belleville	12	Ee	49.06N	2.46 E
Le Pont-de-Claix	11	Li	45.07N	5.42 E
Le Portel	12	Dd	50.42N	1.34 E
Leppävesi	8	Kb	62.15N	25.55 E
Leppävirta	8	Lb	62.29N	27.47 E
Le Prêcheur	51h	Ab	14.48N	61.14W
Lepsøya	8	Bb	62.35N	6.10 E
Lepsy	18	La	46.18N	78.20 E
Lepsy	19	Hf	46.12N	78.55 E
Leptis Magna	33	Bc	32.38N	14.18 E
Le Puy	11	Ji	45.02N	3.53 E
Leqemt (EN) = Nekemt	31	Kh	9.05N	36.33 E
Le Quesnoy	12	Fd	50.15N	3.38 E
Lercara Friddi	14	Hm	37.45N	13.36 E
Lerchenfeld Glacier	66	Af	77.50S	34.50W
Lere	34	Gc	10.23N	8.35 E
Léré	35	Ad	9.39N	14.13 E
Lérida	54	Dc	0.06N	70.43W
Lérida [3]	13	Nc	42.00N	1.10 E
Lérida/Lleida	13	Mc	41.37N	0.37 E
Lérins, Iles de-	11	Nk	43.31N	7.03 E
Lerma	13	Ib	42.02N	3.45W
Lerma, Río-	48	Hg	20.13N	102.46W
Lermontov	16	Mg	44.06N	42.45 E
Le Robert	51h	Bb	14.41N	60.57W
Léros	15	Jl	37.08N	26.50 E
Lerum	7	Ch	57.46N	12.16 E
Lerwick	9	La	60.09N	1.09W
Léry	12	De	49.17N	1.13 E
Les Abrets	11	Li	45.32N	5.35 E
Le Saint-Esprit	51h	Bb	14.34N	60.57W
Les Alberes/Albères, Montes-	11	In	42.28N	2.56 E
Les Allobroges	63b	Dc	16.47S	168.09 E
Les Andelys	11	He	49.15N	1.25 E
Les Anses-d'Arlets	51h	Ac	14.29N	61.05W
Les-Baux-de-Provence	11	Kk	43.45N	4.48 E
Les Borges Blanques/Borjas Blancas	13	Mc	41.31N	0.52 E
Lesbos (EN) = Lésvos	5	Ih	39.10N	26.32 E
L'Escala/La Escala	13	Pb	42.07N	3.08 E
Les Cayes	47	Je	18.12N	73.45W
Les Coëvrons	11	Ff	48.12N	0.10W
Le Serre	14	Kl	38.30N	16.30 E
Les Escoumins	44	Ma	48.25N	69.29W
Les Eyzies-de-Tayac	11	Hj	44.56N	1.01 E
Les Falaises	12	Ce	49.44N	0.21 E
Leshan	27	Hf	29.34N	103.45 E
Les Herbiers	11	Eh	46.52N	1.01W
Lesina, Lago di-	14	Ji	41.55N	15.25 E
Lesja	8	Cb	62.07N	8.52 E
Lesjöfors	7	Dg	59.59N	14.11 E
Leskino	20	Cb	72.25N	79.40 E
Lesko	10	Sg	49.29N	22.21 E
Leskov	66	Ad	56.40S	28.10W
Leskovac	15	Eg	42.59N	21.57 E
Leskoviku	15	Di	40.09N	20.35 E
Les Mangles	51e	Ab	16.23N	61.27W
Les Mauges	11	Fg	47.10N	1.00W
Les Minquiers	9	Km	48.58N	2.08W
Les Monédières	11	Hi	45.30N	1.52 E
Les Mureaux	12	Df	49.00N	1.55 E
Lesnaja	10	Vd	52.55N	25.52 E
Lesnaja	16	Cc	52.11N	23.30 E
Lesneven	11	Bf	48.34N	4.19W
Lešnica	15	Ce	44.39N	19.19 E
Lesnoj [R.S.F.S.R.]	19	Gd	57.01N	67.50 E
Lesnoj [R.S.F.S.R.]	19	Fd	59.49N	52.10 E
Lesnoj, Ostrov-	8	Md	60.02N	28.20 E
Lesný	10	If	50.02N	12.37 E
Lesogorski	8	Mc	61.01N	28.51 E
Lesosibirsk	22	Ld	58.15N	92.30 E
Lesotho [1]	31	Jk	29.30S	28.30 E
Lesozavodsk	20	Ig	45.26N	133.25 E
Lesozavodski	7	Hc	66.45N	32.50 E
Lesparre-Médoc	11	Fi	45.18N	0.56W
L'Espérance Rock	57	Jh	31.26S	178.54W
Les Ponts-de-Cé	11	Fg	47.25N	0.31W
Les Posets	13	Mb	42.39N	0.25 E
Les Sables-d'Olonne	11	Eh	46.30N	1.47W
Lessay	11	Ee	49.13N	1.32W
Lesse	11	Kd	50.14N	4.54 E
Lessebo	7	Dh	56.45N	15.16 E
Lessen/Lessines	12	Fd	50.43N	3.50 E
Les Sept Iles	11	Cf	48.53N	3.28W
Lesser Antilles (EN) = Antillas Menores	38	Mh	15.00N	61.00W
Lesser Caucasus (EN) = Maly Kavkaz	5	Kg	41.00N	44.35 E
Lesser Khingan Range (EN) = Xiao Hinggan Ling	21	Oe	48.45N	127.00 E
Lesser Slave Lake	38	Hd	55.25N	115.30W
Lesser Sunda Islands (EN)	21	Oj	9.13S	121.12 E
Lessines/Lessen	12	Fd	50.43N	3.50 E
Lessini	14	Fe	45.41N	11.13 E
Les Tantes	51p	Bb	12.19N	61.33W
Les Thilliers-en-Vexin	12	De	49.14N	1.36 E
Les Triagoz	11	Cf	48.53N	3.40W
Les Trois-Ilets	51h	Ab	14.33N	61.03W
Lešukonskoje	7	Kd	64.52N	45.40 E
Lésvos = Lesbos (EN)	5	Ih	39.10N	26.32 E
Leszno [2]	10	Me	51.50N	16.35 E
Leszno	10	Me	51.51N	16.35 E
Letälven	8	Fe	59.05N	14.20 E
Le Tanargue	11	Kj	44.37N	4.09 E
Letchworth	12	Bc	51.58N	0.13W
Letea, Ostrovul-	15	Md	45.20N	29.20 E
Le Teil	11	Kj	44.33N	4.41 E
Letenye	10	Mj	46.26N	16.44 E
Lethbridge	39	He	49.42N	110.50W
Lethem	53	Ke	3.20N	59.50W
Le Thillot	11	Mg	47.53N	6.46 E
Leti, Kepulauan- = Leti Islands (EN)	26	Ih	8.13S	127.50 E
Letiahau	30	Jk	21.04S	24.25 E
Leticia	53	Jf	4.09S	69.57W
Leti Islands (EN) = Leti, Kepulauan-	26	Ih	8.13S	127.50 E
Leting	28	Ee	39.25N	118.55 E
Letka	7	Mg	58.59N	50.14 E
Letlhakane	37	Dd	21.25S	25.36 E
Letnerečenski	7	Id	64.19N	34.25 E
Letni Bereg	7	Jd	64.50N	38.20 E
Letohrad	10	Mf	50.03N	16.31 E
Le Touquet-Paris-Plage	11	Hd	50.31N	1.35 E
Letovice	10	Mg	49.33N	16.36 E
Letpadan	25	Je	17.47N	95.45 E
Le Translay	12	De	49.58N	1.41 E
Le Tréport	11	Hd	50.04N	1.22 E
Letsôk-aw Kyun	25	Jf	11.37N	98.15 E
Letterkenny/Leitir = Ceanainn	9	Fg	54.57N	7.44W
Leu	15	Ge	44.11N	24.00 E
Leuca	14	Mk	39.48N	18.21 E
Leucas (EN) = Levkás	15	Dk	38.43N	20.38 E
Leucate	11	Jl	42.55N	3.02 E
Leucate, Étang de-	11	Il	42.51N	3.00 E
Leuk	14	Bd	46.20N	7.38 E
Leukónoikon	24	Ee	35.15N	33.42 E
Leulumoega	65c	Ba	13.49S	171.55W
Leuna	10	Ie	51.19N	12.01 E
Leušeny	15	Lc	46.51N	28.11 E
Leuser, Gunung-	21	Li	3.45N	97.11 E
Leutkirch im Allgäu	10	Gi	47.50N	10.02 E
Leuven/Louvain	11	Kd	50.53N	4.42 E
Leuze-en-Hainaut	12	Fd	50.36N	3.36 E
Levádhia	15	Fk	38.26N	22.53 E
Levaja Hetta	20	Cc	65.15N	73.20 E
Levanger	7	Ce	63.45N	11.18 E
Levante, Riviera di-	14	Df	44.15N	9.30 E
Levanzo	14	Gm	38.00N	12.20 E
Levaši	16	Oh	42.27N	47.20 E
Le Vauclin	51h	Bb	14.33N	60.51W
Levelland	45	Ej	33.35N	102.23W
Lévêque, Cape-	59	Ec	16.25S	122.55 E
Le Verdon-sur-Mer	11	Ei	45.33N	1.04W
Leverkusen	10	Ce	51.01N	6.59 E
Leverkusen-Opladen	10	De	51.04N	7.01 E
Lévèzou	11	Ij	44.09N	2.53 E
Levice	10	Oh	48.13N	18.37 E
Levico Terme	14	Fd	46.01N	11.18 E
Le Vigan	11	Jk	43.59N	3.36 E
Levin	61	Eh	40.37S	175.17 E
Lévis	42	Kg	46.48N	71.10W
Levisa Fork	44	Ff	38.06N	82.37W
Levitha	15	Jm	37.00N	26.28 E
Levittown	44	Je	40.09N	74.50W
Levka/Lefke	24	Ee	35.07N	32.51 E
Levká Óri	15	Gn	35.20N	24.00 E
Levkás	15	Dk	38.50N	20.42 E
Levkás = Leucas (EN)	15	Dk	38.43N	20.38 E

Index Symbols

- [1] Independent Nation
- [2] State, Region
- [3] District, County
- Municipality
- Colony, Dependency
- Continent
- Physical Region
- Historical or Cultural Region
- Mount, Mountain
- Volcano
- Hill
- Mountains, Mountain Range
- Hills, Escarpment
- Plateau, Upland
- Pass, Gap
- Plain, Lowland
- Delta
- Salt Flat
- Valley, Canyon
- Crater, Cave
- Karst Features
- Depression
- Polder
- Desert, Dunes
- Forest, Woods
- Heath, Steppe
- Oasis
- Cape, Point
- Coast, Beach
- Cliff
- Peninsula
- Isthmus
- Sandbank
- Island
- Atoll
- Rock, Reef
- Islands, Archipelago
- Rocks, Reefs
- Coral Reef
- Well, Spring
- Geyser
- River, Stream
- Waterfall Rapids
- River Mouth, Estuary
- Lake
- Salt Lake
- Intermittent Lake
- Reservoir
- Swamp, Pond
- Canal
- Glacier
- Ice Shelf, Pack Ice
- Ocean
- Sea
- Gulf, Bay
- Strait, Fjord
- Lagoon
- Bank
- Seamount
- Tablemount
- Ridge
- Shelf
- Basin
- Escarpment, Sea Scarp
- Fracture
- Trench, Abyss
- National Park, Reserve
- Point of Interest
- Recreation Site
- Cave, Cavern
- Historic Site
- Ruins
- Wall, Walls
- Church, Abbey
- Temple
- Scientific Station
- Airport
- Port
- Lighthouse
- Mine
- Tunnel
- Dam, Bridge

Levkôsia/Lefkosa=Nicosia (EN) 22 Ff 35.10N 33.22 E
Levoča 10 Qg 49.02N 20.35 E
Levroux 11 Hh 46.59N 1.37 E
Levski 15 If 43.22N 25.08 E
Lev Tolstoj 16 Kc 53.12N 39.28 E
Levuka 63d Bb 17.41S 178.50 E
Lévuo/Lévuo 8 Kh 56.02N 24.28 E
Lévuo/Levuo 8 Kh 56.02N 24.28 E
Lewes [De.-U.S.] 44 Jf 38.47N 75.08W
Lewes [Eng.-U.K.] 9 Nk 50.52N 0.01 E
Lewin Brzeski 10 Nf 50.46N 17.37 E
Lewis, Butt of- 9 Gc 58.31N 6.15W
Lewis, Isle of- 5 Fd 58.10N 6.40W
Lewis and Clark Lake 45 He 42.50N 97.45W
Lewisburg 44 Gg 37.49N 80.28W
Lewis Pass 62 Ee 42.24S 172.24 E
Lewis Range 38 He 48.30N 113.15W
Lewis River 46 Dd 45.51N 122.48W
Lewis Smith Lake 44 Dh 34.00N 87.07W
Lewiston [Id.-U.S.] 39 He 46.25N 117.01W
Lewiston [Me.-U.S.] 43 Mc 44.06N 70.13W
Lewistown [Mt.-U.S.] 43 Fb 47.04N 109.26W
Lewistown [Pa.-U.S.] 44 Ie 40.37N 77.36W
Lewisville 45 Jj 33.22N 93.35W
Lexington [Ky.-U.S.] 39 Kf 38.03N 84.30W
Lexington [Nb.-U.S.] 43 Hc 40.47N 99.45W
Lexington [N.C.-U.S.] 44 Gh 35.49N 80.15W
Lexington [Ok.-U.S.] 45 Hi 35.01N 97.20W
Lexington [Va.-U.S.] 44 Hg 37.47N 79.27W
Leygues, Iles- 30 Nm 48.45S 69.30 E
Leyre 11 Ej 44.39N 1.01W
Leysdown-on-Sea 12 Cc 51.23N 0.55 E
Leyte 21 Oh 10.50N 124.50 E
Lez 11 Kj 44.13N 4.43 E
Ležajsk 10 Sf 50.16N 22.24 E
Lézard, Pointe à- 51e Ab 16.08N 61.47W
Lézarde, Rivière- 51h Ab 14.36N 61.01W
Lezha 15 Ch 41.47N 19.39 E
Lézignan-Corbières 11 Ik 43.12N 2.46 E
Lgov 19 De 51.41N 35.17 E
Lhari 27 Fe 30.48N 93.25 E
Lhasa 22 Lg 29.42N 91.07 E
Lhazê 27 Ef 29.13N 87.44 E
Lhazhong 27 Ee 31.28N 86.36 E
Lhokseumawe 26 Ce 5.10N 97.08 E
Lhoksukon 26 Ce 5.03N 97.19 E
L'Hôpital 12 Ie 49.10N 6.44 E
Lhorong 27 Ge 30.45N 95.48 E
L'Hospitalet de l'Infant/Hospitalet del Infante 13 Md 40.59N 0.56 E
Lhozhag 27 Ff 28.18N 90.51 E
Lhünzhub (Poindo) 27 Fe 30.17N 91.20 E
Liádhi 15 Jm 36.55N 26.10 E
Liákoura 15 Fk 38.32N 22.37 E
Liamone 11a Aa 42.04N 8.43 E
Liancheng 27 Kf 25.48N 116.48 E
Liancourt 12 Ee 49.20N 2.28 E
Liane 12 Dd 50.43N 1.36 E
Liangcheng 28 Bd 40.32N 112.28 E
Liangpran, Gunung- 26 Ff 1.04N 114.23 E
Liangshan (Houji) 28 Dg 35.48N 116.07 E
Liangzhou→Wuwei 22 Mf 37.58N 102.48 E
Liangzi Hu 27 Je 30.15N 114.32 E
Lianjiang 27 Jg 21.42N 110.14 E
Lianshui 28 Eh 33.47N 119.16 E
Lianxian 27 Jg 24.48N 112.26 E
Lianyin 27 La 53.26N 123.50 E
Lianyungang 27 Ke 34.38N 119.27 E
Lianyungang (Xinpu) 22 Nf 34.34N 119.15 E
Lianzhou → Hepu 27 Ig 21.40N 109.12 E
Lianzhushan 28 Kb 45.28N 131.45 E
Liaocheng 27 Kd 36.27N 115.58 E
Liaodong Bandao=Liaotung Peninsula (EN) 21 Of 40.00N 122.20 E
Liaodong Wan=Liaotung, Gulf of- (EN) 27 Lc 40.00N 121.30 E
Liao He 21 Oe 40.39N 122.12 E
Liaoning Sheng (Liao-ning Sheng) 27 Lc 41.00N 123.00 E
Liao-ning Sheng→Liaoning Sheng 27 Lc 41.00N 123.00 E
Liaotung, Gulf of- (EN)=Liaodong Wan 27 Lc 40.00N 121.30 E
Liaotung Peninsula (EN)=Liaodong Bandao 21 Of 40.00N 122.20 E
Liaoyang 27 Lc 41.16N 123.10 E
Liaoyuan 22 Oe 42.55N 125.09 E
Liaozhong 28 Gd 41.30N 122.42 E
Liard 38 Gc 61.52N 121.18W
Liard River 42 Ee 59.15N 126.09W
Liat, Pulau- 26 Eg 2.53S 107.05 E
Liatorp 8 Fh 56.40N 14.16 E
Liatroim/Leitrim 9 Eg 54.20N 8.20W
Liban 30 Lh 5.05N 40.05 E
Libano 55 Bm 37.32S 61.18W
Libby 46 Hb 48.23N 115.33W
Libenge 31 Ih 3.39N 18.38 E
Libengé 36 Cb 3.39N 18.38 E
Liberal 43 Gd 37.02N 100.55W
Liberec 10 Lf 50.46N 15.03 E
Liberia 47 Gf 10.38N 85.27W
Liberia 31 Fh 6.00N 10.00W
Libertad [Ur.] 55 Dl 34.38S 56.39W
Libertad [Ven.] 49 Li 8.08N 71.28W
Libertad [Ven.] 54 Eb 8.20N 69.37W
Libertade, Rio- 54 He 9.35S 52.17W
Libertador General Bernardo O'Higgins 56 Fd 33.35S 70.45W
Libertador Gen. San Martin 56 Hb 23.48S 64.48W
Libertador General San Martin, Cumbre del- 52 Jh 24.55S 66.40W
Liberty [Mo.-U.S.] 45 Ig 39.15N 94.25W
Liberty [Tx.-U.S.] 45 Ik 30.03N 94.47W
Lībiyā=Libya (EN) 31 If 27.00N 17.00 E
Lībīyah, Aş Şaḩrā' al-=Libyan Desert (EN) 30 Jf 24.00N 25.00 E
Libo 27 If 25.28N 107.52 E
Libobo, Tanjung- 26 Ig 0.54S 128.28 E
Liboi 36 Hb 0.24N 40.57 E
Libourne 11 Fj 44.55N 0.14W
Libramont-Chevigny 12 He 49.55N 5.23 E
Librazhdi 15 Dh 41.11N 20.19 E
Libreville 31 Hh 0.23N 9.27 E
Libro Point 26 Gd 11.26N 119.29 E
Libya (EN)=Lībiyā 31 If 27.00N 17.00 E
Libyan Desert (EN)=Lībīyah, Aş Şaḩrā' al- 30 Jf 24.00N 25.00 E
Licantén 56 Fe 34.59S 72.00W
Licata 14 Hm 37.06N 13.56 E
Lice 24 Ic 38.28N 40.39 E
Licenciado Matienzo 55 Cm 37.55S 58.54W
Lich 12 Kd 50.31N 8.50 E
Licheng → Jinhu 28 Eh 33.01N 119.01 E
Lichfield 9 Li 52.42N 1.48W
Lichinga 31 Kj 13.20S 35.20 E
Lichtenau 12 Kc 51.37N 8.54 E
Lichtenburg 37 De 26.08S 26.08 E
Lichtenfels 10 Hf 50.09N 11.04 E
Lichtenvoorde 12 Ic 51.59N 6.34 E
Licking River 44 Ef 39.06N 84.30W
Licosa, Punta- 14 Ij 40.15N 14.54 E
Licuare 37 Fc 17.54S 36.49 E
Licun → Laoshan 28 Ff 36.10N 120.25 E
Licungo 37 Fc 17.40S 37.22 E
Lida 19 Ce 53.56N 25.18 E
Lidan 8 Ef 58.31N 13.09 E
Liddel 9 Kf 55.04N 2.57W
Liddon Gulf 42 Gb 75.00N 113.30W
Liden 7 De 62.42N 16.48 E
Lidhorikion 15 Fk 38.32N 22.12 E
Lidhult 8 Eh 56.50N 13.26 E
Lidingö 7 Eg 59.22N 18.08 E
Lidköping 7 Cg 58.30N 13.10 E
Lido 34 Fc 12.54N 3.44 E
Lido, Venezia- 14 Ge 45.25N 12.22 E
Lido di Ostia 14 Gi 41.44N 12.16 E
Lidzbark 10 Pc 53.17N 19.49 E
Lidzbark Warmiński 10 Qb 54.09N 20.35 E
Lié 11 Df 48.00N 2.40W
Liebenau 12 Lb 52.36N 9.06 E
Liebig, Mount- 59 Gd 23.15S 131.20 E
Liechtenstein 6 Gf 47.10N 9.30 E
Liège 12 Hd 50.30N 5.40 E
Liège/Luik 6 Ge 50.38N 5.34 E
Lieksa 7 He 63.19N 30.01 E
Lielupé 7 Fh 57.03N 23.56 E
Lielvarde/Lielvārde 8 Kh 56.40N 24.49 E
Lielvārde/Lielvarde 8 Kh 56.40N 24.49 E
Lienen 12 Jb 52.09N 7.59 E
Lienz 14 Gd 46.50N 12.47 E
Liepaja/Liepāja 6 Id 56.35N 21.01 E
Liepāja/Liepaja 6 Id 56.35N 21.01 E
Liepajas, Ozero-/Liepājas Ezers 8 Ih 56.35N 20.35 E
Liepājas ezers/Liepaja, Ozero- 8 Ih 56.35N 20.35 E
Liepna 8 Lg 57.16N 27.35 E
Liepupe 8 Kg 57.22N 24.22 E
Lier/Lierre 11 Kc 51.08N 4.34 E
Lierbyen 8 De 59.47N 10.14 E
Lierneux 12 Hd 50.17N 5.48 E
Lierre/Lier 11 Kc 51.08N 4.34 E
Liesborn, Wadersloh- 12 Kc 51.43N 8.16 E
Lieser 10 Dg 49.55N 7.01 E
Liesing 14 Jc 47.20N 15.02 E
Liestal 14 Bc 47.29N 7.44 E
Liești 15 Kd 45.37N 27.31 E
Lieto 8 Jd 60.30N 22.27 E
Lietuvos Tarybu Socialistine Respublika/Litovskaja SSR 19 Cd 56.00N 24.00 E
Lietuvos TSR=Lithuanian SSR (EN) 19 Cd 56.00N 24.00 E
Lietvesi 8 Lc 61.30N 28.00 E
Lieurey 12 Ce 49.14N 0.29 E
Lieuvin 11 Ge 49.10N 0.30 E
Lievestuoreenjärvi 8 Lb 62.20N 26.10 E
Liévin 11 Id 50.25N 2.46 E
Lievre, Rivière du- 44 Jc 45.35N 75.25W
Liezen 14 Ic 47.34N 14.14 E
Lifford/Leifear 9 Fg 54.50N 7.29W
Li Fiord 42 Ia 80.17N 94.35W
Lifjell 8 Ce 59.30N 8.52 E
Lifou, Ile- 57 Hg 20.53S 167.13 E
Lifuka 65b Ba 19.48S 174.21W
Ligatne/Līgatne 8 Kg 57.07N 25.00 E
Līgatne/Ligatne 8 Kg 57.07N 25.00 E
Lighthouse Reef 49 De 17.20N 87.32W
Lignano Sabbiadoro 14 He 45.52N 13.09 E
Lignières 11 Ih 46.45N 2.10 E
Lignon 11 Ki 45.44N 4.08 E
Ligny-en-Barrois 11 Lf 48.41N 5.20 E
Ligonha 37 Fc 16.51S 39.09 E
Ligure, Mar-=Ligurian Sea (EN) 5 Gg 43.30N 9.00 E
Liguria 14 Cf 44.30N 8.50 E
Ligurian Sea (EN)=Ligure, Mar- 5 Gg 43.30N 9.00 E
Lihir Group 57 Ge 3.05S 152.40 E
Lihme 8 Ch 56.36N 8.44 E
Lihoslavl 7 Ih 57.09N 35.29 E
Lihou Reefs and Cays 57 Gf 17.25S 151.40 E
Lihue 60 Oc 21.59N 159.22W
Lihula 7 Fg 58.44N 23.49 E
Liinahamari 7 Hb 69.40N 31.22 E
Lijiang (Dayan) 22 Mg 26.56N 100.15 E
Lijin 28 Ef 37.29N 118.15 E
Lika 14 Jf 44.46N 15.10 E
Lika 14 Jf 44.30N 15.30 E
Likasi 31 Jj 10.59S 26.43 E
Likati 36 Db 2.53N 24.03 E
Likati 36 Db 3.21N 23.53 E
Likénai/Likenai 8 Kh 56.11N 24.42 E
Likenaj/Likėnai 8 Kh 56.11N 24.42 E
Likenäs 8 Ed 60.37N 13.02 E
Likhapani 25 Jc 27.19N 95.54 E
Likiep Atoll 57 Hc 9.53N 169.09 E
Likolo 36 Cc 0.43S 19.40 E
Likoma Island 36 Fe 12.04S 34.44 E
Likoto 36 Dc 1.10S 24.45 E
Likouala 36 Cb 2.00N 17.30 E
Likouala 36 Cc 1.13S 16.48 E
Likouala aux Herbes 36 Cc 0.50S 17.11 E
Liku 64k Bb 19.02S 169.47W
L'Ile Rousse 11a Aa 42.38N 8.56 E
Lilibeo, Capo-→Boeo, Capo- 14 Gm 37.34N 12.41 E
Lilienfeld 14 Jb 48.01N 15.38 E
Lilienthal 12 Ka 53.08N 8.55 E
Lilla Edet 7 Cg 58.08N 12.08 E
Lille [Bel.] 12 Gc 51.14N 4.50 E
Lille [Fr.] 6 Ge 50.38N 3.04 E
Lille Bælt=Little Belt (EN) 5 Gd 55.20N 9.45 E
Lillebonne 11 Ge 49.31N 0.33 E
Lille Fiskebanke 8 Bh 56.56N 6.20 E
Lillehammer 7 Cf 61.08N 10.30 E
Lille Hellefiske Bank (EN) 41 Ge 65.05N 54.00W
Lillers 11 Id 50.34N 2.29 E
Lillesand 7 Bg 58.15N 8.24 E
Lillestrøm 8 De 59.57N 11.05 E
Lillhärdal 7 Df 61.51N 14.04 E
Lillie Glacier 66 Kf 70.45S 163.55 E
Lillo 13 Ie 39.43N 3.18W
Lillooet 42 Ff 50.42N 121.56W
Lillooet Range 46 Eb 50.00N 121.45W
Lillooet River 42 Fg 49.15N 122.10W
Lilongwe 31 Kj 13.59S 33.47 E
Liloy 26 He 8.08N 122.40 E
Lim [Afr.] 35 Bd 7.54N 15.46 E
Lim [Yugo.] 14 Ng 43.45N 19.13 E
Lima 13 Dc 41.41N 8.50W
Lima 54 Cf 12.00S 76.35W
Lima [Mt.-U.S.] 46 Id 44.38N 112.36W
Lima [Oh.-U.S.] 43 Kc 40.43N 84.06W
Lima [Par.] 55 Df 23.54S 56.20W
Lima [Peru] 53 Ig 12.03S 77.03W
Lima [Swe.] 8 Ed 60.56N 13.21 E
Lima, Pulau-Pulau- 26 Gg 3.03S 107.24 E
Limagne 11 Jh 46.00N 3.20 E
Limah 24 Qj 25.56N 56.25 E
Liman [R.S.F.S.R.] 16 Og 45.45N 47.14 E
Liman [Ukr.-U.S.S.R.] 15 Md 45.42N 29.46 E
Limanskoje 15 Mc 46.38N 29.54 E
Limari, Rio- 56 Fd 30.44S 71.43W
Limassol/Lemesós 23 Dc 34.40N 33.02 E
Limavady/Léim an Mhadaidh 9 Gf 55.03N 6.57W
Limay 12 Df 48.59N 1.44 E
Limay, Rio- 52 Ji 38.59S 68.00W
Limbara 14 Dj 40.51N 9.10 E
Limbaži 7 Fh 57.31N 24.47 E
Limbé 49 Kd 19.42N 72.24W
Limbe, Blantyre- 36 Gf 15.49S 35.03 E
Limbot 63b Cb 14.12S 167.34 E
Limboto 26 Hf 0.37N 122.57 E
Limbourg 12 Hd 50.37N 5.56 E
Limbourg/Limburg 11 Lc 51.05N 5.40 E
Limburg [Bel.] 12 Hc 51.00N 5.30 E
Limburg [Neth.] 12 Hc 51.14N 5.50 E
Limburg/Limbourg 11 Lc 51.05N 5.40 E
Limburg an der Lahn 10 Ef 50.23N 8.03 E
Limedsforsen 8 Ed 60.54N 13.23 E
Limeira 56 Kb 22.34S 47.24W
Limerick/Luimneach 9 Ei 52.30N 9.00W
Limerick/Luimneach 6 Fe 52.40N 8.38W
Limestone, Hadabat- 33 Fe 24.50N 32.00 E
Limfjorden 5 Gd 56.55N 9.10 E
Limia 13 Dc 41.41N 8.50W
Limingen 7 Cd 64.47N 13.36 E
Liminka 7 Fd 64.49N 25.29 E
Limmat 14 Cc 47.30N 8.15 E
Limmen Bight 59 Hb 14.45S 135.40 E
Limmen Bight River 59 Hc 15.15S 135.30 E
Limni 15 Gk 38.46N 23.19 E
Limnos=Lemnos (EN) 5 Ih 39.55N 25.15 E
Limoeiro 54 Ke 7.52S 35.27W
Limoges 6 Gf 45.51N 1.15 E
Limogne, Causse de- 11 Hj 44.20N 1.55 E
Limon 43 Gd 39.16N 103.41W
Limón 49 Fi 10.00N 83.15W
Limón [C.R.] 39 Kh 10.00N 83.02W
Limón [Hond.] 49 Ef 15.52N 85.33W
Limone Piemonte 14 Bf 44.12N 7.34 E
Limousin 11 Hi 45.30N 1.50 E
Limousin, Plateau du- 11 Hi 45.50N 1.10 E
Limoux 11 Ik 43.04N 2.14 E
Limpopo 30 Jk 25.12S 33.32 E
Limu Ling 27 Ie 19.02N 109.43 E
Limuru 36 Gc 1.06S 36.39 E
Līnah 24 Jh 28.42N 43.48 E
Lin'an 27 Ke 30.14N 119.39 E
Linapacan 26 Gd 11.27N 119.49 E
Linares [Chile] 53 Ii 35.51S 71.36W
Linares [Mex.] 47 Ed 24.52N 99.34W
Linares [Sp.] 13 If 38.05N 3.38W
Linares Viejo 55 Bf 23.09S 61.46W
Linaro, Capo- 14 Fh 42.02N 11.50 E
Lincang 22 Mg 23.48N 100.04 E
Lincheng 28 Cf 37.26N 114.34 E
Lincheng→Xuecheng 28 Dg 34.48N 117.14 E
Lincoln 7 Mh 53.20N 0.30W
Lincoln [Arg.] 56 Hd 34.52S 61.32W
Lincoln [Eng.-U.K.] 9 Mh 53.14N 0.33W
Lincoln [Il.-U.S.] 45 Lf 40.09N 89.22W
Lincoln [Nb.-U.S.] 39 Je 40.48N 96.42W
Lincoln [N.Z.] 62 Ee 43.38S 172.29 E
Lincoln, Mount- 45 Cg 39.21N 106.07W
Lincoln City 46 Cd 44.59N 124.01W
Lincoln Sea 67 Ne 83.00N 56.00W
Lincolnshire 9 Mh 53.00N 0.10W
Lindashalvøya 8 Ad 60.40N 5.15 E
Lindau 10 Fi 47.33N 9.41 E
Linde [Neth.] 12 Hb 52.49N 5.52 E
Linde [R.S.F.S.R.] 20 Hd 64.59N 124.36 E
Linden [Guy.] 54 Gb 6.00N 58.18W
Linden [Tn.-U.S.] 44 Dh 35.37N 87.50W
Lindenows Fjord 41 Hf 60.25N 43.00W
Linderödsåsen 8 Ei 55.53N 13.56 E
Lindesberg 7 Dg 59.35N 15.15 E
Lindesnes 5 Gd 58.00N 7.02 E
Lindhorst 12 Lb 52.22N 9.17 E
Lindhos 15 Lm 36.06N 28.04 E
Lindi 36 Gd 9.30S 38.20 E
Lindi 31 Ki 10.00S 39.43 E
Lindi 30 Jh 0.33N 25.05 E
Lindis Pass 62 Cf 44.35S 169.39 E
Lindlar 12 Jc 51.01N 7.23 E
Lindome 8 Eg 57.34N 12.05 E
Lindong→Bairin Zuoqi 27 Kc 43.59N 119.22 E
Lindsay [Ca.-U.S.] 46 Fh 36.12N 119.05W
Lindsay [Ont.-Can.] 44 Hc 44.21N 78.44W
Lindsdal 8 Gh 56.44N 16.18 E
Line Islands 57 Le 0.01S 157.00W
Linfen 27 Jd 36.03N 111.32 E
Lingayen 26 Oh 16.01N 120.14 E
Lingayen Gulf 26 Hc 16.15N 120.14 E
Lingbi 28 Dh 33.33N 117.33 E
Lingbo 7 Df 61.03N 16.41 E
Lingchuan 28 Bg 35.46N 113.16 E
Lingen (Ems) 10 Dd 52.31N 7.19 E
Lingfield 12 Bc 51.10N 0.01W
Lingga, Kepulauan-=Lingga Archipelago (EN) 21 Mj 0.02S 104.35 E
Lingga, Pulau- 26 Dg 0.12S 104.35 E
Lingga Archipelago (EN)=Lingga, Kepulauan- 21 Mj 0.02S 104.35 E
Linghed 8 Fd 60.47N 15.51 E
Lingling 27 Jf 26.24N 111.41 E
Lingomo 36 Db 0.38N 21.59 E
Lingqiu 28 Ce 39.26N 114.14 E
Lingshan 27 Ig 22.30N 109.17 E
Lingshan Dao 28 Fg 35.45N 120.10 E
Lingshi 28 Af 36.50N 111.46 E
Lingshou 28 Ce 38.18N 114.22 E
Linguère 31 Fg 15.24N 15.07W
Lingwu 27 Id 38.05N 106.20 E
Lingxian 28 Df 37.20N 116.35 E
Lingyuan 28 Ed 41.15N 119.23 E
Linh, Ngoc- 21 Mh 15.04N 107.59 E
Linhai 27 La 51.36N 124.22 E
Linhai (Taizhou) 27 Lf 28.52N 121.08 E
Linhares 54 Jg 19.25S 40.04W
Linhe 27 Ic 40.49N 107.28 E
Linhuaiguan 28 Dh 32.54N 117.39 E
Linjiang 28 Id 41.49N 126.55 E
Linköping 6 Hd 58.25N 15.37 E
Linkou 27 Nb 45.18N 130.18 E
Linkuva 8 Jh 56.02N 23.58 E
Linlü Shan 28 Bf 36.02N 113.42 E
Linn, Mount- 46 Df 40.03N 122.48W
Linneryd 8 Fh 56.40N 15.07 E
Linnhe, Loch- 9 He 56.37N 5.25W
Linnich 12 Id 50.59N 6.16 E
Linosa 14 Go 35.50N 12.50 E
Linovo 10 Ud 52.28N 24.35 E
Linqing 27 Kd 36.48N 115.42 E
Linqu 28 Ef 36.31N 118.32 E
Linquan 28 Ch 33.04N 115.16 E
Linru 28 Bg 34.10N 112.51 E
Lins 56 Kb 21.40S 49.45W
Linsell 8 Eb 62.09N 13.53 E
Linshu (Xiazhuang) 28 Eg 34.56N 118.38 E
Linslade 12 Bc 51.55N 0.40W
Linta 37 Ge 25.02S 44.05 E
Lintao 27 Hd 35.20N 104.00 E
Linthal 14 Cd 46.55N 9.00 E
Linton [Eng.-U.K.] 12 Cb 52.06N 0.16 E
Linton [N.D.-U.S.] 45 Fc 46.16N 100.14W
Linxi [China] 22 Ne 43.36N 118.02 E
Linxi [China] 28 Ee 39.42N 118.26 E
Linxia 22 Mf 35.28N 102.59 E
Linxian 27 Jd 37.57N 111.00 E
Linxiang 28 Bj 29.29N 113.28 E
Linyi [China] 28 Df 37.11N 116.51 E
Linyi [China]' 27 Kd 35.09N 118.15 E
Linz 6 Hf 48.18N 14.18 E
Linze (Shahezhen) 27 Hd 39.10N 100.21 E
Lion, Golfe du-=Lion, Gulf of- (EN) 5 Gg 43.00N 4.00 E
Lion, Gulf of- (EN)=Lion, Golfe du- 5 Gg 43.00N 4.00 E
Lions Den 37 Ec 17.16S 30.02 E
Lion-sur-Mer 12 Be 49.18N 0.19W
Lioppa 26 Ih 7.40S 126.00 E
Lios Mór/Lismore 9 Fi 52.08N 7.55W
Lios na gCearrbhach/Lisburn 9 Gg 54.31N 6.03W
Lios Tuathail/Listovel 9 Di 52.27N 9.29W
Liouesso 36 Cb 1.02N 15.43 E
Lipa 26 Hd 13.57N 121.10 E
Lipany 10 Qg 49.10N 20.58 E
Lipari 14 Il 38.30N 14.55 E
Lipari 14 Il 38.28N 14.57 E
Lipari Islands (EN)=Eolie o Lipari, Isole- 5 Hh 38.35N 14.55 E
Lipeck 6 Je 52.37N 39.35 E
Lipeckaja Oblast 19 De 52.45N 39.10 E
Lipenská přehradní nádrž 10 Kh 48.45N 14.05 E
Liperi 7 Ge 62.32N 29.22 E
Lipez, Cordillera de- 54 Eh 22.00S 66.45W
Liphook 12 Bc 51.04N 0.48W
Lipkani 15 Ja 48.13N 26.48 E
Lipljan 15 Eg 42.32N 21.08 E
Lipno 10 Pd 52.51N 19.10 E
Lipova 15 Ec 46.05N 21.42 E
Lipovcy 20 Ih 44.15N 131.45 E
Lippborg, Lippetal- 12 Kc 51.40N 8.02 E
Lippe 10 Ce 51.39N 6.38 E
Lipper Bergland 12 Kb 52.05N 8.57 E
Lippetal 12 Kc 51.40N 8.13 E
Lippetal-Eickelborn 12 Kc 51.39N 8.13 E
Lippetal-Lippborg 12 Kc 51.40N 8.02 E
Lippischer Wald 12 Kc 51.56N 8.45 E
Lippstadt 10 Ee 51.40N 8.21 E
Lipsko 10 Re 51.09N 21.39 E
Lipsoi 15 Jl 37.20N 26.45 E
Liptako 30 Hg 14.15N 0.02 E
Liptovský Mikuláš 10 Pg 49.05N 19.38 E
Lira 36 Fb 2.15N 32.54 E
Liranga 36 Cc 0.40S 17.36 E
Liri 14 Hi 41.25N 13.52 E
Liria 13 Le 39.38N 0.36W
Lis 13 De 39.53N 8.58W
Lisa 15 Cf 43.08N 19.42 E
Lisac 15 Eg 42.45N 21.56 E
Lisakovsk 19 Ge 52.33N 62.28 E
Lisala 31 Jh 2.09N 21.31 E
Lisboa 13 Ce 39.00N 9.08W
Lisboa=Lisbon (EN) 6 Fh 38.43N 9.08W
Lisbon 45 Hc 46.27N 97.41W
Lisbon (EN)=Lisboa 6 Fh 38.43N 9.08W
Lisbon Canyon (EN) 13 Cf 38.20N 9.20W
Lisburn/Lios na gCearrbhach 9 Gg 54.31N 6.03W
Lisburne, Cape- 40 Fc 68.52N 166.14W
Liscannor Bay/Bá Thuath Reanna 9 Di 52.55N 9.25W
Lisec 10 Uh 48.48N 24.45 E
Li Shan 28 Ag 35.25N 111.58 E
Lishi 27 Jd 37.29N 111.08 E
Lishu 28 Hc 43.19N 124.20 E
Lishui 27 Kf 28.30N 119.55 E
Lisianski Island 57 Jb 26.02N 174.00W
Lisičansk 19 Df 48.53N 38.28 E
Lisieux 11 Ge 49.09N 0.14 E
Liska 15 Dh 41.19N 20.58 E
L'Isle-Adam 12 Ee 49.07N 2.14 E
L'Isle-Jourdain 11 Hk 43.37N 1.05 E
L'Isle sur-la-Sorgue 11 Lk 43.55N 5.03 E
Lismore 58 Gg 28.48S 153.17 E
Lismore/Lios Mór 9 Fi 52.08N 7.55W
Liss 24 Hg 31.14N 38.31 E
Liss 12 Bc 51.02N 0.54W
List 10 Ea 55.01N 8.26 E
Lista 8 Bf 58.10N 6.40 E
Listafjorden 8 Bf 58.10N 6.35 E
Lister, Mount- 66 Kf 78.04S 162.41 E
Lištica 14 Lg 43.23N 17.39 E
Listovel/Lios Tuathail 9 Di 52.27N 9.29W
Listowel 44 Gd 43.44N 80.57W
Liswarta 10 Pe 51.06N 19.01 E
Lit 8 Fa 63.19N 14.49 E
Litang [China] 27 Ig 23.12N 109.05 E
Litang [China] 27 He 30.02N 100.18 E
Litani Rivier 54 Hc 3.18N 54.06W
Litchfield 45 Id 45.08N 94.31W
Lithgow 58 Gh 33.29S 150.09 E
Líthinon, Ákra- 15 Ho 34.55N 24.44 E
Lithuania (EN) 5 Id 56.00N 24.00 E
Lithuanian SSR (EN)=Lietuvos TSR 19 Cd 56.00N 24.00 E
Litókhoron 15 Fi 40.06N 22.30 E
Litoměřice 10 Kf 50.32N 14.08 E
Litovel 10 Ng 49.43N 17.05 E
Litovko 20 Ig 49.17N 135.10 E
Litovskaja Sovetskaja Socialističeskaja Respublika 19 Cd 56.00N 24.00 E
Litovskaja SSR/Lietuvos Tarybu Socialistine Respublika 19 Cd 56.00N 24.00 E
Little Abaco Island 47 Ic 26.53N 77.43W
Little Abitibi River 44 Ha 49.29N 79.32W
Little Aden 23 Fg 12.45N 44.52 E
Little America 46 Kf 41.32N 109.47W
Little Andaman 25 Ih 10.45N 92.30 E
Little Bahama Bank (EN) 47 Ic 26.30N 78.00W
Little Barrier Island 62 Fb 36.10S 175.05 E
Little Beaver Creek 45 Ec 46.17N 103.56W
Little Belt (EN)=Lille Bælt 5 Gd 55.20N 9.45 E
Little Belt Mountains 46 Jc 46.45N 110.35W
Little Blue River 45 Hg 39.41N 96.40W
Little Bow River 46 Ib 49.53N 112.29W
Little Carpathians (EN)=Malé Karpaty 10 Nh 48.30N 17.20 E
Little Cayman 47 He 19.41N 80.03W
Little Colorado River 38 Hc 36.11N 111.48W
Little Current 42 Jg 45.58N 81.56W
Little Current 42 Jf 50.57N 84.36W
Little Dry Creek 46 Lc 47.21N 106.22W
Little Exuma Island 49 Jb 23.27N 75.37W
Little Falls 43 Ib 45.59N 94.21W
Littlefield 45 Ej 33.55N 102.20W
Little Fort 46 Ea 51.25N 120.12W
Little Grand Rapids 42 Hf 52.02N 95.25W
Little Halibut Bank 9 Lc 58.20N 1.15W
Littlehampton 12 Bd 50.48N 0.32W
Little Inagua Island 47 Jd 21.30N 73.00W
Little Karroo (EN)=Klein-Karoo 37 Cf 33.42S 21.20 E
Little Missouri 38 Ie 47.30N 102.25W
Little Namaland (EN)=Namakwaland 37 Be 29.00S 17.00 E
Little Nicobar 25 Ig 7.20N 93.40 E
Little Ouse 9 Ni 52.30N 0.22 E
Littleport 12 Cb 52.27N 0.18 E
Little Powder River 46 Md 45.28N 105.20W
Little Quill Lake 46 Ma 51.55N 104.05W
Little River 62 Ee 43.46S 172.47 E
Little Rock 39 Jf 34.44N 92.15W
Little Rocky Mountains 46 Kb 48.00N 108.45W

Index Symbols

1 Independent Nation
2 State, Region
3 District, County
4 Municipality
5 Colony, Dependency
Continent
Physical Region
Historical or Cultural Region
Mount, Mountain
Volcano
Hill
Mountains, Mountain Range
Hills, Escarpment
Plateau, Upland
Pass, Gap
Plain, Lowland
Delta
Salt Flat
Valley, Canyon
Crater, Cave
Karst Features
Depression
Polder
Desert, Dunes
Forest, Woods
Heath, Steppe
Oasis
Cape, Point
Coast, Beach
Cliff
Peninsula
Isthmus
Sandbank
Island
Atoll
Rock, Reef
Islands, Archipelago
Rocks, Reefs
Coral Reef
Well, Spring
Geyser
River, Stream
Waterfall Rapids
River Mouth, Estuary
Lake
Salt Lake
Intermittent Lake
Reservoir
Swamp, Pond
Canal
Glacier
Ice Shelf, Pack Ice
Ocean
Sea
Gulf, Bay
Strait, Fjord
Lagoon
Bank
Seamount
Tablemount
Ridge
Shelf
Basin
Escarpment, Sea Scarp
Fracture
Trench, Abyss
National Park, Reserve
Point of Interest
Recreation Site
Cave, Cavern
Historic Site
Ruins
Wall, Walls
Church, Abbey
Temple
Scientific Station
Airport
Port
Lighthouse
Mine
Tunnel
Dam, Bridge

Name	Page	Grid	Lat.	Long.
Little Scarcies	34	Cd	8.51N	13.09W
Little Sioux River	45	Hf	41.49N	96.04W
Little Sitkin	40a	Cb	51.55N	178.30 E
Little Smoky	42	Fe	55.39N	117.37W
Little Snake River	45	Bf	40.27N	108.26W
Littleton [Co.-U.S.]	45	Dg	39.37N	105.01W
Littleton [N.H.-U.S.]	44	Lc	44.18N	71.46W
Little White River [Ont.-Can.]	44	Fb	46.15N	83.00W
Little White River [S.D.-U.S.]	45	Fe	43.44N	100.40W
Littoral [3]	34	He	4.30N	10.00 E
Litvinov	10	Jf	50.36N	13.36 E
Liuba	27	Ie	33.39N	106.53 E
Liuhe	27	Mc	42.16N	125.45 E
Liu He [China]	28	Gd	41.48N	122.43 E
Liu He [China]	28	Ic	42.46N	126.13 E
Liuheng Dao	28	Gj	29.43N	122.08 E
Liujia Xia	27	Hd	35.50N	103.00 E
Liukang Tenggaja, Kepulauan-	26	Gh	6.45 S	118.50 E
Liupai → Tian'e	27	If	25.05N	107.12 E
Liupan Shan	27	Id	35.40N	106.15 E
Liuqu He	28	Fd	40.10N	120.15 E
Liuwa Plain	36	De	14.27 S	22.25 E
Liuyang	28	Bj	28.09N	113.38 E
Liuzhangzhen → Yuanqu	27	Jd	35.19N	111.44 E
Liuzhou	22	Mg	24.22N	109.20 E
Līvāni/Livány	7	Gh	56.22N	26.12 E
Livanjsko Polje	14	Kg	43.51N	16.50 E
Livany/Līvāni	7	Gh	56.22N	26.12 E
Livarot	12	Ce	49.01N	0.09 E
Livengood	40	Jc	65.32N	148.33W
Livenza	14	Ge	45.35N	12.51 E
Livenzi	15	Ge	44.14N	23.47 E
Live Oak	44	Fj	30.18N	82.59W
Livermore	46	Eh	37.41N	121.46W
Livermore, Mount-	45	Dk	30.37N	104.08W
Liverpool [Eng.-U.K.]	6	Fe	53.25N	2.55W
Liverpool [N.S.-Can.]	42	Lh	44.02N	64.43W
Liverpool, Cape-	42	Jb	73.38N	78.05W
Liverpool Bay [Can.]	42	Ec	70.00N	129.00W
Liverpool Bay [Eng.-U.K.]	9	Jh	53.30N	3.16W
Liverpool Range	59	Kf	31.40 S	150.30 E
Liverpool River	59	Gb	12.00 S	134.00 E
Livigno	14	Ed	46.32N	10.04 E
Livingston [Guat.]	49	Cf	15.50N	88.45W
Livingston [Mt.-U.S.]	43	Eb	45.40N	110.34W
Livingston [Newf.-Can.]	42	Kf	53.40N	66.10W
Livingston [Tn.-U.S.]	44	Eg	36.23N	85.19W
Livingston [Tx.-U.S.]	45	Ik	30.43N	94.56W
Livingston, Lake-	45	Ik	30.45N	95.15W
Livingstone, Chutes de- = Livingstone Falls (EN)	30	Ii	4.50 S	14.30 E
Livingstone Falls (EN) = Livingstone, Chutes de-	30	Ii	4.50 S	14.30 E
Livingstone Memorial	36	Fe	12.19 S	30.18 E
Livingstone Mountains	36	Fd	9.45 S	34.20 E
Livingstonia	36	Fe	10.36 S	34.07 E
Livingston Island	66	Qe	62.36 S	60.30W
Livno	14	Lg	43.50N	17.01 E
Livny	19	De	52.28N	37.37 E
Livonia	44	Fd	42.25N	83.23W
Livonia (EN)=Livonija	5	Id	58.50N	27.30 E
Livonija=Livonia (EN)	5	Id	58.50N	27.30 E
Livorno=Leghorn (EN)	6	Hg	43.33N	10.19 E
Livradois, Monts du-	11	Ji	45.30N	3.33 E
Livramento do Brumado	54	Jf	13.39 S	41.50W
Livron-sur-Drôme	11	Kj	44.46N	4.51 E
Liwale	36	Gd	9.46 S	37.56 E
Liwiec	10	Rd	52.35N	21.33 E
Liwonde	36	Gf	15.01 S	35.13 E
Lixi	27	Hf	26.21N	102.03 E
Lixian [China]	27	Ie	34.11N	105.02 E
Lixian [China]	27	Jf	29.40N	111.45 E
Lixian [China]	28	Ce	38.29N	115.34 E
Lixin	28	Dh	33.09N	116.12 E
Lixoúrion	15	Dk	38.12N	20.26 E
Liyang	28	Ei	31.26N	119.29 E
Lizard	9	Hl	49.57N	5.13W
Lizard Point	5	Ff	49.56N	5.13W
Lizhu	28	Fj	29.58N	120.26 E
Lizy sur Ourcq	12	Fe	49.01N	3.02 E
Ljady	8	Mf	58.35N	28.55 E
Ljahoviči	16	Ec	53.04N	26.15 E
Ljahovskije Ostrova = Lyakhov Islands (EN)	21	Qb	73.30N	141.00 E
Ljalja	17	Jg	59.10N	61.30 E
Ljamin	17	Of	61.18N	71.45 E
Ljangar	18	Ed	40.23N	65.59 E
Ljangasovo	7	Lg	58.33N	49.29 E
Ljapin	17	Je	63.38N	61.58 E
Ljaskelja	8	Nc	61.39N	31.03 E
Ljaskovec	15	If	43.06N	25.43 E
Ljig	15	De	44.14N	20.15 E
Ljuban [Bye.-U.S.S.R.]	16	Ec	52.48N	27.59 E
Ljuban [R.S.F.S.R.]	7	Hg	59.22N	31.13 E
Ljubar	16	Ee	49.55N	27.44 E
Ljubaševka	15	Nb	47.50N	30.07 E
Ljubelj	14	Id	46.26N	14.16 E
Ljubercy	19	Dd	55.40N	37.55 E
Ljubešov	10	Ve	51.45N	25.37 E
Ljubim	7	Jg	58.22N	40.41 E
Ljubimec	15	Jh	41.50N	26.05 E
Ljubinje	14	Mh	42.57N	18.06 E
Ljubišnja	15	Cf	43.20N	19.07 E
Ljubljana	6	Hf	46.02N	14.30 E
Ljuboml	16	Cd	51.15N	23.59 E
Ljubotin	16	Ie	49.59N	35.55 E
Ljubovija	15	Ce	44.12N	19.22 E
Ljubuški	14	Lg	43.12N	17.33 E
Ljubytino	7	Hg	58.50N	33.25 E
Ljudinovo	19	De	53.51N	34.28 E
Ljugarn	7	Eh	57.19N	18.42 E
Ljungan	5	Hc	62.19N	17.23 E
Ljungaverk	8	Gb	62.29N	16.03 E
Ljungby	7	Ch	56.50N	13.56 E
Ljungbyholm	8	Gh	56.38N	16.10 E
Ljungdalen	7	Ce	62.51N	12.47 E
Ljungsbro	8	Ff	58.31N	15.30 E
Ljungskile	8	Df	58.14N	11.55 E
Ljusdal	7	Df	61.50N	16.05 E
Ljusnan	5	Hc	61.12N	17.08 E
Ljusne	7	Df	61.13N	17.08 E
Ljusterö	8	He	59.30N	18.35 E
Ljuta	8	Mf	58.33N	28.45 E
Llandilo	9	Jj	51.53N	3.59W
Llandovery	9	Jj	51.59N	3.48W
Llandrindod Wells	9	Ji	52.15N	3.23W
Llandudno	9	Jh	53.19N	3.49W
Llanelli	9	Ij	51.42N	4.10W
Llanes	13	Ha	43.25N	4.45W
Llangefni	9	Ih	53.16N	4.18W
Llangollen	9	Ji	52.58N	3.10W
Llano	45	Gk	30.45N	98.41W
Llano Estacado	38	If	33.30N	102.40W
Llano River	45	Gk	30.35N	98.25W
Llanos	52	Je	5.00N	70.00W
Llanos de Sonora	47	Bc	28.20N	111.00W
Llanquihue, Lago-	56	Ff	41.08 S	72.48W
Llata	54	Ce	9.25 S	76.47W
Lleida/Lérida	13	Mc	41.37N	0.37 E
Llerena	13	Ff	38.14N	6.01W
Lleyn	9	Ii	52.54N	4.30W
Llica	54	Eg	19.52 S	68.16W
Llivia	13	Nb	42.28N	1.59 E
Llobregat	13	Oc	41.19N	2.09 E
Lloret de Mar	13	Oc	41.42N	2.51 E
Llorona, Punta-	49	Fi	8.37N	83.44W
Llorri/Orri, Pic d'-	13	Nb	42.23N	1.12 E
Lloydminster	42	Gf	53.17N	110.00W
Lluchmayor	13	Oe	39.29N	2.54 E
Llullaillaco, Volcán-	52	Jh	24.43 S	68.33W
Lo	63b	Ca	13.21 S	166.38 E
Loa	46	Jg	38.24N	111.38W
Loa, Río-	56	Fb	21.26 S	70.04W
Loanatit, Pointe-	63b	Dd	19.21 S	169.14 E
Loange	30	Ji	4.17 S	20.02 E
Loango	36	Bc	4.39 S	11.48 E
Loano	14	Cf	44.08N	8.15 E
Loban	7	Mh	56.59N	51.12 E
Lobatse	31	Jk	25.13 S	25.41 E
Löbau/Lubij	10	Ke	51.06N	14.40 E
Lobaye	30	Ih	3.41N	18.35 E
Lobaye [3]	35	Be	4.00N	17.40 E
Lobenstein	10	Hf	50.27N	11.39 E
Loberia	56	Ie	38.09 S	58.47W
Łobez	10	Lc	53.39N	15.36 E
Lobito	31	Ij	12.22 S	13.34 E
Lobo	34	Dd	6.02N	6.47W
Lobos	56	Ie	35.11 S	59.06W
Lobos	32	Ed	28.45N	13.49W
Lobos, Cabo-	48	Cc	29.55N	112.45W
Lobos, Cay-	49	Ib	22.24N	77.32W
Lobos, Cayo-	48	Ph	18.22N	87.24W
Lobos, Isla-	48	Dd	27.20N	110.36W
Lobos, Islas de-	48	Kg	21.27N	97.15W
Lobos de Afuera, Islas-	54	Be	6.57 S	80.42W
Lobos de Tierra, Isla-	54	Be	6.27 S	80.52W
Lobva	19	Gd	59.12N	60.30 E
Łobżonka	10	Nc	53.07N	17.18 E
Locana	14	Be	45.25N	7.27 E
Locarno	14	Cd	46.10N	8.48 E
Loch Aillionn/Allen, Lough-	9	Eg	54.08N	8.08W
Loch Arabhach/Arrow, Lough-	9	Eg	54.05N	8.20W
Lochboisdale	9	Fd	57.09N	7.19W
Loch Cairlinn/Carlingford Lough	9	Gg	54.05N	6.14W
Loch Ce/Key, Lough-	9	Eg	54.00N	8.15W
Loch Coirib/Corrib, Lough	9	Dh	53.05N	9.10W
Loch Con/Conn, Lough-	9	Dg	54.04N	9.20W
Loch Cuan/Strangford Lough	9	Hg	54.26N	5.36W
Loch Deirgeirt/Derg, Lough-	9	Ei	53.00N	8.20W
Lochearnhead	9	Ie	56.23N	4.18W
Loch Éirne Íochtair/Lower Lough Erne	9	Fg	54.30N	7.50W
Loch Éirne Uachtair/Upper Lough Erne	9	Fg	54.20N	7.30W
Lochem	12	Ib	52.10N	6.25 E
Loches	11	Gg	47.08N	1.00 E
Loch Feabhail/Foyle, Lough-	9	Ff	55.05N	7.10W
Loch Garman/Wexford	6	Fe	52.20N	6.27W
Loch Garman/Wexford [2]	9	Gi	52.20N	6.40W
Lochgilphead	9	He	56.03N	5.26W
Loch Hinninn/Ennell, Lough-	9	Fh	53.28N	7.24W
Lochinver	9	Hc	58.09N	5.15W
Loch Lao/Belfast Lough	9	Hg	54.40N	5.50W
Loch Léin/Leane, Lough-	9	Di	52.05N	9.35W
Loch Leven	9	Je	56.13N	3.10W
Loch Long	9	Ie	56.04N	4.50W
Lochmaddy	9	Fd	57.36N	7.10W
Loch Measca/Mask, Lough-	9	Dh	53.35N	9.20W
Lochnagar	9	Je	56.55N	3.10W
Loch nEathach/Neagh, Lough-	5	Fe	54.38N	6.24W
Loch Ness	9	Id	57.15N	4.30W
Łochów	10	Rd	52.32N	21.48 E
Loch Pholl an Phúca/Poulaphuca Reservoir	9	Gh	53.10N	6.30W
Loch Rí/Ree, Lough-	9	Fh	53.35N	8.00W
Lochsa River	46	Hc	46.08N	115.36W
Loch Sileann/Sheelin, Lough-	9	Fh	53.48N	7.20W
Loch Suili/Swilly, Lough-	9	Ff	55.10N	7.38W
Loch Uí Ghadra/Gara, Lough-	9	Eh	53.55N	8.30W
Lochy	9	He	56.49N	5.06W
Lochy, Loch-	9	Ie	56.55N	4.55W
Lockerbie	9	Jf	55.07N	3.22W
Lockhart	45	Hl	29.53N	97.41W
Lock Haven	44	Ie	41.09N	77.28W
Löcknitz	10	Hc	53.07N	11.16 E
Lockport	44	Hd	43.11N	78.39W
Locminé	11	Dg	47.53N	2.50W
Locri	14	Kl	38.14N	16.16 E
Lod	24	Fg	31.58N	34.54 E
Lodalskåpa	7	Bf	61.47N	7.12 E
Loddon	12	Db	52.32N	1.29 E
Loddon River	59	Ig	36.41 S	143.55 E
Lodejnoje Pole	19	Dc	60.44N	33.33 E
Lodève	11	Jk	43.43N	3.19 E
Lodi [Ca.-U.S.]	46	Eg	38.08N	121.16W
Lodi [It.]	14	De	45.19N	9.30 E
Lødingen	7	Db	68.25N	16.00 E
Lodja	31	Ji	3.29 S	23.26 E
Lodosa	13	Jb	42.25N	2.05W
Lödöse	8	Ef	58.02N	12.08 E
Lodwar	31	Kh	3.07N	35.36 E
Łódź	6	He	51.46N	19.30 E
Łódź [2]	10	Pe	51.45N	19.30 E
Loei	25	Ke	17.32N	101.34 E
Loeriesfontein	37	Bf	30.56 S	19.26 E
Lofanga	65b	Ba	19.50 S	174.33W
Loffa	30	Fh	6.36N	11.05W
Loffa [3]	34	Dd	7.45N	10.00W
Lofoten	5	Hb	68.30N	15.00 E
Lofoten Basin (EN)	5	Ga	70.00N	4.00 E
Lofsdalen	8	Eb	62.07N	13.16 E
Loftahammar	8	Gg	57.52N	16.40 E
Loga	34	Fc	13.37N	3.14 E
Logan [N.M.-U.S.]	45	Ei	35.22N	103.25W
Logan [Oh.-U.S.]	44	Ff	39.32N	82.24W
Logan [Ut.-U.S.]	43	Ec	41.44N	111.50W
Logan [W.V.-U.S.]	44	Gg	37.52N	81.58W
Logan, Mount- [Can.]	38	Ec	60.34N	140.24W
Logan, Mount- [Wa.-U.S.]	46	Eb	48.32N	120.57W
Logan Martin Lake	44	Di	33.40N	86.15W
Logan Mountains	42	Ed	61.00N	128.00W
Logansport	44	De	40.45N	86.21W
Loge	30	Ii	7.49 S	13.06 E
Logojsk	8	Lj	54.12N	27.57 E
Logone	30	Ig	12.06N	15.02 E
Logone Birni	34	Ic	11.47N	15.06 E
Logone Occidental [3]	35	Bd	8.40N	16.00 E
Logone Occidental	35	Bd	9.07N	16.26 E
Logone Oriental [3]	35	Bd	8.20N	16.30 E
Logone Oriental	35	Bd	9.07N	16.26 E
Logroño [3]	13	Jb	42.15N	2.30W
Logroño [Arg.]	55	Bi	29.30 S	61.42W
Logroño [Sp.]	13	Jb	42.28N	2.27W
Logrosán	13	Ge	39.20N	5.29W
Løgstør	7	Bh	56.58N	9.15 E
Logudoro	14	Cj	40.35N	8.40 E
Løgumkloster	8	Ci	55.03N	8.57 E
Lögurinn	7a	Cb	65.15N	14.30W
Lohja/Lojo	7	Ff	60.15N	24.05 E
Lohjanjärvi	8	Jd	60.15N	23.55 E
Lohjanselkä/Lojo åsen	8	Kd	60.15N	24.10 E
Löhme	12	Kc	51.41N	8.42 E
Löhne	10	Ed	52.11N	8.41 E
Lohne	12	Kb	52.40N	8.14 E
Lohra	12	Kd	50.44N	8.38 E
Lohr am Main	10	Ff	49.59N	9.35 E
Lohusuu/Lokusu	8	Lf	58.53N	27.01 E
Lohvica	16	Hd	50.22N	33.15 E
Loi, Phou-	25	Kd	20.16N	103.12 E
Loi-Kaw	25	Je	19.41N	97.13 E
Loile	36	Dc	0.52 S	20.12 E
Loimaa	7	Ff	60.51N	23.03 E
Loimijoki	8	Jc	61.13N	22.38 E
Loing	11	If	48.23N	2.48 E
Loir	11	Fg	47.33N	0.32W
Loir, Vaux du-	11	Gg	47.45N	0.25 E
Loire [3]	11	Ji	45.30N	4.00 E
Loire	5	Ff	47.16N	2.11W
Loire, Canal latéral à la-	11	Jh	46.29N	3.59 E
Loire, Val de-	11	Hg	47.40N	1.35 E
Loire-Atlantique [3]	11	Eg	47.15N	1.50W
Loiret [3]	11	Ig	47.55N	2.20 E
Loir-et-Cher [3]	11	Hg	47.30N	1.30 E
Loisach	10	Hi	47.56N	11.27 E
Loison	12	He	49.30N	5.17 E
Loja [Ec.]	53	If	4.00 S	79.13W
Loja [Sp.]	13	Hg	37.10N	4.09W
Lojo/Lohja	7	Ff	60.15N	24.05 E
Lojo åsen/Lohjanselkä	8	Kd	60.15N	24.10 E
Loka	35	Ee	4.16N	31.01 E
Lokači	10	Uf	50.43N	24.44 E
Lokalahti	8	Id	60.41N	21.28 E
Lokandu	36	Ec	2.31 S	25.47 E
Lokantekojärvi	7	Gc	68.56N	27.40 E
Lokbatan	16	Pi	40.21N	49.42 E
Lokčim	17	Ef	61.48N	51.45 E
Løken	8	De	59.48N	11.29 E
Lokeren	11	Jc	51.06N	4.00 E
Lokichar	36	Gb	2.23N	35.39 E
Lokichokio	36	Fb	4.12N	34.21 E
Lokitaung	36	Gb	4.16N	35.45 E
Løkken [Den.]	8	Cg	57.22N	9.43 E
Løkken [Nor.]	7	Be	63.05N	9.36 E
Loknja	7	Hh	56.49N	30.09 E
Loko	34	Gd	8.00N	7.50 E
Lokoja	34	Gd	7.48N	6.44 E
Lokomo	34	Ie	2.41N	15.19 E
Lokoro	36	Cc	1.43 S	18.23 E
Lokossa	34	Fd	6.38N	1.43 E
Lokot	16	Ic	52.33N	34.31 E
Lokoti	34	Hd	6.22N	14.20 E
Loksa	7	Fg	59.34N	25.44 E
Loks Land	42	Ld	62.27N	64.30W
Lokuru	63a	Cc	8.35 S	157.20 E
Lokusu/Lohusuu	8	Lf	58.53N	27.01 E
Lokwa Kangole	36	Gb	3.32N	35.54 E
Lol	30	Jh	9.13N	28.59 E
Lola	34	Dd	7.48N	8.32W
Lolimi	35	Ee	4.35N	33.59 E
Loliondo	36	Gc	2.03 S	35.37 E
Lolland	5	He	54.45N	11.30 E
Lollar	12	Kd	50.38N	8.42 E
Lolo	36	Db	2.13N	23.00 E
Lolo	36	Bc	0.40 S	12.28 E
Lolodorf	34	He	3.14N	10.44 E
Lolo Pass	46	Hc	46.40N	114.33W
Loloway	63b	Cb	15.17 S	167.58 E
Lom	15	Gf	43.49N	23.14 E
Lom [Afr.]	34	Hd	5.20N	13.24 E
Lom [Bul.]	15	Gf	43.50N	23.15 E
Loma Bonita	48	Lh	18.07N	95.53W
Lomaloma	63d	Cb	17.17 S	178.59W
Lomami	30	Jh	0.46N	24.16 E
Loma Mountains	30	Fh	9.10N	11.07W
Lomas de Vallejos	55	Dh	27.44 S	57.56W
Loma Verde	55	Cl	35.16 S	58.24W
Lomba	36	Df	15.36 S	21.32 E
Lombarda, Serra-	54	Hc	2.50N	51.50W
Lombarde, Prealpi-	14	De	46.00N	9.30 E
Lombardia = Lombardy (EN) [2]	14	De	45.40N	9.30 E
Lombardy (EN) = Lombardia [2]	14	De	45.40N	9.30 E
Lomblen, Pulau-	21	Oj	8.25 S	123.30 E
Lombok, Pulau-	21	Nj	8.45 S	116.30 E
Lombok, Selat-	26	Gh	8.30 S	115.50 E
Lomé	31	Hh	6.08N	1.13 E
Lomela	31	Ji	2.18 S	23.17 E
Lomela	30	Ji	0.14 S	20.42 E
Lomellina	14	Ce	45.15N	8.45 E
Loméméti	63b	Dd	19.30 S	169.27 E
Lomié	34	He	3.10N	13.37 E
Lomlom	63c	Bb	10.19 S	166.16 E
Lomma	8	Ei	55.41N	13.05 E
Lomme	12	Hd	50.08N	5.10 E
Lommel	11	Lc	51.14N	5.18 E
Lomnica	10	Ug	49.02N	24.47 E
Lomond, Loch-	9	Ie	56.08N	4.38W
Lomonosov	19	Cd	59.55N	29.40 E
Lomonosovki	19	Ge	52.50N	66.28 E
Lomonosov Ridge (EN)	67	De	88.00N	140.00 E
Lomont	11	Mg	47.21N	6.36 E
Lompobatang, Gunung-	26	Gh	5.20 S	119.55 E
Lompoc	43	Ce	34.38N	120.27W
Lomsegga	8	Cc	61.49N	8.22 E
Łomża	10	Sc	53.11N	22.05 E
Łomża [2]	10	Sc	53.10N	22.05 E
Lønahorg	8	Bd	60.42N	6.25 E
Loncoche	56	Fe	39.22 S	72.38W
Londa	25	Ee	15.28N	74.31 E
Londerzeel	12	Gc	51.01N	4.18 E
Londiani	36	Gc	0.10 S	35.36 E
Londinières	12	De	49.50N	1.24 E
London [Eng.-U.K.]	6	Fe	51.30N	0.10W
London [Kir.]	64g	Bb	1.58N	157.29W
London [Ky.-U.S.]	44	Eg	37.08N	84.05W
London [Ont.-Can.]	39	Ke	42.59N	81.14W
London-Barnet	12	Bc	51.39N	0.12W
London-Bexley	12	Cc	51.26N	0.09 E
London Bridge	51p	Bb	12.17N	61.35W
London-Bromley	12	Cc	51.25N	0.01 E
London-Croydon	9	Mj	51.23N	0.07W
Londonderry/Doire	6	Fd	55.00N	7.19W
Londonderry, Cape-	59	Fb	13.45 S	126.55 E
London-Ealing	12	Bc	51.30N	0.19W
London-Enfield	12	Bc	51.40N	0.04W
London-Greenwich	9	Mj	51.28N	0.00
London-Haringey	12	Bc	51.36N	0.06W
London-Harrow	12	Bc	51.36N	0.20W
London-Havering	12	Cc	51.36N	0.11 E
London-Hillingdon	12	Bc	51.31N	0.27W
London-Kingston-upon-Thames	9	Mj	51.28N	0.19W
London-Redbridge	12	Cc	51.35N	0.08 E
London-Sutton	12	Bc	51.21N	0.12W
London-Wandsworth	12	Bc	51.27N	0.12W
London-Westminster	12	Bc	51.30N	0.07W
Londrina	53	Kh	23.18 S	51.09W
Lone Pine	46	Fh	36.36N	118.04W
Longa	36	Ce	14.41 S	18.29 E
Longa [Ang.]	36	Cf	16.25 S	19.04 E
Longa [Ang.]	36	Be	10.15 S	13.30 E
Longa, Proliv- = De Long Strait (EN)	21	Tb	70.20N	178.00 E
Longá, Rio-	54	Jd	3.09 S	41.56W
Long Akah	26	Ff	3.19N	114.47 E
Longarone	14	Gd	46.16N	12.18 E
Longbangun	26	Gf	0.36N	115.11 E
Long Bay [Bar.]	51q	Bb	13.04N	59.29W
Long Bay [S.C.-U.S.]	43	Le	33.35N	78.45W
Long Beach [Ca.-U.S.]	39	Hf	33.46N	118.11W
Long Beach [N.Y.-U.S.]	44	Ke	40.35N	73.40W
Long Beach [Wa.-U.S.]	46	Cc	46.21N	124.03W
Long Branch	43	Mc	40.17N	73.59W
Long Buckby	12	Ab	52.18N	1.04W
Long Cay	49	Jb	22.37N	74.20W
Longchuan	27	Kg	24.10N	115.17 E
Long Creek	46	Nb	49.07N	103.00W
Long Eaton	12	Ab	52.54N	1.16W
Longfeng	28	Ha	46.31N	125.02 E
Longford/An Longfort [2]	9	Fh	53.40N	7.40W
Longford/An Longfort	9	Fh	53.44N	7.47W
Long Forties	9	Nd	57.10N	0.05 E
Long Hu	28	Dj	29.37N	116.12 E
Longhua	28	Dd	41.18N	117.44 E
Longido	36	Gc	2.44 S	36.41 E
Long Island [Atg.]	51d	Bb	17.08N	61.45W
Long Island [Bah.]	38	Lg	23.10N	75.10W
Long Island [Can.]	42	Jf	54.50N	79.20W
Long Island [Can.]	44	Nc	44.20N	66.15W
Long Island [Pap.N.Gui.]	57	Fe	5.36 S	148.00 E
Long Island [U.S.]	38	Le	40.50N	73.00W
Long Island Sound	44	Ke	41.05N	72.58W
Longjiang	27	Lb	47.20N	123.09 E
Longjuzhai → Danfeng	27	Je	33.44N	110.22 E
Longkou	27	Ld	37.39N	120.20 E
Longlac	42	Ig	49.50N	86.32W
Long Lake [N.D.-U.S.]	45	Fc	46.43N	100.07W
Long Lake [Ont.-Can.]	45	Mb	49.32N	86.45W
Longmalinau	26	Gf	3.30N	116.31 E
Long Men	27	Je	34.40N	110.30 E
Longmont	45	Df	40.10N	105.06W
Longnan	27	Jg	24.54N	114.48 E
Longobucco	14	Kk	39.27N	16.37 E
Longoz	15	Kf	43.02N	27.41 E
Longping → Luodian	27	If	25.26N	106.47 E
Long Point	44	Gd	42.34N	80.15W
Long Point Bay	44	Gd	42.40N	80.14W
Longpujungan	26	Gf	2.34N	115.40 E
Longquan	27	Kf	28.06N	119.05 E
Long Range Mountains	42	Lg	48.00N	58.30W
Longreach	58	Fg	23.26 S	144.15 E
Long Sand	12	Dc	51.37N	1.10 E
Longs Peak	38	Ie	40.15N	105.37W
Long Sutton	12	Cb	52.47N	0.08 E
Longtan	28	Eh	32.10N	119.03 E
Longtown	9	Kf	55.01N	2.58W
Longué	11	Fg	47.23N	0.07W
Longueau	12	Ee	49.52N	2.21 E
Longueville-sur-Scie	12	De	49.48N	1.06 E
Longuyon	11	Le	49.26N	5.36 E
Long Valley	46	Ji	34.37N	111.16W
Longview [Tx.-U.S.]	43	Ie	32.30N	94.44W
Longview [Wa.-U.S.]	43	Cb	46.08N	122.57W
Longwu	27	Hg	24.07N	102.18 E
Longwy	11	Le	49.31N	5.46 E
Longxi	27	Hd	35.01N	104.38 E
Longxian	27	Id	35.00N	106.53 E
Longxian → Wengyuan	27	Jg	24.21N	114.13 E
Longxi Shan	27	Kf	26.35N	117.17 E
Long Xuyen	25	Lf	10.23N	105.25 E
Longyan	27	Kf	25.06N	117.01 E
Longyao	28	Cf	37.21N	114.46 E
Longyearbyen	67	Kd	78.13N	15.38 E
Longyou	28	Ej	29.01N	119.10 E
Longzhou	27	Ig	22.23N	106.49 E
Lonigo	14	Fe	45.23N	11.23 E
Löningen	10	Dd	52.44N	7.46 E
Lonja	14	Ke	45.27N	16.41 E
Lonjsko Polje	14	Ke	45.24N	16.42 E
Lönsboda	8	Fh	56.24N	14.19 E
Lons-le-Saunier	11	Lh	46.40N	5.33 E
Lontra, Ribeirão-	55	Fe	21.28 S	53.37W
Lookout, Cape- [N.C.-U.S.]	43	Le	34.35N	76.32W
Lookout, Cape- [Or.-U.S.]	46	Dd	45.20N	124.00W
Lookout Mountain	44	Eh	34.40N	85.20W
Lookout Pass	43	Db	47.27N	115.42W
Loolmalasin	36	Gc	3.03 S	35.49 E
Loop Head/Ceann Léime	9	Di	52.34N	9.56W
Loosdrechtse Plassen	12	Hb	52.10N	5.08 E
Lop	27	Dd	37.01N	80.16 E
Lopatina, Gora-	21	Qd	50.52N	143.10 E
Lopatino	16	Nc	52.37N	45.47 E
Lopatka, Mys-	21	Rd	50.52N	156.40 E
Lop Buri	25	Kf	14.48N	100.37 E
Lopča	20	He	55.44N	122.45 E
Lopévi	63b	Dc	16.30 S	168.21 E
Lopez, Cap- = Lopez, Cape- (EN)	30	Hi	0.37 S	8.43 E
Lopez, Cape- (EN) = Lopez, Cap-	30	Hi	0.37 S	8.43 E
Lop Nur	21	Le	40.30N	90.30 E
Lopnur/Yuli	27	Ec	41.22N	86.09 E
Lopori	30	Ih	1.14N	19.49 E
Loppersum	12	Ia	53.19N	6.45 E
Lopphavet	7	Ea	70.25N	22.00 E
Loppi	8	Kd	60.43N	24.27 E
Lopud	14	Lh	42.41N	17.57 E
Łopuszno	10	Qf	50.57N	20.15 E
Lora del Río	13	Gg	37.39N	5.32W
Lorain	43	Kc	41.28N	82.11W
Lorán, Boca-	54	Fb	9.00N	60.45W
Lorca	13	Kg	37.40N	1.42W
Lorch	12	Jd	50.03N	7.49 E
Lord Howe Island	57	Gh	31.35 S	159.05 E
Lord Howe Rise (EN)	3	Jm	32.00 S	162.00 E
Lord Mayor Bay	42	Ic	69.45N	92.00W
Lordsburg	45	Bj	32.21N	108.43W
Loreley	12	Jd	50.08N	7.43 E
Lorena	55	Jf	22.44 S	45.08W
Lorengau	60	Dh	2.01 S	147.17 E
Lorestān [3]	23	Gc	33.30N	48.40 E
Loreto [2]	54	Dd	5.00 S	75.00W
Loreto [Arg.]	55	Dh	27.46 S	57.17W
Loreto [Bol.]	54	Fg	15.13 S	64.40W
Loreto [Braz.]	54	Ie	7.05 S	45.09W
Loreto [It.]	14	Hg	43.26N	13.36 E
Loreto [Mex.]	48	If	22.16N	101.58W
Loreto [Mex.]	47	Bc	26.01N	111.21W
Loreto [Par.]	56	Ib	23.16 S	57.11W
Loreto Aprutino	14	Hh	42.26N	13.59 E
Lorica	54	Cb	9.14N	75.49W
Lorient	6	Ff	47.45N	3.22W
Lőrinci	10	Pi	47.44N	19.41 E
Lorn, Firth of-	9	He	56.20N	5.40W
Lorne	59	Ig	38.33 S	143.59 E
Lörrach	10	Di	47.37N	7.40 E
Lorrain, Plateau-	11	Me	49.00N	6.30 E
Lorrain, Rivière du-	51h	Ab	14.50N	61.03W
Lorraine	11	Lf	49.00N	6.00 E
Lorraine, Plaine-	11	Lf	48.10N	5.50 E
Lorsch	12	Ke	49.39N	8.34 E
Los	7	Df	61.44N	15.10 E
Los, Iles de- = Los Islands (EN)	34	Cd	9.30N	13.48W

Index Symbols

[1] Independent Nation
[2] State, Region
[3] District, County
[4] Municipality
[5] Colony, Dependency
Continent
Physical Region
Historical or Cultural Region
Mount, Mountain
Volcano
Hill
Mountains, Mountain Range
Hills, Escarpment
Plateau, Upland
Pass, Gap
Plain, Lowland
Delta
Salt Flat
Valley, Canyon
Crater, Cave
Karst Features
Depression
Polder
Desert, Dunes
Forest, Woods
Heath, Steppe
Oasis
Cape, Point
Coast, Beach
Cliff
Peninsula
Isthmus
Sandbank
Island
Atoll
Rock, Reef
Islands, Archipelago
Rocks, Reefs
Coral Reef
Well, Spring
Geyser
River, Stream
Waterfall Rapids
River Mouth, Estuary
Lake
Salt Lake
Intermittent Lake
Reservoir
Swamp, Pond
Canal
Glacier
Ice Shelf, Pack Ice
Ocean
Sea
Gulf, Bay
Strait, Fjord
Lagoon
Bank
Seamount
Tablemount
Ridge
Shelf
Basin
Escarpment, Sea Scarp
Fracture
Trench, Abyss
National Park, Reserve
Point of Interest
Recreation Site
Cave, Cavern
Historic Site
Ruins
Wall, Walls
Church, Abbey
Temple
Scientific Station
Airport
Port
Lighthouse
Mine
Tunnel
Dam, Bridge

Los Alamos 39 If 35.53N 106.19W
Los Amates 49 Cf 15.16N 89.06W
Los Amores 55 Ci 28.06S 59.59W
Los Angeles 39 Hf 34.03N 118.15W
Los Ángeles 53 Ii 37.28S 72.21W
Los Angeles Aqueduct 46 Fi 35.22N 118.05W
Losap Atoll 57 Gd 6.54N 152.44 E
Los Banos 46 Eh 37.04N 120.51W
Los Blancos 56 Hb 23.36S 62.36W
Los Charrúas 55 Cj 31.10S 58.11W
Los Chiles 49 Eh 11.02N 84.43W
Los Conquistadores 55 Cj 30.36S 58.28W
Los Frailes, Islas- 50 Eg 11.12N 63.45W
Los Frentones 55 Bh 26.25S 61.25W
Los Gatos 46 Eh 37.14N 121.59W
Losheim 12 Ie 49.31N 6.45 E
Los Hermanos, Islas- 54 Fa 11.45N 64.25W
Łosice 10 Sd 52.14N 22.43 E
Lošinj 14 If 44.35N 14.28 E
Los Islands (EN)=Los, Iles de- 34 Cd 9.30N 13.48W
Los Juries 55 Ai 28.28S 62.06W
Los Lagos 56 Ff 39.51S 72.50W
Los Lagos [2] 56 Ff 41.20S 73.00W
Los Llanos de Aridane 32 Dd 28.39N 17.54W
Los Médanos, Istmo de- 49 Mh 11.35N 69.45W
Los Mochis 39 Ig 25.45N 108.53W
Los Monegros 13 Lc 41.29N 0.03W
Los Monjes, Islas- 54 Da 12.25N 70.55W
Los Navalmorales 13 He 39.43N 4.38W
Loso 36 Ec 1.10S 27.10 E
Los Palacios 49 Fb 22.35N 83.12W
Los Palacios y Villafranca 13 Gg 37.10N 5.56W
Los Pedroches 13 Hf 38.27N 4.45W
Los Pirpintos 55 Ah 26.08S 62.05W
Los Remedios, Río de- 48 Fe 24.41N 106.28W
Los Reyes de Salgado 48 Hh 19.35N 102.29W
Los Roques, Islas- 54 Ea 11.50N 66.45W
Los Roques Basin (EN) 50 Cf 12.20N 67.40W
Los Santos [3] 49 Gj 7.45N 80.30W
Los Santos 49 Gj 7.56N 80.25W
Losser 12 Jb 52.16N 7.01 E
Lossiemouth 9 Jd 57.43N 3.18W
Lossnen 8 Eb 62.30N 12.50 E
Los Taques 49 Lh 11.50N 70.16W
Los Telares 56 Hc 28.59S 63.26W
Los Teques 54 Ea 10.21N 67.02W
Los Testigos, Islas- 54 Fa 11.23N 63.06W
Lost River 46 Ef 41.56N 121.30W
Lost River Range 46 Id 44.10N 113.35W
Lost Trail Pass 43 Eb 45.41N 113.57W
Los Vilos 56 Fd 31.55S 71.31W
Lot 5 Gg 44.18N 0.20 E
Lot [3] 11 Hj 44.30N 1.30 E
Lota 56 Fe 37.05S 73.10W
Lotagipi Swamp 35 Ee 4.36N 34.55 E
Løten 8 Dd 60.49N 11.19 E
Lot-et-Garonne [3] 11 Gj 44.20N 0.30 E
Lothair 37 Ee 26.26S 30.27 E
Lothian [3] 9 Jf 55.55N 3.30W
Lothian 9 Jf 55.55N 3.05W
Loto 36 Dc 2.47S 22.30 E
Lotofaga 65c Ba 13.59S 171.50W
Lotoi 36 Cc 1.35S 18.30 E
Lotru 15 Hd 45.20N 24.16 E
Lotrului, Munții- 15 Gd 45.30N 23.52 E
Lotta 7 Hb 68.39N 30.20 E
Lottefors 8 Gc 61.25N 16.24 E
Löttorp 8 Gg 57.10N 16.59 E
Lotuke, Jabal- 35 Ee 4.07N 33.48 E
Louang Namtha 25 Kd 20.57N 101.25 E
Louangphrabang 22 Mh 19.52N 102.08 E
Loubomo 31 Ii 4.12S 12.41 E
Loučná 10 Lf 50.06N 15.48 E
Loudéac 11 Df 48.10N 2.45W
Loudima 36 Bc 4.07S 13.04 E
Loudon 44 Eh 35.44N 84.20W
Loudun 11 Gh 47.00N 0.04 E
Loué 11 Fg 48.00N 0.09W
Loue 11 Lg 47.01N 5.27 E
Loufan 28 Ae 38.04N 111.47 E
Louga 34 Bb 15.37N 16.13W
Louga [3] 34 Bb 15.00N 15.30W
Louge 11 Hk 43.27N 1.20 E
Loughborough 9 Li 52.47N 1.11W
Lougheed 42 Ha 77.30N 105.00W
Loughrea/Baile Locha Riach 9 Eh 53.12N 8.34W
Louhans 11 Lh 46.38N 5.13 E
Louhi 19 Db 66.04N 33.01 E
Louisa 44 Ff 38.07N 82.36W
Louiseville 44 Kb 46.16N 72.57W
Louisiade Archipelago 57 Gf 11.00S 153.00 E
Louisiana 45 Kg 39.27N 91.03W
Louisiana [2] 43 Ie 31.15N 92.15W
Louis Trichardt 37 Dd 23.01S 29.43 E
Louisville [Ky.-U.S.] 39 Kf 38.16N 85.45W
Louisville [Ms.-U.S.] 45 Lj 33.07N 89.03W
Louis-XIV, Pointe - 42 Jf 54.50N 79.30W
Loukoléla 36 Cc 1.02S 17.07 E
Loulan Yiji 27 Ec 40.32N 89.50 E
Loulé 13 Dg 37.08N 8.02W
Loum 34 Ge 4.43N 9.44 E
Lount Lake 45 Ia 50.10N 94.20W
Louny 10 Jf 50.22N 13.49 E
Loup City 45 Gf 41.17N 98.58W
Loup River 43 Hc 41.24N 97.19W
Loups Marins, Lacs des- 42 Ke 56.40N 74.00W
Lourdes 11 Fk 43.06N 0.03W
Lourenço Marques→Maputo 31 Kk 25.58S 32.34 E
Lousa, Serra da- 13 Dd 40.04N 8.13W
Loushan Guan 27 If 28.02N 106.51 E
Louštín 10 Jf 50.12N 13.48 E
Louth [Austl.] 59 Jf 30.32S 145.07 E
Louth [Eng.-U.K.] 9 Mh 53.22N 0.01W
Louth/Lú [2] 9 Gh 53.55N 6.30W
Loutrá Aidhipsoú 15 Gk 38.51N 23.03 E
Loutrá Killinis 15 El 37.52N 21.07 E
Loutrákion 15 Fl 37.59N 23.00 E
Louvain/Leuven 11 Kd 50.53N 4.42 E
Louvet Point 51k Bb 13.58N 60.53W
Louviers 11 He 49.13N 1.10 E
Lövånger 7 Ed 64.22N 21.18 E
Lovászi 10 Mj 46.33N 16.34 E
Lovat 5 Jd 58.14N 31.28 E
Lovćen 15 Bg 42.24N 18.49 E
Lovec [2] 15 Hf 43.08N 24.43 E
Lovec 15 Hf 43.08N 24.43 E
Loveland 45 Df 40.24N 105.05W
Lovell 43 Fc 44.50N 108.24W
Lovelock 43 Dc 40.11N 118.28W
Lövenich, Köln- 12 Id 50.57N 6.50 E
Lovenske Gorice 14 Jd 46.40N 16.00 E
Lovere 14 Ee 45.49N 10.04 E
Loviisa 7 Gf 60.27N 26.14 E
Loviisa/Lovisa 7 Gf 60.27N 26.14 E
Loving 45 Dj 32.17N 104.06W
Lovington 43 Ge 33.27N 103.21W
Lovisa 7 Gf 60.27N 26.14 E
Lovisa/Loviisa 7 Gf 60.27N 26.14 E
Lovoi 36 Ed 8.05S 26.40 E
Lovosice 10 Kf 50.31N 14.03 E
Lovozero 7 Ib 68.01N 35.01 E
Lovozero, Ozero- 7 Ic 67.50N 35.10 E
Lövstabruk 8 Gd 60.24N 17.53 E
Lövstabukten 8 Gd 60.35N 17.45 E
Lovua 36 Dd 6.07S 20.35 E
Lovua 36 De 11.31S 23.35 E
Low, Cape - 42 Id 63.06N 85.18W
Lowa 30 Ji 1.24S 25.52 E
Lowell 43 Mc 42.39N 71.18W
Löwenberg in der Mark 10 Jd 52.53N 13.09 E
Lower Arrow Lake 46 Fb 49.40N 118.08W
Lower Austria (EN) = Niederösterreich [2] 14 Jb 48.30N 15.45 E
Lower California (EN)=Baja California 38 Hg 28.00N 112.00W
Lower Hutt 62 Fd 41.13S 174.55 E
Lower Lake 46 Ef 41.15N 120.02W
Lower Lake 46 Dg 38.55N 122.36W
Lower Lough Erne/Loch Éirne Íochtair 9 Fg 54.30N 7.50W
Lower Post 42 Ee 59.55N 128.30W
Lower Red Lake 45 Ic 48.00N 94.50W
Lower Rhine (EN) = Neder-Rijn 11 Mc 51.59N 6.20 E
Lower Saxony (EN)= Niedersachsen [2] 10 Fd 52.00N 10.00 E
Lower Trajan's Wall (EN)= Nižni Trajanov Val 15 Ld 45.45N 28.30 E
Lower Tunguska (EN)= Nižnjaja Tunguska 21 Kc 65.48N 88.04 E
Lowestoft 9 Oi 52.29N 1.45 E
Lowestoft Ness 9 Oi 52.28N 1.44 E
Lowgar [3] 23 Kc 33.50N 69.00 E
Łowicz 10 Pd 52.07N 19.56 E
Lowlands 9 Jf 56.00N 4.00W
Lowrah 21 If 31.33N 66.33 E
Lowshān 24 Md 36.39N 49.32 E
Low Tatra (EN) = Nizke Tatry 10 Ph 48.54N 19.40 E
Lowther 42 Hb 74.35N 97.40W
Lowville 44 Jd 43.47N 75.30W
Loxton [Austl.] 59 If 34.27S 140.35 E
Loxton [S.Afr.] 37 Cf 31.30S 22.22 E
Loyalty Islands (EN)= Loyauté, Iles- 57 Hg 21.00S 167.00 E
Loyauté, Iles-=Loyalty Islands (EN) 57 Hg 21.00S 167.00 E
Loyoro 36 Fb 3.21N 34.17 E
Lozère [3] 11 Jj 44.30N 3.30 E
Lozère, Mont- 11 Jj 44.25N 3.46 E
Loznica 15 Ce 44.32N 19.13 E
Lozovaja 19 Df 48.53N 36.15 E
Lozva 19 Gd 59.36N 62.20 E
Lú/Louth [2] 9 Gh 53.55N 6.30W
Lua 36 Cb 2.46N 18.26 E
Luacano 36 De 11.16S 21.38 E
Luachimo 36 Dd 6.33S 20.59 E
Luachimo 31 Ji 7.22S 20.49 E
Luaha-Sibuha 26 Cg 0.31S 98.28 E
Luahoko 65b Ba 19.40S 174.24W
Luala 37 Fc 17.57S 36.30 E
Lualaba 29 Jh 0.26N 25.20 E
Luama 36 Ec 4.46S 26.53 E
Lua Makika 65a Ec 20.35N 156.34W
Luampa 36 De 14.32S 24.10 E
Lu'an 27 Ke 31.44N 116.30 E
Luanda 31 Ii 8.50S 13.15 E
Luanda [3] 36 Bd 8.30S 13.20 E
Luando 30 Ij 10.19S 16.40 E
Luang, Khao- 25 Jg 8.31N 99.47 E
Luang, Thale- 25 Kg 7.30N 100.15 E
Luang Chiang Dao, Doi- 25 Je 19.23N 98.54 E
Luanginga 30 Jj 15.11S 22.55 E
Luang Prabang Range 25 Ke 18.30N 101.15 E
Luangue 36 Dc 4.17S 20.01 E
Luangwa 30 Kj 15.36S 30.25 E
Luan He 21 Nf 39.20N 119.10 E
Luaniva 64h Bb 13.16S 176.07W
Luannan (Bencheng) 28 Ee 39.30N 118.42 E
Luanping (Anjiangying) 28 Dd 40.55N 117.19 E
Luanshya 31 Jj 13.08S 28.25 E
Luanxian 27 Kd 39.45N 118.44 E
Luanza 36 Ed 8.40S 28.40 E
Luao 36 De 10.42S 22.12 E
Luapula 30 Ji 9.26S 28.33 E
Luapula [3] 36 Ee 10.40S 29.15 E
Luarca 13 Fa 43.32N 6.32W
Luashi 36 De 10.56S 23.37 E
Luba 34 Ge 3.28N 8.40 E
Lubaantum 49 Ce 16.17N 88.58W
Lubaczów 10 Tf 50.10N 23.07 E
Lubaczówka 10 Sf 50.08N 22.35 E
Lubalo 36 Cd 7.22S 19.20 E
Lubalo 36 Cd 9.07S 19.15 E
Lubamba 36 Ed 5.14S 26.02 E
Lubań 10 Le 51.08N 15.18 E
Lubāna/Lubana 8 Lh 56.49N 26.49 E
Lubana/Lubāna 8 Lh 56.49N 26.49 E
Lubanas, Ozero-/Lubānas Ezers 8 Lh 56.40N 27.00 E
Lubānas Ezers/Lubanas, Ozero- 8 Lh 56.40N 27.00 E
Lubang Islands 26 Hd 13.45N 120.15 E
Lubango 31 Ij 14.55S 13.28 E
Lubao 31 Ji 5.22S 25.45 E
Lubartów 10 Se 51.28N 22.46 E
Lubawa 10 Pc 53.30N 19.45 E
Lübbecke 10 Ed 52.18N 8.37 E
Lubbeek 12 Gd 50.53N 4.50 E
Lübben/Lubin 10 Je 51.57N 13.54 E
Lübbenau/Lubnjow 10 Je 51.52N 13.58 E
Lubbock 39 If 33.35N 101.51W
Lübeck 6 He 53.52N 10.42 E
Lübecker Bucht 10 Gb 54.00N 10.55 E
Lübeck-Travemünde 10 Gc 53.57N 10.52 E
Lubefu 36 Dc 4.10S 23.00 E
Lubefu 36 Dc 4.43S 24.25 E
Lubei→Jarud Qi 27 Lc 44.30N 120.55 E
Lubelska, Wyżyna- 10 Sf 51.00N 23.00 E
Lubenec 10 Jf 50.08N 13.20 E
Lubenka 16 Sd 50.28N 54.06 E
Lubero 36 Ec 0.06S 29.06 E
Lubéron, Montagne du- 11 Lk 43.48N 5.22 E
Lubi 36 Dc 4.59S 23.26 E
Lubie, Jezioro- 10 Lc 53.30N 15.50 E
Lubień Kujawski 10 Pd 52.25N 19.10 E
Lubij/Löbau 10 Ke 51.06N 14.40 E
Lubilash 29 Ji 6.02S 23.45 E
Lubin 10 Me 51.24N 16.13 E
Lubin/Lübben 10 Je 51.57N 13.54 E
Lublin 6 Ie 51.15N 22.35 E
Lublin [2] 10 Se 51.15N 22.35 E
Lubliniec 10 Of 50.40N 18.41 E
Lubnān=Lebanon (EN) [1] 22 Ff 33.50N 35.50 E
Lubnān, Jabal-=Lebanon Mountains (EN) 23 Ec 34.00N 36.30 E
Lubnjow/Lübbenau 10 Je 51.52N 13.58 E
Lubny 19 De 50.01N 33.00 E
Luboń 10 Md 52.23N 16.54 E
Lubraniec 10 Od 52.33N 18.50 E
Lubsko 10 Ke 51.46N 14.59 E
Lubsza 10 Ke 51.55N 14.45 E
Lubudi [2] 29 Ji 9.13S 25.38 E
Lubudi 36 Ed 9.57S 25.58 E
Lubue 36 Cc 4.10S 19.53 E
Lubuklinggau 26 Dg 3.10S 102.52 E
Lubuksikaping 26 Df 0.08N 100.10 E
Lubumba 36 Ec 3.58S 29.06 E
Lubumbashi 31 Jj 11.40S 27.30 E
Lubuskie, Pojezierze- 10 Ld 52.18N 15.20 E
Lubutu 31 Ji 0.44S 26.35 E
Lucala 36 Bd 6.38S 12.34 E
Lucala 36 Cd 9.16S 15.16 E
Lucania, Mount- 42 Dd 61.01N 140.29W
Lucas 55 Ea 13.05S 55.56W
Lucca 14 Eg 43.50N 10.29 E
Lucea 49 Hd 18.27N 78.10W
Luce Bay 9 Ig 54.47N 4.50W
Lucedale 45 Lk 30.55N 88.35W
Lučegorsk 20 Ig 46.25N 134.20 E
Lucélia 55 Ge 21.44S 51.01W
Lucena [Phil.] 26 Hd 13.56N 121.37 E
Lucena [Sp.] 13 Hg 37.24N 4.29W
Lucena del Cid 13 Ld 40.08N 0.17W
Luc-en-Diois 11 Lj 44.37N 5.27 E
Lučenec 10 Ph 48.20N 19.41 E
Lucera 14 Ji 41.30N 15.20 E
Lucerne (EN) = Luzern 14 Cc 47.05N 8.20 E
Lucerne, Lake- (EN) = Vierwaldstätter-See 14 Cc 47.00N 8.30 E
Lucero 48 Fb 30.49N 106.30W
Lucheng 28 Bf 36.18N 113.15 E
Lucheringo 37 Fb 11.43S 36.15 E
Lucheux 12 Ed 50.12N 2.25 E
Luchico 30 Lj 12.15S 44.25 E
Luchico 36 Cd 6.12S 19.42 E
Lüchow 10 Hd 52.58N 11.09 E
Lüchun 27 Hg 23.02N 102.19 E
Lucipara, Kepulauan- 26 Ih 5.30S 127.33 E
Lucira 36 Be 13.52S 12.32 E
Luck 19 Ce 50.47N 25.20 E
Luckau 10 Je 51.51N 13.43 E
Luckenwalde 10 Jd 52.05N 13.10 E
Lucknow 22 Kg 26.51N 80.55 E
Luçon 11 Eh 46.27N 1.10W
Lucrecia, Cabo- 49 Jc 21.04N 75.37W
Luc-sur-Mer 12 Be 49.19N 0.21W
Lucunga 36 Bd 6.49S 14.35 E
Lucusse 36 De 12.33S 20.51 E
Lüda→Dalian=Dairan (EN) 22 Of 38.55N 121.39 E
Luda Kamčija 15 Kg 43.03N 27.29 E
Ludbreg 14 Kd 46.15N 16.37 E
Lüdenscheid 10 De 51.13N 7.37 E
Lüderitz 31 Ik 26.38S 15.10 E
Lüderitz [3] 37 Be 26.00S 15.00 E
Lüderitz Bay 37 Be 26.35S 15.10 E
Ludhiāna 22 Jf 30.54N 75.51 E
Ludinghausen 10 De 51.46N 7.28 E
Ludington 43 Jc 43.57N 86.27W
Ludlow 9 Ki 52.22N 2.43W
Ludogorije 15 Jf 43.46N 26.56 E
Ludogorsko Plato 15 Kf 43.36N 27.03 E
Luduş 15 Hc 46.29N 24.06 E
Ludvika 7 Df 60.09N 15.11 E
Ludwigsburg 10 Fh 48.54N 9.11 E
Ludwigshafen am Rhein 10 Eg 49.29N 8.27 E
Ludwigslust 10 Hc 53.19N 11.30 E
Ludza 7 Gh 56.32N 27.45 E
Luebo 31 Ji 5.21S 21.25 E
Lueki 36 Ec 3.24S 25.57 E
Lueki 36 Ec 3.22S 25.51 E
Luele 36 Dd 7.55S 20.00 E
Luembé 36 Dd 6.43S 24.11 E
Luembe 36 Dd 6.37S 21.06 E
Luena [Ang.] 36 De 12.31S 22.34 E
Luena [Ang.] 31 Ij 11.48S 19.55 E
Luena [Zaire] 36 Ed 9.27S 25.47 E
Luena [Zam.] 36 Df 15.20S 23.30 E
Luengué 36 Df 16.54S 21.52 E
Luenha 37 Ec 16.24S 33.48 E
Luera Peak 45 Cj 33.47N 107.49W
Lueta 36 Dd 7.04S 21.40 E
Lueyang 27 Ie 33.25N 106.14 E
Lufeng 27 Kg 22.57N 115.41 E
Lufico 36 Bd 6.22S 13.30 E
Lufira 29 Ji 8.16S 26.27 E
Lufira, Chutes de la- 36 Ed 9.50S 27.30 E
Lufkin 43 Ie 31.20N 94.44W
Lug 15 De 44.23N 20.45 E
Luga 19 Cd 59.43N 28.18 E
Luga 19 Cd 58.44N 29.50 E
Lugano 14 Cd 46.00N 8.57 E
Lugano, Lago di- 14 Cd 46.00N 9.00 E
Luganville 58 Hf 15.32S 167.10 E
Lugards Falls 30 Ki 3.03S 38.42 E
Lügde 12 Lc 51.57N 9.15 E
Lugela 37 Fc 16.26S 36.39 E
Lugenda 30 Kj 11.26S 38.33 E
Lugnaquillia 5 Fe 52.58N 6.27W
Lugo [3] 13 Eb 43.00N 7.30W
Lugo [It.] 14 Ff 44.25N 11.54 E
Lugo [Sp.] 13 Ea 43.00N 7.34W
Lugoj 15 Ed 45.41N 21.55 E
Lugovoj [Kaz.-U.S.S.R.] 19 Hg 42.55N 72.47 E
Lugovoj [R.S.F.S.R.] 19 Gd 59.44N 65.55 E
Lugovski 20 Ge 58.05N 112.55 E
Lugulu 36 Ec 2.17S 26.32 E
Luh 7 Kh 56.14N 42.28 E
Luhe 10 Gc 53.18N 10.11 E
Luhe 28 Eh 32.21N 118.50 E
Luhin Sum 27 Kb 46.41N 118.38 E
Luhit 25 Jc 27.48N 95.28 E
Luhovicy 7 Ji 54.59N 39.02 E
Luhuo 27 He 31.21N 100.40 E
Lui 36 Cd 8.41S 17.56 E
Luia 36 Dd 8.26S 21.43 E
Luiana 36 Df 17.22S 22.59 E
Luiana 30 Jj 17.27S 23.14 E
Luie 36 Cc 4.33S 17.41 E
Luik/Liège 6 Ge 50.38N 5.34 E
Luilaka 30 Ji 0.52S 20.12 E
Luilu 36 Dd 6.22S 23.50 E
Luimbale 36 Ce 12.15S 15.19 E
Luimneach/Limerick 6 Fe 52.40N 8.38W
Luimneach/Limerick [2] 9 Ei 52.30N 9.00W
Luing 9 He 56.13N 5.39W
Luino 14 Cd 46.00N 8.44 E
Luio 36 De 13.15S 21.39 E
Lui Pătru, Vîrful- 15 Gd 45.30N 23.30 E
Luis Correia 54 Jd 2.53S 41.40W
Luishia 36 Ee 11.13S 27.07 E
Luitpold Coast 66 Af 78.30S 32.00W
Luiza 36 Dd 7.12S 22.25 E
Luján [Arg.] 56 Gd 32.22S 65.57W
Luján [Arg.] 56 Id 34.34S 59.07W
Lujiang 28 Di 31.15N 117.17 E
Lukafu 36 Ee 10.30S 27.33 E
Lukanga Swamp 36 Ee 14.25S 27.45 E
Lukavac 14 Mf 44.33N 18.32 E
Lukengo 36 Ed 5.46S 29.06 E
Lukenie 30 Ii 2.44S 18.09 E
Lukeville 46 Ik 31.57N 112.50W
Lukojanov 19 Ed 55.02N 44.30 E
Lukolela 36 Cc 1.03S 17.12 E
Lukonzolwa 36 Ed 8.47S 28.39 E
Lukov 10 Ue 51.14N 24.25 E
Lukovit 15 Hf 43.12N 24.10 E
Łuków 10 Se 51.56N 22.23 E
Lukuga 30 Ji 5.40S 26.55 E
Lukula 36 Bd 5.23S 12.57 E
Lukulu 36 De 14.23S 23.15 E
Lukusashi 36 Fe 14.38S 30.00 E
Luleå 6 Ib 65.34N 22.10 E
Luleälven 5 Ib 65.35N 22.03 E
Lüleburgaz 23 Ca 41.24N 27.21 E
Lüliang Shan 21 Nf 37.45N 111.25 E
Lulimba 36 Ec 4.42S 28.38 E
Luling 45 Hl 29.41N 97.39W
Lulong 28 Ee 39.53N 118.52 E
Lulonga 36 Cb 0.37N 18.23 E
Lulonga 30 Ih 0.43N 18.23 E
Lulua 30 Ji 5.02S 21.07 E
Lulu Fakahega, Mount- 64h Bb 13.16S 176.10W
Luma 65c Db 14.14S 169.32W
Lumajang 26 Fh 8.08S 113.13 E
Lumajangdong Co 27 De 34.00N 81.37 E
Lumbala [Ang.] 31 Jj 14.06S 21.25 E
Lumbala [Ang.] 36 De 12.39S 22.32 E
Lumberton 43 Le 34.37N 79.00W
Lumbo 37 Gc 15.00S 40.44 E
Lumbrales 13 Fd 40.56N 6.43W
Lumbres 12 Ed 50.42N 2.08 E
Lumby 46 Fa 50.15N 118.58W
Lumding 25 Ic 25.45N 93.10 E
Lumege 36 De 11.34S 20.48 E
Lumesule 36 Ge 11.14S 38.06 E
Lumi 60 Ch 3.29S 142.03 E
Lummen 12 Hd 50.59N 5.15 E
Lumparland 8 Id 60.10N 20.15 E
Lumphăt 25 Lf 13.30N 106.59 E
Lumsden [N.Z.] 62 Cf 45.44S 168.26 E
Lumsden [Sask.-Can.] 46 Ma 50.34N 104.53W
Lumuna 36 Ec 3.46S 26.24 E
Lumut 26 Df 4.14N 100.38 E
Luna 13 Gb 42.40N 5.49W
Luna, Laguna de- 55 Di 28.06S 56.46W
Lunan Shan 27 Hf 27.00N 102.30 E
Lunayyir, Harrat- 24 Gj 25.10N 37.50 E
Lunca Ilvei 15 Hb 47.22N 24.59 E
Lund 7 Ci 55.42N 13.11 E
Lunda [3] 36 Cd 9.30S 20.00 E
Lundazi 31 Kj 12.19S 33.13 E
Lunde 8 Gb 62.53N 17.51 E
Lundevatn 8 Bf 58.20N 6.35 E
Lundi 30 Kk 21.19S 32.24 E
Lundu 26 Ef 1.40N 109.51 E
Lundy Island 9 Ij 51.10N 4.40W
Lüneburg 10 Gc 53.15N 10.24 E
Lüneburger Heide 10 Gc 53.10N 10.20 E
Lunel 11 Kk 43.41N 4.08 E
Lünen 10 De 51.37N 7.31 E
Lunéville 11 Mf 48.36N 6.30 E
Lunga 30 Jj 14.34S 26.26 E
Lungué-Bungo 37 Jj 28.38S 16.27 E
Lungwebungu 36 De 14.19S 23.14 E
Lūni 25 Ed 24.41N 71.14 E
Lūni 25 Ee 26.00N 73.00 E
Lunigiana 14 Df 44.20N 9.55 E
Luninec 19 Ce 52.16N 26.50 E
Lunino 16 Nc 53.35N 45.14 E
Lunsemfwa 36 Fe 14.54S 30.12 E
Luntai/Bügür 27 Dc 41.46N 84.10 E
Luobei (Fengxiang) 27 Nb 47.36N 130.58 E
Luobuzhuang 27 Ed 39.30N 88.15 E
Luocheng 27 Ig 24.51N 108.53 E
Luodian (Longping) 27 If 25.26N 106.47 E
Luoding 27 Jg 22.43N 111.33 E
Luohe 27 Je 33.30N 114.08 E
Luo He 27 Id 32.18N 109.12 E
Luoma Hu 28 Eg 34.10N 118.12 E
Luonteri 8 Lc 61.35N 27.45 E
Luoping 27 Hg 24.58N 104.19 E
Luopioinen 8 Kc 61.22N 24.40 E
Luoshan 28 Ch 32.13N 114.32 E
Luotian 28 Ci 30.48N 115.23 E
Luoxiao Shan 27 Jf 26.35N 114.00 E
Luoyang 22 Nf 34.41N 112.25 E
Luoyuan 27 Kf 26.31N 119.32 E
Luozi 36 Bc 4.57S 14.08 E
Lupa 36 Fd 8.39S 33.12 E
Lupane 37 Dc 18.56S 27.48 E
Łupawa 10 Nb 54.42N 17.07 E
Lupeni 15 Gd 45.21N 23.14 E
Luperón 49 Ld 19.54N 70.57W
Łupków 10 Sg 49.12N 22.06 E
Luputa 36 Dd 7.10S 23.42 E
Lüq 31 Lh 3.56N 42.32 E
Luqiao 28 Fj 28.39N 120.05 E
Luqu 27 He 34.36N 102.30 E
Luque 56 Ic 25.16S 57.34W
Luquillo 51a Cb 18.22N 65.43W
Luray 44 Hf 38.40N 78.28W
Lure 11 Mg 47.41N 6.30 E
Lure, Montagne de- 11 Lj 44.07N 5.47 E
Luremo 36 Cd 8.30S 17.51 E
Lurgan/An Lorgain 9 Gg 54.28N 6.20W
Lurin 54 Cf 12.17S 76.52W
Lúrio 37 Gb 13.32S 40.30 E
Lúrio 30 Lj 13.31S 40.42 E
Lusaka 31 Jj 15.25S 28.17 E
Lusambo 31 Ji 4.58S 23.27 E
Lusanga 36 Cc 4.44S 18.58 E
Lusangi 36 Ec 4.37S 27.08 E
Lu Shan 27 Kf 29.30N 115.55 E
Lushan [China] 28 Cj 29.33N 115.58 E
Lushan [China] 28 Bh 33.44N 112.54 E
Lushi 27 Je 34.04N 111.02 E
Lushiko 36 Cd 6.12S 19.42 E
Lushnja 15 Ci 40.56N 19.42 E
Lushoto 36 Gc 4.47S 38.17 E
Lu Shui 28 Bj 29.54N 113.39 E
Lushui (Luzhangjie) 27 Gf 26.00N 98.50 E
Lüshun=Port Arthur (EN) 27 Ld 38.50N 121.13 E
Lusignan 11 Gh 46.26N 0.07 E
Lusk 43 Gc 42.46N 104.27W
Lussac-les-Châteaux 11 Gh 46.24N 0.43 E
Lustrafjorden 8 Bc 61.20N 7.20 E
Lūt, Dasht-e-=Lut, Dasht-i- (EN) 21 Hf 33.00N 57.00 E
Lut, Dasht-i- (EN)=Lūt, Dasht-e- 21 Hf 33.00N 57.00 E
Lu Tao 27 Lg 22.35N 121.30 E
Lutembo 36 De 13.28S 21.22 E
Luti 63a Cb 7.14S 157.00 E
Lütjenburg 10 Gb 54.17N 10.35 E
Luton 9 Mj 51.53N 0.25W
Luton Airport 12 Bc 51.50N 0.22W
Lutong 26 Ff 4.28N 114.00 E
Lutshima 36 Cd 5.22S 18.59 E
Lutshima 36 Cd 5.22S 18.59 E
Lutterworth 12 Ab 52.27N 1.12W
Lutuai 36 De 12.40S 20.12 E
Lutugino 16 Ke 48.23N 39.13 E
Lützow-Holmbukta 66 De 69.10S 37.30 E
Lutzputs 37 Ce 28.22S 20.37 E
Luuk 26 He 5.58N 121.18 E
Luverne 45 He 43.39N 96.13W
Luvidjo 36 Ed 6.26S 26.59 E
Luvua 30 Ji 6.46S 26.58 E
Luvuei 36 De 13.06S 21.12 E
Luwegu 30 Ki 8.31S 37.23 E
Luwingu 36 Ee 10.16S 29.54 E
Luwuk 26 Hg 0.56S 122.47 E
Luxembourg [3] 12 He 50.00N 5.30 E
Luxembourg/Luxemburg [1] 6 Gf 49.45N 6.05 E
Luxembourg/Luxemburg 6 Gf 49.45N 6.05 E
Luxemburg/Luxembourg 6 Gf 49.45N 6.05 E
Luxemburg/Luxembourg [1] 6 Gf 49.45N 6.05 E
Luxeuil-les-Bains 11 Mg 47.49N 6.23 E
Luxi 22 Mg 24.34N 103.44 E
Luxi (Mangshi) 27 Gg 24.29N 98.40 E
Luxor (EN)=Al Uqşur 33 Fd 25.41N 32.39 E
Luy 11 Ek 43.39N 1.08W
Luy de Béarn 11 Fk 43.38N 0.47W

Index Symbols

[1] Independent Nation
[2] State, Region
[3] District, County
[4] Municipality
[5] Colony, Dependency
Continent
Physical Region
Historical or Cultural Region
Mount, Mountain
Volcano
Hill
Mountains, Mountain Range
Hills, Escarpment
Plateau, Upland
Pass, Gap
Plain, Lowland
Delta
Salt Flat
Valley, Canyon
Crater, Cave
Karst Features
Depression
Polder
Desert, Dunes
Forest, Woods
Heath, Steppe
Oasis
Cape, Point
Coast, Beach
Cliff
Peninsula
Isthmus
Sandbank
Island
Atoll
Rock, Reef
Islands, Archipelago
Rocks, Reefs
Coral Reef
Well, Spring
Geyser
River, Stream
Waterfall Rapids
River Mouth, Estuary
Lake
Salt Lake
Intermittent Lake
Reservoir
Swamp, Pond
Canal
Glacier
Ice Shelf, Pack Ice
Ocean
Sea
Gulf, Bay
Strait, Fjord
Lagoon
Bank
Seamount
Tablemount
Ridge
Shelf
Basin
Escarpment, Sea Scarp
Fracture
Trench, Abyss
National Park, Reserve
Point of Interest
Recreation Site
Cave, Cavern
Historic Site
Ruins
Wall, Walls
Church, Abbey
Temple
Scientific Station
Airport
Port
Lighthouse
Mine
Tunnel
Dam, Bridge

Luy de France 11 Fk 43.38N 0.47W
Luyi 28 Ch 33.51N 115.28 E
Luz 55 Jd 19.48S 45.41W
Luz, Costa de la- 13 Fh 36.40N 6.20W
Luza 19 Ec 60.39N 47.15 E
Luza 5 Kc 60.40N 46.25 E
Luzarches 12 Ee 49.07N 2.25 E
Luzern [2] 14 Cc 47.05N 8.10 E
Luzern = Lucerne (EN) 14 Cc 47.05N 8.20 E
Luzhai 27 Ig 24.31N 109.46 E
Luzhangjie → Lushui 27 Gf 26.00N 98.50 E
Luzhou 22 Mg 28.55N 105.20 E
Luziânia 54 Ig 16.15S 47.56W
Luzická Nisa 10 Kd 52.04N 14.46 E
Luzilândia 54 Jd 3.28S 42.22W
Lužnice 10 Kg 49.16N 14.25 E
Luzon 21 Oh 16.00N 121.00 E
Luzon Sea 26 Gd 12.30N 119.00 E
Luzon Strait (EN) 21 Og 21.00N 122.00 E
Luz-Saint-Sauveur 11 Gl 42.52N 0.01 E
Lužskaja Guba 8 Me 59.35N 28.25 E
Lužskaja Vozvyšennost 8 Mf 58.15N 28.45 E
Luzy 11 Jh 46.47N 3.58 E
Łużyca 10 Oe 51.33N 18.15 E
Lvov 6 If 49.50N 24.00 E
Lvovskaja Oblast [3] 19 Cf 49.45N 24.00 E
Lwowa 60 Hj 10.44S 165.45 E
Lwówek 10 Md 52.28N 16.10 E
Lwówek Śląski 10 Le 51.07N 15.35 E
Lyakhov Islands (EN) = Ljahovskije Ostrova 21 Qb 73.30N 141.00 E
Lyall, Mount- 62 Bf 45.17S 167.33 E
Lyallpur 22 Jf 31.25N 73.05 E
Lychsele 7 Ed 64.36N 18.40 E
Lycia 15 Mm 36.30N 29.30 E
Lyckeby 8 Fh 56.12N 15.39 E
Lyckebyån 8 Fh 56.11N 15.40 E
Lyčkovo 7 Hh 57.57N 32.24 E
Lydd 9 Nk 50.57N 0.55 E
Lydd Airport 12 Cd 50.58N 0.56 E
Lydenburg 37 Ee 25.10S 30.29 E
Lydia 15 Lk 38.35N 28.30 E
Lygna 8 Bf 58.10N 7.02 E
Lygnern 8 Eg 57.29N 12.20 E
Lyme Bay 9 Kk 50.38N 3.00W
Lyminge 12 Dc 51.07N 1.05 E
Lymington 9 Lk 50.46N 1.33W
Łyna 10 Rb 54.37N 21.14 E
Lynchburg 43 Ld 37.24N 79.09W
Lynd 58 Ff 18.56S 144.30 E
Lynden 46 Db 48.57N 122.27W
Lyndon River 59 Cd 23.29S 114.06 E
Lyngdal 7 Bg 58.08N 7.05 E
Lyngen 7 Eb 69.58N 20.30 E
Lyngør 8 Cf 58.38N 9.10 E
Lyngseidet 7 Eb 69.35N 20.13 E
Lynn 44 Ld 42.28N 70.57W
Lynnaj, Gora- 20 Ld 62.55N 163.58 E
Lynn Canal 40 Le 58.50N 135.15W
Lynn Deeps 12 Cb 52.58N 0.20 E
Lynn Lake 39 Id 56.51N 101.03W
Lyntupy 8 Li 55.02N 26.27 E
Lynx Lake 42 Gd 62.25N 106.20W
Lyon 6 Gf 45.45N 4.51 E
Lyon Inlet 42 Jc 66.20N 83.40W
Lyonnais, Monts du- 11 Ki 45.40N 4.30 E
Lyon River 59 De 25.00S 115.20 E
Lyons [Ga.-U.S.] 44 Fi 32.12N 82.19W
Lyons [Ks.-U.S.] 45 Gg 38.21N 98.12W
Lyons, Forêt de- 12 De 49.25N 1.30 E
Lyons-la-Forêt 12 De 49.24N 1.28 E
Lyra Reef 60 Eh 1.50S 153.35 E
Lys 11 Jc 51.03N 3.43 E
Łysa Góra 10 Nd 52.07N 17.33 E
Lysaja, Gora- 8 Lj 54.12N 27.40 E
Lysá nad Labem 10 Kf 50.12N 14.50 E
Lysefjorden 8 Be 59.00N 6.14 E
Lysekil 7 Cf 58.16N 11.26 E
Lyskovo 19 Ed 56.03N 45.03 E
Lyss 14 Bc 47.04N 7.37 E
Lysva 19 Fd 58.07N 57.47 E
Lytham Saint Anne's 9 Jh 53.45N 3.01W
Lyttelton 62 Ee 43.36S 172.43 E
Lytton 46 Ea 50.14N 121.34W
Lyža 17 Hd 65.42N 56.40 E

M

Ma, Oued el- 32 Fe 24.03N 9.10W
Ma, Song 25 Le 19.45N 105.55 E
Maâdis, Djebel- 13 Qi 35.52N 4.44 E
Maalaea Bay 65a Ec 20.47N 156.29W
Ma'āmīr 24 Mg 30.04N 48.20 E
Ma'ān 23 Ec 30.12N 35.44 E
Ma'ānīyah 24 Jg 30.44N 43.00 E
Maanselkä 5 Ib 68.07N 28.29 E
Maanselkä 7 Ge 63.54N 28.30 E
Ma'anshan 27 Ke 31.38N 118.30 E
Maardu 8 Ke 59.28N 24.56 E
Maarianhamina/Mariehamn 7 Ef 60.06N 19.57 E
Ma 'arrat an Nu 'mān 24 Ge 35.38N 36.40 E
Maarssen 12 Hb 52.08N 5.03 E
Maas = Meuse (EN) 5 Ge 51.49N 5.01 E
Maaseik 11 Lc 51.06N 5.48 E
Maaseik-Neeroeteren 12 Hc 51.05N 5.42 E
Maasin 26 Hd 10.08N 124.50 E
Maasmechelen/Mechelen 12 Hd 50.57N 5.40 E
Maassluis 12 Gc 51.55N 4.17 E
Maastricht 11 Ld 50.52N 5.43 E
Maasupa 63a Ec 9.18S 161.15 E
Ma'āzah, Al Haḑabat al- 33 Fd 27.44N 31.44 E
Mabalane 37 Ed 23.38S 32.31 E
Mabaruma 50 Gh 8.12N 59.47W
Mabechi-Gawa 29 Ga 40.31N 141.31 E
Mabella 45 Lb 48.37N 89.58W
Mabel Lake 46 Fa 50.35N 118.44W
Mablethorpe 9 Nh 53.21N 0.15 E
Mabote 37 Ed 22.03S 34.08 E
Ma'būs Yūsuf 31 Jf 25.45N 21.00 E
Maçaão 13 Ee 39.33N 8.00W
McAdam 42 Kg 45.36N 67.20W
Macajaí, Rio- 54 Fc 2.25N 60.50W
McAllen 43 Hf 26.12N 98.15W
Macaloge 37 Fb 12.25S 35.25 E
Mac Alpine Lake 42 Hc 66.40N 102.50W
Macambará 55 Di 29.08S 56.03W
Macamic 44 Ha 48.48N 79.01W
Macamic, Lac- 44 Ha 48.46N 79.00W
Macao (EN) = Aomen/ Macau [5] 22 Ng 22.10N 113.33 E
Macao (EN) = Aomen/Macau 27 Jg 22.12N 113.33 E
Macao (EN) = Macau/ Aomen [5] 22 Ng 22.10N 113.33 E
Macao (EN) = Macau/Aomen 27 Jg 22.12N 113.33 E
Macapá 53 Ke 0.02N 51.03W
Macará 54 Cd 4.21S 79.56W
Macaracas 49 Gj 7.44N 80.33W
Macareo, Caño- 54 Fb 9.47N 61.36W
McArthur 44 Ff 39.14N 82.29W
Mc Arthur River 59 Hc 15.54S 136.40 E
Maçãs 13 Fc 41.29N 6.39W
Macas 54 Cd 2.18S 78.06W
Macatete, Sierra de- 48 Dd 28.00N 110.05W
Macau 53 Mf 5.07S 36.38W
Macau/Aomen = Macao (EN) 27 Jg 22.12N 113.33 E
Macau/Aomen = Macao (EN) [5] 22 Ng 22.10N 113.33 E
Macaúbas 54 Jf 13.02S 42.42W
Macauley Island 57 Ih 30.13S 178.33W
Macaya, Pic de- 47 Je 18.23N 74.02W
McBeth Fiord 42 Kc 69.43N 69.20W
McCamey 45 Ek 31.08N 102.13W
McCammon 46 Ie 42.39N 112.12W
Mc Carthy 40 Kd 61.26N 142.55W
McClellanville 44 Hi 33.06N 79.28W
MacClenny 44 Fj 30.18N 82.07W
Macclesfield 9 Kh 53.16N 2.07W
Macclesfield Bank (EN) 26 Fc 15.50N 114.20 E
McClintock 42 Ie 57.48N 94.12W
McClintock, Mount- 66 Jg 80.13S 157.26 E
Mc Clintock Channel 38 Ib 71.00N 101.00W
McCluer Gulf (EN) = Berau, Teluk- 26 Jg 2.30S 132.30 E
Mc Clure Strait 38 Hb 74.30N 116.00W
McClusky 45 Fc 47.29N 100.27W
McComb 43 Ie 31.14N 90.27W
McConaughy, Lake- 45 Ff 41.18N 101.46W
McConnelsville 44 Gf 39.39N 81.51W
McCook 43 Gc 40.12N 100.38W
McCormick 44 Fi 33.55N 82.19W
McDame 42 Ee 59.13N 129.14W
McDermitt 46 Gf 41.59N 117.36W
Macdhui, Ben- 9 Jd 57.04N 3.40W
Macdonald, Lake- 59 Fd 23.30S 129.00 E
Mc Donald Islands 30 On 52.59S 72.50 E
McDonald Peak [Ca.-U.S.] 46 Ef 40.58N 120.26W
McDonald Peak [Mt.-U.S.] 46 Ic 47.29N 113.46W
Macdonald Range 46 Hb 49.12N 114.46W
Macdonnell Ranges 57 Eg 23.45S 132.20 E
McDouglas Sound 42 Hd 75.15N 97.30W
Macduff 9 Kd 57.40N 2.29W
Macedo de Cavaleiros 13 Fc 41.32N 6.58W
Macedonia (EN) = Makedhonia 5 Ig 41.00N 23.00 E
Macedonia (EN) = Makedhonia 15 Fh 41.00N 23.00 E
Macedonia (EN) = Makedonija [2] 15 Eh 41.50N 22.00 E
Macedonia (EN) = Makedonija 5 Ig 41.00N 23.00 E
Macedonia (EN) = Makedonija 15 Fh 41.00N 23.00 E
Maceió 53 Mf 9.40S 35.43W
Macenta 34 Dd 8.33N 9.28W
Macerata 14 Hg 43.18N 13.27 E
McGehee 45 Kj 33.38N 91.24W
McGill 46 Hg 39.23N 114.47W
Macgillycuddy's Reeks/Na Cruacha Dubha 9 Di 52.00N 9.50W
McGrath 40 Hd 62.58N 155.38W
MacGregor 45 Gb 49.57N 98.49W
McGregor 45 Jc 46.36N 93.19W
McGregor Lake 46 Ia 50.31N 112.53W
Mc Gregor Range 59 Ie 26.40S 142.45 E
McGuire, Mount- 46 Hd 45.10N 114.36W
Machachi 54 Cd 0.30S 78.34W
Machado 55 Je 21.41S 45.56W
Machagai 56 Hc 26.56S 60.03W
Machaila 37 Ed 22.15S 32.58 E
Machaire na Mumhan/ Golden Vale 9 Fi 52.30N 8.00W
Machaire Rátha/Maghera 9 Gg 54.51N 6.40W
Machakos 36 Gc 1.31S 37.16 E
Machala 54 Cd 3.16S 79.58W
Machaneng 37 Dd 23.12S 27.30 E
Machareti 54 Fh 20.49S 63.24W
Machar Marshes 35 Ed 9.20N 33.10 E
Machattie, Lake- 59 Hd 24.50S 139.48 E
Machault 12 Ge 49.21N 4.30 E
Macheke 37 Ec 18.05S 31.51 E
Macheng 27 Je 31.10N 115.00 E
Machias 44 Nc 44.43N 67.28W
Machida 29 Fd 35.32N 139.27 E
Machilipatnam (Bandar) 25 Ge 16.10N 81.08 E
Machiques 54 Da 10.04N 72.34W
Machona, Laguna- 48 Mh 18.20N 93.40W
Machów 10 Rf 50.34N 21.40 E
Machupicchu 53 Ig 13.07S 72.34W
Macia 37 Ef 25.02S 33.06 E
Mc Ilwraith Range 59 Ib 13.45S 143.20 E
Măcin 15 Ld 45.15N 28.09 E
Macina 30 Gg 14.30N 5.00W
McIntosh 45 Fd 45.55N 101.21W
Macintyre River 59 Je 29.25S 148.45 E
Maçka 24 Hb 40.50N 39.38 E
Mackay [Austl.] 58 Fg 21.09S 149.11 E
Mackay [Id.-U.S.] 46 Ie 43.55N 113.37W
Mackay, Lake- 57 Dg 22.30S 129.00 E
McKay Lake 45 Mb 49.35N 86.22W
McKean Atoll 57 Je 3.36S 174.08W
McKeand 42 Kd 63.00N 65.05W
McKeesport 44 He 40.21N 79.52W
Mackenzie 38 Fc 69.15N 134.08W
McKenzie 44 Cg 36.08N 88.31W
Mackenzie, District of- [3] 42 Gd 65.00N 115.00W
Mackenzie Bay [Ant.] 66 Fe 68.20S 71.15 E
Mackenzie Bay [Can.] 38 Fc 69.00N 136.30W
McKenzie Island 42 If 51.05N 93.48W
Mackenzie King 38 Hb 77.45N 111.00W
Mackenzie Mountains 38 Gc 64.00N 130.00W
McKenzie River 46 Dd 44.07N 123.06W
Mackenzie River 59 Jd 24.00S 149.55 E
McKerrow, Lake- 62 Cf 44.30S 168.05 E
Mackinac, Straits of- 43 Kb 45.49N 82.45W
Mackinaw City 44 Ec 45.47N 84.44W
McKinley, Mount- 38 Dc 63.30N 151.00W
McKinley Park 40 Jd 63.44N 148.54W
McKinney 45 Hj 33.12N 96.37W
Mackinnon Road 36 Gc 3.44S 39.03 E
McLaughlin 45 Fd 45.49N 100.49W
McLean 45 Fi 35.14N 100.36W
McLeans Town 44 Il 26.39N 77.59W
Maclean Strait 42 Ha 77.30N 103.10W
Maclear 37 Df 31.02S 28.23 E
Macleay River 59 Kf 30.52S 153.01 E
Mc Leod, Lake- 57 Cg 24.10S 113.35 E
McLeod Bay 42 Gd 62.53N 110.15W
McLeod Lake 42 Ff 54.59N 123.02W
McLoughlin, Mount- 46 De 42.27N 122.19W
McLure 46 Ea 51.03N 120.14W
Macmillan 42 Ed 62.52N 135.55W
McMillan, Lake- 45 Dj 32.40N 104.20W
McMillan Pass 42 Ed 63.00N 130.00W
McMinnville [Or.-U.S.] 46 Dd 45.13N 123.12W
McMinnville [Tn.-U.S.] 44 Eh 35.41N 85.46W
McMurdo 66 Kf 77.51S 166.37 E
McNaughton Lake 42 Ff 52.40N 117.50W
Macomb 45 Kf 40.27N 90.40W
Macomer 14 Cj 40.16N 8.47 E
Macomia 37 Gb 12.15S 40.08 E
Mâcon 11 Kh 46.18N 4.50 E
Macon [Ga.-U.S.] 39 Kf 32.50N 83.38W
Macon [Mo.-U.S.] 45 Jg 39.44N 92.28W
Macon [Ms.-U.S.] 45 Lj 33.07N 88.34W
Macondo 36 De 12.36S 23.43 E
Mâconnais, Monts du- 11 Kh 46.18N 4.45 E
Macoris, Cabo- 49 Ld 19.47N 70.28W
Macouba 51h Ab 14.52N 61.09W
McPherson 43 Hd 38.22N 97.40W
Mc Pherson Range 59 Ke 28.20S 153.00 E
Macquarie 66 Jd 54.30S 158.30 E
Macquarie Harbour 59 Jh 42.20S 145.25 E
Macquarie Ridge (EN) 3 Jo 57.00S 159.00 E
Macquarie River 57 Fh 30.07S 147.24 E
Mac Robertson Land 66 Fe 70.00S 65.00 E
Macroom/Maigh Chromtha 9 Ej 51.54N 8.57W
Macugnaga 14 Be 45.58N 7.58 E
Macujer 54 Dc 0.24N 73.07W
Macuro 50 Fg 10.39N 61.56W
Macusani 54 Df 14.05S 70.26W
Macuspana 48 Mi 17.48N 92.36W
Mačva 15 Ce 44.49N 19.30 E
McVicar Arm 42 Fc 65.10N 120.30W
Ma'dabā 24 Fg 31.43N 35.48 E
Madagali 34 Hc 10.53N 13.38 E
Madagascar 30 Lj 20.00S 47.00 E
Madagascar (EN) = Madagasikara [1] 31 Lj 19.00S 46.00 E
Madagascar Basin (EN) 3 Fl 27.00S 53.00 E
Madagascar Plateau (EN) 3 Fm 30.00S 45.00 E
Madagasikara = Madagascar (EN) [1] 31 Lj 19.00S 46.00 E
Madā'in Şāliḩ 24 Gi 26.48N 37.53 E
Madalai 64a Ac 7.20N 134.28 E
Madama 34 Ha 21.58N 13.39 E
Madan 15 Hh 41.30N 24.57 E
Madang 58 Fe 5.13S 145.48 E
Madanīyīn 31 Ie 33.21N 10.30 E
Madanīyīn [3] 32 Jc 33.00N 10.45 E
Madaoua 34 Gc 14.05N 5.58 E
Madara 15 Kf 43.17N 27.06 E
Madara-Shima 29 Ae 33.35N 129.45 E
Madaroumfa 34 Gc 13.18N 7.09 E
Madau 63a Ac 9.00S 152.26 E
Madawaska Highlands 44 Hc 45.20N 78.15W
Maddalena 14 Di 41.15N 9.25 E
Maddalena, Colle della- 11 Mj 44.25N 6.53 E
Maddaloni 14 Ii 41.02N 14.23 E
Made, Made en Drimmelen- 12 Gc 51.41N 4.48 E
Made en Drimmelen 12 Gc 51.41N 4.48 E
Made en Drimmelen-Made 12 Gc 51.41N 4.48 E
Madeir 35 Dd 7.50N 29.12 E
Madeira [5] 31 Fe 32.40N 16.45W
Madeira 30 Fe 32.44N 17.00W
Madeira, Arquipélago da- = Madeira Islands (EN) 30 Fe 32.40N 16.45W
Madeira, Rio- 52 Kf 3.22S 58.45W
Madeira Islands (EN) = Madeira, Arquipélago da- 30 Fe 32.40N 16.45W
Madeleine, Ile de la - 42 Lg 47.26N 61.44W
Madeleine, Monts de la- 11 Jh 46.03N 3.50 E
Maden 24 Hc 38.23N 39.40 E
Madenassa Veld 30 Jj 19.00S 25.30 E
Madera [Ca.-U.S.] 46 Eh 36.57N 120.03W
Madera [Mex.] 47 Cc 29.12N 108.07W
Mader-Chih 13 Ri 35.26N 5.07 E
Madero, Puerto del- 13 Jc 41.48N 2.05W
Madesimo 14 Dd 46.26N 9.21 E
Madgaon 25 Ee 15.22N 73.49 E
Madhya Pradesh [3] 25 Fd 22.00N 79.00 E
Madimba 36 Cc 4.58S 15.08 E
Madina do Boé 34 Cc 11.45N 14.13W
Madinani 34 Dd 9.37N 6.57W
Madīnat al Abyār 33 Dc 32.11N 20.36 E
Madīnat ash Sha'b 22 Gh 12.50N 44.56 E
Madingo-Kayes 36 Bc 4.10S 12.18 E
Madingou 36 Bc 4.09S 13.34 E
Madirovalo 37 Hc 16.29S 46.30 E
Madison [Fl.-U.S.] 44 Fj 30.28N 83.25W
Madison [In.-U.S.] 44 Ef 38.44N 85.23W
Madison [Mn.-U.S.] 45 Hd 45.01N 96.11W
Madison [S.D.-U.S.] 45 He 44.00N 97.07W
Madison [Wi.-U.S.] 39 Ke 43.05N 89.22W
Madison [W.V.-U.S.] 44 Gf 38.03N 81.50W
Madison Range 46 Jd 45.15N 111.20W
Madison River 46 Jd 45.56N 111.30W
Madisonville 43 Jd 37.20N 87.30W
Madiun 26 Fh 7.37S 111.31 E
Mado Gashi 36 Gb 0.44N 39.10 E
Madoi (Huangheyan) 22 Lf 35.00N 98.56 E
Madon 11 Mf 48.36N 6.06 E
Madona 7 Gh 56.53N 26.20 E
Madra Dağı 15 Kj 39.23N 27.12 E
Madrakah, Ra's al- 23 If 18.59N 57.45 E
Madranbaba Dağı 15 Ll 37.38N 28.12 E
Madras [India] 22 Kh 13.05N 80.17 E
Madras [Or.-U.S.] 46 Ed 44.38N 121.08W
Madre, Laguna- [Mex.] 47 Ed 25.00N 97.40W
Madre, Laguna- [Tx.-U.S.] 43 Hf 27.00N 97.35W
Madre, Sierra- 38 Jh 15.20N 92.20W
Madre de Dios [2] 54 Df 12.00S 70.15W
Madre de Dios 54 Df 12.36S 69.59W
Madre de Dios, Isla- 52 Ik 50.15S 75.05W
Madre de Dios, Río- 52 Jg 10.59S 66.08W
Madre del Sur, Sierra- = Southern Sierra Madre (EN) 38 Jj 17.00N 100.00W
Madre Occidental, Sierra- = Western Sierra Madre (EN) 38 Ig 25.00N 105.00W
Madre Oriental, Sierra- = Eastern Sierra Madre (EN) 38 Jg 22.00N 99.30W
Madrid [3] 13 Id 40.30N 3.40W
Madrid 6 Fg 40.24N 3.41W
Madrid-Aravaca 13 Id 40.27N 3.47W
Madridejos 13 Ie 39.28N 3.32W
Madrid-El Pardo 13 Id 40.32N 3.46W
Madrid-Vallecas 13 Id 40.23N 3.37W
Madrid-Villaverde 13 Id 40.21N 3.42W
Madrigal de las Altas Torres 13 Hc 41.05N 5.00W
Mad River 46 Cf 40.57N 124.07W
Madriz [3] 49 Dg 13.30N 86.30W
Madrona, Sierra- 13 Hf 38.25N 4.10W
Madula 36 Eb 0.28N 25.23 E
Madura, Palau- 21 Nj 7.00S 113.20 E
Madurai 22 Ji 9.56N 78.07 E
Madvār, Kūh-e- 23 Hc 30.36N 54.52 E
Madwin 33 Cd 28.42N 17.31 E
Madyan 21 Fg 27.40N 35.35 E
Madžalis 16 Oh 42.08N 47.50 E
Maebara 29 Be 33.34N 130.13 E
Maebashi 27 Od 36.23N 139.04 E
Mae Hong Son 25 Je 19.16N 97.56 E
Mæl 8 Ce 59.56N 8.48 E
Mae Nam Khong = Mekong (EN) 21 Mh 10.15N 105.55 E
Maesawa 29 Gb 39.03N 141.07 E
Mae Sot 25 Je 16.40N 98.35 E
Maestra, Sierra- 38 Lh 20.00N 76.45W
Maevatanana 37 Hc 16.56S 46.49 E
Maéwo, Ile- 57 Hf 15.10S 168.10 E
Mafeteng 37 De 29.45S 27.18 E
Mafia Channel 36 Gd 7.50S 39.35 E
Mafia Island 30 Ki 7.50S 39.50 E
Mafikeng 31 Jk 25.53S 25.39 E
Mafra [Braz.] 56 Kc 26.07S 49.49W
Mafra [Port.] 13 Cf 38.56N 9.20W
Magadan 22 Rd 59.34N 150.48 E
Magadanskaja Oblast [3] 20 Kd 62.30N 154.00 E
Magadi 36 Gc 1.54S 36.17 E
Magallanes, Estrecho de- = Magellan, Strait of- (EN) 52 Ik 54.00S 71.00W
Magallanes y Antártica Chilena [2] 56 Fh 51.30S 73.30W
Magangué 54 Db 9.14N 74.46W
Maganik 15 Cg 42.44N 19.16 E
Maganoy 26 He 6.51N 124.31 E
Magaria 34 Gc 12.59N 8.50 E
Magazine Mountain 45 Ji 35.10N 93.38W
Magdagači 20 Hf 53.29N 125.55 E
Magdala 55 Bm 36.06S 61.42W
Magdalena [2] 54 Db 10.00N 74.15W
Magdalena [Arg.] 55 Dl 35.04S 57.32W
Magdalena [Bol.] 54 Ff 13.20S 64.08W
Magdalena [Mex.] 47 Bb 30.38N 110.57W
Magdalena [N.M.-U.S.] 45 Ci 34.07N 107.14W
Magdalena, Bahía- 48 Ce 24.35N 112.00W
Magdalena, Isla- 47 Bd 24.55N 112.15W
Magdalena, Llano de la- 47 Bd 24.30N 111.40W
Magdalena, Río- [Col.] 52 Id 11.06N 74.51W
Magdalena, Río- [Mex.] 48 Cb 30.48N 112.32W
Magda Plateau 42 Jb 72.18N 82.55W
Magdeburg 6 He 52.10N 11.40 E
Magdeburg [2] 10 Hd 52.15N 11.35 E
Magdeburger Börde 10 Hd 52.00N 11.30 E
Magdelaine Cays 57 Gf 16.35S 150.15 E
Magee 45 Lk 31.52N 89.44W
Magee, Island-/Oileán Mhic Aodha 9 Hg 54.50N 5.50W
Magelang 26 Fh 7.28S 110.13 E
Magellan, Strait of- (EN) = Magallanes, Estrecho de- 52 Ik 54.00S 71.00W
Magellan Seamounts (EN) 57 Gc 17.30N 152.00 E
Magenta 14 Ce 45.28N 8.53 E
Magerøya 7 Fa 71.03N 25.45 E
Magetan 26 Fh 7.39S 111.20 E
Maggiorasca 14 Df 44.33N 9.29 E
Maggiore, Lago- 14 Ce 45.55N 8.40 E
Maghāghah 33 Fd 28.39N 30.50 E
Maghama 32 Ef 15.31N 12.50W
Maghera/Machaire Rátha 9 Gg 54.51N 6.40W
Maghnia 32 Gc 34.51N 1.44W
Magic Reservoir 46 He 43.20N 114.18W
Mágina, Sierra- 13 Ig 37.45N 3.30W
Magistralny 20 Fe 56.03N 107.35 E
Maglaj 14 Mf 44.33N 18.06 E
Måglenik 15 Ih 41.20N 25.45 E
Maglie 14 Mj 40.07N 18.18 E
Mägliž 15 Ig 42.36N 25.33 E
Magnetawan River 44 Gc 45.46N 80.37W
Magnetic Island 59 Jc 19.10S 146.50 E
Magnitka 17 Ii 55.21N 59.43 E
Magnitnaja, Gora- 17 Ij 53.10N 59.10 E
Magnitogorsk 6 Le 53.27N 59.04 E
Magnolia 45 Jj 33.16N 93.14W
Magnor 7 Cg 59.57N 12.12 E
Magny-en-Vexin 11 He 49.09N 1.47 E
Mago 20 Jf 53.18N 140.20 E
Magoé 37 Ec 15.48S 31.43 E
Magoebaskloof 37 Ed 23.51S 30.02 E
Magog 44 Kc 45.16N 72.09W
Magosa = Famagusta (EN) 23 Dc 35.07N 33.57 E
Magra [Alg.] 13 Qi 35.29N 4.58 E
Magra [It.] 14 Df 44.03N 9.58 E
Magtā Lahjar 32 Ef 17.50N 13.20W
Maguarinho, Cabo- 54 Id 0.20S 48.20W
Magude 37 Ee 25.02S 32.40 E
Magumeri 34 Hc 12.07N 12.49 E
Magura, Gora- 10 Th 48.50N 23.44 E
Magwe [3] 25 Jd 20.00N 95.00 E
Magwe 22 Lg 20.09N 94.55 E
Magyarország = Hungary (EN) [1] 6 Hf 47.00N 20.00 E
Mahābād 23 Gb 36.45N 45.53 E
Mahabalipuram 25 Gf 12.37N 80.12 E
Mahabe 37 Hc 17.05S 45.20 E
Mahabo 37 Gd 20.21S 44.39 E
Mahačkala 6 Kg 42.58N 47.30 E
Mahadday Wēyne 35 He 3.00N 45.32 E
Mahādeo Range 25 Ee 17.50N 74.15 E
Mahafaly, Plateau- 37 Gd 24.30S 44.00 E
Mahagi 36 Fb 2.18N 30.59 E
Mahajamba 37 Hc 15.33S 47.08 E
Mahājan 25 Ec 28.47N 73.50 E
Mahajanga 31 Lj 15.17S 46.43 E
Mahajanga [3] 37 Hc 16.30S 47.00 E
Mahajilo 37 Hc 19.42S 45.22 E
Mahakam 21 Nj 0.35S 117.17 E
Mahalapye 37 Dd 23.07S 26.46 E
Mahalevona 37 Hc 15.26S 49.55 E
Mahallāt 24 Nf 33.55N 50.27 E
Maḩamid 35 Cb 15.09N 20.25 E
Māhān 24 Qg 30.05N 57.19 E
Mahānadi 21 Kg 20.19N 86.45 E
Mahanoro 37 Hc 19.53S 48.49 E
Maharadze 19 Eg 41.53N 42.01 E
Mahārāshtra [3] 25 Ee 18.00N 75.00 E
Mahārlū, Daryācheh-ye- 24 Oh 29.25N 52.50 E
Maḩās 35 He 4.24N 46.07 E
Maha Sarakham 25 Ke 16.12N 103.16 E
Mahavavy 30 Lj 15.57S 45.54 E
Mahbés 32 Dd 27.10N 9.50W
Maḩḑah 24 Pj 24.24N 55.59 E
Mahdia 54 Gb 5.16N 59.09W
Mahe 25 Ff 11.42N 75.32 E
Mahébourg 37a Bb 20.24S 57.42 E
Mahé Island 30 Mi 4.40S 55.28 E
Mahendra Giri 25 Ge 18.58N 84.21 E
Mahenge 31 Ki 8.41S 36.43 E
Maheno 62 Df 45.10S 170.50 E
Mahi 25 Ed 22.16N 72.58 E
Mahia Peninsula 61 Eg 39.10S 177.55 E
Mahmudabad 24 Lc 39.25N 47.15 E
Mahmūdābād 24 Od 36.38N 52.15 E
Mahmūd-e 'Erāqī 23 Kb 35.01N 69.20 E
Mahmudiye 24 Dc 39.30N 31.00 E
Mahmutşevketpaşa 15 Mh 41.09N 29.11 E
Māhneshān 24 Ld 36.45N 47.38 E
Mahnevo 17 Jg 58.27N 61.42 E
Mahnomen 45 Ic 47.19N 95.59W
Mahón/Mao 13 Qe 39.53N 4.15 E
Mahoré/Mayotte 30 Lj 12.50S 45.10 E
Mahrāt, Jabal- 35 Ib 17.00N 52.00 E
Mahsana 25 Ed 23.36N 72.24 E
Mahuan Dao 27 Kd 10.50N 115.47 E
Mahua Point 63a Fd 10.28S 162.05 E
Maiana Atoll 57 Id 0.55N 173.00 E
Maïao, Ile- (Tubai-Manu) 57 Lf 17.34S 150.35W
Maicao 54 Da 11.23N 72.15W
Maicasagi, Lac- 44 Ia 49.52N 76.48W
Maîche 11 Mg 47.15N 6.48 E
Maicuru, Rio- 54 Hd 2.10S 54.17W
Maidenhead 12 Bc 51.31N 0.42W
Maidstone 9 Nj 51.17N 0.32 E
Maiduguri 31 Ig 11.51N 13.09 E
Maigh Chromtha/Macroom 9 Ej 51.54N 8.57W
Maigudo 35 Fd 7.26N 37.10 E
Maihara 29 Ed 35.20N 136.18 E
Maikala Range 25 Gd 22.30N 81.30 E
Maiko 36 Eb 0.14N 25.33 E
Maikona 36 Gb 2.56N 37.38 E
Maikoor, Pulau- 26 Jh 6.15S 134.15 E
Main 10 Ef 50.00N 8.18 E
Mainalon Óros 15 Fl 37.40N 22.15 E

Index Symbols

[1] Independent Nation
[2] State, Region
[3] District, County
[4] Municipality
[5] Colony, Dependency
Continent
Physical Region
Historical or Cultural Region
Mount, Mountain
Volcano
Hill
Mountains, Mountain Range
Hills, Escarpment
Plateau, Upland
Pass, Gap
Plain, Lowland
Delta
Salt Flat
Valley, Canyon
Crater, Cave
Karst Features
Depression
Polder
Desert, Dunes
Forest, Woods
Heath, Steppe
Oasis
Cape, Point
Coast, Beach
Cliff
Peninsula
Isthmus
Sandbank
Island
Atoll
Rock, Reef
Islands, Archipelago
Rocks, Reefs
Coral Reef
Well, Spring
Geyser
River, Stream
Waterfall Rapids
River Mouth, Estuary
Lake
Salt Lake
Intermittent Lake
Reservoir
Swamp, Pond
Canal
Glacier
Ice Shelf, Pack Ice
Ocean
Sea
Gulf, Bay
Strait, Fjord
Lagoon
Bank
Seamount
Tablemount
Ridge
Shelf
Basin
Escarpment, Sea Scarp
Fracture
Trench, Abyss
National Park, Reserve
Point of Interest
Recreation Site
Cave, Cavern
Historic Site
Ruins
Wall, Walls
Church, Abbey
Temple
Scientific Station
Airport
Port
Lighthouse
Mine
Tunnel
Dam, Bridge

Name	Plate	Grid	Lat	Lon
Main Barrier Range 🅰	59	If	31.25 S	141.25 E
Mainburg	10	Hh	48.39 N	11.47 E
Main Camp	64g	Ba	2.01 N	157.25 W
Main Channel 🖃	44	Gc	45.22 N	81.50 W
Main-Ndombe, Lac- 🖃	30	Ii	2.10 S	18.15 E
Main-Donau-Kanal 🖃	10	Gg	49.55 N	10.50 E
Maindong → Coqên	27	Ee	31.15 N	85.13 E
Maine 🖃	11	Ff	48.15 N	0.10 W
Maine 🖃	43	Nb	45.15 N	69.15 W
Maine [Fr.] 🖼	11	Fg	47.25 N	0.37 W
Maine [Fr.] 🖼	11	Fg	47.09 N	1.27 W
Maine, Gulf of- 🖸	38	Me	43.00 N	68.00 W
Maine-et-Loire 🖃	11	Fg	47.30 N	0.20 W
Mainé-Soroa	34	Hc	13.18 N	12.02 E
Mainistir Fhear Maí/Fermoy	9	Ei	52.08 N	8.16 W
Mainistir na Búille/Boyle	9	Eh	53.58 N	8.18 W
Mainistir na Corann/ Midleton	9	Ej	51.55 N	8.10 W
Mainistir na Féile/ Abbeyfeale	9	Di	52.24 N	9.18 W
Mainit, Lake-	26	Ie	9.26 N	125.32 E
Mainland [Scot.-U.K.] 🖸	5	Fc	60.20 N	1.22 W
Mainland [Scot.-U.K.] 🖸	5	Fd	59.00 N	3.10 W
Maintal	12	Kd	50.08 N	8.51 E
Maintenon	11	Hf	48.35 N	1.35 E
Maintirano	31	Lj	18.03 S	44.03 E
Mainz	10	Gg	50.00 N	8.15 E
Maio	32	Cf	23.10 N	15.10 W
Maio 🖼	30	Eg	15.15 N	23.10 W
Maipo, Volcán- 🅰	52	Ji	34.10 S	69.50 W
Maiquetía	56	Ie	36.52 S	57.52 W
Maira 🖼	14	Bf	44.49 N	7.38 E
Mairi	54	Jf	11.43 S	40.08 W
Mairipotaba	55	Hc	17.21 S	49.31 W
Maisán 🖸	24	Lg	32.00 N	47.00 E
Maisi, Punta- 🖻	47	Jd	20.15 N	74.09 W
Maišiagala/Maišjagala	8	Kj	54.51 N	25.14 E
Maišjagala/Maišiagala	8	Kj	54.51 N	25.14 E
Maiter 🖼	13	Qi	35.23 N	4.17 E
Maitland [Austl.]	59	Hf	34.22 S	137.40 E
Maitland [Austl.]	58	Gh	32.44 S	151.33 E
Maíz, Isla Grande del- 🖸	49	Fg	12.10 N	83.03 W
Maíz, Isla Pequeña del- 🖸	49	Fg	12.18 N	82.59 W
Maíz, Islas del- 🖸	47	Hf	12.15 N	83.00 W
Maizhokunggar	27	Ff	29.50 N	91.40 E
Maizières-lès-Metz	12	Ie	49.13 N	6.09 E
Maizuru	28	Mg	35.27 N	135.20 E
Maizuru-Nishimaizuru	29	Dd	35.28 N	135.19 E
Maizuru-Wan 🖸	29	Dd	35.30 N	135.20 E
Maja 🖼	21	Pd	60.17 N	134.41 E
Majagual	49	Ji	8.35 N	74.37 W
Majakovski	16	Mh	42.02 N	42.47 E
Majangat	27	Fb	48.20 N	91.58 E
Majardah, Wâdî- 🖼	14	Em	37.07 N	10.13 E
Majâz al Bâb	14	Dn	36.39 N	9.37 E
Majdanpek	15	Ee	44.25 N	21.56 E
Majene	22	Nj	3.33 S	118.57 E
Majêrtên = Mijirtein (EN) 🖸	30	Lh	9.00 N	50.00 E
Majevica 🅰	14	Mf	44.40 N	18.40 E
Maji	35	Fd	6.10 N	35.35 E
Majia He 🖼	27	Kd	38.09 N	117.53 E
Majja	20	Id	61.38 N	130.25 E
Majkain	19	Ie	51.27 N	75.52 E
Majkamys	18	Ka	46.34 N	77.37 E
Majkop	6	Kg	44.35 N	40.07 E
Majli-Saj	18	Id	41.15 N	72.30 E
Majma'ah	24	Kj	25.54 N	45.20 E
Majmak	19	Hg	42.40 N	71.14 E
Majmakan 🖼	20	Ie	57.30 N	135.23 E
Majmeča 🖼	20	Fb	71.20 N	104.15 E
Majn 🖼	20	Mc	65.03 N	172.10 E
Majna [R.S.F.S.R.]	20	Ef	53.00 N	91.28 E
Majna [R.S.F.S.R.]	7	Li	54.09 N	47.37 E
Major, Puig- 🅰	13	Oe	39.48 N	2.48 E
Major, Puig-/Mayor, Puig- 🅰	13	Oe	39.48 N	2.48 E
Majorca (EN) = Mallorca 🖼	5	Gh	39.30 N	3.00 E
Majrur 🖼	35	Db	16.40 N	26.53 E
Majski [R.S.F.S.R.]	16	Nh	43.36 N	44.03 E
Majski [R.S.F.S.R.]	20	Hf	52.18 N	129.38 E
Maju, Pulau 🖼	26	If	1.20 N	126.25 E
Majuro Atoll 🖸	57	Id	7.09 N	171.12 E
Makabana	31	Ii	3.28 S	12.36 E
Makaha	65a	Cb	21.29 N	158.13 W
Makahuena Point 🖻	65a	Bb	21.52 N	159.27 W
Makalamabedi	37	Cd	20.20 S	23.53 E
Makale	26	Gg	3.06 S	119.51 E
Makallé	56	Ic	27.13 S	59.17 W
Makalondi	34	Fc	12.50 N	1.41 E
Makamby, Nosy- 🖼	37	Hc	15.42 S	45.54 E
Makančí	19	If	46.51 N	81.57 E
Makanza	36	Cb	1.36 N	19.07 E
Makapala	65a	Fc	20.13 N	155.45 W
Makapu Point 🖻	64k	Ba	18.53 S	169.55 W
Makapuu Head 🖻	65a	Db	21.18 N	157.39 W
Makara, Prohod- 🖼	15	Ih	41.16 N	35.26 E
Mákares 🖼	15	Il	37.05 N	25.42 E
Makarfi	34	Gc	11.23 N	7.53 E
Makari	34	Hc	12.35 N	14.28 E
Makari Mountains 🅰	36	Ed	6.05 S	29.50 E
Makarjev	7	Kh	57.57 N	43.49 E
Makarov	20	Jg	48.39 N	142.51 E
Makarov Basin (EN) 🖼	67	Ce	87.00 N	170.00 E
Makarov Seamount (EN) 🖸	57	Gb	29.30 N	153.30 E
Makarska	14	Lg	43.18 N	17.02 E
Makâ Rüd 🖼	24	Nd	36.21 N	51.16 E
Makasar → Ujung Pandang	22	Nj	5.07 S	119.24 E
Makasar, Selat- = Makassar Strait (EN) 🖸	21	Nj	2.00 S	117.30 E
Makassar Strait (EN) = Makasar, Selat-	21	Nj	2.00 S	117.30 E
Makat	6	Lf	47.40 N	53.28 E
Makatea, Ile- 🖼	57	Mf	15.50 S	148.15 W
Makaw	25	Jc	26.27 N	96.42 E
Makawao	65a	Ec	20.51 N	156.19 W
Makay, Massif du- 🅰	37	Hd	21.15 S	45.15 E

Name	Plate	Grid	Lat	Lon
Makedhonía 🖸	15	Fi	40.40 N	22.30 E
Makedhonía = Macedonia (EN) 🖸	15	Fh	41.00 N	23.00 E
Makedonija = Macedonia (EN) 🖼	5	Ig	41.00 N	23.00 E
Makedonija = Macedonia (EN) 🖼	5	Ig	41.00 N	23.00 E
Makedonija 🖼	15	Eh	41.50 N	22.00 E
Makejevka	16	Jf	48.00 N	37.58 E
Makelulu, Mount- 🖼	64a	Bb	7.34 N	134.35 E
Makemo Atoll 🖸	57	Mf	16.35 S	143.40 W
Makeni	31	Fh	8.53 N	12.03 W
Makgadikgadi Pans 🖸	30	Jk	20.50 S	25.30 E
Makhfar al Busayyah	24	Lg	30.08 N	46.07 E
Makhfar al Hammâm	24	He	35.51 N	38.45 E
Makhmûr	24	Je	35.46 N	43.35 E
Makhyah, Wâdî- 🖼	23	Gf	17.40 N	49.01 E
Maki	29	Fc	37.45 N	138.52 E
Makian, Pulau- 🖼	26	If	0.20 N	127.25 E
Makikihi	62	Df	44.38 S	171.09 E
Makinsk	19	Ie	52.40 N	70.26 E
Makkah = Mecca (EN)	22	Fg	21.27 N	39.49 E
Makkovik	42	Le	55.05 N	59.11 W
Maknassy	32	Ic	34.37 N	9.36 E
Makó	10	Qj	46.13 N	20.29 E
Makokou	31	Ih	0.34 N	12.52 E
Makongai 🖼	63d	Bb	17.27 S	178.58 E
Makongolosi	36	Fd	8.24 S	33.09 E
Makorako 🅰	62	Gc	39.09 S	176.03 E
Makoua	31	Ih	0.01 N	15.39 E
Makoura 🖼	63b	Dc	17.08 S	168.26 E
Makov	10	Og	49.22 N	18.29 E
Maków Mazowiecki	10	Rd	52.52 N	21.06 E
Makrá 🖼	15	Im	36.16 N	25.53 E
Makrān 🖸	21	Hg	26.00 N	60.00 E
Makrónisos 🖼	15	Hl	37.42 N	24.07 E
Maksatiha	7	Ht	57.48 N	35.55 E
Makteir 🖸	30	Ff	21.50 N	11.40 W
Makthar	14	Do	35.50 N	9.13 E
Makthar 🖸	32	Ib	35.51 N	9.12 E
Makü	23	Hd	27.52 N	52.26 E
Makü	24	Kc	39.17 N	44.31 E
Makubetsu	29a	Cb	42.54 N	143.19 E
Makumbato	36	Fd	8.51 S	34.50 E
Makumbi	36	Dd	5.51 S	20.41 E
Makunduchi	36	Gd	6.25 S	39.33 E
Makung	27	Kg	23.35 N	119.35 E
Makurazaki	28	Ki	31.16 N	139.19 E
Makurdi	31	Hh	7.44 N	8.32 E
Makushin Volcano 🅰	40a	Eb	53.53 N	166.50 W
Makušino	19	Gd	55.13 N	67.13 E
Makuyuni	36	Gc	3.33 S	36.06 E
Malá	7	Ed	65.11 N	18.44 E
Mala/Mallow	9	Ei	52.08 N	8.39 W
Mala, Punta- 🖻	47	Ig	7.28 N	80.00 W
Malabang	26	He	7.38 N	124.03 E
Malabar Coast 🖸	21	Jh	10.00 N	76.15 E
Malabo	31	Hh	3.45 N	8.47 E
Malabrigo	55	Ci	29.20 S	59.58 W
Malacca, Strait of- (EN) = Melaka, Selat- 🖸	21	Mi	2.30 N	101.20 E
Malacky	10	Nh	48.27 N	17.01 E
Malad City	46	Ie	42.12 N	112.15 W
Malá Fatra 🅰	10	Og	49.08 N	18.50 E
Málaga 🖸	13	Hh	36.48 N	4.45 W
Málaga [Col.]	54	Db	6.42 N	72.44 W
Málaga [Sp.]	6	Fh	36.43 N	4.25 W
Malagarasi 🖼	30	Ji	5.12 S	29.47 E
Malagón	13	Ie	39.10 N	3.51 W
Malaimbandi	37	Hd	20.20 S	45.36 E
Malaita Island 🖼	57	He	9.00 S	161.00 E
Malaja Kuonamka 🖼	20	Gb	70.50 N	113.20 E
Malaja Ob 🖼	20	Bc	66.08 N	65.50 E
Malaja Sosva 🖼	19	Gc	63.10 N	64.22 E
Malaja Višera	19	Dd	58.52 N	32.14 E
Malaja Viska	16	Ge	48.39 N	31.38 E
Malakál	35	Kh	9.31 N	31.39 E
Malakal Harbor 🖃	64a	Ac	7.20 N	134.26 E
Malakal Pass 🖃	64a	Ac	7.17 N	134.28 E
Mala Kapela 🅰	14	Jf	44.55 N	15.28 E
Malakobi 🖼	63a	Db	7.19 S	158.07 E
Mallamalla Range 🅰	25	Fe	16.17 N	79.29 E
Malang	22	Nj	7.59 S	112.37 E
Malange 🖸	36	Cd	9.30 S	16.30 E
Malange	31	Ii	9.33 S	16.22 E
Malangen 🖃	7	Eb	69.30 N	18.20 E
Malanville	34	Fc	11.52 N	3.23 E
Mala Panew 🖼	63b	Cb	15.10 S	166.51 E
Mälären 🖸	10	Nf	50.44 N	17.52 E
Malargüe	5	Hd	59.30 N	17.15 E
Malartic, Lac- 🖸	56	Ge	35.28 S	69.35 W
Malaspina Glacier 🖼	40	Ke	59.50 N	140.30 W
Malatya	22	Ff	38.21 N	38.19 E
Malávi	24	Lf	33.10 N	47.50 E
Malawi 🖸	31	Kj	13.30 S	34.00 E
Malawi, Lake- 🖸	30	Kj	12.00 S	34.30 E
Malaya 🖸	26	Df	4.00 N	102.00 E
Malaybalay	26	Ie	8.09 N	125.05 E
Maläyer 🖸	24	Me	34.16 N	48.12 E
Maläyer	23	Gc	34.17 N	48.50 E
Malay Peninsula (EN) 🖃	21	Mi	6.00 N	102.00 E
Malaysia 🖸	22	Mi	4.00 N	102.00 E
Malazgirt	24	Jc	39.09 N	42.31 E
Malberg	12	Id	50.03 N	6.35 E
Mälbor 🖼	24	Og	30.45 N	52.05 E
Malbork	10	Pb	54.02 N	19.01 E
Malbrän	56	Hc	29.21 S	62.27 W
Malchin	12	Lb	53.44 N	12.47 E
Maldegem	12	Fc	51.13 N	3.27 E

Name	Plate	Grid	Lat	Lon
Malden	45	Lh	36.34 N	89.57 W
Malden Island 🖼	57	Le	4.03 S	154.59 W
Malditos, Montes-/La Maladeta 🅰	13	Mb	42.40 N	0.50 E
Maldive Islands 🖸	21	Ji	3.15 N	73.00 E
Mal di Ventre 🖼	14	Ck	40.00 N	8.20 E
Maldives 🖸	22	Ji	3.15 N	73.00 E
Maldon	9	Nj	51.45 N	0.40 E
Maldonado 🖸	55	El	34.40 S	54.55 W
Maldonado	56	Jd	34.54 S	54.57 W
Maldonado, Punta- 🖻	48	Ji	16.20 N	98.35 W
Male	22	Ji	4.10 N	73.30 E
Malé	64a	Bb	46.21 N	10.55 E
Mâle, Lac du- 🖃	44	Ja	48.30 N	75.30 W
Malea, Cape- (EN) = Maléas, Ákra- 🖻	15	Gm	36.26 N	23.12 E
Maléas, Ákra- = Malea, Cape- (EN) 🖻	15	Gm	36.26 N	23.12 E
Male Atoll 🖸	21	Ji	4.29 N	73.30 E
Malebo, Pool- 🖼	30	Ii	4.17 S	15.20 E
Mâlegaon	25	Ed	20.33 N	74.32 E
Maléha	34	Dc	11.48 N	9.43 W
Malek	35	Ed	6.04 N	31.36 E
Malé Karpaty = Little Carpathians (EN) 🅰	10	Nh	48.30 N	17.20 E
Malek Kandí	24	Ld	37.09 N	46.06 E
Malékoula, Ile 🖼	57	Hf	16.15 S	167.30 E
Malema	37	Fb	14.57 S	37.25 E
Malemba Nkulu	36	Ed	8.02 S	26.48 E
Malenga	7	Ie	63.50 N	36.25 E
Mâlerus 🖼	15	Id	45.54 N	25.32 E
Malesherbes	11	Hf	48.18 N	2.25 E
Malgobek	16	Nh	43.32 N	44.34 E
Malgomaj 🖼	7	Dd	64.47 N	16.12 E
Malhada	55	Kb	14.21 S	43.47 W
Malhanski Hrebet 🅰	20	Ff	50.30 N	109.00 E
Malhão da Estrêla 🅰	13	Ed	40.19 N	7.37 W
Malha Wells	35	Db	15.08 N	26.12 E
Malheur Lake- 🖸	43	Dc	43.20 N	118.45 W
Malheur River 🖼	46	Gd	44.03 N	116.59 W
Mali 🖸	31	Gg	17.00 N	4.00 W
Mali	34	Cc	12.05 N	12.18 W
Mali 🖼	25	Jc	25.42 N	97.31 E
Mali 🖼	63d	Bb	16.20 S	179.21 E
Mália	15	In	35.17 N	25.28 E
Maliakós Kólpos 🖸	15	Fk	38.52 N	22.38 E
Malik, Wâdî al- 🖼	30	Kg	18.00 N	30.58 E
Mali kanal 🖼	15	Cd	45.42 N	19.19 E
Malik Siah, Küh-i- 🅰	23	Jd	29.51 N	60.52 E
Mâlilla	8	Fg	57.23 N	15.48 E
Mali Lošinj	14	Hf	44.32 N	14.28 E
Malimba, Monts- 🅰	36	Ed	7.32 S	29.30 E
Malin	16	Fd	50.46 N	29.14 E
Malinalco 🖸	48	Jh	18.57 N	99.30 W
Malinaltepec	48	Ji	17.03 N	98.40 W
Malindi	31	Li	3.13 S	40.07 E
Malines/Mechelen	11	Kc	51.02 N	4.29 E
Malin Head/Cionn Mhâlanna 🖻	5	Fd	55.23 N	7.24 W
Malino, Bukit- 🅰	26	Hf	0.45 N	120.47 E
Malinovoje Ozero	20	Cf	51.40 N	79.55 E
Malinyi	36	Gd	8.56 S	36.08 E
Malipo	27	Hg	23.07 N	104.42 E
Maliqi	15	Di	40.43 N	20.41 E
Malita	26	Ie	6.25 N	125.36 E
Maljen 🅰	15	De	44.07 N	20.03 E
Maljovica 🅰	15	Gg	42.11 N	23.22 E
Malka 🖼	16	Nh	43.44 N	44.15 E
Malkara	24	Bb	40.53 N	26.54 E
Malki Lom 🖼	15	Jf	43.39 N	26.04 E
Malko Tãrnovo	15	Kh	41.59 N	27.32 E
Mallacoota	59	Jg	37.30 S	149.50 E
Mallaig	9	Hd	57.00 N	5.50 W
Mallâq, Wâdî- 🖼	14	Cn	36.30 N	8.51 E
Mallawî	33	Hf	27.44 N	30.50 E
Mallery Lake 🖸	42	Hd	64.00 N	98.00 W
Malles Venosta / Mals	14	Ee	46.41 N	10.32 E
Mallet	55	Gg	25.55 S	50.50 W
Mallorca = Majorca (EN) 🖼	5	Gh	39.30 N	3.00 E
Mallow/Mala	9	Ei	52.08 N	8.39 W
Malm	7	Cd	64.04 N	11.13 E
Malmbäck	8	Fg	57.35 N	14.28 E
Malmberget	7	Ec	67.10 N	20.40 E
Malmédy	11	Md	50.26 N	6.02 E
Malmesbury	37	Bf	33.28 S	18.44 E
Malmö	5	Hf	55.36 N	13.00 E
Malmöhus 🖸	7	Ci	55.45 N	13.30 E
Malmön	8	Df	58.20 N	11.20 E
Malmslätt	8	Ff	58.25 N	15.30 E
Malmyž	19	Fd	56.31 N	50.41 E
Malo 🖼	63b	Cb	15.41 S	167.10 E
Maloarhangelsk	16	Jc	52.26 N	36.29 E
Maloelap 🖼	57	Id	8.45 N	171.03 E
Mologgia/Malojapaß 🖸	14	Dd	46.24 N	9.41 E
Malojapaß/Maloggia 🖸	14	Dd	46.24 N	9.41 E
Malojaroslavec	16	Jb	55.02 N	36.28 E
Maloje Polesje 🖸	10	Sf	50.00 N	24.30 E
Mololo 🖼	63d	Ab	17.45 S	177.10 E
Malolos	26	Hd	14.51 N	120.49 E
Malombe, Lake- 🖸	36	Ge	14.38 S	35.12 E
Malone	44	Jc	44.52 N	74.19 W
Malonga	36	De	10.24 S	23.10 E
Malopolska 🖸	10	Pf	50.45 N	20.00 E
Malorita	10	Se	51.48 N	24.05 E
Malošujka	7	Ie	63.47 N	37.22 E
Mâløy	7	Af	61.56 N	5.07 E
Malozemelskaja Tundra 🖸	17	Ec	68.00 N	52.00 E
Malpaso 🖸	48	Mi	17.20 N	93.30 W
Malpelo, Isla de- 🖼	52	Je	3.59 N	81.35 W
Malprabha 🖼	25	Fe	16.12 N	76.03 E
Mals / Malles Venosta	14	Ed	46.41 N	10.32 E
Malschr	12	Kf	48.53 N	8.20 E
Malše 🖼	10	Lh	48.59 N	14.29 E
Malta 🖼	5	Hh	35.50 N	14.30 E
Malta 🖸	6	Hh	35.50 N	14.30 E
Malta [Lat.-U.S.S.R.]	8	Lh	56.18 N	27.15 E
Malta [Mt.-U.S.]	43	Fb	48.21 N	107.52 W

Name	Plate	Grid	Lat	Lon
Malta, Canale di- [Eur.] = Malta Channel (EN) 🖸	14	In	36.30 N	14.30 E
Malta Channel (EN) = Malta, Canale di- [Eur.] 🖸	14	In	36.30 N	14.30 E
Maltahöhe 🖸	37	Bd	25.00 S	16.30 E
Maltahöhe	31	Ik	24.50 S	17.00 E
Maltepe	15	Mi	40.55 N	29.08 E
Malton	9	Mg	54.08 N	0.48 W
Maluku 🖸	26	Ig	4.00 S	128.00 E
Maluku, Kepulauan- = Moluccas (EN) 🖸	57	De	2.00 S	128.00 E
Maluku, Laut- = Molucca Sea (EN) 🖃	21	Oj	0.05 S	125.00 E
Malumfashi	34	Gc	11.48 N	7.37 E
Malunda	26	Gg	3.00 S	118.50 E
Malung	7	Cf	60.40 N	13.44 E
Malungsfors	8	Ed	60.44 N	13.33 E
Malüt	35	Ec	10.26 N	32.12 E
Maluu	63a	Ec	8.21 S	160.38 E
Malvern [Ar.-U.S.]	45	Ji	34.22 N	92.49 W
Malvern [Eng.-U.K.]	9	Ki	52.07 N	2.19 W
Malvinas	55	Ci	29.37 S	58.59 W
Malvinas, Islas-/Falkland Islands 🖸	53	Kk	51.45 S	59.00 W
Malvinas, Islas-/Falkland Islands 🖸	52	Kk	51.45 S	59.00 W
Maly, Ostrov- 🖼	8	Ld	60.02 N	27.58 E
Malya	36	Fc	2.59 S	33.31 E
Maly Anjuj 🖼	20	Lc	68.35 N	161.03 E
Maly Čeremšan 🖼	7	Mi	54.20 N	50.01 E
Maly Dunaj 🖼	10	Nh	48.08 N	17.09 E
Malygina, Proliv- 🖸	20	Cb	73.00 N	70.30 E
Maly Jenisej 🖼	20	Ef	51.40 N	94.26 E
Maly Kavkaz = Lesser Caucasus (EN) 🅰	5	Kg	41.00 N	44.35 E
Maly Ljahovski, Ostrov- 🖼	20	Jb	74.07 N	140.36 E
Maly Tajmyr, Ostrov- 🖼	20	Fa	78.08 N	107.08 E
Maly Uzen 🖼	5	Kf	48.50 N	49.38 E
Mama	20	Ge	58.20 N	112.54 E
Mamadyš	7	Mi	55.45 N	51.24 E
Mamagota	63a	Bb	6.46 S	155.24 E
Mamaia	15	Le	44.17 N	28.37 E
Mamakan	20	Ge	57.48 N	114.05 E
Mamantel	48	Nh	18.33 N	91.05 W
Mamanutha Group 🖸	63d	Ab	17.34 S	177.04 E
Mamaqân	24	Kd	37.51 N	45.59 E
Mambaj	55	Ih	14.28 S	46.07 W
Mambajao	26	He	9.15 N	124.43 E
Mambasa	36	Eb	1.21 N	29.03 E
Mamberé 🖼	35	Be	3.31 N	16.03 E
Mambili 🖼	36	Cb	0.07 N	16.08 E
Mamboré	55	Fa	24.18 S	52.32 W
Mambova	36	Ef	17.44 S	25.11 E
Mambrui	36	Hc	3.07 S	40.09 E
Mamburao	26	He	13.14 N	120.35 E
Mamedkala	16	Ph	42.12 N	48.06 E
Mamer	12	Ie	49.38 N	6.02 E
Mamers	11	Gf	48.21 N	0.23 E
Mamfe	34	Gd	5.46 N	9.17 E
Mamiá, Lago- 🖸	54	Fd	4.15 S	63.05 W
Mamisonski, Pereval- 🖃	16	Mh	42.43 N	43.45 E
Mamljutka	19	Ge	54.57 N	68.35 E
Mammoth Cave	44	Dg	37.10 N	86.08 W
Mammoth Hot Springs	46	Jd	44.59 N	110.43 W
Mamoré, Rio- 🖼	52	Jg	10.23 S	65.53 W
Mamou	31	Fg	10.23 N	12.05 W
Mampikony	37	Hc	16.05 S	47.37 E
Mampodre, Picos de- 🅰	13	Ga	43.02 N	5.12 W
Mampong	34	Ed	7.04 N	1.24 W
Mamry, Jezioro- 🖸	10	Rb	54.08 N	21.42 E
Mamuju	26	Gg	2.41 S	118.54 E
Mamuno	37	Cd	22.17 S	20.02 E
Ma'mürah, Ra's al- 🖻	14	En	36.27 N	10.49 E
Mamurokawa	29	Gc	38.54 N	140.15 E
Mamutzu	37	Hb	12.47 S	45.14 E
Man 🖸	31	Gh	7.24 N	7.33 W
Man 🖸	34	Dd	7.31 N	7.41 W
Man, Calf of- 🖼	9	Ig	54.03 N	4.48 W
Man, Isle of- 🖸	5	Fe	54.15 N	4.30 W
Mana	60	Oc	22.02 N	159.46 W
Mana	54	Ic	5.36 N	53.56 W
Manacapuru	54	Fd	3.18 S	60.37 W
Manacor	13	Pe	39.34 N	3.12 E
Manado	22	Oi	1.29 N	124.51 E
Managua 🖸	49	Eg	12.09 N	86.17 W
Managua	47	Hf	12.09 N	86.20 W
Managua, Lago de- 🖸	47	Gf	12.20 N	86.20 W
Manakara	31	Lk	22.07 S	48.00 E
Manama (EN) = Al Manâmah	22	Hg	26.13 N	50.35 E
Manambolo 🖼	37	Gc	19.19 S	44.17 E
Manam Island 🖼	57	Ge	4.05 S	145.03 E
Manamo, Caño- 🖼	54	Fb	9.55 N	62.16 W
Mananara	37	Hc	16.10 S	49.45 E
Mananara 🖼	37	Hd	23.21 S	47.42 E
Mananjary	31	Lk	21.13 S	48.17 E
Manankoro	34	Dc	10.28 N	7.25 W
Manantenina	37	Hd	24.17 S	47.18 E
Manaoba 🖼	63a	Ec	8.19 S	160.47 E
Manapire, Rio- 🖼	50	Ci	7.42 N	66.07 W
Manapouri	58	Hi	45.34 S	167.36 E
Manapouri, Lake- 🖸	62	Bf	45.30 S	167.30 E
Manâr, Jabal- 🅰	33	Hg	14.04 N	44.18 E
Manas	54	Ke	44.18 N	86.13 E
Manas, Gora- 🅰	18	Hc	42.18 N	71.06 E
Manas Hu 🖸	27	Eb	45.45 N	85.55 E
Manasija, Manastir- 🖸	15	Ee	44.06 N	21.28 E
Manati	49	Ic	21.19 N	76.56 W
Manati	50	Dc	4.49 N	72.17 W
Mâni', Wâdî al- 🖼	24	He	34.16 N	41.02 E
Mania 🖼	37	Hc	19.42 S	45.22 E
Maniago	14	Ge	46.10 N	12.43 E
Manica 🖸	37	Ec	18.56 S	32.53 E
Manica	37	Ec	19.00 S	32.30 E
Manicaland 🖸	37	Ec	19.00 S	32.30 E
Manicoré	53	Jf	5.49 S	61.17 W

Name	Plate	Grid	Lat	Lon
Mancelona	44	Ec	44.54 N	85.04 W
Mancha Real	13	Ig	37.47 N	3.37 W
Manche 🖸	11	Ee	49.00 N	1.10 W
Mancheng	28	Ce	38.57 N	115.19 E
Manchester [Ct.-U.S.]	44	Ke	41.47 N	72.31 W
Manchester [Eng.-U.K.]	6	Fe	53.30 N	2.15 W
Manchester [Ia.-U.S.]	45	Ke	42.29 N	91.27 W
Manchester [Ky.-U.S.]	44	Fg	37.09 N	83.46 W
Manchester [N.H.-U.S.]	43	Mc	42.59 N	71.28 W
Manchester [Tn.-U.S.]	44	Dh	35.29 N	86.05 W
Manchok	34	Gd	9.40 N	8.31 E
Manchuria (EN) 🖸	22	Oe	47.00 N	125.00 E
Manciano	14	Fh	42.35 N	11.31 E
Mand 🖼	23	Hd	28.11 N	51.17 E
Manda [Chad]	35	Bd	9.11 N	18.13 E
Manda [Tan.]	36	Fe	10.28 S	34.35 E
Manda, Jabal- 🅰	35	Cd	8.39 N	24.27 E
Mandabe	37	Gd	21.02 S	44.55 E
Mandaguari	56	Jb	23.32 S	51.42 W
Manda Island 🖼	36	Hc	2.17 S	40.57 E
Mandal	7	Bg	58.02 N	7.27 E
Mandalay 🖸	25	Jd	21.00 N	96.00 E
Mandalay	22	Lg	22.00 N	96.05 E
Mandal-Gobi	27	Ib	45.45 N	106.12 E
Mandalī	24	Kf	33.45 N	45.32 E
Mandalselva 🖼	8	Bf	58.02 N	7.28 E
Mandalt → Sonid Zuoqi	27	Kc	43.50 N	116.45 E
Mandalya körfezi 🖸	24	Bd	37.12 N	27.20 E
Mandan	43	Gb	46.50 N	100.54 W
Mandaon	26	Hd	12.13 N	123.17 E
Mandara, Monts- = Mandara Mountains (EN) 🅰	34	Hc	10.45 N	13.40 E
Mandara Mountains (EN) = Mandara, Monts- 🅰	34	Hc	10.45 N	13.40 E
Mandas	14	Dk	39.38 N	9.07 E
Mandasor	25	Fd	24.04 N	75.04 E
Mandera	31	Lh	3.56 N	41.52 E
Manderscheid	12	Id	50.06 N	6.49 E
Mandeville	49	Id	18.02 N	77.30 W
Mandi	25	Fb	31.43 N	76.55 E
Mandiana	34	Dc	10.38 N	8.41 W
Mandimba	37	Fb	14.21 S	35.39 E
Mandingues, Monts- 🅰	34	Cc	13.00 N	11.00 W
Mandioli, Pulau- 🖼	26	Ig	0.44 S	127.14 E
Mandioré, Laguna- 🖸	55	Dd	18.05 S	57.33 W
Mandirituba	55	Fb	25.46 S	49.19 W
Mandji	36	Bc	1.42 S	10.24 E
Mandla	25	Gd	22.36 N	80.23 E
Mande 🖼	8	Ci	55.15 N	8.35 E
Mandoúdhion	15	Gk	38.48 N	23.29 E
Mandrákion	15	Km	36.36 N	27.08 E
Mandritsara	37	Hc	15.49 S	48.48 E
Manduria	14	Lj	40.24 N	17.38 E
Mândvi	25	Dd	22.50 N	69.22 E
Mandya	25	Ff	12.33 N	76.54 E
Mâne 🖼	8	Ce	59.56 N	8.48 E
Mânciu Ungureni	15	Jd	45.19 N	25.59 E
Manendragarh	25	Gd	23.10 N	82.35 E
Maneromango	36	Gd	7.16 S	38.46 E
Manevići	16	Dd	51.19 N	25.33 E
Manfalüt	33	Fd	27.19 N	30.59 E
Manfredonia	14	Ji	41.38 N	15.55 E
Manfredonia, Golfo di- 🖸	14	Ki	41.35 N	16.05 E
Manga [Afr.]	30	Ig	15.00 N	14.00 E
Manga [Braz.]	54	Jf	14.46 S	43.56 W
Mangabeiras, Chapada das- 🅰	52	Lg	10.00 S	46.30 W
Mangai	36	Cc	4.03 S	19.35 E
Mangaia Island 🖼	57	Lg	21.55 S	157.55 W
Mangakino	62	Fc	38.22 S	175.46 E
Mangalia	15	Lf	43.48 N	28.35 E
Mangalmé	35	Bc	12.21 N	19.37 E
Mangalore	22	Jh	12.52 N	74.53 E
Mangareva, Ile- 🖼	57	Ng	23.07 S	134.57 W
Mangfall 🖼	10	Il	47.51 N	12.08 E
Manggar	26	Eg	2.53 S	108.16 E
Mangin Yoma 🅰	25	Jd	24.20 N	95.42 E
Mangistau 🅰	16	Qg	44.00 N	51.57 E
Mangit	19	Gf	42.07 N	60.01 E
Mangkalihat, Tanjung- 🖻	26	Gf	1.02 N	118.59 E
Manglares, Cabo- 🖻	54	Cc	1.36 N	79.02 W
Mangnai	27	Fd	37.48 N	91.55 E
Mangnia He 🖼	28	Ib	45.10 N	126.58 E
Mango (Fiji) 🖼	63d	Cb	17.27 S	179.09 W
Mango (Ton.] 🖼	65b	Bb	20.20 S	174.43 W
Mangoky 🖼	37	Hd	23.55 S	45.13 E
Mangoky [Mad.] 🖼	37	Gd	21.29 S	43.41 E
Mangole, Pulau- 🖼	26	Ig	1.53 S	125.50 E
Mangonui	62	Ea	34.59 S	173.32 E
Mangrove Cay 🖼	49	Ib	24.15 N	77.38 W
Mangrullo, Cuchilla- 🅰	55	Fk	32.27 S	53.50 W
Mangshi → Luxi	27	Gg	24.29 N	98.40 E
Mangualde	13	Ec	40.36 N	7.46 W
Mangueira, Lagoa- 🖸	52	Kh	33.06 S	52.48 W
Mangueni, Plateau de- 🖸	30	If	22.35 N	12.40 E
Mangui	27	La	52.03 N	122.09 E
Mangum	45	Gi	34.53 N	99.30 W
Mânguredjipa	36	Eb	0.21 N	28.44 E
Mangyšlak	19	Fg	43.40 N	51.15 E
Mangyšlak, Plato- 🖸	17	Fg	43.25 N	53.00 E
Mangyšlakskaja Oblast 🖸	19	Fg	44.00 N	53.00 E
Mangyšlakski Zaliv 🖸	16	Qg	44.45 N	51.00 E
Manhica	37	Ee	25.24 S	32.48 E
Mani	52	Kf	8.25 S	25.20 E
Mani	54	Dc	4.49 N	72.17 W

Manicoré, Rio- 54 Fe 5.51S 61.19W
Manicouagan 42 Kg 49.10N 68.15W
Manicouagan 42 Kf 51.00N 68.20W
Manicouagan, Réservoir- 38 Md 51.30N 68.19W
Manigotagan 45 Ha 51.06N 96.18W
Manihi Atoll 57 Mf 14.24S 145.56W
Manihiki Anchorage 64n Ab 10.23S 161.03W
Manihiki Atoll 57 Kf 10.24S 161.01W
Manika, Plateau de la- 36 Ed 10.00S 26.00 E
Manila [Phil.] 22 Oh 14.35N 121.00 E
Manila [Ut.-U.S.] 46 Kf 40.59N 109.43W
Manila Bay 21 Oh 14.30N 120.45 E
Manilaid/Manilajd 8 Kf 58.08N 24.03 E
Manilajd/Manilaid 8 Kf 58.08N 24.03 E
Manily 20 Ld 62.30N 165.20 E
Maningrida Settlement 59 Gb 12.05S 134.10 E
Maniouro, Pointe- 63b Dc 17.41S 168.35 E
Manipa, Selat- 26 Ig 3.20S 127.23 E
Manipur [3] 25 Id 25.00N 94.00 E
Manipur 25 Id 22.52N 94.05 E
Manisa 23 Cb 38.36N 27.26 E
Manisa Dağı 15 Kk 38.33N 27.28 E
Manises 13 Le 39.29N 0.27W
Manissau a-Missu, Rio- 54 Hf 10.58S 53.20W
Manistee 44 Dc 44.15N 86.18W
Manistee River 44 Dc 44.15N 86.21W
Manistique 43 Jb 45.57N 86.15W
Manitique Lake 44 Eb 46.15N 85.45W
Manitoba [3] 42 Hf 55.00N 97.00W
Manitoba, Lake- 38 Jd 51.00N 98.45W
Manitou Islands 44 Ec 45.10N 86.00W
Manitou Lake 44 Gc 45.48N 82.00W
Manitoulin Island 42 Jg 45.45N 82.30W
Manitou Springs 45 Dg 38.52N 104.55W
Manitouwadge 45 Nb 49.08N 85.47W
Manitowoc 43 Jc 44.06N 87.40W
Manitsoq/Sukkertoppen 41 Ge 65.25N 53.00W
Maniwaki 42 Jg 46.23N 75.58W
Manizales 53 Ie 5.05N 75.32W
Manja 17 Jd 64.23N 60.50 E
Manja 37 Gd 21.23S 44.20 E
Manjača 14 Lf 44.35N 17.05 E
Manjacaze 37 Ed 24.42S 33.33 E
Manjakandriana 37 Hc 18.55S 47.47 E
Manji 29a Bb 43.09N 141.59 E
Manjimup 59 Df 34.14S 116.09 E
Mānjra 25 Fe 18.49N 77.52 E
Män Kät 25 Jd 22.05N 98.01 E
Mankato [Ks.-U.S.] 45 Gg 39.47N 98.12W
Mankato [Mn.-U.S.] 43 Ic 44.10N 94.01W
Mankono 34 Dd 8.04N 6.12W
Mankono [3] 34 Dd 7.58N 6.02W
Mankoya 31 Jj 14.50S 25.00 E
Manley Hot Springs 40 Ic 65.00N 150.37W
Manlleu 13 Ob 42.00N 2.17 E
Manmād 25 Ed 20.15N 74.27 E
Manmanoc, Mount- 26 Hc 17.40N 121.06 E
Manna 26 Dh 4.27S 102.55 E
Mannahill 59 Hf 32.26S 139.59 E
Mannar 25 Fg 8.59N 79.54 E
Mannar, Gulf of- 21 Ji 8.30N 79.00 E
Mannheim 6 Gf 49.29N 8.28 E
Manning [Alta.-Can.] 42 Fe 56.55N 117.33W
Manning [S.C.-U.S.] 44 Gi 33.42N 80.12W
Manning, Cape- 64g Ba 2.02N 157.26W
Manning Strait 63a Db 7.24S 158.04 E
Manningtree 12 Dc 51.57N 1.04 E
Mann Ranges 59 Fe 26.00S 129.30 E
Mann River 59 Gb 12.20S 134.07 E
Mannu, Capo- 14 Cj 40.02N 8.22 E
Mannu, Rio- [It.] 14 Cj 40.50N 8.23 E
Mannu, Rio- [It.] 14 Cj 40.41N 8.59 E
Mano 34 Cd 6.56N 11.31W
Mano [Jap.] 29 Fc 37.58N 138.20 E
Mano [S.L.] 34 Cd 7.55N 12.00W
Manoa 54 Ee 9.40S 65.27W
Man of War, Cayos- 49 Fg 13.02N 83.22W
Manokwari 58 Ee 2.30S 134.36 E
Manombo 37 Gd 22.55S 43.28 E
Manompana 37 Hc 16.41S 49.45 E
Manonga 36 Fc 4.08S 34.12 E
Manono 31 Ji 7.18S 27.25 E
Manono 65c Aa 13.50S 172.05W
Manosque 11 Lk 43.50N 5.47 E
Manouane, Lac- 42 Kf 50.40N 70.45W
Mano-Wan 29 Fc 37.55N 138.15 E
Manp'ojin 28 Id 41.09N 126.17 E
Manra Atoll (Sydney) 57 Je 4.27S 171.15W
Manresa 13 Nc 41.44N 1.50 E
Mansa 31 Jj 11.12S 28.53 E
Mansa Konko 34 Bc 13.28N 15.33W
Mansel 38 Lc 62.00N 79.50W
Mansfield [Austl.] 59 Jg 37.03S 146.05 E
Mansfield [Eng.-U.K.] 9 Lh 53.09N 1.11W
Mansfield [La.-U.S.] 45 Jj 32.02N 93.43W
Mansfield [Oh.-U.S.] 43 Kc 40.46N 82.31W
Mansfield [Pa.-U.S.] 44 Ie 41.47N 77.05W
Mansfield, Mount- 44 Kc 44.33N 72.49W
Mansle 11 Gi 45.52N 0.11 E
Manso, Rio- 55 Db 14.42S 56.16W
Manso, Rio- ou Mortes, Rio das- 52 Kg 11.45S 50.44W
Mansôa 34 Bc 12.04N 15.19W
Mansourah 13 Qh 36.04N 4.28 E
Mansourah, Djebel- 13 Qh 36.02N 4.28 E
Manta 54 Bd 0.57S 80.42W
Manta, Bahia de- 54 Bd 0.50S 80.40W
Mantalingajan, Mount- 26 Ge 8.48N 117.40 E
Manteca 46 Eh 37.48N 121.13W
Mantecal [Ven.] 50 Di 6.52N 65.38W
Mantecal [Ven.] 50 Bi 7.33N 69.09W
Manteigas 13 Ed 40.24N 7.32W
Manteo 44 Jh 35.55N 75.40W
Mantes-la-Jolie 11 Hf 48.59N 1.43 E
Manti 46 Jg 39.16N 111.38W
Mantiqueira, Serra da- 52 Lh 22.00S 44.45W
Manto 49 Df 14.55N 86.23W
Manton 44 Ec 44.24N 85.24W
Mantova 14 Ee 45.09N 10.48 E
Mäntsälä 8 Kd 60.38N 25.20 E
Mänttä 7 Fe 62.02N 24.38 E
Mantua 49 Eb 22.17N 84.17W
Manturovo 19 Ed 58.22N 44.44 E
Mäntyharju 7 Gf 61.25N 26.53 E
Mäntyluoto 8 Ic 61.35N 21.29 E
Manu 54 Df 12.15S 70.50W
Manuae Atoll 57 Lf 19.21S 158.56W
Manua Islands 57 Kf 14.13S 169.35W
Manuangi Atoll 57 Mf 19.12S 141.16W
Manūbah 14 En 36.48N 10.06 E
Manuel 48 Jf 22.44N 98.19W
Manuel Alves, Rio- 54 If 11.19S 48.28W
Manuel Bonavides 48 Hc 29.05N 103.55W
Manuel Derqui 55 Ch 27.50S 58.48W
Manuel J. Cobo 55 Dl 35.49S 57.54W
Manuel Ocampo 55 Bk 33.46S 60.39W
Manuga Reefs 63a Ad 11.00S 153.21 E
Manui, Pulau- 26 Hg 3.35S 123.08 E
Manujān 24 Qi 27.24N 57.32 E
Mānūk, Tell- 24 Hf 33.10N 38.50 E
Manukau 58 Ih 36.56S 174.56 E
Manulu Lagoon 64g Bb 1.56N 157.20W
Manus Island 57 Fe 2.05S 147.00 E
Many 45 Jk 31.34N 93.29W
Manyara, Lake- 36 Gc 3.35S 35.50 E
Manyas 24 Bb 40.02N 27.58 E
Manyč 5 Kf 47.15N 40.00 E
Manyč-Gudilo, Ozero- 5 Kf 46.25N 42.35 E
Manyoni 36 Fd 5.45S 34.50 E
Manzanal, Puerto del- 13 Fb 42.32N 6.10W
Manzanares 13 Ie 39.00N 3.22W
Manzaneda, Cabeza de- 13 Eb 42.20N 7.15W
Manzanilla 13 Fg 37.23N 6.25W
Manzanillo [Cuba] 39 Lg 20.21N 77.07W
Manzanillo [Mex.] 39 Ih 19.03N 104.20W
Manzanillo, Bahia de- [Dom.Rep.] 49 Ld 19.45N 71.46W
Manzanillo, Bahia de- [Mex.] 48 Gh 19.04N 104.25W
Manzanillo, Punta- 49 Hi 9.38N 79.32W
Manzano Mountains 45 Ci 34.45N 106.20W
Manzhouli 22 Ne 49.33N 117.28 E
Manzilah, Buḥayrat al- 24 Eg 31.15N 32.00 E
Manzil Bū Ruqaybah 32 Ib 37.10N 9.48 E
Manzil bū Zalafah 14 En 36.41N 10.35 E
Manzil Tamīn 14 En 36.47N 10.59 E
Manzini 37 Ee 26.29S 31.22 E
Mao 63b Dc 17.29S 168.29 E
Mao [Chad] 31 Ig 14.07N 15.19 E
Mao [Dom.Rep.] 47 Je 19.34N 71.05W
Mao/Mahón 13 Qe 39.53N 4.15 E
Maoke, Pegunungan- 57 Ee 4.00S 138.00 E
Maomao Shan 27 Hd 37.12N 103.10 E
Maoming 22 Ng 21.41N 110.52 E
Maoniu Shan 27 He 32.50N 104.12 E
Maotou Shan 27 Hg 24.31N 100.38 E
Maouri, Dallol- 34 Fc 12.05N 3.32 E
Mapai 37 Ed 22.51S 31.58 E
Mapanda 36 Dd 9.32S 24.16 E
Mapati 36 Bc 3.38S 13.21 E
Mapi 58 Ee 7.07S 139.23 E
Mapi 26 Kh 7.00S 139.16 E
Mapia, Kepulauan- 26 Jf 0.50N 134.20 E
Mapimi, Bolsón de- 38 Ig 27.30N 103.15W
Mapinhane 37 Fd 22.15S 35.07 E
Mapire 50 Di 7.45N 64.42W
Mapiri 54 Eg 15.15S 68.10W
Maple Creek 42 Gg 49.55N 109.27W
Maprik 60 Ch 3.38S 143.03 E
Mapuera, Rio- 54 Gd 1.05S 57.02W
Maputo [3] 37 Ee 26.00S 32.30 E
Maputo (Lourenço Marques) 31 Kk 25.58S 32.34 E
Maputo, Baia de- 30 Kk 26.05S 33.00 E
Maqên (Dawu) 27 He 34.29N 100.01 E
Maqran, Wādī al- 33 Ie 20.55N 47.12 E
Maqu 27 He 34.05N 101.45 E
Maquan He/Damqog Kanbab 27 Df 29.36N 84.09 E
Maquela do Zombo 31 Ii 6.03S 15.08 E
Maquinchao 56 Gf 41.15S 68.44W
Maquoketa 45 Ke 42.04N 90.40W
Mar, Serra do- 52 Lh 25.00S 48.00W
Mara 36 Fc 1.31S 33.56 E
Mara [3] 36 Fc 2.30S 34.00 E
Maraã 54 Ed 1.50S 65.22W
Marab 35 Fc 14.54N 37.55 E
Marabá 54 Ie 5.21S 49.07W
Marabahan 26 Fg 3.00S 114.45 E
Marabá Paulista 55 Gf 22.06S 51.56W
Maraca, Ilha de- 54 Hc 2.05N 50.25W
Maracaibo 53 Id 10.40N 71.37W
Maracaibo, Lago de- = Maracaibo, Lake- (EN) 52 Ie 9.50N 71.30W
Maracaibo, Lake- (EN) = Maracaibo, Lago de- 52 Ie 9.50N 71.30W
Maracaju 54 Gh 21.38S 55.09W
Maracaju, Serra de- [Braz.] 52 Kh 21.00S 55.00W
Maracaju, Serra de- [S.Amer.] 55 Ef 23.57S 55.01W
Maracanã 54 Id 0.46S 47.27W
Maracás 54 Jf 13.26S 40.27W
Maracay 53 Jd 10.15N 67.36W
Marādah 33 Cd 29.14N 19.13 E
Maradi 31 Hg 13.29N 7.06 E
Maradi [2] 34 Gc 14.15N 7.15 E
Marāgheh 23 Gb 37.23N 46.40 E
Marāh 23 Gd 25.04N 45.28 E
Maraho 35 Bb 18.21N 17.28 E
Marahuaca, Cerro- 52 Je 3.34N 65.27W
Marajó, Baia de- 52 Lf 1.00S 48.30W
Marajó, Ilha de- 52 Lf 1.00S 49.30W
Marakei Atoll 57 Id 1.58N 173.25 E
Maralal 36 Gb 1.06N 36.42 E
Maralinga 59 Gf 30.13S 131.35 E
Maralwexi/Bachu 27 Cd 39.46N 78.15 E
Maramag 26 He 7.46N 125.00 E
Maramasike Island 60 Gi 9.30S 161.25 E
Maramba 31 Jj 17.51S 25.52 E
Marampa 34 Cd 8.41N 12.28W
Maramureş [2] 15 Gb 47.40N 24.00 E
Maranchón 13 Jc 41.03N 2.12W
Marānd 23 Gb 38.26N 45.46 E
Marandellas 37 Ec 18.10S 31.36 E
Marang 26 De 5.12N 103.13 E
Maranhão [2] 54 Je 5.00S 45.00W
Maranhão, Rio- 54 If 14.34S 49.02W
Marano, Laguna di- 14 He 45.44N 13.10 E
Maranoa River 59 Je 27.50S 148.37 E
Marañón, Rio- 52 If 4.30S 73.35W
Marans 11 Fh 46.18N 1.00W
Marão 37 Ed 24.18S 34.07 E
Marão, Serra do- 13 Ec 41.15N 7.55W
Maraoué 34 Dd 6.54N 5.31W
Marapanim 54 Id 0.42S 47.42W
Marapi, Gunung- 26 Dg 0.23S 100.28 E
Marargiu, Capo- 14 Cj 40.20N 8.23 E
Marari, Serra do- 55 Gh 27.30S 51.00W
Mara Rosa 55 Ha 13.58S 49.09W
Mărăşeşti 15 Kd 45.53N 27.14 E
Maratea 14 Jk 39.59N 15.43 E
Marathón 15 Gk 38.09N 23.58 E
Marathon 45 Ek 30.12N 103.15W
Marathon 42 Ig 48.46N 86.26W
Maratua, Pulau- 26 Gf 2.15N 118.36 E
Marau 55 Fi 28.27S 52.12W
Maravari 63a Cb 7.54S 156.44 E
Marāveh Tappeh 24 Pd 37.55N 55.57 E
Maravilha 55 Fh 26.47S 53.09W
Maravillas Creek 45 El 29.34N 102.47W
Maravovo 63a Dc 9.17S 159.38 E
Marāwah 33 Dc 32.29N 21.25 E
Marawi 26 He 8.13N 124.15 E
Marawi 35 Eb 18.29N 31.49 E
Marāwiḥ 24 Oj 24.18N 53.18 E
Marayes 56 Gd 31.29S 67.20W
Marbella 13 Hh 36.31N 4.53W
Marble Bar 59 Dd 21.11S 119.44 E
Marble Canyon 46 Jh 36.30N 111.50W
Marble Falls 45 Gk 30.34N 98.17W
Marble Hall 37 Dd 24.57S 29.13 E
Marburg an der Lahn 10 Ef 50.49N 8.46 E
Marca, Ponta da- 30 Ij 16.31S 11.42 E
Marcal 10 Ni 47.38N 17.32 E
Marcala 49 Df 14.07N 88.00W
Marçal Dağları 15 Kl 37.09N 28.00 E
Marcali 10 Nj 46.35N 17.25 E
March 10 Mh 48.10N 16.59 E
March 9 Ni 52.33N 0.06 E
Marche 11 Hh 46.10N 1.30 E
Marche = Marches (EN) [2] 14 Hh 43.30N 13.15 E
Marche, Plateau de la- 11 Hh 46.16N 1.30 E
Marche-en-Famenne 11 Ld 50.14N 5.20 E
Marchena 13 Gg 37.20N 5.24W
Marchena, Isla- 54a Aa 0.20N 90.30W
Marches (EN) = Marche [2] 14 Hh 43.30N 13.15 E
Marchesato 14 Kk 39.05N 17.00 E
Marchfeld 14 Kb 48.15N 16.40 E
Mar Chiquita, Laguna- 55 Dm 37.37S 57.24W
Mar Chiquita, Laguna- 52 Ji 30.42S 62.36W
Marciana Marina 14 Eh 42.48N 10.12 E
Marcigny 11 Kh 46.16N 4.02 E
Marcilly-sur-Eure 12 Df 48.49N 1.21 E
Marcinelle, Charleroi- 12 Gd 50.25N 4.28 E
Marck 12 Dd 50.57N 1.57 E
Marcoing 12 Fd 50.07N 3.11 E
Marcos Juaréz 56 Hd 32.42S 62.06W
Marcus Baker, Mount- 40 Jd 61.26N 147.45W
Marcus Island (EN) = Minami-Tori-Shima 57 Gb 26.32N 142.09 E
Marcy, Mount- 43 Mc 44.07N 73.56W
Mardakert 16 Oi 40.12N 46.52 E
Mardakjan 16 Qi 40.29N 50.12 E
Mardān 25 Eb 34.09N 71.52 E
Mardarovka 15 Mb 47.30N 29.40 E
Mar del Plata 53 Ki 38.01S 57.35W
Marden 12 Cc 51.10N 0.30 E
Mardin 23 Fb 37.18N 40.44 E
Mardin Dağları 24 Id 37.20N 41.00 E
Maré, Ile- 57 Hg 21.30S 168.00 E
Mare, Muntele- 15 Gc 46.29N 23.14 E
Marechal Cândido Rondon 55 Eg 24.34S 54.04W
Maree, Loch- 9 Hd 57.40N 5.30W
Mareeba 59 Jc 17.00S 145.26 E
Mārēg 35 He 3.47N 47.18 E
Maremma 14 Fh 42.30N 11.30 E
Marennes 11 Ei 45.49N 1.07W
Marettimo 14 Gm 37.56N 12.05 E
Mareuil-en-Brie 12 Ff 48.57N 3.45 E
Marfa 43 Ge 30.18N 104.01W
Marfil, Laguna- 55 Bb 15.30S 60.20W
Margai Caka 27 Ed 35.10N 86.55 E
Marganec 19 Df 47.38N 34.40 E
Margaret River 59 Df 33.57S 115.04 E
Margarida 55 De 21.41S 56.44W
Margarita, Isla de- 54 Fa 11.00N 64.00W
Margarita Belén 55 Ch 27.16S 58.58W
Margarition 15 Dj 39.21N 20.26 E
Margate [Eng.-U.K.] 9 Oj 51.24N 1.24 E
Margate [S.Afr.] 37 Ef 30.55S 30.15 E
Margeride, Monts de la- 11 Jj 44.50N 3.25 E
Marghera, Venezia- 14 Ge 45.28N 12.44 E
Margherita di Savoia 14 Ki 41.22N 16.09 E
Marghine, Catena del- 14 Cj 40.20N 8.50 E
Marghita 15 Fb 47.21N 22.20 E
Marghūb, Kūh-e- 24 Qf 33.06N 57.30 E
Margilan 19 Hg 40.28N 71.46 E
Margina 15 Fd 45.51N 22.16 E
Marguerite Bay 66 Qe 68.30S 68.30W
Margut 12 He 49.35N 5.16 E
Marha 20 Hd 60.35N 123.10 E
Marha 21 Nc 63.20N 118.50 E
Mari 24 Ie 34.39N 40.53 E
Mari 24 Ee 34.44N 33.18 E
Maria Atoll [W.F.] 57 Ng 22.00S 136.10W
Maria Atoll [W.F.] 57 Lg 21.48S 154.41W
Maria Cleofas, Isla- 48 Fg 21.16N 106.14W
Maria Elena 56 Gb 22.21S 69.40W
Mariager 8 Ch 56.39N 10.00 E
Mariager Fjord 8 Dh 56.40N 10.20 E
Maria Grande, Arroyo- 55 Ci 29.21S 58.45W
Maria Ignacia 55 Cm 37.24S 59.30W
Maria Island [Austl.] 59 Jh 42.40S 148.05 E
Maria Island [Austl.] 59 Hb 14.55S 135.40 E
Maria Island [St.Luc.] 51k Bb 13.44N 60.56W
Mariakani 36 Gc 3.52S 39.28 E
Maria Laach 12 Jd 50.25N 7.15 E
Maria Madre, Isla- 48 Fg 21.35N 106.33W
Maria Magdalena, Isla- 48 Fg 21.25N 106.25W
Mariana Islands 57 Fc 16.00N 145.30 E
Marianao 47 Hd 23.05N 82.26W
Mariana Trench (EN) 3 Ih 14.00N 147.30 E
Marianna [Ar.-U.S.] 45 Ki 34.46N 90.46W
Marianna [Fl.-U.S.] 44 Ej 30.47N 85.14W
Mariannelund 8 Fg 57.37N 15.34 E
Mariano I. Loza 55 Ci 29.22S 58.12W
Mariánské Lázně 10 Ig 49.58N 12.43 E
Marias, Islas- 38 Ig 21.25N 106.28W
Marias Pass 46 Ib 48.19N 113.21W
Marias River 43 Eb 47.56N 110.30W
Maria Theresa Reef 57 Lh 36.58S 151.23W
Mariato, Punta- 47 Hg 7.13N 80.53W
Maria van Diemen, Cape- 62 Ea 34.29S 172.39 E
Mariazell 14 Jc 47.46N 15.19 E
Ma'rib 23 Gf 15.30N 45.21 E
Maribo 8 Dj 54.46N 11.31 E
Maribor 14 Jd 46.33N 15.39 E
Marica 5 Ig 40.52N 26.12 E
Marica 15 Ig 42.02N 25.50 E
Maricao 51a Bb 18.10N 66.58W
Maricopa 46 Ij 33.04N 112.03W
Maricourt 42 Kd 61.36N 71.57W
Maridi 35 Dd 6.05N 29.24 E
Maridi 35 De 4.55N 29.28 E
Marié, Rio- 54 Ed 0.25S 66.26W
Marie Byrd Land (EN) 66 Nf 80.00S 120.00W
Mariec 7 Lh 56.31N 49.51 E
Marie Galante 47 Le 15.56N 61.16W
Marie-Galante, Canal de- 51e Bc 15.55N 61.25W
Mariehamn/Maarianhamina 7 Ef 60.06N 19.57 E
Marie Louise Island 37b Bb 6.11S 53.09 E
Mariembourg, Couvin- 12 Gd 50.06N 4.31 E
Marienburg 12 Jd 50.04N 7.08 E
Marienmünster 12 Lc 51.50N 9.13 E
Marienstatt 12 Jd 50.40N 7.49 E
Mariental 31 Ik 24.36S 17.59 E
Mariestad 7 Cg 58.43N 13.51 E
Marietta [Ga.-U.S.] 43 Ke 33.57N 84.33W
Marietta [Oh.-U.S.] 44 Gf 39.26N 81.27W
Mariga 34 Gd 9.36N 5.57 E
Marignac 11 Gl 42.55N 0.39 E
Marignane 11 Lk 43.25N 5.13 E
Marigot [Dom.] 50 Fe 15.32N 61.18W
Marigot [Guad.] 50 Ec 18.04N 63.06W
Marigot [Haiti] 49 Kd 18.14N 72.19W
Marigot [Mart.] 51h Ab 14.49N 61.02W
Marigot [St.Luc.] 51k Ab 13.58N 61.02W
Mariinsk 20 De 56.13N 87.45 E
Mariinski Posad 7 Lh 56.08N 47.48 E
Mariinskoje 20 Jf 51.43N 140.19 E
Marijovo 15 Eh 41.04N 21.45 E
Marijskaja ASSR [3] 19 Ed 56.40N 48.00 E
Marilia 56 Jb 22.13S 50.01W
Mariluz 55 Fg 24.02S 53.13W
Marimba 36 Cd 8.22S 17.02 E
Marimbondo, Cachoeira do- 55 He 20.18S 49.10W
Marin 13 Db 42.23N 8.42W
Marin, Cul-de-Sac du- 51h Bc 14.27N 60.53W
Marina di Catanzaro 14 Kl 38.49N 16.36 E
Marina di Gioiosa Ionica 14 Kl 38.18N 16.20 E
Marina di Pisa 14 Eg 43.40N 10.16 E
Marina di Ravenna 14 Gf 44.29N 12.17 E
Marina Gorka 19 Ce 53.31N 28.12 E
Marinduque 26 Hd 13.24N 121.58 E
Marineland 44 Gk 29.43N 81.12W
Marines 12 De 49.09N 1.59 E
Marinette 43 Jb 45.06N 87.38W
Maringá 53 Kh 23.25S 51.55W
Maringa 30 Ih 1.14N 19.48 E
Marinha Grande 13 De 39.45N 8.56W
Marino [It.] 14 Gi 41.46N 12.39 E
Marino [Van.] 63b Db 14.59S 168.03 E
Marins, Pico dos- 55 Jf 22.27S 45.10W
Marinsko 8 Mf 58.46N 28.39 E
Marion 30 Km 46.36S 37.55 E
Marion [Al.-U.S.] 44 Di 32.32N 87.26W
Marion [Ia.-U.S.] 45 Ke 42.02N 91.36W
Marion [Il.-U.S.] 45 Lh 37.44N 88.56W
Marion [In.-U.S.] 44 Ee 40.33N 85.40W
Marion [Oh.-U.S.] 43 Kc 40.35N 83.08W
Marion [S.C.-U.S.] 44 Hh 34.11N 79.23W
Marion [Va.-U.S.] 44 Gg 36.51N 81.30W
Marion, Lake- 44 Gi 33.30N 80.25W
Marion Reefs 57 Gf 19.10S 152.20 E
Maripa 54 Ea 7.26N 65.09W
Mariposa 46 Fh 37.29N 119.58W
Mariquita, Cerro- 48 Jf 23.13N 98.22W
Marisa 26 Hf 0.28N 121.56 E
Mariscala 55 El 34.03S 54.47W
Mariscal Estigarribia 56 Hb 22.02S 60.38W
Maritime [3] 34 Fd 6.30N 1.20 E
Mariusa, Caño 50 Fh 9.43N 61.26W
Mariusa, Isla- 50 Fh 9.39N 61.19W
Marīvan 24 Le 35.31N 46.10 E
Märjamaa/Marjamaa 8 Kf 58.54N 24.21 E
Marjamaa/Märjamaa 8 Kf 58.54N 24.21 E
Marjanovka [R.S.F.S.R.] 19 He 54.58N 72.38 E
Marjanovka [Ukr.-U.S.S.R.] 10 Uf 50.23N 24.55 E
Mark 12 Gc 51.39N 4.39 E
Mark [F.R.G.] 12 Jc 51.13N 7.36 E
Mark [Swe.] 8 Eg 57.35N 12.35 E
Marka 31 Lh 1.43N 44.46 E
Markako, Ozero- 19 If 48.45N 85.50 E
Markala 34 Dc 13.39N 6.05W
Markam (Gartog) 27 Gf 29.32N 98.33 E
Markaryd 7 Ch 56.26N 13.36 E
Marken 12 Hb 52.27N 5.05 E
Markerwaard 12 Hb 52.31N 5.15 E
Market Deeping 12 Bb 52.40N 0.18W
Market Harborough 9 Mi 52.29N 0.55W
Markham, Mount- 66 Kg 82.51S 161.21 E
Markham Bay 42 Kd 63.30N 71.40W
Markham River 59 Ja 6.35S 146.25 E
Marki 10 Rd 52.20N 21.07 E
Märkische Schweiz 10 Jd 52.35N 14.00 E
Markit 27 Cd 38.53N 77.35 E
Markounda 35 Bd 7.37N 16.59 E
Markovac 15 Ee 44.14N 21.06 E
Markovka 16 Ke 49.31N 39.32 E
Markovo 22 Tc 64.40N 170.25 E
Markoye 34 Fc 14.39N 0.02 E
Marksburg 12 Jd 50.16N 7.40 E
Marksville 45 Jk 31.08N 92.04W
Marktoberdorf 10 Gi 47.47N 10.37 E
Marktredwitz 10 If 50.00N 12.05 E
Markulešty 15 Lb 47.51N 28.07 E
Marl 10 De 51.39N 7.05 E
Marlagne 12 Gd 50.25N 4.40 E
Marlborough [2] 62 Ed 41.50S 173.40 E
Marlborough [Austl.] 59 Jd 22.49S 149.53 E
Marlborough [Guy.] 50 Gi 7.29N 58.38W
Marle 11 Je 49.44N 3.46 E
Marlin 45 Hk 31.18N 96.53W
Marlinton 44 Gf 38.14N 80.06W
Marlow [Eng.-U.K.] 12 Bc 51.34N 0.46W
Marlow [Ok.-U.S.] 45 Hi 34.39N 97.57W
Marmande 11 Gj 44.30N 0.10 E
Marmara 24 Bb 40.35N 27.33 E
Marmara, Sea of- (EN) = Marmara Denizi 5 Ig 40.40N 28.15 E
Marmara Adasi 24 Bb 40.38N 27.37 E
Marmara Denizi = Marmara, Sea of- (EN) 5 Ig 40.40N 28.15 E
Marmara Ereğlisi 15 Ki 40.58N 27.57 E
Marmara Gölü 15 Lk 38.37N 28.02 E
Marmarica (EN) = Barqah al Bahrīyah 30 Je 31.40N 24.30 E
Marmaris 23 Cb 36.51N 28.16 E
Marmelos, Rio- 54 Fe 6.08S 61.47W
Marmion Lake 45 Kb 48.54N 91.30W
Marmolada 14 Fd 46.26N 11.51 E
Marmora 44 Ic 44.29N 77.41W
Marmore, Cascata delle- 14 Gh 42.35N 12.45 E
Marne 10 Ec 53.57N 9.00 E
Marne 5 Gf 48.49N 2.24 E
Marne [3] 11 Kf 48.55N 4.10 E
Marne à la Saône, Canal de la- 11 Kf 48.44N 4.36 E
Marne au Rhin, Canal de la- 11 Nf 48.35N 7.47 E
Mårnes 7 Dc 67.09N 14.06 E
Marneuli 16 Ni 41.29N 44.45 E
Maro 35 Bd 8.25N 18.46 E
Maro 35 Bb 19.23N 16.38 E
Maroa 54 Ec 2.43N 67.33W
Maroantsetra 31 Lj 15.27S 49.44 E
Marokau Atoll 61 Mc 18.02S 142.17W
Marolambo 37 Hd 20.04S 48.08 E
Maromandia 37 Hb 14.11S 48.06 E
Maromme 11 He 49.28N 1.02 E
Maromokotro 37 Hb 14.01S 48.58 E
Maroni, Fleuve- 52 Ke 5.45N 53.58W
Marónia 15 Ii 40.55N 25.31 E
Maronne 11 Hi 45.04N 1.56 E
Maroochydore 59 Ke 26.39S 153.06 E
Maro Reef 57 Jb 25.25N 170.35W
Maros 15 Dc 46.15N 20.12 E
Maros 26 Gg 5.00S 119.34 E
Maroua 31 Ig 10.36N 14.20 E
Marovoay 37 Hc 16.06S 46.37 E
Marowijne River 54 Hb 5.45N 53.58W
Marqādah 24 Ie 35.44N 40.46 E
Mar Qu 27 He 31.58N 101.54 E
Marquard 37 De 28.54S 27.28 E
Marquenterre 12 Dd 50.20N 1.41 E
Marquesas Islands (EN) = Marquises, Iles- 57 Ne 9.00S 139.30W
Marquette 43 Jb 46.33N 87.24W
Marquion 12 Fd 50.13N 3.05 E
Marquis [Gren.] 51p Bb 12.06N 61.37W
Marquis [St.Luc.] 51k Ba 14.02N 60.55W
Marquis, Cape- 51k Ba 14.03N 60.54W
Marquise 12 Dd 50.49N 1.42 E
Marquises, Iles- = Marquesas Islands (EN) 57 Ne 9.00S 139.30W
Marracuene 37 Ee 25.44S 32.41 E
Marradi 14 Ff 44.04N 11.37 E
Marrah, Jabal- 30 Jg 13.04N 24.21 E
Marrak 33 Hf 16.26N 41.54 E
Marrakech 31 Ge 31.38N 8.00W
Marrakech [3] 32 Fc 32.00N 8.00W
Marrawah 59 Ih 40.56S 144.41 E
Marree 58 Eg 29.39S 138.04 E
Marreh, Kūh-e- 24 Oh 29.15N 52.20 E
Marrero 45 Kl 29.54N 90.07W
Marresalja 17 Mb 69.44N 66.59 E
Marresalskije Koški, Ostrova- 17 Mb 69.30N 67.10 E
Marromeu 37 Fc 18.17S 35.56 E
Marrti 7 Gc 67.28N 28.22 E
Marrupa 37 Fb 13.12S 37.30 E
Marsá al 'Alam 33 Fd 25.05N 34.54 E
Marsá al Burayqah 33 Cc 30.25N 19.35 E

Index Symbols

[1] Independent Nation
[2] State, Region
[3] District, County
[4] Municipality
[5] Colony, Dependency
Continent
Physical Region
Historical or Cultural Region
Mount, Mountain
Volcano
Hill
Mountains, Mountain Range
Hills, Escarpment
Plateau, Upland
Pass, Gap
Plain, Lowland
Delta
Salt Flat
Valley, Canyon
Crater, Cave
Karst Features
Depression
Polder
Desert, Dunes
Forest, Woods
Heath, Steppe
Oasis
Cape, Point
Coast, Beach
Cliff
Peninsula
Isthmus
Sandbank
Island
Atoll
Rock, Reef
Islands, Archipelago
Rocks, Reefs
Coral Reef
Well, Spring
Geyser
River, Stream
Waterfall Rapids
River Mouth, Estuary
Lake
Salt Lake
Intermittent Lake
Reservoir
Swamp, Pond
Canal
Glacier
Ice Shelf, Pack Ice
Ocean
Sea
Gulf, Bay
Strait, Fjord
Lagoon
Bank
Seamount
Tablemount
Ridge
Shelf
Basin
Escarpment, Sea Scarp
Fracture
Trench, Abyss
National Park, Reserve
Point of Interest
Recreation Site
Cave, Cavern
Historic Site
Ruins
Wall, Walls
Church, Abbey
Temple
Scientific Station
Airport
Port
Lighthouse
Mine
Tunnel
Dam, Bridge

Marsá al Uwayjah	33	Cc	30.55N	17.52 E
Marsa Ben Mehidi	13	Ji	35.05N	2.11W
Marsabit	31	Kh	2.20N	37.59 E
Marsala	14	Gm	37.48N	12.26 E
Marsá Sha'b	35	Fa	22.52N	35.47 E
Marsá Umm Ghayj	24	Fj	25.38N	34.30 E
Marsberg	10	Ee	51.27N	8.51 E
Marsciano	14	Gh	42.54N	12.20 E
Marsdiep	12	Gb	52.58N	4.45 E
Marseille = Marseilles (EN)	6	Gg	43.18N	5.24 E
Marseille-en-Beauvaisis	11	He	49.35N	1.57 E
Marseilles (EN) = Marseille	6	Gg	43.18N	5.24 E
Marshall [Ak.-U.S.]	40	Gd	61.52N	162.04W
Marshall [Ar.-U.S.]	45	Ji	35.55N	92.38W
Marshall [Il.-U.S.]	45	Mg	39.23N	87.42W
Marshall [Lbr.]	34	Cd	6.09N	10.23W
Marshall [Mn.-U.S.]	43	Hc	44.27N	95.47W
Marshall [Mo.-U.S.]	45	Jg	39.07N	93.12W
Marshall [Tx.-U.S.]	43	Ie	32.33N	94.23W
Marshall Islands [5]	58	Hd	9.00N	168.00 E
Marshall Islands	57	Hd	9.00N	168.00 E
Marshall River	59	Hd	22.59S	136.59 E
Marshalltown	43	Ic	42.03N	92.54W
Marshfield	45	Kd	44.40N	90.10W
Marsh Harbour	47	Ic	26.33N	77.03W
Mārshinān, Kūh-e-	24	Of	32.53N	52.24 E
Marsh Island	45	Kl	29.35N	91.53W
Marsica	14	Hi	41.55N	13.35 E
Marsico Nuovo	14	Jj	40.25N	15.44 E
Marsjaty	17	Jf	60.05N	60.29 E
Marsland	45	Ee	42.29N	103.16W
Mars-la-Tour	12	He	49.06N	5.54 E
Marson	12	Gf	48.55N	4.32 E
Märsta	8	Ge	59.37N	17.51 E
Marstal	8	Dj	54.51N	10.31 E
Marstrand	8	Dg	57.53N	11.35 E
Marta	14	Fh	42.14N	11.42 E
Martaban	25	Je	16.32N	97.37 E
Martaban, Gulf of- (EN)	21	Lh	16.30N	97.00 E
Martap	34	Hd	6.54N	13.03 E
Martapura [Indon.]	26	Dg	4.19S	104.22 E
Martapura [Indon.]	26	Fg	3.25S	114.51 E
Martelange/Martelingen	12	He	49.50N	5.44 E
Martelingen/Martelange	12	He	49.50N	5.44 E
Martés, Sierra de-	13	Le	39.20N	0.57W
Martha's Vineyard	43	Mc	41.25N	70.40W
Martigny	14	Bd	46.06N	7.05 E
Martigues	11	Lk	43.24N	5.03 E
Martil	13	Gi	35.37N	5.17W
Martim Vaz, Ilhas-	52	Nh	20.30S	28.51W
Martin	13	Lc	41.18N	0.19W
Martin [Czech.]	10	Og	49.04N	18.55 E
Martin [S.D.-U.S.]	43	Gc	43.10N	101.44W
Martin [Tn.-U.S.]	44	Cg	36.21N	88.51W
Martina Franca	14	Lj	40.42N	17.20 E
Martinez de Hoz	55	Bl	35.19S	61.37W
Martinez de la Torre	48	Kg	20.04N	97.03W
Martín García, Isla-	55	Cl	34.11S	58.15W
Martin Hills	66	Pg	82.04S	88.01W
Martinho Campos	55	Jd	19.20S	45.13W
Martinique	38	Mh	14.40N	61.00W
Martinique [5]	39	Mh	14.40N	61.00W
Martinique, Canal de la- = Martinique Passage (EN)	47	Le	15.10N	61.20W
Martinique Passage	50	Fe	15.10N	61.20W
Martinique Passage (EN) = Martinique, Canal de la-	47	Le	15.10N	61.20W
Martin Lake	44	Ei	32.50N	85.55W
Martin Peninsula	66	Of	74.25S	114.10W
Martinsburg	44	If	39.28N	77.59W
Martins Ferry	44	Ge	40.07N	80.45W
Martinsville [In.-U.S.]	44	Df	39.26N	86.25W
Martinsville [Va.-U.S.]	43	Ld	36.43N	79.53W
Marton	62	Fd	40.05S	175.23 E
Martos	13	Ig	37.43N	3.58W
Martre, Lac la-	42	Fd	63.20N	118.00W
Martuk	19	Fe	50.47N	56.31 E
Martuni	16	Ni	40.06N	45.18 E
Maru	34	Gc	12.21N	6.24 E
Marud	25	Ee	18.19N	72.58 E
Marudi	26	Ff	4.11N	114.19 E
Marudu, Teluk-	26	Ge	6.45N	116.55 E
Marugame	29	Cd	34.18N	133.47 E
Maruko	29	Fc	36.19N	138.15 E
Mārūn	24	Mg	31.02N	49.36 E
Marungu, Monts-	30	Ji	7.42S	30.00 E
Maruoka	29	Ec	36.09N	136.16 E
Maruseppu	29a	Ca	44.01N	143.19 E
Marutea Atoll [W.F.]	57	Ng	21.30S	135.34W
Marutea Atoll [W.F.]	57	Mf	17.00S	143.10W
Maruyama-Gawa	29	Dd	35.40N	134.50 E
Marvão	13	Ee	39.24N	7.23W
Marvast	24	Pg	30.30N	54.15 E
Marvast, Kavir-e-	24	Pg	30.20N	54.25 E
Mårvatn	8	Cd	60.10N	8.15 E
Marv-Dasht	23	Hd	29.50N	52.40 E
Marvejols	11	Jj	44.33N	3.17 E
Marvine, Mount-	46	Jg	38.40N	111.39W
Marx	16	Od	51.42N	46.46 E
Mary	22	If	37.36N	61.50 E
Maryborough [Austl.]	58	Gg	25.32S	152.42 E
Maryborough [Austl.]	59	Ig	37.03S	143.45 E
Marydale	37	Ce	29.23S	22.05 E
Maryjskaja Oblast [3]	19	Gh	37.15N	62.30 E
Maryland [2]	43	Ld	39.00N	76.45W
Maryland [3]	34	De	4.45N	8.00W
Maryport	9	Jg	54.43N	3.30W
Mary River	59	Gb	12.53S	131.38 E
Marysville [Ca.-U.S.]	46	Eg	39.09N	121.35W
Marysville [Ks.-U.S.]	45	Hg	39.51N	96.39W
Marysville [N.B.-Can.]	44	Nc	45.59N	66.35W
Marysville [Oh.-U.S.]	44	Fe	40.13N	83.22W
Marysville [Wa.-U.S.]	46	Db	48.03N	122.11W
Maryville [Mo.-U.S.]	43	Ic	40.21N	94.52W
Maryville [Tn.-U.S.]	44	Fh	35.46N	83.58W
Marzūq	31	If	25.55N	13.55 E
Marzūq, Ḩamādat-	33	Bd	26.00N	12.30 E
Marzuq, Şaḩrā'-	30	If	24.30N	13.00 E
Masachapa	49	Dh	11.47N	86.31W
Masāhīm, Kūh-e-	24	Pg	30.21N	55.20 E
Masai Steppe	30	Ki	4.45S	37.00 E
Masaka	36	Fc	0.20S	31.44 E
Masākin	32	Jb	35.44N	10.35 E
Masalembo, Kepulauan-	26	Fh	5.30S	114.26 E
Masally	19	Eh	39.01N	48.40 E
Masalog, Puntan-	64b	Ba	15.01N	145.41 E
Masan	27	Md	35.11N	128.24 E
Masasi	31	Kj	10.43S	38.48 E
Masaya [3]	49	Dh	12.00N	86.10W
Masaya	47	Gf	11.58N	86.06W
Masbate	21	Oh	12.15N	123.30 E
Masbate	26	Hd	12.10N	123.35 E
Mascara	32	Hb	35.24N	0.08 E
Mascara [3]	32	Hb	35.30N	0.15 E
Mascareignes, Iles-/ Mascarene Islands	30	Mk	21.00S	57.00 E
Mascarene Basin (EN)	3	Fk	15.00S	56.00 E
Mascarene Islands/ Mascareignes, Iles-	30	Mk	21.00S	57.00 E
Mascarene Plateau (EN)	3	Gk	10.00S	60.00 E
Mascota	48	Gg	20.32N	104.49W
Masela, Pulau-	26	Ih	8.09S	129.50 E
Maseru	31	Jk	29.28S	27.29 E
Maşfūt	24	Qk	24.48N	56.06 E
Mashaba	37	Ed	20.02S	30.29 E
Mashābih	24	Gj	25.37N	36.32 E
Mashan	28	Kb	45.12N	130.32 E
Mashhad	22	Hf	36.18N	59.36 E
Mashike	28	Pc	43.51N	141.31 E
Mashiki	29	Be	32.47N	130.50 E
Mashiz	24	Qh	29.56N	56.37 E
Mashkel	21	Ig	28.02N	63.25 E
Mashonaland North [3]	37	Ec	17.00S	31.00 E
Mashonaland South [3]	37	Ec	18.00S	31.00 E
Mashra' ar Raqq	35	Dd	8.25N	29.16 E
Mashū-Ko	29a	Db	43.35N	144.30 E
Masiaca	48	Ed	26.45N	109.18W
Masīlah, Wādī al-	21	Hh	15.10N	51.08 E
Masi-Manimba	36	Cc	4.46S	17.55 E
Masindi	36	Fb	1.42N	31.43 E
Maşīrah, Jazīrat-	21	Hg	20.29N	58.33 E
Maşīrah, Khalīj-	21	Hg	20.15N	57.40 E
Masisi	36	Ec	1.24S	28.49 E
Masjed-Soleymān	23	Gc	31.58N	49.18 E
Mask, Lough-/Loch Measca	9	Dh	53.35N	9.20W
Maskanah	24	Hd	36.01N	38.05 E
Maskelynes, Iles-	63b	Cc	16.32S	167.49 E
Maslovare	14	Lf	44.34N	17.33 E
Masoala, Cap-	30	Mj	15.59S	50.13 E
Masoala, Presqu'île de-	37	Ic	15.40S	50.12 E
Mason	45	Gk	30.45N	99.14W
Mason Bay	62	Bg	46.55S	167.45 E
Mason City	39	Je	43.09N	93.12W
Masovia (EN) = Mazowsze	5	Ie	52.40N	20.20 E
Masparro, Río-	49	Mi	8.04N	69.26W
Masqaţ = Muscat (EN)	22	Hg	23.29N	58.33 E
Massa	14	Ef	44.01N	10.09 E
Massachusetts [2]	43	Mc	42.15N	71.50W
Massachusetts Bay	44	Ld	42.20N	70.50W
Massaciuccoli, Lago di-	14	Eg	43.50N	10.20 E
Massafra	14	Lj	40.35N	17.07 E
Massaguet	35	Bc	12.28N	15.26 E
Massakori	35	Bc	13.00N	15.44 E
Massa Marittima	14	Eg	43.03N	10.53 E
Massangano	36	Bd	9.37S	14.17 E
Massangena	37	Ed	21.32S	32.57 E
Massapê	54	Jd	3.31S	40.19W
Massawa (EN) = Mitsiwa	31	Kg	15.37N	39.39 E
Massena	43	Mc	44.56N	74.57W
Massénya	35	Bc	11.24N	16.10 E
Masset	42	Ef	54.02N	132.09W
Masseube	11	Gk	43.26N	0.35 E
Massey Sound	42	Ia	78.00N	94.00W
Massiac	11	Ji	45.15N	3.13 E
Massiaru	8	Kg	57.52N	24.27 E
Massillon	44	Ge	40.48N	81.32W
Massinga	37	Fd	23.20S	35.22 E
Masson Island	66	Ge	66.08S	96.34 E
Massuma	36	De	14.05S	22.00 E
Mastābah	33	Ge	20.49N	39.26 E
Maštaga	16	Pi	40.32N	49.59 E
Masterton	61	Eh	40.57S	175.39 E
Mastūrah	33	Ge	23.06N	38.50 E
Masuda	27	Ne	34.40N	131.51 E
Māsūleh	24	Md	37.10N	48.59 E
Masurai, Gunung-	26	Dg	2.30S	101.51 E
Masuria (EN)	5	Ie	53.50N	21.30 E
Masurian Lakes (EN)	5	Ie	53.45N	21.45 E
Maşyāf	24	Ge	35.03N	36.21 E
Maszewo	10	Lc	53.29N	15.02 E
Mataabé, Cap-	63b	Cb	15.38S	166.46 E
Matabeleland North [3]	37	Dc	19.00S	27.30 E
Matabeleland South [3]	37	Dd	21.00S	29.30 E
Matachel	13	Ff	38.50N	6.17W
Matachewan	42	Jg	47.56N	80.39W
Matacu	55	Bc	17.21S	61.28W
Matadi	31	Ii	5.49S	13.27 E
Matador	45	Fi	34.01N	100.49W
Matagalpa [3]	49	Eg	13.00N	85.30W
Matagalpa	39	Kh	12.53N	85.57W
Matagami	42	Jg	49.45N	77.35W
Matagami, Lac-	44	Ia	49.54N	77.32W
Mata Gassile	35	Ge	2.30N	42.16 E
Matagorda Bay	45	Hl	28.35N	96.20W
Matagorda Island	43	Hf	28.15N	96.30W
Matagorda Peninsula	45	Hl	28.32N	96.07W
Mataiea	65e	Fc	17.46S	149.25W
Mataiva Atoll	57	Mf	14.53S	148.40W
Mataj	19	Hf	45.51N	78.43 E
Matak, Pulau-	26	Ef	3.18N	106.16 E
Matakana Island	62	Gb	37.35S	176.05 E
Matala	36	Ce	14.43S	15.02 E
Matalaa, Pointe-	64h	Bc	13.20S	176.08W
Matale	25	Gg	7.28N	80.37 E
Mataliele	37	Df	30.24S	28.43 E
Matam	34	Cb	15.40N	13.15W
Matamey	34	Gc	13.26N	8.28 E
Matamoros [Mex.]	47	Dc	25.32N	103.15W
Matamoros [Mex.]	39	Jg	25.53N	97.30W
Matana, Danau-	26	Hg	2.28S	121.20 E
Ma'ţan as Sarra	33	De	21.41N	21.52 E
Matancita	48	De	25.09N	111.59W
Matane	42	Kg	48.51N	67.32W
Matankari	34	Fc	13.46N	4.01 E
Matanza	55	Cl	34.33S	58.35W
Matanzas	39	Kg	23.03N	81.35W
Matanzas [3]	49	Gb	22.40N	81.10W
Matão	55	He	21.35S	48.22W
Matapalo, Cabo-	49	Fi	8.23N	83.19W
Matapan, Cape- (EN) = Tainaron, Ákra-	5	Ih	36.23N	22.29 E
Matape, Río-	48	Dc	28.17N	110.41W
Mata Point	64k	Bb	19.07S	169.50W
Matara	35	Fc	14.35N	39.28 E
Matara	25	Gg	5.56N	80.33 E
Mataram	22	Nj	8.35S	116.07 E
Mataranka	59	Gb	14.56S	133.07 E
Mataró	13	Oc	41.32N	2.27 E
Matarraña/Matarranya	13	Mc	41.14N	0.22 E
Matarranya/Matarraña	13	Mc	41.14N	0.22 E
Mataso	63b	Dc	17.15S	168.25 E
Matatula, Cape-	65c	Cb	14.15S	170.34W
Mataura	62	Cg	46.34S	168.44 E
Mataura	62	Cg	46.12S	168.52 E
Mata-Utu	58	Jf	13.17S	176.08W
Mata-Utu, Baie de-	64h	Bb	13.19S	176.07W
Matavai	61	Gb	13.28S	172.35W
Matavera	64p	Cb	21.13S	159.44W
Mataverj	65d	Ab	27.10S	109.27W
Matawai	62	Gc	38.21S	177.32 E
Matawin, Réservoir-	44	Kb	46.45N	73.50W
Matawin, Rivière-	44	Kb	46.55N	72.55W
Maţāy	24	Dh	28.25N	30.46 E
Maţbakhayn	33	Hf	17.29N	41.48 E
Matca	15	Kd	45.51N	27.32 E
Matemo, Ilha-	37	Gb	12.13S	40.36 E
Matera	14	Kj	40.40N	16.36 E
Matese	14	Ii	41.25N	14.20 E
Mátészalka	10	Si	47.57N	22.20 E
Matfors	7	De	62.21N	17.02 E
Matha	11	Fi	45.52N	0.19W
Mathematicians Seamounts (EN)	47	Be	15.30N	111.00W
Matheson	44	Ga	48.32N	80.28W
Mathis	45	Hl	28.06N	97.50W
Mathrákion	15	Cj	39.46N	19.31 E
Mathura	25	Fc	27.30N	77.41 E
Mati	15	Ch	41.39N	19.34 E
Mati	26	Ie	6.57N	126.13 E
Matias Cardoso	55	Kb	14.52S	43.56W
Matias Romero	47	Ee	16.53N	95.02W
Maticora, Río-	49	Lh	11.01N	71.09W
Matina	49	Fh	10.05N	83.17W
Matinha	54	Id	3.06S	45.02W
Mātīr	32	Ib	37.03N	9.40 E
Matiyure, Río-	50	Ci	7.36N	67.39W
Matkaselkja	8	Nc	61.57N	30.33 E
Mātmāţah	32	Ic	33.33N	9.58 E
Matnog	26	Hd	12.35N	124.05 E
Mato, Cerro-	50	Di	7.15N	65.14W
Mato, Río-	50	Di	7.09N	65.07W
Matočkin Šar, Proliv-	19	Fa	73.30N	54.55 E
Mato Grosso [2]	54	Gf	14.00S	56.00W
Mato Grosso [Braz.]	54	Dd	18.18S	57.20W
Mato Grosso [Braz.]	53	Kg	15.00S	59.57W
Mato Grosso, Planalto do- = Mato Grosso, Plateau of- (EN)	52	Kg	15.30S	56.00W
Mato Grosso, Plateau of- (EN) = Mato Grosso, Planalto do-	52	Kg	15.30S	56.00W
Mato Grosso do Sul [2]	54	Hg	20.00S	55.00W
Matos Costa	55	Gh	26.27S	51.09W
Matosinhos	13	Dc	41.11N	8.42W
Matou	28	Cj	29.50N	115.32 E
Matov → Qiuxian	28	Cf	36.47N	114.30 E
Mátra	5	Hf	47.53N	19.57 E
Maţrah	23	Ie	23.29N	58.31 E
Matrei in Osttirol	14	Gc	47.00N	12.32 E
Maţrūḩ	31	Je	31.21N	27.14 E
Matsiatra	37	Hd	21.25S	45.33 E
Matsudo	28	Og	35.48N	139.55 E
Matsue	27	Nd	35.28N	133.04 E
Matsukawa [Jap.]	29	Gc	37.40N	140.28 E
Matsukawa [Jap.]	29	Ed	35.36N	137.53 E
Matsu Liehtao	27	Kf	26.05N	119.56 E
Matsumae	29a	Bc	41.26N	140.07 E
Matsumae-Hantō	29a	Bc	41.40N	140.15 E
Matsumoto	27	Od	36.14N	137.58 E
Matsuo	29	Gb	39.58N	141.02 E
Matsu-Ōminato	29a	Bc	41.16N	141.09 E
Matsusaka	28	Ng	34.34N	136.32 E
Matsushima	29	Gb	38.22N	141.04 E
Matsutō	29	Ec	36.31N	136.33 E
Matsuura	29	Ae	33.22N	129.42 E
Matsuyama	22	Pf	33.50N	132.45 E
Matsuzaki	29	Fd	34.44N	138.45 E
Mattagami Lake	44	Gb	47.57N	81.35W
Mattagami River	42	Jf	50.43N	81.30W
Mattawa	42	Jg	46.19N	78.42W
Matterhorn [Eur.]	14	Be	45.58N	7.39 E
Matterhorn [Nv.-U.S.]	46	Hf	41.49N	115.23W
Matthew, Ile-	57	Ig	22.20S	171.20 E
Matthews Ridge	54	Fb	7.30N	60.10W
Matthew Town	47	Jd	20.57N	73.40W
Matti, Sabhat-	35	Ia	23.30N	52.00 E
Mattighofen	14	Hb	48.06N	13.09 E
Mattoon	45	Lg	39.29N	88.22W
Matua, Ostrov-	20	Kg	48.00N	153.10 E
Matucana	54	Cf	11.51S	76.24W
Matuku Island	61	Ec	19.10S	179.46 E
Matundu	36	Db	4.21N	23.40 E
Matundu	36	Gd	8.50S	39.30 E
Maturín	53	Je	9.45N	63.11W
Matvejev Kurgan	16	Kf	47.34N	38.55 E
Maúa	37	Fb	13.52S	37.09 E
Maubeuge	11	Jd	50.17N	3.58 E
Ma-ubin	25	Je	16.44N	95.39 E
Maudheimvidda	66	Bf	74.00S	8.00W
Maud Seamount (EN)	66	Ce	65.00S	2.35 E
Maués	54	Gd	3.24S	57.42W
Maués, Rio-	54	Gd	3.22S	57.44W
Mau Escarpment	36	Gc	0.40S	36.02 E
Maug Islands	57	Fb	20.01N	145.13 E
Maui Island	57	Lb	20.45N	156.20W
Mauke Island	57	Lg	20.09S	157.23W
Mau Kyun	25	Jf	12.45N	98.20 E
Mauldre	12	Df	48.59N	1.49 E
Maule [2]	56	Fe	35.45S	72.15W
Mauléon	11	Fh	46.55N	0.45W
Mauléon-Licharre	11	Fk	43.14N	0.53W
Maullín	56	Ff	41.38S	73.37W
Maumee	44	Fe	41.34N	83.39W
Maumere	26	Hh	8.37S	122.14 E
Maun	31	Jj	19.58S	23.26 E
Maun	14	If	44.26N	14.55 E
Mauna Kea	57	Lc	19.50N	155.28W
Maunaloa	65a	Db	21.08N	157.13W
Mauna Loa	65a	Fd	19.28N	155.36W
Maunath	25	Gc	25.40N	82.38 E
Maunawili	65a	Db	21.21N	157.47W
Maunga Roa	64p	Bb	21.13S	159.48W
Maungdaw	25	Id	20.49N	92.22 E
Maunoir, Lac -	42	Fc	67.30N	125.00W
Maupihaa Atoll (Mopelia, Atoll-)	57	Lf	16.50S	153.55W
Maupin	46	Ed	45.11N	121.05W
Maupiti, Ile-	57	Lf	16.27S	152.15W
Maurepas, Lake-	45	Kk	30.15N	90.30W
Maures	11	Mk	43.16N	6.23 E
Mauriac	11	Ii	45.13N	2.20 E
Maurice, Lake-	59	Ge	29.30S	131.00 E
Maurienne	11	Mi	45.13N	6.30 E
Mauritania (EN) = Mūrītāniyā [1]	31	Fg	20.00N	12.00W
Mauriti	54	Ke	7.23S	38.46W
Mauritius	30	Mk	20.17S	57.33 E
Mauritius [1]	31	Mj	18.00S	57.40 E
Mauron	11	Df	48.05N	2.18W
Maurs	11	Ij	44.43N	2.12 E
Mauston	45	Ke	43.48N	90.05W
Mauthausen	14	Ib	48.14N	14.31 E
Mauzé-sur-le-Mignon	11	Fh	46.12N	0.40W
Mavinga	36	Df	15.47S	20.24 E
Mavita	37	Ec	19.32S	33.09 E
Mavrovoúni [Grc.]	15	Fj	39.37N	22.47 E
Mavrovoúni [Grc.]	15	Gh	41.07N	23.08 E
Mawchi	25	Je	18.49N	97.09 E
Mawei	27	Kf	26.02N	119.30 E
Mawlaik	25	Id	23.38N	94.25 E
Mawqaq	24	Ii	27.25N	41.08 E
Mawr, Wādī-	23	Ff	15.41N	42.42 E
Mawson	66	Fe	67.36S	62.53 E
Mawson Coast	66	Fe	67.40S	63.30 E
Mawson Escarpment	66	Ff	73.05S	68.10 E
Maxcanú	47	Fd	20.35N	90.01W
Maxixe	37	Fd	23.51S	35.21 E
Maxwell Bay	42	Ib	74.32N	89.00W
May, Isle of-	9	Ke	56.10N	2.30W
Maya, Pulau-	26	Eg	1.10S	109.35 E
Mayaguana Island	47	Jd	22.23N	72.57W
Mayaguana Passage	49	Kb	22.32N	73.15W
Mayagüez	47	Ke	18.12N	67.09W
Mayahi	34	Gc	13.58N	7.40 E
Mayama	36	Bc	3.51S	14.54 E
Mayāmey	24	Pd	36.24N	55.42 E
Maya Mountains	47	Ge	16.40N	88.50W
Mayapan	47	Gd	20.38N	89.27W
Mayari	49	Jc	20.40N	75.41W
Maybell	45	Bf	40.31N	108.05W
Maychew	35	Fc	12.46N	39.34 E
Mayd	35	Hc	10.57N	47.06 E
Maydān	24	Ke	34.55N	45.37 E
Maydena	59	Jh	42.55S	146.30 E
Maydī	23	Ff	16.18N	42.48 E
Mayen	10	Df	50.20N	7.13 E
Mayenne	11	Ff	48.18N	0.37W
Mayenne	11	Fg	47.30N	0.32W
Mayenne [3]	11	Ff	48.05N	0.40W
Mayfa'ah	35	Hc	14.16N	47.35 E
Mayfield	44	Cg	36.44N	88.38W
May Glacier	66	Ie	67.00S	133.00 E
Mayi He	28	Jb	45.52N	128.46 E
Maymyo	25	Jd	22.02N	96.28 E
Maynas	54	Dd	3.00S	75.00W
Mayo	39	Fc	63.35N	135.54W
Mayo/Muigheo [2]	9	Dh	53.50N	9.30W
Mayo, Mountains of-	9	Dg	54.05N	9.30W
Mayo, Río-	48	Ed	26.45N	109.47W
Mayo Darlé	34	Hd	6.30N	11.55 E
Mayo-Kébbi	35	Ad	9.18N	13.33 E
Mayo-Kébbi [3]	35	Bd	10.00N	15.30 E
Mayoko	36	Bc	2.18S	12.49 E
Mayon, Mount-	21	Oh	13.15N	123.41 E
Mayor, Puig-	13	Oe	39.48N	2.48 E
Mayor, Puig-/Major, Puig-	13	Oe	39.48N	2.48 E
Mayor Island	62	Gb	37.15S	176.15 E
Mayor Pablo Lagerenza	56	Ha	19.58S	60.45W
Mayotte [5]	31	Lj	12.50S	45.10 E
Mayotte/Mahoré	30	Lj	12.50S	45.10 E
May Pen	47	Ie	17.58N	77.14W
Mayraira Point	26	Hc	18.39N	120.51 E
Mayran, Laguna de-	48	He	25.45N	102.45W
Mayreau Island	51n	Bb	12.39N	61.23W
May-sur-Orne	12	Be	49.06N	0.22W
Maysville	44	Ff	38.39N	83.46W
Mayumba [Gabon]	31	Ii	3.25S	10.39 E
Mayumba [Zaire]	36	Ed	7.16S	27.03 E
Mayum La	27	De	30.35N	82.27 E
Mayville	44	Hd	42.15N	79.32W
Mayyit, Al Baḩr al- = Dead Sea (EN)	21	Ff	31.30N	35.30 E
Mazabuka	36	Ef	15.51S	27.46 E
Mazagão	54	Hd	0.07S	51.17W
Mazamet	11	Ik	43.30N	2.24 E
Māzandarān [3]	23	Hb	36.00N	54.00 E
Māzandarān, Daryā-ye- = Caspian Sea (EN)	5	Lg	42.00N	50.30 E
Mazar	27	Cd	36.27N	77.03 E
Mazara del Vallo	14	Gm	37.39N	12.35 E
Mazār-e Sharif	22	If	36.42N	67.06 E
Mazarrón, Golfo de-	13	Kg	37.30N	1.18W
Mazartag	27	Dd	38.29N	80.50 E
Mazaruni River	54	Gb	6.25N	58.38W
Mazatenango	47	Ff	14.32N	91.30W
Mazatlán	39	Ig	23.13N	106.25W
Mažeikiai/Mažejkjaj	7	Fh	56.20N	22.22 E
Mažejkjaj/Mažeikiai	7	Fh	56.20N	22.22 E
Mazḩafah, Jabal-	24	Fh	28.48N	34.57 E
Mazḩūr, 'Irq al-	24	Ji	27.25N	43.55 E
Mazinga	51c	Ab	17.29N	62.58W
Mazirbe	8	Jg	57.40N	22.10 E
Mazoe	37	Ec	17.30S	30.58 E
Mazoe	30	Kj	16.32S	33.25 E
Mazomeno	36	Ec	4.55S	27.13 E
Mazong Shan	27	Gc	41.33N	97.10 E
Mazowsze	10	Qd	52.40N	20.20 E
Mazowsze = Masovia (EN)	5	Ie	52.40N	20.20 E
Mazsalaca	8	Kg	57.45N	24.59 E
Mazunga	37	Dd	21.44S	29.52 E
Mazurskie, Pojezierze-	10	Qc	53.40N	21.00 E
Mazzarino	14	Im	37.18N	14.13 E
Mba	63d	Ab	17.32S	177.42 E
Mbabane	31	Kk	26.18S	31.07 E
Mbabo, Tchabal-	34	Hd	7.16N	12.09 E
Mbacké	34	Bc	14.48N	15.55W
Mbaéré	35	Be	3.47N	17.31 E
Mbaiki	31	Ih	3.53N	18.00 E
Mbakaou	34	Hd	6.19N	12.49 E
Mbakaou, Barrage de-	34	Hd	6.25N	13.00 E
Mbala	31	Ki	8.50S	31.22 E
Mbalam	34	He	2.13N	13.49 E
Mbale	31	Kh	1.05N	34.10 E
Mbali	35	Be	4.27N	18.20 E
Mbalmayo	34	He	3.31N	11.30 E
Mbam	30	Ih	4.24N	11.17 E
Mbamba Bay	36	Fe	11.17S	34.46 E
Mbandaka	31	Ih	0.04N	18.16 E
Mbanga	34	Ge	4.30N	9.34 E
Mbanika	63a	Dc	9.05S	159.12 E
Mbanza Congo	36	Bd	6.16S	14.15 E
Mbanza-Ngungu	31	Ii	5.35S	14.47 E
Mbarangandu	36	Gd	8.57S	37.24 E
Mbarara	36	Fc	0.36S	30.38 E
Mbari	35	Ce	4.34N	22.43 E
Mbatiki	63d	Bb	17.46S	179.08 E
Mbava	63a	Cb	7.49S	156.37 E
Mbé	34	Hd	7.51N	13.36 E
Mbengga	63d	Bc	18.23S	178.08 E
Mbengwi	34	Hd	6.01N	10.00 E
Mbéré	35	Bd	6.40N	16.26 E
Mbeya	31	Ki	8.54S	33.27 E
Mbeya [3]	36	Fd	8.00S	33.30 E
Mbi	35	Be	4.28N	18.07 E
Mbigou	36	Bc	1.53S	11.56 E
Mbinda	31	Ii	2.07S	12.52 E
Mbinga	36	Ge	10.56S	35.01 E
Mbingué	34	Dc	10.00N	5.54W
Mbini	34	Ge	1.34N	9.37 E
Mbini [3]	34	He	1.30N	10.00 E
Mbini	30	Ih	1.30N	10.30 E
Mboki	35	Dd	5.19N	25.58 E
Mbokonimbeti	63a	Ec	8.57S	160.05 E
Mbomo	36	Bb	0.24N	14.44 E
Mbomou = Bomu (EN) [3]	35	Cd	5.30N	23.30 E
Mbomou = Bomu (EN)	30	Jh	4.08N	22.26 E
Mborokua	63a	Dc	9.02S	158.44 E
Mbour	34	Bc	14.24N	16.58W
Mbout	32	Ef	16.01N	12.35W
Mbozi	36	Fd	9.02S	32.56 E
Mbrés	35	Bd	6.40N	19.48 E
M'Bridge	36	Bd	7.14S	12.52 E
Mbua	63d	Bb	16.48S	178.37 E
Mbuji-Mayi	31	Ji	6.09S	23.33 E
Mbulo	63a	Dc	8.46S	158.21 E
Mbulu	36	Gc	3.51S	35.32 E
Mburucuyá	55	Ci	28.03S	58.14W
Mbutha	63d	Bb	16.39S	179.51 E
Mbuyuni	36	Gd	7.23S	36.32 E
Mbwemburu	36	Gd	9.29S	39.39 E
Mcalester	43	He	34.56N	95.46W
Mcensk	19	De	53.17N	36.32 E
M'Chedallah	13	Qh	36.22N	4.16 E
Mcherrah	32	Gd	27.00N	4.30W
Mchinga	36	Gd	9.44S	39.42 E
Mchinji	36	Fe	13.48S	32.54 E
Mdandu	36	Fd	9.09S	34.42 E
M'Daourouch	14	Bn	36.05N	7.49 E
Mdennah	32	Gd	25.00N	4.50W
Mdiq	13	Gi	35.41N	5.19W
Mead	44	Fa	49.29N	83.50W
Mead, Lake-	43	Ed	36.05N	114.25W
Meade	40	Hb	70.50N	156.25W
Meade	45	Fh	37.17N	100.20W
Meade Peak	46	Je	42.30N	111.15W
Meadow Lake	42	Gf	54.07N	108.20W
Meadville	44	Ge	41.38N	80.10W
Me-akan-Dake	29a	Cb	43.23N	143.59 E
Mealhada	13	Dd	40.22N	8.27W

Index Symbols

[1] Independent Nation
[2] State, Region
[3] District, County
[4] Municipality
[5] Colony, Dependency
Continent
Physical Region
Historical or Cultural Region
Mount, Mountain
Volcano
Hill
Mountains, Mountain Range
Hills, Escarpment
Plateau, Upland
Pass, Gap
Plain, Lowland
Delta
Salt Flat
Valley, Canyon
Crater, Cave
Karst Features
Depression
Polder
Desert, Dunes
Forest, Woods
Heath, Steppe
Oasis
Cape, Point
Coast, Beach
Cliff
Peninsula
Isthmus
Sandbank
Island
Atoll
Rock, Reef
Islands, Archipelago
Rocks, Reefs
Coral Reef
Well, Spring
Geyser
River, Stream
Waterfall Rapids
River Mouth, Estuary
Lake
Salt Lake
Intermittent Lake
Reservoir
Swamp, Pond
Canal
Glacier
Ice Shelf, Pack Ice
Ocean
Sea
Gulf, Bay
Strait, Fjord
Lagoon
Bank
Seamount
Tablemount
Ridge
Shelf
Basin
Escarpment, Sea Scarp
Fracture
Trench, Abyss
National Park, Reserve
Point of Interest
Recreation Site
Cave, Cavern
Historic Site
Ruins
Wall, Walls
Church, Abbey
Temple
Scientific Station
Airport
Port
Lighthouse
Mine
Tunnel
Dam, Bridge

Mealy Mountains	42	Lf	53.20N	59.30W
Meama	65b	Ba	19.45S	174.34W
Méan, Havelange-	12	Hd	50.22N	5.20 E
Meander Reef	26	Ge	8.09N	119.14 E
Meander River	42	Fe	59.02N	117.42W
Meanguera, Isla-	49	Dg	13.12N	87.43W
Mearim, Rio-	52	Lf	3.04S	44.35W
Meath/An Mhí [2]	9	Gh	53.35N	6.40W
Meaux	11	If	48.57N	2.52 E
Mecca (EN)=Makkah	22	Fg	21.27N	39.49 E
Mechara	35	Gd	8.34N	40.28 E
Mechelen/Maasmechelen	12	Hd	50.57N	5.40 E
Mechelen/Malines	11	Kc	51.02N	4.29 E
Mecheraa-Asfa	13	Ni	35.24N	1.03 E
Mecheria	32	Gc	33.33N	0.17W
Mechernich	12	Id	50.36N	6.39 E
Mechongué	55	Cn	38.09S	58.13W
Mecidiye	15	Ji	40.38N	26.32 E
Mecitözü	24	Fb	40.31N	35.19 E
Mecklemburgischer Höhenrücken	10	Ic	53.40N	12.10 E
Mecklenburg	10	Hc	53.30N	12.00 E
Mecklenburger Bucht	10	Hb	54.20N	11.40 E
Mecklenburger Schweiz	10	Ic	53.45N	12.35 E
Mecoacán, Laguna-	48	Mh	18.20N	93.10W
Meconta	37	Fb	14.59S	39.50 E
Mecsek	10	Oj	46.10N	18.18 E
Mecubúri	37	Gb	14.10S	40.31 E
Mecúfi	37	Gb	13.17S	40.33 E
Mecula	37	Fb	12.05S	37.39 E
Médala	32	Ff	15.30N	5.37W
Medan	22	Li	3.35N	98.40 E
Médanos [Arg.]	56	He	38.50S	62.41W
Médanos [Arg.]	55	Ck	33.24S	59.05W
Medanosa, Punta-	56	Gg	48.06S	65.55W
Mede	14	Ce	45.06N	8.44 E
Médéa	32	Hb	36.16N	2.45 E
Médéa [3]	32	Hb	36.20N	3.25 E
Medebach	12	Kc	51.12N	8.43 E
Medellin	26	Hd	11.08N	123.58 E
Medellín	53	Ie	6.15N	75.35W
Medelpad	8	Gb	62.35N	16.15 E
Medemblik	12	Hb	52.46N	5.06 E
Medenica	10	Tg	49.21N	23.45 E
Mederdra	32	Df	16.54N	15.40W
Medetzız	24	Fd	37.25N	34.40 E
Medford [Or.-U.S.]	39	Ge	42.19N	122.52W
Medford [Wi.-U.S.]	45	Kd	45.09N	90.20W
Medgidia	15	Le	44.15N	28.17 E
Medi	35	Ed	5.06N	30.44 E
Media Luna, Arrecife de la-	49	Ff	15.13N	82.36W
Medianeira	55	Eg	25.17S	54.05W
Mediaş	15	Hc	46.10N	24.21 E
Medical Lake	46	Gc	47.34N	117.41W
Medicine Bow	46	Lf	41.54N	106.12W
Medicine Bow Mountains	46	Lf	41.10N	106.25W
Medicine Butte	46	Jf	41.29N	110.48W
Medicine Hat	39	Hd	50.03N	110.40W
Medicine Lake	46	Mb	48.28N	104.24W
Medicine Lodge	45	Gh	37.17N	98.35W
Međimurje	14	Kd	46.25N	16.30 E
Medina (EN)=Al Madīnah [Sau.Ar.]	22	Fg	24.28N	39.36 E
Medina Az-Zahra	13	Hg	37.52N	4.50W
Medinaceli	13	Jc	41.10N	2.26W
Medina del Campo	13	Hc	41.18N	4.55W
Medina de Rioseco	13	Gc	41.53N	5.02W
Medina-Sidonia	13	Gh	36.27N	5.55W
Medininkai/Medininkaj	8	Kj	54.32N	25.46 E
Medininkaj/Medininkai	8	Kj	54.32N	25.46 E
Medio, Arroyo del-	55	Bk	33.16S	60.15W
Mediterranean Sea (EN)= Akdeniz	5	Hh	35.00N	20.00 E
Mediterranean Sea (EN)= Khatikhon, Yam-	5	Hh	35.00N	20.00 E
Mediterranean Sea (EN)= Méditerranée, Mer-	5	Hh	35.00N	20.00 E
Mediterranean Sea (EN)= Mediterraneo, Mar-	5	Hh	35.00N	20.00 E
Mediterranean Sea (EN)= Mediterráneo, Mar-	5	Hh	35.00N	20.00 E
Mediterranean Sea (EN)= Mesoyéios Thálassa	5	Hh	35.00N	20.00 E
Mediterranean Sea (EN)= Mutawassiţ, Al Baḩr al-	5	Hh	35.00N	20.00 E
Méditerranée, Mer-= Mediterranean Sea (EN)	5	Hh	35.00N	20.00 E
Mediterráneo, Mar-= Mediterranean Sea (EN)	5	Hh	35.00N	20.00 E
Mediterraneo, Mar-= Mediterranean Sea (EN)	5	Hh	35.00N	20.00 E
Medje	36	Eb	2.25N	27.18 E
Medjerda, Monts de la-	32	Ib	36.35N	8.15 E
Mednogorsk	19	Fe	51.26N	57.40 E
Medny, Ostrov-	20	Lf	54.40N	167.50 E
Médoc	11	Fi	45.00N	1.00W
Mêdog	27	Gf	29.18N	95.27 E
Médouneu	36	Bb	1.01N	10.48 E
Medveđa	15	Eg	42.51N	21.36 E
Medvedica [R.S.F.S.R.]	5	Kf	49.35N	42.41 E
Medvedica [R.S.F.S.R.]	7	Ih	57.05N	37.31 E
Medvednica	14	Je	45.55N	15.58 E
Medvedok	7	Mh	57.24N	50.06 E
Medvenka	16	Jd	51.27N	36.08 E
Medveži, Ostrova-=Bear Islands (EN)	21	Sb	70.52N	161.26 E
Medvežjegorsk	19	Dc	62.56N	34.29 E
Medway	12	Cc	51.23N	0.31 E
Medzilaborce	10	Rg	49.16N	21.55 E
Meekatharra	58	Cg	26.36S	118.29 E
Meeker	45	Cf	40.02N	107.55W
Meerane	10	If	50.51N	12.28 E
Meerbusch	12	Ic	51.16N	6.40 E
Meerut	25	Fc	28.59N	77.42 E
Meeteetse	46	Kd	44.09N	108.52W
Mefarlane, Lake-	59	Hf	32.00S	136.40 E
Mega [Eth.]	31	Kh	4.03N	38.20 E
Mega [Indon.]	26	Jg	0.41S	131.53 E
Mega, Pulau-	26	Dg	4.00S	101.02 E
Megalo	35	Gd	6.52N	40.47 E
Megálon Khorion	15	Km	36.27N	27.21 E
Megalópolis	15	Fl	37.24N	22.08 E
Megálo Sofráno	15	Jm	36.04N	26.25 E
Meganísion	15	Dk	38.38N	20.43 E
Meganom, Mys-	16	Ig	44.48N	35.05 E
Mégara	15	Gk	38.00N	23.21 E
Megève	11	Mi	45.52N	6.37 E
Meghalaya [3]	25	Ic	26.00N	91.00 E
Megid	33	Dd	28.35N	22.10 E
Megion	19	Hc	61.00N	76.15 E
Megiscane, Lac-	44	Ia	48.30N	76.04W
Megri	16	Oj	38.55N	46.15 E
Mehadia	15	Fe	44.54N	22.22 E
Mehaigne	12	Hd	50.32N	5.13 E
Meharry, Mount-	59	Dd	23.00S	118.35 E
Mehdia	13	Ni	35.25N	1.45 E
Mehdīshahr	24	Oe	35.44N	53.22 E
Mehedinţi [2]	15	Fe	44.30N	23.00 E
Mehetia, Ile-	61	Lc	17.52S	148.03W
Mehrabān	24	Lc	38.05N	47.08 E
Mehrān	24	Pi	26.52N	55.24 E
Mehrān	24	Lf	33.07N	46.10 E
Mehrenga	7	Je	63.17N	41.20 E
Mehrīz	24	Pg	31.35N	54.28 E
Mehtar Lām	23	Lc	34.39N	70.10 E
Mehun-sur-Yèvre	11	Ig	47.09N	2.13 E
Meia Meia	36	Gd	5.49S	35.48 E
Meia Ponte, Rio-	54	Ig	18.32S	49.36W
Meiganga	34	Hd	6.31N	14.18 E
Meighen	42	Ha	79.55N	99.00W
Meihekou→Hailong	27	Mc	42.32N	125.37 E
Meiktila	25	Jd	20.52N	95.52 E
Meilü→Wuchuan	27	Jg	21.28N	110.44 E
Meinerzhagen	12	Jc	51.07N	7.39 E
Meiningen	10	Gf	50.33N	10.25 E
Meio, Rio do-	55	Ja	13.20S	44.34W
Meisenheim	12	Je	49.43N	7.40 E
Meishan [China]	27	He	30.05N	103.48 E
Meishan [China]	28	Ei	31.06N	119.43 E
Meishan → Jinzhai	28	Ci	31.40N	115.52 E
Meißen	10	Je	51.09N	13.29 E
Meißner	10	Fe	51.12N	9.50 E
Meitan (Yiquan)	27	If	27.48N	107.32 E
Meixian	27	Kg	24.21N	116.07 E
Meiyukou	28	Bd	40.01N	113.08 E
Méjean, Causse-	11	Jj	44.16N	3.22 E
Mejillones	56	Fb	23.06S	70.27W
Mékambo	36	Bb	1.01N	13.56 E
Mekdela	35	Fc	11.28N	39.20 E
Mekele=Meqele (EN)	31	Kg	13.30N	39.28 E
Mékhé	34	Bb	15.07N	16.38W
Mekherrhane, Sebkha-	30	Hf	26.22N	1.20 E
Meknès [3]	32	Fc	33.00N	5.30W
Meknès	31	Ge	33.54N	5.32W
Mekong (EN)=Lancang Jiang	21	Mh	10.15N	105.55 E
Mekong (EN)=Mae Nam Khong	21	Mh	10.15N	105.55 E
Mekong (EN)=Mékôngk	21	Mh	10.15N	105.55 E
Mekong (EN)=Mènam Khong	21	Mh	10.15N	105.55 E
Mekong Delta (EN)	21	Mi	10.20N	106.40 E
Mekongga, Gunung-	26	Hg	3.35S	121.15 E
Mékôngk=Mekong (EN)	21	Mh	10.15N	105.55 E
Mekoryuk	40	Fd	60.23N	166.12W
Mékrou	34	Fc	12.24N	2.49 E
Mel, Ilha do-	55	Hg	25.31S	48.20W
Melaab	13	Ni	35.43N	1.20 E
Mēladēn	35	Hc	10.25N	49.52 E
Melaka	22	Mi	2.12N	102.15 E
Melaka, Selat-=Malacca, Strait of- (EN)	21	Mi	2.30N	101.20 E
Melamo, Cabo-	30	Lj	14.24S	40.49 E
Melanesia	57	Hf	13.00S	164.00 E
Melanesian Basin (EN)	3	Jj	0.05S	160.35 E
Melawi	26	Ff	0.05N	111.29 E
Melbourne [Ar.-U.S.]	45	Kh	36.04N	91.54W
Melbourne [Austl.]	58	Fh	37.49S	144.58 E
Melbourne [Eng.-U.K.]	12	Ab	52.49N	1.26W
Melbourne [Fl.-U.S.]	43	Kf	28.05N	80.37W
Melbourne-Dandenong	59	Jg	37.59S	145.12 E
Melchor Múzquiz	47	Dc	27.53N	101.31W
Melchor Ocampo	48	Hi	17.59N	102.11W
Meldorf	10	Fb	54.05N	9.05 E
Mele, Capo-	14	Cg	43.57N	8.10 E
Melekeiok	64a	Bc	7.29N	134.38 E
Melela	37	Fc	17.04S	38.36 E
Melenci	15	Dd	45.31N	20.19 E
Melenki	19	Ed	55.23N	41.42 E
Meleto Dağı	24	Ic	38.35N	41.32 E
Meleuz	19	Fe	52.58N	55.59 E
Mélèzes, Rivière aux-	42	Ke	57.00N	69.00W
Melfa	14	Hi	41.30N	13.35 E
Melfi [Chad]	35	Bc	11.04N	17.56 E
Melfi [It.]	14	Jj	41.00N	15.39 E
Melfort	42	Hf	52.52N	104.36W
Melgaço	54	Hd	1.47S	50.44W
Melibocus	10	Eg	49.42N	8.40 E
Melilla [5]	31	Ge	35.19N	2.58W
Melincué, Laguna-	55	Bk	33.42S	61.28W
Melipilla	56	Fd	33.42S	71.13W
Melita	45	Fb	49.16N	101.00W
Melíti	15	Ei	40.50N	21.35 E
Melito di Porto Salvo	14	Jm	37.55N	15.47 E
Melito di Porto Salvo, Punta di-	14	Jm	37.57N	15.45 E
Melitopol	6	Jf	46.50N	35.22 E
Melk	14	Jb	48.13N	15.19 E
Mella	14	Ee	45.13N	10.13 E
Mellakou	13	Ni	35.15N	1.14 E
Mellanfryken	8	Ee	59.40N	13.15 E
Melle [Fr.]	11	Fh	46.13N	0.08W
Melle [F.R.G.]	12	Kb	52.12N	8.21 E
Mellen	45	Kc	46.20N	90.40W
Mellerud	7	Cg	58.42N	12.28 E
Mellish Reef	59	Lc	17.25S	155.50 E
Mellish Seamount (EN)	57	Ia	34.00N	178.15 E
Mellit	35	Dc	14.08N	25.33 E
Mělník	10	Kf	50.21N	14.30 E
Melnik	15	Gh	41.31N	23.24 E
Melo	53	Ki	32.22S	54.11W
Melo, Río-	55	De	21.25S	57.55W
Melrhir, Chott-	30	He	34.20N	6.20 E
Melrose	46	Id	45.38N	112.40W
Melsetter	37	Ec	19.48S	32.50 E
Melsungen	10	Fe	51.08N	9.33 E
Meltaus	7	Fc	66.54N	25.22 E
Melton Constable	12	Db	52.51N	1.02 E
Melton Mowbray	9	Mi	52.46N	0.53W
Meluco	37	Fb	12.33S	39.37 E
Meluli	37	Fc	16.28S	39.44 E
Melun	11	If	48.32N	2.40 E
Melville	38	Ib	75.15N	110.00W
Melville	46	Na	50.55N	102.48W
Melville, Cape-	59	Ib	14.10S	144.30 E
Melville, Lake-	42	Lf	53.42N	59.30W
Melville Bay	59	Hb	12.05S	136.45 E
Melville Bay (EN)=Melville Bugt	67	Od	75.35N	62.30W
Melville Bugt=Melville Bay (EN)	67	Od	75.35N	62.30W
Melville Hills	42	Fc	69.20N	123.00W
Melville Island	57	Ef	11.40S	131.00 E
Melville Peninsula	38	Kc	68.00N	84.00W
Melville Sound	42	Gc	68.05N	107.30W
Melvin, Lough-	9	Eg	54.25N	8.10W
Mélykút	10	Pj	46.13N	19.23 E
Memaliaj	15	Ci	40.20N	19.58 E
Memambetsu	29a	Db	43.55N	144.11 E
Memba, Baía de-	37	Gb	14.11S	40.35 E
Memberamo	26	Kg	1.28S	137.52 E
Memboro	26	Gh	9.22S	119.32 E
Mēmele	8	Kh	56.24N	24.10 E
Memmert	10	Cc	53.39N	6.53 E
Memmingen	10	Gi	47.59N	10.10 E
Mempawan	26	Ef	0.22N	108.58 E
Memphis	33	Fd	29.52N	31.15 E
Memphis [Mo.-U.S.]	45	Jf	40.28N	92.10W
Memphis [Tn.-U.S.]	39	Jf	35.08N	90.03W
Memphis [Tx.-U.S.]	45	Fi	34.44N	100.32W
Memrut Dağı	24	Jc	38.40N	42.12 E
Memuro	28	Qc	42.55N	143.03 E
Memuro-Dake	29a	Cb	42.52N	142.45 E
Mena	35	Gd	5.30N	41.06 E
Mena [Ar.-U.S.]	45	Ii	34.35N	94.15W
Mena [Ukr.-U.S.S.R.]	19	De	51.33N	32.14 E
Menabe	30	Lk	20.00S	44.40 E
Menai Strait	9	Ih	53.12N	4.12W
Ménaka	31	Hg	15.55N	2.26 E
Mènam Khong=Mekong (EN)	21	Mh	10.15N	105.55 E
Menangalaku	26	Gh	9.36S	119.01 E
Menard	45	Gk	30.55N	99.47W
Menawashei	35	Dc	12.40N	25.01 E
Menčul, Gora-	10	Th	48.16N	23:49 E
Mendala, Puncak-	26	Lg	4.44S	140.20 E
Mendanau, Pulau-	26	Eg	2.51S	107.26 E
Mendanha	55	Kd	18.06S	43.30W
Mende	11	Jj	44.31N	3.30 E
Mendebo	30	Kh	6.50N	39.40 E
Mendelejevsk	7	Mi	55.57N	52.22 E
Menden (Sauerland)	10	De	51.26N	7.48 E
Mendes	13	Mi	35.39N	0.52 E
Méndez	48	Je	25.07N	98.34W
Mendi [Eth.]	35	Fd	9.48N	35.05 E
Mendi [Pap.N.Gui.]	60	Ci	6.10S	143.40 E
Mendig	12	Jd	50.22N	7.16 E
Mendip Hills	9	Kj	51.15N	2.40W
Mendocino	46	Dg	39.19N	123.48W
Mendocino, Cape-	38	Ge	40.25N	124.25W
Mendocino Fracture Zone (EN)	3	Lf	40.00N	145.00W
Mendota [Ca.-U.S.]	46	Eh	36.45N	120.23W
Mendota [Il.-U.S.]	45	Lf	41.33N	89.07W
Mendoza	53	Ji	32.54S	68.50W
Mendoza [2]	56	Gd	34.30S	68.30W
Mené, Landes du-	11	Df	48.15N	2.32W
Mene de Mauroa	49	Lh	10.43N	71.01W
Mene Grande	54	Db	9.49S	70.56W
Menemen	24	Bc	38.36N	27.04 E
Menen/Menin	11	Jd	50.48N	3.07 E
Meneng Point	64e	Bb	0.33S	166.57 E
Meneses	55	Dj	30.53S	56.30W
Ménez Hom	11	Bf	48.13N	4.16W
Menfi	14	Gm	37.36N	12.58 E
Mengcheng	27	Ke	33.11N	116.30 E
Mengdingjie	27	Gg	23.31N	99.07 E
Menggala	26	Eg	4.28S	105.17 E
Mengíbar	13	Ig	37.58N	3.48W
Mengjin	28	Bg	34.50N	112.26 E
Mengla	27	Hg	21.30N	101.35 E
Menglangba→Lancang	27	Gg	22.37N	99.57 E
Menglian	27	Gg	22.20N	99.27 E
Mengoun Huizu Zizhixian	28	De	38.04N	117.06 E
Mengyin	28	Dg	35.42N	117.56 E
Mengzi	22	Mg	23.23N	103.34 E
Menihek Lakes	42	Kf	54.00N	66.30W
Menin/Menen	11	Jd	50.48N	3.07 E
Menindee	59	If	32.24S	142.26 E
Menindee Lake	59	If	22.00S	142.23 E
Meningie	59	Hg	35.42S	139.20 E
Menjapa, Gunung-	26	Gf	1.05N	116.05 E
Menno	45	He	43.14N	97.34W
Menoikion Óros	15	Gh	41.11N	23.48 E
Menominee	44	Dc	45.07N	87.39W
Menongue	31	Ij	14.40S	17.39 E
Menor, Mar-	13	Lg	37.43N	0.48W
Menorca=Minorca (EN)	5	Gg	40.00N	4.00 E
Menor do Araguaia, Braço-ou Javaes	54	He	9.50S	50.12W
Mentana	14	Gh	42.02N	12.38 E
Mentasta Lake	40	Kd	62.55N	143.45W
Mentawai, Kepulauan-= Mentawai Islands (EN)	21	Lj	2.00S	99.30 E
Mentawai, Selat-	21	Lj	2.00S	99.30 E
Mentawai Islands (EN)= Mentawai, Kepulauan-	21	Lj	2.00S	99.30 E
Menton	11	Nk	43.47N	7.30 E
Mentougou	28	De	39.56N	116.02 E
Menyuan	27	Hd	37.30N	101.35 E
Menzelinsk	7	Mi	55.45N	53.09 E
Menzies	59	Ee	29.41S	121.02 E
Menzies, Mount-	66	Ff	73.30S	61.50 E
Meon	12	Ad	50.49N	1.15W
Meoqui	47	Cc	28.17N	105.29W
Meponda	37	Eb	13.25S	34.52 E
Meppel	11	Mb	52.42N	6.11 E
Meppen	10	Dd	52.41N	7.19 E
Meqele(EN)=Mekele	31	Kg	13.30N	39.28 E
Mê Qu	27	He	33.58N	102.10 E
Mequinensa, Pantà de-/ Mequinenza, Embalse de-	13	Lc	41.15N	0.02W
Mequinenza, Embalse de-/ Mequinensa, Pantà de-	13	Lc	41.15N	0.02W
Mera	14	Dd	46.11N	9.25 E
Merabello, Gulf of- (EN) = Merabéllou, Kólpos-	15	In	35.14N	25.47 E
Merabéllou, Kólpos- = Merabello, Gulf of- (EN)	15	In	35.14N	25.47 E
Merak	26	Eh	5.56S	106.00 E
Meråker	7	Ce	63.26N	11.45 E
Méralab	63b	Db	14.27S	168.03 E
Meramangye, Lake-	59	Ge	28.25S	132.15 E
Meran / Merano	14	Fd	46.40N	11.09 E
Merano / Meran	14	Fd	46.40N	11.09 E
Meratus, Pegunungan-	26	Gg	2.45S	115.40 E
Merauke	58	Fe	8.28S	140.20 E
Mercadal	13	Qe	39.59N	4.05 E
Mercato Saraceno	14	Gg	43.57N	12.12 E
Merced	43	Cd	37.18N	120.29W
Mercedario, Cerro-	52	Ii	31.59S	70.14W
Mercedes [Arg.]	56	Id	34.39S	59.27W
Mercedes [Arg.]	56	Ic	29.12S	58.05W
Mercedes [Arg.]	53	Ji	33.40S	65.30W
Mercedes [Ur.]	53	Ki	33.16S	58.01W
Merchants Bay	42	Lc	67.10N	62.50W
Merchtem	12	Gd	50.58N	4.14 E
Mercury Islands	62	Fb	36.35S	175.50 E
Mercy, Cape -	42	Ld	64.56N	63.40W
Mercy Bay	42	Fb	74.15N	118.10W
Meredith, Cape-	56	Hh	52.12S	60.38W
Meredith, Lake-	45	Fi	35.36N	101.42W
Meredoua	32	Hd	25.20N	2.05 E
Merefa	19	Df	49.51N	36.00 E
Merelbeke	12	Fd	51.00N	3.45 E
Merenga	20	Kd	61.43N	156.05 E
Mergui	22	Lh	12.26N	98.36 E
Mergui Archipelago	21	Lh	12.00N	98.00 E
Méri	34	Hc	10.47N	14.06 E
Meriç	15	Jh	41.11N	26.25 E
Meriç	24	Bb	40.52N	26.12 E
Mérida [2]	54	Db	8.30N	71.10W
Mérida [Mex.]	39	Kg	20.58N	89.37W
Mérida [Sp.]	13	Ff	38.55N	6.20W
Mérida [Ven.]	53	Ie	8.36N	71.08W
Merida, Cordillera de-	52	Ie	8.40N	71.00W
Meridian	39	Kf	32.22N	88.42W
Mérig	63b	Cb	14.19S	167.48 E
Mérignac	11	Fj	44.50N	0.38W
Merikarvia	7	Ef	61.51N	21.30 E
Merín, Laguna-	56	Jd	32.45S	52.50W
Meringur	59	If	34.24S	141.29 E
Merir Island	57	Ed	4.19N	132.19 E
Merizo	64c	Bb	13.16N	144.40 E
Merke	18	Ic	42.52N	73.12 E
Merkem, Houthulst-	12	Ed	50.57N	2.51 E
Merkine/Merkiné	8	Kj	54.07N	24.20 E
Merkiné/Merkine	8	Kj	54.07N	24.20 E
Merkis/Merkys	7	Fi	54.10N	24.11 E
Merksem, Antwerpen-	12	Gc	51.15N	4.27 E
Merksplas	12	Gc	51.22N	4.52 E
Merkys/Merkis	7	Fi	54.10N	24.11 E
Meroe	35	Eb	16.56N	33.59 E
Meroe	35	Eb	16.05N	33.55 E
Merouane, Chott-	32	Ic	34.00N	6.02 E
Merredin	59	Df	31.29S	118.16 E
Merrick	9	If	55.08N	4.29W
Merrill	43	Jb	45.11N	89.41W
Merriman	45	Fe	42.55N	101.42W
Merritt	42	Ff	50.07N	120.47W
Merritt Island	43	Kf	28.21N	80.42W
Merritt Reservoir	45	Fe	42.35N	100.55W
Mersa Fatma	35	Gc	14.53N	40.19 E
Mersa Teklay	35	Fb	17.25N	38.45 E
Mersea Island	12	Cc	51.47N	0.57 E
Merseburg	10	He	51.22N	12.00 E
Mers el Kebir	13	Li	35.44N	0.43W
Mersey	9	Kh	53.25N	3.00W
Merseyside [3]	9	Kh	53.30N	3.00W
Mersin	23	Db	36.48N	34.38 E
Mersing	26	Df	2.26N	103.50 E
Mers-les-Bains	12	Dd	50.04N	1.23 E
Mērsrags/Mersrags	8	Jg	57.19N	23.01 E
Mersrags/Mērsrags	8	Jg	57.19N	23.01 E
Merta	25	Ec	26.39N	74.02 E
Merta Road	25	Ec	26.43N	73.55 E
Mertert	12	Ie	49.42N	6.29 E
Merthyr Tydfil	9	Jj	51.46N	3.23W
Merti	36	Gb	1.04N	38.40 E
Mértola	13	Eg	37.38N	7.40W
Mertule Maryam	35	Fc	10.50N	38.15 E
Mertvy Kultuk, Sor-	16	Rg	45.30N	53.40 E
Mertz Glacier	66	Je	67.40S	144.45 E
Meru	36	Gb	0.03N	37.39 E
Méru	11	Ie	49.14N	2.08 E
Meru, Mount-	36	Gc	3.14S	36.45 E
Merure	55	Fb	15.33S	53.05W
Merville	12	Ed	50.38N	2.38 E
Merzifon	23	Ea	40.53N	35.29 E
Merzig	10	Cg	49.27N	6.38 E
Meša	7	Li	55.34N	49.24 E
Mesa [Az.-U.S.]	39	Hf	33.25N	111.50W
Mesa [Co.-U.S.]	45	Bg	39.14N	108.08W
Mesabi Range	45	Jc	47.30N	92.50W
Mesagne	14	Lj	40.34N	17.48 E
Mescalero	45	Dj	33.09N	105.46W
Meščera=Moscow Basin	5	Kd	55.00N	40.30 E
Meschede	10	Ee	51.21N	8.17 E
Mescit Dağı	24	Ib	40.22N	41.11 E
Meščovsk	16	Ib	54.19N	35.18 E
Mesegon	64d	Bb	7.09N	151.55 E
Mesfinto	35	Fc	13.28N	37.23 E
Me-Shima	28	Jh	32.01N	128.25 E
Meshkīnshahr	24	Lc	38.24N	47.40 E
Mesima	14	Jl	38.30N	15.55 E
Mesjagutovo	17	Ii	55.35N	58.20 E
Meskiana	14	Bo	35.38N	7.40 E
Meskiana, Oued-	14	Bo	35.48N	7.53 E
Meslo	35	Fd	6.22N	39.50 E
Mesnil-Val, Criel-sur-Mer-	12	Dd	50.03N	1.20 E
Mesola	14	Gf	44.55N	12.14 E
Mesolóngion	15	Ek	38.22N	21.26 E
Mesopotamia	52	Kh	30.00S	58.00W
Mesopotamia (EN)	23	Fc	34.00N	44.00 E
Mesoyéios Thálassa= Mediterranean Sea (EN)	5	Hh	35.00N	20.00 E
Mesquite [Nv.-U.S.]	46	Hh	36.48N	114.04W
Mesquite [Tx.-U.S.]	45	Hj	32.46N	96.36W
Mesra	13	Mi	35.50N	0.10 E
Messaad	32	Hc	34.10N	3.30 E
Messalo	30	Lj	11.40S	40.46 E
Messará, Órmos-	15	Ho	35.00N	24.40 E
Messina [It.]	6	Hh	38.11N	15.34 E
Messina [S.Afr.]	31	Kk	22.23S	30.00 E
Messina, Strait of- (EN) = Messina, Stretto di-	5	Hh	38.15N	15.35 E
Messina, Stretto di- = Messina, Strait of- (EN)	5	Hh	38.15N	15.35 E
Messíni	15	El	37.15N	21.50 E
Messínı	15	Fl	37.03N	22.01 E
Messiniakós Kólpos	15	Fm	36.45N	22.10 E
Messojaha	20	Cc	67.52N	77.27 E
Mesta	15	Hi	40.51N	24.44 E
Mestecăniş, Pasul-	15	Ib	47.28N	25.20 E
Mesters Vig	41	Jd	72.15N	24.20W
Mestia	16	Mh	43.03N	42.43 E
Mestre, Espigão-	54	If	12.30S	46.00W
Mestre, Venezia-	14	Ge	45.29N	12.14 E
Mesuji	26	Eg	4.08S	105.52 E
Meta [2]	54	Dc	3.30N	73.00W
Meta, Río-	52	Je	6.12N	67.28W
Meta Incognita Peninsula	38	Mc	62.40N	68.00W
Metairie	45	Kl	29.59N	90.09W
Metaliferi, Munţii-	15	Fc	46.10N	22.50 E
Metallifere, Colline-	14	Eg	43.10N	10.55 E
Metán	56	Hc	25.29S	64.57W
Metangula	37	Eb	12.43S	34.49 E
Metaponto	14	Kj	40.20N	16.50 E
Metauro	14	Hg	43.50N	13.03 E
Metautu	65c	Ba	13.57S	171.54W
Meteghan	44	Nc	44.11N	66.10W
Metelen	12	Jb	52.09N	7.12 E
Metéora	15	Ej	39.43N	21.40 E
Meteor Seamount (EN)	30	Hm	48.00S	8.30 E
Meteor Trench (EN)	3	Do	55.00S	27.00 E
Méthana	15	Gl	37.35N	23.23 E
Methánon, Khersónisos-	15	Gl	37.36N	23.22 E
Methven	62	De	43.38S	171.38 E
Methwold	12	Cb	52.31N	0.33 E
Metković	14	Lg	43.03N	17.39 E
Metlakatla	40	Me	55.08N	131.35W
Metlika	14	Je	45.39N	15.19 E
Metlili Chaamba	32	Hc	32.16N	3.38 E
Metmárfag	32	Ed	26.26N	13.26W
Metohija	15	Dg	42.40N	20.27 E
Metro	26	Eh	5.05S	105.20 E
Metropolis	45	Lh	37.09N	88.44W
Métsovon	15	Ej	39.46N	21.11 E
Métsovon, Zigós- = Métsovon Pass (EN)	15	Ej	39.47N	21.15 E
Métsovon Pass (EN) = Métsovon, Zigós-	15	Ej	39.47N	21.15 E
Mettet	12	Gd	50.19N	4.40 E
Mettingen	12	Jb	52.19N	7.47 E
Mettlach	12	Ie	49.30N	6.36 E
Mettmann	12	Ic	51.15N	6.58 E
Metu	31	Kh	8.20N	35.38 E
Metuje	10	Lf	50.20N	15.55 E
Metz	6	Gf	49.08N	6.10 E
Metzervisse	12	Ie	49.19N	6.17 E
Meu	11	Ef	48.02N	1.47W
Meulaboh	26	Cf	4.09N	96.08 E
Meulan	12	De	49.01N	1.54 E
Meulebeke	12	Fd	50.57N	3.17 E
Meureudu	26	Ce	5.16N	96.16 E
Meurthe	11	Mf	48.47N	6.09 E
Meurthe-et-Moselle [3]	11	Mf	48.35N	6.10 E
Meuse [3]	11	Lf	49.00N	5.30 E
Meuse	5	Ge	51.49N	5.01 E
Meuse (EN)=Maas	5	Ge	51.49N	5.01 E
Meuse, Côtes de-	11	Le	49.10N	5.30 E
Meuzenti	35	Bb	18.14N	17.06 E
Mexia	45	Hk	31.41N	96.29W
Mexiana, Ilha	54	Ic	0.00	49.35W
Mexıcali	39	Hf	32.40N	115.29W
Mexicana, Altiplanicie-= Mexico, Plateau of- (EN)	38	Ig	25.30N	104.00W
Mexican Hat	46	Kh	37.09N	109.52W
Mexicanos, Laguna de los-	48	Fc	28.09N	106.57W
Mexico	45	Kg	39.10N	91.53W
México [1]	39	Ig	23.00N	102.00W

Index Symbols

[1] Independent Nation
[2] State, Region
[3] District, County
[4] Municipality
[5] Colony, Dependency
Continent
Physical Region
Historical or Cultural Region
Mount, Mountain
Volcano
Hill
Mountains, Mountain Range
Hills, Escarpment
Plateau, Upland
Pass, Gap
Plain, Lowland
Delta
Salt Flat
Valley, Canyon
Crater, Cave
Karst Features
Depression
Polder
Desert, Dunes
Forest, Woods
Heath, Steppe
Oasis
Cape, Point
Coast, Beach
Cliff
Peninsula
Isthmus
Sandbank
Island
Atoll
Rock, Reef
Islands, Archipelago
Rocks, Reefs
Coral Reef
Well, Spring
Geyser
River, Stream
Waterfall Rapids
River Mouth, Estuary
Lake
Salt Lake
Intermittent Lake
Reservoir
Swamp, Pond
Canal
Glacier
Ice Shelf, Pack Ice
Ocean
Sea
Gulf, Bay
Strait, Fjord
Lagoon
Bank
Seamount
Tablemount
Ridge
Shelf
Basin
Escarpment, Sea Scarp
Fracture
Trench, Abyss
National Park, Reserve
Point of Interest
Recreation Site
Cave, Cavern
Historic Site
Ruins
Wall, Walls
Church, Abbey
Temple
Scientific Station
Airport
Port
Lighthouse
Mine
Tunnel
Dam, Bridge

México [2] 47 Ee 19.20N 99.30W
México, Golfo de- = Mexico, Gulf of- (EN) ◧ 38 Kg 25.00N 90.00W
Mexico, Gulf of- (EN) = México, Golfo de- ◧ 38 Kg 25.00N 90.00W
Mexico, Plateau of- (EN) = Mexicana, Altiplanicie- ▬ 38 Ig 25.30N 104.00W
Mexico Basin (EN) ⊔ 3 Bg 25.00N 92.00W
Mexico City (EN) = Ciudad de México 39 Jh 19.24N 99.09W
Meybod 24 Of 32.16N 53.59 E
Meydān-e Gel ▭ 24 Ph 29.04N 54.50 E
Meyísti ◆ 15 Mm 36.08N 29.34 E
Meyísti 15 Mm 36.09N 29.40 E
Meymaneh 22 If 35.55N 64.47 E
Meymeh 24 Nf 33.27N 51.10 E
Meymeh ≈ 24 Lf 32.05N 47.16 E
Meža ≈ 7 Hi 55.43N 31.30 E
Mezcala 48 Ji 17.56N 99.37W
Mezcalapa, Río- ≈ 48 Mh 18.36N 92.39W
Mezdra 15 Gf 43.09N 23.42 E
Meždurečenski 19 Gd 59.36N 65.53 E
Meždušarski, Ostrov- ◆ 19 Fa 71.20N 53.00 E
Mèze 11 Jk 43.25N 3.36 E
Mezen ≈ 5 Kb 66.00N 43.59 E
Mezen 6 Kb 65.50N 44.13 E
Mézenc, Mont- ▲ 11 Kj 44.55N 4.11 E
Meženin 10 Sc 53.07N 22.29 E
Mezenskaja Guba ◧ 5 Kb 66.40N 43.45 E
Mezenskaja Pižma ≈ 7 Ld 64.30N 48.32 E
Mežgorje 10 Th 48.30N 23.37 E
Mežica 14 Id 46.31N 14.52 E
Mézidon-Canon 12 Be 49.05N 0.04W
Mézin 11 Gj 44.03N 0.16 E
Mezőberény 10 Rj 46.49N 21.02 E
Mezőcsát 10 Qi 47.49N 20.55 E
Mezőföld ⧗ 10 Oj 46.55N 18.35 E
Mezőkovácsháza 10 Qj 46.24N 20.55 E
Mezőkövesd 10 Qi 47.49N 20.35 E
Mezőtúr 10 Qi 47.00N 20.38 E
Mežozerny 17 Ii 54.10N 59.25 E
Mežpjanje ⧗ 7 Ki 55.25N 45.00 E
Mezquital 48 Gf 23.29N 104.23W
Mezquital, Río- ≈ 48 Gf 22.55N 104.54W
Mezquitic 48 Hf 22.23N 103.41W
Mgači 20 Jf 51.02N 142.18 E
Mglin 16 Hc 53.04N 32.53 E
Mhow 25 Fd 22.33N 75.46 E
Miahuatlán de Porfirio Díaz 48 Ki 16.20N 96.36W
Miajadas 13 Ge 39.09N 5.54W
Miaméré 35 Bd 9.02N 19.55 E
Miami [Az.-U.S.] 46 Jj 33.24N 110.52W
Miami [Fl.-U.S.] 39 Kg 25.46N 80.12W
Miami [Ok.-U.S.] 43 Id 36.53N 94.53W
Miami Beach 43 Kf 25.47N 80.08W
Mīānābād 24 Qd 37.02N 57.27 E
Mīāndowāb 23 Gb 36.58N 46.06 E
Miandrivazo 37 Hc 19.30S 45.28 E
Mianduhe 27 Lb 49.12N 121.09 E
Mīāneh 23 Gb 37.26N 47.42 E
Miang, Khao- ▲ 25 Ke 17.42N 101.01 E
Miangas, Pulau- ◆ 26 Ie 5.35N 126.35 E
Mianning 27 Hf 28.31N 102.10 E
Miānwāli 25 Eb 32.35N 71.33 E
Mianyang 27 He 31.23N 104.49 E
Mianyang (Xiantaozhen) 28 Bi 30.22N 113.27 E
Miaodao Qundao ❖ 27 Ld 38.10N 120.45 E
Miao'er Shan ▲ 27 Jf 25.50N 110.22 E
Miao Ling ⛰ 27 If 26.05N 108.00 E
Miarinarivo 37 Hc 18.56S 46.54 E
Miass 19 Gd 55.01N 60.06 E
Miass ≈ 19 Gd 56.06N 64.30 E
Miasskoje 17 Ji 55.15N 61.55 E
Miasteczko Krajeńskie 10 Nc 53.06N 17.01 E
Miastko 10 Mb 54.01N 17.00 E
Michael, Mount- ▲ 59 Ja 6.25S 145.20 E
Michajlova Island ◆ 66 Ge 66.30S 85.00 E
Michalovce 10 Rh 48.46N 21.55 E
Michelstadt 12 Le 49.41N 9.01 E
Miches 49 Md 18.59N 69.03W
Michigan [2] 43 Jc 44.00N 85.00W
Michigan, Lake- ◍ 38 Ke 44.00N 87.00W
Michigan City 43 Jc 41.43N 86.54W
Michipicoten Bay ◧ 44 Eb 47.55N 84.56W
Michipicoten Island ◆ 42 Ig 47.45N 85.45W
Michoacán [2] 47 De 19.10N 101.50W
Michów 10 Se 51.32N 22.19 E
Mico, Río- ≈ 49 Eg 12.11N 84.16W
Micoud 51k Bb 13.50N 60.54W
Micronesia ❖ 57 Gc 11.00N 159.00 E
Micronesia, Federated States of- [5] 58 Gd 6.30N 152.00 E
Mičurin 15 Kg 42.10N 27.51 E
Mičurinsk 6 Ke 52.54N 40.31 E
Midai, Pulau- ◆ 26 Ef 3.00N 107.47 E
Midar 32 Gc 34.57N 3.32W
Mid-Atlantic Ridge (EN) ⋀ 3 Di 0.00 20.00W
Middelburg [Neth.] 11 Jc 51.30N 3.37 E
Middelburg [S.Afr.] 37 Cf 31.30S 25.00 E
Middelburg [S.Afr.] 37 De 25.47S 29.28 E
Middelfart 7 Bi 55.30N 9.45 E
Middelharnis 12 Gc 51.45N 4.12 E
Middelkerke 12 Ec 51.11N 2.49 E
Middelkerke-Westende 12 Ec 51.10N 2.46 E
Middle Alkali Lake ◍ 46 Ef 41.28N 120.04W
Middle America Trench (EN) ⊽ 3 Mh 15.00N 95.00W
Middle Andaman ◆ 25 If 12.30N 92.50 E
Middle Atlas (EN) = Moyen Atlas ⛰ 30 Ge 33.30N 4.30W
Middlebury 44 Kc 44.01N 73.10W
Middle Caicos ◆ 49 Lc 21.47N 71.43W
Middle Fork Feather River ≈ 46 Eg 38.47N 121.36W
Middle Island ◆ 37b Ab 9.22S 46.21 E
Middle Loup River ≈ 45 Gf 41.17N 98.23W
Middlemarch 62 Df 45.30S 170.07 E
Middle Reef ❋ 63a Ee 12.35S 160.30 E
Middlesboro 43 Kd 36.36N 83.43W
Middlesbrough 9 Lg 54.35N 1.14W
Middlesex 49 Ce 17.02N 88.31W
Middlesex ⧗ 12 Bc 51.35N 0.10W
Middlesex ▣ 9 Mj 51.30N 0.05W
Middleton ◆ 40 Je 59.25N 146.25W
Middleton Reef ❋ 57 Gg 29.30S 159.10 E
Middletown [Ct.-U.S.] 44 Ke 41.33N 72.39W
Middletown [N.Y.-U.S.] 44 Je 41.26N 74.26W
Middletown [Oh.-U.S.] 44 Ef 39.31N 84.25W
Midelt 32 Gc 32.41N 4.45W
Mid Glamorgan [3] 9 Jj 51.35N 3.35W
Midhordland ⧗ 8 Ad 60.15N 5.55 E
Midhurst 12 Bd 50.59N 0.44W
Midi, Canal du- ═ 5 Gg 43.36N 1.25 E
Midi de Bigorre, Pic du- ▲ 11 Gl 42.56N 0.08 E
Midi d'Ossau, Pic du- ▲ 11 Fl 42.51N 0.26W
Mid-Indian Basin (EN) ⊔ 3 Gj 10.00S 80.00 E
Mid-Indian Ridge (EN) ⋀ 3 Gj 3.00S 75.00 E
Midland [Mi.-U.S.] 44 Ed 43.37N 84.14W
Midland [Ont.-Can.] 42 Jh 44.45N 79.53W
Midland [S.D.-U.S.] 45 Fd 44.04N 101.10W
Midland [Tx.-U.S.] 43 Ge 32.00N 102.05W
Midlands [3] 37 Dc 19.00S 30.00 E
Midlands ⧗ 9 Li 52.40N 1.50W
Midleton/Mainistir na Corann 9 Ej 51.55N 8.10W
Midnapore 25 Hd 22.26N 87.20 E
Midongy du Sud 37 Hd 23.34S 47.01 E
Midou ≈ 11 Fk 43.54N 0.30W
Midouze ≈ 11 Fk 43.48N 0.51W
Mid-Pacific Mountains (EN) ⋀ 3 Jg 20.00N 170.00 E
Midway Islands [5] 58 Jb 28.13N 177.22W
Midway Islands ❖ 57 Jb 28.13N 177.22W
Midwest 46 Le 43.25N 106.16W
Midwest City 45 Hi 35.27N 97.24W
Midyat 24 Id 37.25N 41.23 E
Midžor ▲ 5 Ig 43.24N 22.40 E
Miechów 10 Qf 50.23N 20.01 E
Miedwie, Jezioro- ◍ 10 Kc 53.15N 14.55 E
Międzychód 10 Ld 52.36N 15.53 E
Międzylesie 10 Mf 50.10N 16.40 E
Międzyrzec Podlaski 10 Se 52.00N 22.47 E
Międzyrzecz 10 Ld 52.27N 15.34 E
Międzyrzecze Łomżyńskie ⧗ 10 Rd 52.45N 21.45 E
Miehikkälä 8 Ld 60.40N 27.42 E
Mie Ken [2] 28 Ng 34.35N 136.25 E
Miekojärvi ◍ 7 Fc 66.36N 24.23 E
Mielan 11 Gk 43.26N 0.19 E
Mielec 10 Rf 50.18N 21.25 E
Mielno 10 Mb 54.16N 16.01 E
Mien ◍ 8 Fh 56.25N 14.50 E
Mier 48 Jd 26.26N 99.09W
Miercurea Ciuc 15 Ic 46.21N 25.48 E
Mieres 13 Ga 43.15N 5.46W
Miersig 15 Ec 46.53N 21.51 E
Mier y Noriega 48 If 23.25N 100.07W
Miesbach 10 Hi 47.47N 11.50 E
Mieso 35 Gd 9.15N 40.45 E
Mifune 29 Be 32.43N 130.48 E
Migang Shan ▲ 27 Id 35.32N 106.13 E
Miguel Alamán, Presa- ⊟ 48 Kh 18.13N 96.32W
Miguel Auza 48 He 24.18N 103.25W
Miguel Hidalgo, Presa- ⊟ 48 Ed 26.40N 108.45W
Miha Chakaja 19 Eg 42.17N 42.02 E
Mihăilesti 15 Ie 44.20N 25.54 E
Mihail Kogălniceanu 15 Le 44.22N 28.27 E
Mihajlov 19 De 54.16N 39.03 E
Mihajlovgrad 15 Gf 43.25N 23.13 E
Mihajlovgrad [2] 15 Gf 43.25N 23.13 E
Mihajlovka [Kaz.-U.S.S.R.] 18 Hc 43.01N 71.31 E
Mihajlovka [R.S.F.S.R.] 19 Ee 50.05N 43.15 E
Mihajlovsk 17 Ih 56.29N 59.07 E
Mihalıççık 24 Dc 39.52N 31.30 E
Mihara 29 Cd 34.24N 133.05 E
Mihara-Yama 🌋 29 Fd 34.43N 139.23 E
Mi He ≈ 28 Ef 37.12N 119.10 E
Mihonoseki 29 Cd 35.34N 133.18 E
Miho-Wan ◧ 29 Cd 35.30N 133.20 E
Miiraku 29 Ae 32.45N 128.40 E
Mijaly 16 Re 48.54N 53.50 E
Mijares/Millars ≈ 13 Le 39.55N 0.01W
Mijdaḩah 35 Hc 14.00N 48.26 E
Mijdrecht 12 Gb 52.12N 4.52 E
Mijirtein (EN) = Majĕrtĕn ⧗ 30 Lh 9.00N 50.00 E
Mikasa 28 Pc 43.20N 141.40 E
Mikata 29 Dd 35.34N 135.54 E
Miki 29 Dd 34.17N 134.07 E
Mikínai = Mycenae (EN) ⛬ 15 Fl 37.43N 22.45 E
Mikindani 36 Ge 10.17S 40.07 E
Mikkeli [2] 7 Ge 62.00N 27.30 E
Mikkeli/Sankt Michel 6 Ic 61.41N 27.15 E
Mikomoto-Jima ◆ 29 Fd 34.34N 138.56 E
Mikonos ◆ 15 Il 37.27N 25.23 E
Mikonos 15 Il 37.27N 25.20 E
Mikonou, Stenón- ⋈ 15 Il 37.30N 25.20 E
Mikrá Préspa, Límni- ◍ 15 Ei 40.45N 21.06 E
Mikre 15 Hf 43.02N 24.31 E
Mikró Sofráno ◆ 15 Jm 36.05N 26.24 E
Mikulov 10 Mh 48.49N 16.39 E
Mikumi 36 Gd 7.24S 36.59 E
Mikun 19 Fc 62.21N 50.05 E
Mikuni 29 Ec 36.13N 136.09 E
Mikuni-Sanmyaku ⛰ 28 Of 36.15N 138.40 E
Mikuni-Tōge ⩊ 29 Fc 36.46N 138.50 E
Mikuni-Yama ▲ 29 Dd 35.21N 134.01 E
Mikura-Jima ◆ 27 Oe 33.50N 139.35 E
Milaca 45 Jd 45.45N 93.39W
Miladummadulu Atoll ⊙ 25a Ba 6.15N 73.15 E
Milagro 54 Cd 2.07S 79.36W
Mīlājerd 24 Me 34.37N 49.12 E
Milan [Mo.-U.S.] 45 Jf 40.12N 93.07W
Milan [Tn.-U.S.] 44 Ch 35.55N 88.46W
Milan (EN) = Milano 6 Gf 45.28N 9.12 E
Milange 37 Fc 16.05S 35.47 E
Milano = Milan (EN) 6 Gf 45.28N 9.12 E
Milâs 24 Bd 37.19N 27.47 E
Milazzo 14 Jl 38.13N 15.14 E
Milazzo, Capo di- ► 14 Jl 38.16N 15.14 E
Milazzo, Golfo di- ◧ 14 Jl 38.15N 15.20 E
Milbank 43 Hb 45.13N 96.38W
Mildenhall 12 Cb 52.21N 0.31 E
Mildura 58 Fh 34.12S 142.09 E
Mile 27 Hg 24.28N 103.26 E
Mile ≈ 35 Gc 11.08N 40.55 E
Miléai 15 Gj 39.20N 23.09 E
Miles 58 Gg 26.40S 150.11 E
Miles City 43 Fb 46.25N 105.51W
Milet = Miletus (EN) ⛬ 15 Kl 37.30N 27.16 E
Miletus (EN) = Milet ⛬ 15 Kl 37.30N 27.16 E
Milevec ▲ 15 Fg 42.34N 22.27 E
Milevsko 10 Kg 49.27N 14.22 E
Milford 46 Ig 38.24N 113.01W
Milford Haven 9 Hj 51.44N 5.02W
Milford Lake ◍ 45 Hg 39.15N 97.00W
Milford Sound 61 Ch 44.40S 167.55 E
Milford Sound ⋈ 62 Bf 44.35S 167.50 E
Milgis ≈ 36 Gb 1.48N 38.06 E
Milḩ, Baḩr al- ◍ 23 Fc 32.40N 43.35 E
Milḩ, Ra's al- ► 33 Ec 31.55N 25.02 E
Miliana 13 Oh 36.17N 2.14 E
Mili Atoll ⊙ 57 Id 6.08N 171.55 E
Milicz 10 Ne 51.32N 17.17 E
Milkovo 20 Kf 54.43N 158.43 E
Milk River ≈ 43 Eb 49.09N 112.05W
Milk River 46 Ib 49.09N 112.05W
Milkūh ▲ 23 Jc 32.45N 61.55 E
Mill ◆ 42 Jd 63.57N 78.00W
Millars/Mijares ≈ 13 Le 39.55N 0.01W
Millau 11 Jj 44.06N 3.05 E
Milledgeville 44 Fi 33.04N 83.14W
Mille Lacs, Lac des - ◍ 42 Ig 48.50N 90.30W
Mille Lacs Lake ◍ 43 Ib 46.15N 93.40W
Millen 44 Gi 32.48N 81.57W
Miller [Nb.-U.S.] 45 Gf 40.57N 99.26W
Miller [S.D.-U.S.] 45 Gd 44.31N 98.59W
Millerovo 19 Ef 48.52N 40.25 E
Miller Seamount (EN) ⏏ 40 Kf 53.30N 144.20W
Millerton 62 Dd 41.38S 171.52 E
Millevaches, Plateau de- ▬ 11 Ii 45.45N 2.11 E
Millicent 59 Ig 37.36S 140.22 E
Millington 44 Ch 35.20N 89.54W
Millinocket 44 Mc 45.39N 68.43W
Mill Island ◆ 66 He 65.30S 100.40 E
Millmerran 59 Ke 27.52S 151.16 E
Mills Lake ◍ 42 Fd 61.28N 118.15W
Millstatt 14 Hd 46.48N 13.35 E
Millville 44 Jf 39.24N 75.02W
Millwood Lake ◍ 45 Jj 33.45N 94.00W
Milne Land ⧗ 41 Jd 71.20N 27.30W
Milo ≈ 30 Gg 11.04N 9.14W
Milolii 65a Fd 19.11N 155.55W
Mílos 15 Hm 36.45N 24.26 E
Mílos = Milos (EN) ◆ 15 Hm 36.41N 24.25 E
Milos (EN) = Mílos ◆ 15 Hm 36.41N 24.25 E
Milparinka 59 Ie 29.44S 141.53 E
Miltenberg 10 Fg 49.42N 9.15 E
Milton [Fl.-U.S.] 44 Dj 30.38N 87.03W
Milton [N.Z.] 62 Cg 46.07S 169.58 E
Milton-Freewater 46 Fd 45.56N 118.23W
Milton Keynes 9 Mi 52.03N 0.42W
Miltou 35 Bc 10.14N 17.26 E
Milumbe, Monts- ⛰ 36 Ed 8.00S 27.30 E
Miluo 28 Bj 28.51N 113.05 E
Miluo Jiang ≈ 27 Jf 28.51N 112.59 E
Milwaukee 39 Ke 43.02N 87.55W
Milwaukee Depth (EN) ⊽ 3 Do 55.10S 26.00W
Milwaukee Seamounts (EN) ⋀ 57 Ia 32.28N 171.55 E
Milwaukie 46 Dd 45.27N 122.38W
Mimi-Gawa ≈ 29 Be 32.20N 131.37 E
Mimizan 11 Ej 44.12N 1.14W
Mimoň 10 Kf 50.40N 14.44 E
Mimongo 36 Bc 1.38S 11.39 E
Mimoso 55 Hb 15.10S 48.05W
Mīna ≈ 13 Mi 35.58N 0.31 E
Mina [Mex.] 48 Id 26.01N 100.32W
Mina [Nv.-U.S.] 46 Fg 38.24N 118.07W
Mina, Cerro- △ 49 Ki 8.21N 73.10W
Mīnā' Abd Allāh 24 Mh 29.01N 48.10 E
Mīnā' al Aḩmadī 24 Mh 29.04N 48.09 E
Mīnāb 24 Qi 27.09N 57.05 E
Mīnāb ≈ 24 Qi 27.01N 56.53 E
Mīnā' Barānīs 33 Ge 23.55N 35.28 E
Minahassa = Minahassa Peninsula (EN) ◪ 21 Oi 1.00N 124.35 E
Minahassa Peninsula (EN) = Minahassa ◪ 21 Oi 1.00N 124.35 E
Minakuchi 29 Ed 34.59N 136.11 E
Minamata 28 Kh 32.13N 130.24 E
Minami-Daitō-Jima ◆ 27 Nf 25.50N 131.15 E
Minami-furano 29a Cb 43.10N 142.32 E
Minami-Iō-Jima ◆ 60 Cc 24.14N 141.28 E
Minami-kayabe 29a Bc 41.53N 141.01 E
Minami-Tori-Shima = Marcus Island (EN) ◆ 57 Gb 26.32N 142.09 E
Minas [Cuba] 49 Ic 21.29N 77.37W
Minas [Indon.] 26 Df 0.50N 101.29 E
Minas [Ur.] 53 Ki 34.23S 55.14W
Minas de Ríotinto 13 Fg 37.42N 6.35W
Minas Gerais [2] 54 Jg 18.00S 44.30W
Mīnā' Su'ūd 24 Mh 28.44N 48.24 E
Minatitlán [Mex.] 47 Fe 17.59N 94.31W
Minatitlán [Mex.] 48 Gh 19.22N 104.04W
Minaya 13 Je 39.17N 2.19W
Minbu 25 Id 20.11N 94.53 E
Minbya 25 Id 20.22N 93.16 E
Minchinmávida, Volcan- 🌋 56 Ff 42.49S 72.28W
Mincio ≈ 14 Ee 45.04N 10.59 E
Mindanao ◆ 21 Oi 8.00N 125.00 E
Mindanao Sea ☰ 21 Oi 9.15N 123.40 E
Mindel ≈ 10 Gh 48.31N 10.23 E
Mindelheim 10 Gh 48.03N 10.29 E
Mindelo 31 Eg 16.53N 25.00W
Minden [F.R.G.] 10 Ed 52.17N 8.55 E
Minden [La.-U.S.] 45 Jj 32.37N 93.17W
Minden [Nb.-U.S.] 45 Gf 40.30N 98.57W
Mindif 34 Hc 10.24N 14.26 E
Mindoro ◆ 21 Oh 12.50N 121.05 E
Mindoro Strait ⋈ 26 Hd 12.20N 120.40 E
Mindouli 36 Bc 4.17S 14.21 E
Mindszent 10 Qj 46.32N 20.12 E
Mine 29 Bd 34.12N 131.11 E
Minehead 9 Jj 51.13N 3.29W
Mine Head ► 9 Fj 52.00N 7.35W
Mineiros 54 Hg 17.34S 52.34W
Mineral del Monte 48 Jg 20.08N 98.40W
Mineralnyje Vody 19 Eg 44.12N 43.08 E
Mineral Wells 43 He 32.48N 98.07W
Minerva Reefs ❋ 57 Jg 23.50S 179.00W
Minervino Murge 14 Ki 41.05N 16.05 E
Minervois ⧗ 11 Ik 43.25N 2.45 E
Minfeng/Niya 27 Dd 37.04N 82.46 E
Minga 36 Ee 11.08S 27.56 E
Mingala 35 Cd 5.06N 21.49 E
Mingan 42 Lf 50.18N 64.01W
Mingečaur 16 Oi 40.46N 47.02 E
Mingečaurskoje Vodohranilišče ⊟ 16 Oi 40.55N 46.45 E
Mingenew 59 De 29.11S 115.26 E
Minggang 28 Ci 32.27N 114.02 E
Mingguang → Jiashan 28 Dh 32.47N 118.00 E
Ming He ≈ 28 Cf 37.14N 114.47 E
Minglanilla 13 Ke 39.32N 1.36W
Mingoyo 36 Ge 10.06S 39.38 E
Mingshui 27 Mb 47.15N 125.53 E
Mingshui → Zhangqiu 28 Df 36.44N 117.33 E
Mingteke 27 Bd 37.09N 74.58 E
Mingteke Daban ⩊ 27 Bd 37.00N 74.50 E
Minguez, Puerto- ⩊ 13 Ld 40.50N 0.59W
Mingulay ◆ 9 Fe 56.50N 7.40W
Mingyuegou 28 Jc 43.08N 128.55 E
Minhe 27 Hd 36.20N 102.50 E
Minho ≈ 13 Dc 41.52N 8.51W
Minho ▣ 13 Dc 41.40N 8.30W
Minicoy Island ◆ 21 Ji 8.17N 73.02 E
Minigwal, Lake- ◍ 59 Ee 29.35S 123.10 E
Minija ≈ 8 Ii 55.20N 21.12 E
Minilya 59 Cd 23.51S 113.58 E
Minilya River ≈ 59 Cd 23.56S 113.51 E
Minipi Lake ◍ 42 Lf 52.28N 60.50W
Ministra, Sierra- ⛰ 13 Jc 41.07N 2.30W
Minjar 17 Hi 55.04N 57.33 E
Min Jiang ≈ 21 Mg 28.46N 104.38 E
Minmaya 28 Pd 41.10N 140.28 E
Minna 31 Hh 9.37N 6.33 E
Minna Bluff ◪ 66 Kf 78.32S 166.30 E
Minneapolis [Ks.-U.S.] 45 Hg 39.08N 97.42W
Minneapolis [Mn.-U.S.] 39 Je 44.59N 93.13W
Minnedosa 42 Hf 50.14N 99.51W
Minnedosa River ≈ 45 Fb 49.53N 100.08W
Minnesota [2] 43 Ib 46.00N 94.15W
Minnesota River ≈ 43 Ic 44.54N 93.10W
Miño ≈ 5 Fg 41.52N 8.51W
Mino 29 Ed 35.32N 136.54 E
Minobu 29 Fd 35.22N 138.24 E
Minobu-Sanchi ⛰ 29 Fd 35.15N 138.20 E
Minokamo 29 Ed 35.26N 137.00 E
Mino-Mikawa-Kōgen ▬ 29 Ed 35.10N 137.25 E
Minorca (EN) = Menorca ◆ 5 Gg 40.00N 4.00 E
Minot 39 Ie 48.14N 101.18W
Minqin 27 Hd 38.42N 103.11 E
Minqing 27 Kf 26.15N 118.52 E
Minquan 28 Cg 34.39N 115.08 E
Min Shan ⛰ 27 He 33.35N 103.00 E
Minsk 6 Ie 53.54N 27.34 E
Minskaja Oblast [3] 19 Ce 53.50N 27.40 E
Minskaja Vozvyšennost ▬ 8 Lj 54.00N 27.10 E
Mińsk Mazowiecki 10 Rd 52.11N 21.34 E
Minta 34 He 4.35N 12.48 E
Minto, Lac - ◍ 42 Ke 57.15N 74.50W
Minto, Mount- ▲ 66 Kf 71.47S 168.45 E
Minto Inlet ◧ 42 Fb 71.19N 117.00W
Minto Reef ❋ 57 Gd 8.08N 154.17 E
Minturn 45 Cg 39.35N 106.26W
Mīnūdasht 24 Pd 37.10N 55.25 E
Miñuf 24 Dg 30.28N 30.56 E
Minusinsk 20 Ef 53.43N 91.48 E
Minvoul 36 Bb 2.09N 12.08 E
Minwakh 35 Hb 16.48N 48.06 E
Minxian 27 He 34.26N 104.02 E
Miory 7 Gi 55.39N 27.41 E
Mios Num ◆ 26 Kg 1.30S 135.10 E
Miquan 27 Ec 44.05N 87.33 E
Miquelon 42 Jg 49.00N 76.00W
Mira ≈ 13 Dg 37.43N 8.47W
Mira [It.] 14 Ge 45.26N 12.08 E
Mira [Port.] 13 Dd 40.26N 8.44W
Mira, Peña- ▲ 13 Fc 41.55N 6.28W
Mīrābād 23 Jc 30.25N 61.50 E
Mirabela 55 Jc 16.15S 44.11W
Miracatu 55 Ig 24.17S 47.28W
Miracema 54 Jh 21.25S 42.11W
Mirador, Serra do- ⛰ 55 Hh 26.45S 49.50W
Miraflores [Col.] 54 Db 5.12N 73.12W
Miraflores [Col.] 54 Dc 1.30N 72.16W
Mīrah, Wādī al- ≈ 24 If 32.26N 41.42 E
Miraj 25 Ee 16.50N 74.38 E
Miramar 56 Ie 38.16S 57.51W
Miramar, Laguna- ◍ 48 Ni 16.20N 91.20W
Miramas 11 Kk 43.35N 5.00 E
Mirambeau 11 Fi 45.22N 0.34W
Miramichi Bay ◧ 42 Kg 47.07N 65.10W
Miramont-de-Guyenne 11 Gj 44.36N 0.22 E
Miran 27 Ed 39.15N 88.50 E
Miranda [2] 54 Ea 10.15N 66.25W
Miranda [Arg.] 55 Cm 36.32S 59.09W
Miranda [Braz.] 54 Gh 20.14S 56.22W
Miranda de Corvo 13 Dd 40.06N 8.20W
Miranda de Ebro 13 Jb 42.41N 2.57W
Miranda do Douro 13 Fc 41.30N 6.16W
Mirande 11 Gk 43.31N 0.25 E
Mirandela 13 Ec 41.29N 7.11W
Mirandola 14 Ff 44.53N 11.04 E
Mirandópolis 55 Ge 21.09S 51.06W
Mirante do Paranapanema 55 Gf 22.17S 51.54W
Mira Por Vos ❖ 49 Jb 22.04N 74.38W
Mirapuxi, Rio- ≈ 55 Ga 13.06S 51.10W
Mirassol 55 He 20.46S 49.28W
Miravalles ▲ 13 Fb 42.45N 6.53W
Miravalles, Volcán- 🌋 38 Kh 10.45N 85.10W
Miravete, Puerto de- ⩊ 13 Ge 39.43N 5.43W
Mir-Bašir 16 Oi 40.19N 46.58 E
Mirbāţ 23 Hf 16.58N 54.50 E
Mirdita ⧗ 15 Ch 41.49N 19.56 E
Mirebalais 49 Kd 18.50N 72.06W
Mirebeau 11 Gh 46.47N 0.11 E
Mirecourt 11 Mf 48.18N 6.08 E
Mirepoix 11 Hk 43.05N 1.53 E
Mirgorod 19 Df 50.00N 33.40 E
Miri 22 Ni 4.23N 113.59 E
Miria 34 Gc 13.43N 9.07 E
Mirim, Lagoa- ◠ 52 Ki 32.45S 52.50W
Mirina 15 Ij 39.52N 25.04 E
Miriñay, Esteros del- ≋ 55 Di 28.49S 57.10W
Miriñay, Río- ≈ 55 Dj 30.10S 57.39W
Mirny ⚗ 66 Ge 66.33S 93.01 E
Mirny 22 Nc 62.33N 113.53 E
Mironovka 16 Ge 49.40N 31.01 E
Mirosławiec 10 Mc 53.21N 16.05 E
Mirpur 25 Eb 33.11N 73.46 E
Mīrpur Khās 22 Ig 25.32N 69.00 E
Mirqah Sūr 24 Kd 36.50N 44.19 E
Mīrsāle 35 Hd 5.58N 47.54 E
Mîrşani 15 He 44.01N 24.01 E
Mirtóön Pélagos ☰ 15 Gm 37.00N 24.00 E
Miryang 28 Jg 35.29N 128.45 E
Mirzāpur 25 Gc 25.09N 82.35 E
Misaki 29 Ce 33.23N 132.07 E
Misawa 28 Pd 40.41N 141.24 E
Misery, Mount- ▲ 51c Ab 17.22N 62.48W
Mishan 27 Nb 45.34N 131.50 E
Mishawaka 44 De 41.40N 86.11W
Mi-Shima ◆ 28 Kg 34.47N 131.10 E
Mishima 29 Fd 35.07N 138.54 E
Mishraq, Khashm- ▲ 24 Lj 24.13N 46.18 E
Misilmeri 14 Hl 38.02N 13.27 E
Misima Island ◆ 60 Ej 10.40S 152.45 E
Misiones [3] 55 Dh 27.00S 57.00W
Misiones [2] 56 Jc 27.00S 55.00W
Misiones, Sierra de- ⛰ 55 Eh 26.45S 54.20W
Miski, Enneri- ≈ 35 Bb 18.10N 17.45 E
Miškino 17 Ki 55.20N 63.55 E
Miskitos, Cayos- ⁂ 47 Hf 14.23N 82.46W
Miskolc [2] 10 Qh 48.06N 20.43 E
Miskolc 6 If 48.06N 20.47 E
Mismār 35 Fb 18.13N 35.38 E
Misool, Pulau- ◆ 26 Jg 1.52S 130.10 E
Misquah Hills ⌓ 43 Ib 47.17N 92.00W
Mişr = Egypt (EN) [1] 31 Jf 27.00N 30.00 E
Mişr al Jadīdah, Al Qāhirah- 33 Fc 30.06N 31.20 E
Mişrātah 31 Ie 32.23N 15.06 E
Mişrātah [3] 33 Cd 29.00N 16.00 E
Mişrātah, Ra's- ► 30 Ie 32.25N 15.05 E
Misserghin 13 Li 35.37N 0.44W
Missinaibi ≈ 42 Jf 50.44N 81.30W
Missinaibi Lake ◍ 44 Fa 48.23N 83.40W
Missinipe 42 He 55.36N 104.45W
Mission [S.D.-U.S.] 45 Fe 43.18N 100.40W
Mission [Tx.-U.S.] 45 Gm 26.13N 98.20W
Mission City 46 Db 49.08N 122.18W
Mission Range ⛰ 46 Ic 47.30N 113.55W
Mississippi ≈ 38 Kg 29.00N 89.15W
Mississippi [2] 43 Je 32.50N 89.30W
Mississippi Delta ◣ 38 Kg 29.10N 89.15W
Mississippi Fan (EN) 43 Jf 26.45N 88.30W
Mississippi River ≈ 44 Ic 45.26N 76.16W
Mississippi Sound ⋈ 45 Lk 30.15N 89.00W
Misso 8 Lg 57.33N 27.23 E
Missoula 39 He 46.52N 114.01W
Missour 32 Gc 33.03N 3.59W
Missouri ≈ 38 Jf 38.50N 90.08W
Missouri [2] 43 Id 38.30N 93.30W
Missouri, Coteau du- ⌓ 45 Gc 46.00N 99.30W
Missouri Valley 45 If 41.33N 95.53W
Mistassibi ≈ 42 Kg 48.53N 72.13W
Mistassini 44 Ka 48.58N 72.40W
Mistassini, Lac- ◍ 38 Ld 51.00N 75.00W
Mistassini, Rivière- ≈ 42 Kg 48.42N 72.20W
Mistelbach an der Zaya 14 Kb 48.34N 16.34 E
Misterhult 8 Gg 57.28N 16.33 E
Mistrás ⛬ 15 Fl 37.04N 22.22 E
Mistretta 14 Im 37.56N 14.22 E
Misugi 29 Ed 34.33N 136.15 E
Misumi [Jap.] 29 Bd 34.46N 131.58 E
Misumi [Jap.] 29 Be 32.37N 130.29 E
Mita, Punta- ► 48 Gg 32.04N 105.33W
Mitare, Río- ≈ 49 Mh 11.28N 69.56W
Mitchell [Austl.] 59 Je 26.29S 147.58 E
Mitchell [Or.-U.S.] 46 Ed 44.34N 120.09W
Mitchell [S.D.-U.S.] 43 Hc 43.40N 98.01W
Mitchell, Mount- ▲ 38 Kf 35.46N 82.16W
Mitchell Range ⛰ 59 Hb 12.50S 135.35 E
Mitchell River ≈ 57 Ff 15.12S 141.35 E
Mitchell River Mission 59 Ic 15.28S 141.44 E
Mitchelstown/Baile Mhistéala 9 Ei 52.16N 8.16W
Míthimna 15 Jj 39.22N 26.10 E
Mitiaro Island ◆ 57 Lf 19.49S 157.43W
Mitidja, Plaine de la- ▁ 13 Oh 36.36N 3.00 E
Mitilíni 15 Jj 39.06N 26.33 E
Mitilínis, Stenón- ⋈ 15 Jj 39.10N 26.35 E
Mitla ⛬ 47 Ee 16.55N 96.17W
Mitla, Laguna- ◍ 48 Ii 17.03N 100.25W
Mito 27 Pd 36.22N 140.28 E
Mitomoni 36 Ge 11.32S 35.19 E

Index Symbols

[1] Independent Nation
[2] State, Region
[3] District, County
[4] Municipality
[5] Colony, Dependency
■ Continent
⧗ Physical Region
▣ Historical or Cultural Region
▲ Mount, Mountain
🌋 Volcano
△ Hill
⛰ Mountains, Mountain Range
⌓ Hills, Escarpment
▬ Plateau, Upland
⩊ Pass, Gap
▁ Plain, Lowland
◣ Delta
▭ Salt Flat
∨ Valley, Canyon
○ Crater, Cave
✲ Karst Features
◡ Depression
▦ Polder
∴ Desert, Dunes
🌲 Forest, Woods
ψ Heath, Steppe
🌴 Oasis
► Cape, Point
⌇ Coast, Beach
◨ Cliff
◪ Peninsula
⧖ Isthmus
⏥ Sandbank
◆ Island
⊙ Atoll
✳ Rock, Reef
❖ Islands, Archipelago
⁂ Rocks, Reefs
❋ Coral Reef
◉ Well, Spring
⇑ Geyser
≈ River, Stream
⤓ Waterfall Rapids
⋔ River Mouth, Estuary
◍ Lake
◎ Salt Lake
◌ Intermittent Lake
⊟ Reservoir
≋ Swamp, Pond
═ Canal
❄ Glacier
❅ Ice Shelf, Pack Ice
≣ Ocean
☰ Sea
◧ Gulf, Bay
⋈ Strait, Fjord
◠ Lagoon
▤ Bank
⏏ Seamount
⏍ Tablemount
⋀ Ridge
⊐ Shelf
⊔ Basin
⌐ Escarpment, Sea Scarp
⚡ Fracture
⊽ Trench, Abyss
✿ National Park, Reserve
★ Point of Interest
☺ Recreation Site
∩ Cave, Cavern
⚑ Historic Site
⛬ Ruins
▥ Wall, Walls
✝ Church, Abbey
⛩ Temple
⚗ Scientific Station
✈ Airport
⚓ Port
⛯ Lighthouse
⚒ Mine
⊓ Tunnel
⌿ Dam, Bridge

Mitsamiouli	37	Gb	11.23 S	43.18 E
Mitsinjo	37	Hc	16.00 S	45.52 E
Mitsio, Nosy-	37	Hb	12.54 S	48.36 E
Mitsiwa=Massawa (EN)	31	Kg	15.37 N	39.39 E
Mitsiwa Channel	35	Fb	15.30 N	40.00 E
Mitsuishi	29a	Cb	42.15 N	142.33 E
Mitsukaido	29	Fc	36.01 N	139.59 E
Mitsuke	29	Fc	37.32 N	138.56 E
Mitsushima	29	Ad	34.16 N	129.20 E
Mittelfranken	10	Gg	49.20 N	10.40 E
Mittelland	14	Bd	46.50 N	7.05 E
Mittellandkanal	5	He	52.16 N	11.41 E
Mittelmark	10	Jd	52.20 N	13.20 E
Mittenwald	10	Hi	47.27 N	11.15 E
Mittersheim	12	If	48.52 N	6.56 E
Mittersill	14	Gc	47.16 N	12.29 E
Mittweida	10	If	50.59 N	12.59 E
Mitú	53	Ie	1.08 N	70.03 W
Mitumba, Monts-=Mitumba Range (EN)	30	Ji	6.00 S	29.00 E
Mitumba Range (EN)=Mitumba, Monts-	30	Ji	6.00 S	29.00 E
Mituva	8	Jj	55.00 N	22.45 E
Mitwaba	36	Ed	8.38 S	27.20 E
Mitzic	36	Bb	0.47 N	11.34 E
Miura	29	Fd	35.08 N	139.37 E
Miura-Hantō	29	Fd	35.15 N	139.40 E
Mixco Viejo	49	Bf	14.52 N	90.40 W
Mixian	28	Bg	34.31 N	113.22 E
Mixteco, Río-	48	Jh	18.11 N	98.30 W
Miya-Gawa	29	Ed	34.32 N	136.42 E
Miyagi Ken [2]	28	Pe	38.30 N	140.50 E
Miyagusuku-Jima	29b	Ab	26.22 N	127.59 E
Miyāh, Wādī al- [Eg.]	24	Ej	25.00 N	33.23 E
Miyāh, Wādī al- [Sau. Ar.]	24	Gi	26.06 N	36.31 E
Miyāh, Wādī al- [Syr.]	24	He	34.44 N	39.57 E
Miyake-Jima	27	Oe	34.05 N	139.30 E
Miyako	27	Pd	39.38 N	141.57 E
Miyako-Jima	27	Mg	24.45 N	125.20 E
Miyakonojō	28	Ki	31.44 N	131.04 E
Miyako-Rettō	27	Lg	24.25 N	125.00 E
Miyako-Wan	29	Hb	39.40 N	142.00 E
Miyama	29	Dd	35.17 N	135.34 E
Miyanojō	29	Bf	31.54 N	130.27 E
Miyanoura-Dake	28	Ki	30.20 N	130.29 E
Miyata	29	Be	33.45 N	130.45 E
Miyazaki	27	Ne	31.54 N	131.26 E
Miyazaki Ken [2]	28	Kh	32.05 N	131.20 E
Miyazu	28	Mg	35.32 N	135.11 E
Miyazuka-Yama	29	Fd	34.24 N	139.16 E
Miyazu-Wan	29	Dd	35.35 N	135.13 E
Miyoshi	28	Lg	34.48 N	132.51 E
Miyun	27	Kc	40.22 N	116.53 E
Miyun Shuiku	28	Dd	40.31 N	116.58 E
Mizan Teferi	35	Fd	6.53 N	35.28 E
Mizdah	33	Bc	31.26 N	12.59 E
Mizen Head/Carn Ui Néid	5	Fe	51.27 N	9.49 W
Mizil	15	Je	45.01 N	26.27 E
Mizorām [3]	25	Id	23.00 N	93.00 E
Mizque	54	Eg	17.56 S	65.19 W
Mizuho	29	Cd	34.50 N	132.29 E
Mizuho	66	Ef	70.43 S	40.20 E
Mizunami	29	Ed	35.22 N	137.15 E
Mizusawa	28	Pe	39.08 N	141.08 E
Mjadel	8	Lj	54.54 N	27.03 E
Mjakiševo	8	Mh	56.30 N	28.54 E
Mjakit	20	Kd	61.23 N	152.10 E
Mjällom	8	Ha	62.59 N	18.26 E
Mjaundža	20	Jd	63.02 N	147.13 E
Mjölby	7	Dg	58.19 N	15.08 E
Mjøndalen	8	De	59.45 N	10.01 E
Mjorn	8	Eg	57.54 N	12.25 E
Mjøsa	5	Hc	60.40 N	11.00 E
Mkoani	36	Gd	5.22 S	39.39 E
Mkokotoni	36	Gd	5.52 S	39.15 E
Mkushi Bona	36	Ee	13.37 S	29.23 E
Mkushi River	36	Fe	13.33 S	29.40 E
Mkuze	37	Ee	27.10 S	32.00 E
Mladá Boleslav	10	Kf	50.21 N	14.54 E
Mladenovac	15	De	44.26 N	20.42 E
Mlava	15	Ee	44.45 N	21.14 E
Mława	10	Qc	53.06 N	20.23 E
Mljet	14	Lh	42.45 N	17.30 E
Mljetski kanal	14	Lh	42.48 N	17.35 E
Mmadinare	37	Dd	21.53 S	27.45 E
Mnichovo Hradiště	10	Kf	50.32 N	14.59 E
Mnogoveršinny	20	If	53.55 N	139.50 E
Moa	49	Jc	20.40 N	74.56 W
Moa	34	Cd	6.59 N	11.36 W
Moa, Pulau-	26	Ih	8.10 S	127.56 E
Moab	43	Fd	38.35 N	109.33 W
Moabi	36	Bc	2.24 S	10.59 E
Moala	63d	Bc	18.36 S	179.53 E
Moamba	37	Ee	25.36 S	32.15 E
Moanda [Gabon]	36	Bc	1.34 S	13.11 E
Moanda [Zaïre]	36	Bd	5.56 S	12.21 E
Moatize	37	Ec	16.10 S	33.46 E
Moba	31	Ji	7.03 S	29.47 E
Mobara	29	Gd	35.25 N	140.17 E
Mobārakeh	24	Nf	32.20 N	51.30 E
Mobaye	31	Jh	4.19 N	21.11 E
Mobayi-Mbongo	36	Db	4.18 N	21.11 E
Mobeka	36	Cb	1.53 N	19.46 E
Moberly	43	Id	39.25 N	92.26 W
Mobile	39	Kf	30.42 N	88.05 W
Mobile Bay	43	Je	30.25 N	88.00 W
Mobridge	43	Gb	45.32 N	100.26 W
Mobuto Sese Seko, Lac-=Albert, Lake- (EN)	30	Kh	1.40 N	31.00 E
Moca	49	Ld	19.24 N	70.31 W
Moçambique=Mozambique (EN) [1]	31	Kj	18.15 S	35.00 E
Moçambique=Mozambique (EN)	31	Lk	15.03 S	40.45 E
Moçambique, Canal de-=Mozambique Channel (EN)	30	Lk	20.00 S	43.00 E
Moçâmedes [3]	36	Bf	15.20 S	12.30 E
Moçâmedes	31	Ij	15.12 S	12.10 E
Mocapra, Río-	50	Ci	7.56 N	66.46 W
Mocha, Isla-	56	Fe	38.22 S	73.56 W
Moc Hoa	25	Lf	10.46 N	105.56 E
Mochudi	37	Dd	24.23 S	26.08 E
Mocimboa da Praia	31	Lj	11.20 S	40.21 E
Möckeln	8	Fh	56.40 N	14.10 E
Mockfjärd	8	Fd	60.30 N	14.58 E
Môco, Serra-	30	Ij	12.28 S	15.10 E
Mocoa	54	Cc	1.09 N	76.38 W
Mococa	55	Ie	21.28 S	47.01 W
Mocovi	55	Ci	28.24 S	59.42 W
Moctezuma [Mex.]	47	Cc	29.48 N	109.42 W
Moctezuma [Mex.]	48	If	22.45 N	101.05 W
Moctezuma [Mex.]	48	Fb	30.12 N	106.26 W
Moctezuma, Rio [Mex.]	48	Ec	29.09 N	109.40 W
Moctezuma, Rio- [Mex.]	48	Jg	21.59 N	98.34 W
Mocuba	31	Kj	16.51 S	36.56 E
Mocubúri	37	Fb	14.39 S	38.54 E
Močurica	15	Jg	42.31 N	26.32 E
Modane	11	Mi	45.12 N	6.40 E
Modderrivier	37	Ce	29.02 S	24.37 E
Modena [It.]	14	Ef	44.40 N	10.55 E
Modena [Ut.-U.S.]	46	Ih	37.49 N	113.55 W
Moder	11	Of	48.49 N	8.06 E
Modesto	43	Cd	37.39 N	120.59 W
Modica	14	In	36.52 N	14.46 E
Modjamboli	36	Db	2.28 N	22.06 E
Modjigo	34	Hb	17.09 N	13.12 E
Mödling	14	Kb	48.05 N	16.28 E
Modriča	14	Mf	44.58 N	18.18 E
Modum	8	Ce	59.55 N	10.00 E
Moe	59	Jg	38.10 S	146.15 E
Moelv	7	Cf	60.56 N	10.42 E
Moen	64d	Bb	7.26 N	151.52 E
Moengo	54	Hb	5.37 N	54.24 W
Moen-jo-Daro	25	Dc	27.19 N	68.07 E
Moenkopi Wash	46	Ji	35.54 N	111.26 W
Moerbeke	12	Fc	51.10 N	3.56 E
Moers	10	Ce	51.27 N	6.39 E
Moeskroen/Mouscron	11	Jd	50.44 N	3.13 E
Moffat	9	Jf	55.20 N	3.27 W
Moga	36	Ec	2.21 S	26.49 E
Mogadishu (EN)=Muqdisho	31	Lh	2.03 N	45.22 E
Mogadouro	13	Fc	41.20 N	6.43 W
Mogadouro, Serra do-	13	Fc	41.19 N	6.40 W
Mogāl	24	Nd	36.35 N	50.35 E
Mogalakwena	37	Dd	22.27 S	28.55 E
Mogami	29	Gb	38.45 N	140.30 E
Mogami-Gawa	28	Oe	38.54 N	139.50 E
Mogami Trench (EN)	29	Fb	39.00 N	139.00 E
Mogaung	25	Jc	25.18 N	96.56 E
Mogho	35	Ge	4.49 N	40.19 E
Mogielnica	10	Qe	51.42 N	20.43 E
Mogilev	6	Je	53.56 N	30.18 E
Mogilev-Podolski	16	Ee	48.27 N	27.48 E
Mogilevskaja Oblast [3]	19	De	53.45 N	30.30 E
Mogilno	10	Nd	52.40 N	17.58 E
Mogincual	37	Gc	15.34 S	40.24 E
Mogoča	22	Nd	53.44 N	119.44 E
Mogočin	20	De	57.43 N	83.40 E
Mogogh	35	Ed	8.26 N	31.19 E
Mogojto	20	Gf	54.25 N	110.27 E
Mogojtuj	20	Gf	51.15 N	114.58 E
Mogok	25	Jd	22.55 N	96.30 E
Mogollon Rim	43	Ee	34.20 N	111.00 W
Mogotes, Punta-	55	Dn	38.06 S	57.33 W
Mogotón, Pico-	49	Dg	13.45 N	86.23 W
Mogreïn	31	Ff	25.13 N	11.34 W
Mogroum	35	Bc	11.06 N	15.25 E
Moguer	13	Fg	37.16 N	6.50 W
Mogzon	20	Gf	51.42 N	111.59 E
Mohács	10	Ok	45.59 N	18.42 E
Mohaka	62	Gc	39.07 S	177.12 E
Mohaka	62	Gc	39.07 S	177.12 E
Mohales Hoek	37	Df	30.15 S	27.25 E
Mohall	45	Fb	48.46 N	101.31 W
Moḥammadābād	24	Pg	31.47 N	54.27 E
Mohammadia	13	Mi	35.35 N	0.04 E
Mohammedia	32	Fc	33.42 N	7.24 W
Mohanganj	25	Id	24.54 N	90.59 E
Mohang-ni	28	If	36.46 N	126.08 E
Mohave, Lake-	43	Ed	35.25 N	114.38 W
Mohawk Mountains	46	Ij	32.25 N	113.25 W
Mohe	22	Od	53.27 N	122.18 E
Moheda	8	Fh	57.00 N	14.34 E
Moheli/Mwali	30	Lj	12.15 S	43.45 E
Moher, Cliffs of-/Aillte an Mhothair	9	Di	52.58 N	9.27 W
Mohican, Cape-	40	Fd	60.12 N	167.28 W
Mohinora	38	Ig	26.06 N	107.04 W
Möhnesee	12	Kc	51.29 N	8.05 E
Mohns Ridge (EN)	5	Ga	73.00 N	5.00 E
Moholm	8	Ff	58.37 N	14.02 E
Mohon, Charleville-Mézierès-	12	Ge	49.46 N	4.43 E
Mohon Peak	46	Ii	34.57 N	113.15 W
Mohoro	36	Gd	8.08 S	39.10 E
Mohotani, Ile-	61	Na	9.59 S	138.49 W
Mohovaja	20	Kf	53.01 N	158.38 E
Moi	8	Bf	58.28 N	6.32 E
Moikovac	15	Cg	42.58 N	19.35 E
Moimenta da Beira	13	Ed	40.59 N	7.37 W
Moindou	63b	Be	21.42 S	165.41 E
Moineşti	15	Jc	46.28 N	26.29 E
Moirai	15	Hn	35.03 N	24.52 E
Mo i Rana	6	Hb	66.18 N	14.08 E
Mõisaküla/Myjzakjula	7	Fg	58.07 N	25.10 E
Moisés Ville	55	Bj	30.43 S	61.29 W
Moisie	42	Kf	50.13 N	66.06 W
Moisie	42	Kf	50.11 N	66.06 W
Moissac	11	Hj	44.06 N	1.05 E
Moissala	35	Bd	8.21 N	17.46 E
Moitaco	50	Dh	8.01 N	61.21 W
Mõja	8	He	59.25 N	18.55 E
Mojácar	13	Kg	37.08 N	1.51 W
Mojada, Sierra-	48	Hd	27.15 N	103.45 W
Mojana, Caño-	49	Ji	9.02 N	74.46 W
Mojave	43	Dd	35.03 N	118.10 W
Mojave Desert	38	Hf	35.00 N	117.00 W
Mojiguaçu, Rio-	55	He	20.53 S	48.10 W
Moji Mirim	55	If	22.26 S	46.57 W
Mojjero	20	Fc	68.44 N	103.30 E
Mojo	35	Fd	8.36 N	39.09 E
Mojo	35	Gd	8.00 N	41.50 E
Mojos, Llanos de-	52	Jg	15.00 S	65.00 W
Moju, Rio-	54	Id	1.40 S	48.25 W
Mojynty	19	Hf	47.10 N	73.18 E
Mokambo	36	Ee	12.25 S	28.21 E
Mokapu Peninsula	65a	Db	21.26 N	157.45 W
Mokau	62	Fc	38.42 S	174.35 E
Mokau	61	Dg	38.41 S	174.37 E
Mokhotlong	37	De	29.17 S	29.05 E
Mokil Atoll	57	Gd	6.40 N	159.47 E
Moklakan	20	Gf	54.48 N	118.56 E
Möklinta	8	Gd	60.05 N	16.32 E
Mokochu, Khao-	25	Je	15.56 N	99.06 E
Mokohinau Islands	62	Fa	35.55 S	175.05 E
Mokolo	34	Hc	10.45 N	13.48 E
Mokp'o	22	Of	34.47 N	126.23 E
Mokra Gora	15	Dg	42.50 N	20.25 E
Mokrany	10	Ue	51.48 N	24.23 E
Mokrin	15	Dd	45.56 N	20.25 E
Mokša	5	Ke	54.44 N	41.53 E
Mokwa	34	Gd	9.17 N	5.03 E
Mol	11	Lc	51.11 N	5.07 E
Mola di Bari	14	Li	41.04 N	17.05 E
Molango	48	Jg	20.47 N	98.43 W
Moláoi	15	Fm	36.48 N	22.51 E
Molara	14	Dj	40.50 N	9.45 E
Molas, Punta-	48	Pg	20.35 N	86.44 W
Molat	14	If	44.13 N	14.50 E
Molatón	13	Kf	38.59 N	1.24 W
Moldau (EN)=Vltava	5	He	50.21 N	14.30 E
Moldava nad Bodvou	10	Qh	48.37 N	21.00 E
Moldavia (EN) = Moldova	15	Jc	46.30 N	27.00 E
Moldavia (EN)=Moldova	5	If	46.30 N	27.00 E
Moldavian SSR (EN)=Moldavskaja SSR [2]	19	Cf	47.00 N	29.00 E
Moldavskaja Sovetskaja Socialističeskaja Respublika [2]	19	Cf	47.00 N	29.00 E
Moldavskaja SSR/Respublika Sovetike Sočialiste Moldovenjaske [2]	19	Cf	47.00 N	29.00 E
Moldavskaja SSR=Moldavian SSR (EN) [2]	19	Cf	47.00 N	29.00 E
Molde	6	Gc	62.44 N	7.11 E
Moldefjorden	8	Bb	62.45 N	7.05 E
Moldotau, Hrebet-	18	Jd	40.00 N	74.50 E
Moldova	15	Jc	46.54 N	26.58 E
Moldova = Moldavia (EN)	15	Jc	46.30 N	27.00 E
Moldova = Moldavia (EN)	5	If	46.30 N	27.00 E
Moldova Nouă	15	Ee	44.44 N	21.41 E
Moldoveanu, Vîrful-	5	If	45.36 N	24.44 E
Moldoviţa	15	Ib	47.41 N	25.32 E
Mole	12	Bc	51.24 N	0.20 W
Molène, Ile de-	11	Bf	48.24 N	4.58 W
Molens van Kinderdijk	12	Gc	51.52 N	4.40 E
Molepolole	31	Jk	24.25 S	25.30 E
Môle Saint-Nicolas	49	Kd	19.47 N	73.22 W
Moletai/Molėtaj	8	Ki	55.13 N	25.36 E
Moletaj/Moletai	8	Ki	55.13 N	25.36 E
Molfetta	14	Ki	41.12 N	16.36 E
Molihong Shan	28	Hc	42.11 N	124.43 E
Molina, Parameras de-	13	Jd	40.55 N	2.01 W
Molina de Aragón	13	Kd	40.51 N	1.53 W
Molina de Segura	13	Kf	38.03 N	1.12 W
Moline	45	Kf	41.30 N	90.31 W
Moliniere Point	51p	Bb	12.05 N	61.45 W
Molise [2]	14	Ii	41.40 N	14.30 E
Molkābād	24	Oe	34.32 N	52.35 E
Molkom	8	Ee	59.36 N	13.43 E
Möll	14	Hd	46.50 N	13.26 E
Moll	55	Cl	35.04 S	59.39 W
Mollafeneri	15	Mi	40.54 N	29.30 E
Mölle	8	Eh	56.17 N	12.29 E
Mollendo	53	Ig	17.02 S	72.01 W
Molliens-Dreuil	12	Ee	49.52 N	2.01 E
Mölln	10	Gc	53.38 N	10.41 E
Mollösund	8	Df	58.04 N	11.28 E
Mölndal	7	Ch	57.39 N	12.01 E
Mölnlycke	8	Ef	57.39 N	12.09 E
Moločansk	16	If	47.10 N	35.36 E
Moločny, Liman-	16	If	46.30 N	35.20 E
Molócuè	37	Fc	17.03 S	38.52 E
Molodečno	19	Ce	54.19 N	26.53 E
Molodežnaja	66	Ee	67.40 S	45.51 E
Molodi	8	Mf	58.00 N	28.52 E
Molodogvardejskoje	19	He	54.07 N	70.50 E
Mologa	5	Jd	58.50 N	37.11 E
Molokai Island	57	Lb	21.08 N	157.00 W
Moloma	7	Lg	58.20 N	48.28 E
Molong	59	Jf	33.06 S	148.52 E
Molopo	30	Jk	28.31 S	20.13 E
Moloundou	34	Ie	2.02 N	15.13 E
Molteno	37	Df	31.24 S	26.22 E
Molu, Pulau-	26	Jh	6.45 S	131.33 E
Moluccas (EN)=Maluku, Kepulauan-	57	De	2.00 S	128.00 E
Molucca Sea (EN)=Maluku, Laut-	21	Oj	0.05 S	125.00 E
Molygino	20	Ee	58.11 N	94.45 E
Moma	20	Jc	66.20 N	143.06 E
Moma	37	Fc	16.44 S	39.14 E
Mombaça	54	Ke	5.45 S	39.28 W
Mombasa	31	Ki	4.03 S	39.40 E
Mombo	36	Gc	4.53 S	38.17 E
Momboyo	36	Cc	0.16 S	19.00 E
Mombuca, Serra da-	55	Fd	18.15 S	52.26 W
Momčilgrad	15	Ih	41.32 N	25.25 E
Mömling	12	Le	49.50 N	9.09 E
Momotombo, Volcán-	49	Dg	12.26 N	86.33 W
Mompono	36	Db	0.04 N	21.48 E
Mompós	54	Db	9.14 N	74.27 W
Momski Hrebet	20	Jc	66.00 N	145.00 E
Mon [2]	25	Je	17.22 N	97.20 E
Møn	7	Ci	55.00 N	12.20 E
Mona, Canal de la-=Mona Passage (EN)	38	Mh	18.30 N	67.45 W
Mona, Isla-	47	Ke	18.05 N	67.54 W
Mona, Punta-	49	Fi	9.38 N	82.37 W
Monach Islands	9	Fd	57.32 N	7.40 W
Monaco [1]	6	Gg	43.42 N	7.23 E
Monadhliath Mountains	9	Id	57.15 N	4.10 W
Monagas [2]	54	Fb	9.20 N	63.00 W
Monaghan/Muineachán [2]	9	Gg	54.10 N	7.00 W
Monaghan/Muineachán	9	Gg	54.15 N	6.58 W
Monahans	45	Ek	31.36 N	102.54 W
Mona Passage (EN)=Mona, Canal de la-	38	Mh	18.30 N	67.45 W
Monapo	37	Gb	14.55 S	40.18 E
Monarch Mountain	42	Ef	51.54 N	125.54 W
Monashee Mountains	42	Ff	51.00 N	118.43 W
Monastyrščina	16	Gb	54.19 N	31.48 E
Monatélé	34	He	4.16 N	11.12 E
Monbetsu [Jap.]	28	Qc	42.28 N	142.07 E
Monbetsu [Jap.]	27	Pc	44.21 N	143.22 E
Monbetsu-Shokotsu	29a	Ca	44.23 N	143.16 E
Moncalieri	14	Be	45.00 N	7.41 E
Moncalvo	14	Ce	45.03 N	8.16 E
Monção [Braz.]	54	Id	3.30 S	45.15 W
Monção [Port.]	13	Db	42.05 N	8.29 W
Moncayo	13	Kc	41.46 N	1.50 W
Moncayo, Sierra del-	13	Kc	41.45 N	1.50 W
Mončegorsk	19	Db	67.56 N	32.58 E
Mönchengladbach	10	Ce	51.12 N	6.26 E
Mönchengladbach-Rheydt	12	Ic	51.10 N	6.27 E
Mönchengladbach-Wickrath	12	Ic	51.08 N	6.25 E
Mönchgut	10	Jb	54.20 N	13.40 E
Monchique	13	Dg	37.19 N	8.33 W
Monchique, Serra de-	13	Dg	37.19 N	8.36 W
Monclova	39	Ig	26.54 N	101.25 W
Moncton	39	Me	46.06 N	64.07 W
Mondai	55	Fh	27.05 S	53.25 W
Mondego	13	Dd	40.09 N	8.52 W
Mondego, Cabo-	13	Dd	40.11 N	8.55 W
Mondeville	12	Be	49.10 N	0.19 W
Mondjoko	36	Dc	1.41 S	21.12 E
Mondo	35	Bc	13.43 N	15.32 E
Mondoñedo	13	Ea	43.26 N	7.22 W
Mondorf-les-Bains/Bad Mondorf	12	Ie	49.30 N	6.17 E
Mondoubleau	11	Gg	47.59 N	0.54 E
Mondovi	14	Bf	44.23 N	7.49 E
Mondragone	14	Hi	41.07 N	13.53 E
Mondy	20	Ff	51.40 N	100.59 E
Monemvasia	15	Gm	36.41 N	23.03 E
Monessen	44	He	40.09 N	79.53 W
Monett	45	Jh	36.55 N	93.55 W
Monfalcone	14	He	45.49 N	13.32 E
Monferrato	14	Cf	44.55 N	8.05 E
Monforte	13	Ee	39.03 N	7.26 W
Monforte de Lemos	13	Eb	42.31 N	7.30 W
Monga	36	Db	4.12 N	22.49 E
Mongala	36	Cb	1.53 N	19.46 E
Mongalla	35	Ed	5.12 N	31.46 E
Mongbwalu	36	Fb	1.57 N	30.02 E
Mong Cai	25	Ld	21.32 N	107.58 E
Monger, Lake-	59	De	29.15 S	117.05 E
Mongga	63a	Cb	7.57 S	156.59 E
Monggolküre/Zhaosu	27	Dc	43.10 N	81.07 E
Monghyr	25	Hc	25.23 N	86.28 E
Monginevro, Colle del-	11	Mj	44.56 N	6.44 E
Mongo	31	Ig	12.11 N	18.42 E
Mongo	34	Cd	9.34 N	12.11 W
Mongol Altajn Nuruu→Mongolski Altaj=Mongolian Altai (EN)	21	Le	46.30 N	93.00 E
Mongol Ard-Uls=Mongolia (EN) [1]	22	Me	47.00 N	104.00 E
Mongolia (EN)=Mongol Ard-Uls [1]	22	Me	47.00 N	104.00 E
Mongolian Altai (EN)=Mongol Altajn Nuruu→Mongolski Altaj	21	Le	46.30 N	93.00 E
Mongolian Altai (EN)=Mongolski Altaj (Mongol Altajn Nuruu)	21	Le	46.30 N	93.00 E
Mongolski Altaj (Mongol Altajn Nuruu)=Mongolian Altai (EN)	21	Le	46.30 N	93.00 E
Mongonu	34	Hc	12.41 N	13.36 E
Mongororo	35	Cc	12.01 N	22.28 E
Mongoumba	35	Be	3.38 N	18.36 E
Möng Pan	25	Jd	20.19 N	98.22 E
Mongrove, Punta-	48	Hi	17.56 N	102.11 W
Mongu	31	Jj	15.17 S	23.08 E
Monguel	32	Ef	16.25 N	13.08 W
Möng Yai	25	Jd	22.25 N	98.02 E
Monheim	12	Ic	51.05 N	6.53 E
Mönichkirchen	14	Kc	47.30 N	16.02 E
Mon Idée, Auvillers-lès-Forges-	12	Ge	49.52 N	4.21 E
Monigotes	55	Bj	30.30 S	61.39 W
Moni Hosiou Loukâ	15	Fk	38.24 N	22.49 E
Monistrol-sur-Loire	11	Ki	45.17 N	4.10 E
Monito, Isla-	51a	Ab	18.09 N	67.56 W
Monitor Peak	46	Gg	38.50 N	116.32 W
Monitor Range	46	Gg	38.45 N	116.40 W
Monjolos	55	Jd	18.18 S	44.05 W
Monkayo	26	Ie	7.50 N	126.00 E
Monkey Bay	36	Fe	14.05 S	34.55 E
Monkey Point	49	Fg	11.36 N	83.39 W
Monkey River	49	Ce	16.22 N	88.29 W
Mońki	10	Sc	53.24 N	22.49 E
Monkoto	36	Dc	1.38 S	20.39 E
Monmouth [Il.-U.S.]	45	Kf	40.55 N	90.39 W
Monmouth	9	Kj	51.50 N	3.00 W
Monmouth [Or.-U.S.]	46	Dd	44.51 N	123.14 W
Monmouth [Wales-U.K.]	9	Kj	51.50 N	2.43 W
Monmouth Mountain	46	Da	51.00 N	123.47 W
Mönne	10	De	51.28 N	7.30 E
Monnikendam	12	Hb	52.27 N	5.02 E
Monnow	9	Kj	51.48 N	2.42 W
Mono	63a	Bb	7.20 S	155.35 E
Mono [3]	34	Fd	6.45 N	1.50 E
Monobe-Gawa	29	Ce	33.32 N	133.42 E
Mono Lake	43	Dd	38.00 N	119.00 W
Monólithos	15	Km	36.07 N	27.45 E
Monopoli	14	Lj	40.57 N	17.18 E
Monor	10	Pi	47.21 N	19.27 E
Monou	35	Cb	16.24 N	22.11 E
Monóvar	13	Lf	38.26 N	0.50 W
Monowai, Lake-	62	Bf	45.55 S	167.25 E
Monreal	12	Jd	50.18 N	7.10 E
Monreal del Campo	13	Kd	40.47 N	1.21 W
Monreale	14	Hl	38.05 N	13.17 E
Monroe [Ga.-U.S.]	44	Fi	33.47 N	83.43 W
Monroe [La.-U.S.]	39	Jf	32.33 N	92.07 W
Monroe [Mi.-U.S.]	44	Fe	41.55 N	83.24 W
Monroe [N.C.-U.S.]	44	Gh	34.59 N	80.33 W
Monroe [Or.-U.S.]	46	Dd	44.19 N	123.18 W
Monroe [Wi.-U.S.]	45	Le	42.36 N	89.38 W
Monroe, Lake-	44	Df	39.05 N	86.25 W
Monroe City	45	Kg	39.39 N	91.44 W
Monroeville	44	Dj	31.31 N	87.20 W
Monrovia	31	Fh	6.19 N	10.48 W
Mons/Bergen	11	Jd	50.27 N	3.56 E
Monsanto	13	Ed	40.02 N	7.07 W
Monschau	10	Cf	50.33 N	6.15 E
Monselice	14	Fe	45.14 N	11.45 E
Monserrate, Isla-	48	De	25.41 N	111.05 W
Monsheim	12	Ke	49.38 N	8.12 E
Møns Klint	8	Ej	54.58 N	12.33 E
Mönsterås	7	Dh	57.02 N	16.26 E
Montabaur	10	Df	50.26 N	7.50 E
Montagna Grande	14	Gm	37.56 N	12.44 E
Montagne	11	Jh	46.10 N	3.40 E
Montagu	66	Ad	58.25 S	26.20 W
Montague	40	Je	60.00 N	147.30 W
Montague, Isla-	48	Bb	31.45 N	114.48 W
Montaigu	11	Eh	46.59 N	1.19 W
Montalbán	13	Ld	40.50 N	0.48 W
Montalbano Ionico	14	Kj	40.17 N	16.34 E
Montalcino	14	Fg	43.03 N	11.29 E
Montalegre	13	Ec	41.49 N	7.48 W
Montalto di Castro	14	Fh	42.21 N	11.37 E
Montalto Uffugo	14	Kk	39.24 N	16.09 E
Montalvânia	55	Jb	14.28 S	44.32 W
Montana [2]	43	Eb	47.00 N	110.00 W
Montana	14	Bd	46.18 N	7.30 E
Montánchez	13	Fe	39.13 N	6.09 W
Montánchez, Sierra de-	13	Ge	39.15 N	5.55 W
Montargis	11	Ig	48.00 N	2.45 E
Montataire	12	Ee	49.16 N	2.26 E
Montauban [Fr.]	11	Hj	44.01 N	1.21 E
Montauban [Fr.]	11	Df	48.12 N	2.03 W
Montauk Point	44	Le	41.04 N	71.52 W
Montbard	11	Kg	47.37 N	4.20 E
Montbéliard	11	Mg	47.31 N	6.48 E
Montblanc	13	Nc	41.22 N	1.10 E
Mont Blanc	5	Gf	45.50 N	6.52 E
Montbrison	11	Ki	45.36 N	4.03 E
Montceau-les-Mines	11	Kh	46.40 N	4.22 E
Mont Cenis, Col du-	5	Gf	45.15 N	6.54 E
Montchanin	11	Kh	46.45 N	4.27 E
Mont Darwin	37	Ec	16.46 S	31.35 E
Mont-de-Marsan	11	Fk	43.53 N	0.30 W
Montdidier	11	Ie	49.39 N	2.34 E
Mont Dore	11	Ii	45.34 N	2.49 E
Mont-Dore	63b	Cf	22.17 S	166.35 E
Monte, Laguna del-	55	Am	37.00 S	62.28 W
Monteagudo	54	Fg	19.49 S	63.59 W
Monte Alban	39	Jh	17.02 N	96.45 W
Monte Alegre	54	Hd	2.01 S	54.04 W
Monte Alegre, Rio-	55	Gc	17.16 S	50.41 W
Monte Alegre de Goiás	55	Ia	13.14 S	47.10 W
Montealegre del Castillo	13	Kf	38.47 N	1.19 W
Monte Alegre de Minas	55	Hd	18.52 S	48.52 W
Monte Azul	54	Jg	15.09 S	42.53 W
Montebello	44	Jc	45.39 N	74.56 W
Monte Bello Islands	59	Dd	20.25 S	115.30 E
Monte Carlo	11	Nk	43.44 N	7.25 E
Montecarlo	55	Eh	26.34 S	54.47 W
Monte Carmelo	55	Id	18.43 S	47.29 W
Monte Caseros	56	Id	30.15 S	57.39 W
Montecatini Terme	14	Eg	43.23 N	10.45 E
Montecchio Maggiore	14	Fe	45.30 N	11.24 E
Monte Comán	56	Gd	34.36 S	67.54 W
Montecristi	49	Ld	19.52 N	71.39 W
Montecristo	14	Eh	42.20 N	10.20 E
Monte Cristo	55	Bb	14.43 S	61.14 W
Monte Ermoso	55	Bn	38.55 S	61.33 W
Monte Escobedo	48	Hf	22.18 N	103.35 W
Montefalco	14	Gh	42.52 N	12.39 E
Montefeltro	14	Gg	43.55 N	12.15 E
Montefiascone	14	Gh	42.32 N	12.02 E
Montefrio	13	Hg	37.19 N	4.01 W
Montego Bay	39	Lh	18.30 N	77.55 W
Monteiro	54	Ke	7.53 S	37.07 W
Montelíbano	49	Ji	8.02 N	75.29 W
Montélimar	11	Kj	44.34 N	4.45 E
Monte Lindo, Arroyo-	55	Cg	25.28 S	59.25 W
Monte Lindo, Río-	56	Ib	23.56 S	57.12 W
Monte Lindo Chico, Riacho-	55	Dg	25.53 S	57.53 W

Index Symbols

[1] Independent Nation
[2] State, Region
[3] District, County
Municipality
Colony, Dependency
Continent
Physical Region
Historical or Cultural Region
Mount, Mountain
Volcano
Hill
Mountains, Mountain Range
Hills, Escarpment
Plateau, Upland
Pass, Gap
Plain, Lowland
Delta
Salt Flat
Valley, Canyon
Crater, Cave
Karst Features
Depression
Polder
Desert, Dunes
Forest, Woods
Heath, Steppe
Oasis
Cape, Point
Coast, Beach
Cliff
Peninsula
Isthmus
Sandbank
Island
Atoll
Rock, Reef
Islands, Archipelago
Rocks, Reefs
Coral Reef
Well, Spring
Geyser
River, Stream
Waterfall Rapids
River Mouth, Estuary
Lake
Salt Lake
Intermittent Lake
Reservoir
Swamp, Pond
Canal
Glacier
Ice Shelf, Pack Ice
Ocean
Sea
Gulf, Bay
Strait, Fjord
Lagoon
Bank
Seamount
Tablemount
Ridge
Shelf
Basin
Escarpment, Sea Scarp
Fracture
Trench, Abyss
National Park, Reserve
Point of Interest
Recreation Site
Cave, Cavern
Historic Site
Ruins
Wall, Walls
Church, Abbey
Temple
Scientific Station
Airport
Port
Lighthouse
Mine
Tunnel
Dam, Bridge

Monte Lindo Grande, Riacho- 55 Cg 25.45 S 58.06W
Montello [Nv.-U.S.] 46 Hf 41.16N 114.12W
Montello [Wi.-U.S.] 45 Le 43.48N 89.20W
Montemorelos 47 Ec 25.12N 99.49W
Montemor-o-Novo 13 Df 38.39N 8.13W
Montemor-o-Velho 13 Dd 40.10N 8.41W
Montemuro, Serra de- 13 Dc 40.58N 8.01W
Montenegro 56 Jc 29.42 S 51.28W
Montenegro (EN) = Crna Gora [2] 15 Cg 42.30N 19.18 E
Montenegro (EN)=Crna Gora 15 Cg 42.30N 19.18 E
Monte Plata 49 Md 18.48N 69.47W
Montepuez 37 Gb 12.32 S 40.27 E
Montepuez 37 Fb 13.07 S 39.00 E
Montepulciano 14 Fg 43.05N 11.47 E
Monte Quemado 56 Hc 25.48 S 62.52W
Monte Real 13 De 39.51N 8.52W
Montereale, Passo di- 14 Hh 42.31N 13.13 E
Montereau-Faut-Yonne 11 If 48.23N 2.57 E
Monterey 43 Cd 36.37N 121.55W
Monterey Bay 43 Cd 36.45N 121.55W
Montería 53 Ie 8.46N 75.53W
Montero 54 Fg 17.20 S 63.15W
Monteros 56 Gc 27.10 S 65.30W
Monterotondo 14 Gh 42.03N 12.37 E
Monterrey 39 Ig 25.40N 100.19W
Montesano 46 Dc 46.59N 123.36W
Monte San Savino 14 Fg 43.20N 11.43 E
Monte Sant'Angelo 14 Ji 41.42N 15.57 E
Monte Santu, Capo di- 14 Dj 45.05N 9.44 E
Montes Claros 53 Lg 16.43 S 43.52W
Montes Claros de Goiás 55 Gb 15.54 S 51.13W
Montesilvano 14 Ih 42.31N 14.09 E
Montevarchi 14 Fg 43.31N 11.34 E
Montevideo [2] 55 Dl 34.50 S 56.10W
Montevideo [Mn.-U.S.] 45 Id 44.57N 95.43W
Montevideo [Ur.] 53 Ki 34.53 S 56.11W
Monte Vista 45 Ch 37.35N 106.09W
Montfaucon 12 He 49.17N 5.08 E
Montfort-l'Amaury 12 Df 48.47N 1.49 E
Montfort-sur-Risle 12 Ce 49.18N 0.40 E
Montgenèvre, Col de- 11 Mj 44.56N 6.44 E
Montgomery 39 Kf 32.23N 86.18W
Montgomery Pass 46 Fh 38.00N 118.20W
Montguyon 11 Fi 45.13N 0.11W
Monthermé 12 Ge 49.53N 4.44 E
Monthey 14 Ad 46.15N 6.56 E
Monthois 12 Ge 49.19N 4.43 E
Monticello [Ar.-U.S.] 45 Kj 33.38N 91.47W
Monticello [Fl.-U.S.] 44 Fj 30.33N 83.52W
Monticello [Ia.-U.S.] 45 Ke 42.15N 91.12W
Monticello [In.-U.S.] 44 De 40.45N 86.46W
Monticello [Ky.-U.S.] 44 Eg 36.50N 84.51W
Monticello [N.Y.-U.S.] 44 Je 41.39N 74.41W
Monticello [Ut.-U.S.] 43 Fd 37.52N 109.21W
Montiel 13 Jf 38.42N 2.52W
Montiel, Campo de- 13 Jf 38.46N 2.44W
Montiel, Cuchilla de- 55 Cj 31.05 S 59.10W
Montignac 11 Hi 45.04N 1.10 E
Montigny-le-Roi 11 Lf 48.00N 5.30 E
Montigny-les-Metz 11 Me 49.06N 6.09 E
Montigny-le-Tilleul 12 Gd 50.23N 4.22 E
Montijo [Pan.] 49 Gj 7.59N 81.03W
Montijo [Port.] 13 Df 38.42N 8.58W
Montijo [Sp.] 13 Ff 38.55N 6.37W
Montijo, Golfo de- 49 Gj 7.40N 81.07W
Montilla 13 Hg 37.35N 4.38W
Montividiu 55 Gc 17.24 S 51.14W
Montivilliers 11 Ge 49.33N 0.12 E
Mont Joli 42 Kg 48.35N 68.11W
Mont-Laurier 42 Jg 46.33N 75.30W
Mont Louis 44 Oa 49.15N 65.43W
Mont-Louis 11 Il 42.31N 2.07 E
Montluçon 11 Ih 46.20N 2.36 E
Montmagny 42 Kg 46.59N 70.33W
Montmarault 11 Ih 46.19N 2.57 E
Montmédy 11 Le 49.31N 5.22 E
Montmirail 11 Jf 48.52N 3.32 E
Montmorency 12 Ef 49.00N 2.20 E
Montmorillon 11 Gh 46.26N 0.52 E
Montmort-Lucy 12 Ff 48.55N 3.49 E
Monto 59 Kd 24.52 S 151.07 E
Montoire-sur-le-Loir 11 Gg 47.45N 0.52 E
Montone 14 Gf 44.24N 12.14 E
Montoro 13 Hf 38.01N 4.23W
Montpelier [Id.-U.S.] 43 Ec 42.19N 111.18W
Montpelier [Vt.-U.S.] 39 Le 44.16N 72.35W
Montpellier 6 Gg 43.36N 3.53 E
Montpon-Ménestérol 11 Gi 45.01N 0.10 E
Montréal 39 Le 45.31N 73.34W
Montreal Lake 42 Gf 54.20N 105.40W
Montreal River 44 Hb 47.08N 79.27W
Montréjeau 11 Gk 43.05N 0.35 E
Montreuil [Fr.] 11 Hd 50.28N 1.46 E
Montreuil [Fr.] 12 Ef 48.52N 2.26 E
Montreuil-l'Argillé 12 Cf 48.56N 0.29 E
Montreux 14 Ad 46.26N 6.55 E
Montrose [Co.-U.S.] 43 Fd 38.29N 107.53W
Montrose [Scot.-U.K.] 9 Ke 56.43N 2.29W
Monts, Pointe des- 44 Na 49.19N 67.23W
Mont-Saint-Aignan 12 De 49.28N 1.05 E
Mont-Saint-Michel, Baie du- 11 Ef 48.40N 1.40W
Montsalvy 11 Ij 44.42N 2.30 E
Montsant, Serra del-/Montsant, Sierra de- 13 Mc 41.17N 0.50 E
Montsant, Sierra de-/Montsant, Serra del- 13 Mc 41.17N 0.50 E
Montsec, Serra del-/Montsech, Sierra del- 13 Mb 42.02N 0.50 E
Montsech, Sierra del-/Montsec, Serra del- 13 Mb 42.02N 0.50 E
Montseny/Pallars, Montsent de- 13 Nb 42.29N 1.02 E
Montseny, Sierra de- 13 Oc 41.48N 2.24 E
Montserrado [3] 34 Cd 6.35N 10.35W
Montserrat [5] 39 Mh 16.45N 62.12W
Montserrat, Monasterio de- 13 Nc 41.35N 1.49 E
Montserrat, Monasterio de-/Montserrat, Monèstir de- 13 Nc 41.35N 1.49 E
Montserrat, Monèstir de- 13 Nc 41.35N 1.49 E
Montserrat, Monèstir de-/Montserrat, Monasterio de- 13 Nc 41.35N 1.49 E
Montuosa, Isla- 49 Fj 7.28N 82.14W
Montville 12 De 49.33N 1.07 E
Monument Peak 46 He 42.07N 114.14W
Monument Valley 46 Jh 36.50N 110.20W
Monveda 36 Db 2.57N 21.27 E
Monviso 5 Gg 44.40N 7.07 E
Monywa 25 Jd 22.07N 95.08 E
Monza 14 De 45.35N 9.16 E
Monze 36 Ef 16.16 S 27.29 E
Monzen 29 Ec 37.17N 136.46 E
Monzón 13 Mc 41.55N 0.12 E
Mo'oka 29 Fc 36.27N 139.59 E
Moonbeam 44 Fa 49.25N 82.11W
Moonie 59 Ke 27.40 S 150.19 E
Moonie River 59 Je 29.19 S 148.43 E
Moonta 59 Hf 34.04 S 137.35 E
Moora 58 Ch 30.39 S 116.00 E
Moorcroft 46 Md 44.16N 104.57W
Moore 45 Hi 35.20N 97.29W
Moore, Lake- 57 Cg 29.50 S 117.35 E
Moorea, Ile- 57 Mf 17.32 S 149.50W
Moore's Island 44 Il 26.18N 77.33W
Moorhead 43 Hb 46.53N 96.45W
Moormerland 12 Ja 53.18N 7.26 E
Moormerland-Neermoor 12 Ja 53.18N 7.26 E
Moorreesburg 37 Bf 33.09 S 18.40 E
Moosburg an der Isar 10 Hh 48.28N 11.56 E
Moose 38 Kd 50.48N 81.18W
Moosehead Lake 43 Nb 45.40N 69.40W
Moose Jaw 39 Id 50.23N 105.32W
Moose Jaw River 46 Ma 50.34N 105.17W
Moose Lake 45 Jc 46.25N 92.45W
Mooselookmeguntic Lake 44 Lc 44.53N 70.48W
Moose Mountain 45 Eb 49.45N 102.37W
Moose Mountain Creek 45 Eb 49.12N 102.10W
Moosomin 42 Hf 50.09N 101.40W
Moosonee 39 Kd 51.17N 80.39W
Mopeia 37 Fc 17.59 S 35.43 E
Mopelia, Atoll- → Maupihaa Atoll 57 Lf 16.50 S 153.55W
Mopti 31 Gg 14.30N 4.12W
Mopti [3] 34 Ec 14.40N 4.15W
Moqokorei 35 He 4.04N 46.08 E
Moquegua [2] 54 Dg 16.50 S 70.55W
Moquegua 54 Dg 17.12 S 70.56W
Mór 10 Oi 47.23N 18.12 E
Mor, Glen- 9 Id 57.10N 4.40W
Mora [Cam.] 34 Hc 11.03N 14.09 E
Mora [Port.] 13 Df 38.56N 8.10W
Mora [Sp.] 13 Ie 39.41N 3.46W
Mora [Swe.] 7 Df 61.00N 14.33 E
Morača 15 Cg 42.16N 19.09 E
Morača, Manastir- 15 Cg 42.46N 19.24 E
Morādābād 22 Jg 28.50N 78.47 E
Morada Nova de Minas 55 Jd 18.25 S 45.22W
Móra d'Ebre/Mora de Ebro 13 Mc 41.05N 0.38 E
Mora de Ebro/Móra d'Ebre 13 Mc 41.05N 0.38 E
Mora de Rubielos 13 Ld 40.15N 0.45W
Morafenobe 37 Gc 17.49 S 44.55 E
Morąg 10 Pc 53.56N 19.56 E
Mórahalom 10 Pj 46.13N 19.53 E
Moraleda, Canal- 56 Ff 44.30 S 73.30W
Moraleja 13 Fd 40.04N 6.39W
Morales [Col.] 49 Ki 8.17N 73.52W
Morales [Guat.] 49 Cf 15.29N 88.49W
Morales, Laguna- 48 Kf 23.35N 97.45W
Moramanga 37 Hc 18.57 S 48.11 E
Moran 46 Je 43.50N 110.28W
Morane Atoll 57 Ng 23.10 S 137.07W
Morangas, Ribeirão- 55 Fd 19.39 S 52.19W
Morant Bay 49 Ie 17.53N 76.25W
Morant Cays 47 Ie 17.24N 75.59W
Morant Point 49 Ie 17.55N 76.10W
Morar, Loch- 9 He 56.58N 5.45W
Morarano 37 Hc 17.46 S 48.10 E
Mora River 45 Di 35.44N 104.23W
Moraska, Góra- 10 Md 52.30N 16.52 E
Morat/Murten 14 Bd 46.56N 7.08 E
Morata, Puerto de- 13 Kc 41.29N 1.31W
Moratalla 13 Kf 38.12N 1.53W
Moratuwa 25 Fg 6.46N 79.53 E
Morava 5 Hf 48.10N 16.59 E
Morava=Moravia (EN) 5 Hf 49.30N 17.00 E
Morava=Moravia (EN) 10 Mg 49.30N 17.00 E
Moravia (EN)=Morava 5 Hf 49.30N 17.00 E
Moravia (EN)=Morava 10 Mg 49.30N 17.00 E
Moravian Gate (EN)= Moravská Brána 5 Hf 49.33N 17.42 E
Moravian Upland (EN)= Českomoravská Vrchovina 5 Hf 49.20N 15.30 E
Moravica 15 Df 43.51N 20.05 E
Moravská Brána=Moravian Gate(EN) 5 Hf 49.33N 17.42 E
Moravské Budějovice 10 Lg 49.03N 15.49 E
Morawa 59 De 29.13 S 116.00 E
Morawhanna 54 Gb 8.16N 59.45W
Moray Firth 5 Fd 57.50N 3.30W
Morbach 12 Je 49.49N 7.07 E
Morbihan [3] 11 Dg 47.55N 2.50W
Morbihan 11 Dg 47.35N 2.48W
Morbylånga 7 Dh 56.31N 16.23 E
Morcenx 11 Fj 44.02N 0.55W
Mordāb 24 Md 37.26N 49.25 E
Mordaga 27 La 51.14N 120.43 E
Morden 42 Hg 49.11N 98.05W
Mordovo 16 Lc 52.05N 40.46 E
Mordovskaja ASSR [3] 19 Ee 54.20N 44.30 E
Möre 8 Fh 56.25N 15.55 E
More, Ben- 9 Ie 56.23N 4.31W
Morea 37 Bd 22.41 S 15.54 E
More Assynt, Ben- 9 Ic 58.07N 4.51W
Moreau River 43 Gb 45.18N 100.43W
Morecambe 9 Kg 54.04N 2.53W
Morecambe Bay 9 Kg 54.07N 3.00W
Moree 58 Fg 29.28 S 149.51 E
Morehead [Ky.-U.S.] 44 Ff 38.11N 83.25W
Morehead [Pap.N.Gui.] 60 Ci 8.50 S 141.57 E
Morehead City 39 Lf 34.43N 76.43W
Moreiz, Gora- 19 Gb 69.30N 62.05 E
Moreju 17 Ib 68.20N 59.45 E
Morelia 39 Ih 19.42N 101.07W
Morella 13 Ld 40.37N 0.06W
Morelos 48 Ic 28.25N 100.53W
Morelos [2] 47 Ee 18.45N 99.00W
Morena, Sierra- 5 Fh 38.00N 5.00W
Moreni 15 Ie 44.59N 25.39 E
Møre og Romsdal [2] 7 Be 62.40N 7.50 E
Moresby 42 Ef 52.45N 131.50W
Moreton Bay 59 Ke 27.20 S 153.15 E
Moreton Island 59 Ke 27.10 S 153.25 E
Moret-sur-Loing 11 If 48.22N 2.49 E
Moreuil 11 Ie 49.46N 2.29 E
Morez 11 Mh 46.31N 6.02 E
Morezu 15 Hd 45.09N 24.01 E
Mörfelden 12 Ke 49.59N 8.34 E
Morgan City 45 Kl 29.42N 91.12W
Morganfield 44 Dg 37.41N 87.55W
Morganton 44 Gh 35.45N 81.41W
Morgantown [Ky.-U.S.] 44 Dg 37.14N 86.41W
Morgantown [W.V.-U.S.] 44 Hf 39.38N 79.57W
Morges 14 Ad 46.31N 6.30 E
Morghāb 23 Jb 38.18N 61.12 E
Morhange 11 Mf 48.55N 6.38 E
Mori [China] 27 Fc 43.49N 90.11 E
Mori [Jap.] 28 Pc 42.06N 140.35 E
Moriarty 45 Ci 34.59N 106.03W
Morichal Largo, Río- 50 Eh 9.27N 62.25W
Moriguchi 29 Dd 34.44N 135.34 E
Morin Dawa (Nirji) 27 Lb 48.30N 124.28 E
Morioka 22 Qf 39.42N 141.09 E
Moriyoshi 29 Ga 40.07N 140.22 E
Moriyoshi-Yama 29 Gb 39.59N 140.33 E
Morjärv 7 Fc 66.04N 22.43 E
Morki 7 Lh 56.28N 49.00 E
Morko 8 Gf 59.00N 17.40 E
Morkoka 20 Gc 65.03N 115.40 E
Mørkøv 8 Di 55.40N 11.32 E
Morlaix 11 Cf 48.35N 3.50W
Morlanwelz 12 Gd 50.27N 4.14 E
Mörlunda 8 Fg 57.19N 15.51 E
Mormanno 14 Jk 39.53N 15.59 E
Morne-à-l'Eau 50 Fd 16.21N 61.31W
Morne Diablotin 47 Le 15.30N 61.24W
Mornington, Isla- 56 Eg 49.45 S 75.23W
Mornington Island 59 Hc 16.35 S 139.24 E
Moro 46 Ed 45.29N 120.44W
Morobe 58 Fe 7.45 S 147.37 E
Morocco (EN)=Al Maghrib [1] 31 Ge 32.00N 5.50W
Morogoro 31 Ki 6.49 S 37.40 E
Morogoro [3] 36 Gd 8.20 S 37.00 E
Moro Gulf 26 He 6.51N 123.00 E
Moroleón 48 Ig 20.08N 101.12W
Morombe 31 Lk 21.44 S 43.23 E
Morón [Arg.] 55 Cl 34.39 S 58.37W
Morón [Cuba] 47 Id 22.06N 78.38W
Morón [Ven.] 54 Ea 10.29N 68.11W
Morona, Río- 54 Cd 4.45 S 77.04W
Morondava 31 Lk 20.15 S 44.17 E
Morón de la Frontera 13 Gg 37.08N 5.27W
Morones, Sierra- 48 Hg 21.55N 103.05W
Moroni 31 Lj 11.41 S 43.16 E
Moron Us He 21 Lf 34.42N 94.50 E
Morotai, Pulau- 57 Dd 2.20N 128.25 E
Moroto 31 Kh 2.32N 34.39 E
Morovița 15 Ed 45.16N 21.16 E
Morozov 15 Ig 42.30N 25.10 E
Morozovsk 19 Ef 48.20N 41.50 E
Morpeth 9 Lf 55.10N 1.41W
Morphou/Güzelyurt 24 Ee 35.12N 32.59 E
Morrilton 45 Ji 35.09N 92.45W
Morrinhos 54 Ig 17.44 S 49.07W
Morrinsville 62 Fb 37.39 S 175.32 E
Morris [Il.-U.S.] 45 Lf 41.22N 88.26W
Morris [Man.-Can.] 42 Hg 49.21N 97.22W
Morris [Mn.-U.S.] 45 Id 45.35N 95.55W
Morris, Mount- 59 Ge 26.09 S 131.04 E
Morrisburg 44 Jc 44.54N 75.11W
Morris Jesup, Kap- 67 Me 83.45N 35.50W
Morrison Dennis Cays 49 Ff 14.28N 82.53W
Morristown 44 Fg 36.13N 83.18W
Morrito 49 Eh 11.37N 85.05W
Morro, Punta del- 48 Kh 19.51N 96.27W
Morro Bay 43 Cd 35.22N 120.51W
Morro do Chapéu 54 Jf 11.33 S 41.09W
Morrosquillo, Golfo de- 49 Ji 9.35N 75.40W
Morro Vermelho, Serra do- 55 Jc 17.45 S 45.20W
Mörrum 8 Fh 56.11N 14.45 E
Morrumbala 37 Fc 17.20 S 35.35 E
Morrumbene 37 Fd 23.39 S 35.20 E
Mörrumsån 8 Fh 56.09N 14.44 E
Mors 8 Ch 56.50N 8.45 E
Moršansk 19 Ee 53.26N 41.49 E
Morsbach 12 Jd 50.52N 7.45 E
Morsberg 12 Ke 49.43N 8.54 E
Mörsil 7 Ce 63.19N 13.38 E
Mörskom/Myrskylä 8 Kd 60.40N 25.51 E
Morsott 14 Co 35.40N 8.01 E
Mortagne 11 Mf 48.33N 6.27 E
Mortagne-au-Perche 11 Gf 48.31N 0.33 E
Mortagne-sur-Sèvre 11 Fg 47.00N 0.57W
Mortain 11 Ff 48.39N 0.56W
Mortara 14 Ce 45.15N 8.44 E
Mortcha 30 Jg 16.00N 21.10 E
Morteau 11 Mg 47.04N 6.37 E
Morteaux-Couliboeuf 12 Bf 48.56N 0.04W
Morteros 56 Hd 30.42 S 62.00W
Mortes, Rio das- 55 Je 21.09 S 44.53W
Mortesoro 35 Ec 10.12N 34.09 E
Mortlock Islands 57 Gd 5.27N 153.40 E
Morton 46 Dc 46.33N 122.17W
Mortsel 12 Gc 51.10N 4.28 E
Morumbi 55 Ef 23.46 S 54.06W
Morvan 11 Jg 47.05N 4.00 E
Morven 59 Je 26.25 S 147.07 E
Morvern 9 He 56.35N 5.50W
Morvi 25 Ed 22.49N 70.50 E
Morwell 58 Fh 38.14 S 146.24 E
Morzine 11 Mh 46.11N 6.43 E
Moržovec, Ostrov- 7 Kc 66.45N 42.35 E
Moša 7 Je 62.25N 39.48 E
Mosbach 10 Fg 49.21N 9.09 E
Mosby 8 Bf 58.14N 7.54 E
Moščny, Ostrov- 7 Gg 60.00N 27.50 E
Mosconi 55 Bl 35.44 S 60.34W
Moscos Islands 25 Jf 14.00N 97.45 E
Moscow [Id.-U.S.] 43 Db 46.44N 116.59W
Moscow (EN)=Moskva 5 Jd 55.08N 38.50 E
Moscow (EN)=Moskva [R.S.F.S.R.] 6 Jd 55.45N 37.35 E
Moscow Basin (EN)= Meščera 5 Kd 55.00N 40.30 E
Moscow Canal (EN)= Moskvy, kanal imeni- 5 Jd 56.43N 37.08 E
Moscow Upland (EN)= Moskovskaja Vozvyšennost 5 Jd 56.30N 37.30 E
Mosel=Moselle (EN) 5 Ge 50.22N 7.36 E
Moselberge 12 Ie 49.57N 6.56 E
Moselle [3] 11 Me 49.00N 6.30 E
Moselle 5 Ge 50.22N 7.36 E
Moselle (EN)=Mosel 5 Ge 50.22N 7.36 E
Moses Lake 43 Db 47.08N 119.17W
Mosgiel 61 Di 45.53 S 170.22 E
Moshi 31 Ki 3.21 S 37.20 E
Mosina 10 Md 52.16N 16.51 E
Mosjøen 7 Cd 65.50N 13.12 E
Moskalvo 20 Jf 53.39N 142.37 E
Moskenesøy 7 Cc 67.59N 13.00 E
Moskovskaja Oblast [3] 19 Dd 55.45N 37.45 E
Moskovskaja Vozvyšennost =Moscow Upland (EN) 5 Jd 56.30N 37.30 E
Moskovski 18 Gf 37.40N 69.39 E
Moskva [R.S.F.S.R.] = Moscow (EN) 6 Jd 55.45N 37.35 E
Moskva [Tur.-U.S.S.R.] 18 Ee 38.27N 64.24 E
Moskva=Moscow (EN) 5 Jd 55.08N 38.50 E
Moskva, Pik- 18 He 38.55N 71.52 E
Moskvy, kanal imeni-= Moscow Canal (EN) 5 Jd 56.43N 37.08 E
Moslavačka Gora 14 Ke 45.38N 16.42 E
Moso 63b Dc 17.32 S 168.15 E
Mosomane 37 Dd 24.01 S 26.19 E
Mosoni-Duna 10 Ni 47.44N 17.47 E
Mosonmagyaróvár 10 Ni 47.52N 17.17 E
Mosor 14 Kg 43.30N 16.40 E
Mosquero 45 Ei 35.47N 103.58W
Mosquito, Baie - 42 Jd 60.40N 78.00W
Mosquito Coast (EN)= Mosquitos, Costa de- 38 Kh 13.00N 83.45W
Mosquito, Riacho- 55 Cf 22.12 S 57.57W
Mosquitos, Costa de-= Mosquito Coast (EN) 38 Kh 13.00N 83.45W
Mosquitos, Golfo de los- 38 Ki 9.00N 81.20W
Moss 6 Hd 59.26N 10.42 E
Mossaka 36 Cc 1.13 S 16.48 E
Mossâmedes 55 Gc 16.07 S 50.11W
Mossbank 46 Mb 49.55N 105.59W
Mossburn 61 Ci 45.41 S 168.15 E
Mosselbaai 31 Jl 34.11 S 22.08 E
Mossendjo 36 Bc 2.57 S 12.44 E
Mossman 58 Ff 16.28 S 145.22 E
Mossø 8 Ch 56.05N 9.50 E
Mossoró 53 Mf 5.11 S 37.20W
Moss Point 45 Lk 30.25N 88.29W
Mossuril 37 Gb 14.58 S 40.40 E
Most 10 Jf 50.32N 13.39 E
Mostaganem [3] 32 Hb 35.40N 0.30 E
Mostaganem 31 He 35.56N 0.05 E
Mostar 14 Lg 43.21N 17.49 E
Mostardas 55 Gj 31.06 S 50.57W
Møsting, Kap- 41 Hf 63.45N 41.00W
Mostiska 16 Ce 49.48N 23.09 E
Mostiştea 15 Je 44.15N 26.54 E
Most na Soci 14 Hd 46.09N 13.45 E
Mostovskoj 16 Lg 44.22N 40.48 E
Mosty 19 Ce 53.27N 24.33 E
Mosul (EN)=Al Mawşil 22 Gf 36.20N 43.08 E
Møsvatn 7 Bg 59.50N 8.05 E
Mota 63b Ca 13.40 S 167.42 E
Mota 35 Fc 11.05N 37.53 E
Motaba 36 Cb 2.03N 18.03 E
Motacusito 55 Bc 17.35 S 61.31W
Mota del Marques 13 Gc 41.38N 5.10W
Motagua 38 Kh 15.44N 88.14W
Motajica 14 Le 45.04N 17.40 E
Motala 7 Dg 58.33N 15.03 E
Motala ström 8 Gf 58.38N 16.10 E
Motatán 49 Li 9.24N 70.36W
Motatán, Río- 49 Li 9.32N 71.02W
Motegi 29 Gc 36.32N 140.10 E
Motehuala 47 Dd 23.39N 100.39W
Mothe 63d Cc 18.40 S 178.30W
Motherwell 9 Jf 55.48N 4.00W
Motīhāri 25 Gc 26.39N 84.55 E
Motilla del Palancar 13 Ke 39.34N 1.53W
Motiti Island 62 Gb 37.40 S 176.25 E
Motlav 63b Ca 13.40 S 167.40 E
Motobu 29b Ab 26.40N 127.55 E
Motol 10 Vd 52.17N 25.40 E
Motovski Zaliv 7 Hb 69.30N 32.30 E
Motoyoshi 29 Gb 38.48N 141.31 E
Motozintla de Mendoza 48 Mj 15.22N 92.14W
Motril 13 Ih 36.45N 3.31W
Motru 15 Ge 44.33N 23.27 E
Motru 15 Fe 44.48N 23.00 E
Motsuta-Misaki 29a Ab 42.36N 139.49 E
Mott 45 Ec 46.22N 102.20W
Motteville 12 Ce 49.38N 0.51 E
Motu 62 Gb 37.51 S 177.35 E
Motueka 62 Ed 41.07 S 173.01 E
Motuhora Island 62 Gb 37.50 S 177.00 E
Motu-Iti 65d Ac 27.11 S 109.27W
Motu-Iti → Tupai Atoll 61 Kc 16.17 S 151.50W
Motul 47 Gd 21.06N 89.17W
Motu-Nui 65d Ac 27.12 S 109.28W
Motu One Atoll 57 Lf 15.48 S 154.33W
Motupae 64n Ac 10.27 S 161.02W
Motupena Point 63a Bb 6.32 S 155.09 E
Moturiki 63d Bb 17.46 S 178.45 E
Motutapu 64p Cb 21.14 S 159.43W
Motu Tautara 65d Ab 27.05 S 109.26W
Motutunga Atoll 57 Mf 17.06 S 144.22W
Moubray Bay 66 Kf 72.11 S 170.15 E
Mouchard 11 Lh 46.58N 5.48 E
Mouchoir Bank (EN) 47 Jd 20.57N 70.42W
Mouchoir Passage 49 Lc 21.10N 71.00W
Moudjéria 32 Ef 17.52N 12.20W
Mouila 31 Ii 1.52 S 11.01 E
Mouka 35 Cd 7.16N 21.52 E
Moul 34 Hb 15.03N 13.18 E
Mould Bay 39 Hb 76.15N 119.30W
Moule 50 Fd 16.20N 61.21W
Moule à Chique, Cap- 51k Bb 13.43N 60.57W
Moulins 11 Jh 46.34N 3.20 E
Moulmein 22 Le 16.30N 97.38 E
Moulouya 30 Ge 35.06N 2.20W
Moult 12 Be 49.07N 0.10W
Moultrie 44 Fj 31.11N 83.47W
Moultrie, Lake- 44 Gi 33.20N 80.05W
Mouly, Pointe de- 63b Ce 20.43 S 166.23 E
Moúnda, Ákra- 15 Dk 38.03N 20.47 E
Moundou 31 Ih 8.34N 16.05 E
Moundsville 44 Gf 39.54N 80.44W
Mo'unga'one 65b Ba 19.38 S 174.29W
Moungoudou 36 Bc 2.40 S 12.41 E
Mountainair 45 Ci 34.31N 106.15W
Mountain Grove 45 Jh 37.08N 92.16W
Mountain Home [Ar.-U.S.] 45 Jh 36.21N 92.23W
Mountain Home [Id.-U.S.] 43 Dc 43.08N 115.41W
Mountain Nile (EN)=Jabal, Baḩr al- 30 Kh 9.30N 30.30 E
Mountain Village 40 Gd 62.05N 163.44W
Mount Airy 44 Gg 36.31N 80.37W
Mount Barker 59 Df 34.38 S 117.40 E
Mount Carmel 45 Mf 38.25N 87.46W
Mount Desert Island 44 Mc 44.20N 68.20W
Mount Douglas 58 Fg 21.30 S 146.50 E
Mount Eba 59 Hf 30.12 S 135.40 E
Mount Forest 44 Gd 43.59N 80.44W
Mount Frere 37 Df 31.00 S 28.58 E
Mount Gambier 58 Fh 37.50 S 140.46 E
Mount Hagen 60 Ci 5.52 S 144.13 E
Mount Hope 59 Hf 34.07 S 135.23 E
Mount Isa 58 Eg 20.44 S 139.30 E
Mountlake Terrace 46 Dc 47.47N 122.18W
Mount Lavinia 25 Fg 6.50N 79.52 E
Mount Lebanon 44 Ge 40.23N 80.03W
Mount Lofty Ranges 59 Hg 35.15 S 138.50 E
Mount Magnet 58 Cg 28.04 S 117.49 E
Mount Maunganui 61 Eg 37.38 S 176.12 E
Mount Morgan 59 Kd 23.39 S 150.23 E
Mountnorris Bay 59 Gb 11.20 S 132.45 E
Mount Peck 46 Ha 50.10N 115.02W
Mount Pleasant [Ia.-U.S.] 45 Kf 40.58N 91.33W
Mount Pleasant [Mi.-U.S.] 44 Ed 43.35N 84.47W
Mount Pleasant [S.C.-U.S.] 44 Hi 32.47N 79.52W
Mount Pleasant [Tx.-U.S.] 45 Ij 33.09N 94.58W
Mount Pleasant [Ut.-U.S.] 46 Jg 39.33N 111.27W
Mount's Bay 9 Hk 50.03N 5.25W
Mount Somers 62 De 43.42 S 171.25 E
Mount Sterling [Il.-U.S.] 45 Kg 39.59N 90.45W
Mount Sterling [Ky.-U.S.] .44 Ff 38.04N 83.56W
Mount Vancouver 42 Dd 60.20N 139.41W
Mount Vernon [Al.-U.S.] 44 Cj 31.05N 88.01W
Mount Vernon [Austl.] 59 Dd 24.13 S 118.14 E
Mount Vernon [Il.-U.S.] 43 Jd 38.19N 88.55W
Mount Vernon [In.-U.S.] 44 Dg 37.56N 87.54W
Mount Vernon [Ky.-U.S.] 44 Eg 37.21N 84.20W
Mount Vernon [Oh.-U.S.] 44 Fe 40.23N 82.30W
Mount Vernon [Wa.-U.S.] 43 Cb 48.25N 122.20W
Moura [Austl.] 59 Jd 24.35 S 150.00 E
Moura [Port.] 13 Ef 38.08N 7.27W
Mourão 13 Ef 38.23N 7.21W
Mourdi 35 Cb 17.50N 22.25 E
Mourdi, Dépression du-= Mourdi Depression (EN) 30 Jg 18.10N 23.00 E
Mourdiah 34 Dc 14.26N 7.31W
Mourdi Depression (EN)= Mourdi, Dépression du- 30 Jg 18.10N 23.00 E
Mourmelon-le-Grand 12 Ge 49.08N 4.22 E
Mourne Mountains/Beanna Boirche 9 Gg 54.10N 6.04W
Mouscron/Moeskroen 11 Jd 50.44N 3.13 E
Moussoro 31 Ig 13.39N 16.29 E
Moustiers-Sainte-Marie 11 Mk 43.51N 6.13 E
Moutier/Münster 14 Bc 47.16N 7.22 E
Moutiers 11 Mi 45.29N 6.32 E
Moutong 26 Hf 0.28N 121.13 E
Mouy 12 Ee 49.19N 2.19 E
Mouydir 30 Hf 25.00N 4.10 E
Mouyondzi 36 Bc 3.58 S 13.57 E
Mouzaia 13 Oh 36.28N 2.41 E
Mouzon 12 He 49.36N 5.05 E
Movas 48 Ec 28.10N 109.25W

Index Symbols

[1] Independent Nation
[2] State, Region
[3] District, County
[4] Municipality
[5] Colony, Dependency
Continent
Physical Region
Historical or Cultural Region
Mount, Mountain
Volcano
Hill
Mountains, Mountain Range
Hills, Escarpment
Plateau, Upland
Pass, Gap
Plain, Lowland
Delta
Salt Flat
Valley, Canyon
Crater, Cave
Karst Features
Depression
Polder
Desert, Dunes
Forest, Woods
Heath, Steppe
Oasis
Cape, Point
Coast, Beach
Cliff
Peninsula
Isthmus
Sandbank
Island
Atoll
Rock, Reef
Islands, Archipelago
Rocks, Reefs
Coral Reef
Well, Spring
Geyser
River, Stream
Waterfall Rapids
River Mouth, Estuary
Lake
Salt Lake
Intermittent Lake
Reservoir
Swamp, Pond
Canal
Glacier
Ice Shelf, Pack Ice
Ocean
Sea
Gulf, Bay
Strait, Fjord
Lagoon
Bank
Seamount
Tablemount
Ridge
Shelf
Basin
Escarpment, Sea Scarp
Fracture
Trench, Abyss
National Park, Reserve
Point of Interest
Recreation Site
Cave, Cavern
Historic Site
Ruins
Wall, Walls
Church, Abbey
Temple
Scientific Station
Airport
Port
Lighthouse
Mine
Tunnel
Dam, Bridge

Moxico [3]	36	De	12.00S	20.00 E
Moxico	36	De	11.51S	20.01 E
Moy/An Mhuaidh ∿	9	Dg	54.12N	9.08W
Moyahua	48	Hg	21.16N	103.10W
Moyale [Eth.]	31	Kh	3.32N	39.04 E
Moyale [Kenya]	36	Gb	3.32N	39.03 E
Moyamba	34	Cd	8.10N	12.26W
Moÿ-de-l'Aisne	12	Fe	49.45N	3.22 E
Moyen Atlas=Middle Atlas (EN) ⛰	30	Ge	33.30N	4.30W
Moyen-Chari [3]	35	Bd	9.00N	18.00 E
Moyenne Guinée [3]	34	Cc	11.15N	12.30W
Moÿenneville	12	Dd	50.04N	1.45 E
Moyen-Ogooué [3]	36	Bc	0.30S	10.30 E
Moyeuvre-Grande	12	Ie	49.15N	6.02 E
Moyo	36	Fb	3.40N	31.43 E
Moyo, Pulau- ◆	26	Gh	8.15S	117.34 E
Moyobamba	53	If	6.02S	76.58W
Moyowosi ∿	36	Fc	4.50S	31.24 E
Moyto	35	Bc	12.35N	16.33 E
Moyu/Karakax	27	Cd	37.17N	79.42 E
Možajsk	7	Ii	55.32N	36.02 E
Mozambique (EN)=Moçambique [1]	31	Kj	18.15S	35.00 E
Mozambique (EN)=Moçambique	31	Lk	15.03S	40.45 E
Mozambique, Canal de-=Mozambique Channel (EN) ⇌	30	Lk	20.00S	43.00 E
Mozambique Channel (EN)=Moçambique, Canal de- ⇌	30	Lk	20.00S	43.00 E
Mozambique Channel (EN)=Mozambique, Canal de- ⇌	30	Lk	20.00S	43.00 E
Mozambique Plateau (EN) ⋀	30	Kl	32.00S	35.00 E
Mozdok	19	Eg	43.44N	44.38 E
Možga	19	Fd	56.28N	52.13 E
Mozuli	8	Mh	56.32N	28.14 E
Mozyr	19	Ce	52.02N	29.16 E
Mpala	36	Ed	6.45S	29.31 E
Mpanda	31	Ki	6.22S	31.02 E
Mpigi	36	Fb	0.15N	32.20 E
Mpika	31	Kj	11.50S	31.27 E
Mpoko ∿	35	Be	4.19N	18.33 E
Mporokoso	36	Fd	9.23S	30.08 E
Mpouia	36	Cc	2.37S	16.13 E
Mpui	36	Fd	8.21S	31.50 E
Mpulungu	36	Fd	8.46S	31.07 E
Mpwapwa	36	Gd	6.21S	36.29 E
Mrągowo	10	Rc	53.52N	21.19 E
Mrakovo	17	Hj	52.43N	56.38 E
Mrewa	37	Ec	17.39S	31.47 E
Mrkonjić Grad	14	Lf	44.25N	17.06 E
Mrocza	10	Nc	53.14N	17.36 E
Mroga ∿	10	Pd	52.09N	19.42 E
Msangesi ∿	36	Ge	11.40S	36.45 E
Msid, Djebel- ▲	14	Cn	36.25N	8.04 E
Msif ∿	13	Qi	35.23N	4.45 E
M'Sila ∿	13	Qi	35.31N	4.30 E
M'Sila [3]	32	Hb	35.00N	4.30 E
M'Sila	32	Hb	35.42N	4.33 E
Mšinskaja	8	Nf	58.55N	30.03 E
Msta ∿	5	Jd	58.25N	31.20 E
Mstislavl	16	Gc	53.59N	31.45 E
Mszana Dolna	10	Qg	49.42N	20.05 E
Mtakuja	36	Fd	7.22S	30.37 E
Mtama	36	Ge	10.18S	39.22 E
Mtelo ▲	36	Gb	1.39N	35.23 E
Mtera Reservoir ⊜	36	Gd	7.01S	35.55 E
Mtito Andei	36	Gc	2.41S	38.10 E
Mtoko	37	Ec	17.24S	32.13 E
Mtubatuba	37	Ee	28.30S	32.08 E
Mtwara [3]	36	Ge	10.40S	39.00 E
Mtwara	31	Lj	10.16S	40.11 E
Mu, Cerro- ▲	49	Ki	9.29N	73.07W
Mua	64h	Ac	13.21S	176.10W
Mu'a	65b	Ac	21.11S	175.07W
Mua, Baie de- ◐	64h	Bc	13.23S	176.09W
Muaná	54	Id	1.32S	49.13W
Muang Huon	25	Kd	20.09N	101.27 E
Muang Khammouan	25	Ke	17.24N	104.48 E
Muang Không	25	Lf	14.07N	105.51 E
Muang Khôngxédôn	25	Le	15.34N	105.49 E
Muang Khoua	25	Kd	21.05N	102.31 E
Muang Pak Lay	25	Ke	18.12N	101.25 E
Muang Pakxan	25	Ke	18.22N	103.39 E
Muang Pakxong	25	Le	15.11N	106.14 E
Muang Sing	25	Kd	21.11N	101.09 E
Muang Tahoi	25	Le	16.10N	106.38 E
Muang Thai=Thailand (EN) [1]	22	Lh	15.00N	100.00 E
Muang Vangviang	25	Ke	18.56N	102.27 E
Muang Xaignabouri	25	Ke	19.15N	101.45 E
Muang Xaÿ	25	Kd	20.42N	101.59 E
Muang Xépôn	25	Le	16.41N	106.14 E
Muanzanza	36	Dd	6.32S	20.51 E
Muar	26	Df	2.02N	102.34 E
Muaraaman	26	Dg	3.07S	102.12 E
Muarabungo	26	Dg	1.28S	102.07 E
Muaraenim	26	Dg	3.39S	103.48 E
Muaralasan	26	Gf	1.48N	117.12 E
Muarapajang	26	Gg	1.32S	115.48 E
Muarasiberut	26	Cg	1.36S	99.11 E
Muarasiram	26	Gg	0.46S	116.11 E
Muaratebo	26	Dg	1.30S	102.26 E
Muaratewe	26	Fg	0.57S	114.53 E
Muarawahau	26	Gf	1.02N	116.52 E
Mubarek	18	Ee	39.16N	65.07 E
Mubende	36	Fb	0.35N	31.23 E
Mubi	31	Ig	10.16N	13.16 E
Much	12	Jd	50.55N	7.24 E
Muchinga Escarpment ◧	36	Fe	13.40S	30.00 E
Muchinga Mountains ⛰	30	Kj	12.00S	31.45 E
Muck ◆	9	Ge	56.50N	6.14W
Mücke	12	Ld	50.37N	9.02 E
Mucojo	37	Gb	12.04S	40.28 E
Muconda	36	De	10.34S	21.20 E
Mucua ∿	37	Ec	18.09S	34.58 E
Mucubela	37	Fc	16.54S	37.49 E
Mucuchies	49	Li	8.45N	70.55W
Mucumbura	37	Ec	16.10S	31.42 E
Mucur	24	Fc	39.04N	34.23 E
Mucusso	36	Df	18.00S	21.25 E
Mudan Jang ∿	21	Oe	46.18N	129.31 E
Mudanjiang	22	Oe	44.35N	129.34 E
Mudanya	24	Cb	40.22N	28.52 E
Muddy Gap	46	Le	42.22N	107.27W
Mudgee	59	Jf	32.36S	149.35 E
Mud Lake	46	Ie	43.53N	112.24W
Mud Lake ⬭	46	Gh	37.55N	117.05W
Mudon	25	Je	16.15N	97.44 E
Mudug [3]	35	Hd	6.30N	48.00 E
Mudug ⊠	35	Hd	6.20N	47.00 E
Mudurnu	24	Db	40.28N	31.13 E
Muecate	37	Fb	14.53S	39.38 E
Mueda	37	Fb	11.39S	39.33 E
Muerto, Cayo- ◆	49	Ff	14.34N	82.44W
Muerto, Mar- ◍	48	Li	16.10N	94.10W
Mufulira	31	Jj	12.33S	28.14 E
Mufu Shan ⛰	27	Jf	29.15N	114.20 E
Mufu Shan ▲	27	Jf	29.00N	113.50 E
Mugello ⊠	14	Fg	43.55N	11.25 E
Múggia	14	He	45.36N	13.46 E
Mughshin, Wādī- ∿	35	Ib	19.44N	55.00 E
Mugi	29	De	33.40N	134.25 E
Mu Gia, Deo- ⌵	25	Le	17.40N	105.47 E
Mugila, Monts- ⛰	36	Ed	6.49S	29.08 E
Muğla	23	Cb	37.12N	28.22 E
Mugodžary ⛰	21	He	49.00N	58.40 E
Mugur an Na'ām	24	Ig	31.56N	40.30 E
Muhaiwir	24	If	33.28N	40.59 E
Muḩammad, Ra's- ▶	33	Fd	27.42N	34.13 E
Muḩammad Oawl	35	Fa	20.54N	37.05 E
Muhen	20	Ig	48.10N	136.08 E
Muheza	36	Gd	5.10S	38.47 E
Muhīt, Al Baḩr al-=Atlantic Ocean (EN) ≋	3	Di	2.00N	25.00W
Mühlacker	10	Eh	48.57N	8.50 E
Mühldorf am Inn	10	Ih	48.15N	12.32 E
Mühlhausen in Thüringen	10	Ge	51.13N	10.27 E
Mühlig-Hofmann Gebirge ⛰	66	Cf	72.00S	5.20 E
Mühlviertel ⊠	14	Ib	48.30N	14.10 E
Muhoršibir	20	Ff	51.01N	107.50 E
Muhos	7	Gd	64.50N	26.01 E
Muhu ◆	7	Fg	58.35N	23.15 E
Muhu	8	Jf	58.37N	23.05 E
Muhu, Proliv-/Muhu Väin ⇌	8	Jf	58.45N	23.15 E
Muhulu	36	Ec	1.03S	27.17 E
Muhu Väin/Muhu, Proliv- ⇌	8	Jf	58.45N	23.15 E
Muhuwesi ∿	36	Ge	11.16S	37.58 E
Muiderslot ♜	12	Hb	52.20N	5.06 E
Muigheo/Mayo [2]	9	Dh	53.50N	9.30W
Muikamachi	28	Of	37.04N	138.53 E
Muineachán/Monaghan [2]	9	Gg	54.10N	7.00W
Muineachán/Monaghan	9	Gg	54.15N	6.58W
Muine Bheag	9	Gi	52.42N	6.57W
Muir Bhreatan=Saint George's Channel (EN) ⇌	5	Fe	52.00N	6.00W
Muir Eireann=Irish Sea (EN) ≈	5	Fe	53.30N	5.20W
Muiron Islands ❖	59	Cd	21.35S	114.20 E
Muir Seamount (EN) ⋏	38	Mf	33.41N	63.32W
Muíte	37	Fb	14.02S	39.02 E
Mujeres, Isla- ◆	48	Pg	21.13N	86.43W
Mujezerski	7	He	63.57N	32.01 E
Muji	27	Cd	37.27N	78.33 E
Mujnak	19	Fg	43.44N	59.02 E
Mujnakski Zaliv ◐	18	Bc	43.50N	58.40 E
Mujunkum, Peski- ∴	21	Je	44.00N	70.30 E
Mukačevo	19	Cf	48.26N	22.45 E
Mukah	26	Ff	2.54N	112.06 E
Mukawa	29a	Bb	42.35N	141.55 E
Mu-Kawa ∿	29a	Bb	42.33N	141.53 E
Mukawwar ◆	35	Fa	20.48N	37.13 E
Mukdahan	25	Ke	16.31N	104.42 E
Mukden → Shenyang	22	Oe	41.48N	123.24 E
Mukeru	64a	Bc	7.25N	134.30 E
Mukho	28	Jf	37.33N	129.07 E
Mukinbudin	59	Df	30.54S	118.13 E
Mukojima-Rettō ❖	60	Cb	27.37N	142.10 E
Mukomuko	26	Dg	2.35S	101.07 E
Muksu ∿	18	He	39.17N	71.25 E
Mula ∿	25	Dc	27.57N	67.36 E
Mula	13	Kf	38.03N	1.30W
Mulainagiri ▲	25	Ff	13.24N	75.43 E
Mulaku Atoll ◎	25a	Bb	2.57N	73.34 E
Mulaly	19	Hf	45.27N	78.20 E
Mulan	27	Mb	46.00N	128.02 E
Mulanje ▲	30	Kj	16.03S	35.31 E
Mulanje	36	Gf	16.02S	35.30 E
Mulatre, Point- ▶	51g	Bb	15.17N	61.15W
Mulatupo Sasardí	49	Ii	8.57N	77.45W
Mulchatna ∿	40	Hd	59.39N	157.08W
Mulchén	56	Fe	37.34S	72.14W
Mulda	17	Kc	67.28N	63.34 E
Mulde ∿	10	Ie	51.48N	12.10 E
Mulebreen ❄	66	Ee	67.28S	59.21 E
Mulegé	47	Bc	26.53N	112.01W
Mulegé, Sierra de- ⛰	47	Bc	37.30N	112.40W
Mulenda	36	Dc	4.18S	24.58 E
Muleshoe	45	Ei	34.13N	102.43W
Mulgrave Island ◆	59	Ib	10.05S	142.10 E
Mulhacén ▲	5	Fh	37.03N	3.19W
Mülheim an der Ruhr	12	Ic	51.26N	6.53 E
Mülheim-Kärlich	12	Jd	50.23N	7.30 E
Mulhouse	6	Gf	47.45N	7.20 E
Muli (Bowa)	27	Hf	27.55N	101.13 E
Mulifanua	65c	Aa	13.50S	172.02W
Muling	28	Kb	44.34N	130.12 E
Muling (Bamiantong)	28	Kb	44.55N	130.32 E
Muling Guan ⌵	28	Ef	36.10N	118.46 E
Muling He ∿	28	Lb	45.53N	133.30 E
Mull, Island of- ◆	5	Fd	56.27N	6.00W
Mull, Sound of- ⇌	9	He	56.35N	5.50W
Mullen	45	Fe	42.03N	101.01W
Mullens	44	Gg	37.35N	81.25W
Muller, Pegunungan- ⛰	26	Ff	0.40N	113.50 E
Mullet Peninsula/An Muirthead ⊏	9	Cg	54.15N	10.04W
Mullett Lake ⬭	44	Ec	45.30N	84.30W
Mullewa	59	De	28.33S	115.31 E
Müllheim	10	Di	47.48N	7.38 E
Mullingar/An Muileann gCearr	9	Fh	53.32N	7.20W
Mullsjö	8	Eg	57.55N	13.53 E
Mulobezi	36	Ef	16.47S	25.10 E
Mulock Glacier ❄	66	Jf	79.03S	159.10 E
Mulongo	36	Ed	7.50S	26.57 E
Multān	22	Jf	30.11N	71.29 E
Multé	48	Ni	17.41N	91.24W
Multia	8	Kb	62.25N	24.47 E
Multien ⊠	12	Ee	49.05N	2.55 E
Mulu, Gunong- ▲	26	Ff	4.03N	114.56 E
Mulvane	45	Hh	37.29N	97.14W
Mulymja ∿	17	Lf	60.12N	64.32 E
Mumbué	36	Ce	13.53S	17.19 E
Mumbwa	36	Ee	14.59S	27.04 E
Mumhan/Munster ▣	9	Ei	52.30N	9.00W
Mumra	16	Og	45.43N	47.41 E
Mun ∿	21	Mh	15.19N	105.30 E
Muna	48	Og	20.29N	89.43W
Muna ∿	21	Oc	67.52N	123.10 E
Muna, Pulau- ◆	26	Hg	5.00S	122.30 E
Munābāo	25	Ec	25.45N	70.17 E
Munamägi/Munamjagi △	8	Lg	57.38N	27.10 E
Munamjagi/Munamägi △	8	Lg	57.38N	27.10 E
Munaybarah, Sharm- ⇌	24	Gi	26.04N	36.38 E
Muncar	26	Fh	8.29S	114.21 E
Münchberg	10	Hf	50.12N	11.47 E
München=Munich (EN)	6	Hf	48.09N	11.35 E
Münchhausen	12	Kd	50.57N	8.43 E
Muncho Lake	42	Ee	58.56N	125.46W
Munch'ŏn	28	Ie	39.14N	127.22 E
Muncie	43	Jc	40.11N	85.23W
Munda	63a	Cc	8.19S	157.15 E
Mundaring, Perth-	59	Df	31.54S	116.10 E
Munday	45	Gj	33.27N	99.38W
Mundemba	34	Ge	4.59N	8.40 E
Münden	10	Fe	51.25N	9.41 E
Mundesley	12	Db	52.52N	1.25 E
Mundford	12	Cb	52.30N	0.39 E
Mundiwindi	58	Dg	23.52S	120.09 E
Mundo ∿	13	Kf	38.19N	1.40W
Mundo Novo	54	Jf	11.52S	40.28W
Munellës, Mali i- ▲	15	Dh	41.58N	20.06 E
Munera	13	Je	39.02N	2.28W
Mungana	59	Ic	17.07S	144.24 E
Mungbere	31	Jh	2.38N	28.30 E
Mungindi	59	Je	28.58S	148.59 E
Munhango	36	Ce	12.10S	18.34 E
Munh-Hajrhan-Ula ▲	21	Le	46.40N	91.30 E
Munich (EN)=München	6	Hf	48.09N	11.35 E
Muniesa	13	Lc	41.02N	0.48W
Munīfah	23	Gd	27.38N	49.00 E
Munising	44	Db	46.25N	86.40W
Munkedal	7	Cg	58.29N	11.41 E
Munkfors	7	Cg	59.50N	13.32 E
Munku Sardik, Gora- ▲	21	Md	51.45N	100.20 E
Muñoz Gamero, Peninsula- ⊏	56	Fh	52.30S	73.10W
Munsan	28	If	37.55N	126.22 E
Münsingen	10	Fh	48.25N	9.30 E
Munster	11	Nf	48.03N	7.08 E
Münster [F.R.G.]	12	Ke	49.55N	8.52 E
Münster [F.R.G.]	10	De	51.58N	7.38 E
Münster/Moutier	14	Bc	47.16N	7.22 E
Munster/Mumhan ▣	9	Ei	52.30N	9.00W
Münster-Hiltrup	12	Jc	51.54N	7.38 E
Münsterland [F.R.G.] ⊠	12	Kb	52.45N	8.10 E
Münsterland [F.R.G.] ⊠	10	De	52.00N	7.30 E
Münstermaifeld	12	Jd	50.15N	7.22 E
Muntenia ⊠	15	Ie	44.00N	26.00 E
Munteni Buzău	15	Je	44.38N	26.59 E
Muntok	26	Eg	2.04S	105.11 E
Munzur Dağları ⛰	24	Hc	39.30N	39.10 E
Muojärvi ⬭	7	Gd	65.56N	28.36 E
Muong Sen	25	Ke	19.24N	104.08 E
Muonio	6	Ib	67.57N	23.42 E
Muonioälven Muonionijoki ∿	5	Ib	67.11N	23.34 E
Muping	28	Ff	37.23N	121.36 E
Muqaddam ∿	35	Eb	18.04N	31.30 E
Muqayshiţ ❖	24	Oj	24.10N	53.45 E
Muqdisho=Mogadishu (EN)	31	Lh	2.03N	45.22 E
Mur ∿	5	Hf	46.18N	16.55 E
Mura ∿	5	Hf	46.18N	16.55 E
Muradiye [Tur.]	15	Kk	38.39N	27.24 E
Muradiye [Tur.]	24	Jc	39.00N	43.43 E
Murafa ∿	16	Fe	48.13N	28.14 E
Murakami	28	Oe	38.14N	139.29 E
Murallón, Cerro- ▲	52	Ij	49.48S	73.25W
Muráň	10	Qh	48.45N	20.02 E
Mur'aňyo	35	Ic	11.41N	50.27 E
Muraši	19	Ed	59.24N	48.59 E
Murat ∿	21	Ff	38.52N	38.48 E
Murat	11	Ii	45.07N	2.52 E
Murat Dağı ▲	23	Cb	38.55N	29.43 E
Muratlı [Tur.]	24	Ib	41.29N	41.41 E
Muratlı [Tur.]	15	Kh	41.10N	27.30 E
Murau	14	Ic	47.06N	14.10 E
Muravera	14	Dk	39.25N	9.34 E
Murayama	29	Gb	38.29N	140.23 E
Mürchen Khvort	24	Nf	33.06N	51.30 E
Murchison	62	Ed	41.48S	172.20 E
Murchison, Mount- [Austl.] ▲	59	De	26.46S	116.25 E
Murchison, Mount- [N.Z.] ▲	62	De	43.01S	171.17 E
Murchison River ∿	57	Cg	27.50S	114.00 E
Murcia	6	Fh	37.59N	1.07W
Murcia [3]	13	Kg	38.00N	1.30W
Murcia ▣	13	Kf	38.30N	1.45W
Mur-de-Barrez	11	Ij	44.51N	2.39 E
Murdo	45	Fe	43.53N	100.43W
Mürefte	15	Ki	40.40N	27.14 E
Muren	22	Me	49.38N	100.10 E
Mureş ∿	5	If	46.15N	20.12 E
Mureş [2]	15	Hc	46.30N	24.40 E
Muret	11	Hk	43.28N	1.21 E
Murfreesboro	43	Jd	35.51N	86.23W
Murg ∿	10	Eh	48.55N	8.10 E
Murgab ∿	21	If	38.18N	61.12 E
Murgab [Tad.-U.S.S.R.]	19	Hh	38.10N	73.59 E
Murgab [Tur.-U.S.S.R.]	18	Df	37.32N	62.01 E
Murgaš ▲	15	Gg	42.50N	23.40 E
Murgeni	15	Lc	46.12N	28.01 E
Murgon	59	Ke	26.15S	151.57 E
Muri	64p	Cc	21.15S	159.43W
Muriaé	54	Jh	21.08S	42.22W
Murici	54	Ke	9.19S	35.56W
Muriege	36	Dd	9.53S	21.13 E
Murihiti ◎	64n	Ab	10.23S	161.02W
Murilo Atoll ◎	57	Gd	8.40N	152.11 E
Mūrītāniyā=Mauritania (EN) [1]	31	Fg	20.00N	12.00W
Müritz ⬭	10	Ic	53.25N	12.43 E
Murkong Selek	25	Jc	27.44N	95.18 E
Murmansk	6	Jb	68.58N	33.05 E
Murmanskaja Oblast [3]	19	Db	68.00N	35.30 E
Murmaši	19	Db	68.49N	32.49 E
Murnau	10	Hi	47.41N	11.12 E
Muro	13	Pe	39.44N	3.03 E
Muro, Capo di- ▶	11a	Ab	41.44N	8.40 E
Muro Lucano	14	Jj	40.45N	15.29 E
Murom	6	Kd	55.34N	42.02 E
Muromcevo	19	Hd	56.23N	75.14 E
Muroran	22	Qe	42.18N	140.59 E
Muros	13	Cb	42.47N	9.02W
Muros y Noya, Ría de- ⋖	13	Db	42.45N	9.00W
Muroto	27	Ne	33.18N	134.09 E
Muroto Zaki ▶	28	Mh	33.16N	134.10 E
Murowana Goślina	10	Nd	52.35N	17.01 E
Murphy [Id.-U.S.]	46	Ge	43.13N	116.33W
Murphy [N.C.-U.S.]	44	Eh	35.05N	84.01W
Murphysboro	45	Lh	37.46N	89.20W
Murrah al Kubrá, Al Buḩayrah al- ⬭	24	Eg	30.20N	32.23 E
Murray [Ky.-U.S.]	44	Cg	36.37N	88.19W
Murray [Ut.-U.S.]	46	Jf	40.40N	111.53W
Murray, Lake- [Pap.N.Gui.] ⬭	60	Ci	7.00S	141.30 E
Murray, Lake- [S.C.-U.S.] ⬭	44	Gh	34.04N	81.23W
Murray Bridge	59	Hg	35.07S	139.17 E
Murray Fracture zone (EN) ⚡	3	Lf	34.00N	135.00W
Murray Islands ❖	59	Ia	9.55S	144.05 E
Murray Ridge (EN) ⋀	3	Gg	21.00N	61.50 E
Murray River ∿	57	Eh	35.22S	139.22 E
Murraysburg	37	Cf	31.58S	23.47 E
Murro di Porco, Capo- ▶	14	Jm	37.00N	15.20 E
Murrumbidgee River ∿	57	Fh	34.43S	143.12 E
Murrupula	37	Fc	15.27S	38.47 E
Murska Sobota	14	Kd	46.40N	16.10 E
Murten/Morat	14	Bd	46.56N	7.08 E
Murter ◆	14	Jg	43.47N	15.37 E
Murtle Lake ⬭	46	Fa	52.08N	119.38W
Murud, Gunong- ▲	26	Gf	3.52N	115.30 E
Murupara	62	Gc	38.27S	176.42 E
Mururoa Atoll ◎	57	Ng	21.52S	138.55W
Murwāra	25	Gd	23.51N	80.24 E
Murwillumbah	59	Ke	28.19S	153.24 E
Mürz ∿	14	Jc	47.24N	15.17 E
Mürzzuschlag	14	Jc	47.36N	15.41 E
Muş	23	Fb	38.44N	41.30 E
Muša/Mūša ∿	7	Fh	56.24N	24.12 E
Mūša/Muša ∿	7	Fh	56.24N	24.12 E
Mūsa, Jabal-=Sinai, Mount- (EN) ▲	24	Eh	28.32N	33.59 E
Musa Ali ▲	35	Gc	12.30N	42.27 E
Musāfī	24	Qk	25.18N	56.10 E
Musā'id	33	Ed	31.36N	25.03 E
Musala ▲	5	Ig	42.11N	23.34 E
Musallam	24	Lg	31.53N	46.56 E
Musan	27	Mc	42.14N	129.13 E
Musandam Peninsula ⊏	24	Qi	26.18N	56.24 E
Musay'īd	24	Nj	25.00N	51.33 E
Musaymir	33	Hg	13.27N	44.37 E
Muscat (EN)=Masqaţ	22	Hg	23.29N	58.33 E
Muscat and Oman (EN) → Oman (EN) [1]	22	Hg	21.00N	57.00 E
Muscatine	45	Kf	41.25N	91.03W
Musgrave	58	Ff	14.47S	143.30 E
Musgrave Ranges ⛰	57	Eg	26.10S	131.50 E
Mūshā	24	Di	27.07N	31.14 E
Mus-Haja, Gora- ▲	21	Qc	62.35N	140.50 E
Mushāsh al 'Ashawī	24	Mj	24.12N	48.50 E
Mushāsh Ramlān	24	Mj	24.25N	49.15 E
Mushayrib, Ra's- ▶	24	Nj	24.18N	51.44 E
Mushie	36	Cc	3.01S	16.54 E
Mūsi ∿	25	Ge	15.20N	80.06 E
Musi ∿	21	Mj	2.20S	104.56 E
Mūsiān	24	Lf	32.28N	47.26 E
Musicians Seamounts (EN) ⋏	57	Kb	29.00N	162.00W
Muskegon	43	Jc	43.14N	86.16W
Muskegon Heights	44	Dd	43.12N	86.12W
Muskegon River ∿	44	Dd	43.14N	86.20W
Muskö ◆	8	He	59.00N	18.05 E
Muskogee	43	Hd	35.45N	95.22W
Muskoka, Lake- ⬭	44	Hc	45.00N	79.25W
Musoma	31	Ki	1.30S	33.48 E
Musone ∿	14	Hg	43.28N	13.38 E
Mussaţţaḩah, Al Jazīrah al- ◆	14	Em	37.11N	10.20 E
Mussau Island ◆	60	Dh	1.25S	149.38 E
Musselkanaal, Stadskanaal-	12	Jb	52.56N	7.02 E
Musselshell River ∿	43	Fb	47.21N	107.58W
Mussende	36	Ce	10.31S	16.02 E
Mussidan	11	Gi	45.02N	0.22 E
Mussòmeli	14	Hm	37.35N	13.45 E
Must	27	Fb	46.40N	92.40 E
Muşţafá, Ra's- ▶	14	Fn	36.50N	11.07 E
Mustafakemalpaşa	24	Cb	40.02N	28.24 E
Mustahil	35	Gd	5.15N	44.44 E
Mustāng	25	Gc	29.11N	83.58 E
Mustang Draw ∿	45	Fj	32.00N	101.40W
Mustang Island ◆	45	Hm	28.00N	96.55W
Mustasaari/Korsholm	8	Ia	63.05N	21.43 E
Musters, Lago- ⬭	56	Gg	45.27S	69.13W
Mustique Island ◆	50	Ff	12.39N	61.15W
Mustjala	8	Jf	58.25N	22.04 E
Mustla	7	Fg	58.14N	25.52 E
Mustvee	7	Gg	58.52N	26.59 E
Musu-dan ▶	28	Jd	40.50N	129.43 E
Muswellbrook	59	Kf	32.16S	150.53 E
Muszyna	10	Qg	49.21N	20.54 E
Mut	24	Ed	36.39N	33.27 E
Mūţ	33	Ed	25.29N	28.59 E
Mūtaf, Ra's al- ▶	23	Hd	27.41N	51.27 E
Mutalau	64k	Ba	18.56S	169.50W
Mutarara	31	Kj	17.27S	35.04 E
Mutatá	54	Cb	7.16N	76.32W
Mutawassiţ, Al Baḩr al-=Mediterranean Sea (EN) ≈	5	Hh	35.00N	20.00 E
Mutha	36	Gc	1.48S	38.26 E
Muting	26	Lh	7.23S	140.20 E
Mutis, Gunung- ▲	26	Hh	9.34S	124.14 E
Mutoraj	20	Fd	61.20N	100.20 E
Mutsamudu	31	Lj	12.09S	44.25 E
Mutshatsha	36	De	10.39S	24.27 E
Mutsu	27	Pc	41.05N	140.55 E
Mutsu-Wan ◐	28	Pd	41.10N	140.55 E
Muttaburra	59	Id	22.36S	144.33 E
Mutterstadt	12	Ke	49.27N	8.21 E
Mutton/Oiléan Coarach ◆	9	Di	52.49N	9.31W
Mutton Bird Islands ❖	62	Bg	47.15S	167.25 E
Mutuali	37	Fb	14.53S	37.00 E
Mutún	55	Dd	19.10S	57.54W
Mutunópolis	55	Ha	13.40S	49.15W
Mutusjärvi ⬭	7	Gb	69.31N	26.57 E
Muurame	8	Kb	62.08N	25.40 E
Mu Us Shamo=Ordos Desert (EN) ∴	21	Mf	38.45N	109.10 E
Muxima	36	Bd	9.32S	13.57 E
Muyinga	36	Fc	2.51S	30.20 E
Muy Muy	49	Eg	12.46N	85.38W
Muzaffarābād	25	Eb	34.22N	73.28 E
Muzaffargarh	25	Eb	30.04N	71.12 E
Muzaffarnagar	25	Fc	29.28N	77.41 E
Muzaffarpur	25	Hc	26.07N	85.24 E
Muzambinho	55	Ie	21.22S	46.32W
Muzat He ∿	27	Dc	41.15N	83.27 E
Muži	20	Bc	65.27N	64.40 E
Muzillac	11	Dg	47.33N	2.29W
Mužlja	15	Dd	45.21N	20.25 E
Muztag [China] ▲	21	Kf	35.55N	80.20 E
Muztag [China] ▲	21	Kf	36.25N	87.25 E
Muztagata ▲	27	Cd	38.17N	75.07 E
Mvolo	35	Dd	6.03N	29.56 E
Mvomero	36	Gd	6.20S	37.25 E
Mvoung ∿	36	Bb	0.04N	12.18 E
Mwadingusha	36	Ee	10.45S	27.15 E
Mwali/Mohéli ◆	30	Lj	12.15S	43.45 E
Mwanza [3]	36	Fc	2.30S	32.30 E
Mwanza [Mwi.]	36	Ff	15.37S	34.31 E
Mwanza [Tan.]	31	Ki	2.31S	32.54 E
Mwanza [Zaire]	36	Ed	7.54S	26.45 E
Mwatate	36	Gc	3.30S	38.23 E
Mweelrea ▲	9	Dh	53.38N	9.50W
Mweka	31	Ji	4.51S	21.34 E
Mwene Ditu	31	Ji	7.03S	23.27 E
Mwenga	36	Ec	3.02S	28.26 E
Mweru, Lake- ⬭	30	Ji	9.00S	28.45 E
Mweru Wantipa, Lake- ⬭	36	Ed	8.42S	29.46 E
Mwimbi	36	Fd	8.39S	31.40 E
Mwinilunga	36	De	11.44S	24.26 E
Mya ∿	30	He	31.40N	5.15 E
Myaing	25	Id	21.37N	94.51 E
Myanaung	25	Je	18.17N	95.19 E
Myanma-Nainggan-Daw → Burma [1]	22	Lg	22.00N	98.00 E
Myaungmya	25	Ie	16.36N	94.56 E
Mycenae (EN) = Mikínai ⁖	15	Fl	37.43N	22.45 E
Myebon	25	Id	20.03N	93.22 E
Myingyan	22	Lg	21.28N	95.23 E
Myinmoletkat Taung ▲	25	Jf	13.28N	98.48 E
Myitta	25	Jf	14.10N	98.31 E
Myjava ∿	10	Mh	48.33N	16.58 E
Myjzakjula/Mõisaküla	7	Fg	58.07N	25.10 E
Mykulkin, Mys- ▶	17	Cc	67.48N	46.40 E
Mylius Erichsens Land ⊠	41	Jb	81.40N	24.00W
Myltkyinā	22	Lg	25.23N	97.24 E
Mymensingh	25	Id	24.45N	90.24 E
Mynämäki	7	Ef	60.40N	22.00 E
Mynaral	19	Hf	45.22N	73.39 E
Myōkō-Zan ▲	29	Fc	36.52N	138.06 E
Mýrdalsjökull ❄	7a	Bc	63.40N	19.06W
Myre	7	Db	68.51N	15.05 E
Myrskylä/Mörskom	8	Kd	60.40N	25.51 E
Myrtle Beach	43	Le	33.42N	78.54W
Myrtle Point	46	Ce	43.04N	124.08W
Mysen	7	Cg	59.33N	11.20 E
Mysia ▣	15	Kj	39.30N	28.00 E
Myśla ∿	10	Kd	52.40N	14.29 E
Myślenice	10	Pg	49.51N	19.56 E
Myślibórz	10	Kd	52.55N	14.52 E
Mysore	22	Jh	12.18N	76.39 E
Mysore → Karnataka [3]	25	Ff	13.30N	76.00 E
Mys Saryč ▶	16	Hg	44.23N	33.45 E
Myszków	10	Pf	50.36N	19.20 E
Myszyniec	10	Rc	53.24N	21.21 E
My Tho	22	Mh	10.21N	106.21 E
Mytišči	7	Ii	55.56N	37.46 E
Mývatn ⬭	7a	Cb	65.36N	17.00W

Index Symbols

[1] Independent Nation
[2] State, Region
[3] District, County
[4] Municipality
[5] Colony, Dependency
■ Continent
⊠ Physical Region
▣ Historical or Cultural Region
▲ Mount, Mountain
Δ Volcano
△ Hill
⛰ Mountains, Mountain Range
◭ Hills, Escarpment
▰ Plateau, Upland
⌵ Pass, Gap
▭ Plain, Lowland
◣ Delta
⊟ Salt Flat
∨ Valley, Canyon
◡ Crater, Cave
⌘ Karst Features
⌣ Depression
⊔ Polder
∴ Desert, Dunes
♣ Forest, Woods
⩫ Heath, Steppe
☘ Oasis
▶ Cape, Point
⌇ Coast, Beach
◧ Cliff
⊏ Peninsula
⋈ Isthmus
⋯ Sandbank
◆ Island
◎ Atoll
✱ Rock, Reef
❖ Islands, Archipelago
✲ Rocks, Reefs
✺ Coral Reef
⊙ Well, Spring
⇡ Geyser
∿ River, Stream
⤓ Waterfall Rapids
⋖ River Mouth, Estuary
⬭ Lake
⬬ Salt Lake
◌ Intermittent Lake
⊜ Reservoir
⩸ Swamp, Pond
═ Canal
❄ Glacier
❅ Ice Shelf, Pack Ice
≋ Ocean
≈ Sea
◐ Gulf, Bay
⇌ Strait, Fjord
◍ Lagoon
⊞ Bank
⋏ Seamount
⊓ Tablemount
⋀ Ridge
⌐ Shelf
⊍ Basin
⌟ Escarpment, Sea Scarp
⚡ Fracture
⋎ Trench, Abyss
⚑ National Park, Reserve
★ Point of Interest
⚐ Recreation Site
◚ Cave, Cavern
♜ Historic Site
⁖ Ruins
▥ Wall, Walls
✝ Church, Abbey
⛩ Temple
⚗ Scientific Station
✈ Airport
⚓ Port
☼ Lighthouse
⚒ Mine
∩ Tunnel
⫽ Dam, Bridge

Myzeqeja 15 Ci 41.01N 19.36 E
M'Zab 32 Hc 32.35N 3.20 E
Mže 10 Jg 49.46N 13.24 E
Mziha 36 Gd 5.54S 37.47 E
Mzimba 36 Fe 11.54S 33.36 E
Mzuzu 31 Kj 11.27S 33.55 E

N

Naab 10 Ig 49.01N 12.02 E
Naaldwijk 12 Gc 51.59N 4.12 E
Naalehu 65a Fd 19.04N 155.35W
Naantali/Nådendal 7 Ff 60.27N 22.02 E
Naarden 12 Hb 52.18N 5.10 E
Naas/An Nás 9 Gh 53.13N 6.39W
Nabadid 35 Gd 9.38N 43.29 E
Nabão 13 De 39.31N 8.21W
Nabari 29 Ed 34.37N 136.05 E
Naberera 36 Gc 4.12S 36.56 E
Naberežnyje Čelny 6 Ld 55.42N 52.19 E
Nābha 25 Fb 30.22N 76.09 E
Nabileque, Rio- 55 De 20.55S 57.49W
Nabire 58 Ee 3.22S 135.29 E
Nabī Shu'ayb, Jabal an- 21 Gh 15.17N 43.59 E
Nabq 24 Fh 28.04N 34.25 E
Nābul 31 Ie 36.27N 10.44 E
Nābul 32 Jb 36.45N 10.45 E
Nābulus 24 Ff 32.13N 35.16 E
Nabusanke 36 Fb 0.01N 32.03 E
Nacala 37 Gb 14.33S 40.40 E
Nacala-a-Velha 31 Lj 14.33S 40.36 E
Nacaome 49 Dg 13.31N 87.30W
Nacaroa 37 Fb 14.23S 39.55 E
Nacereddine 13 Ph 36.08N 3.26 E
Nachikatsuura 29 De 33.39N 135.55 E
Nachingwea 36 Ge 10.23S 38.46 E
Nachi-San 29 De 33.42N 135.51 E
Náchod 10 Mf 50.26N 16.10 E
Nachuge 25 If 10.35N 92.28 E
Nachvak Fiord 42 Le 59.03N 63.45W
Nacka 7 Ee 59.18N 18.10 E
Ná Clocha Liatha/ Greystones 9 Gh 53.09N 6.04W
Nacogdoches 45 Ik 31.36N 94.39W
Na Comaraigh/Comeragh Mountains 9 Fi 52.13N 7.35W
Nacori, Sierra- 48 Ec 29.50N 108.50W
Nacozari, Rio- 48 Ec 29.48N 109.42W
Nacozari de Garcia 47 Cb 30.24N 109.39W
Na Cruacha/Blue Stack 9 Eg 54.45N 8.06W
Na Cruacha Dubha/ Macgillycuddy's Reeks 9 Di 52.00N 9.50W
Nacunday, Rio- 55 Eh 26.03S 54.45W
Nada → Danxian 27 Ih 19.38N 109.32 E
Nådendal/Naantali 7 Ff 60.27N 22.02 E
Nadiād 25 Ed 22.42N 72.52 E
Nădlac 15 Dc 46.10N 20.45 E
Nador 32 Gb 35.00N 3.00W
Nador 32 Gb 35.11N 2.56W
Nădusa 15 Fi 40.38N 22.04 E
Nadvoicy 19 Dc 63.52N 34.20 E
Nadvornaja 16 De 48.38N 24.34 E
Nadym 22 Jc 65.35N 72.42 E
Naeba-San 29 Fc 36.51N 138.41 E
Nærbø 8 Af 58.40N 5.39 E
Næstved 7 Ci 55.14N 11.46 E
Nafada 34 Hc 11.06N 11.20 E
Näfels 14 Dc 47.06N 9.04 E
Naftah 14 Dn 36.57N 9.04 E
Naftan Rock 64b Bb 14.50N 145.32 E
Naft-e-Safid 24 Mg 31.40N 49.17 E
Naft-e-Shāh 24 Kf 33.59N 45.30 E
Naft Khāneh 24 Ke 34.02N 45.28 E
Nafūsah, Jabal- 30 Ie 31.50N 12.00 E
Nāg 25 Dc 27.24N 65.08 E
Naga 22 Oh 13.28N 123.39 E
Nāga, Kreb en- 32 Fe 24.00N 6.00W
Nagagami Lake 44 Ea 49.28N 85.02W
Nagagami River 45 Na 50.25N 84.20W
Nagahama [Jap.] 29 Ed 35.23N 136.16 E
Nagahama [Jap.] 29 Ce 33.36N 132.29 E
Nagai 29 Gb 38.06N 140.02 E
Nagai 40 Ge 55.11N 159.55W
Na Gaibhlte/Galty Mountains 9 Ei 52.23N 8.11W
Nāgāland 25 Ic 26.30N 94.00 E
Nagano 22 Pf 36.39N 138.11 E
Nagano Ken 28 Nf 36.10N 138.00 E
Nagano-Matsushiro 29 Fc 36.34N 138.10 E
Nagano-Shinonoi 29 Fc 36.35N 138.06 E
Nagaoka 27 Od 37.27N 138.51 E
Nāgappattinam 25 Ff 10.46N 79.50 E
Nagara-Gawa 29 Ed 35.02N 136.43 E
Nagarote 49 Dg 12.16N 86.34W
Nagarzê 27 Ff 28.59N 90.28 E
Nagasaki 22 Of 32.47N 129.56 E
Nagasaki-Hantō 29 Ae 32.40N 129.45 E
Nagasaki Ken 28 Jh 33.00N 129.50 E
Naga-Shima 29 Ce 33.50N 132.05 E
Nagashima 29 Ed 34.12N 136.19 E
Nagashima 29 Be 32.10N 130.10 E
Naga-Shima-Kaikyō 29 Be 32.15N 130.10 E
Nagato 28 Kg 34.21N 131.10 E
Nagayo 29 Ae 32.50N 129.52 E
Nāgda 25 Fd 23.27N 75.25 E
Nāgercoil 25 Fg 8.10N 77.26 E
Naghora Point 60 Gj 10.50S 162.24 E
Nagichot 35 Ee 4.16N 33.34 E
Nagi-San 29 Dd 35.10N 134.10 E
Nagiso 29 Ed 35.36N 137.36 E
Nago 27 Mf 26.35N 128.01 E
Nagold 10 Eh 48.52N 8.42 E
Nagorno-Karabahskaja Avtonomnaja Oblast 19 Eh 39.55N 46.45 E
Nagorny [R.S.F.S.R.] 20 He 55.45N 124.58 E
Nagorny [R.S.F.S.R.] 20 Md 63.10N 179.05 E
Nagorsk 7 Mg 59.21N 50.48 E
Nago-Wan 29b Ab 26.35N 127.55 E
Nagoya 22 Pf 35.10N 136.55 E
Nāgpur 22 Jg 21.09N 79.06 E
Nagqu 22 Lf 31.30N 92.00 E
Nag's Head 51c Ab 17.13N 62.38W
Nagua 49 Md 19.23N 69.50W
Naguabo 51a Cb 18.13N 65.44W
Nagyatád 10 Nj 46.13N 17.22 E
Nagybajom 10 Mj 46.23N 16.31 E
Nagyecsed 10 Si 47.52N 22.24 E
Nagyhalász 10 Rh 48.08N 21.46 E
Nagykálló 10 Ri 47.53N 21.51 E
Nagykanizsa 10 Mj 46.27N 16.59 E
Nagykáta 10 Pi 47.25N 19.45 E
Nagykőrös 10 Pi 47.02N 19.47 E
Nagykunság 10 Qj 46.55N 20.15 E
Nagy-Milic 10 Rh 48.35N 21.28 E
Naha 22 Og 26.13N 127.40 E
Nahanni Butte 42 Fd 61.04N 123.24W
Nahari 29 De 33.25N 134.01 E
Naharyya 24 Ff 33.00N 35.05 E
Nahāvand 23 Gc 34.12N 48.22 E
Nahe 10 Dg 49.58N 7.57 E
Nahičevan 6 Kh 39.13N 45.27 E
Nahičevanskaja ASSR 19 Eh 39.15N 45.35 E
Na'hīmābād 24 Qg 30.51N 56.31 E
Nahodka 22 Pe 42.48N 132.52 E
Nahr al 'Āsī=Orontes (EN) 23 Eb 36.02N 35.58 E
Nahr Quassel 13 Oi 35.45N 2.46 E
Nahuala, Laguna- 48 Ji 16.50N 99.40W
Nahuel Huapi, Lago- 56 Ff 40.58S 71.30W
Nahunta 44 Gj 31.12N 81.59W
Naie 29a Bb 43.24N 141.52 E
Naiguatá, Pico- 54 Ea 10.33N 66.46W
Naila 10 Hf 50.19N 11.42 E
Naiman Qi (Daqin Tal) 27 Lc 42.49N 120.38 E
Nain 39 Md 57.00N 61.40W
Nā'īn 24 Of 32.52N 53.05 E
Na'ināb̄ād 24 Pd 36.14N 54.39 E
Nairai 63d Bb 17.49S 179.24 E
Nairn 9 Jd 57.35N 3.53W
Nairobi 31 Ki 1.17S 36.49 E
Nairobi 36 Gc 1.17S 36.50 E
Naissaar/Najssar 8 Ke 59.35N 24.25 E
Naitamba 63d Cb 17.01S 179.17W
Naizishan 28 Ic 43.41N 127.27 E
Najafābād 23 Hc 32.37N 51.21 E
Najd 23 Fe 25.00N 44.30 E
Najd 21 Gg 25.00N 44.30 E
Nājera 13 Jb 42.25N 2.44W
Najerilla 13 Jb 42.31N 2.42W
Naj' Ḩammādī 33 Fd 26.03N 32.15 E
Najibābād 25 Fc 29.58N 78.10 E
Najin 27 Nc 42.15N 130.18 E
Najō 29 Ec 35.47N 136.12 E
Najrān 33 Hf 17.30N 44.10 E
Najrān 33 Hf 17.30N 44.10 E
Najssar/Naissaar 8 Ke 59.35N 24.25 E
Najstenjarvi 7 He 62.18N 32.42 E
Naju 28 Ig 35.02N 126.43 E
Najzataš, Pereval- 18 If 37.52N 73.46 E
Nakadōri-Jima 28 Jh 32.58N 129.05 E
Nakagawa 29a Ca 44.47N 142.05 E
Naka-Gawa [Jap.] 29 Gc 36.20N 140.36 E
Naka-Gawa [Jap.] 29 De 33.56N 134.42 E
Nakagusuku-Wan 29b Ab 26.15N 127.50 E
Nakahechi 29 De 33.47N 135.29 E
Naka-Iō-Jima 60 Cc 24.47N 141.20 E
Naka-Jima 29 Ce 33.58N 132.37 E
Nakajō 28 Oe 38.03N 139.24 E
Naka-Koshiki-Jima 29 Af 31.48N 129.50 E
Nakalele Point 65a Eb 21.02N 156.35W
Nakama 29 Be 33.50N 130.43 E
Nakaminato 29 Gc 36.22N 140.36 E
Nakamura 28 Lh 32.59N 132.56 E
Nakanai Mountains 59 Ka 5.35S 151.10 E
Nakano 29 Fc 36.45N 138.22 E
Naka-no-Dake 29 Fc 37.04N 139.06 E
Nakanojō 29 Fc 36.35N 138.51 E
Naka-no-Shima 28 Lf 36.05N 133.04 E
Naka-no- Shima 27 Mf 29.50N 129.50 E
Nakasato 29a Bc 40.58N 140.26 E
Naka-satsunai 29a Cb 42.42N 143.08 E
Nakashibetsu 28 Rc 43.36N 145.00 E
Nakasongola 36 Fb 1.19N 32.28 E
Nakatonbetsu 29a Ca 44.58N 142.17 E
Nakatsu 28 Kh 33.34N 131.13 E
Nakatsugawa 28 Ng 35.29N 137.30 E
Nakfa 35 Fb 16.40N 38.30 E
Nakhon Pathom 25 Kf 13.49N 100.06 E
Nakhon Phanom 25 Mh 17.22N 104.46 E
Nakhon Ratchasima 22 Mh 14.57N 102.09 E
Nakhon Sawan 22 Mh 15.42N 100.06 E
Nakhon Si Thammarat 22 Li 8.26N 99.58 E
Nakijin 29b Ab 26.42N 127.59 E
Nakina 39 Kd 50.10N 86.42W
Nakkila 8 Ic 61.22N 22.00 E
Nakło nad Notecia 10 Nc 53.08N 17.35 E
Naknek 40 He 58.44N 157.02W
Nakonde 36 Fd 9.19S 32.46 E
Nakskov 7 Ci 54.50N 11.09 E
Näkten 8 Fb 62.50N 14.40 E
Naktong-gang 28 Jg 35.07N 128.57 E
Nakuru 31 Ki 0.20S 35.56 E
Nakusp 46 Ga 50.15N 117.48W
Nāl 25 Dc 26.02N 65.29 E
Nalajch → Nalajha 27 Ib 47.45N 107.16 E
Nalajha (Nalajch) 27 Ib 47.45N 107.16 E
Nalčik 6 Kg 43.29N 43.37 E
Nallıhan 24 Db 40.11N 31.21 E
Nālōn 13 Fa 43.32N 6.04W
Nālūt 31 Ie 31.52N 10.59 E
Nalwasha 36 Gc 0.43S 36.26 E
Na Machairi/Brandon Head 9 Ci 52.16N 10.15W
Namacurra 37 Fc 17.29S 37.01 E
Namai Bay 64a Bb 7.32N 134.39 E
Namak, Daryācheh-ye-= Namak Lake (EN) 21 Hf 34.45N 51.36 E
Namak Lake (EN)= Namak, Daryācheh-ye- 21 Hf 34.45N 51.36 E
Namakan Lake 45 Jb 48.27N 92.35W
Namak-e Mighān, Kavīr-e- 24 Me 34.13N 49.49 E
Namakia 37 Hc 15.56S 45.48 E
Namakwaland=Little Namamland (EN) 37 Be 29.00S 17.00 E
Namanga 36 Gc 2.33S 36.47 E
Namangan 22 Je 41.00N 71.40 E
Namanganskaja Oblast 19 Hg 41.00N 71.20 E
Namanyere 36 Fd 7.31S 31.03 E
Namapa 37 Fb 13.43S 39.50 E
Namaqua Seamount (EN) 37 Af 31.30S 11.20 E
Namarrói 37 Fc 15.57S 36.51 E
Namasagali 36 Fb 1.01N 32.57 E
Namasale 36 Fb 1.30N 32.37 E
Namatanai 60 Eh 3.40S 152.27 E
Namathu 63d Bb 17.21S 179.26 E
Nambavatu 63d Bb 16.36S 178.55 E
Namber 26 Jg 1.04S 134.49 E
Nambour 59 Ke 26.38S 152.58 E
Nambouwalu 61 Ec 16.59S 178.42 E
Nam Can 25 Kg 8.46N 104.59 E
Namche Bazar 25 Hc 27.49N 86.43 E
Nam Co 21 Lf 30.45N 90.35 E
Namčy 20 Hd 62.35N 129.40 E
Namdalen 7 Cd 64.38N 12.35 E
Nam Dinh 22 Mg 20.25N 106.10 E
Nāmdö 8 He 59.10N 18.40 E
Nam Du, Quan Dao- 25 Kg 9.42N 104.22 E
Naméche, Andenne- 12 Hd 50.28N 5.00 E
Namelaki Passage 64a Bc 7.24N 134.38 E
Namen/Namur 11 Kd 50.28N 4.52 E
Namerikawa 29 Ec 36.45N 137.20 E
Náměšt nad Oslavou 10 Mg 49.12N 16.09 E
Nametil 37 Fc 15.43S 39.21 E
Namib Desert/ Namibwoestyn 30 Ik 23.00S 15.00 E
Namibia (South West Africa) 31 Ik 22.00S 17.00 E
Namibwoestyn/Namib Desert 30 Ik 23.00S 15.00 E
Namie 28 Pf 37.29N 140.59 E
Namīn 24 Mc 38.25N 48.30 E
Namioka 29 Ga 40.42N 140.35 E
Namiquipa 48 Fc 29.15N 107.40W
Namiranga 37 Gb 10.33S 40.30 E
Namjagbarwa Feng 22 Lg 29.38N 95.04 E
Namja La 27 Df 29.58N 82.34 E
Namkham 25 Jd 23.50N 97.41 E
Namlea 26 Ig 3.18S 127.06 E
Namling 27 Ef 29.44N 89.05 E
Namnoi, Khao- 25 Jf 10.36N 98.38 E
Namoi River 59 Je 30.00S 148.07 E
Namoluk Island 57 Gd 5.55N 153.08 E
Namonuito Atoll 57 Gd 8.46N 150.02 E
Namorik Atoll 57 Hd 5.36N 168.07 E
Namous 32 Gc 30.28N 0.14W
Nampa 43 Dc 43.34N 116.34W
Nampala 34 Db 15.17N 5.33W
Nam Phan=Cochin China (EN) 21 Mg 11.00N 107.00 E
Nam Phong 25 Ke 16.45N 102.52 E
Nampi 28 De 38.02N 116.42 E
Namp'o 27 Md 38.44N 125.25 E
Nampula 37 Fb 15.00S 39.30 E
Nampula 31 Kj 15.07S 39.15 E
Namsê Shankou 27 Df 29.58N 82.34 E
Namsos 6 Hc 64.30N 11.30 E
Namtu 25 Jd 23.05N 97.24 E
Namu 46 Ba 51.49N 127.52W
Namu Atoll 57 Hd 8.00N 168.10 E
Namuka-I-Lau 63d Cc 18.51S 178.38W
Namúli, Serra- 31 Kj 15.21S 37.00 E
Namuno 37 Fb 13.37S 38.48 E
Namur 12 Gd 50.20N 4.50 E
Namur/Namen 11 Kd 50.28N 4.52 E
Namur-Saint Servais 12 Gd 50.28N 4.50 E
Namuruputh 36 Gb 4.34N 35.57 E
Namur-Wépion 12 Gd 50.25N 4.52 E
Namutoni 37 Bc 18.30S 17.55 E
Namwala 36 Ef 15.45S 26.26 E
Namwŏn 28 Ig 35.24N 127.23 E
Namysłów 10 Ne 51.05N 17.42 E
Nan 21 Mh 15.42N 100.09 E
Nan 25 Ke 18.48N 100.46 E
Nana 35 Bd 5.00N 15.50 E
Nana Barya 35 Bd 7.59N 17.43 E
Nanae 29a Bc 41.53N 140.41 E
Nanaimo 42 Fg 49.10N 123.56W
Nanakuli 65a Cb 21.23N 158.08W
Nana-Mambéré 35 Bd 6.00N 16.00 E
Nanango 59 Ke 26.40S 152.00 E
Nanao 27 Od 37.03N 136.58 E
Nanao-Wan 29 Ec 37.10N 137.00 E
Nanatsu-Shima 29 Ec 37.35N 136.50 E
Nancha 27 Mb 47.08N 129.09 E
Nanchang 22 Ng 28.40N 115.58 E
Nancheng 27 Kf 27.32N 116.36 E
Nanchong 22 Mf 30.47N 106.03 E
Nancowry 25 Ig 7.59N 93.32 E
Nancy 6 Gf 48.41N 6.12 E
Nanda Devi 21 Jf 30.23N 79.59 E
Nandaime 49 Dh 11.46N 86.03W
Nandan [China] 27 Ig 24.59N 107.31 E
Nandan [Jap.] 28 Mg 34.15N 134.43 E
Nandaran → Qingyuan 28 Ce 38.46N 115.29 E
Nander 22 Jh 19.09N 77.20 E
Nandewar Range 59 Kf 30.40S 151.10 E
Nandi 61 Ec 17.48S 177.25 E
Nandu Jiang 27 Jg 20.04N 110.22 E
Nanduri 63d Bb 16.27S 179.09 E
Nandyāl 25 Fe 15.29N 78.29 E
Nanfen 28 Gd 41.06N 123.45 E
Nanfeng 27 Kf 27.15N 116.30 E
Nanga-Eboko 34 He 4.41N 12.22 E
Nanga Parbat 21 Jf 35.15N 74.36 E
Nangapinoh 26 Fg 0.20S 111.44 E
Nangarhār 23 Lc 34.15N 70.30 E
Nangatayap 26 Fg 1.32S 110.34 E
Nangis 11 If 48.33N 3.00 E
Nangnim-san 28 Id 40.21N 126.55 E
Nangnim-Sanmaek 28 Id 40.30N 127.00 E
Nangong 27 Kd 37.22N 115.23 E
Nangqên 27 Ge 32.15N 96.13 E
Nanguan 28 Af 36.42N 111.41 E
Nanguantao → Guantao 28 Cf 36.33N 115.18 E
Nangweshi 36 Df 16.26S 23.20 E
Nan Hai=South China Sea (EN) 21 Ni 10.00N 113.00 E
Nanhaoqian → Shangyi 28 Bd 41.06N 113.58 E
Nanhe 28 Cf 36.58N 114.41 E
Nanhua 27 Hf 25.16N 101.18 E
Nanhui 28 Fi 31.03N 121.46 E
Nan Hulsan Hu 27 Gd 36.45N 95.45 E
Nanjian 27 Hf 25.05N 100.32 E
Nanjiang 27 Ie 32.22N 106.45 E
Nanjing=Nanking (EN) 22 Nf 31.59N 118.51 E
Nankai Trough (EN) 27 Ne 32.00N 135.00 E
Nanking (EN)=Nanjing 22 Nf 31.59N 118.51 E
Nankoku 28 Lh 33.39N 133.44 E
Nanle 28 Cf 36.06N 115.12 E
Nanling 28 Ei 30.55N 118.19 E
Nan Ling 21 Ng 25.00N 112.00 E
Nanlou Shan 28 Ic 43.24N 126.40 E
Nanma → Yiyuan 28 Ef 36.11N 118.10 E
Nanning 22 Mg 22.50N 108.18 E
Nannup 59 Df 33.59S 115.45 E
Nanortalik 41 Hf 60.32N 45.45W
Nanpan Jiang 27 Ig 24.56N 106.12 E
Nānpāra 25 Gc 27.52N 81.30 E
Nanping [China] 22 Ng 26.42N 118.09 E
Nanping [China] 27 He 33.15N 104.13 E
Nanpu 28 Ee 39.16N 118.12 E
Nanqiao → Fengxian 28 Fi 30.55N 121.27 E
Nansei-Shotō=Ryukyu Islands (EN) 21 Og 26.30N 128.00 E
Nansen Cordillera (EN) 67 Ge 87.00N 90.00 E
Nansen Land 41 Hb 83.20N 46.00W
Nanshan Islands (EN)= Nansha Qundao 21 Ni 9.40N 113.30 E
Nansha Qundao= Nanshan Islands (EN) 21 Ni 9.40N 113.30E
Nansio 36 Fc 2.08S 33.03 E
Nant 11 Jj 44.01N 3.18 E
Nantais, Lac - 42 Kd 61.00N 73.50W
Nanterre 11 If 48.54N 2.12 E
Nantes 6 Ff 47.13N 1.33W
Nantes à Brest, Can. de- 11 Bf 48.12N 4.06W
Nanteuil-le-Haudouin 12 Ee 49.08N 2.48 E
Nanticoke 44 Je 41.13N 76.00W
Nantō 29 Ed 34.17N 136.29 E
Nantong 27 Le 32.00N 120.52 E
Nantong (Jinsha) 28 Fh 32.06N 120.52 E
Nantou 27 Lg 23.54N 120.51 E
Nantua 11 Lh 46.09N 5.37 E
Nantucket 44 Le 41.17N 70.06W
Nantucket Island 43 Mc 41.16N 70.03W
Nantucket Sound 44 Le 41.30N 70.15W
Nanuku Passage 63d Cb 16.45S 179.15W
Nanuku Reef 63d Cb 16.40S 179.26W
Nanumanga Island 57 Ie 6.18S 176.20 E
Nanumea Atoll 57 Ie 5.43S 176.00 E
Nanuque 54 Jg 17.50S 40.21W
Nanusa, Pulau-Pulau- 26 If 4.42N 127.06 E
Nanwan Shuiku 28 Bh 32.02N 113.57 E
Nanwei Dao 27 Je 8.42N 111.40 E
Nanweng He 27 Ma 51.10N 125.59 E
Nanxian 28 Bj 29.22N 112.25 E
Nanxiang 28 Fi 31.18N 121.17 E
Nanxiong 27 Jf 25.13N 114.18 E
Nanxun 28 Fi 30.53N 120.26 E
Nanyandang Shan 27 Lf 27.37N 120.06 E
Nanyang 22 Nf 32.56N 112.32 E
Nanyang Hu 28 Dg 35.15N 116.39 E
Nanyō 28 Pe 38.03N 140.10 E
Nanyuki 31 Kh 0.01N 37.04 E
Nanzhang 27 Je 31.45N 111.53 E
Nanzhao 27 Je 33.28N 112.29 E
Nao, Cabo de la- 5 Gh 38.44N 0.14 E
Naococane, Lac- 42 Kf 52.50N 70.40W
Naoero/Nauru 58 He 0.31S 166.56 E
Naoetsu 29 Fc 37.11N 138.14 E
Não-me-Toque 55 Fi 28.28S 52.49W
Naours, Souterrains de- 12 Ed 50.05N 2.17 E
Napa 46 Dg 38.18N 122.17W
Napanee 44 Ic 44.15N 76.57W
Napassoq 41 Ge 65.45N 52.38W
Napata 35 Eb 18.29N 31.51 E
Na-Peng 25 Lg 23.10N 98.26 E
Napf 14 Bc 47.01N 7.57 E
Napier 58 Ih 39.30S 176.54 E
Napier, Mount- 59 Fc 17.32S 129.10 E
Napier Mountains 66 Ee 66.30S 53.40 E
Naples [Fl.-U.S.] 43 Kf 26.08N 81.48W
Naples [Id.-U.S.] 46 Gb 48.34N 116.24W
Naples (EN) = Napoli 6 Hg 40.50N 14.15 E
Naples, Gulf of- (EN) = Napoli, Golfo di- 14 Ij 40.45N 14.10 E
Napo 27 Ig 23.25N 105.49 E
Napo, Rio- 52 If 3.20S 72.40W
Napoleon 45 Gc 46.30N 99.46W
Napoli = Naples (EN) 6 Hg 40.50N 14.15 E
Napoli, Golfo di- = Naples, Gulf of- (EN) 14 Ij 40.45N 14.10 E
Napostá 55 An 38.26S 62.15W
Napuka, Ile- 57 Mf 14.12S 141.15W
Naqa 35 Eb 16.16N 33.17 E
Naqadeh 23 Gb 36.57N 45.23 E
Naqsh-e-Rostam 24 Og 30.01N 52.50 E
Nar 9 Ni 52.45N 0.24 E
Nāra 25 Dc 24.07N 69.07 E
Nara [Jap.] 27 Oe 34.41N 135.50 E
Nara [Mali] 34 Db 15.11N 7.15W
Naračenskibani 15 Hh 41.54N 24.45 E
Naracoorte 59 Ig 36.58S 140.44 E
Nara-Ken 28 Mg 34.20N 135.55 E
Naranjo 48 Ee 25.48N 108.31W
Naranjos [Bol.] 55 Cd 18.38S 59.09W
Naranjos [Mex.] 48 Kg 21.21N 97.41W
Narao 29 Ae 32.52N 129.04 E
Narathiwat 25 Kg 6.25N 101.48 E
Nārāyanganj 25 Id 23.37N 90.30 E
Narbonne 11 Ik 43.11N 3.00 E
Narca, Ponta da- 36 Bd 6.07S 12.16 E
Narcea 13 Fa 43.28N 6.06W
Narcondam 25 If 13.15N 94.30 E
Nardò 14 Mj 40.11N 18.02 E
Naré 55 Bj 30.58S 60.28W
Nares Land 41 Hb 82.25N 47.30W
Nares Strait 38 Lb 78.50N 73.00W
Narew 10 Td 52.55N 23.29 E
Narew 10 Qd 52.26N 20.42 E
Narian, Pointe- 63b Be 20.05S 164.00 E
Narin Gol 27 Fd 36.54N 92.51 E
Nariño 54 Cc 1.30N 78.00W
Narita 29 Gd 35.47N 140.18 E
Narjan-Mar 6 Lb 67.39N 53.00 E
Närke 8 Ff 59.05N 15.05 E
Narlı 24 Gd 37.27N 37.09 E
Narmada 21 Jg 21.38N 72.36 E
Narman 24 Ib 40.21N 41.52 E
Närnaul 25 Fc 28.03N 76.06 E
Narni 14 Gh 42.31N 12.31 E
Naroč 8 Lj 54.27N 26.45 E
Naroč 8 Lj 54.57N 26.49 E
Naroč, Ozero- 16 Eb 54.50N 26.45 E
Naroda 17 Jd 64.15N 61.00 E
Narodnaja, Gora- 5 Mb 65.04N 60.09 E
Naro-Fominsk 19 Dd 55.24N 36.43 E
Narok 36 Gc 1.05S 35.52 E
Narovlja 16 Fd 51.48N 29.31 E
Närpes/Närpio 8 Ib 62.28N 21.20 E
Närpio/Närpes 8 Ib 62.28N 21.20 E
Narrabri 59 Jf 30.19S 149.47 E
Narrandera 59 Jf 34.45S 146.33 E
Narrogin 59 Df 32.56S 117.10 E
Narromine 59 Jf 32.14S 148.15 E
Narrows, The- 51c Ab 17.12N 62.38W
Narryer, Mount- 59 De 26.30S 116.25 E
Narsimhapur 25 Fd 22.57N 79.12 E
Narssalik 41 Hf 61.42N 49.11W
Narssaq [Grld.] 41 Hf 61.00N 46.00W
Narssaq [Grld.] 41 Gf 64.00N 51.33W
Narssarssuaq 41 Hf 61.10N 45.15W
Narthákion 15 Fj 39.14N 22.22 E
Nartkala 16 Mh 43.32N 43.47 E
Narubis 37 Be 26.55S 18.35 E
Narugo 29 Gb 38.44N 140.43 E
Nāruja 15 Jd 45.50N 26.47 E
Naru-Shima 29 Ae 32.50N 128.56 E
Naruto 28 Mg 34.11N 134.37 E
Naruto-Kaikyō 29 Dd 34.15N 134.40 E
Narva 7 Gg 59.29N 28.02 E
Narva 6 Id 59.23N 28.11 E
Narva Jõesuu/Narva-Jyesuu 8 Me 59.21N 28.04 E
Narva-Jyesuu/Narva Jõesuu 8 Me 59.21N 28.04 E
Narva laht 7 Gg 59.30N 27.40 E
Narvik 6 Hb 68.26N 17.25 E
Narvski Zaliv 7 Gg 59.30N 27.40 E
Narvskoje Vodohranilišče 8 Me 59.10N 28.30 E
Narym 20 De 58.58N 81.40 E
Naryn 21 Je 40.54N 71.45 E
Naryn 22 Je 41.26N 75.59 E
Naryncol 19 Ig 42.43N 80.08 E
Narynskaja Oblast 19 Hg 41.20N 75.40 E
Nås 7 Df 60.27N 14.29 E
Na Sailtí/Saltee Islands 9 Gi 52.07N 6.36W
Näsåker 7 De 63.23N 16.54 E
Nasarawa 34 Gd 8.32N 7.43 E
Nāsāud 15 Hb 47.17N 24.24 E
Nasawa 63b Db 15.12S 168.06 E
Na Sceirí/Skerries 9 Gh 53.35N 6.07W
Nash Point 9 Jj 51.24N 3.27W
Nashtārud 24 Nd 36.45N 51.02 E
Nashua 44 Ld 42.44N 71.28W
Nashville [Ar.-U.S.] 45 Jj 33.57N 93.51W
Nashville [Ga.-U.S.] 44 Fj 31.12N 83.15W
Nashville [Il.-U.S.] 45 Lg 38.21N 89.23W
Nashville [In.-U.S.] 44 Df 39.12N 86.15W
Nashville [Tn.-U.S.] 39 Kf 36.09N 86.48W
Nashville Seamount (EN) 38 Nf 35.00N 57.20W
Našice 14 Me 45.30N 18.06 E
Nasielsk 10 Qd 52.36N 20.48 E
Näsijärvi 5 Ic 61.35N 23.40 E
Nāsik 22 Jg 20.05N 73.48 E
Nāşir 35 Ed 8.36N 33.04 E
Naskaupi 42 Lf 53.47N 60.51W
Nasorolevu 63d Bb 16.38S 179.24 E
Naşr [Eg.] 24 Dg 30.36N 30.23 E
Naşr [Lib.] 33 Dd 28.59N 21.13 E
Naşrābād 24 Of 32.09N 52.08 E
Nass 42 Ee 55.00N 129.50W
Nassandres 12 Ce 49.07N 0.44 E
Nassandres-La Rivière Thibouville 12 Ce 49.07N 0.44 E
Nassau [Bah.] 39 Lg 25.05N 77.21W
Nassau [F.R.G.] 12 Jd 50.19N 7.48 E
Nassau, Bahía- 56 Gi 55.25S 67.40W
Nassau Island 57 Kf 11.33S 165.25W
Nassau River 59 Ic 15.58S 141.30 E
Nasser, Birkat-=Nasser, Lake-(EN) 30 Kf 22.40N 32.00 E

Index Symbols

Independent Nation · State, Region · District, County · Municipality · Colony, Dependency · Continent · Physical Region · Historical or Cultural Region · Mount, Mountain · Volcano · Hill · Mountains, Mountain Range · Hills, Escarpment · Plateau, Upland · Pass, Gap · Plain, Lowland · Delta · Salt Flat · Valley, Canyon · Crater, Cave · Karst Features · Depression · Polder · Desert, Dunes · Forest, Woods · Heath, Steppe · Oasis · Cape, Point · Coast, Beach · Cliff · Peninsula · Isthmus · Sandbank · Island · Atoll · Rock, Reef · Islands, Archipelago · Rocks, Reefs · Coral Reef · Well, Spring · Geyser · River, Stream · Waterfall Rapids · River Mouth, Estuary · Lake · Salt Lake · Intermittent Lake · Reservoir · Swamp, Pond · Canal · Glacier · Ice Shelf, Pack Ice · Ocean · Sea · Gulf, Bay · Strait, Fjord · Lagoon · Bank · Seamount · Tablemount · Ridge · Shelf · Basin · Escarpment, Sea Scarp · Fracture · Trench, Abyss · National Park, Reserve · Point of Interest · Recreation Site · Cave, Cavern · Historic Site · Ruins · Wall, Walls · Church, Abbey · Temple · Scientific Station · Airport · Port · Lighthouse · Mine · Tunnel · Dam, Bridge

Nasser, Lake-(EN)=Nasser, Birkat- 30 Kf 22.40N 32.00 E
Nassian 34 Ed 9.24N 4.29W
Nässjö 7 Dh 57.39N 14.41 E
Nassogne 12 Hd 50.08N 5.21 E
Na Staighri Dubha/Blackstairs Mountains 9 Gi 52.33N 6.49W
Nastapoka Islands 42 Je 56.50N 76.50W
Nastätten 12 Jd 50.12N 7.52 E
Nastola 8 Kd 60.57N 25.56 E
Nasu 29 Gc 37.02N 140.06 E
Nasu-Dake 29 Fc 37.07N 139.58 E
Näsviken 8 Gc 61.45N 16.52 E
Natá 49 Gi 8.20N 80.31W
Nata 30 Jk 20.14S 26.10 E
Nata 37 Dd 20.13S 26.11 E
Natal [2] 37 Ee 29.00S 30.00 E
Natal [B.C.-Can.] 46 Hb 49.44N 114.50W
Natal [Braz.] 53 Mf 5.47S 35.13W
Natal [Indon.] 26 Cf 0.33N 99.07 E
Natal Basin (EN) 3 Fm 30.00S 40.00 E
Natanz 24 Nf 33.31N 51.54 E
Natashquan 42 Lf 50.09N 61.37W
Natashquan 42 Lf 50.11N 61.49W
Natchez 43 Ie 31.34N 91.23W
Natchitoches 43 Ie 31.46N 93.05W
Natewa Bay 63d Bb 16.35S 179.40 E
Nathorsts Land 41 Jd 72.20N 27.00W
Nathula 63d Ab 16.53S 177.25 E
Natitingou 31 Hg 10.19N 1.22 E
Natityāy, Jabal- 33 Fe 23.01N 34.22 E
Natividad, Isla- 48 Bd 27.55N 115.10W
Natividade 54 If 11.43S 47.47W
Natori 28 Pe 38.11N 140.58 E
Natron, Lake- 30 Ki 2.25S 36.00 E
Naţrūn, Wādī an- 24 Dg 30.25N 30.13 E
Natsudomari-Zaki 29a Bc 41.00N 140.53 E
Nättarö 8 Hf 58.50N 18.10 E
Nättraby 8 Fh 56.12N 15.31 E
Natuna Besar, Pulau- 26 Ef 4.00N 108.15 E
Natuna Islands (EN)=Bunguran, Kepulauan- 21 Mi 2.45N 109.00 E
Naturaliste, Cape- 57 Ch 33.32S 115.01 E
Naturaliste Channel 59 Ce 25.25S 113.00 E
Naturita 45 Bg 38.14N 108.34W
Naturno / Naturns 14 Ed 46.39N 11.00 E
Naturns / Naturno 14 Ed 46.39N 11.00 E
Nau 18 Gd 40.09N 69.22 E
Nau, Cap de la-/Nao, Cabo de la- 5 Gh 38.44N 0.14 E
Naucelle 11 Ij 44.12N 2.21 E
Nauëji-Akmjane/Naujoji-Akmenė 7 Fh 56.21N 22.50 E
Naugo/Nauvo 8 Id 60.10N 21.50 E
Nauhcampatépetl→ Cofre de Perote, Cerro- 48 Kh 19.29N 97.08W
Nauja Bay 42 Kc 68.58N 75.00W
Naujamiestis/Naujamiestis 8 Ki 55.41N 24.09 E
Naujamiestis/Naujamiestis 8 Ki 55.41N 24.09 E
Naujoji-Akmenė/Nauëji-Akmjane 7 Fh 56.21N 22.50 E
Naukluft 37 Bd 24.10S 16.10 E
Naumburg [F.R.G.] 12 Lc 51.15N 9.10 E
Naumburg [G.D.R.] 10 He 51.09N 11.49 E
Nā'ūr 24 Fg 31.53N 35.50 E
Nauru 57 He 0.31S 166.56 E
Nauru/Naoero [1] 58 He 0.31S 166.56 E
Nauški 20 Ff 50.28N 106.07 E
Nausori 61 Ec 18.02S 178.32 E
Nauta 54 Dd 4.32S 73.33W
Nautanwa 25 Gc 27.26N 83.25 E
Nautla 48 Kg 20.13N 96.47W
Nauvo/Naugo 8 Id 60.10N 21.50 E
Nava 48 Ic 28.25N 100.45W
Navacerrada, Puerto de- 13 Id 40.47N 4.00W
Nava del Rey 13 Gc 41.20N 5.05W
Navahermosa 13 He 39.38N 4.28W
Navajo Mountain 46 Jh 37.02N 110.52W
Navajo Reservoir 45 Ch 36.55N 107.30W
Navalmoral de la Mata 13 Ge 39.54N 5.32W
Navan/An Uaimh 9 Gh 53.39N 6.41W
Navarin, Mys- 21 Tc 62.16N 179.10 E
Navarino, Isla- 52 Jk 55.05S 67.40W
Navarra [3] 13 Kb 42.45N 1.40W
Navarra=Navarre (EN) 13 Kb 43.00N 1.30W
Navarre (EN)=Navarra 13 Kb 43.00N 1.30W
Navarro 55 Cl 35.01S 59.16W
Navarro Mills Lake 45 Hk 31.56N 96.45W
Navašino 7 Ki 55.33N 42.12 E
Navasota 45 Hk 30.23N 96.05W
Navasota River 45 Hk 30.20N 96.09W
Navassa 47 Ie 18.24N 75.01W
Navaste Jõgi/Navesti 8 Kf 58.56N 24.58 E
Nävekvarn 8 Gf 58.38N 16.49 E
Naver 9 Ic 58.30N 4.15W
Navesti/Navaste Jõgi 8 Kf 58.56N 24.58 E
Navia 13 Fa 43.32N 6.43W
Navia 13 Fa 43.33N 6.44W
Navidad, Bahía de- 48 Gh 19.10N 104.45W
Navidad Bank (EN) 49 Mc 20.00N 68.50W
Naviti 63d Ab 17.07S 177.15 E
Navlja 16 Ic 52.42N 34.03 E
Navlja 19 De 52.50N 34.31 E
Năvodari 15 Le 44.19N 28.36 E
Navoi 19 Gg 40.10N 65.15 E
Navoja 47 Cc 27.06N 109.26W
Navolato 48 Fe 24.47N 107.42W
Navoloki 7 Jh 57.28N 41.59 E
Návpaktos 15 Ek 38.24N 21.50 E
Návplion 15 Fl 37.34N 22.48 E
Navrongo 34 Ec 10.54N 1.06W
Navsāri 25 Ed 20.55N 72.55 E
Navtilos 15 Gn 35.57N 23.13 E
Navua 63d Bc 18.13S 178.10 E
Navy Board Inlet 42 Jb 73.30N 81.00W
Nawa 24 Gf 32.53N 36.03 E
Nawābshāh 25 Dc 26.15N 68.25 E
Nawāşif, Ḩarrat- 33 He 21.20N 42.10 E
Ņaws, Ra's- 23 If 17.18N 55.16 E
Náxos 15 Il 37.06N 25.23 E
Naxos 14 Jm 37.49N 15.15 E
Náxos=Naxos (EN) 5 Ih 37.02N 25.35 E
Naxos (EN)=Náxos 5 Ih 37.02N 25.35 E
Nayarit [2] 47 Cd 22.00N 105.00W
Nayarit, Sierra- 47 Dd 22.00N 103.50W
Nayau 63d Cb 17.58S 179.03W
Nāy Band [Iran] 24 Oi 27.23N 52.38 E
Nāy Band [Iran] 24 Qf 32.20N 57.34 E
Nāy Band, Ra's-e- 24 Oi 27.23N 52.34 E
Nayoro 27 Pc 44.21N 142.28 E
Nazaré [Braz.] 54 Kf 13.02S 39.00W
Nazaré [Port.] 13 Ce 39.36N 9.04W
Nazareth (EN)=Nazerat 24 Ff 32.42N 35.18 E
Nazarovo 20 Ee 56.01N 90.36 E
Nazas 48 Ge 25.14N 104.08W
Nazas, Rio- 38 Ig 25.35N 105.00W
Nazca 53 Ig 14.50S 74.55W
Nazca Ridge (EN) 3 Nl 22.00S 82.00W
Naze 27 Mf 28.23N 129.30 E
Nazerat=Nazareth (EN) 24 Ff 32.42N 35.18 E
Nazilli 23 Cb 37.55N 28.21 E
Nazimiye 24 Hc 39.11N 39.50 E
Nazimovo 20 Ed 59.30N 90.58 E
Nazino 20 Cd 60.15N 78.58 E
Nazlū 24 Kd 37.42N 45.16 E
Nazran 16 Nh 43.15N 44.46 E
Nazret 35 Fd 8.34N 39.18 E
Nazw'a 23 Ie 22.54N 57.31 E
Nazym 17 Nf 61.12N 68.57 E
Nazyvajevsk 19 Hd 55.34N 71.21 E
Nbâk 32 Ef 17.15N 14.59W
Nchanga 36 Ee 12.31S 27.52 E
Ncheu 36 Fe 14.49S 34.38 E
Ndala 36 Fc 4.46S 33.16 E
Ndalatando 36 Bd 9.18S 14.54 E
Ndali 34 Fd 9.51N 2.43 E
Ndélé 31 Jh 8.24N 20.39 E
Ndélélé 34 He 4.02N 14.56 E
Ndendé 36 Bc 2.23S 11.23 E
Ndindi 36 Bc 3.46S 11.09 E
N'djamena (Fort-Lamy) 31 Ig 12.07N 15.03 E
Ndola 31 Jj 12.58S 28.38 E
Ndouana, Pointe- 63b Dc 16.35S 168.09 E
Ndrhamcha, Sebkha de- 32 Df 18.45N 15.48W
Nduindui 60 Fi 9.48S 159.58 E
Ndui Ndui 63b Cb 15.24S 167.46 E
Né 11 Fi 45.40N 0.23W
Nea 63c Ab 10.51S 165.47 E
Nea 7 Ce 63.13N 11.02 E
Néa Alikarnassós 15 In 35.20N 25.09 E
Néa Artáki 15 Gk 38.31N 23.38 E
Neagari 29 Ec 36.26N 136.26 E
Neagh, Lough-/Loch nEathach 5 Fe 54.38N 6.24W
Neagră, Marea-=Black Sea (EN) 5 Jg 43.00N 35.00 E
Neah Bay 46 Cb 48.22N 124.37W
Néa Ionia 15 Fj 39.23N 22.56 E
Neajlov 15 Je 44.11N 26.12 E
Neale, Lake- 59 Fd 24.20S 130.00 E
Neamţ [2] 15 Jb 47.00N 26.20 E
Neápolis [Grc.] 15 In 35.15N 25.37 E
Neápolis [Grc.] 15 Ei 40.19N 21.23 E
Neápolis [Grc.] 15 Gm 36.31N 23.04 E
Near Islands 38 Bd 52.40N 173.30W
Neath 9 Jj 51.37N 3.50W
Neath 9 Jj 51.40N 3.48W
Néa Zikhni 15 Gh 41.02N 23.50 E
Néba 63b Ae 20.09S 163.55 E
Nebaj 49 Bf 15.24N 91.08W
Nebbou 34 Ec 11.18N 1.53W
Nebit-Dag 22 Hf 39.30N 54.22 E
Neblina, Pico da- 52 Je 1.08N 66.10W
Nebo 59 Jd 21.40S 148.39 E
Nebo, Mount- 46 Jg 39.49N 111.46W
Nebolči 7 Hg 59.08N 33.21 E
Nebraska [2] 43 Gc 41.30N 100.00W
Nebraska City 45 Hc 40.41N 95.52W
Nebrodi (Caronie) 14 Im 37.55N 14.35 E
Necedah 45 Kd 44.02N 90.03W
Nechako 42 Ff 53.55N 122.44W
Nechako Reservoir 42 Ef 53.00N 126.10W
Nechar, Djebel- 13 Qi 35.52N 4.59 E
Neches River 45 Jl 29.55N 93.52W
Nechi 49 Ji 8.07N 74.46W
Nechí, Río- 49 Jj 8.08N 74.46W
Neckako Plateau 42 Ff 53.25N 124.40W
Neckar 10 Eg 49.31N 8.26 E
Neckarsulm 10 Fg 49.11N 9.14 E
Necker Island 57 Kb 23.35N 164.42W
Necochea 53 Ki 38.33S 58.45W
Necy 12 Bf 48.50N 0.07W
Nedeley 35 Bb 15.34N 18.10 E
Nederland 45 Jl 29.58N 93.59W
Nederland=Netherlands (EN) [1] 6 Ge 52.15N 5.30 E
Nederlandse Antillen [5] 50 Ee 18.06N 63.10W
Nederlandse Antillen = Netherlands Antilles (EN) [5] 53 Jd 12.15N 69.00W
Neder-Rijn = Lower Rhine (EN) 11 Mc 51.59N 6.20 E
Nëdong 22 Lg 29.14N 91.46 E
Nedstrand 8 Ae 59.21N 5.51 E
Nedstrandefjorden 8 Ae 59.20N 5.50 E
Neede 12 Ib 52.08N 6.37 E
Needham Market 12 Db 52.09N 1.02 E
Needham's Point 51q Ab 13.05N 59.36W
Needles 43 Ee 34.51N 114.37W
Neembucú [3] 55 Dh 27.00S 58.00W
Neenah 45 Ld 44.11N 88.28W
Neepawa 45 Ga 50.13N 99.29W
Neermoor, Moormerland- 12 Ja 53.18N 7.26 E
Neeroeteren, Maaseik- 12 Hc 51.05N 5.42 E
Neerpelt 12 Hc 51.13N 5.25 E
Nefasit 35 Fb 15.18N 39.04 E
Nefedova 19 Hd 58.48N 72.34 E
Né Finn/Nephin 9 Dg 54.01N 9.22W
Neftah 32 Ic 33.52N 7.53 E
Neftečala 16 Pj 39.19N 49.13 E
Neftegorsk [R.S.F.S.R.] 16 Kg 44.22N 39.42 E
Neftegorsk [R.S.F.S.R.] 20 Jf 53.00N 143.00 E
Neftegorsk [R.S.F.S.R.] 19 Fe 52.45N 51.13 E
Neftejugansk 19 Hc 61.05N 72.45 E
Neftekamsk 19 Fd 56.06N 54.17 E
Neftekumsk 19 Eg 44.43N 44.59 E
Neftjanyje Kamin 16 Qi 40.15N 50.49 E
Negage 36 Cd 7.46S 15.18 E
Negara 26 Fh 8.22S 114.37 E
Negele=Neghelle (EN) 31 Kh 5.20N 39.37 E
Negev Desert (EN)=Hānegev 24 Fg 30.30N 34.55 E
Neghelle (EN)=Negele 31 Kh 5.20N 39.37 E
Negla, Arroyo- 55 Df 22.52S 56.41W
Negola 36 Be 14.10S 14.30 E
Negomano 37 Fb 11.26S 38.33 E
Negombo 25 Fg 7.13N 79.50 E
Negonego Atoll 57 Mf 18.47S 141.48W
Negotin 15 Fe 44.13N 22.32 E
Negotino 15 Fh 41.29N 22.06 E
Negra, Cordillera- 54 Ce 9.25S 77.40W
Negra, Coxilha- 55 Ej 31.02S 55.45W
Negra, Peña- 13 Fb 42.11N 6.30W
Negra, Ponta- 55 Jf 23.21S 44.36W
Negra, Punta- 52 Hf 6.06S 81.10W
Negra, Serra- 55 Fc 16.30S 52.10W
Negra o de los Difuntos, Laguna- 55 Fl 34.03S 53.40W
Negreira 13 Db 42.54N 8.44W
Negreni 15 He 44.34N 24.36 E
Negreşti 15 Gb 47.52N 23.26 E
Negrine 32 Ic 34.29N 7.31 E
Negrinho, Rio- 55 Ed 19.20S 55.05W
Negro, Cabo- 13 Gi 35.41N 5.17W
Negro, Rio- [Arg.] 55 Ch 27.27S 58.54W
Negro, Rio- [Arg.] 52 Jj 41.02S 62.47W
Negro, Rio- [Bol.] 54 Ff 14.11S 63.07W
Negro, Rio- [Braz.] 54 Gg 19.13S 57.17W
Negro, Rio- [Braz.] 56 Jc 26.01S 50.30W
Negro, Rio- [Par.] 56 Ib 24.23S 57.11W
Negro, Rio- [S.Amer.] 52 Kf 3.08S 59.55W
Negro, Rio- [S.Amer.] 55 Ce 20.11S 58.10W
Negro, Rio- [Ur.] 52 Ki 33.24S 58.22W
Negros 21 Oi 10.00N 123.00 E
Negru, Rîu- 15 Id 45.45N 25.46 E
Negru Vodă 15 Lf 43.49N 28.12 E
Nehajevski 16 Ld 50.27N 41.46 E
Nehalem River 46 Dd 45.40N 123.56W
Nehāvand 24 Me 35.56N 49.31 E
Nehe 27 Lb 48.28N 124.53 E
Nehoiu 15 Jd 45.25N 26.17 E
Néhoué, Baie de- 63b Be 20.21S 164.09 E
Neiba 49 Ld 18.28N 71.25W
Neiba, Bahia de- 49 Ld 18.15N 71.02W
Neidin/Kenmare 9 Dj 51.53N 9.35W
Neige, Crêt de la- 11 Lh 46.16N 5.56 E
Neiges, Piton des- 30 Mk 21.05S 55.29 E
Neijiang 22 Mg 29.38N 104.58 E
Neilton 46 Dc 47.25N 123.52W
Nei-meng-ku Tzu-chih-ch'ü→ Nei Monggol Zizhiqu [2] 27 Jc 44.00N 112.00 E
Nei Monggol Gaoyuan 21 Ne 42.00N 111.00 E
Nei Monggol Zizhiqu (Nei-meng-ku Tzu-chih-ch'ü)=Inner Mongolia (EN) [2] 27 Jc 44.00N 112.00 E
Neiqiu 28 Cf 37.17N 114.30 E
Neiva 53 Ie 2.56N 75.18W
Neja 19 Ed 58.19N 43.52 E
Nejanilini Lake 42 He 59.30N 97.50W
Nejdek 10 If 50.19N 12.44 E
Nejo 35 Fd 9.30N 35.32 E
Nejva 17 Kh 57.54N 62.18 E
Nekemt=Leqemt (EN) 31 Kh 9.05N 36.33 E
Neksø 8 Fi 55.04N 15.09 E
Nelemnoje 20 Kc 65.23N 151.08 E
Nelgese 20 Ic 66.40N 136.30 E
Nelichu 35 Ed 6.08N 34.25 E
Nelidovo 19 Dd 56.13N 32.50 E
Neligh 45 Ge 42.08N 98.02W
Neljaty 20 Ge 56.29N 115.50 E
Nelkan 20 Jd 64.15N 143.03 E
Nellore 22 Jh 12.56N 79.08 E
Nelma 20 Ig 47.40N 139.08 E
Nelson [2] 62 Ed 41.45S 172.30 E
Nelson 38 Jd 57.04N 92.30W
Nelson [B.C.-Can.] 42 Fg 49.29N 117.17W
Nelson [N.Z.] 58 Ii 41.16S 173.15 E
Nelson, Cape- [Austl.] 57 Fh 38.26S 141.33 E
Nelson, Cape- [Pap.N.Gui.] 59 Ja 9.00S 149.15 E
Nelson Island 40 Gd 60.35N 164.45W
Nelson's Dockyard 51d Bb 17.00N 61.46W
Nelspruit 31 Kk 25.30S 30.58 E
Néma 31 Gg 16.36N 7.15W
Néma, Dahr- 32 Ff 16.14N 7.30W
Neman 5 Id 55.18N 21.23 E
Neman 7 Fi 55.03N 22.01 E
Nembrala 26 Hi 10.53S 122.50 E
Nemda 7 Kh 57.31N 43.15 E
Neméa 15 Fl 37.49N 22.39 E
Neméa 15 Fl 37.49N 22.40 E
Némĕçkes, Mali i- 15 Di 40.08N 20.24 E
Nemenčinė 8 Kj 54.50N 25.39 E
Nëmërçkes, Mali i- 15 Di 40.08N 20.24 E
Nemira, Vîrful- 15 Jc 46.15N 26.19 E
Nemirov [Ukr.-U.S.S.R.] 10 Tf 50.08N 23.28 E
Nemirov [Ukr.-U.S.S.R.] 16 Fe 48.59N 28.50 E
Némiscau 42 Jf 51.30N 77.00W
Nemjuga 7 Kd 65.29N 43.40 E
Nemours 11 If 48.16N 2.42 E
Nemunas 5 Id 55.18N 21.23 E
Nemunėlis 8 Kh 56.24N 24.10 E
Nemuro 27 Qc 43.20N 145.35 E
Nemuro-Hantō 29a Db 43.20N 145.35 E
Nemuro-Kaikyō=Nemuro Strait (EN) 20 Jh 43.50N 145.30 E
Nemuro Strait (EN)=Kunašírski Proliv 20 Jh 43.50N 145.30 E
Nemuro Strait (EN)=Nemuro-Kaikyō 20 Jh 43.50N 145.30 E
Nemuro-Wan 29a Db 43.25N 145.25 E
Nenagh/An tAonach 9 Ei 52.52N 8.12W
Nenana 40 Jd 64.30N 149.00W
Nenana 40 Jd 64.34N 149.07W
Nendo Island 57 Hf 10.40S 165.54 E
Nene 9 Ni 52.48N 0.13 E
Nenecki Nacionalny Okrug [3] 19 Fb 67.30N 54.00 E
Nenjiang 22 Oe 49.10N 125.12 E
Nen Jiang 21 Oe 45.26N 124.39 E
Neo 29 Ed 35.38N 136.37 E
Neodesha 45 Ih 37.25N 95.41W
Néon Karlovásion 15 Jl 37.47N 26.42 E
Neosho 45 Ih 36.52N 94.22W
Neosho River 45 Ih 35.48N 95.18W
Néouvielle, Massif de- 11 Gl 42.51N 0.07 E
Nepal [1] 22 Kg 28.00N 84.00 E
Nepalganj 25 Gc 28.03N 81.37 E
Nephi 43 Ed 39.43N 111.50W
Nephin/Né Finn 9 Dg 54.01N 9.22W
Nepisiguit River 44 Ob 47.37N 65.38W
Nepoko 30 Jh 1.40N 27.01 E
Nepomuk 10 Jg 49.29N 13.34 E
Ner 10 Od 52.10N 18.40 E
Nera [It.] 14 Gh 42.26N 12.24 E
Nera [Rom.] 15 Ee 44.49N 21.22 E
Nérac 11 Gj 44.08N 0.21 E
Neratovice 10 Kf 50.16N 14.31 E
Nerău 15 Dd 45.58N 20.34 E
Nerča 20 Gf 51.54N 116.30 E
Nerčinsk 20 Gf 51.58N 116.35 E
Nerčinski Zavod 20 Gf 51.17N 119.30 E
Nerehta 19 Ed 57.28N 40.34 E
Nereju 15 Jd 45.42N 26.43 E
Nereta 8 Kh 56.12N 25.24 E
Neretva 14 Lg 43.02N 17.27 E
Neretvanski kanal 14 Lg 43.03N 17.11 E
Nerica 17 Fd 65.20N 52.45 E
Neringa 7 Ei 55.24N 21.05 E
Neringa 7 Ei 55.18N 21.00 E
Neringa-Juodkrante/Neringa-Juodkrantė 8 Ii 55.35N 21.01 E
Neringa-Juodkrantė/Neringa-Juodkrante 8 Ii 55.35N 21.01 E
Neringa-Nida 8 Ii 55.18N 20.53 E
Neringa-Preila/Neringa-Prejla 8 Ii 55.20N 20.59 E
Neringa-Prejla/Neringa-Preila 8 Ii 55.20N 20.59 E
Neriquinha 36 Df 15.45S 21.33 E
Neris/Njaris 8 Kj 54.55N 25.45 E
Nerja 13 Ih 36.44N 3.52W
Nerjungri 20 He 56.40N 124.47 E
Nerl [R.S.F.S.R.] 7 Jh 56.11N 40.34 E
Nerl [R.S.F.S.R.] 7 Ih 57.07N 37.39 E
Nerpio 13 Jf 38.09N 2.18W
Nerussa 16 Hc 52.33N 33.47 E
Nerva 13 Fg 37.42N 6.32W
Nervi, Genova- 14 Df 44.23N 9.02 E
Nervión 13 Ja 43.14N 2.53W
Nes 8 Cd 60.34N 9.59 E
Nes, Ameland- 12 Ha 53.26N 5.48 E
Nesbyen 7 Bf 60.34N 9.06 E
Nesebăr 15 Kg 42.39N 27.44 E
Nesjøen 8 Db 63.00N 12.00 E
Neskaupstaður 7a Db 65.09N 13.42W
Nesle 12 Ee 49.46N 2.45 E
Nesna 7 Cc 66.12N 13.02 E
Ness City 45 Gg 38.27N 99.54W
Nesterov [R.S.F.S.R.] 7 Fi 54.42N 22.34 E
Nesterov [Ukr.-U.S.S.R.] 16 Cd 50.03N 24.00 E
Néstos 15 Hi 40.51N 24.44 E
Nesttun 8 Ad 60.19N 5.20 E
Nesviž 16 Ec 53.13N 26.39 E
Netanya 24 Ff 32.20N 34.51 E
Netcong 44 Je 40.54N 74.43W
Nete 11 Kc 51.10N 4.15 E
Nethe 12 Lc 51.44N 9.23 E
Netherdale 59 Jd 21.08S 148.32 E
Netherlands (EN)=Nederland [1] 6 Ge 52.15N 5.30 E
Netherlands Antilles (EN) = Nederlandse Antillen [5] 53 Jd 12.15N 69.00W
Neto 14 Lk 39.12N 17.09 E
Netphen 12 Kd 50.55N 8.06 E
Nettebach 12 Jd 50.26N 7.28 E
Nettersheim 12 Id 50.30N 6.38 E
Nettetal 12 Ic 51.18N 6.12 E
Nettiling Lake 38 Lc 66.30N 70.40W
Nettuno 14 Gi 41.27N 12.39 E
Netzahualcóyotl, Presa- 48 Mi 17.00N 93.30W
Neubourg, Campagne du- 11 Ge 49.08N 1.00 E
Neubrandenburg 10 Jc 53.34N 13.16 E
Neubrandenburg [2] 10 Jc 53.35N 13.15 E
Neuburg an der Donau 10 Hh 48.44N 11.11 E
Neuchâtel [2] 14 Ac 47.05N 6.50 E
Neuchâtel/Neuenburg 14 Ad 46.59N 6.56 E
Neuchâtel, Lac de- / Neuenburger See 14 Ad 46.55N 6.55 E
Neuenbürg 12 Kf 48.50N 8.35 E
Neuenburg/Neuchâtel 14 Ad 46.59N 6.56 E
Neuenburger See/Neuchâtel, Lac de- 14 Ad 46.55N 6.55 E
Neuenhaus 12 Ib 52.30N 6.58 E
Neuenkirchen 12 Jb 52.15N 7.22 E
Neuerburg 12 Id 50.01N 6.18 E
Neufchâteau [Bel.] 11 Le 49.51N 5.26 E
Neufchâteau [Fr.] 11 Lf 48.21N 5.42 E
Neufchâtel-en-Bray 11 He 49.44N 1.27 E
Neufchâtel-Hardelot 12 Dd 50.37N 1.38 E
Neufchâtel Hardelot-Hardelot Plage 12 Dd 50.38N 1.35 E
Neufchâtel-sur-Aisne 12 Ge 49.26N 4.02 E
Neuffossé, Canal de- 12 Ed 50.45N 2.15 E
Neuhaus am Rennweg 10 Hf 50.31N 11.09 E
Neuilly-en-Thelle 12 Ee 49.13N 2.17 E
Neuilly-Saint-Front 12 Fe 49.10N 3.16 E
Neu-Isenburg 12 Kd 50.03N 8.42 E
Neukirchen-Vluyn 12 Ic 51.27N 6.35 E
Neum 14 Lh 42.55N 17.38 E
Neumagen Dhron 12 Ie 49.51N 6.54 E
Neumarkter Sattel 14 Id 47.06N 14.22 E
Neumarkt in der Oberpfalz 10 Hg 49.17N 11.28 E
Neumünster 10 Fb 54.04N 9.59 E
Neunkirchen [Aus.] 14 Kc 47.43N 16.05 E
Neunkirchen [F.R.G.] 10 Dg 49.21N 7.11 E
Neunkirchen [F.R.G.] 12 Jd 50.51N 7.20 E
Neunkirchen [F.R.G.] 12 Kd 50.48N 8.00 E
Neuquén 53 Ji 39.00S 68.05W
Neuquén [2] 56 Ge 39.00S 70.00W
Neuquén, Río- 52 Ji 38.59S 68.00W
Neurupping 10 Id 52.56N 12.48 E
Neuse River 44 Ih 35.06N 76.30W
Neusiedl am See 14 Kc 47.56N 16.50 E
Neusiedler See (Fertő) 10 Mi 47.50N 16.45 E
Neuß 10 Ce 51.12N 6.42 E
Neustadt (Hessen) 12 Ld 50.51N 9.07 E
Neustadt am Rübenberge 10 Fd 52.30N 9.28 E
Neustadt an der Aisch 10 Gg 49.35N 10.36 E
Neustadt an der Orla 10 Hf 50.44N 11.45 E
Neustadt an der Weinstraße 10 Eg 49.21N 8.09 E
Neustadt bei Coburg 10 Hf 50.19N 11.07 E
Neustadt in Holstein 10 Gb 54.06N 10.49 E
Neustrelitz 10 Jc 53.22N 13.05 E
Neu-Ulm 10 Gh 48.24N 10.01 E
Neuville-les-Dieppe 12 De 49.55N 1.06 E
Neuville-sur-Saône 11 Ki 45.52N 4.51 E
Neuwerk 10 Ec 53.55N 8.30 E
Neuwied 10 Df 50.26N 7.28 E
Neva 5 Jd 59.55N 30.15 E
Nevada [2] 43 Dd 39.00N 117.00W
Nevada [Ia.-U.S.] 45 Je 42.01N 93.27W
Nevada [Mo.-U.S.] 43 Id 37.51N 94.22W
Nevada, Sierra- [Sp.] 5 Fh 37.05N 3.10W
Nevada, Sierra- [U.S.] 38 Hf 38.00N 119.15W
Nevada del Cocuy, Sierra- 52 Ie 6.10N 72.15W
Nevada de Santa Marta, Sierra- 52 Id 10.50N 73.40W
Nevado, Cerro- 52 Ie 3.59N 74.04W
Nevado de Ampato 52 Ig 15.50S 71.52W
Neve, Serra da- 30 Ij 13.52S 13.26 E
Nevel 19 Cd 56.02N 29.55 E
Nevele 12 Fc 51.02N 3.33 E
Nevelsk 20 Jg 46.37N 141.57 E
Neverkino 16 Oc 52.47N 46.48 E
Nevers 11 Jg 46.59N 3.10 E
Nevesinje 14 Mg 43.16N 18.07 E
Nevinnomyssk 19 Eg 44.38N 41.58 E
Nevis 47 Le 17.10N 62.34W
Nevis, Ben- 5 Fd 56.48N 5.01W
Nevis Peak 51c Ab 17.10N 62.34W
Nevjansk 19 Gd 57.32N 60.13 E
Nevşehir 23 Db 38.38N 34.43 E
Nevskoje 28 Lb 45.42N 133.40 E
Newala 36 Ge 10.56S 39.18 E
New Albany [In.-U.S.] 43 Jd 38.18N 85.49W
New Albany [Ms.-U.S.] 45 Li 34.29N 89.00W
New Alresford 12 Ac 51.05N 1.10W
New Amsterdam 53 Ke 6.17N 57.36W
Newark [De.-U.S.] 44 Jf 39.41N 75.45W
Newark [N.J.-U.S.] 43 Mc 40.44N 74.11W
Newark [N.Y.-U.S.] 44 Id 43.03N 77.06W
Newark [Oh.-U.S.] 43 Kc 40.03N 82.25W
Newark-on-Trent 9 Mh 53.05N 0.49W
New Bedford 43 Mc 41.38N 70.56W
New Bern 43 Ld 35.07N 77.03W
Newberry [Mi.-U.S.] 44 Eb 46.21N 85.30W
Newberry [S.C.-U.S.] 44 Gh 34.17N 81.37W
New Braunfels 43 Hf 29.42N 98.08W
New Britain 44 Ke 41.40N 72.47W
New Britain Island 57 Ge 5.40S 151.00 E
New Britain Trench (EN) 60 Ei 6.00S 153.00 E
New Brunswick 44 Je 40.29N 74.27W
New Brunswick [3] 42 Kg 46.30N 66.45W
New Buckenham 12 Db 52.28N 1.05 E
New Buffalo 44 De 41.47N 86.45W
Newburgh 43 Mc 41.30N 74.00W
Newbury 9 Lj 51.25N 1.20W
New Caledonia (EN) = Nouvelle-Calédonie [5] 58 Hg 21.30S 165.30 E
New Caledonia (EN)= Nouvelle-Calédonie 57 Hg 21.30S 165.30 E
New Caledonia Basin (EN) 3 Jm 30.00S 165.00 E
New Carlisle 44 Oa 48.01N 65.20W
New Castile (EN)=Castilla la Nueva 13 Id 40.00N 3.45W
New Castle [In.-U.S.] 44 Ef 39.55N 85.22W
New Castle [Pa.-U.S.] 43 Kc 41.00N 80.22W
Newcastle [Austl.] 58 Gh 32.56S 151.46 E
Newcastle [N.B.-Can.] 42 Kg 47.00N 65.34W
Newcastle [N.Ire.-U.K.] 9 Hg 54.12N 5.54W
Newcastle [S.Afr.] 37 De 27.49S 29.55 E
Newcastle [St.C.N.] 51c Ab 17.13N 62.34W
Newcastle/An Caisleán Nua 9 Hg 54.12N 5.54W
Newcastle Creek 59 Gc 17.20S 133.23 E
Newcastle-under-Lyme 9 Kh 53.00N 2.14W

Index Symbols

[1] Independent Nation
[2] State, Region
[3] District, County
[4] Municipality
[5] Colony, Dependency
Continent
Physical Region
Historical or Cultural Region
Mount, Mountain
Volcano
Hill
Mountains, Mountain Range
Hills, Escarpment
Plateau, Upland
Pass, Gap
Plain, Lowland
Delta
Salt Flat
Valley, Canyon
Crater, Cave
Karst Features
Depression
Polder
Desert, Dunes
Forest, Woods
Heath, Steppe
Oasis
Cape, Point
Coast, Beach
Cliff
Peninsula
Isthmus
Sandbank
Island
Atoll
Rock, Reef
Islands, Archipelago
Rocks, Reefs
Coral Reef
Well, Spring
Geyser
River, Stream
Waterfall Rapids
River Mouth, Estuary
Lake
Salt Lake
Intermittent Lake
Reservoir
Swamp, Pond
Canal
Glacier
Ice Shelf, Pack Ice
Ocean
Sea
Gulf, Bay
Strait, Fjord
Lagoon
Bank
Seamount
Tablemount
Ridge
Shelf
Basin
Escarpment, Sea Scarp
Fracture
Trench, Abyss
National Park, Reserve
Point of Interest
Recreation Site
Cave, Cavern
Historic Site
Ruins
Wall, Walls
Church, Abbey
Temple
Scientific Station
Airport
Port
Lighthouse
Mine
Tunnel
Dam, Bridge

Newcastle-upon-Tyne 6 Fd 54.59N 1.35W
Newcastle Waters 58 Ef 17.24S 133.24 E
Newcastle West/An Caisleán Nua 9 Di 52.27N 9.03W
New Delhi 22 Jg 28.36N 77.12 E
New Denver 46 Ga 50.00N 117.22W
Newell 45 Ed 44.43N 103.25W
Newell, Lake- 46 Ja 50.25N 111.56W
New England 38 Le 44.00N 71.20W
New England Range 57 Gh 30.00S 151.50 E
New England Seamounts (EN) 38 Mf 38.00N 61.00W
Newenham, Cape- 40 Ge 58.37N 162.12W
New Forest 9 Lk 50.55N 1.35W
Newfoundland [3] 42 Lf 52.00N 56.00W
Newfoundland, Island of- 38 Ne 48.30N 56.00W
Newfoundland Basin (EN) 3 De 45.00N 40.00W
New Galloway 9 If 55.05N 4.10W
New Georgia 57 Ge 8.30S 157.20 E
New Georgia Island 60 Fi 8.15S 157.30 E
New Georgia Sound (The Slot) 60 Fi 8.00S 158.10 E
New Glasgow 42 Lg 45.35N 62.39W
New Guinea/Pulau Irian 57 Fe 5.00S 140.00 E
New Guinea Trench (EN) 60 Bg 0.05N 135.50 E
New Hampshire [2] 43 Mc 43.35N 71.40W
New Hampton 45 Je 43.03N 92.19W
New Hanover Island 57 Ge 2.30S 150.15 E
New Harmony 44 Df 38.08N 87.56W
New Haven 39 Le 41.18N 72.56W
Newhaven 9 Nk 50.47N 0.03 E
New Hebrides/Nouvelles Hébrides 57 Hf 16.01S 167.01 E
New Hebrides Trench (EN) 3 Jl 20.00S 168.00 E
New Iberia 43 If 30.00N 91.49W
New Ireland Island 57 Ge 3.20S 152.00 E
New Jersey [2] 43 Mc 40.15N 74.30W
New Kowloon/Julong 22 Ng 22.20N 114.09 E
New Liskeard 42 Jg 47.30N 79.40W
New London 43 Mc 41.21N 72.07W
New Madrid 45 Lh 36.36N 89.32W
Newman 59 Dd 23.15S 119.35 E
Newmarket [Eng.-U.K.] 9 Ni 52.15N 0.25 E
Newmarket [Ont.-Can.] 44 Hc 44.03N 79.28W
New Martinsville 44 Gf 39.39N 80.52W
New Meadows 46 Gd 44.58N 116.32W
New Mexico [2] 43 Fe 34.30N 106.00W
Newnan 44 Ei 33.23N 84.48W
New Norfolk 59 Jh 42.47S 147.03 E
New Orleans 39 Jg 29.58N 90.07W
New Philadelphia 44 Ge 40.30N 81.27W
New Pine Creek 46 Ee 42.01N 120.18W
New-Plymouth 58 Ih 39.04S 174.04 E
Newport [Ar.-U.S.] 45 Ki 35.37N 91.17W
Newport [Eng.-U.K.] 12 Cc 51.59N 0.15 E
Newport [Eng.-U.K.] 9 Lk 50.42N 1.18W
Newport [Fl.-U.S.] 44 Ej 30.14N 84.12W
Newport [Or.-U.S.] 43 Cc 44.38N 124.03W
Newport [R.I.-U.S.] 44 Le 41.30N 71.19W
Newport [Tn.-U.S.] 44 Fh 35.58N 83.11W
Newport [Vt.-U.S.] 44 Kc 44.56N 72.13W
Newport [Wales-U.K.] 9 Kj 51.35N 3.00W
Newport [Wa.-U.S.] 46 Gb 48.11N 117.03W
Newport Beach 43 De 33.37N 117.54W
Newport News 39 Lf 37.04N 76.28W
Newport Pagnell 12 Bb 52.05N 0.43W
New Providence Island 47 Ic 25.02N 77.24W
Newquay 9 Hk 50.25N 5.05W
New Quebec Crater (EN) = Nouveau-Québec, Cratère du- 42 Kd 61.30N 73.55W
New Richmond [Oh.-U.S.] 44 Ef 38.57N 84.16W
New Richmond [Que.-Can.] 44 Oa 48.10N 65.52W
New River [Blz.] 49 Cd 18.22N 88.24W
New River [Guy.] 54 Gc 3.23N 57.36W
New River [U.S.] 44 Ff 38.50N 82.06W
New Rockford 45 Gc 47.41N 99.15W
New Romney 12 Cd 50.59N 0.56 E
New Ross/Ros Mhic Thriúin 9 Gi 52.24N 6.56W
Newry/an t-Iúr 9 Gg 54.11N 6.20W
New Salem 45 Fc 46.51N 101.25W
New Sandy Bay 51n Ba 13.20N 61.08W
New Schwabenland (EN) 66 Cf 72.30S 1.00 E
New Siberia (EN) = Novaja Sibir, Ostrov- 21 Qb 75.00N 149.00 E
New Siberian Islands (EN) = Novosibirskije Ostrova 21 Qb 75.00N 142.00 E
New Smyrna Beach 44 Gk 29.02N 80.56W
New South Wales 59 Jf 33.00S 146.00 E
Newton [Ia.-U.S.] 45 Jf 41.42N 93.03W
Newton [Il.-U.S.] 45 Lg 38.59N 88.10W
Newton [Ks.-U.S.] 43 Hd 38.03N 97.21W
Newton [Ma.-U.S.] 44 Ld 42.21N 71.13W
Newton [Ms.-U.S.] 45 Lj 32.19N 89.10W
Newton [N.J.-U.S.] 44 Je 41.03N 74.45W
Newton Abbot 9 Jk 50.32N 3.36W
Newton Stewart 9 Ig 54.57N 4.29W
Newtontoppen 67 Kd 78.02N 17.30 E
New Town 45 Ec 47.59N 102.30W
Newtown 9 Ji 52.32N 3.19W
Newtownabbey/Baile na Mainistreach 9 Hg 54.42N 5.54W
Newtownards/Baile Nua na hArda 9 Hg 54.36N 5.41W
New Ulm 43 Ic 44.19N 94.28W
New Westminster 42 Fg 49.12N 122.55W
New York 39 Le 40.43N 74.01W
New York [2] 43 Lc 43.00N 75.00W
New York State Barge Canal 44 Hd 43.05N 78.43W
New Zealand [1] 58 Ii 41.00S 174.00 E
New Zealand 57 Ii 41.00S 174.00 E
Nexpa, Río- 48 Hh 18.05N 102.46W
Neyagawa 29 Dd 34.46N 135.36 E
Neyrīz 24 Ph 29.12N 54.19 E
Neyshābūr 23 Ib 36.12N 58.50 E
Nežárka 10 Kg 49.11N 14.43 E
Nežin 19 De 51.02N 31.57 E
Ngabé 36 Cc 3.12S 16.11 E
Ngahere 62 De 42.24S 171.26 E
Ngajangel 64a Ba 8.05N 134.43 E
Ngala 34 Hc 12.20N 14.11 E
Ngaliema, Chutes- = Stanley Falls (EN) 30 Jh 0.30N 25.30 E
Ngamegei Passage 64a Bb 7.44N 134.34 E
Ngami, Lake- 37 Cd 20.37S 22.40 E
Ngamiland [3] 37 Cc 19.09S 22.47 E
Ngamring 27 Ef 29.14N 87.12 E
Ngangala 35 Ee 4.42N 31.55 E
Ngangerabeli Plain 36 Hc 1.30S 40.15 E
Ngangla Ringco 27 De 31.40N 83.00 E
Nganglong Kangri 27 De 32.45N 81.12 E
Nganglong Kangri 21 Kf 32.00N 83.00 E
Ngangzê Co 27 Ee 31.00N 86.55 E
Ngao 25 Je 18.45N 99.59 E
Ngaoundéré 31 Ih 7.19N 13.35 E
Ngapara 62 Df 44.57S 170.45 E
Ngara 35 Fc 2.28S 30.39 E
Ngardmau 64a Bb 7.37N 134.35 E
Ngardmau Bay 64a Bb 7.39N 134.35 E
Ngardololok 64a Ac 7.00N 134.16 E
Ngaregur 64a Bb 7.45N 134.38 E
Ngarekeukl 64a Ac 7.00N 134.14 E
Ngariungs 64a Ba 8.03N 134.43 E
Ngaruangl 64a Ba 8.10N 134.39 E
Ngaruangl Passage 64a Ba 8.07N 134.40 E
Ngaruawahia 62 Fb 37.40S 175.09 E
Ngaruroro 62 Gc 39.34S 176.55 E
Ngatangiia 64p Cb 21.14S 159.43W
Ngatangiia Harbour 64p Cb 21.14S 159.43W
Ngateguil, Point- 64a Bc 7.26N 134.37 E
Ngatik Atoll 57 Gd 5.51N 157.16 E
Ngatpang 64a Bc 7.28N 134.32 E
Ngau Island 63d Bc 18.02S 179.18 E
Ngauruhoe 62 Fc 39.09S 175.38 E
Ngawa/Aba 27 He 32.55N 101.45 E
Ngayu 36 Eb 1.35N 27.13 E
Ngemelis Islands 64a Ac 7.07N 134.15 E
Ngeregong 64a Ac 7.07N 134.22 E
Ngergoi 64a Ac 7.05N 134.17 E
Ngesebus 64a Ac 7.03N 134.16 E
Ngga Pulu 63d Cb 16.46S 179.46W
Nggamea 63d Cb 16.46S 179.46W
Nggatokae 63a Dc 8.46S 158.11 E
Nggela Pile 63a Ec 9.08S 160.20 E
Nggela Sule 63a Ec 9.03S 160.12 E
Nggelelevu 63d Cb 16.05S 179.09W
Ngidinga 36 Cd 5.37S 15.17 E
Ngiro, Ewaso- 36 Gb 0.28N 39.55 E
Ngiva 31 Ij 17.03S 15.47 E
Ngo 36 Cc 2.29S 15.45 E
Ngoangoa 35 Dd 5.58N 25.10 E
Ngobasangel 64a Ac 7.16N 134.20 E
Ngoko 36 Cb 1.40N 16.03 E
Ngola Shankou 27 Gd 35.30N 99.36 E
Ngoma 36 Ef 15.58S 25.56 E
Ngoring Hu 27 Gd 35.00N 97.30 E
Ngorongoro Crater 30 Ki 3.10S 35.35 E
Ngoui 34 Cb 16.09N 13.55W
Ngouna 63b Dc 17.26S 168.21 E
Ngounié [3] 36 Bc 2.00S 11.00 E
Ngounié 36 Bc 0.37S 10.18 E
Ngoura 35 Bc 12.52N 16.27 E
Ngouri 35 Bc 13.38N 15.22 E
Ngourti 34 Hb 15.19N 13.12 E
Ngousoubout, Pointe- 63b Ca 13.58S 167.27 E
Ngudu 36 Fc 2.58S 33.20 E
Nguigmi 31 Ig 14.15N 13.07 E
Ngulu Atoll 57 Ed 8.18N 137.29 E
Nguni 36 Gc 0.50S 38.20 E
Ngunza 31 Ij 11.12S 13.51 E
Nguru 31 Ig 12.53N 10.28 E
Nhachengue 37 Fd 22.51S 35.11 E
Nhamundá 54 Gd 2.14S 56.43W
Nhamundá, Rio- 54 Gd 2.12S 56.41W
Nhandeara 55 Ge 20.40S 50.02W
Nhandutiba 55 Jb 14.37S 44.12W
Nharea 36 Ce 11.28S 16.53 E
Nha Trang 22 Mh 12.15N 109.11 E
Nhecolândia 55 Dd 19.16S 57.04W
Nhia 36 Be 10.15S 14.12 E
Nhulunbuy 58 Ef 12.00S 35.58 E
Niafounké 34 Eb 15.56N 4.00W
Niagara Escarpment 44 Gc 44.30N 80.35W
Niagara Falls 38 Le 43.05N 79.04W
Niagara Falls [N.Y.-U.S.] 43 Lc 43.06N 79.02W
Niagara Falls [Ont.-Can.] 42 Jh 43.06N 79.04W
Niagara River 44 Hd 43.15N 79.04W
Niagassola 34 Dc 12.19N 9.07W
Niah 26 Ff 3.52N 113.44 E
Niakaramandougou 34 Dd 8.40N 5.17W
Niamey 31 Hg 13.31N 2.07 E
Niamey [2] 34 Fc 14.00N 2.00 E
Niandan 34 Dc 10.35N 9.45W
Niangara 31 Jh 3.42N 27.52 E
Niangay, Lac- 34 Eb 15.50N 3.00W
Niangoloko 34 Ec 10.17N 4.55W
Nia-Nia 36 Eb 1.24N 27.36 E
Nianzishan 27 Lb 47.31N 122.50 E
Niao Dao 27 Gd 37.20N 99.50 E
Niaoshu Shan 27 He 34.54N 104.04 E
Niari [3] 36 Bc 4.30S 13.00 E
Niari 36 Bc 3.56S 12.12 E
Nias, Pulau- 21 Li 1.05N 97.35 E
Niassa [3] 37 Fb 13.00S 36.00 E
Niassa, Lago- = Nyasa, Lake- (EN) 30 Kj 12.00S 34.30 E
Niau, Ile- 57 Mf 16.09S 146.21W
Nibāk 24 Nj 24.24N 50.50 E
Nibe 8 Ch 56.59N 9.38 E
Nica 17 Lh 57.29N 64.33 E
Nica/Nīca 8 Ih 56.25N 20.56 E
Nica/Nīca 8 Ih 56.25N 20.56 E
Nicanor Olivera 55 Cn 38.17S 59.12W
Nicaragua [1] 39 Kh 13.00N 85.00W
Nicaragua, Lago de- = Nicaragua, Lake- (EN) 38 Kh 11.35N 85.25W
Nicaragua, Lake- (EN) = Nicaragua, Lago de- 38 Kh 11.35N 85.25W
Nicastro 14 Kl 38.59N 16.19 E
Nice 6 Gg 43.42N 7.15 E
Niceville 44 Dj 30.31N 86.29W
Nichicum, Lac- 42 Kf 53.08N 70.55W
Nichinan [Jap.] 29 Cd 35.10N 133.16 E
Nichinan [Jap.] 28 Ki 31.36N 131.23 E
Nicholas Channel 49 Gb 23.25N 80.05W
Nicholas Channel (EN) = Nicolás, Canal- 47 Hd 23.25N 80.05W
Nicholasville 44 Eg 37.53N 84.34W
Nicholls Town 49 Ia 25.08N 78.00W
Nicholson Range 59 De 27.15S 116.45 E
Nicholson River 57 Ef 17.31S 139.36 E
Nickerson Ice Shelf 66 Mf 75.45S 145.00W
Nickol Bay 59 Dd 20.40S 116.50 E
Nicobar Islands 21 Li 8.00N 93.30 E
Nicocli 49 Ii 8.26N 76.48W
Nicolajevka 15 Nb 47.33N 30.41 E
Nicola River 46 Ea 50.25N 121.18W
Nicolás, Canal- = Nicholas Channel (EN) 47 Hd 23.25N 80.05W
Nicolet 44 Kb 46.14N 72.37W
Nicopolis (EN) = Nikópolis 15 Dj 39.00N 20.45 E
Nicosia 14 Im 37.45N 14.24 E
Nicosia (EN) = Lefkosa/Levkôsia 22 Ff 35.10N 33.22 E
Nicosia (EN) = Levkôsia/Lefkosa 22 Ff 35.10N 33.22 E
Nicotera 14 Jl 38.33N 15.56 E
Nicoya 47 Gf 10.09N 85.27W
Nicoya, Golfo de- 47 Hg 9.47N 84.48W
Nicoya, Peninsula de- = Nicoya Peninsula (EN) 38 Ki 10.00N 85.25W
Nicoya Peninsula (EN) = Nicoya, Peninsula de- 38 Ki 10.00N 85.25W
Nicuadala 37 Fc 17.37S 36.50 E
Niculitel 15 Ld 45.11N 28.29 E
Nida 10 Qf 50.18N 20.52 E
Nidda 12 Ld 50.25N 9.00 E
Nidda 10 Ef 50.06N 8.34 E
Nidder 12 Kd 50.12N 8.47 E
Nideggen 12 Id 50.42N 6.29 E
Nidelva [Nor.] 8 Cf 58.24N 8.48 E
Nidelva [Nor.] 8 Da 63.26N 10.25 E
Nido, Sierra del- 48 Fc 29.30N 106.45W
Nidže 15 Ei 41.00N 21.50 E
Nidzica 10 Qf 50.12N 20.40 E
Nidzica 10 Qc 53.22N 20.26 E
Nidzkie, Jezioro- 10 Rc 53.37N 21.30 E
Niebüll 10 Eb 54.48N 8.50 E
Nied 12 Ie 49.23N 6.40 E
Nieddu 14 Dj 40.44N 9.34 E
Niederbayern 10 Ih 48.35N 12.30 E
Niederbronn-les-Bains 11 Nf 48.58N 7.38 E
Niedere Tauern 14 Hc 47.20N 14.00 E
Niederlausitz 10 Ke 51.40N 14.15 E
Nieder-Olm 12 Ke 49.54N 8.13 E
Niederösterreich = Lower Austria (EN) [2] 14 Jb 48.30N 15.45 E
Niedersachsen = Lower Saxony (EN) [2] 10 Fd 52.00N 10.00 E
Niederwald 10 Df 50.10N 8.00 E
Niederzier 12 Id 50.53N 6.28 E
Niefang 34 He 1.50N 10.14 E
Niegocin, Jezioro- 10 Rb 54.00N 21.50 E
Niel 12 Gc 51.07N 4.20 E
Nielfa, Puerto de- 13 Hf 38.32N 4.23W
Niéllé 34 Dc 10.12N 5.38W
Niellim 35 Bd 9.42N 17.49 E
Niemba 36 Ed 5.57S 28.26 E
Niemba 36 Ed 5.57S 28.26 E
Niemodlin 10 Nf 50.39N 17.37 E
Niéna 34 Dc 11.25N 6.20W
Nienburg (Weser) 10 Fd 52.38N 9.13 E
Niepołomice 10 Qf 50.03N 20.13 E
Niermalak, Pointe- 63b Cb 14.21S 167.24 E
Niers 10 Be 51.43N 5.57 E
Nierstein 12 Ke 49.53N 8.20 E
Niesky/Niska 10 Ke 51.18N 14.49 E
Nieszawa 10 Od 52.50N 18.55 E
Nieuport/Nieuwpoort 11 Ic 51.08N 2.45 E
Nieuw Amsterdam 54 Gb 5.53N 55.05W
Nieuwe-Pekela 12 Ia 53.04N 6.59 E
Nieuweschans 12 Ja 53.11N 7.15 E
Nieuw Milligen, Apeldoorn- 12 Hb 52.14N 5.48 E
Nieuw Nickerie 53 Ke 5.57N 56.59W
Nieuwolda 12 Ia 53.14N 6.59 E
Nieuwoudtville 37 Bf 31.22S 19.06 E
Nieuwpoort/Nieuport 11 Ic 51.08N 2.45 E
Nieuw Weerdinge, Emmen- 12 Jb 52.52N 7.01 E
Nieves 48 He 24.00N 103.01W
Nièvre [3] 11 Jg 47.05N 3.30 E
Nièvre 11 Jh 46.59N 3.10 E
Nigata 28 Lg 34.13N 132.29 E
Niğde 23 Db 37.59N 34.42 E
Nigenān 24 Qe 34.13N 57.19 E
Niger [1] 31 Hg 16.00N 8.00 E
Niger 30 Hh 5.33N 6.33 E
Niger [2] 34 Gd 9.40N 6.00 E
Niger Basin (EN) 30 Gg 15.00N 2.00 E
Niger Delta 30 Hh 4.50N 6.00 E
Nigeria [1] 31 Hh 10.00N 8.00 E
Night Hawk Lake 44 Ga 48.28N 81.00W
Nightingale Island 30 Fi 37.24S 12.28W
Nigrita 15 Gi 40.54N 23.30 E
Nihiru Atoll 57 Mf 16.42S 142.50W
Nihoa Island 57 Kb 23.06N 161.58W
Nihonmatsu 28 Pf 37.35N 140.26 E
Nihuil, Embalse del- 56 Ge 35.05S 68.45W
Niigata 22 Pf 37.55N 139.03 E
Niigata Ken [2] 28 Of 37.30N 138.50 E
Niihama 28 Lh 33.58N 133.16 E
Niihau Island 57 Kb 21.55N 160.10W
Nii-Jima 27 Oe 34.20N 139.15 E
Niikappu-Gawa 29a Cb 42.22N 142.16 E
Niimi 28 Lg 34.59N 133.28 E
Niisato 29 Gb 39.36N 141.49 E
Niitsu 28 Of 37.48N 139.07 E
Nijar 13 Jh 36.58N 2.12W
Nijkerk 12 Hb 52.14N 5.29 E
Nijlen 12 Gc 51.10N 4.39 E
Nijmegen 11 Lc 51.50N 5.50 E
Nijvel/Nivelles 11 Kd 50.36N 4.20 E
Nijverdal, Hellendoorn- 12 Ib 52.22N 6.27 E
Nikel 19 Db 69.24N 30.13 E
Niki 15 Ei 40.55N 21.25 E
Nikitin Seamount (EN) 21 Kj 3.00S 83.00 E
Nikki 34 Fd 9.56N 3.12 E
Nikkō 29 Fc 36.44N 139.35 E
Nikolajev [Ukr.-U.S.S.R.] 16 Ce 49.32N 23.58 E
Nikolajev [Ukr.-U.S.S.R.] 6 Jf 46.58N 32.00 E
Nikolajevka 18 Kc 43.37N 77.01 E
Nikolajevo 8 Mf 58.14N 29.32 E
Nikolajevsk 19 Ee 50.02N 45.31 E
Nikolajevskaja Oblast [3] 19 Df 47.20N 32.00 E
Nikolajevsk 20 Hf 54.50N 129.25 E
Nikolajevsk-na-Amure 22 Qd 53.08N 140.44 E
Nikolsk [R.S.F.S.R.] 19 Ee 53.42N 46.03 E
Nikolsk [R.S.F.S.R.] 19 Ed 59.33N 45.31 E
Nikolski [Ak.-U.S.] 40a Eb 53.15N 168.22W
Nikolski [Kaz.-U.S.S.R.] 19 Gf 47.55N 67.33 E
Nikonga 36 Fc 4.40S 31.28 E
Nikopol [Bul.] 15 Hf 43.42N 24.54 E
Nikopol [Ukr.-U.S.S.R.] 19 Df 47.35N 34.25 E
Nikópolis = Nicopolis (EN) 15 Dj 39.00N 20.45 E
Nīkpey 24 Md 36.50N 48.10 E
Niksar 24 Gb 40.36N 36.58 E
Nikšić 15 Bg 42.46N 18.58 E
Nikumaroro Atoll (Gardner) 57 Je 4.40S 174.32W
Nikunau Island 57 Ie 1.23S 176.26 E
Nīl, Kūh-e- 24 Ng 30.52N 50.49 E
Nīl, Nahr an- = Nile (EN) 30 Ke 30.10N 31.06 E
Nila, Pulau- 26 Ih 6.44S 129.31 E
Nilakka 7 Ge 63.07N 26.33 E
Niland 46 Hj 33.14N 115.31W
Nilandu Atoll 25a Bb 3.00N 72.55 E
Nile [3] 36 Fb 3.00N 31.30 E
Nile (EN) = Nīl, Nahr an- 30 Ke 30.10N 31.06 E
Nile Delta (EN) 30 Ke 31.20N 31.00 E
Nīleh, Kūh-e- 24 Nf 32.59N 50.32 E
Niles 44 De 41.50N 86.15W
Nilgiri Hills 25 Ff 11.30N 76.30 E
Nilka 27 Dc 43.47N 82.20 E
Nīl Kowtal 23 Kc 34.48N 67.22 E
Nilsiä 7 Ge 63.12N 28.05 E
Nilüfer 15 Li 40.18N 28.27 E
Nimba [3] 34 Dd 6.45N 8.45W
Nimba, Monts- = Nimba Mountains (EN) 30 Gh 7.35N 8.28W
Nimba Mountains (EN) = Nimba, Monts- 30 Gh 7.35N 8.28W
Nîmes 6 Gg 43.50N 4.21 E
Nimjad 32 Df 17.25N 15.41W
Nimmitabel 59 Jg 36.31S 149.16 E
Nimpkish River 46 Ba 50.32N 126.59W
Nimrode Glacier 66 Kg 82.27S 161.00 E
Nimrud 24 Jd 36.06N 43.20 E
Nimrūz [3] 23 Jc 30.30N 62.00 E
Nims 12 Ie 49.51N 6.28 E
Nimule 31 Kh 3.36N 32.03 E
Nimún, Punta- 48 Ng 20.46N 90.25W
Nin 14 Jf 44.14N 15.11 E
Nina 37 Bd 22.57S 18.14 E
Nīnawā [3] 24 Je 35.45N 42.45 E
Nīnawā = Nineveh (EN) 23 Fb 36.22N 43.09 E
Nine Degree Channel 21 Ji 9.00N 73.00 E
Ninetyeast Ridge (EN) 3 Gj 10.00S 90.00 E
Ninety Mile Beach [Austl.] 59 Jg 38.15S 147.25 E
Ninety Mile Beach [N.Z.] 62 Ea 34.45S 173.00 E
Nineveh (EN) = Nīnawā 23 Fb 36.22N 43.09 E
Ning'an 27 Mc 44.22N 129.23 E
Ningbo 22 Og 29.55N 121.28 E
Ningcheng (Tianyi) 27 Kc 41.34N 119.25 E
Ningde 27 Kf 26.44N 119.29 E
Ningdu 27 Kf 26.31N 115.59 E
Ningguo 28 Ei 30.39N 119.00 E
Ninghai 28 Fj 29.19N 121.26 E
Ning-hsia-hui-tsu Tzu-chih-ch'ü → Ningxia Huizu Zizhiqu = Ningsia Hui (EN) [2] 27 Id 37.00N 106.00 E
Ningjin [China] 28 Df 37.39N 116.48 E
Ningjin [China] 28 Cf 37.37N 114.55 E
Ningjing Shan 27 Ge 31.45N 97.15 E
Ninglang 27 Hf 27.17N 100.52 E
Ningling 28 Cg 34.27N 115.18 E
Ningnan 27 Hf 27.05N 102.44 E
Ningqiang 27 Ie 32.48N 106.15 E
Ningsia Hui (EN) = Ning-hsia-hui-tsu Tzu-chih-ch'ü → Ningxia Huizu Zizhiqu [2] 27 Id 37.00N 106.00 E
Ningsia Hui (EN) = Ningxia Huizu Zizhiqu (Ning-hsia-hui-tsu Tzu-chih-ch'ü) [2] 27 Id 37.00N 106.00 E
Ningwu 27 Jd 38.59N 112.14 E
Ningxia Huizu Zizhiqu (Ning-hsia-hui-tsu Tzu-chih-ch'ü) = Ningsia Hui (EN) [2] 27 Id 37.00N 106.00 E
Ningxian 27 Id 35.27N 107.50 E
Ningxiang 28 Bj 28.16N 112.33 E
Ningyang 28 Dg 35.45N 116.48 E
Ningyō-Tōge 29 Cd 35.19N 133.56 E
Ninh Binh 25 Ld 20.15N 105.59 E
Ninh Hoa 25 Lf 12.29N 109.08 E
Ninigo Group 57 Fe 1.15S 144.15 E
Niniva 65b Ba 19.46S 174.38W
Ninnis Glacier 66 Je 68.12S 147.12 E
Ninohe 27 Pc 40.16N 141.18 E
Ninove 12 Fd 50.50N 4.00 E
Nioaque 54 Gh 21.08S 55.48W
Niobrara 38 Je 42.45N 98.00W
Niobrara 45 He 42.25N 98.00W
Nioghalvfjerdsfjorden 41 Kc 79.30N 18.45W
Nioki 36 Cc 2.43S 17.41 E
Niono 34 Dc 14.15N 6.00W
Nioro du Rip 34 Bc 13.45N 15.48W
Nioro du Sahel 31 Gg 15.14N 9.37W
Niort 11 Fh 46.19N 0.28W
Nipawin 42 Hf 53.22N 104.00W
Nipe, Bahía de- 49 Jc 20.47N 75.42W
Nipesotsu-Yama 29a Cb 43.27N 143.02 E
Nipigon 39 Ke 49.01N 88.16W
Nipigon, Lake- 38 Ke 49.50N 88.30W
Nipigon Bay 45 Mb 48.53N 87.50W
Nipissing, Lake- 38 Le 46.17N 80.00W
Nippon = Japan (EN) [1] 22 Pf 38.00N 137.00 E
Nippon-Kai = Japan, Sea of- (EN) 21 Pf 40.00N 134.00 E
Nippur 24 Kf 32.10N 45.10 E
Niquelândia 54 If 14.27S 48.27W
Niquero 49 Ic 20.03N 77.35W
Niquitao, Teta de- 49 Li 9.07N 70.30W
Niquivil 56 Gd 30.25S 68.42W
Nīr 24 Lc 38.02N 47.59 E
Nirasaki 29 Fd 35.43N 138.27 E
Nirji → Morin Dawa 27 Lb 48.30N 124.28 E
Nirmal 25 Fe 19.06N 78.21 E
Niš 6 Ig 43.19N 21.54 E
Nisa 13 Ee 39.31N 7.39W
Nīsāb 23 Gg 14.24N 46.38 E
Nisāh, Sha'īb- 24 Lj 24.11N 47.11 E
Nišava 15 Ef 43.22N 21.46 E
Niscemi 14 Im 37.09N 14.23 E
Nishibetsu-Gawa 29a Db 43.23N 145.17 E
Nishikawa 29 Gb 38.26N 140.08 E
Nishiki 29 Bd 34.16N 131.57 E
Nishinomiya 29 Dd 34.43N 135.20 E
Nishino'omote 27 Ne 30.44N 131.00 E
Nishino-Shima 60 Cb 27.30N 140.53 E
Nishi-No-Shima 28 Lf 36.06N 133.00 E
Nishiokoppe 29a Ca 44.20N 142.57 E
Nishi-Sonogi-Hantō 29 Ae 32.55N 129.45 E
Nishiwaki 29 Dd 34.59N 134.58 E
Nisiros 15 Km 36.35N 27.10 E
Niska/Niesky 10 Ke 51.18N 14.49 E
Niška Banja 15 Ff 43.18N 22.01 E
Nisko 10 Sf 50.31N 22.09 E
Nismes, Viroinval- 12 Gd 50.05N 4.33 E
Nisoi Aiyaiou [2] 15 Il 37.40N 25.40 E
Nisporeny 16 Ff 47.06N 28.10 E
Nissan 8 Eh 56.40N 12.51 E
Nissan 63a Ba 4.30S 154.14 E
Nisser 8 Ce 59.10N 8.30 E
Nissum Bredning 8 Ch 56.40N 8.20 E
Nissum Fjord 8 Ch 56.20N 8.15 E
Nita 29 Cd 35.12N 133.00 E
Nitchequon 42 Kf 53.15N 70.44W
Niterói 53 Lh 22.53S 43.07W
Nith 9 Jf 55.00N 3.35W
Nitra 10 Oi 47.46N 18.10 E
Nitra 10 Oh 48.19N 18.05 E
Niuafo'ou Island 57 Jf 15.35S 175.38W
Niuatoputapu Island 57 Jf 15.57S 173.45W
Niue [5] 58 Kf 19.02S 169.55W
Niue Island 57 Kf 19.02S 169.55W
Niu'erhe 27 La 51.30N 121.40 E
Niufu 29a Ca 44.35N 142.35 E
Niulakita Island 57 If 10.45S 179.30 E
Niutaca, Corrente- 55 De 20.42S 57.37W
Niutao Island 57 Ie 6.06S 177.16 E
Niutg, Gunung- 26 Ef 1.00N 109.55 E
Niutoushan 27 Ke 31.00N 119.35 E
Niuzhuang 28 Gd 40.57N 122.30 E
Nivala 7 Fe 63.58N 25.01 E
Nive 11 Ek 43.30N 1.29W
Nivelles/Nijvel 11 Kd 50.36N 4.20 E
Nivernais 11 Jg 47.00N 3.30 E
Nivernais, Canal du- 11 Jg 47.40N 3.40 E
Nivernais, Côtes du- 11 Jg 47.10N 3.30 E
Nivillers 12 Ee 49.28N 2.10 E
Nixon 45 Hl 29.16N 97.46W
Niya/Minfeng 27 Dd 37.04N 82.46 E
Nīyābād 24 Le 35.12N 46.20 E
Niyodo-Gawa 29 Ce 33.28N 133.29 E
Niza 24 Ph 28.25N 55.55 E
Nizāmābad 25 Fe 18.40N 78.07 E
Nižankoviči 10 Sg 49.40N 22.48 E
Nizip 23 Eb 37.01N 37.46 E
Nízke Tatry = Low Tatra (EN) 10 Ph 48.54N 19.40 E
Nízký-Jeseník 10 Ng 49.50N 17.30 E
Nižná 10 Pg 49.19N 19.32 E
Nižneangarsk 22 Md 55.47N 109.33 E
Nižnegorski 16 Ig 45.27N 34.44 E
Nižnejansk 20 Ib 71.24N 136.00 E
Nižnekamsk 19 Fd 55.38N 51.49 E
Nižnekolymsk 20 Lc 68.38N 160.56 E
Nižnetroicki 17 Fi 54.20N 53.41 E
Nižneudinsk 20 Ef 54.54N 99.03 E
Nižnevartovsk 22 Jc 61.00N 77.00 E
Nižni Baskunčak 17 Ef 48.13N 46.50 E
Nižni Bestjah 20 Hd 61.48N 129.55 E
Nižni Casučej 20 Gf 50.27N 115.08 E
Nižnije Serogozy 16 If 46.49N 34.24 E
Nižni Kuranah 20 He 58.40N 125.48 E
Nižni Lomov 19 Ee 53.32N 43.41 E
Nižni Odes 17 Ge 63.40N 54.52 E

Index Symbols

[1] Independent Nation
[2] State, Region
[3] District, County
[4] Municipality
[5] Colony, Dependency
Continent
Physical Region
Historical or Cultural Region
Mount, Mountain
Volcano
Hill
Mountains, Mountain Range
Hills, Escarpment
Plateau, Upland
Pass, Gap
Plain, Lowland
Delta
Salt Flat
Valley, Canyon
Crater, Cave
Karst Features
Depression
Polder
Desert, Dunes
Forest, Woods
Heath, Steppe
Oasis
Cape, Point
Coast, Beach
Cliff
Peninsula
Isthmus
Sandbank
Island
Atoll
Rock, Reef
Islands, Archipelago
Rocks, Reefs
Coral Reef
Well, Spring
Geyser
River, Stream
Waterfall Rapids
River Mouth, Estuary
Lake
Salt Lake
Intermittent Lake
Reservoir
Swamp, Pond
Canal
Glacier
Ice Shelf, Pack Ice
Ocean
Sea
Gulf, Bay
Strait, Fjord
Lagoon
Bank
Seamount
Tablemount
Ridge
Shelf
Basin
Escarpment, Sea Scarp
Fracture
Trench, Abyss
National Park, Reserve
Point of Interest
Recreation Site
Cave, Cavern
Historic Site
Ruins
Wall, Walls
Church, Abbey
Temple
Scientific Station
Airport
Port
Lighthouse
Mine
Tunnel
Dam, Bridge

Nižni Oseredok, Ostrov- ◆	16	Pg	45.45N	48.35 E
Nižni Tagil	6	Ld	57.55N	59.57 E
Nižni Trajanov Val=Lower Trajan's Wall (EN) ⊓	15	Ld	45.45N	28.30 E
Nižnjaja Omra	17	Ge	62.46N	55.46 E
Nižnjaja Peša	19	Eb	66.43N	47.36 E
Nižnjaja Pojma	20	Ee	56.08N	97.18 E
Nižnjaja Salda	17	Jg	58.05N	60.48 E
Nižnjaja Tavda	19	Gd	57.40N	66.12 E
Nižnjaja Tojma ∿	7	Ke	62.22N	44.15 E
Nižnjaja Tunguska=Lower Tunguska (EN) ∿	21	Kc	65.48N	88.04 E
Nižnjaja Tura	17	Ig	58.37N	59.49 E
Nižnjaja Zolotica	7	Jd	65.41N	40.13 E
Nižny Pjandž	18	Gf	37.14N	68.35 E
Nizza Monferrato	14	Cf	44.46N	8.21 E
Njajs ∿	17	Je	62.25N	60.47 E
Njamunas ∿	5	Id	55.18N	21.23 E
Njandoma	19	Ec	61.43N	40.12 E
Njaris/Neris ∿	8	Kj	54.55N	25.45 E
Njazepetrovsk	17	Ih	56.03N	59.38 E
Njazidja/Grande Comore ◆	30	Lj	11.35 S	43.20 E
Njegoš ⛰	15	Bg	42.53N	18.45 E
Njinjo	36	Gd	8.48 S	38.54 E
Njombe ∿	30	Ki	6.56 S	35.06 E
Njombe	31	Ki	9.20 S	34.46 E
Njudung ⊠	8	Fg	57.25N	14.50 E
Njuja	20	Gd	60.32N	116.25 E
Njuk, Ozero- ≈	7	Hd	64.25N	31.45 E
Njuksenica	7	Kf	60.28N	44.15 E
Njukža ∿	20	He	56.30N	121.40 E
Njunes ▲	7	Eb	68.45N	19.30 E
Njurba	22	Nc	63.17N	118.20 E
Njurundabommen	7	De	62.16N	17.22 E
Njutånger	8	Gc	61.37N	17.03 E
Njuvčim	17	Ef	61.22N	50.42 E
Nkai	37	Dc	19.00 S	28.54 E
Nkambe	34	Hd	6.38N	10.40 E
Nkawkaw	34	Ed	6.33N	0.46W
Nkayi	31	Ii	4.05 S	13.18 E
Nkhata Bay	36	Fe	11.36 S	34.18 E
Nkongsamba	31	Hh	4.57N	9.56 E
Nkota Kota	31	Kj	12.55 S	34.18 E
Nkululu ∿	36	Fd	6.26 S	32.49 E
Nkusi ∿	36	Fb	1.07N	30.40 E
Nkwalini	37	Ee	28.45 S	31.30 E
'Nmai ∿	25	Jc	25.42N	97.30 E
Nmaki ∿	24	Pg	31.16N	55.29 E
Nnewi	34	Gd	6.01N	6.55 E
Nō	29	Ec	37.05N	137.59 E
Noailles	12	Ee	49.20N	2.12 E
Noākhāli	25	Id	22.49N	91.06 E
Noatak	40	Gc	67.34N	162.59W
Nobel	44	Gc	45.25N	80.06W
Nobeoka	27	Ne	32.35N	131.40 E
Noblesville	44	Ee	40.03N	86.00W
Noboribetsu	28	Pc	42.25N	141.11 E
Noce ∿	14	Fd	46.09N	11.04 E
Nocra ◆	35	Fc	15.40N	39.55 E
Nodaway River ∿	45	Ig	39.54N	94.58W
Noēn	27	Hc	43.15N	102.20 E
Noeuf, Ile des- ◆	37b	Bb	6.14 S	53.03 E
Noeux-les-Mines	12	Ed	50.29N	2.40 E
Nogajskaja Step ψ	16	Ng	44.15N	46.00 E
Nogales [Az.-U.S.]	43	Ee	31.21N	110.55W
Nogales [Mex.]	39	Hf	31.20N	110.56W
Nogaro	11	Fk	43.46N	0.02W
Nogat ∿	10	Pb	54.11N	19.15 E
Nōgata	29	Be	33.44N	130.44 E
Nogent-le-Rotrou	11	Gf	48.19N	0.50 E
Nogent-sur-Marne	12	Ef	48.50N	2.29 E
Nogent-sur-Oise	12	Ee	49.16N	2.28 E
Nogent-sur-Seine	11	Jf	48.29N	3.30 E
Noginsk [R.S.F.S.R.]	20	Ed	64.25N	91.10 E
Noginsk [R.S.F.S.R.]	19	Dd	55.54N	38.28 E
Nogliki	20	Jf	51.45N	143.15 E
Nōgo-Hakusan ▲	29	Ed	35.46N	136.31 E
Nogoyá	56	Id	32.24 S	59.48W
Nogoya, Arroyo- ∿	55	Ck	32.55 S	59.59W
Nógrád [2]	10	Ph	48.00N	19.35 E
Nogueira, Serra da- ⛰	13	Fc	41.42N	6.52W
Noguera Pallaresa ∿	13	Mb	42.15N	0.54 E
Noguera Ribagorçana/Noguera Ribagorzana ∿	13	Mc	41.40N	0.43 E
Noguera Ribagorzana/Noguera Ribagorçana ∿	13	Mc	41.40N	0.43 E
Noh, Laguna- ≈	48	Nh	18.40N	90.20W
Nohain ∿	11	Ig	47.24N	2.55 E
Noheji	28	Pd	40.52N	141.08 E
Nohfelden	12	Je	49.35N	7.09 E
Noidore, Rio- ∿	55	Fb	14.50 S	52.34W
Noir, Causse- ◠	11	Jj	44.09N	3.15 E
Noire, Montagne- ▲	11	Ik	43.28N	2.18 E
Noires, Montagnes- ⛰	11	Cf	48.09N	3.40W
Noirétable	11	Ji	45.49N	3.46 E
Noirmoutier, Ile de- ◆	11	Dh	46.58N	2.12W
Noirmoutier-en-l'Ile	11	Dg	47.00N	2.15W
Nojima-Zaki ►	29	Fd	34.54N	139.50 E
Nojiri-Ko ≈	29	Fc	36.49N	138.13 E
Noka	63c	Bb	10.40 S	166.03 E
Nokaneng	37	Cc	19.40 S	22.12 E
Nokia	7	Ff	61.28N	23.30 E
Nok Kundi	25	Cc	28.48N	62.46 E
Nokomis	46	Ma	51.30N	105.00W
Nokou	35	Ac	14.35N	14.47 E
Nokra	35	Fb	15.42N	39.56 E
Nol	8	Eg	57.55N	12.03 E
Nola [C.A.R.]	35	Be	3.32N	16.04 E
Nola [It.]	14	Ij	40.55N	14.33 E
Nolin Lake ≈	44	Dg	37.20N	86.10W
Nolinsk	19	Ed	57.33N	50.00 E
Nomad	58	Fe	6.21 S	142.12 E
Noma Omuramba ∿	37	Cc	19.10 S	22.16 E
Noma-Zaki ►	29	Bf	31.25N	130.06 E
Nombre de Dios	48	Gf	23.51N	104.14W
Nome	39	Cc	64.30N	165.24W
Nomeny	12	If	48.54N	6.14 E
Nomo-Saki ►	29	Ae	32.35N	129.45 E
Nomozaki	29	Ae	32.35N	129.45 E
Nomuka ◆	65b	Bb	20.15 S	174.48W
Nomuka Group ❖	57	Jg	20.20 S	174.45W
Nomuka Iki ◆	65b	Bb	20.17 S	174.49W
Nomwin Atoll ◎	57	Gd	8.32N	151.47 E
Nonacho Lake ≈	42	Gd	62.40N	109.30W
Nonancourt	12	Df	48.46N	1.12 E
Nonette ∿	12	Ee	49.12N	2.24 E
Nong'an	27	Mc	44.24N	125.08 E
Nong Han	25	Ke	17.21N	103.06 E
Nong Khai	22	Mh	17.52N	102.45 E
Nongoma	37	Ee	27.53 S	31.38 E
Nonoava	48	Fd	27.28N	106.44W
Nonouti Atoll ◎	57	Ie	0.40 S	174.21 E
Nonsan	28	If	36.12N	127.05 E
Nonsuch Bay ◧	51d	Bb	17.03N	61.42W
Nontron	11	Gi	45.32N	0.40 E
Noord-Beveland ◆	12	Fc	51.35N	3.45 E
Noord-Brabant [3]	12	Gc	51.30N	5.00 E
Noord-Holland [3]	12	Gb	52.40N	4.50 E
Noordhollandskanaal ═	11	Kb	52.55N	4.50 E
Noordoewer	37	Be	28.45 S	17.37 E
Noordoostpolder ⊠	11	Lb	52.42N	5.45 E
Noordoostpolder	12	Hb	52.42N	5.44 E
Noordoostpolder-Emmeloord	12	Hb	52.42N	5.44 E
Noordwijk aan Zee	11	Kb	52.14N	4.26 E
Noordwijk aan Zee, Noordwijk-	12	Gb	52.14N	4.26 E
Noordwijk-Noordwijk aan Zee	12	Gb	52.14N	4.26 E
Noordzee=North Sea (EN) ▤	5	Gd	55.20N	3.00 E
Noordzeekanaal ═	11	Kb	52.30N	4.35 E
Noormarkku/Norrmark	8	Ic	61.35N	21.52 E
Noorvik	40	Gc	66.50N	161.12W
Nootka Island ◆	46	Bb	49.32N	126.42W
Nootka Sound ◧	46	Bb	49.33N	126.38W
Nóqui	36	Bd	5.50 S	13.27 E
Nora [It.]	14	Dk	39.00N	9.02 E
Nora [Swe.]	7	Dg	59.31N	15.02 E
Noranda	42	Jg	48.15N	79.01W
Noraskog ⊠	8	Fe	59.40N	14.50 E
Norberg	8	Fd	60.04N	15.56 E
Norcia	14	Hh	42.48N	13.05 E
Nord	41	Kb	81.45N	17.30W
Nord [Cam.] [3]	34	Hd	9.00N	13.50 E
Nord [Fr.] [3]	11	Jd	50.20N	3.40 E
Nord [U.V.] [3]	34	Ec	13.40N	2.50W
Nord, Canal du- ═	11	Id	49.57N	2.55 E
Nord, Mer du-=North Sea (EN) ▤	5	Gd	55.20N	3.00 E
Nordausques	12	Ed	50.49N	2.05 E
Nordaustlandet ◆	67	Jd	79.48N	22.24 E
Nordborg	8	Ci	55.03N	9.45 E
Nordby	8	Ci	55.27N	8.25 E
Norddeutsches Tiefland=North German Plain (EN) ⊠	5	He	53.00N	11.00 E
Norden	10	Dc	53.36N	7.12 E
Nordenham	10	Ec	53.39N	8.29 E
Nordenskjölda, Ostrova-=Nordenskjöld, Archipelago (EN) ❖	20	Ea	76.50N	96.00 E
Nordenskjöld Archipelago (EN)=Nordenskjölda, Ostrova- ❖	20	Ea	76.50N	96.00 E
Norderney ◆	10	Dc	53.42N	7.10 E
Norderstedt	10	Fc	53.41N	9.58 E
Nordfjord ⊠	8	Bc	61.50N	6.15 E
Nordfjord ▬	7	Af	61.55N	5.10 E
Nordfjordeid	7	Af	61.54N	6.00 E
Nordfold	7	Dc	67.46N	15.12 E
Nordfriesische Inseln=North Frisian Islands (EN) ❖	10	Ea	54.50N	8.30 E
Nordfriesland ⊠	10	Eb	54.40N	8.55 E
Nordgau ⊠	10	Hg	49.15N	11.50 E
Nordgrønland=North Greenland (EN) [2]	41	Gc	79.30N	50.00W
Nordhausen	10	Ge	51.31N	10.48 E
Nordhordland ⊠	8	Ad	60.50N	5.50 E
Nordhorn	10	Dd	52.26N	7.05 E
Nord-Jylland [2]	8	Cg	57.15N	10.00 E
Nordkapp [Nor.] =North Cape (EN) ►	5	Ia	71.11N	25.48 E
Nordkapp [Sval.] ►	41	Nb	80.31N	20.00 E
Nordkinn ⊐	5	Ia	71.08N	27.39 E
Nordkinnhalvøya ⊐	7	Ga	70.55N	27.45 E
Nord-Kvaløy ◆	7	Ea	70.10N	19.11 E
Nordland [3]	7	Cc	67.06N	13.20 E
Nördlingen	10	Gh	48.51N	10.30 E
Nordloher Tief ∿	12	Ja	53.10N	7.45 E
Nordmark	8	Fe	59.50N	14.06 E
Nordmøre ⊠	8	Ca	63.00N	8.30 E
Nordostrundingen ►	67	Le	81.30N	11.00W
Nord-Ostsee Kanal=Kiel Canal (EN) ═	5	Ge	53.53N	9.08 E
Nord-Ouest [3]	34	Hd	6.30N	10.30 E
Nordøyane ❖	8	Bb	62.40N	6.15 E
Nordreisa	7	Eb	69.46N	21.03 E
Nordre Rønner ◆	8	Dg	57.22N	10.56 E
Nordrhein-Westfalen=North Rhine-Westphalia (EN) [2]	10	De	51.30N	7.30 E
Nordsee=North Sea (EN) ▤	5	Gd	55.20N	3.00 E
Nordsjøen=North Sea (EN) ▤	5	Gd	55.20N	3.00 E
Nordskjobotn	7	Eb	69.13N	19.34 E
Nordsøen=North Sea (EN) ▤	5	Gd	55.20N	3.00 E
Nord Strand ◆	10	Eb	54.30N	8.55 E
Nordtiroler Kalkalpen ⛰	10	Hi	47.30N	11.30 E
Nord-Trøndelag [2]	7	Cd	64.25N	12.00 E
Nordwestfjord ▬	41	Jd	71.30N	26.30W
Nore/An Fheoir ∿	9	Gi	52.25N	6.58W
Norefjell ▲	8	Cd	60.16N	9.29 E
Norefjorden ≈	8	Cd	60.10N	9.00 E
Norfolk ▣	9	Oi	52.40N	1.05 E
Norfolk [3]	9	Mi	52.45N	0.40W
Norfolk [Nb.-U.S.]	43	Hc	42.02N	97.25W
Norfolk [Va.-U.S.]	39	Lf	38.40N	76.14W
Norfolk Island [5]	58	Hg	29.05 S	167.59 E
Norfolk Island ◆	57	Hg	29.05 S	167.59 E
Norfolk Ridge (EN) ⋀	57	Hg	29.00 S	168.00 E
Norfork Lake ≈	45	Jh	36.25N	92.10W
Norg	12	Ia	53.04N	6.32 E
Norge=Norway (EN) [1]	6	Gc	62.00N	10.00 E
Norheimsund	7	Bf	60.22N	6.08 E
Norikura-Dake ▲	29	Ec	36.06N	137.33 E
Norilsk	22	Kc	69.20N	88.06 E
Normal	45	Lf	40.31N	88.59W
Norman	43	Hd	35.15N	97.26W
Norman, Lake- ≈	44	Gh	35.35N	81.00W
Normanby Island ◆	60	Ej	10.00 S	151.00 E
Normanby River ∿	59	Ib	14.25 S	144.08 E
Normand, Bocage- ♣	11	Ef	49.00N	1.10W
Normandie=Normandy (EN) ▣	11	Gf	49.00N	0.10 E
Normandie=Normandy (EN) ⊠	5	Gf	49.00N	0.10 E
Normandie, Collines de-=Normandy Hills (EN) ◠	5	Ff	48.50N	0.40W
Normandin	44	Ka	48.52N	72.30W
Normandy (EN)=Normandie ▣	11	Gf	49.00N	0.10 E
Normandy (EN)=Normandie ⊠	5	Gf	49.00N	0.10 E
Normandy Hills (EN)=Normandie, Collines de- ◠	5	Ff	48.50N	0.40W
Norman Island ◆	51a	Db	18.20N	64.37W
Norman River ∿	59	Ic	17.28 S	140.39 E
Normanton	58	Ff	17.40 S	141.05 E
Norman Wells	39	Gc	65.17N	126.51W
Norquinco	56	Ff	41.51 S	70.54W
Norra Dellen ≈	8	Gc	61.55N	16.40 E
Norrahammar	8	Fg	57.42N	14.06 E
Norrala	8	Gc	61.22N	16.59 E
Norra Midsjöbanken ▥	8	Gh	56.10N	17.30 E
Norra Ny	7	Cf	60.24N	13.15 E
Norra Storfjället ▲	7	Dd	65.53N	15.14 E
Norrbotten [2]	7	Ec	67.26N	19.35 E
Nørre Åby	8	Ci	55.27N	9.54 E
Nørre Alslev	8	Dj	54.54N	11.54 E
Nørre-Nebel	8	Ci	55.47N	8.18 E
Norrent-Fontes	12	Ed	50.35N	2.24 E
Nørresundby	7	Bh	57.04N	9.55 E
Norrhult	7	Dh	57.08N	15.10 E
Norris Lake ≈	44	Fg	36.20N	83.55W
Norristown	44	Je	40.07N	75.20W
Norrköping	6	Hd	58.36N	16.11 E
Norrland ⊠	5	Hc	64.27N	17.20 E
Norrland ▣	7	Dd	65.00N	18.00 E
Norrmark/Noormarkku	8	Ic	61.35N	21.52 E
Norrsundet	8	Gd	60.56N	17.08 E
Norrtälje	7	Eg	59.46N	18.42 E
Norseman	58	Dh	32.12 S	121.46 E
Norsewood	62	Gd	40.04 S	176.13 E
Norsjö	7	Ed	64.55N	19.29 E
Norsjø ≈	8	Ce	59.20N	9.20 E
Norsk	20	Hf	52.20N	129.59 E
Norske Havet=Norwegian, Sea (EN) ▤	5	Gc	70.00N	2.00 E
Norske Øer ❖	41	Kc	79.00N	18.00W
Norsoup	63b	Cc	16.04 S	167.23 E
Norte, Baía- ◧	55	Hh	27.30 S	48.35W
Norte, Cabo- [Braz.] ►	54	Ic	1.40N	50.00W
Norte, Cabo- [Pas.] ►	65d	Ab	27.03 S	109.24W
Norte, Canal do- ▬	54	Hc	0.30N	50.30W
Norte, Punta- ►	56	Hf	42.04 S	63.45W
Norte, Serra do- ⛰	54	Gf	11.00 S	59.00W
Norte del Cabo San Antonio, Punta- ►	56	Ie	36.17 S	56.47W
Norte de Santander [2]	54	Db	8.00N	73.00W
Nortelândia	54	Gf	14.25 S	56.48W
North, Cape - ►	42	Lg	47.02N	60.25W
North Adams	44	Kd	42.42N	73.02W
Northallerton	9	Lg	54.20N	1.26W
Northam [Austl.]	58	Ch	31.39 S	116.40 E
Northam [S.Afr.]	37	Dd	24.58 S	27.11 E
North America ■	38	Jf	40.00N	95.00W
North American Basin (EN) ◡	3	Cf	30.00N	60.00W
Northampton ▣	9	Mi	52.30N	1.00W
Northampton [Austl.]	59	Ce	28.21 S	114.37 E
Northampton [Eng.-U.K.]	9	Mi	52.14N	0.54W
Northampton [Ma.-U.S.]	44	Kd	42.19N	72.38W
Northampton Seamounts (EN) ▴	57	Jb	25.20N	172.04W
Northamptonshire [3]	9	Mi	52.25N	0.55W
North Andaman ◆	25	If	13.15N	92.55 E
North Arm ◧	42	Gd	62.00N	114.30W
North Astrolabe Reef ❋	63d	Bc	18.39 S	178.32 E
North Augusta	44	Gi	33.30N	81.58W
North Aulatsivik ◆	42	Le	59.45N	64.04W
North Australian Basin ◡	3	Hk	14.30 S	116.30 E
North Battleford	39	Id	52.47N	108.17W
North Bay	39	Le	46.19N	79.28W
North Belcher Islands ❖	42	Je	56.45N	79.45W
North Berwick	9	Ke	56.04N	2.44W
North Buganda [3]	36	Fb	0.50N	32.10 E
North Caicos ◆	49	Lc	21.56N	71.59W
North Canadian River ∿	43	Hd	35.17N	95.31W
North Cape ►	57	Ih	34.25 S	173.03 E
North Cape (EN)=Nordkapp [Nor.] ►	5	Ia	71.11N	25.48 E
North Caribou Lake ≈	42	If	52.48N	90.45W
North Carolina [2]	43	Ld	35.30N	80.00W
North Channel ▬	42	Jg	46.02N	82.50W
North Channel/Sruth na Maoile ▬	5	Fd	55.10N	5.40W
Northchapel	12	Bc	51.03N	0.38W
North Charleston	44	Hi	32.53N	80.00W
North Chicago	45	Me	42.20N	87.51W
North Cove	46	Cc	46.47N	124.06W
North Dakota [2]	43	Gb	47.30N	100.15W
North Downs ◠	9	Nj	51.20N	0.10 E
North East	44	Hd	42.13N	79.51W
North-East [3]	37	Dd	21.00 S	27.30 E
Northeast Cape	40	Fd	63.18N	168.42W
North-Eastern [3]	36	Hb	1.00N	40.15 E
Northeast Islands ❖	64d	Ba	7.36N	151.57 E
Northeast Pacific Basin (EN) ◡	3	Lg	20.00N	140.00W
Northeast Pass ▬	64d	Ba	7.30N	151.59 E
North East Point ►	64g	Bb	1.57N	157.16W
Northeast Point [Bah.] ►	49	Kc	21.18N	72.54W
Northeast Point [Bah.] ►	49	Kb	22.43N	73.50W
Northeast Providence Channel ▬	47	Ic	25.40N	77.09W
Northeim	10	Fe	51.42N	10.00 E
North Entrance ▬	64a	Bb	7.59N	134.37 E
Northern [Ghana] [3]	34	Ed	9.30N	1.00W
Northern [Mwi.] [3]	36	Fe	11.00 S	34.00 E
Northern [S.L.] [3]	34	Cd	9.15N	11.45W
Northern [Ug.] [3]	36	Fb	2.45N	32.45 E
Northern [Zam.] [3]	36	Fe	11.00 S	31.00 E
Northern Cay ◆	49	De	17.27N	87.28W
Northern Cook Islands ❖	57	Kf	10.00 S	161.00W
Northern Dvina (EN)=Severnaja Dvina ∿	5	Kc	64.32N	40.30 E
Northern Guinea ⊠	30	Gh	8.30N	1.00W
Northern Indian Lake ≈	42	He	57.20N	97.17W
Northern Ireland [2]	9	Gg	54.40N	6.45W
Northern Mariana Islands [5]	58	Fc	16.00N	145.30 E
Northern Sporades (EN)=Vórioi Sporádhes, Nísoi- ❖	5	Ih	39.15N	23.55 E
Northern Territory	59	Gc	20.00 S	134.00 E
Northern Urals (EN)=Severny Ural ⛰	5	Lc	62.00N	59.00 E
Northern Uvals (EN)=Severnyje Uvaly ◠	5	Kd	59.30N	49.00 E
North Esk ∿	9	Ke	56.45N	2.30W
Northfield	45	Jd	44.27N	93.09W
North Fiji Basin (EN) ◡	3	Jk	16.00 S	174.00 E
North Foreland ►	9	Oj	51.23N	1.27 E
North Fork Grand River ∿	45	Ed	45.47N	102.16W
North Fork John Day River ∿	46	Fd	44.45N	119.38W
North Fork Moreau River ∿	45	Ed	45.09N	102.50W
North Fork Pass ⌵	42	Dd	64.00N	138.00W
North Fork Powder River ∿	46	Le	43.40N	106.30W
North Fork Red ∿	45	Gi	34.25N	99.14W
North Fort Myers	44	Gl	26.40N	81.54W
North Frisian Islands (EN)=Nordfriesische Inseln ❖	10	Ea	54.50N	8.30 E
North German Plain (EN)=Norddeutsches Tiefland ⊠	5	He	53.00N	11.00 E
North Greenland (EN) = Nordgrønland [2]	41	Gc	79.30N	50.00W
North Highlands	46	Eg	38.40N	121.23W
North Horr	36	Gb	3.19N	37.04 E
North Island [N.Z.] ◆	57	Ih	39.00 S	176.00 E
North Island [Sey.] ◆	37b	Bc	10.07 S	51.11 E
North Kent ◆	42	Ia	76.40N	90.15W
North Korea (EN)=Chosŏn M.I.K. [1]	22	Oe	40.00N	127.30 E
North Lakhimpur	25	Ic	27.14N	94.07 E
Northland [2]	62	Ea	35.30 S	173.40 E
North Las Vegas	46	Hh	36.12N	115.07W
North Lincoln Land ⊠	42	Ja	76.15N	80.00W
North Little Rock	43	Ie	34.46N	92.14W
North Loup River ∿	45	Gf	41.17N	98.23W
North Magnetic Pole (1980)	67	Qd	77.03N	101.08W
North Malosmadulu Atoll ◎	25a	Ba	5.35N	72.55 E
North Mamm Peak ▲	45	Cg	39.23N	107.52W
North Mayreau Channel	51n	Bb	12.41N	61.20W
North Miami	44	Gm	25.56N	80.09W
North Minch ▬	5	Fd	58.05N	5.55W
North Palisade ▲	46	Fh	37.10N	118.38W
North Pass [F.S.M.] ▬	64d	Ba	7.41N	151.48 E
North Pass [U.S.] ▬	45	Ll	29.10N	89.15W
North Platte	43	Gc	41.08N	100.46W
North Platte ∿	38	Ie	41.15N	100.45W
North Point ►	64n	Ab	10.22 S	161.02W
North Point [Bar.] ►	51q	Ab	13.20N	59.36W
North Pole	67	Ge	90.00N	0.00
Northport	44	Di	33.14N	87.35W
North Powder	46	Gd	45.03N	117.55W
North Raccoon River ∿	45	Jf	41.35N	93.31W
North Reef ❋	63a	Ee	12.13 S	160.04 E
North Rhine-Westphalia (EN)=Nordrhein-Westfalen [2]	10	De	51.30N	7.30 E
North Rim	46	Ih	36.12N	112.03W
North River	42	Ie	58.53N	94.42W
North Rona ◆	9	Hb	59.10N	5.40W
North Ronaldsay ◆	9	Kb	59.25N	2.30W
North Saskatchewan ∿	38	Id	53.15N	105.06W
North Sea ▤	5	Gd	55.20N	3.00 E
North Sea (EN)=Noordzee ▤	5	Gd	55.20N	3.00 E
North Sea (EN)=Nord, Mer du- ▤	5	Gd	55.20N	3.00 E
North Sea (EN)=Nordsee ▤	5	Gd	55.20N	3.00 E
North Sea (EN)=Nordsjøen ▤	5	Gd	55.20N	3.00 E
North Sea (EN)=Nordsøen ▤	5	Gd	55.20N	3.00 E
North Sentinel ◆	25	If	11.33N	92.15 E
North Shoshone Peak ▲	46	Gg	39.10N	117.29W
North Siberian Plain (EN)=Severo-Sibirskaja Niz. ▭	21	Mb	72.00N	104.00 E
North Sound ▬	51d	Bb	17.07N	61.45W
North Sound ◧	49	Gd	19.25N	81.26W
North Stradbroke Island ◆	59	Ke	27.35 S	153.30 E
North Taranaki Bight ◧	62	Fc	38.50 S	174.25 E
North Thompson ∿	42	Ff	50.41N	120.11W
North Tokelau Trough (EN) ∨	3	Kj	3.00 S	165.00W
North Tonawanda	44	Hd	43.02N	78.54W
North Trap ◆	62	Bg	47.20 S	167.55 E
North Tyne ∿	9	Kg	54.59N	2.08W
North Uist ◆	9	Fd	57.37N	7.22W
Northumberland [3]	9	Kf	55.15N	2.10W
Northumberland ▣	9	Kf	55.15N	2.05W
Northumberland Islands ❖	57	Gg	21.40 S	150.00 E
Northumberland Strait ▬	42	Lg	46.00N	63.30W
North Umpqua River ∿	46	De	43.16N	123.27W
North Vancouver	46	Db	49.19N	123.04W
North Walsham	12	Db	52.49N	1.23 E
Northway	40	Kd	62.59N	141.43W
North West Bluff ✱	51c	Bc	16.49N	62.12W
North West Cape ►	57	Cg	21.45 S	114.10 E
North-Western [3]	36	Ee	13.00 S	25.00 E
Northwest Frontier [3]	25	Eb	33.00N	70.30 E
North West Highlands ⌓	5	Fd	57.30N	5.00W
Northwest Pacific Basin (EN) ◡	3	Je	40.00N	155.00 E
North West Point ►	64g	Ab	2.02N	157.30W
Northwest Providence Channel ═	44	Hl	26.10N	78.20W
Northwest Reef ✱	64a	Bb	7.59N	134.33 E
North West River	42	Lf	53.32N	60.09W
Northwest Territories [3]	42	Hc	66.00N	102.00W
Northwich	9	Kh	53.16N	2.32W
North York Moors	9	Mg	54.25N	0.50W
North Yorkshire [3]	9	Lg	54.15N	1.40W
Norton [Ks.-U.S.]	43	Gd	39.50N	100.01W
Norton [Va.-U.S.]	44	Fg	36.56N	82.37W
Norton [Zimb.]	37	Ec	17.53 S	30.41 E
Norton Bay ◧	40	Gd	64.45N	161.15W
Norton Sound ▬	38	Cc	64.45N	161.15W
Norvegia, Kapp- ►	66	Bf	71.25 S	12.18W
Norwalk [Ct.-U.S.]	44	Ke	41.07N	73.27W
Norwalk [Oh.-U.S.]	44	Fe	41.14N	82.37W
Norway	44	Dc	45.47N	87.55W
Norway (EN)=Norge [1]	6	Gc	62.00N	10.00 E
Norway Bay ◧	42	Hb	71.00N	104.35W
Norway House	42	Hf	53.58N	97.50W
Norwegian Basin (EN) ◡	3	Dc	68.00N	2.00W
Norwegian Bay ◧	42	Ij	77.45N	90.30W
Norwegian Sea (EN)=Norske Havet ▤	5	Gc	70.00N	2.00 E
Norwegian Trench (EN) ∨	5	Gd	59.00N	4.30 E
Norwich [Ct.-U.S.]	44	Ke	41.32N	72.05W
Norwich [Eng.-U.K.]	6	Ge	52.38N	1.18 E
Norwich [N.Y.-U.S.]	44	Jd	42.33N	75.33W
Norwich Airport ✈	12	Db	52.40N	1.18 E
Norwood	44	Ef	39.10N	84.28W
Nosappu-Misaki ►	29a	Db	43.23N	145.47 E
Noshappu-Misaki ►	29a	Ba	45.27N	141.39 E
Noshiro	27	Pc	40.12N	140.02 E
Nosovaja	19	Fb	68.15N	54.31 E
Nosovka	19	De	50.54N	31.37 E
Nosratābād	23	Id	29.54N	59.59 E
Nossa Senhora das Candeias	54	Kf	12.40 S	38.33W
Nossa Senhora do Livramento	55	Db	15.48 S	56.22W
Noss Head ►	9	Jc	58.30N	3.05W
Nossob ∿	30	Jk	26.55 S	20.40 E
Nossop ∿	37	Ce	26.55 S	20.40 E
Nosy-Be ◆	30	Lj	13.20 S	48.15 E
Nosy-Be	31	Lj	13.22 S	48.16 E
Nosy-Varika	37	Hd	20.35 S	48.30 E
Nota ∿	7	Hb	68.07N	30.10 E
Notch Peak ▲	46	Ig	39.08N	113.24W
Noteć ∿	10	Ld	52.44N	15.26 E
Notecka, Puszcza- ♣	10	Ld	52.45N	16.00 E
Note Kemopla ►	63c	b	10.55 S	165.51 E
Notengo, Laguna de- ◍	48	Ji	16.15N	98.10W
Notia Píndhos ⛰	15	Ej	39.30N	21.20 E
Nótioi Sporádhes=Dodecanese (EN) ❖	5	Ih	36.00N	27.00 E
Nótios Evvoïkós Kólpos ◧	15	Gk	38.20N	23.50 E
Nötö ◆	8	Ie	60.00N	21.45 E
Noto [It.]	14	Jn	36.53N	15.04 E
Noto [Jap.]	28	Nf	37.18N	137.09 E
Noto, Golfo di- ◧	14	Jn	36.50N	15.10 E
Notodden	7	Bg	59.34N	9.17 E
Noto-Hantō ⊐	27	Od	37.20N	137.00 E
Noto-Jima ◆	29	Ec	37.07N	137.00 E
Notoro-Ko ≈	29a	Da	44.05N	144.10 E
Notoro-Misaki ►	29a	Da	44.07N	144.15 E
Notranjsko ⊠	14	Ie	45.46N	14.26 E
Notre-Dame, Monts- ⛰	38	Me	48.00N	69.00W
Notre Dame Bay ◧	42	Mg	49.50N	55.00W
Notre-Dame-de-Courson	12	Cf	48.59N	0.16 E
Notre-Dame-de-Gravenchon	12	Ce	49.29N	0.35 E
Notre Dame-du-Lac	44	Mb	47.38N	68.49W
Notre-Dame-du-Nord	44	Hb	47.36N	79.29W
Notsé	34	Fd	6.59N	1.12 E
Notsuke-Zaki ►	29a	Db	43.34N	145.19 E
Nottawasaga Bay ◧	44	Gc	44.40N	80.30W
Nottaway ∿	38	Ld	51.25N	79.50W
Notterøy ◆	8	De	59.15N	10.25 E
Nottingham	6	Fe	52.58N	1.10W
Nottingham ◆	42	Jd	63.20N	78.00W
Nottingham ▣	9	Mh	53.05N	1.00W
Nottinghamshire [3]	9	Mh	53.10N	0.55W
Nottoway River ∿	44	Ig	36.33N	76.55W
Nottuln	12	Jc	51.56N	7.21 E
Notukeu Creek ∿	46	Lb	49.55N	106.30W
Nouâdhibou	31	Ff	20.54N	17.01W
Nouâdhibou, Dahklet- ◧	32	De	21.00N	16.50W
Nouâdhibou, Râs-=Blanc Cape- (EN) ►	30	Ff	20.46N	17.03W
Nouakchott	31	Fg	18.07N	15.59W
Nouakchott, District de- [3]	32	Df	18.06N	15.57W
Nouamrhar	32	Df	19.22N	16.31W
Nouméa	58	Hg	22.16 S	166.26 E
Nouna	34	Ec	12.44N	3.52W
Noupoort	37	Cf	31.10 S	24.57 E

Index Symbols

- [1] Independent Nation
- [2] State, Region
- [3] District, County
- [4] Municipality
- [5] Colony, Dependency
- ■ Continent
- ⊠ Physical Region
- ▣ Historical or Cultural Region
- ▲ Mount, Mountain
- △ Volcano
- ⌒ Hill
- ⛰ Mountains, Mountain Range
- ◠ Hills, Escarpment
- ⌓ Plateau, Upland
- ⌵ Pass, Gap
- ▭ Plain, Lowland
- ◣ Delta
- ▱ Salt Flat
- ⋁ Valley, Canyon
- ◌ Crater, Cave
- ⊛ Karst Features
- ⊔ Depression
- ⊡ Polder
- ⁖ Desert, Dunes
- ♣ Forest, Woods
- ψ Heath, Steppe
- ☘ Oasis
- ► Cape, Point
- ⋯ Coast, Beach
- ◨ Cliff
- ⊐ Peninsula
- ⋈ Isthmus
- ▔ Sandbank
- ◆ Island
- ◎ Atoll
- ✱ Rock, Reef
- ❖ Islands, Archipelago
- ✳ Rocks, Reefs
- ❋ Coral Reef
- ⊙ Well, Spring
- ⛲ Geyser
- ∿ River, Stream
- ⤓ Waterfall Rapids
- ⊲ River Mouth, Estuary
- ≈ Lake
- ≋ Salt Lake
- ⊏ Intermittent Lake
- ⊟ Reservoir
- ⩸ Swamp, Pond
- ═ Canal
- ❄ Glacier
- ❅ Ice Shelf, Pack Ice
- ▩ Ocean
- ▤ Sea
- ◧ Gulf, Bay
- ▬ Strait, Fjord
- ◍ Lagoon
- ▥ Bank
- ▴ Seamount
- ⏍ Tablemount
- ⋀ Ridge
- ⏊ Shelf
- ◡ Basin
- ⌇ Escarpment, Sea Scarp
- ⚡ Fracture
- ∨ Trench, Abyss
- ⚑ National Park, Reserve
- ✠ Point of Interest
- ✚ Recreation Site
- ◚ Cave, Cavern
- ⛫ Historic Site
- ⁘ Ruins
- ⊓ Wall, Walls
- ⛪ Church, Abbey
- ⛩ Temple
- ⊗ Scientific Station
- ✈ Airport
- ⚓ Port
- ☗ Lighthouse
- ⚒ Mine
- ∩ Tunnel
- ⌿ Dam, Bridge

Nouveau-Comptoir 42 Jf 52.35N 78.40W
Nouveau-Québec, Cratère du- = New Quebec Crater (EN) 42 Kd 61.30N 73.55W
Nouvelle-Calédonie = New Caledonia (EN) [5] 58 Hg 21.30S 165.30 E
Nouvelle-Calédonie=New Caledonia (EN) 57 Hg 21.30S 165.30 E
Nouvelle-France, Cap de - 42 Kd 62.33N 73.35W
Nouvelles Hébrides/New Hebrides 57 Hf 16.01S 167.01 E
Nouvion 12 Dd 50.12N 1.47 E
Nouzonville 11 Ke 49.49N 4.45 E
Novabad 18 He 39.01N 70.09 E
Nová Baňa 10 Oh 48.26N 18.39 E
Nová Bystřice 10 Lg 49.02N 15.06 E
Nova Cruz 54 Ke 6.28S 35.26W
Nova Esperança 55 Ff 23.08S 52.13W
Nova Friburgo 54 Jh 22.16S 42.32W
Nova Gaia 36 Ce 10.05S 17.32 E
Nova Gorica 14 He 45.57N 13.39 E
Nova Gradiška 14 Le 45.16N 17.23 E
Nova Granada 55 He 20.29S 49.19W
Nova Iguaçu 53 Lh 22.45S 43.27W
Novaja Igirma 20 Fe 57.10N 103.55 E
Novaja-Ivanovka 15 Md 45.59N 29.04 E
Novaja Kahovka 16 Hf 46.43N 33.23 E
Novaja Kazanka 16 Pe 48.58N 49.37 E
Novaja Ladoga 7 Hf 60.05N 32.16 E
Novaja Ljalja 19 Gd 59.03N 60.36 E
Novaja Odessa 16 Gf 47.18N 31.47 E
Novaja Sibir, Ostrov-=New Siberia (EN) 21 Qb 75.00N 149.00 E
Novaja Vodolaga 16 Ie 49.45N 35.52 E
Novaja Zemlja=Novaya Zemlya (EN) 21 Hb 74.00N 57.00 E
Nova Lamego 34 Cc 12.17N 14.13W
Nova Lima 54 Jh 19.59S 43.51W
Nova Londrina 55 Ff 22.45S 53.00W
Nova Mambone 37 Fd 20.58S 35.00 E
Nova Olinda do Norte 54 Gd 3.45S 59.03W
Nová Paka 10 Lf 50.29N 15.31 E
Nova Prata 55 Gi 28.47S 51.36W
Novara 14 Ce 45.28N 8.38 E
Nova Roma 55 Ia 13.51S 46.57W
Nova Russas 54 Jd 4.42S 40.34W
Nova Scotia [3] 42 Lh 45.00N 63.00W
Nova Scotia 38 Me 45.00N 63.00W
Nova Sintra 32 Cf 14.54N 24.40W
Nova Sofala 37 Ed 20.10S 34.44 E
Novato 46 Dg 38.06N 122.34W
Nova Varoš 15 Cf 43.28N 19.49 E
Nova Venécia 54 Jg 18.43S 40.24W
Novaya Zemlya (EN)= Novaja Zemlja 21 Hb 74.00N 57.00 E
Nova Zagora 15 Jg 42.29N 26.01 E
Novelda 13 Lf 38.23N 0.46W
Novellara 14 Ef 44.51N 10.44 E
Nové Mesto nad Váhom 10 Nh 48.46N 17.50 E
Nové Zámky 10 Oi 47.59N 18.11 E
Novgorod 6 Jd 58.31N 31.17 E
Novgorodka 8 Mg 57.00N 28.37 E
Novgorod-Severski 19 De 52.01N 33.16 E
Novgorodskaja Oblast [3] 19 Dd 58.20N 32.40 E
Novi Bečej 15 Dd 45.36N 20.08 E
Novigrad [Yugo.] 14 He 45.19N 13.34 E
Novigrad [Yugo.] 14 Jf 44.11N 15.33 E
Novi Kričim 15 Hg 42.03N 24.28 E
Novi Ligure 14 Cf 44.46N 8.47 E
Novillero 48 Gf 22.21N 105.39W
Novion-Porcien 12 Ge 49.36N 4.25 E
Novi Pazar [Bul.] 15 Kf 43.21N 27.12 E
Novi Pazar [Yugo.] 15 Df 43.08N 20.31 E
Novi Sad 6 Hf 45.15N 19.50 E
Novi Travnik 14 Lf 44.10N 17.39 E
Novi Vinodolski 14 Ie 45.08N 14.47 E
Novoaleksandrovsk 16 Lg 45.24N 41.14 E
Novoaleksejevka [Kaz.-U.S.S.R.] 16 Sd 50.08N 55.42 E
Novoaleksejevka [Ukr.-U.S.S.R.] 16 If 46.16N 34.39 E
Novoaltajsk 20 Df 53.24N 83.58 E
Novoanninski 19 Ee 50.31N 42.45 E
Novoarhangelsk 16 Ge 48.39N 30.50 E
Novo Aripuanã 54 Fe 5.08S 60.22W
Novoazovsk 16 Kf 47.05N 38.05 E
Novobirjusinski 20 Ee 56.58N 97.55 E
Novobogdanovka 16 If 47.05N 35.18 E
Novočeboksarsk 7 Lh 56.08N 47.29 E
Novočeremšansk 7 Mi 54.23N 50.10 E
Novočerkassk 19 Ef 47.25N 40.03 E
Novodevičje 7 Lj 53.35N 48.51 E
Novograd-Volynski 19 Ce 50.36N 27.36 E
Novogrudok 16 Dc 53.37N 25.50 E
Nôvo Hamburgo 56 Jc 29.41S 51.08W
Novohopërsk 16 Ld 51.06N 41.37 E
Novo Horizonte 55 He 21.28S 49.13W
Novoizborsk 8 Mg 57.43N 28.05 E
Novojenisejsk 20 Ee 58.19N 92.27 E
Novojerudinski 20 Ee 59.47N 93.30 E
Novokačalinsk 20 Ig 45.05N 131.59 E
Novokazalinsk 22 Ie 45.50N 62.10 E
Novokubansk 16 Lg 45.06N 41.01 E
Novokujbyševsk 19 Ee 53.08N 49.58 E
Novokuzneck 22 Kd 53.45N 87.06 E
Novolazarevskaja 66 Cf 70.46S 11.50 E
Novolukoml 7 Gi 54.38N 29.07 E
Novo Mesto 14 Je 45.48N 15.10 E
Novomičurinsk 7 Ji 54.02N 39.48 E
Novomihajlovka 20 Ih 44.17N 133.50 E
Novo Miloševo 15 Dd 45.43N 20.18 E
Novomirgorod 16 Ge 48.45N 31.39 E
Novomoskovsk [R.S.F.S.R.] 6 Je 54.05N 38.13 E
Novomoskovsk [Ukr.-U.S.S.R.] 19 Df 48.37N 35.16 E
Novonikolajevski 16 Md 50.55N 42.24 E
Novoorsk 19 Fe 51.24N 58.59 E
Novopokrovskaja 16 Lg 45.56N 40.42 E
Novopolock 19 Cd 55.31N 28.40 E
Novorossijsk 6 Jg 44.45N 37.45 E
Novorybnaja 20 Fb 72.50N 105.45 E
Novoržev 19 Cd 57.02N 29.20 E
Novo-Šahtinsk 19 Df 47.47N 39.54 E
Novoselica 15 Ja 48.13N 26.17 E
Novoselje 8 Mf 58.05N 29.00 E
Novoselki 10 Ud 52.04N 24.25 E
Novoselovo 20 Ef 54.55N 91.00 E
Novosergijevka 19 Fe 52.03N 53.39 E
Novosibirsk 22 Kd 55.02N 82.55 E
Novosibirskaja Oblast [3] 20 Ce 55.30N 80.00 E
Novosibirskije Ostrova= New Siberian Islands (EN) 21 Qb 75.00N 142.00 E
Novosibirskoje Vodohranilišče 20 Df 54.40N 82.35 E
Novosil 16 Jc 52.59N 37.01 E
Novosineglazovski 17 Ji 55.05N 61.25 E
Novosokolniki 19 Dd 56.19N 30.12 E
Novospasskoje 7 Lj 53.09N 47.44 E
Novotroick 19 Fe 51.12N 58.35 E
Novotroickoje 19 Hg 43.39N 73.45 E
Novoukrainka 16 Ge 48.19N 31.32 E
Novouljanovsk 7 Li 54.10N 48.23 E
Novouzensk 19 Ee 50.29N 48.08 E
Novovjatsk 7 Lg 58.31N 49.43 E
Novovolynsk 19 Ce 50.46N 24.09 E
Novovoronežski 16 Kd 51.17N 39.16 E
Novozybkov 19 De 52.32N 32.00 E
Novska 14 Ke 45.20N 16.59 E
Novy Bug 16 Hf 47.43N 32.29 E
Nový Bydžov 10 Lf 50.15N 15.29 E
Novy Jaričev 10 Ug 49.50N 24.21 E
Novyje Aneny 15 Mc 46.53N 29.13 E
Novyje Burasy 16 Oc 52.06N 46.06 E
Nový Jičín 10 Og 49.36N 18.01 E
Novy Oskol 19 De 50.43N 37.54 E
Novy Pogost 8 Li 55.30N 27.32 E
Novy Port 22 Jc 67.40N 72.52 E
Novy Tap 17 Mh 56.55N 67.15 E
Novy Terek 16 Oh 43.37N 47.25 E
Novy Uzen 19 Fg 43.19N 52.55 E
Novy Vasjugan 20 Ce 58.34N 76.29 E
Novy Zaj 7 Mi 55.17N 52.02 E
Nowa Dęba 10 Rf 50.26N 21.46 E
Nowa Huta, Kraków- 10 Qf 50.04N 20.05 E
Nowa Ruda 10 Mf 50.35N 16.31 E
Nowa Sarzyna 10 Sf 50.23N 22.22 E
Nowa Sól 10 Le 51.48N 15.44 E
Now Bandegān 24 Oh 28.52N 53.53 E
Nowbarān 24 Me 35.08N 49.42 E
Nowdesheh 24 Le 35.11N 46.15 E
Nowe 10 Oc 53.40N 18.43 E
Nowe Miasto Lubawskie 10 Pc 53.27N 19.35 E
Nowe Miasto-nad-Pilicą 10 Qe 51.38N 20.35 E
Nowe Warpno 10 Kc 53.44N 14.20 E
Nowfel low Shātow 24 Ne 34.27N 50.55 E
Nowgong 25 Ic 26.21N 92.40 E
Nowogard 10 Lc 53.40N 15.08 E
Nowogród 10 Rc 53.15N 21.53 E
Nowood River 46 Ld 44.17N 107.58W
Nowra 59 Kf 34.53S 150.36 E
Nowshahr 24 Nd 36.39N 51.31 E
Nowy Dwór Gdański 10 Pb 54.13N 19.06 E
Nowy Dwór Mazowiecki 10 Qd 52.26N 20.43 E
Nowy Korczyn 10 Qf 50.20N 20.50 E
Nowy Sącz [2] 10 Qg 49.40N 20.40 E
Nowy Sącz 10 Qg 49.38N 20.42 E
Nowy Targ 10 Qg 49.29N 20.02 E
Nowy Tomyśl 10 Md 52.20N 16.07 E
Noya 13 Db 42.47N 8.53W
Noya/Anoia 13 Nc 41.28N 1.56 E
Noyant 11 Gg 47.31N 0.08 E
Noyon 11 Ie 49.35N 3.00 E
Nozaki-Jima 29 Ae 33.11N 129.08 E
Nozay 11 Eg 47.34N 1.38W
Nsanje 36 Gf 16.55S 35.16 E
Nsawan 34 Ed 5.48N 0.21W
Nschodnia 10 Rf 50.30N 21.18 E
Nsefu 36 Fe 13.03S 32.07 E
Nsukka 34 Gd 6.52N 7.23 E
Ntadembele 36 Cc 2.11S 17.08 E
Ntchisi 36 Fe 13.22S 34.00 E
Ntem 30 Hh 2.10N 9.57 E
Ntoum 36 Ab 0.22N 9.47 E
Ntui 34 He 4.27N 11.38 E
Ntusi 36 Fb 0.03N 31.13 E
Nuageuses, Iles- 30 Nm 48.40S 68.58 E
Nuanetsi 37 Ed 21.22S 30.45 E
Nuanetsi 30 Kk 22.40S 31.49 E
Nūbah, Jibāl an- 30 Kg 12.00N 30.45 E
Nubian Desert (EN)= Nūbiyah, Aş Şaḩrā' an- 30 Kf 20.30N 33.00 E
Nūbiyah, Aş Şaḩrā' an-= Nubian Desert (EN) 30 Kf 20.30N 33.00 E
Nudha 63a Ec 9.32S 160.48 E
Nueces Plain 43 Hf 28.30N 99.15W
Nueces River 43 Hf 27.50N 97.30W
Nueltin Lake 38 Jc 60.50N 99.30W
Nü'er He 28 Fd 41.06N 121.09 E
Nueva Asunción [3] 55 Be 21.00S 60.20W
Nueva Ciudad Guerrero 48 Jd 26.35N 99.15W
Nueva Esparta [2] 54 Fa 11.00N 64.00W
Nueva Germania 55 Df 23.54S 56.34W
Nueva Gerona 47 Hd 21.53N 82.48W
Nueva Imperial 56 Fe 38.44S 72.57W
Nueva Italia de Ruiz 48 Hh 19.01N 102.06W
Nueva Ocotepeque 49 Cf 14.24N 89.13W
Nueva Palmira 55 Ck 33.53S 58.25W
Nueva Rosita 39 Ig 27.57N 101.13W
Nueva San Salvador 47 Gf 13.41N 89.17W
Nueva Segovia [3] 49 Dg 13.40N 86.10W
Nueve de Julio 56 He 35.27S 60.52W
Nuevitas 47 Id 21.33N 77.16W
Nuevitas, Bahía de- 49 Ic 21.30N 77.12W
Nuevo, Cayo- 48 Mg 21.51N 92.05W
Nuevo, Golfo- 52 Jj 42.42S 64.36W
Nuevo Berlín 55 Ck 32.59S 58.03W
Nuevo Casas Grandes 39 If 30.25N 107.55W
Nuevo Laredo 39 Jg 27.30N 99.31W
Nuevo León [2] 47 Ec 25.40N 100.00W
Nuevo Mundo, Cerro- 54 Eh 21.55S 66.53W
Nuevo Rocafuerte 54 Cd 0.56S 75.25W
Nugaal [3] 35 Hd 8.30N 48.00 E
Nugālēd, Dēḥ- 30 Lh 7.58N 49.51 E
Nugālēd, Dōḥo- 35 Hd 8.35N 48.35 E
Nûgâtsiaq 41 Gd 71.39N 53.45W
Nugget Point 62 Cg 46.27S 169.49 E
Nûgssuaq 41 Gd 70.30N 51.30W
Nuguria Islands 57 Ge 3.20S 154.45 E
Nuguš 17 Gj 53.05N 56.00 E
Nuhaka 62 Gc 39.02S 177.45 E
Nui Atoll 57 Ie 7.15S 177.10 E
Nuijama 8 Md 60.58N 28.32 E
Nuiqsut 40 Ib 70.20N 151.00W
Nu Jang 21 Lh 16.31N 97.37 E
Nûk/Godthåb 67 Nc 64.15N 51.40W
Nukapu 63c Ab 10.07S 165.59 E
Nukey Bluff 59 Hf 32.35S 135.40 E
Nukhayb 23 Fc 32.02N 42.15 E
Nukhaylak 31 Jg 19.08N 26.20 E
Nukiki 63a Cb 6.45S 156.29 E
Nukuaéta 64h Ac 13.22S 176.11W
Nuku'alofa 58 Jg 21.08S 175.12W
Nukufetau Atoll 57 Ie 8.00S 178.22 E
Nukufotu 64h Bb 13.11S 176.10W
Nukuhifala 64h Bb 13.17S 176.05W
Nukuhione 64h Bb 13.16S 176.06W
Nuku Hiva, Ile- 57 Me 8.54S 140.06W
Nukulaelae Atoll 57 Ie 9.23S 179.52 E
Nukuloa 64h Bb 13.11S 176.09W
Nukumanu Islands 57 Ge 4.30S 159.30 E
Nukumbasanga 63d Cb 16.18S 179.15W
Nukunonu Atoll 57 Je 9.10S 171.53W
Nukuoro Atoll 57 Gd 3.51N 154.58 E
Nukus 22 He 42.50N 59.29 E
Nukutapu 64h Bb 13.13S 176.08W
Nukuteatea 64h Bb 13.12S 176.08W
Nulato 40 Hd 64.43N 158.06W
Nules 13 Le 39.51N 0.09W
Nullagine 58 Dg 21.53S 120.06 E
Nullagine River 59 Ed 20.43S 120.33 E
Nullarbor 59 Gf 31.26S 130.55 E
Nullarbor Plain 57 Dh 31.00S 129.00 E
Nulu'erhu Shan 27 Kc 41.40N 119.50 E
Numakawa 29a Ba 45.15N 141.51 E
Numan 34 Hd 9.28N 12.02 E
Numancia [Phil.] 26 Ie 9.52N 125.58 E
Numancia [Sp.] 13 Jc 41.47N 2.30W
Numanohata 29a Bb 42.40N 141.41 E
Numata [Jap.] 29a Bb 43.49N 141.55 E
Numata [Jap.] 28 Of 36.38N 139.03 E
Numatinna 35 Dd 7.14N 27.37 E
Numazu 28 Og 35.06N 138.52 E
Nümbrecht 12 Jd 50.54N 7.33 E
Numedal 7 Bf 60.05N 9.05 E
Numena 36 Ee 11.46S 26.31 E
Número Cinco, Canal- 55 Cm 37.14S 58.06W
Número Doce, Canal- 55 Cm 36.30S 59.08W
Número Dos, Canal- 55 Cm 36.51S 58.03W
Número Nueve, Canal- 55 Cm 36.08S 58.36W
Número Once, Canal- 55 Bm 36.28S 60.01W
Número Quince, Canal- 55 Dl 35.55S 57.45W
Número Uno, Canal- 55 Cm 36.40S 58.35W
Numfoor, Pulau- 26 Jg 1.03S 134.54 E
Nuneaton 9 Li 52.32N 1.28W
Nungarin 59 Df 31.11S 118.06 E
Nungnain Sum 27 Kb 45.45N 118.56 E
Nungo 37 Fb 13.25S 37.46 E
Nunivak 38 Cd 60.00N 166.30W
Nunkirchen, Wadern- 12 Ie 49.32N 6.53 E
Nunn 45 Df 40.45N 104.46W
Nunspeet 12 Hb 52.22N 5.46 E
Nunukan Timur, Pulau- 26 Gf 4.05N 117.40 E
Nuomin He 27 Lb 48.21N 124.32 E
Nuorgam 7 Ga 70.05N 27.51 E
Nuoro 6 Gg 40.19N 9.20 E
Nupani 63c Ab 10.04S 165.40 E
Nūq 24 Pg 30.55N 55.35 E
Nuqayr 24 Mi 27.48N 48.21 E
Nuqrah 24 Ij 25.34N 41.24 E
Nuqruş, Jabal- 33 Fe 24.49N 34.36 E
Nuquí 54 Cb 5.43N 77.16W
Nūr 24 Od 36.15N 52.20 E
Nūr 24 Pg 31.25N 54.20 E
Nura 19 Gf 48.57N 62.20 E
Nura 21 Id 50.30N 69.59 E
Nūrābād 24 Ng 30.48N 51.27 E
Nuraghe Santu Antine 14 Cj 40.29N 8.45 E
Nurata 19 Gg 40.34N 65.35 E
Nur Dağları 24 Gd 36.45N 36.20 E
Nure 14 De 45.03N 9.49 E
Nurek 19 Gh 38.25N 69.20 E
Nurhak Dağı 23 Eb 38.04N 37.29 E
Nūrī 35 Eb 18.30N 32.02 E
Nurki 20 Ie 56.42N 138.28 E
Nurlat 19 Fe 54.28N 50.48 E
Nurlati 7 Li 55.38N 48.17 E
Nurmes 7 Ge 63.33N 29.07 E
Nurmijärvi 8 Kd 60.28N 24.48 E
Nurmo 8 Jb 62.50N 22.54 E
Nürnberg 6 Hf 49.27N 11.05 E
Nurra 14 Cj 40.45N 8.15 E
Nurri, Mount- 59 Jf 31.42S 146.02 E
Nurugas 37 Bc 19.11S 18.54 E
Nurzec 10 Sd 52.33N 22.28 E
Nusa Tenggara Barat [3] 26 Gh 8.50S 117.30 E
Nusa Tenggara Timur [3] 26 Hh 9.30S 122.00 E
Nusaybin 24 Id 37.03N 41.13 E
Nushagak 40 He 58.57N 158.29W
Nushan 27 Gf 25.00N 99.00 E
Nu-Shima 29 Dd 34.10N 134.50 E
Nutak 42 Le 57.31N 62.00W
Nuttal 25 Dc 28.45N 68.08 E
Nuutele 65c Bb 14.02S 171.22W
Nuwākot 25 Gc 28.08N 83.53 E
Nuwara 25 Gg 6.58N 80.46 E
Nuwaybi 'al Muzayyinah 33 Fd 28.58N 34.39 E
Nyabing 59 Df 33.32S 118.09 E
Nyagquka/Yajiang 27 He 30.07N 100.58 E
Nyagrong/Xinlong 27 He 30.57N 100.12 E
Nyahanga 36 Fc 2.23S 33.33 E
Nyahua 36 Fc 4.58S 33.34 E
Nyainqêntanglha Feng 27 Fe 30.12N 90.33 E
Nyainqêntanglha Shan 21 Kf 30.10N 90.00 E
Nyakanazi 36 Fc 3.00S 31.15 E
Nyala 31 Jg 12.03N 24.53 E
Nyalam 27 Ef 28.15N 85.55 E
Ny-Ålesund 41 Nc 78.56N 11.57 E
Nyalikungu 36 Fc 3.11S 33.47 E
Nyamandhlovu 37 Dc 19.51S 28.16 E
Nyamapanda 37 Ec 16.55S 32.52 E
Nyamlell 35 Dd 9.07N 26.58 E
Nyamtumbo 36 Ge 10.30S 36.06 E
Nyanding 35 Ed 8.40N 32.41 E
Nyanga 30 Ii 2.58S 10.15 E
Nyanga [3] 36 Bc 3.00S 11.00 E
Nyanza [3] 36 Fc 0.30S 34.30 E
Nyanza-Lac 36 Ec 4.21S 29.36 E
Nyasa, Lake- (EN)=Niassa, Lago- 30 Kj 12.00S 34.30 E
Nyaunglebin 25 Je 17.57N 96.44 E
Nyborg 7 Ci 55.19N 10.48 E
Nybro 7 Dh 56.45N 15.54 E
Nyda 17 Pc 66.40N 72.50 E
Nyda 20 Cc 66.36N 72.54 E
Nyeboe Land 41 Gb 81.45N 56.40W
Nyêmo 27 Ff 29.30N 90.07 E
Nyeri 36 Gc 0.25S 36.57 E
Nyerol 35 Ed 8.41N 32.02 E
Ny Friesland 41 Nc 79.30N 17.00 E
Nyhammar 8 Fd 60.17N 14.58 E
Nyhem 8 Fb 62.54N 15.40 E
Nyika 30 Ki 2.37S 38.44 E
Nyika Plateau 30 Kj 10.40S 33.50 E
Nyikog Qu 27 He 30.24N 100.40 E
Nyimba 36 Fe 14.33S 30.48 E
Nyingchi 27 Ff 29.38N 94.23 E
Nyírbátor 10 Si 47.50N 22.08 E
Nyíregyháza 10 Ri 47.57N 21.43 E
Nyiri Desert 36 Gc 2.20S 37.20 E
Nyiro, Mount- 36 Gb 2.08N 36.51 E
Nyírség 10 Ri 47.50N 21.55 E
Nykøbing [Den.] 7 Ci 54.46N 11.53 E
Nykøbing [Den.] 7 Ci 55.55N 11.41 E
Nykøbing [Den.] 8 Ch 56.48N 8.52 E
Nyköping 7 Dg 58.45N 17.00 E
Nyköpingsån 8 Gf 58.45N 17.01 E
Nykroppa 8 Fe 59.38N 14.18 E
Nyland 8 Ga 63.00N 17.46 E
Nylstroom 37 Dd 24.42S 28.20 E
Nymburk 10 Lf 50.11N 15.03 E
Nymphe Bank (EN) 9 Fj 51.30N 7.05W
Nynäshamn 7 Dg 58.54N 17.57 E
Nyngan 58 Fh 31.34S 147.11 E
Nyon 14 Ad 46.23N 6.15 E
Nyong 30 Hh 3.17N 9.54 E
Nyonga 36 Fd 6.43S 32.04 E
Nyons 11 Lj 44.22N 5.08 E
Nýřany 10 Jg 49.43N 13.13 E
Nyrob 17 Hf 60.42N 56.45 E
Nyš 20 Jf 51.30N 142.49 E
Nysa 10 Nf 50.29N 17.20 E
Nysa Kłodzka 10 Nf 50.49N 17.50 E
Nysa Łużycka 10 Kd 52.04N 14.46 E
Nyslott/Savonlinna 7 Gf 61.52N 28.53 E
Nyssa 46 Ge 43.53N 117.00W
Nystad/Uusikaupunki 7 Ef 60.48N 21.25 E
Nysted 8 Dj 54.40N 11.45 E
Nytva 19 Fd 57.56N 55.20 E
Nyūdō-Zaki 28 Od 40.00N 139.35 E
Nyunzu 36 Ed 5.57S 28.01 E
Nyūzen 29 Ec 36.56N 137.30 E
Nzambi 36 Bc 3.58S 11.16 E
Nzara 35 De 4.40N 28.14 E
Nzega 36 Fc 4.13S 33.11 E
Nzérékoré 31 Gh 7.45N 8.49W
Nzeto 36 Bd 7.05S 12.50 E
Nzi 30 Gh 5.57N 4.50W
Nzilo, Barrage de- 36 Ee 10.35S 25.30 E
Nzo 34 Dd 6.16N 7.03W
Nzoro 36 Eb 3.18N 29.26 E
Nzwali/Anjouan 30 Lj 12.15S 44.25 E

O

Oa, Mull of- 9 Gf 55.35N 6.20W
Oahe, Lake- 38 Ie 45.30N 100.25W
Oahu Island 57 Lb 21.30N 158.00W
O-akan-Dake 29a Db 43.27N 144.10 E
Oakdale [Ca.-U.S.] 46 Eh 37.46N 120.51W
Oakdale [La.-U.S.] 45 Jk 30.49N 92.40W
Oakham 9 Mi 52.40N 0.44W
Oak Harbor 46 Db 48.18N 122.39W
Oak Lake 45 Fb 49.40N 100.45W
Oakland [Ca.-U.S.] 39 Gf 37.47N 122.13W
Oakland [Md.-U.S.] 44 Hf 39.25N 79.24W
Oakley [Id.-U.S.] 46 Ie 42.15N 113.53W
Oakley [Ks.-U.S.] 43 Gd 39.08N 100.51W
Oak Park 45 Mf 41.53N 87.48W
Oak Ridge 43 Kd 36.01N 84.16W
Oakridge 46 De 43.45N 122.28W
Oakville 44 Hd 43.27N 79.41W
Oamaru 61 Di 45.05S 170.59 E
Oancea 15 Ld 45.55N 28.06 E
Oani-Gawa 29 Ga 40.12N 140.16 E
Ōarai 29 Gc 36.18N 140.33 E
Oaro 62 Ee 42.31S 173.30 E
Oasis 46 Hf 41.01N 114.37W
Oasis 32 Hd 26.00N 5.00 E
Oates Coast 66 Jf 70.00S 160.00 E
Oaxaca [2] 47 Ee 17.00N 96.30W
Oaxaca, Sierra Madre de- 48 Ki 17.30N 96.30W
Oaxaca de Juárez 39 Jh 17.03N 96.43W
Ob 21 Ic 66.45N 69.30 E
Oba 42 Jg 48.55N 84.17W
Obala 34 He 4.10N 11.32 E
Obama [Jap.] 28 Mg 35.30N 135.45 E
Obama [Jap.] 29 Be 32.43N 130.13 E
Obama-Wan 29 Dd 35.30N 135.40 E
Oban [N.Z.] 61 Ci 46.52S 168.10 E
Oban [Scot.-U.K.] 9 He 56.25N 5.29W
Obanazawa 28 Pe 38.36N 140.24 E
Obando 53 Je 4.07N 67.45W
Oban Hills 34 Gd 5.30N 8.35 E
Obeliai/Obeljaj 8 Ki 55.58N 25.59 E
Obeljaj/Obeliai 8 Ki 55.58N 25.59 E
Oberá 56 Ic 27.29S 55.08W
Oberbayern 10 Hi 47.50N 11.50 E
Oberderdingen 12 Ke 49.04N 8.48 E
Oberfranken 10 Hf 50.10N 11.30 E
Oberhausen 10 Ce 51.28N 6.51 E
Oberkirchen, Schmallenberg- 12 Kc 51.09N 8.18 E
Oberland [Switz.] 14 Bd 46.35N 7.30 E
Oberland [Switz.] 14 Dd 46.45N 9.05 E
Oberlausitz 10 Ke 51.15N 14.30 E
Oberlin 45 Fg 39.49N 100.32W
Obermoschel 12 Je 49.44N 7.46 E
Obernkirchen 12 Lb 52.16N 9.08 E
Oberösterreich=Upper Austria (EN) [2] 14 Hb 48.15N 14.00 E
Oberpfalz 10 Ig 49.30N 12.10 E
Oberpfälzer Wald= Bohemian Forest (EN) 10 Ig 49.50N 12.30 E
Oberpullendorf 14 Kc 47.30N 16.31 E
Ober-Ramstadt 12 Ke 49.50N 8.45 E
Oberstdorf 10 Gi 47.24N 10.16 E
Oberursel (Taunus) 12 Kd 50.12N 8.35 E
Obervellach 14 Hd 46.56N 13.12 E
Oberwesel 12 Jd 50.06N 7.44 E
Ob Gulf (EN)=Obskaja Guba 21 Jc 69.00N 73.00 E
Obi, Kepulauan- 26 Ig 1.30S 127.45 E
Obi, Pulau- 57 De 1.30S 127.45 E
Obi, Selat- 26 Ig 0.52S 127.33 E
Óbidos [Braz.] 53 Kf 1.55S 55.31W
Óbidos [Port.] 13 Ce 39.22N 9.09W
Obihiro 27 Pc 42.55N 143.12 E
Obilić 15 Eg 42.41N 21.05 E
Obira 29a Ba 44.01N 141.38 E
Obispos 49 Li 8.36N 70.05W
Obispo Trejo 56 Hd 30.46S 63.25W
Obitočnaja Kosa 16 Jf 46.35N 36.15 E
Oblučje 20 Ig 48.59N 131.05 E
Obninsk 19 Dd 55.05N 36.37 E
Obo 31 Jh 5.24N 26.30 E
Obock 35 Gc 11.57N 43.17 E
Obojan 19 De 51.13N 36.16 E
Obokote 36 Ec 0.52S 26.19 E
Obol 7 Gi 55.24N 29.01 E
Oborniki 10 Md 52.39N 16.51 E
Obouya 36 Cc 0.56S 15.43 E
Obozerski 19 Ec 63.28N 40.20 E
Obra 10 Ld 52.36N 15.28 E
Obrenovac 15 De 44.39N 20.12 E
Obrovac 14 Jf 44.12N 15.41 E
Obrovo 10 Vd 52.27N 25.43 E
Obruchev Rise (EN) 20 Lf 52.30N 166.00 E
Obruk Platosu 24 Ec 38.02N 33.30 E
Obšči Syrt 5 Le 51.50N 51.00 E
Obskaja Guba=Ob Gulf (EN) 21 Jc 69.00N 73.00 E
Ob' Tablemount (EN) 30 Ln 52.30S 42.00 E
Ōbu 29 Ed 35.01N 136.58 E
Obuasi 34 Ed 6.12N 1.40W
Obudu 34 Gd 6.40N 9.10 E
Obuhov 16 Gd 50.07N 30.37 E
Obva 17 Gg 58.35N 55.25 E
Obzor 15 Kg 42.49N 27.53 E
Oca 13 Ib 42.46N 3.26W
Oca, Montes de- 13 Ib 42.20N 3.15W
Očakov 19 Df 46.38N 31.33 E
Ocala 43 Kf 29.11N 82.07W
Očamcira 16 Lh 42.46N 41.27 E
Ocampo [Mex.] 48 Hd 27.20N 102.21W
Ocampo [Mex.] 48 Ec 28.11N 108.23W
Ocaña [Col.] 54 Db 8.15N 73.20W
Ocaña [Sp.] 13 Ie 39.56N 3.31W
Occhito, Lago di- 14 Ii 41.35N 14.55 E
Ocean Bight 49 Kc 21.15N 73.15W
Ocean City [Md.-U.S.] 43 Ld 38.20N 75.05W
Ocean City [N.J.-U.S.] 44 Jf 39.16N 74.35W
Ocean Falls 42 Ef 52.21N 127.40W
Oceania 57 Ie 5.00S 175.00E
Ocean Point 44 Il 26.16N 77.03W
Oceanside 43 De 33.12N 117.23W
Ocean Springs 45 Lk 30.25N 88.50W
Ocejón, Pico- 13 Ic 41.07N 3.15W
Očenyrd, Gora- 17 Mb 68.05N 66.20 E
Očer 19 Fd 57.53N 54.45 E
Ochagavia 13 Kb 42.55N 1.05W
Ochiai 29 Cd 35.02N 133.45 E
Ochi-Gata 29 Ec 36.55N 136.48 E
Ochiishi-Misaki 29a Db 43.10N 145.28 E
Ochil Hills 9 Je 56.23N 3.35W
Och'onjang 28 Jd 40.55N 128.50 E
Ocho Rios 49 Id 18.25N 77.07W
Ochsenfurt 10 Gg 49.39N 10.05 E
Ochtrup 12 Jb 52.13N 7.11 E
Ockelbo 7 Dd 60.53N 16.43 E
Öckerö 8 Dg 57.43N 11.39 E
Ocmulgee River 44 Fj 31.58N 82.32W
Ocna Mureş 15 Gc 46.23N 23.51 E

Index Symbols

[1] Independent Nation
[2] State, Region
[3] District, County
[4] Municipality
[5] Colony, Dependency
Continent
Physical Region
Historical or Cultural Region
Mount, Mountain
Volcano
Hill
Mountains, Mountain Range
Hills, Escarpment
Plateau, Upland
Pass, Gap
Plain, Lowland
Delta
Salt Flat
Valley, Canyon
Crater, Cave
Karst Features
Depression
Polder
Desert, Dunes
Forest, Woods
Heath, Steppe
Oasis
Cape, Point
Coast, Beach
Cliff
Peninsula
Isthmus
Sandbank
Island
Atoll
Rock, Reef
Islands, Archipelago
Rocks, Reefs
Coral Reef
Well, Spring
Geyser
River, Stream
Waterfall Rapids
River Mouth, Estuary
Lake
Salt Lake
Intermittent Lake
Reservoir
Swamp, Pond
Canal
Glacier
Ice Shelf, Pack Ice
Ocean
Sea
Gulf, Bay
Strait, Fjord
Lagoon
Bank
Seamount
Tablemount
Ridge
Shelf
Basin
Escarpment, Sea Scarp
Fracture
Trench, Abyss
National Park, Reserve
Point of Interest
Recreation Site
Cave, Cavern
Historic Site
Ruins
Wall, Walls
Church, Abbey
Temple
Scientific Station
Airport
Port
Lighthouse
Mine
Tunnel
Dam, Bridge

Ocna Sibiului	15	Hc	45.53N	24.03 E
Ocoa, Bahía de-	49	Ld	18.22N	70.39W
Oconee River	44	Fj	31.58N	82.32W
Oconto	45	Md	44.55N	87.52W
Ocosingo	48	Mi	17.04N	92.15W
Ocotal	49	Dg	13.38N	86.29W
Ocotepeque [3]	49	Cf	14.30N	89.00W
Ocotlán	47	Dd	20.21N	102.46W
Ocotlán de Morelos	48	Ki	16.48N	96.43W
Ocracoke Inlet	44	Ih	35.10N	76.05W
Ocracoke Island	44	Jh	35.09N	75.53W
Ocreza	13	Ee	39.32N	7.50W
Octeville-sur-Mer	12	Ce	49.33N	0.07 E
October Revolution Island (EN)=Oktjabrskoj Revoljuci, Ostrov-	21	Lb	79.30N	97.00 E
Ocú	49	Gj	7.57N	80.47W
Ocumare del Tuy	50	Cg	10.07N	66.46W
Oda [Ghana]	34	Ed	5.55N	0.59W
Oda [Jap.]	29	Ce	33.34N	132.48 E
Ōda	28	Lg	35.11N	132.30 E
Oda, Jabal-	35	Fa	20.21N	36.39 E
Ódáðahraun	7a	Cb	65.09N	17.00W
Ōdai	29	Ed	34.24N	136.24 E
Odaigahara-San	29	Ed	34.11N	136.06 E
Odalen	8	Dd	60.15N	11.40 E
Ōdate	28	Pd	40.16N	140.34 E
Odawara	28	Og	35.15N	139.10 E
Odda	7	Bf	60.04N	6.33 E
Odder	8	Di	55.58N	10.10 E
Odeleite	13	Eg	37.21N	7.27W
Odemira	13	Dg	37.36N	8.38W
Ödemiş	24	Bc	38.13N	27.59 E
Odendaalsrus	37	De	27.48 S	26.45 E
Odense	6	Hd	55.24N	10.23 E
Odenthal	12	Jc	51.02N	7.07 E
Odenwald	10	Eg	49.40N	9.00 E
Oder [Eur.]	5	He	53.40N	14.33 E
Oder [F.R.G.]	10	Ge	51.40N	10.02 E
Oderbruch	10	Kd	52.40N	14.15 E
Oderské vrchy	10	Ng	49.40N	17.45 E
Oderzo	14	Ge	45.47N	12.29 E
Ödeshög	7	Dg	58.14N	14.39 E
Odessa [Tx.-U.S.]	39	If	31.51N	102.22W
Odessa [Ukr.-U.S.S.R.]	6	Jf	46.28N	30.44 E
Odessa [Wa.-U.S.]	46	Fc	47.20N	118.41W
Odesskaja Oblast [3]	19	Df	46.45N	30.30 E
Odet	11	Bg	47.52N	4.06W
Odiel	13	Fg	37.10N	6.54W
Odienné	31	Gh	9.30N	7.34W
Odienné [3]	34	Dd	9.45N	7.45W
Odivelas	13	Df	38.12N	8.18W
Ödmården	8	Gc	61.05N	16.40 E
Odobeşti	15	Kd	45.46N	27.03 E
Ŏdŏngk	25	Kf	11.48N	104.45 E
Odoorn	12	Ib	52.51N	6.50 E
Odorheiu Secuiesc	15	Ic	46.18N	25.18 E
Ōdose-Zaki	29a	Bc	40.46N	140.03 E
Odra	5	He	53.40N	14.33 E
Ōdwēyne	35	Hd	9.23N	45.04 E
Odžaci	15	Cd	45.31N	19.16 E
Odžak	14	Me	45.01N	18.18 E
Odzi	37	Ec	19.47 S	32.24 E
Oeiras	13	Eg	37.38N	7.40W
Oeiras [Braz.]	54	Je	7.01 S	42.08W
Oeiras [Port.]	13	Cf	38.41N	9.19W
Oelde	12	Kc	51.49N	8.09 E
Oelerbeek	12	Ib	52.21N	6.38 E
Oelrichs	45	Ee	43.15N	103.10W
Oelsnitz	10	If	50.25N	12.10 E
Oelwein	45	Ke	42.41N	91.55W
Oeno Island	57	Ng	23.56 S	130.44W
Oer-Erkenschwick	12	Jc	51.38N	7.15 E
Oeste, Punta-	51a	Ab	18.05N	67.57W
Oeventrop, Arnsberg-	12	Kc	51.24N	8.08 E
Ōe-Yama	29	Dd	35.27N	135.06 E
Of	24	Ib	40.57N	40.16 E
O'Fallon Creek	46	Mc	46.50N	105.09W
Ofanto	14	Ki	41.21N	16.13 E
Ofaqim	24	Fg	31.17N	34.37 E
Offa	34	Fd	8.09N	4.43 E
Offaly/Uíbh Fhailí [2]	9	Fh	53.20N	7.30W
Offenbach am Main	10	Ef	50.06N	8.46 E
Offenbach-Hundheim	12	Je	49.37N	7.33 E
Offenburg	10	Dh	48.29N	7.56 E
Offida	14	Hh	42.56N	13.41 E
Offoué	36	Bc	0.04 S	11.44 E
Offranville	12	De	49.52N	1.03 E
Ofidhoúsa	15	Jm	36.33N	26.09 E
Ofolanga	65b	Ba	19.36 S	174.27W
Ofu	65c	Db	14.11 S	169.42W
Ōfunato	28	Pe	39.04N	141.43 E
Oga	28	Oe	40.43N	141.18 E
Ogachi	29	Gb	39.05N	140.28 E
Ogaden	30	Lh	7.30N	45.00 E
Oga-Hantō	28	Oe	39.55N	139.50 E
Ōgaki	28	Ng	35.21N	136.37 E
Ogallala	43	Gc	41.08N	101.43W
Ogasawara-Shotō=Bonin Islands (EN)	21	Qg	27.00N	142.10 E
Ogawara-Ko	29a	Bc	40.45N	141.20 E
Ogbomosho	31	Hh	8.08N	4.16 E
Ogden	39	He	41.14N	111.58W
Ogdensburg	44	Jc	44.42N	75.31W
Ogeechee River	44	Gj	31.51N	81.06W
Oghāsh	24	Lc	39.10N	46.55 E
Ogi	29	Fc	37.50N	138.16 E
Ogilvie Mountains	42	Dc	65.00N	140.00W
Ogi-no-Sen	29	Dd	35.26N	134.26 E
Oginski Kanal	16	Dc	52.20N	25.55 E
Oglanly	16	Sj	39.50N	54.33 E
Oglethorpe	44	Ei	31.28N	84.04W
Ogliastra	14	Dk	39.55N	9.35 E
Oglio	14	Ee	45.02N	10.39 E
Ognon	11	Lg	47.20N	5.29 E
Ogo	35	Hd	9.48N	45.35 E
Ogoamas, Bulu-	26	Hf	0.40N	120.12 E
Ogodža	20	If	52.48N	132.40 E
Ogoja	34	Gd	6.40N	8.48 E
Ogoki	42	If	51.38N	85.56W
Ogoki	42	If	51.38N	85.55W
Ogoki Reservoir	42	If	51.35N	86.00W
Ogonëk	20	Ie	59.40N	138.01 E
Ogooué	30	Hi	0.49 S	9.00 E
Ogooué-Ivindo [3]	36	Bb	0.30N	13.00 E
Ogooué-Lolo [3]	36	Bc	1.00 S	13.00 E
Ogooué-Maritime [3]	36	Ac	2.00 S	9.30 E
Ogōri [Jap.]	29	Bd	34.06N	131.25 E
Ogōri [Jap.]	29	Be	33.24N	130.34 E
Ogosta	15	Gf	43.45N	23.51 E
Ogražden	15	Fh	41.30N	22.55 E
Ogre	8	Kh	56.42N	24.33 E
Ogre	7	Fh	56.50N	24.39 E
Ogulin	14	Je	45.16N	15.14 E
Ogun [2]	34	Fd	7.00N	3.40 E
Oguni [Jap.]	29	Fb	38.04N	139.45 E
Oguni [Jap.]	29	Be	33.07N	131.04 E
Ogurčinski, Ostrov-	16	Rj	38.55N	53.05 E
Oğuzeli	24	Gd	37.00N	37.30 E
Oha	22	Qd	53.34N	142.56 E
Ohai	62	Bf	45.56 S	167.57 E
Ohakune	62	Fc	39.25 S	175.25 E
Ohanet	32	Id	28.40N	8.50 E
Ohansk	17	Gh	57.42N	55.25 E
Ōhara	29	Gd	35.15N	140.23 E
Ōhasama	29	Gb	39.28N	141.17 E
Ohata	20	Je	59.20N	143.05 E
Ōhata	28	Pd	41.24N	141.10 E
Ohau, Lake-	62	Cf	44.15 S	169.50 E
Ohey	12	Hd	50.26N	5.08 E
O'Higgins, Cabo-	65d	Bb	27.05 S	109.15W
Ohio	38	Kf	36.59N	89.08W
Ohio [2]	43	Kc	40.15N	82.45W
Ohm	10	Ef	50.51N	8.48 E
Ohmberge	10	Ge	51.30N	10.28 E
'Ohonua	65b	Bc	21.20 S	174.57W
Ohopoho	31	Ij	18.03 S	13.45 E
Ohotsk	22	Qd	59.23N	143.18 E
Ohotskoje More=Okhotsk, Sea of- (EN)	21	Qd	53.00N	150.00 E
Ohre	10	Hd	52.18N	11.47 E
Ohře	10	Kf	50.32N	14.08 E
Ohrid	15	Dh	41.07N	20.48 E
Ohrid, Lake- (EN) = Ohridsko Jezero	5	Ig	41.00N	20.45 E
Ohrid, Lake- (EN) = Ohrit, Liqen i-	5	Ig	41.00N	20.45 E
Ohridsko Jezero=Ohrid, Lake- (EN)	5	Ig	41.00N	20.45 E
Öhringen	10	Fg	49.12N	9.30 E
Ohrit, Liqen i- = Ohrid, Lake- (EN)	5	Ig	41.00N	20.45 E
Ohura	62	Fc	38.51 S	174.59 E
Oiapoque	54	Hc	3.50N	51.50W
Oich	9	Id	57.10N	4.45W
Oi-Gawa	29	Fd	34.46N	138.17 E
Oil City	44	He	41.26N	79.44W
Oildale	46	Fi	35.25N	119.01W
Oiléan Baoi/Dursey	9	Cj	51.36N	10.12W
Oileán Ciarraí/Castleisland	9	Di	52.14N	9.27W
Oileán Coarach/Mutton	9	Di	52.49N	9.31W
Oileán Mhic Aodha/Magee, Island-	9	Hg	54.50N	5.50W
Oinoúsai	15	Jk	38.32N	26.13 E
Oinoúsai, Nísoi-	15	Jk	38.31N	26.14 E
Oirschot	12	Hc	51.30N	5.18 E
Oisans	11	Mi	45.02N	6.02 E
Oise [3]	11	Ie	49.30N	2.30 E
Oise	11	Ie	49.00N	2.04 E
Oise à l'Aisne, Canal de l'-	11	Je	49.36N	3.11 E
Oisemont	12	De	49.57N	1.46 E
Oissel	12	De	49.20N	1.06 E
Oisterwijk	12	Hc	51.35N	5.11 E
Oistins	51q	Ab	13.04N	59.32W
Oistins Bay	51q	Ab	13.03N	59.33W
Ōita	27	Ne	33.14N	131.36 E
Ōita Ken [2]	28	Kh	33.15N	131.20 E
Oiti Óros	15	Fk	38.49N	22.17 E
Oituz, Pasul-	15	Jc	46.03N	26.23 E
Oiwake	29a	Bb	42.52N	141.48 E
Ojat	7	Hf	60.31N	33.05 E
Öje	8	Ed	60.49N	13.51 E
Ojestos de Jalisco	48	Ig	21.50N	101.35W
Ojika-Jima	29	Ae	33.13N	129.03 E
O-Jima	29	Be	34.00N	130.45 E
Ojinaga	47	Dc	29.34N	104.25W
Ojiya	28	Of	37.18N	138.48 E
Ojmjakon	20	Jd	63.28N	142.49 E
Ojocaliente	48	Hf	22.34N	102.15W
Ojo Caliente	48	Fb	30.25N	106.33W
Ojos del Salado, Nevado-	52	Jh	27.06 S	68.32W
Ojos Negros	13	Kd	40.44N	1.30W
Ojtal	19	Hg	42.54N	73.21 E
Oka [R.S.F.S.R.]	21	Md	55.00N	102.03 E
Oka [U.S.S.R.]	5	Kd	56.20N	43.59 E
Okaba	26	Kh	8.06 S	139.42 E
Okahandja [3]	37	Bd	21.30 S	17.30 E
Okahandja	31	Ik	21.59 S	16.58 E
Okahukura	62	Fc	38.47 S	175.14 E
Okaihau	62	Ea	35.19 S	173.46 E
Okak Islands	42	Le	57.28N	61.48W
Okanagan Lake	42	Fg	49.55N	119.30W
Okano	36	Bc	0.05 S	10.57 E
Okanogan River	43	Db	48.06N	119.43W
Okapa	59	Ja	6.31 S	145.32 E
Okāra	25	Eb	30.49N	73.27 E
Okarem	19	Fh	38.07N	54.05 E
Okato	62	Ec	39.12 S	173.53 E
Okaukuejo	37	Bc	19.10 S	15.54 E
Okavango	30	Jj	18.53N	22.24 E
Okavango [3]	37	Cc	18.00 S	21.00 E
Okavango Swamp	30	Jj	19.30 S	23.00 E
Ōkawa	29	Be	33.12N	130.23 E
Okaya	28	Of	36.03N	138.03 E
Okayama	22	Pf	34.39N	133.55 E
Okayama Ken [2]	28	Lg	34.50N	133.45 E
Okazaki	28	Ng	34.57N	137.10 E
Okeechobee	44	Gl	27.15N	80.50W
Okeechobee, Lake-	38	Kg	26.55N	80.45W
Okefenokee Swamp	44	Fj	30.42N	82.20W
Okehampton	9	Jk	50.44N	4.00W
Okene	34	Gd	7.33N	6.14 E
Oker	10	Gd	52.30N	10.22 E
Oketo	29a	Cb	43.41N	143.32 E
Okha	25	Dd	22.27N	69.04 E
Ókhi Óros	15	Hk	38.04N	24.28 E
Okhotsk, Sea of- (EN)= Hok-Kai	21	Qd	53.00N	150.00 E
Okhotsk, Sea of- (EN)= Ohotskoje More	21	Qd	53.00N	150.00 E
Okhthonía, Ákra-	15	Hk	38.32N	24.14 E
Oki-Daitō-Jima	27	Ng	24.30N	131.00 E
Okiep	37	Be	29.39 S	17.53 E
Okinawa	29b	Ab	26.20N	127.47 E
Okinawa Islands (EN)= Okinawa-Shotō	21	Og	26.40N	128.00 E
Okinawa-Jima	27	Mf	26.40N	128.20 E
Okinawa Ken [2]	29b	Ab	26.31N	127.59 E
Okinawa-Shotō=Okinawa Islands (EN)	21	Og	26.40N	128.00 E
Okinoerabu-Jima	27	Mf	27.20N	128.35 E
Okino-Shima [Jap.]	29	Ce	32.44N	132.33 E
Okino-Shima [Jap.]	29	Bd	34.15N	130.08 E
Okino-Tori-Shima	21	Pg	20.25N	136.00 E
Oki Ridge (EN)	28	Mf	37.00N	135.00 E
Oki-Shotō	27	Nd	36.00N	132.50 E
Okitipupa	34	Fd	6.30N	4.48 E
Oki Trench (EN)	29	Dc	37.00N	135.30 E
Oklahoma [2]	43	Hd	35.30N	98.00W
Oklahoma City	39	Jf	35.28N	97.32W
Okmulgee	45	Ii	35.37N	95.58W
Oknica	15	Ka	48.22N	27.24 E
Oko	35	Fa	22.20N	35.56 E
Okoko	36	Fb	2.06N	33.53 E
Okolo	36	Fb	2.40N	31.09 E
Okolona	44	Ef	38.08N	85.41W
Okondja	36	Bc	0.41 S	13.47 E
Okonek	10	Mc	53.33N	16.50 E
Okoppe	28	Qb	44.28N	143.08 E
Okotoks	46	Ia	50.44N	113.59W
Okoyo	36	Cc	1.28 S	15.04 E
Okrzeika	10	Re	51.40N	21.30 E
Øksfjord	7	Fa	70.14N	22.22 E
Oksino	17	Fc	67.33N	52.10 E
Okstindane	5	Hb	66.02N	14.10 E
Oktemberjan	16	Ni	40.09N	44.03 E
Oktjabrsk [Kaz.-U.S.S.R.]	6	Lf	48.40N	57.11 E
Oktjabrsk [R.S.F.S.R.]	7	Lj	53.13N	48.40 E
Oktjabrski [Bye.-U.S.S.R.]	16	Fc	52.38N	28.54 E
Oktjabrski [Kaz.-U.S.S.R.]	17	Kj	52.37N	62.43 E
Oktjabrski [R.S.F.S.R.]	20	Ee	56.05N	99.25 E
Oktjabrski [R.S.F.S.R.]	19	Fe	54.31N	53.28 E
Oktjabrski [R.S.F.S.R.]	17	Hh	56.31N	57.12 E
Oktjabrski [R.S.F.S.R.]	7	Kf	61.05N	43.08 E
Oktjabrski [R.S.F.S.R.]	20	Hf	53.00N	128.42 E
Oktjabrski [R.S.F.S.R.]	20	Kf	52.38N	156.15 E
Oktjabrski [R.S.F.S.R.]	16	Mf	47.56N	43.38 E
Oktjabrskoje	19	Gc	62.28N	66.01 E
Oktjabrskoj Revoljuci, Ostrov-=October Revolution Island (EN)	21	Lb	79.30N	97.00 E
Oku	29b	Bb	26.50N	128.17 E
Ōkuchi	28	Kh	32.04N	130.37 E
Okulovka	7	Hg	58.24N	33.18 E
Okushiri	28	Oc	42.09N	139.29 E
Okushiri-Kaikyō	29a	Ab	42.15N	139.40 E
Okushiri-Tō	27	Oc	42.10N	139.25 E
Okuta	34	Fd	9.13N	3.11 E
Oku Tango-Hantō	29	Dd	35.40N	135.10 E
Okwa	30	Jk	22.26 S	22.58 E
Ola	20	Ke	59.37N	151.20 E
Ólafsfjördur	7a	Ba	66.04N	18.39W
Ólafsvík	7a	Ab	64.53N	23.43W
Ola Grande, Punta-	51a	Bc	17.55N	66.08W
Olaiņe/Olajne	7	Fh	56.49N	23.59 E
Olajne/Olaiņe	7	Fh	56.49N	23.59 E
Olancha	46	Gh	36.17N	117.59W
Olanchito	49	Df	15.30N	86.35W
Olancho [3]	49	Ef	14.45N	86.00W
Öland	5	Hd	56.45N	16.40 E
Ölands norra udde	8	Gg	57.22N	17.05 E
Ölands södra grund	8	Gh	55.40N	17.25 E
Ölands södra udde	8	Gh	56.11N	16.24 E
Olanga	7	Hc	66.08N	30.38 E
Olathe	45	Ig	38.53N	94.49W
Olavarría	53	Ji	36.53 S	60.20W
Oława	10	Nf	50.57N	17.17 E
Oława	10	Nf	50.57N	17.17 E
Olbernhau	10	Jf	50.40N	13.20 E
Olbia	6	Gg	40.55N	9.31 E
Olbia, Golfo di-	14	Dj	40.55N	9.40 E
Old Bahama Channel	49	Ib	22.30N	78.05W
Old Bahama Channel (EN)= Bahamas, Canal Viejo de-	49	Ib	22.30N	78.05W
Old Castile (EN)=Castilla la Vieja	13	Ic	41.30N	4.00W
Old Crow	39	Fc	67.35N	139.50W
Oldeani	36	Gc	3.21 S	35.33 E
Oldebroek	12	Hb	52.26N	5.53 E
Oldenburg	10	Ec	53.10N	8.12 E
Oldenburg in Holstein	10	Gb	54.18N	10.53 E
Oldenzaal	11	Mb	52.19N	6.56 E
Old Faithful Geyser	46	Jd	44.30N	110.45W
Old Fletton	12	Bb	52.34N	0.15W
Oldham	9	Kh	53.33N	2.07W
Old Hickory Lake	44	Dg	36.18N	86.30W
Oldman River	46	Jb	49.56N	111.42W
Old Marsh Bed	59	Gd	20.55 S	130.30 E
Old Mkuski	36	Ee	14.22 S	29.22 E
Old Road	51d	Bb	17.01N	61.50W
Old Road Town	51c	Ab	17.19N	62.48W
Olds	42	Gf	51.47N	114.06W
Old Town	44	Mc	44.56N	68.39W
Old Wives Lake	46	Ma	50.06N	106.00W
Olean	44	Hd	42.05N	78.26W
Olecko	10	Sb	54.03N	22.30 E
Oleiros	13	Ee	39.55N	7.55W
Olëkma	21	Oc	60.22N	120.42 E
Olëkminsk	22	Oc	60.30N	120.15 E
Olëkminski Stanovik	20	Gf	54.00N	119.00 E
Ølen	7	Ag	59.36N	5.48 E
Olenegorsk	19	Db	68.10N	33.13 E
Olenëk	21	Nb	73.00N	119.55 E
Olenëkski Zaliv	20	Hb	73.10N	121.00 E
Olenica	7	Ic	66.29N	35.19 E
Olenj, Ostrov-	20	Cb	72.25N	77.45 E
Olenty	16	Re	49.45N	52.10 E
Oléron, Ile d'-	5	Ff	45.56N	1.18W
Olesko	10	Ug	49.53N	24.58 E
Oleśnica	10	Ne	51.13N	17.23 E
Olesno	10	Of	50.53N	18.25 E
Olevsk	16	Ed	51.13N	27.41 E
Olga	20	Ih	43.46N	135.21 E
Olga, Mount-	59	Ge	25.19 S	130.46 E
Olgastretet	41	Oc	78.30N	24.00 E
Ølgod	8	Ci	55.49N	8.37 E
Olhão	13	Eg	37.02N	7.50W
Olhovatka	16	Kd	50.17N	39.17 E
Oli	34	Fd	9.40N	4.29 E
Oliana	13	Nb	42.04N	1.19 E
Olib	14	If	44.23N	14.47 E
Oliena	14	Dj	40.16N	9.24 E
Olifants [Afr.]	30	Kk	24.03 S	32.40 E
Olifants [Nam.]	37	Be	25.30 S	19.30 E
Olifantshoek	37	Ce	27.57 S	22.42 E
Olimarao Atoll	57	Fd	7.42N	145.53 E
Olimbía	15	El	37.39N	21.38 E
Ólimbos	15	Kn	35.44N	27.13 E
Ólimbos, Óros-=Olympus, Mount- (EN)	5	Ig	40.05N	22.21 E
Ólimbos Óros	15	Jj	39.05N	26.20 E
Olímpia	55	He	20.44 S	48.54W
Olinda	54	Le	8.01 S	34.51W
Olite	13	Kb	42.29N	1.39W
Oliva [Arg.]	56	Hd	32.03 S	63.34W
Oliva [Sp.]	13	Lf	38.55N	0.07W
Oliva, Monasterio de la-	13	Kb	42.20N	1.25W
Oliva de la Frontera	13	Ff	38.16N	6.55W
Oliveira	55	Je	20.41 S	44.49W
Oliveira dos Brejinhos	54	Jf	12.19 S	42.54W
Olivença	37	Fb	11.46 S	35.13 E
Olivenza	13	Ef	38.41N	7.06W
Oliver	46	Fb	49.11N	119.33W
Olivet	11	Hg	47.52N	1.54 E
Olivia	45	Id	44.46N	94.59W
Olja	16	Og	45.47N	47.35 E
Olji Moron He	28	Fb	44.16N	121.42 E
Oljutorski, Mys-	21	Td	59.55N	170.25 E
Oljutorski Zaliv	20	Ld	60.00N	168.00 E
Olkusz	10	Pf	50.17N	19.35 E
Ollan	64d	Bb	7.14N	151.38 E
Ollerton	12	Aa	53.13N	1.01W
Olmedo	13	Hc	41.17N	4.41W
Olmos	54	Ce	5.59 S	79.46W
Olney [Eng.-U.K.]	12	Bb	52.09N	0.42W
Olney [Il.-U.S.]	45	Lg	38.44N	88.05W
Olney [Tx.-U.S.]	45	Gj	33.22N	98.45W
Oloči	20	Gf	51.20N	119.53 E
Olofström	7	Dh	56.16N	14.30 E
Oloitokitok	36	Gc	2.56 S	37.30 E
Oloj	20	Kc	66.20N	159.29 E
Olojski Hrebet	20	Lc	65.50N	162.30 E
Olombo	36	Cc	1.18 S	15.53 E
Ólomburi	63a	Ec	8.59 S	161.09 E
Olomouc	6	Hf	49.36N	17.16 E
Olona	14	De	45.06N	9.21 E
Olonec	19	Dc	61.01N	32.58 E
Olonešty	15	Mc	46.29N	29.52 E
Olongapo	22	Oh	14.50N	120.16 E
Oloron, Gave d'-	11	Ek	43.33N	1.05W
Oloron-Sainte-Marie	11	Fk	43.12N	0.36W
Olosega	65c	Db	14.11 S	169.39W
Olot	13	Ob	42.11N	2.29 E
Olovjannaja	20	Gf	50.56N	115.35 E
Olovo	14	Mf	44.07N	18.35 E
Olpe	10	De	51.02N	7.51 E
Olpoy	63b	Cb	14.52 S	166.33 E
Olroyd River	59	Ib	14.10 S	141.50 E
Olsberg	12	Kc	51.21N	8.30 E
Olshammar	8	Ff	58.45N	14.48 E
Olst	12	Ib	52.20N	6.08 E
Olsztyn	6	Ie	53.48N	20.29 E
Olsztyn [2]	10	Qc	53.50N	20.30 E
Olsztynek	10	Qc	53.36N	20.17 E
Olt [2]	15	He	44.25N	24.30 E
Olt	5	If	43.43N	24.51 E
Oltedal	8	Bf	58.50N	6.02 E
Olten	14	Bc	47.22N	7.55 E
Olteni	15	Ie	44.11N	25.17 E
Oltenia	15	Ge	44.30N	23.30 E
Olteniţa	15	Je	44.05N	26.38 E
Olteţ	15	He	44.14N	24.27 E
Oltu	24	Ib	40.33N	41.59 E
Oluanpi	21	Og	21.54N	120.51 E
Olutanga	26	He	7.22N	122.52 E
Olvera	13	Gh	36.56N	5.16W
Olym	16	Kc	52.27N	38.05 E
Olympia	39	Ge	47.03N	122.53W
Olympic Mountains	46	Dc	47.50N	123.45W
Olympus, Mount-	38	Ge	47.48N	123.43W
Olympus, Mount- (EN)= Ólimbos, Óros-	5	Ig	40.05N	22.21 E
Om	20	Cf	54.59N	73.22 E
Ōma	29a	Bc	41.30N	140.55 E
Oma	17	Cc	66.45N	46.20 E
Ōmachi	28	Nf	36.30N	137.52 E
Omae-Zaki	29	Fd	34.36N	138.14 E
Ōmagari	28	Pe	39.27N	140.29 E
Omagh/An Ómaigh	9	Fg	54.36N	7.18W
Omaha	39	Je	41.16N	95.57W
Omak	46	Fb	48.24N	119.31W
Omakau	62	Cf	45.06 S	169.36 E
Omak Lake	46	Fb	48.16N	119.23W
Oman (EN)='Umān [1]	22	Hg	21.00N	57.00 E
Oman, Gulf of- (EN)= 'Umān, Khalīj-	21	Hg	25.00N	58.00 E
Omarama	61	Ch	44.29 S	169.58 E
Omar Gambon	35	He	3.10N	45.47 E
Omaru-Gawa	29	Be	32.07N	131.34 E
Omaruru	37	Bd	21.28 S	15.56 E
Omaruru [3]	37	Bd	21.30 S	15.00 E
Omatako	37	Bd	21.07 S	16.43 E
Omatako, Omuramba-	30	Jj	17.57 S	20.25 E
Omate	54	Dg	16.41 S	70.59W
Ōma-Zaki	29a	Bc	41.32N	140.55 E
Ombai, Selat-	26	Hh	8.30 S	125.00 E
Ombella-Mpoko [3]	35	Bd	5.00N	18.00 E
Omberg	8	Ff	58.20N	14.39 E
Ombo	8	Ae	59.15N	6.00 E
Omboué	36	Ac	1.34 S	9.15 E
Ombrone	14	Fh	42.39N	11.01 E
Ombu	27	Ee	31.18N	86.33 E
Omčak	20	Jd	61.38N	147.55 E
Omdurman (EN)=Umm Durmān	31	Kg	15.38N	32.30 E
Ōme	29	Fd	35.47N	139.15 E
Omegna	14	Ce	45.53N	8.24 E
Omeo	59	Jg	37.06 S	147.36 E
Ömerköy	15	Lj	39.50N	28.04 E
Ometepe, Isla de-	47	Gf	11.30N	85.35W
Ometepec	47	Ee	16.41N	98.25W
Omhajer	35	Fc	14.19N	36.40 E
Ōmihachiman	29	Ed	35.08N	136.05 E
Omihi	62	Ee	43.01 S	172.51 E
Omineca	42	Fe	56.05N	124.05W
Omineca Mountains	42	Ee	56.35N	125.55W
Omiš	14	Kg	43.27N	16.42 E
Ōmi-Shima [Jap.]	29	Bd	34.25N	131.15 E
Ōmi-Shima [Jap.]	29	Cd	34.15N	133.00 E
Omitara	37	Bd	22.18 S	18.01 E
Ōmiya	27	Od	35.54N	139.38 E
Ommanney Bay	42	Hb	73.00N	101.00W
Omme Å	8	Ci	55.55N	8.25 E
Ommen	12	Ib	52.31N	6.25 E
Omo	30	Kh	4.32N	36.04 E
Omø	8	Di	55.10N	11.10 E
Omoa, Bahía de-	49	Cf	15.50N	88.10W
Omodeo, Lago-	14	Cj	40.10N	8.55 E
Omoloj	20	Ib	71.08N	132.01 E
Omolon	21	Rc	68.42N	158.36 E
Omolon	20	Lc	65.12N	160.27 E
Omono-Gawa	29	Gb	39.44N	140.04 E
Omont	12	Ge	49.36N	4.44 E
Omoto-Gawa	29	Gb	39.51N	141.58 E
Omsk	22	Jd	55.00N	73.24 E
Omskaja Oblast [3]	19	Hd	56.00N	72.30 E
Omsukčan	20	Kd	62.27N	155.50 E
Omsukčanski Hrebet	20	Kd	63.00N	155.10 E
Ōmu	28	Qb	44.34N	142.58 E
Omu, Vîrful-	15	Id	45.26N	25.25 E
Omulew	10	Rc	53.05N	21.32 E
Ōmura	28	Jh	32.54N	129.57 E
Ōmura-Wan	29	Ae	33.00N	129.50 E
Omurtag	15	Jf	43.06N	26.25 E
Ōmuta	28	Kh	33.02N	130.27 E
Omutinski	19	Gd	56.31N	67.45 E
Omutninsk	19	Fd	58.43N	52.12 E
Oña	13	Ib	42.44N	3.24W
Onagawa	29	Gb	38.26N	141.27 E
Onakayale	37	Bc	17.30 S	15.01 E
Onaman Lake	45	Ma	50.00N	87.29W
Onamia	45	Jc	46.04N	93.40W
Onamue	64d	Bb	7.21N	151.31 E
Onaping Lake	44	Gb	46.57N	81.30W
Onatchiway, Lac-	44	La	49.03N	71.03W
Onawa	45	He	42.02N	96.06W
Onch'ŏn	28	He	38.49N	125.13 E
Oncócua	36	Bf	16.40 S	13.24 E
Onda	13	Le	39.58N	0.15W
Ondangua	31	Ij	17.55 S	16.00 E
Ondàrroa	13	Ja	43.19N	2.25W
Ondava	10	Rh	48.27N	21.48 E
Ondo [2]	34	Gd	7.00N	5.00 E
Ondo [Jap.]	29	Cd	34.12N	132.32 E
Ondo [Nig.]	34	Fd	7.06N	4.50 E
Ondor Sum	28	Bc	42.30N	113.00 E
Ondozero, Ozero-	7	He	63.40N	33.15 E
One and Half Degree Channel	21	Ji	1.30N	73.10 E
Oneata	63d	Cc	18.27 S	178.29W
Oneata Passage	63d	Cc	18.32 S	178.28W
Onega	6	Jc	63.57N	38.05 E
Onega	5	Jc	63.58N	37.55 E
Onega, Lake- (EN)= Onežskoje Ozero	5	Jc	61.30N	35.45 E
Onega Peninsula (EN)= Onežski Poluostrov	5	Jc	64.35N	38.00 E
One Hundred Mile House	42	Ff	51.38N	121.16W
Oneida	44	Jd	43.04N	75.40W
Oneida Lake	44	Jd	43.13N	76.00W
O'Neil	43	Hc	42.27N	98.39W
Ōnejime	29	Bf	31.14N	130.47 E
Onekotan, Ostrov-	21	Re	49.25N	154.45 E
Oneonta [Al.-U.S.]	44	Di	33.57N	86.29W
Oneonta [N.Y.-U.S.]	44	Jd	42.28N	75.04W
Oneroa	64p	Cb	21.15 S	159.43W
Onežskaja Guba	5	Jc	64.20N	36.30 E
Onežski Poluostrov=Onega Peninsula (EN)	5	Jc	64.35N	38.00 E
Onežskoje Ozero=Onega, Lake- (EN)	5	Jc	61.30N	35.45 E
Ongea Levu	63d	Cc	19.08 S	178.24W

Index Symbols

[1] Independent Nation
[2] State, Region
[3] District, County
[4] Municipality
[5] Colony, Dependency
Continent
Physical Region
Historical or Cultural Region
Mount, Mountain
Volcano
Hill
Mountains, Mountain Range
Hills, Escarpment
Plateau, Upland
Pass, Gap
Plain, Lowland
Delta
Salt Flat
Valley, Canyon
Crater, Cave
Karst Features
Depression
Polder
Desert, Dunes
Forest, Woods
Heath, Steppe
Oasis
Cape, Point
Coast, Beach
Cliff
Peninsula
Isthmus
Sandbank
Island
Atoll
Rock, Reef
Islands, Archipelago
Rocks, Reefs
Coral Reef
Well, Spring
Geyser
River, Stream
Waterfall Rapids
River Mouth, Estuary
Lake
Salt Lake
Intermittent Lake
Reservoir
Swamp, Pond
Canal
Glacier
Ice Shelf, Pack Ice
Ocean
Sea
Gulf, Bay
Strait, Fjord
Lagoon
Bank
Seamount
Tablemount
Ridge
Shelf
Basin
Escarpment, Sea Scarp
Fracture
Trench, Abyss
National Park, Reserve
Point of Interest
Recreation Site
Cave, Cavern
Historic Site
Ruins
Wall, Walls
Church, Abbey
Temple
Scientific Station
Airport
Port
Lighthouse
Mine
Tunnel
Dam, Bridge

Ongijn-Gol	27	Hc	44.30N	103.40 E
Ongjin	27	Md	37.56N	125.22 E
Ongniud Qi (Wudan)	27	Kc	42.58N	119.01 E
Ongole	25	Ge	15.30N	80.03 E
Ongon	27	Jb	45.49N	113.08 E
Onhaye	12	Gd	50.15N	4.50 E
Oni	16	Mh	42.35N	43.27 E
Onigajō-Yama	29	Ce	33.07N	132.41 E
Onilany	30	Lk	23.34S	43.45 E
Onishibetsu	29a	Ca	45.21N	142.06 E
Onitsha	31	Hh	6.10N	6.47 E
Ono	29	Dd	34.51N	134.57 E
Ono	63d	Bc	18.54S	178.29 E
Ōno [Jap.]	28	Ng	35.59N	136.29 E
Ōno [Jap.]	29	Cd	34.18N	132.17 E
Onoda	29	Be	33.59N	131.11 E
Ōno-Gawa	29	Be	33.15N	131.43 E
Ōnohara-Jima	29	Fd	34.02N	139.23 E
Onohoj	20	Ff	51.55N	108.01 E
Ono-i-Lau Islands	57	Jg	20.39S	178.42W
Onojō	29	Be	33.34N	130.29 E
Onomichi	28	Lg	34.25N	133.12 E
Onon	21	Nd	51.42N	115.50 E
Onoto	50	Dh	9.36N	65.12W
Onotoa Atoll	57	Ie	1.52S	175.34 E
Ons, Isla de-	13	Db	42.23N	8.56W
Onsala	7	Ch	57.25N	12.01 E
Onseepkans	37	Be	28.45S	19.17 E
Onslow	58	Cg	21.39S	115.06 E
Onslow Bay	43	Le	34.20N	77.20W
On-Take	29	Bf	31.35N	130.39 E
Ontake-San	29	Ed	35.53N	137.29 E
Ontario [3]	42	If	50.00N	86.00W
Ontario [Ca.-U.S.]	46	Gi	34.04N	117.39W
Ontario [Or.-U.S.]	43	Dc	44.02N	116.58W
Ontario, Lake-	38	Le	43.40N	78.00W
Ontario Peninsula	38	Ke	43.50N	81.00W
Onteniente/Ontinyent	13	Lf	38.49N	0.37W
Ontinyent/Onteniente	13	Lf	38.49N	0.37W
Ontojärvi	7	Gd	64.08N	29.09 E
Ontonagon	44	Cb	46.52N	89.19W
Ontong Java Atoll	57	Ge	5.20S	159.30 E
Ō-Numa	29a	Bc	41.59N	140.41 E
Oodnadatta	58	Eg	27.33S	135.28 E
Ooidonk	12	Fc	51.01N	3.35 E
Ookala	65a	Fc	20.01N	155.17W
Ooldea	58	Eh	30.27S	131.50 E
Oologah Lake	45	Ih	36.39N	95.36W
Ooltgensplaat, Oostflakkee-	12	Gc	51.41N	4.21 E
Oostburg	12	Fc	51.20N	3.30 E
Oostelijk Flevoland	12	Hb	52.30N	5.40 E
Oostende/Ostende	11	Ic	51.14N	2.55 E
Oosterhout	11	Kc	51.38N	4.51 E
Oosterschelde=East Schelde (EN)	11	Jc	51.30N	4.00 E
Oosterwolde, Ooststellingwerf-	12	Ha	53.00N	6.18 E
Oosterzele	12	Fd	50.57N	3.48 E
Oostflakkee	12	Gc	51.41N	4.21 E
Oostflakkee-Ooltgensplaat	12	Gc	51.41N	4.21 E
Oostkamp	12	Fc	51.09N	3.14 E
Oost-Souburg, Vlissingen-	12	Fc	51.28N	3.36 E
Ooststellingwerf	12	Ib	53.00N	6.18 E
Ooststellingwerf-Oosterwolde	12	Ha	53.00N	6.18 E
Oost Vieland, Vieland-	12	Ha	53.17N	5.06 E
Oost-Vlaanderen [3]	12	Fc	51.00N	3.40 E
Ootmarsum	12	Ib	52.25N	6.54 E
Opala	36	Dc	0.37S	24.21 E
Opalenica	10	Md	52.19N	16.23 E
Opanake	25	Gg	6.36N	80.37 E
Opari	35	Ee	3.56N	32.03 E
Oparino	7	Lg	59.53N	48.25 E
Opasatika	44	Fa	49.31N	82.58W
Opasatika Lake	44	Fa	49.06N	83.08W
Opasatika River	44	Fa	50.15N	82.25W
Opatija	14	Ie	45.20N	14.19 E
Opatów	10	Rf	50.49N	21.26 E
Opatówka	10	Rf	50.42N	21.50 E
Opava	10	Ng	49.57N	17.54 E
Opava	10	Og	49.51N	18.17 E
Opelika	43	Je	32.39N	85.23W
Opelousas	45	Jk	30.32N	92.05W
Opémisca, Lac-	44	Ja	49.58N	74.57W
Opheim	46	Lb	48.51N	106.24W
Ophir	40	Hd	63.10N	156.31W
Ophthalmia Range	59	Dd	23.15S	119.30 E
Opienge	36	Eb	0.12N	27.30 E
Opihikao	65a	Gd	19.26N	154.53W
Opinaca	42	Jf	52.14N	78.02W
Opiscotéo, Lac-	42	Kf	53.09N	68.10W
Opladen, Leverkusen-	10	De	51.04N	7.01 E
Opobo	34	Ge	4.34N	7.27 E
Opočka	19	Cd	56.42N	28.41 E
Opoczno	10	Qe	51.23N	20.17 E
Opole [2]	10	Nf	50.40N	17.55 E
Opole	10	Nf	50.41N	17.55 E
Opole Lubelskie	10	Re	51.09N	21.58 E
Oporny	19	Ff	46.13N	54.29 E
Opotiki	62	Gc	38.01S	177.17 E
Opp	44	Dj	31.17N	86.22W
Oppa-Wan	29	Gb	38.35N	141.30 E
Oppdal	7	Be	62.36N	9.40 E
Oppenheim	10	Eg	49.51N	8.21 E
Oppland [2]	7	Bf	61.10N	9.40 E
Opportunity	46	Gc	47.39N	117.15W
Opsa	8	Li	55.31N	26.54 E
Opsterland	12	Ia	53.03N	6.04 E
Opsterland-Beetsterzwaag	12	Ia	53.03N	6.04 E
Opua	61	Dg	35.18S	174.07 E
Opunake	62	Ec	39.27S	173.51 E
Oputo	48	Eb	30.03N	109.20W
Oquossoc	44	Lc	45.04N	70.44W
Or	16	Ud	51.12N	58.33 E
Ōra	33	Cd	28.20N	19.35 E
Oradea	6	If	47.04N	21.56 E
Orahovac	15	Dg	42.24N	20.40 E
Orahovica	14	Le	45.32N	17.53 E
Orai	25	Fc	25.59N	79.28 E
Oraibi Wash	46	Ji	35.26N	110.49W
Oran	31	Ge	35.42N	0.38W
Oran [3]	32	Gb	36.00N	0.35W
Orange [Austl.]	58	Fh	33.17S	149.06 E
Orange [Fr.]	11	Kj	44.08N	4.48 E
Orange [Tx.-U.S.]	43	Ie	30.01N	93.44W
Orange [Va.-U.S.]	44	Hf	38.14N	78.07W
Orange/Oranje	30	Ik	28.38N	16.27 E
Orange, Cabo-	52	Ke	4.24N	51.33W
Orangeburg	43	Ke	33.30N	80.52W
Orange Free State/Oranje Vrystaat [2]	37	De	29.00S	26.00 E
Orange Lake	44	Fk	29.25N	82.13W
Orange Park	44	Gj	30.10N	81.42W
Orangeville	44	Gd	43.55N	80.06W
Orange Walk	47	Ge	18.06N	88.33W
Orango	30	Fg	11.05N	16.08W
Oranienburg	10	Jd	52.45N	13.14 E
Oranje/Orange	30	Ik	28.38N	16.27 E
Oranje Gebergte	54	Hc	3.00N	55.00W
Oranjemund	37	Be	28.38S	16.24 E
Oranjestad	54	Da	12.33N	70.06W
Oranje Vrystaat/Orange Free State [2]	37	De	29.00S	26.00 E
Oranžerei	16	Og	45.50N	47.36 E
Orapa	37	Dd	21.16S	25.22 E
Orăştie	15	Gd	45.50N	23.12 E
Orava	10	Pg	49.08N	19.10 E
Oraviţa	15	Ed	45.02N	21.42 E
Orayská Priehradní Nádrž	10	Pg	49.20N	19.35 E
Orb	11	Jk	43.15N	3.18 E
Orba	14	Cf	44.53N	8.37 E
Orba Co	27	De	34.33N	81.06 E
Ørbæk	8	Di	55.16N	10.41 E
Orbec	12	Ce	49.01N	0.25 E
Orbetello	14	Fh	42.27N	11.13 E
Orbetello, Laguna di-	14	Fh	42.25N	11.15 E
Orbigo	13	Gc	41.58N	5.40W
Orbiquet	12	Ce	49.09N	0.14 E
Orbost	59	Jg	37.42S	148.27 E
Örbyhus	8	Gd	60.14N	17.42 E
Orcadas	66	Re	60.40S	44.30W
Orcas Island	46	Db	48.39N	122.55W
Orchies	12	Fd	50.28N	3.14 E
Orchon → Orhon	21	Md	50.21N	106.05 E
Orcia	14	Fh	42.58N	11.21 E
Orco	14	Be	45.10N	7.52 E
Ord, Mount-	59	Fc	17.20S	125.35 E
Órdenes	13	Da	43.04N	8.24W
Ordos Desert (EN)=Mu Us Shamo	21	Mf	38.45N	109.10 E
Ord River	57	Df	15.30S	128.21 E
Ordu	23	Ea	41.00N	37.53 E
Ordubad	16	Oj	38.55N	46.01 E
Ordynskoje	20	Df	54.22N	81.58 E
Ordžonikidze [Ukr.-U.R.S.S.]	16	If	47.40N	34.04 E
Ordžonikidze [Kaz.-U.S.S.R.]	17	Jj	52.25N	61.45 E
Ordžonikidze [R.S.F.S.R.]	6	Kg	43.03N	44.40 E
Ordžonikidzeabad	19	Gh	38.34N	69.02 E
Ore älv	8	Fc	61.08N	14.35 E
Orebić	14	Lh	42.58N	17.11 E
Örebro	6	Hd	59.17N	15.13 E
Örebro [2]	7	Dg	59.30N	15.00 E
Oredež	8	Nf	58.50N	30.13 E
Oregon	44	Fe	41.38N	83.28W
Oregon [2]	43	Cc	44.00N	121.00W
Oregon City	43	Cb	45.21N	122.36W
Oregon Inlet	44	Jh	35.50N	75.35W
Öregrund	8	Hd	60.20N	18.26 E
Orehov	16	If	47.34N	35.47 E
Orehovo-Zujevo	6	Jd	55.49N	38.59 E
Orel	6	Je	52.59N	36.05 E
Orel	16	Ie	48.31N	34.55 E
Orel, Gora-	20	Jf	53.55N	140.01 E
Orellana [Peru]	54	Ce	6.54S	75.04W
Orellana [Peru]	54	Cd	4.40S	78.10W
Orem	43	Ec	40.19N	111.42W
Ore Mountains (EN)=Erzgebirge	5	He	50.30N	13.15 E
Ore Mountains (EN)=Krušné Hory	5	He	50.30N	13.15 E
Ören	24	Bd	37.18N	29.17 E
Orenbel	24	Hb	40.00N	39.10 E
Orenburg	6	Le	51.54N	55.06 E
Orenburgskaja Oblast [3]	19	Fe	52.00N	55.00 E
Örencik	24	Cc	39.16N	29.34 E
Orense [3]	13	Eb	42.10N	7.30W
Orense [Arg.]	56	Ie	38.40S	59.47W
Orense [Sp.]	13	Eb	42.20N	7.51W
Oreón, Dhiavlos-	15	Fk	38.54N	22.55 E
Orepuki	62	Bg	46.17S	167.44 E
Orestiás	15	Jh	41.30N	26.31 E
Øresund	5	Hd	55.50N	12.40 E
Oreti	62	Cg	46.28S	168.17 E
Orewa	62	Fb	36.35S	174.42 E
Orford	12	Db	52.05N	1.32 E
Orford Ness	9	Oi	52.05N	1.34 E
Orgañá/Organyà	13	Nb	42.13N	1.20 E
Organ Needle	45	Cj	32.21N	106.33W
Organyà/Orgañá	13	Nb	42.13N	1.20 E
Orgaz	13	Ie	39.39N	3.54W
Orgejev	19	Cf	47.23N	28.50 E
Orgelet	11	Lh	46.31N	5.37 E
Orgon Tal	28	Bc	43.20N	112.40 E
Orgosolo	14	Dj	40.12N	9.21 E
Orgūn	23	Kc	32.57N	69.11 E
Orhaneli	15	Lj	39.54N	29.00 E
Orhaneli/Koca Çay	15	Lj	39.56N	28.32 E
Orhangazi	15	Mi	40.30N	29.18 E
Orhomenós	15	Fk	38.35N	22.54 E
Orhon (Orchon)	21	Md	50.21N	106.05 E
Orhy, Pico de-	13	La	42.59N	1.00W
Oria	13	Ja	43.17N	2.08W
Orichuna, Río-	50	Bi	7.30N	68.13W
Orick	46	Cf	41.17N	124.04W
Oriental	48	Kh	19.22N	97.37W
Oriental, Cordillera-	49	Md	18.55N	69.15W
Oriente	56	He	38.44S	60.37W
Orihuela	13	Lf	38.05N	0.57W
Oriku	15	Ci	40.17N	19.25 E
Óri Lekánis	15	Hh	41.08N	24.33 E
Orillia	42	Jh	44.37N	79.25W
Orimattila	7	Ff	60.48N	25.45 E
Orinoco, Río-	52	Je	8.37N	62.15W
Oripää	8	Jd	60.51N	22.41 E
Orissa [3]	25	Gd	21.00N	84.00 E
Orissaare/Orissare	7	Fg	58.34N	23.05 E
Orissare/Orissaare	7	Fg	58.34N	23.05 E
Oristano	14	Ck	39.54N	8.36 E
Oristano, Golfo di-	14	Ck	39.50N	8.30 E
Orituco, Río-	50	Ch	8.45N	67.27W
Orivesi	5	Ic	62.15N	29.25 E
Orivesi	7	Ff	61.41N	24.21 E
Oriximiná	54	Gd	1.45S	55.52W
Orizaba	39	Jh	18.51N	97.06W
Orizaba, Pico de- (Citlaltépetl, Volcán-)	38	Jh	19.01N	97.16W
Orizona	55	Hc	17.03S	48.18W
Orjahovo	15	Gf	43.44N	23.58 E
Ørje	8	De	59.29N	11.39 E
Orjen	15	Bg	42.34N	18.33 E
Orjiva	13	Ih	36.54N	3.25W
Orkanger	7	Be	63.19N	9.52 E
Orkdalen	8	Ca	63.15N	9.50 E
Örkelljunga	8	Eh	56.17N	13.17 E
Orkla	8	Ca	63.18N	9.50 E
Orkney	37	De	27.00S	26.39 E
Orkney [3]	9	Kb	59.00N	3.00W
Orkney Islands	5	Fd	59.00N	3.00W
Orlândia	55	Ie	20.43S	47.53W
Orlando	39	Kg	28.32N	81.23W
Orlando, Capo d'-	14	Il	38.10N	14.45 E
Orlanka	10	Td	52.52N	23.12 E
Orléanais	11	Hf	48.40N	1.20 E
Orléans	6	Gf	47.55N	1.54 E
Orlice	10	Lf	50.12N	15.49 E
Orlické Hory	10	Mf	50.10N	16.30 E
Orlik	20	Ef	52.30N	99.55 E
Orlovskaja Oblast [3]	19	De	52.45N	36.30 E
Orlovski	16	Mf	46.52N	42.06 E
Orlovski, mys-	7	Jc	67.16N	41.18 E
Orly	11	If	48.45N	2.24 E
Ormāra	25	Cc	25.12N	64.38 E
Ormes	12	Ce	49.03N	0.59 E
Ormoc	26	Hd	11.00N	124.37 E
Ormond	62	Gc	38.33S	177.55 E
Ormond Beach	44	Gk	29.17N	81.02W
Ornain	11	Kf	48.46N	4.47 E
Ornans	11	Mg	47.06N	6.09 E
Ornäs	8	Fd	60.31N	15.32 E
Orne [3]	11	Gf	48.40N	0.05 E
Orne [Fr.]	11	Ie	49.17N	6.11 E
Orne [Fr.]	11	Be	49.19N	0.14W
Orne Seamount (EN)	61	Je	27.30S	157.30W
Orneta	10	Qb	54.08N	20.08 E
Ornö	7	Eg	59.05N	18.25 E
Ornsköldsvik	7	Ee	63.18N	18.43 E
Oro	28	Id	40.01N	127.27 E
Oro, Río de-	55	Ch	27.04S	58.34W
Oro, Río del-	48	Ge	25.35N	105.03W
Orocué	54	Dc	4.48N	71.20W
Orodara	34	Ec	10.59N	4.55W
Orofino	46	Gc	46.29N	116.15W
Orogrande	45	Cj	32.23N	106.08W
Orohena, Mont-	65e	Fc	17.31S	149.28W
Oroluk Atoll	57	Gd	7.32N	155.18 E
Orom	36	Fb	3.20N	33.40 E
Oromocto	42	Kg	45.51N	66.29W
Oron	34	Ge	4.50N	8.14 E
Orona Atoll (Hull)	57	Je	4.29S	172.10W
Orongo	65d	Ac	27.10S	109.26W
Oronsay	9	Ge	56.01N	6.14W
Orontes (EN)=Nahr al 'Āsī	23	Eb	36.02N	35.58 E
Oropesa [Sp.]	13	Ge	39.55N	5.10W
Oropesa [Sp.]	13	Ld	40.06N	0.09W
Oroqen Zizhiqi (Alihe)	27	La	50.35N	123.42 E
Oroquieta	26	He	8.29N	123.48 E
Orós	54	Ke	6.15S	38.55W
Orós, Açude-	54	Ke	6.15S	39.05W
Orosei	14	Dj	40.23N	9.42 E
Orosei, Golfo di-	14	Dj	40.15N	9.45 E
Orosháza	10	Qj	46.34N	20.40 E
Oro-Shima	29	Be	33.52N	130.02 E
Oroszlány	10	Oi	47.29N	18.19 E
Orote Peninsula	64c	Bb	13.26N	144.38 E
Orote Point	64c	Bb	13.27N	144.37 E
Orotukan	20	Kd	62.17N	151.50 E
Oroville [Ca.-U.S.]	46	Eg	39.31N	121.33W
Oroville [Wa.-U.S.]	46	Fb	48.56N	119.26W
Orp-Jauche	12	Gd	50.40N	4.57 E
Orqohan	27	Lb	49.36N	121.23 E
Orr	45	Jb	48.03N	92.50W
Orrefors	8	Fh	56.50N	15.45 E
Orri, Pic d'-/Llorri	13	Nb	42.23N	1.12 E
Orša	6	Je	54.30N	30.24 E
Orsa	7	Df	61.07N	14.37 E
Orsasjön	8	Fc	61.05N	14.35 E
Orsay	12	Ef	48.42N	2.11 E
Orsjön	8	Gc	61.35N	16.20 E
Orsk	6	Le	51.12N	58.34 E
Orşova	15	Fe	44.42N	22.25 E
Ørsta	7	Be	62.12N	6.09 E
Örsundsbro	8	Ge	59.44N	17.18 E
Orta, Lago d'-	14	Ce	45.50N	8.25 E
Ortaca	24	Cd	36.49N	28.47 E
Ortakent	15	Kl	37.02N	27.21 E
Ortaklar	15	Kl	37.53N	27.30 E
Orta Nova	14	Ji	41.19N	15.42 E
Orte	14	Gh	42.27N	12.23 E
Ortegal, Cabo-	13	Ea	43.45N	7.53W
Ortenberg	12	Ld	50.21N	9.03 E
Orthez	11	Fk	43.29N	0.46W
Orthon, Río-	54	Ef	10.50S	66.04W
Ortigueira [Braz.]	56	Jb	24.12S	50.55W
Ortigueira [Sp.]	13	Fa	43.34N	6.44W
Ortisei / Sankt Ulrich	14	Fd	46.34N	11.40 E
Ortiz [Mex.]	48	Dc	28.15N	110.43W
Ortiz [Ven.]	50	Ch	9.37N	67.17W
Ortlergruppe/Ortles	14	Ed	46.30N	10.40 E
Ortles/Ortlergruppe	14	Ed	46.30N	10.40 E
Ortolo	11a	Ab	41.30N	8.55 E
Ortona	14	Ih	42.21N	14.24 E
Ortonville	45	Hd	45.19N	96.27W
Orto-Tokoj	18	Kc	42.20N	76.02 E
Örtze	10	Fd	52.40N	9.57 E
Orukuizu	64a	Ac	7.10N	134.17 E
Orūmīyeh	22	Gf	37.33N	45.04 E
Orūmīyeh, Daryācheh-ye-=Urmia, Lake- (EN)	21	Gf	37.40N	45.30 E
Oruro [2]	54	Eg	18.40S	67.30W
Oruro	53	Jg	17.59S	67.09W
Orust	8	Df	58.10N	11.38 E
Orūzgān [3]	23	Kc	33.15N	66.00 E
Orūzgān	23	Kc	32.56N	66.38 E
Orval, Abbaye d'-	12	He	49.38N	5.22 E
Orvault	11	Eg	47.16N	1.37W
Orvieto	14	Gh	42.43N	12.07 E
Orville Escarpment	66	Qf	75.45S	65.30W
Órvilos, Óros-	15	Gh	41.23N	23.36 E
Orwell	12	Dc	51.58N	1.18 E
Orxois	12	Fe	49.08N	3.12 E
Orz	10	Rd	52.50N	21.30 E
Orzinuovi	14	De	45.24N	9.55 E
Orzyc	10	Rd	52.47N	21.13 E
Orzysz	10	Rc	53.49N	21.56 E
Oš	19	Hg	40.32N	72.50 E
Os	7	Ce	62.30N	11.12 E
Osa	19	Fd	57.17N	55.26 E
Oša	8	Lh	56.21N	26.29 E
Osa	10	Oc	53.33N	18.45 E
Osa, Peninsula de-	47	Hg	8.35N	83.33W
Osage	45	Je	43.17N	92.49W
Osage River	43	Id	38.35N	91.57W
Osaka	29	Ed	35.57N	137.14 E
Ōsaka	22	Pf	34.40N	135.30 E
Osaka Bay (EN)=Ōsaka-Wan	28	Mg	34.36N	135.27 E
Ōsaka-Fu [2]	28	Mg	34.45N	135.35 E
Osakarovka	19	He	50.32N	72.39 E
Ōsaka-Wan=Osaka Bay (EN)	28	Mg	34.36N	135.27 E
Osăm	15	Hf	43.42N	24.51 E
Osan	28	If	37.09N	127.04 E
Osasco	55	If	23.32S	46.46W
Osat	14	Nf	44.02N	19.20 E
Osawatomie	45	Ig	38.31N	94.57W
Osborne	45	Gg	39.26N	98.42W
Osburger Hochwald	12	Ie	49.40N	6.50 E
Osby	7	Ch	56.22N	13.59 E
Osceola [Ar.-U.S.]	45	Li	35.42N	89.58W
Osceola [Ia.-U.S.]	43	Ic	41.02N	93.46W
Osceola [Mo.-U.S.]	45	Jh	38.03N	93.42W
Oschatz	10	Je	51.18N	13.07 E
Oschersleben	10	Hd	52.02N	11.15 E
Oschiri	14	Dj	40.43N	9.06 E
Osen	7	Cd	64.18N	10.31 E
Osered	16	Ld	50.01N	40.48 E
Osetr	16	Kb	55.00N	38.45 E
Ōse-Zaki	28	Jh	32.38N	128.42 E
Oshamanbe	28	Pc	42.30N	140.22 E
Oshawa	42	Jh	43.54N	78.51W
Oshekehia Lake	37	Bc	18.08S	15.45 E
Oshika	29	Gb	38.17N	141.31 E
Oshika-Hantō	28	Pe	38.22N	141.27 E
Oshikango	37	Bc	17.22S	15.55 E
Oshima	29	Ce	33.55N	132.11 E
Ō-Shima [Jap.]	29	De	33.28N	135.50 E
Ō-Shima [Jap.]	29	Ae	33.30N	129.33 E
Ō-Shima [Jap.]	29	Ae	32.34N	128.54 E
Ō-Shima [Jap.]	29	Be	33.54N	130.27 E
Ō-Shima [Jap.]	27	Oe	34.45N	139.30 E
Ōshima [Jap.]	29	Fd	34.44N	139.20 E
Ō-Shima [Jap.]	29	Bf	31.32N	131.25 E
Ō-Shima [Jap.]	29	De	33.38N	134.30 E
Ō-Shima [Jap.]	29	Cd	34.10N	133.05 E
Ōshima [Jap.]	29	Ae	33.04N	129.36 E
Ō-Shima [Jap.]	28	Od	41.30N	139.15 E
Ō-Shima [Jap.]	28	Jh	32.04N	128.26 E
Oshima-Hantō	28	Pd	41.40N	140.30 E
Ōshima-Kaikyō	29b	Ba	28.10N	129.15 E
Oshkosh [Nb.-U.S.]	45	Ef	41.24N	102.21W
Oshkosh [Wi.-U.S.]	43	Jc	44.01N	88.33W
Oshnavīyeh	24	Kd	37.02N	45.06 E
Oshogbo	31	Hh	7.46N	4.34 E
Oshtorān Kūh	23	Gc	33.20N	49.16 E
Oshtorīnān	24	Me	34.01N	48.38 E
Oshwe	36	Cc	3.24S	19.30 E
Osich'ŏn-ni	28	Jd	41.25N	128.16 E
Osijek	6	Hf	45.33N	18.42 E
Osilo	14	Cj	40.45N	8.40 E
Osimo	14	Hg	43.28N	13.29 E
Osinki	7	Lj	52.52N	49.31 E
Osinniki	20	Df	53.37N	87.31 E
Osipaonica	15	Ee	44.33N	21.04 E
Osipoviči	16	Fc	53.19N	28.40 E
Osječenica	14	Kf	44.29N	16.17 E
Oskaloosa	45	Jf	41.18N	92.39W
Oskarshamn	7	Dh	57.16N	16.26 E
Oskarström	8	Eh	56.48N	12.58 E
Oskélanéo	44	Ja	48.08N	75.05W
Oskino	20	Fd	60.48N	107.58 E
Öskjuvatn	7a	Cb	65.02N	16.45W
Oskol	16	Je	49.06N	37.25 E
Oskū	24	Ld	37.55N	46.06 E
Oslava	10	Mg	49.05N	16.22 E
Ösling	11	Le	49.55N	6.00 E
Osljanka, Gora-	17	Ig	59.10N	58.33 E
Oslo [2]	7	Cg	59.55N	10.45 E
Oslo	6	Hd	59.55N	10.45 E
Oslofjorden	5	Hd	59.20N	10.35 E
Osmānābād	25	Fe	18.10N	76.03 E
Osmancık	24	Fb	40.59N	34.49 E
Osmaneli	15	Ni	40.22N	30.01 E
Osmaniye	23	Eb	37.05N	36.14 E
Osmino	8	Mf	58.54N	29.15 E
Ošmjanskaja Vozvyšennost	8	Kj	54.30N	26.00 E
Ošmjany	16	Db	54.27N	25.57 E
Ösmo	8	Gf	58.59N	17.54 E
Osmussaar/Osmussar	8	Je	59.20N	23.15 E
Osmussar/Osmussaar	8	Je	59.20N	23.15 E
Osnabrück	6	Ge	52.16N	8.03 E
Osning	12	Kb	52.10N	8.05 E
Oso, Sierra del-	48	Gd	26.00N	105.25W
Osobłoga	10	Nf	50.27N	17.58 E
Osogovske Planine	15	Fg	42.10N	22.30 E
Osor	14	If	44.42N	14.24 E
Osório	56	Jc	29.54S	50.16W
Osorno	53	Ij	40.34S	73.09W
Osoyoos	42	Fg	49.02N	119.28W
Osøyra	7	Af	60.11N	5.28 E
Ospino	50	Bh	9.18N	69.27W
Osprey Reef	57	Ff	13.55S	146.40 E
Oss	11	Lc	51.46N	5.31 E
Ossa, Mount-	57	Fi	41.54S	146.01 E
Óssa, Óros-	15	Fj	39.49N	22.40 E
Ossabaw Island	44	Gj	31.47N	81.06W
Ossa de Montiel	13	Jf	38.58N	2.45W
Osse	11	Gj	44.07N	0.17 E
Ossining	44	Ke	41.10N	73.52W
Ossjøen	8	Dc	61.15N	11.55 E
Oŝskaja Oblast [3]	19	Hg	40.45N	73.20 E
Ossora	20	Le	59.15N	163.02 E
Östanvik	8	Fc	61.10N	15.13 E
Ostaškov	19	Dd	57.09N	33.07 E
Ostbevern	12	Jb	52.03N	7.51 E
Oste	10	Fc	53.33N	9.10 E
Ostende/Oostende	11	Ic	51.14N	2.55 E
Oster	16	Gd	50.55N	30.57 E
Oster [Ukr.-U.S.S.R.]	16	Gd	50.53N	30.55 E
Oster [U.S.S.R.]	16	Gc	53.47N	31.45 E
Osterburg in der Altmark	10	Hd	52.47N	11.44 E
Österbybruk	8	Gd	60.12N	17.54 E
Österdalälven	7	Df	60.33N	15.08 E
Østerdalen	7	Cf	62.00N	10.40 E
Osterfjorden	8	Ad	60.30N	5.20 E
Österforse	8	Ga	63.09N	17.01 E
Östergarnsholm	8	Hg	57.25N	19.00 E
Östergötland	8	Ff	58.25N	15.35 E
Östergötland [2]	7	Dg	58.25N	15.45 E
Osterholz Scharmbeck	10	Ec	53.14N	8.48 E
Österlen	8	Fi	55.30N	14.10 E
Ostermark/Teuva	7	Ee	62.29N	21.44 E
Osterode am Harz	10	Ge	51.44N	10.11 E
Osterøya	7	Af	60.35N	5.35 E
Österreich = Austria (EN) [1]	6	Hf	47.30N	14.00 E
Östersjön=Baltic Sea (EN)	5	Hd	57.00N	19.00 E
Østersøen=Baltic Sea (EN)	5	Hd	57.00N	19.00 E
Östersund	6	Hc	63.11N	14.39 E
Osterwick, Rosendahl-	12	Jb	52.01N	7.12 E
Østfold [2]	7	Cg	59.20N	11.30 E
Ostfriesische Inseln=East Frisian Islands (EN)	10	Dc	53.45N	7.25 E
Ostfriesland=East Friesland (EN)	10	Dc	53.20N	7.40 E
Østgrønland=East Greenland (EN) [2]	41	Id	72.00N	35.00W
Östhammar	7	Ed	60.16N	18.22 E
Osthofen	12	Ke	49.42N	8.20 E
Östmark	8	Ed	60.17N	12.45 E
Ostrach	10	Fh	48.05N	9.25 E
Östra Silen	8	Ee	59.15N	12.20 E
Ostrava	6	Hf	49.50N	18.17 E
Ostrhauderfehn	12	Ja	53.08N	7.37 E
Ostróda	10	Pc	53.43N	19.59 E
Ostrog	16	Ed	50.19N	26.32 E
Ostrogožsk	19	De	50.52N	39.05 E
Ostrołęka [2]	10	Rc	53.05N	21.35 E
Ostrołęka	10	Rc	53.06N	21.34 E
Ostrošicki Gorodok	8	Lj	54.03N	27.46 E
Ostrov [Bye.-U.S.S.R.]	10	Vd	52.48N	26.01 E
Ostrov [Czech.]	10	If	50.18N	12.57 E
Ostrov [Rom.]	15	Ke	44.07N	27.22 E
Ostrov [R.S.F.S.R.]	19	Cd	57.23N	28.22 E
Ostrov [R.S.F.S.R.]	8	Mf	58.28N	28.44 E
Ostrovec	8	Lj	54.38N	26.06 E
Ostrovicës, Mali i-	15	Di	40.34N	20.27 E
Ostrovskoje	7	Kh	57.50N	42.13 E
Ostrov Zmeiny	16	Gg	45.15N	30.12 E
Ostrowiec Świętokrzyski	10	Rf	50.57N	21.23 E
Ostrów Lubelski	10	Se	51.30N	22.52 E
Ostrów Mazowiecka	10	Rd	52.49N	21.54 E
Ostrów Wielkopolski	10	Ne	51.39N	17.49 E
Ostryna	10	Uc	53.41N	24.37 E
Ostrzeszów	10	Ne	51.25N	17.57 E
Ostsee=Baltic Sea (EN)	5	Hd	57.00N	19.00 E
Oststeirisches Hügelland	14	Jd	47.00N	15.45 E
Osttirol	14	Gd	46.55N	12.30 E
Ostuni	14	Lj	40.44N	17.35 E
Osumi	15	Ci	40.48N	19.52 E
Ōsumi	29	Bf	31.36N	130.59 E
Ōsumi-Hantō	29	Bf	31.15N	130.50 E
Osumi Islands (EN)=Ōsumi-Shotō	21	Pf	30.35N	130.59 E
Ōsumi-Shotō=Osumi Islands (EN)	21	Pf	30.35N	130.59 E
Osuna	13	Gg	37.14N	5.07W
Osveja	8	Mi	55.59N	28.10 E
Osvejskoje, Ozero-	8	Mh	56.00N	28.15 E
Oswego	43	Lc	43.27N	76.31W
Oswestry	9	Ji	52.52N	3.04W

Index Symbols

[1] Independent Nation
[2] State, Region
[3] District, County
Municipality
Colony, Dependency
Continent
Physical Region
Historical or Cultural Region
Mount, Mountain
Volcano
Hill
Mountains, Mountain Range
Hills, Escarpment
Plateau, Upland
Pass, Gap
Plain, Lowland
Delta
Salt Flat
Valley, Canyon
Crater, Cave
Karst Features
Depression
Polder
Desert, Dunes
Forest, Woods
Heath, Steppe
Oasis
Cape, Point
Coast, Beach
Cliff
Peninsula
Isthmus
Sandbank
Island
Atoll
Rock, Reef
Islands, Archipelago
Rocks, Reefs
Coral Reef
Well, Spring
Geyser
River, Stream
Waterfall Rapids
River Mouth, Estuary
Lake
Salt Lake
Intermittent Lake
Reservoir
Swamp, Pond
Canal
Glacier
Ice Shelf, Pack Ice
Ocean
Sea
Gulf, Bay
Strait, Fjord
Lagoon
Bank
Seamount
Tablemount
Ridge
Shelf
Basin
Escarpment, Sea Scarp
Fracture
Trench, Abyss
National Park, Reserve
Point of Interest
Recreation Site
Cave, Cavern
Historic Site
Ruins
Wall, Walls
Church, Abbey
Temple
Scientific Station
Airport
Port
Lighthouse
Mine
Tunnel
Dam, Bridge

Oświęcim 10 Pf 50.03N 19.12 E
Osyka 45 Kk 31.00N 90.28W
Ōta 29 Fc 36.18N 139.22 E
Ota 29 Ec 35.56N 136.03 E
Otago [2] 62 Cf 45.00S 169.10 E
Otago Peninsula 62 Df 45.50S 170.45 E
Ōtake 28 Lg 34.12N 132.13 E
Otakeho 62 Fc 39.33S 174.03 E
Otaki 62 Fd 40.45S 175.08 E
Ōtakime-Yama 29 Gc 37.22N 140.42 E
Otanoshike 29a Db 43.01N 144.16 E
Otar 19 Hg 43.31N 75.12 E
Otaru 27 Pc 43.13N 141.00 E
Otautau 62 Bg 46.09S 168.00 E
Otava 10 Kg 49.26N 14.12 E
Otava 8 Lc 61.39N 27.04 E
Otavi 37 Bc 19.39S 17.20 E
Ōtawara 28 Pf 36.52N 140.02 E
Otelu Roşu 15 Fd 45.32N 22.22 E
Otematata 62 Df 44.37S 170.11 E
Otepää/Otepja 7 Gg 58.03N 26.30 E
Otepää, Vozvyšennost-/
Otepää Kõrgustik 8 Lf 58.00N 26.40 E
Otepää Kõrgustik/Otepää,
Vozvyšennost- 8 Lf 58.00N 26.40 E
Otepja/Otepää 7 Gg 58.03N 26.30 E
Oteros 47 Cc 26.55N 108.30W
Othain 12 He 49.31N 5.23 E
Othello 46 Fc 46.50N 119.10W
Othonoi 15 Cj 39.50N 19.25 E
Óthris Óros 15 Fj 39.02N 22.37 E
Oti 30 Hh 7.48N 0.08 E
Otira 62 De 42.51S 171.33 E
Otish, Monts- 38 Md 52.45N 69.15W
Otjikondo 37 Bc 19.50S 15.23 E
Otjimbingwe 37 Bd 22.21S 16.08 E
Otjiwarongo 31 Ik 20.29S 16.36 E
Otjiwarongo [3] 37 Bd 20.30S 17.30 E
Otjosondjou, Omuramba- 30 Ij 19.55S 20.00 E
Otjosondu 37 Bd 21.12S 17.58 E
Otmuchowskie, Jezioro- 10 Nf 50.27N 17.15 E
Otnes 7 Cf 61.46N 11.12 E
Otobe 29a Bc 41.57N 140.08 E
Otočac 14 Jf 44.52N 15.14 E
Otofuke 29a Cb 42.59N 143.10 E
Otofuke-Gawa 29a Cb 42.56N 143.12 E
Otog Qi (Ulan) 27 Id 39.07N 108.00 E
Otoineppu 29a Ca 44.43N 142.16 E
Otok 14 Me 45.09N 18.53 E
Otopeni 15 Je 44.33N 26.04 E
Otorohanga 62 Fc 38.11S 175.12 E
Otorten, Gora- 17 If 61.50N 59.13 E
Ōtoyo 29 Ce 33.46N 133.40 E
Otra 5 Gd 58.09N 8.00 E
Otradnaja 16 Lg 44.23N 41.31 E
Otradnoje, Ozero- 8 Nd 60.50N 30.25 E
Otradny 7 Mj 53.23N 51.24 E
Otranto 14 Mj 40.09N 18.30 E
Otranto, Canale d'- =
Otranto, Strait of- (EN) 5 Hg 40.00N 19.00 E
Otranto, Capo d'- 14 Mj 40.06N 18.31 E
Otranto, Strait of- (EN)=
Otranto, Canale d'- 5 Hg 40.00N 19.00 E
Otranto, Strait of- (EN)=
Otrantos, Kanali i- 15 Bi 40.00N 19.00 E
Otranto, Terra d'- 14 Mj 40.20N 18.15 E
Otrantos, Kanali i-=Otranto,
Strait of- (EN) 15 Bi 40.00N 19.00 E
Ötscher 14 Jc 47.51N 15.12 E
Ōtsu 28 Mg 35.00N 135.52 E
Ōtsuchi 28 Pe 39.21N 141.54 E
Ōtsuki [Jap.] 29 Fd 35.36N 138.54 E
Ōtsuki [Jap.] 29 Ce 32.50N 132.41 E
Otta 8 Cc 61.46N 9.31 E
Otta 7 Bf 61.46N 9.32 E
Otta 64d Bb 7.09N 151.54 E
Ottadalen 8 Bc 61.55N 8.00 E
Ottana 14 Dj 40.15N 9.05 E
Otta Pass 64d Bb 7.09N 151.53 E
Ottawa [Il.-U.S.] 45 Lf 41.21N 88.51W
Ottawa [Ks.-U.S.] 43 Hd 38.37N 95.16W
Ottawa [Oh.-U.S.] 44 Ee 41.02N 84.03W
Ottawa [Ont.-Can.] 39 Le 45.25N 75.42W
Ottawa Islands 38 Kd 59.30N 80.10W
Ottawa River 38 Le 45.20N 73.58W
Ottenby 7 Dh 56.16N 16.24 E
Otterberg 12 Je 49.30N 7.46 E
Otter Creek 44 Fk 29.19N 82.48W
Otterndorf 10 Ec 53.48N 8.54 E
Otterøy 8 Bb 62.40N 6.50 E
Otter Rapids 44 Ga 50.15N 81.45W
Otterup 8 Di 55.31N 10.24 E
Ottumwa 43 Ic 41.01N 92.25W
Ottweiler 12 Je 49.23N 7.10 E
Otukpa 34 Gd 7.05N 7.40 E
Otumpa 55 Ah 27.19S 62.13W
Otuquis, Bañados de- 54 Gg 19.20S 58.30W
Otuquis, Río- 55 Cd 19.41S 58.20W
Oturkpo 34 Gd 7.13N 8.09 E
Otu Tolu Group 65b Bb 20.21S 174.32W
Otuzco 54 Ce 7.54S 78.35W
Otway, Cape- 59 Ig 38.52S 143.31 E
Otwock 10 Rd 52.07N 21.16 E
Otynja 10 Uh 48.40N 24.57 E
Ötz 14 Ec 47.12N 10.54 E
Ötztaler Ache 14 Ec 47.14N 10.50 E
Ötztaler Alpen 10 Gi 46.45N 10.55 E
Ou 25 Kd 20.04N 102.13 E
'O'ua 65b Bb 20.02S 174.41W
Oua 63b Ce 21.14S 167.05 E
Ouachita, Lake- 45 Ji 34.40N 93.25W
Ouachita Mountains 38 Jf 34.40N 94.25W
Ouachita River 43 Ie 31.38N 91.49W
Ouadane 31 Ff 20.57N 11.35W
Ouaddaï [3] 35 Cc 13.00N 21.00 E
Ouaddaï 30 Jg 13.00N 21.00 E
Ouagadougou 31 Gg 12.22N 1.31W
Ouahigouya 31 Gg 13.35N 2.25W
Ouaka [3] 35 Cd 6.00N 21.00 E
Ouaka 30 Ih 4.59N 19.56 E
Oualata 32 Ff 17.18N 7.00W
Oualata, Dahr- 32 Ff 17.48N 7.24W
Oualidia 32 Fc 32.44N 9.02W
Ouallam 34 Fc 14.19N 2.05 E
Ouallene 32 He 24.35N 1.17 E
Ouanda-Djallé 35 Cd 8.54N 22.48 E
Ouandjia 35 Cd 8.35N 23.12 E
Ouandjia 35 Cd 9.35N 21.43 E
Ouango 35 Ce 4.19N 22.33 E
Ouangolodougou 34 Dd 9.58N 5.09W
Ouanne 11 Ig 47.57N 2.47 E
Ouarane 30 Ff 21.00N 10.00W
Ouargaye 34 Fc 11.32N 0.01 E
Ouargla 31 He 31.57N 5.20 E
Ouargla [3] 32 Id 30.00N 6.30 E
Ouarkziz, Jbel- 30 Gf 28.00N 8.20W
Ouarra 30 Jh 5.05N 24.26 E
Ouarsenis, Djebel- 13 Nh 35.53N 1.38 E
Ouarsenis, Massif de l'- 13 Hh 35.50N 2.05 E
Ouarzazate [3] 32 Fc 31.00N 6.30W
Ouarzazate 32 Fc 30.55N 6.55W
Oubangui 30 Ii 0.30S 17.42 E
Ouborré, Pointe- 63b Dd 18.47S 169.16 E
Ouche, Pays d'- 11 Gf 48.55N 0.45 E
Ōuchi 29 Gb 39.27N 140.06 E
Oud Beijerland 12 Gc 51.50N 4.26 E
Oude IJssel 12 Ic 52.00N 6.10 E
Oudenaarde/Audenarde 11 Jd 50.51N 3.36 E
Oudenbosch 12 Gc 51.35N 4.34 E
Oude Rijn 11 Kb 52.05N 4.20 E
Oudon 11 Fg 47.37N 0.42W
Oudtshoorn 31 Jl 33.35S 22.14 E
Oued Ben Tili 32 Fd 25.48N 9.32W
Oued el Abtal 13 Mi 35.27N 0.41 E
Oued Fodda 13 Nh 36.11N 1.32 E
Oued Lili 13 Ni 35.31N 1.16 E
Oued Rhiou 32 Hb 35.58N 0.55 E
Oued-Taria 13 Mi 35.07N 0.05 E
Oued Tlelat 13 Li 35.33N 0.27W
Oued Zem 31 Ge 32.52N 6.34W
Ouégoa 63b Be 20.21S 164.26 E
Ouéllé 34 Ed 7.18N 4.01W
Ouémé 30 Hh 6.29N 2.32 E
Ouémé [3] 34 Fd 7.00N 2.35 E
Ouen 63b Cf 22.26S 166.48 E
Ouenza 32 Ib 35.57N 8.07 E
Ouenza, Djebel- 14 Co 35.57N 8.05 E
Ouessa 34 Ec 11.03N 2.47W
Ouessant, Ile d'- 11 Af 48.28N 5.05W
Ouesso 31 Ih 1.37N 16.04 E
Ouest [3] 34 Hd 5.20N 10.30 E
Ouest, Baie de l'- 64h Ab 13.15S 176.13W
Ouezzane 32 Fc 34.48N 5.36W
Oughter, Lough- 9 Fg 54.00N 7.29W
Ouham [3] 35 Bd 7.00N 18.00 E
Ouham 30 Ih 9.18N 18.14 E
Ouham-Pendé [3] 35 Bd 7.00N 16.00 E
Ouidah 34 Fd 6.22N 2.05 E
Ouistreham 11 Fe 49.17N 0.15W
Ouistreham-Riva Bella 12 Be 49.17N 0.16W
Oujda [3] 32 Gc 33.00N 2.00W
Oujda 31 Ge 34.40N 1.54W
Oujeft 32 Ee 20.02N 13.03W
Oulainen 7 Fd 64.16N 24.57 E
Oulchy-le-Château 12 Fe 49.12N 3.21 E
Ouled Djellal 32 Ic 34.25N 5.04 E
Ouled Nail, Monts des- 32 Hc 34.40N 3.25 E
Oulou, Bahr- 35 Cd 9.48N 21.32 E
Oulu [2] 7 Gd 65.00N 27.00 E
Oulu/Uleåborg 6 Ib 65.01N 25.30 E
Oulu, Lake- (EN)=
Oulujärvi 5 Ic 64.20N 27.15 E
Oulujärvi=Oulu, Lake- (EN) 5 Ic 64.20N 27.15 E
Oulujoki 5 Ib 65.01N 25.25 E
Oum Chalouba 31 Jg 15.48N 20.46 E
Oumé [3] 34 Dd 6.25N 5.30W
Oumé 34 Dd 6.23N 5.25W
Oum el Bouaghi [3] 32 Ib 35.30N 7.10 E
Oum el Bouaghi 32 Ib 35.53N 7.07 E
Oum er Rbia 30 Ge 33.19N 8.20W
Oum Hadjer 35 Bc 13.18N 19.41 E
Oumm ed Droûs Guebli,
Sebkhet- 32 Ee 24.03N 11.45W
Oumm ed Droûs Telli,
Sebkhet- 32 Ee 24.20N 11.30W
Ounasjoki 5 Ib 66.30N 25.45 E
Oundle 12 Bb 52.29N 0.28W
Ounianga 35 Cb 19.10N 20.30 E
Ounianga Kébir 31 Jg 19.04N 20.29 E
Ountivou 34 Fd 7.21N 1.34 E
Ouolossébougou 34 Dc 12.00N 7.55W
Oupeye 12 Hd 50.42N 5.39 E
Oupu 27 Ma 52.45N 126.00 E
Our 12 Ie 49.53N 6.18 E
Ouray 45 Cg 38.01N 107.40W
Ouray, Mount- 45 Cg 38.25N 106.14W
Ource 11 Kf 48.06N 4.23 E
Ourcq 11 Je 49.01N 3.01 E
Ourcq, Canal de l'- 11 If 48.51N 2.22 E
Ourém 54 Id 1.33S 47.06W
Ouricuri 54 Je 7.35S 40.05W
Ourinhos 53 Lh 22.59S 49.52W
Ouro, Rio do- 55 Ha 13.20S 48.59W
Ouro Fino 55 If 22.17S 46.22W
Ouro Prêto 54 Jh 20.23S 43.30W
Ourthe [Bel.] 11 Ld 50.38N 5.35 E
Ourville-en-Caux 12 Ce 49.44N 0.36 E
Ous 19 Gc 60.55N 61.31 E
Ou-Sanmyaku 28 Pe 39.00N 141.00 E
Ouse [Eng.-U.K.] 9 Nk 50.47N 0.03 E
Ouse [Eng.-U.K.] 9 Mh 53.42N 0.41W
Oust 11 Dg 47.35N 2.06W
Outagouna 34 Fb 15.11N 0.43 E
Outaouais, Rivière- 38 Le 45.20N 73.58W
Outardes, Rivière aux- 42 Kg 49.05N 68.23W
Outat Oulad El Hajj 32 Gc 33.21N 3.42W
Outer Dowsing 9 Oh 53.25N 1.05 E
Outer Hebrides 9 Fd 57.50N 7.32W
Outer Santa Barbara
Passage 46 Fj 33.10N 118.30W
Outer Silver Pit 9 Og 54.05N 2.00 E
Outjo 31 Ik 20.08S 16.08 E
Outjo [3] 37 Ac 19.30S 14.30 E
Outlook 46 La 51.30N 107.03W
Outokumpu 7 Ge 62.44N 29.01 E
Outram Mountain 46 Eb 49.19N 121.05W
Outreau 12 Dd 50.42N 1.35 E
Out Skerries 9 Ma 60.30N 0.50W
Outwell 12 Cb 52.37N 0.14 E
Ouvéa, Ile- 57 Hg 20.35S 166.35 E
Ouvèze 11 Kk 43.59N 4.51 E
Ouxian 28 Ej 28.58N 118.53 E
Ouyen 59 Ig 35.04S 142.20 E
Ouyen Bézédinga 34 Hb 16.32N 13.15 E
Ouzera 13 Oh 36.15N 2.51 E
Ovacık [Tur.] 24 Ed 36.11N 33.40 E
Ovacık [Tur.] 24 Hc 39.22N 39.13 E
Ovada 14 Cf 44.38N 8.38 E
Ova Gölü 15 Mm 36.16N 29.22 E
Ovakent 15 Lk 38.06N 28.02 E
Ovalau Island 63d Bb 17.40S 178.48 E
Ovalle 53 Ii 30.36S 71.12W
Oval Peak 46 Eb 48.15N 120.25W
Ovamboland 37 Bc 18.30S 16.00 E
Ovamboland [3] 37 Bc 18.00S 16.00 E
Ovan 36 Bb 0.30N 12.10 E
Ovanåker 7 Df 61.21N 15.54 E
Ovar 13 Dd 40.52N 8.38W
Ovau 63a Cb 6.48S 156.02 E
Ovejas 49 Ji 9.32N 75.14W
Overath 12 Jd 50.57N 7.18 E
Øverbygd 7 Eb 69.01N 19.18 E
Overflakkee 11 Kc 51.45N 4.10 E
Overhalla 7 Cd 64.30N 12.00 E
Overijse 12 Gd 50.46N 4.32 E
Overijssel [3] 12 Ib 52.25N 6.30 E
Överkalix 7 Fc 66.19N 22.50 E
Overland Park 45 Ig 38.59N 94.40W
Övermark/Ylimarkku 8 Ib 62.37N 21.28 E
Overpelt 12 Hc 51.12N 5.25 E
Overri 34 Gd 5.29N 7.02 E
Overton 46 Hh 36.33N 114.27W
Övertorneå 7 Fc 66.23N 23.40 E
Överum 8 Gg 57.59N 16.19 E
Ovidiu 15 Le 44.16N 28.34 E
Oviedo [3] 13 Ga 43.20N 6.00W
Oviedo [Dom.Rep.] 49 Le 17.47N 71.22W
Oviedo [Sp.] 6 Fg 43.22N 5.50W
Oviši 8 Ig 57.34N 21.35 E
Ovo, Capo dell'- 14 Lj 40.18N 17.30 E
Øvre Årdal 7 Bf 61.19N 7.48 E
Övre Fryken 8 Ed 60.00N 13.05 E
Övre Soppero 7 Eb 68.05N 21.41 E
Ovruč 19 Ce 51.19N 28.50 E
Ovsjanka 20 Hf 53.32N 126.58 E
Owaka 62 Cg 46.27S 169.40 E
Owando 31 Ii 0.29S 15.55 E
Ōwani 28 Pd 40.31N 140.35 E
Owase 28 Ng 34.04N 136.12 E
Owatonna 43 Ic 44.05N 93.14W
Owego 44 Id 42.06N 76.16W
Owen, Mount- 62 Ed 41.33S 172.32 E
Owendo 36 Ab 0.17N 9.30 E
Owen Falls Dam 36 Fb 0.24N 33.11 E
Owensboro 43 Jd 37.46N 87.07W
Owens Lake 46 Gh 36.25N 117.56W
Owen Sound 42 Jh 44.34N 80.56W
Owens River 46 Gh 36.31N 117.57W
Owen Stanley Range 57 Fe 9.20S 148.00 E
Owl Creek Mountains 46 Ke 43.30N 108.35W
Ownay, Kowlal-e- 23 Kc 34.27N 68.22 E
Owo 34 Gd 7.11N 5.35 E
Owosso 44 Ed 43.00N 84.10W
Owyhee 46 Gf 41.57N 116.06W
Owyhee, Lake- 46 Ge 43.28N 117.20W
Owyhee Mountains 46 Ge 43.00N 116.45W
Owyhee River [U.S.] 46 Ge 43.40N 117.16W
Owyhee River [U.S.] 43 Dc 43.46N 117.02W
Oxberg 8 Fc 61.07N 14.10 E
Oxbow 45 Eb 49.14N 102.11W
Oxelösund 7 Dg 58.40N 17.06 E
Oxford 9 Lj 51.50N 1.30W
Oxford [Eng.-U.K.] 6 Fe 51.46N 1.15W
Oxford [Ms.-U.S.] 45 Li 34.22N 89.32W
Oxford [N.C.-U.S.] 44 Hg 36.19N 78.35W
Oxford [N.Z.] 62 Ee 43.17S 172.11 E
Oxford Lake 42 Hf 54.50N 95.35W
Oxfordshire [3] 9 Lj 51.50N 1.20W
Oxia 15 Ek 38.18N 21.06 E
Oxkutzcab 48 Og 20.18N 89.25W
Oxnard 43 De 34.12N 119.11W
Ox or Slieve Gamph
Mountains/Sliabh
Gamh 9 Eg 54.10N 8.50W
Oxted 12 Bc 51.14N 0.01W
Oyabe 29 Ec 36.40N 136.52 E
Oyahue 53 Jh 21.08S 68.45W
O-Yama 29 Fd 34.04N 139.31 E
Oyama 28 Of 36.21N 139.50 E
Ōyama 29 Ec 36.35N 137.18 E
Ōyano 29 Be 32.35N 130.27 E
Oyapock, Fleuve- 52 Ke 4.08N 51.40W
Oyem 31 Ih 1.37N 11.35 E
Oyen 46 Ja 51.22N 110.28W
Øyeren 8 De 59.50N 11.14 E
Oykel 9 Id 57.50N 4.25W
Oyo [2] 34 Fd 8.00N 3.50 E
Oyo [Nig.] 34 Fd 7.51N 3.56 E
Oyo [Sud.] 35 Fa 21.55N 36.06 E
Oyodo-Gawa 29 Bf 31.55N 131.28 E
Oyonnax 11 Lh 46.15N 5.40 E
Oyster Bay 59 Jh 42.10S 148.10 E
Øystese 8 Bd 60.23N 6.13 E
Özalp 24 Jc 38.39N 43.59 E
Ozamiz 26 He 8.08N 123.50 E
Ozark 44 Ej 31.28N 85.38W
Ozark Plateau 38 Jf 37.00N 93.00W
Ozark Reservoir 45 Ii 35.25N 94.05W
Ozarks, Lake of the- 43 Id 37.39N 92.50W
Ózd 10 Qh 48.13N 20.18 E
Ozeblin 14 Jf 44.35N 15.53 E
Ozernoj, Zaliv- 20 Le 57.00N 163.20 E
Ozernovski 20 Kf 51.21N 156.32 E
Ozerny 16 Vd 51.08N 60.55 E
Ozersk 8 Ij 54.24N 21.59 E
Ozery [Bye.-U.S.S.R.] 10 Uc 53.38N 24.18 E
Ozery [R.S.F.S.R.] 7 Ji 54.54N 38.32 E
Ožezdy 19 Gf 48.03N 67.09 E
Ozieri 14 Cj 40.35N 9.00 E
Ozinki 19 Ee 51.12N 49.47 E
Ožogina 20 Kc 66.12N 151.05 E
Ozona 43 Ge 30.43N 101.12W
Ozorków 10 Pe 51.58N 19.19 E
Ozouri 36 Ac 0.55S 8.55 E
Ozren [Yugo.] 14 Mf 44.37N 18.15 E
Ozren [Yugo.] 14 Mg 43.59N 18.30 E
Ozren [Yugo.] 15 Ef 43.36N 21.54 E
Ōzu [Jap.] 29 Be 32.52N 130.52 E
Ōzu [Jap.] 28 Lh 33.30N 132.23 E

P

Pääjärvi 8 Kb 62.50N 24.45 E
Paama 63b Dc 16.28S 168.13 E
Pa-an 25 Je 16.53N 97.38 E
Paar 10 Hh 48.45N 11.35 E
Paarl 31 Il 33.45S 18.56 E
Paauilo 65a Fc 20.03N 155.22W
Paavola 7 Fd 64.36N 25.12 E
Pabbay 9 Fd 57.47N 7.20W
Pabellón, Ensenada del- 48 Fe 24.27N 107.36W
Pabianice 10 Pe 51.40N 19.22 E
Pābna 25 Hd 24.00N 89.15 E
Pabradé/Pabrade 7 Fi 54.59N 25.50 E
Pabrade/Pabradé 7 Fi 54.59N 25.50 E
Pacaás Novos, Serra dos- 54 Ff 10.50S 64.00W
Pacajá, Rio- 54 Hd 1.56S 50.55W
Pacajus 54 Kd 4.10S 38.28W
Pacaraima, Serra- 52 Je 4.30N 60.40W
Pacasmayo 54 Ce 7.24S 79.34W
Paceco 14 Gm 37.59N 12.33 E
Pachala 35 Ed 7.10N 34.06 E
Pacheco 48 Eb 30.06N 108.21W
Pachino 14 Jn 36.43N 15.05 E
Pachitea, Río- 54 De 8.46S 74.32W
Pachuca de Soto 47 Ed 20.07N 98.44W
Pacific-Antarctic Ridge (EN) 3 Kp 62.00S 157.00W
Pacific City 46 Dd 45.12N 123.57W
Pacific Grove 46 Eh 36.38N 121.56W
Pacific Islands, Trust
Territory of the- 58 Gc 10.00N 155.00 E
Pacífico, Océano-=Pacific
Ocean (EN) 3 Ki 5.00N 155.00W
Pacific Ocean 3 Ki 5.00N 155.00W
Pacific Ocean (EN)=Kita-
Taiheiyō 60 Ch 22.00N 167.00 E
Pacific Ocean (EN)=
Pacífico, Océano- 3 Ki 5.00N 155.00W
Pacific Ocean (EN)=
Pacifique, Océan- 3 Ki 5.00N 155.00W
Pacific Ocean (EN)=
Taiheiyō 3 Ki 5.00N 155.00W
Pacific Ocean (EN)=Tihi
Okean 3 Ki 5.00N 155.00W
Pacific Ranges 42 Ef 50.55N 125.10W
Pacifique, Océan-=Pacific
Ocean (EN) 3 Ki 5.00N 155.00W
Packsattel 14 Id 46.58N 14.58 E
Pacuí, Rio- 55 Jc 16.46S 45.01W
Pacuneiro, Rio- 55 Fa 13.02S 53.25W
Pacy-sur-Eure 12 De 49.01N 1.23 E
Paczków 10 Mf 50.27N 17.00 E
Padana, Pianura-=Po
Valley (EN) 5 Gf 45.20N 10.00 E
Padang 22 Mj 0.57S 100.21 E
Padangsidempuan 26 Cf 1.22N 99.16 E
Padangtikar, Pulau- 26 Eg 0.50S 109.30 E
Padany 7 He 63.19N 33.25 E
Padasjoki 8 Kc 61.21N 25.17 E
Padauiri, Rio- 54 Fd 0.15S 64.05W
Paddle Prairie 42 Fe 58.02N 117.50W
Paderborn 10 Ee 51.43N 8.46 E
Paderborn-Elsen 12 Kc 51.44N 8.41 E
Paderborn-Schloß Neuhaus 12 Kc 51.44N 8.42 E
Padeş, Vîrful- 15 Fd 45.40N 22.20 E
Padilla 54 Fg 19.19S 64.20W
Padina 15 Ke 44.50N 27.07 E
Padornelo, Portillo del- 13 Fb 42.03N 6.50W
Padova = Padua (EN) 14 Fe 45.25N 11.53 E
Padre, Morro do- 55 Ic 16.48S 47.35W
Padre Bernardo 55 Hb 15.21S 48.30W
Padre Island 43 Hf 27.00N 97.15W
Padrón 13 Db 42.44N 8.40W
Padua (EN) = Padova 14 Fe 45.25N 11.53 E
Paducah [Ky.-U.S.] 39 Kf 37.05N 88.36W
Paducah [Tx.-U.S.] 45 Fi 34.01N 100.18W
Padula 14 Jj 40.20N 15.39 E
Paea 65e Fc 17.41S 149.35W
Paegam-san 28 Id 40.35N 126.15 E
Paengnyong-Do 27 Ld 38.00N 124.40 E
Paeroa 61 Eg 37.23S 175.41 E
Paestum 14 Jj 40.25N 15.01 E
Paeu 63c Bb 11.22S 166.50 E
Pafuri 37 Ed 22.26S 31.20 E
Pag 14 Jf 44.27N 15.03 E
Pag 14 If 44.30N 15.00 E
Pagadian 26 He 7.49N 123.25 E
Pagai, Kepulauan-=Pagai
Islands (EN) 21 Lj 2.45S 100.00 E
Pagai Selatan 26 Dg 3.00S 100.20 E
Pagai Utara 26 Cg 2.42S 100.07 E
Pagan Island 57 Fc 18.07N 145.46 E
Pagasitikós Kólpos 15 Fj 39.15N 23.00 E
Pagatan 26 Gg 3.36S 115.56 E
Pagat Point 64c Bb 13.30N 144.53 E
Page 46 Jh 36.57N 111.27W
Pagėgiai 8 Ii 55.09N 21.54 E
Paget, Mount- 66 Ad 54.26S 36.33W
Pagi Islands (EN)=Pagai,
Kepulauan- 21 Lj 2.45S 100.00 E
Paglia 14 Gh 42.42N 12.11 E
Pago Bay 64c Bb 13.25N 144.48 E
Pagoda Point 21 Lh 15.57N 94.15 E
Pāgodār 24 Qh 28.10N 57.22 E
Pago Pago 58 Jf 14.16S 170.42W
Pago Pago Harbor 65c Cb 14.17S 170.40W
Pago Redondo 55 Ci 29.35S 59.13W
Pagosa Springs 45 Ch 37.16N 107.01W
Pagua Bay 51g Ba 15.32N 61.17W
Pagwa River 45 Na 50.01N 85.10W
Pahači 20 Ld 60.30N 169.00 E
Pahala 65a Fd 19.12N 155.29W
Pàhara, Laguna- 49 Ff 14.18N 83.15W
Pahiatua 62 Fd 40.27S 175.50 E
Pahkaing Bum 21 Lg 26.00N 95.30 E
Pahoa 65a Gd 19.30N 154.57W
Pahokee 44 Gl 26.49N 80.40W
Pahtakor 18 Fd 40.16N 67.55 E
Pahute Mesa 46 Gh 37.20N 116.40W
Paia 63b Dc 16.35S 168.12 E
Paide/Pajde 7 Fg 58.57N 25.35 E
Paignton 9 Jk 50.28N 3.30W
Päijänne 5 Ic 61.35N 23.30 E
Páikon Óros 15 Fi 40.56N 22.21 E
Paila 48 He 25.39N 102.07W
Pailin 25 Kf 12.51N 102.36 E
Pailitas 49 Ki 8.58N 73.38W
Pailolo Channel 65a Eb 21.05N 156.42W
Paimio/Pemar 8 Jd 60.27N 22.42 E
Paimionjoki 8 Jd 60.25N 22.40 E
Paimpol 11 Cf 48.46N 3.03W
Painan 26 Dg 1.21S 100.34 E
Paine, Mount- 66 Mg 86.46S 147.32W
Painel 55 Gh 27.55S 50.06W
Painesville 44 Ge 41.43N 81.15W
Painted Desert 43 Ed 36.00N 111.20W
Paintsville 44 Fg 37.49N 82.48W
País do Vinho 13 Ec 41.15N 7.55W
Paisley 9 If 55.50N 4.26W
Paita 54 Be 5.06S 81.07W
Païta 63b Cf 22.08S 166.22 E
Paiva 13 Dc 41.04N 8.16W
Paj 7 If 61.43N 34.28 E
Pajala 7 Fc 67.12N 23.22 E
Pajares, Puerto de- 13 Ga 43.00N 5.46W
Pajaros, Punta- 48 Ph 19.36N 87.25W
Pajaros Point 51a Db 18.31N 64.18W
Pajatén 54 Ce 7.29S 77.22W
Pajde/Paide 7 Fg 58.57N 25.35 E
Pajęczno 10 Oe 51.09N 19.00 E
Pajer, Gora- 19 Gb 66.40N 64.20 E
Paj-Hoj 5 Mb 69.00N 62.30 E
Pajule 36 Fb 2.58N 32.56 E
Pakanbaru 22 Mi 0.32N 101.27 E
Pakaraima Mountains 54 Fb 4.05N 61.30W
Pakch'on 28 He 39.44N 125.35 E
Pakhiá 15 Im 36.16N 25.50 E
Pakhna 24 Ee 34.46N 32.48 E
Pákhnes 15 Gn 35.18N 23.58 E
Paki 34 Gc 11.30N 8.09 E
Pakima 36 Dc 3.21S 24.06 E
Pakin Atoll 57 Gd 7.04N 157.48 E
Pakistan [1] 22 Ig 30.00N 70.00 E
Pakleni Otoci 14 Kg 43.10N 16.23 E
Pakokku 25 Jd 21.17N 95.06 E
Pakowki Lake 46 Jb 49.22N 110.57W
Pak Phanang 25 Kg 8.21N 100.12 E
Pakrac 14 Le 45.26N 17.12 E
Pakruois/Pakruojis 7 Fi 55.57N 23.50 E
Pakruojis/Pakruois 7 Fi 55.57N 23.50 E
Paks 10 Oj 46.38N 18.52 E
Paktīā [3] 23 Kc 33.30N 69.30 E
Pakwach 36 Fb 2.28N 31.30 E
Pakxé 22 Mh 15.07N 105.47 E
Pakxèng 25 Kd 20.10N 102.40 E
Pala 35 Ad 9.22N 14.54 E
Palacca Point 49 Kc 21.15N 73.26W
Palacios [Arg.] 55 Bj 30.43S 61.37W
Palacios [Tx.-U.S.] 45 Hl 28.42N 96.13W
Palafrugell 13 Pc 41.55N 3.10 E
Palagruža 14 Kh 42.24N 16.15 E
Palaiokastritsa 15 Cj 39.40N 19.41 E
Palaiokhóra 15 Gn 35.14N 23.41 E
Palaiseau 12 Ef 48.43N 2.15 E
Palamás 15 Fj 39.28N 22.05 E
Palamós 13 Pc 41.51N 3.08 E
Palamuse/Palamuze 8 Lf 58.39N 26.35 E
Palamut 15 Kk 38.59N 27.41 E
Palamuze/Palamuse 8 Lf 58.39N 26.35 E
Palana 22 Rd 59.07N 159.58 E
Palancia 13 Le 39.40N 0.12W
Palanga 19 Cd 55.57N 21.05 E
Palangkaraya 26 Fg 2.16S 113.56 E
Pālanpur 25 Ed 24.10N 72.26 E

Index Symbols

[1] Independent Nation
[2] State, Region
[3] District, County
[4] Municipality
[5] Colony, Dependency
Continent
Physical Region
Historical or Cultural Region
Mount, Mountain
Volcano
Hill
Mountains, Mountain Range
Hills, Escarpment
Plateau, Upland
Pass, Gap
Plain, Lowland
Delta
Salt Flat
Valley, Canyon
Crater, Cave
Karst Features
Depression
Polder
Desert, Dunes
Forest, Woods
Heath, Steppe
Oasis
Cape, Point
Coast, Beach
Cliff
Peninsula
Isthmus
Sandbank
Island
Atoll
Rock, Reef
Islands, Archipelago
Rocks, Reefs
Coral Reef
Well, Spring
Geyser
River, Stream
Waterfall Rapids
River Mouth, Estuary
Lake
Salt Lake
Intermittent Lake
Reservoir
Swamp, Pond
Canal
Glacier
Ice Shelf, Pack Ice
Ocean
Sea
Gulf, Bay
Strait, Fjord
Lagoon
Bank
Seamount
Tablemount
Ridge
Shelf
Basin
Escarpment, Sea Scarp
Fracture
Trench, Abyss
National Park, Reserve
Point of Interest
Recreation Site
Cave, Cavern
Historic Site
Ruins
Wall, Walls
Church, Abbey
Temple
Scientific Station
Airport
Port
Lighthouse
Mine
Tunnel
Dam, Bridge

Name	Map	Grid	Lat.	Long.
Palaoa Point ►	65a	Ec	20.44N	156.58W
Palapye	31	Jk	22.33S	27.08 E
Palasa	26	Hf	0.29N	120.24 E
Palatka [Fl.-U.S.]	43	Kf	29.39N	81.38W
Palatka [R.S.F.S.R.]	20	Kd	60.05N	151.00 E
Palau	14	Di	41.11N	9.23 E
Palau ⑤	58	Ed	7.30N	134.30 E
Palau Islands ⁂	57	Ed	7.30N	134.30 E
Palauli	65c	Aa	13.44S	172.16W
Palauli Bay ◖	65c	Aa	13.47S	172.14W
Palau Trench (EN) ⋎	60	Af	6.30N	134.30 E
Palavas-les-Flots	11	Jk	43.32N	3.56 E
Palaw	25	Jf	12.58N	98.39 E
Palawan ◆	21	Ni	9.30N	118.30 E
Palawan Passage ⇌	26	Gd	10.00N	118.00 E
Palayan	26	Hc	15.33N	121.06 E
Pālayankottai	25	Fg	8.43N	77.44 E
Palazzo, Punta- ►	11a	Aa	42.22N	8.33 E
Palazzolo Acreide	14	Im	37.04N	14.54 E
Palazzolo sull'Oglio	14	De	45.36N	9.53 E
Paldiski	19	Cd	59.20N	24.06 E
Pale di San Martino ▲	14	Fd	46.14N	11.53 E
Paleleh	26	Hf	1.04N	121.57 E
Palembang	22	Mj	2.55S	104.45 E
Palena	14	Ii	41.59N	14.08 E
Palencia ③	13	Hb	42.25N	4.30W
Palencia	13	Hb	42.01N	4.32W
Palen Lake ψ	46	Hj	33.46N	115.12W
Palenque ⁘	39	Jh	17.30N	92.00W
Palenque [Mex.]	48	Ni	17.31N	91.58W
Palenque [Pan.]	49	Hi	9.13N	79.41W
Palenque, Punta- ►	49	Ld	18.14N	70.09W
Palermo	6	Hh	38.07N	13.22 E
Palermo, Golfo di- ◖	14	Hl	38.10N	13.25 E
Palestine	43	He	31.46N	95.38W
Palestine (EN) ▣	23	Dc	32.15N	34.47 E
Palestrina	14	Gi	41.50N	12.53 E
Pālghāt	25	Ff	10.47N	76.39 E
Palgrave Point ►	37	Ad	20.28S	13.16 E
Palhoça	55	Hh	27.38S	48.40W
Pāli	25	Ec	25.46N	73.20 E
Palinuro	14	Jj	40.02N	15.17 E
Palinuro, Capo- ►	14	Jj	40.02N	15.16 E
Palisades Reservoir ⊟	46	Je	43.04N	111.26W
Paliseul	12	He	49.54N	5.08 E
Palivere	8	Jf	59.00N	23.45 E
Palizada	48	Mh	18.15N	92.05W
Paljakka ◭	7	Gd	64.45N	28.07 E
Paljavaam ↝	20	Mc	68.50N	170.50 E
Paljenik ▲	5	Hg	44.15N	17.36 E
Pälkäne	8	Kc	61.20N	24.16 E
Palkino	8	Mg	57.29N	28.10 E
Palk Strait ⇌	21	Ji	10.00N	79.45 E
Palla Bianca/Weißkugel ▲	14	Ed	46.48N	10.44 E
Pallars ⊠	13	Mb	42.25N	0.55 E
Pallars, Montsent de-/Montseny ▲	13	Nb	42.29N	1.02 E
Pallasovka	19	Ee	50.03N	46.55 E
Pallastunturi ▲	7	Fb	68.06N	24.02 E
Palliser, Cape- ►	61	Eh	41.37S	175.16 E
Palliser, Iles- ⁂	57	Mf	15.30S	146.30W
Palma [Moz.]	37	Gb	10.46S	40.28 E
Palma [Sp.]	6	Gh	39.34N	2.39 E
Palma, Badia de-/Palma, Bahía de- ◖	13	Oe	39.27N	2.35 E
Palma, Bahía de-/Palma, Badia de- ◖	13	Oe	39.27N	2.35 E
Palma, Rio- ↝	54	If	12.33S	47.52W
Palma, Sierra de la- ⛰	48	Id	26.00N	101.35W
Palma del Río	13	Gg	37.42N	5.17W
Palma di Montechiaro	14	Hm	37.11N	13.46 E
Palmar, Laguna del- ◒	55	Bi	29.35S	60.42W
Palmar, Río- ↝	49	Lh	10.11N	71.52W
Palmar, Salto- ⤓	55	Cg	24.18S	59.18W
Palmares	54	Ke	8.41S	35.36W
Palmares do Sul	55	Gj	30.16S	50.31W
Palmarito	54	Db	7.37N	70.10W
Palmarola ◆	14	Gj	40.55N	12.50 E
Palmar Sur	47	Hg	8.58N	83.29W
Palmas	56	Jc	26.30S	52.00W
Palmas, Cape- ►	30	Gh	4.22N	7.44W
Palmas, Golfo di- ◖	14	Cl	39.00N	8.30 E
Palmas Bellas	49	Gi	9.14N	80.05W
Palma Soriano	47	Id	20.13N	76.00W
Palm Bay	44	Gk	28.01N	80.35W
Palm Beach	43	Kf	26.42N	80.02W
Palmdale	46	Fi	34.35N	118.07W
Palmeira	55	Gg	25.25S	50.00W
Palmeira das Missões	56	Jc	27.55S	53.17W
Palmeira dos Indios	54	Ke	9.25S	36.37W
Palmeirais	54	Je	5.58S	43.04W
Palmeiras, Rio- ↝	55	Gb	15.25S	51.10W
Palmeiras de Goiás	55	Hc	16.47S	49.53W
Palmeirinhas, Ponta das- ►	30	Ii	9.05S	13.00 E
Palmela	13	Df	38.34N	8.54W
Palmer	40	Jd	61.36N	149.07W
Palmer Archipelago ⁂	66	Qe	64.10S	62.00W
Palmer Land (EN) ⊠	66	Qf	71.30S	65.00W
Palmer Station ⚗	66	Qe	64.46S	64.05W
Palmerston	62	Df	45.29S	170.43 E
Palmerston Atoll ◎	57	Kf	18.04S	163.10W
Palmerston North	58	Ii	40.28S	175.17 E
Palmetto Point ►	51d	Ba	17.35N	61.52W
Palmi	14	Jl	38.21N	15.51 E
Palmira [Col.]	53	Ie	3.32N	76.16W
Palmira [Cuba]	49	Gb	22.14N	80.23W
Palm Islands ⁂	59	Jc	18.40S	146.30 E
Palmital	55	Fg	24.39S	52.16W
Palmitas	55	Dk	33.27S	57.48W
Palmito	55	Cd	18.53S	58.22W
Palmitos	55	Fh	27.05S	53.08W
Palm Springs	43	De	33.50N	116.33W
Palmyra ⁘	23	Ec	34.33N	38.17 E
Palmyra Atoll ◎	57	Kd	5.52N	162.06W
Palo Alto	43	Cd	37.27N	122.09W
Paloh	26	Ef	1.43N	109.18 E
Paloich	35	Ec	10.28N	32.32 E
Palomani, Nevado- ↝	52	Jg	14.38S	69.14W
Palomar Mountain ▲	43	De	33.22N	116.50W
Palomera, Sierra- ⛰	13	Kd	40.40N	1.12W
Palopo	22	Oj	3.00S	120.12 E
Palos, Cabo de- ►	5	Fh	37.38N	0.41W
Palo Santo	55	Cg	25.34S	59.21W
Palotina	55	Fg	24.17S	53.50W
Palouse River ↝	46	Fc	46.35N	118.13W
Palpa	54	Cf	14.32S	75.11W
Palsa ↝	8	Lg	57.23N	26.24 E
Pålsboda	8	Fe	59.04N	15.20 E
Paltamo	7	Gd	64.25N	27.50 E
Palu [Indon.]	22	Nj	0.53S	119.53 E
Palu [Tur.]	24	Hc	38.42N	39.57 E
Palu, Pulau- ◆	26	Hh	8.20S	121.43 E
Pam ◆	63b	Be	20.15S	164.17 E
Pama	34	Fc	11.15N	0.42 E
Påmark/Pomarkku	8	Ic	61.42N	22.00 E
Pambarra	37	Fd	21.56S	35.06 E
Pambeguwa	34	Gc	10.40N	8.17 E
Pamekasan	26	Fh	7.10S	113.28 E
Pamiers	11	Hk	43.07N	1.36 E
Pamir ⛰	21	Jf	38.00N	73.00 E
Pamir ↝	19	Hh	37.01N	72.41 E
Pâmiut/Frederikshåb	41	Hf	62.00N	49.45W
Pamlico Sound ⇌	43	Ld	35.20N	75.55W
Pampa	43	Gd	35.32N	100.58W
Pampa del Indio	55	Ch	26.02S	59.55W
Pampa del Infierno	55	Bh	26.31S	61.10W
Pampa de los Guanacos	56	Hc	26.14S	61.51W
Pampas	54	Df	12.24S	74.54W
Pampas ⊠	52	Ji	35.00S	63.00W
Pampeiro	55	Ej	30.38S	55.16W
Pamplona [Col.]	54	Db	7.23N	72.38W
Pamplona [Sp.]	6	Fg	42.49N	1.38W
Pamukkale ★	15	Ml	37.47N	29.04 E
Pamukova	15	Ni	40.31N	30.09 E
Pamunkey River ↝	44	Ig	37.32N	76.48W
Pan, Tierra del- ⊠	13	Gc	41.50N	6.00W
Pana	36	Bc	1.41S	12.39 E
Panagjurište	15	Hg	42.30N	24.11 E
Panaitan, Pulau- ◆	26	Eh	6.36S	105.12 E
Panaitolikón Óros ⛰	15	Ek	38.43N	21.39 E
Panaji (Panjim)	22	Jh	15.29N	73.50 E
Panakhaïkón Óros ▲	15	Ek	38.12N	21.54 E
Panamá ①	39	Li	9.00N	80.00W
Panamá = Panama (EN) ③	49	Hi	9.00N	79.00W
Panamá = Panama City (EN)	39	Li	8.58N	79.31W
Panama (EN) = Panamá ③	49	Hi	9.00N	79.00W
Panamá, Bahia de- ◖	49	Hi	8.50N	79.15W
Panamá, Canal de- = Panama Canal (EN) ═	47	Ig	9.20N	79.55W
Panamá, Golfo de- = Panama, Gulf of- (EN) ◖	38	Li	8.00N	79.10W
Panama, Gulf of- (EN) = Panamá, Golfo de- ◖	38	Li	8.00N	79.10W
Panama, Isthmus of- (EN) = Panamá, Istmo de- ⧓	38	Li	9.20N	79.30W
Panamá, Istmo de- = Panama, Isthmus of- (EN) ⧓	38	Li	9.20N	79.30W
Panama Canal (EN) = Panamá, Canal de- ═	47	Ig	9.20N	79.55W
Panama City [La.-U.S.]	39	Kf	30.10N	85.41W
Panama City (EN) = Panamá	39	Li	8.58N	79.31W
Panamá La Vieja ⁘	49	Hi	9.00N	79.29W
Panambí	55	Fi	28.18S	53.30W
Panamint Range ⛰	46	Gh	36.30N	117.20W
Panao	54	Ce	9.49S	76.00W
Panarea ◆	14	Jl	38.40N	15.05 E
Panaro ↝	14	Ff	44.55N	11.25 E
Pana Tinai ◆	63a	Ad	11.14S	153.10 E
Pana-Wina ◆	63a	Ad	11.11S	153.01 E
Panay ◆	21	Oh	11.15N	122.30 E
Pancake Range ⛰	46	Hg	39.00N	115.45W
Pančevo	15	De	44.52N	20.39 E
Pančičev vrh ▲	15	Df	43.15N	20.45 E
Panciu	15	Kd	45.54N	27.05 E
Pancros	63b	Db	15.58S	168.12 E
Panda	37	Ed	24.03S	34.43 E
Panda ma Tenga	37	Dc	18.32S	25.38 E
Pandan	26	Hd	11.43N	122.06 E
Pan de Azúcar	55	El	34.48S	55.14W
Pandeiros, Ribeirão- ↝	55	Jb	15.42S	44.36W
Pandelis/Pandėlys	8	Kh	56.01N	25.21 E
Pandėlys/Pandelis	8	Kh	56.01N	25.21 E
Pandharpur	25	Fe	17.40N	75.20 E
Pándheon ▲	15	Fi	40.05N	22.20 E
Pāndhurna	25	Fd	21.36N	78.31 E
Pandivere Kõrgustik/Pandivere Vozvyšennost ▬	8	Le	59.00N	26.15 E
Pandivere Vozvyšennost/Pandivere Kõrgustik ▬	8	Le	59.00N	26.15 E
Pando	56	Id	34.43S	55.57W
Pando ②	54	Ef	11.20S	67.40W
Pandokrátor ▲	15	Cj	39.45N	19.52 E
Pandora	49	Fi	9.45N	82.57W
Pandrup	8	Cg	57.14N	9.41 E
Pandu	36	Cb	4.59N	19.16 E
Panevežis/Panevėžys	19	Cd	55.44N	24.22 E
Panevėžys/Panevežis	19	Cd	55.44N	24.22 E
Panfilov	19	Ig	44.08N	80.01 E
Panga	36	Eb	1.51N	26.25 E
Pangai	65b	Ba	19.48S	174.21W
Pangaíon Óros ⛰	15	Hi	40.50N	24.05 E
Pangalanes, Canal de- ═	30	Lk	22.48S	47.50 E
Pangani	36	Gd	5.26S	38.58 E
Pangani or Ruvu ↝	36	Gc	5.26S	38.58 E
Pange	12	Ie	49.05N	6.22 E
Panggoe	58	Ge	7.01S	157.05 E
Pangi	36	Ec	3.11S	26.38 E
Pangkajene	26	Gg	4.50S	119.32 E
Pangkalanberandan	26	Cf	4.01N	98.17 E
Pangkalanbuun	26	Fg	2.41S	111.37 E
Pangkalaseang, Tanjung- ►	26	Hg	0.42S	123.26 E
Pangkalpinang	26	Eg	2.08S	106.08 E
Pangnirtung	39	Mc	66.08N	65.44W
Pang-Pang	63b	Dc	17.41S	168.32 E
Panguitch	43	Ed	37.49N	112.26W
Panguma	34	Cd	8.24N	11.13W
Pangutaran Group ⁂	26	He	6.15N	120.30 E
Panhandle	45	Fi	35.21N	101.23W
Pania Mutombo	36	Dd	5.11S	23.51 E
Paniau ▲	65a	Ab	21.57N	160.05W
Panié, Mont- ▲	61	Bd	20.36S	164.46 E
Pānīpat	25	Fc	29.23N	76.58 E
Paniza, Puerto de- ⋈	13	Kc	41.15N	1.20W
Panjang	26	Eh	5.29S	105.18 E
Panjang, Pulau- ◆	26	Ef	2.44N	108.55 E
Panjgūr	25	Cc	26.58N	64.06 E
Panjim → Panaji	22	Jh	15.29N	73.50 E
Panjwīn	24	Ke	35.36N	45.58 E
Pankow, Berlin-	10	Jd	52.34N	13.24 E
Pankshin	34	Gd	9.20N	9.27 E
P'anmunjŏm	28	If	37.57N	126.40 E
Panopah	26	Fg	1.56S	111.11 E
Panorama	56	Jb	21.21S	51.51W
Panshan	28	Gd	41.12N	122.03 E
Panshi	27	Mc	42.56N	126.02 E
Pant ↝	12	Cc	51.53N	0.39 E
Pantanal ψ	52	Kg	18.00S	56.00W
Pantar, Pulau- ◆	26	Hh	8.25S	124.07 E
Pantego	44	Ih	35.34N	76.36W
Pantelleria	14	Fn	36.50N	11.57 E
Pantelleria ◆	5	Hh	36.45N	12.00 E
Pantelleria, Canale di- ⇌	14	Fn	36.40N	11.45 E
Pante Makassar	26	Hh	9.12S	124.23 E
Pantoja	54	Cd	0.58S	75.10W
Pánuco	48	Jf	22.03N	98.10W
Pánuco ↝	38	Jg	22.16N	97.47W
Panxian	27	Hf	25.45N	104.39 E
Panyam	34	Gd	9.25N	9.13 E
Panzi	36	Cd	7.13S	17.58 E
Panzós	49	Cf	15.24N	89.40W
Pao, Río- [Ven.] ↝	50	Bh	8.33N	68.01W
Pao, Río- [Ven.] ↝	50	Dh	8.06N	64.17W
Paola [It.]	14	Kk	39.21N	16.03 E
Paola [Ks.-U.S.]	45	Ig	38.35N	94.53W
Paoli	44	Df	38.33N	86.28W
Paopao	65e	Fc	17.30S	149.49W
Paoua	35	Bd	7.15N	16.26 E
Pápa	10	Ni	47.20N	17.28 E
Papa	65a	Fd	19.13N	155.52W
Papaaloa	65a	Fd	19.59N	155.13W
Papagaios	55	Jd	19.32S	44.45W
Papagayo, Golfo del- ◖	47	Gf	10.45N	85.45W
Papaikou	65a	Fd	19.47N	155.06W
Papakura	62	Fb	37.03S	174.57 E
Papaloapan, Río- ↝	48	Lh	18.42N	95.38W
Papanduva	55	Gh	26.25S	50.09W
Papangpanjang	26	Dg	0.27S	100.25 E
Papantla de Olarte	47	Ed	20.27N	97.19W
Papar	26	Ge	5.44N	115.56 E
Paparoa Range ⛰	62	De	42.05S	171.35 E
Papa Stour ◆	9	La	60.30N	1.40W
Papa Westray ◆	9	Kb	59.22N	2.54W
Papeete	58	Mf	17.32S	149.34W
Papenburg	10	Dc	53.04N	7.24 E
Papenburg-Aschendorf (Ems)	12	Ja	53.04N	7.22 E
Papenoo	65e	Fc	17.30S	149.25W
Papes Ezers/Papes Ozero ◍	8	Ih	56.15N	20.55 E
Papes Ozero/Papes Ezers ◍	8	Ih	56.15N	20.55 E
Papetoai	65e	Fc	17.30S	149.52W
Papey ◆	7a	Cb	64.36N	14.11W
Paphos/Baf	24	Ee	34.50N	32.35 E
Papija ▲	15	Kg	42.07N	27.51 E
Papíkion Óros ▲	15	Ih	41.15N	25.18 E
Papilė/Papile	8	Jh	56.09N	22.45 E
Papile/Papilė	8	Jh	56.09N	22.45 E
Papillion	45	Hf	41.09N	96.03W
Papua, Gulf of- ◖	57	Fe	8.32S	145.00 E
Papua New Guinea ①	58	Fe	6.00S	150.00 E
Papua Passage ⇌	64p	Bc	21.15S	159.47W
Papuk ⛰	14	Le	45.31N	17.39 E
Papun	25	Je	18.04N	97.27 E
Para ↝	7	Ji	54.23N	40.53 E
Pará ②	54	Hd	4.00S	53.00W
Pará, Rio- ↝	55	Jd	19.13S	45.07W
Para, Rio- ↝	52	Lf	1.30S	48.55W
Parabel ↝	20	De	58.40N	81.30 E
Parabel	20	De	58.43N	81.31 E
Paraburdoo	59	Dd	23.15S	117.45 E
Paracas	54	Cf	13.49S	76.16W
Paracatu	54	Ig	17.13S	46.52W
Paracatu, Rio- [Braz.] ↝	55	Ic	17.30S	46.32W
Paracatu, Rio- [Braz.] ↝	55	Jc	16.30S	45.04W
Paracel Islands (EN) = Xisha Qundao ⁂	21	Nh	16.30N	112.15 E
Pārachinār	25	Eb	33.54N	70.06 E
Paraćin	15	Ef	43.52N	21.25 E
Paracuru	54	Kd	3.24S	39.04W
Parada Km 329	55	Ek	32.30S	55.25W
Paradip	25	Hd	20.19N	86.42 E
Paradise [Ca.-U.S.]	46	Eg	39.46N	121.37W
Paradise [Mi.-U.S.]	44	Eb	46.38N	85.03W
Paragould	45	Kh	36.03N	90.29W
Paragua, Río- ↝	54	Fb	6.55N	62.55W
Paraguá, Rio- ↝	54	Ff	13.34S	61.53W
Paraguaçu, Rio- ↝	52	Mg	12.45S	38.54W
Paraguaçu Paulista	55	Gf	22.25S	50.34W
Paraguai, Rio- ↝	52	Kh	27.18S	58.38W
Paraguaipoa	49	Lh	11.21N	71.57W
Paraguaná, Península de- ◨	52	Jd	11.55N	70.00W
Paraguarí ③	55	Dg	26.00S	57.10W
Paraguarí	56	Ic	25.38S	57.09W
Paraguay ①	53	Kh	23.00S	58.00W
Paraguay, Río- ↝	52	Kh	27.18S	58.38W
Paraíba ②	54	Ke	7.10S	36.30W
Paraíba do Sul, Rio- ↝	52	Lh	21.37S	41.03W
Paraibuna, Represa do- ⊟	55	Jf	23.25S	45.35W
Paraibuna, Rio- ↝	55	Jf	23.22S	45.40W
Parainen/Pargas	7	Ff	60.18N	22.18 E
Paraíso [Braz.]	55	Fd	19.03S	52.59W
Paraíso [Mex.]	48	Mh	18.24N	93.14W
Paraiso, Río- ↝	55	Bb	15.08S	61.52W
Parakou	31	Hh	9.21N	2.37 E
Param ◆	64d	Bb	7.22N	151.48 E
Paramaribo	53	Ke	5.50N	55.10W
Paramera, Sierra de la- ⛰	13	Hd	40.30N	4.46W
Paramithiá	15	Dj	39.28N	20.31 E
Paramušir, Ostrov- ◆	21	Rd	50.25N	155.50 E
Paraná	53	Ji	31.45S	60.30W
Paraná ②	56	Jb	24.00S	51.00W
Paraná, Pico- ▲	55	Hg	25.14S	48.48W
Paraná, Río- ↝	52	Ki	33.43S	59.15W
Paranã, Rio- ↝	52	Lg	12.30S	48.14W
Paraná de las Palmas, Río- ↝	55	Cl	34.18S	58.33W
Paranaguá	53	Lh	25.31S	48.30W
Paraná-Guazú, Río- ↝	55	Ck	34.00S	58.25W
Paranaiba	54	Hg	19.40S	51.11W
Paranaíba, Rio- ↝	52	Kh	20.07S	51.05W
Paranaiguara	55	Gd	18.53S	50.28W
Paranapanema, Rio- ↝	52	Kh	22.40S	53.09W
Paranapiacaba, Serra do- ⛰	52	Lh	24.20S	49.00W
Paranapuã-Guaçu, Ponta do- ►	55	Ig	24.24S	47.00W
Paranavaí	56	Jb	23.04S	52.28W
Parandak	24	Ne	35.21N	50.42 E
Paranéstion	15	Hh	41.16N	24.30 E
Paranhos	55	Ef	23.55S	55.25W
Paraoa Atoll ◎	57	Mf	19.09S	140.43W
Paraopeba	55	Jd	19.18S	44.25W
Paraopeba, Rio- ↝	55	Jd	18.50S	45.11W
Parapara ◆	63b	Ca	13.32S	167.20 E
Paraparaumu	62	Fd	40.55S	175.00 E
Paraspóri ►	15	Kn	35.54N	27.14 E
Parati	55	Jf	23.13S	44.43W
Paratodos, Serra- ⛰	55	Jb	14.40S	44.50W
Paratunka	20	Kf	52.52N	158.12 E
Pārāu, Kūh-e- ▲	24	Le	34.37N	47.05 E
Paraúna	55	Gc	17.02S	50.26W
Paravae ◎	64n	Bc	10.27S	160.58W
Paray-le-Monial	11	Kh	46.27N	4.07 E
Parbati ↝	25	Fc	25.51N	76.36 E
Parbhani	25	Fe	19.16N	76.47 E
Parchim	10	Hc	53.26N	11.51 E
Parczew	10	Se	51.39N	22.54 E
Pardo	55	Cm	36.15S	59.22W
Pardo, Rio- [Braz.] ↝	55	Fi	29.59S	52.23W
Pardo, Rio- [Braz.] ↝	54	Hh	21.46S	52.09W
Pardo, Rio- [Braz.] ↝	55	He	20.10S	48.38W
Pardo, Rio- [Braz.] ↝	55	Hf	22.55S	49.58W
Pardo, Rio- [Braz.] ↝	55	Jb	15.48S	44.48W
Pardo, Rio- [Braz.] ↝	54	Kg	15.39S	38.57W
Pardubice	10	Lf	50.02N	15.45 E
Parea	65e	Eb	16.49S	150.58W
Parecis, Chapada dos- ▬	52	Kg	13.00S	60.00W
Parecis, Rio- ↝	55	Da	12.56S	56.43W
Paredes de Nava	13	Hb	42.09N	4.41W
Parelhas	54	Ke	6.41S	36.39W
Paren	20	Ld	62.28N	163.05 E
Parent	42	Kg	47.55N	74.37W
Parentis-en-Born	11	Ej	44.21N	1.04W
Pareora	62	Df	44.29S	171.13 E
Parepare	22	Nj	4.01S	119.38 E
Párga	15	Dj	39.17N	20.24 E
Pargas/Parainen	7	Ff	60.18N	22.18 E
Pargolovo	8	Nd	60.03N	30.30 E
Parham	51d	Bb	17.05N	61.46W
Parhar	19	Gh	37.31N	69.23 E
Pari, Rio- ↝	55	Db	15.36S	56.08W
Paria, Golfo de-/Paria, Gulf of- ◖	54	Fa	10.20N	62.00W
Paria, Gulf of-/Paria, Golfo de- ◖	54	Fa	10.20N	62.00W
Paria, Peninsula de- ◨	50	Eg	10.40N	62.30W
Pariaguán	54	Fb	8.51N	64.43W
Pariaman	26	Dg	0.38S	100.08 E
Paria River ↝	46	Jh	36.52N	111.36W
Paricutin, Volcán- 🌋	48	Hh	19.28N	102.15W
Parida, Isla- ◆	49	Fi	8.07N	82.20W
Pari das Pedras	55	Ja	12.45S	44.47W
Parigi	26	Hg	0.48S	120.10 E
Parika	54	Gb	6.52N	58.25W
Parikkala	7	Gf	61.33N	29.30 E
Parima, Serra- ⛰	52	Je	3.00N	64.20W
Parinacota	56	Ga	18.12S	69.16W
Pariñas, Punta- ►	52	Hf	4.40S	81.20W
Paringul Mare, Vîrful- ▲	15	Gd	45.20N	23.30 E
Parintins	53	Kf	2.36S	56.44W
Paris [Fr.]	6	Gf	48.52N	2.20 E
Paris [Il.-U.S.]	45	Mg	39.36N	87.42W
Paris [Kir.]	64g	Ab	1.56N	157.31W
Paris [Ky.-U.S.]	44	Ef	38.13N	84.14W
Paris [Tn.-U.S.]	44	Cg	36.19N	88.20W
Paris [Tx.-U.S.]	43	He	33.40N	95.33W
Paris Basin (EN) = Parisien, Bassin- ▁	5	Gf	49.00N	2.00 E
Parisien, Bassin- = Paris Basin (EN) ▁	5	Gf	49.00N	2.00 E
Parita	49	Gi	8.00N	80.31W
Parita, Bahía de- ◖	49	Gi	8.08N	80.24W
Parit Buntar	26	De	5.07N	100.30 E
Parkano	7	Fe	62.01N	23.01 E
Parkent	18	Gd	41.18N	69.40 E
Parker	46	Hi	34.09N	114.17W
Parker, Mount- ▲	59	Fc	17.10S	128.20 E
Parkersburg	43	Kd	39.17N	81.33W
Parker Seamount (EN) ⏶	40	If	52.35N	151.15W
Parkes	58	Fh	33.08S	148.11 E
Park Falls	45	Kd	45.56N	90.32W
Parkland	46	Dc	47.09N	122.26W
Park Range ⛰	43	Fc	40.00N	106.30W
Park Rapids	45	Ic	46.55N	95.04W
Park River	45	Hb	48.24N	97.45W
Park Valley	46	If	41.50N	113.21W
Parma ↝	14	Ef	44.56N	10.26 E
Parma [It.]	6	Hg	44.48N	10.20 E
Parma [Oh.-U.S.]	44	Ge	41.24N	81.44W
Parnaguá	54	Jf	10.13S	44.38W
Parnaíba	53	Lf	2.54S	41.47W
Parnaíba, Rio- ↝	52	Lf	3.00S	41.50W
Parnamirim [Braz.]	54	Ke	8.05S	39.34W
Parnamirim [Braz.]	54	Ke	5.55S	35.15W
Parnarama	54	Je	5.41S	43.06W
Parnassós Óros = Parnassus (EN) ⛰	5	Ih	38.30N	22.37 E
Parnassus	62	Ee	42.43S	173.17 E
Parnassus (EN) = Parnassós Óros ⛰	5	Ih	38.30N	22.37 E
Párnis Óros ▲	15	Gk	38.10N	23.40 E
Párnon Óros ⛰	15	Fl	37.12N	22.38 E
Pärnu/Pjarnu	6	Id	58.24N	24.32 E
Pärnu-Jaagupi/Pjarnu-Jagupi	8	Kf	58.36N	24.25 E
Pärnu Jõgi/Pjarnu ↝	7	Fg	58.23N	24.34 E
Pärnu Laht/Pjarnu, Zaliv- ◖	7	Fg	58.15N	24.25 E
Parola	8	Kc	61.03N	24.22 E
Paroo River ↝	57	Fh	31.28S	143.32 E
Paropamisus/Salseleh-ye Safīd Kūh ⛰	21	If	34.30N	63.30 E
Páros	15	Il	37.05N	25.09 E
Páros ◆	15	Il	37.06N	25.12 E
Parowan	46	Ih	37.51N	112.57W
Parpaillon ⛰	11	Mj	44.35N	6.40 E
Parque Industrial	55	Jd	19.57S	44.01W
Parral	56	Fe	36.09S	71.50W
Parral, Río- ↝	48	Gd	27.35N	105.25W
Parras, Sierra de- ⛰	48	He	25.25N	102.00W
Parras de la Fuente	47	Dc	25.25N	102.11W
Parravicini	55	Dm	36.27S	57.46W
Parrett ↝	9	Jj	51.13N	3.01W
Parrita	49	Ei	9.30N	84.19W
Parry, Cape - ►	42	Fb	70.12N	124.35W
Parry, Kap- [Grld.] ►	41	Jd	72.28N	22.00W
Parry, Kap- [Grld.] ►	41	Ec	77.00N	71.00W
Parry Bay ◖	42	Jc	68.00N	82.00W
Parry Islands ⁂	38	Ib	76.00N	110.00W
Parry Peninsula ◨	42	Fc	69.45N	124.35W
Parry Sound	42	Jg	45.21N	80.02W
Parsęta ↝	10	Lb	54.12N	15.33 E
Parsons [Ks.-U.S.]	43	Hd	37.20N	95.16W
Parsons [W.V.-U.S.]	44	Hf	39.06N	79.43W
Parsons Range ⛰	59	Hb	13.30S	135.15 E
Partanna	14	Gm	37.43N	12.53 E
Parthenay	11	Fh	46.39N	0.15W
Partille	8	Eg	57.44N	12.07 E
Partinico	14	Hl	38.03N	13.07 E
Partizansk	20	Ih	43.13N	133.05 E
Partizánske	10	Oh	48.38N	18.23 E
Partizanskoje	20	Ee	55.30N	94.30 E
Paru, Rio- ↝	52	Kf	1.33S	52.38W
Paru de Este, Rio- ↝	54	Hc	1.10N	54.40W
Paru de Oeste, Rio- ↝	52	Kf	1.30S	56.00W
Paruru	63a	Ec	9.51S	160.49 E
Parvān ③	23	Kb	35.15N	69.30 E
Părvomaj	15	Ig	42.06N	25.13 E
Parys	37	De	27.04S	27.16 E
Paša ↝	7	Hf	60.28N	32.55 E
Pasadena [Ca.-U.S.]	39	Hf	34.09N	118.09W
Pasadena [Tx.-U.S.]	45	Il	29.42N	95.13W
Paşaeli Yarimadası ◨	15	Lh	41.20N	28.25 E
Paşalimani Adası ◆	15	Ki	40.28N	27.37 E
Pasangkaju	26	Gg	1.10S	119.20 E
Pāsārgād ⁘	24	Og	30.17N	52.55 E
Pasarwajo	26	Hh	5.29S	122.50 E
Pascagoula	43	Je	30.23N	88.31W
Paşcani	15	Jb	47.15N	26.44 E
Pasco	43	Db	46.14N	119.06W
Pasco ②	54	Cf	10.30S	75.15W
Pascoal	55	Ba	13.38S	61.06W
Pascoal, Monte- ▲	54	Kg	16.54S	39.24W
Pascua, Isla de-/Rapa Nui = Easter Island (EN) ◆	57	Qg	27.07S	109.22W
Pas-de-Calais ③	11	Id	50.30N	2.20 E
Pas-en-Artois	12	Ed	50.09N	2.30 E
Pasewalk	10	Jc	53.31N	13.59 E
Pasinler	24	Ib	40.00N	41.41 E
Pašino	20	De	55.11N	83.02 E
Pasión, Rio de la- ↝	49	Be	16.28N	90.33W
Pasir Mas	26	De	6.02N	102.08 E
Pasirpengarayan	26	Df	0.51N	100.16 E
Pasir Puteh	26	De	5.50N	102.24 E
Påskallavik	8	Gg	57.10N	16.27 E
Paškovski	16	Kg	45.01N	39.05 E
Pasłęk	10	Pb	54.05N	19.39 E
Pasłęka ↝	10	Pb	54.25N	19.50 E
Pašman ◆	14	Jg	43.57N	15.21 E
Pasni	22	Ig	25.16N	63.28 E
Paso de Indios	56	Gf	43.52S	69.06W
Paso del Cerro	55	Ej	31.31S	55.46W
Paso de los Libres	56	Ic	29.43S	57.05W
Paso de los Toros	56	Id	32.49S	56.31W
Paso Tranqueras	55	Ej	31.12S	55.45W
Passamaquoddy Bay ◖	44	Nc	45.06N	66.59W
Passa Três, Serra- ⛰	55	Hb	14.40S	49.30W
Passau	10	Jh	48.35N	13.29 E
Passero, Capo- ►	14	Jn	36.40N	15.10 E
Passo Fundo	53	Kh	28.15S	52.24W
Passo Fundo, Rio- ↝	55	Fh	27.16S	52.42W
Passos	54	Ig	20.43S	46.37W
Pastaza, Río- ↝	52	If	4.50S	76.25W
Pasteur	56	He	35.08S	62.14W
Pasto	53	Ie	1.13N	77.17W
Pastora Peak ▲	46	Kh	36.47N	109.10W
Pastoría, Laguna de- ◒	48	Ki	16.00N	97.40W
Pastos Bons	54	Je	6.36S	44.05W
Pastrana	13	Jd	40.25N	2.55W
Paštrik ▲	15	Dg	42.14N	20.32 E
Pasubio ▲	14	Fe	45.47N	11.10 E
Pasvalis/Pasvalys	7	Fh	56.02N	24.28 E
Pasvalys/Pasvalis	7	Fh	56.02N	24.28 E
Pásztó	10	Pi	47.55N	19.42 E

Index Symbols

① Independent Nation	▣ Historical or Cultural Region	⋈ Pass, Gap	⊔ Depression	⌇ Coast, Beach	⊞ Rock, Reef	⤓ Waterfall Rapids	═ Canal	◒ Lagoon
② State, Region	▲ Mount, Mountain	▁ Plain, Lowland	⊓ Polder	◧ Cliff	⁂ Islands, Archipelago	⋔ River Mouth, Estuary	❄ Glacier	≣ Bank
③ District, County	🌋 Volcano	◺ Delta	∿ Desert, Dunes	◨ Peninsula	⊕ Rocks, Reefs	◍ Lake	❅ Ice Shelf, Pack Ice	⏶ Seamount
④ Municipality	◭ Hill	░ Salt Flat	♣ Forest, Woods	⧓ Isthmus	❋ Coral Reef	⊜ Salt Lake	≋ Ocean	⊼ Tablemount
⑤ Colony, Dependency	⛰ Mountains, Mountain Range	⋁ Valley, Canyon	⩩ Heath, Steppe	⋯ Sandbank	⊙ Well, Spring	◌ Intermittent Lake	≈ Sea	⌃ Ridge
■ Continent	◠ Hills, Escarpment	◡ Crater, Cave	🌴 Oasis	◆ Island	⌶ Geyser	⊟ Reservoir	◖ Gulf, Bay	⊏ Shelf
⊠ Physical Region	▬ Plateau, Upland	✲ Karst Features	► Cape, Point	◎ Atoll	↝ River, Stream	ψ Swamp, Pond	⇌ Strait, Fjord	⊍ Basin

⟋ Escarpment, Sea Scarp	⌂ Historic Site	⚓ Port
⚡ Fracture	⁘ Ruins	⛯ Lighthouse
⋎ Trench, Abyss	▥ Wall, Walls	⚒ Mine
♠ National Park, Reserve	✝ Church, Abbey	∩ Tunnel
★ Point of Interest	⛩ Temple	⌓ Dam, Bridge
⛱ Recreation Site	⚗ Scientific Station	
◓ Cave, Cavern	✈ Airport	

Patagonia 52 Jj 44.00S 68.00W
Patagonica, Cordillera- 52 Ij 46.00S 71.30W
Patan 25 Hc 27.40N 85.20 E
Pātan 25 Ed 23.50N 72.07 E
Patani 26 If 0.18N 128.48 E
Pata Peninsula 64d Bb 7.23N 151.35 E
Patchogue 44 Ke 40.46N 73.01W
Pate 36 Hc 2.08S 41.00 E
Patea 62 Fc 39.46S 174.29 E
Patea 62 Fc 39.46S 174.30 E
Pategi 34 Gd 8.44N 5.45 E
Patensie 37 Cf 33.46S 24.49 E
Paternò 14 Jm 37.34N 15.54 E
Paterson 43 Mc 40.55N 74.10W
Paterson Inlet 62 Bg 46.55S 168.00 E
Paterson Range 59 Ed 21.45S 122.05 E
Pathānkot 25 Fb 32.17N 75.39 E
Pathfinder Reservoir 46 Le 42.30N 106.50W
Pathfinder Seamount (EN) 40 Kf 50.55N 143.15W
Pathiu 25 Jf 10.41N 99.20 E
Patia, Río- 54 Cc 2.13N 78.40W
Patiāla 25 Fb 30.19N 76.24 E
Patiño, Estero- 55 Cg 24.05S 59.55W
Patio 65e Db 16.35S 151.29W
Pati Point 64c Ba 13.36N 144.57 E
Pătîrlagele 15 Jd 45.19N 26.21 E
Pativilca 54 Cf 10.42S 77.47W
Pátmos 15 Jl 37.19N 26.34 E
Pátmos 15 Jl 37.20N 26.33 E
Patna 22 Kg 25.36N 85.07 E
Patnos 24 Jc 39.14N 42.52 E
Pato Branco 56 Jc 26.13S 52.40W
Patom Plateau (EN) = Patomskoje Nagorje 20 Ge 59.00N 115.30 E
Patomskoje Nagorje = Patom Plateau (EN) 20 Ge 59.00N 115.30 E
Patos 53 Mf 7.01S 37.16W
Patos, Isla de- 50 Fg 10.38N 61.52W
Patos, Lagoa dos- 52 Ki 31.06S 51.15W
Patos, Laguna de los- 55 Aj 30.25S 62.15W
Patos, Ribeirão dos- 55 Gd 18.58S 50.30W
Patos, Rio dos- [Braz.] 55 Da 13.33S 56.29W
Patos, Rio dos- [Braz.] 55 Hb 14.59S 48.46W
Patos de Minas 53 Lg 18.35S 46.32W
Patosi 15 Ci 40.38N 19.39 E
Patquía 56 Gd 30.03S 66.53W
Pátrai 6 Ih 38.15N 21.44 E
Patrai, Gulf of- (EN) = Patraïkós Kólpos 15 Ek 38.15N 21.30 E
Patraïkós Kólpos = Patrai, Gulf of- (EN) 15 Ek 38.15N 21.30 E
Patricio Lynch, Isla- 56 Eg 48.36S 75.26W
Patricios 55 Bl 35.27S 60.42W
Patrocinio 54 Ig 18.57S 46.59W
Patta Island 30 Li 2.07S 41.03 E
Pattani 25 Kg 6.51N 101.16 E
Patteson, Passage- 63b Db 15.26S 168.09 E
Patti 14 Il 38.08N 14.58 E
Patti, Golfo di- 14 Jl 38.10N 15.05 E
Patton Seamount (EN) 38 Dd 54.40N 150.30W
Pattullo, Mount - 42 Ee 56.14N 129.39W
Patu 54 Ke 6.06S 37.38W
Patuākhāli 25 Id 22.16N 90.18 E
Patuca, Punta- 49 Ef 15.51N 84.18W
Patuca, Río- 47 He 15.50N 84.18W
Pătulele 15 Fe 44.21N 22.47 E
Patutahi 62 Gc 38.37S 177.53 E
Patuxent Range 66 Qg 84.43S 64.30W
Pátzcuaro 48 Ih 19.31N 101.36W
Pau 11 Fk 43.18N 0.22W
Pau, Gave de- 11 Ek 43.33N 1.12W
Paucartambo 54 Df 13.18S 71.40W
Paucerne, Río- 55 Ba 13.34S 61.14W
Pau dos Ferros 54 Ke 6.07S 38.10W
Pauillac 11 Fi 45.12N 0.45W
Pauini 54 Ee 7.40S 66.58W
Pauini, Rio- 54 Ee 7.47S 67.15W
Pauksa Taung 25 Ie 19.55N 94.18 E
Paulatuk 39 Gc 69.23N 124.00W
Paulaya, Río- 49 Ef 15.51N 85.06W
Paulding Bay 66 Ie 66.35S 123.00 E
Paulina Peak 46 Ee 43.41N 121.15W
Păuliş 15 Ec 46.07N 21.35 E
Paulistana 54 Je 8.09S 41.09W
Paulo Afonso 53 Mf 9.21S 38.14W
Paulo Afonso, Cachoeira de- 52 Mf 9.24S 38.12W
Pauls Valley 45 Hi 34.44N 97.13W
Paungde 25 Je 18.29N 95.30 E
Pavant Range 46 Ig 39.00N 112.15W
Pāveh 24 Le 35.03N 46.22 E
Pavia 14 De 45.10N 9.10 E
Pavilly 12 Ce 49.34N 0.58 E
Pāvilosta/Pavilosta 7 Eh 56.55N 21.13 E
Pavilosta/Pāvilosta 7 Eh 56.55N 21.13 E
Pavlikeni 15 If 43.14N 25.18 E
Pavlodar 22 Jd 52.18N 76.57 E
Pavlodarskaja Oblast [3] 19 He 52.00N 76.30 E
Pavlof Islands 40 Ge 55.15N 161.20W
Pavlof Volcano 40 Ge 55.24N 161.55W
Pavlograd 16 Ie 48.32N 35.53 E
Pavlovka 17 Hi 55.25N 56.33 E
Pavlovo 19 Ed 55.58N 43.04 E
Pavlov Seamount (EN) 20 Lf 50.40N 162.00 E
Pavlovsk 16 Ld 50.27N 40.08 E
Pavlovskaja 19 Df 46.06N 39.48 E
Pavullo nel Frignano 14 Ef 44.20N 10.50 E
Pavuvu 63a Dc 9.04S 159.08 E
Pawa 63a Ed 10.15S 161.44 E
Pawhuska 45 Hh 36.40N 96.20W
Pawnee 45 Hh 36.20N 96.48W
Pawnee River 45 Gg 38.10N 99.06W
Pawtucket 44 Le 41.53N 71.23W
Paximádhia, Nisídhes- 15 Ho 35.00N 24.35 E
Paxoí 15 Dj 39.12N 20.10 E
Paxson 40 Jd 63.02N 145.30W
Payakumbuk 26 Dg 0.14S 100.38 E
Payas, Cerro- 49 Ef 15.50N 85.00W
Payerne 14 Ad 46.49N 6.58 E
Payette 46 Gd 44.05N 116.57W
Payette 43 Dc 44.05N 116.56W
Payne, Baie- 42 Ke 59.55N 69.35W
Payne, Lac - 42 Ke 59.30N 74.00W
Paysandú [2] 55 Dk 32.00S 57.15W
Paysandú 53 Ki 32.19S 58.05W
Pays de Léon 11 Bf 48.28N 4.30W
Pays d'Othe 11 Jf 48.06N 3.37 E
Payson [Az.-U.S.] 46 Ji 34.14N 111.20W
Payson [Ut.-U.S.] 46 Jf 40.03N 111.44W
Payzawat/Jiashi 27 Cd 39.29N 76.39 E
Pāzanān 24 Mg 30.35N 49.59 E
Pazar 24 Ib 41.11N 40.53 E
Pazarbası Burun 24 Db 41.13N 30.17 E
Pazarcık 24 Gd 37.31N 37.19 E
Pazardžik 15 Hg 42.12N 24.20 E
Pazardžik [2] 15 Hg 42.12N 24.20 E
Pazarköy 15 Kj 39.51N 27.24 E
Pazaryeri 24 Cc 40.00N 29.54 E
Pazin 14 He 45.14N 13.56 E
Pčinja 15 Eh 41.49N 21.40 E
Pea 65b Ac 21.11S 175.14W
Peabirú 55 Ff 23.54S 52.20W
Peace Point 42 Ge 59.12N 112.33W
Peace River 39 Hd 56.14N 117.17W
Peace River [Can.] 38 Hd 56.14N 117.17W
Peace River [Fl.-U.S.] 44 Fl 26.55N 82.05W
Peachland 46 Fb 49.46N 119.44W
Peach Springs 46 Ii 35.32N 113.25W
Peacock Hills 42 Gc 66.05N 110.00W
Peak District 9 Lh 53.17N 1.45W
Peake Creek 59 He 28.05S 136.07 E
Peaked Mountain 44 Mb 46.34N 68.49W
Peale, Mount- 43 Fd 38.26N 109.14W
Pearl 45 Lb 48.42N 88.44W
Pearland 45 Il 29.34N 95.17W
Pearl and Hermes Reef 57 Jb 27.55N 175.45W
Pearl City 65a Db 21.23N 157.58W
Pearl Harbor 65a Cb 21.20N 158.00W
Pearl River 43 Je 30.11N 89.32W
Pearsall 45 Gl 28.53N 99.06W
Pearsoll Peak 46 De 42.18N 123.50W
Peary Channel 42 Ha 79.25N 101.00W
Peary Land 67 Me 82.40N 30.00W
Pease River 45 Gi 34.12N 99.07W
Pebane 37 Fc 17.14S 38.10 E
Pebas 54 Dd 3.20S 71.49W
Peć 15 Dg 42.39N 20.18 E
Peca 14 Id 46.29N 14.48 E
Peças, Ilha das- 55 Hg 25.26S 48.19W
Pecatonica River 45 Le 42.29N 89.03W
Pečenežskoje Vodohranilišče 16 Jd 50.05N 36.50 E
Pečenga 6 Jb 69.33N 31.07 E
Pečenga 7 Hb 69.39N 31.27 E
Pechea 15 Kd 45.38N 27.48 E
Pechora (EN) = Pečora 5 Lb 68.13N 54.10 E
Pechora (EN) = Pečora 6 Lb 65.10N 57.11 E
Pechora Bay (EN) = Pečorskaja Guba 19 Fb 68.40N 54.45 E
Pechora Sea (EN) = Pečorskoje More 19 Fb 69.45N 54.30 E
Pecica 15 Ec 46.10N 21.04 E
Peçin 15 Kl 37.19N 27.45 E
Peckelsheim, Willebadessen- 12 Lc 51.36N 9.08 E
Pečora = Pechora (EN) 6 Lb 65.10N 57.11 E
Pečora = Pechora (EN) 5 Lb 68.13N 54.10 E
Pecora, Capo- 14 Ck 39.27N 8.23 E
Pečorskaja Guba = Pechora Bay (EN) 19 Fb 68.40N 54.45 E
Pečorskoje More = Pechora Sea (EN) 19 Fb 69.45N 54.30 E
Pečory 7 Gh 57.49N 27.38 E
Pecos 43 Ge 31.25N 103.30W
Pecos 38 Ig 29.42N 101.22W
Pecos Plain 43 Ge 33.20N 104.30W
Pécs 6 Hf 46.05N 18.14 E
Pécs [2] 10 Oj 46.06N 18.15 E
Pedasí 49 Gj 7.32N 80.02W
Pedder, Lake- 59 Jh 43.00S 146.15 E
Peddie 37 Df 33.14S 27.07 E
Pededze 8 Lh 56.53N 27.01 E
Pedernales [Dom.Rep.] 49 Ld 18.02N 71.45W
Pedernales [Ven.] 50 Eh 9.58N 62.16W
Pedernales, Salar de- 56 Gc 26.15S 69.10W
Pedja Jõgi 8 Lf 58.20N 26.10 E
Pêdo Shankou 27 Df 29.12N 83.26 E
Pedra Azul 54 Jg 16.01S 41.16W
Pedra Branca 54 Ke 5.27S 39.43W
Pedra do Sino 55 Kf 22.27S 43.03W
Pedra Lume 32 Cf 16.46N 22.54W
Pedras, Rio das- 55 Ia 13.30S 47.09W
Pedras Altas, Coxilha- 55 Fj 31.45S 53.35W
Pedregal 54 Da 11.01N 70.08W
Pedreiras 54 Jd 4.34S 44.39W
Pedriceña 48 He 25.06N 103.47W
Pedrizas, Puerto de las- 13 Hh 36.55N 4.30W
Pedro Afonso 54 Ie 8.59S 48.11W
Pedro Bank (EN) 49 He 17.00N 78.30W
Pedro Betancourt 49 Gb 22.44N 81.17W
Pedro Cays 47 Ie 17.00N 77.50W
Pedro de Valdivia 56 Gb 22.37S 69.38W
Pedro Gomes 55 Ed 18.04S 54.32W
Pedro Gonzáles, Isla- 49 Hi 8.24N 79.06W
Pedro II 54 Jd 4.25S 41.28W
Pedro II, Ilha- 54 Ec 1.10N 66.44W
Pedro Juan Caballero 56 Ib 22.34S 55.37W
Pedro Leopoldo 55 Jd 19.38S 44.03W
Pedro Luro 56 He 39.29S 62.41W
Pedro Lustoza 55 Gg 25.49S 51.51W
Pedro Montoya 48 Jg 21.38N 99.49W
Pedro Osorio 56 Jd 31.51S 52.45W
Pedro R. Fernández 55 Ci 28.45S 58.39W
Pedro Severo 55 Ec 17.40S 54.02W
Pedroso, Sierra del- 13 Gf 38.35N 5.35W
Peebles 9 Jf 55.39N 3.12W
Pee Dee River 38 Lf 33.21N 79.16W
Peekskill 44 Ke 41.18N 73.56W
Peel 38 Fc 67.37N 134.40W
Peel 11 Lc 51.25N 5.50 E
Peel 9 Ig 54.13N 4.40W
Peel Sound 42 Hb 73.00N 96.00W
Peene 10 Jb 54.09N 13.46 E
Peer 12 Hc 51.08N 5.28 E
Peera Peera Poolanna Lake 59 He 26.30S 138.00 E
Peetz 45 Ef 40.58N 103.07W
Pegasus, Port- 62 Bg 47.10S 167.40 E
Pegasus Bay 61 Dh 43.20S 172.50 E
Pegnitz 10 Gg 49.29N 11.00 E
Pegnitz 10 Hg 49.45N 11.33 E
Pego 13 Lf 38.51N 0.07W
Pegtymel 20 Mc 69.47N 174.00 E
Pegu 22 Lh 17.30N 96.30 E
Pegu [3] 25 Je 17.52N 95.40 E
Pegu Yoma 21 Lh 19.00N 95.50 E
Pegwell Bay 12 Dc 51.18N 1.23 E
Pehčevo 15 Fh 41.46N 22.54 E
Pehlivanköy 15 Jh 41.21N 26.55 E
Pehuajó 56 He 35.48S 61.53W
Pei-ching Shih → Beijing Shi [4] 27 Kc 40.15N 116.30 E
Peine 10 Gd 52.19N 10.14 E
Peipsi järv = Peipus, Lake- (EN) 5 Id 58.45N 27.30 E
Peipus, Lake- (EN) = Čudskoje Ozero 5 Id 58.45N 27.30 E
Peipus, Lake- (EN) = Peipsi järv 5 Id 58.45N 27.30 E
Peixe 54 If 12.03S 48.32W
Peixe, Lagoa do- 55 Gj 31.18S 51.00W
Peixe, Rio do- [Braz.] 55 Ge 21.31S 51.58W
Peixe, Rio do- [Braz.] 55 Gb 14.06S 50.51W
Peixe, Rio do- [Braz.] 55 Hc 17.37S 48.29W
Peixe, Rio do- [Braz.] 55 Fc 16.32S 52.38W
Peixe, Rio do- [Braz.] 55 Gh 27.27S 51.54W
Peixe de Couro, Rio- 55 Ec 17.21S 55.29W
Peixes, Rio dos- 55 Hb 15.10S 49.30W
Peixian (Yunhe) 28 Dg 34.44N 116.56 E
Peixoto, Represa de- 54 Ih 20.30S 46.30W
Pejantan, Pulau- 26 Ef 0.07N 107.14 E
Pëjde/Pöide 8 Jf 58.30N 22.50 E
Pek 15 Ee 44.46N 21.33 E
Pekalongan 26 Eh 6.53S 109.40 E
Pekan 26 Df 3.30N 103.25 E
Pekin 43 Jc 40.35N 89.40W
Peking (EN) = Beijing 22 Nf 39.55N 116.23 E
Pekulnei, Hrebet- 20 Mc 66.30N 176.00 E
Pelabuhanratu 26 Eh 6.59S 106.33 E
Pelagie, Isole- 5 Hh 35.40N 12.40 E
Pelagonija 15 Eh 41.05N 21.30 E
Pélagos 15 Hj 39.20N 24.05 E
Pelaihari 26 Fg 3.48S 114.45 E
Pelat, Mont- 11 Mj 44.16N 6.42 E
Pelawanbesar 26 Gf 1.10N 117.54 E
Pélé 63b Dc 17.30S 168.24 E
Peleaga, Vîrful- 15 Fd 45.22N 22.53 E
Peleduj 20 Ge 59.40N 112.38 E
Pelée, Montagne- 47 Le 14.48N 61.10W
Pelee, Point- 44 Fe 41.54N 82.30W
Pelee Island 44 Fe 41.46N 82.39W
Peleliu Island 57 Ed 7.01N 134.15 E
Peleng, Pulau- 26 Hg 1.20S 123.10 E
Pelhřimov 10 Lg 49.26N 15.13 E
Pelican Lake 45 Gb 49.20N 99.35W
Pelicanpunt 37 Ad 22.54S 14.26 E
Peligre, Lac de- 49 Ld 18.52N 71.56W
Pelinaion Óros 15 Ik 38.32N 26.00 E
Pelješac 14 Lh 42.55N 17.25 E
Pelkosenniemi 7 Gc 67.07N 27.30 E
Pella 45 Jf 41.25N 92.55W
Pélla 15 Fi 40.46N 22.34 E
Pellegrini 56 He 36.16S 63.09W
Pellice 14 Bf 44.50N 7.38 E
Pellinge/Pellinki 8 Kd 60.15N 25.50 E
Pellinki/Pellinge 8 Kd 60.15N 25.50 E
Pello 7 Fc 66.47N 24.01 E
Pellworm 10 Eb 54.30N 8.40 E
Pelly 38 Fc 62.47N 137.19W
Pelly Bay 42 Ic 68.50N 90.10W
Pelly Bay 39 Kc 68.52N 89.55W
Pelly Crossing 42 Dd 62.50N 136.35W
Pelly Mountains 42 Ed 61.30N 132.00W
Peloncillo Mountains 46 Kj 32.15N 109.10W
Pelón de Nado, Cerro- 48 Jg 20.05N 99.55W
Peloponnesus (EN) = Pelopónnisos 5 Ih 37.40N 22.00 E
Peloponnesus (EN) = Pelopónnisos 15 El 37.40N 22.00 E
Pelopónnisos [2] 15 El 37.40N 22.00 E
Pelopónnisos = Peloponnesus (EN) 15 El 37.40N 22.00 E
Pelopónnisos = Peloponnesus (EN) 5 Ih 37.40N 22.00 E
Peloritani 14 Jl 38.05N 15.20 E
Peloro, Capo- o Faro, Punta del- 14 Jl 38.16N 15.39 E
Pelotas 53 Ki 31.46S 52.20W
Pelotas, Rio- 56 Jc 27.28S 51.55W
Pelplin 10 Oc 53.56N 18.42 E
Pelvoux, Massif du- 5 Gg 44.55N 6.20 E
Pelym 19 Gd 59.40N 63.05 E
Pelymskí Tuman, Ozero- 17 Kf 60.05N 63.05 E
Pemalang 26 Eh 6.54S 109.22 E
Pemar/Paimio 8 Jd 60.27N 22.42 E
Pematangsiantar 22 Li 2.57N 99.03 E
Pemba [3] 36 Hd 5.02S 40.00 E
Pemba [Moz.] 31 Lj 12.57S 40.30 E
Pemba [Zam.] 36 Ef 16.31S 27.22 E
Pemba Channel 36 Gd 5.10S 39.20 E
Pemba Island 30 Ki 5.10S 39.48 E
Pemberton [Austl.] 59 Df 34.28S 116.01 E
Pemberton [B.C.-Can.] 46 Da 50.20N 122.48W
Pembina 42 Gf 54.45N 114.17W
Pembina 43 Hb 48.58N 97.15W
Pembina River 43 Hb 48.56N 97.15W
Pembroke [Ont.-Can.] 42 Jg 45.49N 77.07W
Pembroke [Wales-U.K.] 9 Ij 51.41N 4.55W
Pembuang 26 Fg 3.24S 112.33 E
Peña, Sierra de la- 13 Lb 42.31N 0.38W
Penafiel 13 Dc 41.12N 8.17W
Peñafiel 13 Hc 41.36N 4.07W
Peñagolosa/Penyagolosa 13 Ld 40.13N 0.21W
Peña Gorda, Cerro- 48 Gg 20.40N 104.55W
Peñalara 13 Id 40.51N 3.57W
Penalva 54 Id 3.18S 45.10W
Penamacor 13 Ed 40.10N 7.10W
Peña Nevada, Cerro- 38 Jg 23.46N 99.52W
Penápolis 55 Ge 21.24S 50.04W
Peñaranda de Bracamonte 13 Gd 40.54N 5.12W
Peñarroya 13 Ld 40.28N 0.43W
Peñarroya-Pueblonuevo 13 Gf 38.18N 5.16W
Peñas, Cabo de- 5 Fg 43.39N 5.51W
Penas, Golfo de- 52 Ij 47.22S 74.50W
Peñas, Punta- 54 Fa 10.44N 61.51W
Peñasco, Río- 45 Dj 32.45N 104.19W
Pendé 35 Ad 9.07N 16.26 E
Pendembu [S.L.] 34 Cd 9.06N 12.12W
Pendembu [S.L.] 34 Cd 8.06N 10.42W
Pendik 15 Mi 40.53N 29.13 E
Pendjari 34 Fc 10.54N 0.51 E
Pendle Hill 9 Kh 53.52N 2.17W
Pendleton 39 He 45.40N 118.47W
Pendolo 26 Hg 2.05S 120.42 E
Pend Oreille Lake 43 Db 48.10N 116.11W
Pend Oreille River 43 Db 49.04N 117.37W
Pendžikent 19 Gh 39.29N 67.38 E
Peneda 13 Dc 41.58N 8.15W
Penedo 54 Kf 10.17S 36.36W
Penetanguishene 44 Hc 44.47N 79.55W
Penganga 25 Fe 19.53N 79.09 E
Pengcheng 27 Jd 36.25N 114.08 E
Penge 36 Dd 5.31S 24.37 E
Pengho Jiao 27 Jc 16.03N 112.35 E
Penghu Liehtao = Pescadores (EN) 27 Kg 23.30N 119.30 E
Penglai (Dengzhou) 27 Ld 37.44N 120.45 E
Pengshui 27 If 29.17N 108.13 E
Pengze 27 Kf 29.52N 116.34 E
Penha 55 Hh 26.46S 48.39W
Penhalonga 37 Ec 18.54S 32.40 E
Penibético, Sistema- 13 Ig 37.00N 3.30W
Peniche 13 Ce 39.21N 9.23W
Penicuik 9 Jf 55.50N 3.14W
Penida, Nusa- 26 Gh 8.44S 115.32 E
Península Ibérica = Iberian Peninsula (EN) 5 Fg 40.00N 4.00W
Peñíscola 13 Md 40.21N 0.25 E
Penisola Salentina = Salentine Peninsula (EN) 5 Hg 40.30N 18.00 E
Penitente, Serra do- 54 Ie 8.45S 46.20W
Pénjamo 48 Ig 20.26N 101.44W
Penju, Kepulauan- 26 Ih 5.22S 127.46 E
Penmarch, Pointe de- 11 Bg 47.48N 4.22W
Penne 14 Hh 42.27N 13.55 E
Penne, Punta- 14 Lj 40.41N 17.56 E
Pennell Coast 66 Kf 71.00S 167.00 E
Penner 21 Kh 14.35N 80.10 E
Penn Hills 44 He 40.28N 79.53W
Pennines 5 Fe 54.10N 2.05W
Pennsylvania [2] 43 Lc 40.45N 77.30W
Penn Yan 44 Id 42.41N 77.03W
Penny Ice Cap 42 Kc 67.00N 65.10W
Penny Strait 42 Ha 76.35N 97.10W
Peno 7 Hh 56.57N 32.45 E
Penobscot Bay 44 Mc 44.15N 68.52W
Penobscot River 43 Nc 44.30N 68.50W
Penola 59 Ig 37.23S 140.50 E
Peñón del Rosario, Cerro- 48 Jh 19.40N 98.12W
Penong 58 Eh 31.55S 133.01 E
Penonomé 47 Hg 8.31N 80.22W
Pénot, Mont- 63b Cc 16.20S 167.31 E
Penrhyn Atoll 57 Le 9.00S 158.00W
Penrith 9 Kg 54.40N 2.44W
Penrith, Sydney- 59 Kf 33.45S 150.42 E
Pensacola 39 Kf 30.25N 87.13W
Pensacola Mountains 66 Rg 83.45S 55.00W
Pensacola Seamount (EN) 57 Lc 18.17N 157.20W
Pensamiento 55 Bb 14.44S 61.35W
Pensiangan 26 Gf 4.33N 116.19 E
Pentecôte, Ile- 57 Hf 15.45S 168.10 E
Penticton 42 Fg 49.30N 119.35W
Pentland 59 Jd 20.32S 145.24 E
Pentland Firth 9 Jc 58.44N 3.13W
Pentland Hills 9 Jf 55.48N 3.23W
Penwith 9 Hk 50.13N 5.40W
Penyagolosa/Peñagolosa 13 Ld 40.13N 0.21W
Penza 6 Ke 53.13N 45.00 E
Penzance 6 Ff 50.07N 5.33W
Penzenskaja Oblast [3] 19 Ee 53.15N 44.40 E
Penzhina Bay (EN) = Penžinskaja Guba 20 Ld 61.00N 163.00 E
Penžina 21 Sc 62.28N 165.18 E
Penžinskaja Guba = Penzhina Bay (EN) 20 Ld 61.00N 163.00 E
Penžinski Hrebet 20 Ld 62.15N 166.35 E
Peoples Creek 46 Kb 48.24N 108.19W
Peoria 39 Ke 40.42N 89.36W
Peoúia 24 Ee 34.53N 32.23 E
Pepa 36 Ed 7.42S 29.47 E
Pepel 34 Cd 8.35N 13.03W
Peperiguaçu, Rio- 55 Fh 27.10S 53.50W
Peqini 15 Ch 41.03N 19.45 E
Pequena, Lagoa- 55 Fj 31.36S 52.04W
Pequiri, Rio- 54 Gg 17.23S 55.38W
Perabumulih 26 Dg 3.27S 104.15 E
Perälä 8 Ib 62.28N 21.36 E
Perales, Puerto de- 13 Fd 40.15N 6.41W
Pérama 15 Hn 35.22N 24.42 E
Peräseinäjoki 8 Jb 62.34N 23.04 E
Perche, Col de la- 11 Il 42.30N 2.06 E
Perche, Collines du- 11 Gf 48.25N 0.40 E
Percival Lakes 59 Ed 21.25S 125.00 E
Percy Islands 59 Kd 21.40S 150.15 E
Perdasdefogu 14 Dk 39.41N 9.26 E
Perdida, Sierra- 48 Hd 27.30N 103.30W
Perdido, Monte- 5 Gg 42.40N 0.05 E
Perdido, Rio- 55 Df 22.10S 57.33W
Perdizes 55 Id 19.21S 47.17W
Perečin 10 Sh 48.44N 22.29 E
Pereginskoje 16 De 48.49N 24.12 E
Pereira 54 Cc 4.48N 75.42W
Pereira Barreto 56 Jb 20.38S 51.07W
Perejaslav-Hmelnicki 16 Gd 50.04N 31.27 E
Perejil, Isla de- 13 Ig 35.55N 5.26W
Pereljub 16 Qd 51.52N 50.20 E
Peremennyj, Cape- 66 He 66.08S 105.30 E
Peremyšliany 10 Ug 49.38N 24.35 E
Perenjori 59 De 29.26S 116.17 E
Pereščepino 16 Ie 48.59N 35.22 E
Pereslavl-Zalesski 7 Jh 56.45N 38.55 E
Peretu 15 Ie 44.03N 25.05 E
Peretyčiha 20 Ig 47.10N 138.35 E
Perevolocki 16 Sd 51.51N 54.15 E
Pergamino 56 Hd 33.53S 60.35W
Pergamon 15 Kj 39.08N 27.13 E
Perge 24 Dd 37.00N 30.10 E
Pergine Valsugana 14 Fd 46.04N 11.14 E
Pergola 14 Gg 43.34N 12.50 E
Perham 45 Ic 46.36N 95.34W
Perho 7 Fe 63.13N 24.25 E
Periam 15 Dc 46.03N 20.52 E
Péribonca, Rivière- 42 Kg 48.44N 72.06W
Perico 56 Hb 24.23S 65.00W
Pericos 48 Fe 25.03N 107.42W
Périgord 11 Gi 45.00N 0.30 E
Perigoso, Canal- 54 Ic 0.05N 49.40W
Périgueux 11 Gi 45.11N 0.43 E
Perijá, Sierra de- 52 Ie 10.00N 73.00W
Peristerá 15 Gj 39.12N 23.59 E
Perito Moreno 53 Ij 46.36S 70.56W
Perkam, Tanjung- = Urville, Cape d'- (EN) 26 Kg 1.28S 137.54 E
Perković 14 Kg 43.41N 16.06 E
Perlas, Archipiélago de las- 47 Ig 8.25N 79.00W
Perlas, Cayos de- 49 Fg 12.28N 83.28W
Perlas, Laguna de- 49 Fg 12.30N 83.40W
Perlas, Punta de- 49 Fg 12.23N 83.30W
Perleberg 10 Hc 53.04N 11.52 E
Perlez 15 Dd 45.12N 20.23 E
Perm 6 Ld 58.00N 56.15 E
Përmeti 15 Di 40.14N 20.21 E
Permskaja Oblast [3] 19 Fd 59.00N 57.00 E
Pernambuco [2] 54 Ke 8.30S 37.30W
Pernik 15 Gg 42.36N 23.02 E
Pernik [2] 15 Fg 42.35N 22.50 E
Perniö/Bjärna 7 Ff 60.12N 23.08 E
Péronne 11 Ie 49.56N 2.56 E
Perote 48 Kh 19.34N 97.14W
Perpignan 6 Gg 42.41N 2.53 E
Perro, Laguna del- 45 Di 34.40N 105.57W
Perros-Guirec 11 Cf 48.49N 3.27W
Perry [Fl.-U.S.] 44 Fj 30.07N 83.35W
Perry [Ga.-U.S.] 44 Fi 32.27N 83.44W
Perry [Ia.-U.S.] 45 If 41.50N 94.06W
Perry [Ok.-U.S.] 45 Hh 36.17N 97.17W
Perry Lake 45 Ig 39.20N 95.30W
Perryton 45 Fh 36.24N 100.48W
Perryville 40 He 55.54N 159.10W
Persan 12 Ee 49.09N 2.16 E
Perşani, Munţii- 15 Id 45.40N 25.15 E
Persberg 8 Fe 59.45N 14.15 E
Persembe 24 Gb 41.04N 37.46 E
Persepolis 24 Oh 29.57N 52.52 E
Perseverancia 54 Ff 14.44S 62.48W
Persian Gulf (EN) = Al-Khalīj al-'Arabi 21 Hg 27.00N 51.00 E
Persian Gulf (EN) = Khalīj-e Fārs 21 Hg 27.00N 51.00 E
Perstorp 8 Eh 56.08N 13.23 E
Pertek 24 Hc 38.50N 39.22 E
Perth [Austl.] 58 Ch 31.56S 115.50 E
Perth [Ont.-Can.] 44 Ic 44.54N 76.15W
Perth [Scot.-U.K.] 9 Je 56.24N 3.28W
Perth Amboy 44 Je 40.32N 74.17W
Perth-Andover 44 Nb 46.44N 67.42W
Perth-Armadale 59 Df 32.09S 116.00 E
Perth-Fremantle 59 Df 32.03S 115.45 E
Perth-Kalamunda 59 Df 31.57S 116.03 E
Perth-Mundaring 59 Df 31.54S 116.10 E
Perthus, Col de-/Portús, Coll del- 13 Ob 42.28N 2.51 E
Perthus, Col du- 13 Ob 42.28N 2.51 E
Pertuis 11 Lk 43.41N 5.30 E
Pertusato, Capo- 11a Bb 41.21N 9.11 E
Perú [1] 53 Ig 10.00S 76.00W
Peru [Il.-U.S.] 45 Lf 41.20N 89.08W
Peru [In.-U.S.] 44 De 40.45N 86.04W
Perú, Altiplano del- 54 Df 15.00S 72.00W
Peruaçu, Rio- 55 Jb 15.11S 44.07W
Peru Basin (EN) 3 Mk 17.00S 90.00W
Peru-Chile Trench (EN) 3 Nl 20.00S 73.00W
Perugia 6 Hg 43.08N 12.22 E
Perugorria 55 Ci 29.20S 58.37W
Peruíbe 55 Ig 24.19S 47.00W
Perušić 14 Jf 44.39N 15.22 E
Péruwelz 12 Fd 50.31N 3.35 E

Index Symbols

[1] Independent Nation
[2] State, Region
[3] District, County
[4] Municipality
[5] Colony, Dependency
Continent
Physical Region
Historical or Cultural Region
Mount, Mountain
Volcano
Hill
Mountains, Mountain Range
Hills, Escarpment
Plateau, Upland
Pass, Gap
Plain, Lowland
Delta
Salt Flat
Valley, Canyon
Crater, Cave
Karst Features
Depression
Polder
Desert, Dunes
Forest, Woods
Heath, Steppe
Oasis
Cape, Point
Coast, Beach
Cliff
Peninsula
Isthmus
Sandbank
Island
Atoll
Rock, Reef
Islands, Archipelago
Rocks, Reefs
Coral Reef
Well, Spring
Geyser
River, Stream
Waterfall Rapids
River Mouth, Estuary
Lake
Salt Lake
Intermittent Lake
Reservoir
Swamp, Pond
Canal
Glacier
Ice Shelf, Pack Ice
Ocean
Sea
Gulf, Bay
Strait, Fjord
Lagoon
Bank
Seamount
Tablemount
Ridge
Shelf
Basin
Escarpment, Sea Scarp
Fracture
Trench, Abyss
National Park, Reserve
Point of Interest
Recreation Site
Cave, Cavern
Historic Site
Ruins
Wall, Walls
Church, Abbey
Temple
Scientific Station
Airport
Port
Lighthouse
Mine
Tunnel
Dam, Bridge

Pervari 24 Jd 37.54N 42.36 E
Pervomajsk [R.S.F.S.R.] 19 Ee 54.52N 43.48 E
Pervomajsk [Ukr.-U.S.S.R.] 16 Ke 48.36N 38.32 E
Pervomajsk [Ukr.-U.S.S.R.] 19 Df 48.03N 30.52 E
Pervomajski [Bye.-U.S.S.R.] 10 Vc 53.52N 25.33 E
Pervomajski [Kaz.-U.S.S.R.] 19 Ie 50.15N 81.59 E
Pervomajski [R.S.F.S.R.] 16 Lc 53.18N 40.15 E
Pervomajski [R.S.F.S.R.] 19 Ec 64.26N 40.48 E
Pervomajski [R.S.F.S.R.] 17 Ji 54.52N 61.08 E
Pervomajski [R.S.F.S.R.] 16 Sd 51.34N 54.59 E
Pervomajski [Ukr.-U.S.S.R.] 16 Je 49.24N 36.15 E
Pervouralsk 19 Fd 57.00N 60.00 E
Pervy Kurilski Proliv 20 Kf 50.50N 156.50 E
Perwez/Perwijs 12 Gd 50.37N 4.49 E
Perwijs/Perwez 12 Gd 50.37N 4.49 E
Pes 7 Ig 59.10N 35.18 E
Peša 17 Cc 66.50N 47.32 E
Pesaro 14 Gg 43.54N 12.55 E
Pescadores (EN)=Penghu Liehtao 27 Kg 23.30N 119.30 E
Pescadores, Punta- 48 Ef 23.45N 109.45W
Pesčany, Mys- 16 Qh 43.10N 51.18 E
Pesčany, Ostrov 20 Gb 74.20N 115.55 E
Pescara 14 Ih 42.28N 14.13 E
Pescara 6 Hg 42.28N 14.13 E
Pescasseroli 14 Hi 41.48N 13.47 E
Peschici 14 Ki 41.57N 16.01 E
Pescia 14 Eg 43.54N 10.41 E
Pescocostanzo 14 Ii 41.53N 14.04 E
Peshāwar 22 Jf 34.01N 71.33 E
Peshkopia 15 Dh 41.41N 20.26 E
Pesio 14 Bf 44.28N 7.53 E
Peskovka 7 Mg 59.03N 52.22 E
Pesmes 11 Lg 47.17N 5.34 E
Pesočny 8 Nd 60.05N 30.20 E
Peso da Régua 13 Ec 41.10N 7.47W
Pesqueira 54 Ke 8.22S 36.42W
Pesqueria, Rio- 48 Je 25.54N 99.11W
Pessac 11 Fj 44.48N 0.37W
Pest [2] 10 Pi 47.25N 19.20 E
Pešter 15 Df 43.05N 20.02 E
Peštera 15 Hg 42.02N 24.18 E
Pestovo 19 Dd 58.36N 35.47 E
Petacalco, Bahia de- 47 De 17.57N 102.05W
Petah Tiqwa 24 Ff 32.05N 34.53 E
Petäjävesi 8 Kb 62.15N 25.12 E
Petal 45 Lk 31.21N 89.17W
Petalioí 15 Hl 38.01N 24.17 E
Petalioí, Gulf of- (EN) = Petalión, Kólpos- 15 Hk 38.00N 24.05 E
Petalión, Kólpos- = Petalioi, Gulf of- (EN) 15 Hk 38.00N 24.05 E
Petaluma 46 Dg 38.14N 122.39W
Pétange/Petingen 12 He 49.33N 5.53 E
Petare 54 Ea 10.29N 66.49W
Petatlán 48 Ii 17.31N 101.16W
Petatlán, Rio- 48 Fd 26.09N 107.45W
Petauke 36 Fe 14.15S 31.20 E
Petén 47 Fe 16.15N 89.50W
Petén [3] 49 Be 16.50N 90.00W
Petén Itzá, Lago- 49 Ce 16.59N 89.50W
Petenwell Lake 45 Ld 44.05N 89.45W
Peterborough [Austl.] 59 Hf 32.58S 138.50 E
Peterborough [Eng.-U.K.] 9 Mi 52.35N 0.15W
Peterborough [Ont.-Can.] 42 Jh 44.18N 78.19W
Peterhead 9 Ld 57.30N 1.46W
Peter I, Oy- 66 Pe 68.47S 90.35W
Peter Island 51a Db 18.22N 64.35W
Peterlee 9 Lg 54.46N 1.19W
Petermann Gletscher 41 Fb 80.45N 61.00W
Petermann Ranges 59 Fd 25.00S 129.45 E
Petermanns Bjerg 67 Md 73.10N 28.00W
Peter Pond Lake 42 Ge 55.55N 108.40W
Petersberg 10 He 51.35N 11.57 E
Petersburg [Ak.-U.S.] 40 Me 56.49N 132.57W
Petersburg [In.-U.S.] 44 Df 38.30N 87.16W
Petersburg [Va.-U.S.] 43 Ld 37.14N 77.24W
Petersburg [W.V.-U.S.] 44 Hf 39.01N 79.09W
Petersfield 9 Mk 51.00N 0.56W
Petershagen 12 Kb 52.23N 8.58 E
Peter the Great Bay (EN)= Petra Velikogo, Zaliv- 21 Pe 42.40N 132.00 E
Petilia Policastro 14 Kk 39.07N 16.47 E
Petingen/Pétange 12 He 49.33N 5.53 E
Petit-Bourg 51eAb 16.12N 61.36W
Petit-Canal 51eBb 16.23N 61.29W
Petit Canouan 51nBb 12.47N 61.17W
Petit Cul-de-Sac Marin 51eAb 16.12N 61.33W
Petite Kabylie 13 Rh 36.35N 5.25 E
Petite Rivière de l'Artibonite 49 Kd 19.08N 72.29W
Petites Pyrénées 11 Hk 43.05N 1.10 E
Petite-Terre, Iles de la- 51eBb 16.10N 61.07W
Petit-Goâve 49 Kd 18.26N 72.52W
Petit Martinique Island 51p Ca 12.32N 61.22W
Petit-Mécatina, Rivière du- 42 Lf 50.39N 59.25W
Petit Morin 11 Jf 48.56N 3.07 E
Petit Mustique Island 51nBb 12.51N 61.13W
Petit Nevis Island 51nBb 12.58N 61.15W
Petitot 42 Fd 60.14N 123.29W
Petit Saint-Bernard, Col du- 14 Ae 45.40N 6.55 E
Petit Saint Vincent Island 51nBb 12.33N 61.23W
Petit Savanne 51gBb 15.15N 61.17W
Petitsikapau Lake 42 Kf 54.40N 66.25W
Petkula 7 Gc 67.40N 26.41 E
Petlalcingo 48 Kh 18.05N 97.54W
Peto 47 Gd 20.08N 88.55W
Petorca 56 Fd 32.15S 71.00W
Petoskey 44 Ec 45.22N 84.57W
Petra 24 Fg 30.19N 35.29 E
Petralia Soprana 14 Im 37.47N 14.06 E
Petra Pervogo, Hrebet- 18 He 39.00N 71.10 E
Petra Velikogo, Zaliv- = Peter the Great Bay (EN) 21 Pe 42.40N 132.00 E
Petre, Point- 44 Id 43.50N 77.09W
Petre Bay 62 Je 43.55S 176.40W
Petrel 66 Re 63.28S 56.17W
Petrela 15 Ch 41.15N 19.51 E
Petrella Tifernina 14 Ii 41.41N 14.42 E
Petrič 15 Gh 41.24N 23.13 E
Pétrie, Récif- 61 Bc 18.30S 164.20 E
Petrikov 16 Fc 52.08N 28.31 E
Petrila 15 Gd 45.27N 23.25 E
Petrinja 14 Ke 45.27N 16.17 E
Petrodvorec 7 Gg 59.53N 29.50 E
Petrólea 54 Db 8.30N 72.35W
Petrolia 44 Fd 42.52N 82.09W
Petrolina 54 Je 9.24S 40.30W
Petrolina de Goiás 55 Hc 16.06S 49.20W
Petronanski prohod 15 Gf 43.08N 23.08 E
Petronell 14 Kb 48.07N 16.51 E
Petropavlovka 20 Ff 50.38N 105.19 E
Petropavlovsk 22 Id 54.54N 69.06 E
Petropavlovsk-Kamčatski 22 Rd 53.01N 158.39 E
Petrópolis 53 Lh 22.31S 43.10W
Petroşani 15 Gd 45.25N 23.22 E
Petrovac [Yugo.] 15 Bg 42.12N 18.57 E
Petrovac [Yugo.] 15 Ee 44.22N 21.25 E
Petrova Gora 14 Je 45.17N 15.47 E
Petrovaradin 15 Cd 45.15N 19.53 E
Petrovka 15 Nc 46.55N 30.40 E
Petrovsk 19 Ee 52.18N 45.23 E
Petrovski Jam 7 Ie 63.18N 35.15 E
Petrovsk-Zabajkalski 22 Md 51.17N 108.50 E
Petrov Val 16 Nd 50.10N 45.12 E
Petrozavodsk 6 Jc 61.47N 34.20 E
Petuhovo 19 Gd 55.06N 67.58 E
Petuški 7 Ji 55.59N 39.28 E
Petworth 12 Bd 50.59N 0.36W
Peuetsagoe, Gunung- 26 Cf 4.55N 96.20 E
Peumo 56 Fd 34.24S 71.10W
Peureulak 26 Cf 4.48N 97.53 E
Pevek 22 Tc 69.42N 170.17 E
Pevensey 12 Cd 50.48N 0.21 E
Pevensey Bay 12 Cd 50.48N 0.22 E
Peza 7 Kd 65.34N 44.33 E
Pézenas 11 Jk 43.27N 3.25 E
Pezinok 10 Nh 48.18N 17.16 E
Pfaffenhofen an der Ilm 10 Hh 48.32N 11.31 E
Pfaffenhoffen 12 Jf 48.51N 7.37 E
Pfalz 12 Je 49.20N 7.57 E
Pfalzel, Trier- 12 Ie 49.46N 6.41 E
Pfälzer Bergland 10 Dg 49.35N 7.30 E
Pfälzer Wald 10 Dg 49.15N 7.50 E
Pfarrkirchen 10 Ih 48.26N 12.52 E
Pfinz 12 Ke 49.11N 8.25 E
Pfinztal 12 Ke 49.02N 8.30 E
Pforzheim an der Enz 10 Eh 48.53N 8.42 E
Pfrimm 12 Ke 49.39N 8.22 E
Pfullendorf 10 Fi 47.55N 9.15 E
Pfunds 14 Ed 46.58N 10.33 E
Pfungstadt 12 Ke 49.48N 8.36 E
Phalaborwa 37 Ed 23.55S 31.13 E
Phalodi 25 Ec 27.08N 72.22 E
Phangan, Ko- 25 Jg 9.45N 100.00 E
Phangnga 25 Jg 8.28N 98.32 E
Phan Ly Cham 25 Lf 11.13N 108.31 E
Phanom 25 Jg 8.49N 98.50 E
Phan Rang 25 Lf 11.34N 108.59 E
Phan Thiet 25 Lf 10.56N 108.06 E
Pharr 45 Gm 26.12N 98.11W
Phatthalung 25 Kg 7.38N 100.04 E
Phayao 25 Ke 18.07N 100.11 E
Phenix City 43 Je 32.29N 85.01W
Phet Buri 25 Jf 13.06N 99.56 E
Phetchabun, Thiu Khao- 25 Ke 16.20N 100.55 E
Phichit 25 Ke 16.24N 100.21 E
Philadelphia [Ms.-U.S.] 45 Lj 32.46N 89.07W
Philadelphia [Pa.-U.S.] 39 Lf 39.57N 75.07W
Philae 33 Fe 23.35N 32.52 E
Philip 45 Fd 44.02N 101.40W
Philippeville 11 Kd 50.12N 4.33 E
Philippi 44 Gf 39.08N 80.03W
Philippi (EN) = Filippoi 15 Hh 41.02N 24.18 E
Philippi, Lake- 59 Hd 24.20S 139.00 E
Philippi Glacier 66 Ge 66.45S 88.20 E
Philippine Basin (EN) 3 Ih 17.00N 132.00 E
Philippine Islands (EN) = Pilipinas 21 Oh 13.00N 122.00 E
Philippines (EN)=Pilipinas [1] 22 Oh 13.00N 122.00 E
Philippine Sea (EN) 21 Oh 20.00N 130.00 E
Philippine Trench (EN) 3 Ii 9.00N 127.00 E
Philippsburg 12 Ke 49.14N 8.27 E
Philipsburg [Mt.-U.S.] 46 Ic 46.20N 113.08W
Philipsburg [Neth.Ant.] 50 Ec 18.01N 63.04W
Philip Smith Mountains 40 Jc 68.30N 148.00W
Philipstown 37 Cf 30.26S 24.29 E
Phillipsburg 45 Gg 39.45N 99.19W
Philpots 42 Jb 74.55N 80.00W
Phitsanulok 22 Mh 16.49N 100.15 E
Phnom Penh (EN)=Phnum Pénh 22 Mh 11.33N 104.55 E
Phnum Pénh=Phnom Penh (EN) 22 Mh 11.33N 104.55 E
Phoenix 39 Hf 33.27N 112.05W
Phoenix→Rawaki Atoll 57 Je 3.43S 170.43W
Phoenix Islands 57 Je 4.00S 172.00W
Phôngsali 25 Kd 21.41N 102.06 E
Phrae 25 Ke 18.07N 100.11 E
Phra Nakhom Si Ayutthaya 22 Mh 14.21N 100.33 E
Phrygia 15 Mk 38.30N 29.50 E
Phu Cuong 25 Lf 10.58N 106.39 E
Phuket 22 Li 7.54N 98.24 E
Phuket, Ko- 21 Li 8.00N 98.20 E
Phulbani 25 Gd 20.28N 84.14 E
Phumĭ Mlu Prey 25 Lf 13.48N 105.16 E
Phumĭ Sâmraông 25 Kf 14.11N 103.31 E
Phu My 25 Lf 14.10N 109.03 E
Phuoc Binh 25 Lf 11.50N 106.58 E
Phu Quoc, Dao- 25 Kf 10.12N 104.00 E
Phu Tho 25 Ld 21.24N 105.13 E
Phu Vinh 25 Lg 9.56N 106.20 E
Piaanu Pass 64d Ab 7.20N 151.26 E
Piacenza 14 De 45.01N 9.40 E
Piana degli Albanesi 14 Hm 37.59N 13.17 E
Piana Mwanga 36 Ed 7.40S 28.10 E
Piancó 54 Ke 7.12S 37.57W
Pianguan 27 Jd 39.28N 111.32 E
Pianosa [It.] 14 Jh 42.15N 15.45 E
Pianosa [It.] 14 Eh 42.35N 10.05 E
Piaseczno 10 Rd 52.05N 21.01 E
Piaski 10 Se 51.08N 22.51 E
Piątek 10 Pd 52.05N 19.28 E
Piatra 15 If 43.49N 25.10 E
Piatra Neamţ 15 Jc 46.55N 26.20 E
Piatra Olt 15 He 44.22N 24.16 E
Piauí [2] 54 Je 7.00S 43.00W
Piauí, Rio- 52 Lf 6.38S 42.42W
Piave 5 Hf 45.32N 12.44 E
Piaxtla, Punta- 48 Ff 23.38N 106.50W
Piaxtla, Rio- 48 Ff 23.42N 106.49W
Piazza Armerina 14 Im 37.23N 14.22 E
Pibor 35 Ed 8.26N 33.13 E
Pibor Post 35 Ed 6.48N 33.08 E
Pica 56 Gb 20.30S 69.21W
Picachos, Cerro dos- 48 Bc 29.25N 114.10W
Picardie = Picardy (EN) 11 Je 50.00N 3.30 E
Picardy (EN) = Picardie 11 Je 50.00N 3.30 E
Picayune 45 Lk 30.26N 89.41W
Picentini, Monti- 14 Jj 40.45N 15.10 E
Pichanal 53 Jh 23.20S 64.15W
Pichilemu 56 Fd 34.23S 72.00W
Pichilingue 48 De 24.20N 110.20W
Pichna 10 Oe 51.50N 18.40 E
Pichones, Cayos- 49 Ff 15.45N 82.55W
Pichucalco 48 Mi 17.31N 93.04W
Pickering 9 Mg 54.14N 0.46W
Pickering, Vale of- 9 Mg 54.10N 0.45W
Pickle Lake 42 If 51.29N 90.10W
Pickwick Lake 44 Ch 34.55N 88.10W
Pico 30 Ee 38.28N 28.20W
Picos 53 Lf 7.05S 41.28W
Pico Truncado 56 Gg 46.48S 67.58W
Picquigny 11 Ie 49.57N 2.09 E
Picton 61 Dh 41.18S 174.00 E
Picton 42 Lg 45.41N 62.43W
Picunda 16 Lh 43.12N 40.21 E
Pidurutalagala 21 Ki 7.00N 80.46 E
Piedecuesta 54 Db 6.59N 73.03W
Piedimonte Matese 14 Ii 41.20N 14.22 E
Piedmont [Al.-U.S.] 44 Ei 33.55N 85.37W
Piedmont [Mo.-U.S.] 45 Kh 37.09N 90.42W
Piedmont (EN) = Piemonte [2] 14 Be 45.00N 8.00 E
Piedmont Plateau 38 Kf 35.00N 81.00W
Piedra 13 Kc 41.19N 1.48W
Piedra, Monasterio de- 13 Kc 41.10N 1.50W
Piedrabuena 13 He 39.02N 4.10W
Piedrafita, Puerto de- 13 Fb 42.36N 6.57W
Piedrahita 13 Gd 40.28N 5.19W
Piedras 54 Cd 3.38S 79.54W
Piedras, Punta- 56 Ie 35.25S 57.08W
Piedras, Rio de las- 54 Ef 12.30S 69.14W
Piedras Negras 39 Ig 28.42N 100.31W
Piedras Negras 49 Be 17.12N 91.15W
Piedra Sola 56 Id 32.04S 56.21W
Piekary Śląskie 10 Of 50.24N 18.58 E
Pieksämäki 7 Ge 62.18N 27.08 E
Pielach 14 Jb 48.15N 15.22 E
Pielavesi 7 Ge 63.14N 26.45 E
Pielinen 5 Ic 63.15N 29.40 E
Piemonte = Piedmont (EN) [2] 14 Be 45.00N 8.00 E
Pieniężno 10 Qb 54.15N 20.08 E
Pieni Salpausselkä 8 Lc 61.10N 27.20 E
Piennes 12 He 49.19N 5.47 E
Pienza 14 Fg 43.04N 11.41 E
Pierce 46 Hc 46.29N 115.48W
Piéria Óri 15 Fi 40.12N 22.07 E
Pierre 39 Ie 44.22N 100.21W
Pierrefitte-sur-Aire 12 Hf 48.54N 5.20 E
Pierrefonds 12 Ee 49.21N 2.59 E
Pierrelatte 11 Kj 44.23N 4.42 E
Pieskehaure 7 Dc 66.57N 16.30 E
Piešťány 10 Nh 48.36N 17.50 E
Pietarsaari/Jakobstad 7 Fe 63.40N 22.42 E
Pietermaritzburg 31 Kk 29.37S 30.16 E
Pietersburg 31 Jk 23.54S 29.25 E
Pietraperzia 14 Im 37.25N 14.08 E
Pietrasanta 14 Eg 43.57N 10.14 E
Piet Retief 37 Ee 27.01S 30.50 E
Pietrii, Vîrful- 15 Fd 45.23N 22.40 E
Pietroşani 15 If 43.43N 25.38 E
Pietrosu, Vîrful- [Rom.] 15 Ib 47.08N 25.11 E
Pietrosu, Vîrful- [Rom.] 5 If 47.23N 25.33 E
Pieve di Cadore 14 Gd 46.26N 12.22 E
Pigeon Island 51k Ba 14.06N 60.58W
Pigeon River 45 Lb 48.02N 89.41W
Piggott 45 Kh 36.23N 90.11W
Pigg's Peak 37 Ee 25.58S 31.15 E
Pigs, Bay of- (EN)= Cochinos, Bahia de- 49 Gb 22.07N 81.10W
Pigüé 55 Am 37.37S 62.25W
Pi He 28 Dh 32.26N 116.34 E
Pihkva järv=Pskov, Lake- (EN) 7 Gg 58.00N 28.00 E
Pihlajavesi 7 Gf 61.45N 28.45 E
Pihlava 8 Ic 61.33N 21.36 E
Pihtipudas 7 Fe 63.23N 25.34 E
Piikkiö 8 Jd 60.26N 22.31 E
Piirisaar/Pirissar 8 Lf 58.23N 27.40 E
Pijijiapan 48 Mj 15.42N 93.14W
Pijol, Pico- 49 Df 15.06N 87.35W
Pikalevo 7 Ig 59.32N 34.03 E
Pikangikum 42 If 51.49N 94.00W
Pikelot Island 57 Fd 8.05N 147.38 E
Pikes Peak 43 Fd 38.51N 105.03W
Piketberg 37 Bf 32.54S 18.46 E
Pikiutdleq 41 Hf 64.45N 40.10W
Pikou 28 Ge 39.24N 122.21 E
Pikounda 36 Cb 0.33N 16.42 E
Piła 10 Mc 53.10N 16.44 E
Piła [2] 10 Mc 53.10N 16.45 E
Pila 55 Cm 36.01S 58.08W
Pila, Sierra de la- 13 Kf 38.16N 1.11W
Pilar [Arg.] 55 Bj 31.27S 61.15W
Pilar [Braz.] 54 Ke 9.36S 35.56W
Pilar [Par.] 56 Ic 26.52S 58.23W
Pilas Group 26 He 6.45N 121.35 E
Pilat, Mont- 11 Ki 45.23N 4.35 E
Pilatus 14 Cd 46.59N 8.20 E
Pilaya, Rio- 54 Fh 20.55S 64.04W
Pilcaniyeu 56 Ff 41.08S 70.40W
Pilcomayo, Rio- 52 Kh 25.21S 57.42W
Pile, Jezioro- 10 Mc 53.35N 16.30 E
Pili 15 Ej 39.28N 21.37 E
Pilibhit 25 Fc 28.38N 79.48 E
Pilica 10 Re 51.52N 21.17 E
Pilion Óros 15 Gj 39.24N 23.05 E
Pilipinas=Philippine Islands (EN) 21 Oh 13.00N 122.00 E
Pilipinas=Philippines (EN) [1] 22 Oh 13.00N 122.00 E
Pilis 10 Oi 47.41N 18.53 E
Pillahuincó, Sierra de- 55 Bn 38.18S 60.45W
Pillar, Cape- 59 Jh 43.15S 148.00 E
Pilna 7 Ki 55.33N 45.55 E
Pilões, Rio- 55 Gc 16.14S 50.54W
Pilões, Serra dos- 55 Ic 17.50S 47.13W
Pilón, Rio- 48 Je 25.32N 99.32W
Pilos 15 Em 36.55N 21.42 E
Pilos = Pylos (EN) 15 Em 36.56N 21.40 E
Pilot Peak 46 Hf 41.02N 114.06W
Pilot Rock 46 Fd 45.29N 118.50W
Pilsen (EN)=Plzeň 6 Hf 49.45N 13.24 E
Piltene 7 Eh 57.15N 21.42 E
Pilzno 10 Rg 49.59N 21.17 E
Pim 19 Hc 61.18N 71.57 E
Pimba 59 Hf 31.15S 136.47 E
Pimenteiras 54 Je 6.14S 41.25W
Pimža Jõgi 8 Lg 57.57N 27.59 E
Pina 13 Lc 41.29N 0.32W
Pinacate, Cerro- 48 Cb 31.45N 113.31W
Pinaki Atoll 57 Nf 19.22S 138.44W
Pinamar 55 Dm 37.07S 56.50W
Piñami, Arroyo- 48 Cd 27.44N 113.47W
Pinar 13 Gh 36.46N 5.26W
Pinarbaşi 24 Gc 38.50N 36.30 E
Pinar del Rio 39 Kg 22.25N 83.42W
Pinar del Rio [3] 49 Eb 22.35N 83.40W
Pinarello 11a Bb 41.41N 9.22 E
Pinarhisar 15 Kh 41.37N 27.30 E
Pinchbeck 12 Bb 52.48N 0.09W
Pincher Creek 42 Gg 49.30N 113.48W
Pinçon, Mont- 11 Ff 48.58N 0.37W
Pincota 15 Ec 46.20N 21.42 E
Pindaiba, Ribeirão 55 Gb 14.48S 52.00W
Pindaré, Rio- 54 Jd 3.17S 44.47W
Pindaré-Mirim 54 Id 3.37S 45.21W
Pindaval 55 Dc 17.08S 56.09W
Pindhos Óros=Pindus Mountains (EN) 5 Ih 39.45N 21.30 E
Pindus Mountains (EN)= Pindhos Óros 5 Ih 39.45N 21.30 E
Pine Bluff 43 Ie 34.13N 92.01W
Pine Bluffs 46 Mf 41.11N 104.04W
Pine Creek 59 Gb 13.49S 131.49 E
Pine Falls 42 Hf 50.35N 96.15W
Pinega 19 Ec 64.42N 43.22 E
Pinega 5 Kc 64.08N 41.54 E
Pine Island Glacier 66 Of 75.00S 101.00W
Pineland 45 Jk 31.15N 93.58W
Pine Mountain [Ga.-U.S.] 44 Ei 32.51N 84.47W
Pine Mountain [U.S.] 44 Fg 36.55N 83.20W
Pine Pass 42 Fe 55.50N 122.30W
Pine Point 39 Hc 61.01N 114.15W
Pine Ridge 45 Ee 43.02N 102.33W
Pinerolo 14 Bf 44.53N 7.21 E
Pines, Isle of- (EN)= Juventud, Isla de la- 38 Kg 21.40N 82.50W
Pines, Isle of- (EN)=Pins, Ile des- 57 Hg 22.37S 167.30 E
Pines, Lake O' The- 45 Ij 32.46N 94.35W
Pinetown 37 Ee 29.52S 30.46 E
Ping 21 Mh 15.42N 100.09 E
Pingbian 27 Hg 22.56N 103.46 E
Pingchang 27 Ie 31.38N 107.06 E
Pingding 28 Bf 37.48N 113.37 E
Pingdingbu → Guyuan 28 Cd 41.40N 115.41 E
Pingding Shan 27 Mb 46.39N 128.30 E
Pingdingshan 27 Je 33.41N 113.27 E
Pingdu 28 Ef 36.47N 119.57 E
Pingelap Atoll 57 Hd 6.13N 160.42 E
Pingelly 59 Df 32.32S 117.05 E
Pinggu 28 Dd 40.08N 117.07 E
Pingguo 27 Ig 23.21N 107.34 E
Pinghu 28 Fi 30.42N 121.02 E
Pingjiang 28 Bj 28.45N 113.37 E
Pingle 27 Jg 24.43N 110.42 E
Pingli 27 Ie 32.27N 109.21 E
Pingliang 22 Mf 35.32N 106.41 E
Pinglu (Jingping) 28 Be 39.32N 112.14 E
Pingluo 22 Mf 38.56N 106.34 E
Pingma → Tiandong 27 Ig 23.40N 107.09 E
Pingnan 27 Jg 23.38N 110.23 E
Pingouins, Ile des- 30 Mm 46.25S 50.19 E
Pingquan 27 Kc 41.00N 118.36 E
Pingshan 28 Ce 38.21N 114.01 E
Pingshun 28 Bf 36.12N 113.26 E
Pingtan 27 Kf 25.31N 119.48 E
Pingtung 27 Lg 22.40N 120.29 E
Pingüicas, Cerro- 48 Jg 21.10N 99.42W
Pingvallavatn 7a Bb 64.15N 21.09W
Pingvellir 7a Bb 64.17N 21.03W
Pingwu 27 He 32.27N 104.35 E
Pingxiang [China] 27 Ig 22.11N 106.46 E
Pingxiang [China] 27 Jf 27.43N 113.48 E
Pingyang 27 Lf 27.40N 120.35 E
Pingyao 27 Jd 37.12N 112.13 E
Pingyi 28 Dg 35.30N 117.38 E
Pingyin 28 Df 36.17N 116.26 E
Pingyu 28 Ci 32.58N 114.36 E
Pingyuan 28 Df 37.10N 116.25 E
Pinhal 55 If 22.12S 46.45W
Pinhão 55 Gg 25.43S 51.38W
Pinheir Machado 55 Fj 31.34S 53.23W
Pinhel 13 Ed 40.46N 7.04W
Pini, Pulau- 26 Cf 0.08N 98.40 E
Piniós [Grc.] 15 Fj 39.53N 22.44 E
Piniós [Grc.] 15 El 37.48N 21.14 E
Pinipel 63a Ba 4.24S 154.08 E
Pinjug 7 Lf 60.16N 47.54 E
Pinka 10 Mi 47.00N 16.35 E
Pink Mountain 42 Fe 56.06N 122.35W
Pinnaroo 59 Ig 35.16S 140.55 E
Pinneberg 10 Fc 53.39N 9.48 E
Pinnes, Ákra- 15 Hi 40.07N 24.18 E
Pinolosean 26 Hf 0.23N 124.07 E
Pinos 48 If 22.18N 101.34W
Pinos, Mount- 38 Hf 34.50N 119.09W
Pinos-Puente 13 Ig 37.15N 3.45W
Pinrang 26 Gg 3.48S 119.38 E
Pins, Cap des- 63b Ce 21.04S 167.28 E
Pins, Ile des-=Pines, Isle of- (EN) 57 Hg 22.37S 167.30 E
Pins, Pointe aux- 44 Gd 42.15N 81.51W
Pinsk 19 Ce 52.08N 26.06 E
Pinta, Isla- 54a Aa 0.35N 90.44W
Pintas, Sierra de las- 48 Bb 31.40N 115.10W
Pinto [Arg.] 56 Hc 29.09S 62.39W
Pinto [Sp.] 13 Id 40.14N 3.41W
Pintwater Range 46 Hh 36.55N 115.30W
Pio 63a Ed 10.12S 161.42 E
Pioche 46 Hh 37.56N 114.27W
Piombino 14 Eh 42.55N 10.32 E
Piombino, Canale di- 14 Eh 42.55N 10.30 E
Pioneer Mountains 46 Id 45.40N 113.00W
Pioner, Ostrov- 21 Lb 79.50N 92.30 E
Pionerski [R.S.F.S.R.] 19 Gc 61.12N 62.57 E
Pionerski [R.S.F.S.R.] 7 Ei 54.57N 20.13 E
Pionki 10 Re 51.30N 21.27 E
Piorini, Lago- 54 Fd 3.35S 63.15W
Piorini, Rio- 54 Fd 3.23S 63.30W
Piotrków [2] 10 Pe 51.25N 19.40 E
Piotrków Trybunalski 10 Pe 51.25N 19.42 E
Piove di Sacco 14 Ge 45.18N 12.02 E
Pipa Dingzi 27 Mc 43.57N 128.14 E
Pipéri 15 Hj 39.19N 24.21 E
Pipestone 45 Hd 44.01N 96.19W
Pipestone Creek 45 Fb 49.42N 100.45W
Pipi 35 Cd 7.27N 22.48 E
Pipinas 55 Dl 35.32S 57.20W
Pipmouacan, Réservoir - 42 Kg 49.40N 70.20W
Piqan → Shanshan 27 Fc 42.52N 90.10 E
Piqua 44 Ee 40.08N 84.14W
Piqueras, Puerto de- 13 Jb 42.03N 2.32W
Piquiri, Rio- 56 Jb 24.03S 54.14W
Piquiri, Serra do- 55 Fg 24.53S 52.25W
Piracanjuba 55 Hc 17.18S 49.01W
Piracanjuba, Rio- [Braz.] 55 Hd 18.14S 48.48W
Piracanjuba, Rio- [Braz.] 55 Hc 17.18S 48.13W
Piracema 55 Je 20.31S 44.29W
Piracicaba 56 Kb 22.43S 47.38W
Piracicaba, Rio- 55 Hf 22.36S 48.19W
Piraçununga 55 Ie 21.59S 47.25W
Piracuruca 54 Jd 3.56S 41.42W
Piraeus (EN) = Piraiévs 6 Ih 37.57N 23.38 E
Pirai do Sul 55 Hg 24.31S 49.56W
Piraiévs = Piraeus (EN) 6 Ih 37.57N 23.38 E
Piraju 55 Hf 23.12S 49.23W
Pirajuí 55 He 21.59S 49.29W
Piramide, Cerro- 52 Ij 49.01S 73.32W
Piran 14 He 45.32N 13.34 E
Pirané 56 Ic 25.43S 59.06W
Piranhas 55 Gc 16.31S 51.51W
Piranhas, Rio- 55 Gc 16.01S 51.52W
Pirān Shahr 24 Kd 36.40N 45.05 E
Pirapora 53 Lg 17.21S 44.56W
Pirarajá 56 Jd 33.44S 54.45W
Pirate Well 49 Kb 22.26N 73.04W
Piratini 55 Fj 31.27S 53.06W
Piratini, Rio- 55 Fk 32.01S 52.25W
Piratinim, Rio- 55 Ei 28.06S 55.27W
Pirdop 15 Hg 42.42N 24.11 E
Pirenópolis 55 Hb 15.51S 48.57W
Pires do Rio 54 Ig 17.18S 48.17W
Pirgos 15 El 37.41N 21.27 E
Pirgós 15 Fi 40.38N 22.44 E
Piriápolis 55 El 34.54S 55.17W
Pirin 15 Gh 41.40N 23.30 E
Pirineos=Pyrenees (EN) 5 Gg 42.40N 1.00 E
Pirineus, Serra dos- 55 Hc 16.15S 49.10W
Piripiri 54 Jd 4.16S 41.47W
Pirissar/Piirisaar 8 Lf 58.23N 27.40 E
Piritu 50 Bh 9.23N 69.12W
Piritu, Islas- 50 Dg 10.10N 64.56W
Pirizal 55 Dc 16.16S 56.23W
Pirjatin 16 Hd 50.14N 32.30 E
Pirmasens 10 Dg 49.12N 7.36 E
Pirna 10 Jf 50.58N 13.56 E
Piron 63a Ad 11.20S 153.27 E
Pirón 13 Hc 41.23N 4.31W
Pirot 15 Ff 43.09N 22.36 E
Pirre, Cerro- 49 Ij 7.49N 77.43W
Pirrit Hills 66 Pg 81.17S 85.21W
Pirsagat 16 Pj 39.53N 49.19 E
Pīr Tāj 24 Me 35.45N 48.07 E
Pirttikyla/Pörtom 8 Ib 62.42N 21.37 E
Piru 26 Ig 3.04S 128.12 E
Pis 64d Ba 7.41N 151.46 E
Pisa 14 Eg 43.43N 10.23 E
Pisa 10 Rc 53.15N 21.52 E
Pisagua 56 Fa 19.36S 70.13W

Index Symbols

[1] Independent Nation
[2] State, Region
[3] District, County
[4] Municipality
[5] Colony, Dependency
Continent
Physical Region
Historical or Cultural Region
Mount, Mountain
Volcano
Hill
Mountains, Mountain Range
Hills, Escarpment
Plateau, Upland
Pass, Gap
Plain, Lowland
Delta
Salt Flat
Valley, Canyon
Crater, Cave
Karst Features
Depression
Polder
Desert, Dunes
Forest, Woods
Heath, Steppe
Oasis
Cape, Point
Coast, Beach
Cliff
Peninsula
Isthmus
Sandbank
Island
Atoll
Rock, Reef
Islands, Archipelago
Rocks, Reefs
Coral Reef
Well, Spring
Geyser
River, Stream
Waterfall Rapids
River Mouth, Estuary
Lake
Salt Lake
Intermittent Lake
Reservoir
Swamp, Pond
Canal
Glacier
Ice Shelf, Pack Ice
Ocean
Sea
Gulf, Bay
Strait, Fjord
Lagoon
Bank
Seamount
Tablemount
Ridge
Shelf
Basin
Escarpment, Sea Scarp
Fracture
Trench, Abyss
National Park, Reserve
Point of Interest
Recreation Site
Cave, Cavern
Historic Site
Ruins
Wall, Walls
Church, Abbey
Temple
Scientific Station
Airport
Port
Lighthouse
Mine
Tunnel
Dam, Bridge

Pisano 14 Eg 43.46N 10.33 E
Pisar 64d Cb 7.19N 152.01 E
Pisciotta 14 Jj 40.06N 15.14 E
Pisco 53 Ig 13.42 S 76.13W
Pişcolt 15 Fb 47.35N 22.18 E
Písek 10 Kg 49.19N 14.10 E
Pishan/Guma 27 Cd 37.38N 78.19 E
Pīsh Qal'eh 24 Qd 37.35N 57.05 E
Pīshvā 24 Ne 35.18N 51.44 E
Piso Firme 55 Ba 13.41 S 61.52W
Pissa 7 Ei 54.39N 21.50 E
Pisshiri-Dake 29a Ba 44.20N 141.55 E
Pista 7 Hd 65.28N 30.45 E
Pisticci 14 Kj 40.23N 16.33 E
Pistoia 14 Eg 43.55N 10.54 E
Pisuerga 13 Hc 41.33N 4.52W
Pisz 10 Rc 53.38N 21.49 E
Pita 34 Cc 11.05N 12.24W
Pitalito 54 Cc 1.53N 76.02W
Pitanga 56 Jb 24.46 S 51.44W
Pitanga, Serra da- 55 Gg 24.52 S 51.48W
Pitangui 55 Jd 19.40 S 44.54W
Pitcairn [5] 58 Og 24.00 S 129.00W
Pitcairn Island 57 Ng 25.04 S 130.05W
Piteå 7 Ed 65.20N 21.30 E
Piteälven 5 Ib 65.14N 21.32 E
Piteşti 6 Ig 44.51N 24.52 E
Pithiviers 11 If 48.10N 2.15 E
Pithorāgarh 25 Gc 29.35N 80.13 E
Piti 36 Fd 7.00 S 32.44 E
Piti 64c Bb 13.28N 144.41 E
Pitiquito 48 Cb 30.42N 112.02W
Pitkjaranta 19 Dc 61.35N 31.31 E
Pitkkala 8 Jc 61.28N 23.34 E
Pitljar 20 Bc 65.52N 65.55 E
Pitlochry 9 Je 56.43N 3.45W
Pitomača 14 Le 45.57N 17.14 E
Piton, Pointe du- 51e Ba 16.30N 61.27W
Pit River 43 Cc 40.45N 122.22W
Pitrufquén 56 Fe 38.59 S 72.39W
Pitt 42 Ef 53.40N 129.50W
Pitt Island 57 Ji 44.20 S 176.10W
Pittsburg 43 Id 37.25N 94.42W
Pittsburgh 39 Le 40.26N 80.00W
Pittsfield [Il.-U.S.] 45 Kg 39.36N 90.48W
Pittsfield [Ma.-U.S.] 44 Kd 42.27N 73.15W
Pittsfield [Me.-U.S.] 44 Mc 44.47N 69.23W
Pitt Strait 62 Jf 44.10 S 176.20W
Pitu 26 If 1.41N 128.01 E
Piūí 55 Je 20.28 S 45.58W
Piura 53 Hf 5.12 S 80.38W
Piura [2] 54 Be 5.00 S 80.20W
Piuthān 25 Gc 28.06N 82.52 E
Piva 15 Bf 43.21N 18.51 E
Pivan 20 If 50.27N 137.05 E
Pivijay 49 Jh 10.28N 74.38W
Pižma [R.S.F.S.R.] 7 Lh 57.36N 48.58 E
Pižma [R.S.F.S.R.] 17 Fd 65.24N 52.05 E
Pizzo 14 Kl 38.44N 16.40 E
Pjakupur 20 Cd 65.00N 77.48 E
Pjalica 7 Jc 66.12N 39.32 E
Pjalma 19 Dc 62.27N 35.53 E
Pjana 7 Ki 55.37N 45.58 E
Pjandž 19 Gh 37.15N 69.07 E
Pjandž 21 If 37.06N 68.20 E
Pjaozero, Ozero- 5 Jb 66.05N 30.55 E
Pjarnu/Pärnu 6 Id 58.24N 24.32 E
Pjarnu/Pärnu Jõgi 7 Fg 58.23N 24.34 E
Pjarnu, Zaliv-/Pärnu Laht 7 Fg 58.15N 24.25 E
Pjarnu-Jagupi/Pärnu-Jaagupi 8 Kf 58.36N 24.25 E
Pjasina 21 Kb 73.47N 87.01 E
Pjasino, Ozero- 20 Dc 69.45N 87.30 E
Pjasinski Zaliv 20 Db 74.00N 85.00 E
Pjatigorsk 6 Kg 44.03N 43.04 E
Pjatihatki 16 He 48.27N 33.40 E
Pjórsá 5 Dc 63.45N 20.50W
Pjussi/Püssi 8 Le 59.17N 26.57 E
Pkulagalid 64a Bb 7.36N 134.33 E
Pkulagasemieg 64a Ac 7.08N 134.23 E
Pkurengel 64a Ac 7.27N 134.28 E
Plá 55 Bl 35.07 S 60.13W
Placentia 42 Mg 47.14N 53.58W
Placentia Bay 38 Ne 47.15N 54.30W
Placer 26 Hd 11.52N 123.55 E
Placerville 46 Eg 38.43N 120.48W
Placetas 47 Id 22.19N 79.40W
Plácido Rosas 55 Fk 32.45 S 53.44W
Plačkovci 15 Ig 42.49N 25.28 E
Plačkovica 15 Fh 41.46N 22.32 E
Plainfield 44 Je 40.37N 74.25W
Plains [Mt.-U.S.] 46 Hc 47.27N 114.53W
Plains [Tx.-U.S.] 45 Ej 33.11N 102.50W
Plainview [Nb.-U.S.] 45 He 42.21N 97.47W
Plainview [Tx.-U.S.] 43 Ge 34.11N 101.43W
Plainville 45 Gg 39.14N 99.18W
Pláka, Ákra- 15 Ii 40.02N 25.25 E
Plake 15 Eh 41.14N 21.02 E
Plampang 26 Gh 8.48 S 117.48 E
Planá 10 Ig 49.52N 12.44 E
Plana Cays 49 Kb 22.37N 73.33W
Plana o Nueva Tabarca, Isla- 13 Lf 38.10N 0.28W
Planco, Peñón- 48 Ge 24.35N 104.15W
Plane, Ile- 13 Li 35.46N 0.54W
Planeta Rica 54 Cb 8.25N 75.35W
Planet Depth (EN) 3 Hi 10.20 S 110.30 E
Planézes 11 Ij 45.00N 2.50 E
Plankinton 45 Ge 43.43N 98.29W
Plantation 44 Gl 26.05N 80.14W
Plantaurel 11 Hk 43.04N 1.30 E
Plant City 44 Fk 28.01N 82.08W
Plasencia 13 Fd 40.02N 6.05W
Plast 19 Ge 54.22N 60.55 E
Plaster Rock 44 Nb 46.54N 67.24W
Plastun 20 Ih 44.48N 136.17 E
Plasy 10 Jg 49.56N 13.24 E
Plata, Río de la- [P.R.] 51a Bb 18.30N 66.14W
Plata, Río de la- [S.Amer.] 52 Ki 35.00 S 57.00W
Plataiaí 15 Gk 38.13N 23.16 E
Platani 14 Hm 37.24N 13.16 E
Plateau [2] 34 Gd 8.50N 9.00 E
Plateau [3] 36 Cc 2.10 S 15.00 E
Plateau, Khorat- 21 Mh 15.30N 102.50 E
Plateaux [3] 34 Fd 7.30N 1.10 E
Platen, Kapp- 41 Ob 80.31N 22.48 E
Platí 15 Fi 40.39N 22.32 E
Plato 54 Db 9.47N 74.47W
Platte 45 Ge 43.23N 98.51W
Platte 38 Je 43.23N 98.51W
Platte Island 30 Mi 5.52 S 55.23 E
Platte River 45 Ig 39.16N 94.50W
Platteville 45 Ke 42.44N 90.29W
Plattsburgh 43 Mc 44.42N 73.29W
Plattsmouth 45 If 41.01N 95.53W
Plau 10 Ic 53.27N 12.16 E
Plauen 10 If 50.30N 12.08 E
Plauer See 10 Ic 53.30N 12.20 E
Plav 15 Cg 42.36N 19.57 E
Plavecký Mikuláš 10 Nh 48.30N 17.18 E
Pļaviņas/Pljavinjas 7 Fh 56.38N 25.46 E
Plavsk 16 Jc 53.43N 37.18 E
Playa Azul 47 De 17.59N 102.24W
Playa Noriega, Laguna- 48 Dc 29.10N 111.50W
Playa Vicente 48 Li 17.50N 95.49W
Playón Chico 49 Hi 9.18N 78.14W
Pleasanton [Ks.-U.S.] 45 Ig 38.11N 94.43W
Pleasanton [Tx.-U.S.] 45 Gl 28.58N 98.29W
Pleasant Point 62 Df 44.16 S 171.08 E
Pleasant Valley 45 Fi 35.15N 101.48W
Plechý 10 Jh 48.49N 13.53 E
Pleiku 25 Lf 13.59N 108.00 E
Pleiße 10 Ie 51.20N 12.22 E
Plekinge 8 Fh 56.20N 15.05 E
Pleniţa 15 Ge 44.13N 23.11 E
Plenty, Bay of- 57 Ih 37.45 S 177.10 E
Plentywood 43 Gb 48.47N 104.34W
Pleščenicy 16 Eb 54.29N 27.55 E
Pleseck 19 Ec 62.44N 40.18 E
Plešivec 10 Qh 48.33N 20.25 E
Pleşu, Vîrful- 15 Fc 46.32N 22.11 E
Pleszew 10 Ne 51.54N 17.48 E
Plétipi, Lac - 42 Kf 51.42N 70.08W
Plettenberg 12 Jc 51.13N 7.53 E
Plettenbergbaai 37 Cf 34.03 S 23.22 E
Pleven [2] 15 Hf 43.25N 24.37 E
Pleven 6 Ig 43.25N 24.37 E
Plibo 34 De 4.35N 7.40W
Pliska 15 Kf 43.22N 27.07 E
Pliszka 10 Kd 52.15N 14.40 E
Plitvice 14 Jf 44.54N 15.36 E
Pljavinjas/Pļaviņas 7 Fh 56.38N 25.46 E
Plješevica 14 Jf 44.45N 15.45 E
Pljevlja 15 Cf 43.21N 19.21 E
Pljusa 7 Gg 58.25N 29.20 E
Pljusa 7 Gg 59.13N 28.11 E
Ploča, Rt- 14 Jg 43.30N 15.58 E
Ploče 14 Lg 43.04N 17.26 E
Płock [2] 10 Pd 52.35N 19.45 E
Płock 10 Pd 52.33N 19.43 E
Ploërmel 11 Dg 47.56N 2.24W
Ploieşti 6 Ig 44.57N 26.01 E
Plomárion 15 Jk 38.59N 26.22 E
Plomb du Cantal 11 Ii 45.03N 2.46 E
Plön 10 Gb 54.10N 10.26 E
Płonia 10 Kc 53.25N 14.36 E
Płonka 10 Qd 52.37N 20.30 E
Płońsk 10 Qd 52.38N 20.23 E
Plopana 15 Kc 46.41N 27.13 E
Płoty 10 Lc 53.50N 15.16 E
Plouguerneau 11 Bf 48.36N 4.30W
Plovdiv [2] 15 Hg 42.09N 24.45 E
Plovdiv 6 Ig 42.09N 24.45 E
Plummer 46 Gc 47.20N 116.53W
Plumridge Lakes 59 Fe 29.30 S 125.25 E
Plumtree 37 Dd 20.31 S 27.48 E
Plungė/Plunge 7 Ei 55.56N 21.48 E
Plunge/Plungė 7 Ei 55.56N 21.48 E
Plymouth [Eng.-U.K.] 6 Fe 50.23N 4.10W
Plymouth [In.-U.S.] 44 De 41.21N 86.19W
Plymouth [Ma.-U.S.] 44 Le 41.58N 70.41W
Plymouth [Mont.] 47 Le 16.42N 62.13W
Plymouth Sound 9 Ik 50.25N 4.05W
Plzeň=Pilsen (EN) 6 Hf 49.45N 13.24 E
Plzeňská pahorkatina 10 Jg 49.50N 13.15 E
Pniewy 10 Md 52.31N 16.15 E
Pô 34 Ec 11.10N 1.09W
Po 5 Hg 44.57N 12.05 E
Po, Colline del- 14 Be 45.05N 7.50 E
Po, Foci del-=Po, Mouths of the- (EN) 14 Gf 44.52N 12.30 E
Po, Mouths of the- (EN)=Po, Foci del- 14 Gf 44.52N 12.30 E
Poarta de Fier a Transilvaniei, Pasul- 15 Fd 45.25N 22.40 E
Poarta Orientală, Pasul- 15 Fd 45.08N 22.20 E
Poás, Volcán- 49 Eh 10.11N 84.13W
Pobé 34 Fd 6.58N 2.41 E
Pobeda, Gora- 21 Qc 65.12N 146.12 E
Pobeda Ice Island 66 Ge 64.30 S 97.00 E
Pobedy, Pik- 21 Ke 42.02N 80.05 E
Pobla de Segur/La Pobla de Segur 13 Mb 42.15N 0.58 E
Poblet, Monasterio de-/Poblet, Monèstir de- 13 Nc 41.20N 1.05 E
Poblet, Monèstir de-/Poblet, Monasterio de- 13 Nc 41.20N 1.05 E
Pobrežije 15 Jf 43.56N 26.21 E
Pocahontas 45 Kh 36.16N 90.58W
Pocatello 39 He 42.52N 112.27W
Počep 16 Hc 52.57N 33.28 E
Pocerina 15 Ce 44.38N 19.35 E
Počinok 19 De 54.23N 32.29 E
Počitelj 14 Lg 43.08N 17.44 E
Pocito, Sierra del- 13 He 39.20N 4.05W
Pocito Casas 48 Dc 28.32N 111.06W
Pocklington Reef 60 Fj 11.00 S 155.00 E
Poções 54 Jf 14.31 S 40.21W
Poço Fundo, Cachoeira- 55 Jc 16.10 S 45.51W
Poconé 54 Gg 16.15 S 56.37W
Pocono Mountains 44 Je 41.10N 75.20W
Poços de Caldas 54 Ih 21.48 S 46.34W
Pocri 49 Gj 7.40N 80.07W
Podborovje [R.S.F.S.R.] 8 Mg 57.51N 28.46 E
Podborovje [R.S.F.S.R.] 7 Ig 59.32N 35.01 E
Podbrezová 10 Ph 48.49N 19.31 E
Podčerje 17 He 63.55N 57.30 E
Poděbrady 10 Lf 50.09N 15.07 E
Podgajcy 10 Vg 49.12N 25.12 E
Podgorina 15 Ce 44.15N 19.56 E
Po di Volano 14 Gf 44.49N 12.15 E
Podjuga 7 Jf 61.07N 40.54 E
Podkamennaja Tunguska=Stony Tunguska (EN) 21 Lc 61.36N 90.18 E
Podlasie 10 Sd 52.30N 23.00 E
Podlaska, Nizina- 10 Sc 53.00N 22.45 E
Podlužje 15 Ce 44.45N 19.55 E
Podolia (EN)=Podolskaja Vozvyšennost 5 If 49.00N 28.00 E
Podolsk 19 Dd 55.27N 37.33 E
Podolskaja Vozvyšennost=Podolia (EN) 5 If 49.00N 28.00 E
Podor 34 Cb 16.40N 14.57W
Podporožje 19 Dc 60.54N 34.09 E
Podravina 14 Le 45.40N 17.40 E
Podravska Slatina 14 Le 45.42N 17.42 E
Podrima 15 Dg 42.24N 20.33 E
Podromanija 14 Mg 43.54N 18.46 E
Podsvilje 8 Mi 55.09N 28.01 E
Podujevo 15 Eg 42.55N 21.12 E
Podunajská nížina 10 Nh 48.00N 17.40 E
Podvološino 20 Fe 58.15N 108.25 E
Poel 10 Hb 54.00N 11.26 E
Poeniţa, Vîrful- 15 Gc 46.15N 23.20 E
Pofadder 37 Be 29.10 S 19.22 E
Pogăniş 15 Ed 45.41N 21.21 E
Pogar 16 Hc 52.33N 33.16 E
Poggibonsi 14 Fg 43.28N 11.09 E
Pöggstall 14 Jb 48.19N 15.11 E
Pogibi 20 Jf 52.15N 141.45 E
Pogny 12 Gf 48.52N 4.29 E
Pogoanele 15 Je 44.55N 27.00 E
Pogórze Karpackie 10 Qg 49.52N 21.00 E
Pogradeci 15 Di 40.54N 20.39 E
Pograničny 20 Ih 44.26N 131.20 E
Pogrebišče 16 Fe 49.29N 29.14 E
Poguba Xoréu, Rio- 55 Ec 16.29 S 54.58W
P'ohang 27 Md 36.02N 129.22 E
Pohja/Pojo 8 Jd 60.06N 23.31 E
Pohjankangas 8 Jc 62.00N 22.30 E
Pohjanlahti=Bothnia, Gulf of- (EN) 5 Hc 63.00N 20.00 E
Pohjanmaa 8 Jb 63.00N 22.30 E
Pohjois-Karjala [2] 7 Ge 63.00N 30.00 E
Pohlheim 12 Kd 50.32N 8.42 E
Pohorje 14 Jd 46.32N 15.28 E
Po Hu 28 Di 30.15N 116.32 E
Pohue Bay 65a Fd 19.01N 155.48W
Pohvistnevo 19 Fe 53.40N 52.08 E
Poiana Mare 15 Gf 43.55N 23.04 E
Poiana Ruscă, Munţii 15 Fd 45.41N 22.30 E
Pöide/Pějde 8 Jf 58.30N 22.50 E
Poie 36 Dc 2.55 S 23.10 E
Poindimié 61 Cd 20.56 S 165.20 E
Poindo → Lhünzhub 27 Fe 30.17N 91.20 E
Poinsett, Cape- 66 He 65.42 S 113.18 E
Poinsett, Lake- 45 Hd 44.34N 97.05W
Point Arena 46 Dg 38.55N 123.41W
Point au Fer Island 45 Kl 29.15N 91.15W
Pointe-à-Pitre 47 Le 16.14N 61.32W
Pointe Duble 51e Bb 16.20N 61.00W
Pointe-Noire 51e Ab 16.14N 61.47W
Pointe Noire 31 Ii 4.48 S 11.51 E
Point Hope 40 Fc 68.21N 166.41W
Point Lake 42 Gc 65.15N 113.00W
Point Lay 40 Gc 69.45N 163.03W
Point Pleasant [N.J.-U.S.] 44 Je 40.06N 74.02W
Point Pleasant [W.V.-U.S.] 44 Ff 38.53N 82.07W
Poisson-Blanc, Lac- 44 Jc 46.00N 75.44W
Poissonnier Point 59 Dc 20.00 S 119.10 E
Poissy 11 If 48.56N 2.03 E
Poitevin, Marais- 11 Eh 46.22N 1.06W
Poitiers 6 Gf 46.35N 0.20 E
Poitou 11 Fh 46.40N 0.30W
Poitou, Plaines et Seuil du- 11 Gh 46.26N 0.17 E
Poivre Islands 37b Bb 5.46 S 53.19 E
Poix-de-Picardie 11 He 49.47N 1.59 E
Poix-Terron 12 Ge 49.39N 4.39 E
Pojarkovo 20 Hg 49.42N 128.50 E
Pojkovski 19 Hc 60.59N 72.00 E
Pojo/Pohja 8 Jd 60.06N 23.31 E
Pojuba, Rio- 55 Ec 16.30 S 54.59W
Pokaran 25 Ec 26.55N 71.55 E
Pokhara 25 Gc 28.14N 83.59 E
Poko 36 Eb 3.09N 26.53 E
Pokoinu 64p Bb 21.12 S 159.49W
Pokój 10 Nf 50.56N 17.50 E
Pokrovka 18 Lc 42.19N 78.01 E
Pokrovsk 20 Hd 61.29N 129.10 E
Pokrovskoje [R.S.F.S.R.] 16 Jc 52.38N 36.51 E
Pokrovskoje [Ukr.-U.S.S.R.] 16 Jf 47.59N 36.13 E
Pokšenga 7 Kd 64.01N 44.15 E
Pokutje 15 Ia 48.20N 25.05 E
Pola 7 Hg 58.05N 31.40 E
Polabí 10 Lf 50.10N 15.10 E
Polacca 46 Ji 35.50N 110.23W
Pola de Laviana 13 Ga 43.15N 5.34W
Pola de Lena 13 Ga 43.10N 5.49W
Pola de Siero 13 Ga 43.23N 5.40W
Polanco 55 Ek 33.54 S 55.09W
Poland 64g Ab 1.52N 157.33W
Poland (EN)=Polska [1] 6 He 52.00N 19.00 E
Polanów 10 Mb 54.08N 16.39 E
Polar Plateau 66 Cg 90.00 S 0.00
Polar Urals (EN)=Poljarny Ural 5 Mb 66.55N 64.30 E
Polatlı 23 Db 39.36N 32.09 E
Polch 12 Jd 50.18N 7.19 E
Połczyn Zdrój 10 Mc 53.46N 16.06 E
Pol-e Khomrī 23 Kb 35.56N 68.43 E
Pole of Inaccessibility (EN) 66 Eg 82.06 S 54.58 E
Pol-e-Safīd 24 Od 36.06N 53.01 E
Polesella 14 Ff 44.58N 11.45 E
Polesie Lubelskie 10 Te 51.30N 23.20 E
Polesine 14 Fe 45.00N 11.45 E
Polesje=Polesye (EN) 5 Ie 52.00N 27.00 E
Polessk 8 Ij 54.51N 21.02 E
Polesskoje 16 Fd 51.16N 29.27 E
Polesye (EN)=Polesje 5 Ie 52.00N 27.00 E
Polevskoj 19 Gd 56.28N 60.11 E
Polewali 26 Gg 3.25 S 119.20 E
Poležan 15 Gh 41.43N 23.30 E
Polgár 10 Ri 47.52N 21.07 E
Pŏlgyo 28 Ig 34.51N 127.21 E
Poli 34 Hd 8.29N 13.15 E
Políaigos 15 Hm 36.46N 24.38 E
Poliçani 15 Di 40.08N 20.21 E
Policastro, Golfo di- 14 Jk 40.00N 15.35 E
Police 10 Kc 53.33N 14.35 E
Policoro 14 Kj 40.13N 16.41 E
Poligny 11 Lh 46.50N 5.43 E
Poligus 20 Ed 61.58N 94.40 E
Políkastron 15 Fh 41.00N 22.34 E
Polikhnítos 15 Jj 39.05N 26.11 E
Polillo Islands 21 Oh 14.50N 122.05 E
Pólis 24 Ee 35.02N 32.25 E
Polist 7 Hg 58.07N 31.32 E
Polistena 14 Kl 38.24N 16.04 E
Políyros 15 Gi 40.23N 23.27 E
Poljarny [R.S.F.S.R.] 19 Db 69.13N 33.28 E
Poljarny [R.S.F.S.R.] 20 Mc 69.01N 178.45 E
Poljarny Ural=Polar Urals (EN) 5 Mb 66.55N 64.30 E
Polkowice 10 Me 51.32N 16.06 E
Pöllau 14 Jc 47.18N 15.50 E
Polle 64d Bb 7.20N 151.15 E
Pollença/Pollensa 13 Pe 39.53N 3.01 E
Pollensa/Pollença 13 Pe 39.53N 3.01 E
Pollino 5 Hh 39.55N 16.10 E
Polochic, Río- 49 Cf 15.28N 89.22W
Polock 19 Cd 55.29N 28.52 E
Polog 15 Dh 42.00N 21.00 E
Pologi 19 Df 47.28N 36.15 E
Polonina 10 Jh 48.30N 23.30 E
Polonnaruwa 25 Gg 7.56N 81.00 E
Polonnoje 16 Ed 50.06N 27.29 E
Polousny Krjaž 20 Jc 69.30N 144.00 E
Polska=Poland (EN) [1] 6 He 52.00N 19.00 E
Polski Gradec 15 Jg 42.11N 26.06 E
Polski Trămbeš 15 If 43.22N 25.38 E
Polson 46 Hc 47.41N 114.09W
Poltár 10 Ph 48.27N 19.48 E
Poltava 6 Jf 49.35N 34.34 E
Poltavka 19 He 54.22N 71.45 E
Poltavskaja Oblast [3] 19 Df 49.45N 33.50 E
Põltsamaa/Pyltsamaa 8 Lf 58.23N 26.08 E
Põltsamaa/Pyltsamaa 7 Fg 58.39N 25.59 E
Poluj 20 Bc 66.30N 66.31 E
Polunočnoje 19 Gc 60.52N 60.25 E
Polūr 24 Oe 32.52N 52.03 E
Põlva/Pylva 7 Gg 58.04N 27.06 E
Polvijärvi 7 Ge 62.51N 29.22 E
Polynesia 57 Le 4.00 S 156.00W
Polynésie Française=French Polynesia (EN) [5] 58 Mf 16.00 S 145.00W
Pom, Laguna de- 48 Mh 18.35N 92.15W
Pomarance 14 Eg 43.18N 10.52 E
Pomarkku/Påmark 8 Ic 61.42N 22.00 E
Pombal [Braz.] 54 Ke 6.46 S 37.47W
Pombal [Port.] 13 De 39.55N 8.38W
Pombo, Rio- 55 Fe 20.53 S 52.23W
Pomerania (EN)=Pommern 5 He 54.00N 16.00 E
Pomerania (EN)=Pommern 10 Lc 54.00N 16.00 E
Pomeranian Bay (EN)=Pommersche Bucht 10 Kb 54.20N 14.20 E
Pomeranian Bay (EN)=Pomorska, Zatoka- 10 Kb 54.20N 14.20 E
Pomeroy 44 Ff 39.03N 82.03W
Pomio 58 Ge 5.32 S 151.30 E
Pomme de Terre Reservoir 45 Jh 37.51N 93.19W
Pommern=Pomerania (EN) 10 Lc 54.00N 16.00 E
Pommern=Pomerania (EN) 5 He 54.00N 16.00 E
Pommersche Bucht=Pomeranian Bay (EN) 10 Kb 54.20N 14.20 E
Pommersfelden 10 Gg 49.46N 10.49 E
Pomona 46 Gi 34.04N 117.45W
Pomona Lake 45 Ig 38.40N 95.35W
Pomorije 15 Kg 42.33N 27.39 E
Pomorska, Zatoka-=Pomeranian Bay (EN) 10 Kb 54.20N 14.20 E
Pomorski Bereg 7 Id 64.00N 36.15 E
Pomorskie, Pojezierze- 10 Mc 53.30N 16.30 E
Pomorski Proliv 19 Eb 68.40N 50.00 E
Pomošnaja 16 Ge 48.14N 31.29 E
Pompano Beach 44 Gl 26.15N 80.07W
Pompei 14 Ij 40.45N 14.30 E
Pompeu 55 Jd 19.12 S 44.59W
Ponape 58 Gd 6.52N 158.15 E
Ponape Island 57 Gd 6.55N 158.15 E
Ponca City 43 Hd 36.42N 97.05W
Ponce 39 Mh 18.01N 66.37W
Poncheville, Lac- 44 Ia 50.12N 76.55W
Pondcreek 45 Hh 36.40N 97.48W
Pondicherry 25 Ff 11.56N 79.53 E
Pondicherry [3] 25 Ff 11.55N 79.45 E
Pond Inlet 39 Lb 72.41N 78.00W
Pond Inlet 42 Jb 72.48N 77.00W
Ponea 64n Ac 10.28 S 161.01W
Ponente, Riviera di- 14 Cf 44.10N 8.20 E
Ponérihouen 63b Be 21.05 S 165.24 E
Pones 64d Bb 7.12N 151.59 E
Ponferrada 13 Fb 42.33N 6.35W
Pongaroa 62 Gd 40.33 S 176.11 E
Pongo 30 Jh 8.42N 27.40 E
Pongola 37 Ee 26.52 S 32.20 E
Pong Qu 27 Ef 26.49N 87.09 E
Poniatowa 10 Se 51.11N 22.05 E
Ponoj 6 Kb 67.05N 41.07 E
Ponoj 5 Kb 66.59N 41.10 E
Ponomarevka 16 Sc 53.09N 54.12 E
Ponorogo 26 Fh 7.52 S 111.27 E
Pons 11 Fi 45.35N 0.33W
Pons/Ponts 13 Nc 41.55N 1.12 E
Ponsul 13 Ee 39.40N 7.31W
Pont-à-Celles 12 Gd 50.30N 4.21 E
Ponta Delgada 31 Ee 37.44N 25.40W
Ponta Delgada [3] 32 Bb 37.48N 25.30W
Ponta Grossa 53 Kh 25.05 S 50.09W
Pont-à-Mousson 11 Mf 48.54N 6.04 E
Ponta Porá 53 Kh 22.32 S 55.43W
Pontarlier 11 Mh 46.54N 6.22 E
Pontassieve 14 Fg 43.46N 11.26 E
Pont-Audemer 11 Ge 49.21N 0.31 E
Pontaut 55 Bm 37.44 S 61.20W
Pontávert 12 Fe 49.25N 3.49 E
Pontchartrain, Lake- 43 Ie 30.10N 90.10W
Pontchâteau 11 Dg 47.26N 2.05W
Pont-de-l'Arche 12 De 49.18N 1.10 E
Pont de Suert 13 Mb 42.24N 0.45 E
Pont-de-Vaux 11 Kh 46.26N 4.56 E
Ponte Alta 55 Gh 27.29 S 50.23W
Ponte Alta, Serra da- 55 Id 19.42 S 47.40W
Ponte Branca 55 Fc 16.27 S 52.40W
Pontecorvo 14 Hi 42.27N 13.40 E
Ponte de Lima 13 Dc 41.46N 8.35W
Ponte de Pedra 55 Ec 17.06 S 54.23W
Ponte de Pedrā 55 Da 13.35 S 57.21W
Pontedera 14 Eg 43.40N 10.38 E
Ponte de Sor 13 De 39.15N 8.01W
Ponte Firme, Chapada da- 55 Id 18.05 S 46.25W
Ponteix 46 Lb 49.49N 107.30W
Ponte Nova 54 Jh 20.24 S 42.54W
Pontés e Lacerda 55 Cb 15.11 S 59.21W
Pontevedra [3] 13 Db 42.30N 8.30W
Pontevedra 13 Db 42.26N 8.38W
Pontevedra, Ría de- 13 Db 42.22N 8.45W
Ponte Vermelha 55 Ed 19.29 S 54.25W
Pont-Farcy 12 Af 48.56N 1.02W
Pontfaverger-Moronvilliers 12 Ge 49.18N 4.19 E
Ponthieu 11 Hd 50.10N 1.55 E
Pontiac [Il.-U.S.] 45 Lf 40.53N 88.38W
Pontiac [Mi.-U.S.] 44 Fd 42.37N 83.18W
Pontianak 22 Mj 0.02 S 109.20 E
Pontian Kechil 26 Df 1.29N 103.23 E
Pontine Islands (EN) = Ponziane, Isole- 14 Gj 40.55N 13.00 E
Pontivy 11 Df 48.04N 2.59W
Pontivy, Pays de- 11 Dg 48.00N 3.00W
Pont-l'Abbé 11 Bg 47.52N 4.13W
Pont-l'Evêque 12 Ce 49.18N 0.11 E
Pontoise 11 Ie 49.03N 2.06 E
Pontorson 11 Ef 48.33N 1.31W
Pontremoli 14 Df 44.22N 9.53 E
Pontresina 14 Dd 46.28N 9.53 E
Ponts/Pons 13 Nc 41.55N 1.12 E
Pont-Sainte-Maxence 12 Ee 49.18N 2.36 E
Pont-Saint-Esprit 11 Kj 44.15N 4.39 E
Pontypool 9 Jj 51.43N 3.02W
Ponza 14 Gj 40.54N 12.58 E
Ponza 14 Gj 40.55N 12.55 E
Ponziane, Isole- = Pontine Islands (EN) 14 Gj 40.55N 13.00 E
Pool [3] 36 Bc 3.30 S 15.00 E
Poole 9 Lk 50.43N 1.59W
Poona → Pune 22 Jh 18.32N 73.52 E
Poopó 54 Eg 18.23 S 66.59W
Poopó, Lago de- = Poopó, Lake- (EN) 52 Jg 18.45 S 67.07W
Poopó, Lake- (EN) = Poopó, Lago de- 52 Jg 18.45 S 67.07W
Poor Knights Islands 62 Fa 35.30 S 174.45 E
Pöösaspea Neem/Pyzaspea 8 Je 59.15N 23.25 E
Popakai 54 Gc 3.22N 55.25W
Popayán 53 Ie 2.27N 76.36W
Poperinge 11 Id 50.51N 2.43 E
Poperinge-Watou 12 Ed 50.51N 2.37 E
Popigaj 20 Gb 71.55N 110.47 E
Popigaj 20 Fb 72.55N 106.00 E
Poplar 46 Mb 48.07N 105.12W
Poplar 42 Hf 53.00N 97.18W
Poplar Bluff 43 Id 36.45N 90.24W
Poplar River 46 Mb 48.05N 105.11W
Popocatépetl, Volcán- 38 Jh 19.02N 98.38W
Popokabaka 36 Cd 5.42 S 16.35 E
Popoli 14 Hh 42.10N 13.50 E
Popomanaseu, Mount- 63a Ec 9.42 S 160.03 E
Popondetta 60 Di 8.46 S 148.14 E
Popovo 15 Jf 43.21N 26.14 E
Poppberg 10 Hg 49.20N 11.45 E
Poppel, Ravels- 12 Hc 51.27N 5.02 E
Poprad 10 Qg 49.38N 20.42 E
Poprad 6 If 49.03N 20.19 E
Poptún 49 Ce 16.21N 89.26W
Por 10 Tf 50.48N 23.01 E
Porangahau 62 Gd 40.18 S 176.38 E

Index Symbols

[1] Independent Nation
[2] State, Region
[3] District, County
[5] Municipality
Colony, Dependency
Continent
Physical Region
Historical or Cultural Region
Mount, Mountain
Volcano
Hill
Mountains, Mountain Range
Hills, Escarpment
Plateau, Upland
Pass, Gap
Plain, Lowland
Delta
Salt Flat
Valley, Canyon
Crater, Cave
Karst Features
Depression
Polder
Desert, Dunes
Forest, Woods
Heath, Steppe
Oasis
Cape, Point
Coast, Beach
Cliff
Peninsula
Isthmus
Sandbank
Island
Atoll
Rock, Reef
Islands, Archipelago
Rocks, Reefs
Coral Reef
Well, Spring
Geyser
River, Stream
Waterfall Rapids
River Mouth, Estuary
Lake
Salt Lake
Intermittent Lake
Reservoir
Swamp, Pond
Canal
Glacier
Ice Shelf, Pack Ice
Ocean
Sea
Gulf, Bay
Strait, Fjord
Lagoon
Bank
Seamount
Tablemount
Ridge
Shelf
Basin
Escarpment, Sea Scarp
Fracture
Trench, Abyss
National Park, Reserve
Point of Interest
Recreation Site
Cave, Cavern
Historic Site
Ruins
Wall, Walls
Church, Abbey
Temple
Scientific Station
Airport
Port
Lighthouse
Mine
Tunnel
Dam, Bridge

Porangatu	55	Ha	13.26S	49.10W
Porbandar	25	Dd	21.38N	69.36 E
Porcien	12	Ge	49.40N	4.20 E
Porcos, Rio dos-	55	Ja	12.42S	45.07W
Porcuna	13	Hg	37.52N	4.11W
Porcupine	38	Ec	66.35N	145.15W
Porcupine	44	Ga	48.32N	81.10W
Porcupine Bank (EN)	5	Ee	53.20N	13.30W
Porcupine Hills	46	Ha	50.05N	114.10W
Porcupine Plain	42	Dc	67.30N	137.30W
Pordenone	14	Ge	45.57N	12.39 E
Poreč	14	He	45.13N	13.37 E
Poreč	15	Fe	44.20N	22.05 E
Porecatú	55	Gf	22.43S	51.24W
Porećje	8	Kk	53.53N	24.08 E
Poreckoje	7	Li	55.13N	46.19 E
Porhov	19	Cd	57.45N	29.32 E
Pori/Björneborg	6	Ic	61.29N	21.47 E
Poríon	15	Gn	35.58N	23.16 E
Porirua	61	Dh	41.08S	174.50 E
Pórisvatn	7a	Bb	64.20N	18.55W
Porjus	7	Ec	66.57N	19.49 E
Porkkala	8	Ke	59.55N	24.25 E
Porlamar	54	Fa	10.57N	63.51W
Porma	13	Gb	42.29N	5.28W
Pornic	11	Dg	47.07N	2.06W
Poronajsk	22	Qe	49.14N	143.04 E
Poronin	10	Qg	49.20N	20.04 E
Póros	15	Gl	37.30N	23.31 E
Póros	15	Gl	37.30N	23.27 E
Poroshiri-Dake	28	Qc	42.42N	142.35 E
Porosozero	7	He	62.44N	32.42 E
Porozovo	10	Ud	52.54N	24.27 E
Porpoise Bay	66	Ie	66.30S	128.30 E
Porquis Junction	44	Ga	48.43N	80.52W
Porrentruy	14	Bc	47.25N	7.10 E
Porreras	13	Oe	39.31N	3.00 E
Porretta, Passo della-	14	Ef	44.02N	10.56 E
Porretta Terme	14	Ef	44.09N	10.59 E
Porsangen	5	Ia	70.50N	26.00 E
Porsangerhalvøya	7	Fa	70.50N	25.00 E
Porsgrunn	7	Bg	59.09N	9.40 E
Pórshöfn	7a	Ca	66.10N	15.20W
Porsuk	24	Dc	39.42N	31.59 E
Portachuelo	54	Fg	17.21S	63.24W
Portadown/Port an Dúnáin	9	Gg	54.26N	6.27W
Portage	45	Le	43.33N	89.28W
Portage la Prairie	42	Hg	49.57N	98.18W
Port Alberni	42	Fg	49.14N	124.48W
Portalegre	13	Ee	39.17N	7.26W
Portalegre [2]	13	Ee	39.15N	7.35W
Portales	43	Ge	34.11N	103.20W
Port-Alfred	42	Kg	48.20N	70.53W
Port Alfred	37	Df	33.36S	26.55 E
Port Alice	42	Ef	50.23N	127.27W
Port Allegany	44	He	41.48N	78.18W
Port an Dúnáin/Portadown	9	Gg	54.26N	6.27W
Port Angeles	43	Cb	48.07N	123.27W
Port Antonio	47	Ie	18.11N	76.28W
Port Arthur [Austl.]	59	Jh	43.09S	147.51 E
Port Arthur [Tx.-U.S.]	39	Jg	29.55N	93.55W
Port Arthur (EN)=Lüshun	27	Ld	38.50N	121.13 E
Port Augusta	58	Eh	32.30S	137.46 E
Port-Au-Prince	39	Lh	18.32N	72.20W
Port-au-Prince, Baie de-	49	Kd	18.40N	72.30W
Port Austin	44	Fc	44.03N	83.01W
Port aux Français	31	Om	49.25S	70.10 E
Porta Westfalica	12	Kb	52.15N	8.56 E
Port-Bergé-Vao Vao	37	Hc	15.33S	47.38 E
Port Blair	22	Lh	11.36N	92.45 E
Port-Bou/Portbou	13	Pb	42.25N	3.10 E
Portbou/Port-Bou	13	Pb	42.25N	3.10 E
Port Burwell [Newf.-Can.]	39	Mc	60.25N	64.49W
Port Burwell [Ont.-Can.]	44	Gd	42.39N	80.49W
Port-Cartier	42	Kf	50.01N	66.53W
Port Chalmers	62	Df	45.49S	170.37 E
Port Charlotte	43	Kf	26.59N	82.06W
Port Clinton	44	Fe	41.30N	82.58W
Port Coquitlam	46	Db	49.16N	122.46W
Port-de-Bouc	11	Kk	43.24N	4.59 E
Port-de-Paix	49	Kd	19.57N	72.50W
Port Dickson	26	Df	2.31N	101.48 E
Port Edward	37	Ef	31.03S	30.13 E
Portel [Braz.]	54	Hd	1.57S	50.49W
Portel [Port.]	13	Ef	38.18N	7.42W
Port Elgin	44	Gc	44.26N	81.24W
Port Elizabeth [S.Afr.]	31	Jl	33.58S	25.40 E
Port Elizabeth [St.Vin.]	51n	Ba	13.00N	61.16W
Port Ellen	9	Gf	55.39N	6.12W
Port-en-Bessin-Huppain	11	Fe	49.21N	0.45W
Port Erin	9	Ig	54.05N	4.43W
Porter Point	51n	Ba	13.23N	61.11W
Porterville [Ca.-U.S.]	43	Dd	36.04N	119.01W
Porterville [S.Afr.]	37	Bf	33.00S	19.00 E
Portete, Bahía de-	49	Lg	12.13N	71.55W
Port Fairy	59	Ig	38.23S	142.14 E
Port Fitzroy	62	Fb	36.10S	175.21 E
Port-Gentil	31	Hi	0.43S	8.47 E
Port Gibson	45	Kk	31.58N	90.58W
Port Harcourt	31	Hh	4.46N	7.01 E
Port Hardy	42	Ef	50.43N	127.29W
Port Hawkesbury	42	Lg	45.37N	61.21W
Porthcawl	9	Jj	51.29N	3.43W
Port Hedland	58	Cg	20.19S	118.34 E
Port Heiden	40	He	56.55N	158.41W
Port Hope Simpson	42	Lf	52.30N	56.17W
Port Huron	43	Kc	42.58N	82.27W
Portile de Fier = Iron Gate (EN)	5	Ig	44.41N	22.31 E
Port-Ilič	16	Pj	38.53N	48.51 E
Portimão	13	Dg	37.08N	8.32W
Port Isabel	45	Hm	26.04N	97.13W
Portiţa	15	Le	44.41N	29.00 E
Port Láirge/Waterford [2]	9	Fi	52.10N	7.40W
Port Láirge/Waterford	6	Fe	52.15N	7.06W
Portland [Austl.]	59	Ig	38.21S	141.36 E
Portland [Eng.-U.K.]	9	Kk	50.33N	2.27W
Portland [In.-U.S.]	44	Ee	40.26N	84.59W
Portland [Me.-U.S.]	39	Le	43.39N	70.17W
Portland [N.D.-U.S.]	45	Hc	47.30N	97.22W
Portland [N.Z.]	62	Fa	35.48S	174.20 E
Portland [Or.-U.S.]	39	Ge	45.33N	122.36W
Portland [Tx.-U.S.]	45	Hm	27.53N	97.20W
Portland, Bill of-	9	Kk	50.31N	2.28W
Portland, Promontoire -	42	Je	58.41N	78.33W
Portland Bight	49	Ie	17.57N	77.08W
Portland Island	62	Gc	39.20S	177.50 E
Portland Point	49	Ie	17.42N	77.11W
Port-la-Nouvelle	11	Jk	43.01N	3.03 E
Portlaoise/Port Laoise	9	Fh	53.02N	7.17W
Port Laoise/Portlaoise	9	Fh	53.02N	7.17W
Port Lavaca	43	Hf	28.37N	96.38W
Port Lincoln	58	Eh	34.44S	135.52 E
Port Loko	34	Cd	8.46N	12.47W
Port Louis	50	Fd	16.25N	61.32W
Port-Louis	31	Mk	20.10S	57.30 E
Port Macquarie	59	Kf	31.26S	152.44 E
Portmadoc	9	Ii	52.55N	4.08W
Port Maria	49	Id	18.22N	76.54W
Port-Menier	42	Lg	49.49N	64.20W
Port Moller	40	Ge	55.59N	160.34W
Port Moody	46	Db	49.17N	122.51W
Port Moresby	58	Fe	9.30S	147.07 E
Port Nelson	42	Ie	57.04N	92.30W
Portneuf, Rivière-	44	Ma	48.37N	69.05W
Port Nolloth	31	Ik	29.17S	16.51 E
Port Nouveau-Québec	39	Md	58.35N	65.59W
Porto [2]	13	Dc	41.15N	8.20W
Porto [Fr.]	11a	Aa	42.16N	8.42 E
Porto [Port.]	6	Fg	41.09N	8.37W
Porto, Golfe de-	11a	Aa	42.16N	8.37 E
Pôrto Acre	54	Ee	9.34S	67.31W
Porto Alegre [Braz.]	53	Ki	30.04S	51.11W
Porto Alegre [SaoT.P.]	34	Ge	0.02N	6.32 E
Porto Alexandre	31	Ij	15.48S	11.52 E
Porto Amboim	31	Ij	10.44S	13.45 E
Porto Azzurro	14	Eh	42.46N	10.24 E
Portobelo	49	Hi	9.33N	79.39W
Pôrto Cedro	55	Ed	18.17S	55.02W
Porto Cervo	14	Di	41.08N	9.35 E
Porto Curupai	55	Ff	22.50S	53.53W
Porto de Moz	53	Kf	1.45S	52.14W
Porto Empedocle	14	Hm	37.17N	13.32 E
Porto Esperança [Braz.]	55	Dd	19.37S	57.27W
Porto Esperança [Braz.]	55	Db	14.02S	56.06W
Porto Esperança [Braz.]	55	Dc	17.47S	57.07W
Porto Esperidião	55	Cb	15.51S	58.28W
Pôrto Estrêla	55	Db	15.20S	57.14W
Portoferraio	14	Eh	42.49N	10.19 E
Port of Ness	9	Gc	58.30N	6.15W
Pôrto Franco	54	Ie	6.20S	47.24W
Port of Spain	53	Jd	10.39N	61.31W
Porto Fundação	55	Ea	13.39S	55.18W
Portogruaro	14	Ge	45.47N	12.50 E
Porto Lucena	55	Eh	27.51S	55.01W
Pörtom/Pirttikyla	8	Ib	62.42N	21.37 E
Portomaggiore	14	Ff	44.42N	11.48 E
Porto Mendes	55	Eg	24.30S	54.20W
Porto Moniz	32	Dc	32.51N	17.10W
Porto Moroco	55	Ea	13.24S	55.35W
Porto Morrinho	55	Dc	16.38S	57.49W
Porto Murtinho	53	Kh	21.42S	57.52W
Porto Novo [Ben.]	31	Hh	6.29N	2.37 E
Porto Novo [C.V.]	32	Bf	17.07N	25.04W
Port Orford	46	Ce	42.45N	124.30W
Porto San Giorgio	14	Hg	43.11N	13.48 E
Pôrto Santana	54	Hd	0.03S	51.11W
Porto Sant'Elpidio	14	Hg	43.15N	13.45 E
Porto Santo	30	Fe	33.04N	16.20W
Porto Santo Stefano	14	Fh	42.26N	11.07 E
Portoscuso	14	Ck	39.12N	8.23 E
Pôrto Seguro	54	Kg	16.26S	39.05W
Porto Tolle	14	Gf	44.56N	12.22 E
Porto Torres	14	Cj	40.50N	8.24 E
Porto União	55	Gh	26.15S	51.05W
Pôrto Válter	54	De	8.15S	72.45W
Porto Vecchio	11a	Bb	41.35N	9.17 E
Porto Velho	53	Jf	8.46S	63.54W
Portoviejo	53	Hf	1.03S	80.27W
Porto Xavier	55	Eh	27.54S	55.08W
Port Phillip Bay	59	Ig	38.05S	144.50 E
Port Pirie	58	Eh	33.11S	138.01 E
Portree	9	Gd	57.24N	6.12W
Port Renfrew	46	Cb	48.33N	124.25W
Port Rois/Portrush	9	Gf	55.12N	6.40W
Port Royal	44	If	38.10N	77.12W
Portrush/Port Rois	9	Gf	55.12N	6.40W
Port Said (EN)=Būr Sa'īd	31	Ke	31.16N	32.18 E
Port Saint Joe	43	Jf	29.49N	85.18W
Port Saint Johns	37	Df	31.38S	29.33 E
Port-Saint-Louis-du-Rhône	11	Kk	43.23N	4.48 E
Port-Salut	49	Kd	18.05N	73.55W
Port Saunders	42	Lf	50.39N	57.18W
Port Shepstone	31	Kl	30.46S	30.22 E
Portsmouth [Dom.]	50	Fe	15.35N	61.28W
Portsmouth [Eng.-U.K.]	9	Lk	50.48N	1.05W
Portsmouth [N.H.-U.S.]	43	Mc	43.03N	70.47W
Portsmouth [Oh.-U.S.]	43	Kd	38.45N	82.59W
Portsmouth [Va.-U.S.]	43	Ld	36.50N	76.26W
Portsmouth City Airport	12	Ad	50.46N	1.04W
Port Sudan (EN)=Būr Sūdān	31	Kg	19.37N	37.14 E
Port Sulphur	45	Ll	29.29N	89.42W
Port Talbot	9	Jj	51.36N	3.47W
Porttipahdantekojärvi	7	Gb	68.06N	26.33 E
Port Townsend	46	Db	48.07N	122.46W
Portugal [1]	6	Fh	39.30N	8.00W
Portugalete	13	Ia	43.19N	3.01W
Portuguesa [2]	54	Eb	9.10N	69.15W
Portuguesa, Río-	54	Eb	7.57N	67.32W
Portuguesa, Sierra de-	50	Bh	9.35N	69.45W
Portuguese Guinea (EN) → Guinea Bissau (EN) [1]	31	Fg	12.00N	15.00W
Portús, Coll del-/Perthus, Col de-	13	Ob	42.28N	2.51 E
Port-Vendres	11	Jl	42.31N	3.07 E
Port-Vila	58	Hf	17.44S	168.19 E
Port Wakefield	59	Hf	34.11S	138.09 E
Port Washington	45	Me	43.23N	87.53W
Porvenir [Bol.]	54	Ef	11.15S	68.41W
Porvenir [Bol.]	55	Ba	13.59S	61.39W
Porvenir [Chile]	56	Fh	53.18S	70.22W
Porvenir [Ur.]	55	Dk	32.23S	57.59W
Porvoo/Borgå	7	Ff	60.24N	25.40 E
Porvoonjoki	8	Kd	60.23N	25.40 E
Porz, Köln-	10	Df	50.53N	7.03 E
Posada, Fiume di-	14	Dj	40.39N	9.45 E
Posadas [Arg.]	53	Kh	27.25S	55.50W
Posadas [Sp.]	13	Gg	37.48N	5.06W
Posavina	15	De	44.33N	20.04 E
Poschiavo	14	Ed	46.20N	10.04 E
Pošehonje-Volodarsk	7	Jg	58.30N	39.08 E
Posht-e Bādām	24	Pf	33.02N	55.23 E
Posio	7	Gc	66.06N	28.09 E
Posjet	28	Kc	42.39N	130.48 E
Poskam/Zepu	27	Cd	38.12N	77.18 E
Poso	22	Oj	1.23S	120.44 E
Poso, Danau-	26	Hg	1.52S	120.35 E
Posof	24	Jb	41.31N	42.42 E
Posŏng	28	Ig	34.46N	127.05 E
Pospeliha	20	Df	52.02N	81.56 E
Posse	54	If	14.05S	46.22W
Possession, Ile de la-	30	Mm	46.14S	49.55 E
Possession Island	37	Be	27.01S	15.30 E
Pößneck	10	Hf	50.42N	11.36 E
Post	45	Fj	33.12N	101.23W
Posta de San Martín	55	Bk	33.09S	60.31W
Postavy	19	Cd	55.07N	26.50 E
Poste-de-la-Baleine	42	Je	55.20N	76.50W
Poste Maurice Cortier/Bidon V	32	He	22.18N	1.05 E
Poste Weygand	32	He	24.29N	0.40 E
Postmasburg	37	Ce	28.18S	23.05 E
Postojna	14	Ie	45.47N	14.14 E
Posto Simões Lopes	55	Eb	14.14S	54.41W
Postville [Ia.-U.S.]	45	Ke	43.05N	91.34W
Postville [Newf.-Can.]	42	Lf	54.55N	59.58W
Potchefstroom	37	De	26.46S	27.01 E
Poteau	45	Ii	35.03N	94.37W
Potenza	14	Hg	43.25N	13.40 E
Potenza	14	Jj	40.38N	15.48 E
Poteriteri, Lake-	62	Bg	46.05S	167.05 E
Potes	13	Ha	43.09N	4.37W
Potgietersrus	37	Dd	24.15S	28.55 E
Potholes Reservoir	46	Fc	47.01N	119.19W
Poti	6	Kg	42.08N	41.39 E
Poti, Rio-	54	Je	5.02S	42.50W
Potigny	12	Bf	48.58N	0.14W
Potiskum	31	Ig	11.43N	11.04 E
Potnarhvin	63b	Dd	18.45S	169.12 E
Potomac	38	Lf	38.00N	76.18W
Potosí [2]	54	Eh	20.40S	67.00W
Potosí [Bol.]	53	Jg	19.35S	65.45W
Potosí [Mex.]	47	Dd	24.51N	100.19W
Potosí, Bahía-	48	Ii	17.35N	101.30W
Potosí, Cerro-	48	Ie	24.52N	100.13W
Pototan	26	Hd	10.55N	122.40 E
Potrerillos	56	Gc	26.26S	69.29W
Potrero, Río-	55	Bc	17.32S	61.35W
Potsdam [2]	10	Id	52.30N	13.00 E
Potsdam [G.D.R.]	10	Jd	52.24N	13.04 E
Potsdam [N.Y.-U.S.]	44	Jc	44.40N	75.01W
Pott	63b	Ad	19.35S	163.36 E
Potters Bar	12	Bc	51.41N	0.10W
Pottstown	44	Je	40.15N	75.38W
Pottsville	44	Ie	40.42N	76.13W
Pouancé	11	Eg	47.45N	1.10W
Pouébo	63b	Be	20.24S	164.34 E
Pouembout	63b	Be	21.08S	164.54 E
Poughkeepsie	44	Ke	41.43N	73.56W
Poulaphuca Reservoir/Loch Pholl an Phúca	9	Gh	53.10N	6.30W
Poum	63b	Be	20.14S	164.01 E
Pourtalé	55	Bm	37.02S	60.36W
Pouso Alegre	54	Ih	22.13S	45.56W
Pouss	34	Ic	10.51N	15.03 E
Poutasi	65c	Bb	14.01S	171.41W
Poŭthĭsăt	25	Kf	12.32N	103.55 E
Poutrincourt, Lac-	44	Ja	49.13N	74.04W
Po Valley (EN)=Padana, Pianura-	5	Gf	45.20N	10.00 E
Považská Bystrica	10	Og	49.07N	18.28 E
Považský Inovec	10	Nh	48.35N	18.00 E
Povenec	7	Ie	62.51N	34.45 E
Poverty Bay	62	Gc	38.45S	178.00 E
Povlen	15	Ce	44.09N	19.44 E
Póvoa de Varzim	13	Dc	41.23N	8.46W
Povorino	16	Md	51.12N	42.17 E
Povungnituk	42	Jd	60.03N	77.16W
Povungnituk	39	Lc	60.02N	77.10W
Powassan	44	Hb	46.05N	79.22W
Powder River [U.S.]	43	Fb	46.44N	105.26W
Powder River [Or.-U.S.]	46	Gd	44.45N	117.03W
Powell	46	Kd	44.45N	108.46W
Powell, Lake- [U.S.]	43	Ed	37.25N	110.45W
Powell Lake [Can.]	46	Ca	50.11N	124.24W
Powell River	42	Fg	49.52N	124.33W
Powers	44	Dc	45.39N	87.32W
Powers Lake	45	Eb	48.34N	102.39W
Powidzkie, Jezioro-	10	Nc	52.24N	17.57 E
Powys [3]	9	Ji	52.25N	3.20W
Poxoréu	54	Hg	15.50S	54.23W
Poxoréu, Rio- [Braz.]	55	Ec	16.32S	54.46W
Poxoréu, Rio- [Braz.]	55	Ec	16.08S	54.14W
Poya	63b	Be	21.21S	165.09 E
Poyang Hu	21	Ng	29.00N	116.25 E
Poza de la Sal	13	Ib	42.40N	3.30W
Pozanti	24	Fd	37.25N	34.52 E
Požarevac	15	Ee	44.37N	21.12 E
Poza Rica de Hidalgo	39	Jg	20.33N	97.27W
Požarskoje	28	Ma	46.16N	134.04 E
Požega	15	Df	43.51N	20.02 E
Poznań [2]	10	Pd	52.25N	19.55 E
Poznań	6	He	52.25N	16.55 E
Pozoblanco	13	Hf	38.22N	4.51W
Pozo Borrado	55	Bi	28.56S	61.41W
Pozo Colorado	55	Cf	23.22S	58.55W
Pozo del Mortero	55	Bg	24.24S	61.02W
Pozo del Tigre	55	Bc	17.34S	61.59W
Pozo Dulce	55	Ai	29.04S	62.02W
Pozos, Punta-	56	Gg	47.57S	65.47W
Pozuelos	54	Fa	10.11N	64.39W
Pozzallo	14	In	36.43N	14.51 E
Pozzuoli	14	Ij	40.49N	14.07 E
Pra [Ghana]	34	Ed	6.27N	1.47W
Pra [R.S.F.S.R.]	7	Ji	54.45N	41.01 E
Prabuty	10	Pc	53.46N	19.10 E
Prachatice	10	Jg	49.01N	14.00 E
Prachin Buri	25	Kf	14.02N	101.22 E
Prachuap Khiri Khan	25	Jf	11.48N	99.47 E
Praděd	10	Nf	50.06N	17.14 E
Prades	11	Il	42.37N	2.26 E
Prado	54	Kg	17.21S	39.13W
Præstø	8	Ei	55.07N	12.03 E
Prague (EN)=Praha	6	He	50.05N	14.26 E
Praha=Prague (EN)	6	He	50.05N	14.26 E
Prahova [2]	15	Id	45.10N	26.00 E
Praia	31	Eg	14.55N	23.31W
Praia a Mare	14	Jk	39.54N	15.47 E
Praia da Rocha	13	Dg	37.07N	8.32W
Praia Rica	55	Eb	14.51S	55.33W
Praid	15	Ic	46.33N	25.08 E
Prainha	54	Hd	1.48S	53.29W
Prairie Dog Town Fork	45	Gi	34.26N	99.21W
Prairie du Chien	45	Ke	43.03N	91.09W
Prangli	8	Ke	59.38N	24.50 E
Prānhita	25	Fe	18.49N	79.55 E
Prapat	26	Cf	2.40N	98.56 E
Prasat	25	Kf	14.38N	103.24 E
Praslin	51k	Bb	13.53N	60.54W
Praslin, Port-	51k	Bb	13.53N	60.54W
Praslin Island	37b	Ca	4.19S	55.44 E
Prasonisíon	15	Kn	35.52N	27.46 E
Prat, Isla-	56	Fg	48.15S	75.00W
Prata	54	Ig	19.18S	48.55W
Prata, Rio da-	55	Hd	18.49S	49.54W
Pratapgarh	25	Ed	24.02N	74.47 E
Prat de Llobregat/El Prat de Llobregat	13	Oc	41.20N	2.06 E
Prato	14	Fg	43.53N	11.06 E
Pratomagno	14	Fg	43.40N	11.40 E
Pratt	43	Hd	37.39N	98.44W
Prättigau	14	Dd	46.55N	9.40 E
Pratt Seamount (EN)	40	Ke	56.10N	142.30W
Prattville	44	Di	32.28N	86.29W
Pratudinho, Rio-	55	Ja	13.58S	45.10W
Pravda	18	Cf	36.50N	60.33 E
Pravda Coast	66	Ge	67.00S	94.00 E
Pravdinsk [R.S.F.S.R.]	8	Ij	54.28N	21.00 E
Pravdinsk [R.S.F.S.R.]	7	Kh	56.33N	43.33 E
Pravia	13	Fa	43.29N	6.07W
Praxedis G. Guerrero	48	Gb	31.22N	106.00W
Praya	26	Gh	8.42S	116.17 E
Prealpi Venete	14	Fd	46.25N	11.50 E
Predazzo	14	Fd	46.19N	11.36 E
Predeal	15	Id	45.30N	25.34 E
Predeal, Pasul-	15	Id	45.28N	25.36 E
Predel	14	Hd	46.25N	13.35 E
Predivinsk	20	Ee	57.04N	93.37 E
Predporožny	20	Jd	65.00N	143.20 E
Pré-en-Pail	11	Ff	48.27N	0.12W
Preetz	10	Gb	54.14N	10.17 E
Pregolia	7	Ei	54.42N	20.24 E
Pregradnaja	16	Lh	43.58N	41.12 E
Preiļi/Prejli	7	Gh	56.19N	26.48 E
Preissac, Lac-	44	Ha	48.25N	78.28W
Prejli/Preiļi	7	Gh	56.19N	26.48 E
Prekmurje	14	Kd	46.45N	16.15 E
Prekornica	15	Cg	42.40N	19.12 E
Prekule/Priekulė	8	Ii	55.36N	21.12 E
Přelouč	10	Lf	50.02N	15.33 E
Premià de Mar/Premiá de Mar	13	Oc	41.29N	2.22 E
Premiá de Mar/Premià de Mar	13	Oc	41.29N	2.22 E
Premnitz	10	Id	52.32N	12.20 E
Premuda	14	If	44.21N	14.37 E
Prenaj/Prienai	7	Fi	54.39N	23.59 E
Prenj	14	Lg	43.32N	17.52 E
Prenjasi	15	Dh	41.04N	20.32 E
Prentice	45	Kd	45.33N	90.17W
Prentiss	45	Lk	31.36N	89.52W
Prenzlau	10	Jc	53.19N	13.52 E
Preobraženije	20	Ih	42.58N	133.55 E
Preobraženka	20	Fd	60.04N	107.58 E
Preparis Island	25	If	14.52N	93.41 E
Preparis North Channel	25	Ie	15.27N	94.05 E
Preparis South Channel	25	If	14.45N	94.05 E
Přerov	10	Ng	49.27N	17.27 E
Prescelly, Mynydd-	9	Ij	51.58N	4.42W
Prescott [Ar.-U.S.]	45	Jj	33.48N	93.23W
Prescott [Az.-U.S.]	43	Ee	34.33N	112.28W
Preševo	15	Eg	42.19N	21.39 E
Presho	45	Fe	43.53N	100.04W
Presicce	14	Mk	39.54N	18.16 E
Presidencia Roque Sáenz Peña	53	Jh	26.50S	60.30W
Presidente Epitácio	56	Jb	21.46S	52.06W
Presidente Frei	66	Re	62.12S	58.55W
Presidente Hayes [3]	55	Cf	24.00S	59.00W
Presidente Juscelino	55	Jd	18.39S	44.05W
Presidente Murtinho	55	Fb	15.39S	53.54W
Presidente Olegário	55	Id	18.25S	46.25W
Presidente Prudente	56	Jb	22.07S	51.22W
Presidente Venceslau	55	Ge	21.52S	51.50W
President Thiers Seamount (EN)	57	Lg	24.39S	145.51W
Presidio	43	Gf	29.33N	104.23W
Presidio, Río del-	48	Ff	23.06N	106.17W
Preslav	15	Jf	43.10N	26.49 E
Presnovka	17	Mi	54.40N	67.09 E
Prešov	10	Rh	49.00N	21.14 E
Prespa	15	Hh	41.43N	24.53 E
Prespa, Lake- (EN)=Prespansko jezero	5	Ig	40.55N	21.00 E
Prespansko jezero=Prespa, Lake- (EN)	5	Ig	40.55N	21.00 E
Presque Isle	43	Nb	46.41N	68.01W
Prestea	34	Ed	5.26N	2.09W
Přeštice	10	Jg	49.35N	13.21 E
Preston [Eng.-U.K.]	9	Kh	53.46N	2.42W
Preston [Id.-U.S.]	43	Ec	42.06N	111.53W
Preston [Ont.-Can.]	44	Gd	43.23N	80.21W
Prestonsburg	44	Fg	37.40N	82.46W
Preststranda	8	Ce	59.06N	9.04 E
Prestwick	9	If	55.30N	4.37W
Prêto, Rio- [Braz.]	54	Jf	11.21S	43.52W
Prêto, Rio- [Braz.]	55	Gd	18.44S	50.23W
Prêto, Rio- [Braz.]	55	Ic	17.00S	46.12W
Prêto, Rio- [Braz.]	55	Ha	13.37S	48.06W
Preto do Igapó Açu, Rio-	54	Gd	4.26S	59.48W
Pretoria	31	Jk	25.45S	28.10 E
Pretty Rock Butte	45	Fc	46.10N	101.42W
Preußisch-Oldendorf	12	Kb	52.18N	8.30 E
Préveza	15	Dk	38.57N	20.45 E
Prey	12	Df	48.58N	1.13 E
Prey Vêng	25	Lf	11.29N	105.19 E
Priangarskoje Plato	20	Ee	57.30N	97.00 E
Priargunsk	20	Gf	50.27N	119.00 E
Pribelski	17	Hi	54.24N	56.29 E
Pribilof Islands	38	Cd	57.00N	170.00W
Priboj	15	Cf	43.35N	19.32 E
Příbram	10	Kg	49.42N	14.01 E
Price [Que.-Can.]	44	Ma	48.39N	68.12W
Price [Ut.-U.S.]	46	Jg	39.36N	110.48W
Price River	46	Jg	39.10N	110.06W
Prichard	44	Cj	30.44N	88.05W
Prickly Pear Cays	51b	Ab	18.16N	63.11W
Prickly Point	51p	Bc	11.59N	61.45W
Pridneprovskaja Vozvyšennost=Dnepr Upland (EN)	5	Jf	49.00N	32.00 E
Priego	13	Jd	40.27N	2.18W
Priego de Córdoba	13	Hg	37.26N	4.11W
Priei, Măgura-	15	Fc	46.58N	22.50 E
Priekule	7	Eh	56.29N	21.37 E
Priekulė/Prekule	8	Ii	55.36N	21.12 E
Prienai/Prenaj	7	Fi	54.39N	23.59 E
Priene	24	Bd	37.40N	27.13 E
Prieska	31	Jk	29.40S	22.42 E
Priest Lake	46	Gb	48.34N	116.52W
Prieta, Peña-	13	Ha	43.01N	4.44W
Prieta, Sierra-	48	Cb	31.15N	112.55W
Prievidza	10	Oh	48.46N	18.39 E
Prignitz	10	Hc	53.00N	12.00 E
Prijedor	14	Kf	44.59N	16.42 E
Prijepolje	15	Cf	43.24N	19.39 E
Prijutovo	19	Fe	53.58N	53.58 E
Prikaspijskaja Nizmennost=Caspian Depression (EN)	5	Lf	48.00N	52.00 E
Prilenskoje Plato = Lena Mountains (EN)	21	Oc	60.45N	125.00 E
Prilep	15	Eh	41.21N	21.34 E
Priluki	19	De	50.36N	32.24 E
Primavera	66	Qe	64.09S	60.57W
Primeira Cruz	54	Jd	2.30S	43.26W
Primorje	8	Hj	54.56N	20.00 E
Primorsk [R.S.F.S.R.]	7	Gf	60.22N	28.36 E
Primorsk [Ukr.-U.S.S.R.]	16	Jf	46.43N	36.22 E
Primorski Hrebet	20	Ff	52.30N	106.00 E
Primorski Kraj [3]	20	Ig	45.30N	135.30 E
Primorsko	15	Kg	42.16N	27.46 E
Primorsko-Ahtarsk	19	Df	46.03N	38.11 E
Primorskoje [R.S.F.S.R.]	8	Ld	60.32N	27.56 E
Primorskoje [Ukr.-U.S.S.R.]	15	Nd	45.59N	30.15 E
Primošten	14	Jg	43.36N	15.55 E
Primrose Lake	42	Gf	54.55N	109.45W
Prims	10	Cg	49.20N	6.44 E
Prince Albert	39	Id	53.12N	104.46W
Prince Albert Mountains	66	Jf	76.00S	161.30 E
Prince Albert Peninsula	42	Fb	72.30N	116.00W
Prince Albert Road	37	Cf	33.13S	22.02 E
Prince Albert Sound	42	Gb	70.25N	115.00W
Prince Alfred, Cape -	42	Fb	74.05N	124.29W
Prince Charles	38	Lc	67.50N	76.00W
Prince Charles Mountains	66	Ff	72.00S	67.00 E
Prince-de-Galles, Cap -	42	Kd	61.36N	71.30W
Prince Edward	30	Km	46.33S	37.57 E
Prince Edward Island [3]	42	Lg	46.30N	63.00W
Prince Edward Island	38	Me	46.30N	63.00W
Prince Edward Islands	30	Km	46.35S	37.56 E
Prince George	39	Gd	53.55N	122.49W
Prince Gustaf Adolf Sea	38	Ib	78.30N	107.00W
Prince of Wales [Ak.-U.S.]	40	Me	55.47N	132.50W
Prince of Wales [Can.]	38	Jb	72.40N	99.00W
Prince of Wales, Cape-	38	Cc	65.40N	168.05W
Prince of Wales Island	59	Ib	10.40S	142.10 E
Prince of Wales Mountains	42	Ja	77.45N	78.00W
Prince of Wales Strait	42	Fb	72.45N	118.00W
Prince Patrick	38	Hb	76.45N	119.30W
Prince Regent Inlet	42	Ib	72.45N	90.30W
Prince Rupert	39	Fd	54.19N	130.19W
Prince Rupert Bay	51g	Ba	15.34N	61.29W
Prince Rupert Bluff	51g	Ba	15.35N	61.29W
Princes Risborough	12	Bc	51.43N	0.49W
Princess Anne	44	Jf	38.12N	75.41W
Princess Charlotte Bay	59	Ib	14.25S	144.00 E
Princess Elizabeth Land	66	Ff	70.00S	80.00 E

Index Symbols

[1] Independent Nation
[2] State, Region
[3] District, County
[4] Municipality
[5] Colony, Dependency
Continent
Physical Region
Historical or Cultural Region
Mount, Mountain
Volcano
Hill
Mountains, Mountain Range
Hills, Escarpment
Plateau, Upland
Pass, Gap
Plain, Lowland
Delta
Salt Flat
Valley, Canyon
Crater, Cave
Karst Features
Depression
Polder
Desert, Dunes
Forest, Woods
Heath, Steppe
Oasis
Cape, Point
Coast, Beach
Cliff
Peninsula
Isthmus
Sandbank
Island
Atoll
Rock, Reef
Islands, Archipelago
Rocks, Reefs
Coral Reef
Well, Spring
Geyser
River, Stream
Waterfall Rapids
River Mouth, Estuary
Lake
Salt Lake
Intermittent Lake
Reservoir
Swamp, Pond
Canal
Glacier
Ice Shelf, Pack Ice
Ocean
Sea
Gulf, Bay
Strait, Fjord
Lagoon
Bank
Seamount
Tablemount
Ridge
Shelf
Basin
Escarpment, Sea Scarp
Fracture
Trench, Abyss
National Park, Reserve
Point of Interest
Recreation Site
Cave, Cavern
Historic Site
Ruins
Wall, Walls
Church, Abbey
Temple
Scientific Station
Airport
Port
Lighthouse
Mine
Tunnel
Dam, Bridge

Princess Margaret Range	42	Ia	79.00N	88.30W
Princess Royal	42	Ef	52.55N	128.50W
Princeton [B.C.-Can.]	42	Fg	49.27N	120.31W
Princeton [Il.-U.S.]	45	Lf	41.23N	89.28W
Princeton [In.-U.S.]	44	Df	38.21N	87.34W
Princeton [Ky.-U.S.]	44	Dg	37.07N	87.53W
Princeton [Mo.-U.S.]	45	Jf	40.24N	93.35W
Prince William Sound	38	Ec	60.40N	147.00W
Príncipe	30	Hh	1.37N	7.25 E
Prineville	46	Ed	44.18N	120.51W
Prineville Reservoir	46	Ed	44.08N	120.42W
Prins Christians Sund	41	Hf	60.00N	43.10W
Prinsesse Astrid Kyst	66	Cf	70.45S	12.30 E
Prinsesse Ragnhild Kyst	66	Df	70.15S	27.30 E
Prins Harald Kyst	66	De	69.30S	36.00 E
Prins Karls Forland	41	Nc	78.32N	11.10 E
Prinzapolka	47	Hf	13.24N	83.34W
Prinzapolka, Río-	49	Fg	13.24N	83.34W
Priora, Mount-	59	Ja	6.51S	145.58 E
Priozersk	19	Dc	61.04N	30.07 E
Pripet Marshes (EN)	5	Ie	52.00N	27.00 E
Pripjat	5	Je	51.21N	30.09 E
Pripoljarny Ural=Subpolar Urals (EN)	5	Lb	65.00N	60.00 E
Prirečny	19	Db	69.02N	30.15 E
Prišib	16	Pj	39.06N	48.38 E
Prislop, Pasul-	15	Hb	47.37N	24.55 E
Pristan-Prževalsk	18	Lc	42.33N	78.18 E
Pristen	16	Jd	51.15N	36.42 E
Priština	15	Eg	42.40N	21.10 E
Pritzwalk	10	Ic	53.09N	12.11 E
Privas	11	Kj	44.44N	4.36 E
Priverno	14	Hi	41.28N	13.11 E
Privolžkaja Vozvyšennost=Volga Hills (EN)	5	Ke	52.00N	46.00 E
Privolžsk	7	Jh	57.27N	41.16 E
Privolžski	16	Od	51.23N	46.02 E
Prizren	15	Dg	42.13N	20.45 E
Prizzi	14	Hm	37.43N	13.26 E
Prjaža	7	Hf	61.43N	33.37 E
Prnjavor	14	Lf	44.52N	17.40 E
Probolinggo	26	Fh	7.45S	113.13 E
Prochowice	10	Me	51.17N	16.22 E
Procida	14	Hj	40.45N	14.00 E
Proctor Reservoir	45	Gj	32.02N	98.32W
Proddatur	25	Ff	14.44N	78.33 E
Profítis Ilías [Grc.]	15	Fm	36.53N	22.22 E
Profítis Ilías [Grc.]	15	Fj	39.50N	22.38 E
Profondeville	12	Gd	50.23N	4.52 E
Progonati	15	Ci	40.13N	19.56 E
Progranični̇k	18	Dg	35.43N	63.12 E
Progreso [Mex.]	39	Kg	21.17N	89.40W
Progreso [Mex.]	48	Id	27.28N	101.04W
Progress	20	Hg	49.41N	129.40 E
Prohladny	16	Nh	43.45N	44.01 E
Prohorovka	16	Jd	51.02N	36.42 E
Prokopjevsk	22	Kd	53.53N	86.45 E
Prokuplje	15	Ef	43.15N	21.36 E
Proletari	7	Hg	58.26N	31.43 E
Proletarsk [R.S.F.S.R.]	19	Ef	46.41N	41.44 E
Proletarsk [Tad.-U.S.S.R.]	18	Gd	40.10N	69.31 E
Proletarski	16	Id	50.51N	35.46 E
Proletarskoje Vodohranilišče	16	Mf	46.30N	42.10 E
Proliv Soela/Soela Väin	8	Jf	58.40N	22.30 E
Prome	22	Lh	18.49N	95.13 E
Promissâe, Reprêsa-	56	Kb	21.32S	49.52W
Promissão	55	He	21.32S	49.52W
Promyšlenny	17	Kc	67.35N	63.55 E
Pronja [Bye.-U.S.S.R.]	16	Gc	53.27N	31.03 E
Pronja [U.S.S.R.]	16	Lb	54.21N	40.24 E
Pronsfeld	12	Id	50.10N	6.20 E
Prophet	42	Fe	58.46N	122.45W
Propriá	54	Kf	10.13S	36.51W
Propriano	11a	Ab	41.40N	8.54 E
Prorva	16	Rg	45.57N	53.13 E
Proserpine	59	Jd	20.24S	148.34 E
Prosna	10	Nd	52.10N	17.39 E
Prosotsáni	15	Gh	41.11N	23.59 E
Prosperidad	26	Ie	8.34N	125.52 E
Prospihino	20	Ee	58.37N	99.20 E
Prosser	46	Fc	46.12N	119.46W
Prostějov	10	Ng	49.29N	17.07 E
Proszowice	10	Qf	50.12N	20.18 E
Próti	15	El	37.03N	21.33 E
Protoka	16	Jg	45.43N	37.46 E
Protva	7	Ii	54.51N	37.16 E
Provadija	15	Kf	43.11N	27.26 E
Prøven	41	Gd	72.15N	55.40W
Provence	11	Lk	44.00N	6.00 E
Provence	5	Gg	44.00N	6.00 E
Providence [Ky.-U.S.]	44	Dg	37.24N	87.39W
Providence [R.I.-U.S.]	39	Le	41.50N	71.25W
Providence, Cape-	62	Bg	46.01S	166.28 E
Providence Bay	44	Fc	45.44N	82.18W
Providence Island	30	Mi	9.14S	51.02 E
Providencia, Isla de-	47	Hf	13.21N	81.22W
Providenciales	49	Kc	21.49N	72.15W
Providenija	22	Uc	64.23N	173.18W
Provincetown	44	Ld	42.03N	70.11W
Provins	11	Jf	48.33N	3.18 E
Provo	39	He	40.14N	111.39W
Prozor	14	Lg	43.49N	17.37 E
Prudentópolis	55	Gg	25.12S	50.57W
Prudhoe Bay	39	Eb	70.20N	148.25W
Prudnik	10	Nf	50.19N	17.34 E
Prüm	12	Ie	49.49N	6.28 E
Prüm	10	Cf	50.13N	6.25 E
Prune Island	51n	Bb	12.35N	61.24W
Prussia (EN)	10	Pc	53.45N	20.00 E
Pruszcz Gdański	10	Ob	54.16N	18.36 E
Pruszków	10	Qd	52.11N	20.48 E
Prut	5	If	45.28N	28.14 E
Pružany	19	Ce	52.36N	24.28 E
Prvić	14	If	44.54N	14.48 E
Prydz Bay	66	Fe	69.00S	76.00 E
Pryor	45	Ih	36.19N	95.19W
Przasnysz	10	Qc	53.01N	20.55 E
Przedbórz	10	Pe	51.06N	19.53 E
Przemyśl [2]	10	Sg	49.45N	22.45 E
Przemyśl	10	Sg	49.47N	22.47 E
Prževalsk	22	Je	42.29N	78.24 E
Przeworsk	10	Sf	50.05N	22.29 E
Przysucha	10	Qe	51.22N	20.38 E
Psakhná	15	Gk	38.35N	23.38 E
Psará	15	Ik	38.35N	25.37 E
Psathoúra	15	Hj	39.30N	24.11 E
Pščišč	16	Kg	45.03N	39.25 E
Psebaj	16	Lg	44.07N	40.47 E
Psël	5	Jf	49.05N	33.30 E
Psérimos	15	Km	36.56N	27.09 E
Psina	10	Of	50.02N	18.16 E
Pšiš, Gora-	16	Lh	43.24N	41.14 E
Pskem	18	Hd	41.38N	70.01 E
Pskent	18	Gd	40.54N	69.23 E
Pskov	6	Id	57.50N	28.20 E
Pskov, Lake- (EN)=Pihkva järv	7	Gg	58.00N	28.00 E
Pskov, Lake- (EN)=Pskovskoje Ozero	5	Id	58.00N	28.00 E
Pskova	8	Mg	57.47N	28.30 E
Pskovskaja Oblast [3]	19	Cd	57.20N	29.20 E
Pskovskoje Ozero=Pskov, Lake- (EN)	5	Id	58.00N	28.00 E
Psunj	14	Le	45.24N	17.20 E
Ptič	16	Fc	52.09N	28.52 E
Ptolemaïs	15	Ei	40.31N	21.41 E
Ptuj	14	Jd	46.25N	15.52 E
Pua-a, Cape-	65c	Aa	13.26S	172.43W
Puah, Pulau-	26	Hg	0.30S	122.34 E
Puapua	65c	Aa	13.34S	172.09W
Pucallpa	53	If	8.20S	74.30W
Pučež	7	Kh	56.59N	43.11 E
Pucheng [China]	27	Kf	27.55N	118.30 E
Pucheng [China]	27	Id	35.00N	109.38 E
Pucho	36	Cf	17.35S	16.30 E
Pucioasa	15	Id	45.05N	25.25 E
Pučišća	14	Kg	43.21N	16.44 E
Puck	10	Ob	54.44N	18.27 E
Pucka, Zatoka-	10	Ob	54.40N	18.35 E
Pudasjärvi	7	Gd	65.23N	27.00 E
Pudož	19	Dc	61.50N	36.32 E
Pudukkottai	25	Ff	10.23N	78.49 E
Puebla [2]	47	Ee	18.50N	98.00W
Puebla, Sierra de-	48	Kh	19.50N	97.00W
Puebla de Alcocer	13	Gf	38.59N	5.15W
Puebla de Don Fabrique	13	Jg	37.58N	2.26W
Puebla de Guzmán	13	Eg	37.37N	7.15W
Puebla de Sanabria	13	Fb	42.03N	6.38W
Puebla de Trives	13	Eb	42.20N	7.15W
Puebla de Zaragoza	39	Jh	19.03N	98.12W
Pueblo	39	If	38.16N	104.37W
Pueblo Libertador	55	Cj	30.13S	59.23W
Pueblo Nuevo [Mex.]	48	Gf	23.23N	105.23W
Pueblo Nuevo [Ven.]	49	Mh	11.58N	69.55W
Pueblo Nuevo Tiquisate	49	Bf	14.17N	91.22W
Pueblo Viejo, Laguna de-	48	Kf	22.10N	97.55W
Puelches	56	Ge	38.09S	65.55W
Puenteáreas	13	Db	42.11N	8.30W
Puente de la Reina	13	Kb	42.40N	1.49W
Puentedeume	13	Da	43.24N	8.10W
Puente-Genil	13	Hg	37.23N	4.47W
Puentelarrá	13	Ib	42.45N	3.03W
Pueo Point	65a	Ab	21.54N	160.04W
Pu'er	27	Hg	23.00N	101.00 E
Puerca, Punta-	51a	Cb	18.15N	65.35W
Puerco, Rio-	45	Ci	34.22N	107.50W
Puerco River	46	Ji	34.52N	110.05W
Puerto Abente	55	Df	22.55S	57.43W
Puerto Acosta	54	Eg	15.32S	69.15W
Puerto Adela	55	Eg	24.33S	54.22W
Puerto Aisén	53	Ij	45.24S	72.42W
Puerto Alegre	54	Ff	13.53S	61.36W
Puerto Ángel	47	Ee	15.40N	96.29W
Puerto Arista	48	Mj	15.56N	93.48W
Puerto Armuelles	47	Hg	8.17N	82.52W
Puerto Asís	54	Cc	0.29N	76.32W
Puerto Ayacucho	53	Je	5.40N	67.35W
Puerto Ayora	54a	Ab	0.45S	90.23W
Puerto Barrios	39	Kh	15.43N	88.36W
Puerto Bermejo	55	Ch	26.56S	58.30W
Puerto Berrío	54	Db	6.30N	74.25W
Puerto Boyacá	54	Db	5.45N	74.29W
Puerto Caballo	55	Ce	20.12S	58.12W
Puerto Cabello	53	Jd	10.28N	68.01W
Puerto Cabezas	47	Hf	14.02N	83.23W
Puerto Carreño	53	Je	6.12N	67.22W
Puerto Casado	56	Ib	20.20S	57.55W
Puerto Colombia	49	Jh	10.59N	74.57W
Puerto Colón	55	Df	23.11S	57.33W
Puerto Constanza	55	Ck	33.50S	59.03W
Puerto Cooper	56	Ib	23.03S	57.43W
Puerto Cortés [C.R.]	49	Fi	8.58N	83.32W
Puerto Cortés [Hond.]	39	Kh	15.48N	87.56W
Puerto Cumarebo	54	Ea	11.29N	69.21W
Puerto de Eten	54	Ce	6.56S	79.52W
Puerto de la Cruz	32	Dd	28.23N	16.33W
Puerto de Lajas, Cerro-	47	Cc	28.59N	107.02W
Puerto del Rosario	32	Ed	28.30N	13.52W
Puerto de Mazarrón	13	Kg	37.34N	1.15W
Puerto de San José	47	Ff	13.55N	90.49W
Puerto Deseado	53	Jj	47.45S	65.55W
Puerto de Sóller	13	Oe	39.48N	2.41 E
Puerto Escondido [Mex.]	47	Ee	15.48N	96.57W
Puerto Escondido [Mex.]	48	De	25.48N	111.20W
Puerto Esperanza [Arg.]	55	Eh	26.01S	54.39W
Puerto Esperanza [Par.]	55	Ce	20.26S	58.06W
Puerto Estrella	49	Lg	12.14N	71.13W
Puerto Fonciere	55	Df	22.29S	57.48W
Puerto Francisco de Orellana	54	Cd	0.27S	76.57W
Puerto Frey	55	Bb	14.42S	61.10W
Puerto Gaitán	54	Dc	4.20N	72.10W
Puerto General Diaz	55	Eg	25.12S	54.32W
Puerto Goya	55	Ci	29.09S	59.20W
Puerto Grether	54	Fg	17.12S	64.21W
Puerto Guaraní	55	De	21.18S	57.55W
Puerto Heath	54	Ef	12.30S	68.40W
Puerto Huasco	56	Fc	28.28S	71.14W
Puerto Huitoto	54	Dc	0.18N	74.03W
Puerto Iguazú	56	Jc	25.34S	54.34W
Puerto Indio	55	Eg	24.52S	54.29W
Puerto Ingeniero Ibañez	56	Fg	46.18S	71.56W
Puerto Isabel	55	Dd	18.11S	57.37W
Puerto Jesús	49	Eh	10.07N	85.16W
Puerto Juárez	39	Kg	21.11N	86.49W
Puerto la Concordia	54	Dc	2.38N	72.47W
Puerto la Cruz	53	Jd	10.13N	64.38W
Puerto Leguízamo	53	If	0.12S	74.46W
Puerto Lempira	49	Ff	15.15N	83.46W
Puerto Libertad	47	Bc	29.55N	112.43W
Puerto Limón [Col.]	54	Cc	1.02N	76.32W
Puerto Limón [Col.]	54	Dc	3.23N	73.30W
Puertollano	13	Hf	38.41N	4.07W
Puerto Lopez	54	Dc	4.06N	72.58W
Puerto López	49	Lh	11.56N	71.17W
Puerto Lumbreras	13	Kg	37.34N	1.49W
Puerto Madero	48	Mj	14.44N	92.25W
Puerto Madryn	56	Gf	42.46S	65.03W
Puerto Magdalena	48	Ce	24.35N	112.05W
Puerto Maldonado	53	Jg	12.36S	69.11W
Puerto Marangatú	55	Eg	24.39S	54.21W
Puerto Mayor Otaño	55	Eh	26.19S	54.44W
Puerto Mihanovich	55	De	20.52S	57.59W
Puerto Monte Lindo	55	Df	23.57S	57.12W
Puerto Montt	53	Ij	41.28S	72.57W
Puerto Morelos	48	Pg	20.50N	86.52W
Puerto Mutis	54	Cb	6.14N	77.25W
Puerto Naranjito	55	Eh	26.57S	55.18W
Puerto Nariño	54	Ec	4.56N	67.48W
Puerto Natales	53	Ik	51.44S	72.31W
Puerto Nuevo	55	Ce	20.33S	58.03W
Puerto Nuevo, Punta-	51a	Bb	18.30N	66.21W
Puerto Ordaz	54	Fb	8.22N	62.41W
Puerto Padre	49	Ic	21.12N	76.36W
Puerto Páez	54	Eb	6.13N	67.28W
Puerto Peñasco	47	Bb	31.20N	113.33W
Puerto Piña	49	Hj	7.35N	78.10W
Puerto Pinasco	56	Ib	22.43S	57.50W
Puerto Píritu	50	Dg	10.04N	65.03W
Puerto Plata	47	Je	19.48N	70.41W
Puerto Presidente Stroessner	55	Eg	25.33S	54.39W
Puerto Princesa	22	Ni	9.44N	118.44 E
Puerto Quijarro	55	Dc	17.47S	57.46W
Puerto Real	13	Fh	36.32N	6.11W
Puerto Rico [5]	39	Mh	18.15N	66.30W
Puerto Rico	38	Mh	18.15N	66.30W
Puerto Rico [Arg.]	56	Jc	26.48S	54.59W
Puerto Rico [Bol.]	54	Ef	11.05S	67.38W
Puerto Rico [Col.]	54	Cc	1.54N	75.10W
Puerto Rico Trench (EN)	3	Bg	20.00N	66.00W
Puerto Rondón	54	Db	6.18N	71.06W
Puerto San José	55	Eg	26.32S	54.50W
Puerto Santa Cruz	53	Jk	50.09S	68.30W
Puerto Sastre	56	Ib	22.06S	57.59W
Puerto Siles	54	Ef	12.48S	65.05W
Puerto Suárez	53	Kg	18.57S	57.51W
Puerto Tacurú Pytá	55	Df	23.49S	57.09W
Puerto Tirol	55	Ch	27.23S	59.05W
Puerto Tres Palmas	55	De	21.43S	57.58W
Puerto Triunfo	55	Eg	26.45S	55.06W
Puerto Vallarta	47	Cd	20.37N	105.15W
Puerto Varas	56	Ff	41.19S	72.59W
Puerto Victoria	55	Eh	26.20S	54.39W
Puerto Viejo	49	Eh	10.26N	83.59W
Puerto Villamizar	49	Ki	8.19N	72.26W
Puerto Villazón	55	Ba	13.32S	61.57W
Puerto Wilches	54	Db	7.20N	73.54W
Puerto Ybapobó	55	Df	23.42S	57.12W
Pueu	65e	Fc	17.44S	149.13W
Pugačev	19	Ee	52.03N	48.48 E
Puget Sound	46	Dc	48.00N	122.30W
Puglia = Apulia (EN) [2]	14	Ki	41.15N	16.15 E
Pu He	28	Gd	41.21N	122.47 E
Puhja	8	Lf	58.13N	26.17 E
Puigcerdá	13	Nb	42.26N	1.56 E
Puigmal	13	Ob	42.23N	2.07 E
Puir	20	Jf	53.10N	141.25 E
Puisaye, Collines de la-	11	Jg	47.35N	3.18 E
Puisieux	12	Ed	50.07N	2.42 E
Pujehum	34	Cd	7.21N	11.42W
Pujeşti	15	Kc	46.25N	27.29 E
Puji → Wugong	27	Ie	34.15N	108.14 E
Pujiang	28	Ei	29.28N	119.53 E
Pujilí	54	Cd	0.57S	78.42W
Puka	15	Cg	42.03N	19.54 E
Pukaki, Lake-	62	Df	44.05S	170.10 E
Pukalani	65a	Ec	20.50N	156.21W
Pukapuka Atoll	57	Kf	10.53S	165.49W
Pukapuka Atoll [W.F.]	57	Nf	14.49S	138.48W
Pukaruha Atoll	57	Nf	18.20S	137.02W
Pukatawagan	42	He	55.44N	101.19W
Pukchin	28	Hd	40.12N	125.45 E
Pukch'ŏng	27	Mc	40.14N	128.19 E
Pukega, Pointe-	64h	Ab	13.17S	176.13W
Pukekohe	62	Fb	37.12S	174.54 E
Pukemiro	62	Fb	37.37S	175.01 E
Pukeuri Junction	62	Df	45.02S	171.02 E
Pukšenga	7	Je	63.36N	41.55 E
Puksoozero	19	Ec	62.38N	40.32 E
Puksubaek-san	28	Id	40.42N	127.15 E
Pula [It.]	14	Ck	39.01N	9.00 E
Pula [Yugo.]	14	Hf	44.52N	13.50 E
Pula, Capo di-	14	Dl	38.59N	9.01 E
Pulandian → Xinjin	27	Ld	39.24N	121.59 E
Pulap Atoll	57	Fd	7.39N	149.25 E
Pulaski [Tn.-U.S.]	44	Dh	35.12N	87.02W
Pulaski [Va.-U.S.]	44	Gg	37.03N	80.47W
Pulau	26	Kh	5.50S	138.15 E
Pulau Halura	26	Hi	10.19S	120.11 E
Pulau Irian/New Guinea	57	Fe	5.00S	140.00 E
Pulau Sapudi	26	Fh	7.06S	114.20 E
Puławy	10	Re	51.25N	21.57 E
Pulborough	12	Bd	50.57N	0.31W
Pulheim	12	Ic	51.00N	6.48 E
Pulkau	14	Kb	48.43N	16.21 E
Pulkkila	7	Fd	64.16N	25.52 E
Pullman	43	Db	46.44N	117.10W
Pulo Anna Island	57	Ed	4.40N	131.58 E
Pulog, Mount-	21	Oh	16.36N	120.54 E
Pulpito, Punta-	48	Dd	26.30N	111.30W
Pulsano	14	Lj	40.23N	17.21 E
Pułtusk	10	Rd	52.43N	21.05 E
Pülümür	24	Hc	39.30N	39.54 E
Pulusuk Island	57	Fd	6.42N	149.19 E
Puluwat Atoll	57	Fd	7.22N	149.11 E
Puma Yumco	27	Ff	28.35N	90.20 E
Pumpėnai/Pumpenaj	8	Ki	55.53N	24.25 E
Pumpenaj/Pumpėnai	8	Ki	55.53N	24.25 E
Pumpkin Creek	46	Mc	46.15N	105.45W
Puná, Isla-	54	Bd	2.50S	80.10W
Punākha	25	Hc	27.37N	89.52 E
Punaluu	65a	Fd	19.08N	155.30W
Pūnch	25	Eb	33.46N	74.06 E
Punda Milia	37	Ed	22.40S	31.05 E
Pune (Poona)	22	Jh	18.32N	73.52 E
Pūnel	24	Md	37.33N	49.07 E
Pungan	18	Hd	40.45N	70.50 E
P'unggi	28	Jf	36.52N	128.32 E
Púngoè	37	Ec	19.50S	34.48 E
P'ungsan	28	Jd	40.40N	128.05 E
Punia	36	Ec	1.28S	26.27 E
Punitaqui	56	Fd	30.50S	71.16W
Punjab [3]	25	Fb	31.00N	76.00 E
Punjab	21	Jf	30.00N	74.00 E
Punjad [3]	25	Eb	30.00N	74.00 E
Punkaharju	8	Mc	61.48N	29.24 E
Punkalaidun	8	Jc	61.07N	23.06 E
Puno	53	Ig	15.50S	70.02W
Puno [2]	54	Ef	15.00S	70.00W
Punta, Cerro de-	47	Ke	18.10N	66.36W
Punta Alta	53	Ji	38.53S	62.04W
Punta Arenas	53	Ik	53.09S	70.55W
Punta Cardón	54	Da	11.38N	70.14W
Punta de Mata	50	Eh	9.43N	63.38W
Punta Gorda [Blz.]	47	Ge	16.07N	88.48W
Punta Gorda [Fl.-U.S.]	44	Fl	26.56N	82.03W
Punta Gorda [Nic.]	49	Fh	11.31N	83.47W
Punta Gorda, Bahía de-	49	Fh	11.15N	83.45W
Punta Gorda, Río-	49	Fh	11.30N	83.47W
Punta Indio	55	Dl	35.16S	57.14W
Punta Prieta	47	Bc	28.58N	114.17W
Puntarenas [3]	49	Ei	9.00N	83.15W
Puntarenas	39	Ki	9.58N	84.50W
Punta Róbalo	49	Fi	9.02N	82.15W
Punto Fijo	54	Da	11.42N	70.13W
Puolanka	7	Gd	64.52N	27.40 E
Puolo Point	65a	Bb	21.54N	159.36W
Puqi	27	Jf	29.43N	113.52 E
Puquio	54	Df	14.42S	74.08W
Purace, Volcán-	54	Cc	2.21N	76.23W
Purari	60	Ci	7.52S	145.10 E
Purcell Mountains	42	Fg	49.55N	116.15W
Purdy Islands	57	Fe	2.53S	146.20 E
Purgatoire River	45	Eg	38.04N	103.10W
Puri	25	He	19.48N	85.51 E
Purificación	47	Ed	23.58N	98.42W
Purikari Neem/Purikarinem	8	Ke	59.36N	25.35 E
Purikarinem/Purikari Neem	8	Ke	59.36N	25.35 E
Purmani/Puurmani	8	Lf	58.30N	26.14 E
Purmerend	11	Kb	52.31N	4.57 E
Purna [India]	25	Fe	19.07N	77.02 E
Purna [India]	25	Fd	21.05N	76.00 E
Purnač	7	Jc	67.00N	40.15 E
Purnea	25	Hc	25.47N	87.28 E
Purukcahu	26	Fg	0.35S	114.35 E
Purūlia	25	Hd	23.20N	86.22 E
Puruni River	50	Gi	6.00N	59.12W
Purus, Rio-	52	Jf	3.42S	61.28W
Puruvesi	7	Gf	61.50N	29.25 E
Purwakarta	26	Eh	6.34S	107.26 E
Purwokerto	26	Eh	7.25S	109.14 E
Pusala Dağı	24	Ed	37.12N	32.54 E
Pusan	22	Of	35.06N	129.03 E
Pusan Si [2]	28	Jg	35.10N	129.05 E
Pushi He	28	Hd	40.17N	124.43 E
Puškin	19	Dd	59.43N	30.24 E
Puškino [Abz.-U.S.S.R.]	16	Pj	39.28N	48.33 E
Puškino [R.S.F.S.R.]	16	Od	51.14N	46.59 E
Puškino [R.S.F.S.R.]	7	Ih	56.02N	37.53 E
Puškinskije Gory	8	Mh	56.59N	28.59 E
Pušlahta	7	Id	64.48N	36.33 E
Püspökladány	10	Ri	47.19N	21.07 E
Püssi/Pjussi	8	Le	59.17N	26.57 E
Pusteci	15	Di	40.47N	20.54 E
Pusteria, Val-/Pustertal	14	Gd	46.45N	12.20 E
Pustertal/Pusteria, Val-	14	Gd	46.45N	12.20 E
Pustomyty	10	Tg	49.37N	23.59 E
Pustoška	7	Gh	56.20N	29.22 E
Putao	25	Jc	27.21N	97.24 E
Putaruru	62	Fc	38.03S	175.47 E
Putian	27	Kf	25.32N	119.01 E
Putignano	14	Lj	40.51N	17.07 E
Putila	15	Ip	48.00N	25.07 E
Putivl	16	Hd	51.22N	33.55 E
Putjatin	28	Lc	42.52N	132.25 E
Putla de Guerrero	48	Ki	17.02N	97.56W
Putna	15	Kd	45.34N	27.30 E
Putna	15	Ib	47.52N	25.37 E
Putnok	10	Qh	48.18N	20.26 E
Puto	63a	Ba	5.41S	154.43 E
Putorana, Plato-=Putoran Mountains (EN)	21	Lc	69.00N	95.00 E
Putoran Mountains (EN)=Putorana, Plato-	21	Lc	69.00N	95.00 E
Puttalam	25	Fg	8.02N	79.49 E
Putte	12	Gc	51.04N	4.38 E
Puttelange-aux-Lacs	12	Ie	49.03N	6.56 E
Putten	12	Hb	52.16N	5.35 E
Putten	12	Gc	51.50N	4.15 E
Puttgarden, Burg auf Fehmarn-	10	Hb	54.30N	11.13 E
Püttlingen	12	Ie	49.17N	6.53 E
Putumayo [2]	54	Cc	0.30N	76.00W
Putumayo, Río-	52	Jf	3.07S	67.58W
Putuo (Shenjiamen)	28	Gj	29.57N	122.18 E
Putussibau	26	Ff	0.50N	112.56 E
Puu Kukui	65a	Ec	20.54N	156.35W
Puulavesi	5	Ic	61.50N	26.40 E
Puumala	7	Gf	61.32N	28.11 E
Puu o Umi	65a	Fc	20.05N	155.42W
Puurmani/Purmani	8	Lf	58.30N	26.14 E
Puurs	12	Gc	51.05N	4.17 E
Puuwai	65a	Ab	21.54N	160.12W
Puyallup	46	Dc	47.11N	122.18W
Puyang	27	Jd	35.41N	115.00 E
Puy-de-Dôme [3]	11	Ii	45.40N	3.00 E
Puy-l'Evêque	11	Hj	44.30N	1.08 E
Puymorens, Col de-	11	Hl	42.34N	1.49 E
Puyo	54	Cd	1.29S	77.58W
Puysegur Point	62	Bg	46.10S	166.37 E
Pwani [3]	36	Gd	7.30S	39.00 E
Pweto	31	Ji	8.28S	28.54 E
Pwllheli	9	Ii	52.53N	4.25W
Pyapon	25	Je	16.17N	95.41 E
Pyhäjärvi	7	Fe	63.40N	25.59 E
Pyhäjärvi [Fin.]	7	Ff	61.00N	22.20 E
Pyhäjärvi [Fin.]	7	Fe	63.35N	25.57 E
Pyhäjärvi [Fin.]	8	Kc	62.45N	25.25 E
Pyhäjärvi [Fin.]	8	Jc	61.30N	23.35 E
Pyhäjoki	7	Fd	64.28N	24.13 E
Pyhäjoki	7	Fd	64.28N	24.14 E
Pyhäntä	7	Gd	64.06N	26.19 E
Pyhäranta	8	Id	60.57N	21.27 E
Pyhäselkä	7	Ge	62.30N	29.40 E
Pyhaselkä	8	Mb	62.26N	29.58 E
Pyhätunturi	7	Gc	67.01N	27.09 E
Pyhävesi	8	Lc	61.25N	26.35 E
Pyhävuori	8	Ib	62.17N	21.38 E
Pyhrnpaß	14	Ic	47.38N	14.18 E
Pyhtää/Pyttis	7	Gf	60.29N	26.32 E
Pyinmana	22	Lh	19.44N	96.13 E
Pylos (EN) = Pílos	15	Em	36.56N	21.40 E
Pyltsamaa/Põltsamaa	8	Lf	58.23N	26.08 E
Pyltsamaa/Põltsamaa	7	Fg	58.39N	25.59 E
Pylva/Põlva	7	Gg	58.04N	27.06 E
Pymatuning Reservoir	44	Ge	41.37N	80.30W
P'yŏngan-Namdo [2]	28	Ie	39.20N	126.00 E
P'yŏngan-Pukto [2]	28	Hd	40.00N	125.15 E
P'yŏnggang	27	Md	38.25N	127.17 E
P'yŏngsan	27	Md	38.20N	126.24 E
P'yongt'aek	28	If	36.59N	127.05 E
P'yŏngyang	22	Of	39.01N	125.45 E
P'yŏngyang Si [2]	28	He	39.04N	125.50 E
Pyramiden	41	Nc	77.54N	16.41 E
Pyramid Lake	43	Dc	40.00N	119.35W
Pyramid Mountains	45	Bj	32.00N	108.30W
Pyrénées=Pyrenees (EN)	5	Gg	42.40N	1.00 E
Pyrenees (EN)=Pirineos	5	Gg	42.40N	1.00 E
Pyrenees (EN)=Pyrénées	5	Gg	42.40N	1.00 E
Pyrenees (EN)=Serralada Pirinenca	5	Gg	42.40N	1.00 E
Pyrénées-Atlantiques [3]	11	Fk	43.15N	0.50W
Pyrénées-Orientales [3]	11	Il	42.30N	2.20 E
Pyrzyce	10	Kc	53.10N	14.55 E
Pyšma	19	Gd	57.08N	66.18 E
Pytalovo	7	Gh	57.06N	27.59 E
Pyttegga	8	Bd	62.13N	7.42 E
Pyttis/Pyhtää	7	Gf	60.29N	26.32 E
Pyu	25	Je	18.29N	96.26 E
Pyzaspea/Põõsaspea Neem	8	Je	59.15N	23.25 E
Pyzdry	10	Nd	52.11N	17.41 E

Q

Qā', Wādī al-	24	Hi	27.04N	38.34 E
Qābis [3]	32	Ic	33.00N	9.30 E
Qābis	31	Ie	33.53N	10.07 E
Qābis, Khalīj-=Gabès, Gulf of-(EN)	30	Ie	34.00N	10.25 E
Qabr Hūd	35	Hb	16.09N	49.34 E
Qāderābād	24	Og	30.17N	53.16 E
Qādır Karam	24	Ke	35.12N	44.53 E
Qāḑub	23	Hg	12.38N	53.57 E
Qā'emshahr	24	Od	36.30N	52.55 E
Qafşah	31	He	34.25N	8.48 E
Qafsah [3]	32	Ic	34.30N	9.00 E
Qa'fūr	14	Dn	36.20N	9.19 E
Qagan	27	Kb	49.16N	118.04 E
Qagan Moron He	28	Ec	43.13N	119.02 E
Qagan Nur	27	Jc	43.20N	112.58 E
Qagan Nur [China]	28	Bd	41.33N	113.48 E
Qagan Nur [China]	27	Jc	43.25N	114.50 E
Qagan Nur [China]	28	Hb	45.14N	124.17 E
Qagan Nur→Zhengxiangbai Qi	27	Jc	42.16N	114.59 E
Qagan Us→Dulan	22	Lf	36.29N	98.29 E
Qagchêng/Xiangcheng	27	Gf	28.56N	99.46 E
Qahar Youyi Houqi (Bayan Qagan)	28	Bd	41.28N	113.10 E
Qahar Youyi Qianqi (Togrog Ul)	28	Bd	40.46N	113.13 E
Qahar Youyi Zhongqi	28	Bd	41.15N	112.36 E
Qahd, Wādī-	24	Ii	26.13N	40.49 E
Qaidam He	27	Gd	36.48N	95.50 E
Qaidam Pendi=Tsaidam Basin (EN)	27	Fd	37.00N	95.00 E

Index Symbols

[1] Independent Nation
[2] State, Region
[3] District, County
[4] Municipality
[5] Colony, Dependency
Continent
Physical Region

Historical or Cultural Region
Mount, Mountain
Volcano
Hill
Mountains, Mountain Range
Hills, Escarpment
Plateau, Upland

Pass, Gap
Plain, Lowland
Delta
Salt Flat
Valley, Canyon
Crater, Cave
Karst Features

Depression
Polder
Desert, Dunes
Forest, Woods
Heath, Steppe
Oasis
Cape, Point

Coast, Beach
Cliff
Peninsula
Isthmus
Sandbank
Island
Atoll

Rock, Reef
Islands, Archipelago
Rocks, Reefs
Coral Reef
Well, Spring
Geyser
River, Stream

Waterfall Rapids
River Mouth, Estuary
Lake
Salt Lake
Intermittent Lake
Reservoir
Swamp, Pond

Canal
Glacier
Ice Shelf, Pack Ice
Ocean
Sea
Gulf, Bay
Strait, Fjord

Lagoon
Bank
Seamount
Tablemount
Ridge
Shelf
Basin

Escarpment, Sea Scarp
Fracture
Trench, Abyss
National Park, Reserve
Point of Interest
Recreation Site
Cave, Cavern

Historic Site
Ruins
Wall, Walls
Church, Abbey
Temple
Scientific Station
Airport

Port
Lighthouse
Mine
Tunnel
Dam, Bridge

Qala'an Naḩl 35 Ec 13.38N 34.57 E
Qalāt 23 Kc 32.07N 66.54 E
Qal'at Abū Ghār 24 Lg 30.25N 46.09 E
Qal'at al Akhḑar 23 Ed 28.06N 37.05 E
Qal 'at al Marqab 24 Fe 35.09N 35.57 E
Qal'at al Mu'aẕẕam 24 Gi 27.45N 37.31 E
Qal'at aş Şanam 14 Co 35.46N 8.21 E
Qal'at Bīshah 22 Gh 20.00N 42.36 E
Qal'at Dīzah 24 Kd 36.11N 45.07 E
Qal'at Şāliḩ 24 Lg 31.31N 47.16 E
Qal'at Sukkar 24 Lg 31.53N 46.56 E
Qal'eh Asgar 24 Qh 29.30N 56.35 E
Qal'eh Kūh 24 Mf 33.00N 49.10 E
Qal'eh Mūreh 24 Pe 35.35N 55.58 E
Qal'eh-ye Now 23 Jc 34.59N 63.08 E
Qal'eh-ye Sahar 24 Mg 31.40N 48.33 E
Qalīb ash Shuyūkh 23 Gd 29.12N 47.55 E
Qallābāt 35 Fc 12.58N 36.09 E
Qalmarz, Godār-e- 24 Qf 33.26N 56.14 E
Qalyūb 24 Dg 30.11N 31.13 E
Qamata 37 Df 31.58S 27.24 E
Qamdo 22 Lf 31.15N 97.12 E
Qamīnis 33 Dc 31.40N 20.01 E
Qamsar 24 Nf 33.45N 51.26 E
Qamūdah 32 Ic 35.00N 9.21 E
Qamūdah [3] 32 Ic 34.50N 9.20 E
Qânâq/Thule 67 Od 77.35N 69.40W
Qandahār [3] 23 Kc 31.00N 65.45 E
Qandahār 22 If 31.35N 65.45 E
Qandala 35 Hc 11.23N 49.53 E
Qangdin Gol 28 Cc 43.27N 115.03 E
Qanţarat al Fahş 14 Dn 36.23N 9.54 E
Qapqal 27 Dc 43.48N 80.47 E
Qaqortoq/Julianehåb 67 Nc 60.50N 46.10W
Qarā Dāgh 24 Lc 38.48N 47.13 E
Qārah 33 Ed 29.37N 26.30 E
Qarah Būlāq 24 Ke 34.32N 45.12 E
Qarah Dagh 24 Jd 37.00N 43.30 E
Qarah Tappah 24 Ke 34.25N 44.56 E
Qarānqū 24 Ld 37.23N 47.43 E
Qardo 31 Lh 9.30N 49.03 E
Qareh Āghāj 24 Ld 36.46N 48.46 E
Qareh Sū [Iran] 23 Ib 37.00N 56.50 E
Qareh Sū [Iran] 24 Hc 34.52N 51.25 E
Qareh Ẕīā'Od Dīn 24 Kc 38.53N 45.02 E
Qarkilik/Ruoqiang 22 Kf 39.02N 88.00 E
Qarnayn, Jazirat al- 24 Oj 24.56N 52.52 E
Qarnayt, Jabal- 23 Fe 21.02N 40.22 E
Qarqan/Qiemo 22 Kf 38.08N 85.32 E
Qarqan He 21 Kf 39.30N 88.15 E
Qarqannah, Juzur-= Kerkennah Islands (EN) 30 Ie 34.44N 11.12 E
Qartājannah 14 En 36.51N 10.20 E
Qārūn, Birkat- 33 Fd 29.28N 30.40 E
Qaryat Abū Nujaym 33 Cc 30.35N 15.24 E
Qaryat al Gharab 24 Kg 31.27N 44.48 E
Qaryat al Qaddāḩiyah 33 Cc 31.22N 15.14 E
Qaryat al 'Ulyā 23 Gd 27.33N 47.42 E
Qaryat az Zarrūq 33 Cc 32.22N 15.09 E
Qaryat az Zuwaytīnah 33 Dc 30.58N 20.07 E
Qaşabah, Ra's al- 24 Fh 28.02N 34.38 E
Qaşabāt, Hanshir al- 14 Dn 36.24N 9.54 E
Qasigiánguit/Christianshåb 41 Ge 68.45N 51.30W
Qaşr al Azraq 24 Gg 31.53N 36.49 E
Qasr Al Hayr 24 Ge 34.23N 37.36 E
Qaşr al Qarahbullī 33 Bc 32.45N 13.43 E
Qaşr 'Amij 24 If 33.30N 41.45 E
Qaşr Bū Hādī 33 Cc 31.03N 16.40 E
Qaşr Burqu' 24 Gf 32.37N 37.58 E
Qasr-e Shīrīn 24 Ke 34.31N 45.35 E
Qaşr Farāfirah 31 Jf 27.15N 28.10 E
Qasr Ḩamān 23 Ge 20.50N 45.50 E
Qaşr Qārūn 24 Dh 29.25N 30.25 E
Qaşş Abū Sa'īd 24 Bi 27.00N 27.35 E
Qatana 24 Gf 33.26N 36.05 E
Qatar 21 Hg 25.30N 51.15 E
Qatar [1] 22 Hg 25.30N 51.15 E
Qatlīsh 24 Qd 37.50N 57.19 E
Qaţrānī, Jabal- 24 Dh 29.41N 30.35 E
Qatrūyeh 24 Ph 29.09N 54.43 E
Qattara Depression (EN)= Qaţţārah, Munkhafaḑ al- 30 Je 30.00N 27.30 E
Qaţţārah, Munkhafaḑ al-= Qattara Depression (EN) 30 Je 30.00N 27.30 E
Qawām al Hamzah 24 Kg 31.43N 44.58 E
Qawz Abu Dulū' 35 Eb 16.55N 32.30 E
Qawz Rajab 35 Fb 16.04N 35.34 E
Qaysān 35 Ec 10.45N 34.48 E
Qayyārah 24 Je 35.48N 43.17 E
Qazvīn [Iran] 22 Gf 36.16N 50.00 E
Qazvīn [Iraq] 24 Je 34.21N 42.05 E
Qeqertarssuaq/Godhavn 67 Nc 69.20N 53.35W
Qeshm 24 Qi 26.58N 56.16 E
Qeshm 23 Id 26.45N 55.45 E
Qeydār 24 Md 36.07N 48.35 E
Qeys, Jazīreh-ye- 24 Hd 26.32N 53.58 E
Qezel Owzan 23 Gb 36.45N 49.22 E
Qian'an [China] 28 Ed 40.01N 118.42 E
Qian'an [China] 28 Hb 44.58N 124.01 E
Qianfangzi 28 Ad 40.01N 111.23 E
Qian Gorlos (Quianguozhen) 27 Lb 45.05N 124.52 E
Qian He 28 Dh 32.55N 117.10 E
Qianjiang [China] 27 Ig 23.37N 108.58 E
Qianjiang [China] 28 Bi 30.25N 112.54 E
Qianjiang [China] 27 If 29.30N 108.45 E
Qianning/Gartar 27 He 30.27N 101.29 E
Qian Shan 27 Lc 40.35N 123.00 E
Qiansuo 27 Hf 25.27N 100.41 E
Qianwei 27 Hf 29.08N 103.56 E
Qianxi [China] 27 If 27.03N 106.04 E
Qianxi [China] 28 Ed 40.08N 118.19 E
Qianyang (Anjiang) 27 If 27.19N 110.13 E
Qiaojia 27 Hf 27.00N 103.00 E
Qiaowan 27 Gc 40.36N 96.42 E
Qibilī 32 Ic 33.42N 8.58 E
Qichun (Caojiahe) 28 Ci 30.15N 115.26 E
Qidaogou 28 Id 41.31N 126.18 E
Qidong 28 Fi 31.48N 121.39 E
Qiemo/Qarqan 22 Kf 38.08N 85.32 E
Qift 24 Ei 26.00N 32.49 E
Qijiang 27 If 29.00N 106.39 E
Qijiaojing 27 Fc 43.28N 91.36 E
Qike → Xunke 27 Mb 49.34N 128.28 E
Qili → Shitai 28 Di 30.12N 117.28 E
Qilian (Babao) 27 Hd 38.14N 100.15 E
Qilian Shan 27 Gd 39.12N 98.35 E
Qilian Shan 21 Lf 38.30N 100.00 E
Qimantag 27 Fd 37.00N 91.00 E
Qimen 27 Kf 29.57N 117.39 E
Qinā 31 Kf 26.10N 32.43 E
Qinā, Wādī- 24 Ei 26.12N 32.44 E
Qin'an 27 Ie 34.50N 105.35 E
Qingchengzi 28 Gd 40.44N 123.36 E
Qingchuan 27 Ie 32.32N 105.11 E
Qingdao=Tsingtao (EN) 22 Of 36.05N 120.21 E
Qingduizi 28 Fd 41.27N 121.52 E
Qingfeng 28 Cg 35.54N 115.07 E
Qinggang 27 Mb 46.41N 126.03 E
Qinggil/Qinghe 27 Fb 46.43N 90.24 E
Qinghai Hu=Koko Nor (EN) 21 Mf 37.00N 100.20 E
Qinghai Sheng (Ch'ing-hai Sheng)=Tsinghai (EN) [2] 27 Gd 36.00N 96.00 E
Qing He 28 Hc 42.16N 124.10 E
Qinghe/Qinggil 27 Fb 46.43N 90.24 E
Qinghe (Gexianzhuang) 28 Cf 37.03N 115.39 E
Qinghemen 28 Fd 41.45N 121.25 E
Qingjian 27 Jd 37.10N 110.09 E
Qingjiang 27 Nf 33.31N 119.03 E
Qing Jiang 27 Je 30.24N 111.30 E
Qingjiang (Zhangshuzhen) 27 Kf 28.02N 115.31 E
Qingkou → Ganyu 28 Eg 34.50N 119.07 E
Qinglong 28 Ed 40.26N 118.58 E
Qinglong He 28 Ee 39.51N 118.51 E
Qingshan 28 Ci 30.39N 114.27 E
Qingshuihe 27 Jd 39.56N 111.41 E
Qingshui Jiang 27 If 27.11N 109.48 E
Qingtian 27 Lf 28.12N 120.17 E
Qingxian 28 De 38.35N 116.48 E
Qingxu 28 Bf 37.36N 112.21 E
Qingyang [China] 27 Id 36.01N 107.48 E
Qingyang [China] 28 Di 30.38N 117.50 E
Qingyuan 27 Lc 42.06N 124.56 E
Qingyuan (Nandaran) 28 Ce 38.46N 115.29 E
Qingyun (Xiejiaji) 28 Df 37.46N 117.22 E
Qing Zang Gaoyuan=Tibet, Plateau of- (EN) 21 Kf 32.30N 87.00 E
Qin He 28 Bg 35.01N 113.25 E
Qinhuangdao 27 Kg 40.00N 119.32 E
Qin Ling 21 Mf 34.00N 108.00 E
Qinshui 28 Bg 35.41N 112.10 E
Qintong 28 Fh 32.39N 120.06 E
Qinxian 28 Bf 36.46N 112.42 E
Qinyang 28 Bg 35.05N 112.56 E
Qinyuan 28 Bf 36.29N 112.20 E
Qinzhou 27 Ig 22.02N 108.30 E
Qionghai (Jiaji) 27 Jh 19.25N 110.28 E
Qionglai 27 He 30.24N 103.28 E
Qiongzhou Haixia 21 Ng 20.10N 110.15 E
Qipan Guan 27 Ie 32.45N 106.11 E
Qiqihar 22 Oe 47.21N 123.58 E
Qīr 24 Oh 28.29N 53.04 E
Qira 27 Dd 37.02N 80.53 E
Qiryat Gat 24 Fg 31.36N 34.46 E
Qiryat Shemona 24 Ff 33.13N 35.34 E
Qiryat Yam 24 Ff 32.51N 35.04 E
Qishn 23 Hf 15.26N 51.40 E
Qi Shui 28 Ci 30.09N 115.22 E
Qishuyan 28 Fi 31.41N 120.04 E
Qitai 22 Ke 44.01N 89.28 E
Qitaihe 27 Nb 45.49N 130.51 E
Qiuxian (Matou) 28 Cf 36.50N 115.10 E
Qixia 28 Ff 37.18N 120.50 E
Qixian [China] 28 Bf 37.23N 112.21 E
Qixian [China] 28 Cg 34.33N 114.46 E
Qixian (Zhaoge) 28 Cg 35.35N 114.12 E
Qiyang 27 Jf 26.44N 111.50 E
Qizhou 28 Ci 30.04N 115.20 E
Qogir Feng=Godwin Austen (EN) 21 Jf 35.53N 76.30 E
Qog Qi 27 Ic 41.31N 107.00 E
Qog Ul 27 Kc 44.50N 116.19 E
Qohrūd, Kūhhā-ye- 21 Hf 32.40N 53.00 E
Qoltag 27 Ec 42.20N 88.45 E
Qom 22 Hf 34.39N 50.54 E
Qom 24 Ne 34.48N 51.02 E
Qomolangma Feng=Everest, Mount- (EN) 21 Kg 27.59N 86.56 E
Qomrud 24 Ne 34.43N 51.04 E
Qomsheh 23 Hc 32.00N 51.50 E
Qondūz [3] 23 Kb 36.45N 68.30 E
Qondūz 23 If 36.45N 68.51 E
Qondūz 23 Kb 37.00N 68.16 E
Qoqek/Tacheng 22 Ke 46.45N 82.57 E
Qôrnoq 41 Gf 64.30N 51.19W
Qorveh 24 Le 35.10N 47.48 E
Qoşbeh-ye Naşşār 23 Gc 30.02N 48.27 E
Qoţbābād [Iran] 24 Oh 28.39N 53.37 E
Qoţbābād [Iran] 24 Qi 27.46N 56.06 E
Qoţūr 24 Kc 38.28N 44.25 E
Qotūr 24 Kc 38.46N 45.16 E
Quadda 31 Jh 8.04N 22.24 E
Quadros, Lagoa dos- 55 Gi 29.42S 50.05W
Quairading 59 Df 32.01S 117.25 E
Quakenbrück 10 Dd 52.41N 7.57 E
Quanah 45 Gi 34.18N 99.44W
Quanbao Shan 27 Je 34.08N 111.26 E
Quang Ngai 25 Le 15.07N 108.48 E
Quang Tri 25 Le 21.02N 106.29 E
Quan He 28 Ch 32.55N 115.52 E
Quanjiao 28 Eh 32.09N 118.16 E
Quan Long 25 Lg 9.11N 105.08 E
Quanzhou [China] 22 Ng 24.57N 118.35 E
Quanzhou [China] 27 Jf 26.01N 111.04 E
Qu'Appelle River 42 Hf 50.27N 101.19W
Quaraí 56 Id 30.23S 56.27W
Quaraí, Rio- 55 Dj 30.12S 57.36W
Quaregnon 12 Fd 50.26N 3.51 E
Quartu Sant'Elena 14 Dk 39.14N 9.11 E
Quartz Lake 42 Jb 70.57N 80.40W
Quartz Mountain 46 De 43.10N 122.40W
Quartzsite 46 Hj 33.40N 114.13W
Quatre, Isle- 51n Bb 12.57N 61.15W
Quatsino Sound 46 Aa 50.25N 128.10W
Qūchān 22 Hf 37.06N 58.30 E
Qué 36 Ce 14.43S 15.06 E
Queanbeyan 59 Jg 35.21S 149.14 E
Québec 39 Le 46.49N 71.13W
Québec [3] 42 Kf 54.00N 72.00W
Quebó 55 Db 14.36S 56.04W
Quebra Anzol, Rio- 55 Id 19.09S 47.38W
Quebracho 55 Dj 31.57S 57.57W
Quebradillas 51a Bb 18.28N 66.56W
Quedas do Iguaçu 55 Fg 25.31S 52.54W
Quedlinburg 10 He 51.47N 11.09 E
Queen, Cape - 42 Jd 64.43N 78.18W
Queen Alexandra Range 66 Jg 84.00S 168.00 E
Queen Bess, Mount - 42 Ff 51.18N 124.33W
Queenborough 12 Cc 51.25N 0.46 E
Queen Charlotte Islands 38 Gd 51.30N 129.00W
Queen Charlotte Sound 42 Ef 51.30N 129.30W
Queen Charlotte Strait 38 Gd 50.40N 127.25W
Queen Elizabeth Islands 38 Ib 79.00N 105.00W
Queen Elizabeth Range 66 Kg 83.20S 162.00 E
Queen Mary Land 66 Ge 69.00S 96.00 E
Queen Maud Gulf 38 Ic 68.25N 102.30W
Queen Maud Land (EN) 66 Cf 72.30S 12.00 E
Queen Maud Range 66 Lg 86.00S 160.00W
Queens Channel [Austl.] 59 Fb 14.45S 129.25 E
Queens Channel [N.W.T.-Can.] 42 Ha 76.11N 96.00W
Queensland 59 Id 22.00S 145.00 E
Queenstown [Austl.] 59 Jh 42.05S 145.33 E
Queenstown [Guy.] 50 Gi 7.12N 58.29W
Queenstown [N.Z.] 62 Cf 45.02S 168.40 E
Queenstown [S.Afr.] 31 Jl 31.52S 26.52 E
Queguay, Cuchilla del- 55 Dj 31.50S 57.30W
Queguay Grande, Río- 55 Ck 32.09S 58.09W
Queich 12 Ke 49.14N 8.23 E
Queimadas 54 Kf 10.58S 39.38W
Queiros 56 Ge 21.49S 50.13W
Quela 36 Cd 9.15S 17.05 E
Quelimane 31 Kj 17.51S 36.52 E
Quemado 45 Bi 34.20N 108.30W
Quemado de Güines 49 Gb 22.48N 80.15W
Quembo 36 De 14.57S 20.22 E
Quemú-Quemú 56 He 36.03S 63.33W
Quepos 49 Ei 9.25N 84.09W
Que Que 31 Jj 18.55S 29.49 E
Quequén 56 Ie 38.32S 58.42W
Quequén Grande, Río- 55 Cn 38.34S 58.43W
Quequén Salado, Río- 55 Bn 38.56S 60.31W
Quercy 11 Hj 44.15N 1.15 E
Querétaro [2] 47 Ed 21.00N 99.55W
Querétaro 39 Ig 20.36N 100.23W
Querobabi 48 Db 30.03N 111.01W
Quesada [C.R.] 49 Eh 10.19N 84.26W
Quesada [Sp.] 13 Ig 37.51N 3.04W
Queshan 27 Je 32.42N 114.02 E
Quesnel 42 Ff 52.59N 122.30W
Quesnel Lake 42 Ff 52.32N 121.05W
Questa 45 Dh 36.42N 105.36W
Quetena 54 Eh 22.10S 67.25W
Quetico Lake 45 Kb 48.37N 91.52W
Quetta 22 If 30.12N 67.00 E
Quevas, Cerro- 48 Dc 29.15N 111.20W
Quevedo 54 Cd 1.02S 79.27W
Queyras 11 Mj 44.44N 6.49 E
Quezaltenango 39 Jh 14.50N 91.31W
Quezaltenango [3] 49 Bf 14.45N 91.40W
Quezon 26 Ge 9.14N 117.56 E
Quezon City 22 Oh 14.38N 121.00 E
Qufu 28 Dg 35.35N 116.59 E
Quianguoshen → Qian Gorlos 27 Lb 45.05N 124.52 E
Quianshan 28 Di 30.38N 116.35 E
Quibala 36 Be 10.44S 14.59 E
Quibaxe 36 Bd 8.30S 14.36 E
Quibdó 54 Cb 5.42N 76.39W
Quiberon, Baie de- 11 Dg 47.32N 3.00W
Quiberon, Presqu'île de- 11 Cg 47.30N 3.08W
Quibor 49 Mi 9.56N 69.37W
Quiché [3] 49 Bf 15.30N 90.55W
Quierschied 12 Je 49.19N 7.03 E
Quiha 35 Fc 13.28N 39.33 E
Quiindy 55 Dh 25.58S 57.16W
Quijarro 55 Cd 19.26S 58.08W
Quilá 48 Fe 24.23N 107.13W
Quilán, Cabo- 56 Ff 43.16S 74.23W
Quillabamba 54 Df 12.49S 72.43W
Quillacollo 54 Eg 17.26S 66.17W
Quillagua 56 Gb 21.39S 69.33W
Quillan 11 Il 42.52N 2.11 E
Quillebeuf-sur-Seine 12 Ce 49.28N 0.31 E
Quillota 56 Fd 32.53S 71.16W
Quilmes 56 Id 34.44S 58.16W
Quilon 25 Fg 8.53N 76.36 E
Quilpie 59 Ie 26.37S 144.15 E
Quilqué 56 Fd 33.03S 71.27W
Quimari, Alto de- 49 Ii 8.07N 76.23W
Quimbele 36 Cd 6.30S 16.14 E
Quimili 56 Hc 27.38S 62.25W
Quimome 55 Bc 17.42S 61.16W
Quimome, Rio- 55 Bc 17.36S 61.09W
Quimper 11 Bf 48.00N 4.06W
Quimperlé 11 Cg 47.52N 3.33W
Quinault River 46 Cc 47.23N 124.18W
Quincy [Ca.-U.S.] 46 Eg 39.56N 120.57W
Quincy [Fl.-U.S.] 44 Ej 30.37N 84.32W
Quincy [Il.-U.S.] 43 Id 39.56N 91.23W
Quincy [Ma.-U.S.] 44 Ld 42.15N 71.01W
Quincy [Wa.-U.S.] 46 Fc 47.14N 119.51W
Quindío [2] 54 Cc 4.30N 75.40W
Quingey 11 Lg 47.06N 5.53 E
Quinhagak 40 Ge 59.45N 161.43W
Qui Nhon 22 Mh 13.46N 109.14 E
Quiñihual 55 Bm 37.47S 61.36W
Quinilubian Group 26 Hd 11.27N 120.48 E
Quinn River 46 Ff 40.25N 119.00W
Quiñones 48 De 24.22N 111.25W
Quintanar de la Orden 13 Ie 39.34N 3.03W
Quintana Roo [2] 47 Ge 19.40N 88.30W
Quinze, Lac des- 44 Hb 47.30N 79.00W
Quionga 37 Gb 10.35S 40.33 E
Quirigua 49 Cf 15.18N 89.07W
Quirihue 56 Fe 36.17S 72.32W
Quirima 36 Ce 10.48S 18.09 E
Quirinópolis 54 Hg 18.32S 50.30W
Quiroga 13 Eb 42.29N 7.16W
Quiros, Cap- 63b Cb 14.56S 167.01 E
Quisiro 49 Lh 10.53N 71.17W
Quissanga 37 Gb 12.25S 40.29 E
Quissico 37 Ed 24.43S 34.45 E
Quita Sueno Bank 47 Hf 14.20N 81.15W
Quitengues 36 Be 14.06S 14.05 E
Quiterage 37 Gb 11.45S 40.27 E
Quitéria, Rio- 55 Ge 20.16S 51.08W
Quitexe 36 Cd 7.56S 15.03 E
Quitilipi 55 Bh 26.52S 60.13W
Quitman [Ga.-U.S.] 44 Fj 30.47N 83.33W
Quitman [Ms.-U.S.] 45 Lj 32.03N 88.43W
Quito 53 If 0.13S 78.30W
Quitovac 48 Cb 31.32N 112.42W
Quixadá 54 Kd 4.58S 39.01W
Quixeramobim 54 Ke 5.12S 39.17W
Qujiang 28 Cj 28.14N 115.46 E
Qu Jiang [China] 27 Kf 29.32N 119.31 E
Qu Jiang [China] 27 Ie 30.01N 106.24 E
Qujing 27 Hf 25.31N 103.45 E
Qul'ān, Jazā'ir- 24 Fj 24.22N 35.23 E
Qulansiyah 23 Hg 12.41N 53.29 E
Qulaybīah 32 Jb 36.51N 11.06 E
Qulbān al 'Isāwīyah 24 Gg 30.38N 37.53 E
Qulbān an Nabk al Gharbī 24 Gg 31.15N 37.26 E
Qumar He 21 Lf 34.42N 94.50 E
Qumarlêb 27 Ge 34.35N 95.18 E
Qunayfidhah, Nafūd- 24 Kj 24.45N 45.30 E
Quoi 64d Ba 7.32N 151.59 E
Quoich 42 Id 63.56N 93.25W
Quorn 59 Hf 32.21S 138.03 E
Quqên/Jinchuan 27 He 31.02N 102.02 E
Quraitu 24 Ke 34.36N 45.30 E
Qurayyāt, Juzur- 32 Jb 35.48N 11.02 E
Qurbah 14 En 36.35N 10.52 E
Qurdūd 35 Dc 10.17N 29.56 E
Qūr Laban 24 Cg 30.23N 28.59 E
Qurunbāliyah 14 En 36.36N 10.30 E
Qūş 33 Fd 25.55N 32.45 E
Quşay'ir 35 Ic 14.55N 50.20 E
Qutdligssat 41 Gd 70.12N 53.00W
Quthing 37 Df 30.24S 27.42 E
Quţū 33 Hf 18.30N 41.04 E
Quwaiz 33 He 20.27N 44.53 E
Quxian 27 Kf 28.54N 118.53 E
Qüxü 27 Ff 29.23N 90.45 E
Quyang 28 Ce 38.37N 114.41 E
Quy Chau 25 Le 19.33N 105.06 E
Quzhou 28 Cf 36.47N 114.56 E
Qyteti Stalin 15 Ci 40.48N 19.54 E

R

Raab 10 Ni 47.41N 17.38 E
Raahe/Brahestad 7 Fd 64.41N 24.29 E
Rääkkylä 8 Mb 62.19N 29.37 E
Raalte 12 Ib 52.23N 6.17 E
Raamsdonk 12 Gc 51.41N 4.54 E
Raanes Peninsula 42 Ia 78.20N 86.20W
Raasay, Island of- 9 Gd 57.25N 6.04W
Raasay, Sound of- 9 Gd 57.25N 6.05W
Raasiku/Raziku 8 Ke 59.22N 25.11 E
Rab 14 If 44.46N 14.59 E
Rab 14 If 44.45N 14.46 E
Rába 10 Ni 47.41N 17.38 E
Raba 10 Qf 50.09N 20.30 E
Raba 22 Nj 8.27S 118.46 E
Rabāble 35 Hd 8.14N 48.18 E
Rabaçal 13 Ec 41.30N 7.12W
Rabat [Malta] 14 Io 35.50N 14.29 E
Rabat [Mor.] 31 Ge 34.02N 6.50W
Rabat-Salé [2] 32 Fc 34.02N 6.50W
Rabaul 58 Ge 4.12S 152.12 E
Rábca 10 Ni 47.41N 17.37 E
Rabenau 12 Kd 50.40N 8.52 E
Rabī', Ash Shallāl ar-= Fourth Cataract (EN) 30 Kg 18.47N 32.03 E
Rabiah 24 Jd 36.47N 42.07 E
Rábida, Monasterio de- 13 Fg 37.12N 6.55W
Rābigh 23 Ee 22.48N 39.02 E
Rabinal 49 Bf 15.06N 90.27W
Rabka 10 Pg 49.36N 19.56 E
Rabočeostrovsk 7 Id 64.59N 34.44 E
Rabyānah, Şaḩrā'- 30 Jf 24.30N 21.00 E
Rabyānah, Wāḩāt al-= Rebiana Oasis (EN) 33 De 24.14N 21.59 E
Răcăciuni 15 Jc 46.20N 26.59 E
Racalmuto 14 Hm 37.24N 13.44 E
Răcăşdia 15 Ee 44.59N 21.38 E
Racconigi 14 Bf 44.46N 7.46 E
Race, Cape- 38 Ne 46.40N 53.10W
Race Point 44 Ld 42.04N 70.14W
Rach Gia 22 Mh 10.01N 105.05 E
Rachid 32 Ef 18.48N 11.41W
Raciąż 10 Qd 52.47N 20.06 E
Racibórz 10 Of 50.06N 18.13 E
Racine 43 Jc 42.43N 87.48W
Ráckeve 10 Oi 47.10N 18.57 E
Racos 15 Ic 46.03N 25.30 E
Råda 8 Ed 60.00N 13.36 E
Radama, Iles- 37 Hb 14.00S 47.47 E
Radan 15 Ef 43.02N 21.30 E
Rădăuţi 15 Ib 47.51N 25.55 E
Radbuza 10 Jg 49.46N 13.24 E
Radeberg 10 Je 51.07N 13.55 E
Radebeul 10 Je 51.06N 13.39 E
Radeče 14 Jd 46.04N 15.11 E
Radehov 10 Uf 50.13N 24.43 E
Radenthein 14 Hd 46.48N 13.43 E
Radevormwald 12 Jc 51.12N 7.22 E
Radew 10 Lb 54.07N 15.50 E
Radford 44 Gg 37.07N 80.34W
Radnevo 15 Ig 42.18N 25.56 E
Radolfzell 10 Ei 47.44N 8.58 E
Radom [2] 10 Re 51.25N 21.10 E
Radom 6 Ie 51.25N 21.10 E
Radomir 15 Fg 42.33N 22.58 E
Radomka 10 Re 51.43N 21.26 E
Radomsko 10 Pe 51.05N 19.25 E
Radomyšl 16 Fd 50.29N 29.14 E
Radomyśl Wielki 10 Rf 50.12N 21.16 E
Radoškoviči 8 Lj 54.12N 27.17 E
Radotín 10 Kg 49.59N 14.22 E
Radovanu 15 Je 44.12N 26.31 E
Radoviš 15 Fh 41.38N 22.28 E
Radøy 8 Ad 60.40N 5.00 E
Radstadt 14 Hc 47.23N 13.27 E
Radun 10 Vb 54.02N 25.07 E
Radunia 10 Ob 54.25N 18.45 E
Raduša 14 Lg 43.52N 17.29 E
Radvaniči 10 Ue 51.59N 24.09 E
Radviliškis 7 Fi 55.50N 23.33 E
Radymno 10 Sg 49.57N 22.48 E
Radziejów 10 Od 52.38N 18.32 E
Radzyń Podlaski 10 Se 51.48N 22.38 E
Rae 42 Fd 62.50N 116.00W
Rāe Bareli 25 Gc 26.13N 81.14 E
Rae Isthmus 42 Ic 66.55N 86.10W
Raesfeld 12 Ic 51.46N 6.51 E
Raeside, Lake- 59 Ee 29.30S 121.50 E
Raetihi 62 Fc 39.26S 175.17 E
Raevavae, Ile- 57 Mg 23.52S 147.40W
Raevski, Groupe- 61 Mc 16.45S 144.14W
Rāf, Jabal- 24 Hh 29.12N 39.48 E
Rafaela 53 Ji 31.17S 61.30W
Rafai 35 Ce 4.58N 23.56 E
Rafḩā' 23 Fd 29.42N 43.30 E
Rafi 34 Fc 13.28N 4.10 E
Rāfkā 24 Qe 35.55N 57.36 E
Rafsanjān 23 Ic 30.24N 56.01 E
Rāfsö/Reposaari 8 Ic 61.37N 21.27 E
Raga 31 Jh 8.28N 25.41 E
Ragay Gulf 26 Hd 13.30N 122.45 E
Ragged Island 49 Jb 22.12N 75.44W
Ragged Island Range 47 Id 22.42N 75.55W
Ragged Point 51q Bb 13.10N 59.25W
Raglan 62 Fb 37.48S 174.52 E
Raguencau 44 Ma 49.04N 68.32W
Ragusa 14 In 36.55N 14.44 E
Raguva 8 Ki 55.30N 24.45 E
Raha 26 Hg 4.51S 122.43 E
Raḩā, Ḩarrat ar- 24 Gi 27.40N 36.40 E
Rahad al Bardī 35 Cc 11.18N 23.53 E
Rahama 34 Gc 10.25N 8.41 E
Rahat, Ḩarrat- 23 He 23.00N 40.05 E
Rahat Dağı 15 Ml 37.08N 29.49 E
Rahden 12 Kb 52.26N 8.37 E
Rāhgāmāti 25 Id 22.38N 92.12 E
Rahīmyār Khan 25 Ec 28.25N 70.18 E
Rahmanovskije Ključi 19 If 49.35N 86.35 E
Rahmet 19 Gf 49.19N 65.16 E
Råholt 8 Dd 60.16N 11.11 E
Rahouia 13 Ni 35.32N 1.01 E
Rahov 16 De 48.02N 24.18 E
Rahrbach, Kirchhundem- 12 Jc 51.02N 7.59 E
Raia 13 Df 39.00N 8.17W
Raiatea, Ile- 57 Lf 16.50S 151.25W
Raices 55 Cj 31.54S 59.16W
Raichūr 25 Jh 16.12N 77.22 E
Raiganj 25 Hc 25.37N 88.07 E
Raigarh 25 Gd 21.54N 83.24 E
Raijua, Pulau- 26 Hi 10.37S 121.36 E
Rainbow Peak 46 Hd 44.55N 115.17W
Rainier, Mount- 38 Ge 46.52N 121.46W
Rainy Lake 43 Ib 48.42N 93.10W
Rainy River 45 Ib 48.43N 94.29W
Rainy River 45 Ib 48.50N 94.41W
Raipur 22 Kg 21.14N 81.38 E
Raisi, Punta- 14 Hl 38.11N 13.06 E
Raisio/Reso 7 Ff 60.29N 22.11 E
Raita Bank (EN) 60 Mb 25.25N 169.30W
Raja Ampat, Kepulauan- 26 Jg 0.50S 130.25 E
Rājahmundry 22 Kh 16.59N 81.47 E
Rajakoski 7 Gb 68.59N 29.07 E
Rajang 21 Ni 2.07N 111.12 E
Rājapālaiyam 25 Fg 9.27N 77.34 E
Rājasthān [3] 25 Ec 26.00N 74.00 E
Rājasthān Canal 25 Eb 31.10N 75.00 E
Rajbiraj 25 Hc 26.30N 86.50 E
Rajčihinsk 20 Hg 49.43N 129.27 E
Rajevski 17 Gi 54.04N 54.56 E
Rajgarh 25 Fc 28.38N 75.23 E
Rajgródzkie, Jezioro- 10 Sc 53.45N 22.38 E
Rajić 10 Ni 48.00N 17.12 E
Rajkot 22 Jg 22.18N 70.47 E
Raj-Nāndgaon 25 Gd 21.06N 81.02 E
Rajony Respublikanskogo Podčinenija [Kirg.-U.S.S.R.] [3] 19 Hg 42.30N 73.50 E
Rajony Respublikanskogo Podčinenija [Tad.-U.S.S.R.] [3] 19 Gh 38.50N 69.30 E

Index Symbols

[1] Independent Nation
[2] State, Region
[3] District, County
[4] Municipality
[5] Colony, Dependency
Continent
Physical Region
Historical or Cultural Region
Mount, Mountain
Volcano
Hill
Mountains, Mountain Range
Hills, Escarpment
Plateau, Upland
Pass, Gap
Plain, Lowland
Delta
Salt Flat
Valley, Canyon
Crater, Cave
Karst Features
Depression
Polder
Desert, Dunes
Forest, Woods
Heath, Steppe
Oasis
Cape, Point
Coast, Beach
Cliff
Peninsula
Isthmus
Sandbank
Island
Atoll
Rock, Reef
Islands, Archipelago
Rocks, Reefs
Coral Reef
Well, Spring
Geyser
River, Stream
Waterfall Rapids
River Mouth, Estuary
Lake
Salt Lake
Intermittent Lake
Reservoir
Swamp, Pond
Canal
Glacier
Ice Shelf, Pack Ice
Ocean
Sea
Gulf, Bay
Strait, Fjord
Lagoon
Bank
Seamount
Tablemount
Ridge
Shelf
Basin
Escarpment, Sea Scarp
Fracture
Trench, Abyss
National Park, Reserve
Point of Interest
Recreation Site
Cave, Cavern
Historic Site
Ruins
Wall, Walls
Church, Abbey
Temple
Scientific Station
Airport
Port
Lighthouse
Mine
Tunnel
Dam, Bridge

Rājshāhi 25 Hd 24.22N 88.36 E
Rakahanga Atoll 57 Kl 10.02S 161.05W
Rakaia 62 Ee 43.54S 172.13 E
Rakaia 62 Ee 43.45S 172.01 E
Rakan, Ra's- 24 Ni 26.10N 51.13 E
Rakata, Pulau- 26 Eh 6.10S 105.26 E
Raka Zangbo 27 Ef 29.24N 87.58 E
Rakhawt, Wādī- 35 Ib 18.16N 51.50 E
Rakht-e Shāh 24 Mf 33.17N 49.23 E
Rakitnoje 28 Mb 45.36N 134.17 E
Rakitovo 15 Hh 41.59N 24.05 E
Rakkestad 8 De 59.26N 11.21 E
Rakoniewice 10 Md 52.10N 16.16 E
Rakops 37 Cd 21.01S 24.20 E
Rakovnicka panev 10 Jf 50.10N 13.30 E
Rakovnik 10 Jf 50.06N 13.43 E
Rakovski 15 Hg 42.18N 24.58 E
Raków 10 Rf 50.42N 21.03 E
Rakušečny, Mys- 16 Qh 42.52N 51.55 E
Råkvåg 7 Ce 63.46N 10.05 E
Rakvere 7 Gg 59.22N 26.22 E
Raleigh [N.C.-U.S.] 39 Lf 35.47N 78.39W
Raleigh [Ont.-Can.] 45 Kb 49.31N 91.56W
Raleigh Bay 44 Ih 35.00N 76.20W
Ralik Chain 57 Hd 8.00N 167.00 E
Rama 47 Hf 12.09N 84.15W
Rama, Río- 49 Eg 12.08N 84.13W
Ramādah 32 Jc 32.19N 10.24 E
Ramaḡīn, Wādī- 24 Ej 24.57N 32.34 E
Ramales de la Victoria 13 Ia 43.15N 3.27W
Ramalho, Serra do- 55 Ja 13.45S 44.00W
Ramapo Bank (EN) 57 Fb 27.15N 145.10 E
Ramatlabama 37 De 25.37S 25.30 E
Ramberg 10 He 51.45N 11.05 E
Rambervillers 11 Mf 48.21N 6.38 E
Rambi 63d Cb 16.30S 179.59W
Rambouillet 11 Hf 48.39N 1.50 E
Rambutyo Island 57 Fe 2.18S 147.48 E
Rāmhormoz 23 Mg 31.16N 49.36 E
Ramigala/Ramygala 8 Ki 55.28N 24.23 E
Ramis 35 Gd 8.02N 41.36 E
Ramla 24 Fg 31.55N 34.52 E
Ramlīyah, 'Aqabat ar- 24 Di 26.01N 30.42 E
Ramlu 35 Gc 13.20N 41.45 E
Ramm, Jabal- 24 Fh 29.35N 35.24 E
Rammāk, Ghurd ar- 24 Ch 29.40N 29.20 E
Rāmnagar 25 Fc 29.24N 79.07 E
Ramnäs 8 Ge 59.46N 16.12 E
Ramón Santamarina 55 Cn 38.26S 59.20W
Ramos 63a Ec 8.16S 160.11 E
Ramos, Río- 48 Ge 25.35N 105.03W
Ramotswa 37 Dd 24.52S 25.50 E
Rāmpur 25 Fc 28.49N 79.02 E
Ramree 25 Ie 19.06N 93.48 E
Rams 24 Qj 25.53N 56.02 E
Rämsar 24 Nd 36.53N 50.41 E
Ramsele 7 De 63.33N 16.29 E
Ramsey [Eng.-U.K.] 12 Bb 52.27N 0.07W
Ramsey [Ont.-Can.] 44 Fb 47.29N 82.24W
Ramsey [U.K.] 9 Ig 54.20N 4.21W
Ramsey Lake 42 Jg 47.20N 83.00W
Ramsgate 9 Oj 51.20N 1.25 E
Rāmshīr 24 Mg 30.50N 49.30 E
Ramsjö 7 De 62.11N 15.39 E
Ramstein-Miesenbach 12 Je 49.27N 7.32 E
Ramsund 7 Db 68.29N 16.32 E
Ramu 60 Di 4.02S 144.41 E
Ramu 36 Hb 3.56N 41.13 E
Ramvik 7 De 62.49N 17.51 E
Ramville, Ilet- 51h Bb 14.42N 60.53W
Ramygala/Ramigala 8 Ki 55.28N 24.23 E
Rana 7 Dc 66.20N 14.08 E
Rañadoiro, Sierra del- 13 Fa 43.20N 6.45W
Ranai 26 Ef 3.55N 108.23 E
Ranakah, Potjo- 26 Hh 8.38S 120.31 E
Rana Kao, Volcán- 65d Ac 27.11S 109.27W
Rana Roi, Volcán- 65d Ab 27.05S 109.23W
Rana Roraka, Volcán- 65d Bb 27.07S 109.18W
Ranau 26 Ge 5.58N 116.41 E
Ranča 14 Lf 44.24N 17.22 E
Rancagua 53 Ii 34.10S 70.45W
Rance 11 Ef 48.31N 1.59W
Rance, Sivry-Rance- 12 Gd 50.09N 4.16 E
Rancharia 55 Gf 22.15S 50.55W
Rancheria, Río- 49 Kh 11.34N 72.54W
Rānchī 22 Kg 23.21N 85.20 E
Ranchos 55 Cl 35.32S 58.22W
Ranco, Lago- 56 Ff 40.14S 72.24W
Randa 35 Gc 11.51N 42.40 E
Randaberg 8 Ae 59.00N 5.36 E
Randazzo 14 Im 37.53N 14.57 E
Randers 7 Ch 56.28N 10.03 E
Randers Fjord 8 Dh 56.35N 10.20 E
Randijaure 7 Ec 66.42N 19.18 E
Randow 10 Kc 53.41N 14.04 E
Randsfjorden 7 Cf 60.25N 10.25 E
Ranérou 34 Cb 15.18N 13.58W
Ranfurly 62 Df 45.08S 170.06 E
Rangasa, Tanjung- 26 Gg 3.33S 118.56 E
Ranger 45 Gj 32.28N 98.41W
Rangiora 62 Ee 43.18S 172.36 E
Rangiroa Atoll 57 Mf 15.10S 147.35W
Rangitaiki 62 Gb 37.55S 176.53 E
Rangitata 62 Df 44.10S 171.30 E
Rangitikei 62 Fd 40.17S 175.13 E
Rangkasbitung 26 Eh 6.21S 106.15 E
Rangoon 22 Lh 16.47N 96.10 E
Rangoon 25 Je 16.40N 95.20 E
Rangpur 25 Hc 25.44N 89.16 E
Rāniyah 24 Kd 36.15N 44.53 E
Rankin Inlet 39 Jc 62.45N 92.10W
Rankoshi 29a Bb 42.47N 140.31 E
Rannoch, Loch- 9 Ie 56.41N 4.20W
Ranobe 37 Gc 17.10S 44.08 E
Ranon 63b Dc 16.09S 168.07 E
Ranong 25 Jg 9.59N 98.40 E
Ranongga Island 60 Fi 8.05S 156.34 E
Ranova 16 Lb 54.07N 40.14 E
Ransaren 7 Dd 65.14N 14.59 E
Rantabe 37 Hc 15.42S 49.39 E
Rantasalmi 8 Mb 62.04N 28.18 E
Rantaupanjang 26 Fg 1.23S 112.04 E
Rantauprapat 26 Cf 2.06N 99.50 E
Rantekombola, Bulu- 21 Oj 3.21S 120.01 E
Rantoul 45 Lf 40.19N 88.09W
Ranua 7 Gd 65.55N 26.32 E
Ranyah, Wādī- 33 He 21.18N 43.20 E
Raohe 27 Nb 46.48N 133.58 E
Raon-l'Étape 11 Mf 48.24N 6.51 E
Raoui, Erg er- 32 Gd 29.15N 2.45W
Raoul Island 57 Jg 29.15S 177.52W
Raoyang 28 Ce 38.14N 115.44 E
Raoyang He 28 Gd 41.13N 122.12 E
Rapa, Ile- 57 Mg 27.36S 144.20W
Rapallo 14 Df 44.21N 9.14 E
Rapang 26 Gg 3.50S 119.48 E
Rapa Nui/Pascua, Isla de-= Easter Island (EN) 57 Qg 27.07S 109.22W
Raper, Cape- 42 Kc 69.41N 67.24W
Rapid City 39 Ie 44.05N 103.14W
Rapid Creek 45 Ee 43.54N 102.37W
Rapid River 44 Dc 45.58N 86.59W
Räpina/Rjapina 8 Lf 58.03N 27.35 E
Rapla 7 Fg 59.02N 24.47 E
Rappahannock River 44 Ig 37.34N 76.18W
Rápulo, Río- 52 Jg 13.43S 65.32W
Rāqūbah 31 If 28.58N 19.02 E
Raraka Atoll 57 Mf 16.10S 144.54W
Raroia Atoll 57 Mf 16.05S 142.26W
Rarotonga Island 57 Lg 21.14S 159.46W
Rasa, Punta- 52 Jj 40.51S 62.19W
Ra's Abū Daraj 24 Eh 29.23N 32.33 E
Ra's Abū Rudays 24 Eh 28.53N 33.11 E
Ra's Abū Shajarah 35 Fa 21.04N 37.14 E
Ra's Ajdīr 33 Bc 33.09N 11.34 E
Ra's al 'Ayn 24 Id 36.51N 40.04 E
Ra's al-Barr 24 Dg 31.31N 31.50 E
Ra's al Ḥikmah 24 Bg 31.08N 27.50 E
Ra's al Jabal 14 Em 37.13N 10.08 E
Ra's al Khafjī 24 Mh 28.25N 48.30 E
Ra's al Khaymah 23 Id 25.47N 55.57 E
Ra's al Mish'āb 24 Mh 28.12N 48.37 E
Ra's al Unūf 33 Cc 30.31N 18.34 E
Ra's an Naqb 24 Fh 30.00N 35.29 E
Ra's as Sidr 24 Eh 29.36N 32.40 E
Ra's at Tannūrah 24 Ni 26.42N 50.10 E
Ras Beddouza 30 Ge 32.22N 9.18W
Ras Dashan 30 Kg 13.19N 38.20 E
Raseiniai/Rasejnjaj 7 Fi 55.23N 23.07 E
Rasejnjaj/Raseiniai 7 Fi 55.23N 23.07 E
Râs el Mâ 34 Eb 16.37N 4.27W
Ras-el-Ma 13 Ji 35.08N 2.29W
Ras el Oued 13 Ri 35.57N 5.02 E
Ra's Ghārib 33 Fd 28.21N 33.06 E
Rashād 35 Ec 11.51N 31.04 E
Rāshayyā 24 Ff 33.30N 35.51 E
Rashīd = Rosetta (EN) 33 Fc 31.24N 30.25 E
Rashīd, Maṣabb- 24 Dg 31.30N 30.20 E
Rasht 22 Gf 37.16N 49.36 E
Rāsiga 'Alūla 35 Ic 11.59N 50.50 E
Rās Jumbo 35 Gf 1.37S 41.31 E
Raška 15 Df 43.18N 20.38 E
Ra's Madhar, Jabal- 24 Gj 25.46N 37.32 E
Ra's Matārimah 24 Eh 29.27N 32.43 E
Rasmussen Basin 42 Hc 67.56N 95.15W
Rason Lake 59 Ee 28.45S 124.20 E
Rasskazovo 19 Ee 52.39N 41.57 E
Rassūa, Ostrov- 20 Kg 47.40N 153.00 E
Rassvet 20 Ee 57.00N 91.32 E
Ras-Tarf, Cap- 13 Ii 35.17N 3.41W
Rastatt 10 Eh 48.51N 8.12 E
Rastede 12 Ka 53.15N 8.12 E
Rastigaissa 7 Ga 70.03N 26.18 E
Råstojaure 7 Eb 68.45N 20.30 E
Ra's Ṭurunbi 24 Fj 25.40N 34.35 E
Rasūl 24 Pi 27.10N 55.30 E
Ra's Zayt 33 Fd 27.56N 33.31 E
Rat 40a Bb 51.55N 178.20 E
Ratak Chain 57 Id 9.00N 171.00 E
Ratangarh 25 Ec 28.05N 74.36 E
Rätansbyn 7 De 62.29N 14.32 E
Rat Buri 25 Jf 13.32N 99.49 E
Rathbun Lake 45 Jf 40.54N 93.05W
Ráth Droma/Rathdrum 9 Gi 52.56N 6.13W
Rathdrum/Ráth Droma 9 Gi 52.56N 6.13W
Rathenow 10 Id 52.36N 12.20 E
Rathlin Island/Reachlainn 9 Gf 55.18N 6.13W
Ráth Luirc/An Ráth 9 Ei 52.21N 8.41W
Rathor, Pik- 18 If 37.55N 72.14 E
Rātikon 14 Dc 47.03N 9.40 E
Ratingen 12 Ic 51.18N 6.51 E
Rätische Alpen=Rhaetian Alps (EN) 14 Dd 46.30N 10.00 E
Rat Islands 38 Ad 52.00N 178.00 E
Ratlām 25 Fd 23.19N 75.04 E
Ratmanova, Ostrov- 20 Lc 55.45N 169.00W
Ratnāgiri 25 Ee 16.59N 73.18 E
Ratnapura 25 Gg 6.41N 80.24 E
Ratno 16 Dd 51.42N 24.31 E
Raton 43 Gd 36.54N 104.24W
Ratqh, Wādī ar- 24 Ie 34.25N 40.55 E
Ratta 20 Dd 63.35N 84.05 E
Rattlesnake Hills 46 Le 42.45N 107.10W
Rattray Head 9 Ld 57.38N 1.46W
Rättvik 7 Df 60.53N 15.06 E
Ratz, Mount- 38 Fd 57.23N 132.19W
Ratzeburg 10 Gc 53.42N 10.46 E
Raub 26 Df 3.48N 101.52 E
Rauch 56 Ie 36.46S 59.06W
Raucourt-et-Flaba 12 Ge 49.36N 4.57 E
Raudeberg 8 Ab 61.59N 5.09 E
Rauer Islands 66 Fe 68.51S 77.50 E
Raufarhöfn 7a Ca 66.27N 15.57W
Raufjellet 8 Dc 61.15N 11.00 E
Raufoss 7 Cf 60.43N 10.37 E
Raukotaha 64n Ac 10.28S 161.01W
Raukumara Range 62 Gc 38.00S 178.00 E
Rauland 8 Be 59.44N 8.00 E
Raúl Leoni, Represa- (Guri) 54 Fb 7.30N 63.00W
Rauma 7 Be 62.33N 7.43 E
Rauma/Raumo 7 Ef 61.08N 21.30 E
Raumo/Rauma 7 Ef 61.08N 21.30 E
Rauna 8 Kg 57.14N 25.39 E
Raunds 12 Bb 52.20N 0.32W
Raurimu 62 Fc 39.07S 175.24 E
Raurkela 22 Kg 22.13N 84.53 E
Rausu 28 Rb 44.01N 145.12 E
Rausu-Dake 29a Da 44.06N 145.07 E
Rautalampi 8 Lb 62.38N 26.50 E
Ravahere Atoll 57 Mf 18.14S 142.09W
Ravan 14 Mf 44.15N 18.16 E
Ravanica, Manastir- 15 Ef 43.58N 21.30 E
Ravānsar 24 Le 34.43N 46.40 E
Ravanusa 14 Hm 37.16N 13.58 E
Rāvar 24 Qg 31.12N 56.53 E
Rava-Russkaja 16 Cd 50.13N 23.37 E
Ravels 12 Gc 51.22N 4.59 E
Ravelsbach 14 Jb 48.30N 15.50 E
Ravels-Poppel 12 Hc 51.27N 5.02 E
Ravenna [It.] 14 Gf 44.25N 12.12 E
Ravenna [Nb.-U.S.] 45 Gf 41.02N 98.55W
Ravensburg 10 Fi 47.47N 9.37 E
Ravenshoe 58 Ff 17.37S 145.29 E
Ravensthorpe 59 Ef 33.35S 120.02 E
Ravi 21 Jf 30.35N 71.49 E
Ravnina 19 Gh 37.57N 62.42 E
Rawaki Atoll (Phoenix) 57 Je 3.43S 170.43W
Rāwalpindi 22 Jf 33.35N 73.03 E
Rawa Mazowiecka 10 Qe 51.46N 20.16 E
Rawāndūz 24 Kd 36.37N 44.31 E
Rawdah 24 Ie 35.15N 41.05 E
Rawene 62 Ea 35.24S 173.30 E
Rawicz 10 Me 51.37N 16.52 E
Rawka 10 Qd 52.07N 20.08 E
Rawlinna 58 Dh 31.01S 125.20 E
Rawlins 43 Fc 41.47N 107.14W
Rawlinson Range 59 Fd 24.50S 128.00 E
Rawson [Arg.] 55 Bl 34.36S 60.04W
Rawson [Arg.] 53 Jj 43.18S 65.06W
Rawura, Ras- 36 He 10.20S 40.30 E
Raxaul 25 Gc 26.59N 84.51 E
Ray, Cape- 42 Lg 47.37N 59.19W
Raya, Bukit- 21 Nj 1.32S 111.05 E
Rayadrug 25 Ff 14.42N 76.52 E
Rayāt 24 Kd 36.40N 44.58 E
Rayleigh 12 Cc 51.35N 0.37 E
Raymond [Alta.-Can.] 46 Ib 49.27N 112.39W
Raymond [Wa.-U.S.] 46 Dc 46.41N 123.44W
Raymondville 45 Hf 26.29N 97.47W
Rayne 45 Jk 30.14N 92.16W
Rayón [Mex.] 48 Jg 21.51N 99.40W
Rayón [Mex.] 48 Dc 29.43N 110.35W
Rayones 48 Ie 25.01N 100.05W
Rayong 25 Kf 12.40N 101.17 E
Raysüt 23 Hf 16.54N 54.02 E
Raytown 45 Ig 39.00N 94.28W
Raz, Pointe du- 11 Bf 48.02N 4.44W
Razan 24 Me 35.23N 49.02 E
Razdan 16 Ni 40.28N 44.43 E
Razdelnaja 16 Gf 46.50N 30.05 E
Razdolinsk 20 Ee 58.25N 94.44 E
Razdolnaja 28 Kc 43.20N 131.49 E
Razdolnoje [R.S.F.S.R.] 28 Kc 43.33N 131.55 E
Razdolnoje [Ukr.-U.S.S.R.] 16 Hg 45.47N 33.30 E
Razgrad 15 Jf 43.32N 26.31 E
Razgrad 15 Jf 43.32N 26.31 E
Razī 24 Mc 38.32N 48.08 E
Raziku/Raasiku 8 Ke 59.22N 25.11 E
Razlog 15 Gh 41.53N 23.28 E
Razo 32 Cf 16.37N 24.36W
Ré, Ile de- 5 Ff 46.12N 1.25W
Reachlainn 9 Gf 55.18N 6.13W
Reachlainn/Rathlin Island 9 Gf 55.18N 6.13W
Reachrainn/Lambay 9 Gh 53.29N 6.01W
Read 42 Gc 69.12N 114.30W
Reading [Eng.-U.K.] 9 Mj 51.28N 0.59W
Reading [Pa.-U.S.] 43 Lc 40.20N 75.55W
Real, Cordillera- [Bol.] 54 Eg 16.30S 68.30W
Real, Cordillera- [Ec.] 52 If 3.00S 78.00W
Real Audiencia 55 Cm 36.11S 58.35W
Real del Castillo 48 Aa 31.58N 116.19W
Realicó 56 He 35.02S 64.15W
Réalmont 11 Ik 43.47N 2.12 E
Reao Atoll 57 Nf 18.31S 136.23W
Rebiana, Monti- 14 Gh 42.35N 12.50 E
Rebais 12 Ff 48.51N 3.14 E
Rebecca, Lake- 59 Ee 29.55S 122.10 E
Rebiana Oasis (EN)= Rabyānah, Wāḥāt al- 33 De 24.14N 21.59 E
Rebollera 13 Hf 38.25N 4.02W
Reboly 7 He 63.52N 30.47 E
Rebord Manambien 37 Hd 24.05S 46.30 E
Rebun 28 Pb 45.23N 141.02 E
Rebun-Dake 29a Ba 45.22N 141.01 E
Rebun-Suidō 29a Ba 45.15N 141.05 E
Rebun-Tō 27 Pb 45.23N 141.10 E
Recalde 55 Bm 36.39S 61.05W
Recanati 14 Hg 43.24N 13.32 E
Recaş 15 Ed 45.48N 21.30 E
Recherche, Archipelago of the- 57 Dh 34.06S 122.45 E
Rečica 19 De 52.22N 30.25 E
Recife 53 Mf 8.03S 34.54W
Recife, Cape- 30 Jl 34.02S 25.45 E
Recke 12 Jb 52.23N 7.43 E
Recklinghausen 10 De 51.37N 7.12 E
Recknitz 10 Ib 54.14N 12.28 E
Recoaro Terme 14 Fe 45.42N 11.13 E
Reconquista 56 Ic 29.09S 59.39W
Recovery Glacier 66 Ag 81.10S 28.00W
Recreo 56 Gc 29.16S 65.04W
Recz 10 Lc 53.16N 15.33 E
Reda 10 Ob 54.38N 18.30 E
Redange 12 He 49.46N 5.54 E
Red Bank 44 Eh 35.07N 85.17W
Red Bay 42 Lf 51.44N 56.25W
Red Bluff 43 Cc 40.11N 122.15W
Red Bluff Reservoir 45 Ek 31.57N 103.56W
Redbridge, London- 12 Cc 51.35N 0.08 E
Red Butte 46 Ii 35.55N 112.03W
Redcar 9 Lg 54.37N 1.04W
Red Cliff 51c Ab 17.05N 62.32W
Redcliff 37 Dc 19.02S 29.50 E
Redcliffe, Mount- 59 Ee 28.25S 121.32 E
Red Cloud 45 Gf 40.05N 98.32W
Red Deer 39 Hd 52.16N 113.48W
Red Deer [Can.] 42 Hf 52.55N 101.27W
Red Deer [Can.] 38 Id 50.56N 109.54W
Redding 39 Ge 40.35N 122.24W
Redditch 9 Li 52.19N 1.56W
Rede 9 Kf 55.08N 2.13W
Redenção 54 Kd 4.13S 38.43W
Redfield 43 Hc 44.53N 98.31W
Red Hill 65a Ec 20.43N 156.15W
Red Hills 45 Gh 37.25N 99.25W
Redkino 7 Ih 56.40N 36.19 E
Red Lake 42 If 51.05N 93.55W
Red Lake 42 If 51.03N 93.49W
Red Lake River 45 Hc 47.55N 97.01W
Red Lakes 43 Ib 48.05N 94.45W
Redlands 46 Gi 34.03N 117.11W
Red Lodge 46 Kd 45.11N 109.15W
Redmond 43 Cc 44.17N 121.11W
Red Mountain [Ca.-U.S.] 46 Df 41.35N 123.06W
Red Mountain [Mt.-U.S.] 46 Ic 47.07N 112.44W
Red Oak 45 If 41.01N 95.14W
Redon 11 Dg 47.39N 2.05W
Redonda 50 Ed 16.55N 62.19W
Redondela 13 Db 42.17N 8.36W
Redondo 13 Ef 38.39N 7.33W
Redondo Beach 46 Fj 33.51N 118.23W
Redoubt Volcano 38 Dc 60.29N 152.45W
Red River [N.Amer.] 38 Jd 50.24N 96.48W
Red River [U.S.] 38 Jf 31.00N 91.40W
Red River (EN)=Hông, Sông- 21 Mg 20.17N 106.34 E
Red River (EN)=Yuan Jiang [Asia] 21 Mg 20.17N 106.34 E
Red Rock, Lake- 45 Jf 41.30N 93.20W
Red Rock River 46 Id 44.59N 112.52W
Redruth 9 Hk 50.13N 5.14W
Red Sea (EN)=Aḥmar, Al Baḥr al- 30 Kf 25.00N 38.00 E
Redstone 42 Fd 64.17N 124.33W
Redstone 46 Da 52.08N 123.42W
Red Volta (EN)=Volta Rouge 30 Gh 10.34N 0.30W
Redwater Creek 46 Mb 48.03N 105.13W
Red Wing 43 Ic 44.34N 92.31W
Redwood City 46 Dh 37.29N 122.13W
Redwood Falls 45 Id 44.32N 95.07W
Ree, Lough-/Loch Rí 9 Fh 53.35N 8.00W
Reed City 44 Ed 43.53N 85.31W
Reedley 46 Fh 36.24N 119.37W
Reeds Peak 45 Cj 33.09N 107.51W
Reedsport 43 Cc 43.42N 124.06W
Reedy Glacier 66 Ng 85.30S 134.00W
Reef Islands 57 Hf 10.15S 166.10 E
Reefton 62 De 42.07S 171.52 E
Reepham 12 Db 52.45N 1.07 E
Rees 12 Ic 51.46N 6.24 E
Reese River 46 Gf 40.39N 116.54W
Refahiye 24 Hc 39.54N 38.46 E
Reforma, Río- 48 Ed 26.56N 108.12W
Reftele 8 Eg 57.11N 13.35 E
Reftinski 17 Jh 57.10N 61.43 E
Refugio 45 Hl 28.18N 97.17W
Refugio, Punta- 48 Cc 29.30N 113.30W
Rega 10 Lb 54.10N 15.18 E
Regar 19 Gh 38.34N 68.13 E
Regen 10 Jh 48.58N 13.08 E
Regen 10 Ig 49.01N 12.06 E
Regensburg 6 Hf 49.01N 12.06 E
Reggane 31 Hf 26.42N 0.10 E
Regge 12 Ib 52.26N 6.29 E
Reggio di Calabria 6 Hh 38.06N 15.39 E
Reggio nell'Emilia 14 Ef 44.43N 10.36 E
Reghin 15 Hc 46.46N 24.42 E
Regina [Fr.Gui.] 54 Hc 4.19N 52.08W
Regina [Sask.-Can.] 39 Id 50.25N 104.39W
Registan (EN)=Rīgestān 21 If 31.00N 65.00 E
Registro 55 Ig 24.30S 47.50W
Registro do Araguaia 55 Gb 15.44S 51.50W
Regnitz 10 Gg 49.54N 10.49 E
Regocijo 48 Gf 23.35N 105.11W
Reguengos de Monsaraz 13 Ef 38.25N 7.32W
Rehburg-Loccum 12 Lb 52.28N 9.14 E
Rehoboth 37 Bd 23.50S 17.00 E
Rehoboth 37 Bd 23.18S 17.03 E
Reḥovot 24 Fg 31.54N 34.49 E
Reichelsheim (Odenwald) 12 Ke 49.43N 8.51 E
Reichenbach 10 If 50.37N 12.18 E
Reichshoffen 12 Jf 48.56N 7.40 E
Reichshoft 12 Jd 50.55N 7.39 E
Reichshoft-Denklingen 12 Jd 50.55N 7.39 E
Reidsville 44 Hg 36.21N 79.40W
Reigate 9 Mj 51.14N 0.13W
Reims 6 Gf 49.15N 4.02 E
Rein=Rhine (EN) 5 Ge 51.52N 6.02 E
Reina Adelaida, Archipiélago- 52 Ik 52.10S 74.25W
Reindeer 42 He 55.34N 103.10W
Reindeer Bank (EN) 51p Ac 11.50N 62.05W
Reindeer Lake 38 Id 57.15N 102.40W
Reineskarvet 8 Cd 60.47N 8.13 E
Reinga, Cape- 62 Ea 34.25S 172.41 E
Reinhardswald 10 Fe 51.30N 9.30 E
Reinheim 12 Je 49.08N 7.11 E
Reinosa 13 Ha 43.00N 4.08W
Reisa 7 Eb 69.48N 21.00 E
Reitoru Atoll 57 Mf 17.52S 143.05W
Reitz 37 De 27.53S 28.31 E
Rejmyra 8 Ff 58.50N 15.55 E
Rejowiec Fabryczny 10 Te 51.08N 23.13 E
Reka Devnja 15 Kf 43.13N 27.36 E
Rekarne 8 Ge 59.20N 16.25 E
Reken 12 Jc 51.48N 7.03 E
Reliance 39 Ic 62.42N 109.08W
Relizane 32 Hb 35.45N 0.33 E
Remagen 12 Jd 50.34N 7.14 E
Remarkable, Mount- 59 Hf 32.48S 138.10 E
Rembang 26 Fh 6.42S 111.20 E
Remedios 49 Gi 8.14N 81.51W
Remedios, Punta- 49 Cg 13.31N 89.49W
Remedios, Río- 49 Mh 11.01N 69.15W
Remich 12 Ie 49.32N 6.22 E
Rémire 54 Hc 4.53N 52.17W
Remiremont 11 Mf 48.01N 6.35 E
Remire Reef 37b Bb 5.05S 53.22 E
Remontnoje 16 Mf 46.33N 43.40 E
Remoulins 11 Kk 43.56N 4.34 E
Remscheid 10 De 51.11N 7.12 E
Rena 7 Cf 61.08N 11.22 E
Rena 8 Dc 61.08N 11.23 E
Renaix/Ronse 11 Jd 50.45N 3.36 E
Renana, Fossa- 5 Gf 48.40N 7.50 E
Renard Islands 63a Ad 10.50S 153.00 E
Renaud Island 66 Qe 65.40S 66.00W
Rende 14 Kk 39.20N 16.11 E
Rendezvous Bay 51b Ab 18.10N 63.07W
Rend Lake 45 Lg 38.05N 88.58W
Rendova Island 60 Fi 8.32S 157.20 E
Rendsburg 10 Fb 54.18N 9.40 E
Renfrew 42 Jg 45.28N 76.41W
Rengat 26 Dg 0.24S 102.33 E
Rengo 56 Fd 34.25S 70.52W
Reni 16 Fg 45.29N 28.18 E
Renko 8 Kd 60.54N 24.17 E
Renkum 12 Hc 51.58N 5.45 E
Renland 41 Jd 71.15N 27.20W
Renmark 58 Fh 34.11S 140.45 E
Rennell, Islas- 56 Fh 52.00S 74.00W
Rennell Island 57 Hf 11.40S 160.10 E
Rennes 6 Ff 48.05N 1.41W
Rennes, Bassin de- 11 Ef 48.05N 1.40W
Rennesøy 8 Ae 59.05N 5.40 E
Rennick Glacier 66 Kf 70.30S 161.45 E
Rennie Lake 42 Gd 61.10N 105.30W
Reno 39 Hf 39.31N 119.48W
Reno 14 Gf 44.38N 12.16 E
Renqiu 28 De 38.42N 116.06 E
Rensselaer [In.-U.S.] 44 De 40.57N 87.09W
Rensselaer [N.Y.-U.S.] 44 Kd 42.37N 73.44W
Renterria 13 Ka 43.19N 1.54W
Renton 46 Dc 47.30N 122.11W
Renwez 12 Ge 49.50N 4.36 E
Renxian 28 Cf 37.07N 114.41 E
Reo 26 Hh 8.19S 120.30 E
Repartimento, Serra do- 55 Jc 17.40S 44.50W
Répce 10 Ni 47.41N 17.02 E
Repino 8 Md 60.10N 29.58 E
Repong, Pulau- 26 Ef 2.22N 105.53 E
Reposaari/Räfsö 8 Ic 61.37N 21.27 E
Republic 46 Fb 48.39N 118.44W
Republican 38 Jf 39.03N 96.48W
Repulse Bay 39 Kc 66.32N 86.15W
Repulse Bay [Austl.] 59 Jd 20.35S 148.45 E
Repulse Bay [Can.] 42 Ic 66.20N 86.00W
Repvåg 7 Fa 70.45N 25.41 E
Requena [Peru] 54 Dd 5.00S 73.50W
Requena [Sp.] 13 Ke 39.29N 1.06W
Requin Bay 51p Bb 12.02N 61.38W
Réquista 11 Ij 44.02N 2.32 E
Reşadiye Yarimadası 15 Km 36.40N 27.45 E
Reschenpass/Resia, Passo di- 14 Ed 46.50N 10.30 E
Resen 15 Eh 41.05N 21.01 E
Reserva 55 Gg 24.38S 50.52W
Reserve 45 Bj 33.43N 108.45W
Reševilovka 16 Ie 49.33N 34.05 E
Reshui 27 Hd 37.38N 100.30 E
Resia, Passo di-/Reschenpass 14 Ed 46.50N 10.30 E
Resistencia 53 Kh 27.30S 58.59W
Reşiţa 15 Ed 45.18N 21.55 E
Resko 10 Lc 53.47N 15.25 E
Reso/Raisio 7 Ff 60.29N 22.11 E
Resolute 39 Jb 74.41N 94.54W
Resolution 38 Mc 61.30N 65.00W
Resolution Island 42 Ld 61.35N 64.39W
Resolution Island 62 Bf 45.40S 166.35 E
Respublikai Soveth Socialisti Todžikiston/Tadžikskaja SSR 19 Hh 39.00N 71.00 E
Respublika Sovetike Sočialiste Moldovenjaske/Moldavskaja SSR 19 Cf 47.00N 29.00 E
Ressa 16 Ib 54.45N 35.10 E
Ressons-sur-Matz 12 Ee 49.33N 2.45 E
Restigouche River 44 Na 48.04N 66.20W
Restinga de Sefton, Isla- 52 Hi 37.00S 83.50W
Restinga Sêca 55 Fi 29.49S 53.23W
Reszel 10 Rb 54.04N 21.09 E
Retalhuleu 49 Bf 14.20N 91.50W
Retalhuleu 47 Ff 14.32N 91.41W
Retavas/Rietavas 8 Ii 55.43N 21.49 E
Retezatului, Munţii- 15 Fd 45.25N 23.00 E
Rethel 11 Ke 49.31N 4.22 E
Rethem (Aller) 12 Lb 52.47N 9.23 E
Réthinnon 15 Hn 35.22N 24.28 E
Retie 12 Hc 51.17N 5.05 E

Index Symbols

Independent Nation; State, Region; District, County; Municipality; Colony, Dependency; Continent; Physical Region
Historical or Cultural Region; Mount, Mountain; Volcano; Hill; Mountains, Mountain Range; Hills, Escarpment; Plateau, Upland
Pass, Gap; Plain, Lowland; Delta; Salt Flat; Valley, Canyon; Crater, Cave; Karst Features
Depression; Polder; Desert, Dunes; Forest, Woods; Heath, Steppe; Oasis; Cape, Point
Coast, Beach; Cliff; Peninsula; Isthmus; Sandbank; Island; Atoll
Rock, Reef; Islands, Archipelago; Rocks, Reefs; Coral Reef; Well, Spring; Geyser; River, Stream
Waterfall Rapids; River Mouth, Estuary; Lake; Salt Lake; Intermittent Lake; Reservoir; Swamp, Pond
Canal; Glacier; Ice Shelf, Pack Ice; Ocean; Sea; Gulf, Bay; Strait, Fjord
Lagoon; Bank; Seamount; Tablemount; Ridge; Shelf; Basin
Escarpment, Sea Scarp; Fracture; Trench, Abyss; National Park, Reserve; Point of Interest; Recreation Site; Cave, Cavern
Historic Site; Ruins; Wall, Walls; Church, Abbey; Temple; Scientific Station; Airport
Port; Lighthouse; Mine; Tunnel; Dam, Bridge

Retourne 12 Ge 49.26N 4.02 E
Rétság 10 Pi 47.56N 19.08 E
Rettihovka 28 Lb 44.10N 132.45 E
Retz 14 Jc 48.45N 15.57 E
Retz, Pays de- 11 Eg 47.07N 1.58W
Réunion=Reunion (EN) 30 Mk 21.06S 55.36 E
Réunion=Reunion (EN) [5] 31 Mk 21.06S 55.36 E
Reunion (EN)=Réunion 30 Mk 21.06S 55.36 E
Reunion (EN)=Réunion [5] 31 Mk 21.06S 55.36 E
Reus 13 Nc 41.09N 1.07 E
Reusel 12 Hc 51.22N 5.10 E
Reuss 14 Cc 47.28N 8.14 E
Reut 16 Ff 47.15N 29.09 E
Reutlingen 10 Fh 48.29N 9.13 E
Reutte 14 Ec 47.29N 10.43 E
Revda [R.S.F.S.R.] 17 Ih 56.48N 59.57 E
Revda [R.S.F.S.R.] 7 Ic 67.57N 34.32 E
Revel 11 Hk 43.28N 2.00 E
Revelstoke 42 Ff 50.59N 118.12W
Revermont 11 Lh 46.27N 5.25 E
Revillagigedo 40 Me 55.35N 131.23W
Revillagigedo, Islas- 38 Hh 19.00N 111.30W
Revin 11 Ke 49.56N 4.38 E
Revoljucii, Pik- 18 Ie 38.33N 72.28 E
Revsundssjön 8 Fb 62.50N 15.15 E
Rewa 63d Bc 18.08S 178.33 E
Rewa 25 Gd 24.32N 81.18 E
Rewāri 25 Fc 28.11N 76.37 E
Rex, Mount- 66 Qf 74.54S 75.57W
Rexburg 46 Je 43.49N 111.47W
Rexpoëde 12 Ed 50.56N 2.32 E
Rey 23 Hb 35.35N 51.25 E
Rey, Arroyo del- 55 Ci 29.12S 59.36W
Rey, Isla del- 47 Ig 8.22N 78.55W
Rey, Laguna del- 48 Hd 27.00N 103.25W
Rey Bouba 34 Hd 8.40N 14.11 E
Reyes, Point- 46 Dg 38.00N 123.01W
Reyhanli 24 Gd 36.18N 36.32 E
Reykjalid 7a Cb 65.39N 16.55W
Reykjanes 5 Dc 63.49N 22.43W
Reykjanes Ridge (EN) 3 Dc 62.00N 27.00W
Reykjavík 6 Dc 64.09N 21.57W
Reynolds Range 59 Gd 22.20S 132.50 E
Reynosa 39 Jg 26.07N 98.18W
Reyssouze 11 Kh 46.27N 4.54 E
Rež 17 Kh 57.54N 62.20 E
Rež 17 Jh 57.23N 61.24 E
Rezé 11 Eg 47.12N 1.34W
Rezekne/Rēzekne 6 Id 56.30N 27.19 E
Rēzekne/Rezekne 6 Id 56.30N 27.19 E
Rezelm, Lacul- 15 Le 44.54N 28.57 E
Rezina 16 Ff 47.43N 28.58 E
Reznas, Ozero-/Rēznas Ezers 8 Lh 56.20N 27.30 E
Rēznas Ezers/Reznas, Ozero- 8 Lh 56.20N 27.30 E
Rezovo 15 Lh 41.59N 28.02 E
Rezvān 24 Qi 27.34N 56.06 E
Rezve 15 Lh 41.59N 28.01 E
Rgotina 15 Fe 44.01N 22.17 E
Rhaetian Alps (EN)=Alpi Retiche 14 Dd 46.30N 10.00 E
Rhaetian Alps (EN)= Rätische Alpen 14 Dd 46.30N 10.00 E
Rhallamane 30 Ff 23.15N 10.00W
Rhauderfehn 12 Ja 53.08N 7.34 E
Rhaunen 12 Je 49.51N 7.21 E
Rheda-Wiedenbrück 10 Ee 51.51N 8.18 E
Rheden 12 Ib 52.01N 6.01 E
Rheden-Dieren 12 Ib 52.03N 6.08 E
Rheider Land 12 Ja 53.13N 7.18 E
Rhein 12 Ke 49.52N 8.07 E
Rhein=Rhine (EN) 5 Ge 51.52N 6.02 E
Rheinberg 12 Ic 51.33N 6.36 E
Rheine 10 Dd 52.17N 7.27 E
Rheinfall 14 Cc 47.41N 8.38 E
Rheinfelden 10 Di 47.34N 7.48 E
Rheingaugebirge 12 Jd 50.05N 8.00 E
Rheinisches Schiefergebirge =Rhenish Slate Mountains (EN) 5 Ge 50.25N 7.10 E
Rheinland-Pfalz=Rhineland-Palatinate (EN) [2] 10 Cf 50.00N 7.00 E
Rheinsberg 10 Ic 53.06N 12.53 E
Rheinstetten 12 Kf 48.58N 8.18 E
Rhenen 12 Hc 51.58N 5.35 E
Rhenish Slate Mountains (EN)=Rheinisches Schiefergebirge 5 Ge 50.25N 7.10 E
Rheris 32 Gc 30.41N 4.57W
Rheydt, Mönchengladbach- 12 Ic 51.10N 6.27 E
Rhin=Rhine (EN) 5 Ge 51.52N 6.02 E
Rhine (EN)=Rein 5 Ge 51.52N 6.02 E
Rhine (EN)=Rhein 5 Ge 51.52N 6.02 E
Rhine (EN)=Rhin 5 Ge 51.52N 6.02 E
Rhine (EN)=Rijn 5 Ge 51.52N 6.02 E
Rhine Bank (EN) 56 Ji 50.30S 53.30W
Rhineland-Palatinate (EN)= Rheinland Pfalz [2] 10 Cf 50.00N 7.00 E
Rhinelander 43 Jb 45.38N 89.25W
Rhinluch 10 Id 52.50N 12.50 E
Rhino Camp 36 Fb 2.58N 31.24 E
Rhiou 13 Mi 35.59N 0.53 E
Rhir, Cap- 32 Fc 30.38N 9.54W
Rho 14 De 45.32N 9.02 E
Rhode Island [2] 43 Mc 41.40N 71.30W
Rhode Island Sound 44 Le 41.25N 71.15W
Rhodes (EN)=Ródhos 6 Ih 36.26N 28.13 E
Rhodes (EN)=Ródhos 5 Ih 36.10N 28.00 E
Rhodesia→Zimbabwe [1] 31 Jj 20.00S 30.00 E
Rhodes Peak 46 Hc 46.41N 114.47W
Rhodope Mountains (EN)= Rodopi 5 Ig 41.30N 24.30 E
Rhomara 13 Hi 35.10N 4.57W
Rhön 10 Gf 50.25N 10.05 E
Rhondda 9 Jj 51.40N 3.30W
Rhône 5 Gg 43.20N 4.50 E
Rhône [3] 11 Ki 46.00N 4.30 E
Rhône au Rhin, Canal du- 11 Lg 47.06N 5.19 E
Rhourd el Baguel 32 Ic 31.24N 6.57 E
Rhue 11 Ii 45.23N 2.29 E
Rhum 9 Ge 57.00N 6.20W
Rhyl 9 Jh 53.19N 3.29W
Riaba 34 Ge 3.24N 8.42 E
Riacho de Santana 54 Jf 13.37S 42.57W
Riangnom 35 Ed 9.55N 30.01 E
Riaño 13 Gb 42.58N 5.01W
Riánsares 13 Ie 39.32N 3.18W
Říany 10 Kg 50.00N 14.39 E
Rias Altas 13 Da 43.30N 8.30W
Rias Bajas 13 Db 42.30N 9.00W
Riau [3] 26 Df 1.00N 102.00 E
Riau Archipelago (EN)= Riau, Kepulauan- 21 Mi 1.00N 104.30 E
Riau Kepulauan-=Riau Archipelago (EN) 21 Mi 1.00N 104.30 E
Riaza 13 Ic 41.17N 3.28W
Riaza 13 Ic 41.42N 3.55W
Ribadavia 13 Db 42.17N 8.08W
Ribadeo 13 Ea 43.32N 7.02W
Ribadesella 13 Ga 43.28N 5.04W
Ribagorza/La Ribagorça 13 Mb 42.15N 0.30 E
Ribamar 54 Jd 2.33S 44.03W
Ribas do Rio Pardo 55 Fe 20.27S 53.46W
Ribatejo 13 De 39.15N 8.30W
Ribáuè 37 Fb 14.57S 38.17 E
Ribble 9 Kh 53.44N 2.50W
Ribe 7 Bi 55.21N 8.46 E
Ribe [2] 8 Ci 55.35N 8.45 E
Ribécourt-Dreslincourt 12 Ee 49.31N 2.55 E
Ribeira [Braz.] 55 Hg 24.39S 49.00W
Ribeira [Sp.] 13 Db 42.33N 9.00W
Ribeira, Rio- 55 Ig 24.40S 47.24W
Ribeira Brava 32 Cf 16.37N 24.18W
Ribeira Grande 32 Bf 17.11N 25.04W
Ribeirão Prêto 53 Lh 21.10S 47.48W
Ribeirãozinho 55 Fc 16.22S 52.36W
Ribeiro Gonçalves 54 Ie 7.32S 45.14W
Ribemont 12 Fe 49.48N 3.28 E
Ribera 14 Hm 37.30N 13.16 E
Ribérac 11 Gi 45.15N 0.20 E
Riberalta 53 Jg 10.59S 66.06W
Ribnica 14 Ie 45.44N 14.44 E
Ribnitz-Damgarten 10 Ib 54.15N 12.28 E
Ricardo Flores Magón 48 Fc 29.58N 106.58W
Riccia 14 Ii 41.29N 14.50 E
Riccione 14 Gg 43.59N 12.39 E
Rice Lake 44 Hc 44.08N 78.13W
Rich 32 Gc 32.15N 4.30W
Richan 45 Jb 49.59N 92.49W
Richard Collinson Inlet 42 Gb 72.45N 113.00W
Richards 42 Ec 69.20N 134.35W
Richard's Bay 31 Kk 28.47S 32.06 E
Richardson 45 Hj 32.57N 96.44W
Richardson Mountains 38 Fc 66.00N 135.20W
Richard Toll 34 Bb 16.28N 15.41W
Richât, Guel er- 32 Ee 21.07N 11.24W
Richel 12 Ha 53.18N 5.10 E
Richel Griend 12 Ha 53.18N 5.15 E
Richelieu 11 Gg 47.01N 0.19 E
Richer 45 Hb 49.39N 96.28W
Richey 46 Mc 47.39N 105.04W
Richfield 43 Ed 38.46N 112.05W
Richibucto 44 Ob 46.41N 64.52W
Richland 43 Db 46.17N 119.18W
Richland Center 45 Ke 43.22N 90.21W
Richmond [Austl.] 59 Id 20.44S 143.08 E
Richmond [Ca.-U.S.] 43 Cd 37.57N 122.22W
Richmond [Eng.-U.K.] 9 Lg 54.24N 1.44W
Richmond [In.-U.S.] 43 Kd 39.50N 84.54W
Richmond [Ky.-U.S.] 43 Kd 37.45N 84.18W
Richmond [N.Z.] 62 Ed 41.21S 173.11 E
Richmond [S.Afr.] 37 Cf 31.23S 23.56 E
Richmond [Tx.-U.S.] 45 Il 29.35N 95.46W
Richmond [Va.-U.S.] 39 Lf 37.30N 77.28W
Richmond, Mount- 62 Ed 41.28S 173.24 E
Richmond Hill 44 Hd 43.52N 79.27W
Richmond Peak 51n Ba 13.17N 61.13W
Richthofen, Mount- 45 Df 40.29N 105.57W
Rickmansworth 12 Bc 51.38N 0.28W
Ricobayo, Embalse de- 13 Gc 41.35N 5.50W
Ridā' 33 Hg 14.25N 44.50 E
Ridderkerk 12 Gc 51.52N 4.36 E
Ridgecrest 46 Gi 35.38N 117.36W
Ridgway 44 He 41.25N 78.45W
Riding Mountain 45 Fa 50.55N 100.25W
Riecito, Rio- 50 Bi 6.50N 68.51W
Ried 12 Ke 49.50N 8.25 E
Ried im Innkreis 14 Hb 48.13N 13.30 E
Riedlingen 10 Fh 48.09N 9.28 E
Riemst 12 Hd 50.48N 5.36 E
Ries 10 Gh 48.55N 10.40 E
Riesa 10 Je 51.18N 13.18 E
Riesco, Isla- 56 Fh 53.00S 72.30W
Riesi 14 Im 37.17N 14.05 E
Riet 30 Jk 29.00S 23.53 E
Rietavas/Retavas 8 Ii 55.43N 21.49 E
Rietberg 12 Kc 51.48N 8.26 E
Rietbron 37 Cf 32.54S 23.09 E
Rietfontein [Nam.] 37 Cd 21.58S 20.58 E
Rietfontein [S.Afr.] 37 Ce 26.44S 20.01 E
Rieti 14 Gh 42.24N 12.51 E
Rif 30 Ge 35.00N 4.00W
Rifle 45 Cg 39.32N 107.47W
Rifstangi 5 Eb 66.32N 16.12W
Rift Valley [3] 36 Gb 0.30N 36.00 E
Rift Valley 30 Kh 0.30N 36.00 E
Riga/Rīga 6 Id 56.57N 24.06 E
Rīga/Riga 6 Id 56.57N 24.06 E
Riga, Gulf of- (EN)=Rīgas Jūras Līcis 5 Id 57.30N 23.35 E
Riga, Gulf of- (EN)=Riia Laht 5 Id 57.30N 23.35 E
Riga, Gulf of- (EN)=Rižski Zaliv 5 Id 57.30N 23.35 E
Rigachikum 34 Gc 10.38N 7.28 E
Rīgas Jūras Līcis=Riga, Gulf of- (EN) 5 Id 57.30N 23.35 E
Rigestān=Registan (EN) 21 If 31.00N 65.00 E
Riggins 46 Gd 45.25N 116.19W
Rigolet 42 Lf 54.10N 58.26W
Rig-Rig 35 Ac 14.16N 14.21 E
Rihand Sagar 25 Hd 24.05N 83.05 E
Riia Laht=Riga, Gulf of- (EN) 5 Id 57.30N 23.35 E
Riihimäki 7 Ff 60.45N 24.46 E
Riiser-Larsen-Halvøya 66 De 68.55S 34.00 E
Riito 48 Ba 32.10N 114.45W
Riječki zaljev = Rijeka, Gulf of- (EN) 14 Ie 45.15N 14.25 E
Rijeka 6 Hf 45.21N 14.24 E
Rijeka, Gulf of- (EN)= Riječki zaljev 14 Ie 45.15N 14.25 E
Rijksmuseum Kröller-Müller 12 Hb 52.06N 5.47 E
Rijn=Rhine (EN) 5 Ge 51.52N 6.02 E
Rijssen 12 Ib 52.18N 6.37 E
Rijswijk 12 Gb 52.03N 4.21 E
Rika 10 Th 48.08N 23.22 E
Rikā, Wādī ar- 33 He 22.25N 44.50 E
Rikubetsu 29a Cb 43.28N 143.43 E
Rikuzentakada 28 Pe 39.01N 141.38 E
Rila 15 Gh 42.08N 23.33 E
Rila 15 Gh 42.08N 23.08 E
Riley 46 Fe 43.32N 119.29W
Riley, Mount- 45 Ck 31.58N 107.05W
Rilski Manastir 15 Gg 42.08N 23.20 E
Rima 30 Hg 13.04N 5.10 E
Rimatara, Ile- 57 Lg 22.38S 152.51W
Rimava 10 Qh 48.15N 20.21 E
Rimavská Sobota 10 Qh 48.23N 20.01 E
Rimbo 7 Eg 59.45N 18.22 E
Rimé 35 Bc 14.02N 18.03 E
Rimforsa 8 Ff 58.08N 15.40 E
Rimini 14 Gf 44.04N 12.34 E
Rimito/Rymättylä 8 Jd 60.25N 21.55 E
Rîmnic 15 Kd 45.32N 27.31 E
Rîmnicu Sărat 15 Kd 45.23N 27.03 E
Rîmnicu Vîlcea 15 Hd 45.06N 24.22 E
Rimouski 39 Me 48.27N 68.32W
Rimše/Rimšė 8 Li 55.30N 26.33 E
Rimšė/Rimše 8 Li 55.30N 26.33 E
Rinbung 27 Ef 29.15N 89.52 E
Rincon 50 Bf 12.14N 68.20W
Rincón 51a Ab 18.21N 67.16W
Rincón, Bahía de- 51a Bc 17.57N 66.19W
Rincón del Bonete, Lago Artificial de- 56 Id 32.45S 56.00W
Rincón de Romos 48 Hf 22.14N 102.18W
Rindal 7 Be 63.03N 9.13 E
Ringe 8 Di 55.14N 10.29 E
Ringebu 8 Dc 61.31N 10.10 E
Ringerike 8 Dd 60.05N 10.15 E
Ringgold Isles 57 Jf 16.15S 179.25W
Ringim 34 Gc 12.09N 9.10 E
Ringkøbing [2] 8 Ch 56.10N 8.45 E
Ringkøbing 7 Bh 56.05N 8.15 E
Ringkøbing Fjord 7 Bi 56.00N 8.15 E
Ringlådes 15 Dj 39.25N 20.04 E
Ringsjön 8 Ei 55.50N 13.30 E
Ringsted 7 Ci 55.27N 11.49 E
Ringvassøy 7 Eb 69.55N 19.15 E
Rinia 15 Il 37.25N 25.13 E
Rinjani, Gunung- 26 Gh 8.24S 116.28 E
Rinn Chathóir/Cahore Point 9 Gi 52.34N 6.11W
Rinn Dúain/Hook Head 9 Gi 52.07N 6.55W
Rinteln 10 Fd 52.11N 9.05 E
Rinya 10 Nk 45.57N 17.27 E
Rio Azul 55 Gg 25.43S 50.47W
Riobamba 53 If 1.40S 78.38W
Rio Branco 53 Jf 9.58S 67.48W
Rio Branco 55 Fk 32.34S 53.25W
Rio Branco do Sul 55 Hg 25.10S 49.18W
Rio Brilhante 55 Hh 21.48S 54.33W
Rio Bueno 56 Ff 40.19S 72.58W
Rio Caribe 54 Fa 10.42N 63.07W
Rio Chico 50 Dg 10.19N 65.59W
Rio Claro [Braz.] 55 If 22.24S 47.33W
Rio Claro [Trin.] 50 Fg 10.18N 61.11W
Rio Colorado 56 He 39.01S 64.05W
Rio Cuarto 53 Ji 33.08S 64.20W
Rio de Janeiro 53 Lh 22.54S 43.15W
Rio de Janeiro [2] 54 Jh 22.30S 42.30W
Rio de Jesús 49 Gj 7.59N 81.10W
Rio de Oro 32 Ee 24.00N 14.00W
Rio de Oro 49 Ki 8.57N 73.23W
Rio de Oro, Bahía de- 32 De 23.45N 15.50W
Rio do Sul 56 Kc 27.13S 49.39W
Rio Fortuna 55 Hi 28.06S 49.07W
Rio Gallegos 53 Jk 51.37S 69.10W
Rio Grande 53 Ki 32.02S 52.05W
Rio Grande [Arg.] 56 Gh 53.47S 67.42W
Rio Grande [Nic.] 49 Dg 12.59N 86.34W
Rio Grande [P.R.] 51a Cb 18.23N 65.50W
Rio Grande City 45 Gm 26.23N 98.49W
Rio Grande de Añasco 51a Ab 18.17N 67.10W
Rio Grande de Manati 51a Bb 18.29N 66.32W
Rio Grande de Matagalpa 47 Hf 12.54N 83.32W
Rio Grande do Norte [2] 54 Ke 5.40S 36.00W
Rio Grande do Sul [2] 56 Jc 30.00S 54.00W
Rio Grande Rise (EN) 3 Cm 31.00S 35.00W
Riohacha 54 Da 11.32N 72.54W
Rio Hato 49 Gi 8.23N 80.10W
Rio Lagartos 48 Og 21.36N 88.10W
Rio Largo 54 Ke 9.29S 35.51W
Riom 11 Ji 45.54N 3.07 E
Rio Maior 13 De 39.20N 8.56W
Rio Mayo 56 Fg 45.41S 70.16W
Riom-ès-Montagnes 11 Ii 45.17N 2.40 E
Rio Miranda 54 Gg 19.25S 57.20W
Rio Mulatos 54 Eg 19.42S 66.47W
Rion 15 Ek 38.18N 21.47 E
Rio Negro [Chile] 56 Ff 40.47S 73.14W
Rio Negro [Arg.] [2] 56 Gf 40.00S 67.00W
Rio Negro [Braz.] 56 Kc 26.06S 49.48W
Rio Negro [Braz.] 55 Dd 19.33S 56.32W
Rio Negro [Ur.] [2] 55 Dk 32.45S 57.20W
Rio Negro, Pantanal do- 54 Gg 18.50S 56.00W
Rionero in Vulture 14 Jj 40.56N 15.40 E
Rioni 16 Lh 42.10N 41.38 E
Rio Novo 55 Dc 16.28S 56.30W
Rio Pardo 56 Jc 29.59S 52.22W
Rio Prêto, Serra do- 55 Gd 18.18S 50.42W
Rio San Juan [3] 49 Eh 11.10N 84.30W
Rio Segundo 56 Hd 31.40S 63.55W
Riosucio 54 Cb 7.27N 77.07W
Rio Tercero 56 Hd 32.11S 64.06W
Rio Tinto 54 Ke 6.48S 35.04W
Rioverde 47 Dd 21.56N 100.01W
Rio Verde 54 Hg 17.43S 50.56W
Rio Verde, Serra do- 55 Fc 17.32S 52.25W
Rio Verde de Mato Grosso 54 Hg 18.56S 54.52W
Rio Verde do Sul 55 Ef 22.54S 55.27W
Rioz 11 Mg 47.25N 6.04 E
Říp 10 Kf 50.24N 14.18 E
Ripanj 15 De 44.38N 20.32 E
Ripley [Eng.-U.K.] 12 Aa 53.02N 1.24W
Ripley [Tn.-U.S.] 44 Ch 35.44N 89.33W
Ripley [W.V.-U.S.] 44 Gf 38.49N 81.44W
Ripoll 13 Ob 42.12N 2.12 E
Ripon 9 Lg 54.08N 1.31W
Riposto 14 Jm 37.44N 15.12 E
Ripple Mountain 46 Gb 49.02N 117.05W
Risan 15 Bg 42.31N 18.42 E
Risaralda [2] 54 Cb 5.00N 75.45W
Risbäck 7 Dd 64.42N 15.32 E
Rīshah, Wādī- 24 Kj 25.33N 44.05 E
Rī Shahr 24 Nh 28.55N 50.50 E
Rishiri 28 Pb 45.11N 141.15 E
Rishiri-Suidō 29a Ba 45.10N 141.30 E
Rishiri-Tō 27 Pb 45.11N 141.15 E
Rishiri-Yama 29a Ba 45.11N 141.15 E
Rishmūk 24 Ng 31.15N 50.20 E
Rishon Leẕiyyon 24 Fg 31.58N 34.48 E
Rising Star 45 Gj 32.06N 98.58W
Risle 11 Ge 49.26N 0.23 E
Risnjak 14 Ie 45.26N 14.37 E
Rîşnov 15 Id 45.35N 25.27 E
Risør 7 Bg 58.43N 9.14 E
Risoux, Mont- 11 Mh 46.36N 6.10 E
Risøyhamn 7 Db 69.00N 15.45 E
Riß 10 Fh 48.17N 9.49 E
Risti 7 Fg 59.03N 24.01 E
Ristiina 8 Lc 61.30N 27.16 E
Ristijarvi 7 Gd 64.30N 28.13 E
Ristna, Mys-/Ristna Neem 8 If 58.55N 21.55 E
Ristna Neem/Ristna, Mys- 8 If 58.55N 21.55 E
Risū 24 Qf 33.52N 57.28 E
Ritchie's Archipelago 25 If 12.14N 93.10 E
Ritidian Point 64c Ba 13.39N 144.51 E
Ritscher-Hochland 66 Bf 73.20S 9.30W
Ritter, Mount- 46 Dd 37.42N 119.20W
Ritterhude 12 Ka 53.11N 8.45 E
Rituerto 13 Jc 41.36N 2.22W
Ritzville 46 Fc 47.08N 118.23W
Riva-Bella, Ouistreham- 12 Be 49.17N 0.16W
Rivadavia [Arg.] 56 Hb 24.11S 62.53W
Rivadavia [Arg.] 56 Gd 33.11S 68.28W
Riva del Garda 14 Ee 45.53N 10.50 E
Rivas 39 Kh 11.26N 85.50W
Rivas [3] 49 Eh 11.25N 85.50W
Rive-de-Gier 11 Ki 45.22N 4.37 E
Rivellata, Punta di a- 11a Aa 42.35N 8.40 E
Rivera [2] 55 Ej 31.30S 55.15W
Rivera [Arg.] 56 He 37.12S 63.14W
Rivera [Ur.] 53 Ki 30.54S 55.31W
River Cess 34 Dd 5.27N 9.35W
Riverdale 45 Fc 47.30N 101.22W
Riverina 59 Jg 35.25S 145.30 E
River Inlet 42 Ef 51.41N 127.15W
Rivers [2] 34 Ge 4.50N 6.30 E
Rivers, Lake of the- 46 Mb 49.45N 105.45W
Riversdale [N.Z.] 62 Cf 45.54S 168.44 E
Riversdale [S.Afr.] 37 Cf 34.07S 21.15 E
Riverside 43 De 33.59N 117.22W
Riverton [N.Z.] 62 Bg 46.21S 168.00 E
Riverton [Wy.-U.S.] 43 Fc 43.02N 108.23W
Rivesaltes 11 Il 42.46N 2.52 E
Riviera Beach 44 Ge 26.47N 80.04W
Rivière-à-Pierre 44 Kb 46.58N 72.11W
Rivière-du-Loup 42 Kg 47.50N 69.32W
Rivière-Pilote 51h Bc 14.29N 60.54W
Rivière-Salée 51h Bb 14.32N 60.59W
Rivoli 14 Be 45.04N 7.31 E
Rivungo 36 Df 16.15S 22.00 E
Riwaka 62 Ed 41.05S 173.00 E
Riwoqê 27 Ge 31.13N 96.29 E
Rixensart 12 Gd 50.43N 4.35 E
Riyadh (EN)=Ar Riyāḍ 22 Gg 24.38N 46.43 E
Rize 23 Fa 41.02N 40.31 E
Rize, Gora- 18 Bf 37.48N 58.13 E
Rize Dağları 24 Ib 40.30N 40.50 E
Rizhao 27 Kd 35.27N 119.28 E
Rizokarpásso/Dipkarpas 24 Fe 35.36N 34.23 E
Rižski Zaliv=Riga, Gulf of- (EN) 5 Id 57.30N 23.35 E
Rizzuto, Capo- 14 Ll 38.53N 17.05 E
Rjabovo 8 Md 60.17N 29.01 E
Rjapina/Räpina 8 Lf 58.03N 27.35 E
Rjazan 6 Je 54.38N 39.44 E
Rjazanovski 7 Ji 55.08N 39.35 E
Rjazanskaja Oblast [3] 19 Ee 54.30N 40.40 E
Rjažsk 6 Ke 53.43N 40.04 E
Rjukan 7 Bg 59.52N 8.34 E
Rjuven 8 Be 59.13N 7.10 E
Rkiz 32 Df 16.50N 15.20W
Rldal 8 Be 59.49N 6.48 E
Roa [Nor.] 8 Dd 60.17N 10.37 E
Roa [Sp.] 13 Ic 41.42N 3.55W
Road Town 47 Le 18.27N 64.37W
Roag, Loch- 9 Gc 58.16N 6.50W
Roan Antelope 36 Ee 13.08S 28.24 E
Roannais 11 Kh 46.05N 4.10 E
Roanne 11 Kh 46.02N 4.04 E
Roanoke 38 Lf 35.56N 76.43W
Roanoke [Al.-U.S.] 44 Ei 33.09N 85.22W
Roanoke [Va.-U.S.] 39 Lf 37.16N 79.57W
Roanoke Rapids 44 Ig 36.28N 77.40W
Roan Plateau 46 Kg 39.35N 108.55W
Roaringwater Bay 9 Dj 51.25N 9.30W
Roatán 49 De 16.18N 86.35W
Roatán, Isla de- 49 De 16.23N 86.30W
Robāt [Iran] 24 Qd 37.35N 57.42 E
Robāt [Iran] 24 Pg 30.04N 54.49 E
Robāt-e-Khān 23 Ic 33.21N 56.02 E
Robāt-e-Kord 24 Qf 33.45N 56.37 E
Robāt Karim 24 Ne 35.28N 51.05 E
Robbie Bank (EN) 61 Fb 11.03S 176.53W
Robe, Mount- 59 If 31.40S 141.20 E
Röbel 10 Ic 53.23N 12.36 E
Robert Lee 45 Fk 31.54N 100.29W
Roberts 55 Bl 35.09S 61.57W
Roberts, Mount- 59 Ke 28.13S 152.28 E
Roberts Creek Mountain 46 Gg 39.52N 116.18W
Robertsfors 7 Ed 64.11N 20.51 E
Robert S. Kerr Lake 45 Ii 35.25N 95.00W
Robertson 37 Bf 33.46S 19.50 E
Robertson Bay 66 Kf 71.25S 170.00 E
Robertson Range 59 Ed 23.10S 121.00 E
Robertsport 34 Cd 6.45N 11.22W
Roberval 42 Kg 48.31N 72.13W
Robi 35 Fd 7.38N 39.52 E
Robinson Crusoe (EN) = Robinson Crusoe, Isla- 52 Ii 33.38S 78.52W
Robinson Crusoe, Isla- = Robinson Crusoe (EN) 52 Ii 33.38S 78.52W
Robinson Range 59 De 25.45S 119.00 E
Robinson River 59 Hc 16.03S 137.16 E
Roboré 53 Kg 18.20S 59.45W
Rob Roy 63a Cb 7.23S 157.36 E
Robson, Mount- 38 Hd 53.07N 119.09W
Robstown 45 Hm 27.27N 97.40W
Roby 45 Fj 32.45N 100.23W
Roca, Cabo da- 5 Fh 38.47N 9.30W
Rocamadour 11 Hj 44.48N 1.38 E
Roca Partida, Isla- 47 Be 19.01N 112.02W
Roca Partida, Punta- 48 Lh 18.42N 95.10W
Rocas, Atol das- 52 Mf 3.52S 33.49W
Roccaraso 14 Ii 41.51N 14.05 E
Ročegda 19 Ec 62.42N 43.23 E
Rocha [2] 55 Fk 34.00S 54.00W
Rocha 56 Jd 34.29S 54.20W
Rochdale 9 Kh 53.38N 2.09W
Rochechouart 11 Gi 45.49N 0.49 E
Rochedo 55 Ed 19.57S 54.52W
Rochefort [Bel.] 11 Ld 50.10N 5.13 E
Rochefort [Fr.] 11 Fi 45.56N 0.59W
Rochefort-Han-sur-Lesse 12 Hd 50.08N 5.11 E
Rochelle 45 Lf 41.56N 89.04W
Rocher River 42 Gd 61.23N 112.45W
Roche's Bluff 51c c 16.42N 62.09W
Rochester [Eng.-U.K.] 9 Nj 51.24N 0.30 E
Rochester [In.-U.S.] 44 De 41.04N 86.13W
Rochester [Mn.-U.S.] 43 Ic 44.02N 92.29W
Rochester [N.H.-U.S.] 44 Ld 43.18N 70.59W
Rochester [N.Y.-U.S.] 39 Le 43.10N 77.36W
Rochlitzer Berg 10 Ie 51.05N 12.48 E
Rocigalgo 13 He 39.35N 4.35W
Rockall 5 Ed 57.35N 13.48W
Rockall Rise (EN) 5 Ed 57.00N 14.00W
Rock Creek Butte 46 Fd 44.49N 118.07W
Rockefeller Plateau 66 Ng 80.00S 135.00W
Rockenhausen 12 Je 49.38N 7.50 E
Rockford 43 Jc 42.17N 89.06W
Rockglen 46 Mb 49.10N 105.57W
Rockhampton 58 Gg 23.23S 150.31 E
Rock Hill 43 Ke 34.55N 81.01W
Rockingham [Austl.] 59 Df 32.17S 115.44 E
Rockingham [N.C.-U.S.] 44 Hh 34.56N 79.46W
Rock Island 43 Ic 41.30N 90.34W
Rockland 43 Nc 44.06N 69.06W
Rocklands Reservoir 59 Ig 37.15S 142.00 E
Rockledge 44 Gk 28.20N 80.43W
Rockneby 8 Gh 56.49N 16.20 E
Rockport 45 Hl 28.01N 97.04W
Rock River 45 Kf 41.29N 90.37W
Rock Sound 47 Im 24.53N 76.09W
Rock Spring 43 Fc 41.35N 109.13W
Rocksprings 45 Fk 30.01N 100.13W
Rockville [In.-U.S.] 44 Df 39.45N 87.15W
Rockville [Md.-U.S.] 44 If 39.05N 77.09W
Rockwood 44 Eh 35.52N 84.41W
Rocky Ford 45 Eg 38.03N 103.43W
Rocky Island Lake 44 Fb 46.56N 83.04W
Rocky Mount 43 Ld 35.56N 77.48W
Rocky Mountain 43 Eb 47.49N 112.49W
Rocky Mountain House 42 Gf 52.22N 114.55W
Rocky Mountains 38 He 48.00N 116.00W
Rocky Point [Blz.] 49 Cd 18.22N 88.06W
Rocky Point [Nam.] 37 Ac 19.01S 12.29 E
Rocroi 12 Ge 49.55N 4.31 E
Rodach 10 Gf 50.08N 10.52 E
Rodalben 12 Je 49.14N 7.38 E
Roda Velha, Rio- 55 Ja 12.27S 45.33W
Rødberg 8 Cd 60.16N 8.58 E
Rødby 8 Dj 54.42N 11.24 E
Rødby Havn, Rødby- 7 Ci 54.39N 11.21 E
Rødby-Rødby Havn 7 Ci 54.39N 11.21 E
Roddickton 42 Lf 50.51N 56.07W
Rødding 8 Ci 55.22N 9.04 E

Index Symbols

[1] Independent Nation
[2] State, Region
[3] District, County
[4] Municipality
[5] Colony, Dependency
Continent
Physical Region
Historical or Cultural Region
Mount, Mountain
Volcano
Hill
Mountains, Mountain Range
Hills, Escarpment
Plateau, Upland
Pass, Gap
Plain, Lowland
Delta
Salt Flat
Valley, Canyon
Crater, Cave
Karst Features
Depression
Polder
Desert, Dunes
Forest, Woods
Heath, Steppe
Oasis
Cape, Point
Coast, Beach
Cliff
Peninsula
Isthmus
Sandbank
Island
Atoll
Rock, Reef
Islands, Archipelago
Rocks, Reefs
Coral Reef
Well, Spring
Geyser
River, Stream
Waterfall Rapids
River Mouth, Estuary
Lake
Salt Lake
Intermittent Lake
Reservoir
Swamp, Pond
Canal
Glacier
Ice Shelf, Pack Ice
Ocean
Sea
Gulf, Bay
Strait, Fjord
Lagoon
Bank
Seamount
Tablemount
Ridge
Shelf
Basin
Escarpment, Sea Scarp
Fracture
Trench, Abyss
National Park, Reserve
Point of Interest
Recreation Site
Cave, Cavern
Historic Site
Ruins
Wall, Walls
Church, Abbey
Temple
Scientific Station
Airport
Port
Lighthouse
Mine
Tunnel
Dam, Bridge

Name	Page	Grid	Lat.	Long.
Rödeby	8	Fh	56.15N	15.36 E
Rodeio Bonito	55	Fh	27.28S	53.10W
Roden	12	Ia	53.09N	6.26 E
Rodeo [Arg.]	56	Gd	30.12S	69.06W
Rodeo [Mex.]	48	Ge	25.11N	104.34W
Rodeo [N.M.-U.S.]	45	Bk	31.50N	109.02W
Röder	10	Je	51.30N	13.25 E
Rodez	11	Ij	44.20N	2.34 E
Rodgau	12	Kd	50.01N	8.53 E
Rodholivos	15	Gi	40.56N	23.59 E
Ródhos = Rhodes (EN)	6	Ih	36.26N	28.13 E
Ródhos = Rhodes (EN)	5	Ih	36.10N	28.00 E
Rodi Garganico	14	Ji	41.55N	15.53 E
Roding	9	Nj	51.31N	0.06 E
Rodna	15	Hb	47.25N	24.49 E
Rodnei, Munții-	15	Hb	47.35N	24.38 E
Rodney, Cape-	40	Fd	64.39N	166.24W
Rodniki	7	Jh	57.07N	41.48 E
Rodonit, Gjiri i-	15	Ch	41.35N	19.30 E
Rodonit, Kep i-	15	Ch	41.35N	19.27 E
Rodopi=Rhodope Mountains (EN)	5	Ig	41.30N	24.30 E
Rodrigues Island	30	Nj	19.42S	63.25 E
Roebourne	59	Dd	20.47S	117.09 E
Roebuck Bay	59	Ec	18.04S	122.15 E
Roer	10	Be	51.12N	5.59 E
Roermond	11	Lc	51.12N	6.00 E
Roeselare/Roulers	11	Jd	50.57N	3.08 E
Roes Welcome Sound	42	Id	64.30N	86.45W
Roetgen	12	Id	50.39N	6.12 E
Rogačev	16	Gc	53.09N	30.06 E
Rogačevka	16	Kd	51.31N	39.34 E
Rogagua, Laguna-	54	Ef	13.45S	66.55W
Rogaguado, Laguna-	54	Ef	12.55S	65.45W
Rogaland [2]	7	Bg	59.00N	6.15 E
Rogaška Slatina	14	Jd	46.15N	15.38 E
Rogatica	14	Ng	43.48N	19.01 E
Rogatin	10	Ug	49.19N	24.40 E
Rogers	45	Ih	36.20N	94.07W
Rogers, Mount-	44	Gg	36.39N	81.33W
Rogers City	44	Fc	45.25N	83.49W
Rogers Lake	46	Gi	34.52N	117.51W
Rogers Peak	46	Jg	38.04N	111.32W
Rogersville	44	Fg	36.25N	82.59W
Roggan	42	Jf	54.24N	79.30W
Roggeveldberge	37	Bf	31.50S	19.50 E
Roggewein, Cabo-	65d	Bb	27.07S	109.15W
Rognan	7	Dc	67.06N	15.23 E
Rogozhina	15	Ch	41.05N	19.40 E
Rogozna	15	Df	43.04N	20.40 E
Rogoźno	10	Md	52.46N	17.00 E
Rogue River	46	Ce	42.26N	124.25W
Rohan, Plateau de-	11	Df	48.10N	3.00W
Rohl	35	Dd	7.05N	29.46 E
Rohrbach in Oberösterreich	14	Hb	48.34N	13.59 E
Rohrbach-lès-Bitche	12	Je	49.03N	7.16 E
Rohri	25	Dc	27.41N	68.54 E
Rohtak	25	Fc	28.54N	76.34 E
Roi, Le Bois du-	11	Kh	46.59N	4.02 E
Roi Et	25	Ke	16.05N	103.42 E
Roi Georges, Iles du-	57	Mf	14.32S	145.08W
Roine	8	Kc	61.25N	24.05 E
Roisel	12	Fe	49.57N	3.06 E
Roja	7	Fh	57.30N	22.51 E
Rojas	56	Hd	34.12S	60.44W
Rojo, Cabo- [Mex.]	47	Ed	21.33N	97.20W
Rojo, Cabo- [P.R.]	49	Nd	18.01N	67.15W
Rokan	26	Df	2.00N	100.52 E
Rokiškis	7	Fi	55.59N	25.37 E
Rokitnoje	16	Ed	51.21N	27.14 E
Rokkasho	29a	Bc	40.58N	141.21 E
Rokycany	10	Jg	49.45N	13.36 E
Rokytná	10	Mg	49.05N	16.21 E
Rola Co	27	Ed	35.25N	88.25 E
Rolândia	55	Gf	23.18S	51.22W
Rolla [Mo.-U.S.]	43	Id	37.57N	91.46W
Rolla [N.D.-U.S.]	45	Gb	48.52N	99.37W
Rolleston	62	Ee	43.35S	172.23 E
Rolvsøya	7	Fa	71.00N	24.00 E
Roma [Austl.]	58	Fg	26.35S	148.47 E
Roma [It.] = Rome (EN)	6	Hg	41.54N	12.29 E
Roma [Swe.]	7	Eh	57.32N	18.26 E
Romagna	14	Gf	44.30N	12.15 E
Romaine	42	Lf	50.18N	63.48W
Roman	15	Jc	46.55N	26.55 E
Romanche	11	Li	45.05N	5.43 E
Romanche Gap (EN)	3	Dj	0.10S	18.15W
Romang	55	Ci	29.30S	59.46W
Romang, Pulau-	26	Ih	7.35S	127.26 E
România=Romania (EN) [1]	6	If	46.00N	25.30 E
Romania (EN)=România [1]	6	If	46.00N	25.30 E
Romanija	14	Mg	43.51N	18.43 E
Roman Koš, Gora-	19	Dg	44.36N	34.16 E
Romano, Cayo-	49	Ib	22.04N	77.50W
Romanovka	20	Gf	53.14N	112.46 E
Romans-sur-Isère	11	Li	45.03N	5.03 E
Romanzof, Cape-	38	Cc	61.49N	166.09W
Romanzof Mountains	40	Kc	69.00N	144.00W
Rombas	12	Ie	49.15N	6.05 E
Romblon	26	Hd	12.35N	122.15 E
Rome [Ga.-U.S.]	43	Je	34.16N	85.11W
Rome [N.Y.-U.S.]	43	Lc	43.13N	75.28W
Rome [Or.-U.S.]	46	Ge	42.50N	117.37W
Rome (EN) = Roma [It.]	6	Hg	41.54N	12.29 E
Romeleåsen	8	Ei	55.34N	13.33 E
Romerike	8	Dd	60.05N	11.10 E
Romilly-sur-Seine	11	Jf	48.31N	3.43 E
Rommani	32	Fc	33.32N	6.36W
Romme	8	Fd	60.26N	15.30 E
Rommerskirchen	12	Ic	51.02N	6.41 E
Romney Marsh	12	Cc	51.02N	0.55 E
Romny	19	De	50.45N	33.29 E
Rømø	7	Bi	55.10N	8.30 E
Romodanovo	7	Ki	54.28N	45.18 E
Romont	14	Ad	46.42N	6.55 E
Romorantin-Lanthenay	11	Hg	47.22N	1.45 E
Romsdal	8	Bb	62.35N	7.50 E
Romsdalen	8	Bb	62.30N	7.55 E
Romsdalsfjorden	8	Bb	62.40N	7.15 E
Romsdalshorn	8	Bd	62.29N	7.50 E
Romsey	9	Lk	50.59N	1.30W
Ronas Hill	9	La	60.38N	1.20W
Ronave	64e	Ba	0.29S	166.56 E
Roncador, Cayos de-	47	Hf	13.32N	80.03W
Roncador, Serra do-	52	Kg	13.00S	51.50W
Roncador Reef	57	Ge	6.13S	159.22 E
Roncesvalles	13	Ka	43.01N	1.19W
Roncesvalles o Ibañeta, Puerto de-	13	Ka	43.01N	1.19W
Ronciglione	14	Gh	42.17N	12.13 E
Ronco	14	Gf	44.24N	12.12 E
Ronda	13	Gh	36.44N	5.10W
Ronda, Serrania de-	13	Gh	36.45N	5.05W
Ronda do Sul	55	Cb	15.57S	59.42W
Rondane	7	Bf	61.55N	9.45 E
Rønde	7	Ch	56.18N	10.29 E
Ronde, Point-	51g	Ba	15.33N	61.29W
Ronde Island	50	Ff	12.18N	61.31W
Rondeslottet	8	Cc	61.55N	9.46 E
Rondon	55	Ff	23.23S	52.48W
Rondón, Pico-	54	Fc	1.36N	63.08W
Rondônia	53	Jg	10.52S	61.57W
Rondônia, Território de- [2]	54	Ff	11.00S	63.00W
Rondonópolis	53	Kg	16.28S	54.38W
Rong'an (Chang'an)	27	If	25.16N	109.23 E
Rongcheng	28	Ce	39.03N	115.52 E
Rongcheng (Yatou)	28	Gf	37.10N	122.25 E
Rongelap Atoll	57	Hc	11.09N	166.50 E
Rongerik Atoll	57	Hc	11.21N	167.26 E
Rongjiang (Guzhou)	27	If	25.58N	108.30 E
Rongxian	27	Jg	22.48N	110.30 E
Rongzhag/Danba	27	He	30.48N	101.54 E
Rønne	7	Di	55.06N	14.42 E
Ronne Bay	66	Qf	72.30S	74.00W
Ronneby	7	Dh	56.12N	15.18 E
Ronnebyån	8	Fh	56.10N	15.18 E
Ronne Ice Shelf	66	Qf	78.30S	61.00W
Ronse/Renaix	11	Jd	50.45N	3.36 E
Ronuro, Rio-	52	Kg	11.56S	53.33W
Roodepoort	37	De	26.11S	27.54 E
Roof Butte	43	Fd	36.28N	109.05W
Rooiboklaagte	37	Cd	20.20S	21.15 E
Roon, Pulau-	26	Jg	2.23S	134.33 E
Rooniu, Mont-	65e	c	17.49S	149.12W
Roorkee	25	Fc	29.52N	77.53 E
Roosendaal	11	Kc	51.32N	4.28 E
Roosevelt [Az.-U.S.]	46	Jj	33.40N	111.09W
Roosevelt [Ut.-U.S.]	46	Kf	40.18N	109.59W
Roosevelt, Mount-	42	Ee	58.23N	125.04W
Roosevelt, Rio-	52	Jf	7.35S	60.20W
Roosevelt Island	66	Lf	79.30S	162.00W
Root Portage	45	Ka	50.53N	91.18W
Ropa	10	Rg	49.46N	21.29 E
Ropar	25	Fb	30.58N	76.20 E
Ropaži	8	Kh	56.58N	24.26 E
Ropczyce	10	Rf	50.03N	21.37 E
Rope, The-	64q	Ab	25.04S	130.05W
Roper River	57	Ef	14.43S	135.27 E
Roquefort	11	Fj	44.02N	0.19W
Roque Pérez	55	Cl	35.25S	59.20W
Roquetas de Mar	13	Jh	36.46N	2.36W
Roraima, Monte-	52	Je	5.12N	60.44W
Roraima, Território de- [2]	54	Fc	1.30N	61.00W
Røros	7	Ce	62.35N	11.24 E
Rorschach	14	Dc	47.30N	9.30 E
Rørvik	7	Cd	64.51N	11.14 E
Ros	16	Ge	49.39N	31.35 E
Rosa, Cap-	14	Cn	36.57N	8.14 E
Rosa, Lake-	49	Kc	20.55N	73.20W
Rosa, Monte-	5	Gf	45.55N	7.53 E
Rošal	7	Ji	55.41N	39.55 E
Rosala	8	Je	59.50N	22.25 E
Rosalia	46	Gc	47.14N	117.22W
Rosalia, Punta-	65d	Bb	27.03S	109.19W
Rosalie	51g	Bb	15.22N	61.16W
Rosalind Bank (EN)	49	Ge	16.30N	80.30W
Rosamond Lake	46	Fi	34.50N	118.04W
Rosamorada	48	Gf	22.08N	105.12W
Rosana	55	Ff	22.36S	53.01W
Rosario [Arg.]	53	Ji	32.57S	60.40W
Rosario [Braz.]	54	Jd	2.57S	44.14W
Rosario [Mex.]	48	Dd	26.27N	111.38W
Rosario [Mex.]	47	Cd	23.00N	105.52W
Rosario [Par.]	56	Ib	24.27S	57.03W
Rosario [Ven.]	49	Kh	10.19N	72.19W
Rosario, Arroyo-	48	Bb	30.03N	115.45W
Rosario, Bahía-	48	Bc	29.50N	115.45W
Rosario, Cayo del-	49	Gc	21.38N	81.53W
Rosario, Islas de-	49	Jh	10.10N	75.46W
Rosario, Sierra del-	48	He	25.35N	103.50W
Rosario de Arriba	47	Ab	30.01N	115.40W
Rosario de la Frontera	56	Hc	25.48S	64.58W
Rosario de Lerma	56	Gb	24.59S	65.35W
Rosario del Tala	55	Ck	32.18S	59.09W
Rosário do Sul	56	Jd	30.15S	54.55W
Rosário Oeste	54	Gf	14.50S	56.25W
Rosarito	48	Bc	28.38N	114.04W
Rosarno	14	Jl	38.29N	15.58 E
Rosas/Roses	13	Pb	42.16N	3.11 E
Rosas, Golfo de-/Roses, Golf de-	13	Pb	42.10N	3.15 E
Rosa Seamount (EN)	47	Bc	26.12N	114.58W
Rosa Zarate	54	Cc	0.18N	79.27W
Roščino	8	Md	60.13N	29.43 E
Roscoe Glacier	66	Ge	66.30S	95.20 E
Ros Comáin/Roscommon [2]	9	Eh	53.40N	8.30W
Ros Comáin/Roscommon	9	Eh	53.38N	8.11W
Roscommon	44	Ec	44.30N	84.35W
Roscommon/Ros Comáin	9	Eh	53.38N	8.11W
Roscommon/Ros Comáin [2]	9	Eh	53.40N	8.30W
Ros Cré/Roscrea	9	Fi	52.57N	7.47W
Roscrea/Ros Cré	9	Fi	52.57N	7.47W
Rose, Pointe de la-	51h	Bb	14.33N	61.03W
Roseau [Dom.]	39	Mh	15.18N	61.24W
Roseau [Dom.]	51g	Bb	15.18N	61.24W
Roseau [Mn.-U.S.]	45	Ib	48.51N	95.46W
Roseau [St.Luc.]	51k	Ab	13.58N	61.02W
Roseau River	45	Hb	49.08N	97.14W
Rosebery	59	Jh	41.46S	145.32 E
Rosebud	46	Lc	46.16N	106.27W
Rosebud Creek	46	Lc	46.16N	106.28W
Rosebud River	46	Ia	51.25N	112.37W
Roseburg	43	Cc	43.13N	123.20W
Rosemary Bank (EN)	9	Cb	59.15N	10.10W
Rosenberg	43	Hf	29.33N	95.48W
Rosendahl	12	Jb	52.01N	7.12 E
Rosendahl-Osterwick	12	Jb	52.01N	7.12 E
Rosendal	7	Bf	59.59N	6.01 E
Rosenheim	10	Ii	47.51N	12.08 E
Rosental	14	Id	46.33N	14.15 E
Roses/Rosas	13	Pb	42.16N	3.11 E
Roses, Golf de-/Rosas, Golfo de-	13	Pb	42.10N	3.15 E
Roseţi	15	Ke	44.13N	27.26 E
Roseto degli Abruzzi	14	Ih	42.41N	14.01 E
Rosetown	42	Gf	51.33N	108.00W
Rosetta (EN)=Rashīd	33	Fc	31.24N	30.25 E
Roseville	46	Eg	38.45N	121.17W
Roshage	7	Bh	57.07N	8.38 E
Rosica	15	If	43.15N	25.42 E
Rosières-en-Santerre	12	Ee	49.49N	2.43 E
Rosignano Solvay	14	Eg	43.23N	10.26 E
Rosignol	54	Gb	6.17N	57.32W
Roşiori de Vede	15	He	44.07N	24.59 E
Roskilde [2]	8	Ei	55.35N	12.10 E
Roskilde	7	Ci	55.39N	12.05 E
Roslagen	8	He	59.30N	18.40 E
Ros Láir/Rosslare	9	Gi	52.17N	6.23W
Roslavl	19	De	53.58N	32.53 E
Roslyn	46	Ec	47.13N	120.59W
Ros Mhic Thriúin/New Ross	9	Gi	52.24N	6.56W
Røsnæs	8	Di	55.45N	10.55 E
Rosny-sur-Seine	12	Df	49.00N	1.38 E
Rösrath	12	Jd	50.54N	7.12 E
Ross	42	Ed	62.00N	132.25W
Ross [Austl.]	59	Jh	42.02S	147.29 E
Ross [Bye.-U.S.S.R.]	10	Uc	53.16N	24.29 E
Ross [N.Z.]	62	De	42.54S	170.49 E
Ross, Cape-	26	Gd	10.56N	119.13 E
Ross, Mount-	30	Nm	49.25S	69.08 E
Rossano	14	Kk	39.34N	16.38 E
Rossan Point/Ceann Ros Eoghain	9	Eg	54.42N	8.48W
Ross Barnett Reservoir	45	Lj	32.30N	90.00W
Rosseau Lake	44	Hc	45.10N	79.35W
Rossel Island	57	Gf	11.26S	154.07 E
Rossell, Cap-	63b	Ce	20.23S	166.36 E
Ross Ice Shelf	66	Lg	81.30S	175.00W
Rossijskaja Sovetskaja Federativnaja Socialističeskaja Respublika (RSFSR) [2]	19	Jc	60.00N	100.00 E
Ross Island	66	Kf	77.30S	168.00 E
Ross Lake	46	Eb	48.53N	121.04W
Rossland	46	Gb	49.05N	117.48W
Rosslare/Ros Láir	9	Gi	52.17N	6.23W
Roßlau	10	Ie	51.53N	12.15 E
Rosso	31	Fg	16.31N	15.49W
Ross-on-Wye	9	Kj	51.55N	2.35W
Rossony	8	Mi	55.53N	28.49 E
Rossoš	19	De	50.11N	39.39 E
Ross River	42	Ed	61.59N	132.27W
Ross Sea (EN)	66	Lf	76.00S	175.00W
Røssvatn	7	Cd	65.45N	14.00 E
Røst	7	Cc	67.31N	12.07 E
Rosta	7	Eb	69.02N	18.40 E
Rostamī	24	Nh	28.52N	51.02 E
Rostan Kalā	24	Od	36.42N	53.27 E
Rösterkopf	12	Ie	49.40N	6.50 E
Rosthern	42	Gf	52.40N	106.20W
Rostock	6	He	54.05N	12.08 E
Rostock [2]	10	Ib	54.10N	12.10 E
Rostock-Warnemünde	10	Ib	54.10N	12.05 E
Rostov	19	Dd	57.13N	39.25 E
Rostov-na-Donu	6	Jf	47.14N	39.42 E
Rostovskaja Oblast [3]	19	Ef	47.45N	41.15 E
Roswell [Ga.-U.S.]	44	Eh	34.03N	84.22W
Roswell [N.M.-U.S.]	39	If	33.24N	104.32W
Rot	8	Fc	61.15N	14.02 E
Rota	13	Fh	36.37N	6.21W
Rota Island	57	Fc	14.10N	145.12 E
Rotenburg (Wümme)	10	Fc	53.07N	9.24 E
Rotenburg an der Fulda	10	Ff	50.59N	9.43 E
Roter Main	10	Hf	50.03N	11.27 E
Roth	10	Hg	49.15N	11.06 E
Rothaargebirge	10	Ee	51.05N	8.15 E
Rothenburg ob der Tauber	10	Gg	49.23N	10.11 E
Rother [Eng.-U.K.]	9	Nk	50.57N	0.45 E
Rother [Eng.-U.K.]	12	Bd	50.57N	0.22W
Rothera	66	Qe	67.46S	68.54W
Rotherham	9	Lh	53.26N	1.20W
Rothesay	9	Hf	55.51N	5.03W
Rothorn	14	Cd	46.47N	8.03 E
Rothschild Island	66	Qe	69.25S	72.30W
Rothwell	12	Bb	52.25N	0.48W
Roti, Pulau-	21	Ok	10.45S	123.10 E
Roti, Selat-	26	Hi	10.25S	123.25 E
Rotja, Punta-	13	Nf	38.38N	1.34 E
Rotnes	8	Dd	60.04N	10.53 E
Roto	59	Jf	33.03S	145.29 E
Rotoiti, Lake-	62	Ed	41.50S	172.50 E
Rotondella	14	Kj	40.10N	16.31 E
Rotondo, Monte-	11a	Ba	42.13N	9.03 E
Rotoroa, Lake-	62	Ed	41.50S	172.40 E
Rotorua	61	Eg	38.09S	176.15 E
Rotorua, Lake-	62	Gc	38.05S	176.15 E
Rotselaar	12	Gd	50.57N	4.43 E
Rott	10	Jh	48.25N	13.20 E
Rottenburg am Neckar	10	Eh	48.28N	8.56 E
Rotterdam	6	Ge	51.55N	4.28 E
Rottnaälven	8	Ed	59.48N	13.07 E
Rottnen	8	Fh	56.45N	15.05 E
Rottneros	8	Ee	59.48N	13.07 E
Rottnest Island	59	Df	32.00S	115.30 E
Rottumerplaat	11	Ma	53.35N	6.30 E
Rottweil	10	Eh	48.10N	8.37 E
Rotuma Island	57	If	12.30S	177.05 E
Roubaix	11	Jd	50.42N	3.10 E
Roubion	11	Kj	44.31N	4.42 E
Roudnice nad Labem	10	Kf	50.26N	14.16 E
Rouen	6	Gf	49.26N	1.05 E
Rouergue	11	Ij	44.30N	2.58 E
Rouge, Rivière-	44	Jc	45.38N	74.42W
Rouillac	11	Fi	45.47N	0.04W
Roulers/Roeselare	11	Jd	50.57N	3.08 E
Roumois	11	Ge	49.30N	0.30 E
Roundup	43	Fb	46.27N	108.33W
Rousay	9	Jb	59.01N	3.02W
Roussillon	11	Ki	45.22N	4.49 E
Roussillon	11	Il	42.30N	2.30 E
Roussin, Cap-	63b	Ce	21.21S	167.59 E
Routot	12	Ce	49.23N	0.44 E
Rouyn	39	Le	48.14N	79.01W
Rovaniemi	6	Ib	66.30N	25.43 E
Rovenskaja Oblast [3]	19	Ce	51.00N	26.30 E
Rovereto	14	Fe	45.53N	11.02 E
Rovigo	14	Fe	45.04N	11.47 E
Rovinari	15	Ge	44.55N	23.11 E
Rovinj	14	He	45.05N	13.38 E
Rovkulskoje, Ozero-	7	Hd	64.00N	31.00 E
Rovno	6	Ie	50.37N	26.15 E
Rovnoje	16	Od	50.47N	46.05 E
Rovuma=Ruvuma (EN)	30	Lj	10.29S	40.28 E
Rowa, Iles-	63b	Ca	13.37S	167.32 E
Rowley	42	Jc	69.05N	78.55W
Rowley Shoals	57	Cf	17.30S	119.00 E
Roxas [Phil.]	26	Gd	10.28N	119.30 E
Roxas [Phil.]	26	Hd	11.35N	122.45 E
Roxboro	44	Hg	36.24N	78.59W
Roxburgh	62	Cf	45.33S	169.19 E
Roxen	8	Ff	58.30N	15.40 E
Roxo, Cap-	30	Fg	12.20N	16.43W
Roy [N.M.-U.S.]	45	Di	35.57N	104.12W
Roy [Ut.-U.S.]	46	If	41.10N	112.02W
Roya	11	Nk	43.48N	7.35 E
Royal Canal	9	Gh	53.21N	6.15W
Royale, Isle-	43	Jb	48.00N	89.00W
Royal Leamington Spa	9	Li	52.18N	1.31W
Royal Society Range	66	Jf	78.10S	162.36 E
Royal Tunbridge Wells	9	Nj	51.08N	0.16 E
Royan	11	Ei	45.38N	1.02W
Royat	11	Ji	45.46N	3.03 E
Royaumont, Abbaye de-	12	Ee	49.17N	2.28 E
Roye	11	Ie	49.42N	2.48 E
Roy Hill	59	Dd	22.38S	119.57 E
Røyken	8	De	59.45N	10.23 E
Royston	9	Mi	52.03N	0.01W
Rožaj	15	Dg	42.51N	20.10 E
Różan	10	Rd	52.53N	21.25 E
Rozdol	10	Ug	49.24N	24.08 E
Rozewie, Przylądek-	10	Ob	54.51N	18.21 E
Rožišče	16	Dd	50.54N	25.19 E
Rožňava	10	Qh	48.40N	20.32 E
Rožniatov	10	Uh	48.51N	24.14 E
Roznov	15	Jc	46.50N	26.31 E
Rožnov pod Radhoštěm	10	Og	49.28N	18.09 E
Rożnów	10	Qg	49.46N	20.42 E
Rożnowskie, Jezioro-	10	Qg	49.39N	20.45 E
Rozoy-sur-Serre	12	Ge	49.43N	4.08 E
Roztocze	5	Ie	50.30N	23.20 E
Rrësheni	15	Ch	41.47N	19.54 E
RSFSR=Russian SFSR (EN) [2]	19	Jc	60.00N	100.00 E
RSFSR→Rossijskaja Sovetskaja Federativnaja Socialističeskaja Respublika [2]	19	Jc	60.00N	100.00 E
Rtanj	15	Ef	43.47N	21.54 E
Rtiščevo	19	Ee	52.16N	43.52 E
Ruacana, Quedas-	30	Jj	17.23S	14.15 E
Ruahine Range	62	Gc	39.50S	176.05 E
Ruapehu	57	Ih	39.17S	175.34 E
Ruapuke Island	61	Ci	46.45S	168.30 E
Rua Sura	63a	Ec	9.30S	160.36 E
Ruatahuna	62	Gc	38.38S	176.58 E
Rubbestadneset	8	Ae	59.49N	5.17 E
Rubcovsk	22	Kd	51.33N	81.10 E
Rubeho Mountains	36	Gd	6.55S	36.30 E
Rubeshibe	28	Qc	43.47N	143.38 E
Rubežnoje	16	Ke	48.59N	38.26 E
Rubi	36	Db	2.48N	23.54 E
Rubiataba	55	Hb	15.08S	49.48W
Rubiku	15	Ch	41.46N	19.45 E
Rubio	54	Db	7.43N	72.22W
Rubio	13	Ic	41.26N	3.47W
Ruby	40	Hd	64.44N	155.30W
Ruby Lake	46	Hf	40.15N	115.30W
Ruby Mountains	46	Hf	40.25N	115.35W
Ruby Range	46	Id	45.15N	112.15W
Rucăr	15	Id	45.24N	25.10 E
Rucava	8	Ih	56.10N	21.00 E
Ruciane Nida	10	Rc	53.39N	21.35 E
Ruda	10	Of	50.10N	18.18 E
Rudabánya	10	Qh	48.23N	20.38 E
Rūdak	24	Nh	35.51N	51.33 E
Rūdān	24	Qi	27.17N	57.13 E
Ruda Śląska	10	Of	50.18N	18.51 E
Rūdbār [Afg.]	23	Jc	30.09N	62.36 E
Rūdbār [Iran]	24	Md	36.48N	49.24 E
Rüdersdorf bei Berlin	10	Jd	52.27N	13.47 E
Rüdesheim am Rhein	12	Je	49.59N	7.55 E
Rudiškes/Rūdiškės	8	Kj	54.30N	24.58 E
Rūdiškės/Rudiškes	8	Kj	54.30N	24.58 E
Rudki	10	Tg	49.34N	23.30 E
Rudkøbing	7	Ci	54.56N	10.43 E
Rudnaja-Pristan	20	Ih	44.25N	135.49 E
Rudničny	7	Mg	59.38N	52.29 E
Rudnik	15	De	44.08N	20.30 E
Rudnik [Bul.]	15	Kg	42.57N	27.46 E
Rudnik [Pol.]	10	Sf	50.28N	22.15 E
Rudnik [Yugo.]	15	De	44.08N	20.31 E
Rudnja [R.S.F.S.R.]	16	Nd	50.49N	44.36 E
Rudnja [R.S.F.S.R.]	7	Hi	54.57N	31.07 E
Rudno	10	Tg	49.44N	23.57 E
Rudny [Kaz.-U.S.S.R.]	19	Ge	52.57N	63.07 E
Rudny [R.S.F.S.R.]	28	Mb	44.28N	135.00 E
Rudolf, Lake-/Turkana, Lake-	30	Kh	3.30N	36.00 E
Rudolstadt	10	Hf	50.43N	11.20 E
Rudong (Juegang)	28	Fh	32.19N	121.11 E
Rudozem	15	Hh	41.29N	24.51 E
Rūd Sar	23	Hb	37.08N	50.18 E
Rudyard	46	Jb	48.34N	110.33W
Rue	11	Hd	50.16N	1.40 E
Ruecas	13	Ge	39.00N	5.55W
Ruelle-sur-Touvre	11	Gi	45.41N	0.14 E
Rufā'ah	35	Ec	14.46N	33.22 E
Ruffec	11	Gh	46.01N	0.12 E
Ruffing Point	51a	Db	18.45N	64.25W
Rufiji	30	Ki	8.00S	39.20 E
Rufino	56	Hd	34.16S	62.42W
Rufisque	34	Bc	14.43N	17.17W
Rufunsa	36	Ef	15.05S	29.40 E
Rugao	28	Fh	32.24N	120.34 E
Rugby [Eng.-U.K.]	9	Li	52.23N	1.15W
Rugby [N.D.-U.S.]	43	Gb	48.22N	99.59W
Rügen	5	He	54.25N	13.24 E
Rugles	12	Cf	48.49N	0.42 E
Ru He	28	Ch	32.55N	114.24 E
Ruhea	25	Hc	26.10N	88.25 E
Ruhengeri	36	Ec	1.30S	29.38 E
Rühlertwist	12	Jb	52.39N	7.06 E
Ruhner Berge	10	Hc	53.17N	11.55 E
Ruhnu, Ostrov-/Ruhnu Saar	7	Fh	57.50N	23.15 E
Ruhnu Saar/Ruhnu, Ostrov-	7	Fh	57.50N	23.15 E
Ruhr	10	Ce	51.27N	6.44 E
Rui'an	27	Lf	27.48N	120.38 E
Ruichang	28	Cj	29.41N	115.38 E
Ruiena/Rūjiena	7	Fh	57.54N	25.17 E
Ruijin	27	Kf	25.59N	116.03 E
Ruili	27	Gg	24.03N	97.46 E
Ruiselede	12	Fc	51.03N	3.24 E
Ruiz	48	Gg	21.57N	105.09W
Ruiz, Nevado del-	54	Cc	4.54N	75.18W
Ruj	15	Fg	42.51N	22.35 E
Ruja/Rūja	8	Kg	57.38N	25.10 E
Rūja/Ruja	8	Kg	57.38N	25.10 E
Rujan	15	Eg	42.23N	21.49 E
Rujen	15	Fg	42.10N	22.31 E
Rūjiena/Ruiena	7	Fh	57.54N	25.17 E
Ruki	30	Ih	0.05N	18.17 E
Rukwa [3]	36	Fd	7.00S	31.20 E
Rukwa, Lake-	30	Ki	8.00S	32.15 E
Rūl Dadnah	24	Qk	25.33N	56.21 E
Rülzheim	12	Ke	49.10N	8.18 E
Ruma	15	Cd	45.01N	19.49 E
Rumaylah	35	Fc	12.57N	35.02 E
Rumbek	31	Jh	6.48N	29.41 E
Rumberpon, Pulau-	26	Jg	1.50S	134.15 E
Rum Cay	47	Jd	23.40N	74.53W
Rumes	12	Fd	50.33N	3.18 E
Rumford	44	Lc	44.33N	70.33W
Rumia	10	Ob	54.35N	18.25 E
Rumigny	12	Ge	49.48N	4.16 E
Rumija	15	Cg	42.06N	19.12 E
Rumilly	11	Li	45.52N	5.57 E
Rum Jungle	59	Gb	13.01S	131.00 E
Rummah, Wādī ar-	24	Ki	26.38N	44.18 E
Rumoi	27	Pc	43.56N	141.39 E
Rumphi	36	Fe	11.01S	33.52 E
Run	12	Hc	51.40N	5.20 E
Runan	28	Ci	33.00N	114.21 E
Runanga	62	De	42.24S	171.15 E
Runaway, Cape-	62	Gb	37.32S	177.59 E
Rundēni/Rundeni	8	Lh	56.14N	27.52 E
Rundeni/Rundēni	8	Lh	56.14N	27.52 E
Rundu	31	Ij	17.55S	19.45 E
Rungu	36	Eb	3.11N	27.52 E
Rungwa	31	Ki	6.57S	33.31 E
Rungwa	36	Fd	7.36S	31.50 E
Runmarö	8	He	59.15N	18.45 E
Runn	8	Fd	60.35N	15.40 E
Ruokolahti	7	Gf	61.17N	28.50 E
Ruoqiang (Qarkilik)	22	Kf	39.02N	88.00 E
Ruo Shui	21	Le	40.20N	99.40 E
Ruotsalainen	8	Kc	61.15N	25.55 E
Ruotsinpyhtää/Strömfors	8	Ld	60.32N	26.27 E
Ruovesi	7	Ff	61.59N	24.05 E
Ruovesi	8	Kc	61.55N	24.10 E
Rupanco	56	Ff	40.46S	72.42W
Rupea	15	Ic	46.02N	25.13 E
Rupel	12	Gc	51.07N	4.19 E
Rupert	42	Jf	51.30N	78.48W
Rupert	46	Ie	42.37N	113.41W
Rupert, Baie de-	42	Jf	51.35N	79.00W
Ruppert Coast	66	Mf	75.45S	141.00W
Rur	10	Be	51.12N	5.59 E
Rurrenabaque	53	Jg	14.28S	67.34W
Rurstausee	12	Id	50.38N	6.24 E
Rurutu, Ile-	57	Lg	22.26S	151.20W
Rušan	19	Hh	37.57N	71.31 E
Rusape	37	Ec	18.32S	32.07 E
Rușayriș, Khazzān ar-=Rusayris, Lake- (EN)	35	Ec	11.40N	34.20 E
Rusayris, Lake- (EN)=Rușayriș, Khazzān ar-	35	Ec	11.40N	34.20 E
Ruse	6	Ig	43.50N	25.57 E
Ruse [2]	15	If	43.50N	25.57 E
Rușețu	15	Ke	44.57N	27.13 E
Rushan (Xiacun)	28	Ff	36.55N	121.30 E
Rushden	12	Bb	52.17N	0.35W
Rushville	45	Kf	40.07N	90.34W
Rusk	45	Ik	31.48N	95.09W

Index Symbols

[1] Independent Nation; [2] State, Region; [3] District, County; [4] Municipality; [5] Colony, Dependency; Continent; Physical Region

Historical or Cultural Region; Mount, Mountain; Volcano; Hill; Mountains, Mountain Range; Hills, Escarpment; Plateau, Upland

Pass, Gap; Plain, Lowland; Delta; Salt Flat; Valley, Canyon; Crater, Cave; Karst Features

Depression; Polder; Desert, Dunes; Forest, Woods; Heath, Steppe; Oasis; Cape, Point

Coast, Beach; Cliff; Peninsula; Isthmus; Sandbank; Island; Atoll

Rock, Reef; Islands, Archipelago; Rocks, Reefs; Coral Reef; Well, Spring; Geyser; River, Stream

Waterfall Rapids; River Mouth, Estuary; Lake; Salt Lake; Intermittent Lake; Reservoir; Swamp, Pond

Canal; Glacier; Ice Shelf, Pack Ice; Ocean; Sea; Gulf, Bay; Strait, Fjord

Lagoon; Bank; Seamount; Tablemount; Ridge; Shelf; Basin

Escarpment, Sea Scarp; Fracture; Trench, Abyss; National Park, Reserve; Point of Interest; Recreation Site; Cave, Cavern

Historic Site; Ruins; Wall, Walls; Church, Abbey; Temple; Scientific Station; Airport

Port; Lighthouse; Mine; Tunnel; Dam, Bridge

Rusken 8 Fg 57.17N 14.20 E
Rusne/Rusnė 8 Ii 55.19N 21.16 E
Rusnė/Rusne 8 Ii 55.19N 21.16 E
Russel 42 Hb 73.55N 98.35W
Russell [Man. Can.] 42 Hf 50.47N 101.15W
Russell [Ks.-U.S.] 45 Gg 38.54N 98.52W
Russell [N.Z.] 62 Fa 35.16S 174.08 E
Russell Islands 60 Fi 9.04S 159.12 E
Russellville [Al.-U.S.] 44 Dh 34.30N 87.44W
Russellville [Ar.-U.S.] 45 Ji 35.17N 93.08W
Russellville [Ky.-U.S.] 44 Dg 36.51N 86.53W
Russel Range 59 Ef 33.25S 123.30 E
Rüsselsheim 10 Eg 50.00N 8.25 E
Russian River 46 Dg 38.27N 123.08W
Russian SFSR (EN) = RSFSR [2] 19 Jc 60.00N 100.00 E
Rust 14 Kc 47.48N 16.40 E
Rustavi 19 Eg 41.33N 45.02 E
Rustenburg 37 De 25.37S 27.08 E
Ruston 43 Ie 32.32N 92.38W
Rutaki Passage 64p Bc 21.15S 159.48W
Rutana 36 Fc 3.55S 30.00 E
Rutanzige, Lac- = Edward, Lake- (EN) 30 Ji 0.25S 29.30 E
Rute 13 Hg 37.19N 4.22W
Ruteng 26 Hh 8.36S 120.27 E
Rutenga 37 Ed 21.15S 30.44 E
Rüthen 12 Kc 51.29N 8.27 E
Rutherfordton 44 Gh 35.22N 81.57W
Ruthin 9 Jh 53.07N 3.18W
Rutland 9 Mi 52.40N 0.40W
Rutland 44 Kd 43.37N 72.59W
Rutland 25 If 11.25N 92.10 E
Rutog 22 Jf 33.29N 79.42 E
Rutshuru 36 Ec 1.11S 29.27 E
Rutter 44 Gb 46.06N 80.40W
Rutul 16 Oi 41.33N 47.29 E
Ruutana 8 Kc 61.31N 24.02 E
Ruvo di Puglia 14 Ki 41.09N 16.29 E
Ruvu 36 Gd 6.48S 38.39 E
Ruvuma [3] 36 Ge 10.30S 35.50 E
Ruvuma 30 Lj 10.29S 40.28 E
Ruvuma (EN) = Rovuma 30 Lj 10.29S 40.28 E
Ruwayshid, Wādī- 24 Hf 32.41N 38.04 E
Ruwenzori 30 Jh 0.23N 29.54 E
Ruwer 12 Ie 49.47N 6.42 E
Ruya 37 Ec 16.34S 33.12 E
Ruyang 28 Bg 34.10N 112.28 E
Ru'yas, Wādī ar- 33 Cd 27.06N 19.24 E
Ruyigi 36 Fc 3.29S 30.15 E
Ruza 7 Ii 55.39N 36.18 E
Ruzajevka [Kaz.-U.S.S.R.] 17 Mj 52.49N 67.01 E
Ruzajevka [R.S.F.S.R.] 19 Ee 54.05N 44.54 E
Ružany 10 Ud 52.48N 24.58 E
Ružomberok 10 Pg 49.05N 19.18 E
Rwanda [1] 31 Ji 2.30S 30.00 E
Ry 8 Ch 56.05N 9.46 E
Ryan 45 Hi 34.01N 97.57W
Rybachi Peninsula (EN) = Rybači, Poluostrov- 5 Jb 69.45N 32.35 E
Rybači 8 Ii 55.09N 20.45 E
Rybači, Poluostrov- = Rybachi Peninsula (EN) 5 Jb 69.45N 32.35 E
Rybačje 19 Hg 42.28N 76.11 E
Rybinsk 6 Jd 58.03N 38.52 E
Rybinskoje Vodohranilišče = Rybinsk Reservoir (EN) 5 Jd 58.30N 38.25 E
Rybinsk Reservoir (EN) = Rybinskoje Vodohranilišče 5 Jd 58.30N 38.25 E
Rybnica 16 Ff 47.45N 29.01 E
Rybnik 10 Of 50.06N 18.32 E
Rybnoje 19 De 54.46N 39.33 E
Rybnovsk 20 Jf 53.15N 141.55 E
Rychnov nad Kněžnou 10 Mf 50.10N 16.17 E
Rychwał 10 Od 52.05N 18.09 E
Ryd 8 Fh 56.28N 14.41 E
Rydaholm 8 Fh 56.59N 14.16 E
Ryde 12 Ad 50.43N 1.10W
Rye 9 Mg 54.10N 0.45W
Rye 9 Nk 50.57N 0.44 E
Rye Bay 12 Cd 50.55N 0.48 E
Ryegate 46 Kc 46.18N 109.15W
Rye Patch Reservoir 46 Ff 40.38N 118.18W
Ryes 12 Be 49.19N 0.37W
Ryfylke 8 Be 59.30N 6.30 E
Ryki 10 Re 51.39N 21.56 E
Rylsk 19 De 51.36N 34.43 E
Rymanów 10 Rg 49.34N 21.53 E
Rymättylä/Rimito 8 Jd 60.25N 21.55 E
Ryn 10 Rc 53.56N 21.33 E
Ryńskie, Jezioro- 10 Rc 53.53N 21.30 E
Ryōhaku-Sanchi 29 Ec 36.05N 136.45 E
Ryōsō-Yosui 29 Gd 35.22N 140.25 E
Ryōtsu 28 Oe 38.05N 138.26 E
Ryōtsu-Wan 29 Fb 38.10N 138.30 E
Ryō-Zen 29 Gc 37.46N 140.41 E
Rypin 10 Pc 53.05N 19.25 E
Ryškany 16 Ef 47.57N 27.32 E
Ryssby 8 Fh 56.52N 14.10 E
Rytterknægten 8 Fi 55.06N 14.54 E
Ryūgasaki 29 Gd 35.54N 140.10 E
Ryukyu Islands (EN) = Nansei-Shotō 21 Og 26.30N 128.00 E
Ryūkyū-Shotō 27 Mf 25.30N 126.30 E
Ryukyu Trench (EN) 3 Ig 25.45N 128.00 E
Rzepin 10 Kd 52.22N 14.50 E
Rzeszów 6 Ie 50.03N 22.00 E
Rzeszów [2] 10 Rf 50.05N 22.00 E
Ržev 6 Jd 56.16N 34.20 E

S

Šaa, Gora- 16 Nh 42.39N 44.43 E
Sa'ādatābād [Iran] 24 Ph 28.02N 55.50 E
Sa'ādatābād [Iran] 24 Og 30.08N 52.38 E
Sa'ādatābād [Iran] 24 Og 30.06N 53.08 E
Sääksjarvi 8 Jc 61.24N 22.24 E
Saalbach 12 Ke 49.15N 8.27 E
Saale 10 He 51.57N 11.55 E
Saaler Bodden 10 Ib 54.20N 12.28 E
Saalfeld 10 Hf 50.39N 11.22 E
Saalfelden am Steinernen Meer 14 Gc 47.25N 12.51 E
Saaminki 8 Mc 61.52N 28.50 E
Saâne 12 Ce 49.54N 0.56 E
Saane 14 Bd 46.59N 7.16 E
Saanen 14 Bd 46.30N 7.15 E
Saar 10 Cg 49.42N 6.34 E
Saar-Bergland 12 Ie 49.27N 6.45 E
Saarbrücken 6 Gf 49.14N 7.00 E
Saarbrücken-Dudweiler 12 Je 49.17N 7.02 E
Saarburg 10 Cg 49.36N 6.33 E
Sääre/Sjare 8 Ig 57.57N 21.53 E
Saaremaa/Sarema 5 Id 58.25N 22.30 E
Saarijärvi 7 Fe 62.43N 25.16 E
Saaristomeri 8 Id 60.20N 21.10 E
Saarland [2] 10 Cg 49.20N 7.00 E
Saarlouis 10 Cg 49.19N 6.45 E
Šaartuz 19 Gh 37.16N 68.06 E
Saarwellingen 12 Ie 49.21N 6.49 E
Saas Fee 14 Bd 46.07N 7.55 E
Saatly 16 Pj 39.57N 48.26 E
Saavedra 55 Am 37.45S 62.22W
Sab, Tônlé- 25 Kf 11.34N 104.57 E
Saba 47 Le 17.38N 63.10W
Saba 8 Me 59.05N 29.10 E
Saba Bank (EN) 50 Ed 17.30N 63.30W
Šabac 15 Ce 44.45N 19.43 E
Sabadell 13 Oc 41.33N 2.06 E
Sabae 28 Ng 35.57N 136.11 E
Sabah [2] 26 Ge 5.30N 117.00 E
Sab'ah, Qārat as- 33 Cd 27.20N 17.10 E
Sabak Bernam 26 Df 3.46N 100.59 E
Sabalān, Kūhhā-ye- 21 Gf 38.15N 47.49 E
Sab'ān 24 Ii 27.04N 41.58 E
Sabana, Archipiélago de- 49 Hb 22.30N 79.00W
Sabana de la Mar 49 Md 19.04N 69.23W
Sabanagrande 49 Dg 13.50N 87.15W
Sabanalarga 54 Da 10.38N 74.56W
Sabancuy 48 Nh 18.58N 91.11W
Sabaneta 49 Ld 19.12N 70.58W
Sabaneta, Puntan- 64b Ba 15.17N 145.49 E
Sabang [Indon.] 26 Gf 0.11N 119.51 E
Sabang [Indon.] 26 Ce 5.55N 95.19 E
Şabanözü 24 Eb 40.29N 33.18 E
Săbăoani 15 Jb 47.01N 26.51 E
Sabarei 36 Gb 4.20N 36.55 E
Sab'Atayn, Ramlat as- 33 If 15.30N 46.10 E
Sabatini, Monti- 14 Gh 42.10N 12.15 E
Sabaudia 14 Hi 41.18N 13.01 E
Sabaudia, Lago di- 14 Hi 41.15N 13.05 E
Şabbāgh, Jabal- 24 Fh 28.12N 34.04 E
Sab 'Bi 'Ār 24 Gf 33.46N 37.41 E
Sabbioneta 14 Ee 45.00N 10.39 E
Sa Bec 25 Lf 10.18N 105.46 E
Sabhā [3] 33 Bd 26.00N 14.00 E
Sabhā 31 If 27.02N 14.26 E
Şabḩā 24 Gf 32.20N 36.30 E
Sābhā, Wāḩāt- = Sebha Oasis (EN) 30 If 27.00N 14.25 E
Sabi 30 Kk 21.00S 35.02 E
Sabidana, Jabal- 35 Fb 18.04N 36.50 E
Sabile 8 Jg 57.05N 22.29 E
Sabina 14 Gh 42.20N 12.45 E
Sabinal 48 Fb 30.57N 107.30W
Sabinal, Peninsula de- 49 Ic 21.40N 77.18W
Sabiñánigo 13 Lb 42.31N 0.22W
Sabinas 47 Dc 27.51N 101.07W
Sabinas, Río- 48 Id 27.37N 100.42W
Sabinas Hidalgo 47 Dc 26.30N 100.10W
Sabine Lake 45 Jl 29.50N 93.50W
Sabine Pass 45 Jl 29.44N 93.52W
Sabine Peninsula 42 Ga 76.25N 109.50W
Sabine River 43 Ie 30.00N 93.45W
Sabini, Monti- 14 Gh 42.15N 12.50 E
Şabir, Jabal- 23 Fg 13.30N 44.03 E
Sabirabad 16 Pj 39.59N 48.29 E
Šabla 15 Lf 43.32N 28.32 E
Sable, Anse de- 51e b 16.07N 61.34W
Sable, Cape- [Can.] 38 Me 43.25N 65.35W
Sable, Cape- [U.S.] 38 Kg 25.12N 81.05W
Sable, Ile de- 57 Gf 19.15S 159.56 E
Sable Island 38 Ne 43.55N 59.55W
Sablé-sur-Sarthe 11 Fg 47.50N 0.20W
Sablūkah, Ash Shallāl as- = Sixth Cataract (EN) 30 Kg 16.20N 32.42 E
Sabonetau, Serra da- 55 Kb 15.20S 43.50W
Sabonkafi 34 Gc 14.38N 8.45 E
Sabór 13 Ec 41.10N 7.07W
Şabrātah 33 Bc 32.47N 12.29 E
Sabres 11 Fj 44.09N 0.44W
Sabrina Coast 66 He 67.00S 119.30 E
Sabtang 26 Hb 20.19N 121.52 E
Sabunči 16 Pi 40.27N 49.57 E
Şabyā 23 Ff 17.09N 42.37 E
Sabzevār 22 Hf 36.13N 57.42 E
Saca, Virful- 15 Ic 46.30N 25.15 E
Sacajawea Peak 43 Db 45.15N 117.17W
Sacalin, Insulă- 15 Me 44.50N 29.39 E
Sacandica 36 Cd 5.58S 15.56 E
Sacatepéquez [3] 49 Bf 14.35N 90.45W
Sacavém 13 Cf 38.46N 9.05W
Sac City 45 Ie 42.25N 95.00W
Sacco 14 Hi 41.31N 13.32 E
Sacedón 13 Jd 40.29N 2.43W
Săcel 15 Hb 47.38N 24.26 E
Săcele 15 Id 45.37N 25.41 E
Sachayoj 55 Bh 26.41S 61.50W
Saĉhere 16 Mh 42.20N 43.22 E
Sachigo 42 Ie 55.05N 89.00W
Sachsen = Saxony (EN) 10 Jf 51.00N 13.30 E
Sachsenhagen 12 Lb 52.24N 9.16 E
Sachs Harbour 42 Eb 72.00N 125.08W
Šack [R.S.F.S.R.] 7 Ji 54.04N 41.42 E
Šack [Ukr.-U.S.S.R.] 10 Je 51.30N 24.00 E
Sackets Harbor 44 Id 43.57N 76.07W
Saco [Me.-U.S.] 44 Ld 43.29N 70.28W
Saco [Mt.-U.S.] 46 Lb 48.28N 107.21W
Sacramento 38 Gf 38.03N 121.56W
Sacramento [Braz.] 54 Ig 19.53S 47.27W
Sacramento [Ca.-U.S.] 39 Gf 38.35N 121.30W
Sacramento, Pampa del- 54 Ce 8.00S 75.50W
Sacramento Mountains 38 If 33.10N 105.50W
Sacramento Valley 43 Cd 39.15N 122.00W
Sacre ou Timalacia, Rio- 55 Ca 13.55S 58.02W
Săcueni 15 Fb 47.21N 22.06 E
Sacuriuiná ou Ponte de Pedra, Rio- 55 Da 13.58S 57.18W
Sádaba 13 Kb 42.17N 1.16W
Sa'dābād 24 Nh 29.23N 51.07 E
Şa'dah 22 Gh 16.57N 43.44 E
Sada-Misaki 29b Ce 33.22N 132.01 E
Sada-Misaki-Hantō 29 Ce 33.25N 132.15 E
Sadani 36 Gd 6.03S 38.47 E
Sadao 25 Kg 6.39N 100.31 E
Sadd al 'Ālī 33 Fe 23.54N 32.52 E
Saddle Mountains 46 Fc 46.50N 119.55W
Saddle Peak [India] 25 If 13.09N 93.01 E
Saddle Peak [Mt.-U.S.] 46 Jd 45.57N 110.58W
Sad-e Eskandar 24 Pd 37.10N 55.00 E
Sadiya 25 Jc 27.50N 95.40 E
Sa'dīyah, Hawr as- 24 Lf 32.00N 46.45 E
Sad Kharv 24 Qd 36.19N 57.05 E
Sado 13 Df 38.29N 8.55W
Sado-Kaikyō 29 Fc 37.55N 138.40 E
Sado-Shima 21 Pf 38.00N 138.25 E
Sadowara 29 Be 32.04N 131.26 E
Šadrinsk 19 Gd 56.05N 63.38 E
Saeby 7 Ch 57.20N 10.32 E
Saeh, Teluk- 26 Gh 8.00S 117.30 E
Saengcheon 28 Ie 39.55N 126.34 E
Saerbeck 12 Jb 52.11N 7.38 E
Şafājah 24 Hi 26.30N 39.30 E
Safājah, Jazīrat- 24 Ei 26.45N 33.59 E
Safané 34 Ec 12.08N 3.13W
Şafāqis = Sfax (EN) [3] 32 Jc 34.30N 10.30 E
Şafāqis = Sfax (EN) 31 Ie 34.44N 10.46 E
Safata Harbour 65c Bb 14.00S 171.50W
Saffānīyah, Ra's as- 23 Gd 27.59N 48.37 E
Säffle 7 Cg 59.08N 12.56 E
Safford 43 Fe 32.50N 109.43W
Saffron Walden 12 Cb 52.01N 0.15 E
Safi 31 Ge 32.18N 9.14W
Safi [3] 32 Fc 31.55N 9.00W
Safia, Hamāda- 34 Ea 23.10N 4.15W
Şafīdābād 24 Qd 36.45N 57.58 E
Safid 23 Hb 37.23N 50.11 E
Safīd, Kūh-e 24 Lf 33.55N 47.30 E
Safīd Kūh, Salseleh-ye- 23 Jc 34.30N 63.30 E
Safonovo [R.S.F.S.R.] 19 Dd 55.06N 33.14 E
Safonovo [R.S.F.S.R.] 7 Ld 65.41N 47.43 E
Şafrā' al Asyāḩ 24 Ji 26.50N 43.57 E
Şafrā' as Sark 24 Kj 25.25N 44.20 E
Safranbolu 24 Eb 41.15N 32.42 E
Şafwān 24 Lg 30.07N 47.43 E
Saga [Jap.] 27 Ne 33.15N 130.18 E
Saga [Jap.] 29 Ce 33.05N 133.06 E
Saga [Kaz.-U.S.S.R.] 19 Fe 50.30N 64.14 E
Saga (Gya'gya) 27 Ef 29.22N 85.15 E
Sagae 29 Gb 38.22N 140.17 E
Sagaing [3] 25 Jd 23.30N 95.30 E
Sagaing 25 Jd 21.52N 95.59 E
Saga Ken [2] 28 Kh 33.15N 130.15 E
Sagamihara 29 Fd 35.34N 139.22 E
Sagami-Nada 29 Fd 35.00N 139.30 E
Sagami-Wan 29 Fd 35.15N 139.20 E
Sagan 35 Fd 5.17N 36.57 E
Šagan 19 He 50.37N 79.15 E
Saganaga Lake 45 Kb 48.14N 90.52W
Saganoseki 29 Be 33.15N 131.53 E
Šagany, Ozero- 15 Md 45.45N 29.55 E
Sāgar [India] 25 Ff 14.10N 75.02 E
Sāgar [India] 22 Jg 23.50N 78.42 E
Sagara 29 Fd 34.40N 138.12 E
Sagaredžo 16 Ni 41.43N 45.16 E
Sagavanirktok 40 Jb 70.20N 148.00W
Sagawa 29 Ce 33.29N 133.16 E
Sage 46 Jf 41.50N 110.56W
Saghād 24 Og 31.12N 52.30 E
Saginaw 43 Kc 43.25N 83.58W
Saginaw Bay 43 Kc 43.50N 83.40W
Sagiz 19 Ff 47.32N 53.45 E
Sagiz [Kaz.-U.S.S.R.] 19 Ff 48.12N 54.56 E
Sagiz [Kaz.-U.S.S.R.] 16 Rf 47.32N 53.27 E
Saglek Bay 42 Le 58.30N 63.00W
Saglouc 39 Lc 62.12N 75.38W
Šagonar 20 Ef 51.32N 92.51 E
Sagone, Golfe de- 11a a 42.06N 8.41 E
Sagres 13 Dg 37.01N 8.56W
Sagres, Ponta de- 13 Dh 37.00N 8.57W
Sagter Ems 12 Ja 53.10N 7.40 E
Şagu 15 Ec 46.03N 21.17 E
Sagu/Sauvo 8 Jd 60.21N 22.42 E
Saguache 45 Cg 38.05N 106.08W
Sagua de Tánamo 49 Jc 20.35N 75.14W
Sagua la Grande 47 Hd 22.49N 80.05W
Saguenay 38 Me 48.10N 69.45W
Saguia el Hamra 32 Ed 26.50N 12.00W
Sagunt/Sagunto 13 Le 39.41N 0.16W
Sagunto/Sagunt 13 Le 39.41N 0.16W
Sagunto-Grao de Sagunto 13 Le 39.40N 0.16W
Sa'gya 27 Ef 28.53N 88.10 E
Sahagún [Col.] 54 Cb 8.57N 75.27W
Sahagún [Sp.] 13 Gb 42.22N 5.02W
Sahalin, Ostrov- = Sakhalin (EN) 21 Qd 51.00N 143.00 E
Sahalinskaja Oblast [3] 20 Jf 50.00N 143.30 E
Sahalinski Zaliv 20 Jf 53.45N 141.30 E
Sahara 30 Hf 21.00N 6.00 E
Saharan Atlas (EN) = Atlas Saharien 30 He 34.00N 2.00 E
Sahāranpur 22 Jg 29.58N 77.23 E
Sahel [3] 34 Ec 14.10N 0.50W
Sahel 30 Gg 15.40N 8.30W
Şahin 15 Jh 41.01N 26.50 E
Sāhīwāl [Pak.] 25 Eb 30.41N 72.57 E
Sāhīwāl [Pak.] 25 Eb 31.58N 72.20 E
Sahlābād 23 Ic 32.10N 59.51 E
Sahneh 24 Le 34.29N 47.41 E
Sahnovščina 16 Ie 49.09N 35.57 E
Sahova Kosa, Mys- 16 Qi 40.13N 50.22 E
Sahrihan 18 Id 40.40N 72.03 E
Šahrisabz 19 Gh 39.03N 66.41 E
Šahristan, Pereval- 18 Ge 39.35N 68.38 E
Šahtersk [R.S.F.S.R.] 20 Jg 49.13N 142.09 E
Šahtersk [Ukr.-U.S.S.R.] 16 Ke 48.01N 38.32 E
Šahterski 20 Md 64.46N 177.47 E
Šahtinsk 19 Hf 49.40N 72.37 E
Šahty 19 Ef 47.42N 40.13 E
Sahuaripa 47 Cc 29.03N 109.14W
Sahuayo de Diaz 47 Dd 20.04N 102.43W
Šahunja 19 Ed 57.43N 46.35 E
Saḩūq, Wādī- 24 Jj 25.18N 42.20 E
Šahy 10 Oh 48.05N 18.58 E
Sahyadri/Western Ghats 21 Jh 14.00N 75.00 E
Sai Buri 25 Kg 6.42N 101.37 E
Saïda [3] 32 Hc 33.35N 0.30 E
Saïda 31 He 34.50N 0.09 E
Saïda, Monts de- 13 Mi 35.10N 0.30 E
Sa'īdābād 23 Id 29.28N 55.42 E
Saidaiji 29 Dd 34.39N 134.02 E
Said Bundas 35 Cd 8.35N 24.30 E
Saïdia 13 Ji 35.04N 2.13W
Saidor 60 Di 5.37S 146.28 E
Saidu 25 Eb 34.45N 72.21 E
Saigō 29 Cc 36.13N 133.20 E
Saigon → Ho Chi Minh 22 Mh 10.45N 106.40 E
Saihan Tal → Sonid Youqi 27 Jc 42.45N 112.36 E
Saihan Toroi 27 Hc 41.54N 100.24 E
Saijō 29 Ce 33.55N 133.10 E
Saikai 29 Ae 33.03N 129.44 E
Sai-Kawa 29 Fc 36.37N 138.14 E
Saiki 28 Kh 32.57N 131.54 E
Saiki-Wan 29 Be 33.00N 131.55 E
Sail Rock 51n Bb 12.37N 61.16W
Saimaa 5 Ic 61.15N 28.15 E
Saimaa Canal (EN) = Sajmenski Kanal 8 Mc 61.05N 28.18 E
Sain Alto 48 Hf 23.35N 103.15W
Sā in Dezh 24 Ld 36.40N 46.33 E
Sains-Richaumont 12 Fe 49.49N 3.42 E
Saint Abb's Head 9 Kf 55.54N 2.09W
Saint-Affrique 11 Ik 43.57N 2.53 E
Saint Agnes Head 9 Hk 50.23N 5.07W
Saint-Agrève 11 Ki 45.01N 4.24 E
Saint Albans [Eng.-U.K.] 9 Mj 51.46N 0.21W
Saint Albans [Vt.-U.S.] 44 Kc 44.49N 73.05W
Saint Albans [W.V.-U.S.] 44 Gf 38.24N 81.53W
Saint Alban's Head 9 Kk 50.34N 2.04W
Saint Albert 42 Gf 53.38N 113.38W
Saint-Amand-les-Eaux 11 Jd 50.26N 3.26 E
Saint-Amand-Mont-Rond 11 Ih 46.43N 2.31 E
Saint-André, Cap- 30 Lj 16.11S 44.27 E
Saint-André, Plaine de- 11 Hf 48.55N 1.10 E
Saint-André-de-Cubzac 11 Fi 45.00N 0.27W
Saint-André-de-l'Eure 12 Df 48.54N 1.17 E
Saint-André-sur-Cailly 12 De 49.33N 1.13 E
Saint Andrews [N.B.-Can.] 44 Nc 45.06N 67.02W
Saint Andrews [Scot.-U.K.] 9 Ke 56.20N 2.48W
Saint Anne 9 Kl 49.40N 2.10W
Saint Ann's Bay 49 Id 18.26N 77.16W
Saint Ann's Head 9 Hj 51.41N 5.10W
Saint Anthony [Id.-U.S.] 46 Je 43.58N 111.41W
Saint Anthony [Newf.-Can.] 42 Lf 51.22N 55.35W
Saint Arnaud 59 Ig 36.37S 143.15 E
Saint-Aubert 44 Lb 47.14N 70.15W
Saint-Aubin-sur-Mer 12 Be 49.20N 0.24W
Saint Augustine 43 Kf 29.51N 81.25W
Saint-Augustin-Saguenay 42 Lf 51.14N 58.39W
Saint Austell 9 Ik 50.20N 4.48W
Saint-Avold 11 Me 49.06N 6.42 E
Saint Barthélemy 47 Le 17.55N 62.50W
Saint-Barthélemy 11 Hl 42.49N 1.45 E
Saint Barthélemy, Canal de- 51b Bb 18.00N 63.00W
Saint Barthélemy, Kanaal Van- 51b Bb 18.00N 63.00W
Saint Bees Head 9 Jg 54.32N 3.38W
Saint-Benoit 37a b 21.02S 55.43 E
Saint-Benoît-sur-Loire 11 Ig 47.49N 2.18 E
Saint-Bonnet 11 Mj 44.41N 6.05 E
Saint-Brévin-les-Pins 11 Dg 47.15N 2.10W
Saint Brides Bay 9 Hj 51.48N 5.15W
Saint-Brieuc 11 Df 48.31N 2.47W
Saint-Brieuc, Baie de- 11 Df 48.38N 2.40W
Saint-Calais 11 Gg 47.55N 0.45 E
Saint-Camille 44 Lb 46.29N 70.12W
Saint Catharines 44 Jd 43.10N 79.15W
Saint Catherine, Monastery of- (EN) = Dayr Kātrīna 33 Fd 28.31N 33.57 E
Saint Catherine, Mount- 51p Bb 12.10N 61.40W
Saint Catherines Island 44 Gj 31.38N 81.10W
Saint Catherine's Point 9 Lk 50.34N 1.15W
Saint-Céré 11 Hj 44.52N 1.54 E
Saint-Chamond 11 Ki 45.28N 4.30 E
Saint Charles 43 Id 38.47N 90.29W
Saint-Chély-d'Apcher 11 Jj 44.48N 3.17 E
Saint-Christol, Plateau de- 11 Lj 44.00N 5.50 E
Saint Christopher/Saint Kitts 38 Mh 17.21N 62.48W
Saint Christopher-Nevis [5] 39 Mh 17.21N 62.48W
Saint-Cirq-Lapopie 11 Hj 44.28N 1.40 E
Saint Clair, Lake- 38 Ke 42.25N 82.41W
Saint Clair River 44 Fd 42.37N 82.31W
Saint Clair Shores 44 Fd 42.30N 82.54W
Saint-Clair-sur-l'Elle 12 Ae 49.12N 1.02W
Saint-Claud 11 Gi 45.54N 0.28 E
Saint-Claude [Fr.] 11 Lh 46.23N 5.52 E
Saint Claude 45 Gb 49.40N 98.22W
Saint-Claude [Guad.] 51e Ab 16.02N 61.42W
Saint Cloud 39 Je 45.33N 94.10W
Saint Croix 47 Le 17.45N 64.45W
Saint Croix Falls 45 Jd 45.24N 92.38W
Saint Croix River 43 Ic 44.45N 92.49W
Saint-Cyr-l'Ecole 12 Ef 48.48N 2.04 E
Saint-Cyr-sur-Loire 11 Gg 47.24N 0.40 E
Saint David Bay 51g Bb 15.26N 61.15W
Saint David's [Gren.] 51p Bb 12.04N 61.39W
Saint David's [Wales-U.K.] 9 Hj 51.54N 5.16W
Saint David's Head 9 Hj 51.55N 5.19W
Saint David's Point 51p Bb 12.01N 61.40W
Saint-Denis [Fr.] 11 If 48.56N 2.22 E
Saint-Denis [May.] 31 Mk 20.52S 55.28 E
Saint-Dié 11 Mf 48.17N 6.57 E
Saint-Dizier 11 Kf 48.38N 4.57 E
Sainte-Adresse 12 Ce 49.30N 0.05 E
Sainte-Anne [Guad.] 51e Bb 16.14N 61.23W
Sainte-Anne [Mart.] 51h Bc 14.26N 60.53W
Sainte-Anne-des-Monts 44 Na 49.07N 66.29W
Sainte Baume, Chaîne de la- 11 Lk 43.20N 5.45 E
Sainte-Énimie 11 Jj 44.22N 3.25 E
Sainte Genevieve 45 Kh 37.59N 90.03W
Sainte-Geneviève 12 Ee 49.17N 2.12 E
Saint Elias, Mount- 38 Ec 60.18N 140.55W
Saint Elias Mountains 38 Fc 60.30N 139.30W
Saint-Elie 54 Hc 4.50N 53.17W
Sainte-Livrade-sur-Lot 11 Gj 44.24N 0.36 E
Saint-Eloy-les-Mines 11 Ih 46.09N 2.50 E
Sainte Luce 37 Hd 24.46S 47.12 E
Sainte-Luce 51h Bc 14.28N 60.56W
Sainte-Lucie, Canal de- = Saint Lucia Channel (EN) 50 Fe 14.09N 60.57W
Sainte-Marcellin 11 Li 45.09N 5.19 E
Sainte-Marie [Guad.] 51e Ab 16.06N 61.34W
Sainte-Marie [Mart.] 51h Ab 14.47N 61.00W
Sainte-Marie, Cap- = Sainte-Marie, Cape- (EN) 30 Lk 25.36S 45.08 E
Sainte-Marie, Cape- (EN) = Sainte-Marie, Cap- 30 Lk 25.36S 45.08 E
Sainte-Marie, Ile- 30 Lj 16.50S 49.55 E
Sainte-Marie-aux-Mines 11 Nf 48.15N 7.11 E
Sainte-Maure-de-Touraine 11 Gg 47.06N 0.37 E
Sainte-Maxime 11 Mk 43.18N 6.38 E
Sainte-Menehould 11 Ke 49.05N 4.54 E
Sainte-Rose 51e Ab 16.20N 61.42W
Sainte-Rose-du-Dégelé 44 Mb 47.33N 68.39W
Sainte Rose du Lac 45 Ga 51.03N 99.32W
Saintes 11 Fi 45.45N 0.38W
Saintes, Canal des- 51e Ac 15.55N 61.40W
Saintes, Iles des- 50 Fe 15.52N 61.37W
Sainte-Savine 11 Kf 48.18N 4.03 E
Saintes-Maries-de-la-Mer 11 Kk 43.27N 4.26 E
Sainte-Thérèse 44 Kc 45.22N 73.15W
Saint-Étienne 6 Gf 45.26N 4.24 E
Saint-Étienne-du-Rouvray 11 He 49.23N 1.06 E
Sainte Victoire, Montagne- 11 Lk 43.32N 5.39 E
Saint-Félicien 44 Ka 48.39N 72.28W
Saint-Florent 11a Ba 42.41N 9.18 E
Saint-Florent, Golfe de- 11a Ba 42.45N 9.16 E
Saint-Florentin 11 Jf 48.00N 3.44 E
Saint-Florent-sur-Cher 11 Ih 46.59N 2.15 E
Saint-Flour 11 Ji 45.02N 3.05 E
Saint Francis 45 Fg 39.46N 101.48W
Saint Francis River 45 Ki 34.38N 90.35W
Saint Francisville 45 Kk 30.47N 91.23W
Saint-François 51e Bb 16.15N 61.17W
Saint François Island 37b Bb 7.10S 52.44 E
Saint Francois Mountains 45 Kh 37.30N 90.35W
Saint-Gaudens 11 Gk 43.07N 0.44 E
Saint George 40 Fe 56.35N 169.35W
Saint George [Austl.] 59 Je 28.02S 148.35 E
Saint George [N.B.-Can.] 44 Nc 45.10N 66.48W
Saint George [Ut.-U.S.] 43 Ed 37.06N 113.35W
Saint George, Cape- [Newf.-Can.] 42 Lm 48.28N 59.16W
Saint George, Cape- [Pap.N.Gui.] 60 Eh 4.52S 152.52 E
Saint George, Point- 46 Cf 41.47N 124.15W
Saint George Harbour 44 Nd 43.15N 66.10W
Saint George Island 44 Ek 29.39N 84.55W
Saint George's 39 Mh 12.03N 61.45W
Saint-Georges 44 Lb 46.10N 70.38W
Saint George's Bay 42 Lg 48.20N 59.00W
Saint George's Channel 5 Fe 52.00N 6.00W
Saint George's Channel (EN) = Muir Bhreatan 5 Fe 52.00N 6.00W
Saint-Georges-du-Vièvre 12 Ce 49.15N 0.35 E
Saint-Germain-en-Laye 11 If 48.54N 2.05 E
Saint-Gervais-d'Auvergne 11 Ih 46.02N 2.49 E
Saint-Gervais-les-Bains 11 Mi 45.54N 6.43 E
Saint-Ghislain 12 Fd 50.27N 3.49 E
Saint-Ghislain-Baudour 12 Fd 50.29N 3.49 E
Saint-Gildas, Pointe de- 11 Dg 47.08N 2.15W
Saint-Gilles 11 Kk 43.41N 4.26 E
Saint-Gilles-Croix-de-Vie 11 Eh 46.41N 1.55W
Saint-Girons 11 Hl 42.59N 1.09 E
Saint-Gobain 12 Fe 49.36N 3.23 E
Saint Gotthard Pass (EN) = San Gottardo/Sankt Gotthard 5 Gf 46.30N 8.30 E
Saint Gotthard Pass (EN) = Sankt Gotthard/San Gottardo 5 Gf 46.30N 8.30 E
Saint Govan's Head 9 Ij 51.36N 4.55W
Saint Helena [5] 31 Gj 15.57S 5.42W
Saint Helena 30 Gj 15.57S 5.42W
Saint Helena Bay 30 Il 32.45S 18.05 E
Saint Helena Island 44 Gi 32.30N 80.30W

Index Symbols

- [1] Independent Nation
- [2] State, Region
- [3] District, County
- [4] Municipality
- [5] Colony, Dependency
- Continent
- Physical Region
- Historical or Cultural Region
- Mount, Mountain
- Volcano
- Hill
- Mountains, Mountain Range
- Hills, Escarpment
- Plateau, Upland
- Pass, Gap
- Plain, Lowland
- Delta
- Salt Flat
- Valley, Canyon
- Crater, Cave
- Karst Features
- Depression
- Polder
- Desert, Dunes
- Forest, Woods
- Heath, Steppe
- Oasis
- Cape, Point
- Coast, Beach
- Cliff
- Peninsula
- Isthmus
- Sandbank
- Island
- Atoll
- Rock, Reef
- Islands, Archipelago
- Rocks, Reefs
- Coral Reef
- Well, Spring
- Geyser
- River, Stream
- Waterfall Rapids
- River Mouth, Estuary
- Lake
- Salt Lake
- Intermittent Lake
- Reservoir
- Swamp, Pond
- Canal
- Glacier
- Ice Shelf, Pack Ice
- Ocean
- Sea
- Gulf, Bay
- Strait, Fjord
- Lagoon
- Bank
- Seamount
- Tablemount
- Ridge
- Shelf
- Basin
- Escarpment, Sea Scarp
- Fracture
- Trench, Abyss
- National Park, Reserve
- Point of Interest
- Recreation Site
- Cave, Cavern
- Historic Site
- Ruins
- Wall, Walls
- Church, Abbey
- Temple
- Scientific Station
- Airport
- Port
- Lighthouse
- Mine
- Tunnel
- Dam, Bridge

Saint Helena Sound 44 Gi 32.27N 80.25W
Saint Helens [Austl.] 59 Jh 41.20S 148.15 E
Saint Helens [Eng.-U.K.] 9 Kh 53.28N 2.44W
Saint Helens [Or.-U.S.] 46 Dd 45.52N 122.48W
Saint Helens, Mount- 46 Dc 46.12N 122.11W
Saint Helier 9 Kl 49.12N 2.07W
Saint-Hubert 12 Hd 50.03N 5.23 E
Saint-Hyacinthe 44 Kc 45.38N 72.57W
Saint Ignace Island 45 Mb 48.48N 87.55W
Saint Ignatius 46 Hc 47.19N 114.06W
Saint Ives [Eng.-U.K.] 9 Hk 50.12N 5.29W
Saint Ives [Eng.-U.K.] 12 Bb 52.18N 0.04W
Saint James 45 Ie 43.59N 94.38W
Saint James, Cape - 42 Ef 51.57N 131.01W
Saint-Jean 42 Kg 45.13N 73.15W
Saint-Jean, Baie de- 51b Bc 17.55N 62.51W
Saint-Jean, Lac- 38 Le 48.35N 72.00W
Saint-Jean-d'Angély 11 Fi 45.57N 0.31W
Saint-Jean-de-Luz 11 Ek 43.23N 1.40W
Saint-Jean-de-Maurienne 11 Mi 45.17N 6.21 E
Saint-Jean-de-Monts 11 Dh 46.47N 2.04W
Saint-Jean-du-Gard 11 Jj 44.06N 3.53 E
Saint-Jean-Pied-de-Port 11 Ek 43.10N 1.14W
Saint-Jérôme [Que.-Can.] 42 Kg 45.46N 74.00W
Saint-Jérôme [Que.-Can.] 44 La 48.26N 71.52W
Saint Joe River 46 Gc 47.21N 116.42W
Saint John 50 Dc 18.20N 64.42W
Saint John [Can.] 38 Me 45.15N 66.04W
Saint John [Ks.-U.S.] 45 Gh 38.00N 98.46W
Saint John [Lbr.] 34 Cd 5.55N 10.05W
Saint John [N.B.-Can.] 39 Me 45.16N 66.03W
Saint John's [Atg.] 47 Le 17.06N 61.51W
Saint Johns [Az.-U.S.] 46 Ki 34.30N 109.22W
Saint Johns [Mi.-U.S.] 44 Ed 43.00N 84.33W
Saint John's [Mont.] 51c Bc 16.48N 62.11W
Saint John's [Newf.-Can.] 39 Ne 47.34N 52.43W
Saint Johnsbury 44 Kc 44.25N 72.01W
Saint Johns River 44 Gj 30.24N 81.24W
Saint Joseph [Dom.] 51g Bb 15.24N 61.26W
Saint Joseph [La.-U.S.] 45 Kk 31.55N 91.14W
Saint-Joseph [Mart.] 51h Ab 14.40N 61.03W
Saint Joseph [Mi.-U.S.] 44 Dd 42.06N 86.29W
Saint Joseph [Mo.-U.S.] 43 Id 39.46N 94.51W
Saint-Joseph [New Caledonia] 63b Ce 20.27S 166.36 E
Saint-Joseph [Reu.] 37a Bb 21.22S 55.37 E
Saint Joseph, Lake- 42 If 51.06N 90.36W
Saint Joseph Island 44 Fb 46.13N 83.57W
Saint Joseph River 44 Dd 42.06N 86.29W
Saint-Junien 11 Gi 45.53N 0.54 E
Saint-Just-en-Chaussée 12 Ee 49.30N 2.26 E
Saint Kilda 9 Ed 57.49N 8.36W
Saint Kitts/Saint Christopher 38 Mh 17.21N 62.48W
Saint-Lary-Soulan 11 Gl 42.49N 0.19 E
Saint Laurent 53 Ke 5.30N 54.02W
Saint Laurent = Saint Lawrence (EN) 38 Me 49.15N 67.00W
Saint Lawrence 38 Bc 63.30N 170.30W
Saint Lawrence 38 Me 49.15N 67.00W
Saint Lawrence (EN) = Saint Laurent 38 Me 49.15N 67.00W
Saint Lawrence, Gulf of- 38 Me 48.00N 62.00W
Saint-Léger-en-Yvelines 12 Df 48.43N 1.46 E
Saint-Léonard 44 Nb 47.10N 67.56W
Saint-Léonard-de-Noblat 11 Hi 45.50N 1.29 E
Saint-Lewis 42 Lf 52.22N 55.58W
Saint-Lô 11 Ee 49.07N 1.05W
Saint Louis 39 Jf 38.38N 90.11W
Saint-Louis [Guad.] 51e Bc 15.57N 61.20W
Saint-Louis [Sen.] 31 Fg 16.02N 16.30W
Saint-Loup-sur-Semouse 11 Mg 47.53N 6.16 E
Saint Lucia 37 Ee 28.23S 32.25 E
Saint Lucia 39 Mh 13.53N 60.58W
Saint Lucia 38 Mh 13.53N 60.58W
Saint Lucia, Cape- 30 Kk 28.32S 32.24 E
Saint Lucia, Lake- 37 Ee 28.00S 32.30 E
Saint Lucia Channel 50 Fe 14.09N 60.57W
Saint Lucia Channel (EN) = Sainte-Lucie, Canal de- 50 Fe 14.09N 60.57W
Saint Magnus Bay 9 La 60.25N 1.35W
Saint-Maixent-l'Ecole 11 Fh 46.25N 0.12W
Saint-Malo 6 Ff 48.39N 2.01W
Saint-Malo, Golfe de- 5 Ff 48.45N 2.00W
Saint-Marc 47 Je 19.06N 72.43W
Saint-Marc, Canal de- 49 Kd 18.50N 72.45W
Saint Margaret's at Cliffe 12 Dc 51.09N 1.19 E
Saint Margaret's Hope 9 Kc 58.49N 2.57W
Saint Maries 46 Gc 47.19N 116.35W
Saint Martin 47 Le 18.04N 63.04W
Saint Martin, Cap- 51h Ab 14.52N 61.13W
Saint-Martin-Boulogne 12 Dd 50.43N 1.40 E
Saint-Martin-de-Ré 11 Eh 46.12N 1.22W
Saint-Martin-des-Besaces 12 Be 49.01N 0.51W
Saint Martins 44 Oc 45.21N 65.32W
Saint-Martin-Vésubie 11 Nj 44.04N 7.15 E
Saint Mary, Cape- 44 Nc 44.05N 66.13W
Saint Mary Peak [Austl.] 59 Hf 31.30S 138.35 E
Saint Mary Peak [U.S.] 46 Hc 46.40N 114.20W
Saint Mary's 9 Gl 49.55N 6.20W
Saint Marys [Austl.] 59 Jh 41.35S 148.10 E
Saint Marys [Oh.-U.S.] 44 Ee 40.32N 84.22W
Saint Marys [W.V.-U.S.] 44 Gf 39.24N 81.13W
Saint Mary's, Cape - 42 Mg 46.49N 54.12W
Saint Mary's Bay [N.S.-Can.] 44 Nc 44.25N 66.10W
Saint Mary's Bay [N.W.T.-Can.] 42 Mg 46.50N 53.47W
Saint Marys River 44 Gj 30.45N 81.30W
Saint-Mathieu, Pointe de- 5 Ff 48.20N 4.46W
Saint Matthew 38 Bb 60.30N 172.45W
Saint Matthias Group 57 Fe 1.30S 149.48 E
Saint-Maur-des-Fossés 11 If 48.48N 2.30 E
Saint-Maurice, Rivière- 42 Kg 46.21N 72.31W
Saint Michael 40 Gd 63.29N 162.02W
Saint Michaels 46 Ki 35.46N 109.04W
Saint-Michel 12 Ge 49.55N 4.08 E
Saint-Mihiel 11 Lf 48.54N 5.33 E
Saint-Nazaire 11 Dg 47.17N 2.12W
Saint Neots 12 Bb 52.13N 0.16W
Saint-Nicolas/Sint Niklaas 11 Kc 51.10N 4.08 E
Saint-Nicolas-d'Aliermont 12 De 49.53N 1.13 E
Saint-Nicolas-de-Port 11 Mf 48.38N 6.18 E
Saint-Omer 11 Id 50.45N 2.15 E
Saintonge 11 Fi 45.50N 0.30W
Saint Patrick's 51c Bc 16.41N 62.12W
Saint Paul 34 Cd 6.23N 10.48W
Saint-Paul 37a Bb 21.00S 55.16 E
Saint Paul 30 Ol 38.55S 77.41 E
Saint Paul [Ak.-U.S.] 40 Ee 57.07N 170.17W
Saint Paul [Alta.-Can.] 42 Gf 53.59N 111.17W
Saint Paul [Mn.-U.S.] 39 Je 44.58N 93.07W
Saint Paul [Nb.-U.S.] 45 Gf 41.13N 98.27W
Saint Paul, Cape- 34 Fd 5.49N 0.57 E
Saint-Paul-lès-Dax 11 Ek 43.44N 1.03W
Saint Paul's 51c Ab 17.24N 62.49W
Saint Paul's Point 64q Ab 25.04S 130.05W
Saint-Péray 11 Kj 44.57N 4.50 E
Saint Peter 45 Jd 44.17N 93.57W
Saint Peter Port 9 Kl 49.27N 2.32W
Saint Peter's 51c Bc 16.46N 62.12W
Saint Petersburg 39 Kg 27.46N 82.38W
Saint Petersburg Beach 44 Fl 27.45N 82.45W
Saint-Pierre [Mart.] 50 Fe 14.45N 61.11W
Saint-Pierre [May.] 31 Mk 21.19S 55.29 E
Saint-Pierre [St.P.M.] 42 Lg 46.46N 56.12W
Saint-Pierre, Lac- 44 Kb 46.10N 72.50W
Saint Pierre and Miquelon (EN) = Saint-Pierre et Miquelon 39 Ne 46.55N 56.10W
Saint-Pierre-en-Port 12 Ce 49.48N 0.29 E
Saint-Pierre et Miquelon 38 Ne 46.55N 56.10W
Saint-Pierre et Miquelon = Saint Pierre and Miquelon (EN) 39 Ne 46.55N 56.10W
Saint Pierre Island 37b Bb 9.19S 50.43 E
Saint-Pierre-sur-Dives 12 Be 49.01N 0.02W
Saint-Pol-de-Léon 11 Cf 48.41N 3.59W
Saint-Pol-sur-Mer 12 Ec 51.02N 2.21 E
Saint-Pol-sur-Ternoise 11 Id 50.23N 2.20 E
Saint-Pons 11 Ik 43.29N 2.46 E
Saint-Pourçain-sur-Sioule 11 Jh 46.18N 3.17 E
Saint-Quentin 11 Je 49.51N 3.17 E
Saint-Quentin, Canal de- 12 Fe 49.36N 3.11 E
Saint-Raphaël 11 Mk 43.25N 6.46 E
Saint-Rémy-de-Provence 11 Kk 43.47N 4.50 E
Saint-Rigaux, Mont- 11 Kh 46.12N 4.29 E
Saint-Riquier 12 Dd 50.08N 1.57 E
Saint Roch Basin 42 Ic 68.50N 95.00W
Saint Rogatien Bank (EN) 60 Mc 24.40N 167.10W
Saint-Romain-de-Colbosc 12 Ce 49.32N 0.22 E
Saint-Saëns 12 De 49.40N 1.17 E
Saint Sauflieu 12 Ee 49.47N 2.15 E
Saint-Savin 11 Gh 46.34N 0.52 E
Saint-Sébastien, Cap- 37 Hb 12.26S 48.44 E
Saint-Seine-l'Abbaye 11 Kg 47.26N 4.47 E
Saint-Servais, Namur- 12 Gd 50.28N 4.50 E
Saint Simon 12 Fe 49.45N 3.10 E
Saint Simons Island 44 Gj 31.14N 81.21W
Saint Stanislas Bay 64g Bb 1.53N 157.30W
Saint Stephen 42 Kg 45.12N 67.17W
Saint-Sylvain 12 Be 49.03N 0.13W
Saint Teresa Beach 44 Ek 29.58N 84.28W
Saint Thomas 44 Gd 42.47N 81.12W
Saint Thomas 47 Le 18.21N 64.55W
Saint-Trond/Sint-Truiden 11 Ld 50.49N 5.12 E
Saint-Tropez 11 Mk 43.16N 6.38 E
Saint-Tropez, Golfe de- 11 Mk 43.17N 6.38 E
Saint-Valéry-en-Caux 11 Ge 49.52N 0.44 E
Saint-Valery-sur-Somme 11 Hd 50.11N 1.38 E
Saint-Vallier 11 Ki 45.10N 4.49 E
Saint-Venant 12 Ed 50.37N 2.33 E
Saint Vincent 14 Be 45.45N 7.39 E
Saint Vincent 38 Mh 13.15N 61.12W
Saint-Vincent, Baie de- 63b Cf 22.00S 166.05 E
Saint Vincent, Cap- 30 Lk 21.57S 43.16 E
Saint Vincent, Gulf- 59 Hf 35.00S 138.05 E
Saint Vincent and the Grenadines 39 Mh 13.15N 61.12W
Saint-Vincent-de-Tyrosse 11 Ek 43.40N 1.18W
Saint Vincent Island 44 Ek 29.40N 85.07W
Saint Vincent Passage 50 Ff 13.30N 61.00W
Saint-Wandrille-Rançon 12 Ce 49.32N 0.46 E
Saint-Yrieix-la-Perche 11 Hi 45.31N 1.12 E
Saipan 64a Ad 6.54N 134.08 E
Saipan Channel 64b Ba 15.05N 145.41 E
Saipan Island 57 Fc 15.12N 145.45 E
Saira 55 Ak 32.24S 62.06W
Sairecabur, Cerro- 54 Eh 22.43S 67.54W
Saitama Ken 28 Of 36.00N 139.50 E
Saito 28 Kh 32.06N 131.24 E
Sajak 19 Hf 46.55N 77.22 E
Sajama 54 Eg 18.07S 69.00W
Sajama, Nevado de- 52 Jg 18.06S 68.54W
Sajānan 14 Dm 37.03N 9.14 E
Sajat 18 De 38.49N 63.51 E
Sajīd 33 Hf 16.52N 41.55 E
Sajir, Ra's- 35 Ib 16.45N 53.35 E
Sajmenski Kanal = Saimaa Canal (EN) 8 Mc 61.05N 28.18 E
Sajn-Sand 22 Ne 44.55N 110.11 E
Sajó 10 Ri 47.56N 21.08 E
Sajószentpéter 10 Qh 48.13N 20.43 E
Sajram 18 Gc 42.18N 69.45 E
Sajzī 24 Of 32.41N 52.07 E
Saka 36 Gc 0.09S 39.20 E
Sakai 28 Mg 34.35N 135.28 E
Sakaide 29 Cd 34.19N 133.51 E
Sakaiminato 29 Cd 35.33N 133.15 E
Sakākah 23 Fd 29.59N 40.06 E
Sakakawea, Lake- 43 Gb 47.50N 102.20W
Sakala, Vozvyšennost-/Sakala Kõrgustik 8 Kf 58.00N 25.30 E
Sakala Kõrgustik/Sakala, Vozvyšennost- 8 Kf 58.00N 25.30 E
Sakami 42 Jf 53.18N 76.45W
Sakami, lac- 42 Jf 53.15N 76.45W
Sâkâne, 'Erg i-n- 34 Ea 20.40N 0.51W
Sakania 36 Ee 12.43S 28.33 E
Sakao 63b Cb 14.58S 167.07 E
Sakar 15 Jh 41.59N 26.16 E
Sakar 18 De 38.59N 63.45 E
Sakaraha 37 Gd 22.54S 44.32 E
Sakar-Čaga 18 Cf 37.39N 61.40 E
Sakārinah, Jabal as- 14 Do 35.45N 9.05 E
Sakartvelos Sabčata Socialisturi Respublica/Gruzinskaja SSR 19 Eg 42.00N 44.00 E
Sakarya 23 Da 41.07N 30.39 E
Sakata 27 Od 38.55N 139.50 E
Sakchu 28 Hd 40.23N 125.02 E
Sakhalin (EN) = Sahalin, Ostrov- 21 Qd 51.00N 143.00 E
Saki 16 Hg 45.07N 33.37 E
Šakiai/Šakjaj 7 Fi 54.57N 23.01 E
Sakishima Islands (EN) = Sakishima-Shotō 21 Og 24.30N 125.00 E
Sakishima-Shotō = Sakishima Islands (EN) 21 Og 24.30N 125.00 E
Sakito 29 Ae 33.02N 129.34 E
Sakiz Boğazı 15 Jk 38.20N 26.12 E
Šakjaj/Šakiai 7 Fi 54.57N 23.01 E
Sakmara 5 Le 51.46N 55.01 E
Sakon Nakhon 25 Ke 17.10N 104.01 E
Sakrivier 37 Cf 30.54S 20.28 E
Šakša 17 Hi 54.47N 56.15 E
Saksaulski 19 Gf 47.05N 61.13 E
Sakskøbing 8 Dj 54.48N 11.39 E
Saku 28 Of 36.09N 138.26 E
Sakuma 29 Ed 35.05N 137.47 E
Sakura 29 Gd 35.43N 140.13 E
Sakurai 29 Dd 34.31N 135.50 E
Sakura-Jima 29 Bf 31.35N 130.40 E
Säkylä 8 Jc 61.02N 22.20 E
Sal 30 Eg 16.45N 22.55W
Sal 19 Ef 47.31N 40.45 E
Sal, Cay- 49 Gb 23.42N 80.24W
Sal, Punta- 49 Df 15.53N 87.37W
Sala 35 Cb 17.00N 20.53 E
Šalá 10 Nh 48.09N 17.53 E
Sala 7 Dg 59.55N 16.36 E
Salabangka, Kepulauan- 26 Hg 3.02S 122.25 E
Salaca 8 Kg 57.39N 24.15 E
Salacgriva/Salacgrīva 7 Fh 57.46N 24.27 E
Salacgrīva/Salacgriva 7 Fh 57.46N 24.27 E
Sala Consilina 14 Jj 40.23N 15.36 E
Salada 48 Hc 28.36N 103.28W
Salada, Laguna- 48 Ba 32.20N 115.40W
Saladas 56 Ic 28.15S 58.38W
Saladillo 56 Ie 35.38S 59.46W
Saladillo, Arroyo- 55 Bj 31.22S 60.30W
Saladillo Amargo, Arroyo- 55 Ci 31.01S 60.19W
Saladillo Dulce, Arroyo- 55 Bj 31.01S 60.19W
Salado, Arroyo- [Arg.] 55 Bm 36.27S 61.06W
Salado, Arroyo- [Mex.] 48 De 24.25N 111.30W
Salado, Riacho- 55 Ch 26.30S 58.18W
Salado, Rio- 45 Ci 34.16N 106.52W
Salado, Rio- 47 Ec 26.52N 99.19W
Salado, Rio- [Arg.] 52 Ji 31.42S 60.44W
Salado, Rio- [Arg.] 56 Ee 38.49S 64.57W
Salado, Rio- [Arg.] 52 Ki 35.44S 57.21W
Salado, Valle- 48 He 24.47N 102.50W
Salaga 34 Ed 8.33N 0.31W
Salagle 35 Ge 1.50N 42.18 E
Salāhuddīn 24 Je 34.40N 44.00 E
Salailua 65c Aa 13.41S 172.34W
Salairski Krjaž 20 Df 54.00N 85.00 E
Sălaj 15 Fb 47.10N 23.00 E
Šalakuša 7 Je 62.15N 40.18 E
Salal 35 Bc 14.51N 17.13 E
Salālah [Oman] 22 Hh 17.05N 54.10 E
Salālah [Sud.] 35 Fa 21.19N 36.13 E
Salamá 49 Bf 15.06N 90.16W
Salamanca 13 Gd 40.50N 6.00W
Salamanca [Chile] 56 Fd 31.47S 70.58W
Salamanca [Mex.] 47 Dd 20.34N 101.12W
Salamanca [N.Y.-U.S.] 44 Hd 42.11N 78.43W
Salamanca [Sp.] 6 Fg 40.58N 5.39W
Salamat 35 Cc 11.00N 20.30 E
Salamat, Bahr- 35 Bd 9.27N 18.06 E
Salamina 49 Jh 10.30N 74.48W
Salamís 15 Gl 37.58N 23.29 E
Salamis 24 Ee 35.10N 33.54 E
Salamis 15 Gl 37.55N 23.30 E
Sālang, Tūnel-e- 23 Kb 35.19N 69.02 E
Salani 65c Bb 14.00S 171.34W
Salantai/Salantaj 8 Ih 56.05N 21.30 E
Salantaj/Salantai 8 Ih 56.05N 21.30 E
Salas 13 Fa 43.24N 6.16W
Salas de los Infantes 13 Ib 42.01N 3.17W
Salat 64d Cb 7.14N 152.01 E
Salat 11 Gk 43.10N 0.58 E
Salatiga 26 Fh 7.19S 110.30 E
Salavat 6 Le 53.25N 55.58 E
Salawati, Pulau- 26 Jg 1.07S 130.52 E
Sala y Gómez 57 Qg 26.28S 105.28W
Sala y Gómez Ridge (EN) 3 Ml 25.00S 98.00W
Salazar 55 Am 36.18S 62.12W
Salbris 11 Ig 47.26N 2.03 E
Salcantay, Nevado de- 52 Ig 13.22S 72.34W
Šalčininkai/Salčininkaj 8 Kj 54.18N 25.30 E
Salčininkaj/Šalčininkai 8 Kj 54.18N 25.30 E
Salda Gölü 15 Ml 37.33N 29.42 E
Saldaña 13 Hb 42.31N 4.44W
Saldanha 31 Il 33.00S 17.56 E
Saldungaray 55 Bn 38.12S 61.47W
Saldus 19 Cd 56.40N 22.31 E
Sale 59 Jg 38.06S 147.04 E
Salé 32 Fc 34.04N 6.48W
Salebabu, Pulau- 26 If 3.55N 126.40 E
Şāleḩābād 24 Me 34.56N 48.20 E
Salehard 22 Ic 66.33N 66.40 E
Saleimoa 65c Ba 13.48S 171.52W
Salelologa 65c Aa 13.44S 172.10W
Salem [Fl.-U.S.] 44 Fk 29.58N 83.28W
Salem [Il.-U.S.] 45 Lg 38.38N 88.57W
Salem [India] 22 Jh 11.39N 78.10 E
Salem [In.-U.S.] 44 Df 38.36N 86.06W
Salem [Ma.-U.S.] 44 Ld 42.31N 70.55W
Salem [Mont.] 51c Bc 16.45N 62.13W
Salem [Mo.-U.S.] 45 Kh 37.39N 91.32W
Salem [N.J.-U.S.] 44 Jf 39.35N 75.28W
Salem [Oh.-U.S.] 44 Ge 40.54N 80.52W
Salem [Or.-U.S.] 39 Ge 44.57N 123.01W
Salem [S.D.-U.S.] 45 He 43.44N 97.23W
Salem [Va.-U.S.] 44 Gg 37.17N 80.03W
Salemi 14 Gm 37.49N 12.48 E
Sälen 8 Ec 61.10N 13.16 E
Salentine Peninsula (EN) = Penisola Salentina 5 Hg 40.30N 18.00 E
Sale Pit 9 Oh 53.40N 1.30 E
Salerno 6 Hg 40.41N 14.47 E
Salerno, Golfo di- 14 Ij 40.30N 14.40 E
Salers 11 Ii 45.08N 2.30 E
Salève, Mont- 11 Mh 46.07N 6.10 E
Salgir 16 Ig 45.38N 35.01 E
Salgótarján 10 Ph 48.07N 19.49 E
Salgueiro 54 Ke 8.04S 39.06W
Salher 25 Ed 20.41N 73.52 E
Salhus 7 Af 60.30N 5.16 E
Sali 14 Jg 43.56N 15.10 E
Šali 16 Nh 43.06N 45.56 E
Salice Terme 14 Df 44.55N 9.01 E
Salida 43 Fd 38.32N 106.00W
Salies-de-Béarn 11 Fk 43.29N 0.55W
Salihli 23 Cb 38.29N 28.09 E
Salima 36 Fe 13.47S 34.26 E
Salīma, Wāḩāt- = Salimah Oasis (EN) 31 Jf 21.22N 29.19 E
Salimah Oasis (EN) = Salīma, Wāḩāt- 31 Jf 21.22N 29.19 E
Salina 14 Il 38.35N 14.50 E
Salina [Ks.-U.S.] 39 Jf 38.50N 97.37W
Salina [Ut.-U.S.] 46 Jg 38.58N 111.51W
Salina Cruz 47 Ee 16.10N 95.12W
Salinas [Ca.-U.S.] 39 Gf 36.40N 121.38W
Salinas [Ec.] 54 Bd 2.13S 80.58W
Salinas [P.R.] 51a Bc 17.59N 66.17W
Salinas, Bahia de- 49 Eh 11.03N 85.43W
Salinas, Cabo de-/Ses Salines, Cap de- 13 Pe 39.16N 3.03 E
Salinas, Punta- [Dom.Rep.] 49 Ld 18.12N 70.34W
Salinas, Punta- [P.R.] 51a Bb 18.29N 66.10W
Salinas, Río- 49 Be 16.28N 90.33W
Salinas de Hidalgo 48 If 22.38N 101.43W
Salinas Peak 45 Cj 33.18N 106.31W
Saline, Point- 50 Fg 12.00N 61.48W
Saline Island 51p Cb 12.26N 61.29W
Saline River [Ks.-U.S.] 45 Hg 38.51N 97.30W
Saline River [U.S.] 45 Jj 33.10N 92.08W
Salines, Pointe des- 51h Bc 14.24N 60.53W
Salinópolis 54 Id 0.37S 47.20W
Salins-les-Bains 11 Lh 46.57N 5.53 E
Salisbury 42 Jd 63.35N 77.00W
Salisbury [Dom.] 51g Bb 15.26N 61.27W
Salisbury [Eng.-U.K.] 9 Lj 51.05N 1.48W
Salisbury [Md.-U.S.] 43 Ld 38.22N 75.36W
Salisbury [N.C.-U.S.] 44 Gh 35.40N 80.29W
Salisbury Plain 9 Lj 51.15N 1.55W
Săliște 15 Gd 45.47N 23.53 E
Šalja 19 Fd 57.15N 58.43 E
Saljany 19 Eh 39.35N 48.59 E
Šalkar, Ozero- 16 Qd 50.35N 51.40 E
Šalkar-Jega-Kara, Ozero- 16 Vd 50.45N 60.55 E
Salkhad 24 Gf 32.29N 36.43 E
Salla 7 Gc 66.50N 28.40 E
Sallent de Gállego 13 Lb 42.46N 0.20W
Salling 8 Ch 56.40N 9.00 E
Salliqueló 56 He 36.45S 62.56W
Sallisaw 45 Ii 35.28N 94.47W
Sallūm 35 Fb 19.23N 37.06 E
Sallūm, Khalīj as- = Salum, Gulf of- (EN) 33 Ec 31.40N 25.20 E
Sallyana 25 Gc 28.22N 82.10 E
Salm 12 Ie 49.51N 6.51 E
Salmās 23 Fb 38.11N 44.47 E
Salmi 7 Hf 61.24N 31.54 E
Salmo 46 Gb 49.12N 117.17W
Salmon 43 Eb 45.11N 113.54W
Salmon Arm 42 Ff 50.42N 119.16W
Salmon Bank (EN) 60 Kb 26.56N 176.28W
Salmon Falls Creek Reservoir 46 He 42.05N 114.45W
Salmon Mountain 46 Hd 45.38N 114.50W
Salmon Mountains 46 Df 41.00N 123.00W
Salmon River 38 He 45.51N 116.46W
Salmon River Mountains 43 Dc 44.45N 115.30W
Salmtal 12 Ie 49.56N 6.48 E
Salmyš 16 Sc 52.01N 55.21 E
Salò 14 Ee 45.36N 10.31 E
Salo [C.A.R.] 35 Be 3.12N 16.07 E
Salo [Fin.] 7 Ff 60.23N 23.08 E
Salobra, Rio- 55 De 20.12S 56.29W
Salobreña 13 Ih 36.44N 3.35W
Salomon, Cap- 51h Ab 14.30N 61.06W
Salon-de-Provence 11 Lk 43.38N 5.06 E
Salonga 30 Ii 0.10S 19.50 E
Salonika (EN) = Thessaloníki 6 Ig 40.38N 22.56 E
Salonika, Gulf of- (EN) = Thermaïkós Kólpos 5 Ig 40.20N 22.45 E
Salonta 15 Ec 46.48N 21.39 E
Salop 9 Ki 52.40N 2.50W
Salop 9 Ki 52.40N 2.50W
Salor 13 Ee 39.39N 7.03W
Salou 13 Nc 41.04N 1.08 E
Salouël 12 Ee 49.52N 2.15 E
Saloum 34 Bc 13.50N 16.45W
Salpausselkä 5 Ic 61.00N 26.30 E
Sal-Rei 32 Cf 16.11N 22.55W
Salsbruket 7 Cd 64.48N 11.52 E
Salseleh-ye Safīd Kūh/Paropamisus 21 If 34.30N 63.30 E
Salsipuedes, Canal de- 48 Cc 28.40N 113.00W
Salsipuedes, Punta- 49 Fi 8.28N 83.37W
Salsk 19 Ef 46.28N 41.29 E
Šalski 7 If 61.48N 36.03 E
Salso [It.] 14 Hm 37.06N 13.57 E
Salso [It.] 14 Im 37.39N 14.49 E
Salsola 14 Ji 41.37N 15.40 E
Salsomaggiore Terme 14 Df 44.49N 9.59 E
Salt 13 Oc 41.59N 2.47 E
Salta 56 Hb 25.00S 64.30W
Salta 53 Jh 24.47S 65.24W
Saltash 9 Ik 50.24N 4.12W
Salt Basin 45 Dk 31.50N 105.00W
Saltburn by the Sea 9 Mg 54.35N 0.58W
Salt Cay 49 Lc 21.20N 71.11W
Salt Creek 46 Gh 36.15N 116.49W
Salt Draw 45 Ek 31.19N 103.28W
Saltee Islands/Na Sailti 9 Gi 52.07N 6.36W
Salten 7 Dc 67.45N 15.31 E
Salt Fork Arkansas River 45 Hh 36.36N 97.03W
Salt Fork Brazos 45 Gj 33.15N 100.00W
Salt Fork Red 45 Gi 34.30N 99.22W
Saltholm 8 Ei 55.40N 12.45 E
Saltillo 39 Ig 25.25N 101.01W
Salt Lake City 39 He 40.46N 111.53W
Salto 55 Dj 31.25S 57.00W
Salto 14 Gh 42.23N 12.54 E
Salto [Arg.] 56 Hd 34.17S 60.15W
Salto [Ur.] 53 Ki 31.23S 57.58W
Salto da Divisa 54 Kg 16.00S 39.57W
Salto Grande 55 Hf 22.54S 49.59W
Salton Sea 38 Hf 33.20N 115.50W
Salt River 43 Ee 33.23N 112.18W
Saltsjöbaden 8 He 59.17N 18.18 E
Saltvik 7 Ef 60.17N 20.03 E
Saluafata Harbour 65c Ba 13.55S 171.38W
Saluda 44 Ig 37.36N 76.36W
Salum, Gulf of- (EN) = Sallūm, Khalīj as- 33 Ec 31.40N 25.20 E
Saluzzo 14 Bf 44.39N 7.29 E
Salvación, Bahía- 56 Eh 50.55S 75.05W
Salvador [Braz.] 53 Mg 12.59S 38.31W
Salvador [Niger] 34 Ha 23.14N 12.05 E
Salvador, Lake- 45 Kl 29.45N 90.15W
Salvador Maza 56 Hb 22.10S 63.43W
Salvaterra de Magos 13 De 39.01N 8.48W
Salvatierra [Mex.] 48 Ig 20.13N 100.53W
Salvatierra [Sp.] 13 Jb 42.51N 2.23W
Salwa, Dawḩat as- 24 Nj 25.30N 50.40 E
Salwá Baḩrī 33 Fe 24.44N 32.56 E
Salween 21 Lh 16.31N 97.37 E
Salyersville 44 Fg 37.45N 83.04W
Salza 14 Ic 47.40N 14.43 E
Salzach 10 Ih 48.12N 12.56 E
Salzburg 6 Hf 47.48N 13.02 E
Salzburg 14 Gc 47.20N 13.00 E
Salzburger Kalkalpen 14 Gc 47.35N 12.55 E
Salzgitter 10 Gd 52.05N 10.20 E
Salzkammergut 14 Hc 47.45N 13.30 E
Salzkotten 12 Kc 51.40N 8.36 E
Salzwedel 10 Hd 52.51N 11.09 E
Samadāy, Ra's- 24 Fj 25.00N 34.56 E
Samagaltaj 20 Ef 50.36N 95.03 E
Samaḩ [Lib.] 33 Cd 28.10N 19.10 E
Samaḩ [Sau.Ar.] 24 Kh 28.52N 45.30 E
Samaipata 54 Fg 18.09S 63.52W
Samalayuca 48 Fb 31.21N 106.28W
Samales Group 26 He 6.00N 121.45 E
Samalga Pass 40a Eb 52.48N 169.25W
Samālūt 33 Fd 28.18N 30.42 E
Samambaia, Rio- 55 Ff 22.45S 53.21W
Samaná 49 Md 19.13N 69.19W
Samaná, Bahía de- 47 Ke 19.10N 69.25W
Samaná, Cabo- 49 Md 19.18N 69.09W
Samana Cay 49 Kb 23.06N 73.42W
Samandağı 24 Fd 36.07N 35.56 E
Samangān 23 Kb 36.15N 67.40 E
Samani 27 Pc 42.07N 142.56 E
Samanli Dağlari 15 Mi 40.32N 29.10 E
Samar 21 Oh 12.00N 125.00 E
Samara [R.S.F.S.R.] 5 Le 53.10N 50.04 E
Samara [Ukr.-U.S.S.R.] 16 Ie 48.33N 35.12 E
Samarai 58 Gf 10.36S 150.39 E
Samarinda 22 Nj 0.30S 117.09 E
Samarkand 22 If 39.40N 66.58 E
Samarkandskaja Oblast 19 Gg 40.10N 66.20 E
Sāmarrā' 23 Fc 34.12N 43.52 E
Samar Sea 26 Hd 11.50N 124.32 E
Samaru 34 Gc 11.10N 7.38 E
Samatan 11 Gk 43.30N 0.56 E
Samate 26 Jg 0.58S 131.04 E
Samba [Zaire] 36 Ec 4.38S 26.22 E
Samba [Zaire] 36 Db 0.14N 21.19 E
Samba Caju 36 Cd 8.45S 15.25 E
Sambalpur 25 Gd 21.27N 83.58 E
Sambar, Tanjung- 26 Fg 2.59S 110.19 E
Sambas 26 Ef 1.20N 109.15 E
Sambava 37 Ib 14.15S 50.10 E
Samber 11 Kd 50.28N 4.52 E
Sāmbhar 25 Fc 26.55N 75.12 E
Sambiase 14 Kl 38.58N 16.17 E
Samboja 26 Gg 1.02S 117.02 E
Sambor 19 Cf 49.32N 23.11 E
Samborombón, Bahía- 56 Ie 36.00S 57.12W
Samborombón, Río- 55 Dl 35.43S 57.20W
Sambre 11 Kd 50.28N 4.52 E
Sambre à l'Oise, Canal de la- 11 Je 49.39N 3.20 E
Samburg 20 Cc 67.00N 78.25 E

Index Symbols

Independent Nation	Historical or Cultural Region	Pass, Gap	Depression	Coast, Beach	Rock, Reef	Waterfall Rapids	Canal	Lagoon	Escarpment, Sea Scarp	Historic Site	Port
State, Region	Mount, Mountain	Plain, Lowland	Polder	Cliff	Islands, Archipelago	River Mouth, Estuary	Glacier	Bank	Fracture	Ruins	Lighthouse
District, County	Volcano	Delta	Desert, Dunes	Peninsula	Rocks, Reefs	Lake	Ice Shelf, Pack Ice	Seamount	Trench, Abyss	Wall, Walls	Mine
Municipality	Hill	Salt Flat	Forest, Woods	Isthmus	Coral Reef	Salt Lake	Ocean	Tablemount	National Park, Reserve	Church, Abbey	Tunnel
Colony, Dependency	Mountains, Mountain Range	Valley, Canyon	Heath, Steppe	Sandbank	Well, Spring	Intermittent Lake	Sea	Ridge	Point of Interest	Temple	Dam, Bridge
Continent	Hills, Escarpment	Crater, Cave	Oasis	Island	Geyser	Reservoir	Gulf, Bay	Shelf	Recreation Site	Scientific Station	
Physical Region	Plateau, Upland	Karst Features	Cape, Point	Atoll	River, Stream	Swamp, Pond	Strait, Fjord	Basin	Cave, Cavern	Airport	

Samch'ök	27	Md	37.27N	129.10 E
Samch'ŏnp'o	27	Me	34.55N	128.04 E
Samdi Dağı ▲	24	Kd	37.19N	44.15 E
Samdŏng-ni	28	Ie	39.21N	126.14 E
Samdŭng	28	Ie	38.59N	126.11 E
Same [Indon.]	26	Ih	8.59S	125.40 E
Same [Tan.]	36	Gc	4.04S	37.44 E
Samer	12	Dd	50.38N	1.45 E
Sam Ford Fiord ◧	42	Kb	70.40N	70.35W
Samfya	36	Ee	11.20S	29.32 E
Šamhor	16	Oi	40.48N	46.01 E
Sámi	15	Dk	38.15N	20.39 E
Sāmī Ghar ▲	23	Kc	31.43N	67.01 E
Samīrah	24	Ji	26.18N	42.05 E
Samisu-Jima ◆	27	Oe	31.40N	140.00 E
Şamli	15	Kj	39.48N	27.51 E
Samnah, Jabal- ▲	24	Ei	26.26N	33.34 E
Samoa I Sisifo = Western Samoa (EN) [1]	58	Jf	13.40S	172.30W
Samoa Islands ⁂	57	Jf	14.00S	171.00W
Samobor	14	Je	45.48N	15.43 E
Samojlovka	16	Md	51.10N	43.43 E
Samokov	15	Gg	42.20N	23.33 E
Samolva	8	Lf	58.16N	27.45 E
Sámos	15	Jl	37.45N	26.58 E
Sámos ◆	5	Ih	37.45N	26.48 E
Samosir, Pulau- ◆	26	Cf	2.35N	98.50 E
Samothrace (EN) = Samothráki ◆	15	Ii	40.27N	25.35 E
Samothráki	15	Ii	40.29N	25.31 E
Samothráki = Samothrace (EN) ◆	15	Ii	40.27N	25.35 E
Sampacho	56	Hd	33.23S	64.43W
Sampaga	26	Gg	2.19S	119.07 E
Sampit ≈	26	Fg	3.00S	113.03 E
Sampit	22	Nj	2.32S	112.57 E
Sampoku	29	Fb	38.30N	139.30 E
Sampwe	36	Ed	9.20S	27.23 E
Sam Rayburn Reservoir ⊟	45	Ik	31.27N	94.37W
Samro, Ozero- ≋	8	Mf	58.55N	28.50 E
Samsjøen ≋	8	Da	63.05N	10.40 E
Samsø ◆	7	Ci	55.50N	10.35 E
Samsø Bælt ⇌	8	Di	55.50N	10.45 E
Sam Son	25	Ld	19.44N	105.54 E
Samsun	22	Fe	41.17N	36.20 E
Samsun Dağı ▲	15	Kl	37.40N	27.15 E
Samtredia	16	Mh	42.11N	42.17 E
Samuel, Mount- ▲	59	Gc	19.41S	134.09 E
Samuhú	55	Bh	27.31S	60.24W
Samui, Ko- ◆	21	Li	9.30N	100.00 E
Samur ≈	16	Pi	41.53N	48.32 E
Samur-Apšeronski Kanal ═	16	Pi	40.35N	49.35 E
Samus	20	De	56.46N	84.44 E
Samut Prakan	25	Kf	13.36N	100.36 E
Samut Sakhon	25	Kf	13.31N	100.15 E
San	31	Gg	13.08N	4.53W
San [Asia] ≈	25	Lf	13.32N	105.57 E
San [Pol.] ≈	10	Rf	50.45N	21.51 E
San'ā'	22	Gh	15.23N	44.12 E
Sana ≈	14	Ke	45.03N	16.23 E
Sanaag [3]	35	Hc	10.10N	47.50 E
Şanabū	24	Di	27.30N	30.47 E
Sanae ⊠	66	Bf	70.18S	2.22W
Sanāfir ◆	24	Fi	27.55N	34.42 E
Sanāg	35	Hd	7.45N	48.00 E
Sanaga ≈	30	Hh	3.35N	9.38 E
San Agustin	55	Cn	38.01S	58.21W
San Agustin, Cabo- ▶	48	Bc	28.05N	115.20W
San Agustin, Cape- ▶	26	Ie	6.16N	126.11 E
Sanak Islands ⁂	40	Gf	54.25N	162.35W
Sanalona, Presa- ⊟	48	Fe	24.53N	107.00W
San Ambrosio, Isla- ◆	56	Ec	26.21S	79.52W
Sanana	26	Ig	2.04S	125.08 E
Sanana, Pulau- ◆	26	Ig	2.12S	125.55 E
Sanandaj	23	Gb	35.19N	47.00 E
San Andreas	46	Eg	38.12N	120.41W
San Andrés [3]	47	Hf	12.35N	81.42W
San Andres, Cerro- ▲	48	Ih	19.48N	100.36W
San Andres, Isla de- ◆	52	Hd	12.32N	81.42W
San Andrés, Laguna de- ◎	48	Kf	22.40N	97.50W
San Andrés de Giles	55	Cl	34.27S	59.27W
San Andrés del Rabanedo	13	Gb	42.37N	5.36W
San Andres Mountains ⛰	43	Fe	32.55N	106.45W
San Andres Peak ▲	45	Cj	32.43N	106.30W
San Andrés Tuxtla	47	Ee	18.27N	95.13W
San Andrés y Providencia [2]	54	Ba	12.30N	81.45W
Sananduva	55	Gh	27.57S	51.48W
San Angelo	43	Ge	31.28N	100.26W
San Antonio [Blz.]	49	Ce	16.30N	89.02W
San Antonio [Chile]	56	Fd	33.35S	71.38W
San Antonio [Tx.-U.S.]	39	Jg	29.28N	98.31W
San Antonio [Ur.]	55	Dj	31.20S	57.45W
San Antonio, Cabo- [Arg.] ▶	52	Ki	36.40S	56.42W
San Antonio, Cabo- [Cuba] ▶	38	Kg	21.52N	84.57W
San Antonio, Cabo de-/Sant Antoni, Cap- ▶	13	Mf	38.48N	0.12 E
San Antonio, Canal- ═	55	Aj	31.42S	62.15W
San Antonio, Punta- ▶	48	Bc	29.45N	115.45W
San Antonio, Sierra de- ⛰	48	Db	30.00N	110.20W
San Antonio Abad	13	Nf	38.58N	1.18 E
San Antonio Bay ◧	45	Hl	28.20N	96.45W
San Antonio de Caparo	49	Lj	7.35N	71.27W
San Antonio de Cortés	49	Cf	15.05N	88.04W
San Antonio de los Baños	49	Fb	22.53N	82.30W
San Antonio de los Cobres	56	Gb	24.11S	66.21W
San Antonio del Táchira	54	Db	7.50N	72.27W
San Antonio de Tamanaco	50	Ch	9.14N	66.03W
San Antonio Oeste	53	Jj	40.44S	64.57W
San Antonio River ≈	43	Hf	28.30N	96.50W
Sanare	49	Mi	9.45N	69.39W
Sanary-sur-Mer	11	Lk	43.07N	5.48 E
San Augustin	53	Ie	1.53N	76.16W
San Augustine	45	Ik	31.32N	94.07W
Sanāw	35	Ib	17.50N	51.05 E
San Bartolomeo in Galdo	14	Ji	41.24N	15.01 E
San Baudilio de Llobregat/Sant Boi de Llobregat	13	Oc	41.21N	2.03 E
San Benedetto del Tronto	14	Hh	42.57N	13.53 E
San Benedetto Po	14	Ee	45.02N	10.55 E
San Benedicto, Isla- ◆	47	Be	19.18N	110.49W
San Benito [Guat.]	49	Ce	16.55N	89.54W
San Benito [Tx.-U.S.]	45	Hm	26.08N	97.38W
San Benito, Islas- ⁂	48	Bc	28.20N	115.35W
San Benito Abad	49	Ji	8.56N	75.02W
San Benito Mountain ▲	46	Eh	36.22N	120.38W
San Bernardino	39	Hf	34.06N	117.17W
San Bernardino, Passo del-/Sankt Bernardin Paß ⌓	14	Dd	46.30N	9.10 E
San Bernardino Mountains ⛰	46	Gi	34.10N	117.00W
San Bernardino Strait ⇌	26	Hd	12.32N	124.10 E
San Bernardo [Arg.]	55	Bh	27.17S	60.42W
San Bernardo [Chile]	56	Fd	33.36S	70.43W
San Bernardo [Mex.]	48	De	25.32N	111.45W
San Bernardo, Islas de- ⁂	49	Ji	9.45N	75.50W
San Bernardo, Punta de- ▶	49	Ji	9.42N	75.42W
San Bernardo del Viento	54	Cb	9.22N	75.57W
San Blas [3]	49	Hi	7.50N	81.10W
San Blas [Mex.]	47	Cd	21.31N	105.16W
San Blas [Mex.]	47	Cc	26.05N	108.46W
San Blas [Mex.]	48	Id	27.25N	101.40W
San Blas, Archipiélago de- ◆	49	Hi	9.30N	78.30W
San Blas, Cape- ▶	43	Jf	29.40N	85.22W
San Blas, Cordillera de- ⛰	49	Hi	9.18N	79.00W
San Blas, Golfo de- ◧	49	Hi	9.30N	79.00W
San Blas, Punta- ▶	49	Hi	9.34N	78.58W
San Borja	54	Ef	14.49S	66.51W
San Borjas, Sierra de- ⛰	48	Cc	28.40N	113.45W
San Buenaventura	48	Id	27.05N	101.32W
Sancai ▲	35	Fc	10.43N	35.40 E
San Carlos [Arg.]	55	Eh	27.45S	55.54W
San Carlos [Chile]	56	Fe	36.25S	71.58W
San Carlos [Mex.]	48	Je	24.35N	98.56W
San Carlos [Mex.]	48	Ic	29.01N	100.51W
San Carlos [Nic.]	49	Eh	11.07N	84.47W
San Carlos [Pan.]	49	Hi	8.29N	79.57W
San Carlos [Par.]	55	Df	22.16S	57.18W
San Carlos [Phil.]	26	Hd	10.30N	123.25 E
San Carlos [Phil.]	26	Hc	15.55N	120.20 E
San Carlos [Ur.]	56	Jd	34.48S	54.55W
San Carlos [Ven.]	54	Eb	9.40N	68.39W
San Carlos, Bahia- ◧	48	Cd	27.55N	112.45W
San Carlos, Mesa de- ⌂	48	Bc	29.40N	115.25W
San Carlos, Punta- ▶	48	Cc	28.00N	112.45W
San Carlos, Riacho- ≈	55	Df	22.49S	57.53W
San Carlos, Río- [C.R.] ≈	49	Eh	10.47N	84.12W
San Carlos, Río- [Ven.] ≈	50	Bh	9.07N	68.25W
San Carlos de Bariloche	53	Ij	41.08S	71.15W
San Carlos de Bolívar	56	He	36.15S	61.06W
San Carlos de la Rápita/Sant Carles de la Ràpita	13	Md	40.37N	0.36 E
San Carlos del Zulia	54	Db	9.01N	71.55W
San Carlos de Río Negro	54	Ec	1.55N	67.04W
San Carlos Reservoir ⊟	46	Jj	33.13N	110.24W
San Cataldo [It.]	14	Mj	40.23N	18.18 E
San Cataldo [It.]	14	Hm	37.29N	13.59 E
San Cayetano	55	Cn	38.20S	59.37W
Sancerre	11	Ig	47.20N	2.50 E
Sancerrois, Collines du- ◭	11	Ig	47.20N	2.30 E
Sanchahe	28	Ib	44.59N	126.03 E
Sánchez	49	Md	19.14N	69.36W
Sánchez Magallanes	48	Mh	18.17N	93.59W
San Clemente [Ca.-U.S.]	43	De	33.26N	117.37W
San Clemente [Sp.]	13	Je	39.24N	2.26W
San Clemente del Tuyú	55	Dm	36.22S	56.43W
San Clemente Island ◆	46	Fj	32.55N	118.30W
Sancois	11	Ih	46.50N	2.55 E
San Cosme	55	Ch	27.22S	58.31W
San Cristóbal [Arg.]	56	Hd	30.19S	61.14W
San Cristóbal [Bol.]	55	Ba	13.56S	61.50W
San Cristóbal [Cuba]	49	Fb	22.43N	83.03W
San Cristóbal [Dom.Rep.]	49	Ld	18.25N	70.06W
San Cristóbal [Mex.]	48	Li	17.49N	94.32W
San Cristóbal [Ven.]	53	Ie	7.46N	72.14W
San Cristobal, Baía de- ◧	48	Bd	27.25N	114.40W
San Cristóbal, Isla- ◆	52	Hf	0.50S	89.26W
San Cristóbal de las Casas	47	Fe	16.45N	92.38W
San Cristóbal Island ◆	57	Hf	10.36S	161.45 E
San Cristóbal Verapaz	49	Bf	15.23N	90.24W
Sancti Spiritus	47	Id	21.56N	79.27W
Sancti Spiritus [3]	49	Hb	22.00N	79.30W
Sancy, Puy de- ▲	11	Ii	45.32N	2.50 E
Sand	7	Bg	59.29N	6.15 E
Sand ≈	37	Ed	22.25S	30.05 E
Sanda	29	Dd	34.53N	135.14 E
Sandai	26	Fg	1.15S	110.31 E
Sandakan	22	Ni	5.50N	118.07 E
Sandal, Baie de- ◧	63b	Ce	20.49S	167.10 E
Sandal, Ozero- ≋	7	Ie	62.25N	34.10 E
Sandane	7	Bf	61.46N	6.13 E
Sandanski	15	Gh	41.34N	23.17 E
Sandaré	34	Cc	14.42N	10.18W
Sandared	8	Eg	57.43N	12.47 E
Sandarne	8	Gc	61.16N	17.10 E
Sanday ◆	9	Kb	59.15N	2.30W
Sande	8	De	59.36N	10.12 E
Sandefjord	7	Cg	59.08N	10.14 E
Sandégué	34	Ed	7.59N	3.33W
Sandeid	7	Ag	59.33N	5.50 E
Sanders	46	Ki	35.13N	109.20W
Sanderson	43	Ge	30.09N	102.24W
Sandersville	44	Fi	32.59N	82.48W
Sandfontein	37	Bd	22.11S	19.58 E
Sandgate	12	Dc	51.04N	1.09 E
Sandhammaren ▶	8	Fi	55.23N	14.12 E
Sandhamn	8	He	59.17N	18.55 E
Sand Hills ⛰	43	Gc	41.45N	102.00W
Sandia	54	Ef	14.17S	69.26W
Sandia Crest ▲	45	Ci	35.13N	106.27W
San Diego [Bol.]	55	Bc	16.04S	60.28W
San Diego [Ca.-U.S.]	39	Hf	32.43N	117.09W
San Diego, Cabo- ▶	52	Jk	54.38S	65.07W
Sandıklı	24	Dc	38.28N	30.17 E
San Dimitri Point ▶	14	In	36.05N	14.05 E
Sand in Taufers / Campo Tures	14	Fd	46.55N	11.57 E
Sand Lake ≋	45	Ia	50.05N	94.39W
Sand Mountain ⛰	44	Dh	34.20N	86.02W
Sandnes	7	Ag	58.51N	5.44 E
Sandnessjøen	7	Cc	66.01N	12.38 E
Sandoa	31	Ji	9.41S	22.52 E
Sandö bank ▦	8	Hf	58.10N	19.15 E
Sandomierska, Kotlina- ▭	10	Rf	50.30N	22.00 E
Sandomierz	10	Rf	50.41N	21.45 E
San Domino ◆	14	Jh	42.05N	15.30 E
Sandoná	54	Cc	1.18N	77.28W
San Donà di Piave	14	Ge	45.38N	12.34 E
Sandoval, Boca de- ⇌	48	Ke	24.58N	97.32W
Sandover River ≈	59	Hd	21.43S	136.32 E
Sandoway	25	Ie	18.28N	94.22 E
Sandown	9	Lk	50.39N	1.09W
Sand Point	40	Ge	55.20N	160.30W
Sandpoint	43	Db	48.16N	116.33W
Sandras Dağı ▲	15	Ll	37.04N	28.51 E
Sandray ◆	9	Fe	56.54N	7.25W
Sandspit	42	Ef	53.15N	131.50W
Sand Springs [Mt.-U.S.]	46	Lc	47.09N	107.27W
Sand Springs [Ok.-U.S.]	45	Hh	36.09N	96.07W
Sandstone [Austl.]	59	De	27.59S	119.17 E
Sandstone [Mn.-U.S.]	45	Jc	46.08N	92.52W
Sandu	27	Jf	26.08N	113.16 E
Sandusky [Mi.-U.S.]	44	Fd	43.25N	82.50W
Sandusky [Oh.-U.S.]	43	Kc	41.27N	82.42W
Sandveld ⁙	37	Cd	21.20S	20.10 E
Sandvig-Allinge	7	Di	55.15N	14.49 E
Sandvika	8	De	59.54N	10.31 E
Sandviken	7	Df	60.37N	16.46 E
Sandwich	9	Oj	51.17N	1.20 E
Sandwich Bay ◧	42	Lf	53.35N	57.15W
Sandy	12	Bb	52.07N	0.17W
Sandy Cape [Austl.] ▶	59	Ih	41.25S	144.45 E
Sandy Cape [Austl.] ▶	57	Gg	24.40S	153.15 E
Sandy Desert ⁙	25	Cc	28.46N	62.30 E
Sandykači	19	Gh	36.32N	62.35 E
Sandy Lake ≋	42	If	53.02N	92.55W
Sandy Lake	42	If	53.02N	93.14W
Sandy Point	44	Il	26.01N	77.24W
Sandy Point Town	50	Ed	17.22N	62.50W
Sandžak ⧓	15	Cf	43.10N	20.00 E
Sanem	12	He	49.33N	5.56 E
San Estanislao	56	Ib	24.39S	56.26W
San Esteban	49	Ef	15.17N	85.52W
San Esteban, Bahía de- ◧	48	Ee	25.40N	109.15W
San Esteban, Isla- ◆	48	Cc	28.42N	112.36W
San Esteban de Gormaz	13	Ic	41.35N	3.12W
San Felice Circeo	14	Hi	41.14N	13.05 E
San Felipe [Chile]	56	Fd	32.45S	70.44W
San Felipe [Col.]	54	Ec	1.55N	67.06W
San Felipe [Mex.]	47	Bb	31.00N	114.52W
San Felipe [Mex.]	48	Ig	21.29N	101.13W
San Felipe [Ven.]	54	Ea	10.20N	68.44W
San Felipe, Cayos de- ⁂	49	Fc	21.58N	83.30W
San Felipe, Cerro de- ▲	13	Kd	40.24N	1.51W
San Felipe Creek ≈	46	Hj	33.09N	115.46W
San Felíu de Guíxols	13	Pc	41.47N	3.02 E
San Felĭu de Llobregat/Sant Feliu de Llobregat	13	Oc	41.23N	2.03 E
San Felix, Isla- ◆	56	Dc	26.17S	80.05W
San Fermin, Punta- ▶	48	Bb	30.25N	114.40W
San Fernando [Chile]	56	Fd	34.35S	71.00W
San Fernando [Mex.]	48	Bb	29.59N	115.17W
San Fernando [Mex.]	47	Ed	24.51N	98.10W
San Fernando [Phil.]	26	Hc	16.37N	120.19 E
San Fernando [Phil.]	26	Hc	15.01N	120.41 E
San Fernando [Sp.]	13	Fh	36.28N	6.12W
San Fernando [Trin.]	54	Fa	10.17N	61.28W
San Fernando, Río- [Bol.] ≈	55	Cc	17.13S	58.23W
San Fernando, Río- [Mex.] ≈	48	Ke	24.55N	97.40W
San Fernando de Apure	53	Je	7.54N	67.28W
San Fernando de Atabapo	54	Ec	4.03N	67.42W
Sanford [Fl.-U.S.]	43	Kf	28.48N	81.16W
Sanford [Me.-U.S.]	44	Ld	43.26N	70.46W
Sanford [N.C.-U.S.]	44	Hh	35.29N	79.10W
Sanford, Mount- ▲	40	Kd	62.13N	144.09W
San Francisco [Arg.]	56	Hd	31.26S	62.05W
San Francisco [Bol.]	55	Cc	17.42S	59.38W
San Francisco [Ca.-U.S.]	39	Gf	37.48N	122.24W
San Francisco [Pan.]	49	Gi	8.15N	80.58W
San Francisco, Isla- ◆	48	De	24.50N	110.35W
San Francisco Bay ◧	38	Gf	37.43N	122.17W
San Francisco Creek ≈	45	El	29.53N	102.19W
San Francisco de Arriba	48	Hd	26.15N	102.50W
San Francisco de Bellocq	55	Bn	38.42S	60.01W
San Francisco de la Paz	49	Df	14.55N	86.14W
San Francisco del Laishi	55	Ch	26.14S	58.38W
San Francisco del Oro	47	Cc	26.52N	105.51W
San Francisco del Rincón	48	Ig	21.01N	101.51W
San Francisco de Macoris	47	Je	19.18N	70.15W
San Francisco Gotera	49	Cg	13.42N	88.06W
San Francisco Javier	13	Nf	38.42N	1.25 E
San Francisco Mountains ⛰	46	Kj	33.45N	109.00W
San Francisco River ≈	46	Kj	32.59N	109.22W
San Fratello	14	Il	38.01N	14.36 E
San Gabriel	55	Di	28.58S	58.12W
San Gabriel, Punta- ▶	48	Cc	28.25N	112.50W
San Gabriel Mountains ⛰	46	Gi	34.20N	117.45W
San Gallán, Isla- ◆	54	Cf	13.50S	76.28W
Sangamon River ≈	45	Kf	40.07N	90.20W
Sangar [Iran]	24	Md	37.08N	49.02 E
Sangar [R.S.F.S.R.]	22	Oc	63.55N	127.31 E
Sangatte	12	Dd	50.56N	1.45 E
San Gavino Monreale	14	Ck	39.33N	8.47 E
Sangay, Volcán- 🌋	52	If	2.00S	78.20W
Sange	36	Ed	7.02S	28.21 E
Sangeang, Pulau- ◆	26	Gh	8.12S	119.04 E
San Gemini	14	Gh	42.37N	12.33 E
Sanger	46	Fh	36.42N	119.27W
Sangerhausen	10	He	51.28N	11.18 E
San Germán [Cuba]	49	Ic	20.36N	76.08W
San Germán [P.R.]	49	Nd	18.05N	67.03W
Sanggan He ≈	28	Cd	40.24N	115.18 E
Sanggau	26	Ff	0.08N	110.36 E
Sangha ≈	30	Ii	1.13S	16.49 E
Sangha [C.A.R.] [3]	35	Be	3.30N	16.00 E
Sangha [Con.] [3]	36	Cb	2.00N	15.00 E
Sangihe, Kepulauan- = Sangihe Islands (EN) ⁂	21	Oi	3.00N	125.30 E
Sangihe, Pulau- ◆	26	If	3.35N	125.32 E
Sangihe Islands (EN) = Sangihe, Kepulauan- ⁂	21	Oi	3.00N	125.30 E
San Gil	54	Db	6.32N	73.08W
San Gimignano	14	Fg	43.28N	11.02 E
San Giovanni in Fiore	14	Kk	39.15N	16.42 E
San Giovanni in Persiceto	14	Ff	44.38N	11.11 E
San Giovanni Rotondo	14	Ji	41.42N	15.44 E
San Giovanni Valdarno	14	Fg	43.34N	11.32 E
Sangju	28	Jf	36.25N	128.10 E
Sāngli	22	Jh	16.52N	74.34 E
Sangmélima	34	He	2.56N	11.59 E
Sangoli	24	Pd	37.25N	54.35 E
San Gorgonio ▲	38	Hf	34.05N	116.50W
San Gottardo/Sankt Gotthard = Saint Gotthard Pass (EN) ⌓	5	Gf	46.30N	8.30 E
Sangradouro Grande, Rio- ≈	55	Dc	16.24S	57.10W
Sangre de Cristo Mountains ⛰	38	If	37.30N	105.15W
San Gregorio	55	Al	34.19S	62.02W
Sangre Grande	50	Fg	10.35N	61.07W
Sangri	27	Ff	29.20N	92.15 E
Sangro ≈	14	Ih	42.14N	14.32 E
Sangue, Rio- ≈	54	Gf	11.00S	58.40W
Sangüesa	13	Kb	42.35N	1.17W
Sanguinaires, Iles- ⁂	11	Ab	41.53N	8.35 E
San Gustavo	55	Cj	30.41S	59.23W
Sangyuan → Wuqiao	28	Df	37.38N	116.23 E
Sangzhi	27	Jf	29.23N	110.11 E
Sanhe [China]	28	Dd	40.00N	117.01 E
Sanhe [China]	27	La	50.30N	120.04 E
Sanhe-San ▲	29	Cd	35.08N	132.37 E
Sanhezhen	28	Di	31.30N	117.15 E
San Hilario [Arg.]	55	Ch	26.02S	58.39W
San Hilario [Mex.]	48	De	24.22N	110.59W
San Hipolito, Bahia- ◧	48	Cd	26.55N	113.55W
San Ignacio [Arg.]	55	Eh	27.16S	55.32W
San Ignacio [Blz.]	47	Ge	17.10N	89.04W
San Ignacio [Bol.]	54	Ef	14.53S	65.36W
San Ignacio [Bol.]	54	Fg	16.23S	60.59W
San Ignacio [Mex.]	48	Ff	25.55N	106.25W
San Ignacio [Mex.]	47	Bc	27.27N	112.51W
San Ignacio [Par.]	56	Ic	26.52S	57.03W
San Ignacio, Isla de- ◆	48	Ee	25.25N	108.55W
San Ignacio, Laguna- ◎	48	Cd	26.55N	113.15W
San Ildefonso, Cape- ▶	26	Hc	16.02N	121.59 E
San Ildefonso, Cerro- ▲	49	Cf	15.31N	88.17W
San Ildefonso o La Granja	13	Id	40.54N	4.00W
Saniquellie	34	Dd	7.22N	8.43W
San Isidro [Arg.]	56	Id	34.27S	58.30W
San Isidro [Phil.]	26	Hd	11.24N	124.21 E
San Isidro de El General	47	Hg	9.22N	83.42W
Sanīyah	24	If	33.49N	42.43 E
San Jacinto	49	Ji	9.50N	75.07W
San Jacinto Peak ▲	46	Gj	33.49N	116.41W
San Jaime	55	Cj	30.20S	58.19W
San Javier [Arg.]	56	Id	30.35S	59.57W
San Javier [Chile]	56	Fe	35.36S	71.45W
San Javier [Sp.]	13	Lg	37.48N	0.51W
San Javier [Ur.]	55	Ck	32.41S	58.08W
San Javier, Río- ≈	55	Bj	31.30S	60.20W
San Jerónimo Taviche	48	Ki	16.44N	96.35W
Sanjiachang	27	Hg	24.45N	101.53 E
Sanjiaocheng → Haiyan	27	Hd	36.58N	100.50 E
Sanjō	28	Of	37.37N	138.57 E
San Joaquin	54	Ff	13.04S	64.49W
San Joaquín, Río- ≈	54	Ff	13.08S	63.41W
San Joaquín, Sierra de- ⛰	55	Eg	24.48S	56.00W
San Joaquin River ≈	46	Eh	36.43N	121.50W
San Joaquin Valley ∨	38	Gf	36.50N	120.10W
San Jon	45	Ei	35.06N	103.20W
San Jorge	56	Hd	31.54S	61.52W
San Jorge, Bahía de- ◧	48	Cb	31.10N	113.15W
San Jorge, Golfe de-/Sant Jordi, Golf de- ◧	13	Md	40.53N	1.00 E
San Jorge, Golfo- ◧	52	Jj	46.00S	67.00W
San Jorge, Río- ≈	49	Ji	9.07N	74.44W
San Jorge, Serranía- ▲	55	Be	20.21S	60.59W
San Jorge Island ◆	63a	Dc	8.27S	159.35 E
San José [2]	55	Dl	34.15S	56.45W
San José [3]	49	Ei	9.40N	84.00W
San José [Arg.]	55	Eh	27.46S	55.47W
San Jose [Ca.-U.S.]	39	Gf	37.20N	121.53W
San José [C.R.]	39	Ki	9.56N	84.05W
San José [Mex.]	48	Dd	27.32N	110.09W
San José [Par.]	55	Dg	25.33S	56.45W
San Jose [Phil.]	26	Hc	15.48N	121.00 E
San Jose [Phil.]	26	Hd	12.21N	121.04 E
San José, Isla- [Mex.] ◆	47	Bc	25.00N	110.38W
San José, Isla- [Pan.] ◆	49	Hi	8.15N	79.07W
San José, Salinas de- ⊜	55	Bd	19.07S	60.54W
San José, Serranía de- ⛰	55	Bc	17.52S	60.49W
San Jose de Buenavista	26	Hd	10.46N	122.30 E
San José de Chiquitos	54	Fg	17.51S	60.47W
San José de Feliciano	55	Cj	30.23S	58.45W
San José de Gracia	48	Fd	26.08N	107.58W
San José de Guanipa	54	Fb	8.54N	64.09W
San José de Jachal	56	Gd	30.14S	68.45W
San José de las Lajas	49	Fb	22.58N	82.09W
San José del Cabo	47	Cd	23.03N	109.41W
San José del Guaviare	53	Ie	2.35N	72.38W
San José del Rosario	55	Dg	24.12S	56.48W
San José de Mayo	56	Id	34.20S	56.42W
San José de Ocuné	54	Dc	4.15N	70.20W
San José de Tiznados	50	Ch	9.23N	67.33W
San Juan [2]	56	Gd	31.00S	69.00W
San Juan [Arg.]	53	Ji	31.30S	68.30W
San Juán [Bol.]	55	Cc	17.52S	59.59W
San Juán [Bol.]	55	Bd	18.08S	60.08W
San Juan [C.Amer.] ≈	38	Kh	10.56N	83.42W
San Juan [Dom.Rep.]	47	Je	18.48N	71.14W
San Juan [P.R.]	39	Mh	18.28N	66.07W
San Juan [U.S.] ≈	38	Hf	37.18N	110.28W
San Juan, Cabezas de- ▶	51a	Cb	18.23N	65.36W
San Juan, Cabo- ▶	30	Hh	1.10N	9.21 E
San Juan, Muela de- ▲	13	Kd	40.26N	1.44W
San Juan, Pico- ▲	47	Hd	21.59N	80.09W
San Juan, Punta- ▶	65d	Ab	27.03S	109.22W
San Juan, Río- [Arg.] ≈	56	Gd	32.17S	67.22W
San Juan, Río- [Mex.] ≈	48	Jd	26.10N	99.00W
San Juan, Río- [Mex.] ≈	48	Lh	18.36N	95.40W
San Juan, Río- [Ven.] ≈	50	Eg	10.14N	62.39W
San Juan, Volcán- 🌋	48	Gg	21.30N	104.57W
San Juan Bautista [Par.]	56	Ic	26.38S	57.10W
San Juan Bautista [Sp.]	13	Ne	39.05N	1.30 E
San Juan Bautista Tuxtepec	48	Kh	18.06N	96.07W
San Juan de Colón	49	Ki	8.02N	72.16W
San Juan de Guadalupe	48	He	24.38N	102.44W
San Juan del César	49	Kh	10.46N	72.59W
San Juan de Lima, Punta- ▶	48	Hh	18.36N	103.42W
San Juan del Norte	47	Hf	10.55N	83.42W
San Juan de los Cayos	54	Ea	11.10N	68.25W
San Juan de los Lagos	48	Hg	21.15N	102.14W
San Juan de los Morros	54	Ea	9.55N	67.21W
San Juan del Río [Mex.]	48	Jg	20.29N	100.00W
San Juan del Rio [Mex.]	48	Ge	24.47N	104.27W
San Juan del Sur	47	Gf	11.15N	85.52W
San Juan de Payara	50	Ci	7.39N	67.36W
San Juanico, Isla- ◆	48	Fg	21.55N	106.40W
San Juanico, Punta- ▶	48	Cd	26.05N	112.15W
San Juan Island ◆	46	Db	48.32N	123.05W
San Juan Mountains ⛰	43	Fd	37.35N	107.10W
San Juan Neembucú	55	Dh	26.39S	57.56W
San Juan Nepomuceno [Col.]	54	Cb	9.57N	75.05W
San Juan Nepomuceno [Par.]	55	Eh	26.06S	55.58W
San Juan y Martínez	49	Fb	22.16N	83.50W
San Julián	53	Jj	49.19S	67.40W
San Just, Sierra de- ⛰	13	Ld	40.46N	0.48W
San Justo	56	Hd	30.47S	60.35W
Sankarani ≈	30	Gg	12.01N	8.19W
Sankt Anton am Arlberg	14	Ec	47.08N	10.16 E
Sankt Augustin	12	Jd	50.47N	7.11 E
Sankt Bernardin Paß/San Bernardino, Passo del- ⌓	14	Dd	46.30N	9.10 E
Sankt Gallen	14	Dc	47.25N	9.25 E
Sankt Gallen [2]	14	Dc	47.20N	9.10 E
Sankt Goar	10	Df	50.09N	7.43 E
Sankt Goarshausen	12	Jd	50.09N	7.44 E
Sankt Gotthard/San Gottardo = Saint Gotthard Pass (EN) ⌓	5	Gf	46.30N	8.30 E
Sankt Ingbert	10	Dg	49.17N	7.07 E
Sankt Johann im Pongau	14	Hc	47.21N	13.12 E
Sankt Michael im Lungau	14	Hc	47.06N	13.38 E
Sankt Michel/Mikkeli	6	If	61.41N	27.15 E
Sankt Moritz	14	Dd	46.30N	9.52 E
Sankt Peter-Ording	10	Eb	54.18N	8.38 E
Sankt Pölten	14	Jb	48.12N	15.38 E
Sankt Ulrich / Ortisei	14	Fd	46.34N	11.40 E
Sankt Veit an der Glan	14	Id	46.46N	14.22 E
Sankt-Vith	11	Md	50.17N	6.08 E
Sankt Wendel	10	Dg	49.28N	7.10 E
Sankt Wolfang im Salzkammergut	14	Hc	47.44N	13.27 E
Sankuru ≈	30	Ji	4.17S	20.25 E
San Lázaro	56	Ib	22.10S	57.55W
San Lázaro, Cabo- ▶	47	Bd	24.48N	112.19W
San Lazaro, Sierra de- ⛰	48	Df	23.25N	110.00W
San Leandro	46	Dh	37.43N	122.09W
San Lorenzo ⛬	47	Fe	17.44N	94.45W
San Lorenzo [Arg.]	55	Bk	32.45S	60.44W
San Lorenzo [Ec.]	53	Ie	1.17N	78.50W
San Lorenzo [Hond.]	49	Dg	13.25N	87.27W
San Lorenzo, Isla- [Mex.] ◆	48	Cc	28.38N	112.51W
San Lorenzo, Isla- [Peru] ◆	54	Cf	12.05S	77.15W
San Lorenzo, Río- [Mex.] ≈	48	Je	25.07N	98.32W
San Lorenzo, Río- [Mex.] ≈	48	Fe	24.15N	107.24W
San Lorenzo de El Escorial	13	Hd	40.35N	4.09W
San Louis Potosí [2]	47	Dd	22.30N	100.30W
Sanlúcar de Barrameda	13	Fh	36.47N	6.21W
Sanlúcar la Mayor	13	Fg	37.23N	6.12W
San Lucas [Mex.]	48	Gf	22.33N	104.24W
San Lucas [Mex.]	47	Cd	22.53N	109.54W
San Lucas, Cabo- ▶	38	Ig	22.50N	109.55W
San Lucas, Serrania de- ⛰	54	Db	8.00N	74.20W
San Lucido	14	Kk	39.18N	16.03 E
San Luis [Arg.]	53	Ji	33.20S	66.20W
San Luis [2]	56	Gd	34.00S	66.00W
San Luis [Bol.]	55	Cc	17.39S	58.42W
San Luis [Cuba]	49	Jc	20.12N	75.51W
San Luis [Guat.]	49	Ce	16.14N	89.27W
San Luis [Mex.]	48	Dc	29.33N	111.05W
San Luis, Isla- ◆	48	Bb	29.58N	114.26W
San Luis, Sierra de- ⛰	49	Mh	11.11N	69.42W
San Luis de la Paz	48	Ig	21.18N	100.31W
San Luis del Palmar	55	Ch	27.31S	58.34W
San Luis de Palenque	54	Db	5.25N	71.40W
San Luis Gonzaga, Bahía- ◧	48	Bc	30.00N	114.25W
San Luis Obispo	39	Gf	35.17N	120.40W
San Luis Pass ⇌	45	Il	29.05N	95.08W
San Luis Peak ▲	45	Ch	37.59N	106.56W
San Luis Potosí	39	Ig	22.09N	100.59W
San Luis Rio Colorado	47	Bb	32.29N	114.48W
San Luis Valley ∨	43	Fd	37.25N	106.00W
Sanluri	14	Ck	39.34N	8.54 E
San Manuel [Arg.]	55	Cm	37.47S	58.50W
San Manuel [Az.-U.S.]	46	Jj	32.36N	110.38W

Index Symbols

[1] Independent Nation
[2] State, Region
[3] District, County
[4] Municipality
[5] Colony, Dependency
■ Continent
⧓ Physical Region
▣ Historical or Cultural Region
▲ Mount, Mountain
🌋 Volcano
△ Hill
⛰ Mountains, Mountain Range
◭ Hills, Escarpment
⌂ Plateau, Upland
⌓ Pass, Gap
▭ Plain, Lowland
◺ Delta
▱ Salt Flat
∨ Valley, Canyon
◡ Crater, Cave
✱ Karst Features
⌴ Depression
⊔ Polder
⁙ Desert, Dunes
♣ Forest, Woods
⩪ Heath, Steppe
☘ Oasis
▶ Cape, Point
⌇ Coast, Beach
▐ Cliff
⊢ Peninsula
⋈ Isthmus
▁ Sandbank
◆ Island
◌ Atoll
✳ Rock, Reef
⁂ Islands, Archipelago
❋ Rocks, Reefs
✿ Coral Reef
⊙ Well, Spring
♨ Geyser
≈ River, Stream
⇊ Waterfall Rapids
⋔ River Mouth, Estuary
≋ Lake
⊜ Salt Lake
◫ Intermittent Lake
⊟ Reservoir
⋓ Swamp, Pond
═ Canal
❄ Glacier
❅ Ice Shelf, Pack Ice
▩ Ocean
▤ Sea
◧ Gulf, Bay
⇌ Strait, Fjord
◎ Lagoon
▦ Bank
⩓ Seamount
⊓ Tablemount
⋀ Ridge
⎍ Shelf
⌣ Basin
⟋ Escarpment, Sea Scarp
⚡ Fracture
∪ Trench, Abyss
⊛ National Park, Reserve
✦ Point of Interest
✚ Recreation Site
◠ Cave, Cavern
⛫ Historic Site
⛬ Ruins
▥ Wall, Walls
⛪ Church, Abbey
⛩ Temple
⊠ Scientific Station
✈ Airport
⚓ Port
⛯ Lighthouse
⚒ Mine
∩ Tunnel
⊼ Dam, Bridge

San Marcial, Punta- 48 De 25.30N 111.00W
San Marco, Capo- 14 Hm 37.30N 13.01 E
San Marcos [3] 49 Bf 15.00N 91.55W
San Marcos [Col.] 54 Cb 8.39N 75.08W
San Marcos [Guat.] 49 Bf 14.58N 91.48W
San Marcos [Hond.] 49 Cf 14.24N 88.56W
San Marcos [Mex.] 48 Gg 20.47N 104.11W
San Marcos [Mex.] 48 Ji 16.48N 99.21W
San Marcos [Nic.] 49 Dh 11.55N 86.12W
San Marcos [Tx.-U.S.] 43 Hf 29.53N 97.57W
San Marcos, Isla- 48 Cd 27.13N 112.06W
San Marcos, Sierra de- 48 Hd 26.30N 101.55W
San Marino 14 Gg 43.55N 12.28 E
San Marino [1] 6 Hg 43.55N 12.28 E
San Martín 56 Gd 33.04S 68.28W
San Martín 66 Qe 68.11S 67.00W
San Martin 48 Ab 30.30N 116.05W
San Martín [2] 54 Ce 7.00S 76.50W
San Martin, Cerro- 48 Lh 18.19N 94.48W
San Martín, Lago- 56 Fg 48.52S 72.40W
San Martín, Río- 54 Ff 13.08S 63.43W
San Martin de los Andes 56 Ff 40.10S 71.21W
San Martín de Valdeiglesias 13 Hd 40.21N 4.24W
San Martino di Castrozza 14 Fd 46.16N 11.48 E
San Mateo [Ca.-U.S.] 46 Dh 37.35N 122.19W
San Mateo [Ven.] 50 Dh 9.45N 64.33W
San Mateo/Sant Mateu del Maestrat 13 Md 40.28N 0.11 E
San Mateo Ixtatán 49 Bf 15.50N 91.29W
San Mateo Mountains 45 Cj 33.10N 107.20W
San Matias 55 Cc 16.22S 58.24W
San Matías, Golfo- 52 Jj 41.30S 64.15W
Sanmen (Haiyou) 27 Lf 29.08N 121.22 E
Sanmen Wan 28 Fj 29.00N 121.45 E
Sanmenxia 27 Je 34.44N 111.19 E
San Miguel [Arg.] 55 Dh 27.59S 57.36W
San Miguel [Bol.] 55 Bc 16.42S 61.01W
San Miguel [Ca.-U.S.] 46 Ei 35.45N 120.42W
San Miguel [ElSal.] 39 Kh 13.29N 88.11W
San Miguel [Pan.] 49 Hi 8.27N 78.56W
San Miguel, Golfo de- 49 Hi 8.22N 78.17W
San Miguel, Río- [Bol.] 52 Jg 13.52S 63.56W
San Miguel, Río- [Mex.] 48 Dc 29.16N 110.53W
San Miguel, Río- [Mex.] 48 Fd 26.59N 107.58W
San Miguel, Río- [S.Amer.] 55 Cd 19.25S 58.20W
San Miguel, Salinas de- 55 Bd 19.12S 60.45W
San Miguel, Volcán de- 47 Gf 13.26N 88.16W
San Miguel Bay 26 Hd 13.50N 123.10 E
San Miguel de Allende 48 Ig 20.55N 100.45W
San Miguel de Horcasitas 48 Dc 29.29N 110.45W
San Miguel del Monte 55 Cl 35.27S 58.48W
San Miguel del Padrón 49 Fb 23.05N 82.19W
San Miguel de Tucumán 53 Jh 26.49S 65.13W
San Miguel Island 46 Ei 34.02N 120.22W
San Miguel Islands 26 Ge 7.45N 118.28 E
San Miguelito 55 Bc 17.20S 60.59W
San Miguel River 45 Bg 38.23N 108.48W
San Miguel Sola de Vega 48 Ki 16.31N 96.59W
San Millán 13 Ib 42.18N 3.12W
Sanming 27 Kf 26.11N 117.37 E
San Miniato 14 Eg 43.41N 10.51 E
Sannan 29 Dd 35.04N 135.03 E
Sannār 31 Kg 13.33N 33.38 E
Sannicandro Garganico 14 Ji 41.50N 15.34 E
San Nicolás, Río- [Bol.] 55 Bc 17.08S 61.17W
San Nicolás, Río- [Mex.] 48 Gh 19.40N 105.14W
San Nicolas de los Arroyos 56 Hd 33.20S 60.13W
San Nicolás de los Garzas 48 Ie 25.45N 100.18W
San Nicolas Island 46 Fj 33.15N 119.31W
Sannikova, Proliv- 20 Ib 74.30N 140.00 E
Sannio 14 Ii 41.20N 14.30 E
San'nohe 29 Ga 40.22N 141.15 E
San'nō-Tōge 29 Fc 37.06N 139.44 E
Sannūr, Wādī- 24 Dh 28.59N 31.03 E
Sanok 10 Sg 49.34N 22.13 E
Sanok-Zagórz 10 Sg 49.31N 22.17 E
San Onofre 54 Cb 9.45N 75.32W
San Pablo 22 Oh 14.04N 121.19 E
San Pablo, Punta- 48 Bd 27.15N 114.30W
San Pedro 56 Ib 24.07S 56.59W
San-Pédro 34 De 4.44N 6.37W
San Pedro [3] 55 Dg 24.15S 56.30W
San Pedro [Arg.] 56 Hb 24.14S 64.52W
San Pedro [Arg.] 55 Ck 33.40S 59.40W
San Pedro [Arg.] 56 Jc 26.38S 54.08W
San Pedro, Río- [Guat.] 49 Be 17.46N 91.26W
San Pedro, Río- [Mex.] 48 Gg 21.45N 105.30W
San Pedro, Sierra de- 13 Fe 39.20N 6.35W
San Pedro Carchá 49 Bf 15.29N 90.16W
San Pedro Channel 46 Fj 33.43N 118.23W
San Pedro de Alcántara 13 Hh 36.29N 5.00W
San Pedro de Atacama 56 Gb 22.55S 68.13W
San Pedro de Lloc 54 Ce 7.26S 79.31W
San Pedro de Macorís 49 Md 18.27N 69.18W
San Pedro Martir, Sierra de- 47 Ab 30.45N 115.13W
San Pedro Nolasco, Isla- 48 Dd 27.58N 111.25W
San Pedro Pochutla 48 Kj 15.44N 96.28W
San Pedros de las Colonias 47 Dc 25.45N 102.59W
San Pedro Sula 39 Kh 15.27N 88.02W
San Pedro Tapanatepec 48 Li 16.21N 94.12W
San Pedro Tututepec 48 Ki 16.09N 97.38W
San Pellegrino Terme 14 De 45.50N 9.40 E
San Pietro 14 Ck 39.10N 8.15 E
San Quentin, Bahía de- 48 Ab 30.20N 116.00W
San Quintín 47 Ab 30.29N 115.57W
San Rafael [Arg.] 53 Ji 34.40S 68.21W
San Rafael [Bol.] 55 Bc 16.45S 60.34W
San Rafael [Ca.-U.S.] 46 Dg 38.00N 122.31W
San Rafael [Mex.] 48 He 24.40N 102.01W
San Rafael [Mex.] 48 Ie 25.01N 100.33W
San Rafael [Ven.] 49 Lh 10.58N 71.44W
San Rafael, Cabo- 49 Md 19.01N 68.57W
San Rafael, Río- 55 Cd 18.26S 59.37W
San Rafael de Atamaica 50 Ci 7.32N 67.24W
San Rafael del Norte 49 Dg 13.12N 86.06W
San Rafael Knob 46 Jg 38.50N 110.48W
San Rafael Mountains 46 Fi 34.45N 119.50W
San Rafael River 46 Jg 38.47N 110.07W
San Ramón [Peru] 54 Cf 11.08S 75.20W
San Ramón [Ur.] 55 El 34.18S 55.58W
San Ramón, Río- 55 Bb 14.03S 61.35W
San Ramón de la Nueva Oran 56 Hb 23.08S 64.20W
San Raymundo, Arroyo- 48 Cd 26.21N 112.37W
San Remo 14 Bg 43.49N 7.46 E
Sanriku 29 Gb 39.08N 141.48 E
San Román, Cabo- 54 Ea 12.12N 70.00W
San Roque [Arg.] 55 Ci 28.34S 58.43W
San Roque [Sp.] 13 Gh 36.13N 5.24W
San Saba 45 Gk 31.12N 98.43W
Sansalé 34 Cc 11.07N 14.51W
San Salvador 13 Pe 39.27N 3.11 E
San Salvador [Arg.] 55 Di 29.16S 57.31W
San Salvador [Arg.] 56 Id 31.37S 58.30W
San Salvador [ElSal.] 39 Kh 13.42N 89.12W
San Salvador [Par.] 55 Dg 25.51S 56.28W
San Salvador (Watling) 47 Jd 24.02N 74.28W
San Salvador, Cuchilla- 55 Dk 33.56S 57.45W
San Salvador, Isla- 52 Gf 0.14S 90.45W
San Salvador, Río- 55 Ck 33.29S 58.23W
San Salvador de Jujuy 53 Jh 24.10S 65.20W
Sansanné-Mango 34 Fc 10.21N 0.28 E
San Sebastián [Col.] 49 Ji 9.13N 74.18W
San Sebastián [P.R.] 51a Bb 18.21N 67.00W
San Sebastián [Sp.] 6 Fg 43.19N 1.59W
San Sebastián, Bahía- 56 Gh 53.15S 68.23W
San Sebastián, Isla- 49 Cg 13.11N 88.26W
San Sebastián de la Gomera 32 Dd 28.06N 17.06W
Sansepolcro 14 Gg 43.34N 12.08 E
San Severo 14 Ji 41.41N 15.23 E
San Silvestre 49 Li 8.15N 70.02W
San Simeon 46 Ei 35.39N 121.11W
Sanski Most 14 Kf 44.46N 16.40 E
Santa Agueda 48 Cd 27.13N 112.20W
Santa Ana 63a Fd 10.50S 162.28 E
Santa Ana [Arg.] 55 Eh 27.22S 55.34W
Santa Ana [Bol.] 55 Bc 16.37S 60.43W
Santa Ana [Bol.] 54 Eg 15.31S 67.30W
Santa Ana [Bol.] 55 Cd 18.43S 58.44W
Santa Ana [Ca.-U.S.] 43 De 33.43N 117.54W
Santa Ana [ElSal.] 39 Kh 13.59N 89.34W
Santa Ana [Mex.] 47 Bb 30.33N 111.07W
Santa Ana [Ven.] 50 Dh 9.19N 64.39W
Santa Ana, Río- 49 Li 9.30N 71.57W
Santa Ana, Volcán de- 38 Kh 13.50N 89.39W
Santa Bárbara [3] 49 Cf 15.10N 88.20W
Santa Barbara 39 Hf 34.03N 118.15W
Santa Bárbara [Hond.] 49 Cf 14.53N 88.14W
Santa Bárbara [Mex.] 47 Cc 26.48N 105.49W
Santa Bárbara [Ven.] 49 Lj 7.47N 71.10W
Santa Bárbara, Puerto de- 13 Lb 42.30N 0.50W
Santa Bárbara, Serra de- 55 Fe 21.45S 53.23W
Santa Barbara Channel 46 Fi 34.15N 119.55W
Santa Catalina 63a Fd 10.54S 162.27 E
Santa Catalina [Col.] 49 Jh 10.37N 75.33W
Santa Catalina [Ven.] 50 Fh 8.33N 61.51W
Santa Catalina, Gulf of- 46 Gj 33.20N 117.45W
Santa Catalina, Isla- 48 De 25.40N 110.45W
Santa Catalina Island 46 Fj 33.23N 118.24W
Santa Catarina 48 Ie 25.41N 100.28W
Santa Catarina [2] 56 Kc 27.00S 50.00W
Santa Catarina, Ilha de- 52 Lh 27.36S 48.30W
Santa Catarina, Sierra- 48 Fc 29.40N 107.30W
Santa Cecília 55 Gh 26.56S 50.27W
Santa Cesarea Terme 14 Mj 40.02N 18.28 E
Santa Clara [Ca.-U.S.] 46 Eh 37.21N 121.59W
Santa Clara [Cuba] 39 Lg 22.24N 79.58W
Santa Clara [Gabon] 36 Ab 0.34N 9.17 E
Santa Clara [Mex.] 48 Fc 29.17N 107.01W
Santa Clara [Ur.] 55 Ek 32.55S 54.58W
Santa Clara, Barragem do- 13 Dg 37.30N 8.20W
Santa Clara, Isla- 56 Ed 33.42S 79.00W
Santa Clara de Saguier 55 Bj 31.21S 61.50W
Santa Coloma de Farners/Santa Coloma de Farnés 13 Oc 41.52N 2.40 E
Santa Coloma de Farnés/Santa Coloma de Farners 13 Oc 41.52N 2.40 E
Santa Coloma de Gramanet 13 Oc 41.27N 2.13 E
Santa Coloma de Queralt 13 Nc 41.32N 1.23 E
Santa Comba 13 Da 43.02N 8.49W
Santa Croce Camerina 14 In 36.50N 14.31 E
Santa Cruz [Arg.] [2] 56 Gg 49.00S 70.00W
Santa Cruz [Azr.] 32 Bb 39.05N 28.01W
Santa Cruz [Azr.] 32 Ab 39.27N 31.07W
Santa Cruz [Bol.] 53 Jg 17.48S 63.10W
Santa Cruz [Bol.] [2] 54 Fg 17.30S 61.30W
Santa Cruz [Braz.] 54 Id 0.36S 49.11W
Santa Cruz [Braz.] 55 Dd 18.32S 57.12W
Santa Cruz [Ca.-U.S.] 43 Cd 36.58N 122.01W
Santa Cruz [Chile] 56 Fd 34.38S 71.22W
Santa Cruz [C.R.] 49 Eh 10.01N 84.02W
Santa Cruz [Phil.] 26 Hd 14.01N 121.21 E
Santa Cruz, Isla- 52 Gf 0.38S 90.23W
Santa Cruz, Isla de- 48 De 25.17N 110.43W
Santa Cruz, Río- 56 Gh 50.08S 68.20W
Santa Cruz, Serra da- 55 Jc 17.05S 45.17W
Santa Cruz Cabrália 54 Kg 16.17S 39.02W
Santa Cruz de la Palma 32 Dd 28.41N 17.45W
Santa Cruz de la Zarza 13 Ie 39.58N 3.10W
Santa Cruz del Quiché 49 Bf 15.02N 91.08W
Santa Cruz del Sur 47 Id 20.43N 78.00W
Santa Cruz de Mudela 13 If 38.38N 3.28W
Santa Cruz de Tenerife [3] 32 Dd 28.10N 17.20W
Santa Cruz de Tenerife 31 Ff 28.27N 16.14W
Santa Cruz do Rio Pardo 55 Hf 22.55S 49.37W
Santa Cruz do Sul 56 Jc 29.43S 52.26W
Santa Cruz Island 46 Fi 34.01N 119.45W
Santa Cruz Islands 57 Hf 10.45S 165.55 E
Santadi 14 Ck 39.05N 8.43 E
Santa Elena [Arg.] 55 Bm 37.21S 60.37W
Santa Elena [Arg.] 56 Id 30.57S 59.48W
Santa Elena [Ec.] 54 Bd 2.14S 80.52W
Santa Elena, Bahía de- [C.R.] 49 Eh 10.59N 85.50W
Santa Elena, Bahía de- [Ec.] 54 Bd 2.05S 80.55W
Santa Elena, Cabo- 47 Gf 10.55N 85.57W
Santa Elena de Uairén 54 Fc 4.37N 61.08W
Santa Eulalia 13 Kd 40.34N 1.19W
Santa Eulalia del Río 13 Nf 38.59N 1.31 E
Santa Fé 49 Fc 21.45N 82.45W
Santa Fe [2] 56 Hd 31.00S 61.00W
Santafé 13 Ig 37.11N 3.43W
Santa Fe [Arg.] 53 Ji 31.40S 60.40W
Santa Fe [N.M.-U.S.] 39 If 35.42N 106.57W
Santa Fé de Minas 55 Jc 16.41S 45.28W
Santa Fé do Sul 55 Ge 20.13S 50.56W
Sant'Agata di Militello 14 Il 38.04N 14.38 E
Santa Helena [Braz.] 55 Eg 24.56S 54.23W
Santa Helena [Braz.] 54 Id 2.14S 45.18W
Santa Helena de Goiás 54 Hg 17.43S 50.35W
Santa Inês 54 Id 3.39S 45.22W
Santa Inés 49 Mh 10.37N 69.18W
Santa Ines, Bahía- 48 Dd 27.00N 111.55W
Santa Inés, Isla- 52 Ik 53.45S 72.45W
Santa Isabel [Arg.] 55 Bk 33.54S 61.42W
Santa Isabel [Arg.] 56 Ge 36.15S 66.56W
Santa Isabel [Braz.] 55 Ba 13.40S 60.44W
Santa Isabel [P.R.] 51a Bc 17.58N 66.25W
Santa Isabel, Pico de- 34 Ge 3.35N 8.46 E
Santa Isabel Island 57 Ge 8.00S 159.00 E
Santa Izabel do Ivaí 55 Ff 22.58S 53.14W
Santa Juliana 55 Id 19.19S 47.32W
Santa Lucia [Arg.] 56 Gd 31.32S 68.29W
Santa Lucía [Ur.] 55 Dl 34.27S 56.24W
Santa Lucía, Esteros del- 55 Ci 28.15S 58.20W
Santa Lucía, Río- [Arg.] 55 Ci 29.05S 59.13W
Santa Lucía, Río- [Ur.] 55 Dl 34.48S 56.22W
Santa Lucía Cotzumalguapa 49 Bf 14.20N 91.01W
Santa Lucia Range 43 Cd 36.00N 121.20W
Santa Luzia 32 Cf 16.46N 24.45W
Santa Luzia, Ribeirão- 55 Fe 21.31S 53.53W
Santa Margarita 55 Bi 28.18S 61.33W
Santa Margarita, Isla de- 47 Bd 24.27N 111.50W
Santa Margherita Ligure 14 Df 44.20N 9.12 E
Santa Maria [Braz.] 53 Kh 29.41S 53.48W
Santa Maria 30 Ee 36.58N 25.06W
Santa Maria [Ca.-U.S.] 43 Ce 34.57N 120.26W
Santa María 56 Gc 26.41S 66.02W
Santa María 47 Cb 31.00N 107.14W
Santa María 55 Bc 17.08S 61.01W
Santa María, Bahía de- 48 Ee 25.05N 108.10W
Santa Maria, Cabo de- [Ang.] 30 Ij 13.25S 12.32 E
Santa Maria, Cabo de- [Port.] 13 Eh 36.58N 7.54W
Santa Maria, Cape- 49 Jb 23.41N 75.19W
Santa María, Cayo- 49 Hb 22.40N 79.00W
Santa María, Isla- [Chile] 56 Fe 37.02S 73.33W
Santa María, Isla- [Ec.] 54a Ab 1.15S 90.25W
Santa María, Laguna de- 48 Fb 31.10N 107.15W
Santa María, Río- [Mex.] 48 Jg 21.37N 99.15W
Santa María, Río- [Pan.] 49 Gi 8.06N 80.29W
Santa Maria, Rio- [Braz.] 55 Ee 21.50S 54.53W
Santa Maria, Rio- [Braz.] 55 Ib 14.19S 46.49W
Santa María Asunción Tlaxiaco 48 Ki 17.16N 97.41W
Santa Maria Capua Vetere 14 Ii 41.05N 14.15 E
Santa Maria da Vitória 55 Ja 13.24S 44.12W
Santa María de Cuevas 48 Fd 27.55N 106.23W
Santa María de Ipire 50 Dh 8.49N 65.19W
Santa María del Oro 48 Ge 25.56N 105.22W
Santa María del Río 48 Ig 21.48N 100.45W
Santa Maria di Leuca, Capo- 5 Hh 39.47N 18.22 E
Santa María la Real de Nieva 13 Hc 41.04N 4.24W
Santa María Zacatepec 48 Ki 16.46N 98.00W
Santa Marinella 14 Fh 42.02N 11.51 E
Santa Marta 53 Id 11.15N 74.13W
Santa Marta, Cabo de- 36 Be 13.52S 12.25 E
Santa Marta, Ría de- 13 Ea 43.42N 7.51W
Santa Marta Grande, Cabo de- 55 Hi 28.38S 48.45W
Santa Monica 43 De 34.01N 118.30W
Santan 26 Gg 0.03S 117.28 E
Santana 55 Ja 12.59S 44.03W
Santana, Coxilha de- 55 Ej 31.15S 55.15W
Santana, Rio- 55 Gd 19.43S 51.02W
Santana da Boa Vista 55 Fj 30.52S 53.07W
Santana do Livramento 56 Id 30.53S 55.31W
Santander [3] 13 Ia 43.10N 4.00W
Santander [2] 54 Db 6.35N 73.20W
Santander [Col.] 54 Cc 3.01N 76.29W
Santander [Phil.] 26 He 9.25N 123.20 E
Santander [Sp.] 6 Fg 43.28N 3.48W
Santander, Bahía de- 13 Ia 43.27N 3.48W
Santander Jiménez 47 Ed 24.13N 98.28W
Sant'Andrea 14 Lj 40.05N 17.55 E
Sant'Antioco 14 Ck 39.04N 8.27 E
Sant'Antioco 5 Gh 39.05N 8.25 E
Sant Antoni, Cap-/San Antonio, Cabo de- 13 Mf 38.48N 0.12 E
Santañy 13 Pe 39.22N 3.07 E
Santa Olalla 13 Hd 40.01N 4.26W
Santa Olalla del Cala 13 Fg 37.54N 6.13W
Santa Paula 46 Fi 34.21N 119.04W
Santa Pola 13 Lf 38.11N 0.33W
Sant'Arcangelo 14 Kj 40.15N 16.16 E
Santarcangelo di Romagna 14 Gf 44.04N 12.27 E
Santarém [2] 13 De 39.15N 8.35W
Santarém [Braz.] 53 Kf 2.26S 54.42W
Santarém [Port.] 13 De 39.14N 8.41W
Santaren Channel 47 Id 24.00N 79.30W
Santa Rita [Braz.] 55 Cc 16.15S 59.00W
Santa Rita [Col.] 54 Ec 4.55N 68.20W
Santa Rita [Guam] 64c Bb 13.23N 144.40 E
Santa Rita [Hond.] 49 Df 15.09N 87.53W
Santa Rita [Ven.] 50 Ch 8.08N 66.16W
Santa Rita [Ven.] 49 Lh 10.32N 71.32W
Santa Rita do Araguaia 55 Fc 17.20S 53.12W
Santa Rosa [3] 49 Bf 14.10N 90.18W
Santa Rosa [Arg.] 56 Gd 31.31S 65.04W
Santa Rosa [Arg.] 53 Ji 36.40S 64.15W
Santa Rosa [Braz.] 56 Jc 27.52S 54.29W
Santa Rosa [Ca.-U.S.] 43 Cd 38.26N 122.43W
Santa Rosa [Ec.] 54 Cd 3.27S 79.58W
Santa Rosa [N.M.-U.S.] 43 Ge 34.57N 104.41W
Santa Rosa [Par.] 55 Dh 26.52S 56.49W
Santa Rosa [Ven.] 49 Mi 8.26N 69.42W
Santa Rosa [Ven.] 50 Dh 9.38N 64.18W
Santa Rosa, Mount- 64c Ba 13.32N 144.55 E
Santa Rosa de Copán 49 Cf 14.47N 88.46W
Santa Rosa de la Roca 55 Bc 16.04S 61.32W
Santa Rosa Island 46 Ej 33.58N 120.06W
Santa Rosalia 39 Hg 27.19N 112.17W
Santa Rosalía 50 Bh 9.02N 69.01W
Santa Rosalia, Punta- 48 Bc 28.40N 114.20W
Santa Rosa Range 46 Gf 41.00N 117.40W
Santa Rosa Wash 46 Ij 33.10N 112.05W
Šantarskije Ostrova = Shantar Islands (EN) 21 Pd 55.00N 137.36 E
Santas Creus/Santes Creus 13 Nc 41.19N 1.18 E
Santa Sylvina 56 Hc 27.49S 61.09W
Santa Teresa [Arg.] 55 Bk 33.26S 60.47W
Santa Teresa [Mex.] 48 Ke 25.17N 97.51W
Santa Teresa [Peru] 54 Df 13.01S 72.39W
Santa Teresa, Rio- 55 Ha 12.40S 48.47W
Santa Teresa di Riva 14 Jm 37.57N 15.22 E
Santa Teresa Gallura 14 Di 41.14N 9.11 E
Santa Teresita 55 Dm 36.32S 56.41W
Santa Vitória do Palmar 56 Jd 33.31S 53.21W
Santa Vitória 55 Gd 18.50S 50.08W
Sant Barbara Island 46 Fj 33.23N 119.01W
Sant Boi de Llobregat/San Baudilio de Llobregat 13 Oc 41.21N 2.03 E
Sant Carles de la Ràpita/San Carlos de la Rápita 13 Md 40.37N 0.36 E
Santee River 43 Le 33.14N 79.28W
Santeh 24 Ld 36.10N 46.32 E
San Telmo 48 Ab 30.58N 116.06W
San Telmo, Bahía de- 48 Hh 18.45N 103.40W
San Telmo, Punta- 47 De 18.19N 103.30W
Santerno 14 Ff 44.34N 11.58 E
Santerre 11 Ie 49.55N 2.30 E
Santes Creus/Santas Creus 13 Nc 41.19N 1.18 E
Sant'Eufemia, Golfo di- 14 Kl 38.50N 16.05 E
Sant'Eufemia Lamezia 14 Kl 38.55N 16.15 E
Sant Feliu de Llobregat/San Feliũ de Llobregat 13 Oc 41.23N 2.03 E
Santhià 14 Ce 45.22N 8.10 E
Santiago [2] 56 Fd 33.30S 70.50W
Santiago [Bol.] 54 Gg 18.19S 59.34W
Santiago [Bol.] 55 Bd 19.22S 60.51W
Santiago [Braz.] 56 Jc 29.11S 54.53W
Santiago [Chile] 53 Ii 33.27S 70.40W
Santiago [Dom.Rep.] 39 Lh 19.27N 70.42W
Santiago [Mex.] 48 Ie 25.25N 100.09W
Santiago [Mex.] 48 Cd 27.32N 112.49W
Santiago [Pan.] 39 Ki 8.05N 80.59W
Santiago [Par.] 55 Dh 27.09S 56.47W
Santiago, Cerro- 49 Gi 8.33N 81.44W
Santiago, Río- 54 Cd 4.27S 77.36W
Santiago, Río de- 48 Ge 25.11N 105.26W
Santiago, Serranía- 55 Cd 18.25S 59.25W
Santiago de Chuco 54 Ce 8.09S 78.11W
Santiago de Compostela 13 Db 42.53N 8.33W
Santiago de Cuba 39 Lg 20.01N 75.49W
Santiago de Cuba [3] 49 Ic 20.10N 76.10W
Santiago de la Ribera 13 Lg 37.48N 0.48W
Santiago del Estero 53 Jh 27.50S 64.15W
Santiago del Estero [2] 56 Hc 28.00S 63.30W
Santiago de Papasquiaro 48 Ge 25.03N 105.25W
Santiago do Cacém 13 Df 38.01N 8.42W
Santiago Ixcuintla 47 Cd 21.49N 105.13W
Santiago Mountains 45 El 29.40N 103.15W
Santiago Pinotepa Nacional 47 Ee 16.19N 98.01W
Santiaguillo, Isla- 48 Lh 19.05N 95.50W
Santiaguillo, Laguna de- 48 Ge 24.50N 104.50W
Santiam River 46 Dd 44.42N 123.55W
Santillana 13 Ha 43.23N 4.06W
San Timoteo 49 Li 9.48N 71.04W
Säntis 14 Dc 47.15N 9.20 E
Santisteban del Puerto 13 If 38.15N 3.12W
Sant Jordi, Golf de-/San Jorge, Golfe de- 13 Md 40.53N 1.00 E
Sant Mateu del Maestrat/San Mateo 13 Md 40.28N 0.11 E
Santo, Ile- 57 Hf 15.15S 166.50 E
Santo Anastácio 55 Ge 21.58S 51.39W
Santo André 55 If 23.40S 46.31W
Santo Ângelo 56 Jc 28.18S 54.16W
Santo Antão 30 Eg 17.05N 25.10W
Santo Antônio 56 Jc 26.03S 53.12W
Santo Antonio 34 Ge 1.39N 7.25 E
Santo Antônio de Jesus 54 Kf 12.58S 39.16W
Santo Antônio do Içá 54 Ed 3.05S 67.57W
Santo Antônio do Leverger 54 Gg 15.52S 56.05W
Santo Corazón 54 Gg 17.59S 58.51W
Santo Corazón, Río- 55 Cc 17.23S 58.23W
Santo Domingo [Cuba] 49 Gb 22.35N 80.15W
Santo Domingo [Dom.Rep.] 39 Mh 18.28N 69.54W
Santo Domingo [Mex.] 48 Bb 30.43N 115.56W
Santo Domingo [Mex.] 48 Bc 28.12N 114.02W
Santo Domingo [Mex.] 48 If 23.20N 101.44W
Santo Domingo [Nic.] 49 Eg 12.16N 85.05W
Santo Domingo, Cay- 49 Jc 21.42N 75.46W
Santo Domingo, Punta- 48 Cd 26.20N 112.40W
Santo Domingo, Río- [Mex.] 48 Kh 18.10N 96.08W
Santo Domingo, Río- [Ven.] 49 Mi 8.01N 69.33W
Santo Domingo de la Calzada 13 Jb 42.26N 2.57W
Santo Domingo de los Colorados 54 Cd 0.15S 79.10W
Santo Domingo de Silos 13 Ic 41.58N 3.25W
Santo Domingo Pueblo 45 Ci 35.31N 106.22W
San Tomé 50 Dh 8.58N 64.08W
Santoña 13 Ia 43.27N 3.27W
Santos 53 Lh 23.57S 46.20W
Santos, Sierra de los- 13 Gf 38.15N 5.20W
Santos Dumont 55 Ke 21.28S 43.34W
Santos Unzué 55 Bl 35.45S 60.51W
Santo Tirso 13 Dc 41.21N 8.28W
Santo Tomás [Bol.] 55 Cc 17.46S 58.55W
Santo Tomás [Mex.] 48 Ab 31.33N 116.24W
Santo Tomás [Nic.] 49 Eg 12.04N 85.05W
Santo Tomás, Punta- 48 Ab 31.34N 116.42W
Santo Tomé 56 Ic 28.33S 56.03W
Santu Lussurgiu 14 Cj 40.08N 8.39 E
Santurce-Antiguo 13 Ia 43.20N 3.02W
Sanuki-Sanmyaku 29 Cd 34.05N 134.00 E
San Valentín, Cerro- 52 Ij 46.36S 73.20W
San Vicente [Arg.] 55 Cl 35.01S 58.25W
San Vicente [Mex.] 48 Ab 31.20N 116.15W
San Vicente [Phil.] 26 Hc 18.30N 122.09 E
San Vicente, Sierra de- 13 Hd 40.10N 4.45W
San Vicente de Cañete 54 Cf 13.05S 79.24W
San Vicente de la Barquera 13 Ha 43.26N 4.24W
San Vicente del Caguán 54 Dc 2.07N 74.46W
San Vicente de Raspeig 13 Lf 38.24N 0.31W
San Vincente 47 Gf 13.38N 88.48W
San Vincenzo 14 Eg 43.06N 10.32 E
San Vito [C.R.] 49 Fi 8.50N 82.58W
San Vito [It.] 14 Dk 39.26N 9.32 E
San Vito, Capo- 14 Gl 38.11N 12.44 E
Sanya → Yaxian 22 Mh 18.27N 109.28 E
Sanyati 37 Dc 16.49S 28.45 E
San'yō 29 Bd 34.03N 131.10 E
Sanza 14 Jj 40.15N 15.33 E
Sanza Pombo 36 Cd 7.20S 16.00 E
São Bartoloméu, Rio- 55 Ic 16.48S 47.55W
São Benedito 54 Jd 4.03S 40.53W
São Bento 54 Jd 2.42S 44.50W
São Bento do Sul 55 Hh 26.15S 49.23W
São Borja 56 Ic 28.39S 56.00W
São Brás de Alportel 13 Eg 37.09N 7.53W
São Caetano do Sul 56 Kb 23.36S 46.34W
São Carlos [Braz.] 56 Kb 22.01S 47.54W
São Carlos [Braz.] 55 Ej 33.47N 55.30W
São Domingos [Braz.] 55 Ia 13.24S 46.19W
São Domingos [Gui.Bis.] 34 Bc 12.24N 16.12W
São Domingos, Rio- [Braz.] 55 Fe 20.03S 53.13W
São Domingos, Rio- [Braz.] 55 Ia 13.24S 47.12W
São Domingos, Rio- [Braz.] 55 Gd 19.13S 50.44W
São Domingos, Rio- [Braz.] 55 Ib 15.37S 46.14W
São Felix 54 Hf 11.36S 50.39W
São Félix do Xingu 54 He 6.38S 51.59W
São Filipe 32 Cf 14.54N 24.31W
São Francisco [Braz.] 54 Jg 15.57S 44.52W
São Francisco [Braz.] 55 Dd 18.45S 56.55W
São Francisco, Ilha de- 52 Lh 26.18S 48.37W
São Francisco, Rio- 52 Mg 10.30S 36.24W
São Francisco de Assis 55 Ei 29.33S 55.08W
São Francisco de Paula 55 Gi 29.27S 50.35W
São Francisco de Sales 55 Hd 19.52S 49.46W
São Francisco do Sul 56 Kc 26.14S 48.39W
São Gabriel 56 Jd 30.20S 54.19W
São Gonçalo 54 Jh 22.51S 43.04W
São Gonçalo, Canal de- 55 Fk 32.10S 52.38W
São Gonçalo do Abaete 55 Jd 18.20S 45.49W
São Gonçalo do Sapucaí 55 Je 21.54S 45.36W
São Gotardo 55 Id 19.19S 46.03W
Sao Hill 36 Gd 8.20S 35.12 E
São Jerônimo, Serra de- 55 Ec 16.20S 54.55W
São João da Barra 54 Jh 21.38S 41.03W
São João da Boa Vista 55 Ie 21.58S 46.47W
São João d'Aliança 55 Ib 14.42S 47.31W
São João da Madeira 13 Dd 40.54N 8.30W
São João da Ponte 55 Kb 15.56S 44.01W
São João del Rei 54 Jh 21.09S 44.16W
São João de Meriti 55 Kf 22.48S 43.22W
São João do Araguaia 54 Ie 5.23S 48.46W
São João do Piauí 54 Je 8.21S 42.15W
São João dos Patos 54 Je 6.30S 43.42W
São João do Triunfo 55 Gg 25.41S 50.18W
São Joaquim 56 Kc 28.18S 49.56W
São Joaquim da Barra 55 Ie 20.35S 47.53W
São Jorge 30 Ee 38.38N 28.03W
São José da Serra 55 Eb 15.40S 55.18W
São José do Cerrito 55 Gh 27.40S 50.35W
São José do Norte 55 Fk 32.01S 52.03W
São José do Rio Pardo 56 Kb 21.36S 46.54W
São José do Rio Prêto 53 Lh 20.48S 49.23W
São José dos Campos 56 Kb 23.11S 45.53W
São José dos Dourados, Rio- 55 Ge 20.22S 51.21W
Saolat, Buku- 26 If 0.45N 127.59 E
São Leopoldo 56 Jc 29.46S 51.09W
São Lourenço 55 Ec 16.32S 55.02W
São Lourenço, Pantanal de- 54 Gg 17.45S 56.15W
São Lourenço, Rio- 54 Gg 17.53S 57.27W
São Lourenço, Serra de- 55 Ec 17.30S 54.50W
São Lourenço do Sul 56 Jd 31.22S 51.58W
São Luís 53 Lf 2.31S 44.16W
São Luis Gonzaga 56 Jc 28.24S 54.58W
São Mamede, Serra de- 13 Ee 39.19N 7.19W
São Manuel 55 Hf 22.44S 48.34W
São Marcos 55 Gi 28.58S 51.04W
São Marcos, Baía de- 52 Lf 2.30S 44.30W
São Marcos, Rio- 55 Id 18.15S 47.37W
São Mateus 54 Kg 18.44S 39.51W
São Mateus [Braz.] 55 Gg 25.52S 50.23W

Index Symbols

[1] Independent Nation
[2] State, Region
[3] District, County
[4] Municipality
[5] Colony, Dependency
Continent
Physical Region
Historical or Cultural Region
Mount, Mountain
Volcano
Hill
Mountains, Mountain Range
Hills, Escarpment
Plateau, Upland
Pass, Gap
Plain, Lowland
Delta
Salt Flat
Valley, Canyon
Crater, Cave
Karst Features
Depression
Polder
Desert, Dunes
Forest, Woods
Heath, Steppe
Oasis
Cape, Point
Coast, Beach
Cliff
Peninsula
Isthmus
Sandbank
Island
Atoll
Rock, Reef
Islands, Archipelago
Rocks, Reefs
Coral Reef
Well, Spring
Geyser
River, Stream
Waterfall Rapids
River Mouth, Estuary
Lake
Salt Lake
Intermittent Lake
Reservoir
Swamp, Pond
Canal
Glacier
Ice Shelf, Pack Ice
Ocean
Sea
Gulf, Bay
Strait, Fjord
Lagoon
Bank
Seamount
Tablemount
Ridge
Shelf
Basin
Escarpment, Sea Scarp
Fracture
Trench, Abyss
National Park, Reserve
Point of Interest
Recreation Site
Cave, Cavern
Historic Site
Ruins
Wall, Walls
Church, Abbey
Temple
Scientific Station
Airport
Port
Lighthouse
Mine
Tunnel
Dam, Bridge

São Mateus, Rio- 55 Ia 13.48S 46.54W
São Miguel 30 Ee 37.47N 25.30W
São Miguel, Rio- 55 Ic 16.03S 46.07W
São Miguel do Araguaia 55 Ga 13.19S 50.13W
São Miguel d'Oeste 55 Fh 26.45S 53.34W
Saona, Isla- 49 Md 18.09N 68.40W
Saône 5 Gf 45.44N 4.50 E
Saône-et-Loire [3] 11 Kh 46.40N 4.30 E
Saonek 26 Jg 0.28S 130.47 E
São Nicolau 30 Eg 16.35N 24.15W
São Nicolau [Ang.] 36 Be 14.15S 12.24 E
São Nicolau [Braz.] 55 Ei 28.11S 55.16W
São Patricio, Rio- 55 Hb 15.02S 49.15W
São Paulo 53 Lh 23.32S 46.37W
São Paulo [2] 56 Kb 22.00S 49.00W
São Paulo de Olivença 54 Ed 3.27S 68.48W
São Pedro, Ribeirão 55 Ic 16.54S 46.32W
São Pedro do Sul [Braz.] 55 Ei 29.37S 54.10W
São Pedro do Sul [Port.] 13 Dd 40.45N 8.04W
São Pedro e São Paulo, Penedos de- 52 Ne 0.56N 29.22W
São Raimundo Nonato 54 Je 9.01S 42.42W
São Romão [Braz.] 55 Ed 18.33S 54.27W
São Romão [Braz.] 54 Ig 16.22S 45.04W
São Roque 55 De 21.43S 57.46W
São Roque, Cabo de- 52 Mf 5.29S 35.16W
São Roque, Serra de- 55 Ib 14.40S 46.50W
São Sebastião 55 Jf 23.48S 45.25W
São Sebastião, Ilha de- 52 Lh 23.50S 45.18W
São Sebastião, Ponta- 30 Kk 22.05S 35.24 E
São Sebastião da Boa Vista 54 Id 1.42S 49.31W
São Sebastião do Paraiso 54 Ih 20.55S 47.00W
São Sepé 55 Fj 30.10S 53.34W
São Simão 54 Hg 18.56S 50.30W
São Tiago 30 Eg 15.05N 23.40W
São Tomé 30 Hh 0.12N 6.39 E
São Tomé 31 Hh 0.20N 6.44 E
São Tomé, Cabo de- 54 Jh 22.00S 40.59W
Sao Tome and Principe (EN) = São Tomé e Principe [1] 31 Hh 1.00N 7.00 E
São Tomé e Principe = Sao Tome and Principe (EN) [1] 31 Hh 1.00N 7.00 E
Saoura 32 Gd 27.50N 2.50W
Saoura 30 Gf 28.48N 0.50W
São Vicente 30 Eg 16.50N 25.00W
São Vicente [Braz.] 55 Ia 13.38S 46.31W
São Vicente [Braz.] 56 Kb 23.58S 46.23W
São Vicente, Cabo de- 5 Fh 37.01N 9.00W
São Xavier, Serra de- 55 Ei 29.15S 54.15W
Sápai 15 Ih 41.02N 25.42 E
Sapanca 15 Ni 40.41N 30.16 E
Sapanca Gölü 15 Ni 40.43N 30.15 E
Sape [Braz.] 54 Ke 7.06S 35.13W
Sape [Indon.] 26 Gh 8.34S 118.59 E
Sape, Selat- 26 Gh 8.39S 119.18 E
Sapele 34 Gd 5.55N 5.42 E
Sapelo Island 44 Gj 31.28N 81.15W
Şaphane 15 Mj 39.01N 29.14 E
Şaphane Dağı 15 Mj 39.03N 29.16 E
Sapiéntza 15 Em 36.45N 21.42 E
Šapkina 17 Fc 66.44N 52.25 E
Sapo, Serrania del- 49 Hi 7.50N 78.17W
Saponé 34 Ec 12.03N 1.36W
Sapopema 55 Gf 23.55S 50.35W
Saposoa 54 Ce 6.56S 76.48W
Sapphire Mountains 46 Ic 46.20N 113.45W
Sapporo 22 Qe 43.03N 141.21 E
Sapri 14 Jj 40.04N 15.38 E
Sapucai, Rio- 55 He 20.08S 48.27W
Sapulpa 43 Hd 36.00N 96.06W
Sapulut 26 Gf 4.42N 116.29 E
Sāqiyat Sīdī Yūsuf 14 Cn 36.13N 8.21 E
Saqqez 23 Gb 36.14N 46.16 E
Sarāb 23 Gb 37.56N 47.32 E
Saraburi 25 Kf 14.30N 100.55 E
Saraf Doungous 35 Bc 12.33N 19.42 E
Sarafjagān 24 Ne 34.28N 50.28 E
Saragmatha = Everest, Mount- (EN) 21 Kg 27.59N 86.56 E
Saragossa (EN) = Zaragoza [Sp.] 6 Fg 41.38N 0.53W
Sarai 7 Jj 53.44N 41.03 E
Sarajevo 6 Hg 43.50N 18.25 E
Saraji Mine 59 Jd 22.30S 148.20 E
Sarakhs 23 Jb 36.32N 61.11 E
Sarakiná 15 Hk 38.40N 24.37 E
Šarakol 17 Kj 52.03N 62.47 E
Saraktaš 19 Fe 51.47N 56.18 E
Saraland 44 Cj 30.49N 88.02W
Saramati 25 Jc 25.44N 95.02 E
Saran 19 Hf 49.46N 72.52 E
Saran, Gunung- 26 Fg 0.25S 111.18 E
Saranac Lake 44 Jc 44.20N 74.08W
Saranci 15 Gg 42.43N 23.46 E
Saranda 15 Cj 39.52N 20.00 E
Sarandi 55 Fh 27.56S 52.55W
Sarandi, Arroyo- 55 Cj 30.13S 59.19W
Sarandi del Yi 55 Ek 33.21S 55.38W
Sarandi Grande 55 Dk 33.44S 56.20W
Šaranga 7 Lh 57.12N 46.34 E
Sarangani Bay 26 Ie 5.57N 125.11 E
Sarangani Islands 26 Ie 5.25N 125.26 E
Saranley 35 Ge 2.23N 42.16 E
Saransk 6 Ke 54.11N 45.11 E
Sarapul 6 Ld 56.28N 53.48 E
Sarapulskoje 20 Ig 48.50N 135.58 E
Sarare 49 Mi 9.47N 69.10W
Sararé, Rio- 55 Cb 14.51S 59.58W
Sarasota 43 Kf 27.20N 82.34W
Sarata 16 Ff 46.01N 29.41 E
Sărăţel 15 Kb 47.03N 27.25 E
Saratoga 46 Lf 41.27N 106.48W
Saratoga Springs 43 Mc 43.04N 73.47W
Saratok 26 Ff 1.24N 111.31 E
Saratov 6 Ke 51.34N 46.02 E
Saratov Reservoir (EN) = Saratovskoje Vodohranilišče 5 Ke 52.50N 47.50 E
Saratovskaja Oblast [3] 19 Ee 51.30N 47.00 E
Saratovskoje Vodohranilišče = Saratov Reservoir (EN) 5 Ke 52.50N 47.50 E
Saravan 25 Le 15.43N 106.25 E
Sarawak [2] 26 Ff 2.30N 113.30 E
Saray 24 Bb 41.26N 27.55 E
Saraya 34 Cc 12.50N 11.45W
Sarāyā 24 Fe 35.47N 35.58 E
Sarayköy 24 Cd 37.55N 28.56 E
Sarbāz 23 Jd 26.39N 61.15 E
Sárbogárd 10 Oj 46.53N 18.38 E
Sarca 14 Ee 45.52N 10.52 E
Sarcelle, Passe de la- 63b Cf 22.28S 167.13 E
Sarcelles 12 Ef 49.00N 2.23 E
Sarcidano 14 Dk 39.40N 9.15 E
Sardara 14 Ck 39.37N 8.49 E
Sar Dasht [Iran] 24 Mf 32.32N 48.52 E
Sar Dasht [Iran] 24 Kd 36.09N 45.28 E
Sardegna [2] 14 Cj 40.00N 9.00 E
Sardegna = Sardinia (EN) 5 Gh 40.00N 9.00 E
Sardegna, Mar di- 14 Bk 40.00N 7.30 E
Sardes 15 Lk 38.29N 28.03 E
Sardinal 49 Eh 10.31N 85.39W
Sardinata 54 Db 8.07N 72.48W
Sardinia (EN) = Sardegna 5 Gh 40.00N 9.00 E
Sardis Lake 45 Li 34.27N 89.43W
Sarektjåkkå 7 Dc 67.25N 17.46 E
Sarema/Saaremaa 5 Id 58.25N 22.30 E
Sar-e Pol 23 Kb 36.14N 65.55 E
Sar Eskand Khān 24 Ld 37.29N 47.04 E
Sar-e Yazd 24 Pg 31.36N 54.35 E
Sargasso Sea 38 Mg 29.00N 65.00W
Sargatskoje 19 Hd 55.37N 73.30 E
Sargodha 25 Eb 32.05N 72.40 E
Šargun 18 Fe 38.31N 67.59 E
Sarh 31 Ih 9.09N 18.23 E
Sarhe 11 Fg 47.30N 0.32W
Sarhro, Jebel- 32 Fc 31.00N 6.00W
Sāri [Iran] 22 Hf 36.34N 53.04 E
Sāri [Iraq] 24 Je 34.42N 44.44 E
Sariá 15 Kn 35.50N 27.15 E
Sariçakaya 24 Db 40.02N 30.31 E
Sarigan Island 57 Fc 16.42N 145.47 E
Sarigöl 24 Cc 38.14N 28.43 E
Sarikamiş 24 Jb 40.15N 42.35 E
Sarikaya 24 Fc 39.48N 35.24 E
Sarikei 26 Ff 2.07N 111.31 E
Sariköy 15 Ki 40.12N 27.36 E
Sarina 59 Jd 21.26S 149.13 E
Sarine 14 Bd 46.59N 7.16 E
Sariñena 13 Lc 41.48N 0.10W
Sarioğlan 24 Fc 39.05N 35.59 E
Sarir 33 Dd 27.30N 22.30 E
Sariwŏn 27 Md 38.30N 125.45 E
Sarıyer 24 Cb 41.10N 29.03 E
Sarj, Jabal as- 14 Do 35.56N 9.32 E
Šarja 6 Kd 58.24N 45.30 E
Sark 9 Kl 49.26N 2.21W
Sarkad 10 Rj 46.45N 21.23 E
Sarkand 19 Hf 45.25N 79.54 E
Şarkikaraağaç 24 Dc 38.04N 31.23 E
Sarkışla 24 Gc 39.21N 36.26 E
Šarkovščina 8 Li 55.22N 27.32 E
Şarköy 24 Bb 40.37N 27.06 E
Sarlat-la-Canéda 11 Hj 44.53N 1.13 E
Šarlyk 16 Sc 52.54N 54.42 E
Sarmi 58 Ee 1.51S 138.44 E
Sarmiento 53 Jj 45.35S 69.05W
Sarmizegetuza 15 Fd 45.31N 22.47 E
Särna 8 Ec 61.41N 13.08 E
Sarnen 14 Cd 46.54N 8.15 E
Sărnena Gora 15 Ig 42.35N 25.30 E
Sarnia 43 Kc 42.58N 82.23W
Sarny 19 Ce 51.21N 26.36 E
Saroako 26 Hg 2.31S 121.22 E
Sarolangun 26 Dg 2.18S 102.42 E
Saroma 29a Ca 44.02N 143.45 E
Saroma-Ko 28 Qb 44.10N 143.40 E
Šaromy 20 Kf 54.23N 158.14 E
Saronic Gulf (EN) = Saronikós Kólpos 15 Gl 37.45N 23.30 E
Saronikós Kólpos = Saronic Gulf (EN) 15 Gl 37.45N 23.30 E
Saronno 14 De 45.38N 9.02 E
Saros, Gulf of- (EN) = Saros Körfezi 24 Bb 40.30N 26.20 E
Saros Körfezi = Saros, Gulf of- (EN) 24 Bb 40.30N 26.20 E
Sárospatak 10 Rh 48.19N 21.35 E
Sar Passage 64a Ac 7.12N 134.23 E
Sarpinskije Ozera 16 Nf 47.45N 45.00 E
Šar Planina 15 Dg 42.05N 20.50 E
Sarpsborg 8 De 59.17N 11.07 E
Sarqaq 41 Gd 70.00N 51.39W
Sarrabus 14 Dk 39.20N 9.30 E
Sarralbe 11 Ne 49.00N 7.01 E
Sarrāt, Wādī- 14 Co 35.59N 8.23 E
Sarre 10 Cg 49.42N 6.34 E
Sarrebourg 11 Nf 48.44N 7.03 E
Sarreguemines 11 Ne 49.06N 7.03 E
Sarre-Union 12 Jf 48.56N 7.05 E
Sarria 13 Eb 42.47N 7.24W
Sarstún, Rio- 49 Cf 15.54N 88.54W
Sartang 21 Oc 67.30N 133.20 E
Sartène 11a Ab 41.37N 8.59 E
Sarthe [3] 11 Gf 48.00N 0.05 E
Sartu → Anda 28 Ha 46.35N 125.00 E
Sarufutsu 29a Ca 45.18N 142.13 E
Saru-Gawa 29a Cb 42.30N 142.00 E
Saruhanlı 24 Bc 38.44N 27.34 E
Sarukaishi-Gawa 29 Gb 39.25N 141.08 E
Sārūq 24 Me 34.25N 49.30 E
Saruyama-Misaki 29 Ec 37.18N 136.43 E
Sárvár 10 Mi 47.15N 16.56 E
Sarvestān 24 Oh 29.16N 53.13 E
Sárvíz 10 Oj 46.22N 18.48 E
Saryagač 18 Gd 41.28N 69.11 E
Sarybarak 18 Hc 43.24N 71.29 E
Sary-Bulak 18 Jd 41.54N 75.47 E
Saryč, Mys- 5 Jg 44.23N 33.45 E
Saryg-Sep 20 Ef 51.30N 95.40 E
Sary-Išikotrau 18 Kb 45.15N 76.25 E
Sarykamys 19 Ff 46.00N 53.41 E
Sarykamyšskoje, Ozero- 19 Fg 41.58N 57.58 E
Sarykolski Hrebet 18 Je 38.30N 74.15 E
Šaryn-Gol 27 Ib 49.20N 106.30 E
Saryozek 19 Hg 44.22N 77.54 E
Saryšagan 19 Hf 46.05N 73.38 E
Saryšiganak, Zaliv- 18 Ca 46.35N 61.25 E
Sarysu 21 Ie 45.12N 66.36 E
Sary-Taš 19 Hh 39.44N 73.16 E
Saryžaz 18 Lc 42.54N 79.31 E
Sarzana 14 Df 44.07N 9.58 E
Sasabe 48 Db 31.27N 111.31W
Sasabeneh 35 Gd 8.00N 43.44 E
Sasa-ga-Mine 29 Ce 33.49N 133.17 E
Sasago-Tōge 29 Fd 35.37N 138.45 E
Sasamungga 63a Cb 7.02S 156.47 E
Sasarām 25 Gd 24.57N 84.02 E
Sasari, Mount- 63a Dc 8.11S 159.33 E
Sascut 15 Kc 46.11N 27.04 E
Sásd 10 Oj 46.15N 18.07 E
Sasebo 27 Me 33.12N 129.44 E
Saseginaga, Lac- 44 Hb 47.05N 78.34W
Saskatchewan [3] 42 Gf 54.00N 106.00W
Saskatchewan 38 Jd 53.12N 99.16W
Saskatoon 39 Id 52.07N 106.38W
Saskylah 20 Gb 72.00N 114.00 E
Saslaya, Cerro- 49 Eg 13.45N 85.03W
Sasovo 19 Ee 54.22N 41.54 E
Sassafras Mountain 44 Fh 35.03N 82.48W
Sassandra 30 Gh 4.58N 6.05W
Sassandra [3] 34 Dd 5.20N 6.10W
Sassandra 31 Gh 4.57N 6.05W
Sassari 6 Gg 40.43N 8.34 E
Sassenberg 12 Kc 51.59N 8.03 E
Sassenheim 12 Gb 52.14N 4.33 E
Sassetot-le-Mauconduit 12 Ce 49.48N 0.32 E
Saßnitz 10 Jb 54.31N 13.39 E
Sasso Marconi 14 Ff 44.24N 11.15 E
Sassuolo 14 Ef 44.33N 10.47 E
Sastobe 18 Hc 42.34N 70.03 E
Sastre 55 Bj 31.45S 61.50W
Sasyk, Ozero- (Kunduk) 16 Fg 45.45N 29.40 E
Sasykkol, Ozero- 19 If 46.40N 81.00 E
Sata 29 Bf 31.04N 130.42 E
Sata, Cape- (EN) = Sata Misaki 21 Pf 30.59N 130.37 E
Satakunta 8 Jc 61.30N 23.00 E
Sata-Misaki = Sata, Cape- (EN) 21 Pf 30.59N 130.37 E
Satan, Pointe de- 63b Dd 19.00S 169.17 E
Sātāra 25 Ee 17.41N 73.59 E
Sataua 65c Aa 13.28S 172.40W
Satawal Island 57 Fd 7.21N 147.02 E
Satawan Atoll 57 Gd 5.25N 153.35 E
Satellite Bay 42 Fa 77.25N 117.15W
Säter 7 Df 60.21N 15.45 E
Satihaure 7 Ec 67.30N 18.45 E
Satipo 54 Df 11.16S 74.37W
Satīt 35 Fc 14.20N 35.50 E
Satka 19 Fd 55.03N 59.01 E
Šatki 7 Ki 55.11N 44.08 E
Sātmāla Range 25 Fe 19.30N 78.45 E
Satna 25 Gd 24.35N 80.50 E
Šator 14 Kf 44.09N 16.37 E
Sátoraljaújhely 10 Rh 48.24N 21.40 E
Sātpura Range 21 Jg 21.25N 76.10 E
Satsuma-Hantō 29 Bf 31.25N 130.25 E
Satsunai-Gawa 29a Cb 42.55N 143.15 E
Satsunan-Shotō 27 Mf 29.00N 130.00 E
Sattahip 25 Kf 12.39N 100.54 E
Satulung 15 Gb 47.34N 23.26 E
Satu Mare 15 Fb 47.48N 22.53 E
Satu Mare [2] 15 Fb 47.46N 22.56 E
Satun 25 Kg 6.39N 100.03 E
Saturninà ou Papagaio, Rio- 55 Ca 13.55S 58.18W
Saualpe 14 Id 46.50N 14.40 E
Sauce 56 Ic 30.00S 58.46W
Sauce Corto, Arroyo- 55 Bm 36.55S 61.48W
Sauceda Mountains 46 Ij 32.30N 112.30W
Sauce Grande, Rio- 55 Bn 38.59S 61.07W
Saucillo 47 Cc 28.01N 105.17W
Sauda 8 Be 59.39N 6.20 E
Saudade, Serra da- [Braz.] 55 Jd 19.20S 45.50W
Saudade, Serra da- [Braz.] 55 Fc 16.20S 53.53W
Saudarkrókur 7a Bb 65.45N 19.39W
Saudi Arabia (EN) = Al 'Arabīyah As-Su'ūdīyah [1] 22 Gg 25.00N 45.00 E
Sauer [Eur.] 10 Cg 49.44N 6.31 E
Sauer [Fr.] 12 Kf 48.55N 8.10 E
Sauerland 10 De 51.10N 8.00 E
Sauêruiná, Rio- 54 Gf 12.00S 58.40W
Sauga Jõgi 8 Kf 58.19N 24.25 E
Saugatuck 44 Dd 42.40N 86.12W
Saugues 11 Jj 44.58N 3.33 E
Sauk Centre 45 Id 45.44N 94.57W
Sauk Rapids 45 Id 45.34N 94.09W
Saül 54 Hc 3.37N 53.12W
Šaulder 18 Gc 42.47N 68.24 E
Sauldre 11 Hg 47.16N 1.30 E
Saulieu 11 Kg 47.16N 4.14 E
Saulkrasti/Saulkrasty 7 Fh 57.17N 24.29 E
Saulkrasty/Saulkrasti 7 Fh 57.17N 24.29 E
Saulnois 12 If 48.52N 6.30 E
Sault 11 Lj 44.05N 5.25 E
Sault Sainte Marie [Mi.-U.S.] 43 Kb 46.30N 84.21W
Sault Sainte Marie [Ont.-Can.] 39 Ke 46.31N 84.20W
Saumarez Reefs 57 Gg 21.50S 153.40 E
Saumâtre, Étang- 49 Kd 18.35N 72.00W
Saumlaki 26 Jh 7.57S 131.19 E
Saumur 11 Fg 47.16N 0.05W
Saunders 66 Ad 57.47S 26.27W
Saunders Coast 66 Mf 77.45S 150.00W
Saurimo 31 Ji 9.38S 20.24 E
Sauro 14 Kj 40.18N 16.21 E
Sautar 36 Ce 11.09S 18.25 E
Sauteurs 51p Bb 12.14N 61.38W
Sauveterre, Causse de- 11 Jj 44.22N 3.17 E
Sauveterre-de-Guyenne 11 Fj 44.42N 0.05W
Sauvo/Sagu 8 Jd 60.21N 22.42 E
Sauwald 14 Hb 48.28N 13.40 E
Sava 5 Ig 44.50N 20.28 E
Savage River 59 Jh 41.33S 145.09 E
Savai'i Island 57 Jf 13.35S 172.25W
Savala 16 Ld 51.06N 41.29 E
Savalou 34 Fd 7.56N 1.58 E
Savanes [3] 34 Fc 10.30N 0.30 E
Savan Island 51n Bb 12.48N 61.12W
Savanna 45 Ke 42.05N 90.08W
Savannah 38 Kf 32.02N 80.53W
Savannah [Ga.-U.S.] 39 Kf 32.04N 81.05W
Savannah [Tn.-U.S.] 44 Ch 35.14N 88.14W
Savannah Beach 44 Gi 32.01N 80.51W
Savannakhét 22 Mh 16.33N 104.45 E
Savanna-la-Mar 47 Ie 18.13N 78.08W
Savanne 45 Kb 48.59N 90.12W
Savannes Bay 51k Bb 13.45N 60.56W
Savant Lake 42 If 50.15N 90.42W
Savant Lake 45 Ka 50.30N 90.20W
Savaştepe 24 Bc 39.22N 27.40 E
Savdiri 35 Dc 14.25N 29.05 E
Savé 31 Hh 8.02N 2.29 E
Save [Afr.] 30 Kk 21.00S 35.02 E
Save [Fr.] 11 Hk 43.47N 1.17 E
Saveån 8 Dg 57.43N 11.59 E
Sāveh 23 Hb 35.01N 50.20 E
Săveni 15 Jb 47.57N 26.52 E
Saverdun 11 Hk 43.14N 1.35 E
Saverne 11 Nf 48.44N 7.22 E
Savigliano 14 Bf 44.38N 7.40 E
Savigsivik 41 Fc 76.00N 64.45W
Săvineşti 15 Jc 46.51N 26.28 E
Savinjske Alpe 14 Id 46.20N 14.30 E
Savinski 19 Ec 62.57N 40.13 E
Savio 14 Gf 44.19N 12.20 E
Săvîrşin 15 Fc 46.01N 22.14 E
Savitaipale 7 Gf 61.12N 27.42 E
Šavnik 15 Cg 42.57N 19.06 E
Savo 63a Dc 9.08S 159.48 E
Savo 8 Lb 62.30N 27.30 E
Savoie [3] 11 Mi 45.30N 6.25 E
Savoie = Savoy (EN) 11 Mi 45.24N 6.30 E
Savona 14 Cf 44.17N 8.30 E
Savonlinna/Nyslott 7 Gf 61.52N 28.53 E
Savonranta 7 Ge 62.11N 29.12 E
Savonselkä 8 Lb 62.05N 27.20 E
Savoonga 40 Ed 63.42N 170.27W
Savoy (EN) = Savoie 11 Mi 45.24N 6.30 E
Şavşat 24 Jb 41.15N 42.20 E
Savsjö 7 Dh 57.25N 14.40 E
Savudrija, Rt- 14 He 45.30N 13.31 E
Savukoski 7 Gc 67.17N 28.10 E
Savur 24 Id 37.33N 40.53 E
Savusavu 61 Ec 17.34S 178.15 E
Savusavu Bay 63d Bb 16.45S 179.15 E
Savu Sea (EN) = Sawu, Laut- 21 Oj 9.40S 122.00 E
Savuto 14 Kk 39.02N 16.06 E
Sawahlunto 26 Dg 0.40S 100.47 E
Sawai Mādhopur 25 Fc 25.59N 76.22 E
Sawākin 31 Kg 19.07N 37.20 E
Sawākin, Jazā'ir- = Suakin Archipelago (EN) 30 Kg 19.07N 37.20 E
Sawankhalok 25 Je 17.19N 99.54 E
Sawara 29 Gd 35.53N 140.29 E
Sawasaki-Hana 28 Of 37.47N 138.12 E
Sawatch Range 45 Cg 39.10N 106.25W
Sawbā = Sobat (EN) 30 Kh 9.45N 31.45 E
Sawbridgeworth 12 Cc 51.49N 0.09 E
Sawdā', Jabal as- 33 Cd 28.40N 15.30 E
Sawfajjin 33 Cc 31.54N 15.07 E
Sawhāj = Sohag (EN) 31 Kf 26.33N 31.42 E
Sawkanah 33 Cd 29.04N 15.47 E
Sawla 34 Ed 9.17N 2.25W
Sawqirah 23 If 18.10N 56.30 E
Şawqirah, Ghubbat- 23 If 18.35N 56.45 E
Sawtooth Mountains 46 He 44.00N 115.00W
Sawu, Kepulauan- 26 Hi 10.30S 121.50 E
Sawu, Laut- = Savu Sea (EN) 21 Oj 9.40S 122.00 E
Sawu, Pulau- 21 Ok 10.30S 121.54 E
Şawwān, Ard as- 24 Gg 31.00N 37.00 E
Sax 13 Lf 38.32N 0.49W
Saxby River 59 Ic 18.25S 140.53 E
Saxmundham 12 Db 52.13N 1.30 E
Saxony (EN) = Sachsen 10 Jf 51.00N 13.30 E
Say 34 Fc 13.07N 2.21 E
Sayabec 44 Na 48.36N 67.37W
Saya de Malha Bank (EN) 30 Nj 11.00S 61.00 E
Sayago 13 Fc 41.20N 6.10W
Sayan 54 Cf 11.08S 77.12W
Sayang, Pulau- 26 If 0.18N 129.54 E
Sayaxché 49 Be 16.31N 90.10W
Saydā 23 Ec 33.33N 35.22 E
Sayḥūt 22 Hh 15.12N 51.14 E
Saylorville Lake 45 Jf 41.48N 93.46W
Säynätsalo 8 Kb 62.08N 25.46 E
Sayō 29 Dd 35.01N 134.22 E
Sayram Hu 27 Dc 44.35N 81.10 E
Sayula 48 Hh 19.52N 103.37W
Saywūn 35 Hb 15.56N 48.47 E
Sazanit, Ishull i- 15 Ci 40.30N 19.16 E
Sázava 10 Kg 49.53N 14.24 E
Sázava 10 Kg 49.52N 14.54 E
Sbaa 32 Gd 28.13N 0.10W
Sbisseb 13 Pi 35.42N 3.51 E
Sbruč 16 Ee 48.32N 26.25 E
Scaër 11 Cf 48.02N 3.42W
Scafell Pike 9 Jg 54.27N 3.12W
Scalea 14 Jk 39.49N 15.47 E
Scalone, Passo dello- 14 Jk 39.38N 15.57 E
Scammon, Laguna- 48 Bd 27.45N 114.15W
Scammon Bay 40 Fd 61.53N 165.38W
Scandinavia (EN) 5 Hc 65.00N 16.00 E
Scanno 14 Hi 41.54N 13.53 E
Scansano 14 Fh 42.41N 11.20 E
Scapa Flow 9 Jc 58.54N 3.05W
Scapegoat Mountain 46 Ic 47.19N 112.50W
Ščapino 20 Ke 55.15N 159.25 E
Ščara 16 Dc 53.27N 24.44 E
Scaramia, Capo- 14 In 36.47N 14.29 E
Scarba 9 He 56.11N 5.42W
Scarborough [Eng.-U.K.] 9 Mg 54.17N 0.24W
Scarborough [Trin.] 54 Fa 11.11N 60.44W
Scarpe 11 Jd 50.30N 3.27 E
Ščastje 16 Ke 48.44N 39.14 E
Sceaux 12 Ef 48.47N 2.17 E
Ščekino 16 Jb 54.01N 37.29 E
Ščekurja 17 Jd 64.15N 60.52 E
Ščeljajur 19 Fb 65.21N 53.25 E
Scenic 45 Ee 43.47N 102.30W
Ščerbakty 19 He 52.29N 78.14 E
Schaalsee 10 Gc 53.35N 10.57 E
Schaarbeek/Schaerbeek 12 Gd 50.51N 4.23 E
Schaerbeek/Schaarbeek 12 Gd 50.51N 4.23 E
Schaffhausen [2] 14 Cc 47.45N 8.40 E
Schaffhausen 14 Cc 47.40N 8.40 E
Schagen 12 Gb 52.48N 4.48 E
Schärding 14 Hb 48.27N 13.26 E
Scharmützelsee 10 Kd 52.15N 14.03 E
Scharnhörn 10 Ec 53.57N 8.25 E
Scheeßel 12 La 53.10N 9.29 E
Schefferville 39 Md 54.47N 64.49W
Scheibbs 14 Jb 48.00N 15.10 E
Schela 15 Gd 45.10N 23.18 E
Schelde 11 Kc 51.22N 4.15 E
Schelde (EN) = Escaut 11 Kc 51.22N 4.15 E
Schell Creek Range 43 Ed 39.10N 114.40W
Schenectady 43 Mc 42.48N 73.57W
Scheno 35 Fd 9.35N 39.25 E
Scherfede, Warburg- 12 Lc 51.32N 9.02 E
Scherpenheuvel-Zichem 12 Gd 50.59N 4.59 E
Scheveningen, 's-Gravenhage- 11 Kb 52.06N 4.18 E
Schiedam 11 Kc 51.55N 4.24 E
Schiermonnikoog 11 Ma 53.28N 6.15 E
Schifferstadt 12 Ke 49.23N 8.22 E
Schiffgraben 10 Hd 52.02N 11.10 E
Schifflange 12 Ie 49.30N 6.01 E
Schijndel 12 Hc 51.37N 5.28 E
Schiltigheim 11 Nf 48.36N 7.45 E
Schio 14 Fe 45.43N 11.21 E
Schipbeek 12 Ib 52.15N 6.14 E
Schladming 14 Hc 47.23N 13.41 E
Schlei 10 Fb 54.35N 9.50 E
Schleiden 10 Cf 50.32N 6.28 E
Schleiz 10 Hf 50.35N 11.49 E
Schleswig 10 Fb 54.31N 9.33 E
Schleswig Holstein [2] 10 Gb 54.00N 10.30 E
Schlitz 10 Ff 50.40N 9.34 E
Schloß Holte-Stukenbrock 12 Kc 51.55N 8.38 E
Schloß Neuhaus, Paderborn- 12 Kc 51.44N 8.42 E
Schluchsee 10 Ei 47.49N 8.10 E
Schlüchtern 10 Ff 50.21N 9.31 E
Schmallenberg 12 Kc 51.09N 8.18 E
Schmallenberg-Bödefeld-Freiheit 12 Kc 51.15N 8.24 E
Schmallenberg-Oberkirchen 12 Kc 51.09N 8.18 E
Schmelz 12 Ie 49.26N 6.51 E
Schmida 14 Kb 48.20N 16.14 E
Schneeberg 10 If 50.36N 12.38 E
Schneeberg [Aus.] 14 Jc 47.46N 15.52 E
Schneeberg [F.R.G.] 10 Hf 50.00N 11.51 E
Schneifel 12 Id 50.16N 6.23 E
Schoberpaß 14 Ic 47.27N 14.40 E
Schoberspitze 14 Ic 47.17N 14.09 E
Schœlcher 51h Ab 14.37N 61.06W
Schönebeck 10 Hd 52.01N 11.45 E
Schönecken 12 Id 50.10N 6.28 E
Schongau 10 Gi 47.49N 10.54 E
Schöningen 10 Gd 52.08N 10.57 E
Schoondijke 12 Fc 51.21N 3.33 E
Schoonebeek 12 Ib 52.40N 6.53 E
Schoonhoven 12 Gc 51.55N 4.51 E
Schorfheide 10 Jd 52.55N 13.35 E
Schoten 12 Gc 51.15N 4.30 E
Schotten 12 Ld 50.30N 9.08 E
Schouten Islands 57 Fe 3.30S 144.30 E
Schouwen 11 Jc 51.43N 3.50 E
Schramberg 10 Eh 48.14N 8.23 E
Schreiber 42 Ig 48.48N 87.15W
Schriesheim 12 Ke 49.29N 8.40 E
Schrobenhausen 10 Hh 48.33N 11.16 E
Schruns 14 Dc 47.04N 9.55 E
Schuls / Scuol 14 Ed 46.48N 10.17 E
Schultz Lake 42 Hd 64.45N 97.30W
Schurz 46 Fg 38.58N 118.46W
Schussen 10 Fi 47.37N 9.32 E
Schüttorf 12 Jb 52.19N 7.14 E
Schwabach 10 Hg 49.20N 11.02 E
Schwaben = Swabia (EN) 10 Gh 48.20N 10.30 E
Schwäbisch-Bayerisches Alpenvorland = Swabian-Bavarian Plateau (EN) 5 Hf 48.15N 10.30 E
Schwäbische Alb = Swabian Jura (EN) 5 Gf 48.25N 9.30 E

Index Symbols

[1] Independent Nation
[2] State, Region
[3] District, County
Municipality
Colony, Dependency
Continent
Physical Region
Historical or Cultural Region
Mount, Mountain
Volcano
Hill
Mountains, Mountain Range
Hills, Escarpment
Plateau, Upland
Pass, Gap
Plain, Lowland
Delta
Salt Flat
Valley, Canyon
Crater, Cave
Karst Features
Depression
Polder
Desert, Dunes
Forest, Woods
Heath, Steppe
Oasis
Cape, Point
Coast, Beach
Cliff
Peninsula
Isthmus
Sandbank
Island
Atoll
Rock, Reef
Islands, Archipelago
Rocks, Reefs
Coral Reef
Well, Spring
Geyser
River, Stream
Waterfall Rapids
River Mouth, Estuary
Lake
Salt Lake
Intermittent Lake
Reservoir
Swamp, Pond
Canal
Glacier
Ice Shelf, Pack Ice
Ocean
Sea
Gulf, Bay
Strait, Fjord
Lagoon
Bank
Seamount
Tablemount
Ridge
Shelf
Basin
Escarpment, Sea Scarp
Fracture
Trench, Abyss
National Park, Reserve
Point of Interest
Recreation Site
Cave, Cavern
Historic Site
Ruins
Wall, Walls
Church, Abbey
Temple
Scientific Station
Airport
Port
Lighthouse
Mine
Tunnel
Dam, Bridge

Schwäbisch Gmünd	10	Fh	48.48N	9.47 E
Schwäbisch Hall	10	Fg	49.06N	9.44 E
Schwalbach (Saar)	12	Ie	49.18N	6.49 E
Schwalm	12	Lc	51.07N	9.24 E
Schwalm	10	Ff	50.45N	9.25 E
Schwalmstadt	10	Ff	50.55N	9.12 E
Schwalmtal	12	Ic	51.15N	6.15 E
Schwandorf	10	Ig	49.20N	12.07 E
Schwaner, Pegunungan-	26	Fg	0.40S	112.40 E
Schwanewede	12	Ka	53.14N	8.36 E
Schwarzach	10	Ig	49.30N	12.10 E
Schwarzbach	12	Je	49.17N	7.40 E
Schwarze Elster	10	Ie	51.49N	12.51 E
Schwarzer Mann	12	Id	50.15N	6.22 E
Schwarzrand	37	Be	26.00S	17.10 E
Schwarzwald=Black Forest (EN)	5	Gf	48.00N	8.15 E
Schwarzwalder Hochwald	12	Ie	49.39N	6.55 E
Schwatka Mountains	40	Hc	67.25N	157.00W
Schwaz	14	Fc	47.20N	11.42 E
Schwechat	14	Kb	48.08N	16.28 E
Schwechat	14	Kb	48.08N	16.28 E
Schwedt	10	Kc	53.04N	14.18 E
Schweich	12	Ie	49.49N	6.45 E
Schweinfurt	10	Gf	50.03N	10.14 E
Schweiz / Suisse / Svizra / Svizzera = Switzerland (EN) [1]	6	Gf	46.00N	8.30 E
Schweizer-Reneke	37	De	27.11S	25.18 E
Schwelm	12	Jc	51.17N	7.17 E
Schwerin [2]	10	Hc	53.35N	11.25 E
Schwerin	10	Hc	53.38N	11.23 E
Schweriner See	10	Hc	53.45N	11.28 E
Schwerte	12	Jc	51.27N	7.34 E
Schwetzingen	12	Ke	49.23N	8.34 E
Schwielochsee	10	Kd	52.03N	14.12 E
Schwyz [2]	14	Cc	47.10N	8.50 E
Schwyz	14	Cc	47.03N	8.40 E
Sciacca	14	Hm	37.31N	13.03 E
Scicli	14	In	36.47N	14.42 E
Ščigry	19	De	51.53N	36.55 E
Scilly, Isles of-	5	Ff	49.57N	6.15W
Scioto River	44	Ff	38.44N	83.01W
Ščirec	10	Tg	49.34N	23.54 E
Scobey	46	Mb	48.47N	105.25W
Scordia	14	Im	37.18N	14.51 E
Scoresby Land	41	Jd	71.45N	26.30W
Scoresbysund	67	Md	70.35N	21.40W
Scoresby Sund	67	Md	70.20N	23.30W
Scorff	11	Cg	47.46N	3.21W
Ščors	19	De	51.48N	31.59 E
Scotia Ridge (EN)	3	Co	57.00S	45.00W
Scotia Sea (EN)	52	Mk	57.00S	40.00W
Scotland [2]	9	Ie	56.30N	4.30W
Scotland	5	Fd	56.30N	4.30W
Scotlandville	45	Kk	30.31N	91.11W
Scotstown	44	Lc	45.31N	71.17W
Scott	42	Gf	52.27N	108.23W
Scott, Cape- [Austl.]	59	Fb	13.30S	129.50 E
Scott, Cape - [B.C.-Can.]	42	Ef	50.47N	128.25W
Scott, Mount-	46	De	42.56N	122.01W
Scott Base	66	Kf	77.51S	166.46 E
Scottburgh	37	Ef	30.19S	30.40 E
Scott Channel	46	Aa	50.45N	128.30W
Scott City	45	Fg	38.29N	100.54W
Scott Coast	66	Kf	76.30S	162.30 E
Scott Glacier [Ant.]	66	He	66.15S	100.05 E
Scott Glacier [Ant.]	66	Mg	85.45S	153.00W
Scott Inlet	42	Kb	71.05N	71.05W
Scott Island	66	Le	67.24S	179.55W
Scott Islands	46	Aa	50.48N	128.40W
Scott Peak	46	Id	44.21N	112.50W
Scott Reef	59	Eb	14.00S	121.50 E
Scottsbluff	39	Ie	41.52N	103.40W
Scottsboro	44	Dh	34.40N	86.01W
Scottsburg	44	Ef	38.41N	85.46W
Scottsdale [Austl.]	59	Jh	41.10S	147.31 E
Scottsdale [Az.-U.S.]	43	Ee	33.30N	111.56W
Scotts Head	51g	Bb	15.13N	61.23W
Scottsville	44	Dg	36.45N	86.11W
Scottville	44	Dd	43.59N	86.17W
Scranton	39	Le	41.24N	75.40W
Scrivia	14	Ce	45.03N	8.54 E
Scrub Cays	49	Ia	24.07N	76.55W
Scrub Island	51b	Bb	18.17N	62.57W
Ščučin	16	Dc	53.39N	24.48 E
Ščučinsk	19	He	53.00N	70.11 E
Ščučja	17	Nc	66.45N	68.20 E
Ščučje	19	Gd	55.15N	62.43 E
Scugog, Lake-	44	Hc	44.10N	78.51W
Ščugor	17	Hd	64.12N	57.32 E
Scunthorpe	9	Mh	53.36N	0.38W
Scuol / Schuls	14	Ed	46.48N	10.17 E
Scutari, Lake- (EN)= Shkodrës, Liqen i-	5	Hg	42.10N	19.20 E
Scutari, Lake- (EN)= Skadarsko Jezero	5	Hg	42.10N	19.20 E
Seaford	9	Nk	50.46N	0.06 E
Seahorse Point	42	Jd	63.47N	80.10W
Sea Islands	43	Ke	31.20N	81.20W
Seal	42	Ie	59.04N	94.47W
Seal Island	44	Nd	43.30N	66.01W
Sealpunt	30	Jl	34.06S	23.24 E
Searcy	45	Ki	35.15N	91.44W
Searles Lake	46	Gi	35.43N	117.20W
Seaside [Ca.-U.S.]	46	Eh	36.37N	121.50W
Seaside [Or.-U.S.]	46	Dc	46.01N	123.55W
Seattle	39	Ge	47.36N	122.20W
Seaward Kaikoura Range	62	Ee	42.15S	173.35 E
Seba	26	Hi	10.29S	121.50 E
Sébaco	49	Dg	12.51N	86.06W
Sebago Lake	44	Ld	43.50N	70.35W
Sebaiera	32	Ee	24.51N	13.02W
Sebaou	13	Ph	36.55N	3.51 E
Sebastian, Cape-	46	Ce	42.19N	124.26W
Sebastián Vizcaíno, Bahía-	38	Hg	28.00N	114.30W
Sebastopol	46	Dg	38.24N	122.49W
Sebatik, Pulau-	26	Gf	4.10N	117.45 E
Sebba	34	Fc	13.26N	0.32 E
Sebderat	35	Fb	15.27N	36.39 E
Sébé	36	Bc	1.02S	13.06 E
Šebekino	19	De	50.27N	37.00 E
Sébékoro	34	Dc	12.49N	8.50W
Seberi	55	Fh	27.29S	53.24W
Sebeş	15	Gd	45.58N	23.34 E
Sebeş	15	Gd	46.00N	23.34 E
Sebes-Körös	15	Dc	46.55N	20.59 E
Sebeşului, Munţii-	15	Gd	45.38N	23.27 E
Sebewaing	44	Fd	43.44N	83.27W
Sebež	19	Cd	56.19N	28.31 E
Sebha Oasis (EN)=Sabhā, Wāḩāt	30	If	27.00N	14.25 E
Şebınkaranhisar	24	Hb	40.18N	38.26 E
Sebiş	15	Fc	46.22N	22.07 E
Sebou	30	Ge	34.16N	6.41W
Sebring	44	Gl	27.30N	81.26W
Sebugal	13	Ed	40.21N	7.05W
Sebuku, Pulau-	26	Gg	3.30S	116.22 E
Šebunino	20	Jg	46.24N	141.56 E
Secas, Islas-	49	Gi	7.58N	82.02W
Secchia	14	Ee	45.04N	11.00 E
Sechura	54	Be	5.33S	80.51W
Sechura, Bahía de-	54	Be	5.40S	81.00W
Sechura, Desierto de-	54	Be	6.00S	80.30W
Seckau	14	Ic	47.16N	14.47 E
Seclin	12	Fd	50.33N	3.02 E
Secondigny	11	Fh	46.37N	0.25W
Secos, Ilhéus-	32	Cf	14.58N	24.40W
Secretary Island	62	Bf	45.15S	166.55 E
Sécure, Río-	54	Fg	15.10S	64.52W
Seda	8	Kg	57.38N	25.12 E
Sêda	13	Df	38.56N	8.03W
Seda [Lat.-U.S.S.R.]	8	Kg	57.32N	25.43 E
Seda [Lith.-U.S.S.R.]	8	Jh	56.10N	22.00 E
Sedalia	43	Id	38.42N	93.14W
Sedan	11	Ke	49.42N	4.57 E
Sedanka	40a	Eb	53.50N	166.10W
Sedano	13	Ib	42.43N	3.45W
Sedbergh	9	Kg	54.20N	2.31W
Seddenga	35	Ea	20.33N	30.18 E
Seddon	62	Fd	41.40S	174.04 E
Seddon, Kap-	41	Gc	75.20N	58.45W
Seddonville	62	Dd	41.33S	171.59 E
Seddülbahir	15	Ji	40.03N	26.10 E
Sedelnikovo	19	Hd	56.57N	75.18 E
Séderon	11	Lj	44.12N	5.32 E
Sédhiou	34	Bc	12.44N	15.33W
Sedini	14	Ci	40.51N	8.49 E
Šedok	16	Lg	44.13N	40.52 E
Sedom	24	Fg	31.04N	35.24 E
Sedona	46	Ji	34.52N	111.46W
Sedrada	14	Bn	36.08N	7.32 E
Šédro	14	Kg	43.05N	16.42 E
Sedro Woolley	46	Db	48.30N	122.14W
Šeduva	7	Fi	55.48N	23.45 E
Sée	11	Ef	48.39N	1.26W
Seeheim [F.R.G.]	12	Ke	49.46N	8.40 E
Seeheim [Nam.]	37	Be	26.50S	17.45 E
Seeis	37	Bd	22.29S	17.39 E
Seeland	14	Bc	47.05N	7.05 E
Seeling, Mount-	66	Og	82.28S	103.00W
Seelow	10	Kd	52.31N	14.23 E
Sées	11	Gf	48.36N	0.10 E
Seesen	10	Ge	51.54N	10.11 E
Seewarte Seamounts (EN)	30	Ee	33.00N	28.30W
Şefaatli	24	Fc	39.31N	34.46 E
Sefadu	34	Cd	8.39N	10.59W
Seferihisar	24	Bc	38.11N	26.51 E
Séféto	34	Dc	14.08N	9.51W
Sefid Dasht	24	Nf	32.09N	51.10 E
Sefrou	32	Gc	33.50N	4.50W
Sefuri-San	29	Be	33.26N	130.22 E
Segaf, Kepulauan-	26	Jg	2.10S	130.28 E
Ségalas	11	Ij	44.09N	2.30 E
Segamat	26	Df	2.30N	102.49 E
Segangane	13	Ii	35.10N	3.01W
Şegarcea	15	Ge	44.06N	23.45 E
Šegarka	20	De	57.16N	84.02 E
Segbana	34	Fc	10.56N	3.42 E
Segeg	35	Gd	7.40N	42.50 E
Segesta	14	Gm	37.55N	12.50 E
Segeža	6	Jc	63.44N	34.19 E
Seghe	63a	Cc	8.25S	157.51 E
Seglinge	8	Id	60.15N	20.40 E
Segmon	8	Ee	59.17N	13.01 E
Segorbe	13	Le	39.51N	0.29W
Ségou [3]	34	Dc	14.00N	6.20W
Ségou	31	Gg	13.27N	6.15W
Segovia	13	Hd	40.57N	4.07W
Segovia [3]	13	Ic	41.10N	4.00W
Segozero, Ozero-	5	Jc	63.18N	33.45 E
Segré	11	Fg	47.41N	0.52W
Segre	13	Mc	41.40N	0.43 E
Seguam	40a	Db	52.17N	172.30W
Séguédine	34	Ha	20.12N	12.59 E
Séguéla	34	Dd	7.57N	6.40W
Séguéla [3]	34	Dd	8.05N	6.32W
Seguin	43	Hf	29.34N	97.58W
Segula	40a	Bb	52.01N	178.07 E
Segura	13	Lf	38.06N	0.38W
Segura, Sierra de-	13	Jf	38.00N	2.45W
Segura de la Sierra	13	Jf	38.18N	2.39W
Sehithwa	37	Cd	20.27S	22.42 E
Seia	13	Ed	40.25N	7.42W
Seibal	49	Be	16.27N	90.05W
Seiche	11	Eg	48.00N	1.46W
Seiland	7	Fa	70.25N	23.15 E
Seiling	45	Gh	36.09N	98.56W
Seille [Fr.]	11	Me	49.07N	6.11 E
Seille [Fr.]	11	Kh	46.31N	4.56 E
Sein, Ile de-	11	Bf	48.02N	4.51W
Seinäjoki	7	Fe	62.47N	22.50 E
Seine	5	Gf	49.26N	0.26 E
Seine, Baie de la-=Seine, Bay of the- (EN)	5	Ff	49.30N	0.30W
Seine, Bay of the- (EN)= Seine, Baie de la-	5	Ff	49.30N	0.30W
Seine, Val de-	11	Jf	48.30N	3.20 E
Seine-et-Marne [3]	11	If	48.30N	3.00 E
Seine-Maritime [3]	11	Ge	49.45N	1.00 E
Seine-Saint-Denis [3]	11	If	48.55N	2.30 E
Seine Seamount (EN)	5	Ei	33.45N	14.25W
Seini	15	Gb	47.45N	23.17 E
Seistan (EN)=Sīstān	21	If	30.30N	62.00 E
Seixal	13	Cf	38.38N	9.06W
Sējaha	20	Cb	70.10N	72.30 E
Sejerø	8	Di	55.55N	11.10 E
Sejerø Bugt	8	Di	55.50N	11.15 E
Sejm	5	Je	51.27N	32.34 E
Sejmčan	20	Kd	62.52N	152.27 E
Sejny	10	Tb	54.07N	23.20 E
Sekakes	37	Df	30.04S	28.21 E
Sekenke	36	Fc	4.16S	34.10 E
Šeki	19	Eg	41.10N	47.11 E
Seki [Jap.]	29	Ed	35.28N	136.54 E
Seki [Tur.]	24	Cd	36.44N	29.33 E
Sekincau, Gunung-	26	Dh	5.05S	104.18 E
Seki-Zaki	29b	Be	33.16N	131.54 E
Sekoma	37	Cd	24.36S	23.58 E
Sekondi-Takoradi	31	Gh	4.53N	1.45W
Sekota	35	Fc	12.37N	39.03 E
Šeksna	19	Dd	59.13N	38.32 E
Šelagski, Mys-	20	Mb	70.10N	170.45 E
Selah	46	Ec	46.39N	120.32W
Selajar, Pulau-	26	Hh	6.05S	120.30 E
Selajar, Selat-	26	Hh	5.42S	120.28 E
Selaön	8	Ge	59.25N	17.10 E
Selaru, Pulau-	26	Jh	8.09S	131.00 E
Selatan, Cape- (EN)= Selatan, Tanjung-	21	Nj	4.10S	113.48 E
Selatan, Tanjung-=Selatan, Cape- (EN)	21	Nj	4.10S	113.48 E
Selawik	40	Gc	66.37N	160.03W
Selawik Lake	40	Hc	66.30N	160.40W
Selb	10	If	50.10N	12.08 E
Selbjørn	8	Ae	60.00N	5.10 E
Selbjørnsfjorden	8	Ae	59.55N	5.10 E
Selbu	8	Da	63.13N	11.02 E
Selbukta	66	Bf	71.40S	12.25W
Selbusjøen	8	Da	63.15N	10.55 E
Selby [Eng.-U.K.]	9	Lh	53.48N	1.04W
Selby [S.D.-U.S.]	45	Fd	45.31N	100.02W
Selco	16	Ic	53.23N	34.05 E
Selçuk	24	Bd	37.56N	27.22 E
Seldovia	40	Ie	59.27N	151.43W
Sele	14	Ij	40.29N	14.56 E
Sele, Piana del-	14	Ij	40.30N	14.55 E
Selebi-Pikwe	31	Jk	22.13S	27.58 E
Selečka Planina	15	Eh	41.05N	21.35 E
Šelehov	20	Ff	52.10N	104.01 E
Selemdža	21	Od	51.49N	128.53 E
Selencia	24	Kf	33.04N	44.33 E
Selendi	15	Lk	38.40N	28.41 E
Selendi	15	Lk	38.45N	28.53 E
Selenduma	20	Ff	50.55N	106.10 E
Selenga (Selenge)	21	Md	52.16N	106.16 E
Selenge [Mong.]	27	Hb	49.25N	103.59 E
Selenge [Zaire]	36	Cc	1.58S	18.11 E
Selenge → Selenga	21	Md	52.16N	106.16 E
Selenginsk	20	Ff	51.59N	106.57 E
Selenica	15	Ci	40.32N	19.38 E
Selennjah	20	Jc	67.55N	145.00 E
Sélestat	11	Nf	48.16N	7.27 E
Selety	19	He	53.06N	73.00 E
Seletyteniz, Ozero-	19	He	53.15N	73.15 E
Selevac	15	De	44.30N	20.53 E
Seleznevo	8	Md	60.44N	28.37 E
Selfoss	7a	Bc	63.56N	21.00W
Seli	34	Cd	8.33N	12.48W
Sélibabi	32	Ef	15.10N	12.11W
Seliger, Ozero-	19	Dd	57.20N	33.05 E
Seligman	46	Ii	35.20N	112.53W
Šelihova, Zaliv-=Shelikhov Gulf (EN)	21	Rc	60.00N	158.00 E
Selimağa	15	Lj	39.35N	28.33 E
Selimiye	24	Bd	37.24N	27.40 E
Selingenstadt	12	Kd	50.03N	8.59 E
Selinunte	14	Gm	37.35N	12.48 E
Seližarovo	7	Hh	56.51N	33.29 E
Seljatin	15	Ib	47.52N	25.14 E
Selje	8	Ab	62.03N	5.22 E
Seljord	7	Bg	59.29N	8.37 E
Selkirk [Man.-Can.]	45	Ha	50.09N	96.52W
Selkirk [Scot.-U.K.]	9	Kf	55.33N	2.50W
Selkirk Mountains	42	Ff	50.00N	117.00W
Sella	13	Ga	43.28N	5.04W
Sellasía	15	Fl	37.10N	22.25 E
Selle	12	Fd	50.19N	3.23 E
Selles-sur-Cher	11	Hg	47.16N	1.33 E
Sells	46	Jk	31.55N	111.53W
Selm	12	Jc	51.42N	7.28 E
Selma [Al.-U.S.]	43	Je	32.25N	87.01W
Selma [Ca.-U.S.]	46	Fh	36.34N	119.37W
Selmer	44	Ch	35.11N	88.36W
Selmęt Wielki, Jezioro-	10	Sc	53.50N	22.30 E
Šelon	7	Hg	58.14N	30.50 E
Selong	26	Gh	8.39S	116.32 E
Selsey	12	Bd	50.44N	0.47W
Selsey Bill	9	Mk	50.43N	0.48W
Seltz	12	Kf	48.53N	8.06 E
Selu, Pulau-	26	Jh	7.32S	130.54 E
Selukwe	37	Dc	19.40S	30.00 E
Sélune	11	Ef	48.39N	1.26W
Selva	55	Ai	29.46S	62.03W
Selvagens, Ilhas-	30	Fe	30.05N	15.55W
Selvānā	24	Kd	37.25N	44.51 E
Selvas	52	Jf	5.00S	68.00W
Selway River	46	Hc	46.08N	115.36W
Selwyn, Détroit de-	63b	Dc	16.04S	168.11 E
Selwyn Lake	42	He	60.00N	104.30W
Selwyn Mountains	38	Fc	63.10N	130.20W
Selwyn Range	57	Fg	21.35S	140.35 E
Selz	12	Ke	49.59N	8.02 E
Šemaha	16	Pi	40.39N	48.38 E
Semani	15	Ci	40.54N	19.26 E
Semara	31	Ff	26.44N	11.41W
Semarang	22	Nj	6.58S	110.25 E
Sematan	26	Ef	1.48N	109.46 E
Semau, Pulau-	26	Hi	10.13S	123.22 E
Sembakung	26	Gf	3.47N	117.30 E
Sembé	36	Bb	1.39N	14.36 E
Semberija	14	Nf	44.45N	19.10 E
Sembuan	26	Gg	0.19S	115.30 E
Semenicului, Munţii-	15	Fd	45.05N	22.05 E
Semenov	7	Kh	56.49N	44.29 E
Semenovka	16	Hc	52.11N	32.40 E
Semeru, Gunung-	21	Nj	7.58S	113.35 E
Semichi Islands	40a	Db	52.42N	174.00 E
Semidi Islands	40	He	56.07N	156.44W
Semiluki	19	De	51.43N	39.02 E
Semily	10	Lf	50.36N	15.20 E
Seminoe Reservoir	46	Le	42.00N	106.50W
Seminole [Ok.-U.S.]	45	Hi	35.14N	96.14W
Seminole [Tx.-U.S.]	45	Ej	32.43N	102.39W
Seminole, Lake-	43	Ke	30.46N	84.50W
Semipalatinsk	22	Kd	50.28N	80.13 E
Semipalatinskaja Oblast [3]	19	If	48.30N	80.10 E
Semirara Islands	26	Hd	11.57N	121.27 E
Semīrom	24	Ng	31.22N	51.47 E
Semisopochnoi	40a	Cb	52.00N	179.35 E
Semitau	26	Ff	0.33N	111.58 E
Semiun, Pulau-	26	Ef	4.31N	107.44 E
Semizbugy	19	He	50.12N	74.48 E
Semliki	30	Kh	1.14N	30.28 E
Semmering	14	Jc	47.38N	15.49 E
Semnām [3]	23	Hb	35.00N	53.30 E
Semnān	22	Hf	35.33N	53.24 E
Semnon	11	Eg	47.54N	1.45W
Semois	11	Ke	49.53N	4.45 E
Šemonaiha	19	Ie	50.39N	81.54 E
Semporna	26	Gf	4.28N	118.36 E
Semuda	26	Fg	2.51S	112.58 E
Semur-en-Auxois	11	Kg	47.29N	4.20 E
Sên	25	Kf	12.32N	104.28 E
Senador Mourão	55	Kc	17.51S	43.22W
Senador Pompeu	54	Ke	5.35S	39.22W
Senaja	26	Ge	6.45N	117.03 E
Sena Madureira	54	Ee	9.04S	68.40W
Senanga	36	Df	16.07S	23.16 E
Senarpont	12	De	49.53N	1.43 E
Senatobia	45	Li	34.39N	89.58W
Sendai [Jap.]	28	Ki	31.49N	130.18 E
Sendai [Jap.]	22	Qf	38.15N	140.53 E
Sendai-Gawa [Jap.]	29	Bf	31.51N	130.12 E
Sendai-Gawa [Jap.]	29	Dd	35.34N	134.11 E
Sendai-Wan	28	Pe	38.10N	141.15 E
Senden	12	Jc	51.51N	7.30 E
Sendenhorst	12	Jc	51.50N	7.50 E
Senderg	24	Qi	26.52N	57.37 E
Seneca	45	Hg	39.50N	96.04W
Seneca Lake	44	Id	42.40N	76.57W
Sénégal=Senegal (EN)	30	Fg	15.48N	16.32W
Sénégal=Senegal (EN) [1]	31	Fg	14.00N	14.00W
Senegal (EN)=Sénégal [1]	31	Fg	14.00N	14.00W
Senegal (EN)=Sénégal	30	Fg	15.48N	16.32W
Sénégal Oriental [3]	34	Cc	13.30N	13.00W
Senekal	37	De	28.30S	27.32 E
Senetosa, Punta di-	11a	Ab	41.33N	8.47 E
Seney	44	Eb	46.21N	85.56W
Senftenberg/Zły Komorow	10	Ke	51.31N	14.01 E
Sengata	22	Ni	0.28N	117.33 E
Sengilej	7	Lj	53.58N	48.46 E
Senguerr, Río-	56	Gg	45.32S	68.54W
Sengwa	37	Dc	17.05S	28.03 E
Senhor do Bonfim	53	Lg	10.27S	40.11W
Senica	10	Nh	48.41N	17.23 E
Senigallia	14	Hg	43.43N	13.13 E
Senirkent	24	Dc	38.07N	30.33 E
Senj	14	If	45.00N	14.54 E
Senja	5	Hb	69.20N	17.30 E
Senjsko Bilo	14	Jf	44.55N	15.03 E
Senkaku-Shotō	27	Lf	25.45N	124.00 E
Şenkaya	24	Jb	40.35N	42.21 E
Senkevičevka	10	Vf	50.29N	25.05 E
Šenkursk	19	Ec	62.08N	42.53 E
Senlin Shan	28	Kc	43.12N	130.38 E
Senlis	11	Ie	49.12N	2.35 E
Senmonorom	25	Lf	12.27N	107.12 E
Senn, Dahr Ou-	32	Ef	17.55N	11.00W
Sennestadt, Bielefeld-	12	Kc	51.57N	8.35 E
Senneterre	42	Jg	48.24N	77.14W
Senno	7	Gi	54.47N	29.41 E
Sennoj	16	Oc	52.07N	46.59 E
Senorbì	14	Dk	39.32N	9.08 E
Senqu	37	Be	28.38S	16.27 E
Sens	11	Jf	48.12N	3.17 E
Sensée	12	Fd	50.16N	3.06 E
Sensuntepeque	49	Cg	13.52N	88.38W
Senta	15	Dd	45.56N	20.05 E
Sentinel Peak	42	Ff	54.58N	122.00W
Sentinel Range	66	Pf	78.10S	85.30W
Senyavin Islands	57	Gd	6.55N	158.00 E
Şenyurt	24	Id	37.06N	40.40 E
Senzaki-Wan	29	Bd	34.25N	131.20 E
Senžarka	17	Mi	54.45N	67.50 E
Seo de Urgel/La Seu d'Urgell	13	Nb	42.21N	1.28 E
Seoni	25	Fd	22.05N	79.32 E
Seoul (EN)=Sŏul	22	Of	37.34N	127.00 E
Séoune	11	Gj	44.10N	0.41 E
Sepanjang, Pulau-	26	Gh	7.10S	115.50 E
Separation Point	62	Ed	40.47S	173.00 E
Sepetovka	19	Ce	50.12N	27.04 E
Sepik River	57	Fe	3.51S	144.34 E
Sępólno Krajeńskie	10	Nc	53.28N	17.32 E
Sępopol	10	Qb	54.15N	21.00 E
Sępopolska, Nizina-	10	Rb	54.15N	21.10 E
Septemvri	15	Hg	42.13N	24.06 E
Septentrional, Cordillera-	49	Ld	19.35N	70.45W
Septeuil	12	Df	48.54N	1.41 E
Sept-Iles	39	Md	50.12N	66.23W
Sepúlveda	13	Ic	41.18N	3.45W
Sequeros	13	Fd	40.31N	6.01W
Sequillo	13	Gc	41.45N	5.30W
Sera	29	Cd	34.36N	133.01 E
Sera, Pulau-	26	Jh	7.40S	131.05 E
Šerabad	19	Gh	37.43N	66.59 E
Šerabad	18	Ff	37.22N	67.03 E
Serafettın Dağları	24	Ic	39.05N	41.10 E
Serafimovič	16	Me	49.36N	42.47 E
Serahs	19	Gh	36.30N	61.13 E
Seraidi	14	Bn	36.55N	7.40 E
Seraing	11	Ld	50.36N	5.31 E
Seram	57	De	3.00S	129.00 E
Seram, Laut-=Ceram Sea (EN)	57	De	2.30S	128.00 E
Serang	26	Eh	6.07S	106.09 E
Serasan, Pulau-	26	Ef	2.30N	109.03 E
Serasan, Selat-	26	Ef	2.20S	109.00 E
Serbia (EN) = Srbija [2]	15	Df	44.00N	21.00 E
Serbia (EN) = Srbija	5	Ig	43.00N	21.00 E
Serbia (EN)=Srbija	15	Df	44.00N	21.00 E
Şercaia	15	Id	45.50N	25.08 E
Serchio	14	Eg	43.47N	10.16 E
Serdo	35	Gc	11.58N	41.18 E
Serdoba	16	Nc	52.34N	44.01 E
Serdobsk	19	Ee	52.29N	44.16 E
Sereba	35	Gc	13.12N	40.32 E
Serebrjansk	19	If	49.43N	83.20 E
Serebrjanski	7	Ib	68.52N	35.32 E
Sered'	10	Nh	48.17N	17.45 E
Seredka	8	Mf	58.10N	28.25 E
Şereflikoçhisar	24	Ec	38.56N	33.33 E
Serein	11	Jg	47.55N	3.31 E
Seremban	26	Df	2.43N	101.56 E
Serengeti Plain	36	Fc	2.50S	35.00 E
Serenje	36	Fe	13.14S	30.14 E
Šereševo	10	Ud	52.31N	24.19 E
Seret	16	De	48.38N	25.52 E
Serfopoúla	15	Hl	37.15N	24.36 E
Sergač	19	Ed	55.33N	45.28 E
Sergeievka	28	Lc	43.23N	133.22 E
Sergeja Kirova, Ostrova-	20	Da	77.10N	90.00 E
Sergejevka [Kaz.-U.S.S.R.]	19	Ge	53.51N	67.28 E
Sergejevka [R.S.F.S.R.]	28	Kb	44.20N	131.40 E
Sergino	22	Ic	62.30N	65.40 E
Sergipe [2]	54	Kf	10.30S	37.10W
Sergokala	16	Oh	42.30N	47.40 E
Sergozero, Ozero-	7	Ic	66.45N	36.50 E
Seria	26	Ff	4.37N	114.19 E
Serian	26	Ff	1.10N	110.34 E
Seriana, Val-	14	De	45.50N	9.50 E
Seribu, Kepulauan-	26	Fh	5.36S	106.33 E
Sérifontaine	12	De	49.21N	1.46 E
Sérifos	15	Hl	37.09N	24.30 E
Sérifos	15	Hl	37.10N	24.30 E
Serifou, Stenón-	15	Hl	37.15N	24.30 E
Serik	24	Dd	36.55N	31.06 E
Seringapatam Reef	59	Eb	13.40S	122.05 E
Serio	14	De	45.16N	9.45 E
Šerlovaja Gora	20	Gf	50.34N	116.18 E
Sermata, Kepulauan-	26	Ih	8.10S	128.40 E
Sermilik	41	Ie	66.00N	38.45W
Sernovodsk	7	Mj	53.54N	51.09 E
Sernur	7	Lh	56.57N	49.11 E
Sernyje Vody	7	Mj	53.53N	50.59 E
Sero	24	Kd	37.33N	44.40 E
Serock	10	Rd	52.31N	21.03 E
Serodino	55	Bk	32.37S	60.57W
Serov	22	Id	59.29N	60.31 E
Serowe	31	Jk	22.23S	26.43 E
Serpa	13	Eg	37.56N	7.36W
Serpent, Vallée du-	34	Dc	14.50N	8.00W
Serpentine Lakes	59	Fe	28.30S	129.10 E
Serpent's Mouth/Serpiente, Boca de la-	54	Fa	10.10N	61.58W
Serpiente, Boca de la-/ Serpent's Mouth	54	Fa	10.10N	61.58W
Serpis	13	Lf	38.59N	0.09W
Serpnevoje	15	Lc	46.23N	28.59 E
Serpuhov	6	Je	54.55N	37.25 E
Serra, Aparados da-	55	Hi	28.45S	49.45W
Serra Bonita	55	Ib	15.13S	46.49W
Serra das Araras	55	Jb	15.30S	45.21W
Serra do Navio	53	Ke	0.59N	52.03W
Serra do Salitre	55	Id	19.06S	46.41W
Serra Dourada	55	Ka	12.50S	43.56W
Sérrai	15	Gh	41.05N	23.33 E
Serralada Litoral Catalana/ Cadena Costero Catalana= Catalan Coastal Range (EN)	5	Gg	41.35N	1.40 E
Serralada Pirinenca= Pyrenees (EN)	5	Gg	42.40N	1.00 E
Serrana Bank	47	Hf	14.23N	80.12W
Serranilla Bank	47	Ie	15.50N	79.50W
Serranópolis	55	Fd	18.16S	52.00W
Serra San Bruno	14	Kl	38.35N	16.20 E
Serrat, Cap-	32	Ib	37.14N	9.13 E
Serra Talhada	54	Ke	7.59S	38.18W
Serre	11	Je	49.41N	3.23 E
Serre, Massif de la-	11	Lg	47.10N	5.35 E
Serre-Ponçon, Réservoir de-	11	Mj	44.27N	6.16 E
Serres	11	Lj	44.26N	5.43 E
Serrezuela	56	Gd	30.38S	65.23W
Serrinha	54	Kf	11.39S	39.00W
Serriola, Bocca-	14	Gg	43.31N	12.21 E
Serro	55	Kd	18.37S	43.23W
Serrota	13	Gd	40.30N	5.04W
Serrote, Rio-	55	Ee	21.27S	54.40W

Index Symbols

- [1] Independent Nation
- [2] State, Region
- [3] District, County
- [4] Municipality
- [5] Colony, Dependency
- Continent
- Physical Region
- Historical or Cultural Region
- Mount, Mountain
- Volcano
- Hill
- Mountains, Mountain Range
- Hills, Escarpment
- Plateau, Upland
- Pass, Gap
- Plain, Lowland
- Delta
- Salt Flat
- Valley, Canyon
- Crater, Cave
- Karst Features
- Depression
- Polder
- Desert, Dunes
- Forest, Woods
- Heath, Steppe
- Oasis
- Cape, Point
- Coast, Beach
- Cliff
- Peninsula
- Isthmus
- Sandbank
- Island
- Atoll
- Rock, Reef
- Islands, Archipelago
- Rocks, Reefs
- Coral Reef
- Well, Spring
- Geyser
- River, Stream
- Waterfall Rapids
- River Mouth, Estuary
- Lake
- Salt Lake
- Intermittent Lake
- Reservoir
- Swamp, Pond
- Canal
- Glacier
- Ice Shelf, Pack Ice
- Ocean
- Sea
- Gulf, Bay
- Strait, Fjord
- Lagoon
- Bank
- Seamount
- Tablemount
- Ridge
- Shelf
- Basin
- Escarpment, Sea Scarp
- Fracture
- Trench, Abyss
- National Park, Reserve
- Point of Interest
- Recreation Site
- Cave, Cavern
- Historic Site
- Ruins
- Wall, Walls
- Church, Abbey
- Temple
- Scientific Station
- Airport
- Port
- Lighthouse
- Mine
- Tunnel
- Dam, Bridge

Sersou, Plateau du- 13 Ni 35.30N 2.00 E
Sertã 13 De 39.48N 8.06W
Sertão 52 Lg 10.00S 41.00W
Sertãozinho 55 Ie 21.08S 47.59W
Sêrtar 27 He 32.20N 100.20 E
Serti 34 Hd 7.30N 11.22 E
Serua, Pulau- 26 Jh 6.18S 130.01 E
Serui 26 Kg 1.53S 136.14 E
Serule 37 Dd 21.55S 27.19 E
Sérvia 15 Ei 40.11N 22.00 E
Sêrxü 27 Ge 32.56N 98.02 E
Seryitsi 15 Ii 40.00N 25.10 E
Seryševo 20 Hf 51.02N 128.25 E
Sesayap 26 Gf 3.36N 117.15 E
Sese 36 Eb 2.11N 25.47 E
Seseganaga Lake 45 Ka 50.10N 90.15W
Sese Islands 36 Fc 0.20S 32.20 E
Sesfontein 37 Ac 19.07S 13.39 E
Sesheke 36 Df 17.29S 24.18 E
Sesia 14 Ce 45.05N 8.37 E
Sesibi 35 Ea 20.05N 30.31 E
Sesimbra 13 Cf 38.26N 9.06W
Šešma 7 Mi 55.20N 51.12 E
Sesnut 8 Be 59.42N 7.21 E
Sessa Aurunca 14 Hi 41.14N 13.56 E
Ses Salines, Cap de-/Salinas, Cabo de- 13 Pe 39.16N 3.03 E
Sestao 13 Ja 43.18N 3.00W
Sesto Fiorentino 14 Fg 43.50N 11.12 E
Sesto San Giovanni 14 De 45.32N 9.14 E
Sestriere 14 Af 44.57N 6.53 E
Sestri Levante 14 Df 44.16N 9.24 E
Sestroreck 7 Gf 60.06N 29.59 E
Šešupė 7 Fi 55.00N 22.10 E
Šešuvis 8 Ji 55.12N 22.31 E
Sesvenna, Piz- 14 Ed 46.42N 10.25 E
Sesvete 14 Ke 45.50N 16.07 E
Šeta/Šeta 8 Ki 55.14N 24.18 E
Šeta/Šeta 8 Ki 55.14N 24.18 E
Setaka 29 Be 33.09N 130.28 E
Setana 28 Oc 42.26N 139.51 E
Sète 11 Jk 43.24N 3.41 E
Sete de Setembro, Rio- 55 Fa 12.56S 52.51W
Sete Lagoas 54 Jg 19.27S 44.14W
Setenil 13 Gh 36.51N 5.11W
Sete Quedas, Saltos das-=Guaira Falls (EN) 56 Jb 24.02S 54.16W
Setermoen 7 Eb 68.52N 18.28 E
Setesdal 8 Bg 59.05N 7.35 E
Setesdalsheiane 8 Be 59.30N 7.10 E
Seti 25 Gc 28.58N 81.06 E
Sétif [3] 32 Ib 36.05N 5.00 E
Sétif 31 He 36.12N 5.24 E
Seto 29 Ed 35.13N 137.05 E
Setonaikai=Inland Sea (EN) 21 Pf 34.10N 133.00 E
Setouchi 29b Ba 28.08N 129.20 E
Šetpe 19 Fg 44.06N 52.02 E
Settat 32 Fc 33.00N 7.37W
Settat [3] 32 Fc 33.00N 7.30W
Setté Cama 36 Ac 2.32S 9.45 E
Sette-Daban, Hrebet- 20 Id 62.00N 138.00 E
Settle 9 Kg 54.04N 2.16W
Setúbal [2] 13 Df 38.20N 8.30W
Setúbal 6 Fh 38.32N 8.54W
Setúbal, Baía de- 13 Df 38.27N 8.53W
Setúbal o de Guadalupe, Laguna- 55 Bj 31.33S 60.35W
Seudre 11 Ei 45.48N 1.09W
Seugne 11 Fi 45.42N 0.32W
Seui 14 Dk 39.50N 9.19 E
Seuil-d'Argonne 12 Hf 48.58N 5.03 E
Seul, Lac- 38 Jd 50.20N 92.30W
Seulles 12 Be 49.20N 0.27W
Seurre 11 Lg 47.00N 5.09 E
Sevan 19 Eg 40.32N 44.57 E
Sevan, Lake- (EN)=Sevan, Ozero- 5 Kg 40.20N 45.20 E
Sevan, Ozero-=Sevan, Lake- (EN) 5 Kg 40.20N 45.20 E
Sévaré 34 Ec 14.32N 4.06W
Sevastopol 6 Jg 44.36N 33.32 E
Ševčenko 22 He 43.35N 51.05 E
Ševčenko, Zaliv- 18 Ca 46.30N 60.15 E
Sevenoaks 9 Nj 51.16N 0.12 E
Sever 13 Ee 39.40N 7.32W
Sévérac-le-Château 11 Jj 44.19N 3.04 E
Severn 9 Kj 51.20N 3.10W
Severn [Can.] 38 Kd 56.02N 87.36W
Severn [U.K.] 9 Kj 51.35N 2.40W
Severnaja Dvina=Northern Dvina (EN) 5 Kc 64.32N 40.30 E
Severnaja Keltma 17 Ff 61.30N 54.00 E
Severnaja Pseašho, Gora- 16 Lh 43.47N 40.30 E
Severnaja Sosva 19 Gc 64.10N 65.28 E
Severnaja Zemlja=Severnaya Zemlya (EN) 21 Lb 79.30N 98.00 E
Severnaya Zemlya (EN)=Severnaja Zemlja 21 Lb 79.30N 98.00 E
Severn Lake 42 If 53.52N 90.58W
Severnoje [R.S.F.S.R.] 16 Rb 54.05N 52.32 E
Severnoje [R.S.F.S.R.] 20 Ce 56.21N 78.23 E
Severny 19 Gb 67.38N 64.06 E
Severnyje Uvaly=Northern Uvals (EN) 5 Kd 59.30N 49.00 E
Severny Kommunar 17 Gg 58.23N 54.02 E
Severny Ledovity Okean=Arctic Ocean (EN) 67 Be 85.00N 170.00 E
Severny Ural=Northern Urals (EN) 5 Lc 62.00N 59.00 E
Severobajkalsk 20 Fe 55.40N 109.25 E
Severočeský kraj [3] 10 Kf 50.35N 14.15 E
Severodoneck 16 Ke 48.57N 38.31 E
Severodvinsk 6 Jc 64.34N 39.50 E
Severo-Jenisejski 20 Ed 60.28N 93.01 E
Severo-Kazahstanskaja Oblast [3] 19 Ge 54.30N 68.00 E
Severo-Krymski Kanal 16 Ig 45.30N 34.35 E
Severo-Kurilsk 22 Rd 50.40N 156.08 E
Severomoravský kraj [3] 10 Ng 49.45N 17.50 E
Severomorsk 19 Db 69.04N 33.24 E
Severo-Osetinskaja ASSR [3] 19 Eg 43.00N 44.10 E
Severo-Sibirskaja Nizmennost=North Siberian Plain (EN) 21 Mb 72.00N 104.00 E
Severouralsk 19 Gc 60.09N 60.01 E
Sevier 46 Ig 38.35N 112.14W
Sevier Bridge Reservoir 46 Jg 39.21N 111.57W
Sevier Desert 46 Ig 39.25N 112.50W
Sevier Lake 43 Ed 38.55N 113.09W
Sevier River 43 Ed 39.04N 113.06W
Sevilla [3] 13 Gg 37.30N 5.30W
Sevilla [Col.] 54 Cc 4.16N 75.53W
Sevilla [Sp.]=Seville (EN) 6 Fh 37.23N 5.59W
Sevilla, Isla- 49 Fi 8.14N 82.24W
Seville (EN)=Sevilla [Sp.] 6 Fh 37.23N 5.59W
Sevlijevo 15 If 43.01N 25.06 E
Sèvre Nantaise 11 Eg 47.12N 1.33W
Sèvre Niortaise 11 Eh 46.18N 1.08W
Sevron 11 Lh 46.32N 5.16 E
Sevsk 16 Ic 52.08N 34.30 E
Sewa 34 Cd 7.18N 12.08W
Seward [Ak.-U.S.] 39 Ec 60.06N 149.26W
Seward [Nb.-U.S.] 45 Hf 40.55N 97.06W
Seward Peninsula 38 Cc 65.00N 164.00W
Sewell 56 Fd 34.05S 70.21W
Seyāhkal 24 Md 37.09N 49.52 E
Seybaplaya 48 Nh 19.39N 90.40W
Seybaplaya, Punta- 48 Nh 19.45N 90.42W
Seybouse, Oued- 14 Bn 36.53N 7.46 E
Seychelles [1] 31 Mi 8.00S 55.00 E
Seychelles Islands 30 Mi 4.35S 55.40 E
Seydān 24 Og 30.01N 53.01 E
Seydişehir 24 Dd 37.25N 31.51 E
Seyðisfjörður 6 Eb 65.16N 14.00W
Seyfe Gölü 24 Fc 39.13N 34.23 E
Seyf Ţāleh 24 Le 35.57N 46.19 E
Seyhan 23 Db 36.43N 34.53 E
Seyitgazi 24 Dc 39.27N 30.43 E
Seyitömer 15 Mj 39.34N 29.52 E
Seyla' 35 Gc 11.21N 43.30 E
Seymour [Austl.] 59 Jg 37.02S 145.08 E
Seymour [In.-U.S.] 44 Ef 38.58N 85.53W
Seymour [Mo.-U.S.] 45 Jh 37.09N 92.46W
Seymour [S.Afr.] 37 Df 32.33S 26.46 E
Seymour [Tx.-U.S.] 43 He 33.35N 99.16W
Sezana 14 He 45.42N 13.52 E
Sézanne 11 Jf 48.43N 3.43 E
Sfaktiria 15 Em 36.56N 21.40 E
Sfax (EN)=Şafāqis [3] 32 Jc 34.30N 10.30 E
Sfax (EN)=Şafāqis 31 Ie 34.44N 10.46 E
Sferracavallo, Capo- 14 Dk 39.43N 9.40 E
Sfîntu Gheorghe [Rom.] 15 Me 44.53N 29.26 E
Sfîntu Gheorghe [Rom.] 15 Id 45.52N 25.47 E
Sfîntu Gheorghe, Braţul- 15 Me 44.53N 29.36 E
Sfîntu Gheorghe, Ostrovul- 15 Md 45.07N 29.22 E
Sfizef 13 Li 35.14N 0.15W
's-Gravenhage/Den Haag=The Hague (EN) 6 Ge 52.06N 4.18 E
's-Gravenhage-Scheveningen 11 Kb 52.06N 4.18 E
Shaan-hsi Sheng→Shaanxi Sheng=Shensi (EN) [2] 27 Id 36.00N 109.00 E
Shaanxi Sheng (Shaan-hsi Sheng)=Shensi (EN) [2] 27 Id 36.00N 109.00 E
Shaba [2] 36 Ed 8.30S 25.00 E
Sha'bah, Wādī ash- 24 Ij 25.59N 41.55 E
Shabani 37 Ed 20.19S 30.04 E
Shabeellaha Dhexe [3] 35 He 3.00N 46.00 E
Shabellaha Hoose [3] 35 Ge 2.00N 44.40 E
Shabēlle, Webi-=Shebeli Webi (EN) 30 Lh 0.12S 42.45 E
Shabestar 24 Kc 38.11N 45.42 E
Shabunda 36 Ec 2.42S 27.20 E
Shache/Yarkant 27 Cd 38.24N 77.15 E
Shacheng→Huailai 27 Kc 40.29N 115.30 E
Shackleton Coast 66 Kg 82.00S 162.00 E
Shackleton Glacier 66 Lg 84.35S 176.15W
Shackleton Ice Shelf 66 He 66.00S 101.00 E
Shackleton Range 66 Ag 80.40S 26.00W
Shaddādī 24 Id 36.02N 40.45 E
Shādegān 24 Mg 30.40N 48.38 E
Shadwān, Jazīrat- 33 Fd 27.30N 33.55 E
Shaftesbury 9 Kk 51.01N 2.12W
Shagedu→Jungar Qi 27 Jd 39.37N 110.58 E
Shāghir Bazar 24 Id 36.52N 40.53 E
Shag Rocks 66 Rd 54.26S 36.33W
Shāh'Abbās 24 Oe 34.44N 52.10 E
Shah Alam 26 Df 3.05N 101.29 E
Shahdol 25 Gd 23.13N 81.18 E
Sha He [China] 28 Ch 33.39N 114.38 E
Sha He [China] 28 Cf 37.09N 114.46 E
Shahezhen→Linze 27 Hd 39.10N 100.21 E
Shah Jahān, Kūh-e- 24 Qd 37.02N 57.54 E
Shahjahānpur 25 Fc 27.53N 79.55 E
Shah Kūh 23 Hb 36.35N 54.31 E
Shahmīrzād 24 Oe 35.47N 53.20 E
Shāhpūr 24 Nh 32.50N 51.45 E
Shāhpūr 24 Nh 29.39N 51.03 E
Shahrak 24 Nd 36.14N 50.40 E
Shahr-e-Bābak 24 Pg 30.10N 55.09 E
Shahr-e Khafr 24 Oh 28.56N 53.14 E
Shahr Kord 23 Hc 32.19N 50.50 E
Shāhrūd 24 Md 37.17N 48.43 E
Shahu, Kūh-e- 24 Le 34.45N 46.30 E
Shāh Zeyd 24 Od 36.13N 52.22 E
Shā'īb al Banāt, Jabal- 30 Kf 26.59N 33.29 E
Sha'īt, Wādī- 24 Ej 24.33N 33.01 E
Shakaga-Dake 29 Be 33.11N 130.53 E
Shakawe 31 Ji 18.23S 21.51 E
Shak Bay (Denham) 59 Ce 25.55S 113.32 E
Shaker Heights 44 Ge 41.29N 81.36W
Shaki 34 Fd 8.40N 3.23 E
Shakotan-Dake 29a Bb 43.16N 140.26 E
Shakotan-Hantō 29a Bb 43.15N 140.30 E
Shakotan-Misaki 29a Bb 43.23N 140.28 E
Shaktoolik 40 Gd 64.20N 161.09W
Shāl 24 Me 35.54N 49.46 E
Shala, Lake- 35 Fd 7.29N 38.32 E
Shalamzār 24 Nf 32.02N 50.49 E
Shalānbōd 35 Ge 1.40N 44.42 E
Shaler Mountains 42 Gb 71.45N 111.00W
Shaliuhe→Gangca 27 Hd 37.30N 100.14 E
Shaluli Shan 21 Lf 30.45N 99.45 E
Shām, Bādiyat ash-=Syrian Desert (EN) 21 Ff 32.00N 40.00 E
Shām, Jabal ash- 21 Hg 23.10N 57.20 E
Shamattawa 42 Ie 55.52N 92.05W
Shambe 35 Ed 7.07N 30.46 E
Shambu 35 Fd 9.33N 37.07 E
Shamīl 24 Qi 27.30N 56.53 E
Shāmīyah 21 Ff 34.00N 39.59 E
Shammar, Jabal- 21 Gg 27.20N 41.45 E
Shamo, Lake- 35 Fd 5.50N 37.40 E
Shamokin 44 Ie 40.47N 76.34W
Shamrock 45 Fi 35.13N 100.15W
Shams 24 Pg 31.04N 55.02 E
Shamsī 35 Db 19.03N 29.54 E
Shamwa 37 Ec 17.18S 31.34 E
Shan [2] 25 Jd 22.00N 98.00 E
Shandī 31 Kg 16.42N 33.26 E
Shandian He 28 Dc 42.20N 116.20 E
Shandong Bandao=Shantung Peninsula (EN) 21 Of 37.00N 121.00 E
Shandong Sheng (Shan-tung Sheng)=Shantung (EN) [2] 27 Kd 36.00N 119.00 E
Shandūr Pass 25 Ea 36.04N 72.31 E
Shangani 37 Dc 19.42S 29.22 E
Shangani 37 Dc 18.30S 27.11 E
Shangbahe 28 Ci 30.39N 115.06 E
Shangcai 28 Ch 33.16N 114.15 E
Shangcheng 28 Ci 31.49N 115.24 E
Shangdu 27 Jc 41.31N 113.32 E
Shanggao 28 Cj 28.15N 114.55 E
Shanghai 22 Of 31.14N 121.28 E
Shanghai Shi (Shang-hai Shih) [4] 27 Le 31.14N 121.28 E
Shang-hai Shih→Shanghai Shi [4] 27 Le 31.14N 121.28 E
Shanghang 27 Kf 25.04N 116.21 E
Shanghe 28 Df 37.19N 117.09 E
Shanghekou 27 Lc 40.26N 124.51 E
Shangpaihe→Feixi 28 Di 31.42N 117.09 E
Shangqiu (Zhuji) 27 Ke 34.24N 115.37 E
Shangrao 27 Kf 28.29N 117.59 E
Shan Guan 27 Kf 27.28N 117.05 E
Shangxian 27 Ie 33.55N 109.57 E
Shangyi (Nanhaoqian) 28 Bd 41.06N 113.58 E
Shangyu (Baiguan) 28 Fi 30.01N 120.53 E
Shangzhi 27 Mb 45.13N 127.55 E
Shanhaiguan 28 Ed 40.01N 119.45 E
Shanhetun 28 Ib 44.43N 127.14 E
Shan-hsi Sheng→Shanxi Sheng=Shansi (EN) [2] 27 Jd 37.00N 112.00 E
Shanklin 12 Ad 50.37N 1.11W
Shanmatang Ding 27 Jg 24.45N 111.50 E
Shannon 41 Kc 75.20N 18.10W
Shannon 62 Fd 40.33S 175.25 E
Shannon/Aerfort na Sionainne 9 Ei 52.42N 8.57W
Shannon/An tSionainn 5 Fe 52.36N 9.41W
Shannon, Mount- 59 Ie 29.58S 141.30 E
Shannon, Mouth of the- 9 Di 52.30N 9.53W
Shanshan (Piqan) 27 Fc 42.52N 90.10 E
Shansi (EN)=Shan-hsi Sheng→Shanxi Sheng [2] 27 Jd 37.00N 112.00 E
Shansi (EN)=Shanxi Sheng (Shan-hsi Sheng) [2] 27 Jd 37.00N 112.00 E
Shansonggang 28 Ic 42.30N 126.13 E
Shanţah, Ra's- 24 Qi 26.22N 56.26 E
Shantar Islands (EN)=Šantarskije Ostrova 21 Pd 55.00N 137.36 E
Shantou 22 Ng 23.26N 116.42 E
Shantung (EN)=Shandong Sheng (Shan-tung Sheng) [2] 27 Kd 36.00N 119.00 E
Shantung (EN)=Shan-tung Sheng→Shandong Sheng [2] 27 Kd 36.00N 119.00 E
Shantung Peninsula (EN)=Shandong Bandao 21 Of 37.00N 121.00 E
Shan-tung Sheng→Shandong Sheng=Shantung (EN) [2] 27 Kd 36.00N 119.00 E
Shanxian 28 Dg 34.47N 116.05 E
Shanxi Sheng (Shan-hsi Sheng)=Shansi (EN) [2] 27 Jd 37.00N 112.00 E
Shanyin (Daiyue) 28 Be 39.30N 112.48 E
Shanyincheng 28 Be 39.27N 112.56 E
Shaoguan 22 Ng 24.57N 113.34 E
Shaoshan 27 Jf 27.55N 112.32 E
Shaowu 27 Kf 27.21N 117.29 E
Shaoxing 22 Og 30.00N 120.30 E
Shaoyang 22 Ng 27.13N 111.31 E
Shapinsay 9 Kb 59.03N 2.51W
Shaqlāwah 24 Kd 36.23N 44.18 E
Shaqq al Ju'ayfir 35 Db 15.16N 26.00 E
Shaqrā' 23 Gg 13.21N 45.42 E
Shaqū 24 Qi 27.14N 56.22 E
Sharāf 24 Jg 30.37N 43.45 E
Sharafah 35 Dc 12.04N 27.07 E
Sharafkhāneh 24 Kc 38.11N 45.29 E
Sharāh, Jibāl ash- 24 Fg 30.10N 35.30 E
Sharā 'Iwah 24 Oj 25.02N 52.14 E
Shareh 24 Kd 37.38N 44.50 E
Shari 27 Pc 43.55N 144.40 E
Shārī, Buḩayrat- 24 Ke 34.23N 44.07 E
Shari-Dake 29a Db 43.46N 144.43 E
Sharifābād [Iran] 24 Nd 36.12N 50.08 E
Sharifābād [Iran] 24 Ne 35.25N 51.47 E
Shark Bay 57 Cg 25.30S 113.30 E
Sharm ash Shaykh 33 Fd 27.50N 34.16 E
Sharon 44 Ge 41.16N 80.30W
Sharon Springs 45 Fg 38.54N 101.45W
Sharp 9 Fc 58.05N 7.05W
Sharqīyah, Aş Şaḩrā' ash-=Arabian Desert (EN) 30 Kf 28.00N 32.00 E
Sharshar, Jabal- 24 Dk 23.52N 30.20 E
Shary 23 Fd 27.15N 43.27 E
Shashe 37 Dd 21.24S 27.27 E
Shashemene 35 Fd 7.13N 38.36 E
Shashi 22 Nf 30.22N 112.11 E
Shashi 30 Jk 22.12S 29.21 E
Shasta, Mount- 38 Ge 41.20N 122.20W
Shasta Lake 43 Cc 40.50N 122.25W
Shāţī', Wādī ash- 33 Bd 27.10N 13.25 E
Shattuck 45 Gh 36.16N 99.53W
Shaunavon 42 Gg 49.40N 108.25W
Shawan 27 Ec 44.21N 85.37 E
Shawano 45 Ld 44.47N 88.36W
Shawinigan 42 Kg 46.33N 72.45W
Shawnee 43 Hd 35.20N 96.55W
Shawneetown 45 Lh 37.42N 88.08W
Shaw River 59 Dd 20.20S 119.17 E
Shāwshāw, Jabal- 24 Ci 26.03N 28.56 E
Shayang 28 Bi 30.42N 112.34 E
Shaybārā 24 Gj 25.25N 36.51 E
Shaykh Aḩmad 24 Lf 32.53N 46.26 E
Shaykh Fāris 24 Lf 32.05N 47.36 E
Shaykh Sa'd 24 Lf 32.34N 46.17 E
Shaykh 'Uthmān 23 Fg 12.52N 44.59 E
Shebar, Kowtal-e- 23 Kc 34.54N 68.14 E
Shebele, Wabe-=Shebeli Webi (EN) 30 Lh 0.12S 42.45 E
Shebeli Webi (EN)=Shabēlle, Webi- 30 Lh 0.12S 42.45 E
Shebeli Webi (EN)=Shebele, Wabe- 30 Lh 0.12S 42.45 E
Sheberghān 22 If 36.41N 65.45 E
Sheboygan 45 Me 43.46N 87.44W
Shebshi Mountains 30 Ih 8.30N 11.45 E
Shedin Peak 42 Ee 55.50N 127.00W
Sheelin, Lough-/Loch Sileann 9 Fh 53.48N 7.20W
Sheenjek 40 Kc 66.45N 144.33W
Sheep Haven/Cuan na gCaorach 9 Ff 55.10N 7.52W
Sheep Mountain 46 Hj 32.32N 114.14W
Sheep Range 46 Hh 36.45N 115.05W
's Heerenberg, Bergh- 12 Ic 51.53N 6.16 E
Sheerness 9 Nj 51.27N 0.45 E
Sheffield [Al.-U.S.] 44 Dh 34.46N 87.40W
Sheffield [Eng.-U.K.] 6 Fe 53.23N 1.30W
Sheffield [Tx.-U.S.] 45 Fk 30.43N 101.50W
Shefford 12 Bb 52.02N 0.20W
Shek Hasan 35 Fc 12.04N 35.53 E
Shek Husen 35 Gd 7.45N 40.42 E
Shelburne [N.S.-Can.] 42 Kh 43.46N 65.19W
Shelburne [Ont.-Can.] 44 Gc 44.04N 80.12W
Shelby [Mt.-U.S.] 43 Eb 48.30N 111.51W
Shelby [N.C.-U.S.] 44 Gh 35.17N 81.32W
Shelbyville [Il.-U.S.] 45 Lg 39.24N 88.48W
Shelbyville [In.-U.S.] 44 Ef 39.31N 85.47W
Shelbyville [Tn.-U.S.] 44 Dh 35.29N 86.27W
Shelbyville, Lake- 45 Lg 39.30N 88.40W
Sheldon 45 Ie 43.11N 95.51W
Sheldon Point 40 Gd 63.32N 164.52W
Shelikhov Gulf (EN)=Šelihova, Zaliv- 21 Rc 60.00N 158.00 E
Shelikof Strait 40 Ie 57.30N 155.00W
Shell 46 Ld 44.33N 107.44W
Shellbrook 42 Gf 53.13N 106.24W
Shellharbour 58 Gh 34.35S 150.52 E
Shelter Point 62 Cg 47.06S 168.13 E
Shelton 46 Dc 47.13N 123.06W
Shenandoah 45 If 40.46N 95.22W
Shenandoah Mountain 44 Hf 38.58N 79.00W
Shenandoah Valley 44 Hf 38.45N 78.45W
Shenchi 28 Be 39.05N 112.11 E
Shendam 34 Gd 8.53N 9.32 E
Shending Shan 27 Nb 46.34N 133.27 E
Shenge 34 Cd 7.55N 12.57W
Shëngjini 15 Ch 41.49N 19.35 E
Shengsi (Caiyuanzhen) 28 Gi 30.42N 122.29 E
Shengsi Liedao 27 Le 30.45N 122.40 E
Shengxian 27 Lf 29.35N 120.45 E
Shengze 28 Fi 30.55N 120.39 E
Shenjiamen→Putuo 28 Gj 29.57N 122.18 E
Shenmu 27 Jd 38.52N 110.35 E
Shenqiu (Huaidian) 27 Ke 33.27N 115.05 E
Shensi (EN)=Shaan-hsi Sheng→Shaanxi Sheng [2] 27 Id 36.00N 109.00 E
Shensi (EN)=Shaanxi Sheng (Shaan-hsi Sheng) [2] 27 Id 36.00N 109.00 E
Shenton, Mount- 59 Ee 28.00S 123.22 E
Shenxian 28 Ce 38.01N 115.33 E
Shenyang (Mukden) 22 Oe 41.48N 123.24 E
Shenze 28 Ce 38.11N 115.11 E
Shepherd, Iles-=Shepherd Islands (EN) 63b Dc 16.55S 168.35 E
Shepherd Islands (EN)=Shepherd, Iles- 63b Dc 16.55S 168.35 E
Shepparton 58 Fh 36.23S 145.25 E
Sheppey 9 Nj 51.24N 0.50 E
Shepshed 12 Ab 52.45N 1.17W
Sheqi 28 Bh 33.04N 112.56 E
Sherard, Cape- 42 Jb 74.36N 80.10W
Sherard Osborn Fjord 41 Gb 82.10N 51.30W
Sherborne 9 Kk 50.57N 2.31W
Sherbro Island 30 Fh 7.33N 12.42W
Sherbrooke 39 Le 45.24N 71.54W
Sherda 35 Ba 20.08N 16.45 E
Shere Hill 34 Gd 9.57N 9.03 E
Sheridan [Mt.-U.S.] 46 Id 45.27N 112.12W
Sheridan [Wy.-U.S.] 39 Ie 44.48N 106.58W
Sheridan Lake 45 Eg 38.30N 102.15W
Sheringham 9 Oi 52.57N 1.12 E
Sherman 43 He 33.38N 96.36W
Sherman Station 44 Mc 45.54N 68.26W
Sherridon 42 He 55.07N 101.05W
's-Hertogenbosch/Den Bosch 11 Lc 51.41N 5.19 E
Sherwood Forest 9 Lh 53.10N 1.10W
She Shui 28 Ci 30.52N 114.22 E
Shetland [3] 9 La 60.30N 1.30W
Shetland Islands (Zetland) 5 Fc 60.30N 1.30W
Shewa [3] 35 Fd 9.20N 38.55 E
Shewa Gimira 35 Fd 7.00N 35.50 E
Shexian 28 Bf 36.33N 113.40 E
Shexian (Huicheng) 28 Ej 29.53N 118.27 E
Sheyang (Hede) 28 Fh 33.47N 120.15 E
Sheyenne River 43 Hb 47.05N 96.50W
Shiant Islands 9 Gd 57.54N 6.30W
Shibām 35 Hb 15.56N 48.38 E
Shibamīnah, Wādī- 23 Ie 22.12N 55.30 E
Shibata [Jap.] 28 Of 37.57N 139.20 E
Shibata [Jap.] 29 Gb 38.05N 140.50 E
Shibayama-Gata 29 Ec 36.21N 136.23 E
Shibazhan 27 Ma 42.28N 125.20 E
Shibecha 28 Rc 43.17N 144.36 E
Shibetsu [Jap.] 28 Rc 43.40N 145.08 E
Shibetsu [Jap.] 27 Pc 44.10N 142.23 E
Shibetsu-Gawa 29a Db 43.40N 145.06 E
Shibīn al Kawm 33 Fc 30.33N 31.01 E
Shibiutan 29a Ca 44.42N 142.35 E
Shibi-Zan 29 Bf 31.59N 130.22 E
Shīb Kūh 23 Hd 27.20N 52.40 E
Shibukawa 28 Of 36.29N 139.00 E
Shibushi 29 Bf 31.28N 131.07 E
Shibushi-Wan 28 Ki 31.25N 131.12 E
Shichinohe 29 Ga 40.41N 141.10 E
Shichiyo Islands 64d Bb 7.23N 151.40 E
Shidao 27 Ld 36.51N 122.18 E
Shido 29 Dd 34.19N 134.10 E
Shidongsi→Gaolan 27 Hd 36.23N 103.55 E
Shiel, Loch- 9 He 56.50N 5.50W
Shiga Ken [2] 28 Ng 35.15N 136.10 E
Shigu 27 Gf 26.54N 99.44 E
Shi He 28 Ch 32.32N 115.52 E
Shihezi 27 Ec 44.18N 86.02 E
Shiiba 29 Be 32.28N 131.09 E
Shijaku 15 Ch 41.20N 19.34 E
Shijiazhuang 22 Nf 38.00N 114.30 E
Shijiusuo 28 Eg 35.24N 119.32 E
Shika 29 Ec 37.01N 136.46 E
Shikabe 29a Bb 42.02N 140.47 E
Shikārpur 25 Dc 27.57N 68.38 E
Shiki Islands 64d Bb 7.24N 151.53 E
Shikine-Jima 29 Fd 34.19N 139.13 E
Shikoku 21 Pf 33.30N 133.30 E
Shikoku Basin (EN) 27 Oe 30.00N 135.30 E
Shikoku-Sanchi 29 Ce 33.45N 133.35 E
Shikotsu-Ko 28 Pc 42.45N 141.20 E
Shilabo 35 Gd 6.05N 44.45 E
Shiliu→Changjiang 27 Ih 19.20N 109.03 E
Shilla 25 Fb 32.24N 78.12 E
Shillong 22 Lg 25.34N 91.53 E
Shimabara 28 Kh 32.47N 130.22 E
Shimabara-Hantō 29 Be 32.45N 130.15 E
Shimabara-Wan 29 Be 32.50N 130.30 E
Shimada 29 Fd 34.49N 138.09 E
Shima-Hantō 29 Ed 34.25N 136.45 E
Shimane-Hantō 29 Cd 35.30N 133.00 E
Shimane Ken [2] 28 Lg 35.00N 132.20 E
Shimanto-Gawa 29 Ce 32.56N 133.00 E
Shimaura-Tō 29 Bd 34.50N 131.50 E
Shimian 27 Hf 29.10N 102.26 E
Shimizu [Jap.] 29a Cb 43.01N 142.51 E
Shimizu [Jap.] 29 Og 35.01N 138.29 E
Shimizu-Tōge 29 Fc 36.53N 138.55 E
Shimoda 28 Og 34.40N 138.57 E
Shimodate 29 Fc 36.19N 139.58 E
Shimoga 22 Jh 13.55N 75.34 E
Shimo-Jima 29 Be 32.25N 130.05 E
Shimokawa 29a Ca 44.18N 142.38 E
Shimokita-Hantō 29a Bc 41.15N 141.05 E
Shimo-Koshiki-Jima 29 Af 31.40N 129.40 E
Shimo la Tewa 36 Gc 3.57S 39.44 E
Shimoni 36 Gc 4.39S 39.23 E
Shimonoseki 27 Ne 33.57N 130.57 E
Shimono-Shima 29 Ad 34.15N 129.15 E
Shimotsu 29 Dd 34.07N 135.08 E
Shimotsuma 29 Fc 36.11N 139.58 E
Shin, Loch- 9 Ic 58.07N 4.32W
Shinano 29 Fc 36.47N 138.10 E
Shinano-Gawa 29 Fc 37.57N 139.04 E
Shināş 24 Qj 24.43N 56.27 E
Shindand 23 Jc 33.18N 62.08 E
Shinga 36 Dc 3.16S 24.38 E
Shingbwiyang 25 Jc 26.41N 96.13 E
Shingū 27 Oe 33.44N 135.59 E
Shingwidzi 37 Ed 23.01S 30.43 E
Shinji 29 Cd 35.24N 132.54 E
Shinji-Ko 28 Lg 35.27N 133.02 E
Shinjō 27 Pd 38.46N 140.18 E
Shinkafe 34 Gc 13.05N 6.31 E
Shinminato 29 Ec 36.47N 137.04 E
Shinnanyō 29 Bd 34.05N 131.45 E
Shinshiro 29 Ed 34.53N 137.30 E
Shintoku 28 Qc 43.12N 142.55 E
Shintotsugawa 29a Bb 43.32N 141.40 E
Shinyanga 31 Ki 3.40S 33.26 E
Shinyanga [3] 36 Fc 3.30S 33.00 E
Shiogama 29 Gb 38.19N 141.01 E
Shiojiri 28 Nf 36.06N 137.58 E
Shiokubi-Misaki 29a Bc 41.43N 140.57 E
Shio-no-Misaki 27 Oe 33.25N 135.45 E
Shipai→Huaining 28 Di 30.25N 116.39 E

Index Symbols

[1] Independent Nation
[2] State, Region
[3] District, County
[4] Municipality
[5] Colony, Dependency
Continent
Physical Region
Historical or Cultural Region
Mount, Mountain
Volcano
Hill
Mountains, Mountain Range
Hills, Escarpment
Plateau, Upland
Pass, Gap
Plain, Lowland
Delta
Salt Flat
Valley, Canyon
Crater, Cave
Karst Features
Depression
Polder
Desert, Dunes
Forest, Woods
Heath, Steppe
Oasis
Cape, Point
Coast, Beach
Cliff
Peninsula
Isthmus
Sandbank
Island
Atoll
Rock, Reef
Islands, Archipelago
Rocks, Reefs
Coral Reef
Well, Spring
Geyser
River, Stream
Waterfall Rapids
River Mouth, Estuary
Lake
Salt Lake
Intermittent Lake
Reservoir
Swamp, Pond
Canal
Glacier
Ice Shelf, Pack Ice
Ocean
Sea
Gulf, Bay
Strait, Fjord
Lagoon
Bank
Seamount
Tablemount
Ridge
Shelf
Basin
Escarpment, Sea Scarp
Fracture
Trench, Abyss
National Park, Reserve
Point of Interest
Recreation Site
Cave, Cavern
Historic Site
Ruins
Wall, Walls
Church, Abbey
Temple
Scientific Station
Airport
Port
Lighthouse
Mine
Tunnel
Dam, Bridge

Name	Page	Grid	Lat.	Long.
Shiping	27	Hg	23.44N	102.28 E
Shipki La	27	Ce	31.49N	78.45 E
Shippegan	42	Lg	47.45N	64.42W
Shiprock	45	Bh	36.47N	108.41W
Shipshaw, Rivière-	44	La	48.30N	71.15W
Shipu	28	Fj	29.17N	121.57 E
Shipugi Shankou	27	Ce	31.49N	78.45 E
Shiquan	27	Ie	33.05N	108.15 E
Shiquanhe	22	Jf	32.24N	79.52 E
Shiquan He	27	Ce	32.28N	79.44 E
Shiragami Dake	29	Ga	40.30N	140.01 E
Shiragami-Misaki	28	Pd	41.25N	140.12 E
Shirahama	29	De	33.40N	135.20 E
Shirakawa [Jap.]	29	Ed	35.36N	137.12 E
Shirakawa [Jap.]	29	Ec	36.17N	136.53 E
Shirakawa [Jap.]	28	Pf	37.07N	140.13 E
Shirane-San [Jap.]	27	Od	36.48N	139.22 E
Shirane-San [Jap.]	29	Fd	35.40N	138.13 E
Shirane-San [Jap.]	29	Fc	36.38N	138.32 E
Shiranuka	28	Rc	42.57N	144.05 E
Shiraoi	28	Pc	42.31N	141.16 E
Shirase Coast	66	Mf	78.30S	156.00W
Shirataka	29	Gb	38.11N	140.06 E
Shirataki	29a	Cb	43.53N	143.09 E
Shīrāz	22	Hg	29.36N	52.32 E
Shirbīn	24	Dg	31.11N	31.32 E
Shire	30	Kj	17.42S	35.19 E
Shiren	28	Id	41.54N	126.34 E
Shiretoko-Dake	29a	Da	44.15N	145.14 E
Shiretoko-Hantō	29a	Da	44.00N	145.00 E
Shiretoko-Misaki	27	Qc	44.21N	145.20 E
Shīrgāh	24	Od	36.17N	52.54 E
Shiribetsu-Gawa	29a	Bb	42.52N	140.21 E
Shiriha-Misaki	29a	Db	42.56N	144.45 E
Shirikishinai	29a	Bc	41.48N	141.05 E
Shīrīn	24	Qi	27.10N	56.41 E
Shīrīn sū	24	Me	35.29N	48.27 E
Shiriya-Zaki	27	Pc	41.26N	141.28 E
Shīr Kūh	21	Hf	31.37N	54.04 E
Shirley Mountains	46	Le	42.15N	106.30W
Shiroishi	28	Pe	38.00N	140.37 E
Shirone	29	Fc	37.46N	139.00 E
Shirotori	29	Ed	35.53N	136.52 E
Shirouma-Dake	29	Ec	36.45N	137.46 E
Shirshov Ridge (EN)	20	Me	57.30N	171.00 E
Shīrvān	24	Lf	33.33N	46.49 E
Shirwan Mazīn	24	Kd	37.03N	44.10 E
Shishaldin Volcano	38	Cd	54.45N	163.57W
Shishi-Jima	29	Be	32.17N	130.15 E
Shishmaref	40	Fc	66.14N	166.09W
Shishou	27	Jf	29.42N	112.23 E
Shitai (Qili)	28	Di	30.12N	117.28 E
Shitara	29	Ed	35.05N	137.34 E
Shitou Shan	27	Ma	51.02N	125.12 E
Shivwits Plateau	46	Ih	36.10N	113.40W
Shiwa	28	Pe	39.33N	141.35 E
Shiwan Dashan	27	Ig	21.45N	107.35 E
Shiwa Ngandu	36	Fe	11.12S	31.43 E
Shiwpuri	25	Fc	25.26N	77.39 E
Shixian	28	Jc	43.05N	129.46 E
Shiyan	27	Je	32.34N	110.48 E
Shiyang He	27	Hd	39.00N	103.25 E
Shizilu → Junan	28	Eg	35.10N	118.50 E
Shizugawa	29	Gb	38.40N	141.28 E
Shizui	28	Ic	43.03N	126.09 E
Shizuishan (Dawukou)	27	Id	39.03N	106.24 E
Shizukuishi	29	Gb	39.42N	140.59 E
Shizunai	28	Qc	42.20N	142.22 E
Shizunai-Gawa	29a	Cb	42.20N	142.22 E
Shizuoka	22	Pf	34.58N	138.23 E
Shizuoka Ken [2]	28	Og	35.00N	138.25 E
Shkodra	6	Hg	42.05N	19.30 E
Shkodrës, Liqen i-=Scutari, Lake- (EN)	5	Hg	42.10N	19.20 E
Shkumbini	15	Ch	41.01N	19.26 E
Shoal Lake	45	Fa	50.26N	100.34W
Shoal Lake	45	Ib	49.32N	95.00W
Shoal Lakes	45	Ha	50.20N	97.40W
Shōbara	28	Lg	34.51N	133.01 E
Shodo-Shima	29	Dd	34.30N	134.15 E
Shō-Gawa	29	Ec	36.47N	137.04 E
Shokanbetsu-Dake	29a	Bb	43.43N	141.31 E
Shokotsu-Gawa	29a	Ca	44.23N	143.17 E
Sholāpur	22	Jh	17.41N	75.55 E
Shoqān	24	Qd	37.20N	56.58 E
Shoranūr	25	Ff	10.46N	76.17 E
Shoreham-by-Sea	9	Mk	50.49N	0.16W
Shortland Islands	60	Fi	6.55S	155.53 E
Shosambetsu	29a	Ba	44.32N	141.46 E
Shoshone	46	He	42.56N	114.24W
Shoshone Mountains	43	Dd	39.15N	117.25W
Shoshone Peak	46	Gh	36.56N	116.16W
Shoshone River	46	Kd	44.52N	108.11W
Shoshong	37	Dd	23.02S	26.31 E
Shoshoni	46	Ke	43.14N	108.07W
Shotor Khūn	23	Jc	34.20N	64.55 E
Shouchang	28	Ej	29.23N	119.12 E
Shouguang	28	Ef	36.53N	118.44 E
Shouxian (Shouyang)	28	Dh	32.35N	116.47 E
Shouyang → Shouxian	28	Dh	32.35N	116.47 E
Shōwa	29	Gb	39.51N	140.03 E
Show Low	46	Ji	34.15N	110.02W
Shqiperia=Albania (EN) [1]	6	Hg	41.00N	20.00 E
Shreveport	39	Jf	32.30N	93.45W
Shrewsbury	9	Ki	52.43N	2.45W
Shuangcheng	27	Mb	45.21N	126.17 E
Shuangjiang	27	Gg	23.27N	99.50 E
Shuangjiang → Tongdao	27	If	26.14N	109.45 E
Shuangliao	27	Lc	43.30N	123.30 E
Shuangyang	27	Mc	43.31N	125.28 E
Shuangyashan	22	Pe	46.37N	131.10 E
Shucheng	28	Di	31.28N	116.57 E
Shufu	27	Cd	39.27N	75.52 E
Shuguri Falls	36	Gd	8.31S	37.23 E
Shu He	28	Eg	34.07N	118.30 E
Shuicheng	27	Hf	26.34N	104.52 E
Shuiding → Huocheng	27	Dc	44.03N	80.49 E
Shuiji → Laixi	28	Ff	36.52N	120.31 E
Shuijiahu → Changfeng	28	Dh	32.29N	117.10 E
Shuikou → Jianghua	27	Jg	24.58N	111.56 E
Shuiye	28	Cf	36.08N	114.06 E
Shuizhai → Xiangcheng	28	Ch	33.27N	114.53 E
Shūl	24	Ng	30.10N	51.38 E
Shulan	27	Mc	44.26N	126.55 E
Shule	27	Cd	39.25N	76.06 E
Shule He	21	Le	40.20N	92.50 E
Shulu (Xinji)	28	Cf	37.56N	115.14 E
Shumagin Islands	40	He	55.07N	159.45W
Shumarinai-Ko	29a	Ca	44.20N	142.13 E
Shunayn, Sabkhat-	33	Dc	30.10N	21.00 E
Shungnak	40	Hc	66.53N	157.02W
Shunyi	28	Dd	40.09N	116.38 E
Shuolong	27	Ig	22.51N	106.55 E
Shuoxian	27	Jd	39.18N	112.25 E
Shūr [Iran]	24	Pi	26.59N	55.47 E
Shūr [Iran]	24	Oh	28.12N	52.09 E
Shūr [Iran]	24	Ne	35.09N	51.30 E
Shūr [Iran]	24	Oh	28.33N	53.12 E
Shūr Āb	24	Pg	31.45N	55.15 E
Shurāb	23	Ic	33.07N	55.18 E
Shūsf	23	Jc	31.48N	60.01 E
Shūsh	24	Mf	32.12N	48.17 E
Shushica	15	Ci	40.34N	19.34 E
Shūshtar	23	Gc	32.03N	48.51 E
Shuswap Lake	46	Fa	50.57N	119.15W
Shūt	24	Oe	34.44N	52.53 E
Shuwak	35	Fc	14.23N	35.52 E
Shuyang	27	Ke	34.01N	118.52 E
Shuzenji	29	Fd	34.58N	138.55 E
Shwebo	25	Jd	22.34N	95.42 E
Shwell	25	Jd	23.56N	96.17 E
Shyok	25	Fa	35.13N	75.53 E
Sia	26	Jh	6.49S	134.19 E
Siagne	11	Mk	43.32N	6.57 E
Siāh Band	23	Kc	33.25N	65.21 E
Sīah-Chashmeh	24	Kc	39.04N	44.23 E
Sīāh-Kūh	24	Oe	34.38N	52.16 E
Siak	26	Df	1.13N	102.09 E
Sialkot [Pak.]	25	Ea	35.15N	73.17 E
Sialkot [Pak.]	22	Jf	32.30N	74.31 E
Sianów	10	Mb	54.15N	16.16 E
Siantan, Pulau-	26	Ef	3.10N	106.15 E
Siargao	26	Ie	9.53N	126.02 E
Šiaškotan, Ostrov-	21	Re	48.49N	154.06 E
Siátista	15	Ei	40.16N	21.33 E
Siau, Pulau-	26	If	2.42N	125.24 E
Šiauliai/Šjauljaj	6	Id	55.53N	23.19 E
Siavonga	36	Ef	16.32S	28.43 E
Siazan	19	Eg	41.04N	49.06 E
Sibā'ī, Jabal as-	33	Fd	25.43N	34.09 E
Sibaj	19	Fe	52.42N	58.39 E
Sibari	14	Kk	39.45N	16.27 E
Sibasa	37	Ed	22.56S	30.29 E
Šibenik	14	Jg	43.44N	15.53 E
Siberimanua	26	Cg	2.09S	99.34 E
Siberut, Pulau-	21	Lj	1.20S	98.55 E
Siberut, Selat-	26	Cg	0.42S	98.35 E
Sibi	25	Dc	29.33N	67.53 E
Sibigo	26	Cf	2.51N	95.55 E
Sibillini, Monti-	14	Hh	42.55N	13.15 E
Sibircatajaha	17	Lb	69.05N	64.43 E
Sibircevo	20	Ih	44.16N	132.20 E
Sibirjakova, Ostrov-	20	Cb	72.50N	79.00 E
Sibiti	36	Bc	3.41S	13.21 E
Sibiu [2]	15	Hd	45.46N	24.12 E
Sibiu	6	If	45.48N	24.09 E
Sibolga	22	Li	1.45N	98.48 E
Sibsāgar	25	Ic	26.59N	94.38 E
Sibu	22	Ni	2.18N	111.49 E
Sibuguey Bay	26	He	7.30N	122.40 E
Sibut	31	Ih	5.44N	19.05 E
Sibutu Islands	26	Gf	4.45N	119.20 E
Sibutu Passage	26	Gf	4.56N	119.36 E
Sibuyan	26	Hd	12.25N	122.34 E
Sibuyan Sea	26	Hd	12.50N	122.40 E
Siby	34	Dc	12.22N	8.22W
Sibyllenstein	10	Ke	51.12N	14.05 E
Sicani, Monti-	14	Hm	37.40N	13.15 E
Sicasica	54	Eg	17.22S	67.45W
Si Chon	25	Jg	9.00N	99.56 E
Sichuan Pendi	21	Mf	30.01N	105.00 E
Sichuan Sheng (Ssu-ch'uan Sheng)=Szechwan (EN) [2]	27	He	30.00N	103.00 E
Sicilia [2]	14	Im	37.45N	14.15 E
Sicilia = Sicily (EN)	5	Hh	37.30N	14.00 E
Sicilia, Canale di-=Sicily, Strait of- (EN)	5	Hh	37.20N	11.20 E
Sicilia, Mar di-	14	Gn	36.30N	13.00 E
Sicily (EN) = Sicilia	5	Hh	37.30N	14.00 E
Sicily, Strait of- (EN)= Sicilia, Canale di-	5	Hh	37.20N	11.20 E
Sicily, Strait of- (EN)= Tūnis, Canal de-	5	Hh	37.20N	11.20 E
Sico Tinto, Río-	49	Ef	15.58N	84.58W
Sicuani	53	Ig	14.15S	71.15W
Šid	15	Cd	45.08N	19.14 E
Sidamo [3]	35	Fd	5.48N	38.50 E
Siddipet	25	Fe	18.06N	78.51 E
Side	24	Dd	36.46N	31.22 E
Sidéradougou	34	Ec	10.40N	4.15W
Siderno	14	Kl	38.16N	16.18 E
Siders/Sierre	14	Bd	46.17N	7.32 E
Šiderty	19	He	52.32N	74.50 E
Šiderty	19	He	51.40N	74.50 E
Sidheros, Ákra-	15	Jn	35.19N	26.19 E
Sidhirókastron	15	Gh	41.14N	23.23 E
Sīdī 'Abd ar Raḩmān	24	Cg	30.58N	28.44 E
Sidi Aïch	13	Qh	36.37N	4.41 E
Sidi-Akacha	13	Nh	36.28N	1.18 E
Sidi Ali	13	Mh	36.06N	0.25 E
Sīdī'Alī al Makkī, Ra's-	14	Em	37.11N	10.17 E
Sīdī Barrānī	33	Ec	31.36N	25.55 E
Sidi Bel Abbes [3]	32	Gc	34.45N	0.35W
Sidi Bel Abbes	32	Gb	35.12N	0.38W
Sidi Bennour	32	Fc	32.39N	8.26W
Sidi di Daoud	13	Ph	36.51N	3.52 E
Sidi Ifni	31	Ff	29.33N	10.10W
Sidi Kacem	32	Fc	34.13N	5.42W
Sidikalang	26	Cf	2.45N	98.19 E
Sidi Lakhdar	13	Mh	36.10N	0.27 E
Sīdī Zayd, Jabal-	14	En	36.29N	10.20 E
Sidlaw Hills	9	Ke	56.30N	3.00W
Sidmouth	9	Jk	50.41N	3.15W
Sidney [B.C.-Can.]	42	Fg	48.39N	123.24W
Sidney [Mt.-U.S.]	43	Gb	47.43N	104.09W
Sidney [Nb.-U.S.]	43	Gc	41.09N	102.59W
Sidney [Oh.-U.S.]	44	Ee	40.16N	84.10W
Sidney Lanier, Lake-	44	Fh	34.15N	83.57W
Sidobre	11	Ik	43.40N	2.30 E
Sidorovsk	20	Dc	66.35N	82.30 E
Sidra	10	Tc	53.33N	23.30 E
Sidra, Gulf of-(EN)=Surt, Khalīj-	30	Ie	31.30N	18.00 E
Sidrolândia	55	Ee	20.55S	54.58W
Siedlce [2]	10	Sd	52.10N	22.15 E
Siedlce	10	Sd	52.11N	22.16 E
Siedlecka, Wysoczyzna-	10	Sd	52.10N	22.15 E
Sieg [F.R.G.]	10	Df	50.45N	7.05 E
Sieg [F.R.G.]	12	Kd	50.55N	8.01 E
Siegburg	10	Df	50.48N	7.12 E
Siegen	10	Ef	50.52N	8.02 E
Siemiatycze	10	Sd	52.26N	22.53 E
Siĕmréab	25	Kf	13.22N	103.51 E
Siena	14	Fg	43.19N	11.21 E
Sieniawa	10	Sf	50.11N	22.36 E
Sienne	11	Ee	49.00N	1.34W
Sieradz	10	Oe	51.36N	18.45 E
Sieradz [2]	10	Oe	51.35N	18.45 E
Sieradzka, Niecka-	10	Oe	51.35N	18.50 E
Sierck-les-Bains	12	Ie	49.26N	6.21 E
Sierpc	10	Pd	52.52N	19.41 E
Sierra Blanca	45	Dk	31.11N	105.21W
Sierra Blanca Peak	43	Fe	33.23N	105.48W
Sierra Colorada	56	Gf	40.35S	67.48W
Sierra Leone [1]	31	Fh	8.30N	11.30W
Sierra Leone Basin (EN)	3	Di	5.00N	17.00W
Sierra Leone Rise (EN)	3	Di	5.30N	21.00W
Sierra Madre	21	Oh	16.20N	122.00 E
Sierra Mojada	47	Dc	27.17N	103.42W
Sierre/Siders	14	Bd	46.17N	7.32 E
Siete Palmas	55	Cg	25.13S	58.20W
Siete Puntas, Río-	55	Df	23.34S	57.20W
Şieu	15	Hb	47.11N	24.13 E
Sifié	34	Dd	7.59N	6.55W
Sífnos	15	Hm	37.00N	24.40 E
Sig	32	Gb	35.32N	0.11W
Siğacik Körfezi	15	Jk	38.12N	26.45 E
Sigean	11	Ik	43.02N	2.59 E
Sighetu Marmaţiei	15	Gb	47.56N	23.53 E
Sighişoara	15	Hc	46.13N	24.48 E
Sigli	26	Ce	5.23N	95.57 E
Siglufjördur	7a	Ba	66.09N	18.55W
Sigmaringen	10	Fh	48.05N	9.13 E
Signal Peak	46	Hj	33.22N	114.03W
Signy Island	66	Re	60.43S	45.38W
Signy-l'Abbaye	12	Ge	49.42N	4.25 E
Signy-le-Petit	12	Ge	49.54N	4.17 E
Sigtuna	7	Dg	59.37N	17.43 E
Siguanea, Ensenada de la-	49	Fc	21.38N	83.05W
Siguatepeque	49	Df	14.32N	87.49W
Sigüenza	13	Jc	41.04N	2.38W
Siguiri	31	Gg	11.25N	9.10W
Sigulda	7	Fh	57.09N	24.53 E
Si He	28	Dg	35.11N	116.42 E
Sihong	28	Eh	33.28N	118.13 E
Sihote-Alin	21	Pe	48.00N	138.00 E
Sihou → Changdao	28	Ff	37.56N	120.42 E
Sihuas	54	Ce	8.34S	77.37W
Siikainen	8	Ic	61.52N	21.50 E
Siilinjärvi	7	Ge	63.02N	27.40 E
Siirt	23	Fb	37.56N	41.57 E
Sijunjung	26	Dg	0.42S	100.58 E
Sikaiana	63a	Fc	8.22S	162.45 E
Sikakap	26	Dg	2.46S	100.13 E
Sikanni Chief	42	Fe	58.17N	121.46W
Sīkar	25	Fc	27.37N	75.09 E
Sikasso	31	Gg	11.20N	5.40W
Sikasso [3]	34	Dc	10.55N	7.00W
Sikéa [Grc.]	15	Fm	36.46N	22.56 E
Sikéa [Grc.]	15	Gi	40.03N	23.58 E
Sikeston	43	Jd	36.53N	89.35W
Síkinos	15	Im	36.50N	25.05 E
Sikkim [3]	25	Hc	27.50N	88.30 E
Siklós	10	Ok	45.51N	18.18 E
Sikonge	36	Fd	5.38S	32.46 E
Šikotan, Ostrov/Tō, Shikotan-	20	Jh	43.47N	146.45 E
Siktjah	20	Hc	69.55N	125.10 E
Sil	13	Eb	42.27N	7.43W
Sila Grande	14	Kk	39.20N	16.30 E
Sila Greca	14	Kk	39.30N	16.30 E
Šilale/Šilalė	7	Fi	55.29N	22.12 E
Šilalė/Šilale	7	Fi	55.29N	22.12 E
Silao	48	Ig	20.56N	101.26W
Silaogou	28	Be	39.59N	113.03 E
Sila Piccola	14	Kk	39.05N	16.35 E
Silba	14	If	44.23N	14.42 E
Silchar	25	Id	24.49N	92.48 E
Šilda	16	Ud	51.47N	59.50 E
Sildagapet	8	Ab	62.05N	5.10 E
Sile	14	Ge	45.28N	12.35 E
Şile	24	Cb	41.05N	29.35 E
Šilega	19	Ec	64.03N	44.02 E
Silesia (EN)=Śląsk	10	Me	51.00N	16.45 E
Silesia (EN)=Śląsk	5	He	51.00N	16.45 E
Silet	32	He	22.39N	4.35 E
Silhouette Island	37b	Ca	4.29S	55.14 E
Silifke	23	Db	36.22N	33.56 E
Siligir	20	Gc	68.27N	114.50 E
Silīguri	22	Kg	26.42N	88.26 E
Siling Co	21	Kf	31.50N	89.00 E
Siling Jiao	27	Ke	8.20N	115.27 E
Silisili, Mauga-	65c	Aa	13.35S	172.27W
Silistra [2]	15	Kf	44.07N	27.16 E
Silistra	15	Ke	44.07N	27.16 E
Silivri	24	Cb	41.04N	28.15 E
Siljan	7	Df	60.50N	14.45 E
Šilka	20	Gf	51.51N	116.02 E
Šilka	21	Od	53.22N	121.32 E
Silkeborg	7	Bh	56.10N	9.34 E
Sillamäe/Sillamjae	7	Gg	59.24N	27.43 E
Sillamjae/Sillamäe	7	Gg	59.24N	27.43 E
Sillaro	14	Ff	44.34N	11.51 E
Silleiro, Cabo-	13	Db	42.07N	8.54W
Sillé-le-Guillaume	11	Ff	48.12N	0.08W
Sillian	14	Gd	46.45N	12.25 E
Sillil	35	Gc	11.00N	43.26 E
Siloam Springs	45	Ih	36.11N	94.32W
Siloana Plains	36	Df	17.15S	23.10 E
Šilovo	19	Ee	54.24N	40.52 E
Silsbee	45	Ik	30.21N	94.11W
Siltou	35	Bb	16.52N	15.43 E
Šilutė/Šilute	19	Cd	55.21N	21.30 E
Šilute/Šilutė	19	Cd	55.21N	21.30 E
Silvan	24	Ic	38.08N	41.01 E
Silvassa	25	Ed	20.20N	73.05 E
Silver Bank (EN)	49	Mc	20.30N	69.45W
Silver Bay	43	Ib	47.17N	91.16W
Silver City	43	Fe	32.46N	108.17W
Silverdalen	8	Fg	57.32N	15.44 E
Silver Lake	46	Ee	43.06N	120.53W
Silver Spring	44	If	39.02N	77.03W
Silver Springs	46	Fg	39.25N	119.13W
Silverthrone Mountain	46	Ba	51.31N	126.06W
Silverton [Co.-U.S.]	45	Ch	37.49N	107.40W
Silverton [Tx.-U.S.]	45	Fi	34.28N	101.19W
Silves [Braz.]	54	Gd	2.54S	58.27W
Silves [Port.]	13	Dg	37.11N	8.26W
Silvi	14	Ih	42.34N	14.06 E
Silvia	54	Cc	2.37N	76.24W
Silviers River	46	Fe	43.22N	118.48W
Silvretta	14	Ed	46.50N	10.15 E
Silyānah [3]	32	Ib	36.00N	9.30 E
Silyānah	32	Ib	36.05N	9.22 E
Silyānah, Wādī-	14	Dn	36.33N	9.25 E
Sim	17	Hi	54.59N	57.41 E
Sim	17	Hi	54.32N	56.30 E
Sim, Cap-	32	Fc	31.23N	9.51W
Simanggang	26	Ff	1.15N	111.26 E
Šimanovsk	20	Hf	52.01N	127.36 E
Simao	27	Hg	22.40N	101.02 E
Simard, Lac-	44	Hb	47.38N	78.40W
Sīmareh	24	Mf	32.08N	48.03 E
Simav	23	Ca	40.23N	28.31 E
Simav	24	Cc	39.05N	28.59 E
Simav Dağ	15	Lj	39.04N	28.54 E
Simav Gölü	15	Lj	39.09N	28.55 E
Simayama-Jima	29	Ae	32.40N	128.38 E
Simba	36	Db	0.36N	22.55 E
Simbo	36	Fc	4.53S	29.44 E
Simbo	63a	Cc	8.18S	156.34 E
Simbruini, Monti-	14	Hj	41.55N	13.15 E
Simcoe	44	Gd	42.50N	80.18W
Simcoe, Lake -	42	Jh	44.27N	79.20W
Simen	35	Fc	13.25N	38.00 E
Simenti	34	Cc	13.00N	13.25W
Simeria	15	Gd	45.51N	23.01 E
Simeto	14	Jm	37.24N	15.06 E
Simeulue, Pulau-	21	Li	2.35N	96.05 E
Simferopol	6	Jf	44.57N	34.06 E
Simhah, Jabal-	23	Hf	17.20N	54.50 E
Simi	15	Km	36.36N	27.50 E
Simi	15	Km	36.35N	27.50 E
Simití	49	Kj	7.58N	73.58W
Simitli	15	Gh	41.53N	23.06 E
Simla	22	Jf	31.06N	77.10 E
Şimleu Silvaniei	15	Fb	47.14N	22.48 E
Simmental	14	Bd	46.35N	7.25 E
Simmerath	12	Id	50.36N	6.18 E
Simmerbach	12	Je	49.48N	7.31 E
Simmern	10	Dg	49.59N	7.31 E
Simmertal	12	Je	49.48N	7.33 E
Simnas	8	Jj	54.20N	23.45 E
Simo	7	Fd	65.39N	24.55 E
Simojärvi	7	Gc	66.06N	27.03 E
Simojoki	7	Fd	65.37N	25.03 E
Simojovel de Allende	48	Mi	17.12N	92.38W
Simonstown	37	Bf	34.14S	18.26 E
Simpele	7	Gf	61.26N	29.22 E
Simpelejärvi	8	Mc	61.30N	29.25 E
Simplon	14	Bd	46.15N	8.00 E
Simpson Desert	57	Eg	25.00S	137.00 E
Simpson Hill	59	Fe	26.30S	126.30 E
Simpson Peninsula	42	Ic	68.45N	89.10W
Simrishamn	7	Di	55.33N	14.20 E
Simsonbaai	51b	Ab	18.02N	63.08W
Simušir, Ostrov-	21	Re	46.58N	152.02 E
Sina	25	Fe	17.22N	75.54 E
Sīnā'=Sinai Peninsula (EN)	30	Kf	29.30N	34.00 E
Sinabang	26	Cf	2.29N	96.23 E
Sinaḍaqo	35	Hd	5.22N	46.22 E
Sinai, Mount- (EN)=Mūsa, Jabal-	24	Eh	28.32N	33.59 E
Sinaia	15	Id	45.21N	25.33 E
Sinai Peninsula (EN)= Sīnā'	30	Kf	29.30N	34.00 E
Sinajana	64c	Bb	13.28N	144.45W
Sinaloa [2]	47	Cc	25.00N	107.30W
Sinaloa, Llanos de-	47	Cc	25.00N	107.30W
Sinaloa, Río-	48	Ee	25.18N	108.30W
Sinaloa de Leyva	48	Ee	25.50N	108.14W
Sinalunga	14	Fg	43.12N	11.44 E
Sinamaica	54	Da	11.05N	71.51W
Sinan	27	If	27.56N	108.11 E
Sinara	17	Kh	56.17N	62.23 E
Sīnāwin	33	Bc	31.02N	10.36 E
Sinazongwe	36	Ef	17.15S	27.28 E
Şincai	15	Hc	46.39N	24.23 E
Sincanli	24	Dc	38.45N	30.15 E
Sincé	49	Ji	9.14N	75.06W
Sincelejo	53	Ie	9.18N	75.24W
Sinch'am	28	Jc	42.07N	129.25 E
Sinch'ang	28	Jd	40.07N	128.28 E
Sinch'on	28	He	38.28N	125.27 E
Sinclair, Lake-	44	Fi	33.11N	83.16W
Sind [3]	25	Cc	25.30N	69.00 E
Sind	21	Ig	25.30N	69.00 E
Sindal	8	Dg	57.28N	10.13 E
Sindangbarang	26	Eh	7.27S	107.08 E
Sindara	36	Bc	1.02S	10.40 E
Sindelfingen-Böblingen	10	Fh	48.41N	9.01 E
Sindfeld	12	Kc	51.32N	8.48 E
Sindi	7	Fg	58.24N	24.42 E
Sındırgı	24	Cc	39.14N	28.10 E
Sindirgi Geçidi	15	Lj	39.10N	28.04 E
Sîndominic	15	Ic	46.35N	25.47 E
Sindri	25	Hd	23.42N	86.29 E
Sinegorje	20	Kd	62.03N	150.25 E
Sinegorski	16	Le	48.00N	40.53 E
Šine-Ider	27	Gb	48.56N	99.33 E
Sinekli	15	Lh	41.14N	28.12 E
Sinelnikovo	16	Ie	48.18N	35.31 E
Sines	13	Dg	37.57N	8.52W
Sines, Cabo de-	13	Dg	37.57N	8.53W
Sine-Saloum [3]	34	Bc	14.00N	15.50W
Singako	35	Bd	9.50N	19.29 E
Singapore / Singapura	22	Mi	1.17N	103.51 E
Singapore Strait (EN)= Singapura, Selat-	26	Df	1.15N	104.00 E
Singapura / Singapore	22	Mi	1.17N	103.51 E
Singapura, Selat-= Singapore Strait (EN)	26	Df	1.15N	104.00 E
Singaraja	26	Gh	8.07S	115.06 E
Singatoka	63d	Ac	18.08S	177.30 E
Sing Buri	25	Kf	14.53N	100.25 E
Singen	10	Ei	47.46N	8.50 E
Sîngeroz Băi	15	Hb	47.22N	24.41 E
Singida [3]	36	Fd	5.30S	34.30 E
Singida	31	Ki	4.49S	34.45 E
Singitic Gulf (EN) = Singitikós Kólpos	15	Gi	40.10N	23.55 E
Singitikós Kólpos = Singitic Gulf (EN)	15	Gi	40.10N	23.55 E
Singkaling Hkamti	25	Jc	26.00N	95.42 E
Singkang	26	Hg	4.08S	120.01 E
Singkawang	26	Ef	0.54N	109.00 E
Singkep, Pulau-	26	Dg	0.30S	104.25 E
Singkil	26	Cf	2.17N	97.49 E
Singleton [Austl.]	59	Kf	32.34S	151.10 E
Singleton [Eng.-U.K.]	12	Bd	50.55N	0.44W
Singleton, Mount-	59	De	29.28S	117.18 E
Singö	8	Hd	60.10N	18.45 E
Siniscola	14	Dj	40.34N	9.41 E
Sini vrăh	15	Ih	41.51N	25.01 E
Sinj	14	Kg	43.42N	16.38 E
Sinjah	35	Ec	13.09N	33.56 E
Sinjai	26	Hh	5.07S	120.15 E
Sinjaja	8	Mg	57.05N	28.33 E
Sinjajevina	15	Cf	43.00N	19.18 E
Sinjār	24	Id	36.19N	41.52 E
Sinjār, Jabal-	24	Id	36.23N	41.52 E
Sinjuža	16	Ge	48.03N	30.50 E
Sinkiang (EN)= Hsin-chiang-wei-wu-erh Tzu-chih-ch'ü → Xinjiang Uygur Zizhiqu [2]	27	Ec	42.00N	86.00 E
Sinkiang (EN)= Xinjiang Uygur Zizhiqu (Hsin-chiang-wei-wu-erh Tzu-chih-ch'ü) [2]	27	Ec	42.00N	86.00 E
Sin-le-Noble	12	Fd	50.22N	3.07 E
Sinmi-Do	28	He	39.33N	124.53 E
Sinn	12	Kd	50.39N	8.20 E
Sinn al Kadhdhāb	33	Fe	23.30N	32.05 E
Sinnamary	54	Hb	5.23N	53.00W
Sinni	14	Kj	40.08N	16.41 E
Sînnicolau Mare	15	Dc	46.05N	20.38 E
Sinnūris	24	Dh	29.25N	30.52 E
Sinnyŏng	28	Jf	36.02N	128.47 E
Sinoe [3]	34	Dd	5.20N	8.40W
Sinoe, Lacul-	15	Le	44.38N	28.53 E
Sinoia	31	Kj	17.22S	30.12 E
Sinop	23	Ea	41.59N	35.09 E
Sinop Burun	24	Fa	42.02N	35.12 E
Sinp'o	28	Jd	40.02N	128.12 E
Sinsang	28	Ie	39.39N	127.25 E
Sinsheim	10	Eg	49.15N	8.53 E
Sint-Amandsberg, Gent-	12	Fc	51.04N	3.45 E
Sîntana	15	Ec	46.21N	21.30 E
Sint-Andries, Brugge-	12	Fc	51.12N	3.10 E
Sintang	26	Ff	0.04N	111.30 E
Sint Eustatius	47	Le	17.30N	62.59W
Sint-Gillis-Waas	12	Gc	51.13N	4.08 E
Sint Kruis	50	Bf	12.18N	69.08W
Sint Laureins	12	Fc	51.15N	3.31 E
Sint Maarten	50	Ec	18.04N	63.04W
Sint Nicolaas	50	Bf	12.26N	69.55W
Sint Niklaas/Saint-Nicolas	11	Kc	51.10N	4.08 E
Sint-Oedenrode	12	Hc	51.34N	5.28 E
Sinton	45	Hl	28.02N	97.33W
Sint-Pieters-Leeuw	12	Gd	50.47N	4.14 E
Sintra	13	Cf	38.48N	9.23W
Sint-Truiden/Saint-Trond	11	Ld	50.49N	5.12 E
Sintu	35	Fd	8.12N	36.56 E
Sinú, Río-	49	Ji	9.24N	75.49W
Sinŭiju	22	Oe	40.06N	124.24 E
Sinujīf	35	Hd	8.30N	48.59 E
Sinzig	12	Jd	50.33N	7.15 E
Sió	10	Oj	46.23N	18.40 E
Siocon	26	He	7.42N	122.08 E
Siófok	10	Oj	46.54N	18.03 E
Sioma	36	Df	16.40S	23.35 E

Index Symbols

[1] Independent Nation
[2] State, Region
[3] District, County
[4] Municipality
[5] Colony, Dependency
Continent
Physical Region
Historical or Cultural Region
Mount, Mountain
Volcano
Hill
Mountains, Mountain Range
Hills, Escarpment
Plateau, Upland
Pass, Gap
Plain, Lowland
Delta
Salt Flat
Valley, Canyon
Crater, Cave
Karst Features
Depression
Polder
Desert, Dunes
Forest, Woods
Heath, Steppe
Oasis
Cape, Point
Coast, Beach
Cliff
Peninsula
Isthmus
Sandbank
Island
Atoll
Rock, Reef
Islands, Archipelago
Rocks, Reefs
Coral Reef
Well, Spring
Geyser
River, Stream
Waterfall Rapids
River Mouth, Estuary
Lake
Salt Lake
Intermittent Lake
Reservoir
Swamp, Pond
Canal
Glacier
Ice Shelf, Pack Ice
Ocean
Sea
Gulf, Bay
Strait, Fjord
Lagoon
Bank
Seamount
Tablemount
Ridge
Shelf
Basin
Escarpment, Sea Scarp
Fracture
Trench, Abyss
National Park, Reserve
Point of Interest
Recreation Site
Cave, Cavern
Historic Site
Ruins
Wall, Walls
Church, Abbey
Temple
Scientific Station
Airport
Port
Lighthouse
Mine
Tunnel
Dam, Bridge

Sion/Sitten	14	Bd	46.15N	7.20 E
Siorapaluk	41	Ec	77.39N	71.00W
Sioule	11	Jh	46.22N	3.19 E
Sioux City	39	Je	42.30N	96.23W
Sioux Falls	39	Je	43.32N	96.44W
Sioux Lookout	42	If	50.06N	91.55W
Sipalay	26	He	9.45N	122.24 E
Šipan	14	Lh	42.43N	17.54 E
Siparia	50	Fg	10.08N	61.30W
Šipčenski prohod	15	Ig	42.46N	25.19 E
Siping	22	Oe	43.11N	124.24 E
Sipiwesk	42	He	55.27N	97.24W
Sipiwesk Lake	42	He	55.05N	97.35W
Siple, Mount-	66	Nf	73.15 S	126.06W
Siple Coast	66	Mg	82.00 S	153.00W
Siple Island	66	Nf	73.39 S	125.00W
Siple Station	66	Pf	75.55 S	83.55W
Sipolilo	37	Ec	16.39 S	30.42 E
Sipora, Pulau-	26	Cg	2.12 S	99.40 E
Sippola	8	Ld	60.44N	27.00 E
Siqueira Campos	55	Hf	23.42 S	49.50W
Siquia, Río-	49	Eg	12.09N	84.13W
Siquijor	26	He	9.13N	123.31 E
Siquisique	54	Ea	10.34N	69.42W
Šira	20	Ef	54.29N	90.02 E
Sira	8	Be	58.17N	6.24 E
Sira	7	Bg	58.25N	6.38 E
Şīr Abū Nu'Ayr	24	Pj	25.13N	54.13 E
Si Racha	25	Kf	13.10N	100.57 E
Siracusa=Syracuse (EN)	6	Hh	37.04N	15.18 E
Sir Alexander, Mount -	42	Ff	53.56N	120.23W
Sirasso	34	Dd	9.16N	6.06W
Şirāţ, Jabal-	33	Hf	17.00N	43.50 E
Sirba	34	Fc	13.46N	1.40 E
Şīr Banī Yās	24	Oj	24.19N	52.37 E
Sirdalen	8	Bf	58.50N	6.40 E
Sirdalsvatn	8	Bf	58.35N	6.40 E
Sire [Eth.]	35	Fd	8.58N	37.00 E
Sire [Eth.]	35	Fd	8.16N	39.30 E
Sir Edward Pellew Group	59	Hc	15.40 S	136.50 E
Siret	5	If	45.24N	28.01 E
Siret	15	Jb	47.57N	26.04 E
Sirevåg	7	Ag	58.30N	5.47 E
Sīrīk	23	Id	26.29N	57.09 E
Sirik, Tanjong-	26	Ff	2.46N	111.19 E
Sirina	15	Jm	36.21N	26.41 E
Sirino	14	Jj	40.07N	15.50 E
Sirius Seamount (EN)	40	Gf	52.00N	160.50W
Širjajevo	16	Gf	47.24N	30.13 E
Sir James Mac Brian, Mount-	42	Ed	62.08N	127.40W
Sirjān, Kavīr-e-	24	Ph	29.30N	55.30 E
Sirmione	14	Ee	45.29N	10.36 E
Şırnak	24	Jd	37.32N	42.28 E
Širokaja Pad	20	Jf	50.15N	142.11 E
Široki	20	Jd	63.04N	148.01 E
Širokoje	16	Hf	47.38N	33.14 E
Sironcha	25	Fe	18.50N	79.58 E
Siros	15	Hl	37.26N	24.55 E
Sirpsindiği	15	Jh	41.50N	26.29 E
Sirr, Nafūd as-	24	Kj	25.15N	44.45 E
Sirrayn	33	Hf	19.38N	40.36 E
Sirretta Peak	46	Fi	35.59N	118.20W
Sīrrī, Jazīreh-ye-	24	Pj	25.55N	54.32 E
Sirsa	25	Fc	29.32N	75.01 E
Sir Sandford, Mount-	46	Ga	51.40N	117.52W
Sirte Desert (EN)=As Sidrah	30	Ie	30.30N	17.30 E
Sir Thomas, Mount-	59	Fe	27.11 S	129.46 E
Širvintos	7	Fi	55.03N	25.01 E
Sir Wilfrid Laurier, Mount -	42	Ff	52.48N	119.45W
Sisak	14	Ke	45.29N	16.22 E
Si Sa Ket	25	Ke	15.07N	104.19 E
Sīsakht	24	Ng	30.47N	51.33 E
Sisal	48	Ng	21.10N	90.02W
Sisante	13	Je	39.25N	2.13W
Sisargas, Islas-	13	Da	43.22N	8.50W
Šišchid-Gol	27	Ga	51.30N	97.10 E
Sishen	37	Ce	27.55 S	22.59 E
Sishui	28	Dg	35.40N	117.17 E
Sisian	16	Oj	39.31N	46.03 E
Sisili	34	Ec	10.16N	1.15W
Sisimiut/Holsteinsborg	67	Nc	67.05N	53.45W
Siskiyou Mountains	46	Df	41.55N	123.15W
Sisŏphŏn	25	Kf	13.35N	102.59 E
Sissano	60	Ch	3.00 S	142.03 E
Sisseton	45	Hd	45.40N	97.03W
Sissonne	12	Fe	49.34N	3.54 E
Sīstān=Seistan (EN)	21	If	30.30N	62.00 E
Sistema Central	5	Fg	40.30N	5.00W
Sistema Ibérico=Iberian Mountains (EN)	5	Fg	41.30N	2.30W
Sistemas Béticos	5	Fh	37.35N	3.30W
Sisteron	11	Lj	44.12N	5.56 E
Sisters	46	Ed	44.17N	121.33W
Sistranda	7	Be	63.43N	8.50 E
Sitāpur	25	Gc	27.34N	80.41 E
Sitasjaure	7	Dc	68.00N	17.25 E
Siteki	37	Ee	26.27 S	31.57 E
Sitges	13	Nc	41.14N	1.49 E
Sithonía	15	Gi	40.05N	23.55 E
Sitia	15	Jn	35.12N	26.07 E
Sitio d'Abadia	55	Ib	14.48 S	46.16W
Sitio Nuevo	49	Jh	10.46N	74.43W
Sitka	39	Fd	57.03N	135.14W
Sitkalidak	40	Ie	57.10N	153.14W
Sitna	15	Kb	47.30N	27.10 E
Sitnica	15	Dg	42.53N	20.52 E
Sitona	35	Fc	14.23N	37.22 E
Sitrah [Bhr.]	24	Ni	26.10N	50.40 E
Sitrah [Eg.]	24	Bh	28.42N	26.54 E
Sittang	25	Je	17.10N	96.58 E
Sittard	11	Ld	51.00N	5.53 E
Sittee Point	49	Ce	16.48N	88.15W
Sitten/Sion	14	Bd	46.15N	7.20 E
Sittingbourne	12	Cc	51.20N	0.45 E
Sittwe (Akyab)	22	Lg	20.09N	92.54 E
Siuna	49	Eg	13.44N	84.46W
Siuslaw River	46	Cd	44.01N	124.08W
Siva	7	Mh	56.49N	53.55 E
Sivac	15	Cd	45.42N	19.23 E
Sivaki	20	Hf	52.38N	126.45 E
Sivas	22	Ff	39.50N	37.03 E
Sivaš, Ozero-	16	Ig	45.50N	34.40 E
Sivasli	15	Mk	38.30N	29.42 E
Šiveluč, Vulkan-	20	Le	56.33N	161.25 E
Sivera, Ozero-/Sivera Ezers	8	Li	55.58N	27.25 E
Sivera Ezers/Sivera, Ozero-	8	Li	55.58N	27.25 E
Siverek	23	Eb	37.45N	39.19 E
Siverski	7	Hg	59.22N	30.02 E
Sivomaskinski	17	Kc	66.40N	62.31 E
Sivrice	24	Hc	38.27N	39.19 E
Sivrihisar	24	Dc	39.27N	31.34 E
Sivry-Rance	12	Gd	50.10N	4.16 E
Sivry Rance-Rance	12	Gd	50.09N	4.16 E
Sivry-sur-Meuse	12	He	49.19N	5.16 E
Sīwah	31	Jf	29.12N	25.31 E
Sīwah, Wāḩāt-=Siwa Oasis (EN)	30	Jf	29.10N	25.40 E
Siwalik Range	21	Jg	29.00N	80.00 E
Siwān	25	Gc	26.13N	84.22 E
Siwa Oasis (EN)=Sīwah, Wāḩāt-	30	Jf	29.10N	25.40 E
Sixaola, Río-	49	Fi	9.35N	82.34W
Six Cross Road	51q	Bb	13.07N	59.28W
Six-Fours-la-Plage	11	Lk	43.06N	5.51 E
Sixian	28	Dh	33.29N	117.53 E
Six Men's Bay	51q	Ab	13.16N	59.38W
Sixth Cataract (EN)=Sablūkah, Ash Shallāl as-	30	Kg	16.20N	32.42 E
Siyah-Chaman	24	Ld	37.35N	47.10 E
Siyang (Zhongxing)	28	Eh	33.43N	118.40 E
Siziwang Qi (Ulan Hua)	28	Ad	41.31N	111.41 E
Sjaelland=Zealand (EN)	5	Hd	55.30N	11.45 E
Sjamozero, Ozero-	7	Hf	61.55N	33.15 E
Sjare/Sääre	8	Ig	57.57N	21.53 E
Sjas	7	Hf	60.10N	32.31 E
Sjasstroj	7	Hf	60.09N	32.36 E
Šjašupe	7	Fi	55.00N	22.10 E
Šjauljaj/Šiauliai	6	Id	55.53N	23.19 E
Sjenica	15	Cf	43.16N	20.00 E
Sjnjaja	20	Hd	61.00N	126.57 E
Sjoa	8	Cc	61.41N	9.33 E
Sjöbo	8	Ei	55.38N	13.42 E
Sjøholt	7	Be	62.29N	6.50 E
Sjujutlijka	15	Ig	42.17N	25.55 E
Sjun	17	Gi	55.43N	54.17 E
Sjuøyane	41	Ob	80.43N	20.45 E
Skadarsko Jezero=Scutari, Lake- (EN)	5	Hg	42.10N	19.20 E
Skadovsk	19	Df	46.07N	32.56 E
Skælskør	8	Di	55.15N	11.19 E
Skærbæk	8	Ci	55.09N	8.46 E
Skagatá	7a	Ba	66.07N	20.06W
Skagen	7	Ch	57.44N	10.36 E
Skagern	8	Ff	59.00N	14.15 E
Skagerrak	5	Gd	57.45N	9.00 E
Skaget	8	Cc	61.17N	9.12 E
Skagit River	46	Db	48.20N	122.25W
Skagway	39	Fd	59.28N	135.19W
Skaidi	7	Fa	70.26N	24.30 E
Skaland	7	Db	69.27N	17.18 E
Skälderviken	8	Eh	56.20N	12.40 E
Skålevik	8	Bf	58.04N	8.00 E
Skalisty Golec, Gora- [R.S.F.S.R.]	20	Ge	56.20N	119.10 E
Skalisty Golec, Gora- [R.S.F.S.R.]	20	Ie	55.55N	130.35 E
Skanderborg	7	Bh	56.02N	9.56 E
Skåne	5	Hd	56.00N	13.30 E
Skånevik	8	Ae	59.44N	5.59 E
Skänninge	8	Ff	58.24N	15.05 E
Skanör	8	Ei	55.25N	12.52 E
Skántzoura	15	Hj	39.05N	24.07 E
Skara	7	Cg	58.22N	13.25 E
Skaraborg [2]	7	Cg	58.20N	13.30 E
Skärblacka	8	Ff	58.34N	15.54 E
Skārdu	25	Fa	35.18N	75.37 E
Skärhamn	8	Dg	57.59N	11.33 E
Skarnes	8	Dd	60.15N	11.41 E
Skarsstind	8	Cb	62.03N	8.35 E
Skarsvåg	7	Fa	71.06N	25.56 E
Skarszewy	10	Ob	54.05N	18.27 E
Skarvdalsegga	8	Cb	62.09N	8.03 E
Skaryszew	10	Re	51.19N	21.15 E
Skarżysko-Kamienna	10	Qe	51.08N	20.53 E
Skasøy	8	Ca	63.20N	8.35 E
Skăt	15	Gf	43.44N	23.51 E
Skattkärr	8	Ee	59.25N	13.41 E
Skattungbyn	8	Fc	61.12N	14.52 E
Skaudvile/Skaudvilė	7	Fi	55.27N	22.33 E
Skaudvilė/Skaudvile	7	Fi	55.27N	22.33 E
Skaulen	8	Be	59.38N	6.35 E
Skawa	10	Pf	50.02N	19.26 E
Skawina	10	Pg	49.59N	19.49 E
Skee	8	Df	58.56N	11.19 E
Skeena	38	Fd	54.09N	130.02W
Skeena Mountains	42	Ee	56.45N	128.40W
Skegness	9	Nh	53.10N	0.21 E
Skeidararsandur	7a	Cc	63.54N	17.14W
Skeldon	54	Gb	5.53N	57.08W
Skeleton Coast	37	Ac	17.50 S	12.45 E
Skellefteå	6	Ic	64.46N	20.57 E
Skellefteälven	5	Ic	64.42N	21.06 E
Skelleftehamn	7	Ed	64.41N	21.14 E
Skëndërbeut, Mali i-	15	Ch	41.35N	19.50 E
Skene	8	Eg	57.29N	12.38 E
Skerki Bank (EN)	32	Jb	37.45N	10.50 E
Skerries/Na Sceiri	9	Gh	53.35N	6.07W
Skerryvore	9	Fe	56.20N	7.05W
Skhíza	15	Em	36.44N	21.46 E
Skhoinoúsa	15	Im	36.50N	25.30 E
Ski	7	Cg	59.43N	10.50 E
Skiathos	15	Gj	39.10N	23.28 E
Skíathos	15	Gj	39.10N	23.29 E
Skibbereen/An Sciobairin	9	Dj	51.33N	9.15W
Skibotn	7	Eb	69.24N	20.16 E
Skidel	16	Dc	53.38N	24.17 E
Skien	6	Gd	59.12N	9.36 E
Skierniewice	10	Qe	51.58N	20.08 E
Skierniewice [2]	10	Qe	52.00N	20.10 E
Skiftet/Kihti	8	Id	60.15N	21.05 E
Skikda	31	He	36.52N	6.54 E
Skikda [3]	32	Ib	36.45N	6.50 E
Skillet Fork	45	Lg	38.08N	88.07W
Skillingaryd	8	Fg	57.26N	14.05 E
Skinári, Ákra-	15	Dl	37.56N	20.42 E
Skinnskatteberg	8	Fe	59.50N	15.41 E
Skipton	9	Kh	53.58N	2.01W
Skiptvet	8	De	59.28N	11.11 E
Skiropoúla	15	Hk	38.50N	24.21 E
Skíros	15	Hk	38.54N	24.34 E
Skiros	15	Hk	38.53N	24.32 E
Skive	7	Bh	56.34N	9.02 E
Skive Å	8	Ch	56.34N	9.04 E
Skjærhalden	8	De	59.02N	11.02 E
Skjåk	8	Cc	61.52N	8.22 E
Skjálfandafljót	7a	Cb	65.59N	17.38W
Skjeberg	8	De	59.14N	11.12 E
Skjern	7	Bi	55.57N	8.30 E
Skjern Å	7	Bi	55.55N	8.24 E
Skjervøy	7	Ea	70.02N	20.59 E
Skjoldungen	41	Hf	63.20N	41.20W
Sklad	20	Hb	71.52N	123.35 E
Šklov	16	Gb	54.14N	30.18 E
Skobeleva, Pik-	18	Ie	39.51N	72.47 E
Skœrfjorden	41	Kc	77.30N	19.10W
Škofja Loka	14	Id	46.10N	14.18 E
Skog	8	Gc	61.10N	16.55 E
Skógafoss	7a	Bc	63.32N	19.31W
Skoghall	8	Ee	59.19N	13.26 E
Skogshorn	8	Cd	60.53N	8.42 E
Skokie	45	Me	42.02N	87.46W
Skole	10	Th	48.58N	23.32 E
Skópelos	15	Gj	39.07N	23.44 E
Skópelos	15	Gj	39.10N	23.40 E
Skopí	15	Jn	35.11N	26.02 E
Skopin	7	Jj	53.52N	39.37 E
Skopje	6	Ig	42.00N	21.29 E
Skórcz	10	Oc	53.48N	18.32 E
Skorovatn	7	Cd	64.39N	13.07 E
Skorpa	8	Ac	61.35N	4.50 E
Skørping	8	Ch	56.50N	9.53 E
Skorpiós	15	Dk	38.42N	20.45 E
Škotovo	28	Lc	43.20N	132.21 E
Skotselv	8	Ce	59.51N	9.53 E
Skoura	32	Fc	31.04N	6.43W
Skövde	7	Cg	58.24N	13.50 E
Skovorodino	22	Od	53.59N	123.55 E
Skowhegan	44	Mc	44.46N	69.43W
Skradin	14	Jg	43.49N	15.56 E
Skreia	8	Dd	60.34N	11.04 E
Skreia	8	Dd	60.39N	10.56 E
Skrekken	8	Bd	60.13N	7.49 E
Skridulaupen	8	Bc	61.55N	7.35 E
Skrimkolla	8	Cb	62.23N	9.04 E
Skrīveri/Skriveri	8	Kh	56.37N	25.10 E
Skriveri/Skrīveri	8	Kh	56.37N	25.10 E
Skrunda	7	Eh	56.41N	22.00 E
Skrwa	10	Pd	52.33N	19.32 E
Skudenesfjorden	8	Ae	59.05N	5.20 E
Skudeneshavn	7	Ag	59.09N	5.17 E
Skuodas	7	Eh	56.17N	21.31 E
Skurup	8	Ei	55.28N	13.30 E
Skutskär	8	Gd	60.38N	17.25 E
Skvira	16	Fe	49.44N	29.42 E
Skwierzyna	10	Ld	52.35N	15.30 E
Skye, Island of-	5	Fd	57.15N	6.10W
Slagelse	7	Ci	55.24N	11.22 E
Slagnäs	7	Ed	65.36N	18.10 E
Slamet, Gunung-	21	Mj	7.14 S	109.12 E
Slaná	10	Ri	47.56N	21.08 E
Slancy	19	Cd	59.08N	28.02 E
Slaney/An tSláine	9	Gi	52.21N	6.30W
Slănic	15	Id	45.15N	25.56 E
Slănic Moldova	15	Jc	46.12N	26.26 E
Slannik	15	Jf	43.06N	26.13 E
Slano	14	Lh	42.47N	17.54 E
Slaný	10	Kf	50.14N	14.06 E
Śląsk=Silesia (EN)	10	Me	51.00N	16.45 E
Śląsk=Silesia (EN)	5	He	51.00N	16.45 E
Śląska, Wyżyna-	10	Of	50.28N	18.40 E
Slate Islands	45	Mb	48.34N	86.45W
Slatina	15	He	44.26N	24.22 E
Slatina	10	Ph	48.32N	19.10 E
Slaton	45	Fj	33.26N	101.39W
Slave Coast	30	Hh	6.00N	3.30 E
Slave Lake	42	Ge	55.17N	114.46W
Slave River	38	Hc	61.18N	113.39W
Slavgorod [Bye.-U.S.S.R.]	16	Gc	53.27N	31.01 E
Slavgorod [R.S.F.S.R.]	20	Cf	53.03N	78.48 E
Slavičín	10	Ng	49.06N	17.53 E
Slavjanka	20	Ih	42.55N	131.20 E
Slavjanka	15	Gh	41.23N	23.36 E
Slavjansk	6	Jf	48.52N	37.37 E
Slavjansk-na-Kubani	19	Df	45.15N	38.08 E
Slavkoje	10	Th	48.45N	23.31 E
Slavkoviči	8	Mg	57.37N	29.10 E
Slavonia (EN) = Slavonija	5	Hf	45.00N	18.00 E
Slavonia (EN)=Slavonija	14	Le	45.00N	18.00 E
Slavonija=Slavonia (EN)	14	Le	45.00N	18.00 E
Slavonija = Slavonia (EN)	5	Hf	45.00N	18.00 E
Slavonska Požega	14	Le	45.20N	17.41 E
Slavonski Brod	14	Me	45.09N	18.02 E
Slavsk	8	Ii	55.01N	21.37 E
Slavuta	19	Ce	50.18N	26.52 E
Sława	10	Me	51.53N	16.04 E
Sławatycze	10	Te	51.43N	23.30 E
Sławno	10	Mb	54.22N	16.40 E
Slayton	45	Id	44.01N	95.45W
Sleaford	9	Mh	53.00N	0.24W
Slea Head/Ceann Sléibhe	9	Ci	52.06N	10.27W
Sleat, Sound of-	9	Hd	57.10N	5.50W
Sleen	12	Ib	52.47N	6.49 E
Sleeper Islands	42	Je	57.25N	79.50W
Sléibhte Chill Mhantáin/Wicklow Mountains	9	Gh	53.02N	6.24W
Sleidinge, Evergem-	12	Fc	51.08N	3.41 E
Slesin	10	Od	52.23N	18.19 E
Slessor Glacier	66	Af	79.50 S	28.30W
Slessor Peak	66	Qe	66.31 S	64.58W
Slettefjell	8	Cc	61.13N	8.44 E
Sletterhage	8	Dh	56.06N	10.31 E
Ślęża	10	Me	51.10N	16.58 E
Ślęża	10	Mf	50.52N	16.45 E
Sliabh Bearnach/Slieve Bernagh	9	Ei	52.50N	8.35W
Sliabh Bladhma/Slieve Bloom	9	Fh	53.10N	7.35W
Sliabh Eachtaí/Slieve Aughty	9	Eh	53.10N	8.30W
Sliabh Gamh/Ox or Slieve Gamph Mountains	9	Eg	54.10N	8.50W
Sliabh Mis/Slieve Mish	9	Di	52.10N	9.50W
Sliabh Speirín/Sperrin Mountains	9	Fg	54.50N	7.05W
Slidell	45	Lk	30.17N	89.47W
Slide Mountain	44	Jd	42.00N	74.23W
Slidre	8	Cc	61.10N	9.00 E
Sliedrecht	12	Gc	51.50N	4.46 E
Slieve Aughty/Sliabh Eachtaí	9	Eh	53.10N	8.30W
Slieve Bernagh/Sliabh Bearnach	9	Ei	52.50N	8.35W
Slieve Bloom/Sliabh Bladhma	9	Fh	53.10N	7.35W
Slievefelim Mountains	9	Ei	52.45N	8.15W
Slieve Mish/Sliabh Mis	9	Di	52.10N	9.50W
Sligeach/Sligo [2]	9	Eg	54.10N	8.40W
Sligeach/Sligo	6	Fe	54.17N	8.28W
Sligo/Sligeach [2]	9	Eg	54.10N	8.40W
Sligo/Sligeach	6	Fe	54.17N	8.28W
Sligo Bay/Cuan Shligigh	9	Eg	54.20N	8.40W
Slinge	12	Ib	52.08N	6.31 E
Slingebeek	12	Ic	51.59N	6.18 E
Slite	8	Hg	57.43N	18.48 E
Sliven	15	Jg	42.40N	26.19 E
Sliven [2]	15	Jg	42.40N	26.19 E
Slivnica	15	Gg	42.51N	23.02 E
Sljudjanka	20	Ff	51.38N	103.40 E
Slobodka	15	Mb	47.54N	29.12 E
Slobodskoj	19	Fd	58.47N	50.12 E
Slobodzeja	16	Ff	46.43N	29.43 E
Slobozia [Rom.]	15	Ke	44.34N	27.22 E
Slobozia [Rom.]	15	Ie	44.30N	25.11 E
Slochteren	12	Ia	53.12N	6.50 E
Slocum Mountain	46	Gi	35.18N	117.13W
Slonim	19	Ce	53.05N	25.18 E
Sloten	12	Hb	52.54N	5.40 E
Slotermeer	12	Hb	52.55N	5.40 E
Slough	9	Mj	51.31N	0.36W
Slovakia (EN)=Slovensko	10	Ph	48.45N	19.30 E
Slovakia (EN)=Slovensko	5	Hf	48.45N	19.30 E
Slovečna	16	Fd	51.41N	29.42 E
Slovenia (EN) = Slovenija	5	Hf	46.00N	15.00 E
Slovenia (EN) = Slovenija	14	Id	46.00N	15.00 E
Slovenia (EN) = Slovenija [2]	14	Id	46.00N	15.00 E
Slovenija=Slovenia (EN) [2]	14	Id	46.00N	15.00 E
Slovenija = Slovenia (EN)	14	Id	46.00N	15.00 E
Slovenija = Slovenia (EN)	5	Hf	46.00N	15.00 E
Slovenska Bistrica	14	Jd	46.24N	15.34 E
Slovenske Gorice	14	Jd	46.35N	15.55 E
Slovenské rudohorie	10	Ph	48.45N	20.00 E
Slovensko [2]	10	Ph	48.45N	19.30 E
Slovensko=Slovakia (EN)	5	Hf	48.45N	19.30 E
Slovensko=Slovakia (EN)	10	Ph	48.45N	19.30 E
Slovenský kras	10	Qh	48.35N	20.40 E
Słubice	10	Kd	52.20N	14.35 E
Sluč [Bye.-U.S.S.R.]	16	Ec	52.08N	27.32 E
Sluč [Ukr.-U.S.S.R.]	16	Ed	51.37N	26.38 E
Sluck	19	Ce	53.02N	27.31 E
Slunj	14	Je	45.07N	15.35 E
Słupca	10	Nd	52.19N	17.52 E
Słupia	10	Mb	54.35N	16.50 E
Słupsk	10	Nb	54.28N	17.01 E
Słupsk [2]	10	Mb	54.30N	17.00 E
Slyne Head/Ceann Gólaim	9	Ch	53.24N	10.13W
Småland	7	Dh	57.20N	15.05 E
Smålandsfarvandet	8	Di	55.06N	11.20 E
Smålandsstenar	8	Eg	57.10N	13.24 E
Smalininkai/Smalininkaj	8	Ji	55.01N	22.32 E
Smalininkaj/Smalininkai	8	Ji	55.01N	22.32 E
Smallingerland-Drachten	11	Ma	53.06N	6.05 E
Smallwood Reservoir	38	Md	54.00N	64.30W
Smederevo	15	De	44.39N	20.56 E
Smederevska Palanka	15	De	44.22N	20.58 E
Smedjebacken	7	Df	60.08N	15.25 E
Smela	19	Df	49.13N	31.53 E
Smidovič	20	Ig	48.36N	133.50 E
Šmidta, Mys-	20	Nc	68.45N	178.40W
Šmidta, Ostrov-	21	La	81.08N	90.48 E
Šmidta, Poluostrov-	20	Jf	54.15N	142.40 E
Śmigiel	10	Md	52.01N	16.32 E
Smilde	12	Ib	52.56N	6.28 E
Smiltene	7	Fh	57.28N	25.56 E
Smirnovo	17	Ni	54.31N	69.28 E
Smirnyh	20	Jg	49.45N	142.53 E
Smith	55	Bl	35.30 S	61.36W
Smith Arm	42	Fc	66.15N	124.00W
Smith Bay [Ak.-U.S.]	40	Ib	70.51N	154.25W
Smith Bay [Can.]	42	Ja	77.15N	79.00W
Smith Center	45	Gg	39.47N	98.47W
Smithers	42	Ef	54.47N	127.10W
Smithfield [S.Afr.]	37	Df	30.09 S	26.30 E
Smithfield [Ut.-U.S.]	46	Jf	41.50N	111.50W
Smith Knoll	9	Pi	52.50N	2.10 E
Smith Mountain Lake	44	Hg	37.10N	79.40W
Smith Peak	46	Gb	48.50N	116.39W
Smith River	46	Jc	47.25N	111.29W
Smiths Falls	42	Jh	44.54N	76.01W
Smith Sound	46	Ba	51.18N	127.48W
Smithton	58	Fi	40.51 S	145.07 E
Smjadovo	15	Kf	43.04N	27.01 E
Smjörfjoll	7a	Cb	65.35N	14.46W
Smögen	8	Df	58.21N	11.13 E
Smoke Creek Desert	46	Ff	40.30N	119.40W
Smokey Dome	46	He	43.29N	114.56W
Smoky Bay	59	Gf	32.20 S	133.45 E
Smoky Cape	59	Kf	30.56 S	153.05 E
Smoky Falls	42	Jf	50.03N	82.10W
Smoky Hill	38	Jf	39.03N	96.48W
Smoky Hills	45	Gg	39.15N	99.00W
Smoky River	42	Fe	56.11N	117.19W
Smøla	7	Be	63.25N	8.00 E
Smolensk	6	Je	54.47N	32.03 E
Smolenskaja Oblast [3]	19	De	55.00N	33.00 E
Smolenskaja Vozvyšennost =Smolensk Upland (EN)	5	Je	54.40N	33.00 E
Smolensk Upland (EN)= Smolenskaja Vozvyšennost	5	Je	54.40N	33.00 E
Smoleviči	16	Fb	54.03N	28.02 E
Smolianica	10	Ud	52.40N	24.40 E
Smólikas Óros	5	Ig	40.06N	20.55 E
Smoljan	15	Hh	41.35N	24.41 E
Smoljan [2]	15	Hh	41.40N	24.40 E
Smooth Rock Falls	44	Ga	49.20N	81.39W
Smorgon	19	Ce	54.31N	26.23 E
Smørstabbren	8	Cc	61.32N	8.06 E
Smrdeš	15	Fh	41.34N	22.28 E
Smygehamn	8	Ei	55.21N	13.22 E
Smygehuk	8	Ei	55.21N	13.23 E
Smyley, Cape-	66	Qf	72.00 S	78.50W
Smyrna	44	Ei	33.53N	84.31W
Smyrna (EN)=İzmir	22	Ef	38.25N	27.09 E
Smyšljajevka	7	Mj	53.17N	50.24 E
Smythe, Mount-	38	Gd	57.50N	124.59W
Snacke Point	51b	Bb	18.17N	62.58W
Snæfell	7a	Cb	64.48N	15.34W
Snaefell	9	Ig	54.16N	4.27W
Snæfellsjökull	7a	Ab	64.49N	23.46W
Snag	42	Dd	62.23N	140.22W
Snake Bay Settlement	59	Gb	11.25 S	130.40 E
Snake Range	46	Hg	39.00N	114.15W
Snake River [Can.]	42	Ec	65.57N	134.13W
Snake River [U.S.]	38	He	46.12N	119.02W
Snake River Plain	43	Ec	42.45N	114.30W
Snare	42	Fd	63.15N	116.08W
Snares Islands	61	Ci	48.00 S	166.35 E
Snarumselva	8	Cc	59.57N	9.58 E
Snåsa	7	Cd	64.15N	12.22 E
Sneek	11	La	53.02N	5.40 E
Snekermeer	11	La	52.59N	5.40 E
Snežnaja, Gora-	20	Lc	65.18N	165.30 E
Snežnik	14	Ie	45.26N	14.36 E
Snežnogorsk	20	Dc	68.15N	87.35 E
Šnežnoje	16	Kf	47.59N	38.50 E
Śniardwy, Jezioro-	10	Rc	53.46N	21.44 E
Śnieżka	5	He	50.45N	15.43 E
Śnieżnik	10	Mf	50.12N	16.50 E
Snigirevka	16	Hf	47.04N	32.45 E
Snillfjord	8	Ca	63.24N	9.30 E
Snina	10	Sh	48.59N	22.08 E
Snizort, Loch-	9	Gd	57.30N	6.25W
Snjatyn	16	De	48.29N	25.34 E
Snøhetta	5	Gc	62.20N	9.17 E
Snohomish	46	Dc	47.55N	122.06W
Snønuten	8	Be	59.31N	6.54 E
Snøonipa	8	Bc	61.42N	6.41 E
Snota	8	Cb	62.51N	9.06 E
Snov	16	Gd	51.32N	31.33 E
Snowbird Lake	42	Hd	60.40N	102.50W
Snowdon	5	Fe	53.04N	4.05W
Snowdonia	9	Jh	53.05N	3.55W
Snowdrift	42	Gd	62.23N	110.47W
Snowflake	46	Ji	34.30N	110.05W
Snow Hill	44	Jf	38.11N	75.24W
Snow Lake	42	Hf	54.53N	100.02W
Snow Mountain	43	Cd	39.23N	122.46W
Snowshoe Peak	46	Hb	48.13N	115.41W
Snowville	46	If	41.58N	112.43W
Snowy Mountain [B.C.-Can.]	46	Fb	49.02N	119.57W
Snowy Mountain [N.Y.-U.S.]	44	Jd	43.42N	74.23W
Snowy Mountains	59	Jg	36.30 S	148.20 E
Snowy River	59	Jg	37.48 S	148.32 E
Snudy, Ozero-	8	Li	55.40N	27.15 E
Snug Corner	49	Kb	22.32N	73.53W
Snuŏl	25	Lf	12.04N	106.26 E
Snyder	43	Ge	32.44N	100.55W
Soalala	37	Hc	16.07 S	45.21 E
Soalara	37	Gd	23.35 S	43.44 E
Soanierana-Ivongo	37	Hc	16.54 S	49.34 E
Soar	12	Ab	52.52N	1.17W
Şoarş	15	Hd	45.56N	24.55 E
Soavinandriana	37	Hc	19.10 S	46.43 E
Sob [R.S.F.S.R.]	17	Mc	66.20N	66.02 E

Index Symbols

- [1] Independent Nation
- [2] State, Region
- [3] District, County
- [4] Municipality
- [5] Colony, Dependency
- Continent
- Physical Region
- Historical or Cultural Region
- Mount, Mountain
- Volcano
- Hill
- Mountains, Mountain Range
- Hills, Escarpment
- Plateau, Upland
- Pass, Gap
- Plain, Lowland
- Delta
- Salt Flat
- Valley, Canyon
- Crater, Cave
- Karst Features
- Depression
- Polder
- Desert, Dunes
- Forest, Woods
- Heath, Steppe
- Oasis
- Cape, Point
- Coast, Beach
- Cliff
- Peninsula
- Isthmus
- Sandbank
- Island
- Atoll
- Rock, Reef
- Islands, Archipelago
- Rocks, Reefs
- Coral Reef
- Well, Spring
- Geyser
- River, Stream
- Waterfall Rapids
- River Mouth, Estuary
- Lake
- Salt Lake
- Intermittent Lake
- Reservoir
- Swamp, Pond
- Canal
- Glacier
- Ice Shelf, Pack Ice
- Ocean
- Sea
- Gulf, Bay
- Strait, Fjord
- Lagoon
- Bank
- Seamount
- Tablemount
- Ridge
- Shelf
- Basin
- Escarpment, Sea Scarp
- Fracture
- Trench, Abyss
- National Park, Reserve
- Point of Interest
- Recreation Site
- Cave, Cavern
- Historic Site
- Ruins
- Wall, Walls
- Church, Abbey
- Temple
- Scientific Station
- Airport
- Port
- Lighthouse
- Mine
- Tunnel
- Dam, Bridge

Sob [Ukr.-U.S.S.R.]	16	Fe	48.41N	29.17 E
Soba	34	Gc	10.59N	8.04 E
Sobaek-Sanmaek	28	Jf	36.00N	128.00 E
Sobat (EN)=Sawbā	30	Kh	9.45N	31.45 E
Sobernheim	12	Je	49.48N	7.39 E
Soběslav	10	Kg	49.16N	14.44 E
Sōbetsu	29a	Bb	42.33N	140.51 E
Sobinka	7	Jh	56.01N	40.07 E
Sobolevo [R.S.F.S.R.]	16	Qd	51.59N	51.48 E
Sobolevo [R.S.F.S.R.]	20	Kf	54.17N	156.00 E
Sobolew	10	Re	51.41N	21.40 E
Sobo-San	29	Be	32.47N	131.21 E
Sobradinho	55	Fi	29.24S	53.03W
Sobral	53	Lf	3.42S	40.21W
Sobrarbe	13	Mb	42.20N	0.05 E
Soca	55	El	34.41S	55.41W
Soča=Isonzo (EN)	14	He	45.43N	13.33 E
Sochaczew	10	Qd	52.14N	20.14 E
Soči	6	Jg	43.35N	39.45 E
Société, Iles de la-=Society Islands (EN)	57	Lf	17.00S	150.00W
Society Islands (EN)= Société, Iles de la-	57	Lf	17.00S	150.00W
Socompa, Paso-	52	Jh	24.27S	68.18W
Socorro [Col.]	54	Db	6.27N	73.16W
Socorro [N.M.-U.S.]	43	Fe	34.04N	106.54W
Socorro, Isla-	47	Be	18.45N	110.58W
Socotra (EN)=Suquṭrā	21	Hh	12.30N	54.00 E
Socuéllamos	13	Je	39.17N	2.48W
Soda Lake	46	Gi	35.08N	116.04W
Sodankylä	7	Gc	67.25N	26.36 E
Soda Springs	46	Je	42.39N	111.36W
Söderåsen	8	Eh	56.04N	13.05 E
Söderfors	7	Df	60.23N	17.14 E
Söderhamn	7	Df	61.18N	17.03 E
Söderköping	8	Gf	58.29N	16.18 E
Södermanland	8	Ge	59.10N	16.50 E
Södermanland [2]	7	Dg	59.15N	16.40 E
Söderslätt	8	Ei	55.30N	13.15 E
Södertälje	7	Dg	59.12N	17.37 E
Södertörn	8	Ge	59.05N	18.00 E
Sodo	35	Fd	6.51N	37.45 E
Södra Dellen	8	Gc	61.50N	16.45 E
Södra Gloppet	8	Ia	63.05N	21.00 E
Södra Kvarken	8	Hd	60.20N	19.08 E
Södra-Midsjöbanken	8	Gi	55.40N	17.20 E
Södra Vi	8	Fg	57.45N	15.48 E
Soe	26	Hh	9.52S	124.17 E
Soekmekaar	37	Dd	23.28S	29.58 E
Soela, Proliv-/Soela Väin	8	Jf	58.40N	22.30 E
Soela Väin/Soela, Proliv-	8	Jf	58.40N	22.30 E
Soest [F.R.G.]	10	Ee	51.35N	8.07 E
Soest [Neth.]	12	Hb	52.10N	5.20 E
Soeste	12	Ja	53.10N	7.44 E
Soester Borde	12	Kc	51.38N	8.03 E
Soestwetering	12	Ib	51.30N	6.09 E
Sofádhes	15	Fj	39.20N	22.06 E
Sofala [3]	37	Ec	19.30S	34.40 E
Sofala, Baia de-	30	Kk	20.11S	34.45 E
Sofia	37	Hc	15.27S	47.23 E
Sofia [Bul.] [2]	15	Gg	42.43N	23.25 E
Sofia [Grc.] [2]	15	Gg	42.41N	23.19 E
Sofia (EN)=Sofija	6	Ig	42.41N	23.19 E
Sofija=Sofia (EN)	6	Ig	42.41N	23.19 E
Sofijsk	20	If	52.20N	134.01 E
Sofporog	19	Db	65.48N	31.28 E
Sofrána, Nisidhes-	15	Jm	36.04N	26.24 E
Sōfu-Gan	27	Pf	29.50N	140.20 E
Sogamoso	54	Db	5.43N	72.56W
Soganlı	24	Eb	41.11N	32.38 E
Sogara, Lake-	36	Fd	5.15S	31.00 E
Sogda	20	If	50.24N	132.18 E
Sögel	10	Dd	52.51N	7.31 E
Sogeri	60	Di	9.10S	147.32 E
Sogn	8	Ac	61.05N	5.55 E
Sogndalsfjøra	8	Bc	61.14N	7.06 E
Søgne	8	Bf	58.05N	7.49 E
Sognefjell	8	Bc	61.35N	7.55 E
Sognefjorden	5	Gc	61.05N	5.10 E
Sognesjøen	8	Ac	61.05N	5.00 E
Sogn og Fjordane [2]	7	Bf	61.30N	6.50 E
Sogod	26	Hd	10.23N	124.59 E
Sogo Nur	27	Hc	42.20N	101.20 E
Sogoža	7	Jg	58.30N	39.06 E
Söğüt	15	Nj	40.00N	30.11 E
Söğütalan	15	Li	40.03N	28.34 E
Söğüt Gölü	24	Cd	37.03N	29.53 E
Sog Xian	27	Fe	31.51N	93.42 E
Soh	18	He	39.57N	71.08 E
Sohag (EN)=Sawhāj	31	Kf	26.33N	31.42 E
Sohano	60	Ei	5.29S	154.41 E
Sohŭksan-Do	28	Hg	34.04N	125.07 E
Soignies/Zinnik	11	Kd	50.35N	4.04 E
Soini	8	Kb	62.52N	24.13 E
Soisalo	8	Mb	62.40N	28.10 E
Soissonnais, Plateau du-	11	Je	49.15N	3.10 E
Soissons	11	Je	49.22N	3.20 E
Sōja	29	Cd	34.40N	133.44 E
Sojana	7	Kd	65.53N	43.30 E
Sojma	17	Ec	67.00N	51.00 E
Šojna	17	Bc	67.52N	44.08 E
Sŏjosŏn-man=Korea Bay (EN)	21	Of	39.15N	125.00 E
Sojuznoje	16	Vd	50.50N	60.10 E
Sojuz Sovetskih Socialističeskih Respublik =USSR (EN) [1]	22	Jd	60.00N	80.00 E
Sojuz Sovetskih Socialističeskih Respublik (SSSR) [1]	22	Jd	60.00N	80.00 E
Sok	19	Fe	53.25N	50.10 E
Sokal	16	Dd	50.29N	24.17 E
Šokalskogo, Proliv-	20	Ea	79.00N	100.00 E
Sokch'o	27	Md	38.12N	128.36 E
Söke	23	Cb	37.45N	27.24 E
Sokele	36	Dd	9.55S	24.36 E
Sokirjany	16	Ee	48.28N	27.25 E
Sokna	7	Bf	60.14N	9.54 E
Soko Banja	15	Ef	43.39N	21.53 E
Sokodé	31	Hh	8.59N	1.08 E
Sokol	19	Ed	59.29N	40.13 E
Sokol	15	Ce	44.18N	19.25 E
Sokółka	10	Tc	53.25N	23.31 E
Sokolo	34	Dc	14.44N	6.07W
Sokolov	10	If	50.11N	12.38 E
Sokołów Podlaski	10	Sd	52.25N	22.15 E
Sokone	34	Bc	13.53N	16.22W
Sokosti	7	Gb	68.20N	28.01 E
Sokoto	30	Hg	11.24N	4.07 E
Sokoto [2]	34	Gc	12.20N	5.20 E
Sokoto	31	Hg	13.04N	5.15 E
Sokourala	34	Dd	9.13N	8.05W
Sōl	35	Hd	9.20N	49.25 E
Sōl	35	Hd	9.40N	48.30 E
Sol, Costa del-	13	Ih	36.46N	3.55W
Sol, Pico do-	55	Ke	20.07S	43.28W
Soła	10	Pf	50.04N	19.13 E
Sola	63b	Ca	13.53S	167.33 E
Solai	36	Gb	0.02N	36.09 E
Solakrossen	8	Af	58.53N	5.36 E
Solander Island	61	Ci	46.35S	166.50 E
Solanet	55	Cm	36.51S	58.31W
Solbad Hall in Tirol	14	Fc	47.17N	11.31 E
Solcy	19	Dd	58.09N	30.20 E
Sölden	14	Ed	46.58N	11.00 E
Soldier Point	51d	Bb	17.02N	61.41W
Soldotna	40	Id	60.29N	151.04W
Solec Kujawski	10	Oc	53.06N	18.14 E
Soledad [Arg.]	55	Bj	30.37S	60.55W
Soledad [Ca.-U.S.]	46	Eh	36.26N	121.19W
Soledad [Col.]	54	Da	10.55N	74.46W
Soledad [Ven.]	54	Fb	8.10N	63.34W
Soledad, Boca de-	48	Ce	25.17N	112.09W
Soledad, Isla-/East Falkland	52	Kk	51.45S	58.50W
Soledade	56	Jc	28.50S	52.30W
Sølen	8	Dc	61.55N	11.30 E
Sølensjøen	8	Dc	61.55N	11.35 E
Solentiname, Archipiélago de-	49	Fh	11.10N	85.00W
Solenzara	11a	Bb	41.51N	9.24 E
Solesmes	12	Fd	50.11N	3.30 E
Solferino	14	Ee	45.23N	10.34 E
Solgen	8	Fg	57.33N	15.07 E
Solgne	12	Ie	48.58N	6.18 E
Soligalič	7	Kg	59.07N	42.13 E
Soligorsk	19	Ce	52.49N	27.31 E
Solihull	9	Li	52.25N	1.45W
Solikamsk	19	Fd	59.39N	56.47 E
Sol-lleck	6	Le	51.12N	55.03 E
Solimán, Punta-	48	Ph	19.50N	87.27W
Solimoes→Amazonas, Rio- =Amazon (EN)	52	Lf	0.10S	49.00W
Solingen	10	De	51.11N	7.05 E
Solińskie, Jezioro-	10	Sg	49.22N	22.30 E
Solis, Presa-	48	Ig	20.05N	100.36W
Sollebrunn	8	Ef	58.07N	12.32 E
Sollefteå	7	De	63.10N	17.16 E
Sollentuna	8	Ge	59.28N	17.54 E
Söller	13	Oe	39.46N	2.42 E
Sollerön	8	Fd	60.55N	14.37 E
Solling	10	Fe	51.45N	9.35 E
Solms	12	Kd	50.46N	9.36 E
Solna	8	He	59.22N	18.01 E
Solnečnogorsk	7	Ih	56.10N	37.00 E
Solnečny	20	Id	60.10N	137.35 E
Sologne	11	Hg	47.50N	2.00 E
Sologne Bourbonnaise	11	Jh	46.40N	3.30 E
Solok	26	Dg	0.48S	100.39 E
Sololá [3]	49	Bf	14.40N	91.15W
Sololá	49	Bf	14.46N	91.11W
Solomon Basin (EN)	60	Ei	7.00S	152.00 E
Solomon Islands [1]	58	Ge	8.00S	159.00 E
Solomon Islands	57	Ge	8.00S	159.00 E
Solomon Islands (British Solomon Islands) [1]	58	Ge	8.00S	159.00 E
Solomon River	43	Hd	38.54N	97.22W
Solomon Sea	57	Ge	8.00S	155.00 E
Solon Springs	45	Kc	46.22N	91.48W
Solør	8	Dd	60.30N	11.55 E
Solor, Kepulauan-	26	Hh	8.25S	123.30 E
Solothurn	14	Bc	47.15N	7.30 E
Solothurn [2]	14	Bc	47.20N	7.40 E
Solotvin	10	Uh	48.38N	24.31 E
Soloveckije Ostrova	7	Id	65.05N	35.45 E
Solovjevka	8	Nd	60.44N	30.20 E
Solovjevsk [R.S.F.S.R.]	20	Hf	54.15N	124.30 E
Solovjevsk [R.S.F.S.R.]	20	Gg	49.54N	115.43 E
Sölöz	15	Mi	40.23N	29.25 E
Solre-le-Château	12	Gd	50.10N	4.05 E
Solsona	13	Nc	41.59N	1.31 E
Solt	10	Oj	46.48N	19.00 E
Šolta	14	Kg	43.23N	16.17 E
Soltānābād [Iran]	24	Mg	31.03N	49.42 E
Soltānābād [Iran]	24	Rd	36.23N	58.02 E
Solṭānī, Khowr-e-	24	Nh	29.00N	50.50 E
Soltāniyeh	24	Md	36.26N	48.48 E
Soltau	10	Fd	52.59N	9.50 E
Soltvadkert	10	Pj	46.35N	19.23 E
Solvang	46	Ei	34.36N	120.08W
Sölvesborg	7	Dh	56.03N	14.33 E
Solvyčegodsk	7	Lf	61.21N	46.52 E
Solway Firth	9	Jg	54.50N	3.35W
Solwezi	31	Jj	12.11S	26.24 E
Sōma	28	Pf	37.48N	140.57 E
Soma	24	Bc	39.10N	27.36 E
Somain	12	Fd	50.22N	3.17 E
Somalia (EN)= Soomaaliya [1]	31	Lh	10.00N	49.00 E
Somali Basin (EN)	3	Fi	0.00	52.00 E
Sombo	36	Dd	8.42S	20.57 E
Sombor	15	Cd	45.46N	19.07 E
Sombrerete	47	Dd	23.38N	103.39W
Sombrero	47	Le	18.36N	63.26W
Sombrero Channel	25	Ig	7.41N	93.35 E
Sombrio	55	Hi	29.07S	49.40W
Sombrio, Lagoa do-	55	Hi	29.12S	49.42W
Somcuţa Mare	15	Gb	47.31N	23.28 E
Someren	12	Hc	51.23N	5.43 E
Somero	8	Jd	60.37N	23.32 E
Somerset	38	Jb	73.30N	93.30W
Somerset [3]	9	Jk	51.10N	3.10W
Somerset	9	Kj	51.00N	3.00W
Somerset [Austl.]	59	Ib	10.35S	142.15 E
Somerset [Ky.-U.S.]	43	Kd	37.05N	84.36W
Somerset [Pa.-U.S.]	44	He	40.02N	79.05W
Somerset East	37	Df	32.42S	25.35 E
Somerton	46	Hj	32.36N	114.43W
Somerville Lake	45	Hk	30.18N	96.40W
Someş	15	Fa	48.07N	22.20 E
Someşu Mare	15	Gb	47.09N	23.55 E
Someşu Mic	15	Gb	47.09N	23.55 E
Somme [3]	11	Id	49.55N	2.30 E
Somme	11	Hd	50.11N	1.39 E
Somme, Baie de-	12	Dd	50.14N	1.33 E
Somme, Bassurelle de la-	12	Dd	50.15N	1.10 E
Somme, Canal de la-	11	He	50.11N	1.39 E
Somme-Leuze	12	Hd	50.20N	5.22 E
Somme-Leuze-Hogne	12	Hd	50.15N	5.17 E
Sommen	7	Dh	58.00N	15.15 E
Sommen	8	Ff	58.08N	14.58 E
Sommepy-Tahure	12	Ge	49.15N	4.33 E
Sömmerda	10	He	51.09N	11.06 E
Somogy [2]	10	Nj	46.25N	17.35 E
Somontano	13	Lc	42.02N	0.20W
Somosierra, Puerto de-	13	Ic	41.09N	3.35W
Somosomo Strait	63d	Bb	16.47S	179.58 E
Somotillo	49	Dg	13.02N	86.53W
Somoto	47	Gf	13.28N	86.35W
Somovo	16	Kd	51.45N	39.25 E
Sompolno	10	Od	52.24N	18.31 E
Somport, Puerto de-	13	Lb	42.48N	0.31W
Son	21	Kg	25.25N	84.55 E
Sona	10	Qd	52.33N	20.35 E
Soná	49	Gi	8.01N	81.19W
Sonaguera	49	Df	15.38N	86.20W
Sonári, Ákra	15	Lm	36.27N	28.13 E
Sŏnch'ŏn	28	He	39.48N	124.55 E
Søndeled	7	Bg	58.46N	9.05 E
Sønderborg	7	Bi	54.55N	9.47 E
Sønder-Jylland [2]	8	Ci	55.00N	9.00 E
Sønder-Omme	8	Ci	55.50N	8.54 E
Sondershausen	10	Ge	51.22N	10.52 E
Søndre Strømfjord	67	Nc	66.59N	50.40W
Søndre Strømfjord	41	Ge	66.10N	53.10W
Søndre Upernavik	41	Gd	72.10N	55.38W
Sondrio	14	Dd	46.10N	9.52 E
Sonepat	25	Fc	28.59N	77.01 E
Song	34	Hd	9.50N	12.37 E
Songa	8	Be	59.47N	7.43 E
Songavatn	8	Be	59.50N	7.35 E
Song Cau	25	Lf	13.27N	109.13 E
Songe	8	Cf	58.41N	9.01 E
Songea	31	Kj	10.41S	35.39 E
Songeons	12	De	49.33N	1.52 E
Songhua Hu	28	Ic	43.30N	126.51 E
Songhua Jiang=Sungari (EN)	21	Pe	47.42N	132.30 E
Songjiang	27	Le	31.01N	121.14 E
Songjiang → Antu	28	Jc	42.33N	128.20 E
Songjianghe	28	Ic	42.10N	127.30 E
Songjin→Kimch'aek	27	Mc	40.41N	129.12 E
Songjŏng	28	Ig	35.08N	126.48 E
Songkhla	22	Mi	7.13N	100.34 E
Songling	27	Lb	48.02N	121.08 E
Songnim	28	He	38.44N	125.38 E
Songo [Ang.]	36	Bd	7.21S	14.50 E
Songo [Moz.]	37	Ec	15.33S	32.48 E
Songololo	36	Bd	5.42S	14.02 E
Songpan (Sungqu)	27	He	32.37N	103.34 E
Songsa-dong	28	Hd	39.49N	124.49 E
Song Shan	27	Je	34.31N	113.00 E
Songshuzhen	28	Ic	42.01N	127.09 E
Songueur	13	Ni	35.11N	1.30 E
Songxian	28	Bg	34.12N	112.09 E
Songzi (Xinjiangkou)	28	Ai	30.10N	116.46 E
Sonid Youqi (Saihan Tal)	27	Jc	42.45N	112.36 E
Sonid Zuoqi (Mandalt)	27	Kc	43.50N	116.45 E
Sonkari	8	Lb	62.50N	26.35 E
Sonkël, Ozero-	18	Jd	41.50N	75.10 E
Sonkovo	7	Ih	57.47N	37.09 E
Son La	22	Mg	21.19N	103.54 E
Sonmiāni Bay	25	Dc	25.15N	66.30 E
Sonneberg	10	Hf	50.21N	11.10 E
Sono, Rio do- [Braz.]	55	Jc	17.02S	45.32W
Sono, Rio do- [Braz.]	54	Ie	9.00S	48.11W
Sonobe	29	Dd	35.07N	135.28 E
Sonoita	47	Bb	31.51N	112.50W
Sonoma Peak	46	Gf	40.52N	117.36W
Sonora [2]	47	Bc	29.20N	110.40W
Sonora	47	Bc	28.48N	111.49W
Sonora [Ca.-U.S.]	46	Eh	37.59N	120.23W
Sonora [Tx.-U.S.]	45	Fk	30.34N	100.39W
Sonqor	24	Le	34.47N	47.36 E
Sonsbeck	12	Ic	51.37N	6.22 E
Sonsonate	47	Gf	13.43N	89.44W
Sonsorol Islands	57	Ed	5.20N	132.13 E
Sonthofen	10	Gi	47.31N	10.17 E
Sontra	10	Fe	51.04N	9.56 E
Soomaaliya=Somalia (EN) [1]	31	Lh	10.00N	49.00 E
Soomenlaht=Finland, Gulf of- (EN)	5	Ic	60.00N	27.00 E
Soonwald	12	Je	49.56N	7.35 E
Søorværøy	7	Cc	67.38N	12.40 E
Sopi, Tanjung-	26	If	2.39N	128.34 E
Sopo	35	Dd	8.51N	26.11 E
Sopockin	10	Tc	53.50N	23.42 E
Sopot [Bul.]	15	Hg	42.39N	24.45 E
Sopot [Pol.]	10	Ob	54.28N	18.34 E
Sopron	10	Mi	47.41N	16.36 E
Sopur	25	Eb	34.18N	74.28 E
Sor	13	De	39.00N	8.17W
Sora	14	Hi	41.43N	13.37 E
Sorachi-Gawa	29a	Bb	43.32N	141.52 E
Soråker	8	Gb	62.31N	17.30 E
Sorak-san	27	Md	38.07N	128.28 E
Sorano	14	Fh	42.41N	11.43 E
Soratteld	12	Kc	51.40N	8.55 E
Sorbas	13	Jg	37.07N	2.07W
Sorbe	13	Id	40.51N	3.08W
Sörberget	8	Gb	62.31N	17.22 E
Sore	11	Fj	44.19N	0.35W
Sorel	42	Kg	46.03N	73.07W
Sorell, Cape-	59	Jh	42.10S	145.10 E
Soresina	14	De	45.17N	9.51 E
Sorezaru Point	63a	Cb	7.37S	156.38 E
Sørfjorden	8	Bd	60.25N	6.40 E
Sørfold	7	Dc	67.28N	15.28 E
Sorgues	11	Kj	44.00N	4.52 E
Sorgun	24	Fc	39.50N	35.19 E
Soria [3]	13	Jc	41.40N	2.40W
Soria	13	Jc	41.46N	2.28W
Soriano [2]	55	Dk	33.30S	57.45W
Sørkapp	67	Kd	76.28N	16.36 E
Sorkh, Godār-e-	24	Pf	33.05N	55.05 E
Sorkh, Kūh-e-	24	Pf	33.05N	55.05 E
Sorkheh	24	Oe	35.28N	53.13 E
Sorø	8	Di	55.26N	11.34 E
Sorocaba	53	Lh	23.29S	47.27W
Soroči Gory	7	Li	55.24N	49.55 E
Soročinsk	19	Fe	52.26N	53.10 E
Soroki	16	Fe	48.07N	28.16 E
Sorol Atoll	57	Fd	8.08N	140.23 E
Sorong	58	Ee	0.53S	131.15 E
Soroti	31	Kh	1.43N	33.37 E
Sørøya	5	Ia	70.36N	22.46 E
Sørøyane	8	Ab	62.20N	5.45 E
Sorraia	13	Df	38.56N	8.53W
Sørreisa	7	Eb	69.09N	18.10 E
Sorrentina, Penisola-	14	Ij	40.35N	14.30 E
Sorrento	14	Ij	40.37N	14.22 E
Sør Rondane	66	Df	72.00S	25.00 E
Sorsatunturi	7	Gc	67.24N	29.38 E
Sorsavesi	8	Lb	62.30N	27.35 E
Sorsele	7	Dd	65.32N	17.30 E
Sorsk	20	Ef	54.00N	90.20 E
Sorso	14	Cj	40.48N	8.34 E
Sorsogon	26	Hd	12.58N	124.00 E
Sort	13	Nb	42.24N	1.08 E
Šortandi	19	He	51.42N	71.05 E
Sortavala	19	Dc	61.44N	30.41 E
Sortland	7	Db	68.42N	15.24 E
Sør-Trøndelag [2]	7	Ce	63.00N	10.40 E
Sorum	17	Ne	63.50N	68.05 E
Sørumsand	8	De	59.58N	11.15 E
Šoša	7	Ih	56.33N	36.09 E
Sŏsan	28	If	36.47N	126.27 E
Sösdala	8	Eh	56.02N	13.40 E
Sos del Rey Católico	13	Kb	42.30N	1.13W
Sosna	16	Kc	52.42N	38.55 E
Sosnogorsk	6	Lc	63.37N	53.51 E
Sosnovka [R.S.F.S.R.]	16	Lc	53.14N	41.22 E
Sosnovka [R.S.F.S.R.]	7	Mh	56.18N	51.17 E
Sosnovka [R.S.F.S.R.]	7	Jc	66.31N	40.33 E
Sosnovka [Ukr.-U.S.S.R.]	16	Dd	50.15N	24.13 E
Sosnovo	8	Nd	60.31N	30.29 E
Sosnovo-Ozerskoje	20	Gf	52.31N	111.35 E
Sosnovy Bor	8	Me	59.48N	29.10 E
Sosnowiec	10	Pf	50.18N	19.08 E
Sospel	11	Nk	43.53N	7.27 E
Šostka	19	De	51.52N	33.31 E
Sosumav	37	Hb	13.03S	48.54 E
Sosva	19	Gd	59.32N	62.20 E
Sosva [R.S.F.S.R.]	19	Gc	63.40N	62.02 E
Sosva [R.S.F.S.R.]	19	Gd	59.10N	61.50 E
Sotavento [3]	32	Cf	14.40N	23.25W
Sotavento, Islas de- = Windward Islands (EN)	52	Jd	11.10N	67.00W
Sotik	36	Gc	0.41S	35.07 E
Sotkamo	7	Gd	64.08N	28.25 E
Soto la Marina	48	Jf	23.48N	98.13W
Soto la Marina, Rio-	48	Kf	23.45N	97.45W
Sotonera, Embalse de la-	13	Lb	42.05N	0.48W
Sotouboua	34	Fd	8.34N	0.59 E
Sotra	8	Ad	60.20N	5.05 E
Sotsudaka-Zaki	29b	Ba	28.15N	129.10 E
Sottern	8	Fe	59.05N	15.30 E
Sotteville-lès-Rouen	11	He	49.25N	1.06 E
Sottrum	12	La	53.07N	9.14 E
Sottunga	8	Id	60.10N	20.40 E
Sotuf, Adrar-	32	De	21.42N	15.36W
Sotuta	48	Og	20.36N	89.01W
Souanké	36	Bb	2.05N	14.03 E
Soubré	34	Dd	5.47N	6.36W
Soubré [3]	34	Dd	5.47N	6.38W
Soúdha	15	Hn	35.29N	24.04 E
Souf	30	He	33.25N	6.50 E
Soufflenheim	12	Jf	48.50N	7.58 E
Souflion	15	Jh	41.12N	26.18 E
Soufrière	50	Ff	13.52N	61.04W
Soufrière [Guad.]	47	Le	16.03N	61.40W
Soufrière [St.Vin.]	47	Lf	13.21N	61.11W
Soufrière Bay	51g	Bb	15.13N	61.22W
Soufrière Hills	51c	Bc	16.43N	62.10W
Souillac	11	Hj	44.54N	1.29 E
Souilly	11	Le	49.01N	5.17 E
Souk Ahras	32	Ib	36.17N	7.57 E
Souk el Arba du Rharb	32	Fc	34.41N	5.59W
Sŏul=Seoul (EN)	22	Of	37.34N	127.00 E
Soulac-sur-Mer	11	Ei	45.30N	1.06W
Sŏul Si [2]	28	If	37.35N	127.00 E
Soultz-sous-Forêts	12	Jf	48.56N	7.53 E
Soumagne	12	Hd	50.37N	5.45 E
Soummam	13	Rh	36.44N	5.04 E
Sounding Creek	46	Ja	52.06N	110.28W
Soúnion	15	Hl	37.39N	24.02 E
Soúnion, Ákra-	15	Hl	37.39N	24.01 E
Sources, Mont aux-	30	Jk	28.46S	28.52 E
Soure [Braz.]	54	Id	0.44S	48.31W
Soure [Port.]	13	Dd	40.03N	8.38W
Sour el Ghozlane	32	Hb	36.09N	3.41 E
Souris	42	Hg	49.38N	100.15W
Souris	38	Je	49.39N	99.34W
Sous	32	Fc	30.22N	9.37W
Sous	32	Fc	30.25N	9.30W
Sousa	53	Mf	6.45S	38.14W
Sousel	13	Ef	38.57N	7.40W
Sous le Vent, Iles-= Leeward Islands (EN)	57	Lf	16.38S	151.30W
Sousse (EN)=Sūsah [3]	32	Jb	35.45N	10.30 E
Sousse (EN)=Sūsah [Tun.]	31	Ie	35.49N	10.38 E
Sout	37	Cf	33.03S	23.29 E
South Africa / Suid Africa [1]	31	Jl	30.00S	26.00 E
South Alligator River	59	Gb	12.15S	132.24 E
Southam	12	Ab	52.15N	1.23W
South America (EN)	52	Jg	15.00S	60.00W
Southampton	38	Kc	64.20N	84.40W
Southampton [Eng.-U.K.]	6	Fe	50.55N	1.25W
Southampton [N.Y.-U.S.]	44	Ke	40.54N	72.23W
Southampton, Cape-	42	Jd	62.08N	83.44W
Southampton Airport	12	Ad	50.55N	1.23W
Southampton Water	12	Ad	50.52N	1.20W
South Andaman	25	If	11.45N	92.45 E
Southard, Cape-	66	Ie	66.33S	122.04 E
South Auckland-Bay of Plenty [2]	62	Fb	38.00S	176.00 E
South Aulatsivik	42	Le	56.47N	61.30W
South Australia [2]	59	Ge	30.00S	135.00 E
South Australian Basin (EN)	3	Im	40.00S	128.00 E
Southaven	45	Li	35.00N	90.00W
South Baldy	45	Cj	33.59N	107.11W
South Bay	42	Jd	64.00N	83.25W
South Bend	43	Jc	41.41N	86.15W
South Benfleet	12	Cc	51.32N	0.33 E
Southborough	12	Cc	51.09N	0.15 E
South Boston	44	Hg	36.42N	78.58W
Southbridge	62	Ee	43.48S	172.15 E
South Buganda [3]	36	Fc	0.30S	32.00 E
South Caicos	49	Lc	21.31N	71.30W
South Carolina [2]	43	Ke	34.00N	81.00W
South China Basin (EN)	3	Hh	15.00N	115.00 E
South China Sea (EN)=Bien Dong	21	Ni	10.00N	113.00 E
South China Sea (EN)=Cina Selatan, Laut-	21	Ni	10.00N	113.00 E
South China Sea (EN)=Nan Hai	21	Ni	10.00N	113.00 E
South Dakota [2]	43	Gc	44.15N	100.00W
South Downs	9	Mk	50.55N	0.25W
South-East [3]	37	De	25.00S	25.45 E
South East Cape	57	Fi	43.39S	146.50 E
Southeast Indian Ridge (EN)	3	Ho	50.00S	110.00 E
Southeast Pacific Basin (EN)	3	Mp	60.00S	115.00W
South East Point [Austl.]	57	Fh	39.00S	146.20 E
South East Point [Kir.]	64g	Bb	1.40N	157.10W
Southend	42	He	56.20N	103.14W
Southend-on-Sea	9	Nj	51.33N	0.43 E
Southern [Bots.] [3]	37	Cd	24.45S	24.00 E
Southern [Mwi.] [3]	36	Gf	15.30S	35.00 E
Southern [S.L.] [3]	34	Cd	7.40N	12.15W
Southern [Ug.] [3]	36	Fc	0.30S	30.30 E
Southern [Zam.] [3]	36	Ef	16.00S	27.00 E
Southern Alps	57	Ii	43.30S	170.35 E
Southern Cook Islands	57	Lg	20.00S	159.00W
Southern Cross	58	Ch	31.13S	119.19 E
Southern Desert (EN)= Janūbīyah, Aş Şaḥrā' al-	30	Jf	24.00N	30.00 E
Southern Ghats	25	Ff	10.00N	76.50 E
Southern Gilbert Islands	60	Jh	1.30S	175.30 E
Southern Indian Lake	38	Jd	57.10N	98.40W
Southern Pines	44	Hh	35.11N	79.24W
Southern Region (EN)= Iglim al Janūbīyah [2]	35	Dd	6.00N	30.00 E
Southern Sierra Madre (EN) =Madre del Sur, Sierra-	38	Jj	17.00N	100.00W
Southern Uplands	5	Fd	55.30N	3.30W
Southern Urals (EN)=Južny Ural	5	Le	54.00N	58.30 E
Southern Yemen (EN) → Yemen, People's Democratic Republic of- (EN) [1]	22	Gh	14.00N	46.00 E
South Esk	9	Ke	56.43N	2.28W
South Fiji Basin (EN)	3	Jl	26.00S	175.00 E
South Foreland	9	Oj	51.09N	1.23 E
South Fork	46	Ge	42.26N	116.53W
South Fork Flathead River	46	Ib	48.07N	113.45W
South Fork Grand River	45	Ed	45.43N	102.17W
South Fork Kern River	46	Fi	35.40N	118.27W
South Fork Moreau River	45	Ed	45.09N	102.50W
South Fork Powder River	46	Le	43.40N	106.30W
South Fork Republican River	45	Ff	40.03N	101.31W
South Georgia/Georgia del Sur, Islas-	66	Ad	54.15S	36.45W
South Glamorgan [3]	9	Jj	51.30N	3.15W
South Haven	44	Dd	42.24N	86.16W
South Honshu Ridge (EN)	3	Ig	24.00N	142.00 E
South Horr	36	Gb	2.06N	36.55 E
South Indian Basin (EN)	3	Ho	60.00S	120.00 E
South Island [F.S.M.]	64d	Bc	6.59N	151.59 E
South Island [Kenya]	36	Gb	2.38N	36.36 E
South Island [N.Z.]	57	Ii	44.00S	171.00 E
South Island [Sey.]	37b	Ab	9.26S	46.23 E
South Island [Sey.]	37b	Bc	10.10S	51.10 E

Index Symbols

[1] Independent Nation
[2] State, Region
[3] District, County
[4] Municipality
[5] Colony, Dependency
Continent
Physical Region
Historical or Cultural Region
Mount, Mountain
Volcano
Hill
Mountains, Mountain Range
Hills, Escarpment
Plateau, Upland
Pass, Gap
Plain, Lowland
Delta
Salt Flat
Valley, Canyon
Crater, Cave
Karst Features
Depression
Polder
Desert, Dunes
Forest, Woods
Heath, Steppe
Oasis
Cape, Point
Coast, Beach
Cliff
Peninsula
Isthmus
Sandbank
Island
Atoll
Rock, Reef
Islands, Archipelago
Rocks, Reefs
Coral Reef
Well, Spring
Geyser
River, Stream
Waterfall Rapids
River Mouth, Estuary
Lake
Salt Lake
Intermittent Lake
Reservoir
Swamp, Pond
Canal
Glacier
Ice Shelf, Pack Ice
Ocean
Sea
Gulf, Bay
Strait, Fjord
Lagoon
Bank
Seamount
Tablemount
Ridge
Shelf
Basin
Escarpment, Sea Scarp
Fracture
Trench, Abyss
National Park, Reserve
Point of Interest
Recreation Site
Cave, Cavern
Historic Site
Ruins
Wall, Walls
Church, Abbey
Temple
Scientific Station
Airport
Port
Lighthouse
Mine
Tunnel
Dam, Bridge

South Korea (EN)=Taehan-Min' guk [1] 22 Of 38.00N 127.30 E
South Lake Tahoe 46 Eg 38.57N 120.01W
Southland [2] 62 Bf 45.45S 168.00 E
South Loup River 45 Gf 41.04N 98.40W
South Lueti 36 Df 16.14S 23.12 E
South Magnetic Pole (1980) 66 Ie 65.08S 139.03 E
South Malosmadulu Atoll [5] 25a Ba 5.10N 72.58 E
South Mountain 46 Ge 42.44N 116.54W
South Nahanni 42 Fd 61.03N 123.22W
South Negril Point 47 Ie 18.16N 78.22W
South Orkney Islands 66 Re 60.35S 45.30W
South Pass 38 Ie 42.22N 108.55W
South Pass [F.S.M.] 64d Bb 7.14N 151.48 E
South Pass [U.S.] 45 Ll 28.55N 89.20W
South Platte 38 Ie 41.07N 100.42W
South Point 51q Ab 13.02N 59.31W
South Pole 66 Bg 90.00S 0.00
South Porcupine 44 Ga 48.28N 81.13W
Southport [Eng.-U.K.] 9 Jh 53.39N 3.01W
Southport [N.C.-U.S.] 44 Hi 33.55N 78.01W
South Reef 63a Ee 13.00S 160.32 E
South Ronaldsay 9 Kc 58.46N 2.50W
South Rukuru 36 Fe 10.44S 34.14 E
South Saint Paul 45 Jd 44.52N 93.02W
South Sandwich Islands 66 Ad 56.00S 26.30W
South Sandwich Trench (EN) 3 Do 56.30S 25.00W
South Saskatchewan River 38 Id 53.15N 105.05W
South Shetland Islands 66 Re 62.00S 58.00W
South Shields 9 Lg 55.00N 1.25W
South Sioux City 45 He 42.28N 96.24W
South Sister 46 Ed 44.12N 121.45W
South Taranaki Bight 62 Fc 39.40S 174.15 E
South Trap 62 Bg 47.30S 167.55 E
South Tyne 9 Kg 54.59N 2.08W
South Uist 9 Fd 57.15N 7.24W
South Umpqua River 46 De 43.20N 123.25W
*Southwell 12 Ba 53.04N 0.57W
South Wellesley Islands 59 Hc 17.05S 139.25 E
South West Africa→Namibia [1] 31 Ik 22.00S 17.00 E
Southwest Cape 57 Hi 47.17S 167.27 E
South West Cape 59 Jh 43.34S 146.02 E
Southwest Cape 51a Dc 17.42N 64.53W
Southwest Indian Ridge (EN) 3 Fm 32.00S 55.00 E
Southwest Miramichi River 44 Ob 46.50N 65.45W
Southwest Pacific Basin (EN) 3 Km 40.00S 150.00W
Southwest Pass 45 Ll 29.00N 89.20W
Southwest Point 49 Jb 22.10N 74.10W
South West Point 64g Ab 1.52N 157.33W
South West Point 51p Cb 12.27N 61.30W
Southwold 9 Oi 52.20N 1.40 E
South Yorkshire [3] 9 Lh 53.30N 1.25W
Soutpansberg 37 Dd 22.58S 29.50 E
Soverato 14 Kl 38.41N 16.33 E
Sovetabad 18 Gd 40.14N 69.42 E
Sovetsk [R.S.F.S.R.] 19 Ed 57.36N 48.58 E
Sovetsk [R.S.F.S.R.] 19 Cd 55.05N 21.52 E
Sovetskaja Gavan 22 Qe 48.58N 140.18 E
Sovetski [R.S.F.S.R.] 7 Lh 56.47N 48.30 E
Sovetski [R.S.F.S.R.] 8 Md 60.29N 28.40 E
Sovetski [R.S.F.S.R.] 19 Gc 61.20N 63.29 E
Sovetskoje 19 Ef 47.17N 44.30 E
Soviet Union (EN)→Union of Soviet Socialist Republics(EN) 22 Jd 60.00N 80.00 E
Şowghān 24 Qh 28.20N 56.54 E
Sowie, Góry- 10 Mf 50.38N 16.30 E
Sōya 29a Ba 45.28N 141.53 E
Sōya-Kaikyō=La Perouse Strait (EN) 21 Qe 45.30N 142.00 E
Sōya-Misaki 27 Pb 45.31N 141.56 E
Soyatita 48 Fe 25.45N 107.22W
Soyo 36 Bd 6.05S 12.20 E
Sož 5 Je 51.57N 30.48 E
Sozopol 15 Kg 42.25N 27.42 E
Spa 11 Ld 50.29N 5.52 E
Spain (EN)=España [1] 6 Fg 40.00N 4.00W
Špakovskoje 16 Lg 45.06N 42.00 E
Spalding 9 Mi 52.47N 0.10W
Spanish Fork 46 Jf 40.07N 111.39W
Spanish Peak 46 Fd 44.24N 119.46W
Spanish Point 51d Ba 17.33N 61.44W
Spanish Sahara (EN) →Western Sahara (EN) [5] 31 Ff 24.30N 13.00W
Spanish Town [B.V.I.] 51a Db 18.27N 64.26W
Spanish Town [Jam.] 47 Ie 17.59N 76.57W
Sparbu 7 Ce 63.55N 11.28 E
Spargi, Isola- 14 Di 41.15N 9.20 E
Sparks 43 Dd 39.32N 119.45W
Sparreholm 8 Ge 59.04N 16.49 E
Sparta [Il.-U.S.] 45 Lg 38.07N 89.42W
Sparta [N.C.-U.S.] 44 Gg 36.30N 81.07W
Sparta [Tn.-U.S.] 44 Eh 35.56N 85.29W
Sparta [Wi.-U.S.] 45 Ke 43.57N 90.47W
Sparta (EN)=Spárti 15 Fl 37.05N 22.26 E
Spartanburg 43 Ke 34.57N 81.55W
Spartel, Cap- 30 Ge 35.48N 5.56W
Spárti=Sparta (EN) 15 Fl 37.05N 22.26 E
Spartivento, Capo- [It.] 14 Cl 38.53N 8.50 E
Spartivento, Capo- [It.] 14 Hh 37.55N 16.04 E
Spas-Demensk 16 Ib 54.24N 34.01 E
Spas-Klepiki 7 Ji 55.10N 40.13 E
Spassk-Rjazanski 7 Ji 54.27N 40.22 E
Spátha, Ákra-=Spatha, Cape- (EN) 15 Gn 35.42N 23.44 E
Spatha, Cape- (EN)=Spátha, Ákra- 15 Gn 35.42N 23.44 E
Spearfish 43 Gc 44.30N 103.52W
Spearman 45 Fh 36.12N 101.12W
Speedway 44 Df 39.47N 86.15W
Speicher 12 Ie 49.56N 6.38 E
Speightstown 50 Gf 13.15N 59.39W
Speke Gulf 36 Fc 2.20S 33.15 E
Spello 14 Gh 42.59N 12.40 E
Spenard 40 Jd 61.11N 149.55W
Spence Bay 39 Jc 69.32N 93.31W
Spencer [Ia.-U.S.] 43 Hc 43.09N 95.09W
Spencer [In.-U.S.] 44 Df 39.17N 86.46W
Spencer [Nb.-U.S.] 45 Ge 42.53N 98.42W
Spencer [W.V.-U.S.] 44 Gf 38.48N 81.22W
Spencer, Cape- 59 Hg 35.18S 136.53 E
Spencer Gulf 57 Eh 34.00S 137.00 E
Spenge 12 Kb 52.08N 8.29 E
Spenser Mountains 62 Ee 42.10S 172.35 E
Sperillen 8 Dd 60.30N 10.05 E
Sperkhiós 15 Fk 38.52N 22.34 E
Sperlonga 14 Hi 41.15N 13.26 E
Sperone, Capo- 14 Cl 38.55N 8.25 E
Sperrin Mountains/Sliabh Speirin 9 Fg 54.50N 7.05W
Spessart 10 Fg 49.55N 9.30 E
Spétsai 15 Gl 37.16N 23.09 E
Spétsai 15 Gl 37.16N 23.08 E
Spey 9 Jd 57.40N 3.06W
Spey Bay 9 Jd 57.40N 3.05W
Speyer 10 Eg 49.19N 8.26 E
Speyer-bach 12 Ke 49.19N 8.27 E
Speyside 50 Fg 11.18N 60.32W
Spezzano Albanese 14 Kk 39.40N 16.19 E
Spicer Islands 42 Jc 68.10N 79.00W
Spiekeroog 10 Dc 53.46N 7.42 E
Spiez 14 Bd 46.41N 7.42 E
Spijkenisse 12 Gc 51.51N 4.21 E
Spilimbergo 14 Gd 46.07N 12.54 E
Spilion 15 Hn 35.13N 24.32 E
Spilsby 12 Ca 53.11N 0.06 E
Spina 14 Gf 44.42N 12.08 E
Spinazzola 14 Kj 40.58N 16.05 E
Spincourt 12 He 49.20N 5.40 E
Spirit River 42 Fe 55.47N 118.50W
Spirovo 7 Ih 57.27N 35.01 E
Spiš 10 Qg 49.05N 20.30 E
Spišská Nová Ves 10 Qh 48.57N 20.34 E
Spitak 16 Ni 40.49N 44.14 E
Spitsbergen 67 Kd 78.00N 19.00 E
Spitsbergen 67 Kd 78.45N 16.00 E
Spittal an der Drau 14 Hd 46.48N 13.30 E
Spitzbergen Bank (EN) 41 Oc 76.00N 23.00 E
Spjelkavik 7 Be 62.28N 6.23 E
Split 6 Hg 43.31N 16.26 E
Split Lake 42 He 56.10N 96.10W
Spluga, Passo dello- 14 Dd 46.29N 9.20 E
Splügenpaß 14 Dd 46.29N 9.20 E
Spógi/Špogi 8 Lh 56.02N 26.52 E
Špogi/Spógi 8 Lh 56.02N 26.52 E
Spokane 39 He 47.40N 117.23W
Spokane, Mount- 46 Gc 47.55N 117.07W
Spokane River 46 Fc 47.44N 118.20W
Špola 19 Df 49.01N 31.24 E
Spoleto 14 Gh 42.44N 12.44 E
Spooner 45 Kd 45.50N 91.53W
Spoon River 45 Kf 40.18N 90.04W
Sporovo 10 Vd 52.25N 25.27 E
Spotsylvania 44 If 38.12N 77.35W
Sprague 46 Gc 47.18N 117.59W
Sprague River 46 Ee 42.34N 121.51W
Spray 46 Fd 44.50N 119.48W
Spreča 14 Mf 44.44N 18.06 E
Spree 10 Jd 52.32N 13.13 E
Spreewald 10 Je 51.55N 14.00 E
Spremberg/Grodk 10 Ke 51.33N 14.22 E
Sprengisandur 7a Bb 64.40N 18.07W
Springbok 31 Ik 29.43S 17.15 E
Spring Creek 45 Fd 45.45N 100.18W
Springdale 45 Ih 36.11N 94.08W
Springe 10 Fd 52.13N 9.33 E
Springer 45 Dh 36.22N 104.36W
Springer, Mount- 44 Ja 49.48N 74.51W
Springerville 46 Ki 34.08N 109.17W
Springfield [Co.-U.S.] 45 Eh 37.24N 102.37W
Springfield [Il.-U.S.] 39 Kf 39.47N 89.40W
Springfield [Ma.-U.S.] 43 Mc 42.07N 72.36W
Springfield [Mn.-U.S.] 45 Id 44.14N 94.59W
Springfield [Mo.-U.S.] 39 Jf 37.14N 93.17W
Springfield [N.Z.] 62 De 43.20S 171.56 E
Springfield [Oh.-U.S.] 43 Kd 39.55N 83.48W
Springfield [Or.-U.S.] 43 Cc 44.03N 123.01W
Springfield [S.D.-U.S.] 45 He 42.49N 97.54W
Springfield [Tn.-U.S.] 44 Dg 36.31N 86.52W
Springfontein 37 Df 30.19S 25.36 E
Spring Garden 50 Gd 6.59N 58.31W
Spring Hall 51q Ab 13.19N 59.36W
Springhill [La.-U.S.] 45 Jj 33.00N 93.28W
Springhill [N.S.-Can.] 42 Lg 45.39N 64.03W
Spring Mountains 46 Hh 36.10N 115.40W
Springs 37 De 26.13S 28.25 E
Springsure 59 Jd 24.07S 148.05 E
Spring Valley 46 Hg 39.10N 114.30W
Spring Valley 45 Je 43.41N 92.23W
Springville 46 Jf 40.10N 111.37W
Spruce Knob 38 Lf 38.42N 79.32W
Spruce Mountain [Az.-U.S.] 46 Ii 34.28N 112.24W
Spruce Mountain [Nv.-U.S.] 46 Hf 40.33N 114.49W
Spulico, Capo- 14 Kk 39.58N 16.38 E
Spurn Head 9 Nh 53.34N 0.07 E
Squamish 42 Fg 49.42N 123.09W
Squillace 14 Kl 38.47N 16.31 E
Squillace, Golfo di- 14 Kl 38.45N 16.50 E
Squinzano 14 Mj 40.26N 18.02 E
Srbica 15 Dg 42.45N 20.47 E
Srbija=Serbia (EN) 15 Df 44.00N 21.00 E
Srbija=Serbia (EN) [2] 15 Df 44.00N 21.00 E
Srbija=Serbia (EN) 5 Ig 43.00N 21.00 E
Srbobran 15 Cd 45.33N 19.48 E
Srē Âmběl 25 Kf 11.07N 103.46 E
Sredinny Hrebet 21 Rd 56.00N 158.00 E
Sredna Gora 15 Hg 42.30N 25.00 E
Srednekolymsk 20 Kc 67.27N 153.41 E
Srednerusskaja Vozvyšennost'=Central Russian Uplands (EN) 5 Je 52.00N 38.00 E
Srednesatyginski Tuman, Ozero- 17 Lg 59.45N 65.25 E
Srednesibirskoje Ploskogorje=Central Siberian Uplands (EN) 21 Mc 65.00N 105.00 E
Sredni Kujto, Ozero- 7 Hd 65.05N 31.30 E
Sredni Ural=Central Urals (EN) 5 Ld 58.00N 59.00 E
Sredni Urgal 20 If 51.13N 132.58 E
Sredni Verecki, Pereval- 16 Ce 48.49N 23.07 E
Srednjaja Ahtuba 16 Ne 48.43N 44.52 E
Srednjaja Olëkma 20 He 55.26N 120.40 E
Śrem 10 Nd 52.08N 17.01 E
Sremska Mitrovica 15 Ce 44.58N 19.37 E
Sremski Karlovci 15 Cd 45.12N 19.56 E
Sretensk 22 Nd 52.15N 117.43 E
Sri Gangānagar 25 Ec 29.55N 73.53 E
Srijem 15 Cd 45.00N 19.40 E
Srīkākulam 25 Ge 18.18N 83.54 E
Srī Lanka (Ceylon) [1] 22 Ki 7.40N 80.50 E
Srīnagar 22 Jf 34.05N 74.49 E
Srivardhan 25 Ee 18.02N 73.01 E
Środa Śląska 10 Me 51.10N 16.36 E
Środa Wielkopolska 10 Nd 52.14N 17.17 E
Srpska Crnja 15 Dd 45.43N 20.42 E
Sruth na Maoile/North Channel 5 Fd 55.10N 5.40W
SSSR=Union of Soviet Socialist Republics (USSR) (EN) [1] 22 Jd 60.00N 80.00 E
SSSR→Sojuz Sovetskih Socialističeskih Respublik [1] 22 Jd 60.00N 80.00 E
Ssu-ch'uan Sheng→Sichuan Sheng=Szechwan (EN) [2] 27 He 30.00N 103.00 E
Staaten River 59 Ic 16.24S 141.17 E
Stabroek 12 Gc 51.20N 4.22 E
Stack Skerry 9 Ib 59.02N 4.30W
Stade 10 Fc 53.36N 9.29 E
Staden 12 Fd 50.59N 3.01 E
Stadhavet 8 Ab 62.15N 5.05 E
Städjan 8 Ec 61.58N 12.52 E
Stadlandet 8 Ab 62.05N 5.20 E
Stadskanaal 11 Ma 53.00N 6.55 E
Stadskanaal-Musselkanaal 12 Jb 52.56N 7.02 E
Stadthagen 12 Lb 52.19N 9.12 E
Stadtkyll 12 Id 50.21N 6.32 E
Stadtlohn 12 Ic 51.59N 6.56 E
Stadtoldendorf 10 Fe 51.54N 9.39 E
Staffa 9 Ge 56.25N 6.10W
Staffanstorp 8 Ei 55.38N 13.13 E
Staffelsee 10 Hi 47.42N 11.10 E
Staffora 14 De 45.04N 9.01 E
Stafford 9 Li 52.50N 2.00W
Stafford 9 Ki 52.48N 2.07W
Staffordshire [3] 9 Li 52.55N 2.00W
Staicele/Stajcele 8 Kg 57.44N 24.39 E
Stainach 14 Ic 47.32N 14.06 E
Staines 12 Bc 51.26N 0.31W
Stajcele/Staicele 8 Kg 57.44N 24.39 E
Stakčín 10 Sg 49.00N 22.13 E
Stalać 15 Ef 43.40N 21.25 E
Stalham 12 Db 52.46N 1.31 E
Stalingrad→Volgograd 6 Kf 48.44N 44.25 E
Ställdalen 8 Fe 59.56N 14.56 E
Stalowa Wola 10 Sf 50.35N 22.02 E
Stamberger See 10 Ii 47.55N 12.20 E
Stamford [Ct.-U.S.] 44 Ke 41.03N 73.32W
Stamford [Eng.-U.K.] 9 Mi 52.39N 0.29W
Stamford [Tx.-U.S.] 45 Gj 32.57N 99.48W
Stamford, Lake- 45 Gj 33.05N 99.35W
Stampriet 37 Bd 24.20S 18.28 E
Stamsund 7 Cb 68.08N 13.51 E
Stanberry 45 If 40.13N 94.35W
Stancija Jakkabag 18 Fe 38.59N 66.42 E
Stancija-Karakul 19 Gh 39.30N 63.50 E
Standerton 37 De 26.58S 29.07 E
Standish 44 Fd 44.00N 83.57W
Stanford 46 Jc 47.09N 110.13W
Stånga 8 Hg 57.17N 18.28 E
Stångån 8 Ff 58.27N 15.37 E
Stange 8 Dd 60.43N 11.11 E
Stanger 37 Ee 29.27S 31.14 E
Stanke Dimitrov 15 Gg 42.16N 23.07 E
Stanley [Austl.] 59 Jh 40.46S 145.18 E
Stanley [Falk. Is.] 53 Kk 51.42S 57.51W
Stanley [N.D.-U.S.] 45 Eb 48.19N 102.23W
Stanley Falls (EN)=Ngaliema, Chutes- 30 Jh 0.30N 25.30 E
Stann Creek 49 Ce 16.50N 88.30W
Stanovoje Nagorje=Stanovoy Upland (EN) 21 Nd 56.00N 114.00 E
Stanovoj Hrebet=Stanovoy Range (EN) 21 Od 56.20N 126.00 E
Stanovoy Upland (EN)=Stanovoje Nagorje 21 Nd 56.00N 114.00 E
Stans 14 Cd 46.58N 8.22 E
Stansted Airport 12 Cc 51.54N 0.13 E
Stansted Mountfitchet 12 Cc 51.54N 0.12 E
Stanthorpe 59 Ke 28.39S 151.57 E
Stanton Banks 9 Fe 56.15N 7.50W
Staphorst 12 Ib 52.38N 6.14 E
Staples 45 Ic 46.21N 94.48W
Stapleton 45 Ff 41.29N 100.31W
Stąporków 10 Qe 51.09N 20.34 E
Starachowice 10 Re 51.03N 21.04 E
Staraja Majna 7 Li 54.36N 48.59 E
Staraja Russa 19 Dd 57.59N 31.23 E
Staraja-Vyževka 10 Ue 51.27N 24.34 E
Stará L'ubovňa 10 Qg 49.18N 20.42 E
Stara Moravica 15 Cd 45.52N 19.28 E
Stara Pazova 15 De 44.59N 20.10 E
Stara Planina = Balkan Mountains (EN) 5 Ig 43.15N 25.00 E
Stara Zagora [2] 15 Ig 42.25N 25.38 E
Stara Zagora 6 Ig 42.25N 25.38 E
Starbuck Island 57 Le 5.37S 155.53W
Staretina 14 Kf 44.02N 16.43 E
Stargard Szczeciński 10 Lc 53.20N 15.02 E
Stari Begejski kanal 15 Dd 45.29N 20.25 E
Starica 7 Ih 56.30N 34.56 E
Starigrad 14 Kg 43.11N 16.36 E
Stari Vlah 15 Df 43.23N 20.10 E
Starke 44 Fk 29.57N 82.07W
Starkville 45 Lj 33.28N 88.48W
Starnberg 10 Hh 48.00N 11.21 E
Starobelsk 19 Df 49.15N 38.58 E
Starodub 19 De 52.35N 32.46 E
Starogard Gdański 10 Oc 53.59N 18.33 E
Starokonstantinov 16 Ee 49.43N 27.13 E
Starominskaja 19 Df 46.31N 39.06 E
Staroščerbinovskaja 16 Kf 46.37N 38.42 E
Starosubhangulovo 17 Hj 53.06N 57.20 E
Starotimoškino 7 Lj 53.43N 47.32 E
Start Point 9 Jk 50.13N 3.38W
Staryje Dorogi 16 Fc 53.02N 28.17 E
Stary Krym 16 Ig 45.02N 35.05 E
Stary Oskol 19 De 51.18N 37.51 E
Stary Sambor 16 Ce 49.29N 23.01 E
Stary Terek 16 Og 44.01N 47.24 E
Staßfurt 10 He 51.52N 11.35 E
Staszów 10 Rf 50.34N 21.10 E
State College 44 Ie 40.48N 77.52W
Staten Island (EN)=Estados, Isla de los- 52 Jk 54.47S 64.15W
Statesboro 44 Gi 32.27N 81.47W
Statesville 44 Gh 35.47N 80.53W
Stathelle 8 Ce 59.03N 9.41 E
Stathmós Krioneriou 15 Ek 38.20N 21.35 E
Statland 7 Cd 64.30N 11.08 E
Staunton 43 Ld 38.10N 79.05W
Stavanger 6 Gd 58.58N 5.45 E
Stavelot 12 Hd 50.23N 5.56 E
Staveren 11 Lb 52.53N 5.22 E
Stavern 8 Df 59.00N 10.02 E
Stavnoje 10 Sh 48.59N 22.45 E
Stavropol 6 Kf 45.02N 41.59 E
Stavropolskaja Vozvyšennost 16 Mg 45.10N 43.00 E
Stavropolski Kraj [3] 19 Eg 45.00N 43.15 E
Stavrós [Grc.] 15 Fj 39.19N 22.14 E
Stavrós [Grc.] 15 Gi 40.40N 23.42 E
Stavroúpolis 15 Hh 41.12N 24.42 E
Stawell 59 Ig 37.04S 142.46 E
Stawiski 10 Sc 53.23N 22.09 E
Stawiszyn 10 Oe 51.55N 18.07 E
Stayton 46 Dd 44.48N 122.48W
Steamboat Springs 43 Fc 40.29N 106.50W
Stebnik 10 Tg 49.14N 23.34 E
Stedingen 12 Ka 53.10N 8.30 E
Steele 45 Gc 46.51N 99.55W
Steelpoort 37 Ed 24.48S 30.12 E
Steenbergen 12 Gc 51.35N 4.19 E
Steen River 42 Fe 59.38N 117.06W
Steensby Inlet 42 Jb 70.10N 78.25W
Steenstrups Gletscher 41 Gc 75.15N 57.30W
Steenvoorde 12 Ed 50.48N 2.35 E
Steenwijk 11 Mb 52.47N 6.08 E
Ştefăneşti 15 Kb 47.48N 27.12 E
Stefanie, Lake- (EN)=Chew Bahir 30 Kh 4.38N 36.50 E
Stefansson 42 Gb 73.30N 105.30W
Ştefleşti, Vîrful- 15 Gd 45.32N 23.48 E
Stege 8 Ej 54.59N 12.18 E
Steiermark = Styria (EN) 14 Ic 47.15N 15.00 E
Steiermark = Styria (EN) [2] 14 Ic 47.15N 15.00 E
Steigerwald 10 Gg 49.40N 10.20 E
Steilrandberge 37 Ac 17.53S 13.20 E
Steinach 14 Fc 47.05N 11.28 E
Steinbach 42 Hg 49.32N 96.41W
Steinen, Rio- 54 Hf 12.05S 53.46W
Steinfeld (Oldenburg) 12 Kb 52.36N 8.13 E
Steinfort/Steinfurt 12 He 49.40N 5.55 E
Steinfurt 10 Dd 52.09N 7.20 E
Steinfurt/Steinfort 12 He 49.40N 5.55 E
Steinfurt-Borghorst 12 Jb 52.08N 7.25 E
Steinhagen 12 Kb 52.01N 8.24 E
Steinhausen 37 Bd 21.49S 18.20 E
Steinheim 12 Lc 51.51N 9.06 E
Steinhuder Meer 10 Fd 52.28N 9.19 E
Steinkjer 7 Cd 64.01N 11.30 E
Steinkopf 37 Be 29.18S 17.43 E
Steinshamn 8 Bb 62.47N 6.29 E
Steinsøy 7 Ac 61.00N 4.30 E
Steirisch-Niederösterreichische Kalkalpen 14 Jc 47.45N 15.30 E
Stekene 12 Gc 51.12N 4.02 E
Stekolny 20 Ke 60.00N 150.50 E
Stella 37 Ce 26.33S 24.53 E
Stellenbosch 37 Bf 33.58S 18.50 E
Stello 11a Ba 42.47N 9.25 E
Stelvio, Passo dello-/Stilfser Joch 14 Ed 46.32N 10.27 E
Stemwede 12 Kb 52.26N 8.26 E
Stenay 11 Le 49.29N 5.11 E
Stendal 10 Hd 52.36N 11.51 E
Stende 8 Jg 57.10N 22.28 E
Stende 8 Ig 57.40N 21.57 E
Stenhouse Bay 59 Hg 35.17S 136.56 E
Stenstorp 8 Ef 58.16N 13.43 E
Stenungsund 7 Cg 58.05N 11.49 E
Stepanakert 6 Kh 39.49N 46.44 E
Stepanavan 16 Ni 40.59N 44.20 E
Stephens, Cape- 62 Ed 40.42S 173.57 E
Stephens, Mount- 66 Rg 83.23S 51.27W
Stephens Passage 40 Me 57.50N 133.50W
Stephenville [Newf.-Can.] 42 Lg 48.33N 58.35W
Stephenville [Tx.-U.S.] 45 Gj 32.13N 98.12W
Steps Point 65c Cb 14.22S 170.45W
Sterea Ellás kai Évvoia [2] 15 Hk 38.20N 24.30 E
Sterkstroom 37 Df 31.32S 26.32 E
Sterlibaševo 17 Gj 53.28N 55.15 E
Sterling [Co.-U.S.] 43 Gc 40.37N 103.13W
Sterling [Il.-U.S.] 45 Lf 41.48N 89.42W
Sterling City 45 Fk 31.50N 100.59W
Sterlitamak 6 Le 53.37N 55.58 E
Šternberk 10 Ng 49.44N 17.19 E
Sterzing / Vipiteno 14 Fd 46.54N 11.26 E
Stettin (EN)=Szczecin 6 He 53.24N 14.32 E
Stettiner Haff 10 Kc 53.46N 14.14 E
Stettler 42 Gf 52.19N 112.43W
Steubenville 43 Kc 40.22N 80.39W
Stevenage 9 Mj 51.54N 0.11W
Stevenson Entrance 40 Ie 57.45N 152.20W
Stevens Point 43 Jc 44.31N 89.34W
Stewart 42 Dd 63.18N 139.24W
Stewart 42 Ee 55.56N 129.59W
Stewart Crossing 42 Dd 63.19N 136.33W
Stewart Island 57 Hi 47.00S 167.50 E
Stewart Islands 57 He 8.20S 162.40 E
Steyerberg 12 Lb 52.34N 9.02 E
Steyning 12 Bd 50.53N 0.20W
Steynsburg 37 Df 31.15S 25.49 E
Steyr 14 Ib 48.02N 14.25 E
Steyr 14 Ib 48.03N 14.25 E
Štiavnické vrchy 10 Oh 48.15N 18.50 E
Stidia 13 Li 35.50N 0.05W
Stiene 8 Kg 57.19N 24.28 E
Stiens, Leeuwarderadeel- 12 Ha 53.16N 5.46 E
Stigliano 14 Kj 40.24N 16.14 E
St. Ignace 43 Kb 45.52N 84.43W
Stigtomta 8 Gf 58.48N 16.47 E
Stikine 38 Fd 56.40N 132.30W
Stikine Ranges 42 Ee 57.35N 131.00W
Stilfer Joch/Stelvio, Passo dello- 14 Ed 46.32N 10.27 E
Stilfontein 37 De 26.50S 26.50 E
Stilis 15 Fk 38.55N 22.37 E
Stillwater [Mn.-U.S.] 43 Jd 45.04N 92.49W
Stillwater [Ok.-U.S.] 43 Hd 36.07N 97.04W
Stillwater Range 46 Fg 39.50N 118.15W
Stilo 14 Kl 38.29N 16.28 E
Stilo, Punta- 14 Kl 38.27N 16.35 E
Štimlje 15 Eg 42.26N 21.03 E
Stînişoarei, Munţii- 15 Ib 47.20N 26.00 E
Stinnett 45 Fi 35.50N 101.27W
Štip 15 Fh 41.44N 22.12 E
Stirling 9 Je 56.07N 3.57W
Stirling Range 59 Df 34.25S 117.50 E
Stjernøya 7 Fa 70.18N 22.45 E
Stjørdalshalsen 7 Ce 63.28N 10.44 E
Stobi 15 Eh 41.33N 21.59 E
Stobrawa 10 Nf 50.50N 17.32 E
Stocka 8 Gc 61.54N 17.20 E
Stockach 10 Fi 47.51N 9.01 E
Stockbridge 12 Ac 51.06N 1.29W
Stockerau 14 Kb 48.23N 16.13 E
Stockholm [2] 7 Dg 59.20N 18.00 E
Stockholm 6 Hd 59.20N 18.03 E
Stockport 9 Kh 53.25N 2.10W
Stocks Seamount (EN) 52 Mg 12.15S 32.00W
Stockton [Ca.-U.S.] 39 Gf 37.57N 121.17W
Stockton [Mo.-U.S.] 45 Jh 37.42N 93.48W
Stockton Lake 45 Jh 37.40N 93.45W
Stockton-on-Tees 9 Lg 54.34N 1.19W
Stockton Plateau 43 Ge 30.30N 102.30W
Stoczek Łukowski 10 Re 51.58N 21.58 E
Stöde 7 De 62.25N 16.35 E
Stoĕng Trĕng 25 Lf 13.31N 105.58 E
Stoer, Point of- 9 Hc 58.20N 5.25W
Stogovo 15 Dh 41.29N 20.39 E
Stohod 10 Ve 51.52N 25.44 E
Stoholm 8 Ch 56.29N 9.10 E
Stoj, Gora- 16 Ce 48.39N 23.15 E
Stojba 22 Pd 52.49N 131.43 E
Stoke-on-Trent 9 Kh 53.00N 2.10W
Stokksnes 7a Cb 64.14N 14.58W
Stokmarknes 7 Db 68.34N 14.55 E
Stol 15 Fe 44.11N 22.09 E
Stolac 14 Lg 43.05N 17.58 E
Stolbcy 16 Ec 53.31N 26.43 E
Stolberg 10 Cf 50.46N 6.14 E
Stolbovoj, Ostrov- 20 Ib 74.05N 136.00 E
Stolin 16 Ed 51.57N 26.52 E
Stolzenau 12 Lb 52.31N 9.04 E
Ston 14 Lh 42.50N 17.42 E
Stone 9 Ki 52.54N 2.10W
Stonehaven 9 Ke 56.58N 2.13W
Stonehenge 9 Lj 51.11N 1.49W
Stonehenge 59 Id 24.22S 143.17 E
Stoner 45 Bh 37.37N 108.19W
Stonewall 45 Ha 50.09N 97.21W
Stony 40 Hd 61.45N 156.35W
Stony Rapids 42 Ge 59.16N 105.50W
Stony River 40 Hd 61.47N 156.41W
Stony Stratford 12 Bb 52.03N 0.51W
Stony Tunguska (EN)=Podkamennaja Tunguska 21 Lc 61.36N 90.18 E
Stör 10 Fc 53.50N 9.25 E
Storå 8 Ch 56.19N 8.19 E
Storå 8 Fe 59.43N 15.08 E
Storå/Isojoki 7 Ee 62.07N 21.58 E
Stora Gla 8 Ee 59.30N 12.30 E
Stora Le 8 De 59.05N 11.55 E
Stora Lulevatten 7 Ec 67.08N 19.20 E
Storavan 7 Ed 65.42N 18.12 E
Storby 8 Hd 60.13N 19.34 E
Stord 7 Ag 59.55N 5.25 E
Storđa 7 Ee 62.07N 21.58 E
Stordal 8 Bb 62.23N 7.01 E

Index Symbols

[1] Independent Nation
[2] State, Region
[3] District, County
[4] Municipality
[5] Colony, Dependency
Continent
Physical Region
Historical or Cultural Region
Mount, Mountain
Volcano
Hill
Mountains, Mountain Range
Hills, Escarpment
Plateau, Upland
Pass, Gap
Plain, Lowland
Delta
Salt Flat
Valley, Canyon
Crater, Cave
Karst Features
Depression
Polder
Desert, Dunes
Forest, Woods
Heath, Steppe
Oasis
Cape, Point
Coast, Beach
Cliff
Peninsula
Isthmus
Sandbank
Island
Atoll
Rock, Reef
Islands, Archipelago
Rocks, Reefs
Coral Reef
Well, Spring
Geyser
River, Stream
Waterfall Rapids
River Mouth, Estuary
Lake
Salt Lake
Intermittent Lake
Reservoir
Swamp, Pond
Canal
Glacier
Ice Shelf, Pack Ice
Ocean
Sea
Gulf, Bay
Strait, Fjord
Lagoon
Bank
Seamount
Tablemount
Ridge
Shelf
Basin
Escarpment, Sea Scarp
Fracture
Trench, Abyss
National Park, Reserve
Point of Interest
Recreation Site
Cave, Cavern
Historic Site
Ruins
Wall, Walls
Church, Abbey
Temple
Scientific Station
Airport
Port
Lighthouse
Mine
Tunnel
Dam, Bridge

Store Bælt = Great Belt (EN) 5 Hd 55.30N 11.00 E
Storebro 8 Fg 57.35N 15.51 E
Storefiskbank 9 Qe 56.50N 4.00 E
Store Heddinge 8 Ei 55.19N 12.25 E
Store Hellefiske Bank (EN) 41 Ge 67.30N 55.00W
Store Koldewey 41 Kc 76.20N 18.30W
Store Kvien 8 Dc 61.34N 10.33 E
Støren 7 Ce 63.02N 10.18 E
Store Nupsfonn 8 Be 59.54N 7.08 E
Store Sølnkletten 8 Dc 61.59N 10.18 E
Storfjorden [Nor.] 8 Bb 62.25N 6.30 E
Storfjorden [Sval.] 41 Nc 77.30N 20.00 E
Storfors 8 Fe 59.32N 14.16 E
Storis Passage 42 Hc 67.40N 98.30W
Storkerson Bay 42 Fb 73.00N 124.00W
Storkerson Peninsula 42 Gb 73.00N 106.30W
Storlien 7 Ce 63.19N 12.06 E
Stormarn 10 Gc 53.45N 10.20 E
Storm Bay 59 Jh 43.10S 147.30 E
Storm Lake 43 Hc 42.39N 95.13W
Stornoway 9 Gc 58.12N 6.23W
Storøya 41 Ob 80.08N 27.50 E
Storožinec 16 De 48.10N 25.46 E
Storsjøen [Nor.] 8 Dd 60.25N 11.40 E
Storsjøen [Nor.] 8 Dd 61.35N 11.15 E
Storsjön [Swe.] 8 Gd 60.35N 16.45 E
Storsjön [Swe.] 5 Hc 63.15N 14.20 E
Storsteinfjellet 7 Db 68.14N 17.52 E
Storstrøm 8 Dj 55.00N 11.50 E
Storstrømmen 41 Jc 77.20N 23.00W
Storsudret 8 Hh 57.00N 18.15 E
Storuman 7 Dd 65.14N 16.54 E
Storuman 6 Hb 65.06N 17.06 E
Storvätteshågna 8 Eb 62.07N 12.27 E
Storvigelen 8 Eb 62.32N 12.04 E
Storvik 8 Gd 60.35N 16.32 E
Storvreta 8 Ge 59.58N 17.42 E
Stöttingfjället 7 Dd 64.38N 17.44 E
Stoughton 46 Nb 49.41N 103.03W
Stour [Eng.-U.K.] 9 Lk 50.43N 1.46W
Stour [Eng.-U.K.] 9 Oj 51.52N 1.16 E
Stourbridge 9 Ki 52.27N 2.09W
Støvring 8 Ch 56.53N 9.51 E
Stowmarket 12 Cb 52.11N 0.59 E
Strabane/An Srath Bán 9 Fg 54.49N 7.27W
Stradella 14 De 45.05N 9.18 E
Straelen 12 Ic 51.27N 6.16 E
Strakonice 10 Jg 49.16N 13.55 E
Straldža 15 Jg 42.36N 26.41 E
Stralsund 6 He 54.18N 13.06 E
Strand 37 Bf 34.06S 18.50 E
Stranda 7 Be 62.19N 6.54 E
Strand Bay 42 Ia 79.00N 94.00W
Strangford Lough/Loch Cuan 9 Hg 54.26N 5.36W
Strängnäs 8 Ge 59.23N 17.02 E
Stranraer 9 Hg 54.54N 5.02W
Strasbourg [Fr.] 6 Gf 48.35N 7.45 E
Strasbourg [Sask.-Can.] 46 Ma 51.04N 104.57W
Strašeny 16 Ff 47.06N 28.34 E
Straßwalchen 14 Hc 47.59N 13.15 E
Stratford [N.Z.] 62 Fc 39.21S 174.17 E
Stratford [Ont.-Can.] 44 Gd 43.22N 80.57W
Stratford [Tx.-U.S.] 45 Eh 36.20N 102.04W
Stratford-upon-Avon 9 Li 52.12N 1.41W
Strathclyde 9 If 55.50N 4.50W
Strathgordon 59 Jh 42.54S 146.10 E
Strathmore 9 Je 56.40N 3.05W
Strathmore 46 Ia 51.03N 113.23W
Strathroy 44 Gd 42.57N 81.38W
Strathy Point 9 Ic 58.35N 4.01W
Straubenhardt 12 Kf 48.50N 8.34 E
Straubing 10 Ih 48.53N 12.34 E
Straumnes 7a Aa 66.26N 23.08W
Straumsjøen 7 Db 68.41N 14.30 E
Strausberg 10 Jd 52.35N 13.53 E
Strawberry Mountain 46 Fd 44.19N 118.43W
Strawberry River 46 Jf 40.10N 110.24W
Straža 15 Fg 42.15N 22.14 E
Stražica 15 If 43.14N 25.58 E
Strážiště 10 Kg 49.32N 14.58 E
Strážovské vrchy 10 Oh 48.55N 18.30 E
Streaky Bay 59 Gf 32.48S 134.13 E
Streaky Bay 59 Gf 32.35S 134.10 E
Streator 45 Lf 41.07N 88.50W
Středočeská pahorkatina 10 Kg 49.30N 14.15 E
Středočeský kraj 10 Kg 49.55N 14.30 E
Středoslovenský kraj 10 Ph 48.50N 19.10 E
Strehaia 15 Ge 44.37N 23.12 E
Strei 15 Gd 45.51N 23.03 E
Střela 10 Jg 49.54N 13.32 E
Strelasund 10 Jb 54.20N 13.05 E
Strelka 20 Ee 58.03N 93.05 E
Strelna 7 Jc 66.04N 38.39 E
Strenči 7 Fh 57.39N 25.38 E
Stresa 14 Ce 45.53N 8.32 E
Streževoj 20 Cd 60.42N 77.35 E
Stříbro 10 Ig 49.46N 13.00 E
Strickland River 59 Ia 6.00S 142.05 E
Strîmbeni 15 He 44.28N 24.58 E
Strimón 15 Gi 40.47N 23.51 E
Strimonikós Kólpos 15 Gi 40.40N 23.50 E
Strjama 15 Hg 42.10N 24.56 E
Strofádhes, Nisoi- 15 Dl 37.15N 21.00 E
Ströhen, Wagenfeld- 12 Kb 52.32N 8.39 E
Stromberg 12 Je 49.57N 7.46 E
Stromboli 14 Jl 38.45N 15.15 E
Strömfors/Ruotsinpyhtää 8 Ld 60.32N 26.27 E
Stromness 9 Jc 58.57N 3.18W
Strömsbro 8 Gd 60.42N 17.10 E
Strömsbruk 7 Dc 61.53N 17.19 E
Strömsnäsbruk 8 Eh 56.33N 13.43 E
Strömstad 7 Cf 58.56N 11.10 E
Strömsund 7 De 63.51N 15.35 E
Strongili 15 Hm 36.58N 24.55 E
Ströngoli 14 Lk 39.16N 17.03 E
Stronsay 9 Kb 59.08N 2.38W
Stropkov 10 Rg 49.12N 21.40 E
Stroud 9 Kj 51.45N 2.12W
Struer 7 Bh 56.29N 8.37 E
Struga 15 Dh 41.11N 20.41 E
Strugi-Krasnyje 7 Gg 58.17N 29.08 E
Strule 9 Fg 54.40N 7.20W
Struma 5 Ig 40.47N 23.51 E
Strumble Head 9 Hi 52.02N 5.04W
Strumica 15 Fh 41.26N 22.39 E
Stry 16 De 49.24N 24.13 E
Stry 19 Cf 49.14N 23.49 E
Strydenburg 37 Ce 29.58S 23.40 E
Stryn 7 Bf 61.55N 6.47 E
Strynsvatn 8 Bc 61.55N 7.05 E
Strzegom 10 Mf 50.57N 16.21 E
Strzegomka 10 Me 51.08N 16.50 E
Strzelce Krajeńskie 10 Ld 52.53N 15.32 E
Strzelce Opolskie 10 Of 50.31N 18.19 E
Strzelin 10 Nf 50.47N 17.03 E
Strzelno 10 Od 52.38N 18.11 E
Strzyżów 10 Rg 49.52N 21.47 E
Stuart 40 Gd 63.35N 162.30W
Stuart, Mount- 46 Ec 47.29N 120.54W
Stuart Bluff Range 59 Gd 22.45S 132.15 E
Stuart Lake 42 Ff 54.33N 124.35W
Stuart Range 59 Ge 29.10S 134.55 E
Stubaier Alpen 14 Fc 47.10N 11.05 E
Stubbekøbing 8 Ej 54.43N 12.03 E
Stubbenkammer 10 Jb 54.35N 13.40 E
Stubbs Bay 51n Ba 13.08N 61.10W
Štubik 15 Fe 44.18N 22.21 E
Stucka 7 Fh 56.36N 25.17 E
Studenica, Manastir- 15 Df 43.28N 20.37 E
Studholme Junction 62 Df 44.44S 171.08 E
Stugun 7 De 63.10N 15.36 E
Stuhr 12 Ka 53.02N 8.45 E
Stupino 7 Ji 54.57N 38.03 E
Stura di Demonte 14 Bf 44.40N 7.53 E
Stura di Lanzo 14 Be 45.06N 7.44 E
Sturge Island 66 Ke 67.27S 164.18 E
Sturgeon Bay 45 Md 44.50N 87.23W
Sturgeon Falls 42 Jg 46.22N 79.55W
Sturgeon Lake 45 Kb 50.00N 90.45W
Sturgis [Mi.-U.S.] 44 Ee 41.48N 85.25W
Sturgis [S.D.-U.S.] 45 Ed 44.25N 103.31W
Sturkö 8 Fh 56.05N 15.40 E
Sturt Creek 59 Fd 20.08S 127.24 E
Sturt Desert 59 Ie 28.30S 141.00 E
Stutterheim 37 Df 32.33S 27.28 E
Stuttgart [Ar.-U.S.] 45 Ki 34.30N 91.33W
Stuttgart [F.R.G.] 6 Gf 48.46N 9.11 E
Stviga 16 Ec 52.04N 27.55 E
Stykkishólmur 7a Ab 65.04N 22.44W
Styr 19 Ce 52.07N 26.35 E
Styria (EN) = Steiermark 14 Ic 47.15N 15.00 E
Styria (EN) = Steiermark 14 Ic 47.15N 15.00 E
Styrsö 8 Dg 57.37N 11.46 E
Suafa Point 63a Ec 8.19S 160.41 E
Suai 26 Ih 9.21S 125.17 E
Suakin Archipelago (EN) = Sawākin, Jazā'ir- 30 Kg 19.07N 37.20 E
Suao 27 Lg 24.36N 121.51 E
Suardi 55 Bj 30.32S 61.58W
Suavanao 60 Fi 7.34S 158.44 E
Subačius/Subačjus 8 Ki 55.44N 24.53 E
Subačjus/Subačius 8 Ki 55.44N 24.53 E
Subang 26 Eh 6.34S 107.45 E
Subansiri 25 Jc 26.48N 93.49 E
Subao Ding 27 Jf 27.10N 110.18 E
Šubarkuduk 19 Ff 49.09N 56.31 E
Šubarši 16 Te 48.38N 57.12 E
Subate 8 Lh 56.01N 26.04 E
Subay', 'Urūq- 33 He 22.15N 43.05 E
Subaytilah 30 Ic 35.14N 9.08 E
Subbético, Sistema- 13 Jf 38.30N 2.30W
Subei (Dangchengwan) 27 Fd 39.36N 94.58 E
Subi, Pulau- 26 Ef 2.55N 108.50 E
Subiaco 14 Hi 41.55N 13.06 E
Sublette 45 Fh 37.29N 100.50W
Submeseta Norte 5 Fg 42.20N 4.50W
Submeseta Sur 5 Fh 39.30N 3.30W
Subotica 15 Cc 46.06N 19.40 E
Subpolar Urals (EN) = Pripoljarny Ural 5 Lb 65.00N 60.00 E
Subugo 36 Gc 1.40S 35.49 E
Suceava 15 Jb 47.32N 26.32 E
Suceava 15 Ib 47.40N 25.45 E
Suceava 15 Jb 47.38N 26.15 E
Sucha Beskidzka 10 Pg 49.44N 19.36 E
Süchbaatar → Suhe-Bator 22 Md 50.15N 106.12 E
Suchedniów 10 Qe 51.03N 20.51 E
Suchiapa, Río- 48 Mi 16.36N 93.01W
Suchitepéquez 49 Bf 14.25N 91.20W
Sucia, Bahía- 51a Ac 17.57N 67.10W
Sucio, Río- 49 Ij 7.27N 77.07W
Suck/An tSuca 9 Eh 53.16N 8.03W
Suckling, Mount- 59 Ja 9.45S 148.55 E
Sucre [Bol.] 53 Jg 19.02S 65.17W
Sucre [Col.] 54 Db 9.00N 75.00W
Sucre [Col.] 54 Db 8.50N 74.43W
Sucre [Ven.] 54 Fa 10.25N 63.30W
Suçuarana, Serra da- 55 Jb 14.25S 45.00W
Sucunduri, Rio- 54 Ge 5.30S 59.40W
Sućuraj 14 Lg 43.08N 17.12 E
Sucuriú, Rio- 54 Hh 20.47S 51.38W
Sud, Canal du- 49 Kd 18.40N 73.05W
Sud, Massif du- 49 Kd 18.25N 73.55W
Suda 7 Ig 59.11N 37.33 E
Suda 7 Ig 59.12N 37.30 E
Sudak 19 Dg 44.50N 34.59 E
Sudan 30 Ig 11.30N 15.00 E
Sudan (EN) = As Sūdān 31 Jg 15.00N 30.00 E
Sudbury [Eng.-U.K.] 9 Ni 52.02N 0.44 E
Sudbury [Ont.-Can.] 39 Ke 46.30N 81.00W
Suddie 50 Gi 7.07N 58.29W
Sude 10 Gc 53.22N 10.45 E
Sudeten (EN) 5 He 50.30N 16.00 E
Sudirman, Pegunungan- 26 Kg 4.12S 137.00 E
Sudočje, Ozero- 18 Bc 43.25N 58.30 E
Sudogda 7 Ji 55.59N 40.50 E
Sudost 16 Hc 52.19N 33.24 E
Sud-Ouest [Cam.] 34 Gd 5.20N 9.20 E
Sud-Ouest [U.V.] 34 Ec 10.30N 3.15W
Sudovaja Višnja 10 Tg 49.43N 23.26 E
Südradde 12 Jb 52.41N 7.34 E
Südtirol / Trentino-Alto Adige 14 Fd 46.30N 11.20 E
Sudža 16 Id 51.13N 35.16 E
Sue 30 Jh 7.41N 28.03 E
Sueca 13 Le 39.12N 0.19W
Suess Land 41 Jd 72.45N 26.00W
Suez (EN) = As Suways 31 Kf 29.58N 32.33 E
Suez, Gulf of- (EN) = Suways, Khalīj as- 30 Kf 28.10N 33.27 E
Suez Canal (EN) = Suways, Qanāt as- 30 Ke 29.55N 32.33 E
Suffolk 9 Ni 52.25N 1.00 E
Suffolk 43 Ld 36.44N 76.37W
Suffolk 9 Li 52.10N 1.05W
Sufián 24 Kc 38.17N 45.59 E
Sugana, Val- 14 Fd 46.00N 11.40 E
Suga-no-Sen 29 Dd 35.22N 134.31 E
Sugar Island 44 Eb 46.25N 84.12W
Sugarloaf Mountain 44 Lc 45.01N 70.22W
Suğla Gölü 24 Ed 37.20N 32.02 E
Sugoj 20 Kd 64.15N 154.29 E
Suguta 36 Gb 2.03N 36.33 E
Suha 15 Ke 44.08N 27.36 E
Suhai Hu 27 Fd 38.55N 94.05 E
Şuḩār 23 Ie 24.22N 56.45 E
Suhe-Bator (Süchbaatar) 22 Md 50.15N 106.12 E
Suhiniči 16 Ib 54.06N 35.20 E
Suhl 10 Gf 50.36N 10.42 E
Suhl 10 Gf 50.35N 10.40 E
Suhodolskoje, Ozero- 8 Nd 60.35N 30.30 E
Suhoj Log 17 Kh 56.55N 62.01 E
Suhona 5 Kc 60.46N 46.24 E
Suhr 14 Cc 47.25N 8.04 E
Suhumi 6 Kg 43.01N 41.02 E
Suhurlui 15 Kd 45.25N 27.35 E
Suiá-Missu, Rio- 54 Hf 11.13S 53.15W
Suibara 29 Fc 37.50N 139.12 E
Suichang 27 Kf 28.34N 119.15 E
Suid Africa / South Africa 31 Jl 30.00S 26.00 E
Suide 27 Jd 37.28N 110.15 E
Suifen He 28 Kc 43.20N 131.49 E
Suifenhe 27 Nc 44.25N 131.09 E
Sui He 28 Eh 33.29N 118.06 E
Suihua 27 Mb 46.38N 126.57 E
Suijiang 27 Hf 28.37N 104.00 E
Suileng 27 Mb 47.17N 127.08 E
Suining [China] 27 Ie 30.30N 105.34 E
Suining [China] 28 Dh 33.54N 117.56 E
Suipacha 55 Cl 34.45S 59.41W
Suiping 28 Bh 33.09N 113.59 E
Suippe 12 Je 49.25N 3.57 E
Suippes 11 Ke 49.08N 4.32 E
Suir/An tSiúir 9 Gi 52.15N 7.00W
Suisse / Svizra / Svizzera / Schweiz = Switzerland (EN) 6 Gf 46.00N 8.30 E
Suisse Normande 12 Bf 48.53N 0.50W
Suita 29 Dd 34.45N 135.32 E
Suixi 28 Dh 33.55N 116.47 E
Suixian [China] 28 Cg 34.25N 115.04 E
Suixian [China] 27 Je 31.44N 113.25 E
Suiyang 28 Kb 44.26N 130.53 E
Suizhong 27 Lc 40.21N 120.20 E
Suj 27 Ic 42.12N 108.01 E
Šuja 7 If 61.54N 34.15 E
Šuja [R.S.F.S.R.] 7 If 61.59N 34.15 E
Šuja [R.S.F.S.R.] 19 Ed 56.52N 41.23 E
Sujer 17 Li 55.59N 65.47 E
Suji → Haixing 28 De 38.10N 117.29 E
Sujstamo 8 Nc 61.49N 31.05 E
Sukabumi 26 Eh 6.55S 106.56 E
Sukadana 26 Eg 1.15S 109.57 E
Sukagawa 28 Pf 37.17N 140.23 E
Sukaja 26 Fg 7.27S 108.12 E
Sukeva 7 Ge 63.54N 27.26 E
Sukhothai 25 Je 17.01N 99.49 E
Suki 35 Ec 13.23N 33.58 E
Sukkertoppen/Manitsoq 41 Ge 65.25N 53.00W
Sukkozero 19 Dc 63.09N 32.23 E
Sukkur 22 Ig 27.42N 68.52 E
Sukon 26 Hg 0.56S 123.10 E
Sukses 37 Bd 21.01S 16.52 E
Suksun 17 Hh 57.07N 57.24 E
Sukumo 27 Ne 32.56N 132.44 E
Sukumo-Wan 29 Ce 32.55N 132.40 E
Sul, Baia- 55 Hh 27.40S 48.35W
Sul, Canal do- 54 Id 0.10S 49.30W
Sula [Nor.] 7 Af 61.10N 4.55 E
Sula [Nor.] 8 Bb 62.25N 6.10 E
Sula [R.S.F.S.R.] 7 Ld 64.41N 47.46 E
Sula [R.S.F.S.R.] 17 Fc 67.16N 52.07 E
Sula [Ukr.-U.S.S.R.] 16 He 49.40N 32.43 E
Sula, Kepulauan- = Sulu Islands (EN) 57 De 1.52S 125.22 E
Sulaimāniya 23 Gb 35.33N 45.26 E
Sūlaimaniya 24 Ke 35.40N 45.30 E
Sulaimān Range 21 Jf 30.30N 70.10 E
Sulak 16 Oh 43.17N 47.31 E
Sulak 19 Eg 43.17N 47.34 E
Sula Sgeir 9 Gb 59.05N 6.10W
Sulawesi/Celebes 21 Oj 2.00S 121.10 E
Sulawesi, Laut- = Celebes Sea (EN) 21 Oj 3.00N 122.00 E
Sulawesi Selatan 26 Gg 4.00S 120.00 E
Sulawesi Tengah 26 Hg 1.00S 121.00 E
Sulawesi Tenggara 26 Hg 4.00S 122.30 E
Sulawesi Utara 26 Hf 1.00N 123.00 E
Sulaymān 14 Eh 36.42N 10.30 E
Sulb 35 Ea 20.26N 30.20 E
Sulcis 14 Ck 39.05N 8.40 E
Suldalsvatn 8 Be 59.35N 6.45 E
Süldeh 24 Od 36.34N 52.01 E
Sulechów 10 Ld 52.06N 15.37 E
Sulęcin 10 Ld 52.26N 15.08 E
Suleja 17 Ii 55.11N 58.50 E
Sulejów 10 Pe 51.22N 19.53 E
Süleoğlu 15 Jh 41.46N 26.55 E
Sule Skerry 9 Ib 59.10N 4.10W
Sulima 34 Cd 6.58N 11.35W
Sulina 15 Md 45.09N 29.40 E
Sulina, Braţul- 15 Md 45.09N 29.41 E
Sulingen 10 Ed 52.41N 8.48 E
Sulitjelma 7 Dc 67.09N 16.03 E
Sulitjelma 7 Dc 67.08N 16.24 E
Suljukta 19 Gh 39.56N 69.37 E
Sulkava 7 Gf 61.47N 28.23 E
Sullana 53 Hf 4.53S 80.42W
Süller 15 Mk 38.09N 29.29 E
Sullivan [In.-U.S.] 44 Df 39.06N 87.24W
Sullivan [Mo.-U.S.] 45 Kg 38.13N 91.10W
Sullivan Lake 46 Ja 52.00N 112.00W
Sully-sur-Loire 11 Ig 47.46N 2.22 E
Sulmona 14 Hh 42.03N 13.55 E
Sulphur [La.-U.S.] 45 Jk 30.14N 93.23W
Sulphur [Ok.-U.S.] 45 Hi 34.31N 96.58W
Sulphur Creek 45 Ed 44.46N 102.25W
Sulphur River 45 Jj 33.07N 93.52W
Sulphur Springs 45 Ij 33.08N 95.36W
Sulphur Springs Draw 45 Fj 32.12N 101.36W
Sultandağı 24 Dc 38.32N 31.14 E
Sultan Dağları 24 Dc 38.20N 31.20 E
Sultanhanı 24 Ec 38.15N 33.33 E
Sultanhisar 15 Ll 37.53N 28.10 E
Sultānpur 25 Gc 26.16N 82.04 E
Sulu Archipelago 21 Oi 6.00N 121.00 E
Sulu Basin (EN) 26 Ge 8.00N 121.30 E
Sulu Islands (EN) = Sula, Kepulauan- 57 De 1.52S 125.22 E
Suluova 24 Fb 40.47N 35.42 E
Sulūq 33 Dc 31.40N 20.15 E
Sulu Sea 21 Ni 9.00N 120.00 E
Sulz am Neckar 10 Eh 48.21N 8.37 E
Sulzbach (Saar) 12 Je 49.18N 7.04 E
Sulzbach-Rosenberg 10 Hg 49.30N 11.45 E
Sulzberger Bay 66 Mf 77.00S 152.00W
Šumadija 15 De 44.20N 20.40 E
Sumalata 26 Hf 0.59N 122.30 E
Sumāmus 24 Nd 36.50N 50.30 E
Šumanaj 18 Bc 42.37N 58.55 E
Sumatera = Sumatra (EN) 21 Mj 0.01N 102.00 E
Sumatera Barat 26 Dg 1.00S 100.30 E
Sumatera Selatan 26 Dg 3.30S 104.00 E
Sumatera Utara 26 Cf 2.00N 99.00 E
Sumatra (EN) = Sumatera 21 Mj 0.01N 102.00 E
Šumava = Bohemian Forest (EN) 5 Hf 49.00N 13.30 E
Sumayr 33 Hf 17.47N 41.26 E
Sumba, Pulau- 21 Nj 10.00S 120.00 E
Sumba, Selat- = Sumba Strait (EN) 26 Hh 9.05S 120.00 E
Sumbar 16 Jj 38.00N 55.15 E
Sumba Strait (EN) = Sumba, Selat- 26 Hh 9.05S 120.00 E
Sumbawa, Pulau- 21 Nj 8.40S 118.00 E
Sumbawa Besar 26 Gh 8.30S 117.26 E
Sumbawanga 36 Fd 7.58S 31.37 E
Sumber 27 Ib 46.21N 108.20 E
Sumbi Point 63a Cb 7.19S 157.04 E
Sumbu 36 Fd 8.31S 30.29 E
Sumburgh Head 9 Lb 59.51N 1.16W
Sumedang 26 Eh 6.52S 107.55 E
Šume'eh Sarā 24 Md 37.18N 49.19 E
Sümeg 10 Nj 46.59N 17.17 E
Šumen 15 Jf 43.16N 26.55 E
Šumen 15 Jf 43.20N 27.00 E
Sumenep 26 Fh 7.01S 113.52 E
Šumerlja 6 Kd 55.30N 46.26 E
Sumgait 16 Pi 40.37N 49.37 E
Sumgait 6 Kg 40.33N 49.40 E
Sumidouro, Rio- 55 Da 13.28S 56.39W
Šumiha 19 Gd 55.14N 63.19 E
Sumkino 19 Gd 58.09N 68.21 E
Summer, Lake- [N.M.-U.S.] 45 Di 34.38N 104.26W
Summer, Lake- [N.Z.] 62 Ee 42.40S 172.15 E
Summer Lake 46 Ee 42.50N 120.45W
Summerland 46 Fb 49.39N 119.33W
Summerside 42 Lg 46.24N 63.47W
Summersville 44 Gf 38.17N 80.52W
Summerville 44 Eh 34.29N 85.21W
Summit Lake 42 Fe 54.17N 122.38W
Summit Mountain 46 Gg 39.23N 116.28W
Summit Peak 45 Ch 37.21N 106.42W
Sumoto 29 Dd 34.20N 134.54 E
Šumperk 10 Mg 49.58N 16.59 E
Sumprabum 25 Jc 26.33N 97.34 E
Sumsar 18 Hd 41.13N 71.23 E
Sumskaja Oblast 19 De 51.00N 34.15 E
Šumšu, Ostrov- 20 Kf 50.45N 156.20 E
Sumter 43 Ke 33.55N 80.20W
Sumusţā al Waqf 24 Dh 28.55N 30.51 E
Sumy 6 Je 50.54N 34.48 E
Suna 7 Mh 57.53N 50.07 E
Suna 7 Ie 62.08N 34.12 E
Sunagawa 28 Pc 43.29N 145.55 E
Šunak, Gora- 19 Hf 47.05N 72.35 E
Sunan 28 He 39.15N 125.40 E
Sunan (Hongwansi) 27 Gd 38.59N 99.25 E
Sunart, Loch- 9 He 56.45N 5.45W
Sunaysilah 24 Ie 35.35N 41.53 E
Sunburst 46 Jb 48.53N 111.55W
Sunbury 44 Ie 40.52N 76.47W
Sunchales 56 Hd 30.56S 61.34W
Suncho Corral 56 Hc 27.56S 63.27W
Sunch'ŏn [N. Kor.] 27 Me 34.57N 127.29 E
Sunch'ŏn [S. Kor.] 27 Md 39.25N 125.56 E
Sun City 46 Ij 33.36N 112.17W
Suncun → Xinwen 27 Kd 35.49N 117.38 E
Sunda, Selat- = Sunda Strait (EN) 21 Mj 6.00S 105.45 E
Sundance 46 Md 44.24N 104.23W
Sundarbans 25 Hd 22.00N 89.00 E
Sundargarh 25 Gd 22.07N 84.02 E
Sunda Strait (EN) = Sunda, Selat- 21 Mj 6.00S 105.45 E
Sunday Strait 59 Ec 16.20S 123.15 E
Sundborn 8 Fd 60.39N 15.46 E
Sundbron 8 Ha 63.01N 18.11 E
Sundbyberg 8 Ge 59.22N 17.58 E
Sunde 7 Ag 59.50N 5.43 E
Sunderland 9 Lg 54.55N 1.23W
Sundern (Sauerland) 12 Kc 51.20N 8.00 E
Sundgau 11 Ng 47.40N 7.15 E
Sündiken Dağları 24 Dc 39.55N 31.00 E
Sundridge 44 Hc 45.46N 79.24W
Sundsvall 6 Hc 62.23N 17.18 E
Sundsvallsbukten 8 Gb 62.20N 17.35 E
Sunflower, Mount- 45 Eg 39.04N 102.01W
Sungaidareh 26 Dg 0.58S 101.30 E
Sungaigerong 26 Dg 2.59S 104.52 E
Sungaiguntung 26 Df 0.18N 103.37 E
Sungai Kolok 25 Kg 6.02N 101.58 E
Sungai Lembing 26 Df 3.55N 103.02 E
Sungailiat 26 Eg 1.51S 106.08 E
Sungaipenuh 26 Dg 2.05S 101.23 E
Sungai Petani 26 De 5.39N 100.30 E
Sungai Siput 26 Df 4.49N 101.04 E
Sungari (EN) = Songhua Jiang 21 Pe 47.42N 132.30 E
Sungqu → Songpan 27 He 32.37N 103.34 E
Sungurlu 24 Fb 40.10N 34.23 E
Sunharon Roads 64b Bb 14.57N 145.36 E
Suning 28 Ce 38.25N 115.50 E
Sunja 14 Ke 45.21N 16.33 E
Sunjiapuzi 28 Ic 42.02N 126.34 E
Sunkar, Gora- 18 Ib 44.12N 73.55 E
Sun Kosi 25 Hc 26.55N 87.09 E
Sunnadalsøra 7 Be 62.40N 8.33 E
Sunnan 7 Cd 64.04N 11.38 E
Sunndalen 8 Cb 62.40N 8.45 E
Sunndalsfjorden 8 Cb 62.45N 8.25 E
Sunne 7 Cg 59.50N 13.09 E
Sunnerbo 8 Eh 56.45N 13.50 E
Sunnersta 8 Ge 59.48N 17.39 E
Sunnfjord 8 Ac 61.25N 5.20 E
Sunnhordland 8 Ae 59.55N 6.00 E
Sunnmøre 8 Bb 62.20N 6.40 E
Sunnyside 46 Fc 46.20N 120.00W
Sunnyvale 46 Dh 37.23N 122.01W
Su-no-Zaki 29 Fd 34.58N 139.45 E
Sun River 46 Jc 47.30N 111.25W
Sunsas, Serrania de- 55 Cc 17.57S 59.35W
Suntar 20 Gd 62.04N 117.40 E
Suntar-Hajata, Hrebet- = Suntar-Khayata Range (EN) 21 Qc 62.00N 143.00 E
Suntar-Khayata Range (EN) = Suntar-Hajata, Hrebet- 21 Qc 62.00N 143.00 E
Suntaži 8 Kh 56.49N 24.57 E
Sun Valley 43 Ec 43.42N 114.21W
Sunwu 27 Mb 49.27N 127.19 E
Sunyani 31 Gh 7.20N 2.20W
Sunža 19 Eg 43.26N 46.08 E
Suojarvi 19 Dc 62.04N 32.21 E
Suokonmäki 8 Kb 62.47N 24.30 E
Suolahti 7 Fe 62.34N 25.52 E
Suomenlahti = Finland, Gulf of- (EN) 5 Ic 60.00N 27.00 E
Suomenniemi 8 Lc 61.19N 27.27 E
Suomenselkä 5 Ic 62.50N 25.00 E
Suomi/Finland 6 Ic 64.00N 26.00 E
Suomussalmi 7 Gd 64.54N 29.00 E
Suō-Nada 29 Be 33.50N 131.30 E
Suonenjoki 7 Ge 62.37N 27.08 E
Suontee 8 Lc 61.40N 26.35 E
Suordah 20 Ic 66.43N 132.04 E
Suozhen → Huantai 28 Ef 36.57N 118.05 E
Supamo, Rio- 50 Fi 6.48N 61.50W
Superior [Az.-U.S.] 46 Jj 33.18N 110.06W
Superior [Mt.-U.S.] 46 Hc 47.12N 114.53W
Superior [Nb.-U.S.] 45 Gf 40.01N 98.04W
Superior [Wi.-U.S.] 39 Je 46.44N 92.05W
Superior, Lake- 38 Ke 48.00N 88.00W
Suphan Buri 25 Kf 14.29N 100.10 E
Süphan Dağı 23 Fb 38.54N 42.48 E
Supiori, Pulau- 26 Kg 0.45S 135.30 E
Supoj 16 Ge 49.38N 31.50 E
Support Force Glacier 66 Rg 83.05S 47.30W
Supraśl 10 Tc 53.13N 23.20 E
Supraśl 10 Sc 53.12N 22.55 E
Sup'ung 27 Lc 40.27N 124.57 E
Sup'ung-chosuji 28 Hd 40.30N 125.05 E
Suq ash Shuyūkh 24 Lg 30.53N 46.28 E
Suqian 27 Ke 33.55N 118.13 E
Sūq Suwayq 24 Hj 24.23N 38.27 E
Suquṭrā = Socotra (EN) 21 Hh 12.30N 54.00 E
Sūr 22 Hg 22.31N 59.30 E
Şūr 23 Ec 33.16N 35.11 E
Sur, Cabo- 65d Ac 27.12S 109.26W
Sur, Point- 46 Eh 36.18N 121.54W
Sura 16 Nc 53.53N 45.44 E
Sura 5 Kd 56.06N 46.00 E
Šurab 18 Hd 40.03N 70.33 E
Surabaya 22 Nj 7.15S 112.45 E

Index Symbols

1 Independent Nation
2 State, Region
3 District, County
5 Municipality
6 Colony, Dependency
Continent
Physical Region
Historical or Cultural Region
Mount, Mountain
Volcano
Hill
Mountains, Mountain Range
Hills, Escarpment
Plateau, Upland
Pass, Gap
Plain, Lowland
Delta
Salt Flat
Valley, Canyon
Crater, Cave
Karst Features
Depression
Polder
Desert, Dunes
Forest, Woods
Heath, Steppe
Oasis
Cape, Point
Coast, Beach
Cliff
Peninsula
Isthmus
Sandbank
Island
Atoll
Rock, Reef
Islands, Archipelago
Rocks, Reefs
Coral Reef
Well, Spring
Geyser
River, Stream
Waterfall Rapids
River Mouth, Estuary
Lake
Salt Lake
Intermittent Lake
Reservoir
Swamp, Pond
Canal
Glacier
Ice Shelf, Pack Ice
Ocean
Sea
Gulf, Bay
Strait, Fjord
Lagoon
Bank
Seamount
Tablemount
Ridge
Shelf
Basin
Escarpment, Sea Scarp
Fracture
Trench, Abyss
National Park, Reserve
Point of Interest
Recreation Site
Cave, Cavern
Historic Site
Ruins
Wall, Walls
Church, Abbey
Temple
Scientific Station
Airport
Port
Lighthouse
Mine
Tunnel
Dam, Bridge

Surahammar 8 Ge 59.43N 16.13 E
Sūrak 23 Id 25.43N 58.48 E
Surakarta 22 Nj 7.35 S 110.50 E
Şūrān 24 Ge 35.17N 36.45 E
Šurany 10 Oh 48.06N 18.11 E
Surar 35 Gd 7.29N 40.54 E
Surat 22 Jg 21.10N 72.50 E
Surat Thani 22 Li 9.06N 99.20 E
Suraž [Bye.-U.S.S.R.] 7 Hi 55.26N 30.43 E
Suraž [R.S.F.S.R.] 19 De 53.02N 32.29 E
Surčin 15 De 44.47N 20.17 E
Sur del Cabo San Antonio, Punta- ▶ 56 Ie 36.52 S 56.40W
Surduc 15 Gb 47.15N 23.21 E
Sûre ≈ 10 Cg 49.44N 6.31 E
Surendranagar 25 Ed 22.42N 71.41 E
Surgères 11 Fh 46.06N 0.45W
Surgut 22 Jc 61.14N 73.20 E
Surgutiha 20 Dd 63.47N 87.20 E
Surhandarinskaja Oblast [3] 19 Gh 38.00N 67.30 E
Surhandarja ≈ 18 Ff 37.14N 67.20 E
Surhob ≈ 19 Hh 38.54N 70.04 E
Surigao 26 Ie 9.45N 125.30 E
Surin 25 Kf 14.53N 103.30 E
Suriname [1] 53 Ke 4.00N 56.00W
Suripá, Río- ≈ 49 Mj 7.47N 69.53W
Sūrīyah=Syria (EN) [1] 22 Ff 35.00N 38.00 E
Sūrmaq 24 Og 31.03N 52.48 E
Surmelin ≈ 12 Fe 49.04N 3.31 E
Sürmene 24 Ib 40.55N 40.07 E
Surna ≈ 8 Cb 62.59N 8.40 E
Surnadalsøra 8 Cb 62.59N 8.39 E
Surovikino 19 Ef 48.36N 42.54 E
Surovo 20 Fe 55.39N 105.36 E
Sur-Pakri/Suur-Pakri ◆ 8 Je 59.50N 23.45 E
Surprise, Ile- ◆ 63b Ad 18.32 S 163.02 E
Surprise, Lac- ◍ 44 Ja 49.20N 74.57W
Surrey [3] 9 Mj 51.25N 0.30W
Surrey ▣ 9 Mj 51.20N 0.05W
Sursee 14 Cc 47.10N 8.07 E
Sursk 16 Nc 53.04N 45.42 E
Surskoje 7 Li 54.31N 46.44 E
Surt 31 Ie 31.13N 16.35 E
Surt, Khalīj-=Sidra, Gulf of-(EN) ◖ 30 Ie 31.30N 18.00 E
Surte 8 Eg 57.49N 12.01 E
Surtsey ◆ 7a Bc 63.20N 20.38W
Sürüç 24 Hd 36.58N 38.24 E
Surud Ad ▲ 30 Lg 10.42N 47.09 E
Suruga-Wan ◖ 28 Og 34.55N 138.35 E
Surulangun 26 Dg 2.37 S 102.45 E
Survey Pass ⩗ 40 Ic 67.52N 154.10W
Sur-Vjajn/Suur Väin ⇌ 8 Jf 58.30N 23.20 E
Surwold 12 Jb 52.57N 7.31 E
Suså ≈ 8 Di 55.11N 11.46 E
Šuša 16 Oj 39.43N 46.44 E
Susa [It.] 14 Be 45.08N 7.03 E
Susa [Jap.] 29 Bd 34.37N 131.36 E
Susa, Val di- ∨ 14 Be 45.10N 7.10 E
Sušac ◆ 14 Kh 42.46N 16.30 E
Sūsah [Lib.] 33 Dc 32.54N 21.58 E
Sūsah [Tun.] =Sousse (EN) 31 Ie 35.49N 10.38 E
Sūsah=Sousse (EN) [3] 32 Jb 35.45N 10.30 E
Susak 14 If 44.31N 14.18 E
Susaki 27 Ne 33.22N 133.17 E
Susami 29 De 33.33N 135.29 E
Susamyr 18 Ic 42.09N 73.59 E
Susanville 43 Cc 40.25N 120.39W
Suşehri 24 Hb 40.11N 38.06 E
Suseja ≈ 8 Kh 56.23N 25.00 E
Šušenskoje 20 Ef 53.19N 92.01 E
Sušice 10 Jg 49.14N 13.30 E
Susitna ≈ 40 Id 61.16N 150.30W
Suslonger 7 Lh 56.18N 48.12 E
Susoh 26 Cf 3.43N 96.50 E
Susong 28 Di 30.10N 116.06 E
Suspiro 55 Ej 30.38 S 54.22W
Suspiro del Moro, Puerto del- ⩗ 13 Ig 37.08N 3.40W
Susquehanna River ≈ 43 Ld 39.33N 76.05W
Susques 56 Gb 23.25 S 66.29W
Sussex ▣ 9 Mk 50.55N 0.30W
Sussex 44 Oc 45.43N 65.31W
Sussex, Vale of- ∨ 9 Mk 51.00N 0.15W
Susubona 63a Dc 8.19 S 159.27 E
Susuman 22 Qc 62.47N 148.10 E
Susurluk 24 Cc 39.54N 28.10 E
Susuzmüsellim 15 Kh 41.06N 27.03 E
Šušvė ≈ 8 Ji 55.08N 23.53 E
Susz 10 Pc 53.44N 19.20 E
Suţeşti 15 Kd 45.13N 27.26 E
Sutherland 37 Cf 32.24 S 20.40 E
Sutherland Falls ⇣ 62 Bf 44.48 S 167.44 E
Sutherlin 46 De 43.25N 123.19W
Sutla ≈ 14 Je 45.51N 15.41 E
Sutlej ≈ 21 Jg 29.23N 71.02 E
Sutton 44 Gf 38.41N 80.43W
Sutton, London- 12 Bc 51.21N 0.12W
Sutton Bridge 12 Cb 52.46N 0.11 E
Sutton in Ashfield 12 Aa 53.07N 1.16W
Sutton Scotney 12 Ac 51.09N 1.20W
Suttor River ≈ 59 Jd 21.25 S 147.45 E
Suttsu 28 Pc 42.48N 140.14 E
Sütşler 24 Dd 37.30N 30.59 E
Sutwik ◆ 40 He 56.34N 157.05W
Su'uholo 63a Ec 9.46 S 161.58 E
Suunduk ≈ 16 Ud 51.46N 58.46 E
Suure-Jaani 7 Fg 58.31N 25.29 E
Suur-Pakri/Sur-Pakri ◆ 8 Je 59.50N 23.45 E
Suur Väin/Sur-Vjajn ⇌ 8 Jf 58.30N 23.20 E
Suva 58 If 18.08 S 178.25 E
Suvadiva Atoll ◎ 21 Ji 0.30N 73.13 E
Suva Gora ⛰ 15 Eh 41.51N 21.03 E
Suva Planina ⛰ 15 Ff 43.08N 22.13 E
Suvasvesi ◍ 7 Ge 62.40N 28.10 E
Suvorov 16 Jb 54.08N 36.32 E
Suvorovo [Mold.-U.S.S.R.] 15 Mc 46.33N 29.35 E
Suvorovo [Ukr.-U.S.S.R.] 15 Ld 45.35N 29.00 E
Suvorovskaja 16 Mg 44.10N 42.38 E
Suwa 28 Of 36.02N 138.08 E
Suwa-Ko ◍ 29 Fc 36.03N 138.05 E
Suwałki 10 Sb 54.07N 22.56 E
Suwałki [2] 10 Sb 54.05N 22.55 E
Suwalskie, Pojezierze- ⊠ 10 Sb 54.15N 23.00 E
Suwannee River ≈ 44 Fk 29.18N 83.09W
Suwanose-Jima ◆ 27 Mf 29.40N 129.45 E
Suwarrow Atoll ◎ 57 Kf 13.15 S 163.05W
Suwayqīyah, Hawr as- ◍ 24 Lf 32.40N 46.03 E
Suways, Khalīj as-=Suez, Gulf of-(EN) ◖ 30 Kf 28.10N 33.27 E
Suways, Qanāt as-=Suez Canal (EN) ═ 30 Ke 29.55N 32.33 E
Suwŏn 27 Md 37.16N 127.01 E
Suxian 27 Ke 33.36N 116.58 E
Suzaka 29 Fc 36.39N 138.18 E
Suzdal 7 Jh 56.28N 40.27 E
Suzhou 22 Of 31.16N 120.37 E
Suzhou/Jiuquan 22 Lf 39.46N 98.34 E
Suzi He ≈ 28 Hd 41.56N 124.20 E
Suzu 27 Od 37.25N 137.17 E
Suzuka 29 Ed 34.51N 136.35 E
Suzuka-Sanmyaku ⛰ 29 Ed 35.10N 136.20 E
Suzu-Misaki ▶ 28 Nf 37.28N 137.20 E
Suzun 20 Df 53.47N 82.19 E
Suzzara 14 Ef 45.00N 10.45 E
Særholthalvøya ▰ 7 Ga 70.30N 26.05 E
Svågan ≈ 8 Gc 61.54N 16.33 E
Svalbard [5] 67 Kd 78.00N 20.00 E
Svaljava 16 Ce 48.32N 22.59 E
Svalöv 8 Ei 55.55N 13.06 E
Svaneholm 8 Ee 59.11N 12.33 E
Svaneke 7 Di 55.08N 15.09 E
Svängsta 8 Fh 56.16N 14.46 E
Svanøy ◆ 8 Ac 61.30N 5.05 E
Svapa ≈ 16 Id 51.44N 34.59 E
Svappavaara 7 Ec 67.39N 21.04 E
Svärdsjö 8 Fd 60.45N 15.55 E
Svartå 8 Fe 59.08N 14.31 E
Svartälven ≈ 8 Fe 59.20N 14.35 E
Svartån [Swe.] ≈ 8 Fe 59.17N 15.15 E
Svartån [Swe.] ≈ 8 Ff 58.28N 15.33 E
Svartån [Swe.] ≈ 8 Ge 59.37N 16.33 E
Svartenhuk Halvø=Svartenhuk Peninsula (EN) ▰ 41 Gd 71.30N 55.20W
Svartenhuk Peninsula (EN)=Svartenhuk, Halvø ▰ 41 Gd 71.30N 55.20W
Svartisen ❄ 7 Cc 66.38N 13.58 E
Svatoj Nos, Mys- ▶ 20 Jb 72.45N 140.45 E
Svatovo 19 Df 49.24N 38.13 E
Svay Riĕng 25 Lf 11.05N 105.48 E
Sveabreen ❄ 66 Cf 72.08 S 1.53 E
Sveagruva 41 Nc 78.39N 16.25 E
Svealand ▣ 7 Dd 60.30N 15.30 E
Svealand ⊠ 5 Hc 60.30N 15.30 E
Svedala 8 Ei 55.30N 13.14 E
Sveg 7 De 62.02N 14.21 E
Švėkšna 8 Ii 55.32N 21.30 E
Svelgen 7 Af 61.45N 5.18 E
Svelvik 8 De 59.37N 10.24 E
Švenčėneljaj/Švenčioneliai 7 Gi 55.09N 26.02 E
Švenčėnis/Švenčionys 7 Gi 55.07N 26.12 E
Švenčioneliai/Švenčėneljaj 7 Gi 55.09N 26.02 E
Švenčionys/Švenčėnis 7 Gi 55.07N 26.12 E
Svendborg 7 Ci 55.03N 10.37 E
Svendsen Peninsula ▰ 42 Ja 77.50N 84.00W
Svenljunga 7 Ch 57.30N 13.07 E
Svenska högarna ⁑ 8 He 59.35N 19.35 E
Svenskøya ◆ 41 Oc 78.43N 26.30 E
Svenstavik 7 De 62.46N 14.27 E
Šventoj/Šventoji 8 Ih 56.04N 20.59 E
Šventoji ≈ 7 Fi 55.05N 24.24 E
Šventoji/Šventoj 8 Ih 56.04N 20.59 E
Sverdlovsk 22 Id 56.51N 60.36 E
Sverdlovskaja Oblast [3] 19 Gd 59.00N 62.00 E
Sverdrup, Ostrov- ◆ 20 Cb 74.30N 79.35 E
Sverdrup Channel ⇌ 42 Ha 80.00N 96.30W
Sverdrup Islands ◆ 38 Jb 79.00N 98.00W
Sverige=Sweden (EN) [1] 6 Hc 62.00N 15.00 E
Svetac ◆ 14 Jg 43.02N 15.45 E
Svēte/Svete ≈ 8 Jh 56.40N 23.38 E
Svete/Svēte ≈ 8 Jh 56.40N 23.38 E
Sveti Naum ✝ 15 Di 40.55N 20.45 E
Sveti Nikola, Prohod- ⩗ 15 Ff 43.27N 22.36 E
Sveti Nikole 15 Eh 41.52N 21.57 E
Sveti Stefan 15 Bg 42.16N 18.54 E
Svetlaja 20 Ig 46.31N 138.18 E
Svetli 20 Ge 58.34N 116.00 E
Svetlogorsk [Bye.-U.S.S.R.] 19 Ce 52.38N 29.42 E
Svetlogorsk [R.S.F.S.R.] 8 Ij 54.55N 20.08 E
Svetlograd 19 Ef 45.19N 42.40 E
Svetlovodsk 16 He 49.02N 33.15 E
Svetly [R.S.F.S.R.] 19 Ge 50.51N 60.53 E
Svetly [R.S.F.S.R.] 7 Ei 54.41N 20.08 E
Svetly Jar 16 Ne 48.29N 44.46 E
Svetogorsk 7 Gf 61.07N 28.58 E
Svetozarevo 15 Ef 43.59N 21.15 E
Sviča ≈ 10 Ug 49.04N 24.06 E
Svid ≈ 7 Jf 61.13N 38.45 E
Svidník 10 Rg 49.18N 21.35 E
Svidník ▲ 10 Kg 49.23N 14.58 E
Svijaga ≈ 19 Ed 55.39N 48.28 E
Svilaja ⛰ 14 Kg 43.50N 16.26 E
Svilengrad 15 Jh 41.46N 26.12 E
Svincovy Rudnik 18 Ff 37.52N 66.28 E
Svinecea Mare, Vîrful- ▲ 15 Fe 44.48N 22.09 E
Svir ≈ 5 Jc 60.30N 32.48 E
Svir 8 Lj 54.50N 26.34 E
Svirica 7 Hf 60.30N 32.54 E
Svirsk 20 Ff 53.04N 103.18 E
Svisloč ≈ 16 Fc 53.27N 28.59 E
Svisloč 16 Dc 53.03N 24.07 E
Svištov 15 If 43.37N 25.20 E
Svit 10 Qg 49.03N 20.12 E
Svitava ≈ 10 Mg 49.11N 16.38 E
Svitavy 10 Mg 49.46N 16.27 E
Svizra / Svizzera / Schweiz / Suisse = Switzerland (EN) [1] 6 Gf 46.00N 8.30 E
Svizzera / Schweiz / Suisse / Svizra = Switzerland (EN) [1] 6 Gf 46.00N 8.30 E
Svjatoj Nos, Mys- ▶ 5 Jb 68.10N 39.43 E
Svobodny 22 Od 51.24N 128.07 E
Svoge 15 Gg 42.58N 23.21 E
Svolvær 7 Db 68.14N 14.34 E
Svratka ≈ 10 Mh 48.52N 16.38 E
Svrljig 15 Ff 43.25N 22.08 E
Svulrya 8 Ed 60.25N 12.24 E
Svytaya Anna Trough (EN) ⊻ 67 He 80.00N 70.00 E
Swabia (EN)=Schwaben ⊠ 10 Gh 48.20N 10.30 E
Swabian-Bavarian Plateau (EN)=Schwäbisch-Bayerisches Alpenvorland ▭ 5 Hf 48.15N 10.30 E
Swabian Jura (EN)=Schwäbische Alb ⛰ 5 Gf 48.25N 9.30 E
Swaffham 12 Cb 52.39N 0.41 E
Swain Reefs ✺ 57 Gg 21.40 S 152.15 E
Swains Atoll ◎ 57 Jf 11.03 S 171.05W
Swainsboro 44 Fi 32.36N 82.20W
Swakop ≈ 37 Ad 22.41 S 14.31 E
Swakopmund [3] 37 Ad 22.30 S 15.00 E
Swakopmund 31 Ik 22.41 S 14.34 E
Swale ≈ 9 Lg 54.06N 1.20W
Swalmen 12 Ic 51.14N 6.02 E
Swanage 9 Lk 50.37N 1.58W
Swan Hill 59 Ig 35.21 S 143.34 E
Swan Range ⛰ 46 Ic 47.50N 113.40W
Swan River 42 Hf 52.06N 101.16W
Swansboro 44 Ih 34.36N 77.07W
Swansea [Austl.] 59 Jh 42.08 S 148.04 E
Swansea [Wales-U.K.] 6 Fe 51.38N 3.57W
Swansea Bay ◖ 9 Jj 51.35N 3.52W
Swans Island ◆ 44 Mc 44.10N 68.25W
Swanson Lake ◍ 45 Ff 40.09N 101.06W
Swan Valley 46 Je 43.28N 111.20W
Swartberge ⛰ 30 Jl 33.23 S 21.48 E
Swarzędz 10 Nd 52.26N 17.05 E
Swastika 44 Ga 48.07N 80.12W
Swaziland [1] 31 Kk 26.30 S 31.10 E
Sweden (EN)=Sverige [1] 6 Hc 62.00N 15.00 E
Swedru 34 Ed 5.32N 0.42W
Sweet Grass Hills ⌓ 46 Jb 48.55N 111.30W
Sweet Home 46 Dd 44.24N 122.44W
Sweetwater 43 Ge 32.28N 100.25W
Sweetwater River ≈ 43 Fc 42.31N 107.02W
Swellendam 37 Cf 34.02 S 20.26 E
Świder ≈ 10 Rd 52.08N 21.12 E
Świdnica 10 Mf 50.51N 16.29 E
Świdnik 10 Se 51.14N 22.41 E
Świdwin 10 Lc 53.47N 15.47 E
Świebodzin 10 Ld 52.15N 15.32 E
Świecie 10 Oc 53.25N 18.28 E
Świętej Anny, Góra- ▲ 10 Of 50.28N 18.13 E
Świętokrzyskie, Góry- ▲ 10 Qf 50.55N 21.00 E
Swift Current 42 Gf 50.17N 107.50W
Swift Current Creek ≈ 46 La 50.40N 107.44W
Swift River 42 Ed 60.05N 131.11W
Swilly, Lough-/Loch Suili ◖ 9 Ff 55.10N 7.38W
Swinburne, Cape - ▶ 42 Hb 71.14N 98.33W
Swindon 9 Lj 51.34N 1.47W
Swinford/Béal Átha na Muice 9 Eh 53.57N 8.57W
Świnoujście 10 Kc 53.53N 14.14 E
Swischenahner Meer ◍ 12 Ka 53.12N 8.01 E
Swisttal 12 Id 50.44N 6.54 E
Switzerland (EN) = Schweiz / Suisse / Svizra / Svizzera [1] 6 Gf 46.00N 8.30 E
Switzerland (EN) = Suisse / Svizra / Svizzera / Schweiz [1] 6 Gf 46.00N 8.30 E
Switzerland (EN) = Svizra / Svizzera / Schweiz / Suisse [1] 6 Gf 46.00N 8.30 E
Switzerland (EN) = Svizzera / Schweiz / Suisse / Svizra [1] 6 Gf 46.00N 8.30 E
Syčevka 16 Ib 55.51N 34.15 E
Syców 10 Ne 51.19N 17.43 E
Sydfalster-Gedser 7 Ci 54.35N 11.57 E
Sydkap Ice Cap ❄ 42 Ja 76.30N 85.00W
Sydney [Austl.] 58 Gh 33.52 S 151.13 E
Sydney [N.S.-Can.] 39 Me 46.09N 60.11W
Sydney→Manra Atoll ◎ 57 Je 4.27 S 171.15W
Sydney-Campbelltown 59 Kf 34.04 S 150.49 E
Sydney Lake ◍ 45 Ia 50.40N 94.24W
Sydney Mines 42 Lg 46.14N 60.12W
Sydney-Penrith 59 Kf 33.45 S 150.42 E
Syktyvkar 6 Lc 61.40N 50.46 E
Sylacauga 44 Di 33.10N 86.15W
Sylane ▲ 7 Ce 63.02N 12.13 E
Sylarna ▲ 7 Ce 63.02N 12.13 E
Sylhet 25 Id 24.54N 91.52 E
Sylling 8 De 59.54N 10.17 E
Sylt ◆ 10 Eb 54.55N 8.20 E
Sylva ≈ 17 Hh 57.40N 56.57 E
Sylvania 44 Gi 32.45N 81.38W
Sylvania Tablemount (EN) ⊤ 60 Ge 11.58N 165.00 E
Sylvan Pass ⩗ 43 Ec 44.28N 110.08W
Sylvester 44 Fj 31.32N 83.49W
Sylvester, Lake- ◍ 59 Hc 18.50 S 135.50 E
Sym ≈ 20 Ed 60.15N 90.02 E
Syndassko 20 Fb 73.14N 108.05 E
Synja ≈ 17 Ld 65.12N 64.45 E
Synnfjell ▲ 8 Cc 61.05N 9.45 E
Syowa ⚗ 66 De 69.00 S 39.35 E
Syracuse [Ks.-U.S.] 45 Fh 37.59N 101.45W
Syracuse [N.Y.-U.S.] 39 Le 43.03N 76.09W
Syracuse (EN)=Siracusa 6 Hh 37.04N 15.18 E
Syrdarinskaja Oblast [3] 19 Gg 40.30N 68.40 E
Syrdarja 19 Gg 40.52N 68.38 E
Syrdarja=Syr Darya (EN) ≈ 21 Ie 46.03N 61.00 E
Syr Darya (EN)=Syrdarja ≈ 21 Ie 46.03N 61.00 E
Syria (EN) ⊠ 21 Ff 35.00N 38.00 E
Syria (EN)=Sūrīyah [1] 22 Ff 35.00N 38.00 E
Syriam 25 Je 16.46N 96.15 E
Syrian Desert- (EN)=Shām, Bādiyat ash- ∴ 21 Ff 32.00N 40.00 E
Syrkovoje, Ozero- ◍ 17 Lf 60.40N 65.00 E
Syrski 16 Kc 52.36N 39.28 E
Sysert 17 Jh 56.31N 60.49 E
Sysmä 7 Ff 61.30N 25.41 E
Sysola ≈ 19 Fc 61.42N 50.58 E
Sysslebäck 8 Ed 60.44N 12.52 E
Sysulp, Gora- ▲ 15 Ha 48.29N 24.17 E
Syverma, Plato- ▭ 21 Lc 67.00N 99.00 E
Syzran 6 Ke 53.09N 48.27 E
Szabolcs-Szatmár [2] 10 Sh 48.00N 22.10 E
Szamocin 10 Nc 53.02N 17.08 E
Szamos ≈ 15 Fa 48.07N 22.20 E
Szamotuły 10 Md 52.37N 16.35 E
Szarvas 10 Qj 46.52N 20.33 E
Szczawnica Krościenko 10 Qg 49.26N 20.30 E
Szczebrzeszyn 10 Sf 50.42N 22.59 E
Szczecin [2] 10 Kc 52.35N 14.30 E
Szczecin=Stettin (EN) 6 He 53.24N 14.32 E
Szczecinek 10 Mc 53.43N 16.42 E
Szczeciński, Zalew- ◖ 10 Kc 53.46N 14.14 E
Szczekociny 10 Pf 50.38N 19.50 E
Szczerców 10 Pe 51.18N 19.09 E
Szczucin 10 Rf 50.18N 21.04 E
Szczuczyn 10 Sc 53.34N 22.18 E
Szczytno 10 Qc 53.34N 21.00 E
Szechwan (EN)=Sichuan Sheng (Ssu-ch'uan Sheng) [2] 27 He 30.00N 103.00 E
Szechwan (EN)=Ssu-ch'uan Sheng→Sichuan Sheng [2] 27 He 30.00N 103.00 E
Szécsény 10 Ph 48.05N 19.31 E
Szeged 6 If 46.15N 20.10 E
Szeged [2] 10 Qj 46.16N 20.08 E
Szeghalom 10 Ri 47.02N 21.10 E
Székesfehérvár 6 Hf 47.12N 18.25 E
Szekszárd 10 Oj 46.21N 18.43 E
Szendrő 10 Qh 48.24N 20.44 E
Szentendre 10 Pi 47.40N 19.05 E
Szentes 10 Qj 46.39N 20.16 E
Szentgotthárd 10 Mj 46.57N 16.17 E
Szérencs 10 Rh 48.10N 21.12 E
Szeskie Wzgórza ▲ 10 Sb 54.14N 22.22 E
Szigetvár 10 Nj 46.03N 17.48 E
Szkwa ≈ 10 Rc 53.10N 21.45 E
Szlichtyngowa 10 Me 51.43N 16.15 E
Szob 10 Oi 47.49N 18.52 E
Szolnok 10 Qi 47.11N 20.12 E
Szolnok [2] 10 Qi 47.15N 20.30 E
Szombathely 10 Mi 47.14N 16.37 E
Szprotawa 10 Le 51.34N 15.33 E
Szreniawa ≈ 10 Qf 50.10N 20.35 E
Sztum 10 Pc 53.56N 19.01 E
Szubin 10 Nc 53.00N 17.44 E
Szydłów 10 Rf 50.35N 21.01 E
Szydłowiec 10 Qe 51.14N 20.51 E

T

Taakoka ◆ 64p Cc 21.15 S 159.43W
Taalintendas/Dalsbruk 8 Jd 60.02N 22.31 E
Taavetti 8 Ld 60.55N 27.34 E
Tab 10 Oj 46.44N 18.02 E
Tabacal 56 Hb 23.16 S 64.15W
Ţābah 24 Ji 27.02N 42.08 E
Tabaqah 24 He 35.52N 38.34 E
Tabar Islands ◈ 57 Ge 2.50 S 152.00 E
Ţabarqah 32 Ib 36.57N 8.45 E
Ţabas 24 Qf 33.36N 56.54 E
Tabasará, Serranía de- ⛰ 49 Gi 8.33N 81.40W
Tabasco [2] 47 Fe 18.00N 92.40W
Tabasco y Campeche, Llanos de- ▁ 47 Fe 18.15N 91.00W
Tabašino 7 Lh 56.59N 47.43 E
Tābask, Kūh-e- ▲ 24 Nh 29.52N 51.49 E
Tabay 55 Ci 28.18 S 58.17W
Tabelbala 32 Gd 29.24N 3.15W
Taber 42 Gg 49.47N 112.08W
Taberg 8 Fg 57.41N 14.05 E
Taberg ▲ 8 Fg 57.41N 14.05 E
Tabernacle 51c Ab 17.23N 62.46W
Tabernas 13 Jg 37.03N 2.23W
Tabernes de Valldigna 13 Le 39.04N 0.16W
Tabiteuea Atoll ◎ 57 Ie 1.20 S 174.50 E
Tabla 34 Fc 13.46N 3.01 E
Tablas ◆ 26 Hd 12.24N 122.02 E
Tablas Strait ⇌ 26 Hd 12.40N 121.48 E
Tablat 13 Ph 36.25N 3.19 E
Tablazo, Bahía del- ◖ 49 Lh 10.52N 71.35W
Table Cape ▶ 62 Gc 39.06 S 178.00 E
Table Rock Lake ◍ 45 Jh 36.35N 93.30W
Tabocas 55 Jb 14.39 S 45.28W
Taboco, Rio- ≈ 55 Ed 19.53 S 55.58W
Tabola ≈ 16 Pg 45.53N 48.20 E
Tábor 10 Kg 49.25N 14.41 E
Tabora 31 Ki 5.01 S 32.48 E
Tabora [3] 36 Fd 5.20 S 32.30 E
Tabory 17 Lg 58.31N 64.33 E
Tabou 31 Gh 4.25N 7.21W
Tabrīz 22 Gf 38.05N 46.18 E
Tábua 13 Dd 40.21N 8.02W
Tabuaeran Atoll (Fanning) ◎ 57 Ld 3.52N 159.20W
Tabūk 22 Fg 28.23N 36.35 E
Tabuk 26 Hc 17.24N 121.25 E
Ţaburbah 14 Dn 36.50N 9.50 E
Tabursuq 14 Dn 36.28N 9.15 E
Tabursuq, Monts de- ⛰ 14 Dn 36.25N 9.05 E
Tabusintac 44 Ob 47.24N 65.02W
Tabwemasana ▲ 63b Cb 15.22 S 166.45 E
Täby 7 Eg 59.30N 18.03 E
Tacámbaro de Codallos 48 Ih 19.14N 101.28W
Tacarcuna, Cerro- ▲ 49 Ij 8.05N 77.17W
Tacarigua, Laguna de- ⊂ 50 Dg 10.15N 65.50W
Tacheng/Qoqek 22 Ke 46.45N 82.57 E
Tachibana-Wan ◖ 29 Be 32.45N 130.05 E
Tachichilte, Isla de- ◆ 48 Ee 24.59N 108.04W
Tachikawa [Jap.] 29 Fd 35.42N 139.23 E
Tachikawa [Jap.] 29 Fb 38.48N 139.58 E
Táchira [2] 54 Db 7.50N 72.05W
Tachiumet 33 Bd 26.19N 10.03 E
Tachov 10 Ig 49.48N 12.40 E
Tachungnya 64b Bb 14.58N 145.36 E
Tacinski 16 Le 48.13N 41.17 E
Tacir 15 Mi 40.32N 29.44 E
Tacloban 22 Oh 11.15N 125.00 E
Tacna 53 Ig 18.01 S 70.15W
Tacna [2] 54 Dg 17.40 S 70.20W
Tacoma 39 Ge 47.15N 122.27W
Tacotalpa, Río- ≈ 48 Mi 17.50N 92.52W
Tacuaral 55 Cd 18.59 S 58.07W
Tacuarembó [2] 55 Ek 32.10 S 55.30W
Tacuarembó, Río- ≈ 55 Ek 32.25 S 55.29W
Tacuarí, Río- ≈ 55 Fk 32.46 S 53.18W
Tacuati 55 Df 23.27 S 56.35W
Tadami 29 Fc 37.21N 139.17 E
Tadami-Gawa ≈ 29 Fc 37.38N 139.45 E
Tadarimana, Rio- ≈ 55 Ec 16.29 S 54.31W
Tademaït, Plateau du- ▭ 30 Hf 28.30N 2.15 E
Tadine 63b Ce 21.33 S 167.53 E
Tadjeraout ≈ 32 He 21.17N 1.20 E
Tadjetaret ≈ 32 Ie 22.00N 7.30 E
Tadjourah 35 Gc 11.45N 42.54 E
Tadjourah, Golfe de- ◖ 35 Gc 11.45N 43.00 E
Tadoule Lake ◍ 42 He 58.35N 98.20W
Tadoussac 44 Ma 48.09N 69.43W
Tadzhik SSR (EN)=Tadžikskaja SSR [2] 19 Hh 39.00N 71.00 E
Tadžikskaja Sovetskaja Socialističeskaja Respublika [2] 19 Hh 39.00N 71.00 E
Tadžikskaja SSR/Respublikai Soveth Socialisti Todžikiston [2] 19 Hh 39.00N 71.00 E
Tadžikskaja SSR=Tadzhik SSR (EN) [2] 19 Hh 39.00N 71.00 E
T'aebaek-Sanmaek ⛰ 21 Of 37.40N 128.50 E
Taechon 28 If 36.21N 126.36 E
T'aech'on 28 He 39.55N 125.30 E
Taedong-gang ≈ 28 He 38.42N 125.15 E
Taegu 22 Of 35.52N 128.36 E
Taeha-dong 28 Kf 37.31N 130.48 E
Taehan-Haehyŏp=Korea Strait (EN) ⇌ 21 Of 34.40N 129.00 E
Taehan-Min' guk=South Korea (EN) [1] 22 Of 38.00N 127.30 E
Taehuksan-Do ◆ 28 Hg 34.40N 125.25 E
Taejŏn 22 Of 36.20N 127.26 E
Tafahi Island ◆ 57 Jf 15.52 S 173.55W
Tafalla 13 Kb 42.31N 1.40W
Tafassasset ≈ 30 If 21.56N 10.12 E
Tafassasset, Ténéré du- ⊠ 34 Ha 21.20N 11.00 E
Taff ≈ 9 Jj 51.27N 3.09W
Tafilalt 🌴 32 Gc 31.18N 4.18W
Tafiré 34 Dd 9.04N 5.10W
Tafi Viejo 56 Gc 26.44 S 65.16W
Taflan 24 Gb 41.25N 36.09 E
Tafna ≈ 13 Ki 35.18N 1.28W
Tafraout 32 Fd 29.43N 9.00W
Tafresh 24 Ne 34.41N 50.01 E
Taft 24 Pg 31.45N 54.14 E
Taftān, Kuh-e- ▲ 21 Ig 28.36N 61.06 E
Taftanāz 24 Ge 35.59N 36.47 E
Taga 65c Aa 13.46 S 172.28W
Taga Dzong 25 Hc 27.04N 89.53 E
Tagajō 29 Gb 38.18N 140.58 E
Tagama ⊠ 30 Hg 15.50N 8.12 E
Taganrog 6 Jf 47.12N 38.56 E
Taganrogski Zaliv ◖ 16 Kf 46.50N 38.25 E
Tagant [3] 32 Ef 18.30N 10.30W
Tagant ▲ 30 Fg 17.31N 12.07W
Tagarev, Gora- ▲ 18 Ae 38.19N 57.18 E
Tagawa 29 Be 33.39N 130.48 E
Tagbilaran 26 He 9.39N 123.51 E
Tageru, Jabal- ▲ 35 Db 16.25N 27.10 E
Taggia 14 Bg 43.52N 7.51 E
Taghit 32 Gc 30.55N 2.02W
Tagil ≈ 17 Kg 58.33N 62.30 E
Tagish Lake ◍ 42 Ed 60.00N 134.00W
Tagliamento ≈ 14 He 45.38N 13.06 E
Taglio di Po 14 Ge 45.00N 12.12 E
Tagomago, Isla de- ◆ 13 Ne 39.02N 1.39 E
Tagounit 32 Fd 29.58N 5.35W
Tagpochau, Ogso- ▲ 64b Ba 15.11N 145.45 E
Tāgrīfat 33 Cd 29.12N 17.21 E
Taguatinga 54 If 12.25 S 46.26W
Taguersimet 32 De 24.09N 15.07W
Tagula 63a Ad 11.20 S 153.00 E
Tagula Island ◆ 57 Gf 11.30 S 153.30 E
Tagum 26 Ie 7.21N 125.50 E
Tagus (EN)=Tajo ≈ 5 Fh 38.40N 9.24W
Tagus (EN)=Tejo ≈ 5 Fh 38.40N 9.24W
Tah 32 Ed 27.37N 12.50W
Tahaa, Ile- ◆ 61 Kc 16.38 S 151.30W
Tahakopa 62 Cg 46.31 S 169.23 E
Tahan, Gunong- ▲ 21 Mi 4.39N 102.14 E
Tahanea Atoll ◎ 57 Mf 16.52 S 144.45W

Index Symbols

[1] Independent Nation
[2] State, Region
[3] District, County
[4] Municipality
[5] Colony, Dependency
■ Continent
⊠ Physical Region
▣ Historical or Cultural Region
▲ Mount, Mountain
🌋 Volcano
⌒ Hill
⛰ Mountains, Mountain Range
⌓ Hills, Escarpment
▭ Plateau, Upland
⩗ Pass, Gap
▁ Plain, Lowland
◺ Delta
░ Salt Flat
∨ Valley, Canyon
◡ Crater, Cave
✷ Karst Features
⊔ Depression
⊓ Polder
∴ Desert, Dunes
♣ Forest, Woods
⁂ Heath, Steppe
🌴 Oasis
▶ Cape, Point
⌇ Coast, Beach
▌ Cliff
▰ Peninsula
⋈ Isthmus
⋯ Sandbank
◆ Island
◎ Atoll
✳ Rock, Reef
◈ Islands, Archipelago
⁑ Rocks, Reefs
✺ Coral Reef
⊙ Well, Spring
⛲ Geyser
≈ River, Stream
⇣ Waterfall Rapids
⋔ River Mouth, Estuary
◍ Lake
◌ Salt Lake
◯ Intermittent Lake
⊜ Reservoir
⩩ Swamp, Pond
═ Canal
❄ Glacier
❅ Ice Shelf, Pack Ice
🌊 Ocean
∽ Sea
◖ Gulf, Bay
⇌ Strait, Fjord
⊂ Lagoon
▤ Bank
⊼ Seamount
⊤ Tablemount
⋀ Ridge
⊐ Shelf
⊍ Basin
⌐ Escarpment, Sea Scarp
⚡ Fracture
⊻ Trench, Abyss
♠ National Park, Reserve
✔ Point of Interest
⚑ Recreation Site
◗ Cave, Cavern
⌂ Historic Site
⌘ Ruins
▥ Wall, Walls
✝ Church, Abbey
⛩ Temple
⚗ Scientific Station
✈ Airport
⚓ Port
☼ Lighthouse
⚒ Mine
∩ Tunnel
⌿ Dam, Bridge

Tahat ▲	30	Hf	23.18N	5.32 E
Tahe	27	La	52.22N	124.48 E
Ţāherī	24	Oi	27.42N	52.21 E
Tahgong, Puntan- ▶	64b	Ba	15.06N	145.39 E
Tahiataš	18	Bc	42.20N	59.33 E
Tahifet	32	Ie	22.56N	5.59 E
Tahir Geçidi ⌣	24	Jc	39.52N	42.20 E
Tahiti, Ile- ◆	57	Mf	17.37 S	149.27W
Tahkuna Neem/Takuna, Mys- ▶	8	Je	59.05N	22.30 E
Tahlequah	45	Ii	35.55N	94.58W
Tahoe, Lake- ≈	46	Fg	38.54N	120.00W
Tahoua [2]	34	Gb	16.00N	5.30 E
Tahoua	31	Hg	14.54N	5.16 E
Ţahţā	33	Fd	26.46N	31.28 E
Tahta-Bazar	18	Dg	35.55N	62.55 E
Tahtabrod	19	Ge	52.40N	67.35 E
Tahtakarača Pereval ⌣	18	Fe	39.17N	66.55 E
Tahtaköprü	15	Mj	39.57N	29.39 E
Tahtakupyr	19	Gg	43.01N	60.22 E
Tahtali Dağları ⛰	24	Gc	38.46N	36.47 E
Tahtamygda	20	Hf	54.09N	123.38 E
Tahuata, Ile- ◆	57	Ne	9.57 S	139.05W
Tahulandang, Pulau- ◆	26	If	2.20N	125.25 E
Tahuna	26	If	3.37N	125.29 E
Taï	34	Dd	5.52N	7.27W
Tai'an [China]	28	Gd	41.24N	122.27 E
Tai'an [China]	27	Kd	36.09N	117.05 E
Taiarapu, Presqu'île de- ▬	65e	Fc	17.47 S	149.14W
Taibai Shan ▲	27	Ie	33.57N	107.40 E
Taibilla, Canal del- ═	13	Kg	37.43N	1.22W
Taibilla, Sierra de- ⛰	13	Jf	38.10N	2.10W
Taibus Qi (Baochang)	27	Kc	41.55N	115.22 E
Taicang	28	Fi	31.26N	121.06 E
Taichung	22	Og	24.09N	120.41 E
Taieri ∿	62	Dg	46.03 S	170.12 E
Taiga	20	De	56.04N	85.37 E
Taigonos Peninsula (EN)= Tajgonos, Poluostrov- ▬	20	Ld	61.35N	161.00 E
Taigu	28	Bf	37.26N	112.33 E
Taihang Shan ⛰	21	Nf	37.00N	114.00 E
Taihape	62	Fc	39.41 S	175.48 E
Taihe [China]	28	Ch	33.11N	115.38 E
Taihe [China]	27	Jf	26.50N	114.52 E
Taiheiyō=Pacific Ocean (EN) ≣	3	Ki	5.00N	155.00W
Tai Hu ≈	21	Of	31.15N	120.10 E
Taihu	27	Ke	30.26N	116.10 E
Taikang	27	Je	34.00N	114.56 E
Taiki	29a	Cb	42.30N	143.16 E
Tailai	27	Lb	46.24N	123.26 E
Tailles, Plateau des- ⏥	12	Hd	50.15N	5.45 E
Taim	55	Fk	32.30 S	52.35W
Tain	9	Id	57.48N	4.04W
Tainan	22	Og	23.00N	120.11 E
Taínaron, Ákra-=Matapan, Cape- (EN) ▶	5	Ih	36.23N	22.29 E
Taiof ◆	63a	Ba	5.31 S	154.39 E
Taipei	22	Og	25.03N	121.30 E
Taiping	26	Df	4.51N	100.44 E
Taiping (Gantang)	28	Ei	30.18N	118.07 E
Taipingchuan	28	Gb	44.24N	123.11 E
Taiping Dao ◆	27	Jd	10.15N	113.42 E
Taiping Ling ▲	27	Lb	47.36N	120.12 E
Tairadate	29a	Bc	41.09N	140.38 E
Tairadate-Kaikyō ≍	29a	Bc	41.10N	140.40 E
Taisei	29a	Ab	42.14N	139.49 E
Taisetsu-Zan ▲	21	Qe	43.40N	142.48 E
Taisha	29	Cd	35.24N	132.40 E
Taishaku-San ▲	29	Fc	36.58N	139.28 E
Tai Shan ⛰	21	Nf	36.30N	117.20 E
Taishō	29	Ce	33.12N	132.57 E
Taitao, Península de- = Taitao Peninsula (EN) ▬	52	Ij	46.30 S	74.25W
Taitao Peninsula (EN) = Taitao, Península de- ▬	52	Ij	46.30 S	74.25W
Taitung	27	Lg	22.45N	121.09 E
Taiwa	29	Gb	38.26N	140.52 E
Taiwan [1]	22	Og	23.30N	121.00 E
Taiwan Haixia=Formosa Strait (EN) ≍	21	Ng	24.00N	119.00 E
Taixian	28	Fh	32.31N	120.08 E
Taixing	28	Fh	32.10N	120.00 E
Taiyang Shan ▲	27	Ie	33.37N	106.26 E
Taíyetos Óros- ⛰	15	Fl	37.06N	22.18 E
Taiyuan	22	Nf	37.50N	112.37 E
Taiyue Shan ⛰	28	Bf	36.48N	112.00 E
Taizhou	28	Eh	32.29N	119.55 E
Taizhou → Linhai	27	Lf	28.52N	121.08 E
Taizhou Wan ◧	28	Fj	28.40N	121.37 E
Taizi He ∿	28	Gd	41.00N	122.23 E
Ta'izz	22	Gh	13.38N	44.02 E
Tājābād	24	Pg	30.02N	54.24 E
Tajarḩī	33	Be	24.21N	14.28 E
Tajgonos, Mys- ▶	20	Ld	60.35N	160.10 E
Tajgonos, Poluostrov-= Taigonos Peninsula (EN) ▬	20	Ld	61.35N	161.00 E
Tajima	28	Of	37.12N	139.46 E
Tajimi	29	Ed	35.19N	137.08 E
Tājirwīn	14	Co	35.54N	8.33 E
Tajito	48	Cb	30.58N	112.18W
Tajmba	20	Ed	60.22N	98.50 E
Tajmyr	20	Ea	76.05N	98.55 E
Tajmyr, Ozero- ≈	21	Mb	74.30N	102.30 E
Tajmyr, Poluostrov-= Taymyr Peninsula (EN) ▬	21	Mb	76.00N	104.00 E
Tajmyra ∿	21	Lb	76.00N	99.40 E
Tajmyrlur	20	Hb	72.30N	121.39 E
Tajmyrski (Dolgano-Nenecki) Nacionalny okrug [3]	20	Eb	72.00N	95.00 E
Tajo=Tagus (EN) ∿	5	Fh	38.40N	9.24W
Tajo-Segura, Canal de Trasvase- ═	13	Je	39.30N	2.05W
Tajrīsh	23	Hb	38.48N	51.25 E
Tajšet	22	Ld	55.57N	98.00 E
Tajumulco, Volcán- 🌋	38	Jh	15.02N	91.54W
Tajuña ∿	13	Id	40.07N	3.35W
Tak	25	Je	16.52N	99.08 E
Taka Atoll ≈	3	Ii	4.00N	146.45 E
Takāb	24	Ld	36.24N	47.07 E
Takaba	36	Hb	3.27N	40.14 E
Takahagi	28	Pf	36.42N	140.41 E
Takahama	29	Dd	35.29N	135.33 E
Takahara-Gawa ∿	29	Ec	36.27N	137.15 E
Takaharu	29	Bf	31.55N	130.59 E
Takahashi	28	Lg	34.47N	133.37 E
Takahashi-Gawa ∿	29	Cd	34.32N	133.42 E
Takahata	29	Gc	38.00N	140.12 E
Takahe, Mount- ▲	66	Of	76.17 S	112.05W
Takaka	62	Ed	40.51 S	172.48 E
Takakuma-Yama ▲	29	Bf	31.28N	130.49 E
Takalar	26	Gh	5.28 S	119.24 E
Takalous ∿	32	Ie	23.25N	7.02 E
Takamatsu	27	Ne	34.21N	134.03 E
Takamori	29	Be	32.48N	131.08 E
Takanabe	29	Be	32.08N	131.31 E
Takanawa-Hantō ▬	29	Ce	34.00N	132.55 E
Takanawa-San ▲	29	Ce	33.57N	132.50 E
Takanosu	29	Ga	40.14N	140.22 E
Takaoka [Jap.]	28	Nf	36.45N	137.01 E
Takaoka [Jap.]	29	Bf	31.57N	131.17 E
Takapoto Atoll ◎	61	Lb	15.00 S	148.10W
Takapuna	62	Fb	36.48 S	174.47 E
Takara-Jima ◆	27	Mf	29.10N	129.05 E
Takarazuka	29	Dd	34.49N	135.21 E
Takaroa Atoll ◎	61	Mb	14.28 S	144.58W
Takasaki	28	Of	36.20N	139.01 E
Taka-Shima [Jap.] ◆	29	Be	32.40N	131.50 E
Taka-Shima [Jap.] ◆	29	Af	31.26N	129.45 E
Takatshwane	37	Cd	22.36 S	21.55 E
Takatsu-Gawa ∿	29	Bd	34.42N	131.49 E
Takatsuki	28	Mg	34.51N	135.37 E
Takayama	28	Nf	36.08N	137.15 E
Takebe	29	Cd	34.53N	133.54 E
Takefu	28	Ng	35.54N	136.10 E
Takehara	29	Cd	34.21N	132.54 E
Takeo	29	Ae	33.12N	130.00 E
Tåkern ≈	8	Ff	58.20N	14.50 E
Take-Shima ◆	28	Kf	37.22N	131.58 E
Tākestān	23	Gb	36.05N	49.14 E
Taketa	29	Be	32.58N	131.24 E
Takêv	25	Kf	10.59N	104.47 E
Takhādīd	24	Kh	29.59N	44.30 E
Takhār [3]	23	Kb	36.30N	69.30 E
Takhmaret	13	Mi	35.06N	0.41 E
Takht-e Soleimān ▲	24	Nd	36.20N	51.00 E
Taki [Jap.]	29	Cd	35.16N	132.38 E
Taki [Pap.N.Gui.]	63a	Bb	6.29 S	155.50 E
Takijuq Lake ≈	42	Gc	66.05N	113.00W
Takikawa	28	Pc	43.33N	141.54 E
Takingeun	26	Cf	4.38N	96.50 E
Takinoue	29a	Ca	44.13N	143.03 E
Takko	29	Ga	40.20N	141.09 E
Takla Lake ≈	42	Ee	55.30N	126.00W
Takla Landing	42	Ee	55.29N	125.58W
Takla Makan (EN)= Taklimakan Shamo ◢	21	Kf	39.00N	83.00 E
Taklimakan Shamo=Takla Makan (EN) ◢	21	Kf	39.00N	83.00 E
Takob	18	Ge	38.51N	69.00 E
Tako-Bana ▶	29	Cd	35.35N	133.05 E
Takolokouzet, Massif de- ⛰	34	Gb	18.40N	9.30 E
Taku	29	Be	33.19N	130.06 E
Takuan, Mount- ▲	63a	Bb	6.27 S	155.36 E
Takua Pa	25	Jg	8.52N	98.21 E
Takum	34	Gd	7.16N	9.59 E
Takuma	29	Cd	34.14N	133.40 E
Takume Atoll ◎	57	Mf	15.49 S	142.12W
Takuna, Mys-/Tahkuna Neem ▶	8	Je	59.05N	22.30 E
Takutea Island ◆	57	Lf	19.49 S	158.18W
Tala	48	Hg	20.40N	103.42W
Tālah	32	Ib	35.35N	8.40 E
Talaimmannar	25	Fg	9.05N	79.44 E
Talāīyeh	24	Kd	37.50N	45.00 E
Talaja	20	Kd	61.03N	152.30 E
Talak ⧗	30	Hg	18.20N	6.00 E
Talamanca, Cordillera de- ⛰	49	Fi	9.30N	83.40W
Talara	53	Hf	4.35 S	81.25W
Talas	19	Hg	42.29N	72.14 E
Talas ∿	18	Ic	44.05N	70.20 E
Talasea	59	Ka	5.20 S	150.05 E
Talasski Alatau, Hrebet- ⛰	18	Hc	42.10N	72.00 E
Talata Mafara	34	Gc	12.34N	6.04 E
Talaud, Kepulauan-=Talaud Islands (EN) ❖	21	Oi	4.20N	126.50 E
Talaud Islands (EN)= Talaud, Kepulauan- ❖	21	Oi	4.20N	126.50 E
Talavera, Isla- ◆	55	Dh	27.32 S	56.26W
Talavera de la Reina	13	He	39.57N	4.50W
Talawdī	35	Ec	10.38N	30.23 E
Talbot Inlet ◧	42	Ja	77.55N	77.35W
Talca	53	Ii	35.26 S	71.40W
Talcahuano	53	Ii	36.43 S	73.07W
Tālcher	25	Hd	20.57N	85.13 E
Taldom	7	Ih	56.45N	37.32 E
Taldy-Kurgan	22	Je	44.59N	78.23 E
Taldy-Kurganskaja Oblast [3]	19	Hf	44.00N	78.00 E
Talēḩ	35	Hd	9.09N	48.26 E
Tal-e Khosravī	24	Ng	30.47N	51.29 E
Talence	11	Fj	44.49N	0.36W
Ţalesh, Kūhhā-Ye- ⌓	24	Md	37.35N	48.38 E
Talgar	19	Hg	43.18N	77.13 E
Taliabu, Pulau- ◆	26	Hg	1.48 S	124.48 E
Talica	19	Gd	57.01N	63.43 E
Talimardžan	19	Gh	38.21N	65.31 E
Tali Post	35	Ed	5.54N	30.47 E
Talisajan	22	Ni	1.37N	118.11 E
Taliwang	26	Gh	8.44 S	116.52 E
Talkeetna	40	Id	62.20N	150.07W
Talkeetna Mountains ⛰	40	Jd	62.10N	148.15W
Talkheh ∿	24	Kd	37.40N	45.46 E
Talladega	44	Di	33.26N	86.06W
Tall 'Afar	23	Fb	36.22N	42.27 E
Tallah	24	Dh	28.05N	30.44 E
Tallahassee	39	Kf	30.25N	84.16W
Tallahatchie River ∿	45	Kj	33.33N	90.10W
Tall al Abyaḑ	24	Hd	36.41N	38.57 E
Tallapoosa River ∿	44	Di	32.30N	86.16W
Tallard	11	Mj	44.28N	6.03 E
Tällberg	8	Fd	60.49N	15.00 E
Tall Birāk at Taḩtānī	24	Id	36.38N	41.05 E
Tallinn	6	Id	59.25N	24.45 E
Tall Kayf	24	Jd	36.29N	43.08 E
Tall Kūshik	24	Jd	36.48N	42.04 E
Tallulah	45	Kj	32.25N	91.11W
Tălmaciu	15	Hd	45.39N	24.16 E
Talmenka	20	Df	53.51N	83.45 E
Talmest	32	Fc	31.09N	9.00W
Talnah	20	Dc	69.30N	88.15 E
Talnoje	16	Ge	48.53N	30.42 E
Talo ▲	30	Kg	10.44N	37.55 E
Talofofo	64c	Bb	13.20N	144.46 E
Talon	20	Je	59.48N	148.50 E
Tāloqān	23	Kb	36.44N	69.33 E
Talovaja	16	Ld	51.06N	40.48 E
Talpa de Allende	48	Gg	20.23N	104.51W
Talsi	7	Fh	57.17N	22.37 E
Taltal	53	Ih	25.24 S	70.29W
Taltson ∿	42	Gd	61.24N	112.45W
Taluk	26	Dg	0.32 S	101.35 E
Talvik	7	Fa	70.03N	22.58 E
Talwār ∿	24	Md	36.00N	48.00 E
Tama ⧗	35	Cc	14.45N	22.25 E
Tamaghzah	32	Ic	34.23N	7.57 E
Tamala	16	Mc	52.33N	43.18 E
Tamalameque	49	Ki	8.52N	73.38W
Tamale	31	Gh	9.24N	0.50W
Tamames	13	Fd	40.39N	6.06W
Tamana	29	Be	32.55N	130.33 E
Tamanaco, Río- ∿	50	Dh	9.25N	65.23W
Tamana Island ◆	57	Ie	2.29 S	175.59 E
Tamano	28	Lg	34.30N	133.56 E
Tamanoura	29	Ae	32.38N	128.37 E
Tamanrasset ∿	30	Hf	22.03N	0.10 E
Tamanrasset	31	Hf	22.47N	5.31 E
Tamanrasset [3]	32	Ie	23.00N	5.30 E
Tamar ∿	9	Ik	50.22N	4.10W
Tamara	15	Cg	42.27N	19.33 E
Támara	54	Db	5.50N	72.10W
Tamarit de Llitera/Tamarite de Litera	13	Mc	41.52N	0.26 E
Tamarite de Litera/Tamarit de Llitera	13	Mc	41.52N	0.26 E
Tamarro ∿	14	Ii	41.09N	14.50 E
Tamarugal, Pampa del- ▭	56	Gb	21.00 S	69.25W
Tamási	10	Oj	46.38N	18.17 E
Tamassoumit	32	Ef	18.35N	12.39W
Tamaulipas [2]	47	Ed	24.00N	98.45W
Tamaulipas, Llanos de- ▭	47	Ed	25.00N	98.25W
Tamaulipas, Sierra de- ⛰	48	Jf	23.30N	98.30W
Tamayama	29	Gb	39.50N	141.11 E
Tamazula de Gordiano	48	Hh	19.38N	103.15W
Tamazunchale	47	Ed	21.16N	98.47W
Tambach	36	Gb	0.36N	35.31 E
Tambacounda	31	Fg	13.12N	15.48W
Tambara	37	Ec	16.44 S	34.15 E
Tambelan, Kepulauan-= Tambelan Islands (EN) ❖	26	Ef	1.00N	107.30 E
Tambelan, Pulau- ◆	26	Ef	0.58N	107.34 E
Tambelan Islands (EN)= Tambelan, Kepulauan- ❖	26	Ef	1.00N	107.30 E
Tambo	59	Jd	24.53 S	146.15 E
Tambohorano	37	Gc	17.29 S	43.58 E
Tambora, Gunung- ▲	26	Gh	8.14 S	117.55 E
Tambores	55	Dj	31.52 S	56.16W
Tambov	6	Ke	52.43N	41.27 E
Tambovskaja Oblast [3]	19	Ee	52.45N	41.40 E
Tambre ∿	13	Db	42.49N	8.53W
Tambunan	26	Ge	5.40N	116.22 E
Tambura	31	Jh	5.36N	27.28 E
Tamchaket	32	Ef	17.20N	10.40W
Tame	54	Db	6.27N	71.45W
Tâmega ∿	13	Dc	41.05N	8.21W
Támega ∿	13	Dc	41.05N	8.21W
Tamel Aike	56	Fg	48.19 S	70.58W
Tamesi ∿	47	Ed	22.13N	97.52W
Tamesnar ⧗	30	Hg	18.25N	3.33 E
Tamgak, Monts- ⛰	30	Hg	19.11N	8.42 E
Tamgue, Massif du- ⛰	30	Fg	12.00N	12.18W
Tamiahua	48	Kg	21.16N	97.27W
Tamiahua, Laguna de- ⊙	47	Ed	21.35N	97.35W
Tamianglajang	26	Gg	2.07 S	115.10 E
Tamil Nādu [3]	25	Ff	11.00N	78.00 E
Tamiš ∿	15	De	44.51N	20.39 E
Tamise/Temse	12	Gc	51.08N	4.13 E
Tamitatoala, Rio- ∿	54	Hf	11.56 S	53.36W
Ţāmiyah	24	Dh	29.29N	30.58 E
Tam Ky	25	Le	15.34N	108.29 E
Tammela	8	Jd	60.48N	23.46 E
Tammerfors/Tampere	6	Ic	61.30N	23.45 E
Tammisaari/Ekenäs	7	Fg	59.58N	23.26 E
Tämnaren ≈	8	Gd	60.10N	17.20 E
Tamnava ⧗	15	De	44.25N	20.05 E
Tamou	34	Fc	12.45N	2.11 E
Tampa	39	Kg	27.57N	82.27W
Tampa Bay ◧	43	Kf	27.45N	82.35W
Tampake-Misaki ▶	29a	Bb	43.43N	141.20 E
Tampere/Tammerfors	6	Ic	61.30N	23.45 E
Tampico	39	Jg	22.13N	97.51W
Tampin	26	Df	2.28N	102.14 E
Tamri	32	Fc	30.43N	9.50 E
Tamsag-Bulak	27	Kb	47.14N	117.21 E
Tamsalu	7	Gg	59.10N	26.07 E
Tamsweg	14	Hc	47.08N	13.48 E
Tamu	25	Id	24.13N	94.19 E
Tamuín	48	Jg	21.59N	98.45W
Tamuín ⁘	47	Ed	22.00N	98.44W
Tamuín, Río- ∿	48	Jg	21.47N	98.28W
Tamworth [Austl.]	58	Gh	31.05 S	150.55 E
Tamworth [Eng.-U.K.]	9	Li	52.39N	1.40W
Tamyang	28	Ig	35.19N	126.59 E
Tana [Eur.] ∿	5	Ia	70.28N	28.18 E
Tana [Kenya] ∿	30	Li	2.32 S	40.31 E
Tana, Lake- ≈	30	Kg	12.00N	37.20 E
Tanabe	28	Mh	33.42N	135.44 E
Tana bru	7	Ga	70.16N	28.10 E
Tanacross	40	Kd	63.23N	143.21W
Tanafjorden ≍	7	Ga	70.54N	28.40 E
Tanaga ◆	40a	Cb	51.50N	178.00W
Tanagro ∿	14	Jj	40.38N	15.14 E
Tanagura	29	Gc	37.02N	140.23 E
Tanahbala, Pulau- ◆	26	Cg	0.25 S	98.25 E
Tanahgrogot	26	Gg	1.55 S	116.12 E
Tanahjampea, Pulau- ◆	26	Hh	7.05 S	120.42 E
Tanahmasa, Pulau- ◆	26	Cg	0.12 S	98.27 E
Tanah Merah	26	De	5.48N	102.09 E
Tanahmerah	26	Lh	6.05 S	140.17 E
Tanakpur	25	Gc	29.05N	80.07 E
Tanalyk ∿	17	Ij	51.46N	58.45 E
Tanami	59	Fc	19.59 S	129.43 E
Tanami Desert ◢	57	Eg	20.00 S	132.00 E
Tan An	25	Lf	10.32N	106.25 E
Tanana	40	Ic	65.10N	152.05W
Tanana ∿	38	Dc	65.09N	151.55W
Tanapag	64b	Ba	15.14N	145.45 E
Tanapag, Puetton- ⊙	64b	Ba	15.14N	145.44 E
Tanāqīb, Ra's at- ▬	24	Mi	27.50N	48.53 E
Tanaro ∿	14	Ce	45.01N	8.47 E
Tanba-Sanchi ⛰	29	Dd	35.15N	135.35 E
Tancheng	28	Eg	34.37N	118.20 E
Tanch'ŏn	27	Mc	40.25N	128.57 E
Tancitaro, Pico de- ▲	47	De	19.26N	102.18W
Tanda	34	Ed	7.48N	3.10W
Tanda, Lac- ≈	34	Eb	15.45N	4.42W
Tandag	26	Ie	9.04N	126.12 E
Tandaltī	35	Ec	13.01N	31.52 E
Tăndărei	15	Ke	44.39N	27.40 E
Tandijungbalai	26	Cf	2.58N	99.48 E
Tandil	53	Ki	37.20 S	59.05W
Tandil, Sierras del- ⛰	55	Cm	37.24 S	59.06W
Tandjilé [3]	35	Bd	9.30N	16.30 E
Tando Ādam	25	Dc	25.46N	68.40 E
Tandsjöborg	7	Df	61.42N	14.43 E
Tanḑubāyah	35	Db	18.40N	28.37 E
Taneatua	62	Gc	38.04 S	177.00 E
Tane-Ga-Shima ◆	27	Ne	30.40N	131.00 E
Taneichi	29	Ga	40.24N	141.43 E
Tan Emellel	32	Id	27.28N	9.45 E
Tanew ∿	10	Sf	50.27N	22.16 E
Tanezrouft ◢	30	Gf	24.00N	0.45W
Tanezzuft ∿	33	Bd	25.51N	10.19 E
Tanf, Jabal at- ◠	24	Hf	33.30N	38.42 E
Tanga [3]	36	Gd	5.30 S	38.00 E
Tanga	31	Ki	5.04 S	39.06 E
Tangail	25	Hd	24.15N	89.55 E
Tanga Islands ❖	57	Ge	3.30 S	153.15 E
Tangalla	25	Gg	6.01N	80.48 E
Tanganyika [2]	36	Fd	6.00 S	35.00 E
Tanganyika, Lac-= Tanganyika, Lake- (EN) ≈	30	Ji	6.00 S	29.30 E
Tanganyika, Lake- ≈	30	Ji	6.00 S	29.30 E
Tanganyika, Lake- (EN)= Tanganyika, Lac- ≈	30	Ji	6.00 S	29.30 E
Tangará	54	Ke	6.11 S	35.49W
Tangarare	63a	Dc	9.35 S	159.39 E
Tangdan → Dongchuan	27	Hf	26.07N	103.05 E
Tāngehgol	24	Pd	37.25N	55.50 E
Tanger=Tangier (EN) [3]	32	Fb	35.45N	5.45W
Tanger=Tangier (EN)	31	Ge	35.48N	5.48W
Tangerang	26	Eh	6.11 S	106.37 E
Tangermünde	10	Hd	52.33N	11.57 E
Tanggu	27	Kd	39.00N	117.36 E
Tanggula Shan (Dangla Shan) ⛰	21	Lf	33.00N	92.00 E
Tanggula Shankou ⌣	27	Fe	32.42N	92.27 E
Tanggulashanqu/Tuotuohe	22	Lf	34.15N	92.29 E
Tang He ∿	28	Bh	32.10N	112.20 E
Tanghe	27	Je	32.37N	112.57 E
Tangier (EN)=Tanger	31	Ge	35.48N	5.48W
Tangier (EN)=Tanger [3]	32	Fb	35.45N	5.45W
Tang La ⌣	21	Kg	28.00N	89.15 E
Tango	29	Dd	35.44N	135.05 E
Tangra Yumco ≈	21	Kf	31.00N	86.25 E
Tangshan	22	Nf	39.35N	118.09 E
Tanguiéta	34	Fc	10.37N	1.16 E
Tanguro, Rio- ∿	55	Fa	12.36 S	52.56W
Tangxian	28	Ce	38.46N	114.58 E
Tangyin	28	Cg	35.54N	114.21 E
Tangyuan	27	Mb	46.45N	129.53 E
Tanhoj	20	Ff	51.33N	105.07 E
Tanhuijo, Arrecife- ✱	48	Kg	21.07N	97.17W
Taniantaweng Shan ⛰	27	Ge	30.00N	98.00 E
Tanimbar, Kepulauan-= Tanimbar Islands (EN) ❖	57	Ee	7.30 S	131.30 E
Tanimbar Islands (EN)= Tanimbar, Kepulauan- ❖	57	Ee	7.30 S	131.30 E
Tanjung [Indon.]	26	Gg	2.11 S	115.23 E
Tanjung [Indon.]	26	Dg	1.23 S	103.58 E
Tanjungpandan	26	Eg	2.45 S	107.39 E
Tanjungpinang	26	Df	0.55N	104.27 E
Tanjungredep	26	Gf	2.09N	117.29 E
Tanjungselor	26	Gf	2.51N	117.22 E
Tankenberg ◠	12	Ib	52.21N	6.58 E
Tanna, Ile- ◆	57	Hf	19.30 S	169.20 E
Tännäs	7	Ce	62.27N	12.40 E
Tanner, Mount- ▲	46	Fb	49.40N	118.34W
Tannis Bugt ◧	8	Dg	57.40N	10.15 E
Tannu-Ola ⛰	21	Ld	51.00N	94.00 E
Tano ∿	34	Ed	5.07N	2.56W
Tanout	31	Hg	14.58N	8.53 E
Ţanţā	31	Ke	30.47N	31.00 E
Tan Tan	32	Ed	28.30N	11.02W
Tan-Tan [3]	32	Ed	28.30N	11.00W
Tan Tan Plage	32	Ed	28.26N	11.15W
Tantoyuca	48	Jg	21.21N	98.14W
Tanum	7	Cg	58.43N	11.20 E
Tanzania [1]	31	Ki	6.00 S	35.00 E
Tao, Ko- ◆	25	Jf	10.05N	99.52 E
Tao'an (Taonan)	27	Lb	45.20N	122.46 E
Tao'er He ∿	21	Oe	45.42N	124.05 E
Taoghe ∿	37	Cd	20.37 S	22.35 E
Tao He ∿	27	Hd	35.50N	103.20 E
Taojiang	28	Bj	28.33N	112.05 E
Taonan → Tao'an	27	Lb	45.20N	122.46 E
Taongi Atoll ◎	57	Hc	14.37N	168.58 E
Taormina	14	Jm	37.51N	15.17 E
Taos	43	Fd	36.24N	105.24W
Taoudenni	31	Gf	22.42N	3.56W
Taougrite	13	Mh	36.15N	0.55 E
Taounate	32	Gc	34.33N	4.39W
Taounate [3]	32	Gc	34.04N	4.06W
Taoura	14	Cn	36.10N	8.02 E
Taourirt	32	Gc	34.25N	2.54W
Taouz	32	Gc	31.00N	4.00W
Taoyuan	27	Lg	25.00N	121.18 E
Tapa	19	Cd	59.15N	25.59 E
Tapachula	39	Jh	14.54N	92.17W
Tapaga, Cape- ▶	65c	Bb	14.01 S	171.23W
Tapah	26	Df	4.11N	101.16 E
Tapajera	55	Fi	28.09 S	52.01W
Tapajós, Rio- ∿	52	Kf	2.24 S	54.41W
Tapaktuan	26	Cf	3.16N	97.11 E
Tapalqué	55	Bm	36.21 S	60.01W
Tapan	26	Dg	2.10 S	101.04 E
Tapanahoni Rivier ∿	54	Hc	4.22N	54.27W
Tapanlieh	27	Lg	21.58N	120.47 E
Tapanui	62	Cf	45.57 S	169.16 E
Tapauá	54	Fe	5.45 S	64.23W
Tapauá, Rio- ∿	52	Jf	5.40 S	64.21W
Tapenagá, Río- ∿	55	Ci	28.04 S	59.10W
Taperas	55	Bc	17.54 S	60.23W
Tapes	56	Jd	30.40 S	51.23W
Tapes, Serra do- ⛰	55	Fj	30.25 S	51.55W
Tapeta	34	Dd	6.29N	8.51W
Taphan Hin	25	Ke	16.12N	100.26 E
Tapili	36	Eb	3.25N	27.40 E
Tapini	60	Di	8.19 S	146.59 E
Tapiola, Espoo-	8	Kd	60.11N	24.49 E
Tapiraí	55	Id	19.52 S	46.01W
Tapirapuã	55	Db	14.51 S	57.45W
Tapolca	10	Nj	46.53N	17.26 E
Tappahannock	44	Ig	37.55N	76.54W
Tappi-Zaki ▶	28	Pd	41.18N	140.22 E
Tappu	29a	Ba	44.04N	141.52 E
Tapsuj ∿	17	Je	62.20N	61.30 E
Tāpti ∿	21	Jg	21.06N	72.41 E
Tapul Group ❖	26	He	5.30N	121.00 E
Tapurucuara	54	Ed	0.24 S	65.02W
Taputapu, Cape- ▶	65c	Cb	14.19 S	170.50W
Tāqbostān	24	Le	34.30N	46.58 E
Ţaqţaq	24	Ke	35.53N	44.35 E
Taquara	56	Jc	29.39 S	50.47W
Taquaral, Serra do- ∿	55	Fb	15.42 S	52.30W
Taquarí	55	Fc	17.50 S	53.17W
Taquari, Pantanal de- ⩫	54	Gg	18.10 S	56.30W
Taquari, Rio- [Braz.] ∿	55	Gi	29.56 S	51.44W
Taquari, Rio- [Braz.] ∿	55	Hf	23.16 S	49.12W
Taquari, Rio- [Braz.] ∿	52	Kg	19.15 S	57.17W
Taquari, Serra do- ⛰	55	Fd	18.18 S	53.49W
Taquaritinga	55	He	21.24 S	48.30W
Taquarituba	55	Hf	23.31 S	49.15W
Taquaruçu, Rio- ∿	55	Fe	21.35 S	52.08W
Tar ∿	18	Id	40.38N	73.26 E
Tara ⛰	15	Cf	43.55N	19.25 E
Tara ⁘	9	Gh	53.34N	6.35W
Tara [Austl.]	59	Ke	27.17 S	150.28 E
Tara [Jap.]	29	Be	33.02N	130.11 E
Tara [R.S.F.S.R.] ∿	20	Ce	56.40N	74.50 E
Tara [R.S.F.S.R.]	19	Hd	56.54N	74.22 E
Tara [Yugo.] ∿	15	Bf	43.21N	18.51 E
Taraba ∿	34	Hd	8.34N	10.15 E
Tarabuco	54	Fg	19.10 S	64.57W
Ţarābulus=Tripoli (EN) [3]	33	Bc	32.40N	13.15 E
Ţarābulus [Leb.]=Tripoli (EN)	23	Ec	34.26N	35.51 E
Ţarābulus [Lib.]=Tripoli (EN)	31	Ie	32.54N	13.11 E
Ţarābulus=Tripolitania (EN) ⧗	30	Ie	31.00N	14.00 E
Ţarābulus=Tripolitania (EN) ▣	33	Bc	30.00N	15.00 E
Taradale	62	Gc	39.32 S	176.51 E
Tarāghin	33	Bd	25.59N	14.26 E
Tarahumara, Sierra- ⛰	47	Cc	28.26N	106.50W
Tarakan	22	Ni	3.18N	117.38 E
Tarakan, Pulau- ◆	26	Gf	3.21N	117.36 E
Taraklija	16	Fg	45.57N	28.41 E
Tarama Jima ◆	27	Lg	24.40N	124.40 E
Taran, Mys- ▶	7	Ei	54.57N	19.59 E
Taranaki [2]	62	Fc	39.10 S	174.40 E
Tarancón	13	Jd	40.01N	3.00W
Taranga Island ◆	62	Fa	36.00 S	174.45 E
Taransay ◆	9	Fd	57.55N	7.10W
Taranto	6	Hg	40.28N	17.14 E
Taranto, Golfo di- = Taranto, Gulf of- (EN) ◧	5	Hg	40.10N	17.20 E
Taranto, Gulf of- (EN) = Taranto, Golfo di- ◧	5	Hg	40.10N	17.20 E
Tarapacá [2]	56	Ga	20.00 S	69.20W
Tarapacá	56	Ga	19.55 S	69.31W
Tarapaina	63a	Ec	9.23 S	161.24 E
Tarapoto	54	Ce	6.30 S	76.25W
Taraquá	54	Ec	0.06N	68.28W
Tarara	63a	Bb	6.02 S	155.24 E
Tarare	11	Ki	45.54N	4.26 E
Tararua Range ⛰	62	Fd	40.40 S	175.25 E
Tarašča	16	Ge	49.34N	30.31 E
Tarascon	11	Kk	43.48N	4.40 E
Tarascon-sur-Ariège	11	Hl	42.51N	1.36 E
Tarat	32	Id	26.08N	9.21 E
Tarata	54	Dg	17.27 S	70.02W

Index Symbols

- [1] Independent Nation
- [2] State, Region
- [3] District, County
- [4] Municipality
- [5] Colony, Dependency
- ■ Continent
- ⧗ Physical Region
- ▣ Historical or Cultural Region
- ▲ Mount, Mountain
- 🌋 Volcano
- ◠ Hill
- ⛰ Mountains, Mountain Range
- ⌓ Hills, Escarpment
- ⏥ Plateau, Upland
- ⌣ Pass, Gap
- ▭ Plain, Lowland
- Δ Delta
- ⊟ Salt Flat
- ∨ Valley, Canyon
- ◡ Crater, Cave
- ⌬ Karst Features
- ⊔ Depression
- ⊥ Polder
- ◢ Desert, Dunes
- ♣ Forest, Woods
- ⩗ Heath, Steppe
- ✾ Oasis
- ▶ Cape, Point
- ⌇ Coast, Beach
- ▐ Cliff
- ▬ Peninsula
- ⋈ Isthmus
- ∺ Sandbank
- ◆ Island
- ◎ Atoll
- ✱ Rock, Reef
- ❖ Islands, Archipelago
- ✳ Rocks, Reefs
- ✺ Coral Reef
- ⊡ Well, Spring
- ⛲ Geyser
- ∿ River, Stream
- ⥥ Waterfall Rapids
- ⋎ River Mouth, Estuary
- ≈ Lake
- ⊜ Salt Lake
- ◌ Intermittent Lake
- ⊞ Reservoir
- ⩫ Swamp, Pond
- ═ Canal
- ❄ Glacier
- ⧊ Ice Shelf, Pack Ice
- ≣ Ocean
- ≡ Sea
- ◧ Gulf, Bay
- ≍ Strait, Fjord
- ⊙ Lagoon
- ⊏ Bank
- ⊼ Seamount
- ⊓ Tablemount
- ⋀ Ridge
- ⊐ Shelf
- ⊍ Basin
- ⌐ Escarpment, Sea Scarp
- ↯ Fracture
- ⊽ Trench, Abyss
- ♧ National Park, Reserve
- ★ Point of Interest
- ☼ Recreation Site
- ◒ Cave, Cavern
- ⌂ Historic Site
- ⁘ Ruins
- ▦ Wall, Walls
- ✝ Church, Abbey
- ⛩ Temple
- ⚛ Scientific Station
- ✈ Airport
- ⚓ Port
- ⛯ Lighthouse
- ⚒ Mine
- ∩ Tunnel
- ⌿ Dam, Bridge

Tarauacá 54 De 8.10S 70.46W
Tarauacá, Rio 52 Jf 6.42S 69.48W
Taravao 65eFc 17.44S 149.19W
Taravao, Baie de- 65eFc 17.43S 149.17W
Taravo 11a Ab 41.42N 8.48 E
Tarawa Atoll 57 Id 1.25N 173.00 E
Tarawera 62 Gc 39.02S 176.35 E
Tarazi 24 Mg 31.05N 48.18 E
Tarazona 13 Kc 41.54N 1.44W
Tarazona de la Mancha 13 Ke 39.15N 1.55W
Tarbagataj, Hrebet 21 Ke 47.10N 83.00 E
Tarbagatay Shan 27 Db 47.10N 83.00 E
Tarbat Ness 9 Jd 57.50N 3.40W
Tarbert [Scot.-U.K.] 9 Gd 57.54N 6.49W
Tarbert [Scot.-U.K.] 9 Hf 55.52N 5.26W
Tarbes 11 Gk 43.14N 0.05 E
Tarboro 44 Ih 35.54N 77.32W
Tarcăului, Munţii- 15 Jc 46.45N 26.20 E
Tarcoola 59 Gf 30.41S 134.33 E
Tardenois 12 Fe 49.12N 3.40 E
Tardienta 13 Lc 41.59N 0.32W
Tardoire 11 Gi 45.52N 0.14 E
Tardoki-Jani, Gora- 20 Ig 48.50N 137.55 E
Taree 58 Gh 31.54S 152.28 E
Taremert-n-Akli 32 Id 25.53N 5.18 E
Tarentaise 11 Mi 45.30N 6.30 E
Ţarfā', Ra's aţ- 33 Hf 17.02N 42.22 E
Ţarfā', Wādī aţ- 24 Dh 28.38N 30.43 E
Ţarfah, Jazīrat aţ- 33 Hg 14.37N 42.55 E
Tarfaya 31 Ff 27.57N 12.55W
Targa 13 Qi 35.41N 4.09 E
Tărgoviški prohod 15 Jf 43.12N 26.30 E
Tărgovište 15 Jf 43.15N 26.34 E
Tărgovište [2] 15 Jf 43.15N 26.34 E
Tarhankut, Mys- 16 Hg 45.21N 32.30 E
Tarhaus, Virful- 15 Jc 46.38N 26.10 E
Tarhūnah 33 Bc 32.26N 13.38 E
Tarhūni, Jabal at- 33 De 22.12N 22.25 E
Táriba 49 Kj 7.49N 72.13W
Tarif 23 He 24.01N 53.45 E
Tarifa 13 Gh 36.01N 5.36W
Tarifa, Punta de- 13 Ih 36.00N 3.37W
Tarija 53 Jh 21.31S 64.45W
Tarija [2] 54 Fh 21.30S 64.00W
Tarik 64d Bb 7.21N 151.47 E
Tariku 26 Kg 2.55S 138.26 E
Tarīm [P.D.R.Y.] 23 Gf 16.03N 49.00 E
Tarīm [Sau.Ar.] 24 Fi 27.54N 35.24 E
Tarim Basin (EN)=Tarim Pendi 21 Ke 41.00N 84.00 E
Tarime 36 Fc 1.21S 34.22 E
Tarim He 21 Ke 41.05N 86.40 E
Tarim Pendi=Tarim Basin (EN) 21 Ke 41.00N 84.00 E
Tarin Kowt 23 Kc 32.52N 65.38 E
Taritatu 26 Kg 2.54S 138.27 E
Tarjalan 27 Hb 49.38N 101.59 E
Tarjannevesi 8 Kb 62.10N 24.05 E
Tarjat 27 Gb 48.10N 99.40 E
Tarka, Vallée de- 34 Gc 14.30N 6.30 E
Tarkastad 37 Df 32.00S 26.16 E
Tarkio 45 If 40.27N 95.23W
Tarko-Sale 20 Cd 64.55N 78.05 E
Tarkwa 34 Ed 5.18N 1.59W
Tarlac 22 Oh 15.29N 120.35 E
Tarm 8 Ci 55.55N 8.32 E
Tarma 54 Cf 11.25S 75.42W
Tarn 11 Hj 44.06N 1.02 E
Tarn [3] 11 Hk 43.50N 2.00 E
Tarna 10 Pi 47.31N 19.59 E
Tärnaby 7 Dd 65.43N 15.16 E
Tarn-et-Garonne [3] 11 Hj 44.00N 1.10 E
Tarnica 10 Sg 49.06N 22.47 E
Tarnobrzeg 10 Rf 50.35N 21.41 E
Tarnobrzeg [2] 10 Rf 50.35N 21.40 E
Tarnogród 10 Sf 50.23N 22.45 E
Tarnos 11 Ek 43.32N 1.28W
Tarnów 6 Ie 50.01N 21.00 E
Tarnów [2] 10 Qf 50.00N 21.00 E
Tarnowskie Góry 10 Of 50.27N 18.52 E
Tärnsjö 8 Gd 60.09N 16.56 E
Taro 14 Ef 45.00N 10.15 E
Taron 63a Aa 4.28S 153.04 E
Taroom 58 Fg 25.39S 149.49 E
Taroudant 32 Fc 30.29N 8.52W
Tarpon Springs 44 Fk 28.09N 82.45W
Tarquinia 14 Fh 42.15N 11.45 E
Tarra, Rio- 49 Ki 9.04N 72.27W
Tarrafal 32 Cf 15.17N 23.46W
Tarragona 6 Gg 41.07N 1.15 E
Tarragona [3] 13 Mc 41.10N 1.00 E
Tarraleah 59 Jh 42.10S 146.30 E
Tarrant 44 Di 33.38N 86.46W
Tarrasa 13 Oc 41.34N 2.01 E
Tàrrega 13 Nc 41.39N 1.09 E
Tarsus 23 Db 36.55N 34.53 E
Tart 27 Fd 37.07N 92.57 E
Tartagal 56 Hb 22.32S 63.49W
Tartaro 14 Fe 45.02N 11.30 E
Tartas 11 Fk 43.50N 0.48W
Tartas 20 Ce 55.37N 76.44 E
Tartu 6 Id 58.23N 26.45 E
Tartūs 23 Ec 34.53N 35.53 E
Tarumae-Yama 29a Bb 42.41N 141.23 E
Tarumizu 28 Ki 31.29N 130.42 E
Tarusa 16 Jb 54.43N 37.11 E
Tārūt 24 Ni 26.34N 50.04 E
Tarutau, Ko- 25 Jg 6.35N 99.40 E
Tarutino 16 Ff 46.12N 29.09 E
Tarutung 26 Cf 2.01N 98.58 E
Tarvisio 14 Hd 46.30N 13.35 E
Tarvo 55 Bb 15.06S 60.34W
Tarvo, Rio- 55 Bb 14.47S 61.03W
Tasajera, Sierra- 48 Gc 29.35N 105.35W
Tašanta 20 Dg 49.43N 89.11 E
Tasaral, Ostrov- 18 Ja 46.15N 74.05 E
Tašauz 19 Fg 41.52N 59.59 E
Tašauzskaja Oblast [3] 19 Fg 41.00N 58.40 E
Tasāwah 33 Bd 25.59N 13.29 E
Tasbuget 19 Gg 44.38N 65.38 E
Tasejeva 20 Ee 58.06N 94.01 E
Taseko Lake 46 Da 51.15N 123.35W
Tasendjanet 32 Hd 25.40N 0.59 E
Tashk, Daryācheh-ye- 23 Hd 29.45N 53.35 E
Tasikmalaya 22 Mj 7.20S 108.12 E
Tåsinge 8 Di 55.00N 10.36 E
Tasiussaq 41 Gd 73.18N 56.00W
Taskan 20 Kd 62.58N 150.20 E
Taškent 22 Ie 41.20N 69.18 E
Taškentskaja Oblast [3] 19 Gg 41.20N 69.40 E
Taškepri 19 Gh 36.17N 62.38 E
Taškeprinskoje, Vodohranilišče- 18 Df 36.15N 62.40 E
Tasker 34 Hb 15.04N 10.42 E
Taşköprü 24 Fb 41.30N 34.14 E
Taš-Kumyr 19 Hg 41.20N 72.14 E
Taşlıçay 24 Jc 39.38N 43.23 E
Tasman, Mount- 62 De 43.34S 170.09 E
Tasman Basin (EN) 3 Jn 43.00S 158.00 E
Tasman Bay 61 Dh 41.10S 173.15 E
Tasmania 59 Jh 43.00S 147.00 E
Tasmania 57 Fi 43.00S 147.00 E
Tasman Peninsula 59 Jh 43.05S 147.50 E
Tasman Plateau (EN) 3 In 48.00S 148.00 E
Tasman Sea 57 Hh 40.00S 163.00 E
Tăşnad 15 Fb 47.29N 22.35 E
Taşova 24 Gb 40.46N 36.20 E
Tassah, Wādī- 14 Cn 36.35N 8.54 E
Tassara 34 Gb 16.01N 5.39 E
Taštagol 20 Df 52.47N 88.00 E
Tåstrup 8 Ei 55.39N 12.19 E
Tastūr 14 Dn 36.33N 9.27 E
Tasty-Taldy 19 Ge 50.47N 66.31 E
Ţasūj 24 Kc 38.19N 45.21 E
Taşuou 24 Ed 36.19N 33.53 E
Tata [3] 32 Fd 29.40N 8.00W
Tata [Hun.] 10 Oi 47.39N 18.19 E
Tata [Mor.] 32 Fd 29.45N 7.59W
Tataba 26 Hg 1.18S 122.49 E
Tatabánya 10 Oi 47.34N 18.25 E
Tatakoto Atoll 57 Nf 17.20S 138.23W
Tata Mailau 26 Ih 8.55S 125.30 E
Tatarbunary 16 Fg 45.49N 29.35 E
Tatarsk 22 Jd 55.13N 75.58 E
Tatarskaja ASSR [3] 19 Fd 55.20N 50.50 E
Tatarski Proliv=Tatar Strait (EN) 21 Qd 50.00N 141.15 E
Tatar Strait (EN)=Tatarski Proliv 21 Qd 50.00N 141.15 E
Tatau 26 Ff 2.53N 112.51 E
Taţāwin 32 Jc 32.56N 10.27 E
Tateyama 28 Og 34.59N 139.52 E
Tathlina Lake 42 Fd 60.30N 117.30W
Tathlith 23 Ff 19.32N 43.30 E
Tatiščevo 16 Nd 51.40N 45.35 E
Tatla Lake 46 Ca 51.58N 124.25W
Tatla Lake 46 Ca 51.55N 124.36W
Tatlow, Mount- 46 Da 51.23N 123.52W
Tatnam, Cape - 42 Ie 57.16N 91.00W
Tatra Mountains (EN) 5 Hf 49.15N 20.00 E
Tatsuno [Jap.] 29 Dd 34.52N 134.33 E
Tatsuno [Jap.] 29 Ed 35.58N 137.58 E
Tatsuruhama 29 Ec 37.04N 136.53 E
Tatta 25 Dd 24.45N 67.55 E
Tatui 55 If 23.21S 47.51W
Tatum 45 Ej 33.16N 103.19W
Tatvan 23 Fb 38.30N 42.16 E
Tau 8 Ae 59.04N 5.54 E
Tau [Am.Sam.] 65c Db 14.15S 169.30W
Tau [Ton.] 65b Bc 21.01S 175.00W
Tauá 54 Je 6.01S 40.26W
Taubaté 53 Lh 23.02S 45.33W
Tauberbischofsheim 10 Fg 49.37N 9.40 E
Taučik 19 Fg 44.15N 51.20 E
Tauere Atoll 57 Mf 17.22S 141.30W
Tauern 5 Hf 47.15N 13.15 E
Taufstein 10 Ff 50.31N 9.14 E
Tauhunu 64n Ac 10.25S 161.03W
Tauhunu 64n Ac 10.25S 161.03W
Taujsk 20 Je 59.46N 149.20 E
Taujskaja Guba 20 Je 59.15N 150.00 E
Taukum 18 Jb 44.50N 75.30 E
Taumako 63c Ba 9.57S 167.13 E
Taumarunui 62 Fc 38.52S 175.15 E
Taum Sauk Mountain 45 Kh 37.34N 90.44W
Taunay 55 De 20.18S 56.05W
Taung 37 Ce 27.33S 24.47 E
Taungdwingyi 25 Jd 20.01N 95.33 E
Taunggyi 25 Jd 20.47N 97.02 E
Taungthonlon 25 Jd 24.58N 95.48 E
Taungup 25 Ie 18.51N 94.14 E
Taunton [Eng.-U.K.] 9 Jj 51.01N 3.06W
Taunton [Ma.-U.S.] 44 Le 41.54N 71.06W
Taunus 10 Ef 50.10N 8.15 E
Taunusstein 12 Kd 50.08N 8.10 E
Taupo 61 Eg 38.41S 176.05 E
Taupo, Lake- 61 Eg 38.50S 175.55 E
Tauragė/Taurage 7 Fi 55.16N 22.19 E
Taurage/Tauragė 7 Fi 55.16N 22.19 E
Tauranga 58 Ih 37.42S 176.10 E
Taurianova 14 Kl 38.21N 16.01 E
Taurion 11 Hi 45.53N 1.24 E
Taurisano 14 Mk 39.57N 18.13 E
Tauroa Point 62 Ea 35.10S 173.04 E
Taurus Mountains (EN)= Toros Dağları 21 Ff 37.00N 33.00 E
Tauste 13 Kc 41.55N 1.15W
Tauu Islands 57 Ge 4.45S 157.00 E
Tauz 19 Eg 41.01N 45.35 E
Ţavālesh, Kūhhā-Ye- 24 Mc 38.42N 48.18 E
Tavas [Tur.] 24 Dc 39.54N 30.03 E
Tavas [Tur.] 24 Cd 37.34N 29.04 E
Tavas Ovasi 15 Ll 37.30N 28.55 E
Tavastehus/Hämeenlinna 7 Ff 61.00N 24.27 E
Tavau/Davos 14 Dd 46.47N 9.50 E
Tavda 19 Gd 58.03N 65.15 E
Tavda 21 Id 57.47N 67.16 E
Tavendroua 63b Cc 16.21S 167.22 E
Taveta 36 Gc 3.24S 37.41 E
Taveuni Island 61 Fc 16.51S 179.58W
Taviano 14 Mk 39.59N 18.05 E
Tavignano 11a Ba 42.06N 9.33 E
Tavira 13 Eg 37.07N 7.39W
Tavistock 9 Ik 50.33N 4.08W
Tavolara 14 Dj 40.55N 9.40 E
Tavoliere 14 Ji 41.35N 15.25 E
Tavolžan 19 He 52.44N 77.30 E
Tavoy 22 Lh 14.05N 98.12 E
Tavričanka 28 Kc 43.20N 131.52 E
Tavropóu, Tekhnití Límni- 15 Ej 39.15N 21.40 E
Tavşan Adalari 15 Jj 39.55N 26.05 E
Tavşanlı 24 Cc 39.35N 29.30 E
Tavua 61 Ec 17.27S 177.51 E
Taw 9 Ij 51.04N 4.11W
Tawakoni, Lake- 45 Ij 32.55N 96.00W
Tawas City 43 Kc 44.16N 83.31W
Tawau 22 Ni 4.15N 117.54 E
Tawfiqiyah 35 Ed 9.26N 31.37 E
Ţawīlah, Juzur- 24 Ei 27.35N 33.46 E
Tawitawi Group 26 He 5.10N 120.15 E
Ţawkar 31 Kg 18.26N 37.44 E
Ţāwūq 24 Ke 35.08N 44.27 E
Tawūq Chāy 24 Ke 34.35N 44.31 E
Tāwurghā', Sabkhat- 33 Cc 31.10N 15.15 E
Tawzar 32 Ic 33.55N 8.08 E
Taxco de Alarcón 48 Jh 18.33N 99.36W
Taxkorgan 27 Cd 37.47N 75.14 E
Tay 9 Je 56.30N 3.30W
Tay, Firth of- 9 Ke 56.28N 3.00W
Tay, Loch- 9 Ie 56.30N 4.10W
Tayandu, Kepulauan- 26 Jh 5.30S 132.15 E
Tayēgle 35 Ge 4.02N 44.36 E
Taylor [Nb.-U.S.] 45 Gf 41.46N 99.23W
Taylor [Tx.-U.S.] 43 He 30.34N 97.25W
Taylor, Mount- 43 Fd 35.14N 107.37W
Taylorville 45 Lg 39.33N 89.18W
Taymā' 23 Ed 27.38N 38.29 E
Taymyr Peninsula (EN)= Tajmyr, Poluostrov- 21 Mb 76.00N 104.00 E
Tay Ninh 25 Lf 11.18N 106.06 E
Tayside [3] 9 Je 56.30N 3.40W
Taytay 26 Gd 10.49N 119.31 E
Taza [3] 32 Gc 34.00N 4.00W
Taza [Mor.] 31 Ge 34.13N 4.01W
Taza [R.S.F.S.R.] 20 Gf 54.55N 111.05 E
Tāzah Khurmātū 24 Ke 35.18N 44.20 E
Tazawa-Ko 29 Gb 39.43N 140.40 E
Tazawako 29 Gb 39.42N 140.44 E
Tazenakht 32 Fc 30.35N 7.12W
Tazerbo Oasis (EN)= Tāzirbū, Wāḥāt al- 30 Jf 25.45N 21.00 E
Tazewell [Tn.-U.S.] 44 Fg 36.27N 83.34W
Tazewell [Va.-U.S.] 44 Gg 37.07N 81.34W
Tāziāzet 32 De 20.55N 15.40W
Tazin Lake 42 Ge 59.48N 109.05W
Tāzirbū, Wāḥāt al-=Tazerbo Oasis (EN) 30 Jf 25.45N 21.00 E
Tazlău 15 Jc 46.16N 26.47 E
Tazmalt 13 Qh 36.43N 4.08 E
Tazouikert 34 Ea 21.46N 1.13W
Tazovskaja Guba 17 Qb 69.05N 76.00 E
Tazovski 20 Cc 67.28N 78.42 E
Tazrouk 32 Ie 23.27N 6.14 E
Tazumal 49 Cg 14.00N 89.40W
Tbilisi 6 Kg 41.43N 44.49 E
Tchad=Chad (EN) [1] 31 Ig 15.00N 19.00 E
Tchad, Lac-=Chad, Lake- (EN) 30 Ig 13.20N 14.00 E
Tchamba [Cam.] 34 Hd 8.37N 12.48 E
Tchamba [Togo] 34 Fd 9.02N 1.25 E
Tchibanga 36 Bc 2.51S 11.02 E
Tchien 34 Dd 6.04N 8.08W
Tchigaï, Plateau du- 30 If 21.30N 14.50 E
Tchin Tabaraden 34 Gb 15.58N 5.50 E
Tcholliré 34 Hd 8.24N 14.10 E
Tczew 10 Ob 54.06N 18.47 E
Tea, Rio- 54 Ed 0.30S 65.09W
Teaca 15 Hc 46.55N 24.31 E
Teacapán 48 Gf 22.33N 105.45W
Teaiti Point 64p Bb 21.11S 159.47W
Te Anau 62 Bf 45.25S 167.43 E
Te Anau, Lake- 61 Ci 45.15S 167.45 E
Teano 14 Ii 41.15N 14.04 E
Teapa 48 Mi 17.33N 92.57W
Te Araroa 61 Eg 37.38S 178.22 E
Te Aroha 62 Fb 37.32S 175.42 E
Tea Tree 59 Gd 22.11S 133.17 E
Te Atu Kura 64p Bb 21.14S 159.45W
Te Awamutu 62 Fc 38.00S 175.19 E
Teberda 16 Lh 43.28N 41.43 E
Tébessa 31 He 35.24N 8.07 E
Tébessa [3] 32 Ic 35.00N 7.45 E
Tébessa, Oued- 14 Bo 35.48N 7.53 E
Tebicuary, Río- [Par.] 55 Ch 26.36S 58.16W
Tebicuary, Río- [Par.] 55 Dh 26.26S 56.51W
Tebingtinggi [Indon.] 26 Dg 3.36S 103.05 E
Tebingtinggi [Indon.] 26 Cf 3.20N 99.09 E
Tebulosmta, Gora- 16 Nh 42.33N 45.16 E
Teča 17 Kh 56.17N 62.59 E
Tecate 47 Ab 32.34N 116.38W
Tecer Dağları 24 Gc 39.27N 37.11 E
Techirghiol 15 Le 44.03N 28.36 E
Tecka 56 Ff 43.29S 70.48W
Tecklenburg 12 Jb 52.13N 7.50 E
Tecomán 47 De 18.55N 103.53W
Tecomate, Laguna- 48 Ji 16.45N 99.25W
Tecoripa 48 Ec 28.37N 109.57W
Tecpan de Galeana 47 De 17.15N 100.41W
Tecuala 47 Cd 22.23N 105.27W
Tecuci 15 Kd 45.52N 27.25 E
Tedegra 35 Ba 20.46N 19.34 E
Tedori-Gawa 29 Ec 36.29N 136.28 E
Tedžen 21 If 37.24N 60.38 E
Tedženstroj 19 Gh 36.54N 60.53 E
Teeli 20 Ef 50.57N 90.18 E
Teenuse Jõgi/Tenuze 7 Jf 58.44N 23.58 E
Tees 9 Lg 54.34N 1.16W
Tees Bay 9 Lg 54.35N 1.05W
Teesside 6 Fe 54.35N 1.14W
Tefé 53 Jf 3.22S 64.42W
Tefé, Rio- 54 Fd 3.35S 64.47W
Tefedest 32 Ie 24.40N 5.30 E
Tefenni 24 Cd 37.18N 29.47 E
Tegal 22 Mj 6.52S 109.08 E
Tegea (EN) = Teyéa 15 Fl 37.27N 22.25 E
Tegelen 12 Ic 51.20N 6.08 E
Tegernsee 10 Hi 47.43N 11.46 E
Tegina 34 Gc 10.04N 6.11 E
Tégoua 63b Ca 13.15S 166.37 E
Tegucigalpa 39 Kh 14.06N 87.13W
Teguidda I-n-Tessoum 34 Gb 17.26N 6.39 E
Teguldet 20 De 57.20N 88.20 E
Tehachapi 46 Fi 35.08N 118.27W
Tehachapi Mountains 46 Fi 34.56N 118.40W
Tehamiyam 35 Fb 18.20N 36.32 E
Te Hapua 61 Df 34.30S 172.55 E
Tehaupoo 65eFc 17.49S 149.18W
Tehek Lake 42 Hd 64.55N 95.30W
Téhini 34 Ed 9.36N 3.40W
Tehi-n-Isser 32 Ie 24.48N 8.08 E
Tehoru 26 Ig 3.23S 129.30 E
Tehrān 22 Hf 35.40N 51.26 E
Tehrān [3] 23 Hb 35.30N 51.30 E
Tehuacán 47 Ee 18.27N 97.23W
Tehuantepec 47 Ee 16.20N 95.14W
Tehuantepec, Golfo de-= Tehuantepec, Gulf of- (EN) 38 Jh 16.00N 94.50W
Tehuantepec, Gulf of- (EN) =Tehuantepec, Golfo de- 38 Jh 16.00N 94.50W
Tehuantepec, Isthmus of- (EN)=Tehuantepec, Istmo de- 38 Jh 17.00N 94.30W
Tehuantepec, Istmo de-= Tehuantepec, Isthmus of- (EN) 38 Jh 17.00N 94.30W
Tehuantepec Ridge (EN) 47 Ef 13.30N 98.00W
Tehuata Atoll 57 Mf 16.50S 141.55W
Teiga Plateau 35 Db 15.38N 25.40 E
Teignmouth 9 Jk 50.33N 3.30W
Teili/Delet 8 Id 60.15N 20.35 E
Teith 9 Ie 56.14N 4.20W
Teiuş 15 Gc 46.12N 23.41 E
Teixeira Pinto 34 Bc 12.04N 16.02W
Teja 20 Ed 60.27N 92.38 E
Tejkovo 19 Ed 56.50N 40.34 E
Tejo=Tagus (EN) 5 Fh 38.40N 9.24W
Teju 25 Jc 27.55N 96.10 E
Te Kaha 62 Gb 37.44S 177.41 E
Te Kao 62 Ea 34.39S 172.58 E
Tekapo, Lake- 62 De 43.50S 170.30 E
Te Karaka 62 Gc 38.28S 177.52 E
Tekax 48 Og 20.12N 89.17W
Teke 15 Mh 41.04N 29.39 E
Teke 15 Jh 41.21N 26.57 E
Teke Burun [Tur.] 15 Ji 40.02N 26.10 E
Teke Burun [Tur.] 15 Jk 38.05N 26.36 E
Tekeli 19 Hg 44.48N 78.57 E
Tekes 27 Dc 43.10N 81.43 E
Tekes He 27 Dc 43.35N 82.30 E
Tekeze 35 Fc 14.20N 35.50 E
Tekija 15 Fe 44.41N 22.25 E
Tekiliktag 27 Dd 36.35N 80.20 E
Tekirdağ 23 Ca 40.59N 27.31 E
Tekman 24 Ic 39.38N 41.31 E
Te Kopuru 62 Eb 36.02S 173.55 E
Te Kou 64p Bb 21.14S 159.46W
Tekouiat 32 He 22.20N 2.30 E
Tekro 35 Cb 19.34N 20.57 E
Te Kuiti 62 Fc 38.20S 175.10 E
Tela 47 Ge 15.44N 87.27W
Telagh 32 Gc 34.47N 0.34W
Telatai 34 Fb 16.31N 1.30 E
Telavåg 7 Af 60.16N 4.49 E
Telavi 19 Eg 41.55N 45.29 E
Tel Aviv-Yafo 22 Ff 32.04N 34.46 E
Telč 10 Lg 49.11N 15.27 E
Telchac Puerto 48 Og 21.21N 89.16W
Telciu 15 Hb 47.26N 24.24 E
Tele 36 Db 2.48N 23.54 E
Teleac 15 Hc 46.41N 24.48 E
Telečkoje Ozero 20 Df 51.30N 87.45 E
Telefomin 60 Ci 5.08S 141.31 E
Telegraph Creek 42 Ee 57.54N 131.09W
Telekitonga 65b Bb 20.24S 174.32W
Telekivavu'u 65b Bb 20.19S 174.32W
Telêmaco Borba 55 Gg 24.23S 50.28W
Telemark [2] 7 Bg 59.30N 8.40 E
Telemark 8 Ce 59.30N 8.45 E
Telén 56 Ge 36.16S 65.30W
Telen 26 Gf 0.26N 116.42 E
Telenešty 15 Lb 47.30N 28.16 E
Teleno 13 Fb 42.21N 6.23W
Teleorman 15 If 43.52N 25.26 E
Teleorman [2] 15 If 44.10N 25.15 E
Telerhteba, Djebel- 32 Ie 24.10N 6.51 E
Telescope Peak 46 Gh 36.10N 117.05W
Telescope Point 51p Bb 12.08N 61.36W
Telese 14 Ii 41.13N 14.32 E
Teles Pires, Rio- o São Manuel, Rio- 52 Kf 7.21S 58.03W
Telfān, Hadjer- 35 Bc 12.05N 18.57 E
Telford 9 Ki 52.40N 2.30W
Telgte 12 Jc 51.59N 7.47 E
Télimélé 34 Cc 10.54N 13.02W
Teljo, Jabal- 35 Dc 14.42N 25.56 E
Tell al Ubaid 24 Lg 30.59N 46.01 E
Tellaro 14 Jn 36.50N 15.06 E
Tell Atlas (EN)=Atlas Tellien 30 He 36.00N 2.00 E
Tell City 44 Dg 37.57N 86.46W
Teller 40 Fc 65.16N 166.22W
Telok Anson 26 Df 4.02N 101.01 E
Teloloapan 48 Jh 18.21N 99.51W
Telposiz, Gora- 5 Lc 63.54N 59.10 E
Telsen 56 Gf 42.24S 66.57W
Telšiai/Telšjaj 19 Cd 55.59N 22.17 E
Telšjaj/Telšiai 19 Cd 55.59N 22.17 E
Teltow 10 Jd 52.24N 13.16 E
Telukbetung 22 Mj 5.27S 105.16 E
Telukbutun 26 Ef 4.13N 108.12 E
Telukdalem 26 Cf 0.34N 97.49 E
Téma 31 Gh 5.37N 0.01W
Temacine 32 Ic 33.01N 6.01 E
Te Manga 64p Bb 21.13S 159.45W
Tematangi Atoll 57 Mg 21.41S 140.40W
Tembenči 20 Ed 64.36N 99.58 E
Témbi 15 Fj 39.53N 22.35 E
Tembilahan 26 Dg 0.19S 103.09 E
Temblador 50 Eh 8.59N 62.44W
Tembleque 13 Ie 39.42N 3.30W
Temblor Range 46 Fi 35.30N 119.55W
Tembo 36 Cd 7.42S 17.17 E
Tembo, Chutes- 30 Ii 8.50S 15.20 E
Tembo, Mont- 36 Bb 1.50N 12.00 E
Tembué 37 Eb 14.51S 32.50 E
Teme 9 Ki 52.09N 2.18W
Temerin 15 Cd 45.25N 19.53 E
Temerloh 26 Df 3.27N 102.25 E
Teminabuan 26 Jg 1.26S 132.01 E
Temir 19 Ff 49.08N 57.09 E
Temir 16 Te 48.31N 57.29 E
Temirlanovka 18 Gc 42.36N 69.17 E
Temirtau 22 Jd 50.05N 72.56 E
Témiscaming 44 Hb 46.44N 79.06W
Témiscouata, Lac- 44 Mb 47.40N 68.50W
Temki 35 Bc 11.29N 18.13 E
Temnikov 7 Ki 54.40N 43.13 E
Temo 14 Cj 40.17N 8.28 E
Temoe, Ile- 57 Ng 23.20S 134.29W
Temores 48 Ed 27.16N 108.15W
Tempe 46 Jj 33.25N 111.56W
Tempio Pausania 14 Dj 40.54N 9.06 E
Temple 43 He 31.06N 97.21W
Templeman, Mount- 46 Ga 50.43N 117.14W
Templemore/An Teampall Mór 9 Fi 52.48N 7.50W
Templin 10 Jc 53.07N 13.30 E
Tempoal, Río- 48 Jg 21.47N 98.27W
Tempué 36 Ce 13.27S 18.53 E
Temrjuk 16 Jg 45.15N 37.23 E
Temse/Tamise 12 Gc 51.08N 4.13 E
Temuco 53 Ii 38.44S 72.36W
Temuka 62 Df 44.15S 171.16 E
Tena 54 Cd 0.59S 77.48W
Tenacatita, Bahía de- 48 Gh 19.20N 104.50W
Tenala/Tenhola 8 Jd 60.04N 23.18 E
Tenāli 25 Ge 16.15N 80.35 E
Tenancingo de Degollado 48 Jh 18.58N 99.36W
Tenasserim [3] 25 Jf 13.00N 99.00 E
Tenasserim 25 Jf 12.05N 99.01 E
Tenasserim 25 Jf 12.24N 98.37 E
Tenasserim 21 Lh 12.35N 97.52 E
Tenby 9 Ij 51.41N 4.43W
Tence 11 Ki 45.07N 4.17 E
Tench Island 60 Eh 1.38S 150.42 E
Tenda, Col di- 14 Bf 44.09N 7.34 E
Tendaho 35 Gc 11.38N 41.00 E
Tende 11 Nj 44.05N 7.36 E
Tende, Col de- 14 Bf 44.09N 7.34 E
Ten Degree Channel 21 Lh 10.00N 92.30 E
Tendō 29 Gb 38.22N 140.22 E
Tendrara 32 Gc 33.03N 2.00W
Tendre, Mont- 14 Ad 46.36N 6.19 E
Tendrovskaja Kosa 16 Gf 46.15N 31.45 E
Ténenkou 34 Ec 14.28N 4.55W
Tenente Lira, Rio- 55 Db 15.56S 57.39W
Ténéré 30 Ig 17.35N 10.55 E
Ténéré, 'Erg du- 34 Hb 17.35N 10.55 E
Tenerife 30 Ff 28.19N 16.34W
Ténès 32 Hb 36.31N 1.18 E
Ténès, Cap- 13 Nh 36.33N 1.21 E
Teng 25 Je 19.52N 97.45 E
Tengah, Kepulauan- 26 Gh 7.30S 117.30 E
Tengchong 27 Gg 24.59N 98.32 E
Te Nggano, Lake- 60 Gj 11.45S 160.25 E
Tenggarong 26 Gg 0.24S 116.58 E
Tengger Shamo 21 Mf 38.00N 104.10 E
Tengiz, Ozero- 21 Id 50.25N 69.00 E
Tengréla 34 Dc 10.29N 6.24W
Tengréla [3] 34 Dc 10.27N 6.25W
Tengxian [China] 27 Jg 23.18N 110.49 E
Tengxian [China] 28 Dg 35.07N 117.10 E
Tenhola/Tenala 8 Jd 60.04N 23.18 E
Teniente General Rosendo M. Fraga 55 Af 23.45S 62.09W
Tenkāsi 25 Fg 8.58N 77.18 E
Tenke 36 Ee 10.33S 26.08 E
Tenkeli 20 Jb 70.01N 140.55 E
Tenkodogo 34 Ec 11.47N 0.22W
Tenna 14 Hg 43.14N 13.47 E
Tennant Creek 58 Ef 19.40S 134.10 E
Tennessee 38 Kf 37.04N 88.33W
Tennessee [2] 43 Jd 35.50N 85.30W
Tenneville 12 Hd 50.06N 5.32 E
Tenoioki 7 Ga 70.28N 28.18 E
Tenom 26 Ge 5.08N 115.57 E
Tenosique de Pino Suárez 47 Fe 17.29N 91.26W
Tenri 29 Dd 34.36N 135.49 E
Tenryū 29 Ed 34.52N 137.47 E
Tenryū-Gawa 28 Ng 34.35N 137.48 E
Tensift 32 Fc 32.02N 9.21W
Ten Sleep 46 Ld 44.02N 107.27W
Tenterden 12 Cc 51.03N 0.42 E

Index Symbols

[1] Independent Nation
[2] State, Region
[3] District, County
[4] Municipality
[5] Colony, Dependency
Continent
Physical Region
Historical or Cultural Region
Mount, Mountain
Volcano
Hill
Mountains, Mountain Range
Hills, Escarpment
Plateau, Upland
Pass, Gap
Plain, Lowland
Delta
Salt Flat
Valley, Canyon
Crater, Cave
Karst Features
Depression
Polder
Desert, Dunes
Forest, Woods
Heath, Steppe
Oasis
Cape, Point
Coast, Beach
Cliff
Peninsula
Isthmus
Sandbank
Island
Atoll
Rock, Reef
Islands, Archipelago
Rocks, Reefs
Coral Reef
Well, Spring
Geyser
River, Stream
Waterfall Rapids
River Mouth, Estuary
Lake
Salt Lake
Intermittent Lake
Reservoir
Swamp, Pond
Canal
Glacier
Ice Shelf, Pack Ice
Ocean
Sea
Gulf, Bay
Strait, Fjord
Lagoon
Bank
Seamount
Tablemount
Ridge
Shelf
Basin
Escarpment, Sea Scarp
Fracture
Trench, Abyss
National Park, Reserve
Point of Interest
Recreation Site
Cave, Cavern
Historic Site
Ruins
Wall, Walls
Church, Abbey
Temple
Scientific Station
Airport
Port
Lighthouse
Mine
Tunnel
Dam, Bridge

Tenterfield 59 Ke 29.03S 152.01 E
Tenuku 25 Ge 81.40N 16.45 E
Tenuze/Teenuse Jõgi 7 Jf 58.44N 23.58 E
Ten-Zan 29 Be 33.20N 130.08 E
Teocaltiche 48 Hg 21.26N 102.35W
Teodelina 55 Bl 34.11S 61.32W
Teodoro Sampaio 55 Ff 22.31S 52.10W
Teófilo Otoni 53 Lg 17.51S 41.30W
Teotepec, Cerro- 38 Ih 16.50N 100.50W
Teotihuacan 47 Ee 19.44N 98.50W
Teotilán del Camino 48 Kh 18.08N 97.05W
Tepa [Indon.] 26 Ih 7.52S 129.31 E
Tepa [W.F.] 64h Bb 13.19S 176.09W
Te Pae Roa Ngake o Tuko 64n Bb 10.23S 161.00W
Tepako, Pointe- 64h Bb 13.16S 176.08W
Tepalcatepec, Río- 48 Ih 18.35N 101.59W
Tepa Point 64k Bb 19.07S 169.56W
Tepatitlán de Morelos 48 Hg 20.49N 102.44W
Tepehuanes 47 Cc 25.21N 105.44W
Tepehuanes, Río- 48 Ge 25.11N 105.26W
Tepehuanes, Sierra de- 47 Cc 25.00N 105.40W
Tepelena 15 Di 40.18N 20.01 E
Tepi 35 Fd 7.03N 35.30 E
Tepic 39 Ig 21.30N 104.54W
Teplá 10 Ig 49.59N 12.52 E
Teplá 10 If 50.14N 12.52 E
Teplice 10 Jf 50.39N 13.50 E
Tepoca, Bahía de- 48 Cb 30.15N 112.50W
Tepopa, Cabo- 48 Cc 29.20N 112.25W
Te Puka 64n Ac 10.26S 161.02W
Te Puke 62 Gb 37.47S 176.20 E
Tequepa, Bahía de- 48 Ii 17.17N 101.05W
Tequila 48 Hg 20.54N 103.47W
Tequisquiapan 48 Jg 20.31N 99.52W
Ter 13 Pb 42.01N 3.12 E
Téra 31 Hg 14.01N 0.45 E
Tera [Port.] 13 Df 38.56N 8.03W
Tera [Sp.] 13 Gc 41.54N 5.44W
Teradomari 29 Fc 37.38N 138.45 E
Terai 21 Kg 26.30N 85.15 E
Teraina Island (Washington) 57 Kd 4.43N 160.24W
Terakeka 35 Ed 5.26N 31.45 E
Teramo 14 Hh 42.39N 13.42 E
Terampa 26 Ef 3.14N 106.14 E
Ter Apel, Vlagtwedde- 12 Jb 52.52N 7.06 E
Terborg, Wisch- 12 Ic 51.55N 6.22 E
Tercan 24 Ic 39.47N 40.24 E
Terceira 30 Ee 38.43N 27.13W
Tercero, Río- 56 Hd 32.55S 62.19W
Terebovlja 16 De 49.18N 25.42 E
Terehovka 28 Kc 43.38N 131.55 E
Terek 16 Nh 43.29N 44.08 E
Terek 5 Kg 43.44N 47.30 E
Térékolé 34 Cb 15.07N 10.53W
Terek-Saj 18 Hd 41.29N 71.13 E
Terenos 55 Ee 20.26S 54.50W
Teresa Cristina 55 Gg 24.48S 51.07W
Teresina 53 Lf 5.05S 42.49W
Teresinha 54 Hc 0.58N 52.02W
Tereška 16 Od 51.50N 46.45 E
Terespol 10 Td 52.05N 23.36 E
Teressa 25 Ig 8.15N 93.10 E
Teresva 16 Cf 47.59N 23.15 E
Terevaka, Cerro- 65d Ab 27.05S 109.23W
Tergnier 11 Je 49.39N 3.18 E
Terhazza 34 Ea 23.36N 4.56W
Teriberka 7 Ib 69.10N 35.10 E
Teriberka 7 Ib 69.09N 35.08 E
Terlingua Creek 45 El 29.10N 103.36W
Termas de Río Hondo 56 Hc 27.29S 64.52W
Terme 24 Gb 41.12N 36.59 E
Termez 22 If 37.14N 67.16 E
Termini Imerese 14 Hm 37.59N 13.42 E
Termini Imerese, Golfo di- 14 Hl 38.00N 13.45 E
Terminillo 14 Hh 42.28N 13.01 E
Términos, Laguna de- 47 Fe 18.37N 91.33W
Termit, Massif de- 34 Hb 16.15N 11.17 E
Termit-Kaoboul 34 Hb 15.43N 11.37 E
Termoli 14 Ii 42.00N 15.00 E
Termonde/Dendermonde 12 Gc 51.02N 4.07 E
Ternaard, Westdongeradeel- 12 Ha 53.23N 5.58 E
Ternate 25 If 0.48N 127.24 E
Ternej 20 Ig 45.05N 136.35 E
Terneuzen 11 Jc 51.20N 3.50 E
Terni 14 Gh 42.34N 12.37 E
Ternitz 14 Kc 47.43N 16.02 E
Ternois 12 Ed 50.25N 2.19 E
Ternopol 6 If 49.34N 25.38 E
Ternopolskaja Oblast [3] 19 Cf 49.20N 25.35 E
Terpenija, Mys- 20 Jg 48.38N 144.40 E
Terpenija, Zaliv- 21 Qe 49.00N 143.30 E
Terrace 42 Ef 54.31N 128.35W
Terrace Bay 45 Mb 48.47N 87.09W
Terracina 14 Hi 41.17N 13.15 E
Terra de Basto 13 Ec 41.25N 8.00W
Terra Firma 37 Ce 25.36S 23.24 E
Terråk 7 Cd 65.05N 12.25 E
Terralba 14 Ck 39.43N 8.39 E
Terra Rica 55 Ff 22.43S 52.38W
Terrebonne Bay 45 Kl 29.09N 90.35W
Terre-de-Bas 51e Ac 15.51N 61.39W
Terre-de-Haut 51e Ac 15.58N 61.35W
Terre Froides 11 Li 45.30N 5.30 E
Terre Haute 43 Jd 39.28N 87.24W
Terrell 45 Hj 32.44N 96.17W
Terre Plaine 11 Jg 47.25N 4.00 E
Terril 13 Gh 37.00N 5.11W
Territoire de Belfort [3] 11 Mg 47.45N 7.00 E
Terruca 13 Fc 41.45N 6.25W
Terry 46 Mc 46.47N 105.19W
Tersa 16 Nd 50.46N 44.42 E
Terschelling 12 Ha 53.21N 5.13 E
Terschelling 11 La 53.24N 5.20 E
Terschelling-West-Terschelling 12 Ha 53.21N 5.13 E
Tersef 35 Bc 12.55N 16.49 E
Terskej-Alatau, Hrebet- 19 Hg 42.10N 78.45 E
Terski Bereg 7 Jc 66.10N 39.30 E
Tersko-Kumski Kanal 16 Ng 44.47N 44.37 E
Terter 16 Oi 40.27N 47.16 E
Teruel 13 Kd 40.21N 1.06W
Teruel [3] 13 Ld 40.40N 0.40W
Tervakoski 8 Kd 60.48N 24.37 E
Tervel 15 Kf 43.45N 27.24 E
Tervo 8 Lb 62.57N 26.45 E
Tervola 7 Fc 66.05N 24.48 E
Tes 27 Fa 50.27N 93.30 E
Teša 7 Ki 55.38N 42.10 E
Tesalia 54 Cc 2.29N 75.44W
Tesaret 32 Hd 25.40N 2.43 E
Tesdrero, Cerro- 48 Hf 22.47N 103.04W
Teseney 35 Fb 15.07N 36.40 E
Teshekpuk Lake 40 Ib 70.35N 153.30W
Teshikaga 28 Rc 43.29N 144.28 E
Teshio 28 Pb 44.53N 141.44 E
Teshio-Dake 28 Qc 43.58N 142.50 E
Teshio-Gawa 28 Pb 44.53N 141.44 E
Teshio-Sanchi 29a Ba 44.20N 142.00 E
Tesijn → Tesijn Gol 21 Ld 50.28N 93.04 E
Tesijn Gol (Tesijn) 21 Ld 50.28N 93.04 E
Teslić 14 Lf 44.37N 17.52 E
Teslin 42 Ed 61.34N 134.50W
Teslin 42 Ed 60.09N 132.45W
Teslin Lake 42 Ed 60.00N 132.30W
Teslui 15 He 44.09N 24.29 E
Tesocoma 48 Ed 27.41N 109.16W
Tesouras, Rio- 55 Gb 14.36S 50.51W
Tesouro 55 Fc 16.04S 53.34W
Tessala, Monts du- 13 Li 35.15N 0.45W
Tessalit 31 Hf 20.14N 0.59 E
Tessaoua 34 Gc 13.45N 7.59 E
Tessenderlo 12 Hc 51.04N 5.05 E
Test 9 Lk 50.55N 1.29W
Test, Tizi n'- 32 Fc 30.50N 8.20W
Testa, Capo- 14 Di 41.14N 9.08 E
Têt 11 Jl 42.44N 3.02 E
Tetari, Cerro- 49 Ki 9.59N 72.55W
Tetas, Punta- 56 Fc 23.31S 70.38W
Tete 31 Kj 16.10S 33.36 E
Tete [3] 37 Ec 15.30S 33.00 E
Te Teko 62 Gc 38.02S 176.48 E
Tetepare Island 63a Cc 8.45S 157.35 E
Téterchen 12 Ie 49.14N 6.34 E
Tetere 63a Ec 9.25S 160.15 E
Teterev 16 Gd 51.01N 30.08 E
Teterow 10 Ic 53.47N 12.34 E
Teteven 15 Hg 42.55N 24.16 E
Tetiaroa Atoll 57 Mf 17.05S 149.32W
Tetijev 16 Fe 49.23N 29.41 E
Tetjuši 7 Li 54.57N 48.49 E
Teton Peak 46 Ic 47.55N 112.48W
Teton Range 46 Je 43.50N 110.55W
Teton River 46 Jc 47.56N 110.31W
Tétouan 31 Ge 35.34N 5.22W
Tétouan [3] 32 Fb 35.35N 5.30W
Tetovo 15 Dg 42.01N 20.59 E
Tetri-Ckaro 16 Ni 41.33N 44.27 E
Teuco, Río- 55 Bg 25.38S 60.12W
Teufelskopf 12 Ie 49.36N 6.49 E
Teulada 14 Cl 38.58N 8.46 E
Teulada, Capo- 5 Gh 38.52N 8.38 E
Téul de Gonzales Ortega 48 Hg 21.28N 103.29W
Teun, Pulau- 26 Ih 6.59S 129.08 E
Teupasenti 49 Df 14.13N 86.42W
Teuquito, Río- 55 Bg 24.22S 61.09W
Teuri-Tō 29a Ba 44.25N 141.20 E
Teutoburger Wald 10 Ee 52.10N 8.15 E
Teuva/Ostermark 7 Ee 62.29N 21.44 E
Teuz 15 Ec 46.39N 21.33 E
Tevai 63c Bb 11.37S 166.55 E
Tevaïtoa 65e Db 16.46S 151.28W
Tevere = Tiber (EN) 5 Hg 41.44N 12.14 E
Teverya 24 Ff 32.47N 35.32 E
Teviot 9 Kf 55.36N 2.26W
Tevli 10 Ud 52.19N 24.23 E
Tevriz 19 Hd 57.34N 72.24 E
Tevšruleh 27 Hb 47.25N 101.55 E
Te Waewae Bay 62 Bg 46.15S 167.30 E
Tewkesbury 9 Kj 51.59N 2.09W
Têwo (Dêngkagoin) 27 He 34.03N 103.21 E
Texada Island 46 Cb 49.40N 124.24W
Texarkana [Ar.-U.S.] 43 Ie 33.26N 94.02W
Texarkana [Tx.-U.S.] 39 Jf 33.26N 94.03W
Texas 59 Ke 28.51S 151.11 E
Texas [2] 43 He 31.30N 99.00W
Texas City 43 If 29.23N 94.54W
Texcoco 48 Jh 19.31N 98.53W
Texel 12 Ga 53.03N 4.47 E
Texel 11 Ka 53.05N 4.45 E
Texel-De Koog 12 Ga 53.07N 4.46 E
Texel-Den Burg 12 Ga 53.03N 4.47 E
Texoma, Lake- 43 He 33.55N 96.37W
Teyéa = Tegea (EN) 15 Fl 37.27N 22.25 E
Teza 7 Jh 56.32N 41.57 E
Teze-Jel 19 Gh 37.55N 60.22 E
Teziutlán 47 Ee 19.49N 97.21W
Tezpur 25 Ic 26.38N 92.48 E
Tha-anne 42 Id 60.31N 94.37W
Thabana Ntlenyana 30 Jk 29.30S 29.15 E
Thabazimbi 37 Dd 24.41S 27.21 E
Thai, Ao- = Thailand, Gulf of- (EN) 21 Mh 10.00N 102.00 E
Thai Binh 25 Ld 20.27N 106.20 E
Thailand (EN) = Muang Thai [1] 22 Mh 15.00N 100.00 E
Thailand, Gulf of- (EN) = Thai, Ao- 21 Mh 10.00N 102.00 E
Thai Nguyen 25 Ld 21.36N 105.50 E
Thal 25 Eb 31.30N 71.40 E
Thālith, Ash Shallāl ath- = Third Cataract (EN) 30 Kg 19.49N 30.19 E
Thamad Bū Ḩashīshah 33 Cd 25.50N 18.05 E
Thamarīd 35 Ib 17.39N 54.02 E
Thame 12 Bc 51.45N 0.59W
Thames 61 Eg 37.08S 175.33 E
Thames 5 Ge 51.28N 0.43 E
Thames River 44 Fd 42.19N 82.28W
Thamūd 23 Gf 17.15N 49.54 E
Thāna 22 Jh 19.12N 72.58 E
Thandaung 25 Je 19.04N 96.41 E
Thanh Hoa 22 Mh 19.48N 105.46 E
Thanjāvūr 25 Ff 10.48N 79.09 E
Thann 11 Ng 47.49N 7.05 E
Thaon-les-Vosges 11 Mf 48.15N 6.25 E
Thap Sakae 25 Jf 11.14N 99.31 E
Thar/Great Indian Desert 21 Ig 27.00N 70.00 E
Thargomindah 59 Ie 28.00S 143.49 E
Tharrawaddy 25 Je 17.39N 95.48 E
Tharros 14 Ck 39.54N 8.28 E
Tharthār, Baḩr ath- 23 Fc 33.59N 43.12 E
Tharthār, Wādī ath- 23 Fc 33.59N 43.12 E
Thasi Gang Dzong 25 Ic 27.19N 91.34 E
Thásos 5 Ig 40.49N 24.42 E
Thásos 15 Hi 40.47N 24.43 E
Thásou, Dhíavlos- 15 Hi 40.49N 24.42 E
Thathlīth, Wādī- 33 He 20.25N 44.55 E
Thau, Bassin de- 11 Jk 43.23N 3.36 E
Thaxted 12 Cc 51.57N 0.22 E
Thaya 10 Mh 48.37N 16.56 E
Thayetchaung 25 Jf 13.52N 98.16 E
Thayetmyo 25 Je 19.19N 95.11 E
Thaywthadangyi Kyun 25 Jf 12.20N 98.00 E
The Alberga River 59 He 27.06S 135.33 E
The Aldermen Islands 62 Gb 37.00S 176.05 E
Thebai = Thebes (EN) 33 Fd 25.43N 32.35 E
Thebes (EN) = Thebai 33 Fd 25.43N 32.35 E
Thebes (EN) = Thívai 15 Gk 38.19N 23.19 E
The Black Sugarloaf 59 Kf 31.20S 151.33 E
The Borders 9 Kf 55.35N 2.50W
The Bottom 50 Ed 17.38N 63.15W
The Broads 9 Oi 52.40N 1.30 E
The Cheviot 9 Kf 55.28N 2.09W
The Cheviot Hills 9 Kf 55.30N 2.10W
The Crane 51q Bb 13.06N 59.26W
The Dalles 43 Cb 45.36N 121.10W
Thedford 43 Gc 41.59N 100.35W
The Entrance 59 Kf 33.21S 151.30 E
The Everglades 43 Kf 26.00N 81.00W
The Fens 9 Mi 5.24N 0.02W
The Gap 46 Jh 36.25N 111.30W
The Granites 59 Gd 20.35S 130.21 E
The Hague (EN) = Den Haag /'s-Gravenhage 6 Ge 52.06N 4.18 E
The Hague (EN) = 's-Gravenhage/Den Haag 6 Ge 52.06N 4.18 E
The Knob 44 He 41.14N 78.22W
The Little Minch 9 Gd 57.35N 6.55W
Thelle 12 De 49.23N 1.51 E
Thelon 38 Jc 64.16N 96.05W
The Macumba River 57 Eg 27.45S 136.50 E
The Merse 9 Kf 55.50N 2.10W
The Naze 12 Dc 51.42N 1.47 E
The Neales River 59 He 28.08S 136.47 E
The Needles 9 Lk 50.39N 1.34W
Theniet el Had 13 Oi 35.32N 2.01 E
Theodore 59 Kd 24.57S 150.05 E
Theológos 15 Hi 40.40N 24.42 E
The Pas 39 Id 53.50N 101.15W
The Pillories 51n Bb 12.54N 61.12W
Thérain 11 Ie 49.15N 2.27 E
Thermaïkós Kólpos = Salonika, Gulf of- (EN) 5 Ig 40.20N 22.45 E
Thermopílai = Thermopylae (EN) 15 Fk 38.48N 22.32 E
Thermopolis 43 Fc 43.39N 108.13W
Thermopylae (EN) = Thermopílai 15 Fk 38.48N 22.32 E
Thérouanne 12 Ed 50.38N 2.15 E
The Round Mountain 59 Kf 30.27S 152.16 E
The Sandlings 9 Oi 52.10N 1.30 E
Thesiger Bay 42 Fb 71.30N 124.00W
The Slot → New Georgia Sound 60 Fi 8.00S 158.10 E
The Solent Spithead 9 Lk 50.46N 1.20W
Thessalia [2] 15 Fj 39.30N 22.10 E
Thessalia = Thessaly (EN) 5 Ih 39.30N 22.10 E
Thessalia = Thessaly (EN) 15 Fj 39.30N 22.10 E
Thessalon 44 Fb 46.15N 83.34W
Thessaloníki = Salonika (EN) 6 Ig 40.38N 22.56 E
Thessaly (EN) = Thessalia 15 Fj 39.30N 22.10 E
Thessaly (EN) = Thessalia 5 Ih 39.30N 22.10 E
The Stevenson River 59 He 27.06S 135.33 E
Thet 12 Cb 52.24N 0.45 E
Thetford 9 Ni 52.25N 0.45 E
Thetford Mines 44 Lb 46.05N 71.18W
The Twins 62 Ed 41.14S 172.40 E
Theux 12 Hd 50.33N 5.49 E
The Valley 47 Le 18.03N 63.04W
The Warburton River 59 He 27.55S 137.28 E
The Wash 5 Ge 52.55N 0.15 E
The Weald 9 Nj 51.05N 0.05 E
The Witties 49 Ff 14.10N 82.45W
The Wolds 9 Mh 53.20N 0.10W
Thiaucourt-Regniéville 12 Hf 48.57N 5.52 E
Thiberville 12 Ce 49.08N 0.27 E
Thibodaux 45 Kl 29.48N 90.49W
Thief River Falls 43 Hb 48.07N 96.10W
Thiel Mountains 66 Pg 85.15S 91.00W
Thiene 14 Fe 45.42N 11.29 E
Thiérache, Collines de la- 11 Je 49.48N 3.55 E
Thiers 11 Ji 45.51N 3.34 E
Thiès 31 Fg 14.48N 16.56W
Thiès [3] 34 Bc 14.45N 16.50W
Thiesi 14 Cj 40.31N 8.43 E
Thika 36 Gc 1.03S 37.05 E
Thikombia 61 Fc 15.44S 179.55W
Thimerais 11 Hf 48.40N 1.20 E
Thimphu 22 Kg 27.28N 89.39 E
Thio 61 Cd 21.37S 166.14 E
Thionville 11 Me 49.22N 6.10 E
Thiou 34 Ec 13.48N 2.40W
Thíra 15 Im 36.25N 25.26 E
Thíra = Thira (EN) 15 Im 36.24N 25.26 E
Thira (EN) = Thíra 15 Im 36.24N 25.26 E
Thirasia 15 Im 36.25N 25.20 E
Third Cataract (EN) = Thālith, Ash Shallāl ath- 30 Kg 19.49N 30.19 E
Thirsk 9 Lg 54.14N 1.20W
Thisted 7 Bh 56.57N 8.42 E
Thithia 63d Cb 17.45S 179.18W
Thiu Khao Phetchabun 25 Ke 16.20N 100.55 E
Thívai = Thebes (EN) 15 Gk 38.19N 23.19 E
Thiviers 11 Gi 45.25N 0.55 E
Thlewiaza 42 Id 60.28N 94.42W
Thoa 42 Gd 60.31N 109.45W
Tho Chu, Dao- 25 Kg 9.00N 103.50 E
Thoen 25 Je 17.41N 99.14 E
Tholen 12 Gc 51.32N 4.13 E
Tholen 11 Kc 51.35N 4.05 E
Tholey 12 Je 49.29N 7.04 E
Thomasset, Rocher- 57 Nf 10.21S 138.25W
Thomaston 44 Ei 32.54N 84.20W
Thomasville [Al.-U.S.] 44 Dj 32.18N 87.47W
Thomasville [Ga.-U.S.] 43 Ke 30.50N 83.59W
Thomasville [N.C.-U.S.] 44 Gh 35.53N 80.05W
Thompson 42 He 55.45N 97.45W
Thompson Falls 46 Hc 47.36N 115.21W
Thompson River 45 Jg 39.45N 93.36W
Thompson Sound 62 Bf 45.10S 167.00 E
Thomsen 42 Fb 73.40N 119.30W
Thomson 44 Fi 33.28N 82.30W
Thomson River 59 Ie 25.11S 142.53 E
Thomson's Falls 36 Gb 0.02N 36.22 E
Thon 12 Fe 49.53N 3.55 E
Thon Buri 22 Mh 13.43N 100.24 E
Thong Pha Phum 25 Jf 14.44N 98.38 E
Thongwa 25 Je 16.46N 96.32 E
Thonon-les-Bains 11 Mh 46.22N 6.29 E
Thoreau 45 Bi 35.24N 108.13W
Thornaby-on-Tees 9 Lg 54.34N 1.18W
Thornbury 61 Ci 46.17S 168.06 E
Thorney 12 Bb 52.37N 0.06W
Thornhill 9 Jf 55.18N 3.40W
Thorshavn 6 Fc 62.01N 6.46W
Thouars 11 Fh 46.58N 0.13W
Thouet 11 Fg 47.17N 0.06W
Thrace (EN) = Thráki 15 Jh 41.20N 26.45 E
Thrace (EN) = Thráki 5 Ig 41.20N 26.45 E
Thrace (EN) = Trakya 15 Jh 41.20N 26.45 E
Thrace (EN) = Trakya 5 Ig 41.20N 26.45 E
Thráki [2] 15 Ih 41.10N 25.30 E
Thráki = Thrace (EN) 5 Ig 41.20N 26.45 E
Thráki = Thrace (EN) 15 Jh 41.20N 26.45 E
Thrakikón Pélagos 15 Hi 40.30N 25.00 E
Thrapston 12 Bb 52.24N 0.32W
Three Forks 43 Eb 45.54N 111.33W
Three Kings Islands 57 Ih 34.10S 172.10 E
Three Kings Trough (EN) 3 Jm 32.00S 170.30 E
Three Points, Cape- 30 Gh 4.45N 2.06W
Three Rivers 44 Ee 41.57N 85.38W
Three Sisters Islands 63a Ed 10.10S 161.57 E
Throckmorton 45 Gj 33.11N 99.11W
Throssel, Lake- 59 Ee 27.25S 124.15 E
Thua 36 Gc 1.17S 40.00 E
Thuin 11 Kd 50.20N 4.17 E
Thule 66 Ad 59.27S 27.19W
Thule/Qânâq 67 Od 77.35N 69.40W
Thule, Mount - 42 Jb 73.00N 78.27W
Thun 14 Bd 46.45N 7.40 E
Thunder Bay 39 Ke 48.23N 89.15W
Thunder Bay [Mi.-U.S.] 44 Fc 45.04N 83.25W
Thunder Bay [Ont.-Can.] 45 Lb 48.24N 89.00W
Thunder Butte 45 Fd 45.19N 101.53W
Thuner See 14 Bd 46.40N 7.45 E
Thung Song 25 Jg 8.11N 99.41 E
Thur 14 Cc 47.36N 8.35 E
Thurgau [2] 14 Dc 47.40N 9.10 E
Thüringen 10 Gf 50.40N 11.00 E
Thüringer Wald = Thuringian Forest (EN) 5 He 50.30N 11.00 E
Thuringian Forest (EN) = Thüringer Wald 5 He 50.30N 11.00 E
Thurles/Durlas 9 Fi 52.41N 7.49W
Thurrock 9 Nj 51.28N 0.20 E
Thursday Island 59 Ib 10.35S 142.13 E
Thurso 6 Fd 58.35N 3.32W
Thurso 9 Jc 58.35N 3.30W
Thurston Island 66 Pf 72.06S 99.00W
Thury-Harcourt 12 Bf 48.59N 0.29W
Thusis/Tusaun 14 Dd 46.42N 9.26 E
Thuwayrāt, Nafūd ath- 24 Kj 26.00N 44.50 E
Thuy Phong 25 Lf 11.14N 108.43 E
Thwaites Iceberg Tongue 66 Of 74.00S 108.30W
Thy 8 Ch 57.00N 8.30 E
Thyborøn 8 Ch 56.42N 8.13 E
Tianbaoshan 28 Jc 42.57N 128.57 E
Tianchang 27 Ke 32.37N 119.00 E
Tiandong (Pingma) 27 Ig 23.40N 107.09 E
Tian'e (Liupai) 27 If 25.05N 107.12 E
Tianguá 54 Jd 3.44S 40.59W
Tianjin = Tientsin (EN) 22 Nf 39.08N 117.12 E
Tianjin Shi (T'ien-chin Shih) [4] 27 Kd 39.08N 117.12 E
Tianjun (Xinyuan) 22 Lf 37.18N 99.15 E
Tianlin (Leli) 27 Ig 24.22N 106.11 E
Tian Ling 28 Kb 44.24N 130.10 E
Tianmen 27 Je 30.40N 113.10 E
Tianmu Shan 28 Ei 30.31N 119.36 E
Tianmu Xi 28 Ej 29.59N 119.24 E
Tianqiaoling 27 Mc 43.35N 129.35 E
Tian Shan 21 Ke 42.00N 80.01 E
Tianshan → Ar Horqin Qi 27 Lc 43.55N 120.05 E
Tianshifu 27 Lc 41.15N 124.20 E
Tianshui 22 Mf 34.35N 105.43 E
Tiantal 28 Fj 29.08N 121.00 E
Tianwangsi 28 Ei 31.45N 119.12 E
Tianyi → Ningcheng 27 Kc 41.34N 119.25 E
Tianzhen 28 Cd 40.24N 114.05 E
Tianzhen → Gaoqing 28 Df 37.10N 117.50 E
Tianzhuangtai 28 Gd 40.49N 122.06 E
Tiaraju 55 Ej 30.15S 54.23W
Tiarei 65e Fc 17.32S 149.20W
Tiaret [3] 32 Hc 34.50N 1.30 E
Tiaret 31 He 35.20N 1.14 E
Tiaret, Monts de- 13 Ni 35.26N 1.15 E
Tiassalé 34 Ed 5.54N 4.50W
Tiavea 65c Ba 13.57S 171.24W
Ţīb, Ra's Aţ- = Bon, Cape- (EN) 30 Ie 37.05N 11.03 E
Tibaji 55 Gg 24.30S 50.24W
Tibaji, Rio- 55 Gf 22.47S 51.01W
Tibasti, Sarīr- 30 If 24.00N 17.00 E
Tibati 31 Ih 6.28N 12.38 E
Tiber (EN) = Tevere 5 Hg 41.44N 12.14 E
Tiberina, Val- 14 Gg 43.30N 12.10 E
Tibesti 30 If 21.30N 17.30 E
Tibet (EN) = Xizang Zizhiqu (Hsi-tsang Tzu-chih-ch'ü) [2] 27 Ee 32.00N 90.00 E
Tibet, Plateau of- (EN) = Qing Zang Gaoyuan 21 Kf 32.30N 87.00 E
Tibidabo 13 Oc 41.25N 2.07 E
Tibni 24 He 35.35N 30.49 E
Tibro 8 Ff 58.26N 14.10 E
Tibú 49 Ki 8.40N 72.42W
Tibugà, Golfo de- 54 Cb 5.45N 77.20W
Tiburón, Capo- 49 Ii 8.42N 77.21W
Tiburon, Isla- 47 Bc 29.00N 112.25W
Ticao 26 Hd 12.31N 123.42 E
Tice 44 Gl 26.41N 81.49W
Tichá Orlice 10 Mf 50.09N 16.05 E
Tichît 31 Gg 18.26N 9.31W
Tichît, Dahr- 32 Ff 18.30N 9.25W
Tichka, Tizı n'- 32 Fc 31.17N 7.21W
Tichla 32 Ee 21.36N 14.58W
Ticino [2] 14 Cd 46.20N 9.00 E
Ticino 14 De 45.09N 9.14 E
Ticul 47 Gd 20.24N 89.32W
Tidaholm 7 Cg 58.11N 13.57 E
Tidan 8 Ef 58.42N 13.48 E
Tiddim 25 Id 23.22N 93.40 E
Tidikelt, Plaine du- 30 Hf 27.00N 1.30 E
Tidirhine 32 Gc 34.51N 4.31W
Tidjikja 31 Fg 18.32N 11.27W
Tidore 26 If 0.40N 127.26 E
Tidra, Ile- 30 Fg 19.44N 16.24W
Tiebissou 34 Dd 7.10N 5.13W
Tiechang 28 Id 41.40N 126.12 E
Tiel 11 Lc 51.54N 5.25 E
Tieli 27 Mb 47.04N 128.02 E
Tieling 28 Gc 42.18N 123.51 E
Tielt 11 Jc 51.00N 3.20 E
Tienba 34 Dd 8.30N 7.10W
T'ien-chin Shih → Tianjin Shi [4] 27 Kd 39.08N 117.12 E
Tienen/Tirlemont 12 Gd 50.48N 4.57 E
Tiengemeten 12 Gc 51.45N 5.20 E
Tientsin (EN) = Tianjin 22 Nf 39.08N 117.12 E
Tieroko, Tarso- 35 Ba 20.45N 17.52 E
Tierp 7 Df 60.20N 17.30 E
Tierra Amarilla [Chile] 56 Fc 27.29S 70.17W
Tierra Amarilla [N.M.-U.S.] 45 Ch 36.42N 106.33W
Tierra Blanca 47 Ee 18.27N 96.21W
Tierra Colorada 48 Ji 17.10N 99.35W
Tierra del Fuego [2] 56 Gh 54.00S 67.00W
Tierra del Fuego (EN) = Tierra del Fuego, Isla Grande de- 52 Jk 54.00S 69.00W
Tierra del Fuego, Isla Grande de- = Tierra del Fuego (EN) 52 Jk 54.00S 69.00W
Tierralta 54 Cb 8.10N 76.04W
Tiétar 13 Fe 39.50N 6.01W
Tietê, Rio- 52 Kh 20.40S 51.35W
Tietjerksteradeel 12 Ia 53.12N 6.00 E
Tietjerksteradeel-Bergum 12 Hb 52.17N 5.58 E
Tifariti 32 Ed 26.09N 10.33W
Tiffany Mountain 46 Fb 48.40N 119.56W
Tiffin 44 Fe 41.07N 83.11W
Tifton 43 Ke 31.27N 83.31W
Tiga 63b Ce 21.08S 167.49 E
Tigalda 40a Fb 54.05N 165.05W
Tigăneşti 15 If 43.54N 25.22 E
Tighennif 13 Mi 35.25N 0.15 E
Tigil 20 Ke 57.57N 158.20 E
Tigil 20 Ke 57.48N 158.40 E
Tignère 34 Hd 7.22N 12.39 E
Tigray [3] 35 Fc 14.00N 39.00 E
Tigre 48 Hh 19.53N 102.59W
Tigre, Cerro del- 48 Jf 23.03N 99.16W
Tigre, Río- [S.Amer.] 52 If 4.30S 74.10W
Tigre, Río- [Ven.] 50 Eh 9.20N 62.30W
Tigris (EN) = Dicle 21 Gf 31.00N 47.25 E
Tigris (EN) = Dijlah 21 Gf 31.00N 47.25 E
Tigrovy Hvost, Mys- 18 Bc 43.57N 58.45 E
Tiguent 32 Df 17.15N 16.00W
Tiguentourine 32 Id 27.43N 9.33 E
Tigui 35 Bb 18.38N 18.47 E
Tigzirt 13 Qh 36.54N 4.07 E
Tīh, Jabal at- 33 Fd 29.35N 34.00 E
Tīh, Şaḩrā' at- = At Tih Desert (EN) 33 Fc 30.05N 34.00 E
Tihāmat 23 Ff 18.30N 41.30 E
Tihāmat Ash Shām 33 Hf 19.15N 41.10 E

Index Symbols

- [1] Independent Nation
- [2] State, Region
- [3] District, County
- [4] Municipality
- [5] Colony, Dependency
- Continent
- Physical Region
- Historical or Cultural Region
- Mount, Mountain
- Volcano
- Hill
- Mountains, Mountain Range
- Hills, Escarpment
- Plateau, Upland
- Pass, Gap
- Plain, Lowland
- Delta
- Salt Flat
- Valley, Canyon
- Crater, Cave
- Karst Features
- Depression
- Polder
- Desert, Dunes
- Forest, Woods
- Heath, Steppe
- Oasis
- Cape, Point
- Coast, Beach
- Cliff
- Peninsula
- Isthmus
- Sandbank
- Island
- Atoll
- Rock, Reef
- Islands, Archipelago
- Rocks, Reefs
- Coral Reef
- Well, Spring
- Geyser
- River, Stream
- Waterfall Rapids
- River Mouth, Estuary
- Lake
- Salt Lake
- Intermittent Lake
- Reservoir
- Swamp, Pond
- Canal
- Glacier
- Ice Shelf, Pack Ice
- Ocean
- Sea
- Gulf, Bay
- Strait, Fjord
- Lagoon
- Bank
- Seamount
- Tablemount
- Ridge
- Shelf
- Basin
- Escarpment, Sea Scarp
- Fracture
- Trench, Abyss
- National Park, Reserve
- Point of Interest
- Recreation Site
- Cave, Cavern
- Historic Site
- Ruins
- Wall, Walls
- Church, Abbey
- Temple
- Scientific Station
- Airport
- Port
- Lighthouse
- Mine
- Tunnel
- Dam, Bridge

Tihāmat ʿAsīr 33 Hf 17.30N 42.20 E
Tihi Okean=Pacific Ocean (EN) 3 Ki 5.00N 155.00W
Tihoreck 6 Kf 45.51N 40.09 E
Tihuţa, Pasul- 15 Hb 47.15N 25.00 E
Tihvin 19 Dd 59.38N 33.31 E
Tiirismaa 8 Kc 61.01N 25.31 E
Tiji 33 Bc 32.01N 11.22 E
Tijirīt 32 Ee 20.30N 15.00W
Tijuana 39 Hf 32.32N 117.01W
Tijucas 55 Hh 27.14S 48.38W
Tijucas, Baia do- 55 Hh 27.15S 48.31W
Tijucas, Rio- 55 Hh 27.15S 48.38W
Tijucas, Serra do- 55 Hh 27.16S 49.10W
Tijucas do Sul 55 Hg 25.56S 49.10W
Tijuco, Rio- 55 Gd 18.40S 50.05W
Tikal 39 Kh 17.20N 89.39W
Tikanlik 27 Ec 40.42N 87.38 E
Tikchik Lakes 40 Hd 60.07N 158.35W
Tikehau Atoll 61 Lb 15.00S 148.10W
Tikei, Ile- 61 Mb 14.58S 144.32W
Tikitiki 62 Hb 37.47S 178.25 E
Tikkakoski 8 Kb 62.24N 25.38 E
Tikkurila 8 Kd 60.18N 25.03 E
Tiko 34 Ge 4.05N 9.22 E
Tikopia Island 57 Hf 12.19S 168.49 E
Tikrit 23 Fc 34.36N 43.42 E
Tikšeozero, Ozero- 7 Hc 66.15N 31.45 E
Tiksi 22 Ob 71.36N 128.48 E
Tiladummati Atoll 25a Ba 6.50N 73.05 E
Tilamuta 26 Hf 0.30N 122.20 E
Tilburg 11 Lc 51.34N 5.05 E
Tilbury, Gravesend- 9 Nj 51.28N 0.23 E
Tilcara 56 Gb 23.34S 65.22W
Til-Châtel 11 Lg 47.31N 5.10 E
Tileagd 15 Fb 47.04N 22.12 E
Tilemsès 34 Fb 15.37N 4.44 E
Tilemsi, Vallée du- 30 Hg 19.00N 0.02 E
Tilia 32 Gd 27.22N 0.02W
Tiličiki 20 Ld 60.20N 166.03 E
Tiligul 16 Gf 47.07N 30.57 E
Tiligulski Liman 16 Gf 46.50N 31.10 E
Till 9 Kf 55.41N 2.12W
Tillabéry 34 Fc 14.13N 1.27 E
Tillamook 46 Dd 45.27N 123.51W
Tillamook Bay 46 Dd 45.30N 123.53W
Tillanchong 25 Ig 8.30N 93.37 E
Tillberga 8 Ge 59.41N 16.37 E
Tille 11 Lg 47.07N 5.21 E
Tillia 34 Fb 16.08N 4.47 E
Tillières-sur-Avre 12 Df 48.46N 1.04 E
Tillingham 12 Cd 50.58N 0.44 E
Tillsonburg 44 Gd 42.51N 80.44W
Tilly-sur-Seulles 12 Be 49.11N 0.37W
Tiloa 34 Fb 15.04N 2.03 E
Tilos 15 Km 36.25N 27.25 E
Tilpa 59 If 30.57S 144.24 E
Tim 16 Jd 51.37N 37.11 E
Tim 16 Jc 52.15N 37.22 E
Ţimā 33 Fd 26.54N 31.26 E
Timagami 44 Gb 47.00N 80.05W
Timagami, Lake- 42 Jg 46.57N 80.05W
Timane, Rio- 55 Be 20.16S 60.08W
Timan Ridge (EN)= Timanski Krjaž 5 Lc 65.00N 51.00 E
Timanski Bereg 17 Eb 68.20N 51.45 E
Timanski Krjaž=Timan Ridge (EN) 5 Lc 65.00N 51.00 E
Timaru 58 Ii 44.24S 171.15 E
Timaševsk 19 Df 45.35N 38.58 E
Timbalier Bay 45 Kl 29.10N 90.20W
Timbalier Island 45 Kl 29.04N 90.28W
Timbaúba 54 Ke 7.31S 35.19W
Timbédra 32 Ff 16.14N 8.10W
Timbó 55 Hh 26.50S 49.18W
Timbuktu (EN)= Tombouctou 31 Gg 16.46N 2.59W
Timedouine, Ras- 13 Oi 36.28N 4.09 E
Timétrine 34 Eb 19.20N 0.42W
Timétrine 34 Eb 19.27N 0.26W
Timfi Óros 15 Dj 39.57N 20.50 E
Timfristós 15 Ek 38.57N 21.49 E
Timia 34 Gb 18.04N 8.40 E
Timimoun 31 Hf 29.15N 0.15 E
Timimoun, Sebkha de- 32 Hd 29.00N 0.05 E
Timiris, Cap- 32 Df 19.23N 16.32W
Timirjazevo 19 Ge 53.45N 66.33 E
Timiş 15 De 44.51N 20.39 E
Timiş [2] 15 Ed 45.38N 21.13 E
Timiskaming, Lake- 44 Hb 47.35N 79.35W
Timişoara 6 If 45.45N 21.13 E
Ti-m-Merhsoï 34 Gb 18.00N 5.40 E
Timmins 39 Ke 48.28N 81.20W
Timmoudi 32 Gd 29.19N 1.08W
Timms Hill 45 Kd 45.27N 90.11W
Timok 15 Fe 44.13N 22.40 E
Timon 54 Je 5.06S 42.49W
Timor, Laut-=Timor Sea (EN) 57 Df 11.00S 128.00 E
Timor, Pulau- 21 Oj 8.50S 126.00 E
Timor Sea (EN)=Timor, Laut- 57 Df 11.00S 128.00 E
Timor Timur [3] 26 Ih 8.35S 126.00 E
Timor Trough (EN) 3 Ij 9.50S 126.00 E
Timote 56 He 35.21S 62.14W
Timotes 54 Db 8.59N 70.44W
Timpton 20 He 58.43N 127.12 E
Timrå 7 De 62.29N 17.18 E
Tims Ford Lake 44 Dh 35.15N 86.10W
Tin, Ra's at- 33 Dc 32.37N 23.08 E
Tinaca Point 21 Oi 5.33N 125.20 E
Tinaco 50 Bh 9.42N 68.26W
Tinakula 63c Ab 10.24S 165.47 E
Ti-n-Alkoum 32 Je 24.34N 10.11 E
Ti-n-Amzi [Alg.] 32 He 20.32N 4.37 E
Ti-n-Amzi [Niger] 34 Fb 17.54N 4.32 E
Tinaquillo 50 Bh 9.55N 68.18W
Tinchebray 12 Bf 48.46N 0.44W
Tindalo 35 Ed 5.39N 31.03 E
Tindari 14 Jl 38.10N 15.04 E
Tindila 34 Dc 10.16N 8.15W
Tindouf 31 Gf 27.42N 8.09W
Tindouf, Hamada de- 32 Fd 27.45N 8.25W
Tindouf, Sebkha de- 32 Fd 27.45N 7.35W
Tinée 11 Nk 43.55N 7.11 E
Tineo 13 Fa 43.20N 6.25W
Ti-n-Essako 34 Fb 18.27N 2.29 E
Tin Fouye 32 Id 28.15N 7.45 E
Tinghert, Ḥamādat- 30 Hf 28.50N 10.00 E
Tinglev 8 Cj 54.56N 9.15 E
Tingmiarmiut 41 Hf 62.25N 42.15W
Tingo Maria 54 Ce 9.10S 76.00W
Tingri (Xêgar) 27 Ef 28.41N 87.00 E
Tingsryd 7 Dh 56.32N 14.59 E
Tingstäde 8 Hg 57.44N 18.36 E
Tingvoll 7 Be 62.54N 8.12 E
Tinian Channel 64b Bb 14.54N 145.37 E
Tinian Island 57 Fc 15.00N 145.38 E
Tini Wells 35 Cb 15.02N 22.48 E
Tinkisso 34 Dc 11.21N 9.10W
Tinnelva 8 Ce 59.34N 9.15 E
Tinniswood, Mount- 46 Da 50.19N 123.50W
Tinnoset 8 Ce 59.43N 9.02 E
Tinnsjo 8 Ce 59.54N 8.55 E
Tinogasta 56 Gc 28.04S 67.34W
Tinos 15 Il 37.35N 25.10 E
Tinos 15 Il 37.32N 25.10 E
Tinou, Stenón- 15 Il 37.38N 25.10 E
Tinrhert, Hamada de- 30 Hf 28.50N 10.00 E
Tinrhir 32 Fc 31.31N 5.32W
Tinsukia 25 Jc 27.30N 95.22 E
Tintagel Head 9 Ik 50.41N 4.46W
Tintamarre, Ile- 51b Bb 18.07N 63.00W
Ti-n-Tarabine 32 Ie 21.16N 7.24 E
Tintăreni 15 Ge 44.36N 23.29 E
Tintina 56 Hc 27.02S 62.43W
Tinto 13 Fg 37.12N 6.55W
Ti-n-toumma 30 Ig 16.04N 12.40 E
Tinwald 62 De 43.55S 171.43 E
Ti-n-Zaouâtene 31 Hg 19.56N 2.55 E
Tiobraid Árann/Tipperary 9 Ei 52.29N 8.10W
Tiobraid Árann/Tipperary [2] 9 Ei 52.40N 8.20W
Tioga 45 Eb 48.24N 102.56W
Tioman, Pulau- 26 Df 2.48N 104.11 E
Tione di Trento 14 Ed 46.02N 10.43 E
Tioro, Selat-=Tioro, Strait (EN) 26 Hg 4.40S 122.20 E
Tioro Strait (EN)=Tioro, Selat- 26 Hg 4.40S 122.20 E
Tiøtta 7 Cd 65.50N 12.24 E
Tiouilit 32 Df 18.52N 16.10W
Tipasa 13 Oh 36.35N 2.27 E
Tipitapa 47 Gf 12.12N 86.06W
Tipperary/Tiobraid Árann 9 Ei 52.29N 8.10W
Tipperary/Tiobraid Árann [2] 9 Ei 52.40N 8.20W
Tipton, Mount- 46 Hi 35.32N 114.12W
Tip Top Mountain 45 Nb 48.16N 85.59W
Tiptree 12 Cc 51.49N 0.45 E
Tiracambu, Serra do- 54 Id 3.15S 46.30W
Tirahart 32 He 23.45N 2.30 E
Tirān 24 Nf 32.42N 51.09 E
Tirān, Maḍīq- 24 Fi 27.55N 34.28 E
Tirana 6 Hg 41.20N 19.50 E
Tirania 32 Ie 23.08N 9.01 E
Tirano 14 Ed 46.13N 10.10 E
Tiraspol 19 Cf 46.50N 29.37 E
Tirat Karmel 24 Ff 32.46N 34.58 E
Tire 23 Cb 38.04N 27.45 E
Tirebolu 24 Hb 41.00N 38.50 E
Tiree 9 Ge 56.31N 6.49W
Tiree, Passage of- 9 Ge 56.30N 6.30W
Tîrgovişte 15 Ie 44.56N 25.27 E
Tîrgu Bujor 15 Kd 45.52N 27.54 E
Tîrgu Cărbuneşti 15 Ge 44.57N 23.31 E
Tîrgu Frumos 15 Jb 47.12N 27.00 E
Tîrgu Jiu 15 Gd 45.03N 23.17 E
Tîrgu Lăpuş 15 Gb 47.27N 23.52 E
Tîrgu Mureş 6 If 46.33N 24.34 E
Tîrgu Neamţ 15 Jb 47.12N 26.22 E
Tîrgu Ocna 15 Jc 46.17N 26.37 E
Tîrgu Secuiesc 15 Jd 46.00N 26.08 E
Tîrguşor 15 Le 44.27N 28.25 E
Tirich Mir 21 Jf 36.15N 71.50 E
Tirins 15 Fl 37.36N 22.48 E
Tiririca, Serra da- 55 Ic 17.06S 47.06W
Tiris 30 Ff 23.10N 13.30W
Tiris Zemmour [3] 32 Fe 24.00N 10.00W
Tirlemont/Tienen 12 Gd 50.48N 4.57 E
Tirljanski 17 Ii 54.12N 58.33 E
Tîrnava Mare 15 Gc 46.09N 23.42 E
Tîrnava Mică 15 Gc 46.11N 23.55 E
Tîrnăveni 15 Hc 46.20N 24.17 E
Tirnavos 15 Fj 39.45N 22.17 E
Tiro 34 Cd 9.45N 10.39W
Tirol/Tirolo=Tyrol (EN) 14 Fd 47.00N 11.20 E
Tirol=Tyrol (EN) [2] 14 Fc 47.10N 11.25 E
Tirolo/Tirol=Tyrol (EN) 14 Fd 47.00N 11.20 E
Tiros 55 Jd 19.00S 45.58W
Tirreno, Mar-=Tyrrhenian Sea (EN) 5 Hh 40.00N 12.00 E
Tirschenreuth 10 Ig 49.53N 12.21 E
Tirso 14 Ck 39.53N 8.32 E
Tirstrup 8 Dh 56.18N 10.42 E
Tirua Point 62 Fc 38.23S 174.38 E
Tiruchchirappalli 22 Jh 10.49N 78.41 E
Tiruliai/Tiruliaj 8 Ji 55.44N 23.18 E
Tiruliaj/Tiruliai 8 Ji 55.44N 23.18 E
Tirunelveli 22 Ji 8.44N 77.42 E
Tirupati 25 Ff 13.39N 79.25 E
Tirza 8 Lg 57.09N 26.37 E
Tisa=Tisza (EN) 5 If 45.15N 20.17 E
Tis Abay 35 Fc 11.20N 37.40 E
Tisdale 42 Hf 52.51N 104.04W
Tisnaren 8 Ff 58.55N 15.55 E
Tisovec 10 Ph 48.42N 19.57 E
Tissemsilt 32 Hb 35.36N 1.49 E
Tissø 8 Di 55.35N 11.20 E
Tisza 5 If 45.15N 20.17 E
Tisza (EN)=Tisa 5 If 45.15N 20.17 E
Tiszaföldvár 10 Qj 46.59N 20.15 E
Tiszafüred 10 Qi 47.37N 20.46 E
Tiszakécske 10 Qj 46.56N 20.06 E
Tiszántúl 10 Qj 47.00N 21.00 E
Tiszavasvári 10 Ri 47.58N 21.21 E
Titao 34 Ec 13.46N 2.04W
Titarisios 15 Fj 39.47N 22.23 E
Tit-Ary 20 Hb 71.55N 127.01 E
Titicaca, Lago- 52 Jg 15.50S 69.20W
Titikaveka 64p Bc 21.15S 159.45W
Titlagarh 25 Gd 20.18N 83.09 E
Titlis 14 Cd 46.47N 8.26 E
Titograd 6 Hg 42.26N 19.16 E
Titova Korenica 14 Jf 44.45N 15.42 E
Titovo Užice 15 Cf 43.52N 19.51 E
Titov Veles 15 Eh 41.42N 21.48 E
Titov vrh 15 Dh 41.58N 20.50 E
Titran 7 Be 63.40N 8.18 E
Titteri 13 Pi 35.59N 3.15 E
Titule 36 Eb 3.17N 25.32 E
Titusville [Fl.-U.S.] 43 Kf 28.37N 80.49W
Titusville [Pa.-U.S.] 44 He 41.37N 79.42W
Tituvenaj/Tytuvėnai 8 Ji 55.33N 23.09 E
Tiva 36 Gc 2.20S 39.55 E
Tivaouane 34 Bc 14.57N 16.49W
Tiveden 8 Ff 58.45N 14.40 E
Tiverton 9 Jk 50.55N 3.29W
Tivoli [Gren.] 51p Bb 12.10N 61.37W
Tivoli [It.] 14 Gi 41.58N 12.48 E
Ţiwāl 35 Cc 10.22N 22.43 E
Tiwi 36 Gc 4.14S 39.35 E
Tiyo 35 Gc 14.41N 40.57 E
Tizatlán 48 Jh 19.21N 98.15W
Tizimin 47 Gd 21.09N 88.09W
Tizi Ouzou [3] 32 Hb 36.35N 4.05 E
Tizi Ouzou 32 Hb 36.42N 4.03 E
Tiznados, Rio- 50 Ch 8.16N 67.47W
Tiznit 32 Fd 29.43N 9.43W
Tiznit [3] 32 Fd 29.07N 9.04W
Tjačev 10 Th 48.02N 23.36 E
Tjanšan 27 Dc 42.00N 80.01 E
Tjasmin 16 He 49.03N 32.50 E
Tjeggelvas 7 Dc 66.35N 17.40 E
Tjeukemeer 11 Lb 52.54N 5.50 E
Tjolotjo 37 Dc 19.46S 27.45 E
Tjøme 8 De 59.10N 10.25 E
Tjorn 8 Df 58.00N 11.38 E
Tjub-Karagan, Mys- 16 Qg 44.38N 50.20 E
Tjubuk 17 Jh 56.03N 60.58 E
Tjuhtet 20 De 56.32N 89.29 E
Tjukalinsk 19 Hd 55.52N 72.12 E
Tjuleni, Ostrov- 16 Og 44.30N 47.30 E
Tjuleni, Ostrova- 16 Qg 44.55N 50.10 E
Tjulgan 19 Fe 52.22N 56.12 E
Tjumen 22 Id 57.09N 65.32 E
Tjumenskaja Oblast [3] 19 Gd 57.00N 69.00 E
Tjung 20 Hd 63.42N 121.30 E
Tjup 18 Lc 42.44N 78.20 E
Tjuri/Türi 7 Fg 58.50N 25.27 E
Tjust 8 Gg 57.50N 16.15 E
Tjuters Maly, Ostrov- 8 Le 59.45N 26.53 E
Tjuzašu, Pereval- 18 Ic 42.19N 73.50 E
Tkibuli 16 Mh 42.19N 42.59 E
Tkvarčeli 19 Eg 42.52N 41.40 E
Tlacolula 48 Ki 16.57N 96.29W
Tlacotalpan 48 Lh 18.37N 95.40W
Tlahualilo, Sierra del- 48 Hd 26.30N 103.20W
Tlalnepantla 48 Jh 19.33N 99.12W
Tlapa de Comonfort 48 Ji 17.33N 98.33W
Tlapaneco, Rio- 48 Jh 18.00N 98.48W
Tlaquepaque 48 Hg 20.39N 103.19W
Tlaxcala [2] 47 Ee 19.25N 98.10W
Tlaxcala 47 Ee 19.19N 98.14W
Tlemcen 32 Gc 34.52N 1.19W
Tlemcen [3] 32 Gc 34.45N 1.30W
Tleń 10 Oc 53.38N 18.20 E
Tleta Rissana 13 Gi 35.14N 5.59W
Tletat ed Douair 13 Oi 35.59N 2.55 E
Tljarata 16 Oh 42.06N 46.22 E
Tlumač 10 Vh 48.46N 25.06 E
Tłuszcz 10 Rd 52.26N 21.26 E
Tmassah 33 Cd 26.22N 15.48 E
Tō, Shikotan-/Šikotan, Ostrov- 20 Jh 43.47N 146.45 E
Toaca, Vîrful- 15 Ic 46.55N 25.59 E
Toagel Mlungui 64a Ab 7.32N 134.28 E
Toamasina 31 Lj 18.10S 49.24 E
Toamasina [3] 37 Hc 18.00S 48.40 E
Toau Atoll 61 Lc 15.55S 146.00W
Toay 56 He 36.40S 64.21W
Toba 28 Ng 34.29N 136.51 E
Toba, Danau-=Toba, Lake- (EN) 26 Li 2.35N 98.50 E
Toba, Lake- (EN)=Toba, Danau- 26 Li 2.35N 98.50 E
Tobago 52 Jd 11.15N 60.40W
Tobago Basin (EN) 50 Ff 12.30N 60.30W
Tobago Cays 51n Bb 12.39N 61.22W
Toba Kākar Range 25 Db 31.15N 68.00 E
Tobarra 13 Kf 38.35N 1.41W
Tobe 29 Ce 33.44N 132.47 E
Tobejuba, Isla- 50 Fh 9.20N 60.52W
Tobelo 26 If 1.25N 127.31 E
Tobermory [Ont.-Can.] 44 Gc 45.15N 81.40W
Tobermory [Scot.-U.K.] 9 Ge 56.37N 6.05W
Tōbetsu 29a Bb 43.14N 141.29 E
Tobi Island 57 Ed 3.00N 131.10 E
Tobin, Kap- 41 Jd 70.30N 21.30W
Tobin, Mount- 46 Gf 40.22N 117.32W
Tobin Lake [Austl.] 59 Fd 21.45S 125.50 E
Tobin Lake [Sask.-Can.] 42 Hf 53.40N 103.20W
Tobi-Shima 29 Fb 39.12N 139.32 E
Toblach / Dobbiaco 14 Gd 46.44N 12.14 E
Toboali 26 Eg 3.00S 106.30 E
Tobol 19 Ge 52.40N 62.39 E
Tobol 21 Id 58.10N 68.12 E
Tobolsk 22 Id 58.12N 68.16 E
Tobruk (EN)=Ţubruq 31 Je 32.05N 23.59 E
Tobseda 19 Fb 68.36N 52.20 E
Tobyš 17 Ed 65.30N 51.00 E
Tocantinópolis 53 Lf 6.20S 47.25W
Tocantins, Rio- 52 Lf 1.45S 49.10W
Tocantinzinho, Rio- 55 Ha 13.57S 48.20W
Toccoa 44 Fh 34.35N 83.19W
Toce 14 Ce 45.56N 8.29 E
Tochigi 29 Fc 36.23N 139.44 E
Tochigi Ken [2] 28 Of 36.50N 139.50 E
Tochio 29 Fc 37.29N 138.58 E
Töcksfors 8 De 59.31N 11.50 E
Toco 50 Fg 10.50N 60.57W
Tocoa 49 Df 15.41N 86.03W
Toconao 56 Gb 23.11S 68.01W
Tocopilla 53 Ih 22.05S 70.12W
Tocumen 49 Hi 9.05N 79.23W
Tocuyo, Rio- 49 Mh 11.03N 68.20W
Todd Mountain 44 Nb 46.32N 66.43W
Todi 14 Gh 42.47N 12.24 E
Tödi 14 Cd 46.49N 8.55 E
Todo-ga-Saki 27 Pd 39.33N 142.05 E
Todos os Santos, Baia de- 52 Mg 12.48S 38.38W
Todos Santos 47 Bd 23.27N 110.13W
Todos Santos, Bahía- 48 Ab 31.48N 116.42W
Tofino 42 Eg 49.09N 125.54W
Tofte 8 De 59.33N 10.34 E
Toftlund 8 Ci 55.11N 9.04 E
Tofua Island 61 Fc 19.45S 175.05W
Toga 63b Ca 13.26S 166.41 E
Tōgane 29 Gd 35.33N 140.21 E
Tog Ḍarōr 35 Hc 10.25N 50.00 E
Togdere 35 Hd 9.01N 47.07 E
Tog-Dheer [3] 35 Hd 9.50N 45.50 E
Togi 29 Ec 37.08N 136.43 E
Togiak 40 Ge 59.04N 160.24W
Togian, Kepulauan-=Togian Islands (EN) 26 Hg 0.20S 122.00 E
Togian Islands (EN)= Togian, Kepulauan- 26 Hg 0.20S 122.00 E
Togliatti 6 Ke 53.31N 49.26 E
Togni 35 Fb 18.05N 35.10 E
Togo [1] 31 Hh 8.00N 1.10 E
Togrog Ul → Qahar Youyi Qianqi 28 Bd 40.46N 113.13 E
Togtoh 27 Jc 40.17N 111.15 E
Togučin 20 De 55.16N 84.33 E
Toguzak 17 Ki 54.05N 62.48 E
Togwotee Pass 43 Ec 43.45N 110.04W
Tohen 35 Ic 11.44N 51.15 E
Tohma 24 Hc 38.31N 38.25 E
Tohmajärvi 7 He 62.11N 30.23 E
Tohopekaliga, Lake- 44 Gk 28.12N 81.23W
Toi 29 Fd 34.54N 138.47 E
Toijala 7 Ff 61.10N 23.52 E
Toi-Misaki 28 Ki 31.26N 131.19 E
Toisvesi 8 Jb 62.20N 23.45 E
Tōjō 29 Cd 34.53N 133.16 E
Tojtepa 18 Gd 41.03N 69.22 E
Tok 10 Jg 49.43N 13.50 E
Tok 16 Rc 52.46N 52.22 E
Tok 40 Kd 63.20N 142.59W
Tokachi-Dake 29a Cb 43.25N 142.41 E
Tokachi-Gawa 29a Cb 42.41N 143.37 E
Tokachi-Heiya 29a Cb 43.00N 143.20 E
Tokachimitsumata 29a Cb 43.31N 143.07 E
Tōkai [Jap.] 29 Gc 36.27N 140.34 E
Tōkai [Jap.] 29 Ed 35.01N 136.51 E
Tokaj 16 Ld 51.18N 41.04 E
Tokaj 10 Rh 48.07N 21.25 E
Tōkamachi 28 Of 37.08N 138.46 E
Tokanui 62 Cg 46.34S 168.57 E
Tokara Islands (EN)= Tokara-Rettō 21 Og 29.35N 129.45 E
Tokara-Kaikyō 28 Ki 30.10N 130.15 E
Tokara-Rettō=Tokara Islands (EN) 21 Og 29.35N 129.45 E
Tokashiki-Jima 29b Ab 26.13N 127.21 E
Tokat 23 Ea 40.19N 36.34 E
Tŏkch'ŏn 28 Ie 39.45N 126.15 E
Tok-Do 28 Kf 37.22N 131.58 E
Tokelau [5] 58 Je 9.00S 171.46W
Tokelau/Union Islands 57 Je 9.00S 171.45W
Toki 29 Ed 35.22N 137.11 E
Tokke 8 Ce 59.00N 9.15 E
Tokke 8 Be 59.27N 7.58 E
Tokkuztara/Gongliu 27 Dc 43.30N 82.15 E
Tokmak [Kirg.-U.S.S.R.] 19 Hg 42.49N 75.19 E
Tokmak [Ukr.-U.S.S.R.] 19 Df 47.13N 35.43 E
Tokomaru Bay 61 Eg 38.08S 178.20 E
Tokoname 29 Ed 34.53N 136.49 E
Tokoro 29a Da 44.08N 144.03 E
Tokoroa 61 Eg 38.13S 175.52 E
Tokoro-Gawa 29a Da 44.08N 144.04 E
Toksovo 8 Nd 60.10N 30.42 E
Toksu/Xinhe 27 Dc 41.34N 82.38 E
Toksun 27 Ec 42.47N 88.38 E
Toktogul 19 Hg 41.50N 73.01 E
Toktogulskoje Vodohranilišče 18 Id 41.45N 73.00 E
Tokuji 29 Bd 34.11N 131.39 E
Tokulu 65b Bb 20.06S 174.48W
Toku-no-Shima 27 Mf 27.45N 128.50 E
Tokunoshima 29b Bb 27.45N 129.00 E
Tokur 20 If 53.09N 132.50 E
Tokushima 27 Ne 34.04N 134.34 E
Tokushima Ken [2] 28 Mh 33.50N 134.10 E
Tokuyama [Jap.] 28 Ed 35.43N 136.27 E
Tokuyama [Jap.] 28 Kg 34.03N 131.49 E
Tokwe 37 Ed 20.09S 31.54 E
Tōkyō 22 Pf 35.40N 139.46 E
Tokyo Bay (EN)=Tōkyō-Wan 28 Og 35.38N 139.57 E
Tōkyō To [2] 28 Og 35.40N 139.20 E
Tōkyō-Wan=Tokyo Bay (EN) 28 Og 35.38N 139.57 E
Tola 21 Me 48.57N 104.48 E
Tolaga Bay 62 Hc 38.22S 178.18 E
Tolbazy 17 Gi 54.02N 55.59 E
Tolbuhin [2] 15 Kf 43.34N 27.50 E
Tolbuhin 15 Kf 43.34N 27.50 E
Toledo [3] 13 Ie 39.50N 4.00W
Toledo [Blz.] 49 Ce 16.25N 88.50W
Toledo [Braz.] 56 Jb 24.44S 53.45W
Toledo [Oh.-U.S.] 39 Ke 41.39N 83.32W
Toledo [Phil.] 26 Hd 10.23N 123.38 E
Toledo [Sp.] 6 Fh 39.52N 4.01W
Toledo, Montes de- 13 He 39.35N 4.20W
Toledo Bend Reservoir 43 Ie 31.30N 93.45W
Tolentino 14 Hg 43.12N 13.17 E
Tolfa 14 Fh 42.09N 11.56 E
Tolfa, Monti della- 14 Fh 42.10N 11.55 E
Tolga 7 Ce 62.25N 11.00 E
Toli 27 Db 45.57N 83.37 E
Toliary [3] 37 Gd 22.00S 44.00 E
Toliary 31 Lk 23.21S 43.39 E
Tolima [2] 54 Cc 3.45N 75.15W
Tolima, Nevado del- 52 Ie 4.40N 75.19W
Toling → Zanda 27 Ce 31.28N 79.50 E
Tolitoli 26 Hf 1.02N 120.49 E
Toll 64d Bb 7.22N 151.37 E
Tollarp 8 Ei 55.56N 13.59 E
Tollja, Zaliv- 20 Ea 76.40N 100.00 E
Tolmačevo 8 Nf 58.48N 30.01 E
Tolmezzo 14 Hd 46.24N 13.01 E
Tolmin 14 Hd 46.11N 13.44 E
Tolna 10 Oj 46.26N 18.47 E
Tolna [2] 10 Oj 46.30N 18.35 E
Tolo 36 Cc 2.56S 18.34 E
Tolo, Gulf of- (EN)=Tolo, Teluk- 21 Oj 2.00S 122.30 E
Tolo, Teluk-=Tolo, Gulf of- (EN) 21 Oj 2.00S 122.30 E
Toločin 7 Gi 54.25N 29.41 E
Tolosa 13 Ja 43.08N 2.04W
Tolstoj, Mys- 5 Rd 59.10N 155.05 E
Toltén 56 Fe 39.13S 73.14W
Tolú 54 Cb 9.32N 75.34W
Toluca, Nevado de- 38 Jh 19.08N 99.44W
Toluca de Lerdo 39 Jh 19.17N 99.40W
Tom 21 Kd 56.50N 84.27 E
Toma 34 Ec 12.46N 2.53W
Tomah 45 Ke 43.59N 90.30W
Tomakomai 27 Pc 42.38N 141.36 E
Tomamae 29a Ba 44.18N 141.39 E
Tomanivi 63d Bb 17.37S 178.01 E
Tomar 13 De 39.36N 8.25W
Tómaros 15 Dj 39.32N 20.45 E
Tomaševka 16 Cd 51.33N 23.40 E
Tomás Young 55 Ai 28.36S 62.11W
Tomaszów Lubelski 10 Tf 50.28N 23.25 E
Tomaszów Mazowiecki 10 Qe 51.32N 20.01 E
Tomatlán 48 Gh 19.56N 105.15W
Tombador, Serra dos- 54 Gf 12.00S 57.40W
Tombigbee River 43 Je 31.04N 87.58W
Tomboco 36 Bd 6.45S 13.18 E
Tombouctou=Timbuktu (EN) 31 Gg 16.46N 2.59W
Tombstone 46 Jk 31.43N 110.04W
Tomé 56 Fe 36.37S 72.57W
Tomé-Açu 54 Id 2.25S 48.09W
Tomelilla 7 Ci 55.33N 13.57 E
Tomelloso 13 Ie 39.10N 3.01W
Tomichi Creek 45 Cg 38.31N 106.58W
Tomie 29 Ae 32.37N 128.46 E
Tominé 34 Cc 10.53N 13.18W
Tomini, Gulf of- (EN)= Tomini, Teluk- 21 Oj 0.20S 121.00 E
Tomini, Teluk-=Tomini, Gulf of- (EN) 21 Oj 0.20S 121.00 E
Tominian 34 Ec 13.17N 4.35W
Tomioka [Jap.] 29 Gc 37.20N 140.59 E
Tomioka [Jap.] 29 Fc 36.15N 138.52 E
Tomkinson Ranges 59 Fe 26.10S 129.05 E
Tomma 7 Cc 66.15N 12.48 E
Tomo, Rio- 54 Eb 5.20N 67.48W
Tomochic 48 Fc 28.20N 107.51W
Tomorit, Mali i- 15 Di 40.40N 20.09 E
Tomotu Neo 63c Ab 10.41S 165.47 E
Tomotu Noi 63c Bb 10.50S 166.02 E
Tompa 10 Pj 46.12N 19.33 E
Tompe 26 Gg 0.12S 119.48 E
Tompo 20 Id 62.50N 134.47 E
Tompo 20 Id 64.00N 136.00 E
Tom Price 59 Dd 22.40S 117.55 E
Tomsk 22 Kd 56.30N 84.58 E
Tomskaja Oblast [3] 20 De 58.20N 81.30 E
Tomtabacken 8 Fg 57.30N 14.28 E
Tomur Feng 21 Ke 42.02N 80.05 E
Tom White, Mount- 40 Kd 60.40N 143.40W
Tonaki-Shima 29b Ab 26.21N 127.09 E
Tonalá 47 Fe 16.04N 93.45W
Tonale, Passo del- 14 Ed 46.16N 10.35 E
Tonami 29 Ec 36.38N 136.57 E
Tonara 14 Dj 40.02N 9.10 E
Tonasket 46 Fb 48.42N 119.26W
Tonb-e Bozorg 24 Pi 26.15N 55.03 E
Tonbetsu-Gawa 29a Ca 45.08N 142.23 E
Tonbridge 9 Nj 51.12N 0.16 E
Tondano 26 Hf 1.19N 124.54 E
Tondela 13 Dd 40.31N 8.05W
Tønder 7 Bi 54.56N 8.54 E
Tone-Gawa 29 Gd 35.44N 140.51 E
Tonekābon 23 Hb 36.53N 50.56 E
Toney 66 Of 75.48S 115.48W
Tonga [1] 58 Jf 20.00S 175.00W
Tonga 35 Ed 9.28N 31.03 E

Index Symbols

[1] Independent Nation
[2] State, Region
[3] District, County
[4] Municipality
[5] Colony, Dependency
Continent
Physical Region
Historical or Cultural Region
Mount, Mountain
Volcano
Hill
Mountains, Mountain Range
Hills, Escarpment
Plateau, Upland
Pass, Gap
Plain, Lowland
Delta
Salt Flat
Valley, Canyon
Crater, Cave
Karst Features
Depression
Polder
Desert, Dunes
Forest, Woods
Heath, Steppe
Oasis
Cape, Point
Coast, Beach
Cliff
Peninsula
Isthmus
Sandbank
Island
Atoll
Rock, Reef
Islands, Archipelago
Rocks, Reefs
Coral Reef
Well, Spring
Geyser
River, Stream
Waterfall Rapids
River Mouth, Estuary
Lake
Salt Lake
Intermittent Lake
Reservoir
Swamp, Pond
Canal
Glacier
Ice Shelf, Pack Ice
Ocean
Sea
Gulf, Bay
Strait, Fjord
Lagoon
Bank
Seamount
Tablemount
Ridge
Shelf
Basin
Escarpment, Sea Scarp
Fracture
Trench, Abyss
National Park, Reserve
Point of Interest
Recreation Site
Cave, Cavern
Historic Site
Ruins
Wall, Walls
Church, Abbey
Temple
Scientific Station
Airport
Port
Lighthouse
Mine
Tunnel
Dam, Bridge

Tongaat	37	Ee	29.37S	31.03 E
Tonga Islands ❖	57	Jf	20.00S	175.00W
Tonga Ridge (EN) ⋀	57	Jg	21.00S	175.00W
Tongariki ◆	63b	Dc	17.01S	168.37 E
Tongatapu Group ❖	57	Jg	21.10S	175.10W
Tongatapu Island ◆	61	Fd	21.10S	175.10W
Tonga Trench (EN) ⩂	3	Kl	20.00S	173.00W
Tongbai	28	Bh	32.21N	113.24 E
Tongbai Shan ▲	27	Je	32.20N	113.14 E
Tongcheng [China]	28	Bj	29.15N	113.49 E
Tongcheng [China]	28	Di	31.04N	116.56 E
Tongcheng → Dong'e	28	Df	36.19N	116.14 E
Tongchuan	27	Id	35.10N	109.03 E
Tongdao (Shuangjiang)	27	If	26.14N	109.45 E
Tongde	27	Hd	35.29N	100.32 E
Tongeren/Tongres	11	Ld	50.47N	5.28 E
Tonggu	28	Cj	28.33N	114.21 E
Tongguzbasti	27	Dd	38.23N	82.00 E
Tonggu Zhang ▲	27	Kg	24.12N	116.22 E
Tong-Hae = Japan, Sea of- (EN) ≋	21	Pf	40.00N	134.00 E
Tonghai	22	Mg	24.15N	102.45 E
Tonghe	27	Mb	46.01N	128.42 E
Tonghua	22	Oe	41.43N	125.55 E
Tongjiang	27	Nb	47.39N	132.30 E
Tongjosŏn-man ◐	21	Of	39.30N	128.00 E
Tongliao	22	Oe	43.37N	122.15 E
Tongling	27	Ke	30.49N	117.47 E
Tonglu	28	Ej	29.48N	119.39 E
Tongmun'gŏ-ri	27	Mc	40.58N	127.08 E
Tongoa ◆	63b	Dc	16.54S	168.33 E
Tongoy	56	Fd	30.15S	71.30W
Tongren [China]	27	If	27.45N	109.09 E
Tongren [China]	27	Hd	35.40N	102.07 E
Tongres/Tongeren	11	Ld	50.47N	5.28 E
Tongsa Dzong	25	Ic	27.31N	90.30 E
Tongshan	28	Cj	29.36N	114.30 E
Tongta	25	Jd	21.20N	99.16 E
Tongtian He/Zhi Qu 〰	21	Lf	33.26N	96.36 E
Tongue	9	Ic	58.28N	4.25W
Tongue of the Ocean ⇌	49	Ia	24.12N	77.10W
Tongue River 〰	43	Fb	46.24N	105.52W
Tongxian	27	Kd	39.52N	116.38 E
Tongxin	27	Id	36.59N	105.50 E
Tongxu	28	Cg	34.29N	114.27 E
Tongyu (Kaitong)	27	Lc	44.47N	123.05 E
Tongyu Yunhe ═	28	Eg	34.46N	119.51 E
Tongzi	27	If	28.09N	106.50 E
Tonichi	48	Ec	28.35N	109.34W
Tönisvorst	12	Ic	51.19N	6.28 E
Tonj	35	Dd	7.17N	28.45 E
Tonj 〰	30	Jh	7.31N	29.25 E
Tonk	25	Fc	26.10N	75.47 E
Tonkin (EN) = Bac-Phan ⧗	21	Mg	22.00N	105.00 E
Tonkin, Gulf of- (EN) = Beibu Wan ◐	21	Mh	20.00N	108.00 E
Tonkin, Gulf of- (EN) = Vinh Bac Phan ◐	21	Mh	20.00N	108.00 E
Tônlé Sab, Bœ̆ng- = Tonle Sap (EN) ≈	21	Mh	13.00N	104.00 E
Tonle Sap (EN) = Tônlé Sab, Bœ̆ng- ≈	21	Mh	13.00N	104.00 E
Tonnay-Charente	11	Fi	45.57N	0.54W
Tonneins	11	Gj	44.23N	0.19 E
Tönning	10	Eb	54.19N	8.57 E
Tōno	28	Pe	39.19N	141.32 E
Tonopah	43	Dd	38.04N	117.14W
Tonoshō	29	Dd	34.29N	134.11 E
Tonosí	49	Gj	7.24N	80.27W
Tønsberg	7	Cg	59.17N	10.25 E
Tonstad	7	Bg	58.40N	6.43 E
Tonumeia ◆	65b	Bb	20.28S	174.46W
Tonya	24	Hb	40.53N	39.16 E
Tooele	43	Ec	40.32N	112.18W
Toora-Hem	20	Ef	52.28N	96.22 E
Tootsi	8	Kf	58.34N	24.43 E
Toovoomba	58	Gg	27.33S	151.57 E
Topalu	15	Le	44.33N	28.03 E
Topa Taung ▲	25	Jd	21.08N	95.12 E
Topeka	39	Jf	39.03N	95.41W
Topki	20	De	55.18N	85.40 E
Topko, Gora- ▲	20	Ie	57.00N	137.23 E
Topl'a 〰	10	Rh	48.45N	21.45 E
Topleţ	15	Fe	44.48N	22.24 E
Toplica 〰	15	Ef	43.13N	21.51 E
Topliţa	15	Ic	46.55N	25.20 E
Topola	15	De	44.16N	20.42 E
Topol'čany	10	Oh	48.34N	18.10 E
Topolnica 〰	15	Hg	42.11N	24.18 E
Topolobampo	47	Cc	25.36N	109.03W
Topolobampo, Bahía de- ◐	48	Ee	25.30N	109.05W
Topolog 〰	15	Hd	44.56N	24.16 E
Topolovgrad	15	Jg	42.05N	26.20 E
Topozero, Ozero- ≈	5	Jb	65.40N	32.00 E
Toppenish	46	Ec	46.23N	120.19W
Toprakkale	24	Gd	37.06N	36.07 E
Top Springs	59	Gc	16.38S	131.50 E
Toquepala	54	Eg	17.38S	69.56W
Tor	35	Ed	7.51N	33.36 E
Tora ◆	64d	Ba	7.39N	151.53 E
Toraigh/Tory Island ◆	9	Ef	55.16N	8.13W
Tora Island Pass ⇌	64d	Ba	7.39N	151.53 E
Toråker	8	Gd	60.31N	16.29 E
Torbalı	24	Bc	38.10N	27.21 E
Torbat-e Heydarīyeh	22	Hf	35.16N	59.13 E
Torbat-e Jam	23	Jb	35.14N	60.36 E
Torbay	9	Jk	50.28N	3.30W
Torbert, Mount- ▲	40	Id	61.25N	152.24W
Torch Lake ≈	44	Ec	45.00N	85.19W
Torčin	10	Vf	50.44N	25.05 E
Tordesillas	13	Hc	41.30N	5.00W
Tordino 〰	14	Hh	42.44N	13.59 E
Töre	7	Fd	65.54N	22.39 E
Töreboda	7	Dg	58.43N	14.08 E
Torekov	8	Eh	56.26N	12.37 E
Torenberg ∩	11	Lb	52.15N	5.55 E
Torez	16	Kf	47.59N	38.41 E
Torgau	10	Ie	51.34N	13.00 E
Torgelow	10	Kc	53.38N	14.01 E
Torgun 〰	16	Od	50.10N	46.20 E
Torhamn	8	Fh	56.05N	15.50 E
Torhout	11	Jc	51.04N	3.06 E
Toribulu	26	Hg	0.19S	120.01 E
Torigni-sur-Vire	12	Be	49.05N	0.59W
Torii-Tōge ⌣	29	Ed	35.59N	137.49 E
Tori-Jima ◆	29b	Ab	26.35N	126.50 E
Torino = Turin (EN)	6	Gf	45.03N	7.40 E
Toriparu	55	Fc	16.20S	53.55W
Tori-Shima [Jap.] ◆	27	Pe	30.25N	140.15 E
Tori-Shima [Jap.] ◆	29b	Bb	27.52N	128.14 E
Torit	35	Ee	4.24N	32.34 E
Torixoreu	54	Hg	16.15S	52.26W
Torkoviči	7	Hg	58.53N	30.20 E
Törmänen	7	Gb	68.36N	27.29 E
Tormes 〰	13	Fc	41.18N	6.29W
Tornado Mountain ▲	46	Hb	49.58N	114.39W
Tornavacas, Puerto de- ⌣	13	Gd	40.16N	5.37W
Torneå/Tornio	7	Fd	65.51N	24.08 E
Torneälven 〰	5	Ib	65.48N	24.08 E
Torneträsk ≈	7	Eb	68.22N	19.06 E
Torngat Mountains ⛰	38	Md	59.00N	64.00W
Tornio/Torneå	7	Fd	65.51N	24.08 E
Tornionjoki 〰	5	Ib	65.48N	24.08 E
Tornquist	55	An	38.06S	62.14W
Toro	13	Gc	41.31N	5.24W
Toro ◆	8	Gf	58.50N	17.50 E
Toro, Cerro del- ▲	52	Jh	29.08S	69.48W
Toro, Isla del- ◆	48	Kg	21.35N	97.32W
Toro, Monte- ▲	13	Qe	39.59N	4.07 E
Toroiaga, Vîrful- ▲	15	Hb	47.44N	24.43 E
Torokina	63a	Bb	6.14S	155.03 E
Tōro-Ko ≈	29a	Db	43.08N	144.30 E
Törökszentmiklós	10	Qi	47.11N	20.25 E
Torola, Río- 〰	49	Cg	13.52N	88.30W
Toronto	39	Le	43.39N	79.23W
Toropec	19	Dd	56.31N	31.39 E
Tororo	36	Fb	0.41N	34.11 E
Toros Dağları = Taurus Mountains (EN) ⛰	21	Ff	37.00N	33.00 E
Torquato Severo	55	Ej	31.02S	54.11W
Torquay	9	Jk	50.29N	3.29W
Torrá, Cerro- ▲	52	Ie	4.38N	76.15W
Torrance	46	Fj	33.50N	118.19W
Torre Annunziata	14	Ij	40.45N	14.27 E
Torreblanca	13	Md	40.13N	0.12 E
Torrecilla ▲	13	Hh	36.41N	5.00W
Torrecilla en Cameros	13	Jb	42.16N	2.37W
Torre del Greco	14	Ij	40.47N	14.22 E
Torre del Mar	13	Hh	36.44N	4.06W
Torredembarra	13	Nc	41.09N	1.24 E
Torre de Moncorvo	13	Ec	41.10N	7.03W
Torre de' Passeri	14	Hh	42.14N	13.56 E
Torredonjimeno	13	Ig	37.46N	3.57W
Torrejón de Ardoz	13	Id	40.27N	3.29W
Torrelaguna	13	Id	40.50N	3.32W
Torrelavega	13	Ha	43.21N	4.03W
Torre Miró, Puerto de- ⌣	13	Ld	40.42N	0.05W
Torremolinos	13	Hh	36.37N	4.30W
Torrens, Lake- ≈	57	Eh	31.00S	137.50 E
Torrens Creek	59	Jd	20.46S	145.02 E
Torrent de l'Horta/Torrente	13	Le	39.26N	0.28W
Torrente/Torrent de l'Horta	13	Le	39.26N	0.28W
Torrenueva	13	If	38.38N	3.22W
Torreón	39	Ig	25.33N	103.26W
Torre-Pacheco	13	Lg	37.44N	0.57W
Torre Pellice	14	Bf	44.49N	7.13 E
Torres ◆	64d	Ab	7.19N	151.27 E
Tôrres	56	Kc	29.21S	49.44W
Torrès, Iles- = Torres Islands (EN) ❖	57	Hf	13.15S	166.37 E
Torres Islands (EN) = Torrès, Iles- ❖	57	Hf	13.15S	166.37 E
Torres Novas	13	De	39.29N	8.32W
Torres Strait ⇌	57	Ff	10.25S	142.10 E
Torres Vedras	13	Ce	39.06N	9.16W
Torrevieja	13	Lg	37.59N	0.41W
Torridon, Loch- ⇌	9	Hd	57.35N	5.50W
Torriglia	14	Df	44.31N	9.10 E
Torrijos	13	He	39.59N	4.17W
Torrington [Ct.-U.S.]	44	Ke	41.48N	73.08W
Torrington [Wy.-U.S.]	43	Gc	42.04N	104.11W
Torroella de Montgrí	13	Pb	42.02N	3.08 E
Torröjen ≈	7	Cf	63.55N	12.56 E
Torrox	13	Ih	36.46N	3.58W
Torsås	7	Dh	56.24N	16.00 E
Torsby	7	Cf	60.08N	13.00 E
Torshälla	8	Ge	59.25N	16.28 E
Torsken	7	Db	69.20N	17.06 E
Torsö ❖	7	Cg	58.50N	13.50 E
Torto 〰	14	Hm	37.58N	13.46 E
Tortola ◆	47	Le	18.27N	64.36W
Tortoli	14	Dk	39.55N	9.39 E
Tortona	14	Cf	44.54N	8.52 E
Tortorici	14	Il	38.02N	14.49 E
Tortosa	13	Md	40.48N	0.31 E
Tortosa, Cabo de-/Tortosa, Cap de- ►	13	Md	40.43N	0.55 E
Tortosa, Cap de-/Tortosa, Cabo de- ►	13	Md	40.43N	0.55 E
Tortue, Ile de la- ◆	47	Jd	20.04N	72.49W
Tortuga, Isla- ◆	48	Dd	27.26N	111.55W
Tortum	24	Ib	40.19N	41.35 E
Torud	24	Pe	35.26N	55.07 E
Torugart, Pereval- ⌣	21	Je	40.32N	75.24 E
Torul	24	Hb	40.35N	39.18 E
Toruń [2]	10	Oc	53.00N	18.35 E
Toruń	10	Oc	53.02N	18.35 E
Torunos	49	Li	8.30N	70.04W
Toruńska, Kotlina- ⧗	10	Oc	53.00N	18.30 E
Torup	7	Ch	56.58N	13.05 E
Tõrva/Tyrva	7	Fg	58.01N	25.59 E
Tory Island/Toraigh ◆	9	Ef	55.16N	8.13W
Torysa 〰	10	Rh	48.39N	21.21 E
Toržok	19	Dd	57.03N	35.01 E
Tosa	28	Lh	33.29N	133.25 E
Tosas, Puerto de-/Toses, Port de- ⌣	13	Ob	42.20N	2.01 E
Tosashimizu	28	Lh	32.46N	132.57 E
Tosa-Wan ◐	28	Lh	33.25N	133.35 E
Tosa-yamada	29	Ce	33.36N	133.40 E
Toscana = Tuscany (EN) [2]	14	Eg	43.25N	11.00 E
Toses, Port de-/Tosas, Puerto de- ⌣	13	Ob	42.20N	2.01 E
Toshibetsu-Gawa [Jap.] 〰	29a	Cb	42.54N	143.25 E
Toshibetsu-Gawa [Jap.] 〰	29a	Ab	42.25N	139.48 E
Tōshi-Jima ◆	29	Ed	34.31N	136.52 E
To-Shima ◆	29	Fd	34.31N	139.17 E
Tosno	7	Hg	59.34N	30.50 E
Toson-Cengel	27	Gb	48.47N	98.15 E
Toson Hu ≈	27	Gd	37.08N	96.52 E
Töss 〰	14	Cc	47.33N	8.33 E
Tossa de Mar	13	Oc	41.43N	2.56 E
Tostado	56	Hc	29.14S	61.46W
Tõstamaa/Tystama	8	Jf	58.17N	23.52 E
Tosu	29	Be	33.22N	130.30 E
Tosya	24	Fb	41.01N	34.02 E
Totak ≈	8	Be	59.40N	7.55 E
Totana	13	Kg	37.46N	1.30W
Toten ⧗	8	Dd	60.40N	10.50 E
Toteng	37	Cd	20.23S	22.59 E
Tôtes	11	He	49.41N	1.03 E
Totes Gebirge ⛰	14	Hc	47.42N	13.55 E
Tōtias	35	Ge	3.57N	43.58 E
Totland	12	Ad	50.40N	1.32W
Totma	19	Ed	60.00N	42.45 E
Totness	54	Gb	5.53N	56.19W
Toto	36	Bd	7.10S	14.25 E
Totonicapán [3]	49	Bf	15.00N	91.20W
Totonicapán	47	Ff	14.55N	91.22W
Totora	54	Eg	17.42S	65.09W
Totoras	55	Bk	32.35S	61.11W
Totota	34	Dd	6.49N	9.56W
Totoya ◆	63d	Cc	18.57S	179.50W
Totten Glacier ❄	66	He	66.45S	116.10 E
Totton	12	Ad	50.55N	1.29W
Tottori	27	Nd	35.30N	134.14 E
Tottori Ken [2]	28	Lg	35.25N	133.50 E
Tou, Motu- ◆	64p	Bb	21.11S	159.48W
Touâjil	32	Ee	21.45N	12.35W
Touat ⧗	30	Gf	27.40N	0.01W
Touba [3]	34	Dd	8.15N	7.45W
Touba	34	Dd	8.17N	7.41W
Toubkal, Jebel- ▲	30	Ge	31.03N	7.55W
Touch 〰	11	Hk	43.38N	1.24 E
Toucy	11	Jg	47.44N	3.18 E
Tougan	34	Ec	13.04N	3.04W
Touggourt	31	He	33.06N	6.04 E
Tougué	34	Cc	11.27N	11.41W
Touho	63b	Be	20.47S	165.14 E
Touil 〰	32	Hb	35.33N	2.36 E
Toûil 〰	13	Oi	35.33N	2.36 E
Toukoto	34	Dc	13.28N	9.52W
Toul	11	Lf	48.41N	5.54 E
Toulépleu	34	Dd	6.35N	8.25W
Toulon	6	Gg	43.07N	5.56 E
Toulouse	6	Gg	43.36N	1.26 E
Toulumne River 〰	46	Eh	37.36N	121.10W
Toumodi	34	Dd	6.33N	5.01W
Tounassine, Hamada- ◢	32	Fd	28.36N	5.10W
Toungo	34	Hd	8.07N	12.03 E
Toungoo	22	Lh	18.56N	96.26 E
Touques 〰	11	Ge	49.22N	0.06 E
Toura	35	Bc	10.30N	15.19 E
Touraine ⊟	11	Hg	47.12N	1.30 E
Touraine, Val de- ⋁	11	Hg	47.20N	1.30 E
Tourcoing	11	Jd	50.43N	3.09 E
Touriñan, Cabo de- ►	13	Ca	43.03N	9.18W
Tourine	32	Ee	22.00N	12.15W
Tournai/Doornik	11	Jd	50.36N	3.23 E
Tournai-Kain	12	Fd	50.38N	3.22 E
Tournon	11	Ki	45.04N	4.50 E
Tournus	11	Kh	46.34N	4.54 E
Touros	54	Ke	5.12S	35.28W
Tours	6	Gf	47.23N	0.41 E
Tourteron	12	Ge	49.32N	4.39 E
Toury	11	Hf	48.12N	1.56 E
Touside, Pic- ▲	35	Ba	21.02N	16.25 E
Toussoro ▲	35	Cd	9.02N	23.55 E
Toutouba ◆	63b	Cb	15.34S	167.16 E
Touwsrivier	37	Cf	33.20S	20.00 E
Toužim	10	If	50.04N	12.59 E
Tovar	49	Li	8.20N	71.46W
Tovarkovski	16	Kc	53.43N	38.13 E
Tovdalselva 〰	8	Cf	58.12N	8.06 E
Tove 〰	12	Bb	52.04N	0.50W
Tōwa	29	Gb	39.23N	141.15 E
Towada	28	Pd	40.35N	141.13 E
Towada-Kō ≈	29	Ga	40.28N	140.55 E
Towanda	44	Ie	41.46N	76.27W
Tower	45	Jc	47.48N	92.17W
Towner	45	Fb	48.21N	100.25W
Townsend	46	Jc	46.19N	111.31W
Townshend, Cape- ►	59	Kd	22.15S	150.30 E
Townsville	58	Ff	19.16S	146.48 E
Towot	35	Ed	6.12N	34.25 E
Towson	44	If	39.24N	76.36W
Towuti, Danau- ≈	26	Hg	2.45S	121.32 E
Toxkan He 〰	27	Dc	41.08N	80.11 E
Tōya	29a	Bb	42.39N	140.48 E
Toyah Creek 〰	45	Ek	31.18N	103.27W
Tōya-Ko ≈	28	Pc	42.33N	140.50 E
Toyama	22	Pf	36.41N	137.13 E
Toyama Ken [2]	28	Nf	30.40N	137.10 E
Toyama Trench (EN) ⩂	29	Ec	38.00N	138.00 E
Toyama-Wan ◐	28	Nf	37.00N	137.15 E
Tōyō	28	Mh	33.22N	134.18 E
Toyohashi	27	Oe	34.46N	137.23 E
Toyokoro	29a	Cb	42.48N	143.28 E
Toyonaka	29	Dd	34.47N	135.28 E
Toyo'oka	27	Od	35.33N	137.54 E
Toyosaka	29	Fc	37.55N	139.12 E
Toyota	28	Ng	35.05N	137.09 E
Toyotama	29	Ad	34.27N	129.19 E
Toyotomi	29a	Ba	45.08N	141.47 E
Toyoura	29	Bd	34.10N	130.55 E
Trabancos 〰	13	Gc	41.27N	5.11W
Traben Trabach	12	Je	49.57N	7.07 E
Trabzon	22	Fe	40.59N	39.43 E
Traer	45	Je	42.12N	92.28W
Trafalgar, Cabo- ►	13	Fh	36.11N	6.02W
Tragacete	13	Kd	40.21N	1.51W
Traiguén	56	Fe	38.15S	72.41W
Trail	39	He	49.06N	117.43W
Traill ◆	41	Jd	72.45N	24.00W
Traíras, Rio- 〰	55	Hb	14.07S	48.31W
Trairi	54	Kd	3.17S	39.15W
Traisen 〰	14	Jb	48.22N	15.46 E
Trakai/Trakaj	7	Fi	54.38N	24.57 E
Trakaj/Trakai	7	Fi	54.38N	24.57 E
Trakt	17	Ee	62.44N	51.11 E
Trakya = Thrace (EN) ⊟	15	Jh	41.20N	26.45 E
Trakya = Thrace (EN) ⧗	5	Ig	41.20N	26.45 E
Tralee/Trá Lí	9	Di	52.16N	9.42W
Tralee Bay/Bá Thrá Lí ◐	9	Di	52.15N	9.59W
Trá Lí/Tralee	9	Di	52.16N	9.42W
Trá Mhór/Tramore	9	Fi	52.10N	7.10W
Tramore/Trá Mhór	9	Fi	52.10N	7.10W
Tramping Lake ≈	46	Ka	52.10N	108.48W
Trăn	15	Fg	42.50N	22.39 E
Tranås	7	Dg	58.03N	14.59 E
Trancoso	13	Ed	40.47N	7.21W
Tranebjerg	8	Di	55.50N	10.36 E
Tranemo	8	Eg	57.29N	13.21 E
Trang	22	Li	7.33N	99.36 E
Trani	14	Ki	41.17N	16.25 E
Transantarctic Mountains (EN) ⛰	66	Lg	85.00S	175.00W
Transcaucasia (EN) ⧗	5	Kg	41.00N	45.00 E
Transilvania = Transylvania (EN) ⊟	15	Hc	46.30N	25.00 E
Transilvania = Transylvania (EN) ⧗	5	If	46.30N	25.00 E
Transkei ⧗	30	Jl	31.30S	29.00 E
Transkei ⊟	37	Df	32.45S	28.30 E
Transtrand	8	Ec	61.05N	13.19 E
Transtrandsfjällen ▲	8	Ec	61.15N	12.58 E
Transvaal [2]	37	Dd	25.00S	30.00 E
Transylvania (EN) = Transilvania ⊟	15	Hc	46.30N	25.00 E
Transylvania (EN) = Transilvania ⧗	5	If	46.30N	25.00 E
Transylvanian Alps (EN) = Carpăţii Meridionali ⛰	5	If	45.30N	24.15 E
Trants Bay ◐	51c	Bc	16.46N	62.09W
Trapani	6	Hh	38.01N	12.29 E
Trapper Peak ▲	46	Hd	45.54N	114.18W
Trappes	12	Ef	48.47N	2.01 E
Traralgon	59	Jg	38.12S	146.32 E
Trarza [3]	32	Ef	18.00N	15.00W
Trarza ⧗	30	Fg	17.20N	14.40W
Traşcăului, Munţii- ⛰	15	Gc	46.23N	23.33 E
Trasimeno, Lago- ≈	14	Gg	43.10N	12.05 E
Träslövsläge	8	Eg	57.04N	12.16 E
Trás os Montes e Alto Douro ⊟	13	Ec	41.30N	7.15W
Trat	25	Kf	12.13N	102.16 E
Traun	14	Ib	48.13N	14.14 E
Traun 〰	14	Ib	48.16N	14.22 E
Traunsee ≈	14	Hc	47.52N	13.48 E
Traunstein	10	Ii	47.53N	12.39 E
Trave 〰	10	Gc	53.54N	10.50 E
Travemünde, Lübeck-	10	Gc	53.57N	10.52 E
Travers, Mount- ▲	61	Dh	42.01S	172.44 E
Traverse, Lake- ≈	45	Hd	45.43N	96.40W
Traverse City	43	Jc	44.46N	85.37W
Traverse Islands ❖	66	Ad	56.36S	27.43W
Travers Reservoir ⊡	46	Ia	50.14N	112.51W
Travesía ⁙	49	Df	15.20N	87.53W
Travis, Lake- ≈	45	Hk	30.27N	98.00W
Travnik	23	Ff	44.14N	17.40 E
Travo 〰	11a	Bb	41.54N	9.24 E
Trbovlje	14	Jd	46.10N	15.03 E
Treasurers ◆	63c	Ba	9.53S	167.09 E
Treasury Islands ❖	63a	Bb	7.22S	155.37 E
Trebbia 〰	14	De	45.04N	9.41 E
Třebíč	10	Lg	49.13N	15.53 E
Trebinje	14	Mh	42.43N	18.21 E
Trebisacce	14	Kk	39.52N	16.32 E
Trebišnjica 〰	14	Lg	43.01N	17.47 E
Trebišov	10	Rh	48.40N	21.43 E
Treblinka	10	Sd	52.40N	22.03 E
Trebnje	14	Je	45.54N	15.01 E
Třeboň	10	Kg	49.01N	14.48 E
Třeboňska pánev ⧗	10	Kg	49.00N	14.50 E
Trégorrois ⧗	11	Cf	48.45N	3.15W
Tregrosse Islets ❖	57	Gf	17.40S	150.45 E
Tréguier	11	Cf	48.47N	3.14W
Treherne	45	Gb	49.38N	98.41W
Treignac	11	Hi	45.32N	1.48 E
Treinta y Tres [2]	55	Ek	33.00S	54.15W
Treinta y Tres	56	Jd	33.14S	54.23W
Treis-Karden	12	Jd	50.11N	7.17 E
Trélazé	11	Fg	47.27N	0.28W
Trelew	56	Gf	43.15S	65.18W
Trelleborg	6	Hd	55.22N	13.10 E
Trélon	12	Gd	50.04N	4.06 E
Tremadoc Bay ◐	9	Ii	52.40N	4.10W
Tremblant, Mount- ▲	38	Le	46.15N	74.34W
Tremiti, Isole- = Tremiti Islands (EN) ❖	5	Hg	42.10N	15.30 E
Tremiti Islands (EN) = Tremiti, Isole- ❖	5	Hg	42.10N	15.30 E
Tremonton	46	If	41.43N	112.10W
Tremp	13	Mb	42.10N	0.54 E
Třemšín ▲	10	Jg	49.33N	13.48 E
Trenche, Rivière- 〰	44	Kb	47.35N	72.58W
Trenčín	10	Oh	48.54N	18.04 E
Trenque Lauguen	56	He	35.58S	62.42W
Trent 〰	9	Mh	53.42N	0.41W
Trent, Vale of- ⋁	9	Li	52.45N	1.50W
Trentino-Alto Adige / Südtirol [2]	14	Fd	46.30N	11.20 E
Trento	14	Fd	46.04N	11.08 E
Trenton [Mo.-U.S.]	45	Jf	40.05N	93.37W
Trenton [N.J.-U.S.]	39	Le	40.13N	74.45W
Trenton [Ont.-Can.]	44	Ic	44.06N	77.35W
Tréon	12	Df	48.41N	1.20 E
Trepassey	42	Mg	46.44N	53.22W
Tres Arboles [Ur.]	56	Id	32.24S	56.43W
Tres Arroyos	53	Ji	38.22S	60.15W
Tres Bocas	55	Ck	32.44S	59.45W
Tres Carações	54	Ih	21.42S	45.16W
Tres Cruces, Cerro- ▲	48	Mj	15.28N	92.24W
Três de Maio	55	Eh	27.47S	54.14W
Tres Esquinas	54	Cc	0.43N	75.15W
Tres Isletas	55	Bh	26.21S	60.26W
Treska 〰	15	Eh	41.59N	21.19 E
Treskavica ⛰	14	Mg	43.35N	18.24 E
Três Lagoas	53	Kh	20.48S	51.43W
Três Marias, Represa- ⊡	54	Ig	18.15S	45.15W
Tres Montes, Peninsula- ⊐	56	Eg	46.50S	75.30W
Três Passos	56	Jc	27.27S	53.56W
Tres Picos, Cerro- [Arg.] ▲	52	Ji	38.09S	61.57W
Tres Picos, Cerro- [Mex.] ▲	48	Li	16.36N	94.13W
Três Pontas	55	Je	21.22S	45.31W
Tres Puntas, Cabo- [Arg.] ►	52	Jj	47.06S	65.53W
Tres Puntas, Cabo- [Guat.] ►	49	Cf	15.58N	88.37W
Três Ranchos	55	Id	18.22S	47.47W
Três Rios	55	Kf	22.07S	43.12W
Třešť	10	Lg	49.18N	15.28 E
Tres Valles	48	Kh	18.15N	96.08W
Tres Zapotes ⁙	47	Ee	18.28N	95.24W
Tretten	7	Cf	61.19N	10.19 E
Treuer Range ⛰	59	Gd	22.15S	130.50 E
Treungen	8	Ce	59.02N	8.33 E
Trêve, Lac la- ≈	44	Ja	49.58N	75.31W
Trevi	14	Gh	42.52N	12.45 E
Trévières	12	Be	49.19N	0.54W
Treviglio	14	De	45.31N	9.35 E
Trevinca, Peña- ▲	13	Fb	42.15N	6.46W
Treviño	13	Jb	42.44N	2.45W
Treviso	14	Ge	45.40N	12.15 E
Trevose Head ►	9	Hk	50.33N	5.01W
Trgovište	15	Fg	42.21N	22.06 E
Triánda	15	Lm	36.24N	28.10 E
Triangle	37	Ed	21.02S	31.28 E
Triángulos, Arrecifes- ✵	48	Mg	20.57N	92.16W
Trianísia ◆	15	Jm	36.18N	26.45 E
Tribeč ⛰	10	Oh	48.27N	18.15 E
Tribune	45	Fg	38.28N	101.45W
Tricarico	14	Kj	40.37N	16.09 E
Tricase	14	Mk	39.56N	18.22 E
Trichūr	25	Ff	10.31N	76.13 E
Tri City	46	De	43.02N	123.15W
Trie-Château	12	De	49.17N	1.50 E
Triel-sur-Seine	12	Ef	48.59N	2.01 E
Trier	10	Cg	49.45N	6.38 E
Trier-Ehrang	12	Ie	49.49N	6.41 E
Trier-Pfalzel	12	Ie	49.46N	6.41 E
Trieste	6	Hf	45.40N	13.46 E
Trieste, Golfo di- ◐	14	He	45.40N	13.30 E
Trieux 〰	11	Cf	48.50N	3.03W
Trifels 🏛	12	Je	49.11N	7.59 E
Triglav ▲	5	Hf	46.23N	13.50 E
Trigno 〰	14	Ih	42.04N	14.48 E
Trikala	15	Ej	39.33N	21.46 E
Trikhonis, Límni- ≈	15	Ek	38.34N	21.30 E
Trikomo/Trikomon	24	Ee	35.17N	33.52 E
Trikomon/Trikomo	24	Ee	35.17N	33.52 E
Trikora, Puncak- ▲	26	Kg	4.15S	138.45 E
Trilport	12	Ef	48.57N	2.57 E
Trim/Baile Átha Troim	9	Gh	53.34N	6.47W
Trincheras	48	Gc	28.55N	104.18W
Trincomalee	22	Ki	8.34N	81.14 E
Trindade	54	Ig	16.40S	49.30W
Trindade, Ilha da- ◆	52	Nh	20.31S	29.19W
Třinec	10	Og	49.41N	18.42 E
Tring	12	Bc	51.47N	0.39W
Tringía ▲	15	Ej	39.38N	21.25 E
Trinidad ◆	52	Jd	10.30N	61.15W
Trinidad [Bol.]	53	Jg	14.47S	64.47W
Trinidad [Ca.-U.S.]	46	Cf	41.07N	124.07W
Trinidad [Co.-U.S.]	39	If	37.10N	104.31W
Trinidad [Cuba]	47	Id	21.48N	79.59W
Trinidad [Mex.]	48	Ec	28.25N	109.06W
Trinidad [Ur.]	56	Id	33.32S	56.54W
Trinidad, Golfo- ◐	56	Eg	49.55S	75.25W
Trinidad, Isla- ◆	55	Bn	39.08S	61.58W
Trinidad, Laguna- ≈	55	Be	20.21S	61.35W
Trinidad and Tobago [1]	53	Jd	11.00N	61.00W
Trinidade Spur (EN) ⋀	3	Cl	21.00S	35.00W
Trinitapoli	14	Ki	41.21N	16.05 E
Trinity	45	Ik	30.57N	95.22W
Trinity 〰	38	Jg	29.47N	94.42W
Trinity Bay [Austl.] ◐	59	Jc	16.25S	145.35 E
Trinity Bay [Can.] ◐	42	Mg	48.15N	53.10W
Trinity Islands ❖	40	Ie	56.33N	154.25W
Trinity Range ⛰	46	Ff	40.20N	118.45W
Trinity River 〰	46	Df	41.11N	123.42W
Trinkitat	35	Fb	18.41N	37.43 E
Trino	14	Ce	45.12N	8.18 E
Trionto 〰	14	Kk	39.37N	16.45 E
Trionto, Capo- ►	14	Kk	39.37N	16.45 E
Triora	14	Bf	43.59N	7.46 E
Tripoli (EN) = Ţarābulus [3]	33	Bc	32.40N	13.15 E
Tripoli (EN) = Ţarābulus [Leb.]	23	Ec	34.26N	35.51 E
Tripoli (EN) = Ţarābulus [Lib.]	31	Ie	32.54N	13.11 E
Trípolis	15	Fl	37.31N	22.22 E
Tripolitania (EN) = Tarabulus ⧗	30	Ie	31.00N	14.00 E
Tripolitania (EN) = Ţarābulus ⊟	33	Bc	30.00N	15.00 E

Index Symbols

- [1] Independent Nation
- [2] State, Region
- [3] District, County
- [4] Municipality
- [5] Colony, Dependency
- ■ Continent
- ⧗ Physical Region
- ⊟ Historical or Cultural Region
- ▲ Mount, Mountain
- 🌋 Volcano
- ∩ Hill
- ⛰ Mountains, Mountain Range
- ⌒ Hills, Escarpment
- ⏢ Plateau, Upland
- ⌣ Pass, Gap
- ▭ Plain, Lowland
- ◺ Delta
- ▤ Salt Flat
- ⋁ Valley, Canyon
- ◡ Crater, Cave
- ✲ Karst Features
- ⊍ Depression
- ⊔ Polder
- ◢ Desert, Dunes
- 🌲 Forest, Woods
- ⩔ Heath, Steppe
- 🌴 Oasis
- ► Cape, Point
- ⛱ Coast, Beach
- ◧ Cliff
- ⊐ Peninsula
- ⋈ Isthmus
- ⊥ Sandbank
- ◆ Island
- ◎ Atoll
- ✳ Rock, Reef
- ❖ Islands, Archipelago
- ✵ Rocks, Reefs
- ✿ Coral Reef
- ⊙ Well, Spring
- ⛲ Geyser
- 〰 River, Stream
- ⧹ Waterfall Rapids
- ⥇ River Mouth, Estuary
- ≈ Lake
- ◍ Salt Lake
- ◔ Intermittent Lake
- ⊡ Reservoir
- ⩋ Swamp, Pond
- ═ Canal
- ❄ Glacier
- 🧊 Ice Shelf, Pack Ice
- 🌊 Ocean
- ≋ Sea
- ◐ Gulf, Bay
- ⇌ Strait, Fjord
- ⊖ Lagoon
- ≡ Bank
- ⩘ Seamount
- ⊼ Tablemount
- ⋀ Ridge
- ⊤ Shelf
- ∪ Basin
- ⌐ Escarpment, Sea Scarp
- ⚡ Fracture
- ⩂ Trench, Abyss
- 🏞 National Park, Reserve
- ★ Point of Interest
- ⚑ Recreation Site
- ⌓ Cave, Cavern
- 🏛 Historic Site
- ⁙ Ruins
- 🧱 Wall, Walls
- ⛪ Church, Abbey
- ⛩ Temple
- ⚗ Scientific Station
- ✈ Airport
- ⚓ Port
- 🗼 Lighthouse
- ⚒ Mine
- ⊓ Tunnel
- ⟋ Dam, Bridge

Name	Map	Grid	Lat.	Long.
Tripura [3]	25	Id	24.00N	92.00 E
Trisanna	14	Ec	47.07N	10.30 E
Tristan da Cunha	30	Fi	37.05 S	12.17W
Tristan da Cunha Group	30	Fi	37.15 S	12.30W
Triste, Golfo-	50	Bg	10.40N	68.10W
Triunfo	55	Ee	20.46 S	55.47W
Trivandrum	22	Ji	8.29N	76.55 E
Trivento	14	Ii	41.47N	14.33 E
Trjavna	15	Ig	42.52N	25.30 E
Trnava	10	Nh	48.22N	17.35 E
Troarn	12	Be	49.11N	0.11W
Trobriand Islands	57	Ge	8.30 S	151.05 E
Trödje	8	Gd	60.49N	17.12 E
Trofors	7	Cd	65.34N	13.25 E
Trögd	8	Ge	59.30N	17.15 E
Trogir	14	Kg	43.32N	16.15 E
Troglav [Yugo.]	14	Kg	43.58N	16.36 E
Troglav [Yugo.]	14	Mg	43.02N	18.33 E
Trøgstad	8	De	59.38N	11.18 E
Troia	14	Ji	41.22N	15.18 E
Troick [R.S.F.S.R.]	22	Id	54.06N	61.35 E
Troick [R.S.F.S.R.]	20	Ee	57.23N	94.55 E
Troickoje [R.S.F.S.R.]	20	Df	52.58N	84.45 E
Troickoje [R.S.F.S.R.]	20	Ig	49.30N	136.32 E
Troickoje [Ukr.-U.S.S.R.]	15	Nb	47.38N	30.12 E
Troicko Pečorsk	19	Fc	62.44N	56.06 E
Troina	14	Im	37.47N	14.36 E
Troisdorf	12	Jd	50.49N	7.10 E
Trois Fourches, Cap des-	32	Gb	35.26N	2.58W
Trois-Pistoles	44	Ma	48.07N	69.10W
Trois Pitons, Morne-	51g	Bb	15.22N	61.20W
Trois-Ponts	12	Hd	50.22N	5.52 E
Trois-Rivières [Guad.]	51e	Ac	15.59N	61.39W
Trois-Rivières [Que.-Can.]	39	Le	46.21N	72.33W
Troissereux	12	Ee	49.29N	2.03 E
Troisvierges/Ulflingen	12	Hd	50.07N	6.00 E
Trojah	15	Hg	42.53N	24.43 E
Trojanovka	10	Ve	51.21N	25.25 E
Trojanski Manastir	15	Hg	42.53N	24.48 E
Trojanski prohod	15	Hg	42.48N	24.40 E
Trojebratski	19	Ge	54.25N	66.03 E
Trollhättan	7	Cg	58.16N	12.18 E
Trollheimen	7	Be	62.50N	9.05 E
Trollhetta	8	Cb	62.51N	9.19 E
Trolltindane	8	Bd	62.29N	7.43 E
Tromba	55	Ha	13.28 S	48.45W
Trombetas, Rio-	52	Kf	1.55 S	55.35W
Tromelin	30	Mj	15.52 S	54.25 E
Tromøya	8	Cf	58.30N	8.50 E
Troms [3]	7	Eb	69.07N	19.15 E
Tromsø	6	Hb	69.40N	19.00 E
Tron	8	Db	62.10N	10.43 E
Tronador, Monte-	52	Ij	41.10 S	71.54W
Trondheim	6	Hc	63.25N	10.25 E
Trondheimsfjorden	5	Hc	63.40N	10.50 E
Tronto	14	Hh	42.54N	13.55 E
Tropea	14	Jl	38.41N	15.54 E
Tropeiros, Serra dos-	55	Jb	14.43 S	44.33W
Tropoja	15	Dg	42.24N	20.10 E
Trosa	7	Dg	58.54N	17.33 E
Troškūnai/Troškunaj	8	Ki	55.32N	24.59 E
Troškunaj/Troškūnai	8	Ki	55.32N	24.59 E
Trostberg	10	Ih	48.02N	12.33 E
Trostjanec	16	Id	50.29N	34.59 E
Trotuş	15	Kc	46.03N	27.14 E
Trou Gras Point	51k	Bb	13.52N	60.53W
Troumasse	51k	Bb	13.49N	60.54W
Trout Lake [Mi.-U.S.]	44	Eb	46.12N	85.01W
Trout Lake [N.W.T.-Can.]	42	Fd	60.35N	121.10W
Trout Lake [Ont.-Can.]	42	If	51.12N	93.19W
Trout Lake [Ont.-Can.]	42	If	53.54N	89.56W
Trout Peak	46	Kd	44.36N	109.32W
Trout River	42	Lg	49.29N	58.08W
Trouville-sur-Mer	11	Ge	49.22N	0.05 E
Trowbridge	9	Kj	51.20N	2.13W
Troy [Al.-U.S.]	43	Je	31.48N	85.58W
Troy [Mo.-U.S.]	45	Kg	38.59N	90.59W
Troy [Mt.-U.S.]	46	Hb	48.28N	115.53W
Troy [N.Y.-U.S.]	43	Mc	42.43N	73.40W
Troy [Oh.-U.S.]	44	Ee	40.02N	84.12W
Troy (EN)=Truva	24	Bc	39.57N	26.15 E
Troyes	6	Gf	48.18N	4.05 E
Troy Peak	43	Dd	38.19N	115.30W
Trstenik	15	Df	43.37N	21.00 E
Trubčevsk	19	De	52.36N	33.46 E
Truc Giang	25	Lf	10.14N	106.23 E
Truchas Peak	45	Di	35.58N	105.39W
Trucial Coast (EN)	21	Hg	24.00N	53.00 E
Trucial States (EN)→United Arab Emirates (EN) [1]	22	Hg	24.00N	54.00 E
Truckee	46	Eg	39.20N	120.11W
Trudfront	16	Og	45.56N	47.41 E
Trudovoje	20	Ih	43.18N	132.05 E
Trufanova	7	Kd	64.29N	44.05 E
Trujillo [2]	54	Db	9.25N	70.30W
Trujillo [Hond.]	47	Ge	15.55N	86.00W
Trujillo [Peru]	53	If	8.10 S	79.02W
Trujillo [Sp.]	13	Ge	39.28N	5.53W
Trujillo [Ven.]	54	Db	9.22N	70.26W
Trujillo, Río-	48	Hf	23.39N	103.08W
Truk Islands	57	Gd	7.25N	151.47 E
Trumann	45	Ki	35.41N	90.31W
Trumbull, Mount-	43	Ed	36.25N	113.10W
Trun	12	Gf	48.51N	0.02 E
Trung Phan=Annam (EN)	21	Me	15.00N	108.00 E
Truro [Eng.-U.K.]	9	Hk	50.16N	5.03W
Truro [N.S.-Can.]	39	Me	45.22N	63.16W
Truskavec	16	Ce	49.17N	23.34 E
Truth or Consequences (Hot Springs)	43	Fe	33.08N	107.15W
Trutnov	10	Lf	50.34N	15.54 E
Truva=Troy (EN)	24	Bc	39.57N	26.15 E
Truyère	11	Ij	44.38N	2.34 E
Trysil	8	Ec	61.25N	12.25 E
Trysil	7	Cf	61.18N	12.16 E
Trysilelva	5	Hd	59.23N	13.32 E
Trysilfjellet	8	Ec	61.18N	12.11 E
Trzcianka	10	Mc	53.03N	16.28 E
Trzcińsko Zdrój	10	Kd	52.58N	14.35 E
Trzebiatów	10	Lb	54.04N	15.14 E
Trzebież	10	Kc	53.42N	14.31 E
Trzebinia-Siersza	10	Pf	50.11N	19.25 E
Trzebnica	10	Ne	51.19N	17.03 E
Trzebnicki, Wał-	10	Me	51.30N	16.20 E
Trzebnickie, Wzgórza-	10	Me	51.15N	17.00 E
Trzemeszno	10	Nd	52.35N	17.50 E
Tsaidam Basin (EN)= Qaidam Pendi	27	Fd	37.00N	95.00 E
Tsamandá, Óri-	15	Dj	39.48N	20.21 E
Tsarap	25	Fb	33.31N	76.56 E
Tsaratanana	37	Hc	16.46 S	47.38 E
Tsaratanana (EN)= Tsaratanana, Massif du-	30	Lj	14.00 S	49.00 E
Tsaratanana, Massif du-= Tsaratanana (EN)	30	Lj	14.00 S	49.00 E
Tsau	37	Cd	20.10 S	22.27 E
Tsavo	36	Gc	2.59 S	38.28 E
Tses	37	Be	25.58 S	18.08 E
Tsévié	34	Fd	6.25N	1.13 E
Tshabong	31	Jk	26.02 S	22.06 E
Tshane	31	Jk	24.01 S	21.43 E
Tshangalele, Lac-	36	Ee	10.55 S	27.03 E
Tshela	31	Ii	4.59 S	12.56 E
Tshesebe	37	Dd	20.43 S	27.37 E
Tshibala	36	Dd	6.56 S	21.28 E
Tshibamba	36	Dd	9.06 S	22.34 E
Tshikapa	31	Ji	6.25 S	20.48 E
Tshilenge	36	Dd	6.15 S	23.46 E
Tshimbalanga	36	Dd	9.43 S	23.06 E
Tshimbulu	36	Dd	6.29 S	22.51 E
Tshinsenda	36	Ee	12.16 S	27.55 E
Tshofa	36	Ed	5.14 S	25.15 E
Tshopo	36	Eb	0.33N	25.07 E
Tshuapa	30	Ji	0.14 S	20.42 E
Tshwaane	37	Cd	22.38 S	22.05 E
Tsiafajavona	37	Hc	19.21 S	47.15 E
Tsihombe	37	He	25.17 S	45.30 E
Tsimlyansk Reservoir (EN)= Cimljanskoje Vodohranilišče	5	Kf	48.00N	43.00 E
Tsinan (EN)=Jinan	22	Nf	36.35N	117.00 E
Tsinghai (EN)=Ch'ing-hai Sheng→Qinghai Sheng [2]	27	Gd	36.00N	96.00 E
Tsinghai (EN)=Qinghai Sheng (Ch'ing-hai Sheng) [2]	27	Gd	36.00N	96.00 E
Tsingtao (EN)=Qingdao	22	Of	36.05N	120.21 E
Tsiribihina	37	Gc	19.42 S	44.31 E
Tsiroanomandidy	37	Hc	18.50 S	46.00 E
Tsis	64d	Bb	7.18N	151.50 E
Tsjokkarassa	7	Fb	69.59N	24.32 E
Tsodilo Hill	37	Cc	18.50 S	21.45 E
Tsu	27	Oe	34.43N	136.31 E
Tsubame	29	Fc	37.39N	138.56 E
Tsubata	28	Nf	36.40N	136.44 E
Tsubetsu	29a	Db	43.43N	144.01 E
Tsuchiura	28	Pf	36.05N	140.12 E
Tsugaru-Hantō	29a	Bc	41.00N	140.30 E
Tsugaru-Kaikyō=Tsugaru Strait (EN)	21	Qe	41.40N	140.55 E
Tsugaru Strait (EN)= Tsugaru-Kaikyō	21	Qe	41.40N	140.55 E
Tsuken-Jima	29b	Ab	26.15N	127.57 E
Tsukidate	29	Gb	38.44N	141.01 E
Tsukigata	29a	Bb	43.20N	141.39 E
Tsukuba-San	29	Gc	36.13N	140.06 E
Tsukumi	29	Be	33.04N	131.52 E
Tsukura-Se	29	Af	31.18N	129.47 E
Tsukushi-Sanchi	29	Be	33.25N	130.30 E
Tsumeb	31	Ij	19.13 S	17.42 E
Tsumeb [3]	37	Bc	19.00 S	17.30 E
Tsumkwe	37	Cc	19.32 S	20.30 E
Tsuna	29	Dd	34.26N	134.54 E
Tsuno-Shima	29	Bd	34.22N	130.52 E
Tsuru	29	Fd	35.35N	138.50 E
Tsuruga	27	Od	35.39N	136.04 E
Tsuruga-Wan	29	Ed	35.45N	136.05 E
Tsurugi	29	Ec	36.26N	136.37 E
Tsurugi-San	29	De	33.51N	134.03 E
Tsurui	29a	Db	43.14N	144.21 E
Tsurumi-Dake	29	Be	33.18N	131.27 E
Tsurumi-Saki	29	Ce	32.56N	132.05 E
Tsuruoka	28	Oe	38.44N	139.50 E
Tsuruta	29	Ga	40.44N	140.26 E
Tsushima	21	Of	34.30N	129.20 E
Tsushima [Jap.]	29	Ce	33.07N	132.30 E
Tsushima [Jap.]	29	Ed	35.10N	136.43 E
Tsushima-Kaikyō=Korea, Strait (EN)	21	Of	34.40N	129.00 E
Tsuwano	29	Bd	34.28N	131.46 E
Tsuyama	28	Lg	35.03N	134.00 E
Tua	13	Ec	41.13N	7.26W
Tuai	62	Gc	38.49 S	177.08 E
Tuaim/Tuam	9	Eh	53.31N	8.50W
Tuakau	62	Fb	37.15 S	174.57 E
Tual	26	Jh	5.40 S	132.45 E
Tuam/Tuaim	9	Eh	53.31N	8.50W
Tuamotu, Iles-=Tuamotu Archipelago (EN)	57	Mf	19.00 S	142.00W
Tuamotu Archipelago (EN) =Tuamotu, Iles-	57	Mf	19.00 S	142.00W
Tuamotu Ridge (EN)	3	Ll	20.00 S	145.00W
Tuapa	64k	Ba	18.57 S	169.54W
Tuapse	6	Jg	44.07N	39.05 E
Tuaran	26	Ge	6.11N	116.14 E
Tuasivi	65c	Aa	13.40 S	172.07W
Tuasivi, Cape-	65c	Aa	13.40 S	172.07W
Tuatapere	61	Ci	46.08 S	167.41 E
Tuba	20	Ef	54.00N	91.40 E
Tuba City	46	Jh	36.08N	111.14W
Tubaï, Ile-	57	Mg	23.18 S	149.30W
Tubai-Manu→Maïao, Ile-	57	Lf	17.34 S	150.35W
Tubal, Wādī at-	24	Jf	32.19N	42.13 E
Tuban	26	Fh	6.54 S	112.03 E
Tubarão	56	Kc	28.30 S	49.01W
Ţubayq, Jabal at-	24	Gh	29.32N	37.30 E
Tubbataha Reefs	26	Ge	8.51N	119.56 E
Tubeke/Tubize	12	Gd	50.41N	4.12 E
Tübingen	10	Fh	48.32N	9.03 E
Tubize/Tubeke	12	Gd	50.41N	4.12 E
Ţubruq=Tobruk (EN)	31	Je	32.05N	23.59 E
Tubuaï, Iles-/Australes, Iles- =Tubuai Islands (EN)	57	Lg	23.00 S	150.00W
Tubuai Islands (EN)= Australes, Iles-/Tubuaï, Iles-	57	Lg	23.00 S	150.00W
Tubuai Islands (EN)= Tubuaï, Iles-/Australes, Iles-	57	Lg	23.00 S	150.00W
Tubutama	48	Db	30.53N	111.29W
Tucacas	54	Ea	10.48N	68.19W
Tucacas, Punta-	49	Mh	10.52N	68.13W
Tucavaca	55	Cd	18.36 S	58.55W
Tucavaca, Río-	55	Cd	18.37 S	58.59W
Tuchola	10	Nc	53.35N	17.50 E
Tucholska, Równina-	10	Oc	53.40N	18.30 E
Tuchów	10	Rg	49.54N	21.03 E
Tucker Glacier	66	Kf	72.35 S	169.20 E
Tucson	39	Hf	32.13N	110.58W
Tucuarembó	56	Id	31.44 S	55.59W
Tucumán [2]	56	Gc	27.00 S	65.30W
Tucumcari	43	Gd	35.10N	103.44W
Tucunuí	54	Id	3.42 S	49.27W
Tucupido	54	Eb	9.17N	65.47W
Tucupita	54	Fb	9.04N	62.03W
Tudela	13	Kb	42.05N	1.36W
Tudía, Sierra de-	13	Ff	38.05N	6.20W
Tudmur	23	Ec	34.33N	38.17 E
Tudora	15	Jb	47.31N	26.38 E
Tuela	13	Ec	41.30N	7.12W
Tuensang	25	Ic	26.17N	94.40 E
Tuerto	13	Gb	42.18N	5.53W
Tufanbeyli	24	Gc	38.18N	36.11 E
Tufi	58	Fe	9.08 S	149.20 E
Tugela	30	Kk	29.14 S	31.30 E
Tug Fork	44	Ff	38.25N	82.35W
Tuguegarao	26	Hc	17.37N	121.44 E
Tugulym	17	Lh	57.04N	64.39 E
Tugur	20	If	53.51N	136.52 E
Tuhai He	28	Ee	38.05N	118.13 E
Tujiabu → Yongxiu	27	Kf	29.05N	115.49 E
Tujmazy	19	Fe	54.36N	53.42 E
Tukan	17	Hj	53.50N	57.31 E
Tukangbesi, Kepulauan-= Tukangbesi Islands (EN)	26	Hh	5.40 S	123.50 E
Tukangbesi Islands (EN)= Tukangbesi, Kepulauan-	26	Hh	5.40 S	123.50 E
Tukayel	35	Hd	8.05N	45.20 E
Tukayyid	24	Kh	29.47N	45.36 E
Tukituki	62	Gc	39.36 S	176.56 E
Tuko Village	64n	Ab	10.22 S	161.02W
Tūkrah	33	Dc	32.32N	20.34 E
Tuktoyaktuk	39	Fc	69.27N	133.02W
Tukums	7	Fh	56.59N	23.10 E
Tukuringra, Hrebet-	20	Hf	54.30N	126.00 E
Tukuyu	36	Fd	9.15 S	33.39 E
Tula	47	Ed	20.06N	99.19W
Tula	36	Gc	0.50 S	39.51 E
Tula [Mex.]	48	Jf	23.00N	99.43W
Tula [R.S.F.S.R.]	6	Je	54.12N	37.37 E
Tula de Allende	48	Jg	20.03N	99.21W
Tula Mountains	66	Ee	66.54 S	51.06 E
Tulancingo	47	Ed	20.05N	98.22W
Tulare	46	Fh	36.13N	119.21W
Tulare Lake Bed	46	Fh	36.03N	119.49W
Tularosa	45	Cj	33.04N	106.01W
Tularosa Valley	45	Cj	32.45N	106.10W
Tulcán	54	Cc	0.48N	77.43W
Tulcea [2]	15	Md	45.12N	29.10 E
Tulcea	15	Ld	45.10N	28.48 E
Tulčin	16	Fe	48.39N	28.52 E
Tulelake	46	Ef	41.57N	121.29W
Tulemalu Lake	42	Hd	62.55N	99.25W
Tulgheş	15	Ic	46.57N	25.46 E
Tuli	37	Dd	21.55 S	29.12 E
Tuli	37	Dd	21.48 S	29.04 E
Tulia	45	Fi	34.32N	101.46W
Tulihe	27	La	50.30N	121.51 E
Tullahoma	44	Dh	35.22N	86.11W
Tullamore/An Tulach Mhór	9	Fh	53.16N	7.30W
Tulle	11	Hi	45.16N	1.46 E
Tulln	14	Kb	48.22N	16.03 E
Tulln	14	Kb	48.20N	16.03 E
Tullner Becken	14	Jb	48.25N	15.55 E
Tullow/An Tulach	9	Gi	52.48N	6.44W
Tullus	35	Cc	11.03N	24.33 E
Tully	59	Jc	17.56 S	145.56 E
Ţulmaythah	33	Dc	32.43N	20.57 E
Tuloma	5	Jb	68.52N	32.49 E
Tulos, Ozero-	7	He	63.35N	30.35 E
Tulsa	39	Jf	36.09N	95.58W
Tulskaja Oblast [3]	19	De	54.00N	37.30 E
Tuluá	54	Cc	4.05N	76.12W
Tuluksak	40	Gd	61.06N	160.58W
Tulum	47	Gd	20.15N	87.27W
Tulum	48	Pg	20.13N	87.28W
Tulun	22	Md	54.35N	100.33 E
Tulungagung	26	Fh	8.04 S	111.54 E
Tuma	7	Ji	55.10N	40.36 E
Tuma, Río-	49	Eg	13.03N	84.44W
Tumaco	53	Ie	1.49N	78.46W
Tumaco, Rada de-	54	Cc	1.50N	78.40W
Tumacuarí, Pico-	54	Fc	1.15N	64.40W
Tuman-gang	28	Kc	42.18N	130.41 E
Tumba	8	Ge	59.12N	17.49 E
Tumbarumba	59	Jg	35.47 S	148.01 E
Tumbes [2]	54	Bd	3.50 S	80.30W
Tumbes	53	Hf	4.05 S	80.35W
Tumča	7	Hc	66.35N	31.45 E
Tumd Youqi	27	Jc	40.33N	110.32 E
Tumd Zuoqi	27	Jc	40.43N	111.06 E
Tumen	22	Oe	42.58N	129.49 E
Tumen Jiang	28	Kc	42.18N	130.41 E
Tumeremo	54	Fb	7.18N	61.30W
Tumkur	25	Ff	13.21N	77.05 E
Tummel	9	Je	56.43N	3.44W
Tummo	33	Be	23.00N	14.10 E
Tumon Bay	64c	Ba	13.31N	144.48 E
Tumpat	26	De	6.12N	102.10 E
Tumu	34	Ec	10.52N	1.59W
Tumucumaque, Serra-	52	Ke	2.20N	55.00W
Tumwater	46	Dc	47.01N	122.54W
Tuna, Punta-	51a	Cc	18.00N	65.52W
Tunapuna	50	Fg	10.38N	61.23W
Tunas	55	Hg	24.58 S	49.06W
Tunas, Sierra de las-	48	Fc	29.40N	107.15W
Tunas Chicas, Laguna-	55	Am	36.01 S	62.20W
Tunaydah	24	Cj	25.31N	29.21 E
Tunçbilek	15	Mj	39.37N	29.29 E
Tunduma	36	Fd	9.18 S	32.46 E
Tunduru	36	Ge	11.07 S	37.21 E
Tundža	15	Jh	41.40N	26.34 E
Tunga	34	Gd	8.07N	9.12 E
Tungabhadra	25	Fe	15.57N	78.15 E
Tungaru	35	Ec	10.14N	30.42 E
Tungnaá	7a	Bb	64.10N	19.34W
Tungokočen	20	Gf	53.33N	115.34 E
Tungsten	42	Ed	62.05N	127.42W
Tungua	65b	Bb	20.01 S	174.46W
Tuni	25	Ge	17.21N	82.33 E
Tūnis=Tunis (EN) [3]	32	Jb	36.30N	10.00 E
Tūnis=Tunis (EN)	31	Ie	36.48N	10.11 E
Tūnis=Tunisia (EN) [1]	31	He	34.00N	9.00 E
Tunis (EN)=Tūnis	31	Ie	36.48N	10.11 E
Tunis (EN)=Tūnis [3]	32	Jb	36.30N	10.00 E
Tūnis, Canal de-=Sicily, Strait of- (EN)	5	Hh	37.20N	11.20 E
Tūnis, Khalīj-	32	Jb	37.00N	10.30 E
Tunisia (EN)=Tūnis [1]	31	He	34.00N	9.00 E
Tunja	53	Ie	5.31N	73.22W
Tunkhannock	44	Je	41.32N	75.57W
Tunliu	28	Bf	36.18N	112.53 E
Tunnhovdfjorden	8	Cd	60.25N	8.55 E
Tunø	8	Di	55.55N	10.25 E
Tunumuk	42	Ec	69.00N	134.57W
Tununak	40	Fd	60.35N	165.16W
Tunungayualok	42	Le	56.05N	61.05W
Tunxi	27	Kf	29.45N	118.15 E
Tuo He	28	Dh	33.16N	117.45 E
Tuo Jang	27	If	28.55N	105.26 E
Tuostah	20	Ic	67.50N	135.40 E
Tuotuo He	27	Fe	34.03N	92.46 E
Tuotuohe/Tanggulashanqu	22	Lf	34.15N	92.29 E
Tupã	56	Jb	21.56 S	50.30W
Tupaciguara	55	Hd	18.35 S	48.42W
Tupai Atoll (Motu-Iti)	61	Kc	16.17 S	151.50W
Tupanciretã	56	Jc	29.05 S	53.51W
Tupelo	43	Je	34.16N	88.43W
Tupik	20	Gf	54.28N	119.57 E
Tupinambarana, Ilha-	54	Gd	3.00 S	58.00W
Tupiraçaba	55	Hb	14.29 S	48.34W
Tupper Lake	44	Jc	44.13N	74.29W
Tupungato, Cerro-	56	Gd	33.22 S	69.47W
Tuquan	27	Lb	45.22N	121.33 E
Túquerres	54	Cc	1.06N	77.37W
Tur	15	Fa	48.04N	22.33 E
Tura	19	Gd	57.12N	66.56 E
Tura [India]	25	Ic	25.31N	90.13 E
Tura [R.S.F.S.R.]	22	Mc	64.17N	100.15 E
Turabah [Sau.Ar.]	23	Fe	21.13N	41.39 E
Turabah [Sau.Ar.]	23	Fd	28.13N	42.59 E
Turagua, Serranías-	50	Di	7.20N	64.35W
Turakina	62	Fd	40.02 S	175.13 E
Turān	24	Qe	35.40N	56.50 E
Turan	20	Ef	52.08N	93.55 E
Turana, Hrebet-	20	If	51.30N	132.00 E
Turangi	62	Fc	38.59 S	175.48 E
Turano	14	Gh	42.26N	12.47 E
Turanskaja Nizmennost	21	Ie	44.30N	63.00 E
Turawa	10	Of	50.45N	18.05 E
Turawskie, Jezioro-	10	Of	50.43N	18.10 E
Turbaco	49	Jh	10.19N	75.25W
Turbat	25	Cc	25.59N	63.04 E
Turbo	53	Ie	8.06N	76.43W
Turcoaia	15	Ld	45.07N	28.11 E
Turda	15	Gc	46.34N	23.47 E
Tūreh	24	Me	34.02N	49.17 E
Tureia Atoll	57	Ng	20.50 S	138.32W
Turek	10	Od	52.02N	18.30 E
Turenki	8	Kd	60.55N	24.38 E
Turfan Depression (EN)= Turpan Pendi	21	Ke	42.30N	89.30 E
Turgai Gates (EN)= Turgajskaja Ložbina	21	Id	51.00N	64.30 E
Turgai Upland (EN)= Turgajskoje Plato	21	Id	51.00N	64.00 E
Turgaj [Kaz.-U.S.S.R.]	19	Gf	49.38N	63.28 E
Turgaj [U.S.S.R.]	21	Ie	48.01N	62.45 E
Turgajskaja Ložbina=Turgai Gates (EN)	21	Id	51.00N	64.30 E
Turgajskaja Oblast [3]	19	Ge	50.30N	66.00 E
Turgajskoje Plato=Turgai Upland (EN)	21	Id	51.00N	64.00 E
Turgeon, Rivière-	44	Ha	50.00N	78.55W
Turgutlu	24	Bc	38.30N	27.50 E
Turhal	24	Gb	40.24N	36.06 E
Türi/Tjuri	7	Fg	58.50N	25.27 E
Turia	13	Le	39.27N	0.19W
Turiaçu, Baía de-	54	Id	1.30 S	45.15W
Turiec	10	Og	49.06N	18.52 E
Turijsk	10	Ue	51.10N	24.37 E
Turimiquire, Cerro-	54	Fa	10.03N	64.00W
Turin (EN) = Torino	6	Gf	45.03N	7.40 E
Turinsk	19	Gd	58.03N	63.42 E
Turja	16	Dd	51.48N	24.52 E
Turka [R.S.F.S.R.]	20	Ff	52.57N	108.13 E
Turka [Ukr.-U.S.S.R.]	10	Tg	49.07N	23.01 E
Turkana	36	Gb	4.00N	35.30 E
Turkana, Lake-/Rudolf, Lake-	30	Kh	3.30N	36.00 E
Türkeli	24	Fb	41.57N	34.21 E
Turkenstanski Hrebet	19	Gh	39.35N	69.00 E
Turkestan	22	Ie	43.18N	68.15 E
Túrkeve	10	Qi	47.06N	20.45 E
Turkey (EN)=Türkiye [1]	22	Fg	39.00N	35.00 E
Turkey Creek	59	Fc	17.02 S	128.12 E
Turki	16	Mc	52.01N	43.16 E
Türkiye=Turkey (EN) [1]	22	Fg	39.00N	35.00 E
Turkmenistan Sovet Socialistik Respublikasy/ Turkmenskaja SSR [2]	19	Fh	40.00N	60.00 E
Turkmen-Kala	18	Df	37.26N	62.19 E
Turkmenskaja Sovetskaja Socialističeskaja Respublika [2]	19	Fh	40.00N	60.00 E
Turkmenskaja SSR/ Turkmenistan Sovet Socialistik Respublikasy [2]	19	Fh	40.00N	60.00 E
Turkmenskaja SSR= Turkmen SSR (EN) [2]	19	Fh	40.00N	60.00 E
Turkmenski Zaliv	16	Ff	39.00N	53.30 E
Turkmen SSR (EN)= Turkmenskaja SSR [2]	19	Fh	40.00N	60.00 E
Türkoğlu	24	Gd	37.31N	36.49 E
Turks and Caicos Islands [5]	39	Ff	21.45N	71.35W
Turks Island Passage	49	Lc	21.25N	71.19W
Turks Islands	47	Jd	21.24N	71.07W
Turku/Åbo	6	Ic	60.27N	22.17 E
Turku-Pori [2]	7	Ff	61.00N	22.30 E
Turkwel	36	Gb	3.06N	36.06 E
Turlock	46	Eh	37.30N	120.51W
Turmantas	8	Li	55.42N	26.34 E
Turnagain, Cape-	62	Gd	40.30 S	176.37 E
Turneffe Islands	47	Ge	17.22N	87.51W
Turnhout	11	Kc	51.19N	4.57 E
Turnov	10	Lf	50.35N	15.09 E
Turnu Roşu, Pasul-	15	Hd	45.33N	24.16 E
Turnu Uăgurele	15	Hf	43.45N	24.52 E
Turočak	20	Df	52.16N	87.05 E
Turó de L'Home	13	Oc	41.45N	2.25 E
Turopolje	14	Ke	45.38N	16.07 E
Turpan	22	Ke	42.56N	89.10 E
Turpan Pendi=Turfan Depression	21	Ke	42.30N	89.30 E
Turquino, Pico-	47	Ie	19.59N	76.51W
Turrialba	49	Fi	9.54N	83.41W
Tursuntski Tuman, Ozero-	17	Kf	60.35N	63.55 E
Turtas	17	Ng	58.57N	69.10 E
Turtas	17	Ng	59.06N	68.50 E
Turtkul	19	Gg	41.35N	61.00 E
Turtle Mountain	45	Fb	49.05N	100.15W
Turugart Shankou	21	Je	40.32N	75.24 E
Turuhan	20	Dc	65.56N	87.42 E
Turuhansk	20	Dc	65.49N	87.59 E
Turvânia	55	Gc	16.39 S	50.09W
Turvo	55	Hi	28.56 S	49.41W
Turvo, Rio- [Braz.]	55	Hd	19.56 S	49.55W
Turvo, Rio- [Braz.]	55	Gc	17.46 S	50.12W
Tusaun/Thusis	14	Dd	46.42N	9.26 E
Tuscaloosa	43	Je	33.13N	87.33W
Tuscan Archipelago (EN)= Arcipelago Toscano	5	Hg	42.45N	10.20 E
Tuscania	14	Fh	42.25N	11.52 E
Tuscany (EN) = Toscana [2]	14	Eg	43.25N	11.00 E
Tuscarora Mountain	44	Ie	40.10N	77.45W
Tuscarora Mountains	46	Gf	41.00N	116.20W
Tuščibas, Zaliv-	18	Ba	46.10N	59.45 E
Tuscola	45	Lg	39.48N	88.17W
Tusenøyane	41	Oc	77.05N	22.00 E
Tuskar	16	Jd	51.40N	36.15 E
Tuskegee	44	Ei	32.26N	85.42W
Tuşnad Băi	15	Ic	46.09N	25.51 E
Tustna	8	Ca	63.10N	8.05 E
Tuszymka	10	Rf	50.09N	21.30 E
Tuszyn	10	Pe	51.37N	19.34 E
Tutajev	19	Dd	57.52N	39.32 E
Tutak	24	Jc	39.32N	42.46 E
Tuticorin	25	Fg	8.47N	78.08 E
Tutira	62	Gc	39.12 S	176.53 E
Tutóia	54	Jd	2.45 S	42.16W
Tutoko Peak	62	Bf	44.36 S	167.58 E
Tutončana	20	Ed	64.05N	93.50 E
Tutova	15	Kc	46.06N	27.32 E
Tutrakan	15	Je	44.03N	26.37 E
Tuttle Creek Lake	45	Hg	39.22N	96.40W
Tuttlingen	10	Ei	47.59N	8.49 E
Tutuala	26	Ih	8.24 S	127.15 E
Tutuila Island	57	Jf	14.18 S	170.42W
Tutupaca, Volcán-	54	Dg	17.01 S	70.22W
Tuupovaara	8	Nb	62.29N	30.36 E
Tuusniemi	7	Ge	62.49N	28.30 E
Tuvalu (Ellice Islands) [1]	58	Ie	8.00 S	178.00 E
Tuvalu Islands	57	Ie	8.00 S	178.00 E
Tuvana-i-Ra Island	61	Fd	21.00 S	178.43W
Tuvana-i-Tholo Island	57	Ig	21.02 S	178.49W
Tuvinskaja ASSR [3]	20	Ef	51.30N	94.00 E
Tuvutha	63d	Cb	17.40 S	178.48W
Tuwayq, Jabal-	21	Gg	25.30N	46.20 E
Tuxer Alpen	14	Fc	47.10N	11.45 E
Tuxford	12	Ba	53.13N	0.53W
Tuxpan	48	Hh	19.33N	103.24W
Tuxpán	47	Cd	21.57N	105.18W
Tuxpan, Arrecife-	48	Kg	21.02N	97.13W
Tuxpan, Río-	48	Kg	20.53N	97.18W
Tuxpán de Rodríguez Cano	47	Ed	20.57N	97.24W
Tuxtla Gutiérrez	39	Jh	16.45N	93.07W
Túy	13	Db	42.03N	8.38W
Tuy, Río-	50	Dg	10.24N	65.59W
Tuy An	25	Lf	13.17N	109.16 E

Index Symbols

[1] Independent Nation
[2] State, Region
[3] District, County
[4] Municipality
[5] Colony, Dependency
Continent
Physical Region
Historical or Cultural Region
Mount, Mountain
Volcano
Hill
Mountains, Mountain Range
Hills, Escarpment
Plateau, Upland
Pass, Gap
Plain, Lowland
Delta
Salt Flat
Valley, Canyon
Crater, Cave
Karst Features
Depression
Polder
Desert, Dunes
Forest, Woods
Heath, Steppe
Oasis
Cape, Point
Coast, Beach
Cliff
Peninsula
Isthmus
Sandbank
Island
Atoll
Rock, Reef
Islands, Archipelago
Rocks, Reefs
Coral Reef
Well, Spring
Geyser
River, Stream
Waterfall Rapids
River Mouth, Estuary
Lake
Salt Lake
Intermittent Lake
Reservoir
Swamp, Pond
Canal
Glacier
Ice Shelf, Pack Ice
Ocean
Sea
Gulf, Bay
Strait, Fjord
Lagoon
Bank
Seamount
Tablemount
Ridge
Shelf
Basin
Escarpment, Sea Scarp
Fracture
Trench, Abyss
National Park, Reserve
Point of Interest
Recreation Site
Cave, Cavern
Historic Site
Ruins
Wall, Walls
Church, Abbey
Temple
Scientific Station
Airport
Port
Lighthouse
Mine
Tunnel
Dam, Bridge

Tuy Hoa 25 Lf 13.05N 109.18 E
Tüyserkän 24 Me 34.33N 48.27 E
Tuz, Lake- (EN)=Tuz Gölü 21 Ff 38.45N 33.25 E
Tuz Gölü=Tuz, Lake- (EN) 21 Ff 38.45N 33.25 E
Tuzkan, Ozero- 18 Fd 40.35N 67.30 E
Tüz Khurmätü 23 Fc 34.53N 44.38 E
Tuzla 14 Mf 44.33N 18.41 E
Tuzlov 16 Lf 47.23N 40.08 E
Tuzluca 24 Jb 40.03N 43.39 E
Tuzly 15 Nd 45.56N 30.05 E
Tväåker 8 Eg 57.03N 12.24 E
Tvărdica 15 Ig 42.42N 25.54 E
Tvedestrand 7 Bg 58.37N 8.55 E
Tverca 7 Ih 56.52N 35.59 E
Tweed 9 Lf 55.46N 2.00W
Tweedsmuir Hills 9 Jf 55.30N 3.22W
Tweerivier 37 Be 25.35S 19.37 E
Twello, Voorst- 12 Ib 52.14N 6.07 E
Twente 11 Mb 52.17N 6.40 E
Twentekanaal 12 Ib 52.13N 6.53 E
Twilight Cove 59 Ff 32.20S 126.00 E
Twin Buttes Reservoir 45 Fk 31.20N 100.35W
Twin Falls 39 He 42.34N 114.28W
Twin Islands 42 Jf 53.50N 80.00W
Twin Peaks 46 Hd 44.35N 114.29W
Twisp 46 Eb 48.22N 120.07W
Twiste 12 Lc 51.29N 9.09 E
Twistringen 10 Ed 52.48N 8.39 E
Two Butte Creek 45 Eg 38.02N 102.08W
Two Harbors 45 Kc 47.01N 91.40W
Two Rivers 45 Md 44.09N 87.34W
Two Thumb Range 62 De 43.45S 170.40 E
Tychy 10 Of 50.09N 18.59 E
Tyczyn 10 Sg 49.58N 22.02 E
Tydal 7 Ce 63.04N 11.34 E
Tygda 20 Hf 53.07N 126.20 E
Tyin 8 Cc 61.15N 8.15 E
Tyin 8 Cc 61.14N 8.14 E
Tyler 43 He 32.21N 95.18W
Tylertown 45 Kk 31.07N 90.09W
Tylösand 8 Eh 56.39N 12.44 E
Tylöskog 8 Ff 58.40N 15.10 E
Tym 20 De 59.30N 80.07 E
Tymovskoje 20 Jf 50.50N 142.41 E
Tympákion 15 Hn 35.06N 24.45 E
Tynda 22 Od 53.07N 126.20 E
Tyne 9 Lf 55.01N 1.26W
Tyne and Wear [3] 9 Lg 55.00N 1.35W
Tynemouth 9 Lf 55.01N 1.24W
Týn nad Vltavou 10 Kg 49.14N 14.26 E
Tynset 7 Ce 62.17N 10.47 E
Tyra, Cayos- 49 Fg 12.50N 83.20W
Tyrifjorden 8 De 60.05N 10.10 E
Tyringe 8 Eh 56.10N 13.35 E
Tyrma 20 If 50.01N 132.10 E
Tyrnyauz 16 Mh 43.23N 42.56 E
Tyrol (EN)=Tirol [2] 14 Fc 47.10N 11.25 E
Tyrol (EN)=Tirol/Tirolo 14 Fd 47.00N 11.20 E
Tyrol (EN)=Tirolo/Tirol 14 Fd 47.00N 11.20 E
Tyrone 44 He 40.41N 78.15W
Tyrrell, Lake- 59 Ig 35.20S 142.50 E
Tyrrel Lake 42 Gd 63.05N 105.30W
Tyrrhenian Basin (EN) 5 Hh 40.00N 13.00 E
Tyrrhenian Sea (EN)= Tirreno, Mar- 5 Hh 40.00N 12.00 E
Tyrva/Tõrva 7 Fg 58.01N 25.59 E
Tyrvää 8 Jc 61.21N 22.53 E
Tysmenica 10 Uh 48.49N 24.56 E
Tyśmienica 10 Se 51.33N 22.30 E
Tysnesøy 7 Af 60.00N 5.35 E
Tysse 8 Ad 60.22N 5.45 E
Tyssedal 8 Bd 60.07N 6.34 E
Tystama/Tõstamaa 8 Jf 58.17N 23.52 E
Tystberga 8 Gf 58.52N 17.15 E
Tyszowce 10 Tf 50.36N 23.41 E
Tytuvėnai/Tituvenaj 8 Ji 55.33N 23.09 E
Tywyn 9 Ii 52.35N 4.05W
Tzanconeja, Río- 48 Ni 16.51N 91.47W
Tzaneen 37 Ed 23.50S 30.09 E
Tzintzuntzan 48 Ih 19.38N 101.34W
Tzucacab 48 Og 20.04N 89.05W

U

Uaboe 64e Ab 0.31S 166.54 E
Uacurizal, Ilha do- 55 Dc 16.25S 56.05W
Ua Huka, Ile- 57 Ne 8.54S 139.33W
Uanukuhahaki 65b Ba 19.58S 174.29W
Ua Pou, Ile- 57 Me 9.23S 140.03W
Uaroo 59 Dd 23.00S 115.10 E
Uatumã, Rio- 52 Kf 2.26S 57.37W
Uaupés 53 Jf 0.08S 67.05W
Uaupés, Rio- 52 Je 0.02N 67.16W
Uaxactún 47 Ge 17.25N 89.29W
Ub 15 De 44.27N 20.05 E
Ubá 54 Jh 21.07S 42.56W
Übach-Palenberg [F.R.G.] 10 Cf 50.56N 6.05 E
Ubagan 19 Ge 54.23N 64.40 E
Ubaila 24 If 33.06N 40.15 E
Ubaitaba 54 Kf 14.18S 39.20W
Ubajay 55 Cj 31.47S 58.18W
Ubangi 30 Ii 0.30S 17.42 E
Ubatuba 55 Jf 23.26S 45.04W
Ubay 26 Hd 10.03N 124.28 E
Ubaye 11 Mj 44.28N 6.18 E
Ubayyiḍ, Wādī al- 22 Fc 32.34N 43.48 E
Ube 28 Kh 33.56N 131.15 E
Ubeda 13 If 38.01N 3.22W
Ubekendt Ejland 41 Gd 71.10N 53.45W
Uberaba 53 Lg 19.45S 47.55W
Uberaba, Lagoa- 55 Dc 17.30S 57.45W
Uberlândia 53 Lg 18.56S 48.18W
Überlingen 10 Fi 47.46N 9.10 E
Ubiaja 34 Gd 6.39N 6.23 E
Ubiña, Peña- 13 Ga 43.01N 5.57W
Ubiratã 55 Fg 24.32S 52.56W
Ubon Ratchathani 22 Mh 15.15N 104.54 E
Ubort 16 Fc 52.06N 28.30 E
Ubrique 13 Gh 36.41N 5.27W
Ubsu-Nur (Uvs nuur) 21 Ld 50.20N 92.45 E
Ubundu 31 Ji 0.21S 25.29 E
Učaly 19 Fe 54.20N 59.31 E
Učami 20 Ed 63.50N 96.39 E
Učaral 19 If 46.08N 80.52 E
Ucayali, Río- 52 If 4.30S 73.30W
Uccle/Ukkel 12 Gd 50.48N 4.19 E
Üçdoruk Tepe 24 Ib 40.45N 41.05 E
Ucero 13 Ic 41.31N 3.04W
Uchiko 29 Ce 33.34N 132.38 E
Uchi Lake 45 Ja 51.05N 92.35W
Uchinomi 29 Dd 34.30N 134.19 E
Uchinoura 29 Bf 31.16N 131.05 E
Uchiura-Wan 28 Pc 42.18N 140.35 E
Uchte 10 Ed 52.30N 8.55 E
Učka 14 Ie 45.17N 14.12 E
Uckange 12 Ie 49.18N 6.09 E
Uckermark 10 Jc 53.10N 13.35 E
Uckfield 12 Cd 50.58N 0.06 E
Učkuduk 19 Gg 42.10N 63.30 E
Učkurgan 18 Id 41.01N 72.04 E
Ucrainskaja Sovetskaja Socialističeskaja Respublika [2] 19 Df 49.00N 32.00 E
Ucross 46 Ld 44.33N 106.31W
Ucua 36 Bd 8.40S 14.12 E
Učur 21 Pd 58.48N 130.35 E
Uda [R.S.F.S.R.] 21 Pd 54.42N 135.14 E
Uda [R.S.F.S.R.] 20 Ff 51.45N 107.25 E
Uda [R.S.F.S.R.] 20 Ee 56.05N 99.34 E
Udačny 20 Gc 66.25N 112.20 E
Udaipur 22 Jg 24.35N 73.41 E
Udaj 16 Hd 50.05N 33.07 E
Udaquiola 55 Cm 36.34S 58.31W
Udbina 14 Jf 44.32N 15.46 E
Uddevalla 7 Cg 58.21N 11.55 E
Uddjaure 5 Hb 65.58N 17.50 E
Uden 12 Hc 51.40N 5.37 E
Udgir 25 Fe 18.23N 77.07 E
Udhampur 25 Fb 32.56N 75.08 E
Udimski 7 Kf 61.09N 45.52 E
Udine 14 Hd 46.03N 13.14 E
Udipi 25 Ef 13.21N 74.45 E
Udmurtskaja ASSR [3] 19 Fd 57.20N 52.50 E
Udoha 8 Mg 57.58N 29.50 E
Udomlja 7 Ih 57.56N 35.02 E
Udone-Jima 29 Fd 34.28N 139.17 E
Udon Thani 25 Ke 17.25N 102.48 E
Udot 64d Bb 7.23N 151.43 E
Udskaja Guba 21 Pd 55.00N 136.00 E
Udskoje 20 If 54.36N 134.30 E
Udy 16 Je 49.47N 36.35 E
Udžary 16 Oi 40.31N 47.40 E
Udzungwa Range 36 Gd 8.05S 35.50 E
Uebonti 26 Hg 0.55S 121.38 E
Uecker 10 Kc 53.45N 14.04 E
Ueckermünde 10 Kc 53.44N 14.03 E
Ueda 27 Od 36.24N 138.16 E
Uele 30 Jh 4.09N 22.26 E
Uelen 20 Oc 66.13N 169.48W
Uelzen 10 Gd 52.58N 10.33 E
Ueno 29 Ed 34.46N 136.06 E
Uere 30 Jh 3.42N 25.24 E
Ufa 5 Le 54.40N 56.00 E
Ufa 6 Le 54.44N 55.56 E
Uftjuga 7 Lf 61.28N 46.12 E
Ugab 30 Ik 21.12S 13.38 E
Ugale/Ugāle 8 Ig 57.19N 21.52 E
Ugāle/Ugale 8 Ig 57.19N 21.52 E
Ugalla 36 Fd 5.08S 30.42 E
Uganda [1] 31 Kh 1.00N 32.00 E
Ugărčin 15 Hf 43.06N 24.25 E
Ugashik 40 He 57.32N 157.25W
Ughelli 34 Gd 5.30N 5.59 E
Ugijar 13 Ih 36.57N 3.03W
Uglegorsk 20 Jg 49.05N 142.06 E
Uglekamensk 20 Ih 43.18N 133.08 E
Ugleuralski 17 Hg 58.59N 57.38 E
Uglič 20 Dd 57.33N 38.23 E
Ugljan 14 Jf 44.05N 15.10 E
Uglovoje 28 Lc 43.20N 132.06 E
Ugnev 10 Tf 50.20N 23.45 E
Ugo 29 Gb 39.13N 140.23 E
Ugolnyje Kopi 20 Md 64.42N 177.50 E
Ugoma 36 Ec 4.55S 26.50 E
Ugra 19 De 54.30N 36.07 E
Ugtal-Cajdam 27 Ib 48.25N 105.30 E
Uh 10 Rh 48.33N 22.00 E
Uherské Hradiště 10 Ng 49.04N 17.27 E
Úhlava 10 Jg 49.45N 13.23 E
Uhlenhorst 37 Bd 23.45S 17.55 E
Uhta 6 Lc 63.33N 53.40 E
Uibh Fhaili/Offaly [2] 9 Fh 53.20N 7.30W
Uig 9 Gd 57.30N 6.20W
Uige 31 Ii 7.35S 15.04 E
Uíge [3] 36 Cd 7.00S 15.30 E
'Uiha 65b Ba 19.54S 174.25W
Uijec 64d Bb 7.10N 151.57 E
Ŭijŏngbu 28 If 37.44N 127.02 E
Uiju 28 Hd 40.12N 124.32 E
Uil 19 Ff 48.36N 52.30 E
Uil 19 Ff 49.04N 54.42 E
Uilpata, Gora- 16 Mh 42.47N 43.44 E
Uinta Mountains 43 Ec 40.45N 110.05W
Uinta River 46 Kf 40.14N 109.51W
Uis 37 Ad 21.08S 14.49 E
Ŭisŏng 28 Jf 36.21N 128.42 E
Uitenhage 31 Jl 33.40S 25.28 E
Uithoorn 12 Gb 52.14N 4.52 E
Uithuizen 12 Ia 53.25N 6.42 E
Uithuizerwad 12 Ia 53.30N 6.40 E
Ujae Atoll 57 Hd 9.05N 165.40 E
Ūjān 24 Og 30.45N 52.05 E
Ujandina 20 Jc 68.23N 145.50 E
Ujar 20 Ee 55.48N 94.20 E
Ujarrás 49 Fi 9.50N 83.40W
Ujedinenija, Ostrov- 20 Da 77.30N 82.30 E
Ujelang Atoll 57 Hd 9.49N 160.55 E
Újfehértó 10 Ri 47.48N 21.41 E
Uji 29 Dd 34.53N 135.47 E
Uji 19 Ge 54.20N 63.58 E
Uji-Guntō 28 Ji 31.10N 129.28 E
Ujiie 29 Fc 36.41N 139.57 E
Ujiji 31 Ji 4.55S 29.41 E
Ujjain 22 Jg 23.11N 75.46 E
Ujunglamuru 26 Gg 4.40S 119.58 E
Ujung Pandang (Makasar) 22 Nj 5.07S 119.24 E
Uk 20 Ee 55.04N 98.52 E
Ukata 34 Gc 10.50N 5.50 E
Ukeng, Bukit- 26 Gf 1.45N 115.08 E
Ukerewe Island 36 Fc 2.03S 33.00 E
Uke-Shima 29b Ba 28.02N 129.15 E
Ukhaydir 24 Jf 32.26N 43.36 E
Ukiah [Ca.-U.S.] 43 Cd 39.09N 123.13W
Ukiah [Or.-U.S.] 46 Fd 45.08N 118.56W
Uki Ni Masi 63a Ed 10.15S 161.44 E
Ukkel/Uccle 12 Gd 50.48N 4.19 E
Ukmergė/Ukmerge 7 Fi 55.14N 24.47 E
Ukmerge/Ukmergė 7 Fi 55.14N 24.47 E
Ukraine (EN) 5 Jf 49.00N 32.00 E
Ukrainian SSR (EN)= Ukrainskaja SSR [2] 19 Df 49.00N 32.00 E
Ukrainskaja SSR/Ukrainska Radyanska Socialistična Respublika [2] 19 Df 49.00N 32.00 E
Ukrainskaja SSR=Ukrainian SSR (EN) [2] 19 Df 49.00N 32.00 E
Ukrainska Radyanska Socialistična Respublika/ Ukrainskaja SSR [2] 19 Df 49.00N 32.00 E
Ukrina 14 Le 45.05N 17.56 E
Uku-Jima 29 Ae 33.16N 129.07 E
Ula 24 Cd 37.05N 28.26 E
Ulah Lake 45 Hh 36.58N 96.10W
Ulaidh/Ulster 9 Gg 54.30N 7.00W
Ulalu 64d Bb 7.25N 151.40 E
Ulan (Xiligou) 27 Gd 36.55N 98.16 E
Ulan→Otog Qi 27 Id 39.07N 108.00 E
Ulanbaatar→Ulan-Bator 22 Me 47.55N 106.53 E
Ulan-Badrah 28 Ac 43.58N 110.37 E
Ulan-Bator (Ulaanbaatar) 22 Me 47.55N 106.53 E
Ulanbel 19 Hg 44.49N 71.10 E
Ulan-Burgasy, Hrebet- 20 Ff 52.30N 108.30 E
Ulangom 22 Le 49.58N 92.02 E
Ulanhad/Chifeng 27 Kc 42.16N 118.57 E
Ulan Hol 19 Ef 45.27N 46.46 E
Ulan Hot/Horqin Youyi Qianqi 22 Oe 46.04N 122.00 E
Ulan Hua → Siziwang Qi 28 Ad 41.31N 111.41 E
Ulan-Hus 27 Eb 49.02N 89.23 E
Ulanów 10 Sf 50.30N 22.16 E
Ulansuhai Nur 27 Ic 40.56N 108.49 E
Ulan-Tajga 27 Ga 50.45N 98.30 E
Ulan-Ude 22 Md 51.50N 107.37 E
Ulan Ul Hu 27 Fe 34.45N 90.25 E
Ulas 24 Gc 39.27N 37.03 E
Ulawa Island 60 Gi 9.46S 161.57 E
Ulbeja 20 Je 59.20N 144.25 E
Ulchin 28 Jf 36.59N 129.24 E
Ulcinj 15 Ch 41.56N 19.13 E
Uleåborg/Oulu 6 Ib 65.01N 25.30 E
Ulefoss 7 Bg 59.17N 9.16 E
Ulegej 22 Ke 48.56N 89.57 E
Ulety 20 Gf 51.22N 112.30 E
Uleza 15 Ch 41.40N 19.53 E
Ulfborg 8 Ch 56.16N 8.20 E
Ulflingen/Troisvierges 12 Hd 50.07N 6.00 E
Ulft, Gendringen- 12 Ic 51.54N 6.24 E
Ulgain Gol 27 Kb 45.31N 117.50 E
Ulhāsnagar 25 Ee 19.10N 73.07 E
Uliastai→Dong Ujimqin Qi 27 Kc 45.31N 116.58 E
Uliga 58 Id 7.09N 171.13 E
Ulindi 30 Ji 1.40S 25.52 E
Ulithi Atoll 57 Ed 9.58N 139.40 E
Ulja 20 Je 58.48N 141.40 E
Uljanovka [R.S.F.S.R.] 8 Ne 59.37N 30.55 E
Uljanovka [Ukr.-U.S.S.R.] 16 Ge 48.20N 30.13 E
Uljanovsk 6 Ke 54.20N 48.24 E
Uljanovskaja Oblast [3] 19 Ee 54.00N 48.00 E
Uljanovski 19 He 50.05N 73.45 E
Uljasutaj 22 Le 47.45N 96.49 E
Ulkan 20 Fe 55.55N 107.55 E
Ulla 13 Db 42.39N 8.44W
Ullapool 9 Hd 57.54N 5.10W
Ullared 7 Ch 57.08N 12.43 E
Ulldecona 13 Md 40.36N 0.27 E
Ullsfjorden 7 Eb 69.58N 20.00 E
Ullswater 9 Kg 54.34N 2.54W
Ullüng-Do 27 Nd 37.29N 130.52 E
Ullvettern 8 Fe 59.25N 14.15 E
Ulm 10 Fh 48.25N 10.00 E
Ulmen 12 Id 50.13N 6.59 E
Ulmeni 15 Jd 45.04N 26.39 E
Ulmu 15 Je 44.16N 26.55 E
Ulongwé 37 Eb 14.43S 34.21 E
Ulricehamn 7 Ch 57.47N 13.25 E
Ulrichstein 12 Ld 50.35N 9.12 E
Ulrum 12 Ia 53.22N 6.20 E
Ulrum-Zoutkamp 12 Ia 53.20N 6.18 E
Ulsan 27 Md 35.33N 129.19 E
Ulsteinvik 7 Ae 62.20N 5.53 E
Ulster 10 Ff 50.51N 9.59 E
Ulster/Ulaidh 9 Gg 54.30N 7.00W
Ulster Canal 9 Gg 54.27N 6.40W
Ulu 35 Ec 10.43N 33.29 E
Ulu/Uulu 8 Kf 58.13N 24.29 E
Ulúa, Río- 47 Ge 15.56N 87.43W
Ulubat Gölü 24 Cb 40.10N 28.35 E
Ulubey 24 Cc 38.09N 29.33 E
Uludağ 23 Ca 40.04N 29.13 E
Uludere 24 Jd 37.27N 42.51 E
Ulugqat/Wuqia 27 Cd 39.40N 75.07 E
Ulukışla 24 Fd 37.33N 34.30 E
Ulungur He 21 Ke 46.58N 87.28 E
Ulungur Hu 27 Eb 47.20N 87.10 E
Ulus 24 Eb 41.35N 32.39 E
Ulus Dağ 15 Lj 39.18N 28.24 E
Ulva 9 Ge 56.28N 6.12W
Ulverston 9 Jg 54.12N 3.06W
Ulverstone 59 Jh 41.09S 146.10 E
Ulvik 8 Bd 60.34N 6.54 E
Ulvön 8 Ha 63.05N 18.40 E
Ulysses 45 Fh 37.35N 101.22W
Ulytau 19 Gf 48.35N 67.05 E
Ulytau, Gora- 19 Gf 48.45N 67.00 E
Uly-Žilanšik 19 Gf 48.51N 63.47 E
Uma 27 La 52.36N 120.38 E
Umag 14 He 45.25N 13.32 E
Umala 54 Eg 17.24S 67.58W
Umán 48 Og 20.53N 89.45W
Uman 64d Bb 7.18N 151.53 E
Uman 19 Df 48.47N 30.09 E
'Umān 22 Hg 22.10N 58.00 E
'Umān=Oman (EN) [1] 22 Hg 21.00N 57.00 E
'Umān, Khalīj-=Oman, Gulf of- (EN) 21 Hg 25.00N 58.00 E
Umanak 41 Gd 70.36N 52.15W
Ūmánarssuaq/Farvel, Kap- 67 Nb 59.50N 43.50W
Umatac 64c Bb 13.18N 144.40 E
Umba 19 Db 66.41N 34.17 E
Umbelasha 35 Cd 9.51N 24.50 E
Umbertide 14 Gg 43.18N 12.20 E
Umberto de Campos 54 Jd 2.37S 43.27W
Umboi Island 57 Fe 5.36S 148.00 E
Umbozero, Ozero- 7 Ic 67.45N 34.20 E
Umbria [2] 14 Gh 43.00N 12.30 E
Ume 37 Dc 17.15S 28.20 E
Umeå 6 Ic 63.50N 20.15 E
Umeälven 5 Ic 63.47N 20.16 E
Umm al Arānib 33 Bd 26.08N 14.45 E
Umm al Hayf, Wādī- 23 Hf 18.37N 53.59 E
Umm al Jamāajim 24 Ki 26.59N 45.19 E
Umm al Qaywayn 23 Id 25.35N 55.34 E
Ummanz 10 Jb 54.30N 13.10 E
Umm ar Rizam 33 Dc 32.32N 23.00 E
Umm as Samīm 23 Ie 21.30N 56.45 E
Umm Bāb 24 Nj 25.12N 50.48 E
Umm Bel 35 Dc 13.32N 28.04 E
Umm Buru 35 Cb 15.01N 23.36 E
Umm Dhibbān 35 Dc 14.14N 29.37 E
Umm Durmān=Omdurman (EN) 31 Kg 15.38N 32.30 E
Umm Inderaba 35 Eb 15.12N 31.54 E
Umm Kaddādah 35 Dc 13.36N 26.42 E
Umm Lajj 23 Ed 25.04N 37.13 E
Umm Naqqāt, Jabal- 24 Fj 25.30N 34.14 E
Umm Qam'ul 24 Pj 24.47N 54.42 E
Umm Ruwābah 31 Kg 12.54N 31.13 E
Umm Sayyālah 35 Ec 14.25N 31.00 E
Umm Urūmah 24 Gj 25.46N 36.33 E
Umnak 38 Cd 58.25N 168.10W
Umne-Gobi 27 Fb 49.06N 91.43 E
Umpqua River 46 Ce 43.42N 124.03W
Umpulu 36 Ce 12.42S 17.40 E
Umsini, Gunung- 26 Jg 1.35S 133.30 E
Umtata 31 Kj 18.58S 32.40 E
Umtata 31 Jl 31.35S 28.47 E
Umuarama 56 Jb 23.45S 53.20W
Umurbey 15 Ji 40.14N 26.36 E
Umvukwes 37 Ec 17.01S 30.52 E
Umvuma 37 Ec 19.19S 30.35 E
Umzingwani 37 Dd 22.12S 29.56 E
Una 14 Ke 45.16N 16.55 E
Unabetsu-Dake 29a Db 43.52N 144.51 E
Unac 14 Kf 44.29N 16.08 E
Unaí 54 Ig 16.23S 46.53W
Unalakleet 40 Gd 63.53N 160.47W
Unalaska 38 Cd 53.45N 166.45W
Unare, Río- 50 Dg 10.06N 65.12W
Unauna, Pulau- 26 Hg 0.10S 121.35 E
'Unayzah [Jor.] 24 Fg 30.29N 35.48 E
'Unayzah [Sau. Ar.] 22 Gg 26.06N 43.56 E
Uncia 54 Eg 18.27S 66.37W
Uncompahgre Peak 43 Fd 38.04N 107.28W
Uncompahgre Plateau 45 Bg 38.30N 108.25W
Unden 8 Ff 58.45N 14.25 E
Underberg 37 De 29.50S 29.22 E
Under-Han 22 Ne 47.19N 110.39 E
Undjuljung 20 Hc 66.20N 124.40 E
Undu Point 63d Cb 16.08S 179.57W
Undva Neem/Kiprarenukk, Mys- 8 If 58.25N 21.45 E
Uneča 16 Hc 52.50N 32.44 E
'Ung, Jabal al- 14 Dn 36.45N 9.35 E
Unga 40 Ge 55.15N 160.45W
Ungava, Péninsule d'-= Ungava Peninsula (EN) 38 Lc 60.00N 74.00W
Ungava Bay 38 Md 59.30N 67.30W
Ungava Peninsula (EN)= Ungava, Péninsule d'- 38 Lc 60.00N 74.00W
Ungeny 16 Ef 47.13N 27.50 E
Unggi 28 Kc 42.21N 130.23 E
Ungureni 15 Jb 47.53N 26.47 E
Ungwatiri 35 Fb 16.55N 36.05 E
União 54 Jd 4.35S 42.52W
União da Vitória 56 Jc 26.13S 51.05W
União dos Palmares 54 Ke 9.10S 36.02W
Uničov 10 Ng 49.49N 17.07 E
Uniejów 10 Oe 51.58N 18.49 E
Unije 14 If 44.38N 14.15 E
Unimak 38 Cd 54.50N 164.00W
Unimak Pass 40 Gf 54.35N 164.43W
Unini, Rio- 54 Fd 1.41S 61.30W
Union [Mo.-U.S.] 45 Kg 38.27N 91.00W
Union [S.C.-U.S.] 44 Gh 34.42N 81.37W
Union City 44 Cg 36.26N 89.03W
Uniondale 37 Cf 33.40S 23.08 E
Unión de Reyes 49 Gb 22.48N 81.32W
Unión de Tula 48 Gh 19.58N 104.16W
Union Island 50 Ff 12.36N 61.26W
Union Islands/Tokelau 57 Je 9.00S 171.45W
Union of Soviet Socialist Republics (USSR) (EN)= SSSR [1] 22 Jd 60.00N 80.00 E
Union Seamount (EN) 42 Eg 49.35N 132.45W
Union Springs 44 Ei 32.09N 85.49W
Uniontown 44 Hf 39.54N 79.44W
Unionville 45 Jf 40.29N 93.01W
United Arab Emirates (EN) =Al Imārāt al 'Arabīyah al Muttaḥidah [1] 22 Hg 24.00N 54.00 E
United Arab Republic (EN) → Egypt (EN) [1] 31 Jf 27.00N 30.00 E
United Kingdom [1] 6 Fe 54.00N 2.00W
United Kingdom of Great Britain and Northern Ireland [1] 6 Fe 54.00N 2.00W
United States [1] 39 Jf 38.00N 97.00W
United States of America [1] 39 Jf 38.00N 97.00W
Unity [Or.-U.S.] 46 Fd 44.29N 118.13W
Unity [Sask.-Can.] 42 Gf 52.27N 109.10W
Universales, Montes- 13 Kd 40.18N 1.33W
University City 45 Kg 38.39N 90.19W
Unna 10 De 51.32N 7.41 E
Unnāb, Wādī al- 24 Gg 30.11N 36.39 E
Unnukka 8 Lb 62.25N 27.55 E
Unst 5 Fc 60.45N 0.55W
Unstrut 10 He 51.10N 11.48 E
Unterfranken 10 Fg 50.00N 10.00 E
Unterwalden-Nidwalden [2] 14 Cd 46.55N 8.30 E
Unterwalden-Obwalden [2] 14 Cd 46.50N 8.20 E
Unuli Horog 27 Fd 35.12N 91.58 E
Ünye 23 Ea 41.08N 37.17 E
Unža 5 Kd 57.20N 43.08 E
Unzen-Dake 29 Be 32.45N 130.17 E
Uoleva 65b Ba 19.51S 174.24W
Uozu 28 Nf 36.48N 137.24 E
Úpa 15 Lf 50.22N 15.54 E
Upata 54 Fb 8.01N 62.24W
Upemba, Lac- 36 Ed 8.36S 26.26 E
Upernavik 41 Gd 72.20N 56.00W
Upin 26 Ig 2.56S 129.11 E
Upington 31 Jk 28.25S 21.15 E
Upland 12 Kc 51.18N 8.42 E
Upolu Island 57 Jf 13.55S 171.45W
Upolu Point 60 Oc 20.16N 155.52W
Upper [3] 34 Ec 10.30N 1.30W
Upper Arlington 44 Fe 40.01N 83.03W
Upper Arrow Lake 46 Ga 50.30N 117.55W
Upper Austria (EN) = Oberösterreich [2] 14 Hb 48.15N 14.00 E
Upper Hutt 62 Fd 41.07S 175.04 E
Upper Klamath Lake 43 Cc 42.23N 122.00W
Upper Lake 46 Ef 41.44N 120.08W
Upper Lough Erne/Loch Éirne Uachtair 9 Fg 54.20N 7.30W
Upper Red Lake 45 Ib 48.10N 94.40W
Upper Sandusky 44 Fe 40.48N 83.17W
Upper Sheik 35 Hd 9.57N 45.09 E
Upper Thames Valley 9 Lj 51.40N 1.40W
Upper Trajan's Wall (EN)= Verhni Traijanov Val 15 Lc 46.40N 29.00 E
Upper Volta (EN)=Haute-Volta [1] 31 Gg 13.00N 2.00W
Uppingham 12 Bb 52.35N 0.43W
Uppland 8 Gd 60.00N 17.50 E
Upplands Väsby 8 Ge 59.31N 17.54 E
Uppsala [2] 7 Df 60.00N 17.45 E
Uppsala 6 Hd 59.52N 17.38 E
Upsala 45 Kb 49.02N 90.29W
Upshi 25 Fb 33.50N 77.49 E
Upton 46 Md 44.06N 104.38W
Uqbān 33 Hf 15.30N 42.23 E
'Uqlat aş Şuqūr 24 Jj 25.53N 42.15 E
Uqturpan/Wushi 27 Cc 41.10N 79.16 E
Ur 23 Gc 30.58N 46.06 E
Urabá, Golfo de- 54 Cb 8.25N 77.00W
Uracoa 50 Eh 9.00N 62.21W
Uracoa, Río- 50 Eh 9.08N 62.20W
Uradarja 18 Fe 38.51N 66.02 E
Urad Qianqi 27 Ic 40.49N 108.37 E
Urad Zhonghou Lianheqi (Haliut) 27 Ic 41.34N 108.32 E
Uraga-Suido 29 Fd 35.15N 139.45 E
Ura-Guba 7 Hb 69.18N 32.48 E
Urahoro 29a Cb 42.48N 143.38 E
Urahoro-Gawa 29a Cb 42.44N 143.40 E
Uraj 19 Gc 60.08N 64.40 E
Urakawa 28 Qc 42.09N 142.47 E
Ural 5 Lf 47.00N 51.48 E
Ural Mountains (EN)= Uralskije Gory 5 Ld 57.00N 60.00 E
Uralsk 6 Le 51.14N 51.22 E
Uralskaja Oblast [3] 19 Ff 49.45N 51.00 E
Uralskije Gory=Ural Mountains (EN) 5 Ld 57.00N 60.00 E
Urambo 36 Fd 5.04S 32.03 E
Uranium City 39 Id 59.34N 108.36W
Uraricoera 54 Fc 3.27N 60.59W
Uraricoera, Rio- 52 Je 3.02N 60.30W
Ura-Tjube 19 Gh 39.53N 69.01 E
Urawa 28 Og 35.51N 139.39 E
'Uray'irah 24 Mj 25.57N 48.53 E
Urayq, Nafūd al- 24 Jj 25.17N 42.25 E
Urbana [Il.-U.S.] 45 Lf 40.07N 88.12W
Urbana [Oh.-U.S.] 44 Fe 40.06N 83.45W
Urbandale 45 Jf 41.38N 93.48W
Urbania 14 Gg 43.40N 12.31 E

Index Symbols

[1] Independent Nation
[2] State, Region
[3] District, County
[4] Municipality
[5] Colony, Dependency
Continent
Physical Region
Historical or Cultural Region
Mount, Mountain
Volcano
Hill
Mountains, Mountain Range
Hills, Escarpment
Plateau, Upland
Pass, Gap
Plain, Lowland
Delta
Salt Flat
Valley, Canyon
Crater, Cave
Karst Features
Depression
Polder
Desert, Dunes
Forest, Woods
Heath, Steppe
Oasis
Cape, Point
Coast, Beach
Cliff
Peninsula
Isthmus
Sandbank
Island
Atoll
Rock, Reef
Islands, Archipelago
Rocks, Reefs
Coral Reef
Well, Spring
Geyser
River, Stream
Waterfall Rapids
River Mouth, Estuary
Lake
Salt Lake
Intermittent Lake
Reservoir
Swamp, Pond
Canal
Glacier
Ice Shelf, Pack Ice
Ocean
Sea
Gulf, Bay
Strait, Fjord
Lagoon
Bank
Seamount
Tablemount
Ridge
Shelf
Basin
Escarpment, Sea Scarp
Fracture
Trench, Abyss
National Park, Reserve
Point of Interest
Recreation Site
Cave, Cavern
Historic Site
Ruins
Wall, Walls
Church, Abbey
Temple
Scientific Station
Airport
Port
Lighthouse
Mine
Tunnel
Dam, Bridge

Urbano Santos 54 Jd 3.12S 43.23W
Urbino 14 Gg 43.43N 12.38 E
Urbino, Étang d'- 11a Ba 42.02N 9.28 E
Urbión, Picos de- 13 Jb 42.01N 2.52W
Urcel 12 Fe 49.30N 3.33 E
Urcos 54 Df 13.42S 71.38W
Urdinarrain 55 Ck 32.41S 58.53W
Urdoma 7 Lf 61.47N 48.29 E
Urdžar 19 If 47.05N 81.37 E
Ure 9 Lg 54.01N 1.12W
Uré 49 Jj 7.46N 75.31W
Uren 19 Ed 57.29N 45.48 E
Urenui 62 Fc 39.00S 174.23 E
Ures 47 Bc 29.26N 110.24W
Ureshino 29 Ab 33.06N 129.59 E
'Urf, Jabal al- 24 Ei 27.49N 32.55 E
Urfa 23 Eb 37.08N 38.46 E
Urfa Platosu 24 Hd 37.10N 38.50 E
Urgal 20 If 51.00N 132.50 E
Urgel, Llanos de- 13 Lc 41.25N 0.36W
Urgel, Llanos de-/Urgell, Pla d'- 13 Lc 41.25N 0.36W
Urgell, Pla d'- 13 Lc 41.25N 0.36W
Urgell, Pla d'-/Urgel, Llanos de- 13 Lc 41.25N 0.36W
Urgen 28 Ab 44.45N 110.40 E
Urgenč 22 Ie 41.33N 60.38 E
Ürgüp 24 Fc 38.38N 35.56 E
Urgut 19 Gh 39.23N 67.14 E
Uri 25 Eb 34.05N 74.02 E
Uri [2] 14 Cd 46.40N 8.30 E
Uribia 54 Da 11.42N 72.17W
Uricki 19 Ge 53.19N 65.34 E
Urique, Río- 48 Fd 26.29N 107.58W
Urjala 8 Jc 61.05N 23.32 E
Urjupinsk 19 Ee 50.48N 42.02 E
Urk 11 Lb 52.39N 5.36 E
Urkan 20 Hf 53.27N 126.56 E
Urla 24 Bc 38.18N 26.46 E
Urlaţi 15 Je 44.59N 26.14 E
Urluk 20 Ff 50.03N 107.55 E
Urmi 20 Ig 48.43N 134.16 E
Urmia, Lake- (EN)= Orūmīyeh, Daryācheh-ye 21 Gf 37.40N 45.30 E
Uromi 34 Gd 6.42N 6.20 E
Uroševac 15 Eg 42.22N 21.10 E
Urshult 8 Fh 56.32N 14.47 E
Ursus 10 Qd 52.12N 20.53 E
Urtazym 17 Ij 52.15N 58.50 E
Urtigueira, Serra da- 55 Gg 24.15S 51.00W
Uru, Rio- 55 Hb 15.24S 49.36W
Uruaçu 54 If 14.30S 49.10W
Uruana 55 Hb 15.30S 49.41W
Uruapan del Progreso 47 De 19.25N 101.58W
Uruará, Rio- 54 Hd 2.00S 53.38W
Urubamba, Río- 52 Ig 10.43S 73.48W
Urubici 55 Hi 28.02S 49.37W
Urubú, Cachoeira do- 55 Ha 12.52S 48.13W
Urucará 54 Gd 2.32S 57.45W
Uruçui 54 Je 7.14S 44.33W
Urucuia, Rio- [Braz.] 55 Ib 15.38S 46.10W
Urucuia, Rio- [Braz.] 55 Jc 16.08S 45.05W
Urucum, Serra do- 55 Dd 19.13S 57.33W
Urucurituba 54 Gd 2.41S 57.40W
Uruguai, Rio- 52 Ki 34.12S 58.18W
Uruguaiana 53 Kh 29.45S 57.05W
Uruguay [1] 53 Ki 33.00S 56.00W
Uruguay, Río- 52 Ki 34.12S 58.18W
Urukthapel 64a Ac 7.15N 134.24 E
Urumbaba Dağı 15 Lj 38.25N 28.49 E
Ürümqi 22 Ke 43.48N 87.35 E
Urup 16 Lg 44.59N 41.10 E
Urup, Ostrov- 21 Qe 46.00N 150.00 E
Uruša 20 Hf 54.03N 122.55 E
Urussu 7 Mi 54.38N 53.24 E
Uruwira 36 Fd 6.27S 31.21 E
Urville, Cape D'- (EN)= Perkam, Tanjung- 26 Kg 1.28S 137.54 E
Uryū 29a Bb 43.39N 141.51 E
Uryū-Gawa 29a Bb 43.40N 141.54 E
Urziceni 15 Je 44.43N 26.38 E
Uržum 19 Fd 57.10N 50.01 E
Usa 29 Be 33.31N 131.22 E
Usa [R.S.F.S.R.] 16 Nc 53.02N 45.18 E
Usa [R.S.F.S.R.] 5 Lb 65.57N 56.55 E
Uşak 23 Cb 38.41N 29.25 E
Usakos 37 Bd 22.01S 15.32 E
Ušakovo 20 Hf 51.54N 126.35 E
Ušakovskoje 20 Nb 71.00N 178.35W
Usambara Mountains 30 Ki 4.45S 38.30 E
Usarp Mountains 66 Jf 71.10S 160.00 E
Usas Escarpment 66 Nf 76.00S 125.00W
Ušba, Gora- 16 Mh 43.06N 42.40 E
Usborne, Mount- 56 Ih 51.42S 58.50W
Ušće 15 Df 43.29N 20.38 E
Usedom 10 Jb 54.00N 14.00 E
Useldange 12 He 49.46N 5.59 E
'Ushayrah [Sau. Ar.] 33 He 21.46N 40.38 E
'Ushayrah [Sau. Ar.] 24 Kj 25.35N 45.46 E
Ushibuka 29 Be 32.13N 130.01 E
Ushikubi-Misaki 29a Bc 41.08N 140.48 E
Ushimado 29 Dd 34.37N 134.09 E
'Ushsh, Wādī al- 24 Fd 27.18N 42.15 E
Ushuaia 53 Jk 54.47S 68.20W
Usingen 12 Kd 50.20N 8.32 E
Usinsk 19 Fb 65.57N 57.29 E
Usküdar 24 Cb 41.01N 29.03 E
Üsküp 15 Kh 41.44N 27.24 E
Uslar 10 Fe 51.40N 9.39 E
Úslava 10 Jg 49.54N 13.32 E
Usman 16 Kd 51.54N 39.20 E
Usman 19 De 52.00N 39.43 E
Usmas, Ozero-/Usmas Ezers 8 Ig 57.13N 22.00 E
Usmas Ezers/Usmas, Ozero- 8 Ig 57.13N 22.00 E
Usogorsk 19 Ec 63.28N 48.35 E
Usoke 36 Fd 5.06S 32.20 E
Usolje 19 Fd 59.25N 56.41 E
Usolje-Sibirskoje 20 Ff 52.47N 103.38 E
Usora 14 Mf 44.43N 18.04 E
Ussel 11 Ii 45.33N 2.19 E
USSR (EN)=Sojuz Sovetskih Socialističeskih Respublik [1] 22 Jd 60.00N 80.00 E
Ussuri 21 Pe 48.28N 135.02 E
Ussurijsk 22 Pe 43.48N 131.59 E
Usta 7 Kh 56.53N 45.28 E
Ust-Barguzin 20 Ff 53.27N 108.59 E
Ust-Bolšereck 20 Kf 52.40N 156.18 E
Ust-Cilma 19 Fb 65.27N 52.06 E
Ust-Čorna 10 Uh 48.17N 24.02 E
Ust-Donecki 16 Lf 47.39N 40.55 E
Ust-Džeguta 16 Mg 44.05N 42.01 E
Uster 14 Cc 47.20N 8.43 E
Ustevatn 8 Bd 60.30N 8.00 E
Ust-Hajrjuzovo 20 Ke 57.04N 156.50 E
Ustica 5 Hh 38.40N 13.10 E
Ustica 14 Hl 38.42N 13.11 E
Ust-Ilimsk 22 Md 58.03N 102.43 E
Ustilug 10 Uf 50.50N 24.09 E
Ústí nad Labem 10 Kf 50.40N 14.02 E
Ústí nad Orlicí 10 Mg 49.58N 16.24 E
Ust-Išim 19 Hd 57.44N 71.10 E
Ustja 19 Ec 61.33N 42.36 E
Ust-Judoma 20 Ie 59.10N 135.02 E
Ustjurt, Plato 21 He 43.00N 56.00 E
Ustjužna 7 Ig 58.53N 36.28 E
Ustka 10 Mb 54.35N 16.50 E
Ust-Kamčatsk 22 Sd 56.15N 162.30 E
Ust-Kamenogorsk 22 Ke 49.58N 82.38 E
Ust-Kan 20 Df 50.57N 84.55 E
Ust-Kara 19 Gb 69.15N 64.59 E
Ust-Karsk 20 Gf 52.41N 118.45 E
Ust-Katav 17 Ii 54.56N 58.10 E
Ust-Kujga 22 Pc 70.00N 135.36 E
Ust-Kut 22 Md 56.46N 105.40 E
Ust-Labinsk 19 Df 45.13N 39.40 E
Ust-Luga 7 Gg 59.39N 28.15 E
Ust-Maya 22 Pc 60.25N 134.32 E
Ust-Muja 20 Ge 56.28N 115.30 E
Ust-Nera 22 Qc 64.34N 143.12 E
Ust-Njukža 20 He 56.30N 121.48 E
Uštobe 19 Hf 45.13N 77.59 E
Ust-Olenëk 20 Gb 72.58N 119.42 E
Ust-Omčug 20 Jd 61.05N 149.30 E
Ust-Ordynski 20 Ff 52.48N 104.45 E
Ust-Ordynski Burjatski Nacionalny okrug [3] 20 Ff 53.30N 104.00 E
Ustovo 15 Hh 41.34N 24.47 E
Ust-Pinega 7 Jd 64.10N 41.58 E
Ust-Pit 20 Ee 58.59N 92.00 E
Ust-Port 20 Dc 69.45N 84.25 E
Ust-Požva 17 Hg 59.05N 56.05 E
Ustrzyki Dolne 10 Sg 49.26N 22.37 E
Ust-Sobolevka 20 Ig 46.10N 137.59 E
Ust-Šonoša 7 Jf 61.11N 41.20 E
Ust-Uda 20 Ff 54.10N 103.03 E
Ust-Ujskoje 17 Ki 54.15N 63.57 E
Ust-Umalta 20 If 51.42N 133.18 E
Ustupo 49 Ii 9.08N 77.56W
Usú 22 Ke 44.27N 84.37 E
Usui-Tōge 29 Fc 36.22N 138.38 E
Usuki 28 Kh 33.08N 131.49 E
Usuki-Wan 29 Be 33.10N 131.50 E
Usulután 49 Cg 13.21N 88.27W
Usumacinta 38 Jh 18.22N 92.40W
Ušumun 20 Hf 52.46N 126.37 E
Usu-San 29a Bb 42.32N 140.49 E
Usva 17 Hg 58.40N 57.35 E
Usva 17 Hg 58.17N 57.47 E
Utah [2] 43 Ed 39.30N 111.30W
Utah Lake 43 Ec 40.13N 111.49W
Utajärvi 7 Gd 64.45N 26.23 E
Utashinai 29a Cb 43.31N 142.03 E
Utata 20 Ff 50.51N 102.45 E
Ute Creek 45 Ei 35.21N 103.50W
Utembo 30 Jj 17.06S 22.01 E
Utena 7 Fi 55.29N 25.40 E
Ute Reservoir 45 Ei 35.21N 103.31W
Utete 36 Gd 7.59S 38.47 E
Uthai Thani 25 Ke 15.20N 100.02 E
Utiariti 55 Ca 13.02S 58.17W
Utica 43 Lc 43.06N 75.15W
Utiel 13 Ke 39.34N 1.12W
Utiel, Sierra de- 13 Ke 39.36N 1.08W
Utila 49 De 16.06N 86.54W
Utila, Isla de- 49 De 16.06N 86.56W
Utique 14 Em 37.04N 10.04 E
Utirik Atoll 57 Hc 11.15N 169.48 E
Utlängan 8 Fh 56.00N 15.45 E
Utljukski Liman 16 If 46.20N 35.15 E
Uto 28 Kh 32.40N 130.41 E
Utö [Fin.] 8 Ie 59.45N 21.25 E
Utö [Swe.] 7 Eg 58.55N 18.15 E
Utoro 29a Da 44.06N 144.58 E
Utrata 10 Qd 52.13N 20.15 E
Utrecht [3] 12 Hb 52.05N 5.08 E
Utrecht [Neth.] 6 Ge 52.05N 5.08 E
Utrecht [S.Afr.] 37 Ee 27.28S 30.20 E
Utrera 13 Gg 37.11N 5.47W
Utsira 8 Ae 59.20N 4.55 E
Utsjoki 7 Gb 69.53N 27.00 E
Utsunomiya 22 Pf 36.33N 139.52 E
Uttaradit 25 Ke 17.38N 100.06 E
Uttar Pradesh [3] 25 Fc 28.00N 80.00 E
Utuado 49 Nd 18.16N 66.42W
Utukok 40 Gb 70.04N 162.18W
Utuloa 64h Ab 13.16S 176.11W
Utupua Island 57 Hf 11.20S 166.36 E
Uturoa 65e Db 16.44S 151.26W
Utva 16 Rd 51.29N 52.40 E
Uudenmaa [2] 7 Ff 60.30N 25.00 E
Uukuniemi 8 Nc 61.47N 30.01 E
Uulu/Ulu 8 Kf 58.13N 24.29 E
Uusikaupunki/Nystad 7 Ef 60.48N 21.25 E
Uusimaa 8 Kd 60.30N 25.00 E
Uva 19 Fd 56.58N 52.14 E
Uvac 15 Cf 43.36N 19.30 E
Uvalde 43 Hf 29.13N 99.47W
Uvarovo 19 Ee 52.00N 42.15 E
Uvdal 8 Cd 60.20N 8.30 E
Uvéa, Ile- 57 Jf 13.18S 176.10W
Uvelka 17 Ji 54.05N 61.35 E
Uvelski 17 Ji 54.26N 61.27 E
Uvildy, Ozero- 17 Ji 55.35N 60.30 E
Uvinza 36 Fd 5.06S 30.22 E
Uvira 31 Ji 3.24S 29.08 E
Uvs nuur→Ubsu-Nur 21 Ld 50.20N 92.45 E
Uwa 29 Ce 33.21N 132.30 E
Uwajima 27 Ne 33.13N 132.34 E
Uwajima-Wan 29 Ce 33.15N 132.30 E
Uwa-Kai 29 Ce 33.20N 132.15 E
Uwayl 35 Dd 8.46N 27.24 E
'Uwaynāt, Jabal al-= Uweinat, Gebel- (EN) 30 Jf 21.54N 24.58 E
'Uwaynat Wannīn 33 Bd 28.05N 12.59 E
Uweinat, Gebel- (EN)= 'Uwaynāt, Jabal al- 30 Jf 21.54N 24.58 E
Uwekuli 26 Hg 1.25S 121.06 E
Uwi, Pulau- 26 Ef 1.05N 107.24 E
Uxin Qi (Dabqig) 27 Id 38.27N 109.08 E
Uxmal 39 Kg 20.20N 89.46W
Uyo 34 Gd 5.07N 7.57 E
Uyuni 53 Jh 20.28S 66.50W
Uyuni, Salar de- 52 Jh 20.20S 67.42W
Už [Eur.] 10 Rh 48.33N 22.00 E
Už [Ukr.-U.S.S.R.] 16 Gd 51.15N 30.12 E
Uza 8 Mg 57.47N 29.38 E
Uzbekiston Sovet Socialistik Respublikasy/Uzbekskaja SSR [2] 19 Gg 41.00N 64.00 E
Uzbekskaja Sovetskaja Socialističeskaja Respublika [2] 19 Gg 41.00N 64.00 E
Uzbekskaja SSR/Uzbekiston Sovet Socialistik Respublikasy [2] 19 Gg 41.00N 64.00 E
Uzbekskaja SSR=Uzbek SSR (EN) [2] 19 Gg 41.00N 64.00 E
Uzbek SSR (EN)= Uzbekskaja SSR [2] 19 Gg 41.00N 64.00 E
Uzbel Shankou 27 Bd 38.42N 73.48 E
Uzen 19 Fg 43.22N 52.50 E
Uzerche 11 Hi 45.25N 1.34 E
Uzès 11 Kj 44.01N 4.25 E
Uzgen 18 Id 40.44N 73.21 E
Užgorod 19 Cf 48.37N 22.22 E
Uzin 16 Ge 49.52N 30.27 E
Uzlovaja 16 Kb 54.01N 38.12 E
Uzlovoje 10 Sh 48.23N 22.27 E
Užokski, pereval- 16 Ce 49.02N 22.58 E
Uzümlü 15 Mm 36.44N 29.14 E
Uzun Ada 15 Jk 38.28N 26.42 E
Uzunagač [Kaz.-U.S.S.R.] 18 Kc 43.08N 76.20 E
Uzunagač [Kaz.-U.S.S.R.] 18 Kc 43.36N 76.19 E
Uzunköprü 24 Bb 41.16N 26.41 E
Užur 20 De 55.20N 90.00 E
Užventis 8 Ji 55.44N 22.37 E
Uzynkair, Mys- 18 Bb 45.47N 59.20 E

V

Vääksy 8 Kc 61.11N 25.33 E
Vaal 30 Jk 29.24S 23.38 E
Vaala 7 Gd 64.34N 26.50 E
Vaals 12 Id 50.46N 6.01 E
Vaalwater 37 Dd 24.20S 28.03 E
Vaasa [2] 7 Fe 63.12N 23.00 E
Vaasa/Vasa 6 Ic 63.06N 21.36 E
Vaassen, Epe- 12 Hb 52.17N 5.58 E
Vabalninkas 8 Ki 55.58N 24.49 E
Vác 10 Pi 47.47N 19.08 E
Vacacaí, Rio- 55 Fi 29.55S 53.06W
Vacaria 56 Jc 28.30S 50.56W
Vacaria, Rio- 55 Fe 21.55S 53.59W
Vacaville 46 Eg 38.21N 121.59W
Vaccarès, Étang de- 11 Kk 43.32N 4.34 E
Vache, Ile à- 49 Kd 18.04N 73.38W
Väddö 8 Hd 60.00N 18.50 E
Vadehavet 8 Ci 55.15N 8.40 E
Vădeni 15 Kd 45.22N 27.56 E
Vadheim 8 Ac 61.13N 5.49 E
Vadodara 22 Jg 22.18N 73.12 E
Vado Ligure 14 Cf 44.17N 8.27 E
Vadsø 6 Ia 70.05N 29.46 E
Vadstena 7 Dg 58.27N 14.54 E
Vaduz 6 Gf 47.08N 9.30 E
Værlandet 8 Ac 61.20N 4.45 E
Vaga 5 Kc 62.48N 42.56 E
Vagaj 17 Mh 56.28N 67.18 E
Vagaj 17 Nh 57.55N 69.01 E
Vågåmo 7 Bf 61.53N 9.06 E
Vaganjski vrh 14 Jf 44.21N 15.30 E
Vågåvatn 8 Cc 61.50N 8.50 E
Vaggeryd 7 Dh 57.30N 14.07 E
Vaghena 63a Cb 7.25S 157.43 E
Vagil 17 Kg 59.45N 62.40 E
Vagis, Gora- 20 Jf 52.20N 142.15 E
Vagnhärad 8 Gf 58.57N 17.31 E
Vågsøy 8 Ac 62.00N 5.05 E
Váh 10 Ni 47.55N 18.00 E
Vah 21 Jc 60.45N 76.45 E
Vahitahi Atoll 57 Nf 18.44S 138.52W
Vahruši 7 Mg 58.43N 50.02 E
Vahš 18 Gf 37.43N 68.49 E
Vahsel Bay→Herzog-Ernst-Bucht 66 Af 77.48S 34.39W
Vahtan 7 Lh 57.59N 46.42 E
Vaïaau 65e Db 16.52S 151.28W
Vaigat 41 Gd 70.30N 54.00W
Vaihingen an der Enz 12 Kf 48.56N 8.58 E
Vaihú 65d Ab 27.10S 109.23W
Väike-Maarja/Vjaike-Maarja 8 Le 59.04N 26.12 E
Väike-Pakri/Vjajke-Pakri 8 Je 59.50N 23.50 E
Väike Väin/Vjajke-Vjajn 8 Jf 58.30N 23.10 E
Vailala 64h Bb 13.13S 176.09W
Vailala, Pointe- 64h Ab 13.13S 176.10W
Vaileka 63d Bb 17.23S 178.09 E
Vailheu, Récif- 37 Gb 11.48S 43.04 E
Vailly-sur-Aisne 12 Fe 49.25N 3.31 E
Vainikkala 8 Md 60.52N 28.18 E
Vainode/Vajnëde 8 Ih 56.26N 21.45 E
Vairaatea Atoll 57 Nf 19.19S 139.20W
Vaison-la-Romaine 11 Lj 44.14N 5.04 E
Vaïtape 65e Db 16.31S 151.45W
Vaïtoare 65e Db 16.41S 151.28W
Vaitupu Island 57 Ie 7.28S 178.41 E
Vajgač, Ostrov- 5 La 70.00N 59.30 E
Vajnëde/Vainode 8 Ih 56.26N 21.45 E
Vakaga [3] 35 Cd 10.00N 23.30 E
Vakfıkebir 24 Hb 41.03N 39.20 E
Vaksdal 8 Ad 60.29N 5.44 E
Val 20 Jf 52.19N 143.09 E
Vala 7 Mh 56.59N 51.16 E
Valaam 7 Hf 61.24N 30.59 E
Valaam, Ostrov- 8 Nc 61.20N 31.05 E
Valahia = Walachia (EN) 15 He 44.00N 25.00 E
Valahia = Walachia (EN) 5 Ig 44.00N 25.00 E
Valais [2] 14 Bd 46.15N 7.30 E
Valamares, Mali i- 15 Di 40.47N 20.28 E
Valamaz 7 Mh 57.36N 52.14 E
Valandovo 15 Fh 41.19N 22.34 E
Valašské Meziříčí 10 Ng 49.29N 17.58 E
Valáxa 15 Hk 38.49N 24.29 E
Vålberg 8 Ee 59.24N 13.12 E
Valburg 12 Hc 51.55N 5.49 E
Valcabra 13 Jg 37.30N 2.43W
Vălčedrăm 15 Gf 43.42N 23.27 E
Valcheta 56 Gf 40.42S 66.09W
Valdagno 14 Fe 45.39N 11.18 E
Valdahon 11 Mg 47.09N 6.21 E
Valdai Hills (EN)= Valdajskaja Vozvyšennost 5 Jd 57.00N 33.30 E
Valdaj 19 Dd 57.59N 33.14 E
Valdajskaja Vozvyšennost= Valdai Hills (EN) 5 Jd 57.00N 33.30 E
Valdarno 14 Fg 43.45N 11.15 E
Valdavia 13 Hb 42.24N 4.16W
Valdecañas, Embalse de- 13 Ge 39.45N 5.30W
Valdeganga 13 Ke 39.09N 1.40W
Val-de-Marne [3] 11 If 48.47N 2.29 E
Valdemārpils/Valdemarpils 7 Fh 57.24N 22.39 E
Valdemarpils/Valdemārpils 7 Fh 57.24N 22.39 E
Valdemarsvik 7 Dg 58.12N 16.32 E
Valdepeñas 13 If 38.46N 3.23W
Valderaduey 13 Gc 41.31N 5.42W
Valderas 13 Gb 42.05N 5.27W
Valderrama, Cienaga de- 49 Ki 8.56N 72.10W
Valderrobres/Vall-de-roures 13 Ld 40.53N 0.09W
Valdés, Península- 52 Jj 42.30S 64.00W
Valdez 39 Ec 61.07N 146.16W
Val d'Isère 11 Mi 45.27N 6.59 E
Valdivia 53 Ii 39.48S 73.14W
Valdivia Seamount (EN) 30 Hk 25.20S 6.15 E
Valdobbiadene 14 Fe 45.54N 12.00 E
Val-d'Oise [3] 11 Ie 49.10N 2.10 E
Val-d'Or 39 Le 48.07N 77.47W
Valdosta 39 Kf 30.50N 83.17W
Valdres 8 Cc 60.55N 9.10 E
Vale [Geo.-U.S.S.R.] 16 Mi 41.36N 42.51 E
Vale [Or.-U.S.] 46 Gd 44.01N 117.15W
Valea Ierii 15 Gc 46.39N 23.21 E
Valea lui Mihai 15 Fb 47.31N 22.09 E
Valea Vişeului 15 Hb 47.51N 24.10 E
Valença [Braz.] 55 Kf 22.15S 43.43W
Valença [Braz.] 54 Kf 13.22S 39.05W
Valença do Minho 13 Db 42.02N 8.38W
Valença do Piauí 54 Je 6.24S 41.45W
Valençay 11 Hg 47.09N 1.34 E
Valence [Fr.] 11 Gj 44.06N 0.55 E
Valence [Fr.] 11 Kj 44.56N 4.54 E
Valencia 6 Fh 39.28N 0.22W
Valencia [3] 13 Le 39.20N 0.50W
Valencia 13 Le 39.30N 0.40W
València/Valencia 6 Fh 39.28N 0.22W
Valencia/València 6 Fh 39.28N 0.22W
València, Golf de-/Valencia, Golfo de- 5 Fh 39.30N 0.00
Valencia, Golfo de-/ València, Golf de- 5 Fh 39.30N 0.00
Valencia, Lago de- 50 Cg 10.11N 67.45W
Valencia de Alcántara 13 Ee 39.25N 7.14W
Valencia de Don Juan 13 Gb 42.18N 5.31W
Valencia-El Grao 13 Le 39.27N 0.20W
Valenciennes 11 Jd 50.21N 3.32 E
Vălenii de Munte 15 Jd 45.11N 26.02 E
Valentia/Dairbhre 9 Cj 51.55N 10.20W
Valentin 28 Mc 43.07N 134.19 E
Valentine 43 Gc 42.52N 100.33W
Valenza 14 Ce 45.01N 8.38 E
Våler 7 Cf 60.40N 11.50 E
Valera 54 Db 9.19N 70.37W
Valerie Seamount (EN) 57 Ki 42.00S 163.30W
Valga 19 Cd 57.49N 26.05 E
Valge Jõgi 8 Ke 59.32N 25.36 E
Valhalla Mountains 46 Gb 49.45N 117.48W
Valiente, Península- 49 Gi 9.05N 81.51W
Valier 46 Ib 48.18N 112.15W
Valinco, Golfe de- 11a Ab 41.40N 8.49 E
Valjevo 15 Ce 44.16N 19.53 E
Valka 7 Gh 57.47N 26.01 E
Valkeakoski 7 Ff 61.16N 24.02 E
Valkeala 8 Ld 60.57N 26.48 E
Valkenswaard 12 Hc 51.21N 5.28 E
Valkininkai/Valkininkaj 8 Kj 54.18N 25.55 E
Valkininkaj/Valkininkai 8 Kj 54.18N 25.55 E
Valko/Valkom 8 Ld 60.25N 26.15 E
Valkom/Valko 8 Ld 60.25N 26.15 E
Valkumej 20 Mc 69.41N 170.30 E
Valladolid [3] 13 Hc 41.35N 4.40W
Valladolid [Mex.] 47 Gd 20.41N 88.12W
Valladolid [Sp.] 6 Fg 41.39N 4.43W
Valldal 8 Bb 62.20N 7.21 E
Vall-de-Roures/Valderrobres 13 Ld 40.53N 0.09W
Vall de Uxó 13 Le 39.49N 0.14W
Valle [2] 54 Cc 3.40N 76.30W
Valle [3] 49 Dg 13.30N 87.35W
Valle 7 Bg 59.12N 7.32 E
Vallecas, Madrid- 13 Id 40.23N 3.37W
Valle d'Aosta / Vallée d'Aoste [2] 14 Be 45.45N 7.15 E
Valle de Cabuerniga 13 Ha 43.14N 4.18W
Valle de Guanape 50 Dh 9.54N 65.41W
Valle dei Templi 14 Hm 37.18N 13.35 E
Valle de la Pascua 54 Eb 9.13N 66.00W
Valle de Santiago 48 Ig 20.23N 101.12W
Valle de Topia 48 Fe 25.13N 106.25W
Valle de Zaragoza 48 Gd 27.28N 105.49W
Valledupar 54 Da 10.28N 73.15W
Vallée d'Aoste / Valle d'Aosta [2] 14 Be 45.45N 7.15 E
Vallée Jonction 44 Lb 46.23N 70.55W
Valle Hermoso 48 Ke 25.39N 97.52W
Vallejera, Puerto de- 13 Gd 40.30N 5.42W
Vallejo 43 Cd 38.07N 122.14W
Vallejo, Sierra de- 48 Gg 20.55N 105.20W
Valle Nacional 48 Ki 17.47N 96.19W
Vallenar 53 Ih 28.35S 70.46W
Vallentuna 8 He 59.32N 18.05 E
Valles/El Valles 13 Oc 41.35N 2.15 E
Valles de los Daidos 13 Hd 40.39N 4.09W
Valletta 6 Hh 35.54N 14.31 E
Valley City 43 Hb 46.55N 97.59W
Valley Falls 46 Ee 42.31N 120.15W
Valleyfield 42 Kg 45.15N 74.08W
Valley Station 44 Ef 38.06N 85.52W
Valleyview 42 Fe 55.02N 117.08W
Vallgrund 7 Ee 63.12N 21.14 E
Vallhagar 8 Hg 57.20N 18.10 E
Vallimanca 55 Bm 36.21S 61.02W
Vallimanca, Arroyo- 55 Bl 35.40S 60.02W
Vallo della Lucania 14 Jj 40.14N 15.16 E
Valloires, Abbaye de- 12 Dd 50.20N 1.47 E
Vallorbe 14 Ad 46.43N 6.23 E
Valls 13 Nc 41.17N 1.15 E
Valls d'Andorra → Andorra [1] 6 Gg 42.30N 1.30 E
Vallsta 8 Gc 61.32N 16.22 E
Vallvik 8 Gc 61.11N 17.11 E
Valmaseda 13 Ia 43.12N 3.12W
Valmiera 19 Cd 57.32N 25.29 E
Valmont 12 Ce 49.44N 0.31 E
Valnera 13 Ia 43.10N 3.45W
Valognes 11 Ee 49.31N 1.28W
Valois, Plaine du- 11 Ie 49.10N 2.45 E
Valoria la Buena 13 Hc 41.48N 4.32W
Valpaços 13 Ec 41.36N 7.19W
Valparaiso 44 De 41.28N 87.03W
Valparaíso [Braz.] 55 Ge 21.13S 50.51W
Valparaíso [Chile] 53 Ii 33.02S 71.38W
Valparaíso [Mex.] 48 Hf 22.46N 103.34W
Valpovo 14 Me 45.39N 18.25 E
Valréas 11 Kj 44.23N 4.59 E
Vals 30 Jk 27.23S 26.31 E
Vals, Tanjung- 26 Kh 8.26S 137.38 E
Valsjöbyn 7 Dd 64.04N 14.08 E
Valtellina 14 Dd 46.10N 9.55 E
Valtimo 7 Ge 63.40N 28.48 E
Váltou, Óri- 15 Ej 39.10N 21.20 E
Valujki 19 De 50.12N 38.08 E
Valul-Lui Traian 15 Le 44.15N 28.30 E
Valverde 32 Dd 27.48N 17.55W
Valverde de Júcar 13 Je 39.43N 2.12W
Valverde del Camino 13 Fg 37.34N 6.45W
Valverde del Fresno 13 Ff 40.13N 6.52W
Vamdrup 8 Ci 55.25N 9.17 E
Våmhus 7 Df 61.08N 14.28 E
Vamizi, Ilha- 37 Gb 11.02S 40.40 E
Vammala 7 Ff 61.20N 22.54 E
Vámos 15 Hn 35.25N 24.12 E
Van 23 Fb 38.28N 43.20 E
Van, Lake- (EN)=Van Gölü 21 Gf 38.33N 42.46 E
Vanajanselkä 7 Ff 61.09N 24.15 E
Vanak 24 Ng 31.41N 50.52 E
Vanak 24 Ng 31.32N 51.19 E
Vanån 8 Fd 60.31N 14.14 E
Vanault-les-Dames 12 Gf 48.51N 4.46 E
Vanavana Atoll 57 Ng 20.47S 139.09W
Vanavara 20 Fd 60.22N 102.16 E
Van Buren [Ar.-U.S.] 45 Ii 35.26N 94.21W
Van Buren [Me.-U.S.] 44 Nb 47.09N 67.56W
Vanč 18 He 38.23N 71.29 E
Vanceburg 44 Ff 38.36N 83.19W
Vancouver [B.C.-Can.] 39 Ge 49.16N 123.07W
Vancouver [Wa.-U.S.] 43 Cb 45.39N 122.40W
Vancouver Island 38 Ge 49.45N 126.00W
Vandalia [Il.-U.S.] 45 Lg 38.58N 89.06W
Vandalia [Oh.-U.S.] 44 Ef 39.53N 84.12W
Vanderbijl Park 37 De 26.42S 27.54 E
Vanderhoof 42 Ff 54.01N 124.01W
Vanderlin Island 59 Hc 15.45S 137.00 E
Van Diemen, Cape- 59 Gb 11.10S 130.25 E
Van Diemen Gulf 59 Gb 11.50S 132.00 E
Vandmtor, Ozero- 17 Le 62.15N 65.45 E
Vändra/Vjandra 7 Fg 58.40N 25.01 E
Vänern 5 Hd 58.55N 13.30 E
Vänersborg 7 Cg 58.22N 12.19 E

Index Symbols

[1] Independent Nation
[2] State, Region
[3] District, County
[4] Municipality
[5] Colony, Dependency
Continent
Physical Region
Historical or Cultural Region
Mount, Mountain
Volcano
Hill
Mountains, Mountain Range
Hills, Escarpment
Plateau, Upland
Pass, Gap
Plain, Lowland
Delta
Salt Flat
Valley, Canyon
Crater, Cave
Karst Features
Depression
Polder
Desert, Dunes
Forest, Woods
Heath, Steppe
Oasis
Cape, Point
Coast, Beach
Cliff
Peninsula
Isthmus
Sandbank
Island
Atoll
Rock, Reef
Islands, Archipelago
Rocks, Reefs
Coral Reef
Well, Spring
Geyser
River, Stream
Waterfall Rapids
River Mouth, Estuary
Lake
Salt Lake
Intermittent Lake
Reservoir
Swamp, Pond
Canal
Glacier
Ice Shelf, Pack Ice
Ocean
Sea
Gulf, Bay
Strait, Fjord
Lagoon
Bank
Seamount
Tablemount
Ridge
Shelf
Basin
Escarpment, Sea Scarp
Fracture
Trench, Abyss
National Park, Reserve
Point of Interest
Recreation Site
Cave, Cavern
Historic Site
Ruins
Wall, Walls
Church, Abbey
Temple
Scientific Station
Airport
Port
Lighthouse
Mine
Tunnel
Dam, Bridge

Vang 8 Cc 61.08N 8.35 E
Vangaindrano 37 Hd 23.23S 47.33 E
Van Gölü=Van, Lake- (EN) 21 Gf 38.33N 42.46 E
Vangunu Island 57 Ge 8.40S 158.05 E
Van Horn 43 Ge 31.03N 104.50W
Vanick, Rio- 55 Fa 13.06S 52.52W
Vanier 42 Ha 76.00N 103.50W
Vanikolo 63c Bb 11.37S 166.58 E
Vanikolo Islands 57 Hf 11.37S 167.03 E
Vanimo 60 Ch 2.40S 141.18 E
Vanino 20 Jg 49.11N 140.19 E
Vankavesi 8 Jc 61.50N 23.50 E
Vanna 7 Ea 70.09N 19.51 E
Vännäs 7 Ee 63.55N 19.45 E
Vanne 11 Jf 48.12N 3.16 E
Vannes 11 Dg 47.40N 2.45W
Van Ninh 25 Lf 12.42N 109.14 E
Vannsjø 8 De 59.25N 10.50 E
Vanoise, Massif de la- 11 Mi 45.20N 6.40 E
Vanona Lava, Ile- 57 Hf 14.00S 167.30 E
Van Phong, Vung- 25 Lf 12.33N 109.18 E
Van Rees, Pegunungan- 26 Kg 2.35S 138.15 E
Vanrhynsdorp 37 Bf 31.36S 18.44 E
Vansbro 7 Df 60.31N 14.13 E
Vanse 8 Bf 58.07N 6.42 E
Vansittart 42 Jc 65.50N 84.00W
Vantaa 8 Kd 60.13N 24.59 E
Vänte Litets grund 8 Hb 62.35N 18.12 E
Vanua Levu 57 If 17.28S 177.03 E
Vanua Mbalavu 61 Fc 17.14S 178.57W
Vanuatu [1] 58 Hf 16.00S 167.00 E
Vanua Vatu 63d Cc 18.22S 179.16W
Van Wert 44 Ee 40.53N 84.36W
Van Wyksvlei 37 Cf 30.18S 21.49 E
Vanzylsrus 37 Ce 26.52S 22.04 E
Vao 63b Cf 22.40S 167.29 E
Vao, Nosy- 37 Gc 17.30S 43.45 E
Vão das Almas 55 Ia 13.42S 47.27W
Vapnjarka 16 Fe 48.32N 28.46 E
Var [3] 11 Mk 43.30N 6.20 E
Var 11 Nk 43.39N 7.12 E
Vara 14 Df 44.09N 9.53 E
Vara 8 Ef 58.16N 12.57 E
Varaita 14 Bf 44.49N 7.36 E
Varaklāni/Varakljany 7 Gh 56.36N 26.48 E
Varakljany/Varaklāni 7 Gh 56.36N 26.48 E
Varaldsøy 8 Ad 60.10N 6.00 E
Varalé 34 Ed 9.40N 3.17W
Varallo 14 Ce 45.49N 8.15 E
Varāmīn 24 Ne 35.20N 51.39 E
Vārānasi (Benares) 22 Kg 25.20N 83.00 E
Varangerfjorden 5 Ia 70.00N 30.00 E
Varangerhalvøya=Varanger Peninsula (EN) 5 Ia 70.25N 29.30 E
Varanger Peninsula (EN)= Varangerhalvøya 5 Ia 70.25N 29.30 E
Varano, Lago di- 14 Ji 41.53N 15.45 E
Varāvī 24 Oi 27.25N 53.06 E
Varaždin 14 Kd 46.18N 16.20 E
Varazze 14 Cf 44.22N 8.34 E
Varberg 7 Ch 57.06N 12.15 E
Vardak [3] 23 Kc 34.15N 68.00 E
Vardar 5 Ig 40.35N 22.50 E
Varde 7 Bi 55.38N 8.29 E
Varde Å 8 Ci 55.35N 8.20 E
Vardhoúsia Óri 15 Fk 38.40N 22.10 E
Vårdö 8 Id 60.15N 20.20 E
Vardø 7 Ha 70.22N 31.06 E
Varel 10 Ec 53.24N 8.08 E
Varéna/Varena 7 Fi 54.15N 24.39 E
Varena/Varéna 7 Fi 54.15N 24.39 E
Värend 8 Fh 56.45N 14.55 E
Varengeville-sur-Mer 12 Ce 49.55N 0.59 E
Varenikovskaja 16 Jg 45.06N 37.37 E
Varenne 11 Ff 48.24N 0.39W
Varennes-en-Argonne 12 He 49.14N 5.02 E
Varennes-sur-Allier 11 Jh 46.19N 3.24 E
Vareš 14 Mf 44.10N 18.20 E
Varese 14 Ce 45.48N 8.50 E
Varese, Lago di- 14 Ce 45.50N 8.45 E
Vårgårda 8 Ef 58.02N 12.48 E
Vargaši 19 Gd 55.23N 65.48 E
Vargem Grande 54 Jd 3.33S 43.56W
Varginha 54 Ih 21.33S 45.26W
Vargön 8 Ef 58.21N 12.22 E
Varhaug 8 Af 58.37N 5.39 E
Varjão 55 Hc 17.03S 49.37W
Varkaus 6 Ic 62.19N 27.55 E
Värmdö 8 He 59.20N 18.35 E
Värmeln 8 Ee 59.30N 12.55 E
Värmland 8 Ee 59.50N 13.05 E
Värmland [2] 7 Cg 59.45N 13.15 E
Värmlandsnäs 8 Ee 59.00N 13.10 E
Varna [2] 15 Kf 43.10N 27.35 E
Varna [Bul.] 6 Ig 43.13N 27.55 E
Varna [R.S.F.S.R.] 17 Jj 53.24N 60.58 E
Värnamo 7 Dh 57.11N 14.02 E
Varnenski Zaliv 15 Kf 43.11N 27.56 E
Varniai/Varnjaj 8 Ji 55.44N 22.17 E
Varnjaj/Varniai 8 Ji 55.44N 22.17 E
Varnsdorf 10 Kf 50.54N 14.38 E
Várpalota 10 Oi 47.12N 18.08 E
Varšec 15 Gf 43.12N 23.17 E
Varsinais-Suomi/Egentliga Finland 8 Jd 60.40N 22.30 E
Värska 8 Lg 57.58N 27.38 E
Vartašen 16 Oi 41.05N 47.29 E
Varto 24 Ic 39.10N 41.28 E
Vartofta 8 Ef 58.06N 13.38 E
Värtsilä 8 Nb 62.15N 30.40 E
Varzaneh 24 Of 32.25N 52.39 E
Varzaqān 24 Lc 38.31N 46.39 E
Varzarīn, Kūh-e- 23 Gc 33.24N 46.48 E
Várzea, Rio da- 55 Fh 27.13S 53.19W
Várzea da Palma 55 Jc 17.36S 44.44W
Varzea Grande 54 Gg 15.39S 56.08W
Varzelândia 55 Jb 15.42S 44.02W
Varzi 14 Df 44.49N 9.12 E
Varzuga 7 Ic 66.17N 36.50 E
Varzy 11 Jg 47.22N 3.23 E
Vas [2] 10 Mi 47.10N 16.45 E
Vasa/Vaasa 6 Ic 63.06N 21.36 E
Vasai (Bassein) 25 Ee 19.21N 72.48 E
Vasalemma/Vazalemma 8 Ke 59.15N 24.11 E
Vásárosnamény 10 Sh 48.08N 22.19 E
Vascão 13 Eg 37.31N 7.31W
Vaşcău 15 Fc 46.28N 22.28 E
Vascoeuil 12 De 49.27N 1.23 E
Vascongadas/Euzkadi= Basque Provinces (EN) 13 Ja 43.00N 2.30W
Vascos, Montes- 13 Jb 42.50N 2.10W
Vasgün 24 Qe 34.55N 56.30 E
Vasileviči 16 Fc 52.14N 29.47 E
Vasiliká 15 Gi 40.28N 23.08 E
Vasiljevka 16 If 47.23N 35.18 E
Vasilkov 19 De 50.12N 30.22 E
Vasilkovka 16 Je 48.13N 36.03 E
Vasiss 19 Hd 57.30N 74.55 E
Vasjugan 20 De 59.10N 80.50 E
Vasjuganje 21 Jd 58.00N 77.00 E
Vaška 19 Ec 64.53N 45.47 E
Vaškovcy 15 Ia 48.16N 25.34 E
Vaslui 15 Kc 46.38N 27.44 E
Vaslui 15 Kc 46.37N 27.44 E
Vaslui [2] 15 Kc 46.41N 27.43 E
Väsman 8 Fd 60.11N 15.04 E
Vassako 35 Bd 8.36N 19.07 E
Vassdalsegga 7 Bg 59.46N 7.07 E
Vassy 12 Bf 48.51N 0.40W
Västeras 6 Hd 59.37N 16.33 E
Västerbotten [2] 7 Dd 64.58N 17.28 E
Västerdalälven 7 Df 60.33N 15.08 E
Västergötland 8 Eg 58.00N 13.05 E
Västerhaninge 8 He 59.07N 18.06 E
Västernorrland [2] 7 De 63.00N 17.30 E
Västervik 7 Dh 57.45N 16.38 E
Västmanland 8 Fe 59.40N 15.15 E
Västmanland [2] 7 Dg 59.45N 16.20 E
Vasto 14 Ih 42.07N 14.42 E
Västra Silen 8 Ee 59.15N 12.10 E
Vasvár 10 Mi 47.03N 16.48 E
Vatan 11 Hg 47.04N 1.49 E
Vatersay 9 Fe 56.53N 7.28W
Vatican City (EN) = Città del Vaticano [1] 6 Hg 41.54N 12.27 E
Vaticano, Capo- 14 Jl 38.37N 15.50 E
Vatilau 63a Ec 8.53S 160.01 E
Vatnajökull 5 Ec 64.24N 16.48W
Vatneyri 7a Ab 65.35N 24.00W
Vatoa Island 57 Jf 19.50S 178.13W
Vatomandry 37 Hc 19.20S 48.59 E
Vatra Dornei 15 Ib 47.21N 25.22 E
Vättern 5 Hd 58.25N 14.35 E
Vatu-i-Ra Channel 63d Bb 17.24S 178.29 E
Vatulele 63d Ac 18.33S 177.38 E
Vatutino 16 Ge 49.02N 31.09 E
Vatu Vara 61 Fc 17.26S 179.32W
Vaubecourt 12 Hf 48.56N 5.07 E
Vauclin, Pointe du- 51h Bb 14.34N 60.50W
Vaucluse [3] 11 Lj 44.00N 5.10 E
Vaucluse, Montagne du- 11 Lk 44.32N 5.11 E
Vaucouleurs 11 Lf 48.36N 5.40 E
Vaud [2] 14 Ad 46.35N 6.30 E
Vaudemont, Butte de- 11 Lf 48.25N 6.00 E
Vaughn 43 Fe 34.36N 105.13W
Vaupés [2] 54 Dc 1.00N 71.00W
Vaupés, Rio- 52 Je 0.02N 67.16W
Vauvilliers 63b Ce 21.09S 167.35 E
Vaux 12 Ge 49.31N 4.17 E
Vaux-le-Vicomte 11 If 48.34N 2.43 E
Vavatenina 37 Hc 17.26S 49.22 E
Vava'u Group 57 Jf 18.40S 174.00W
Vava'u Island 61 Gc 18.36S 174.00W
Vavoua 34 Dd 7.23N 6.29W
Vavuniya 25 Gg 8.45N 80.30 E
Vaxholm 8 He 59.24N 18.20 E
Växjö 6 Hd 56.53N 14.49 E
Vaza-Barris, Rio- 54 Kf 11.10S 37.10W
Vazalemma/Vasalemma 8 Ke 59.15N 24.11 E
Vazante 54 Ig 18.00S 46.54W
Vazuza 16 Ia 56.10N 34.35 E
Vding Skovhøj 8 Ch 56.01N 9.48 E
Veadeiros, Chapada dos- 54 If 14.05S 47.28W
Vecht 10 Cd 52.35N 6.05 E
Vechta 10 Ed 52.43N 8.17 E
Vechte 10 Cd 52.35N 6.05 E
Vecpiebalga 8 Kh 56.57N 25.50 E
Vecsés 10 Pi 47.24N 19.17 E
Vedavågen 8 Ae 59.19N 5.12 E
Veddige 8 Eg 57.16N 12.19 E
Vedea 15 He 44.47N 24.37 E
Vedea 15 Ie 43.59N 25.59 E
Vedeno 16 Oh 42.57N 46.05 E
Vedia 55 Bl 34.30S 61.32W
Vedrà Isla- 13 Nf 38.52N 1.12 E
Veendam 11 Ma 53.06N 6.58 E
Veenendaal 12 Hb 52.02N 5.35 E
Veere 12 Fc 51.33N 3.40 E
Vega 7 Cd 65.39N 11.50 E
Vega 45 Ei 35.15N 102.26W
Vega Baja 51a Bb 18.25N 66.23W
Veganj 14 Kg 43.50N 16.45 E
Vegår 8 Cf 58.48N 8.47 E
Vegårshei 8 Cf 58.46N 8.48 E
Veghel 12 Hc 51.37N 5.32 E
Veglie 14 Lj 40.20N 17.58 E
Vegorritis, Límni- 15 Ei 40.45N 21.48 E
Vègre 11 Fg 47.51N 0.14W
Vegreville 42 Gf 53.30N 112.03W
Vehmersalmi 8 Mb 62.46N 28.02 E
Vehnemoor 12 Ka 53.04N 8.02 E
Veinge 8 Eh 56.34N 13.05 E
Veinticinco de Mayo [Arg.] 56 He 35.26S 60.10W
Veinticinco de Mayo [Ur.] 55 Dl 34.12S 56.22W
Veio 14 Gh 42.02N 12.23 E
Veisiejai/Vejsejaj 8 Jj 54.03N 23.46 E
Vejen 7 Bi 55.29N 9.09 E
Vejer de la Frontera 13 Gh 36.15N 5.58W
Vejle [2] 8 Ci 55.45N 9.20 E
Vejle 7 Bi 55.42N 9.32 E
Vejsejaj/Veisiejai 8 Jj 54.03N 23.46 E
Vel 7 Kf 61.06N 42.10 E
Vela, Cabo de la- 49 Kg 12.13N 72.11W
Vela Luka 14 Kh 42.58N 16.44 E
Velas 32 Bb 38.41N 28.13W
Velas, Cabo- 49 Eh 10.22N 85.53W
Velásquez 55 El 34.02S 54.17W
Velay, Plateaux du- 11 Ji 45.10N 3.50 E
Velaz 55 Ch 26.42S 58.40W
Velbăždski prohod 15 Fg 42.14N 22.28 E
Velbert 10 De 51.20N 7.02 E
Velddrif 37 Bf 32.47S 18.10 E
Velden am Wörthersee 14 Id 46.37N 14.03 E
Veldhoven 12 Hc 51.24N 5.24 E
Velebit 5 Hg 44.17N 15.12 E
Velebitski kanal 14 If 44.45N 14.50 E
Veleka 15 Kg 42.04N 27.58 E
Velencei-tó 10 Oi 47.13N 18.36 E
Velenje 14 Jd 46.22N 15.07 E
Velestinon 15 Fj 39.23N 22.45 E
Veleta 13 Ig 37.04N 3.22W
Velež 14 Lg 43.20N 18.00 E
Vélez Blanco 13 Jg 37.41N 2.05W
Vélez de La Gomera, Peñón de- 13 Hi 35.11N 4.54W
Vélez-Málaga 13 Hh 36.47N 4.06W
Vélez Rubio 13 Jg 37.39N 2.04W
Velhas, Rio das- 52 Lg 17.13S 44.49W
Velika Gorica 14 Ke 45.44N 16.04 E
Velikaja 20 Md 64.35N 176.03 E
Velikaja-Gluša 10 Ve 51.49N 25.11 E
Velikaja Guba 7 Ie 62.17N 35.06 E
Velikaja Kema 20 Ig 45.29N 137.08 E
Velikaja Lepetiha 16 Hf 47.09N 33.59 E
Velikaja Mihajlovka 16 Ff 47.04N 29.52 E
Velika Kapela 14 Je 45.13N 15.02 E
Velika Kladuša 14 Je 45.11N 15.49 E
Velika Morava 15 Ee 44.43N 21.03 E
Velika Plana 15 Ee 44.20N 21.05 E
Veliki Berezny 10 Sh 48.54N 22.30 E
Veliki Byčkov 10 Ui 47.58N 24.04 E
Veliki Drvenik 14 Kg 43.27N 16.09 E
Veliki Jastrebac 15 Ef 43.24N 21.26 E
Velikije Luki 6 Jd 56.20N 30.32 E
Velikije Mosty 10 Uf 50.10N 24.12 E
Veliki kanal 15 Bd 45.52N 18.52 E
Veliki Ljuben 10 Tg 49.37N 23.45 E
Veliki Trnovac 15 Eg 42.29N 21.45 E
Veliki Ustjug 6 Kc 60.46N 46.20 E
Velikodolinskoje 15 Nc 46.20N 30.29 E
Veliko Gradište 15 Ee 44.46N 21.32 E
Veliko Târnovo [2] 15 If 43.04N 25.39 E
Veliko Târnovo 6 Ig 43.04N 25.39 E
Velikovisočnoje 19 Fb 67.16N 52.01 E
Veli Lošinj 14 If 44.31N 14.31 E
Vélingara 34 Cc 13.09N 14.07W
Velingrad 15 Gg 42.01N 24.00 E
Velino 14 Hh 42.09N 13.23 E
Velino 14 Gh 42.33N 12.43 E
Veliž 16 Gb 55.36N 31.12 E
Vel'ká Fatra 10 Ph 49.00N 19.05 E
Velké Meziříčí 10 Lg 49.21N 16.00 E
Vel'ký Krtiš 10 Ph 48.13N 19.20 E
Vella Lavella Island 57 Ge 7.45S 156.40 E
Velletri 14 Gi 41.41N 12.47 E
Vellinge 8 Ei 55.28N 13.01 E
Vellore 22 Jh 14.26N 79.58 E
Velmerstot 10 Ee 51.50N 9.00 E
Velmo 20 Ed 61.43N 92.25 E
Velopoúla 15 Gm 36.55N 23.28 E
Vels 17 If 60.45N 58.45 E
Velsen-IJmuiden [Neth.] 11 Kb 52.27N 4.39 E
Velsen-IJmuiden [Neth.] 12 Gb 52.28N 4.35 E
Velsk 19 Ec 61.05N 42.05 E
Veluwe 11 Lb 52.20N 5.50 E
Veluwemeer 12 Hb 52.23N 5.40 E
Velva 45 Fb 48.04N 100.56W
Velvendós 15 Fi 40.15N 22.04 E
Veman 8 Fb 62.02N 14.16 E
Vema Seamount (EN) 30 Hl 31.38S 8.19 E
Vemdalen 8 Eb 62.27N 13.52 E
Ven 8 Ei 55.55N 12.40 E
Venable Ice Shelf 66 Pf 73.03S 87.20W
Venado 48 If 22.56N 101.05W
Venado, Cerro- 50 Ei 6.17N 62.45W
Venado Tuerto 56 Hd 33.45S 61.58W
Venafro 14 Ii 41.29N 14.02 E
Venamo, Rio- 50 Fi 6.43N 61.07W
Vence 11 Nk 43.43N 7.07 E
Venceslau Brás 55 Hf 23.51S 49.48W
Venda 37 Ed 22.35S 30.45 E
Venda Nova 54 Jg 19.45S 43.50W
Vendas Novas 13 Df 38.41N 8.27W
Vendée [3] 11 Eh 46.40N 1.20W
Vendée 11 Hh 46.40N 1.10 E
Vendée 11 Fh 46.19N 0.58W
Vendéen, Bocage- 11 Eh 46.50N 1.20W
Vendéenne, Plaine- 11 Eh 46.40N 1.20W
Vendel 8 Gd 60.10N 17.36 E
Vendeuvre-sur-Barse 11 Kf 48.14N 4.29 E
Vendôme 11 Hg 47.48N 1.04 E
Vendrell/El Vendrell 13 Nc 41.13N 1.32 E
Vendsyssel 8 Cg 57.20N 10.00 E
Venetia (EN) = Veneto [2] 14 Fe 45.30N 12.00 E
Venétiko [Grc.] 15 Jk 38.08N 26.01 E
Venétiko [Grc.] 15 Em 36.42N 21.53 E
Veneto = Venetia (EN) [2] 14 Fe 45.30N 12.00 E
Venev 16 Kb 54.22N 38.18 E
Venezia = Venice (EN) 6 Hf 45.27N 12.21 E
Venezia, Golfo di- = Venice, Gulf of- (EN) 5 Hf 45.15N 13.00 E
Venezia-Lido 14 Ge 45.25N 12.22 E
Venezia-Marghera 14 Ge 45.28N 12.44 E
Venezia-Mestre 14 Ge 45.29N 12.14 E
Venezuela [1] 53 Je 8.00N 65.00W
Venezuela, Golfo de- = Venezuela, Gulf of- (EN) 52 Id 11.30N 71.00W
Venezuela, Gulf of- (EN) = Venezuela, Golfo de- 52 Id 11.30N 71.00W
Venezuelan Basin (EN) 38 Mh 15.00N 68.00W
Vengerovo 20 Ce 55.41N 76.55 E
Veniaminof, Mount- 40 He 56.13N 159.18W
Venice 44 Fl 27.06N 82.27W
Venice (EN) = Venezia 6 Hf 45.27N 12.21 E
Venice, Gulf of- (EN) = Venezia, Golfo di- 5 Hf 45.15N 13.00 E
Vénissieux 11 Ki 45.41N 4.53 E
Venjan 8 Ed 60.57N 13.55 E
Venjansjön 8 Ed 60.55N 14.00 E
Venlo 11 Mc 51.24N 6.10 E
Venlock River 59 Ib 12.15S 142.00 E
Vennesla 7 Bg 58.17N 7.59 E
Venosa 14 Jj 40.58N 15.49 E
Venosta, Val-/Vintschgau 14 Ed 46.40N 10.35 E
Venraij 11 Lc 51.32N 5.59 E
Vent, Canal du- = Windward Passage (EN) 49 Lh 20.00N 73.50W
Vent, Iles du- = Windward Islands (EN) 57 Mf 17.30S 149.30W
Venta 7 Eh 57.23N 21.32 E
Venta de Baños 13 Hc 41.55N 4.30W
Ventana, Cerro- 48 Fe 24.15N 106.20W
Ventersdorp 37 De 26.17S 26.48 E
Venterstad 37 Df 30.47S 25.48 E
Venticinco de Diciembre 55 Dg 24.42S 56.33W
Ventimiglia 14 Bg 43.47N 7.36 E
Ventnor 12 Ad 50.36N 1.11W
Ventotene 14 Hj 40.45N 13.25 E
Ventoux, Mont- 11 Lj 44.10N 5.17 E
Ventspils 19 Cd 57.24N 21.33 E
Ventuari, Rio- 52 Je 3.58N 67.02W
Ventura 43 De 34.17N 119.18W
Vénus, Pointe- 65e Fc 17.29S 149.29W
Venus Bay 59 Jg 38.40S 145.45 E
Venustiano Carranza 48 Mi 16.21N 92.33W
Venustiano Carranza, Presa- 48 Id 27.30N 100.40W
Ver 12 Bc 51.31N 0.27W
Vera [Arg.] 56 Hc 29.28S 60.13W
Vera [Sp.] 13 Kg 37.15N 1.52W
Verá, Laguna- 55 Dh 26.05S 57.39W
Veracruz [2] 47 Ee 19.20N 96.40W
Veracruz Llave 39 Jh 19.12N 96.08W
Veraguas [3] 49 Gj 8.30N 81.00W
Verāval 25 Ed 20.54N 70.22 E
Vera y Pintado 55 Bj 30.09S 60.21W
Verbania 14 Ce 45.56N 8.33 E
Verbovski 7 Ji 55.29N 41.59 E
Vercelli 14 Ce 45.19N 8.25 E
Vercors 11 Lj 44.57N 5.25 E
Verdalsøra 7 Ce 63.48N 11.29 E
Verde, Cape- 49 Jb 22.50N 74.52W
Verde, Cay- 49 Jb 22.02N 75.12W
Verde, Costa- 13 Ga 43.40N 5.40W
Verde, Rio- 52 Kh 23.09S 57.37W
Verde, Rio- [Braz.] 54 Hh 21.12S 51.53W
Verde, Rio- [Braz.] 55 Hb 15.07S 48.40W
Verde, Rio- [Braz.] 55 Hd 19.50S 49.45W
Verde, Rio- [Braz.] 55 Ge 21.12S 51.53W
Verde, Rio- [Braz.] 55 Gd 18.01S 50.14W
Verde, Rio- [Braz.] 55 Je 21.27S 45.40W
Verde, Rio- [Braz.] 55 Ca 13.33S 58.01W
Verde, Rio- [Braz.] 54 Gf 11.54S 55.50W
Verde, Rio- [Braz.] 54 Hg 19.11S 50.44W
Verde, Rio- [Mex.] 48 Jg 21.37N 99.15W
Verde, Rio- [Mex.] 48 Hg 20.42N 103.14W
Verde, Rio- [S.Amer.] 55 Ba 13.59S 60.20W
Verde Grande, Rio- 55 Kb 14.35S 43.53W
Verden (Aller) 10 Fd 52.55N 9.14 E
Verde River 43 Ee 33.33N 111.40W
Verdigris River 45 Ii 35.48N 95.18W
Verdinho, Rio- 55 Gc 17.29S 50.27W
Verdon 11 Lk 43.43N 5.46 E
Verdun [Fr.] 11 Le 49.10N 5.23 E
Verdun [Que.-Can.] 44 Kc 45.28N 73.34W
Verdura 14 Hm 37.28N 13.12 E
Vereeniging 37 De 26.38S 27.57 E
Vereščagino 19 Fd 58.05N 54.40 E
Verga, Cap- 34 Cc 10.12N 14.27W
Vergara [Arg.] 55 Dl 35.23S 57.48W
Vergara [Sp.] 13 Ja 43.07N 2.25W
Vergara [Ur.] 55 Fk 32.56S 53.57W
Vergato 14 Ff 44.17N 11.07 E
Verhnedneprovsk 16 Ie 48.39N 34.21 E
Verhnedneprovski 16 Hb 55.01N 33.21 E
Verhnedvinsk 7 Gi 55.46N 27.59 E
Verhneimbatsk 20 Dd 63.02N 88.00 E
Verhne-Karabahski Kanal 16 Oi 39.44N 47.57 E
Verhnespasskoje 7 Kg 58.45N 45.28 E
Verhnetulomski 7 Hb 68.38N 31.48 E
Verhnetulomskoje Vodohranilišče 7 Hb 68.35N 31.00 E
Verhneuralsk 17 Ij 53.53N 59.13 E
Verhneviljujsk 20 Hd 63.20N 120.25 E
Verhni At-Urjah 20 Kd 62.38N 150.03 E
Verhni Avzjan 17 Hj 53.32N 57.33 E
Verhni Kujto, Ozero- 7 Hd 65.00N 30.40 E
Verhni Most 8 Mg 57.29N 29.00 E
Verhni Tagil 17 Jh 57.22N 60.01 E
Verhni Trajanov Val=Upper Trajan's Wall (EN) 15 Lc 46.40N 29.00 E
Verhni Ufalej 19 Gd 56.04N 60.14 E
Verhnjaja Inta 17 Jd 65.59N 60.29 E
Verhnjaja Pyšma 17 Jh 56.59N 60.37 E
Verhnjaja Salda 17 Jg 58.02N 60.33 E
Verhnjaja Tojma 19 Ec 62.13N 45.01 E
Verhnjaja Tura 17 Ig 58.22N 59.49 E
Verhnj Uslon 7 Li 55.47N 48.58 E
Verhnoje Sinevidnoje 10 Tg 49.02N 23.36 E
Verhojansk 22 Pc 67.35N 133.27 E
Verhojanski Hrebet= Verhoyansk Mountains (EN) 21 Oc 67.00N 129.00 E
Verhoturje 17 Jg 58.52N 60.48 E
Verhovcevo 16 Ie 48.31N 34.12 E
Verhovina 15 Ha 48.08N 24.48 E
Verhovje 16 Jc 52.49N 37.14 E
Verhoyansk Mountains (EN)= Verhojanski Hrebet 21 Oc 67.00N 129.00 E
Verin 13 Ec 41.56N 7.26W
Veriora 8 Lg 58.00N 27.21 E
Verissimo, Rio- 55 Hd 18.23S 48.20W
Verissimo, Serra do- 55 Hd 19.33S 48.25W
Verl 12 Kc 51.53N 8.31 E
Vermand 12 Fe 49.52N 3.09 E
Vermeille, Côte- 11 Jl 42.30N 3.20 E
Vermelho, Rio- [Braz.] 55 Ib 14.26S 46.26W
Vermelho, Rio- [Braz.] 55 Ed 19.36S 55.58W
Vermelho, Rio- [Braz.] 55 Gb 14.54S 51.06W
Vermenton 11 Jg 47.40N 3.44 E
Vermilion Bay 42 Ig 49.51N 93.24W
Vermilion Cliffs 46 Ih 37.10N 112.35W
Vermilion Lake 45 Jc 47.53N 92.25W
Vermilion River 44 Gb 46.16N 81.41W
Vermillion 45 He 42.47N 96.56W
Vermillion River 45 He 42.44N 96.53W
Vermillon, Rivière- 44 Kb 47.38N 72.59W
Vérmion Óros 15 Ei 40.30N 22.00 E
Vermont [2] 43 Mc 43.50N 72.45W
Vernal 43 Fc 40.27N 109.32W
Verneuil-sur-Avre 11 Gf 48.44N 0.56 E
Vernhi Baskunčak 16 Oe 48.14N 46.42 E
Vernon [B.C.-Can.] 42 Ff 50.16N 119.16W
Vernon [Fr.] 11 He 49.05N 1.29 E
Vernon [Tx.-U.S.] 43 He 34.09N 99.17W
Vérnon Óros 15 Ei 40.39N 21.22 E
Vernou 51e Ab 16.11N 61.39W
Verny 12 Ie 49.01N 6.12 E
Vero 13 Mb 42.00N 0.10 E
Vero Beach 43 Kf 27.38N 80.24W
Véroia 15 Fi 40.31N 22.12 E
Verona 6 Hf 45.27N 11.00 E
Verónica 56 Ie 35.22S 57.20W
Versailles [Fr.] 11 If 48.48N 2.08 E
Versailles [In.-U.S.] 44 Ef 39.04N 85.15W
Versilia 14 Eg 43.55N 10.15 E
Veršino-Darasunski 20 Gf 52.18N 115.32 E
Veršino-Šahtaminski 20 Gf 51.16N 117.55 E
Versmold 12 Kb 52.03N 8.09 E
Verson 12 Be 49.09N 0.27W
Vert, Cap- = Vert, Cape- (EN) 30 Fg 14.43N 17.30W
Vert, Cape- (EN) = Vert, Cap- 30 Fg 14.43N 17.30W
Vertentes, Serra das- 55 Je 20.56S 44.00W
Vértes 10 Oi 47.25N 18.20 E
Vertientes 49 Hc 21.16N 78.09W
Vertiskos Óros 15 Gi 40.50N 23.19 E
Verviers 11 Ld 50.36N 5.52 E
Vervins 12 Fe 49.50N 3.54 E
Vesanto 8 Lb 62.56N 26.25 E
Vescovato 11a Ba 42.29N 9.26 E
Vesder/Vesdre 12 Hd 50.37N 5.37 E
Vesdre/Vesder 12 Hd 50.37N 5.37 E
Veseli nad Lužnici 10 Kg 49.11N 14.43 E
Veselovskoje Vodohranilišče 16 Lf 47.00N 41.15 E
Vešenskaja 19 Ef 49.38N 41.46 E
Vesgre 12 Df 48.53N 1.28 E
Vesijarvi 8 Kc 61.05N 25.30 E
Vesjegonsk 7 Ig 58.41N 37.16 E
Veškajma 7 Li 54.03N 47.08 E
Vesle 11 Je 49.23N 3.28 E
Vesljana 17 Gf 60.20N 54.03 E
Vesoul 11 Mg 47.38N 6.10 E
Vessigebro 8 Eh 56.59N 12.39 E
Vest-Agder [2] 7 Bg 58.30N 7.10 E
Vestbygd 7 Bg 58.06N 6.35 E
Vesterålen 5 Hb 68.45N 15.00 E
Vesterøhavn 8 Dg 57.18N 10.56 E
Vestfjorden 5 Hb 68.35N 14.30 E
Vestfold [2] 7 Cg 59.15N 10.10 E
Vestfonna 41 Oc 79.58N 20.15 E
Vestgrønland = West Greenland (EN) [2] 41 He 69.00N 49.30W
Véstia 55 Ge 20.23S 51.25W
Vestmannaeyjar 7a Bc 63.26N 20.16W
Vestnes 8 Bb 62.38N 7.06 E
Vestre Jakobselv 7 Ga 70.07N 29.25 E
Vestsjælland [2] 8 Di 55.30N 11.30 E
Vestvågøy 7 Cb 68.15N 13.50 E
Vésubie 11 Nk 43.52N 7.12 E
Vesuvio = Vesuvius (EN) 5 Hg 40.49N 14.26 E
Vesuvius (EN) = Vesuvio 5 Hg 40.49N 14.26 E
Veszprém [2] 10 Ni 47.10N 17.40 E
Veszprém 10 Ni 47.06N 17.55 E
Vésztő 10 Rj 46.55N 21.16 E
Vétaoundé, Ile- 57 Hf 13.15S 167.38 E
Vetauua 63d Ca 15.57S 179.24W
Vêtê, Pointe- 63b Ca 13.27S 166.41 E
Vetka 16 Gc 52.34N 31.13 E
Vetlanda 7 Dh 57.26N 15.04 E
Vetljanka 7 Mj 52.52N 51.09 E
Vetluga 5 Kd 56.18N 46.24 E
Vetluga 7 Kh 57.52N 45.46 E

Index Symbols

[1] Independent Nation
[2] State, Region
[3] District, County
[4] Municipality
[5] Colony, Dependency
Continent
Physical Region
Historical or Cultural Region
Mount, Mountain
Volcano
Hill
Mountains, Mountain Range
Hills, Escarpment
Plateau, Upland
Pass, Gap
Plain, Lowland
Delta
Salt Flat
Valley, Canyon
Crater, Cave
Karst Features
Depression
Polder
Desert, Dunes
Forest, Woods
Heath, Steppe
Oasis
Cape, Point
Coast, Beach
Cliff
Peninsula
Isthmus
Sandbank
Island
Atoll
Rock, Reef
Islands, Archipelago
Rocks, Reefs
Coral Reef
Well, Spring
Geyser
River, Stream
Waterfall Rapids
River Mouth, Estuary
Lake
Salt Lake
Intermittent Lake
Reservoir
Swamp, Pond
Canal
Glacier
Ice Shelf, Pack Ice
Ocean
Sea
Gulf, Bay
Strait, Fjord
Lagoon
Bank
Seamount
Tablemount
Ridge
Shelf
Basin
Escarpment, Sea Scarp
Fracture
Trench, Abyss
National Park, Reserve
Point of Interest
Recreation Site
Cave, Cavern
Historic Site
Ruins
Wall, Walls
Church, Abbey
Temple
Scientific Station
Airport
Port
Lighthouse
Mine
Tunnel
Dam, Bridge

Vetlužski [R.S.F.S.R.]	7	Kh	57.11N	45.07 E
Vetlužski [R.S.F.S.R.]	7	Kg	58.26N	45.28 E
Vetreny	20	Jd	61.43N	149.40 E
Vetreny Pojas, Krjaž-	7	Ie	63.20N	37.30 E
Vetrino	8	Mi	55.25N	28.31 E
Vetschau/Wětošow	10	Ke	51.47N	14.04 E
Vettore	14	Hh	42.49N	13.16 E
Vetzstein	10	Hf	50.25N	11.25 E
Veules-les-Roses	12	Ce	49.52N	0.48 E
Veulettes-sur-Mer	12	Ce	49.51N	0.36 E
Veurne/Furnes	11	Ic	51.04N	2.40 E
Vevey	14	Ad	46.28N	6.50 E
Vevis/Vievis	8	Kj	54.45N	24.58 E
Vexin	11	He	49.10N	1.40 E
Veynes	11	Lj	44.32N	5.49 E
Vézelay	11	Jg	47.28N	3.44 E
Vežen	15	Hg	42.45N	24.24 E
Vézère	11	Gj	44.53N	0.53 E
Vezirköprü	24	Fb	41.09N	35.28 E
Viadana	14	Ef	44.56N	10.31 E
Viale	55	Bj	31.53 S	60.01W
Viana	54	Jd	3.13 S	45.00W
Viana del Bollo	13	Eb	42.11N	7.06W
Viana do Alentejo	13	Ef	38.20N	8.00W
Viana do Castelo	13	Dc	41.42N	8.50W
Viana do Castelo [2]	13	Dc	41.55N	8.25W
Vianden	12	Ie	49.55N	6.16 E
Viangchan (Vientiane)	22	Mh	17.58N	102.36 E
Vianópolis	55	Hc	16.45 S	48.32W
Viar	13	Gg	37.36N	5.50W
Viareggio	14	Eg	43.52N	10.14 E
Viarmes	12	Ee	49.08N	2.22 E
Viaur	11	Hj	44.08N	1.58 E
Viborg [2]	8	Ch	56.30N	9.30 E
Viborg	7	Bh	56.26N	9.24 E
Vibo Valentia	14	Kl	38.40N	16.06 E
Vic	13	Oc	41.56N	2.15 E
Vicari	14	Hm	37.49N	13.34 E
Vicecomodoro Marambio	66	Re	64.16 S	56.44W
Vicente Guerrero	47	Dd	23.45N	103.59W
Vicenza	14	Fe	45.33N	11.33 E
Vichada [2]	54	Ec	5.00N	69.30W
Vichada, Río-	52	Je	4.55N	67.50W
Vichadero	55	Ej	31.48 S	54.43W
Vichy	11	Jh	46.07N	3.25 E
Vicksburg	43	Ie	32.14N	90.56W
Vico, Lago di-	14	Gh	42.19N	12.10 E
Vic-sur-Aisne	12	Fe	49.24N	3.07 E
Vic-sur-Cère	11	Ij	44.59N	2.37 E
Victor Bay	66	Ie	66.20 S	136.30 E
Victor Harbour	59	Hg	35.34 S	138.37 E
Victoria	38	Hb	71.00N	114.00W
Victoria [3]	37	Ed	21.00 S	31.00 E
Victoria [Arg.]	56	Hd	32.37 S	60.10W
Victoria [Austl.]	59	Ig	38.00 S	145.00 E
Victoria [B.C.-Can.]	39	Ge	48.25N	123.22W
Victoria [Cam.]	34	Ge	4.01N	9.12 E
Victoria [Chile]	56	Fe	38.13 S	72.20W
Victoria [Gren.]	50	Ff	12.12N	61.42W
Victoria [Mala.]	26	Ge	5.17N	115.15 E
Victoria [Malta]	14	In	36.02N	14.14 E
Victoria [Rom.]	15	Hd	45.44N	24.41 E
Victoria [Sey.]	31	Mi	4.38 S	55.27 E
Victoria [Tx.-U.S.]	39	Jg	28.48N	97.00W
Victoria/Ying zhan	22	Ng	22.17N	114.09 E
Victoria, Lake- [Afr.]	30	Ki	1.00 S	33.00 E
Victoria, Lake- [Austl.]	59	If	34.00 S	141.15 E
Victoria, Mount- [Bur.]	21	Lg	21.14N	93.55 E
Victoria, Mount- [Pap.N.Gui.]	57	Fe	8.53 S	147.33 E
Victoria, Sierra de la-	55	Fg	25.55 S	54.00W
Victoria and Albert Mountains	42	Ka	79.00N	75.00W
Victoria de Durango	39	Ig	24.02N	104.40W
Victoria de las Tunas	47	Id	20.58N	76.57W
Victoria Falls	31	Jj	17.56 S	25.50 E
Victoria Falls	30	Jj	17.55 S	25.21 E
Victoria Fjord	41	Hb	82.20N	48.00W
Victoria Land (EN)	66	Jf	75.00 S	159.00 E
Victoria Nile	30	Kh	2.14N	31.26 E
Victoria Peak [B.C.-Can.]	46	Ba	50.03N	126.06W
Victoria Peak [Blz.]	49	Ce	16.48N	88.37W
Victoria River	57	Df	15.12 S	129.43 E
Victoria River Downs	59	Gc	16.24 S	131.00 E
Victoria Strait	42	Hc	69.30N	100.00W
Victoriaville	42	Kg	46.03N	71.58W
Victoria West	37	Cf	31.25 S	23.04 E
Victorija	41	Pb	80.10N	36.45 E
Victorville	46	Gi	34.32N	117.18W
Victory, Mount-	59	Ja	9.10 S	149.05 E
Vičuga	19	Ed	57.15N	42.00 E
Vicuña	56	Fc	29.59 S	70.44W
Vicuña Mackenna	56	Hd	33.54 S	64.23W
Vidå	8	Cj	54.58N	8.41 E
Vidal	46	Hi	34.11N	114.34W
Vidalia	45	Kk	31.34N	91.26W
Videbæk	8	Ch	56.05N	8.38 E
Videira	56	Jc	27.00 S	51.08W
Videla	55	Bj	30.56 S	60.39W
Videle	15	Ie	44.17N	25.31 E
Vidigueira	13	Ef	38.13N	7.48W
Vidin [2]	15	Ff	43.59N	22.52 E
Vidin	15	Ff	43.59N	22.52 E
Vidisha	25	Fd	23.42N	77.47 E
Vidlič	15	Ff	43.08N	22.47 E
Vidojevica	15	Ef	43.10N	21.32 E
Vidöstern	8	Fg	57.04N	14.01 E
Vidourle	11	Kk	43.32N	4.08 E
Vidra [Rom.]	15	Jd	45.55N	26.54 E
Vidra [Rom.]	15	Je	44.16N	26.09 E
Vidsel	7	Ed	65.49N	20.31 E
Viduša	14	Mh	42.54N	18.18 E
Vidzeme	8	Kg	57.10N	26.00 E
Vidzemes Augstiene/ Vidzemskaja Vozvyšennost	8	Kh	56.45N	26.00 E
Vidzemskaja Vozvyšennost/ Vidzemes Augstiene	8	Kh	56.45N	26.00 E
Vidzy	8	Li	55.23N	26.47 E
Vie	12	Be	49.09N	0.04W
Viechtach	10	Ig	49.05N	12.53 E
Viedma	53	Jj	40.50 S	63.00W
Viedma, Lago-	52	Ij	49.35 S	72.35W
Vieille Case	51g	Ba	15.36N	61.24W
Vieja, Sierra-	45	Dk	30.30N	104.40W
Viejo, Cerro-	47	Bb	30.20N	112.15W
Viekšniai/Viekšnjai	8	Jh	56.14N	22.28 E
Viekšnjai/Viekšniai	8	Jh	56.14N	22.28 E
Viella	13	Mb	42.42N	0.48 E
Vielsalm	12	Hd	50.17N	5.55 E
Viels-Maisons	12	Ff	48.54N	3.24 E
Vienna [Mo.-U.S.]	45	Kg	38.11N	91.57W
Vienna [W.V.-U.S.]	44	Gf	39.20N	81.33W
Vienna (EN) = Wien	6	Hf	48.12N	16.22 E
Vienna Woods (EN) = Wienerwald	14	Jb	48.10N	16.00 E
Vienne	11	Ki	45.31N	4.52 E
Vienne [3]	11	Gh	46.30N	0.30 E
Vienne	5	Gf	47.13N	0.05 E
Vientiane → Viangchan	22	Mh	17.58N	102.36 E
Vientos, Paso de los- = Windward Passage (EN)	38	Lh	20.00N	73.50W
Vieques, Isla de-	47	Ke	18.08N	65.25W
Vieques, Pasaje de-	51a	Cb	18.08N	65.40W
Vieques, Sonda de-	51a	Cb	18.17N	65.25W
Vierge Point	51k	Bb	13.49N	60.53W
Viersen	10	Ce	51.15N	6.23 E
Vierville-sur-Mer	12	Be	49.22N	0.54W
Vierwaldstätter-See = Lucerne, Lake- (EN)	14	Cc	47.00N	8.30 E
Vierzon	11	Ig	47.13N	2.05 E
Viesca	48	He	25.21N	102.48W
Viesite/Viesīte	8	Kh	56.20N	25.38 E
Viesīte/Viesite	8	Kh	56.20N	25.38 E
Vieste	14	Ki	41.53N	16.10 E
Viet Nam [1]	22	Mh	13.00N	108.00 E
Viet Tri	25	Ld	21.18N	105.26 E
Vieux Fort	50	Ff	13.44N	60.57W
Vieux-Fort, Pointe du-	51e	Ac	15.57N	61.43W
Vieux Fort Bay	51k	Bb	13.44N	60.58W
Vieux-Habitants	51e	Ab	16.04N	61.46W
Vievis/Vevis	8	Kj	54.45N	24.58 E
Viga	7	Kg	59.15N	43.42 E
Vigala	8	Kf	58.43N	24.22 E
Vigan	26	Hc	17.34N	120.23 E
Vigeland	8	Bf	58.05N	7.18 E
Vigevano	14	Ce	45.19N	8.51 E
Vigia	54	Id	0.48 S	48.08W
Vigía Chico	48	Ph	19.46N	87.35W
Vignacourt	12	Ed	50.01N	2.12 E
Vignemale	13	Lb	42.46N	0.08W
Vigneulles-lès-Hattonchâtel	12	Hf	48.59N	5.43 E
Vignoble	11	Lh	46.50N	5.30 E
Vignola	14	Ef	44.29N	11.00 E
Vigny	12	De	49.05N	1.56 E
Vigo	6	Fg	42.14N	8.43W
Vigo, Ría de-	13	Db	42.15N	8.45W
Vigra	8	Bb	62.30N	6.05 E
Vigrestad	8	Af	58.34N	5.42 E
Vihanti	7	Fd	64.30N	25.00 E
Vihiers	11	Fg	47.09N	0.32W
Vihorevka	20	Fe	56.12N	101.09 E
Vihorlat	10	Sh	48.55N	22.10 E
Vihren	15	Gh	41.46N	23.24 E
Vihti	7	Ff	60.25N	24.20 E
Viiala	8	Jc	61.13N	23.47 E
Viinijärvi	8	Mb	62.45N	29.15 E
Viinijärvi	8	Mb	62.39N	29.14 E
Viitasaari	7	Fe	63.04N	25.52 E
Viivikonna/Vijvikonna	8	Le	59.14N	27.41 E
Vijayawāda	22	Kh	16.31N	80.37 E
Vijvikonna/Viivikonna	8	Le	59.14N	27.41 E
Vík	7a	Bc	63.25N	19.01W
Vika	8	Fd	60.57N	14.27 E
Vikarbyn	8	Fd	60.55N	15.01 E
Vikbolandet	8	Gf	58.30N	16.40 E
Viken	8	Eh	56.09N	12.34 E
Viken	8	Ff	58.40N	14.20 E
Vikenara Point	63a	Dc	8.34 S	159.53 E
Vikersund	8	De	59.59N	10.02 E
Vikingbanken	9	Pa	60.20N	2.30 E
Vikmanshyttan	8	Fd	60.17N	15.49 E
Vikna	7	Cd	64.53N	10.58 E
Vikna	7	Cd	64.54N	11.00 E
Viksoyri	7	Bf	61.05N	6.34 E
Vila da Bispo	13	Dg	37.05N	8.55W
Vila da Maganja	37	Fc	17.18 S	37.31 E
Vila de Rei	13	De	39.40N	8.09W
Vila do Conde	13	Dc	41.21N	8.45W
Vila do Porto	32	Bb	36.56N	25.09W
Vila Flor	13	Ec	41.18N	7.09W
Vilafranca del Penedès/ Villafranca del Panadés	13	Nc	41.21N	1.42 E
Vila Franca de Xira	13	Df	38.57N	8.59W
Vila Franca do Campo	32	Bb	37.43N	25.26W
Vila Franca do Save	37	Ed	21.09 S	34.32 E
Vila Gamito	37	Eb	14.10 S	32.59 E
Vila Gouveia	37	Ec	18.03 S	33.11 E
Vilaine	11	Dg	49.23N	2.27W
Viļaka/Viljaka	7	Gh	57.14N	27.46 E
Vila Machado	37	Ec	19.17 S	34.12 E
Vilanculos	31	Kk	22.00 S	35.19 E
Viļani/Viljani	7	Gh	56.33N	26.59 E
Vila Nova	36	Ce	12.38 S	16.04 E
Vila Nova da Cerveira	13	Dc	41.56N	8.45W
Vila Nova de Famalicão	13	Dc	41.25N	8.32W
Vila Nova de Foz Côa	13	Ec	41.05N	7.12W
Vila Nova de Gaia	13	Dc	41.08N	8.37W
Vila Nova do Sales	36	Be	11.25 S	14.18 E
Vilanova i la Geltrú/ Villanueva y Geltrú	13	Nc	41.14N	1.44 E
Vila Paiva de Andrada	37	Ec	18.41 S	34.04 E
Vila Pouca de Aguiar	13	Ec	41.30N	7.39W
Vila Real [2]	13	Ec	41.35N	7.35W
Vila Real	13	Ec	41.18N	7.45W
Vila-Real de los Infantes/ Villarreal de los Infantes	13	Le	39.56N	0.06W
Vila Real de Santo António	13	Eg	37.12N	7.25W
Vilar Formoso	13	Fd	40.37N	6.50W
Vila Velha	54	Jh	20.20 S	40.17W
Vila Velha de Ródão	13	Ee	39.40N	7.42W
Vila Viçosa	13	Ef	38.47N	7.25W
Vîlcea [2]	15	He	45.10N	24.10 E
Vilches	13	If	38.12N	3.30W
Vildbjerg	8	Ch	56.12N	8.46 E
Viled	7	Lf	61.22N	47.15 E
Vilejka	19	Ce	54.30N	26.53 E
Vilhelmina	7	Dd	64.37N	16.39 E
Vilhena	53	Jg	12.43 S	60.07W
Vilija	16	Db	54.55N	25.40 E
Viljaka/Viļaka	7	Gh	57.14N	27.46 E
Viljandi	19	Cd	58.22N	25.35 E
Viljany/Viļani	7	Gh	56.33N	26.59 E
Viljuj	21	Oc	64.24N	126.26 E
Viljujsk	20	Hd	63.40N	121.33 E
Viljujskoje Plato = Vilyui Range (EN)	21	Mc	66.00N	108.00 E
Viljujskoje Vodohranilišče	20	Gd	62.30N	111.00 E
Vilkaviškis	7	Fi	54.43N	23.02 E
Vilkickogo, Ostrov- [R.S.F.S.R.]	20	Cb	73.30N	76.00 E
Vilkickogo, Ostrov- [R.S.F.S.R.]	20	Ka	75.40N	152.30 E
Vilkickogo, Proliv- = Vilkitski Strait (EN)	21	Mb	77.55N	103.00 E
Vilkija	7	Fi	55.03N	23.35 E
Vilkitski Strait (EN) = Vilkickogo, Proliv-	21	Mb	77.55N	103.00 E
Vilkovo	16	Fg	45.23N	29.35 E
Villa Aberastain	56	Gd	31.39 S	68.35W
Villa Ahumada	47	Cb	30.37N	106.31W
Villa Altagracia	49	Ld	18.40N	70.10W
Villa Ana	55	Ci	28.29 S	59.37W
Villa Angela	56	Hc	27.35 S	60.43W
Villa Atuel	56	Gd	34.50 S	67.54W
Villa Berthet	55	Bh	27.17 S	60.25W
Villablino	13	Fb	42.56N	6.19W
Villa Bruzual	54	Eb	9.20N	69.06W
Villa Cañás	55	Bk	34.00 S	61.36W
Villacañas	13	Ie	39.38N	3.20W
Villacarrillo	13	If	38.07N	3.05W
Villacastín	13	Hd	40.47N	4.25W
Villach	14	Hd	46.36N	13.50 E
Villacidro	14	Ck	39.27N	8.44 E
Villa Clara	55	Cj	31.50 S	58.49W
Villaclara [3]	49	Hb	22.30N	80.00W
Villa Constitución [Arg.]	56	Hd	33.14 S	60.20W
Villa Constitución [Mex.]	47	Bc	25.09N	111.43W
Villa Coronado	48	Gd	26.45N	105.10W
Villada	13	Hb	42.15N	4.58W
Villa de Arriaga	48	Ig	21.54N	101.23W
Villa de Cos	48	Hf	23.17N	102.21W
Villa de Cura	50	Cg	10.02N	67.29W
Villa de Maria	56	Hc	29.54 S	63.43W
Villa de Reyes	48	Ig	21.48N	100.56W
Villa de San Antonio	49	Df	14.16N	87.36W
Villadiego	13	Ib	42.31N	4.00W
Villa Dolores	56	Gd	31.56 S	65.12W
Villa Elisa	55	Ck	32.10 S	58.24W
Villa Flores	48	Mi	16.14N	93.14W
Villa Florida	55	Dh	26.23 S	57.09W
Villafranca del Bierzo	13	Fb	42.36N	6.48W
Villafranca del Cid	13	Ld	40.25N	0.15W
Villafranca de los Barros	13	Ff	38.34N	6.20W
Villafranca del Panadés/ Vilafranca del Penedès	13	Nc	41.21N	1.42 E
Villafranca di Verona	14	Ee	45.21N	10.50 E
Villa Frontera	47	Dc	26.56N	101.27W
Villagarcía de Arosa	13	Db	42.36N	8.45W
Villa General Roca	56	Gd	32.39 S	66.28W
Villa Gesell	55	Dm	37.15 S	56.55W
Villagrán	48	Je	24.29N	99.29W
Villaguay	56	Id	31.51 S	59.01W
Villa Guillermina	55	Ci	28.14 S	59.28W
Villa Hayes	56	Ic	25.06 S	57.34W
Villa Hermandarias	55	Cj	31.13 S	59.59W
Villahermosa	39	Jh	17.59N	92.55W
Villa Hidalgo	48	Gd	26.16N	104.54W
Villa Huidobro	56	Hd	34.50 S	64.35W
Villajoyosa/La Vila Jojosa	13	Lf	38.30N	0.14W
Villalba	13	Ea	43.18N	7.41W
Villaldama	48	Id	26.30N	100.26W
Villalón de Campos	13	Gb	42.06N	5.02W
Villalpando	13	Gc	41.52N	5.24W
Villamalea	13	Ke	39.22N	1.35W
Villamanrique	13	Jf	38.33N	3.00W
Villa Maria	53	Ji	32.25 S	63.15W
Villamartin	13	Gh	36.52N	5.38W
Villa Matamoros	48	Gd	26.50N	105.35W
Villa Media Agua	56	Gd	31.59 S	68.25W
Villamil	54a	Ab	0.56 S	91.01W
Villa Minetti	55	Bi	28.37 S	61.39W
Villa Montes	53	Jh	21.15 S	63.30W
Villandraut	11	Fj	44.28N	0.22W
Villa Nueva	56	Gd	32.54 S	68.47W
Villanueva	49	Kh	10.37N	72.59W
Villanueva [Mex.]	48	Hf	22.21N	102.53W
Villanueva [N.M.-U.S.]	45	Di	35.17N	105.23W
Villanueva de Córdoba	13	Hf	38.20N	4.37W
Villanueva del Arzobispo	13	Jf	38.10N	3.00W
Villanueva de la Serena	13	Gf	38.58N	5.48W
Villanueva del Fresno	13	Ef	38.23N	7.10W
Villanueva de los Infantes	13	If	38.44N	3.01W
Villanueva del Río y Minas	13	Gg	37.39N	5.42W
Villanueva y Geltrú/Vilanova i la Geltrú	13	Nc	41.14N	1.44 E
Villa Ocampo [Arg.]	56	Ic	28.28 S	59.22W
Villa Ocampo [Mex.]	47	Cc	26.27N	105.31W
Villa Ojo de Agua	56	Hc	29.31 S	63.42W
Villa Oliva	55	Dh	26.01 S	57.53W
Villa Pesqueira	48	Ec	29.08N	109.58W
Villaputzu	14	Dk	39.26N	9.34 E
Villa Ramírez	55	Bk	32.11 S	60.12W
Villarcayo	13	Ib	42.56N	3.34W
Villar del Arzobispo	13	Le	39.44N	0.49W
Villa Regina	56	Ge	39.06 S	67.04W
Villarica [Chile]	56	Fe	39.16 S	72.16W
Villarica [Par.]	53	Kh	25.45 S	56.26W
Villa Rosario	54	Db	7.50N	72.29W
Villarreal de los Infantes/ Vila-Real de los Infantes	13	Le	39.56N	0.06W
Villarrobledo	13	Je	39.16N	2.36W
Villasalto	14	Dk	39.29N	9.23 E
Villa San Giovanni	14	Jl	38.13N	15.38 E
Villa San Martin	56	Hc	28.18 S	64.12W
Villasimius	14	Dk	39.08N	9.31 E
Villatoro, Puerto de-	13	Gd	40.33N	5.10W
Villa Unión [Mex.]	47	Cd	23.12N	106.16W
Villa Unión [Mex.]	48	Ic	28.15N	100.43W
Villaverde, Madrid-	13	Id	40.21N	3.42W
Villavicencio	53	Ie	4.09N	73.37W
Villaviciosa	13	Ga	43.29N	5.26W
Villazón	54	Eh	22.06 S	65.36W
Ville-de-Laval	44	Kc	45.33N	73.44W
Ville de Paris [3]	11	If	48.52N	2.20 E
Ville de Toulouse Bank (EN)	38	Hh	11.30N	117.00W
Villedieu-les-Poêles	11	Ef	48.50N	1.13W
Ville-en-Tardenois	12	Fe	49.11N	3.48 E
Villefranche-de-Lauragais	11	Hk	43.24N	1.44 E
Villefranche-de-Rouergue	11	Ij	44.21N	2.03 E
Villefranche-sur-Saône	11	Ki	45.59N	4.43 E
Ville-Marie	44	Hb	47.20N	79.26W
Villemur-sur-Tarn	11	Hk	43.52N	1.31 E
Villena	13	Lf	38.38N	0.51W
Villeneuve d'Ascq	12	Fd	50.38N	3.09 E
Villeneuve-Saint-Georges	12	Ef	48.44N	2.27 E
Villeneuve-sur-Lot	11	Gj	44.24N	0.43 E
Villeneuve-sur-Yonne	11	Jf	48.05N	3.18 E
Ville Platte	45	Jk	30.42N	92.16W
Villers-Bocage [Fr.]	12	Be	49.05N	0.39W
Villers-Bocage [Fr.]	12	Ee	50.00N	2.20 E
Villers-Bretonneux	12	Ee	49.52N	2.31 E
Villers-Carbonnel	12	Ee	49.52N	2.54 E
Villers-Cotterêts	12	Fe	49.15N	3.05 E
Villers-la-Ville	12	Gd	50.35N	4.32 E
Villers-sur-Mer	12	Be	49.19N	0.01W
Villerupt	11	Le	49.28N	5.56 E
Villerville	12	Ce	49.24N	0.08 E
Ville-sur-Tourbe	12	Ge	49.11N	4.47 E
Villeurbanne	11	Ki	45.59N	4.43 E
Villiersdorp	37	Bf	33.59 S	19.17 E
Villingen-Schwenningen	10	Eh	48.04N	8.28 E
Villmanstrand/Lappeenranta	6	Ic	61.04N	28.11 E
Villmar	12	Kd	50.23N	8.12 E
Vilnius/Vilnjus	6	Ie	54.41N	25.19 E
Vilnjus/Vilnius	6	Ie	54.41N	25.19 E
Vilok	10	Sh	48.08N	22.50 E
Vilppula	8	Kb	62.01N	24.31 E
Vils [F.R.G.]	10	Jh	48.35N	13.10 E
Vils [F.R.G.]	10	Hg	49.10N	11.59 E
Vilsandi	8	If	58.20N	21.45 E
Vilsbiburg	10	Ih	48.27N	12.21 E
Vilshofen	10	Jh	48.38N	13.11 E
Vilusi	15	Bg	42.44N	18.36 E
Vilvoorde/Vilvorde	11	Kd	50.56N	4.26 E
Vilvorde/Vilvoorde	11	Kd	50.56N	4.26 E
Vilyui Range (EN) = Viljujskoje Plato	21	Mc	66.00N	108.00 E
Vimeu	12	Dd	50.05N	1.35 E
Vimianzo	13	Ca	43.07N	9.02W
Vimmerby	7	Dh	57.40N	15.51 E
Vimoutiers	11	Gf	48.55N	0.12 E
Vimperk	10	Jg	49.03N	13.47 E
Vimy	12	Ed	50.22N	2.49 E
Vina	34	Id	7.45N	15.36 E
Viña del Mar	53	Ii	33.02 S	71.34W
Vinalhaven Island	44	Mc	44.05N	68.52W
Vinalopo	13	Lf	38.11N	0.36W
Vinaros/Vinaroz	13	Md	40.28N	0.29 E
Vinaroz/Vinaros	13	Md	40.28N	0.29 E
Vînători	15	Hc	46.14N	24.56 E
Vincennes	43	Jd	38.41N	87.32W
Vincennes Bay	66	He	66.30 S	109.30 E
Vincente, Puntan-	64b	Bb	14.56N	145.40 E
Vinci	14	Eg	43.47N	10.55 E
Vindafjorden	8	Ae	59.20N	5.55 E
Vindelälven	7	Ee	63.54N	19.52 E
Vindeln	7	Ed	64.12N	19.44 E
Vinderup	8	Ch	56.29N	8.47 E
Vindhya Range	21	Kg	24.37N	82.00 E
Vindö	8	He	59.20N	18.40 E
Vineland	44	Jf	39.29N	75.02W
Vingåker	7	Dg	59.02N	15.52 E
Vingeanne	11	Lg	47.45N	5.18 E
Vinh	22	Mh	18.40N	105.40 E
Vinhais	13	Fc	41.50N	7.00W
Vinh Bac Phan = Tonkin, Gulf of- (EN)	21	Mh	20.00N	108.00 E
Vinh Linh	25	Le	17.04N	107.02 E
Vinica [Yugo.]	14	Jg	45.28N	77.00 E
Vinica [Yugo.]	15	Fh	41.53N	22.30 E
Vinita	45	Ih	36.39N	95.09W
Vînju Mare	15	Fe	44.25N	22.52 E
Vinkovci	14	Me	45.17N	18.49 E
Vinnica	6	If	49.14N	28.29 E
Vinnickaja Oblast [3]	19	Cf	49.00N	28.50 E
Vinniki	16	De	49.48N	24.11 E
Vino, Tierra del-	13	Gc	41.30N	5.30W
Vinogradov	16	Ce	48.09N	23.02 E
Vinslöv	8	Eh	56.06N	13.55 E
Vinson Massif	66	Pf	78.35 S	85.25W
Vinstervåtn	8	Cc	61.20N	9.00 E
Vinstra	7	Bf	61.36N	9.45 E
Vinstra	8	Cc	61.36N	9.45 E
Vintilă Vodă	15	Jd	45.28N	26.43 E
Vintjärn	8	Gd	60.50N	16.03 E
Vinton	45	Ke	42.10N	92.00W
Vintschgau/Venosta, Val-	14	Ed	46.40N	10.35 E
Vipiteno / Sterzing	14	Fd	46.54N	11.26 E
Vipya Plateau	36	Fe	11.09 S	34.00 E
Viqueque	26	Ih	8.52 S	126.22 E
Vir	14	Jf	44.18N	15.03 E
Virac	26	Hd	13.35N	124.15 E
Viramgām	25	Ed	23.07N	72.02 E
Virandozero	7	Id	64.01N	36.03 E
Viranşehir	24	Hd	37.13N	39.45 E
Virbalis	8	Jj	54.37N	22.49 E
Vircava	8	Jh	56.35N	23.43 E
Virden	42	Hg	49.51N	100.55W
Virdois/Virrat	7	Fe	62.14N	23.47 E
Vire	11	Ff	48.50N	0.53W
Vire	11	Ee	49.20N	1.07W
Virei	36	Bf	15.43 S	12.54 E
Vireux-Wallerand	12	Gd	50.05N	4.44 E
Virgenes, Cabo-	52	Jk	52.19 S	68.21W
Virgin Gorda	50	Dc	18.30N	64.25W
Virginia [2]	43	Ld	37.30N	78.45W
Virginia [Mn.-U.S.]	43	Ib	47.31N	92.32W
Virginia [S.Afr.]	37	De	28.12 S	26.49 E
Virginia Beach	43	Ld	36.51N	75.59W
Virginia City	46	Fg	39.19N	119.39W
Virgin Islands	38	Mg	18.20N	66.45W
Virgin Islands of the United States [5]	39	Mh	18.20N	64.52W
Virgin Mountains	46	Ih	36.40N	113.50W
Virgin Passage	51a	Cb	18.20N	65.10W
Virgin River	46	Hh	36.35N	114.18W
Virihaure	7	Dc	67.22N	16.33 E
Virkby/Virkkala	8	Kd	60.13N	24.01 E
Virkkala/Virkby	8	Kd	60.13N	24.01 E
Virmasvesi	8	Lb	62.50N	26.55 E
Virôchey	25	Lf	13.59N	106.49 E
Viroin	11	Kd	50.05N	4.43 E
Viroinval	12	Gd	50.05N	4.33 E
Viroinval-Nismes	12	Gd	50.05N	4.33 E
Virojoki	7	Gf	60.35N	27.42 E
Viroqua	45	Ke	43.34N	90.53W
Virovitica	14	Le	45.50N	17.23 E
Virpazar	15	Cg	42.15N	19.06 E
Virrat/Virdois	7	Fe	62.14N	23.47 E
Virserum	7	Dh	57.19N	15.35 E
Virsko More	14	If	44.20N	15.00 E
Virton	11	Le	49.34N	5.32 E
Virton-Ethe	12	He	49.35N	5.35 E
Virtsu	7	Fg	58.37N	23.31 E
Virudanagar	25	Fg	9.36N	77.58 E
Virvičja/Virvyčia	8	Jh	56.14N	22.30 E
Virvyčia/Virvičja	8	Jh	56.14N	22.30 E
Vis	14	Kg	43.02N	16.10 E
Vis	14	Kg	43.03N	16.12 E
Visalia	43	Dd	36.20N	119.18W
Visayan Sea	26	Hd	11.35N	123.51 E
Visby	7	Eh	57.38N	18.18 E
Viscount Melville Sound	38	Hb	74.10N	113.00W
Visé/Wezet	12	Hd	50.44N	5.42 E
Višegrad	15	Jh	41.59N	26.20 E
Višegrad	14	Ng	43.48N	19.17 E
Višera [R.S.F.S.R.]	19	Fc	61.57N	52.25 E
Višera [R.S.F.S.R.]	5	Ld	59.55N	56.50 E
Viseu [2]	13	Ed	40.45N	7.50W
Viseu [Braz.]	54	Id	1.12 S	46.07W
Viseu [Port.]	13	Ed	40.39N	7.55W
Vişeu de Sus	15	Hb	47.43N	24.26 E
Vishākhapatnam	22	Kh	17.42N	83.18 E
Visingsö	8	Ff	58.03N	14.20 E
Viskafors	8	Eg	57.38N	12.50 E
Viskan	7	Cg	57.14N	12.12 E
Viški Kanal	14	Kg	43.07N	16.17 E
Vislanda	7	Dh	56.47N	14.27 E
Vislinski Zaliv	10	Pb	54.27N	19.40 E
Visnes	8	Ae	59.21N	5.14 E
Višnevka	15	Lc	46.22N	28.27 E
Visoki Dečani	15	Dg	42.33N	20.16 E
Visoko	14	Mg	43.59N	18.11 E
Visokoi	66	Ad	56.42 S	27.12W
Visonggo	63d	Bb	16.13 S	179.40 E
Visp	14	Bd	46.17N	7.53 E
Vissefjärda	8	Fh	56.32N	15.35 E
Vista	46	Gj	33.12N	117.15W
Visten	8	Ee	59.40N	13.20 E
Vistonías, Órmos-	15	Ii	40.58N	25.05 E
Vistonís, Límni-	15	Ih	41.03N	25.07 E
Vistula (EN) = Wisła	5	He	54.22N	18.55 E
Vištytis	8	Jj	54.27N	22.44 E
Visuvisu Point	63a	Cb	7.57 S	157.31 E
Vit	15	Hf	43.41N	24.45 E
Vitebsk	6	Jd	55.12N	30.11 E
Vitebskaja Oblast [3]	19	Cd	55.20N	29.00 E
Viterbo	14	Gh	42.25N	12.06 E
Vithkuqi	15	Di	40.31N	20.35 E
Vitichi	54	Eh	20.13 S	65.29W
Vitigudino	13	Fc	41.01N	6.26W
Viti Levu	57	If	18.00 S	178.00 E
Vitim	20	Ge	59.33N	112.28 E
Vitim	21	Nd	59.26N	112.34 E
Vitimski	20	Ge	58.18N	113.18 E
Vitimskoje Ploskogorje	20	Gf	54.00N	114.00 E
Vitinja	15	Gg	42.47N	23.45 E
Vitjaz Strait	60	Di	5.35 S	147.00 E
Vitolište	15	Eh	41.11N	21.50 E
Vitoria	13	Jb	42.51N	2.40W
Vitória	53	Lh	20.19 S	40.21W
Vitória da Conquista	53	Lg	14.51 S	40.51W
Vitória de Santo Antão	54	Ke	8.07 S	35.18W
Vitorog	14	Lf	44.08N	17.03 E
Vitosa	15	Gg	42.33N	23.15 E
Vitré	11	Ef	48.08N	1.12W
Vitry-en-Artois	12	Ed	50.20N	2.59 E
Vitry-le-François	11	Kf	48.44N	4.35 E
Vitsi	15	Ei	40.39N	21.23 E

Index Symbols

- [1] Independent Nation
- [2] State, Region
- [3] District, County
- [4] Municipality
- [5] Colony, Dependency
- Continent
- Physical Region
- Historical or Cultural Region
- Mount, Mountain
- Volcano
- Hill
- Mountains, Mountain Range
- Hills, Escarpment
- Plateau, Upland
- Pass, Gap
- Plain, Lowland
- Delta
- Salt Flat
- Valley, Canyon
- Crater, Cave
- Karst Features
- Depression
- Polder
- Desert, Dunes
- Forest, Woods
- Heath, Steppe
- Oasis
- Cape, Point
- Coast, Beach
- Cliff
- Peninsula
- Isthmus
- Sandbank
- Island
- Atoll
- Rock, Reef
- Islands, Archipelago
- Rocks, Reefs
- Coral Reef
- Well, Spring
- Geyser
- River, Stream
- Waterfall Rapids
- River Mouth, Estuary
- Lake
- Salt Lake
- Intermittent Lake
- Reservoir
- Swamp, Pond
- Canal
- Glacier
- Ice Shelf, Pack Ice
- Ocean
- Sea
- Gulf, Bay
- Strait, Fjord
- Lagoon
- Bank
- Seamount
- Tablemount
- Ridge
- Shelf
- Basin
- Escarpment, Sea Scarp
- Fracture
- Trench, Abyss
- National Park, Reserve
- Point of Interest
- Recreation Site
- Cave, Cavern
- Historic Site
- Ruins
- Wall, Walls
- Church, Abbey
- Temple
- Scientific Station
- Airport
- Port
- Lighthouse
- Mine
- Tunnel
- Dam, Bridge

International Map Index

Vittangi	7	Ec	67.41N	21.39 E
Vitteaux	11	Kg	47.24N	4.32 E
Vittel	11	Lf	48.12N	5.57 E
Vittinge	8	Ge	59.54N	17.04 E
Vittoria	14	In	36.57N	14.32 E
Vittorio Veneto	14	Ge	45.59N	12.18 E
Vityaz Depth (EN) ⌐	3	Je	44.00N	151.00 E
Vityaz i Depth (EN) ⌐	3	Ih	11.20N	141.30 E
Vityaz II Depth (EN) ⌐	3	Kl	23.27 S	175.00W
Vityaz III Depth (EN) ⌐	3	Km	32.00 S	178.00W
Vityaz Seamount (EN) ⌐	57	Jc	13.30N	173.15W
Vityaz Trench (EN) ⌐	3	Jj	10.00 S	170.00 E
Vivarais, Monts du- ⌐	11	Ki	44.55N	4.15 E
Vivarais, Plateaux du- ⌐	11	Kj	44.50N	4.45 E
Viver	13	Le	39.55N	0.36W
Vivero	13	Ea	43.40N	7.35W
Viverone, Lago di-	14	Ce	45.25N	8.05 E
Vivi	20	Ed	63.52N	97.50 E
Vivian	45	Jj	32.53N	93.59W
Viviers	11	Kj	44.29N	4.41 E
Vivo	37	Dd	23.03 S	29.17 E
Vivoratá	55	Dm	37.40 S	57.39W
Vivorillo, Cayos- ⌐	49	Ff	15.50N	83.18W
Viwa ⌐	63d	Ab	17.08 S	176.56 E
Vizcaíno, Desierto de- ⌐	47	Bc	27.40N	114.40W
Vizcaíno, Sierra- ⌐	48	Bd	27.20N	114.00W
Vizcaya [3]	13	Ja	43.15N	2.55W
Vizcaya, Golfo de- ⌐	5	Fg	44.00N	4.00W
Vize	15	Kh	41.34N	27.45 E
Vize, Ostrov ⌐	21	Jb	79.30N	77.00 E
Vizianagaram	25	Ge	18.07N	83.25 E
Vizille	11	Li	45.05N	5.46 E
Vizinga	19	Fc	61.05N	50.10 E
Viziru	15	Kd	45.00N	27.42 E
Vižnica	16	De	48.14N	25.12 E
Vizzini	14	Im	37.10N	14.45 E
Vjake-Maarja/Väike-Maarja	8	Le	59.04N	26.12 E
Vjajke-Pakri/Väike-Pakri ⌐	8	Je	59.50N	23.50 E
Vjajke-Vjajn/Väik Vain ⌐	8	Jf	58.30N	23.10 E
Vjalje, Ozero- ⌐	8	Ne	59.00N	30.20 E
Vjalozero, Ozero- ⌐	7	Ic	66.50N	35.10 E
Vjandra/Vändra	7	Fg	58.40N	25.01 E
Vjartsilja	7	He	62.10N	30.48 E
Vjatka ⌐	5	Ld	55.36N	51.30 E
Vjatskije Poljany	19	Fd	56.14N	51.04 E
Vjatski Uval ⌐	7	Lg	58.00N	49.00 E
Vjazemski	20	Ig	47.31N	134.45 E
Vjazma	6	Jd	55.13N	34.18 E
Vjazniki	7	Kh	56.15N	42.12 E
Vjejo, Rio- ⌐	49	Dg	12.17N	86.54W
Vjosa ⌐	15	Ci	40.37N	19.20 E
Vlaamse Banken ⌐	12	Ec	51.15N	2.30 E
Vlaanderen/Flandres = Flanders (EN) ⌐	5	Ge	51.00N	3.20 E
Vlaanderen/Flandres = Flanders (EN) ⌐	11	Jc	51.00N	3.20 E
Vlaardingen	11	Kc	51.54N	4.21 E
Vlădeasa, Virful- ⌐	15	Fc	46.45N	22.48 E
Vlădeni	15	Kb	47.25N	27.02 E
Vladičin Han	15	Fg	42.43N	22.04 E
Vladimir	6	Kd	56.10N	40.25 E
Vladimirskaja Oblast [3]	19	Ed	56.00N	40.40 E
Vladimirski Tupik	16	Hb	55.42N	33.18 E
Vladimir-Volynski	19	Ce	50.51N	24.22 E
Vladivostok	22	Pe	43.10N	131.56 E
Vlad Țepeș	15	Ke	44.21N	27.05 E
Vlagtwedde	12	Ja	53.02N	7.08 E
Vlagtwedde-Ter Apel	12	Jb	52.52N	7.06 E
Vlahina ⌐	15	Fi	41.54N	22.52 E
Vlăhița	15	Ic	46.21N	25.31 E
Vlamse Vlakte = Flanders Plain (EN) ⌐	11	Id	50.40N	2.50 E
Vlasenica	14	Mf	44.11N	18.57 E
Vlašic [Yugo.] ⌐	14	Lf	44.19N	17.40 E
Vlašim	10	Kg	49.42N	14.54 E
Vlasotince	15	Fg	42.58N	22.08 E
Vlasovo	20	Ib	70.40N	134.35 E
Vlieland ⌐	11	Ka	53.15N	5.00 E
Vlieland	11	Ka	53.15N	5.06 E
Vlieland-Oost Vlieland	12	Ha	53.17 N	5.06 E
Vliestroom ⌐	11	Ka	53.17N	5.10 E
Vlissingen	11	Jc	51.26N	3.35 E
Vlissingen-Oost-Souburg	12	Fc	51.28N	3.37 E
Vloesberg/Flobecq	12	Fd	50.44N	3.44 E
Vlora	6	Hg	40.27N	19.30 E
Vlorës, Gjiri i- ⌐	15	Ci	40.25N	19.25 E
Vlotho	12	Kb	52.10N	8.51 E
Vltava = Moldau (EN) ⌐	5	Ne	50.21N	14.30 E
Vöcklabruck	14	Hb	48.01N	13.39 E
Vodice	14	Jg	43.46N	15.47 E
Vodla ⌐	7	If	61.49N	36.00 E
Vodlozero, Ozero- ⌐	7	Ie	62.20N	37.00 E
Vodňany	10	Kg	49.09N	14.11 E
Vodnjan	14	Hf	44.57N	13.51 E
Vodny	17	Fe	63.32N	53.20 E
Voerde (Niederrhein)	10	Ce	51.35N	6.41 E
Voeren/Fouron	12	Hd	50.45N	5.48 E
Vogel Peak ⌐	34	Hd	8.24N	11.47 E
Vogelsberg ⌐	10	Ff	50.30N	9.15 E
Voghera	14	Df	44.59N	9.01 E
Vogtland ⌐	10	If	50.30N	12.05 E
Voh	63b	Be	20.58 S	164.42 E
Võhandu Jõgi/Vyhandu ⌐	8	Lf	58.03N	27.40 E
Vohémar	37	Ib	13.22 S	50.00 E
Vohipeno	37	Hd	22.20 S	47.52 E
Vöhl	12	Kc	51.12N	8.56 E
Vohma ⌐	7	Lg	58.45N	46.36 E
Vohma	8	Ld	58.58N	46.45 E
Voi	31	Ki	3.23 S	38.34 E
Voikoski	8	Le	61.16N	26.48 E
Voinjama	31	Qh	8.25N	9.45W
Vóion Óros ⌐	15	Ei	40.15N	21.03 E
Voire ⌐	11	Kf	48.27N	4.25 E
Voiron	11	Li	45.22N	5.35 E
Voitsberg	14	Jc	47.02N	15.09 E
Voiviis, Limni- ⌐	15	Fj	39.32N	22.45 E
Vojens	8	Ci	55.15N	9.19 E
Vojkar ⌐	17	Ld	65.38N	64.40 E
Vojmsjön ⌐	7	Dd	65.00N	16.24 E
Vojnić	14	Je	45.19N	15.42 E
Vojnilov	10	Ug	49.04N	24.33 E
Vojvodina [3]	15	Cd	45.00N	20.00 E
Voj-Vož	19	Fc	62.56N	54.59 E
Voknavolok	7	Hd	64.57N	30.31 E
Vokré, Hoséré- ⌐	30	Ih	8.21N	13.15 E
Volary	10	Jg	48.55N	13.54 E
Volcán	49	Fi	8.46N	82.38W
Volcanica, Cordillera- ⌐	38	Ih	18.00N	101.00W
Volcano	65a	Fd	19.26N	155.20W
Volcano Islands (EN) = Iō/ Kazan-Rettō ⌐	21	Qg	25.00N	141.00 E
Volcano Islands (EN) = Kazan-Rettō/Iō ⌐	21	Qg	25.00N	141.00 E
Volcán Rana Roi ⌐	65d	Ab	27.05 S	109.23W
Volčansk [R.S.F.S.R.]	17	Jg	59.59N	60.04 E
Volčansk [Ukr.-U.S.S.R.]	16	Jd	50.16N	37.01 E
Volčiha	20	Df	52.02N	80.23 E
Volda	7	Be	62.09N	6.06 E
Voldafjorden ⌐	8	Ab	62.10N	6.00 E
Volga ⌐	7	Jh	57.57N	38.25 E
Volga-Baltic Canal (EN) = Volgo-Baltijski vodny put imeni V. I. Lenina ⌐	5	Jd	59.58N	37.10 E
Volga Delta (EN) ⌐	5	Kf	46.30N	47.00 E
Volga Hills (EN) = Privolžkaja ⌐	5	Ke	52.00N	46.00 E
Volgo-Baltijski vodny put imeni V.I. Lenina = Volga-Baltic Canal (EN) ⌐	5	Jd	59.58N	37.10 E
Volgodonsk	19	Ef	47.33N	42.08 E
Volgo-Donskoj sudohodny kanal imeni V. I. Lenina = Lenin Canal (EN) ⌐	5	Kf	48.40N	43.37 E
Volgograd (Stalingrad)	6	Kf	48.44N	44.25 E
Volgograd Reservoir (EN) = Volgogradskoje Vodohranilišče ⌐	5	Kf	49.20N	45.00 E
Volgogradskaja Oblast [3]	19	Ef	49.30N	44.30 E
Volgogradskoje Vodohranilišče = Volgograd Reservoir (EN) ⌐	5	Kf	49.20N	45.00 E
Volhov ⌐	5	Jc	60.08N	32.20 E
Volhov	6	Jd	59.55N	32.20 E
Volhynia ⌐	5	Ie	51.00N	25.00 E
Volja ⌐	17	Je	63.11N	61.16 E
Volka	10	Vd	52.43N	25.43 E
Völkermarkt	14	Id	46.39N	14.38 E
Völklingen	10	Cg	49.15N	6.51 E
Volkmarsen	12	Lc	51.24N	9.07 E
Volkovysk	16	Dc	53.10N	24.31 E
Volkovysskaja Vozvyšennost ⌐	10	Kc	53.10N	24.30 E
Volksrust	37	De	27.24 S	29.53 E
Vollenhove	12	Hb	52.40N	5.58 E
Vollsjö	8	Ei	55.42N	13.46 E
Volma, Gora- ⌐	12	Jc	51.24N	7.21 E
Volna, Gora- ⌐	20	Kd	63.30N	154.57 E
Volnjansk	16	If	47.54N	35.29 E
Volnovaha	16	If	47.37N	37.36 E
Voločajevka 2-ja	20	Ig	48.36N	134.36 E
Voločisk	16	Ee	49.31N	26.13 E
Volodarsk	7	Kh	56.14N	43.13 E
Volodarski	16	Pf	46.26N	48.31 E
Volodarskoje	19	Ge	53.18N	68.08 E
Vologda	6	Jd	59.12N	39.55 E
Vologodskaja Oblast [3]	19	Ed	60.00N	41.00 E
Volokolamsk	7	Ih	56.03N	35.58 E
Volokonovka	16	Id	50.29N	37.52 E
Vólos	6	Ih	39.22N	22.57 E
Vološka ⌐	7	Jf	61.42N	39.15 E
Vološka	7	Jf	61.21N	40.03 E
Volosovo	8	Nf	59.28N	29.31 E
Volovec	10	Jh	48.42N	23.17 E
Volovo	16	Ic	53.34N	38.00 E
Voložin	16	Eb	54.06N	26.32 E
Volquart Boons Kyst ⌐	41	Jd	70.20N	24.20W
Volsini, Monti- ⌐	14	Fh	42.40N	11.55 E
Volsk	19	Ee	52.02N	47.23 E
Volta [3]	30	Hh	5.46N	0.41 E
Volta ⌐	34	Fd	7.00N	0.30 E
Volta Blanche = White Volta (EN) ⌐	30	Gh	8.38N	0.59W
Volta Lake ⌐	30	Hh	7.30N	0.15 E
Volta Noire = Black Volta (EN) ⌐	30	Gh	8.38N	1.30W
Volta Noire = Black Volta (EN) [3]	34	Ec	12.30N	4.00W
Volta Redonda	53	Lh	22.32 S	44.07W
Volta Rouge = Red Volta (EN) ⌐	30	Gh	10.34N	0.30W
Volterra	14	Eg	43.24N	10.51 E
Voltoya ⌐	13	Hc	41.13N	4.31W
Voltri, Genova-	14	Cf	44.26N	8.45 E
Volturno ⌐	14	Hi	41.01N	13.55 E
Volubilis ⌐	32	Fc	34.04N	5.33W
Vólvi, Limni- ⌐	15	Gi	40.41N	23.28 E
Volynskaja Grjada ⌐	10	Ue	51.05N	25.00 E
Volynskaja Oblast [3]	19	Ce	51.10N	25.00 E
Volynskaja Vozvyšennost ⌐	16	Dd	50.55N	25.00 E
Volžsk	19	Ed	55.55N	48.19 E
Volžski [R.S.F.S.R.]	6	Kf	48.48N	44.45 E
Volžski [R.S.F.S.R.]	7	Mj	53.28N	50.08 E
Vomano ⌐	14	Gg	42.41N	14.04 E
Vomano	14	Ih	42.39N	14.02 E
Vonavona ⌐	63a	Cc	8.12 S	157.05 E
Vónitsa	15	Dk	38.55N	20.53 E
Vonne ⌐	11	Gh	46.25N	0.15 E
Võnnu/Vynnu	8	Lf	58.15N	27.10 E
Voorne ⌐	12	Gc	51.52N	4.05 E
Voorschoten	12	Gb	52.08N	4.28 E
Voorst	12	Ib	52.10N	6.09 E
Voorst-Twello	12	Ib	52.14N	6.07 E
Vop ⌐	16	Ha	54.56N	32.44 E
Vopnafjördur	7a	Cb	65.45N	14.50W
Vora	15	Ch	41.23N	19.40 E
Vörä/Vöyri	8	Ja	63.09N	22.15 E
Vorarlberg [2]	14	Dc	47.15N	9.50 E
Vóras Óros ⌐	15	Ei	41.00N	21.50 E
Vorau	14	Jc	47.24N	15.53 E
Vorden	12	Ib	52.06N	6.20 E
Vorderrhein ⌐	14	Dd	46.49N	9.26 E
Vordingborg	7	Ci	55.01N	11.55 E
Voreifel ⌐	12	Jd	50.10N	7.00 E
Vorga Šor	17	Kc	67.35N	63.40 E
Voria Pindhos ⌐	15	Dj	40.20N	20.55 E
Vórioi Sporádhes, Nísoi- = Northern Sporades (EN) ⌐	5	Ih	39.15N	23.55 E
Vórios Evvoïkós Kólpos = Évvoia, Gulf of- (EN) ⌐	15	Gk	38.45N	23.10 E
Vorkuta	6	Mb	67.27N	63.58 E
Vorma ⌐	7	Cf	60.09N	11.27 E
Vormsi ⌐	8	Je	59.02N	23.05 E
Vormsi	7	Fg	59.00N	23.15 E
Vorniceni	15	Jb	47.59N	26.40 E
Vorogovo	20	Dd	60.58N	89.28 E
Vorona ⌐	16	Md	51.22N	42.03 E
Voroncovo [R.S.F.S.R.]	20	Db	71.40N	83.40 E
Voroncovo [R.S.F.S.R.]	8	Mg	57.15N	28.49 E
Voronež ⌐	6	Je	51.40N	39.10 E
Voronež ⌐	16	Kd	51.31N	39.05 E
Voronežskaja Oblast [3]	19	Ee	51.00N	40.15 E
Voronin Trough (EN) ⌐	67	Ge	80.00N	85.00 E
Voronja ⌐	7	Ib	69.09N	35.47 E
Voronovo	8	Kj	54.09N	25.19 E
Voropajevo	8	Li	55.07N	27.19 E
Vorošilovgrad	6	Jf	48.34N	39.20 E
Vorošilovgradskaja Oblast [3]	19	Df	49.00N	39.10 E
Vorotan ⌐	16	Oj	39.15N	46.43 E
Vorotynec	7	Kh	56.02N	45.52 E
Vorskla ⌐	16	Id	50.10N	34.11 E
Vorsma	7	Ki	55.58N	43.17 E
Vörts Järv/Vyrtsjarv, Ozero-	7	Gg	58.15N	26.05 E
Võru/Vyru	19	Cd	57.52N	27.05 E
Voruh	18	He	39.52N	70.35 E
Vosges ⌐	5	Gf	48.30N	7.10 E
Vosges [3]	11	Mf	48.10N	6.20 E
Voskresensk	7	Ji	55.22N	38.42 E
Voskresenskoje	7	Kh	56.51N	45.27 E
Voss ⌐	8	Bd	60.40N	6.30 E
Vossa ⌐	8	Ad	60.39N	5.42 E
Vossevangen	7	Bd	60.39N	6.26 E
Vostočno-Kazahstanskaja Oblast [3]	19	Jf	49.00N	84.00 E
Vostočno-Kounradski	19	Hf	46.58N	75.07 E
Vostočno Sibirskoje More = East Siberian Sea (EN) ⌐	67	Cd	74.00N	166.00 E
Vostočny [R.S.F.S.R.]	20	Jg	48.19N	142.40 E
Vostočny [R.S.F.S.R.]	7	Mj	58.48N	61.52 E
Vostočny, Hrebet- ⌐	20	Lf	55.00N	160.30 E
Vostočny Sajan = Eastern Sayans (EN) ⌐	21	Ld	53.00N	97.00 E
Vostok	66	Hf	78.28 S	106.48 E
Vostok Island ⌐	57	Lf	10.06 S	152.23W
Vostrecovo	20	Ig	45.56N	134.59 E
Vošu/Vyzu	8	Ke	59.30N	25.50 E
Votkinskoje Vodohranilišče = Votkinsk Reservoir (EN)	5	Ld	57.30N	55.10 E
Votkinsk Reservoir (EN) = Votkinskoje Vodohranilišče ⌐	5	Ld	57.30N	55.10 E
Votuporanga	55	He	20.24 S	49.59W
Vouga ⌐	36	Ce	12.14 S	16.48 E
Vouga	13	Dd	40.41N	8.40W
Vouillé	11	Gh	46.38N	0.10 E
Voulgára ⌐	15	Ej	39.06N	21.54 E
Vouliagméni	15	Gl	37.49N	23.47 E
Voúrinos Óros ⌐	15	Ei	40.11N	21.40 E
Voúxa, Ákra- ⌐	15	Gn	35.38N	23.36 E
Vouziers	11	Kf	49.24N	4.42 E
Voves	11	Hf	48.16N	1.38 E
Vovodo ⌐	35	Cd	5.40N	24.21 E
Voxna ⌐	8	Gc	61.21N	15.34 E
Voxnan ⌐	8	Gc	61.17N	16.26 E
Voyeykov Ice Shelf ⌐	66	Ie	66.20 S	124.38 E
Vöyri/Vörä	8	Ja	63.09N	22.15 E
Vože, Ozero- ⌐	7	Jf	60.35N	39.05 E
Vožega ⌐	7	Jf	60.33N	39.13 E
Vožega	7	Jf	60.30N	40.12 E
Vožega	7	If	61.01N	35.27 E
Voznesenje	18	Bb	45.05N	59.15 E
Voznesensk	19	Df	47.35N	31.20 E
Vozroždenija, Ostrov- ⌐	18	Bb	45.05N	59.15 E
Vraca [2]	15	Gf	43.12N	23.33 E
Vraca ⌐	15	Gf	43.12N	23.33 E
Vraca	15	Ah	41.54N	20.45 E
Vradijevka	16	Gf	47.51N	30.36 E
Vrakhiónas ⌐	15	Dl	37.48N	20.45 E
Vran ⌐	14	Lg	43.39N	17.27 E
Vrancea [2]	15	Jd	45.50N	26.42 E
Vranica ⌐	14	Lg	43.57N	17.44 E
Vranje	15	Fg	42.33N	21.54 E
Vranov nad Topľou	10	Rh	48.54N	21.41 E
Vráška čuka, Prohod- ⌐	15	Ff	43.52N	22.27 E
Vratnik, prohod- ⌐	15	Jg	42.49N	26.10 E
Vratnik, prohod- ⌐	15	Dk	38.55N	20.53 E
Vrbas ⌐	14	Mf	45.08N	17.31 E
Vrbas	15	Cd	45.34N	19.39 E
Vrbno pod Pradědem	10	Nf	50.08N	17.23 E
Vrbovsko	14	Je	45.22N	15.05 E
Vrchlabí	10	Lf	50.38N	15.37 E
Vrede	37	De	27.30 S	29.06 E
Vreden	12	Ib	52.02N	6.50 E
Vredenburg	37	Bf	32.54 S	17.59 E
Vredendal	37	Bf	31.41 S	18.35 E
Vresse, Vresse-sur-Semois-	12	Ge	49.52N	4.56 E
Vresse-sur-Semois	12	Ge	49.52N	4.56 E
Vresse-sur-Semois-Vresse	12	Ge	49.52N	4.56 E
Vretstorp	8	Fe	59.02N	14.52 E
Vrhnika	14	Ie	45.58N	14.18 E
Vries	12	Ia	53.05N	6.36 E
Vriezenveen	12	Ib	52.26N	6.36 E
Vrigstad	8	Fg	57.21N	14.28 E
Vron	12	Dd	50.19N	1.45 E
Vršac	15	Ed	45.07N	21.18 E
Vryburg	37	Jk	26.55 S	24.45 E
Vryheid	37	Ee	27.52 S	30.38 E
Vsetin	10	Ng	49.21N	18.00 E
Vsevidof, Mount- ⌐	40a	Eb	53.07N	168.43W
Vsevoložsk	7	Hd	60.04N	30.41 E
Vstrečny	20	Lc	68.00N	165.58 E
Vtaćnik ⌐	10	Oh	48.42N	18.37 E
Vuanggava ⌐	63d	Cc	18.52 S	178.54W
Vučitrn	15	Eg	42.49N	20.58 E
Vučjak ⌐	15	Fh	41.28N	22.20 E
Vuka ⌐	14	Me	45.21N	19.00 E
Vukovar	14	Me	45.21N	19.00 E
Vuktyl	19	Fc	63.50N	57.25 E
Vulavu	63a	Dc	8.31 S	159.48 E
Vulcan	15	Gd	45.23N	23.16 E
Vulcan, Virful- ⌐	15	Fc	46.14N	22.58 E
Vulcano ⌐	14	Il	38.25N	15.00 E
Vulkanešty	16	Fg	45.38N	28.27 E
Vulture ⌐	14	Jj	40.57N	15.38 E
Vung Tau	25	Lf	10.21N	107.04 E
Vunindawa	63d	Bb	17.49 S	178.19 E
Vunisea Station	61	Ec	19.03 S	178.09 E
Vuohijarvi ⌐	8	Lc	61.10N	26.40 E
Vuoksa ⌐	8	Nd	60.35N	30.42 E
Vuoksa, Ozero- [R.S.F.S.R.] ⌐	8	Mc	61.00N	30.00 E
Vuoksa, Ozero- [R.S.F.S.R.] ⌐	8	Md	60.38N	29.55 E
Vuollerim	7	Ec	66.25N	20.36 E
Vuosjärvi ⌐	8	Ka	63.00N	25.30 E
Vuotso	7	Gb	68.06N	27.08 E
Vuranimala	63a	Ec	9.05 S	160.51 E
Vyborg	6	Ic	60.42N	28.45 E
Vyčegda ⌐	5	Kc	61.18N	46.36 E
Vyčegodski	7	Lf	61.17N	46.48 E
Východočeský kraj [3]	10	Lf	50.10N	16.00 E
Východoslovenska nižina [3]	10	Rh	48.35N	21.50 E
Východoslovenský kraj [3]	10	Rg	49.00N	21.15 E
Vyg ⌐	7	Ie	63.17N	35.17 E
Vygoda [Ukr.-U.S.S.R.]	15	Mc	46.38N	30.24 E
Vygoda [Ukr.-U.S.S.R.]	10	Uh	48.52N	24.01 E
Vygozero, Ozero- ⌐	5	Jc	63.35N	34.45 E
Vyhandu/Võhandu Jõgi ⌐	8	Lf	58.03N	27.40 E
Vyja ⌐	7	Le	62.46N	46.42 E
Vyksa	19	Ed	55.20N	42.12 E
Vym ⌐	19	Fc	62.13N	50.25 E
Vynnu/Võnnu	8	Lf	58.15N	27.10 E
Vyrica	19	Dd	59.24N	30.19 E
Vyrnwy ⌐	9	Ki	52.45N	2.50W
Vyrtsjarv, Ozero-/Vörts Järv ⌐	7	Gg	58.15N	26.05 E
Vyru/Võru	19	Cd	57.52N	27.05 E
Vyša ⌐	16	Mb	54.53N	42.06 E
Vyšgorod	16	Ge	50.38N	30.28 E
Vyšgorodok	8	Mh	56.55N	28.05 E
Vyškov	10	Mg	49.17N	17.00 E
Vyškovsk, pereval ⌐	10	Th	48.38N	23.45 E
Vyšni Voloček	19	Dd	57.37N	34.32 E
Vysock	7	Gf	60.36N	28.36 E
Vysoké Tatry = High Tatra (EN) ⌐	10	Pg	49.10N	20.00 E
Vysokogorny	20	If	50.07N	139.10 E
Vysokogorsk	28	Mb	44.23N	135.23 E
Vysokovsk	7	Ih	56.21N	36.29 E
Vyšši Brod	10	Kh	48.37N	14.18 E
Vytebet ⌐	16	Ic	53.53N	35.38 E
Vytegra	19	Dc	61.01N	36.28 E
Vyvenka ⌐	20	Ld	60.10N	165.20 E
Vyzu/Vošu	8	Ke	59.30N	25.50 E
Vzmorje	20	Jg	47.45N	142.30 E
W				
Wa	34	Ec	10.03N	2.29W
Waal ⌐	11	Kc	51.55N	4.30 E
Waalre	12	Hc	51.23N	5.27 E
Waalwijk	12	Hc	51.41N	5.04 E
Waar, Meos- ⌐	26	Jg	2.05 S	134.23 E
Waardgronden ⌐	12	Ha	53.12N	5.05 E
Waarschoot	12	Fc	51.09N	3.36 E
Wabana	42	Mg	47.38N	52.57W
Wabao, Cap- ⌐	63b	Cc	21.36 S	167.51 E
Wabasca ⌐	42	Ge	56.00N	113.53W
Wabasca	44	Cb	55.57N	113.50W
Wabash ⌐	38	Kf	37.46N	88.02W
Wabash	44	Ge	40.48N	85.49W
Wabasha	44	Bd	44.23N	92.02W
Wabash River ⌐	45	Lh	37.46N	88.02W
Wabowden	42	Hf	54.55N	98.38W
Wabrzeźno	10	Oc	53.17N	18.57 E
Wabu Hu ⌐	28	Ke	32.20N	116.55 E
Wachau ⌐	14	Jb	48.20N	15.25 E
Wachile	35	Fe	4.33N	39.03 E
Wachusett Seamount (EN) ⌐	57	Lh	32.00 S	151.20W
Waco	39	Jf	31.55N	97.08W
Waconda Lake ⌐	45	Gg	39.30N	98.30W
Wadayama	29	Dd	35.20N	134.51 E
Wad Bandah	35	Dc	13.06N	27.57 E
Waddän	33	Cd	29.10N	16.08 E
Waddän, Jabal- ⌐	33	Cd	29.20N	16.20 E
Waddeneilanden = West Frisian Islands (EN) ⌐	11	Ka	53.30N	5.00 E
Waddenzee ⌐	12	Ha	53.20N	5.30 E
Waddington, Mount- ⌐	38	Gd	51.23N	125.15W
Wadena	45	Ic	46.26N	95.08W
Wadern	12	Ie	49.32N	6.53 E
Wadern-Nunkirchen	12	Ie	49.32N	6.53 E
Wadersloh	12	Kc	51.44N	8.15 E
Wadsern-Liesborn	12	Kc	51.43N	8.16 E
Wadesboro	44	Gh	34.58N	80.04W
Wadhams	46	Ba	51.30N	127.31W
Wādī Bishah ⌐	23	Fe	21.24N	43.26 E
Wādī Fajr ⌐	23	Ec	30.17N	38.18 E
Wādī Ḥalfā'	31	Kf	21.56N	31.20 E
Wādī Jimāl, Jazīrat- ⌐	24	Fj	24.40N	35.10 E
Wādī Mūsā	24	Fg	30.19N	35.29 E
Wādī Shiḥan ⌐	35	Ib	18.10N	52.57 E
Wādī Madanī	31	Kg	14.24N	33.32 E
Wad Nimr	35	Ec	14.32N	32.08 E
Wadowice	10	Pg	49.53N	19.30 E
Wadsworth	46	Fg	39.38N	119.17W
Wafangdian → Fuxian	27	Ld	39.38N	121.59 E
Wafrah	23	Gd	28.25N	47.56 E
Waga-Gawa ⌐	29	Gb	39.18N	141.07 E
Wagenfeld	12	Kb	52.33N	8.35 E
Wagenfeld-Ströhen	12	Kb	52.33N	8.39 E
Wageningen	12	Hc	51.57N	5.41 E
Wagėr, Qar- ⌐	35	Hc	10.01N	45.30 E
Wager Bay ⌐	38	Kc	65.26N	88.40W
Wagga Wagga	58	Fh	35.07 S	147.22 E
Waghäusel	12	Ke	49.15N	8.30 E
Waghäusel	58	Ch	33.18 S	117.21 E
Waginger See ⌐	10	Ii	47.58N	12.50 E
Wagoner	45	Ii	35.58N	95.22W
Wagon Mound	45	Dh	36.01N	104.42W
Wagontire Mountain ⌐	46	Fe	43.21N	119.53W
Wagrien ⌐	10	Gb	54.15N	10.45 E
Wągrowiec	10	Nc	52.49N	17.11 E
Wah	25	Eb	33.48N	72.42 E
Waha	31	If	30.19N	19.57 E
Wahai	26	Ig	2.48 S	129.30 E
Wahiawa	60	Oc	21.30N	158.02W
Wahoo	45	Hf	41.13N	96.37W
Wahpeton	45	Hc	46.16N	96.36W
Waialeale, Mount- ⌐	65a	Ba	22.04N	159.30W
Waialua	65a	Cb	21.35N	158.08W
Waianae	65a	Cb	21.27N	158.12W
Waiau ⌐	62	Ee	42.47 S	173.22 E
Waiau	61	Df	39.23 S	173.03 E
Waiblingen	10	Fh	48.50N	9.18 E
Waibstadt	12	Ke	49.18N	8.56 E
Waidhofen an der Thaya	14	Jb	48.49N	15.17 E
Waidhofen an der Ybbs	14	Jc	47.58N	14.46 E
Waigame	26	Ig	1.50 S	129.49 E
Waigeo, Pulau- ⌐	57	Ee	0.14 S	130.45 E
Waihi	62	Fb	37.24 S	175.50 E
Waihou ⌐	62	Fb	37.10 S	175.33 E
Waikabubak	26	Gh	9.38 S	119.25 E
Waikare, Lake- ⌐	62	Fb	37.25 S	175.10 E
Waikaremoana, Lake- ⌐	61	Fb	38.45 S	177.05 E
Waikari	62	Fb	37.23 S	174.43 E
Waikawa	62	Fb	46.38 S	169.08 E
Waikouaiti	62	Cf	45.36 S	170.41 E
Wailangilala ⌐	63d	Cb	16.45 S	179.06W
Wailua	65a	Ba	22.03 S	159.20W
Wailuku	60	Oc	20.53N	156.30W
Waimamaku	62	Ea	35.34 S	173.29 E
Waimanalo Beach	65a	Db	21.20N	157.42W
Waimangaroa	62	Dd	41.43 S	171.46 E
Waimate	62	Df	44.45 S	171.03 E
Waimea	65a	Fc	20.02N	155.40W
Wainfleet All Saints	9	Ni	53.07N	0.15 E
Waingangā ⌐	25	Fd	19.36N	79.48 E
Waingapu	26	Hh	9.39 S	120.16 E
Waini Point ⌐	50	Ba	8.24N	59.49W
Waini River ⌐	50	Ba	8.24N	59.51W
Wainwright [Ak.-U.S.]	40	Gb	70.38N	160.01W
Wainwright [Alta.-Can.]	42	Gf	52.49N	110.52W
Waiouru	61	Eg	39.29 S	175.40 E
Waipahu	65a	Cb	21.23N	158.01W
Waipara	62	Ee	43.03 S	172.45 E
Waipawa	62	Gc	39.56 S	176.35 E
Waipiro	62	Hc	38.02 S	178.20 E
Waipu	62	Fa	35.59 S	174.26 E
Waipukurau	62	Gd	40.00 S	176.33 E
Wairakei	62	Gc	38.37 S	176.05 E
Wairarapa, Lake- ⌐	62	Fd	41.15 S	175.15 E
Wairau ⌐	61	Fd	41.31 S	174.03 E
Wairoa	61	Fg	39.03 S	177.26 E
Wairoa ⌐	62	Fa	36.11 S	174.02 E
Waitaki ⌐	62	Df	44.56 S	171.09 E
Waitangi	61	Fh	43.56 S	176.34W
Waitara	61	Dg	39.00 S	174.14 E
Waitati	62	Cf	45.45 S	170.34 E
Waitotara	62	Fc	39.48 S	174.44 E
Waiwerang	26	Hh	8.23 S	123.09 E
Waiwerang	61	Fc	16.48 S	179.59W
Wäjid	35	Ge	3.50N	43.14 E
Wajima	28	Nf	37.24N	136.54 E
Wajir	31	Lh	1.42N	40.04 E
Waka [Eth.]	35	Fd	7.09N	37.19 E
Waka [Zaire]	36	Db	1.01N	20.13 E
Wakamatsu-Shima ⌐	29	Ae	32.54N	129.02 E
Wakatipu, Lake- ⌐	61	Ci	45.05 S	168.35 E
Wakaya ⌐	63d	Bb	17.37 S	179.00 E
Wakayama	22	Ne	34.13N	135.11 E
Wakayama Ken [2]	28	Mh	33.55N	135.20 E
Wa Keeney	45	Gg	39.01N	99.53W
Wakefield [Eng.-U.K.]	9	Lh	53.42N	1.29W
Wakefield [N.Z.]	62	Ed	41.24 S	173.03 E

Wake Island [5] 58 Jd 19.18N 166.36W
Wake Island 57 Hc 19.18N 166.36 E
Wakkanai 22 Qe 45.25N 141.40 E
Wakunai 63a Ba 5.52S 155.13 E
Wakuya 29 Gb 38.33N 141.05 E
Wala 36 Fd 5.46S 32.04 E
Walachia (EN) = Valahia 5 Ig 44.00N 25.00 E
Walachia (EN) = Valahia 15 He 44.00N 25.00 E
Wałbrzych [2] 10 Mf 50.45N 16.15 E
Wałbrzych 6 He 50.46N 16.17 E
Walchensee 10 Hi 47.35N 11.20 E
Walcheren 11 Jc 51.33N 3.35 E
Walcott, Lake- 46 Ie 42.40N 113.23W
Walcourt 12 Gd 50.15N 4.25 E
Walcourt-Fraire 12 Gd 50.16N 4.30 E
Wałcz 10 Mc 53.17N 16.28 E
Waldböckelheim 12 Je 49.49N 7.43 E
Waldbröl 10 Df 50.53N 7.37 E
Waldeck 12 Kc 51.17N 8.50 E
Waldeck 12 Lc 51.12N 9.05 E
Waldems 12 Kd 50.15N 8.18 E
Walden 45 Cf 40.44N 106.17W
Waldfischbach-Burgalben 12 Je 49.17N 7.40 E
Waldkirchen 10 Jh 48.44N 13.36 E
Waldkraiburg 10 Ih 48.12N 12.25 E
Wald-Michelbach 12 Ke 49.34N 8.49 E
Waldnaab 10 Ig 49.35N 12.07 E
Waldorf 44 If 38.37N 76.54W
Waldrach 12 Ie 49.45N 6.45 E
Waldron 45 Ii 34.54N 94.05W
Waldshut 10 Ei 47.37N 8.13 E
Waldviertel 14 Jb 48.30N 15.30 E
Waleabahi, Pulau- 26 Hg 0.15S 122.20 E
Wales 40 Fc 65.36N 168.05W
Wales 42 Ic 67.50N 86.40W
Wales 5 Fe 52.30N 3.30W
Wales [2] 9 Ji 52.30N 3.30W
Walewale 34 Ec 10.21N 0.48W
Walferdange 12 Ie 49.39N 6.08 E
Walgett 58 Fh 30.01S 148.07 E
Walgreen Coast 66 Of 75.15S 105.00W
Walhalla 45 Hb 48.55N 97.55W
Walikale 36 Ec 1.25S 28.03 E
Walker 45 Ic 47.06N 94.35W
Walker Lake 43 Dd 38.40N 118.43W
Walkerston 59 Jd 21.10S 149.10 E
Wall 45 Ed 44.01N 102.14W
Wallace 46 Hc 47.28N 115.56W
Wallaceburg 44 Fd 42.36N 82.23W
Wallangarra 59 Ke 28.56S 151.56 E
Wallaroo 59 Hf 33.56S 137.38 E
Wallary Island 59 Ic 15.05S 141.50 E
Wallasey 9 Jh 53.26N 3.03W
Walla Walla 43 Db 46.08N 118.20W
Walldorf 12 Ke 49.20N 8.39 E
Wallenhorst 12 Kb 52.21N 8.01 E
Wallibu 51n Ba 13.19N 61.15W
Wallingford 12 Ac 51.36N 1.08W
Wallis, Iles-=Wallis Islands (EN) 57 Jf 13.18S 176.10W
Wallis and Futuna (EN)= Wallis-et-Futuna, Iles-[5] 58 Jf 14.00S 177.00W
Walliser Alpen/Alpes Valaisannes 14 Bd 46.10N 7.30 E
Wallis-et-Futuna, Iles-= Wallis and Futuna (EN) [5] 58 Jf 14.00S 177.00W
Wallis Islands (EN)=Wallis, Iles- 57 Jf 13.18S 176.10W
Wallowa 46 Gd 45.34N 117.32W
Wallowa Mountains 46 Gd 45.10N 117.30W
Walmer 12 Dc 51.12N 1.24 E
Walney, Isle of- 9 Jg 54.07N 3.15W
Walnut Ridge 43 Id 36.04N 90.57W
Walpole, Ile- 57 Hg 22.37S 168.57 E
Walrus Islands 40 Ge 58.45N 160.20W
Walsall 9 Li 52.35N 1.58W
Walsenburg 43 Gd 37.37N 104.47W
Walsrode 10 Fd 52.52N 9.35 E
Walterboro 44 Gi 32.54N 80.39W
Walter F. George Lake 44 Ej 31.49N 85.08W
Walter Lake 43 Dd 38.44N 118.43W
Walters 45 Gi 34.22N 98.19W
Waltershausen 10 Gf 50.54N 10.34 E
Waltham 44 Ic 45.58N 76.57W
Walton-on-the-Naze 12 Dc 51.51N 1.17 E
Waltrop 12 Jc 51.38N 7.24 E
Walvisbaai/Walvis Bay [3] 37 Ad 23.00S 14.30 E
Walvisbaai=Walvis Bay (EN) 31 Ik 22.59S 14.31 E
Walvisbaai=Walvis Bay (EN) [5] 31 Ik 22.59S 14.31 E
Walvisbaai=Walvis Bay (EN) 30 Ik 22.57S 14.30 E
Walvis Bay/Walvisbaai [3] 37 Ad 23.00S 14.30 E
Walvis Bay (EN)= Walvisbaai 30 Ik 22.57S 14.30 E
Walvis Bay (EN)= Walvisbaai [5] 31 Ik 22.59S 14.31 E
Walvis Bay (EN)= Walvisbaai 31 Ik 22.59S 14.31 E
Walvis Ridge (EN) 3 El 28.00S 3.00 E
Wamba 30 Ii 3.56S 17.12 E
Wamba [Kenya] 36 Gb 0.59N 37.19 E
Wamba [Nig.] 34 Gd 8.56N 8.36 E
Wamba [Zaire] 36 Eb 2.09N 28.00 E
Wamena 26 Kg 4.00S 138.57 E
Wami 30 Ki 6.08S 38.49 E
Wampusirpi 49 Ef 15.15N 84.37W
Wamsutter 46 Lf 41.40N 107.58W
Wan 26 Kh 8.23S 137.56 E
Wana 25 Db 32.17N 69.35 E
Wanaka 58 Hi 44.42S 169.08 E
Wanaka, Lake- 62 Cf 44.30S 169.10 E
Wan'an 27 Jf 26.32N 114.48 E
Wanapiri 26 Kg 4.33S 135.59 E
Wanapitei Lake 44 Gb 46.45N 80.45W
Wandel Hav=Wandel Sea (EN) 41 Gb 83.00N 15.00W
Wandel Sea (EN)=Wandel Hav 41 Gb 83.00N 15.00W
Wandsworth, London- 12 Bc 51.27N 0.12W
Wanganui 62 Fc 39.58S 175.00 E
Wanganui 61 Eg 39.56S 175.02 E
Wangaratta 59 Jg 36.22S 146.20 E
Wangcun [China] 28 Df 36.41N 117.42 E
Wangcun [China] 27 Jd 39.58N 112.53 E
Wangda/Zogang 27 Gf 29.37N 97.58 E
Wangdu 28 Ce 38.43N 115.09 E
Wangen in Allgäu 10 Fi 47.41N 9.50 E
Wangerooge 10 Dc 53.46N 7.55 E
Wanggameti, Gunung- 26 Hi 10.07S 120.14 E
Wanggezhuang → Jiaonan 28 Eg 35.53N 119.58 E
Wangiwangi, Pulau- 26 Hh 5.20S 123.35 E
Wangjiang 28 Di 30.08N 116.41 E
Wangkui 27 Mb 46.50N 126.29 E
Wangpan Yang 21 Of 30.33N 121.26 E
Wangping 27 Mc 43.18N 129.46 E
Wangying → Huaiyin 28 Eh 33.35N 119.02 E
Waní, Laguna- 49 Ff 14.50N 83.25W
Wanie-Rukula 36 Eb 0.14N 25.34 E
Wanitsuka-Yama 29 Bf 31.45N 131.17 E
Wankie 31 Jj 18.21S 26.30 E
Wanlewëyn 35 Ge 2.35N 44.55 E
Wan Namton 25 Jd 22.03N 99.33 E
Wannian (Chenying) 28 Dj 28.42N 117.04 E
Wanning 27 Jh 18.59N 110.24 E
Wanquan 28 Cd 40.52N 114.44 E
Wansbeck 9 Lf 55.10N 1.34W
Wan Shui 28 Di 30.30N 117.01 E
Wanxian 22 Mf 30.48N 108.21 E
Wanyuan 27 Ie 32.03N 108.04 E
Wanzai 28 Cj 28.06N 114.27 E
Wanzhi → Wuhu 28 Ei 31.21N 118.23 E
Wapato 46 Ec 46.27N 120.25W
Wapiti 46 Kd 44.28N 109.28W
Wapiti 42 Fe 55.08N 118.19W
Wapsipinicon River 45 Kf 41.44N 90.20W
Waqooyi Galbeed [3] 35 Gc 10.00N 44.00 E
Warangal 22 Jh 18.18N 79.35 E
Waratah Bay 59 Jg 38.50S 146.05 E
Warburg 10 Fe 51.30N 9.10 E
Warburger Borde 12 Lc 51.35N 9.12 E
Warburg-Scherfede 12 Lc 51.32N 9.02 E
Warburton Bay 42 Gd 63.50N 111.30W
Warburton Mission 59 Fe 26.10S 126.35 E
Warburton Range 59 Fe 26.10S 126.40 E
Ward 62 Fd 41.50S 174.08 E
Warden 37 De 27.56S 29.00 E
Wardenburg 12 Ka 53.04N 8.12 E
Wardha 25 Fd 20.45N 78.37 E
Ward Hunt Strait 59 Ja 9.25S 149.55 E
Ware [B.C.-Can.] 42 Ee 57.27N 125.38W
Ware [Eng.-U.K.] 12 Bc 51.49N 0.01W
Waregem 12 Fd 50.53N 3.25 E
Waremme/Borgworm 11 Ld 50.42N 5.15 E
Waren [G.D.R.] 10 Ic 53.31N 12.41 E
Waren [Indon.] 58 Ee 2.16S 136.20 E
Warendorf 10 De 51.57N 7.59 E
Warin Chamrap 25 Ke 15.14N 104.52 E
Warka 10 Re 51.47N 21.10 E
Warkworth 62 Fb 36.24S 174.40 E
Warmbad [3] 37 Be 28.00S 18.30 E
Warmbad [Nam.] 37 Be 28.29S 18.41 E
Warmbad [S.Afr.] 37 Dd 24.53S 28.17 E
Warming Land 41 Gb 81.50N 52.45W
Warmington 12 Ab 52.08N 1.24W
Warminster 9 Kj 51.13N 2.12W
Warm Springs [Nv.-U.S.] 46 Gg 38.13N 116.20W
Warm Springs [Or.-U.S.] 46 Ed 44.46N 121.16W
Warnemünde, Rostock- 10 Ib 54.10N 12.05 E
Warner, Mount- 46 Da 51.03N 123.12W
Warner Mountains 43 Cc 41.40N 120.20W
Warner Peak 46 Fe 42.27N 119.44W
Warner Robins 43 Ke 32.37N 83.36W
Warner Valley 46 Fe 42.30N 119.55W
Warnes 54 Fg 17.30S 63.10W
Warnow 10 Ib 54.06N 12.09 E
Waroona 59 Df 32.50S 115.55 E
Warragul 59 Jg 38.10S 145.56 E
Warrego Range 59 Je 25.00S 145.45 E
Warrego River 57 Fh 30.24S 145.21 E
Warren [Ar.-U.S.] 45 Jj 33.38N 92.05W
Warren [Mi.-U.S.] 44 Fd 42.28N 83.01W
Warren [Mn.-U.S.] 45 Hb 48.12N 96.46W
Warren [Oh.-U.S.] 43 Kc 41.15N 80.49W
Warren [Pa.-U.S.] 44 He 41.52N 79.09W
Warrenpoint/An Pointe 9 Gg 54.06N 6.15W
Warrensburg 45 Jg 38.46N 93.44W
Warrenton 37 Ce 28.09S 24.47 E
Warri 34 Gd 5.31N 5.45 E
Warrington [Eng.-U.K.] 9 Kh 53.24N 2.37W
Warrington [Fl.-U.S.] 44 Dj 30.23N 87.16W
Warrior Reefs 59 Ia 9.35S 143.10 E
Warrnambool 58 Fh 38.23S 142.29 E
Warroad 43 Hb 48.54N 95.19W
Warrumbungle Range 59 Jf 31.30S 149.40 E
Warsaw [In.-U.S.] 44 Ee 41.14N 85.51W
Warsaw [Mo.-U.S.] 45 Jg 38.15N 93.23W
Warsaw [N.Y.-U.S.] 44 Hd 42.45N 78.07W
Warsaw (EN)=Warszawa 6 Ie 52.15N 21.00 E
Warshikh 35 He 2.18N 45.48 E
Warstein 12 Kc 51.27N 8.22 E
Warstein-Belecke 12 Kc 51.29N 8.20 E
Warszawa [2] 10 Qd 52.15N 21.00 E
Warszawa=Warsaw (EN) 6 Ie 52.15N 21.00 E
Warta 5 He 52.35N 14.39 E
Waru 26 Jg 3.24S 130.40 E
Warwick 59 Ke 28.13S 152.02 E
Warwick 9 Li 52.25N 1.30W
Warwick [Eng.-U.K.] 9 Li 52.17N 1.34W
Warwick [R.I.-U.S.] 44 Le 41.42N 71.23W
Warwickshire [3] 9 Li 52.10N 1.35W
Wasagu 34 Gc 11.22N 5.48 E
Wasatch Range 38 He 41.15N 111.30W
Wascana Creek 46 Ma 50.40N 104.55W
Wasco 46 Fi 35.36N 119.20W
Waseca 45 Jd 44.05N 93.30W
Washburn 45 Fc 47.17N 101.02W
Washess Bay 64g Ab 1.49N 157.31W
Wāshim 25 Fd 20.10N 76.58 E
Washington [2] 43 Cb 47.30N 120.30W
Washington [D.C.-U.S.] 39 Lf 38.54N 77.01W
Washington [Eng.-U.K.] 9 Lg 54.54N 1.31W
Washington [Ga.-U.S.] 44 Fi 33.44N 82.44W
Washington [Ia.-U.S.] 45 Kf 41.18N 91.42W
Washington [In.-U.S.] 44 Df 38.40N 87.10W
Washington [N.C.-U.S.] 44 Ih 35.33N 77.03W
Washington [Pa.-U.S.] 44 Ge 40.11N 80.16W
Washington → Teraina Island 57 Kd 4.43N 160.24W
Washington, Mount- 38 Le 44.15N 71.15W
Washington Court House 44 Ff 39.32N 83.29W
Washington Island 45 Md 45.23N 86.55W
Washington Land 41 Fb 80.15N 65.00W
Washita River 45 Hi 34.12N 96.50W
Washtucna 46 Fc 46.45N 118.19W
Wasile 26 If 1.04N 127.59 E
Wasilków 10 Tc 53.12N 23.12 E
Wasior 26 Jg 2.43S 134.30 E
Wāsiţ [3] 24 Lf 32.35N 46.00 E
Wāsiţ 24 Lf 32.11N 46.18 E
Wąsosz 10 Me 51.34N 16.42 E
Waspán 47 Hf 14.44N 83.58W
Wassamu 29a Ca 44.02N 142.24 E
Wassenaar 12 Gb 52.09N 4.24 E
Wassenberg 12 Ic 51.06N 6.09 E
Wasserburg am Inn 10 Ih 48.04N 12.14 E
Wasserkuppe 10 Ff 50.30N 9.56 E
Wassigny 12 Fd 50.01N 3.36 E
Wassuk Range 46 Fg 38.40N 118.50W
Wassy 11 Kf 48.30N 4.57 E
Waswanipi, Lac- 44 Ia 49.32N 76.29W
Watampone 22 Oj 4.32S 120.20 E
Watansoppeng 26 Gg 4.21S 119.53 E
Watari 29 Gb 38.02N 140.51 E
Waterbeach 12 Cb 52.16N 0.12 E
Waterberg 37 Bd 20.25S 17.15 E
Waterbury 43 Mc 41.33N 73.02W
Water Cays 49 Ib 23.40N 77.45W
Wateree Pond 44 Gh 34.25N 80.50W
Waterford/Port Láirge 6 Fe 52.15N 7.06W
Waterford/Port Láirge [2] 9 Fi 52.10N 7.40W
Waterford Harbour/Cuan Phort Láirge 9 Gi 52.10N 6.57W
Wateringues 11 Ic 51.00N 2.30 E
Waterloo [Bel.] 11 Kd 50.43N 4.24 E
Waterloo [Ia.-U.S.] 43 Ic 42.30N 92.20W
Waterloo [Il.-U.S.] 45 Kg 38.20N 90.09W
Waterlooville 12 Ad 50.52N 1.01W
Watersmeet 44 Cb 46.18N 89.11W
Watertown [N.Y.-U.S.] 43 Lc 43.57N 75.56W
Watertown [S.D.-U.S.] 43 Hc 44.54N 97.07W
Watertown [Wi.-U.S.] 45 Le 43.12N 88.43W
Waterville 43 Nc 44.33N 69.38W
Watford 9 Mj 51.40N 0.25W
Watford City 45 Ec 47.48N 103.17W
Wa'th 35 Ed 8.10N 32.07 E
Watheroo 59 Df 30.17S 116.04 E
Watir, Wādi- 24 Fh 29.01N 34.40 E
Watkins Glen 44 Id 42.23N 76.53W
Watling → San Salvador 47 Jd 24.02N 74.28W
Watlington 12 Ac 51.38N 1.00W
Watonga 45 Gi 35.51N 98.25W
Watou, Poperinge- 12 Ed 50.51N 2.37 E
Watrous 42 Gf 51.40N 105.28W
Watsa 31 Jh 3.03N 29.32 E
Watseka 45 Mf 40.47N 87.44W
Watsi [C.R.] 49 Fi 9.37N 82.52W
Watsi [Zaire] 36 Dc 0.19S 21.04 E
Watsi Kengo 36 Dc 0.48S 20.33 E
Watson Lake 39 Gc 60.07N 128.48W
Watsonville 46 Eh 36.55N 121.45W
Watt, Morne- 51g Bb 15.19N 61.19W
Watton 12 Cb 52.34N 0.50 E
Watts Bar Lake 44 Eh 35.48N 84.39W
Wattwil 14 Dc 47.18N 9.05 E
Watubela, Kepulauan- 26 Jg 4.35S 131.40 E
Wau 59 Ja 7.20S 146.45 E
Waubay Lake 45 Hd 45.25N 97.25W
Wauchope 59 Kf 31.27S 152.44 E
Wauchula 44 Gl 27.33N 81.49W
Waucoba Mountain 46 Fh 37.00N 118.01W
Waukara, Gunung- 26 Gg 1.15S 119.42 E
Waukarlycarly, Lake- 59 Ed 21.25S 121.50 E
Waukegan 43 Jc 42.22N 87.50W
Waukesha 45 Le 43.01N 88.14W
Waupaca 45 Ld 44.21N 89.05W
Wausau 43 Jc 44.59N 89.39W
Wauseon 44 Ee 41.33N 84.09W
Wauwatosa 45 Me 43.03N 88.00W
Wave Hill 59 Gc 17.29S 130.57 E
Waveney 9 Oi 52.28N 1.45 E
Waver/Wavre 12 Kd 50.43N 4.37 E
Waverly [Ia.-U.S.] 45 Je 42.44N 92.29W
Waverly [Oh.-U.S.] 44 Ff 39.07N 82.59W
Waverly [Tn.-U.S.] 44 Dg 36.05N 87.48W
Waves 44 Jh 35.37N 75.29W
Wavre/Waver 12 Kd 50.43N 4.37 E
Wāw 31 Jh 7.42N 28.00 E
Wawa [Nig.] 34 Fd 9.55N 4.27 E
Wawa [Ont.-Can.] 42 Jg 47.59N 84.47W
Wawa, Rio- 49 Fg 13.53N 83.28W
Wāw al Kabīr 31 If 25.20N 16.43 E
Wāw an Nāmūs 33 Ce 24.55N 19.45 E
Wāw Nahr 35 Dd 7.03N 27.13 E
Wawo 26 Hg 3.41S 121.02 E
Wawotobi 26 Hg 3.51S 122.06 E
Waxahachie 45 Hj 32.24N 96.51W
Waxweiler 12 Id 50.06N 6.22 E
Waxxari 27 Ed 38.37N 87.22 E
Way, Lake- 59 Ee 26.50S 120.20 E
Waya 63d Ab 17.18S 177.08 E
Wayabula 26 If 2.17N 128.12 E
Wayan 46 Je 43.00N 111.22W
Waycross 43 Ke 31.13N 82.21W
Wayne [Nb.-U.S.] 45 He 42.14N 97.01W
Wayne [W.V.-U.S.] 44 Ff 38.14N 82.27W
Waynesboro [Ga.-U.S.] 44 Fi 33.06N 82.01W
Waynesboro [Ms.-U.S.] 45 Lk 31.40N 88.39W
Waynesboro [Pa.-U.S.] 44 If 39.45N 77.36W
Waynesboro [Va.-U.S.] 44 Hf 38.04N 78.54W
Waynesville [Mo.-U.S.] 45 Jh 37.50N 92.12W
Waynesville [N.C.-U.S.] 44 Fh 35.29N 83.00W
Waynoka 45 Gh 36.35N 98.53W
Waziers 12 Fd 50.23N 3.07 E
Wda 10 Oc 53.25N 18.29 E
Wdzydze, Jezioro- 10 Nc 54.00N 17.50 E
Wé 61 Cd 20.55S 167.16 E
We, Pulau- 26 Ce 5.51N 95.18 E
Wear 9 Lg 54.55N 1.22W
Weatherford [Ok.-U.S.] 45 Gi 35.32N 98.42W
Weatherford [Tx.-U.S.] 43 He 32.46N 97.48W
Weaverville 46 Df 40.44N 122.56W
Weber 62 Gd 40.24S 176.20 E
Webster 45 Hd 45.20N 97.31W
Webster City 45 Je 42.28N 93.49W
Webster Springs 44 Gf 38.29N 80.25W
Weda 26 If 0.21N 127.52 E
Weda, Teluk- 26 If 0.20N 128.00 E
Weddell Island 56 Hh 51.50S 61.00W
Weddel Sea (EN) 66 Rf 72.00S 45.00W
Wedel 10 Fc 53.35N 9.41 E
Wedgeport 44 Od 43.44N 65.59W
Wedza 37 Ec 18.35S 31.35 E
Weed 46 Df 41.25N 122.27W
Weener 10 Dc 53.10N 7.21 E
Weerdinge, Emmen- 12 Ib 52.49N 6.57 E
Weert 11 Lc 51.15N 5.43 E
Weesp 12 Hb 52.18N 5.02 E
Wegberg 12 Ic 51.09N 6.16 E
Węgliniec 10 Le 51.17N 15.13 E
Węgorzewo 10 Rb 54.14N 21.44 E
Węgrów 10 Sd 52.25N 22.01 E
Wehni 35 Fc 12.40N 36.42 E
Weichang (Zhuizishan) 28 Kc 41.55N 117.45 E
Weida 10 If 50.46N 12.04 E
Weiden in der Oberpfalz 10 Ig 49.41N 12.10 E
Weifang 22 Nf 36.43N 119.06 E
Weihai 27 Ld 37.27N 122.02 E
Weihe 28 Jb 44.55N 128.23 E
Wei He 21 Nf 34.36N 110.10 E
Weilburg 10 Ef 50.29N 8.15 E
Weilerbach 12 Je 49.29N 7.38 E
Weilerswist 12 Id 50.46N 6.50 E
Weilheim in Oberbayern 10 Hi 47.50N 11.09 E
Weilmünster 12 Kd 50.26N 8.21 E
Weimar [F.R.G.] 12 Kd 50.46N 8.43 E
Weimar [G.D.R.] 10 Hf 50.59N 11.19 E
Weinan 27 Ie 34.30N 109.34 E
Weingarten 10 Fi 47.48N 9.38 E
Weinheim 10 Eg 49.33N 8.40 E
Weining 27 Hf 26.46N 104.18 E
Weinsberger Wald 14 Ib 48.25N 15.00 E
Weinstraße 12 Ke 49.20N 8.05 E
Weinviertel 14 Kb 48.35N 16.30 E
Weipa 58 Ff 12.41S 141.52 E
Weirton 44 Ge 40.24N 80.37W
Weiser 46 Gd 44.15N 116.58W
Weiser River 46 Gd 44.15N 116.59W
Weishan Hu 27 Ke 34.35N 117.15 E
Weishi 28 Cg 34.25N 114.10 E
Weishui → Jingxing 28 Ce 38.03N 114.09 E
Weiße Elster 10 He 51.26N 11.57 E
Weißenberg 12 Je 49.15N 7.49 E
Weißenburg in Bayern 10 Gg 49.02N 10.59 E
Weißenfels 10 He 51.12N 11.58 E
Weißer Main 10 Hf 50.05N 11.24 E
Weißerstein 12 Id 50.24N 6.22 E
Weißkugel/Palla Bianca 14 Ed 46.48N 10.44 E
Weiss Lake 44 Eh 34.15N 85.35W
Weißwasser/Běła Woda 10 Ke 51.31N 14.38 E
Weitra 14 Ib 48.42N 14.53 E
Weixi 27 Gf 27.13N 99.19 E
Weixian 28 Cf 36.59N 115.15 E
Weixin (Zhaxi) 27 If 27.46N 105.04 E
Weiz 14 Jc 47.13N 15.37 E
Wejherowo 10 Ob 54.37N 18.15 E
Welbourn Hill 58 Eg 27.21S 134.06 E
Welch 44 Gg 37.26N 81.36W
Weldiya 35 Fc 11.48N 39.35 E
Weld Range 59 De 26.55S 117.25 E
Welega [3] 35 Fd 8.38N 35.40 E
Welel 35 Ed 8.56N 34.52 E
Weligama 25 Gg 5.58N 80.25 E
Welkenraedt 12 Hd 50.39N 5.58 E
Welker Seamount (EN) 40 Ke 55.07N 140.20W
Welkite 35 Fd 8.17N 37.49 E
Welkom 31 Jk 27.59S 26.45 E
Welland 42 Jh 42.59N 79.15W
Welland 9 Ni 52.53N 0.02 E
Welland Canal 44 Hd 43.14N 79.13W
Wellesley Islands 57 Ef 16.45S 139.30 E
Wellin 12 Hd 50.05N 5.07 E
Wellingborough 9 Mi 52.19N 0.42W
Wellington [2] 62 Fd 40.10S 175.30 E
Wellington [Austl.] 59 Jf 32.33S 148.57 E
Wellington [Eng.-U.K.] 9 Jk 50.59N 3.14W
Wellington [Ks.-U.S.] 45 Hh 37.16N 97.24W
Wellington [Nv.-U.S.] 46 Fg 38.45N 119.22W
Wellington [N.Z.] 58 Ii 41.17S 174.46 E
Wellington, Isla- 52 Ij 49.20S 74.40W
Wellington, Lake- 59 Jg 38.10S 147.15 E
Wellington Channel 42 Ia 75.10N 93.00W
Wells [Eng.-U.K.] 9 Kj 51.13N 2.39W
Wells [Nv.-U.S.] 43 Dc 41.07N 115.01W
Wells, Lake- 59 Ee 26.45S 123.15 E
Wells, Mount- 59 Fc 17.26S 127.14 E
Wellsboro 44 Ie 41.45N 77.18W
Wellsford 62 Fb 36.18S 174.31 E
Wells-next-the-Sea 9 Ni 52.58N 0.51 E
Wellton 46 Hj 32.40N 114.08W
Welmel 35 Gd 5.35N 40.55 E
Wełna 10 Md 52.36N 16.50 E
Welo [3] 35 Fc 12.00N 40.00 E
Wels 14 Ib 48.10N 14.02 E
Welshpool 9 Ji 52.40N 3.09W
Welver 12 Jc 51.37N 7.58 E
Welwitschia 37 Ad 20.21S 14.57 E
Welwyn Garden City 9 Mj 51.48N 0.13W
Wema 36 Dc 0.26S 21.38 E
Wemding 10 Gh 48.52N 10.43 E
Wen'an 28 De 38.52N 116.30 E
Wenatchee 43 Cb 47.25N 120.19W
Wenatchee Mountains 46 Ec 47.20N 120.45W
Wenchang 27 Jh 19.43N 110.44 E
Wenchi 34 Ed 7.44N 2.06W
Wenchit 35 Fc 10.03N 38.35 E
Wenden 12 Jd 50.58N 7.52 E
Wendeng 27 Ld 37.10N 122.01 E
Wendland 10 Gc 53.10N 11.00 E
Wendo 35 Fd 6.37N 38.25 E
Wengyuan (Longxian) 27 Jg 24.21N 114.13 E
Wen He 28 Ef 37.06N 119.29 E
Wenling 27 Lf 28.23N 121.22 E
Wenquan 27 Fe 33.15N 91.55 E
Wenquan/Arixang 27 Dc 44.59N 81.04 E
Wenshan 27 Hg 23.22N 104.23 E
Wenshui 28 Bf 37.26N 112.01 E
Wensu 27 Dc 41.15N 80.14 E
Wensum 12 Db 52.37N 1.22 E
Wentworth 59 If 34.07S 141.55 E
Wenxian 27 He 32.52N 104.40 E
Wenzhou 22 Og 27.57N 120.38 E
Wenzhu 27 Jf 27.00N 114.00 E
Wepener 37 De 29.46S 27.00 E
Wépion, Namur- 12 Gd 50.25N 4.52 E
Werda 37 Ce 25.16S 23.17 E
Werder 31 Lh 7.00N 45.21 E
Werder 10 Jc 53.40N 13.25 E
Werdohl 12 Jc 51.16N 7.46 E
Were Ilu 35 Fc 10.38N 39.23 E
Werkendam 12 Gc 51.49N 4.55 E
Werl 12 Jc 51.33N 7.55 E
Werlte 12 Jb 52.51N 7.41 E
Wermelskirchen 12 Jc 51.09N 7.13 E
Werne 12 Jc 51.40N 7.38 E
Wernigerode 10 Ge 51.50N 10.47 E
Werra 5 Ge 51.26N 9.39 E
Werribee 59 Ig 37.54S 144.40 E
Werris Creek 59 Kf 31.21S 150.39 E
Werse 12 Jb 52.02N 7.41 E
Wertach 10 Gh 48.24N 10.53 E
Wertheim 10 Fg 49.45N 9.31 E
Wesel 10 Ce 51.40N 6.37 E
Weser 5 Ge 53.32N 8.34 E
Weserbergland 10 Fe 51.55N 9.30 E
Wesergebirge 10 Fd 52.15N 9.10 E
Weslaco 45 Gm 26.09N 98.01W
Wesley 51g Ba 15.34N 61.19W
Wesleyville 42 Mg 49.09N 53.34W
Wessel, Cape- 59 Hb 11.00S 136.45 E
Wesseling 12 Id 50.50N 6.59 E
Wessel Islands 57 Ef 12.00S 136.45 E
Wessington Springs 45 Gd 44.05N 98.34W
West Allis 45 Me 43.01N 88.00W
West Baines River 59 Gc 15.26S 130.08 E
West Bay 45 Ll 29.00N 89.30W
West Bend 45 Le 43.25N 88.11W
West Bengal [3] 25 Hd 24.00N 88.00 E
West Berlin (EN)=Berlin (West) 6 He 52.31N 13.24 E
West Branch 44 Ec 44.17N 84.14W
West Bridgford 12 Ab 52.55N 1.07W
West Bromwich 9 Li 52.31N 1.59W
Westbrook 44 Ld 43.41N 70.21W
West Burra 9 La 60.05N 1.10W
West Caicos 49 Kc 21.47N 72.17W
West Cape 57 Hi 45.55S 166.26 E
West Caroline Basin (EN) 3 Ii 4.00N 138.00 E
West Carpathians (EN)= Západné Karpaty 10 Og 49.30N 19.00 E
West Des Moines 45 Jf 41.35N 93.43W
Westdongeradeel 12 Ha 53.23N 5.58 E
Westdongeradeel-Holwerd 12 Ha 53.22N 5.54 E
Westdongeradeel-Ternaard 12 Ha 53.23N 5.58 E
Westeinderplassen 12 Gb 52.15N 4.30 E
West Elk Mountains 45 Cg 38.40N 107.15W
West End 44 Hl 26.41N 78.58W
Westende, Middelkerke- 12 Ec 51.10N 2.46 E
West End Village 51b Ab 18.11N 63.09W
West Entrance 64a Bb 7.57N 134.30 E
Westerbork 12 Ib 52.51N 6.36 E
Westerburg 12 Jd 50.34N 7.59 E
Westerland 10 Eb 54.54N 8.18 E
Westerlo 12 Gc 51.05N 4.55 E
Western [Ghana] [3] 34 Ed 5.30N 2.30W
Western [Kenya] [3] 36 Fb 0.30N 34.35 E
Western [S.L.] [3] 34 Cd 8.20N 13.00W
Western [Ug.] [3] 36 Fb 1.00N 31.00 E
Western [Zam.] [3] 36 Df 15.00S 24.00 E
Western Australia [2] 59 Ed 25.00S 122.00 E
Western Desert (EN)= Gharbīyah, Aş Şaḩrā' Al- 30 Jf 27.30N 28.00 E
Western Dvina (EN)= Zapadnaja Dvina 5 Id 57.04N 24.03 E
Western Entrance 63a Bb 6.55S 155.40 E
Western Ghats/Sahyadri 21 Jh 14.00N 75.00 E
Western Isles [3] 9 Fd 57.40N 7.10W
Western Port 59 Jg 38.25S 145.10 E
Western River 42 Gc 66.22N 107.15W
Western Sahara (EN) [5] 31 Ff 24.30N 13.00W

Index Symbols

[1] Independent Nation
[2] State, Region
[3] District, County
[4] Municipality
[5] Colony, Dependency
Continent
Physical Region

Historical or Cultural Region
Mount, Mountain
Volcano
Hill
Mountains, Mountain Range
Hills, Escarpment
Plateau, Upland

Pass, Gap
Plain, Lowland
Delta
Salt Flat
Valley, Canyon
Crater, Cave
Karst Features

Depression
Polder
Desert, Dunes
Forest, Woods
Heath, Steppe
Oasis
Cape, Point

Coast, Beach
Cliff
Peninsula
Isthmus
Sandbank
Island
Atoll

Rock, Reef
Islands, Archipelago
Rocks, Reefs
Coral Reef
Well, Spring
Geyser
River, Stream

Waterfall Rapids
River Mouth, Estuary
Lake
Salt Lake
Intermittent Lake
Reservoir
Swamp, Pond

Canal
Glacier
Ice Shelf, Pack Ice
Ocean
Sea
Gulf, Bay
Strait, Fjord

Lagoon
Bank
Seamount
Tablemount
Ridge
Shelf
Basin

Escarpment, Sea Scarp
Fracture
Trench, Abyss
National Park, Reserve
Point of Interest
Recreation Site
Cave, Cavern

Historic Site
Ruins
Wall, Walls
Church, Abbey
Temple
Scientific Station
Airport

Port
Lighthouse
Mine
Tunnel
Dam, Bridge

Western Samoa (EN)= Samoa I Sisifo [1] 58 Jf 13.40S 172.30W
Western Sayans (EN)= Zapadnyj Sajan 21 Ld 53.00N 94.00 E
Western Sierra Madre (EN) =Madre Occidental, Sierra- 38 Ig 25.00N 105.00W
Western Turkistan (EN) 21 He 41.00N 60.00 E
Westerschelde=West Schelde (EN) 11 Jc 51.25N 3.45 E
Westerschouwen 12 Fc 51.41N 3.43 E
Westerschouwen-Haamstede 12 Fc 51.42N 3.45 E
Westerstede 10 Dc 53.15N 7.56 E
Westerwald 10 Df 50.40N 7.55 E
Westerwoldse A 12 Ja 53.10N 7.10 E
West European Basin (EN) 3 De 47.00N 15.00W
West Falkland 52 Kk 51.40S 60.00W
West Falkland/Gran Malvina, Isla- 52 Kk 51.40S 60.00W
West Fayu Island 57 Fd 8.05N 146.44 E
West Fork Big Blue River 45 Hf 40.42N 96.59W
Westfriesland=West Friesland (EN) 11 Kb 52.45N 4.50 E
West Friesland (EN)= Westfriesland 11 Kb 52.45N 4.50 E
West Frisian Islands (EN)= Waddeneilanden 11 Ka 53.30N 5.00 E
Westgate-on-Sea 12 Dc 51.22N 1.21 E
West Glacier 46 Ib 48.30N 113.59W
West Glamorgan [3] 9 Jj 51.40N 3.55W
West Grand Lake 44 Nc 45.15N 67.52W
West Greenland (EN) = Vestgrønland [2] 41 He 69.00N 49.30W
West Helena 45 Ki 34.33N 90.39W
West Hollywood 44 Gm 25.59N 80.11W
Westhope 45 Fb 48.55N 101.01W
West Ice Shelf 66 Gf 67.00S 85.00 E
West Indies 47 Je 19.00N 70.00W
West Indies (EN)=Indias Occidentales 47 Je 19.00N 70.00W
West Island 37b Ab 9.22S 46.13 E
Westkapelle 12 Fc 51.31N 3.26 E
Westkapelle, Knokke- 12 Fc 51.19N 3.18 E
West Lafayette 44 De 40.27N 86.55W
Westland [2] 62 De 43.10S 170.30 E
West Liberty 44 Fg 37.55N 83.16W
Westlock 42 Gf 54.09N 113.52W
West Lunga 36 De 13.06S 24.39 E
Westmalle 12 Gc 51.18N 4.41 E
West Mariana Basin (EN) 3 Ih 15.00N 137.00 E
Westmeath/An Iarmhí [2] 9 Fh 53.30N 7.30W
West Melanesian Trench (EN) 60 Dh 1.00S 150.00 E
West Memphis 43 Id 35.08N 90.11W
West Mersea 12 Cc 51.46N 0.54 E
West Midlands [3] 9 Li 52.30N 2.00W
Westminster 44 If 39.35N 76.59W
Westminster, London- 12 Bc 51.30N 0.07W
West Monroe 45 Jj 32.31N 92.09W
Westmorland 9 Kg 54.30N 2.40W
West Nicholson 31 Jk 21.03S 29.22 E
West Nueces River 45 Gl 29.16N 99.56W
Weston [Mala.] 26 Ge 5.13N 115.36 E
Weston [W.V.-U.S.] 44 Gf 39.03N 80.28W
Weston [Wy.-U.S.] 46 Md 44.42N 105.18W
Weston-super-Mare 9 Kj 51.21N 2.59W
Westoverledingen 12 Ja 53.10N 7.27 E
Westoverledingen - Ihrhove 12 Ja 53.10N 7.27 E
West Palm Beach 39 Kg 26.43N 80.04W
West Pensacola 44 Dj 30.27N 87.15W
West Plains 43 Id 36.44N 91.51W
West Point [Ms.-U.S.] 45 Lj 33.36N 88.39W
West Point [Nb.-U.S.] 45 Hf 41.51N 96.43W
Westport 58 Ii 41.45S 171.36 E
Westport/Cathair na Mart 9 Dh 53.48N 9.32W
Westray 9 Kb 59.20N 3.00W
Westree 44 Gb 47.27N 81.32W
Westrich 12 Je 49.20N 7.25 E
West Road 12 Cd 50.52N 0.50 E
West Schelde (EN)= Westerschelde 11 Jc 51.25N 3.45 E
West Scotia Basin (EN) 52 Kk 57.00S 53.00W
West Siberian Plain (EN)= Zapadno Sibirskaja Ravnina 21 Jc 60.00N 75.00 E
Weststellingwerf 12 Ib 52.53N 6.00 E
Weststellingwerf-Wolvega 12 Ib 52.53N 6.00 E
West Sussex [3] 9 Mk 51.00N 0.40W
West Tavaputs Plateau 46 Jf 40.00N 110.25W
West-Terschelling, Terschelling- 12 Ha 53.21N 5.13 E
West Union [Ia.-U.S.] 45 Ke 42.57N 91.49W
West Union [Oh.-U.S.] 44 Ff 38.48N 83.33W
West Virginia [2] 43 Kd 38.45N 80.30W
West-Vlaanderen [3] 12 Ec 51.00N 3.00 E
Westwood 46 Ef 40.18N 121.00W
West Wyalong 59 Jf 33.55S 147.13 E
West Yellowstone 43 Eb 44.30N 111.05W
West Yorkshire [3] 9 Lh 53.40N 1.30W
Wetar, Pulau- 57 De 7.48S 126.18 E
Wetaskiwin 42 Gf 52.58N 113.22W
Wete 36 Gd 5.04S 39.43 E
Wětošow/Vetschau 10 Ke 51.47N 14.04 E
Wetter 12 Kd 50.18N 8.49 E
Wetter (Hessen) 12 Kd 50.54N 8.43 E
Wetter (Ruhr) 12 Jc 51.23N 7.24 E
Wetterau 10 Ef 50.15N 8.50 E
Wetteren 11 Jc 51.00N 3.53 E
Wetzlar 10 Ef 50.33N 8.30 E
Wevelgem 12 Fd 50.48N 3.10 E
Wewahitchka 44 Ej 30.07N 85.12W
Wewak 58 Fe 3.34S 143.38 E
Wexford/Loch Garman [2] 9 Gi 52.20N 6.40W
Wexford/Loch Garman 6 Fe 52.20N 6.27W
Wexford Harbour/Cuan Loch Garman 9 Gi 52.20N 6.25W
Wey 9 Mj 51.23N 0.28W
Weyburn 42 Hg 49.41N 103.52W
Weyhe 12 Kb 52.59N 8.52 E
Weyhe-Leeste 12 Kb 52.59N 8.50 E
Weymouth 9 Kk 50.36N 2.28W
Wezet/Visé 12 Hd 50.44N 5.42 E
Whakatane 61 Eg 37.58S 177.00 E
Whale Cove 42 Id 62.14N 92.10W
Whalsay 9 Ma 60.22N 0.59W
Whangarei 58 Ih 35.43S 174.19 E
Wharfe 9 Lh 53.51N 1.07W
Wharton 45 Hl 29.19N 96.06W
Wharton Basin (EN) 3 Hk 19.00S 100.00 E
Wharton Lake 42 Hd 64.00N 99.55W
Whataroa 62 De 43.16S 170.22 E
Wheatland 46 Me 42.03N 104.57W
Wheat Ridge 45 Dg 39.46N 105.07W
Wheeler 42 Ke 57.02N 67.14W
Wheeler 46 Dd 45.42N 123.52W
Wheeler Lake 44 Dh 34.40N 87.05W
Wheeler Peak [N.M.-U.S.] 43 Fd 36.34N 105.25W
Wheeler Peak [U.S.] 38 Hf 38.59N 114.19W
Wheeling 43 Kc 40.05N 80.43W
Whidbey Island 46 Db 48.15N 122.40W
Whitby 9 Mg 54.29N 0.37W
Whitchurch [Eng.-U.K.] 9 Ki 52.58N 2.41W
Whitchurch [Eng.-U.K.] 12 Bc 51.53N 0.50W
Whitchurch [Eng.-U.K.] 12 Ac 51.13N 1.20W
White 42 Jc 65.50N 85.00W
White, Lake- 59 Fd 21.05S 129.00 E
White Bay 38 Nd 50.00N 56.30W
White Bear Lake 45 Jd 45.04N 93.01W
White Butte 45 Ec 46.23N 103.19W
White Carpathians (EN) = Bílé Karpaty 10 Nh 48.55N 17.50 E
White Cliffs 59 If 30.51S 143.05 E
White Cloud 44 Ed 43.33N 85.46W
Whitecourt 42 Ff 54.09N 115.41W
Whitefish 43 Eb 48.25N 114.20W
Whitefish Bay 43 Kb 46.40N 84.50W
Whitefish Point 44 Eb 46.45N 85.00W
Whitefish Range 46 Hb 48.40N 114.26W
Whitehall [Mi.-U.S.] 44 Dd 43.24N 86.21W
Whitehall [Mt.-U.S.] 46 Id 45.52N 112.06W
Whitehall [Oh.-U.S.] 44 Ff 39.58N 82.54W
Whitehall [Wi.-U.S.] 45 Kd 44.22N 91.19W
Whitehaven 9 Jg 54.33N 3.35W
Whitehorse 39 Fc 60.43N 135.03W
White Island [Ant.] 66 Ee 66.44S 48.35 E
White Island [N.Z.] 62 Gb 37.30S 177.10 E
White Lake 45 Jl 29.45N 92.30W
White Lake (EN)=Beloje Ozero 5 Jc 60.11N 37.35 E
Whiteman Range 59 Ja 5.50S 149.55 E
Whitemark 59 Jh 40.07S 148.01 E
White Mountain 40 Db 64.35N 163.04W
White Mountain Peak 43 Dd 37.38N 118.15W
White Mountains [Ak.-U.S.] 40 Jc 65.30N 147.00W
White Mountains [U.S.] 46 Fh 37.30N 118.15W
White Mountains [U.S.] 43 Mc 44.10N 71.35W
Whitemouth Lake 45 Ib 49.14N 95.40W
Whitemouth River 45 Ha 50.07N 96.02W
White Nile (EN)=Abyaḍ, Al Baḥr al- 30 Kg 15.38N 32.31 E
White Nile (EN)=Abyaḍ, Al Baḥr al- [3] 35 Ec 12.40N 32.30 E
White Pass [N.Amer.] 40 Le 59.37N 135.08W
White Pass [Wa.-U.S.] 46 Ec 46.38N 121.24W
Whiteriver 46 Kj 33.50N 109.58W
White River [In.-U.S.] 44 Df 38.25N 87.44W
White River [Nv.-U.S.] 46 Hh 37.18N 115.08W
White River [Ont.-Can.] 42 Ig 48.35N 85.17W
White River [S.D.-U.S.] 45 Fe 43.34N 100.45W
White River [Tx.-U.S.] 45 Fj 33.14N 100.56W
White River [U.S.] 46 Kf 40.04N 109.41W
White River [U.S.] 43 Hc 43.45N 99.30W
White River [U.S.] 38 Jf 33.53N 91.03W
White River [Yuk.-Can.] 42 Dd 63.10N 139.32W
White Salmon 46 Ed 45.44N 121.29W
Whitesand Bay 9 Ik 50.20N 4.35W
White Sea (EN)=Beloje More 5 Kb 66.00N 44.00 E
White sea-Baltic Canal (EN) =Belomorsko-Baltijski Kanal 5 Jc 63.30N 34.48 E
White Settlement 45 Hj 32.45N 97.27W
White Sulphur Springs 46 Jc 46.33N 110.54W
Whiteville 44 Hh 34.20N 78.42W
White Volta 30 Gh 8.38N 0.59W
White Volta (EN)=Volta Blanche 30 Gh 8.38N 0.59W
Whitewater 45 Bg 38.59N 108.27W
Whitewater Baldy 45 Bj 33.20N 108.39W
Whitewater Bay 44 Gm 25.16N 81.00W
Whitewater Lake 45 La 50.50N 89.10W
Whitewood 45 Ea 50.20N 102.15W
Whitianga 62 Fb 36.50S 175.42 E
Whitmore Mountains 66 Og 82.35S 104.30W
Whitney 44 Hc 45.30N 78.14W
Whitney, Lake- 45 Hk 31.55N 97.23W
Whitney, Mount- 38 Hf 36.35N 118.18W
Whitstable 12 Dc 51.21N 1.06 E
Whitsunday Island 59 Jd 20.15S 149.00 E
Whittier 40 Jd 60.46N 148.41W
Whittlesea 59 Jg 37.31S 145.07 E
Whittlesey 12 Bb 52.33N 0.08W
Wholdaia Lake 42 Hd 60.45N 104.10W
Whyalla 59 Hf 33.02S 137.35 E
Wiarton 44 Gc 44.45N 81.09W
Wiawso 34 Ed 6.12N 2.29W
Wibaux 46 Mc 46.59N 104.11W
Wichita 39 Jf 37.41N 97.20W
Wichita Falls 39 Jf 33.54N 98.30W
Wichita Mountains 45 Gi 34.45N 98.40W
Wichita River 45 Gi 34.07N 98.10W
Wick 9 Jc 58.26N 3.06W
Wick 9 Jc 58.25N 3.05W
Wickenburg 46 Ij 33.58N 112.44W
Wickepin 59 Df 32.46S 117.30 E
Wickham 12 Ad 50.54N 1.10W
Wickham Market 12 Db 52.09N 1.22 E
Wickiup Reservoir 46 Ee 43.40N 121.43W
Wickliffe 44 Cg 36.58N 89.05W
Wicklow/Cill Mhantáin [2] 9 Gi 53.00N 6.30W
Wicklow/Cill Mhantáin 9 Gi 52.59N 6.03W
Wicklow Head/Ceann Chill Mhantáin 9 Hi 52.58N 6.00W
Wicklow Mountains/ Sléibhte Chill Mhantáin 9 Gh 53.02N 6.24W
Wicko, Jezioro- 10 Mb 54.33N 16.35 E
Wickrath, Mönchengladbach- 12 Ic 51.08N 6.25 E
Widawa 10 Me 51.13N 16.55 E
Wide Bay 59 Ka 5.05S 152.05 E
Widefield 45 Dg 38.42N 104.40W
Widgiemooltha 59 Ef 31.30S 121.34 E
Wi-Do 28 Ig 35.38N 126.17 E
Więcbork 10 Nc 53.22N 17.30 E
Wied 12 Jd 50.27N 7.28 E
Wiedenbrück 12 Kc 50.51N 8.19 E
Wiehengebirge 10 Ed 52.20N 8.40 E
Wiehl 12 Jd 50.57N 7.32 E
Wieliczka 10 Qg 49.59N 20.04 E
Wielimie, Jezioro- 10 Mc 53.47N 16.50 E
Wielki Dział 10 Tf 50.18N 23.25 E
Wielkopolska 10 Ne 51.50N 17.20 E
Wielkopolskie-Kujawskie, Pojezierze- 10 Md 52.25N 16.30 E
Wieluń 10 Oe 51.14N 18.34 E
Wien [2] 14 Kb 48.15N 16.25 E
Wien = Vienna (EN) 6 Hf 48.12N 16.22 E
Wiener Becken 14 Kc 48.00N 16.28 E
Wiener Neustadt 14 Kc 47.48N 16.15 E
Wienerwald=Vienna Woods (EN) 14 Jb 48.10N 16.00 E
Wieprz 10 Re 51.32N 21.49 E
Wieprza 10 Mb 54.26N 16.22 E
Wieprz-Krzna, Kanał- 10 Se 51.56N 22.56 E
Wierden 12 Ib 52.22N 6.36 E
Wieringen 12 Hb 52.56N 5.02 E
Wieringen-Den Oever 12 Hb 52.56N 5.02 E
Wieringen-Hippolytushoef 12 Gb 52.54N 4.59 E
Wieringermeer 12 Hb 52.51N 5.01 E
Wieringermeer Polder 12 Gb 52.50N 5.00 E
Wieringermeer-Wieringerwerf 12 Hb 52.51N 5.01 E
Wieringerwerf, Wieringermeer- 12 Hb 52.51N 5.01 E
Wieruszów 10 Oe 51.18N 18.08 E
Wierzchowo, Jezioro- 10 Mc 53.50N 16.45 E
Wierzyca 10 Oc 53.51N 18.50 E
Wiesbaden 6 Ge 50.05N 8.15 E
Wiese 10 Di 47.35N 7.35 E
Wieslautern 12 Je 49.05N 7.49 E
Wiesloch 10 Eg 49.18N 8.42 E
Wietingsmoor 12 Kb 52.39N 8.39 E
Wietmarschen 12 Jb 52.32N 7.08 E
Wieżyca 10 Ob 54.17N 18.10 E
Wigan 9 Kh 53.32N 2.35W
Wigger 14 Bc 47.15N 7.55 E
Wiggins 45 Lk 30.51N 89.08W
Wight, Isle of- 5 Fe 50.40N 1.20W
Wigry, Jezioro- 10 Tb 54.05N 23.07 E
Wigston 12 Ab 52.35N 1.06W
Wigtown 9 Ig 54.52N 4.26W
Wigtown Bay 9 Ig 54.46N 4.15W
Wijchen 12 Hc 51.48N 5.44 E
Wijdefjorden 41 Nc 79.50N 15.30 E
Wijk bij Duurstede 12 Hc 51.59N 5.22 E
Wil 14 Dc 47.27N 9.05 E
Wilbur 46 Fc 47.46N 118.42W
Wilburton 45 Ii 34.55N 95.19W
Wilcannia 58 Fh 31.34S 143.23 E
Wild Coast 30 Jl 32.00S 29.50 E
Wilder Seamount (EN) 57 Jd 9.00N 173.00W
Wildeshausen 10 Ed 52.54N 8.26 E
Wild Horse 46 Jb 49.01N 110.12W
Wildspitze 14 Ed 46.53N 10.52 E
Wilga 10 Re 51.50N 21.20 E
Wilhelm-II-Land 66 Ge 69.00S 90.00 E
Wilhelminakanaal 12 Gc 51.43N 4.53 E
Wilhelm-Pieck-Stadt-Guben 10 Ke 51.57N 14.43 E
Wilhelmshaven 10 Ec 53.31N 8.08 E
Wilhelmstal 37 Bd 21.54S 16.20 E
Wilkes-Barre 43 Lc 41.15N 75.50W
Wilkesboro 44 Gg 36.09N 81.09W
Wilkes Land (EN) 66 Hf 71.00S 120.00 E
Wilkins Coast 66 Qe 69.40S 63.00W
Wilkins Sound 66 Qf 70.15S 73.00W
Willamette River 46 Dd 45.39N 122.46W
Willandra Billabong Creek 59 If 33.08S 144.06 E
Willapa Bay 46 Dc 46.37N 124.00W
Willard 45 Ci 34.36N 106.02W
Willards, Punta- 48 Cc 28.50N 112.35W
Willcox 46 Kj 32.15N 109.50W
Willebadessen 12 Lc 51.38N 9.02 E
Willebadessen-Peckelsheim 12 Lc 51.36N 9.08 E
Willebroek 12 Gc 51.04N 4.22 E
Willemstad [Neth.] 12 Gc 51.41N 4.26 E
Willemstad [Neth.Ant.] 53 Jd 12.06N 68.56W
Willeroo 59 Gc 15.17S 131.35 E
William Bill Dannelly Reservoir 44 Di 32.15N 86.45W
Williams 43 Ed 35.15N 112.11W
Williamsburg [Ky.-U.S.] 44 Eg 36.44N 84.10W
Williamsburg [Va.-U.S.] 44 Ig 37.17N 76.43W
Williams Lake 42 Ff 52.08N 122.09W
Williamson Glacier 66 He 66.30S 114.30 E
Williamsport 43 Lc 41.16N 77.03W
Williamston 44 Ih 35.50N 77.06W
Williamstown 44 Ef 38.38N 84.34W
Willich 12 Ic 51.16N 6.33 E
Willikie's 51d Bb 17.03N 61.42W
Willingdon, Mount- 46 Ga 51.48N 116.17W
Willis Group 57 Gf 16.20S 150.00 E
Williston [N.D.-U.S.] 43 Gb 48.09N 103.37W
Williston [S.Afr.] 37 Cf 31.20S 20.53 E
Williston Lake 38 Gd 50.57N 122.23W
Willits 46 Dg 39.25N 123.21W
Willmar 43 Hb 45.07N 95.03W
Willoughby Bay 51d Bb 17.02N 61.44W
Willow Bunch Lake 46 Mb 49.27N 105.28W
Willowlake 42 Fd 62.42N 123.08W
Willowmore 37 Cf 33.17S 23.29 E
Willows 46 Dg 39.31N 122.12W
Willow Springs 45 Kh 36.59N 91.58W
Wills, Lake- 59 Fd 21.20S 128.40 E
Wills Point 45 Ij 32.43N 95.57W
Wilma Glacier 66 Ee 67.12S 56.00 E
Wilmington [De.-U.S.] 43 Ld 39.44N 75.33W
Wilmington [N.C.-U.S.] 39 Lf 34.13N 77.55W
Wilmington [Oh.-U.S.] 44 Ff 39.28N 83.50W
Wilnsdorf 12 Kd 50.49N 8.06 E
Wilseder Berg 10 Fc 53.10N 9.56 E
Wilson 43 Ld 35.44N 77.55W
Wilson, Cape - 42 Jc 66.59N 81.27W
Wilson, Mount- 45 Ch 37.51N 107.59W
Wilson Bluff 66 Ff 74.20S 66.47 E
Wilson Lake [Al.-U.S.] 44 Dh 34.49N 87.30W
Wilson Lake [Ks.-U.S.] 45 Gg 38.57N 98.40W
Wilsons Promontory 59 Jg 38.55S 146.20 E
Wilton River 59 Gb 14.45S 134.33 E
Wilts 9 Lj 51.20N 2.00W
Wiltshire [3] 9 Lj 51.30N 2.00W
Wiltz 11 Le 49.58N 5.55 E
Wiluna 59 Ee 26.36S 120.13 E
Wimereux 12 Dd 50.46N 1.37 E
Winamac 44 De 41.03N 86.36W
Winburg 37 De 28.37S 27.00 E
Winchelsea 12 Cd 50.55N 0.43 E
Winchester [Eng.-U.K.] 9 Lj 51.04N 1.19W
Winchester [In.-U.S.] 44 Ee 40.10N 84.59W
Winchester [Ky.-U.S.] 44 Ef 38.01N 84.11W
Winchester [Va.-U.S.] 43 Ld 39.11N 78.12W
Windeck 12 Jd 50.49N 7.34 E
Windemin, Pointe- 63b Ce 16.34S 167.27 E
Winder 44 Fi 34.00N 83.47W
Windermere 9 Kg 54.22N 2.56W
Windermere [B.C.-Can.] 46 Ha 50.30N 115.58W
Windermere [Eng.-U.K.] 9 Kg 54.23N 2.54W
Windhoek 31 Ik 22.34S 17.06 E
Windhoek [3] 37 Bd 22.30S 17.00 E
Windischgarsten 14 Ic 47.43N 14.20 E
Wind Mountain 45 Dj 32.02N 105.34W
Windom 45 Ie 43.52N 95.07W
Windom Mountain 45 Ch 37.37N 107.35W
Windorah 59 Ie 25.26S 142.39 E
Window Rock 46 Ki 35.41N 109.03W
Wind River 46 Ke 43.08N 108.12W
Wind River Peak 46 Ke 42.42N 109.07W
Wind River Range 43 Fc 43.05N 109.25W
Windrush 9 Lj 51.42N 1.25W
Windsor [Eng.-U.K.] 9 Mj 51.29N 0.38W
Windsor [N.S.-Can.] 42 Lh 44.59N 64.09W
Windsor [Ont.-Can.] 42 Jh 42.18N 83.01W
Windsor Forest 44 Gj 31.58N 81.10W
Windward Islands 47 Lf 13.00N 61.00W
Windward Islands (EN)= Barlovento, Islas de- 38 Mh 15.00N 61.00W
Windward Islands (EN) = Sotavento, Islas de- 52 Jd 11.10N 67.00W
Windward Islands (EN)= Vent, Iles du- 57 Mf 17.30S 149.30W
Windward Passage (EN)= Vent, Canal du- 49 Lh 20.00N 73.50W
Windward Passage (EN)= Vientos, Paso de los- 38 Lh 20.00N 73.50W
Winfield [Al.-U.S.] 44 Di 33.56N 87.49W
Winfield [Ks.-U.S.] 43 Hd 37.15N 96.59W
Wingene 12 Fc 51.04N 3.16 E
Wingen-sur-Moder 12 Jf 48.55N 7.22 E
Winisk 38 Kd 55.17N 85.05W
Winisk 39 Kd 55.15N 85.12W
Winisk Lake 42 If 52.55N 87.20W
Winkler 45 Hb 49.11N 97.56W
Winklern 14 Gd 46.52N 12.52 E
Winneba 34 Ed 5.20N 0.37W
Winnebago, Lake- 43 Jc 44.00N 88.25W
Winnemucca 43 Dc 40.58N 117.44W
Winnemucca Lake 46 Ff 40.10N 119.20W
Winner 43 Hc 43.22N 99.51W
Winnett 46 Kc 47.00N 108.21W
Winnfield 45 Jk 31.55N 92.38W
Winnibigoshish, Lake- 45 Ic 47.27N 94.12W
Winnipeg 39 Je 49.53N 97.09W
Winnipeg 38 Jd 50.38N 96.19W
Winnipeg, Lake- 38 Jd 52.00N 97.00W
Winnipeg Beach 45 Ha 50.31N 96.58W
Winnipegosis 42 Hf 51.39N 99.56W
Winnipegosis, Lake- 38 Jd 52.30N 100.00W
Winnipesaukee, Lake- 44 Ld 43.35N 71.20W
Winnsboro 45 Kj 32.10N 91.43W
Winnweiler 12 Je 49.34N 7.51 E
Winona [Mn.-U.S.] 43 Ic 44.03N 91.39W
Winona [Mo.-U.S.] 45 Kh 37.06N 91.19W
Winona [Ms.-U.S.] 45 Lj 33.29N 89.44W
Winschoten 11 Na 53.08N 7.02 E
Winsen 10 Gc 53.22N 10.13 E
Winslow [Az.-U.S.] 43 Ed 35.01N 110.42W
Winslow [Eng.-U.K.] 12 Bc 51.57N 0.52W
Winslow Reef 57 Je 1.36S 174.57W
Winston-Salem 43 Kd 36.06N 80.15W
Winterberg 10 Ee 51.12N 8.32 E
Winter Harbour 42 Gb 74.46N 110.40W
Winter Haven 43 Kf 28.01N 81.44W
Winter Park [Co.-U.S.] 45 Dg 39.47N 105.45W
Winter Park [Fl.-U.S.] 44 Gk 28.36N 81.20W
Winters 45 Gk 31.57N 99.58W
Winterset 45 If 41.20N 94.01W
Winterswijk 11 Mc 51.58N 6.44 E
Winterthur 14 Cc 47.30N 8.45 E
Winton [Austl.] 58 Fg 22.23S 143.02 E
Winton [N.C.-U.S.] 44 Ig 36.24N 76.56W
Winton [N.Z.] 62 Cg 46.09S 168.20 E
Wipper [G.D.R.] 10 He 51.47N 11.42 E
Wipper [G.D.R.] 10 He 51.20N 11.10 E
Wisbech 9 Ni 52.40N 0.10 E
Wiscasset 44 Mc 44.00N 69.40W
Wisch 12 Ic 51.55N 6.22 E
Wisch-Terborg 12 Ic 51.55N 6.22 E
Wisconsin [2] 43 Jc 44.45N 89.30W
Wisconsin 38 Je 43.00N 91.15W
Wisconsin Range 66 Ng 85.45S 125.00W
Wisconsin Rapids 43 Jc 44.23N 89.49W
Wiseman 40 Ic 67.25N 150.06W
Wisła 10 Og 49.39N 18.50 E
Wisła=Vistula (EN) 5 He 54.22N 18.55 E
Wiślana, Mierzeja- 10 Pb 54.25N 19.30 E
Wiślane, Żuławy- 10 Ob 54.10N 19.00 E
Wiślany, Zalew- 10 Pb 54.27N 19.40 E
Wisłok 10 Sf 50.13N 22.32 E
Wisłoka 10 Rf 50.27N 21.23 E
Wismar 10 Hc 53.54N 11.28 E
Wismarbucht 10 Hc 53.57N 11.25 E
Wissant 12 Dd 50.53N 1.40 E
Wissembourg 11 Ne 49.02N 7.57 E
Wissen 10 Df 50.47N 7.45 E
Wissenkerke 12 Fc 51.35N 3.45 E
Wissey 12 Cb 52.34N 0.21 E
Witbank 31 Jk 25.56S 29.07 E
Witchekar Lake 45 Fb 49.15N 100.16W
Witdraai 37 Ce 26.58S 20.41 E
Witham 12 Cc 51.47N 0.38 E
Witham 9 Ni 52.56N 0.04 E
Withernsea 9 Nh 53.44N 0.02 E
Witkowo 10 Nd 52.27N 17.47 E
Witmarsum, Wonseradeel- 12 Ha 53.06N 5.28 E
Witney 9 Lj 51.48N 1.29W
Witnica 10 Kd 52.40N 14.55 E
Witputz 37 Be 27.37S 16.42 E
Witten 10 De 51.26N 7.20 E
Wittenberg [G.D.R.] 10 Ie 51.52N 12.39 E
Wittenberg [Wi.-U.S.] 45 Ld 44.49N 89.10W
Wittenberge 10 Hc 53.00N 11.45 E
Wittenoom 59 Dd 22.17S 118.19 E
Wittingen 10 Gd 52.44N 10.43 E
Wittlich 10 Cg 49.59N 6.53 E
Wittmund 10 Dc 53.34N 7.47 E
Wittow 10 Jb 54.38N 13.19 E
Wittstock 10 Ic 53.09N 12.30 E
Witu 36 Hc 2.23S 40.26 E
Witu Islands 60 Dh 4.40S 149.18 E
Witvlei 37 Bd 22.23S 18.32 E
Witzenhausen 10 Fe 51.20N 9.52 E
Wivenhoe 12 Cc 51.51N 0.58 E
Wizard Reef 30 Mi 8.57S 51.01 E
Wizna 10 Sc 53.13N 22.26 E
Wjdawka 10 Oe 51.32N 18.52 E
W. J. Van Blommestein Meer 54 Hc 4.45N 55.00W
Wkra 10 Qd 52.27N 20.44 E
Władysławowo 10 Ob 54.49N 18.25 E
Włocławek 10 Pd 52.39N 19.02 E
Włocławek [2] 10 Od 52.40N 19.00 E
Włodawa 10 Te 51.34N 23.32 E
Włoszczowa 10 Pf 50.25N 19.59 E
Wodonga 59 Jg 36.17S 146.54 E
Wodzisław Śląski 10 Of 50.00N 18.28 E
Woensdrecht 12 Gc 51.25N 4.18 E
Woerden 12 Gb 52.05N 4.52 E
Woerth 12 Jf 48.56N 7.45 E
Woëvre, Plaine de la- 11 Le 49.15N 5.50 E
Wohlthat-Massif 66 Cf 71.35S 12.20 E
Woippy 12 Ie 49.09N 6.09 E
Wojerecy/Hoyerswerda 10 Ke 51.26N 14.15 E
Wokam, Pulau- 26 Jh 5.37S 134.30 E
Woken He 28 Ja 46.19N 129.34 E
Woking 9 Mj 51.20N 0.34W
Wokingham 12 Bc 51.25N 0.50W
Wolbrom 10 Pf 50.24N 19.46 E
Wolcott 44 Id 43.13N 76.42W
Wołczyn 10 Oe 51.01N 18.03 E
Woldberg 12 Hb 52.55N 5.55 E
Woleai Atoll 57 Fd 7.21N 143.52 E
Woleu-Ntem [3] 36 Bb 2.00N 12.00 E
Wolf, Isla- 54a Aa 1.23N 91.49W
Wolf, Volcán- 54a Ab 0.01S 91.20W
Wolfach 10 Eh 48.18N 8.13 E
Wolf Creek 45 Gh 36.35N 99.30W
Wolf Creek 46 Ic 47.00N 112.04W
Wolfen 10 Ie 51.40N 12.17 E
Wolfenbüttel 10 Gd 52.10N 10.33 E
Wolfhagen 10 Fe 51.19N 9.10 E
Wolf Point 43 Fb 48.05N 105.39W
Wolfratshausen 10 Hi 47.54N 11.25 E
Wolf River 45 Ld 44.11N 88.48W
Wolfsberg 14 Id 46.50N 14.50 E
Wolfsburg 10 Gd 52.26N 10.48 E
Wolfstein 12 Je 49.35N 7.36 E
Wolgast 10 Jb 54.03N 13.46 E
Wolica 10 Tf 50.30N 23.12 E
Wolin 10 Kc 53.51N 14.38 E
Wolin 10 Kc 53.50N 14.35 E
Wollaston 12 Bb 52.15N 0.40W
Wollaston, Islas- 56 Gi 55.40S 67.30W
Wollaston Forland 41 Jd 74.35N 20.15W
Wollaston Lake 38 Id 58.15N 103.20W
Wollaston Lake 42 He 58.05N 103.38W
Wollaston Peninsula 38 Hc 70.00N 115.00W
Wollongong 58 Gh 34.25S 150.54 E
Wöllstein 12 Je 49.49N 7.58 E
Wolmaransstad 37 De 27.12S 26.13 E
Wołomin 10 Rd 52.21N 21.14 E
Wołów 10 Me 51.29N 16.55 E

Index Symbols

[1] Independent Nation
[2] State, Region
[3] District, County
[4] Municipality
[5] Colony, Dependency
Continent
Physical Region
Historical or Cultural Region
Mount, Mountain
Volcano
Hill
Mountains, Mountain Range
Hills, Escarpment
Plateau, Upland
Pass, Gap
Plain, Lowland
Delta
Salt Flat
Valley, Canyon
Crater, Cave
Karst Features
Depression
Polder
Desert, Dunes
Forest, Woods
Heath, Steppe
Oasis
Cape, Point
Coast, Beach
Cliff
Peninsula
Isthmus
Sandbank
Island
Atoll
Rock, Reef
Islands, Archipelago
Rocks, Reefs
Coral Reef
Well, Spring
Geyser
River, Stream
Waterfall Rapids
River Mouth, Estuary
Lake
Salt Lake
Intermittent Lake
Reservoir
Swamp, Pond
Canal
Glacier
Ice Shelf, Pack Ice
Ocean
Sea
Gulf, Bay
Strait, Fjord
Lagoon
Bank
Seamount
Tablemount
Ridge
Shelf
Basin
Escarpment, Sea Scarp
Fracture
Trench, Abyss
National Park, Reserve
Point of Interest
Recreation Site
Cave, Cavern
Historic Site
Ruins
Wall, Walls
Church, Abbey
Temple
Scientific Station
Airport
Port
Lighthouse
Mine
Tunnel
Dam, Bridge

Wolseley 42 Hf 50.25N 103.19W
Wolstenholme, Cap - 42 Jd 62.34N 77.30W
Wolstenholme Fjord 41 Ec 76.40N 69.45W
Wolsztyn 10 Md 52.08N 16.06 E
Wolvega, Weststellingwerf- 12 Ib 52.53N 6.00 E
Wolverhampton 9 Ki 52.36N 2.08W
Wolverton 9 Mi 52.04N 0.50W
Wŏnju 27 Md 37.21N 127.58 E
Wŏnsan 22 Of 39.10N 127.26 E
Wonseradeel 12 Ha 53.06N 5.28 E
Wonseradeel-Witmarsum 12 Ha 53.06N 5.28 E
Wonthaggi 59 Jg 38.36S 145.35 E
Woodall Mountain 45 Li 34.45N 88.11W
Woodbridge 9 Oi 52.06N 1.19 E
Woodbridge Bay 51g Bb 15.19N 61.25W
Woodhall Spa 12 Ba 53.09N 0.13W
Woodland [Ca.-U.S.] 46 Eg 38.41N 121.46W
Woodland [Wa.-U.S.] 46 Dd 45.54N 122.45W
Woodlark Island 57 Ge 9.05S 152.50 E
Wood Mountain 46 Lb 49.14N 106.20W
Woodridge 45 Hb 49.17N 96.09W
Wood River 46 Lb 50.08N 106.10W
Wood River Lakes 40 He 59.30N 158.45W
Woodroffe, Mount- 59 Ge 26.20S 131.45 E
Woods, Lake- 59 Gc 17.50S 133.30 E
Woods, Lake of the- 38 Je 49.15N 94.45W
Woods Hole 44 Le 41.31N 70.40W
Woodside 46 Jg 39.21N 110.18W
Woodstock [Eng.-U.K.] 9 Lj 51.52N 1.21W
Woodstock [N.B.-Can.] 42 Kg 46.09N 67.34W
Woodstock [Ont.-Can.] 44 Gd 43.08N 80.45W
Woodstock [Vt.-U.S.] 44 Kd 43.37N 72.31W
Woodville [Ms.-U.S.] 45 Kk 31.01N 91.18W
Woodville [N.Z.] 62 Fd 40.20S 175.52 E
Woodville [Tx.-U.S.] 45 Ik 30.46N 94.25W
Woodward 43 Hd 36.26N 99.24W
Wooler 9 Kf 55.33N 2.01W
Woomera 59 Hf 31.11S 137.10 E
Wooramel River 59 Ce 25.47S 114.10 E
Wooster 44 Ge 40.46N 81.57W
Worcester 9 Ki 52.15N 2.10W
Worcester [Eng.-U.K.] 9 Ki 52.11N 2.13W
Worcester [Ma.-U.S.] 43 Mc 42.16N 71.48W
Worcester [S.Afr.] 31 Il 33.39S 19.27 E
Worcester Range 66 Jf 78.50S 161.00 E
Wörgl 14 Gc 47.29N 12.04 E
Workai, Pulau- 26 Jh 6.40S 134.40 E
Workington 9 Jg 54.39N 3.33W
Worksop 9 Lh 53.18N 1.07W
Workum 12 Hb 52.59N 5.27 E
Worland 43 Fc 44.01N 107.57W
Wormer 12 Gb 52.30N 4.52 E
Wormhout 12 Ed 50.53N 2.28 E
Worms 10 Eg 49.38N 8.21 E
Worms Head 9 Ij 51.34N 4.20W
Wörrstadt 12 Ke 49.50N 8.06 E
Wörth am Rhein 12 Ke 49.03N 8.16 E
Wörther-See 14 Id 46.37N 14.10 E
Worthing 9 Mk 50.48N 0.23W
Worthington 43 Hc 43.37N 95.36W
Wosi 26 Ig 0.11S 127.58 E
Wotho Atoll 57 Hc 10.06N 165.59 E
Wotje Atoll 57 Id 9.27N 170.02 E
Woudenberg 12 Hb 52.05N 5.25 E
Wounnioné, Pointe- 63b Db 14.54S 168.02 E
Wounta, Laguna de- 49 Fg 13.38N 83.34W
Wour 35 Ba 21.21N 15.57 E
Wousi 63b Cb 15.22S 166.39 E
Wowoni, Pulau- 26 Hg 4.08S 123.06 E
Woy Woy 59 Kf 33.30S 151.20 E
Wrangel, Ostrov-=Wrangel Island (EN) 21 Tb 71.00N 179.30 E
Wrangel Island (EN)= Wrangel, Ostrov- 21 Tb 71.00N 179.30 E
Wrangell 39 Fd 56.28N 132.23W
Wrangell, Cape- 40a Ab 52.50N 172.26 E
Wrangell Mountains 38 Ec 62.00N 143.00W
Wrath, Cape- 9 Fd 58.37N 5.01W
Wray 45 Gc 40.05N 102.13W
Wreake 12 Ab 52.41N 1.05W
Wreck Reef 57 Gg 22.15S 155.10 E
Wrecks, Bay of- 64g Bb 1.52N 157.17W
Wrexham 9 Kh 53.03N 3.00W
Wright Island 66 Of 74.03S 116.45W
Wright Patman Lake 45 Ij 33.16N 94.14W
Wrightson, Mount- 46 Jk 31.42N 110.50W
Wrigley 42 Fd 63.19N 123.38W
Wrigley Gulf 66 Nf 74.00S 129.00W
Wrocław [2] 10 Me 51.05N 17.00 E
Wrocław=Breslau (EN) 6 He 51.06N 17.00 E
Wronki 10 Md 52.43N 16.23 E
Wrotham 12 Cc 51.18N 0.19 E
Wroxham 12 Db 52.42N 1.24 E
Września 10 Nd 52.20N 17.34 E
Wschowa 10 Me 51.48N 16.19 E
Wu'an 28 Cf 36.42N 114.12 E
Wuchale 35 Fc 11.31N 39.37 E
Wuchang 28 Ib 44.55N 127.11 E
Wuchang, Wuhan- 28 Ci 30.32N 114.18 E
Wucheng (Jiucheng) 28 Df 37.12N 116.04 E
Wuchiu Hsu 27 Kg 25.00N 119.27 E
Wuchuan 28 Ad 41.08N 111.25 E
Wuchuan (Duru) 27 If 28.28N 107.57 E
Wuchuan (Meilü) 27 Jg 21.28N 110.44 E
Wuda 27 Id 39.30N 106.33 E
Wudan → Ongniud Qi 27 Kc 42.58N 119.01 E
Wudao 27 Ld 39.28N 121.30 E
Wudaoliang 27 Fd 35.15N 93.14 E
Wudi 28 Df 37.44N 117.36 E
Wudil 34 Gc 11.49N 8.51 E
Wuding 27 Hf 25.36N 102.27 E
Wudu 27 He 33.24N 105.00 E
Wugang 27 Jf 26.48N 110.32 E
Wugong (Puji) 27 Ie 34.15N 108.14 E
Wuhai 27 Id 39.32N 106.55 E
Wuhan 22 Nf 30.30N 114.20 E
Wuhan-Hankou 28 Ci 30.35N 114.16 E
Wuhan-Hanyang 28 Ci 30.33N 114.16 E
Wuhan- Wuchang 28 Ci 30.32N 114.18 E
Wuhe 27 Ke 33.08N 117.51 E
Wuhu 22 Nf 31.18N 118.27 E
Wuhu (Wanzhi) 28 Ei 31.21N 118.23 E
Wujia He 27 Ic 40.56N 108.52 E
Wu Jiang 21 Mg 29.43N 107.24 E
Wujiang 28 Fi 31.09N 120.38 E
Wukari 31 Hh 7.51N 9.47 E
Wukro 35 Fc 13.48N 39.37 E
Wular 25 Eb 34.30N 74.30 E
Wulff Land 41 Hb 82.19N 50.00W
Wulian (Hongning) 28 Eg 35.45N 119.13 E
Wuliang Shan 27 Hg 24.00N 101.00 E
Wuliaru, Pulau- 26 Jh 7.27S 131.04 E
Wuling Shan 21 Mg 28.20N 110.00 E
Wulongbei 28 Hd 40.15N 124.16 E
Wulongji → Huaibin 28 Ci 32.27N 115.23 E
Wulur 26 Ih 7.09S 128.39 E
Wum 34 Hd 6.23N 10.04 E
Wumei Shan 28 Cj 28.47N 114.50 E
Wümme 12 Ka 53.10N 8.40 E
Wuning 28 Cj 29.17N 115.05 E
Wünnenberg 12 Kc 51.31N 8.42 E
Wünnenberg-Haaren 12 Kc 51.34N 8.44 E
Wunnummin Lake 42 If 52.55N 89.10W
Wun Rog 35 Dd 9.00N 28.21 E
Wunstrof 10 Fd 52.26N 9.25 E
Wuntho 25 Jd 23.54N 95.41 E
Wupper 10 Ce 51.05N 7.00 E
Wuppertal 10 De 51.16N 7.11 E
Wuqi 27 Id 36.57N 108.15 E
Wuqia/Ulugqat 27 Cd 39.40N 75.07 E
Wuqiao (Sangyuan) 28 Df 37.38N 116.23 E
Wuqing (Yangcun) 28 De 39.23N 117.04 E
Würm 12 Kf 48.53N 8.42 E
Wurno 34 Gc 13.18N 5.26 E
Würselen 12 Id 50.49N 6.08 E
Würzburg 6 Gf 49.48N 9.56 E
Wurzen 10 Ie 51.22N 12.44 E
Wu Shan 27 Ie 31.00N 110.00 E
Wushaoling 27 Hd 37.15N 102.50 E
Wuski/Uqturpan 27 Cc 41.10N 79.16 E
Wusong 28 Fi 31.23N 121.29 E
Wüst Seamount (EN) 30 Gl 34.00S 3.40W
Wusuli Jiang 27 Ob 48.28N 135.02 E
Wutach 10 Ei 47.37N 8.15 E
Wutai [China] 28 Be 38.43N 113.14 E
Wutai [China] 27 Dc 44.38N 82.06 E
Wutai Shan 27 Jd 39.04N 113.28 E
Wuustwezel 12 Gc 51.23N 4.36 E
Wuvulu Island 57 Fe 1.43S 142.50 E
Wuwei 28 Di 31.17N 117.54 E
Wuwei (Liangzhou) 22 Mf 37.58N 102.48 E
Wuxi [China] 22 Of 31.32N 120.18 E
Wuxi [China] 27 Ie 31.27N 109.34 E
Wu Xia 27 Je 31.02N 110.10 E
Wuxiang (Duancun) 28 Bf 36.50N 112.51 E
Wuxing (Huzhou) 27 Le 30.47N 120.07 E
Wuxue→Guangji 27 Kf 29.58N 115.32 E
Wuyang [China] 28 Bh 33.26N 113.35 E
Wuyang [China] 27 Jd 36.29N 113.07 E
Wuyang → Zhenyuan 27 If 27.05N 108.26 E
Wuyi [China] 28 Cf 37.49N 115.54 E
Wuyi [China] 28 Ej 28.54N 119.50 E
Wuyiling 27 Mb 48.37N 129.20 E
Wuyi Shan 21 Ng 27.00N 117.00 E
Wuyuan [China] 22 Me 41.08N 108.17 E
Wuyuan [China] 28 Dj 29.15N 117.52 E
Wuyuanzhen→Haiyan 28 Fi 30.31N 120.56 E
Wuzhai 28 Ae 38.54N 111.49 E
Wuzhen 28 Ai 31.42N 112.00 E
Wuzhi Shan [China] 28 Ed 40.31N 118.02 E
Wuzhi Shan [China] 27 Ih 18.54N 109.40 E
Wuzhong 27 Id 38.00N 106.10 E
Wuzhou 22 Ng 23.32N 111.21 E
Wyalkatchem 59 Df 31.10S 117.22 E
Wyandotte 44 Fd 42.12N 83.10W
Wyandra 59 Je 27.15S 145.59 E
Wye 9 Kj 51.37N 2.39W
Wye 12 Cc 51.11N 0.56 E
Wyemandoo, Mount- 59 De 28.31S 118.32 E
Wyk auf Föhr 10 Eb 54.42N 8.34 E
Wylie, Lake- 44 Gh 35.07N 81.02W
Wymondham 9 Oi 52.34N 1.07 E
Wyndham [Austl.] 58 Df 15.28S 128.06 E
Wyndham [N.Z.] 62 Cg 46.20S 168.51 E
Wyndmere 45 Hc 46.16N 97.08W
Wynne 45 Ki 35.14N 90.47W
Wynniatt Bay 42 Gb 72.50N 111.00W
Wynyard [Austl.] 59 Jh 40.59S 145.41 E
Wynyard [Sask.-Can.] 42 Hf 51.47N 104.10W
Wyoming 44 Ed 42.54N 85.42W
Wyoming [2] 43 Fc 43.00N 107.30W
Wyoming Peak 43 Ec 42.36N 110.37W
Wyśmierzyce 10 Qe 51.38N 20.49 E
Wysoka 10 Nc 53.11N 17.05 E
Wysokie Mazowieckie 10 Sd 52.56N 22.32 E
Wyszków 10 Rd 52.36N 21.28 E
Wyszogród 10 Qd 52.23N 20.11 E
Wytheville 44 Gg 36.57N 81.07W
Wyville Thomson Ridge (EN) 9 Fa 60.10N 8.00W
Wyvis, Ben- 9 Id 57.42N 4.30W

X

Xaintrie 11 Ii 45.00N 2.10 E
Xainza 27 Ee 30.50N 88.37 E
Xaitongmoin 27 Ef 29.26N 88.08 E
Xai-Xai 31 Kk 25.04S 33.39 E
Xamba→Hanggin Houqi 27 Ic 40.59N 107.07 E
Xam Nua 25 Kd 20.25N 104.02 E
Xangongo 31 Ij 16.46S 14.59 E
Xang Qu 27 Ef 29.22N 89.09 E
Xanten 10 Ce 51.40N 6.27 E
Xánthi 15 Hh 41.08N 24.53 E
Xanthos 24 Cd 36.20N 29.20 E
Xanxerê 56 Jc 26.53S 52.23W
Xapuri 54 Ef 10.39S 68.31W
Xar Hudag 27 Jb 45.06N 114.30 E
Xar Moron 28 Ac 42.37N 111.02 E
Xar Moron He 27 Lc 43.24N 120.39 E
Xarrama 13 Df 38.14N 8.20W
Xàtiva/Játiva 13 Lf 38.59N 0.31W
Xau, Lake- 37 Cd 21.15S 24.44 E
Xavantes, Represa de- 55 Hf 23.20S 49.35W
Xavantina 55 Fe 21.15S 52.48W
Xayar 27 Dc 41.15N 82.50 E
Xebert 28 Fc 44.00N 122.00 E
Xêgar → Tingri 27 Ef 28.41N 87.00 E
Xenia 44 Ff 39.41N 83.56W
Xiabin Ansha 27 Ke 9.48N 116.38 E
Xiachengzi 28 Kb 44.41N 130.26 E
Xiacun → Rushan 28 Ff 36.55N 121.30 E
Xiaguan 27 Hf 25.32N 100.12 E
Xiahe (Labrang) 27 Hd 35.18N 102.30 E
Xiajin 28 Cf 36.57N 116.00 E
Xiamen 22 Ng 24.32N 118.06 E
Xi'an 22 Mf 34.15N 108.50 E
Xianfeng 27 If 29.41N 109.09 E
Xiangcheng 28 Bh 33.51N 113.29 E
Xiangcheng/Qagchêng 27 Gf 28.56N 99.46 E
Xiangcheng (Shuizhai) 28 Ch 33.27N 114.53 E
Xiangfan 22 Nf 32.03N 112.05 E
Xianggang/Hong Kong [5] 22 Ng 22.15N 114.10 E
Xianghua Ling 27 Jf 25.26N 112.32 E
Xianghuang Qi (Xin Bulag) 27 Jc 42.12N 113.59 E
Xiang Jang 21 Ng 29.26N 113.08 E
Xiangkhoang 25 Ke 19.20N 103.22 E
Xiangkhoang, Plateau de- 25 Ke 19.30N 103.10 E
Xiangquan He 27 Ce 32.05N 79.20 E
Xiangshan (Dancheng) 27 Lf 29.29N 121.52 E
Xiangshan Gang 28 Fj 29.35N 121.38 E
Xiangtan 22 Ng 27.54N 112.55 E
Xiangtang 28 Cj 28.26N 115.59 E
Xiangyin 28 Bj 28.41N 112.53 E
Xiangyuan 28 Bf 36.32N 113.02 E
Xianju 27 Lf 28.50N 120.42 E
Xianning 28 Cj 29.52N 114.17 E
Xiannümiao→Jiangdu 28 Eh 32.30N 119.33 E
Xiantaozhen → Mianyang 28 Bi 30.22N 113.27 E
Xianxia Ling 27 Kf 28.24N 118.40 E
Xianxian 28 De 38.12N 116.07 E
Xianyang 27 Ie 34.26N 108.40 E
Xiaobole Shan 27 La 51.46N 124.09 E
Xiao'ergou 27 Lb 49.10N 123.43 E
Xiaogan 27 Je 30.52N 113.58 E
Xiao He 28 Bf 37.38N 112.24 E
Xiao Hinggan Ling=Lesser Khingan Range (EN) 21 Oe 48.45N 127.00 E
Xiaoling He 28 Fd 40.55N 121.12 E
Xiaoluan He 28 Dd 41.36N 117.05 E
Xiaoqing He 28 Ef 37.19N 118.59 E
Xiaowutai Shan 28 Ce 39.57N 114.59 E
Xiaoxian 28 Dg 34.11N 116.56 E
Xiaoyi 28 Af 37.07N 111.48 E
Xiaoyi → Gongxian 28 Bg 34.46N 112.57 E
Xiapu 27 Kf 26.57N 119.59 E
Xiawa 28 Fc 42.36N 120.33 E
Xiayi 28 Dg 34.14N 116.07 E
Xiazhuang → Linshu 28 Eg 34.56N 118.38 E
Xicalango, Punta- 48 Nh 19.41N 92.00W
Xichang 22 Mg 27.52N 102.15 E
Xicheng → Yangyuan 28 Cd 40.08N 114.10 E
Xicoténcatl 48 Jf 23.00N 98.56W
Xicotepec de Juárez 48 Kg 20.17N 97.57W
Xiejiaji → Qingyun 28 Df 37.46N 117.22 E
Xifei He 28 Dh 32.38N 116.39 E
Xifeng 28 Hc 42.45N 124.44 E
Xifengzhen 27 Id 35.40N 107.42 E
Xigazê 22 Kg 29.15N 88.52 E
Xi He [China] 27 Hc 42.23N 101.03 E
Xi He [China] 28 Dj 29.38N 116.53 E
Xiheying 28 Ce 39.53N 114.42 E
Xihua 28 Ch 33.48N 114.31 E
Xi Jang 21 Ng 23.05N 114.23 E
Xiji [China] 27 Id 35.52N 105.35 E
Xiji [China] 28 Ia 46.09N 127.08 E
Xi Jiang 27 Jg 23.05N 114.23 E
Xijir Ulan Hu 27 Fd 35.12N 90.18 E
Xikouzi 27 La 42.58N 120.29 E
Xiligou → Ulan 27 Gd 36.55N 98.16 E
Xilin 27 Ig 24.30N 105.05 E
Xilin Gol 28 Dc 43.55N 116.05 E
Xilin Hot→Abagnar Qi 22 Ne 43.58N 116.08 E
Xilitla 48 Jg 21.20N 98.58W
Xilókastron 15 Fk 38.05N 22.38 E
Ximiao 27 Hc 41.04N 100.14 E
Xin'an 28 Bg 34.43N 112.09 E
Xin'anjiang 28 Ei 29.27N 119.15 E
Xin'anjiang Shuiku 27 Kf 29.25N 119.05 E
Xin'anzhen → Guannan 28 Eg 34.04N 119.21 E
Xin'anzhen → Xinyi 27 Ke 34.17N 118.14 E
Xin Barag Youqi (Altan-Emel) 27 Kb 48.41N 116.47 E
Xin Barag Zuoqi (Amgalang) 27 Kb 48.13N 118.14 E
Xinbin 28 Hd 41.44N 125.02 E
Xin Bulag→Xianghuang Qi 27 Jc 42.12N 113.59 E
Xincai 27 Je 32.40N 114.57 E
Xinchang 28 Fj 29.30N 120.54 E
Xincheng [China] 28 Bf 37.57N 112.33 E
Xincheng [China] 27 Ig 24.04N 108.39 E
Xincheng [China] 27 Id 38.33N 106.10 E
Xincheng (Gaobeidian) 28 Ce 39.20N 115.50 E
Xindi → Honghu 28 Bj 29.50N 113.28 E
Xing'an→Ankang 22 Mf 32.37N 109.03 E
Xingcheng 28 Fd 40.38N 120.43 E
Xingguo 27 Kf 26.22N 115.21 E
Xinghai 27 Gd 35.45N 99.59 E
Xinghe 27 Jc 40.52N 113.56 E
Xinghua 28 Eh 32.56N 119.49 E
Xingkai Hu=Khanka Lake (EN) 21 Pe 45.00N 132.24 E
Xinglong 28 Dd 40.25N 117.31 E
Xinglongzhen 28 Ia 46.26N 127.03 E
Xingren 27 If 25.26N 105.08 E
Xingtai 22 Nf 37.00N 114.30 E
Xingtang 28 Ce 38.26N 114.33 E
Xingu, Rio- 52 Kf 1.30S 51.53W
Xingxingxia 27 Gc 41.47N 95.07 E
Xingyang 28 Bg 34.47N 113.21 E
Xinryi (Huangcaoba) 27 Hf 25.03N 104.55 E
Xingzi 28 Dj 29.28N 116.03 E
Xinhe 28 Cf 37.32N 115.14 E
Xinhe/Toksu 27 Dc 41.34N 82.38 E
Xin Hot→Abag Qi 27 Jc 44.01N 114.59 E
Xinhuai He 28 Fg 34.23N 120.05 E
Xinhui → Aohan Qi 28 Ec 42.18N 119.53 E
Xining 22 Mf 36.37N 101.46 E
Xinji → Shulu 28 Cf 37.56N 115.14 E
Xinjian 28 Cj 28.41N 115.50 E
Xin Jiang 28 Dj 28.37N 116.40 E
Xinjiangkou → Songzi 28 Ai 30.10N 116.46 E
Xinjiang Uygur Zizhiqu (Hsin-chiang-wei-wu-erh Tzu-chih-ch'ü)=Sinkiang (EN) [2] 27 Ec 42.00N 86.00 E
Xinjin 27 He 30.25N 103.46 E
Xinjin (Pulandian) 27 Ld 39.24N 121.59 E
Xinkai He 28 Gc 43.36N 122.31 E
Xinle 28 Ce 38.15N 114.40 E
Xinlin 28 Ec 43.58N 118.03 E
Xinlitun [China] 27 Ma 50.58N 126.39 E
Xinlitun [China] 28 Gc 42.01N 122.11 E
Xinlong/Nyagrong 27 He 30.57N 100.12 E
Xinmin 28 Gc 42.00N 122.50 E
Xinpu→Lianyungang 22 Nf 34.34N 119.15 E
Xinqing 27 Mb 48.15N 129.31 E
Xintai 28 Dg 35.54N 117.44 E
Xinwen (Suncun) 27 Kd 35.49N 117.38 E
Xinxian [China] 27 Jd 38.24N 112.43 E
Xinxian [China] 28 Ci 31.42N 114.50 E
Xinxiang 22 Nf 35.17N 113.50 E
Xinyang 27 Je 32.05N 114.07 E
Xinye 28 Bh 32.30N 112.22 E
Xinyi (Xin'anzhen) 27 Ke 34.17N 118.14 E
Xinyi He 28 Eg 34.29N 119.49 E
Xinyuan/Künes 27 Dc 43.24N 83.18 E
Xinyuan→Tianjun 22 Lf 37.18N 99.15 E
Xinzhan 28 Ic 43.52N 127.20 E
Xin Zhen→Hanggin Qi 27 Id 39.54N 108.55 E
Xinzheng 28 Bg 34.25N 113.46 E
Xinzhou 28 Ci 30.51N 114.49 E
Xioashan 28 Fi 30.10N 120.16 E
Xiong Xian 28 De 38.59N 116.06 E
Xionyuecheng 28 Gd 40.12N 122.08 E
Xiping [China] 28 Ej 28.27N 119.29 E
Xiping [China] 28 Bh 33.22N 114.00 E
Xisha Qundao=Paracel Islands (EN) 21 Nh 16.30N 112.15 E
Xishuangbanna 27 Gg 22.15N 100.00 E
Xishuanghe → Kenli 28 Ef 37.35N 118.30 E
Xishui 28 Ci 30.28N 115.15 E
Xitianmu Shan 27 Ke 30.21N 119.25 E
Xiuanzi → Chongli 28 Cd 40.57N 115.12 E
Xi Ujimqin Qi (Bayan Ul Hot) 27 Kc 44.31N 117.33 E
Xiuning 28 Ej 29.47N 118.11 E
Xiushan 27 If 28.29N 108.58 E
Xiu Shui 28 Cj 29.13N 116.00 E
Xiushui 27 Jf 29.02N 114.33 E
Xiuwu 28 Bg 35.13N 113.27 E
Xiuyan 27 Lc 40.18N 123.10 E
Xiwanzi→Chongli 28 Cf 36.50N 115.10 E
Xixabangma Feng 27 Ef 28.21N 85.47 E
Xixian 28 Ch 32.21N 114.43 E
Xixiang 27 Ie 32.58N 107.45 E
Xiyang 28 Bf 37.38N 113.41 E
Xizang Zizhiqu (Hsi-tsang Tzu-chih-ch'ü)=Tibet (EN) [2] 27 Ee 32.00N 90.00 E
Xizhong Dao 28 Fe 39.25N 121.18 E
Xi Taijnar Hu 27 Fd 37.15N 93.30 E
Xochicalco 48 Jh 18.45N 99.20W
Xochimilco 48 Jh 19.16N 99.06W
Xorkol 27 Fd 39.04N 91.05 E
Xpujil 48 Oh 18.35N 89.25W
Xuancheng 28 Ei 30.56N 118.44 E
Xuande Qundao 26 Fc 17.08N 111.30 E
Xuan'en 27 Ie 30.02N 109.30 E
Xuanhan 27 Ie 31.23N 107.39 E
Xuanhua 27 Kc 40.39N 115.05 E
Xuanwei 27 Hf 26.19N 104.05 E
Xuchang 22 Nf 34.00N 113.58 E
Xuecheng (Lincheng) 28 Dg 34.38N 117.14 E
Xuefeng Shan 27 Jf 27.30N 110.50 E
Xue Shan 27 Gf 27.30N 99.55 E
Xugezhuang → Fengnan 28 Ee 39.34N 118.05 E
Xugou 28 Eg 34.37N 119.08 E
Xugui 27 Gd 35.45N 96.08 E
Xuguit Qi (Yakeshi) 27 Lb 49.16N 120.41 E
Xümatang 27 Ge 33.57N 97.00 E
Xun Jiang 23 Hf 23.28N 111.18 E
Xunke (Qike) 27 Mb 49.34N 128.28 E
Xunwu 27 Kg 24.59N 115.33 E
Xunxian 28 Cg 35.40N 114.33 E
Xupu 27 Jf 27.54N 110.35 E
Xúquer/Júcar 5 Fh 39.09N 0.14W
Xushui 28 Ce 39.02N 115.40 E
Xuwen 27 Jg 20.22N 110.10 E
Xuyi 27 Ke 32.58N 118.33 E
Xuyong (Yongning) 27 If 28.13N 105.26 E
Xuzhou 22 Nf 34.12N 117.13 E

Y

Ya'an 22 Mg 30.00N 102.57 E
Yabassi 34 Ge 4.28N 9.58 E
Yabe 29 Be 32.42N 130.59 E
Yabebyry 55 Dh 27.24S 57.11W
Yabelo 35 Fe 4.53N 38.07 E
Yablonovy Range (EN)= Jablonovy Hrebet 21 Nd 53.30N 115.00 E
Yabrai Shan 27 Hc 40.00N 103.10 E
Yabrīn 35 Ha 23.15N 48.59 E
Yabrūd 24 Gf 33.58N 36.40 E
Yabucoa 51a Cb 18.03N 65.53W
Yabuli 27 Mc 44.56N 128.37 E
Yabulu 59 Jc 19.00S 146.40 E
Yacaré Cururú, Cuchilla- 55 Dj 30.30S 56.33W
Yacaré Norte, Riacho- 55 Cf 22.43S 58.14W
Yacaré Sur, Riacho- 55 Cf 22.43S 58.14W
Yachats 46 Cd 44.20N 124.03W
Yacuma, Rio- 54 Ef 13.38S 65.23W
Yacyretá, Isla- 55 Dh 27.25S 56.30W
Yadé, Massif du- 35 Bd 7.00N 15.30 E
Yādgīr 25 Fe 16.46N 77.08 E
Yadong/Chomo 27 Ef 27.38N 89.03 E
Yae-Dake 29b Ab 26.38N 127.56 E
Yaeyama-Rettō 27 Lg 24.20N 124.00 E
Yafran 33 Bc 32.04N 12.31 E
Yağcilar 15 Lj 39.25N 28.23 E
Yagishiri-Tō 29a Ba 44.26N 141.25 E
Yagoua 34 Ic 10.20N 15.14 E
Yagradagzê Shan 27 Gd 35.09N 95.39 E
Yaguajay 49 Hb 22.19N 79.14W
Yaguari 55 Ej 31.31S 54.58W
Yaguari, Arroyo- 55 Di 29.44S 57.37W
Yahalica de Gonzáles Gallo 48 Hg 21.08N 102.51W
Yahuma 36 Db 1.06N 23.10 E
Yaita 29 Fc 36.50N 139.55 E
Yaizu 29 Fd 34.51N 138.19 E
Yajiang/Nyagquka 27 He 30.07N 100.58 E
Yakacik 24 Ed 36.05N 32.45 E
Yake-Dake 29 Ec 36.14N 137.35 E
Yakeishi-Dake 29 Gb 39.10N 140.50 E
Yakeshi → Xuguit Qi 27 Lb 49.16N 120.41 E
Yake-Yama 29 Gb 39.58N 140.48 E
Yakima 39 Ge 46.36N 120.31W
Yakima River 46 Fc 46.15N 119.02W
Yako 34 Ec 12.58N 2.16W
Yakumo 27 Pc 42.15N 140.16 E
Yaku-Shima 27 Ne 30.20N 130.30 E
Yakutat 40 Le 59.33N 139.44W
Yakutat Bay 40 Ke 59.45N 140.45W
Yala 25 Kg 6.32N 101.19 E
Yalahán, Laguna de- 48 Pg 21.30N 87.15W
Yalcubul, Punta- 48 Og 21.35N 88.35W
Yale Point 46 Kh 36.25N 109.48W
Yalewa Kalou 63d Ab 16.40S 177.46 E
Yalgoo 59 De 28.20S 116.41 E
Yalikavak 15 Kl 37.06N 27.18 E
Yaliköy 15 Lh 41.29N 28.17 E
Yalinga 35 Cd 6.31N 23.13 E
Yaloké 35 Bd 5.19N 17.05 E
Yalong Jiang 21 Mg 26.37N 101.48 E
Yalova 24 Cb 40.39N 29.15 E
Yalu Jiang 21 Of 39.55N 124.20 E
Yalvaç 24 Dc 38.17N 31.11 E
Yām, Ramlat- 33 If 17.42N 45.09 E
Yamada [Jap.] 28 Pe 39.28N 141.57 E
Yamada [Jap.] 29 Be 33.33N 130.45 E
Yamada-Wan 29 Hb 39.30N 142.00 E
Yamaga 29 Be 33.01N 130.41 E
Yamagata 27 Pd 38.15N 140.15 E
Yamagata Ken [2] 28 Pe 38.30N 140.00 E
Yamagawa 29 Bf 31.12N 130.39 E
Yamaguchi 27 Ne 34.10N 131.29 E
Yamaguchi Ken [2] 28 Kh 34.10N 131.30 E
Yamakuni 29 Be 33.24N 131.02 E
Yamal Peninsula (EN)= Jamal, Poluostrov- 21 Ib 70.00N 70.00 E
Yamamoto 29 Ga 40.06N 140.03 E
Yamanaka 29 Ec 36.15N 136.22 E
Yamanashi Ken [2] 28 Og 35.30N 138.45 E
Yamashiro 29 Ce 33.57N 133.43 E
Yamato Rise (EN) 28 Me 39.30N 134.30 E
Yamatsuri 29 Gc 36.53N 140.25 E
Yamazaki 29 Dd 35.00N 134.33 E
Yambi, Mesa de- 54 Dc 1.30N 71.20W
Yambio 31 Jh 4.34N 28.23 E
Yambo 35 Fd 8.25N 36.00 E
Yambu Head 51n Ba 13.09N 61.09W
Yambuya 36 Db 1.16N 24.33 E
Yame 29 Be 33.13N 130.34 E
Yamethin 25 Jd 20.26N 96.09 E
Yamma Yamma, Lake- 59 Ie 26.20S 141.25 E
Yamoto 29 Gb 38.25N 141.13 E
Yamoussoukro 34 Dd 6.49N 5.17W
Yampa River 43 Fc 40.32N 108.59W
Yampi Sound 59 Ec 16.11S 123.40 E
Yamuna 21 Kg 25.30N 81.53 E
Yamunanagar 25 Fb 30.08N 76.59 E
Yamzho Yumco 27 Ff 29.00N 90.40 E
Yanagawa 29 Be 33.10N 130.24 E
Yanahara 29 Dd 34.57N 134.05 E
Yanahuanca 54 Cf 10.30S 76.30W
Yanai 29 Ce 33.58N 132.07 E
Yanam 25 Ge 16.51N 82.15 E
Yan'an 22 Mf 36.36N 109.30 E
Yanaoca 54 Df 14.13S 71.26W
Yanbian 27 Hf 26.51N 101.32 E
Yanbu' 23 Ee 24.05N 38.03 E
Yanchang 27 Jd 36.39N 110.03 E
Yancheng [China] 28 Bh 33.35N 114.00 E
Yancheng [China] 28 Le 33.16N 120.10 E
Yanchi 27 Id 37.47N 107.24 E
Yandé 63b Ae 20.03S 163.48 E
Yandina 63a Dc 9.07S 159.13 E
Yandja 36 Cc 1.41S 17.43 E

Index Symbols

[1] Independent Nation
[2] State, Region
[3] District, County
[4] Municipality
[5] Colony, Dependency
Continent
Physical Region
Historical or Cultural Region
Mount, Mountain
Volcano
Hill
Mountains, Mountain Range
Hills, Escarpment
Plateau, Upland
Pass, Gap
Plain, Lowland
Delta
Salt Flat
Valley, Canyon
Crater, Cave
Karst Features
Depression
Polder
Desert, Dunes
Forest, Woods
Heath, Steppe
Oasis
Cape, Point
Coast, Beach
Cliff
Peninsula
Isthmus
Sandbank
Island
Atoll
Rock, Reef
Islands, Archipelago
Rocks, Reefs
Coral Reef
Well, Spring
Geyser
River, Stream
Waterfall Rapids
River Mouth, Estuary
Lake
Salt Lake
Intermittent Lake
Reservoir
Swamp, Pond
Canal
Glacier
Ice Shelf, Pack Ice
Ocean
Sea
Gulf, Bay
Strait, Fjord
Lagoon
Bank
Seamount
Tablemount
Ridge
Shelf
Basin
Escarpment, Sea Scarp
Fracture
Trench, Abyss
National Park, Reserve
Point of Interest
Recreation Site
Cave, Cavern
Historic Site
Ruins
Wall, Walls
Church, Abbey
Temple
Scientific Station
Airport
Port
Lighthouse
Mine
Tunnel
Dam, Bridge

International Map Index

Yandua ⊕ 63d Bb 16.49 S 178.18 E
Yanfolila 34 Dc 11.11 N 8.08 W
Yangalia 35 Cd 6.58 N 21.01 E
Yangambi 31 Jh 0.47 N 24.28 E
Yangcheng 28 Bg 35.32 N 112.36 E
Yangchun 27 Jg 22.11 N 111.48 E
Yangcun → Wuqing 28 De 39.23 N 117.04 E
Yangdóg-úp 28 Ie 39.13 N 126.39 E
Yangganga ⊕ 63d Bb 16.35 S 178.35 E
Yanggang-Do ② 28 Jd 41.15 N 128.00 E
Yanggao 27 Jc 40.21 N 113.47 E
Yanggeta ⊕ 63d Bb 16.47 S 177.20 E
Yanggu 28 Cf 36.08 N 115.48 E
Yang He ⌐ 28 Cd 40.24 N 115.18 E
Yangi 15 Mm 36.55 N 29.01 E
Yangjiang 27 Jg 21.59 N 111.59 E
Yangjiazhangzi 28 Fd 40.48 N 120.30 E
Yangor 64e Ab 0.32 S 166.54 E
Yangqu (Huangzhai) 28 Be 38.05 N 112.37 E
Yangquan 27 Jd 37.49 N 113.34 E
Yangquanqu 27 Jd 37.04 N 111.30 E
Yangshuo 27 Jg 24.46 N 110.28 E
Yang Sin, Chu- ▲ 25 Lf 12.24 N 108.26 E
Yangtze Kiang → Chang
  Jiang ⌐ 21 Of 31.48 N 121.10 E
Yangxian 27 Ie 33.20 N 107.35 E
Yangxin [China] 28 Df 37.39 N 117.34 E
Yangxin [China] 27 Kf 29.50 N 115.11 E
Yangyuan (Xicheng) 28 Cd 40.08 N 114.10 E
Yangzhou 27 Ke 32.20 N 119.25 E
Yanhe (Heping) 27 If 28.31 N 108.28 E
Yanji 27 Mc 42.56 N 129.30 E
Yanjin 28 Cg 35.09 N 114.11 E
Yankton 43 Hc 42.53 N 97.23 W
Yanling 28 Cg 34.07 N 114.11 E
Yanqi 22 Ke 42.04 N 86.34 E
Yanqing 28 Cd 40.28 N 115.57 E
Yan Shan ▲ 21 Ne 40.18 N 117.36 E
Yanshan [China] 28 De 38.03 N 117.12 E
Yanshan [China] 27 Hg 23.38 N 104.24 E
Yanshan (Hekou) 28 Dj 28.18 N 117.41 E
Yanshi 28 Bg 34.44 N 112.47 E
Yanshou 28 Jb 45.28 N 128.19 E
Yantai 22 Of 37.28 N 121.24 E
Yanutha ⊕ 63d Ac 16.14 S 178.00 E
Yanweigang 28 Eg 34.28 N 119.46 E
Yanyuan 27 Hf 27.26 N 101.32 E
Yanzhou 27 Kd 35.33 N 116.49 E
Yao [Chad] 35 Bc 12.51 N 17.34 E
Yao [Jap.] 29 Dd 34.38 N 135.36 E
Yaodu → Dongzhi 28 Di 30.06 N 117.01 E
Yaoundé 31 Jh 3.52 N 11.31 E
Yapei 34 Ed 9.10 N 1.10 W
Yapen, Pulau- ⊕ 57 Le 1.45 S 136.15 E
Yapen, Selat- ⌐ 26 Kg 1.30 S 136.10 E
Yapeyú 55 Di 29.28 S 56.49 W
Yap Islands ◻ 57 Ed 9.32 N 138.08 E
Yapraklı 24 Eb 40.46 N 33.47 E
Yap Trench (EN) ⌐ 60 Bf 8.30 N 138.00 E
Yapu 25 Jf 14.51 N 98.03 E
Yaqian → Yuexi 28 Di 30.51 N 116.22 E
Yaque del Norte, Río- ⌐ 49 Ld 19.51 N 71.41 W
Yaque del Sur, Río- ⌐ 48 Ld 18.17 N 71.06 W
Yaqueling 28 Ai 30.40 N 111.36 E
Yaqui ⌐ 38 Hg 27.37 N 110.39 W
Yaracuy ② 54 La 10.20 N 68.45 W
Yaraka 58 Fg 24.53 S 144.04 E
Yaralıgöz ▲ 24 Fh 41.45 N 34.10 E
Yare ⌐ 9 Oi 52.35 N 1.44 E
Yaren 64e Ab 0.33 S 166.54 E
Yari, Río- ⌐ 52 If 0.23 S 72.16 W
Yariga-Take ▲ 29 Ec 36.20 N 137.39 E
Yarim 23 Fq 14.21 N 44.22 E
Yaritagua 54 Ea 10.05 N 69.08 W
Yarkant/Shache 27 Cd 38.24 N 77.15 E
Yarkant He ⌐ 21 Ke 40.28 N 80.52 E
Yarlung Zangbo Jiang ⌐ 21 Jg 24.02 N 90.59 E
Yarmouth [Eng.-U.K.] 12 Ad 50.41 N 1.30 W
Yarmouth [N.S.-Can.] 39 Me 43.50 N 66.07 W
Yarram 59 Jg 38.33 S 146.41 E
Yarumal 54 Cb 6.58 N 75.25 W
Yasawa ⊕ 63d Ab 16.47 S 177.31 E
Yasawa Group ◻ 57 If 17.00 S 177.23 E
Yashi 34 Gc 12.22 N 7.55 E
Ya-Shima ⊕ 29 Ce 33.45 N 132.10 E
Yashima 29 Gb 39.09 N 140.10 E
Yashiro-Jima ⊕ 29 Ce 33.55 N 132.15 E
Yasothon 25 Ke 15.46 N 104.12 E
Yass 59 Jf 34.50 S 148.55 E
Yassiören 15 Lh 41.18 N 28.35 E
Yasugi 29 Cd 35.26 N 133.15 E
Yâsüj 23 Hc 30.45 N 51.33 E
Yasun Burnu ⌐ 24 Gb 41.09 N 37.41 E
Yatate Tóge ⌐ 29 Ga 40.26 N 140.37 E
Yatate-Yama ▲ 29 Gb 40.26 N 140.37 E
Yatenga ② 34 Ec 13.48 N 2.10 W
Yaté-Village 61 Cd 22.09 S 166.57 E
Yathata ⊕ 63d Cb 17.15 S 179.32 W
Yathkyed Lake ⌐ 42 Hd 62.40 N 98.00 W
Yatolema 36 Db 0.21 N 24.33 E
Yatou → Rongcheng 28 Gf 37.10 N 122.25 E
Yatsu-ga-Take ▲ 29 Fd 35.59 N 138.23 E
Yatsushiro 27 Ne 32.30 N 130.36 E
Yatsushiro-Kai
  ⌐ 29 Be 32.20 N 130.25 E
Yatta Plateau ▲ 36 Gc 2.00 S 38.00 E
Yauco 49 Nd 18.02 N 66.51 W
Yauri 54 Df 14.47 S 71.29 W
Yauyos 54 Cf 12.24 S 75.54 W
Yavari, Río- ⌐ 54 Dd 4.21 S 70.02 W
Yavi, Cerro- ▲ 52 Bb 5.32 N 65.59 W
Yaviza 49 Ii 8.11 N 77.41 W
Yawatahama 28 Lh 33.27 N 132.24 E
Yaxchilán ⌐ 47 Fe 16.54 N 90.58 W
Yaxian (Sanya) 22 Mh 18.27 N 109.28 E
Yayalı 24 Fc 38.05 N 35.25 E

Yayladağı 24 Ge 35.56 N 36.01 E
Yazd 22 Hf 31.53 N 54.25 E
Yazd ③ 23 Hc 31.30 N 54.30 E
Yazoo City 45 Kj 32.51 N 90.28 W
Yazoo River ⌐ 45 Kj 32.22 N 91.00 W
Ybbs ⌐ 14 Jb 48.10 N 15.06 E
Ybbs an der Donau 14 Jb 48.10 N 15.05 E
Ydre ⊞ 8 Fg 57.52 N 15.15 E
Ydstebøhamn 8 Ae 59.03 N 5.25 E
Ye 22 Lh 15.15 N 97.51 E
Yebaishou → Jianping 27 Kc 41.55 N 119.37 E
Yebbi Bou 35 Ba 20.58 N 18.04 E
Yébigé ⌐ 35 Ba 22.04 N 17.49 E
Yecheng/Kargilik 22 Jf 37.54 N 77.26 E
Yech'ŏn 28 Jf 36.39 N 128.27 E
Yecla 13 Kf 38.37 N 1.07 W
Yécora 47 Cc 28.20 N 108.58 W
Yêd 35 Ge 4.48 N 43.02 E
Yedi Burun ⌐ 15 Mm 36.23 N 29.05 E
Yedseram ⌐ 34 Hc 12.16 N 14.09 E
Yegros 55 Dh 26.24 S 56.25 W
Yeha ⊠ 35 Fc 14.21 N 39.05 E
Yei 35 Ee 4.05 N 30.40 E
Yei ⌐ 35 Ee 4.40 N 30.30 E
Yeji [China] 28 Ci 31.51 N 115.55 E
Yeji [Ghana] 34 Ed 8.13 N 0.39 W
Yekepa 34 Dd 7.35 N 8.32 W
Yelgu 35 Gc 10.01 N 32.31 E
Yélimané 34 Cb 15.07 N 10.36 W
Yell ⊕ 5 Fc 60.35 N 1.05 W
Yellice Dağı ▲ 15 Mj 39.23 N 29.57 E
Yellowhead Pass ⌐ 42 Ff 52.50 N 117.55 W
Yellowknife 42 Gd 62.23 N 114.20 W
Yellowknife 39 Hc 62.27 N 114.21 W
Yellow River (EN) = Huang
  He ⌐ 21 Nf 37.32 N 118.19 E
Yellow Sea (EN) = Huang
  Hai ⌐ 21 Of 36.00 N 124.00 E
Yellow Sea (EN) = Hwang-
  Hae ⌐ 21 Of 36.00 N 124.00 E
Yellowstone ⌐ 38 Ie 47.58 N 103.59 W
Yellowstone Lake ⌐ 38 He 44.25 N 110.22 W
Yellowstone National
  Park ⌐ 46 Jd 44.58 N 110.42 W
Yell Sound ⌐ 9 La 60.33 N 1.15 W
Yeltes ⌐ 13 Hd 40.56 N 6.31 W
Yelwa [Nig.] 34 Gd 8.51 N 9.37 E
Yelwa [Nig.] 34 Fc 10.50 N 4.44 E
Yemen (EN) = Al Yaman ① 22 Gh 15.00 N 44.00 E
Yemen, People's Democratic
  Republic of- (EN) = Al
  Yaman ad Dimuqrāţīyah ① 22 Gh 14.00 N 46.00 E
Yenagoa 34 Ge 4.55 N 6.16 E
Yenangyaung 25 Id 20.28 N 94.53 E
Yen Bay 25 Kd 21.42 N 104.52 E
Yendi 34 Ed 9.26 N 0.01 W
Yenge ⌐ 36 Dc 0.55 S 20.40 E
Yengisar 27 Cd 38.56 N 76.09 E
Yengo 36 Cb 0.22 N 15.29 E
Yenice [Tur.] 24 Ef 37.36 N 35.35 E
Yenice [Tur.] 15 Kj 39.55 N 27.18 E
Yenice [Tur.] 15 Mj 39.58 N 35.03 E
Yenice [Tur.] ⌐ 24 Eb 41.18 N 32.08 E
Yeniçoa 15 Jk 38.44 N 26.51 E
Yenihisar 15 Kl 37.22 N 27.15 E
Yenimahalle 24 Ec 39.56 N 32.52 E
Yenipazar 15 Ll 37.48 N 28.12 E
Yenişehir 24 Cb 40.16 N 29.39 E
Yenisey (EN)=Jenisej ⌐ 21 Kb 71.50 N 82.40 E
Yenisey Bay (EN)=
  Jenisejski Zaliv ⌐ 20 Db 72.00 N 81.00 E
Yenisey Ridge (EN)=
  Jenisejski Krjaž ⌐ 21 Ld 59.00 N 92.30 E
Yennádhion 15 Km 36.01 N 27.56 E
Yeo, Lake- ⌐ 59 Ee 28.05 S 124.25 E
Yeovil 9 Kk 50.57 N 2.39 W
Yeppoon 59 Kd 23.08 S 150.45 E
Yerákion 15 Fm 37.00 N 22.42 E
Yerbabuena ⌐ 48 Hf 20.08 N 103.30 W
Yerer ⌐ 35 Gd 7.32 N 42.05 E
Yerington 46 Cf 38.59 N 119.10 W
Yerkesik 15 Ll 37.09 N 28.17 E
Yerköy 24 Fc 39.38 N 34.29 E
Yerlisu 15 Ji 40.46 N 26.39 E
Yermak Plateau (EN) ▲ 41 Mb 82.00 N 6.00 E
Yeroham 24 Fg 31.00 N 34.55 E
Yerres ⌐ 11 Id 48.43 N 2.27 E
Yerupaja, Nevado- ▲ 52 Ig 10.16 S 76.54 W
Yerushalayim = Jerusalem
  (EN) 22 Ff 31.46 N 35.14 E
Yerville 12 Ce 49.40 N 0.54 E
Yerwa 24 Cd 37.20 N 28.09 E
Yesa, Embalse de- ⌐ 13 Kb 42.36 N 1.09 W
Yesan 28 If 36.41 N 126.51 E
Yeşilhisar 24 Fc 38.21 N 35.06 E
Yeşilırmak ⌐ 24 Fb 41.24 N 36.35 E
Yeşilköy 24 Cb 40.57 N 29.49 E
Yeşilova 15 Ml 37.30 N 29.46 E
Yeşilyurt 15 Ll 37.31 N 28.17 E
Yeso 55 Cj 30.56 S 59.28 W
Yeste 13 Jf 38.22 N 2.19 W
Yetti ⊠ 30 Gf 26.10 N 7.50 W
Ye-u 25 Jd 22.46 N 95.26 E
Yeu, Ile d'- ⊕ 11 Dh 46.43 N 2.20 W
Yexian [China] 28 Ef 37.11 N 119.58 E
Yexian [China] 28 Bh 33.38 N 113.21 E
Yguazú, Río- ⌐ 55 Eg 25.20 S 55.00 W
Yhú 55 Dg 25.00 S 55.00 W
Yí, Río- ⌐ 55 Dk 33.07 S 57.08 W

Yichang 22 Nf 30.42 N 111.22 E
Yicheng [China] 28 Ag 35.44 N 111.43 E
Yicheng [China] 28 Bi 31.42 N 112.16 E
Yichuan 27 Jd 36.00 N 110.06 E
Yichun [China] 27 Jf 27.47 N 114.25 E
Yichun [China] 22 Mb 47.41 N 128.55 E
Yidilzeli 24 Gc 39.52 N 36.38 E
Yidu [China] 27 Ge 30.23 N 111.28 E
Yidu [China] 27 Kd 36.41 N 118.29 E
Yidun (Dagxoi) 27 Ge 30.25 N 99.28 E
Yifag 35 Fc 12.02 N 37.41 E
Yifeng 27 Cj 28.25 N 114.47 E
Yığılca 24 Db 40.58 N 31.27 E
Yigo 64c Ba 13.32 N 144.53 W
Yildiz Dağı ▲ 28 Gg 34.07 N 118.15 E
Yıldız Dağları ▲ 24 Bi 41.50 N 27.10 E
Yiliang 27 Hg 24.59 N 103.08 E
Yimianpo 28 Jb 45.04 N 128.03 E
Yimin He ⌐ 27 Kb 49.15 N 119.42 E
Yinan (Jiehu) 28 Eg 35.33 N 118.27 E
Yinchuan 22 Mf 38.28 N 106.19 E
Yindarlgooda, Lake- 59 Ef 30.45 S 121.55 E
Yingcheng [China] 28 Hb 44.08 N 125.54 E
Yingcheng [China] 28 Bi 30.57 N 113.33 E
Ying He ⌐ 28 Ch 32.30 N 116.31 E
Yingjiang 27 Gg 24.45 N 97.58 E
Yingjin He ⌐ 28 Ec 42.20 N 119.19 E
Yingkou 22 Oe 40.40 N 122.12 E
Yingkou (Dashiqiao) 28 Gd 40.39 N 122.31 E
Yingshan 28 Ci 30.45 N 115.40 E
Yingshang 28 Dh 32.38 N 116.16 E
Yingshouyingzi 28 Dd 40.30 N 117.37 E
Yingtan 28 Dj 28.13 N 117.00 E
Yingxian 28 Be 39.33 N 113.10 E
Ying zhan/Victoria 22 Ng 22.17 N 114.09 E
Yining/Gulja 27 Dc 43.54 N 81.21 E
Yinma He ⌐ 28 Hb 44.50 N 125.45 E
Yinqing Qunjiao ⊞ 26 Fe 8.55 N 112.35 E
Yīn Shan ▲ 21 Me 41.30 N 109.00 E
Yi'ong Zangbo ⌐ 27 Gf 29.56 N 95.10 E
Yioúra ⊕ 15 Hj 39.24 N 24.10 E
Yipinglang 27 Hf 25.13 N 101.55 E
Yiqian → Meitan 27 If 27.48 N 107.32 E
Yirga Alem 35 Fd 6.44 N 38.24 E
Yirol 35 Ed 6.33 N 30.30 E
Yirshi 27 Kb 47.17 N 119.55 E
Yishui 28 Eg 35.47 N 118.38 E
Yisra'el = Israel (EN) ① 22 Ff 31.30 N 35.00 E
Yíthion 15 Fm 36.45 N 22.34 E
Yitong 28 Hc 43.20 N 125.17 E
Yitong He ⌐ 28 Hb 44.45 N 125.40 E
Yitulihe 27 La 50.39 N 121.30 E
Yiwu 27 Fj 29.19 N 120.04 E
Yiwu/Aratürük 27 Fc 43.15 N 94.35 E
Yixian [China] 28 Ce 39.21 N 115.30 E
Yixian [China] 28 Dj 29.56 N 117.56 E
Yixian [China] 27 Fd 41.33 N 121.14 E
Yixing 28 Ei 31.21 N 119.48 E
Yixun He ⌐ 28 Dd 40.10 N 117.41 E
Yiyang [China] 27 Jf 28.41 N 112.20 E
Yiyang [China] 28 Dj 28.24 N 117.24 E
Yiyang [China] 28 Bg 34.30 N 112.10 E
Yiyuan (Nanma) 28 Ef 36.11 N 118.10 E
Yizheng 28 Jf 32.16 N 119.10 E
Yläne 8 Jd 60.53 N 22.25 E
Ylikitka ⌐ 7 Gc 66.08 N 28.30 E
Yli-Li 7 Fd 65.22 N 25.50 E
Ylimarkku/Övermark 8 Ib 62.37 N 21.28 E
Ylistaro 7 Fc 62.57 N 22.31 E
Ylitornio 7 Fc 66.18 N 23.40 E
Ylivieska 7 Fd 64.05 N 24.33 E
Ylöjärvi 8 Jc 61.33 N 23.36 E
Ymers ⊞ 41 Jd 73.20 N 25.00 W
Yngaren ⌐ 8 Gf 58.50 N 16.35 E
Yngen ⌐ 8 Fe 59.45 N 14.20 E
Ynykčanski 20 Id 60.08 N 137.47 E
Yoboki 35 Gc 11.28 N 42.06 E
Yobuko 29 Ae 33.33 N 129.54 E
Yodo-Gawa ⌐ 29 Dd 34.41 N 135.25 E
Yogan, Cerro- ▲ 52 Jk 54.38 S 69.29 W
Yogoum 35 Bb 17.27 N 19.31 E
Yoğuntaş 15 Kh 41.50 N 27.04 E
Yogyakarta 22 Nj 7.48 S 110.22 E
Yoichi 28 Pc 43.12 N 140.41 E
Yojoa, Lago de- ⌐ 49 Df 14.50 N 88.00 W
Yōju 28 If 37.18 N 127.38 E
Yokadouma 31 Jh 3.31 N 15.03 E
Yōkaichi 29 Ed 35.07 N 136.11 E
Yōkaichiba 29 Gd 35.40 N 140.28 E
Yokkaichi 29 Ed 34.58 N 136.37 E
Yoko 34 Hd 5.32 N 12.19 E
Yokoate-Jima ⊕ 27 Mf 28.50 N 129.00 E
Yokohama 22 Pf 35.27 N 139.39 E
Yokosuka 28 Pf 35.18 N 139.40 E
Yokote 28 Pd 39.18 N 140.34 E
Yola 31 Ih 9.12 N 12.29 E
Yolania, Serranías de- ▲ 49 Fh 11.40 N 84.20 W
Yolombo 36 Dc 1.32 S 23.15 E
Yom ⌐ 25 Kc 15.52 N 100.16 E
Yōmju 28 He 39.50 N 124.33 E
Yomou 34 Dd 7.34 N 9.16 W
Yomra 24 Hb 40.58 N 39.54 E
Yon ⌐ 11 Eh 46.30 N 1.18 W
Yona 64c Ba 13.25 N 144.47 E
Yonago 28 Lg 35.26 N 133.20 E
Yonaguni-Jima ⊕ 28 Lf 24.27 N 123.00 E
Yonaha-Dake ▲ 29b Ab 26.43 N 128.13 E
Yoneshiro-Gawa ⌐ 29 Ga 40.10 N 140.00 E
Yonezawa 28 Pd 37.55 N 140.07 E
Yŏngan 34 Mc 44.15 N 129.30 E
Yŏngan 27 Ee 33.55 N 87.05 E

Yongchang 27 Hd 38.17 N 102.07 E
Yongcheng 28 Dh 33.56 N 116.21 E
Yongch'on 28 Jg 35.59 N 127.59 E
Yongchuan 27 If 29.22 N 105.59 E
Yongch'u-gap ⌐ 28 Jf 37.03 N 129.26 E
Yongding He ⌐ 27 Hd 36.44 N 103.24 E
Yŏngdŏk 27 Kd 30.23 N 117.04 E
Yŏngdŏk 28 Jf 36.24 N 129.22 E
Yongding He ⌐ 27 Kd 36.41 N 118.29 E
Yonghung 28 Ie 39.33 N 127.14 E
Yongji (Kouqian) 28 Ic 43.40 N 126.30 E
Yongjing 27 Hd 36.00 N 103.17 E
Yŏngju 28 Md 36.49 N 128.37 E
Yongle Qundao ◻ 26 Fc 16.35 N 111.40 E
Yongnian (Linmingguan) 28 Cf 36.47 N 114.30 E
Yongning 27 If 28.13 N 105.26 E
Yongqing 28 De 39.19 N 116.29 E
Yŏngsanp'o 28 Ig 35.00 N 126.43 E
Yongsheng 27 Hf 26.41 N 100.45 E
Yongshu Jiao ⊞ 26 Fe 9.35 N 112.50 E
Yŏngwŏl 28 Jf 37.11 N 128.28 E
Yongxiu (Tujiabu) 27 Kf 29.05 N 115.49 E
Yonibana 34 Cd 8.29 N 12.14 W
Yonkers 44 Ke 40.56 N 73.54 W
Yonne ③ 11 Jg 47.55 N 3.45 E
Yonne ⌐ 11 If 48.23 N 2.58 E
Yopal 54 Db 5.23 N 72.23 W
Yopurga 27 Cd 39.15 N 76.45 E
York 9 Lg 54.10 N 1.30 W
York [Al.-U.S.] 44 Ci 32.29 N 88.18 W
York [Austl.] 59 Df 31.53 S 116.46 E
York [Eng.-U.K.] 3 Lg 53.58 N 1.05 W
York [Nb.-U.S.] 45 Hf 40.52 N 97.36 W
York [Pa.-U.S.] 43 Ld 39.57 N 76.44 W
York, Cape- ⌐ 57 Ff 10.40 S 142.30 E
York, Kap- ⌐ 67 Od 76.05 N 67.05 W
York, Vale of- ⌐ 9 Lg 54.10 N 1.20 W
Yorke Peninsula ⌐ 59 Hf 35.00 S 137.30 E
Yorkshire Dales ⌐ 9 Kg 54.15 N 2.10 W
Yorkshire Wolds ⌐ 9 Mh 54.00 N 0.40 W
York Sound ⌐ 59 Fb 14.50 S 125.05 E
Yorkton 39 Id 51.13 N 102.28 W
Yorktown 44 Ig 37.14 N 76.32 W
Yoro ③ 49 Df 15.15 N 87.15 W
Yoro 49 Df 15.09 N 87.07 W
Yoron-Jima ⊕ 29b Bb 27.03 N 128.26 E
Yoro-Shima ⊕ 29b Ba 28.02 N 129.10 E
Yorosso 34 Ed 12.21 N 4.47 W
Yorubaland Plateau ▲ 34 Fd 8.00 N 4.30 E
Yörük 15 Ki 40.56 N 27.04 E
Yosemite National Park ⌐ 46 De 37.45 N 119.35 W
Yosemite Rock ⊞ 52 Hi 31.58 S 83.15 W
Yoshida [China] 26 Jb 33.36 N 132.32 E
Yoshida [Jap.] 29 Ce 34.40 N 132.42 E
Yoshii 28 Ae 33.28 N 129.40 E
Yoshii-Gawa ⌐ 29 Dd 34.36 N 134.02 E
Yoshino-Gawa ⌐ 29 Dd 34.05 N 134.36 E
Yōsu 27 Me 34.44 N 127.44 E
Yotaú 54 Fg 16.03 S 63.03 W
Yôtei-Zan ▲ 29a Bg 40.49 N 140.47 E
Yotvata 24 Fh 29.53 N 35.03 E
Youghal/Eochaill 9 Fj 51.57 N 7.50 W
Youghal Harbour/Cuan
  Eochaille ⌐ 9 Fj 51.52 N 7.50 W
You Jiang ⌐ 21 Mg 22.50 N 108.06 E
Youllemmedene ⌐ 30 Ng 16.00 N 1.00 E
Young [Austl.] 59 Jf 34.19 S 148.18 E
Young, Cape- ⌐ 62 Je 43.42 S 176.37 W
Younghusband Peninsula ⌐ 59 Hg 36.00 S 139.30 E
Young Island ⊕ 66 Ke 66.25 S 162.30 E
Young's Island 51n Ba 13.08 N 61.13 W
Youngs Rock ⊞ 64a Ab 25.23 S 130.06 W
Youngstown 43 Kc 41.05 N 80.40 W
Youshashan 27 Fd 38.04 N 90.53 E
Youssoufia 30 Fc 32.15 N 8.32 W
Youyang 27 If 28.49 N 108.45 E
Yozgat 23 Db 39.50 N 34.48 E
Ypacaraí 56 Ic 25.23 S 57.16 W
Ypacarai, Laguna- ⌐ 55 Dg 25.17 S 57.20 W
Ypané, Río- ⌐ 55 Df 23.29 S 57.19 W
Ypé Jhú 55 Ef 23.54 S 55.20 W
Ypoá, Lago- ⌐ 55 Dg 26.00 S 57.28 W
Yport 12 Ce 49.44 N 0.19 E
Ypres/Ieper 11 Id 50.51 N 2.53 E
Yreka 46 Cc 41.44 N 122.42 W
Yser ⌐ 11 Ic 51.09 N 2.43 E
Yssingeaux 11 Kj 45.08 N 4.07 E
Ystad 7 Ci 55.25 N 13.49 E
Ytambey, Río- ⌐ 55 Ld 24.56 S 54.24 W
Ythan ⌐ 9 Ld 57.25 N 2.00 W
Ytre Arna 8 Ad 60.28 N 5.26 E
Ytre Sula ⊕ 8 Ac 61.05 N 4.40 E
Ytterhogdal 8 Fb 62.11 N 14.56 E
Ytterlännäs 7 Gb 63.01 N 17.41 E
Yttermalung 8 Ee 60.38 N 13.50 E
Ytyk-Kjuël 20 Id 62.28 N 133.25 E
Yu 'Alliq, Jabal- ▲ 24 Eg 30.22 N 33.31 E
Yuan'an 28 Ai 31.04 N 111.39 E
Yuanbaoshan 28 Ed 42.19 N 119.19 E
Yuanbao Shan ▲ 27 If 25.24 N 109.11 E
Yuan Jiang [Asia] = Red
  River (EN) ⌐ 21 Mg 20.17 N 106.34 E
Yuanjiang [China] 28 Bj 28.50 N 112.23 E
Yuan Jiang [China] 21 Mg 28.20 N 102.26 E
Yuan Jiang [China] 21 Ng 28.58 N 111.49 E
Yuanmou 27 Jf 28.05 N 101.54 E
Yuanqu (Liuzhangzhen) 28 Ag 35.19 N 111.44 E
Yuanshan → Lianping 27 Jf 35.45 N 114.30 E
Yuba City 46 Cd 39.08 N 121.37 W

Yuba River ⌐ 46 Eg 39.07 N 121.36 W
Yubdo 35 Fd 8.58 N 35.27 E
Yūbetsu 28 Qb 43.13 N 144.05 E
Yūbetsu-Gawa ⌐ 29a Ca 44.14 N 143.37 E
Yucatán ② 47 Gd 20.50 N 89.00 W
Yucatán, Canal de- ⌐ 38 Kg 21.45 N 85.45 W
Yucatán, Peninsula de- ⌐ 38 Kh 19.30 N 89.00 W
Yucatan Basin (EN) ⌐ 47 Ge 20.00 N 84.00 W
Yucatan Channel (EN) = 38 Kg 21.45 N 85.45 W
Yucatán, Canal de-
Yucatan Peninsula (EN) = 38 Kh 19.30 N 89.00 W
  Yucatán, Peninsula de- ⌐
Yucheng 28 Df 36.56 N 116.39 E
Yuci 28 Be 37.41 N 112.49 E
Yucuyácua, Cerro- ▲ 47 Ee 17.07 N 97.40 W
Yuda 29 Gb 39.19 N 140.48 E
Yudi Shan ▲ 21 Lb 52.17 N 121.52 E
Yueliang Pao ⌐ 28 Gb 45.44 N 123.55 E
Yueqing 27 Lf 28.08 N 120.58 E
Yuexi 27 Hf 28.37 N 102.36 E
Yuexi 28 Di 30.51 N 116.22 E
Yueyang 27 Jf 29.18 N 113.12 E
Yufu-Dake ▲ 29 Be 33.17 N 131.23 E
Yugan 27 Kf 28.42 N 116.39 E
Yugoslavia (EN) =
  Jugoslavija ① 6 Id 44.00 N 19.00 E
Yu He ⌐ 28 Be 39.51 N 113.26 E
Yuhuang Ding ▲ 28 Df 36.20 N 117.01 E
Yuki [Jap.] 29 Cd 34.29 N 132.16 E
Yuki [Zaire] 36 Cc 3.55 S 19.25 E
Yukon 45 Hi 35.31 N 97.44 W
Yukon ⌐ 38 Cc 62.33 N 163.59 W
Yukon Flats ⌐ 40 Gc 66.35 N 146.00 W
Yukon Plateau ⌐ 38 Fc 61.30 N 135.40 W
Yukon Territory ③ 42 Dd 63.00 N 136.00 W
Yūksekova 24 Kd 37.19 N 44.10 E
Yukuhashi 29 Be 33.44 N 130.58 E
Yule River ⌐ 59 Db 20.41 S 118.17 E
Yuli/Iopnur 27 Ec 41.22 N 86.09 E
Yulin [China] 22 Mf 38.14 N 109.48 E
Yuling Guan 27 Ke 30.59 N 118.53 E
Yulin [China] 22 Mf 38.14 N 109.48 E
Yulin Jiao ⌐ 21 Mh 17.50 N 109.30 E
Yulongxue Shan ▲ 27 Hf 27.09 N 100.12 E
Yuma [Az.-U.S.] 38 Gf 32.43 N 114.37 W
Yuma [Co.-U.S.] 45 Ef 40.08 N 102.43 W
Yumare 49 Md 10.37 N 68.41 W
Yumbe 50 Bg 10.37 N 68.41 W
Yumbe 35 Fb 3.28 N 31.15 E
Yumbi [Zaire] 36 Cc 1.14 S 26.14 E
Yumbi [Zaire] 36 Cc 1.53 S 16.32 E
Yumen (Laojunmiao) 22 Lf 39.50 N 97.44 E
Yumenkou 27 Jd 35.43 N 110.37 E
Yumenzhen 27 Gd 40.17 N 97.12 E
Yumin 27 Db 45.59 N 82.28 E
Yumurtalik 24 Fd 36.49 N 35.45 E
Yuna, Río- ⌐ 49 Md 19.12 N 69.37 W
Yunaska ⊕ 40a Db 52.40 N 170.50 W
Yuncheng 27 Jd 35.03 N 111.00 E
Yuncheng [China] 28 Cg 35.35 N 115.56 E
Yungas ⊠ 52 Jg 16.20 S 66.45 W
Yungay 56 Fe 37.07 S 72.01 W
Yungui Gaoyuan ▲ 21 Mg 26.00 N 105.00 E
Yunhe → Peixian 28 Dg 34.44 N 116.56 E
Yuni 29a Bb 42.59 N 141.46 E
Yunjinghong → Jinghong 27 Hg 21.59 N 100.48 E
Yunkai Dashan ▲ 27 Jg 22.30 N 111.00 E
Yunlin ② 28 Lg 23.43 N 120.33 E
Yun Ling ▲ 21 Lf 27.00 N 99.30 E
Yunmeng 28 Bi 31.01 N 113.45 E
Yunnan Sheng (Yün-nan
  Sheng) ③ 22 Lg 25.00 N 102.00 E
Yün-nan Sheng = Yunnan
  Sheng ③ 22 Lg 25.00 N 102.00 E
Yunomae 29 Be 32.15 N 130.57 E
Yunotsu 29 Cd 35.05 N 132.21 E
Yun Shui ⌐ 28 Bi 30.43 N 113.57 E
Yunxi 27 Ie 32.59 N 110.50 E
Yunxiao 27 Kg 24.05 N 117.18 E
Yunzhong Shan ▲ 28 Be 38.50 N 112.27 E
Yuquan 28 Ib 45.27 N 127.08 E
Yuqueri 55 Dj 28.53 S 58.02 W
Yura 54 Dg 16.12 S 71.42 W
Yura-Gawa ⌐ 29 Dd 35.31 N 135.17 E
Yurimaguas 53 If 5.54 S 76.05 W
Yuriria 48 Ie 20.12 N 101.09 W
Yururari, Río- ⌐ 50 Fi 6.44 N 61.40 W
Yurungkax He ⌐ 27 Dd 38.05 N 80.20 E
Yuscarán 49 Dg 13.55 N 86.51 W
Yushan 28 Dj 23.30 N 121.00 E
Yu Shan ▲ 27 Kf 27.00 N 116.00 E
Yushan 28 Dj 28.41 N 118.15 E
Yushanzhen 28 If 28.41 N 118.15 E
Yushu 20 Eg 33.01 N 96.50 E
Yushu 28 Ib 44.50 N 126.33 E
Yushutun 27 Lb 47.06 N 123.41 E
Yūsuf, Baḥr- ⌐ 24 Dh 29.19 N 30.50 E
Yusufeli 24 Ab 40.50 N 41.33 E
Yutai (Guting) 28 Dg 35.00 N 116.40 E
Yutian 27 Dd 36.52 N 81.40 E
Yutian/Keriya 22 Kf 36.52 N 81.42 E
Yuty 55 Dg 26.32 S 56.18 W
Yutz 12 Ie 49.21 N 6.11 E
Yuwan-Dake ▲ 29b Ba 28.18 N 129.18 E
Yuxi 27 Hg 24.27 N 102.34 E
Yuxian [China] 28 Cd 38.03 N 113.28 E
Yuxian [China] 28 Bg 34.09 N 113.29 E
Yuxian [China] 28 Be 39.50 N 114.33 E
Yuxikou 27 Ke 31.26 N 118.18 E
Yuyao 28 Fi 30.04 N 121.10 E
Yuya-Wan ⌐ 29a Ab 30.34 N 130.35 E
Yuza 29 Fb 39.01 N 139.53 E
Yuzawa [Jap.] 28 Pe 39.10 N 140.30 E

Yuzawa [Jap.] 29 Fc 36.56N 138.47 E
Yuzhou → Chongqing = Chungking (EN) 22 Mg 29.34N 106.27 E
Yvel 11 Dg 47.59N 2.23W
Yvelines [3] 11 Hf 48.50N 1.50 E
Yverdon 14 Ad 46.46N 6.40 E
Yvetot 11 Ge 49.37N 0.46 E
Yvette 12 Ef 48.40N 2.20 E
Yxlan 8 He 59.40N 18.50 E
Yxningen 8 Gf 58.15N 16.20 E

Z

Zaajatskaja 17 Jj 52.53N 61.35 E
Zaalajski Hrebet 18 Ie 39.25N 72.50 E
Zaanstad 11 Kb 52.26N 4.49 E
Žabaj 17 Nj 51.42N 68.22 E
Zabajkalsk 20 Gg 49.40N 117.21 E
Zabarjad 33 Ge 23.37N 36.12 E
Zāb-e Kūchek 24 Ke 36.00N 45.15 E
Zabīb, Ra's az- 14 Em 37.16N 10.04 E
Zabīd 23 Fg 14.12N 43.18 E
Zabīd, Wādī- 23 Fg 14.07N 43.06 E
Žabinka 16 Dc 52.13N 24.01 E
Ząbkowice Śląskie 10 Mf 50.36N 16.53 E
Žabljak 15 Cf 43.09N 19.08 E
Zabłudów 10 Tc 53.01N 23.20 E
Zabok 14 Jd 46.02N 15.55 E
Zābol [3] 23 Kc 32.00N 67.15 E
Zabolotje [Bye.-U.S.S.R.] 8 Kk 53.56N 24.46 E
Zabolotje [Ukr.-U.S.S.R.] 10 Ue 51.37N 24.26 E
Zabolotov 15 Ia 48.25N 25.23 E
Zabré 34 Ec 11.10N 0.38W
Zábřeh 10 Mg 49.53N 16.52 E
Zabrze 10 Of 50.18N 18.46 E
Zacapa [3] 49 Cf 15.00N 89.30W
Zacapa 47 Gf 14.58N 89.32W
Zacapu 48 Ih 19.50N 101.43W
Zacatecas 39 Ig 22.47N 102.35W
Zacatecas [2] 47 Dd 23.00N 103.00W
Zacatecoluca 49 Cg 13.30N 88.52W
Zacatepec 48 Jh 18.39N 99.12W
Zacatlán 48 Kh 19.56N 97.58W
Zaccar, Djebel- 13 Oh 36.20N 2.13 E
Zacoalco de Torres 48 Hg 20.14N 103.35W
Zacualtipán 48 Jg 20.39N 98.36W
Zaculeu 49 Bf 15.21N 91.29W
Zadar 6 Hg 44.07N 15.15 E
Zadarski Kanal 14 Jf 44.10N 15.10 E
Zadetkyi Kyun 25 Jg 9.58N 98.13 E
Zadi 36 Bc 4.46 S 14.52 E
Zadoi 27 Fe 33.10N 94.58 E
Zadonsk 16 Kc 52.23N 38.58 E
Za'farānah 33 Fd 29.07N 32.33 E
Zafferano, Capo- 14 Hl 38.07N 13.32 E
Zafir 23 He 23.07N 53.46 E
Zafra 13 Ff 38.25N 6.25W
Żagań 10 Le 51.37N 15.19 E
Zagare/Žagarė 8 Jh 56.19N 23.14 E
Žagarė/Zagare 8 Jh 56.19N 23.14 E
Zāgheh 24 Mf 33.30N 48.42 E
Zāgh Marz 24 Od 36.47N 53.17 E
Zaghrah, Wādī- 24 Fh 28.40N 34.20 E
Zaghwān 32 Jb 36.24N 10.09 E
Zaghwān [3] 32 Jb 36.25N 10.10 E
Zaghwān, Jabal- 14 En 36.21N 10.07 E
Zagora 31 Ge 30.19N 5.50W
Zagora 14 Kg 43.40N 16.15 E
Zagória 15 Dj 39.45N 20.50 E
Zagorje 14 Jd 46.05N 16.00 E
Zagorodje 10 Vd 52.15N 25.30 E
Zagórów 10 Nd 52.11N 17.55 E
Zagorsk 6 Jd 56.18N 38.08 E
Zagórz, Sanok- 10 Sg 49.31N 22.17 E
Zagreb 6 Hf 45.48N 16.00 E
Zāgros, Kūhhā-ye- = Zagros Mountains (EN) 21 Gf 33.40N 47.00 E
Zagros Mountains (EN) = Zāgros, Kūhhā-ye- 21 Gf 33.40N 47.00 E
Žagubica 15 Ee 44.12N 21.48 E
Za'gya Zangbo 27 Ee 31.55N 88.58 E
Zagyva 10 Qi 47.10N 20.12 E
Zāhedān 22 Ig 29.30N 60.52 E
Zahlah 24 Ff 33.51N 35.53 E
Zahmet 19 Gh 37.48N 62.29 E
Zahrān 33 Hf 17.40N 43.30 E
Zahrez Chergui 13 Pi 35.14N 3.32 E
Zailijski Alatau, Hrebet- 18 Kc 43.00N 77.00 E
Žailma 19 Ge 51.32N 61.40 E
Zaire 30 Ii 6.04 S 12.24 E
Zaire 30 Ii 6.04 S 12.24 E
Zaire [3] 36 Bd 6.30 S 13.30 E
Zaïre (Congo, Dem. Rep. of the-) [1] 31 Ji 1.00 S 25.00 E
Zaisan, Lake- (EN) = Zajsan, Ozero- 21 Ke 48.10N 83.50 E
Zaj 7 Mi 55.36N 51.40 E
Zaječar 15 Ff 43.54N 22.17 E
Zajsan 22 Ke 47.30N 84.55 E
Zajsan, Ozero- = Zaisan, Lake- (EN) 21 Ke 48.10N 83.50 E
Zak 30 Jk 29.39 S 21.11 E
Zaka 37 Ed 20.20 S 31.29 E
Zakamensk 20 Ff 50.23N 103.20 E
Zakarpatskaja Oblast [3] 19 Cf 48.20N 23.20 E
Zakataly 19 Eg 41.38N 46.37 E
Zākhāro 15 El 37.29N 21.39 E
Zākhū 23 Fb 37.08N 42.41 E
Zákinthos 15 Dl 37.47N 20.54 E
Zákinthos = Zante (EN) 5 Ih 37.47N 20.47 E
Zákinthou Dhiavlos- 15 Dl 37.50N 21.00 E
Zakopane 10 Pg 49.19N 19.57 E
Zakouma 35 Bc 10.54N 19.49 E
Žaksy 19 Ge 51.53N 67.20 E
Zala [2] 10 Mj 46.40N 16.50 E
Zala 10 Nj 46.43N 17.16 E
Zālābiyah 24 He 35.39N 39.51 E
Zalaegerszeg 10 Mj 46.50N 16.51 E
Zalāf 24 Gf 32.55N 37.20 E
Zalalövő 10 Mj 46.51N 16.36 E
Zalamea de la Serena 13 Gf 38.39N 5.39W
Zalamea la Real 13 Fg 37.41N 6.39W
Zalantun → Butha Qi 27 Lb 48.02N 122.42 E
Zalari 20 Ff 53.36N 102.32 E
Zalaszentgrót 10 Nj 46.57N 17.05 E
Zalău 15 Gb 47.12N 23.03 E
Zaleščiki 16 De 48.39N 25.44 E
Zalim 23 Fe 22.43N 42.10 E
Zalingei 35 Cc 12.54N 23.29 E
Zaltan 33 Cd 28.55N 19.50 E
Zaltbommel 12 Hc 51.49N 5.17 E
Žaltidjal 15 Ih 41.30N 25.05 E
Žaltyr 19 Ge 51.35N 69.58 E
Žaltyr, Ozero- 16 Qf 47.25N 51.05 E
Zamakh 23 Gf 16.28N 47.35 E
Zamami-Shima 29b Ab 26.15N 127.18 E
Zamarkh 33 If 16.30N 47.18 E
Zambeze = Zambezi (EN) 30 Kj 18.50N 36.17 E
Zambezi (EN) = Zambeze 30 Kj 18.50N 36.17 E
Zambézia [3] 37 Fc 17.00 S 37.00 E
Zambezi Escarpment 37 Ec 16.15 S 30.10 E
Zambia [1] 31 Jj 15.00 S 30.00 E
Zamboanga 22 Oi 6.54N 122.04 E
Zamboanga Peninsula 26 He 7.32N 122.16 E
Zambrah, Jazirat- 32 Jb 37.08N 10.48 E
Zambrano 49 Ji 9.45N 74.49W
Zambrów 10 Sd 53.00N 22.15 E
Zambué 37 Ec 15.07 S 30.49 E
Zamfara 34 Fc 12.02N 4.03 E
Zamkova, Gora- 10 Vc 53.34N 25.53 E
Zamkowa, Góra- 10 Qb 54.25N 20.25 E
Zammar 24 Jd 36.47N 42.40 E
Zamora [3] 13 Gc 41.45N 6.00W
Zamora [Ec.] 54 Cd 4.04 S 78.52W
Zamora [Sp.] 13 Gc 41.30N 5.45W
Zamora, Rio- 54 Cd 2.59 S 78.15W
Zamora de Hidalgo 47 De 19.59N 102.16W
Zamość [2] 10 Tf 50.44N 23.15 E
Zamość 10 Tf 50.44N 23.15 E
Zampa-Misaki 29b Ab 26.26N 127.43 E
Zamtang (Gamda) 27 He 32.23N 101.05 E
Zamuro, Punta- 49 Mh 11.26N 68.50W
Zamzam 33 Cc 31.24N 15.17 E
Zanaga 36 Bc 2.51 S 13.50 E
Žanatas 19 Gg 43.36N 69.43 E
Zancara 13 Ie 39.18N 3.18W
Zanda (Toling) 27 Ce 31.28N 79.50 E
Zandvoort 11 Kb 52.22N 4.32 E
Zanesville 43 Kd 39.55N 82.02W
Zangelan 16 Oj 39.05N 46.38 E
Zanhuang 28 Cf 37.38N 114.26 E
Zanjān [3] 23 Gb 36.35N 48.15 E
Zanjān 23 Gb 36.40N 48.29 E
Zanjānrūd 24 Ld 37.08N 47.47 E
Zannone 14 Hj 40.55N 13.05 E
Zante (EN) = Zákinthos 5 Ih 37.47N 20.47 E
Zanthus 59 Ef 31.02 S 123.34 E
Zanzibar 31 Ki 6.10 S 39.11 E
Zanzibar [3] 36 Gd 6.00 S 39.50 E
Zanzibar [2] 36 Gd 6.10 S 39.20 E
Zanzibar Channel 36 Gd 6.00 S 39.00 E
Zanzibar Island 30 Ki 6.10 S 39.20 E
Zaolin 27 Jd 39.09N 113.03 E
Zaō-San 29 Gb 38.08N 140.28 E
Zaouatallaz 32 Ie 24.52N 8.26 E
Zaousfana 32 Gc 30.30N 2.18W
Zaoyang 27 Je 32.08N 112.45 E
Zaozerny 20 Ee 55.57N 94.42 E
Zaozhuang 27 Ke 34.58N 117.34 E
Zapacos Norte, Rio- 55 Ac 17.03 S 62.23W
Zapacos Sur, Rio- 55 Ac 17.03 S 62.23W
Zapadnaja Dvina 7 Hh 56.17N 32.03 E
Zapadnaja Dvina = Western Dvina (EN) 5 Id 57.04N 24.03 E
Západná Morava 15 Ef 43.41N 21.24 E
Západné Karpaty = West Carpathians (EN) 10 Og 49.30N 19.00 E
Zapadni Rodopi 15 Hh 41.45N 24.05 E
Zapadno-Karelskaja Vozvyšennost 7 He 63.40N 31.40 E
Zapadno Sibirskaja Ravnina = West Siberian Plain (EN) 21 Jc 60.00N 75.00 E
Zapadny Sajan = Western Sayans (EN) 21 Ld 53.00N 94.00 E
Západočeský kraj [3] 10 Ig 49.45N 13.00 E
Západoslovenský kraj [3] 10 Nh 48.20N 18.00 E
Zapala 53 Ii 38.55 S 70.05W
Zapardiel 13 Gc 41.29N 5.02W
Zapata 45 Gm 26.52N 99.19W
Zapata, Peninsula de- 49 Gb 22.20N 81.35W
Zapatera, Isla- 49 Eh 11.45N 85.50W
Zapatosa, Cienaga de- 49 Ki 9.05N 73.50W
Zapljusje 8 Mf 58.24N 29.56 E
Zapoljarny 19 Db 69.26N 30.48 E
Zapopan 48 Hg 20.43N 103.24W
Zaporožje 6 Jf 47.50N 35.10 E
Zaporožskaja Oblast [3] 19 Df 47.15N 35.50 E
Zapotitlán, Punta- 48 Lh 18.33N 94.49W
Zapovednik Beloveźskaja Pušča 10 Kd 52.45N 24.15 E
Za Qu 27 Ge 32.00N 96.55 E
Zara 24 Gc 39.55N 37.48 E
Zarāf, Baḥr az- 35 Ed 9.25N 31.10 E
Zarafšan 19 Gg 41.39N 64.10 E
Zaragoza [3] 13 Lc 41.35N 1.00W
Zaragoza [Col.] 54 Db 7.30N 74.52W
Zaragoza [Mex.] 48 Jf 23.58N 99.46W
Zaragoza [Mex.] 48 Ic 28.29N 100.55W
Zaragoza [Mex.] 48 If 22.02N 100.44W
Zaragoza [Sp.] = Saragossa (EN) 6 Fg 41.38N 0.53W
Zarajsk 7 Ji 54.47N 38.53 E
Zarand [Iran] 24 Qg 30.48N 56.53 E
Zarand [Iran] 24 Me 35.08N 49.00 E
Zarand-e-Kohneh 24 Ne 35.17N 50.30 E
Zărandului, Munţii- 15 Fc 46.10N 22.15 E
Zaranj 22 If 31.06N 61.53 E
Zarasai/Zarasaj 7 Gi 55.43N 26.19 E
Zarasaj/Zarasai 7 Gi 55.43N 26.19 E
Zárate 53 Ki 34.05 S 59.02W
Zarauz 13 Ja 43.17N 2.10W
Zaraza 54 Eb 9.21N 65.19W
Žarcovski 7 Hi 55.53N 32.16 E
Zard Kūh 21 Hf 32.22N 50.04 E
Zardob 16 Oi 40.14N 47.42 E
Zarečensk 7 Hc 66.40N 31.23 E
Zarghat 24 Ii 26.32N 40.29 E
Zarghun 25 Db 30.31N 68.50 E
Zarghūn Shahr 23 Kc 32.51N 68.25 E
Zaria 31 Hg 11.04N 7.42 E
Žarkamys 19 Ff 47.59N 56.29 E
Žarma 19 If 48.48N 80.55 E
Zărneşti 15 Id 45.33N 25.18 E
Zarqān 24 Oh 29.46N 52.43 E
Zarrīneh 24 Kd 37.05N 45.40 E
Zarrīnshahr 24 Nf 32.30N 51.25 E
Zaruma 54 Cd 3.42 S 79.38W
Zarumilla 54 Bd 3.30 S 80.16W
Žary 10 Le 51.38N 15.09 E
Žaryk 19 Hf 48.52N 72.54 E
Zarzaïtine 32 Id 28.05N 9.45 E
Zasa 8 Lh 56.15N 26.01 E
Zāskar 25 Fb 34.10N 77.20 E
Zaškov 16 Ge 49.15N 30.09 E
Zaslavl 8 Lj 54.00N 27.22 E
Zaslavskoje Vodohranilišče 8 Lj 54.00N 27.30 E
Zastavna 15 Ia 48.25N 25.49 E
Zastron 37 Df 30.18 S 27.07 E
Žatec 10 Jf 50.20N 13.33 E
Zatišje 15 Mb 47.47N 29.48 E
Zatobolsk 17 Kj 53.12N 63.43 E
Zatoka 15 Nc 46.07N 30.25 E
Zauche 10 Id 52.15N 12.35 E
Žavadovskogo Island 66 Ge 66.30 S 86.00 E
Zavāreh 24 Of 33.30N 52.29 E
Zaventem 12 Gd 50.53N 4.28 E
Zavety Ilića 20 Jg 49.02N 140.19 E
Zavidoviči 14 Mf 44.27N 18.09 E
Zavitinsk 20 Hg 50.01N 129.26 E
Zavodoukovsk 19 Gd 56.33N 66.32 E
Zavodovski 66 Ad 56.20 S 27.35W
Zavolžje 7 Kh 56.38N 43.21 E
Zavolžsk 7 Kh 57.32N 42.10 E
Zawidów 10 Le 51.01N 15.02 E
Zawiercie 10 Pf 50.30N 19.25 E
Zawilah 33 Cd 26.10N 15.07 E
Zāwiyat al Mukhaylá 33 Dc 32.10N 22.17 E
Zāwiyat Masūs 33 Dc 31.35N 21.01 E
Zāwiyat Qirzah 33 Bc 31.00N 14.20 E
Zāwiyat Shammās 24 Bg 31.31N 26.24 E
Zawr, Ra's az- 24 Mi 27.26N 49.19 E
Zaya 14 Kb 48.31N 16.55 E
Zāyandeh 24 Of 32.20N 52.50 E
Zaydūn, Wādī- 24 Ej 25.53N 33.04 E
Zayū (Gyigang) 27 Gf 28.42N 97.35 E
Zaza, Rio- 49 Hc 21.37N 79.32W
Zazir 32 If 19.50N 5.13 E
Zbaraž 16 De 49.42N 25.47 E
Zbąszyń 10 Ld 52.16N 15.55 E
Zborov 10 Vg 49.37N 25.09 E
Zdanichý les 10 Mg 49.05N 16.50 E
Ždanov 6 Jf 47.06N 37.33 E
Ždanovsk 16 Oj 39.45N 47.33 E
Žď'árské vrchy 10 Mg 49.35N 16.03 E
Ždiar 10 Qg 49.16N 20.15 E
Zdolbunov 16 Ed 50.33N 26.15 E
Zduńska Wola 10 Oe 51.36N 18.57 E
Zealand (EN) = Sjælland 5 Hd 55.30N 11.45 E
Zebediela 37 Dd 24.19 S 29.16 E
Zebēs, Mali i- 15 Dh 41.55N 20.14 E
Zebil 15 Le 44.57N 28.46 E
Zeča 14 If 44.46N 14.19 E
Zeddine 13 Nh 36.12N 1.50 E
Zedelgem 12 Fc 51.09N 3.08 E
Zeehan 58 Fi 41.53 S 145.20 E
Zeeland 11 Jc 51.27N 3.45 E
Zeeland [3] 12 Fc 51.27N 3.45 E
Zeerust 37 De 25.33 S 26.06 E
Zefat 24 Ff 32.58N 35.30 E
Zegrzyńskie, Jezioro- 10 Rd 52.30N 21.05 E
Zehdenick 10 Jd 52.59N 13.20 E
Zeil, Mount- 59 Gd 23.25 S 132.25 E
Žeimelis/Zeimjalis 8 Jh 56.14N 23.58 E
Žeimena/Žejmena 7 Fi 54.54N 23.53 E
Zeimjalis/Žeimelis 8 Jh 56.14N 23.58 E
Zeist 11 Lb 52.05N 5.15 E
Zeitz 10 Ie 51.03N 12.09 E
Zeja 21 Od 50.13N 127.35 E
Zeja 22 Od 53.45N 127.15 E
Žejmena/Žeimena 7 Fi 54.54N 23.53 E
Zejskoje Vodohranilišče 20 Hf 54.40N 127.30 E
Zēkog 27 Hd 35.00N 101.35 E
Zelanija, Mys- 21 Ib 76.57N 68.35 E
Zelaya [3] 49 Eg 13.00N 84.00W
Želča 8 Lf 58.18N 27.50 E
Zele 12 Gc 51.04N 4.02 E
Želechów 10 Re 51.49N 21.54 E
Zelee, Cape- 63a Ec 9.44 S 161.34 E
Zelenaja Rošča 8 Md 60.08N 29.14 E
Zelenčukskaja 16 Lh 43.51N 41.34 E
Zelengora 14 Mg 43.22N 18.35 E
Zelenoborsk 19 Gc 61.29N 63.59 E
Zelenoborski 19 Db 66.50N 32.18 E
Zelenodolsk 19 Ed 55.53N 48.31 E
Zelenogorsk 19 Cc 60.12N 29.42 E
Zelenograd 7 Ih 56.01N 37.12 E
Zelenogradsk 8 Ij 54.57N 20.27 E
Zelenokumsk 19 Eg 44.23N 43.53 E
Zeletin 15 Kc 46.03N 27.23 E
Železné hory 10 Lg 49.50N 15.45 E
Zeleznik 15 De 44.43N 20.23 E
Železnodorožny [R.S.F.S.R.] 20 Fe 57.55N 102.50 E
Železnodorožny [R.S.F.S.R.] 7 Ei 54.23N 21.19 E
Železnodorožny [R.S.F.S.R.] 19 Fc 62.37N 50.55 E
Železnogorsk 19 De 52.21N 35.23 E
Železnogorsk-Ilimski 20 Fe 56.40N 104.05 E
Železnovodsk 16 Mg 44.08N 43.00 E
Zelfana 32 Hc 32.24N 4.14 E
Želiezovce 10 Oh 48.03N 18.40 E
Želivka 10 Lg 49.43N 15.06 E
Željin 15 Df 43.29N 20.48 E
Zell am See 14 Gc 47.19N 12.47 E
Zell am Ziller 14 Fc 47.14N 11.53 E
Zelów 10 Pe 51.28N 19.13 E
Želtau Ajtau 18 Ib 44.30N 74.00 E
Žéltyje Vody 16 He 48.23N 33.31 E
Želudok 10 Vc 53.33N 25.07 E
Želva 8 Ki 55.13N 25.13 E
Želva 10 Uc 53.04N 24.54 E
Zelzate 11 Jc 51.12N 3.49 E
Žemaičiu Aukštuma/Žemajtskaja Vozvyšennost 8 Ji 55.45N 22.30 E
Žemaiciy-Naumiestis/Žemajčju-Naumiestis 8 Ii 55.21N 21.37 E
Žemaitija 8 Ji 55.55N 22.30 E
Žemajčju-Naumiestis/Žemaiciy-Naumiestis 8 Ii 55.21N 21.37 E
Žemajtskaja Vozvyšennost/Žemaičiu Aukštuma 8 Ji 55.45N 22.30 E
Zembin 8 Mj 54.24N 28.19 E
Zembretta, Ile- 14 Em 37.07N 10.53 E
Zemetčino 16 Mc 53.31N 42.38 E
Zemgale 8 Kh 56.30N 25.00 E
Zémio 35 Dd 5.19N 25.08 E
Zemmora 13 Mi 35.43N 0.45 E
Zemmour 30 Ff 25.30N 12.00W
Zemplinska Širava, údolná nádrž- 10 Sh 48.50N 22.02 E
Zempoala 47 Ee 19.27N 96.23W
Zempoaltepec 38 Jh 17.00N 96.50W
Zemra, Djebel- 13 Pi 35.14N 3.54 E
Zemst 12 Gd 50.59N 4.28 E
Zemun, Beograd- 15 De 44.53N 20.25 E
Zengfeng Shan 28 Jc 42.25N 128.44 E
Zenica 23 Ff 44.13N 17.55 E
Zenkov 16 Id 50.13N 34.22 E
Zenne 12 Gc 51.04N 4.26 E
Zenobia Peak 45 Bf 40.40N 108.48W
Zentsūji 29 Cd 34.14N 133.47 E
Zenzach 13 Pi 35.21N 3.22 E
Zenza do Itombe 36 Bd 9.16 S 14.13 E
Žepče 14 Mf 44.26N 18.03 E
Zepu/Poskam 27 Cd 38.12N 77.18 E
Zéralda 13 Oh 36.43N 2.50 E
Zeravšan 17 If 39.22N 63.45 E
Zeravšan 18 Ge 39.10N 68.40 E
Zeravšanski Hrebet 19 Gh 39.15N 68.30 E
Zerbst 10 Ie 51.58N 12.05 E
Žerdevka 19 Ee 51.53N 41.28 E
Zerind 15 Ec 46.37N 21.31 E
Zermatt 14 Bd 46.02N 7.44 E
Zernez 14 Ed 46.42N 10.07 E
Zernograd 19 Ef 46.48N 40.19 E
Zeroua 13 Ph 36.22N 3.21 E
Žešart 17 De 62.05N 49.31 E
Zestafoni 16 Mh 42.07N 43.02 E
Zeta 15 Cg 42.28N 19.16 E
Zetland → Shetland Islands 5 Fc 60.30N 1.30W
Žetybaj 19 Fg 43.34N 52.04 E
Žetykol Ozero- 16 Vd 51.05N 60.55 E
Zeune Islands 63a Bb 6.18 S 155.50 E
Zeven 10 Fc 53.18N 9.17 E
Zevenaar 12 Ic 51.55N 6.05 E
Zevenbergen 12 Gc 51.38N 4.36 E
Zeydābād 24 Ph 29.37N 55.33 E
Zeydār 24 Pd 36.20N 55.53 E
Zeytinbaği 15 Li 40.23N 28.47 E
Zeytindağ 15 Kk 38.58N 27.04 E
Zêzere 13 De 39.28N 8.20W
Žežmarjaj/Žiežmariai 8 Kj 54.47N 24.36 E
Zgharta 24 Fe 34.24N 35.54 E
Zgierz 10 Pe 51.52N 19.25 E
Zgorzelec 10 Le 51.12N 15.01 E
Zhabdun → Zhongba 22 Kg 29.41N 84.10 E
Zhag'yab 27 Ge 30.40N 97.40 E
Zhangbei 27 Jc 41.13N 114.43 E
Zhangde → Anyang 22 Nf 36.01N 114.25 E
Zhangdian → Zibo 27 Kd 36.48N 118.04 E
Zhangguangcai 28 Jb 45.00N 129.00 E
Zhang He 28 Cf 36.27N 114.42 E
Zhangjiakou 22 Ne 40.49N 114.57 E
Zhangjiapan → Jingbian 27 Id 37.32N 108.45 E
Zhangling 27 La 52.39N 123.31 E
Zhanglou 28 Dh 32.40N 116.47 E
Zhangping 27 Kf 25.25N 117.27 E
Zhangqiu (Mingshui) 28 Df 36.44N 117.33 E
Zhangshuzhen → Qingjiang 27 Kf 28.02N 115.31 E
Zhangwei Xinhe 28 Dg 38.13N 117.48 E
Zhangwu 27 Lc 42.23N 122.33 E
Zhangye 22 Mf 38.57N 100.28 E
Zhangzhou 22 Ng 24.38N 117.39 E
Zhangzi 27 Jd 36.04N 112.53 E
Zhan He 27 Mb 49.21N 128.07 E
Zhanhua (Fuguo) 28 Ef 37.42N 118.08 E
Zhanjiang 22 Ng 21.13N 110.23 E
Zhanyi 27 Hf 25.40N 103.46 E
Zhao'an 27 Kg 23.49N 117.10 E
Zhaodong 27 Mb 46.04N 125.56 E
Zhaoge → Qixian 28 Cg 35.35N 114.12 E
Zhaojue 27 Hf 28.02N 102.50 E
Zhaoqing 27 Jg 23.04N 112.28 E
Zhaosu/Monggolküre 27 Dc 43.10N 81.07 E
Zhaosutai He 28 Gc 42.42N 123.35 E
Zhaotong 22 Mg 27.20N 103.46 E
Zhaoxian 28 Cf 37.46N 114.46 E
Zhaoyang Hu 28 Dg 35.00N 116.48 E
Zhaoyuan [China] 28 Ff 37.22N 120.23 E
Zhaoyuan [China] 28 Hb 45.30N 125.06 E
Zhaozhou 28 Hb 45.42N 125.15 E
Zhari Namco 27 Ee 31.05N 85.35 E
Zhaxi → Weixin 27 If 27.46N 105.04 E
Zhaxi Co 27 Ee 32.12N 85.10 E
Zhecheng 28 Cg 34.05N 115.17 E
Zheduo Shankou 27 He 30.06N 101.48 E
Zhejiang Sheng (Che-Chiang Sheng) [2] 27 Kf 29.00N 120.00 E
Zhen'an 27 Ie 33.27N 109.10 E
Zhenba 27 Ie 32.37N 107.50 E
Zhenghe 27 Kf 27.20N 118.58 E
Zhenghe Qunjiao 26 Fd 10.20N 114.20 E
Zhenglan Qi (Dund Hot) 28 Cc 42.14N 115.59 E
Zhengxiangbai Qi (Qagan Nur) 27 Jc 42.16N 114.59 E
Zhengyang 28 Ci 32.36N 114.23 E
Zhengzhou 22 Nf 34.42N 113.41 E
Zhenhai 28 Fj 29.57N 121.43 E
Zhenjiang 27 Ke 32.03N 119.26 E
Zhenkang (Fengweiba) 27 Gg 23.54N 99.00 E
Zhenlai 27 Lb 45.50N 123.14 E
Zhenning 27 If 26.05N 105.46 E
Zhenping 28 Bh 33.02N 112.14 E
Zhenxiong 27 Hf 27.28N 104.52 E
Zhenyuan 27 Hg 23.52N 100.53 E
Zhenyuan (Wuyang) 27 If 27.05N 108.26 E
Zhicheng 27 Je 30.17N 111.29 E
Zhidan (Bao'an) 27 Id 36.48N 108.46 E
Zhidoi 27 Ge 34.46N 95.46 E
Zhijiang 27 If 27.32N 109.42 E
Zhi Qu/Tongtian He 21 Lf 33.26N 96.36 E
Zhiziluo → Bijiang 27 Gf 26.39N 99.00 E
Zhob 25 Db 32.04N 69.50 E
Zhongba (Zhabdun) 22 Kg 29.41N 84.10 E
Zhongba → Jiangyou 27 He 31.48N 104.39 E
Zhongdian 27 Gf 27.42N 99.41 E
Zhōngguó 21 Mg 35.00N 105.00 E
Zhonghua Renmin Gongheguo = China (EN) [1] 22 Mf 35.00N 105.00 E
Zhongjian Dao 26 Fc 15.52N 111.13 E
Zhongmou 28 Cg 34.45N 114.01 E
Zhongning 27 Id 37.28N 105.41 E
Zhongshan 27 Jg 22.31N 113.23 E
Zhongwei 22 Mf 37.30N 105.09 E
Zhongxian 27 Ie 30.20N 108.02 E
Zhongxiang 27 Je 31.10N 112.38 E
Zhongxing → Siyang 28 Eh 33.43N 118.40 E
Zhongyaozhan 27 Ma 50.46N 125.53 E
Zhongye Qundao 26 Fd 11.20N 114.30 E
Zhoukoudianzhen 28 Ce 39.41N 115.55 E
Zhoukouzhen 27 Je 33.32N 114.40 E
Zhoushan Dao 28 Gi 30.00N 122.00 E
Zhoushan Qundao 21 Of 30.00N 122.00 E
Zhuanghe 27 Ld 39.42N 122.58 E
Zhucheng 27 Kd 35.58N 119.28 E
Zhu Dao 28 Fe 39.05N 121.10 E
Zhugqu 27 He 33.46N 104.18 E
Zhuhe 28 Bj 29.44N 113.07 E
Zhuizishan → Weichang 27 Kc 41.55N 117.39 E
Zhuji 28 Fj 29.43N 120.13 E
Zhuji → Shangqiu 27 Ke 34.24N 115.37 E
Zhujiang Kou 27 Jg 22.20N 113.45 E
Zhumadian 27 Je 32.54N 114.03 E
Zhuolu 28 Cd 40.23N 115.13 E
Zhuoxian 27 Kd 39.26N 116.00 E
Zhuozhang He 28 Bf 36.36N 113.10 E
Zhuozi 28 Bd 40.52N 112.33 E
Zhuozi Shan 27 Id 39.36N 107.00 E
Zhushan 27 Je 32.16N 110.12 E
Zhuzhou 22 Ng 27.52N 113.12 E
Ziama Mansouria 32 Ib 36.40N 5.29 E
Ziar nad Hronom 10 Oh 48.36N 18.52 E
Žibā' 23 Ed 27.21N 35.40 E
Zibo (Zhangdian) 27 Kd 36.48N 118.04 E
Zicavo 11a Bb 41.54N 9.08 E
Židačov 10 Ug 49.17N 24.12 E
Zielona Góra 10 Le 51.56N 15.31 E
Zielona Góra [2] 10 Le 51.55N 15.30 E
Zierikzee 11 Jc 51.38N 3.55 E
Žiežmariai/Žežmarjaj 8 Kj 54.47N 24.36 E
Ziftā 24 Dg 30.43N 31.15 E
Žigalovo 20 Ff 54.48N 105.08 E
Zigana Geçidi 24 Hb 40.38N 39.25 E
Žigansk 20 Hc 66.45N 123.30 E
Zigey 35 Bc 14.43N 15.47 E
Zighan, Wāḥāt- 33 Dd 25.35N 22.06 E
Zigong 22 Mg 29.20N 104.48 E
Zigui 27 Je 31.01N 110.42 E
Ziguinchor 31 Fg 12.35N 16.16W
Žigulevsk 19 Ee 53.27N 49.29 E
Zihuatanejo 47 De 17.38N 101.33W
Zijing Shan 27 Jd 37.12N 112.50 E
Zijpenberg 12 Hb 52.04N 6.00 E
Zilālet 34 Gb 18.28N 7.48 E
Zile 23 Ea 40.18N 35.54 E
Žilina 6 Hf 49.14N 18.45 E
Žilino 8 Ij 54.55N 21.48 E
Zillah 31 If 28.33N 17.35 E
Ziller 14 Fc 47.24N 11.50 E
Zillertaler Alpen 10 Hi 47.00N 11.55 E
Žiloj 16 Qi 40.19N 50.33 E
Zilupe 7 Gh 56.25N 28.07 E
Zima 22 Md 53.55N 102.04 E
Zimapán 48 Jg 20.45N 99.21W
Zimatlán de Alvarez 48 Ki 16.52N 96.47W
Zimba 36 Ef 17.02S 26.30 E
Zimbabwe 37 Ed 20.16 S 30.55 E
Zimbabwe (Rhodesia) [1] 31 Jj 20.00 S 30.00 E

Index Symbols

[1] Independent Nation
[2] State, Region
[3] District, County
[4] Municipality
[5] Colony, Dependency
Continent
Physical Region
Historical or Cultural Region
Mount, Mountain
Volcano
Hill
Mountains, Mountain Range
Hills, Escarpment
Plateau, Upland
Pass, Gap
Plain, Lowland
Delta
Salt Flat
Valley, Canyon
Crater, Cave
Karst Features
Depression
Polder
Desert, Dunes
Forest, Woods
Heath, Steppe
Oasis
Cape, Point
Coast, Beach
Cliff
Peninsula
Isthmus
Sandbank
Island
Atoll
Rock, Reef
Islands, Archipelago
Rocks, Reefs
Coral Reef
Well, Spring
Geyser
River, Stream
Waterfall Rapids
River Mouth, Estuary
Lake
Salt Lake
Intermittent Lake
Reservoir
Swamp, Pond
Canal
Glacier
Ice Shelf, Pack Ice
Ocean
Sea
Gulf, Bay
Strait, Fjord
Lagoon
Bank
Seamount
Tablemount
Ridge
Shelf
Basin
Escarpment, Sea Scarp
Fracture
Trench, Abyss
National Park, Reserve
Point of Interest
Recreation Site
Cave, Cavern
Historic Site
Ruins
Wall, Walls
Church, Abbey
Temple
Scientific Station
Airport
Port
Lighthouse
Mine
Tunnel
Dam, Bridge

International Map Index

Zimbor	15 Gc 47.00N 23.16 E	Zlatibor ▲	15 Cf 43.40N 19.43 E	Zoločev [Ukr.-U.S.S.R.]	19 Cf 49.49N 24.58 E	Zuénoula	34 Dd 7.26N 6.03W	Zürich	6 Gf 47.20N 8.35 E
Zimi	34 Cd 7.19N 11.18W	Zlatica	15 Hg 42.43N 24.08 E	Zolotaja Gora	20 Hf 54.21N 126.41 E	Zuénoula [3]	34 Dd 7.22N 6.12W	Zurich, Lake- (EN) =
Zimni Bereg ▣	7 Jd 66.00N 40.45 E	Zlatica ◥	15 Hg 42.43N 24.08 E	Zolotoje	16 Ke 48.40N 38.30 E	Zuera	13 Lc 41.52N 0.47W	Zürichsee ▣	14 Cc 47.15N 8.45 E
Zimnicea	15 If 43.40N 25.22 E	Zlatijata ◰	15 Gf 43.40N 23.36 E	Zolotonoša	16 He 49.40N 32.02 E	Zufâf ◈	33 Hf 16.43N 41.46 E	Zürichsee = Zurich, Lake-
Zimovniki	16 Mf 47.08N 42.29 E	Zlatiški prohod ▱	15 Hg 42.45N 24.05 E	Zolotuhino	16 Jc 52.07N 36.25 E	Zufallspitze/Cevedale ▲	14 Ed 46.27N 10.37 E	(EN) ▣	14 Cc 47.15N 8.45 E
Zina	34 Hc 11.16N 14.58 E	Zlatna	15 Gc 46.07N 23.13 E	Žolymbet	19 He 51.45N 71.44 E	Zufār ◰	21 Hh 17.30N 54.00 E	Zurmi	34 Gc 12.47N 6.47 E
Zincirli ◳	24 Gd 37.00N 36.41 E	Zlatograd	15 Ih 41.23N 25.06 E	Zomba	31 Kj 15.23S 35.20 E	Zug [2]	14 Cc 47.10N 8.40 E	Żuromin	10 Pc 53.04N 19.55 E
Zinder	31 Hg 13.48N 8.59 E	Zlatoust	6 Ld 55.10N 59.40 E	Zongga → Gyirong	27 Ef 28.57N 85.12 E	Zug [Switz.]	14 Cc 47.10N 8.30 E	Zuru	34 Gc 11.26N 5.14 E
Zinder [2]	34 Hb 15.00N 10.00 E	Zlatoustovsk	20 If 52.59N 133.41 E	Zongo	36 Cb 4.21N 18.36 E	Zug [W.Sah.]	32 Ee 21.36N 14.09W	Zuša ◥	16 Jc 53.27N 36.25 E
Zinga	35 Be 3.43N 18.35 E	Zletovo	15 Fh 41.59N 22.15 E	Zonguldak	23 Da 41.27N 31.49 E	Zugdidi	19 Eg 42.29N 41.48 E	Zusam ◥	14 Ig 48.42N 10.45 E
Zingst ▣	10 Ib 54.25N 12.50 E	Zlîtan	33 Bc 32.28N 14.34 E	Zongyang	28 Di 30.42N 117.12 E	Zugersee ▣	14 Cc 47.10N 8.30 E	Žut ◈	14 Jg 43.52N 15.19 E
Zinjibâr	33 Ig 13.08N 45.23 E	Złobin	19 De 52.59N 30.03 E	Zonkwa	34 Gd 9.47N 8.17 E	Zugspitze ▲	10 Gi 47.25N 10.59 E	Zutiua, Rio- ◥	54 Id 3.43S 45.30W
Zinnik/Soignies	11 Kd 50.35N 4.04 E	Złocieniec	10 Mc 53.33N 16.01 E	Zonnebeke	12 Ed 50.52N 2.59 E	Zuid Beveland ◈	12 Fc 51.25N 3.45 E	Zutphen	11 Mb 52.08N 6.12 E
Zinsel du Nord ◥	12 Jf 48.49N 7.44 E	Złoczew	10 Oe 51.25N 18.36 E	Zontehuitz, Cerro- ▲	48 Mi 16.50N 92.38W	Zuidelijke Flevoland ◳	12 Hb 52.25N 5.20 E	Zuwārah	33 Bc 32.56N 12.06 E
Zion [Il.-U.S.]	45 Me 42.27N 87.50W	Zlot	15 Ge 44.01N 21.59 E	Zonūz	24 Kc 38.35N 45.50 E	Zuid-Holland [3]	12 Gc 52.00N 4.30 E	Zvenigorodka	16 Ge 49.04N 30.59 E
Zion [St.C.N.]	51c Ab 17.09N 62.32W	Złotoryja	10 Le 51.08N 15.55 E	Zonza	11a Bb 41.44N 9.10 E	Zuid-Ijsselmeerpolders [3]	12 Hb 52.20N 5.20 E	Zverinogolovskoje	17 Li 54.28N 64.50 E
Zipaquirá	54 Db 5.02N 74.01W	Złotów	10 Nc 53.22N 17.02 E	Zorita	13 Ge 39.17N 5.42W	Zuidlaren	12 Ia 53.06N 6.42 E	Zvezdny	20 Fe 56.40N 106.30 E
Zirc	10 Ni 47.16N 17.52 E	Zły Komorow/Senftenberg	10 Kc 51.31N 14.01 E	Zorkassa, Gora- ▲	18 Ge 38.01N 68.10 E	Zuid-Willemsvaart ▤	12 Hd 50.50N 5.41 E	Zvičina ▲	10 Lf 50.25N 15.41 E
Žirje ◈	14 Jg 43.39N 15.40 E	Zlynka	16 Gc 52.27N 31.44 E	Zorleni	15 Kc 46.16N 27.43 E	Zuidwolde	12 Ib 52.40N 6.25 E	Zvirca	10 Uf 50.24N 24.16 E
Zirkel, Mount- ▲	45 Cf 40.52N 106.36W	Zmeinogorsk	20 Df 51.10N 82.13 E	Zorritos	54 Bd 3.40S 80.40W	Zvolen	13 Gf 38.50N 5.20W	Zvolen	14 Nf 44.23N 19.07 E
Žirnovsk	19 Ee 51.01N 44.48 E	Žmerinka	19 Cf 49.02N 28.05 E	Zorzor	34 Dd 7.47N 9.26W	Zújar, Embalse del- ◱	13 Gf 38.50N 5.20W	Zvornik	14 Nf 44.23N 19.07 E
Ziro	25 Ic 27.32N 93.32 E	Żmigród	10 Me 51.29N 16.55 E	Zottegem	12 Fd 50.52N 3.48 E	Zujevka	19 Fd 58.26N 51.12 E	Zwardoń	13 Og 49.30N 18.59 E
Zi Shui ◥	27 Jf 28.41N 112.43 E	Zmijev	16 Je 49.41N 36.20 E	Zou [3]	34 Fd 8.00N 2.15 E	Žukovka	19 De 53.33N 33.47 E	Zwarte Bank = Black Bank
Žitava ◥	10 Oi 47.53N 18.11 E	Zmijevka	16 Jc 52.40N 36.24 E	Zouar	31 If 20.27N 16.32 E	Žukovski	7 Ji 55.37N 38.12 E		12 Fa 53.15N 3.55 E
Žitkoviči	16 Fc 52.16N 28.02 E	Zna ▣	7 Ih 57.33N 34.25 E	Zouïrât	31 Ff 22.46N 12.27W	Zula	35 Fb 15.14N 39.40 E	Zweibrücken	14 Bd 46.34N 7.25 E
Zitkovo	7 Gf 60.42N 29.23 E	Znamenka [R.S.F.S.R.]	16 Lc 52.24N 41.28 E	Zoutkamp, Ulrum-	12 Ia 53.20N 6.18 E	Zulia [2]	54 Db 10.00N 72.10W	Zweisimmen	14 Bd 46.34N 7.25 E
Žitomir	6 Ie 50.16N 28.40 E	Znamenka [Ukr.-U.S.S.R.]	16 He 48.41N 32.40 E	Zouxian	28 Dg 35.24N 116.59 E	Zulia, Rio- ◥	49 Ki 9.04N 72.18W	Zwesten	12 Lc 51.03N 9.11 E
Žitomirskaja Oblast [3]	19 Ce 50.40N 28.30 E	Znamensk	8 Ij 54.39N 21.15 E	Zovten	15 Nb 47.14N 30.14 E	Zülpich	12 Id 50.42N 6.39 E	Zwettl in Niederösterreich	14 Jb 48.37N 15.10 E
Zittau	10 Kf 50.54N 14.50 E	Znamenskoje	19 Hd 57.08N 73.55 E	Žovtnevoje	16 Hf 46.52N 32.02 E	Zumbo	37 Ec 15.36S 30.25 E	Zwickau	10 Ie 50.44N 12.30 E
Zitterwald ▲	12 Id 50.27N 6.25 E	Žnin	10 Nd 52.52N 17.43 E	Zpouping	28 Df 36.53N 117.44 E	Zundert	12 Gc 51.29N 4.40 E	Zwickauer Mulde ◥	10 Ie 51.10N 12.48 E
Zitundo	37 Ee 26.44S 32.49 E	Znojmo	10 Mh 48.51N 16.03 E	Zrenjanin	15 Dd 45.23N 20.23 E	Zungeru	34 Gd 9.48N 6.09 E	Zwickau	10 Sf 50.37N 22.58 E
Živinice	14 Mf 44.27N 18.39 E	Zobia	36 Eb 2.53N 26.02 E	Zrinska Gora ▲	14 Ke 45.10N 16.15 E	Zunhua	28 Dd 40.12N 117.58 E	Zwiesel	10 Jg 49.01N 13.14 E
Ziwa Magharibi [3]	36 Fc 2.00S 31.30 E	Zóbuè	37 Ec 15.36S 34.26 E	Zrmanja ◥	14 Jf 44.12N 15.35 E	Zuni	45 Bi 35.04N 108.51W	Zwijndrecht	12 Gc 51.50N 4.41 E
Ziway, Lake- ▣	35 Fd 8.00N 38.48 E	Žodino	16 Fb 54.07N 28.19 E	Zruč nad Sázavou	10 Lg 49.45N 15.07 E	Zuni River ◥	46 Ki 34.39N 109.40W	Zwischenahn	10 Dc 53.11N 8.00 E
Ziya He ◥	28 De 38.39N 117.33 E	Žodiški	8 Lj 54.40N 26.33 E	Zschopau ◥	10 Je 51.08N 13.03 E	Zunyi	22 Mg 27.40N 106.56 E	Zwoleń	10 Re 51.22N 21.35 E
Ziyang	27 Ie 32.34N 108.37 E	Zoetermeer	12 Gb 52.04N 4.30 E	Žuantobe	19 Gg 44.47N 68.52 E	Zuoquan	28 Bf 37.05N 113.22 E	Zwolle	11 Mb 52.30N 6.05 E
Ziz ◥	32 Gc 30.29N 4.26W	Zogang/Wangda	27 Gf 29.37N 97.58 E	Zuata, Rio- ◥	50 Di 7.52N 65.22W	Zuoyun	28 Be 39.58N 112.40 E	Żychlin	10 Pd 52.15N 19.39 E
Žizdra	16 Ic 53.45N 34.43 E	Žohova, Ostrov- ◈	20 Ka 76.10N 153.05 E	Zubayr, Jazā'ir az- ◈	33 Hf 15.05N 42.08 E	Županja	14 Me 45.04N 18.42 E	Żyrardów	10 Qd 52.04N 20.25 E
Žizdra ◥	16 Jb 54.14N 36.12 E	Zohreh ◥	24 Mg 30.04N 49.34 E	Zubcov	16 Ib 56.10N 34.31 E	Zuqāq ◈	33 Hf 18.04N 40.48 E	Zyrjanka	20 Kc 65.45N 105.51 E
Zlatar ▲	15 Cf 43.23N 19.51 E	Zolgê	27 He 33.38N 103.00 E	Zubova Poljana	7 Ki 54.05N 42.50 E	Zurak	34 Hd 9.14N 10.34 E	Zyrjanovsk	19 If 49.45N 84.16 E
Zlaté Moravce	10 Oh 48.23N 18.24 E	Zoločev [Ukr.-U.S.S.R.]	16 Id 50.18N 35.59 E	Zudáñez	54 Fg 19.06S 64.44W	Zürich [2]	14 Cc 47.30N 8.30 E	Żywiec	10 Pg 49.41N 19.12 E

Index Symbols

[1] Independent Nation	▱ Pass, Gap	▱ Depression	▣ Coast, Beach	▦ Rock, Reef	◥ Waterfall Rapids	▱ Canal	◳ Lagoon	▰ Escarpment, Sea Scarp	▲ Historic Site	◳ Port
[2] State, Region	▲ Mount, Mountain	▱ Plain, Lowland	▱ Polder	▱ Cliff	◥ River Mouth, Estuary	◱ Glacier	◳ Bank	▱ Fracture	▱ Ruins	▱ Lighthouse
[3] District, County	▲ Volcano	▲ Delta	▱ Desert, Dunes	▱ Peninsula	▣ Lake	▱ Ice Shelf, Pack Ice	▱ Seamount	▰ Trench, Abyss	◰ Wall, Walls	◳ Mine
[5] Municipality	▲ Hill	▱ Salt Flat	▱ Forest, Woods	▱ Isthmus	▣ Salt Lake	▱ Ocean	▱ Tablemount	▱ National Park, Reserve	▱ Church, Abbey	◻ Tunnel
▣ Colony, Dependency	▲ Mountains, Mountain Range	▱ Valley, Canyon	▱ Heath, Steppe	▱ Sandbank	◳ Well, Spring	◰ Intermittent Lake	▱ Sea	▱ Point of Interest	▲ Temple	◳ Dam, Bridge
▣ Continent	▱ Hills, Escarpment	◳ Crater, Cave	▱ Oasis	◳ Island	◳ Geyser	▱ Reservoir	▱ Gulf, Bay	▰ Recreation Site	◳ Scientific Station	
◳ Physical Region	▱ Plateau, Upland	◳ Karst Features	▱ Cape, Point	◳ Atoll	◥ River, Stream	▱ Swamp, Pond	▱ Basin	▲ Cave, Cavern	◳ Airport	